The *South American Handbook* is accompanied by exclusive website content, to help you get the most out of your travels without weighing you down. The site includes a wealth of background information on South America, accompanying photographs and special features. Enter the site at www.footprinttravelguides.com/guide.

Footprint
South American Handbook

BEN BOX

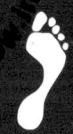

This is
South America

If your system is jaded, South America will uplift your senses with the tropical sun rising over a palm-fringed beach, or a bracing wind blowing off the southern ice fields. Light can be blinding on the high-altitude salt flats, or dense and green in the rainforest. The gentle scent of ripe guava fills the countryside, but the fire of chilli from that innocent-looking jar will electrify your taste buds.

As capybara wade through wetland shallows in the Pantanal, the spectacled bear struggles for survival in secret places in the Andes. Penguins congregate in the lee of glaciers, while tiny swifts dart through mighty waterfalls and their eternal rainbows. Volcanoes come to life and the earth trembles, yet elsewhere there are ancient, immovable tabletop plateaux. But surpassing all is the Amazon Basin, the Earth's greatest jungle, where the immensity of the trees and the smallest details of the wildlife are truly amazing.

You can explore the cities of prehispanic civilizations and the churches of colonial times, or you can immerse yourself in the present with its celebrations and its social dilemmas. Where past and present mix, there are festivals, crafts and gastronomy, from the humble potato in its umpteen varieties to the most sophisticated of wines.

If you are looking for something more active, throw yourself off a giant sand dune into a lake, or climb the highest mountain. Walk in the tree-tops of the rainforest, at eye level with birds and monkeys. Help homeless street kids gain a better life, or learn the martial arts of slaves. Dance in an Andean village square to a solo violin, or to techno brega in a warehouse-sized club in Belém. Whatever South America inspires you to do, you will find that there is no limit to the passion that it fires within you.

In this era of countless websites which bring images and information from every barrio and pueblito, the *South American Handbook* gives the details on how to navigate between each place, big or small. It is a celebration of the spirit of adventure and independence that characterizes travel in this part of the world. Drawing on the expertise of correspondents in the region and the experiences of travellers, the Handbook provides the thread from Acandí to Ushuaia and everywhere you may wish to stop off in between.

Ben Box

Best of
South America
top things to do and see

❶ Buenos Aires

The capital of Argentina, on the southern shore of the River Plate, is a city of historic and fashionable districts, of elegant buildings, atmospheric bars, football and that most nostalgic of dances, the tango. Nearby excursions include the delta of the River Paraná and the endless pampas of the gauchos. Page 50.

❷ Iguazú/Iguaçu

Argentina and Brazil share 275 spectacular waterfalls that tumble over a horseshoe-shaped precipice into a rock-filled canyon. Swifts dart through the torrents and rainbows play in the mists. Walkways take visitors to the very edge and through the spray at the foot, and all around is flower- and bird-filled jungle. Pages 163 and 518.

❸ Lake District

Where the Andes stride through Patagonia, beautiful lakes are overlooked by forests and volcanoes on both the Chilean and Argentine sides. Many of these lakes and their surroundings are protected by national parks and there are countless opportunities for hiking and riding in summer and skiing in winter. Pages 170 and 772.

❹ Lake Titicaca

The border between Peru and Bolivia splits the world's highest navigable lake, a superb destination for boat trips to islands and excursions to villages rich in traditional culture. Ancient tombs and the prehispanic city of Tiwanaku are within easy reach and the celebrations of Puno and Copacabana are not to be missed. Pages 282 and 1399.

❺ Salar de Uyuni

Vast salt flats surrounded by stark volcanoes create some of South America's most iconic landscapes. Add to that flamingos sifting the waters of multicoloured lakes, surreal deserts and high-altitude hot springs and you have one of Bolivia's most memorable attractions. Page 303.

❻ Salvador

Brazil's party city and cultural treasure trove, Salvador de Bahia was the country's first capital. It conjures up images of winding streets lined with pastel-painted houses, ornate baroque churches, Afro-Brazilian ceremonies, gymnastic martial arts, the aroma of spices and palm-fringed tropical beaches. Page 524.

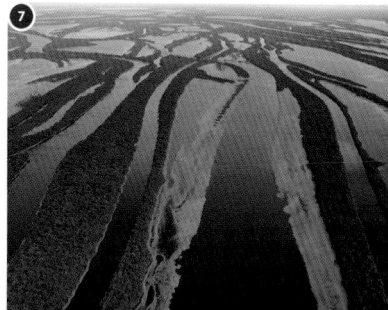

7 Anavilhanas Archipelago

Over 350 islands in the black waters of Brazil's Rio Negro form the largest river archipelago in the world. Just 80 km upstream from the Amazon's greatest city, Manaus, this is a beautiful labyrinth of forest and water best seen at sunset from a cruise boat. Page 614.

8 Pantanal

On the borders of Brazil, Paraguay and Bolivia is an enormous wetland that floods entirely for almost half the year. It is one of the best places in South America to see wildlife, especially birds, but also mammals such as capybara and otters, reptiles and fish. Page 647.

9 Torres del Paine

Without a doubt this is one of the world's best national parks, providing hard-core trekking between basalt towers and pinnacles, around azure lakes and glaciers, at the very foot of the Chilean Andes. Your every step will be watched by condors, black-necked swans, rheas and guanacos. Page 851.

10 Cartagena

Colombia's Caribbean jewel: wander the fortified old centre with its narrow streets and historic buildings, then laze on the beautiful beaches nearby. This is the ideal base for further explorations on the coast or up the Río Magdalena. Page 918.

⓫ Cotopaxi

The perfect snow-capped volcanic peak and one of several mountains that grace the skyline of Ecuador's Avenue of the Volcanoes. A popular climb itself, Cotopaxi is also at the centre of a region of haciendas, treks and train rides. Page 1076.

⓬ Galápagos Islands

Almost 1000 km from mainland South America, the Galápagos Islands have evolved as marine and terrestrial environments like nowhere else on Earth. A visit to this foremost wildlife sanctuary and its almost fearless wildlife is an unforgettable experience. Page 1172.

⓭ Nazca Lines

In the stony desert of Peru's coastal plain, mysterious figures – whale, spider, hummingbird, monkey – great spirals and dead-straight lines were etched on the ground by the Nazca people from about 400 BC. Many theories have tried to explain the culture that made them, as yet without success. Page 1368.

⑭ Machu Picchu

The Inca mountain-top city is Peru's top attraction, and deservedly so. It's the goal of many a hiking challenge and of tourists who want to go by luxury train, but its predominance is rivalled by many other archaeological sites and treks in the Sacred Valley. Page 1453.

⑮ Canaima

Out of Venezuela's Gran Sabana rise the strange, lost worlds of the tepuis, tabletop mountains with unique microclimates. It is a land of age-old rocks and tumbling waterfalls. Canaima camp is a favourite place to stay beside a tannin-brown lagoon. Page 1663.

⑯ Kaieteur Falls

The Potaro River dives 228 m off the edge of a forested plateau at Guyana's majestic falls. Wildlife includes cock-of-the-rock, Makonaima swifts and tiny golden frogs. You can get there by small plane or by a five-day overland adventure. Page 1695.

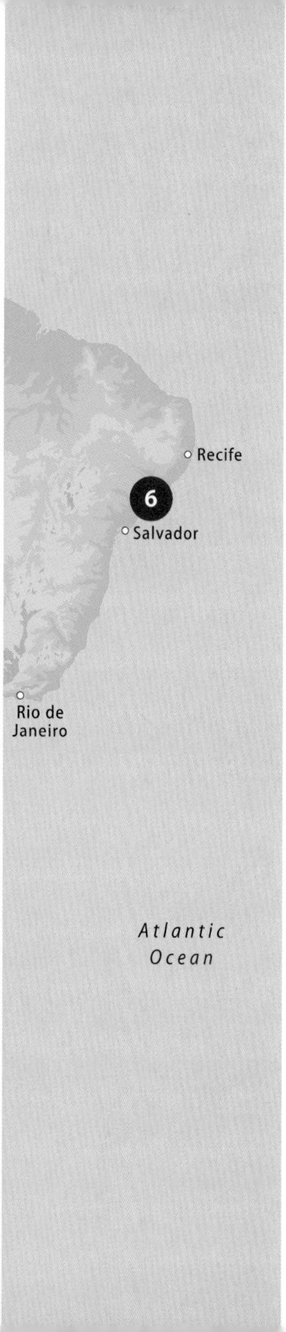
Recife
6
Salvador
Rio de Janeiro
Atlantic Ocean

1 Buenos Aires 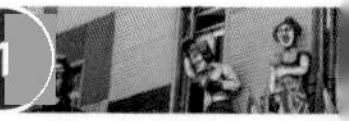

2 Iguazú/Iguaçu 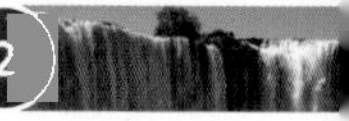

3 Lake District 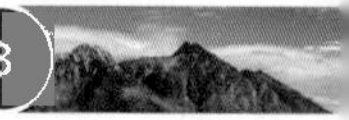

4 Lake Titicaca 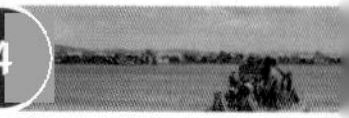

5 Salar de Uyuni 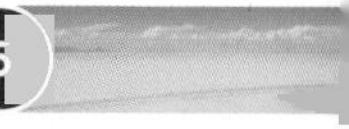

6 Salvador 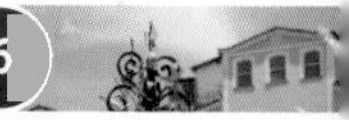

7 Anavilhanas Archipelago 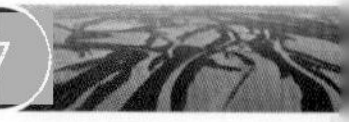

8 Pantanal 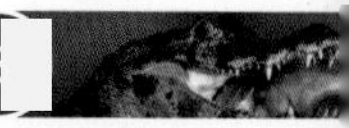

9 Torres del Paine

10 Cartagena 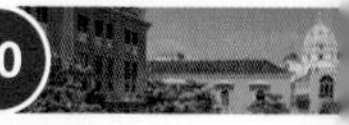

11 Cotopaxi 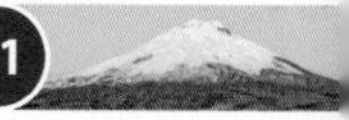

12 Galápagos Islands 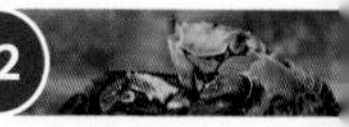

13 Nazca Lines 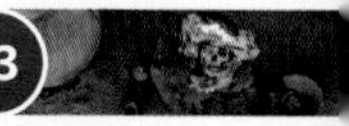

14 Machu Picchu 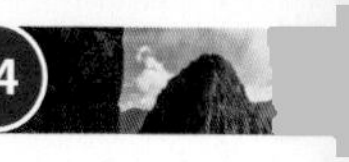

15 Canaima 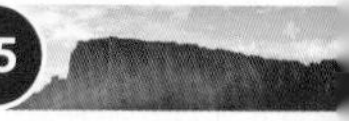

16 Kaieteur Falls 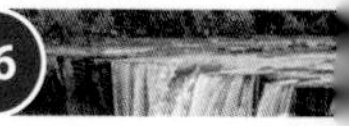

Route
planner

South America is a magnificently varied part of the world and tremendously hospitable. It is a tantalizing mixture of enticing images and ambiguous press reports, inspiring an air of mystery and a certain amount of trepidation. In common with many other places, South America suffers from meteorological, geological and social uncertainties. Within that context you will find some of the most dramatic landscapes on Earth, biological diversity in a range of habitats, historical monuments of strength and elegance and a deep cultural resilience.

The Andes

canyons, condors and the Inca heartland

Down the length of South America runs the Andean mountain chain, which starts in the north overlooking the Caribbean and ends in the south in the fabulous towers and spires of the Chaitén Massif and the Torres del Paine National Park. Condors patrol its deep canyons and strata of rocks display colours you never knew existed in stone. Out of Lake Titicaca, the highest navigable lake in the world, strode the Inca dynasty, founding Cuzco, which has metamorphosed into the gringo capital of South America. Further south, beautiful lakes in Chile and Argentina shelter beneath snow-capped peaks. On their shores are resorts for summer water sports, fishing and winter skiing. Unlike its treeless Argentine counterpart, Chilean Patagonia is a wet and windy confusion of fjords, channels and ancient woodlands.

Forests and wetlands

lungs of the Earth

In the heart of the continent, the Amazon Basin contains 20% of the world's plant and bird species, 10% of the mammals and an inestimable number of insects. In the waters live some 2000 species of fish,

Right: Andes near La Paz, Bolivia
Opposite page: Machu Picchu, Peru

Driving distances

Cartagena–Medellín	652
Medellín–Bogotá	440
Bogotá–Ipiales	948
Ipiales/Tulcán–Quito	240
Quito–Guayaquil	420
Guayaquil–Tumbes	280
Tumbes–Lima	1320
Lima–Arequipa	1011
Lima–Cuzco	1105
Arequipa–Cuzco	521
Cuzco–La Paz	651
Lima–Arica	1348
La Paz–Arica	503
Arica–Santiago	2062
Santiago–Puerto Montt	1016
Santiago–Buenos Aires	1129
Buenos Aires–Ushuaia	3070
Buenos Aires–Asunción	1325
Asunción–Foz do Iguaçu	350
Buenos Aires–Montevideo	577
Montevideo–Porto Alegre	867
Porto Alegre–São Paulo	1123
Foz do Iguaçu–São Paulo	1045
São Paulo–Rio de Janeiro	429
Rio de Janeiro–Salvador	1726
Salvador–Belém	2149
Caracas–Manaus	2399
Caracas–Bogotá	1528

Driving distances in kms 1km = 0.62 miles

plus shy giant otters, caiman and two species of freshwater dolphin. There are trees that strangle their neighbours, palms with a million thorns, plants that heal and vines that will blow your mind. Stalking in the undergrowth is the mythical jaguar, whose influence has spread through almost every religion that has come into contact with the rainforest. On its perimeter, cattle and cowboys share the land with wild birds and animals in the llanos of the Orinoco and the wetlands of the Brazilian/Bolivian Pantanal, while mysterious ecosystems hide on tabletop mountains on the Venezuela/Brazil border and in Bolivia.

Islands and beaches

from the Galápagos to Tierra del Fuego

On the Pacific, at islands such as the Ballestas (Peru) and Isla de la Plata (Ecuador) you can see much marine life, but the destination par excellence is the Galápagos. On the peaks of massive volcanoes, which jut into the ocean, albatross, boobies, giant tortoises and iguanas have evolved with little instinctive fear of man, a paradise for naturalists. Meanwhile, the Atlantic coast of Brazil, all 7408 km of it, is an endless succession of beaches, in wooded coves, dotted with islands in the south, palm tree- and dune-fringed in the north.

Above: Sea lions, Islas Ballestas, Peru
Below: Costa Verde near Paraty, Brazil
Opposite: Macaw, Amazon forest

Itineraries

South America is a big place, so it's important not to be too ambitious on a first visit. Decide what type of holiday you want and research which countries offer what you are interested in. Then work out an itinerary in which the places you want to see and the distance between them coincides with the amount of time you have available. Over the years a Gringo Trail has become firmly established, a network of places to which foreigners tended to gravitate for reasons of shared interests, lower prices, safety in numbers and so on. Some of these places have passed into legend, others are still going strong. New places are added as fashions change or transport links are opened.

Three to four weeks

rivers, waterfalls and lakes

While three to four weeks will give plenty of time to do some exploration in any of the countries of South America, there are many itineraries covering more than one. Starting in Buenos Aires, where you will want to spend a couple of days to attune yourself, you can head west to the wine and adventure sports region of Mendoza, then cross the Andes to Valparaíso on the Pacific. Alternatively, go north to Iguazú Falls and venture into Brazil or Paraguay. Across the Río de la Plata is Uruguay, with its beaches and estancias. If you fly south there are many options for flitting between Argentina and Chile, in the Lake District, in the magnificent trekking territory of Torres del Paine and the Chaitén Massif and Tierra del Fuego. Northwest Argentina, with Salta as a base, opens up opportunities for crossing the altiplano into Chile's Atacama or into southwest Bolivia with its multicoloured lakes and

Above: Medellin, Colombia
Right: Mendoza vineyard, Argentina
Opposite page: The notorious North
Yungas road to Coroico, Bolivia

volcanoes. Another ideal base is Cuzco,
for Machu Picchu and Peru's southeastern
jungle, the circuit around Arequipa and
the Nazca Lines and the route around or
across Lake Titicaca to Bolivia. Further
up the Andean chain, northern Peru,
with its pre-Inca archaeological sites and
beaches, combines well with Ecuador's
avenue of volcanoes and easily reachable
Amazonian jungles and Pacific beaches.
Brazil, often dubbed a continent in itself,
has more than enough for a month-long
trip: combinations of Rio de Janeiro,
Salvador, the beaches north and south,
the dunes of the Lençóis Maranhenses,
the Amazon, the Pantanal wetlands. But
just as Iguazú fits with Argentina, so it
does with southeastern Brazilian trips. At
the other extreme, from Manaus on the
Amazon a road heads north to the Sabana
Grande of Venezuela, with its tabletop
mountains and waterfalls, and on to the
Caribbean. Caracas and Maracaibo are

further gateways, for Venezuela's coast and the northernmost reaches of the Andean
chain, leading into Colombia and its colonial jewel on the sea, Cartagena.

Six to eight weeks

treks and wildlife tours

To see a variety of South American destinations in less than a month, some flights
will be inevitable because of the distances involved. With more time, you need not
leave the ground for the above suggestions and you can add on more destinations,
particularly those that require a set number of days. For instance, to appreciate fully
wildlife watching in the Iberá marshes in northeast Argentina, or staying on an estancia
in the pampas, Patagonia or Uruguay, allow a couple of days. Climbing in the Andes
(eg Aconcagua) and long-distance trekking in the Lake District or Patagonia will take
up a good four days minimum (and may require acclimatization). Likewise, the many
trails in the Inca heartland. Other good trekking options include many national parks
in Ecuador, the Andes in Colombia and Venezuela, and the Chapada Diamantina in
Brazil. Any boat journey on the Amazon takes a few days, while trips to jungle lodges,
with accompanying river journeys, also require about four days. Shorter wildlife tours
can be found in the Venezuelan Llanos. The basic Salar de Uyuni tour in Bolivia is three

days. From the highlands of Bolivia heading east, the steep valleys of the Yungas offer welcome warmth before the Amazonian lowlands and an array of national parks.

From the eastern city of Santa Cruz, take the train to Brazil and the Pantanal, or the new roads across the Chaco into Paraguay. From Asunción, Iguazú and the neighbouring Jesuit missions are not too far. In the north, the Guianas have some of the least spoiled swathes of rainforest, as well as savannahs and waterfalls. On their own they can be visited in under a month, but they fit well with northern Brazil, especially Belém and the mouth of the Amazon. Don't forget that if your Spanish or Portuguese needs some encouragement, a week's intensive course is a good introduction to your trip.

Three months

In three months you can travel the length of the Andes, with plenty of side trips along the way. Some highlights might include San Agustín and Popayán in Colombia; Otavalo in northern Ecuador, with visits to birdwatching lodges; Quito and the volcanoes to the south, plus the Quilotoa circuit. Preferable crossings into Peru are at Macará for Piura and on to the fascinating archaeological and birdwatching zone at Chiclayo, or south of Loja and Vilcabamba through to Chachapoyas, another area of prehispanic riches. It is simplest to take the coastal Panamerican Highway to Trujillo, then head up into the mountains and the trekking mecca of Huaraz. Spend a few days recharging your batteries in Lima then take the train up to Huancayo and the Central Andes, or the coast road to Nazca. Either way, your goal will be Cuzco, the Sacred Valley and a rainforest trip to Manu or Tambopata, before heading into Bolivia via Lake Titicaca. An Andean journey would then pass the Salar de Uyuni before descending to Northwest Argentina or the Chilean Pacific deserts. By the time you reach the far south (time this for the warmer months) meandering through channels and fjords, boating on lakes in ancient forests, scaling mountain passes and taking remote border crossings between Chile and Argentina will easily fill the three months. You can also cross South America from east to west. The Amazon river is a major transport route as far as Iquitos in Peru, from where you can head further via Pucallpa to the Central Highlands and over to the Pacific at Pisco or Lima, or to the Cordillera Blanca via La Unión. Alternatively boats from Iquitos go to Yurimaguas for the climb up to Chachapoyas and on to Chiclayo. A more southerly route would take in some of the new Interoceánica road through the far western state of Acre, to Puerto Maldonado in Peru (for Tambopata) and then to Cuzco.

Right: Sucre, Bolivia
Opposite page top: Cuzco, Peru
Opposite page bottom: Chapada
Diamantina National Park, Brazil

Best
treks

Los Alerces

Los Alerces National Park in Argentina's southern Lake District is a magnificent expanse of wilderness, with ancient alerce trees that grow in forests on the mountain slopes above vivid blue and emerald lakes. There are many good hikes, from self-guided walks of a few hours, to one- to three-day treks through the forest. Treks can combine with boat trips. Park rangers have maps and give out advice. Always consult them before setting out as some trails may be closed. Page 189.

Sorata

Nestled at the foot of Mount Illampu, below the Bolivian altiplano, this colonial town is a great place to base yourself for day hikes to lakes and caves. It is also the ideal starting point for excellent long-distance treks around some of the Andes' most majestic peaks. You need to be prepared for high altitude, cold nights and difficult trails, but these challenging circuits and trans-cordillera treks are some of the best in the South American sierras. Page 290.

Chapada Diamantina

This Brazilian national park is one of the highlights of inland Bahia. A series of escarpments is covered in cerrado and tropical forest, with waterfalls and caves. Various trails cut through the park offering hikes from a few hours to a few days and many leave from the charming colonial town of Lençóis. As it is easy to get lost, a guide is essential, but there are plenty offering their services in town. Page 540.

Ciudad Perdida

Located in the far north of Colombia, on the Caribbean-facing slopes of the Sierra Nevada de Santa Marta, is Teyuna, the Lost City of the Tayrona. It can only be reached on a six-day trek, one of the classic South American adventures. The archaeological site has a complex system of paths and steps linking terraces and platforms. The walk there, which must be done with an official tour operator, is perhaps as spectacular, challenging in parts but always rewarding. Page 944.

Quilotoa Circuit

On this 200-km route from Latacunga in the sierras of Ecuador, there is ample scope for trekking from hostel to hostel. Among the highlights are the walk around the rim of the Quilotoa volcano itself, canyons and lovely villages, any of which make a good base for day walks if you wish to stay in one spot. The less-experienced may wish to hire a guide and conditions may become tricky when the fog rolls in, but this is a beautiful diversion from the main north–south route. Page 1083.

Choquequirao

This Inca city in Peru is as marvellously sited as Machu Picchu but far less visited. The four- to five-day hike starts at the village of Cachora at 2875 m, descends into the Apurímac canyon at 1500 m and climbs back up to Choquequirao at 3000 m. That's a lot of climbing up and down. Do this trek before the cable car is built across the canyon. For the more experienced, there are longer trekking routes from Choquequirao to Huancacalle near Vilcabamba, or Santa Teresa near Machu Picchu. Page 1442.

Above left: Ciudad Perdida, Colombia
Above right: Quilotoa Circuit, Ecuador
Opposite page: Los Alerces, Argentina

Best
wildlife

Valdés Peninsula, Argentina
Experience a close encounter with the largest mammals on the planet, whale watching off Argentina's Valdés Peninsula. Southern right whales breed in the Patagonian waters every year, and the almost uninhabited area is home to a host of other wildlife. Whales are present June-December. Also to be seen at different times are elephant seals, sea lions, orcas, penguins and, on land, guanacos, rheas, armadillos and Patagonian hares. Page 200.

Emas National Park, Brazil
Emas remains a stronghold of the seldom seen maned wolf and giant anteater. It also possesses the greatest concentration of termite mounds on the planet, which is paradise if you're an anteater!

At the beginning of the rainy season (September-October) the termite larvae glow and the night time savannah lights up with its own bioluminescent response to the Manhattan skyline. Page 639.

Galápagos Islands, Ecuador
The joy of the Galápagos for the visitor is the closeness of the animals. On liveaboard cruisers you travel from island to island, seeing the different birds, reptiles and marine mammals which live on or beside the waters of this volcanic archipelago. The albatross, boobies, marine iguanas and giant tortoises have no instinctive fear of humans. Add to that the chance to snorkel in the icy seas with seals, sea lions and hammerhead sharks and you have an unforgettable experience. Page 1172.

Manu Biosphere Reserve, Peru

Manu, in Peru's southeastern jungle, is one of the largest conservation units on Earth, with an unsurpassed diversity of rainforest flora and fauna. Rising from 200 to 4100 m above sea level, the reserve's oxbow lakes are home to giant otters and black caiman while in its lowland forests are jaguar, ocelot and tapir. There are 13 species of primate and almost 1000 species of bird. Access is strictly controlled but, being within easy reach of Cuzco, it is one of the finest places to see wildlife. In addition, projects involving indigenous communities are developing. Page 1500.

Iwokrama Rainforest Reserve, Guyana

Guyana is one of the final frontiers of Latin America, with few visitors. The Iwokrama Rainforest Reserve is a

pioneering project for research and sustainable development, one of the best places to catch a glimpse of the elusive jaguar. Alternatively there's the Rupununi Savannah for cowboy fantasies and wildlife watching. Imagine a tropical version of the American Wild West and add the chance to meet some of South America's few remaining giant otters and harpy eagles. Page 1696.

Right: Iwokrama Rainforest Reserve, Guyana
Below: Manu Biosphere Reserve, Peru
Opposite left: Valdés Peninsula, Argentina
Opposite right: Galápagos Islands, Ecuador

When to go

… and when not to

Making the best choice of when to visit South America depends on latitude as much as on the weather. For example, the far south of Argentina and Chile is busiest in the southern hemisphere summer, December-February; in winter, June-August, it is cold and snow and rain can disrupt transport. The further north you go the more the seasons fall into wet and dry. The Peruvian and Bolivian Andes are dry (and very cold at night) April-October, the rest of the year is rainy. The sierras of Ecuador and Colombia are wet February-May and October-November. East of the Andes is wet November-April, wettest March-May in the Amazon Basin. Each chapter details the intricacies of the weather, but changes in world climate and periodic phenomena such as El Niño can play havoc with the general rules. See the individual chapters for more detailed information on the weather and festivals.

Key events

24 January to first week in February Alacitas Fair, La Paz, Bolivia, a celebration of Ekeko, the household god of good fortune.

February/March Carnaval is celebrated almost everywhere, most famously at Oruro and Santa Cruz de la Sierra (Bolivia), Rio de Janeiro, Salvador da Bahia, São Paulo and Recife/Olinda (Brazil), Barranquilla (Colombia), Montevideo (Uruguay), Carúpano (Venezuela) and Guyane.

March/April Semana Santa is also continent-wide, but there are particularly beautiful celebrations in Ayacucho and Arequipa, Peru, while in Montevideo, Uruguay, it coincides with Semana Criolla, a traditional gaucho festival. The biannual Festival de Música Renacentista y Barroca Americana takes place every other April in the Chiquitania region of Bolivia.

June Festas Juninhas, Bumba-meu-boi and Festa do Boi in Brazil, to Los San Juanes in Ecuador, Corpus Christi, Q'Olloriti and Inti Raymi in the Cuzco region of Peru, and San Juan Bautista on the Barlovento coast of Venezuela.

10-16 July La Tirana, near Iquique, Chile, attracts 150,000 pilgrims to the festival of La Virgen del Carmen.

Last week of September Festival de la Primavera, Trujillo, Peru (and the National Marinera contest at the end of January).

October/November In Guyana and Suriname, Diwali, the Hindu festival of light.

8 December La Inmaculada Concepción, Caacupé, is Paraguay's religious festival.

31 December Reveillon, on many beaches in Brazil, especially Rio de Janeiro, is a massive party to celebrate New Year. A number of places hold the more solemn festival of flowers, boats and candles in honour of Yemenjá, the Afro-Brazilian goddess of the sea.

What to do

from surfing or trekking to wildlife watching

Bird and wildlife watching *See also page 22.*

Argentina At least 980 of the 2926 species of birds registered in South America exist in Argentina. Enthusiasts head for Península Valdés, Patagonia (to see marine mammals as well as birds), the subtropical forests in the northwest, or the Iberá Marshes and Chaco savanna in the northeast. The pampas, too, have rich birdlife, characterized by the oven birds, horneros, which build oven-shaped nests six times as big as themselves on the top of telegraph and fence posts. Contact www.avesargentinas.org.ar.

Bolivia Bolivia has more than 40 well-defined ecological regions and the transition zones between them. On a trip to the Salar de Uyuni you will see Andean birdlife but also landscapes of unmatched, stark beauty. For lowland birds and animals, the main options are Rurrenabaque in the lowlands of the river Beni and the Parque Nacional Amboró, three hours west of Santa Cruz, containing ecosystems of the Amazon basin, Andean foothills and the savannahs of the Chaco plain. For table-top mountains, forests, *cerrado*, wetlands and a stunning array of wildlife, make the effort to get to Parque Nacional Noel Kempff Mercado.

Brazil Brazil's habitats include Amazonian rainforest, the Pantanal wetlands, the subtropical forest at Iguaçu, the *cerrado* of the central plateau, the arid northeast, the Lagoa dos Patos of Rio Grande do Sul and the few remaining pockets of Mata Atlântica of the east coast. None is difficult to get to and a variety of birds can be seen, including many endemics. National parks and protected areas, including those offshore (Abrolhos, Fernando de Noronha), are designed to allow access to Brazil's areas of outstanding beauty. Whales, eg off Santa Catarina, can be seen May-November. For serious birdwatching, contact **Pantanal Bird Club** ⓘ *www.pantanalbirdclub.org*, and **Birding Brazil Tours** ⓘ *www.birdingbraziltours.com*.

Chile In Chile birdwatching opportunities vary from the flamingos and wildfowl of the altiplano, as in the Parque Nacional Lauca in the far north, to the birds of the forests in the south, to the condors, geese and other species in the Torres del Paine. Mammals include llama, alpaca, vicuña and guanaco, and the rare deer, pudú and huemul. The trees of Chile are another attraction: many deciduous varieties, the araucaria, or monkey-puzzle tree, and areas of very ancient forest. Also, the flowering of the desert is a sight to look out for.

Colombia Colombia claims to have more birds than any other country in a wide variety of habitats. Some of the more easily accessible areas are the Parque Nacional Tayrona, the marshes between Santa Marta and Barranquilla, several good spots around the capital, Parque Nacional Los Nevados, the Laguna de Sonso, near Buga, and the road from Cali to Buenaventura, around Popayán, Puracé and San Agustín, La Planada Reserve near Pasto, some routes into the eastern Llanos (eg Garzón to Florencia and Pasto to Mocoa) and around Leticia (eg the Parque Nacional Amacayacu). Contact www.proaves.org. For migratory species, not just birds, but also whales and turtles, visit the Pacific coast between July and October.

Ecuador The Galápagos Islands are the top destination for reliably seeing wildlife close-up, but a number of the species from the Galápagos may also be seen in the Parque Nacional Machalilla and on other parts of the coast. An added bonus on the mainland coast is the opportunity to watch whales from June to September. A huge number of bird species in a great variety of habitats and microclimates may easily be seen. There are five general regions: western lowlands and lower foothills, western Andes, Inter-Andean forests and *páramos*, eastern Andes and Oriente jungle. The **Jocotoco Foundation** ⓘ *www.fjocotoco.org*, specializes in buying up critical bird habitat in Ecuador.

Paraguay Paraguay's main asset is its wildlife. It's a birdwatcher's paradise, with 687 species, many of them endangered. National parks and reserves are the best places to go. Those in the Chaco have the rarest wildlife, but they are hard to get to. For details of NGOs and foundations working for the conservation of birds, and of national parks and reserves, see Paraguay, page 1216.

Peru Nearly 19% of all the bird species in the world and 45% of all neotropical birds are found in Peru. A birding trip is possible during any month as birds breed all year round. The peak in breeding activity occurs just before the rains come in October. The key sites, out of many, are the Manu Biosphere Reserve, Tambopata National Reserve, Abra Málaga, Iquitos, Paracas, Lomas de Lachay, the Colca Canyon, the Huascarán Biosphere Reserve and northern Peru, with its Tumbesian dry forest and Pacific slopes of the Andes. Before arranging any trip, consult **PromPerú** ⓘ *www. peru.travel* (Spanish, English and other languages).

Uruguay Birdwatching is possible throughout Uruguay, but is best in the east where a number of national parks have been set up in the coastal zones: the sand dunes at Cabo Polonio, lakes, marshes and forest reserves on the Atlantic, Santa Teresa and offshore islands. Some also include marine mammals. As most Uruguayan land is farmed, nature reserves are small, but many estancias offer wildlife-watching options. For birdwatching information, contact **Aves Uruguay** ⓘ *www.avesuruguay.org.uy* (in Spanish), or the Ministry of Tourism.

Venezuela Venezuela's Llanos are a prime wildlife destination, but you should plan the timing carefully to make the most of your trip. Amazonas and the Orinoco Delta offer wildlife possibilities, but in the latter case tours can be expensive and poorly organized. The Gran Sabana does not have quite the extent of wildlife that you will find in the Llanos, but is unmatched for open landscapes. In the Andes, too, the scenery is the key, and throughout the *páramo* the unusual *frailejón* plant (felt-leaved and with a yellow bloom) is a common sight. You may also be lucky enough to see the condor. Another significant birdwatching site is the Parque Nacional Henri Pittier in the coastal mountains between Maracay and the Caribbean.

Guianas In Guyana, habitats range from undisturbed rain- and other types of forest to savannahs, wetlands and coastal areas. The country's checklist of birds numbers over 815, including a fantastic range of Guianan Shield endemics and Amazon species including harpy eagle, red siskin and Guianan cock-of-the-rock. See **Guyana Birding Tourism Program** ⓘ *www.guyanabirding.com*, for comprehensive lists and details. Birding sites include Iwokrama (which also has a high incidence of jaguar sightings), Surama, various ranches in the Rupununi, Woweta Cock-of-the-Rock Trail, Kaieteur Falls and Shell Beach, famous for its marine turtle nesting grounds and colonies of scarlet ibis. The 1.6 million-ha **Central Suriname Nature Reserve** has a variety of pristine ecosystems with a high diversity of plant life, significant populations of jaguar, giant armadillo, giant river otter, tapir, sloths, eight species of primates, and 400 of the 576 bird species recorded in the country.

Falkland Islands/Islas Malvinas On the Falkland Islands/Islas Malvinas five types of penguins are the main attraction, but albatross, giant petrels, geese, ducks and many other species (total 227) can be seen close to. Marine mammals, too, are easy to see: sea lions and elephant seals on the beaches, orca and other whales and dolphins off shore. See **Falklands Conservation** ⓘ *www.falklandsconservation.com*.

Climbing
Argentina Among the most popular peaks in Argentina are Aconcagua, in Mendoza province, Pissis in Catamarca, and Lanín and Tronador, reached from the Lake District. The northern part of Los Glaciares National Park, around El Chaltén, has some spectacular peaks with very difficult mountaineering. There are climbing clubs in Mendoza, Bariloche, Esquel, Junín de los Andes, Ushuaia and other cities, and in some places equipment can be hired.

Bolivia Some of the world's best mountaineering can be found in Bolivia. With a dozen peaks at or above 6000 m and almost a thousand over 5000 m, most levels of skill can find something to tempt them. The season is May to September, with usually stable conditions June to August. The Cordillera Real has 600 mountains over 5000 m, including six at 6000 m or above (Huayna Potosí is the most popular). Quimza Cruz, southeast of La Paz, is less accessible but offers some excellent possibilities. The volcanic Cordillera Occidental contains Bolivia's highest peak, Sajama (6542 m). The Apolobamba range, northwest of La Paz, has many peaks over 5000 m.

Brazil The most popular form of climbing in Brazil is rock-face climbing, *escalada*. In the heart of Rio, you can see, or join, climbers scaling the rocks at the base of Pão de Açúcar and on the Sugar Loaf itself. Not too far away, the Serra dos Órgãos provides plenty of challenges, not least the Dedo de Deus (God's Finger).

Chile In Chile, some volcanoes and high mountains are difficult to get to. Others, such as Villarrica and Osorno, are popular excursions, although access is controlled by CONAF (see Tourist information in Essentials A-Z of the Chile chapter) and you need permission to climb.

Colombia The best climbing in Colombia is in the national parks of Los Nevados (eg Nevado del Ruiz, Nevado de Tolima) and Sierra Nevada del Cocuy (check conditions and permitted access before setting out). For rock and ice climbing, the Nevados and Cocuy offer some technical challenges and Suesca, north of Bogotá near Nemocón, is considered the most important centre for rock climbing in the country.

Ecuador Ecuador offers some exceptional high-altitude climbing, with 10 mountains over 5000 m – most with easy access. The three most frequently climbed are Cotopaxi, Chimborazo and Iliniza Norte. Of the other seven, Iliniza Sur, Antisana, El Altar, Sangay, Carihuairazo and Cayambe vary in degree of difficulty and/or danger. Sangay is technically easy, but extremely dangerous from the falling rocks being ejected from the volcano. Tungurahua, which is currently erupting, is closed to climbers (as is Cotopaxi – 2017). Many other mountains can be climbed and climbing clubs, guiding agencies and tour operators will give advice. There are two seasons: June to August for the western cordillera and December to February for the eastern cordillera.

Peru In Peru, the Cordillera Blanca, with Huaraz as a base, is an ice climber's paradise. Over 50 summits are between 5000 and 6000 m and over 20 exceed 6000 m. There is a wide range of difficulty and no peak fees are charged (although national park entrance has to be paid in the Cordillera Blanca). The Cordillera Huayhuash, southeast of Huaraz, is a bit more remote, with fewer facilities, but has some of the most spectacular ice walls in Peru. In the south of the country, the Cordilleras Vilcabamba and Vilcanota are the main destinations, but Cuzco is not developed for climbing. Climbing equipment can be hired in Huaraz but the quality can be poor.

Venezuela The heart of Venezuelan mountaineering and trekking is the Andes, with Mérida as the base. A number of important peaks can be scaled and there are some superb hikes in the highlands.

Fishing

Argentina The main areas for fishing in Argentina are in the Lake District, around Junín de los Andes (south to Bariloche), and around Esquel, and further south around Río Gallegos and Río Grande. The best time for fishing is at the beginning of the season, in November and December (the season runs from early November to the end of March).

Brazil There is enormous potential for fishing in Brazil. Freshwater fishing can be practised in so many places that the best bet is to make local enquiries on arrival. Favoured rivers include tributaries of the Amazon, those in the Pantanal and the Rio Araguaia, but there are many others. Agencies can arrange fishing trips.

Chile In Chile, the lakes and rivers of Araucania, Los Lagos and Aisén offer great opportunities for trout and salmon fishing. The season runs from mid-November to the first Sunday in May (or from mid-September on Lago Llanquihue). Some of the world's best fishing is in the Lake District, which is a very popular region. Less heavily fished are the lakes and rivers south of Puerto Montt. Sea fishing is popular between Puerto Saavedra (Araucania) and Maullín (Los Lagos).

Colombia In Colombia, fishing is particularly good at Girardot, Santa Marta and Barranquilla; marlin is fished off Barranquilla. There is trout fishing, in season, in the lakes in the Bogotá area and at Lago de Tota in Boyacá. Travel agencies in Bogotá and Medellín can arrange fishing trips.

Venezuela Deep-sea fishing, mainly for white and blue marlin, is exceptional in the Venezuelan Caribbean, but there is also good fishing closer to shore. Here again, Los Roques is a good destination, while Macuto and Río Chico on the mainland are popular. Freshwater fishing is possible in the lakes in the Andes and in the rivers in the Llanos.

Falkland Islands/Islas Malvinas Fishing for brown/sea trout and mullet is a Falkland Islands speciality. For information see www.falklandislands.com.

Horse riding

Argentina and Uruguay In Argentina, many estancias offer horse riding, as well as fishing, canoeing, walking and birdwatching. Since estancias fall into four main categories, there is much variety in the type of country you can ride through. In the pampas, estancias tend to be cattle ranches extending for thousands of hectares; in the west they often have vineyards; northeastern estancias border swamps;

those in Patagonia are sheep farms at the foot of the mountains or beside lakes. There is also horse riding on estancias in Uruguay.

Brazil In Brazil some of the best trails for horse riding are the routes that used to be taken by the mule trains that transported goods between the coast and the interior.

Chile Treks in the mountains of Chile can be organized in Santiago, but south of Concepción and north, the Elqui and Hurtado valleys, there are more opportunities and a number of companies organize riding holidays.

Ecuador In Ecuador horse rentals are available in many popular resort areas including Otavalo, Baños and Vilcabamba. Throughout the country, haciendas also usually offer horse riding.

Mountain biking

Argentina and Chile There are lots of opportunities in the mountains and Lake Districts of Argentina and Chile. The Carretera Austral is also a great ride. Bikes are manufactured locally, but quality is variable.

Bolivia In Bolivia, hard-core, experienced, fit and acclimatized riders can choose from a huge range of possibilities. Either take a gamble and figure it out from a map, or find a guide and tackle the real adventure rides. Some popular rides in the La Paz region, achievable by all levels of riders, are La Cumbre to Coroico, down the so-called 'world's most dangerous road'; the Zongo Valley descent into the Yungas; Chacaltaya to La Paz, down from the (ex) world's highest ski-slope; Hasta Sorata, to the trekking paradise of Sorata. If you plan on bringing your own bike and doing some hard riding, be prepared for difficult conditions, an almost complete absence of spare parts and very few good bike mechanics. There are now a number of operators offering guided mountain biking tours, but only a few rent good quality, safe machines. Choose a reputable company, guides who speak your language and only opt for the best, US-made bikes.

Colombia In Colombia, cycling is a major sport, but because some remote parts are unsafe, it is not wise to venture off the beaten track and you should enquire locally about the security situation before setting out. A good specialist agency in Bogotá can give details, or ask at popular travellers' hotels.

Ecuador Ecuador is growing in popularity as there are boundless opportunities in the Sierra, on coastal roads and in the upper Amazon basin. Agencies which offer tours, rent equipment and can help plan routes are listed under Quito and other cities.

Peru This is a relatively new sport in Peru, but dedicated cyclists are opening up routes which offer some magnificent possibilities. Peru has many kilometres of

trails, dirt roads and single track, but very few maps to show you where to go. There is equipment for hire and tours in the Huaraz and Cuzco areas or join an organized group to get the best equipment and guiding.

Surfing

Brazil In Brazil the best waves are at Cacimba do Padre beach, Fernando de Noronha (the archipelago, 345 km out in the Atlantic). International surf championships are held here annually. Other good waves are found in the south, where long stretches of the Atlantic, often facing the swell head-on, give some excellent and varied breaks. Many Brazilian mainland surf spots are firmly on the international championship circuit, including Saquarema, in Rio de Janeiro state. Best waves in Rio de Janeiro city are at Joatinga, Prainha or Grumari beaches. One of the best states for surfing is Santa Catarina (for information visit www.brazilsurftravel.com).

Ecuador In Ecuador there are a few, select surfing spots, such as Mompiche, San Mateo, Montañita and Playas, near Guayaquil. Surf is best December to March, except at Playas where the season is June to September. In the Galápagos there is good surfing at Playa Punta Carola, outside Puerto Baquerizo Moreno on San Cristóbal.

Peru Peru is a top international surfing destination. Its main draws are the variety of waves and the year-round action. The main seasons are September to February in the north and March to December in the south, though May is often ideal south of Lima. The biggest wave is at Pico Alto (sometimes 6 m in May), south of Lima, and the largest break is 800 m at Chicama, near Trujillo.

Shopping tips

Handicrafts, like food, enjoy regional distinctiveness, especially in items such as textiles. In the Andes, weaving has a spiritual significance, as well as a practical one. Each region, even every village, has its own distinct pattern or style of cloth, so the choice is enormous. Reproductions of pre-Columbian designs can be found in pottery and jewellery and many artisans make delightful gold and silver items. Musical instruments (eg from Bolivia), gaucho wear, the *mate* drinking gourd and silver straw (*bombilla*), soapstone carvings and ceramics are just some things you take home. Remember that handicrafts are almost invariably cheaper away from the capital. **Gemstones** are good in Brazil; emeralds in Colombia. Leather goods are best in Argentina, Uruguay, Brazil and Colombia, while Peru markets native cotton. Buy **beachwear** in Brazil; it is matchless. **Bargaining** seems to be the general rule in most street markets, but don't make a fool of yourself by bargaining over what, to you, is a small amount of money.

Trekking *See also page 20.*

Argentina There is ample scope for short and long-distance trekking in Argentina. The best locations are in the foothills and higher up in the Andes. Some suggestions are the valleys around Salta; San Juan and La Rioja; Mendoza and Malargüe; and in the national parks of the Lake District. Around El Chaltén in Los Glaciares National Park there is some of the best trekking on the continent.

Bolivia There are many opportunities for trekking in Bolivia, from gentle one-day hikes in foothills and valleys to challenging walks of several days from highlands to lowlands on Inca or gold-diggers trails. The best known are: the Choro, Takesi and Yunga Cruz hikes, all of whose starting points can be reached from La Paz; the Illampu Circuit from Sorata; and the Apolobamba treks in the northwest. Various treks are outlined in the text, especially near La Paz and from Sorata.

Brazil In Brazil trekking is very popular, especially in Rio de Janeiro, São Paulo, Minas Gerais, Paraná and Rio Grande do Sul. There are plenty of hiking agencies which handle tours. Trails are frequently graded according to difficulty; this is noticeably so in areas where *trilhas ecológicas* have been laid out in forests or other sites close to busy tourist areas. Many national parks and protected areas provide good opportunities for trekking (eg the Chapada Diamantina in Bahia). The latest area to come under the trekker's gaze is Jalapão in Tocantins.

Chile In Chile, trekking possibilities are endless, from short, signposted trails in national parks to hikes of several days, such as the world-renowned circuit of the Parque Nacional Torres del Paine.

Colombia Trekking is popular in Colombia with walks ranging from one-day excursions out of Bogotá, or at San Agustín, to three- to four-day hikes. Good places for longer treks include the national parks of Los Nevados (from Ibagué, Manizales or Pereira), Sierra Nevada del Cocuy in the northeast, and Puracé (between Popayán and San Agustín). Well-trodden is the path to the Ciudad Perdida in the Sierra Nevada de Santa Marta, which has one of the country's main archaeological sites. In the departments of Boyacá and Santander there are many colonial *caminos reales*. Sources of information include tourist offices and **Ministerio del Medio Ambiente, Vivienda y Desarrollo Territorial** (see National parks, in Colombia chapter). See also Bogotá, What to do.

Ecuador In Ecuador, the varied landscape, diverse environments and friendly villages make travelling on foot a refreshing change from crowded buses. Hiking in the Sierra is mostly across high-elevation *páramo*, through agricultural lands and past indigenous communities. There are outstanding views of glaciated peaks in the north and pre-Columbian ruins in the south. In the tropical rainforests of the Oriente, local guides are often required because of the difficulty in navigation and because you will be walking on land owned by local indigenous tribes. The Andean slopes are steep and often covered by virtually impenetrable cloudforests and it rains a lot. Many ancient trading routes head down the river valleys. Some of these trails are still used. Others may be overgrown and difficult to follow but offer the reward of intact ecosystems.

Peru In Peru there are some fabulous circuits around the peaks of the Cordillera Blanca (eg Llanganuco to Santa Cruz, and the treks out of Caraz) and Cordillera Huayhuash. The Ausangate trek near Cuzco is also good. A second type of trek is walking among, or to, ruins. The prime example is the Inca Trail to Machu Picchu, but others include those to Vilcabamba (the Incas' last home) and Choquequirao, and the treks in the Chachapoyas region. The Colca and Cotahuasi canyons also offer superb trekking. See www.trekkingperu.org.

Venezuela In Venezuela there are popular treks in the Sierra Nevada de Mérida, Roraima and other national parks, even in the Parque Nacional El Avila, just outside Caracas.

Volunteering in South America

There is some overlap between volunteering and gap-year or career-break tourism as many people who make this type of trip do some form of work. There is an increasing amount of help for students on a gap year and, at the same time, the career-break market is growing fast and here, too, there is plenty of online assistance. See www. gapyear.com, www.goabroad.com (studying, volunteering, internships and much more), www.yearoutgroup.org and www.thecareerbreaksite.com. More specific (but not limited to South America) are www.rainforestconcern.org (Rainforest Concern), http://handsupholidays.com, www.madventurer.com, www.questoverseas.com (Quest Overseas, which also organizes expeditions), www.lattitude.org.uk (volunteering in Argentina and Ecuador), www.outreachinternational.co.uk (Outreach, in Ecuador and the Galápagos), www.projects-abroad.co.uk, located in Argentina, Bolivia, Ecuador and Peru, and https://visionsserviceadventures.com (international community service summer programmes in Ecuador, Galápagos and Peru). An excellent place to start for low- and zero-cost volunteer programmes in South America is Steve McElhinney's website, www.volunteersouthamerica.net. See also www.volunteerlatinamerica.com. For more options in the continent, see the projects supported by the LATA Foundation ① *www.latafoundation.org*.

Bolivia In Bolivia, see http://boliviainternships.com/.

Brazil In Brazil, for a website with information on volunteering, see www.socio motiva.com, in Portuguese.

Colombia In Colombia, Peace Brigades International ① *http://pbicolombia.org/*, which protects human rights and promotes non-violent transformation of conflicts, employs foreign nationals who often work as human rights' monitors and observers. Fluent Spanish is essential.

Ecuador In Ecuador, 'voluntourism' attracts many visitors. Several language schools operate volunteering schemes in conjunction with Spanish classes. Fundación Jatun Sacha ① *www.jatunsacha.org*, has many different sites at which volunteers can work, all in exceptional natural areas.

Peru In Peru, in Cuzco the **HoPe Foundation** ① *http://hopeperu.org/wp/*, accepts volunteers, as does the **Amauta Spanish School** ① *www.amautaspanish.com*. In Huanchaco, near Trujillo, **Otra Cosa Network** ① *http://otracosa.org/*, arranges a wide range of volunteer placements in the north of the country. Projects which aim to get children away from the street and into education include **Seeds of Hope** ① *www.seedsofhope.pe*, in Huaraz and **Luz de Esperanza** ① *www. peruluzdeesperanza.com*, in Huancayo.

Teaching If looking for paid work, visit the **International Career and Employment Center** ① *www.internationaljobs.org*. To teach in international Baccalaureate (IB) schools, you need to be a qualified subject teacher (primary or secondary level) with one to two years' experience. See **www.ibo.org** for a list of bilingual schools. You don't have to speak Spanish to work in a bilingual school. Most schools offer private health care packages and annual flights home. See also **http://thelajoblist. blogspot.co.uk**for information on teaching English in Latin America. Other resources are books by Susan Griffith, including: *Work your Way around the World*, 17th edition, 2017, and *Gap Years for Grown Ups*, 4th edition, 2011.

Whitewater rafting

Argentina In Argentina there are some good whitewater rafting runs in Mendoza province, near the provincial capital, and near San Rafael and Malargüe. In the Lake District there are possibilities in the Lanín, Nahuel Huapi and Los Alerces national parks.

Brazil In Brazil companies offer whitewater rafting trips in São Paulo state (eg on the Rios Juquiá, Jaguarí, do Peixe, Paraibuna), in Rio de Janeiro (also on the Paraibuna, at Três Rios in the Serra dos Órgãos), Paraná (Rio Ribeira), Santa Catarina (Rio Itajaí) and Rio Grande do Sul (Três Coroas). The Rio Novo, Jalapão, Tocantins, is an excellent, new destination.

Chile In Chile over 20 rivers between Santiago and Tierra del Fuego are excellent for whitewater rafting. Some run through spectacular mountain scenery, such as the Río Petrohué, which flows through temperate rainforest beneath the Osorno and Calbuco volcanoes. Rafting is generally well organized and equipment is usually of a high standard. Access to headwaters of most rivers is easy. For beginners, many agencies in Santiago, Puerto Varas and Pucón offer half-day trips on grade III rivers. The best grade IV and V rafting is in Futaleufú, near Chaitén.

Colombia In Colombia whitewater rafting is growing in popularity and is at present based at San Gil (Santander), Villeta and Utica (Cundinamarca) and less developed in San Agustín (Huila).

Ecuador Ecuador is a whitewater paradise with dozens of accessible rivers, warm waters and tropical rainforest; regional rainy seasons differ so that throughout the year there is always a river to run. The majority of Ecuador's whitewater rivers share a number of characteristics. Plunging off the Andes, the upper sections are very steep creeks offering, if they're runnable at all, serious technical grade V, suitable for experts only. As the creeks join on the lower slopes they form rivers that are less steep, with more volume. Some of these rivers offer up to 100 km of continuous grade III-IV whitewater, before flattening out to rush towards the Pacific Ocean on one side of the ranges or deep into the Amazon Basin on the other. Of the rivers descending to the Pacific coast, the Blanco and its tributaries are the most frequently run. They are within easy reach of Quito, as is the Quijos on the eastern side of the Sierra. In the Oriente, the main rivers are the Aguarico and its tributary the Dué, the Napo, Pastaza and Upano.

Peru Peru has some of the finest whitewater rivers in the world. Availability is almost year-round and all levels of difficulty can be enjoyed. Cuzco is probably the rafting capital and the Río Urubamba has some very popular trips. Further afield is the Río Apurímac, which has some of the best whitewater rafting, including a trip at the source of the Amazon. In the southeastern jungle, a trip on the Río Tambopata to the Tambopata-Candamo Reserved Zone involves four days of white-water followed by two of drifting through virgin forest; an excellent adventure which must be booked up in advance. Around Arequipa is some first-class, technical rafting in the Cotahuasi and Colca canyons and some less-demanding trips on the Río Majes. Other destinations are the Río Santa near Huaraz and the Río Cañete, south of Lima.

Where to stay

from hotels to hammocks

Hotels and hostels

Sleeping accommodation for independent travellers can be roughly divided into two types: hotels and hostels. Within each group there is wide variation of type and price. Choice is greater, and costs often higher, in big cities and popular tourist destinations. A decent hotel room may cost US$25-50, but can be more than this, especially when you get into the self-styled 'boutique' range. Hostel prices also vary, from US$10-25 per person in a shared room, but most also have dearer private rooms. For those on a really tight budget, it is a good idea to ask for a boarding house – *casa de huéspedes*, *hospedaje*, *pensión*, *casa familial* or *residencial* (according to country) – they are normally to be found in abundance near bus and railway stations and markets. There are often great seasonal variations in hotel prices in resorts. Remember, cheaper hotels don't always supply soap, towels and toilet paper; in colder (higher) regions they may not supply enough blankets, so take a sleeping bag. To avoid price hikes for gringos, ask if there is a cheaper room.

Tip...

Many hotels, restaurants and bars have inadequate water supplies. Almost without exception used toilet paper should not be flushed down the pan, but placed in the receptacle provided. This applies even in expensive hotels. Failing to do this will block the pan or drain.

Price codes

Where to stay	Restaurants
$$$$ over US$150	$$$ over US$12
$$$ US$66-150	$$ US$7-12
$$ US$30-65	$ US$6 and under
$ under US$30	

Price of a double room in high season, including taxes.

Price for a two-course meal for one person, excluding drinks or service charge.

Unless otherwise stated, all places to stay listed in this edition have shower and toilet, phone, TV and luggage storage. They are clean and friendly and offer breakfast. All but the most basic places have Wi-Fi and internet in common areas if not rooms. Hostels aimed at the backpacker market have a communal kitchen. In any class, hotel rooms facing the street may be noisy: always ask for the best, quietest room.

Tip...

If using a site like Booking.com to reserve a room in a hotel or hostel and it says 'no rooms available', it is worth checking the establishment's own website because they may keep a few rooms off the general booking site and at a better price (direct payments avoid the booking site's commission charges).

The electric showers used in many hotels should be checked for obvious flaws in the wiring; try not to touch the rose while it is producing hot water. Cockroaches are ubiquitous and unpleasant, but not dangerous. Take some insecticide powder if staying in cheap hotels.

B&Bs and other lodgings

Alternatives to hotels and hostels are popular in South America. For bed-and-breakfast accommodation, see the website www.bedandbreakfast.com. Short-term room rentals can be found on AirBnB ① www.airbnb.com. Travel networking is widespread. Visit www.couchsurfing.org, www.tripping.com, www.stay4free.com, or one of many similar sites. Many language schools offer lodging with families as part of the course.

Youth hostels

Organizations affiliated to the youth hostels movement exist in Bolivia, Brazil, Chile, Peru and Uruguay. There are associated hostels in Colombia and Paraguay. More information in individual countries and from Hostelling International ① www.hihostels.com. Independent sites on hostelling are the Internet Guide to Hostelling ① www.hostels.com, www.hosteltrail.com, geared to hostels and budget lodging in South America, www.hostelworld.com, www.hostelsclub.com and Ho.La Hostels ① www.holahostels.com, with an extensive list of hostels in Latin America.

Camping

Organized campsites are referred to in the text immediately below hotel lists, under each town. If there is no organized site in town, a football pitch or gravel pit might serve. Do obey the following rules for wild camping: (1) arrive in daylight and pitch your tent as it gets dark; (2) ask permission to camp from the parish priest, or the fire chief, or the police, or a farmer regarding his own property; (3) never ask a group of people – especially young people; (4) never camp on a beach (because of sandflies and thieves). If you can't get information from anyone, camp in a spot where you can't be seen from the nearest inhabited place, or road, and make sure no one saw you go there. In Argentina and Brazil, it is common to camp at gas/petrol stations. As Béatrice Völkle of Gampelen, Switzerland, adds, camping wild may be preferable to those organized sites which are treated as discos, with only the afternoon reserved for sleeping.

If taking a cooker, the most frequent recommendation is a multifuel stove (eg MSR International, Coleman Peak 1), which will burn unleaded petrol or, if that is not available, kerosene, benzina blanca, etc. Alcohol-burning stoves are simple, reliable, but slow and you have to carry a lot of fuel: for a methylated spirit-burning stove, the following fuels apply, *alcohol desnaturalizado*, *alcohol metílico*, *alcohol puro (de caña)* or *alcohol para quemar*. Ask for 95%, but 70% will suffice. In all countries fuel can usually be found in chemists/pharmacies. Gas cylinders and bottles are usually exchangeable, but if not can be recharged; specify whether you use butane or propane. Gas canisters are not always available. The **Camping Clube do Brasil** gives 50% discounts to holders of international campers' cards.

Food
& drink

Food in South America is enticingly varied and regionally based. Within one country you cannot guarantee that what you enjoyed on the coast will be available in the sierras. It is impossible to list here what is on offer in each country and there is a section on food and drink in each chapter's Practicalities section. Chinese restaurants tend to offer good value and where there are large immigrant communities you'll find excellent Japanese or Italian restaurants. Pizza is ubiquitous, sometimes genuine, sometimes anything but. Then there's fruit, fruit and more fruit in all the tropical regions, eaten fresh or as ice cream, or as a juice.

In all countries except Brazil and Chile (where cold meats, cheese, eggs, fruit, etc, generally figure) breakfast usually means coffee or tea with rolls and butter, and anything more costs extra. In Colombia and Ecuador breakfast usually means eggs, a roll, fruit juice and a mug of milk with coffee. Most restaurants serve a daily special meal, usually at lunchtime, which is cheap and good.

Vegetarians should be able to list all the foods they cannot eat; saying "*soy vegetariano/a*" (I'm a vegetarian) or "*no como carne*" (I don't eat meat) is often not enough.

This is Argentina

Argentina is a hugely varied country, from the blistering heat of the Chaco in the north to the storms of Tierra del Fuego in the south. In between these extremes, there is so much to enjoy – from nights tangoing in the chic quarters of Buenos Aires to long days riding with *gauchos* in the grasslands of the pampas. You can climb to the roof of the Americas and raft Andean rivers. You can visit the birthplace of Che Guevara and the resting place of a dinosaur known to have been bigger than T Rex. In the northwest, canyons of rocks eroded into unimaginable shapes lead to sleepy villages and staging posts on the colonial trade routes. At the northern border with Brazil, 275 waterfalls cascade into a great gorge at Iguazú. Swifts dart behind the torrents of water and birds and butterflies are easy to see in the surrounding forest. Endangered mammals, giant storks and anacondas live side by side in the Iberá marshes. In the dried-up river beds of San Juan, there are exotic rock forms at Talampaya and Ischigualasto. On the Patagonian coast at Península Valdés, Southern right whales and elephant seals come to breed in the sheltered bays, while estuaries are home to colonies of penguins and pods of dolphin. Lonely roads cross the empty plateau inland, leading to the Andes' jagged finale at the peaks and glaciers of the Chaltén Massif. To set the taste buds tingling, the vineyards of Mendoza and the Welsh tearooms of the Chubut valley hang out the welcome sign. And (vegetarians look away), don't forget the meat, barbecued on an open wood fire at the end of the day.

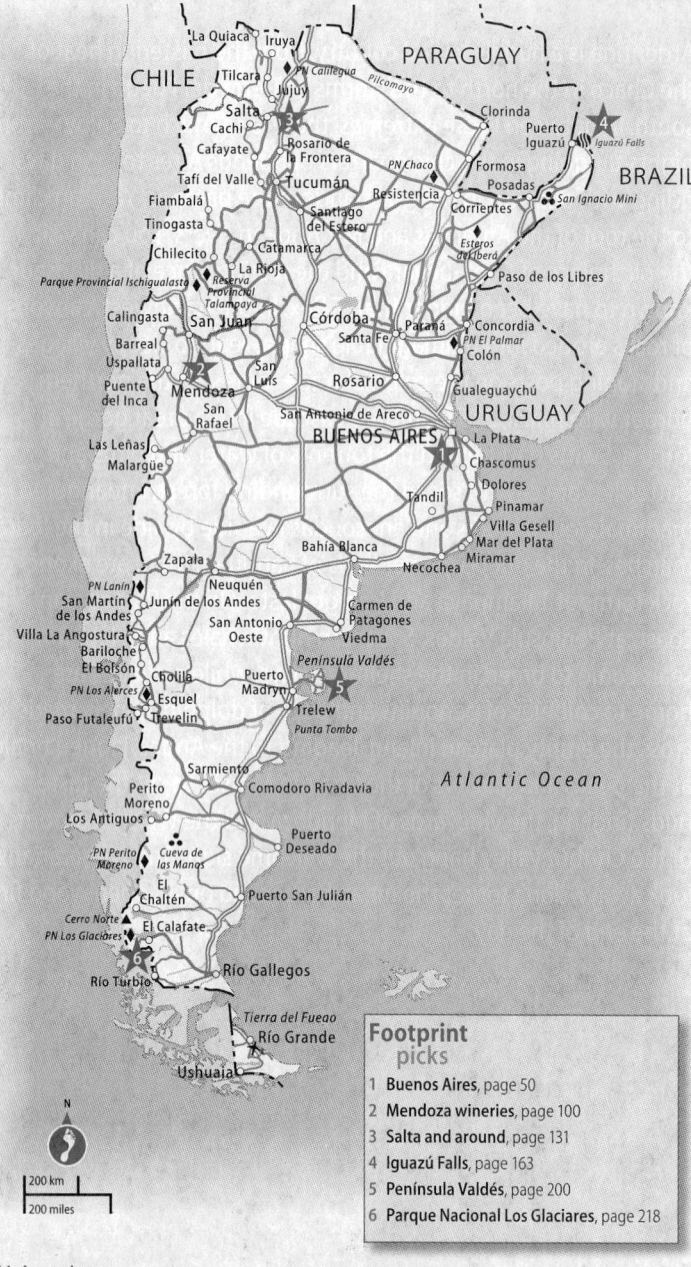

CHILE

PARAGUAY

La Quiaca
Iruya
Tilcara
Jujuy
PN Calilegua
Pilcomayo

Salta
Cachi
Cafayate
Rosario de la Frontera
Tucumán
PN Chaco

Clorinda
Puerto Iguazú
Iguazú Falls

BRAZIL

Formosa
Posadas
Resistencia
Corrientes
San Ignacio Mini

Tafí del Valle
Fiambalá
Tinogasta
Chilecito
Santiago del Estero
Catamarca
La Rioja
Esteros del Iberá

Parque Provincial Ischigualasto
Reserva Provincial Talampaya
Calingasta
Barreal
Uspallata
San Juan
Córdoba
Santa Fe
Paraná
Paso de los Libres

Concordia
PN El Palmar
Colón

Puente del Inca
Mendoza
San Rafael
San Luis
Rosario

Gualeguaychú

San Antonio de Areco

URUGUAY

Las Leñas
Malargüe

BUENOS AIRES
La Plata
Chascomus
Dolores
Pinamar
Villa Gesell
Mar del Plata
Miramar

Tandil

Bahía Blanca
Necochea

Zapala
PN Lanín
San Martín de los Andes
Junín de los Andes
Neuquén
San Antonio Oeste
Carmen de Patagones
Viedma

Villa La Angostura
Bariloche
El Bolsón
Cholila
Puerto Madryn
Península Valdés

PN Los Alerces
Esquel
Trevelin
Paso Futaleufú

Trelew
Punta Tombo

Sarmiento
Comodoro Rivadavia

Perito Moreno
Los Antiguos

Puerto Deseado

PN Perito Moreno
Cueva de las Manos
El Chaltén
Puerto San Julián

Cerro Norte
El Calafate

PN Los Glaciares
Río Gallegos

Río Turbio

Atlantic Ocean

Tierra del Fuego
Río Grande

Ushuaia

N

200 km
200 miles

Footprint picks

1 **Buenos Aires**, page 50
2 **Mendoza wineries**, page 100
3 **Salta and around**, page 131
4 **Iguazú Falls**, page 163
5 **Península Valdés**, page 200
6 **Parque Nacional Los Glaciares**, page 218

Footprint
picks

★ **Buenos Aires**, page 50
Soak up the atmosphere of one
of the world's great cities.

★ **Mendoza wineries**, page 100
Visit bodegas in the foothills of the Andes.

★ **Salta and around**, page 131
Explore ancient cultures around this charismatic city.

★ **Iguazú Falls**, page 163
Don't miss the spectacular sight of 275 converging waterfalls.

★ **Península Valdés**, page 200
See whales, penguins and harems of sea lions on the Atlantic coast.

★ **Parque Nacional Los Glaciares**, page 218
Witness the majesty of the glaciers on foot or by boat.

Route
planner

Two weeks

city lights, waterfalls and glaciers

Buenos Aires is a great first port of call, whether you want to see the football, try tango or shop till you drop, and to get any sense of the city you need a minimum of three days. Then take an overnight bus (16 hours), or a more expensive but much quicker flight, to **Iguazú Falls**. These are the country's star attraction and should not be missed. Two days is sufficient to see both the Argentine and Brazilian sides of the falls, or better still allow two days to explore the larger Argentine park in more detail. Return to Buenos Aires in order to relax in the **delta river system** just north of the city or to spend the weekend at one of the province's grandiose **estancias**.

Then fly to **El Calafate** in Patagonia for breathtaking views of the southern ice field. Spend at least a day staring at the 60-m-high ice walls of the immense **Perito Moreno Glacier**, then catch the four-hour bus to **El Chaltén** to enjoy the hikes into the mountains. Return to Buenos Aires for a night before your journey home. Note that this itinerary is best suited to the warmer months (November to March); if you visit the glacier at other times take plenty of warm clothes!

One month

land of contrast

Start in Buenos Aires, where you'll have time to explore chic **Palermo Viejo** and old **San Telmo** with its cobbled streets. You could also visit the delta river system just north of the city. Heading north, your trip to the **Iguazú Falls** should be combined with a visit to the ruined **Jesuit mission reducciones**, or time in a lodge in the **Esteros del Iberá wetlands**. After Iguazú, fly south to **El Calafate** as before. From November to March head over to **El Chaltén** for a few days' hiking, or cross the border into Chile to trek in the **Torres del Paine National Park**.

From El Calafate you have time to drive or take a bus along the lonely **Ruta 40** north to Bariloche in Ernesto 'Che' Guevara's tyre tracks, stopping off at the **Cueva de las Manos** to see the prehistoric cave paintings. Alternatively, continue south from El Calafate to **Ushuaia** to visit **Tierra del Fuego**. Take a boat trip along the Beagle Channel to feel like a true explorer, take the world's southernmost steam train and visit one of the world's most southerly ski fields. From Ushuaia, take a flight to picturesque **Bariloche**, where you'll find chalet-style hotels, chocolate shops and a backdrop of peaks. The next few days should be spent exploring the **Lake District** on foot and by car: enjoy the serene lakeside setting of **San Martín de Los Andes**; fish for giant trout at **Junín de los Andes**, or head south to laid-back **El Bolsón** for superb hiking in the 2000-year-old forests of **Los Alerces National Park** or to catch the **Old Patagonian Express** cross the steppe.

Moving on, head north by bus to **Mendoza** to visit the nearby vineyards and do a winery tour. Not far away are the fantastic, weather-worn landforms of the Ischigualasto and Talampaya national parks. Travel on to **Córdoba** to marvel at the colonial architecture and the restored **Jesuit missions** of the lovely Sierras. Finally, make your way up to **Salta** in the northwest to discover its rich indigenous culture and ancient civilizations. The city's colonial splendour contrasts perfectly with the traditions of the puna, where Pachamama festivities are a glimpse of another time. Hire a car here or catch a local bus to **Quebrada de Humahuaca**, a vast red gorge connecting a string of little villages. Stay at the HI hostel in **Tilcara** for priceless views, or head to exclusive **Purmamarca** for a luxury resort. From Salta you should also visit the timeless **Valles Calchaquíes**, where high-altitude wine is grown in rugged landscapes. Fly back to Buenos Aires and spend one last night drinking local wine and eating *dulce de leche* pancakes.

Essential Argentina

Finding your feet

Argentina is the second largest country in South America, extending across the continent some 1580 km from east to west and 3460 km from north to south. The capital, Buenos Aires, lies on the eastern side of the country, across the Río de la Plata from Uruguay. North of Buenos Aires are the river systems of the Paraná basin, including the Tigre delta and the Iberá Marshes. In the northeast, sandwiched between Brazil and Paraguay, Misiones Province is named after its ruined Jesuit missions, but is also the location of the magnificent Iguazú Falls. West of Buenos Aires stretch the vast grasslands of the pampas, home of the *gaucho* (cowboy). A string of cities give access to the Andean foothills and the higher peaks, including Córdoba, Santiago del Estero and Tucumán. In the far northwest, the fine city of Salta is an ideal centre for exploring remote valleys and high-altitude communities; there are routes from here to Bolivia, Chile and Paraguay. The iconic and often remote Ruta 40 runs the length of the country beside the Andes, whose peaks form the western border with Chile. The road passes the city of Mendoza, with its vineyards, climbing and skiing centres, and the strange lunar landscapes of San Juan province. It traverses the Lake District, renowned for lovely scenery around San Martín de los Andes and Bariloche, continuing south across the Patagonian steppe to the stunning peaks and glaciers of Los Glaciares national park. On the other side of the country, the Argentine coast stretches over 2000 km along the Atlantic. There are popular coastal resorts south of Buenos Aires and important wildlife areas further south in Patagonia. Río Gallegos is the most southerly town of any size on the mainland; travel south from here to reach the Argentine side of Tierra del Fuego.

Getting around

Distances are huge, and it's time consuming to get around. There are daily flights to all the major destinations but most go via Buenos Aires, so flying between the north and south of the country will take a full day out of your itinerary. Bus travel is cheaper than flying, and the network of long-distance services is extensive, efficient and safe. However you choose to travel, take account of holiday periods (December/January, Easter and July/August), when seats on aircraft and buses sell out fast; book as far in advance as possible at these times. If you've plenty of time, then hiring a car is a great way to explore the country in more depth, but be mindful of the distances and the poor quality of many roads.

When to go

Climate ranges from subtropical in the north to cold temperate in Tierra del Fuego. The densely populated central zone is temperate. From mid-December to the end of February, Buenos Aires can be oppressively hot and humid, with temperatures of 27-35°C (80-95°F) and an average humidity of 70%. The city virtually shuts down in late December and early January as people escape on holiday. Autumn (March-May) can be a good time to visit, and spring in

Weather Buenos Aires

January	February	March	April	May	June
30°C 20°C 100mm	29°C 19°C 100mm	26°C 17°C 100mm	23°C 14°C 80mm	19°C 10°C 70mm	16°C 8°C 50mm

July	August	September	October	November	December
15°C 7°C 50mm	17°C 9°C 50mm	19°C 10°C 60mm	23°C 13°C 100mm	25°C 16°C 90mm	28°C 18°C 80mm

Buenos Aires (September-October) is often very pleasant. Northeast Argentina is best visited in winter (June-August) when it is cooler and drier; Corrientes and Misiones provinces are increasingly wet from September. The winter is also a good time to visit the Northwest, although routes to Chile across the Andes may be closed by snow at this time, so spring and autumn may be better. Spring and autumn are the best seasons for visiting the Lake District. Ideally Patagonia should be visited in December or February-April, avoiding the winter months when the weather is cold, many establishments are closed, transport can be restricted and routes across the Andes are likely to be blocked by snow. There are also

school holidays in July when some facilities, such as youth hostels, may be heavily booked. Note that Bariloche is very popular with school groups in July and December/early January.

Time required

Two to six weeks.

Fact file
Location 34.6000° S, 58.3833° W
Capital Buenos Aires
Time zone GMT -3 hrs
Telephone country code +54
Currency Argentine peso ($)

Buenos Aires city
& province

★With its elegant architecture and fashion-conscious inhabitants, Buenos Aires is often seen as more European than South American. Among its fine boulevards, neat plazas, parks, museums and theatres, there are chic shops and superb restaurants. However, the enormous steaks and passionate tango are distinctly Argentine and to understand the country, you have to know its capital. South and west of Buenos Aires the flat, fertile lands of the *pampa húmeda* stretch seemingly without end, the horizon broken only by a lonely windpump or a line of poplar trees. This is home to the gaucho, whose traditions of music and craftsmanship remain alive.

Sights   Colour map 8, B5.

European style, Argentine passion and international ambition

The capital has been virtually rebuilt since the beginning of the 20th century, and its oldest buildings mostly date from the early 1900s, with some elegant examples from the 1920s and 1930s. The centre has maintained the original layout since its foundation and so the streets are often narrow and one way. Its original name, 'Santa María del Buen Ayre' was in recognition of the favourable winds which brought sailors across the ocean.

Around Plaza de Mayo

The heart of the city is the **Plaza de Mayo**. On the east side is the **Casa de Gobierno**, known as the Casa Rosada because it is pink. It contains the offices of the President of the Republic and is notable for its statuary and the rich furnishing of its halls. The **Museo Casa Rosada** ⓘ *Paseo Colón 100, T011-4344 3802, www.casarosada.gob.ar, Wed-Sun and holidays 1000-1800, free*, in the Fuerte de Buenos Aires and Aduana Taylor, covers the period 1810-2010 with historical exhibits and art exhibitions, permanent and temporary. **Antiguo Congreso Nacional** (Old Congress Hall, 1864-1905) ⓘ *Balcarce 139, guided tours Mon, Tue, Thu, Fri at 1230 and 1700, closed Jan, free*, on the south of the Plaza, is a National Monument. The **Cathedral** ⓘ *San Martín 27, T011-4331 2845, www.catedralbuenosaires. org.ar, Mon-Fri 0800-1900, Sat-Sun 0900-1930; guided visits to San Martín's Mausoleum and Crypt, religious artefacts, and Temple and Crypt; Mass is held daily, check times*, on the north of Plaza, stands on the site of the first church in Buenos Aires. The current structure dates from 1753-1822 (its portico was built in 1827), but the 18th-century towers were never rebuilt. The imposing **tomb** (1880) of the Liberator, Gen José de San Martín ⓘ *Mon-Fri 0900-1900*, is guarded by soldiers in fancy uniforms. A small exhibition to the left of the main nave displays items related to Pope Francis, former archbishop of Buenos Aires.

    Museo del Cabildo y la Revolución de Mayo ⓘ *Bolívar 65, T011-4334 1782, http://cabildonacional. cultura.gob.ar, Tue, Wed, Fri 1030-1700, Thu 1030-2000, Sat-Sun and holidays 1030-1800, guided visits in English Oct-Mar, free*, is in the old Cabildo where the movement for independence from Spain was first planned. It's worth a visit for the paintings of old Buenos Aires, the documents and maps recording the May 1810 revolution, and memorabilia of the 1806 British attack; also Jesuit art. In the patio is a café and restaurant and stalls selling handicrafts (Thursday-Friday 1100-1800). Also on the

Best for
Boat trips ▪ Estancias ▪ Nightlife ▪ Riding ▪ Shopping

Essential Buenos Aires

Finding your feet

Greater Buenos Aires has a population of 12.8 million (including the Federal District and 24 neighbouring districts – 2010 census). The city is served by two **airports**, **Ezeiza**, for international and few domestic flights, and **Aeroparque**, for domestic flights, most services to Uruguay and some to Brazil and Chile. Ezeiza is 35 km southwest of the centre, while Aeroparque is 4 km north of the city centre on the riverside. All international and interprovincial buses use the Retiro **bus terminal** at Ramos Mejía y Antártida Argentina, which is next to the Retiro **railway station**.

Getting around

The commercial heart of the city, from Retiro station and Plaza San Martín through Plaza de Mayo to San Telmo, east of Avenida 9 de Julio, can be explored on foot, and you'll probably want to take a couple of days to explore its museums, shops and markets. Many places of interest lie outside this zone, so you will need to use public transport. City **buses** (*colectivos*) are plentiful, and the **metro**, or Subte, is fast and clean. Yellow and black **taxis** can be hailed on the street, but if possible, book a radio or a remise taxi by phone. See Transport, page 72, for details and fares.

Street numbers start from the dock side rising from east to west, but north/south streets are numbered from Avenida Rivadavia, one block north of Avenida de Mayo rising in both directions. Avenida Roque Sáenz Peña and Avenida Julio A Roca are commonly referred to as Diagonal Norte and Diagonal Sur respectively.

Guided tours are organized by the city authorities, including a Pope Francis tour throughout the city and bike tours in Palermo parks (weekends and holidays only). Other suggested circuits are given on the city website.

Safety

When walking in the centre of the city, especially at night, but even by day, always be on the alert for pickpockets and street crime. Areas to take most care are around Retiro and Plaza San Martín, on Calle Florida and in San Telmo. La Boca is reportedly up-and-coming and less dangerous than in recent years, but always ask about safety. Travel by radio taxi (US$5 one way to La Boca from the centre or San Telmo).

Plaza is the Palacio de Gobierno de la Ciudad (City Hall). Within a few blocks north of the Plaza are the main banks and business houses, such as the **Banco de la Nación**, opposite the Casa Rosada, with an impressively huge main hall and topped by a massive marble dome 50 m in diameter.

On the Plaza de Mayo, the **Mothers of the Plaza de Mayo** march in remembrance of their children who disappeared during the 'dirty war' of the 1970s (their addresses are H Yrigoyen 1584, T011-4383 0377, www.madres.org, and Piedras 153, T011-4343 1926, http://madresfundadoras.blogspot.co.uk). The Mothers march anti-clockwise round the central monument every Thursday at 1530, with photos of their disappeared loved-ones pinned to their chests.

West of Plaza de Mayo

Running west from the Plaza, the Avenida de Mayo leads 1.5 km to the **Palacio del Congreso** (Congress Hall) ① *Plaza del Congreso, Av Rivadavia 1864, T011-6310 7222 for 1-hr guided visits, Sat at 1600 and 1700, Sun at 1100 and 1600, www.congreso.gov.ar; passport essential*. This huge Greco-Roman building houses the seat of the legislature. Avenida de Mayo has several examples of fine architecture of the early 20th century, such as the sumptuous **La Prensa** building (No 575, free guided visits at weekends), the traditional **Café Tortoni** (No 825, www.cafetortoni.com.ar), or the eclectic **Palacio Barolo** (No 1370, www.pbarolo.com.ar), and many others of faded grandeur.

Avenida de Mayo crosses the **Avenida 9 de Julio**, one of the widest avenues in the world, which consists of three major carriageways with heavy traffic, separated in some parts by wide grass borders. Five blocks north of Avenida de Mayo the great **Plaza de la República**, with a 67-m obelisk commemorating the 400th anniversary of the city's founding, is at the junction of Avenida 9 de Julio with Avenidas Roque Sáenz Peña and Corrientes.

Teatro Colón ① *Cerrito 628, entrance for guided visits Tucumán 1171, T011-4378 7109, www.teatrocolon.org.ar*, is one of the world's great opera houses. The interior is resplendent with red plush and gilt; the stage is huge and salons, dressing rooms and banquet halls are equally sumptuous. Consult the website for details of performances, tickets and guided visits. Close by is the **Museo Judío** ① *Libertad 769, T011-4123 0832, www.judaica.org.ar; for visits make an appointment with the rabbi (take identification)*, which has religious objects relating to Jewish presence in Argentina in a 19th-century synagogue. Not far away is **Museo del Holocausto** (Shoah Museum) ① *Montevideo 919, T011-4811 3588, www.museodelholocausto.org.ar, Mon-Thu 1100-1900, Fri 1000-1600, US$4.50 (ID required)*, a permanent exhibition of pictures, personal and religious items with texts in Spanish on the Holocaust, antisemitism in Argentina and the lives of many Argentine Jews in the pre- and post-war periods. **La Chacarita** ① *Guzmán 670, daily 0730-1700, take Subte Line B to the Federico Lacroze station*, is a well-known cemetery with the lovingly tended tomb of Carlos Gardel, the tango singer.

North of Plaza de Mayo
The city's traditional shopping centre, Calle Florida, is reserved for pedestrians, with clothes and souvenir shops, restaurants and the elegant **Galerías Pacífico** ① *Florida entre Córdoba y Viamonte, www.galeriaspacifico.com.ar, guided visits from the fountain on lower ground floor, Mon-Fri, 1130, 1630*, a beautiful mall with fine murals and architecture, many exclusive shops and good food outlets. More shops are to be found on Avenida Santa Fe, which crosses Florida at Plaza San Martín. Avenida Corrientes, a street of theatres, bookshops, restaurants and cafés, and nearby Calle Lavalle (partly

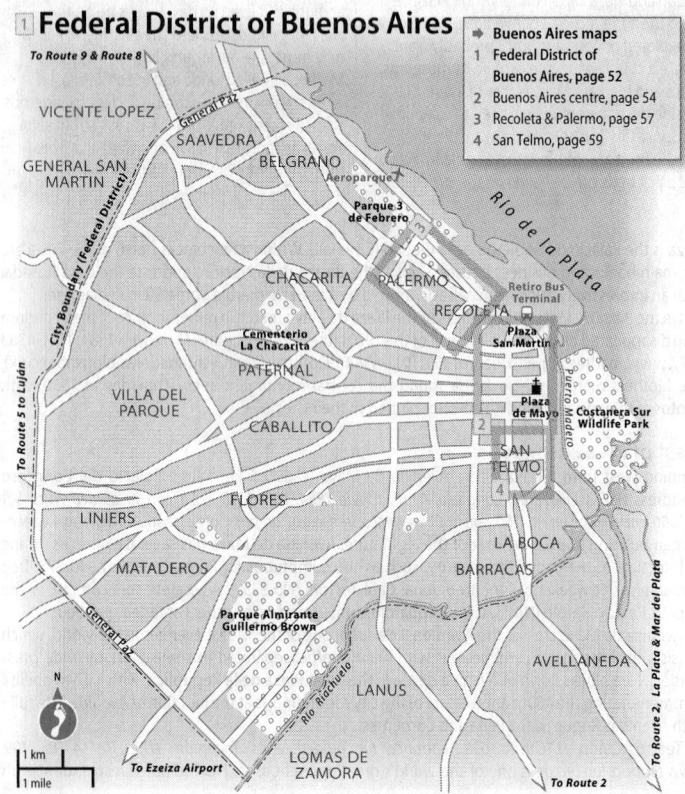

① Federal District of Buenos Aires

➡ Buenos Aires maps
1 Federal District of Buenos Aires, page 52
2 Buenos Aires centre, page 54
3 Recoleta & Palermo, page 57
4 San Telmo, page 59

To Route 9 & Route 8

VICENTE LOPEZ

General Paz

SAAVEDRA

GENERAL SAN MARTIN

BELGRANO

Aeroparque

Parque 3 de Febrero

Río de la Plata

City Boundary (Federal District)

CHACARITA

PALERMO

Retiro Bus Terminal

RECOLETA

Plaza San Martín

To Route 5 to Luján

Cementerio La Chacarita

PATERNAL

Puerto Madero

VILLA DEL PARQUE

CABALLITO

Plaza de Mayo

Costanera Sur Wildlife Park

2

SAN TELMO

4

FLORES

LA BOCA

LINIERS

MATADEROS

BARRACAS

To Route 2, La Plata & Mar del Plata

General Paz

Parque Almirante Guillermo Brown

AVELLANEDA

N

LANUS

Río Riachuelo

1 km
1 mile

To Ezeiza Airport

LOMAS DE ZAMORA

To Route 2

reserved for pedestrians), used to be the entertainment centre, but both are now regarded as faded, since Recoleta, Palermo and Puerto Madero have become much more fashionable (see below).

The **Basílica Nuestra Señora de La Merced** ⓘ *J D Perón y Reconquista 207, Mass times, Wed 1730, Sun 1130,* founded 1604, rebuilt for the third time in the 18th century, has a beautiful interior with baroque and rococo features. In 1807 it was a command post against the invading British. **Museo y Biblioteca Mitre** ⓘ *San Martín 336, T011-4394 8240, www.museomitre.gov.ar, Mon-Fri 1300-1730, US$1.30,* preserves intact the household of President Bartolomé Mitre; has a coin and map collection and historical archives.

The **Plaza San Martín** has a monument to San Martín at the western corner of the main park and, at the north end, a memorial with an eternal flame to those who fell in the Falklands/Malvinas War of 1982. On the plaza is **Palacio San Martín** ⓘ *Arenales 761, T011-4819 7297, www. mrecic.gov.ar, Tue and Thu 1500 free tours in Spanish and English.* Built 1905-1909, it is three houses linked together, now the Foreign Ministry. It has collections of prehispanic and 20th-century art. On the opposite side of the plaza is the opulent **Palacio Paz** (Círculo Militar) ⓘ *Av Santa Fe 750, T011-4311 1071, www.circulomilitar.org, guided tours Tue-Fri 1100, 1500 (1100 only on Wed), tours in English on Thu at 1530, US$10.* The Círculo Militar includes **Museo de Armas** ⓘ *Av Santa Fe 702, Mon-Fri 1300-1900, US$2.60.* It has all kinds of weaponry related to Argentine history, including the 1982 Falklands/ Malvinas War, plus Oriental weapons.

Plaza Fuerza Aérea Argentina (formerly Plaza Británica) has the clock tower presented by British and Anglo-Argentine residents, while in the **Plaza Canadá** (in front of the Retiro Station) there is a Pacific Northwest Indian totem pole, donated by the Canadian government. Behind Retiro station is **Museo Nacional Ferroviario** ⓘ *Av del Libertador 405, T011-4318 3343, daily 1000-1800 (closed on holidays), free.* For railway fans: locomotives, machinery, documents of the Argentine system's history; the building is in very poor condition. In a warehouse beside is the workshop of the sculptor Carlos Regazzoni who recycles refuse material from railways.

Museo de Arte Hispanoamericano Isaac Fernández Blanco ⓘ *Suipacha 1422 (3 blocks west of Retiro), T011-4327 0228, www.museos.buenosaires.gob.ar/mifb.htm, Tue-Fri, 1300-1900, Sat, Sun and holidays 1100-1900, Wed free, US$0.65,* is one of the city's best museums. It contains a fascinating collection of colonial art, especially paintings and silver, also temporary exhibitions of Latin American art, in a beautiful neocolonial mansion (Palacio Noel, 1920s) with Spanish gardens; weekend concerts.

Recoleta

☆**Recoleta cemetery** ⓘ *entrance at Junín 1790, near Museo de Bellas Artes (see below), www. cementeriorecoleta.com.ar, 0700-1745, tours in Spanish and English are available Tue-Fri at 1100, Sat-Sun at 1100 and 1500 (visitasguiadasrecoleta@buenosaires.gob.ar),* is one of the unmissable sights of Buenos Aires. With its streets and alleys separating family mausoleums built in every imaginable architectural style, La Recoleta is often compared to a miniature city. Among the famous names from Argentine history is Evita Perón who lies in the Duarte family mausoleum: to find it from the entrance go to the first tree-filled plaza; turn left and where this avenue meets a main avenue (go just beyond the Turriaca tomb), turn right; then take the third passage on the left. On Saturday and Sunday there is a good craft market in the park on Plaza Francia outside the cemetery (1000-1800), with street artists and performers. Next to the cemetery, the **Centro Cultural Recoleta** ⓘ *T011-4803 1040, www.centroculturalrecoleta.org, Tue-Fri 1330-2030, Sat, Sun, holidays 1130-2030,* specializes in contemporary local art.

Adjoining the cemetery, **Nuestra Señora del Pilar**, Junín 1898, is a jewel of colonial architecture dating from 1732 (renovated in later centuries), facing onto the public gardens of Recoleta. A fine wooden image of San Pedro de Alcántara, attributed to the famous 17th-century Spanish sculptor Alonso Cano, is preserved in a side chapel on the left, and there are stunning gold altars. Upstairs is an interesting museum of religious art.

Museo de Bellas Artes (National Gallery) ⓘ *Av del Libertador 1473, T011-5288 9999, www.mnba. org.ar, Tue-Fri 1130-1930, Sat-Sun 0930-1930, free,* is an excellent museum that gives a taste of Argentine art, as well as having a fine collection of European works, particularly post-Impressionist. There are superb Argentine 19th and 20th-century paintings, sculpture and wooden carvings; also films, classical music concerts and art courses.

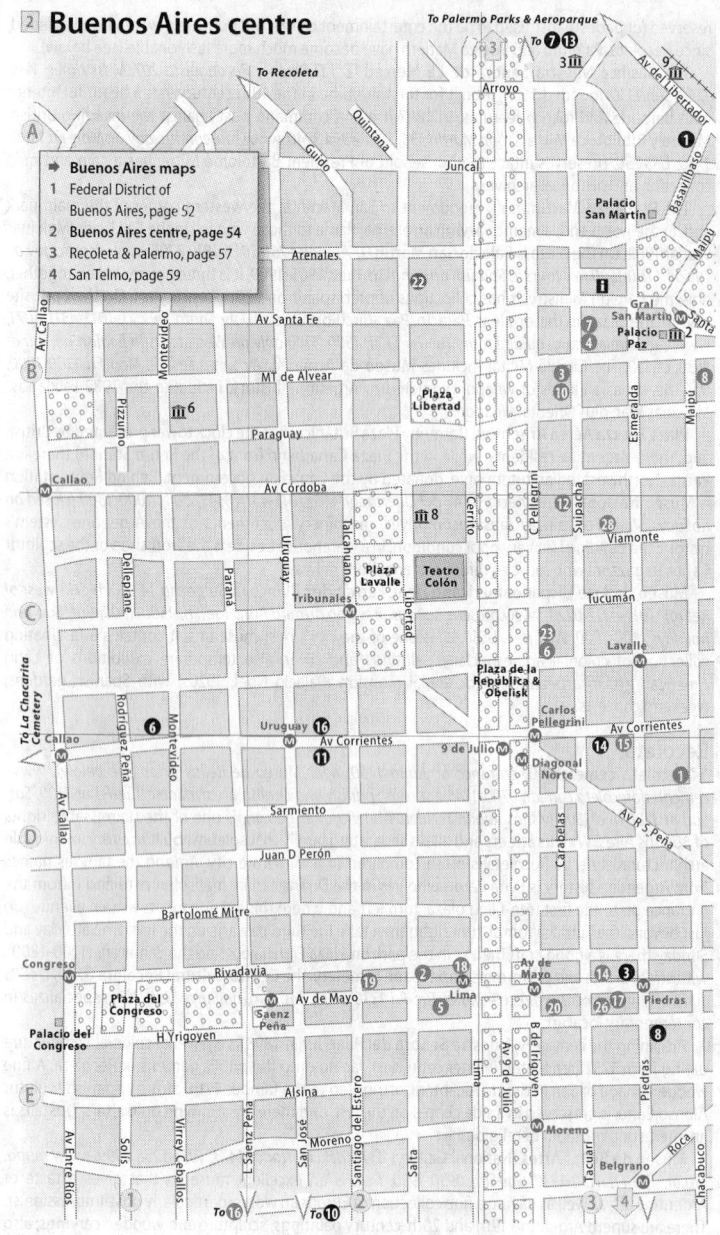

To Palermo Parks & Aeroparque

To Recoleta

Buenos Aires maps
1 Federal District of
   Buenos Aires, page 52
2 Buenos Aires centre, page 54
3 Recoleta & Palermo, page 57
4 San Telmo, page 59

Palacio San Martín

Gral
San Martín
Palacio
Paz

Plaza
Libertad

Plaza
Lavalle

Teatro
Colón

Plaza de la
República &
Obelisk

Carlos
Pellegrini

Diagonal
Norte

To La Chacarita
Cemetery

Plaza del
Congreso

Palacio del
Congreso

Av de
Mayo

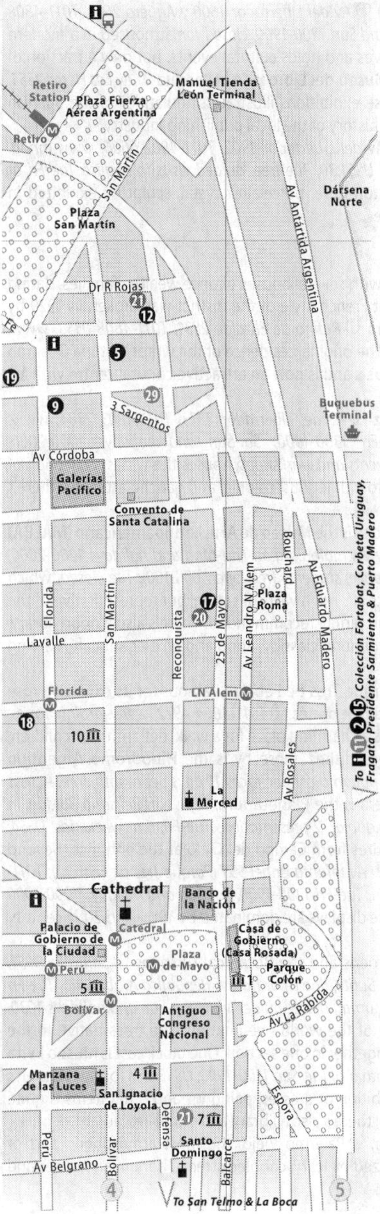

Retiro
Station
Retiro

Plaza Fuerza
Aérea Argentina

Manuel Tienda
León Terminal

Plaza
San Martín

Dársena
Norte

Dr R Rojas

3 Sargentos

Av Córdoba

Galerías
Pacífico

Buquebus
Terminal

Convento de
Santa Catalina

Florida

San Martín

Plaza
Roma

Reconquista

25 de Mayo

Bouchard

N E Anchorena

Av Leandro N Alem

Eduardo Madero

Lavalle

Florida

LN Alem

10 🏛

To 🏠 1 🏠 2 🏛 15 Colección Fortabat, Corbeta Uruguay,
Fragata Presidente Sarmiento & Puerto Madero

Av Rosales

La
Merced

Cathedral

Palacio de
Gobierno de
la Ciudad

Catedral

Perú

Banco de
la Nación

Casa de
Gobierno
(Casa Rosada)

Plaza
de Mayo

Parque
Colón

Bolívar

Antiguo
Congreso
Nacional

Av La Rábida

5 🏛

Manzana
de las Luces

Perú

4 🏛

San Ignacio
de Loyola

Bolívar

Defensa

21 7 🏛

Santo
Domingo

Av Belgrano

Balcarce

To San Telmo & La Boca

200 metres
200 yards

N

Where to stay 🏠
1 06 Central D3
2 BA Stop D2
3 Bisonte Palace B3
4 Casa Calma B3
5 Castelar E2
6 Colón C3
7 Dolmen B3
8 Dorá B3
10 El Conquistador B3
11 Faena C5
12 Goya C3
14 Hispano D3
15 Hostel Suites
   Obelisco D3
16 Kilca Hostel &
   Backpacker E1
17 La Argentina E3
18 Limehouse Hostel D2
19 Marbella E2
20 Milhouse Hostel E3
21 Moreno E4
23 Panamericano &
   Tomo 1 restaurant C3
26 Portal del Sur E3
28 V&S C3
29 Waldorf B4

Restaurants 🍴
1 BASA A3
2 Cabaña Las Lilas D5
3 Café Tortoni D3
4 Clásica y Moderna B1
5 Dadá B4
6 El Gato Negro C1
7 El Mirasol de
   la Recova A3
8 Fika E3
9 Florida Garden B4
10 Gijón E2
11 Güerrín D2
12 Gianni's B4

13 Juana M A3
14 Las Cuartetas D3
15 Le Grill D5
16 Los Inmortales C2
17 Sam Bucherie C4
18 Sorrento C4
19 Tancat B4

Bars & clubs 🍸
20 Bahrein C4
21 Druid In B4
22 Gran Bar Danzón B2

Museums 🏛
1 Museo Casa Rosada E5
2 Museo de Armas B3
3 Museo de Arte
   Hispanoamericano
   Isaac Fernández
   Blanco A3
4 Museo de la Ciudad E4
5 Museo del Cabildo
   y la Revolución
   de Mayo E4
6 Museo del
   Holocausto B1
7 Museo Etnográfico
   JB Ambrosetti E4
8 Museo Judío C2
9 Museo Nacional
   Ferroviario A3
10 Museo y Biblioteca
   Mitre D4

The **Biblioteca Nacional** (National Library) ① *Av del Libertador 1600 y Agüero 2502, T011-4808 6000, www.bn.gov.ar, Mon-Fri 0900-2100, Sat and Sun 1200-1900, closed Jan*, is housed in a modern building. It has an art gallery, periodical archives and holds cultural events, but only a fraction of the extensive stock can be seen. Next to it is **Museo del Libro y de la Lengua** ① *Av Las Heras 2555, T011-4808 0090, Tue-Sun 1400-1900, free*, whose exhibitions illustrate singularities of the Spanish (castellano) spoken in Argentina and trace the history of the local publishing industry.

Museo Nacional de Arte Decorativo ① *Av del Libertador 1902, T011-4802 6606, www.mnad. org.ar, Tue-Sun 1400-1900 (closed Sun in Jan), US$1.30, Tue free, guided visits in English Tue-Fri at 1430, US$4*, contains collections of painting, furniture, porcelain, crystal, sculpture exhibited in sumptuous halls; it was once a family residence.

☆Palermo

Palermo Chico is a delightful residential area with several houses of once wealthy families, dating from the early 20th century. The predominant French style of the district was broken in 1929 by the rationalist lines of the **Casa de la Cultura** ① *Rufino de Elizalde 2831, T011-4808 0553, www. fnartes.gov.ar, Tue-Sun 1500-2000 (Jan closed)*. The original residence of the writer Victoria Ocampo was a gathering place for artists and intellectuals and is now an attractive cultural centre with art exhibitions and occasional concerts.

Museo de Arte Popular José Hernández ① *Av del Libertador 2373, T011-4803 2384, www. buenosaires.gob.ar/museojosehernandez, Tue-Fri 1300-1900, Sat-Sun and holidays 1000-2000, US$0.65, free Wed; see website for exhibitions, events and workshops*, houses the widest collection of Argentine folkloric art, with rooms dedicated to indigenous, colonial and gaucho artefacts; there's a handicraft shop and a library.

One of the most important museums in the city is the **Museo de Arte Latinoamericano (MALBA)** ① *Av Figueroa Alcorta 3415, T011-4808 6500, www.malba.org.ar, Thu-Mon and holidays 1200-2000, US$5.50, students and seniors US$3 (Wed half price, students free, open till 2100); Tue closed*, which houses renowned Latin American artists' works. It's not a vast collection, but representative of the best from the continent: powerful, moving and highly recommended. There's also a good library, cinema (showing art house films as well as Argentine classics), shop and an elegant café, serving delicious food and cakes.

Of the fine Palermo Parks, the largest is **Parque Tres de Febrero**, famous for its extensive rose garden, Andalusian Patio, and delightful **Jardín Japonés** ① *T011-4804 4922, www.jardinjapones. org.ar, daily 1000-1800, US$4.50, seniors free*. It is a charming place for a walk, delightful for children, and with a good café serving some Japanese dishes. Close by is the **Hipódromo Argentino** (Palermo racecourse) ① *T011-4778 2800, www.palermo.com.ar, races 10 days per month, free*. Across Avenida Sarmiento from Parque Tres de Febrero is the **Planetarium** ① *just off Belisario Roldán in Palermo Park, T011-4771 6629, www.planetario.gob.ar, 2 presentations Tue-Fri, 6 at weekends, US$4; small museum*. There are several large meteorites from Campo del Cielo at the entrance. Beyond is **Museo de Artes Plásticas Eduardo Sívori** ① *Av Infanta Isabel 555 (Parque Tres de Febrero), T011-4774 9452, www.buenosaires.gob.ar/museosivori, Tue-Fri 1200-1900, Sat-Sun and holidays 1000-1900 (1800 in winter), US$1.60, Wed and Fri free*, whose displays are dominated by 19th- and 20th-century Argentine art, sculpture and tapestry.

South of the parks are the Zoological Gardens and the **Botanical Gardens** ① *Santa Fe 3951, T011-4831 4527, entrance from Plaza Italia (take Subte, line D) or from C República Arabe Siria, Tue-Fri 0800-1745, Sat-Sun 0930-1745 (closes at 1845 in summer), free guided visits Sat-Sun and holidays 1030, 1500*, which contain characteristic specimens of the world's vegetation. The trees native to the different provinces of Argentina are brought together in one section. One block east is **Museo Evita** ① *Lafinur 2988, T011-4807 0306, www.museoevita.org, Tue-Sun 1100-1900, US$5*, in a former women's shelter run by Fundación Eva Perón. The exhibition of dresses, paintings and other items is quite interesting though lacks the expected passion; there's also a library and a café-restaurant.

Southwest of here, around Plaza Cortázar, is Palermo Viejo, the most atmospheric part of Palermo. It's a very seductive place, characterized by leafy, cobbled streets, bohemian houses and chic eateries and shops.

3 Recoleta & Palermo

To Belgrano, Museo Histórico Sarmiento, Museo de Arte Español Enrique Larreta & Museo Casa de Yrurtia

To Museo de Artes Plásticas Eduardo Sívori

Planetarium

To 9 11 14, Palermo Metro Station & Las Cañitas

To Aeroparque

Plaza Italia

PALERMO

Botanical Gardens

Zoological Gardens

Japanese Garden

Palermo Parks (Parque Tres de Febrero)

Museo Evita

200 metres
200 yards

Paseo Alcorta Shopping Mall

To Plaza Cortázar & Palermo Soho Restaurants

MALBA

Museo de Motivos Populares Argentinos José Hernández

➡ Buenos Aires maps

1 Federal District of Buenos Aires, page 52
2 Buenos Aires centre, page 54
3 Recoleta & Palermo, page 57
4 San Telmo, page 59

Casa de la Cultura

Museo de Arte Popular José Hernández

Where to stay

1 A Hotel
2 Alvear Palace
3 Back in BA
4 Bo Bo
8 Hostel Suites Palermo
9 Krista
10 Legado Mítico
11 Magnolia
12 Play Hostel
13 Querido
14 Solar Soler

Museo del Libro y de la Lengua

Biblioteca Nacional

RECOLETA

Museo de Bellas Artes

Restaurants

1 Al paso y algo más
2 Arkakao
3 Bröet
4 Clásico y Moderna
5 Como en Casa
6 El Mirasol de la Recova
7 Juana M
8 La Madeleine
9 María de Bambi
10 Persicco
11 Rodi Bar

Centro Cultural Recoleta

Cemetery of the Recoleta

Nuestra Señora del Pilar

Recoleta Mall

Bars & clubs

12 Buller Brewing Company
13 Milion
14 Notorious
15 The Shamrock

Patio Bullrich Shopping Centre

Plaza V. López

Plaza R Peña

To Retiro Station & City Centre

Belgrano

Northeast of Palermo in Belgrano is the **Museo de Arte Español Enrique Larreta** ⓘ *Juramento 2291, T011-4784 4040, www.buenosaires.gob.ar/museolarreta, Mon-Fri, 1200-1900, Sat-Sun 1000-2000, guided visits Mon-Fri 1430, Sat-Sun 1600, 1800, US$0.65, Thu free*. The home of the writer Larreta has paintings and religious art from the 14th to the 20th century and is surrounded by a beautiful garden. There are two other worthwhile museums in this district: **Museo Histórico Sarmiento** ⓘ *Juramento 2180, T011-4782 2354, www.museosarmiento.cultura.gob.ar*, and **Museo Casa de Yrurtia** ⓘ *O'Higgins 2390, T011-4781 0385, www.museoyrurtia.cultura.gob.ar, closed for restoration in 2017*.

South of Plaza de Mayo

The church of **San Ignacio de Loyola**, begun 1664, is the oldest colonial building in Buenos Aires (renovated in 18th and 19th centuries). It stands in a block of Jesuit origin, called the **Manzana de las Luces** (Enlightenment Block – Moreno, Alsina, Perú and Bolívar). Also in this block are the **Colegio Nacional de Buenos Aires** ⓘ *Bolívar 263, T011-4331 0734, www.cnba.uba.ar*, formerly the site of the Jesuits' Colegio Máximo, the Procuraduría de las Misiones (today the Mercado de las Luces, a crafts market) and 18th-century **tunnels** ⓘ *T011-4343 3260, www.manzanadelasluces.gov.ar, guided tours from Perú 272, Mon-Fri 1500, Sat and Sun 1500, 1630, 1800 in Spanish (in English by prior arrangement), arrive 15 mins before tour, US$3.25; the tours explore the tunnels and visit the buildings on C Perú*. For centuries the whole block was the centre of intellectual activity, though little remains today but a small **cultural centre** with art courses, concerts, plays and film shows. The **Museo de la Ciudad** ⓘ *Alsina 412, T011-4343 2123, daily 1100-1900, US$0.30, free on Mon and Wed*, has a permanent exhibition covering social history and popular culture, as well as special exhibitions on daily life in Buenos Aires which are changed every two months and a reference library open to the public.

Santo Domingo ⓘ *Defensa y Belgrano, T011-4331 1668, Mon-Fri 0700-1800, Sat afternoon only, Sun 1000-1300*, was founded in 1751. During the British attack on Buenos Aires in 1806 some of Whitelocke's soldiers took refuge in the church. The local forces bombarded it, the British capitulated and their regimental colours were preserved in the church. General Belgrano is buried here. The church holds occasional concerts.

Museo Etnográfico JB Ambrosetti ⓘ *Moreno 350, T011-4345 8196, see Facebook, Tue-Fri 1300-1900, Sat-Sun 1500-1900 (closed Jan), US$2, guided visits Sat-Sun 1600*, displays anthropological and ethnographic collections from Patagonian and Argentina's northwest cultures (the latter a rich collection displayed on the first floor); there's also a small international room with a magnificent Japanese Buddhist altar.

☆San Telmo

One of the few places which still has late colonial and Rosista buildings (mostly renovated in the 20th century) is the barrio of San Telmo, south of Plaza de Mayo. It's an atmospheric place, with lots of cafés, antique shops and little art galleries. On Sundays, it has a great atmosphere, with an antiques market at the Plaza Dorrego (see page 70), free tango shows (1000-1800) and live music. **Museo de Arte Moderno de Buenos Aires (MAMBA)** ⓘ *Av San Juan 350, T011-4361 6919, www.buenosaires.gob.ar/museoartemoderno, Tue-Fri 1100-1900, Sat, Sun and holidays 1100-2000, US$1.30, Tue free*, has temporary art exhibitions from local and foreign artists. Next door is **Museo de Arte Contemporáneo de Buenos Aires (MACBA)** ⓘ *T011-5299 2010, www.macba.com.ar, Mon-Fri 1100-1900 (closed Tue), Sat, Sun 1100-1930, US$4 (Wed US$2.60)*, focusing on geometric abstraction.

La Boca

East of the Plaza de Mayo, behind the Casa Rosada, Paseo Colón runs south towards San Telmo and then, as Avenida Almirante Brown, continues to the old port district of La Boca, where the Riachuelo flows into the Plata. The much-photographed, brightly painted tin and wooden houses cover one block of the pedestrianized Caminito. La Boca is the poorest and roughest area within central Buenos Aires, so tourists are usually limited to this little street running from the Plaza La Vuelta de Rocha. You can also visit **Fundación Proa** ⓘ *Av Pedro de Mendoza 1929, T011-4104 1000, www.proa.org, Tue-Sun 1100-1800*, for varied art exhibitions, cultural events and for its café-restaurant with a view, the Usina del Arte ⓘ *A Caffarena 1 y Av Pedro de Mendoza, T011-4909 2076, www.buenosaires.gob.ar/usinadelarte*, with temporary art exhibitions, plays, live music, film shows in an impressive 1910s converted power station which also offers guided visits, and the **Museo de Bellas Artes Benito Quinquela Martín** ① *Av Pedro de Mendoza 1835, T011-4301 1080, www.buenosaires.gob.ar/museoquinquelamartin, Tue-Fri 1000-1800, Sat, Sun and holidays 1100-1800, US$2,* with over 1000 works by Argentine artists, particularly Benito Quinquela Martín (1890-1977), who painted La Boca port life. Sculptures and figureheads rescued from ships are also on display. La Boca is very rowdy when the Boca Juniors football club is playing at home. At Boca Juniors stadium is **Museo de la Pasión Boquense** ① *Brandsen 805, T011-4362 1100, www.museoboquense.com, daily 1000-1800, US$9, guided tour of the stadium in Spanish or English, 1000-1800, plus ticket to the museum, US$12.*

Puerto Madero

The Puerto Madero dock area has been renovated and is an attractive place for a stroll; the 19th-century warehouses now house restaurants and bars, making it a popular nightspot. **Fragata Presidente Sarmiento** ① *dock 3, Av Alicia Moreau de Justo 980, Puerto Madero, T011-4334 9386,* was a naval training ship until 1961 and is now a museum. Nearby is the **Corbeta Uruguay** ① *dock 4, T011-4314 1090, for both ships see www.ara.mil.ar, daily 1000-1900, entry by donation,* the ship that rescued Otto Nordenskjold's Antarctic expedition in 1903. Also in dock 4

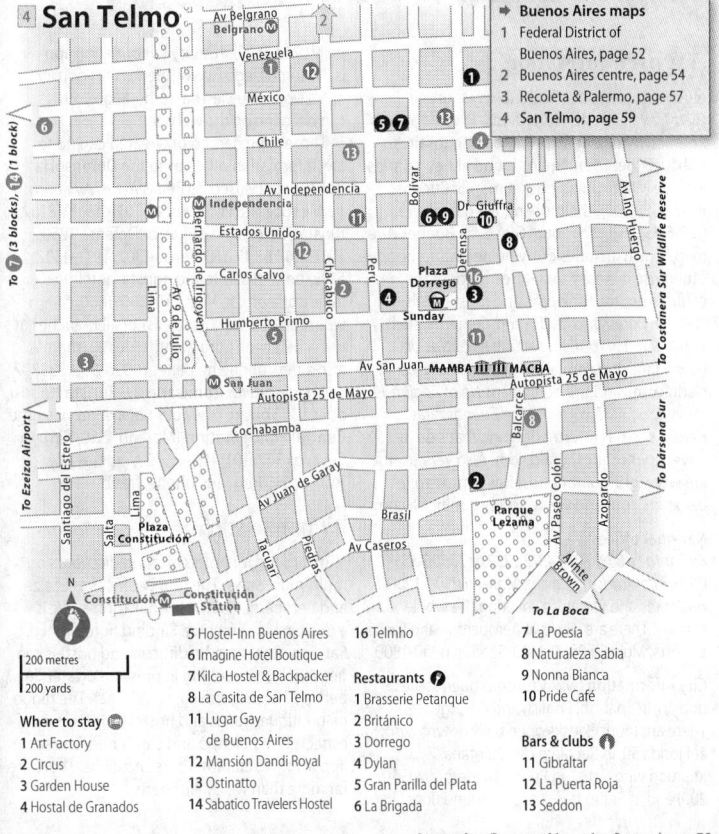

▣ 4 San Telmo

➡ **Buenos Aires maps**
1 Federal District of Buenos Aires, page 52
2 Buenos Aires centre, page 54
3 Recoleta & Palermo, page 57
4 San Telmo, page 59

200 metres
200 yards

Where to stay ▣
1 Art Factory
2 Circus
3 Garden House
4 Hostal de Granados
5 Hostel-Inn Buenos Aires
6 Imagine Hotel Boutique
7 Kilca Hostel & Backpacker
8 La Casita de San Telmo
11 Lugar Gay de Buenos Aires
12 Mansión Dandi Royal
13 Ostinatto
14 Sabatico Travelers Hostel
16 Telmho

Restaurants ❼
1 Brasserie Petanque
2 Británico
3 Dorrego
4 Dylan
5 Gran Parilla del Plata
6 La Brigada
7 La Poesía
8 Naturaleza Sabia
9 Nonna Bianca
10 Pride Café

Bars & clubs ❶
11 Gibraltar
12 La Puerta Roja
13 Seddon

is **Colección Fortabat** ① *Olga Cossettini 141, T011-4310 6600, www.coleccionfortabat.org.ar, Tue-Sun 1200-2000, US$4.50*, which houses a great art collection.

Costanera Sur

East of San Telmo on the far side of the docks, the Avenida Costanera runs as a long, spacious boulevard. A stretch of marshland reclaimed from the river forms the interesting **Costanera Sur Wildlife Reserve** ① *entrances at Av Tristán Achával Rodríguez 1550 (take Estados Unidos east from San Telmo) or next to the Buquebús ferry terminal (take Av Córdoba east), T0800-444 5343; for pedestrians and bikers only, Tue-Sun 0800-1800 (in summer, closes at 1900), free, take colectivos 4, 130 or 152*, where over 150 species of birds have been spotted over the past few years. There are free guided tours at weekends and holidays 0930, 1600 (1030, 1530 in winter), from the administration next to the southern entrance, but much can be seen from the road before then (binoculars useful). There are also free nocturnal visits every month on the Friday closest to the full moon (book Monday before, visitasguiadas_recs@buenosaires.gob.ar). It's half an hour's walk from the entrance to the river shore and about three hours to walk the whole perimeter. In summer it's very hot with little shade. For details (particularly birdwatching) contact **Aves Argentinas/AOP** (see page 71), or see www.reservacostanera.com.ar (English version).

Listings Buenos Aires *maps pages 52, 54, 57 and 59.*

Tourist information

A good guide to bus and subway routes is *Guía T*, available at newsstands. There is also an interactive map at http://mapa.buenosaires. gob.ar. Other useful maps found at newsstands include Mapa-Guía's pocket map of Buenos Aires (US$3.50), the more detailed city map (US$6.75) and the robust GBA Gran Buenos Aires map, which includes outlying neighbourhoods; otherwise it is easy to get free maps of the centre from tourist kiosks and most hotels. The daily press has useful supplements, such as the Sunday tourism section in *La Nación* (www.lanacion.com.ar), *Sí* in *Clarín* (www.si. clarin.com), and the equivalent *No* of *Página 12* (www.pagina12.com.ar). The *Buenos Aires Herald* also has information on what's on at www.buenosairesherald.com. Also very useful are www.gringoinbuenosaires.com, http:// baexpats.com and www.goodmorningba.com.

National office

Av Santa Fe 883, T011-4312 2232 or T0800-555 0016, info@turismo.gov.ar. Mon-Fri 0900-1900. Has maps and literature covering the whole country. There are kiosks at Aeroparque and Ezeiza airports, Mon-Fri 0900-1700, Sat-Sun 0900-1800.

City information (www.turismo.buenosaires. gob.ar), in Spanish, English and Portuguese. There are tourist kiosks open daily downtown at Florida 50, in Recoleta (Av Quintana 596, junction with Ortiz), in Puerto Madero (JM Gorriti 200) and at Retiro bus station (ground floor,

daily 0730-1630). The city's information app is BA Cómo Llego (www.buenosaires.gob.ar/ aplicacionesmoviles/ba-como-llego); others can be found on the website

Those overcharged or cheated can go to any information office or to the **Defensoría del Turista** (Museo de Bellas Artes, Av Pedro de Mendoza 1835 (La Boca), T011-4302 7816, turista@defensoria.org.ar, or Defensa 1250, T011-2017 6845 or Defensa 1302, T011-4307 5102, both in San Telmo, turistasantelmo@ defensoria.org.ar, Mon-Fri 1000-1800, weekends 1100-1800; full list of all branches at www.defensoria.org.ar/subsedes1/); there is also a free-phone helpline: T0800-999-283887. See page 246 for **Comisaría del Turista** (tourist police). If you are the victim of a crime, visit the **Central Police Station** (Moreno 1550, Virrey Cevallos 362, T011-4346 5700; emergency, T101 or 911 from any phone, free).

Where to stay

Shop around for hotels offering discounts on multi-night stays. The tourist offices at Ezeiza and Aeroparque airports book rooms. A/c is a must in high summer. Finding hotels for Fri, Sat, Sun nights can be difficult and hostels can get very busy, resulting in pressure on staff. A bed in a hostel dorm costs US$11-21. The range of 'boutique' hotels and hostels is impressive, especially in Palermo and San Telmo. The same applies to restaurants, bars and clubs. There are far more than we can list here.

There are fine examples of the **Four Seasons** (www.fourseasons.com/buenosaires), **Hilton** (www.hilton.com), **Hyatt** (www.buenosaires. park.hyatt.com), **Marriott** (www.marriott.com), **NH** (www.nh-hoteles.com), **Pestana** (www. pestana.com), **Sofitel** (www.sofitel.com) and **Unique Hotels** (www.uniquehotels.com.ar) chains. Hotels will store luggage, and most have English-speaking staff.

Centre

$$$$ Casa Calma
Suipacha 1015, T011-4312 5000,
www.casacalmahotel.com.
A relaxing haven in a downtown setting, homely yet luxurious, with a wellness centre and honesty bar.

$$$$ Faena
Martha Salotti 445 (Puerto Madero),
T011-4010 9000, www.faena.com.
Set in a 100-year-old silo, renovated by Philippe Starck, this is not for all budgets or tastes. Eclectic decoration, staff trained to be perfect.

$$$$-$$$ Castelar
Av de Mayo 1152, T011-4383 5000,
www.castelarhotel.com.ar.
A wonderfully elegant 1920s hotel which retains all the original features in the grand entrance and bar. Cosy bedrooms, charming staff, and excellent value. Also a spa with Turkish baths and massage. Highly recommended.

$$$$-$$$ Dolmen
Suipacha 1079, T011-4315 7117,
www.hoteldolmen.com.
Good location, smart spacious entrance lobby, with a calm relaxing atmosphere, good professional service, modern, comfortable well-designed rooms, small pool.

$$$$-$$$ El Conquistador
Suipacha 948, T011-4328 3012,
www.elconquistador.com.ar.
Stylish 1970s hotel, which retains the wood and chrome foyer, but has bright modern rooms, and a lovely light restaurant on the 10th floor with great views. Well situated, good value.

$$$$-$$$ Panamericano
Carlos Pellegrini 551, T011-4348 5000,
www.panamericano.us.
Very smart and modern hotel, with luxurious and tasteful rooms, covered rooftop pool, and superb restaurant, *Tomo 1*. Excellent service too. Also has properties in Bariloche

(www.panamericanobariloche.com) and El Calafate (www.casalossauces.com).

$$$ Bisonte Palace
MT de Alvear 902, T011-4390 7830,
www.bisontepalace.com.
Charming, with calm entrance foyer, which remains gracious thanks to courteous staff. Plain but spacious rooms, ample breakfast, good location. Very good value.

$$$ Colón
Carlos Pellegrini 507, T011-4320 3500,
www.exehotelcolon.com.
Splendid location overlooking Av 9 de Julio and Teatro Colón, extremely good value. Charming bedrooms, comfortable, gym, great breakfasts, and perfect service. Highly recommended.

$$$ Dorá
Maipú 963, T011-4312 7391, www.dorahotel.com.ar.
Charming and old-fashioned with comfortable rooms, good service, attractive lounge with paintings. Warmly recommended.

$$$ Goya
Suipacha 748, T011-4322 9269,
www.goyahotel.com.ar.
Welcoming and central, worth paying more for superior rooms, though all are comfortable. Good breakfast, English spoken.

$$$ Hispano
Av de Mayo 861, T011-4345 2020,
www.hhispano.com.ar.
Plain but comfortable rooms in this hotel which has been welcoming travellers since the 1950s, courtyard and small garden, central.

$$$ Marbella
Av de Mayo 1261, T011-4383 3573,
www.hotelmarbella.com.ar.
Modernized, and central, though quiet, multilingual. Recommended.

$$$ Moreno
Moreno 376, T011-4831 6831,
www.morenobuenosaires.com.
150 m from the Plaza de Mayo, decorated in dark, rich tones, large rooms, good value, jacuzzi, gym and chic bar, winery and restaurant.

$$$ Waldorf
Paraguay 450, T011-4312 2071,
www.waldorf-hotel.com.ar.
Welcoming staff and a comfortable mixture of traditional and modern in this centrally located hotel. Good value, with a buffet breakfast, English spoken. Recommended.

$ La Argentina
Av de Mayo 860, T011-4342 0078.
Cheap, central and rickety, but it stands the
test of time. Amazing old building, bringing
new meaning to the term 'high-ceilinged';
can be noisy if your room is near the 'slam-the-
door-shut' elevator. Good, cheap and cheerful
restaurant attached, doing very affordable *menú
del día*. Recommended.

Youth hostels

$ pp 06 Central
*Maipú 306, T011-5219 0052,
www.06centralhostel.com.*
A few metres from the Obelisco and
Av Corrientes, simple, spacious dorms, nicely
decorated doubles ($$), cosy communal area.

$ pp BA Stop
*Rivadavia 1194, T011-6091 2156,
www.bastop.com.*
In a lovely converted 1900s corner block, dorms
for 4-8 people, 11 private rooms ($$ double),
TV, table tennis, English spoken, safe, very
helpful staff can organize tours, Spanish classes.
Repeatedly recommended; the best hostel in
the centre.

$ pp Hostel Suites Obelisco
*Av Corrientes 830, T011-4328 4040,
www.hostelsuites.com.*
Elegant hostel built in a completely restored
old building in the heart of the city. Dorms,
doubles and private apartments ($$), DVD room,
laundry service. Free transfer from Ezeiza airport.

$ pp Limehouse Hostel
Lima 11, T011-4383 4561, www.limehouse.com.ar.
Dorms for up to 12 and doubles with and without
bath ($$), popular, typical city hostel with bar,
roof terrace, 'chilled', great if you like the party
atmosphere, efficient staff. Recommended.

$ pp Milhouse Hostel
*Hipólito Yrigoyen 959, T011-4345 9604,
www.milhousehostel.com.*
In 1890 house, lovely rooms ($$$ in double) and
dorms, comfortable, laundry, tango lessons, very
popular so reconfirm bookings at all times.

$ pp Portal del Sur
*Hipólito Yrigoyen 855, T011-4342 8788,
www.portaldelsurba.com.ar.*
Nice dorms and especially lovely doubles ($$)
and singles in a converted 19th-century building.
Recommended for single travellers.

$ pp V&S
*Viamonte 887, T011-4322 0994,
www.hostelclub.com.*
Central popular hostel ($$ in attractive double
room, bath), café, tango classes, tours, warm
atmosphere, welcoming. Recommended.

Palermo

$$$$ Alvear Palace
*Av Alvear 1891, T011-4808 2100,
www.alvearpalace.com.*
The height of elegance, an impeccably
preserved 1920s Recoleta palace, sumptuous
marble foyer, with Louis XV-style chairs, and a
charming orangery where you can take tea with
superb patisseries. Antique-filled bedrooms.
Recommended.

$$$$ Legado Mítico
*Gurruchaga 1848, T011-4833 1300,
www.legadomitico.com.*
Stylish small hotel with 11 rooms named after
Argentine cultural legends. They use local designs
and products. Luxurious and recommended.

$$$$ Magnolia
*Julián Alvarez 1746, T011-4867 4900,
www.magnoliahotelboutique.com.*
Lovely boutique hotel in a quiet area. This
refurbished early 20th-century house has
attractively designed rooms opening onto
the street or to inner courtyards and a perfect
retreat on its rooftop terrace.

$$$$ Querido
*Juan Ramírez de Velazco 934, T011-4854 6297,
www.queridobuenosaires.com.*
Purpose-built, designed and cared for by a
Brazilian-English couple. 7 rooms, 4 of which
have balconies, for a comfortable stay in Villa
Crespo area, a few blocks from Palermo Soho
and from the subway.

$$$$-$$$ Bo Bo
*Guatemala 4882, T011-4774 0505,
www.bobohotel.com.*
On a leafy street, 15 rooms decorated in
contemporary style, some with private
balconies, excellent restaurant.

$$$$-$$$ Krista
*Bonpland 1665, T011-4771 4697,
www.kristahotel.com.ar.*
Intimate, hidden behind the plain façade of an
elegant townhouse, well placed for restaurants.
Good value, comfortable, individually designed
spacious rooms, wheelchair access.

$$$ A Hotel
Azcuénaga 1268, T011-4821 6248,
www.ahotel.com.ar.
Charming boutique hotel on a quiet residential
street, only a few blocks from Recoleta or
Av Santa Fe, simply but warmly decorated, good
service, solarium, compact standard rooms.

$$$ Solar Soler
Soler 5676, T011-4776 7494,
www.solarsoler.com.ar.
Welcoming B&B in Palermo Hollywood, excellent
service. Recommended.

Youth hostels

$ pp Back in BA
El Salvador 5115, T011-4774 2859,
www.backinba.com.
Small hostel with dorms for up to 6 and private
rooms ($$), lockers with charging points, patio,
bar, information, tours and classes can be
arranged, good Palermo Soho location.

$ pp Hostel Suites Palermo
Charcas 4752, T011-4773 0806,
www.suitespalermo.com.
A beautiful century-old residence with the
original grandeur partially preserved and a quiet
atmosphere. Comfortable renovated dorms and
private rooms with bath ($$ doubles), good service,
small travel agency, free internet, Wi-Fi, cooking
and laundry facilities, DVD room and breakfast
included. Free transfer from Ezeiza airport.

$ Play Hostel
Guatemala 3646, T011-4832 4257,
www.playhostel.com.
Popular option with dorms for 4-10 people.
Wi-Fi, laundry service, bike hire, tourist info
and tango classes.

San Telmo and around

$$$$ Mansión Dandi Royal
Piedras 922, T011-4361 3537,
www.hotelmansiondandiroyal.com.
A wonderfully restored 1903 residence,
small upmarket hotel with an elegant tango
atmosphere, small pool, good value. Daily
tango lessons and *milonga* every Fri at 2130.

$$$$-$$$ Imagine Hotel Boutique
México 1330, T011-4383 2230,
www.imaginehotelboutique.com.
9 suites in a beautifully restored 1820s house,
each room individually designed, quiet, buffet
breakfast, parking. Recommended.

$$$ La Casita de San Telmo
Cochabamba 286, T011-4307 5073,
www.lacasitadesantelmo.com.
7 rooms in restored 1840s house, most
open onto a garden with a beautiful fig
tree, owners are tango fans; rooms rented
by day, week or month.

$$$ Lugar Gay de Buenos Aires
Defensa 1120 (no sign), T011-4300 4747,
www.lugargay.com.ar.
A men-only gay B&B with 8 comfortable
rooms, video room, jacuzzi, a stone's throw
from Plaza Dorrego.

$$$ Telmho
Defensa 1086, T011-4116 5467,
www.telmho-hotel.com.ar.
Smart rooms overlooking Plaza Dorrego, huge
beds, modern bathrooms, lovely roof garden,
helpful staff.

Youth hostels

$ pp Art Factory
Piedras 545, T011-4343 1463,
www.artfactoryba.com.ar.
Large, early 1900s house converted into a hostel,
informal atmosphere with individually designed
and brightly painted private rooms (some with
bath, $$), dorms, halfway between the centre
and San Telmo.

$ pp Circus
Chacabuco 1020, T011-4300 4983,
www.hostelcircus.com.
Stylish rooms for 2 ($$) to 4 people, tastefully
renovated building, small heated swimming pool,
bar and restaurant.

$ pp Garden House
Av San Juan 1271, T011-4304 1824,
www.gardenhouseba.com.ar.
Small, welcoming independent hostel for
those who don't want a party atmosphere;
good barbecues on the terrace. Dorms and
some doubles ($$). Recommended.

$ pp Hostal de Granados
Chile 374, T011-4362 5600,
www.hostaldegranados.com.ar.
Small, light, well-equipped rooms in an
interesting building on a popular street,
rooms for 2 ($$), dorms for 4 to 8, laundry.

$ pp Hostel-Inn Buenos Aires
Humberto Primo 820, T011-4300 7992,
www.hibuenosaires.com.

An old 2-storey mansion with dorms for up to 8 people and also private rooms (**$$**), activities, loud parties, individual lockers in every room. HI discount.

$ pp Kilca Hostel & Backpacker
México 1545, between Sáenz Peña and Virrey Cevallos, T011-4381 1166, www.kilcabackpacker.com.
In a restored 19th-century house with attractive landscaped patios. A variety of rooms from dorms to doubles; all bathrooms shared, but 1 double with bath (**$$**).Offers a host of guest services including bike rental, pub crawl, tango classes, Spanish lessons, football tickets and more.

$ pp Ostinatto
Chile 680, T011-4362 9639, www.ostinatto.com.
Minimalist contemporary design in a 1920s building, promotes the arts, music, piano bar, movie room, tango lessons, arranges events, rooftop terrace. Shared rooms, also has double rooms with and without bath (**$$**), and apartments for rent.

$ pp Sabatico Travelers Hostel
México 1410, T011-4381 1138, www.sabaticohostel.com.ar.
Hostel in a good location, with dorms and double rooms with and without bath (**$$**). It offers a full range of services and information, a rooftop barbecue, mini pool and bar.

Apartments/self catering/homestays

ArgenHomes
T011-4044 5978, www.argenhomes.com.
For those who like attentive, personalized service, this is the best apartment-rental option. A limited selection of charming flats in San Telmo, Recoleta, Belgrano, Palermo and even Tigre. Accepts dollars, euros, pounds and pesos; no credit cards.

B&T Argentina
T011-4876 5000, www.bytargentina.com.
Accommodation in student residences and host families; also furnished flats. Reputable.

Bahouse
T011-5811 3832, www.bahouse.com.ar.
Very good flats, by the week or month, all furnished and well-located in San Telmo, Retiro, Recoleta, Belgrano, Palermo and the centre.

Casa 34
Nicaragua 6045, T011-4775 0207, www.casa34.com.
Helpful, with a big range.

Restaurants

Eating out in Buenos Aires is one of the city's great pleasures, with a huge variety of restaurants from the chic to the cheap. To try some of Argentina's excellent steak, choose from one of the many *parrillas*, where your huge slab of lean meat will be expertly cooked over a wood fire. If in doubt about where to eat, head for Puerto Madero, the revamped docks area, an attractive place to stroll along the waterfront before dinner. There are good places here, generally in stylish interiors, serving international as well as local cuisine, with good service if a little overpriced. Less expensive yet just as delicious and longer-standing *parrillas* can be found in San Telmo. Take a radio taxi to Palermo or Las Cañitas for a wide range of excellent restaurants all within strolling distance. For more information on the gastronomy of Buenos Aires see: www.guiaoleo.com.ar, restaurant guide in Spanish.

There is a growing interest in less conventional eating out, from secret, or *puerta cerrada*, restaurants, to local eateries off the normal restaurant circuit, exploring local markets and so on. Food-oriented blogs in English are: www.saltshaker.net, chef Dan Perlman who also runs a highly recommended private restaurant in his house, see website for details; www.buenosairesfoodies.com; and http://pickupthefork.com, whose scope is wider than just Buenos Aires. Another highly regarded closed door option can be found at **The Argentine Experience**, http://theargentineexperience.com, while tours are run by **Parrilla Tour Buenos Aires**, http://parrillatour.com/.

Some restaurants are *tenedor libre*: eat as much as you like for a fixed price. Most cafés serve tea or coffee plus *facturas*, or pastries, for breakfast.

Centre

$$$ Dadá
San Martín 941.
A restaurant and bar with eclectic decoration. Good for gourmet lunches.

$$$ Sorrento
Av Corrientes 668 (just off Florida), www.sorrentorestaurant.com.ar.
Intimate, elegant atmosphere, one of the most traditional places in the centre for very good pastas and seafood.

$$$ Tancat
Paraguay 645, www.tancatrestaurante.com.
Delicious Spanish food, very popular
at lunchtime.

$$$-$$ Gijón
Chile y San José.
Very good value *parrilla* at this popular *bodegón*,
south of Congreso district.

$$ Fikä
Hipólito Yrigoyen 782. See Facebook.
Mon-Fri till 1700.
Popular at lunchtime with a varied menu, is also
attractive for a coffee break or a drink.

$$ Gianni´s
Reconquista 1028, www.giannisonline.com.ar.
Open till 1700.
The set menu with the meal-of-the-day
makes an ideal lunch. Good risottos and
salads. Slow service.

$$ Güerrín
Av Corrientes 1368, www.pizzeriaguerrin.com.
A Buenos Aires institution. Serves filling pizza
and *faina* (chick pea polenta) which you eat
standing up at a bar, or at tables, though you
miss out on the colourful local life that way.
For an extra service fee, upstairs room is less
crowded or noisy.

$$ Las Cuartetas
Av Corrientes 838, www.lascuartetas.com.
A local institution open early to very late for
fantastic pizza, can be busy and noisy as it's
so popular.

$$ Los Inmortales
Corrientes 1369, www.losinmortales.com.
Opposite **Güerrín**, this does some of the city's
other best pizza (with a thinner crust). It's also
a *parrilla*.

$$ Sam Bucherie
25 de Mayo 562. Open till 1800.
The most imaginative sandwiches and
salads downtown.

Cafés

Café Tortoni
Av de Mayo 825-9.
This most famous Buenos Aires café has been
the elegant haunt of artists and writers for over
100 years, with marble columns, stained-glass
ceilings, old leather chairs, and photographs of its
famous clientele on the walls. Live tango. Packed
with tourists, pricey, but still worth a visit.

El Gato Negro
Av Corrientes 1669, see Facebook.
A beautiful tearoom, serving a choice of coffees
and teas, and good cakes. Delightfully scented
from the wide range of spices on sale.

Florida Garden
Florida y Paraguay, www.floridagarden.com.ar.
Another well-known café, popular for lunch,
and tea.

Ice cream
The Italian ice cream tradition has been marked
for decades by *heladerías* such as **Cadore**
(Av Corrientes 1695, www.heladeriacadore.
com.ar), or **El Vesuvio** (Av Corrientes 1181),
the oldest of all.

North of Plaza de Mayo
3 blocks west of Plaza San Martín, under the
flyover at the northern end of Av 9 de Julio,
between Arroyo and Av del Libertador in La
Recova, are several recommended restaurants.

$$$ BASA
Basavilbaso 1328, www.basabar.com.ar.
Great food and smart cocktails in ultra-chic
surroundings. Same owners as other upscale
hangout **Gran Bar Danzón**, see Bars and clubs,
page 67.

$$$ El Mirasol de la Recova
Posadas 1032, elmirasol.com.ar.
Serves top-quality *parrilla* in an elegant atmosphere.

$$$ Juana M
Carlos Pellegrini 1535 (downstairs),
www.juanam.com.
Excellent choice, popular with locals for its good
range of dishes, and its very good salad bar.

Recoleta

$$$ Rodi Bar
Vicente López 1900.
Excellent *bife* and other dishes in this typical
bodegón, welcoming and unpretentious.

$$$-$$ La Madeleine
Av Santa Fe 1726.
Bright and cheerful choice, quite good pastas.

$$$-$$ María de Bambi
Ayacucho 1821 (with a small branch at
Arenales 920). Open till 2200 (2300 Fri
and Sat), closed on Sun.
This small, quiet place is probably the best value
in the area, serving very good and simple meals,
also *salón de té* and patisserie.

$$ Al paso y algo más
Juncal 2684, www.alpasoyalgomas.com.
Recommended choice for *choripán* and *churrasquito* sandwiches plus other meat dishes.

Tea rooms, café-bars

Bröet
Azcuénaga 1144, see Facebook.
Austrian-owned artisanal bakery with traditionally made bread from around the world.

Clásica y Moderna
Av Callao 892, T4812 8707, www.clasicaymoderna.com.
One of the city's most welcoming cafés, with a bookshop, great atmosphere, good breakfast through to drinks at night, daily live music and varied shows.

Como en casa
Av Quintana 2, Riobamba 1239, Laprida 1782 and at Céspedes 2647 (Belgrano), www.tortascomoencasa.com.
Very popular in the afternoon for its varied and delicious cakes and fruit pies.

Ice cream

Arkakao
Av Quintana 188, www.arkakao.com.ar.
Great ice creams at this elegant tea room.

Freddo, and **Un'Altra Volta**, both with several branches in the city.

Palermo

This area of Buenos Aires is very popular, with many chic restaurants and bars in Palermo Viejo (referred to as 'Palermo Soho' for the area next to Plaza Cortázar and 'Palermo Hollywood' for the area beyond the railways and Av Juan B Justo) and the Las Cañitas district. It's a sprawling district, so you could take a taxi to one of these restaurants, and walk around before deciding where to eat. It's also a great place to stop for lunch, with cobbled streets, and 1900s buildings, now housing chic clothes shops. Las Cañitas is fashionable, with a wide range of interesting restaurants mostly along Báez:

$$$ Bio
Humboldt 2192, T011-4774 3880, www.biorestaurant.com.ar. Daily.
Delicious gourmet organic food, on a sunny corner.

$$$ Campobravo
Báez y Arévalo and Honduras y Fitz Roy, www.campobravo.com.ar.
Stylish, minimalist, superb steaks and vegetables on the *parrilla*. Popular and recommended, can be noisy.

$$$ Don Julio
Guatemala 4691, www.parrilladonjulio.com.ar.
Regarded, along with **La Brigada** in San Telmo, as one of the best *parrillas* in the city. The *entraña* (skirt steak) has a sterling reputation.

$$$ El Manto
Costa Rica 5801, T011-4774 2409, www.elmanto.com.
Genuine Armenian dishes, relaxed, good for a quiet evening.

$$$ El Preferido de Palermo
Borges y Guatemala, T011-4774 6585.
Very popular *bodegón* serving both Argentine and Spanish-style dishes.

$$$ Janio
Malabia 1805, T011-4833 6540. Open for breakfast through to the early hours.
One of Palermo's first restaurants, sophisticated Argentine cuisine in the evening.

$$$ Morelia
Baez 260 and Humboldt 2005, http://morelia.com.ar.
Cooks superb pizzas on the *parrilla*, and has a lovely roof terrace for summer.

$$$ Siamo nel forno
Costa Rica 5886, see Facebook.
Excellent true Italian pizzas, recommended tiramisu.

$$$ Social Paraíso
Honduras 5182, see Facebook. Closed Sun evening and Mon.
Simple delicious dishes in a relaxed chic atmosphere, with a lovely patio at the back. Good fish and tasty salads.

$$$-$$ El Tejano
Honduras 4416, T011-4833 3545, www.eltejanoba.com.ar.
A delight for those who like to compare and contrast traditional Argentine *asado* with authentic US barbecue. This small eatery showcases expat owner Larry's hot sauces and smoked meats, a model of Texas hospitality.

$$$-$$ La Fábrica del Taco
Gorriti 5062, www.lafabricadeltaco.com.
While not on par with the Real McCoy, it's
some of the most authentic Mexican food
in South America.

$$ Krishna
Malabia 1833, www.krishnaveggie.com.
A small, intimate place serving Indian-flavoured
vegetarian dishes.

Cafés and ice cream

Palermo has good cafés opposite the park on
Av del Libertador.

Persicco
Honduras 4900 and many other locations,
www.persicco.com.
The grandsons of **Freddo**'s founders also offer
excellent ice cream.

San Telmo

$$$ Brasserie Petanque
Defensa y Mexico, www.brasseriepetanque.com.
Very attractive, informal French restaurant
offering a varied menu with very good, creative
dishes. Excellent value for their set lunch menus.

$$$ Gran Parrilla del Plata
Chile 594, T011-4300 8858,
www.parrilladelplata.com.
Popular, good value *parrilla* on a historic corner.

$$$ La Brigada
Estados Unidos 465, T011-4361 5557,
www.parrillalabrigada.com.ar.
Excellent *parrilla*, serving Argentine cuisine and
wines. Very popular, expensive. Always reserve.

$$$-$$ Naturaleza Sabia
Balcarce 958, www.naturalezasabia.com.ar.
Tasty vegetarian and vegan dishes in an
attractive ambience.

Tea rooms, café-bars and ice cream

Británico
Brasil y Defensa 399. 24 hrs.
A historic place with a good atmosphere
at lunchtime.

Dorrego
Humberto Primo y Defensa.
Bar/café with great atmosphere, seating on plaza
outside, good for late-night coffee or drinks.

Dylan
Perú 1086, see Facebook.
Very good ice cream.

La Poesía
Chile y Bolívar, www.cafelapoesia.com.ar.
Ideal for a coffee break on the sunny sidewalk.

Nonna Bianca
Estados Unidos 425.
For ice cream in an internet café.

Pride Café
Balcarce y Giuffra, see Facebook.
Wonderful sandwiches, juices, salads and
brownies, with lots of magazines to read.

Puerto Madero

$$$ Cabaña Las Lilas
Av Moreau de Justo 516, T011-4313 1336,
www.restaurantlaslilas.com.ar.
A solid upscale *parrilla* with a good
reputation, pricey and popular with
foreigners and business people.

$$$ Le Grill
Av Moreau de Justo 876, T011-4331 0454,
www.legrill.com.ar/esp.
A gourmet touch at a sophisticated *parrilla* which
includes dry-aged beef, pork and lamb on its menu.

Bars and clubs

Generally it is not worth going to clubs before
0230 at weekends. Dress is usually smart. Entry
can be from US$10-15, sometimes including a
drink. A good way to visit some of the best bars
is to join a pub crawl, eg **The Buenos Aires Pub
Crawl**, www.buenosairespubcrawl.com, whose
daily crawls are a safe night out.

Bars

Buller Brewing Company
Roberto M Ortiz 1827, Recoleta, www.bullerpub.com.
Brew pub which also serves international food.

Chez Juanito
Cabrera 5083, Palermo Soho.
Drinks, snacks, pizzas, cheerful, popular, good for
a relaxed evening.

Gibraltar
Perú 895, www.thegibraltarbar.com.
An inauthentic British pub that somehow does
everything right. Popular San Telmo option and a
great place to shoot pool.

Gran Bar Danzón
Libertad 1161, www.granbardanzon.com.ar.
Original BA swank and a good dark ambience for
a cocktail and romance. Same owners as **BASA**
(see Restaurants, page 65).

La Puerta Roja
Chacabuco 733 (upstairs).
The 'Red Door' is San Telmo's best dive.

Milion
Paraná 1048.
In a beautifully restored mansion with unique (almost unsettling) art on the walls, supposedly once a favourite haunt of Borges' widow. Great bartenders, also serves tapas. Recommended Fri after midnight.

Mundo Bizarro
Serrano 1222, Palermo Viejo, see Facebook.
Famous for its weird films, cocktails, American-style food, electronic and pop music.

Seddon
Defensa y Chile, hbarseddon.blogspot.com.ar.
Traditional bar open till late with live music on Fri.

Sugar
Costa Rica 4619, Palermo Viejo,
www.sugarbuenosaires.com.
Welcoming bar with cheap beer and drinks, happy hour nightly, Thu is ladies' night, shows international sports.

The corner of Reconquista and Marcelo T de Alvear in Retiro is the centre of the small 'Irish' pub district, overcrowded on St Patrick's Day, 17 Mar. **Druid In** (Reconquista 1040, Centre), is by far the most attractive choice there, open for lunch and with live music weekly. **The Shamrock** (Rodríguez Peña 1220, in Recoleta, www.theshamrock.com.ar), is another Irish-run, popular bar, happy hour for ISIC holders.

Clubs

Bahrein
Lavalle 345, Centre, www.bahreinba.com.
Funky and electronic.

L'Arc
Niceto Vega 5452, Palermo Viejo.
Hosts The X Club weekly, with a cocktail bar and live bands.

Niceto Club
Niceto Vega 5510, Palermo, T011-4779 9396,
www.nicetoclub.com.
Early live shows and dancing afterwards, cheap and cheerful. Club 69 weekly parties for house, electronic, hip hop and funk music.

Gay clubs Most gay clubs charge from US$10 entry. **Amerika** (Gascón 1040, Almagro, www. ameri-k.com.ar. Fri-Sun, attracting over 2000 party-goers over 3 floors. **Bach Bar** (Cabrera 4390, www.bach-bar.com.ar). Friendly lesbian bar in Palermo Viejo, Fri-Sun. **Sitges** (Av Córdoba 4119, Palermo, T011-4861 3763, see Facebook, Thu-Sun). Gay and lesbian bar.

Jazz clubs **Notorious** (Av Callao 966, T011-4813 6888, www.notorious.com.ar). Live jazz at a music shop with bar and restaurant. **Thelonious** (Salguero 1884, T011-4829 1562, www.thelonious. com.ar). Live jazz and DJs. **Virasoro Bar** (Guatemala 4328, T011-4831 8918, www.virasorobar.com.ar). Live jazz in a 1920s art deco house.

Salsa clubs La Salsera (Yatay 961, Palermo Viejo, T011-4866 1829, www.lasalsera.com). Highly regarded.

Entertainment

For entertainments, see www.vuenosairez.com, or www.wipe.com.ar. At carnival time, look for the **Programa Carnaval Porteño** (it's on Facebook).

Cinemas
The selection of films is excellent, ranging from new Hollywood releases to Argentine and world cinema; details are listed daily in main newspapers. Films are shown uncensored and most foreign films (other than animated films) are subtitled. Tickets best booked early afternoon to ensure good seats (average price US$10, some chains offer discounts on Wed or with membership card).

Independent foreign and national films are shown during the **Festival de Cine Independiente** (BAFICI, http://festivales. buenosaires.gob.ar), held every Apr.

Cultural events
Centro Cultural Borges, *Galerías Pacífico, Viamonte y San Martín, p 1, T011-5555 5359, www.ccborges.org.ar.* Art exhibitions, concerts, film shows and ballet; some student discounts.
Ciudad Cultural Konex, *Sarmiento 3131 (Abasto), T011-4864 3200, www.ciudadculturalkonex.org.* A converted oil factory hosts this huge complex holding plays, live music shows, summer film projections under the stars, modern ballet, puppet theatre and, occasionally, massive parties.
Fototeca Latinoamericana, *Godoy Cruz 2626, Arcos (near Palermo metro station), http://fola. com.ar. Thu-Tue 1200-2000, US$4.50.* With a permanent collection of photography from the continent, plus temporary exhibitions.
Villa Ocampo, *Elortondo 1811, Beccar, Partido de San Isidro, T011-4732 4988, www.villaocampo.org.*

Former residence of writer and founder of Revista Sur Victoria Ocampo, now owned by UNESCO, in northern suburbs, Thu-Sun and holidays 1230-1800, US$3.25 entry, open for visits, courses, exhibitions and meals at its café/restaurant.

See also **Alliance Française**, www.alianzafrancesa.org.ar, **British Arts Centre**, www.britishartscentre.org.ar, **Goethe Institut**, www.goethe.de, and **Instituto Cultural Argentino Norteamericano**, www.icana.org.ar.

Tango shows

There are 2 ways to enjoy tango: you can watch the dancing at a tango show. Most pride themselves on very high standards and, although they are not cheap (show only US$50-90, show and dinner US$75-150), this is tango at its best. Most prices include drinks and hotel transfers. Or you can learn to dance at a class and try your steps at a *milonga* (tango club). The Tango page on www.turismo.buenosaires.gob.ar lists *tanguerías* for tango shows, classes and *milongas*.

See also the websites **www.tangocity.com** and **www.todotango.com**.

Every Aug there is a tango dancing competition, **Festival y Mundial de Baile**, open to both locals and foreigners.

Bar Sur, *Estados Unidos 299, T011-4362 6086, www.bar-sur.com.ar. Open 2000-0200.* Price with or without dinner. Good fun, public sometimes join the professional dancers.

El Querandí, *Perú 302, T011-5199 1770, www.querandi.com.ar. Daily shows, with or without dinner, also open for lunch.* Tango show restaurant, dating back to 1920s.

El Viejo Almacén, *Independencia y Balcarce, T011-4307 7388, www.viejoalmacen.com.ar. Daily, dinner from 2000, show 2200.* Impressive dancing and singing. Recommended.

Esquina Carlos Gardel, *Carlos Gardel 3200 y Anchorena, T011-4867 6363, www.esquinacarlos gardel.com.ar.* Opposite the former Mercado del Abasto, this is the most popular venue in Gardel's own neighbourhood; dinner at 2030, show at 2230. Recommended.

Esquina Homero Manzi, *Av San Juan 3601 (Subte Boedo), T011-4957 8488, www.esquinahomero manzi.com.ar.* Traditional show at 2200 with excellent musicians and dancers, dinner (2100) and show available, tango school. Recommended.

Piazzolla Tango, *Florida 165 (basement), Galería Güemes, T011-4344 8201, www.piazzollatango.com.* A beautifully restored belle époque hall hosts a smart tango show; dinner at 2045, show at 2215.

Milongas These are very popular with younger Porteños. You can take a class and get a feel for the music before the dancing starts a couple of hours later. Both tango and *milonga* (the music that contributed to the origins of tango and is more cheerful) are played. Cost is from US$8; even beginners are welcome.

Centro Cultural Torquato Tasso, *Defensa 1575, T011-4307 6506, www.torquatotasso.com.ar.* See web for programme and prices (daily lessons), English spoken.

La Viruta (at Centro Armenio), *Armenia 1366, Palermo Viejo, T011-4774 6357, www.lavirutatango.com.* Very popular, classes every day except Mon, entry US$7 (check website for times), also salsa and rock dancing classes, with restaurant.

Theatre

About 20 commercial theatres play all year and there are many amateur theatres. The main theatre street is Av Corrientes.

Complejo Teatral de Buenos Aires, *Corrientes 1530, T011-4371 0111/8, http://complejoteatral.gob.ar.* A group of 5 theatres with many cultural activities. Book seats for theatre, ballet and opera as early as possible. Tickets for most popular shows (including rock and pop concerts) are sold also through **Ticketek** (T011-5237 7200, www.ticketek.com.ar). See also www.alternativateatral.com and www.mundoteatral.com.ar. For live Argentine and Latin American bands, best venues are: **La Trastienda** (Balcarce 460, San Telmo, www.latrastienda.com), theatre/café with lots of live events, also serving meals and drinks from breakfast to dinner, great music; or **ND Teatro** (Paraguay 918, www.ndteatro.com.ar).

Shopping

The main, fashionable shopping streets are Florida and Santa Fe (from Av 9 de Julio to Av Pueyrredón). Palermo is the best area for chic boutiques and well-known international fashion labels; head for C Honduras and C El Salvador, between Malabia and Serrano. C Defensa in San Telmo is known for its antique shops. It also has a few craft stalls around C Alsina, Fri 1000-1700. **Pasaje de la Defensa**, Defensa 1179, is a beautifully restored 1880s house containing small shops.

Bookshops

Buenos Aires is renowned for its bookshops and was UNESCO's World Book Capital in 2011. Many shops are along Florida, Av Corrientes (from Av 9 de Julio to Callao) or Av Santa Fe, and in shopping malls. Second-hand and discount bookshops are mostly along Av Corrientes and Av de Mayo. Rare books are sold in several specialized stores in the Microcentro (the area enclosed by Suipacha, Esmeralda, Tucumán and Paraguay). The main chains of bookshops, usually selling a small selection of foreign books are: **Cúspide** (www.cuspide.com); **Distal** (www.distalnet.com); **Kel** (www.distalnet.com), imported books, mostly in English; and **Yenny-El Ateneo** (www.yenny-elateneo.com), whose biggest store is on Av Santa Fe 1860, in an old theatre; there is café where the stage used to be.

Eterna Cadencia, *Honduras 5574, T011-4774 4100, www.eternacadencia.com.* Has an excellent selection and a good café.

Walrus Books, *Estados Unidos 617, San Telmo, T011-4300 7135, www.walrus-books.com.ar.* Sells second-hand books in English, including Latin American authors, good children's section.

Handicrafts

In Dec there is a **Feria Internacional de Artesanías** (see Facebook).

Arte y Esperanza, *Balcarce 234 and Suipacha 892, www.arteyesperanza.com.ar.* Crafts made by indigenous communities, sold by a Fairtrade organization.

Artesanías Argentinas, *Montevideo 1386.* Aboriginal crafts and other traditional items sold by a Fairtrade organization.

El Boyero, *Florida 753 (Galerías Pacífico) and 953, T011-4312 3564, https://elboyero.com.* High-quality silver, leather, woodwork and other typical Argentine handicrafts.

Martín Fierro, *Santa Fe 992.* Good handicrafts, stonework, etc. Recommended.

Plata Nativa, *Galería del Sol, Florida 860, local 41, www.platanativa.com.* For Latin American folk handicrafts and high-quality jewellery.

Leather goods

Several shops are concentrated along Florida next to Plaza San Martín and also in Suipacha (900 block).

Aida, *Galería de la Flor, local 30, Florida 670.* Quality, inexpensive leather products, can make a leather jacket to measure in the same day.

Casa López, *MT de Alvear 640/658, www.casalopez.com.ar.* The most traditional and finest leather shop, expensive but worth it.

Dalla Fontana, *Reconquista 735, see Facebook.* Leather factory, fast, efficient and reasonably priced for made-to-measure clothes.

Galería del Caminante, *Florida 844.* Has a variety of good shops with leather goods, arts and crafts, souvenirs, etc.

Prüne, *Florida 963 and in many shopping centres, www.prune.com.ar.* Fashionable designs for women, many options in leather and not very expensive.

Markets and malls

Markets can be found in many of the city's parks and plazas, which hold weekend fairs. You will find they all sell pretty much the same sort of handicrafts. The following offer something different:

Feria de Mataderos, *Lisandro de la Torre y Av de los Corrales, T011-4342 9629, www.feriade mataderos.com.ar, subte E to end of line then taxi, or buses 36, 55, 63, 80, 92, 103, 117, 126, 141, 155, 180, 185. Sat from 1800 (Jan-Feb), Sun 1100-2000 (Mar-Dec).* Long way but few tourists, fair of Argentine handicrafts and traditions, music and dance festivals, gaucho horsemanship skills; nearby **Museo Criollo de los Corrales** (Av de los Corrales 6436, T011-4687 1949, Sun 1200-1830, US$0.10).

Mercado Andino, *José León Suárez entre Rivadavia e Ibarrola, Liniers (as far out as Feria de Mataderos, 20 mins by train from Once/ Plaza Miserere).* Mon-Sat 0800-2000. Huge market for Bolivian and Peruvian vegetables, spices, fruit and other products. Go early and take care of your belongings. If you go there, visit also the Carrefour supermarket at Av Juan B Justo y Alvarez Jonte to see Alfredo Segatori's 11 portraits on the wall (see http://buenosairesstreetart.com).

Mercado de las Luces, *Manzana de las Luces, Perú y Alsina. Mon-Fri 1030-1930, Sun 1400-1930.* Handicrafts, second-hand books, plastic arts.

Parque Centenario, *Av Díaz Vélez y L Marechal, see Facebook. Sat-Sun and holidays 1100-2000.* Local crafts, cheap handmade clothes, used items of all sorts.

Parque Rivadavia, *Av Rivadavia 4900, see Facebook. Daily 1100-2000.* Second-hand books, stamps, coins, records, tapes, CDs and magazines.

Plaza Dorrego, *San Telmo, www.feriadesantelmo. com. Sun 1000-1700.* For souvenirs, antiques, etc, with free tango performances and live music, wonderfully atmospheric, and an array of 'antiques'.

Plaza Italia, *Santa Fe y Uriarte (Palermo). Sat-Sun 1200-2030.* Second-hand textbooks and magazines (daily), handicrafts market.

The city has many fine shopping malls, including **Alto Palermo** (Santa Fe 3253, www.altopalermo.com.ar, Subte line D at Bulnes), the most popular and fashionable mall in the city. There's also **Abasto de Buenos Aires** (Av Corrientes 3247, www.abasto-shopping.com.ar, nearest Subte: Carlos Gardel, line B), in the city's impressive, art deco former fruit and vegetable market building, and **Patio Bullrich** (Av del Libertador 750 and Posadas 1245, www.shoppingbullrich.com.ar, nearest Subte: 8 blocks from Plaza San Martín, line C).

What to do

Birdwatching
Aves Argentinas/AOP, *Matheu 1246, T011-4943 7216, www.avesargentinas.org.ar.* For information on birdwatching and specialist tours. Also has a good library Mon-Fri 1030-1330 and 1430-2030 (closed Jan). A BirdLife International partner.

Cricket
Asociación Argentina de Cricket, *Juan María Gutiérrez 3829, T011-3974 9593, www.cricket argentina.com, for information.* Cricket is played Sep-Apr.

Cycle hire and tours
La Bicicleta Naranja, *Pasaje Giuffra 308, San Telmo and Nicaragua 4825, Palermo, T011-4362 1104, www.labicicletanaranja.com.ar.* Bike hire and tours to all parts of the city, 3-4 hrs.
Lan&Kramer Bike Tours, *San Martín 910 p 6, T011-4311 5199, www.biketours.com.ar.* Daily at 0930 and 1400 next to the monument of San Martín (Plaza San Martín), 3½- to 4-hr cycle tours to the south or the north of the city; also to San Isidro and Tigre, 4½-5 hrs and full day tours, plus summer evening tours downtown; also, bike rental.
Urban biking, *Esmeralda 1084, T011-4314 2325, www.urbanbiking.com.* 4½-hr tours either to the south or to the north of the centre, starting daily 0900 and 1400 from Av Santa Fe y Esmeralda. Full day tours (7 hrs) and tours to Tigre (including kayaking in the Delta (8 hrs), or occasionally to the Pampas. Also rents bikes.

Football and rugby
Football fans should see **Boca Juniors**, matches every other Sun at their stadium (La Bombonera, Brandsen 805, La Boca, www.bocajuniors.com.ar, tickets for non-members only through tour operators, or the museum – see the murals), or their arch-rivals, **River Plate** (Av Figueroa Alcorta 7597, T011-4789 1200, www.cariverplate.com.ar). Football season Feb-Jun, and Aug-Dec, most matches on Sun. Buy tickets from stadiums, sports stores near the grounds, ticket agencies or hostels and hotels, which may arrange guide/transport (don't take a bus if travelling alone, phone a radio taxi; see also **Tangol**, below). Rugby season Apr-Oct/Nov. For more information, **Unión de Rugby de Buenos Aires** (www.urba.org.ar), or **Unión Argentina de Rugby** (T011-4898 8500, www.uar.com.ar).

Language schools
Academia Buenos Aires, *Hipólito Yrigoyen 571, p 4, T011-4345 5954, www.academia buenosaires.com.*
All-Spanish, *Talcahuano 77 p 1, T011-4832 7794, www.all-spanish.com.ar.* One-to-one classes.
Amauta Spanish School, *Av de Mayo 1370, p 3 of 10, T011-4383 7706, www.amautaspanish.com.* Spanish classes, one-to-one or small groups, centres in Buenos Aires and Bariloche.
Argentina I.L.E.E, *T011-4782 7173, www.argentina ilee.com.* Recommended by individuals and organizations alike, with a school in Bariloche.
Bue Spanish School, *Av Belgrano 1431, p 2, apt18, T011-4381 6347, www.buespanish.com.ar.* Intensive and regular Spanish courses, culture programme, free materials.
Cedic, *Reconquista 715, p 11 E, T011-4312 1016, www.cedic.com.ar.* Recommended.
Elebaires, *Av de Mayo 1370, of 10, p 3, T011-4383 7706, www.elebaires.com.* Small school with

focused classes, also offers one-to-one lessons and excursions. Recommended.

Expanish, *Av 25 de Mayo 457 p 4, T011-5252 3040, www.expanish.com*. Well-organized courses which can involve excursions, accommodation and Spanish lessons in sister schools in Peru and Chile. Highly recommended.

IBL (Argentina Spanish School), *Florida 165, p 3, of 328, T011-4331 4250, www.ibl.com.ar*. Group and one-to-one lessons, all levels, recommended.

Laboratorio de Idiomas (Universidad de Buenos Aires), *25 de Mayo 221 (also other branches), T011-4343 5981, www.idiomas.filo. uba.ar*. Offers cheap, coherent courses, including summer intensive courses.

Mundo Lingo, *http://mundolingo.org*. Buenos Aires branch of international language exchange set-up, meets in bars in centre, Mon, and Palermo, Wed, Fri. For other schools teaching Spanish and for private tutors look in *Buenos Aires Herald* in the classified advertisements. Enquire also at **Almundo** (see Transport, below).

Polo

The high handicap season is Sep-Dec, but it is played all year round. Argentina has the top polo players in the world. A visit to the national finals at Palermo in Nov and Dec is recommended. For information, **Asociación Argentina de Polo** (T011-4777 6444, www.aapolo.com).

Tour operators and travel agents

An excellent way of seeing Buenos Aires is by a 3-hr tour. Longer tours may include dinner and a tango show, or a boat trip in the Delta, or a gaucho fiesta at a ranch (great food and dancing). Bookable through most travel agents. See also **BA Free Tour** (www.bafreetour.com), www.buenosairesfreewalks.com and www. buenosaireslocaltours.com, for free walking tours. For another type of walking tour, see **BA Street Art** (http://buenosairesstreetart.com), and **Graffitimundo** (http://graffitimundo.com), who offer tours of the city's best graffiti, see websites for prices and times.

Anda, *T011-3221 0833, www.andatravel. com.ar*. Operator specializing in socially and environmentally responsible tourism in Buenos Aires and around the country, including volunteering opportunities.

Argentina Excepción, *Sinclair 3244 p 9, T011-4772 6620, www.argentina-excepcion.com*. French/Argentine agency offering tailor-made, upper end tours, fly-drives, themed trips and other services. Also has a Santiago branch, www.chile-excepcion.com.

Buenos Aires Bus (Bus Turístico), *www.buenos airesbus.com*. Open yellow double-decker buses follow 2 routes every 10-20 mins covering main sights from La Boca to Núñez with multilingual recorded tours. 1-day (US$24) and 2-day (US$32) hop-on/hop-off tickets can be purchased online or onboard. Find bus stops on website or on map provided at city's tourist offices.

Buenos Aires Vision, *Esmeralda 356, p 8, T011-4394 4682, www.buenosaires-vision.com.ar*. City tours, Tigre and Delta, Tango (cheaper without dinner) and **Fiesta Gaucha**.

Cultour, *T011-5624 7368, www.cultour.com.ar*. A highly recommended walking tour of the city, 3-4 hrs led by a group of Argentine history/ tourism graduates. In English and Spanish.

Eternautas, *Av Julio A Roca 584 p 7, T011-5031 9916, www.eternautas.com*. Historical, cultural and artistic tours of the city and pampas guided in English, French or Spanish by academics from the University of Buenos Aires, flexible.

Kallpa, *Tucumán 861, p 2, T011-5278 8010, www. kallpatour.com*. Tailor-made tours to natural and cultural destinations throughout the country, with an emphasis on adventure, conservation and golf.

Mai10, *Av Córdoba 657, p 3, T011-4314 3390, www. mai10.com.ar*. High-end, personalized tours for groups and individuals, covers the whole country, special interests include art, cuisine, estancias, photo safaris, fishing and many more.

Say Hueque, *branches in Palermo at Thames 2062, T011-5258 8740, and in San Telmo at Chile 557, T011-4307 3451, www.sayhueque.com*. Recommended travel agency offering good-value tours aimed at independent travellers, friendly English-speaking staff.

Tangol, *Florida 971, ground floor, shop 31, and Defensa 831, T011-4363 6000, www.tangol.com*. Friendly, independent agency specializing in football and tango, plus various sports, such as polo and paragliding. Can arrange tours, plane and bus tickets, accommodation. English spoken. Discounts for students. Overland tours in Patagonia Oct-Apr.

Transport

Air

Ezeiza (officially Ministro Pistarini, T011-5480 6111, www.aa2000.com.ar), the international airport, is 35 km southwest of the centre (also handles some domestic flights). The airport has 3 terminals: 'A', 'B' and 'C'. There are duty free shops (expensive), ATM and exchange facilities at Banco Nación (terminal 'A') (only change the very minimum to get you into the city), a **Ministerio de Turismo** desk, and a post office (Mon-Fri 1000-1800, Sat 1000-1300). No hotels nearby, but there is an attractive B&B 5 mins away with transfer included: $$$ Bernie's (Estrada 186, Barrio Uno, T011-4480 0420, www. posadabernies.com), book in advance. There is a **Devolución IVA/Tax Free** desk (return of VAT) for purchases over the value of AR$70 (ask for a Global Refund check plus the invoice from the shop when you buy). Hotel booking service at Tourist Information desk – helpful, but prices are higher if booked in this way.

Airport buses A display in immigration shows choices and prices of transport into the city. A good dual carriageway links with the General Paz highway which circles the city. The safest way between airport and city is by an airport bus service run every 30 mins, 0500-2100, by **Manuel Tienda León** (office in front of you as you arrive), company office and terminal at Av Madero 1299 and San Martín, behind Sheraton Hotel in Retiro (take a taxi from the terminal; do not walk outside), T0818-888-5366, www.tiendaleon.com.ar. The bus costs US$13 one way to Puerto Madero, US$13.50 to Aeroparque, pay by pesos, credit card, euros or dollars (change given in pesos). **Manuel Tienda León** will also collect passengers from addresses in centre for a small extra fee, book the previous day. Remise taxis for up to 4 passengers (**Manuel Tienda León, Taxi Ezeiza**, www.taxiezeiza.com.ar, and other counters at Ezeiza) charge US$30-40 airport to town, but less from city to airport. Radio taxis charge US$40 minimum (make sure you pay for your taxi at the booth and then wait in the queue), see Taxis, page 75, for more details. On no account take an unmarked car at Ezeiza, no matter how attractive the fare may sound. Drivers are adept at separating you from far more money than you can possibly owe them. Always ask to see the taxi driver's licence. If you take an ordinary taxi the Policía de Seguridad Aeroportuaria on duty notes down the car's licence and time of departure.

Aeroparque (Jorge Newbery Airport), 4 km north of the centre, T011-5480 6111, www.aa2000. com.ar, handles all internal flights, and some flights to neighbouring countries. On the 1st floor there is a *patio de comidas* and many shops. At the airport also tourist information, car rental, bus companies, ATM, public phones and luggage deposit (ask at information desk in sector B). **Manuel Tienda León** buses to Aeroparque (see above for address), more-or-less hourly, 24 hrs a day, 20-min journey, US$6. Local bus 45 runs from outside the airport to the Retiro railway station. No 37 goes to **Palermo** and **Recoleta** and No 160 to **Palermo** and **Almagro**. If going to the airport, make sure it goes to Aeroparque by asking the driver. Remise taxis to **Ezeiza**, operated by **Manuel Tienda León**, US$50; to the city centre US$18. Taxi to centre US$10. **Manuel Tienda León** operates buses between Ezeiza and Aeroparque airports, US$13.50.

The helpful **Argentine Youth and Student Travel Organization** (Almundo) runs a Student Flight Centre, Florida 835, p 3, oficina 320, T0810-4328 7907, www.almundo. com.ar, Mon-Fri 0900-2000, Sat 0900-1500 (with many branches in BA and around the country). Booking for flights, hotels and travel; information for all South America, noticeboard for travellers, English and French spoken. Cheap fares also at TIJE, San Martín 601, T011-5272 8453 or branches at Av Santa Fe 898, T011-5272 8450, and elsewhere in the city, Argentina, Uruguay and Chile, www.tije.com.

Bus

Local City buses are called *colectivos* and cover a very wide radius. They are clean, frequent, efficient and very fast. *Colectivo* fares are calculated in 3-km sections, US$0.50, and should be paid for with a pre-paid smart card called *Sube* (see www.xcolectivo.com.ar for details of how and where to buy a *Sube* card; you must show passport or identification). If not using a smart card, have coins ready for ticket machine as drivers do not sell tickets, but may give change. The bus number is not always sufficient indication of destination, as each number may have a variety of routes, but bus stops display routes of buses stopping there and little plaques are displayed in the driver's window. A rapid transit system, **Metrobús**, incorporating existing bus routes, is being implemented: 5 lines, including along Av 9 de Julio, are in operation. See www.omnilineas.com.ar and page 242, for city guides listing bus routes.

Long distance Bus terminal for all international and interprovincial buses is at Ramos Mejía y Antártida Argentina (Subte Line C), behind Retiro station, T011-4310 0700, www. tebasa.com.ar. The terminal is on 3 floors.

Bus information is at the Ramos Mejía entrance on the middle floor. Ticket offices are on the upper floor, but there are hundreds of them so you'll need to consult the list of companies and their office numbers at the top of the escalator. They are organized by region and are colour coded. Buenos Aires city information desk is on the upper floor. It is advisable to go to the bus station the day before you travel to get to know where the platforms are so that when you are fully laden you know exactly where to go. At the basement and ground levels there are left luggage lockers, tokens sold in kiosks; for large baggage, there's a *guarda equipaje* on the lower floor. For further details of bus services and fares, look under proposed destinations. There are no direct buses to either of the airports.

International buses International services are run by both local and foreign companies; heavily booked Dec-Mar (especially at weekends), when most fares usually rise sharply. Do not buy Uruguayan bus tickets in Buenos Aires; wait till you get to Colonia or Montevideo. To **Montevideo**, Bus del Carrera/Cita (www. busdedlacarrera.com.uy or www.cita.com.uy), **Belgrano** (T011-4018 0010, www.gralbelgrano. com.ar), **Cauvi** (cauvibue@hotmail.com) and **Cóndor Estrella** (www.condorestrella.com.ar), US$48-53, 8 hrs; see Ferry, below. To **Bolivia**, most Argentine companies only reach the border, where you can change buses at **La Quiaca** or **Aguas Blancas**. Alternatively, change buses at **San Salvador de Jujuy** or at **Orán**, busier transport hubs. Some companies go across the border to **Santa Cruz de la Sierra**, 39 hrs via **Yacuiba**. Also **Trans Americano** direct to **Tarija**, Tue, Thu, Sat 1100, US$100. Direct buses to **Brazil** by Pluma, T011-4313 3880, and **Crucero del Norte**, T011-5258 5000, eg to **Porto Alegre**, 20 hrs, **Florianópolis**, 27 hrs, **Curitiba**, 34 hrs, **São Paulo**, 34-38 hrs and **Rio de Janeiro**, 40 hrs. Crucero del Norte and Flecha Bus operate summer services to southern Brazil beach resorts. The route across the Río de la Plata and through Uruguay is a bit cheaper and offers a variety of transport and journey breaks.

Direct buses to **Santiago** (Chile), 1400 km, with Ahumada, **CATA** and **Pullman del Sur** daily, 20 hrs. To **Asunción** (Paraguay), 1370 km via Clorinda (toll bridge): several bus companies, around 18 hrs. Also to **Ciudad del Este** (16½ hrs), **Encarnación** (13 hrs) and other destinations in Paraguay. To **Peru**: 4 companies including **Ormeño** (T011-4313 2259), direct service to **Lima** (only stops for meals, not included in the price), 3 days. If you need a visa for Chile, get one before travelling.

Driving

Driving in Buenos Aires is no problem, provided you have eyes in the back of your head and good nerves. Traffic fines are high and police look out for drivers without the correct papers. Car hire is cheaper if you arrange it when you arrive rather than from home. Companies include **Localiza**, Cerrito 1575, T0800-999 2999, www.localiza.com/ argentina/es-ar; **Ruta Sur**, T011-5238 4071, www. rutasur.eu, rents 4WDs and motorhomes; and **Sixt**, Cerrito 1314, www.sixt.com.ar. Motoring Associations: see **ACA**, page 243.

Ferry

To **Montevideo** and **Colonia** from Terminal Dársena Norte, Av Antártida Argentina 821 (2 blocks from Av Córdoba y Alem). **Buquebus**, T011-4316 6530, www.buquebus.com (tickets from Terminal, from offices at Av Córdoba 867, Posadas 1452, elsewhere in the city and other cities, by phone or online – the cheapest method): **1)** Direct to **Montevideo**, 1-4 a day, 3 hrs, from US$100 tourist class, one way, also carries vehicles and motorcycles. **2)** To **Colonia**, services by 3 companies: **Buquebus**: minimum 5 crossings a day, from 1-3 hrs, US$34 tourist class one way on slower vessel, US$50 tourist class on faster vessel, with bus connection to **Montevideo**. (Buquebus also offers flights to Uruguay and Brazil with onward connections, www.flybqb.com.uy.) Colonia Express, www. coloniaexpress.com, makes 4-5 crossings a day between Buenos Aires and Colonia in a fast catamaran (no vehicles carried), 50 mins, prices range from US$22 to US$45 one way, depending on type of service and where bought. Office is at Av Córdoba 753, T011-4317 4100; Terminal Fluvial is at Av Pedro de Mendoza 330. You must go there by taxi, US$6-8 from Retiro. Seacat, www. seacatcolonia.com, 3 fast ferries to Colonia, 1 hr, US$34-67 one way, from the same terminal as Buquebus, with bus to Montevideo (US$36-74) and Punta del Este on most crossings. Office: Av Córdoba 772, phone sales: T011-4314 5100. See under Tigre, page 77, for services to Carmelo and Nueva Palmira.

Metro (Subte)

7 lines link the outer parts of the city to the centre. **Line 'A'** runs under Av Rivadavia, from Plaza de Mayo to San Pedrito (Flores). **Line 'B'** from central Post Office, on Av L N Alem, under Av Corrientes to Federico Lacroze railway station at Chacarita, ending at Juan Manuel de Rosas (Villa Urquiza). **Line 'C'** links Plaza Constitución with the Retiro railway station, and provides

connections with all the other lines but 'H'.
Line 'D' runs from Plaza de Mayo (Catedral), under Av Roque Sáenz Peña (Diagonal Norte), Córdoba, Santa Fe and Palermo to Congreso de Tucumán (Belgrano). **Line 'E'** runs from Plaza de Mayo (Cabildo, on C Bolívar) through San Juan to Plaza de los Virreyes (connection to Line 'P' or Premetro train service to the southwest end of the city). **Line 'H'** runs from Corrientes, via Once to Hospitales (Parque Patricios), under Av Jujuy and Av Almafuerte. Note that 3 stations, 9 de Julio (Line 'D'), Diagonal Norte (Line 'C') and Carlos Pellegrini (Line 'B') are linked by pedestrian tunnels. The fare is US$0.30, the same for any direct trip or combination between lines; magnetic cards (for 1, 2, 5, 10, or 30 journeys) must be bought at the station before boarding; only pesos accepted. You can also pay by *Sube* card. Trains are operated by **Metrovías**, T0800-555 1616, www.metrovias.com.ar, and run Mon-Sat 0500-2200/2300 (Sun 0800-2230). Line A, the oldest was built in 1913, the earliest in South America. Backpacks and luggage allowed. Free map (if available) from stations and tourist office.

Taxi
Taxis are painted yellow and black, and carry Taxi flags. Fares are shown in pesos. The meter starts at US$1.40 when the flag goes down; make sure it isn't running when you get in. A fixed rate of US$0.15 for every 200 m or 1-min wait is charged thereafter. The fare from 2200 to 0600 starts at US$1.70, plus US$0.18 for every 200 m or 1-min wait. A charge is sometimes made for each piece of hand baggage (ask first). Tipping isn't mandatory, but rounding the change up is appreciated. For security, take a remise or radio taxi booked by phone or at the company's office. Check that the driver's licence is displayed. Lock doors on the inside. The 2 airports and Retiro bus station are notorious for unlicensed taxi crime; use the airport buses and remises listed above, and taxis from the official rank in the bus terminal which are registered with police and safe.

Radio taxis are managed by several different companies. Phone a radio taxi from your hotel (they can make recommendations), a phone box or *locutorio*, giving the address where you are, and you'll usually be collected within 10 mins. **City**, T011-4585 5544; **Porteño**, T011-4566 5777, www.radiotaxiportenio.com; **Premium**, T011-5238 0000, www.taxipremium.com; **Tiempo**, T011-4854 3838, www.radiotaxitiemposrl.com.

ar. Remise taxis operate all over the city, run from an office and have no meter. The companies are identified by signs on the pavement. Fares are fixed and can be cheaper than regular taxis, can be verified by phoning the office, and items left in the car can easily be reclaimed. **Universal**, T011-4105 5555, www.remisesuniversal.com.

Train
There are 4 main terminals: **1) Retiro** 3 lines: **Mitre**, **Belgrano** and **San Martín** in separate buildings. The state of services changes all the time, owing largely to poor maintenance. The independent website, www.sateliteferroviario.com.ar, is a good source of information on all services. Urban and suburban services include: Mitre line (T0800-222 8736) to **Belgrano**, **Mitre** (connection to Tren de la Costa, see page 77), **Olivos**, **San Isidro**, and **Tigre** (see below); long-distance services to **Rosario Norte**, **Tucumán** and **Córdoba**, times and fares are given under destinations (for information on all these services, **Trenes Argentinos**, T0800-222 8736, www.sofse.gob.ar, ticket office 0700-2200). Belgrano line to northwestern suburbs, including **Villa Rosa**, run by **Ferrovías**, T0800-777 3377, www.ferrovias.com.ar. San Martín line for services to **Pilar** and **Cabred** and long-distance services to **Junín** and **Alberdi** (see www.ferrobaires.gba.gov.ar).

2) Constitución, Roca line urban and suburban services to La Plata, Ezeiza, Ranelagh and Quilmes (Trenes Argentinos). Long-distance services run by **Ferrobaires** (T011-4304 0038, www.ferrobaires.gba.gov.ar) to **Bahía Blanca** Mar del Plata and **Tandil** were suspended in 2017.

3) Federico Lacroze, Urquiza line and Metro headquarters (run by **Metrovías**, T0800-555 1616, www.metrovias.com.ar). Suburban services: to **General Lemos**.

4) Once, Sarmiento line, urban and suburban services to **Moreno**, with connection to **Luján** and **Mercedes** (details from Trenes Argentinos, above).

Tram
Old-fashioned trams operate Mar-Nov on Sat and holidays 1600-1930 and Sun 1000-1300, 1600-1930 and Dec-Feb on Sat and holidays 1700-2030, Sun 1000-1300, 1700-2030, free, on a circular route along the streets of Caballito district, from C Emilio Mitre 500, Subte Primera Junta (Line A) or Emilio Mitre (Line E), no stops en route. Operated by **Asociación Amigos del Tranvía**, T011-4431 1073, www.tranvia.org.ar.

☆Tigre

This touristy little town, 32 km northwest of Buenos Aires, is a popular weekend destination lying on the lush, jungly banks of the Río Luján, with a fun fair and an excellent fruit and handicrafts **market** ① *Puerto de Frutos, access from C Sarmiento or C Perú, Mon-Fri 1000-1800, Sat, Sun and holidays 1000-1900.* There are restaurants on the waterfront across the Río Tigre from the railway line, along Lavalle and Paseo Victorica; cheaper places can be found on Italia and Cazón on the near side, or at the Puerto de Frutos. **Museo Naval** ① *Paseo Victorica 602, T011-4749 0608, Tue-Fri 0830-1730, Sat-Sun and holidays 1030-1830 (voluntary fee),* is worth a visit to see the displays on the Argentine navy. There are also relics of the 1982 Falklands/Malvinas War. **Museo de Arte** ① *Paseo Victorica 972, T011-4512 4528, www.mat.gov.ar, Wed-Fri 0900-1900, Sat-Sun 1200-1900, US$2.75,* has a collection of Argentine figurative art in the former Tigre Club Casino, a beautiful belle époque building. **Museo del Mate** ① *Lavalle 289, T011-4506 9594, www.elmuseodelmate.com, Wed-Sun 1100-1800 (1100-1900 in spring and summer), US$3,* tells the history of mate and has an interesting collection of the associated paraphernalia.

North of the town is the delta of the **Río Paraná**: innumerable canals and rivulets, with holiday homes and restaurants on the banks and a fruit-growing centre. The fishing is excellent and the peace is only disturbed by motor-boats at weekends. Regattas are held in November. Take a trip from the wharf (Estación Fluvial) on one of the regular launch services (*lanchas colectivas*) which run to all parts of the delta, including taxi launches – watch prices for these. You can also hire kayaks, canoes or rowing boats, rent houses, or visit *recreos*, little resorts with swimming pools, tennis courts, bar and restaurant.

> **Tip...**
> **Bus Turístico** (T011-4731 1300, www.busturisticotigre.com.ar) runs one-hour tours on an open-top bus every 30 minutes from 1040, US$6.55, US$9 at weekends, with 10 stops starting at the railway station.

Isla Martín García

This island in the Río de la Plata (Juan Díaz de Solís' landfall in 1516) used to be a military base. Now it is an ecological/historical centre and an ideal excursion from the capital, with many trails through the cane brakes, trees and rocky outcrops – interesting birds and flowers. There are boat trips from Tigre (Lavalle 520), four weekly at 0830, returning 2000, US$50 return including lunch, *asado* and guide, or US$90 including overnight full board accommodation. Reservations only through **Cacciola** (address under Tigre, Transport, below), who also handle bookings for the inn and restaurant on the island. There is also a campsite.

Listings Around Buenos Aires

Tourist information

Centro de Guías de Tigre y Delta
Av Cazón, T011-4731 3555,
www.guiastigreydelta.com.ar.
For guided walks and launch trips.

Tigre tourist office
By the Estación Fluvial, Mitre 345, T011-4512 4497, http://vivitigre.gob.ar, also at Juncal 1600, T0800-8888 4473, and the Puerto de Frutos.
Has a full list of houses to rent, activities, etc.

Where to stay

Tigre

$$$$ La Becasina
Arroyo Las Cañas (Delta islands second section), T011-4328 2687, www.labecasina.com.
One of Argentina's most delightful places to stay, an hour by launch from Tigre, buried deep from the outside world, with 15 individual lodges on stilts in the water, connected by wooden walkways, all comforts and luxuries provided and

tasteful decor, with intimate dining room, jacuzzi and pool amidst the trees. Full board, excellent food and service. Recommended.

$$$$ Villa Julia
Paseo Victorica 800, in Tigre itself, T011-4749 0642, www.villajuliaresort.com.ar.
A 1906 villa converted into a chic hotel, beautifully restored fittings, comfortable, good restaurant open to non-residents.

$$$ Los Pecanes
On Arroyo Felicaria, T011-4728 1932, www.hosterialospecanes.com.
On a secluded island visited regularly by hummingbirds. Ana and Richard offer a few comfortable rooms and delicious food. Ideal base for boat excursions and birdwatching. Cheaper Mon-Fri.

$$$-$ Posada de 1860
Av Libertador 190, T011-4749 4034, www.tigrehostel.com.ar.
A beautiful stylish villa with suites and an associated **Hostel Tigre** at No 137 (same phone and website) with dorms for up to 6 ($ pp), and private rooms ($$$ double).

$$ TAMET
Río Carapachay Km 24, T011-4728 0055, www.tamet.com.ar.
For a relaxing stay on an island with sandy beaches and quite comfortable premises, with breakfast, games and canoes. Also has camping.

What to do

Tigre
Many companies run daily services on tourist catamarans. Trips of 1-2 hrs costing US$10-14 and full-day group tours (minimum 20 passengers) depart from Lavalle 500 on Río Tigre, T011-4731 0261/63, www.tigreencatamaran.com.ar. 1½-hr trips (3 trips a day Mon-Fri, 2 a day Sat-Sun), US$13, from Puerto de Frutos; also **Río Tur** (T011-4731 0280, www.rioturcatamaranes.com.ar).

Sturla, *Estación Fluvial, of 10, T011-4731 1300, www.sturlaviajes.com.ar.* Runs 1-hr catamaran trips, US$16 (includes a ride on **Bus Turístico**); they also have trips with lunch, night-time boat trips, full-day excursions from the centre of Buenos Aires, commuting services to Puerto Madero, and more. **Bus Turístico** (T011-4731 1300, www.busturisticotigre.com.ar) runs 1-hr tours, US$5.25, every hour on an open-top bus with 10 stops, starting at 1040 at the railway station.

Sudeste, *T011-15-3860 4018, www.sudeste-kayak.com.ar (Martin Schoo).* Guided kayak trips in the Delta, includes transfer from Tigre to the islands, full instruction, English spoken.

Transport

Tigre
Bus From central **Buenos Aires**, take No 60 from Constitución; the 60 'bajo' takes a little longer than the 60 'alto' but is better for sightseeing.

Ferry To **Carmelo** (Uruguay) from Terminal Internacional, Lavalle 520, Tigre with **Cacciola** (T011-4749 0931, www.cacciolaviajes.com; in Buenos Aires at Av Córdoba 755, T011-5353 9005), 1 a day, 2½ hrs, US$33. To Montevideo (bus from Carmelo), 3½ hrs, US$40 (cheaper online). **Líneas Delta Argentino**, B Mitre 305, or at the Muelle Internacional, Lavalle 520, T011-4731 1236, http://lineasdelta.com, to **Nueva Palmira** (Uruguay) from Muelle Internacional, 0730, 3 hrs, US$50 return. **Note** Argentine port taxes are generally included in the fares for Argentine departures.

Train Trenes Argentinos operates the Mitre line direct from Retiro in **Buenos Aires** and the **Tren de la Costa**, T011-3220 6300, www.trendelacosta.com.ar, US$1.30 one way from Maipú station (reached by Mitre line from Retiro) to Delta station (Tigre) every 30 mins. (Buses to Tren de la Costa are 60 from Constitución, 19 or 71 from Once, 152 from centre.) Terminus, Estación Delta, has the huge fun fair, El Parque de la Costa, and a casino.

Argentina's agricultural heartland is punctuated by quiet pioneer towns, such as Chascomús, and the houses of grand estancias. Argentina's former wealth lay in these splendid places, where you can stay as a guest, go horse riding and get a great insight into the country's history and gaucho culture.

Luján

This is a place of pilgrimage for devout Catholics throughout Argentina. In 1630 an image of the Virgin brought by ship from Brazil was being transported to its new owner in Santiago del Estero by ox cart, when the cart got stuck, despite strenuous efforts by men and oxen to move it. This was taken as a sign that the Virgin willed she should stay there. A chapel was built for the image, and around it grew Luján. The chapel has long since been superseded by an impressive neo-Gothic basilica and the Virgin now stands on the High Altar. Luján is a very popular spot at weekends, and there are huge pilgrimages on the last weekend of September (La Peregrinación Gaucho), the first weekend of October (**Peregrinación Juvenil**), 8 May (the saint's day) and 8 December (**Inmaculada Concepción**), when the town is completely packed.

Complejo Museográfico Provincial Enrique Udaondo ① *T02323-420245, museoudaondo on Facebook, Wed 1300-1630, Thu-Fri 1130-1630, Sat-Sun 1030-1730, US$0.70*, in the old Cabildo building, is one of the most interesting museums in the country. Exhibits illustrate its historical and political development. General Beresford, the commander of the British troops which seized Buenos Aires in 1806, was a prisoner here, as were Generals Mitre, Paz and Belgrano in later years. Next to it are museums devoted to transport and to motor vehicles. Behind the Cabildo is the river, with river walks, cruises and restaurants.

Some 20 km before Luján, near General Rodríguez, is **Eco Yoga Park** ① *T011-6507 0577, www. ecoyogapark.com.ar*, a spiritual centre and farm with volunteering opportunities, yoga, meditation, organic gardens and vegetarian food. See website for day and weekend packages. Take Luján bus (see Transport, below), get off at La Serenísima, then take taxi US$8-10.

☆San Antonio de Areco *Colour map 8, B5.*

San Antonio de Areco, 113 km northwest of Buenos Aires, is a completely authentic, late 19th-century town, with single-storey buildings around a plaza filled with palms and plane trees, streets lined with orange trees, and an attractive *costanera* along the river bank. There are several estancias and a couple of villages with accommodation nearby and the town itself has historical *boliches* (combined bar and provisions store, eg Los Principios, Moreno y Mitre). The gaucho traditions are maintained in silver, textiles and leather handicrafts of the highest quality, as well as frequent gaucho activities, the most important of which is the **Day of Tradition** in the second week of November (book accommodation ahead), with traditional parades, gaucho games, events on horseback, music and dance. Ricardo Güiraldes, the writer whose best-known book, *Don Segundo Sombra*, celebrates the gaucho, lived in the **Estancia La Porteña** ① *8 km from town, T011-15-5626 7347, www.laporteniadeareco.com*, which dates from 1823. It is a national historic monument and offers day visits and accommodation in three palatial houses ($$$$, huge banquets with lots of meat). The **Museo Gauchesco Ricardo Güiraldes** ① *Camino Güiraldes, T02326-455839, museoguiraldes@areco.gob.ar, 1000-1700*, is a replica of a typical estancia of the late 19th century and is dedicated to the life of the writer. Superb gaucho silverwork is for sale at the workshop and **museum of Juan José Draghi** ① *Lavalle 387, T02326-454219, www.draghiplaterosorfebres.com, Mon-Thu 0930-1300 and 1600-1900, Fri-Sat 1000-1300 and 1600-1900, Sun 1000-1230, US$5 for a guided visit*. There are excellent chocolates at **La Olla de Cobre** ① *Matheu 433, T02326-453105, www.laolladecobre.com.ar*, with a charming little café for drinking chocolate and the most amazing home-made *alfajores*. There is a large Parque San Martín spanning the river near the **tourist information centre**. The **Centro Cultural y Museo Usina Vieja** ① *Alsina 66, T02326-454722, www.sanantoniodeareco.com/centro-cultural-y-museo-usina-vieja, Tue-Sun 1100-1700, free*, is the city museum. There are ATMs on the plaza. The **tourist office** ① *Zerboni y Arellano, T02326-453165, www.sanantoniodeareco.com*, is by the river.

La Plata *Colour map 8, B5.*

La Plata (population 732,000), near the mouth of the Río de la Plata, was founded in 1882 as capital of Buenos Aires province and is now an important administrative centre, with an excellent university. It's a well-planned city, with the French-style **legislature** and the elegant **Casa de Gobierno** on Plaza San Martín, central in a series of plazas along the spine of the city. On **Plaza Moreno** to the south there's an impressive Italianate palace housing the **Municipalidad**, and the **Cathedral** ⓘ *www.catedraldelaplata.com, Mon-Sat 0900-1900, Sun 0900-2000*, a striking neo-Gothic brick construction. North of Plaza San Martín is La Plata's splendid park, the **Paseo del Bosque**, with mature trees, a zoo and a botanical garden, a boating lake and the **Museo de La Plata** ⓘ *T0221-425 7744, www.fcnym. unlp.edu.ar, Tue-Sun 1000-1800 and holiday Mon, closed 1 Jan, 1 May, 24, 25, 31 Dec, US$2*, one of the most famous museums in Latin America. It is particularly outstanding on anthropology and archaeology, with a huge collection of pre-Columbian artefacts including pre-Incan ceramics from Peru, beautiful ceramics from northwest Argentina and fine preserved animal and dinosaur sections. The **Parque Ecológico** ⓘ *Camino Centenario y San Luis, Villa Elisa, T0221-473 2449, www.parquecologico.laplata.gov.ar, 0900-1900, free, take bus 273 D or 6*, is a good place for families, with native *tala* forest and plenty of birds.

Municipal tourist offices ⓘ *Diagonal 79 entre 5 y 56, Palacio Campodónico, T0221-422 9764, Mon-Fri 0900-1700, and Pasaje Dardo Rocha, T0221-427 1535, daily 1000-2000, www.laplata.gov.ar.* The latter, in an Italianate palace, also houses a gallery of contemporary **Latin American art** ⓘ *C 50 entre 6 y 7, T0221-427 1843, www.macla.com.ar, Tue-Fri 1000-2000, Sat-Sun 1400-2100 (1600-2200 in summer), free.*

☆Chascomús and around

To get to the heart of the pampas, stay in one of many estancias scattered over the plains. There are several accessible from the main roads to the coast, fast Ruta 2 (be prepared for tolls) and Ruta 11. On Ruta 2, **Chascomús** is a beautifully preserved town from the 1900s, with a rather Wild West feel to it. Built on a huge lake, it is perfect for fishing and water sports. There's a great little museum **Museo Pampeano** ⓘ *Av Lastra y Muñiz, T02241-430982, Mon-Fri 0900-1900, US$1*, with gaucho artefacts, old maps and fabulous antique furniture. **Tourist office** ⓘ *Av Costanera by the pier, T02241-430405, daily 0900-1900, www.chascomus.gob.ar/turismo.html.*

Further south on Ruta 2, **Dolores** is a delightful small town, like stepping back in time to the 1900s, very tranquil (http://dolores.gov.ar). **Museo Libres del Sur** ⓘ *Wed-Sun 1000-1700*, is an old house in Parque Libres del Sur, full of gaucho silver, plaited leather *talero*, branding irons, and a huge cart from 1868.

Listings The pampas

Where to stay

San Antonio de Areco
Most hotels offer discounts Mon-Thu or Fri.

$$$ Antigua Casona
Segundo Sombra 495, T02325-15-416030, www.antiguacasona.com.
Charmingly restored 1897 house with 5 rooms opening onto a delightful patio and exuberant garden, relaxing and romantic. Bikes to borrow.

$$$ Paradores Draghi
Matheu 380, T02326-455583, www.paradoresdraghi.com.ar.
Traditional-style, comfortable rooms face a manicured lawn with a pool. Just metres away

Draghi family has its silversmith workshop. Recommended.

$$$ Patio de Moreno
Moreno 251, T02326-455197, www.patiodemoreno.com.
The top hotel in town is a stylish place with spacious, minimalist rooms, a large patio with a pool and great service.

$$ Hostal de Areco
Zapiola 25, T02326-456118, www.hostaldeareco.com.ar.
Popular, with a warm welcome, good value.

$$ Los Abuelos
Zerboni y Zapiola T02326-456390, see Facebook.
Very good, welcoming, small pool, plain but comfortable rooms, facing riverside park.

☆ Estancias

Some of the province's finest estancias are within easy reach for day visits, offering horse riding, an *asado* lunch, and other activities. Stay overnight to really appreciate the peace and beauty of these historical places. See also **Estancia La Porteña**, above. Look online at: www.sanantonio deareco.com/turismo/estancias/index.htm.

$$$$ El Ombú
T02326-492080, T011-4737 0436 (Buenos Aires office), www.estanciaelombu.com.
Fine house with magnificent terrace dating from 1890, comfortable rooms, horse riding, English-speaking owners; price includes full board and activities but not transfer. Recommended.

$$$$ La Bamba
T02326-454895, www.labambadeareco.com.
Dating from 1830, in grand parkland, charming rooms, English-speaking owners who have lived here for generations, superb meals, price is for full board. Recommended.

La Plata

$$$ La Plata Hotel
Av 51 No 783, T0221-422 9090, www.weblaplatahotel.com.ar.
Modern, well furnished, comfortable, spacious rooms and nice bathrooms. Price includes a dinner (drinks extra).

$ pp La Plata Hostel
C 50 No 1066, T0221-457 1424, www.laplata-hostel.com.ar.
Well-organized, convenient hostel in a historic house, high ceilings, small garden, simple but comfortable dorms for 4 or 8.

☆ Estancias

$$$$ Casa de Campo La China
60 km from La Plata on Ruta 11, T0221-421 2931, www.casadecampolachina.com.ar.
A charming 1930s adobe house set in eucalyptus woods, with beautifully decorated spacious rooms off an open gallery, group day visits (US$45, minimum 15 people) to ride horses, or in carriages, eat *asado*, or stay the night, guests of Cecilia and Marcelo, who speak perfect English. Delicious food, meals included in price. Highly recommended.

Chascomús and around

For a full list see www.chascomus.com.ar.

$$$ Chascomús
Av Lastra 367, T02241-422968, www.chascomus.com.ar (under 'hoteles').
The town's most comfortable hotel, atmospheric, welcoming, with stylish turn-of-the-20th-century public rooms and lovely terrace.

$$$ La Posada
Costanera España 18, T02241-423503, www. acechascomus.com.ar/ace-la_ posada.
On the laguna, delightful, very comfortable *cabañas* with cooking facilities.

$$$ Roble Blanco
Mazzini 130, T02241-436235, www.robleblanco.com.ar.
A very good choice, in a refurbished 100-year-old house, modern comfortable rooms, a large heated pool with attractive deck and welcoming common areas. Also has a spa. Recommended.

$$ Laguna
Libres del Sur y Maipú, T02241-426113, www.lagunahotel.com.ar.
Old-fashioned, sleepy hotel by the station. Pleasant, quiet rooms.

☆ Estancias

$$$ La Horqueta
3 km from Chascomús on Ruta 20, T011-4777 0150, www.lahorqueta.com.
Full board, mansion in lovely grounds with lake for fishing, horse riding, bikes, English-speaking hosts, safe gardens especially good for children, plain food. Will collect guests from Chascomús.

$$$$ Estancia Dos Talas
10 km from Dolores, T02245-443020, www.dostalas.com.ar. Nov to early Apr.
One of the oldest and most beautiful estancias, you are truly the owners' guests here. The rooms and the service are impeccable, the food exquisite; stay for days and relax completely. Pool, riding, English spoken.

Restaurants

San Antonio de Areco
Many *parrillas* on the bank of the Río Areco.

$$ Almacén de Ramos Generales
Zapiola 143, T02326-456376 (best to book ahead).
Perfect place, popular with locals, very atmospheric, superb meat, very good pastas and a long wine list.

$$ Café de las Artes
Bolívar 70, T02326-456398 (better book ahead; see Facebook).
In a hidden spot, this cosy place serves delicious pastas with a large wine selection.

$$ La Costa
Zerboni y Belgrano, T02326-452481 (on the riverside park).
A very good traditional *parrilla* with an attractive terrace.

$$ La Ochava de Cocota
Alsina y Alem, T02326-454852.
Relaxing, attractive, excellent service, superb *empanadas* and vegetable pies. It is also a café.

$ La Esquina de Merti
Arellano y Segundo Sombra, T02326-456705.
The ideal place for a beer on the main plaza. Go early to get a table outside.

La Plata

$$ Akari Sushi Bar
Diagonal 74 No 1531, T0221-422 7549, www.akari-sushi.com.ar.
The most popular sushi spot in the city. Makes a nice change from so much beef.

$$ Cervecería Modelo
C 54 y C5, T0221-421 1321, www.cerveceriamodelo.com.ar.
Traditional German-style *cervecería*, with good menu and beer.

$$ Don Quijote
Plaza Paso 146, T0221-483 3653, www.rdonquijote.com.ar.
Delicious food in lovely surroundings, well known.

Confitería París
C 7 y 48, T0221-482 8840.
The best croissants, and a lovely place for coffee.

Chascomús

$$ Colonial
Estados Unidos y Artigas, T02241-430322.
Great food, pastas and cakes are recommended.

Horse riding
All estancias offer horse riding. Other operators can be contacted from the hotels in the pampas towns.

Luján
Bus From **Buenos Aires** Bus 57 **Empresa Atlántida** either from Plaza Once, route O (the fastest), or from Plaza Italia, routes C and D; US$2-3. To **San Antonio de Areco**, several a day, US$4, Empresa Argentina, 1 hr.

San Antonio de Areco
Bus From **Buenos Aires** (Retiro bus terminal), 1½-2 hrs, US$7-8, every hour with Chevallier or Autotransportes San Juan.

Remise taxis Sol, San Martín y Alsina, T455444.

La Plata
Bus Terminal at C 42 entre 3 y 4 T0221-427 3198, www.laplataterminal.com. To **Buenos Aires**, very frequent during the day, hourly at night, **Costera Metropolitana** and **Plaza**, 1 hr 10 mins either to Retiro terminal or to Centro (stops along Av 9 de Julio), US$2.60. To **Mar del Plata** US$30 with **El Rápido**.

Train To/from **Buenos Aires** (Constitución), frequent, US$0.70, 1 hr 20 mins.

Chascomús
Bus Frequent service, several per day to **Buenos Aires**, 2 hrs, US$10, **La Plata**, **Mar del Plata**, and daily to **Bahía Blanca** and **Villa Gesell**; terminal T02241-426300.

Train Station T02241-422220. Services with Ferrobaires, www.ferrobaires.gba.gov.ar, to **Buenos Aires** (Constitución) and to **Mar del Plata**, passing **Dolores** en route, were suspended in 2017.

Among the 500 km of resorts stretching from to San Clemente de Tuyú to Monte Hermoso, the most attractive is upmarket Pinamar, with the chic Cariló next door. Villa Gesell is relaxed and friendly but past its best, while, next to it are the quiet, beautiful Mar Azul and Mar de las Pampas. Mar del Plata, Argentina's most famous resort, is a huge city with packed beaches, popular for its lively nightlife and casino; it's much more appealing in winter. Next to it, tranquil Miramar is great for young families, and Necochea has wild expanses of dunes to explore. Near the port of Bahía Blanca is the Sierra de la Ventana, the highest range of hills in the pampas, a great place for hiking.

Pinamar and Cariló

The two most desirable resorts on the coast are next to each other, 340 km from Buenos Aires, via Ruta 11. **Pinamar** is one of the most attractive resorts on the whole coast, with stylish architecture and mature trees lining its avenues. It is great for young people and families, with smart *balnearios,* ranging from chic, quiet places with superb restaurants to very trendy spots with loud music, beach parties and live bands at night. There are golf courses and tennis courts, and fine hotels and smart restaurants all along the main street, Avenida Bunge. Explore the dunes at **Reserva Dunícola**, 13 km north, by horse or 4WD.

Cariló, the most exclusive beach resort in Argentina, has a huge area of mature woodland, where its luxury apart-hotels and *cabañas* are all tastefully concealed. The *balnearios* are neat and exclusive and there are good restaurants and shops around the tiny centre. See www.carilo.com and www.parquecarilo.com.

Villa Gesell and around

Villa Gesell, 22 km south of Pinamar, is set amid thousands of trees planted by its German founder. In contrast to elite Cariló, it has grown from an ecological tourist retreat into a thriving tourist town, with dated holiday homes and a highly commercialized main street, Avenida 3. In January, it's overrun by Argentine youth; it's far quieter in late February and March.

Some 5 km south are two of the most tranquil and charming beach retreats: idyllic and wooded **Mar de las Pampas** and **Mar Azul**. The beach here is broad and uncrowded; there is less to do than in Pinamar or Mar del Plata and no nightlife to speak of, but you can completely relax and enjoy the sea in peace. In January you'll find traffic jams and queues at restaurants.

Mar del Plata *Colour map 8, C5.*

The oldest and most famous Argentine resort has lost much of its charm since it was built in 1874. It's now a huge city (population 650,000) offering great nightlife in summer. There are hundreds of hotels, all busy (and double the price) in January and February, although winter can be pleasantly quiet. If you like some space on the beach, it's best to go elsewhere, as there are plenty of better beaches on this stretch of coast.

The city centre is around **Playa Bristol**, with the huge casino, and **Plaza San Martín**, with pedestrian streets Rivadavia and San Martín, busy in summer with shoppers. Some 10 blocks southwest, the area of Los Troncos contains some remarkable mansions dating from Mar del Plata's heyday, from mock Tudor **Villa Blaquier** to **Villa Ortiz Basualdo** (1909), inspired by Loire chateaux, now the **Museo Municipal de Arte** ① *Av Colón 1189, T0223-486 1636, daily in summer 1700-2200, Mon, Wed-Fri 1400-2000, Sat-Sun 1500-2000, US$1, including guided tour,* which has rooms furnished in period style. The **Centro Cultural Victoria Ocampo** ① *Matheu 1851, T0223-494 2878, Wed-Mon 1200-1800, US$2,* is a beautiful 1900s wooden house in lovely gardens where the famous author entertained illustrious literary figures; concerts are held in the grounds in summer. Nearby is the **Museo Roberto T Barili Villa Mitre** ① *Lamadrid 3870, T0223-495 1200, Mon-Fri 0900-1500, Sat-Sun 1400-1800, US$2, free Tue.* Donated by a descendent of Bartolomé Mitre to the municipality, it is a museum containing the Historical Archive and holds cultural events.

Beaches include fashionable **Playa Grande**, where the best hotels and shops are located, as well as the famous golf course; there are private *balnearios* for wealthy Porteños and a small area open to the public. **Playa La Perla** is now packed and pretty grim; **Playa Punta Mogotes**, further west, and the beaches stretching along the road to Miramar are by far the most appealing. The **port area**, south of Playa Grande, is interesting when the old orange fishing boats come in, and also at night for its seafood restaurants. A sea lion colony basks on rusting wrecks by the Escollera Sur (southern breakwater) and fishing is good all along the coast. There are one-hour **boat trips** ① *from Dársena B, Muelle de Guardacostas in the port, T0223-496 2000, www.cruceroanamora.com.ar, US$19.50, children US$11,* along the city coast on the *Anamora,* several times daily in summer, weekends only in winter.

Miramar *Colour map 8, C5.*
Miramar, 47 km southwest of Mar del Plata, along the coast road, is a charming small resort, known as the 'city of bicycles', and oriented towards families. It has a big leafy plaza at its centre, a good stretch of beach with soft sand and a relaxed atmosphere; a quieter, low-key alternative to Mar del Plata. The most attractive area of the town is away from the high-rise buildings on the sea front, at the **Vivero Dunícola Florentino Ameghino**, a 502-ha forest park on the beach, with lots of walks, restaurants and picnic places for *asado* among the mature trees. In town there are lots of restaurants along Calle 21, and good cafés at *balnearios* on the seafront.

Necochea *Colour map 8, C5.*
Necochea is a well-established resort, famous for its long stretch of beach. The central area is built up and busy in the summer. Further west there are beautiful empty beaches and high sand dunes. There's also a fine golf club and rafting nearby on the river Quequén. The **Parque Miguel Lillo** (named after the Argentine botanist) starts three blocks west of Plaza San Martín and stretches along the seafront, a wonderful dense forest of over 600 ha. There are lovely walks along paths, many campsites and picnic spots, a train ride (www.trendelparque.com.ar), lots of restaurants, and places to practise various sports. West of Necochea, there's a natural arch of rock at the **Cueva del Tigre**, and beyond it stretches a vast empty beach, separated from the land by sand dunes up to 100 m high, the **Médano Blanco**. This is an exhilarating area for walking or horse riding and the dunes are popular for 4WD riding and sandboarding.

Towards Bahía Blanca
There's an established resort at **Monte Hermoso**, 106 km east of Bahía Blanca, with hotels, a well-organized campsite and wonderful beaches. It's one of the few places on the coast where the sun rises and sets over the sea. **Pehuén-Có**, 84 km east of Bahía Blanca, has a wild and untouristy feel, with very few hotels, some apartment rentals, several campsites well shaded, and a couple of places to eat. See www.visitapehuenco.com.ar. There's a long stretch of relatively empty and unspoilt sandy beaches with dunes (beware of jellyfish when wind is in the south), signposted from the main road 24 km from Bahía Blanca.

Bahía Blanca and around *Colour map 8, C4.*
The province's most important port and naval base, Bahía Blanca is a quiet, attractive city. It's a good starting point for exploring **Sierra de la Ventana**, 100 km north, or relaxing on beaches an hour to the east. The architecture is remarkable with many fine buildings especially around the central **Plaza Rivadavia**, notably the ornate, Italianate **Municipalidad** of 1904 and the French-style **Banco de la Nación** (1927). Three blocks north on the main shopping street, at Alsina 425, is the classical **Teatro Municipal** (1922). The **Museo Histórico** ① *at the side of the Teatro Municipal, Dorrego 116, T0291-456 3117, http://mhistorico.bahiablanca.gov.ar, Mon-Fri 0900-1200, Sat-Sun 1430-1630,* has sections on the pre-Hispanic period and interesting photos of early Bahía Blanca. Not to be missed, though, is the **Museo del Puerto** ① *Torres y Cárrega, T0291-457 3006, 7 km away in the port area at Ingeniero White, Mon-Fri 0830-1230, weekends 1530-1930, free; getting there: bus 500A or 504 from plaza, taxi US$14.50.* It houses entertaining and imaginative displays on immigrant life in the early 20th century, and has a quaint *confitería* on Sunday.

☆Sierra de la Ventana
The magnificent Sierra de la Ventana, the highest range of hills in the pampas, lies 100 km north of Bahía Blanca within easy reach for a day or weekend visit. They hills are good for long hikes, with stunning views from their craggy peaks. There are daily trips and *combis* from Bahía Blanca, or you could base yourself at **Tornquist**, a quaint, non-touristy place 70 km north of Bahía Blanca by Ruta 33.

The sierras are accessed through **Parque Provincial Ernesto Tornquist**, 25 km northeast of Tornquist on Ruta 76. There are two main points of entry, one at the foot of Cerro Ventana and the other, further east, at the foot of Cerro Bahía Blanca. To enter the Cerro Ventana section, turn left (signposted) after the massive ornate gates from the Tornquist family home. Nearby is **Campamento Base** ① *T0291-15-649 5304*, camping, basic dormitory, hot showers. At the entrance to the park itself, there's a car park and a **guardaparques station** ① *Dec-Easter 0800-1700*, where you register for longer walks; they also give advice. From here it's a three-hour walk to the summit of **Cerro de la Ventana**, which has fantastic views from the 'window' (which gives the range its name), in the summit ridge; it's a clearly marked path but with no shade; ascents only permitted till 1200 and in good weather. There are also easier walks to waterfalls.

To enter the Cerro Bahía Blanca section, continue 4 km further along Ruta 76. There's a car park and **interpretation centre** ① *T0291-491 0039, Dec-Easter 0900-1700*, with *guardaparques*, who can advise on walks. From here you can go on a guided visit (only with own vehicle, four to five hours), to natural caves and to the **Cueva de las Pinturas**, which contains petroglyphs. Also from here, an hour-long trail goes to Cerro Bahía Blanca.

Villa Ventana, 10 km further, is a pretty, wooded settlement with excellent teashop, Casa de Heidi, and good food at Las Golondrinas. The town of **Sierra de la Ventana**, further east, is a good centre for exploring the hills, with a greater choice of hotels than Villa Ventana, and wonderful open landscapes all around.

Listings Atlantic coast

Tourist information

Pinamar

Tourist office
Av Bunge y Libertador, T02254-517020, www.pinamar.gov.ar, www.pinamar turismo.com.ar. Daily 0800-2300.
English spoken, helpful, can book accommodation.

Villa Gesell

Main tourist office
Av 3 No 820 entre Paseos 108 y 109, T02255-478042, www.gesell.gob.ar. Daily 0800-2000 (till 2300 high season).
Very helpful, English spoken. Also in the bus terminal and 2 other locations. There is also a tourist office in Mar de las Pampas (Mercedes Sosa y El Lucero, T02255-452823, summer 0900-2200); see also www.mardelaspampas.com.ar, for more information.

Mar del Plata

Tourist office
Next to the Casino Central on Blvd Marítimo 2270, T0223-495 1777, daily 0800-2000, www.turismomardelplata. gov.ar.
Very helpful and can provide good leaflets on events, information on bus routes and lists of hotels and apartment/chalet letting agents, including family homes (when everywhere else is full). There are also tourist offices at the airport and the bus station.
For what's on, see www.mardelplata.com (English/Spanish).

Miramar

Tourist office
Av Costanera y 21, T02291-420190, www.miramar.tur.ar. Daily 0800-2200.
Helpful, with listings and maps.

Necochea

Tourist office
On the beachfront at Av 79 y Av 2, T02262-438333, www.necochea.tur.ar.
English spoken, list of apartments for rent.
See also www.necocheanet.com.ar.

Towards Bahía Blanca

Tourist office
Faro Recalada y Pedro de Mendoza, Monte Hermoso, T02921-481123, http://montehermoso.porinternet.com.ar.

Bahía Blanca

Tourist office
Drago 1900, p 1 of bus terminal, T0291-481 8944, http://turismo.bahiablanca.gob.ar. Mon-Fri 0800-1500.

Very helpful. Also at Drago 45, T0291-500 1564, in the centre.

Sierra de la Ventana
There is a helpful tourist office on the edge of Villa Ventana (T0291-491 0095, www.villaventana.com) and another in Sierra de la Ventana (Av Roca 19, just before railway track, T0291-491 5303, www.sierradelaventana.org.ar).

Where to stay

Since accommodation is plentiful all along the coast, only a small selection is listed here. All the resorts have a wide selection of campsites; most are well-equipped and many have *cabañas* as well as tent sites. Most resorts have *balnearios*, private beaches, where you pay US$25-50 per day for family/group use of a sunshade or beach hut, showers, toilets and restaurants. Avoid Jan when the whole coast is packed out.

Pinamar
There are plenty of hotels in Pinamar, of a high standard, all 4-stars have a pool. Some hotels are a long way from the beach. Book ahead in Jan and Feb. All those listed are recommended.

$$$$-$$$ Del Bosque
Av Bunge 1550 y Júpiter, T011-4394 9605,
www.hotel-delbosque.com.
Very attractive, in woods, not on the beach, a smart 4-star with a wide range of rooms and seasonal prices, pool, tennis courts, nice restaurant, good service.

$$$ La Posada
Del Tuyú y Del Odiseo, T02254-482267,
www.laposadapinamar.com.ar.
Very comfortable, small, quiet, with spacious rooms, next to sea and town centre, pretty gardens where breakfast is served. An excellent choice.

$$$ Viejo Hotel Ostende
Biarritz y El Cairo, T02254-486081, www.
viejohotelostende.com.ar. Summer only.
Attractive, smallish hotel, open since 1913. Although it has been renovated, it retains some historic flavour in the old wing, comfortable in a simple way, excellent service. There's a pool and private *balneario*. Breakfast, dinner and a beach hut are all included.

Villa Gesell and around

$$$ De la Plaza
Av 2 entre 103 y 104, T02255-468793,
www.delaplazahotel.com.
Small, spotless, with excellent service, open all year round. Rooms are plain but very comfortable, good value.

$$ Hostería Gran Chalet
Paseo 105 No 447 entre Av 4-5, T02255-462913,
www.gesell.com.ar/granchalet.
Warm welcome, comfortable large rooms, good breakfast. Closed off season.

$ pp Hostel El Galeón
Av 5 No 834 (entre Paseos 108 y 109), T02255-453785, www.galeongesell.com.ar.
Popular hostel, can accommodate from singles to groups of 8 but no dorms, some rooms have kitchen, DVDs, laundry service, cooking facilities, good communal areas, convenient.

Mar del Plata
Busy traffic makes it impossible to move along the coast in summer: choose a hotel near the beach you want.

$$$$ Costa Galana
Bv Marítimo 5725, T0223-410 5000,
www.hotelcostagalana.com.
The best by far, a 5-star modern tower, all luxury facilities, at Playa Grande.

$$$ Dos Reyes
Av Colón 2129, T0223-491 0383,
www.dosreyes.com.ar.
Long-established but modernized town centre hotel with smart, well-equipped rooms. Guests have access to a *balneario*. Good value off season, big breakfast.

$$$-$$ Selent
Arenales 2347, T0223-494 0878,
www.hotelselent.com.ar. Open all year.
Quiet with neat rooms, warm welcome, great value. Recommended.

$$ Abra Marina
Alsina 2444, T0223-486 4646, http://users.
copetel.com.ar/abramarinacafehotel.
Open all year round.
A good budget choice, simple rooms, all services, café/bar, central.

$$ Los Troncos
Rodríguez Peña 1561, T0223-451 8882,
www.hotellostroncos.com.ar.

Small, chalet-style hotel in quiet residential area, handy for Güemes bars and restaurants, garden.

Miramar

Dozens of hotels and apartments between Av 26 and the sea. For a full list see www.miramar-digital.com.ar.

$$ Brisas del Mar
C 29 No 557, T0291-420334, www.
brisasdelmarhotel.com.ar. Summer only.
Sea front, family-run, neat rooms, cheery restaurant, attentive, good value.

Necochea

Most hotels are in the seafront area just north of Av 2. There are at least 100 within 700 m of the beach. Many close off season, when you can bargain with those still open.

$$$ Hostería del Bosque
C 89 No 350, T02262-420002,
www.hosteria-delbosque.com.ar.
5 blocks from beach, quiet, comfortable, lovely atmosphere in this renovated former residence of an exiled Russian princess, great restaurant.

$$$ Presidente
C 4 No 4040, T02262-423800,
www.presinec.com.ar. Mostly closed
in winter; open some weekends.
A 4 star large hotel recommended for excellent service, comfortable rooms and pool, price depends on room category and season.

$$ Bahía
Diagonal San Martín 731, T02262-423353,
hotelbahia@necocheanet.com.ar.
Really kind owners, comfortable rooms, pool in neat gardens. Recommended.

$$ San Miguel
C 85 No 301, T02262-521433, www.hotel-
sanmiguel.com.ar. Open all year.
Good service and value, comfortable.

Towards Bahía Blanca

$$ Petit Hotel
Av Argentina 244, Monte Hermoso, T02921-
481818, www.petitfrentealmar.com.ar.
Simple, modernized 1950s style, family-run, on the beach, restaurant, breakfast extra, cooking facilities. Recommended.

Bahía Blanca and around

$$$ Argos
España 149, T0291-455 0404, www.hotelargos.com.
3 blocks from plaza, 4-star business hotel, smart, Wi-Fi, good breakfast, restaurant.

$$ Bahía Blanca
Chiclana 227, T0291-455 3050,
www.bahia-hotel.com.ar.
Business hotel, good value, well-equipped comfortable rooms, bright bar and *confitería*. Recommended.

$$ Barne
H Yrigoyen 270, T0291-453 0294,
www.hotelbarne.bvconline.com.ar.
Family-run, low-key, good value, welcoming.

$ Hostel Bahía Blanca
Soler 701, T0291-452 6802,
www.hostelbahiablanca.com.
Light, spacious dorms from US$11 and doubles with and without bath in this old building. Close to town, offers lots of travel advice.

Sierra de la Ventana

Tornquist

$ La Casona
Rawson 232, T0291-494 0693,
http://com-tur.com.ar/lacasona/.
A renovated house with plain rooms.

$ San José
Güemes 138, T0291-494 0152, www.
hotelsanjose1.wix.com/hotelsanjose.
Small, central, with plain, faded rooms.

Villa Ventana

Lots of accommodation in *cabañas*; municipal campsite by river with all facilities. See www.sierralaventana.org.ar.

$$$ El Mirador
On RP 76 Km 226, T0291-494 1338,
www.complejoelmirador.com.ar.
Great location right at the foot of Cerro de la Ventana, comfortable rooms, some with tremendous views, very peaceful, good restaurant.

Sierra de la Ventana town

$$$ Cabañas La Caledonia
Los Robles y Ombúes in Villa Arcadia, a couple of blocks over the railway track, T0291-491 5268, www.lacaledonia.com.ar.

Well-equipped, comfortable small cabins in pretty gardens with a pool. Price is for a cabin for up to 4 people.

$$$ Las Vertientes
RP 76, Km 221, signposted just west of the turning to Villa Ventana, T011-4773 6647, http://com-tur.com.ar/lasvertientes/.
Very welcoming ranch with a house for rent (price is for 6 people; breakfast extra) in lovely surroundings, relaxing, horse riding, mountain biking, trekking, day visits.

$$ Alihuen
Tornquist y Balneario, T0291-491 5074, http://com-tur.com.ar/alihuen.
A delightful old place near the river, dining room, garden, pool, good value.

Camping

Yamila
Access on C Tornquist, T0291-154 189266, www.campingyamila.8m.com.
Camping and small cabins with bunks, **$**. Lovely shady site by river, hot showers, food shop.

Restaurants

Mar del Plata
The seafood restaurants in the Centro Comercial Puerto are brightly lit and not atmospheric. 2 other areas have become popular for smaller shops, bars and restaurants: Around C Güemes and around Alem, next to the cemetery, where there lots of pubs and bars serving traditional favourites.

$$ Almacén El Condal
Alsina y Garay.
Charming old street-corner bar, serving *picadas* and drinks, popular with young crowd.

$$ Manolo
Rivadavia 2371 and on the coast at Blv Marítimo y Castelli, as well as Leandro N Alem y Almafuerte, www.churrosmanolo.com.
Famous for *churros* and hot chocolate in the early hours, popular with post-party people.

$$ Pehuén
Bernardo de Irigoyen 3666, see Facebook.
Very good and popular *parrilla*.

$$ Taberna Baska
12 de Octubre 3301.
Seafood and Basque country dishes, next to the port.

$$ Tisiano
San Lorenzo 1332.
Good pasta restaurant in a leafy patio.

Necochea
There are some excellent seafood restaurants.

$$ Chimichurri
C 83 No 345, T02262-420642.
Recommended for *parrilla*.

$$ Parrilla El Loco
Av 10 y 65, T02262-422761.
A classic *parrilla*, deservedly popular for superb steaks.

$$ Sotavento
Av Costanera y Pinolandia.
On the beach, varied menu, can get very busy but good value.

$ Pizzería Tempo
C 83 No 310, T02262-425100.
A lively traditional place serving good pizzas.

Towards Bahía Blanca

$$ Marfil
Valle Encantado 91, Monte Hermoso.
The smartest, delicious fish and pastas.

$ Pizza Jet
Valle Encantado e Int Majluf, Monte Hermoso, see Facebook.
Hugely popular for all kinds of food, arrive before 2130 to get a table.

Bahía Blanca

$$ Micho
Guillermo Torres 3875, T0291-457 0346.
A superb chic fish restaurant at the port (take bus 500 or 501, but go there by taxi at night, as it's in an insalubrious area).

$$ Santino
Dorrego 38, see Facebook.
Italian-influenced, quiet sophisticated atmosphere, good value. Recommended.

$ El Mundo de la Pizza
Dorrego 55, see Facebook.
Fabulous pizzas, lots of choice, the city's favourite.

Cafés

Café del Angel
Paseo del Angel, entrances at O'Higgins 71 and Drago 63.
Good value lunches, friendly place.

Muñoz
O'Higgins y Drago.
Sophisticated café, good for reading the papers.

Piazza
On the corner of the plaza at O'Higgins y Chiclana.
Great coffee, buzzing atmosphere, good salads, and cakes too.

Festivals

Mar del Plata
Late Jan National fishing festival.
Nov International film festival, www.mardel plataflmfest.com.
Mid-Dec Fiesta del Mar.

Transport

Pinamar
Bus Terminal 20 mins' walk from the beach at Av Bunge e Intermédanos, T02254-403500. To **Buenos Aires**, US$29-42, 4-5 hrs, several companies.

Villa Gesell and around
Bus Terminal at Av 3 y Paseo 140, T02255-477253. Direct to **Buenos Aires**, many companies, 5 hrs, US$30-44. To **Mar del Plata** see below.

Mar del Plata
Air Astor Piazzolla airport in Camet, T0223-478 5811, 7 km north of town. Several flights daily to **Buenos Aires**, and LADE to many Patagonian towns once or twice a week. Remise taxi from airport to town, US$10, also bus 542 (signed Aeropuerto) US$0.50 (payable with a magnetic card).

Bus For information T0223-561 3743. The combined bus and train station, Terminal Ferroautomotora, is Av Luro y San Juan; bus No 541 to the centre, Nos 511, 512 and 512B continuing south to beaches (US$0.50 only with top-up card). To **Buenos Aires**, 5-6 hrs, US$28-47, many companies. El Rápido (T0223-494 2507, www.el-rapido.com.ar) run several services a day to most coastal towns: to **Villa Gesell**, 2 hrs, US$11.50; to **Pinamar**, 2 hrs, US$12.50; to **Miramar**, 30 mins, US$5.75; to **Necochea**, US$12.50 (also Río Paraná, T0223-561 3907, Cóndor Estrella, T0223-561 3999); to **Bahía Blanca**, 8 hrs, US$45. To **Bariloche**, Via Bariloche, El Rápido Argentino, 19-20 hrs, US$118-135. To all Patagonian towns along RN 3, ending at **Comodoro Rivadavia**, 23 hrs,

US$142-162, with **Transportadora Patagónica**. To **Mendoza**, Rápido Argentino or San Juan Mar del Plata, daily, 20-22 hrs, US$77-114.

Train To/from **Buenos Aires** (Constitución), enquire beforehand if any trains are running. See www.nuevaterminalmardel.com.ar for train and bus information.

Miramar
Bus Terminals at C 34 y Av 23, T02291-423359, at Fortunato de la Plaza y C 19, and a few others. To **Buenos Aires**, 6½-7 hrs, US$40-45.

Necochea
Bus Terminal at Av 58 y Jesuita Cardiel, T422470, 3 km from the beach area; bus 513 from outside the terminal to the beach. Taxi to beach area US$5. To **Buenos Aires**, 6½-8½ hrs, US$35-50. To **Bahía Blanca**, US$30.

Towards Bahía Blanca
Bus From Monte Hermoso either to **Buenos Aires** or **Bahía Blanca** (US$7) with Cóndor Estrella, also several combis or minibuses to **Bahía Blanca**. From Pehuén-Có to Bahía Blanca, with La Patagonia, T0291-455 3215.

Bahía Blanca
Air Airport Comandante Espora, T0291-486 0300, lies 11 km northeast of centre, US$10 in a taxi. Daily flights to **Buenos Aires**. LADE (T0291-452 1063) has weekly flights to **Buenos Aires**, Necochea, Mar del Plata and Patagonian coastal towns.

Bus Terminal in old railway station 2 km from centre, at Estados Unidos y Brown, T0291-481 9615, connected by buses 512, 514, or taxi US$4-5, no hotels nearby; information office Mon-Fri 0600-1200. To **Buenos Aires** frequent, several companies, 8-10 hrs, US$59-67, shop around. A comfortable option is **Plusmar** suite bus, with flat beds (0291-T456 0616). To **Mar del Plata**, see above. To **Córdoba**, 13-15 hrs, US$73-84. To **Bariloche**, El Valle, Vía Bariloche, 11-13 hrs, US$66-75. To **Puerto Madryn**, Transportadora Patagónica, Don Otto, Cóndor Estrella, 9-10½ hrs, US$58-65. To **Tornquist**, US$5.75, Cóndor Estrella, T0291-481 4846, www. condorestrella.com.ar, 1 hr 20 mins; to **Sierra de la Ventana** (town) Cóndor Estrella and Expreso Cabildo, 2 hr 20 mins, US$10.20. Also minibus to Tornquist with Cerro, T0291-494 1129.

Train Station at Av Gral Cerri 750, T0291-452 9196. To/from **Buenos Aires**, trains suspended in 2017.

West of
Buenos Aires

Rising out of the flat arid pampa, the Sierras of Córdoba and San Luis provide a dramatic backdrop to popular holiday towns and mountain retreats. Beyond the plains, fertile valleys stretch along the length of the Andean precordillera and climb up to the heights of Aconcagua and its neighbours. The western provinces of Mendoza, San Juan, La Rioja and Catamarca cover extreme contrasts, but Mendoza and the surrounding area to the south is popular for its excellent wines, climbing and superb ski and adventure resorts such as Malargüe.

Córdoba   *Colour map 8, A3.*

less hectic than Buenos Aires and just as vibrant

Córdoba, the capital Córdoba Province, is the second largest city in the country with a population of 1.5 million. It was founded in 1573 and has some fine historic buildings as well as a lively university population. In fact, it was the Jesuits in Córdoba who established the first university in the whole country in 1613. (Today, the city boasts two universities.) Córdoba is also an important transport centre and vital industrial hub, as it is the home of Argentina's motor industry. It is also a busy modern metropolis with a flourishing shopping centre.

☆Old city

At the city's heart is **Plaza San Martín**, with a statue of the Liberator. On the west side is the old **Cabildo** ① *Independencia 30, free, except for entry to exhibitions, 0900-2100 (Mon 1400-2100).* Built around two internal patios, the building now houses the tourist office, a small gallery and a bookshop. Next to it stands the **Cathedral** ① *T0351-422 3446, 0800-1300, 1630-2000,* the oldest in Argentina (begun 1640, consecrated 1671), with attractive stained glass windows and a richly decorated ceiling. Look out for statues of angels resembling Native Americans. Behind the cathedral is the pleasant Plaza del Fundador, with a statue to the city's founder, Jerónimo Luis de Cabrera.

One of the features of this part of the city is its old churches. Near Plaza San Martín at Independencia 122 is the 16th-century **Carmelo Convent** and chapel of **Santa Teresa** ① *Mon-Sat, 0700-1430, 1730-1930,* whose rooms and beautiful patio form the **Museo de Arte Religioso Juan de Tejeda** ① *www.museotejeda.com, Mon-Fri 0900-1600, Sat 1000-1330, US$1, US$1.25 on Sat, guided visits also in English and French.* This houses one of the finest collections of religious art in the country. The **Manzana Jesuítica** ① *contained within Av Vélez Sarsfield, Caseros, Duarte Quirós and Obispo Trejo,* has been declared a World Heritage Site by UNESCO. La Compañía (Obispo Trejo y Caseros, built between 1640 and 1676) has a vaulted ceiling reminiscent of a ship's hull. Behind it, on Caseros, is the beautiful **Capilla Doméstica**, a private 17th-century Jesuit chapel (guided visits only). Next to it are two former Jesuit institutions: the main building of the **Universidad Nacional de Córdoba** ① *T0351-433 2075, Mon-Sat 0900-1830, US$2 by guided tour only,* housing one of the most valuable libraries in the country; and the **Colegio Nacional de Montserrat. Guided tours** ① *US$2, daily at 1000 and 1700, available in English,* of the church, chapel, university (called Museo Histórico) and school leave from Obispo Trejo 242. The **Basílica de La Merced** ① *25 de Mayo 83,* was built in the early 19th century, though its fine gilt wooden pulpit dates from the colonial period. On its exterior, overlooking Rivadavia, are fine murals in ceramic by local artist Armando Sica. Further east,

Best for
Adventure tourism ▪ Colonial cities ▪ Wine

at Boulevard J D Perón, is the magnificent late 19th-century **Mitre railway station** ① *daily 0900-1700*, with its beautiful tiled *confitería*, still used for Sunday evening tango shows.

Formerly the house of Rafael Núñez, governor of Córdoba, **Museo Marqués de Sobremonte** ① *Rosario de Santa Fe 218, 1 block east of San Martín, T0351-433 1661, Mon-Fri 0900-1200, 1800-2000, US$1, texts in English and German*, is now the only surviving colonial family residence in the city. The museum displays 18th- and 19th-century provincial history. **Museo Municipal de Bellas Artes** ① *Av General Paz 33, T0351-434 1636, Tue-Sun 1000-2000, free*, has a permanent collection of contemporary art by celebrated Argentine artists in an early 20th-century mansion.

Nuevo Córdoba
South of Plaza San Martín, in the hip **Nuevo Córdoba** district, are two more fine art museums: **Bellas Artes Palacio Ferreyra** ① *Av H Yrigoyen 511, T0351-434 3636, Tue-Sun 1000-2000 (in Jan 1000-1300 and 1800-2100), US$1, Wed free*, with 12 salons of Argentine and international works, and **Museo**

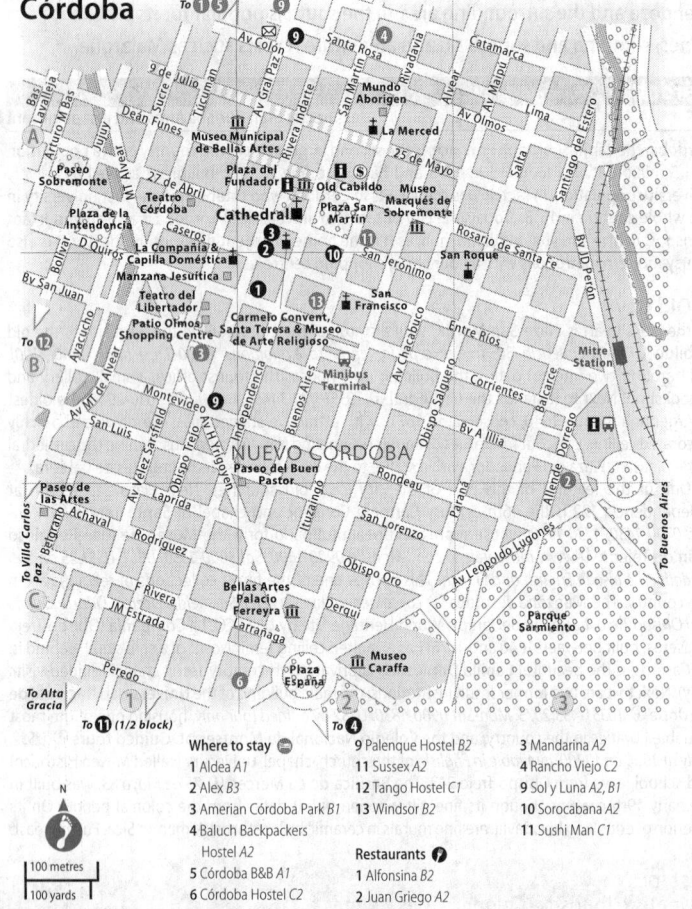

Córdoba

Where to stay
1 Aldea *A1*
2 Alex *B3*
3 Amerian Córdoba Park *B1*
4 Baluch Backpackers
 Hostel *A2*
5 Córdoba B&B *A1*
6 Córdoba Hostel *C2*
9 Palenque Hostel *B2*
11 Sussex *A2*
12 Tango Hostel *C1*
13 Windsor *B2*

Restaurants
1 Alfonsina *B2*
2 Juan Griego *A2*
3 Mandarina *A2*
4 Rancho Viejo *C2*
9 Sol y Luna *A2, B1*
10 Sorocabana *A2*
11 Sushi Man *C1*

100 metres
100 yards

Caraffa ⓘ *Av Poeta Lugones 411, T0351-434 3348, www.museocaraffa.org.ar, Tue-Sun 1000-2000 (in Jan 1000-1300 and 1800-2100), US$1, Wed free (near 50% discount when buying tickets for both Bellas Artes and Museo Caraffa),* showing art from Córdoba. Also in this district is the **Paseo del Buen Pastor** ⓘ *Av H Yrigoyen 325,* on the site of a women's prison, which now has a cultural centre, art gallery, fountains, bookshop and café.

Listings Córdoba *map page 90.*

Tourist information

Agencia Córdoba Turismo old Cabildo
Independencia 30, in the Cabildo, T0351-434 1200, www2.cordoba.gov.ar/turismo/. Daily 0800-2000. Also at the bus terminal, *T0351-433 1982, daily 0700-2100,* and at the airport, *T0351-434 8390, daily 0800-2000.*
All have useful city maps and information on guided walks and cycle tours. See also www.cordobaturismo.gov.ar.

Córdoba City Tour
T0351-15-537 8687, www2.cordoba.gov.ar/turismo/city-tour/.
A big red bus departs daily except Wed 1800, plus 1600 Mon and Fri, 1000 Fri, Sat and Sun, from outside the cathedral, US$9.55, children 4-10 US$3.20.

Where to stay

$$$ Amerian Córdoba Park
Blvd San Juan 165, T0351-526 6600, www.amerian.com.
Swish, modern hotel with marbled foyer and professional service. Comfortable, superb breakfast, convenient and reliable. Also has a business centre, gym, spa and pool.

$$$ Windsor
Buenos Aires 214, T0351-422 4012, www.windsortower.com.
Small, smart, warm, large breakfast, sauna, gym, pool. Excellent white tablecloth dining at the expensive Sibaris restaurant.

$$ Alex
Blvd Illia 742, T0351-421 4350, www.alexhotel.com.ar.
Good value, modern, cosy despite a slightly off-putting exterior. All rooms include a *mate* kit, helpful staff, close to the bus station.

$$ Córdoba B&B
Tucumán 440, T0351-423 0973, www.cordobabyb.com.ar.
Sparsely decorated but pleasant doubles and triples, central, parking, good value.

$$ Sussex
San Jerónimo 125, T0351-422 9070, www.hotelsussexcba.com.ar.
Well kept, with family welcome, small pool, buffet breakfast.

$ pp Aldea
Santa Rosa 447, T0351-426 1312, www.aldeahostel.com.
Nicely designed and decorated, welcoming, terrace with sofas, games, dorm prices depend on number sharing, quite central.

$ pp Baluch Backpackers Hostel
San Martín 338, T0351-422 3977, www.baluchbackpackers.com.
Inviting dorms for 4-6 (US$10-12) and nice doubles (**$$**). Owned and run by backpackers,

central, information and bus tickets, many services, organizes various activities.

$ pp Córdoba Hostel
Ituzaingó 1070, T0351-468 7359, www.cordobahostel.com.ar.
In Nueva Córdoba district, small rooms (US$12.50 in dorms, US$30 in double), quite noisy, private lockers in rooms. Small discount for HI members.

$ pp Palenque Hostel
Av Gral Paz 371, T0351-423 7588, see Facebook.
Lovely hostel in a 100-year-old building, spacious common areas, small dorms, doubles with TV.

$ pp Tango Hostel
Bolívar 613, T0351-425 6023, www.tangohostelcordoba.com.
Good hostel in Nueva Córdoba student district, clubs and bars all around, rooms for 4-11 (US$10.50-13.50), doubles (US$40), library, free coffee/*mate*, local trips arranged.

Estancia
Estancia Los Potreros
Casilla de Correo 64, 5111 Río Ceballos (no phone, contact through the website or via Buenos Aires T011-6091 2692), www.estancialospotreros.com.
An exclusive 2428-ha working cattle farm in the wild and scenic Córdoba hills. High standard of accommodation, with warm hospitality and attention to detail in keeping with a time past. The 'riders' estancia', unrivalled in its fabulous horses (impeccably trained and calm farm horses). Non-equestrians can relax by the pool, go birdwatching (best Oct-Mar), walking or just enjoy the peaceful hilltop setting and savour the delicious food and wines – all included in the price: 3 nights' minimum stay (from US$1110 all inclusive). Highly recommended. Transfers, from Córdoba airport (1 hr) or the local town, Río Ceballos, are included in the rates.

Restaurants

$$$-$$ Juan Griego
Obispo Trejo 104, T0351-570 6577, www.juangriegorestobar.com. Mon-Fri 0800-1600.
On the 7th floor of the Colegio de Escribanos with a view of the Manzana Jesuítica, this modern Argentine restaurant is unmissable. Open for breakfast and lunch.

$$ Rancho Viejo
Martínez 1900, Parque Sarmiento, T0351-468 3685.
Popular *parrilla* in rustic surroundings in the park.

$$-$ Sol y Luna
Gral Paz 278, T0351-425 1189, www.solylunaonline.com.ar. Mon-Sat 1200-1530.
Vegetarian with a change of menu daily, fresh food, lunchtime specials, good desserts. 2nd branch at Montevideo 66, Nueva Córdoba, T0351-421 1863.

$$-$ Sushi Man
Independencia1181, Nueva Córdoba, T0351-4603586, www.sushimanweb.com.
Those who have had their fill of meat and would like to order in can opt for this chain restaurant offering decent sushi options; several branches.

$ Alfonsina
Duarte Quirós 66, T0351-427 2847, see Facebook. Daily 0800-0300.
Rural style in an old house, simple meals, pizzas and *empanadas* or breakfasts with home-made bread, piano and guitar music, popular.

Cafés
Mandarina
Obispo Trejo 171, T0351-426 4909, www.mandarinaresto.com.ar.
Central, welcoming, leafy, lots of great breakfasts, good for lunch and dinner. Highly recommended.

Sorocabana
San Jerónimo 91, T0351-422 7872, see Facebook. Daily 24 hrs.
Great breakfasts, popular, good views of Plaza San Martín.

Bars and clubs

There are plenty of bars, pubs and *boliches* in which to wet one's whistle and dance the night away in Córdoba. See www.nochecordobacapital.com.ar.

In **Nuevo Córdoba** head to Calles Rondeau, Larrañaga or Cañada. C Buenos Aires between Centro and Nuevo Córdoba has many trendy nightspots as well. **El Abasto** district, on the river (about 8 blocks north of Plaza San Martín) has several good, cheap places. Another popular nightlife area lies further northwest in **Chateau Carreras**.

Entertainment

See free listings in the local newspaper *La Voz del Interior* (www.vos.com.ar), for events.

Cinema
Many including **Cineclub Municipal** (Bv San Juna 49), **Teatro Córdoba** (27 de Abril 275), both

showing independent and foreign language films, and the theatre in **Shopping Patio Olmos**, a mall in a wonderful old palace with a stylish food area, with new releases.

Music

Cuarteto is a Cordobés style with an enthusiastic following. See www.kuarteto.com for groups, news and shows.

Tango

There are free tango shows in Plaza San Martin Sat, 2100, and at the plaza of Shopping Patio Olmos, Sun, 2000.

Theatre

Teatro del Libertador, *Av Vélez Sarsfield 365, T0351-433 2323*. Traditional and sumptuous, with a rich history. Several other smaller theatres.

Shopping

The main shopping area is along the pedestrian streets north of the plaza. **Shopping Patio Olmos** (Av Vélez Sarsfield and Blv San Juan, www.patioolmos.com) is the city's best mall, located in a wonderful old palace with a stylish food area. There's a weekend handicraft market at **Paseo de las Artes** (Achával Rodríguez y Belgrano, Sat-Sun 1700-2200), selling ceramics, leather, wood and metalware. At other times visit **Mundo Aborigen** (Rivadavia 155, see Facebook), an NGO promoting indigenous communities.

Transport

Air Pajas Blancas airport is 12 km northwest of city, T0351-475 0877, has shops, post office, a good restaurant and a *casa de cambio* (open Mon-Fri 1000-1500). The bus service can be unreliable; a regular or remise taxi charges around US$12-14. **AR/Austral** run a shuttle service several times a day to/from **Buenos Aires**, about 2 hrs. **LATAM** also flies to Buenos Aires. Most major Argentine cities are served by AR without having to go via Buenos Aires. International flights to **Peru**, **Brazil**, **Uruguay** and **Chile** direct, others via Buenos Aires.

Bus Municipal buses and electric buses (trolleys) do not accept cash. You have to Red 33Bus buy cards from kiosks, US$2 per card, normal fare US$0.60.

Minibuses to nearby towns stop at the main terminal and then stop at the minibus terminal, Bv Illia 155, T0351-425 2854.

The bus terminal is at Blv Perón 380, 8 blocks east of main Plaza (taxi US$4), T0351-434 1692, www.terminaldecordoba.com. It has restaurants, supermarket, internet, left-luggage lockers, ATM, remise taxi desk and tourist office. To **Buenos Aires**, several companies, 9-11 hrs, US$50 *semi cama*, US$55-70 *cama/suite*. To **Salta**, 12 hrs, US$79-83 (*semi cama* and *ejecutivo*), US$96-101 (*suite*). To **Mendoza**, 9-12 hrs, frequent, US$60-69 (*semi cama* and *ejecutivo*). To **La Rioja**, 6-7 hrs, US$38. To **Catamarca**, 6 hrs, US$31.50. **TAC** and **Andesmar** have connecting services to several destinations in **Patagonia**. See towns below for buses to the Sierras de Córdoba.

Train Station at Bv Perón 100, T0351-426 3565. Train from **Buenos Aires** Mon, Fri 1900, arrives 1240, returns Thu, Sun 1335, arrives 0650; fares US$19, US$23 and US$67 for a berth. Ticket office open Mon-Tue 0830-1800, Wed-Sun 1000-1800, www.sofse.gob.ar.

Sierras de Córdoba
go beyond the suburban sprawl to find beautiful mountain landscapes

The Sierras de Córdoba offer beautiful mountain landscapes with many rivers and streams, plus the advantage of good infrastructure and accessibility. Adventure tourism has really taken off here, so there's something for everyone in the hills and valleys. Popular for tourism among the upper classes in the late 19th century, the Sierras de Córdoba were opened up for mass tourism in the 1940s with the building of lots of hotels. The most visited sights lie along the valleys of Punilla, Traslasierra and Calamuchita, and on the east side of the Sierra Chica, north of Córdoba.

Punilla Valley

The Punilla Valley, situated between the Sierras Chicas to the east and the Sierra Grande to the west, was the first area of the sierras to be developed for weekend and summer visitors. Sadly, the once-idyllic retreats have now become a string of built-up areas alongside Ruta 38. The whole valley is unbearably busy and best avoided during the Argentine holiday period; at other times of year head straight for La Cumbre further north, where there's a more civilized pace of life and plenty of appealing places to stay.

Villa Carlos Paz to La Falda The nearest resort to Córdoba is Villa Carlos Paz, a large, modern town 36 km west that is crammed with hotels. Trips on artificial Lago San Roque are offered in all kinds of water-vehicles and a chair-lift runs to the summit of Cerro de la Cruz. **Cosquín**, 26 km north of Villa Carlos Paz, is the site of the country's most important **folklore festival**, in the last two weeks in January (www.aquicosquin.org), followed by a popular rock festival in early February in Santa Maria, the next town over (www.cosquinrock.net). Located 82 km north of Córdoba, La Falda is not an attractive town but is a good base for walking. To the west, an 80-km rough winding road goes to La Higuera, across the Cumbres de Gaspar. It crosses the vast **Pampa de Olaén**, a 1100-m-high grass-covered plateau with the tiny, 18th-century chapel of **Santa Bárbara** (20 km from La Falda) and the **Cascadas de Olaén**, with three waterfalls, 2 km south of the chapel.

☆**La Cumbre** North of La Falda, La Cumbre is located at the highest point in the Punilla Valley, a 1½-hour drive from Córdoba. Founded by British engineers and workers who built the railway here in 1900, it is an attractive place with tree-lined avenues. It has classy shops, good places to eat and have tea, a golf course and, nearby, the paragliding centre of **Cuchi Corral** (see What to do, page 97). It's the best place to visit if you want to avoid the major resorts to the south. Located 11 km from La Cumbre is the **Centro de Rescate, Rehabilitación y Conservación de Primates** (**Center for Rescue, Rehabilitacion and Care of Primates**) ① *www.proyectocaraya. com.ar, daily 1000-1630, US$10 (US$3.50 for children)*, where visitors can see a wide array of howler monkeys (*carayá*) in their natural environment. Guided tours available. To get there, take a taxi from La Cumbre (US$15).

Capilla del Monte About 106 km north of Córdoba in the heart of the Sierras, Capilla del Monte is a good centre for trekking, paragliding and exploring. Excursions in the hills are recommended, particularly to Cerro Uritorco (1979 m), a four-hour climb (no shade, entry US$13.50). The hike is via La Toma where there are medicinal waters and from where there are further walking opportunities. There is horse riding and tours to meditation and 'energy' centres, where many UFOs sightings have taken place. The area is popular for 'mystical tourism' and holds an annual **Festival Alienígena** in February.

Along Ruta 9

Head north on Route 9, named by the tourist board as the Camino de la Historia, to visit Jesús María and the Jesuit estancias. Jesuit missionaries established huge, enterprising estancias in the countryside here in order to finance their educational and artistic work in Córdoba city. The elegant residences and beautiful chapels built for the priests still remain, complete with some wonderful art and walled gardens, recognized by UNESCO as World Heritage sites.

Jesús María and the estancias (Colour map 8, A3; www.jesusmaria.gov.ar). Located 51 km north of Córdoba on Ruta 9, the town holds a popular gaucho and folklore festival each January, lasting 10 nights from second week. Mainly, however, it is associated with the former **Jesuit Estancia de Jesús María** ① *T03525-420126, see Facebook, Tue-Fri 0900-1900, Sat-Sun 1000-1200, 1400-1800, US$1.75, easy 15-min walk from bus station.* Dating from the 17th century, the estancia has the remains of its once famous winery, reputed to have produced the first wine in the Americas, which was served to the Spanish royal family. In the cloister is an excellent **Museo Jesuítico**, where Cuzco-style paintings, religious objects and a curious collection of plates are exhibited. South of Jesús María is **Estancia Caroya** ① *T03525-426701, Tue-Fri 0900-1900, Sat-Sun 0900-1200, 1700-2000, US$1,* dating from 1616. The largest of the estancias is **Santa Catalina** ① *70 km northwest of Jesús María, T0351-15-550 3752, www.santacatalina.info, Tue-Sun 1000-1300, 1430-1900 in summer, 1400-1800 in winter, US$1,* a splendid place that is still in private hands. Some 4 km from Jesús María is **Sinsacate**, a fine colonial posting inn, now a museum, with chapel attached.

Cerro Colorado An unpaved road branches off Ruta 9 at Santa Elena, 104 km north of Jesús María, to Cerro Colorado, 157 km north of Córdoba, the former home of the late Argentine folklore singer and composer Atahualpa Yupanqui. His house is a **museum** ① *Fundación Atahualpa Yupanqui, T011-15-6685 3900, www.fundacionyupanqui.com.ar, daily 0900-1300, 1600-2000, US$2.75, at the end of the winding road to Agua Escondida, also offers guided tours,* lush grounds, with chance of spotting armadillos. There are about 35,000 rock paintings by the indigenous Comechingones in the nearby **Reserva Natural y Cultural Cerro Colorado** ① *www.cba.gov.ar/reserva-cultural-y-natural-cerro-colorado, Tue-Sun 0900-1300, 1600-2000. The park can only be visited as part of a guided tour which lasts 1½ hours and is included in the entry.* The **Museo Arqueológico** ① *daily 1000-1700 (closes early on Mon)*, at the foot of Cerro Intihuasi, has information on the site itself.

Traslasierra Valley

A scenic road southwest from Villa Carlos Paz passes **Icho Cruz**, before climbing into the Sierra Grande and crossing the Pampa de Achala, a huge granite plateau at 2000 m.

Parque Nacional Quebrada del Condorito ① *Administration at Av JS Bach 504 y Drago, Barrio Costa Azul, Villa Carlos Paz, T03541-484511, www.parquesnacionales.gov.ar, open 0800-2000 (Oct-Mar), 0900-1800 (Apr-Sep), free.* At La Pampilla, 60 km from Villa Carlos Paz, is the entrance to this national park, which covers 37,344 ha of the Pampa de Achala and surrounding slopes. This is the easternmost habitat of the condor and an ideal flying school for the younger birds. Sightings are not guaranteed, but there's great trekking on the *pastizal de altura* (sierran grassland). **Balcón Norte**, 7 km on foot from the car park at the visitors centre, has a marked trail, about three hours, and is linked to the Balcón Sur viewpoint, a further two hours. Tours go from Villa Carlos Paz, or Ciudad de Córdoba and TAC buses from Villa Carlos Paz can stop at La Pampilla on their way to Mina Clavero (one hour, US$5).

Mina Clavero (Colour map 8, A3) This is a good centre, 40 km west of Córdoba, for exploring the high *sierra* and the Traslasierra Valley. There is an intriguing museum, **Museo Rocsen** ① *13 km south and about 5 km east of the village of Nono, T03544-498065, www.museorocsen.org, daily 0900 till sunset, US$6.50, take a taxi.* The personal collection of Sr Bouchón, it is a wonderfully bizarre mix of subjects, including furniture, minerals, instruments, archaeology and animals. There are many hotels, *hosterías, hospedajes*, campsites and restaurants in and around Mina Clavero.

Calamuchita Valley: Alta Gracia *Colour map 8, A3.*

Alta Gracia, 39 km southwest of Córdoba beside Lago Tajamar, is the location of ☆**Estancia Jesuítica Alta Gracia** ① *Plaza Solares, Av Padre Viera 41, T03547-421303, www.museoliniers.org.ar, summer Tue-Fri 0900-1300 and 1500-1900, Sat-Sun 0930-1230 and 1530-1830, closed 1 Jan, 1 May and 25 Dec, US$1.25, free Wed, excellent guided visits included in the price but phone in advance for English tours*, a UNESCO World Heritage Site. If you visit only one Jesuit estancia in the Córdoba region, make it this one. The main buildings of the estancia are situated around the plaza. The church, completed in 1762, with a baroque façade but no tower, is open for services only. To the north of the church is the former Residence, built round a cloister and housing the **Museo Casa del Virrey Liniers**.

Che Guevara grew up in Alta Gracia after his parents left Rosario to live in the more refreshing environment in the foothills of the Andes. He had started to suffer from asthma, which would plague him for the rest of his life. See page 151. The house where he lived 1935-1937 and 1939-1943 before going to Córdoba is preserved as the **Museo Casa de Ernesto Che Guevara** ① *in Villa Nydia, Avellaneda 501, T03547-428579, Tue-Sun 0900-1845, Mon 1400-1845, US$5 (US$3 for students), from the Sierras Hotel, go north along C Vélez Sarsfield-Quintana and turn left on C Avellaneda.* There are plenty of personal belongings from his childhood and youth, plus the letter addressed to Fidel Castro in which Che resigns from his position in Cuba. Texts in Spanish and other languages. The ticket also gives entry to the home of Spanish composer Manuel de Falla (Carlos Pellegrini 1011, T03547-429292), the French sculptor who lived in Alta Gracia from 1932 until 1968, and the **Museo de Arte Gabriel Dubois**.

☆Villa General Belgrano and around

This completely German town, 85 km south of Córdoba, was founded by the surviving interned seamen from the *Graf Spee*, some of whom still live here. It is a good centre for excursions in the surrounding mountains. Genuine German cakes and smoked sausages are sold, there is an Oktoberfest, a **Fiesta de la Masa Vienesa** in Easter week (for lovers of Viennese-style pastries), and the **Fiesta del Chocolate Alpino** during the July holidays. **La Cumbrecita** is a charming German village 30 km west, from where lots of outdoor excursions can be made; see www.lacumbrecita.gov.ar.

Tourist information

Punilla Valley

Information is available from the tourist office in each town: **Villa Carlos Paz** (Av San Martín 400, T0810-888 2729, www.villacarlospaz.gov.ar); **Cosquín** (Av San Martín 590, Plaza Nacional del Folclore, T03541-454644, www.cosquinturismo. gob.ar); **La Falda** (Av Edén 93, T03548-423007, www.turismolafalda.gob.ar); **La Cumbre** (Av Caraffa 300, in the old train station, T03548-452966, www.lacumbre.gob.ar); many of the friendly staff speak English; **Capilla del Monte** (RN 38 y F Alcorta, T03548-482200, www. capilladelmonte.gov.ar, daily 0830-2030).

Traslasierra Valley

There's a tourist office (with ATM) in **Mina Clavero** (Plazoleta Merlo, T03544-470171, www.minaclavero.gov.ar, daily 0900-2200).

Alta Gracia

Tourist office El Molino y Av del Tajamar, T03547-428128, www.altagracia.gov.ar.

Villa General Belgrano

The **tourist office** (Av Roca 168, T03546-461215, http://vgb.gov.ar, daily 0900-2100) has helpful German- and English-speaking staff. See also www.vgb.com.ar.

Where to stay

In all towns, municipal websites have lists of accommodation and places to eat. There are campsites at all the main tourist centres, but summer rainstorms may cause sudden floods along riversides so choose a pitch with care.

Punilla Valley

Cosquín

$$$ La Puerta del Sol
Perón 820, T03541-452045,
www.lapuertadelsolhotel.com.ar.
$$$$ in high season. A decent choice, pool, car hire, half board available.

$$ Siempreverde
Santa Fe 525, behind Plaza Molina, T03541-450093, http://hosteriasiempreverde.com.

Spotless, welcoming and informative owner, some rooms small, comfortable, gorgeous garden.

La Falda

All 80 hotels are full in Dec-Feb.

$$$ L'Hirondelle
Av Edén 861, T03548-422825,
www.lhirondellehostal.com.
Lovely building, some rooms retain their original parquet floor and there's a large garden with a pool, and a restaurant. Welcoming owners.

$$ La Asturiana
Av Edén 835, T03548-422923.
Simple, comfortable rooms, pool, superb breakfast.

La Cumbre

There are plenty of hotels but *cabañas* here are high quality and in attractive settings, ideal for larger groups who want the flexibility of self-catering. **Cruz Chica** is a lovely place to stay, but you'll need a car or taxi to get there.

$$ Hotel La Viña
Caraffa 48, T03548-451388,
www.hotellavina.com.ar.
Nice budget option, with cosy flowery rooms, a large pool and pleasant gardens.

$ pp Hostel La Cumbre
Av San Martín 282, T03548-451368,
www.hostellacumbre.com.
Dorms, rooms for up to 6 and doubles (**$$**). Family-owned, HI member, historic building with garden and pool, occasional *asados*, laundry, information and activities. Recommended.

Capilla del Monte

$$$ Montecassino
La Pampa 107, T03548-482572,
www.hotelmontecassino.com.ar.
Beautiful building from 1901, with lovely rooms, cable TV, jacuzzi and pool with stunning views.

$$ Petit Sierras
Pueyrredón 622 y Salta, T03548-481667,
www.hotelpetitsierras.com.ar.
Renovated hotel with comfortable rooms. The owners run the restaurant **Zarzamora** (**$$**), at the access to town (discounts and free transport for guests).

Traslasierra Valley

Mina Clavero
Several close in low season.

$ pp Hostel Andamundos
San Martín 554, T03544-470249,
www.andamundoshostel.com.ar.
Doubles **$$**, dorms US$10-14. Centrally located,
well-maintained and bright, great atmosphere,
HI discount. They can organize local excursions.

$ pp Oh La La!! Hostel
Villanueva 1192, T03544-472634,
www.ohlalahostel.com.ar.
Youth hostel (dorms US$10-15; double rooms **$$**),
shared bathrooms, tourist information, pool
and gardens.

Calamuchita Valley: Alta Gracia

$$$$-$$$ El Potrerillo de Larreta
On the road to Los Paredones, 3 km
from Alta Gracia, T03547-439033,
www.potrerillodelarreta.com.
Old-fashioned, fabulous 1918 resort and country
club in gorgeous gardens with wonderful views.
Tennis courts, 18-hole golf course, swimming
pool. Great service.

$$$ 279 Boutique Bed & Breakfast
Giorello 279, T03547-15-459493,
www.279altagracia.com.
This small, immaculate bed and breakfast is
the best place to stay in town. A short stroll
to the centre of town, quiet. Recommended.

$ pp Alta Gracia Hostel
Paraguay 218, T03547-428810,
www.altagraciahostel.com.ar.
Family-run hostel, with dorm beds
(US$13, breakfast extra), nice bathrooms
and kitchen. 3 blocks from the main street.
Highly recommended.

Villa General Belgrano and around
Many *cabaña* complexes and chalet-style hotels,
often family-orientated. Book ahead Jan-Feb, Jul
and Easter.

$$ La Posada de Akasha
Los Manantiales 60, T03546-462440,
www.laposadadeakasha.com.
Extremely comfortable, spotless chalet-style
house, with small pool, welcoming.

$ pp El Rincón
Fleming 347, T03546-461323,
www.hostelelrincon.com.ar.

The only hostel in town is beautifully set in dense
forests and green clearings 10-min walk from bus
terminal. Dorms (US$10-12), doubles or singles
with bath (**$$** pp) and camping (US$6-8 pp).
US$3.50 for superb breakfasts. HI discounts, half
price for children under 16. In high season rates
are higher and the hostel is usually full. 10-min
walk from terminal. Recommended.

Camping

Camping Granja Ecológica Veilchen Tal
Ruta Provincial 201 Camino a La Cumbrecita
Km 7, T03546-15-513449, http://facebook.com/
veilchental.
5 mins from town, US$9.65 pp, tent rental
available, showers, meals.

La Cumbrecita
Various hotels and *cabañas*, prices **$$$-$$**.

$$ El Ceibo
T03546-481060, www.hosteriaelceibo.com.
Neat rooms for 2-4, near the entrance to the
town, great views, access to the river.

What to do

Climbing
Club Andino Córdoba, *27 de Abril 2050, Barrio*
Alto Alberdi, Córdoba, T0351-480 5126, www.club
andinocordoba.com.ar. Information on climbing
and trekking throughout the region. It has *refugios*
in the Tanti area, northwest of Villa Carlos Paz.
    For Cerro Champaquí (2790m), near Villa
General Belgrano, contact operators like **Alto**
Rumbo in Córdoba (www.champaqui.com.ar),
or ask at the information offices in Villa Alpina
(T03547-15-595163, www.villaalpinacordoba.
com.ar), or Villa Yacanto (www.turismocordoba.
com.ar/villayacanto/).

Paragliding
The world-renowned paragliding site of Cuchi
Corral is 9 km west of La Cumbre on an unpaved
road; **Escuela de Parapentes** (*Ruta 38, Km 65,*
T03548-15-637130, www.cordobaserrana.com.
ar/parapente.htm). Several local companies offer
flights, which start at US$100 for your 1st flight,
the *Vuelo Bautismo*, 20 mins, accompanied by a
trained paragliding instructor in tandem.

Transport

Punilla Valley
Bus Villa Carlos Paz is a transport hub with
frequent buses to **Buenos Aires** and other

main destinations, as well as to the towns in the Punilla and Traslasierra valleys. To/from **Córdoba** with **CoataCórdoba** (T0351-442 3660, www.coata-cordoba.com.ar), 45 mins, US$2. There are also buses from Córdoba and Villa Carlos Paz to Cosquín, La Falda and Capilla del Monte. From **Villa Carlos Paz** to Mina Clavero, with **CoataCórdoba**, 2¼ hrs, US$6; **Córdoba** to **Mina Clavero**, same company, 3 hrs US$9.

Train The *Tren de las Sierras* (www.sofse. gob.ar) runs twice daily, with an extra train at weekends, between **Cosquín** and **Alta**

Córdoba, via **La Calera** and **Rodríguez del Busto**, 2½ hrs, US$0.50.

Calamuchita Valley: Alta Gracia
Bus **Córdoba** to Alta Gracia, 1 hr, US$2.

Villa General Belgrano and around
Bus **Córdoba** to **Villa General Belgrano**, 2 hrs, US$6.50, **Sierras de Calamuchita** (T0800-555 3928, www.sierrasdecalamuchita.com) and others. To **La Cumbrecita** with **Pájaro Blanco**, Av San Martín 105, T03546-461709, every 2-4 hrs, 1½ hrs, US$5.50. La Cumbrecita to Córdoba, 2½ hrs, US$6.50.

a great base for visiting wineries in the foothills of the Andes

At the foot of the Andes, Mendoza is a dynamic and attractive city, surrounded by vineyards and bodegas. The city was colonized from Chile in 1561, and it played an important role in gaining independence from Spain when the Liberator José de San Martín set out to cross the Andes from here to help in the liberation of Chile. Mendoza was completely destroyed by fire and earthquake in 1861, so today it is essentially a modern city of low buildings and wide avenues (as a precaution against earthquakes), thickly planted with trees and gardens.

Sights
In the centre of the city is the **Plaza Independencia**, in the middle of which is the small **Museo Municipal de Arte Moderno** ⓘ *T0261-425 7279, mmamm@ciudaddemendoza.gov.ar, closed for renovation 2017*, with temporary exhibitions, and on the east side, leafy streets lined with cafés. Mendoza's interesting history can be traced at the **Museo del Pasado Cuyano** ⓘ *Montevideo 544, T0261-423 6031, Mon-Fri 0900-1300, US$1.25*, housed in a beautiful 1873 mansionowned by the Civit family, with San Martín memorabilia in one of its rooms and an exquisite Spanish 17th-century carved altarpiece; excellent tours. Among the pleasant squares nearby is **Plaza España**, attractively tiled and with a mural illustrating the epic gaucho poem, *Martín Fierro*. **Plaza Pellegrini** (Avenida Alem y Avenida San Juan) is a beautiful small square where wedding photos are taken on Friday and Saturday nights, and a small antiques market (Thursday-Saturday). By the Plaza San Martín is the **Basílica de San Francisco** (España y Necochea), 1893, in which is the mausoleum of the family of General San Martín.

North of the centre is **Museo del Area Fundacional** ⓘ *Beltrán y Videla Castillo, T0261-425 6927, Tue-Sat 0900-2000, Sun 1200-2000, holidays 1000-1900, US$2 (valid also 24 hrs for Museo Municipal de Arte Moderno – when open – and Aquarium), getting there: from C Chile buses 5 (line 54) and 3 (line 112); it is also one of the Bus Turístico stops*. It has displays of the city pre-earthquake, with original foundations revealed, and the ruins of Jesuit church **San Francisco** opposite, the informative free tour includes museum, an interesting underground chamber and church.

On the west side of the city is the great **Parque San Martín** ⓘ *information office next to the gates, 10 blocks west of the Plaza Independencia, reached by bus 3 (line 112) from Plaza Independencia, or the trolley 'Parque' from Sarmiento y 9 de Julio, daily 0900-1800*, beautifully designed, with views of the Andes rising in a blue-black perpendicular wall, topped off in winter with dazzling snow, into a china-blue sky. The park has many areas for sports and picnics, and a large lake, where regattas are held. Also here is the **Museo de Ciencias Naturales y Antropológicas** ⓘ *T0261-428 7666, Tue-Fri 0900-1845, Sat-Sun 1500-1845*, which has a female mummy among its fossils and stuffed animals. **Cerro de la Gloria** is a hill

Fact...
Banks are open 0800-1245. *Casas de cambio* (many along San Martín, corner of Espejo/Catamarca) are usually open till 2000 on weekdays, some open Saturday morning.

in the park crowned by an astonishing monument to San Martín, with bas-reliefs depicting various episodes in the equipping of the Army of the Andes and the actual crossing. Bus Turístico and El Oro Negro tourist buses run to the top of the Cerro de la Gloria from the city centre, otherwise it's a 45-minute walk from the park gates.

In the southern suburb of Luján de Cuyo is the city's best art gallery, **Museo Provincial de Bellas Artes**, with a small collection of Argentine paintings. It is housed in the **Casa de Fader** ① *Carril San Martín 3651, Mayor Drummond, T0261-496 0224, closed for remodeling in 2017, getting there: bus 1 (line 19) from C La Rioja, between Catamarca and Garibaldi, 40 mins*, where Fernando Fader painted decorative murals. There are sculptures in the gardens.

Where to stay 🛏
1 Alamo Hostel & Suites *B1*
2 Campo Base *B1*
3 Chimbas Hostel *C3*
4 Confluencia *A2*
5 Damajuana *C1*
6 Hostel Internacional
  Mendoza *C2*
8 InterContinental *C3*
9 Mendoza Backpackers *C2*
10 Mendoza Inn *C1*
11 NH *B1*
12 Nutibara *C1*
13 Park Hyatt *B1*
14 Sheraton *B2*

Restaurants 🍴
1 Anna Bistro *A1*
2 Azafrán *B1*
3 Facundo *B1*
4 Ferruccio Soppelsa *A2*
5 Francesco Barbera *B1*
6 Gio Bar *B1*
7 La Marchigiana *A2*
9 Las Tinajas *B2*
10 Liverpool *B2*
11 Mesón Español *C2*
13 Montecatini *A1*
15 Por Acá *B1*
16 Quinta Norte *B1*
17 Vía Civit *B1*

★Bodegas

Zona Alta del Río Mendoza Situated immediately south of the city, this is the oldest wine-producing area in Mendoza province. The bodegas around the sprawling centres of Maipú and Luján de Cuyo produce wines with a high concentration of fruit. Malbec, particularly, thrives here, in altitudes between 650 m and 1050 m. Many bodegas welcome visitors and offer tastings without pressure to buy. Rent a bicycle and make a day of it, but since the wineries are spread out along pretty country roads with few signs to guide you, it's worth taking a map and contacting the bodegas ahead of your visit. Grape harvesting season is March/April.

In the suburb of Godoy Cruz are **Bodegas Escorihuela Gascón** ① *Belgrano 1108, T0261-424 2744, www.escorihuelagascon.com.ar, Mon-Fri 0900-1800, getting there: take any bus going south along Av San Martín to Alvear, then go east 1 block, or take a taxi, 5 mins*, which has an excellent restaurant (see below). In Coquimbito, east of Maipú, are **Bodega La Rural (San Felipe)** ① *Montecaseros 2625, Coquimbito, T0261-497 2013, www.bodegalarural.com.ar; getting there: bus 10 (subnumber 173) from La Rioja y Garibaldi*, recently modernized, with a **Museo del Vino** ① *Mon-Sat 0900-1730, last tour 1600*; **Tempus Alba** ① *Perito Moreno 572, Coquimbito, T0261-481 3501, www.tempusalba.com*, a modern bodega owned by the Biondolillo family; and **Viña El Cerno** ① *Perito Moreno 631, Coquimbito, T0261-481 1567, www.elcerno-wines.com.ar*, in a lovely country house, with restaurant and olive groves. Quite a long way east of Maipú and 35 km east of Mendoza is **Familia Zuccardi** ① *R33, Las Margaritas, Km 7.5, San Roque, T0261-441 0000, www.familiazuccardi.com, Mon-Sat 0900-1630, Sun 1000-1530*, a large, exceptionally welcoming winery. There's a good restaurant, extensive wine tasting, a tea room, occasional concerts and cookery lessons. South of Maipú is **Carinae** ① *Videla Aranda 2899, Cruz de Piedra, T0261-499 0470, www.carinaevinos.com, daily 1000-1700*. The French owners have an interest in astronomy as well as fine wines.

There are several bodegas in or near **Luján de Cuyo**; booking a visit is advisable here, and a fee is charged in most cases. Larger ones include **Catena Zapata** ① *T0261-413 1100, www.catenawines.com*, and **Séptima** ① *T0261-498 9558, www.bodegaseptima.com, Mon-Fri 1000-1800, Sat 1000-1400, with sunset tastings on Thu in summer*. **Tapiz** ① *C Pedro Molina, Russell, T0261-490 0202, www.tapiz.com.ar*, is not only a winery, but also a 1890s house converted into a superb hotel ($$$$) with restaurant to match. Also with a hotel (La Posada) is **Carlos Pulenta-Vistalba** ① *RS Peña 3135, Vistalba, T0261-498 9400, www.carlospulentawines.com*.

Famed for its Malbec is **Renacer** ① *Brandsen 1863, Perdriel, T0261-524 4416, www.bodegarenacer.com.ar*. Also in Perdriel is **Achával Ferrer** ① *C Cobos 2601, T0261-15-553 5565, www.achaval-ferrer.com*, a boutique bodega which has won many prizes. **El Lagar de Carmelo Patti** ① *Av San Martín 2614, Mayor Drummond, T0261-498 1379, Mon-Sat 1100-1300, 1500-1700*, has tours and tastings led by the owner (by appointment and in Spanish only).

Uco Valley The vineyards of the Uco Valley around the towns of Tupungato and Tunuyán, about 80 km south of Mendoza, are increasingly relevant as producers of high-altitude wines. Several wineries welcome visitors, of which **Bodegas Salentein** ① *Ruta 89 Km 14, Los Árboles, Tunuyán, T02622-429500 ext 3200, www.bodegasalentein.com*, and the **Vines of Mendoza** ① *Ruta 94 Km 11, Tunuyán, T0261-632 1768, www.vinesofmendoza.com*, are among the finest examples.

Listings Mendoza and around

Tourist information

Mendoza

City tourist office
Garibaldi y San Martín, T0261-420 1333, www.ciudaddemendoza.gov.ar. Daily 0900-2100.
The main tourist office, which provides tourist and cultural information for the city. There's a useful booth on the street outside. Also at the **Municipalidad** (9 de Julio 500, 7th floor, T0261-449 5185, Mon-Fri 0800-1400), and 2 small, helpful kiosks at the airport and at the bus terminal, and another at the entrance to **Parque San Martín** (daily 0800-1800). All hand out maps and lists of accommodation, including private lodgings in high season, also lists of bodegas and advice on buses. The city also runs free walking tours and the **Bus Turístico**.

Provincial tourist office
Av San Martín 1143, T0261-413 2101,
www.turismo.mendoza.gov.ar.
Information on the whole province.

Unidad Policial de Asistencia al Turista
Av San Martín 1143, T0261-413 2135.
Assistance available 24 hrs.

Bodegas

For general information on the wines of the region, visit: www.turismo.mendoza.gov.ar (with maps and information on the Camino del Vino); www.mendoza.com (in English with lots of information); www.vendimia2016.mendoza.gov.ar (covering the annual wine harvest festival in Mendoza); www.welcometomendoza.com (designed in English by expats with a good general overview). The tourist office in **Luján de Cuyo** (Roque Sáenz Peña 1000, T0261-498 1912, www.lujandecuyo.gov.ar) is also a good source of information.

Where to stay

Hostels charge about US$11-18 pp and advertise themselves outside the tourist office in town, offering free transfers and lots of extras; don't be pressurized into something you don't want. The **Hyatt** (www.mendoza.park.hyatt.com), **InterContinental** (www.intercontinental.com), **Sheraton** (www.starwoodhotels.com) and **NH** (www.nh-hotels.com) chains have good hotels in the city.

$$$ Nutibara
Mitre 867, T0261-429 5428, www.nutibara.com.ar.
In the need of renovation of its small rooms, but still a good choice for its central though quiet location and its pool.

$ pp Alamo Hostel & Suites
Necochea 740, T0261-429 5565,
www.hostelalamo.com.
Beautiful hostel in a very well-kept 1940s residence with dorms for 4 to 8 and doubles with or without bath (**$$**). Bike rental and tiny pool in a pleasant patio. Recommended for a quiet, yet sociable stay.

$ pp Campo Base
Mitre 946, T0261-429 0707,
www.hostelcampobase.com.ar.
A lively place, discounts for HI members, cramped rooms and private doubles (**$$**), lots of parties and barbecues, popular with mountain climbers, excursions run by YTA agency.

Tip...
Hotels fill up fast and prices rise at Easter, in July (the ski season) and around mid-September (Chilean holidays).

$ pp Chimbas Hostel
Cobos 92 y Acceso Este, T0261-431 4191,
www.chimbashostel.com.ar.
Cheaper without bath and in triples, also private doubles with bath (**$$**), close to bus station (phone in advance for pick-up), 20 mins walk to centre, swimming pool, gym, pleasant, quiet atmosphere.

$ pp Confluencia
España 1512, T0261-429 0430,
www.hostalconfluencia.com.ar.
Slightly more expensive than other hostels, but a convenient choice for groups who care for tidiness and a central location. Rooms for 2 to 4 (private doubles **$$**), some en suite.

$ pp Damajuana
Arístides Villanueva 282, T0261-425 5858,
www.damajuanahostel.com.ar.
A great hostel, comfortable stylish dorms with bath, also double rooms (**$$**), pool and garden.

$ pp Hostel Internacional Mendoza
España 343, T0261-424 0018,
www.hostelmendoza.net.
A comfortable hostel, HI discount, 15-min walk south of Plaza Independencia, small rooms for 4 and 6 with bath (cheaper without a/c), doubles with bath (**$$**), warm atmosphere, good value dinners on offer, barbecues on Fri, bike rental, huge range of excursions run by **BackPackers Travel & Adventure** agency. Warmly recommended.

$ pp Mendoza Backpackers
San Lorenzo 19, T0261-429 4941,
www.mendozabackpackers.com.
Well-run central hostel with an attractive lounge and terrace bar, dorms for 4 and 6, some with bath. HI discounts. Excursions run by **BackPackers Travel & Adventure** agency.

$ pp Mendoza Inn
Arístides Villanueva 470, T0261-420 2486,
www.mendozahostel.com.
In the lively bar area, small dorms for 4 to 8, some with bath, and a private double (**$$**), large garden with a tiny pool, dinner extra, HI discounts. Excursions run by **BackPackers Travel & Adventure** agency.

Camping

Camping Suizo
Av Champagnat, El Challao, 8 km from city,
www.campingsuizo.com.ar.
Modern, shady, with pool, barbecues, hot
showers and *cabañas* for 4 and 6. Recommended.

Zona Alta del Rio Mendoza

$$$$ Cavas Wine Lodge
Costaflores, Alto Agrelo, Luján de Cuyo,
T0261-456 1748, www.cavaswinelodge.com.
A pricey but heavenly experience, ideal for
a romantic and wonderfully relaxing stay.
Spacious rooms in a beautifully restored rural
mansion, with restaurant and spa. Each room
has a fireplace and terrace, swimming pool,
wonderful views. Highly recommended.

$$$ Parador del Ángel
Jorge Newberry 5418, 100 m from main plaza,
Chacras de Coria, Luján de Cuyo, T0261-496 2201,
www.paradordelangel.com.ar.
Restored 100-year old house, tastefully
decorated, very relaxing, gardens, pool,
owner is an experienced mountain climber.

$$$ Tikay Killa Lodge & Wines
Montecaseros 3543, Coquimbito, Maipú,
T0261-15-368 5170, www.tikaykilla.com.ar.
Small lodge in the Ruta del Vino, white rooms,
parking, garden, wine tours and other activities
organized, helpful English-speaking manager.

Restaurants

There are many open-air cafés for lunch on
Peatonal Sarmiento and restaurants around
Las Heras. Arístides Villanueva, the extension
of Colón heading west, has good restaurants
and bars, eg the microbrewery Antares at
No 153, www.cervezaantares.com (as well as
hostels). La Alameda (Av San Martín, north of
C Córdoba) is another pleasant bar area with
some basic restaurants open at lunchtime. For
a special occasion, many of the wineries have
excellent restaurants.

$$$ 1884 Francis Mallman
Bodega Escorihuela, Belgrano 1188, Godoy Cruz,
T0261-424 2698, http://1884restaurante.com.ar.
Open for dinner only, reservation is advisable.
The place to go for a really special dinner.
Mallman is one of the country's great chefs, exotic
and imaginative menu. Highly recommended.

$$$ Anna Bistró
Av Juan B Justo 161, T0261-425 1818, www.anna
bistro.com. Open from breakfast to a late dinner.
One of the most attractive restaurants in town,
informal, French-owned, very welcoming, good
food and drink, French and Italian flavours, open
from breakfast to a late dinner, excellent value.
Recommended

$$$ Azafrán
Sarmiento 765, T0261-429 4200,
http://azafranresto.com.ar.
A fine-wine lover's heaven, with an extensive
range from all the best bodegas, expert advice
on wines and a fabulous delicatessen where you
can enjoy superb *picadas*. Its menu changes with
the season. Recommended.

$$$ El Mesón Español
Montevideo 244, T0261-429 6175, see Facebook.
Spanish food, including great paella,
live music Wed-Sat.

$$$ Facundo
Sarmiento 641, T0261-420 2866.
Good modern *parrilla*, lots of other choices
including Italian, good salad bar.

$$$ Francesco Barbera
Chile 1268, T0261-425 3912,
www.francescoristorante.com.ar.
Smart old town house with a wonderful
garden, excellent Italian food, choose from
over 350 different wines.

$$$ La Marchigiana
Patricias Mendocinas 1550, T0261-423 0751,
www.marchigiana.com.ar.
One of Mendoza's best restaurants and great
value. Italian food served in spacious surroundings
with charming old-fashioned service.

$$$ Montecatini
Gral Paz 370, T0261-425 2111,
http://montecatiniristo.com.ar.
Good Italian food, seafood and *parrilla*, more
tourist oriented, popular with families.

$$ Gio Bar
Chile 1288, T0261 420 4107, http://giobar.com.ar.
Attractively set and casual, a good choice for
Italian-style sandwiches, pizzas and salads.

$$ Las Tinajas
Lavalle 38, T0261-429 1174, www.lastinajas.com.
Large buffet-style/all-you-can-eat at very
reasonable prices, wide selection of pastas, grills,
Chinese, desserts and so on. Cheap wine, too.

$$ Por Acá
Arístides Villanueva 557, see Facebook.
Open 2100 till late.
Bar for pizzas and drinks, popular, noisy.

$$ Quinta Norte
Mitre 1206, see Facebook.
Cheap deals and generous portions in an elegant mansion on Plaza Independencia.

$$ Vía Civit
Emilio Civit 277. Open from 0630 onwards.
For first-class sandwiches, tarts and pastries in a relaxed, elegant traditional bakery.

$ Las Heras
Mon-Sat 0830-1300, 1700-2100, Sun 0930-1300.
The atmospheric indoor market has cheap pizza, *parrilla* and pasta. A few food stalls remain open 0830-2300.

$ Liverpool
San Martín y Rivadavia, www.publiverpool.net.
Pub food, sandwiches, burgers, Beatles memorabilia and European football matches on the screen.

Ferruccio Soppelsa
Espejo y Patricias Mendocinas, with several branches, www.soppelsahelados.com.
The best place for ice cream (even wine flavours!). Recommended.

Festivals

Early Mar Fiesta de la Vendimia. The riotous wine harvesting festival is held in the amphitheatre of the Parque San Martín. See www.vendimia2017.mendoza.gov.ar.
Mid-Mar Vendimia Obrera. A more modest affair when vineyard workers, many of whom are of Bolivian origin, recover the roots of the original celebration with live music, wine and food in Cordón del Plata, a village in the Uco valley.
Dec Local wine festivals. A parallel event is the less-promoted but equally entertaining **Gay Vendimia Festival**, featuring parties, shows and the crowning of the Festival Queen, see Facebook: vendimiaparatodosoficial.

Shopping

Handicrafts
The main shopping area is along San Martín and Las Heras, with good clothes, souvenir, leather and handicraft shops as well as vast sports emporia. Cheap shops include: **El Turista** (Las Heras 351), and **Las Viñas** (Las Heras 399,

www.lasvinas.com.ar). For higher quality head to **Raíces** (Peatonal Sarmiento 162), or **Alpataco** (www.alpatacoweb.com.ar) next door. The **Mercado Artesanal** (San Martín 1133, Mon-Fri 0800-1800, Sat 0900-1300) is good for traditional leather, baskets, weaving; there's also a weekend market on Plaza Independencia.

Wine
Good choice of wines at *vinotecas*, such as **Winery** (Chile 898, T0261-420 2840).

What to do

Climbing
Aconcagua Spirit, *Rivadavia 345, Maipú, T0261-559 2819, www.aconcaguaspirit.com.ar.* Arranges treks and climbing on Aconcagua, mule hire, lodging and meal service for expeditions. Recommended for their 6-day horseback expeditions across the Andes.
Club Andinista Mendoza, *F L Beltrán 357, Guaymallén, T0261-431 9870, see Facebook.* Treks and climbs are also run by the famous climber Sr Fernando Grajales (T1(310)-402 2388(US), www.grajales.net). See page 108 for Aconcagua.
Inka Expediciones, *Juan B Justo 345, T0261-425 0871, www.inka.com.ar.* Climbing expeditions, including Aconcagua, highly professional, fixed departure dates, mules for hire.

Cycling
For bike tours and rentals, contact **Internacional Mendoza** (Pedro Molina 63, T0261-423 2103, www.intermza.com). See also **BackPackers Travel & Adventure** below for bike tours and rentals, or shop around a handful of agencies along C Urquiza in Coquimbito, Maipú, such as **Mr Hugo** (Urquiza 2288, Coquimbito, Maipú, T0261-497 4067, www.mrhugobikes.com).

Language schools
Intercultural, *República de Siria 241, T0261-429 0269, www.spanishcourses.com.ar.*

Rafting
Popular on the Río Mendoza; ask agencies for details.
Argentina Rafting, *office in Mendoza at Amigorena 86, T0261-429 6325, www.argentinarafting.com.* Varied activities from its base camp in Potrerillos.

Sightseeing
Bus Turístico, *www.mendozacitytour.com.* Open double-decker bus for city's sightseeing with 18 stops including Cerro de la Gloria. Hourly departures from Peatonal Sarmiento y Av San

Martín 1000-1900, tickets (US$10, hop on/hop off, valid 24 hrs) sold at city's tourist offices.

El Oro Negro, *T0261-498 0510, www.bateatour. com.ar*. Open bus for 2½ hrs bilingual city tours (US$8) including Cerro de la Gloria, 3 daily departures from Plaza Independencia (on C Chile), or 1½ hrs Parque San Martín and Cerro de la Gloria bilingual tours (US$5), 3-4 daily departures from same point.

Trekking and tours

Many agencies, especially on Peatonal Sarmiento, run trekking, riding and rafting expeditions, as well as traditional tours to Alta Montaña and bodegas.

BackPackers Travel & Adventure, *San Lorenzo 19, T0261-429 0707, www.backpackerstravel.com.ar*. Bilingual trips and bike rides through vineyards (US$27 pp). Occasional treks in Aconcagua area. Discounts for hostel network guests. Make sure about extra costs.

Huentata, *Perú 1485, p 2, T0261-425 8950, www.huentata.com.ar*. Conventional tours including Villavicencio and Cañón del Atuel. Recommended.

Mendoza Viajes, *Peatonal Sarmiento 129, T0261-461 0210, www.mendozaviajes.com*. Imaginative tours in comfortable coaches, professional, cheap deals available.

Trekking Travel, *Adolfo C 4171, Villa Nueva, Guaymallén, T0261-421 0450, www.trekking-travel.com.ar*. From easy horse riding to the Andes crossing; trekking in the Aconcagua and Cordón del Plata.

Wine tours

Bus Vitivinícola, *www.busvitivinicola.com*. 4 weekly departures from top hotels and Av San Martín y Garibaldi for visiting Luján de Cuyo's main wineries in 2 alternative circuits, half or full day tours, hop on/hop off, US$17.

Kahuak, *Rivadavia 234, T0261-423 8409, www. kahuak.com.ar*. Mainly focused on a wide range of wine tours. Recommended.

Transport

Air El Plumerillo airport, 8 km northeast of centre, T0261-520 6000, has money exchange, tourist information, shops, restaurant and *locutorio*, but no left luggage. Reached from the centre along San Juan, Av Alem and Salta by bus 6 (line 63 'Mosconi'), hourly, 40 mins journey. Taxi to/from centre US$8-10. Daily flights to **Buenos Aires** and **Santiago de Chile**. Also to **Córdoba**, **Bariloche**, **Iguazú** and a few other national destinations.

Bus Most local services have 2 numbers, a general number and a 'subnumber' in brackets which indicates the specific route. Buses within and near the city are paid with **Red Bus** magnetic cards (trips from US$0.40), which are topped up. They are sold for US$1 at designated outlets, where you can also top up. There are 6 trolley bus routes, plus a streetcar 'Metrotranvía' that runs along Av Belgrano in the centre from Mendoza station to Gutiérrez station, in Maipú, in 30 mins, US$0.40, and a tourist bus decorated as a streetcar runs along the main commercial avenues (US$0.40).

Long distance The huge bus terminal is on the east side of Av Videla, 15 mins' walk from centre (go via Av Alem, which has pedestrian tunnel to gates opposite platforms 38-39), with shops, *locutorio*, tourist information, ATMs, a good café, left luggage (opposite platform 53) and toilets. It's not a place to linger at night. Taxi to/from centre US$2-3, prepare for long queues.

To **Buenos Aires**, 13-17 hrs, US$59-104, many companies. To **Bariloche**, 17 hrs, US$75-107, with **Cata**. To **Córdoba**, 9-12 hrs, US$60-69, several companies.To/from **San Juan**, US$12-17, 2-2½ hrs. To **La Rioja**, US$49-65, 8-9½ hrs. To **Catamarca** 10-11½ hrs, US$61-81. To **Tucumán**, 13-20 hrs, US$79-106. To **Salta**, 18 hrs, US$100-135, via Tucumán or Córdoba. To **Potrerillos**, 1 hr, US$2.25 with **Buttini** (opposite platform 56), which goes on to **Uspallata**, US$5.75, 2¼ hrs and up to **Las Cuevas**, twice a day, US$7, 4 hrs. To **Tupungato**, US$4.50-5.50, 1½-2 hrs, with TBMitre/Cata. To **San Rafael**, US$9, 3-3½ hrs, with Cata and Iselin. To **Malargüe**, direct with **Viento Sur** minibuses, US$18, 5 hrs, or with **Cata**, 6½ hrs, US$18; alternatively with **Cata** or **Iselin**, for connection in San Rafael.

Transport to Santiago, Chile Minibuses (6-7 hrs) and buses (8 hrs) runto Santiago daily, US$35-47. Many companies, from *semi-cama* without service to **Royal Suite**. Most buses and minibuses are comfortable enough, but it's worth paying for a good service as waiting time at the border can be several hours. Buses also go daily to **Viña del Mar** and **Valparaíso**. Information at Mendoza bus terminal: shop around. Book at least 1 day ahead. Passport required, tourist cards given on bus. The ride is spectacular.

There are also direct services, though not daily, to **Lima** (Perú) with **Ormeño** and **El Rápido Internacional**, to **Santa Cruz de la Sierra** (Bolivia) with **Quirquincho**, and to **Montevideo** (Uruguay), with **El Rápido Internacional**.

Car hire Most companies have their offices along C P de la Reta (900 block), next to Plaza Pellegrini.

wine, snow and stars

San Rafael and around *Colour map 8, B2.*

San Rafael, 236 km south of Mendoza, is a tranquil, leafy town in the heart of fertile land which is irrigated by snowmelt from the Andes to produce fine wines and fruit. A road runs southwest over El Pehuenche or Maule pass to Talca (Chile). Several bodegas and olive oil factories can be visited (check opening times at tourist office), including the impressive champagnerie at **Bianchi** ① *Ruta 143, 9 km west of centre, T0260-444 9600, www.vbianchi.com,* whose vineyard and champagne house can be visited on a commercialized tour. They also have a traditional bodega in town, at Comandante Torres 500, T0260-444 8500, which offers an excellent and detailed tour. Some 3 km west is the more intimate **Jean Rivier** ① *H Yrigoyen 2385, T0260-443 2675, www.jeanrivier.com.* At a walking distance from town is **La Abeja** ① *Av H Yrigoyen 1900, T0260-443 9804, www.bodegalaabeja.com.ar,* San Rafael's oldest winery. On the way out to Malargüe, around 20 km southwest of San Rafael is **Algodón Wine Estates** ① *on Ruta 144, Cuadro Benegas, www.algodonwineestates.com,* a state-of-the-art winery with pricey accommodation, restaurant, tennis courts and a golf course. A small but interesting **natural history museum** ① *daily 0800-1900, US$0.50; Iselin bus along Av JA Balloffet,* is 6 km southwest of town at Isla Río Diamante. **Tourist office** ① *Av H Yrigoyen 775 y Balloffet, T0260-443 7860, www.sanrafaelturismo. gov.ar, and in bus terminal (mornings only).*

Southwest of San Rafael, 35 km, is the **Cañón del Atuel**, a spectacular gorge 55 km long with strange polychrome rock formations, home of the Andean condor. It is famous as a rafting centre. Daily buses, Iselin (see Transport), go to the Valle Grande dam at the near end of the canyon, returning in the evening, US$2.75. Remise taxis from San Rafael to Valle Grande charge about US$20. Here there is plenty of accommodation, campsites, river rafting, zip-lining, paragliding and horse riding. The only public transport through the entire gorge up to El Nihuil is Iselin bus at weekends in summer.

☆Towards Las Leñas

At 154 km southwest of San Rafael, Route 222 heads west into the Andes from RN 40 to the chic (expensive) ski resort of Las Leñas. It passes **Los Molles**, at Km 30, where there are thermal springs and an increasing number of accommodation and eating choices. Further along the Las Leñas road is the **Pozo de las Animas**, two natural pits filled with water where the wind makes a ghostly wail, hence the name (Well of the Spirits). At the end of Valle de Los Molles is **Las Leñas** ① *T011-4819 6060, or T0800-222 5362, www.laslenas.com, ski season mid-Jun to end-Oct,* in a spectacular setting at 2240 m with excellent skiing over 170 sq km on 29 pistes, with a maximum drop of 1200 m. It offers many summer adventure activities, too. Beyond Las Leñas the road continues into Valle Hermoso, accessible December to March only.

Malargüe *Colour map 8, B2.*

Further south on Ruta 40, Malargüe is developing as a base for excursions and outdoor activities in the stunning open landscapes nearby. Furthermore, Malargüe has gained the interest of astrophysicists by hosting the world's largest **Pierre Auger Cosmic Ray Observatory** ① *Av San Martín (Norte) 304, T0260-447 1562, www.auger.org, Mon-Fri 0900-1230, 1530-1830, Sat-Sun 1530-1830 (ask in advance for English presentations).* A visit is recommended, together with the excellent **Planetarium** ① *Cdte Rodríguez (Oeste) 207, T0260-447 2116, www.planetariomalargue.com.ar, free guided visits and daily shows.* At the northern access and by a large park with beautiful shade (site of the first estancia) is the helpful **tourist office** ① *Ruta 40 Norte, T0260-447 1659, www.malargue. gov.ar (Facebook: TurismoMalargue), 0800-2030,* also at the bus station.

The most remarkable scenery around Malargüe is in ☆**La Payunia Reserve** ① *access only by guided tour from the guardaparques, 100 km south,* an area of vast grasslands and stark volcanoes where thousands of guanacos roam. Other natural attractions include **Caverna de las Brujas**, to the southwest, which has extraordinary underground cave formations, and **Laguna Llancanelo**, 75 km southeast, which is usually filled with a great variety of birdlife in spring, including nesting Chilean flamingos. There are some magnificent high Andean valleys west of Malargüe and the unusual rock formations of **Volcán Malacara** and **Castillos de Pincheira**.

Where to stay

San Rafael

$$ Nuevo Mundo
Av Balloffet 725, T0260-444 5666,
www.hnmsanrafael.com.
Small business hotel, a little out of
town, with pool, restaurant and spa.

$$ Francia
Francia 248, T0260-442 9351,
www.alojamientofrancia.com.ar.
A lovely place on a quiet street in town
with simple, functional rooms in a manicured
garden; excellent value.

$$ Regine
Independencia 623, T0260-442 1470,
www.hotelregine.com.ar.
Some 8 blocks from centre, a comfortable choice
with good rooms, restaurant and a large pool in
an attractive garden. Very good value.

$$ San Rafael
C Day 30, T0260-443 0127,
www.hotelsanrafael.com.ar.
A decent and reasonably priced option with
plain rooms yet in need of renovation.

$ pp Tierrasoles Hostel
Pellegrini 248, T0260-443 3449,
www.tierrasoles.com.ar.
7 blocks from bus station, small dorms for
6 to 8 and doubles ($$) in a nice residence
with a courtyard.

$ pp Trotamundos Hostel
Barcala 298, T0260-443 2795,
www.trotamundoshostel.com.ar.
On a quiet area next to main streets, a lively
hostel with a nice patio, small dorms for 3 to 6
and a private double ($$).

Towards Las Leñas

There are several plush hotels in Las Leñas,
all $$$$-$$$, and most with pool (see www.
laslenas.com). The resort also has a disco, a
ski shop for renting equipment and several
restaurants. For cheaper accommodation stay
in Los Molles or Malargüe.

Los Molles

$$$ Complejo Los Molles
T0260-15-459 1654, www.complejolosmolles.com.
Wood and stone detached houses, plain and
comfortable, for 4 up to 8 people with breakfast.
Restaurant and ski rental.

$$$ Hotel Termas Lahuen-Có
T0260-449 9700, www.hotellahuenco.com.
Dating from 1930s, and now rather kitsch,
with thermal baths, meals.

$$$ La Valtellina
T0260-15-440 2761, www.lavaltellina.com.ar.
Attractively rustic Alpine cottages, Italian
owned and run, with an excellent restaurant
and tea house.

Malargüe

$$$ Malargüe
Av San Martín (Norte) 1230, T0260-447 2300,
www.hotelmalarguesuite.com.
On the northern access to town, this comfortable
4-star hotel has a new wing with slightly bigger
rooms, an indoor pool, restaurant, spa and a casino.

$$ Rioma
Fray Inalicán (Oeste) 127, T0260-447 1065,
www.hotelrioma.com.ar.
Small, family-run and spotless place with basic
facilities. Convenient for its pool and proximity
to bus station.

$ pp Eco Hostel Malargüe
Prol Constitución Nacional (Finca No 65), Colonia
Pehuenche, 5 km from centre, T0260-447 0391,
www.hostelmalargue.com.
Eco-hostel built with an enhanced traditional
quincha method, in rural surroundings, on
dairy farm with organic fruit and veg, good
meals, basic, comfortable dorms and rooms
($$), cheaper without bath and HI discount,
Choique travel agency.

Restaurants

San Rafael

An area of attractive open-air cafés and small
restaurants lies along C Pellegrini between Chile
and Day in town.

$$$ El Rey del Chivo
Av H Yrigoyen 651.

A good and basic place for the regional speciality, *chivito* (kid).

$$$ Pettra
Av H Yrigoyen 1750.
Very good choice for a great range of meals in an area full of restaurants.

$$$-$$ Las Duelas
Pellegrini 190.
For tasty sandwiches and salads.

$$ Nina
Av San Martín y Olascoaga.
A casual place on a central corner for a light meal, including fine salads, and an open-air café open till late.

La Delicia del Boulevard
Av H Yrigoyen 1594, www.ladeliciaboulevard.com.ar.
Very good ice cream on the way to wineries.

Malargüe

$$$ La Cima
Av San Martín (Norte) 886.
Parrilla and more elaborate meals, including fish. Good value.

$$$-$$ El Chuma
Illescas (Oeste) 155.
The place for trying *chivito*.

$$ Bonafide
Av San Martín (Sur) 364, see Facebook.
Very good café open till late, serving also simple meals, including good pizza.

$$ La Posta
Av Roca (Este) 174, see Facebook.
Popular *parrilla*, offering pastas and pizza too.

What to do

San Rafael
Tour operators charge similar prices for same conventional excursions, including the most popular day tour to Cañón del Atuel for about US$25-30 pp (lunch and extra activities are not included). Ask in advance for tours in English.
Atuel Travel, *Buenos Aires 31, T0260-4429282, www.atueltravel.com.ar.* A recommended agency.
Raffeish, *in Valle Grande, T0260-443 6996, www.raffeish.com.ar.* Recommended as most professional rafting company.
Renta Bike, *Day 487, T0260-15-440 1236, www.renta-bike.com.ar.* Bike rental, wine tours and excursions along Cañón del Atuel.

Malargüe
Tour operators charge similar rates for same excursions (eg Payunia for about US$80-90 pp), which take a full day in most cases and may include a light meal. 2-day trekking in Payunia, fly-fishing, rafting and several-day horse rides in the Andes, including the approach to the remains of the crashed Uruguayan airplane (described in the film *Alive!*) are also available, though some activities are in summer only. Ask in advance for tours in English. A recommended range of tours is offered by **Choique** (Av San Martín Sur 33, T0260-447 0391, www.choique.com), and **Karen Travel** (Av San Martín Sur 54, T0260-447 2226, www.karen travel.com.ar).

Some 30 km south of Malargüe, in the Cuesta del Chihuido area on Ruta 40, are **Manqui Malal** (T0260-447 2567), and **Turcará** (T0260-15-453 5908, www.turcara.com), where trekking, zip-lining, camping and meals are offered.

Transport

San Rafael
Air Airport 7 km west of town. Buttini bus, US$1.20. Remise taxis, US$7. To/from **Buenos Aires** with **Aerolíneas Argentinas/Austral**.

Bus Terminal at General Paz y Paunero, 10-min walk to centre. To/from **Mendoza**, 3-3½ hrs, many daily, US$9; **Neuquén**, US$41-60, 7-9½ hrs. To **Buenos Aires**, 12½-14 hrs, US$94-109. To **Valle Grande**, 1-1½ hrs, US$2.75, with **Iselin**. To **Las Leñas** and **Malargüe**, see below.

For wineries west of town, take **Buttini** bus (destination 25 de Mayo) along C Avellaneda and then Av H Yrigoyen, and tell the driver the bodega you want to visit.

Las Leñas
Bus From **Mendoza**, change bus in **San Rafael**. From San Rafael, 1 a day in winter holidays (3 weekly rest of year) with **Iselín**, US$7; **Cata** buses and transfer services from Malargüe in winter holidays only.

Malargüe
Air Chartered flights from Buenos Aires and São Paulo (Brazil) in the skiing season only.

Bus Terminal at Aldao y Beltrán. To **Mendoza**, direct daily with **Viento Sur** minibuses, 5 hrs, US$18; or with **Cata**, 6½ hrs, US$18; alternatively with bus connection in San Rafael. To **San Rafael**, 2½-3 hrs, US$7, with **Buttini** (Corrientes 494, San

Rafael, T0260-442 1413, www.abuttini.com), **Cata** or **Iselin**. **Cata** leaves twice weekly either to **Agua Escondida**, on La Pampa border (across Payunia), and to **Barrancas**, on Neuquén border (along Ruta 40).

To **Neuquén** (via Ruta 40 and Rincón de los Sauces), Sun-Fri 2115, with **Leader/Rincón** from **Los Amigos** bar, Av San Martín (Sur) 765, by the clock tower.

Mendoza to Chile

travel in the shadow of mighty Aconcagua

From Mendoza to the Chilean border is 210 km on Ruta 7, the only route for motorists. Leave the city south on Avenida Pedro Molina/Rondeau, Acceso Este, Acceso Sur/Ruta 40, to the junction where Ruta 7 turns west; then follow signs to Potrerillos, Uspallata and Chile. The road through the mountains is spectacular but may be blocked by snow and ice in winter; if travelling by car in June to October enquire about road conditions and requirements for snow chains and a shovel in Mendoza before setting out (www.vialidad.mendoza.gov.ar and www.gendarmeria.gov.ar).

Potrerillos and Uspallata *Colour map 8, B1.*

Potrerillos is a pretty village and a good base for horse riding, walking and rafting. In summer a two-day hike passing from desert steppe to scenic peaks goes from Potrerillos to **Vallecitos**, a tiny ski resort 26 km from Potrerillos along a winding *ripio* road (season July-September). Another recommended stopping point is the picturesque village of **Uspallata** ① *52 km from Potrerillos.* From here you can explore the mysterious white, egg-shaped domes of Las Bóvedas (2 km on RN 149 north; entry US$2), built in the early 19th century to smelt metals, where there is a small, interesting museum. From Uspallata, the RN 149 leads north to Barreal and Calingasta (see page 112); it's unpaved for its first part, rough and tricky when the snow melts and floods it in summer. West of Uspallata, **Los Penitentes** ① *187 km west of Mendoza, on the road to Chile, T02624-420356, www.penitentesweb.com,* is a charming family ski resort at 2600 m, named after its majestic mass of pinnacled rocks, looking like a horde of cowled monks. Both Vallecitos (see above) and Los Penitentes are used as acclimatization areas before attempting the ascent of Aconcagua.

Puente del Inca and around *Colour map 8, B2.*

The road that leads from Uspallata to cross the border to Chile is one of the most dramatic in Argentina, climbing through a gorge of richly coloured rock. Surrounded by mountains of great grandeur, Puente del Inca, 72 km west of Uspallata at 2718 m, is a good base for trekking or exploring on horseback. The natural bridge after which the place is named is one of the wonders of South America. Bright ochre yellow, it crosses the Río de las Cuevas at a height of 27 m, has a span of 48 m, and is 28 m wide, and seems to have been formed by sulphur-bearing hot springs. The bridge itself cannot be crossed. There are the remains of a thermal bath complex at the river just under the bridge. Horse treks go to Los Penitentes.

Los Horcones, the Argentine customs post (dealing with all Argentine entry formalities), is 1 km west of Puente del Inca. Some 2 km further west is the access to Parque Provincial Aconcagua (see below). Five kilometres west of Puente del Inca is **Los Puquios** ① *www.puquios.com,* a small family-oriented ski centre, which in summer provides assistance to climbing expeditions, including a camping ground.

☆Aconcagua *Colour map 8, B1.*

West of Puente del Inca on the right, there is a good view of Aconcagua, the highest peak in the Americas at 6959 m, sharply silhouetted against the blue sky. In 1985, a complete Inca mummy was discovered at 5300 m on the mountain. The best time for climbing Aconcagua is from mid-November to mid-February. For camping, trekking or climbing it is first necessary to obtain a **permit**, which must be bought, in person only, from the **Centro de Visitantes** (Subsecretaría de Turismo) ① *Av San Martín 1143, p 1, Mendoza, T0261-425 8751, Nov-Apr Mon-Fri 0800-1800, Sat-Sun and holidays 0900-1300, May-Oct Mon-Fri 0800-1300.* An ascent permit lasts for 20 consecutive

> **Fact...**
> The best time for climbing Aconcagua is from mid-November to mid-February.

days from the moment it is stamped at the park entrance, and prices vary according to season, the chosen access route and whether you are going alone or with a guide. A permit for foreigners to climb Aconcagua in summer cost from US$726 to US$1133 in 2016-2017 (winter US$944). There are also permits for seven-day treks (US$261-305 summer, US$305 winter) and three-day treks (US$131-160). Treks may not go beyond base camps. All information, regulations and advice can be found on the official website: www.aconcagua.mendoza.gov.ar.

There are two access routes to Aconcagua: Río Horcones and Río Vacas, which lead to the two main base camps, Plaza de Mulas and Plaza Argentina respectively. About 70% of climbers use the Río Horcones route, which starts a few kilometres west of Puente del Inca, where a road leads over 1 km north to the Horcones ranger station (open 0800-2000). From here you can walk to the green lake of Laguna de Horcones (US$2.50 entry) for excellent views of Aconcagua, especially in the morning. The trail continues to Plaza de Mulas (4370 m) for the North Face, or Plaza Francia (4200 m) for the South Face. The intermediate camp for either is Confluencia (3300 m), four hours from Horcones.

Río Vacas is the access for those wishing to climb the highly risky Polish Glacier. The Plaza Argentina base camp (4200 m) is three days from Punta de Vacas and the intermediate camps are Pampa de Leñas and Casa de Piedra. From Puente del Inca, mules (US$220-440 per mule for 60 kg of gear, price is one way only, www.aconcaguaspirit.com.ar) are available to take you to Plaza de Mulas, where there is a refuge and camping area (crowded in summer). Aconcagua Spirit arranges full-board lodging at Plaza de Mulas (US$89), Confluencia (US$79 pp per day) and Plaza Argentina (US$99), and at Refugio Cerro Aconcagua in Los Penitentes (US$45, half-board).

An accident prevention and medical assistance service is offered at Plaza de Mulas (climbing season only) and Plaza Argentina (high season only). Climbers should make use of this service to check for early symptoms of mountain sickness and oedema.

Take a tent able to withstand 100 mph/160 kph winds, and clothing and sleeping gear for temperatures below -40°C. Allow at least eight to 10 days for acclimatization at lower altitudes before attempting the summit (four days ideally from Plaza de Mulas).

You can book programmes, which include trekking, or climbing to the summit, with all equipment and camping included in Mendoza (see Tour operators, above). A full list of authorized guides and agencies is published on Aconcagua's official website.

Border with Chile The road to the Chilean border, fully paved, goes through the 3.1-km Cristo Redentor road tunnel (open 24 hours; US$2 toll for cars; a second tunnel is planned). The last settlement before the tunnel is tiny forlorn **Las Cuevas**, 16 km from Puente del Inca, with hostel accommodation, two restaurants, a basic café and a *kiosko*. In summer you can follow the old road over La Cumbre pass to the statue of El Cristo Redentor (Christ the Redeemer), a 7-m statue erected jointly by Chile and Argentina in 1904 to celebrate the settlement of their boundary dispute. It's an all day excursion from Mendoza, or you can drive in a 4WD after the snow has melted, or walk from Las Cuevas (4½ hours up, two hours down – only to be attempted by the fit, in good weather).

The Chilean border is beyond Las Cuevas. All Argentine exit formalities for cars and buses are dealt with at the Chilean customs post, open 24 hours in summer or 0800-2000 in winter. The Chilean consulate in Mendoza is at Belgrano 1080, T0261-425 5024, http://chile.gob.cl/mendoza.

Tip...
Cyclists are not allowed to ride through the tunnel; ask the officials to help you get a lift.

Where to stay

Potrerillos and Uspallata

\$\$\$ Gran Hotel Uspallata
On RN 7, Km 1149, towards Chile, T02624-420003,
www.granhoteluspallata.com.ar.
Lovely location, spacious and modern in big
gardens away from the centre, pool, good
value, restaurant.

\$\$\$ Los Cóndores
Las Heras s/n, Uspallata, T02624-420002,
www.loscondoreshotel.com.ar.
Low season prices, bright, neat rooms, good
restaurant (dinners only), heated pool.

\$\$\$ Silver Cord B&B
Valle del Sol, Potrerillos, T02624-481083,
www.silvercordbb.com.ar.
With breakfast, internet, laundry service,
lots of outdoor activities and 4WD trips,
guides speak English.

\$\$\$ Valle Andino
Ruta 7, Uspallata, T02624-420095,
www.hotelvalleandino.com.
Modern airy place, good rooms, heated pool,
restaurant, breakfast included.

\$ pp Campo Base Penitentes
T0261-425 5511, www.penitentes.com.ar.
Open all year.
A lively place and a cheap ski resort option, with
slightly cramped dorms, shared bath, restaurant,
bar and minibus service to Mendoza. Offers ski
programmes in season.

\$ pp Mountain Chill Out Hostel (officially
Hostel Internacional Uspallata)
RN 7, Km 1141.5, Uspallata, T0261-575 9204,
www.hosteluspallata.com.ar.
Dorms for 4 to 6 with or without bath, private
rooms sleep 1-6, with bath (**\$\$\$-\$\$**), also
comfortable cabins for up to 5, discounts for
HI members, bar, restaurant, tours arranged,
bike and ski rental, attractive surroundings.

Camping
Excellent **ACA** site in Potrerillos, T02624-482013.
Shady, hot water after 1800, pool, clean.

Puente del Inca and around

\$\$\$ Hostería Puente del Inca
RN7, Km 175, T0810-220 0031, http://
hosteriapuentedelinca.onlinetravel.com.ar.
Next to the small ski centre at Los Puquios. Full-
board available, huge cosy dining room, advice on
Aconcagua, helpful owners, great atmosphere.

Camping
At Los Puquios.

Restaurants

Potrerillos and Uspallata

\$\$\$ La Estancia de Elías
Km 1146, Uspallata, opposite petrol station.
A good and crowded *parrilla*.

\$\$\$-\$\$ Lo de Pato
RN7 Km 1148, Uspallata.
The town's classic, popular *parrilla* and also pasta;
takeaway food plus bakery.

\$\$\$-\$\$ Tomillo
Av Los Cóndores, El Salto, Potrerillos, T02624-
483072, www.tomillorestaurant.com.ar.
All day (closed Tue and Wed in low season).
Excellent home-made cooking, including trout.
Also simple and warm accommodation in private
doubles (**\$\$**).

What to do

Potrerillos and Uspallata
Argentina Rafting, *base camp at Ruta Perilago,*
Potrerillos, T02624-482037 (office at Amigorena 86,
T0261-429 6325, Mendoza), www.argentinarafting.
com. Reliable company, organizes good trips
with climbing, hiking, kayaking and other
adventure sports.
Desnivel Aventura, *Ruta 7, by the YPF petrol*
station, Uspallata, T0261-15-554 8872, www.
desnivelaventura.com. Offers rafting, riding,
mountain biking, trekking, climbing, skiing.

Transport

Bus **Buttini** from Mendoza several a day for
Potrerillos, 1 hr, US$2.25, **Uspallata**, 2¼ hrs,
US$5.75 and Las Cuevas; 2 a day to Horcones and
1 a day to **Puente del Inca**, US$7, 4 hrs (Uspallata
to Puente del Inca, US$3.75). Buses going to Chile
do not pick up passengers on the way.

San Juan and around *Colour map 8, A2.*

San Juan, 177 km north of Mendoza, was founded in 1562 and is capital of its namesake province. Nearly destroyed by a 1944 earthquake, the modern centre is well laid-out but lacks Mendoza's charm and sophistication. You're most likely to visit on the way to the national parks further north, but there are some bodegas worth visiting; see www.travelsanjuan.com.ar/vino.html for suggestions.

Sights **Museo Casa Natal de Sarmiento** ① *Sarmiento Sur 21, T0264-422 4603, Tue-Fri and Sun 0900-1900, Mon and Sat 0900-1500, US$2 (free Sun)*, is the birthplace of Domingo Sarmiento (President of the Republic, 1868-1874). **Museo Histórico Celda de San Martín** ① *Laprida 57 Este, daily 1000-1300, 1600-1900, US$2*, includes the restored cloisters and two cells of the Convent of Santo Domingo. San Martín slept in one of these cells on his way to lead the crossing of the Andes. Opposite Plaza 25 de Mayo, take the lift to the top of the Cathedral's campanile (53 m) for **city views** ① *daily 0930-1300, 1830-2130, US$1*.

The University of San Juan's **Museo Arqueológico** ① *Ruta 40, lateral este, entre C 5 y Progreso, Rawson, a few km south of the centre, T0264-424 1424, www.ffha.unsj.edu.ar, Mon-Fri 0800-2000, Sat 1000-1800, US$2, getting there: buses 15, 49, 50 from centre*, contains an outstanding collection of prehispanic indigenous artefacts, including several well-preserved mummies.

Vallecito East of the city by 64 km is the famous shrine to the **Difunta Correa**, Argentina's most loved unofficial saint, whose infant, according to legend, survived at her breast even after the mother's death from thirst in the desert. At roadsides everywhere you'll see mounds of plastic bottles left as offerings to ask for safe journeys, and during Holy Week 100,000 pilgrims visit the site. There is a remarkable collection of personal items left in tribute in several elaborate shrines; also cafés, toilets and souvenir stalls. Buses from San Juan to La Rioja stop here for five minutes, or Vallecito runs a couple of services a day.

San Juan

To Calingasta, Barreal, Jáchal & La Serena (Chile)

Museo de Ciencias Naturales
Mercado Artesanal Tradicional

To Airport, Difunta Correa, Valle Fértil, San Luis & La Rioja

To 4
To Calingasta
To 2

Maipú, Pedro Echagüe, 25 de Mayo, San Luis, Av Libertador Gral San Martín, Plaza Laprida, Laprida, Rivadavia, Av José Ignacio de la Roza, Mitre, Santa Fe, Córdoba, Gral Paz, 9 de Julio

España, Salta, Catamarca, Alem, Sarmiento, Entre Ríos, Mendoza, Gral M Acha, Tucumán, Rioja, Jujuy, Aberastain, Caseros, Güemes, Rawson

Maipú

Plaza Gertrudis Funes

Museo Histórico Celda de San Martín
Museo Casa Natal de Sarmiento
Cambio Santiago

Cathedral
Plaza 25 de Mayo

Plaza Aberastain
Palacio Municipal

Santiago del Estero

To Bus Terminal
To 3

To Mendoza & Museo Arqueológico

N
300 metres
300 yards

Where to stay		
1 Albertina	5 San Juan Hostel	2 Remolacha
2 Alkázar	6 Zonda	3 Soychú
3 América		4 Tagore
4 Gran Hotel Provincial	**Restaurants**	
	1 Club Sirio Libanés 'El Palito'	

Calingasta
Tourist office: Av Argentina s/n, T02648-441066, www.calingastaturismo.gob.ar.

Calingasta, 170 km west of San Juan, is an idyllic, secluded village in a green valley with stunning striped rocks (cider festival in April). To reach Calingasta you go north of San Juan towards Talacasto, then take the paved Quebrada de las Burras road (Rutas 436, then 149) to Pachaco, where a bridge crosses the Río San Juan. Cyclists should note that there is no shade on these roads; fill up with water at every opportunity and consult the police before setting out.

Barreal and around
Tourist office: Av Roca y Las Heras, T02648-441066, daily 0900-2100.

Barreal, 40 km south of Calingasta on the road to Uspallata, is a tranquil place between the Andes and the *precordillera*. It has become a very attractive base for exploring the nearby mountains on foot, horseback or 4WD vehicles, including Cerro Mercedario (6770 m), the Ansilta and Tontal mountain ranges plus a handful of peaks over 6000 m. The village itself is ideal for bike riding along peaceful rural roads, where dogs rarely bark, beneath the shade of willow and poplar trees, and with views of distant Aconcagua from higher sites. As well as visits to a small winery (www.entre tapias.com) and a herb farm (www.demicampo.com.ar), you can go rafting, fishing and even blokart sailing (land yachting/*carrovelismo*) on the vast plain of Leoncito, 20 km to the south.

From Barreal there is access to **Parque Nacional El Leoncito** ⓘ *26 km from Barreal, office in Barreal at Cordillera de Ansilta s/n, T02648-441240, www.elleoncito.gob.ar, free*, with an arid environment, an easy 2-km trail, a small waterfall, a four-hour trek to El Leoncito peak and interesting wildlife (including pumas), ranger post and a basic site for free camping with toilets (take food and water). Most notably, the park has two observatories: **Cesco** ⓘ *T02648-441087, centrohugomira@yahoo.com.ar, daily visits 1000-1200, 1600-1800 (US$3), nocturnal visits with small telescopes from sunset (US$6)*, and **CASLEO** ⓘ *T02648-441088, www.casleo.gov.ar, mid-Sep to mid-Mar daily 1000-1200, 1430-1700 (1500-1730 in summer), US$1, phone in advance for night visits from 1700 (US$16), also with dinner and accommodation (US$60 pp)*. There are no buses to the park; take a tour from Barreal or San Juan.

☆Parque Nacional Ischigualasto *Colour map 8, A2.*
www.ischigualasto.gob.ar. Apr-Sep daily 0900-1600; Oct-Mar daily 0800-1700. US$16.25, with reduced rates for Argentines and students.

Ruta 141 runs across the south of the province towards La Rioja province and Córdoba. Just after Marayes (133 km), paved Ruta 510 (poor in parts) goes north 114 km to **San Agustín del Valle Fértil** ⓘ *tourist office at Gral Achá 52, T02646-420104, www.ischigualastovallefertil.org*. In town, the Museo de Ciencias Naturales ⓘ *España y Maipú, T421 6774, US$2.55*, displays the bones and fossils of the dinosaurs found in the **Parque Provincial Ischigualasto**. To reach the park itself, travel 56 km north from San Agustín by paved road to a police checkpoint, where a side road goes northwest for 17 km to the park entrance.

The 62,000 ha park (a UNESCO World Heritage Site), also known as **Valle de la Luna**, occupies an immense basin, which was once filled by a lake, between the scarlet red Barrancas Coloradas to the east and the green, black and grey rocks of Los Rastros to the west. The vegetation is arid scrub and bushes. For many, the attraction lies in the bizarre sculptural desert landforms dotted throughout the park's other-worldly terrain. They have been named after things that they resemble. The park's other fascination lies in the 250 million years of strata that you can see in the eroded cliffs where fossils from the Triassic period have been found. Here the skeletons of the oldest known dinosaurs have been discovered (230 million years old).

Tours and access to Ischigualasto park There is one tour route, lasting three hours, visiting part of the park but encompassing the most interesting sites. You can follow a ranger in your own vehicle (guide US$2), or go by taxi, minibus or *colectivo*, US$9.75-13. It can be crowded at holiday times. There are also three- to four-hour treks and bicycle routes (both US$9.75) and full-moon visits (US$16.25). Full-day tours are available from San Juan and San Agustín (food and entry fee extra);

ask at the tourist offices. You can camp opposite the ranger station, US$6.50, which has a small museum and an expensive *confitería*, but bring all food and water.

Parque Nacional Talampaya *Colour map 8, A2.*

Office in Villa Unión, T03825-470356, www.parquesnacionales.gob.ar. Oct-Feb daily 0800-1700; Mar-Sep daily 0830-1630. US$16.25 for foreigners (valid 2 days), reductions for Argentines. For tours of the park, see What to do, page 116.

Just beyond the turning to **Ischigualasto**, near Los Baldecitos, paved Ruta 150 heads east to Patquía through the attractive rock formations of El Chiflón park en route to La Rioja or Chilecito. Heading north from Los Baldecitos, Ruta 76 leads to Villa Unión (see page 117). Some 61 km along this route a paved road goes 14 km east to the 215,000-ha **Parque Nacional Talampaya**, another collection of spectacular desert landforms and a UNESCO World Heritage Site.

Tip...
The best time to visit is in the morning for the natural light and to avoid strong afternoon winds.

The park occupies the site of an ancient lake, where sediments have been eroded by water and wind for some 200 million years, forming a dramatic landscape of pale red hills. Numerous fossils have been found and some 600 year-old petroglyphs can be seen not far from the access to the gorge. The centerpiece of the park is the the **Cañon de Talampaya**, where extraordinary structures have been given popular names. At one point, the gorge narrows to 80 m and rises to 143 m. A refreshing leafy spot in the centre of the gorge, the 'botanical garden' has amazingly diverse plants and trees. The end of the *cañón* is marked by the imposing cliffs of the 'cathedral' and the curious 'king on a camel'. The 'chessboard' and the 'monk', 53 m high, lie not far beyond the gorge, marking the end of the **Cañón de Talampaya**. The **Circuito Los Cajones** continues in the same direction up to '*los pizarrones*', an enormous wall of rock, covered with petroglyphs, and then to '*los cajones*', a narrow pass between rock walls. El Sendero del Triásico includes 16 life-sized replicas of dinosaurs.

Circuito Ciudad Perdida, an area of high cliffs and a large number of breathtaking rock formations, and **Circuito Arco Iris**, a multicoloured canyon, can be reached by organized tours from Ruta 76, Km 133 (south of the main access).

Tours and access to Talampaya park Tour operators in San Agustín (and some in La Rioja and Chilecito) combine Talampaya with Ischigualasto; check if guide's fee and entrance is included. Independent access is also possible: buses/combis linking La Rioja and Villa Unión stop at the park entrance (from where it's a 14-km walk to the *administración*) and at Pagancillo (a village 30 km north); most of the park wardens live at Pagancillo and offer free transfer to the park early in the morning. No private vehicles are allowed beyond the administration (which has a small restaurant, toilets and public telephones); the park can only be visited on tours arranged at the *administración*. For details of these, see What to do, page 116.

La Rioja *Colour map 8, A2.*

Located at the edge of the plains, with views of Sierra de Velasco, La Rioja can be oppressively hot from November to March but comes alive after the daily siesta and during the annual carnival, **Chaya**, in February. The city was founded in 1591, but its main buildings and plazas date from the late 19th century. The **Church and Convent of San Francisco** ① *25 de Mayo y Bazán y Bustos, Tue-Sun 0700-1300, 1700-2100, free*, contains the Niño Alcalde, a remarkable image of the infant Jesus. At 25 de Mayo 218, you can see the cell (*celda*) in which San Francisco Solano lived and the orange tree, now dead, which he planted in 1592. San Francisco helped to bring peace between the Spaniards and the indigenous people in 1593, an event celebrated at the annual Tinkunaco festival, beginning on New Year's Eve and lasting four days. The **Convent of Santo Domingo** ① *Luna y Lamadrid*, dates from 1623 and is said to be the oldest surviving church in Argentina. **Museo Arqueológico Inca Huasi** ① *Alberdi 650, T0380-443 9268, Tue-Fri 0900-1300 and 1800-2100, open some weekends, call beforehand, US$1*, owned by the Franciscan Order, contains a huge collection of fine Diaguita indigenous ceramics, considered among the most important pre-Hispanic artefacts in the country. The **Mercado Artesanal** ⓘ *Luna 782, Tue-Sat 1000-1200, 1600-2000*, has expensive handicrafts. In a beautiful and well-kept house, the **Museo Folklórico** ⓘ *Luna 802, T0380-442 8500, Tue-Sat 1000-1200, 1600-2000, US$1.25, free guided visits*, gives a fascinating insight into traditional La Rioja life, with a superb collection of native deities, rustic wine-making machinery and delicate silver *mates*. Its leafy patio is also worth a visit.

Listings San Juan and La Rioja *map page 111.*

Tourist information

San Juan

Tourist office
Sarmiento Sur 24 y San Martín, T0264-421 0004, www.sanjuanlaestrelladelosandes.com. Mon-Fri 0700-2030, Sat-Sun and holidays 0900-2000.
There are also a tourist desks at the airport and bus station.

La Rioja

Municipal tourist office
Av Santa Fe 950, T0380-447 0001, and on plaza opposite the Cathedral daily 0800-2100.

Provincial tourist office
Av Ortiz de Ocampo y Av Félix de la Colina (opposite bus terminal), T0380-442 6345. Daily 0800-2100, www.turismolarioja.gov.ar.

Where to stay

San Juan

$$$ Alkázar
Laprida 82 Este, T0264-421 4965, www.alkazarhotel.com.ar.
Comfortable rooms, sauna, pool, gym, well run, central, excellent restaurant.

$$$ América
9 de Julio 1052 Este, T0264-427 2701, www.hotel-america.com.ar.
A good, quite comfortable choice if you need to be next to bus station.

$$$ Gran Hotel Provincial
Av J I de la Roza 132 Este, T0264-430 9999, www.granhotel provincial.com.
Large, central, good rooms, pool, gym, restaurant.

$$$-$$ Albertina
Mitre 31 Este, T0264-421 4222, www.hotelalbertina.com.

Next to cinema on plaza, a small hotel with comfortable rooms, restaurant and jacuzzi in the junior suites, no parking. Very good value.

$ pp San Juan Hostel
Av Córdoba 317 Este, T0264-420 1835, www.sanjuanhostel.com.
Kindly run by its owner, central, with dorms for 4 to 10, and private rooms with and without bath ($$-$), barbecues on rooftop, bike rental, tours arranged.

$ pp Zonda
Caseros 486 Sur, T0264-420 1009, www.zondahostel.com.ar.
Simple, light rooms, for 2-6, shared bath, room for 4 with bath ($$). Trips and Spanish lessons arranged. HI member discount.

Barreal and around

$$$ Eco Posada El Mercedario
Av Roca y C de los Enamorados (Las Tres Esquinas), T0264-15-509 0907 or 02648-441167, www.elmercedario.com.ar.
Built in 1928 on the northern edge of town, this lovely adobe building preserves a traditional atmosphere with renovated comfort in its good rooms; solar heated water, good value restaurant, a tiny pool in a large garden. Bike tours and rental, horse riding, photography and 4WD excursions to the Andes foothills and Precordillera. Recommended.

$$$ El Alemán
Los Huarpes s/n, T02648-441193, www.elalemanbarreal.com.
Run by Perla, Bernhard and their daughter, very functional apartments for 2 to 4 (with solar heated water) facing a neat garden in a rural area next to the river. Restaurant with some German specialities.

$$$ Posada de Campo La Querencia
T0264-15-436 4699, www.laquerenciaposada.com.
A few spotless comfortable rooms in a homely place south of town run by very attentive owners.

Delicious breakfast, manicured park with a pool and magnificent views of the Andes.

$$$ Posada Paso de los Patos
Patricias Mendocinas y Gualino, T0264-463 4727, www.posadapasolospatos.com.ar.
In a lovely location south of town with grand views, a stylish building with 10 well-equipped rooms facing the Andes, restaurant, pool, full and half-day bike rides to the nearby mountains.

$$$-$$ Posada San Eduardo
Av San Martín s/n, T0264-441046, www.posada-saneduardo.com.
Charming colonial-style house, simple rooms around a courtyard, superior rooms with fireplace, relaxing, beautiful park with a large pool, restaurant, horse rides.

$ pp Hostel Barreal
Av San Martín s/n, T0264-15 415 7147, www.hostelbarreal.com.
Neat, rooms with bath, lovely garden. Rafting, kayaks and excursions organized.

$ pp Hostel Don Lisandro
Av San Martín s/n, T0264-15-5059122, www.donlisandro.com.ar.
In a house built in 1908, a few dorms in rustic style for 3 and 4 and doubles with or without bath ($$-$). Its table football is a gem. Trekking and excursions organized, including blokarting.

Camping

Municipal campsite
C Belgrano, T0264-15-672 3914. Open all year.
Shady, well-maintained, pool.

Parque Nacional Ischigualasto

San Agustín del Valle Fértil

$$$-$$ Cabañas Valle Pintado
Tucumán y Mitre, T0264-434 5737, www.vallepintado.com.ar.
Incredibly good-value option with cabins for up to 6 people also available. Basic, clean rooms, with a large swimming pool surrounded by trees.

$$$ Hostería Valle Fértil
Rivadavia s/n, T02646-420015, www.hosteriavallefertil.com.
Good, a/c, smart, very comfortable, with fine views, also has *cabañas*, pool and good restaurant open to non-residents.

$ pp Campo Base
Tucumán entre Libertador y San Luis, T02646-420063, www.hostelvalledelaluna.com.ar.

HI affiliated, cheerful, private doubles ($$), small basic dorms for 4 to 8 (cheaper without a/c), shared bath, backyard with small pool, tours combining the 2 parks.

$ pp Los Olivos
Santa Fe y Tucumán, T02646-420115, posada_losolivos@hotmail.com.
Welcoming and simple hostel accommodation in dorms and a private double ($$), tours arranged.

Camping
There are several campsites, of which the most highly recommended is **La Majadita** in a lovely spot on the river 8 km to the west of town with hot showers and great views. There's a municipal campsite in the town on Calle Rivadavia, 5 blocks from the plaza, T0264-15 520 1185 (municipal office for information on both sites).

Parque Nacional Talampaya
Several basic places in **Pagancillo**, but many more and better options in Villa Unión (see below). There's a basic campsite next to *administración*, US$4.

La Rioja
A/c or fan are essential for summer nights. High season is during Jul winter holidays.

$$$ Plaza
San Nicolás de Bari y 9 de Julio (on Plaza 25 de Mayo), T443 6290, www.plazahotel-larioja.com.
Functional 4-star, pool on top floor, breakfast included, a/c. Superior rooms have balconies on plaza.

$$$ Vincent Apart Hotel
Santiago del Estero 10, T0380-443 2326, www.vincentaparthotel.com.ar.
Spotless flats for up to 4, a/c, with dining room, kitchen and fridge, breakfast included, excellent value.

$$ Savoy
San Nicolás de Bari y Roque A Luna, T0380-442 6894, www.hotelsavoylarioja.com.ar.
In a quiet residential area, tidy, comfortable, a/c, 2nd floor is best.

$ pp Apacheta Hostel
San Nicolás de Bari 669, T0380-15-444 5445, see Facebook.
Cheerfully decorated, well-run central hostel with dorms for 5 to 8 and a private double ($$).

Restaurants

San Juan

A lively area of bars and restaurants lies along Av San Martín Oeste (west of 1500 block).

$$$ Club Sirio Libanés ' Restaurant Palito'
Entre Ríos 533 Sur, see Facebook.
Pleasant, long-established, tasty food, some Middle Eastern dishes, including its 'arab potpourri', buffet. Recommended.

$$ Remolacha
Av de la Roza y Sarmiento, T0264-422 7070.
Stylish, warm atmosphere, great terrace on C Sarmiento, superb Italian-inspired menu, delicious steaks and pastas. Recommended.

$$ Soychú
Av de la Roza 223 Oeste, T0264-422 1939.
Great value vegetarian food.
Highly recommended.

$$ Tagore
Av San Martín 1556, T0264-426 2702, see Facebook.
Vegetarian meals for takeaway.

Barreal

$$ Cordón de Ansilta
Capitán Giachino s/n, T02648-441067.
Good food, but not cheap, local dishes.

$$ Isidoro
Pres Roca s/n.
In the middle of the village, for local dishes and wines, good value.

La Rioja

$$$ El Nuevo Corral
Av Quiroga y Rivadavia.
Traditional rustic *comidas de campo* and good local wines.

$$$ La Vieja Casona
Rivadavia 457, www.lacasonalunch.com.ar.
Smart *parrilla*, offering *chivito* (kid).

$$ La Aldea de la Virgen de Luján
Rivadavia 756.
Lively atmosphere, cheap and popular small place, including some Middle Eastern dishes.

Shopping

San Juan

San Juan is known for its fine bedspreads, blankets, saddle cloths and other items made from sheep and llama wool, fine leather, wooden plates and mortars and, of course, its wines.
Mercado Artesanal Tradicional (Av España 330 Norte), sells woven blankets/saddlebags, knives and ponchos.

What to do

San Juan

CH Travel, *General Acha 714 Sur, T0264-427 4160, www.chtraveltur.com.* Recommended for its tours to Barreal, Valle de la Luna and 4-day expeditions to Parque Nacional San Guillermo, in the remote northern San Juan high plateau. All great experiences at full moon.
Nerja Tours, *Mendoza 353 Sur, T0264-421 5214, www.nerja-tours.com.ar.* Good for local day trips and adventure tourism inside the national parks.

Barreal

Baho Aventura, *T0264-524 3234, bahoaventura@ gmail.com and on Facebook.* 4WD trips, trekking and quad bikes.
Don Lisandro Expediciones, *Av San Martín s/n, T0264-15-5059122, www.donlisandro.com.ar.* Full-day to several-day high altitude treks in the Andes, including Laguna Blanca and Balcón de los Seis Mil. Combined visit to astronomical observatories and blokarting on Pampa del Leoncito. Check available activities in winter. Recommended.
Fortuna Viajes, *Av Roca s/n (at Posada Don Ramón, northern outskirts), T0264-15-404 0913.* 1-week horseback crossing of the Andes led by expert Ramón Ossa. Also trekking in the Andes and 4WD excursions in Precordillera.

Parque Nacionl Talampaya

Asociación de Guías, *T03825-15-479 0000, talampaya.acg@gmail.com.* Runs guided walks from the administration to Quebrada Don Eduardo, a secondary gorge, next to the canyon (2½ hrs, US$16 pp) and the canyon itself (2½-6 hrs, US$38 pp), also full-moon walks; guided bike rides (2½ hrs, US$20 pp, cycle/ helmet provided); combined bike and trekking (4½ hrs, US$32 pp).
Cooperativa de Transporte Talampaya, *T03825-15-512367, cooperativatalampaya@gmail.com.*

Runs vehicle tours to Ciudad Perdida, 3½ hrs, and Arco Iris, 2¾ hrs

Rolling Travel, *T0351-570 9909, www.talampaya. com.* Runs vehicle guided visits for Cañón de Talampaya (2½ hrs, US$30 pp), Cañón de Talampaya and Cajones de Shimpa (3 hrs, US$35 pp), and Cañón de Talampaya from a truck top (3 hrs, US$35 pp).

Runacay, *T03825-470368, www.runacay.com.* Runs treks to Quebrada Don Eduardo (2½ hrs), tours to Ciudad Perdida (3½ hrs) and full moon tours to Cañón de Talampaya.

La Rioja

Corona del Inca, *PB Luna 914, T0380-445 0054, www.coronadelinca.com.ar.* Wide range of tours to Talampaya, Valle de la Luna, Laguna Brava, Corona del Inca crater, horse riding in Velasco mountains and further afield, English spoken.

San Juan

Air Chacritas Airport, 11 km southeast on RN 20. Daily to/from **Buenos Aires** with **Aerolíneas Argentinas/Austral**. Radio taxi to centre, about US$10.

Bus Terminal at Estados Unidos y Santa Fe, 9 blocks east of centre, T0264-422 1604 (with almost all buses going through the centre). **La Rioja**, 5½-7 hrs, US$36-47, many daily. **Chilecito**, 8 hrs, US$29, daily with **Vallecito**. **Tucumán**, many daily, 11-14 hrs, US$66-87. **Córdoba**, many daily, 8-14 hrs, US$33-55. **Buenos Aires**, 14-17 hrs, US$92-110 (**Autotransportes San Juan**, San Juan Mar del Plata). **San Agustín** with

Vallecito, 3 a day (2 on Sun), 4 hrs, US$12. Hourly departures to and from **Mendoza**, fares above. Also to **Barreal** (3½ hrs, US$13) and **Calingasta** (3 hrs, US$12), 2 a day with **El Triunfo**, T421 4532 (tell the driver your accommodation in Barreal, as the bus stops en route).

Car hire **Trébol**, Laprida 82 Este, T0264-422 5935, www.trebolrentacar.com.ar

Barreal

Bus See above for San Juan; **El Triunfo** bus stops en route along main road (Av Roca); tickets sold at YPF station, return to San Juan at 0300 (not on Sun), 1600 (and 1700 Mon and Fri only).

Parque Nacional Ischigualasto

Bus **Vallecito** runs 3 services a day (2 on Sun) between San Agustín del Valle Fértil and **San Juan**, see above. 3 buses a week from San Agustín to **La Rioja**, 4 hrs, US$11.

La Rioja

Air Airport 5 km northeast, via San Nicolás de Bari, RP5, T0380-446 2160. To **Buenos Aires** daily with Austral.

Bus Terminal is several kilometres from the centre, T0380-442 5453; Minibus and bus No 2 takes 15 mins, US$0.40, taxi US$4, or 45 mins' walk. To **Mendoza**, US$49-65, 8-9½ hrs, many companies, and **San Juan** (see above). To **Tucumán**, US$30-40, 5-7 hrs. To **Villa Unión**, 4 companies daily, 4 hrs, US$12. To **Chilecito**, several daily, 3 hrs, US$8. Minibuses run provincial services, faster and more frequent than buses, but costing a little more. They have their own terminal at Artigas y España.

Ruta 40 north of San Juan

remote settlements off the beaten track

Ruta 40, the principal tourist route on the east Andean slope, heads north from San Juan towards Cafayate and Salta. At Talacasto, 57 km from San Juan, Ruta 436 branches toward Las Flores; after 23 km it joins Ruta 149. From Las Flores, 180 km from San Juan, Ruta 150 goes up to the Chilean border at the Agua Negra pass (4765 m). The border is officially open 0800-1800, but is frequently closed by snow. Immigration, customs and ACA are at Las Flores (T02647-497047).

Villa Unión to Reserva Provincial Laguna Brava *Colour map 8, A2.*

San José de Jachal, 99 km north of Talacasto is a wine- and olive-growing centre with many adobe buildings. From here, the undulating Ruta 40, mostly paved, crosses dozens of dry watercourses. It continues paved to **Villa Unión** (www.turismovillaunion.gob.ar), an alternative base for visiting Parque Nacional Talampaya. The town has hotels, a campsite behind the ACA station and places to eat. From here excursions can be made by four-wheel drive vehicle to the remote **Reserva Provincial Laguna Brava**, 180 km north. The road goes through **Vinchina** and Jagüe (both have basic facilities). As you climb, the Portezuelo del Peñón salt lake becomes visible with some of the mightiest volcanoes on earth in the background. Vicuña and flamingos may be seen in the reserve. Tours are run by **Runacay** ① *in Villa Unión, T03825-470368, www.runacay.com (also has Hostel Laguna Brava in town)*, and by La Rioja and Chilecito operators.

Villa Unión to Chilecito *Colour map 8, A2.*
Ruta 40 heads east from Villa Unión through the Cuesta de Miranda (2020 m) before descending through a deep narrow canyon in a series of hairpins to Nonogasta (92 km from Villa Unión). Chilecito, 16 km north of Nonogasta, is La Rioja province's second town. Founded in 1715, it has good views of Sierra de Famatina, especially from the top of El Portezuelo, an easy climb from the end of Calle El Maestro. The region is famous for its wines, olives and walnuts. **Finca Samay Huasi** ① *3 km south, T03825-422629, Mon-Fri 0800-1900, Sat-Sun 0800-1200, 1400-1800 (closed 22 Dec-6 Jan), US$1*, was the house of Joaquín V González, founder of La Plata University. He designed the gardens with native trees and strange stone monoliths expressing his love of ancient cultures; there's also a small natural history museum. It's an attractive place for a relaxing day; overnight guests welcome (book in advance). At the **Cooperativa La Riojana** ① *La Plata 646, T03825-423150, www.lariojana.com.ar*, there are free guided visits (45 minutes) and you can watch local grapes being processed to make a wide variety of wines, including organic products. There's also a smart wine shop open in the mornings. A nearby attraction is the beautiful botanical garden at **Chirau Mita** ① *Av Primera Junta, Km 0.25, take Arturo Marasso northwards, turning right at Primera Junta; it's on the way to La Puntilla*, with a collection of over 1500 cacti and succulent plants growing on terraces on the rocky slopes. At **Santa Florentina** (8 km northwest), there are the impressive remains of a huge early 20th century foundry, linked to Chilecito and La Mejicana mine by cable car. **Tourist office** ① *Castro y Bazán 52, T03825-429665, daily 0800-2200*, also at the bus station.

North of Chilecito and La Rioja
From Chilecito it's 126 km to the junction with Ruta 60 at the Catamarca/La Rioja border. Beyond, the desert is spectacular, with a distinct culture and remote untouristy towns. From La Rioja city it's most easily reached by the paved Ruta 75 to **Aimogasta** (41 km south of the Ruta 40 junction). In Catamarca province, the small settlement of **Tinogasta** is in an oasis of vineyards, olive groves, and poplars. It is the starting point for expeditions to **Ojos del Salado** (6891 m) and **Pissis** (6795 m), the second and third highest mountains in the Western hemisphere. **Fiambalá** is 49 km north of Tinogasta, a peaceful place in a vine-filled valley, with the **Termas de Fiambalá** hot springs situated 16 km east (take a taxi; make sure fare includes wait and return). 4WD vehicles may be hired for approaching the Pissis-Ojos del Salado region; ask at the Intendencia. Both Tinogasta and Fiambalá are useful staging posts if taking the Paso San Francisco to Chile, or travelling north on Ruta 40 to Belén.

> **Tip...**
> The *Zonda*, a strong, dry mountain wind, can cause dramatic temperature increases in this area.

Border with Chile: Paso San Francisco Paso San Francisco (4726 m) is 203 km northwest of Fiambalá along a paved road. In summer the customs post is open 24 hours, T03837-498001. On the Chilean side roads run to El Salvador and Copiapó. This route is closed by snow June to October; take enough fuel for at least 400 km as there are no service stations from Fiambalá to just before Copiapó.

Belén *Colour map 6, C3.*
Back on Ruta 40, the road is paved via **Londres**, a quiet, pretty village, to Belén. There are important prehispanic ruins at **El Shincal** ① *7 km from Londres, daily 0700-1900*; Cóndor buses, several times daily from Belén, stop 100 m from the ruins, US$2; taxi about US$20 with wait. The setting is superb, in a flat area between a crown of mountains and the river. Tours are run by **Ampujaco Tur** (General Roca 190, Belén, T03835-461189), or at **Hotel Belén**.

Belén is an intimate little town, famous for its ponchos, saddlebags and rugs, which you can see being woven. The museum, **Cóndor Huasi** ① *San Martín y Belgrano, 1st floor, 08 00-1200 daily*, contains fascinating Diaguita artefacts, and there is a newly constructed Virgen (the last one was struck by lightning) on the Cerro de Nuestra Señora de Belén above town; good views. Important festival: **Nuestra Señora de Belén**, 24 December-6 January. **Tourist information** ⓘ *bus terminal, near plaza, Rivadavia y Lavalle, T03835-461304, http://belencunadelponchoturismo.blogspot.co.uk.*

North of Belén

Ruta 40, partially paved, runs another 176 km northeast from Belén to Santa María at the provincial border with Tucumán and on to Cafayate (page 127). From El Eje north of Belén, a paved road branches off the Ruta 43 as it heads 222 km north, mostly paved, through the Puna de Catamarca. It passes the breathtaking **Reserva Natural Laguna Blanca** (a Ramsar site), the distant enormous crater of Volcán Galán and **El Peñón** en route to tiny remote **Antofagasta de la Sierra** (with a *hostería*) and onwards to San Antonio de los Cobres in Salta. Trips to this region are run by Socompa, see page 137.

Listings Ruta 40 north of San Juan

Where to stay

Villa Unión

See also **Hostel Laguna Brava** of **Runacay**, page 117.

$$$ Cañón de Talampaya
On Ruta 76 Km 202 (on southern access), T03825-470753, www.hotelcanontalampaya.com.
Comfortable rooms in rustic style with a/c, restaurant serving some organic products, and a pool.

$$$ Hotel Pircas Negras
On Ruta 76 (on southern access), T03825-470611, www.hotelpircasnegras.com.
Large modern building, comfortable rooms, restaurant and pool, excursions organized.

$$ Chakana
In Banda Florida, T03825-15-51 0168, www.chakanahospedajerural.blogspot.com.ar.
In rural surroundings across the river from Villa Unión, this charming little hotel is carefully run by Natalia and Martín, who also prepare very good meals.

$$ Hotel Noryanepat
JV González 150, T03825-470133.
Small rooms with a/c, good.

Chilecito

$$$ Chilecito (ACA)
T Gordillo y A G Ocampo, T03825-422201, hotelchilecito@aca.org.ar.
Comfortable, renovated rooms, parking, pool, cheap set menus.

$$$ Hotel Ruta 40
Libertad 68, T03825-422804.

Family-run hotel with all services, including kitchen and laundry, bicycles, local produce for breakfast.

$$$ Posada del Sendero
Pasaje Spilimbergo, San Miguel, T03825-15-414041, www.posadadelsendero.com.ar.
In peaceful Chilecito's rural suburbs, a pleasant family-run place with simple rooms with a/c on a lovely park with pool. Excursions with own **Salir del Cráter** agency.

$$ Hostal Mary Pérez
Florencio Dávila 280, T03825-423156, hostal_mp@hotmail.com.
Good value, comfortable, welcoming atmosphere, good breakfast. Recommended.

North of Chilecito and La Rioja

Tinogasta

$$$ Hotel de Adobe Casagrande
Moreno 801, T03837-421140, www.casagrandetour.com.
Individually designed rooms, bar, restaurant, pool, jacuzzi, can arrange tours and activities.

$$ Hotel Nicolás
Perón 231, T03837-420028.
Small, long-established hotel with breakfast, a/c, Wi-Fi, laundry, parking.

Fiambalá

$$ Hostería Municipal
Almagro s/n, T03837-496291.
Good value, also restaurant.

$ pp Complejo Turístico
At the Termas, Fiambalá, bookings at tourist office T03837-496250.
With cabins, restaurant, also camping.

Belén

$$$ Belén
Belgrano y Cubas, T03835-461501,
www.belen cat.com.ar.
Comfortable, restaurant, prices depend on day of
arrival and excursions taken.

$$ Samai
Urquiza 349, T03835-461320, see Facebook.
Old fashioned but welcoming, homely little
rooms with bath and fan.

North of Belén

$$$ Hostería del Altura El Peñón
El Peñón,T0387-15-517 1252,
www.hosteriaelpenon.com.
With bath, breakfast, restaurant, bar, Wi-Fi.

Restaurants

Chilecito

$$$-$$ El Rancho de Ferrito
PB Luna 647, T03825-422481.
Popular *parrilla*, with local wines.

$$ La Rosa
Ocampo 149, T03825-424693.
Relaxing atmosphere, huge variety of pizzas,
more extensive menu Fri and Sat.

What to do

Chilecito
This is an excellent base for amazing treks in the
Famatina mountains and 1-day trips to Talampaya
and Valle de la Luna.

Salir del Cráter, *T03825-15 679620, www.*
salirdelcrater.com.ar. Trekking and 4WD
trips around Chilecito, plus excursions
to neighbouring provinces.

Transport

Chilecito
Bus Terminal on Av Perón, on south access to
town. To **San Juan** with **Vallecito**, 8 hrs, US$29;
to **La Rioja**, several times daily, US$8, 3 hrs. To
Córdoba, US$34-38, 7-8 hrs, and **Buenos Aires**,
US$82, 17 hrs, **Rápido Argentino** to Córdoba,
then change.

North of Chilecito

Tinogasta
Bus To **Catamarca**, Empresa Gutiérrez
(connection to Buenos Aires) and **Robledo**,
4-5 hrs, US$16.

Fiambalá
Bus Empresa Gutiérrez to **Catamarca** via
Tinogasta. For **Belén**, change at Aimogasta.

Belén
Bus From Belén to **Santa María**, San Cayetano
and **Parra** (connections there to Cafayate and
Salta), daily, 4-5 hrs, US$11-15. **Tinogasta**,
Robledo, 4 weekly, 2-3 hrs, US$8. To **El Peñón**
and **Antofagasta de la Sierra**, El Antofagasteño,
T03837-461152, Mon-Tue, return Mon, Fri,
minimum 6 hrs to El Peñón, US$12, 11 hrs
to Antofagasta, US$19. For more frequent
services to **Catamarca** or **La Rioja**, take
bus to Aimogasta, 2½ hrs, US$5.

Northwest
Argentina

Two of the oldest cities in Argentina, Santiago del Estero and Tucumán, are at the start of the route to the fascinating Northwest. Both have some good museums and other sites of interest, but the summer heat may urge you to press on to the mountains. Of the two routes to the atmospheric city of Salta, the more beautiful is via Tafí del Valle, the wine-producing town of Cafayate and the dramatic canyon of the Quebrada de las Conchas or the equally enchanting Valles Calchaquíes. Pretty towns in arid landscapes, archaeological remains and the Andes in the distance make for a memorable journey.

Santiago del Estero *Colour map 6, C4.*

Argentina's oldest city

Located 395 km north of Córdoba and 159 km southeast of Tucumán, Santiago del Estero was founded in 1553 by *conquistadores* pushing south from Peru. It is the oldest Argentine city, but little of its history is visible today. It's rather run down, but the people are relaxed and welcoming.

Sights

On the **Plaza Libertad** stand the **Municipalidad** and the **Cathedral** (the fifth on the site, dating from 1877), with the Cabildo-like Prefectura of Police. In the convent of **Santo Domingo**, Urquiza y 25 de Mayo, is one of two copies of the 'Turin Shroud', given by Philip II to his 'beloved colonies of America'. On Plaza Lugones is the church of **San Francisco**, the oldest surviving church in the city, founded in 1565, with the cell of San Francisco Solano, patron saint of Tucumán, who stayed here in 1593. Beyond it is the pleasant **Parque Francisco de Aguirre**.

Centro Cultural del Bicentenario de Santiago del Estero ⓘ *Libertad 439, T0385-422 4858, Facebook: CCBdeSantiagodelEstero, with café, 0800-2400*, acts as an umbrella organization for all cultural activities in the city. The highly recommended museum, **Museo de Ciencias Antropológicas y Naturales**, can be found on the first floor. It has an eclectic collection of prehispanic artefacts, exquisitely painted funerary urns, flattened skulls, anthropomorphic ceramics and musical instruments; fascinating. Also here is the **Museo Histórico Provincial** ⓘ *museums open Mon 1800-2200, Tue-Fri 0900-2100, Sat-Sun 1000-2100, free*, with 18th- and 19th-century artefacts from wealthy local families.

Tourist office ⓘ *Plaza Libertad 417, T0385-421 3253, www.turismosantiago.gob.ar.* See also www.sde.gov.ar.

Where to stay

Santiago del Estero

$$$ Carlos V
Independencia 110, T0385-424 0303,
www.carlosvhotel.com.
Corner of the plaza, the city's most luxurious hotel, elegant rooms, pool, good restaurant, still good value for its range.

$$$ Centro
9 de Julio 131, T0385-421 9502,
www.hotelcentro.com.ar.
Nice decor, very comfortable, airy restaurant. Recommended.

$$$ Libertador
Catamarca 47, T0385-421 9252,
www.hotellibertadorsrl.com.ar.
Smart and relaxing, spacious lounge, plain rooms, patio with pool (summer only), elegant restaurant, 5 blocks south of plaza in the better part of town.

$$$ Savoy
Peatonal Tucumán 39, T0385-421 1234,
www.savoysantiago.com.ar.

Good option, characterful, art nouveau grandeur, swirling stairwell, large airy rooms, small pool.

$ pp Res Emaus
Av Moreno Sur 675, T0385-421 5893.
Good cheap choice, with bath and TV, helpful.

Restaurants

Santiago del Estero

$$ Mia Mamma
On the main plaza at 24 de Septiembre 15.
A cheery place for *parrilla* and tasty pastas, with good salad for starters.

Transport

Santiago del Estero

Air Airport on northwest outskirts, T0385-434 3654. Flights to **Buenos Aires** and **Tucumán**.

Bus At Perú y Chacabuco, bus information, T0385-422 7091, www.tosde.com.ar. Terminal has toilets, *locutorio*, café, bar and kiosks. **Córdoba**, 6 hrs, US$37-41; **Salta**, 6-7 hrs, US$54; **Buenos Aires**, 12½-15½ hrs, 5 companies, US$92-122.

Tucumán and around *Colour map 6, C3.*

escape the urban heat and head for the hills

San Miguel de Tucumán was founded by Spaniards coming south from Peru in 1565. Capital of a province rich in sugar, tobacco and citrus fruits, it is the biggest city in the north. It stands on a plain and is sweltering hot in summer (a 1230-1630 siesta is strictly observed); so retreat to the cooler mountain town of Tafí del Valle in the Sierra de Aconquija.

Sights

On the west side of the main Plaza Independencia is the ornate **Casa de Gobierno** and the **Museo Casa Padilla** ① *25 de Mayo 36, see Facebook, Tue-Fri 0830-1230, 1530-1930, Sat-Sun 1530-1930, free,* with a small collection of art and antiques. Nearby, the church of **San Francisco**, has a picturesque façade. On the south side of Plaza Independencia is the **Cathedral**. A block south, the **Museo de Bellas Artes Timoteo Navarro** ① *9 de Julio 36, T0381-422 7300,* in a wonderfully restored building, has a large collection local and national art. Two blocks south is the interesting **Casa Histórica** ① *Congreso 151, T0381-431 0826, temporarily closed 2017,* where, in 1816, the country's Declaration of Independence was drawn up.

East of the centre is the **Parque de Julio**, one of the finest urban parks in Argentina. Extending over 400 ha, it contains a wide range of sub-tropical trees as well as a lake and sports facilities. The **Museo de la Industria Azucarera** ① *see Facebook, Tue-Fri 0900-1300, 1500-1800, Sat-Sun 1000-1330, 1430-1900, free,* traces the development of the local sugar industry.

Tafí del Valle

Southwest of Tucumán at Acheral on RN38, Ruta 307 heads northwest out of the sugar cane fields to zigzag up through forested hills to a treeless plateau, before reaching El Mollar and the Embalse

La Angostura. Here the valley is greener and you descend gradually to Tafí del Valle at 1976 m, a small town and popular weekend retreat from the heat of Tucumán in the summer (106 km). It has a cool microclimate and makes a good base for walking, with several peaks of the Sierra de Aconquija providing satisfying day-hikes. There's some excellent, if pricey, accommodation and a cheese festival in early February, with live music. **Tourist information** ⓘ *Peotonal Los Farores, T0381-15-643 8337, daily 0800-2200; see also www.tafidelvalle.com and www.tafidelvalle. travel.* Map US$1.40. Visit the **Capilla Jesuítica y Museo de La Banda** ⓘ *T03867-421685, daily 0800-1800, US$1, includes a guided tour,* southwest of town across bridge over Río Tafí, 500 m on left, an 18th-century chapel and 19th-century estancia, with museum of archaeology and religious art. **Museo de Mitos y Leyendas Casa Duende** ⓘ *R 307, Km 58 T0381-156 408500, Facebook: museocasaduende, daily 1000-1900, US$2 for guided visit,* is a private museum concentrating on the gods, beliefs and environment of the people of the Valles Calchaquíes.

Amaicha del Valle and around

From Tafí the road runs 56 km northwest over the 3040 m Infiernillo Pass (Km 85) with spectacular views and through grand arid landscape to **Amaicha del Valle** ⓘ *tourist information T03892-421198,* at 1997 m. The popular **Complejo Pachamama museum** ⓘ *T03892-421004, daily 0900-1800, www.museopachamama.com, US$5.50, explanations in English, guided tour in Spanish,* is highly recommended; it gives an overview of the Calchaquí culture and geology, and has tapestry for sale by Héctor Cruz, a well-known Argentine artist. From Amaicha the paved road continues north 15 km to the junction with Ruta 40.

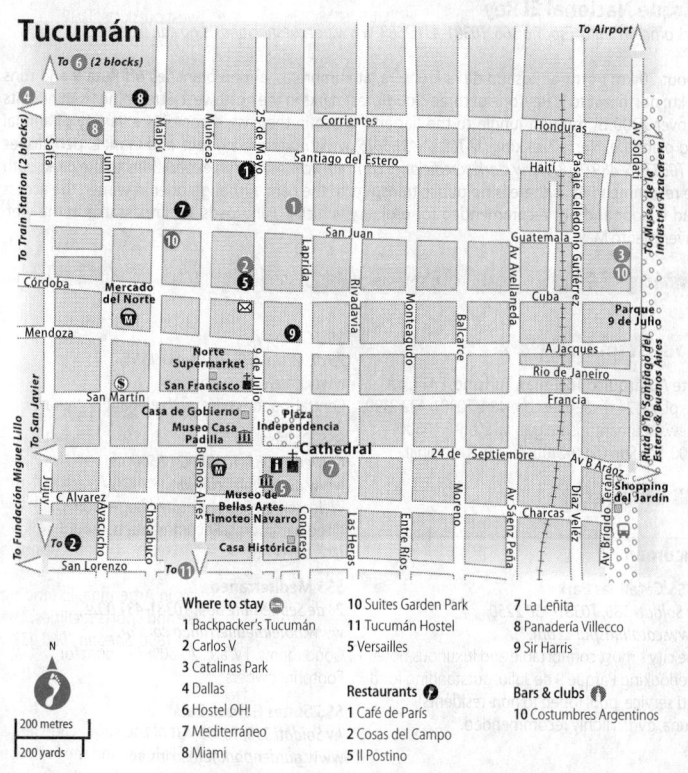

Tucumán

Where to stay
1 Backpacker's Tucumán
2 Carlos V
3 Catalinas Park
4 Dallas
6 Hostel OH!
7 Mediterráneo
8 Miami
10 Suites Garden Park
11 Tucumán Hostel
5 Versailles

Restaurants
1 Café de París
2 Cosas del Campo
5 Il Postino
7 La Leñita
8 Panadería Villecco
9 Sir Harris

Bars & clubs
10 Costumbres Argentinos

Some 35 km north, and 5 km off the main road, are the striking ruins of **Quilmes** ⓘ *daily 1000-1800, US$4, includes guided tour, with café, huge gift shop (check the site is open before going).* The setting is amazing: an intricate web of walls built into the mountain side, where 5000 members of a Diaguita tribe lived, resisting Inca and then Spanish domination, before being marched off to Córdoba and to the Quilmes in Buenos Aires where the beer comes from. For a day's visit take 0600 Aconquija bus from Cafayate to Santa María, and alight after an hour at the stop 5 km from site, or take 0700 El Indio bus (not on Thursday) from Santa María and take the 1130 bus back to Cafayate, US$3; otherwise tours run from Cafayate.

Santa María, 22 km south of Amaicha by paved road, is a delightful, untouristy small town with an interesting archaeology museum at the **Centro Cultural Yokavil** ⓘ *corner of plaza, 0900-1300, 1600-1900, donation requested*, pleasant hotels and a municipal campsite. A helpful **tourist kiosk** ⓘ *T03838-421870*, is on the plaza, with map and list of accommodation; also a *locutorio* and internet places, ATM on Mitre at Banco de la Nación (only one for miles). South of Santa María, Ruta 40 goes to Belén, see page 118.

Tucumán to Salta

The speedy route to Salta is via Rosario de la Frontera and Güemes. **Rosario de la Frontera**, 130 km north of Tucumán, is a convenient place for a stop, with thermal springs 8 km away (www.hoteltermasalta.com.ar; also **ACA** *hostería*, www.aca.org.ar). About 20 km north is the historical post house, **Posta de Yatasto**, with a museum, 2 km east of the main road and a campsite.

Parque Nacional El Rey
Park office in Salta, España 366, T0381-431 2683, www.parquesnacionales.gov.ar, free.

About 70 km north of Rosario de la Frontera, at Lumbreras, a road branches off Ruta 9 and runs 90 km northeast to El Rey, one of three cloudforest parks in the northwest. Stretching from heights of over 2300 m through jungle to the flat arid Chaco in the east, it contains a variety of animal and plant life. **Norte Trekking** ⓘ *T0387-431 6616, www.nortetrekking.com*, and **Clark Expediciones** ⓘ *T0387-15-489 0118, www.clarkexpediciones.com*, are licensed to run expeditions to the park; both are recommended as there is no public transport to the park. Although drier in winter, the access road is poor and not recommended for ordinary vehicles. Park roads are impassable in the wet, November to May.

Listings Tucumán and around *map page 123.*

Tourist information

Ente Autárquico Tucumán Turismo, EATT, on the plaza, 24 de Septiembre 484, T0381-422 2199, www.tucumanturismo.gob.ar. Mon-Fri 0800-2200, Sat-Sun 0900-2100. Also bus terminal.

Where to stay

Tucumán

$$$$ Catalinas Park
Av Soldati 380, T0381-450 2250,
www.catalinaspark.com.
The city's most comfortable and luxurious hotel, overlooking Parque 9 de Julio, outstanding food and service, pool (open to non-residents), sauna, gym. Highly recommended.

$$$ Carlos V
25 de Mayo 330, T0381-431 1666,
www.hotelcarlosv.com.ar.
Central, good service, with elegant restaurant.

$$$ Dallas
Corrientes 985, T0381-421 8500,
www.dallashotel.com.ar.
Welcoming, nicely furnished large rooms, good bathrooms. Recommended, though far from centre.

$$$ Mediterráneo
24 de Septiembre 364, T0381-431 0025,
www.hotelmediterraneo.com.ar.
Good rooms, TV, a/c. 20-30% discount for Footprint owners.

$$$ Suites Garden Park
Av Soldati 330, T0381-431 0700,
www.gardenparkhotel.com.ar.

Smart, welcoming 4-star, views over Parque 9 de Julio, pool, gym, sauna, restaurant. Also apartments.

$$$-$$ Miami
Junín 580, 8 blocks from plaza, T0381-431 0265,
www.hotelmiamitucuman.com.ar.
Good modern hotel, refurbished rooms, pool.

$$$-$$ Versailles
Crisóstomo Alvarez 481, T0381-422 9760,
www.hotelversailles tuc.com.ar.
Comfortable beds though rooms a bit small, good service, price depends on season. Recommended.

$ pp Backpacker's Tucumán
Laprida 456, T0381-430 2716,
www.backpackerstucuman.com.
Youth hostel with HI discounts in restored house with quiet atmosphere, lovely patio, basic dorms (US$12.50-15), English spoken, good. Plus **$$-$** double room with bath.

$ pp Hostel OH!
Santa Fé 930, T0381-430 8849,
http://hostelohtucuman.com.ar.
Neat, modern hostel with shared (US$12-15 pp) or private rooms (**$$**), quiet, *parrilla*, pool, games, garden.

$ pp Tucumán Hostel
Buenos Aires 669, T0381-420 1584,
www.tucumanhostel.com.
HI hostel in a refurbished building. Large, high-ceiling dorms (US$12-16), double room with bath **$$**, **$** without. Slightly unkempt but chilled garden. Recommended.

Tafí del Valle
Many places, including hotels, close out of season.

$$$ Hostería Tafí del Valle
Av San Martín y Gdor Campero,
T03867-421027, www.soldelvalle.com.ar.
Right at the top of the town, with splendid views, good restaurant, luxurious small rooms, pool.

$$$ La Rosada
Belgrano 322, T03867-421323.
Spacious rooms, well decorated, plenty of hot water, comfortable, excellent breakfast included, helpful staff, lots of expeditions on offer and free use of cycles.

$$$ Lunahuana
Av Critto 540, T03867-421330,
www.lunahuana.com.ar.

Stylish comfortable rooms with good views, spacious duplexes for families.

$$$ Mirador del Tafí
R 307, Km 61.2, T03867-421219,
www.miradordeltafi.com.ar.
Warm attractive rooms and spacious lounge, superb restaurant, excellent views, look for midweek offers. Highly recommended.

$ pp La Cumbre
Av Perón 120, T03867-421768,
www.lacumbretafidelvalle.com.
Basic, cramped rooms, but central, helpful owner is a tour operator with wide range of activities (see What to do, below).

Estancias

$$$ Estancia Las Carreras
R 325, 13 km southwest of Tafí, T03867-421473, www.estancialascarreras.com.
A fine working estancia with lodging and a restaurant serving its own produce (including cheeses). It offers many activities, such as riding, trekking, mountain biking and farm visits.

$$ Los Cuartos
Av Gob Critto y Av Juan Calchaquí s/n, T0381-15-587 4230, www.estancialoscuartos.com.
Old estancia in town, rooms full of character, charming hosts. Recommended. Also offer a day at the estancia, with lunch. Delicious *té criollo*, US$7-9, lunch, US$16, and farm cheese can be bought here.

Tucumán
Many popular restaurants and cafés along 25 de Mayo, north from Plaza Independencia, and on Plaza Hipólito Yrigoyen.

$$$-$$ La Leñita
San Juan 633, T0381-422 0855,
Facebook: lalenitaparrillada.
Recommended for *parrilla*, superb salads, live folk music at weekends.

$$ Il Postino
25 de Mayo y Córdoba.
Attractive buzzing pizza place, plus tapas and *tortillas* too, stylish decor. Recommended.

$ Sir Harris
Laprida y Mendoza.
A Tucumán institution, cosy with good quality *tenedor libre*, some veggie dishes. Recommended.

Cafés

Café de París
*Santiago del Estero 502 y 25 de Mayo,
see Facebook.*
Tapas bar and stylish little restaurant.

Cosas del Campo
*Lavalle 857 (south of centre, next to Plaza San
Martín), T420 1758.*
Renowned for its *empanadas*, also for take-away.

Panadería Villecco
Corrientes 751.
Exceptional bread, also wholemeal (*integral*)
and pastries.

Tafí del Valle
Many places along Av Perón.

$$ Parrilla Don Pepito
Av Perón 193.
Very good food, excellent *empanadas*.

Bars and clubs

Tucumán

Costumbres Argentinos
*San Juan 666 y Maipú, Facebook:
costumbresargentinas.bar.*
Intimate place, good atmosphere, for late drinks.

Festivals

Tucumán
9 Jul Independence Day. Has huge
processions/parties.
Early Sep Fiesta Nacional de la Empanada,
in Famaillá, 35 km from Tucumán, 3 days of
baking, eating and folk music.
24 Sep Battle of Tucumán, with
processions/parties.

Shopping

Tucumán
Handicrafts
Mercado Artesanal, *24 de Septiembre 565.
Daily 0800-1300, 1700-2200 (in summer, mornings
only).* Lace, wood and leatherwork, in the same
building as the Museo Folklórico Provincial,
T0381-421 8250, see Facebook, Tue-Fri 0900-
1230, 1530-1930, Sat-Sun 1530-1730.

Mercado del Norte, *Maipú between Mendoza and
Córdoba, Mon-Sat 0900-1400, 1630-2100.* Indoor
market and bazaar featuring cheap regional
foods, meat and local produce.
Regionales del Jardín, *Congreso 18.* Good
selection of local jams, *alfajores*, etc.

What to do

Tucumán
Bike Shop, *San Juan 984, T0381-431 3121.* Good.

Tafí del Valle
La Cumbre, *see Where to stay, above.* Energetic
and helpful company, offering full day walks to
nearby peaks, waterfalls and ruins, or to Cerro
Muñoz, with an *asado* at the summit (4437 m),
has open-sided truck.

Transport

Tucumán
Air Airport at Benjamín Matienzo, 10 km east
of town. Bus No 120 from terminal (pre-paid
cards required, sold in kiosks). Taxi US$10. Minibus
transfer from airport to Plaza Independencia,
US$2, to hotel US$7-9. Flights to **Buenos Aires**
via **Córdoba**.

Bus Local buses use pre-paid cards, US$1.85
or US$3, which you have to buy in advance in
kiosks. Bus terminal Av Brig Terán 250, T0381-400
2000/5000, www.terminaltuc.com, 7 blocks
east of Plaza Independencia. For long-distance
buses. Has a shopping complex, left luggage
lockers, excellent tourist information office (by
boletería 1), lots of *locutorios*, toilets and banks
(with ATM). Bus 4 from outside terminal to San
Lorenzo y 9 de Julio in centre. Taxi to centre
US$3-4. To **Buenos Aires**, many companies,
14-16 hrs, US$106-140. To/from **Santiago del
Estero**, 2 hrs, US$13-15. To **Salta** direct (not via
Cafayate), 4-4½ hrs, several companies US$29-33.
To **Cafayate** direct with **Aconquija** (T0381-422
7620) US$21-23, or go from Tafí del Valle: see
below. To **Mendoza**, 13-14 hrs, US$79-106, via
Catamarca, La Rioja, and San Juan. To **Córdoba**,
8 hrs, US$51-64.

Car hire Movil Renta, San Lorenzo 370, T0381-
431 0550, www.movilrenta.com.ar, and at airport.

Train Station at Corrientes 1045, ticket office
open daily except Sun from 0600 or 0700,

different hours each day. Train from Retiro, Buenos Aires at 0930 Mon and 1900 Thu, arrives 1256 and 2226; returns Wed 0817, Sat 1420, fares US$24, US$29 and US$84 for berth; www.sofse.gob.ar.

Tafí del Valle

Bus Smart **Aconquija** terminal on Av Crito, with café, toilets, helpful information, T03867-421025. To/from **Tucumán**, **Aconquija** (http://transporteaconquija.com.ar), 10 daily (6 on Sun), 2½ hrs, US$8. To **Cafayate**, 4 a day, 2½ hrs, US$17.

Cafayate and around *Colour map 6, C3.*

sample the wine, then head north through the beautiful Valles Calchaquíes

Cafayate is a popular town for daytrippers and tourists, attracted by its dry sunny climate, its picturesque setting against the backdrop of the Andes and its excellent wines, of which the fruity white *Torrontés* is unique to Argentina. Cerro San Isidro (five hours return) gives you a view of the Aconquija chain in the south and Nevado de Cachi in the north.

Sights

The **Museo de la Vid y El Vino** ① *Güemes Sur y F Perdiguero, www.museodelavidyelvino.gov.ar, Tue-Sun 1000-1930, US$2*, in a new building, tells the history of wine through old wine-making equipment. The tiny **Museo Arqueológico Rodolfo I Bravo** ① *Calchaquí y Colón 191, T03868-421054, Mon-Sat 0830-1230, 1300-1900, free*, has beautiful funerary urns, worth seeing if you haven't come across them elsewhere, and some Inca items.

☆Bodegas

Six bodegas can be visited, including **El Esteco** ① *at the junction of Rutas 68 and 40, T011-5198 8000, or 03868-566019, www.elesteco.com.ar*, which offers superb wines in a splendid setting. Next door is the sumptuous Patios de Cafayate spa (see Where to stay, below), a great place for lunch. **Etchart** ① *2 km south on Ruta 40, T03868-421310, www.bodegasetchart.com, tours daily on demand, open Jan, Feb, Jul, closed for lunch, book in advance*, produces high-quality wines. The boutique bodega, **San Pedro de Yacochuya** ① *7 km behind Cafayate, T011-4313 6470, www.sanpedrodeyacochuya.com. ar, phone to arrange a tour, Mon-Fri 1000-1700, Sat-Sun 1000-1300*, has a beautiful hillside setting. **Vasija Secreta** ① *on outskirts, T03868-421850, www.vasijasecreta.com (next to ACA hostería, T03868-421296, www.aca.tur.ar)*, is one of the oldest in the valley, English spoken. One block from the plaza is **Nanni** ① *Chavarría 151, T03868-421527, www.bodegananni.com, US2.50*, a very traditional, family-owned bodega, with good tastings of organic wines and a restaurant. There are more vineyards at Tombolón, to the south. In all cases check visiting times as they vary and can be quite precise. The quality of tours and tastings also varies.

Ruta 68 to Salta

Ruta 68 goes northeast from Cafayate to Salta. Six kilometres out of town is the rather unexpected landscape of Los Médanos (dunes), whose sand is constantly moving through thickets. The road then goes through the dramatic gorge of the Río de las Conchas (also known as the **Quebrada de Cafayate**) with fascinating rock formations of differing colours, all signposted. The road goes through wild and semi-arid landscapes. The vegetation becomes gradually denser as you near Salta, and a pretty river winds by your side with tempting picnic spots.

☆Valles Calchaquíes

A longer alternative to Salta is to take the RN40 north of Cafayate through the stunningly varied landscape of the Valles Calchaquíes to Cachi. The mainly *ripio* road (difficult after rain) winds from the spectacular rock formations of the arid **Quebrada de las Flechas** up through Andean-foothills with lush little oases and tiny unspoilt villages with limited bus services: **San Carlos** has a helpful tourist office on the plaza; **Angastaco** is a small, modern town with a petrol station, bus service and lodging options at the main plaza; and **Molinos** has a mid-18th century church (**San Pedro de Nolasco**) with a cactus-wood ceiling.

Cachi *Colour map 6, C3.*

Cachi is a beautiful town, set at 2280 m in a valley made fertile by pre-Inca irrigation, against a backdrop of arid mountains and the majestic Nevado del Cachi (6380 m). Its rich Diaguita history, starting long before the Incas arrived in 1450, is well presented in the **Museo Arqueológico** ① *T03868-491080, Tue-Sun 0900-1800,*

US$1.25, with painted funerary urns and intriguing petroglyphs. The simple Iglesia San José next door has a roof and lecterns made of cactus wood. In the plaza is the **tourist office** ① *T03868-491902, www.cachi.todowebsalta.com.ar, Mon-Fri 0900-2100, Sat-Sun 0900-1300, 1700-2100,* and a handicrafts market. There are panoramic views from the hill-top cemetery, 20 minutes' walk from the plaza, and a satisfying walk to **La Aguada** (6 km southwest). A longer walk (four hours each way) goes to the barely excavated ruins at **Las Pailas**, 16 km northwest. A 12-km track leads from the main road (slow and rough for cars) to a farmstead from where it's 15 minutes on foot to the ruins; the young man at the farm will offer to guide you. Otherwise, take a guide from Cachi. The view from the ruins is breathtaking, with huge cacti set against snow-topped Andean peaks.

Cachi to Salta

From Cachi follow Ruta 40 for 11 km north to Payogasta (Hotel y Bodega Sala de Payogasta ① *T03868-496754, www.saladepayogasta.com*), then turn right onto Ruta 33. The road climbs continuously up the Cuesta del Obispo, passing a dead-straight 19-km stretch known as La Recta del Tin-Tin through the magnificent **Los Cardones National Park** ① *administration office in Payogasta, 11 km from Cachi, T03868-15 414365, loscardones@apn.gov.ar,* with huge candelabra cacti up to 6 m in height. Paving ends at the end of national park. The road reaches the summit at Piedra de Molino (3347 m) after 43 km then plunges down through the Quebrada de Escoipe, a breathtaking valley between olive green mountains, one of Argentina's great routes. The road rejoins Ruta 68 at El Carril, from where it is 37 km to Salta.

Listings Cafayate and around

Tourist information

Cafayate

Tourist office
20 de Febrero, T03868-422442/422223, www.cafayate.todowebsalta.com.ar. Daily 0800-2200.
At the northeast corner of the plaza. They have a basic map showing bodegas and an accommodation list.

Where to stay

Cafayate

Accommodation is hard to find at holiday periods (Jan, Easter, late Jul), but there are many places to stay. Off season, prices are much lower. All those listed are recommended.

$$$$ Patios de Cafayate
El Esteco, T03868-422229, www.patiosdecafayate.com.
Formerly part of a bodega, now a stunning hotel with luxury spa.

$$$$-$$$ Viñas de Cafayate
R21, Camino al Divisadero, T03868-422272/282, www.cafayatewineresort.com.
On a hillside above Cafayate, colonial style, calm, welcoming with pretty, spacious bedrooms, some with views. Excellent restaurant with local delicacies, open to non-residents with reservation, full buffet breakfast.

$$$ Killa
Colón 47, T03868-422254, www.killacafayate.com.ar.
A delightfully restored colonial house with pleasing views. Delightful owner, who has a fascinating garden, tranquil, comfortable, good breakfasts.

$$$ Portal del Santo
Silvero Chavarria 250, T03868-422400, www.portaldelsanto.todowebsalta.com.ar.
Family-run hotel with lovely large rooms overlooking a beautiful pool and garden.

$$$ Villa Vicuña
Belgrano 76, T03868-422145, www.villavicuna.com.ar.
Half a block from the main plaza, 2 colourful patios, bright rooms, pleasant and calm.

Afternoon tea with home-made pastries served on demand.

$$ Hostal del Valle
San Martín 243, T03868-421039.
Well-kept big rooms around leafy patio, charming owner. Living room at the top has superb views over the valley (as do upper floor rooms).

$ pp El Hospedaje
Quintana de Niño y Salta, T03868-421680, www.elhospedaje.todowebsalta.com.ar.
Simple but pleasant rooms in colonial-style house, wonderful pool, good value, heater in room, HI discount.

$ Hostel Ruta 40
Güermes Sur 178, T03868-421689, www.hostel-ruta40.com.
Very sociable place to stay, dorms US$17, private room $$. Discount for HI members.

$ Rusty K Hostal
Rivadavia 281, T03868-422031, www. rustykhostal.todowebsalta.com.ar.
Neat, basic rooms and a great garden with BBQ. 2 blocks from the main plaza. Lots of activities to enjoy by bike.

Camping

Luz y Fuerza
Ruta Nacional 40, south of town, T03868-421568.
Camping with pool, games, grills showers and a buffet.

Valles Calchaquíes

$$$$ Colomé
20 km west of Molinos, T0387-421 9132, www.bodegacolome.com.
Leave town via the vicuña farm and follow signs, or phone for directions from Cafayate. Recommended as one of the best places to stay in Argentina, winery in a beautiful setting with delightful rooms, fine art, horse riding, tastings of excellent wines, all food is organic, power is hydroelectric.

$$$$-$$$ Hacienda de Molinos
A Cornejo (by the river), Molinos, T03868-494094, www.haciendademolinos.com.ar. Open all year round.
Stunning 18th-century hacienda, with rooms around a courtyard. Great attention to detail, the rooms are an oasis of calm. Swimming pool with a view of the Cachi mountains.

$ pp Hostal San Agustín
Sarmiento y A Cornejo at the Colegio Infantil, Molinos, T03868-494015.
Small but spotless rooms, some with private bath, run by nuns (who don't like to advertise the place, ask around discreetly for "las monjas" and someone will come and give you a key).

Cachi

$$$$-$$$ Finca Santana
Take the road to Cachi Adentro, and ask for Camino to Finca San Miguel, on right at top, T54-9 3868 638762, www.fincasantana.com.
2 rooms in boutique B&B in the heart of the valley, spectacular views, and complete sense of privacy and silence. Welcoming, spacious living room, terrace and garden, gourmet breakfast, trekking can be arranged. Wonderful.

$$$ ACA Hostería Cachi
At the top of Juan Manuel Castilla, T03868-491904, www.hosteriacachi.com.ar.
Smart modern rooms (with wheelchair access), great views, good restaurant, non-residents can use the pool if they eat lunch.

$$$ Casa de Campo La Paya
12 km south of Cachi at La Paya, clearly signposted from the road, T03868-491139, see Facebook.
A restored 18th-century house, pool, elegant rooms, excellent dinners, hospitable. Recommended.

$$$ El Cortijo
Opposite the ACA hotel, on Av Automóvil Club s/n, T03868-491034, http://elcortijohotel.com.
Lovely peaceful rooms, each with its own style, warm hospitality, original art works. Recommended.

$$$ Llaqta Mawk'a
Ruiz de Los Llanos s/n, up from Plaza, T03868-491016.
Traditional frontage hides modern block, garden/ terrace, view of the Nevado de Cachi, pool. Comfy rooms, ample breakfast, good value, popular with tourists (street parking). Horse riding with Ariel Villar arranged.

$$ Hospedaje Don Arturo
Bustamante s/n, T03868-491087, hospedajedonarturo.blogspot.com.
Homely, small rooms, quiet street, charming owners.

$ Hospedaje El Nevado de Cachi
Ruiz de los Llanos y F Suárez, T03868-491912.
Impeccable small rooms around a courtyard,
hot water, *comedor*.

$ Viracocha Art Hostel
F Suárez y Ruiz de los Llanos, T03868-491713,
www.hostelcachi.com.ar.
Good central option offering bike hire, private
with and without bath and shared rooms.
Also has a restaurant.

Camping

Municipal campsite
Av Automóvil Club Argentina s/n, T03868-491902.
With pool and sports complex, also *cabañas*
and *albergue*.

Restaurants

Cafayate

$$ Baco
Güemes Norte y Rivadavia, T0387-15 573 5831,
see Facebook.
Parrilla, *pasta casera*, pizzas, regional dishes,
empanadas and *picadas*. Seating inside and
on street, attractive corner, lively atmosphere.
Good selection of local wines and beers.

$$ El Rancho
Toscano 4, T03868-421256.
Traditional restaurant on plaza, serving meats,
regional dishes.

$$ El Terruño
Güemes Sur 28, T03868-422460,
www.terruno.todowebsalta.com.ar.
Meat and fish dishes, including local specialities,
good service.

$$ La Carreta de Don Olegario
Güemes, on Plaza, T03868-421004,
www.lacarretaolegario.com.
Huge and brightly lit, good set menus including
the usual meat dishes and pastas.

$$-$ La Casa de Las Empanadas
Mitre 24, T03868-15-454111,
www.casadelaempanada.com.ar.
Cosy place with exposed brick and wooden
tables featuring local specialities like *humitas*
and the titular *empanadas*.

Cafés

Helados Miranda
Güemes Norte 170.

Fabulous home-made ice cream, including
wine flavour.

Cachi

$$$-$$ La Merced del Alto
Fuerte Alto, T03868-490030,
www.lamerceddelalto.com.
Set in luscious surroundings, this is a treat to your
taste buds and your eyes. Make sure you try a
local wine.

$$-$ Ashpamanta
Bustamante – Cachi 4417, T0387-15-578 2244.
Just off the main plaza, this little restaurant
serves traditional Argentine favorites like pizza
and pasta, plus some regional gems such as
quinoa risotto.

$ Oliver Café
Ruiz de Los Llanos 160, on the plaza.
Tiny café for ice creams, coffee, breakfasts,
fruit juices, sandwiches and pizza.

Shopping

Cafayate

Handicrafts

Apart from the rather general souvenir shops,
there are some fine handicrafts. See the
Calchaquí tapestry exhibition of **Miguel Nanni**
(Güemes 65 on the main plaza) and the silver
work at **Jorge Barraco** (Colón 157, T03868-
421244). Local pottery, woollen goods, etc are
sold in the **Mercado de Artesanos Cafayetanos**
on the plaza (small, pricey).

What to do

Cafayate

Turismo Cordillerana, *Güemes Sur 178, T03868-
421689, www.turismocordillerano.com.* Tours,
trekking, horses, bike hire.

Cycle hire

Many places, ask tourist office for list.

Cachi

Fernando Gamarra, *Benjamín Zorrilla y
Güemes, T0387-431 7305, fg_serviciosturisticos@
yahoo.com.ar.* Local guide for conventional trips
around Cachi.
Santiago Casimiro, *T03868-15-638545.*
Recommended for mountain hikes; he's a nurse
trained in mountain rescue.

Tourism Urkupiña, *Benjamin Zorrilla s/n, T03868-491317, uk_cachi@hotmail.com*. Local agency for tours and bus tickets.

Cafayate

Bus El Indio on Belgrano, ½ block from plaza, T03868-421002, to **Santa María** (for Quilmes) 4 daily, US$5; also to **Salta**. To **Angastaco**, El Indio, 1 daily Mon-Fri, US$5, 1½ hrs (but does not continue to Molinos and Cachi). To/from **Tucumán**, **Aconquija** at Güemes Norte y Alvarado, T03868-421052 (open only when buses are due), 4 daily, 5½ hrs, US$21-23; to **Tafí del Valle**, 4 daily, US$17, 3 hrs (more via **Santa María**, 5½ hrs); and to **Salta** US$25-30.

Cachi

Bus To **Salta**, Ale, T0387-423 1811, www.alehnos.com.ar, daily, 4 hrs, US$12. Also to **Molinos**, Mon, Wed, Fri, Sun at 1130, 2 hrs, US$4.75.

Salta and around *Colour map 6, C3.*

the northwest's most appealing and intriguing city

★Founded in 1582, Salta, 1600 km north of Buenos Aires, is an atmospheric city, with many fine 19th-century buildings, elegant plazas, stirring folkloric music and fabulous food. It lies in the broad Lerma valley, surrounded by steep and forested mountains, and is a good base for exploring the Andean regions, Cachi in the Calchaquí valleys to the south (described above) and the Quebrada de Humahuaca north of Jujuy (described in the next section).

Sights

Salta is a fascinating city to explore on foot; in a couple of hours you can get a feel for its wonderful architecture. The heart of Salta, is **Plaza 9 de Julio**, planted with tall palms and surrounded by colonial buildings. On the plaza, the **Cabildo**, 1783, one of the few to be found intact in the country, houses the impressive **Museo Histórico del Norte** ⓘ *Caseros 549, Tue-Sat 0900-1800, US$2, free Wed*. The museum has displays on pre-Columbian and colonial history, independence wars, and a fine 18th-century pulpit. Opposite the Cabildo is the 19th-century **Cathedral** (open mornings and evenings), painted pink and cream and reflected in the blue plate glass of a bank next door. It contains a huge late baroque altar (1807) and the much venerated images of the Virgin Mary and of the Cristo del Milagro, sent from Spain in 1592. The miracle was the sudden cessation of a terrifying series of earthquakes when the images were paraded through the streets on 15 September 1692. They still are, each September. The **Museo de Arqueología de Alta Montaña** (MAAM) ⓘ *Mitre 77, T0387-437 0592, www.maam.gob.ar, Tue-Sun 1100-1930, US$2.50, shop and café*, has a collection of exhibits from high-altitude shrines, including mummies of child sacrifices, video material in Spanish and English, also temporary exhibits. Controversy surrounds the discovery of the mummies and their display. They are exhibited with sensitivity; visitors can choose whether or not to view them. Opposite MAAM on the other side of the plaza is the interesting **Museo de Arte Contemporáneo** ⓘ *Zuviría 90, T0387-437 3036, www.macsaltamuseo.org, Tue-Sun 0900-1900*, which is also worth a look.

A block southwest of the Plaza is the **Museo de la Ciudad 'Casa de Hernández'** ⓘ *Florida 97 y Alvarado, T0387-437 3352, www.museociudadsalta.gov.ar, Mon-Fri 0900-1300, 1600-2030, Sat 1600-2030, free*. This fine 18th-century mansion includes furniture and portraits, but a marvellous painting of Güemes. The magnificent façade of **San Francisco** church ⓘ *on Caseros, 0900-2000*, rises above the skyline with its splendid tower, ornately decorated in plum red and gold. Further along Caseros, the Convent of **San Bernardo**, rebuilt in colonial style in the mid-19th century, has a beautifully carved wooden portal of 1762, but is not open to visitors as nuns still live there. They will open up the small shop for you, selling quaint handicrafts.

At the end of Caseros is the **Cerro San Bernardo** (1458 m) ⓘ *accessible by cable car (teleférico) from Parque San Martín, www.telefericosanbernardo.com, daily 1000-1900, US$10 return, US$5.50 children over 5, fine views, 45 mins' walk up, depending on fitness*. At the summit are gardens, waterfalls, a café, a silver collection and playground. Further along Avenida H Yrigoyen is an impressive **statue to General Güemes**, whose *gaucho* troops repelled seven powerful Spanish invasions from Bolivia between 1814 and 1821.

Up beyond the Güemes statue is the **Museo Antropológico** ⓘ *Paseo Güemes, T0387-422 2960, www.antropologico.gov.ar, closed in 2017*. Fascinating displays on pre-Inca cultures include painted urns, intriguing board-flattened skulls (meant to confer superiority), a mummy discovered high in the Andes and many objects from Tastil (see below). **Museo de Ciencias Naturales** ① *Parque San Martín, T0387-431 8086, Tue-Sun 1530-1930, US$0.25*, displays a bewildering number of stuffed animals and birds; the armadillo collection is interesting.

Dique Cabra Corral
The Dique Cabra Corral is one of the largest artificial lakes in Argentina. It's popular with locals for fishing *pejerrey*, water-skiing, camping and restaurants. Catamarans can be hired for fishing and meals. The nearest town is **Coronel Moldes**, which has processions of gauchos at its Fiesta

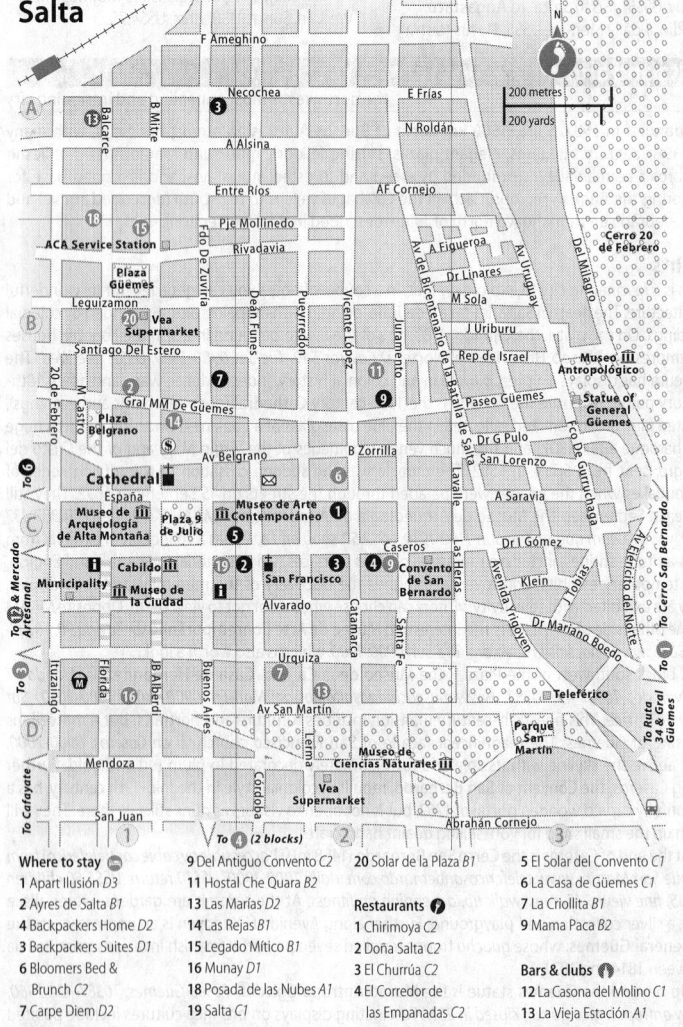

Salta

Where to stay 🛏
1 Apart Ilusión *D3*
2 Ayres de Salta *B1*
3 Backpackers Home *D2*
3 Backpackers Suites *D1*
6 Bloomers Bed & Brunch *C2*
7 Carpe Diem *D2*
9 Del Antiguo Convento *C2*
11 Hostal Che Quara *B2*
13 Las Marías *D2*
14 Las Rejas *B1*
15 Legado Mítico *B1*
16 Munay *D1*
18 Posada de las Nubes *A1*
19 Salta *C1*
20 Solar de la Plaza *B1*

Restaurants 🍽
1 Chirimoya *C2*
2 Doña Salta *C2*
3 El Churrúa *C2*
4 El Corredor de las Empanadas *C2*
5 El Solar del Convento *C1*
6 La Casa de Güemes *C1*
7 La Criollita *B1*
9 Mama Paca *B2*

Bars & clubs 🍸
12 La Casona del Molino *C1*
13 La Vieja Estación *A1*

Cloud line

One of the great railway journeys of South America is the *Tren a las Nubes* (Train to the Clouds). Engineered by Richard Maury, of Pennsylvania (who is commemorated by the station at Km 78 which bears his name) this remarkable project was built in stages between 1921 and 1948, by which time developments in road and air transport had already reduced its importance. The line includes 21 tunnels, 13 viaducts, 29 bridges, 2 loops and 2 zig-zags. From Salta the line climbs gently to Campo Quijano (Km 40, 1520 m), where it enters the Quebrada del Toro, an impressive rock-strewn gorge. At El Alisal (Km 50) and Chorrillos (Km 66) there are zig-zags as the line climbs the side of the gorge before turning north into the valley of the Río Rosario near Puerto Tastil (Km 101, 2675 m), missing the archaeological areas around Santa Rosa de Tastil. At Km 122 and Km 129 the line goes into 360° loops before reaching Diego de Almagro (3304 m). At Abra Muñano (3952 m) the road to San Antonio can be seen zig-zagging its way up the end-wall of the Quebrada del Toro below. From Muñano (3936 m) the line drops slightly to San Antonio, Km 196. The spectacular viaduct at La Polvorilla is 21 km further at 4190 m, just beyond the branch line to the mines at La Concordia. The highest point on the line is reached at Abra Chorrillos (4475 m, Km 231). From here the line runs on another 335 km across a rocky barren plateau 3500-4300 m above sea level before reaching Socompa (3865 m).

As a tourist trip this was a comfortable ride, but a long day out and subject to frequent closures. In 2016 the Tren a las Nubes excursion was reconfigured so that the majority of the journey is done by bus between Salta and San Antonio de los Cobres. The route passes through the Quebrada del Toro. As you climb through the gorge the landscape changes from forested mountains to farmland to arid red rock dotted with giant cactii. Eventually you reach the beautiful *puna*. On the way up breakfast is taken at the community of El Alfarcito and on the return a stop is made at the museum in Santa Rosa de Tastil. The actual train ride comprises the section from San Antonio to the viaduct al La Polvorilla, with a 30-minute stop at the viaduct. The fare includes bilingual guides, breakfast, lunch and medical assistance should altitude sickness hit. At the stops at El Alfarcito, La Polvorilla and Santa Rosa there are opportunities to buy local handicrafts and sample local produce. Don't bother haggling for the shawls and hats; they are beautifully made and the people's only source of income.

Patronal (1 August). Ale Hermanos bus No 5 goes to the Puente across the narrows of the lake (bungee jumping is offered here). Some 95 km from Salta on the Río Juramento outlet from the lake, **Salta Rafting** ⓘ *R 47, Km 43, T0387-421 3216, www.saltarafting.com*, has year-round rafting, kayaking and a zip-line (a fun day out).

☆Salta to Chile

The famous **Tren a las Nubes** is a narrow-gauge railway running from Salta 570 km through the town of San Antonio de los Cobres to Socompa, on the Chilean border (see box, opposite). San Antonio and the border can also be reached by Ruta 51 from Salta. From **Campo Quijano**, the road runs along the floor of the Quebrada del Toro before climbing to Alto Blanco (paved section). At **Santa Rosa de Tastil** there are important prehispanic ruins and a small **museum** ⓘ *Tue-Sun 0900-1900, Mon 0900-1500, free,* recommended. (To get there, take El Quebradeño bus, a tour from Salta, or share a taxi.) Sitting in the vast emptiness of the *puna* at 3775 m, San Antonio de los Cobres, 168 km by road from Salta, is a simple, remote mining town of adobe houses with a friendly Coya community. West of town Ruta 51 leads 20 km to La Polvorilla railway viaduct; ask in town for details and beware sudden changes in the weather.

Border with Chile Beyond San Antonio de los Cobres Ruta 51 continues to **San Pedro de Atacama** in Chile using the **Sico Paso** (4079 m). It's a spectacular route, crossing white salt lakes dotted with flamingos and vast expanses of desert. The first 110 km are paved. This route has largely been replaced by that over Paso de Jama (see page 140), but there is a customs post at Paso Sico (T0387-

498 2001, open 24 hours), where you may be allowed to spend the night: check first in San Antonio de los Cobres if it is open. On the Chilean side continue via Mina Laco and Socaire to Toconao (road may be bad between these two points). Customs and immigration are at Hito Cajón, on the Bolivian border near San Pedro de Atacama. Note that fruit, vegetables and dairy products may not be taken into Chile (search 20 km after Paso Sico). Gasoline is available in San Pedro and Calama. Obtain sufficient drinking water for the trip in San Antonio and do not underestimate the effects of altitude.

> **Tip...**
> In San Antonio, try the *quesillo de cabra* (goat's cheese) from Estancia Las Cuevas. The Huaira Huasi restaurant, used by tour groups, also has a good menu.

Listings Salta *map page 132.*

Tourist information

Cámara de Turismo
Gral Güemes 15 y Av del Bicentenario de la Batalla de Salta, T0387-421 0698, www.turismoensalta.com.

Municipal tourist office
Caseros 711, T0800-777 0300, or 0387-422 7798, www.saltalinda.gov.ar. Mon-Fri 0800-2100, Sat-Sun 0900-2100.
For Salta city only, small but helpful.

Provincial tourist office
Buenos Aires 93 (1 block from main plaza), T0387-431 0950, http://turismo.salta.gov.ar. Weekdays 0800-2100, weekends 0900-2000.
Very helpful, provides good maps, gives advice on tours and arranges accommodation in private houses in high season (Jul) if hotels are fully booked.

Where to stay

All hotels and hostels listed are recommended. Book ahead in Jul holidays and around 10-16 Sep during celebrations of Cristo del Milagro.

$$$$ Legado Mítico
Mitre 647, T0387-422 8786, www.legadomitico.com.
This small, welcoming hotel is absolutely lovely: luxurious rooms each with its own personality. The personalized pre-ordered breakfasts are a fantastic way to start the day.

$$$$ Solar de la Plaza
Juan M Leguizamon 669, T0387-431 5111, www.solardelaplaza.com.ar.
Elegant old former Salteño family home, faultless service, sumptuous rooms, great restaurant and a pool.

$$$$-$$$ Ayres de Salta
Gral Güemes 650, T0387-422 1616, www.ayresdesalta.com.ar.
Spacious, central 4-star hotel near Plaza Belgrano. Everything you would expect in this price range: spacious rooms, heated pool, great views from roof terrace.

$$$ Apart Ilusión (Sweet Dreams)
José Luis Fuentes 743, Portezuelo Norte, T0387-15 539 3198, see Faceb ook.
On the slopes of Cerro San Bernardo, well-equipped self-catering apartments for 2-4, decorated with local handicrafts, beautiful views. English-speaking owner, Sonia Alvarez, is welcoming. Breakfast and parking available, good value.

$$$ Bloomers Bed & Brunch
Vicente López 129, T0387-422 7449, www.bloomers-salta.com.ar. Closed mid-May to mid-Jun.
In a refurbished colonial house, 5 spacious non-smoking rooms individually decorated, and one apartment. Use of kitchen and library. The brunch menu, different each day, is their speciality.

$$$ Carpe Diem
Urquiza 329, T0387-421 8736, www.bedandbreakfastsalta.com.
Welcoming B&B, beautifully furnished, convenient, comfortable public areas, German/Italian-owned, no children under 14.

$$$ Salta
Buenos Aires 1, on main plaza, T0387-426 7500, www.hotelsalta.com.
A Salta institution with neocolonial public rooms, refurbished bedrooms, marvellous suites overlooking plaza, *confitería* and honorary membership of the **Polo and Golf Club**.

$$ Del Antiguo Convento
Caseros 113, T0387-422 7267, www.hoteldelconvento.com.ar.

Small, convenient, with old-fashioned rooms around a neat patio, very helpful, a good choice.

$$ Las Marías
Lerma 255, T0387-422 4193,
www.saltaguia.com/lasmarias.
Central hostel, $ pp in shared rooms, close to Parque San Martín.

$$ Las Rejas
General Güemes 569, T0387-422 7959,
www.lasrejashostel.com.ar.
2 houses converted into a small B&B and a hostel (US$15-17 pp), comfortable, central, helpful owners.

$$ Munay
San Martín 656, T0387-422 4936,
www.munayhotel.com.ar.
Good choice, smart rooms for 2-5 with good bathrooms, warm welcome. Also have hotels of the same standard in Cafayate, Humahuaca, Jujuy and La Quiaca.

$$ Posada de las Nubes
Balcarce 639, T0387-432 1776,
www.posadadelas nubes.com.ar.
Charming, small, with simply decorated rooms around a central patio. Great location for Balcarce nightlife; might be a little too loud at weekends.

$ Backpackers Home
Buenos Aires 930, T0387-423 5910; Backpackers Suites, Urquiza 1045, T0387-431 8944,
www.backpackerssalta.com.
HI-affiliated hostels, well run, with dorms and private rooms ($$, cheaper for HI members), with laundry and budget travel information. Crowded and popular.

$ Hostal Che Quara
Santiago del Estero 125, T0387-422 0392,
www.hostalquara.com.ar.
Dorms US$13-14, also doubles with and without bath, with heating, TV room, drinks for sale. The helpful staff can organize tours.

Estancias
Among Salta's most desirable places to stay are its colonial-style estancias, known locally as fincas. All those listed are recommended for their individual style, setting, comfort, food and activities, especially horse riding. All are in the **$$$$-$$$** price range, mostly pp.

Finca El Bordo de las Lanzas
45 km east of Salta, T054-9-387-5534 6942,
http://estanciaelbordo.com.

Finca Los Los
Chicoana, 40 km from Salta at the entrance to the Valles Calchaquíes, T0387-15-683 3121. Mar-Dec.

Finca Santa Anita
Coronel Moldes, 60 km from Salta, on the way to Cafayate, T0387-490 5050, www.santaanita. com.ar.

Finca Valentina
Ruta 51, Km 11, La Merced Chica, T0387-15-415 3490, www.finca-valentina.com.ar.
Associated with recommended tour operator **Socompa**, below.

La Casa de los Jazmines
R51, Km 6 south towards La Silleta, T0387-497 2002, www.houseofjasmines.com.

Selva Montana
C Alfonsina Storni 2315, San Lorenzo, T0387-492 1184, www.hostal-selvamontana.com.ar.

Salta to Chile

Campo Quijano

$$$ Hostería Punta Callejas
T0387-490 4086, www.puntacallejas.com.ar.
Very comfortable, pool, tennis, riding, excursions.

Camping
Several sites, including municipal campsite, at entrance to Quebrada del Toro gorge, lovely spot with good facilities, hot showers, bungalows.

San Antonio de los Cobres

$$$ Hostería de las Nubes
Edge of San Antonio on Salta road T0387-490 9059, www.hoteldelasnubes.com.
Smart, comfortable, modern and spacious. Recommended.

$$ Hostería El Palenque
Belgrano s/n, T0387-490 9019,
www.hostalelpalenque.com.
Basic, hot showers, cable TV.

There are other lodgings. Ask at the **Municipalidad** (Belgrano s/n, T0387-490 9045), about dorm and double room at the tourist information office (**$**) and minibus tours to salt flats and Purmamarca.

Restaurants

Salta has delicious and distinctive cuisine: try the *locro, humitas* and *tamales*, served in the municipal market at San Martín y Florida. There are lots of cafés on Plaza 9 de Julio; it's a great place to sit and people watch, eg New Time and Plaza Café; the 2 cafés outside MAAM, **Havana** and **El Palacio**, are very touristy.

$$$ El Solar del Convento
Caseros 444, half a block from plaza, T0387-421 5124.
Elegant and not expensive, champagne when you arrive, delicious steaks. Recommended.

$$ Chirimoya
España 211, T0387-431 2857, see Facebook.
Those looking to get away from the *carne* can opt for this café a few blocks off the main plaza. It offers veggie twists on pastas, sandwiches and *milanesas*. There's even a 'raw ravioli'.

$$ Doña Salta
Córdoba 46 (opposite San Francisco convent library), T0387-432 1921.
Excellent regional dishes and pleasant, rustic atmosphere, good value.

$$ El Charrúa
Caseros 221, T0387-432 2222, www.parrillaelcharrua.com.ar.
A good, brightly lit family place with a reasonably priced and simple menu where *parrilla* is particularly recommended.

$$ La Casa de Güemes
España 730.
Popular, local dishes and *parrilla*, traditionally cooked in the house where General Güemes lived. Also has shows.

$ El Corredor de las Empanadas
Caseros 117 and Zuviría 913.
Delicious *empanadas* and tasty local dishes in airy surroundings.

$ La Criollita
Zuviría 306.
Small and unpretentious, a traditional place for tasty *empanadas*.

$ Mama Paca
Gral Güemes 118.
Recommended by locals, traditional restaurant for seafood from Chile and home-made pastas.

Bars and clubs

Visit a *peña* to hear passionate folklore music live. There are many *peñas*, with excellent live bands, on Balcarce towards railway station, a great place to go Thu-Sat from 1900 (taxi US$1.50).

Los Cardones (885 Balcarce, T0387-432 0909) has good food and a good nightly show; **La Vieja Estación** (877 Balcarce, T0387-421 7727, www.la-viejaestacion.com.ar) has a great atmosphere and good food. This area also has a number of popular rock and jazz bars, such as **Macondo** or **Café del Tiempo** (both on Facebook), as well as intimate restaurants and nightclubs.

West of the centre **La Casona del Molino** (Luis Burela 1, T0387-434 2835, see Facebook; take taxi) is the most authentic, in a crumbling old colonial house, serving good food and drink.

Festivals

Feb Salta celebrates **Carnival** with processions and dancers on the 4 weekends before Ash Wed at the *corsódromo*, located on Av Gato Mancha near the convention centre (US$4).
16-17 Jun Commemoration of the death of General Martín Güemes: folk music in evening and gaucho parade in morning around the Güemes statue.
15 Sep Cristo del Milagro. Salta's biggest event.
24 Sep Battles of Tucumán and Salta.

Shopping

Handicrafts
Arts and handicrafts are often cheaper in surrounding villages, but don't miss the **Mercado Artesanal** on the western outskirts, in the Casa El Alto Molino (San Martín 2555, T0387-434 2808, daily 0900-2100; take bus 2, 3, or 7 from Av San Martín in centre and get off as bus crosses the railway line). It has an excellent range and high quality in a lovely 18th-century mansion. Opposite is a cheaper tourist market for similar items, but factory-made. **Mercado Municipal** (San Martín y Florida) sells meat, fish, vegetables and other produce and handicrafts, closed 1300-1700 and Sun.

What to do

There are many tour operators, mostly on Buenos Aires, offering adventure trips and excursions; staff give out flyers on the street. Out of season, tours often run only if there is sufficient demand; check carefully that tour will run on the day you want. All agencies charge similar prices for tours (though some charge extra for credit card payments). City tour US$20; Valles Calchaquíes US$75 (2 days); Cachi US$47; Puna and salt lakes US$85. The tourist office gives reports on agencies and their service.

Clark Expediciones, *Mariano Moreno 1950, T0387-15-489 0118, www.clarkexpediciones.com.*

Specialist birding tours, eco-safaris and treks. English spoken.

Dexotic, *Güemes 569, T0387-421 5971, www.dexotic.com*. Company specializing in various excursions and adventure packages including to Valle Calchaquíes, Cachi, Puna, the salt lakes and Humahuaca. Also horse riding, rafting, bungee jumping and more. Friendly staff, professional.

Movitrack, *Caseros 468, T0387-431 6749, www.movitrack.com.ar*. Entertaining safaris in a 4WD truck, to San Antonio de los Cobres, Humahuaca, Cafayate, adventure trips, German, English spoken, expensive. They also have an **OxyBus** for high-altitude journeys.

New Sendas, *in Chicoana, 47 km south, T0387-490 7009, www.newsendas.com*. Expert guide Martín Pekarek offers adventure excursions and horses for hire, English and German spoken. Also with lodging at Hostería de Chicoana.

Norte Trekking, *Gral Güemes 265, T0387-431 6616, www.nortetrekking.com. Mon-Fri 0900-1400, 1500-1900*. Excellent tours in 4WDs and minivans all over Salta and Jujuy, to Iruya, over Jama Pass to San Pedro de Atacama, hiking, horse riding, excursions to El Rey national park with experienced guide Federico Norte, knowledgeable, speaks English. Tailors tours to your interest and budget.

Puna Expediciones, *Agustín Usandivaras 230, T0387-416 9313, www.punaexpeditions.com.ar*. Qualified and experienced guide Luis H Aguilar organizes treks in remote areas of Salta and Jujuy and safaris further afield. Recommended.

Sayta, *Chicoana, 49 km from Salta, T0387-15 683 6565, see Facebook*. An estancia specializing in horse riding, for all levels of experience, good horses and attention, great *asados*, also has lodging for overnight stays, adventure and rural tourism. Recommended.

Socompa, *Balcarce 998, p 1, T0387-431 5974, www.socompa.com*. Excellent company specializing in trips to salt flats and volcanoes in the puna, 3 days to the beautiful, remote hamlet of Tolar Grande; can be extended to 12 days to include Atacama and Puna of Catamarca; 4 days to Puna of Catamarca. English and Italian spoken, knowledgeable guides. Highly recommended.

Transport

Air The airport (*T0387-424 3115, www.aa2000.com.ar*) is 12 km southwest, served by minibuses, US$3.50, or take a remise taxi, US$8. Bus on Corredor 8A to airport from San Martín, US$0.30. Flights to **Buenos Aires** (2¼ hrs) and **Córdoba**.

Bus Local buses in the city charge US$0.30 (www.saetasalta.com.ar). Long distance terminal is 8 blocks east of the main plaza, T0387-401 1143 for information, www.terminalsalta.com. Taxi to centre US$2-3. Toilets, *locutorio*, café, *panadería*, kiosks. To **Buenos Aires**, several companies daily, US$147-170, 19-20 hrs. To **Córdoba**, several companies daily, 12 hrs, US$79-83. To **Santiago del Estero**, 6-7 hrs, US$54. To **Tucumán**, 4 hrs, several companies, US$29-33. To **Mendoza** via Tucumán, 2 companies daily, US$100-135, 18-20 hrs. To **Jujuy**, frequent service, US$11, 2½ hrs. To **San Antonio de los Cobres**, 5 hrs, El Quebradeño, daily, US$10-12.

To **Cachi** 0700, 1330, US$12, 4 hrs, with Ale Hnos, T0387-423 1811. To **Cafayate**, US$25-30, with El Indio, T0387-422 9393, and Aconquija.

International buses To **Paraguay**: travel to **Resistencia**, daily, 12 hrs, US$70-75, Tigre Iguazú, or to **Formosa**, US$77-90, 16 hrs, then change to a direct bus to Asunción. To **Chile**: Services to **Calama** and **San Pedro de Atacama** with Géminis, T0387-431 7778, Pullman, T0387-422 1366 (3 a week each), and Andesmar 2 a week, but check days as they change, via Jujuy and the Jama Pass, US$42-60, 11 hrs. Géminis and Pullman offices are at booths 15 and 16 in the terminal. Frontera del Norte runs from Salta to **Iquique** via San Pedro. To **Bolivia**: to **La Quiaca**, on Bolivian border, Balut, 7½ hrs, US$23. To **Aguas Blancas** US$28, 5 hrs, or **Pocitos** (both on the Bolivian border, see pages 142 and 143), US$28-39, 8 hrs, 2 companies daily. Direct bus Salta–Tarija, Juárez, Mon and Fri 2230, US$43-56, take photocopy of passport when buying ticket. Or ask at Dragón Rojo, C Alberdi entre La Rioja y San Luis, T0387-414 0227, for their daily service direct to Tarija (mixed reports in 2016). Alternatively, take a bus to Aguas Blancas, or to Orán and change for Aguas Blancas, cross border and take a shared taxi to Tarija. With an early start you can get to Tarija in a day.

Car hire Avis, Caseros 420 and, T0387-421 2181 and at the airport, Ruta 51, T0387-424 2289, salta@avis.com.ar. Efficient and very helpful, recommended. **NOA**, Buenos Aires 1, T0387-431 7080, www.noarentacar.com, in Hotel Salta, helpful, also mountain bike, US$13 per day. Many others.

Train Station at 20 de Febrero y Ameghino, 9 blocks north of Plaza 9 de Julio. The only train service is the **Tren a las Nubes** (see box, page 133), which, since 2016, does not in fact run from Salta. The route is from Salta station to San

Antonio de los Cobres by bus at 0700, transfer to the train at 1200 for the 4-hr journey to the Polvorilla viaduct and back, then bus back to Salta, arriving at 2000. The excursion usually runs Tue, Thu and Sat (Tue and Sat in Jan-Mar), with extra trains at holiday times. The fare (bus, train, bus) is US$126, or US$78 train only, US$140 (US$91 train only) in Semana Santa and Jul to end-Dec, discount for Argentines and minors. Contact T0387-422 8021, www.trenalasnubes.com.ar.

Jujuy city Colour map 6, C3.

soak up the Andean atmosphere

Though it lacks Salta's elegance, since there are few colonial buildings remaining, the historical city of Jujuy is the starting point for some of the country's most spectacular scenery and it has a distinctly Andean feel, evident in its food and music. With extremely varied landscapes, the area is rich in both contemporary and ancient culture, with prehispanic ruins at Tilcara, delightful villages and excursions.

San Salvador de Jujuy (pronounced Choo-Chooey, with ch as in Scottish loch) often referred to by locals as San Salvador, is the capital of Jujuy province and sits in a bowl ringed by lushly wooded mountains. The city was finally established in 1593, after earlier attempts met resistance from local indigenous groups, but the city was plagued by earthquakes, sacking and the Calchaquíes Wars for the next 200 years. It struggled to prosper, then in August 1812 General Belgrano, commanding the republican troops, ordered the city to be evacuated and destroyed before the advancing Spanish army. This extraordinary sacrifice is marked on 23-24 August by festivities known as El Exodo Jujeño with gaucho processions and military parades.

Sights

Away from the busy shopping streets, in the eastern part of the city, is the **Plaza Belgrano**, a wide square planted with tall palms and orange trees. It's lined with impressive buildings, including the elaborate French baroque-style **Casa de Gobierno** ⓘ *daily 0800-2100*, containing the famous flag Belgrano presented to the city. On the west side is the late 19th-century **Cathedral** (the original, 1598-1653, was destroyed by earthquake in 1843) containing one of Argentina's finest colonial treasures: a gold-plated wooden pulpit, carved by *indígenas* in the Jesuit missions, depicting gilded angels mounting the stairs. The modern church of **San Francisco** ⓘ *Belgrano y Lavalle, 2 blocks west of the plaza, daily 0730-1200, 1700-2100*, contains another fine gilded colonial pulpit, with ceramic angels around it, like that at Yavi. Don't miss the **Museo Arqueológico Provincial** ⓘ *Lavalle 434, T0388-422315, Mon-Fri 0800-2000, US$1*, with beautiful ceramics from the Yavi and Humahuaca cultures, haphazardly displayed, a mummified infant, and a 2500-year-old sculpture of a goddess giving birth.

There are hot springs 19 km west at **Termas de Reyes** ⓘ *1 hr by bus Etap (línea 1C) from bus terminal or corner of Gorriti and Urquiza, US$0.75, municipal baths and pool US$3.25*; also cabins with thermal water set among magnificent mountains. The Hotel Termas de Reyes ⓘ *T0388-492 2522, www.termasdereyes.com*, charges US$63 for day visitors to its spa (various treatments), and there are packages from one to seven nights.

Listings Jujuy city

Tourist information

Tourist office
Gorriti 295, on the plaza, T0388-422 1343, www.turismo.jujuy.gov.ar. Mon-Fri 0700-2200, Sat-Sun 0800-2200.
Has an accommodation leaflet and a map. Also at bus terminal, T0388-428 9012, daily 0700-1400, 1600-2100.

Where to stay

$$$ El Arribo
Belgrano 1263, T0388-422 2539, www.elarribo.com.
Attractive, well-located *posada* set in a restored colonial house with swimming pool, smiling staff. Highly recommended.

$$$ Gregorio I
Independencia 829, T0388-424 4747,
www.gregoriohotel.com.
Wonderful, small boutique hotel with 20 rooms.
Smart, modern style, with local art scattered
throughout. Recommended.

$$ El Trébol Hostel
Gorriti 000, on the plaza, T0388-422 9608,
trebolhostel@gmail.com.
Central, private rooms and dorms for 6 to 8
(US$10 pp), all with shared bath, includes breakfast,
Tienda de Cerveza pub with microbrews.

$$ Sumay
Otero 232, T0388-423 5065,
www.sumayhotel.com.ar.
Rather dark, but clean, carpeted rooms, a/c,
very central, helpful staff.

$ pp Aldea Luna
Tilquiza, 1 hr from Jujuy, 3 hrs from Salta, T0388-
15-509 4602, www.aldealuna.com.ar.
Very peaceful, set in the Yungas reserve. Solar-
powered stone cottages with bathroomsn
shared cabin US$20 pp (discount with 4-night
stay), private room US$28 pp. Spanish classes
offered; volunteers welcome. Call to arrange a
pick up from Jujuy US$37 for up to 4 people, or
from Salta US$120 for up to 4. Restaurant with
vegetarian food.

$ pp Club Hostel
San Martín 132, 2½ blocks from plaza, T0388-
423 7565, www.clubhosteljujuy.com.ar.
Dorms and doubles $$; with jacuzzi, patio, lots
of information, welcoming, has a good Noroeste
travel agency.

$ pp Hostal Casa de Barro
Otero 294, T0388-422 9578,
www.hostalcasadebarro.com.ar.
Double, triple and quadruple rooms from
US$14 pp, whitewashed with simple decorations,
shared bathrooms and a nice area for eating and
relaxing. Simple breakfast, showing its age, but
helpful staff. Recommended.

Camping

$ pp El Refugio
Yala, Km 14, Av Libertador 2327, T0388-490 9344,
www.elrefugiodeyala.com.ar.
Pretty spot on riverbank 14 km north of city,
is closest, also has youth hostel, pool, and

restaurant, horse riding and treks organized.
Highly recommended, great place to relax.

Restaurants

$$$ Krysys
Balcarce 272.
Popular bistro-style *parrilla*, excellent steaks.

$$ Chung King
Alvear 627. Closed Sun.
Atmospheric, serving regional food for over
60 years; with pizzería at No 631.

$$ Madre Tierra
Belgrano 619. Mon-Sat 1130-1430.
Vegetarian café, behind a wholemeal bakery,
delicious food.

$$ Manos Jujeños
Sen Pérez 381. See Facebook.
Tue-Sun 1200-1500, 2000-2330.
Regional specialities, the best *humitas*, charming,
good for the *peña* at weekends.

$$ Ruta 9
Belgrano 743 and Costa Rica 968.
Great places for regional dishes such as *locro* and
tamales, also a few Bolivian dishes.

$ Tío Bigote
Pérez y Belgrano. Closed Mon and Sun evening.
Very popular café and pizzería.

Cafés

Sociedad Española
Belgrano y Sen Pérez. Closed Sun.
Good cheap set menus with a Spanish flavour.

Shopping

Handicrafts
There are stalls near the cathedral. Also **Paseo de
las Artesanías**, on the west side of the plaza.

Market
For food, you can't beat the Municipal market
at Dorrego y Alem. Outside, women sell home-
baked *empanadas* and *tamales*, delicious goat's
cheese and all kinds of herbal cures.

What to do

Tour operators offer full-day trips from Jujuy into
the *puna* and the Quebrada de Humahuaca, but
if you have the time it's far better to take at least a
couple of days to explore both areas properly.

Transport

Air Airport at El Cadillal, 32 km southeast, T0388-491 1102, minibus US$12 to AR office in town, taxi US$25-30. Flights to **Salta** and **Buenos Aires**.

Bus Large modern Terminal Terrestre 4 km south of the centre along highway to Salta, T0388-498 3337. Remise to centre US$6.50; micro 24 or 29, US$0.50, 45 mins. There are services to **Buenos Aires**, 21-24 hrs, **Tucumán**, 6 hrs, and **Córdoba**. To **Salta**, see page 137. To **La Quiaca**, 5 hrs, US$12.50, **Balut**; several others. Several rigorous luggage checks en route for drugs, including coca leaves. To **Humahuaca**, **Balut**, US$5, 2½ hrs, several daily, via Tilcara 1½ hrs, US$3.50. To **Purmamarca**, take buses to Susques or to Humahuaca (those calling at Purmamarca village). To **Susques**, **Purmamarca** and **Andes**

Bus, US$11, 4-6½ hrs, daily (except Mon). To **Calilegua**: see Transport, Northeast of Jujuy, page 146. To **Orán** and **Aguas Blancas** (border with Bolivia), US$20, 4½ hrs, daily 0300 with **Balut**. All other services to Aguas Blancas (several companies) depart from Salta and do not pass through Jujuy. Connections can be made in San Pedro or San Martín, both of which have frequent service from Jujuy. To **Pocitos** (border with Bolivia), **Flecha Bus** 0400, 0735, 1620, US$21-30, 7 hrs. All **Pocitos** or **Orán** buses pass through Libertador San Martín.

To Chile: via the **Jama** pass (4400 m), the route taken by most traffic, including trucks, crossing to northern Chile; hours 0800-2200. **Géminis** bus tickets sold at **Paisajes del Noroeste**, San Martin 134, www.paisajesdelnoroeste.tur.ar.

Jujuy to the Chilean and Bolivian borders

head north of Jujuy for colourful geology and culture

☆Ruta 9, the Pan-American Highway, runs through the beautiful Quebrada de Humahuaca, a vast gorge of vividly coloured rock, with giant cactii in the higher parts and emerald green oasis villages on the river below. The whole area is very rich culturally: there are fine 16th-century churches and riotous pre-Lent carnival celebrations throughout the Quebrada and pre-Inca ruins at Tilcara. To the west Ruta 52 crosses the remote Puna Jujeña to Chile, while Ruta 34 runs northeast of Jujuy to remote cloudforest parks and the border with Bolivia.

Alert...

From January to March ask highway police about flooding on the roads in this area. Drivers should note that service stations are far apart: at Jujuy, Tilcara, Humahuaca, Abra Pampa and La Quiaca. Spare fuel and water must be carried.

Purmamarca to Chile

Beyond Tumbaya, where there's a restored 17th-century church, Ruta 52 runs 3 km west to **Purmamarca**, a quiet, picturesque village, much visited for its spectacular mountain of seven colours, striped strata from terracotta to green (best seen in the morning), a lovely church with remarkable paintings and a good handicrafts market. It's worth staying the night in Purmamarca to appreciate the town's quiet rhythm.

From Purmamarca paved Ruta 52 leads through another *quebrada* over the 4164 m Abra Potrerillos to the Salinas Grandes salt flats at about 3400 m on the altiplano (fantastic views especially at sunset). From here roads lead southwest past spectacular rock formations along the east side of the salt flats to San Antonio de los Cobres, and west across the salt flats via Susques to the Paso de Jama (4400 m) and Chile. The only place with lodging beyond Purmamarca is **Susques**, which has an outstanding church.

Border with Chile There is a large modern complex at Paso de Jama shared by officials of both countries. Formalities are relatively efficient but require 1-2 hours for buses. There are no services, ATMs or money exchange at the border, which is open 0800-2300. This is the route taken by most passenger and truck traffic from Salta or Jujuy to San Pedro de Atacama. There is a Chilean consulate in Salta (Santiago del Estero 965, T0387-421 5757, http://chile.gob.cl/salta, Monday-Friday 0830-1330) and an Honorary Consulate in Jujuy (Pacara 50, Barrio Los Perales, T0388-426 1905).

Tip...

Salta–San Pedro de Atacama buses can be boarded in Purmamarca; book at **Hotel Manantial del Silencio** a day ahead.

Tilcara and around *Colour map 6, B3.*

About 7 km north of the Purmamarca turning is **La Posta de Hornillos** ⓘ *open, in theory, Wed-Mon 0830-1800, free,* a museum in a restored colonial posting house where Belgrano stayed, also the scene of several battles. About 2 km further is **Maimará** with its brightly striped rock, known as the 'Artist's Palette', and huge cemetery, decorated with flowers at Easter. Tilcara lies 22 km north of the turn-off to Purmamarca. It's the liveliest Quebrada village and the best base for exploring the area. It has an excellent handicrafts market around its pleasant plaza and plenty of places to stay and to eat. Visit the **Pucará** ⓘ *daily 0900-1800,* a restored prehispanic hilltop settlement, with panoramic views of the gorge, and the superb **Museo Arqueológico** ⓘ *Belgrano 445, daily 0900-1800, US$4 for both and the Jardín Botánico,* with a fine collection of pre-Columbian ceramics, masks and mummies. There are four art museums in town and good walks in all directions. There's an ATM on the plaza, taking most international cards.

The road continues through **Huacalera** and **Uquía**, which has one of the most impressive churches in the valley (from 1691), with extraordinary Cuzqueño paintings of angels in 17th-century battledress and other works of art.

Humahuaca *Colour map 6, B3.*

Although Humahuaca, 129 km north of Jujuy, dates from 1591, it was almost entirely rebuilt in the mid-19th century. Now it is visited by daily coach trips. It still has a distinctive culture of its own, though, and is a useful stopping point for travelling north up to the *puna,* or to Iruya.

On the little plaza is the church, **San Antonio**, originally of 1631, rebuilt 1873-80, containing a statue of the Virgen de la Candelaria, gold retables and 12 fine Cuzqueño paintings. Also on the plaza, tourists gather at 1200 daily to watch a mechanical figure of San Francisco Solano blessing the town from **El Cabildo**, the neocolonial town hall, which dispenses **tourist information** ⓘ *Tucumán y Jujuy, office hours, donations accepted.* (ATM on main plaza, all major credit cards.) Overlooking the town is the massive **Monumento a la Independencia Argentina**, commemorating the heaviest fighting in the country during the Wars of Independence.

At **Coctaca**, 10 km northeast, there is an impressive and extensive (40 ha) series of pre-colonial agricultural terraces.

☆ Towards Iruya *Colour map 6, B3.*

A rough *ripio* road 25 km north of Humahuaca runs northeast from the Panamericana (RN9) 8 km to Iturbe (also called Hipólito Irigoyen), and then up over the 4000 m Abra del Cóndor before dropping steeply, around many hairpin bends, into the Quebrada de Iruya. The road is very rough and unsuited to small hire cars, but is one of Argentina's most amazing drives. Iruya, 66 km from Humahuaca, is a beautiful hamlet wedged on a hillside with warm, friendly inhabitants. It is worth spending a few days here to go horse riding or walking: the hike (seven hours return) to remote **San Isidro** is unforgettable. At Titiconte 4 km away, there are unrestored pre-Inca ruins (guide necessary). Iruya has no ATM. The tourist office is on San Martín (irregular hours), and there is a *locutorio,* post office and a few food and handicraft shops. See www.iruyaonline.com.

Abra Pampa and around

Some 62 km north of Humahuaca on the Panamericana is Tres Cruces, where customs searches are made on vehicles from Bolivia. **Abra Pampa**, 91 km north of Humahuaca, is a mining town. From a point 4 km north of Abra Pampa roads branch west to Cochinoca (25 km) and southwest to **Casabindo** (62 km). Casabindo's church is a magnificent building, with twin bell towers, and a superb series of 16th-century angels in armour paintings inside. Most visitors arrive on day trips from Tilcara.

Monumento Natural Laguna de los Pozuelos ⓘ *50 km northwest of Abra Pampa, park office, Rivadavia 339, Abra Pampa, T03887-491349,* is a nature reserve at 3650 m with a lake at its centre visited by huge colonies of flamingos. There is a ranger station at the southern end of the park, with a campsite nearby. The Laguna is 5 km from the road, reached by a very rough route: high clearance is recommended and you have to walk the last 800 m to reach the edge of the lagoon. There is no bus transport, so it's best to go with a guide. Check with the park office before going, as the lake can be dry with no birds (eg in September) and temperatures can drop to -25°C in winter.

La Quiaca and around *Colour map 6, B3.*

A concrete bridge links the typical border town of La Quiaca with Villazón on the Bolivian side. Warm clothing is essential particularly in winter when temperatures can drop to -15°C, though care should be taken against sunburn during the day. In mid-October, villagers from the far reaches of the remote altiplano come to exchange ceramic pots, sheepskins and vegetables, in the colourful three-day **Fiesta de la Olla**,

Fact...
La Quiaca is 5121 km from Ushuaia. There are two ATMs, but no facilities for changing cash, although there are plenty of *cambios* in Villazón.

which also involves much high-spirited dancing and drinking. **Yavi** is 16 km east of La Quiaca. Its **church of San Francisco** (1690) ① *Mon 1500-1800, Tue-Fri 0900-1200, 1500-1800, Sat-Sun 0900-1200*, is one of Argentina's treasures, with a magnificent gold retable and pulpit and windows of onyx. Caretaker Lydia lives opposite the police station and will show you round the church.

Border with Bolivia Do not photograph the border area. The border bridge is 10 blocks from La Quiaca bus terminal, 15 minutes' walk (taxi US$2). Argentine office open 0700-2400. If leaving Argentina for a short stroll into Villazón, show your passport, but do not let it be stamped by Migración, otherwise you will have to wait 24 hours before being allowed back into Argentina. Formalities on entering Argentina are usually brief at the border but thorough customs searches are made 100 km south at Tres Cruces. Leaving Argentina is very straightforward, but if you need a visa to enter Bolivia, it is best to get it before arriving in La Quiaca. There are **Bolivian consulates** ① *in La Quiaca (9 de Julio 100 y República Arabe Siria, T03885-422283, Mon-Fri 0700-1830 in theory); in Salta (Mariano Boedo 34, T0387-421 1040, coliviansalta@yahoo.com.ar, Mon-Fri 0830-1400, 1430-1800), and in Jujuy (Independencia 1098, T0388-424 0501, Mon-Fri 0830-1400, 1700-2000).*

Tip...
Argentine time is one hour later than Bolivia, or two hours when Buenos Aires adopts daylight saving.

Northeast of Jujuy

Libertador General San Martín (also known as Libertador, San Martín and Ledesma) is a stifling-hot, spread out sugar mill town, the largest in Argentina. It is 113 km northeast of Jujuy on Ruta 34 to southeastern Bolivia. It is the closest base for exploring **Parque Nacional Calilegua** ① *Park office: San Lorenzo s/n, Calilegua, T03886-422046, calilegua@apn.gov.ar; see also www.calilegua.com.* This area of peaks over 3000 m and deep valleys is covered in cloudforest and has a huge variety of wildlife, including 300-400 species of bird (estimates vary) and 60 species of mammals (you may spot tapirs, pumas, tarucas, Andean deer and even jaguars here). The lowest part of the park is hot, with many biting insects. The entrance and ranger station are at Aguas Negras, 12 km along a dirt road (4WD essential when wet) from Libertador. A nearby campsite has toilets but no other facilities. Beyond Aguas Negras the road climbs through the park and over a pass, 36 km to the friendly village of San Francisco and beyond to Valle Grande (basic accommodation and shops), 90 km from Libertador. There are six marked trails of various lengths, five starting at or near Aguas Negras. November to March is the warmest but also the wettest time of year here.

At 1500 m, San Francisco has a delightfully fresh climate, great hiking and birdwatching opportunities, a municipal campground and several *alojamientos familiares* ($$-$). It makes a good base for exploring the area, increasingly popular with Argentines. There is a small **tourist office** ① *T0388-659 8800, quispepablo02@hotmail.com,* by the bus stop.

Routes to Bolivia

From Libertador, Ruta 34 runs northeast for 244 km, passing through **Embarcación** and **Tartagal**, with a good regional museum, to the Bolivian border at **Pocitos** (also called **Salvador Mazza**). In Pocitos is a **Bolivian consulate** ① *Av San Martín 446, T03875-471336, Mon-Fri 0800-1200, 1500-1800,* and **Hotel Buen Gusto**, just tolerable. There are no *casas de cambio* here. The border is open 24 hours. From Yacuiba, on the Bolivian side of the border, buses go to Santa Cruz de la Sierra and Tarija. Several bus companies have services from the border to Salta and Tucumán.

Another route to Bolivia is via Aguas Blancas. At Pichanal, 85 km northeast of Libertador, Ruta 50 (being dualled) heads north via **Orán**, an uninteresting place with a **Bolivian consulate** ⓘ *Av San Martín 134, Orán, T03878-421969, Mon-Fri 0730-1530,* and tourist information at the bus terminal. **Aguas Blancas** is 53 km further on and has restaurants, many shops but no accommodation. There are two border crossings to Bermejo, Bolivia. Puerto Chalana is 150 m from the small bus station, where immigration facilities on the Argentine side (open 0700-1900 Argentine time) are shared by officials of both countries, and small boats cross the river to Bolivia (US$0.60 pp). Puente El Tinglado (customs open 24 hours) is several kilometres away, used mostly by private vehicles and trucks. Argentine and Bolivian immigration on this route are in one complex at Puesto 28 (23 km south of Aguas Blancas, 18 km north of Orán). Taxis between El Tinglado and Orán (US$8; US$2 shared) wait at immigration. See Tip box, opposite, for time differences.

Listings Jujuy to the Chilean and Bolivian borders

Tourist information

Purmamarca has a helpful, tiny **tourist office** (daily 0700-1800) on the plaza, T0388-490 8443, with a list of accommodation, maps and bus tickets. The little Tilcara **tourist office** (Belgrano 590, T0388-4955720, daily 0800-2100) also has very helpful staff; a new office on Ruta 9 was due to open in 2017.

Where to stay

Purmamarca to Chile

Purmamarca

$$$$ El Manantial del Silencio
Ruta 52 Km 3.5, T0388-490 8080,
www.hotelmanantialdelsilencio.com.
Signposted from the road into Purmamarca. Luxurious rooms, modern building, wonderful views, spacious living rooms with huge fire, charming hosts, includes breakfast, heating, riding, pool, superb restaurant (guests only).

$$$ Casa de Piedra
Pantaleon Cruz 6, T0388-490 8092,
www.postadelsol.com.
Well-situated new hotel made of stone and adobe with very comfortable rooms.

$$$ La Posta
C Santa Rosa de Lima 4 blocks up from plaza, T0388-490 8029, www.postadepurmamarca.com.ar.
Beautiful setting by the mountain, comfortable rooms, helpful owner. Highly recommended.

$$ El Viejo Algarrobo
C Salta behind the church, T0388-490 8286,
www.hotelviejoalgarrobo.com.ar.
Small but pleasant rooms, cheaper with shared bath, helpful, good value and quality regional dishes in its restaurant ($).

$ El Pequeño Inti
C Florida 10 m from plaza, T0388-490 8089.
Small, modern rooms around a little courtyard, breakfast, hot water, good value. Recommended.

Susques

$$ El Unquillar
R52, Km 219 (1 km west of Susques), T03887-490201,www.hotelelunquillar.com.ar.
Attractive, with local weavings, good rooms. Restaurant open to public. Phone for pick-up.

$ Res La Vicuñita
San Martín 221, T03887-490207,
see Facebook, opposite the church.
Without bath, hot water, breakfast available, simple and welcoming.

Tilcara

Book ahead during carnival and around Easter when Tilcara is very busy. All those listed are recommended.

$$$ Alas de Alma
Dr Padilla 437, T0388-495 5572, www.alas.travel.
Central, relaxed atmosphere, spacious doubles, and *cabañas* for up to 4 people. 2 mins from the main street.

$$$ Posada con los Angeles
Gorriti 156 (sign-posted from access to town),
T0388-495 5153, www.posadaconlosangeles.
com.ar.
A much-recommended favourite with charming rooms, each in a different colour, all with fireplace and door to the garden with beautiful views.

$$$ Quinta La Paceña
Padilla 660 at Ambrosetti, T0388-495 5098,
www.quintalapacena.com.ar.
This architect-designed traditional adobe house is a peaceful haven. The garden is gorgeous and wonderfully kept.

$ Casa los Molles
Belgrano 155, T0388-495 5410,
www.casalosmolles.com.ar.
Not really a hostel, this affordable *casa de campo* offers simple dorms in a friendly atmosphere (US$12-13 pp), as well as a charming double ($$-$) and 2 comfortable *cabañas* ($$$ for up to 4 people). Small and central, book in advance.

$ pp Malka
San Martín s/n, 5 blocks from plaza up steep hill,
T0388-495 5197, www.malkahostel.com.
A superb youth hostel, one of the country's best. It has beautifully situated rustic *cabañas* ($$$ up to 8), dorms for 5 people, US$20 pp, and doubles with bath ($$$). Catch a taxi from town or walk for 20 mins.

$ Tilcara Hostel
Bolivar 166, T0388-15-585 5994, see Facebook.
This hostel is welcoming with dorms at US$8pp. Also offer doubles and comfortable cabins ($$).

Camping

Camping El Jardín
Access on Belgrano, T0388-495 5128,
www.eljardintilcara.com.ar.
Hot showers, also hotel and basic hostel.

Maimará

$$$ La Casa del Tata
Belgrano s/n, T0388-499 7389,
www.lacasadeltata.com.ar.
Nicely decorated and welcoming *hostería* serving great breakfasts which include home-baked pastries. Rooms have cable TV and good bathrooms with hot water. They also serve a fantastic afternoon tea with several varieties of cakes.

$$$ Posta del Sol
Martín Rodríguez y San Martín, T0388-499 7156,
www.postadelsol.com.
Comfortable, rooms and cabins, with good restaurant, owner is tourist guide and has helpful information.

Huacalera

$$$ Hotel Huacalera
Ruta 9, Km 1790, T0388-15-581 3417,
www.hotelhuacalera.com.
Upscale resort situated in the *puna*, it offers colourful rooms with terraces, spa, swimming pool and nature excursions.

$$$ Solar del Trópico
T0388-15-4 78 5021, www.solardeltropico.com.
2 km from Huacalera, Argentine/French-owned B&B who will cook fusion food on request. Rustic, spacious bedrooms, organic gardens, artist's studio; workshops are run regularly. Tours offered. Call to arrange a pick-up beforehand.

Humahuaca

$$ Hostal Azul
B Medalla Milagrosa, La Banda, T0388-421107.
Across the river, smart, welcoming, pleasant, simple rooms, good restaurant and wine list, parking. Recommended.

$ pp El Sol
Medalla Milagrosa s/n, over bridge from terminal,
then 520 m, follow signs, T0388-421466.
Quiet rural area, shared rooms or private ($$) in a warm welcoming place, laundry, horse riding, owner will collect from bus station if called in advance. HI affiliated. Recommended.

Iruya

$$$ Hostería de Iruya
San Martín 641, T03887-15-533 8482,
www.hoteliruya.com.
A special place, extremely comfortable, with good food, and great views from the top of the village. Highly recommended.

$$$-$$ Mirador de Iruya
La Banda s/n, T03887-427123,
www.elmiradordeiruya.com.ar.
Cross the river and climb a little to this *hostal*. Doubles, triples and quads available. Fantastic views from the terrace.

$ Hospedaje Asunta
Belgrano s/n (up the hill), T0387-15-404 5113.

Friendly hostel with 28 beds. Fantastic views. Recommended.

Abra Pampa and around

$ Residencial El Norte
Sarmiento 530, T03887-491315.
Private or shared room, hot water, good food.

Residencial y restaurante Cesarito
Pérez 200, T03887-491125, 1 block from main plaza.

La Quiaca and around

$$ Munay
Belgrano 51-61, T03885-423924,
www.munayhotel.com.ar.
In same group as Munay in Salta, rooms with heating and fan, parking.

$ Hostel Copacabana
Pellegrini 141, T03885-423875,
www.hostelcopacabana.com.ar.
Only a few blocks from the bus terminal and the plaza. Clean dorms, and doubles and comfortable living areas.

Yavi

$$ Hostal de Yavi
Güemes 222, www.hostaldeyavi.blogspot.com.
Simple bedrooms with bath, and some hostel space. Cosy sitting room, good food. Tours also arranged: to see cave paintings; moonlight walks; trekking; and trips to the Laguna de los Pozuelos. Recommended.

$ La Casona
Sen Pérez y San Martín, T03887-422316.
Welcoming, with and without bath, breakfast.

Northeast of Jujuy

$$$ Finca Portal de Piedra
Villa Monte, Santa Bárbara, T03886-156 820564,
www.ecoportaldepiedra.com.
17 km north of Libertador General San Martín. Eco-run finca in its own reserve (Las Lancitas), convenient for PNs Calilegua and El Rey, guesthouse and cabin, simple food, horse riding, trekking, birdwatching and other excursions, from Jujuy take a bus via San Pedro and Palma Sola (which is 12 km north of the finca).

$$$ Posada del Sol
Los Ceibos 747 at Pucará, Libertador
General San Martín, T03886-424900,
www.posadadelsoljujuy.com.ar.

Comfortable, functional hotel, with gardens and pool, has advice on local trips.

$$ El Jardín Colonial
C San Lorenzo, Calilegua town (just outside Libertador, not the national park), T0388-643 0334, eljardincolonial@hotmail.com
Comfortable *hostería* in an old *casona* on ample grounds, meals available, can organize excursions to the national park.

$$-$ Hostería Real Victoria
Av Libertad 2098, opposite the bus station, Libertador, T0388-643 0004, hosteriarealvictoria@gmail.com.
Small rooms with bath, a/c, very basic breakfast, parking.

Restaurants

Tilcara and around

$$ El Patio
Lavalle 352, T0388-495 5044.
Great range, lovely patio at the back, popular, very good.

$ CApEC (Bar del Centro)
Belgrano 547, T0388-495 5318, see Facebook.
Small restaurant/café serving local dishes in the patio. Not always open. Both the restaurant and crafts shop next door sustain an NGO that organizes free art and music workshops for local children.

Cafés

El Cafecito de Tukuta
Rivadavia, on the plaza.
For a taste of Tilcara's culture, don't miss this place, good coffee and locally grown herbal teas, *peña* at weekends from celebrated local musicians.

La Peña de Carlitos
Lavalle 397, on the plaza, see Facebook.
With music from the charismatic and delightful Carlitos, also cheap *menú del día*, *empanadas*, and drinks.

Humahuaca

$$-$ El Portillo
Tucumán 69, T0387-421288.
A simply decorated room, serving slightly more elaborate regional meals than the usual.

$$-$ La Cacharpaya
Jujuy 317, T0387-421016.

This brightly lit, large place lacks sophistication, but it's central and the food is good.

Festivals

Tilcara
Mar/Apr During **Semana Santa** pictures of the Passion are made of flowers and seeds and a traditional procession on the night of **Holy Wed** is accompanied by thousands of pan-pipe musicians. Book accommodation well in advance.

Humahuaca
1-2 Feb **La Candelaria** festival.
Feb **Jueves de Comadres, Festival de las Coplas y de la Chicha**, at the Thu before carnival is animated, lots of drinking and throwing flour and water around. Book accommodation ahead.

Iruya
Mar/Apr **Easter**, a lively festival, when accommodation is booked up in advance.
1st Sun Oct A colourful **Rosario** festival is held.

Abra Pampa and around
3rd week Jan Important Huancar folklore festival.
15 Aug **El Toreo de la Vincha** at Casabindo. The last and only running with bulls (*corrida de toros*) in Argentina is held on the local saint's day, amidst a colourful popular celebration in front of the church, where a bull defies onlookers to take a ribbon and medal which it carries.

Transport

Purmamarca
Buses to **Jujuy** 1½ hrs, US$3.50; to **Tilcara** US$1.

Tilcara
Bus Balut bus to **Jujuy**, multiple daily, US$3.50, 1½-2 hrs; to **La Quiaca** daily with **Balut**, 40-50 mins, US$2. **Jama Bus** runs between Tilcara, Humahuaca and La Quiaca.

Humahuaca
Bus To all places along the Quebrada from the terminal (toilets, *confitería*, fruit and sandwich

sellers outside), to **Iruya** (see below) and to **La Quiaca**, with **Balut** and La Quiaqueña (more comfortable), several daily, 2½ hrs, US$7.

Iruya
Bus Daily from **Humahuaca**, Iruya SA, 0820, 1030 daily, and Sun-Fri 1600, 3-3½ hrs, US$5 one way, returning 0600 (not on Sun), 1300, 1600. Also trips of several days organized by tour operators.

La Quiaca
Bus Terminal, **España y Belgrano**, luggage storage. Several buses daily to **Salta** (US$23) with **Balut** (7½ hrs) and others. Several daily to **Humahuaca** and **Jujuy**, schedules above. Take own food, as sometimes long delays. Buses are stopped for routine border police controls and rigorous searches for drugs. **Note** If your bus arrives in the early morning when no restaurants are open and it is freezing cold outside, wrap up warm and stay in the terminal until daylight as the streets are unsafe in the dark. No buses go to Yavi. You can take a remise taxi for US$2 each way. **Remisería Acuario**, España y 25 de Mayo s/n, T03885-423333.

Northeast of Jujuy
All buses to Pocitos or Orán pass through Libertador General San Martín. Libertador to **Aguas Blancas**, Veloz del Norte at 0400, 0440, 0910, US$14, 3 hrs. For Parque Nacional Calilegua, a bus leaves Libertador daily at 0830 for **Valle Grande**, U$6.50, 5 hrs, passing **Aguas Negras**, US$1.50, 1 hr, and **San Francisco**, US$3.50, 3 hrs, returns from Valle Grande at 1500, passes San Francisco about 1700 and Aguas Negras about 1830. Remises charge about US$10 from Libertador to Aguas Negras.

Routes to Bolivia
Bus See under Salta for buses to **Orán, Aguas Blancas** and a twice-weekly **Salta-Tarija** service. Between Aguas Blancas and **Orán** San Antonio buses run every 45 mins, US$2.25, pay on bus. Buses and vans run from Bermejo, across the river, to Tarija, 3-4 hrs, US$4-5.75. To **Jujuy** from Aguas Blancas with **Balut**, 1 daily, US$20, also 1 daily from Orán.

Northeast
Argentina

The river systems of the Paraná, Paraguay and Uruguay, with hundreds of minor tributaries, small lakes and marshlands, dominate the Northeast. Between the Paraná and Uruguay rivers is Argentine Mesopotamia containing the provinces of Entre Ríos, Corrientes and Misiones, this last named after Jesuit foundations, whose red stone ruins have been rescued from the jungle. The great attraction of this region is undoubtedly the Iguazú Falls, which tumble into a gorge on a tributary of the Alto Paraná on the border with Brazil. But the region offers other opportunities for wildlife watching, such as the flooded plains of the Esteros del Iberá. This is also the region of *mate* tea, sentimental *chamamé* music and tiny *chipá* bread.

Up the Río Uruguay

riverside promenades, sandy beaches, hot springs and palm forests

This river forms the frontier with Uruguay and has many crossings as you head upstream to the point where Argentina, Uruguay and Brazil meet.

☆ Gualeguaychú *Colour map 8, B5.*
Tourist office: Paseo del Puerto, T03446-422900, www.gualeguaychuturismo.com. Daily 0800-2000 (0800-2200 in summer).

On the Río Gualeguaychú, 19 km above its confluence with the Río Uruguay and 236 km north of Buenos Aires, this is a pleasant town with a massive **pre-Lenten carnival** ⓘ *http://carnavaldelpais.com.ar for details of participating groups, tickets US$12.50-15.75 in 2017.* Parades are held in the Corsódromo. Nice walks can be taken along the *costanera* between the bridge and the small port, from where short boat excursions and city tours leave (some also leave from the *balneario norte*). **El Patio del Mate** ⓘ *G Méndez y Costanera, T03446-424371, www.elpatiodelmate. com.ar, daily 0830-2000 (2100 in summer),* is a workshop dedicated to the *mate* gourd. On the outskirts are thermal pools at **Termas del Guaychú** ⓘ *Ruta 14 Km 63.5, www.termasdelguaychu.com.ar,* and **Termas del Gualeguaychú** ⓘ *Ruta 42 Km 2.5, T03446-15 607620.*

Border with Uruguay Some 33 km east, the Libertador Gral San Martín Bridge (5.4 km long) provides the most southerly route across the Río Uruguay, to Fray Bentos. Pedestrians and cyclists may cross only on vehicles US$8; officials may arrange lifts. There is a **Uruguayan consulate in Guayleguaychú** ⓘ *Luis N Palma 500, T03446-426168, conuruguale@entrerios.net.*

Concepción del Uruguay *Colour map 8, B5.*
Tourist office: Galarza y Supremo Entrerriano, T03442-425820, www.concepcionentrerios.tur.ar; also at Galarza y Daniel Elías, T03442-440812, daily 0800-2000 (0700-2200 in high season).

The first Argentine port of any size on the Río Uruguay was founded in 1783. Overlooking Plaza Ramírez is the church of the Immaculate Conception which contains the remains of General Urquiza.

Best for
River trips ▪ Ruins ▪ Waterfalls ▪ Wildlife

ON THE ROAD

True brew

Yerba mate (ilex paraguayensis) is made into a tea which is widely drunk in Argentina, Paraguay, Brazil and Uruguay. Traditionally associated with the gauchos, the modern mate paraphernalia is a common sight anywhere: the gourd (un mate) in which the tea leaves are steeped, the straw (usually silver) and a thermos of hot water to top up the gourd. It was the Jesuits who first grew yerba mate in plantations, inspiring one of the drink's names: té de jesuitas. Also used has been té de Paraguay, but now just mate or yerba will do. In southern Brazil it is called ximarão; in Paraguay tereré, when drunk cold with digestive herbs.

Palacio San José ① *32 km west of town, T03442-432620, Mon-Fri 0800-1900, Sat-Sun 0900-1800, US$2.50, free guided visits throughout the day, and night visits at Easter, Jan-Feb (on Fri) and Oct-Dec (1 Sat a month).* Urquiza's former mansion, set in beautiful grounds with a lake, is now a museum, with artefacts from his life and a collection of period furniture. To get there take Ruta 39 west and turn right after Caseros train station. Buses to Paraná or Rosario del Tala stop at El Cruce or Caseros, 4 or 8 km away respectively, so it's best to take a remise.

Colón *Colour map 8, A5.*
Tourist office: Av Costanera Quirós y Gouchón, T03447-421233, www.colonturismo.gov.ar. Daily 0700-2100.

Founded in 1863, Colón is 45 km north of Concepción del Uruguay. It has shady streets, an attractive *costanera* and long sandy beaches. The Artigas Bridge (US$6 toll, open 24 hours) crosses the river to Paysandú; all formalities are dealt with on Uruguayan side. *Migraciones* officials board the bus, but non-Argentines/Uruguayans should get off the bus for their stamp. There is a **Uruguayan consulate** ① *San Martín 417, T03447-421999, consulado@grouarnetbyz.com.ar,* in town.

Parque Nacional El Palmar
Entrance off Ruta 14, 58 km north of Colón, T03447-493049, www.elpalmarapn.com.ar. US$16.50 entry, US$7 pp to camp (www.campingelpalmar.com.ar).

This park of 8500 ha is on the Río Uruguay and is very popular at weekends in summer. You'll be given a map and information on walks at the entrance. The park contains varied scenery with a mature palm forest, sandy beaches on the Uruguay river, indigenous tombs and the remains of an 18th-century quarry and port, a good museum and many rheas and other birds. The Yatay palms grow up to 12 m and some are hundreds of years old. It is best to stay overnight as wildlife is more easily seen in the early morning or at sunset. There are camping facilities, a restaurant and shop.

Opposite the Parque Nacional El Palmar **is Refugio de Vida Silvestre La Aurora del Palmar** ① *3 km south of Ubajay at Km 202 Ruta 14, T0345-490 5725, www.auroradelpalmar. com.ar, free,* a private reserve protecting a similar environment to that of its neighbour. La Aurora covers 1300 ha, of which 200 are covered with a mature palm forest. There are also gallery forests along the streams and patches of *espinal* or scrub. Birds are easily seen, as are capybaras along the streams. The administration centre is only 500 m from Ruta 14 and services are well organized. There are guided excursions on horseback, by 4WD and on foot combined, or by canoe. Camping is permitted and there are private rooms at **$$$ Casona La Estación** (rate for four people) or **$$$-$$** in doubles or dorms in old railway carriages.

Concordia *Colour map 8, A5.*
Tourist office: Pellegrini y Bartolomé Mitre, T0345-4213905. Daily 0800-2100.

Just downriver from Salto in Uruguay, Concordia, 120 km north of Colón, is a large city with few fine turn-of-the-20th century buildings and a beautiful 70-ha riverside park, northeast of town. About 20 km upriver Salto Grande international hydroelectric dam provides road and railway crossings to Uruguay. There's a **Uruguayan consulate** ① *Catamarca 20, p 1, T0345-422 1426, conurucon@arnet. com.ar,* in town.

Monte Caseros and further north *Colour map 8, A5.*

Upstream from Concordia in the province of Corrientes is the port of **Monte Caseros**, with the Uruguayan town of Bella Unión on the Brazilian border, almost opposite. An international bridge is planned; in the meantime, small launches provide the border crossing (four a day, not on Sunday). A less adventurous crossing is via the two international bridges at Paso de los Libres and Santo Tomé to the north, the former being very busy and used by most bus companies crossing to Uruguaiana and Brazilian tourist destinations.

Listings Up the Río Uruguay

Where to stay

Gualeguaychú

Accommodation is scarce during carnival. Prices 25% higher Dec-Mar, Easter and long weekends. The tourist office can contact estate agents for short stays in private flats.

$$$ Puerto Sol
San Lorenzo 477, T03446-434017,
www.hotelpuertosol.com.ar.
Good rooms, next to the port, has a small resort on a nearby island (transfer included) for relaxing drink.

$$$ Tykuá
Luis N Palma 150, T03446-422625,
www.tykuahotel.com.ar.
3 blocks from the bridge, with all services including safe.

Camping

Several sites on riverside, others next to the bridge and north of it.

El Ñandubaysal
T03446-423298.
The smartest, on the Río Uruguay,
15 km southeast.

Concepción del Uruguay

$$$$-$$ Grand Hotel Casino
Eva Perón 114, T03442-425586,
www.grandhotelcasino.com.ar.
Originally a French-style mansion with adjacent theatre, superior rooms have a/c and TV, VIP rooms have new bathrooms.

$$$ Antigua Posta del Torreón
España y Almafuerte, T03442-432618,
www.postadeltorreon.com.ar.
9 confortable rooms in a stylish boutique hotel with a pool.

$$ Nuevo Residencial Centro
Moreno 130, T03442-427429, see Facebook.

One of the cheapest options in town. Basic rooms, some with a/c, in a traditional 19th-century building with a lovely patio, 1.5 blocks from the plaza. No breakfast.

Colón

$$$ Holimasú
Belgrano 28, T03447-421305,
www.hotelholimasu.com.ar.
Nice patio, a/c extra, **$$** in low season.

$$$ Hostería Restaurant del Puerto
Alejo Peyret 158, T03447-422698,
www.hosteriadecolon.com.ar.
Great value, lovely atmosphere in old house, pool, no credit cards.

$$ La Posada de David
Alejo Peyret 97, T03447-423930.
Nice family house, garden, welcoming, good double rooms, great value.

Camping

Several sites, some with cabins, on river bank, from US$5 daily.

Restaurants

Concepción del Uruguay

$$$ El Conventillo de Baco
España 193, T03442-433809.
A refined choice with some outside tables and a chance to try fish from the river.

Colón

$$$ Chiva Chiva
Gral Urquiza y Brown.
An artist's refuge; her inspiration is in the meals and drinks and in the pottery on display.

$$$ La Cosquilla del Angel
San Martín 304, T03447-423711 (see Facebook).
The smartest place in town, meals include fish, set menu, live piano music in evenings.

$$$ Viejo Almacén
Gral Urquiza y Paso.
Cosy, very good cooking and excellent service.

Transport

Gualeguaychú
Bus Terminal at Bv Artigas y Bv Jurado, T03446-440688 (30-min walk to centre, remise taxi US$3-4). To **Concepción del Uruguay**, 1 hr, US$4. To **Buenos Aires**, US$21, 3½ hrs, several daily. To **Fray Bentos**, US$5.75, 1½ hrs, and **Mercedes**, US$10, 2 hrs, **Ciudad de Gualeguay** and **ETA CUT** (not Sun). To **Montevideo**, from US$35, 6½ hrs, **Plus Ultra**.

Concepción del Uruguay
Bus Terminal at Rocamora y Los Constituyentes (remise, US$2). To **Buenos Aires**, frequent, 4-4½ hrs, US$25. To **Colón**, 1 hr, US$3.

Colón
Bus Terminal at Paysandú y Sourigues (10 blocks north of main plaza), T421716, left luggage at **Remises Base** (opposite Terminal) on 9 de Julio. Not all long distance buses enter Colón. **Buenos Aires**, US$21-26, 5-6 hrs. **Mercedes** (for Iberá), several companies, 7-8 hrs, US$30. **Paraná**, 4-6 hrs, US$13. To **Uruguay** Bus to **Paysandú**, **Copay** and **Río Uruguay**, US$5, 1 hr.

Parque Nacional El Palmar
Bus Buses from Colón, 1 hr, US$3, will drop you at the entrance and it may be possible to hitch the 12 km to the park administration. For **Refugio de Vida Silvestre La Aurora del Palmar** tell the bus driver you are going to La Aurora del Palmar (ask for Ruta 14 Kilómetro 202) to avoid confusion with the national park. Nearest town is Ubajay, 6 km, where buses stop; local services by **JoviBus**. Remise taxis can be taken from there, about US$10; ask at Parador Gastiazoro where buses stop. Remises also from Colón and Concordia. Otherwise take a tour.

Concordia
Bus Terminal at Justo y Yrigoyen, T4217235, 15 blocks northwest of Plaza 25 de Mayo (reached by No 2 bus). **Buenos Aires**, US$33-38, 5-7½ hrs. **Paraná** US$13.50, 4½ hrs.

To Uruguay By **ferry** to Salto, US$5, 15 mins, 4 a day, not Sun. Port is 15 blocks southeast of centre. The **bus** service via the Salto Grande dam, US$5.50, 1½ hrs, is run by **Flecha Bus** and **Chadre**, 2 day each, not Sun; all formalities on the Argentine side, open 24 hrs. Passengers have to get off the bus to go through immigration. **Bikes** are not allowed to cross the international bridge but officials will help cyclists find a lift.

Up the Río Paraná

historic cities on the banks of the Paraná

Rosario *Colour map 8, B5.*
Rosario is the largest city in the province of Santa Fe and the third largest city in Argentina (population 1.3 million). It lies 295 km northwest of Buenos Aires and is a great industrial and export centre. It has a lively cultural scene with several theatres and bars where there are daily shows. At weekends (daily in summer) boats go to dozens of riverside resorts on the islands and sandbars opposite the city.

Sights The old city centre is Plaza 25 de Mayo. Around it are the **cathedral** and the **Palacio Municipal**. On the north side is the **Museo de Arte Decorativo** ① *Santa Fe 748, T0341-480 2547, www. museoestevez.gob.ar, Wed-Sun 0900-1300, in winter to 1700, US$1.* This sumptuous former residence houses a valuable private collection of paintings, furniture, tapestries sculptures and silverwork, brought mainly from Europe. Left of the cathedral, the **Pasaje Juramento** opens the pedestrian way to the imposing ☆**Monumento a la Bandera** ① *T0341-480 2238, www.monumentoalabandera. gov.ar, daily 0900-1800, US$1 (tower, last entry 1730), free (Salón de las Banderas).* This commemorates the site on which, in 1812, General Belgrano, on his way to fight the Spaniards in Jujuy, raised the Argentine flag for the first time. A 70-m tower has excellent panoramic views. In the first half of November in the Parque a la Bandera (opposite the monument) Fiesta de las Colectividades lasts 10 nights, with folk music, dances and food stalls. From Plaza 25 de Mayo, Córdoba leads west towards Plaza San Martín and beyond, the Boulevard Oroño. These 14 blocks, the **Paseo del Siglo**, have the largest concentration of late 19th- and early 20th-century buildings in the city. **Museo de Bellas Artes J B Castagnino** ① *Av Pellegrini 2202, T0341-480 2542, www.museocastagnino.org.ar, open 1400-2000, closed Tue, US$1,* lies just outside the 126-ha Parque Independencia. It has an impressive collection of French impressionist, Italian baroque and Flemish works, and one of best collections of Argentine paintings and sculpture.

Upriver is the **Museo de Arte Contemporáneo** (MACRO) ① *Blvd Oroño on the river shore, T0341-480 4981, www.macromuseo.org.ar, Thu-Tue 1400-2000 (1500-2100 in summer), US$1*. Inside a massive old silo, this remarkable museum is 10 levels high with a small gallery on each level, and at the top is a viewing deck.

Che Guevara was born here in 1928. The large white house at Entre Ríos y Urquiza where he lived for the first two years of his life, before his family moved to Alta Gracia, near Córdoba (see page 95), is now an insurance company office.

Paraná *Colour map 8, A5.*

The capital of Entre Ríos was, from 1854 to 1861, capital of the Republic. It lies about 30 km southeast of Santa Fe with a hill at its centre offering views over the Río Paraná and beyond to Santa Fe. Around **Plaza Primero de Mayo** are the **Municipalidad**, the **Cathedral** and the Colegio del Huerto, seat of the Senate of the Argentine Confederation between 1854 and 1861. Take pedestrianized San Martín, and half a block west of the corner with 25 de Junio you'll come to the fine **Teatro 3 de Febrero** (1908). Two blocks north is the **Plaza Alvear**; on the west side of which is the **Museo de Bellas Artes** ① *Buenos Aires 355, T0343-420 7868, Tue-Fri 0800-1300, 1500-2000, Sat 1000-1200, 1600-1900, Sun 1000-1200, free with donation.* It houses a vast collection of Argentine artists' work, with many by painter Cesario Bernaldo de Quirós. The city's glory is **Parque Urquiza**, along the cliffs above the Río Paraná.

Santa Fe *Colour map 8, A5.*

From Paraná to Santa Fe, the road goes under the Río Paraná by the Herandarias tunnel (toll) and then crosses a number of bridges (bus service, US$3, 50 minutes). Santa Fe, capital of its province, was founded by settlers from Asunción in 1573, though its present site was not occupied until 1653. The south part of the city, around the **Plaza 25 de Mayo** is the historic centre. On the Plaza itself is the majestic **Casa de Gobierno**, built in 1911-1917 in French style on the site of the historic Cabildo, in which the 1853 constitution was drafted. Opposite is the **Cathedral**. Across San Martín is the extensive Parque General Belgrano. **Museo Histórico Provincial** ① *San Martín 1490, T0342-457 3529, www.museobrigadierlopez. gob.ar, all year Tue-Fri 0830-1200, 1530-1900, Sat-Sun 0830-1200 (afternoon hours change frequently), donation expected,* is housed in a building dating from 1690, making it one of the oldest surviving civil buildings in the country. About 100 m south is the **Iglesia y Convento de San Francisco** (1673 to 1695), with fine wooden ceilings, built from timber floated down the river from Paraguay, carved by indigenous craftsmen and fitted without the use of nails. On the opposite side of the park is the superb **Museo Etnográfico y Colonial** ① *25 de Mayo 1470, T0342-457 3550, http://museojuandegaray. gob.ar, Tue-Fri 0830-1200, 1530-1900, Sat-Sun evening only, donation expected,* with a chronologically ordered exhibition of artefacts from 2000 BC to the first Spanish settlers of Santa Fe la Vieja.

North of Paraná

Heading north from Paraná along the Río Paraná, you can take monotonous Route 11 to Resistencia on the western bank, or Route 12 north to Corrientes, which closely follows the eastern banks of the river through varied landscapes giving access to two attractive small towns on the coast with good fishing: Santa Elena and La Paz.

Corrientes *Colour map 6, C6.*

Corrientes, founded in 1588, is some 30 km below the confluence of the Ríos Paraguay and Alto Paraná. The river can make the air moist and oppressive, but in winter the climate is pleasant. The city, known as the capital of Carnaval in Argentina, is the setting for Graham Greene's novel, *The Honorary Consul*.

Sights On the **Plaza 25 de Mayo**, one of the best preserved in Argentina, are the **Jefatura de Policía**, built in 19th-century French style, the Italianate **Casa de Gobierno** and the church of **La Merced**. The **Museo de Artesanías** ① *Quintana 905, Mon-Fri 0800-1200, 1600-2000, Sat 0800-1300, free,* is a large old house with an exhibition of handicrafts made from the most diverse materials imaginable, by indigenous groups and contemporary urban and rural artisans. Six blocks south is the leafy Plaza de la Cruz, on which is the church of **La Cruz de los Milagros** (1897). Inside, the Santo Madero cross was placed there by the founder of the city, Juan Torres de Vera; *indígenas* who tried to burn it were killed by lightning from a cloudless sky. The **Museo de Ciencias Naturales 'Amadeo Bonpland'** ① *San Martín 850, Mon-Sat 0800-1200, 1600-2000,* contains botanical, zoological, archaeological and mineralogical collections including 5800 insects and huge wasp nest. A beautiful walk eastwards, along the Avenida Costanera, beside the Paraná river leads to **Parque Mitre**, from where there are views of sunset. There are sandy beaches near the 2.75-km General Belgrano bridge (toll), which crosses the Río Paraná to Resistencia (25 km).

Listings Up the Río Paraná

Tourist information

Rosario

Tourist office
Av Belgrano y Buenos Aires, T0341-480 2230,
www.rosarioturismo.com.
On the riverside park next to the Monumento a la Bandera, efficient staff, some of whom speak English. See www.viarosario.com, for the latest events information.

Paraná
There are 4 tourist offices: at **Parque Urquiza** (Av Laurencena y Juan de San Martín, T0343-420 1837); at the **bus terminal** (T0343-420 1862); at San Martín y Urquiza, Plaza 1 de Mayo, and at the Hernandarias tunnel.

Santa Fe
Santa Fe Turismo (T0800-777 5000, www. santafeturismo.gov.ar) has offices at the **bus terminal** (T0342-457 4124, Mon-Fri 0700-2000, Sat-Sun 0800-2000), opposite the **Teatro Municipal** (San Martín 2020); at Bulevar Gálvez 1150 and Santiago del Estero 3100, all good. There's also a **provincial office** (San Martín 1399, T0343-458 9477, www.turismosantafe.com.ar).

Corrientes
Provincial tourist office (25 de Mayo 1330, T0379-442 7200, www.corrientes.gov.ar, Mon-Fri 0800-1200, 1600-2000), and on the Costanera at 9 de Julio and at the **bus station**. City tourist office (Punta Tacuara, at Av Costanera y Av 9 de Julio, T0379-447 4702, http://corrientesturismo. gob.ar, daily 0700-1200, 1600-2000; guided walks around the city every Sat at 1600. Also at Plaza Cabral and at the bus station).

Where to stay

Rosario
Rosario has a good range of business hotels (eg 4 in the **Solans** group, www.solans.com) and a number of hostels at the budget end.

$$$ Esplendor Savoy Rosario
San Lorenzo 1022, T0341-429 6000,
www.esplendorsavoyrosario.com.
Early 20th-century mansion, once Rosario's best, now completely remodelled as a luxury hotel with all modern services. Gym, business centre, Wi-Fi, etc.

$$$ Majestic
San Lorenzo 980, T0341-440 5872,
www.hotelmajestic.com.ar.
Modern, inviting 3-star, well designed rooms in an ornate turn-of-the-20th-century building, stylish.

$ Cool Raul
San Lorenzo 1670, T0341-679 3039,
www.coolraulhostel.com.
Down the street from La Lechuza, this hostel has its rock & roll theme painted on the walls. Good for big groups, sociable, party hostel.

$ Hostel Point
Catamarca 1837, T0341-440 9337,
www.hostelpoint.com.ar.
Central, nicely designed, brightly coloured dorms (US$12.50-13.65) and a lovely double. Recommended.

$ pp La Lechuza
San Lorenzo 1786, T0341-424 1040,
www.lalechuzahostel.com.ar.
Welcoming, sociable hostel with helpful owner, dorms from US$11, private rooms **$$**, with bar, central, good meeting point. Chef makes an excellent breakfast (included) and dinner (not included). Recommended.

Paraná

$$$ Gran Hotel Paraná
Urquiza 976, T0343-422 3900,
www.hotelesparana.com.ar.
Overlooking Plaza Primero de Mayo, 3 room categories, smart restaurant **La Fourchette**, gym.

$$ San Jorge
Belgrano 368, T0343-422 1685,
www.sanjorgehotel.com.ar.
Renovated house, helpful staff, nice decor, Wi-Fi in lobby only. Good mid-range option. Recommended.

$$-$ Paraná Hostel
Andrés Pazos 159, T0343-422 8233.
Small, central, nice living room with cable TV and comfy sofas. Smart dorms and private rooms. Best budget option in the area.

Santa Fe

$$$-$$ Hostal Santa Fe de la Veracruz
San Martín 2954, T0342-455 1740,
www.hostalsf.com.
Traditional favourite, 2 types of room, both good value, large breakfast, restaurant, sauna (extra).

$$ Castelar
25 de Mayo 2349, T0342-456 0999,
www.castelarsantafe.com.ar.
On a small plaza, 1930s hotel, good value, comfortable, breakfast included, restaurant.

Corrientes

$$$ La Alondra
2 de abril 827, T0379-443 0555,
www.laalondra.com.ar.
The best place to stay in town. 8 beautiful rooms and a wonderful communal area. Antique furniture throughout, exquisite styling and a homely feel. Lovely patio and 12-m pool.

$ pp Bienvenida Golondrina
La Rioja 455, T0379-443 5316, www.
hostelbienvenidagolondrina.com.
The only hostel in the city. Half a block from the port, in a beautifully remodelled old building. Bright dorms, private rooms (**$$**), all rooms with a/c, a roof-top terrace and lots of internal patios to relax in. Also organizes fishing and kayaking trips to Iberá.

Restaurants

Rosario

$$$ Escauriza
Bajada Escauriza y Paseo Ribereño,
La Florida, 30 mins' drive from centre, near
bridge over the Paraná, T0341-454 1777,
www.escaurizaparrilla.com.ar.
Said to be the 'oldest and best' fish restaurant, with terrace overlooking the river.

$$ Amarra 2
Av Belgrano y Buenos Aires, T0341-447 7550,
see Facebook.
Good food, including fish and seafood, quite formal, cheap set menus Mon-Fri noon. Also offers wine classes.

$$ La Estancia
Av Pellegrini 1510 y Paraguay, T0341-440 7373.
Recommended by a local *asador* as the best *parrilla* in town. Very popular with locals, a few blocks east of Parque Independencia.

$$ Rock'n'Feller's
Oroño y Jujuy, www.rockandfellers.com.ar.
Popular restobar, upmarket, international fare including Tex-Mex options. Popular at night too.

$$-$ Pizza Piazza
Santa Fe and Cafferata, T0341-437 4384,
www.pizzapiazzaweb.com.ar.
Popular pizzeria with unique, regional twists on sandwiches and hot dogs.

$ New Taipei
Laprida 1121, T0341-449 8508, see Facebook.
Decent Chinese food for a change from the usual Argentine fare.

Cafés and bars

There are many discos in Barrio Pichincha, most only getting busy at 0130-0200; eg **MDM**, Brown 3126, Barrio Pichincha (see Facebook), big and loud, like any self-respecting Argentine disco should be.

Antares
Callao 286, T0341-437 0945, see Facebook.
Daily 1830.
A good choice of their own label beers, happy hour, serves good pub grub.

El Born
Pellegrini 1574, T0341-449 5196, see Facebook.
Daily from 1800.
Tapas bar, also has a clothes shop.

Kaffa
Córdoba 1473.
Good coffee served inside the large bookshop **El Ateneo Yenny**.

La Maltería del Siglo
Santa Fé 1601, T0341-425 1846. Daily.
Food, drinks and background music. Livens up when major football matches are on.

Moore
At the Fluvial next to the Monumento de Bandera.
Regarded as the place to be at weekends and one of the best discos in town.

Verde Que Te Quiero Verde
Córdoba 1358, T0341-530 4419.
Open 0800-2100, closed Sun.
Great vegetarian café, serving a fantastic brunch and lots of good veggie options. Recommended.

Victoria
Jujuy and Blvd Oroño.
One of the oldest cafés in town and the most traditional.

Santa Fe
Many places in the centre close on Sun.

$$ El Quincho de Chiquito
Av Almirante Brown y Obispo Príncipe (Costanera Oeste).
Classic fish restaurant, excellent food, generous helpings and good value.

$$ España
San Martín 2644, T0342-412 2096, www.lineaverdedehoteles.com.ar.
An elegant place, specializing in seafood and fish.

$ Club Sirio Libanés
25 de Mayo 2740.
Very good Middle Eastern food, popular Sun lunch for families.

$ El Brigadier
San Martín 1670.
This colonial-style place next to the Plaza 25 de Mayo serves superb *surubí al paquete* (stuffed fish) and many *parrilla* dishes.

Corrientes

$ Martha de Bianchetti
9 de Julio y Mendoza.
Smart café and bakery.

Panambí
Junín near Córdoba.
A traditional, central *confitería*, serving good pastries and regional breads.

What to do

North of Paraná
Los Troperos al Galope, *Estancia La Rosita, 18 km from Esquina, which is north of La Paz, T011-15-6052 5566, www.estanciasride.com.ar.* A 7-day horse riding programme between 4 estancias with lots of other activities, wildlife-watching, local culture, some riding ability necessary.

Corrientes
Experiencia Corrientes, *T011-15-3688 6999, www.experienciacorrientes.com.* Experienced guide Pablo runs fishing and kayaking excursions in Corrientes and Iberá. Ask at **Bienvenida Golondrina** hostel.

Transport

Rosario
Air Airport at Fisherton, 15 km west of centre, T0341-451 3220, www.aeropuertorosario.com. Remises charge US$14-16. Daily flights to **Buenos Aires**.

Bike hire and repair Bike House, San Juan 973, T0341-424 5280, info@bikehouse.com.ar (see Facebook). **Speedway Bike Center**, Roca 1269, T0341-426 8415, www.speedwaybikecenter. com.ar.

Bus Terminal at Santa Fe y Cafferata, about 30 blocks west of the Monumento de la Bandera, T0341-437 3030, www.terminalrosario.gov.ar. For local buses you must buy a rechargeable magnetic card sold at kiosks in the centre or near bus stops (US$3 for card and 1st journey), several bus lines to centre with stops on Córdoba (eg 101, 102, 115); from centre, take buses on Plaza 25 de Mayo, via C Santa Fe. Remise US$4-6. **Buenos Aires**, 4 hrs, US$19.50-26. **Córdoba**, 6 hrs, US$30-34. **Santa Fe**, 2½ hrs, US$11.75.

Train There are 2 stations: Rosario Norte station, Av del Valle 2750, and Terminal Rosario Sur, Av San Martín y Batlle y Ordóñez, which is the stop before Rosario Norte on the line from **Buenos Aires**, operated by **Trenes Argentinos**, T0800-222 8736, www.sofse.gob.ar, ticket office at the station Mon-Fri 0830-0100 or 0500, Sat 1630-0030, Sun 0900-0100 (Terminal Sur open 1830-0130). From **Buenos Aires** daily 1640, arrive 0010, return at 0105, arriving at Retiro 0830; 1st class US$13.75, Pullman US$16.55. Trains from **Buenos Aires** to Córdoba and Tucumán pass through Rosario Norte: to **Córdoba** Tue and Sat 0230, US$6-7.25; to **Tucumán** Mon 1700 and Fri 0230, US$10.50-12.7 5, bunk US$36.50.

Paraná
Bus Terminal at Av Ramírez 2350 (10 blocks southeast of Plaza Primero de Mayo), T0343-422 1282, left luggage from 0700, closed Sun. Buses 1, 4 to/from centre, US$0.60. Remise US$2-3. To **Colón** on Río Uruguay, 4-5 hrs, US$13. To **Buenos Aires**, 7-8 hrs, US$39.

Santa Fe
Air Airport at Sauce Viejo, 17 km south, T0342-499 5064. Taxi US$8-9 from bus terminal. Daily flights to and from **Buenos Aires**.

Bus Terminal near the centre, Gen M Belgrano 2910, T0342-457 4124, www.terminalsantafe.com.

To **Córdoba**, US$24-36, 5 hrs. Many buses to **Buenos Aires** US$36-42, 6 hrs; to **Paraná** frequent service US$2, 50 mins.

Corrientes
Air **Camba Punta Airport**, 10 km east of city, T0379-448 3336 (remise US$12). Flights to/from **Buenos Aires**.

Bus Terminal: Av Maipú 3100, 5 km southeast of centre, T0379-447 7600, bus No 103 (ask the driver if it goes to terminal as same line has many different routes), 20 mins, US$0.40. To **Resistencia**, 1 hr, US$1. To **Posadas** US$24-28, 3½-4 hrs, several companies. To **Buenos Aires**, several companies, 11-12 hrs, US$75-100. **El Pulqui** and **NS de la Asunción** run Corrientes-Resistencia-**Asunción** (Paraguay), US$16.25-21.

Esteros del Iberá

wonderful wetlands rich in wildlife

☆The Reserva Natural del Iberá protects nearly 13,000 sq km of the wetlands known as the Esteros del Iberá, which are similar to the Pantanal in Brazil. Over 60 small lakes, no more than a few metres deep, cover 20-30% of the protected area, which is rich in aquatic plants. In the *lagunas* are *embalsados*, islands of floating vegetation thick enough to support large animals and trees. Wildlife includes black caiman, marsh deer, capybara and about 370 species of bird, among them the *yabirú* or *Juan Grande*, the largest stork in the western hemisphere. More difficult to see are the endangered maned wolf, the 3-m-long yellow anaconda, the *yacaré ñato* and the river otter.

Mercedes
Mercedes, 250 km southeast of Corrientes, is the most convenient access point for Colonia Carlos Pellegrini and the eastern side of the Esteros del Iberá. A chirpy little town, with some quaint 1900s buildings, it has a few restaurants, ATMs and a small tourist office (Sarmiento 650, T03773-420100). The surrounding countryside is mostly grassy pampas, where rheas can be seen, with rocks emerging from the plains from time to time.

Carlos Pellegrini
T03773-15-459110, www.ibera.gob.ar.

With a remote setting on the beautiful Laguna Iberá 120 km northeast of Mercedes, the sprawling village of Pellegrini is the base for visiting the Esteros del Iberá. It's a quiet, very laid-back place with only 900 inhabitants and earth roads. There are not many restaurants or shops and no ATMs, so bring

> **Tip...**
> Bring a hat, mosquito repellent, plenty of sunblock, binoculars and a torch.

everything you may need, including extra money as few places accept credit cards. The rangers' office and reserve visitor centre, **Aguas Brillantes** ⓘ *Mbigua and Yacare, daily 0730-1200, 1400-1800*, is just by the bridge as you come into town on the right. Here, you can study a map of the natural reserve and get more information on the flora and fauna. They also sell an excellent guide to all the plants, birds and animals you'll find here. A one-day visit allows for a three-hour boat excursion on Laguna Iberá to visit areas where there are lots of birds, alligators and capybaras (US$40 per person if not included in hotel rates); some hotels offer more activities for longer stays.

Western Iberá
The western side of Iberá, some two hours from Corrientes by road, has several access points, including Portal San Nicolás, which is on a reserve owned by the **Conservation Land Trust (CLT)** ⓘ *www.proyectoibera.org*. The Trust's aim is integrate its lands into the publicly owned national reserve. San Nicolás, reached from San Miguel (160 km from Corrientes) has a *guardaparques* post and a campsite. From the jetty it's 45 minutes by boat to CLT's **San Alonso** lodge (see Where to stay), which can also be reached by a two-day, one-night ride. Another access point is Portal Yahaveré, southwest of San Nicolás.

Parque Nacional Mburucuyá

12 km east of the town of Mburucuyá, T03782-498907, www.pnmburucuya.gob.ar, free; buses San Antonio from Corrientes go daily to Mburucuyá, 2½ hrs, US$11; remises to the park and back, US$57.

Covering 17,660 ha between Iberá and Corrientes, this park stretches north from the marshes of the Río Santa Lucía and includes savanna with *yatay* palms, 'islands' of wet Chaco forest, and *esteros*. Wildlife is easy to see, making it a good alternative for those who don't have time to visit Iberá. The land was donated by Danish botanist Troels Myndel Pedersen and his wife Nina Sinding; Pederson identified 1300 different plants here. Provincial route 86 (unpaved) crosses the park for 18 km to the information centre and free campsite at Estancia Santa Teresa. There are three self-guided walking trails.

Listings Esteros del Iberá

Where to stay

Mercedes

$$$$ Iberá Lodge
Ruta Provincial 29, Km 50, 70 km north of Mercedes, T03773-15-475114, www.iberalodge.com.
Fishing lodge at the southern access to Lago Iberá, very close to the wetlands, also offers boat trips, riding, kayak, snorkelling and scuba, welcomes families.

$$ La Casa de China
Mitre y Fray L Beltrán, call for directions, T03773-15-627269, lacasadechina@hotmail.com.
A delightful historical old house with clean rooms and a lovely patio. Recommended.

$$ Sol
San Martín 519 (entre Batalla de Salta y B Mitre), T03773-420283, www.corrientes.com.ar/hotelsolmercedes/.
Comfortable rooms around a wonderful patio with black and white tiles, and lots of plants. Lovely.

Carlos Pellegrini

Rates are generally full board and include water and/or land-based excursions.

$$$$ pp Posada Aguapé
T03773-499412, www.iberawetlands.com.
On a lagoon with a garden and pool, comfortable rooms, attractive dining room. Recommended.

$$$$ pp Posada de la Laguna
T03773-499413, www.posadadelalaguna.com.
A beautiful place run by Elsa Güiraldes (granddaughter of famous Argentine novelist, Ricardo Güiraldes) and set on the lake, very comfortable, large neat garden and a swimming pool, English and some French spoken, excellent country cooking. Highly recommended.

$$$$ pp Rincón del Socorro
T03773-475114, www.rincondelsocorro.com (Conservation Land Trust).
Incredibly luxurious, beautifully set in its own 12,000 ha 35 km south of Carlos Pellegrini, with 6 spacious bedrooms, each with a little sitting room, 1 double bungalow, and elegant sitting rooms and dining rooms. Delicious home-produced organic food, bilingual guides, *asados* at lunchtime, night safaris and horse riding. Gorgeous gardens, pool with superb views all around. Highly recommended.

$$$$-$$$ Ecoposada del Estero
T03773-15-443602, www.ecoposada delestero.com.ar.
2-room bungalows and restaurant, associated with **Iberá Expediciones** (Yaguarete y Pindó, www.iberaexpediciones.com), who run guided treks, horse riding, 4WD trips, birdwatching, lots of information.

$$$$-$$$ Irupé Lodge
T03752-438312 or 03773-402193, www.ibera-argentina.com.
Rustic, simple rooms, great views of the laguna from dining room, offers conventional and alternative trips, camping on islands, diving, fishing, several languages spoken. Offers combined Iberá and Iguazú tours.

$$$ pp Casa Santa Ana del Iberá
Capivara entre Pehuajó y Caraguatá, T03773-15-475114, www.casadelibera.com.
Price includes one excursion a day, packages from 1-7 nights available. Comfortable, simple lodge with grounds leading to the lakeshore, white rooms, in local style and with lots of experience of the region, living room, pool and deck.

$$$ pp Hostería Ñandé Retá
T03773-499411, www.nandereta.com.

Large old wooden house in a shady grove, play room, full board, home cooking.

$$$ pp Posada Ypá Sapukai
Sarmiento 212, T03773-1551 4212, www.ypasapukai.com.ar.
Private rooms and shared single rates $ pp. Good value, nice atmosphere, excellent staff.

$$$ Rancho Iberá
Caraguatá y Aguará, T03783-1531 8594, www.posadaranchoibera.com.ar.
Designed like an old Argentine country house, *posada* with double and triple bedrooms and a well-maintained garden. Also has a cottage for 5.

$$$ Rancho Inambú
T03773-1543 6159, Yeruti, entre Aguapé y Pehuajó, www.ranchoinambu.com.ar.
Nice rustic rooms set in lush garden, lovely common area and a great bar (open to non-guests).

$$$ pp San Lorenzo
At Galarza, T03756-487084, www.rincontreslagunas.com.
Next to 2 lakes on the northeast edge of the region, splendid for wildlife watching, only 3 rooms. Access from Gob Virasoro (90 km), via Rutas 37 and 41. Transfer can be arranged to/from Virasoro or Posadas for an extra charge. Closed Jan-Feb. See also associated tour company, Rincón Tres Lagunas, T03756-15-511931, same website, for birdwatching, nighttime boat excursions, tours to Misiones and more.

$ pp Don Justino Hostel
Curupi y Yaguareté, T03773-15-628823.
Small hostel 3 blocks from the lake, 2 from the plaza. Organizes tours and boat trips.

Camping

Municipal campsite
T03773-15-629656.
Hot showers, jetty for boat trips, also riding and other guided tours.

Western Iberá

$$$$ San Alonso
45 mins by boat from San Nicolás, T03773-475114.
Conservation Land Trust runs 2-night programmes at the lodge including rustic rooms, criollo food and all excursions.

Transport

Bus Empresa Turismo Iberá (T03773-15-407588), Rayo Bus (T03773-420184) and **Empresa Ortiz** (T03773-15-467644) run minibus services from Mercedes to **Carlos Pellegrini** Mon-Fri leaving at 1200, 4-5 hrs, US$10-12; return from Pellegrini at 1600, book by 2200 the night before at the local grocery (ask for directions). Mercedes to **Buenos Aires**, 9-10 hrs, US$59-78. Mercedes to **Corrientes**, 3 hrs, US$18. To **Puerto Iguazú**, best to go via Corrientes, otherwise via any important town along Ruta 14, eg Paso de los Libres, 130 km southeast. There is sometimes a direct bus from Carlos Pellegrini to **Posadas**.

The Chaco

venture onto the vast lowland plains

The Chaco has two distinct natural zones. The Wet Chaco spreads along the Ríos Paraná and Paraguay covered mainly by marshlands with savanna and groves of caranday palms, where birdwatching is excellent. Further west, as rainfall diminishes, scrubland of *algarrobo*, white *quebracho*, *palo borracho* and various types of cacti characterize the Dry Chaco, where South America's highest temperatures, exceeding 45°C, have been recorded. Winters are mild, with only an occasional touch of frost in the south. The Chaco is one of the main centres of indigenous population in Argentina: the Qom/Toba are settled in towns by the Río Paraná and the semi-nomadic Wichí live in the western region. Less numerous are the Mocoví in Chaco and the Pilagá in central Formosa. For introductory articles see http://pueblos-originarios-argentina.wikispaces.com, www.pocnolec.blogspot.co.uk/ and www.chacolinks.org.uk.

Much of the Chaco is inaccessible because of poor roads (many of them impassable during summer rains) and lack of public transport, but it has two attractive national parks which are reachable all year round. Resistencia and Formosa are the main cities at the eastern end, from where Rutas 16 and 81 respectively go west almost straight across the plains to the hills in Salta province. (Buses to Salta take Ruta 16.) Presidencia Roque Sáenz Peña, 170 km northwest of Resistencia, is a reasonable place to stop over.

Resistencia *Colour map 6, C6.*

The hot and energetic capital of the Province of Chaco, Resistencia is 6.5 km up the Barranqueras stream on the west bank of the Paraná and 544 km north of Santa Fe. It is known as the 'city of the statues', there being over 200 of them in the streets. Four blocks from the central Plaza 25 de Mayo is the **Fogón de los Arrieros** ① *Brown 350 (between López y Planes and French), T0362-442 6418, open to non-members Mon-Sat 0800-1200, Tue-Wed 2100-2300, US$1.50 (free for those taking the free city tour that leaves the Casa de Cultura on the plaza every day except Mon at 0945).* This famous club and informal cultural centre deserves a visit for its occasional exhibitions and meetings. The **Museo Del Hombre Chaqueño** ① *Juan B Justo 280, T0362-445 3005, Mon-Fri 0800-1300, 1500-1900, free,* is a small anthropological museum with an exhibition of Wichí, Toba and Mocoví handicrafts. It has a fascinating mythology section in which small statues represent Guaraní beliefs. There are banks and *cambios* in the centre for exchange.

Parque Nacional Chaco *Colour map 6, C5.*
115 km northwest of Resistencia, T03725-499161, chaco@apn.gov.ar. Open 0800-1900 autumn and winter, 0700-2000 spring and summer, free. Best visited between Apr-Oct to avoid intense summer heat and voracious mosquitoes.

The park extends over 15,000 ha and protects one of the last remaining untouched areas of the Wet Chaco with exceptional *quebracho colorado* trees, *caranday* palms and dense riverine forests with orchids along the banks of the Río Negro. Some 340 species of bird have been sighted in the park. Mammals include *carayá* monkeys and, much harder to see, collared peccary, puma and jaguarundi. The visitors centre is 300 m from the entrance; there's also a free campsite with hot showers and electricity. The paved Ruta 16 goes northwest from Resistencia and, after about 60 km, Ruta 9 branches off, leading north to Colonia Elisa and Capitán Solari, 5 km east of the park entrance, via a dirt road. La Estrella run daily buses Resistencia–Capitán Solari, where a minibus runs to the park. Tour operators run day-long excursions to the park from Resistencia.

Formosa to the border *Colour map 6, C6.*
The capital of Formosa Province, 186 km north of Corrientes on the RN 11, is the only Argentine port of any note on the Río Paraguay. It is oppressively hot from November to March. RN 11 heads north from Formosa for 117 km to **Clorinda** on the border with Paraguay.

Border with Paraguay The easiest crossing is by road over the Río Pilcomayo via the Puente Loyola, 4 km north of Clorinda to Puerto Falcón, at the Paraguayan end of the bridge; from here the road runs 40 km to Asunción, crossing the Río Paraguay. The crossing is open 24 hours. **Immigration** formalities for entering Argentina are dealt with at the Argentine end, those for leaving Argentina at the Paraguayan end. From Clorinda take a bus to Puerto Falcón, US$1, and then from Falcón to Asunción, with Empresa Falcón every hour, US$1.25; last bus to the centre of Asunción 1830 (there is a direct bus as well). Paraguayan consulate ① *José F Cancio 1393 esq Rivadavia, T03718-421988, consulpar_clorinda@yahoo.com.ar, Mon-Fri 0700-1700.*

Parque Nacional Río Pilcomayo
Administration centre in Laguna Blanca, Av Pueyrredón y Ruta 86, T03718-470045, riopilcomayo@apn. gov.ar, Mon-Fri 0800-1600, Sat-Sun 0800-1800. Access to the park is free.

Covering some 48,000 ha, 65 km northwest of Clorinda, this natural wetland has lakes, marshes and low-lying parts which flood in the rainy season. The remainder is grassland with caranday palm forests and Chaco woodland. Among the protected species are aguará-guazú, giant anteaters and coatis. Caimans, black howler monkeys, rheas and a variety of birds can also be seen. The park has two entrances: Laguna Blanca has an information point, a free campsite with electricity and cold water, and a footpath to the biggest lake in the park; a bit further is the area of Estero Poí, with another information point and a campsite without facilities. Godoy buses run from Formosa or Resistencia to the small towns of Laguna Naineck, 5 km from the park (for Laguna Blanca) and Laguna Blanca, 8 km from the park (for Estero Poí). Remise taxis from both towns charge US$8-10 for these short journeys on unpaved roads. There are police controls on the way to the park.

Tourist information

Resistencia

Provincial tourist office
Av Sarmiento 2155, T0362-447 9118, www.chaco.
travel. Mon-Fri 0900-2000, Sat-Sun 1000-2000.
Also at bus terminal, T0362-441 6820, Mon-Fri
0700-2000, Sat-Sun 0700-0930, 1800-2030.

Tourist office
Plaza 25 de Mayo, T0362-445 8289.
Daily 0800-1200, 1700-2000.
Helpful, many maps.

Formosa

Tourist office
José M Uriburu 820 (Plaza San Martín), T0370-
442 5192, www.formosa.gob.ar/turismo.
Mon-Fri 0700-1300, 1600-2100.
Ask about guided excursions and
accommodation at estancias.

Where to stay

Resistencia

$$$ Covadonga
Güemes 200, T0362-444 4444,
www.hotelcovadonga.com.ar.
Comfortable, swimming pool, sauna and gym.

$$$-$$ Niyat Urban Hotel
Hipólito Yrigoyen 83, T0362-444 8451,
www.niyaturban.com.ar.
The newest and best hotel in town. Modern,
spacious and stylish rooms overlooking the
park, efficient staff.

$$-$ Bariloche
Obligado 239, T0362-442 0685,
residencialbariloche@hotmail.com.
Good budget choice, welcoming owner, decent
rooms with a/c. No breakfast, but there's a nearby
café at **Gran Hotel Royal**.

Formosa

$$ Colón
Belgrano 1068, T0370-442 6547, see Facebook.
Central, comfortable rooms, all regular services.

$$ Plaza
José M Uriburu 920, T0370-442 6767,
plaza_formosa@hotmail.com.

On Plaza, pool, very helpful, some English spoken,
secure parking.

$ El Extranjero
Av Gutnisky 2660, T0370-452276.
Opposite bus terminal, OK, with a/c.

Festivals

Formosa

Mar/Apr The world's longest **Via Crucis**
pilgrimage with 14 stops along Ruta 81
(registered in the *Guinness Book of Records*) takes
place every Easter week, starting in Formosa and
ending at the border with the province of Salta,
501 km northwest.
Jul Festival de la Caña con Ruda is held on
the last night of the month, when Paraguayan
caña flavoured by the *ruda* plant is drunk as a
protection against the mid-winter blues. A good
chance to try regional dishes.
Nov Festival Provincial de Folclore. Held at
Pirané (115 km northwest), the major music
festival in the northeast, attracting national stars.

Transport

Resistencia

Air Airport 8 km west of town
(taxi US$14-15), T0362-444 6009.
Flights to/from **Buenos Aires**, 1¼ hrs.

Bus Modern terminal on Av Malvinas Argentinas
y Av Maclean in western outskirts (bus 3 or 10
from Oro y Perón, 1 block west of plaza, 20 mins,
US$0.40, paid with card). Remise taxis leave from
Obligado y Frondizi, US$2. To **Buenos Aires** 12-
13 hrs, US$75-100 several companies. To **Formosa**
2-2½ hrs, US$9-15. To **Iguazú**, 8-10½ hrs, US$39-
55, several companies, some require change
of bus in **Posadas**, 5½ hrs, US$22-29. To **Salta**,
Exreso Tigre Iguazú, 12½ hrs, US$70-75. To
Asunción 3 companies, 6 hrs, US$16-21.

Formosa

Air El Pucu airport, 5 km southwest, T0370-
445 0521; remise, US$3. Flights to/from **Buenos
Aires**, 1½ hrs.

Bus Terminal at Av Gutnisky 2615, 15 blocks
west of Plaza San Martín, T0370-445 1766
(remise US$3). **Asunción**, 3 hrs, US$17.
Buenos Aires 15-17 hrs, US$88-116.

Posadas is one of the main crossing points to Paraguay, but most people will head northeast from here, through the province of the Jesuit Missions, towards Iguazú.

Posadas *Colour map 7, C1.*

This is the main Argentine port on the south bank of the Alto Paraná, 377 km above Corrientes, and the capital of the province of Misiones. On the opposite bank of the river lies the Paraguayan town of Encarnación, reached by the San Roque bridge. The city's centre is **Plaza 9 de Julio**, on which stand the Cathedral and the **Gobernación**, in imitation French style. The riverside and adjacent districts are good for a stroll. Follow Rivadavia or Buenos Aires north to Avenida Andrés Guaçurarí (referred also to as Roque Pérez), a pleasant boulevard, lively at night with several bars. Immediately north of it is the small and hilly **Bajada Vieja** or old port district. There is a good **Museo Regional Aníbal Cambas** ① *Alberdi 600 in the Parque República del Paraguay, 11 blocks north of Plaza 9 de Julio, T0376-444 7539, Mon-Fri 0800-1200, 1500-1900, free*; its permanent exhibition of Guaraní artefacts and pieces collected from the nearby Jesuit missions is worth seeing.

Border with Paraguay Argentine immigration and customs are on the Argentine side of the bridge to Encarnación. Buses across the bridge (see Transport, page 163) do not stop for formalities; you must get exit stamps, so get off the bus, keep your ticket and luggage, and catch a later bus. Pedestrians and cyclists are not allowed to cross; cyclists must ask officials for assistance. Taxis (US$5.50-7) and mototaxis (US$3.50) cross 24 hours, or take the train (see Transport, below). **Paraguayan consulate** ① *San Lorenzo 1561, Posadas, T0376-442 3858, Mon-Fri 0800-1400*, issues visas on same day. **Dirección Nacional de Migraciones** ① *Buenos Aires 1633, Posadas, T0376-442 7414, Mon-Fri 0630-1330.*

☆San Ignacio *Colour map 7, C1.*

The little town of San Ignacio, 63 km northeast of Posadas, is the site of the most impressive Jesuit ruins in the region. San Ignacio Miní, together with the missions of Santa Ana and Loreto, is a UNESCO World Heritage Site. There are heavy rains in February. Mosquitoes can be a problem. The local festival is 30-31 July.

> **Tip...**
> Go early to avoid the crowds and for the best light for pictures. There's good birdwatching around the site.

San Ignacio Miní ① *T0376-447 0186, daily 0700-1800, US$13 with tour (ask for English version), leaves from entrance every 30 mins. Allow 1½ hrs. Son et lumière show daily 1930 (weather permitting), US$13.* The mission was founded on its present site in 1696. The 100-sq-m, grass-covered plaza is flanked north, east and west by 30 parallel blocks of stone buildings with four to 10 small, one-room dwellings in each block. The roofs have gone, but the massive metre-thick walls are still standing except where they have been torn down by the *ibapoi* trees. The public buildings, some of them 10 m high, are on the south side of the plaza. In the centre are the ruins of a large church finished about 1724. The masonry, sandstone from the Río Paraná, was held together by mud. Inside the entrance, 200 m from the ruins, is the **Centro de Interpretación Jesuítico-Guaraní**, with displays on the lives of the Guaraníes before the arrival of the Spanish, the work of the Jesuits and the consequences of their expulsion, as well as a fine model of the mission. The **Museo Provincial Miguel Nadasdy** ① *Sarmiento 557, Sat 0700-1900, Sun 0900-1200, 1500-1800*, contains a collection of artefacts from the Guaraní and Jesuits of the missions, some beautiful examples of stone carving and a bas-relief of San Ignacio de Loyola, founder of the Jesuit order.

Around San Ignacio

The ruins of two other Jesuit missions are worth visiting. **Loreto** ① *10 km south of San Ignacio, daily 0700-1800, included with San Ignacio within 15 days*, can be reached by a 3-km dirt road (signposted) which turns off Ruta 12. Little remains other than a few walls; excavations are in progress. There is no public transport to Loreto, but you can take a tour from San Ignacio with Misiones Excursions or catch one of the Henning buses that pass along Sarmiento (0600-2000); ask the driver to drop you outside the mission. **Santa Ana** ① *16 km south of San Ignacio, daily 0700-*

1800, included with San Ignacio ticket, buses stop on Ruta 12, was the site of the Jesuit iron foundry. Impressive high walls still stand and beautiful steps lead from the church to the wide open plaza. The ruins are 700 m along a path from Ruta 12 (signposted).

Near San Ignacio is the **Casa de Horacio Quiroga** ⓘ *T0376-470124, daily 0700-1700, US$3 (includes 40-min guided tour; ask in advance for English); take C San Martín (opposite direction to the ruins) to the Gendarmería HQ; turn right and on your right are 2 attractive wood and stone houses; after 200 m the road turns left and 300 m later, a signposted narrow road branches off.* The Uruguayan writer lived part of his tragic life here as a farmer and carpenter between 1910 and 1916 and again in the 1930s. Many of his short stories were inspired by the subtropical environment and its inhabitants.

San Ignacio to Puerto Iguazú

Ruta 12 continues northeast, running parallel to Río Alto Paraná, towards Puerto Iguazú. With its bright red soil and lush vegetation, this attractive route is known as the Región de las Flores. You get a good view of the local economy: plantations of *yerba mate*, manioc and citrus fruits, timber yards, manioc mills and *yerba mate* factories. The road passes through several small modern towns including Eldorado, with accommodation, campsites, places to eat and regular bus services. Just outside Eldorado, **Estancia Las Mercedes** ⓘ *T03751-1541 8224, www.estancialasmercedes.com*, is an old *yerba mate* farm with period furnishings, open for day visits with activities like riding, boating, and for overnight stays with full board ($$$). **Wanda**, 50 km north of Eldorado, was named after a Polish princess and is famous as the site of open-cast amethyst and quartz mines which sell gems. There are guided tours to two of them: **Tierra Colorada** and **Compañía Minera Wanda** ⓘ *daily 0700-1900.*

Gran Salto del Moconá

For 3 km the waters of the Río Uruguay in a remote part of Misiones create magnificent falls (known in Brazil as Yucumã) up to 20 m high. They are surrounded by dense woodland protected by the Parque Estadual do Turvo in Brazil and by the Parque Provincial Moconá, the Reserva Provincial Esmeralda and the Reserva de la Biósfera Yabotí in Argentina (one of the last remaining areas of Selva Paranaense). Moconá has roads, footpaths and accommodation where outdoor activities can be arranged, such as excursions to the falls, trekking in the forests, kayaking, birdwatching and 4WD trips. Alternative bases are El Soberbio (70 km southwest) or San Pedro (92 km northwest). From the former a paved road runs to the park entrance; from the latter the road is impassable after heavy rain. If the river is high (May-October) the falls may be underwater.

Listings Misiones Province

Tourist information

Posadas tourist office
Colón 1985, T0376-444 7539, www.misiones.tur.ar. Mon-Fri 0800-1300, 1500-2000.
Small office at bus station Mon-Sat 0800-1200, 1600-2000.

San Ignacio tourist office
Independencia 605, T0376-447 0130.
There is another tourist office on RN12 at the entrance to town, daily 0600-2100.

Where to stay

Posadas

$$$ Julio César
Entre Ríos 1951, T0376-442 7930, www.juliocesarhotel.com.
4-star hotel, pool and gym, spacious reasonably priced rooms, some with river views. Recommended.

$$ City
Colón 1754, T0376-433901, www.misionescityhotel.com.ar.
Good rooms, some overlooking plaza, restaurant on 1st floor, parking.

$$ Le Petit
Santiago del Estero 1630, T0376-443 6031, www.hotellepetit.com.ar.
Good value, small, a short walk from centre on a quiet street.

$$ Residencial Colón
Colón 2169, T0376-442 5085, www.residencialcolon.blogspot.com.
Small but affordable rooms, parking. Also apartments for up to 6 people.

$ pp Hostel Posadeña Linda
Bolívar 1439, T0376-443 9238,
www.hostelposadasmisiones.com.
Central, good value, very pleasant, with all
hostel facilities and tourist information.

San Ignacio

$$ La Toscana
H Irigoyen y Uruguay, T0376-447 0777,
see Facebook.
Family-run, 12-bedroom hotel with rustic, inviting
rooms and a wonderful pool with a terrace. It's an
easy 10-min walk from the tourist office and main
plaza. Highly recommended.

$$ San Ignacio
San Martín 823, T0376-447 0422.
Rooms with a/c and self-catering apartments for
4-5 people. Breakfast extra. Phone booths and an
interesting view of town from the reception.

$ pp Adventure Hostel
Independencia 469, T0376-447 0955, see Facebook.
Large hostel with a fantastic pool and a games
area. Spacious communal areas, comfortable
double rooms ($$). Camping available. Short walk
to centre of town.

$ Hostel El Jesuita
San Martín 1291, T0376-447 0542,
www.eljesuita.hostoi.com.
Welcoming owners, spacious double rooms with
their own exit to the garden, small comfortable
dorm (US$10), laundry, Wi-Fi, 1½ blocks from the
ruins. Lots of travel advice, can organize tours.
Camping, US$4.50. Recommended.

Camping

Complejo Los Jesuitas
C Emilia Mayer, T0376-446 0847,
www.complejolosjesuitas.com.ar.
Campsite and cabins for 4 people.

Gran Salto del Moconá

There are other lodges in the vicinity, for
example: www.donenriquelodge.com.ar, www.
lodgelamision.com.ar, www.posadalabonita.net.

$$$ Don Moconá Virgin Lodge
7 km from the falls, inside the Yabotí Reserve,
www.donmoconavirginlodge.com.
Rustic rooms for 2-4 with shared bath, restaurant
and bar. Many activities, including trekking,
kayaking and zip-line, even a night bonfire.
Transfer to and from San Pedro, 2 hrs, is extra and
run through a local company Thu-Sun, 2 hrs.

$$ Hostería Puesta del Sol
C Suipacha s/n, El Soberbio, T03755-495161.
A splendid vantage point overlooking town, with
a swimming pool and restaurant. Comfortable
rooms, full board available. They also run boat
excursions to the falls, 7-8 hrs, landing and meal
included (minimum 4 people), via Brazil or on the
Argentine side.

Restaurants

Posadas

Most places offer *espeto corrido*, eat-as-much-as-
you-can *parrilla* with meat brought to the table.

$$ La Querencia
Bolívar 1849 (on Plaza 9 de Julio).
A large traditional restaurant offering *parrilla*,
surubí and pastas.

$$ Mendieta
Corrientes y Centenario, T0376-443 3844
(see Facebook).
Popular parrilla.

$$ Plaza Café
Bolívar 1979 just outside the shopping centre.
Great salads and large mains. Busy during the
day and busier at night. Highly recommended.

$ Bar Español
Bolívar 2085.
Open since 1958, this restaurant has tasty
Spanish-influenced food. Have an ice cream
for dessert next door at **Duomo**.

$ Café Vitrage
Colón y Bolívar.
Good pizzas, sandwiches and coffee, nice view
of the plaza.

San Ignacio

There are several restaurants catering for tourists
on the streets by the Jesuit ruins.

What to do

Posadas

Abra, *Salta 1848, T0376-442 2221, www.abratours.*
com.ar. Tours to San Ignacio, including Santa Ana
Jesuit ruins, also those in Paraguay and in Brazil,
plus tours to waterfalls.
Guayrá, *San Lorenzo 2208, T03752-433415,*
www.guayra.com.ar. Tours to Iberá, to Saltos
del Moconá, to both sites in a 5-day excursion,
and to other sites in Misiones, also car rental and
transfer to Carlos Pellegrini (for Iberá).

San Ignacio

Misiones Excursions, *Ruta Nacional and Sarmiento*, T0376-437 3448, www.misionesexcursions.blogspot. com.ar. Excellent, small company with its office in the tourist information centre. Personalized tours around San Ignacio, including visits to Santa Ana and Loreto, local Guaraní villages and a *yerba estancia*. All cost US$20 pp. They also organize kayaking trips, cycling excursions and can organize full day trips into Paraguay to Trinidad (US$50), as well as to Saltos del Mocona (US$90 pp). If you contact then in advance they can organize 2-night excursions to the Esteros de Iberá, including luxury accommodation, breakfast, a boat trip on the wetlands and personal 4WD transfers, for US$130 pp. Recommended.

Transport

Posadas

Air **Gen San Martín Airport**, 12 km west, T0376-445 7413, reached by remise US$11-12. To **Buenos Aires**, direct, 1 hr 35 mins.

Bus Terminal about 5 km out of the city at Av Santa Catalina y Av Quaranta (T0376-445 6106), municipal tourist office), on the road to Corrientes. Remise US$7. For bus into town, cross the street from the terminal and look for Nos 14, 15, 21 or 8 to the centre, US$0.75. Travel agencies in the centre can book bus tickets in advance. To **Buenos Aires**, 12-13 hrs, US$77-102. Frequent services to **San Ignacio Miní**, 1 hr, US$4.25, and **Puerto Iguazú**, US$25, 5-6 hrs.

    International To **Encarnación** (Paraguay), Servicio Internacional, 50 mins, US$1.35 in pesos or guaraníes, 0500-2200 from platforms 11 and 12 (lower level), tickets on bus. To **Brazil** and the Jesuit Missions in Rio Grande do Sul, take an **Aguila Dorada** or **Horianski** bus from Posadas to **San Javier**, 124 km, then a ferry, US$2, to Porto Xavier, from where buses run to Santo Ângelo, 4 hrs (see Rio Grande do Sul in the Brazil chapter). Immigration is at either end of the ferry crossing.

Train To **Encarnación** 0615-1715, 8 mins crossing, every 30 mins, US$1.25, must show passport.

San Ignacio

Buses stop in front of the church, leaving almost hourly to **Posadas** or to **Puerto Iguazú** (US$19). Do not rely on bus terminal at the end of Av Sarmiento, where only a few stop. More buses stop on Ruta 12 at the access road (Av Sarmiento).

    To **Paraguay**, a ferry crosses the Río Paraná at **Corpus** (20 km from San Ignacio) to **Bella Vista**, foot passengers US$2.50, also takes a few cars, 5 mins' crossing. This is a good route to the Paraguayan Jesuit missions. There are immigration and customs facilities on either side, but no money changing facilities. Hours change frequently. In late 2016 the border was closed at lunchtime, and on Sat, Sun and holidays.

Gran Salto del Mocona

Regular bus service from Posadas to El Soberbio or San Pedro, and from Puerto Iguazú to San Pedro. **Eldorado** bus company has a direct Puerto Iguazú–Mocona service, once a day, leaving Iguazú at 0700, returning 1800, 3 hrs 40 mins.

Iguazú Falls *Colour map 7, C1.*

mind-blowing and unmissable

★The mighty Iguazú Falls are the most overwhelmingly magnificent in all of South America. So impressive are they that Eleanor Roosevelt remarked "poor Niagara" on witnessing them (they are four times wider). In 2012 they were confirmed as one of the New7Wonders of Nature. Iguazú is a Guaraní phrase, meaning 'big water'.

The falls are located on the Argentina-Brazil border, 19 km upstream from the confluence of the Río Iguazú with the Río Alto Paraná. The Río Iguazú rises in the Brazilian hills near Curitiba and receives the waters of some 30 rivers as it crosses the plateau. Above the main falls, the river is dotted with wooded islets and opens out to a width of 4 km, with rapids for 3.5 km. The main falls consist of a 74-m precipice over which the water plunges in 275 falls over a frontage of 2470 m, at a rate of 1750 cu m a second (rising to 12,750 cu m in the rainy season).

    Viewed from below, the tumbling water is majestically beautiful in its setting of begonias, orchids, ferns and palms. Toucans, flocks of parrots and cacique birds and great dusky swifts dodge in and out, along with myriad butterflies (there are at least 500 different species). Above the impact of the water on the basalt rocks hovers a perpetual 30-m-high cloud of mist in which the sun creates blazing rainbows.

There are national parks on both sides of the falls. Transport between the two parks is via the Puente Tancredo Neves (see below) as there is no crossing at the falls themselves. The Brazilian park offers a superb panoramic view of the whole falls and is best visited in the morning when the light is better for photography. Tourist facilities (including restaurants, toilets, shops and a locutorio) in both parks are constantly being improved and being made more accessible for the disabled. The Argentine visitor centre has information and photographs of the flora and fauna, as well as books for sale. In the rainy season, when water levels are high, waterproof coats or swimming costumes are advisable for some of the lower catwalks and for boat trips. Cameras should be carried in a plastic bag. Busiest times are holidays and Sundays.

Tip...

Brazil is one hour ahead of Argentina from October to May (exact daylight saving dates change each year).

Admission

The falls are open daily 0800-1800 (tickets sold till 1630). Entry is US$32.50, payable in pesos only. Argentines, Mercosur and Misiones inhabitants and children aged 6-12 pay less. Entry next day is half price with same ticket, which you must get stamped at the end of the first day.

Tip...

Every month on the five nights of full moon, there are 1½-hour guided walks (bilingual) that may include dinner at the Restaurant La Selva, depending on the time of departure (US$55 with dinner; US$39 without). See www.iguazuargentina.com for details and reservations or call T03757-491469. Boards at the bus terminal advertise the full-moon tour.

Parque Nacional Iguazú

The Argentine national park covers an area of 67,620 ha and requires at least a day to explore properly. Compared to the Brazilian side, it offers closer views of the individual falls in their forest setting with its wildlife and butterflies, though to appreciate these properly you need to go early and get well away from the main visitor areas. The fauna includes jaguars, tapirs, brown capuchin monkeys, collared anteaters and coatimundis, but these are rarely seen around the falls. There is a huge variety of birds; among the butterflies are shiny blue morphos and red/black heliconius.

From the visitor centre ① T0800-266 4482, or 03757-491469, www.iguazuargentina.com, a small gas-run train, the **Tren de la Selva**, runs every 30 minutes taking visitors on a free 25-minute trip through the jungle to the Estación del Diablo, where it's a 1-km walk along catwalks across the Río Iguazú to the park's centrepiece, the **Garanta del Diablo**. A visit here is particularly recommended in the evening when the light is best and the swifts are returning to roost on the cliffs, some behind the water.

However, if you want to see the falls from a distance first (recommended), there are excellent views from the two well-marked trails, the **Circuito Superior** (1.75 km) and **Circuito Inferior** (1.6 km), each taking 1½ to two hours. To reach these, get off the train at the **Estación Cataratas** (after 10 minutes' journey) and walk down the **Sendero Verde**. The Circuito Superior is a level path which takes you along the easternmost line of falls – Dos Hermanas, Bossetti, Bernabé Mandez, Mbiguá (Guaraní for cormorant) and San Martín – allowing you to see these falls from above. This path is safe for those with walking difficulties, wheelchairs and pushchairs, though you should wear supportive non-slippery shoes. The Circuito Inferior takes you down to the water's edge via a series of steep stairs and walkways with superb views of Dos Hermanas, Bossetti, Alvar Núñez and San Martín falls and, from a distance, the Garganta del Diablo. Wheelchair users, pram pushers, and those who aren't good with steps should go down by the exit route for a smooth and easy descent. At the very bottom of the Circuito Inferior, a free ferry runs 0930-1530 every 15 minutes, or on demand to the small, hilly **Isla San Martín** where trails lead to miradors with good close views of the San Martín falls. You could then return to the Estación Cataratas to take the train to Estación Garganta, at 10 and 40 minutes past the hour, and see the main falls close up.

The park has two further trails. **Sendero Macuco** (7 km return; allow at least three hours) starts from near the visitor centre and leads to the river via a natural pool, El Pozón, fed by a slender waterfall, **Salto Arrechea**. This is the only place for bathing in the park. **Sendero Yacaratiá** starts from the same place but reaches the river by a different route and ends at Puerto Macuco. This trail is really for vehicles (30 km in total) and is best followed on an organized safari.

Fact...
There are ATMs at **Macro** (Misiones y Bonpland), **Banco de la Nación** (Avenida Aguirre 179), and **Banco Santander Río**, Avenida República Argentina 45. Also at the entrance to and within the park and at the airport. Good exchange rates at the Brazilian border.

Puerto Iguazú and around *Colour map 7, C1.*

This modern town is 18 km northwest of the falls high above the river near the confluence of the Ríos Iguazú and Alto Paraná. It serves mainly as a centre for visitors to the falls. The port lies to the north of the town centre at the foot of a hill; see What to do and Transport, page 169, for boat trips and ferry. From the port a road climbs up alongside the Río Iguazú to the Hito-Tres Fronteras, a *mirador* with views over neighbouring Brazil and Paraguay at the point where the Ríos Iguazú and Alto Paraná meet. There is a water feature with constantly playing fountains around the blue and white border post, souvenir shops, toilets and cafés; bus US$0.50. **La Aripuca** ① *T03757-423488, www.aripuca. com.ar, US$5, turn off Ruta 12 just after Hotel Cataratas, entrance after 250 m, 0830-1830, English and German spoken*, is a large wooden structure housing a centre for the appreciation of the native tree species and their environment. **Güirá Oga** ① *Casa de los Pájaros, US$11 (children 4-10 US$6.50, under 4 free), daily 0900-1700, turn off Ruta 12 at Hotel Orquídeas Palace, entrance is 800 m further along the road from Aripuca; T03757-423980, www.guiraoga.com.ar*, is a sanctuary for birds that have been injured, including exquisite parrots and magnificent birds of prey. They are treated and reintroduced to the wild. There is also a trail in the forest and a breeding centre for endangered species.

Border with Brazil Crossing via the Puente Tancredo Neves is straightforward. Border open 24 hours. Both Argentine and Brazilian officials stamp you in and out, even if only for a day visit. Buses from Puerto Iguazú (see Transport, page 169) stop at the Argentine border post, but not the Brazilian. Whether you are entering Brazil for the first time, or leaving and returning after a day in Argentina, you must insist on getting off the bus to get the required stamp and entry card. The bus does not wait for those who need stamps, so you must get a ticket from the driver in order to catch the next one. Tickets between companies are not interchangeable, although you can catch any bus if you pay the fare again. **Brazilian consulate** ① *Av Córdoba 278, T03757-420192, http://puerto iguazu.itamaraty.gov.br, Mon-Fri 0800-1400.*

Border with Paraguay The road crossing to Paraguay is via the Puente Tancredo Neves to Brazil and then via the Puente de la Amistad to Ciudad del Este. Brazilian entry and exit stamps are not required: direct buses between Puerto Iguazú and Ciudad del Este do not stop in Brazil (if you wish to visit Brazil, you must take a bus going to Foz). Buses stop for formalities at Argentine immigration, but only briefly at Paraguayan immigration. You must get off with your luggage to get a Paraguayan entry stamp. If necessary, wait for the next bus. There is also a ferry service (US$2.25 per person, US$8 per car, US$4 per motorbike) more or less hourly 0830-1700 from the port in Puerto Iguazú (see above) to Presidente Franco, just south of Ciudad del Este. There is an immigration post next to the ticket office. See also Transport, below. **Paraguayan consulate** ① *Perito Moreno 236, T03757-424230, page 169, consulpar-iguazu@arnet.com.ar, Mon-Fri 0800-1500.*

Tourist information

As well as the visitor centre at the falls, information is available from the **tourist office** (Av Victoria Aguirre 337, Puerto Iguazú, T03757-423951), the **municipal office** (Av Victoria Aguirre y Balbino Brañas, T03757-423002, 0800-1400, 1600-2100, www.iguazuturismo.gob.ar) and the **national park office** (Victoria Aguirre 66, T03757-420722, iguazu@apn.gov.ar, Mon-Fri 0700-1330, in park, T03757-420180, daily 0700-1400, 1430-1900). See also www.iguazuargentina. com. Note that a municipal "ecotourist tax" of about US$1.30 must be paid by all visitors to Puerto Iguazú. If you do not keep and show your receipt, you will be charged again.

Where to stay

Puerto Iguazú and around

$$$$ Panoramic Grand
Paraguay 372, T03757-498100,
www.panoramicgrand.com.
On a hill overlooking the river, this hotel is stunning. Serene outdoor pool with great views, large well-designed rooms and all 5-star inclusions.

$$$$ Posada Puerto Bemberg
Fundadores Bemberg s/n, Puerto Libertad
(some 35 km south of Iguazú), T03757-496500,
www.donpuertobemberglodge.com.
Wonderful luxury accommodation and gourmet cuisine in Posada and **Casa Puerto Bemberg**, dating from 1940s, surrounded by lush gardens. Huge living areas, beautifully decorated rooms and helpful staff. Good birdwatching with resident naturalist. Highly recommended.

1 Around the Iguazú Falls

➡ **Iguazú Falls maps**
1 Around the Iguazú Falls, page 166
2 Puerto Iguazú, page 168

To Itaipu
To BR-277 & Curitiba
Ponte da Amizade / Puente de la Amistad
Foz do Iguaçu Rodoviária
Foz do Iguaçu Terminal Urbana
BRAZIL
Aeroporto Internacional de Cataratas
Foz do Iguaçu
Av Das Cataratas
Ciudad del Este
PARAGUAY
Rio Iguazú inferior
Ponte Tancredo Neves
Porto Meira
Border Control
Brazilian Frontier Marker
Mirador Trés Fronteras
Paraguayan Frontier Marker
Puerto Iguazú Bus Terminal
Argentine Frontier
Cabalgatas por la Selva
Saltos del Monday
Rio Monday
Puerto Iguazú
La Aripuca
Ruta Nacional 12
PARAGUAY
ARGENTINA
To Posadas

Where to stay
2 Hostel Inn Iguazú
6 Posada 21 Oranges
8 Sheraton Iguazú Resort & Spa

$$$$ Sheraton Iguazú Resort and Spa
T03757-491800, www.sheraton.com/iguazu.
Fine position overlooking the falls, excellent, good restaurant and breakfast, sports facilities and spa. Taxi to airport available. Recommended.

$$$$ Yacutinga Lodge
30 km from town, pick up by jeep, contact by email, www.yacutinga.com.
A beautiful lodge in the middle of the rainforest, with 2-4 night packages, learning about the bird and plant life and Guaraní culture. Accommodation is in rustic adobe houses in tropical gardens, superb food and drinks included, as well as boat trips and walks.

$$$ Iguazú Jungle Lodge
Hipólito Iyrigoyen y San Lorenzo, T03757-420600, www.iguazujunglelodge.com.
A well-designed complex of lofts and family suites, 7 blocks from the centre, by a river, with lovely pool. Comfortable and stylish, DVDs, great service, restaurant. Warmly recommended.

$$$ Posada 21 Oranges
C Montecarlo y Av los Inmigrantes, T03757-494014, www.21oranges.com.
10 simple but comfortable rooms set around a pool, lovely large garden, welcoming, stocked minifridge in room. US$6 taxi ride or 30-min walk to town. Recommended.

$$$ Secret Garden
Los Lapachos 623, T03757-423099, www.secretgardeniguazu.com.
Small B&B with attentive owner, fern garden surrounding the house. Spacious rooms, good breakfast and cocktails, relaxing atmosphere.

$$$-$$ Hostería Casa Blanca
Guaraní 121, near bus station, T03757-421320, www.casablancaiguazu.com.ar.
Family run, large rooms, good showers, with a large unfinished building in front and a modern foyer.

$$ Petit Hotel Sí Mi Capitán
Las Guayabas 228, T03757 424012, www.petithotelsimicapitan.com.
3 blocks from the town centre, with 2 standards of room and bungalows, safe in room, can arrange transfers, packed lunches, tourist information, parking, swimming pool, bar

$ pp Garden Stone
Av Córdoba 441, T03757-420425, www.gardenstonehostel.com.
Lovely hostel with a homely feel set in nice gardens, with a large outdoor eating area, swimming pool. Recommended for a tranquil stay.

$ pp Hostel Inn Iguazú
R 12, Km 5, www.hiiguazu.com.
20% discount to HI members. Large, well-organized hostel which used to be a casino. Huge pool, games and a range of free DVDs to watch.

$ pp Tango Inn Hostel Downtown
Av Córdoba 154, T03757-425559, www.tangoinn.com.
The biggest and most central hostel in town, right in front of the bus station, a/c doubles $$, dorm beds US$14.75, with lockers. Nice pool, outdoor bar and cinema.

$ pp Noelia
Fray Luis Beltrán 119, T03757-420729, www.hostelnoelia.com.
Cheap, well-kept and helpful, good breakfast, family-run, good value.

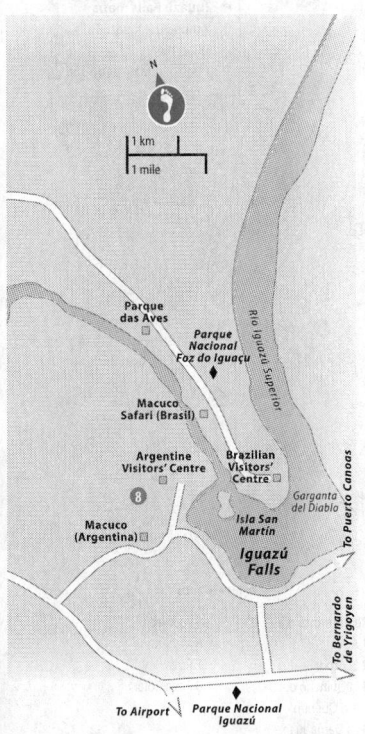

$ pp Peter Pan
Av Córdoba 267, T03757-423616,
www.peterpanhostel.com.
Just down the hill from the bus station, spotless,
central pool and large open kitchen. The doubles
(**$$**) are lovely. Helpful staff.

Restaurants

Puerto Iguazú
Av Córdoba, from the bus terminal to Av Victoria
Aguirre, is almost all restaurants, almost all
parrilla/pasta/pizza places in our **$$$-$$** range.
At the junction of Av Brasil, Misiones and San
Martín is Siete Bocas, a roundabout with food
stalls, *parrillas* and other food vendors, including
a branch of the Freddo ice cream parlour chain.

$$$-$$ Aqva
Av Córdoba y Carlos Thays, T03757-422064,
www.aqvarestaurant.com.

Just down from the bus station, this lovely
restaurant serves dishes made with ingredients
from the area.

$$$-$$ La Dama Juana
Córdoba 42, T03757-424051.
Restaurant and wine bar; same food as
elsewhere and similar prices, but nice
atmosphere and you can have just a glass
of wine if you want.

$$$-$$ La Rueda
Córdoba 28, T03757-422531,
www.larueda1975.com.ar.
Good food and prices, fish, steaks and pastas, often
with mellow live music. Highly recommended.

$$$-$$ Pizza Color
Córdoba 135, T03757-420206,
www.parrillapizzacolor.com.
Popular for pizza and *parrilla*.

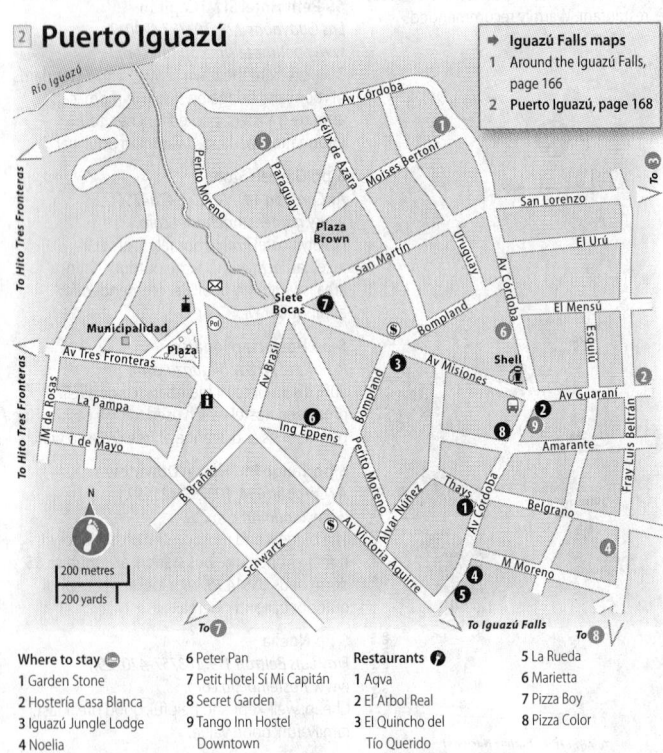

2 **Puerto Iguazú**

➡ **Iguazú Falls maps**
1 Around the Iguazú Falls, page 166
2 Puerto Iguazú, page 168

Where to stay
1 Garden Stone
2 Hostería Casa Blanca
3 Iguazú Jungle Lodge
4 Noelia
5 Panoramic Grand
6 Peter Pan
7 Petit Hotel Sí Mi Capitán
8 Secret Garden
9 Tango Inn Hostel
  Downtown

Restaurants
1 Aqva
2 El Arbol Real
3 El Quincho del
  Tío Querido
4 La Dama Juana
5 La Rueda
6 Marietta
7 Pizza Boy
8 Pizza Color

$$ El Quincho del Tío Querido
Perón 159, T03757-420151,
www.eltioquerido.com.ar.
Recommended for *parrilla* and local fish,
very popular, great value.

$$ Marietta
G Eppens 244, daily 1200-1500, 2000-0000.
Cheaper than many, unpretentious but pleasant,
much the same fare as elsewhere (meat, fish,
pizzas) but also *minutas*, eg tortillas, sandwiches,
desserts, Wi-Fi, takes credit cards.

$$-$ Pizza Boy
Misiones 294, T03757 421466 (see Facebook).
Good budget options with decent thin-crust pizza.
Great-value *milanesas* and generous portions.

$ El Arbol Real
Córdoba 248 y Guaraní, opposite bus station.
Open 24 hrs.
Panadería, confitería and by kg café, shop,
very popular.

What to do

Iguazú Falls
Jungle Explorer, *T03757-421696, www.iguazu*
jungle.com. Runs a series of boat trips, all highly
recommended, eg **Aventura Náutica**, an
exhilarating journey by launch along the lower Río
Iguazú, from opposite Isla San Martín right up to
the San Martín falls and then into the Garganta del
Diablo, completely drenching passengers in the
mighty spray. Great fun; not for the faint-hearted,
12 mins. On **Paseo Ecológico** you float silently for
2.5 km from Estación Garganta to appreciate the
wildlife on the river banks, 30 mins, US$9. **Gran
Aventura** combines the Aventura Náutica with
a longer boat trip along rapids in the lower Río
Iguazú to Puerto Macuco, followed by a jeep trip
along the Yacaratiá trail, 1 hr, US$38.

Puerto Iguazú
Agencies arrange day tours to the Brazilian side
(lunch in Foz), Itaipú and Ciudad del Este. Some
include the duty free mall on the Argentine
side. Tours to the Jesuit ruins at San Ignacio
Miní also visit a gem mine at Wanda (you don't
see as much of the ruins as you do if staying
overnight). There are also horse riding trips
(eg **Cabalgatas Ecológicas**, T03757-15-50942,
www.cabalgatasecologicas.com). At the dock is
an office for boat trips on the river below the falls,
Paseos Naúticos, T03757-15558151, from 0900-
1630, every 30 mins, 1-hr trip, US$10 pp.

Aguas Grandes, *Entre Ríos 66, T03757-425500.*
Tours to both sides of the falls and further afield,
activities in the forest, abseiling down waterfalls,
good fun.
Explorador Expediciones, *T03757-491469,*
www.rainforest.iguazuargentina.com.
Offers small-group safaris, 3-day packages,
birdwatching trips, adventure tours, tours to
Moconá. Recommended.
Iguazú Forest, *Perito Moreno 58, T03757-421140,*
www.iguazuforest.com. Runs a ½- or full-day's
adventure in the jungle offering the chance to
try canopying, climbing waterfalls, rapelling and
mountain biking. Great for kids and teenagers.

Transport

Iguazú Falls
A public *Cataratas/Waterfalls* bus (Río Uruguay
company, www.riouruguaybus.com.ar) runs every
15 mins 0720-1920. It starts at Hito Tres Fronteras
and stops at Puerto Iguazú bus terminal 10 mins
after departure, at the park entrance for the
purchase of entry tickets, then continues to the
visitor centre, US$8.45 return, journey time 45 mins.
Return buses from the park run 0815-1915. You
can get on or off the bus at any point en route.
Cars are not allowed beyond visitor centre.

Puerto Iguazú
Air Airport is 20 km southeast of Puerto Iguazú
near the Falls, T03757-422013. **Four Tourist Travel**
bus service between airport and bus terminal,
US$4.50, will also drop off/collect you from your
hotel. Taxi US$20-22. Direct flights to **Buenos
Aires**, 1½ hrs.

Bus The bus terminal, at Av Córdoba y Av Misiones,
T03757-423006, has a phone office, restaurant
(**$ Estación y Sabores**), various tour company
desks and bus offices. To **Buenos Aires**, 16-18 hrs,
US$98-129, several companies. To **Posadas**, some
direct, others stopping at San Ignacio Miní, frequent,
5-6 hrs, US$25; to **San Ignacio Miní**, US$19. To **Foz
do Iguaçu (Brazil)**, 3 companies from platform 7,
each hourly, daily 0630-1830, US$1.30. Río Uruguay
has a direct bus to the Brazilian side of the Falls,
0830-1430 hourly, return 1000-1700, US$5.25 return
(these buses wait at immigration on both sides
of the frontier). To **Ciudad del Este (Paraguay)**,
direct buses with 3 companies (non-stop in Brazil)
leave Puerto Iguazú terminal 0630-1745, 9 a day,
US$2.25, pay on bus.

Taxi T03757-15-457065. Fares in town US$3-4,
to the border US$20-25.

Lake
District

★The Lake District contains a series of great lakes strung along the foot of the Andes from above 40°S to below 50°S latitude. This chapter covers the northern lakes in Neuquén, Rio Negro and Chubut provinces. The area is dramatic, beautiful and unspoilt, offering superb trekking, fishing, watersports, climbing and skiing. Off season, from mid-April to June and mid-August to mid-November, many excursions, boat trips and tours run on a limited schedule, if at all. Public transport is also limited. For the southernmost lakes and Los Glaciares national park, see Patagonia (page 196). For the lakes on the western side of the Andes, see the Lake District section of the Chile chapter; these can be visited through various passes.

Neuquén and around Colour map 8, C2.

follow the fossilized dino prints

Founded in 1904 on the west side of the confluence of the Ríos Limay and Neuquén, Neuquén is a pleasant provincial capital and a major stop en route from the east coast to the northern lakes and Bariloche. It serves both the oilfields to the west and the surrounding fruit orchards. There are also wine bodegas nearby. The area west of Neuquén is rich in dinosaur fossils.

The city was home to the **Museo Paleontológico de la Universidad Nacional del Comahue**, which is closed indefinitely. In the centre of town is the Parque Central, where the railway station used to be, with open spaces, museums and cultural activities (annual **Feria Artesanal** in November). Avenida Argentina, the main commercial street, with ATMs and a weekend handicrafts market, runs north to Plaza de las Banderas and Parque Centenario.

Tip...
All the towns in the area celebrate the **Fiesta Nacional de la Manzana** (apples are the main local crop) in early February.

Villa El Chocón
Tourist office, acceso a la Villa Ruta 237, T0299-552 0760, Mon-Fri 0800-1500.

Red sedimentary rocks here have preserved, in relatively good condition, bones and footprints of the animals that lived in this region during the Cretaceous period about 100 million years ago. The **Museo Paleontológico Ernesto Bachmann** ① *civic centre, T0299-490 1223, daily 0800-1830, US$1.50*, displays the fossils of a giant carnivore (*Giganotosaurus carolinii*); the museum guides give good tours. Near the Embalse Ezequiel Ramos Mexía, 18 km south of Villa El Chocón, are pedestals of eroded pink rock coming out of the blue water. There are two walks beside the lake to see dinosaur footprints.

Zapala Colour map 8, C2.
Tourist office, Ruta Nacional 22, Km 1392, T02942-424296, daily 0700-210 in summer, closes earlier of season.

Best for
Adventure tourism ▪Lakes ▪Volcanoes

Just over 100 km west of Neuquén, at Plaza Huincul, **Museo Carmen Funes** ① *RN 22 y RP 17, T0299-496 5486, Mon-Fri 0900-1900, Sat-Sun 1030-2030, US\$1.75*, has, among its exhibits, remains of the largest herbivore ever found. In Zapala itself, 185 km west of Neuquén, the excellent geology museum, **Museo Mineralógico Dr Juan Olsacher** ① *Etcheluz 52 (by bus terminal), T02942-422928, Mon-Fri 0900-1930, free*, has collections of minerals, fossils, shells, rocks and a complete crocodile jaw, believed to be 80 million years old.

Listings Neuquén and around

Tourist information

Consult the **regional tourist office** (Félix San Martín 182, T0299-442 4089, www.neuquentur. gob.ar, Mon-Sun 0800-2100), regarding exhibitions of dinosaur fossils found in the region. Also try the **municipal office** (Av Argentina y Roca 8300, T0299-15-576 4264, www.ciudad deneuquen.gob.ar/turismo/, Mon-Fri 0700-1400 – summer, 0800-1500 – winter), with a desk at the bus terminal, T0299-449 1200 ext 4354. See also www.neuquen.com.

Where to stay

Neuquén

\$\$\$\$ Del Comahue
Av Argentina 377, T0299-443 2040,
www.hoteldelcomahue.com.
4-star, extremely comfortable, spa, pool, good service, wine bar and excellent restaurant specializing in Patagonian fare, **1900 Cuatro**.

\$\$\$ Hostal del Caminante
JJ Lastra (Ruta 22, Km 1227), 13 km southwest of Neuquén, towards Zapala, T0299-444 0118,
www.hostaldelcaminante.com.
A comfortable suburban place set among fruit plantations with garden, pool and restaurant.

\$\$\$ Royal
Av Argentina 143, T0299-448 8902,
www.hotelroyal.com.ar.
Central hotel with all services, free continental breakfast, parking.

\$ Hostel Punto Patagónico
Periodistas Neuquinos 94, T0299-447 9940,
www.puntopatagonico.com.
A bit out of the centre, good hostel, breakfast, rustic furniture. Recommended.

Villa El Chocón

\$\$\$ La Posada del Dinosaurio
Costa del Lago, Barrio 1, T0299-490 1201,
www.posadadeldinosaurio.com.ar.
Comfortable, modern, all rooms have lake view.

Zapala

\$\$\$ Hue Melén
Brown 929, T02942-422407,
www.hotelhuemelen.com.ar.
Good value, decent rooms and restaurant with the best food in town. Try your luck in the downstairs casino.

\$\$ Coliqueo
Etcheluz 159, opposite bus terminal, T02942-421308.
Convenient and fair.

\$\$ Pehuén
Elena de la Vega y Etcheluz, 1 block from bus terminal, T02942-423135.
Comfortable and recommended.

Restaurants

Neuquén

\$\$\$-\$\$ La Toscana
Lastra 176, T0299 447 3322,
www.latoscanarestaurante.com.
Rustic cuisine in chic surroundings. Extensive wine list.

\$\$ El Ciervo
Argentina 219.
Good central option featuring an abundance of fresh seafood dishes.

Transport

Neuquén

Air Airport 7 km west of centre, T0299-440 0245, www.anqn.com.ar. Taxi US\$8-10; also served by city buses. Flights to **Buenos Aires** and **Comodoro Rivadavia**; LADE flies to **Bariloche**. Schedules change frequently.

Bus City buses, **Indalo**, take rechargeable magnetic cards, sold at bus terminal and elsewhere, from US$1.75. Terminal at Ruta 22 y Solalique, on Ruta 22, 4 km west of town, T0299-445 2300. Taxi US$4-5. Many companies to **Buenos Aires**, daily, 15-19 hrs, US$88-100. To **Zapala** daily, 3 hrs, US$12-16. To **Junín de los Andes**, 5-6 hrs, US$23-36, **Albus**, T0810-333 7575, www.albus.com.ar. To **San Martín de los Andes**, 7 hrs, US$25-40, **Albus**. To **Bariloche**, many companies, 5-6 hrs, US$25-39, sit on left. To **Mendoza**, several companies, daily, 12-13 hrs, US$52-75. **To Chile**: several companies run to **Temuco**, US$28, 12-14 hrs, also from Zapala. Buy Chilean pesos before leaving.

Zapala

Bus to **San Martín de los Andes**, 4 hrs, US$20-25, via Junín de los Andes. To **Bariloche**, change at San Martín.

Parque Nacional Lanín

sparkling lakes, wooded valleys and one of Argentina's most striking peaks

Junín de los Andes *Colour map 8, C1.*

Known as the trout capital of Argentina, Junín de los Andes is a relaxed, pretty town on the broad Río Chimehuín, with many trout-filled rivers and lakes nearby. It's a less touristy option than San Martín and the best base for trekking in Parque Nacional Lanín. Its small **Museo Mapuche** ① *Ginés Ponte y Nogueira, Mon-Fri 0900-1400, 1600-1930*, has a collection of items from the Mapuche culture, and there are impressive sculptures at **Vía Christi** on the hilljust west of town. The **Fiesta Provincia de Puestero** (www.fiestadelpuestero.org.ar), in mid-February, with the election of the queen handicrafts, *asados* with local foods and fabulous gaucho riding, is one of the most important country fiestas in southern Argentina.

Lago Huechulafquen and around

Lago Huechulafquen provides the easiest access to the beautifully situated lakes in the centre of the park. To get there, travel northwest fo 25 km on Route 61 from Junín de los Andes a good dirt road, as far as the guardaparque office at the eastern end of the lake, where you can get free maps and information on hikes The lakes of **Huechulafquen** and **Paimún** are unspoilt, beautiful, and easily accessible fo superb walking and fishing, with *hosterías* and camping all along the lakeside. From Puerto Canoa on the north shore of Huechulafquen there is a boat excursion to **Lago Epulafquen** on the catamaran José Julián ① *T02972-428029 www.catamaranjosejulian.com.ar, 4 trips daily in summer (Dec-Mar), for other months ask locally US$32, coffee and chocolate on board.*

Volcán Lanín and Paso Mamuil Mala

Snow-capped, extinct Lanín is one of the world' most beautiful mountains and, geologically, it is one of the youngest in the Andes. It's challenging and popular climb, starting nea Seccional de Guardaparques (VHF 15567. or T02972-491270) at Paso Mamuil Malal (se below) where you must register and all climbing equipment and experience are checked Crampons and ice axes are essential, as protection against strong, cold winds. There ar three *refugios*, the first of which is a five-hour walk. It's a six- to seven-hour walk to the base of the volcano and back. Before setting off, seek advice from the Lanín National Park office.

Border with Chile **Paso Mamuil Malal** (formerly Tromen) is 64 km northwest of Junín de los Andes, reached by *ripio* Route 60 which runs from Tropezón on Route 23, through Parque Nacional Lanín. The border is open daily 0900-2000, but is closed in winter and during heavy rain or snow (phone the *gendarmería* to check, T02972-427339, www.gendarmeria.gob.ar/pasos-chile/mamuil-mamal.html). Formalities are carried out on the Argentine side of the pass. The route runs through glorious scenery to Pucón (135 km) on Lago Villarrica in Chile. Parts are narrow and steep. (For details of the Chilean side, see Puesco.) International buses may not pick up passengers at the pass or on the Chilean part of the route.

San Martín de los Andes and around *Colour map 8, C1.*
This picturesque and upmarket tourist town, 40 km southwest of Junín, with its chocolate-box, chalet-style architecture, is spectacularly set at the east end of Lago Lácar. Surrounded by lakes and mountains, it is the main tourist centre in the park, very busy in summer. Mirador Bandurrias, a 45-minute walk from the centre, offers good views.

The most popular excursions are south along the **Seven Lakes Drive** (see below), north to the thermal baths at **Termas de Lahuen-Co** (also reached on foot after two days from Lagos Huechulafquen and Paimún) and to **Lagos Lolog** and **Lácar**. There's a *ripio* track along the north side of Lago Lácar with beaches and rafting at **Hua Hum**, and along the south to quieter and beautiful **Quila Quina**. A good walk from Quila Quina goes along a nature trail to a lovely waterfall, or there's a two-hour walk to a quiet Mapuche community in the hills above the lake. Boats from San Martín's pier, T02972-428427, travel to Hua Hum three daily in season, US$64 return; and to Quila Quina, hourly, 30 minutes, US$21. Cyclists can complete a circuit around Lago Lácar, or take the cable car up to Cerro Chapelco to the southeast and come back down the paths.

Border with Chile: Paso Hua Hum The *ripio* road along the north shore of Lago Lácar continues to the border at Paso Hua Hum. The border is open daily 0800-1900 (www.gendarmeria.gob.ar/pasos-chile/hua-hum.html). The road continues to Puerto Pirihueico in Chile, where a boat crosses Lago Pirihueico; bikes can be taken (foot passengers US$1.35; for information, https://barcazahuahum.com). Ko Ko Bus ① T02972-427422, goes to the pass, two hours, and **Lafit** continues to Panguipulli (Chile); contact Ko Ko Bus for the schedule. For connections from Puerto Pirihueico to Panguipulli and beyond, see Chile chapter.

Listings Parque Nacional Lanín

Tourist information

Junín de los Andes

Tourist office
Plaza at Col Suárez y Padre Milanesio, T02972-491160, https://junindelosandesturismo. wordpress.com. Daily 0800-2100 (0800-2000 in winter).
There is a **Parque Nacional Lanín office** (T02972-492748) in the same building. Both very helpful.

San Martín de los Andes

Tourist office
San Martín y Rosas, T02972-427347, www.sanmartindelosandes.gov.ar/turismo. Daily 0800-2000.

For maps, accommodation lists and prices, English and Portuguese spoken.

Where to stay

Junín de los Andes

$$$$ Río Dorado Lodge & Fly shop
Pedro Illera 378, T02972-492451, www.riodoradolodge.com.
Comfortable rooms in log cabin-style fishing lodge, big American breakfast, good fly shop, fishing excursions to many rivers and lakes, lovely gardens, attentive service.

$$$ Caleufu Travel Lodge
JA Roca 1323 (on Ruta 234), T02972-492757, www.caleufutravellodge.com.ar.

Excellent value, welcoming, very good, homey rooms, neat garden, also comfortable apartments for up to 5 people, 3-6 night packages and fly fishing. Owner Jorge speaks English. Recommended.

$$ Hostería Chimehuín
Col Suárez y 25 de Mayo, T02972-491132, www.hosteriachimehuin.com.ar. Closed May.
Cosy, quaint fishing lodge by the river, fishing and mountain guides. Recommended.

$$ Res Marisa
JM de Rosas 360 (on Ruta 234), T02972-491175, residencialmarisa@hotmail.com.
A simple place with helpful owners, breakfast extra, very good value.

$ pp Tromen
Lonquimay 195, T02972-491498, www.hosteltromen.com.ar.
Small house with dorms and private rooms for up to 4 people. At night take a taxi from the bus station as the streets in the area have no signs or lights.

Lago Huechulafquen and around

$$$ Hostería Paimun
Ruta 61, T02972-491758, www.hosteriapaimun.com.ar.
Basic, comfortable rooms, private beach, fly fishing guide, lake excursions, cosy restaurant, stunning views all around

$$$ Huechulafquen
Ruta 61, Km 55, T02972-427598, www. hosteriahuechulafquen.com. Nov-May.
Half board, comfortable cabin-like rooms, gardens, expert fly fishing guide, restaurant open to non-residents in high season.

Camping
Several sites in beautiful surroundings on Lagos Huechulafquen and Paimún. The most recommended are: **Bahía Cañicul** (48 km from Junín), **Camping Lafquen-co** (53 km from Junín) and **Piedra Mala** (65 km from Junín; last 2 US$4.25 pp (US$1 extra for hot water). There are 3 more campsites beyond Hostería Paimún, including **Mawizache** (T02972-492150, Raúl and Carmen Hernández, both very knowledgeable), just beyond the picturesque little chapel. Offers fishing trips with expert, good restaurant. Open all year.

San Martín de los Andes and around
Single rooms are expensive. There are 2 high seasons, when rates are much higher: Jan/Feb and Jul/Aug. *Cabañas* are available in 2 main areas: up Perito Moreno on the hill to the north of town, and down by the lakeside. Prices increase in high season but are good value for families or groups. When everywhere else is full, tourist office provides a list of private addresses in high season. See www.sanmartindelosandes. gov.ar for a full list of places to stay. All listed are recommended.

$$$$ La Casa de Eugenia
Coronel Díaz 1186, T02972-427206, www.lacasadeeugenia.com.ar.
B&B in a beautifully renovated 1900s house, very welcoming and relaxing, cosy rooms, huge breakfast, charming hosts.

$$$$ Le Châtelet
Villegas 650, T02972-428294, www.lechatelethotel.com.
Chic and luxurious, beautiful chalet-style hotel with excellent service to pamper you. Wood-panelled living room, gorgeous bedrooms and suites, buffet breakfast, spa and pool with massage and facial treatments. Also, welcome glass of wine.

$$$ Arco Iris
Los Cipreses 1850, T02972-428450, www.arcoirisar.com.
Comfortable, well-equipped *cabañas* in a quiet area of town, each has a cosy living room, spacious kitchen, Wi-Fi and cable TV. Own access to the river, so you can fish before breakfast or enjoy a drink on the water side in the evening.

$$$ Hostería Bärenhaus
Los Alamos 156, Barrio Chapelco (8370), T02972-422775, www.baerenhaus.com.ar.
5 km outside town, pick-up from bus terminal and airport arranged. Welcoming young owners, very comfortable rooms with heating, English and German spoken.

$$$ Hostería Walkirias
Villegas 815, T02972-428307, www.laswalkirias.com. Open all year.
A lovely place, smart, tasteful rooms with big bathrooms. Sauna and pool room. Buffet breakfast. Great value off season and for longer stays.

$$$ Plaza Mayor
Cnel Pérez 1199, T02972-427302, www.hosteriaplazamayor.com.ar.
A chic and homely *hostería* in a quiet residential area, with traditional touches in the simple

elegant rooms, excellent home-made breakfast, heated pool with solarium, BBQ, parking.

$$ Crismalú
Rudecindo Roca 975, T02972-427283,
www.interpatagonia.com/crismalu.
Simple rooms in attractive chalet-style converted home, good value.

$$ Hostería Las Lucarnas
Cnel Pérez 632, T02972-427085,
www.hosterialaslucarnas.com.
Great value, centrally located, pretty place with simple comfortable rooms, English-speaking owner, breakfast included. Discounts for more than 5 nights, open all year.

$ pp Puma
A Fosbery 535 (north along Rivadavia, 2 blocks beyond bridge), T02972-422443, www.pumahostel.com.ar.
Discount for ISIC members, small dorms with bath and a double room with view, laundry, bikes for hire, very well run by mountain guide owner, good value.

$ pp Rukalhue
Juez del Valle 682 (3 blocks from terminal), T02972-427431, www.rukalhue.com.ar.
Large camp-style accommodation with 1 section full of dorm rooms (US$15-21) and 1 section with doubles, triples and apartments ($$$-$$). Also has apartments with private bath and kitchenette.

Camping

ACA Camping
Av Koessler 2175, T02972-429430,
www.interpatagonia.com/aca.
With hot water and laundry facilities, also *cabañas*.

Camping Quila Quina
T02972-411919, www.campingquilaquina. com.ar. Open only in summer until Easter.
Lovely site on a stream near Lago Lácar, 18 km from San Martín, with beaches, immaculate toilet blocks, restaurant and shop, access to boats and treks.

Restaurants

Junín de los Andes

$$$ Ruca Hueney
Col Suárez y Milanesio, T02972-491113,
www.ruca-hueney.com.ar.

Good steak, roast lamb, trout and pasta dishes, popular, great atmosphere.

$ La Nueva Posta de Junín
JM de Rosas 160 (on Ruta 234), T02972-492080.
Parrilla with good service and wine list; also trout, pizza and pastas.

San Martín de los Andes

$$$ 54 La Vaca
Rivadavia y San Martín, T02972-422564,
Facebook: parrilla54.
A traditional Argentine *parrilla*, great atmosphere.

$$ El Regional
San Martín y Mascardi, T02972-414600,
www.elregionalpatagonia.com.ar.
Popular for regional specialities – smoked trout, venison, wild boar, pâtés and hams, El Bolsón's home-made beer, cheerful German-style decor.

$$ La Costa del Pueblo
Costanera opposite pier, T02972-429289,
www.lacostadelpueblo.com.ar.
Overlooking the lake, huge range of pastas, chicken and trout dishes, generous portions, good service, cheerful.

$$ La Tasca
Mariano Moreno 866, T02972-428663.
Good for venison, trout and home-made pastas, varied wine list.

Cafés

Beigier
Av Costanera 815.
Hidden cottage with views of the bay serving a fantastic home-made afternoon tea with home-made goodies.

Vieja Deli
Villegas y Juez del Valle, T02972-428631.
Affordable place with views of the bay and nice salads, pastas and pizzas.

Shopping

San Martín de los Andes
There are also many clothing, camping and handicraft shops in San Martín.
Abuela Goye, *San Martín 807.* Sells delicious chocolates and runs a good café serving gorgeous cakes and delicious ice creams.
Mamusia, *San Martín 601, see Facebook.*
Recommended chocolate shop, also sells home-made jams.

San Martín de los Andes

There are facilities for water skiing, windsurfing and sailing on Lago Lácar.

Cycling

Many places in the centre rent mountain and normal bikes, US$10-20 per day, maps provided. **HG Rodados**, *San Martín 1061, T02972-427345, hgrodados@smandes.com.ar (also Facebook)*. Arranges trips, rents mountain bikes, also spare parts and expertise.

Fishing

Licence, US$26 for a day, to US$104 for a season, with extra charges for trolling. Contact the tourist office for a list of fishing guides or the national park office.
Jorge Cardillo Pesca, *Villegas 1061, T02972-428372, www.jorgecardillo.com*. Fly shop, sells equipment, fishing licences and offers excursions.
Jorge Trucco, *based in Patagonia Outfitters, Pérez 662, T02972-429561, www.jorgetrucco.com*. Expert and professional trips, good advice and many years of experience.

Skiing

Southeast of San Martín, Cerro Chapelco has 29 km of pistes, many of them challenging, with an overall drop of 730 m. Very good slopes and snow conditions from Jul to Sep make this a popular resort with foreigners and wealthier Argentines. Details, passes, equipment hire from office at M Moreno 859, loc B y C, T02972-427845; see www.chapelco.com. At the foot of the mountain are a restaurant and a café, with 4 more restaurants and a lodge on the mountain and a café at the top.

Tours

Prices for conventional tours are similar in most agencies. Most tours operate from 2 Jan:

eg Villa la Angostura via Seven Lakes; Lakes Huechulafquen and Paimún. 1 day's rafting at Hua Hum, US$60-70; many other options.
El Claro, *Col Díaz 751, T02972-428876, www.elclaroturismo.com.ar*. For conventional tours, horse riding, mountain biking and trekking.
El Refugio, *Villegas 698 y Cnel Pérez, upstairs, T02972-425140, www.elrefugioturismo.com.ar*. Bilingual guides, conventional tours, boat trips, also mountain bike hire, rafting, horse riding and trekking. Recommended.

Junín de los Andes

Air Chapelco airport 19 km southwest towards San Martín, served by **AR** from **Buenos Aires**. LADE office in bus terminal, San Martín de los Andes, T02972-427672. Taxi to centre US$20.

Bus Terminal at Olavarria y F San Martín, T02972-492038. To **San Martín**, **Albus**, **Ko Ko** and others, 50 mins, US$3-4. To **Buenos Aires**, 20-21 hrs, US$130. To **Chile** (via Paso Mamuil Malal), see below.

San Martín de los Andes

Air Chapelco airport, 23 km away, transfer US$8.50. See under Junín de los Andes, above.

Bus Terminal at Villegas 251 y Juez del Valle, T02972-427044, has café, left luggage, toilets and a *locutorio*. To **Buenos Aires**, 21-22 hrs, US$135, daily. To **Villa La Angostura**, **Albus** 2 a day, US$9. To **Bariloche**, 3½-4 hrs, US$14 (not via 7 Lagos), **Vía Bariloche** and **Ko Ko**. **To Chile**: Pucón, **Villarrica** and **Valdivia** via Junín de los Andes and Mamuil Malal, US$23, 5 hrs to Pucón with **San Martín**, heavily booked in summer. See above for route via Hua Hum Pass.

Parque Nacional Nahuel Huapi
explore the magnificent scenery by car, by boat or on foot

Covering 709,000 ha and stretching along the Chilean border, this is the oldest national park in Argentina, with lakes, rivers, glaciers, waterfalls, torrents, rapids, valleys, forest, bare mountains and snow-clad peaks. There are many kinds of wild animals living in the region, including the pudú, the endangered huemul (both deer) as well as river otters, cougars and guanacos. Bird life, particularly swans, geese and ducks, is abundant. The outstanding feature is the splendour of the lakes. The largest is Lago Nahuel Huapi, 531 sq km and 460 m deep in places, particularly magnificent to explore by boat since the lake is very irregular in shape and long arms of water, or *brazos*, stretch far into the land. The southern part of the national park, centred around the tourist town and trekking centre of Bariloche, is covered in its own section, below.

Seven Lakes Drive and Lago Traful

The paved road known as the '**Seven Lakes Drive**' runs south from San Martín to Bariloche on Route 234 through the Lanín and Nahuel Huapi national parks, passing seven magnificent lakes, all flanked by mixed natural forest; it is particularly attractive in autumn (April to May) when the forested slopes turn red and yellow. There are several places to stay, open summer only. Round-trip excursions, five hours, are operated by several companies, but it's better in your own transport. North of Villa Angostura, **Lagos Correntoso** and **Espejo** both offer stunning scenery and tranquil places to stay and walk.

Essential Nahuel Huapi

The park fee is US$16.50. Access to the park from the north is along the Seven Lakes Drive or by a fully paved and faster but less scenic route via **Confluencia** (ACA service station and a hotel). The tourist town of Bariloche (see page 179) on the southern shore of Lago Nahuel Huapi is the main tourist centre in the national park, with plentiful accommodation and opportunities for hiking, rafting, tours and boat trips.

A detour to the east will bring you to navy blue **Lago Traful**. This lake can also be reached directly from Villa La Angostura or from the main Neuquén–Bariloche highway on a road which follows the Río Limay through the fantastic rock formations of the Valle Encantado. **Villa Traful** on the southern shore is the perfect place to escape to, with fishing, camping, walking and a tourist office ① *Lafitte s/n, off Ruta Provincial 65, T0294-15-483 8974.*

Villa La Angostura and around *Colour map 8, C1.*

This pretty town, 80 km northwest of Bariloche on Lago Nahuel Huapi, is a popular holiday resort with wealthier Argentines; there are countless restaurants, hotels and *cabaña* complexes around the centre, **El Cruce** and along Ruta 231 between Correntoso and Puerto Manzano. The picturesque port, known as **La Villa**, is 3 km away at the neck of the Quetrihué Peninsula. At its end is exquisite **Parque Nacional Los Arrayanes** ① *12 km from Villa La Angostura, entry US$16.50*, with 300-year-old specimens of the rare *arrayán* tree, whose flaky bark is cinnamon-coloured. The park can be reached on foot or by bike (for a return walk start out between 0900 and 1400), or you could take the boat back. Catamarans run at least twice daily in summer from Bahía Mansa and Bahía Brava in La Villa, US$38-42 (plus the national park entry fee); go to the national parks office by the Bahía Mansa jetty. See also below for tours by boat from Bariloche.

Border with Chile: Paso Samoré (formerly Puyehue) A spectacular six-hour drive takes you from Bariloche to Chile. A good broad paved road, RN 40 then RN 231, goes around the east end of Lago Nahuel Huapi, then follows the north side of the lake through Villa La Angostura. The road is rough *ripio* from there on, with the occasional paved stretch. It passes the junction with 'Ruta de Los Siete Lagos' for San Martín at Km 90 (see above), Argentine customs at El Rincón, Km 105, and the pass at Km 122 at an elevation of about 1314 m. Chilean customs is at **Pajarito**, Km 145, in the middle of a forest. The border is open 0900-1900 (0800-1800 from Chile) but liable to be closed after snowfalls; contact the *gendarmería* in Bariloche (T0294-442 2711). The **Chilean consulate** ① *España 275, Bariloche, T0294-442 3050, http://chile.gob.cl/bariloche, Mon-Fri 0900-1300, 1400-1730,* is also helpful. There is an absolute ban in Chile on importing any fresh food from Argentina. You are advised to get rid of all your Argentine pesos before leaving Argentina; it is useful to have some Chilean pesos before you cross into Chile from Bariloche, though you can buy them at a reasonable rate at the Chilean border post. Further information on border crossings in the Lake District will be found in the Chile chapter.

Listings Parque Nacional Nahuel Huapi

Tourist information

Information is available from the **Nahuel Huapi national park office** (San Martín 24, Bariloche, T0294-442 3111, www.nahuelhuapi.gov.ar, daily 0900-1400), or from the **tourist office in Villa La Angostura** (Av Arrayanes 9, T0294-449 4124, www.villalaangostura.gov.ar; also near the bus terminal, Av Siete Lagos 93, high season daily 0800-2200, low season 0800-2000), which is helpful, lots of information, very busy in summer, English spoken.

Where to stay

Lago Traful

$$$ Hostería Villa Traful
Villa Traful, T0294-447 9005,
www.hosteriavillatraful.com.
A cosy house with a tea room by the lake, also *cabañas* for 4-6 people, pretty gardens, good value. The owner's son, Andrés organizes fishing and boat trips.

$$ Cabañas Aiken
Villa Traful, T0294-447 9048, www.aiken.com.ar.
Well-decorated *cabañas* in beautiful surroundings near the lake (close to the tourist office), each with its own *parrillada*, also has a restaurant. Recommended.

$ pp Vulcanche Hostel
Ruta Provincial 61, Villa Traful, T0294-15-469 2314, www.vulcanche.com.
Chalet-style hostel in gardens with good views, with good dorms and **$$** doubles, breakfast extra, large park for camping.

Villa La Angostura

$$$$ La Escondida
Av Arrayanes 7014, T0294-482 6110,
www.hosterialaescondida.com.ar.
Wonderful setting, right on the lake, 14 rooms, heated pool, offers mid-week, weekend and long-stay specials. Recommended.

$$$$ La Posada
R 231, Km 64.5, C Las Balsas s/n, T0294-449 4450,
www.hosterialaposada.com.
In a splendid elevated position off the road with clear views over the lake, welcoming, beautifully maintained hotel in lovely gardens, with pool, spa, fine restaurant; a perfect place to relax.

$$$$ Las Balsas
On Bahía Las Balsas (signposted from Av Arrayanes), T0294-449 4308, www.lasbalsas.com.
One of the best small hotels in Argentina, with fabulous cosy rooms, warm relaxed public areas, fine cuisine, impeccable service, and a wonderfully intimate atmosphere in a great lakeside location with its own secluded beach.

Lakeside heated swimming pools, spa, trips and excursions arranged. Highly recommended.

$$$ Hostería ACA al Sur
Av Arrayanes 8 (behind the petrol station), T0294-448 8412, www.aca.tur.ar/hoteles.
Modern, attractive single-storey hotel with well-designed rooms in the centre of town.

$$$ Hostería Le Lac
Av de los 7 Lagos 2350, T0294-448 8029,
www.hosterialelac.com.ar.
3-star, 8 rooms, some with jacuzzi and DVD, gardens, lake view, can arrange lots of activities, several languages spoken by owner.

$$$ Hotel Angostura
Nahuel Huapi 1911, at La Villa, T0294-449 4224, www.hotelangostura.com.
Built in 1938, this traditional hotel has a lovely lakeside setting and a good restaurant and tea room, **Viejo Coihue**. Also has 3 cabins for 6 (**$$$$**). Arrange boat excursions along the nearby shore.

$$ Bajo Cero
Av 7 Lagos al 1200, T0294-449 5454,
www.bajocerohostel.com.
Well-situated, rooms for 2-6, can arrange trekking, cycling and other excursions.

$ pp Hostel La Angostura
Barbagelata 157, 150 m up road
behind tourist office, T0294-449 4834,
www.hostellaangostura.com.ar.
A warm, luxurious hostel, all small dorms have bathrooms (US$21), good doubles (US$60), HI discounts, welcoming owners organize trips and rent bikes. Recommended.

$ pp Italian Hostel
Los Maquis 215 (5 blocks from terminal), T0294-449 4376. Closed in Apr-Oct.
Welcoming, small, with dorms and doubles (**$$**), rustic, functional and nice, run by a biker. Fireplace and orchard from where you can pick berries and herbs for your meals. Recommended.

Camping

Osa Mayor
Signposted off main road, close to town, T0294-449 4304, www.campingosamayor.com.ar.
Well-designed leafy and level site, US$8-10, all facilities, also rustic *cabañas* **$$$** for up to 4 people, and dorms **$$$** for up to 6 people, helpful owner.

Restaurants

Lago Traful

$$ Ñancu Lahuen
Villa Traful.
A chocolate shop, tea room and restaurant serving local trout. Delightful and cosy, with big open fire, delicious food and reasonably priced.

Villa La Angostura

$$$ Cocina Waldhaus
Av Arrayanes 6431, T0294-447 5323, see Facebook.
Very recommended, this is 'auteur cuisine' with gorgeous local delicacies created by Chef Leo Morsea, served in a charming chalet-style building.

$$ El Esquiador
Las Retamas 146 (behind the bus terminal), T0294-449 4331, see Facebook.
Good, popular *parrilla* has an all-you-can-eat choice of cold starters, a main meal and a dessert.

$$ Los Pioneros
Av Arrayanes 267, T0294-449 5525.
Famous for fine local dishes in a chalet-style building and great Argentine steaks. Great pizza place next door run by the same owners. They also serve locally brewed beers.

$ Jardín Patagonia
Av Arrayanes 4.
Popular pizzeria and *parrilla*.

$ TemaTyCo
Ruta 231 y Mirlo, T0294-447 5211.
Chic tearoom with a wide range of teas and delicious cakes.

What to do

Villa La Angostura

There is lots to do here: bicycle hire, US$15-20 per day, and mountain biking (**Bayo Abajo**, Av Siete Lagos 94, T0294-448 8383, bayoabajo@argentina. com; Taquari Bici Shop, Av Arrayanes 259, T0294-448 8415, see Facebook), boat trips, canopying, climbing, fishing, horse riding and trekking (**Alma Sur**, T0294-15-456 4724, www.almasur.com). There is a small ski resort at **Cerro Bayo** (www. cerrobayoweb.com, 1-day ski pass US$68 for adults) with summer activities too.

Transport

Villa La Angostura

Bus Terminal at Av 7 Lagos y Av Arrayanes, opposite ACA service station, has left luggage store. Urban buses, **15 de Mayo**, US$1, link El Cruce (main bus stop on main road, 50 m from tourist office), La Villa, Correntoso and Puerto Manzano, and go up to Lago Espejo and Cerro Bayo in high season. To/from **Bariloche**, 1¼ hrs, US$5, several companies. If going on to **Osorno** in Chile, 3½ hrs, you can arrange for the bus company to pick you up in La Angostura.

Bariloche and around *Colour map 8, C1.*

the best centre for exploring Parque Nacional Nahuel Huapi

☆Beautifully situated on the south shore of Lago Nahuel Huapi, at the foot of Cerro Otto, San Carlos de Bariloche is an attractive tourist town. There are many good hotels, restaurants and chocolate shops among its chalet-style stone and wooden buildings. Others along the lake shore have splendid views. Spectacular mountains surround the town, making for great trekking and skiing country.

Sights

At the heart of the city is the **Centro Cívico**, built in 'Bariloche Alpine style' and separated from the lake by Avenida Rosas. It includes the **Museo de La Patagonia** ① *T0294-442 2309, Tue-Fri 1000-1230, 1400-1900, Sat 1000-1700, entry by donation*, which, apart from the region's fauna (stuffed), has indigenous artefacts and material from the lives of the first white settlers. The **cathedral**, built in 1946, lies six blocks east of here, with the main commercial area on Mitre in between. Opposite the main entrance to the

Fact...

At peak holiday times (July and December to January), Bariloche is heaving with holidaymakers and students. The best times to visit are in the spring (September to November) and autumn (March to April), when the forests are in their glory, or February for camping and walking and August for skiing.

cathedral there is a huge rock left in this spot by a glacier during the last glacial period. On the lakeshore is the **Museo Paleontológico** ① *12 de Octubre y Sarmiento, T0294-15-461 1210, Mon-Sat 1600-1900, US$1.25, children US$0.75*, which displays fossils mainly from Patagonia, including an ichthyosaur and replicas of a giant spider and shark's jaws.

West of town
Avenida Bustillo runs parallel to the lakeshore west of Bariloche towards Puerto Pañuelo (Km 25.5, for boat trips, see below) and the Llao Llao peninsula, with access to the mountains above. At Km 5, a cable car (*teleférico*) goes up to **Cerro Otto** (1405 m) with its revolving restaurant and splendid views (see What to do, page 186). At Km 17.7 a chairlift goes up to **Cerro Campanario** (1049 m) ① *daily 0900-1800, 7 mins, US$4*, with fine views of Isla Victoria and Puerto Pañuelo. At Km 18.3 **Circuito Chico** begins – a 60-km circular route around Lago Moreno Oeste, past Punto Panorámico and through Puerto Pañuelo to **Llao Llao**, Argentina's most famous hotel (see Where to stay, below); take bus No 20 (no 21 for return), 45 minutes, US$1, or it's a half-day drive or tour with agency, or a full day's cycle. You could also extend this circuit, returning via **Colonia Suiza** and **Cerro Catedral** (2388 m) one of South America's most important ski centres (see What to do, page 185).

Boat trips
Boat trips run from Puerto Pañuelo (bus 10, 20/21, or transfer with tour operator, US$12 return) across Lago Nahuel Huapi to **Isla Victoria** (the largest island on the lake, with its idyllic hotel) and **Bosque de Arrayanes**, on the Quetrihué Peninsula for US$52, not including park entry, with Turisur ① *T0294-442 6109, www.turisur.com.ar*, on the 1937 boat *Modesta Victoria* or more modern boats, and with **Espacio** ① *T0294-443 1372, www.islavictoriayarrayanes.com, take picnic lunch if you don't want to buy food sold on board*, on the modern *Cau Cau*. Turisur also run a highly recommended all-day trip to **Puerto Blest** (US$52), in native Valdivian rainforest at the far western extremity of the lake. From Puerto Pañuelo, sail down to Puerto Blest (hotel, restaurant), continue by short bus ride to Puerto Alegre and again

1 Bariloche – the road to Llao Llao

Where to stay 🛏	5 El Yeti	9 Llao-Llao
1 Alaska	6 Hostería Santa Rita	10 Petunia
2 Aldebaran	7 Katy	11 Selva Negra
3 Departamentos Bellevue	8 La Caleta	12 Tunquelén

by launch to Puerto Frías. From Puerto Blest, you can walk through forest to the Cascada and Laguna de los Cántaros (1½ hours). Another boat trip goes from Puerto Pañuelo to Brazo Tristeza, at the southwest tip of the lake, one of several trips on the *Kaikén Patagonia* (www.kaikenpatagonia.com.ar).

Bariloche to Puerto Varas via Lago Todos Los Santos The route is Bariloche to Puerto Pañuelo by road (30 minutes, departure 0900), Puerto Pañuelo to Puerto Blest by boat (one hour), Puerto Blest to Puerto Alegre on Lago Frías by bus (15 minutes), cross the lake to Puerto Frías by boat (20 minutes), then two hours by road to Peulla in Chile. Leave for Petrohué in the afternoon by boat (one hour 40 minutes), cross Lago Todos Los Santos, passing the Osorno volcano, then by bus to Puerto Varas (two hours). This route is beautiful, but the weather is often wet. The journey can be done in one day, US$280 (US$230 April-July), or two days with an overnight stop in Peulla (lodging and food in Peulla are not included in the price, see under Peulla, Chile). **Cruce Andino** ① *in Bariloche see Turisur, below, www.cruceandino.com*, has the monopoly on this crossing. Book in advance during the high season. The only day the trip does not run is 1 May.

Listings Bariloche and around *maps below and page 182.*

Tourist information

Club Andino Bariloche (CAB)
20 de Febrero 30, T0294-442 2266, www. clubandino.org. Mon-Fri 0900-1300, plus 1500-1930 high season.
Very useful for information on hiking. You can also contact the **Association of Guides**, all of whom are trained, and know the geography, flora and fauna. They sell excellent maps showing walks, with average walking times, and *refugios*, and can advise on which have room. Ask for the *Sendas y Bosques* (walks and forests) series (www.guiasendasybosques.com.ar), which are 1:200,000, laminated and easy to read, with good books containing English summaries of the walks, the detailed *Active Patagonia* map

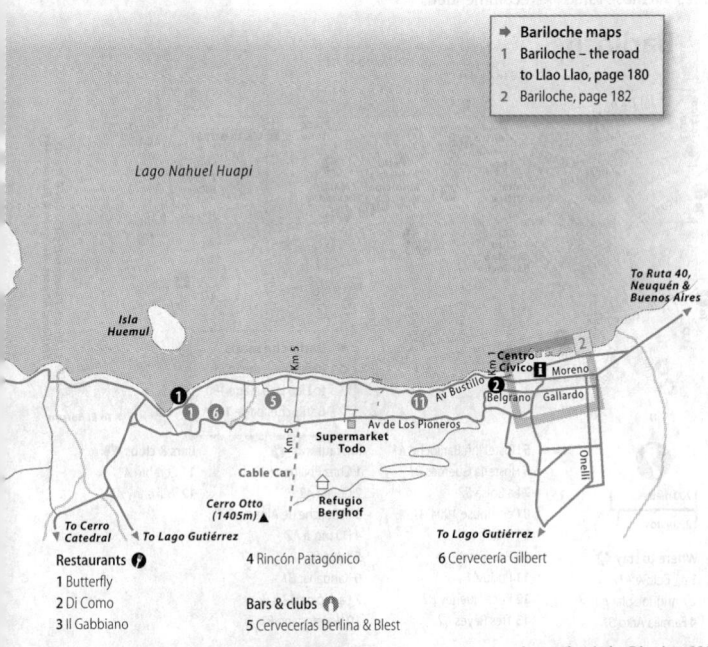

➡ **Bariloche maps**
1 Bariloche – the road to Llao Llao, page 180
2 Bariloche, page 182

Lago Nahuel Huapi

Isla Huemul

To Ruta 40, Neuquén & Buenos Aires

Av Bustillo

Centro Cívico **i**
Moreno
Belgrano Gallardo

Onelli

Av de Los Pioneros
Supermarket Todo

Cable Car

Cerro Otto (1405m) ▲
Refugio Berghof

To Cerro Catedral   *To Lago Gutiérrez*

To Lago Gutiérrez

Restaurants 🍴
1 Butterfly
2 Di Como
3 Il Gabbiano

4 Rincón Patagónico

Bars & clubs 🍸
5 Cervecerías Berlina & Blest

6 Cervecería Gilbert

and the *Carta de Refugios, Senderos y Picadas* for Bariloche. They can also tell you about transport, which varies from year to year and between high and low season.

Oficina Municipal de Turismo
Centro Cívico p 6, T0294-442 9850, http://barilocheturismo.gob.ar. Daily 0800-2100.
Full information on all there is to do in Bariloche by season, where to stay and eat, transport details.

Provincial office
12 de Octubre 605, T0294-442 3188.

Where to stay

Prices rise in 2 peak seasons: Jul-Aug for skiing, and mid-Dec to Mar for summer holidays. If you arrive in the high season without a reservation, consult the listing published by the tourist office (address above). In 2017 the municipality introduced an Eco-Tax on overnight stays from 1 to 3 nights; the tax varies from AR$60 (US$3.90) in 5-star hotels to AR$10 (US$0.65) in guesthouses, B&Bs, hostels and 1-stars. Campsites should charge AR$5. This selection gives lake-view, high-season prices where applicable. In low season you pay half of these prices in most cases. All those listed are recommended.

$$$ Premier
Rolando 263, T0294-442 6168, www.hotelpremier.com.
Good central choice (very good value in low season), small 'classic' rooms and larger superior rooms, English spoken.

$$$ Tres Reyes
12 de Octubre 135, T0294-442 6121, www.hotel3reyes.com.ar.
Traditional lakeside hotel with spacious rooms, splendid views, all services, gardens.

$$ Antiguo Solar
A Gallardo 360, T0294-440 0337, www.antiguosolar.com.ar.
Not far from the centre, nice simple B&B on the upper level of an attractive residential building, with parking, breakfast includes fresh biscuits and local jams.

$$ Hostería Güemes
Güemes 715, T0294-442 4785, www.hosteriaguemes.com.ar.
Lovely, quiet, lots of space in living areas, very pleasant, big breakfast included, owner is a fishing expert and very knowledgeable about the area.

2 Bariloche

Lago Nahuel Huapi

N
200 metres
200 yards

Where to stay
1 41 Below *A1*
2 Antiguo Solar *B2*
4 Familia Arko *B1*
5 Hostel Inn Bariloche *A1*
6 Hostería Güemes *B1*
7 La Bolsa *B2*
8 Penthouse 1004 *A1*
9 Periko's *B1*
10 Premier *A2*
11 Pudu *A1*
12 Ruca Hueney *B2*
13 Tres Reyes *A2*

Restaurants
1 Chez Philippe *B1*
2 Covita *A3*
3 El Boliche de Alberto *B2*
4 Huang Ji *A2*
5 Jauja *B2*
6 Kandahar *B1*
7 La Alpina *A2*
10 Vegetariano *B1*

Bars & clubs
11 Cerebro *A1*
12 Wilkenny *A1*

→ Bariloche maps
1 Bariloche – the road to Llao Llao, page 180
2 Bariloche, page 182

$ pp 41 Below
Pasaje Juramento 94, T0294-443 6433,
www.hostel41below.com.
Central, quiet, relaxing atmosphere, good light
rooms for 4-6 (US$16-18) and an apartment ($$).

$ Familia Arko
Güemes 685, T0294-442 3109,
arko@eco-family.com.
English and German spoken, helpful, good
trekking information, beautiful garden.

$ pp Hostel Inn Bariloche
Salta 308, T0294-442 6084,
www.hostelbariloche.com.
Large, well-designed hostel with great views of
the lake from the communal areas and rooms.
Comfortable beds, in dorm US$15 pp); also
doubles ($$), discount for HI members. The
best feature is the great deck with a view in the
garden. Neighbouring **Marco Polo Inn** (T440
0105), is in the same group.

$ pp La Bolsa
Palacios 405 y Elflein, T0294-442 3529,
www.labolsadeldeporte.com.ar.
Relaxed atmosphere, rustic rooms with duvets,
1 double with bath, some rooms with views,
deck to sit out on.

$ pp Penthouse 1004
San Martín 127, 10th floor, T0294-443 2228,
www.penthouse1004.com.ar.
Welcoming hostel at the top of a block of
apartments with amazing views. Helpful
staff, cosy rooms, dorms US$18-19, doubles $$.
Big communal area for chilling and watching
the sunset.

$ pp Periko's
Morales 555, T0294-452 2326, www.perikos.com.
Welcoming, quiet, nice atmosphere, dorms
US$13-17, and doubles $$ (price depends on
season), breakfast included, washing machine.
Arranges tours, including to Ruta 40. Reserve in
advance by email.

$ pp Pudu
Salta 459, T0294-442 9738, www.hostelpudu.com.
"A gem". Irish/Argentine-run, dorms US$17
and doubles $$ with spectacular lake views,
downstairs is a small garden and a bar.
Long term rates available.

$ pp Ruca Hueney
Elflein 396, T0294-443 3986, www.rucahueney.com.
Lovely, calm, comfortable beds with duvets, rooms
for 2 to 6 people, great view, very kind owners.

West of town

$$$$ Aldebaran
*On Península San Pedro, reached from
Av Bustillo Km 20.4, T0294-444 8678,
www.aldebaranpatagonia.com.*
Not in chalet style, but tasteful rooms in this
modern boutique hotel on the lake shore, superb
views. Rustic-style restaurant, sauna and spa with
outdoor pool, so you can bask under the stars.
Great service from helpful bilingual staff.

$$$$ Llao-Llao
*Av Bustillo Km 25, T0294-444 5700/8530,
www.llaollao.com.*
Deservedly famous, superb location,
complete luxury, golf course, pool, spa,
water sports, restaurant.

$$$$ Tunquelén
*Av Bustillo, Km 24.5, T0294-444 8400/8600,
www.tunquelen.com.*
4-star, comfortable, splendid views, feels quite
secluded, superb restaurant, attentive service.

$$$ Departamentos Bellevue
*Av Bustillo, Km 24.6, T0294-444 8389,
www.bellevue.com.ar. Open year-round.*
A famous tea room with beautiful views also
offers accommodation with high-quality
furnishings, very comfortable, well-equipped
self-catering *cabañas*, delicious breakfast
included. Access to beaches on Lake Moreno,
lovely gardens.

$$$ Hostería Santa Rita
*Av Bustillo, Km 7.2, T0294-446 1028,
www.santarita.com.ar. Bus 10, 20/21 to Km 7.5.*
Peaceful lakeside views, comfortable, lovely
terrace, great service.

$$$ Katy
*Av Bustillo, Km 24.3, T0294-444 8023,
www.gringospatagonia.com.*
Delightful, peaceful, garden full of flowers,
charming Slovenian family Kastelic (also half-
board, $$$$). Also offers adventure tourism.

$$$ La Caleta
*Av Bustillo, Km 1.95, T0294-15-460 7727,
www.bungalows-bariloche.com.ar.*
Cabañas sleep 4, open fire, excellent value,
minimum booking 3 nights (7 in high season). Also
owns **San Isidro** *cabañas* at Km 5.7, further west.

$ pp Alaska
*Lilinquen 328 (buses 10, 20/21, get
off at La Florida, Av Bustillo Km 7.5),
T0294-446 1564, www.alaska-hostel.com.*

Well run, cosy with shared rustic rooms for 4, US$14 pp, also doubles **$$** (cheaper without bath), nice garden, washing machine, organizes horse riding and rafting, rents mountain bikes. Recommended.

Camping

List of sites from tourist office. These are recommended among the many along Bustillo. **Petunia** (Km 13.5, T0294-446 1969, www. campingpetunia.com). A lovely shady site going down to lakeside with all facilities. Shops and restaurants on most sites; these are closed outside Jan-Mar. **Selva Negra** (Km 2.95, T0294-444 1013, www.campingselvanegra.alojar. com.ar). Very good, discounts for long stay. **El Yeti** (Km 5.7, T0294-444 2073, www.elyeti. alojar.com.ar). All facilities, *cabañas*. **Complejo Los Coihues**, 13 km from Bariloche at PN Lihuel Calel 156, Villa Los Coihues, near Lago Gutiérrez (see Trekking, below), T0294-446 7481, www. campingloscoihues.com.ar. Camping US$7.70, also has hostel with dorms (US$19.25 pp), breakfast included, other meals available, open all year, kayaking, rafting, horse riding and trekking.

(see Trekking, below)

Restaurants

Bariloche is blessed with superb food, much of it locally produced, including smoked trout and salmon, wild boar and other delicacies, not least fine chocolate and, in season, delicious berries. There are many good delicatessens.

$$$ Chez Philippe
Primera Junta 1080, T0294-442 7291.
Delicious local delicacies and fondue, fine French-influenced cuisine.

$$$ Jauja
Elflein 148, T442 2952.
Recommended for delicious local dishes, quiet and welcoming, good value.

$$$ Kandahar
20 de Febrero 698, T0294-442 4702.
Dinner only, reserve in high season.
Atmospheric, warm and intimate, with exquisite food, run by ski champion Marta Peirono de Barber, superb wines and *pisco sour*. Highly recommended.

$$ Covita
Rolando 172, T0294-442 1708.
Mon-Sat for lunch, Thu-Sat for dinner.
Vegetarian restaurant (also serves fish), offering curries, masalas and pastas.

$$ El Boliche de Alberto
Villegas 347, T0294-443 1433,
www.elbolichedealberto.com.
Very good pasta, huge portions, popular after 2000 (queues in summer). There is a 2nd location at Bustillo Km 8800 that specializes in grilled meats.

$$ Vegetariano
20 de Febrero 730, T0294-442 1820,
www.vegetarianpatagonia.com.ar.
Also fish, excellent food, beautifully served, warm atmosphere, take-away available. Highly recommended.

$ Huang Ji
Rolando 268, T0294-442 8168.
Good Chinese, next to a bowling alley.

La Alpina
Moreno 98.
Old-fashioned café serving delicious cakes, good for tea, Wi-Fi, charming.

West of town

$$$ Butterfly
Hua Huan 7831, just off Av Bustillo Km 7.9, T0294-446 1441, www.thebutterflygroup.com.ar.
2 seatings: 1945 and 2130. German/Argentine/Irish-owned, an elite dining experience, tasting menus using only local ingredients, carefully selected wines, art exhibitions, only 6 tables. Reserve in advance and discuss the menu with the chef.

$$$ Il Gabbiano
Av Bustillo Km 24.3, T0294-444 8346,
www.gabbiano.com.ar. Closed Wed.
Delicious Italian lunches and dinners. Booking essential (no credit cards).

$$$ Rincón Patagónico
Av Bustillo, Km 14, Paraje Laguna Fantasma, T0294-446 3063, www.rinconpatagonico.com.ar.
Traditional *parrilla* with Patagonian lamb cooked *al palo*, huge menu but service can be minimal at busy times.

$$ Di Como
Av Bustillo, Km 0.8, T0294-452 2118.
A 10-min walk from town. Good pizza and pasta, terrace and great views of the lake.

Bars and clubs

Cerebro
JM de Rosas 406, www.cerebro.com.ar. Jun-Dec.
The party starts at 0130, Fri best.

Cervecería Berlina
Ruta 79 y F Goye, T0294-445 4393,
www.cervezaberlina.com. Open 1200-0100
(until last person has left).
3 good brews. They have a diverse menu ($$) at
their restaurant at Av Bustillo Km 11.750, with a
deck for watching the sunset.

Cervecería Blest
Av Bustillo Km 11.6, T0294-446 1026,
www.cervezablest.com.ar.
Wonderful brewery with delicious beers, serving
imaginative local and German dishes and steak
and kidney pie ($$$-$$). Recommended.

Cervecería Gilbert
Km 24, Barrio Las Cartas, Circuito Chico,
T0294-445 4292. Daily 1100-2300.
Popular beers and simple meals ($$).

Wilkenny
San Martín 435, T0294-442 4444.
Lively Irish pub with expensive food but it really
gets busy around 2400. Great place to watch
televized sports.

Shopping

The main shopping area is on Mitre between the
Centro Cívico and Beschtedt, also on San Martín.
Local chocolate is excellent. Local wines, from the
Alto Río Negro, are also good.

Chocolate
Several shops on Mitre.
Abuela Goye, *Mitre 258 and Quaglia 219, www.*
abuelagoye.com. First rate chocolatier, also with
café in the Quaglia branch (2 other branches and
outlets nationwide).
Fenoglio, *Av Bustillo 1200, Mitre 76 and others.*
Daily 1100-1900. Chocolate production with
tastings, a good shop and museum.
Mamuschka, *Mitre y Rolando, www.mamuschka.*
com. Considered the best chocolate here, also
with café.

Handicrafts
Feria Artesanal Municipal, *Moreno y Villegas.*

What to do

Climbing
Note that at higher levels, winter snow
storms can begin as early as Apr, making
climbing dangerous.
Club Andino Bariloche, *see Tourist information,*
page 181. The club can contact mountain guides
and provide information.

Cycling
Bikes can be hired at many places in high season.
Circuito Chico, *Av Bustillo 18300, T0294-459 5608,*
www.circuitochicobikes.com. Rents mountain
bikes, with road assistance service, and kayaks.
Dirty Bikes, *Lonquimay 3908, T0294-444 2743,*
www.dirtybikes.com.ar. Very helpful for repairs,
tours and bike rentals (US$6-45 per day).

Horse riding
Ariane Patagonia, *T0294-452 3488, www.*
arianepatagonia.com.ar. Horse-riding trips, visits
to farms and estancias, personalized service.
Bastion del Manso, *Av Bustillo 13491, T0294-445*
6111, www.bastiondelmanso.com. Relaxed
place with tuition and full-day's riding offered,
including rafting and longer treks.
Estancia Peuma Hue, *see under Bariloche to*
El Bolsón, Where to stay, below.

Kayaking
Patagonia Infinita, *T0294-15-455 3954, www.*
patagoniainfinita.com.ar. Kayaking and trekking
trips in Parque Nacional Nahuel Huapi.
Pura Vida Patagonia, *T0294-15-441 4053, www.*
puravidapatagonia.com. Informative, attentive
guides, good value, trips from 1-9 days in
Nahuel Huapi.

Language schools
Academia Bariloche, *Mitre 17-2A, T0294-442 9307,*
www.academiabariloche.com.
ILEE, *www.argentinailee.com.* Arranges classes
and homestay.
La Montaña, *Elflein 251, T0294-452 4212,*
www.lamontana.com. Spanish courses,
family lodging, activities and volunteering.

Paragliding
There are several paragliding schools. Take-offs
are usually from Cerro Otto, but there are other
starting points, 10- to 40-min tandem flights.

Skiing
Cerro Catedral, *T0294-440 9000, www.catedral*
altapatagonia.com. Mid-Jun to end-Sep, busiest
from mid-Jun to mid-Aug for school holidays,
ski lifts: 0900-1630. It has 120 km of slopes
of all grades, allowing a total drop of 1010 m,
and 52 km of cross country (Nordic) skiing
routes. There are also snowboarding areas
and a well-equipped base with hotels,
restaurants and equipment hire, ski schools
and nursery care for children. Bus, labelled
'Catedral' (3 de Mayo company), leaves from
the bus terminal and Moreno entre Beschtedt
y Palacios every 90 mins, 35 mins, US$3,

taxi US$25. The cable car for Catedral costs US$25 round trip.

Cerro Otto, *T0294-444 1035, www.teleferico barilochle.com.ar*. Cable car and funicular passengers can take a bus leaving from Mitre y Villegas, hourly 1000-1930 in summer, returning hourly, US$8.75.

Tours

Check what your tour includes; cable cars and chair lifts usually extra. Tours get booked up in season. Most travel agencies will pick you up from your hotel and charge roughly the same prices: Circuito Chico US$19, half-day; Isla Victoria and Bosque de Arrayanes, full-day boat trip (see above); Tronador, Ventisquero Negro and Pampa Linda, US$40 plus National Park entry via Lago Mascardi by boat; El Bolsón US$35, full-day, including Lago Puelo; several other tours.

Aguas Blancas, *Morales 564, T0294-443 2799, www.aguasblancas.com.ar*. Rafting on the Río Manso, all grades, with expert guides, and all equipment provided, also 'duckies' – inflatable kayaks for beginners.

Canopy, *Colonia Suiza, Cerro López, T0294-440 0286, www.canopybariloche.com*. Zip-line adventure in the forest, including 4WD ride to get there and night descents.

Eco Family, *20 de Junio 728, T0294-442 8995, www.eco-family.com*. Riding, walking, skiing, other adventures, bilingual guides. Highly recommended.

Senza Limiti Adventures, *J Cortázar 5050, T0294-452 0597, www.slimiti.com*. Adventure travel company, including kayaking, mountain-biking, hut-to-hut treks and much more, licensed by National Parks Administration.

Tronador Turismo, *Quaglia 283, T0294-442 5644, www.tronadorturismo.com.ar*. Conventional tours, trekking and rafting. Also to Refugio Neumeyer and to Chilean border. Great adventurous wintersports options.

Turisur, *Mitre 219, T0294-442 6109, www.turisur. com.ar*. Boat trips to Bosque de Arrayanes, Isla Victoria on a 1937 ship and to Tronador via Lago Mascardi. Licensee for the Cruce Andino trip to Puerto Montt. Always reserve 1 day ahead.

Warning...
Horseflies (*tábanos*) infest the lakeshore and lower areas in summer.

Trekking

There's a network of paths and several *refugios* in the mountains, allowing for treks over several days. *Refugios* are leased by **Club Andino Bariloche**. On treks to *refugios* remember to add costs of ski lifts, buses, food at *refugios* and lodging (in **Club Andino** *refugios*: US$10-20 per night, plus US$8-20 for food. Take a good sleeping bag. Among the many great treks possible are: from Llao Llao a delightful, easy circuit in Valdivian (temperate) rainforest (2 hrs), also climb the small hill for wonderful views. Up to privately owned **Refugio López** (2076 m, bus 10 to Colonia Suiza and López, check return times), 5 hrs return, from southeastern tip of Lago Moreno up Arroyo López, for fabulous views. From Cerro Catedral to **Refugio Frey** (1700 m), beautiful setting on small lake, via Arroyo Piedritas (4 hrs each way), or via cable car to **Refugio Lynch** and via Punta Nevada (only experienced walkers). To beautiful Lago Gutiérrez, 2 km downhill from Cerro Catedral, along lakeshore to the road from El Bolsón and walk back to Bariloche (4 hrs), or Bus 50. From **Pampa Linda**, idyllic (*hosterías*, campsite), walk up to **Refugio Otto Meiling** (5 hrs each way), to tranquil Laguna Ilon (5½ hrs each way), or across Paso de las Nubes to Puerto Frías, boat back to Bariloche (2 days: closed when boggy). Bus to Pampa Linda from outside **Club Andino Bariloche** (0830 in summer), **Expreso Meiling** (T0294-452 9875), or from **Transitando lo Natural** (20 de Febrero 25, T0294-452 7926), 2¼ hrs. Contact **CAB** for maps, guidebooks and to check if walks are open (see under Tourist information, above).

Andescross, *T0294-15-463 3581, www.andescross. com*. Expert guides, all included. Trekking to Chile across the Andes, via Pampa Linda, Lago Frías, Peulla.

Transport

Air Airport is 15 km east of town, with access from Ruta 40, 7 km east of centre, T0294-440 5016; bus service 72 from town centre; also *colectivos* and taxis (US$10). If staying on the road to Llao Llao, west of town, expect to pay more for transport to your hotel. Car rental agencies, internet, exchange, ATM, café at the cramped airport. Many flights a day to **Buenos Aires**. AR also flies to **El Calafate** in summer only. **LADE** to **Buenos Aires**, **Comodoro Rivadavia**, **Esquel** and several other destinations in Patagonia.

Bus Station 3 km east of centre; urban buses 'Mascardo', 'Manso', 20, 21, 22, to/from centre; also bus 10, 11, 72. City buses run by **3 de Mayo**, Moreno 480, also at terminal, http://3demayobariloche.com.ar. Buy rechargeable ticket before travelling. Taxi US$5-8. Bus info at terminal T0294-443 2860, http://terminaldebariloche.com.ar. Toilets, small *confitería*, *kiosko*, *locutorio* with internet, tourist information desk. Bus company offices in town (purchase tickets there or at terminal): **Vía Bariloche/El Valle/Don Otto/TAC**, Mitre 321, T0294-442 9012, terminal T0294-443 2444; **Chevallier/Flechabus**, Moreno 107, T0294-442 3090. At terminal: **Andesmar/Tramat**, T0294-443 0211; **Ko Ko**, T0294-443 1135. **Buenos Aires**, 7 companies daily, 19-22 hrs, US$123-140. To **Bahía Blanca**, 5 companies, 14 hrs, US$76-87. To **Mendoza**, US$100-115, **Andesmar** and **Cata**, 17-19 hrs. To **Esquel**, via **El Bolsón**, fares and schedules given below. To **San Martín de los Andes**, and **Villa La Angostura**, see above. To **Comodoro Rivadavia**, US$57-77, **Don Otto**, 14 hrs, and **Marga** who continue to **Río Gallegos**, US$130, 23 hrs. In Río Gallegos make other onward connections to El Calafate and Ushuaia. To **El Chaltén** and **El Calafate** take

Chaltén Travel's 3-day trip via El Bolsón, Esquel, Perito Moreno and Los Antiguos on Ruta 40, www.chaltentravel.com (page 204), US$174, depart 0745 on odd-numbered days mid-Nov to mid-Apr, office at Mitre 422, loc 10, T0294-489 0463. **Taqsa/Marga** (T02944-423081, www.taqsa.com.ar) may run a service to El Chaltén and El Calafate on Ruta 40 in high season, otherwise they have connecting services via Perito Moreno and Río Gallegos which take about 30 hrs and cost about US$175. **To Chile**: Vía Bariloche and Transaustral run daily services via Samoré pass to **Osorno**, 5 hrs, US$25, and **Puerto Montt** (6-7½ hrs, US$26); **Andesmar** goes to **Valdivia** via Osorno, US$28, not daily. Take passport when booking. Sit on left side for best views.

Car hire Rates are US$60-130 per day. **Lagos**, Mitre 83, T0294-442 8880, www.lagosrentacar.com.ar, among many others. To enter Chile, a permit is necessary; it's generally included in the price. State when booking car, allow 24 hrs.

Train The *Tren Patagónico* runs from **Bariloche** to **Viedma** usually on Sun; check the website www.trenpatagonico-sa.com.ar for latest information. See under Viedma, page 198, for more details. Bariloche station, T02944-423172.

South of Bariloche

ancient trees, fabulous fishing and the Old Patagonian Express

More wild and beautiful scenery can be explored along the Andes, with a few tourist centres such as El Bolsón and Esquel giving access to lakes and national parks. There is trekking, rafting, skiing and fishing on offer, a train ride on the famous La Trochita and the magnificent Los Alerces national park to explore.

South and west of Bariloche

Paved Ruta 258 runs from Bariloche to El Bolsón, 126 km south, passing the beautiful lakes **Gutiérrez**, **Mascardi** and **Guillelmo**, which offer horse riding, trekking and world-class rafting along the **Río Manso**. From the southern end of Lago Mascardi, 35 km south of Bariloche, a *ripio* road (note one-way system) runs west towards **Pampa Linda**, in the most blissfully isolated location, with spectacular views of **Cerro Tronador** (3478 m) towering above. Whole-day trips from Bariloche to these destinations also include visits to the strange **Ventisquero Negro** (black glacier) and to the **Garganta del Diablo** at the road's end. If you want to spend more time in the area, Pampa Linda is the starting point for excellent trekking including the two-day walk over Paso de los Nubes to Laguna Frías (see Trekking, opposite, and Where to stay, page 190).

Back on Ruta 258, stop off at beautiful **Río Villegas**, about 70 km south of Bariloche.

El Bolsón and around *Colour map 8, C1.*

El Bolsón is an attractive town in a broad fertile valley, surrounded by the mountains of the cordillera and dominated by the dramatic peak of **Cerro Piltriquitrón** (2284 m), hence the town's name: the 'big bag'. Its magical setting attracted thousands of hippies to create an ideological community here in the 1970s; they now produce the handicrafts, beers, fruit and jams, sold at the market on Tuesday, Thursday and Saturday, 0900-1800. There are many mountain walks and waterfalls nearby, and good fishing at Lagos Puelo (see below) and Epuyén (40 km southeast of El Bolsón, off Ruta 40).

Walks around El Bolsón East of town, a pleasant hour-long walk will take you to the top of **Cerro Amigo**, with lovely views; follow Calle General Roca east until it becomes Islas Malvinas and continue up the hill. Better still are the panoramic views from Cerro Piltriquitrón: drive, join a tour or take a taxi 10 km up winding earth roads; then it's an hour's walk to the **Bosque Tallado**, where sculptures have been carved from fallen trees; food and shelter are available at the *refugio* (1400 m), and from there it's three hours' walk to the summit (six- to seven-hour round trip walking all the way). You can also do paragliding from here. There are also good views from **Cabeza del Indio**, so called because the rock's profile resembles a face, a good 6-km drive or bike ride from the centre. From the rock, there's a waymarked walk throught the woods north to **Cascada Escondida**, an impressive sweep of waterfalls, 10 km northwest of El Bolsón. There are rather less exciting falls at **Cataratas Mallín Ahogado**, a little further north; see the tourist office map for details.

There is also wonderful trekking in the mountains and valleys west of town on an excellent network of trails with well-equipped and staffed *refugios* in superb locations (see Where to stay, page 192). Additional information and compulsory registration at the **Club Andino Piltriquitrón** ⓘ *Sarmiento y Roca, T0294-449 2600, www.capiltriquitron.com.ar, Mon-Fri 1800-2000,* or tourist office in El Bolsón. In high season there are minibuses to the trailheads, at other times hitch or take a remise taxi.

Parque Nacional Lago Puelo At **Lago Puelo**, 15 km south of El Bolsón, there are gentle walks on marked paths, boat trips across the lake on the *Juana de Arco* (T0294-449 8946, www.interpatagonia.com/juanadearco), and canoes for rent. Wardens at the park entrance (US$16.50) can advise on these and on a three-day trek through magnificent scenery to the Chilean border. Buses (US$1-2) go from Avenida San Martín y Dorrego in El Bolsón to the lake via Villa Lago Puelo.

> **Tip...**
> Gorgeous home-made *alfajores* are sold in a fairytale setting at **El Bolsonero** (www.elbolsonero.bolsonweb.com/quienes.htm) on the old road to Lago Puelo.

Cholila and around

This peaceful, sprawling village lies 76 km south of El Bolsón, with superb views at Lago Cholila (17 km west), crowned by the Matterhorn-like mountains of **Cerros Dos** and **Tres Picos** (where there's a campsite and expensive **Hostería El Pedregoso**). There's excellent fishing, canoeing and kayaking on rivers nearby. Along Valle de Cholila (Ruta 71) are several old brick and wooden houses and barns, including the **wooden cabins** where Butch Cassidy, the Sundance Kid and Etta Place lived between 1901 and 1905. The cabins, which have been renovated, controversially, are 13 km north of Cholila, east of the road, opposite a police station (officially US$1.50 entry, if anyone's around to charge you). One kilometre west of the road is the **Casa de Piedra** teahouse serving *té galés* and offering basic accommodation.

Villa Lago Rivadavia, 15 km south of Cholila, lies next to the northern gates of Parque Nacional Los Alerces, with an increasing number of *cabañas*.

Esquel *Colour map 9, A1.*

Esquel, 293 km south of Bariloche, was originally an offshoot of the Welsh colony at Chubut, 650 km to the east, and still has a pioneer feel. A breezy open town in a fertile valley, with a backdrop of mountains, Esquel is the base for visiting the Parque Nacional Los Alerces and for skiing at **La Hoya** in winter (15 km, good 6½-hour trek in summer). There are good walks from the town to **Laguna La Zeta**, 5 km, and to **Cerro La Cruz**, two hours (one way). It's also the departure point for the famous narrow-gauge railway, **La Trochita** (see box, opposite, and Transport, page 195).

Trevelin *Colour map 9, A1.*

Welsh is still spoken in the pretty village of Trevelin, 24 km southwest of Esquel, which was an offshoot of the Welsh Chubut colony (see box, page 206). It has a Welsh chapel (built 1910, closed) and tea rooms. The **Museo Regional** ⓘ *daily 1100-2000, US$4,* in the old mill (1918) includes artefacts from the Welsh colony. The **Museo Cartref Taid** ⓘ *daily 1600-2000, US$4 (ask for directions in the tourist office),* is the house of John Evans, one of Trevelin's first pioneers, full of his belongings, and provides a great insight into the local Welsh history. There's also a touching memorial of Evans' life

The Old Patagonian Express

Esquel is the terminus of a 402-km branch-line from Ingeniero Jacobacci, a junction on the old Buenos Aires-Bariloche mainline, 194 km east of Bariloche. This narrow-gauge line (0.75 m wide) took 23 years to build, being finally opened in 1945. It was made famous outside Argentina by Paul Theroux who described it in his book *The Old Patagonian Express*. The 1922 Henschel and Baldwin steam locomotives (from Germany and USA respectively) are powered by fuel oil and use 100 litres of water every kilometre. Water has to be taken on at least every 40 km along the route. A replica is used when there are strong winds. Most of the coaches are Belgian and also date from 1922. If you want to see the engines, go to El Maitén where the workshops are.

Until the Argentine government handed responsibility for railways over to the provincial governments in 1994, regular services ran the length of the line. Since then, tourist services have been maintained out of Esquel and El Maitén by the provincial government of Chubut.

at **El Tumbo del Caballo Malacara** ⓘ *200 m from the main plaza, guided tours US$4*, a private garden containing the remains of Evans' horse, Malacara, who once saved his life. **Nant-y-fall Falls** ⓘ *17 km southwest on the road to the border, US$38 pp including guide to the falls*, are a series of impressive cascades in lovely forest.

Border with Chile: Paso Futaleufú Route 259 runs from Trevelín to the Chilean border at the spectacularly beautiful Paso Futaleufú. The border is crossed by a bridge over the Río Futaleufú. Argentine customs and a campsite (**Camping Puerto Ciprés**) are on the Argentine side of river, 70 km southwest of Esquel; Chilean customs is 1 km on the other side of river (one hour for all formalities). The Chilean town of Futaleufú is 9 km west of the border. There are buses from Esquel via Trevelin to **Paso Futaleufú** (see page 195), but very little traffic for hitching.

☆ **Parque Nacional Los Alerces** *Colour map 9, A1.*
33 km west of Esquel, T02945-471015, http://losalercesparquenacional.blogspot.com, US$16.50; see also www.parquesnacionales.gob.ar.

One of the most appealing and untouched expanses in the Andes region, this relatively undeveloped national park has several lakes, including **Lago Futalaufquen**, which has some of the best fishing in the area; **Lago Menéndez**, which can be crossed by boat to visit rare and impressive *alerce* trees (Fitzroya cupressoides), some of which are over 2000 years old, and the green waters of **Lago Verde**. Access is possible only to the east side of the park, via a *ripio* road (which is also an alternative way from Esquel to El Bolsón) with many camping spots and *hosterías*. Helpful *guardaparques* give out maps and advice on walks at the visitor centre in **Villa Futalaufquen** (southern end of Lago Futulaufquen, open 0800-2000), where there's also a service station food shops, *locutorio* and a restaurant. Fishing licences are available from food shops, the *kiosko* or Hosterías Cume Hué and Futalaufquen, or from petrol stations in Esquel. There is another entrance at the north end of Lago Rivadavia, 55 km north of Villa Futalaufquen (open 0800-2000), and a southern entrance, 50 km south (open 0800-1400), which gives access to the Complejo Hidroeléctrico Fautaleufú, www.chfutaleufu.com.ar.

Trekking and tours The west half of the park is inaccessible, but there are splendid walks along footpaths on the southern shore of Lago Futalaufquen, with several waterfalls, and near Lago Verde further north. Treks at Los Alerces range from an hour to two or three days. All long treks require previous registration with the *guardaparques*; some paths are closed in autumn and winter.

At Lago Futalaufquen's northern end, walk across the bridge over Río Arrayanes to Lago Verde. A longer more difficult trek is to **Cerro El Dedal** (1916 m), either returning the way you came from Villa Futalaufquen, eight hours, or making an eight- to 10-hour loop through

Tip...
Some of the long-distance trails in the park are closed each year, mainly because of fires; ask the *guardaparques* which are open.

Puerto Limonao. Walkers must register with the *guardaparques* and you're required to start before 1000. Carry plenty of water. There's also a two- to three-day hike through *coihue* forest to the tip of beautiful, secluded **Lago Krügger**. **Cerros Alto El Petiso** and **La Torta** can be climbed and there is a trekkers' shelter at the base of **Cerro Cocinero**. **Boat trips** go to El Alerzal, from Puerto Limonao, across Lago Futalaufquen along the pea-green **Río Arrayanes**, lined with extraordinary cinnamon-barked trees, to Puerto Mermoud on Lago Verde. A short walk leads to Puerto Chucao, on **Lago Menéndez**, where another boat makes the unforgettable trip to see the majestic 2600-year-old alerce trees, walking to silent Lago Cisne, past the white waters of Río Cisne. A cheaper alternative is to get to Puerto Chucao on your own and take the boat there. Boats run frequently in high season; fares start at US$35. Book through Esquel, Tour operators, below.

South of Esquel

South of Esquel, Ruta 40 is paved through the towns of **Tecka** and **Gobernador Costa** in Chubut province (the latter has a couple of hotels and *cabañas* and a municipal campsite). At 38 km south of Gobernador Costa, gravelled Ruta 40 forks southwest through the town of Alto Río Senguer, while provincial Ruta 20 heads almost directly south for 141 km, before turning east towards Sarmiento and Comodoro Rivadavia. At La Puerta del Diablo, in the valley of the lower Río Senguer, Ruta 20 intersects provincial Ruta 22, which joins with Ruta 40 at the town of Río Mayo (see page 215). This latter route is completely paved and preferable to Ruta 40 for long-distance motorists; there are good informal campsites on the west side of the bridge across the Río Senguer.

Listings South of Bariloche

Tourist information

El Bolsón tourist office
Av San Martín y Roca, T0294-449 2604, www.turismoelbolson.gob.ar. Open 0900-2100 all year, until 2400 in high summer.
Extremely helpful with maps, treks to *refugios* and accommodation, English spoken.

Cholila tourist information hut
Opposite petrol station at El Rincón. Summer only.

Municipalidad
Cholila, T02945-498040.
Basic information.

Esquel tourist office
Av Alvear y Sarmiento, T02945-451927, www.esquel.tur.ar. Daily 0800-2200.

Trevelin tourist office
In the central plaza, T02945-480120, www.trevelin.gob.ar. Mon-Fri 0800-2000, Sat-Sun 0900-2000.
Has maps, accommodation booking service, helpful, English spoken.

Where to stay

$$$$ El Retorno
Villa Los Coihues, on the shore of Lago Gutiérrez, T0294-446 7333, www.hosteriaelretorno.com.

Stunning lakeside position, comfortable hunting lodge style, family run, with a beach, tennis, very comfortable rooms ($$$ in low season) and self-catering apartments (Bus 50, follow signs from the road to El Bolsón).

$$$$ Estancia Peuma Hue
Ruta 40, Km 2014, T0294-15-450 1030, www.peuma-hue.com.
Best comfort in a homely environment, on the southern shores of Lago Gutiérrez, below Cerro Catedral Sur. Charming owner Evelyn Hoter and dedicated staff make it all work perfectly, tasty home-made food, superb horse riding and other activities, health treatments, yoga, meditation, etc, candlelit concerts. All inclusive, varied accommodation. Highly recommended.

$$$ Hostería Pampa Linda
T0294-449 0517, www.hosteria pampalinda.com.ar.
A comfortable, peaceful base for climbing Tronador and many other treks (plus horse riding, trekking and climbing courses), simple rooms, all with stunning views, restaurant, full board optional, packed lunches available for hikes. Charming owners, Sebastián de la Cruz is one of the area's most experienced mountaineers. Highly recommended. Nearby is **Refugio Pampa Linda** and **Camping Río Manso**.

$$$ pp Hotel Tronador
T0294-449 0556, www.hoteltronador.com.

60 km from Bariloche, on the narrow road from Villa Mascardi to Pampa Linda (there are restricted times for going in each direction: check with tourist office), Nov-Apr, full board, lakeside paradise, lovely rooms with lake view, beautiful gardens, charming owner, also riding, fishing and lake excursions. Also camping **La Querencia.**

Camping

Camping La Cascada
At Mallín Ahogado, near La Cascada Escondida, T0294-483 5304, Camping-La-Cascada on Facebook.
Lovely setting, helpful owner, camping and *cabañas*, organic vegetables, home-made bread and beer. Recommended.

Camping Las Carpitas
RN 40, 33 km from Bariloche, T0294-449 0527, www.campinglascarpitas.com.ar.
Great location, all facilities, also *cabañas*.

Camping Los Rápidos
After crossing the Río Manso to Pampa Linda, T0294-15-431 7028, www.losrapidos.com.ar.
All facilities, attractive shaded site going down to lake, *confitería*, open all year.

Camping Los Vuriloches
Pampa Linda, T0294-446 2131, www. pampalindatere@hotmail.com.
Idyllic spacious lakeside site with trees, good meals, food shop.

El Bolsón
Difficult to find accommodation in the high season: book ahead.

$$$ Amancay
Av San Martín 3207, T0294-449 2222, www.hotelamancayelbolson.com.
Good, comfortable and light rooms, though small and a bit old-fashioned, breakfast included.

$$$ La Posada de Hamelin
Int Granollers 2179, T0294-449 2030, www.posadadehamelin.com.ar.
Charming rooms, welcoming atmosphere, huge breakfasts with home-made jams and cakes, German spoken. Highly recommended.

$$ El Refugio del Lago
T02945-499025, www.elrefugiodellago.com.ar.
Buses between El Bolsón and Esquel stop (briefly) at Lago Epuyén, though some don't enter the village itself. Transfers available on request. Relaxed, comfortable rooms in a lovely wooden house a short walk from the lakeshore,

also cabins, dorms (US$19), with breakfast, good meals. Camping US$6-7 pp. Recommended.

$$ La Casona de Odile
Barrio Luján, T0294-449 2753, www.odile.com.ar.
Private rooms and 3-6-bed dorms (US$17 pp) by stream, delicious home cooking, bicycle rental. Recommended.

$ pp Altos del Sur
Villa Turismo, T0294-449 8730, www.altosdelsur.bolsonweb.com.
Peaceful hostel in a lovely setting, HI member, shared rooms and private doubles, dinner available, will collect from bus station if you call ahead.

$ pp El Pueblito
4 km north in Barrio Luján, 1 km off Ruta 40 (take bus from Plaza Principal, US$0.50), T0294-449 3560, www.elpueblitohostel.com.ar.
Wooden building in open country, dorms (US$12-15 depending on season and if with breakfast), also has cabins (**$$**, laundry facilities, shop, open fire. Recommended.

$ pp Hostel La Casa del Viajero
Libertad y Las Flores, Barrio Usina, T0294-449 3092, www.lacasadelviajero.com.ar.
A little out of the centre, in a beautful setting. Surrounded by organic gardens, simple, comfortable rooms (dorms – US$15, and private – US$25). Call them for pick up from the centre of town.

$ pp Refugio Patagónico
Islas Malvinas y Pastorino, T0294-448 3628, www.refugiopatagonico.com.
Basic hostel, with small dorms (US$12.50) and doubles (**$$**), in a spacious house set in open fields, views of Piltriquitrón, 5 blocks from the plaza.

Camping

La Chacra
Av Belgrano 1128, T0294-449 2111, www.campinglachacra.com.ar.
15 mins' walk from town, well shaded, good facilities, lively atmosphere in season.

Quem-Quem
On river bank Río Quemquemtreu, T0294-449 3550, www.quem-quem.com.ar.
Lovely site, hot showers, good walks, free pickup from town.

There are many *cabañas* in picturesque settings with lovely views in the Villa Turismo, about US$60-100 for 2 people.

Around El Bolsón

Club Andino Piltriquitrón
T0294-449 2600, www.capiltriquitron.com.ar, manages some 10 refugios in the mountains around El Bolsón. Most open Oct-Mar.
Most offer simple accommodation (US$10-12 per person, sleeping bag required), a hearty breakfast (US$3.75), other meals (US$5-7.50), basic supplies (including home-baked bread and home-brewed beer), camping and hot showers. They have radio communication with each other and with town.

$$$ Frontera
Ruta Nacional 40, 9 km from Lago Puelo, isolated in woodland, off the main road heading for Esquel, T0294-447 3092, www.frontera-patagonia.com.ar.
Cabañas for 4 and *hostería*, in native forest, furnished to a very high standard, delicious breakfasts and dinner if required.

$$$ Lodge Casa Puelo
R16, Km 10, T0294-449 9539, www.casapuelo.com.ar.
Cabañas for up to 6. Beautifully designed rooms and self-catering cabins right against forested mountains where you can walk, good service, English-speaking owner Miguel, who knows the local area intimately. Very comfortable, dinner offered. Recommended.

$$$-$$ Cabañas Cerro La Momia
Ruta 71, Villa Lago Rivadavia T011-4964 2586.
Very good *cabañas* for up to 6, picturesque setting among fruit orchards and wooded slopes. Restaurant, excursions arranged.

$$$-$$ La Yoica
Just off R16, Km 5, T0294-449 9200, www.layoica.com.ar.
Charming Scottish owners make you feel at home in these traditional *cabañas* set in lovely countryside with great views. Price for up to 4 people.

$ pp La Pasarela
2 km from town, T0294-449 9061, www.lpuelo.com.ar.
Dorms (US$10 pp), cabins and camping US$7.50, shops, fuel.

Esquel
Ask at tourist office for lodgings in private houses.

$$$ Angelina
Av Alvear 758, T02945-452763, www.hosteriaangelina.com.ar.
Good value, welcoming, big breakfast, English and Italian spoken, open high season only.

$$$ Canela
Los Notros y Los Radales, Villa Ayelén, on road to Trevelin, T02945-453890, www.canelaesquel.com.
Bed and breakfast and tea room in a lovely, quiet residential area, English spoken, owner knowledgeable about Patagonia.

$$$ Cumbres Blancas
Av Ameghino 1683, T02945-455100, www.cumbres blancas.com.ar.
Attractive modern building, a little out of centre, very comfortable, spacious rooms, sauna, gym, airy restaurant. Recommended.

$$$-$$ La Chacra
Km 5 on Ruta 259 towards Trevelin, T02945-452802, www.lachacrapatagonia.com.
Relaxing, spacious rooms, huge breakfast, Welsh and English spoken.

$$ La Posada
Chacabuco 905, T02945-454095, www.laposadaesquel.blogspot.com.ar.
Tasteful B&B in quiet part of town, lovely lounge, very comfortable, excellent value.

$$ La Tour D'Argent
San Martín 1063, T02945-454612, www.latourdargent.com.ar.
Bright, comfortable, family-run, very good value.

$ pp Anochecer Andino
Av Ameghino 482, 4 blocks from the commercial centre and 2 from the mountains, T02945-450498.
Basic, helpful, can organize ski passes and excursions. They also can provide dinner and have a bar.

$ pp Casa del Pueblo
San Martín 661, T02945-450581, www.esquelcasadel pueblo.com.ar.
Smallish rooms but good atmosphere ($$ double), laundry, HI discounts, organizes adventure activities.

$ pp Hospedaje Rowlands
behind Rivadavia 330, T02945-452578, gales01@hotmail.com.
Warm family welcome, Welsh spoken, breakfast extra, basic rooms with shared bath and a double with bath ($), good value.

$ pp Planeta Hostel
Roca 458, T02945-456846, www.planetahostel.com.
4- to 6-bed dorms (US$15-18), doubles $$, shared bath, specialize in snowboarding, climbing and mountain biking, English spoken.

$ Res El Cisne
Chacabuco 778, T02945-452256.
Basic small rooms, hot water, quiet, well kept, good value, breakfast extra.

Camping

Millalen
Av Ameghino 2063 (5 blocks from bus terminal), T02945-456164.
Good services and cabins.

Trevelin

$$$ Casa de Piedra
Almirante Brown 244, T02945-480357, www.casadepiedratrevelin.com.
Stone and wood cottage in the suburbs. King-size beds, heating and a charming common area, popular.

$$ Pezzi
Sarmiento 351, T02945-480146, hpezzi@intramed.net.
Charming family house with a beautiful garden, English spoken. Recommended.

$ pp Casa Verde Hostal
Los Alerces s/n (9203), T02945-480091, www.casaverdehostel.com.ar.
Charming owners, spacious log cabin with panoramic views, comfortable dorms for 4-6 and doubles ($$), laundry, HI member, breakfast extra. English and Welsh spoken, excursions into Los Alerces, bikes for hire. Highly recommended.

Camping

Many sites, especially on the road to Futaleufú and Chile; also many *cabañas*; ask for full list at tourist office.

Parque Nacional Los Alerces

East side of Lago Futalaufquen

$$$$ El Aura
Lago Verde Wilderness Resort, T011-4816 5348 (Buenos Aires), www.elaurapatagonia.com.
Exquisite taste in these 3 stone cabins and a guesthouse on the shore of Lago Verde. Luxury in every respect, attention to detail, ecologically friendly. Impressive place.

$$$ Hostería Quime Quipan
T02945-425 423, www.hosteriaquimequipan.com.ar.
Comfortable rooms with lake views, dinner included. Recommended.

$$ Bahía Rosales
T02945-15-403413, www.bahiarosales.com.
Comfortable *cabaña* for 6 with kitchenette and bath, $ pp in small basic cabin without bath, and camping in open ground, hot showers, restaurant, all recommended.

$$ Cabañas Tejas Negras
Next to Pucón Pai, T02945-471046, www.tejasnegras.com.ar.
Really comfortable *cabañas* for 4, also good camp site, and tea room.

$$ Motel Pucón Pai
T02945-451425.
Slightly spartan rooms, but good restaurant, recommended for fishing; basic campsite with hot showers.

Camping

Several campsites at Villa Futalaufquen (eg **Nahuel Pan**), Lagos Rivadavia, Verde and Río Arrayanes.

Restaurants

El Bolsón

$$$ Pasiones Argentinas
Av Belgrano y Berutti, T0294-448 3616, www.facebook.com/pasiones.restaurant.
Traditional Argentine food in a wonderful cosy setting.

$$ Amancay
San Martín 3217, T0294-449 2222, www.hotelamancaybolson.com.
Good *parrilla* and home-made pastas.

$$ Arcimbaldo
Av San Martin 2790, T0294-449 2137.
Good-value *tenedor libre*, smoked fish and draft beer, open for breakfast.

$$ Jauja
Av San Martín 2867, T0294-449 2448.
The best restaurant in town is a great meeting place, serving delicious fish and pasta. It also makes outstanding ice cream from organic milk and local berries: there are 11 varieties of chocolate alone. English spoken.

$$ Martin Sheffield
Av San Martín 2760, T0294-449 1920.
Central, good food, Patagonian specialities, menu of the day, with or without a drink.

Cafés

Cerveza El Bolsón
RN 258, Km 123.9, T0294-449 2595,
www.cervezaselbolson.com.
Microbrewery where you can see how the beer
is made and sample the 18 varieties. *Picadas* are
served with beer, and you can sit outside in the
gardens. Highly recommended.

El Rey de Sandwich
Roca 345.
Good-value sandwiches at this *rotisería*, next to
Via Bariloche bus terminal.

Esquel

\$\$ Don Chiquino
Behind Av Ameghino 1641, T02945-450035.
Delicious pastas in a fun atmosphere with plenty
of games brought to the tables by magician
owner Tito. Recommended.

\$\$ La Española
Rivadavia 740, T02945-451509.
Excellent beef, salad bar and tasty pasta.
Recommended.

\$\$ Vascongada
9 de Julio y Mitre, T02945-452229.
Traditional style, trout and other local specialities.

\$ La Tour D'Argent
San Martín 1063, T02945-454612,
www.latourdargent.com.ar.
Delicious local specialities, good-value set
meals and a warm ambience in this popular,
traditional restaurant.

Cafés

María Castaña
Rivadavia y 25 de Mayo.
Popular, good coffee.

Trevelin

\$\$ Parrilla Oregon
Av San Martín y JM Thomas, T02945-480408,
www.oregontrevelin.com.ar/restaurante.html.
Large meals (particularly breakfasts), set menus
based on *parrilla* and pastas.

\$ Nain Maggie
Perito Moreno 179, T02945-480232,
nainmaggieguia patagonia.net.
Tea room, offering *té galés* and *torta negra*,
expensive but good.

Heladería Artesanal Serenata y Chocolatería Mizke
Rotonda 28 de Julio 190, T02945-48012.
Decent chocolates and ice cream on the
central plaza.

What to do

El Bolsón
Grado 42, *Av Belgrano 406, T0294-449 3124,*
www.grado42.com. Tours to El Maitén to take
La Trochita, 7 hrs; also short excursions in the
surroundings and day trips to Parque Nacional
Los Alerces, as well as wide range of adventure
activities. Recommended.

Esquel

Fishing
Tourist office has a list of guides and companies
hiring out equipment.

Skiing
One of Argentina's cheapest, with laid back
family atmosphere, **La Hoya**, 15 km north, has
22 km of pistes, 8 ski-lifts. For skiing information
ask at **Club Andino Esquel** (Pellegrini 787,
T02945-453248); travel agencies run 3 daily
minibuses to La Hoya from Esquel. Details
of facilities, lifts and passes can be found on
www.patagoniaexpress.com/la_hoya.html,
or phone **CAM** (La Hoya, T02945-451927).

Tour operators
Frontera Sur, *Sarmiento 784, T02945-450505,*
www.fronterasur.net. Good company offering
adventure tourism of all sorts, as well as more
traditional excursions, ski equipment and trekking.
Patagonia Verde, *9 de Julio 926, T02945-454396,*
www.patagonia-verde.com.ar. Boat trips to
El Alerzal on Lago Menéndez, rafting on
Río Corcovado, tickets for *La Trochita* and for
Ruta 40 to El Calafate. Also range of adventure
activities, horse riding, short local excursions
and ski passes. Ask about lodging at **Lago
Verde**. English spoken. Excellent company,
very professional.

Transport

El Bolsón
Bus Several daily from **Bariloche** and **Esquel**,
with **Don Otto**, **TAC**, **Via Bariloche**. Check
with **Vía Bariloche**, T0800-333 7575, www.
viabariloche.com.ar, for timings. Heavily over-

booked in high season: US$9.50-11, 2 hrs to **Bariloche**; US$13.50 El Bolsón-**Esquel**, 2½-3 hrs. Other destinations from these 2 towns. Buses to **Lago Puelo** with **Vía Bariloche** every 2 hrs, 4 on Sun, 45 mins, US$5. To **Parque Nacional Los Alerces** (highly recommended route), with **Transportes Esquel** (from ACA service station), once a day, US$10, 4-5 hrs, via Cholila and Epuyen.

Esquel

Air Airport, 20 km east of Esquel, T02945-451676, by paved road, US$20 by taxi, US$14 by bus. To **Buenos Aires**, **Comodora Rivadavia** and **Trelew**. LADE (Av Alvear 1085, T02945-452124) to **Bariloche**, **Comodora Rivadavia**, **El Calafate**, **Mar del Plata** and several other destinations in Patagonia; weekly departures.

Bus Terminal at Av Alvear 1871, T02945-451584, US$2.50 by taxi from centre, it has toilets, *kiosko*, *locutorio* with internet, café, tourist information desk, left luggage. To **Buenos Aires** change in Bariloche, with **Andesmar**, T02945-450143, or **Vía Bariloche**, T02945-454676, US$152-162. To **Bariloche** (via El Bolsón, 2½ hrs), 4-5 hrs, US$13-15, **Don Otto** (T02945-453012), **Vía Bariloche**, **TAC** and others. To **Puerto Madryn**, 9 hrs, US$68, **Ejecutivo de Chubut**. To **Trelew**, US$45-50, 8-9 hrs overnight, **Don Otto** and **Ejecutivo de Chubut**. To **Río Gallegos** (for connections to El Calafate or Ushuaia), take a bus to Trelew and change there. To **Trevelin**, **Vía Trevelin** (T02945-455222) and **Jacobsen** (T02945-454676, www. transportejacobsen.com.ar), Mon-Fri, hourly 0600-2300, fewer, from 0730, at weekends, 30 mins, US$1. To **Paso Futaleufú** (Chilean border) via Trevelin, **Jacobsen** 0900, 1900 Mon, Wed and Fri (Tue and Thu 1800 only), return 0800, 1800, US$7. Buses connect there for Chaitén.

Car hire Los Alerces, Sarmiento 763, T02945-456008, www.losalercesrentacar.com.ar. Good value, good cars, top service.

Train *La Trochita* (which Paul Theroux called the Old Patagonian Express) runs from Esquel to Nahuel Pan (19 km). In 2017 it ran Mon-Sat at 1000 and 1400 in Jan-Feb, Tue-Sat at 1000 in Mar and Sat only at 1000 in Apr. Additional services usually in high season, Carnaval, Easter, Jul, summer from Nov. See website below for 2017-2018 schedule. It takes 2½ hrs, US$49 return, children under 5 free. At remote Nahuel Pan, there is just a small terrace of houses, home to a Mapuche community, who sell delicious cakes and display their knitwear, some of it very fine quality. In high season a service runs on Sat from El Maitén at the northernmost end of the line to **Desvío Thomae** (55 km), US$44; occasional additional services midweek. Information, in English including schedules in El Maitén, T02945-495190, and in Esquel T02945-451403. See www. patagoniaexpress.com/el_trochita.htm. Tickets from tour operators, or from Esquel station office, Urquiza y Roggero.

Parque Nacional Los Alerces

Bus From **Esquel** (Jacobsen, see above) runs daily at 0700 and 1330 from Esquel to Lago Puelo, US$15, along the east side of Lago Futalaufquen. It returns at 1500. From **Trevelin**, **Martín** at 1730, return 2030, US$15-20.

Patagonia

Patagonia is the vast, windy, mostly treeless plateau covering all of southern Argentina south of the Río Colorado. The Atlantic coast is rich in marine life; penguins, whales and seals can all be seen around Puerto Madryn. The far south offers spectacular scenery in the Parque Nacional Los Glaciares, with the mighty Perito Moreno and Upsala glaciers, as well as challenging trekking around Mount Fitz Roy. The contrasts are extreme: thousands of prehistoric handprints can be found in the Cueva de las Manos, but in most of Patagonia there's less than one person to each square kilometre; far from the densely wooded Andes, there are petrified forests in the deserts; and one legacy of brave early pioneers is the over-abundance of tea and cakes served up by Argentina's Welsh community in the Chubut valley.

Patagonia's appeal lies in its emptiness. Vegetation is sparse, since a relentless dry wind blows continually from the west, raising a haze of dust in summer, which can turn to mud in winter. Rainfall is high only in the foothills of the Andes, where dense virgin beech forests run from Neuquén to Tierra del Fuego. During a brief period in spring, after the snows melt, there is grass on the plateau, but in the desert-like expanses of eastern Patagonia, water can be pumped only in the deep crevices which intersect the land from west to east. This is where the great sheep estancias lie, sheltered from the wind. There is little agriculture except in the north, in the valleys of the Colorado and Negro rivers, where alfalfa is grown and cattle are raised. Centres of population are tiny and most of the towns are small ports on the Atlantic coast. Only Comodoro Rivadavia has a population over 100,000, thanks to its oil industry. Patagonia has attracted many generations of people getting away from it all, from Welsh religious pioneers to Butch Cassidy and the Sundance Kid, and tourism is an increasingly important source of income.

South of Bahía Blanca

the doorstep to Patagonia

Viedma and Carmen de Patagones *Colour map 8, C4.*

These two pleasant towns lie on opposite banks of the Río Negro, about 27 km from its mouth and 270 km south of Bahía Blanca. **Carmen de Patagones** (population 40,000) was founded in 1779 and many early pioneer buildings remain in the pretty streets winding down to the river. There's a fascinating museum, **Museo Histórico Regional "Emma Nozzi"** ① *JJ Biedma 64, T02920-462729, Mon-Fri 1000-1200, 1500-1700, Sat-Sun and bank holidays 1700-1900*, with artefacts of the indigenous

Essential Patagonia

Getting there and around

Air

There are daily flights from Buenos Aires to Viedma, Trelew, Puerto Madryn, Comodoro Rivadavia, Río Gallegos, Río Grande, El Calafate's airport, Lago Argentino, and Ushuaia. **Aerolíneas Argentinas** (AR) and **LADE** fly these routes and it is vital that you book flights well ahead in the summer (December to February) and the winter ski season for Ushuaia (July and August). At other times of year, flights can be booked with just a few days' notice. **LATAM**, flies to Ushuaia from Argentine destinations as well as in summer. Even if a flight is sold out, check again on the day of departure.

Flying between Patagonian towns is complicated without flying all the way back to Buenos Aires, since there are often only weekly fights with **LADE**. The baggage allowance is 15 kg. Overnight buses may be more convenient.

Road

The principal roads in Patagonia are the Ruta 3, which runs down the Atlantic coast, and the Ruta 40 on the west. One of Argentina's main arteries, Ruta 3 runs from Buenos Aires to Ushuaia, interrupted by the car ferry crossing through Chilean territory across the Magellan Strait to Tierra del Fuego. It is paved in Argentine territory, but sections on Chilean Tierra del Fuego (Cerro Sombrero to San Sebastán) are *ripio*. Regular buses run along the whole stretch, more frequently between October and April, and there are towns with services and accommodation every few hundred km. Ruta 40, which was at the time of writing slowly being paved, zigzags across the moors from Zapala to Lago Argentino, near El Calafate, ending at Cabo Vírgenes. It's by far the more interesting road, lonely and bleak, offering fine views of the Andes and plenty of wildlife as well as giving access to many national parks. A number of companies run daily tourist bus services in summer between Los Antiguos and El Chaltén. The east–west road across Patagonia, from south of Esquel in the Lake District to Comodoro Rivadavia, is paved, and there's a good paved highway running from Bariloche through Neuquén to San Antonio Oeste.

Although they are increasingly being paved, many of the roads in southern Argentina are still *ripio* (graveled), limiting maximum speeds to 60 kph, or less where surfaces are poor, very hard on low-clearance vehicles. Strong winds can also be a hazard. Windscreen and headlight protection is a good idea (expensive to buy, but can be improvised with wire mesh for windscreen, strips cut from plastic bottles for lights). There are cattle grids (*guardaganados*), even on main highways, usually signposted; cross them very slowly. Always carry plenty of fuel, as service stations may be as much as 300 km apart and as a precaution in case of a breakdown, carry warm clothing and make sure your car has anti-freeze. Petrol prices in Chubut, Santa Cruz and Tierra del Fuego provinces are 40% cheaper than in the rest of the country (10-15% for diesel).

Accommodation

In summer hotel prices are very high, especially in El Calafate and El Chaltén. From November onwards you must reserve hotels a week or more in advance. Camping is increasingly popular and estancias may be hospitable to travellers who are stuck for a bed. Many estancias, especially in Santa Cruz province, offer transport, excursions and food as well as accommodation: see www.estanciasdesantacruz.com and www.interpatagonia.com/estancias. **ACA** establishments, which charge roughly the same prices all over Argentina, are good value in Patagonia.

inhabitants, missionaries and gauchos; good guided tours. On 7 March the Battle of Patagones (1827) is celebrated in a week-long colourful fiesta of horse displays and fine food.

Although Patagones is older and more charming, most services are in **Viedma** (population 60,000), capital of Río Negro Province. A quiet place, its main attraction is the perfect bathing area along the shaded south bank of the river. The two towns are linked by two bridges and a four-minute frequent ferry crossing (US$1).

Along the coast

El Condór is a beautiful beach 30 km south of Viedma (six buses daily in summer), with hotels, restaurants, shops and free camping on the beach 2 km south (most facilities have reduced hours or close entirely after February). The sealion colony, **Lobería Punta Bermeja**, is 30 km further southwest; there's a daily bus from Viedma in summer and hitching is easy.

Bahía San Blas is an attractive small resort and renowned shark fishing area, 100 km from Patagones (tourist information at www.vivesanblas.com.ar in Spanish), with plentiful accommodation.

Listings South of Bahía Blanca

Tourist information

Viedma has the **provincial tourist office** (Av Caseros 1425, T02920-422150, www. rionegrotur.gob.ar (Spanish only), Mon-Fri 0700-1400, 1800-2000) and a helpful **municipal tourist office** (Av Francisco de Viedma 51, T02920-427171, www.viedma.gov.ar/turismo/, Mon-Fri 0800-2000, Sat-Sun in winter 1200-1800; longer hrs in summer). Also helpful is the **tourist office** in Patagones (Mitre 84, T02920-464819, www.patagones.gov.ar, Mon-Fri 0800-2000, Sat-Sun 0930-1330, 1530-1930). Another office is open Mon-Fri 0900-1900, Sat-Sun 1200-1800 at Balneario El Cóndor, T02920-497148.

Where to stay

Viedma

$$$ Nijar
Mitre 490, T02920-422833, www.hotelnijar.com.
Most comfortable, smart, modern, good service.

$$ Peumayen
Buenos Aires 334, T02920-425222,
www.hotelpeumayen.com.ar.
Old-fashioned friendly place on the plaza.

$$ Res Roca
Roca 347, T02920-431241.
A cheap option with comfortable beds, helpful staff, breakfast included.

Transport

Viedma

Air Airport 5 km south. **LADE** (Saavedra 576, T02920-424420, www.lade.com.ar) fly to **Buenos Aires**, **Mar del Plata**, **Bahía Blanca**, **Comodoro Rivadavia** and other Patagonian destinations.

Bus Terminal in Viedma at Av Pte Perón y Guido, 15 blocks from plaza (www.terminalpatagonia. com.ar); taxi US$3.50. To **Buenos Aires** 13 hrs, daily, US$80-100, **Don Otto** and others. To **Puerto Madryn**, 6½ hrs, several daily, US$35-40, **Don Otto** and others. To **Bahía Blanca**, 4 hrs, many daily, US$15-25.

Ferry Between Viedma and **Carmen de Patagones**, small boat, every 15 mins, 4-min crossing US$0.40.

Train The Tren Patagónico runs from Viedma to **Bariloche** usually on Fri, returning usually on Sun; check the website www.trenpatagonico-sa.com.ar for latest information. It's a comfortable overnight service with 3 classes: 1st US$61, Pullman US$72 and sleeper US$103. Viedma station, T02920-422130. There are several intermediate stops, including San Antonio Oeste (T02934-421313) and Ingeniero Jacobacci (T02940-432125). Always check in advance if the service is running.

Puerto Madryn is a seaside town 250 km south of San Antonio Oeste. It stands on the wide bay of Golfo Nuevo, the perfect base for the Península Valdés and its extraordinary array of wildlife, just 70 km east. It was the site of the first Welsh landing in 1865 and is named after the Welsh home of the colonist, Jones Parry.

The area around Puerto Madryn, especially the Península Valdés, is a spectacular region for wildlife. There are **elephant seal** and **sea lion** colonies at the base of chalky cliffs; breeding grounds for **Southern right whales** in the sheltered Golfo Nuevo and the Golfo San José; and **guanacos**, **rheas**, **maras** (a large rodent, sometimes called the **Patagonian hare**) and **armadillos** everywhere on land. Whales can be seen from June to mid-December but are particularly interesting with their young in September-October. The sea lion breeding season runs from early December to mid-February, but visiting is good up to late April.

> **Tip...**
> When taking boat trips be certain that you and the operator understand what you are paying for.

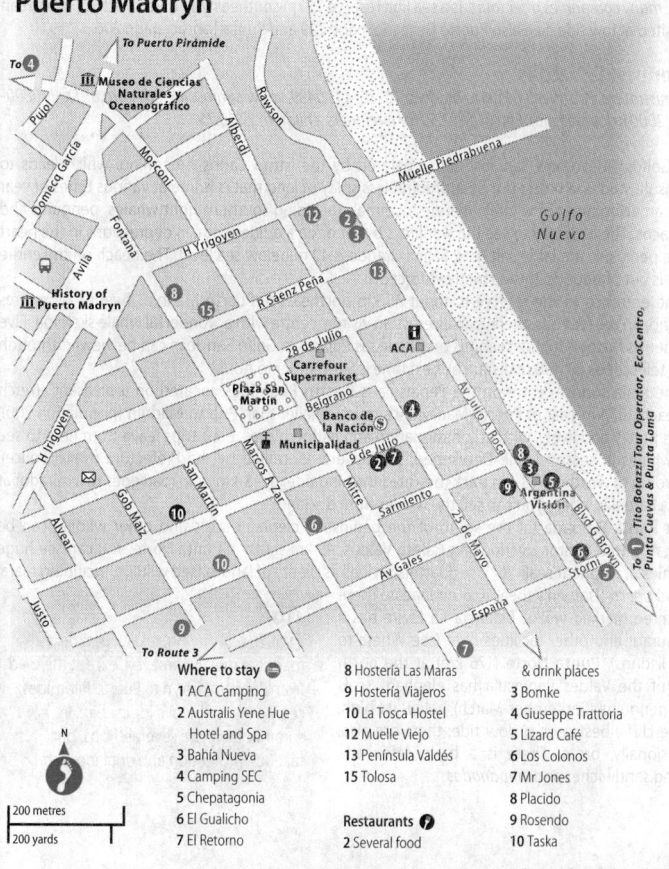

Puerto Madryn

To Puerto Pirámide

To 4

III Museo de Ciencias Naturales y Oceanográfico

Puijol

Domeca García

Alberdi

Mosconi

Rawson

Muelle Piedrabuena

Golfo Nuevo

Fontana

Avila

H Yrigoyen

History of III Puerto Madryn

R Sáenz Peña

28 de Julio

Carrefour Supermarket

Plaza San Martín

Belgrano

Banco de la Nación

Municipalidad

9 de Julio

ACA

Av Julio A Roca

Tito Botazzi Tour Operator, EcoCentro, Punta Cuevas & Punta Loma

H Yrigoyen

Gob Maíz

San Martín

Marcos A Zar

Mitre

Sarmiento

25 de Mayo

Argentina Visión

Blvd G Brown

Alvear

Justo

Av Gales

Storni

Av Gales

España

To Route 3

N

200 metres	
200 yards	

Where to stay
1 ACA Camping
2 Australis Yene Hue Hotel and Spa
3 Bahía Nueva
4 Camping SEC
5 Chepatagonia
6 El Gualicho
7 El Retorno

8 Hostería Las Maras
9 Hostería Viajeros
10 La Tosca Hostel
12 Muelle Viejo
13 Península Valdés
15 Tolosa

Restaurants
2 Several food

& drink places
3 Bomke
4 Giuseppe Trattoria
5 Lizard Café
6 Los Colonos
7 Mr Jones
8 Placido
9 Rosendo
10 Taska

Bull elephant seals begin to claim their territory in late August and the breeding season is late September/early November. They return to sea for a month then are back on land mid-December-March to change skin. Orcas can be seen attacking seals at Punta Norte in February/March.

Sights

There is a popular beach in the town itself, and sea lions can be seen in Puerto Madryn harbour. **EcoCentro** ① *Julio Verne 3784, T0280-488 3173, www.ecocentro.org.ar, Wed-Mon 1500-2000 (2100 high season), US$9.50*, is an inspired interactive sea life information centre, art gallery, reading room and café, perched on a cliff at the south end of town, with fantastic views of the whole bay. Staff at the EcoCentro study the marine ecosystems. **Museo de Ciencias Naturales y Oceanográfico** ① *Domecq García y J Menéndez, T0280-445 1139, Mon-Fri 1000-1600, Sat 1500-1900, US$0.75*, is an informative museum with displays of local flora and fauna. Run by the same museum is a **study centre and small museum** ① *Mon-Fri 0830-1130*, of the history of Puerto Madryn, housed in the old railway station, next door to the current bus station (Dr Ávila 350). There is a handicraft market on the main plaza.

You can often spot whales directly from the coast at the long beach of **Playa El Doradillo**, 16 km northeast (June-October). **Punta Loma** ① *0800-2000; US$7.50, children US$3.75, information and video, many companies offer tours*, is a sea lion reserve 15 km southeast of Puerto Madryn, which can be visited at low tide. See also Puerto Deseado, page 209 and Punta Tombo, page 206.

★Península Valdés

Administration, Fournier 54, Puerto Madryn, T0280-445 0489, www.peninsulavaldes.org.ar. Daily 0800-2100 (2000 in low season). Entry US$21.50 for foreigners, children US$10.75.

The Golfos Nuevo and San José are separated by the Istmo Carlos Ameghino, which leads to Península Valdés, a bleak, but beautiful treeless splay of land that is home at various times of year to an amazing array of wildlife: marine mammals including southern right whales, penguins and guanacos. The best way to see the wildlife is by car or on a guided tour. In depressions in the heart of the peninsula are large salt flats; Salina Grande is 42 m below sea level. The beach on the entire coast is out of bounds; this is strictly enforced.

The entrance to the reserve is about 45 km northeast of Puerto Madryn. Twenty kilometres beyond, on the isthmus, there is an interesting visitors centre with a wonderful whale skeleton. Five kilometres further on, the seabirds on Isla de los Pájaros in Golfo San Jose can be viewed through fixed telescopes (at 400 m distance); best time is September to April.

The main tourist centre on the Peninsula is **Puerto Pirámide**s, located on a pleasant stretch of beach 107 km east of Puerto Madryn. It's much smaller than Puerto Madryn (population 700), but is pretty and lively, with accommodation and eating places. Boat trips leave from here to see the whales in season (June-December); sailings are controlled by the Prefectura (Naval Police), according to weather. A 3-km track (beware incoming tide) or 15-km *ripio* road goes to a mirador at Punta Pardelas where you can see the whales from dry land

At **Punta Delgada** (at the south of the peninsula) elephant seals and other wildlife can be seen. At Punta Cantor, overlooking **Caleta Valdés**, 45 km south of Punta Norte, you can see huge colonies of elephant seals at close quarters, as well as plenty of land-based wildlife, including mara, *ñandú petiso* (Darwin's rhea) and guanacos. There are three marked walks. **Estancia La Elvira** has a restaurant and other facilities here (see Where to stay listings). **Punta Norte** (176 km) at the north end of the Valdés Peninsula has elephant seals and penguins (September-March) below its high, white cliffs, best seen at low tide; there are also, occasionally, orcas. There is a basic café here, selling sandwiches and *empanadas*.

Tip...
If you're self-driving, take your time, as roads are mostly unpaved, except the road from Puerto Madryn to Puerto Pirámides; see Transport, below, for car hire. In summer there are several shops, but take sun protection and drinking water.

Tourist information

The **tourist office** in Puerto Madryn (Av Roca 223, T0280-445 3504, www.madryn.travel, daily 0700-2100 (Dec-Feb from 0800); also at the bus station, daily 0700-2100), is extremely helpful. There is another office in Puerto Pirámides (Av de las Ballenas s/n, T0280-449 5048, www.puertopiramides.gov.ar).

Where to stay

Puerto Madryn
Book ahead in summer, and whale season.

$$$$ Australis Yene Hue Hotel and Spa
Roca 33, T0280-445 2937,
www.hotelesaustralis.com.ar.
Luxury hotel on the beachfront with a small spa, modern rooms, and nice buffet breakfast. Ask for a room with a view.

$$$$-$$$ Península Valdés
Av Roca 155, T0280-447 1292,
www.hotelpeninsula.com.ar.
Luxurious seafront hotel with great views. Spa, sauna, gym.

$$$ Bahía Nueva
Av Roca 67, T0280-445 1677,
www.bahianueva.com.ar.
One of the best sea front hotels, quite small but comfortable rooms, professional staff, cheaper in low season.

$$$ Hostería Las Maras
Marcos A Zar 64, T0280-445 3215.
Nice modern place, well-decorated rooms with large beds, cheaper with fan, parking.

$$$ Tolosa
Roque Sáenz Peña 253, T0280-447 1850,
www.hoteltolosa.com.ar.
Extremely comfortable, modern, great breakfasts. Disabled access. Recommended.

$$ Hostería Viajeros
Gob Maíz 545, T0280-445 6457,
www.hostelviajeros.com.ar.
Rooms for 2, 3 and 4 people, big kitchen/dining room, lawn, parking, new superior rooms on 2nd floor (**$$$**), helpful, family-run.

$$ Muelle Viejo
H Yrigoyen 38, T0280-447 1284,
www.muelleviejo.com.
Ask for the comfortable modernized rooms in this funny old place. Rooms for 4 are excellent value.

$ pp Chepatagonia
Alfonsina Storni 16, T0280-445 5783,
www.chepatagoniahostel.com.ar.
Good view of the beach (and whales in season), helpful owners, mixed and single dorms, doubles with shared bath (**$$**), lockers, bicycle hire and many other services. A good choice.

$ pp El Gualicho
Marcos A Zar 480, T0280-445 4163,
www.elgualicho.com.ar.
Decent budget option, some double rooms (**$$**), HI discounts, enthusiastic staff, English-speaking staff, heating, free pick up from bus terminal, *parrilla*, garden, bikes for hire, runs tours, parking, pool table. Recommended.

$ El Retorno
Bartolomé Mitre 798, T0280-445 6044,
www.elretornohostel.com.ar.
3 blocks from beach, hot water, lockers, cosy common area, free bus terminal pick-up. Double rooms available (**$$**). Also rents apartments with seaview (**$$$**).

$ pp La Tosca Hostel
Sarmiento 437, T0280-445 6133,
www.latoscahostel.com.
Private rooms for 2-4 people with all mod cons, dorms also have bathrooms, free pick-up from bus station if you call them, helpful and welcoming. Organizes tours and provides advice about the area. Kitchen with *parrilla* open 24 hrs, big breakfast included in price. Highly recommended.

Camping

ACA
Blvd Brown 3869, 4 km south of town at Punta Cuevas, T0280-488 3485, www.acamadryn. com.ar. Open year-round. Cheaper rates Apr-Nov.
Hot showers, café, shop, also duplexes for 4-6, no kitchen facilities, shady trees, close to the sea. US$10 per night.

Camping SEC
Río Mayo 800, 5 km from town centre, T0280-447 3015.
Basic campsite from US$6 per night.

Península Valdés

Puerto Pirámides

$$$$-$$$ Las Restingas
1ra Bajada al Mar, T0280-449 5101,
www.lasrestingas.com.
Exclusive, 8 rooms with sea views, very comfortable, with sophisticated regional restaurant. Good deals available in low season.

$$$ ACA Motel
Julio A Roca s/n, T0280-449 5004,
www.motelacapiramides.com.
Welcoming, handy for the beach, with good seafood restaurant (you might spot whales from its terrace). There is also an **ACA** service station (daily) with good café and shop.

$$$ Cabañas en el Mar
Av de las Ballenas y 1ra Bajada al Mar,
T0280-449 5049, www.piramides.net.
Comfortable, well-equipped 2- to 6-bed *cabañas* with sea view.

$$$ Del Nómade
Av de las Ballenas s/n, T0280-449 5044,
www.ecohosteria.com.ar.
Eco lodge using solar power and water recycling, buffet breakfast, heating, café, specializes in wildlife watching, nature and underwater photography, kayaking, scuba diving, adventure sports, courses offered. Discounts via the website.

$$$ The Paradise
2da Bajada al Mar, T0280-449 5030,
www.hosteriaparadise.com.ar.
Large comfortable rooms, suites with jacuzzis, fine seafood restaurant.

$$ La Nube del Angel
2da Bajada al Mar, T0280-449 5070, www.
lanubedelangel.com.ar. Open all year.
Lovely owners, small *cabañas* for 2-6 people, quiet, 5 mins' walk from the beach.

Camping

Municipal campsite by the black sand beach (T0280-15-420 2760). Hot showers in evening, good, get there early to secure a place, US$6 per night. Do not camp on the beach: people have been swept away by the incoming tide.

Estancias

The peninsula is dotted with large estancias, 56 in total, mostly dedicated to sheep farming, but some with accommodation and rural tourism activities.

$$$$ El Pedral
Punta Ninfas, T0280-15-457 2551,
www.reservaelpedral.com. Open all year.
By a pebble beach, with lots of wildlife-watching opportunities, farm activities, horse riding, zodiac trips (extra), guesthouse with en suite rooms, restaurant and bar, swimming pool.

$$$$ Faro Punta Delgada
Punta Delgada, T0280-445 8444,
www.puntadelgada.com.
Next to a lighthouse, amazing setting, half and full board, excellent food, very helpful. Recommended; book in advance, no credit cards.

$$$ La Elvira
Caleta Valdés, near Punta Cantor, T0280-
445 8444 (contact Gonzalo Hernández).
Traditional Patagonian dishes and comfortable accommodation (B&B, half and full board available).

$$$ San Lorenzo
On RP3, 20 km southwest of Punta Norte,
T0280-445 8444 (contact through Argentina
Visión in Puerto Madryn, see Tour operators).
Great for day excursions to a beautiful stretch of coast to see penguins and fossils and do birdwatching and horse treks.

Restaurants

Puerto Madryn

Excellent seafood restaurants, mostly charging similar prices, but quality varies. There are also less-touristy takeaways. 1 block in 9 de Julio between 25 de Mayo and Mitre has an interesting mix of food and drink places, including a winebar, a craft beer pub and several restaurants.

$$$ Placido
Av Roca 506, T0280-445 5991, www.placido.com.ar.
On the beach, great location and service, but food can be hit and miss. Seafood and vegetarian options, also cheaper pasta dishes.

$$$ Taska
9 de Julio 461, T0280-447 4003.
Excellent food, with Basque influence – book ahead. Highly recommended.

$$ Giuseppe Trattoria
25 de Mayo 388, T0280-456 891.
With its red-checkered tablecloths and cosy family vibe, this pizza and pasta restaurant is quite popular with locals. The large portions certainly don't hurt.

$$ Los Colonos
Av Roca y A Storni, T0280-445 8486.
Quirky restaurant built into the wooden hull of a boat, plenty of maritime heritage, cosy, *parrilla*, seafood and pastas.

$ Rosendo
Av Roca 549, 1st floor, T0280-445 0062.
Open lunchtime and evenings in high season, from 1700 in low season.
Snack bar/café overlooking the main street. Excellent home-made *empanadas*, snacks, cocktails and wines. Reading and games room. Recommended.

Cafés

Bomke
Av Roca 540, T0280-447 4094,
www.bomke.com.ar. Open late.
Popular ice cream place with outdoor seating at the back. Excellent ice creams. Recommended.

Lizard Café
Av Roca y Av Galés, near the seafront.
Lively funky place with friendly people. Good for plentiful pizzas or for late night drinks.

Mr Jones
9 de Julio 116, T0280-447 5368 (see Facebook).
With over 25 Argentine and imported beers, this pub is a popular hang-out. The pub food is good value and there is a great atmosphere.

Puerto Pirámides
There are many restaurants on the main street in Puerto Pirámides.

$$ Quimey Quipan
Primera Bajada opposite Las Restingas, T0280-445 8609.
By the beach and next to **Tito Bottazzi**, this family-run place specializes in delicious seafood with rice and has a cheap set menu. Always open for lunch, ring to reserve for dinner.

Towanda
1ra Bajada al Mar s/n, T0280-422 1460.
Quirky café and snack bar with outside seating overlooking the main street and beach. Friendly staff, recommended.

Puerto Madryn

Diving
Puerto Madryn is a diving centre, with several shipwrecked boats in the Golfo Nuevo. A 1st dive ('bautismo') for beginners costs about US$90 pp.
Aquatours, *Av Roca 550, T0280-445 1954, www. aquatours.com.ar.* A variety of options, including PADI courses, good value.
Lobo Larsen, *Roca 885, loc 2 (also Bv Brown 860), T0280-447 0277, www.lobolarsen.com.* Friendly company that specializes in diving with the sea lion colony at Punta Lomas. Wide variety of courses offered.
Puerto Madryn Buceo, *Blvd Brown, 3rd round-about in Balneario Nativo Sur, T0280-15-456 4422, www.madrynbuceo.com.* Courses of all kinds from beginners' dives to a week-long PADI course, around US$160 for diving/snorkelling with sea lions.
Scuba Duba, *Blvd Brown 893, T0280-445 2699, www.scubaduba.com.ar.* Professional and good fun, diving with sea lions at Punta Loma, pick-up from hotel, offer a hot drink and warm clothes after the dive, good equipment, instructor Javier A Crespi is very responsible.

Mountain bike hire
From US$10. At **El Gualicho**, see Where to stay.

Tours
Many agencies do similar 7- and 9-hr tours to the Península Valdés, about US$50-60 pp, plus the entrance to the Peninsula. They include the interpretation centre, Puerto Pirámides (the whales boat trip is US$70 extra), Punta Delgada and Caleta Valdés. Shop around to find out how long you'll spend at each place, how big the group is, and if your guide speaks English. On all excursions take binoculars. Most tour companies stay about 1 hr on location. Tours to see the penguins at Punta Tombo and Welsh villages are better from Trelew. Tours do not run after heavy rain in the low season. Many of the agencies below also have offices at the bus terminal (Dr Avila 350). Recommended for Península Valdés:
Alora Viaggio, *Av Roca 27, T0280-445 5106, www.aloraviaggio.com.* Helpful company, also has an office in Buenos Aires (T011-4827 1591, 0800-1300).
Argentina Visión, *Av Roca 536, T0280-445 5888, www.argentinavision.com.* Also 4WD adventure trips and estancia accommodation, English and French spoken.

Chaltén Travel, *Av Roca 115, T0280-445 4906, www.chaltentravel.com.* Local office of the El Calafate-based operator.

Cuyun Có, *Av Roca 165, T0280-445 1845, www.cuyunco.com.ar.* Offers a friendly, personal service and a huge range of conventional and more imaginative tours: guided walks with local experts, 4WD expeditions, and can arrange estancia accommodation. Bilingual guides.

Tito Botazzi, *Blvd Brown y Martín Fierro, T0280-447 4110, www.titobottazzi.com, and at Puerto Pirámide (T0280-449 5050).* Particularly recommended for small groups and well-informed bilingual guides; very popular for whale watching.

Península Valdés

Puerto Pirámides

Hydrosport, *1ra Bajada, al Mar, T0280-449 5065, www.hydrosport.com.ar.* Rents scuba equipment and boats, and organizes land and sea wildlife tours to see whales and dolphins.

Whales Argentina, *1ra Bajada al Mar, T0280-449 5015, www.whalesargentina.com.ar.* Recommended for whale watching.

Puerto Madryn

Air El Tehuelche Airport 8 km west, T0280-445 6774; taxi US$10-13. Daily flights from **Buenos Aires** in high season, with more flights to **Bariloche**, Buenos Aires, and El Calafate from Trelew. Limited **LADE** flights to **Buenos Aires**, **Bahía Blanca**, **Viedma**, **Trelew**, **Comodoro Rivadavia** and other Patagonian airports (in low season Mon and Fri departures only). Buses to Trelew stop at entrance to airport if asked.

Bus Terminal at Av Dr Ávila, entre Necochea e Independencia, T0280-445 1789. To **Buenos Aires**, 18-19 hrs, several companies, US$150. To **Bahía Blanca**, 9½ hrs with **Don Otto** and others, US$80. To **Comodoro Rivadavia**, 6 hrs, US$45 with **Don Otto** and **Andesmar**. To **Río Gallegos**, 18 hrs, US$130, **Andesmar**. To **Trelew**, 1 hr, every hour, US$4 with **28 de Julio/Mar y Valle**.

Car hire Expensive, US$100 per day, and note large excess for turning car over. Drive slowly on unpaved *ripio* roads; best to hire 4WD. Many agencies on Av Roca. **Dubrovnik**, Av Roca 19, T0280-445 0030, www.rentacardubrovnik.com. Reliable company with offices in El Calafate and Bariloche. **Wild Skies**, Morgan 2274, p 1, Depto 6 B Sur, T0280-15-467 6233, www.wildskies.com.ar. Efficient service, English spoken, recommended.

Taxi There are taxis outside the bus terminal, T0280-445 2966/447 4177, and on the main plaza.

Península Valdés

Bus Mar y Valle bus company from **Puerto Madryn** to **Puerto Pirámides**, daily at 0630, 0945 and 1600, and returning at 0815, 0945 and 1800, 1½ hrs, US$5.50 each way (on Sat and Sun there is only 1 daily bus, leaving at 0945).

Trelew and around   *Colour map 9, A3.*

a Little Wales beyond Wales

The Río Chubut is one of the most important rivers in Patagonia, flowing a massive 820 km from the eastern foothills of the Andes into the Atlantic at Bahía Engaño. It's thanks to the Río Chubut that the Welsh pioneers came to this part of the world in 1865, and their irrigation of the arid land around it enabled them to survive and prosper. You can trace their history west along the valley from the pleasant airy town of Trelew. From here, there's also access to colonies of penguins, south along the coast.

Sights

Trelew, pronounced 'Trel-e-Oo', is a busy town, with an excellent museum and a shady plaza, which hosts a small handicraft market every Saturday 0900-1800. Evidence of Welsh settlement still remains in a few brick buildings: the 1889 **Capilla Tabernacl**, on Belgrano, between San Martín and 25 de Mayo, and the **Salón San David**, a 1913 Welsh meeting hall. The latter has a **mini-museum** ① *Mon-Fri 0900-1300 (all day during Sep-Oct)*, of objects donated by descendants of the Welsh settlers, also organizes Welsh language and traditional dance classes. On the road to Rawson, 3 km south, is one of the oldest standing Welsh chapels, **Capilla Moriah**, from 1880,

Tip...
Visit mid-October to see the **Eisteddfod** (Welsh festival of arts – five of them are held throughout Welsh Patagonia, September-October).

with a simple interior and graves of many original settlers in the cemetery. Don't miss the **Museo Paleontológico Egidio Feruglio** ⓘ *Fontana 140, T0280-442 0012, www.mef.org.ar, Sep-Mar daily 0900-1900, otherwise Mon-Fri 1000-1800, Sat-Sun 1000-1900, US$7.50, full disabled access and guides for the blind.* This is an excellent museum, which presents the origins of life and dynamically poised dinosaur skeletons. It has good information in Spanish and free tours in English, German and Italian; also a café and shop, as well as information about **Parque Paleontológico Bryn-Gwyn**, 8 km from Gaiman (see below). In the old 1889 railway station is the **Museo Regional Pueblo de Luis** ⓘ *Fontana y Lewis Jones 9100, T0280-442 4062, Mon-Fri 0800-2000, US$2.50.* It has displays on indigenous societies, failed Spanish attempts at settlement and on Welsh colonization. The **Museo Municipal de Artes Visuales (MMAV)** ⓘ *Mitre 350, T0280-443 3774, Mon-Fri 0800-1900, Sat-Sun 1400-1900, US$1,* is in an attractive wooden building, with exhibitions of local artists.

Gaiman and the Chubut Valley *Colour map 9, A3.*

A small pretty place with old brick houses retaining the Welsh pioneer feel, Gaiman hosts an annual Eisteddfod (Welsh festival of arts) in September. It's renowned for delicious Welsh teas and its fascinating tiny museum, **Museo Histórico Regional Galés** ⓘ *Sarmiento y 28 de Julio, T0280-15-456 9372, US$1, daily 1500-1900,* revealing the spartan lives of the idealistic Welsh pioneers. There are also several Welsh chapels here, on the banks of the Río Chubut. **Geoparque Bryn Gwyn** ⓘ *8 km south of town, T0280-442 0012, www.mef.org.ar, Tue-Sun 1000-1600 US$3, children US$1.50, taxi from Gaiman US$5,* encompasses a series of fossil beds that are 40 million years old. They are shown on a good guided tour, and there is a visitor centre offering try-outs in paleontology fieldwork.

Dolavon, founded in 1919, is a quiet settlement, with a few buildings reminiscent of the Welsh past. The main street, Avenida Roca, runs parallel to the irrigation canal built by the settlers, where willow trees now trail into the water, and there's a Welsh chapel, **Capilla Carmel** at one

Trelew

Where to stay
1 Galicia
2 Libertador
3 Rayentray
4 Rivadavia
5 Touring Club

Restaurants 🍴
1 Bulevú
2 Café de mi Ciudad
3 Café Verdi
5 La Bodeguita
6 La Casona
7 Miguel Angel

Keeping up with the Joneses

On 28 July 1865, 153 Welsh immigrants landed at Puerto Madryn, then a deserted beach deep in *indígena* country. After three weeks they pushed, on foot, across the parched pampa and into the Chubut river valley, where there is flat cultivable land along the riverside for a distance of 80 km upstream. Here, maintained in part by the Argentine government, they settled, but it was three years before they realized the land was barren unless watered. They drew water from the river, which is higher than the surrounding flats, and built a fine system of irrigation canals. The colony, reinforced later by immigrants from Wales and from the US, prospered, but in 1899 a great flood drowned the valley and some of the immigrants left for Canada. The last Welsh contingent arrived in 1911. The object of the colony had been to create a 'Little Wales beyond Wales', and for four generations they kept the Welsh language alive. The language has, however, been dying out from the fifth generation. There is an offshoot of the colony of Chubut at Trevelin, at the foot of the Andes nearly 650 km to the west, settled in 1888 (see page 188). It is interesting that this distant land gave to the Welsh language one of its most endearing classics: *Dringo'r Andes* (Climbing the Andes), written by one of the early women settlers.

end. The **old flour mill** ① *Tue-Sun 1100-1600, US$2*, at Maipú y Roca dates from 1927 and can be visited. There's Autoservicio Belgrano at the far end of San Martín, for food supplies, one tea room, El Molienda ① *Maipú 61, T0280-449 2290, www.molinoharinerodolavon.com, US$7.50*, but nowhere to stay. The municipal campsite, two blocks north of the river, is free, with good facilities.

In the irrigated valley between Dolavon and Gaiman, you'll see more Welsh chapels tucked away among fringes of tall *álamo* (poplar) trees and silver birches; most easily visited in your own transport. The **San David chapel** (1917) is a beautifully preserved brick construction, with an elegant bell tower and sturdy oak-studded door, in a quiet spot surrounded by birches.

Paved Ruta 25 runs from Dolavon west to the upper Chubut Valley, passing near the **Florentino Ameghino** dam, a leafy spot for a picnic. The stretch from Ameghino to Tecka (on Ruta 40 south of Trevelín) is one of the most beautiful routes across Patagonia to the Andes, with lots of wildlife to see. It goes through Las Plumas (mind the bridge if driving), Los Altares, which has an ACA motel ($$, Ruta 25, km 321, dep_6076@aca.org.ar, restaurant, bar), camping 400 m behind service station (very basic), fuel and some shops, and Paso de Indios.

South of Trelew

The nature reserve at **Punta Tombo** ① *125 km south of Trelew, access from Ruta 1, a ripio road between Trelew and Camarones, daily 0800-1800 (high season), entry US$14, children US$7*, is open from September, when huge numbers of Magellanic penguins come here to breed, making it the largest single penguin colony on the South American subcontinent. It's best visited between September and March. Chicks can be seen from mid-November; they take to the water January to February. It's fascinating to see these creatures up close. There are tours from Trelew and Puerto Madryn (US$70, 45 minutes at the site, plus a stop at Gaiman), but to avoid tourist crowds, go in the afternoon. You'll see guanacos, hares and rheas on the way.

There's another well-known penguin colony with 100,000 birds and lots more species of marine life, including whales (March-November) and orcas (October-April), and, onland, lesser rheas, guanacos and maras, at **Reserva Natural Cabo Dos Bahías** ① *35 km southeast of Camarones, daily*.

Some 90 km south of Camarones along the coast is **Bahía Bustamante**, a settlement of seaweed harvesters and sheep ranchers on Golfo San Jorge (180 km north of Comodoro Rivadavia). Its main attractions are the coastal and steppe landscapes of the surrounding **Patagonia Austral Marine national park**, which offers exceptional opportunities to see birds (including 100,000 penguins), marine and land mammals. An award-winning resort (T011-4156 7788/T0297-480 1000, www.bahiabustamante.com, electricity 1900 to 2400, closed mid-April to August, or September) offers full-board and self-catering accommodation, plus hiking, cycling, riding and kayaking; guides are on hand.

Tourist information

Information on the Chubut Valley is available from the **tourist office in Trelew** (on the plaza, Mitre 387, T0280-442 4039, Mon-Fri 0800-2000, Sat-Sun 0900-2100) and at the airport when flights arrive. See also **Entretur** (www.trelewpatagonia.gov.ar). The **tourist office in Gaiman** (Belgrano 574, T0280-449 1571, www.gaiman.gov.ar, Mon-Sat 0900-1900, Sun 1100-1800 – shorter hours in low season), is very helpful, with knowledgeable staff and a good map of the area, marking all the Welsh sites.

Where to stay

Trelew

$$$$ La Casona del Río
Chacra 105, Capitán Murga, 5 km from town, T0280-443 8343, www.lacasonadelrio.com.ar. Feb-Jul.
Pick-up arranged, attractive, family-run B&B with heating, TV, meals available, bicycles, massage, laundry, tennis and bowls, English and French spoken.

$$$ Galicia
9 de Julio 214, T0280-443 3802, www.hotelgalicia.com.ar.
Central, grand entrance, comfortable rooms, excellent value. Recommended.

$$$ Libertador
Rivadavia 31, T0280-442 0220, www.hotellibertadortw.com.
Modern hotel, highly recommended for service and comfortable bedrooms.

$$$ Rayentray
Belgrano 397, at San Martín, T0280-443 4702, www.cadenarayentray.com.ar.
Large, modern, comfortable rooms, professional staff, pool.

$$ Rivadavia
Rivadavia 55, T0280-443 4472, www.rivadaviahotel.com.ar.
Simple, comfortable rooms, breakfast extra.

$$ Touring Club
Fontana 240, Peatonal Luis Gazín, T0280-443 3997.
Gorgeous 1920s bar and elegant meeting room at the back (ask to see it), Butch Cassidy stayed here for a while, simple rooms, great value, breakfast

included. Open from breakfast until 0030 for sandwiches and drinks. Wi-Fi in rooms and bar. Recommended.

Camping

Camping Sero
Play Unión, 25 km from Trelew, T0280-449 6982.
In the quaint seaside village of Playa Unión, from US$7.50 per night.

Gaiman

$$$$-$$$ Posada Los Mimbres
Chacra 211, 6 km west of Gaiman, T0280-449 1299, www.posadalosmimbres.com.ar.
Rooms in the old farmhouse or in modern building, good food, very relaxing, $$$ in Apr-Aug.

$$$-$$ Ty Gwyn
9 de Julio 111, T0280-449 1009, tygwyn@tygwyn.com.ar.
Neat, comfortable, above the tea rooms, excellent value.

$$ Hostería Ty'r Haul
Sarmiento 121, T0280-449 1880.
Historic building, rooms are comfortable and well-lit.

$$ Plas y Coed
Yrigoyen 320, T0280-449 1133, www.plasycoed.com.ar.
Ana Rees' delightful tea shop has double and twin rooms in an annex next door. Highly recommended.

Camping

Municipal site, **Camping de los Bomberos** (fire brigade).

South of Trelew

$$$-$$ Complejo Indalo Inn
Sarmiento and Roca, Camarones, T0297-496 3004, www.indaloinn.com.ar.
Simple but clean, doubles and singles with en suite. Good food. Owner runs trips to the peguin colony.

$$$-$$ El Faro
Brown s/n, Camarones, T0297-414 5510, www.elfaro-patagonia.com.ar. Open all year.
2 fully equipped cabins for up to 5 with kitchen, living rom and bedroom, and 4 double rooms with bath, ocean front.

Restaurants

Trelew

$$ La Bodeguita
Belgrano 374, T0280-443 7777.
Delicious pastas and pizzas. Reasonable wine list. Recommended.

$$ La Casona
Pasaje Jujuy and Lewis Jones,
near Plaza Centenario.
Patagonian lamb, *parrilla*, good lunchtime venue.

$$ Miguel Angel
Fontana 246, next door to Touring Club,
in Peatonal Luis Gazín, Av Fontana.
Good standard fare of meat and pasta dishes.

Cafés

Bulevú
San Martín 412, T0280-443 6601 (see Facebook).
Cosy café featuring an array of healthy dishes including sandwiches, salads and fresh juices. Mouth-watering bakery. Great for vegetarians.

Café de mi Ciudad
Belgrano 394.
Smart café serving great coffee; read the papers here. Also has Wi-Fi.

Café Verdi
Attached to Teatro Verdi, San Martín 130.
Home-made waffles, pizzas and pasta, drinks.

Gaiman
Welsh teas are served from 1400-1900, US$15-20, by several tea rooms.

Casa de Té Gaiman
Av Yrigoyen 738, T0280-449 1633,
amaliaj51@hotmail.com.
One of the few tea houses in Gaiman still run by the original Welsh descendents.

Plas Y Coed
See Where to stay, above.
The best and oldest tea room; Ana Rees learned to cook at the feet of her grandmother, Marta, one of the best cooks in Gaiman.

Siop Bara
Tello y 25 de Mayo.
Welsh cakes and ice creams.

Ty Gwyn
9 de Julio 111, see Where to stay. Opens 1400.

Large tea room, more modern than some, welcoming; generous teas. Recommended.

What to do

Trelew
Agencies run tours to Punta Tombo, Chubut Valley (half- and full-day). Tours to Península Valdés are best done from Puerto Madryn.
Explore Patagonia, *Roca 94, T0280-443 7860, www.explore-patagonia.com.ar.* Operator offering tours to prominent local sites. Also has office in Puerto Madryn.
Nieve Mar, *Italia 20, T0280-443 4114, www. nievemartours.com.ar.* Punta Tombo and Valdés, bilingual guides (reserve ahead), organized and efficient. Has a branch in Puerto Madryn (Av Roca 493).

Transport

Trelew
Air Airport is 5 km north of centre; taxis about US$7. Local buses to/from Puerto Madryn stop at the airport entrance if asked, turning is 10 mins' walk, US$8. Flights to/from **Buenos Aires**, **Bariloche**, **El Calafate** and **Ushuaia**. **LADE (**Italia 170, T0280-443 5740) flies to Patagonian airports.

Bus The terminal is on the east side of Plaza Centenario in Urquiza y Lewis Jones, T0280-442 0121.
　Local 28 de Julio goes frequently to **Gaiman**, 30-45 mins (buy tickets from Mar y Valle, buses take different routes, some on unpaved roads); US$1, and **Dolavon** 1 hr, US$3.50, to **Puerto Madryn**, 1hr, US$4. To **Puerto Pirámides**, 2½ hrs, US$7, daily, Mar y Valle/28 de Julio.
　Long distance Buenos Aires, 19-20 hrs; US$100-140, several companies go daily. Ñandú buses to **Camarones** Mon, Wed and Fri, 3½ hrs, departs 0800, returns same day 1600, US$17 one-way, US$23 return. To **Comodoro Rivadavia**, 5 hrs, US$30-37, many departures; to **Río Gallegos**, 17 hrs, US$90-105 (with connections to El Calafate, Puerto Natales, Punta Arenas), many companies. To **Esquel**, 9-10 hrs, US$45-50, Don Otto.

Car hire Expensive. Airport desks are staffed only at flight arrival times and cars are snapped up quickly. All have offices in town.

Comodoro Rivadavia

Located 375 km south of Trelew, Comodoro Rivadavia the largest city in the province of Chubut. Oil was discovered here in 1907, but the city now looks rather unkempt, reflecting changing fortunes in the industry. The town and surroundings were seriously damaged by floods caused by heavy rain in April 2017. The history of oil in the region is described at the **Museo del Petroleo** ① *3 km north, San Lorenzo 250, T0297-455 9558, Mon-Fri 0900-1700, Sat 1500-1800, US$4.* There's a beach at Rada Tilly, 8 km south, (buses every 30 minutes, US$1); walk along beach at low tide to see sea lions.

Sarmiento   *Colour map 9, A2.*

If you're keen to explore the petrified forests and the Cueva de las Manos near Perito Moreno, take the road to Chile running west from Comodoro Rivadavia for 156 km to Colonia Sarmiento (known as Sarmiento). This is a quiet relaxed place, sitting just south of two large lakes, Musters and Colhué Huapi. Every second week in February it holds a three-day **Festival Interprovincial de Doma y Folclore**, featuring music, gaucho parades and local crafts. It is the best base for seeing the 70 million-year-old **petrified forests** of fallen araucaria trees. Most accessible is the **Bosque Petrificado José Ormachea** ① *30 km south of Sarmiento on a ripio road; contact Sr Juan José Valero, the park ranger, for guided tours: Uruguay 43, T0297-489 8282/15-464 0659 (Ivan), Apr-Sep 1000-1800, Oct-Mar 0800-2000, free.* Less easy to reach is the bleaker **Víctor Szlapelis** petrified forest, some 40 km further southwest along the same road (follow signposts, road from Sarmiento in good condition). From December to March a combi service runs twice daily, or there are taxis: contact Sarmiento tourist office for details (see below).

South of Comodoro Rivadavia

Caleta Olivia lies on the Bahía San Jorge, 74 km south of Comodoro Rivadávia and is a convenient place to break long bus journeys, with hotels (one opposite the bus station is good) and a municipal campsite near the beach (tourist information: Güemes y San Martín, T0297-485 0988).

In a bizarre lunar landscape surrounding the Laguna Grande is the country's largest area of petrified trees, **Monumento Natural Bosques Petrificados** ① *access by Ruta 49 which branches off RN 3, 91 km south of Fitz Roy;* tours from Puerto Deseado with **Los Vikingos** (see page 211). The araucarias, 140 million years old, lie in a desert which was once, astonishingly, a forest. There is a museum and a well-documented 1-km trail that passes the most impressive specimens. There's no charge but donations are accepted; please do not remove 'souvenirs'. There are no facilities at the site and the nearest campsite is at **Estancia La Paloma**, on Ruta 49, 24 km before the entrance, T0297-444 3503.

Puerto Deseado and around   *Colour map 9, B3.*

This is a pleasant fishing port on the estuary of the Río Deseado, which drains, strangely, into the Lago Buenos Aires in the west. Surrounding the port is a stunning stretch of coastline, and the estuary is a wonderful nature reserve, with Magellanic penguins, cormorants, and breeding grounds of the beautiful Commerson's dolphin. **Cabo Blanco**, 72 km north, is the site of the largest fur seal colony in Patagonia; the breeding season is December-January. **Tourist office** ① *Vagón Histórico, San Martín y Almte Brown, http://deseado.gob.ar.*

Puerto San Julián   *Colour map 9, B2.*

Quiet Puerto San Julián is the best place for breaking the 778 km run from Comodoro Rivadavia to Río Gallegos. It has a fascinating history, little of which is visible today. The first Mass in Argentina was held here in 1520, after Magellan had executed a member of his mutinous crew. Francis Drake also put in here in 1578 to behead Thomas Doughty, after amiably dining with him. There is much wildlife in the area: red and grey foxes, guanacos, wildcats in the mountains, rheas and an impressive array of marine life in the coastal **Reserva San Julián**. A recommended zodiac boat trip is run by **Excursiones Pinocho** ① *T02962-454600, www.pinochoexcursions.com.ar,* to see Magellanic penguins (September-March), cormorants and Commerson's dolphins (best in December). Ceramics are made at the **Escuela de Cerámica**, a good handicraft centre at Moreno y San Martín. There is also a regional museum at the end of San Martín on the waterfront. **Tourist office** ① *Av San Martín 1570 at the bus terminal, T02962-454396/452301, http://sanjulian.gob.ar.*

Piedrabuena and around *Colour map 9, B2.*

Piedrabuena on Ruta 3 is 125 km south of San Julián on the Río Santa Cruz. On Isla Pavón, south of town on Ruta 3 at the bridge over Río Santa Cruz, is a tourist complex, with popular wooded campsite and wildlife park, liable to get crowded in good weather. There's a **national trout festival** in March. **Tourist office** ① *Av G Ibáñez 157 (bus station), T02962-15-573065.* A turn off 9 km south of Piedrabuena leads to **Santa Cruz**, which has the **Museo Regional Carlos Borgialli**, with a range of local exhibits. There is a **tourist information centre** ① *Av Piedra Buena y San Martin, T02962-498700,* and a municipal campsite.

Some 24 km further south, a dirt road branches 22 km to **Parque Nacional Monte León** ① *office at Belgrano y 9 de Julio, Puerto de Santa Cruz, T02962-489184, monteleon@apn.gov.ar,* which includes the Isla Monte León, an important breeding area for cormorants and terns, where there is also a penguin colony and sea lions. There are impressive rock formations and wide isolated beaches at low tide.

Listings Comodoro Rivadavia and inland

Tourist information

Comodoro Rivadavia

Chilean consulate
Almte Brown 456, entrepiso, of 3, T0297-446 2414, www.chile.gob.cl/comodoro-rivadavia/en.

Tourist office
Dr Scocco y Abasolo, T0297-444 0664, www.comodoroturismo.gob.ar. Mon-Fri 0800-2000, Sat 0900-2000, Sun 1000-2000.
English spoken, very helpful.

Sarmiento

Tourist office
Pietrobelli 388, T0297-489 2105. Open 0700-1100 in high season, 1100-1900 in low season.
Another office in the bus terminal. Both are helpful, with map of town and information on transport to forests, English spoken.

Where to stay

Comodoro Rivadavia

$$$ Lucania Palazzo
Moreno 676, T0297-449 9300, www.lucania-palazzo.com.
Most luxurious business hotel, superb rooms, sea views, good value, huge American breakfast, sauna and gym included. Recommended.

$$ Azul
Sarmiento 724, T0297-446 7539, www.hotelazul.com.ar.
Breakfast extra, quiet old place with lovely bright rooms, kind, great views from the *confitería.*

$$ Hospedaje Cari Hue
Belgrano 563, T0297-447 2946, see Facebook.
Sweet rooms, with separate bathrooms, breakfast extra. Probably the cheapest place to stay that's half-way safe.

Sarmiento

$$$ Chacra Labrador
10 km from Sarmiento, T0297-489 3329, agna@coopsar.com.ar.
Excellent small estancia, breakfast included, other meals extra and available for non-residents, English and Dutch spoken, runs tours to petrified forests at good prices, will collect guests from Sarmiento (same price as taxi).

$$ El Molle
Roca337, T0297-489 3637, www.elmollehotelboutique.com.
Private bathroom, Wi-Fi, laundry service, breakfast included. Good central option.

$ Colón
Perito Moreno 645, T0297-489 4212.
One of the better cheap places in town.

$ Los Lagos
Roca y Alberdi, T0297-489 3046.
Good, heating, restaurant.

Camping

Río Senguer
1 km from centre on the left where the road branches off at the river, T0297-489 8482.

SGPCH
Río Senger, 1 km from centre, on the right where the road branches off at the river, T0297-489 7112.

South of Comodoro Rivadavia

Puerto Deseado

$$ Isla Chaffers
San Martín y Mariano Moreno, T0297-487 2246, administracion@hotelislachaffers.com.ar.
Modern, central.

$$ Los Acantilados
Pueyrredón y España, T0297-487 2167, reservas.losacantilados@gmail.com.
Beautifully located, good breakfast, but some rooms reported dingy and run-down.

Puerto San Julián

$$$ Bahía
San Martín 1075, T02962-453144, www.hotelbahiasanjulian.com.ar.
Modern, comfortable, good value. Recommended.

$$$ Estancia La María
150 km northwest of Puerto San Julián.
Offers transport, lodging, meals, visits to caves with paintings of human hands, guanacos, etc, 4000-12,000 years old, less visited than Cueva de las Manos. Contact Fernando Behm in San Julián, Saavedra 1163, T02962-452328.

$$ Municipal Costanera
25 de Mayo y Urquiza, T02962-452300, www.costanerahotel.com.
Very nice, well run, good value, no restaurant.

$$ Sada
San Martín 1112, T02962-452013.
Fine, on busy main road.

Camping

Municipal campsite
Magallanes 650, T454506.
Repeatedly recommended, all facilities.

Piedrabuena and around

$$$$ Hostería Estancia Monte León
Ruta 3, Km 2399, T011-4621 4780 (Buenos Aires), www.monteleon-patagonia.com. Nov-Apr.

A good base for visiting the national park. 4 tasteful rooms, plus library, living room and small museum.

Restaurants

Comodoro Rivadavia

$$ Cayo Coco
Rivadavia 102, T0297-4097 3033.
Bistro with excellent pizzas, good service. Also Cayo Coco del Mar, Av Costanera 1051.

$$ Maldito Peperoni
Sarmiento 581, T0297-446 9683.
Cheerful, modern, pastas.

Puerto Deseado

$$ Puerto Cristal
España 1698, T0297-487 0387.
Panoramic views of the port, a great place for Patagonian lamb, *parrilla* and seafood.

Puerto San Julián
Also bars and tearooms.

$$ La Rural
Ameghino 811.
Good, but not before 2100.

What to do

Puerto Deseado

Darwin Expediciones, *España 2551, T0297-15-624 7554, www.darwin-expeditions.com.* Excursions by boat to Ría Deseado reserve and trips to the Monumento Natural Bosques Petrificados.
Los Vikingos, *Prefectura Naval s/n, T0297-15-624 5141/487 0020, www.losvikingos.com.ar.* Excursions by boat to Ría Deseado reserve and Reserva Provincial Isla Pingüino, bilingual guides, customized tours.

Transport

Comodoro Rivadavia
Air Airport, 13 km north. Palazzo buses from bus terminal, hourly (45 mins), US$0.50. Taxi to airport, US$17. Regular flights to **Buenos Aires** and **Bariloche**. LADE flies to all Patagonian destinations.

Bus Terminal in centre at Pellegrini 730, T0297-446 7305; has luggage store, *confitería*, toilets, some kiosks. In summer buses usually arrive full; book ahead. Services to **Buenos Aires** several daily, 24-28 hrs, US$135-155. To **Bariloche**, 14½ hrs, US$57-77, **Don Otto**, T0297-447 0450, **Marga**, **Andesmar** (T0297-446 8894). To **Esquel** (paved road) 9 hrs direct with **EETAP**, T0297-447 4841, and **Don Otto**, US$45-50. To **Río Gallegos**, daily, 10-12 hrs, US$60-70. To **Puerto Madryn** and **Trelew**, see above. To/from **Sarmiento** and **Caleta Olivia**, see below. To **Puerto Deseado**, **Sportman**, 2 a day, US$25.

Sarmiento

Bus 4 daily to/from **Comodoro Rivadavia**, US$11, 2½ hrs. From Sarmiento you can reach **Esquel** (448 km north along Rutas 20 and 40); overnight buses on Sun stop at Río Mayo, take food for journey.

South of Comodoro Rivadavia

Caleta Olivia

Bus To **Río Gallegos**, **Andesmar**, **Sportman** and others, US$54-71, 9½ hrs. Many buses to/from **Comodoro Rivadavia**, 1 hr, US$5-8, **Sportman**. To **Perito Moreno**, US$24; to **Los Antiguos**, 3-5 hrs, US$30, 3 a day, **Andesmar**, **Sportman** and **Taqsa**.

Puerto Deseado

Bus 2 daily to **Caleta Olivia**, 2½-3 hrs, US$18, with **Sportman**.

Puerto San Julián

Bus Many companies to both **Comodoro Rivadavia**, US$30-40, and **Río Gallegos**, 6 hrs, US$21-29.

a staging post for the glaciers or Tierra del Fuego

The capital of Santa Cruz Province is located 232 km south of Piedrabuena, on the estuary of the Río Gallegos. The pleasant, open town was founded in 1885 as a centre for the trade in wool and sheepskins, and boasts a few smart shops and some excellent restaurants.

Sights

The delightful Plaza San Martín, two blocks south of the main street, Avenida Roca, has an interesting collection of trees, many planted by the early pioneers, and a tiny corrugated iron cathedral, with a wood-panelled ceiling in the chancel and stained glass windows. The small **Museo de los Pioneros** ① *Elcano y Alberdi, daily 1000-1700, free,* is worth a visit: an interesting tour is given by the English-speaking owner, a descendent of the Scottish pioneers, and there are great photos of the first sheep-farming settlers, who came here in 1884 from the Malvinas/Falkland Islands. **Museo de Arte Eduardo Minichelli** ① *Maipú 13, T02966-436323, Mon 0800-1300, Tue-Fri 0800-1900, Sat-Sun 1500-1900,* has work by local artists. Also stimulating is the **Museo Malvinas Argentinas** ① *Pasteur 72, T02966-437618, Mon-Fri 1100-1600, Sat-Sun 1000-1700,* which aims to inform visitors, with historical and geographical evidence, why the Malvinas are Argentine.

Tip...

Change money or withdraw cash from ATMs here as it is difficult in El Calafate. **Cambios El Pingüino**, Zapiola 469, and **Thaler**, Fagnano 20, will change Chilean pesos as well as US$. There's a Chilean consulate at Mariano Moreno 148, T02966-422364, www.chile.gob.cl/rio-gallegos/, Monday-Friday 0800-1300, 1400-1700.

Cabo Vírgenes

134 km south of Río Gallegos. Access from ripio Ruta 1, 3½ hrs. Entry free. Tours cost from US$60.

This nature reserve protects the second largest colony of Magellanic penguins in Patagonia. There's an informative self-guided walk that takes you to see nests among the *calafate* and *mata verde* bushes. It's best to visit between November, when the chicks are born, and January. There are great views from Cabo Vírgenes lighthouse, and a *confitería* close by with snacks and souvenirs.

Tourist information

Information is available from the **municipal office** (Av Beccar 126, T02966-436920, http://www.turismo.mrg.gov.ar, Mon-Fri 0800-1700, Sat-Sun 0800-1200, 1600-2000), from the **provincial tourist office** (Ruta 3 y Charlotte Fairchild, T02966-442159, Mon-Fri 0700-2200, Sat-Sun 0700-1400, 1600-2000); and from the **Carretón Municipal** (Kirchner 863), a helpful information caravan open in high season Mon-Fri 1300-2200, Sat-Sun 0800-2200; English spoken. It has a list of estancias, and the staff will phone round hotels for you. There's also a small desk at the **bus terminal** (T02966-442159, Mon-Fri 0700-2000, Sat-Sun 0800-1300, 1500-2000).

Where to stay

Río Gallegos

$$$ Santa Cruz
Kirchner 701, T02966-420601, www.hotelsantacruzrgl.com.ar.
Good value, spacious rooms with good beds, full buffet breakfast. Recommended.

$$$-$$ Sehuen
Rawson 160, T02966-425683, www.hotelsehuen.com.
Good, cosy, helpful.

$$ Comercio
Kirchner 1302, T02966-420209, www.hotelcomercio.com.ar.
Good value, including breakfast, nice design, comfortable, cheap *confitería*.

Río Gallegos

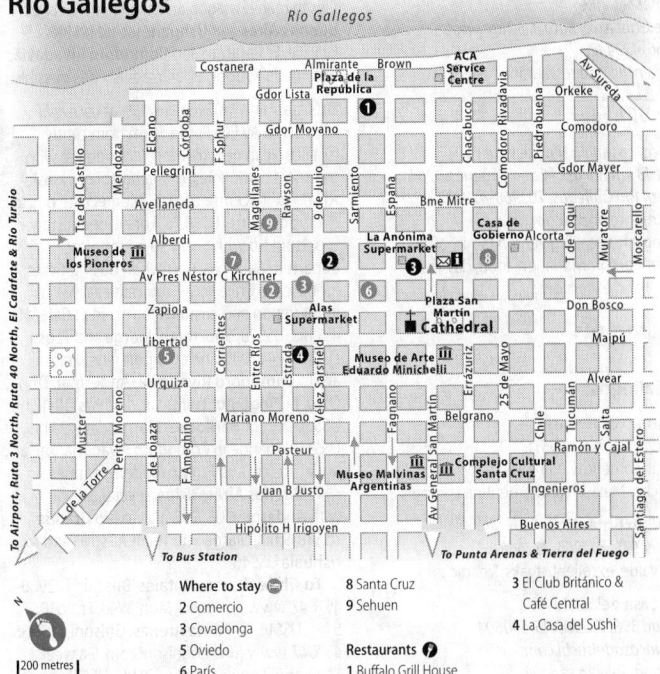

Río Gallegos

Where to stay
2 Comercio
3 Covadonga
5 Oviedo
6 París
7 Punta Arenas
8 Santa Cruz
9 Sehuen

Restaurants
1 Buffalo Grill House
2 El Chino
3 El Club Británico & Café Central
4 La Casa del Sushi

200 metres
200 yards

$$ Covadonga
Kirchner 1244, T02966-420190,
www.hotel-alonso.com.ar.
Small rooms, attractive old building, breakfast
extra. Same owner as **Hotel Alonso** at
Corrientes 33.

$$ París
Kirchner 1040, T02966-420111,
www.hotelparisrg.com.ar.
Simple rooms, shared bath, good value.

$$ Punta Arenas
F Sphur 55, T02966-427743,
www.hotelpuntaarenas.com.
Rooms with shared bath cheaper. Smart, rooms in
new wing cost more. **Something Café** attached.

$ Oviedo
Libertad 746, T02966-420118,
www.hoteloviedo.com.ar.
A cheaper budget option, breakfast extra,
laundry facilities, café, parking.

Camping

Club Pescazaike
Paraje Guer Aike, Ruta 3, 30 km west,
T02966-423442.
Also *quincho* and restaurant.

Cabo Vírgenes

$$$$ pp Estancia Monte Dinero
About 13 km north of Cabo Vírgenes, 120 km
south of Río Gallegos, T02966-428922,
www.montedinero.com.ar.
The English-speaking Fenton family offers
excellent accommodation, food, day visits
(US$60) and excursions.

Río Gallegos

$$ Buffalo Grill House
Lista 198, T02966-439511.
Popular, somehow manages to mix North
American, Mexican and Argentine cuisine.

$$ El Club Británico
Kirchner 935, T02966-432668.
Good value, excellent steaks, "magic".

$$ La Casa del Sushi
Libertad 398, T02966-15-590604,
www.lacasadelsushi.com.
Sushi and Chilean sandwiches.

$ El Chino
9 de Julio 27.
Varied *tenedor libre.*

Café Central
Kirchner 923.
Smart and popular.

Río Gallegos

Maca Tobiano Turismo, *Av San Martín 1093,*
T02966-422466, macatobiano@macatobiano.com.
Air tickets and tours to Pingüinero Cabo Vírgenes
(see above) and to Estancia Monte León, as well as
tickets to El Calafate and Ushuaia. Recommended.

Río Gallegos

Air Airport 10 km from centre. Taxi (remise) to/
from town US$10-12, see below. Regular flights
to/from **Buenos Aires** and **Ushuaia** direct. LADE
flies to many Patagonian destinations between
Buenos Aires and **Ushuaia**, including Río
Grande, **El Calafate** and **Comodoro Rivadavia**,
but not daily. Book as far in advance as possible.

Bus Terminal, T02966-442159, at corner of
Ruta 3 and Av Eva Perón, 3 km from centre
(small, so can get crowded, left luggage with
transport companies, *confitería*, toilets, kiosk,
ATM); taxi to centre US$4-5, Montecristo bus to
and from centre, US$0.75. For all long distance
trips, turn up with ticket 30 mins before
departure. Take passport when buying ticket;
for buses to Chile some companies give out
immigration and customs forms. To **El Calafate**,
4-5 hrs, US$28, **Sportman**, **Marga** and **Taqsa**
(T02966-442003, and at airport, www.taqsa.com.
ar). To **Comodoro Rivadavia**, **Andesmar**, **Don
Otto**, **El Pingüino**, **Tramat** and others, 10-12 hrs,
US$60-70. For **Bariloche**, **Marga**, daily, 24 hrs,
US$130, change in Comodoro Rivadavia. See also
under Trelew and Puerto Madryn for fares.

To **Buenos Aires**, 36 hrs, several daily
with **Andesmar**, US$202-212. To **Río Grande**
US$38, 9 hrs, **Marga** and Tecni Austral, and to
Ushuaia US$46.

To **Chile** **Puerto Natales**, Bus Sur, T02966-
457047, www.bus-sur.cl, Mon, Wed, Fri 1630,
5 hrs, US$16. To **Punta Arenas**, Ghisoni, T02966-
457047, www.turismoghisoni.com, 5 a week at
1200, and Pingüino, daily, 6-8 hrs, US$23.

Car hire Localiza, Sarmiento 245, T02966-436717, www.localiza.com. **Cristina**, Libertad 123, T02966-425709. **Avis** at the airport. Essential to book rental in advance in season.

Taxi Taxi ranks plentiful, rates controlled, remise slightly cheaper. **Note** Remise meters show metres travelled, refer to card for price; taxi meters show cost in pesos.

Tip...
If travelling to Chile by car, make sure your papers are in order: go first to the tourist office for necessary documents, then to the customs office at the port, at the end of San Martín. It's very uncomplicated. For road details, see Tierra del Fuego sections on page 229 and in Chile.

Ruta 40 to the glaciers

travel the iconic road alongside the Andes

☆Ruta 40 was at the time of writing in the process of being paved, but this project may take some time (see www.turismoruta40.com.ar), consequently high-clearance vehicles are still advised. There is no public transport and very few other vehicles even in mid-summer, but several tour operators cover the whole route (see What to do, page 227).

Río Mayo
Set in beautifully bleak landscape by the meandering Río Mayo, this very rural town has little of tourist interest except fuel and hotels, but it's an important junction at the intersection of Ruta 40 and Ruta 26, as well as provincial routes 20 and 22 (the last of these is paved and branches southwest 74 km west of Sarmiento). On the third weekend in January, it holds the Fiesta Nacional de la Esquila (national sheep-shearing competition).

Border with Chile From Río Mayo, there are two roads crossing the border into Chile. **Coyhaique Alto** is reached by a 133-km road (87 km *ripio*, then dirt) that branches off Ruta 40 about 7 km north of Río Mayo. Further south at Km 31, a turning off Ruta 40 leads west to Lago Blanco, **Paso Huemules** and Balmaceda (border open 0800-2200 in summer, 0900-2000 in winter, www.gendarmeria.gov.ar).

Perito Moreno and the Cueva de las Manos *Colour map 9, B2.*
Not to be confused with the famous glacier of the same name near El Calafate, nor with nearby Parque Nacional Perito Moreno, this provincial town has some interesting historical houses and plenty of character. It lies 25 km east of Lago Buenos Aires, the second largest lake in South America, and to the southwest is Parque Laguna, which has varied birdlife and fishing. The town calls itself the 'archaeological capital of Santa Cruz' because it is the main access point for the famous **Cueva de las Manos** ① *US$9 for foreigners, reduction for locals, under 12 free, access by compulsory guided tour with informative rangers, daily 0900-1900 (1000-1800 May-Oct).* Some 88 km south of Perito Moreno, a signed road runs 28 km east to the site in a beautiful volcanic canyon, where a series of rock galleries contain an exceptional assemblage of cave art, executed between 13,000 and 9500 years ago: paintings of human hands and animals in red, orange, black, white and green. It was declared a World Heritage Site in 1999. The best time to visit is early morning or evening (in summer, morning is best to beat the crowds). There is another access road, 46 km long, at Km 124. Tours run from Perito Moreno (eg **Zoyen**, San Martín y Saavedra, T02963-432207 or 0297-15-623 8811, www.zoyenturismo.com.ar) and Los Antiguos (Chelenco, 11 de Julio 548, T02963-491198, www.chelencoturs.com.ar).

Fact...
Perito Moreno is very remote: Bariloche 823 km, El Chaltén 582 km, El Calafate 619 km. It is nearly impossible to hitchhike between Perito Moreno and El Calafate as there is hardly any traffic and few services. US dollars, euros and Chilean pesos can be changed at **Banco Santa Cruz**, Avenida San Martín 1385, T02963-432028.

Los Antiguos
To see the Cueva de las Manos, you'll probably stop in Perito Moreno for at least one night, but if you're staying in the area for longer, consider going the extra 56 km west to Los Antiguos, especially

if you're heading for Chile Chico. From Perito Moreno Ruta 43 (paved) runs south of Lago Buenos Aires to this oasis set on the lake, in the middle of a desert, 2 km from the Chilean border. Blessed by a lovely climate and famous for its cherries (**Fiesta Nacional de la Cereza** in early January attracts national *folclore* stars) and great views, Los Antiguos is an increasingly popular tourist town. It is developing fast, with modern hotels, restaurants, bus terminal, internet and other services, ideal for a couple of days' rest and for stocking up on the basics before journeying on. It is also the headquarters for the 52,811-ha Parque Nacional Patagonia, which protects Patagonian steppe on the meseta of Lago Buenos Aires, with volcanoes, lakes and plants and animals specific to the region (administration Avenida Costanera s/n, dpto 2, T02966-15-622852, pnpatagonia@apn.gov.ar). There is an ATM on Avenida 11 de Julio.

Border with Chile The village of Chile Chico is 8 km west of Los Antiguos. The main reason to enter Chile here is either to explore the beautiful southern shore of Lago General Carrera, or to take the ferry over the lake north to Puerto Ibáñez for connections to Coyhaique (see the Chile chapter).

Bajo Caracoles to Tres Lagos
After hours of spectacular emptiness, even tiny **Bajo Caracoles** (population 100) is a relief: a few houses with a grocery store selling uninspiring *empanadas* and very expensive fuel. From here Ruta 41 goes 99 km northwest to **Paso Roballos**, continuing to Cochrane in Chile.

South of Bajo Caracoles, 101 km, is a crossroads: Ruta 40 heads southeast while the turning northwest goes to remote **Parque Nacional Perito Moreno** ⓘ *free, open 0900-2100, park office in Gobernador Gregores at 9 de Julio 610, T02962-491477,* at the end of a 90-km *ripio* track, accessible only by private high-clearance transport. There is trekking and abundant wildlife among the large, interconnected system of lakes below glaciated peaks, though much of the park is dedicated to scientific study only. Lago Belgrano, the biggest lake, is a vivid turquoise, its surrounding mountains streaked with a mass of differing colours.

Ammonite fossils can be found. The park ranger, 10 km beyond the park entrance, has maps and information on walks and wildlife, none in English. Camping is free, but there are no facilities, and fires are not permitted.

Tip...
The website www.turismoruta40.com.ar has good information on the park in Spanish.

From the Parque Moreno junction to Tres Lagos, Ruta 40 improves considerably. East of the junction (7 km) is **Hotel Las Horquetas** (closed) and 15 km beyond is Tamel Aike village (police station, water). After another 34 km Ruta 40 turns sharply southwest, but if you need fuel before Tres Lagos, you must make a 72 km detour to **Gobernador Gregores** (always carry spare).

At **Tres Lagos** a road turns off northwest to Lago San Martín. On the southern shore, 120 km from Tres Lagos, is **Estancia El Cóndor** (T011-5272 0343, www.cielospatagonicos.com, open October-April, rooms with bath, home-produced food, riding and gaucho activities, trekking, fishing). From Tres Lagos Ruta 40 deteriorates again and remains very rugged until the turnoff to the Fitz Roy sector of Parque Nacional Los Glaciares. The bridge over the Río La Leona is 21 km along this road, with delightful **Hotel La Leona Roadhouse and Country Lodge**, a great place to stay and sample local cuisine. Nearby are petrified tree trunks 30 m long, protected in a natural reserve.

Listings Ruta 40 to the glaciers

Tourist information

The website www.rutanacional40.com has good information in Spanish.

There are **tourist offices** in Río Mayo (Av Argentina s/n, T02903-420058, www.turismoriomayo.gob.ar, daily 0800-1200,

1500-1800), Los Antiguos (Buenos Aires 59, T02963-491261, www.losantiguos.tur.ar, 0800-2400 Dec-Easter, 0800-2000 rest of year) and, most usefully, Perito Moreno (Av San Martín 2005, http://peritomoreno.tur.ar, daily 0700-1200). The staff here can advise on tours to the Cueva de las Manos and also have information on Patagonian estancias in English.

Río Mayo

$$$$ Estancia Don José
3 km west of Río Mayo, T02903-420015 or T0297-15-624 9155, www.turismoguenguel.com.ar.
Excellent estancia, with superb food, 2 rooms and 1 cabin. The family business involves sustainable production of guanaco fibre.

$$ Hotel Aka-Ta
San Martín 640, T02903-420054, hotelacata@gmail.com.
One of a couple hotels in town that could pass for a chalet in Normandy. Cosy, well-furnished rooms, welcoming, great vibe. Restaurant open in high season.

$$-$ El Viejo Covadonga
San Martín 573, T02903-420020, elviejocovadonga@hotmail.com.
The other chalet-style lodging, with beautiful, expansive reception area. Run by 2 helpful sisters, all rooms have hot water and Wi-Fi. Recommended.

$$-$ San Martín
San Martín s/n, T02903-420066.
Decent hotel noteworthy mostly for its good restaurant.

Perito Moreno and Cueva de las Manos

$$ Americano
San Martín 1327, T02963-432074, www.hotelamericanoweb.com.ar.
12 pleasant rooms, some superior, recommended restaurant.

$$ Belgrano
San Martín 1001, T02963-432019.
This hotel is often booked by Ruta 40 long-distance bus companies, basic, not always clean, 1 key fits all rooms, helpful owner, breakfast extra, excellent restaurant.

$$ Hotel El Austral
San Martín 1381, T02963-432605, hotelaustral@speedy.com.ar.
Similar to others on the main street, but clean.

$ El Viejo Bar
San Martín 991, T02963 432538.
This good *parrilla* also rents rooms.

$ Hospedaje Las Formoseñas
O'Higgins 943, T02963-432123.
The only true budget hostel in town. Bunks with thin mattresses from US$10 per night. Still, the owner is friendly and you stand to save hundreds of pesos by lodging here than at other hotels.

Camping

Municipal site at Paseo Roca y Mariano Moreno, near Laguna de los Cisnes, T02963-432130.
Also 2 *cabaña* places near the river on Ruta 43: **Cabañas Las Moras**, T02963-15-400 7549, and **Turístico Río Fénix**, T02963-432458.

Estancias

$$$ Hostería Cueva de Las Manos
20 km from the cave at Estancia Los Toldos, 60 km south, 7 km off the road to Perito Moreno, T02963-432207 or T0297-15-623 8811, www.cuevadelasmanos.net. 1 Nov-5 Apr, closed Christmas and New Year.
Private rooms and dorms, runs tours to the caves, horse riding, meals extra and expensive.

$$ Estancia Turística Casa de Piedra
80 km south of Perito Moreno on Ruta 40, in Perito Moreno ask for Sr Sabella, Av Perón 941, T02963-432199.
Price is for rooms, camping, hot showers, home-made bread, use of kitchen, excursions to Cueva de las Manos and volcanoes by car or horse.

Los Antiguos

$$$ Antigua Patagonia
Ruta 43, T02963-491055, www.antiguapatagonia.com.ar.
Luxurious rooms with beautiful views, excellent restaurant. Tours to Cueva de las Manos and nearby Monte Zevallos.

$$$-$ Mora
Av Costanera 1064, T02963-15-540 2444, www.hotelmorapatagonia.com.
Rooms range from simple to 1st class with private bath, parking, lake views, corporate rates, multi-purpose room.

$$ Sol de Mayo
Av 11 de Julio 1300, T02963-491232, chacrasoldemayo@hotmail.com.
Basic rooms with shared bath, kitchen, also has cabins for rent, about 20 mins' walk from centre.

$ pp Albergue Padilla
San Martín 44 (just off main street), T02963-491140.
Comfortable dorms, doubles (**$$**); *quincho* and garden. Also camping. El Chaltén travel tickets.

Camping

An outstanding **Camping Municipal**, 2 km from centre on Ruta Provincial 43, T02963-491265, with hot showers, US\$4 pp, also has cabins for 4 (no linen).

Bajo Caracoles to Tres Lagos

\$\$\$ Estancia La Oriental
T02962-407197, laorientalpatagonia@ yahoo.com.ar. Nov-Mar.
Full board. Nearest accommodation to the Perito Moreno national park. Splendid setting, with comfortable rooms. With horse riding, trekking.

\$\$\$ pp La Angostura
55 km from Gobernador Gregores, T02962-491501, www.estancialaangostura.com.ar.
Offers horse riding, trekking and fishing. Recommended.

\$\$ Estancia La Siberia
Between Ruta 40 and Lago Cardiel some 90 km south of the turning to Gobernador Gregores, T02966-426972, www.lasiberia.8k.com, see Facebook: estancia.lasiberia. Oct-Apr.
This is a lunch stop on the El Calafate–Bariloche bus route, but also has rooms.

\$\$ Hotel Bajo Caracoles
Bajo Caracoles, T02963-490100.
Old-fashioned but hospitable, meals.

Camping
At **Estancia La Lucia**, near Tres Lagos, US\$2.50, water, barbecue, "a little, green paradise"; supermarket, fuel.

Restaurants

Los Antiguos
There are several other places in town.

Viva El Viento
11 de Julio 477, T02963-491109, www.vivael viento.com. Daily in high season 0900-2100.
Dutch-owned, great vibe, food and coffee, also has Wi-Fi and lots of information on the area. Live music Tue. Recommended.

Transport

Río Mayo
Bus To **Sarmiento** once a day (1900) with **Etap**, US\$11, 2 hrs. To **Perito Moreno**, 3 weekly (2100), **Etap**, US\$11.

Perito Moreno
Bus Terminal on edge of town next to petrol station, T02963-432177, open only when buses arrive or depart. If crossing from Chile at Los Antiguos, 2 buses daily in summer, 1 hr, US\$7, **Sportman**, T02963-432177. To **El Chaltén** and **El Calafate**, **Chaltén Travel**, see under Los Antiguos Transport, below, at 0700; also **Cal-Tur**.

Car Several mechanics on C Rivadavia and Av San Martín, good for repairs.

Taxi Parada El Turista, Av San Martín y Rivadavia, T02963-432592.

Los Antiguos
Bus Bus terminal on Av Tehuelches with large café/restaurant, free Wi-Fi. Most bus companies will store the luggage. Minibuses from Chile arrive at this terminal. To **Comodoro Rivadavia**, Etap (T0297-491078) and **Sportman** (T0297-442983) 2 daily, US\$34. To **El Chaltén** (10 hrs) and **El Calafate** (12 hrs), **Chaltén Travel**, www.chalten travel.com, daily at 2000, via Perito Moreno (departs 2100), US\$107 from Los Antiguos, also north to **Bariloche**, every even day 0700 (0800 Perito Moreno), US\$67 (US\$102 if not part of the Ruta 40 package), mid-Nov to mid-Apr, at **Hotel Belgrano**. **Cal-Tur** (see page 228) also runs direct services **El Calafate/ El Chaltén** to **Los Antiguos** and **Perito Moreno**. **To Chile**: frequent minibus service in summer, 0800-2200, US\$7 (for routes from Chile Chico to Coyhaique, see Chile chapter).

Parque Nacional Los Glaciares

glorious glaciers and tremendous trekking

★This park, the second largest in Argentina and a UNESCO World Heritage Site, extends over 724,000 ha. Forty per cent of it is covered by ice fields (*hielos continentales*) from which 13 major glaciers descend into two great lakes, Lago Argentino and, further north, Lago Viedma. They are linked by the Río La Leona, flowing south from Lago Viedma. The only accessible areas of the park are the southern area around Lago Argentino, reached from El Calafate, and the northern area around Cerro El Chaltén (Fitz Roy). Access to the central area is difficult and there are no tourist facilities.

Essential Parque Nacional Los Glaciares

Finding your feet

Access to the southern part of the park is 50 km west of El Calafate, US$33 for non-Argentines. An informative talk about the national park and its paths is given to all incoming bus passengers at the **national park office**, Avenida del Libertador 1302, El Calafate, T02902-491005, www.losglaciares.com, January-February daily 0800-2100, March to Semana Santa and December daily till 2000, August-October daily till 1800, Semana Santa to July daily till 1600. The staff are helpful and speak English. They hand out helpful trekking maps of the area, with paths and campsites marked, distances and walking times.

Similar services are offered at the park office in **El Chaltén**, across the bridge at the entrance to the town, T02963-493004 (opening times as above), for access to the northern part of the park around Cerro Fitz Roy. It is best to take cash to the park as high commission is charged on exchange. In 2016 in both El Calafate and El Chaltén few ATMs accepted new-style bank cards with smart chips. There are only two ATMs in El Calafate that accepted such cards: Banco Patagonia, Avenida del Libertador 1355, and at the airport. There are two 24-hour ATMs in El Chaltén, one in the bus station and the other a block away at Banco de la Nación (Monday-Friday 0800-1300). There are no *casas de cambio* in El Calafate, but some hotels may change money.

When to visit

The hotel, restaurant and transport situation in this region changes greatly between high and low season. El Calafate and El Chaltén may be packed out in January and February, when you should book all transport and accommodation in advance, but they are empty and quiet in winter.

Many hotels are open only from September or October to April or May. Out of season trips to the glaciers may be difficult to arrange. The best months to visit are October, November, March and April when it is less crowded and less expensive, but services are running normally.

Trekking

Most paths are very clear and well worn, but a map is essential, even on short walks, available from the park information centre, tourist offices and hotels. If you wish to buy maps, the best are by *Zagier and Urruty* (www.patagoniashop.net, 1:50,000, US$10-13); they're updated quite regularly and available in shops in El Calafate and El Chaltén. Walking here is only really viable from mid-October to April, with the best months usually March to early April when the weather is generally stable and not very cold, and the autumn colours of the beech forest are stunning. Midsummer (December and January) and spring (September to October) are generally very windy.

Climbing

Base camp for Fitz Roy (3405 m) is Campamento Río Blanco (see above). Other peaks include Cerro Torre (3102 m), Torre Egger (2900 m), Cerro Solo (2121 m), Poincenot (3002 m), Guillaumet (2579 m), Saint-Exupery (2558 m), Aguja Bífida (2394 m) and Cordón Adela (2938 m): most of these are for very experienced climbers. Generally the best time is mid February to end March; November-December is very windy; January is fair; winter is extremely cold, but weather is unpredictable and it all depends on the specific route being climbed. Permits for climbing are available at the national park information office. Guides are available in El Chaltén.

El Calafate and around *Colour map 9, B1.*

This town sits on the south shore of **Lago Argentino** and exists almost entirely as a tourist centre for the **Parque Nacional los Glaciares**, 50 km away. In both El Calafate and El Chaltén most of the inhabitants hail from Buenos Aires and other provincial cities. With the recent decline in tourism as a result of global recession, many people have returned north and the local population has fallen. It's certainly not cheap, but pleasant enough, with picturesque wooden architecture and a bustling main drag. Lago Argentino's stunning turquoise waters nearby add further charm.

At **Punta Gualicho** (or Walichu) on the shores of Lago Argentino 7 km east of town, there are cave paintings (badly deteriorated). Just west of the town centre is Bahía Redonda, a shallow part of Lago Argentino that's good for birdwatching; it freezes in winter, when ice-skating and skiing are possible. At the eastern edge of the bay, **Laguna Nímez** ① *high season daily 0900-2000,* *low season daily 0900-1800, US$7*, is a bird reserve where there are flamingos, black-necked swans and ducks; the 2.5-km self-guided trail with multilingual leaflets is recommended. To get there from the Intendencia del Parque at Avenida del Libertador 1302, follow Calle Bustillo up the road to cross the bridge and keep heading north through a residential area: the laguna is signposted. On the way back, stop at the **Centro de Interpretación Histórica** ⓘ *Av Brown y Bonarelli, US$7, children half price*, which has a very informative anthropological and historical exhibition about the region, with pictures and bilingual texts. There's also a very relaxing café/library. The **Glaciarium** ⓘ *6 km from town on R 11, www.glaciarium.com, daily 0900-2000 (Apr-Aug 1100-1900), US$20, US$8 for under-12s, free bus from provincial tourist office hourly*, is a modern museum dedicated to Patagonian ice and glaciers, with an ice-bar (*daily 1100-2000, US$11.75, US$6 for under-16s, cash only, for 20 mins, includes drink*), café and shop.

There are several estancias within reach, offering a day on a working farm, *asado al palo*, horse riding and accommodation. Among them is Estancia Alice '**El Galpón del Glaciar**' ⓘ *T02902-497503, www.elgalpondelglaciar.com.ar*, which offers 'El Dia del Campo', and Estancia Nibepo Aike ⓘ *book at Av Libertador 1215 p 1A, T02902-499904, Buenos Aires T011-5272 0341, www.nibepoaike.com.ar*, in a beautiful, remote setting 55 km southwest of town on the Brazo Sur of Lago Argentina. This traditional estancia has original furniture and is largely self-sustainable; delightful meals are served, and trekking, riding and other rural pursuits are offered within the national park. Trekking, 4WD or horse-riding trips to the top of Cerro Frías (1030 m), 25 km west, for fantastic views of Mount

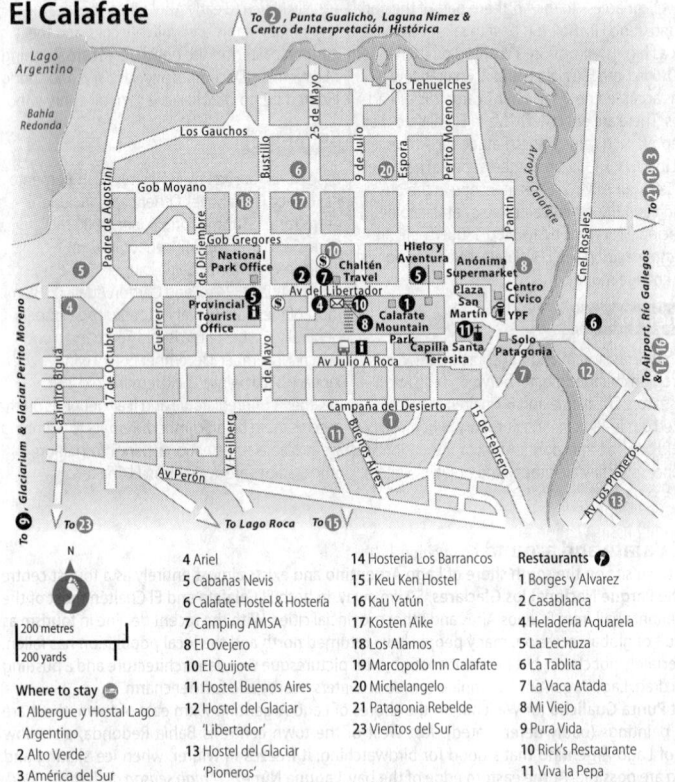

El Calafate

Where to stay 🛏
1 Albergue y Hostal Lago Argentino
2 Alto Verde
3 América del Sur
4 Ariel
5 Cabañas Nevis
6 Calafate Hostel & Hostería
7 Camping AMSA
8 El Ovejero
10 El Quijote
11 Hostel Buenos Aires
12 Hostel del Glaciar 'Libertador'
13 Hostel del Glaciar 'Pioneros'
14 Hosteria Los Barrancos
15 i Keu Ken Hostel
16 Kau Yatún
17 Kosten Aike
18 Los Alamos
19 Marcopolo Inn Calafate
20 Michelangelo
21 Patagonia Rebelde
23 Vientos del Sur

Restaurants 🍴
1 Borges y Alvarez
2 Casablanca
4 Heladería Aquarela
5 La Lechuza
6 La Tablita
7 La Vaca Atada
8 Mi Viejo
9 Pura Vida
10 Rick's Restaurante
11 Viva la Pepa

Fitz Roy, Paine and Lago Argentino, are organized by **Cerro Frías** ① *Libertador 1857, T02902-492808,* *www.cerrofrias.com, US$63 (US$41 without lunch).* See also **Helsingfors**, in Where to stay, page 223.

☆Glaciar Perito Moreno

At the western end of Lago Argentino (80 km from El Calafate) the major attraction is the Glaciar Perito Moreno, one of the few glaciers in the world that is both moving and maintaining its size, despite climate change. It descends to the surface of the water over a 5-km frontage and a height of about 70 m. Several times in the past, the glacier has advanced across the lake, cutting the Brazo Rico off from the Canal de los Témpanos; when this occurs the pressure of water in the Brazo Rico eventually breaks through the ice and reopens the channel, a spectacular rupture that last occurred in March 2016.

The glacier can be seen close up from a series of walkways descending from the car park (reached by bus or guided tour from El Calafate). A 45-minute catamaran trip departs from near the entrance to the walkways and gets closer to the glacier's face, US$17.50; this can be arranged independently through **Solo Patagonia** or is offered with regular excursions. Other boat trips are combined with a mini-trek on the glacier itself (see What to do, page 227). Marvel at the vivid blue hues of the ice floes and listen to the dull roar as pieces break off and float away as icebergs from the snout; it's an unforgettable experience, especially at sunset, but note that the weather may be rough.

☆Glaciar Upsala

At the northwest end of Lago Argentino, 60 km long and 4 km wide, Upsala Glacier is a stunning expanse of untouched beauty. The glacier itself, unlike its cousin Perito Moreno, is suffering badly from the changing climate. When large parts break from the main mass of ice, access by lake may be blocked. Normally it can be reached by motor-boat from Punta Bandera, 50 km west of El Calafate, on a trip that also goes to Lago Onelli and Spegazzini glaciers. Small Lago Onelli is quiet and very beautiful, with beech trees on one side and ice-covered mountains on the other. The lake is full of icebergs of every size and sculpted shape.

El Chaltén and around *Colour map 9, B1.*

This small tourist town lies 217 km northwest of El Calafate via a paved road, at the foot of the jagged peaks of the spectacular Fitz Roy massif, which soars steeply from the Patagonian steppe, its sides too steep for snow to stick. Chaltén is a Tehuelche name meaning the 'smoking mountain'; occasionally at sunrise the mountains are briefly lit up bright red for a few seconds, a phenomenon known as the 'sunrise of fire', or '*amanecer de fuego*'. The town is windy, with an Alpine feel. It's a neat place, but incredibly expensive. Nevertheless you should not let the acute commercialism detract from the fact that it offers amazing views of the nearby peaks, is the base for some of the country's finest trekking and has some very good restaurants and places to sleep. If you haven't got a tent, you can easily rent all you'll need.

☆Trekking routes

Laguna Torre (three hours each way). This is one of the most popular walks. After one to 1½ hours you'll come to Mirador Laguna Torre with great views of Cerro Torre and Fitz Roy; it's 1¼ hours more to busy **Camping De Agostini** near the lake, where you have fantastic views. A longer route is via Laguna Capri (see below): between Camping Capri and Camping Poincenot a path branches off south, passing Lagunas Madre e Hija, and reaches the path to Laguna Torre, west of the Mirador, after two hours. From El Chaltén to Laguna Torre along this route takes about seven hours one way.

Laguna de los Tres (four hours each way). Walk 1¾ hours up to Camping Capri on Laguna Capri for great views of Fitz Roy, then another hour to **Camping Poincenot**. Just beyond it is **Camping Río Blanco** (only for climbers, registration at the national park office required). From Río Blanco you can walk another hour, very steep, to Laguna de los Tres where you'll get a spectacular view (not a good walk if it's cloudy).

Loma del Pliegue Tumbado (four hours each way). A recommended day walk is to this viewpoint from where you can see both *cordones* and Lago Viedma. There's a marked path from the *guardería* with excellent panoramic views, best in clear weather. The onward trek to Laguna Toro, a glacial lake on the route across the ice cap (seven hours each way) is for more experienced trekkers.

Up the Río Blanco to Piedra del Fraile (seven hours each way, two hours each way from the road to Lago del Desierto). A beautiful walk out of the national park to a campsite with facilities, and Refugio Piedra del Fraile, neither is free. Recommended.

Short walks The best options are the miradors on the way to both Laguna Capri and Mirador Laguna Torre, after an hour or so (see above). Alternatively, there's a one-hour hike to Chorillo del Salto, a small but pristine waterfall; take the road to Lago del Desierto for about 30 minutes, then follow the marked path. No guide is necessary.

Lago del Desierto to Chile

There are excursions from El Chaltén to **Lago del Desierto**, 37 km north, surrounded by forests in a stunning virgin landscape. A short walk to a mirador at the end of the road gives fine views. There's a campsite at the southern end of the lake (sometimes no food, although there is a kiosk that sells, soda, beer and *choripán*), and a *refugio* at its northern end. There is also the secluded **Aguas Arriba Lodge** ① T011-4152 5697, www.aguasarribalodge.com, reached only by boat, 15 mins, or by a 3-hr walk with guide (luggage goes by boat), open mid-Oct to end-Mar, 2 nights minimum, price includes full board and guided activities which include treks and fishing. Chaltén Travel run to the lake daily in summer, or **Las Lengas** runs a minibus twice daily to Lago del Desierto (see El Chaltén, What to do, page 227).

Border with Chile To get to **Villa O'Higgins** (Chile), the southernmost town on the Carretera Austral, take the Las Lengas transfer, or JR minibus to Lago del Desierto, then a 45-minute boat trip to the northern end (US$43), or walk up a path along the east shores, 4½ hours to reach the northern end. From Argentine immigration at Punta Norte it's a demanding 5-km hike to the border, then 14 km to Chilean immigration, 1km from Puerto Candelario Mancilla on Lago O'Higgins. This can be done on foot, on horseback, or by 4WD service (US$35 for two to four passengers and luggage, or US$15.50 luggage only), or you can take a horse for the whole 19 km from Punta Norte, US$47 per horse with guide. Overnight at Estancia Candelario Mancilla, then take a boat from Candelario Mancilla to Bahía Bahamóndez (three hours, US$65), and a bus to Villa O'Higgins (7 km, US$4). The border is closed from April/May to November (check at www.villaohiggins.com for dates, tours and boat availability and see Chile chapter, **Villa O'Higgins**, for more details).

El Calafate to Chile

If travelling from El Calafate to Torres del Paine by car or bike, you'll cross this bleak area of steppe. About 40 km before reaching the border there are small lagoons and salt flats with flamingos (between El Calafate and Punta Arenas it is also possible to see guanacos and condors). From Calafate you can take the paved combination of Ruta 11, RN 40 and RN 5 to **La Esperanza** (165 km), where there's fuel, a campsite and a large but expensive *confitería* (lodging $$ with bath). From La Esperanza, Ruta 7 heads west (not completely paved) along the valley of the Río Coyle. A shorter route (closed in winter) missing La Esperanza, turns off at El Cerrito and joins Ruta 7 at Estancia Tapi Aike. For bus services along this route see under El Calafate.

Border with Chile: Paso Río Don Guillermo (Cancha Carrera) Ruta 7 continues west to the border, 48 km north of Río Turbio. This is the most convenient crossing for Parque Nacional Torres del Paine and is open all year, 0900-2300. Argentine customs are fast and friendly. On the Chilean side the road continues 7 km to the border post at Cerro Castillo, where it joins the road between Torres del Paine (20 km north) and Puerto Natales (63 km south).

Río Turbio *Colour map 9, C2.*

You're most likely to visit this charmless town, 267 km west of Río Gallegos and 30 km from Puerto Natales (Chile), en route to or from Torres del Paine. The site of Argentina's largest coalfield hasn't recovered from the depression hitting the industry in the 1990s. It has a cargo railway, connecting it with Punta Loyola; Mina 1 is where the first mine was opened. There is a ski centre, **Valdelén** ① Club Andino Río Turbio, T02902-421900, for more info, with six pistes that are ideal for beginners, also scope for cross-country skiing between early June and late September. **Tourist information** ① in the municipality, Plazoleta Castillo, T02902-421950.

Border with Chile As well as Cancha Carrera to the north (see above), there are two other crossings, both of which join the main Puerto Natales–Punta Arenas road on the Chilean side of the border: **Paso Mina Uno/Dorotea** is 5 km south of Río Turbio, open all year, 0900-2300; **Paso Casas Viejas/Laurita** is 33 km south of Río Turbio via 28 de Noviembre, open all year, 0900-0100. All crossings may have different hours in winter; see www.gendarmeria.gov.ar.

Listings Parque Nacional Los Glaciares *map page 220.*

Tourist information

El Calafate

In addition to the national park office (see Essential box, page 219), there are very helpful **tourist offices** in the bus station (T02902-491476), at Bajada de Palma 44 (T02902-491090) and at Anfiteatro del Bosque, Libertador 1400 (T02902-496497), all daily 0800-2000, www.elcalafate.tur.ar; municipal site is www.elcalafate.gov.ar); the staff speak several languages.

El Chaltén

The **tourist office** is at the bus terminal (T02962-493370, daily 0800-2200 in high season, otherwise 0800-1500). The website, www.elchalten.com, is excellent with accommodation listed.

Where to stay

Parque Nacional Los Glaciares

$$$$ Estancia Cristina
Office at 9 de Julio 69, El Calafate, T02902-491133 (T011-4218 2333 ext 106/107 in Buenos Aires), www.estanciacristina.com.
Located at the northern tip of Lago Argentina, this remote estancia offers unrivalled access to the Upsala glacier and its surroundings. 20 comfortable rooms available in 5 lodges. Boat transfers from El Calafate are included.

$$$$ Estancia Helsingfors
73 km northwest of La Leona, on Lago Viedma, in BsAs: T011-5277 0195, reservations T02966-675753, www.helsingfors.com.ar. Nov-Apr.
Fabulous place in splendid position on Lago Viedma, stylish rooms, welcoming lounge, delicious food (full board), and excursions directly to glaciers and to Laguna Azul, by horse or trekking, plus boat trips.

El Calafate

Prepare to pay more for accommodation here than elsewhere in Argentina.

$$$$ El Quijote
Gob Gregores 1191, T02902-491017, www.quijotehotel.com.ar.
A very good hotel, spacious, well designed with traditional touches, tasteful rooms with TV, restaurant **Sancho**, stylish lobby bar, English and Italian spoken.

$$$$ Kau Yatún
Estancia 25 de Mayo (10 blocks from centre, east of arroyo Calafate), T02902-491059, www.kauyatun.com/index.php/en.
Renovated main house of a former estancia, well-kept grounds, 2 excellent restaurants, only half board or all inclusive packages that include excursions in the national park.

$$$$ Kosten Aike
Gob Moyano 1243, T02902-492424, www.kostenaike.com.ar. Open year-round.
Relaxed yet stylish, elegant spacious rooms (some superior), jacuzzi, gym, excellent restaurant, **Ariskaiken** (open to non residents), cosy bar, garden, English spoken. Recommended.

$$$$ Los Alamos
Guatti 1135, T02902-491144, www.posadalosalamos.com. Cheaper in low season.
Very comfortable, charming rooms, good service, lovely gardens, good bar and without doubt the best restaurant in town, **La Posta**.

$$$ Alto Verde
Zupic 138, T02902-491326, www.welcomeargentina.com/altoverde.
$$ in low season. Top quality, spotless, spacious, helpful, also with apartments for 4.

$$$ Cabañas Nevis
Av del Libertador 1696, T02902-493180, www.cabanasnevis.com.ar.
Owner Mr Patterson offers very nice cabins for 5 and 8 (price quoted is for 5), some with lake view, great value.

$$$ Hostería Los Barrancos
Villa Parque Los Glaciares, T02902-491380, www.hosterialosbarrancos.com.

Light rooms with heating, lounge and terrace with lovely views, safe, laundry service, parking, English spoken.

$$$ Michelangelo
Espora y Gob Moyano, T02902-491045,
www.michelangelocalafate.com.
Lovely, quiet, welcoming, restaurant. Recommended.

$$$ Patagonia Rebelde
José Haro 442, T02902-494495 (in Buenos Aires T015-5890 1276), www.patagoniarebelde.com.
Charming new building in traditional Patagonian style, like an old inn with rustic decor, good comfort with well-heated bedrooms and comfy sitting-rooms.

$$$ Vientos del Sur
Up the hill at Río Santa Cruz 2317, T02902-493563, www.vientosdelsur.com.
Very hospitable, calm, comfortable, good views, kind family attention.

$$$-$$ Ariel
Av Libertador 1693, T02902-493131,
www.hotelariel.com.ar.
Modern, functional, well maintained. Breakfast included.

$$ Hostel Buenos Aires
Buenos Aires 296, 200 m from terminal, T02902-491147, www.glaciarescalafate.com.
Quiet, kind owner, helpful, comfortable with doubles, cheaper without bath, good hot showers, laundry service, luggage store, bikes for hire.

$$-$ pp Albergue y Hostal Lago Argentino
Campaña del Desierto 1050-61 (near bus terminal), T02902-491423, www.lago argentinohostel.com.ar.
$ pp shared dorms, too few showers when full, nice atmosphere, good flats, *cabañas* and **$$** doubles on a neat garden and also in building on opposite side of road.

$$-$ pp Calafate Hostel & Hostería
Gob Moyano 1226, T02902-492450,
www.calafatehostels.com.
A huge log cabin with good rooms: dorms with or without bath, breakfast extra, **$$** doubles with bath and breakfast. Book a month ahead for Jan-Feb, HI discounts, travel agency, **Always Glacier**, and restaurant **Isabel** on premises.

$$-$ pp Marcopolo Inn Calafate
Los Lagos 82, T02902-493899,
www.marcopoloinncalafate.com.

Part of Hostelling International. **$** pp in dorms. Laundry facilities, various activities and tours on offer.

$ pp América del Sur
Puerto Deseado 153, T02902-493525,
www.americahostel.com.ar.
Panoramic views from this comfortable, relaxed hostel, welcoming, well-heated rooms (dorms for 4, **$$** doubles with views, 1 room adapted for wheelchair users), chill-out area, fireplace. Warmly recommended, but can be noisy.

$ pp Hostel del Glaciar 'Libertador'
Av del Libertador 587 (next to the bridge), T02902-492492, www.glaciar.com. HI discounts. Sep-Apr.
Smaller and pricier than 'Pioneros', rooms are good and well-heated, all with bath and safe box (US$20 pp dorms for 4 and **$$$-$$** doubles), breakfast included for private rooms, laundry service. Owners run **Patagonia Backpackers** (see below under What to do). Recommended.

$ pp Hostel del Glaciar 'Pioneros'
Los Pioneros 255, T02902-491243,
www.glaciar.com. 1 Nov to end-Feb.
Accommodation for all budgets: standard **$$** doubles (also for 3 and 4) with bath and safe box, shared dorms up to 4 beds, US$17 pp. Many languages spoken, lots of bathrooms, breakfast extra, only for guests in private rooms, laundry service. Arranges tours to glaciers and Navimag boat trips in Chile. Very popular, so book well in advance and double-check.

$ pp i Keu Ken Hostel
F M Pontoriero 171, T02902-495482,
www.patagoniaikeuken.com.ar.
On a hill, very helpful, flexible staff, hot water, heating, luggage store, good.

Camping

AMSA
Olavarría 65 (50 m off the main road, turning south at the fire station), T02902-492247.
Hot water, open in summer, US$7 pp.

El Huala
42 km from El Calafate, on the road to Lago Roca. Open all year round
Free with basic facilities.

El Ovejero
José Pantin 64, near the river, T02902-493 422, www.campingelovejero.com.ar.
US$7.25 pp, also has dorm (**$$**)

Lago Roca
50 km from El Calafate, T02902-499500,
www.campinglagoroca.com.ar. Oct-Apr.
Beautifully situated, US$11 pp, bike hire, fishing licences, restaurant/confitería. (**Ferretería Chuar**, 1 block from bus terminal, sells camping gas.)

El Chaltén
In high season places are full: you must book ahead. Most places close in low season.

$$$$ Hostería El Puma
Lionel Terray 212, T02962-493095,
www.hosteriaelpuma.com.ar.
A little apart, splendid views, lounge with log fire, tasteful stylish furnishings, comfortable, transfers and big American breakfast included. Recommended.

$$$$ Los Cerros
Av San Martín 260, T02962-493182,
www.loscerrosdelchalten.com.
Stylish and sophisticated, in a stunning setting with mountain views, sauna, whirlpool and massage. Half-board and all-inclusive packages with excursions available.

$$$$ Senderos
Perito Moreno 35, T02962-493336,
www.senderoshosteria.com.ar.
4 types of room and suite in a new, wood-framed structure, comfortable, warm, can arrange excursions, excellent restaurant.

$$$ El Pilar
R23, Km 17, T02962-493002,
www.hosteriaelpilar.com.ar.
Country house in a spectacular setting at the meeting of Ríos Blanco and de las Vueltas, with clear views of Fitz Roy. A chance to sample the simple life with access to less-visited northern part of the park. Simple comfortable rooms, great food, breakfast and return transfers included.

$$$ Lunajuim
Trevisán 45, T02962-493047, www.lunajuim.com.
Stylish yet relaxed, comfortable (duvets on the beds), lounge with wood fire. Recommended.

$$$ Nothofagus
Hensen y Riquelme, T493087,
www.nothofagusbb.com.ar.
Cosy bed and breakfast, simple rooms, cheaper without bath and in low season, Oct and Apr (**$$**), good value. Recommended.

$$ Hospedaje La Base
Calle 10 H 16, T02962-493031, see Facebook.

Good rooms for 2, 3 and 4, tiny kitchen, self service breakfast, great video lounge. Recommended.

$ pp Albergue Patagonia
Av San Martín 493, T02962-493019, www.
patagoniahostel.com.ar. Closed Jun-Sep.
HI-affiliated, cheaper for members, small and cosy with rooms for 2 with own bath (**$$**) or for 2 (**$$**), 4, 5 or 6 with shared bath, also has cabins, video lounge, bike hire, laundry, luggage store and lockers, restaurant, very welcoming. Helpful information on Chaltén, also run excursions to Lago del Desierto.

$ pp Albergue Rancho Grande
San Martín 724, T02962-493005,
www.ranchograndehostel.com.
HI-affiliated, in a great position at the end of town with good open views and attractive restaurant and lounge, rooms for 4, with shared bath, breakfast extra. Also **$$** doubles, breakfast extra. Helpful, English spoken. Recommended. Reservations in **Calafate Hostel/Chaltén Travel**, Calafate.

$ pp Cóndor de los Andes
Av Río de las Vueltas y Halvorsen, T02962-
493101, www.condordelosandes.com.
Nice little rooms for up to 6 with bath, sheets included, breakfast extra apart from bread and tea/coffee, also doubles with bath (**$$$-$$**), laundry service, quiet, HI affiliated, helpful.

Camping
In the national park there are campsites at Poincenot, Capri, Laguna Toro and Laguna Torre. None has services, but it is possible to rent equipment in El Chaltén; ask at park office or Rancho Grande. All river water is drinkable. A gas/ alcohol stove is essential for camping as open fires are prohibited in the national park. Take plenty of warm clothes and a good sleeping bag. Pack up all rubbish and take it back to town; do not wash within 70 m of rivers. **Camping Los Troncos/ Piedra del Fraile** on Río Eléctrico is beyond the park boundary and privately owned, with facilities.

Camping del Lago
Lago del Desierto 135, T02962-493245.
Centrally located with hot showers.

Lago Desierto to Chile

$$$$ Aguas Arriba Lodge
On shore of Lago Desierto, T011-4152 5697, www.
aguasarribalodge.com. Mid-Oct to end-Mar.
Reached only by boat, 15 mins, or by a 3-hr walk with guide (luggage goes by boat), 2 nights

minimum, price includes full board, boat transfers and guided activities which include treks and fishing, no Wi-Fi or TV but has internet, hot water, electricity, no children under 12. The lodge can held with logistics for the crossing to Villa O'Higgins. Special promotions with Bahía Bustamante (see page 206).

Río Turbio

$$ Nazó
Gob Moyano 464, T02902-421800,
www.hotelnazo.com.ar.
Modern building, rooms for 2-4, laundry service, restaurant and bar.

$ Hostería Capipe
Paraje Julia Dufour, 9 km from town,
T02902-482935, see Facebook.
Simple, with restaurant.

Restaurants

El Calafate

$$ La Lechuza
Av del Libertador 1301, see Facebook.
Good-quality pizzas, pasta, salad and meat dishes. Excellent wine list. Has another branch up the road at No 935.

$$ La Tablita
Cnel Rosales 28 (near the bridge),
www.la-tablita.com.ar.
Typical *parrilla*, generous portions and quality beef. Recommended.

$$ La Vaca Atada
Av del Libertador 1176.
Good home-made pastas and more elaborate and expensive dishes based on salmon and king crab.

$$ Mi Viejo
Av del Libertador 1111. Closed Tue.
Popular *parrilla*.

$$ Pura Vida
Av Libertador 1876, near C 17, see Facebook.
Open 1930-2330 only, closed Wed.
Comfortable sofas, home-made Argentine food, vegetarian options, lovely atmosphere, lake view (reserve table). Recommended.

$$ Rick's Restaurante
Av del Libertador 1091.
Lively *parrilla* with good atmosphere.

$$ Viva la Pepa
Emilio Amado 833, see Facebook.
Mon-Sat 1200-2100.
A mainly vegetarian café with great sandwiches and crêpes filled with special toppings. Wi-Fi, craft beers. Child-friendly.

Cafés

Borges y Alvarez
Av del Libertador 1015 (Galería de los Gnomos).
Daily till 0200.
A lively, friendly book-bar open daily till 0400. Excellent place to hang out. Recommended.

Casablanca
25 de Mayo y Av del Libertador.
Jolly place for omelettes, hamburgers, vegetarian, 30 varieties of pizza.

Heladería Aquarela
Av del Libertador 1197.
The best ice cream – try the *calafate*. Also home-made chocolates and local produce.

El Chaltén

$$ Estepa
Cerro Solo y Antonio Rojo, www.esteparestobar.com.
Small, intimate place with good, varied meals, friendly staff.

$$ Fuegia
San Martín 342. Dinner only.
Pastas, trout, meat and vegetarian dishes. Recommended.

$$ Josh Aike
Lago de Desierto 105.
Excellent *chocolatería*, home-made food, beautiful building. Recommended.

$$ Pangea
Lago del Desierto 330 y San Martín. Open for lunch and dinner, drinks and coffee.
Calm, good music, varied menu. Recommended.

$$ Patagonicus
Güemes y Madsen. Midday to midnight.
Lovely warm place with salads, *pastas caseras* and fabulous pizzas for 2, US$3-8. Recommended.

$$-$ Ahonikenk Chaltén
Av Martín M de Güemes 23, T02962-493070.
Restaurant and pizzería, good home-made pastas.

$$-$ B&B Burger Joint
San Martín between Calle 6 and Terray.
Great burgers, microbrews and pub grub.

$ Domo Blanco
San Martín 164.
Delicious ice cream.

Bars and clubs

El Chaltén

Cervecería Artesanal El Chaltén
San Martín 564, T02962-493109.
Brews its own excellent beer, also local dishes and pizzas, coffee and cakes, English spoken. Recommended.

Lagula de Los Tres
Trevisan 45 (see Facebook).
Newer bar, live music, artesanal beer, sandwiches and pizzas. Free salsa classes on Thu.

Shopping

El Calafate

Plenty of touristy shops in main street Av del Libertador. Recommended for home-made local produce, especially Patagonian fruit teas, sweets and liqueurs is **Estancia El Tranquilo** (Av del Libertador 935, www.eltranquilo.com.ar).

El Chaltén

Several outdoor shops. Supermarkets are all expensive, with little fresh food available. Fuel is available next to the bridge.

What to do

El Calafate

Most agencies charge the same rates and run similar excursions: minibus tours to the Perito Moreno glacier (park entry not included), US$31; minitrekking tours (transport plus a 2½-hr walk on the glacier), US$105. Note that in winter boat trips can be limited by bad weather, even cancelled.
Calafate Mountain Park, *Av del Libertador 1037, T02902-491446, www.calafatemountainpark.com.*
Excursions in 4WD to panoramic views, 3-6 hrs. Summer and winter experiences including kayaking, quad biking, skiing and more.
Chaltén Travel, *Av del Libertador 1174, T02902-492212, also Av Güemes 7, T02902-493092, El Chaltén, www.chaltentravel.com.* Huge range of tours (has a monopoly on some): glaciers, estancias, trekking, and bus to El Chaltén. Has daily bus service at 1800 to Perito Moreno, US$98, and Los Antiguos, US$107, and a service along

the Ruta 40 via Perito Moreno and Los Antiguos to Bariloche, departures 0600 on odd-numbered days (0800 from El Chaltén) mid-Nov to Apr, overnight in Perito Moreno (cheaper to book your own accommodation), 36 hrs, English spoken.
Hielo y Aventura, *Av del Libertador 935, T02902-492205, www.hieloyaventura.com.* Mini-trekking includes walk through forests and 2½-hr trek on Moreno glacier (crampons included); Big Ice full-day tour includes a 4-hr trek on the glacier. Also half-day boat excursion to Brazo Sur for a view of stunning glaciers, including Moreno. Recommended.
Lago San Martín, *Av del Libertador 1215, p 1 A, T02902-492858, www.lagosanmartin.com.*
Operates with **Estancias Turísticas de Santa Cruz**, specializing in arranging estancia visits, helpful.
Mar Patag, *Av del Libertador 1319, loc 7, T02902-492118, www.crucerosmarpatag.com.*
Exclusive 2-day boat excursion to Upsala, Spegazzini and Moreno glaciers, with full board. Also does a shorter full-day cruise with gourmet lunch included.
Mundo Austral, *Av del Libertador 1080, p 1, T02902-492365, www.mundoaustral.com.ar.*
For all bus travel and cheaper trips to the glaciers, helpful bilingual guides.
Patagonia Backpackers, *at Hosteles del Glaciar, T02902-492492, www.patagonia-backpackers. com.* Alternative glacier tour takes a more scenic route and is the only one that treks off the tourist trail on the south side of the glacier, entertaining, informative, includes walking, US$52, park entrance extra. Recommended constantly.
Solo Patagonia, *Av del Libertador 867, T02902-491155, www.solopatagonia.com.* This company runs 2 7-hr trips taking in Upsala, Onelli and Spegazzini glaciers, US$92.

El Chaltén

There are daily boat trips on Lago Viedma to pass Glaciar Viedma, with ice trekking optional in the day-long tour. **Hostería El Pilar** (see Where to stay) is a base for trekking up Río Blanco or Río Eléctrico, or try the multi activity adventure circuit. In summer **Las Lengas**, see below, runs a regular minibus to Lago del Desierto, via El Pilar, US$33, and to Río Eléctrico, 3 a day, US$8.50, for several of the hikes mentioned above. Highly recommended.
Casa De Guías, *Av San Martín s/n, T02962-493118, www.casadeguias.com.ar.* Experienced climbers who lead groups to nearby peaks, to the Campo de Hielo Continental and easier trek.
El Relincho, *San Martín s/n, T02962-493007, www.elrelinchopatagonia.com.ar.* For trekking

on horseback with guides, also trekking, accommodation and rural activities.

Fitz Roy Expediciones, *San Martín 56, T02962-493178, www.fitzroyexpediciones.com.ar*. Organizes trekking and adventure trips including on the Campo de Hielo Continental, ice climbing schools, and fabulous longer trips. Climbers must be fit, but no technical experience required; equipment provided. Email with lots of notice to reserve. Also has ecocamp with 8 wilderness cabins. Highly recommended.

Patagonia Aventura, *San Martín 56, T02962-493110, www.patagonia-aventura.com*. Has various ice trekking and other tours to Lago and Glaciar Viedma, also to Lago del Desierto.

Transport

El Calafate
Air Airport, T02902-491220, 23 km east of town, **Transpatagonia Expeditions**, T02902-494355, runs service from town to meet flights, US$7 (US$8.50 from airport). Taxi (T02902-491850), US$18. Daily flights to/from **Buenos Aires**. Many more flights in summer to **Bariloche, Ushuaia** and **Trelew**. LADE flies to **Ushuaia, Comodoro Rivadavia, Río Gallegos** and other Patagonian airports (office at J Mermoz 160, T02902-491262). Note that a boarding fee of US$20.50, not included in the airline ticket price, has to be paid at El Calafate.

Bike hire **Patagonia Shop**, Av del Libertador 995, also at 9 de Julio 29.

Bus Terminal on Roca 1004, 1 block up stairs from Av del Libertador, T02902-491476. Terminal fee US$0.35, always included in bus ticket price. Some bus companies will store luggage for a fee. To **Perito Moreno** glacier, **Taqsa**, US$32 return, or on a minibus tour (see above). To **Río Gallegos** daily with 4-5 hrs, US$28-33, **Taqsa** (T02902-491843). To **Puerto Madryn** with **Red Patagonia** (T02902 494250) 2 per day, 0300, 1330, US$112. To **El Chaltén** daily with **Taqsa**, US$30, **Chaltén Travel** (T02902-492212, at 0800, 1800), **Los Glaciares**, **Cal-Tur** (Av El Libertador 1080, T02902-491368, www.caltur.com.ar, who run many other services and tours), 3 hrs. To **Bariloche**, see page 187 for **Chaltén Travel**'s buses via Los Antiguos and Perito Moreno, also **Cal-Tur**. **Marga** may run a bus to Bariloche via Los Antiguos, 36 hrs, frequency depends on demand. To **Ushuaia** take bus to Río Gallegos for connections.

Direct bus services to Chile (Take passport when booking bus tickets to Chile.) To **Puerto Natales**, daily in summer with **Cootra** (T02902-491444), via Río Turbio, 8½ hrs, US$36, daily 0830, **Turismo Zaahj** (T02902-491631), 3 a week, fewer off season, 5 hrs, US$36, or Bus Sur, Tue, Thu, Sat 1630, US$18 (advance booking recommended, tedious customs check at border). **Note** Argentine pesos cannot be exchanged in Torres del Paine.

Car hire Average price under US$65 per day for small car with insurance but usually only 200 free km. **Avis**, Av del Libertador 1078, T02902-492877, www.avis.com.ar. **Localiza**, Av del Libertador 687, T02902-491398, www.localiza.com.ar. **Nunatak**, Gob Gregores 1075, T02902-491987, www.nunatakrentacar.com.ar. All vehicles have a permit for crossing to Chile, included in the fee, but cars are poor.

Taxi There is small taxi stand outside the bus terminal. Taxis to the glacier cost about US$90 for 4 passengers round trip including wait of 3-4 hrs at the glacier. Reliable companies include **El Tehuelche**, T02902-491 850, **La Terminal**, T02902-490 933 and **Calafate**, T02902-492 005.

El Chaltén
Bus Tax of US$1.15 is charged at the terminal. In summer, buses fill quickly: book ahead. Fewer services off season. Daily buses to **El Calafate**, 3 hrs (most stop at El Calafate airtport), companies and price given above, for El Chaltén phone numbers: **Chaltén Travel**, see above for address, **Cal Tur**, Av San Martín 520, T02962-493079. **Taqsa**, T02962-493130. (See page 187 for **Chaltén Travel** to Los Antiguos and Bariloche.) **Las Lengas** (Viedma 95, opposite tourist office, T02962-493023, laslengaselchalten@yahoo.com.ar) run to El Calafate airport 6 times a day in high season, 3 hrs, US$28, reserve in advance.

To **Piedrabuena** on Ruta 3, for connections to Río Gallegos and north to Comodoro Rivadavia and Puerto Madryn, Taqsa, 3 daily in high season.

Taxi Taxi/rent Oxalis, T02962-493343.

Río Turbio
Bus To **Puerto Natales**, 2 hrs, US$12, hourly with **Cootra** (Tte del Castillo 01, T02902-421448), and other companies. To **El Calafate**, via La Esperanza, **Taqsa**, 4 hrs, US$17-20. **Río Gallegos**, 5 hrs, US$28 (**Taqsa/Marga**, T02902-421422).

Tierra del Fuego

The island at the extreme south of South America is divided between Argentina and Chile, with the tail end of the Andes cordillera providing dramatic mountain scenery along the southern fringe of both countries. There are lakes and forests, mostly still wild and undeveloped, offering good trekking in summer and downhill or cross-country skiing in winter. Until a century ago, the island was inhabited by four ethnic groups, Selk'nam (or Ona), Alacaluf (Kaweskar), Haush (Manekenk) and Yámana (Yahgan). They were removed by settlers, who occupied their land to introduce sheep, and many died from disease. Their descendants (except for the extinct Haush) are very few in number and live on the islands. Many of the sheep farming estancias that replaced the indigenous people can be visited. Ushuaia, the island's main city, is an attractive base for exploring the southwest's small national park, and for boat trips along the Beagle channel to Harberton, a fascinating pioneer estancia. There's good trout and salmon fishing, and a tremendous variety of birdlife in summer.

Río Grande to Ushuaia *Colour map 9, C2.*

trout fishing and pastries on the way to Ushuaia

Río Grande is a sprawling modern town in windy, dust-laden sheep-grazing and oil-bearing plains. (The oil is refined at San Sebastián in the smallest and most southerly refinery in the world.) Government tax incentives to companies in the 1970s led to a rapid growth in population. Although incentives were withdrawn, it continues to expand, most recently into mobile phone and white goods assembly. Nearby estancias can be visited, notably María Behety (15 km), with a vast sheep-shearing shed, but the area's main claim to fame is sport-fishing, especially for trout.

Sights

The city was founded by Fagnano's Salesian mission in 1893; you can visit the original building **La Candelaria** ① *11 km north, T02964-421642, Mon-Sat 1000-1230, 1500-1900, US$2, afternoon teas, US$3, getting there: taxi US$8 with wait.* The museum has displays of indigenous artefacts and natural history. Río Grande's **Museo Virginia Choquintel** ① *Alberdi 555, T02964-430647, Mon-Fri 0900-1700, Sat 1500-1900,* is also recommended for its history of the Selk'nam, the pioneers, missions and oil. Next door is a handicraft shop called **Kren** (meaning 'sun' in Selk'nam), which sells good local products. There are banks with ATMs on San Martín by junction with Avenida 9 de Julio.

Best for
Boat trips ▪ Cross-country skiing ▪ Fishing ▪ Isolation ▪ Trekking

Essential Tierra del Fuego

Getting there

There are no road/ferry crossings between the Argentine mainland and Argentine Tierra del Fuego. You have to go through Chilean territory. From Río Gallegos, Ruta 3 reaches the Chilean border at Monte Aymond (67 km; open 24 hours summer, 0900-2300 April to October), passing Laguna Azul. For bus passengers the border crossing is easy, although you have about a 30-minute wait at each border post as luggage is checked and documents are stamped. Hire cars need a document for permission to cross the border. (From the border, it's two more hours to Punta Arenas.) Some 30 km into Chile is **Kamiri Aike**, with a dock 16 km east at **Punta Delgada** for the 20-minute ferry crossing over the Primera Angostura (First Narrows) to **Bahía Azul**. At Punta Delgada is **Hostería El Faro** for food and drinks. Three boats work continuously, 0830-2400, US$23 per vehicle, foot passengers US$2.65, www.tabsa.cl. The road is paved to Cerro Sombrero, from where *ripio* (unsurfaced) roads run southeast to Chilean **San Sebastián** (130-140 km from ferry, depending on route taken). Chilean San Sebastián is just a few houses with **Hostería La Frontera** 500 m from the border. It's 15 km east, across the border (24 hours, 0800-2200 April to October), to Argentine San Sebastián, not much bigger, with a seven-room **ACA hostería** ($$), T02964-425542; service station open 0700-2300. From here the road is paved to Río Grande and Ushuaia.

The other ferry crossing is **Punta Arenas–Porvenir**. RN255 from Kamiri Aike goes southwest 116 km to the intersection with the Punta Arenas–-Puerto Natales road, from where it is 53 km to Punta Arenas. The ferry dock is 5 km north of Punta Arenas centre, at Tres Puentes. The ferry crosses to Bahía Chilota, 5 km west of Porvenir Tuesday to Sunday mostly (subject to tides, **Transportadora Austral Broom**, www.tabsa.cl, publishes timetable a month in advance), 2½ hours, US$62 per vehicle, foot passengers US$10. From Porvenir a 234 km *ripio* road runs east to Río Grande (six hours, no public transport) via San Sebastián. See also Transport, page 241. For details of transport and hotels on Chilean territory, see the Chile chapter.

Tip...

There are Chilean consulates in Río Grande (Belgrano 369, T02964-430523, http://chile.gob.cl/rio-grande/, Monday-Friday 0830-1330), and Ushuaia (Jainén 50, T02901-430909, http://chile.gob.cl/ushuaia, Monday-Friday 0900-1300).

When to visit

March to April is a good time because of the spectacular autumn colours and the most stable weather. November has the strongest winds (not good for sailing to Antarctica). Most visitors arrive in January. Accommodation, planes and buses fill up quickly from November to March, so it's essential to book ahead. Summer temperatures average at about 15°C, but exceed 20° more frequently than in the past. Likewise, there has been a reduction in snowfall in winter (average temperature 0°C). Lots of Brazilians come to ski, so there is a mini high season in July-August. European skiers also come to train in the northern hemisphere summer.

Tip...

Fruit and meat may not be taken onto the island, nor between Argentina and Chile.

South of Río Grande

About 20 km south of Río Grande, trees begin to appear on the steppe while the road, Ruta 3, runs parallel to the seashore. On Sunday people drive out to the woods for picnics, go fishing or look for shellfish on the mudflats. The road is mostly very good as it approaches the mountains to the south.

Tolhuin, known as 'la corazón de la isla', at the eastern tip of Lago Fagnano, is 1¼ hours from Río Grande. The small town caters for horse riders, anglers, mountain bikers and trekkers. There are cabins, hostels and campsites. On Sunday it is crammed with day-trippers. The **Panificadora La Unión** in the centre is renowned for its breads, pastries and chocolate and is an obligatory stop. Líder and Montiel minibuses break the Río Grande–Ushuaia journey here.

The road leaves Lago Fagnano and passes *lenga* forest destroyed by fire in 1978 before climbing into healthier forests. After small Lago Verde and fjord-like Lago Escondido, the road crosses the cordillera at Paso Garibaldi. It then descends to the Cerro Castor winter sports complex and the Tierra Mayor recreation area (see Ushuaia What to do, below). There is a police control just as you enter the Ushuaia city limits; passports may be checked.

Listings Río Grande and around

Tourist information

There are **tourist offices** in both Río Grande (Rosales 350, on Plaza Almte Brown, T02964-430516, www.riogrande.gob.ar/ciudad/informacion-turistica/, Mon-Fri 0900-2000) and Tolhuin (Av de los Shelknam 80, T02901-492380, dir.turismo@tolhuin.gob.ar). Río Grande also has the provincial office (Av Belgrano 319, T02946-422887, infuerg1@tierradelfuego.org.ar).

Where to stay

Book ahead, as there are few decent choices. Several estancias offer full board, and some, mainly on the northern rivers, have expensive fishing lodges; others offer horse riding. See www.tierradelfuego.org.ar for a full list.

Río Grande

$$$$ pp Estancia Viamonte
40 km southeast on the coast, T02964-430861, www.estanciaviamonte.com.
For an authentic experience of Tierra del Fuego. Built in 1902 by pioneer Lucas Bridges, writer of *Uttermost Part of the Earth*, to protect the Selk'nam/Ona people, this working estancia has simple and beautifully furnished rooms in a spacious cottage. Price is for full board and all activities: riding and trekking; cheaper for dinner, bed and breakfast only. Delicious meals. Book a week ahead.

$$$ Posada de los Sauces
Elcano 839, T02964-430868, www.laposadadelossauces.com.ar.
Best by far, with breakfast, beautifully decorated, comfortable, good restaurant (trout recommended), cosy bar, very helpful staff.

$$$ Villa
Av San Martín 281, T02964-424998, hotelvilla@live.com.
Central, modern, restaurant/*confitería*, parking, discount given for cash.

South of Rio Grande

$$$ Cabañas Khami
On Lago Fagnano, 8 km from Tolhuin, T02964-15-611243, www.cabaniaskhami.com.ar.
Well-equipped, rustic cabins, good value with linen. Price given for 6 people, 3-night weekend rates available.

Camping Hain
Tolhuin, T02964-15-603606, Facebook: camping.hain. Oct-May.
Full of character, camping US$4.50 pp, shelter available, *refugios* for 7, or 3 people ($$$-$$).

Restaurants

Río Grande

$$ El Rincón de Julio
Next to Posada de los Sauces, Elcano 800 block.
For excellent *parrilla*.

$$ La Nueva Colonial
Av Belgrano 489.
Delicious pasta, warm family atmosphere.

Cafés

El Roca (sic)
Espora 643, ½ block from Plaza.
Confitería and bar in historic premises (the original cinema), good and popular.

Tío Willy
Alberdi 279.
Serves *cerveza artesanal* (micro brewery).

Festivals

Río Grande
Jan Sheep shearing festival.
2nd week Feb Rural exhibition and handicrafts.
1st week Mar Shepherd's Day, with impressive sheepdog display.

Transport

Río Grande
Air Airport 4 km west of town, T02964-420600. Taxi US$3. To **Buenos Aires**, daily, 3½ hrs direct. **LADE** flies to **Río Gallegos**.

Bus To **Punta Arenas**, Chile, via Punta Delgada, 7-9 hrs, **Pacheco** (Finocchio 1194, T02964-425611, daily except Sun) and **Tecni Austral** (Moyano 516, T02964-430610) and others en route from Ushuaia, US$25-33. To **Río Gallegos**, Tecni Austral, Mon-Sat, 8 hrs; **Marga/Taqsa** (Mackinley 545, T02964-434316), daily, 0815, US$38, connection to El Calafate and Comodoro Rivadavia. To **Ushuaia**, 3½-4 hrs, **Montiel** (25 de Mayo 712, T02964-420997) and **Líder** (Perito Moreno 635, T02964-420003, www.lidertdf.com.ar), US$33. Both use small buses, frequent departures. They stop en route at Tolhuin. Also Tecni Austral, between 1600 and 1730 (bus has come from Punta Arenas), **Marga** and **Pacheco**, US$23.

Ushuaia and around *Colour map 9, C2.*

experience pioneer life at the end of the world

Situated 212 km southwest of Río Grande, Ushuaia is beautifully positioned on the northern shore of the Beagle Channel, named after the ship in which Darwin sailed here in 1832. This is the most southerly town in Argentina, and it's growing fast. The streets climb steeply towards snow-covered Cerro Martial and there are fine views to neighbouring mountains and over the Beagle Channel to the jagged peaks of Isla Navarino (Chile). First settled in 1884 by missionary Thomas Bridges, whose son Lucas became a great defender of the indigenous peoples here, Ushuaia's fascinating history is still visible in its old buildings and at Estancia Harberton, 85 km west (see below). The town has a number of excellent museums.

☆Sights

A penal colony for many years, the old prison, **Presidio** ① *Yaganes y Gob Paz, at the back of the Naval Base, daily 0900-2000, US$14 for foreigners, tours in Spanish 1130, 1630,1730, English 1400,* houses the small **Museo Marítimo**, with models and artefacts from seafaring days, and, in the cells of most of the huge five wings, the **Museo Penitenciario**, which details the history of the prison and of the pioneers who came to the area. There are also temporary exhibitions, a shop and a café; highly recommended.

Fact...
Banks are open 1000-1500 in summer. ATMs are plentiful all along San Martín, but may be empty at weekends and holidays. **Agencia de Cambio Thaler**, San Martín 209, T02901-421911, Monday-Friday 1000-1500, in high season Monday-Saturday 1000-2000.

Museo del Fin del Mundo ① *Maipú y Rivadavia, T02901-421863, Mon-Fri 1000-1900, Sat, Sun and bank holidays 1400-2000, US$9, guided tours 1100, 1400, 1700, fewer in winter,* is housed in the 1912 bank building and has small displays on indigenous peoples, missionaries and first settlers, as well as nearly all the birds of Tierra del Fuego (stuffed); recommended. The building also contains an excellent library with helpful staff. On the same ticket is the **Antigua Casa de Gobierno** ① *Maipú 465, same hours,* with an exhibition on the history of the city and temporary exhibitions. Recently opened, the **Galería Temática** ① *San Martín 152, PB, 1er y 2do p, T02901-422245, www.historiafueguina.com, Mon-Sat 1200-2000, US$10,* has numerous life-size displays which take you through an informative history of Tierra del Fuego. There's a useful audioguide in different languages, and a themed garden at the back, reached through a huge souvenir shop with good knitwear and other goods.

Around Ushuaia

Cerro Martial About 7 km behind the town, this mountain offers fine views down the Beagle Channel and to the north. Take a **chair lift** (*aerosilla*) ① *daily ascents 1000-1615 (last down 1730), US$10, tariffs change in winter, closed for repair for a time in Apr*, to the summit where there's a basic *refugio* with no electricity. To reach the chairlift, follow Magallanes out of town, allow 1½ hours. Several companies run minibus services from the corner of Maipú and Fadul, with frequent departures daily in summer, US$4. Taxis charge US$7.50-9 to the base, from where you can walk all the way back. At the base are the **Cumbres de Martial cabañas** and a splendid tea shop. Also by the lower platform is the **Canopy** ① *T02901-15-510307, www.canopyushuaia.com.ar, US$35, US$25 for a shorter run, US$28 and US$20 under 12s*, a series of 11 zip-lines and bridges in the trees. All visitors are accompanied by staff: safe and good fun. There are several marked trails from 600 m to 1 km – a leaflet is given out at the lower platform – including to a viewpoint (one hour) and to **Glaciar Martial** itself.

Tren del Fin del Mundo ① *T02901-431600, www.trendelfindelmundo.com.ar, 4-5 departures daily, US$45 tourist, US$77 1st class return, US$100 premium, with reductions for residents, 6-17 year olds and seniors, plus park entry (cheaper in winter)*. This is the world's southernmost steam train, running new locomotives and carriages on track first laid by prisoners to carry wood to Ushuaia. It's a totally touristy experience with commentary in English and Spanish (written material in other languages). The 50-minute ride is from the Fin del Mundo station, 8 km west of Ushuaia, into Tierra del Fuego national park (see below); sit on the left on the outbound journey for the best views. There is one stop at Estación Macarena after 15 minutes, for a view of the river and a walk up to Macarena waterfall. In first class you can buy food and drinks at the station *confitería* to eat at your table. Tickets are available at the station, the port or from travel agencies.

☆**Estancia Harberton** ① *85 km from Ushuaia on Ruta J (2 hrs' drive), T02901-422742, www.estancia harberton.com. US$13. 15 Oct-15 Apr daily 1000-1900, except 25 Dec, 1 Jan and Easter*. The oldest estancia on the island is run by descendants of British missionary, Thomas Bridges, whose family protected the indigenous peoples here. It's a beautiful place, offering a wide variety of guided walks through protected forest. The impressive **Museo Acatushún** ① *www.acatushun.org*, has skeletons of South American sea mammals and birds, the result of 25 years' scientific investigation in Tierra del Fuego, with excellent tours in English. You can camp free, with permission from the owners, or stay in cottages. Access is from a good unpaved road which branches off Ruta 3, 40 km east of Ushuaia and runs 45 km through forest before the open country around Harberton with marvellous views (no petrol outside Ushuaia and Tolhuin). The road passes Laguna Victoria, where there is a good chance of seeing condors, and the turning to Puerto Almanza fishing port. See What to do, page 239, for visits to penguin colonies on nearby Isla Martillo/Yécapasela.

> **Tip...**
> Hearty lunches and delicious teas are served in the **Mánacatush** *casa de té* (0930-1830) or there's lunch in the **Acawaia** restaurant overlooking the bay (1200-1530).

☆**Beagle Channel** Short boat excursions from Ushuaia are highly recommended, though the Beagle Channel can be very rough. These can be booked through most agencies and leave from the **Muelle Turístico**, where all operators have ticket booths and representatives (**Tolkeyen** also at JM de Rosas 160, and **Rumbo Sur**, San Martín 350). All passengers must pay US$1.25 port tax; this is not included in tickets. Operators offer slight variations on a basic theme of trips to Isla de los Lobos, Isla de los Pájaros, Les Eclaireurs lighthouse and Harberton. See under What to do below for details of these and of longer sea trips.

☆Parque Nacional Tierra del Fuego

National Park Office, San Martín 1395, Ushuaia, T02901-421315, tierradelfuego@apn.gov.ar. Mon-Fri 0900-1600. Entry to the park US$23 (valid for 48 hrs). For buses see Transport, page 241.

Covering 63,000 ha of mountains, lakes, rivers and deep valleys, this small but beautiful park stretches west to the Chilean border and north to Lago Fagnano, though large areas are closed to tourists. It's best to go in the early morning or afternoon to avoid the tour buses. You'll see geese, the torrent duck, Magellanic woodpeckers and austral parakeets. Remember that the weather can be cold, damp and unpredictable, even in summer, and that winter days are short.

Fact...
There are no legal crossing points to Chile.

Public access is allowed from the park entrance 12 km west of Ushuaia, where you'll be given the basic map with marked walks. Buses run into the park, stopping at various points, and the Tren del Fin del Mundo (see above) stops 2 km west of the entrance. There's a helpful *guardaparque* (ranger) at Lago Acigami (formerly Lago Roca), as well as the park's main campsite; see below for details of this and other sites.

On the coast, southwest of the entrance, is Ensenada from where a **boat** ① *1st at 1000, last back at 1700, US$52 return*, goes to Isla Redonda, a provincial Reserva Natural, and on to Lapataia. There are four trails on the island, a *refugio* for sleeping, hot water and a post office, open end October to beginning of April.

Walks The following are recommended 1) **Senda Costera** (8 km, three hours each way). Start at Ensenada (where boat trips depart) and follow the forested shoreline west. Rejoin the road briefly to cross broad green Río Lapataia and a second stretch of water (where there's a small camping spot and the gendarmería), after which there are more short paths to follow. 2) **Senda Hito XXIV** (3.5 km, 90 minutes one way). This starts at the bus stop for Lago Acigami and follows the northeast shore of the lake to the Chilean frontier, with lots of birdlife to spot along the way. 3) **Cerro Guanaco** (4 km, four hours one way). A challenging hike up through forest to splendid views at 1106 m. The path branches off Senda Hito XXIV (see above) after crossing Arroyo Guanaco. 4) **Senda Pampa Alta** (4.9 km via a *mirador* or 3.7 km via the road). To Río Pipo.

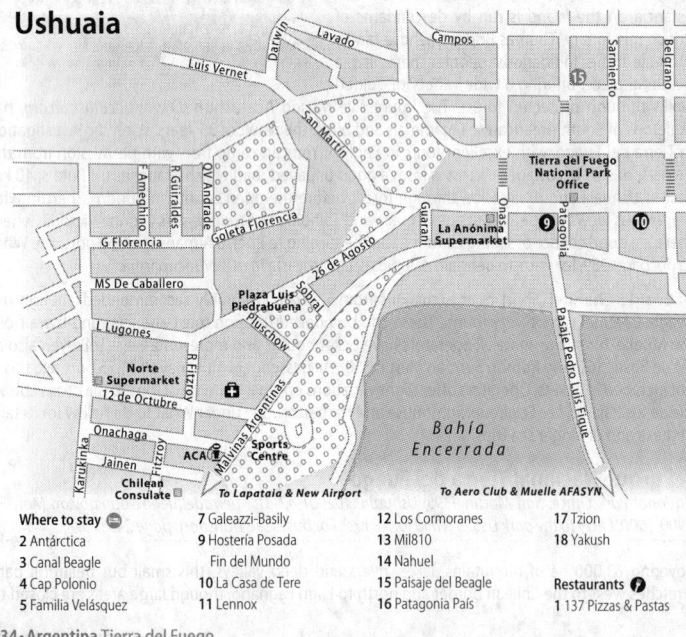

Ushuaia

Where to stay 🛏	7 Galeazzi-Basily	12 Los Cormoranes	17 Tzion
2 Antártica	9 Hostería Posada	13 Mil810	18 Yakush
3 Canal Beagle	Fin del Mundo	14 Nahuel	
4 Cap Polonio	10 La Casa de Tere	15 Paisaje del Beagle	**Restaurants** 🍴
5 Familia Velásquez	11 Lennox	16 Patagonia País	1 137 Pizzas & Pastas

Tourist information

Dirección Nacional de Migraciones
Fuegia Basket 187, T02901-422334.

Oficina Antártica
*Maipú 510, at entrance to port, T02901-430015,
antartida@tierradelfuego.org.ar. Mon-Fri 0900-
1700 (Nov-Mar 0800-1800, Sat-Sun 0900-1800).*
Has information on Antarctica and a small
library with navigational charts. Ushuaia
is the main centre for Antarctic trips with
occasional good last-minute deals to be
had (see What to do listings).

Tourist office
*San Martín 674, esq Fadul, T02901-424550,
www.turismoushuaia.com. Oct-Mar daily
1700-2100, Apr-Sep daily 0900-2000.*
Helpful English-speaking staff, who find
accommodation in summer; information
available in English, French, Portuguese
and German. There are also offices at the **Muelle
Turístico** (T02901-437666, Oct-Mar

daily 0800-1700, closed Apr-Sep), with free
Wi-Fi and toilets; and at the airport, T02901-
423970, open when there are flights arriving.
The Secretaría de Turismo is at Prefectura
Naval 470, T02901-432000.

Other sources of information include the
provincial **tourist office** (Maipú 505, T02901-
421423, info@tierradelfuego.org.ar) and the
Biblioteca Popular Sarmiento (San Martín 1589,
T02901-423103, Mon-Fri 1000-2000), a library
with a good range of books about the area.

Where to stay

The tourist office has a comprehensive list of all
officially registered accommodation and will
help with rooms in private homes, campsites,
etc. An excellent choice is to stay with Ushuaia
families on a B&B basis. The range of lodging
is growing at all budget levels, from the very
chic, to *cabañas*, to the basic B&B, in the centre
and the suburbs. There are too many to list
here. Despite the expansion, you must book in
advance in high season.

2 Bodegón Fueguino
3 Café Bar Banana
5 Café Tante Sara
6 Chicho's
8 El Bambú
9 El Turco
10 Gadget Café
12 Laguna Negra
13 Martinica
14 Moustacchio
15 Mr Jones Ushuaia
16 Parrilla La Rueda
17 Ramos Generales
18 Sandwichería Kami
19 Tante Sara
20 Tía Elvira
21 Volver

Ushuaia

$$$$ Canal Beagle
Maipú y 25 de Mayo, T02901-432303,
www.hotelcanalbeagle.com.ar.
ACA hotel (discounts for members), $$$ Apr-Oct,
comfortable and well-attended, with a small
pool, gym, spa, business centre, some rooms with
channel views (others overlook the container
dock), good restaurant.

$$$$ Cap Polonio
San Martín 746, T02901-422140,
www.hotelcappolonio.com.ar.
Smart, central, modern, comfortable, popular
restaurant/café **Marcopolo**.

$$$$ Lennox
San Martín 776, T02901-436430,
www.lennoxhotels.com.
Boutique hotel on the main street, with
breakfast, services include hydromassage,
minibar, restaurant and confitería on 4th floor.
Laundry service.

$$$$ Mil810
25 de Mayo 245, T02901-437714,
www.hotel1810.com.
City hotel with 30 standard rooms, 1 with
disabled access, no restaurant but breakfast and
confitería, all rooms with minibar, safe, quite small
but cosy, calm colours, good views, business
centre and multiple use room where you can
hang out while waiting for flight.

$$$ Galeazzi-Basily
Gob Valdez 323, T02901-423213,
www.avesdelsur.com.ar.
Among the best, beautiful family home,
incredible welcome, in pleasant area
5 blocks from centre, 4 rooms with shared
bath. Also excellent *cabañas* in the garden.
Highly recommended.

$$$ Hostería Posada Fin del Mundo
Rivadavia 610, T02901-437345,
www.posadafindelmundo.com.ar.
Family atmosphere, comfortable rooms,
good value, has character.

$$$ Paisaje del Beagle
Gob Paz 1347, T02901-421214,
www.paisajedelbeagle.com.ar.
Family-run, quiet, with a cosy dining area for
good breakfast, laundry service. Recommended.

$$$ Tzion
Gob Valdez 468, T02901-432290,
tzion_byb@hotmail.com.
B&B with 3 rooms, 1 with bath, high above
town, 10 mins' walk from centre, nice family
atmosphere, cheaper low season, laundry
service, English and French spoken. Great
views, highly recommended.

$$ pp La Casa de Tere
Rivadavia 620, T02901-422312,
www.lacasadetere.com.ar.
Shared or private bath, use of kitchen facilities,
freshly baked bread, open fire, singles, doubles
and triples, hot water, helpful owner.

$$ Nahuel
25 de Mayo 440, T02901-423068,
www.bybnahuel.com.
Charming Sra Navarrete has a comfortable B&B
with channel views from the upper rooms and
the terrace, good value, but noisy street.

$$-$ Familia Velásquez
Juana Fadul 361, T02901-421719,
losnokis_figueroa@hotmail.com.
Cosy, welcoming house of a pioneer, with
basic rooms, breakfast, cooking and laundry
facilities, good.

$ pp Antártica
Antártida Argentina 270, T02901-435774,
www.antarcticahostel.com.
Central, welcoming, spacious chill-out room,
excellent 24-hr bar, dorms for 6 and large
doubles, breakfast included, game night Thu
with good prizes. Recommended.

$ pp Los Cormoranes
Kamshén 788 y Alem, T02901-423459,
www.loscormoranes.com.
Large hostel, with good views, cosy rooms, with
lockers, OK bathrooms. Doubles ($$) available.
They can book tours. HI member discount.

$ Patagonia País
Alem 152, T02901-431886,
patagoniapais@gmail.com.
Just above the centre, this welcoming,
family-run hostel is a good meeting point.
Dorms from US$17, laundry service, parrilla,
tour and excursion info. Under same ownership
is **$ Patagonia Onas**, Onas 176, T02901-433389.
More central, less of a party hostel. Also has
doubles with shared bath ($$).

$ pp Yakush
Piedrabuena 118 y San Martín, T02901-435807.
Very well-run, central with spacious dorms,
also doubles ($$, cheaper without bath),
book exchange and library, dining room,

steep garden with views. In-house tour op organizes excursions.

Camping

La Pista del Andino
Leandro N Alem 2873, T02901-435890.
Set in the Club Andino ski premises in a woodland area, it has wonderful views over the channel. Electricity, hot showers, tea room and grocery store, very helpful. Recommended.

Around Ushuaia
The following all are recommended.

$$$$ Cabañas del Beagle
Las Aljabas 375, T02901-432785, www.cabanasdelbeagle.com.
3 rustic-style cabins 1.3 km above the city, fully equipped with kitchen, hydromassage, fireplace, heating, phone, self-service breakfast, very comfortable, personal attention.

$$$$ Cumbres del Martial
Luis F Martial 3560, 7 km from town, T02901-424779, www.cumbresdelmartial.com.ar.
At the foot of the *aerosilla* to Glaciar Martial, 4 *cabañas* and 6 rooms, beautifully set in the woods, charming, very comfortable, cabins have whirlpool baths. Small spa (massage extra) with saunas and gym. The tearoom, with disabled access, is open all year, restaurant with traditional fondues.

$$$$ Finisterris Lodge Relax
Monte Susana, Ladera Este, 7 km from city, T02901-15-612121, www.finisterrislodge.com.
In 17 ha of forest, 5-star luxury in individual cabins, with top-of-the-range fittings, hydromassage and private spa (massage arranged, extra), rustic style but spacious, 'home-from-home' atmosphere, 24-hr attention from owner, given mobile phone on arrival. Meals can be ordered in, or private chef and sommelier can be booked for you.

$$$$ Las Hayas
Luis Martial 1650 (road to Glaciar Martial), T02901-430710, www.lashayashotel.com.
4 standards of room, all very good with TV, safe, 3 types of view, channel, mountains or forest. 2 restaurants: **Martial** for lunch and dinner, **Drake** for breakfast. Everything is included in room price except massages and hairdresser. A fine hotel.

$$$$ Los Acebos
Luis F Martial 1911, T02901-442200, www.losacebos.com.ar.
Run by the same company as Las Hayas. All rooms with channel view, safe, games room, **Rêve d'Orange** restaurant independent of hotel. Golf days organized.Very comfy, as expected, but less characterful than Las Hayas.

$$$$ Los Cauquenes
At Bahía Cauquen, De La Ermita 3462, T02901-441300, www.loscauquenes.com.
High-quality 5-star hotel overlooking Beagle Channel, price varies according to size and view, spa, very tastefully decorated, prize-winning restaurant, regional food on dinner menu, wine bar with over 100 Argentine wines.

$$$$ Los Yámanas
Costa de los Yámanas 2850, western suburbs, T02901-446809, www.hotelyamanas.com.ar.
In the same group as Canoero tour operator, all rooms with Channel view, spacious, well-decorated, hydromassage, fitness centre, spa and conference centre outside in wooded grounds, shuttle to town. Very pleasant.

$$$$ Tierra de Leyendas
Tierra de Vientos 2448, T02901-446565, www.tierradeleyendas.com.ar.
In the western suburbs. 5 very comfortable rooms with views of the Beagle Channel, or the mountains at the back, 1 room with jacuzzi, all others with shower, excellent restaurant serving regional specialities, open only for guests for breakfast and dinner. No cable TV, but DVDs, living room with games, library, deck overlooking Río Pipo's outflow. Only for non smokers. Recommended and award-winning.

$$$$-$$ pp Estancia Harberton
T02901-422742, www.estanciaharberton.com. Mid-Oct to mid-Apr.
2 restored buildings on the estancia (see above), simple rooms, wonderful views, heating. Price includes walking tour and entry to museum. Shepherd's House (Ovejeros) has 2 rooms with bath, full or half-board. Foreman's House (Capataz) has hostel accommodation, shared bath, **$$** pp B&B, kitchenette for tea and coffee. Lunch and dinner extra. No credit cards.

Parque Nacional Tierra del Fuego

Camping

Camping Lago Roca
T02901-433313, 21 km from Ushuaia, by forested shore of Lago Acigami (Roca), a beautiful site with good facilities, reached by bus Jan-Feb.

It has a backpackers' *refugio*, toilets, showers, restaurant and confitería, expensive small shop; camping equipment for hire with deposit. There are also campsites with facilities at **Río Pipo** 16 km from Ushuaia and at **Laguna Verde**, 20 km, near Lapataia, and **Bahía Ensenada** with no facilities.

Restaurants

Ushuaia

Lots of restaurants along San Martín and Maipú. Be aware that most open 1200-1500 and again from 1900 at the earliest. Several cafés are open all the time. Ask around for currently available seafood, especially *centolla* (king crab) and *cholga* (giant mussels); much cheaper if you prepare your own meal, but note *centolla* may not be fished Nov-Dec. Beer drinkers should try the handcrafted brews of the **Cape Horn** brewery, Pilsen, Pale Ale and Stout.

$$$ Bodegón Fueguino
San Martín 859. Open 1230-1500, 2000-2400, closed Mon.
Snacks, home-made pastas and good roast lamb with varied sauces in a renovated 1896 *casa de pioneros*.

$$$ Tía Elvira
Maipú 349. Mon-Sat 1200-1500, 1900-2300.
Excellent seafood.

$$$ Volver
Maipú 37.
Delicious seafood and fish in atmospheric 1896 house, with ancient newspaper all over the walls. Recommended.

$$$-$$ Moustacchio
San Martín 298.
Long established, good for seafood and meat, all-you-can-eat branch US$13.

$$$-$$ Parrilla La Rueda
San Martín y Rivadavia.
Good *tenedor libre* (US$24 with dessert) for beef, lamb and great salads. Recommended for freshness.

$$ 137 Pizzas and Pastas
San Martín 137.
Tasty filling versions of exactly what the name says, plus excellent *empanadas*, elegant decor.

$$ Chicho's
Rivadavia 72, T02901-423469.
Bright, cheerful place just off the main street, friendly staff, kitchen open to view. Fish, meat and chicken dishes, pastas, wide range of *entradas*.

$$ El Turco
San Martín 1410.
A very popular place, serving generous milanesas, pastas, pizzas, seafood and meat. Very tasty *empanadas*.

$$-$ Martinica
San Martín entre Antártida Argentina y Yaganes.
Cheap, small, busy, sit at the bar facing the *parrilla* and point to your favourite beef cut. Takeaway (T432134) and good meals of the day, also pizzas and *empanadas*.

Cafés

Café Bar Banana
San Martín 273, T02901-424021.
Quite small, always busy, pool table, offers good fast food, such as burgers, small pizzas, puddings, breakfasts and an all-day *menú* for US$7.50.

El Bambú
Piedrabuena 276. Open 1100-1700.
One of few purely vegetarian places in town, take-away only, home-made food, delicious and good value.

Gadget Café
Av San Martín 1256, www.gadgettugelateria. com.ar.
The best ice cream parlour in town, multiple flavours, friendly. Recommended.

Laguna Negra
San Martín 513.
Mainly a shop selling chocolate and other fine produce, catering to the cruise ship passengers, but has a good little café at the back for hot chocolate and coffee. Also has a bigger branch at Libertador 1250, El Calafate. Sells postcards and stamps, too.

Ramos Generales
Maipú 749, T02901-424317. Daily 0900-2400 in high season.
An old warehouse, with wooden floor and a collection of historic objects. Sells breads, pastries, wines and drinks, also cold cuts, sandwiches, salads, ice cream, Argentine mate and coffee. Not cheap but atmospheric. Recommended.

Sandwichería Kami
San Martín 54. Open 0800-2100.
Friendly, simple sandwich shop, selling rolls, baguettes and *pan de miga*.

Tante Sara
San Martín 701.

Opposite the tourist office, is very good, smart café, good coffee, tasty sandwiches, always busy. Also has restaurant and *panadería* at San Martín 175, selling breads, sandwiches, chocolates, *empanadas* and snacks, coffee, lots of choice.

Shopping

Ushuaia

Ushuaia's tax free status doesn't produce as many bargains as you might hope. Lots of souvenir shops on San Martín and several offering good quality leather and silverware. The **Pasaje de Artesanías**, by the Muelle Turístico, sells local arts and crafts. **Atlántico Sur** (San Martín 627) is the (not especially cheap) duty free shop. **Boutique del Libro** (San Martín 1120, T02901-424750, www.boutiquedellibro.com.ar, Mon-Sat 1000-1300 and 1530-2030 year-round) has an excellent selection of books, including several in English and other languages on Tierra del Fuego. CDs and DVDs upstairs. (Branches throughout Argentina, see website for details).

Festivals

Ushuaia
Early Apr Classical Music Festival (www.festivaldeushuaia.com).
20-21 Jun Winter solstice, with a torch-light procession and fireworks.
Aug Annual sled dog race and **Marcha Blanca**, a ski trek from Lago Escondido to Tierra Mayor valley (www.marchablanca.com).

What to do

Ushuaia

Boat trips
All short boat trips leave from the Muelle Turístico. Take your time to choose the size and style of boat you want. Representatives from the offices are polite and helpful. All have a morning and afternoon sailing and include **Isla de los Lobos, Isla de los Pájaros** and **Les Eclaireurs lighthouse**, with guides and some form of refreshment. Note that weather conditions may affect sailings, prices can change and that port tax is not included. See also **Rumbo Sur** and **Tolkeyen**, below.
Canoero, *T02901-433893, www.catamaranes canoero.com.ar.* Catamarans for 130 passengers (Ushuaia's biggest fleet), 2½- to 3-hr trips to the 3 main sites and Isla Bridges, US$54. They also

have a 4½-hr trip almost daily to the Pingüinera on Isla Martillo near Estancia Harberton (Oct-Mar only), boats stay for 1 hr, but you cannot land on Martillo, US$80 (US$90 including Harberton – entry extra). Also longer tours to Estancia Harberton and Lapataia Bay.
Patagonia Adventure Explorer, *T02901-15-465842, www.patagoniaadvent.com.ar.* Has a sailing boat and motor boats for the standard trip, plus Isla Bridges: US$60 sailing boat. Good guides.
Pira-Tour, *T02901-435557, www.piratour.com.ar and www.piratour.net.* Runs 2-3 buses a day to Harberton, from where a boat goes to the Pingüinera on Isla Martillo/Yécapasela: 20 people allowed to land (maximum 80 per day – the only company licensed to do this). US$110 with entrance to Harberton.
Tres Marías, *T02901-436416, www.tresmariasweb. com.* The only company licensed to visit Isla H, which has archaeological sites, cormorants, other birds and plants. Departures 1000 and 1500, 4 hrs. Also has sailing boat, no more than 10 passengers; specialist guide, café on board, US$60 on *Tres Marías*, US$80 on sailing boat. Highly recommended.

Cruises
Ushuaia is the starting point, or the last stop, en route to Antarctica for several cruises from Oct-Mar that usually sail for 9 to 21 days along the western shores of the Antarctic peninsula and the South Shetland Islands. Other trips include stops at Falkland/Malvinas archipelago and at South Georgia. Go to **Oficina Antártica** for advice (see page 235). Agencies sell 'last minute tickets', but the price is entirely dependent on demand. Coordinator for trips is **Turismo Ushuaia** (Gob Paz 865, T02901-436003, www.ushuaiaturismoevt. com.ar), which operates with IAATO members only. See the website for prices for the upcoming season. Port tax is US$15 per passenger and an exit tax of US$10 is also charged.
Freestyle Adventure Travel, *Gob Paz 866, T02901-15-609792, www.freestyleadventuretravel. com.* Organizes trips to Antarctica, particularly good for last-minute deals. 7- to 22-day cruises, wide variety of itineraries. Cape Horn expeditions also available.
Polar Latitudes, *sales@polar-latitudes.com, www. polar-latitudes.com.* Antarctic cruises aboard small expedition vessels, some itineraries take in the Falklands/Malvinas and South Georgia. All-suite accommodation onboard.
To Chile Australis Cruises, www.australis.com, operates luxury cruise ships between Ushuaia

and **Punta Arenas**, with a visit to Cape Horn, highly recommended. Full details are given under Punta Arenas, Tour operators. Check-in at JM de Rosas 160, T02901-437073. For crossings to Puerto Williams on Isla Navarino, see Transport, below. At **Muelle AFASYN**, near the old airport, T02901-435805, ask about possible crossings with a club member to Puerto Williams, about 4 hrs, or if any foreign sailing boat is going to Cabo de Hornos or Antarctica.

Fishing

Trout season is Nov to mid-Apr, licences US$21 per day (an extra fee is charged for some rivers and lakes). **Asociación de Caza y Pesca** (Maipú 822, T02901-423168, cazaypescaushuaia@speedy. com.ar, Mon-Fri 1600-2000), sells licences, with list on door of other places that sell it.

Hiking and climbing

The winter sports resorts along Ruta 3 (see below) are an excellent base for summer trekking and many arrange excursions.
Club Andino, *Fadul 50, T02901-422335*. For advice, Mon-Fri 0930-1230, 1600-2000. Sells maps and trekking guidebooks; free guided walks once a month in summer; also offers classes in yoga, dancing, karate-do and has excercise bikes.
Nunatak, *25 de Mayo 296, T02901-430329, www.antartur.com.ar*. Organizes treks, canoeing, mountain biking and 4WD trips to Lagos Escondido and Fagnano. Good winter excursions.

Horse riding

Centro Hípico, *Ruta 3, Km 3021, T02901-15-569099, www.horseridingtierradelfuego.com*. Rides through woods, on Monte Susana, along coast and through river, 2 hrs, US$40; 4-hr ride with light lunch, US$80; 7-hr ride with *asado*, US$105. Gentle horses, well-cared for, all guides have first-aid training. Very friendly and helpful. All rides include transfer from town and insurance. Hats provided for children. They can arrange long-distance rides of several days, eg on Península Mitre.

Tours operators

Lots of companies offer imaginative adventure tourism expeditions. All agencies charge the same fees for excursions; ask tourist office for a complete list: Tierra del Fuego National Park, 4 hrs, US$50 (entry fee US$23 extra); Lagos Escondido and Fagnano, 7 hrs, US$70 without lunch. With 3 or 4 people it might be worth hiring a remise taxi.
All Patagonia, *Juana Fadul 58, T02901-433622, www.allpatagonia.com*. Trekking, ice climbing, and tours; trips to Cabo de Hornos and Antarctica.

Canal, *Roca 136, T02901-435777, www.canalfun. com*. Huge range of activities, trekking, canoeing, riding, 4WD excursions. Recommended.
Compañía de Guías de Patagonia, *San Martín 628, T02901-437753, www.companiadeguias. com.ar*. The best agency for walking guides, expeditions for all levels, rock and ice climbing (training provided), also diving, sailing, riding, 7-day crossing of Tierra del Fuego on foot and conventional tours. Recommended.
Rumbo Sur, *San Martín 350, T02901-421139, www.rumbosur.com.ar*. Flights, buses, conventional tours on land and sea, including to Harberton, plus Antarctic expeditions, mid-Nov to mid-Mar, English spoken.
Tolkar, *Roca 157, T02901-431412, www. tolkarturismo.com.ar*. Flights, bus tickets to Argentina and Punta Arenas/Puerto Natales, conventional and adventure tourism, canoeing and mountain biking to Lago Fagnano.
Tolkeyen, *JM de Rosas 160, T02901-437073, www.tolkeyenpatagonia.com*. Bus and flight tickets, catamaran trips (50-300 passengers), including to Harberton (Tue, Thu, Sat-Sun, US$94) and Parque Nacional, large company.
Travel Lab, *San Martín 1444, T02901-436555, www.travellab.com.ar*. Conventional and unconventional tours, mountain biking, trekking etc, English and French spoken, helpful.

Winter sports

Ushuaia is becoming popular as a winter resort with 11 centres for skiing, snowboarding and husky sledging. Cerro Castor on Ruta 3 is the only centre for Alpine skiing; the other centres along Ruta 3 at 18-36 km east of Ushuaia offer excellent cross country skiing (and alternative activities in summer).
Cerro Castor, *Ruta 3, Km 26, T02901-499301, www.cerrocastor.com*. 24 km of pistes, a vertical drop of 800 m and powder snow. Attractive centre with complete equipment rental, also for snowboarding and snowshoeing.
Kawi Shiken at *Las Cotorras, Ruta 3, Km 26, T02901-444152, siberianfuego@hotmail.com*. Specializes in sled dogs, with 90 Alaskan and Siberian huskies, with winter rides on snow and summer rides in a dog cart.
Tierra Mayor, *Ruta 3, 20 km from town, T02901-437454*. The largest and most recommended ski centre. Lies in a beautiful wide valley between steep-sided mountains. It offers half and full day excursions on sledges with huskies, as well as cross country skiing and snowshoeing. Equipment hire and restaurant.

Ushuaia

Air Airport 4 km from town, T02901-431232. Book ahead in summer; flights fill up fast. In winter flights are often delayed. Taxi to airport US$5-7 (no bus). Schedules tend to change from season to season. Airport tourist information only at flight times, T02901-423970. To **Buenos Aires** (Aeroparque or Ezeiza), 3½ hrs; to **El Calafate**, 1 hr, and **Río Gallegos**, 1 hr; also to **Río Grande**, 1 hr, several a week (but check with agents). In summer DAP an d **LATAM** fly to **Punta Arenas** twice a week. The **Aeroclub de Ushuaia** flies to **Puerto Williams** and organizes flight tours of Tierra del Fuego from the downtown airport, www.aeroclubushuaia.com.

Boat Fernández Campbell have a 1½-hr crossing to **Puerto Williams (Isla Navarino)**, Fri, Sat, Sun 1000, return 1500, US$125 for foreigners, tickets sold at **Zenit Explorer** (Juana Fadul 126, Ushuaia, T02901-433232, www. fernandezcampbell.com), and at **Naviera RFC** in Puerto Williams. **Ushuaia Boating** (Gob Paz 233, T02901-436193, or at the Muelle Turístico, www.ushuaiaboating.com) operates a year-round channel crossing to Puerto Navarino (Isla Navarino), 30-90 mins depending on weather, and then bus to Puerto Williams, 1 hr, US$125 one way, not including taxes. From Puerto Williams a ferry goes once a week to Punta Arenas. For cruises to Chile and Antarctica, see What to do, above.

Bus   Local Urban buses from west to east across town, most stops along Maipú, US$0.50. Tourist office provides a list of minibus companies that run daily from town (stops along Maipú) to nearby attractions.

To the **national park**, buses and minibuses leave from the bus stop on Maipú at the bottom of Fadul in summer. **Transporte Lautaro** and **Transporte Santa Lucía**, 3 a day each, hourly

from 0900, last return 1900, US$19 return (US$12.50 one way). From same bus stop, many other *colectivos* go to the *Tren del Fin del Mundo* station (0900 and 1400, return 1200, 1700 and 1745), Lago Escondido, Lago Fagnano (1000 and 1100, return 1400 and 2200) and Glaciar Martial (1000 and 1200, return 1400 and 1600). For **Harberton**, check the noticeboards at the station at Maipú y Fadul; the only regular bus is run by **Pira-Tur**, see What to do, above.

Long distance Passport needed when booking international bus tickets. Buses always booked up Nov-Mar; buy your ticket to leave as soon as you arrive. To **Río Grande**, 3½-4 hrs, combis **Líder** (Gob Paz 921, T02901-436421), and **Montiel** (Gob Paz 605, T02901-421366), US$33. Also buses en route to Río Gallegos and Punta Arenas. To **Río Gallegos**, **Tecni Austral**, 0500, 13 hrs, US$46 (book through Tolkar), and **Marga/ Taqsa** (Gob Godoy 41), daily at 0500. To **Punta Arenas**, US$38-52, **Tecni Austral**, Mon, Wed, Fri, 0500, 11-12 hrs (book through Tolkar); **Pacheco**, Tue, Thu, Sat 1000, 12-13 hrs, book through **Tolkeyen** (JM de Rosas 160, T02901-437073), Ghisoni, Mon, Wed, Fri 0500, **Bus Sur** (JM de Rosas 160, Juana Fadul 126, or Gob Paz 601) Mon, Wed, Sat, change in Río Grande.

Car hire Most companies charge minimum US$60-70 per day, including insurance and 200 km per day, special promotions available. **Localiza**, Maipu 768, T02901-437780, www. localiza.com. Cars can be hired in Ushuaia to be driven through Chile and then left in any Localiza office in Argentina, but you must buy a one-off customs document for US$50, to use as many times as you like to cross borders. Must reserve well in advance and pay a drop-off fee. **Budget**, Godoy 49, T02901-437373.

Taxi Cheaper than remises, T02901-422007, T02901-422400. Taxi stand by the Muelle Turístico. **Remises Carlitos y Bahía Hermosa**, San Martín y Rosas, T02901-422222.

Practicalities
Getting around

Air

Internal air services are run by **Aerolíneas Argentinas (AR)** ① *T0810-222 86527, www.aerolineas. com.ar*, **Austral** (part of AR), **LATAM** ① *T0810-999 9526, within Chile T600-526 2000, www.latam.com*, and the army airline **LADE** (in Patagonia, Buenos Aires, Córdoba and Paraná) ① *T0810-810 5233, www.lade.com.ar;* its flights are always heavily booked. **Andes** ① *T0810-777-26337, www.andes online.com*, based in Salta, flies between Buenos Aires and Salta, Jujuy and Puerto Madryn. The low-cost carrier, Norwegian Air Shuttle, was due to enter the market at end-2017. Some airlines operate during the high season, or are air taxis on a semi-regular schedule. Children under three travel free. Seats on all domestic flights are reserved well in advance, especially for travel during December and January. Reconfirmation of all flights 24 hours in advance (online if possible) is essential. Check in at least two hours before the flight.

Aerolíneas Argentinas has a Visite Argentina airpass which offers domestic flights at cheaper rates than those bought individually. Details can be found on **www.aerolineas.com.ar**. You can buy from three to 12 coupons for a maximum of 90 days. Coupons cost from US$47 to US$195 each, depending on whether for North and Central Argentina, or for Patagonia. It is unwise to set too tight a schedule because of delays caused by bad weather, or flight cancellations or postponements.

Road

Bus

Long-distance buses are the cheapest way to get around. *Coche cama* or *semi cama* buses between cities are more expensive than the *comunes*, but well worth the extra money for the comfort of reclining seats and fewer stops. Fares vary according to time of year: advance booking is essential December-March, Easter, July and long weekends. The biggest bus companies are: **Andesmar** ① *T0810-122 1122, www.andesmar.com;* **Chevallier** ① *T011-4000 5255, www.nuevachevallier.com.ar;* **Flecha Bus** ① *T011-4000 5200, www.flechabus.com.ar;* **Vía Bariloche** ① *T0810-333 7575, www. viabariloche.com.ar*. Long-distance tickets can be bought online or over the phone. At www. plataforma10.com, www.omnilineas.com.ar and www.xcolectivo.com.ar (all also in English) you can check bus prices and times and book tickets throughout the country. Note that if you buy a bus ticket with a credit card online, you must show the receipt and your identity (eg passport) when you collect your ticket. Student discounts of 20% are sometimes available – always ask. Buses have strong a/c, even more so in summer; take a sweater for night journeys. On long-distance journeys, meals are included. They can vary from a sandwich to a full meal, so take your own food and drink for longer journeys. Note that luggage is handled by *maleteros*, who expect a tip (US$0.35 or less is acceptable) though many Argentines refuse to pay.

Taxi

Licensed taxis known as *Radio Taxi* can be hired on the street, or can be called in advance and are safer. Remise is a commonly used system, where car and driver are booked from an office and operate with a fixed fare; they cost more than a regular taxi.

TRAVEL TIP

Driving in Argentina

Roads Only 30% of Argentina's roads are paved and a further 17% improved. Most main roads are rather narrow but roadside services are good. To avoid flying stones on gravel roads (called *ripio* on maps) and dirt roads, don't follow trucks too closely, overtake with plenty of room, and pull over and slow down for oncoming vehicles. Most main roads have private tolls about every 100 km, US$0. 70-2.15. Unprivatized secondary roads are generally poor. Internal checkpoints prevent food, vegetable and meat products entering Patagonia, Mendoza, San Juan, Catamarca, Tucumán, Salta and Jujuy provinces.

Safety All motorists are required to carry two warning triangles, a fire-extinguisher, a tow rope or chain, and a first aid kit. The handbrake must be fully operative and seat belts must be worn if fitted. Headlights must be on in the daytime on roads in Buenos Aires province.

Documents Full car documentation must be carried (including an invoice for the most recently paid insurance premium) together with international driving licence (for non-residents). For drivers of private vehicles entering Argentina from Chile, there is a special *salida y admisión temporal de vehículos* form.

Organizations Automóvil Club Argentino (ACA), Avenida Libertador Gen San Martín 1850, Buenos Aires, T011-4808 4000 or T0800-888-3777, www.aca.org.ar, has a travel documents service, car service facilities, and road maps (including online). Foreign automobile clubs with reciprocity with ACA are allowed to use ACA facilities and discounts (with a membership card). ACA accommodation comprises: Motel, Hostería, Hotel, Centro Recreativo, and campsites. All have meal facilities.

Car hire The minimum age for renting is usually 21-25 (private arrangements may be possible). A credit card is required. Prices range from US$55-130 a day; highest prices are in Patagonia. Discounts available for weekly rental. 4WD vehicles offered in some agencies. At tourist centres such as Salta, Posadas, Bariloche or Mendoza it may be more economical to hire a taxi with driver, which includes a guide, fuel, insurance and a mechanic.

Fuel Petrol/gasoline (*nafta*) costs on average US$1.24-1.40 per litre and diesel US$1.13-1.32. Octane ratings: regular petrol (*común*) 85; *súper* 93-95, *premium* 98-100 (oil companies have different grades). Unleaded fuel is widely available. Cars are being converted to *gas natural comprimido* (GNC), which costs about 25% of *nafta*, but filling stations are further apart. Always refuel when you can in less developed areas like Chaco and Formosa and in parts of Patagonia as even petrol stations are infrequent.

Maps

Several road maps are available including those of the **ACA** (best and most up-to-date), **Firestone** (also accurate and detailed), and **Automapa** ① *www.automapa.com.ar* (regional maps, Michelin-style, high quality). Topographical maps are issued by the **Instituto Geográfico Nacional** ① *Av Cabildo 381, Buenos Aires, T011-4576 5576, Mon-Fri 0800-1400, www.ign.gob.ar*. Some maps may be bought online, others only at the office. Take passport if buying maps there. For walkers, the **Sendas y Bosques** series (www.guiasendasybosques.com.ar) is recommended: 1:200,000, laminated and easy to read, with good books containing English summaries.

Where to stay

Hotels

It is often cheaper to book a room at reception, rather than over the internet. If you pay in cash (pesos) you may get a discount, but more expensive hotels sometimes have more expensive rates for non-Argentines. See Tax, below, on VAT on hotel bills and the Planning your trip chapter for our hotel price guide.

Camping

Camping is very popular in Argentina and there are many superbly situated sites, most with good services, whether municipal or private. Some are family-oriented, others are livelier and frequented by younger people (often near beaches), with partying till the small hours. Prices vary widely, from US$5 to US$10 per tent. Camping is almost impossible in Buenos Aires and many sites are closed off-season. Camping is allowed at the side of major highways (not recommended) and in most national parks (not at Iguazú Falls). Many ACA and YPF service stations have an area for campers (usually free) and owners are generally friendly, but ask first. Most service stations have hot showers. A list of camping sites is available from ACA (for members, but easily available) and from the national tourist office in Buenos Aires. See www.acampante.com and www.solocampings.com.ar for lists of campsites and other information.

If you are planning a long trip, renting a motorhome is a good idea. A recommended company is **Andean Roads Motorhome Rentals**, see www.andeanroads.com for contact details and rates (starting at US$110-200 per day for three weeks or more).

Estancias

An estancia is, generally speaking, a farm, but the term covers a wide variety of establishments. Accommodation for visitors is often pricey but most estancias are extremely comfortable and offer an insight into traditional country life. In the pampas, they tend to be cattle ranches extending for thousands of hectares; in the west they often have vineyards; northeastern estancias border swamps; those in Patagonia are sheep farms at the foot of the mountains or beside lakes. Many also offer horse riding, fishing, canoeing or birdwatching. The national tourist board website lists all estancias: www.turismo.gov.ar (look for *alojamiento rural* under each province).

Youth hostels

Hostelling International Argentina ① *Florida 835 of 107, Buenos Aires, T011-4511 8723, www.hostels. org.ar*, offers discounts to cardholders at their network of hostels throughout Argentina, and for buses and backpacker tours. It also has its own travel agency, www.hitravel.com.ar. An HI card in Argentina costs US$20 (US$30 for two years). See www.hostelsuites.com for a chain of HI-affiliated hostels. Very few Argentine hostels have laundry facilities, which may be tricky if you have expensive trekking gear to wash carefully.

Food & drink

Eating out

The cheapest option is always to have the set lunch as your main meal of the day and then find cheap, wholesome snacks for breakfast and supper. Also good value are *tenedor libre* restaurants where you can eat all you want for a fixed price. Restaurants are open 1200-1500 and again in the evening; most Argentines have lunch around 1300, then go to a *confitería* for tea, sandwiches and cakes at about 1700. Cafés are open all day and may stay open until 0200. Dinner is generally eaten between 2000 and 2300. See the Planning your trip chapter for our restaurant price guide.

> **Tip...**
> Extras such as chips or *puré* (mashed potato) are ordered and served separately.

Food

National dishes are based upon plentiful supplies of beef. Many dishes are distinctive and excellent: the *asado*, a roast cooked on an open fire or grill; *puchero*, a stew, very good indeed; *bife de chorizo*, rump steak; *bife de lomo*, fillet steak; *bife a caballo*, steak topped with a fried egg; *carbonada*, onions, tomatoes and minced beef (particularly good in Buenos Aires); *churrasco*, a thick grilled steak; *parrillada*, a mixed grill (usually enough for two or more people) consisting of roast meat, offal and sausages (*chorizos*), including *morcilla* (blood sausage). *Locro* is a thick stew made of maize, white beans, beef, sausages, pumpkin and herbs. A *choripán* is a roll with a *chorizo* inside. *Empanada* is a tasty meat pie; *empanadas de humita* are filled with a thick paste of cooked corn/maize, onions, cheese and flour. Other alternatives to beef include *milanesa (de pollo)*, a breaded veal (or chicken) cutlet, and *noquis* (gnocchi), potato dumplings normally served with meat and tomato sauce. These are tasty and often the cheapest item on the menu; they are also a good vegetarian option when served either *al tuco* or with Argentine Roquefort. (Note that a few places only serve *noquis* on the 29th of the month, when you should put a coin under your plate for luck.) Pizzas come in all sorts of exotic flavours, both savoury and sweet.

A popular sweet is *dulce de leche* (especially from Chascomús), milk and sugar evaporated to a pale, soft fudge. Other popular desserts are *almendrado*, ice cream rolled in crushed almonds; *dulce de batata*, sweet potato preserve; *dulce de membrillo*, quince preserve; *dulce de zapallo*, pumpkin in syrup; these *dulces* are often eaten with cheese. Also try *postre balcarce*, a cream and meringue cake, and *alfajores*, wheat-flour biscuits filled with *dulce de leche* or apricot jam. Note that *al natural* in reference to fruit means canned without sugar; fresh fruit is *al fresco*. Croissants (known as *media lunas*) come in two varieties: *de grasa* (dry) and *de manteca* (rich and fluffy).

Drink

It is best not to drink tap water; in the main cities it is safe, but often heavily chlorinated. Never drink tap water in the northwest, where it is notoriously poor. It is usual to drink soda or mineral water at restaurants, and many Argentines mix it with cheap wine and with ice. Argentine wines (a subject in themselves) are sound in all price ranges. The ordinary *vinos de la casa*, or *comunes* are wholesome and relatively cheap; the reds are better than the whites. In restaurants wine is quite expensive. *Clericó* is a white-wine *sangría* drunk in summer. **Vineyards** can be visited in Mendoza and San Juan provinces and Cafayate (in the south of Salta province). The local beers, mainly lager, are quite acceptable. If invited to drink *mate* (pronounced 'mattay'), always accept; it's the essential Argentine drink, usually shared as a social ritual between friends or colleagues. *Mate* is a stimulating green tea made from the yerba mate plant, slightly bitter in taste, drunk from a cup or seasoned gourd through a silver, perforated straw.

Essentials A-Z

Accident and emergency

Police T911or 101. **Fire department**, T100.
Urgent medical service T107. If robbed or
attacked, call the tourist police, **Comisaría del
Turista**, Av Corrientes 436, Buenos Aires, T011-
4346 5748 (24 hrs) or T0800-999 5000, turista@
policiafederal.gov.ar, English, Italian, French,
Portuguese, Japanese and Ukrainian spoken.

Electricity

220 volts (and 110 too in some hotels), 50 cycles,
AC, European Continental-type plugs in old
buildings, Australian 3-pin flat-type in the new.
Adaptors can be purchased locally for either type
(ie from new 3-pin to old 2-pin and vice-versa).

Embassies and consulates

For all Argentine embassies and consulates abroad
and for all foreign embassies and consulates in
Argentina, see http://embassy.goabroad.com.

Health

Medical services
For medical emergencies, call T107. For further
advice on the nearest or best hospital, ask at
your hotel.
Buenos Aires For free municipal ambulance
service to an emergency ward, call T107 (SAME,
www.buenosaires.gob.ar/same). **Centros
Médicos Stamboulian** (25 de Mayo 464,
T011-4515 3000, www.stamboulian.com.ar)
gives private health advice for travellers and
inoculations; also in Belgrano, Villa Crespo, Villa
Urquiza, Barrio Norte and Flores. **Hospital Juan A
Fernández** (Cerviño 3356 entre Ruggieri y Bulnes,
T011-4808 2600, www.hospitalfernandez.org)
provides probably the best free medical attention
in the city. The **British Hospital** (Perdriel 74, T011-
4309 6400, www.hospitalbritanico.org.ar) has a
first-aid centre (*centros asistenciales*) as do other
main hospitals.
Bariloche Hospital Zonal, Moreno 601,
T0294-442 6119, www.hospitalbariloche.com.ar.
Córdoba Hospital Córdoba, Libertad 2050,
T0351-433 9021. **Hospital Clínicas**, Santa Rosa
1564, T0351-433 7046. For both, www.fcm.unc.
edu.ar.
Mendoza Central hospital near bus terminal
at Alem 410, T0261-449 0684. **Lagomaggiore**,

Timoteo Gordillo s/n, T0261-520 4600, www.
hospitallagomaggiore.com, public general
hospital with good reputation.
Salta Hospital San Bernardo, Tobias 69, T0387-
432 0300, www.hospitalsanbernardo.com.ar.

Money

US$1 = 16.19 pesos; €1 = 18.12 pesos (Jun 2017).
The currency is the Argentine peso (ARS or $;
we use AR$), divided into 100 centavos. Peso
notes in circulation: 2, 5, 10, 20, 50 and 100.
Coins in circulation: 5, 10, 25 and 50 centavos,
1 and 2 pesos.
Always pay the exact amount of a bill as small
change is in short supply. Foreigners can use
credit cards to withdraw cash and for making
payments. You will need to show your passport
with your card. ATMs can be found in every
town and city. They are usually Banelco or Link,
accepting international cards, but they dispense
only pesos, impose withdrawal and daily limits
and a charge per transaction (limits change,
check on arrival). You will also have to add any
commission imposed by your card's issuing
company. Note that fake notes circulate, mostly
AR$100, 20 and 10. Check that the green numbers
showing the value of the note (on the left hand
top corner) shimmer; that there is a watermark;
that there is a continuous line from the top of the
note to the bottom about ¾ of the way along.
US dollar bills are often scanned electronically
for forgeries.

Credit cards
Visa, MasterCard, American Express and Diners
Club cards are all widely accepted in the major
cities and provincial capitals, though less so
outside these. There is a high surcharge on credit
card transactions in many establishments; many
hotels offer reductions for cash.

Cost of travelling
You can find comfortable accommodation with
a private bathroom and breakfast for around
US$45-60 for 2 people, while a good dinner in the
average restaurant will be around US$12-20 pp.
Prices are cheaper away from the main touristy
areas: El Calafate, Ushuaia and Buenos Aires can
be particularly pricey. For travellers on a budget,
hostels usually cost between US$10-20 pp in a
shared dorm. A cheap, insubstantial breakfast

costs US$4-5 and set meals at lunchtime about US$8-10 including drink, US$10 in Buenos Aires. Fares on long-distance buses increase annually and very long journeys are quite expensive. Even so it's worth splashing out an extra 20% for coche cama service on overnight journeys. The average cost of internet use is US$0.50-2 per hr.

National parks

Argentina has 47 protected areas, covering most of the country's natural environments. Best represented are the northwestern highlands and Patagonian forests. **Administración de Parques Nacionales** (APN; Santa Fe 690, opposite Pl San Martín, Buenos Aires, T011-4311 0303, www.parquesnacionales.gov.ar, Mon-Fri 1000-1700), has information and advice. The website **www.patrimonionatural.com** also has information on Argentina's national parks, natural reserves, UN-recognized and RAMSAR sites.

Opening hours

There is much variation nationally, but banks, government offices and businesses are not open on Sat. Office hours are usually 0800 or 0900 to between 1700 and 2100, with an hour break for lunch. **Bank** opening hours vary according to city and sometimes according to the season. **Shops** are open 0900-1800, but many close at 1300 on Sat, and, outside the main cities, many close at 1300 daily for the afternoon siesta, reopening at about 1700. Shopping malls are usually open 1000-2200.

Post

Correo Central, **Correos Argentinos**, T011-4891 9191 for enquiries, www.correoargentino.com.ar, Mon-Fri 0900-1800. **Centro Postal Internacional**, for all parcels over 2 kg for mailing abroad, at Av Comodoro Py y Antártida Argentina 1100, near Retiro station, Buenos Aires, helpful, many languages spoken, packing materials available, Mon-Fri 0900-1600.

Public holidays and festivals

No work may be done on the national holidays (1 Jan, Good Fri, 1 May, 25 May, 10 Jun, 20 Jun, 9 Jul, 17 Aug, 12 Oct and 25 Dec) except where specifically established by law. There are limited bus services on 25 and 31 Dec. On Holy Thu and 8 Dec employers decide whether their employees should work, but banks and public offices are closed. Banks are also closed on 31 Dec. There are gaucho parades in San Antonio de Areco (110 km from Buenos Aires) and throughout Argentina, with fabulous displays of horsemanship and with traditional music, on the days leading up to the Día de la Tradición, 10 Nov. On 30 Dec there is a ticker-tape tradition in downtown Buenos Aires: it snows paper and the crowds stuff passing cars and buses with long streamers. Details of local festivals can be found throughout the text.

Safety

Argentina is generally a safe country. All travellers should, however, remain on their guard in big cities, especially Buenos Aires, where petty crime is a problem. Trickery occurs, as does robbery, sometimes violent, with high-value items like top-of-the-range mountain bikes a common target.

Tax

Airport tax By law airport taxes must be included in the price of your air ticket. There is a 5% tax on the purchase of air tickets.
VAT/IVA 21%; VAT is not levied on medicines, books and some foodstuffs. Foreign tourists are exempt from VAT on hotel bills if they pay with a foreign credit or debit card.

Telephone and Wi-Fi

Country code +54.
Ringing: equal tones with long pauses. Engaged: equal tones with equal pauses. Note that area phone codes are constantly being changed. If you don't have your own phone, then *locutorios*, phone centres with private booths, are the best places to make phone calls. The price of the call appears on a screen as you talk. They often have internet, fax and photocopying services as well. Phone cards can be used for making calls from landlines, but not usually from *locutorios*. It is easy to buy a SIM card for an unlocked tri-or quad-band mobile phone. You can also buy a pay-as-you-go mobile phone relatively cheaply. For other options with your own device, check with your provider about roaming costs abroad. To call a mobile phone in Argentina, dial the city code followed by 15, then the mobile's number (eg 011-15-xxxx xxxx in Buenos Aires). To call a Argentine mobile from abroad, dial the country code, then 9, then the city code and number, omitting 15 (eg +54-9-11-xxxx xxxx). In the text we give the number for calling within Argentina.

Wi-Fi is widely available and can be found in almost every hotel and hostel, frequently free. It is also available in many public spaces. Skype and similar services are therefore a good way to keep in touch.

Time

GMT -3 hrs.

Tipping

10% in restaurants and cafés. Porters and ushers are usually tipped.

Tourist information

Tourism is handled by the national office of the **Ministerio de Turismo**, whose central information office is at Av Santa Fe 883, Buenos Aires, T011-4312-2232, www.turismo.gov.ar. For tourist information abroad, contact Argentine embassies and consulates.

Each province has a tourist office, or Casa de Provincia, in Buenos Aires (the majority have Facebook pages): **Buenos Aires Province**, Av Callao 237, T011-5300 9500, www.casaprov. gba.gov.ar, www.turismo.gba.gov.ar and www. buenosaires.tur.ar (official sites of province of Buenos Aires tourism); **Catamarca**, Av Córdoba 2080, T011-4374 6891, www.cataweb.com.ar; **Chaco**, Av Callao 328, T011-4372 3045, casa.del. chaco@ecomchaco.com.ar; **Chubut**, Sarmiento 1172, T011-4382 2009, www.chubut.gov.ar; **Córdoba**, Av Callao 332, T011-4371 1668, casadecordoba@cba.gov.ar; **Corrientes**, Maipú 271, T011-4394 7418, casadecorrientes@argentina. com; **Entre Ríos**, Suipacha 844, T011-4312 3697, www.casadeentrerios.gov.ar; **Formosa**, Hipólito Yrigoyen 1429, T011-4384 8443, casadeformosa@ formosa.gob.ar; **Jujuy**, Av Santa Fe 967, T011-4393 1295, http://casadejujuy.jujuy.gob.ar; **La Pampa**, Suipacha 346, T011-4326 0511, www. casa.lapampa.gov.ar; **La Rioja**, Av Callao 745, T011-4816 7068, www.turismolarioja.gov.ar; **Mendoza**, Av Callao 445, T011-5077 8509, http:// casamendoza.mendoza.gov.ar; **Misiones**, Santa Fe 989, T011-4317 3700, see casa.dem isiones Facebook page; **Neuquén**, Maipú 48, T011-4343 2324, casanqn_turismoycultura@neuquen.gov.ar; **Río Negro**, Tucumán 1916, T011-4371 7273, www. casa.rionegro.gov.ar; **Salta**, Av Roque Saenz Peña 933, T011-4326 2456, Facebook: casadesalta; **San Juan**, Sarmiento 1251, T011-4382 5580, Facebook: casadesanjuanenbsas ; **San Luis**,

Azcuénaga 1087, T011-5778 1621, Facebook: casadesanluis; **Santa Cruz**, 25 de Mayo 279, T011-4343 8478, www.casadesantacruz.gov.ar; **Santa Fé**, 25 de Mayo 178, T011-4342 0408, casadesantafeencaba@santafe.gov.ar; **Santiago del Estero**, Florida 274, T011-4326 9418, www.casadesantiago.gob.ar; **Tierra del Fuego**, Sarmiento 745, T011-4322 7324, http:// representacionbsas.tierradelfuego.gov.ar; **Tucumán**, Suipacha 140, T011-4322 0562, casaenbsas@tucumanturismo.gob.ar.

Websites

www.infobae.com An Argentine online newspaper, in Spanish.
www.buenosairesherald.com *Buenos Aires Herald*, English language newspaper.
www.ypf.com/guia/Paginas/Home.aspx Site of the YPF fuel company, with travel and tourist information.
www.patagonia.com.ar, **www.patagonia-argentina.com** and **www.interpatagonia.com** Tourist information for Patagonia.
www.smn.gov.ar Useful website for forecasts and weather satellite images.
www.tageblatt.com.ar *Argentinisches Tageblatt*, German-language weekly, very informative.
www.welcomeargentina.com Online travel guide to the whole country.

Visas and immigration

Passports are not required by citizens of South American countries who hold identity cards issued by their own governments. No visa is necessary for British citizens, nationals of western European countries, Central American and some Caribbean countries, plus citizens of Australia, Canada, Croatia, Hong Kong, Israel, Japan, New Zealand, Russia, Singapore, South Africa, Turkey and USA, who are given a tourist card ('tarjeta de entrada') on entry and may stay for 3 months; the card can be renewed only once for another 3 months (fee AR$900/US$59) at the **Dirección Nacional de Migraciones**, Av Antártida Argentina 1355 (Retiro), Buenos Aires, T011-4317 0234, Mon-Fri 0800-1400, or any other delegation of the **Dirección Nacional de Migraciones** (www.migraciones.gov.ar). For all others there are 3 forms of visa: a tourist visa (multiple entry, valid for 3 months; onward ticket and proof of adequate funds must be provided; fees vary depending on the country of origin; can be extended 90 days), a business visa and a transit visa. If leaving Argentina on a short trip, check on re-entry that border officials look at the correct expiry date on your visa, otherwise they will give only 30 days. Carry your passport at all times; backpackers are often targets for thorough searches – just stay calm; it is illegal not to have identification to hand.

At land borders if you don't need a visa, 90 days' permission to stay is usually given without proof of transportation out of Argentina. Make sure you are given a tourist card, otherwise you will have to obtain one before leaving the country. If you need a 90-day extension for your stay then leave the country (eg at Iguazú), and 90 further days will be given on return. Visa extensions may also be obtained from the address above, ask for 'Prórrogas de residencia'. No renewals are given after the expiry date. If, after 10 days of expiry, you have not left the country you must go to **Dirección Nacional de Migraciones** to authorize departure at a cost of AR$1500.

Reciprocal fees: in 2010 Argentina introduced entry fees for citizens of countries which require Argentines to obtain a visa and pay an entry fee, namely Australia (US$100, valid 1 year) and Canada (US$92, multiple entry). The fee is only payable by credit card online before arrival. You must print the receipt and present it to immigration wherever you enter the country. Go to www.migraciones.gov.ar, Tasa Reciprocidad page for instructions. There is also www.ivisa.com/visa-argentina-reciprocity-fee to help you. The reciprocity fee for US citizens (US$160) was revoked in Aug 2016.

Weights and measures

Metric.

This is
Bolivia

Like its luminescent sky, Bolivia remains largely unpolluted and, in an age of rampant Disneyfication, stands out for its authenticity. There are over 17 million hectares of protected natural areas, but isolation is what best protects the intense and often bizarre beauty of Bolivia's landscapes. For the same reason, the cultural integrity of its peoples remains intact. Even though Evo Morales' government is bringing municipalities closer together, paving roads and building communal facilities, it takes time and patience to travel from one place to the next.

No matter how far you travel in Bolivia, no matter how close you think you are to figuring it out, it will catch you off guard. Amazing new experiences will leave you humbled and in awe of this remarkable country. These are just a few of the author's favourites, gathered on journeys around the country: a guide playing his charango in a cathedral-like cave near Torotoro; listening to the choir practise baroque music in San José de Chiquitos; admiring Tunupa reflected in a flooded salar; bathing in hot springs at Laguna Blanca and not wanting to get out because the air is almost zero; gliding down the river Yacuma being watched by countless caiman and cackled at by family after family of prehistoric hoatzin.

From the shores of Titicaca, the world's highest navigable lake, to the 'Lost World' table-lands of Noel Kempff Mercado National Park, following the footsteps of dinosaurs, bandits and revolutionaries, there are endless opportunities for off-the-beaten path exploration. Along the way are rest-stop cities and towns where travellers can indulge in creature comforts and recount tall tales of their adventures.

BRAZIL

Assis Brasil
Brasiléia
Cobija
Puerto Rico
Riberalta
Guayaramerín

PERU

Puerto Pardo
Puerto Heath
El Chorro

Parque Nacional Madidi
Reyes
Rurrenabaque
Yucumo

Sta Ana de Yacuma
San Joaquín
Magdalena

Parque Nacional Noel Kempff Mercado

Pilón Lajas Biosphere Reserve
San Borja
San Ignacio de Moxos
San Javier
Trinidad
Caimanes
Casarebe
Perseverancia

Lake Titicaca
Guanay
Sorata
Carabuco
Copacabana
Tiwanaku
LA PAZ

Parque Nacional Sajama

Caranavi
Coroico
Chulumani
Villa Tunari
Cochabamba
Puerto Villarroel

San Pablo
San Javier
Concepción
Santa Ana

Baía Grande
San Ignacio de Velasco
San Matías

Tambo Quemado
Oruro
Huanuni
Challapata
Parque Nacional Torotoro
Totora
Aiquile
Samaipata

Parque Nacional Amboró
Buena Vista
San Ramón
Montero
Santa Cruz de la Sierra

San Miguel
San Rafael
San José de Chiquitos
Roboré
Quijarro/ Puerto Suárez

Sacabaya
Lago Poopó
Sabaya
Llica
Salar de Uyuni
Colchane
Uyuni

Sucre
La Higuera
Potosí
Tarabuco
Monteagudo

Parque Nacional Kaa-Iya
Abapó

Avaroa/Ollagüe
Alota
Reserva Eduardo Avaroa
San Vicente
Tupiza

Cerdas
Camargo
Villamontes
Camiri
Boyuibe
Hito Villazón
Ibibobo

PARAGUAY

Laguna Colorada
Hito Cajones
Laguna Verde
Tarija
Yacuiba
Villazón
Pocitos
Bermejo
Fortín Infante Rivarola

ARGENTINA

N

100 km
100 miles

Footprint picks

★ **La Diablada festival, Oruro**, page 257

Dance with the devil at Bolivia's world-renowned carnival.

★ **Copacabana**, page 283

Picturesque little town on beautiful Lake Titicaca.

★ **Salar de Uyuni and Reserva Eduardo Avaroa**, pages 303 and 305

The largest and highest salt lake in the world, together with some of Bolivia's most stunning, remote landscapes.

★ **Parque Nacional Torotoro**, page 345

A geologist's paradise, with magnificent rock formations, fossils from the ocean bed and dinosaur tracks.

★ **Chiquitania missions**, page 362

Remarkable colonial churches in a sparsely populated plain.

★ **Parque Nacional Madidi**, page 372

Possibly the world's most biodiverse region with pristine jungle and abundant wildlife.

Route
planner

One to two weeks

base camp

Your best bet is to stay within reach of **La Paz**, whose centre can be explored on foot in a couple of days. There are several worthwhile museums to visit; the warren of streets running uphill from El Prado leads you into a strange and fascinating world, and the cable cars to **El Alto** and **Zona Sur** give a wonderful overview of the city. Trailheads of several good day-walks can be reached by public transport and specialist tour companies can take you on exciting mountain-bike rides. An enlightening excursion from La Paz is the archaeological site of **Tiwanaku**. **Lake Titicaca** can also be visited in a day, but it is much more rewarding to stay overnight at the lakeside and visit **Isla del Sol** the following day. A day or two could easily be spent in the subtropical town of **Coroico**, 2½ hours from La Paz on a spectacular and hair-raising road. Three hours from La Paz is **Sorata**, another small town surrounded by beautiful mountain scenery and a major climbing, trekking and biking centre.

If you have a few more days, you might consider taking a four-day tour to either the **Salar de Uyuni** or to the jungle near **Rurrenabaque** (see below).

Two to three weeks: Salar–Cochabamba circuit

salt lakes and colonial cities

After a couple of days in **La Paz**, making the most of the city while acclimatizing to the altitude, take a bus to Oruro. Continue by road or train to **Uyuni** or **Tupiza**. Either is a good place to start a tour to the **Salar de Uyuni** and its dramatic, volcanic surroundings in **Reserva Eduaro Avaroa**. It takes at least four days to enjoy this world-class attraction properly, but you could easily spend more time in the vast and magnificent area. If short of time you can fly to Uyuni from La Paz. Paved roads run from Uyuni and Tupiza to **Potosí** to visit the mines and the Mint. From there buses and train run to **Sucre**, the nation's capital and most distinguished city. From Sucre you could fly or take a bus back to La Paz, or extend the circuit to **Cochabamba** by short flight or long bus journey, to enjoy the city, the surrounding colonial towns, nearby **Parque Nacional Tunari** and, if time permits, **Parque Nacional Torotoro** (four days). Both Sucre and Torotoro are great places to see dinosaur tracks.

Two to three weeks: Jesuit missions and Samaipata
religious art and a cool resort

From **Santa Cruz de la Sierra**, one of Bolivia's international gateways, begin your travels by bus to **San Javier**, the closest of the Jesuit mission towns. The missions circuit needs at least five days and involves seven towns, six of which have UNESCO World-Heritage-status churches, perhaps the finest examples of religious art and craftsmanship in the country. From **San José de Chiquitos** you can return to Santa Cruz by bus or train. After the heat and dust of Chiquitania, head up to the refreshingly cool resort of **Samaipata**, only 2½ hours from Santa Cruz on a good paved road. It's a great place to relax and nearby is **El Fuerte** archaeological site, once the easternmost stronghold of the Inca Empire. North of Samaipata is **Parque Nacional Amboró**, one of Bolivia's richest wildlife reserves, and southwest is the **Che Guevara trail**, a significant element of Latin American history.

Two to three weeks: Yungas to Amazon
adrenalin fix and jungle trips

After a few days in **La Paz**, ride the infamous road down to **Coroico** by bike or minibus. Once you have recovered in the delightful surroundings of the **Yungas**, take a shared taxi to **Caranavi** where you can break your journey again before starting the rough 12-hour bus ride to **Rurrenabaque**. Alternative ways to get to Rurre are to fly in, or to go by mountain bike and boat from **Sorata** via **Guanay** (two hours from Caranavi) – tour operators offer this route. In Rurre, there are two types of tour: selva into the **Parque Nacional Madidi** and pampas into the **Beni lowlands**. Allow at least three days for each; there are many agencies to choose from. Instead of a marathon bus ride back to La Paz, consider flying and taking in the breathtaking views as you soar over the top of the Cordillera Real.

Essential Bolivia

Finding your feet

International flights to Bolivia arrive either at La Paz (LPB) or Santa Cruz de la Sierra (VVI). There are frequent domestic flights between La Paz and Santa Cruz, as well as plentiful bus services. If you are arriving overland, Bolivia has numerous borders with Argentina, Brazil, Chile, Paraguay and Peru.

Fact file

Location 16.7120° S, 64.6660° W
Capital Sucre (constitutional)/
La Paz (administrative)
Time zone GMT -4 hrs
Telephone country code +591
Currency Boliviano (Bs)

Getting around

Many internal flights radiate from La Paz, Santa Cruz or Cochabamba. A growing percentage of Bolivian roads are paved, the rest are gravel-surfaced or earth. Any road, whatever its surface, may be closed in the rainy season (December-March). The main paved road axis of Bolivia runs from the Peruvian border at Desaguadero (also Copacabana) via La Paz and Oruro to Cochabamba and Santa Cruz, continuing to the Brazilian border at Arroyo Concepción. Be mindful that distances are long and land transport is slow.

When to go

The dry season is May to September, July and August see the most tourists, while some of the best festivals, eg Carnaval and Holy Week, fall during the wet season -- generally December to March. The country has four climatic zones:

• **The Puna and altiplano** Average temperature, 10°C, but above 4000 m may drop as low as -30°C at night from June to August. By day, the tropical sun raises temperatures to above 20°C. Rainfall on the northern altiplano is 400-700 mm, much less further south. Little rain falls upon the western plateau between May and November, but the rest of the year can be wet.

• **The Yungas** North of La Paz and Cochabamba, among the spurs of the Cordillera; altitude, 750-1500 m; average temperature 24°C. Rainfall in the Yungas is 700-800 mm a year, with high humidity.

• **The Valles** The high valleys and basins gouged out by the rivers of the Puna; average temperature 19°C.

• **The tropical lowlands** Altitude 150 m to 750 m; rainfall is high but seasonal (heaviest November to March, but can fall at any time); large areas suffer from alternate flooding and drought. The climate is hot, ranging from 23° to 25°C in the south and to 30°C in the north. Occasional cold winds from the south, the *surazos*, can lower the temperature suddenly and considerably.

Time required

Two to three weeks is just enough time to acclimatize in La Paz and then do any of the itineraries suggested above. A month or more will allow you to experience the finest activity Bolivia has to offer – genuine exploration.

Weather La Paz

January	February	March	April	May	June
15°C 4°C 137mm	15°C 4°C 83mm	15°C 3°C 82mm	15°C 2°C 32mm	15°C -2°C 8mm	14°C -4°C 10mm

July	August	September	October	November	December
14°C -4°C 6mm	15°C -3°C 30mm	16°C -1°C 28mm	16°C 2°C 40mm	17°C 2°C 50mm	16°C 4°C 77mm

★La Diablada

If you are in Bolivia in the period before Lent, you should make every effort to visit Oruro (see page 297) to witness one of South America's most distinctive festivals. Starting on the Saturday before Ash Wednesday, Los Carnavales de Oruro include the famous **Diablada** ceremony in homage to the miraculous Virgen del Socavón, patroness of miners, and in gratitude to Pachamama, the Earth Mother. The carnival is especially notable for its fantastically elaborate and imaginative costumes. The Diablada was traditionally performed by indigenous miners, but several other guilds have taken up the custom.

The **Sábado de Peregrinación** starts its 5 km route through the town at 0700, finishing at the Sanctuary of the Virgen del Socavón, and continues into the early hours of Sunday. There the dancers invoke blessings and ask for pardon.

At dawn on Sunday, **El Alba** is a competition of all participating musicians at Plaza del Folklore near the Santuario, an amazing battle of the bands. The **Gran Corso** or **La Entrada** starts at 0800 on the Sunday, a more informal parade (many leave their masks off) along the same route.

Monday is **El Día del Diablo y del Moreno** in which the Diablos and Morenos, with their bands, bid farewell to the Virgin. Arches decorated with colourful woven cloths and silverware are set up on the road leading to the Santuario, where a Mass is held. In the morning, at Avenida Cívica, the Diablada companies participate in a play of the Seven Deadly Sins. This is followed by a play about the meeting of the Inca Atahualpa with Pizarro. On Tuesday, **Martes de Chall'a**, families get together, with ch'alla rituals to invoke ancestors, unite with Pachamama and bless personal possessions. The Friday before Carnaval, traditional miners' ceremonies are held at mines, including the sacrifice of a llama. Visitors may only attend with advance permission.

Preparations for Carnaval begin four months before the actual event, on the first Sunday of November, and rehearsals are held every Sunday until one week before Carnaval, when a plain clothes rehearsal takes place, preceded by a Mass for participants. In honour of its syncretism of ancestral Andean traditions and Catholic faith, the Oruro Carnaval has been included on UNESCO's Heritage of Humanity list.

Seating Stands are erected along the entire route. Tickets are for Saturday and Sunday, there is no discount if you stay only one day. Some stands have a cover for shade or rain. A prime location is around Plaza 10 de Febrero where the companies perform in front of the authorities. Along Avenida 6 de Agosto a sought-after location is by TV cameras, where performers put on their best. Seats cost US$35-70.

Where to stay During Carnaval, accommodation costs as much as five times more than normal and must be booked well in advance. Hotels charge for Friday, Saturday and Sunday nights. You can stay for only one night, but you'll be charged for three. Locals also offer places to stay in their homes, expect to pay at least US$12 per person per night.

Transport When demand is at its peak, posted prices are ignored and buses from La Paz charge three or more times the usual fare. Buses fill quickly starting Friday and tickets are not sold in advance. Many agencies in La Paz organize day-trips for the Saturday parade. They leave around 0430 and return late. Trips in 2017 cost US$150 and up (much more for seats on the plaza) for transport, breakfast, box lunch, drinks and seats for the parade.

La Paz

The minute you arrive in La Paz, the highest seat of government in the world, you realize this is no ordinary place. El Alto airport is at a staggering 4061 m above sea level. The sight of the city, lying hundreds of metres below, at the bottom of a steep canyon and ringed by snow-peaked mountains, takes your breath away – literally – for at this altitude breathing can be a problem.

The Spaniards chose this odd place for a city on 20 October 1548, to avoid the chill winds of the plateau, and because they had found gold in the Río Choqueyapu, which runs through the canyon. The centre of the city, Plaza Murillo, is at 3636 m, about 400 m below the level of the altiplano and the sprawling city of El Alto, perched dramatically on the rim of the canyon.

Sights   *Colour map 3, B2.*

the centre has lively markets and some worthwhile museums

There are few colonial buildings left in La Paz; probably the best examples are in Calle Jaén (see below). Late 19th- and early 20th-century architecture, often displaying European influence, can be found in the streets around Plaza Murillo, but much of La Paz is modern. The Plaza del Estudiante (Plaza Franz Tamayo), or a bit above it, marks a contrast between old and new styles, between the commercial and the more elegant. El Prado itself is lined with high-rise blocks dating from the 1960s and 1970s and new ones were being built in 2017.

Around Plaza Murillo

Plaza Murillo Three blocks north of El Prado, this is the traditional centre. Facing its formal gardens are the **Cathedral**, the **Palacio Presidencial** in Italian Renaissance style, known as the **Palacio Quemado** (burnt palace) twice gutted by fire in its stormy 130-year history and, on the east side, the **Congreso Nacional**. In front of the Palacio Quemado is a statue of former President Gualberto Villarroel who was dragged into the plaza by a mob and hanged in 1946. Across from the Cathedral on Calle Socabaya is the **Palacio de los Condes de Arana** (built 1775), with beautiful exterior and patio. It houses the **Museo Nacional de Arte** ① *T02-240 8600, www.mna.org.bo, Tue-Fri 0930-1230, 1500-1900, Sat 1000-1730, Sun 1000-1330, US$3.* It has a fine collection of colonial paintings including many works by Melchor Pérez Holguín, considered one of the masters of Andean colonial art, and which also exhibits the works of contemporary local artists. Calle Comercio, running east-west across the Plaza, has many stores. West of Plaza Murillo, at Ingavi 916, in the palace of the Marqueses de Villaverde is the **Museo Nacional de Etnografía y Folklore** ① *T02-240 8640, www.musef.org.bo, Mon-Fri 0900-1230, 1500-1900, Sat 0900-1630, Sun 0900-1230, US$3, photos cost US$3, filming an extra US$6.* Various sections show the cultural richness of Bolivia by region through textiles and other items. It has a *videoteca* (video library).

Calle Jaén Northwest of Plaza Murillo is Calle Jaén, a picturesque colonial street with a café, craft shops, good views and several museums housed in colonial buildings. **Museo Costumbrista Juan de Vargas** ① *on Plaza Riosinio, at the top of Jaén, T02-228 0758, US$0.60, Tue-Fri 0930-1230, 1500-1900, Sat-Sun 1000-1230,* has miniature displays depicting incidents in the history of La Paz and well-known Paceños, as well as miniature replicas of reed rafts used by the Norwegian Thor Heyerdahl, and the Spaniard Kitin Muñoz, to prove their theories of ancient migrations. The following three museums are known as **Museos Municipales** ① *Tue-Fri 0930-1230, 1500-1900, Sat 1000-1700,*

Essential La Paz

Finding your feet

La Paz has the highest commercial **airport** in the world, high above the city at El Alto. A taxi from the airport to or from the centre takes between 30 minutes and one hour.

Orientation

The city's main street runs from **Plaza San Francisco** as Avenida Mariscal Santa Cruz, then changes to Avenida 16 de Julio (more commonly known as El Prado) and ends at **Plaza del Estudiante**. The business quarter, government offices, central university (UMSA) and many of the main hotels and restaurants are in this area. Banks and exchange houses are clustered on Calle Camacho, between Loayza and Colón, not far from **Plaza Murillo**, the traditional heart of the city. From the Plaza del Estudiante, Avenida Villazón splits into Avenida Arce, which runs southeast towards the wealthier residential districts of **Zona Sur**, in the valley, 15 minutes away; and Avenida 6 de Agosto which runs through **Sopocachi**, an area full of restaurants, bars and clubs. Zona Sur has shopping centres, supermarkets with imported items and some of the best restaurants and bars in La Paz (see pages 270 and 273).

Tip...

Travellers arriving in La Paz, especially when flying directly from sea level, may experience mild altitude sickness. If your symptoms are severe, consult a physician. See Health, page 384.

Getting around

There are three main **bus terminals**: the bus station at Plaza Antofagasta, the cemetery district for Sorata, Copacabana and Tiwanaku, and Minasa bus station in Villa Fátima for the Yungas, including Coroico, and northern jungle.

A system of cable cars (*teleféricos*) is under construction. Four lines were in operation at the time of writing, the red line, between El Alto and Vita, west of the main bus station, the yellow line

from Ciudad Satélite (El Alto) to Sopocachi and Obrajes, and the green line, which continues from Obrajes to Calacoto, near Irpavi (Zona Sur) and the blue line in El Alto, from Ciudad Satélite to Río Seco. There are three types of city bus: *puma katari* (a fleet of new buses with defined stops), *micros* (small, old buses) and faster, more plentiful minibuses. *Trufis* are fixed-route collective taxis, with a sign with their route on the windscreen. Taxis come in three types: regular honest taxis, fake taxis and radio taxis, the safest, which have a dome light and number.

When to go

The weather is cool all year; locals say that the city experiences all the seasons in one day. The sun is strong, but the moment you go into the shade, the temperature falls. From December to March, the summer, it rains most afternoons, making it feel colder than it actually is. Temperatures are even lower in winter, June-August, when the sky is always clear.

It is good to visit La Paz at any time. The two most important festivals, when the city gets particularly busy, are **Alasitas** (four weeks starting 24 January) and **Festividad del Señor del Gran Poder** (end May/early June). See Festivals, page 274.

Safety

La Paz is in general a safe city, but like any metropolis it is not crime-free. Areas where you must take care are around Plaza Murillo and the Cemetery neighbourhood where local buses serve Copacabana and Tiwanaku. **Tourist police** (T02-222 5016) now patrol these bus stops during the daytime, but caution is still advised. Also beware of fake police who work the main bus terminal. **Warning for ATM users**: scams to get card numbers and PINs have flourished, especially in La Paz. The tourist police post warnings in hotels. See also Safety, page 386.

Time required

Two to three days to acclimatize to the altitude and see the city's highlights; one to two weeks for excursions and treks.

1 La Paz

➡ La Paz maps
1 La Paz, page 260
2 La Paz centre, page 262
3 Sopocachi, page 264

To ① ② ⑭, Bus Station, El Alto, Airport,
Titicaca, Tiwanaku & Oruro

Plaza
Riosinio
Plaza
de la Alianza

Museo Costumbrista
& other museums

TAM

Museo de
Instrumentos
Musicales

Teatro
Municipal

Plaza
Mendoza

Plaza
Vicente
Eguino

Evaristo Valle

Lanza

Plaza Pérez
Velasco

Plaza San
Francisco

Plaza
Murillo

Cathedral

San
Francisco

Palacio
Presidencial

Negro

Main
Market Area

Electronics

Rodríguez

Av Camacho

Plaza
Venezuela

Calderón

Plaza
San Pedro   Sucre

San Pedro
Prison

Where to stay 🛏

1 Adventure Brew B&B *A2*
2 Adventure Brew
  Hostel *A2*
3 Arthy's Guesthouse *A2*
4 Bacoo *A3*
5 Casa Prado *C4*
6 El Rey Palace *D4*
7 Estrella Andina *B2*
8 Europa *C4*
9 Hostal República *B4*
10 Hostel 3600 *D4*
11 Onkell Inn 1886 *C3*
12 Rosario & Tambo
   Colonial Restaurant *B2*
13 Sol Andino *B2*
14 Tambo de Oro *A3*
15 Wild Rover
   Backpackers Hostel *B4*

🚡 Teleférico station

Restaurants 🍴

1 Alexander Coffee *C4*
2 Café Urbano *C4*
3 Ken-Chan *D4*
4 Paladar *C6*
5 Potokos *A6*
6 The Writer's Coffee *B4*
7 Vienna *D4*
8 Wist'u Piku *D4*

Bars & clubs 🍸

9 Etno Café *A3*

N

100 metres
100 yards

Plaza
Israel

Plaza
Confederación

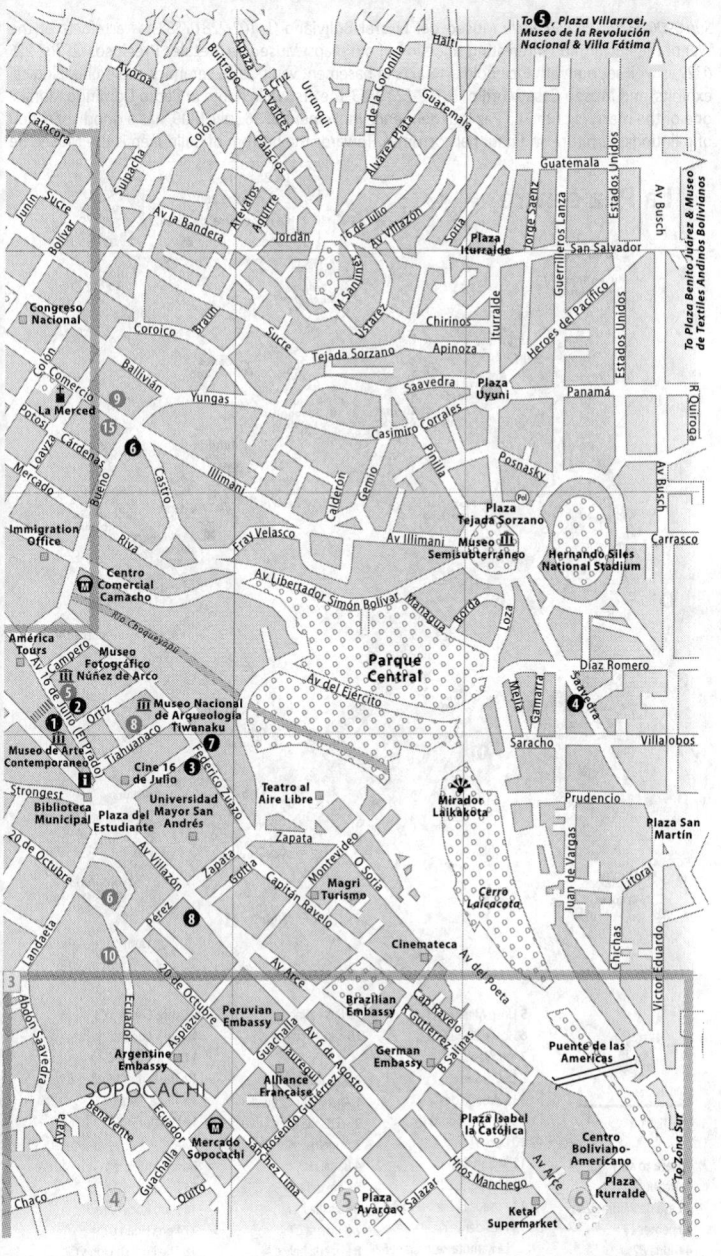

Sun 0900-1330, US$1.50 each: **Museo del Litoral Boliviano** ① *T02-228 0758*, has artefacts of the War of the Pacific, and interesting selection of old maps; **Museo de Metales Preciosos** ① *T02-228 0329*, is well set out with Inca gold artefacts in basement vaults, also ceramics and archaeological exhibits; and **Museo Casa Murillo** ① *T02-228 0553*, the erstwhile home of Pedro Domingo Murillo, one of the martyrs of the La Paz independence movement of 16 July 1809, has a good collection of paintings, furniture and national costumes. Towards the bottom of Calle Jaén is the **Museo de**

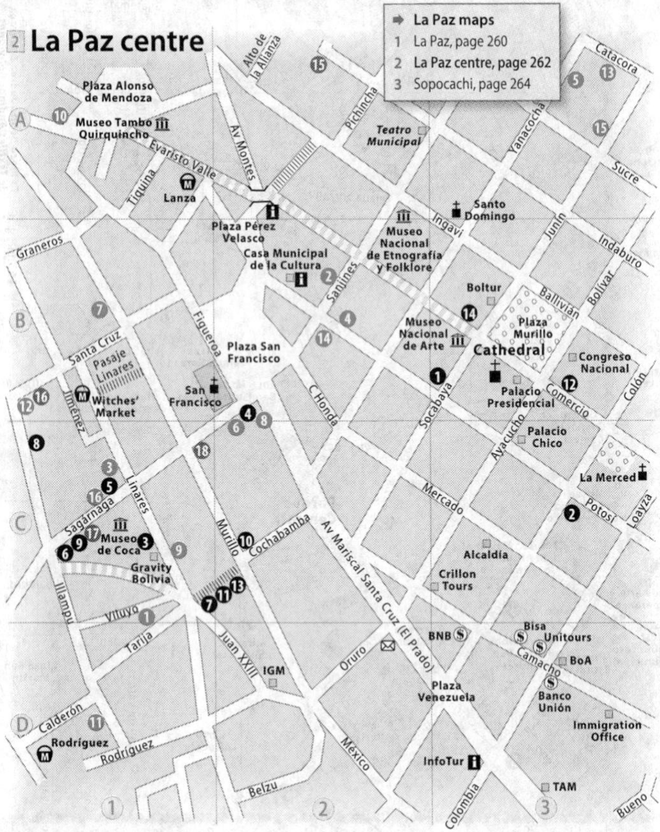

2 La Paz centre

➡ **La Paz maps**
1 La Paz, page 260
2 La Paz centre, page 262
3 Sopocachi, page 264

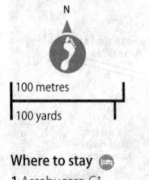

N

100 metres
100 yards

Where to stay 🛏
1 Arcabucero *C1*
2 Casa de Piedra *B2*
3 Fuentes *C1*
4 Gloria *B2*
5 Hosp Milenio *A3*
6 Hostal Naira *C2*
7 Inti Wasi *B1*
8 La Casona *B2*
9 La Posada de la
   Abuela Obdulia *C1*
10 Loki *A1*
11 Milton *D1*
12 Muzungu *B1*
13 Posada El Carretero *A3*
14 Presidente &
   La Kantuta Restaurant *B2*
15 Res Latino *A3*
16 Sagárnaga *C1*

Restaurants 🍴
1 Alexander Coffee *B3*
2 Ali Pacha *C3*
3 Angelo Colonial *C1*
4 Banais *B2*
5 Café del Mundo *C1*
6 Kalakitas *C1*
7 K'umara *C1*
8 Pizzería Italy *C1*
9 Sabor Cubano *C1*
10 Sol y Luna *C2*
11 Steakhouse *C2*
12 The Writer's Coffee *B3*
13 Tierra Sana *C2*
14 Wist'u Piku *B3*

Bars & clubs 🍸
15 Bocaisapo *A2*
16 Hard Rock Café *B1*
17 Peña Huari *C1*
18 The English Lion's *C2*

Instrumentos Musicales ① *C Jaén 711 e Indaburo, T02-240 8177, Mon-Sat 0930-1330,1430-1830, Sun 0930-1830, US$1.40,* founded by Ernesto Cavour and based on 30 years of research. The **Teatro del Charango** ① *Sat 1930-2130,* is within the museum, also the **International Charango Association** is based here and lessons are available.

Museo Tambo Quirquincho ① *C Evaristo Valle, south of Jaén, Plaza Alonso de Mendoza, T02-239 0969, Tue-Fri, 0930-1230, 1500-1900, Sat-Sun, 0900-1300, US$1.20,* displays modern painting and sculpture, carnival masks, silver, early 20th-century photography and city plans, and is recommended.

Plaza San Francisco up to the cemetery district

☆**Church and monastery of San Francisco** ① *Plaza San Francisco, open for Mass at 0700, 0900, 1100 and 1900, Mon-Sat, and also at 0800, 1000 and 1200 on Sun.* At the upper end of Avenida Mcal Santa Cruz, this church and monastery, dating from 1549, is one of the finest examples of colonial religious architecture in South America and well worth seeing. The **Centro Cultural Museo San Francisco** ① *Plaza San Francisco 503, T02-231 8472, Mon-Sat 0900-1800, US$2.80, allow 1½-2 hrs, free guides available but tip appreciated, some speak English and French,* offers access to various areas of the church and convent including the choir, crypt (open 1400-1730), roof, various chapels and gardens. Fine art includes religious paintings from the 17th, 18th and 19th centuries, plus visiting exhibits and a hall devoted to the works of Tito Yupanqui, the indigenous sculptor of the Virgen de Copacabana. There is a pricey but good café at entrance.

Behind the San Francisco church a network of narrow cobbled streets rise steeply up the canyon walls. Much of this area is a ☆**street market**. Handicraft shops, travel agencies, hotels and restaurants line the lower part of **Calle Sagárnaga** (here you find the highest concentration of tourists and pick-pockets). The **Mercado de Brujas**, 'witchcraft market', on Calles Melchor Jiménez and Linares, which cross Santa Cruz above San Francisco, sells charms, herbs and more gruesome items like llama foetuses. The small **Museo de la Coca** ① *Linares 906, T02-231 1998, www. cocamuseum.com, Mon-Sat 1000-1900, Sun 1000-1600, US$2.15,* is devoted to the coca plant, its history, cultural significance, medical values and political implications. A guidebook in English is available and there's a shop selling coca products.

Further up, from Illampu to Rodríguez and in neighbouring streets, is the produce-based **Rodríguez market** ① *daily, but best on Sat and Sun mornings.* Turning right on Max Paredes, heading north, is **Avenida Buenos Aires**, where small workshops turn out the costumes and masks for the Gran Poder festival, and with great views of Illimani, especially at sunset. Continuing west along Max Paredes towards the **cemetery district**, the streets are crammed with stalls selling every imaginable item. Transport converges on the cemetery district. See also Safety, page 386.

El Prado, Sopocachi, Miraflores and Zona Sur

El Prado The **Museo de Arte Contemporáneo Plaza** ① *Av 16 de Julio 1698, T02-233 5905, daily 1000-1900, US$2.20,* in a 19th-century house that has been declared a national monument, exhibits a selection of contemporary art from national and international artists.

Nearby, the ☆**Museo Nacional de Arqueología** or **Tiahuanaco (Tiwanaku)** ① *Tiwanacu 93 entre Bravo y F Zuazo, T02-233 1633, www.minculturas.gob.bo, Thu-Fri 0830-1230, 1500-1900, Sat-Sun 0900-1300,* just off El Prado (down the flight of stairs near the Maria Auxiliadora church), contains good collections of the arts and crafts of ancient Tiwanaku and items from the eastern jungles. It also has an exhibition of gold statuettes and objects found in Lake Titicaca. Further north, on Avenida Camacho is the **Centro Comercial Camacho**, with produce market, restaurants, a popular food court, gym and an area for entertainment. To the east, the continuation of Camacho is Avenida Libertador Simón Bolívar, from where there are views of Mount Illimani; along it is the large **Parque Central**.

☆**Sopocachi** To the south of Plaza del Estudiante, Sopocachi is a combination of older stately homes (many now house shops or offices) and high-rise buildings. **Plaza Avaroa**, where a number of the city's cultural activities take place, is the centre of the neighbourhood. Uphill from Plaza Avaroa is the smaller **Plaza España**, near which is a station on the yellow line of the ☆**Teleférico**, and next to it **El Montículo**, a lovely park with more great views of the city. From Plaza España, Avenida Ecuador leads north towards San Pedro and downtown. Along it is the **Casa Museo Marina Núñez del Prado** ① *Ecuador 2034, T02-242 4175, www.bolivian.com/cmnp, daily 0930-1300, Tue-Fri*

1500-1900 (may be closed afternoons and weekends), US$0.75, students US$0.30, which houses an excellent collection of Marina Núñez's sculptures in the family mansion.

Miraflores Downhill from Plaza Avaroa along Calle Pedro Salazar, at the intersection with Avenida Arce, is **Plaza Isabel La Católica**. Avenida Arce leads to the Zona Sur, the continuation of Salazar leads to Miraflores via the **Puente de las Américas**, which offers more excellent views of Illimani.

In the residential district of Miraflores, east of the centre, on Plaza Tejada Sorzano, outside the Hernán Siles national football stadium is the **Museo Semisubterráneo**, a sunken garden full of replicas of statues and artefacts from Tiwanaku, but difficult to get to because of the traffic. At the north end of Avenida Busch are Plaza Villarroel and **Museo del la Revolución Nacional** ① *Tue-Fri 0930-1200, 1500-1800, Sat-Sun 1000-1200, US$0.15*, a memorial of the 1952 revolution and a mausoleum with tombs of former presidents. East of Avenida Busch, on Calles Cuba and Guatemala, are Plaza Benito Juárez and the **Museo de Textiles Andinos Bolivianos** ① *Plaza Benito Juárez 488, T02-224 3601, Mon-Sat 0900-1230, 1500-1830, US$1.25*, with good displays of textiles from around the country, detailed explanations and a knowledgeable owner.

Zona Sur The Zona Sur, in the valley 15 minutes south of the city, includes the wealthier suburbs of La Paz with various upmarket hotels, restaurants and shopping centres.

③ **Sopocachi**

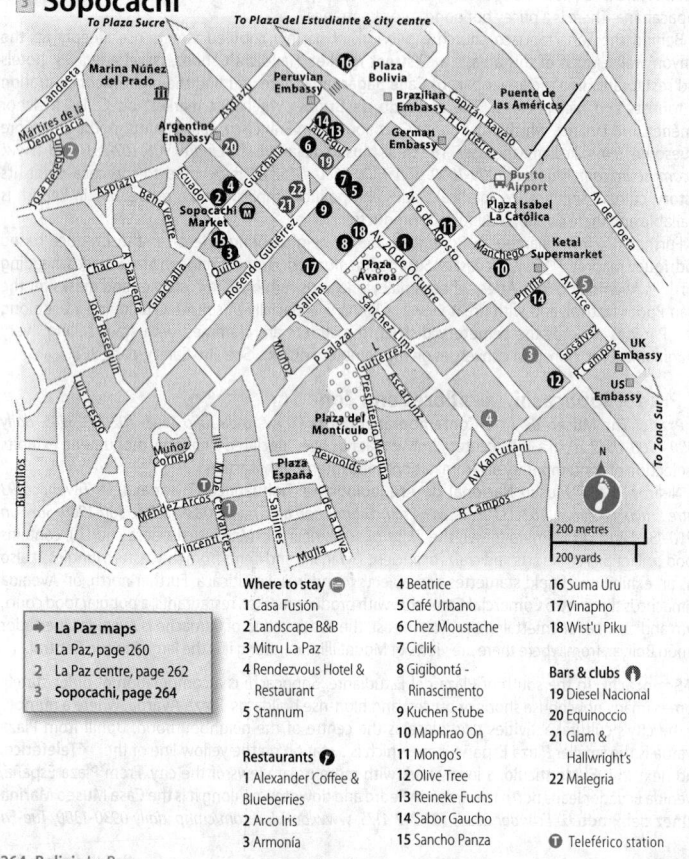

La Paz maps	
1	La Paz, page 260
2	La Paz centre, page 262
3	**Sopocachi, page 264**

Where to stay 🛏
1 Casa Fusión
2 Landscape B&B
3 Mitru La Paz
4 Rendezvous Hotel & Restaurant
5 Stannum

Restaurants 🍴
1 Alexander Coffee & Blueberries
2 Arco Iris
3 Armonía
4 Beatrice
5 Café Urbano
6 Chez Moustache
7 Ciclik
8 Gigibontá - Rinascimento
9 Kuchen Stube
10 Maphrao On
11 Mongo's
12 Olive Tree
13 Reineke Fuchs
14 Sabor Gaucho
15 Sancho Panza
16 Suma Uru
17 Vinapho
18 Wist'u Piku

Bars & clubs 🎷
19 Diesel Nacional
20 Equinoccio
21 Glam & Hallwright's
22 Malegria

🚠 Teleférico station

Tiny treats

One of the most intriguing items for sale in Andean markets is Ekeko, the god of good fortune and plenty and one of the most endearing of the Aymara folk legends. He is a cheery, avuncular little chap, with a happy face, a pot belly and short legs. His image is laden with various household items, as well as sweets, confetti and streamers, food, and with a cigarette dangling from his lower lip. Believers say that these statues only bring luck if they are received as gifts. The Ekeko occupies a central role in the festival of Alasitas, the Feast of Plenty, which takes place in La Paz for a month starting 24 January. Everything under the sun can be bought in miniature: houses, trucks, buses, suitcases, university diplomas. The idea is to have your mini-purchase blessed by a *yatiri*, an Aymara priest, and the real thing will be yours within the year.

Excursions from La Paz

day trips, and treks once you've acclimatized

South of La Paz

Beyond Calacoto is the **Valle de la Luna**, or 'Valley of the Moon' (US$7), with impressive eroded hills; the climate in this valley is always much warmer than in the city. For transport details see page 280. About 3 km from the bridge at Calacoto the road forks, get out of the minibus at the turning and walk a few minutes east to the Valle entrance, or get out at the football field which is by the entrance. Take good shoes and water, but do not go alone, armed robbery has occurred. Just past the Valle de la Luna is **Mallasa** where horses and motorcycles can be rented and there are several small roadside restaurants and cafés and the **Hotel Oberland** (see page 269). To the south of the city are dry hills of many colours, topped by the **Muela del Diablo**, a striking outcrop reached through El Pedregal neighbourbood (take minibus 288); **Gravity Bolivia** (see page 276) offers cycling tours here.

El Alto

Sprawled around the rim of the canyon is El Alto, Bolivia's second-largest city (after Santa Cruz, La Paz is third). Its population (about 1 million) is mostly indigenous migrants from the countryside and its economic and political influence has grown rapidly. Of interest in El Alto are 'cholets' or 'nueva arquitectura andina', glitzy and colourful mansions of the new rich; a blend of modern architecture and traditional Aymara styles. See Shopping, Markets, page 274, for details of the ☆**Feria 16 de Julio**, the largest market in the department of La Paz.

El Alto is connected to La Paz by the ☆**Teleférico** and by a motorway (toll US$0.25) as well as by a road to Obrajes and the Zona Sur. Minibuses from Plaza Eguino leave regularly for Plaza 16 de Julio, El Alto; more leave from Plaza Pérez Velasco for La Ceja, the edge of El Alto. See Transport, page 279, for full details.

Trekking and climbing near La Paz

Three so-called 'Inca Trails' link the altiplano with the Yungas, taking you from the high Andes to the subtropics, with dramatic changes in weather, temperature and vegetation. Each has excellent sections of stonework and they vary in difficulty from relatively straightforward to quite hard-going. In the rainy season going can be particularly tough. For details of how to reach the starting point of each trail, see Transport sections on page 280.

Takesi Trail Start at **Ventilla**, walk up the valley for about three hours passing the village of **Choquekhota** until the track crosses the river and to the right of the road, there is a falling-down brick wall with a map painted on it. The Takesi and **Alto Takesi** trails start here, following the path to the right of the wall. The road continues to Mina San Francisco. In the first hour's climb from the wall is excellent stone paving which is Inca or pre-Inca, depending on who you believe, either side of the pass at 4630 m. There are camping possibilities at **Estancia Takesi** and near the village of **Kakapi** where there is an *albergue*. Be prepared for bridges to be washed away periodically. You also have to pass the unpleasant mining settlement of **Chojlla**. Between Chojlla and Yanacachi is a gate where it is necessary to register and often pay a small 'fee'. **Yanacachi** has a couple of places to stay, several good hikes and an orphanage you can help at. The **Fundación Pueblo** ① *on the plaza, T02-212 4413, www. fundacionpueblo.org,* has information; they organize clean-ups of the trail each year. Buy a minibus ticket on arrival in Yanacachi or walk 45 minutes down to the La Paz–Chulumani road for transport.

The trek can be done in one long day, especially if you organize a jeep to the start of the trail, but is more relaxing in two or three days. If you take it slowly, though, you'll have to carry camping kit. Hire mules in Choquekhota for US$10 per day plus up to US$10 for the muleteer.

A two- to three-day alternative is from Mina San Francisco to El Castillo and the village of Chaco on the La Paz–Chulumani road. This trek is called **La Reconquistada** and has the distinction of including a 200-m disused mining tunnel (torch essential).

Choro Trail (La Cumbre to Coroico) Immediately before the road drops down from La Cumbre to start the descent to Las Yungas, there is a good dirt road leading up to the *apacheta* (narrow pass) where the trail starts properly. Cloud and bad weather are normal at La Cumbre (4660 m): you have to sign in at the Guardaparque post on the way to the pass. The trail passes **Samaña Pampa** (small shop, sign in again, camping), **Chucura** (pay US$1.50 fee, another shop, camping), **Challapampa** (camping possible, US$1.20, small shop), the **Choro bridge** and the **Río Jacun-Manini** (fill up with water at both river crossings). At **Sandillani** is a lodge ($$-$). There is good paving down to **Villa Esmeralda**, after which is **Chairo** (lodging and camping), then to **Yolosa**. It takes three days to trek from La Cumbre to Chairo, from where you can take a truck to Puente Yolosita, the turn-off for Coroico on the new road. From Puente Yolosita minibuses and trucks run uphill to Coroico when they fill, US$0.50, 15 minutes.

Huayna Potosí Huayna Potosí (6088 m) is normally climbed in two days, with one night in a basic shelter at 5300 m or camped on a glacier at 5600 m. Acclimatization and experience on ice are essential, and the mountain is dangerous out of season. There are four shelters: a community-run shelter 10 minutes up from the pass, one by the lake, very cold; Refugio Huayna Potosí at 4780 m, with toilets and shower, run by the tour operator of the same name, and a basic shelter at 5300 m owned by the same operator. Average cost is US$185 per person for a two-day tour for three people including all equipment except sleeping bag; US$215 for three days. Private three-day tours run about US$100 more. **Refugio Huayna Potosí** charges US$150 for two days, US$170 for three days with exclusive use of its base camp. Park entrance fee of US$2.10 is not included. The starting point for the normal route is at **Zongo**. See Climbing, hiking and trekking, page 275, for tour operators.

Listings La Paz *maps pages 260, 262 and 264.*

Tourist information

Gobierno Municipal de La Paz (www.lapaz.bo) has information centres at:

Bus terminal
T228 5858. Mon-Fri 0830-1200, 1430-1900, Sat-Sun 1000-1400, holidays 0800-1200, 1600-2000.

El Prado InfoTur
Mariscal Santa Cruz y Colombia, T02-265 1677, Facebook: LaPazMaravillosa. Mon-Fri 0830-1830.

Plaza del Estudiante
Lower end of El Prado between 16 de Julio and México, T02-237 1044. Mon-Fri 0830-1200, 1430-1900.
Very helpful, English and French spoken.

Plaza Pérez Velasco
Opposite San Francisco, under the pedestrian walkway. Mon-Fri 0830-1200, 1430-1900.

Boltur (Boliviana de Turismo)
Plaza Murillo 551, T2-218 5999 and 9011 05296, www.boltur.gob.bo. Mon-Fri 0830-1230, 1430-1830, Sat 1000-1200.
State tourism agency, offering a limited number of tours throughout the country.

Tomás Katari
Av Bautista y José María Aliaga, by the cemetery. Mon-Fri 0900-1700, Sat-Sun 1000-1800.
Specifically for tourists going to and from Tiwanaku and Titicaca, has luggage store. They also have information booths at the Plaza Alonso de Mendoza, Angelo Colonial on C Linares, at the Casa de la Cultura and Parque Metropolitano Laikacota.

See also www.turismolapaz.com and http://lapaz.metro-blog.com. For news and information pick up a copy of the free *Bolivian Express* magazine, www.bolivianexpress.org.

Tourist Police
Plaza Stadium, Edif Olimpya, Miraflores, next to Love City Chinese restaurant, T800-140081. Daily 0800-1800.
For police report for insurance claims after theft. Officers are on call for emergencies outside office hours.

El Alto

Unidad de Turismo
Av Bolivia, C 1, Plaza de la Cruz (also at arrivals in airport and at El Alto bus terminal area), T02-283 3341. Mon-Fri 0800-1800.

Where to stay

Around Plaza Murillo

$$$$ Presidente
Potosí 920 y Sanjines, T02-240 6666, www.hotelpresidente.com.bo.
The "highest 5-star in the world". Excellent service, comfortable, heating, 2 good restaurants, gym and sauna, pool, all open to non-residents, bar. See also **Urban Rush**, under What to do, page 278.

$$$ Casa de Piedra
Sanjinés 451, T02-290 6674, http://casadepiedrahb.com.
In a historic *posada* in the centre, wooden floors, beautiful ceilings above the inner balcony, objets d'art, 15 rooms with heating and all facilities, includes buffet breakfast, restaurant open 0700-2145, airport transfers extra.

$$$ Gloria
Potosí 909, T02-240 7070, www.hotelgloria.com.bo.
Modern rooms and suites, good central location, includes buffet breakfast, good service, runs **Gloria Tours** (www.gloriatours.com.bo) and also owns Gloria hotels in Coroico, Copacabana and Urmiri (resort 2 hrs from La Paz). Recommended.

$$-$ Hostal República
Comercio 1455, T02-220 2742, www.hostalrepublica.com.
Old house of former president, with and without bath, also apartment for 5, good café, quiet garden, book ahead and ask for room on upper floor.

$$-$ Residencial Latino
Junín 857, T02-228 5463, www.residenciallatino.com.
Centrally located hotel, simple rooms with private bath, those with shared bath have no TV, basic breakfast included, heating, book exchange.

$ Adventure Brew Bed & Breakfast
Av Montes 533, T02-291 5896, www.theadventurebrewhostel.com.
Mostly private rooms with bath, cheaper in dorms for 4 or 8, includes buffet breakfast, 1 free beer from microbrewery every night, rooftop bar with great views and spa, BBQ on Fri night, good value, popular meeting place.

$ Adventure Brew Hostel
Av Montes 503, T02-291 5896, www.theadventurebrewhostel.com.
More economical than the B&B above, 8-bed dorm with bath and 8- to 20-bed dorms with shared hot showers, includes buffet breakfast and a free beer every night, rooftop terrace with great views of the city and Illimani, basement bar, pool table, travel agency and bank, lively young crowd, convenient to the bus station, associated with **Gravity Bolivia** (see What to do, page 276).

$ Arthy's Guesthouse
Montes 693, T02-228 1439, on Facebook. 2400 curfew.
Shared bath, warm water, safe, no breakfast, helpful, popular with bikers, English spoken.

$ Bacoo
Calle Alto de la Alianza 693, T02-228 0679, www.bacoohostel.com.
Some rooms with private bath, cheaper in 6- to 18-bed dorms, restaurant and bar, beautiful garden, ping-pong and pool, arrange tours.

$ Hospedaje Milenio
Yanacocha 860, T02-228 1263, www.hospedajemilenio.blogspot.com.
Economical, shared bath, electric shower, basic, family house, homely and welcoming, popular, helpful owner, quiet, kitchen, breakfast extra, security boxes, great value.

$ Loki
Av América 120, esq Plaza Alonso de Mendoza, T245 7300, www.lokihostel.com.
Members of a chain of popular party hostels. Private double rooms and 4- to 10-bed dorms, TV room, computer room, bar (meals available), tour operator.

$ Posada El Carretero
Catacora 1056, entre Yanacocha y Junín, T228 5271, on Facebook.
Very economical single and double rooms (cheaper with shared bath), also dorms, hot showers, kitchen facilities, terrace, helpful staff, good atmosphere and value.

$ Tambo de Oro
Armentia 367, T02-228 1565, on Facebook.
Near bus station, private or shared bath, showers, good value if a bit run down, safe for luggage.

$ Wild Rover Backpackers Hostel
Comercio 1476, T02-211 6903,
http://wildroverhostels.com.
Party chain hostel in renovated colonial-style house with courtyard and high-ceilings, dorms with 4-10 beds with shared bath, Irish bar, TV room, book exchange, breakfast included, other meals available, helpful staff speak English.

Plaza San Francisco up to the cemetery district

$$$$-$$$ La Casona
Av Mcal Santa Cruz 938, T02-290 0505,
www.lacasonahotelboutique.com.
Boutique hotel in beautifully restored former San Francisco convent dating to 1860, nice rooms (those in front get street noise), suite has jacuzzi, includes buffet breakfast (0700-1000 or continental breakfast 0300-0700) and some museum entry fees, heating, safe box, terrace and cupola with nice views, very good restaurant.

$$$ Rosario
Illampu 704, T02-245 1658,
www.gruporosario.travel.
Tasteful rooms, buffet breakfast included, good restaurant also serves dinner, stores luggage, no smoking, very helpful staff. Highly recommended. **Turisbus** travel agency downstairs (see Tour operators, page 278), **Cultural Interpretation Centre** explains items for sale in nearby 'witches' market'.

$$ Estrella Andina
Illampu 716, T02-245 6421,
www.estrellaandina.com.
Cheaper in low season, all rooms have a safe and are decorated individually, includes buffet breakfast, English spoken, family-run, comfortable, tidy, helpful, roof terrace, game room, pool table, computer room, heaters, money exchange, very nice. Also owns **$$ Sol Andino** (Aroma 6) and **$ Cruz de los Andes** (Aroma 216, T02-245 1401); both in the same style, but the latter shares premises with a car garage.

$$ Hostal Naira
Sagárnaga 161, T02-235 5645,
www.hostalnaira.com.
Comfortable but pricey, rooms around courtyard, some are dark, price includes good buffet breakfast in **Café Banais** (see page 271), restaurant, safety deposit boxes.

$$ La Posada de la Abuela Obdulia
C Linares 947, T02-233 2285,
http://hostalabuelaposada.com.
Very pleasant inn, rooms for 2-4 people around a courtyard in an early 20th-century building, café, includes buffet breakfast, computer room.

$$-$ Milton
Illampu 1126-1130, T02-236 8003,
www.hotelmiltonbolivia.com.
Popular hotel refurbished in 2016, restaurant, excellent views from roof.

$$-$ Onkel Inn 1886
Colombia 257, T02-249 0456, www.onkelinn.com.
Hostel in a remodelled 19th-century house, private rooms with bath and 6- to 9-bed dorms. Sauna, laundry facilities, café and bar, pool table, computer room. HI affiliated. Also in Copacabana.

$$-$ Sagárnaga
Sagárnaga 326, T02-235 0252,
www.hotel-sagarnaga.com.
Rooms on the ground floor with smaller beds are cheaper, solar hot water, includes buffet breakfast, 2 ATMs, English spoken, *peña*, popular with tour groups, helpful owner.

$ Arcabucero
C Viluyo 307 y Linares, T02-231 3473,
arcabucero-bolivia@hotmail.com.
Price rises in high season, pleasant new rooms in converted colonial house, excellent value but check the beds, no breakfast, kitchen facilities.

$ Fuentes
Linares 888, T02-231 3966,
www.hotelfuentes.com.bo.
Private or shared bath, hot water, variety of rooms and prices, nice colonial style, comfortable, includes simple breakfast, sauna, good value, family-run.

$ Inti Wasi
Murillo 776, T02-236 7963,
intiwasi.bolivia@gmail.com.
Central economical hostel, private rooms and 6-bed dorms all with shared bath, kitchen facilities, terrace, medical services, taxi and travel agency, good value, gets crowded.

$ Muzungu Hostel
Illampu 441, T02-2451640, muzunguhostel@ hotmail.com, on Facebook.
Rooms with 1-4 beds, with and without bath and cheaper rate (US$6.50-10 pp) for dorms, several common areas, bar, breakfast and a

welcome drink included, ping pong and pool tables, games, videos, baggage storage, safety box, book exchange, English and German spoken.

El Prado, Sopocachi, Miraflores and Zona Sur

$$$$ Atix
C 16 8052 y Sánchez Bustamante, Calacoto, T02-277 6500, www.atixhotel.com.
Luxury modern hotel decorated with Gastón Ugalde's art (a renowned Bolivian artist). Ample rooms and suites with excellent views, some have bathtubs and balconies. Very good gourmet restaurant on the ground floor and popular rooftop bar, also pool, gym and spa. Opened in 2016.

$$$$ Casa Grande
Av Ballivián 1000 y C 17, T02-279 5511, and C 16 8009, T02-277 4000, both in Calacoto, www.casa-grande.com.bo.
Beautiful, top-quality suites, those on C 16 are under a greenhouse dome, buffet breakfast, business centre, gym, pool and spa, airport transfers at night only, restaurants, ice cream parlour, very good service.

$$$$ Europa
Tiahuanacu 64, T02-231 5656, www.hoteleuropa.com.bo.
Next to the Museo Nacional de Arqueología. Excellent facilities and plenty of frills, health club, several restaurants, parking. Recommended.

$$$$ Stannum
Av Arce 2631, Torre Multicine, p 12, T02-214 8393, www.stannumhotels.com.
Boutique hotel on the 12th floor of an office building with lovely views of Illimani and the city, above mall and cinema complex. Comfortable rooms with minimalist decor, includes breakfast, bathtub, heating, a/c, fridge, restaurant, bar, business centre, gym, spa, airport transfers, no smoking anywhere on the premises.

$$$ Casa Fusión
Miguel de Cervantes 2725, Sopocachi, T02-214 0933, www.casafusion.com.bo.
Lovely hotel with modern comfortable rooms, predominantly white, good fittings, includes buffet breakfast, heating, meeting room, restaurant serves set lunches, bakery, good value, no smoking. Near Plaza España Teleférico station.

$$$ Casa Prado
Av 16 de Julio (El Prado) 1615, entre Campero y Ortiz, T02-231 2094, www.casapradolapaz.com.bo.

'Boutique'-style hotel in a renovated old building, plain rooms and suites with colourful furnishings, simple breakfast included, airport transfer arranged.

$$$ El Rey Palace
Av 20 de Octubre 1947, Sopocachi, T02-241 8541 or toll free T800-100013, www.reypalacehotel.com.
Large suites and rooms with heating, buffet breakfast included, excellent restaurant, business centre, parking.

$$$ Mitru La Paz
6 de Agosto 2628, Edif Torre Girasoles, Sopocachi, T02-243 2242, www.hotelmitrulapaz.com.
Modern hotel on the 1st 3 floors of the highest building in La Paz (37 storeys). Includes breakfast and complimentary hot drinks, comfortable, bright ample rooms and suites most with bathtubs, heating, safe boxes, fridge, parking, convenient location for Sopocachi dining, excellent value for its price category, helpful staff. Recommended.

$$ Rendezvous
Sargento Carranza 461, side street at the end of Sánchez Lima, Sopocachi, T02-291 2459, www.rendezvouslapaz.com.
Delightful rooms in small hotel above the restaurant of the same name (see below), family atmosphere, roof terrace with good view, communal area with DVD library, kitchen, safe, garden. Recommended.

$$-$ Landscape B&B
Reseguín 1945 entre Aspiazu y Harington, Sopocachi, T7066 0542, Facebook: landscape.bolivia.
Like a family home, use whatever you like except the washing machine (laundry service provided), 5 rooms, private or shared bath, also 4-8-bed dorms, all you can eat breakfast for US$2.50, nice bar, backyard for smokers, popular. Also has another house at Reseguín 1981 and an apartment on Av Arce.

$ Hostel 3600
Ecuador 1982, Sopocachi, T02-212 0478, www.3600hostel.com.
Converted Republican-era home, gender specific and mixed dorms for 6 with privacy curtains on bunk beds, includes simple breakfast, nice patio bar and pizzeria with heaters, attentive service, opened in 2016.

South of La Paz

$$$ Oberland
Av Florida, C 2, Mallasa, 12 km from La Paz centre, T02-274 5040, www.h-oberland.com.

A Swiss-owned, chalet-style restaurant (excellent, not cheap) and hotel (also good) with rooms and suites and older resort facilities, lovely gardens, spa, sauna, covered pool (open to public – US$4.30-5.70 – very hot water), volleyball, tennis. Welcomes campers with or without vehicle. Recommended.

$$$-$$ Allkamari
Near Valle de las Animas, 30 mins from town on the road to Palca, T02-277 2711, www.boliviamistica.com.
Reservations required, cabins for up to 8 in a lovely valley between the Palca and La Animas canyons, a place to relax and star-gaze, $ pp in dorm, solar heating, breakfast and jacuzzi included, other meals on request, lots of packages available, horse and bike rentals, massage, acupuncture and other therapies, shamanic rituals, taxi from Calacoto US$7, bus No 42 from the cemetery to within 1 km.

$$-$ Colibrí Camping
C 4, Jupapina, near Mallasa, 30 mins from La Paz, T7629 5658, http://colibricamping.com.
Cabins, teepee, tents and sleeping bags for hire or set up your own tent for US$7 pp, nice views, details about transport on their website.

El Alto

$$-$ Alexander Palace
Av Jorge Carrasco 61 y C 3, Ceja, Zona 12 de Octubre, T02-282 3376, www.alexanderpalacehotel.com.bo.
Modern, heated rooms, with buffet breakfast, restaurant, parking, disco, karaoke.

$ Orquídea
C 1 N°22 y Av 6 de Marzo, Villa Bolívar, near long distance bus stations, T02-282 6487.
Comfortable heated rooms, private or shared bath, electric showers, includes simple breakfast, good value. Better than others in the area. 2nd, more expensive ($$), location in Ciudad Satélite, Av Satélite 632, T02-2812283, www.hotelesorquidea.com, includes buffet breakfast.

Restaurants

Around Plaza Murillo

$$$ Ali Pacha
Colón 1306 y Potosí, T02-220 2366, www.alipacha.com. Mon-Sat 1200-1500, Wed-Sat 1900-2200.
Upmarket restaurant with open kitchen, an offshoot of **Gustu** (see Zona Sur, below). Signature vegan cuisine focusing on ingredients, dishes are elaborate and gorgeous but small, nice atmosphere, good service, rotating surprise menu, all members of a party must order the same meal.

$$ La Kantuta
In Hotel Presidente, Potosí 920, T02-240 6666. Daily 0600-2300.
Excellent food, good service, lunch buffet 1200-1500. **La Bella Vista** on the top floor is fancier, open 1200-1500, 1900-2300.

Cafés

Alexander Coffee
Potosí 1091.
Part of a chain (see El Prado below), sandwiches, salads, coffee, pastries.

The Writer's Coffee
Comercio 1270, at Librería Gisbert, http://thewriterscoffee.com. Mon-Fri 0830-1930, Sat 0900-1230.
Gourmet café inside a bookstore, decorated with antique typewriters. Wide selection of fair-trade Bolivian coffee and other hot and cold drinks, proceeds from sale of pastries go to development projects. 2nd location on Av Illimani corner Bueno.

Wist'u Piku
Comercio 1057, half a block from Plaza Murillo; also at 6 de Agosto 2048, near the university, and 20 de Octubre 2463, Sopocachi and other locations. Mon-Sat 0700-2230, Sun 0830-2030.
A Cochabamba chain, now in other cities, with a variety of *empanadas* and other Bolivian snacks, fruit juices and *api* (a warm corn-flour drink).

Plaza San Francisco up to the cemetery district

$$$-$$ Steakhouse
Psje Tarija 243B, T02-214 8864, www.4cornerslapaz.com. Daily 1200-2400.
Good cuts of meat, large variety of sauces and a great salad bar in a modern environment.

$$$-$$ Tambo Colonial
In Hotel Rosario (see page 268). Daily 0630-0930, 1800-2130.
Excellent local and international cuisine, good salad bar, buffet breakfast open to the public.

$$ Pizzería Italy
Illampu 809, T02-246 3229. Daily 1000-2300.
Thin-crust pizza, pasta, also meat, fish and other dishes.

$$-$ Angelo Colonial
Linares 922, T02-215 9633. Daily 0730-2300.
Breakfast, many vegetarian options, good music, internet, can get busy with slow service. 2nd location and *hostal* at Av Mariscal Santa Cruz 1066.

$$-$ Kalakitas
Sagárnaga 363, T7756 0 770. Mon-Fri 1200-2300
Small, brightly decorated Mexican restaurant, good food, drinks, popular.

$$-$ Sabor Cubano
Sagárnaga 357, entre Linares y Illampu, T02-245 1797. Mon-Sat 1200-2400.
Almuerzo for US$4.30, but it runs out fast, also other choices of good Cuban food, good value. Live Cuban music Thu-Sat night.

$$-$ Sol y Luna
Murillo 999 y Cochabamba, T02-211 5323, www.solyluna-lapaz.com. Daily 0700-2400.
Dutch-run, breakfast, *almuerzo* and international menu, coffees and teas, full wine and cocktail list, live music Sun and Thu, movies, Wi-Fi, guide books for sale, book exchange.

$$-$ Tierra Sana
Tarija 213 corner Murillo, T02-212 0101, Facebook: tierrasanalapaz. Daily 0800-2300.
Nice modern restaurant with a Bolivian touch. Excellent healthy and vegetarian food, extensive menu, sandwiches, salads, mains, set lunches and a meal of the day, fresh juices, good service.

Cafés

Banais
Sagárnaga 161, same entrance as Hostal Naira. Mon-Fri 0700-2200, Sat-Sun until 2300.
Coffee, sandwiches and juices, buffet breakfast, set lunch, à la carte dishes in $$ range, laid-back music and Wi-Fi.

Café del Mundo
Sagárnaga 324. Daily 0630-2130.
Swedish-owned, breakfasts, pancakes, waffles, sandwiches, coffees, teas and chocolate.

K'umara
Pasaje Tarija casi Linares. Daily 0800-2000.
Small café serving breakfasts, cereals, juices, sandwiches, omelettes, soups and drinks, organic produce, Wi-Fi.

El Prado, Sopocachi, Miraflores and Zona Sur
Restaurants listed are in Sopocachi unless noted otherwise.

$$$ Chalet la Suisse
Av Muñoz Reyes 1710, Cota Cota, T02-279 3160, www.chaletlasuisse.com. Mon-Fri 1200-1430, 1900-0030, Sat 1900-0030, Sun 1200-1530, booking is essential on Fri.
Serves excellent fondue, steaks, seafood.

$$$ Gustu
C 10 No 300, Calacoto, T02-211 7491, www.gustu.bo. Mon-Sat 1200-1500, 1830-2300.
Upmarket restaurant with remarkable food and cookery school. Part of the Nordic cuisine pioneers, aimed at stimulating Bolivian gastronomy and giving opportunities to vulnerable people through the **Melting Pot Foundation**, www.meltingpot-bolivia.org. Also has a street food tour, Suma Phayata.

$$$-$$ Maphrao On
Hnos Manchego 2586, near Plaza Isabel La Católica, T02-243 4682. Sun-Mon 1900-2200, Tue-Sat 1200-1600, 1900-2400.
Thai and Southeast Asian food, ask for seatting upstairs, warm atmosphere, good music.

$$$-$$ Rendezvous
Sargento Carranza 461, end of Sánchez Lima, T02-291 8459. Mon-Sat 1800-2300.
Classic French cuisine and Mediterranean food, excellent variety and quality.

$$$-$$ Sabor Gaucho
F Guachalla 319 entre Av 6 de Agosto y 20 de Octubre, and Pinilla 273 entre Av 6 de Agosto y Arce, T02-244 0844, www.elsaborgaucho.com. Daily 1200-2400, Pinilla location till 1600 on Sun.
Argentine meat dishes, excellent *parrillada*, also has salad bar, wine list, good service.

$$$-$$ Sancho Panza
Av Ecuador 738 y Gutiérrez, T02-242 6490. Tue-Sat 1200-2300.
Mediterranean and Spanish tapas, *tablas* and daily specials, also good-value set lunches (no credit cards or US dollars).

$$ Beatrice
F Guachalla 510 y Ecuador, opposite Sopocachi market, T02 2417168, www.beatricepastas.com. Open 1100-2200, Sat-Sun 1100-1600, closed Tue.
Excellent home-made pasta, good value and very popular with locals.

$$ Chez Moustache
F Guachalla399 esq Av 20 de Octubre, at Alliance Française, Chez-Moustache on Facebook. Mon-Sat 1100-1530, 1900-2300.

French restaurant with good food, extensive wine list and fun atmosphere.

$$ Ciclik
Rosendo Gutiérrez y 20 de Octubre, T02-212 4557, on Facebook. Daily 0800-2300.
Popular modern café-restaurant with wide range of international dishes, good coffee and baked goods.

$$ Ken-Chan
Bat Colorados 98 y F Suazo, p 2 of Japanese Cultural Centre, T02-244 2292. Tue-Sun 1130-1500, 1800-2200.
Japanese restaurant with wide variety of dishes, popular.

$$ Mongo's
Hnos Manchego 2444, near Plaza Isabel La Católica, T02-244 0714. Tue-Sat 1200-1500, 2000-0300. Live music Tue-Wed (cover US$4) salsa lessons Tue, club after midnight.
Excellent Mexican fare and steaks, open fires, bar (cocktails can be pricey), popular with gringos and locals.

$$ Paladar
Av Saavedra 1984, Edif Cristembo, Miraflores, T02-224 1520, and C Ferrecio B-28 in San Miguel. Open 1200-1630, Mon-Sat in Miraflores, Tue-Sun in San Miguel.
Brazilian dishes, daily specials, popular and good value.

$$ Reineke Fuchs
Pje Jauregui 2241, Sopocachi, T02-244 2979, www.reinekefuchs.com; Av Montenegro y C 18, San Miguel, T02-277 2103. Both locations open Mon-Sat 1800-2400. Also at Centro Comercial Camacho, Av Camacho y Bueno, daily 1200-2230.
German-style bar/restaurant, microbrews and many imported German beers, also set lunch from US$5.

$$ Suma Uru
Av Arce 2177 in Real Plaza Hotel, T02-244 1111. Daily 24 hrs.
Almuerzo Mon-Fri for US$9 and excellent buffet on Sun 1200-1500, US$13.60. Friendly to backpackers.

$$-$ Potokos
Costa Rica 1346, T02-224 4306, Potokos on Facebook. Only Sat-Sun 1200-1630.
Potosino food, traditional dishes, very good.

$$-$ Vienna
Federico Zuazo 1905, T02-244 1660, www.restaurantvienna.com. Mon-Fri 1200-1400, 1830-2200, Sun 1200-1430.
Good Austrian, international and local food, great atmosphere and service, live piano music, popular.

$$-$ Vinapho
Sánchez Lima 2326, T02-242 4619. Mon-Sat 1200-1600, 1700-2200, Sun 1200-1500.
Very good Vietnamese, Thai and other Asian food, their *almuerzo* (US$5.50) is very popular.

$ Armonía
Av Ecuador 2284, above bookstore, T02-2418458. Mon-Sat 1200-1430.
Nice varied vegetarian buffet with organic produce from proprietors' farm. Recommended.

$ Olive Tree
Campos 334, Edif Iturri, T02-243 1552. Mon-Fri 1130-2200.
Good salads, soups and sandwiches, attentive service.

Cafés

Alexander Coffee
Av 16 de Julio 1832, El Prado, also at 20 de Octubre 2463 Plaza Avaroa, Av Arce 2631 (Multicine), Av Montenegro 1336, San Miguel, and at the airport (16 branches in all). Daily 0730-2300; Fri-Sat till 0130 at Av Arce and Av Montenegro.
Excellent coffee, smoothies, muffins, cakes and good salads and sandwiches, Wi-Fi.

Arco Iris
F Guachalla 554 y Sánchez Lima, Sopocachi. Also in Achumani, C 16 by the market. Mon-Sat 0700-2015.
Bakery and handicraft outlet of **Fundación Arco Iris** (www.arcoirisbolivia.org), which works with street children, good variety of breads, pastries, meats and cheeses.

Blueberries
Av 20 de Octubre 2475, Plaza Avaroa, T02-243 3402. Mon-Sat 0815-2245, Sun 1330-2100.
Relaxed quiet café with outdoor seating in small front patio. Good coffee and juice selection, a variety of dishes, cakes and desserts, Wi-Fi.

Café Urbano
16 de Julio 1615, El Prado; and 20 de Octubre 2331, Sopocachi, T02-242 2009. Mon-Sat 0730-2400, Sun 2000-2200.
Excellent sandwiches and coffee, pancakes, breakfasts, Wi-Fi.

Gigibontá-Rinascimento
20 de Octubre 927, Plaza Avaroa, see gigibonta. bolivia on Facebook. Daily 1100-2130.
Authentic Italian ice creams, delicious flavours.

Kuchen Stube
Rosendo Gutiérrez 461, Sopocachi,
T02-2424089. Daily 0900-2100.
Excellent cakes, coffee and German specialities,
breakfast, also *almuerzo* Mon-Fri, US$5.

Bars and clubs

The epicentre for nightlife in La Paz is currently
Plaza Avaroa in Sopocachi. Clubs are clustered
around here and crowds gather Fri and Sat nights.

Around Plaza Murillo

Etno Café
Jaén 722, T02-228 0343. Mon-Sat 1130-0300.
Small café/bar with cultural programmes
including readings and concerts, popular, serves
artisanal and fair trade drinks (alcoholic or not).

Plaza San Francisco up to the cemetery district

Hard Rock Café
Santa Cruz 399 e Illampu, T02-211 9318.
Daily 2100-0400. Cover US$5.
Turns into nightclub around 2400, popular with
locals and tourists, especially on Sun.

The English Lion's
Sagárnaga 189, T02-2231682. Daily 0800-0300.
English-style pub serving breakfast from 0800,
sandwiches, fish and chips, bangers and mash,
sports channels, music, party atmosphere at
night with 2 for 1 drinks.

El Prado, Sopocachi, Miraflores and Zona Sur

Diesel Nacional
Av 20 de Octubre 2271, T70155405.
Mon-Sat 1900-0200.
Unique bar-lounge decorated with the remains
of trains and airplanes. Wide range of great
cocktails, food available.

Equinoccio
Sánchez Lima 2191, Sopocachi. Thu-Sat
2130-0330, cover charge US$3.60, or more
for popular bands.
Top venue for live rock music and bar.

Glam
Sánchez Lima 2237, T7061 6000.
Thu-Sat from 2100.
Good place to go dancing, live salsa on Fri,
electronic music on Sat.

Hallwrights
Sánchez Lima 2235, T6706 3699.
Mon-Sat 1700-2400.
The only wine bar in La Paz.

Malegria
Pje Medinacelli 2282. Thu-Sat 2130-0300.
Bar and club, good pizza, varied music for
dancing. Live *saya* (Afrobolivian dance)
performances Thu at 2200 and 2300. Popular
with Bolivians and foreigners of all ages.

Entertainment

For current information on cinemas and shows,
check *La Prensa* or *La Razón* on Fri, or visit www.
laprensa.com.bo or www.la-razon.com. Also look
for *Bolivian Express* (in English) and *Mañana*, both
free monthly magazines with listings of concerts,
exhibits, festivals, etc.

Cinemas
Most films are dubbed into Spanish, so look for
those in English with Spanish subtitles, they
cost around US$5-6, some cinemas have 2 for
the price of 1 promotions on Wed. See www.
cinecenter.com.bo, http://megacenter.irpavi.
com (their VIP lounge has very comfortable seats
and most films are in English with subtitles) and
www.multicine.com.bo (in Sopocachi, also has
very comfortable halls). **Cinemateca Boliviana**,
Oscar Soria (prolong Federico Zuazo) y Rosendo
Gutiérrez, T02-244 4090. Municipal theatre with
emphasis on independent productions.

Peñas
Bocaisapo, *Indaburo 654 y Jaén, T7774 3456.*
Tue-Thu 2030-0200, Fri-Sat 2030-0300. Live music
in a bar; no cover charge, popular.
Peña Huari, *Sagárnaga 339, T02-231 6225. Daily*
1900-2200. Good shows of traditional music and
dance at 2000 (if there are at least 8 clients), also
serves food and drink.

Theatre
Teatro Municipal Alberto Saavedra Pérez,
Sanjinés e Indaburo, T02-240 6183, has a regular
schedule of plays, opera, ballet and classical
concerts. The National Symphony Orchestra is
very good and gives inexpensive concerts. Next
door is the **Teatro Municipal de Cámara**, which
shows dance, drama, music and poetry. **Casa
Municipal de la Cultura 'Franz Tamayo'**, almost
opposite Plaza San Francisco, hosts a variety of
exhibitions, paintings, sculpture, photography,
etc, mostly free. Free monthly guide to cultural
events at information desk at entrance. The

Palacio Chico, *Ayacucho y Potosí, Mon-Fri 0830-1230, 1430-1830*, in old Correo, operated by the Secretaría Nacional de Cultura, also has free exhibitions (good for modern art), concerts and ballet.

Festivals

24 Jan (continuing for 4 weeks), **Alasitas** (see Tiny treats, page 265), in Parque Central up from Av del Ejército, also in Plaza Sucre/San Pedro, recommended.
Feb/Mar Carnaval.
End May/early Jun Festividad del Señor del Gran Poder, the most important festival of the year, with a huge procession of costumed and masked dancers on the 3rd Sat after Trinity.
Jul Fiestas de Julio, a month of concerts and performances at the Teatro Municipal, with a variety of music, including the University Folkloric Festival.
8 Dec Festival around **Plaza España**, colourful and noisy.
31 Dec New Year's Eve, fireworks displays; view from higher up.
See page 385 for national holidays and festivals outside La Paz.

Shopping

Camping equipment
Several shops on Illampu between Sagárnaga and Tarija sell camping equipment. **Ayni Sport Bolivia** (Jiménez 806). Rents and sometimes sells camping equipment and mountain gear (trekking shoes, fleeces, climbing equipment etc). **Camping Bolivia** (Edif Handal Center, No 9, Av Mcal Santa Cruz y Socabaya, T6557 5899). Outdoor equipment. Camping stove fuel is imported and expensive, enquire at the shops on Illampu or **Emita Tours** on Sagárnaga.

Handicrafts
Behind San Francisco church is the **Mercado Artesanal** with many handicraft stalls. Above Plaza San Francisco (see page 263), up C Sagárnaga, are booths and small stores with interesting local items of all sorts. The lower end of Sagárnaga is best for antiques. On Linares, between Sagárnaga and Santa Cruz, high-quality alpaca goods are priced in US$. Also in this area are many places making fleece jackets, gloves and hats, but shop around for value and service. **Galería Doryan** (Sagárnaga 177), is an entire gallery of handicraft shops; includes: **Comart Tukuypaj** (also at Linares 958, T02-231 2686 and Galería Centro de Moda, Local 4B, C 21, Calacoto, www.comart-tukuypaj.com), high-quality textiles from an artisan community association; and **Tejidos Wari** (unit 12), for high-quality alpaca goods, will make to measure, English spoken. **Alpaca Style** (C 22 No 14, Achumani, T02-271 1233). Upmarket shop selling alpaca and leather clothing. **Arte y Diseño** (Illampu 833, T7128 0696). Makes typical clothing to your own specifications in 24 hrs. The shop at Illampu 857 sells *tejidos* (material) by the metre. **Artesanía Sorata** (Sagárnaga 303 y Linares, T02-245 4728, and Sagárnaga 363, www.artesaniasorata.com). Specializes in dolls, sweaters and weavings. **Ayni** (Illampu 704, www.aynibolivia.com). Fairtrade shop in Hotel Rosario, featuring Aymara work. **Jiwitaki Art Shop** (Jaén 705, T7725 4042, Mon-Fri 1100-1300, 1500-1800). Run by local artists selling sketches, paintings, sculptures, literature, etc. **LAM** shops on Sagárnaga and Linares. Good quality alpaca goods. **Millma** (Sagárnaga 225, T02-231 1338, and Claudio Aliaga 1202, Bloque L-1, San Miguel, closed Sat afternoon and Sun). High-quality alpaca knitwear and woven items and, in the San Miguel shop, a permanent exhibition of ceremonial 19th and 20th century Aymara and Quechua textiles (free). **Mistura**, Sagárnaga 163, www.misturabolivia.com. Clothing, hats, bags, wine and other produce, jewellery and scents, high-end design incorporating traditional features. **Mother Earth** (Linares 870, T02-239 1911, daily 0930-1930). High-quality alpaca sweaters with natural dyes. **Toshy** on Sagárnaga. Top-quality knitwear.

Jewellery
Good jewellery stores with native and modern designs include **King's** (Loayza 261, between Camacho and Mercado also at Torre Ketal, C 15, Calacoto).

Maps
IGM (head office at Estado Mayor, Av Saavedra 2303, Miraflores, T02-214 9484, Mon-Thu 0900-1200, 1500-1800, Fri 0900-1200, take passport to buy maps. Also office in Edif Murillo, Final Rodríguez y Juan XXIII, T02-237 0116, Mon-Fri 0830-1230, 1430-1830), some stock or will get maps from HQ in 24 hrs. **Librería IMAS** (Av Mcal Santa Cruz entre Loayza y Colón, Edif Colón, T02-235 8234). Ask to see the map collection. Maps are also sold in the Post Office on the stalls opposite the Poste Restante counter.

Markets
In addition to those mentioned in the Plaza San Francisco section (page 263), the 5-sq-km **Feria 16 de Julio, El Alto** market is on Thu and

Sun (the latter is bigger). The best way to get there is on the red line of the Teleférico, the terminus (Estación 16 de Julio) is by the market. Alternatively, take any minibus that says La Ceja and get off at overpass after toll booth (follow crowd of people or tell driver you're going to La Feria), or take 16 de Julio minibus from Plaza Eguino. Arrive around 0900; most good items are sold by 1200. Goods are cheap, especially on Thu. Absolutely everything imaginable is sold here. Be watchful for pickpockets, just take a bin liner to carry your purchases. **Mercado Sopocachi**, Guachalla y Ecuador, a well-stocked covered market selling foodstuffs, kitchen supplies, etc, closes 1400 on Sun. Produce also available at **Centro Comercial Camacho** near El Prado.

Musical instruments

Many shops on Pasaje Linares, the stairs off C Linares, also on Sagárnaga/Linares, eg **Walata 855**.

What to do

City tours

The red and yellow lines of the **Teleférico** give a spectacular overview of La Paz (see Transport , page 279), **Red Cap** (see Tour operators, below) offer tours on the Teleférico. **Sightseeing**, www. lapazcitytour.net, city tours on a double-decker bus, 2 circuits, downtown and Zona Sur with Valle de la Luna (1 morning and 1 afternoon departure to each), departs from Plaza Isabel La Católica and can hop on at Plaza San Francisco, tour recorded in 7 languages, US$8.60 for both circuits, daily at 0900 and 1500 (city), 1030 and 1330 (Zona Sur). City tours also with **Gloria Tours**; for walking tours see **La Paz On Foot**, **Magri Turismo** and **Red Cap**; for El Alto market and wrestling cholitas tours, see **Andean Secrets** and **Red Cap**; all under Tour operators, below.

Climbing, hiking and trekking

Guides must be hired through a tour company. The Asociación de Guías de Montaña y Trekking (AGMTB) runs a mountain rescue group, **Socorro Andino Boliviano**, contact Jenaro Yupanqui, T7158 1118 or 02-239 5891. See www. boliviaclimbinginfo.org for climbing information. **Altitud 6000**, Sagárnaga 389, T02-245 3935. Mon-Sun 1000-1230, 1400-1830. Climbing tours in Bolivia, Argentina, Chile, Ecuador and Peru. Well organized, very good guides and excellent food. **Andean Base Camp**, Illampu 1037, T02-246 3782. Mon-Sat 0900-1200, 1500-1900. Climbing and trekking, Swiss staff, good reports, also equipment rentals.

Andean Summits, Muñoz Cornejo 1009 y Sotomayor, Sopocachi, T02-242 2106, www. andeansummits.com. Mon-Fri 0900-1200, 1500-1900. For mountaineering and other trips off the beaten track, contact in advance.
Bolivian Mountain Guides, Sagárnaga 348, T7758 0433, www.bolivianmountainguides.com. Mon-Fri 0800-2000, Sat-Sun 0900-1900. For private climbs and treks in the Cordillera and around La Paz.
Bolivian Mountains, Rigoberto Paredes 1401 y Colombia, p 3, San Pedro, T02-249 2775, www. bolivianmountains.com (in UK T01273-746545). High-quality mountaineering with experienced guides and good equipment, not cheap.
Climbing South America, Linares 940, T02-297 1543, www.climbingsouthamerica.com. Mon-Fri 0900-1900, Sat 0900-1300. Climbing, trekking, hiking and multi-activity trips, 4WD and cultural tours, Australian-run.
Refugio Huayna Potosí, Sagárnaga 398, T02-231 7324, www.huayna-potosi.com. Mon-Fri 0900-1900, Sat 0900-1500. Climbing and trekking tours, run 2 mountain shelters on Huayna Potosí and a climbing school. Check equipment before using.

Football

Popular and played on Wed and Sun at the **Siles Stadium** in Miraflores (Micro A), which is shared by both La Paz's main teams, Bolívar and The Strongest. There are reserved seats.

Golf

Mallasilla, T02-274-5124, is the world's highest golf course, at 3318 m. Non-members can play here on weekdays, US$85 plus equipment rental.

Language schools

Instituto Exclusivo (IE), Av 20 de Octubre 2315, Edif Mechita, T02-242 1072, www.instituto-exclusivo. com. Spanish lessons for individual and groups (US$10 per hr), accredited by Ministry of Education.

Tour operators

America Tours, Av 16 de Julio 1490 (El Prado), Edif Avenida pb, No 9, T02-237 4204, www.america-ecotours.com. Mon-Fri 0900-1800. Ecotourism and adventure trips in Bolivia and Peru. Specialists in the Amazon jungle and pampas, Lake Titicaca and Salar de Uyuni. Highly professional and recommended.
Andean Secrets, Av Saavedra 1135 (at Hotel Topaz), Miraflores, T7729 4590, www.andean-secrets.com. Mon-Fri 1500-1900, Sat 0900-1730, Sun 1000-1400. Mountain guide Denys Sanjines specializes in the Cordillera Quimsa Cruz. She also arranges visits to El Alto to see the Wrestling

Cholitas. Arrange hotel pick-up, go on your own or book through a Red Cap tour (see below).

Barracuda Biking Company, *Linares 971, of 5, T7672 8881, www.barracudabiking.com. Mon-Fri 1000-1830, Sat 1000-1500.* Bike trips to Coroico at a lower price than the upmarket companies.

Crillon Tours, *Camacho 1223, T02-233 7533, http://crillontours.com. Mon-Fri 0900-1200, 1430-1830, Sat 0900-1200.* A company with over 50 years' experience. Trips throughout Bolivia, including the Yungas, Sajama and Lauca, community and adventure tourism, tours combining Bolivia and Peru. Fixed departures and luxury camper service to Salar de Uyuni (www.uyuni.travel). Full details of their Lake Titicaca services on page 288. ATM for cash. Recommended.

Deep Rainforest, *Av América 121, T02-215 0385, www.deep-rainforest.com. Mon-Sat 1000-1400, 1500-1900, Sun 1000-1900.* Off-the-beaten-track trekking, canoe trips from Guanay to Rurrenabaque, rainforest and pampas trips.

Enjoy Bolivia, *Plaza Isabel La Católica, Edif Presidente Bush, of 2, T02-243 5162, www.enjoybolivia.org. Mon-Thu 0900-1900, Fri 0900-1800.* Wide selection of tours and transport service. Transfers to bus terminal and airport (US$20), van service to Oruro (US$108 shared between 4-8 passengers). Attentive service.

Fremen Tours, *Av 20 de Octubre 2396, Edif María Haydee, p 10, T02-242 1258, www.andes-amazonia.com. Mon-Fri 0900-1230, 1430-1830, Sat 0900-1200.* Customized tours and special interest travel throughout Bolivia, including Salar de Uyuni and Reina de Enín riverboat.

Gloria Tours, *Potosí 909, T02-240 7070, www.gloriatours.com.bo. Mon-Fri 0900-1230, 1430-1900, Sat 0900-1300.* Good service for ½ to full-day city tours, excursions further afield and tours throughout Bolivia. See **Hotel Gloria**, page 267.

Gravity Bolivia, *Linares 940, p 1, between Tarija and Sagárnaga, T02-231 0218, after hours T7720 8356, www.gravitybolivia.com (book on website). Mon-Fri 0900-1900.* A wide variety of mountain-biking tours throughout Bolivia, including the world-famous downhill ride to Coroico. They offer a zip-line at the end of the ride, or independently (www.ziplinebolivia.com). Also more challenging bike rides, including single-track and high-speed dirt roads, with coaching and safety equipment, and customized bike tours. They have cycle spares, very knowledgeable service. Also offer a ride and river tour from La Paz to Rurrenabaque and run **ScreeRush** on some of the world's highest scree slopes near Huyana Potosí. Book in advance at the office or by phone (T7721 9634), until 1900. Recommended.

Kanoo Tours, *Illampu 828 entre Sagárnaga y Santa Cruz, T02-246 0003, www.kanootours.com. Mon-Fri 0900-1800.* Also at **Adventure Brew Hostel** (open Sat). Sells **Gravity Bolivia** tours (see above), plus Salar de Uyuni, Rurrenabaque jungle trips and Peru.

La Paz On Foot, *882-B Linares, T7154 3918, www.lapazonfoot.com.* Walking city tours, including murals and urban art, trips on Titicaca, tours to Salar de Uyuni, multi-day treks in the Yungas and Apolobamba and regional tours focused on Andean food and biodiversity, which also include Peru, northern Chile and Argentina. Also works with the **Tarapari Biodiversity Garden and Guesthouse** in Chulumani, see page 295. Recommended.

Lipiko Tours, *Pedro Salazar, Edif Santa Martha, p13, Sopocachi, T7910 3555, http://lipiko.com. Mon-Fri 0900-1700, Sat 0900-1300.* Tailor-made tours for all budgets, 4WD tours, trekking, climbing and adventure sport, trips to Amazon and national parks. Also runs trips to Peru, Chile and Argentina.

Magri Turismo, *Capitán Ravelo 2101, T02-244 2727, www.magriturismo.com. Mon-Fri 0830-1215, 1430-1830, Sat 0900-1200.* Recommended for tours throughout Bolivia, flight tickets. Own **La Estancia** hotel on the Isla del Sol. They also have a city walking tour led by shoeshine boys.
Moto Andina, *Urb La Colina N°6 C 25, Calacoto, T7129 9329, www.moto-andina.com (in French).* Motorcycle tours of varying difficulty in Bolivia, contact Maurice Manco.
Mundo Quechua, *Av Circunvalación 43, Achumani, Zona Sur, T02-279 6145, www. mundoquechua.com.* Daily tours to the Cordillera Real, private transport in and around La Paz, custom made climbing, trekking and 4WD tours throughout Bolivia. Also extensions to Peru and Argentina and tours to **La Encantada Lodge** in Yungas. English, French and Portuguese spoken, good service.
Peru Bolivian Tours, *C23 No 7875, Edif Magnolia, PB of 1, Calacoto, T02-279 9501, www.perubolivian. com. Mon-Fri 0900-1230, 1430-1830, Sat 0900-1200.* More than 28 years' experience, arranges special programmes throughout Bolivia and Peru.
Pure! Bolivia, *Lisimaco Gutiérrez 481 y 20 de Octubre, Sopocachi, T02-243 4455 (6701 1344 24 hrs), info@bolivia-pure.com.* Member of the **Pure! Travel Group** (www.pure-travelgroup.com). Offering tailor-made, conventional, special interest and adventure tours in Bolivia.
Red Cap, *Linares 940, upstairs, T7628 5738, www. redcapwalkingtours.com. Mon-Fri 0900-1830.* La Paz walking tours daily at 1100 and 1400 from Plaza San Pedro, 2½ hrs, US$3, look for the guide with a red cap; also private half-day city tour and full-day adventure tours; local food tours (4 hrs of tasting and learning about local dishes US$30); extended tours off the beaten track; custom-tailored tours; and, on Thu and Sun, to El Alto market with option to see Wrestling Cholitas (extra cost, see Andean Secrets, above).
Topas Travel, *Carlos Bravo 299 (behind Hotel Plaza), T02-211 1082, www.topas.bo. Mon-Fri 0900-1700, Sat 0900-1200.* Joint venture of **Akhamani Trek** (Bolivia), **Topas** (Denmark) and the Danish embassy, offering trekking, overland truck trips, jungle trips and climbing, English spoken, also accommodations.
Transturin, *C6 N°100, Achumani (prolongación C 20, Calacoto), T02-242 2222 or 800-10TRANSTURIN, www.transturin.com. Mon-Fri 0900-1900.* Full travel services for over 40 years with tours in La Paz and

great walks
great guides
great memories

La Paz on foot
882-B Calle Linares
La Paz Bolivia
+591-71543918
lapazonfoot.com

TUPIZA TOURS
We are the first and the best
Turism Operater in Bolivia

Offices in: **LA PAZ - TARIJA UYUNI - TUPIZA**

We advise, desing, organize the trip of your dreams in Bolivia

info@tupizatours.com
info_groups@tupizatours.com

+591 70152537
TupizaTours@TupizaToursOficial

www.tupizatours.com

throughout Bolivia. Details of their Lake Titicaca services on page 288. Also extensions to Peru, Chile and Argentina.

Tupiza Tours, *Villalobos 625 y Av Saavedra, Edif Girasoles, ground floor, Miraflores, T02-224 5254, www.tupizatours.com. Mon-Fri 0900-1300, 1500-1900.* La Paz office of the recommended Tupiza agency, also have an office in Tarija. Specialize in the Salar de Uyuni, Reserva Avaroa and southwest Bolivia, but also offer tours around La Paz and throughout the country.

Turisbus, *Av Illampu 704, T02-245 1341, also C 10 y Av Costanera 501, Calacoto, www.gruporosario. com. Mon-Fri 0900-1200, 1500-1900, Sat 1600-1900.* Lake Titicaca and Isla del Sol, Salar de Uyuni, Rurrenbaque, trekking and Bolivian tours. Also airport transfers (US$12 pp), city tours and tours and tickets to Puno and Cuzco.

Turismo Balsa, *Av 6 de Agosto y Pinilla, Pje Pascoe 3, Sopocachi, T02-244 0620, www. turismobalsa.com.* City and tours throughout Bolivia. Owns **Hotel Las Balsas**, in beautiful lakeside setting at Puerto Pérez on Lake Titicaca, T02-289 5147, 72 km from La Paz, with excellent restaurant.

Urban Rush, *T7629 7222, www.urbanrushbolivia. com.* Go to **Hotel Presidente** (17th floor, 1200-1800) for abseiling or rap jumping from one of the tallest buildings in La Paz, US$30 for 1 jump, US$36 for 2, US$13 for each extra jump.

Transport

Air

La Paz has the highest commercial **airport** in the world, at El Alto (4061 m); T02-215 7300, www.sabsa.aero. **Cotranstur** minibuses, T02-231 2032, white with 'Cotranstur' and 'Aeropuerto' written on the side and back, go from Plaza Isabel La Católica, stopping all along El Prado and Av Mcal Santa Cruz to the airport, 0610-2130, US$0.55 (allow about 1 hr), best to buy an extra seat for your luggage, departures every 15 mins. Shared transport from Plaza Isabel La Católica, US$4 pp, carrying 4 passengers, also private transfers from **Enjoy Bolivia** and **Turisbus**, see Tour operators, above and page 288. Radio-taxi is US$8-10 to centre and Sopocachi, US$11-15 to Zona Sur. Prices are displayed at the airport terminal exit. If your luggage is small, outside rush hour you can save time by riding the **Teleférico** (see below) to El Alto and a taxi from there (US$2 from Estación Mirador on the yellow line, less from Estación 16 de Julio, the junction of the red and blue lines, or Estación Plaza Libertad

on the blue line). There is an **Info Tur** office in arrivals (daily 0500-2100) with a *casa de cambio* next to it (dollars, euros and cash, poor rates; open 0530-1300, 1700-0300, closed Sun evening). Several ATMs in the departures hall. There are also food outlets and shops (prices of handicrafts in the duty-free area are ridiculously high). The international and domestic departures hall is the main concourse, with all check-in desks. There are separate domestic and international arrivals. For details of air services, see under destinations.

Bus

City buses There are 3 types of city bus: the modern *puma katari* (www.lapazbus.bo), with 6 routes, mostly from El Alto through the centre to the Zona Sur, US$0.25-0.30 depending on route, US$0.42-0.50 at night, for frequent use you can buy a card for US$2.85, which can then be topped up; *micros* (small, old buses), which charge US$0.25 a journey; and minibuses (small vans), US$0.30-0.40 depending on the journey. *Trufis* are fixed-route collective taxis, with a sign with their route on the windscreen, US$0.50 pp in the centre, US$0.60 outside.

Long distance For information, T02-228 5858. Buses (called *flotas*) to: **Oruro**, **Potosí**, **Sucre**, **Cochabamba**, **Santa Cruz**, **Tarija**, **Uyuni**, **Tupiza** and **Villazón**, leave from the main terminal at Plaza Antofagasta (a couple of blocks from Estación Central on the red line of the Teleférico or micros 2, M, CH or 130); see under each destination for details. Taxi to central hotels should be US$1.50-2.50 and US$3-4 to hotels in Sopocachi and Zona Sur. Take Taxi Terminal, or Taxi Magnífico for best service. The terminal (open 0400-2300) has a tourist booth by the main entrance, ATMs, internet, a post office, **Entel**, restaurant, luggage store and travel agencies. Touts find passengers the most convenient bus and are paid commission by the bus company; feel free to choose your own. Unless they depart full, buses stop at their own terminals in El Alto (sector Terminal off Av 6 de Marzo) and may wait to fill. There are also buses that depart from El Alto, so it can be faster to catch a bus there. Buses entering La Paz stop in El Alto to unload before going to La Paz terminal; this can take some time. If not staying in La Paz you can save time by changing buses in El Alto. To **Oruro** van service with **Enjoy Bolivia**, see Tour operators, page 276, US$13 pp shared, US$90 private. To **Copacabana**, several bus companies (tourist service) pick-up travellers at their hotels (in the centre) and also stop at the main terminal, tickets from booths at the terminal (cheaper) or agencies in town. They all leave about 0800 (**Titicaca Bolivia** also at 1400), 3½ hrs, US$3-4.50 one way, return from Copacabana about 1330. When there are not enough passengers for each company, they pool them. **Diana Tours**, T02-235 0252, **Titicaca Bolivia**, T02-246 2655, many others. You can also book this service all the way to Puno, US$8, or Cuzco (US$14-22).

Public buses to the Lake Titicaca area: **Copacabana**, **Tiwanaku**, **Desaguadero** (border with Peru) and **Sorata**, leave from the Cemetery district. To get there, take any bus or minibus marked 'Cementerio' going up C Santa Cruz or the red line of the Teleférico to Estación Cementerio. On Plaza Tomás Katari are **Manco Kapac**, and **2 de Febrero** buses and **6 de Junio** vans, for **Copacabana** and **Tiquina**. From the Plaza go up Av Kollasuyo and at the 2nd street on the right (Manuel Bustillos) is the terminal for minibuses to **Achacachi**, **Huatajata** and **Huarina**, as well as **Trans Unificada** and **Flor del Illampu** minibuses for **Sorata**. Several micros (20, J, 10) and minibuses (223, 252, 270, 7) go up Kollasuyo. Taxi US$2 from downtown, US$4.30 from Zona Sur. After La Paz, all the above transport stops at **Terminal Interprovincial El Alto** or **Terminal del Altiplano** in Villa Esperanza, El Alto; you can save time by riding the Teleférico to El Alto, Estación UPEA on the blue line is near this terminal. Buses to **Coroico**, the **Yungas** and **northern jungle** leave from **Terminal Minasa** in Villa Fátima (25 mins by micros B, V, X, K, 131, 135, or 136, or *trufis* 2 or 9, which pass Pérez Velasco coming down from Plaza Mendoza, and get off at Puente Minasa; once operational, Estación Busch on the white line of the Teleférico will be a couple of blocks from the terminal). See Safety, page 386.

International buses From main bus terminal: to **Puno** and **Cuzco**, luxury and indirect services, see above and under Lake Titicaca, page 289. Also **Bolivia Hop**, www.boliviahop.com, which runs a hop-on, hop-off service from La Paz to Cuzco or Arequipa and on to Lima, via Copacabana and Puno, daily 0700, from Copacabana daily except Sat at 1700, packages start at US$39. To Puno via Desaguadero, **Nuevo Continente** at 0730, US$21.60, 5 hrs. To Cuzco **Trans Salvador**, at 1630 via Desaguadero, US$22-29 *cama*, US$26-33 VIP. To **Lima**, **Ormeño** Wed and Sat at 0700, US$60-70, 27 hrs. To **Buenos Aires** via Villazón, with **Río Paraguay**, 3 a week, US$75, or **Trans Americano**, daily at 1300, US$135

Alternatively, go to Villazón and change buses in Argentina. To **Arica** via the frontier at Tambo Quemado and Chungará, **Pullmanbus** at 0630 (good), **Cuevas** at 0700, **Zuleta** at 0600, **Nuevo Continente** at 0600 except Sat.

The main route to **Chile** is via Tambo Quemado (see page 298), but an alternative route, on which there are no trucks, is to go by good road direct from La Paz via Viacha to **Santiago de Machaco** (130 km, petrol); then 120 km on a very bad road to the border at **Charaña** (basic **Alojamiento Aranda**; immigration behind railway station). From Visviri, on the Chilean side of the frontier (no services), a regular road runs to Putre. A motorized railway car also runs from Viacha to Charaña on Mon and Thu at 0800 (4 hrs, US$4.30), returning Tue and Fri at 1200. There is no train service on the Chilean side.

Cable car

Teleférico An impressive system of cable cars (www.miteleferico.bo) joins El Alto along the edge of the altiplano with the centre of the city and the Zona Sur. Each ride costs US$0.45 (pay again if connecting to another line), for frequent use you can buy a card which can then be topped up and gives you a discount on connecting lines. Opening hours are Mon-Sat 0630-2300 (until 2330 on the yellow and green lines), Sun 0700-2100; enter at least 15 mins before closing time. There are long queues at rush hour (especially 0700-1000 down from El Alto and 1800-2000 up from La Paz and on the red line Sun 1300-2000); you cannot take luggage at these times. 4 lines are operating: **Línea Roja** (red line) from Zona 16 de Julio, La Ceja in El Alto, to the old train station, 3 blocks above Plaza Eguino, in an area known as Vita in the northwest of the city, via Av Entre Ríos in the cemetery district; **Línea Amarilla** (yellow line) from Parque Mirador, Ciudad Satélite in Al Alto, to Curva de Holguín, Av Libertador at the border between Sopocachi and Alto Obrajes, via Av Buenos Aires and Plaza España in Sopocachi; **Línea Verde** (green line) from Curva de Holguín (yellow line terminus) to Zona Sur: Calle 12 and 13 in Calacoto, entrance to Irpavi, via Alto Obrajes and Calle 17 de Obrajes; **Línea Azul** (blue line, open Mon-Sat 0630-2300, Sun 0700-2100), all in El Alto, from 16 de Julio (red line terminus) to Río Seco, Av Juan Pablo II, the road leading to Lake Titicaca, via Plaza Libertad, Plaza La Paz and UPEA (Villa Esperanza). A 5th line, **Línea Blanca** (white line), running through Miraflores and connecting it with San Jorge, Av del Poeta, by Parque Central, is due to start operating by the end of 2017. 6 additional lines are planned.

Car hire

Budget, Capitan Ravelo 2130 and at the airport, T02-291 1925, www.budget.bo. **Europcar**, at the airport, T02-220 2933, www.europcar. com. **Imbex**, C15 esquina Los Sauces, Calacoto, T02-212 1010, www.imbex.com. Wide range of well-maintained vehicles; Suzuki jeeps from US$60 per day, including 200 km free for 4-person 4WD. Also office in Santa Cruz, T03-311001. Recommended. **Petita Rent-a-car**, Valentín Abecia 2031, Sopocachi Alto, T6740 1468, www.rentacarpetita.com. Recommended for personalized service and well-maintained 4WD jeeps, minimum rental 1 week. Their vehicles can also be taken outside Bolivia. Also offer adventure tours (English spoken).

Taxi

Taxis are often, but not always, white. Taxi drivers are not tipped. There are 3 types: **standard taxis**, which may take several passengers at once (US$0.45-1.75 for short trips within city limits), **fake taxis**, which have been involved in robberies (a recurring problem for those arriving at the cemetery district), and **radio taxis**, which take only one group of passengers at a time. Since it is impossible to distinguish between the first two, it is best to pay a bit more for a radio taxi, especially at night. These have a dome light, a unique number (note this when getting in) and radio communication (eg **Servisur**, T02-279 9999; **Taxi Terminal** at the bus station; **Taxi Magnífico** T02-277 1717; **Taxi Diplomático**, T02-222 4343). They charge US$1.50-2.50 in the centre, more to suburbs and at night.

> **Tip...**
> Taxi ranks outside malls, cinemas, etc operate with radio taxis and are more expensive than the ones you flag down on the street, but are good places to find the safer option.

Train

Ferroviaria Andina (FCA), T02-218 4555, or 800-119000, www.fca.com.bo, runs the **Oruro–Uyunui–Tupiza–Villazón** line; see schedule and fares under Oruro Transport (page 302). Tickets are sold online or at the Oruro station. The 2nd Sun of each month, FCA runs a **tourist train** from El Alto to **Guaqui**, with a 1½-hr stop at Tiwanaku and 2 hrs at Guaqui. The station is

at C 8, 3 blocks from Av 6 de Marzo, by Cuartel Ingavi, departs 0800, returns 1320, arrives in El Alto 1915, US$11.50 *ejecutivo*, US$3 *salón*. Confirm all details in advance.

South of La Paz

For **Valle de la Luna**, Minibuses 231, 273 and 902 can be caught on C México, the Prado or Av 6 de Agosto. Alternatively take Micro 11 ('Aranjuez' large bus) or ones that say 'Mallasa' or 'Mallasilla' along the Prado or Av 6 de Agosto, US$0.75, and ask driver where to get off. You can also catch these minibuses and micros at Curva de Holguín, the southern terminus of the yellow line of the Teleférico. Most of the local travel agents organize tours to the **Valle de la Luna**. Some are a brief, 5-min stop for photos in a US$15 tour of La Paz and surroundings, but longer tours and cycling trips are also available.

Takesi Trail

Take a **Líneas Ingavi** bus from C Gral Luis Lara esq Venacio Burgoa near Plaza Líbano, San Pedro, going to **Pariguaya** (2 hrs past Chuñavi), several daily, US$3.55, 2 hrs. On Sun, also minibuses from C Gral Luis Lara y Boquerón, hourly 0700-1500. To **Mina San Francisco**: hire a **jeep** from La Paz; US$85, takes about 2 hrs. **Veloz del Norte** (T02-221 8279) leaves from Ocabaya 495 in Villa Fátima, T02-221 8279, 0900 daily, and 1400 Thu-Sun, US$3.55, 3½ hrs, continuing to Chojlla. From **Chojlla** to La Paz daily at 0500, 1300 also on Thu-Sun, passing **Yanacachi** 15 mins later. You can also catch a bus to La Paz from La Florida on the main Yungas road, US$3.55.

Choro Trail

To the *apacheta* pass beyond **La Cumbre**, take a **taxi** from central La Paz for US$20, 45 mins, stopping to register at the Guardaparque hut. Alternatively, buses from Villa Fátima to Coroico and Chulumani pass La Cumbre. Tell driver where you are going, US$3. The trail is signed.

Huayna Potosí

The mountain can be reached by transport arranged through tourist agencies (US$100) or the *refugio*, **taxi** US$45. **Minibus Trans Zongo**, Av Chacaltaya e Ingavi, Ballivián, El Alto, daily 0600, 2½ hrs, US$2 to Zongo, check on return time. Also minibuses from the Ballivián area that leave when full (few on Sun). If camping in the Zongo Pass area, stay at the site near the white house above the cross.

Around La Paz
& Lake Titicaca

Within striking distance of La Paz are an enormous variety of landscapes, extraordinary historical sites and potential for adventure. The most popular excursion is to the remarkable site of Tiwanaku, 72 km west of the city. Rising out of the vast flatness of the altiplano are the remains of pyramids and temples, of a great civilization that predated the Incas by a thousand years.

No visit to Bolivia would be complete without seeing the sapphire-blue waters of mystical Lake Titicaca and its beautiful islands. Covering 8000 sq km, Titicaca is the highest navigable lake in the world at over 3800 m above sea level.

Tiwanaku *Colour map 3, B2.*

Bolivia's best-known archaeological site is a must-see trip

☆This remarkable archaeological site, 72 km west of La Paz, near the southern end of Lake Titicaca, takes its name from one of the most important pre-Columbian civilizations in South America. It is the most popular excursion from La Paz, with good facilities for the visitor.

The site
The site is open 0900-1700, US$12, including entry to museums. Allow 4 hrs to see the ruins and village. See also Transport, opposite.

Many archaeologists believe that Tiwanaku existed as early as 1200 BC, while the complex visible today probably dates from the eight to the 10th centuries AD. The site may have been a ceremonial complex and political centre, the nucleus of an empire which is thought to have covered most of Bolivia, southern Peru, northern Chile and northwest Argentina. It was also a hub of trans-Andean trade. The demise of the Tiwanaku civilization remains a mystery, but heading the list of theories is that some form of major change in the climate, most probably drought, meant that the area's extensive system of raised fields (*sukakollu*), which at one stage were capable of sustaining many thousands of people, failed to feed the population and, more importantly, the elites. As a result, some time around 1000-1100 AD the main culture collapsed and disappeared. The Pumapunku section, 1 km south of the main complex, may have been a port, as the waters of the lake used to be much higher than they are today. The raised field system is once again being used in parts locally.

Kalasasaya One of the main structures is the Kalasasaya, meaning 'standing stones', referring to the statues found in that part: two of them, the Ponce monolith (centre of inner patio) and the Fraile monolith (southwest corner), have been re-erected.

Puerta del Sol In the northwest corner is the Puerta del Sol, originally at Pumapunku. Its carvings are thought to be either a depiction of the creator god, or a calendar. The motifs are exactly the same as those around the Ponce monolith.

Templo Semisubterráneo This is a sunken temple whose walls are lined with faces, all different. According to some theories they depict states of health, the temple being a house of healing; another theory is that the faces display all the ethnicities of the world.

Best for
Archaeology ■ Cycling ■ Islands ■ Trekking ■ Wildlife

Essential Around La Paz and Lake Titicaca

Getting around

Tiwanaku village, Copacabana, Sorata and other towns in the area are all linked by minibuses from La Paz. A paved road (being dualled in 2017, expect delays) runs from La Paz to the southeastern shore of the lake. One branch continues north along the eastern shore, another branch goes to the Straits of Tiquina (114 km El Alto–San Pablo) and Copacabana. A third road goes to Guaqui and Desaguadero on the southwestern shore. Ferries cross the Straits of Tiquina and go to islands in the lake. See also Transport, below.

When to go

Cool all year; rainy season December to March.

Time required

One day for Tiwanaku, two to four days for Copacabana or Sorata, two to three weeks for the more remote areas.

Akapana Originally a pyramid (said to have been the second largest in the world, covering over 28,000 sq m), the Akapana still has some ruins on it.

Pumapunku A natural disaster may have put a sudden end to the construction at Pumapunku before it was finished; some of the blocks weigh 100 to 150 tonnes.

Museums There is a small **Museo Lítico** at the ticket office, with several large stone pieces and, at the site, the **Museo Regional Arqueológico**, contains a well-illustrated explanation of the raised field system of agriculture. Many other artefacts are in the **Museo Nacional de Arqueología** in La Paz.

Tiwanaku village

Nearby Tiwanaku village, with several basic hotels and eateries, still has remnants from the time of independence and the 16th-century church was built using pre-Columbian masonry. In fact, Tiwanaku for a long while was the 'quarry' for the altiplano. For the Willkakuti, winter solstice festival on 21 June, there is an all-night vigil and colourful dances. There is also a colourful local festival on the Sunday after Carnaval.

Listings Tiwanaku

Transport

Tours to Tiwanaku cost US$10-12, not including entry fee or lunch. If not on a tour take the red line of the **Teleférico** to Estación Cementerio or any **minibus** marked 'Cementerio' in La Paz, get out at Plaza Félix Reyes Ortiz, on Mariano Bautista (north side of cemetery), go north up Aliaga, 1 block east of Asín to find Tiwanaku vans, US$2, 1½ hrs, every 30 mins, 0600 to 1500. Tickets can be bought in advance. You can also take the red and blue lines of the Teleférico to Estación UPEA in El Alto and go to the Terminal del Altiplano to get a minibus to Tiwanaku. **Taxi** from La Paz costs US$30-55 return (shop around), with 2 hrs

at site. Some **buses** go on from Tiwanaku to Desaguadero; virtually all Desaguadero buses stop at the access road to Tiwanaku, 20-min walk from the site. Return buses (last back 1700) leave from south side of the Plaza in village. Minibuses (vans) to **Desaguadero**, from José María Asín y P Eyzaguirre (Cemetery district) US$2, 2 hrs, most movement on Tue and Fri when there is a market at the border.

Note When returning from Tiwanaku (ruins or village) to La Paz, do not take an empty minibus. We have received reports of travellers being taken to El Alto and robbed at gun point. Wait for a public bus with paying passengers in it.

Lake Titicaca   *Colour map 3, B2.*

superb views, altiplano life and trips on the lake

★Lake Titicaca is two lakes joined by the Straits of Tiquina: the larger, northern lake (Lago Mayor, or Chucuito) contains the Islas del Sol and de la Luna; the smaller lake (Lago Menor, or Huiñamarca) has several small islands. The waters are a beautiful blue, reflecting the hills and the distant cordillera in the shallows of Huiñamarca, mirroring the sky in the rarified air and changing colour when it is cloudy or raining. A boat trip on the lake is a must.

La Paz to Copacabana

The main road from La Paz to Copacabana (being dualled in 2017) reaches the east side of the Straits of Tiquina at **San Pablo**. On the west side is **San Pedro**, the main Bolivian naval base, from where a paved road goes to Copacabana. Vehicles across on barges, US$5. Passengers cross separately, US$0.20 (not included in bus fares) and passports and visas may be checked (do not leave your documents on the bus or in your hotel in La Paz). Expect delays during rough weather, when it can get very cold.

★Copacabana

A popular little resort town on Lake Titicaca, 158 km from La Paz by paved road, Copacabana (population 5515, altitude 3850 m) is set on a lovely bay and surrounded by scenic hills. **Centro de Información Turística** ① *Av 6 de Agosto esq 16 de Julio, Mon-Fri 080-1200, 1400-1800, Sat 0800-1200*, English spoken, provides pamphlets and maps of Copacabana and Isla del Sol. Next door, **Apthapi Red de Turismo Comunitario** ① *Av 6 de Agosto y 16 de Julio, T7729 9088, www.titicacaturismo.com, Mon-Sat 0800-1200, 1300-1900, Sun 0900-1800*, a group of five communities around the lake and on the islands, day trips and multi-day tours on offer. ATMs in town run out of money at busy times, best take some cash.

Copacabana has a heavily restored, Moorish-style **basilica** ① *open 0700-2000; minimum 5 people at a time to visit museum, Tue-Sat 1000-1100, 1500-1600, Sun 1000-1100, US$2.50, no photos allowed.* It contains a famous 16th-century miracle-working Virgen Morena (Black Madonna), also known as the Virgen de Candelaria, one of the patron saints of Bolivia. The basilica is clean, white, with coloured tiles decorating the exterior arches, cupolas and chapels. It is notable for its spacious atrium with four small chapels; the main chapel has one of the finest gilt altars in Bolivia. There are 17th- and 18th-century paintings and statues in the sanctuary. Vehicles decorated with flowers and confetti are blessed in front of the church at weekends and other special days (eg Semana Santa).

On the headland which overlooks the town and port, **Cerro Calvario**, are the Stations of the Cross (a steep 45-minute climb – leave plenty of time if going to see the sunset). On the hill behind the town is the **Horca del Inca** ① *entry US$1.45*, two pillars of rock with another laid across them;

Copacabana

Where to stay 🛏
1 Ecolodge
2 Emperador
3 Gloria Copacabana
4 Kantutas
5 Kotha Kahuaña
6 La Cúpula
7 Las Olas
8 Leyenda
9 Rosario del Lago
10 Sonia
11 Utama
12 Wendy Mar

Restaurants 🍴
1 Aransaya
2 Café Bistrot Copacabana
3 El Cóndor & The Eagle
4 La Orilla
5 Mauraz
6 Panamericano Café
7 Snack 6 de Agosto
8 Sujna Wasi

200 metres
200 yards

probably a solar calendar, the Inti Watana, now covered in graffiti. There is a path marked by arrows; boys will offer to guide you, but fix a price in advance.

There are many great hikes in the hills surrounding Copacabana. North of town is the **Yampupata Peninsula**. It is a beautiful 17-km (six-hour) walk to the village of Yampupata at the tip of the peninsula, either via **Sicuani** on the southwest shore or **Sampaya** (with a lodge, part of Apthapi) on the northeast shore, both picturesque little towns. There are also minibuses from Copacabana to Yampupata, where you can hire a motorboat or rowboat to Isla del Sol or Isla de la Luna; boats are also available from Sampaya to Isla de la Luna (US$21 for a motorboat, US$14 for a rowing boat).

☆Isla del Sol

The site of the main Inca creation myth (there are other versions) is a place of exceptional natural beauty and spiritual interest. Legend has it that Viracocha, the creator god, had his children, Manco Kapac and Mama Ocllo, spring from the waters of the lake to found Cuzco and the Inca dynasty. **La Roca Sagrada** (sacred rock) at the island's northwest end is worshipped as their birthplace. Near the rock are the impressive ruins of **Chincana**, the labyrinth, a 25-minute walk from the village of **Challapampa**, with a basic **Museo de Oro** ① *US$2.15 includes landing fee and entry to Chincana*, displaying ceramics (the gold figures are now in **Museo de Metales Preciosos** in La Paz). Challapampa (part of Apthapi) is beautifully set along two sandy bays, separated by an isthmus. Near the centre of the island is the community of Challa on a secluded bay with an **ethnographic museum** ① *US$2.15, includes trail fees*. Towards the south end of the island is the **Fuente del Inca**, a spring reached by Inca steps, Las Mil Gradas, leading up from the lake and continuing up to **Yumani**. The village is spread out along a steep slope between the port and a ridge 200 m above. Near the southeast tip of the island, 2 km from the spring, are the ruins of **Pilcocaina** ① *US$2.15, includes landing fees*, the Temple of the Sun, a two-storey building with false domes and nice views over the water. You must pay the fees even if you don't visit the museums or ruins. Keep all entry tickets, you may be asked for them at other locations. Several restored pre-Columbian roads cross the island from north to south.

The three communities are along the east shore of the island. All have electricity (Yumani also has internet), accommodation and simple places to eat. The island is heavily touristed and gets crowded in high season. Touts and beggars can be persistent, especially in Yumani. Tour operators in Copacabana offer half- and full-day 'tours' (many are just transport, see page 288) but an overnight stay at least is recommended to appreciate fully the island and to enjoy the spectacular walk from north to south (or vice-versa), about 11 km, at a comfortable pace. In a day trip, you will barely have time for a quick look at Chincana and you will see Pilcocaina from the boat; see more details in Transport, below. Note that it is a steep climb from the pier to the town of Yumani. Local guides are available in Challapampa and Yumani.

Isla de la Luna Southeast of Isla del Sol is the smaller Isla de la Luna (or Coati), which may also be visited on a tour or with private transport. The community of Coati (part of Apthapi) is located on the west shore, the ruins of the Inca **Palacio de Iña Kuyu** ① *US$1.45 community fee for ruins and landing*, on the east shore.

Border with Peru

West side of Lake Titicaca The road goes from La Paz 91 km west to the former port of **Guaqui** (passports may be inspected at the military checkpoint here and at other spots along the road). The road crosses the border at **Desaguadero**, 22 km further west, and runs along the shore of the lake to Puno. Bolivian and Peruvian immigration offices, open 0800-2030 (0700-1930 Peruvian time, one hour earlier than Bolivia) are on either side of the international bridge over the Río Desaguadero, Lake Titicaca's outflow. Peruvian visas should be arranged in La Paz. There are a few hotels and restaurants on both sides of the border; very basic in Bolivia, slightly better in Peru. Money changers on the Peruvian side give reasonable rates. Market days are Friday and Tuesday, otherwise the town is dead.

Via Copacabana From Copacabana a paved road leads 8 km south to the frontier at Kasani, then to Yunguyo, Peru. For bus services on this route, see page 289, and for boat trips, see What to do, page 288. The border is open 0830-2000 Bolivian time (0700-1930 Peruvian time). International tourist buses stop at both sides of the border; if using local transport walk 300 m between the two posts. Going to Peru, money can be changed at the Peruvian side of the border or in Yunguyo. Coming into Bolivia, the best rates for US dollars are at Copacabana.

East side of Lake Titicaca From Huarina, a road heads northwest to **Achacachi** (Sunday market; fiesta 14 September). Here, one road goes north across a tremendous marsh to **Warisata**, then crosses the altiplano to Sorata (see below). At Achacachi, another road runs roughly parallel to the shore of Lake Titicaca, through **Ancoraimes** (Sunday market, the church hosts a community project making dolls and alpaca sweaters, also has dorms), **Carabuco** (with a colonial church), **Escoma** (which has an Aymara market every Sunday morning) to **Puerto Acosta**, 10 km from the Peruvian border. It is a pleasant, friendly town with a large plaza and several simple places to stay and eat. The area around Puerto Acosta is good walking country. From La Paz to Puerto Acosta the road is paved as far as Escoma, then good until Puerto Acosta (best in the dry season, approximately May to October). North of Puerto Acosta towards Peru the road deteriorates and should not be attempted except in the dry season. There is a smugglers' market at the border on Wednesday and Saturday, the only days when transport is plentiful. Bolivian immigration, open 0800-2000 (0700-1900 Peruvian time) is before the international bridge. Peruvian customs is 2 km from the border and 2 km before Tilali, where Peruvian immigration is on the plaza.

Listings Lake Titicaca *map page 283.*

Where to stay

La Paz to Copacabana

$$ Hotel Titicaca
Between Huatajata and Huarina, Km 80 from La Paz, T02-289 5180 (in La Paz T02-290 7000).
Beautiful views, sauna, pool, good restaurant. It's very quiet during the week.

$ Máximo Catari's Inti Karka Hotel
Huatajata, on the lakeshore, T7197 8959, erikcatari@hotmail.com.
Rooms are cheaper with shared bath. Also restaurant, open daily ($$-$), and tours to islands (see What to do, below).

Copacabana

$$$ Gloria Copacabana
Av 16 de Julio, T02-862 2094, La Paz T02-240 7070, www.hotelgloria.com.bo.
On the lakeshore. Full board available, bar, café and restaurant with international and vegetarian food, gardens, mini-golf, racquetball, parking. Same group as **Gloria** in La Paz.

$$$ Rosario del Lago
Rigoberto Paredes y Av Costanera, T02-862 2141, reservations La Paz T02-244 1756, www.hotelrosario.com/lago.
Comfortable rooms with lake views, beautifully furnished, good restaurant (0730-0930, 1230-1430, 1830-2100), small museum, **Turisbus** tour operator, parking. Efficient and attentive service.

$$ Ecolodge
2 km south along the lakeshore, T02-862 2500 (or T02-245 1626, Hostal Copacabana, La Paz).
Small comfortable cabins in a quiet out-of-the way location, nice grounds. Only breakfast available, solar hot water, helpful owner.

$$ Las Olas
lake-end of Pje Michel Pérez past La Cúpula, T7250 8668, www.hostallasolas.com.
Tastefully decorated suites, each in its own style. All have kitchenettes, heaters, lovely grounds and views, outdoor solar-heated jacuzzi, a special treat. Warmly recommended.

$$ Utama
Pje Michel Pérez, T02-862 2013, www.utamahotel.com.
Comfortable rooms, hot water, good showers, restaurant, book exchange.

$$ Wendy Mar
Av 16 de Julio, opposite Gloria, T02-862 2124.
Very clean, bright rooms in pastel colours, large modern building, conveniently placed, terrace, cheaper in low season.

$$-$ La Cúpula
Pje Michel Pérez 1-3, 5 mins' walk from centre, T6708 8464, www.hotelcupula.com.
Variety of rooms and prices from suite with jacuzzi to comfortable rooms with shared bath, reliable hot water, sitting room with TV and video, fully equipped kitchen, garden with hammocks and lake view, library, book exchange, attentive service, excellent restaurant ($$ with

vegetarian options, great breakfast, open 0730-1500, 1800-2230, closed Tue lunch). Popular, advance booking advised. Highly recommended.

$ Emperador
C Murillo 235, T02-862 2083.
Very economical, even cheaper without bath, electric showers, newer rooms at the back, popular, helpful, tours arranged.

$ Kantutas
Av Jauregui esq Bolívar, on Plaza Sucre, T6730 5804, hostalkantutas@entel.bo.
Good rooms, a decent option in the middle price range, convenient location for transport, includes breakfast.

$ Kotha Kahuaña
Av Busch 15, T7652 3760, evelinn996@gmail.com.
Very economical, with or without bath, also 4-11-bed shared rooms (US$3.60 pp) simple kitchen facilities, quiet, hospitable, basic but good value.

$ Leyenda
Av Costanera y Germán Busch, T7067 4097, hostel.leyenda@gmail.com.
Lakeshore hotel with eclectic decor, rooms elaborately decorated with local motifs, electric shower.

$ Sonia
Murillo 253, T7196 8441.
Rooms are cheaper without bath, good beds, big windows, roof terrace, laundry facilities, breakfast in bed on request, very helpful, good value.

Isla del Sol
La Posada del Inca, a restored colonial hacienda, owned by **Crillon Tours**, is only available as part of a tour with Crillon, see page 288.
Magri Turismo also owns a hotel on the island, **La Estancia** (www.ecolodge-laketiticaca.com).

See page 277. See also **Transturin's** overnight options on page 288.

Yumani
The majority of *posadas* are in the south of the island, most in the upper part of Yumani. For those unable to walk a long way up the steps there are *hostales* and *cabañas* between Yumani port and higher up the village. Quality varies; ignore the touts and shop around for yourself. Please conserve water, it is hauled up the steep hill by donkeys.

$$ Puerto Alegre
100m from the port, T7195 8015.
Nice hotel with good rooms and views, private bath, opened 2016.

$ Hostal Utama
Almost at the top of the hill, T7300 3268.
In a pleasant location, rooms with or without bath, breakfast and restaurant, small garden, helpful and good value.

$ Inti Kala
At the top of the hill, T7197 3878, javierintikala@hotmail.com.
Upstairs rooms (remodelled in 2016) have stunning lake views and terrace, bath, electric shower, comforters, nice views also from breakfast/common area, good quality.

$ Mirador del Inca
Access from the port along the steps to the south of the main Inca steps, at the same level as the Fuente del Inca.
Simple but nice hostel with lake views, cheaper rooms with shared bath, electric showers, breakfast extra.

$ Palacio del Inca
10 min walk from the port, T7304 0579.
Small rooms with nice views, private or shared bath, new in 2016.

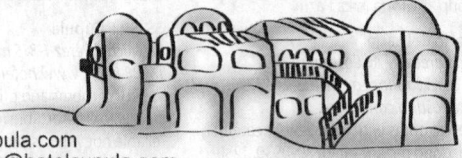

$ Templo del Sol
At the top of the hill, T7351 8970.
Comfortable rooms, cheaper without bath,
electric shower, great views, comfy beds, meals
available on request, good value.

Challa

Located mid-island on the east shore, about
200 m below the main north-south trail. Most
hostels are on the beach, the town is uphill.

$ Inca Beach
On the beach, T7353 0309.
Simple rooms with bath, electric shower, kitchen
and laundry facilities, meals available, nice
common area, camping possible, good value.

$ Qhumpuri
On hillside above beach.
Simple 2-room units with nice views, private toilet,
shared electric shower, tasty meals available.

Challapampa

$$-$ Cumri Hostal
*On the northern (2nd) bay, along a lane 100 m
from the trail to the ruin; a 5-min walk from
the port.*
Nice hotel with good infrastructure, rooms with
bath with solar heated water, nice views, cheaper
without breakfast, a good choice.

$ Manco Kapac
By the dock, T6706 2400.
Basic clean and well maintained rooms, shared
bath, electric shower, economical, camping
possible, does not include breakfast.

$ Mirador del Sol
*At north end of southern bay, past the docks,
T7370 6536.*
Simple rooms with great views, shared bath,
electric shower, no breakfast. Fancier rooms
with bath nearing completion in 2017.

Camping

Camping is permitted along the beach of the
northern bay.

Restaurants

La Paz to Copacabana

$$-$ Inti Raymi
Next to Inca Utama hotel, Huatajata.
With fresh fish and boat trips. There are other
restaurants of varying standard, most lively at
weekends and in the high season.

Copacabana

Excellent restaurants at hotels **Rosario del Lago**
and **La Cúpula**. Many touristy places on Av 6 de
Agosto toward the lakeshore, all similar.

$$ Café Bistrot Copacabana
*Av Busch y Costanera, near the lake.
Daily 0800-1430, 1730-2130.*
Varied menu, international dishes, vegetarian
and vegan options, good service, French and
English spoken.

$$-$ La Orilla
Av 6 de Agosto, close to lake. Daily 1800-2200.
Warm, atmospheric, tasty food with local and
international choices.

$$-$ Mauraz
*Av 6 de Agosto, 1 block from Plaza Sucre toward
the lake. Open 0730-2230.*
A good choice for food (pizza, fast food,
breakfasts) and drinks, has a happy hour, music.

$ Aransaya
Av 6 de Agosto 121. Daily 0830-2100.
Good restaurant and café serving local dishes,
including trout.

$ El Cóndor & The Eagle
*Av 6 de Agosto, 1 block from Plaza Sucre toward the
lake, in Residencial París. Only open for breakfast.*
Good food, sandwiches, cakes, teas and coffee,
friendly, English spoken.

$ Snack 6 de Agosto
Av 6 de Agosto, 2 branches. Daily 0800-2200.
Good trout, big portions, some vegetarian dishes,
serves breakfast.

$ Sujna Wasi
Jauregui 127. Daily 0730-2300.
Serves breakfast, vegetarian lunch, wide range
of books on Bolivia, slow service.

Panamericano Café
*Avaroa at Plaza 2 de Febrero (near the Basílica).
Daily 1000-1900, closed Wed-Thu.*
Small café with great coffee, teas, pastries,
sandwiches, quiche, pizza, also take-away.
English spoken.

Isla del Sol

Yumani

$$ Las Velas
*Yumani, near the top of the hill behind a
eucalyptus grove, follow the signs.*
Great views, especially at sunset, take a torch for
the way back. Lovely candle-lit atmosphere, small

choice of excellent meals, all freshly prepared, slow service, but worth the wait.

Festivals

Copacabana

Note At these times hotel prices quadruple; book in advance.

24 Jan Alacitas, held on Cerro Calvario and at Plaza Colquepata, is when miniature houses, cars and the like are sold and blessed.

1-3 Feb Virgen de la Candelaria, massive procession, folk dancing, fireworks, bullfights.

Mar/Apr Easter, with candlelight procession on Good Friday.

3 May Fiesta del Señor de la Cruz de Colquepata, held on the weekend nearest 3 May, very colourful with dances in typical costumes.

21 Jun Aymara New Year, celebrated throughout the Titicaca region.

4-6 Aug Virgen de la Candelaria and **Bolivian Independence Day**, a large fair selling trinkets, without much cultural activity, fireworks and partying on 4-5 Aug.

What to do

Lake Titicaca

Lago Huiñamarca In Huatajata, Máximo Catari (see Where to stay, above) and Paulino Esteban (east end of Huatajata, T7196 7383) arrange trips to the islands in Lago Huiñamarca for US$58 for up to 10 people. Includes a visit to **Museo Titi** (entry US$2), with information about reed boats.

Crillon Tours, *La Paz, see page 276*. A very experienced company which runs a hydrofoil service on Lake Titicaca with excellent bilingual guides. Tours stop at their Andean Roots cultural complex at Inca Utama. The **Inca Utama Hotel and Spa ($$$)** has a health spa based on natural remedies and Kallawaya medicine; the rooms are comfortable, with heating, electric blankets, good service, bar, restaurant, Wi-Fi, reservations through **Crillon Tours** in La Paz. Crillon is Bolivia's oldest travel agency and is consistently recommended. Also at **Inca Utama** is an observatory (*alajpacha*) with 2 telescopes and retractable roof for viewing the night sky, an altiplano museum, a floating restaurant and bar on the lake (**La Choza Náutica**), a 252-sq-m floating island and examples of different altiplano cultures. Health, astronomical, mystic and ecological programmes are offered. The hydrofoil trips include visits to Andean Roots complex, Copacabana, Islas del Sol and de la Luna, Straits of Tiquina and the Cocotoni community. See Isla del Sol, Where to stay, for **La Posada del Inca**. Crillon has a sustainable tourism project with Urus-Iruitos people from the Río Desaguadero area on floating islands by the Isla Quewaya. Trips can be arranged to/from Puno and Juli (bus and hydrofoil excursion to Isla del Sol) and from Copacabana via Isla del Sol to Cuzco and Machu Picchu. Other combinations of hydrofoil and land-based excursions can be arranged (also highland, Eastern lowland, jungle and adventure tours). See http://crillontours.com and www.uyuni.travel for details. All facilities and modes of transport connected by radio.

Transturin, *www.transturin.com, see also page 277*. Run catamarans on Lake Titicaca, either for sightseeing or as part of the La Paz-Puno route. The catamarans are more leisurely than the hydrofoils, there is more room and time for on-board meals and entertainment, with bar, video and sun deck. From their dock at Chúa, catamarans run full-day and 2-day/1-night cruises starting either in La Paz or Copacabana. Puno may also be the starting point for trips. Overnight cruises involve staying in a cabin on the catamaran, moored at the Isla del Sol, with lots of activities. On the island, Transturin has the Inti Wata cultural complex which has restored Inca terraces, an Aymara house, the underground Ekeko museum and cultural demonstrations and activities. There is also a 30-passenger totora reed boat for trips to the Pilcocaina Inca palace. All island-based activities are community-led and for catamaran clients only. Transturin runs through services to Puno without many of the formalities at the border. They also offer last-minute programmes in Puno, Cuzco and La Paz, if booked 6 days prior to departure only. You can book by phone or by email, but ask first, as availability depends on date.

Turisbus, *www.gruporosario.com/turisbus-tours, see La Paz, Tour operators, page 278, and Hoteles Rosario, La Paz, page 268, and Rosario del Lago, Copacabana*. Offer full-day guided tours in the fast launches *Titicaca Explorer I* (28 passengers) and *II* (8 passengers) to the Isla del Sol, and 2-day tours with an overnight at **Hotel Rosario del Lago** and the option to include Isla de la Luna.

Copacabana

The town is filled with agencies, all offering trips to floating islands on imitation reed vessels, and tours to Isla del Sol (see Transport, below). Kayak and pedal-boat rentals on the beach, US$3 per hr.

La Paz to Copacabana: Huatajata

Bus La Paz–Huatajata, US$1, frequent minibuses from Bustillos y Kollasuyo, Cementerio district, daily 0400-1800, continuing to **Tiquina**. Also from Terminal del Altiplano, El Alto.

Copacabana

If arriving in Bolivia at Copacabana and going to La Paz, it is best to arrive in the city before dark.

Bus To/from **La Paz**, US$3 plus US$0.30 for Tiquina crossing, 4 hrs (expect delays due to road construction and a shorter trip once it is completed), throughout the day from Plaza Sucre with **Manco Kapac** and **2 de Febrero**; also **6 de Junio** vans, US$3.60. In La Paz at Plaza Tomás Katari, near entrance to cemetery (see La Paz Transport). In El Alto from Terminal del Altiplano. Buy ticket in advance at weekends and on holidays. Tourist bus services are run by **Trans Titicaca** (www.titicacabolivia.com), **Vicuña Travel**, **Diana Tours** and others, daily from Plaza Sucre, 16 de Julio y 6 de Agosto, US$3.50-4.50. **Trans Titicaca** takes you to the main bus terminal, the others to Sagárnaga e Illampu in the tourist district, but they will not drop you off at your hotel. (See also Border with Peru via Copacabana, page 284.)

Isla del Sol

Boat 4 boat companies have ticket booths at the beach, by the bottom of Av 6 de Agosto; there are also agencies selling boat and bus tickets along Av 6 de Agosto. All companies depart at 0830 to **Yumani** (south end of the island, 1½ hrs) and Unión Marinos continues to **Challapampa** (north end, 2 hrs). Afternoon boats depart at 1330 and go only to Yumani. At busy times (holidays and some weekends) Unión Marinos departs for Challapampa at 0900, 1000 and 1100. Boats return from Yumani at 1100 and 1530; from Challapampa at 1330. The latter stop at floating islands off the Yampupata peninsula on the way to Copacabana. Some boats make a short stop at the Pilcocaina ruins on the return trip. A full-day return ticket including Yumani and Challapampa costs US$5; full- or half-day return ticket to Yumani only, US$3.50. Return tickets are only valid on the same day; get a one way fare if you plan to stay overnight. One way to Yumani costs US$2.90, to Challapampa US$3.60. If you wish to walk, you can be dropped off at Challapampa around 1030-1100 and picked up at Yumani at 1530 (boats leave punctually, so you

will have to walk quickly to see the ruins in the north and then hike south to Yumani and down to the pier). **Wilka** boats also run from **Challa** to Copacabana Wed, Sat, Sun at 0700, returning 1330, US$2.80 one way. From **Yampupata** to Yumani by motorboat, US$15 per boat (US$5 pp by rowing boat).

There is no public boat service to **Isla de la Luna**. A private boat Copacabana-Coati costs US$72 return; Copacabana-Yumani-Coati-Copacabana, US$86; Yumani-Coati-Yumani, US$22. To Coati from the village of Sampaya (Yampupata Penisula), US$21 for a motorboat, US$14 for a rowing boat.

Taxi Copacabana–Sampaya US$11.50 or take Yampupata transport and get out at the turn-off, 4 km before the village. **Apthapi** runs tours to **Isla de la Luna**.

Border with Peru

West side of Lake Titicaca

Bus Road paved all the way to Peru. Buses from La Paz to Guaqui and Desaguadero depart from J M Asín y P Eyzaguirre, Cementerio, from 0500, US$1.50, shared taxi US$3, 2 hrs. Also from Terminal del Altiplano in El Alto. From Desaguadero to **La Paz** buses depart 4 blocks from bridge, last vehicle 2000.

Via Copacabana

Bus Several agencies go from La Paz to **Puno**, with a stop for lunch at Copacabana, or with an open ticket for continuing to Puno later. Some companies require change of bus at Copacabana. They charge US$8 and depart La Paz around 0800 (**Titicaca Bolivia** also at 1400), pick-up from hotel. From Copacabana they continue to the Peruvian border at Kasani and on to Puno, stopping for immigration formalities and changing money (better rates in Puno). From Copacabana to Puno (US$5-7, 3 hrs), continuing to **Cuzco** (US$16-23, 12 hrs from Copacabana); **Trans Titicaca** (www.titicacabolivia.com) at 0900, 1330, 1830, **Huayruro Tours** at 1800, and other agencies at 1330, offices on Av 6 de Agosto; **Trans Titicaca** and **Huayruro Tours** do not require a transfer in Puno, other companies may. Both **Crillon Tours** (page 288) and **Transturin** (page 288) have direct luxury services to Puno without a change of bus at Copacabana. Also **Bolivia Hop**, www.boliviahop.com, hop-on, hop-off service La Paz–Copacabana–Puno–Cuzco 4 days a week. If you are not on a direct bus to **Cuzco**, you will have to change in Puno where the tour company arranges connections, which may involve a long wait, check details (US$14-22 La Paz–Cuzco). In high season, book at least a day in advance. It is always cheaper, if less convenient, to buy only the next segment of your journey directly from local bus companies and cross the border on your own. *Colectivo* taxi Copacabana (Plaza Sucre)–**Kasani** US$0.70 pp, minivan US$0.60, taxi US$2.90, 15 mins, Kasani–**Yunguyo**, where Peruvian buses start, US$0.30 pp.

East side of Lake Titicaca
Bus La Paz (Reyes Cardona 772, Cancha Tejar, Cementerio district, T02-238 2239)–**Puerto Acosta**, 5 hrs, US$4, Tue-Sun 0500. Transport past Puerto Acosta only operates on market days, Wed and Sat, and is mostly cargo trucks. Bus Puerto Acosta–La Paz at about 1500. There are frequent minivans to La Paz from **Escoma**, 25 km from Puerto Acosta; trucks from the border may take you this far.

Cordillera north of La Paz
go trekking and biking in wonderful mountain scenery

Sorata *Colour map 3, B2.*
This beautiful colonial town (population 2523, altitude 2700 m), 163 km from La Paz along a paved road, is nestled at the foot of Mount Illampu; all around it are views over steep lush valleys. The climate is milder and more humid than the altiplano. Nearby are some challenging long-distance

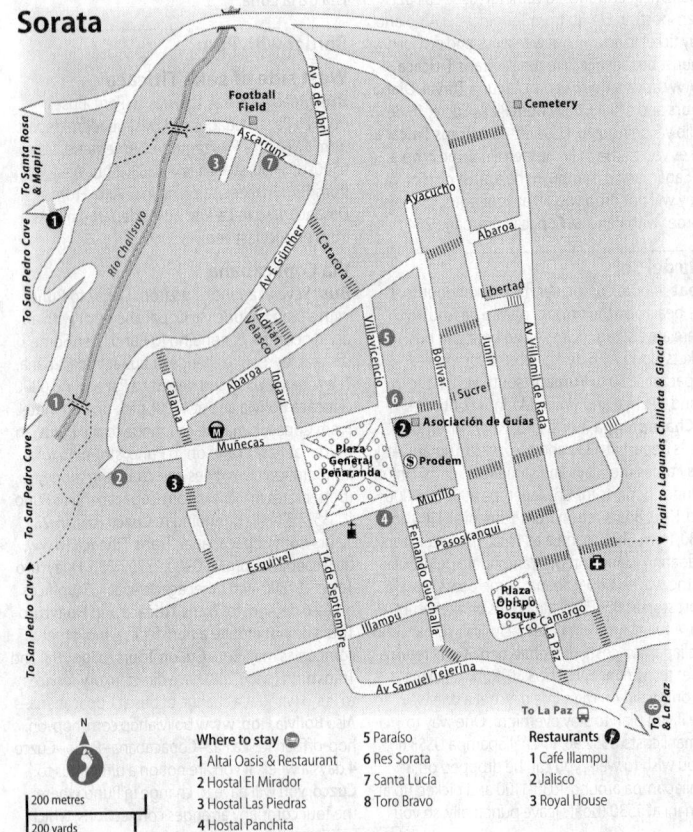

Sorata

Where to stay
1 Altai Oasis & Restaurant
2 Hostal El Mirador
3 Hostal Las Piedras
4 Hostal Panchita
5 Paraíso
6 Res Sorata
7 Santa Lucía
8 Toro Bravo

Restaurants
1 Café Illampu
2 Jalisco
3 Royal House

treks and mountain-bike adventures, as well as great day-hikes. The town has a charming plaza, with views of the snow-capped summit of Illampu on a clear day. The main fiesta is 14 September.

Tip...
There is no ATM in Sorata so take enough cash. Prodem changes US dollars and gives cash advances on Visa and Mastercard for 5% commission.

A popular excursion is to **San Pedro cave** ① *0800-1700, US$3*, beyond the village of San Pedro. The cave has an underground lake (no swimming allowed) and is lit. It is reached either by road, a 12 km walk (three hours each way), or by a path high above the Río San Cristóbal (about four hours, impassable during the rainy season and not easy at any time). Get clear directions before setting out and take sun protection, food, water, etc. Taxis and pick-ups from the plaza, 0600-2200, US$11 with a 30-minute wait. The **Mirador del Iminapi** (above the community of Laripata) offers excellent views of town and the Larecaja tropical valleys. It is a nice day-walk or take a taxi, 20 minutes, US$11 return.

Trekking and climbing from Sorata

Sorata is the starting point for climbing **Illampu** and **Ancohuma**. All routes out of the town are difficult, owing to the number of paths and the very steep ascent. Experience and full equipment are necessary. You can hire trekking guides and mules (see What to do, page 292). The three- to four-day trek to **Lagunas Chillata and Glaciar** is the most common and gets busy during high season. Laguna Chillata can also be reached by road or on a long day-hike with light gear, but mind the difficult navigation and take warm clothing. Laguna Chillata has been heavily impacted by tourism (remove all trash, do not throw it in the pits around the lake) and groups frequently camp there. The ☆**Illampu Circuit**, a six- to seven-day high-altitude trek (three passes over 4000 m, one over 5000 m) around Illampu, is excellent. It can get very cold and it is a hard walk, though very beautiful with nice campsites. Some food can be bought in Cocoyo on the third day. You must be acclimatized before setting out. Another option is the **Trans-Cordillera Trek**, 10-12 days from Sorata to Huayna Potosí, or longer, all the way to Illimani at the opposite (south) end of the Cordillera Real. Some communities charge visitors fees along the way.

☆Cordillera Apolobamba

The Area Protegida Apolobamba forms part of the Cordillera Apolobamba, the north extension of the Cordillera Real. The range itself has many 5000-m-plus peaks, while the conservation area of some 560,000 ha protects herds of vicuña, huge flocks of flamingos and many condors. The area adjoins the Parque Nacional Madidi (see page 372).

This is great trekking country and the four- to six-day **Charazani to Pelechuco** (or vice versa) mountain trek is one of the best in the country (see Footprint's *Bolivia Handbook* for details). It passes traditional villages and the peaks of the southern Cordillera Apolobamba.

Charazani is the biggest village in the region (3200 m), with hot springs (US$0.75). Its three-day fiesta is around 16 July. There are some cheap *alojamientos*, restaurants and shops. **Pelechuco** (3600 m) is a smaller village, also with cheap *alojamientos*, cafés and shops. The road to Pelechuco goes through the Area Protegida, passing the community of Ulla Ulla, 5 km outside of which are the reserve's HQ at La Cabaña. Visitors are welcome to see the orphaned vicuñas. There are economical community hostels at the villages of Lagunillas and Agua Blanca. Basic food is available in the communities. For information, contact SERNAP ① *www.sernap.gob.bo*.

Listings Cordillera north of La Paz *map page 290.*

Where to stay

Sorata

$$ Altai Oasis
T02-213 3895, www.altaioasis.com.
At the bottom of the valley in a beautiful setting, a 15-min steep downhill walk from town, or

taxi US$2. Cabins, rooms with bath (cheaper with shared bath), 3-bed dorms (US$12 pp) and camping (US$4.30 pp). Very good restaurant (**$$**) uses organic vegetables from own garden, bar with fireplace, kitchen facilities, lovely grounds, pool, peaceful, very welcoming, family-run by the Resnikowskis, English and German spoken. Warmly recommended.

$ Hostal El Mirador
Muñecas 400, T7350 5453, on Facebook.
Cheaper with shared bath, hot water, kitchen,
laundry facilities, terrace.

$ Hostal Las Piedras
Just off Ascarrunz, T7191 6341,
http://sorata-laspiedras.com.
Rooms with and without bath, good mattresses,
electric shower, very nice, good breakfast and
meals with home-made products available, very
helpful. Recommended.

$ Hostal Panchita
On plaza, T7192 0879, on Facebook.
Simple rooms, newer ones with private bath,
cheaper with shared bath, electric shower, sunny
courtyard, kitchen and washing facilities, does
not include breakfast, good value.

$ Paraíso
Villavicencio 117, ½block from plaza, T7127 7057.
With electric shower, basic rooms, terrace,
breakfast available.

$ Residencial Sorata
On plaza, T02-213 6672.
Cheaper without bath, electric shower,
restaurant, large but scruffy grounds, poor beds,
a bit run-down overall but still adequate.

$ Santa Lucía
Ascarrunz, T02-213 6686.
Rooms are cheaper with shared bath, electric
shower, carpeted rooms, patio, does not include
breakfast, not always open.

$ Toro Bravo
Below petrol station at entrance to town,
T7725 5255.
With electric shower, ample grounds and rooms
(upstairs rooms are better), small pool, restaurant,
a bit faded but good value.

Restaurants

Sorata
There are several **$$-$** Italian places on the plaza,
all quite similar.

$$-$ Jalisco
On plaza.
Mexican and Italian dishes, sidewalk seating.

$ Royal House
Off Muñecas by the market.
Decent set lunch, friendly.

Café Illampu
15 mins' walk on the way to San Pedro cave.
Closed Tue and Dec-Mar.
Excellent breakfast, sandwiches, bread and
cakes. Camping possible, also offers tours
with own 4WD vehicle. Swiss-run, English
and German spoken.

Festivals

Sorata
**14 Sep Fiesta Patronal del Señor de la
Columna**, is the main festival.

What to do

Sorata

Guides for trekking
It may be cheaper to go to Sorata and arrange
trekking there than to book a trek with an agency
in La Paz. Buy necessary foods and supplies in
La Paz, Sorata shops have basic items.
Asociación de Guías, *Sucre 302 y Guachalla,
leave message at Residencial Sorata (T02-213 6672).*
Hires guides, porters and mules. Prices vary:
guides approximately US$30 per day, mules
US$15 per day. Porters take maximum 2 mules,
remember you have to feed your guide/porter.
Eduardo Chura, *T7157 8671, guiasorata@yahoo.
com.* Is an independent local trekking guide.

Mountain biking
Sorata is an increasingly popular destination for
mountain biking, especially for long-distance
routes from the mountains and gold-mining
communities above Sorata, down to the
town of Consata and then on to Mapiri in the
lowlands. From Mapiri the route continues
by jeep or boat to Guanay, from where you
can return to La Paz, or carry on by boat to
Rurrenabaque. See **Gravity**, page 276, for a
company offering this adventure.

Transport

Sorata
Bus Minibuses throughout the day 0400-1800
from **La Paz** with **Trans Unificada** (C Manuel
Bustillos 683 y Av Kollasuyo in the Cementerio
district, T02-238 1693); also **Perla del Illampu**
(Manuel Bustillos 615, T02-238 0548), US$2.50,
3½ hrs. Booking recommended on Fri. You can
also board at Terminal del Altiplano in El Alto. In
Sorata they leave from C Samuel Tejerina, near
the exit to La Paz. To or from **Copacabana** and

Peru, change buses at Huarina but they are often full so start early and be prepared for a long wait.

Jeep, boat and motorcycle Jeeps run from La Paz (C Chorolque y Tarapacá, T02-245 0296, often full), via Sorata to **Santa Rosa** (US$15, 13 hrs), on the road to **Mapiri** and **Guanay**, a rough route with interesting vegetation and stunning scenery. Onward transport can be found in Santa Rosa. From Guanay private boats may be arranged to **Rurrenabaque**, and vehicles run to Caranavi and thence to Coroico. Sorata–Coroico by this route is excellent for off-road motorcycling. (See also Mountain biking, above.)

If travelling by public transport it is easier to go La Paz–Coroico–Caranavi–Guanay–Santa Rosa–Sorata–La Paz, than vice versa.

Cordillera Apolobamba

Charazani

Bus From C Reyes Cardona 732, off Av Kollasuyo, Cemetery district, **La Paz**, daily with **Trans Altiplano**, 0600-0630, 7 hrs, US$3.50, very crowded. Return to La Paz at 1800; also has 0900 on Sat and 1200 Mon and Fri.

Pelechuco

Bus From **La Paz Trans Provincias del Norte** leaves daily 0600-0700 from Ex Tranca de Río Seco in El Alto, passing through Qutapampa, Ulla Ulla and Agua Blanca to Pelechuco, 10-12 hrs, US$5, sometimes on sale 24 hrs before departure at the booking office in C Reyes Cardona. Return to La Paz between 0300 and 0400 most days.

The Yungas

a 3500-m drop to the green subtropical forest in 70 km

☆Only a few hours from La Paz are the subtropical valleys known as the Yungas. These steep, forested slopes, squeezed in between the Cordillera and the Amazon Lowlands, provide a welcome escape from the chill of the capital. They have become a centre for adrenaline sports including mountain biking, zip-lines, rappelling, a via ferrata, paragliding and more. The warm climate of the Yungas is also ideal for growing citrus fruit, bananas, coffee and especially coca.

La Paz to the Yungas

The roads from La Paz to Nor- and Sud-Yungas go via **La Cumbre**, a pass at 4725 m about one hour northeast of the city. The road out of La Paz circles cloudwards over La Cumbre; all around are towering snow-capped peaks. The first village after the pass is **Unduavi**, where there is a checkpoint, a petrol station and roadside stalls. Beyond Unduavi a road (being paved in 2017, with temporary closures until completion) branches right 75 km to Chulumani and the Sud-Yungas (see below). Beyond Sud-Yungas, to the southeast, are the **Yungas de Inquisivi**, see Quime, page 297. The main road continues to Cotapata, where it again divides: right is the old unpaved road to Yolosa, the junction 8 km from Coroico (this is the popular cycling route). To the left, the main paved road goes via Chuspipata and Puente Yolosita, where a paved side road climbs steeply to Coroico. Between Yolosita and Yolosa (see below) is **Senda Verde** ① *T7472 2825, www.sendaverde.com, open 1000-1700, 1-hr tours at 1000, 1100, 1200 and 1500, US$14.50,* an animal refuge, ecolodge ($$) and restaurant with opportunities for volunteering. In addition, from Puente Villa on the Unduavi–Chulumani road, an unpaved road runs to Coripata and Coroico. For the La Cumbre–Coroico hike (Choro), see page 266.

☆All roads to Coroico drop some 3500 m to the green subtropical forest in 70 km. The best views are in May to June, when there is less chance of fog and rain. The old road, the so-called '**World's Most Dangerous Road**', is steep, twisting, clinging to the side of sheer cliffs. It is a breathtaking descent (best not to look over the edge if you don't like heights) and its reputation for danger is more than matched by the beauty of the scenery. It passes through **Parque Cotapata** ① *www.sernap.gob. bo,* and there is a community tax of US$3.55 to enter. Many tourists go on a mountain-bike tour: it is your responsibility to choose top-quality bikes (with hydraulic disc brakes) and a reputable company which offers bilingual guides, helmet, gloves, vehicle support throughout the day (see La Paz, Tour operators, page 275). Many bike companies take riders back to La Paz the same day, but Coroico is worth more of your time. In **Yolosa**, at the end of the bike ride, is a three-segment zip-line (total 1555 m) operated by **Gravity Bolivia** (see page 276 and www.ziplinebolivia.com; T02-231 3849 or book through La Paz agencies).

> **Tip...**
> The road is especially dangerous when it is raining (mid-December to mid-February).

★ Coroico Colour map 3, B2.

The little town of Coroico (population 2903, altitude 1750 m), capital of the Nor-Yungas region, is perched on a hill amid beautiful scenery. The hillside is covered with orange and banana groves and coffee plantations. Coroico is a first-class place to relax with several good walks. A colourful four-day festival is held 19-22 October. On 2 November, All Souls' Day, the cemetery is festooned with black ribbons.

A good walk is up to the waterfalls, starting from **El Calvario**. Follow the stations of the cross by the cemetery, off Calle Julio Zuazo Cuenca, which leads steeply uphill from the plaza. Facing the chapel at El Calvario, with your back to the town, look for the path on your left. This leads to the falls which are the town's water supply (Toma de Agua) and, beyond, to two more falls. **Cerro Uchumachi**, the mountain behind El Calvario, can be climbed following the same stations of the cross, but then look for the faded red and white antenna behind the chapel. From there it's about two hours' steep walk to the top (take water). A third walk goes to the pools in the **Río Vagante**, 7 km off the road to Coripata; it takes about three hours. With the Yungas so close to La Paz, you get the chance to see the production of crops which cannot be grown at high altitude and some farms welcome visitors to their fruit, coffee or coca leaf plantations. In the interests of personal safety, women in particular should not hike alone in this area. There are two ATMs on the plaza and the hospital is the best in the Yungas.

Caranavi Colour map 3, B2.

From the junction at Puente Yolosita, the paved road (under construction in 2017, see Transport, below) follows the river 11 km to Santa Bárbara, then 23 km to Puente San Pedro, access to La Encantada Reserve ① www. ecoparquelaencantada.com, with a system of trails to waterfalls, cabins ($$) and camping. A further 42 km ahead is Caranavi (population 21,883, altitude 600 m), an uninspiring town 156 km from La Paz. Market days are Friday and Saturday. There is a range of hotels and alojamientos and buses from La Paz (Villa Fátima) to Rurrenabaque pass through. From Caranavi an unpaved road continues, at times following a picturesque gorge, 70 km to **Guanay** at the junction of the Tipuani and Mapiri rivers (see also under Sorata, Mountain biking, page 292), where the road divides, one branch goes north to Apolo and the second towards the settled area of the Alto Beni and beyond to Yucumo in the Department of Beni. Here it divides again, one branch goes northeast to San Borja, San Ignacio de Moxos and Trinidad (pages 376), the second branch goes northwest to Rurrenabaque (page 371), then north to Santa Rosa and El Triángulo. Here it divides once again, northeast to Riberalta (page 378) and northwest to Cobija (page 378).

Sud-Yungas

The capital of Sud-Yungas is **Chulumani**, a small town (population 3650), 124 km from La Paz, with beautiful views. There are many birds in the area and good hiking. The Fiesta de San Bartolomé (24 August) lasts 10 days and there is a lively market every weekend. There is no ATM in Chulumani, take cash. **Irupana**, a friendly little colonial village (altitude 1900 m, irupana.bolivia on Facebook), is 31 km east of Chulumani (minibus or shared taxi US$2) and has a lovely location, delightful climate, more good walking and birdwatching, and a couple of very nice places to stay.

Listings The Yungas

Tourist information

Coroico
A good independent website is www.coroico. info. **Gobernación** (corner of the main plaza).

Chulumani

Tourist office
In the main plaza. Open irregular hours, mostly weekends.

Where to stay

Coroico
Hotel rooms are hard to find at holiday weekends and prices are higher.

$$$-$$ El Viejo Molino
1 km on road to Santa Bárbara, T02-243 0020, www.hotelviejomolino.com.
Upmarket hotel and spa, offers massage, pool, gym, games room, rafting and other tours, restaurant with set menu lunch and dinner.

$$$-$$ Gloria
C Kennedy 1, T02-289 5554,
www.hotelgloria.com.bo.
Traditional resort hotel, full board, pool,
restaurant with set lunches and à la carte,
internet, transport from plaza at extra charge.

$$ Esmeralda
On the edge of town, C Julio Suazo 10 mins uphill
from plaza (see website for transport), T02-213
6017, www.hotelesmeraldacoroico.com.
Most rooms include breakfast, cheaper in dorms,
prices rise at weekends, hot showers, satellite TV
and DVD, book exchange, good buffet restaurant,
sauna, garden, pool, camping, can arrange local
tours and transport to/from La Paz, free pick-up
from Coroico bus stop or Plaza.

$$ Sol y Luna
Carretera Apanto Alto, 15-20 mins beyond Hotel
Esmeralda, T7156 1626, www.solyluna-bolivia.com.
Excellent accommodation in fully equipped
cabins, apartments and rooms with and without
bath, splendid views, restaurant (vegetarian
specialities), camping US$6.50 pp (not suitable
for cars), garden, pool, hot tub US$13, shiatsu
massage and yoga available, good value, Sigrid
(owner) speaks English, French, German, Spanish.

$$-$ Bella Vista
C Héroes del Chaco 7 (2 blocks from main plaza),
T02-213 6059.
Beautiful rooms and views, includes breakfast,
cheaper without bath, racquetball court, terrace,
bike hire, restaurant.

$$-$ Hostal Kory
At top of steps leading down from the plaza,
T02-243 1234/7156 4050, info@hostalkory.com.
Rooms with and without bath, electric showers,
restaurant, huge pool, terrace, good value but
basic, helpful.

$ Don Quijote
500 m out of town, on road to Coripata,
T02-213 6007.
Economical, electric shower, pool, quiet,
nice views.

$ El Cafetal
Miranda, next to the hospital, a 10-min walk from
town, T7193 3979.
Rooms with and without bath, very nice, great
views, pool, restaurant with excellent French/Indian/
vegetarian cuisine, French-run, a good choice.

$ Los Tunqui Eye
Iturralde 4043, T7350 0081.

Simple rooms with and without bath, hot water,
good value.

$ Matsu
1 km from town on road to El Calvario
(call for free pick-up, taxi US$2), T7069 2219,
ecolodgematsu@hotmail.com.
Economical, has restaurant, pool, views,
quiet, helpful.

$ Residencial de la Torre
Julio Zuazo Cuenca, ½ block from plaza,
T02-289 5542.
Welcoming place with courtyard, cheap sparse
rooms, no alcoholic drinks allowed.

Sud-Yungas

Chulumani
Chulumani suffers from water shortages, check if
your hotel has a reserve tank.

$$ Monarca
Av Circunvalación, T772 6 6353.
Good hotel, largest in the area, with pool,
gardens, restaurant, parking.

$$ San Bartolomé
T02-244 1111, plaza@plazabolivia.com.bo.
Comfortable rooms and cabins in a rural setting,
pool, sports field, games room, mini-golf,
restaurant and bar.

$ Country House
400 m out of town on road to cemetery,
T7528 2212, La Paz T02-274 5584,
countryhouse.chulumani on Facebook.
Rooms with hot water, lovely tranquil setting,
pool and gardens, library, video room, restaurant,
bar, family-run. Enthusiastic owner Xavier Sarabia
is hospitable and offers hiking advice and tours,
English spoken.

$ Tarapari
On the outskirts, 10 mins' walk from centre,
T7651 5088.
Guesthouse in a biodiversity garden, butterfly
sanctuary and organic coffee farm, 3 rooms,
shared bath, price is per person, breakfast
included, use of kitchen extra, also tours,
workshops and treks. Base of **La Paz on Foot**'s
Sud Yungas tours (see www.lapazonfoot.com
and page 276).

Irupana

$ Nirvana Inn
Uphill at the edge of town past the football field,
T02-213 6154.

Comfortable cabins on beautiful grounds with great views, pool, sauna, parking, flower and orchid gardens lovingly tended by the owners. Includes breakfast, other meals on request.

Restaurants

Coroico

$$ Bamboos
Iturralde y Ortiz.
Good Mexican food and pleasant atmosphere, live music some nights with cover charge. Happy hour 1800-1900.

$$-$ Carla's Garden Pub and Pastelería Alemana Back-stube
Pasaje Adalid Linares, 50 m from the main plaza, T7207 5620. Wed-Sun 1200-2230.
Sandwiches, snacks, pasta and international food, vegetarian options, German dishes, coffee, groups catered for at weekends. Lots of music, live music at weekends. Garden, hammocks, games, book exchange, terrace with panoramic views, nice atmosphere, tourist information.

$ Pizzería Italia
2 with same name on the plaza. Daily 1000-2300.
Pizza, pasta, snacks.

Chulumani

There are a couple of other places around the plaza, all closed Mon. Basic eateries up the hill by bus stops.

$ La Cabaña Yungeña
C Sucre 2 blocks below plaza. Tue-Sun.
Simple set lunch and dinner.

What to do

Coroico

Coffee production

Café Munaipata, *Camino a Carmen Pampa Km 4, T7204 2824, www.cafemunaipata.com.*
Visits to a finca producing high-altitude coffee. Recommended. They also have an outlet in the San Pedro district of La Paz, T02-249 0356.

Cycling

CXC, *T7157 3015, cxc_mtb@yahoo.com.* Contact 2 days in advance by phone or email. Good bikes, US$25 for 6 hrs including packed lunch, a bit disorganized but good fun and helpful, English and German spoken.

Horse riding

El Relincho, *Don Reynaldo, 100 m past Hotel Esmeralda (enquire here).* Rides from 2 hrs to 2 days; average price US$30 for 4 hrs.

Language classes

Siria León Domínguez, *T7195 5431.* US$6.50 per hr, also rents rooms, makes silver jewellery and gives language classes in Coroico and La Paz, excellent English.

Transport

Coroico

Bus From La Paz all companies are at Minasa terminal, Puente Minasa, in Villa Fátima: minibuses and buses (less often) leave throughout the day US$3-4.50, 2½ hrs on the paved road: **Turbus Totaí**, **Palmeras**, **Yungueña** and several others. Services return to La Paz from the small terminal down the hill in Coroico, across from the football field. All are heavily booked at weekends and on holidays.

To **Rurrenabaque**: take a pick-up from the small mirador at Pacheco y Sagárnaga that go to **Puente Yolosita**, 15 mins, US$0.70. Here you can try to catch a bus, but they are usually full. Ask at **Turbus Totaí** or others in the Coroico terminal if you can reserve a seat to Rurre (US$9). There are also *trufis* (US$3.25) and trucks from Yolosita to **Caranavi**, where La Paz–Rurre buses pass through in the evening, often full. Note that in 2017 the Yolosita-Caranavi road was closed for construction Mon-Sat 0700-1700. After Caranavi the road goes to Sapecho and then Yucumo, from where *trufis* go to Rurre. Caranavi–Rurre 12 hrs minimum, US$7, **Flota Yungueña**, at 1800-1900, **Turbus Totaí** 2100-2200, and others. See also **Gravity** and **Deep Rainforest**, La Paz (page 276). For Guanay to **Sorata** via **Mapiri** and **Santa Rosa**, see page 293.

Sud-Yungas

Bus From **La Paz** to Chulumani, several companies from Virgen del Carmen y San Borja, Villa Fátima, leave when full, US$4, 4 hrs: eg **San Cristóbal** and **24 de Agosto**, both also go to Irupana. In Chulumani most buses leave from the top of the hill by the petrol station; minibuses and taxis to local villages from plaza.

Southwest
Bolivia

The mining town of Oruro, shimmering salt flats, coloured lakes and surrealistic rock formations combine to make this one of the most fascinating regions of Bolivia. Add some of the country's most celebrated festivals and the last hideout of Butch Cassidy and the Sundance Kid and you have the elements for some great and varied adventures. The journey across the altiplano from Uyuni to San Pedro de Atacama is a popular route to Chile and there are other routes south to Argentina.

Oruro and around   *Colour map 3, B3. See map, page 299.*

dancing devils and old tin mines

★Oruro (population 264,943) is the gateway to the altiplano of southwest Bolivia. It's a somewhat drab, dirty, functional place, the commercial centre for the mining communities of the altiplano. Once a year, it explodes into life with its famous carnival, symbolized by La Diablada (see box, page 257). To the west is the national park encompassing Bolivia's highest peak, Sajama.

Sights

The Plaza 10 de Febrero and surroundings are well maintained and several buildings in the centre hint at the city's former importance. The **Museo Sacro, Folklórico, Arqueológico y Minero** ① *inside the Church of the Virgen del Socavón, T02-525 0616, entry via the church daily 0900-1145, 1500-1800, US$1.50, guided tours every 45 mins*, contains religious art, clothing and jewellery and, after passing through old mining tunnels and displays of mining techniques, a representation of El Tío (the god of the underworld). **Museo Antropológico Eduardo López Rivas** ① *south of centre on Av España y Urquidi, T02-527 4020, daily 0800-1200, 1400-1800, US$0.75, guide mandatory, getting there: take micro A heading south or any trufi going south*. It has a unique collection of stone llama heads as well as impressive carnival masks.

Quime

North of Oruro, 2½ hours by bus (233 km, four hours south of La Paz) is the junction at Konani, where there are a few simple places to stay and eat. From here a beautiful road, mostly paved, runs over the altiplano to the **Tres Cruces pass** (over 5000 m) before dropping a spectacular 2000 m to Quime (founded 1887, population 3000), a town in the Yungas de Inquisivi at the southern edge of the Cordillera Quimsa Cruz. It can also be reached along scenic secondary roads from Chulumani in Sud-Yungas and Cochabamba. It's an increasingly popular escape from La Paz, to relax or hike in the *cordillera*. Excursions include to Aymara mining communities and waterfalls and mountain-biking trips, including a downhill from Tres Cruces. The main festival is 24-25 July (Apóstol Santiago). There are basic services, internet in the Biblioteca Municipal (open Sunday-Thursday) in the Alcaldía at the Plaza, but no ATMs.

Essential Southwest Bolivia

Getting around

The only airport serving the region is at Uyuni, with expensive flights to/from La Paz. The area can also be reached along roads from Potosí and Tarija, both of which have airports. Tupiza is reached from Potosí, Tarija or Argentina. The road from La Paz to Oruro is a dual carriageway, which has paved connections to Cochabamba and Chile and from Oruro to Potosí From Oruro to Sucre via Ravelo is being paved. From Potosí and Oruro to Uyuni there are good paved roads. With better roads, bus service is also improving but the train remains a viable alternative.

When to go

The altiplano can be bitterly cold at night, especially in the drier months of May to September. Sunny days can be dazzling and warm and protection against the sun is essential. The rainy season is November to March, when travel can be disrupted. The high season is June to August, but in the wet season there is a popular market for rapid tours to see the Salar de Uyuni as a mirror, in and out in a day.

Time required

Except at carnival time, Oruro itself merits a day or so, but once you head south into the *salares*, the minimum you should spend is four days. Most tours of the Salar de Uyuni area are this long, but you can easily extend this for further exploration. If you continue to Tupiza or start there, add another two or three days, but bear in mind the time required for transport into and out of the region.

☆Parque Nacional Sajama

Park HQ in Sajama village, T02-513 5526 (in Oruro, Potosí 5238 entre 1 de Noviembre y León, in La Paz T02-242 6268, or 252 8080), also see www.biobol.org. US$4.25 payable to community of Sajama.

A one-day drive to the west of Oruro, Parque Nacional Sajama was established in 1939. Covering 100,230 ha, it contains the world's highest forest, consisting mainly of the rare queñual tree (*Polylepis tarapacana*) which grows up to an altitude of 5500 m. The scenery is wonderful with views of several volcanoes, including Sajama – Bolivia's highest peak at 6542 m – Parinacota and Pomerape (jointly called Payachatas). The road is paved and leads across the border into the Parque Nacional Lauca in Chile. You can trek in the park, with or without porters and mules, but once you move away from the Río Sajama or its major tributaries, lack of water is a problem. There is basic accommodation in Sajama village (see below) as well as a more comfortable and expensive option at **Tomarapi** on the north side of the mountain; see page 301.

Sajama village In Sajama village (population 500, altitude 4200 m), visitors are billeted in basic family-run *alojamientos* on a rotating basis (about US$4.50 per person). All are basic to very basic, especially the sanitary facilities; no showers or electricity, solar power for lighting only. *Alojamientos* may provide limited food, or take your own supplies. It can be very windy and cold at night; a good sleeping bag, gloves and hat are essential. Crampons, ice axe and rope are needed for climbing the volcanoes and can be hired in the village. Maps are hard to find. Local guides charge US$50-70 per day. Pack animals can be hired for US$10 per day including guide. Good bathing is available at the Manasaya thermal complex, 6 km northwest of the village (entry US$4.25). Many villagers sell alpaca woollen items.

By road to Chile

The shortest and most widely used route from La Paz to Chile is the road to **Arica** via the border at **Tambo Quemado** (Bolivia) and **Chungará** (Chile). From La Paz take the highway south towards Oruro. Immediately before Patacamaya (see above), turn right at a green road sign to Puerto Japonés on the Río Desaguadero, then on to Tambo Quemado.

Bolivian **customs and immigration** are at Tambo Quemado, where there are a couple of very basic places to stay and eat. Border control is open daily 0800-2000. Shops change bolivianos

> **Tip...**
> Take extra petrol (none available after Chilean border until Arica), food and water.

Chilean pesos and US dollars. From Tambo Quemado there is a stretch of about 7 km of 'no-man's land' before you reach the Chilean frontier at Chungará. Here the border crossing, which is set against the most spectacular scenic backdrop of Lago Chungará and Volcán Parinacota, is thorough but efficient; open 0800-2000. Expect a long wait at weekends and any day behind lines of lorries. Drivers must fill in 'Relaciones de Pasajeros', US$0.25 from a kiosk at border, giving details of driver, vehicle and passengers. Do not take any livestock, plants, fruit, vegetables, coca or dairy products into Chile.

An alternative crossing from Oruro: several bus companies travel southwest to Iquique, via the border posts of **Pisiga** (Bolivia) and **Colchane** (Chile). The road is paved from Oruro to Toledo (32 km) and from Opoquari to Pisiga via Huachachalla (about 100 km). The rest of the 170-km road in Bolivia

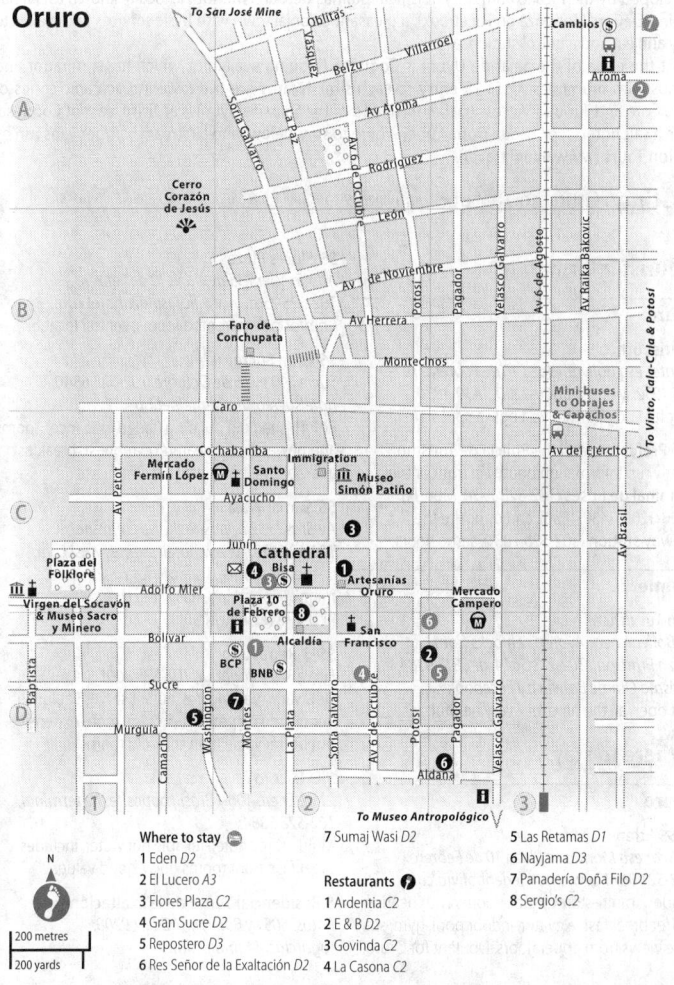

Oruro

To San José Mine
Oblitas
Vásquez
Belzu
Villarroel
Cambios
Aroma
Sofía Galvarro
La Paz
Av de Octubre
Av Aroma
Rodriguez
Cerro
Corazón
de Jesús
León
Av Raúl de Noviembre
Potosí
Pagador
Velasco Galvarro
Av 6 de Agosto
Av Raúk Bakovic
To Vinto, Cala-Cala & Potosí
Faro de
Conchupata
Av Herrera
Montecinos
Caro
Mini-buses
to Obrajes
& Capachos
Av del Ejército
Cochabamba
Immigration
Mercado
Fermín López
Santo
Domingo
Museo
Simón Patiño
Ayacucho
Junín
Cathedral
Plaza del
Folklore
Bisa
Artesanías
Oruro
Virgen del Socavón
& Museo Sacro
y Minero
Adolfo Mier
Plaza 10
de Febrero
Mercado
Campero
Bolívar
Alcaldía
San
Francisco
BCP
BNB
Sucre
Murguía
Baptista
Camacho
Washington
Montes
La Plata
Sofía Galvarro
Av 6 de Octubre
Potosí
Pagador
Velasco Galvarro
Aldana
To Museo Antropológico
To Brasil

N
200 metres
200 yards

Where to stay
1 Eden D2
2 El Lucero A3
3 Flores Plaza C2
4 Gran Sucre D2
5 Repostero D3
6 Res Señor de la Exaltación D2
7 Sumaj Wasi D2

Restaurants
1 Ardentia C2
2 E & B D2
3 Govinda C2
4 La Casona C2
5 Las Retamas D1
6 Nayjama D3
7 Panadería Doña Filo D2
8 Sergio's C2

is due to be paved; on the Chilean side it's paved all the way to Iquique, 250 km. There is also service from Oruro to Arica via Patacamaya and Tambo Quemado.

South of Oruro

Salar de Coipasa and around   Reached via the Oruro–Pisiga–Iquique road (turn off at **Sabaya**), is the **Salar de Coipasa**, 225 km from Oruro. It is smaller and less visited than the Salar de Uyuni, and has a turquoise lake in the middle of the salt pan surrounded by mountains with gorgeous views and large cacti.

Coipasa is northwest of the Salar de Uyuni and travel from one to the other is possible with a private vehicle along the impressive **Ruta Intersalar**. Along the way are tombs, terracing and ancient irrigation canals at the archaeological site of **Alcaya** ① *US$1.25*, gradually being developed by the local community. It is near **Salinas de Garci Mendoza**, locally known as Salinas (SalinasDeGarciMendoza on Facebook), a pleasant colonial town with basic services and places to stay and eat and a petrol station.

At the edge of the Salar de Uyuni is **Coquesa** (lodging available), which has a mirador and tombs with mummies (US$1.25 entry to each site). Nearby are the towering volcanic cones of Cora Cora and Tunupa. Access to the north end of the Salar de Uyuni is at **Jirira**, east of Coquesa, with a salt hotel (see **Posada Doña Lupe**, Where to stay, below) and airstream camper vans run by **Crillon Tours** (www.uyuni.travel).

Listings Oruro and around *map page 299.*

Tourist information

Oruro

Tourist office
Montes esq Bolívar, Plaza 10 de Febrero, T02-525 1932. Mon-Fri 0800-1200, 1430-1830.
Helpful and informative, English spoken.

The **Prefectura** and the **Policía de Turismo** jointly run information booths in front of the **Terminal de Buses** (T02-528 7774, Mon-Fri 0800-1200, 1430-1830); and opposite the **railway station** (T02-525 7881), same hours.

Quime

Info Tur office
Av Bolívar, near Avaroa, 2 blocks from Plaza Principal, T02-213 5644, or 6813 0384, Turismo Quime Bolivia on Facebook.
Not open all the time, but very helpful.

Where to stay

Oruro

$$$$ Eden
Bolívar esq Montes at Plaza 10 de Febrero, T02-521 0671, www.hoteledenbolivia.com.
Modern multi-storey hotel. Rooms with heating, buffet breakfast, elevator, indoor pool, gym, spa, nice views from upper floors. Opulent for Oruro.

$$ Flores Plaza
Adolfo Mier 735 at Plaza 10 de Febrero, T02-525 2561, www.floresplazahotel.com.
Comfortable carpeted rooms, central location.

$$ Gran Sucre
Sucre 510 esq 6 de Octubre, T02-527 6800, hotelsucreoruro@entelnet.bo.
Refurbished old building (faded elegance), rooms and newer suites, heaters on request, breakfast available, helpful staff.

$$ Sumaj Wasi
Av Brasil 232 opposite the bus terminal, T02-527 6737, www.hotelessamaywasi.com.
Carpeted rooms, discount for IYHF members, parking, has a 2nd branch in Uyuni (Av Potosí 965).

$$-$ Repostero
Sucre 370 y Pagador, T02-525 8001.
Hot water, parking, restaurant serves set lunch. Renovated carpeted rooms are more expensive but better value than their old rooms.

$ El Lucero
21 de Enero 106 y Brasil, opposite the terminal, T02-528 5884.
Multi-storey hotel, reliable hot water, includes breakfast, front rooms noisy, good value.

$ Residencial Señor de la Exaltación
Potosí 6051 y Bolívar, T02-527 9200, rogarciach@gmail.com.

Simple family run place, modest rooms with private bath, cheaper with shared bath, friendly owner, good economy option.

Quime

There are various other basic, slightly cheaper *alojamientos* in town (eg of the Helguero family, in an old house, nice, clean; also Santiago).

$ Hostal Rancho Colibrí
4 steep blocks uphill from main plaza (ask directions or see website, it's not easy to spot), T6976 4476, http://ranchocolibri.wordpress.com.
8 simple rooms with shared bath, meals available, fully equipped kitchen, most guests do their own cooking.

$ Quime
Close to Plaza Principal, T02-213 3342.
Big, basic place. Rooms with private bath, cheaper with shared bath, electric shower, could be cleaner but adequate.

Parque Nacional Sajama

$$ Tomarapi Ecolodge
North of Sajama in Tomarapi community, near Caripe, ecotomarapi@yahoo.es (see tomarapi on Facebook), represented by Millenarian Tourism & Travel, Av Sánchez Lima 2193, La Paz, T02-241 4753, www.boliviamilenaria.com.
Including full board (good food) and guiding service with climbing shelter at 4900 m, helpful staff, simple but comfortable, with hot water, heating.

South of Oruro

$ Alojamiento Paraíso
Sabaya.
Take a sleeping bag, shared bath, cold water, meals on request or take own food. Sells petrol.

$ Doña Wadi
Salinas de Garci Mendoza, C Germán Busch, near main plaza, T02-513 8015.
Shared bath, hot water, basic but clean, meals available.

$ Posada Doña Lupe
Jirira.
Partly made of salt, hot water, cheaper without bath, use of kitchen but bring your own food, no meals available, caters to tour groups, pleasant, comfortable.

$ Zuk'arani
On a hillside overlooking Salinas de Garci Mendoza and the salar, T02-513 7086, zukarani@hotmail.com.
2 cabins for 4, with bath, hot water, cheaper with shared bath, hot water, meals on request.

Restaurants

Oruro

$$ E & B
Potosí 6135 y Bolívar, T02-525 7042. Mon-Sat 1200-1400, 1800-2300, Sun 1200-1400.
Good set meals at lunchtime, local and international dishes *à la carte* at night, generous portions, pleasant atmosphere.

$$ Nayjama
Aldana 1880.
Good regional specialities, very popular for lunch, huge portions.

$$-$ Las Retamas
Murguía 930 esq Washington. Mon-Sat 0930-2330, Sun 0930-1430.
Excellent quality and value for set lunches ($), Bolivian and international dishes à la carte, very good pastries at **Kuchen Haus**, pleasant atmosphere, attentive service, a bit out of the way but well worth the trip. Recommended.

$ Ardentia
Sorria Galvarro y Junín. Open 1900-2200.
Home cooking, tasty pasta and meat dishes.

$ Govinda
Junín 533 entre 6 de Octubre y Soria Galvarino. Mon-Sat 1200-1400, 1600-2130.
Good vegetarian set meals and *à la carte*.

$ La Casona
Pres Montes 5970, opposite Post Office. Closed midday.
Salteñas in the morning. Good *pizzería* at night.

$ Sergio's
La Plata y Mier, at Plaza 10 de Febrero.
Very good pizza, hamburgers, snacks; also pastries in the afternoon, good service.

Panadería Doña Filo
Montes 1720 y Sucre. Mon-Sat 0800-1300, 1430-2000.
Bakery and small café serving excellent sweets and savoury snacks, wide variety of temptations. Recommended.

Shopping

Oruro

Camping equipment
Camping Oruro, *Pagador 1660, T02-528 1829,* camping_oruro@hotmail.com.

Crafts
On Av La Paz the blocks between León and Belzu are largely given over to workshops producing masks and costumes for Carnaval.
Artesanías Oruro, *A Mier 599, esq S Galvarro.* Lovely selection of regional handicrafts produced by 6 rural community cooperatives; nice sweaters, carpets, wall-hangings.

Markets
C Bolívar is the main shopping street.
Global, *Junín y La Plata.* A well-stocked supermarket.
Irupana, *S Galvarra y A Mier.* Sells natural food and snacks.
Mercado Campero, *V Galvarro esq Bolívar.* Sells everything, also *brujería* section for magical concoctions.
Mercado Fermín López, *C Ayacucho y Montes.* Sells food and hardware.
Mercado Kantuta, *Tacna entre Beni y D, north of the bus terminal; take minibus from northeast corner of Plaza 10 de Febrero.* A *campesino* market on Tue and Fri.

What to do

Oruro

Asociación de Guías Mineros, *contact Gustavo Peña, T02-523 2446.* Arranges visits to San José mine, US$7-10.
Freddy Barrón, *T02-527 6776,* lufba@hotmail. com. Custom-made tours and transport, speaks German and some English.

Transport

Oruro

Bus Bus terminal 10 blocks north of centre at Bakovic and Aroma, T02-527 5070/9554, US$0.25 terminal use fee, luggage store, ATMs, *casas de cambio.* Micro 2 to centre, or any saying 'Plaza 10 de Febrero'. Vans (*surubís*) to several destinations leave as they fill from Bakovic y Aroma, outside the terminal, faster and more expensive than buses. To **Challapata** and **Huari**: several companies go about every hour, US$1, 1¾ hrs, and Huari, US$1.25, 2 hrs, last bus back leaves

Huari about 1630. You can also take a bus to Challapata and a shared taxi from there to Huari US$0.30. Daily services to: **La Paz** (along a 4-lane motorway) at least every hour 0400-2200, US$4-6, 3-4 hrs; also tourist van service with **Enjoy Bolivia**, see La Paz Tour operators, page 276. **Cochabamba**, US$3-4.50, 4 hrs, frequent; vans US$7. **Potosí**, US$5.50-7.50, 5 hrs, several daily; vans US$8.50, 4 hrs. **Sucre**, all buses around 2000, US$9-12, 8 hrs. **Tarija**, 2 departures at 2030, US$11.50, and US$16-20, 10-11 hrs. To **Uyuni** on a fully paved road, several companies, US$4.50, 4½ hrs; vans US$8.50, 3½ hrs. **Todo Turismo**, offers a tourist bus departing from La Paz at 2100, arrange ahead for pick-up in Oruro at midnight, US$28, office Rodríguez 134 entre 6 de Agosto y Bakovic, T02-511 1889. To **Tupiza**, via Potosí, **Boquerón** at 1230, **Illimani** at 1630 and 2000, US$13, 11-12 hrs, continuing to Villazón, US$14.50, 13-14 hrs. **Santa Cruz, Bolívar** at 2000, US$12, *bus cama* at 2130, US$17, 11 hrs. To **Pisiga** (Chilean border), **Trans Pisiga**, Av Dehene y España, T02-526 2241, at 2000 and 2030, or with Iquique bound buses, US$5, 3-4 hrs; vans US$8.50.

International buses (US$2 to cross border): to **Iquique** via Pisiga, **InterBus** at 0400, 1000, 2030, US$10, 8 hrs. **Arica** via Patacamaya and Tambo Quemado, several companies daily around 1100-1300 and 2300, US$25 normal, US$30 *semi-cama*, US$37 *cama*, 8 hrs, some continue to Iquique, 12 hrs.

Train The station is at Av Velasco Galvarro y Aldana, T02-527 4605, ticket office Mon-Fri 0800-1200, 1430-1800, Sun 0830-1120, 1530-1800. Tickets can also be purchased on line from Ferroviaria Andina (FCA, www.fca.com. bo). Services from Oruro to **Uyuni**, **Tupiza** and **Villazón**. Expreso del Sur runs Tue and Fri at 1430, arriving in Uyuni at 2120, and **Wara Wara** on Sun and Wed at 1900, arriving in Uyuni at 0220.

Fares Expreso del Sur to **Uyuni**, *Ejecutivo* US$17, *Salón* US$8.50; **Tupiza**, 12½ hrs: US$34.50, US$15.50; **Villazón**, 15½ hrs, US$40, US$18. **Wara Wara del Sur** to **Uyuni**: *Ejecutivo* US$14.50 *Salón* US$6.75; **Tupiza**, 13½-14 hrs: US$26, US$11.50 respectively; **Villazón**, 17 hrs: US$31.50, US$14.50

Quime

Bus To get to Quime, take any bus from La Paz to Oruro or Cochabamba and get out at Konani, 2-3 hrs, US$2 (likewise get out at Konani coming from Oruro or Cochabamba). Change to a bus, minibus (*surubí*) or taxi to Quime (wait till full),

1½ hrs, US$3.75. Direct buses from La Paz to Quime, 5 hrs, are **Inquisivi** (T02-282 4732) from the bus terminal at 0600 and **Apóstol Santiago** from C 1, Villa Bolívar A, El Alto (T7585 2090, Quime T6900 6854), 5 daily, US$3-5, some continue to Inquisivi and other destinations in Yungas. All transport stops on the Alameda in Quime.

Parque Nacional Sajama
Bus To get to the park, take a La Paz–Oruro bus and change at Patacamaya. Minivans from Patacamaya to Sajama Sun-Fri 1200, 3 hrs, US$2.75. Sajama to **Patacamaya** Mon-Fri 0600, some days via **Tambo Quemado**, confirm details and weekend schedule locally. From Tambo Quemado to Sajama about 1530 daily,

1 hr, US$0.75. Or take a La Paz–Arica bus, ask for Sajama, try to pay half the fare, but you may be charged full fare.

South of Oruro
Bus To **Coipasa** ask if **Trans Pisiga** (see above) is running a fortnightly service. If not, you can take one of the buses for Iquique and get off at the turn-off, but it's difficult to hire a private vehicle for onward transportation in this sparsely populated area. Salinas de Garci Mendoza from **Oruro**, **Trans Cabrera**, C Tejerina y Caro, daily except Sat (Mon, Wed Fri, Sun 1900, Tue, Thu 0830, Sun also at 0730). Return to Oruro same days, US$3.40, 7 hrs. Also **Trans Thunupa**, daily 1800, 1900, office at Tarapacá 1144 entre Caro y Montesinos, T7231 6471.

Salar de Uyuni and around   Colour map 3, C2.
shimmering salt flats and luminous lakes

★Crossing the Salar de Uyuni, the largest and highest salt lake in the world, is one of the great Bolivian trips. Driving across it is a fantastic experience, especially during June and July when the bright blue skies contrast with the blinding-white salt crust. Further south, and included on most tours of the region, is the Reserva Eduardo Avaroa (REA, see page 305) with the towering volcanoes, multicoloured lakes with abundant birdlife, weird rock formations, thermal activity and endless *puna* that make up some of most fabulous landscapes in South America. For information on the north shore of the *salar*, see South of Oruro, page 300.

The Salar de Uyuni contains what may be the world's largest lithium deposits and concern has been expressed about the impact of proposed extensive lithium mining.

Uyuni   See map, page 305.
Uyuni (population 18,000, altitude 3670 m) lies near the eastern edge of the Salar de Uyuni and is one of the jumping-off points for trips to the salt flats, volcanoes and lakes of southwest Bolivia. Still a commercial and communication centre, Uyuni was, for much of the 20th century, important as a major railway junction.

Two monuments dominate Avenida Ferroviaria: one of a railway worker, erected after the 1952 Revolution, and the other commemorating those who died in the Chaco War. **Museo Arqueológico y Antropológico de los Andes Meridionales** ① *Arce y Potosí, Mon-Fri 0830-1200, 1430-1830, Sat-Sun 0900-1300, US$0.70*, is a small museum with local artefacts. The market is at Potosí y Bolívar, a larger Thursday market is held near the bus stations, and the town's fiesta is 11 July. There is a Railway Cemetery outside town with engines from 1907 to the 1950s, now rusting hulks. **Pulacayo**, 25 km from Uyuni on the road to Potosí, is a town at the site of a 19th-century silver mine. The train cemetery here is more interesting with Bolivia's first locomotive and the train robbed by Butch Cassidy and the Sundance Kid.

Trips to the Salar de Uyuni
Trips to the Salar de Uyuni originating in Uyuni enter via the *terraplén* (ramp) at **Colchani**, which has a **Museo de la Llama y de la Sal** selling souvenirs. Tours include stops to see traditional salt-mining techniques and the Ojos del Agua, where salt water bubbles to the surface of the salt flat, perhaps a call at a salt hotel (see Where to stay, page 308) and a visit to the **Isla Incahuasi** ① *entry US$4.30*. This is a coral island, raised up from the ocean bed, covered in tall cacti. There is a walking trail with superb views, a café, basic lodging and toilets. If on an extended tour (see below), you may leave the *salar* by another *terraplén*, eg Puerto Chuvica in the southwest. Some tours also include **Gruta de la Galaxia** ① *entry US$2.80*, an interesting cave at the edge of the *salar*. Private

Essential Salar de Uyuni

Finding your feet

The Salar de Uyuni and Reserva Eduardo Avaroa (REA) are best visited on a tour, these generally start in Uyuni or Tupiza. Uyuni is reached by air from La Paz; by bus from La Paz, Oruro or Potosí; or by train from Oruro. Tupiza is reached by air on a flight La Paz–Tarija and a bus from there; by bus from La Paz, Oruro, Potosí, Tarija or Salta (Argentina); or by train from Oruro. Special arrangements are required to drive to the Salar de Uyuni from Oruro via the Salar de Coipasa (intersalar route), to drive across the Salar de Uyuni and to access it from San Pedro de Atacama (Chile). Villages along the perimeter of the Salar are reached by infrequent buses.

Getting around

Travel is in 4WD Landcruisers, cramped for those on the back seat, but the staggering scenery makes up for any discomfort.

Safety

Getting stranded out on the altiplano or, worse yet on the *salar* itself, is dangerous because of extreme temperatures and total lack of drinking water. It is best to visit this area with a tour operator. Travellers with their own vehicles should be aware that the edges of the *salares* are soft and only established entry points or ramps (*terraplenes*) should be used to cross onto or off the salt. The intersalar route (Oruro–Coipasa–Uyuni) should only be attempted following extensive local inquiry or after taking on a guide to avoid becoming lost or bogged.

Booking a tour

Always check the itinerary, the vehicle, language of guiding, group numbers, the menu (especially vegetarians), what is included in the price. The most popular trips are three to four days: Salar de Uyuni, Reserva Eduardo Avaroa, and back to Uyuni or on to San Pedro de Atacama (Chile); or Tupiza to Uyuni, San Pedro de Atacama or back to Tupiza. There are also one- to two-day tours and five-day tours which include additional attractions or climbing a volcano. Prices per person start at US$50 for a day tour, US$100 for a three-day tour and US$190 for four days plus park fee of Bs 150 (US$21) and entry fees to some attractions (total of up to US$12). Prices rise in high season, when better guides are scarce and

Tip...

There are a couple of ATMs in Uyuni and Tupiza, but they may not always have funds. *Casas de cambio* in both towns give poor rates. Best take cash bolivianos.

English guiding may not be available on some tours. The cheapest tours are not recommended (vehicles in poor condition have been involved in fatal accidents). The best value is at the mid-to high-end, where you can assemble your own tour for four or five passengers, with driver, cook and good equipment. Private star- and sunrise-watching tours cost US$150-250, for two or three hours, for one or two passengers.

Three factors often lead to misunderstandings between what is offered and what is actually delivered by the tour operator: 1) agencies pool clients when there are not enough passengers to fill a vehicle. 2) Agencies all over Bolivia sell *salar* tours, but booking from far away may not give full information on the local operator. 3) Many drivers work for multiple agencies and may cut tours short. If the tour seriously fails to match the contract and the operator refuses any redress, complaints can be taken to the **Subprefectura de Potosí** in Uyuni (see page 307) but don't expect a quick refund or apology. Try to speak to travellers who have just returned from a tour before booking your own, and ignore touts on the street and at the rail or bus stations. For tour operators, see Uyuni, page 310, and Tupiza, page 314.

When to go

In direct sun temperatures can reach 30°C in the summer (December to April), but it is much cooler in the shade and can fall well below freezing at night, with record low temperatures of -30°C registered in the winter (June to September). The average temperature is 6°C.

During the rainy season (December to April), water can cover part or all of the *salar* turning it into an immense mirror. The *salar* is beautiful with a few millimetres of water on its surface. If there is too much water, however, driving on it is not possible, it can only be admired from the shore and tour routes must be altered. After the rains, the intense solar radiation and the wind dry the surface and a pure white crust is formed. Beneath this layer, the salt is still wet. As the surface crust cracks, the salt crystallizes as it dries up, forming polygons on the surface. *Ojos de agua* are round holes that allow you to see water welling up from under the salt crust.

star- and sunrise-watching *salar* tours go for a few hours to an area flooded year round, where you can appreciate the mirror effect.

San Cristóbal

The original village of San Cristóbal, southwest of Uyuni, was relocated in 2002 to make way for a huge open-pit mine, said to be one of the largest silver deposits in South America. The original church (1650) had been declared a national monument and was therefore rebuilt in its entirety. Ask at the Fundación San Cristóbal Office for the church to be opened as the interior artwork, restored by Italian techniques, is worth seeing. The fiesta is 27-28 July.

★ Reserva Nacional de Fauna Andina Eduardo Avaroa (REA)

SERNAP office in Quetena Chico, T7237 8318 and at Colón y Avaroa, Uyuni, T02-693 2225, www.boliviarea.com or www.biobol.org, Mon-Fri 0830-1230, 1430-1800; entry to reserve US$21 (not included in tour prices; pay in bolivianos) Entry fees charged by communities can add up to US$32, depending which places are visited. Park ranger/entry points are near Laguna Colorada and Laguna Verde, close to the Chilean border, and at Sol de Mañana, near Quetena Chico. There is public transport from Uyuni into the region, but rarely more than 1 bus a week, with several hours rough travelling. If travelling independently, note that there are countless tracks and no signposts.

In the far southwest of Bolivia, in the López region, is the 714,745-ha Reserva Nacional Eduardo Avaroa (REA). There are two access routes: one from Uyuni via the *salar* and one from Tupiza. This is one of Bolivia's prime attractions and tour vehicles criss-cross the *puna* every day, some on the route from Uyuni to San Pedro de Atacama (Chile). Roads are still unmarked rugged

Where to stay		
1 Avenida	8 Piedra Blanca	**Restaurants**
2 El Viajero	Backpackers	2 Home Chicken
3 Jardines de Uyuni	9 Tambo Aymara	3 Kactus
4 Julia	10 Toñito &	4 Pizzería Donna Isabella
5 Le Ciel	Minuteman Pizza	5 Sal Negra
6 Los Girasoles	11 Vieli	
7 Mágia de Uyuni		**Bars & clubs**
		6 Extreme Fun Pub

tracks, however, and may be impassable in the wet season.

☆ **Laguna Colorada** at 4278 m, 346 km southwest of Uyuni, is just one of the highlights of the reserve, its shores and shallows encrusted with borax and salt, an arctic white counterpoint to the flaming red, algae-coloured waters in which the rare James flamingos, along with the more common Chilean and Andean flamingos, breed and live. **Laguna Verde** (lifeless because it is laden with arsenic) and its neighbour **Laguna Blanca**, near the Chilean border, are at the foot of Volcán Licancábur, 5868 m. Between Lagunas Colorada and Verde there are thermal pools at Laguna Blanca (blissful water, a challenge to get out into the bitter wind – no facilities) and at **Polques** ① *entry US$0.85*, on the shores of Río Amargo/Laguna Salada by the Salar de Chalviri. A *centro comunal* at Polques has a dining room, changing room and toilets.

Tip...
Be prepared for the altitude, intense solar radiation and lack of drinking water.

All these places are on the 'classic' tour route, across the Salar de Uyuni to **San Juan**, which has a museum of local *chullpas*, and is where most tour companies stop (there are plenty of lodgings). Other tours stop at **Culpina K**. Then you go to the Salar de Chiguana, Mirador del Volcán de Ollagüe, Cinco Lagunas, a chain of small, flamingo-specked lagoons, the much-photographed Arbol de Piedra in the Siloli desert, then Laguna Colorada (spend the second night here: **Hospedaje Laguna Colorada**, the newer and better $ **Don Humberto** in Huayllajara, and Campamento Ende). From Colorada you go over the Cuesta del Pabellón, 4850 m, to the **Sol de Mañana** geysers (not to be confused with the Sol de Mañana entry point); the **Desierto de Dalí**, a pure sandy desert as much Daliesque for the spacing of the rocks, with snow-covered peaks behind, as for the shape of the rocks themselves; and **Laguna Verde** (4400 m).

Jurisdiction of the reserve belongs to the villages of **Quetena Chico** and **Quetena Grande**, to the east of Laguna Colorada. The villagers run lodging in the reserve: Quetena Chico runs *hospedajes* at Laguna Colorada. Quetena Grande runs **La Cabaña** at Hito Cajones (see below). In Quetena Chico is the reserve's visitors centre, **Centro Ecológico Ch'aska** ① *daily 0730-1800*, with informative displays about the region's geology, vulcanology, fauna, flora and human history; a worthwhile stop. The village has two cheap *hospedajes* (**Piedra Preciosa** and **Hostal Quetena**, hot water extra), and places to eat. With the exception of Quetena Chico, *alojamientos* in the villages on the tour routes cannot be booked. You turn up and search for a room. All provide kitchen space for the tour's cook or independent traveller to prepare meals, take your own stove, though.

Sadly, lakes in the reserve are gradually drying up, most noticeably Laguna Verde. This has been attributed to global climate change but the real reason may be massive underground water consumption by Bolivian, Chilean and Argentine mines.

From Tupiza Tour operators in Tupiza (see page 314) run trips to the REA and Salar de Uyuni and go to places not included on tours from Uyuni. These may include the beautiful **Lagunas Celeste** and **Negra** below Cerro Uturunco, which is near Quetena Chico; the **Valle de las Rocas**, 4260 m, between the villages of **Alota** and **Villa Mar** (a vast extension of rocks eroded into fantastic configurations, with polylepis trees in sheltered corners); **Ciudad Roma** rock formations near the village of **Guadalupe**; and isolated communities in the *puna*. The high-altitude scenery is out of this world. An alternative access to this area from the south is from **Villazón** (see page 312), along a wide gravel road.

Crossing into Chile

There is a REA ranger station near Lagunas Blanca and Verde: if going from Bolivia, have your park entry receipt at hand, if crossing from Chile pay the entry fee here. Alongside is a *refugio*, La Cabaña; US$7 per person in comfortable but very cold dorms, solar-powered lighting, hot water seldom works, cooking facilities (in high season book in advance – tour agencies can do this).

There is good climbing and hiking in the area with outstanding views. You must register at the ranger station before heading out and they may insist that you take a guide (eg to climb Licancábur, US$100 for guide plus US$30 for transport unless it is part of your tour).

From the ranger station it's 5 km to the border at **Hito Cajones** (on the Chilean side called Hito Cajón), 4500 m. Bolivian immigration open 0800-2000, charges US$2 in any currency. There are no services or facilities at the border. A further 6 km along a good dirt road into Chile is the intersection with the fully paved road from San Pedro de Atacama to **Paso de Jama**, the border between Chile and Argentina. From here it's 40 km (2000 m downhill) to San Pedro. Chilean customs and immigration at Hito Cajón are open 0800-2000.

There is also a border crossing at **Avaroa/Ollagüe**, used by buses between Uyuni and **Calama**, see Transport, below. Bolivian immigration (US$2 fee) is open 0830-1230, 1430-1630 Bolivian time. Chilean immigration and customs are 4 km further, open 0800-2000 Chilean time. Expect thorough searches and long delays when entering Chile.

Listings Salar de Uyuni and around *map page 305.*

Tourist information

Uyuni

Dirección de Turismo Uyuni
InfoTur, Av Potosí y Arce, opposite the clock tower,
T02-693 3666. Mon-Fri 0800-1200, 1430-1830.

Subprefectura de Potosí
Colón y Sucre, T693 3563. Mon-Fri 0800-1200,
1430-1800, Sat 0800-1200.
Departmental information office, the place to file any complaints in writing.

Where to stay

Uyuni
Many hotels fill early, reservations are advised in high season. Be conservative with water use, this is a very dry area, water is scarce and supplied at limited hours (better hotels have reserve tanks).

$$$ Jardines de Uyuni
Av Potosí 113, T02-693 2989, reservations T02-622 9515, www.hotelesrusticosjardines.com.
Tastefully decorated with lovely common areas (refurbished in 2016), comfortable rooms, heating, open fire in the lounge, buffet breakfast, restaurant, small pool, sauna, parking.

$$$ Mágia de Uyuni
Av Colón 432, T02-693 2541,
www.magiauyuni.com.
Nice ample rooms and suites upstairs with central heating, cheaper in older rooms downstairs (ask for a heater), both with buffet breakfast, parking.

$$$ Tambo Aymara
Camacho s/n y Colón, T02-693 2227,
bookings through tamboaymara@gmail.com,
www.hoteltamboaymara.com.
Lovely colonial-style modern hotel, large comfortable rooms, heating, buffet breakfast, parking, Belgian-owned.

$$$-$$ Los Girasoles
Santa Cruz 155, T693 3323,
www.girasoleshotel.hostel.com.
Buffet breakfast, bright and warm (especially 2nd floor), comfortable, nice decor, heaters, cheaper in old section.

$$$-$$ Toñito
Av Ferroviaria 60, T02-693 3186,
www.tonitouyuni.com.
Spacious rooms with good beds, solar-powered showers and heating, refurbished in 2016, **Minuteman Pizza** restaurant, parking, book exchange, tours.

TAMBO AYMARA
Calle Camacho - Uyuni

www.hoteltamboaymara.com
phone: 00591/2/6932227
mail: tamboaymara@gmail.com

$$ Julia
Ferroviaria 314 y Arce, T02-693 2134.
Spacious rooms, cheaper with shared bath, solar hot water, central heating at night.

$$-$ Le Ciel
Sucre 35 y Potosí, T02-693 2885,
leciel.contacto@gmail.com.
Upstairs in a multi-storey building, rooms with private bath (cheaper without), electric shower, small lounge, attentive staff.

$$-$ Piedra Blanca Backpackers
Tomás Frías y Loa, T7643 7643,
piedrablanca_hostel@hotmail.com.
Warm, comfortable, private rooms, some with bath, and dorms (US$11 pp), kitchen, terrace, luggage store extra, simple breakfast.

$ Avenida
Av Ferroviaria 11, near train station,
T02-693 2078.
Simple but well maintained, cheaper with shared bath, hot water (shared showers 0700-2100), long covered patio with laundry facilities, family-run, helpful, good value, popular and often full.

$ El Viajero
Cabrera 334 y 6 de Agosto, T02-693 3549.
Basic rooms, cheaper with shared bath, electric shower, cement patio, helpful owner, parking.

$ Vieli
Sucre 257 entre Colón y Cabrera, T02-693 2377,
hostalvieli@hotmail.com.
Rooms around a covered patio, private bath (cheaper without), good value, away from the tourist crowds and convenient for bus stations.

Salar de Uyuni and Reserva Eduardo Avaroa
These *hoteles de sal* are generally visited on tours, seldom independently.

$$$$ Palacio de Sal
On the edge of the salar, near the ramp outside Colchani, T6482 0888, www.palaciodesal.com.bo.
Book through **Hidalgo Tours** (Potosí, T02-622 9512). Spacious, luxury salt hotel, decorated with large salt sculptures, heating, sauna, lookout on 2nd storey with views of the *salar*.

$$$$-$$$ Luna Salada
5 km north of Colchani near the edge of the salar, T7121 2007, La Paz T02-277 0885,
www.lunasaladahotel.com.bo.
Lovely salt hotel, comfortable rooms, hot water, ample common areas with fabulous views of the *salar*, salt floors, skylights make it warm and cosy, reserve ahead.

$$$ Mallku Cueva
Outside Villa Mar, along the route from Tupiza to the reserve, T02-693 2989,
www.hotelesrusticosjardines.com.
Nicely decorated upmarket hotel with all services, including Wi-Fi. Run by **Hidalgo Tours**, see What to do, below.

$$$ Tayka
Uyuni office: Sucre 7715 entre Uruguay y México, T02-693 2987, La Paz T02-241 3065,
www.taykahoteles.com.
A chain of 4 upmarket hotels in Salar de Uyuni-REA area, operating in conjunction with local communities. The hotels have comfortable rooms with bath, hot water, heating and restaurant, price includes breakfast, discounts in low season. The **Hotel de Sal** (salt hotel) is in Tahua, on the north shore of the *salar*; the **Hotel de Piedra** (stone hotel) is in San Pedro de Quemes, on the south shore of the *salar*; the **Hotel del Desierto** (desert hotel) is in Ojo de Perdiz in the Siloli Desert, north of Laguna Colorada; the **Hotel de los Volcanes** (volcanoes hotel) is in San Pablo de Lípez, between Uturunco Volcano and Tupiza.

San Cristóbal

There are also a couple of inexpensive *alojamientos* in town.

$$ Hotel San Cristóbal
In centre, T7264 2117.
Purpose-built and owned by the community. The bar is inside a huge oil drum, all metal furnishings. The rest is comfortable if simple, hot water, good breakfast, evening meal extra.

Restaurants

Uyuni
Plaza Arce has various tourist restaurants serving mostly mediocre pizza.

$$ Pizzería Donna Isabella
Ferrovaria y Camacho. Daily 1800-2200.
Variety of tasty pizzas, made with either wheat flour or *quinua* crust.

$$-$ Kactus
Bolívar y Ferrovaria. Daily 0730-1500, 1700-2200.
Set lunches and international food à la carte, also sells whole-wheat bread, slow service.

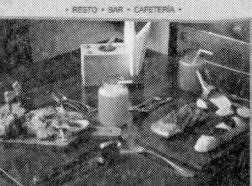

$$-$ Minuteman Pizza
Pizza restaurant attached to Toñito Hotel (see above).
Good pizzas and soups, also serves breakfast.

$$-$ Sal Negra
Potosí y Bolívar, upstairs. Daily 0730-2000.
Set lunch and *à la carte*, varied menu.

$ Home Chicken
Sucre esq Cabrera. Daily 1200-1400, 1800-2200.
Economical set lunch and *à la carte* at night, popular with locals, go early.

Bars and clubs

Uyuni

$ Extreme Fun Pub
Potosí 9.
Pleasant atmosphere, good service, videos, friendly owner is very knowledgeable about Bolivia.

What to do

Uyuni

Tour operators
In 2017 there were over 100 registered tour operators in Uyuni, plus countless unofficial agencies. Touts work the streets, especially Av Ferroviaria in the afternoons. See also Booking a tour, page 304.
Cordillera Traveller, *Av Ferroviaria entre Arce y Sucre, T02-693 3304, www.cordilleratraveller.com.* Salar tours and transfers to San Perdo de Atacama (Chile).
Creative Tours, *Sucre 362, T02-693 3543, Cochabamba T04-403 2941, www.creativetours. com.bo.* Long-established company, partners in the **Tayka** chain of hotels, see above. Premium tours in the region and throughout the country, with representatives in the main cities.
Esmeralda, *Arce y Av Ferroviaria, T7387 3605, www.esmeraldatoursuyuni.com.* At the more economical end of market, tours from 1 to 4 days.
Hidalgo Tours, *Av Potosí 113 at Hotel Jardines de Uyuni, www.salardeuyuni.net.* Well-established *salar*/REA operator, also runs **Palacio de Sal** and **Mallku Cueva** hotels (see above); also in Potosí.
Mammut, *Peú y Sucre, T7240 4720.* 1-, 2- and 3-day tours to the salt flats and Reserva Eduardo Avaroa, transfers to San Pedro de Atacama and express service to La Paz, Tupiza and other cities. Spanish-speaking guides.

Red Planet, *Av Ferroviaria entre Sucre y Camacho, T7240 3896, www.redplanetexpedition.com.* Tours to the *salar*, 1, 2 and 3 days, also from Potosí, transport from La Paz for groups. English-speaking guides.

San Cristóbal
Llama Mama, *T7240 0309.* 60 km of exclusive bicycle trails descending 2-3 or 4 hrs, depending on skill, 3 grades, all-inclusive, taken up by car, with guide and communication.

Transport

Uyuni
Air To/from **La Paz**, **Amazonas** (Arce y Potosí, T02-693 3333) and **Boa** (Potosí y Sucre, T02-693 3674), 2 daily each, US$75-150.

Bus Most offices are on Av Arce and Cabrera. Many roads to Uyuni have been paved and bus transport is more efficient and reliable than in the past. Vans to Oruro and Potosí leave as they fill throughout the day. To **La Paz**, US$14.50-21.50, 9 hrs, with **Panasur** (www.uyunipanasur. com), **Cruz del Norte**, and **Trans Omar** (www. transomar.com); all overnight. To travel by day transfer in Oruro. Tourist buses with **Todo Turismo**, Cabrera 158, T02-693 3337, www. todobturismo.com, daily at 2000, US$34 (La Paz office, Av Uruguay 102, Edif Paola, p1 of 6, opposite the bus terminal, T02-211 9418, daily to Uyuni at 2100). **Oruro**, several companies, US$4.50, 4½ hrs; vans US$8.50, 3½ hrs. To **Cochabamba** with **Trans Omar** at 1930, US$14.50, 9 hrs. To **Potosí**, several companies, frequent service, US$4.50, 4 hrs; vans US$7, 3 hrs; spectacular scenery. To **Sucre**, 6 de Octubre at 2200 and 11 de Julio at 2130, both direct, US$8-14, 8 hrs; or transfer in Potosí. To **Tupiza** US$6-7, 6-7 hrs, via **Atocha** (US$3.50, 3 hrs), several companies daily at 0600 and 2000. The Uyuni–Tupiza road was being paved in 2017. To **Villazón** on the Argentine border, 3 daily, US$9.50-12, 7 hrs. For **Tarija** change in Potosí or Tupiza. Regional services to villages in **Nor-** and **Sud-López** operate about 3 times a week, confirm details locally. To **Pulacayo**, US$0.75, 30 mins, take any bus for Potosí. To **Calama** and **San Pedro Atacama**, see Crossing into Chile, below.

Car Advance preparations are required to drive across the *salar* and REA. Fuel is not easily available in the López region, so you must take jerrycans (a permit from the Dirección General de Substancias Controladas in La Paz is required to fill them). Fuel for vehicles with foreign plates may be considerably more expensive.

Train With the road from Oruro to Uyuni now paved, rail service is slower than buses and receives fewer passengers, but it remains a good option. **Expreso del Sur** train leaves for **Oruro** on Thu and Sun at 0005, arriving 0710. **Wara Wara del Sur** leaves on Tue and Fri at 0145, arriving 0910 (prices for both under Oruro, page 402). To **Atocha**, **Tupiza** and **Villazón Expreso del Sur** leaves Uyuni on Tue and Fri at 2140, arriving, respectively, at 2345, 0300 and 0605. **Wara Wara** leaves on Mon and Thu at 0250, arriving 0500, 0835 and 1205. The ticket office (T02-693 2153) opens Mon-Fri 0900-1200, 1500-1800, Sat 0900-1100, and 1 hr before the trains leave.

Crossing into Chile

On a tour The easiest way is to go to San Pedro de Atacama as part of your tour to the *salar* and REA (see above). **Colque Tours** (www. colquetours.com) runs 1 minibus daily from near the ranger station at Hito Cajones to San Pedro de Atacama, departing 1000, US$10, 1 hr including stop at immigration. At other times onward transport to San Pedro must be arranged by your agency, this costs US$10-15 for shared service if it is an add-on to your tour, or US$120-160 per vehicle for private service.

Tip...
In 2016 Chile was one hour later than Bolivian time all year (previously daylight saving was from mid-October-March only). Chile does not allow coca, dairy produce, tea bags, fruit or vegetables to be brought in.

By bus Cruz del Norte (T02-693 3896), **Frontera del Norte** (T7243 3598), and **11 de Julio** offer service from their stations in Uyuni (Arce y Cabrera) to **Calama** via the border at Avaroa (Bolivia)/Ollagüe(Chile). From Calama there are frequent buses to **San Pedro de Atacama**. Cruz del Norte is recommended for good vehicles and daily direct service, departing 0400, US$21.50, 7-8 hrs plus several hours for border delays. The other companies run 4-5 times per week, US$12, and change buses at the border (11 de Julio changes to Atacama 2000 in Chile).

By car Good wide unpaved roads run south of the Salar, 215 km, 3 hrs, from Uyuni, via **Culpina** and **Alota**, to the border at Avaroa/Ollagüe; no fuel or services on route. Some food and bottled water is sold at the border when buses pass through in the early morning but best take your own. It is 180 km further to **Calama**, 4-5 hrs on rough partly paved roads, no fuel or services. For border formalities see page 382.

Tupiza and the far south *Colour map 3, C3.*

last hideout of Butch Cassidy and the Sundance Kid

☆Set in a landscape of colourful, eroded mountains and stands of huge cacti (usually flowering November-December), Tupiza, 200 km south of Uyuni, is a pleasant town (population 25,709) with a lower altitude (2975 m) and milder climate, making it a good alternative for visits to the Reserva Eduardo Avaroa and the *salar*.

Several Tupiza operators offer *salar*, REA and local tours. Beautiful sunsets over the fertile Tupiza valley can be seen from the foot of a statue of Christ on a hill behind the plaza.

There are two ATMs in Tupiza. Don't rely on them, though; take cash. There is a public hospital on Calle Suipacha, opposite the bus terminal.

Around Tupiza

There is good hiking around Tupiza but be prepared for sudden changes of climate including hailstorms, and note that dry gullies are prone to flash flooding. The routes are very scenic and the villages are tranquil. A worthwhile excursion is to **Quebrada Palala**, with the nearby 'Stone Forest'. Here is the hamlet of **Torre Huayco**, part of a community tourism project. **Oploca**, a small town 17 km northwest of Tupiza with a lovely colonial church, is also part of the project, as is **Chuquiago**, 30 km south of Tupiza, along the rail line. Each has a small *eco-albergue* ($ per person, with breakfast, simple comfortable rooms, kitchen) and guides (US$6.50 per person). A circuit can be done in one to three days by bicycle, horse, trekking, jeep, or a combination of these (US$35-50 per day, ask tour operators in Tupiza).

Butch Cassidy and the Sundance Kid tours Tupiza's statue in the main plaza is to **José Avelino Aramayo** (1809-1882), of the 19th-century mining dynasty. Butch and Sundance's last holdup was of an Aramayo company payroll at Huaca Huañusca on 4 November 1908. They are believed by some (see *Digging Up Butch and Sundance*, by Anne Meadows, Bison Books, 2003) to have died soon afterwards at the hands of a military patrol in **San Vicente**, a tiny mining camp at 4500 m, but no grave in the San Vicente cemetery has yet to be positively identified as theirs. There is a small museum with local artifacts and a basic hotel but no other services. Visits can be arranged by Tupiza agencies.

South to the Argentine border

Villazón The Argentine border is at Villazón (population 44,645, altitude 3443 m), 81 km south of Tupiza. At Plaza 6 de Agosto are the municipal museum about the Chicha culture and tourist information office. Of traditional villages in the surroundings, those to the west, like Berque, are known for their pottery, rock art is found in Yanalpa, to the east, and San Pedro in the centre, has colonial haciendas. Many *casas de cambio* on Avenida República de Argentina, leading to the border, change US dollars, pesos and euros, all at poor rates. There are banks and three ATMs near the main plaza. Tour operators are near the old bus terminal. The border area must not be photographed.

Border with Argentina **Migración Conjunta**, a joint immigration complex, is on the Argentine side of the international bridge, open 0700-2100 Bolivian time (0800-2200 Argentine standard time, see below); longer hours during July and December school holidays, 0600-2200 Bolivian time (0700-2300 Argentine standard time). Exit and entry stamps for both countries are issued at

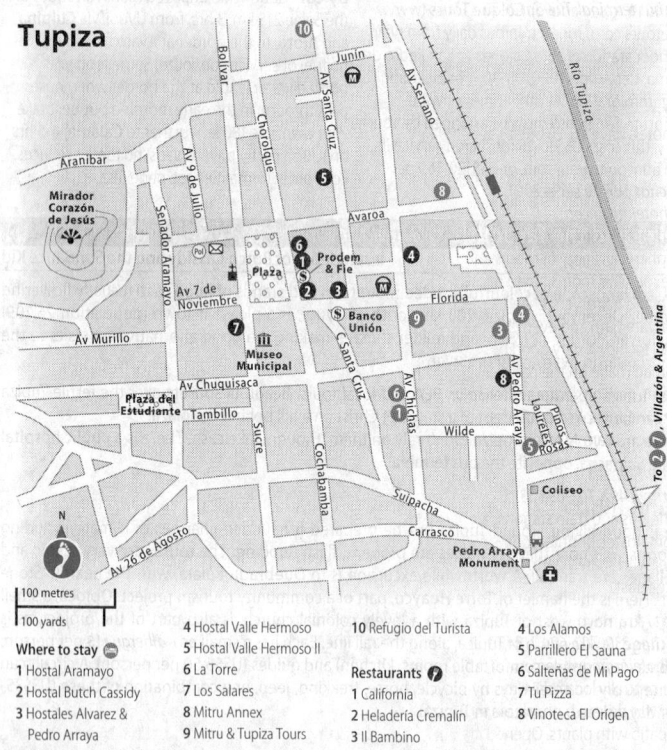

Tupiza

Where to stay		10 Refugio del Turista	4 Los Alamos
1 Hostal Aramayo	**4** Hostal Valle Hermoso		**5** Parrillero El Sauna
2 Hostal Butch Cassidy	**5** Hostal Valle Hermoso II	**Restaurants**	**6** Salteñas de Mi Pago
3 Hostales Alvarez &	**6** La Torre	**1** California	**7** Tu Pizza
Pedro Arraya	**7** Los Salares	**2** Heladería Cremalín	**8** Vinoteca El Origen
	8 Mitru Annex	**3** Il Bambino	
	9 Mitru & Tupiza Tours		

the corresponding booths in the same complex. If entering Argentina, you have to proceed to a customs control after getting your entry stamp; there is no customs control entering Bolivia. Queuing begins at 0600 and there may be long

Tip...
Change all your bolivianos in Villazón as there is nowhere to do so in La Quiaca or beyond.

delays, especially entering Argentina. Allow several hours if crossing with your own vehicle. The border is four blocks along Avenida República de Argentina from Plaza 6 de Agosto, Villazón's main square, five blocks from the old bus station (taxi US$0.70) and 10 blocks from the train station. A new Villazón bus station, 3 km from the border, was not yet operating in early 2017. The border is 10 blocks from La Quiaca (Argentina) bus terminal (taxi US$1.50). Taxis do not cross the bridge. Entering Bolivia, boys offer to wheel your bags uphill to the bus or train station, US$1-1.50 (but they will ask for more). The Argentine consulate is at Plaza 6 de Agosto 111, T02-597 2011, Monday-Friday 0800-1500. **Note** Argentine time is one hour later than Bolivia, two hours when Buenos Aires adopts daylight saving.

Listings Tupiza and the far south *map page 312.*

Tourist information

Tourist office
There is a small tourist information office at the Tupiza bus terminal, Tue-Sat 0800-1200, 1600-1930.

Where to stay

Tupiza
Most hotels have Wi-Fi, but it's very slow.

$$-$ Mitru
Av Chichas 187, T02-694 3001,
www.hotelmitru.com.
Pleasant ample grounds with heated pool, nice atmosphere, a variety of rooms and prices, the more expensive rooms have king-size beds, a/c, heating and hairdryers, cheaper in older section with private bath and even cheaper with shared bath. All include a very good buffet breakfast with bread made on the premises, reliable solar hot water, parking, luggage store. Very helpful and knowledgeable, popular, reserve ahead in high season. Warmly recommended.

$ Hostal Alvarez
Av P Arraya 492, T02-694 5327.
Near the bus and train stations, good small 10-room hostel, brighter rooms on 2nd storey, cheaper with shared bath, extra charge for a/c and breakfast.

$ Hostal Aramayo
Av Chichas 230, T02-694 2184,
http://hotelaramayo.com.
Simple centrally located 24-room hotel, most rooms with private bath, pleasant common areas, patio with plants. Opened in 2016.

$ Hostal Butch Cassidy
Av José Luis San Juan s/n, the main road in Chajrahuasi, T7183 6651.
Modern 12-room hostel, ample rooms with private bath, kitchen, parking. On the opposite bank of the river from town, can be cold in the winter when it is windy. Good value and service.

$ Hostal Pedro Arraya
Av P Arraya 494, T02-694 2734.
Convenient to bus and train stations, small rooms, cheaper with shared bath, hot water, breakfast available, laundry facilities, terrace, family-run.

$ Hostal Valle Hermoso
Av Pedro Arraya 478, T02-694 3441,
www.vallehermosotours.com.
Breakfast available, private or shared bath, US$6 pp in dorm. TV/breakfast room, book exchange, motorbike parking. 2nd location, **Valle Hermoso II**, Av Pedro Arraya 585, near the bus station, 3 simple rooms with bath, several dorms with bunk beds, same prices as No 1.

$ La Torre
Av Chichas 220, T02-694 2633,
www.latorretours-tupiza.com.
Lovely refurbished house, newer rooms at back, comfortable, cheaper with shared bath and no TV, great service, good value. Recommended.

$ Los Salares
C Ecuador s/n, Zona Chajrahuasi,
behind petrol station, T02-694 5813,
www.lossalares.hostel.com.
Small simple hotel with 9 rooms, private bath, kitchen, sauna (extra), parking. On the opposite bank of the river from town, can be cold in the

winter when it is windy. A bit out of the way but good value.

$ Mitru Annex
Avaroa 20, T02-694 3002, www.hotelmitru.com.
Nicely refurbished older hotel, buffet breakfast, cheaper with shared bath, good hot showers, use of pool at **Hotel Mitru** (see above).

$ Refugio del Turista
Av Santa Cruz 240, T02-694 3155, www.hotelmitru.com.
Refurbished home with garden, shared bath, reliable hot water, well-equipped kitchen, laundry facilities, use of pool and Wi-Fi at **Hotel Mitru**, parking and electric outlet for camper vans, popular budget option, good value.

Villazón
Hotels in Villazón do not have Wi-Fi.

$ Center
Plaza 6 de Agosto 125, T02-596 5472.
Rooms with private or shared bath, includes simple breakfast, parking.

$ Grand Palace
C 25 de Mayo 52 T02-596 5333.
Simple rooms with private or shared bath, no breakfast.

$ Olimpo
Av República Argentina 116 y Chorolque, T02-597 2219,olimpogranhotel@gmail.com.
Among the better hotels in town, private or shared bath, heating, includes simple breakfast, restaurant, parking.

Restaurants

Tupiza
Not the culinary capital of Bolivia. There are several touristy pizza places (**$$-$**) on C Florida with slow service and variable quality. The best options are just outside town (all **$$-$**), they serve grilled meat and good regional specialities like *picante de cabrito* (spicy goat) but open only Sat or Sun 1200 – go early. These include: **La Campiña**, in Tambillo Alto, 45 mins' walk north along the river. There are food stalls upstairs in the market serving tasty local fare, but mind the cleanliness.

$$-$ Parrillero El Sauna
Av Santa Cruz entre Avaroa y Junín.
Tue-Sun from 1700.

Very good *parrilladas*, Argentine meat on request, salad bar.

$$-$ Tu Pizza
Sucre y 7 de Noviembre, on Plaza.
Mon-Sat 1830-2300.
Cute name, variety of pizzas, very slow service.

$ California
Cochabamba 413, 2nd floor.
Set lunches, hamburgers and snacks in the evening when service is slow.

$ Il Bambino
Florida y Santa Cruz. Open 1100-1400.
Serves a decent set lunch.

$ Los Alamos
Av Chichas 157. Open 0800-2400.
Local and international dishes, good atmosphere, average food, good juices, large portions, popular with tourists.

Heladería Cremalín
Cochabamba y Florida, on Plaza.
Ice cream, juices and fruit shakes.

Salteñas de Mi Pago
Cochabamba, on Plaza. Tue-Sun 0900-1300.
Tasty *salteñas* every morning, popular.

Vinoteca El Orígen
Pedro Arraya y Chuquisaca. Mon-Sat 0900-1230, 1500-2300, Sun 1700-2300.
Selection of wines and snacks, also juices and breakfast, sells crafts.

Villazón
Restaurants are clustered 2 blocks around the main plaza.

$$-$ Rincón Salteño
C Suipacha 135. Open 1100-2300.
Good Argentine style *parrillada* and a variety of pizzas.

What to do

Tupiza
Tour operators in Tupiza run trips to the REA and Salar de Uyuni and go to places not included on tours from Uyuni.

Tours on offer include 1-day jeep tours US$35 pp for group of 5; 2-day San Vicente plus colonial town of Portugalete US$80 pp (plus lodging); horse riding 3-, 5- and 7-hr tours, US$6-10 per hr, multi-day tours US$70 per day; Salar de Uyuni and REA, 4 days with Spanish-speaking guide, US$190 pp for a group of 5, US$230 pp in high season, plus Bs150 (US$21) park fee and US$12 total entry fees to other attractions. Add US$28 pp for English-speaking guides. Longer tours (5 days or more) are available and include climbing volcanoes and attractions not covered in standard excursions.

Aventurista Off Road, *Pedro Arraya 86, T7181 3654, www.aventuristaoffroad.com.* Mountain bike, motorcycle and quadritrack rentals plus a wide variety of tours. Knowledgeable owner, English spoken.

La Torre Tours, *in Hotel La Torre (see above), T02-694 4816. Salar/REA tours and local trips on jeep, bicycle, walking or horse riding.*

Tupiza Tours, *in Hotel Mitru (see above), T02-694 4816, www.tupizatours.com.* Highly experienced and well organized for *salar*/REA and local tours. Their daily van tours cover 4 different routes to regional attractions with the option of returning by horse, bicycle or walking; US$29-60 depending on selected options. Also 2-day tours, staying overnight in a local community, US$82 all included. Have offices in La Paz and Tarija, and offer tours in all regions of Bolivia. Highly recommended.

Valle Hermoso Tours, *in Hostal Valle Hermoso 1 (see above), www.vallehermosotours.com.* Offers similar tours on horse or jeep, as do several other agencies and most Tupiza hotels.

Villazón

Aventuras del Sur, *C 20 de Mayo 544, T02-5973224, carlosalvarez_26@hotmail.es.* Jeep, cycling and walking tours to communities around Villazón, also Salar and REA tours.

Imperio Inca, *C Suipacha 546, T02-5965744, www.imperinca.com.* Tours throughout Bolivia, also in Argentina, Chile and Peru.

Transport

Tupiza

Bus There is a small, well-organized bus terminal at the south end of Av Pedro Arraya; vans and shared taxis (*rapiditos*) leave as they fill from across the street. To **Villazón** *rapiditos* 0500-2100, US$3.50, 1¼hrs. To **Potosí**, several companies (**Oglobo** and **Expreso Tupiza** are good), US$4.50-7, 5 hrs; vans and *rapiditos*, US$11.50, 3½hrs. To **Sucre**, several companies, all overnight, US$7-11.50, 8 hrs; or transfer in Potosí. To **Tarija**, **Juárez** at 1000, 2000, 2200, US$6 regular, US$7-12 *semicama*, US$14 *cama*, 6 hrs (impressive scenery). To **Uyuni**, several companies around 1000 and 1800, US$6-7, 6-7 hrs; road being paved in 2017. To **Oruro**, several companies, US$10-14.50, 12 hrs; **Trans Illimani** at 1300 and 1730 continues to **Cochabamba**, US$13-19, 14-16 hrs. To **La Paz** several companies, US$11.50-17, 14-15 hrs. To **Santa Cruz**, change buses in Tarija.

To **Argentina**, agents for Argentine companies (eg **Balut** and **Andesmar**) at terminal sell tickets to Jujuy, Salta, Buenos Aires or Córdoba (local transport to the border at Villazón, then change to Argentine bus), but beware overcharging or buy tickets directly from Argentine companies once in Argentina.

Train Train station ticket office, T02-694 2529, open Mon-Sat 0800-1100, 1530-1730, and early morning half an hour before trains arrive. To **Villazón**: Expreso del Sur Wed and Sat at 0310;

Wara Wara Mon and Thu at 0905. To **Atocha, Uyuni** and **Oruro: Expreso del Sur** Wed and Sat at 1825; **Wara Wara** Mon and Thu at 1905. Fares are given under Oruro, page 302.

Villazón

Bus Bus terminal is near the plaza, 5 blocks from the border. Taxi to border, US$0.70 or hire a porter, US$1, and walk. A new terminal, 2.6 km northeast of the centre, on Av Tumulsa by the ring-road was not yet operating in early 2017. To **La Paz**, several companies, US$15-23, *bus cama* US$23, depart **Villazón** 0830-1000 and 1500-1900 (eg Illimani *bus cama* at 1500 and 1900). To **Tupiza**, several daily buses, vans and cars, see Tupiza Transport, above. To **Potosí** several buses between 0800-0900 and 1830-1900, US$6-10, 8 hrs; vans US$8, 7 hrs; cars (*rapiditos*) US$9-15 (according to demand), 6 hrs. To **Uyuni**, at 0900, 1100 and 1500, US$9.50-12, 7 hrs. To **Tarija**,

3 companies, US$6, 6 hrs, change here for **Santa Cruz**. To **Sucre**, at 1100, 1500 and 2030, US$10-14, 11 hrs. Tickets for buses in **Argentina** are sold in Villazón but beware of scams and overcharging. Buy only from company offices, never from sellers in the street and allow extra time for border formalities. Safer still, cross to La Quiaca and buy onward tickets there.

Car The road north from Villazón through Tupiza, Potosí and Sucre to Cochabamba is paved. 2 scenic roads lead to Tarija, 1 from Villazón (about 40% paved) and one from Tupiza (about 50% paved).

Train Station about 1 km north of border on main road, T02-597 2565, ticket sales Mon-Sat 0800-1100, 1530-1730. To **Tupiza, Atocha, Uyuni** and **Oruro: Expreso del Sur** Wed and Sat at 1530; **Wara Wara** Mon and Thu at 1530. Fares are given under Oruro, page 302.

Central & southern highlands

This region boasts two World Cultural Heritage Sites, Sucre, the white city and Bolivia's official capital, and the mining city of Potosí, the source of great wealth for colonial Spain and of indescribable hardship for many Bolivians. In the south, Tarija is known for its fruit and wines, and for its traditions which set it apart from the rest of the country.

Sucre and around   *Colour map 3, C3. See map, page 319.*

a white colonial masterpiece and the world's largest palaeontological site

Sucre is sometimes referred to as La Ciudad Blanca, owing to the tradition that all buildings in the centre are painted in their original colonial white. This works to beautiful effect and in 1991 UNESCO declared the city a World Heritage Site.

With a population of 338,281, there are four universities, the older dating from 1624. Founded in 1538 as La Plata, it became capital of the Audiencia of Charcas in 1559. Its name was later changed to Chuquisaca before the present name was adopted in 1825 in honour of the second president of the new republic. From 1825 to 1899 Sucre was the only capital of Bolivia; it remains the constitutional capital as it is home to Bolivia's judicial branch although La Paz is the administrative one.

Sights

Plaza 25 de Mayo Plaza 25 de Mayo is large, spacious, full of trees and surrounded by elegant buildings. Among these are the **Casa de la Libertad** ① *T04-645 4200, Tue-Sat 0915-1145, 1445-1745 Sun 0915-1115, US$2.15 with tour (in Spanish, English, French or Quechua); US$5.80 video.* Formerly the Assembly Hall of the Jesuit University, where the country's Declaration of Independence was signed, this house contains a famous portrait of Simón Bolívar by the Peruvian artist Gil de Castro, admired for its likeness. Also on the plaza are the beautiful 17th-century **cathedral** and **Museo Eclesiástico** ① *Ortiz 61, T04-645 2257, Mon-Fri 1000-1200, 1500-1700, US$1.45.* Worth seeing are the famous jewel-encrusted Virgin of Guadalupe, 1601, and works by Viti, the first great painter of the New World, who studied under Raphael. On the north side of the plaza is the **Museo del Tesoro** ① *Plaza 25 de Mayo 59, T04-675 3500, www.museodeltesoro. com, Mon-Fri 0830-1230, 1500-1830 (with reservations on weekends and holidays), US$3.60, cafeteria, gift shop.* Housed in the former home of ex-president Aniceto Arce, it displays the history of Bolivian precious metals and gems and the techniques used until today in creating works of art. Recommended.

South of the plaza Visits to **San Felipe Neri** ① *entrance through school, Ortiz 165 y Azurduy, T04-645 4333, Mon-Sat 1600-1800, US$1.45 (extra charge for photos),* include the neoclassical church with its courtyard, the crypt and the roof (note the penitents' benches), which offers fine views over the city. The monastery is used as a school. Diagonally opposite is the church of **La Merced** ① *C Pérez 1, T04-645 1355, Mon-Sat 1430-1730, US$1.45,* which is notable for its gilded central and side altars. The **Museo Universitario Charcas** ① *Bolívar 698, T04-645 3285, Mon-Fri 0900-1200, 1430-1830, Sat 0930-1200, US$0.50, photos extra,* has anthropological, archaeological and folkloric exhibits, and colonial collections and presidential and modern-art galleries.

East of the plaza San Lázaro (1538) ① *Padilla 198 y Calvo, T04-645 1448, Mass daily 0700, Sun also 1000 and 1900,* is regarded as the first cathedral of La Plata (Sucre). On the nave walls are

---

Best for
Colonial history ■ Fossils ■ Textiles ■ Wine

Essential Sucre

Finding your feet

Sucre's airport, 31 km southeast of town, has regular services to and from La Paz, Santa Cruz, Cochabamba and Tarija. Access by road to Potosí is straightforward and quite quick. To get elsewhere by road takes time, but there are daily bus services to all major cities. The bus terminal is on the northern outskirts of town, 3 km from the centre. See also Transport, page 324.

When to go

Sucre has a pleasant climate. In winter, May-August, days are sunny and mild, nights are cold (temperatures can drop below freezing in June to July). December-March there is rain, but also many sunny days.

Safety

Caution is advised after 2200 and in market areas.

Time required

Two or three days but many visitors stay longer for a period of language study or volunteering.

six paintings attributed to Zurbarán; it has fine silverwork and alabaster in the baptistery. San Miguel, San Francisco and San Lázaro are only open during Mass. The **Monasterio de Santa Clara** ① *Calvo 212, church at Calvo 202, Mass daily 1600, Sun also 0800, museum open Mon-Fri 1400-1800, Sat 1400-1730, US$2, good guided tours in Spanish*, displays paintings by Bitti, sculptures, books, vestments, some silver and musical instruments (including a 1664 organ). Small items made by the nuns are on sale. The excellent **Museo de Arte Indígena ASUR (Museo Téxtil Etnográfico)** ① *Pasaje Iturricha 314, opposite Casa Kolping in La Recoleta, T04-645 6651, www.asur.org.bo, Mon-Fri 0900-1200, 1430-1830, Sat 0930-1200, 1400-1800, US$3, English and French-speaking guides*, displays regional textiles and traditional techniques, shop sells crafts. Near the main plaza is the **Museo Nacional de Etnografía y Folklore (MUSEF)** ① *España 74 y San Alberto, T04-645 5293, www.musef.org.bo, Tue-Fri 0930-1230, 1430-1830, Sat 0930-1230, free*, with an impressive display of masks and an exhibition on the Uru-Chipaya culture. Nearby, the **Museo Costumbrista** ① *San Alberto 156, T04-641 4030, Mon-Fri 0930-1230, 1500-1900, Sat 0930-1200, US$2.90*, at Casa Deheza, depicts urban life in the late 19th- and early 20th-century.

North of the plaza **San Miguel** ① *Arenales 10, T04-645 1026, Mass Mon-Sat 0800 and 1915, Sun 1100, no shorts, short skirts or short sleeves allowed*, completed in 1628, has been restored and is very beautiful with Moorish-style carved and painted ceilings, alfarjes (early 17th century), pure-white walls and gold and silver altar. Some early sculpture can be seen in the sacristy. Nearby **Santa Mónica** ① *Arenales y Junín, Mass Sun 1830*, is one of the finest gems of Spanish architecture in the Americas, but has been converted into the theatre and hall for the Colegio Sagrado Corazón. Near the Mercado Central, **San Francisco** (1581) ① *Ravelo y Arce, Mass daily 1900, Sun 0700, 1000, 1700 and 1800*, has altars coated in gold leaf and 17th-century ceilings; one of its bells summoned the people of Sucre to struggle for independence.

Four blocks northwest of Plaza 25 de Mayo is the **Corte Suprema de Justicia** ① *Luis Paz Arce 352, Mon-Fri 1000-1200, 1500-1800, free*, the seat of Bolivia's national judiciary and what remains of the city's official status as capital of Bolivia. To enter you must be smartly dressed and leave your passport with the guard; guides can be found in the public relations office. The nearby **Parque Bolívar** contains a monument and a miniature of the Eiffel Tower and Arc de Triomphe in honour of one of Bolivia's richest 20th-century tin barons, Francisco Argandoña, who created much of Sucre's splendour. At the downhill-end of the park is the **Fuente del Bicentenario**, where a **sound and light show** ① *Thu-Sun 1900-2100*, is displayed. The **obelisk** opposite the Teatro Gran Mariscal, in Plazuela Libertad, was erected with money raised by fining bakers who cheated on the size and weight of their bread. Also on this plaza is the Hospital Santa Bárbara (1574).

Around Sucre

North of Sucre Some 3 km north of Sucre is ☆**Cal Orcko**, considered the world's largest palaeontological site, where tracks from eight types of dinosaur have been identified (inside the

Fancesa cement works). Nearby is **Parque Cretácico** ① *T04-645 7392, http://parquecretacicosucre. com, Tue-Fri 0900-1700, Sat, Sun and holidays 1000-1800, visit to the tracks 1200-1300, US$4.30, children US$0.75*, crowded at weekends, with fibreglass dinosaurs, recorded growls, a 30-minute guided tour and binoculars through which (for an extra US$0.30) you can look at the prints on Cal Orcko, 300 m away. The **Sauromóvil** bus leaves daily 0930, 1200, 1430, the Dinobus daily 1100-1500, both from corner of cathedral, US$1.75 return, or take Micros 4 or H from Calle Arenales y Junín.

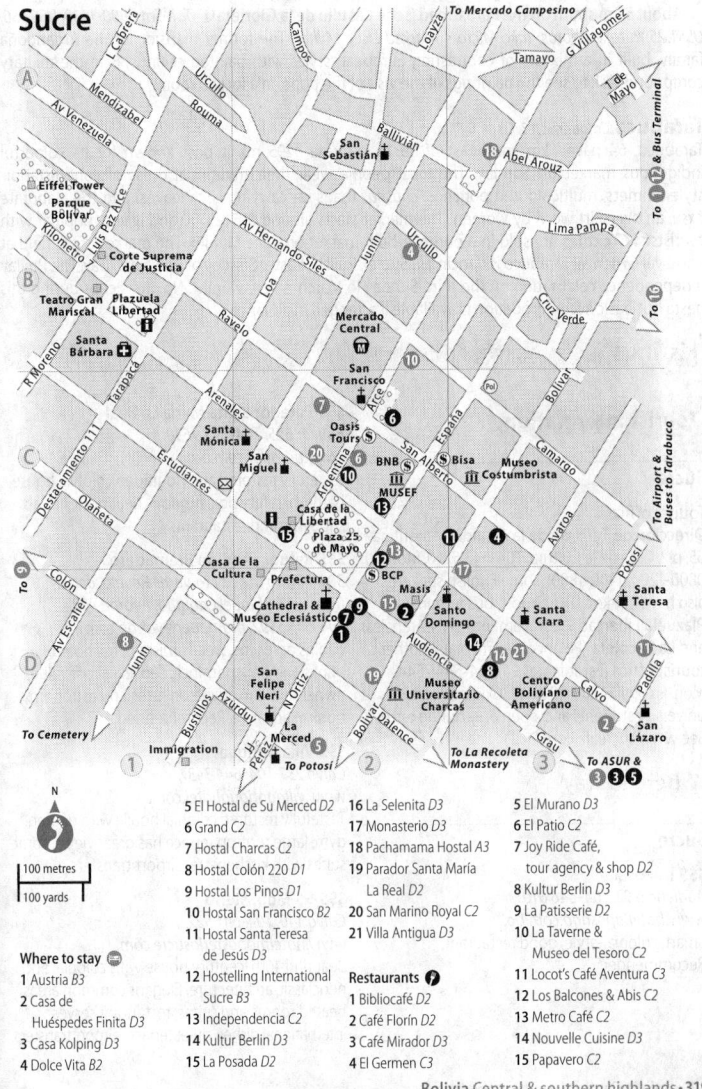

Sucre

Where to stay 🛏
1 Austria *B3*
2 Casa de
   Huéspedes Finita *D3*
3 Casa Kolping *D3*
4 Dolce Vita *B2*

5 El Hostal de Su Merced *D2*
6 Grand *C2*
7 Hostal Charcas *C2*
8 Hostal Colón 220 *D1*
9 Hostal Los Pinos *D1*
10 Hostal San Francisco *B2*
11 Hostal Santa Teresa
   de Jesús *D3*
12 Hostelling International
   Sucre *B3*
13 Independencia *C2*
14 Kultur Berlin *D3*
15 La Posada *D2*

16 La Selenita *D3*
17 Monasterio *D3*
18 Pachamama Hostal *A3*
19 Parador Santa María
   La Real *D2*
20 San Marino Royal *C2*
21 Villa Antigua *D3*

Restaurants 🍴
1 Bibliocafé *D2*
2 Café Florín *D2*
3 Café Mirador *D3*
4 El Germen *C3*

5 El Murano *D3*
6 El Patio *C2*
7 Joy Ride Café,
   tour agency & shop *D2*
8 Kultur Berlin *D3*
9 La Patisserie *D2*
10 La Taverne &
   Museo del Tesoro *C2*
11 Locot's Café Aventura *C3*
12 Los Balcones & Abis *C2*
13 Metro Café *C2*
14 Nouvelle Cuisine *D3*
15 Papavero *C2*

South of Sucre Southeast of the centre, at the top of Dalence is **La Recoleta**, a lookout with arches offering good views over the city. Here, within the Franciscan convent of La Recoleta is the **Museo de la Recoleta** ① *Plaza Pedro de Anzúrez, T04-645 1658, Mon-Fri 0900-1130, 1430-1630, Sat 1500-1700, US$2.15 for entrance to all collections, guided tours only*, notable mainly for the beauty of its cloisters and gardens; the carved wooden choir stalls above the nave of the church are especially fine (see the martyrs transfixed by lances). In the grounds is the Cedro Milenario, a 1400-year-old cedar. Behind Recoleta monastery a road flanked by Stations of the Cross ascends an attractive hill **Cerro Churuquella**, with large eucalyptus trees on its slopes, to a statue of Christ at the top.

About 5 km south on the Potosí road is the **Castillo de la Glorieta** ① *Tue-Sat 0900-1630, US$2.50, US$1.25 to take photos, take Micro 4 marked Liceo Militar*. The former mansion of the Argandoña family, built in a mixture of contrasting European styles with painted ceilings, is in the military compound. Ask to see the paintings of the visit of the pope, in a locked room.

Tarabuco *Colour map 3, C3.*

Tarabuco, 64 paved km southeast of Sucre (altitude 3295 m), is best known for its colourful indigenous market on Sunday. The local people wear their traditional dress of conquistador-style helmets, multicoloured ponchos, *chuspas* (bags for carrying coca leaves) and the elaborate *axsu*, an overskirt worn by women. The market starts around 0930-1000 and is very popular with tourists. ☆ **Textiles** are sold in a purpose-built market on Calle Murillo. The market is not held at Carnaval (when all Tarabuco is dancing in Sucre), Pujllay, Easter Sunday or All Saints' Day. The Pujllay independence celebration on the third Sunday in March is very vibrant. No one sleeps during this fiesta but basic accommodation is available if arranged in advance.

Listings Sucre and around *map page 319.*

Tourist information

Sucre

Tourist office
Dirección de Turismo de la Alcaldía (Argentina 65, p 2, Casa de la Cultura, T04-643 5240, Mon-Fri 0800-1200, 1400-1800), some English spoken; also have kiosks at the airport, bus terminal, **Plazuela Libertad** (Destacamento 111 y Arenales) and **La Recoleta** (Polanco e Iturrichia). Another **tourist office** (Estudiantes 25, T04-644 7644, Mon-Fri 0900-1200, 1500-1830) is staffed by university students and open only during term. See www.sucrelife.com.

Where to stay

Sucre

$$$ La Posada
Audiencia 92, T04-646 0101,
www.hotellaposada.com.bo.
Smart, colonial-style, good restaurant. Recommended.

$$$ Parador Santa María La Real
Bolívar 625, T04-643 9630,
www.parador.com.bo.
Tastefully restored and upgraded colonial house, bathtub, safety box, frigobar, heating. It has a shop, spa and restaurant.

$$$ Refugio Andino Bramadero
30 km from the city towards Ravelo, details from Raul y Mabel Cagigao, Avaroa 472, T04-645 5592, bramader@yahoo.com,
Cabins or rooms, well-furnished, full board, drinks and transport included, excellent value, owner Raúl can advise on hikes and astronomy, book in advance. Recommended.

$$$ Villa Antigua
Calvo 237, T04-644 3437,
www.villaantiguahotel.com.
Tastefully restored colonial house with garden, gym, large rooftop terrace has great views, some suites with kitchenette, airport transfers.

$$$-$$ Monasterio
Calvo 140, T04-641 5222,
www.hotelmonasteriosucre.com.
Beautiful 16th-century house with colonial and neoclassic architecture. Elegant common areas, heated rooms and suites, restaurant serves international dishes, quiet terrace, airport transfers.

$$ Casa Kolping
Pasaje Iturricha 265, La Recoleta, T04-642 3891.
Pleasant, lovely location with nice views, good
Munay Pata restaurant (**$$-$**), internet lounge,
wheelchair access, parking. Part of the **Kolping
International** network (www.kolping.net).

$$ El Hostal de Su Merced
Azurduy 16, T04-644 2706,
www.desumerced.com.
Beautifully restored colonial building, lots
of character, owner and staff speak French
and English, good breakfast buffet, sun
terrace, restaurant. Airport transfer US$7.50.
Recommended.

$$ Hostal Santa Teresa de Jesús
San Alberto 431, T04-645 4189,
www.santateresahostal.com.
Refurbished colonial house, restaurant,
comfortable, garage. Recommended.

$$ Independencia
Calvo 31, T04-644 2256,
www.independenciahotel.com.
Historic colonial house, opulent salon, spiral
stairs, lovely garden, comfortable, some rooms
with bathtub, café, attentive service.

$$ La Selenita
J Mostajo 145, T7285 9993, www.laselenita.com.
Pleasant guesthouse with 4 cabins for
2-3 persons, 2 types of breakfast with home-
made bread and jam available, nice gardens,
quiet, panoramic views of the colonial city,
French/Belgian-run.

$$ San Marino Royal
Arenales 13, T04-645 1646, www.
sanmarinoroyalhotel.com.bo.
Nicely converted colonial house, frigobar,
cafeteria, **$$$** for suite.

$$-$ Austria
Av Ostria Gutiérrez 506, by bus station,
T04-645 4202, on Facebook.
Hot showers, good beds and carpeted rooms,
cafeteria, parking, cheaper with shared bath
and no breakfast, parking extra.

$$-$ Hostelling International Sucre
G Loayza 119 y Ostria Gutiérrez, T04-644 0471,
www.hosteltrail.com/hostels/hisucre.
Functional hostel 1½ blocks from bus terminal,
cheaper without bath and in dorms, breakfast
available, garden, internet extra, parking, Spanish
language classes, discount for HI members.

$$-$ Kultur Berlin
Avaroa 326, T646 6854, http://kulturberlin.com.
Associated with the Kultur Berlin café and the
Insituto Cultural Boliviano-Alemán, imaginatively
designed, spotless rooms with solar hot water,
some with kitchenette. Recommended.

$ Casa de Huéspedes Finita
Padilla 233 (no sign), T04-645 3220.
Rooms with private or shared bath, heaters,
garden, terrace, family run, also apartments
with fully equipped kitchens for longer stays.

$ Dolce Vita
Urcullo 342 y Junín, T04-691 2014,
www.dolcevitasucre.com.
Small family-run guesthouse with brightly
painted rooms with or without bath, kitchen
facilities, breakfast extra, terrace, book exchange,
Swiss-French run.

$ Grand
Arce 61, T04-645 2461.
Older hotel but well maintained, comfortable
(ask for room 18), ground floor at the back is
noisy, some rooms dark, electric showers, good-
value lunch in **Arcos** restaurant, Wi-Fi in patio.

$ Hostal Charcas
Ravelo 62, T04-645 3972,
hostalcharcas@yahoo.com.
Cheaper without bath or TV, good value, huge
breakfast extra, hot showers, at times runs bus
to Tarabuco on Sun.

$ Hostal Colón 220
Colón 220, T04-645 5823.
Very nice guesthouse, cheaper with shared
bath, laundry, helpful owner speaks English and
German and has tourist information, coffee room.

$ Hostal los Pinos
Colón 502, T04-645 5639.
Comfortable, hot showers, garden, quiet,
peaceful, parking.

$ Hostal San Francisco
Av Arce 191 y Camargo, T04-645 2117.
Colonial building, electric showers, breakfast
available, quiet, patio, good value.

$ Pachamama Hostal
Arce 452, T04-645 3673, hostal_pachamama@
hotmail.com.
Simple rooms with bath, electric shower,
pleasant patio, parking, good value.

Restaurants

Sucre
Sausages and chocolates are among the locally produced specialities.

$$ El Huerto
Ladislao Cabrera 86, San Matías, T04-645 1538.
Tue-Sun 1200-1500 and with reservations for groups of 12 or more also1830-2100.
International food with salad bar, good *almuerzo*, in a beautiful garden. Take a taxi there at night.

$$ El Murano
Grau 458 entre Padilla y Oruro, T04-645 4738.
Daily 1200-1430, Tue-Sat also 1900-2300.
Upmarket restaurant with an open patio, located between the main plaza and La Recoleta. French-Bolivian ownership and cuisine, also set lunch ($).

$$ Papavero
Estudiantes 1, on Facebook. Daily 1230-1400, 1900-2200.
Popular restaurant at Plaza 25 de Mayo. Pizzeria and drinks on the ground floor and extensive Italian menu on the upper level with views of the plaza; also set lunch ($) and good natural fruit juices. Pleasant atmosphere, good food and service.

$$ La Taverne
In the Alliance Française, Arce 35, T04-645 5719, www.lataverne.com.bo. Mon-Sat 0830-2300, Sun 1900-2200.
Lovely terrace seating, weekly lunch specials, international food, also regular cultural events.

$$-$ El Germen
San Alberto 231. Mon-Sat 0800-2200.
Mostly vegetarian, set lunches, excellent breakfast, German pastries, book exchange, German magazines. Recommended.

$$-$ Los Balcones
Plaza 25 de Mayo 34, upstairs. Open 1200-2400.
Good food, popular with locals, set lunch with salad bar, views over plaza.

$$-$ Nouvelle Cuisine
Avaroa 537. Daily 1130-1430, 1800-2300.
Excellent *churrasquería* (grill), set lunch and *à la carte* in the evening, good value.

Tip...
Llama meat contains parasites, so make sure it has been properly cooked, and be especially careful of raw salads as many tourists experience gastrointestinal upsets.

Cafés

Abis
Plaza 25 de Mayo 32.
Belgian-owned café and *heladería*, with coffees, breakfasts, sandwiches, light meals, ice cream.

Bibliocafé
N Ortiz 50, near plaza. Open 1200-1500, 1800-0200, Sun 1900-2400.
Pasta and light meals. Music and drinks, Wi-Fi.

Café Florín
Bolívar 567. Daily 0730-0200, weekends to 0300.
Breakfast, sandwiches, snacks and international meals ($$), large portions, microbrews. Sunny patio, Wi-Fi, tour bookings, cosy atmosphere, Dutch-run.

Café Mirador
Pasaje Iturricha 297, La Recoleta. Open 0930-2000.
Very good garden café, fine views, good juices, snacks and music, popular.

El Patio
San Alberto 18.
Small place for delicious *salteñas/empanadas*.

Joy Ride Café
N Ortiz 14, www.joyridebol.com. Daily 0730-2300.
Great international food and drink, music, Wi-Fi, very popular, upstairs lounge shows films, also cultural events. Joy Ride has a new hostel ($) at Avaroa 431, T04-645 0035.

Kultur Berlin
Avaroa 326, T646 6854, http://kulturberlin.com.
German, Bolivian and international dishes, themed evenings and other events.

La Patisserie
Audiencia 17. Open 0830-1230, 1530-2030.
French-owned, popular for crêpes, salads and puddings.

Locot's Café Aventura
Bolívar 465, T04-691 5958. Mon-Sat 0800-2400, Sun 1100-2300.
Bar serving international and Mexican food, live music and theatre, Wi-Fi, also offer many types of adventure sports: mountain biking, hiking, riding, paragliding.

Metro Café
Calvo y España on Plaza 25 de Mayo.
A variety of coffees, sandwiches, breakfasts, pastries, desserts, juices; delicious and good service.

Bars and clubs

Sucre

Mitos
F Cerro 60, near Junín, Disco-Mitos on Facebook.
Thu-Sat 2100-0300.
Disco, popular with travellers.

Stigma
Bolívar 128 y Camargo.
Varied music, young crowd.

Festivals

Sucre

24-26 May Independence celebrations, most
services, museums and restaurants closed on 25.
8 Sep Virgen de Guadalupe, 2-day fiesta.
21 Sep Día del Estudiante, music around
main plaza.
Oct/Nov Festival Internacional de la Cultura,
2nd week, shared with Potosí.

Shopping

Sucre

Handicrafts
ASUR (opposite Casa Kolping in La Recoleta) sells
weavings from around Tarabuco and from the
Jalq'a. More expensive, but of higher quality than
elsewhere. Several shops on C Arce, 100th block.
Alpaca Andina (Calvo 64), fair-trade crafts,
has many nice items. **Centro Cultural Masis**
(Bolívar 591, T04-645 3403, www.losmasis.com),
teaches local youth traditional music and culture
and has items for sale; visitors are welcome at
events and exhibitions. **Inca Pallay** (Audiencia 97
y Bolívar, T04-646 1936, www.incapallay.org),
a not-for-profit association and Fairtrade shop,
sells textiles by Tarabuco and Jalq'a weavers,
clothing, gifts, bags and household items;
also in La Paz. Artisans sell their wares at the
La Recoleta lookout. **Chocolates Para Tí**
(Arenales 7, Audiencia 68, at the airport and bus
terminal), is one of the best chocolate shops in
Sucre. **Taboada** (Arce y Arenales, Daniel Campos
82, at airport and bus terminal, www.taboada.
com.bo) is also very good for chocolates.

Markets
The central market is colourful with some stalls
selling *artesanía*, but beware of theft.

What to do

Sucre

Language classes
Academia Latinoamericana de Español, *Bolivar
490 y Calvo*,T04-642 7085, www.latinoschool.com.
Professional, good extracurricular activities.
Alianza Francesa, *Aniceto Arce 35*, T04-645 3599,
www.sucre.alianzafrancesa.org.bo. Spanish and
French classes.
Bolivian Spanish School, *Dalence 109*, at
Colours House Hostel, T04-644 3841, www.
bolivianspanishschool.com. Pleasant school,
good value, excellent teachers.
Centro Boliviano Americano, *Calvo 301*, T04-
644 1608, www.cbasucre.org. Recommended for
language courses. These centres run cultural
events, have libraries and branches in La Paz.
Continental Spanish School, *Olañeta 224*,
T04-643 8093, www.schoolcontinental.com.
Good teachers and fun activities.
Fox Academy, *Av Destacamento Chuquisaca
134*, T04-644 0688, www.foxacademysucre.com.
Spanish and Quechua classes, US$5 per hr,
non-profit, proceeds go to teaching English
to children, volunteering arranged.
**Instituto Cultural Boliviano-Alemán (ICBA,
Goethe Institute)**, *Bolívar 609*, T04-645 2091,
www.icba-sucre.edu.bo. Spanish, German,
Portuguese and Quechua courses, US$7.50 pp
per lesson; also has an Ecomuseum.
Sucre Spanish School, *Calvo 350*, T04-643 6727,
www.sucrespanishschool.com. US$6.50 per hr,
friendly and flexible, home stays or lodging at
Kultur Berlin, can arrange tours and volunteering.

Tour operators
Bolivia Specialist, *N Ortiz 30*, T04-643 7389, www.
boliviaspecialist.com. Dutchman Dirk Dekker's
agency for local hikes, horse riding and 4WD
trips, tours in Bolivia and Peru; also bus and plane
tickets and information.
Candelaria Tours, *JJ Pérez 301 y Colón*, T04-
644 0340, www.candelariatours.com. Hikes
around Sucre, tours to weaving communities,
English spoken.
Cóndor Trekkers, *Calvo 102 y Bolívar*, T7289 1740,
www.condortrekkers.org. Not-for-profit trekking
company using local guides supported by
volunteers, city walks and treks around Sucre,
proceeds go to social projects, first-aid carried.
Also has an excellent vegetarian café (T7343 3392),
good value, some English spoken, free Wi-Fi.

Joy Ride Tourism, *N Ortiz 26, at corner of Plaza, T04-645 7603, www.joyridebol.com*. Mountain- and motorbiking, hiking, climbing, horse riding, paragliding, tours to Potosí and Salar de Uyuni.
Leyton's Magical Bolivian Historic Tours, *no storefront, T6967 9569, arturoleytonv@gmail. com, on Facebook*. Historic tours in and around Sucre and Potosí, run and guided by historian Luis Arturo Leyton, English spoken. Recommended.
Oasis Tours, *Arce 95, of 2, T04-643 2438, www. oasistours-bo.com*. City walking tour, indigenous communities, Chataquila, Inca trail. Also sell bus tickets and have their own office in Uyuni for *salar* trips. Very helpful owner.
San Martín, *Estudiantes 18, T04-646 6550, info@ sanmartinviajes.com*. Flight ticket sales, tours in and around Sucre. Good service.

Transport

Sucre
Air Alcantarí airport (T04-693 3112) is 31 km southeast of town on the road to Tarabuco. Direct flights to **La Paz**, **Santa Cruz**, **Cochabamba** and **Tarija** with BoA (Audiencia 21, T04-646 6600) and Ecojet (Dalence 138, T04-691 4711); to **La Paz** and **Santa Cruz** with **Amaszonas**. Airport tax US$1.60. Taxi to/from centre about US$10, 30-40 mins, or city bus from Av Gregorio Donoso y Av Jaime Mendoza, 1.4 km southeast of Plaza 25 de Mayo. Departure points for transport to the airport were in dispute in 2017; check in advance.

Bus Bus terminal is on north outskirts of town, 3 km from centre on Ostria Gutiérrez, T04-644 1292; taxi US$1.15; Micro A or 3. Daily to/from

La Paz several companies at 1700-2000, 12 hrs, regular US$12.75, *semi-cama* US$17.75, *cama* US$25.50. To **Cochabamba**: several companies daily at 1830-1930, 9 hrs via Aiquile (paved road); at 2100 via Oruro, 12 hrs, US$9.65, *semi-cama* US$12.50, *cama* US$19.50. To **Potosí**: frequent departures between 0630 and 1800, US$3-6, 3 hrs. Shared taxis with pick-up service: **Cielito Lindo**, T04-644 1014, **Cielito Express**, T04-643 1000 and **Expreso Dinos**, T04-643 7444, all outside the bus terminal, 2½ hrs, US$7 pp. To **Oruro**: 2000-2200, 4 companies via Potosí, 8 hrs, US$9-12. To **Tarija**: several companies, most at 1500-1600, also 4 daily with TNT (www. transportetnt.com), US$10 regular, US$11.50-14 semicama, US$14-22 cama, 11 hrs. To **Uyuni**: direct at 0830 with **6 de Octubre** and 0900 with **11 de Julio**, US$8-14, 8 hrs, or transfer in Potosí. To **Villazón** via Potosí and Tupiza: at 1330, 1730, **6 de Octubre** (with *bus cama*), 10 hrs, US$10-14; to **Tupiza**, 8 hrs, US$7-11.50. To **Santa Cruz**: many companies 1600-1730, 15 hrs, US$13.75; *semi-cama* US$18, *cama* US$24.

To Tarabuco Minivans leave when full from C Túpac Yupanqui (Parada de Tarabuco), daily starting 0630, US$1, 1¼ hrs on a good paved road. To get to the Parada take a micro "C" or "7" from the Mercado Central. Also buses to Tarabuco from Av de las Américas y Jaime Mendoza, same fare and times. Tourist buses from the cathedral on Sun at 0830, US$5 round-trip, reserve at **Oasis Tours** (address above); also **Real Audiencia**, depart San Alberto 181 y España, T04-644 3119, at 0830, return 1330; you must use the same bus you went on. Shared taxi with **Cielito Lindo** (see Transport to Potosí, above), Sun at 0900, US$5 return.

Potosí *Colour map 3, C3.*
one of the most beautiful, saddest and fascinating places you'll ever experience

Potosí is the highest city of its size in the world (population 175,562, altitude 3977 m). It was founded by the Spaniards on 10 April 1545, after they had discovered indigenous mine workings at Cerro Rico (4824 m), which dominates the city. Immense amounts of silver were once extracted. In Spain *'es un Potosí'* (it's a Potosí) is still used for anything superlatively rich.

By the early 17th century Potosí was the largest city in the Americas, but over the next two centuries, as its lodes began to deteriorate and silver was found elsewhere, Potosí became little more than a ghost town. It was the demand for tin – a metal the Spaniards ignored – that saved the city from absolute poverty in the early 20th century, until the price slumped because of over-supply. Mining continues in Cerro Rico (mainly tin, zinc, lead, antimony and wolfram) to this day.

Sights
Plaza 10 de Noviembre and around Large parts of Potosí are colonial, with twisting streets and an occasional great mansion with its coat of arms over the doorway. The city is a UNESCO World Heritage Site. Some of the best buildings are grouped round the Plaza 10 de Noviembre. The old Cabildo and

the Royal Treasury – Las Cajas Reales – are both here, converted to other uses. The massive cathedral faces Plaza 10 de Noviembre.

West of the plaza The ☆**Casa Nacional de Moneda (Mint)** ① *C Ayacucho, T02-622 2777, www.bolivian.com/cnm, Tue-Sat 0900-1230, 1430-1830, Sun 0900-1230, entry US$6, plus US$3 to take photos, US$6 for video, entry by regular, 2-hr guided tour only (in English or French if there are 10 or more people, at 0900, 1030, 1430 and 1630),* is near the plaza. Founded in 1572, rebuilt 1759-1773, it is one of the chief monuments of civil building in Hispanic America. Thirty of its 160 rooms are a museum with sections on mineralogy, silverware and an art gallery in a splendid salon on the first floor. One section is dedicated to the works of the acclaimed 17th- to 18th-century religious painter Melchor Pérez de Holguín. Elsewhere are coin dies and huge wooden presses which made the silver strips from which coins were cut. The smelting houses have carved altarpieces from Potosí's ruined churches. You can't fail to notice the huge, grinning mask of Bacchus over an archway between two principal courtyards. Erected in 1865, its smile is said to be ironic and aimed at the departing Spanish. Wear warm clothes; it's cold inside.

Potosí has many outstanding colonial churches. Among its baroque churches, typical of 18th-century Andean or 'mestizo' architecture, are the Jesuit **Compañía de Jesús church and bell-gable** ① *Ayacucho entre Bustillos y Oruro,* whose beautiful façade hides the modern tourist office building, and whose tower has a **mirador** ① *0800-1200, 1400-1800, 30 mins later Sat-Sun, US$1.40.*

Further west, the **Convento y Museo de Santa Teresa** ① *Santa Teresa y Ayacucho, T02-622 3847, http://museosantateresa.blogspot.co.uk, only by guided tour in Spanish or English, Mon-Sat 0900-1230, 1500-1800; Sun 0900-1200, 1500-1800, museum is closed Tue and Sun morning; US$3, US$1.50 to take photos, US$25 for video,* has an impressive amount of giltwork inside and an interesting collection of colonial and religious art.

South of the plaza Another interesting church, **San Francisco** ① *Tarija y Nogales, T02-622 2539, Mon-Fri 0900-1100, 1430-1700, Sat 0900-1100, US$2.15,* has a fine organ and is worthwhile for the views from the tower and roof, the museum of ecclesiastical art and an underground tunnel system.

Three blocks east, the **Museo del Ingenio de San Marcos** ① *La Paz 1565 y Betanzos, T02-622 6717, 1000-1500, US$1.40; textiles museum and shop Mon-Sat 1430-2200; restaurant 1000-1530, 1830-2200,* is a well-preserved example of the city's industrial past, with machinery used in grinding down the silver ore. It also has cultural activities and an exhibition of Calcha textiles.

North of the plaza On the north side of the Plaza 6 de Agosto, the **Teatro Omiste** has an imposing façade.

To the east are the churches of **La Merced** ① *Hoyos y Millares, US$1.40 for museo sacro and mirador, US$0.70 for mirador only (with café),* with great views of Cerro Rico and the city, and **San Martín** ① *Hoyos, T02-622 3682, Mon-Sat 1000-1200, 1500-1830, free,* which has an uninviting exterior, but is beautiful inside. It is normally closed for fear of theft so ask the German Redemptorist Fathers to show you around; their office is just to the left of the church.

Essential Potosí

Finding your feet

The airport, 6 km out of town on the Sucre road, has scheduled flights to Cochabamba with BoA. The bus terminal (Nueva Terminal) is on Avenida de las Banderas at the north end of the city. Frequent buses go to Oruro and La Paz and there are good roads to Uyuni, Sucre and Tarija. Cochabamba is a long bus ride with connections on to Santa Cruz. See also Transport, page 330.

When to go

Bring warm clothes at any time of year; the average temperature is 9°C and there are 130 sub-zero nights a year. The dampest months are October to March.

Time required

Two to three days to visit the city.

Tip...

Take it easy on arrival; remember Potosí is even higher than La Paz.

Directly north of the plaza, the **Museo Universitario** ① *C Bolívar 54 y Sucre, T02-622 7310, Mon-Fri 0800-1200, 1400-1800, US$0.70*, displays archaeology, fossils, costumes, musical instruments and some good modern Bolivian painting. Guided tour to the mirador (tower) offers great views, US$0.70. Nearby is the church of **San Agustín** ① *Bolívar y Quijarro, open only for Mass*, which has crypts and catacombs (much of the city was interconnected by tunnels in colonial times), and **San Lorenzo** (1728-1744) ① *Héroes del Chaco y Bustillos, Mass 0700-1000*, with a rich portal and fine views from the tower.

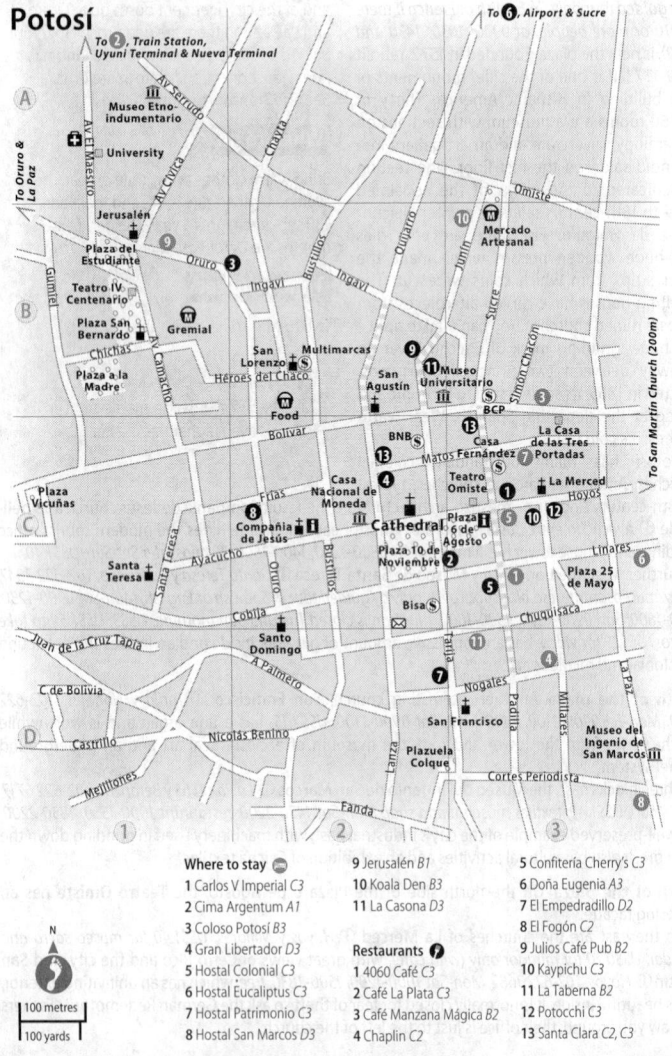

Potosí

Where to stay 🛏
1 Carlos V Imperial *C3*
2 Cima Argentum *A1*
3 Coloso Potosí *B3*
4 Gran Libertador *D3*
5 Hostal Colonial *C3*
6 Hostal Eucaliptus *C3*
7 Hostal Patrimonio *C3*
8 Hostal San Marcos *D3*
9 Jerusalén *B1*
10 Koala Den *B3*
11 La Casona *D3*

Restaurants 🍴
1 4060 Café *C3*
2 Café La Plata *C3*
3 Café Manzana Mágica *B2*
4 Chaplin *C2*
5 Confitería Cherry's *C3*
6 Doña Eugenia *A3*
7 El Empedradillo *D2*
8 El Fogón *C2*
9 Julios Café Pub *B2*
10 Kaypichu *C3*
11 La Taberna *B2*
12 Potocchi *C3*
13 Santa Clara *C2, C3*

Further north, the fascinating **Museo Etno-indumentario** ① *Av Serrudo 152, T02-622 3258, Mon-Fri 0930-1200, 1430-1800, Sat 0930-1200, US$1.40, includes tour,* displays in detail the dress, customs and histories of Potosí department's 16 provinces.

City centre architecture In Potosí, 2000 colonial buildings have been catalogued. Among the better preserved examples is the house of the **Marqués de Otavi**, now the BNB bank, on Junín between Matos and Bolívar. Next to Hotel Gran Libertador, on Millares between Nogales and Chuquisaca, is a doorway with two rampant lions in low relief on the lintel. The **Casa de las Tres Portadas** (house of the three arches), on Bolívar near La Paz, is a *hostal*.

☆Mine tours

For many, the main reason for being in Potosí is to visit the mines of Cerro Rico. The state mines were closed in the 1980s and are now worked as cooperatives by small groups of miners in conditions which are, if anything, more dangerous than in colonial times. An estimated 14,000 miners work in 49 cooperatives, some 800 are children. *The Devil's Miner* is a recommended documentary film about child labour in the mines, shown regularly by Potosí agencies and Sucre cafés.

A tour to the mines and ore-processing plant involves meeting miners and seeing them at work first-hand. Mine entrances are above 4000 m and temperatures inside can reach 40°C, with noxious dust and gasses. You should be acclimatized, fit and have no heart or breathing problems, such as asthma. Tours last up to five hours and their difficulty varies; you can ask for a shorter, less gruelling, visit if you wish. Not all tours visit the processing plant.

Guided tours are conducted by former miners; by law all guides have to work with a tour agency and carry an ID card issued by the Prefectura. Essential equipment is provided: helmet, lamp and usually protective clothing but large-size boots may not be available. Wear old clothes and take a torch and a handkerchief or mask to filter the dusty air. The smaller the tour group, the better. Some are as large as 20 people, which is excessive. Tours cost about US$10.50-13 per person and include transport. Many agencies say they give part of their proceeds to miners but such claims are difficult to verify. You can also contribute directly, for example by taking medicines to the health centre (Posta Sanitaria) on Cerro Rico. Saturday and Sunday are the quietest days (Sunday is the miners' day off). **Note** Tourists are not allowed to buy dynamite to give to miners.

Museo Histórico Minero Diego Huallpa ① *by Mina Pailaviri on Cerro Rico, city buses P, Q, 70 and others, T02-623 1143, Mon-Sat 0900-1200, 1430-1800, Sun 0900-1500, US$10,* has exhibits of minerals and mining techniques, two-hour visits include mine tunnels with mannequins instead of real miners.

Tarapaya

A good place to freshen up after visiting the mines (or to spend a day relaxing) is Tarapaya, 21 km on the road to Oruro, where there are **thermal baths** ① *public pools US$0.50 and private baths US$1.20 per hr (see complejorecreacional.detarapaya on Facebook), and cabins for rent ($) and camping, US$4.25.* On the other side of the river from Tarapaya is a 60-m-diameter crater lake, which has a temperature of 30-34°C; take sun protection. Below the crater lake are boiling ponds, not fit for swimming. **Balneario Miraflores** (25 km) ① *pools US$0.35, private baths US$2.80,* has hotter water than Tarapaya, but is not as clean. Minibuses run to both *balnearios* from outside Chuquimia market on Avenida Universitaria, 0600-1800, US$0.75; taxi US$9. The last vehicle back to Potosí from Miraflores is at 1800.

South of Potosí

A paved road runs south of Potosí. At Ingenio Cucho (Km 38) the road splits. One branch continues south to Cotagaita, Tupiza and Villazón. The other road goes east to the next valley then south to Camargo and the Valle de Cinti to El Puente, where it climbs to the altiplano before descending eventually to Tarija. Both branches are paved.

The tranquil colonial town of **Camargo** (population 14,200, altitude 2406 m) is surrounded by vineyards and fruit orchards, 186 km south of Potosí. Straddling the Río Chico and flanked by crumbling red sandstone cliffs on one side and rolling hills on the other, the town has a very pretty setting. The church is by the main **Plaza 6 de Agosto**. The bus terminal and a small market are along Avenida Chuquisaca, closer to **Plazuela Avaroa**. The main market is at the opposite end of town past the main plaza. Also along Avenida Chuquisaca is the **Alcaldía**, where you can get information about the area. Places to stay include **Hostal Plaza** ($$ Grau 13, T04-629 2977, hostalplaza.camargo@outlook.es, modern, family-run, very hospitable) and **Villa Sofía** ($ Potosí 17, T04-629 2047, on Facebook, old house and new sections, big garden, family-run, very nice). Many shops sell excellent fruit preserves, singani and wine. Many vineyards nearby can be visited and there is **Museo Etno Antropológico de Cinti** ① *Comunidad El Chical, just south of Camargo, T04-629 2092, US$1.50, with toilets.*

The main road runs south from Camargo, between the Río Chico and towering red cliffs, 42 km to **Villa Abecia**, a lovely small town surrounded by vineyards and fruit orchards on the banks of the Río Grande ($$-$ Hostal Cepas de Mi Abuelo, near the plaza, T7299 0111, is a delightful hotel with traditional linen and home-made and home-grown produce). Beyond Villa Abecia is **Las Carreras**, in the far southern reaches of the department of Chuquisaca, where a small bodega, **La Casa de Barro**, is denominated a **Museo de Sitio Vivo**, with its vines clambering over molle and chañar trees. Next is **El Puente**, where the road turns east and crosses the Río San Juan de Oro into the department of Tarija. From here it climbs steeply along cacti-covered slopes with beautiful views to the **Altiplano de Tarija**, a high plateau at about 3500 m. After the **Falda la Queñua** tunnel is a vertiginous 1900-m descent to the flat valley north of Tarija.

Listings Potosí *map page 326.*

Tourist information

Infotur
Ayacucho s/n, Torre de la Compañía,
T02-623 1021, www.potosy.com.bo.
Also at the bus terminal.

Where to stay

Unless otherwise stated hotels have no heating.

$$$ Coloso Potosí
Bolívar 965, T02-622 2627, www.potosihotel.com.
Comfortable modern rooms with frigobar, heating, bath tubs and nice views. Small indoor pool, sauna, parking.

$$$-$$ Cima Argentum
Av Villazón 239, T02-622 9538,
www.hca-potosi.com.
Modern comfortable rooms and suites all with safe. Warm and bright, heating, frigobar.

$$$-$$ Hostal Patrimonio
Matos 62, T02-622 2659,
www.hostalpatrimonio.com.
Bright, warm, modern hotel. Heating, frigobar and safe in each room, sauna and jacuzzi (suites each have their own).

$$ Hostal Colonial
Hoyos 8, T02-622 4809, www.
hostalcolonialpotosi.com.bo.
Older place but well located, breakfast extra, carpeted, heating, bathtubs, frigobar.

$$ Hotel Gran Libertador
Millares 58, T02-622 7877,
www.hotelgranlibertador.com.
Colonial-style hotel, good buffet breakfast, cafeteria, comfortable rooms, central heating, quiet, helpful, parking.

$$-$ Jerusalén
Oruro 143, T02-622 4633, http://hoteljerusalen.es.tl.
HI affiliated, private rooms and dorms, near Mercado Gremial, family-run, money exchange, book exchange, common and TV room, laundry service, café.

$ Carlos V Imperial
Linares 42, T02-623 1010.
Cheaper rooms without bath, hot water, kitchen facilities.

$ Hostal Eucaliptus
Linares 88A, T7240 1884, part of Koala Tours
(see below).
Pleasant bright rooms, cheaper with shared bath, heating, good breakfast, 350 m from main plaza.

$ Hostal San Marcos
La Paz 1626 y Periodista, T02-623 001.
Colonial house, nice comfortable rooms, heating, cooking facilities.

$ Koala Den
Junín 56, T02-622 6467, papaimilla@
hotmail.com (Koala-Den on Facebook).
Private rooms with bath and breakfast (cheaper in dorm), heating, TV and video, use of kitchen, popular and often full.

$ La Casona
Chuquisaca 460, T02-623 0523,
www.hotelpotosi.com.
Cheaper with shared bath and in dorm,
courtyard, kitchen facilities.

Restaurants

$$ 4060 Café
Hoyos y Sucre. Open 1600-late, food until 2300.
Restaurant/bar serving good meals, varied
menu, large portions, nice atmosphere, heating.
Recommended.

$$ El Empedradillo
Tarija 43, T02-262 8130. Daily from 1200.
Local and international cuisine in a colonial
setting; best known for its Calapurcka soup,
served with a hot rock which helps keep it warm.
Good ambiance and service.

$$ El Fogón
Frías 58 y Oruro. Daily 1200-2300.
Restaurant/grill, good food and atmosphere.

$$-$ Julios Café Pub
Junín 17, T02-623 1362. Open all day.
Popular for sandwiches, hamburgers (meat or
vegetarian) and its unique llama meat salteñas
served in the morning; also breakfast, Bolivian and
international dishes, hot drinks, pub at night with
occasional live music. Popular with travellers.

$$-$ Kaypichu
Millares 16. Tue-Sun 0700-1300, 1700-2300.
Breakfast, vegetarian options, *peña* in
high season.

$$-$ La Taberna
Junín 12, T02-6230123, www.lataverne.com.bo.
Mon-Sat 0830-2300, Sun 1900-2200.
Bolivian and international food with a French
touch, set lunch and à la carte in the evening,
good service.

$$-$ Potocchi
Millares 24, T622 2759. Open 0800-2230.
International and local dishes, can accommodate
special diets with advance notice, *peña* in
high season.

$ Doña Eugenia
Santa Cruz y Ortega. Open 0900-1300.
Typical food such as the warming *kalapurca* soup
with corn and meat (be careful it is hot) and
chicharrón de cerdo, pork crackling.

Cafés

Café La Plata
Tarija y Linares at Plaza 10 de Noviembre.
Mon-Sat 1000-2200.
Upmarket place for coffee, sweets and drinks.
Nice atmosphere, English and French spoken.

Café Manzana Mágica
Oruro 239.
Meat-free meals only, a popular, small café.

Chaplin
Matos y Quijarro. Mon-Fri 0830-1200.
Breakfasts and excellent *tucumanas*
(fried *empanadas*).

Confitería Cherry's
Padilla 8. Open 0800-2230.
Small economical place, good cakes, breakfast.

Santa Clara
Quijarro 32 y Matos, also Sucre 33 y Bolívar and
other locations. Mon-Sat 0700-2300.
Popular with locals for afternoon snacks.

Festivals

Potosí is sometimes called the 'Ciudad de las
Costumbres', especially at Corpus Cristi, Todos
Santos and Carnaval, when special sweets are
prepared, families go visiting friends, etc.

Jan/Feb Carnaval Minero, 2 weeks before
Carnaval in Oruro, includes **Tata Ckascho**, when
miners dance down Cerro Rico and El Tío (the
Dios Minero) is paraded.
End May/beginning Jun Fiesta de Manquiri:
on 3 consecutive Sat llama sacrifices are made at
the cooperative mines in honour of Pachamama.
Aug San Bartolomé, or **Chutillos**, is held from
the middle of Aug, with the main event being
processions of dancers on the weekend closest
to the 24-26 Aug; Sat features Potosino, and Sun
national, groups. Costumes can be hired in the
artesanía market on C Sucre. Hotel and transport
prices go up by 30% for the whole of that weekend.
10 Nov Fiesta Aniversiario de Potosí.

Shopping

Mercado Artesanal, *Sucre y Omiste. Mon-Sat*
0830-1230, 1430-1830. Sells handwoven cloth and
regional handicrafts. There are several craft shops
on C Sucre between Omiste and Bustillos.
Mercado Central, *Bustillos y Bolívar.* Sells mainly
meat and some produce.
Mercado Gremial, *between Av Camacho*
and Oruro. For household goods.

What to do

All agencies offer mine tours (see page 327), trips to the Salar de Uyuni (see page 303) and REA (see page 305) and trekking at Kari Kari lakes, the artificial water sources for the city and mines.

Claudia Tours, *Ayacucho 7, T02-622 5000, www. turismoclaudia.com.* City tours, mines and trekking; also in Uyuni, Av Ferroviaria opposite Hotel Avenida.
Hidalgo Tours, *La Paz 1133, T02-622 9512, www. salardeuyuni.net; also in Uyuni.* Specialized services in Potosí and to Salar de Uyuni. Pioneering tour operator for the Uyuni salt flats and the lagoons, having the first salt hotel in the world, the **Palacio de Sal**; see page 308.
Koala Tours, *Ayacucho 3, T02-622 2092, koalabolivia@hotmail.com.* Owner Eduardo Garnica speaks English and French. Their mine tours are popular and have been recommended.
Leyton's Magical Bolivian Historic Tours, see Sucre Tour operators, page 324.
Silver Tours, *Quijarro 12, T02-622 3600.* Economical mine tours.
Sin Fronteras, *Ayacucho 17 y Bustillos, T02-622 4058, frontpoi@entelnet.bo, on Facebook.* Owner Juan Carlos Gonzales speaks English and French and is very helpful. Mine tours, full-day private or shared tours from Potosí to Salar de Uyuni, ending in Uyuni or Potosí. Also sells flight and bus tickets (national and international), arranges private transport and hires camping gear.

Transport

Air The airport, Capitán Nicolás Rojas, is 6 km from Potosí on the road to Sucre. **BoA** flies daily direct to **Cochabamba** (US$41-51) with connection to **La Paz** (US$59-76) and direct to **Santa Cruz** (US$56-62).

Bus Large modern bus terminal (Nueva Terminal, Av Las Banderas, use fee US$0.30) with ATMs, luggage store, information office, tourist police and food court. **Note** it is far from the centre: taxi US$2; city buses F, I, 150, US$0.20, but there are no city buses or taxis late at night; not safe to go out on the street, try to arrive by day or wait inside until morning. Daily services: **La Paz** several companies 1900-2230, US$9-13, 10 hrs by paved road; *bus cama* US$18.25 (departures from La Paz 1830-2030). To travel by day, go to **Oruro**, several daily, US$5.50-7.50, 5 hrs; vans US$8.50, 4 hrs. Buses to **Uyuni** leave from the old bus terminal, Av Universitaria beyond the train station, 1000-1200 and 1800-2000, US$6, 3-4 hrs on a paved road, superb scenery; book in advance. **Cochabamba** several companies 1830-2030, US$9-13, *bus cama* US$18.75, 10 hrs. **Sucre** frequent service 0630-1800, US$3-6, 3 hrs; also shared taxis from behind the old bus terminal, **Cielito Lindo**, T02-624 3381, 2½ hrs, US$7 pp, drop-off at your hotel. For **Santa Cruz** change in Sucre or Cochabamba. **Tupiza** several companies (**Oglobo** and **Expreso Tupiza** are good), US$4.50-7.50, 5 hrs; continuing to **Villazón**, US$6-10, 6 hrs. Also vans (*minibuses*) and cars (*rapiditos*), US$11.50, 3½ hrs to Tupiza; to Villazón vans US$8, 5 hrs; cars (*rapiditos*) US$9-15, 5 hrs. **Tarija** several companies 1800-1830, US$6-7 *semicama*, US$9 *cama*, 7-8 hrs, spectacular journey; to go by day, take transport to Camargo and transfer; also cars throughout the day from Potosí, US$14.50, 5½ hrs. Camargo buses leave from offices outside main terminal.

Train Station is at Av Sevilla y Villazón, T02-622 3101, www.fca.com.bo. A 25-passenger railcar to **Sucre** leaves on Tue, Thu, Sat 0800, 6 hrs, US$3.60; confirm details in advance.

Tarija and around *Colour map 3, C4.*

a warm easy-going city with shady parks and flower-filled plazas

☆This pleasant city on the banks of the Río Guadalquivir, with streets and plazas planted with flowering trees, is blessed with plenty of sun and a spring-like climate almost all year-round. Tarija is known for the fruit and wines of the fertile Valle Central in which it sits.

Founded 4 July 1574 by Capitán Luis de Fuentes y Vargas, Tarija declared itself independent of Spain in 1807, and in 1825 it opted to join Bolivia. With a population of 234,422, the city has a strong cultural heritage which sets it apart from the rest of the country. Since 2005 it has experienced an economic boom thanks to the development of natural gas in the department.

Sights

The oldest and most interesting church in the city is the **Basílica de San Francisco** ① *corner of La Madrid y Daniel Campos, 0700-1000, 1800-2000, Sun 0630-1200, 1800-2000.* It is beautifully painted inside, with praying angels depicted on the ceiling and the four evangelists at the four corners below the dome. The library is divided into old and new sections, the old containing some 15,000 volumes, the new a further 5000. To see the library, go to the door at Ingavi O-0137. Behind the church is the **Museo Fray Francisco Miguel de Mari** ⓘ *Colón 641, entre La Madrid e Ingavi, T04-6661767, www.franciscanosdetarija.com, Mon-Fri 1500-1800, US$2.15*, with colonial and contemporary art collections, colonial books, the oldest of which is a 1501 Iliad, 19th-century photograph albums and other items.

The **Casa Dorada** ⓘ *Ingavi 370 entre Trigo y Sucre, T04-664 4606 http://casadelaculturatarija.com, guided tours Mon-Fri at 0900, 1000, 1100, 1500, 1600, and 1700, Sat 0900, 1000, 1100, US$0.70, free cultural events nightly at 1900*, begun in 1886, is also known as the Maison d'Or and is now part of the Casa de la Cultura. It belonged to importer/exporter Moisés Navajas and his wife Esperanza Morales and has been beautifully restored inside and out.

Tarija's **Museo de Arqueología y Paleontología** ⓘ *Trigo 402 y Lema, T04-663 6680, Mon-Fri 0800-1200, 1500-1800, Sat 0900-1200, 1500-1800, US$0.70 minimum contribution*, contains a palaeontological collection (fossils, remains of several Andean elephants of the Pleistocene), as well as smaller mineralogical, ethnographic and anthropological collections. The outskirts of the city can be a good place to look for **fossils**, but report any finds to the university.

Valle Central

The Valle Central, which surrounds Tarija, offers many opportunities for excursions in pleasant countryside at about 1800 m. As well as the fossil deposits, there are vineyards and bodegas (wineries), riverside beaches, waterfalls and colonial towns. It is this zone which inspires the nickname Andalucía of Bolivia because of its fruit and berry production, vegetables, ham cured Serrano-style, goat's cheese, preserves and honey. You can buy local produce at **Las Duelas Calamuchita** ⓘ *opposite the sports field in village of Calamuchita near Valle de la Concepción, T04-666 8943, Mon-Sat 0900-1200, 1430-1645*, a shop and small winery, selling mostly artisanal wines and singani from nine producers, wine-tasting (pay what you consume) and regional preserves, ham and other items. In Tarija itself **La Vinoteca** and **La Rotisería** (see Shopping, page 335) sell regional wines and other products.

☆Wineries

Tarija is proud of its **wine** and **singani** (clear brandy) production, the best in Bolivia. There are two distinct wine-producing regions near Tarija. The first is in the Valle de Cinti, which can easily be reached from Tarija. The best option is to take a tour (see What to do, page 336), which provides transport and allows you to visit several different bodegas on the same day. The same applies to the second region, south of town in the Valle Central. See box, page 332, for a selection of wine producers. The main centres are Santa Ana and La Concepción.

Finding your feet

Daily scheduled flights to La Paz, Cochabamba, Sucre and Santa Cruz. There are paved roads to Potosí, where good connections can be made elsewhere, and Bermejo on the Argentine border. Roads west to Tupiza and east to the Chaco for the route to Santa Cruz are being improved – slowly.

Getting around

Note that blocks west of Calle Colón have a small O before number (oeste), and all blocks east have an E (este); blocks are numbered from Colón outwards. All streets north of Avenida Las Américas are preceded by N (norte).

When to go

The best time to visit is from December to April, when the fruit is in season, but September, after the spring rains begin, is also nice. The months when most rain falls are October to March.

Time required

Two to three days in the city and surroundings, but if travelling onwards overland, allow another day to get to your next destination.

Immigration

Avenida La Paz 892 esquina Oruro, Parque Bolívar, T04-664 3594, Monday-Friday 0830-1230, 1430-1830. Visa renewals take up to three days.

ON THE ROAD

Tarija wineries

Aranjuez, *T04-664 2552, gcomercial@vinosaranjuez.com*. Bodega at Avenida Dr A Baldivieso E-1976, Barrio Aranjuez, across the river within walking distance of town is open to visitors. A large bodega producing only wine.

Bodegas Magnus, *Ingavi 244, T04-611 2462 (bodega), www.bodegasmagnus.com*. A small winery since 2000, which is open to tourists, concentrating on reds and rosé, in Valle de la Concepción.

Campos de Solana, *15 de Abril E-0259 entre Suipacha y Méndez (tienda), T04-664 8482, www. camposdesolana.com*. Increasingly recognized for their selection of fine wines (the Malbec is highly regarded), as well as the popular Casa Real brand of singani (same company, same shop but different bodega, T04-664 5498, http://casa-real.com). The Campos de Solana bodega is in El Portillo, 6 km on road to Bermejo and the Casa Real bodega (T6737 0868, visitas@casa-real.com) is in Santa Ana, about 15 km off the road to Bermejo. Vineyards and bodegas are open to visitors.

Casa Vieja, *Trigo casi Corrado (shop), T04-666 2605, www.lacasavieja.info, Mon-Sun 1000-1600*. A traditional *bodega artesanal*, small-scale winery, located in Valle de la Concepción, 25 km from Tarija. Interesting and recommended. It also has a popular restaurant overlooking the vines, open daily for lunch (dishes US$3-7) and, on Sunday, live music and roast suckling pig (*chancho a la cruz*), US$10.

Kohlberg, *Av Francisco Lazcano, Barrio San Jorge No 1, T04-666 6366, http://kohlberg.com.bo*. Bodega La Cabaña in Santa Ana, 15 km from town off the road to Bermejo. The first industrial winery and now the largest. Specializes in table wines, their Syrah is well regarded.

La Concepción, *Colón entre 15 de Abril y La Madrid (shop), T04-664 5040, T04-666 3787 (bodega), 7870 9646, www.laconcepcion.bo*. Wines (try their Cabernet Sauvignon) and Rujero singani, bodega in Valle de la Concepción.

North of Tarija

About 15 km north of the centre is the charming town of **San Lorenzo**. Just off the plaza is the **Museo Méndez** ① *T04-664 1194, Tue-Sun 0900-1230, 1500-1830, suggested contribution US$0.70*, the house of the independence hero Eustaquio Méndez, 'El Moto'. The small museum exhibits his weapons, his bed and his 'testimonio'. At lunchtime on Sunday, many courtyards serve cheap meals. Minibuses from Domingo Paz y J M Saracho leave every five minutes, US$0.75. The road to San Lorenzo passes **Tomatitas** (5 km), now almost a suburb of Tarija, a popular picnic and river-bathing area, from where a good day trip is to the waterfalls at **Coimata**. **Rincón de la Victoria**, 14 km from Tarija, has a similar setting.

There is a challenging one- to two-day trek along a **Camino del Inca** from Pujzara (community hostel) in **Reserva de Sama** to **Pinos Sud**, from where public transport can take you back to the city. At least two days are recommended to appreciate a few of the many wonders of the reserve, bird-rich lakes in the *altiplano* and beautiful cloud forest at lower elevations. For information contact SERNAP ① *Av Jaime Paz 1171, T04-665 0850*. Tours offered by Tarija operators.

To Argentina

The Argentine Consulate is at Ballivián N 0699 y Bolívar, T04-664 3273, open Mon-Fri 0830-1230. The quickest route is via Bermejo, which is easily reached from Tarija; 210 km all paved, the views are also spectacular (sit on the right). This road gives access to Reserva Tariquía, protecting *selva tucumano-boliviana* (humid forest). **Bermejo** (population 21,500, altitude 415 m) is well supplied with places to sleep and eat and there are many *casas de cambio* (including in the bus terminal); it's very hot. Tourist information office at bus terminal (Mon-Fri 0730-1200, 1500-1830).

Tip...
Bolivia is one or two hours behind Argentina, depending on the time of year.

An international bridge (El Tinglado), 2.5 km from Bermejo (taxi US$1.50), crosses the river to **Aguas Blancas**, Argentina, this route, open 24 hours, is used by through buses and private vehicles. If driving from Tarija, the access to the bridge is at La Tranca, before reaching Bermejo. On the Argentine side of the bridge is Argentine customs, where all incoming luggage is x-rayed. Both Bolivian and Argentine immigration are in one complex at Puesto 28 (23 km south of Aguas Blancas, 18 km north of Orán). You can also cross the river from Bermejo to Puerto Chalana by launch (US$0.60), which takes you directly to another combined Bolivian-Argentine immigration post, open 0600-1800 Bolivian time, 150 m from the Aguas Blancas bus station. Bermejo's bus terminal is at the opposite end of town from the international bridge (taxi port-terminal US$0.60 per person). Another option from Tarija is the road to Villazón (see page 312), which is the shortest route to Argentina, 189 km, but it's a tiring trip along a winding, scenic mountain road. A third option, from Tarija to the Yacuiba/Pocitos border (see page 361), is 290 km away.

Listings Tarija and around

Tourist information

Tarija

Dirección de Turismo
Gral Trigo entre 15 de Abril y La Madrid, T04-667 2633, www.turismo.tarija.gob.bo. Mon-Fri 0800-1200, 1500-1900, Sat-Sun 0900-1200, also at airport Mon-Fri same hours.
Helpful, and they provide a city and departmental map.

Dirección Municipal de Turismo
C 15 de Abril y Mcal Sucre, T04-663 3581. Mon-Fri 0800-1200, 1430-1830.
Helpful, city map, some English spoken; also has a booth at the Nueva Terminal de Buses, T04-666 7701, Mon-Fri 0800-1200, 1430-1830, Sat-Sun 1600-2030. The municipal office is on the south side of the Plaza Luis de Fuentes, which also contains the Patio del Cabildo, where events and concerts are held.

Where to stay

Tarija
Some hotels may offer low-season discounts, May-Aug.

$$$$-$$$ Los Parrales Resort
Urbanización Carmen de Aranjuez Km 3.5, T04-664 8444, www.losparraleshotel.com.
Large luxury hotel offering fine views over the city and surrounding hills. Includes buffet breakfast, pool, spa, gym, Wi-Fi in communal areas. Non-guests can pay US$7 to use the pool and other facilities.

$$$ Altiplano
Belgrano 1640 entre Lazcano y Gral Sosa, T04-666 3550, www.altiplanohotel.com.

A high-standard B&B owned by a couple from New Zealand, a bit of a walk from the centre, cosy elegant, contemporary design with traditional fabrics, delightful rooms, very comfortable, good breakfast, thoughtful service with attention to detail. Warmly recommended.

$$$ Terravina
Bolívar E 525 entre Santa Cruz y Junín, T04-666 8673, terravinatarija@gmail.com.
Modern boutique hotel with a wine theme, rooms with fridge and heating and fully furnished 1- and 2-bedroom apartments, 2 rooms on the ground floor are equipped for disabled guests, includes buffet breakfast.

$$ Hostal Carmen
Ingavi O-0784, T04-664 3372, www.hostalcarmentarija.com.
Older place but well maintained, excellent buffet breakfast, hot water, heating, airport transfers available. Often full, advance booking advised, very helpful, good value. Recommended.

$$ Mitru Tarija
Avaroa 450, entre Isaac Attie y Delgadillo, T04-664 3930, www.hotelmitrutarija.com.
Modern hotel built around a central garden, convenient, large comfortable rooms with a/c, heating, frigobar and safe, also family rooms, light and airy, includes excellent buffet breakfast, parking. In the same group as, and with the same high standards as the Mitru hotels in Tupiza and La Paz.

$ Hostel Casa Blanca
Ingavi 645 entre Juan Misael Saracho y Ballivian, T04-664 2909, luiszilvetiali@gmail.com (see also Facebook HostelCasaBlancaTarija).
Good cheap option, popular with foreign travellers, conveniently placed 3 blocks from the main plaza, English spoken, lots of information, café.

$ Residencial Rosario
Ingavi O-0777, T04-664 2942.
Simple rooms, cheaper with shared bath, hot water, good budget option, family atmosphere, helpful.

Valle Central

$ Hostería Valle d'Vino
Verdiguera y 6 de Julio, Valle de la Concepción, T04-665 1056, www.valledivinotarija.com.
Hostel with private rooms with bath and dorms, breakfast extra, idiosyncratic place with the small **Infiernillo Bodega** with wine for sale and weekend fiestas, a museum with a mish-mash of items from flat irons and stoves to fossils and animal skins, a 'tunnel of love' and other oddities (tour of the property US$1.50).

$ Las Lomas
C Final Campo Ferial, Valle de la Concepción, T7454 9394.
Small hotel with views of vineyards, nice ample rooms with private or shared bath, good beds, patio, breakfast available with advanced notice.

To Argentina

$$-$ París
La Paz y Tarija, Bermejo, T04-696 1022.
Central hotel with bath and a/c, cheaper with fan, electric shower, includes breakfast, parking.

$ Alojamiento San Roque
Opposite the bus terminal, Bermejo, T7453 4024.
Adequate lodging, private or shared bath, fan, no breakfast.

Restaurants

Tarija
Many restaurants (and much else in town) close between 1400 and 1600.

$$$-$$ Don Pepe Rodizio
D Campos N-0138, near Av Las Américas.
Stylish restaurant serving tasty daily set lunch, all-you-can-eat *rodizio* at weekends for US$10.

$$$-$$ El Fogón del Gringo
La Madrid O-1053, Plaza Uriondo. Daily 1200-1430, 1900-2300.
Upmarket *parrillada* includes excellent salad bar.

$$$-$$ La Taberna
Sucre 508 y 15 de Abril, T04-665 4880, www.lataverne.com.bo. Daily 0800-2300.

In the former Club Social, a traditional setting on the main plaza, serves international food, seafood (including ceviche) and meat dishes, also set lunch.

$$ El Marqués
La Madrid entre Trigo y Sucre, on the main plaza. Daily 0830-2300.
In the beautiful historic Casa El Marqués de Tojo, specializing in international food, seafood and fish, caters for events, popular.

$$ Guten
15 de Abril y Colón, Plaza Sucre, T04-6676445. Mon-Sat 0800-2400, Sun 0800-1700.
Limited menu of meat and fish dishes with a German touch, pasta and a snack menu, breakfast, desserts, set lunch ($), also bar, sports TV screens, low-key, good for a light meal.

$$ La Taberna Gattopardo
La Madrid y Sucre, on main plaza. Daily 0800-2100.
Pizza, *parrillada* with Argentine beef, local wines, desserts, snacks, excellent salads, popular meeting place.

$$ Sabores del Río
Av Jaime Paz 2313 esq Romero, T04-665 2686. Daily 0800-2200.
A very good fish restaurant not far from the entrance to the airport, set lunch ($) Mon-Fri.

$ El Guapito Pizza
Suipacha esq Alejandro del Carpio. Mon-Fri 1200-1430, 1930-2300, Sat-Sun1930-2300.
Good set lunch, pizza and pasta in the evening. Pleasant ambiance, attentive service.

$ El Patio
Sucre N-0458. Mon-Sat.
Good set lunch with small salad bar, also great *tucumanas al horno*.

$ Guadalquivir
Oruro entre O'Connor y Carlos Paz, on Parque Bolívar opposite the monument. Daily.
Economical restaurant offering daily *almuerzos* and a salad buffet.

$ Miiga Comida Coreana
Cochabamba 813 y Ballivian. Every night except Tue.
Good sushi with salmon and a small but tasty range of Korean dishes.

$ Verde que te quiero
Ballivián esq Bolivar, T6870 6635. Mon-Sat 1200-1400.

Excellent vegetarian buffet with ample selection. Popular, go early. Recommended.

Cafés

Café Belén
Colón N536 y Madrid. Mon-Sat 1630-2200.
Coffee, natural juices, healthy sandwiches, pastries, desserts.

DeliGelato
Suipacha 0462, Plaza Sucre. Daily until 2130.
Good ice cream.

Nobu
Gral Trigo on the main plaza.
Serving coffee, juices, sandwiches, ice cream, cakes and some meals.

To Argentina

$$-$ La Casona
C Barranqueras near the river, Bermejo.
A/c upmarket restaurant with a choice of Bolivian and international dishes.

Festivals

Tarija
Tarija is known for its fiestas.
Feb/Mar **Carnaval Chapaco** is lively and colourful; **Compadres**, celebrated on the Thu 2 weeks before carnival, and **Comadres**, celebrated on the Thu preceding carnival, are an important part of the tradition.
Apr **Abril en Tarija**, cultural events are held throughout the month; programme available at **Casa Dorada**.
15 Aug-14 Sep **La Virgen de Chaguaya**, a 45-km pilgrimage from the city to the Santuario Chaguaya, south of El Valle. For less devoted souls, Línea P *trufi* from Plaza Sucre, Tarija, to Padcaya, US$1.30; during the festival bus to Chaguaya and Padcaya from terminal daily, 0700, returns 1700, US$1.35; at other times, vans (*surubis*) as they fill, to Padcaya US$1.30, a different van to Chaguaya, US$0.60.
16 Aug-1st week Sep **San Roque**, Tarija's main festival. *Chunchos*, male devotees of the saint wearing tall, brightly stripped turbans, veils, colourful shawls and calf-length robes, carry the image of San Roque and dance to the tunes of unusual instruments. These processions take place throughout the 1st week of Sep. A different church is visited every day and on the main day, the 1st Sun, the procession with the richly dressed saint's statue goes to all the churches and ends in the church of San Roque. No alcohol is consumed.
Dec Christmas is the time of the Adoraciones, when children dance around a pole to the music of *tambores y quenas* (drums and flutes).

Around Tarija
Feb/Mar **Fiesta de la Vendimia**, Valle de la Concepción, 25 km from Tarija, is a week-long wine vintage festival. 10 days before La Vendimia is the Encuentro El Arte y El Vino, with music, theatre, painting, sculpture, workshops for children. The artworks remain with the Municipio.
Mar/Apr **Easter week**, communities such as San Lorenzo and Padcaya welcome visitors with colourful arches and flowers to **La Pascua Florida** processions.
2nd Sun in Oct The flower festival commemorates the **Virgen del Rosario** (celebrations in the surrounding towns are recommended, eg San Lorenzo and Padcaya).

Shopping

Tarija

Handicrafts
Arte y Hogar, *Gen Trigo entre Corrado y Fray Manuel Mingo*. For leatherwork, embroidered blouses, knitted sweaters.
Artesanías Bolivia, *Sucre 952 entre D Paz y Corrado, T04-664 6947*. For local handicrafts and musical instruments.
Tejidos de Tajzara, *Gen Trigo, same block as Arte y Hogar*. Womens cooperative selling knitted goods.

Local produce and wine
See Valle Central, page 331, for additional shops selling local produce and wine.
La Rotisería, *Gral Trigo y Bolívar*. For meats, cheeses and wines.
La Vinoteca, *Ingavi O-0731 y Gral Trigo. Mon-Sat 0900-1200, 1500-1900*. Sells wine at bodega prices, cheese and ham.

Markets
The main market is in the block between Domingo Paz, Sucre, Bolívar and Trigo. In early 2017 it was being rebuilt and was due for completion the same year. There is also a **book market** on Pasaje Baldiviezo next to the Cathedral. The Mercado Campesino, wholesale market, is on the road heading north out of town towards San Lorenzo, open daily.

Tarija

Tour operators

There are several tour operators in the city, offering wine tours (all about US$22), tours of surroundings (Campiña Chapaca: San Lorenzo, Coimata and San Jacinto, about US$22), a combined wine and Campiña full-day tour (US$44), city tours, and the Camino del Inca. Most operators require advanced booking.

Bolivian Wine Tours, *Méndez 175, T7187 1626/7022 5715, www.bolivianwinetours.com.* Speciality tours to vineyards and wine cellars (*bodegas*) in the Valle Central and Valle de Cinti, focusing not only on the production of high-altitude wines but also on local culture. Ask here also about trips to the Reserva Biológica Cordillera de Sama and the Camino del Inca.

Educación y Futuro, *at the Ecosol shop, Virgino Lema y Méndez, near Plazuela Sucre, T04-666 4973, www.educacionyfuturo.com.* An NGO giving information on homestays with rural families, cheese making and guided trekking in the Valle de Los Cóndores.

Explora Tarija, *no storefront, T7619 7685, exploratarija@hotmail.com.* Daily bus tours to wineries or Campiña depart from the main plaza, corner Sucre y Madrid, at 0900 and 1430, minimum 2 passengers, tickets on sale at restaurants around the plaza.

Sur Bike, *Ingavi 0289 y Ballivián, T7619 4200, surbike_1002@hotmail.com.* Bike rentals US$11.50 per day.

Tupiza Tours, *at Hotel Mitru, T04-664 3930, www.tupizatours.com.* A branch of the Tupiza operator offering local tours to wineries and surroundings. Also innovative 'salt and wine' private trips of 3 or more days combining Tarija and its

attractions with Tupiza, Reserva Avaroa and Salar de Uyuni; tours can start or end in Potosí, San Pedro de Atacama, Villazón, Tupiza or Tarija.

VTB, *Ingavi 784 entre Ballivian y R Rojas, at Hostal Carmen (see Where to stay, above), T04-664 4341, www.vtbtourtarija.com.* Trips of 4- to 6-hrs including bodegas; comprehensive 10-hr 'Tarija and surroundings in 1 day'; you can also try your hand at excavation with a palaeontology specialist! Good vehicles, recommended.

Viva Tours, *Bolívar 251, entre Sucre y Daniel Campos, Edif Ex Hansa p 2, of 6, T04-663 8325, auriventur@hotmail.com, on Facebook.* Vineyard tours US$30 with lunch, Campiña tours, nighttime city tour.

Transport

Tarija

Air BoA (General Trigo 327 entre V Lema y A del Carpio, T04-611 2787) flies to **Cochabamba**, **La Paz**, **Sucre** and **Santa Cruz**. TAM (La Madrid O-0470 entre Trigo y Campero, T04-664 2734), to **La Paz**, **Sucre**, **Santa Cruz** or **Yacuiba**, depending on day of week. Amaszonas (Trigo y Lema, T04-667 6800) has daily flights to **Santa Cruz** via **Yacuiba**. Ecojet (La Madrid 590 esq Colón, T04-611 3427), to **Santa Cruz** on Mon, Wed and Fri.

Bus Most buses and vans leave from the **Nueva Terminal de Buses** in Torrecillas, 7 km south of the centre, T04-666 7701; taxi US$1.50-2 or micro Z or 6 from Palacio de Justicia or Plazuela Sucre. To **La Paz** (935 km), direct service with **Platinum** (new buses with toilet, heating, a/c, food service, Wi-Fi) at 1900 (same time from La Paz), US$28 *semicama*, US$38 *cama*, 12-13 hrs; several companies via Potosí and **Oruro** (US$11.50, 10-11 hrs) around 1700-1800, **Villa del Norte** also at 0730, 1300, 2030, US$16-20, 13-14 hrs. To **Potosí**, several additional departures

1630-2200, US$6-7 *semicama*, US$9 *cama*,
7-8 hrs; also cars throughout the day, US$14.50,
5½ hrs. To Camargo, vans from **Parada del
Norte** (Carretera a Tomatitas, past the wholesale
market), US$5, 2½ hrs, or any Potosí bound car
(US$7) or bus (US$ 4.30 *semicama*, US$6 *cama*).

To **Sucre** several companies at 1730-1930,
also 4 daily with **TNT** (www.transportetnt.com),
US$10 regular, US$11.50-14 *semicama*, US$14-22
cama, 11 hrs. To **Tupiza** (impressive scenery)
several companies around 1930-2100, US$6
regular, US$7-12 *semicama*, US$14 *cama*, 6 hrs;
most comfortable service with **Juárez** at 2100;
for daytime service, **Sama** and **Juárez** at 0930
and **Narváez** at 1000; cars US$14, minimum
6 passengers. To **Villazón**, US$6, 6 hrs, with
Narváez at 1000 and 2100, **Trans Tarija** at 2000,
Sama at 2030. To **Cochabamba** via Potosí
and Oruro, 3 weekly at 1730 with **Platinum**,
semicama US$26, several other companies
1630-1830, US$13-16, 14-16 hrs. To **Santa Cruz**
via Villamontes, with **Platinum** at 1800, US$26,
several other companies 1600-1800, US$13-15,
12-14 hrs. Vans and cars to **Entre Ríos**, US$4.50,
and **Villamontes**, US$14.50, leave as they fill
from **Parada del Chaco** (east end of Av Las
Américas); also cars from the Nueva Terminal or
take a Santa Cruz bound bus.

To Argentina: to **Villazón**, see above. To
Bermejo, **El Chapaco** and **Gran Chaco**, US$4,
4 hrs; vans and cars leave as they fill, US$5.75, 3 hrs.
To **Salta**: US$43 *semicama*, US$56 *cama*, 9-11 hrs
(shorter northbound), with **Juárez**, Sun, Thu 1930
(from Salta Mon, Fri at 2230), take photocopy
of passport when booking, no change of bus at
border; and **Dragón Rojo** (mixed reports in 2016),
C Sucre N-0235 y Avaroa, T04-666 5014, Mon-Fri
1900, Sat-Sun 1700, transfer to shared taxis or
a different bus once in Argentina. To **Yacuiba**
several companies at 1900-1930, Narváez also at
0900, US$5-7, 7-8 hrs; vans US$14.50, 6-7 hrs. To
Buenos Aires, with **Trans Americano**, Tue, Thu,
Sat 0900, US$100, 28-30 hrs (from Buenos Aires
same days at 1100 Argentine time).

Taxi Within the city centre, journeys start at
about US$0.55.

Valle Central

From Tarija to **Valle de la Concepción**, micros
run from Corrado entre Trigo y Campero, all day
to 1800, US$0.85 pp. Taxis leave from Corrado y
JM Saracho.

North of Tarija

From Tarija to **San Lorenzo**, from Domingo Paz y
JM Saracho, US$0.85, all day.

Cochabamba &
central Bolivia

Set in a bowl of rolling hills at a comfortable altitude (2570 m), Cochabamba enjoys a wonderfully warm, dry and sunny climate. Its parks and plazas are a riot of colour, from the striking purple of the bougainvillea to the subtler tones of jasmine, magnolia and jacaranda.

Markets, colonial towns and archaeological sites such as little-known Incallacta – the largest Inca ruins in Bolivia – are all close by. Conquering Cerro Tunari is a challenge for all adventurers. Further afield, the dinosaur tracks and great scenery at Torotoro National Park are worth the trip. The paved lowland route to Santa Cruz de la Sierra has much more transport than the rough old road over the mountains via Comarapa and Samaipata. Both offer access to Carrasco and Amboró national parks.

Cochabamba and around Colour map 3, B3.

eat, drink and be merry in this appealing city

☆ Bolivia's fourth largest city (population 650,038) was founded in 1571 and in colonial times it was the 'breadbasket' of Bolivia, providing food for the great mining community of Potosí. Today it is an important commercial centre. Many visitors particularly enjoy La Cancha market, one of the largest in Bolivia, as well as Cochabamba's very good dining and nightlife.

Sights

At the heart of the old city is the arcaded **Plaza 14 de Septiembre** with the **Cathedral** ⓘ *Mon-Fri 0800-1000, 1500-1800, Sat-Sun 0800-1200*, dating from 1701, but much added to. Of the colonial churches nearby, the **Convent and Museum of Santa Teresa** ⓘ *Baptista y Ecuador, T04-422 1252, guided tours only Mon-Fri 1430, 1530, 1630, US$2.50, camera US$3 extra*, original construction 1760-1790, has a lovely courtyard, a Sala Capitular with painted walls, many other paintings and a beautiful Coro (being restored in 2017). There are spectacular views from the roof.

Museo Arqueológico ⓘ *Jordán E-199 y Aguirre, T04-425 0010, www.museo.umss.edu.bo, Mon-Fri 0800-1800, Sat 0800-1200, US$3.50, guided tours in English at no extra cost, Mon-Fri from 1300*, is part of the Universidad de San Simón. The museum displays some 40,000 artefacts including Amerindian hieroglyphic scripts, mummies, and pre-Inca textiles, through to the colonial era. There is a lot to appreciate, but descriptions are only in Spanish and the presentation is a bit dated. **Casona Santiváñez** ⓘ *Santiváñez O-0156, Mon-Fri 0900-1200, 1430-1800, free*, has a nice colonial patio (open 1700-1845), and exhibition of paintings and historic photographs.

From Plaza Colón, at the north end of the old town, the wide **Avenida Ballivián** (known as **El Prado**) runs northwest to the wealthy modern residential areas; along it you can find restaurants and bars. Also in the north is the Patiño family's **Palacio Portales** ⓘ *Av Potosí 1450, T04-448 9666, Mon-Fri 1500-1830, Sat-Sun 1000-1200, entry US$2; guided tours in Spanish Tue-Fri 1500, 1530, 1630, 1730, 1800, in English or French 1600, 1700, 1830, Sat in Spanish at 1000, 1100, 1200, English or French 1030, 1130; the gardens are open Tue-Fri 1500-1830, Sat-Sun 1000-1200, no charge*. Built in French

Best for
Fossils ■ Inca ruins ■ Markets ■ Nightlife

Renaissance style, furnished from Europe and set in 10 ha of gardens inspired by Versailles, the Patiño mansion was finished in 1927 but never occupied. It is now the **Centro Cultural Simón I Patiño** ① http://portal.fundacionpatino.org, with an excellent art gallery in the basement. To get there, take a taxi (five minutes from the centre) or micro G from Avenida San Martín. Next to Palacio Portales is the interesting **Museo de Historia Natural Alcide d'Orbigny** ① *Av Potosí 1458 y Buenos Aires, T04-448 6969, Mon-Fri 0900-1200, 1500-1800, US$0.65,* named after the famous 19th-century French naturalist. It houses well-presented natural history collections of international importance.

East of the centre is **Cerro de San Pedro**, at the top of which stands an enormous statue of **Cristo de la Concordia**. A modern **cable car** ① *Tue-Sat 1000-1800, Sun 0900-1800, US$1.50 return,* will whizz you to the top from the east end of Heroínas. Steps up to the statue are reasonably safe in daylight hours, but if you go in the afternoon, take a taxi, US$1.50. The 34.2-m, 2200-ton statue, finished in 1994, is claimed to be the biggest depiction of Christ in the world. It gives a 360° view over the city and its bowl-like setting. North of Cerro de San Pedro is the **Jardín Botánico Martín Cárdenas** ① *Av Gral Galindo y R Rivera, Mon-Fri 0930-1630, Sat-Sun 1000-1630,* with over 250 species of cactus and pleasant tree-lined avenues.

To the south of the old town lie the bus terminal and former train station and one of the best markets in Bolivia. The huge and fascinating **Mercado La Cancha** ① *between Aguirre, Punata, República and Pulacayo,* is open all week but best on Wednesday and Saturday when it is packed with *campesinos* and trading spills over into surrounding streets. It has four main sections and various offshoots, with a vast array of foodstuffs and local goods. Souvenirs can be found mainly in the San Antonio section, Avenida Esteban Arze y Punata, but you can find things of interest everywhere inside.

The **Parque de la Familia**, ① *entre Av Rafael Urquidi y Puente Cobija, in the Costanera district, 5 mins by taxi from the centre, Tue-Fri 1500-2200, show at 2000, Sat-Sun 1000-2300, shows at 2000 and 2130,* is an interesting park with 20-m-high dancing fountains, a Bolivian culture show projected with music on a wall of water, and places to eat and meet.

Essential Cochabamba and central Bolivia

Finding your feet

The city is served by paved roads from La Paz, Sucre and Santa Cruz. Neither airport, nor bus station are far from the centre. Buses and taxis serve both.

Getting around

The city is divided into four quadrants based on the intersection of Avenida Las Heroínas running west to east, and Avenida Ayacucho running north to south. In all longitudinal streets north of Heroínas the letter N (Norte) precedes the four numbers. South of Heroínas the numbers are preceded by S (Sur). In all transversal streets west of Ayacucho the letter O (Oeste) precedes the numbers and all streets running east are preceded by E (Este). The first two numbers refer to the block, 01 being closest to Ayacucho or Heroínas; the last two refer to the building's number. See also Transport, page 345.

Safety

Do not venture into any of the hills around town on foot (including San Sebastián, La Coronilla and San Pedro with the Cristo de la Concordia, although at the Cristo itself there are usually plenty of people about). At night take only radio taxis (marked with stickers on the back doors). Take usual precautions with your belongings in markets, on public transport and other crowded places. In the main towns in the coca-growing region of Chapare tourists are reasonably safe, but don't go off the beaten track alone. See also Safety, page 386.

When to go

Cochabamba city can be visited at any time of year, rainy season December-March. At this time roads to outlying areas can become difficult.

Time required

Three or four days for the city and a day excursion, of which there are a few. There are other two-day trips and Torotoro requires three to four days. Stopping on the overland route to Santa Cruz can add a couple more days to a visit to this region.

Cochabamba

To ③⑦ To ⑨

To Palacio Portales & ①②⑤③④
⑧⑩⑬⑯

Pedro Borda

To Jardín Botánico
Martín Cárdenas

La Paz

José de la Reza

Av Ballaván El Prado

⑫

⑨

Av Salamanca

Paccieri

⑰

José Martí

México

⑤ ⑩ ⑪ ④
⑦ ⑥

Plaza
Colón
ℹ

Paccieri

⑪

Mayor Rocha

⑮

Venezuela

A

Convent of
Santa Teresa

Spitting
Llama

⑧

②

To
Parque de
la Familia

Ecuador

Bolivia
Cultura

Ecuador

⑭

⑥

Colombia

Hamiraya

Junín

Av Ayacucho

Baptista

España

Av Las Heroínas

Av Oquendo

To Cerro de San Pedro
& Cristo de la Concordia

B

To La Paz & Oruro

✉

La Compañía ✝

①

San
Francisco ✝

Bolívar

General Achá

Casona
Santiváñez ⅏

Plaza 14 de
Septiembre
ℹ

Av San Martín

Lanza

Antezana

16 de Julio

Sucre

IGM

Santiváñez

Santo
Domingo ▪

Cathedral ✝

Cnl Jordán

Museo ⅏
Arqueológico

Ⓢ FIE

C

Ⓢ BoA

BNB Ⓢ

Aguirre

Esteban Arze

25 de Mayo

Calama

Cabrera

Uruguay

Plazuela
de San Sebastián

Av Aroma

Brasil

Brasil

D

Av Ayacucho

R López

Montes

Local Buses to
Tarata & Cliza

Av República

To Airport

ℹ

Colina de San
Sebastián
La Coronilla ①

To La Cancha Market ①

To La Cancha Market ②

To La Cancha Market
& Local Buses for Punata,
Totora & Torotoro
(Av 6 de Agosto, approx 6
blocks) ②

Av 9 de Abril

Micros to
Villa Tunari ③

N

↓

100 metres
100 yards

Where to stay 🛏
1 Apart Hotel Anteus A3
2 Aranjuez A3
3 El Jardín Suites A1
4 Gina's A2
5 Gran Hotel Cochabamba A3
6 Hostal Maya B1
7 Jaguar House Hostel A1
8 Monserrat A2
9 Regina A2
10 Running Chaski Hostel A2
11 Violetta's Apart Hotel A3

Restaurants 🍴
1 Café París B2
2 Casablanca A2
3 Casa de Campo A3
4 Churrasquería Tunari A3
5 El Palacio del Silpancho A2
6 Gopal A2, B2
7 La Cantonata A2
8 La Estancia Steakhouse A2
9 Los Castores A2
10 Modena Café A3
11 Oasis de Dalí A2

12 Restaurante Tunari A2
13 Sole Mio A3

Bars & clubs 🍸
14 Cocafé Arte B3
15 El Caracol A2
16 La Muela del Diablo A3
17 Na Cúnna A3

Parque Nacional Tunari

SERNAP office, Av Atahuallpa 2367, T04-445 2534, www.sernap.gob.bo, http://parquetunari.blogspot.com, www.biobol.org.

Despite the proximity of this national park (300,000 ha, just outside Cochabamba), it remains a beautiful unspoilt natural area and a good place for trekking and acclimatization to altitude. There are traditional communities, *kewiña* forests, llamas and alpacas above 4000 m and even the occasional condor. The highest point in the park, **Cerro Tunari** (5035 m), offers magnificent views, even as far as Illimani. The peak can be climbed in a day trip, but it is easy to get lost and a guide is required. Access to Cerro Tunari is from Tawa Cruz reached by taxi from Quillacollo (see below), or take a tour with a Cochabamba operator (see page 344) or Berghotel Carolina (see Where to stay, below). Another park entrance, which does not provide access to Cerro Tunari, is along a marked trail from Avenida Circunvalación in the north of Cochabamba, but it is not recommended because armed attacks on visitors have taken place here.

West of Cochabamba

Quillacollo Thirteen kilometres west of the city, Quillacollo has a Sunday produce market and a famous festival (see page 344). Take any micro or *trufi* marked "Quillacollo" along Avenida Heroínas. Some 8 km beyond town is the turn-off to the beautiful **Hacienda Pairumani** ⓘ *Mon-Fri 1500-1600, Sat 0900-1100, T04-401 0470, http://portal.fundacionpatino.org*, centre of the Patiño agricultural foundation. Also known as **Villa Albina**, it was built in 1925-1932, furnished from Europe and inhabited by Patiño's wife, Albina. From the main square of Quillacollo take *trufi* 211 with a red flag marked "Iskaypata".

Listings Cochabamba and around *map page 340.*

Tourist information

Cochabamba

Centro de Información Turística Virtual (CITV)
Plaza Colón 448, T04-466 2277.
Mon-Fri 0800-1200, 1430-1830.
This is the municipal office and the best option. Other offices at the bus station (Mon-Fri 0730-1130, 1730-2230) and Jorge Wilstermann airport (Mon-Fri 0800-1200, 1430-1630). There is a kiosk behind the cathedral (Pasaje Catedral, Esteban Arze y Sucre, Mon-Fri 0900-1200, 1430-1800).

Immigration office
Av J Rodríguez entre C Sanata Cruz y C Potosí, T04-450 7080.

Tourist police
Plaza 14 de Septiembre, north side, T04-450 3880.

Where to stay

Cochabamba
However attractive their prices, places to stay south of Av Aroma and near the bus station are unsafe at all times.

$$$ Apart Hotel Anteus
Potosí 1365, T04-424 5067, www.hotelanteus.com.
Very nice hotel in a good residential area, a few steps from supermarket and shopping area. Comfortable rooms and common areas, includes buffet breakfast.

$$$ Aranjuez
Av Buenos Aires E-0563, T04-428 0076, www.aranjuezhotel.com.
The most beautiful of the luxury hotels with a nice garden and lots of style, 4-star, small, good restaurant and bar, small swimming pool. Recommended.

$$$ Gran Hotel Cochabamba
Plaza de la Recoleta E-0415, T04-448 9520, www.granhotelcochabamba.com.
One of the best hotels in Cochabamba, pool, tennis courts, business centre, airport transfers, parking.

$$ El Jardín Suites
C Baptista 722 casi La Paz, T04-452 3821, danielwestlopez@yahoo.com.
Very good location just behind the Prado. Large clean rooms with private bath and frigobar, well-equipped common kitchen.

\$\$ Gina's
México 346 entre España y 25 de Mayo,
T04-422 2925.
Has a variety of rooms for 1-5 persons, includes
simple breakfast, safe box in rooms, convenient
location in the heart of the city.

\$\$ Monserrat
España 0342, T04-452 1011,
http://hotelmonserrat.com.
Older-style hotel near many bars and restaurants,
helpful, good service, convenient, cafetería,
buffet breakfast.

\$\$ Regina
Reza 0359, T04-425 4629,
www.hotelreginabolivia.com.
Excellent spacious and efficient hotel,
with breakfast, restaurant.

\$\$ Violetta's Apart Hotel
Lanza 0464, T04-452 0257, www.violettas.com.
Good central hotel, comfortable rooms and
furnished apartments, transfers available.

\$\$-\$ Jaguar House Hostel
Baptista 746, entre Tte Arevalo y La Paz,
T04-459 1813, www.jaguarhousehostel.com.
Tipical backpackers' hostel with private rooms
and dorms, good location near restaurants, bars,
supermarket, and other services.

\$\$-\$ Running Chaski Hostel
España 449 casi México, T04-425 0559,
www.runningchaski.com.bo.
Popular hostel in the nightlife zone, private
rooms with bath, and dorms for girls only and
mixed (US\$11 pp), each dorm has bathroom
and lockers with electric sockets. Kitchen,
movie room, balcony with views, garden with
hammocks, lots of information and activities.

\$ Hostal Maya
Colombia 710 y Suipacha, T04-425 9701.
Includes basic breakfast, simple rooms with
private bath, hot water, quiet area. Decent
economy option.

Parque Nacional Tunari

\$\$\$ Berghotel Carolina
Pairumani, at the foot of the Cerro Tunari,
T7213 0003, www.berghotelcarolina.com.
Arranges private transport, 45 mins from
Cochabamba, 25 mins from Plaza Bolívar in
Quillacollo. Intimate mountain lodge with
5 comfortable rooms with private bath and
2 with shared bath, restaurant, bar, living room

with fireplace, sauna and large terrace, family run,
wonderful atmosphere. Organizes guided 2-day
walking tours with tent to the Laguna Cajón
(4100 m), Cerro Tunari and other peaks in Parque
Tunari. Walking trails start right from the lodge.
Warmly recommended.

Quillacollo

\$\$ El Poncho Eco Center
Quillacollo Marquina, T04-439 2283,
www.elponcho.org.
Ecological cabins in a lovely setting, camping,
restaurant, pool and various outdoor activities.

Restaurants

Cochabamba
North of the Río Rocha on the Pasaje Boulevard
de la Recoleta and Av Pando is a group of
restaurants and bars.

\$\$\$-\$\$ Casa de Campo
Pasaje Boulevard de la Recoleta 618,
T04-424 3937. Mon-Sun 1230-0200.
One of the best in town. Large menu of mostly
local dishes, all-in-one price, very popular,
half-portions available, also has *peña*, book
at weekend evenings.

\$\$\$-\$\$ Churrasquería Tunari
Pasaje Boulevard de la Recoleta, T04-
448 8153. Tue-Sat 1830-2300, Fri-Sat
also 1200-1500, Sun 1200-1500 only.
The most delicious meat you can find
in Cochabamba.

\$\$\$-\$\$ La Estancia Steakhouse
Pasaje Boulevard de la Recoleta 786, T04-
424 9262. Mon-Sun 1200-1500, 1800-2330.
Best steak in town, salads and international food
in this traditional restaurant.

\$\$\$-\$\$ Restaurante Tunari
Av Ballivián 676 y La Paz, T04-452 8588.
Mon-Sat 0930-2230, Sun 0930-1530.
Family-run restaurant specializing in local meat
dishes (half-portions available), good filling food,
also sandwiches.

\$\$ La Cantonata
España y Mayor Rocha 409, T04-425 9222.
Mon-Sat 1200-1430, 1830-2330, Sun 1200-1500,
1900-2230.
Pleasant Italian restaurant with good food and
service, no smoking. Recommended.

$$ Sole Mio
*Av América 826 y Pando, T04-428 3379.
Tue-Fri 1730-2400, Sat-Sun also 1200-1430.*
A smart Neapolitan pizza restaurant with wood-burning pizza oven, delicious, also good for desserts. Attentive service.

$$-$ El Palacio del Silpancho
Baptista 434, T04-422 2732. Mon-Sun 1100-2400.
The place for Cochabamba's most typical dish, ultra-thin fried breaded beef, likely to overflow the plate.

$ Gopal
España 250, and Mayor Rocha 375 near Plaza Colón. Mon-Sat 1100-1400.
Bolivian Hare-Krishna, good quality and value vegetarian buffet lunch, nice garden setting (at España 250), popular, go early.

Cafés
There are several cafés at the junction of the Pasaje Catedral and Esteban Arze.

Café París
Bolívar, corner of Plaza 14 de Septiembre.
Serves good coffee and crêpes, traditional atmosphere.

Casablanca
25 de Mayo entre Venezuela y Ecuador.
Attractive, buzzing, good food, mostly pastas, pizzas and Mexican, and a wide selection of coffee, popular for wine and cocktails in the evening, indoor games and music.

Los Castores
Ballivián 790 y Oruro, several other branches. Open 0745-1330.
Popular, good for *salteñas*, 4 different kinds including an extra spicy variety.

Modena Café
Beni 508 esquina Potosí, in La Recoleta.
Variety of coffees, sweet and savoury snacks, drinks and ice cream.

Oasis de Dalí
España 428.
Great music, good food, nice atmosphere, try the *café helado* (ice coffee).

Bars and clubs

Cochabamba
The main nightlife district is on España, Ecuador, Mayor Rocha and Av Ballivian (El Prado) with lots of bars and a few restaurants. Wander around and see what takes your fancy.

Cocafé Arte
Ecuador y Antezana 279.
Friendly, family atmosphere, snacks, good place for foreigners to meet. Street musicians always pass by to show off their skills.

El Caracol
Mayor Rocha entre Baptista y España.
High ceilings, Mediterranean-themed dishes, desserts, lots of drinks and coffees.

La Muela del Diablo
Potosí 1392 y Portales, next to Palacio Portales. Mon-Fri 1100-2330, Sat 1800-0100.
Bolivian rock music, theatre groups, German beer, variety of wines, pastas, good pizzas and desserts.

Na Cúnna
Av Salamanca 577. Tue-Thu 1900-2400, Fri-Sat 1900-0230.
Irish pub and restaurant, live music. They also serve Guinness.

Entertainment

Cochabamba

Art galleries
There are several art galleries in the centre, such as **Salón Municipal de Verano** (Plaza 14 de Septiembre) and **Galería Walter Terrazas** (Av Heroínas y España, T04-422 7561).

Theatre and cinema
For cinema, see www.cinecenter.com.bo.
mARTadero, *Av 27 de Agosto entre Ollantay y Ladislao Cabrera, micros/trufis P, Q, and 212 to Plaza de los Arrieros, T04-458 8778, www.martadero.org. Daily 1500-1800.* Cultural and artistic centre for local and international artists, exhibitions, and events, in a refurbished slaughterhouse.
Teatro Achá, *España 280 entre Heroínas y Bolívar, T04-425 8054.* The city's oldest cultural centre, with monthly presentations.
Teatro Hecho a Mano, *Av Uyuni 635 entre Puente Recoleta y Potosí, T04-448 5528, Hecho-a-Mano on Facebook.* Theatre school.

Festivals

Cochabamba
Feb Carnaval is celebrated 15 days before **Lent**. Rival groups (*comparsas*) compete in music, dancing, and fancy dress, culminating in

El Corso de Corsos on the last Sat of the Carnaval; crowded, go very early to buy seats.
14 Sep Día de Cochabamba.

Quillacollo
14-15 Aug Fiesta de la Virgen de Urkupiña (www.urcupina.com), in Quillacollo. There's plenty of transport from Cochabamba, hotels are all full. Be there before 0900 to be sure of a seat, as you are not allowed to stand in the street. The 1st day is the most colourful with all the groups in costumes and masks, parading and dancing in the streets till late at night. Many groups have left by the 2nd day and dancing stops earlier. The 3rd day is dedicated to the pilgrimage.

Shopping

Cochabamba

Camping gear, maps, etc
Camping Oruro, *Sucre entre 25 de Mayo y San Martín in Shoping Sucre*. Good quality outdoor gear.
IGM, *16 de Julio S-237, T04-425 5503, Mon-Thu 0800-1200, 1430-1800, Fri 0800-1200*. Sells topographic maps of Cochabamba department.
The Spitting Llama, *España N-615 y Ecuador, T04-489 4540, www.thespittingllama.com*. Travel shop.

Handicrafts
Artesanos Andinos, *Pasaje Catedral, T04-450 8367*. An artisans' association selling textiles.
Fotrama, *Bolívar 0349, entre San Martín y 25 de Mayo*. High-quality alpaca clothing.

What to do

Adventure sports and tours
Cochabamba is growing in popularity for parapenting, with several outfits offering tandem jumps starting at US$50, as well as courses.

AndesXtremo, *La Paz 138 entre Ayacucho y Junín, T04-452 3392, www.andesxtremo.com*. Adventure sports company specializing in parapenting, also offers climbing, rafting and trekking, good value, professional staff. Recommended.
Bolivia Cultura, *Ecuador 342 entre 25 de Mayo y España, T04-452 7272, www.boliviacultura.com*. Tours to Torotoro. They run year-round tours for 3 and 4 days to all the major sites and can arrange longer trips. Tours also to other local destinations.
Bolivia Motors, *no storefront, T 6740 1468, www.boliviamotors.com*. Reliable motorcycle tours and rentals, Kiwi owned and operated.
D'Orbigny Travel, *Pasaje de la Promotora 344 entre España y Heroínas, T04-451 1367*. Run by an enthusiastic Bolivian couple, sell flight tickets and excursions in Cochabamba department and throughout Bolivia.
El Mundo Verde Travel, *no storefront, T6534 4272, www.elmundoverdetravel.com*. Great for local information, regional experts offer tours to Torotoro, Pico Tunari, Inkallajta and Chimboata village. Also rafting, zip-lines, jungle trips in Chapare and throughout Bolivia; day trips and adventure tours. Dutch/Bolivian-run, very enthusiastic and informative. Also 4WD tours to Samaipata and Sucre. English, Dutch and Spanish spoken. Warmly recommended.
Río Kayaks Bolivia, *Melchor Pérez de Holgín entre Dorbigny y 15 de agosto, T6534 4272, riokayaks@gmail.com, www.facebook.com/RioKayaksBolivia/*. Offer kayaking, alone or combined with other adventure sports.

Language classes
There are many qualified language teachers in the city.
Beyond Bolivia, *www.beyondsouthamerica.com*. Dutch organization which offers Spanish/Portuguese language classes, homestays

and recommended volunteer programmes and internships.

Bolivia Sostenible, *Julio Arauco Prado 230, Zona Las Cuadras, T04-423 3786, www.bolivia sostenible.org*. Offers homestays and paid placements for volunteers.

Centro de Idiomas Kori Simi, *Lanza 727, entre La Paz y Chuquisaca, T04-425 7248*. Spanish and Quechua school run by staff from Switzerland, Germany and Bolivia, also offers activity programme, homestays and volunteer placements.

Juntucha, *T7976 1679, info@juntucha.org*. Spanish school run by a Dutchman, funds are donated to a charity, www.casadelaalegria.nl.

Runawasi, *Maurice Lefebvre 0470, Villa Juan XXIII, Av Blanco Galindo Km 4.5, T04-424 8923, www.runawasi.org*. Spanish, Quechua and Aymara, also has accommodation.

Volunteer Bolivia, *Ecuador E-0342, T04-452 6028, www.volunteerbolivia.org*. Bolivian/US-run organization which offers language classes, homestays and a recommended volunteer programme.

Cochabamba

Air Jorge Wilstermann airport, T04-412 0400; modern, with places to eat, *casas de cambio* and ATMs. Airport bus is Micro B from Heroínas y Ayacucho, US$0.40; taxis from airport to centre US$4. Arrive 2 hrs ahead for international flights. Cochabamba is an air transport hub with several daily flights to/from **La Paz** (35 mins) and **Santa Cruz** (40 mins) with **Amaszonas**, Av Libertador Bolívar 1509, Edif El Solar, PB, T04-479 4200, **Boliviana de Aviación**, Jordán 202 y Nataniel Aguirre, T04-414 0873 or 901-105010, and **TAM** Militar, Buenos Aires entre Av Santa Cruz y América, T04-441 1545. **Ecojet**, Plazuela Constitución 0879 entre 16 de Julio y Chuquisaca, T04-412 3700, to **Sucre**, **Tarija**, **Trinidad** and

other northern cities. **TAM** has flights to **Trinidad**, with connections to other northern cities.

Bus *Micros* and *colectivos*, US$0.30; *trufis*, US$0.30. Anything marked 'San Antonio' goes to the market. *Trufis* C and 10 go from bus terminal to the city centre.

Regional *Trufis* leave from Av Barrientos y Manuripi, or Barrientos y Guayaramerin, south of La Cancha, for **Tarata**, US$1. From Av Barrientos y Av 6 de Agosto, for **Cliza**, US$0.85. From Av 6 de Agosto y Av República y Av República to **Punata**, US$1.15, and **Totora**, US$2 (minibus). Av Oquendo y 9 de Abril (be careful in this area), to **Villa Tunari**, US$4.50, 4-5 hrs, from 0400 to 2000; **Puerto Villarroel**, US$7, 6 hrs (from 0800 when full, daily).

Long distance The main bus terminal is on Ayacucho y Tarata (T04-422 0550). To **Santa Cruz**, almost hourly 0600-2130, 10-11 hrs; **Trans Copacabana** *semi-cama*, 2130, US$13; **Bolívar** *bus-cama*, US$18.50; all via the paved lowland road through Villa Tunari. See next page. To/from **La Paz** almost hourly 0500-2200, 6-7 hrs, *semi-cama* US$10.50, *bus-cama* US$15. To **Oruro**, 0500-2200, 4 hrs, *semi-cama* US$5, *bus-cama* US$8. To **Potosí**, departures 1900-2130 *semi-cama* US$9, *bus-cama* US$15 with **Bolívar** and **Trans Copacabana**, 10 hrs. Daily to **Sucre**, 8-9 hrs, several companies (**Bolívar** and **Trans Copacabana** at 1900-2130), *semi-cama* US$12.50, *bus-cama* US$20. To **Sucre** by day; go to Aiquile by bus (several from Av 6 de Agosto entre Av República y Av Barrientos, US$4, none before 1200) or **Ferrobús**, then a bus at 0200-0300 passing en route to Sucre, or Fri and Sun, 2000. To **Tarija** via Oruro and Potosí, US$13-16, 14-16 hrs, also 3 weekly direct buses with **Platinum** (new buses with toilet, heating, a/c, food service, Wi-Fi), US$26.

Taxi About US$1 from anywhere to the plaza, more expensive to cross the river; double after dark.

caves, canyons, waterfalls, wildlife and stunning scenery

☆Parque Nacional Torotoro

Entry US$4.50 for foreigners, payable at the Dirección de Turismo, Calle Cochabamba, Main Plaza, T7227 0968, open 0730-1200, 1400-1700, all visitors must register here. SERNAP office on Calle del Olvido, 3 blocks southwest of the plaza, next to Rosas T'ika.

In the department of Potosí, but best reached from Cochabamba (136 km), is **Torotoro**, a small town, set amid dramatic canyonlands in the centre of the Parque Nacional Torotoro, covering an area of 21,744 ha.

Attractions in the park include caves, canyons, waterfalls, ruins, rock paintings, fossils and thousands of incredible fossilized dinosaur tracks, some of which can be seen by the Río Torotoro just outside the village. Near the community of **Wayra K'asa**, about 8 km northwest of Torotoro, **Umajalanta cave**, the largest in Bolivia, has many stalactites, stalagmites and a lake with endemic blind fish; 7 km have been explored and are open to caving. Head torch and helmet are required and for hire at the entrance, US$1-2; it's not recommended for claustrophobics. Beyond the cave, 21 km from Torotoro village, is **Ciudad de Itas**, in the community of Ovejerías, a circular walk on top of and within an unusual rock formation with caves (some resemble gothic cathedrals) and rock paintings. The **Cementerio de Tortugas** (turtle cemetery) is 3.5 km southeast of the town, with fossilized remains of sea turtles (Cheloniidae family). Other sites of interest include the **Cañón de Torotoro** for birdwatching (including the critically endangered Red-fronted Macaw), **Vergel** for bathing and **Chiflon Q'aqa** for rappelling.

Tours or day trips must be organized by the **Asociación de Guías (Guiaventura)** ① *Main Plaza across from the Oficina de Turismo, T7435 9152, open 0730-1130, 1330-1630. You can reserve a guide in advance, otherwise the person at the desk will phone for a guide; guides charge US$14.50 per route for 1 to 6 people (a little more to Itas).* 4WD tours are also offered by **El Mundo Verde Travel** ① *www. elmundoverdetravel.com*, which can also provide transport from Sucre (eight hours), and other Cochabamba agencies; and vehicles with driver can be hired in Torotoro town.

Cochabamba to Santa Cruz: the lowland road

Villa Tunari The lowland road from Cochabamba through Villa Tunari to Santa Cruz is partly paved and prone to landslides after heavy rain. Villa Tunari is a relaxing place and holds an annual Fish Fair the first weekend of August, with music, dancing and food. The Facebook page, villatunarituristica, has a lot of information. At **La Hormiga** ① *contact through El Mundo Verde, see page 344*, Rolando Mamani leads jungle walks, with good chance of seeing monkeys, birds, insects and snakes, about which he educates local farmers.

Parque Ecoturístico Machía Just outside Villa Tunari, Parque Ecoturístico Machía is managed by **Inti Wara Yassi** ① *T04-413 6572, www.intiwarayassi.org, entrance of US$0.90 payable to the municipality, donations welcome, open Tue-Sun 0930-1600 (not open when raining).* This 36-ha park includes a well-signposted 3-km interpretive trail and other trails through semi-tropical forest. The park is run by an animal rescue organization that operates two other parks, one about halfway between Santa Cruz and Trinidad and another near Rurrenabaque (mixed reports for the latter). Contact them for volunteer opportunities.

☆**Parque Nacional Carrasco** ① *Information from SERNAP, Av Atahuallpa 2367, Cochabamba, T04-445 6633 www.sernap.gob.bo.* Southeast of Villa Tunari, this park covers 622,600 ha between 300 and 4500 m. It has 11 ecological life zones, superb birdwatching and many rivers, waterfalls, canyons and pools.

Access is from Villa Tunari, Totora and Monte Punku – Sehuencas; taking a guide is advised. From the park entrance 20 km from Villa Tunari, a cable car takes you across the Río San Mateo for a 2½-hour walking circuit to the **Cavernas de Repechón** (oilbird caves) and bat caves. Guides may be hired from the **Kawsay Wasi community** ① *T7939 0894, www.tusoco.com.* Julián (T7480 9714) and Sebastián (T6852 1150) are recommended.

Cochabamba to Santa Cruz: the highland road

The 500-km highland road from Cochabamba to Santa Cruz is very scenic. Some sections are unpaved and the newer lowland route is preferred by most transport. Between Monte Punku (Km 119) and Epizana is the turn-off to Pocona and Inkallajta. It is 13 km from Pocona as far as the village of Collpa, then take the left fork for a further 10 km; see Transport, below. Tours are offered by Cochabamba operators.

The ruins of ☆**Inkallajta** (1463-1472, rebuilt 1525), on a flat spur of land at the mouth of a steep valley, are the largest Inca archaeological site in Bolivia and the main structure may have been the largest roofed Inca building anywhere. There are several good camping sites near the river and some basic facilities but take all food and supplies.

The highland Cochabamba-Santa Cruz road continues to **Epizana**, junction for the partly paved road to Sucre via the beautiful colonial village of **Totora** (14 km) and the more modern town of

Aiquile. Past Epizana the road from Cochabamba goes on to **Pojo** and Comarapa (being paved), thence to Samaipata (see page 356).

Aiquile is also on the new, beautiful, fully paved route from Cochabamba to Sucre via Vacas and Mizque. At Aiquile an alternative route to Samaipata joins the highland route at La Palizada, 22 km east of Comarapa; this road is being paved.

Listings Beyond Cochabamba

Where to stay

Parque Nacional Torotoro
There are over 15 hotels in Torotoro, more than we can list, but during holidays they all fill.

$$ El Molino
1.5 km from the village,T04-243 633, T7647 5999, www.elmolinotorotoro.com.
Beautiful Spanish-style country house surrounded by mountains and a river, comfortable rooms with private bath, nice common areas including facilities for events, fireplace, bar, pool table, indoor patio. All-inclusive 2- to 4-day tours from Cochabamba arranged.

$$ Villa Etelvina
C Sucre, 15-min walk from plaza, T6752 2004, www.villaetelvina.com.
Bungalow for 4 and rooms with private bath, includes breakfast, other meals available, beautiful garden, camping possible, parking, can arrange tours and activities.

$$-$ Eco-albergue Ujalanta
In the community of Wayra K'asa, 10 km from Torotoro town, T6742 2461, ecoalbergue.umajalanta@gmail.com.
Comfortable cabins with private bath, built in rustic style using local materials and administered by the local community. Great location, spectacular views, includes breakfast, other meals on request.

$ El Vergel
Arteche y Charcas, T6747 6325.
Rooms with and without bath, breakfast available.

$ Hostal Edén
Opposite the market, T7376 6465.
Good clean hostal in the middle of town, rooms with private bath, opened in 2016.

$ Hostal Las Hermanas
C Cochabamba, ½ block from the plaza, T7221 1257.

Basic rooms, cheaper with shared bath, Doña Lily serves delicious food and is very attentive.

$ Hostal Palacio Asteria
Guadalupe y El Olvido, 2 blocks from Plaza, T6817 2374.
Colonial-style hotel, comfortable rooms with private bath, good café **Como en Casa**, beautiful patio.

$ Hostal Santa Bárbara
Calle Santa Bárbara, T7278 1307.
A nice house in the centre of town, cheaper with shared bath, good economy option, parking.

Villa Tunari

$$$-$$ Victoria Resort
Km 156 on the road to Santa Cruz, 4 km before Villa Tunari on the right, T04-413 6538, www.victoria-resort.com.
Modern, *cabaña* style, 500 m from the main road in the middle of the forest, quiet, large pool, breakfast buffet.

$$ El Puente Jungle Hotel
Av de la Integración, 4 km from town, T04-458 0085, www.hotelelpuente.com.bo (or book in advance through Creative Tours in Sucre, see page 310).
Cabins from 2 persons to family-size surrounded by tropical vegetation, with breakfast and bath, pool, zip-line, stream and natural swimming pools, nature treks. Very good restaurant.

$$ Los Tucanes Casa de Campo
On the mainroad after the 2nd bridge, T04-413 6506, www.lostucaneshotel.com.
Clean rooms with a/c, 2 pools, buffet breakfast.

Totora

$$-$ Casa de Huéspedes Villa Eva
On main road, Totora, contact César T7647 6291.
Well-furnished country house with large living room, fully equipped kitchen, and comfortable rooms with private bath.

Restaurants

Parque Nacional Torotoro
Several small restaurants in Torotoro town include **El Comedo**r, at the food market 2 blocks above the main plaza, good for a typical breakfast; and **El Dinosaurio**, C Sáens opposite the market, serves pasta, pizza and local fare, as well as drinks, helpful owner Franz.

Villa Tunari
There are several eating places in Villa Tunari on both sides of the main road to Santa Cruz. The more expensive ones are on the riverside (**San Silvestre** is recommended). The more popular food stalls 1 block from the bus terminal serve different fish dishes and have also a cheap daily menu. Upstairs at the market (breakfast and lunch) is a very cheap option.

Festivals

Aiquile
2 Feb **La Virgen de la Candelaria**, Aiquile.
Oct/Nov **Feria del Charango**, Aiquile.

Shopping

Parque Nacional Torotoro
Rosas T'ika, *Asociación de Mujeres, C del Olvido, 3 blocks southwest of Plaza Principal, 0800-1200,* *1400-1800, closed Tue.* Sells beautiful, locally made textiles, clothing and bags, mostly sheep's wool, some of llama wool.

Transport

Parque Nacional Torotoro
Bus Trans del Norte (Cochabamba T7078 6818) from Av República y Pje Mairana, daily at 1800; return to Cochabamba Mon-Sat at 0600, Sun at 1300; US$3.50, 4-5 hrs in the dry season, 5-6 hrs in the wet. Also **Torotoro Turístico** minibuses (*surubís*), Pje Mairana y Av República (Cochabamba T7144 2073, Torotoro T7147 7601), leave when full daily 0500-1800, US$5. There is no bus service from Sucre, it takes 14 hrs in a private vehicle.

Inkallajta
Take a *trufi* from 0500 onwards from 6 de Agosto y Manuripi (Av República) in Cochabamba (ask for the "Parada Pocona"). For 3 people the *trufi* will drop you off at the entrance to the Inca ruins (US$4 pp). Arrange with the driver to pick you up at a specific time to return to Cochabamba. *Trufis* return from Pocona to Cochabamba when full till 1600. Taxis from Pocona charge around US$15 one way to the ruins.

Santa Cruz &
eastern lowlands

In contrast to the highlands of the Andes and the gorges of the Yungas, eastern Bolivia is made up of vast plains stretching to the Chaco of Paraguay and the Pantanal wetlands of Brazil. Agriculture is well developed and other natural resources are fully exploited, bringing prosperity to the region. There are a number of national parks with great biodiversity, such as Amboró and Noel Kempff Mercado. Historical interest lies in the pre-Inca ceremonial site at Samaipata, the beautiful Jesuit missions of Chiquitania and, of much more recent date, the trails and villages where Che Guevara made his final attempt to bring revolution to Bolivia.

Santa Cruz Colour map 3, B4. See map, page 352.

Bolivia's largest city, gateway to one of the most fascinating parts of the country

Sights

The Plaza 24 de Septiembre is the city's main square with the huge **cathedral** (**Basílica de San Lorenzo**) ① *Museum, T03-332 4683, Mon-Sat 0730-1200, 1500-2030, Sun 0700-1200, 1500-2130, US$1.50*. You can climb to a mirador in the cathedral **bell tower** ① *daily 0800-1200, 1500-1900, US$0.50*, with nice views of the city. The block behind the cathedral, **Manzana Uno** ① *Tue-Sat 1000-1230, 1600-2100, Sun 1600-2100*, has been set aside for rotating art and cultural exhibits. **El Casco Viejo**, the heart of the city, with its arcaded streets and buildings with low, red-tiled roofs and overhanging eaves, retains a slight colonial feel, despite the profusion of modern, air-conditioned shops and restaurants. The **Museo de Historia** ① *Junín 141, T03-336 5533, Mon-Fri 0800-1200, 1500-1830, free*, has several displays including archaeological pieces from the Chané and Guaraní cultures and explorers' routes. The **Museo de Arte Contemporáneo** ① *Sucre y Potosí, T03-334 0926, Mon-Fri 1000-1200, 1500-1900, free*, houses contemporary Bolivian and international art in a nicely restored old house.

Around Santa Cruz

At Km 8 on the road to Cotoca are the **Botanical Gardens** ① *micro or trufi from C Suárez Arana, 15 mins, T03-362 3101, open Mon-Fri 0900-1700, entry US$0.50*, a bit run-down but with many walking trails, birds and several forest habitats.

Parque Ecológico Yvaga Guazu ① *Km 12.5 Doble Vía a La Guardia, taxi US$5, T03-352 7971, daily 0800-1600, US$10 for 2-hr guided tour in Spanish (more for English-speaking guide)*, 14 ha of tropical gardens with native and exotic species, plants for sale, restaurant serves Sunday buffet lunch. **Biocentro Güembé** ① *Km 5 Camino a Porongo, taxi US$7, T03-370 0700, www.biocentroguembe.com, daily 0830-1800, US$18.75 includes guided tour in Spanish or English*, is a resort with accommodation ('$$$ range), restaurant, butterfly farm, walk-in aviary, swimming pools and other family recreation.

Best for
Archaeology ▪ Religious architecture ▪ Wildlife

Essential Santa Cruz and eastern lowlands

Finding your feet

The international airport is at Viru-Viru, 13 km from the centre of Santa Cruz, reached by taxi or micro. Regional flights operate from El Trompillo airport, south of the centre on the Segundo Anillo. Long-distance and regional buses leave from the combined bus/train terminal, Terminal Bimodal, Avenida Montes on the Tercer Anillo. There are two train lines, to Quijarro on the Brazilian border and, of much less importance, to Yacuiba on the Argentine border.

Getting around

The city has 12 ring roads, Anillos 1, 2, 3, 4 and so on, the first three of which contain most sites of interest to visitors. The neighbourhood of Equipetrol, where many upscale hotels, restaurants and bars are situated, is northwest of the centre in the Tercer (3rd) Anillo.

Medical services

Santa Cruz is an important medical centre with many hospitals and private clinics. See page 384.

> **Tip...**
> Dengue fever outbreaks are common during the wet season (December to March), take mosquito precautions.

When to go

It is hot most of the year. The rainy season runs from December to March.

Time required

One or two days for Santa Cruz itself; two or three days for Samaipata or Parque Nacional Amboró, one week for Chiquitania, two to three weeks for remote areas.

Listings Santa Cruz *map page 352.*

Tourist information

APAC
*Av Busch 552 (2nd Anillo), T03-333 2287,
www.festivalesapac.com.*
Has information about cultural events in the department of Santa Cruz. See also www.destinosantacruz.com.

Fundación Amigos de la Naturaleza (FAN)
*Km 7.5 Vía a La Guadria, T03-355 6800,
www.fan-bo.org.*

InfoTur
*Sucre y Potosí, inside the Museo de Arte,
T03-336 9581, Mon-Fri 0800-1200, 1500-1900.
There is a departamental tourist desk at Viru-Viru
airport, 0700-2000.*

Municipal Tourism and Culture Office
*Libertad 65, on Plaza 24 de Septiembre T03-337
8493, Mon-Sat 0900-1900, and at Plaza del
Estudiante, Av Cañoto y Av Mons Rivero, Biblioteca
Municipal, T03-337 8493, www.gmsantacruz.
gob.bo, see also Dirección-Municipal-de-
Cultura-Patrimonio-y-Turismo on Facebook.*

SERNAP
*C 9 Oeste 138, frente a la Plaza Italia,
Barrio Equipetrol, T03-339 4311.
Mon-Fri 0800-1200, 1400-1800.*

Where to stay

$$$$ Los Tajibos
*Av San Martín 455, Barrio Equipetrol,
T03-342 1000, www.lostajiboshotel.com.*
Set in 6 ha of lush gardens, one of several hotels in this price bracket in the city and the most traditional, all facilities including business centre, art gallery, restaurants and spa. Weekend discounts.

$$$ Cortez
*Cristóbal de Mendoza 280 (2do Anillo),
T03-333 1234, www.hotelcortez.com.*
Traditional tropical hotel with restaurant, pool, gardens, meeting rooms, parking, good for dining and nightlife.

$$$ Royal Lodge
*Av San Martín 200, Equipetrol, T03-343 8000,
www.royalhotel.com.bo.*
With restaurant and bar, pool, airport transfers. Excellent option for its location and price range.

BACKGROUND

Santa Cruz

A little over 50 years ago, what is now Bolivia's largest city (population 1,566,000) was a remote backwater, but rail, road and air links ended its isolation. The exploitation of oil and gas in the Departments of Santa Cruz and Tarija and a burgeoning agribusiness sector helped fuel rapid development. Since the election of Evo Morales in 2006, however, *cruceños* have been concerned about the impact of his economic policies, perceived as favouring the highlands. There is considerable local opposition to the national government and Santa Cruz has spearheaded the eastern lowland departments' drive for greater autonomy from La Paz. The city is modern and busy, far removed from most travellers' perceptions of Bolivia. The centre still retains a bit of its former air, however, and the main plaza – 24 de Septiembre – is well cared for and a popular meeting place. During the extended lunchtime hiatus, locals (who call themselves *cambas*) take refuge in their homes from the heat or rain and the gridlock traffic eases. December to March is the hottest and rainiest time of the year.

\$\$\$ Senses
Sucre y 24 de Septiembre, just off main plaza,
T03-339 6666, www.sensescorp.com.
Self-styled boutique hotel in the heart of the city, minimalist decor, includes all services.

\$\$ Villa Magna
Barrón 70, T03-339 9700,
www.villamagna-aparthotel.com.
Fully furnished apartments with small pool, Wi-Fi, parking, attentive owner and staff, English and German spoken, from daily to monthly rates.

\$ Hotel Bolivia
C Libertad 365, T03-333-6292,
www.hotelbolivia.com.bo.
Good 3-star accommodations in the primer anillo. No nonsense, very helpful, attentive service. Will hold luggage and arrange airport transfers.

\$ Bibosi
Junín 218, T03-334 8548, htlbibosi@hotmail.com.
Central, nothing fancy, electric shower, a/c, cheaper with fan, Wi-Fi in lobby, good value.

\$ Copacabana
Junín 217, T03-336 2770,
www.hotelcopacabanabolivia.com.
Very good, popular with European tour groups, rooms cheaper without a/c, restaurant.

\$\$-\$ Hostal Río Magdalena
Arenales 653 (no sign), T03-339 3011,
www.hostalriomagdalena.com.
Comfortable rooms, downstairs ones are dark, with a/c or fan, small yard and pool, popular.

\$\$-\$ Jodanga
C El Fuerte 1380, Zona Parque Urbano, Barrio Los Chóferes, T03-339 6542, www.jodanga.com.
Good backpacker option 10 mins' walk from Terminal Bimodal, cheaper with fan and without bath, cheaper still in dorm, kitchen, bar, swimming pool, billiards, DVDs, nice communal areas, laundry, helpful owner and multilingual staff.

\$\$-\$ Residencial Bolívar
Sucre 131, T03-334 2500.
Includes good breakfast, cheaper with shared bath and in dorm, lovely courtyard with hammocks, rooms can get hot, alcohol prohibited, popular.

\$ Milán
René Moreno 70, T03-339 7500.
Some rooms with a/c, hot water, central.

\$ Sarah
C Sara 85, T03-332 2425, Facebook: HotelSarah.
Simple rooms which cost less without a/c, screened windows, small patio, good value.

Restaurants

Av San Martín in Barrio Equipetrol, and Av Monseñor Rivero are the areas for upmarket restaurants and nightlife. Both are away from the centre, take a taxi at night. Some restaurants close Mon.

\$\$\$-\$\$ La Bella Napoli
Independencia 635, T03-332 5402. Daily 1200-2200.
Genuine Neopolitan restaurant where the owner makes his own wine and liqueurs and greets customers every evening. Attractive décor, famed for pastas, pizzas and salads.

Tip...
Santa Cruz has the best meat in Bolivia, try a local *churrasquería* (grill).

$$$-$$ La Creperie
Arenales 135, T03 333-9053. Mon-Sat 1900-2300.
Serves crêpes, fondues, salads, pastas and seafood.

$$$-$$ Los Hierros
Av Monseñor Rivero 300 y Castelnau.
Daily 1200-1500, 1900-2400.
Popular upmarket grill with salad bar.

$$$-$$ Michelangelo
Chuquisaca 502. Mon-Fri 1200-1430,
1900-2330, Sat evenings only.
Excellent Italian cuisine, a/c.

$$ Ken
Uruguay 730 (1er Anillo), T03-333 3728.
Open 1130-1430, 1800-2300, closed Wed.

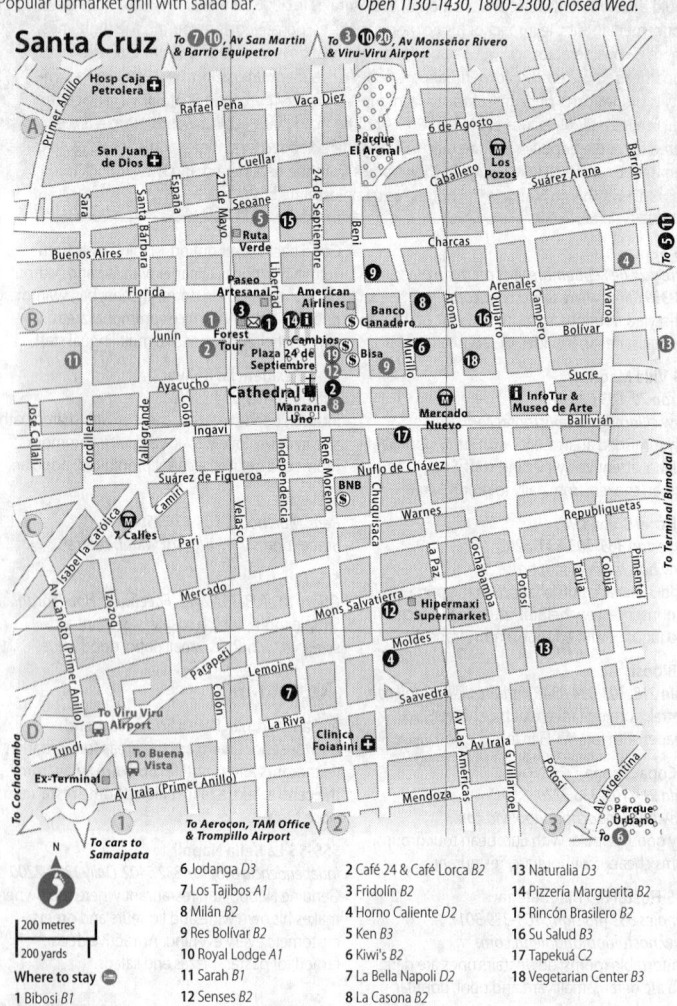

Santa Cruz

Where to stay
1 Bibosi *B1*
2 Copacabana *B1*
3 Cortez *A2*
4 Hostal Río Magdalena *B3*
5 Hotel Bolivia *B2*
6 Jodanga *D3*
7 Los Tajibos *A1*
8 Milán *B2*
9 Res Bolívar *B2*
10 Royal Lodge *A1*
11 Sarah *B1*
12 Senses *B2*
13 Villa Magna *B3*

Restaurants
1 Alexander Coffee *B2*
2 Café 24 & Café Lorca *B2*
3 Fridolín *B2*
4 Horno Caliente *D2*
5 Ken *B3*
6 Kiwi's *B2*
7 La Bella Napoli *D2*
8 La Casona *B2*
9 La Creperie *B2*
10 Los Hierros *A2*
11 Los Lomitos *B3*
12 Michelangelo *C2*
13 Naturalia *D3*
14 Pizzería Marguerita *B2*
15 Rincón Brasilero *B2*
16 Su Salud *B3*
17 Tapekuá *C2*
18 Vegetarian Center *B3*

Bars & clubs
19 Café Irlandés *B2*
20 Med Resto Bar *A2*

Sushi and authentic Japanese food, popular.

$$ La Casona
Arenales 222, T03-337 8495.
Open 1130-1500, 1900-2400.
German-run restaurant, very good food.

$$ Los Lomitos
Uruguay 758 (1er Anillo), T03-332 8696.
Daily 0800-2400.
Traditional *churrasquería* with unpretentious local atmosphere, excellent Argentine-style beef, also pastas, sandwiches and desserts.

$$ Pizzería Marguerita
Junín y Libertad, northwest corner of the plaza.
Open 0930-2400, from 1600 on Sat-Sun.
A/c, good service, coffee, bar. Popular with expats, Finnish owner speaks English and German.

$$ Rincón Brasilero
Libertad 358. Daily 1130-1430, 1930-2330.
Brazilian-style buffet for lunch, pay by weight, very good quality and variety, popular; pizza and a la carte at night. Recommended.

$$ Tapekuá
Ballivián y La Paz, T03-334 5905.
French and international food, good service, live entertainment some evenings.

$-$ Kiwi's Café Restaurant
Bolívar 208, T03-330 1410,
facebook: KiwisCafeRestaurant.
2 blocks from main plaza, eclectic inexpensive lunches and dinners (buffalo wings, peanut soup, *picante de pollo*, etc), occasional tango lessons, popular, run by a New Zealander.

$-$ Naturalia
Potosí 648, T03-333 4374, Facebook:
Naturalia-202835006418807.
Specializes in organic gourmet and health foods, café and deli on premises, popular, has 2 other locations.

$-$ Vegetarian Center
Aroma 64, entre Bolívar y Sucre.
Mon-Sat 0900-1500.
Set lunch or pay-by-weight buffet, vegan options, massive salad bar.

Su Salud
Quijarro 115. Mon-Thu 0800-2100,
Fri and Sun 0800-1700.

Tasty vegetarian food, filling lunches, sells vegetarian products.

Cafés

There are lots of very pleasant a/c cafés where you can get coffee, ice cream, drinks and snacks.

Alexander Coffee
Junín y Libertad near main plaza, and
Av Monseñor Rivero 400 y Santa Fe.
For good coffee and people-watching.

Café 24
Downstairs at René Moreno y Sucre,
on the main plaza. Daily 0830-0200.
Breakfast, juices, international meals, wine rack, nice atmosphere, Wi-Fi.

Café Lorca
Upstairs at Sucre 8 y René Moreno,
on the main plaza. Daily 0900-1600
for lunch, 1600-2300 for dinner.
Meals and drinks, Spanish wines, central patio, small balcony with views over plaza, live music most nights 2030-0130, lounge Wed-Sat 1600-0300.

Fridolín
21 de Mayo 168, Pari 254, Av Cañoto y Florida,
and Monseñor Rivero y Cañada Strongest.
All good places for coffee and pastries.

Horno Caliente
Chuquisaca 604 y Moldes, also 24 de
Septiembre 653.
Salteñas 0730-1230, traditional local snacks and sweets 1530-1930. Popular and very good.

Bars and clubs

Shamrock Irish Pub
3er Anillo Interno 1216, entre Av Banzer y
Zoológico), www.irishpub.com.bo.
Irish-themed pub, food available, Irish owner, live music Wed, Fri and Sat evenings. Also **Café Irlandés** (Plaza 24 de Septiembre, Shopping Bolívar), overlooking main plaza. Popular.

Med Resto Bar
Cañada Strongest y Mons Rivero (2do anillo),
T03-335 2848. Daily 1130-1500, 1830-2330.
Great local dishes, salads and grill by day, and a variety of pop, rock and tropical bands at night. Inside-outside seating, very popular with *cruceños* and foreigners alike, crowded on weekends.

Entertainment

Cinema

Cine Center, *Av El Trompillo – 2do Anillo – entre Monseñor Santiesteban y René Moreno, www. cinecenter.com.bo.*

Cultural centres with events and programmes

Centro Cultural Santa Cruz (René Moreno 369, T03-335 6941, www.culturabcb.org.bo); **Centro Simón I Patiño** (Independencia y Suárez de Figueroa 89, T03-337 2425, www. fundacionpatino.org), with exhibitions, galleries, and bookstore on Bolivian cultures; **Centro Boliviano Americano** (Potosí 78, T03-334 2299, www.cba.com.bo); **Centro Cultural Franco Alemán** (24 de Septiembre 36, on main plaza, T03-335 0142, www.ccfrancoaleman.org); **Centro de Formación de la Cooperación Española** (Arenales 583, T03-335 1311, www.aecid-cf.bo).

Festivals

Cruceños are famous as fun-lovers and their music, the *carnavalitos*, can be heard all over South America.

Feb Of the various festivals, the brightest is **Carnaval**, renowned for riotous behaviour, celebrated for the 15 days before Lent. There's music in the streets, dancing, fancy dress and the coronation of a queen. Water and paint throwing is common – no one is exempt.

Apr/May **Festival de Música Renacentista y Barroca Americana 'Misiones de Chiquitos'** is held in late Apr through early May every even year (next in 2018) in Santa Cruz and the Jesuit mission towns of the Chiquitania. It is organized by **Asociación Pro Arte y Cultura** (**APAC**), Av Busch 552, Santa Cruz, T03-333 2287, www.festivalesapac.com, and celebrates the wealth of sacred music written by Europeans and indigenous composers in the 17th and 18th centuries. APAC sells books, CDs and videos and also offers – in both Santa Cruz and the mission towns – a schedule of musical programmes. The festival is very popular: book hotels at least 2-3 weeks in advance.

Festival Internacional de Teatro, also organized by **APAC** (see above) is held every odd year (next in 2019).

Aug and Dec **Festival de la Temporada** in Santa Cruz and major towns of Chiquitania, featuring *música misional* with local performers.

24 Sep The local holiday of Santa Cruz city and department.

Shopping

Handicrafts

Bolivian Souvenirs, *Shopping Bolívar, local 10 and 11, on main plaza, T03-333 7805; also at Viru-Viru airport.* Expensive knitwear and crafts from all over Bolivia.

Paseo Artesanal La Recova, *off Libertad, ½ block from Plaza.* Many different kiosks selling crafts.

Vicuñita Handicrafts, *Ingavi e Independencia, T03-333 4711.* Wide variety of crafts from the lowlands and the altiplano, very good.

Jewellery

Carrasco, *Velasco 23, T03-336 2841, and other branches.* For gemstones.

RC Joyas, *Bolívar 262, T03-333 2725.* Jewellery and Bolivian gems.

Markets

Los Pozos, *between Quijarro, Campero, Suárez Arana and 6 de Agosto.* A sprawling street market for all kinds of produce.

Mercado Nuevo, *at Sucre y Cochabamba.*

Siete Calles, *Isabel la Católica y Vallegrande.* Mainly clothing.

What to do

Bird Bolivia, *T03-356 3636, www.birdbolivia.com.* Specializes in organized birding tours, English spoken.

Forest Tour, *Junín y 21 de Mayo, Galería Casco Viejo, upstairs, No 115, T03-337 2042, www.forest bolivia.com.* Environmentally sensitive tours to Refugio los Volcanes, birdwatching, national parks Chiquitania and Salar de Uyuni. English spoken.

Magri Turismo, *Velarde 49 y Irala, T03-334 4559, www.magriturismo.com.* Long-established agency for airline tickets and tours.

Misional Tours, *Los Motojobobos 2515, T03-360 1985, www.misionaltours.com.* Covers all of Bolivia, specializing in Chiquitania, Amboró, and Santa Cruz. Tours in various languages.

Nick's Adventures, *Equipetrol 8 Este, No 11, T7845 8046, www.nicksadventuresbolivia.com.* Australian/Bolivian-owned company offering tours locally and throughout Bolivia, with a strong emphasis on wildlife conservation.

Ruta Verde, *21 de Mayo 318, T03-339 6470, www. rutaverdebolivia.com.* Offers national parks, Jesuit missions, Ruta del Che, Amazonian boat trips, Salar de Uyuni, and tailor-made tours, Dutch/ Bolivian-owned, English and German also spoken, knowledgeable and helpful.

Transport

Air Viru-Viru, T03-338 5000, open 24 hrs, airline counters from 0600; *casa de cambio* changing cash US$ and euros at poor rates, 0630-2100; various ATMs; luggage lockers 0600-2200, US$5.50 for 24 hrs; ENTEL for phones and internet, plus a few eateries. Taxi US$10, micro from Ex-Terminal (see below), or El Trompillo, US$1, 45 mins. From airport take micro to Ex-Terminal then taxi to centre. Domestic flights with **Boliviana de Aviación (BoA)**, T03-311 6247), **Amaszonas** (T03-311 5393), **Ecojet** (T03-311 7039) and **TAM** (Bolivia, T03-352 9669), to **La Paz**, **Cochabamba**, **Sucre**, **Tarija** and **Cobija**. International flights to **Asunción**, **Buenos Aires**, **Salta**, **Lima**, **Madrid**, **Miami**, **Washington**, **Santiago** and **São Paulo**.

El Trompillo is the regional airport operating daily 0500-1900, T352 6600, located south of the centre on the 2do Anillo. It has a phone office and kiosk selling drinks, but no other services. Taxi US$1.50, many micros. **TAM** has flights throughout the country, different destinations on different days.

Bus Regional buses and vans These leave either from behind the Terminal Bimodal (use pedestrian tunnel under the rail tracks) or from near the Ex-Terminal (the old bus station, Av Irala y Av Cañoto, 1er Anillo, which is no longer functioning).

Long distance Most long-distance buses leave from the combined bus/train terminal, **Terminal Bimodal**, Av Montes on the 3er Anillo, 03-348 8382; police check passports and search luggage here; taxi to centre, US$1.50. Terminal fee, US$0.50, left luggage US$0.50, there are ATMs and *cambios*.

To **Cochabamba**, via the lowland route, many depart 0600-0930 and 1630-2130, US$9-12. 75, *bus-cama* US$18.55, 8-10 hrs, also **Trans Carrasco** vans leave when full across the street from the Terminal Bimodal, US$20; via the old highland route, **Trans Carrasco**, depart from the main plaza in El Torno, 30 km west of Santa Cruz, daily at 1200 (from Mairana daily at 0800 and 1500), US$8, 14 hrs. Direct to **Sucre** via Aiquile, around 1600, US$13.50-18, 12-13hrs. To **Oruro**, US$15-21, 14-15 hrs, and **La Paz** between 1630-1900, US$15.50-22.75, *bus-cama* US$31.25, 15-16 hrs;

change in Cochabamba for daytime travel. To **Camiri** (US$5, 4-5 hrs), **Yacuiba** (border with Argentina), US$8.50-13, 8 hrs and **Tarija**, US$26 with **Platinum**(new buses with toilet, heating, a/c, food service, Wi-Fi), several others for US$13-15, 12-14 hrs. To **Trinidad**, several daily after 2000, 9 hrs, US$9-13. To **San José de Chiquitos**, US$7-10, 5 hrs, **Roboré**, US$7-10, 7 hrs, and **Quijarro** (border with Brazil), at 1030 and between 1700-2000, US$12-22, 8-10 hrs. Also vans to San José, leave when full, US$10, 4½ hrs. To **San Ignacio de Velasco**, US$10, 10 hrs; **Jenecherú** *bus-cama* US$18; also **Expreso San Ignacio** vans leave when full, US$20, 8 hrs.

International Terminal fee US$1.50. To **Asunción**, US$52-64, 20-24 hrs via Villamontes and the Chaco, at 1930, with **Yacyretá**, T03-362 5557, Mon, Tue, Thu, Sat; **Stel Turismo**, T03-349 7762, daily; **Pycazú**, daily, and **Palma Loma**. Other companies are less reliable. See page 361 for the route to Paraguay across the Chaco. To **Buenos Aires** daily departures around 1900, US$158, 36 hrs, several companies. To **São Paulo** via Puerto Suárez, with **La Preferida**, T03-364 7160, Mon, Wed, Fri, 2 days.

Car hire Avis, Carretera al Norte Km. 3.5, T03-343 3939, www.avis.com.bo. **A Barron's**, Av Alemana 50 y Tajibos, T03-342 0160, www. abarrons.com. Outstanding service and completely trustworthy. **IMBEX**, 3er Anillo Interno, entre Bush y N Ortiz, T03-311 1000, www.imbex.com.

Taxi About US$1-1.50 inside 1er Anillo (more at night), US$2 inside 3er Anillo, fix fare in advance. Use radio-taxis at night.

Train Ferroviaria Oriental, at Terminal Bimodal, T03-338 7300, www.fo.com.bo, runs east to **San José de Chiquitos**, **Roboré** and **Quijarro** on the Brazilian border. The **Ferrobús** (a rail-car with the fastest most luxurious service) leaves Santa Cruz Tue, Thu, Sun 1800, arriving Quijarro 0700 next day, US$29.50; **Expreso Oriental** (an express train), Mon, Wed, Fri 1320, arriving 0602, US$12.50. There is also little-used weekly train service south to **Yacuiba** on the Argentine frontier, Thu 1530, arrives 0805 next day, US$6, returns Fri 1700; buses are much faster.

West of Santa Cruz

a sacred rock, a revolutionary trail and a wildlife hotspot

The highlights of this area, known as Los Valles Cruceños, are southwest of Santa Cruz: the pre-Inca site of El Fuerte by the pleasant resort town of Samaipata, nearby Parque Nacional Amboró and the Che Guevara Trail, on which you can follow in the final, fatal footsteps of the revolutionary.

☆Samaipata *Colour map 3, B4.*

From Santa Cruz the old mountain road to Cochabamba runs along the Piray gorge and up into th
highlands. Some 120 km from Santa Cruz is Samaipata (population 10,470), a great place to rela
midweek, with good lodging, restaurants, hikes and riding, and a growing ex-pat community. ,
two-hour walk takes you to the top of Cerro de La Patria, just east of town, with nice views of th
surrounding valleys. Local *artesanías* include ceramics, paintings and sculpture. At weekends th
town bursts into life as crowds of Cruceños come to escape the city heat and to party. See www
samaipata.info. There is a Banco Unión ATM at Calle Campero s/n, between Warnes and Saavedra.

The **Museo de Arqueología** ① *2 blocks east, 1 north from the plaza, Mon-Fri 0800-1200, 140C
1800, Sat-Sun 0800-1600, US$1 (for museum only, US$8 for El Fuerte and museum),* houses the touris
information office and a collection of ceramics with anthropomorphic designs, dating from 200 B
to AD 300, and provides information on the nearby pre-Inca ceremonial site commonly calle
El Fuerte.

☆El Fuerte

*Daily 0900-1630, US$8 for El Fuerte and Museum, ticket valid 3 days, Spanish- and English-speakin
guides available, US$12.*

A UNESCO World Heritage Site, El Fuerte is 9 km from Samaipata; 3 km along the highway to Sant
Cruz, then 6 km up a rough, signposted road (taxi from Plaza Principal US$7.50 one way, US$1
return with two hours' wait); two to three hours' walk one way. Pleasant bathing is possible in a rive
on the way to El Fuerte.

This sacred structure (altitude 1990 m)
consists of a complex system of channels, basins,
high-relief sculptures, etc, carved out of one
vast slab of rock. Some suggest that Amazonian
people created it around 1500 BC, but it could be

Tip...
It is not permitted to walk on the rock, so visit
the museum first to see the excellent model.

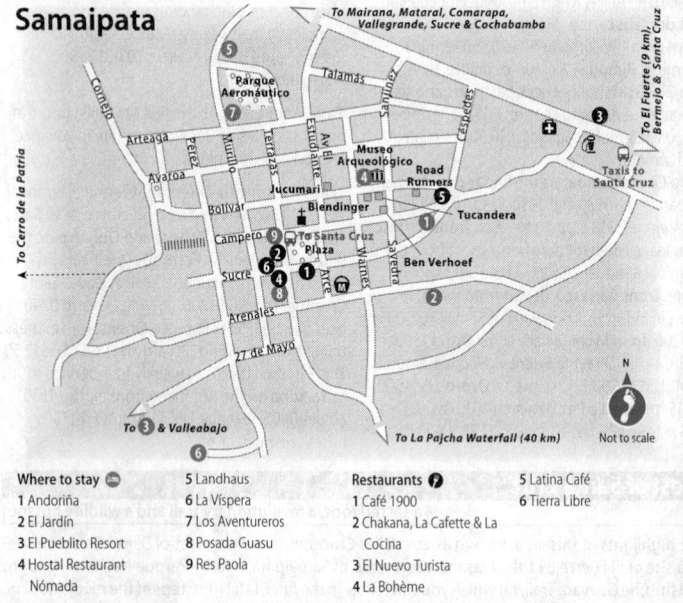

Samaipata

*To Mairana, Mataral, Comarapa,
Vallegrande, Sucre & Cochabamba*

To El Fuerte (9 km),
Bermejo & Santa Cruz

Parque
Aeronáutico

Museo
Arqueológico

Road
Runners

Taxis to
Santa Cruz

Plaza

To Santa Cruz

Tucandera

Biendinger

Ben Verhoef

To Cerro de la Patria

Streets: Cornelio, Arteaga, Petza, Avaroa, Murillo, Terrazas, Av J Estudiante, Talamas, Santuney, Cespedes, Jucumari, Bolívar, Campero, Sucre, Warnes, Saavedra, Arce, Arenales, 27 de Mayo

To ③ & Valleabajo

To La Pajcha Waterfall (40 km)

Not to scale

N

Where to stay 🛏
1 Andoriña
2 El Jardín
3 El Pueblito Resort
4 Hostal Restaurant
   Nómada

5 Landhaus
6 La Víspera
7 Los Aventureros
8 Posada Guasu
9 Res Paola

Restaurants 🍴
1 Café 1900
2 Chakana, La Cafette & La
   Cocina
3 El Nuevo Turista
4 La Bohème

5 Latina Café
6 Tierra Libre

later. There is evidence of subsequent occupations and that it was the nethermost outpost of the Incas' Kollasuyo (their eastern empire). Behind the rock are poorly excavated remains of a city.

Around Samaipata

In addition to tours to El Fuerte and the Ruta del Che (see below), many other worthwhile excursions can be made in the Samaipata area. Impressive forests of giant ferns can be visited around **Cerro La Mina** and elsewhere in the Amboró buffer zone. Also **Cuevas**, 20 km east of town, with waterfalls and pools, often visited together with El Fuerte. Further east are forest and sandstone mountains at **Bella Vista/Codo de los Andes**. There is a wonderful hike up to the **Loma de Cóndores**, with many condors and nearby the the 25-m-high **La Pajcha** waterfall, 40 km south of Samaipata. **Postrervalle** is a quaint hamlet with many interesting walks and mountain bike trails. There is good birdwatching throughout the region, especially around Mataral (see below). Tour operators in Samaipata can arrange all of the above trips.

The little village of **Bermejo**, 40 km east of Samaipata on the road to Santa Cruz, provides access to the strikingly beautiful **Serranía Volcanes** region, abutting on Parque Nacional Amboró. Here is the excellent **Refugio Los Volcanes** ① *T7688 0800, or 03-337 2042, www.refugiovolcanes.net*, a small lodge with a 15-km trail system, with good birdwatching, orchids and bromeliads. Ginger's Paradise, some 2 km from Bermejo (T6777 4772, www.gingersparadise.com), offers an organic, communal alternative, popular with backpackers (you can work to offset some room costs).

Comarapa and the old road to Cochabamba

Past Samaipata the road from Santa Cruz continues west 17 km to Mairana, a hot dusty roadside town where long-distance buses make their meal stops and there is daily service to Cochabamba (see Santa Cruz transport, page 355). It is 51 km further to Mataral, where there are petroglyphs. The paved road to Vallegrande (51 km, see below) branches south here.

Another 57 km west is Comarapa (population 15,875, altitude 1800 m), a tranquil agricultural centre halfway between Santa Cruz and Cochabamba. The town provides access to several lovely natural areas including **Laguna Verde** (12 km, taxi US\$11.50 with two hours' wait, or walk back over the hills), surrounded by cloudforest bordering Parque Nacional Amboró; and the **Jardín de Cactáceas de Bolivia**, where the huge *carparí* cactus and 25 other endemic species may be seen (entry US\$0.75, take a *trufi* from Comarapa to Pulquina Abajo, US\$1). The *jardín* itself is run-down but there are many more impressive cacti, good walking and birdwatching throughout the area. Beyond Comarapa the road is unpaved and very scenic. It climbs through cloudforest past the village of **La Siberia** to the pass at El Churo and enters the department of Cochabamba (see page 338).

Vallegrande and La Higuera

Some 115 km south of the Santa Cruz–Cochabamba road is La Higuera, where Che Guevara was killed. On 8 October each year, visitors, most from outside Bolivia, gather there to celebrate his memory. La Higuera is reached through the town of Vallegrande (population 17,200) where, at Hospital Nuestro Señor de Malta ① *no fee, but voluntary donation to the health station*, you can see the old laundry building where Che's body was shown to the international press on 9 October 1967. Near Vallegrande's airstrip you can see the results of excavations carried out in 1997 which finally unearthed his physical remains (now in Cuba); ask an airport attendant to see the site. Vallegrande has a small **archaeological museum** ① *Mon-Fri 1000-1200, 1400-1700, US\$1.50*, above which is the **Che Guevara Room** ① *entry US\$4.50*. Another **museum** ① *T03-942 2003*, owned by René Villegas, opens on advance request.

The schoolhouse in La Higuera (60 km south of Vallegrande) where Che was executed is now a museum. Guides, including Pedro Calzadillo, headmaster of the school, will show visitors to the ravine of El Churo (or Yuro), where Che was captured on 8 October 1967.

☆La Ruta del Che tours organized by agencies in Santa Cruz (three days, two nights) and Samaipata (two days, one night) follow some of the last movements of Che and his band.

☆Parque Nacional Amboró *Colour map 3, B4.*

The park is administered by SERNAP, C 9 Oeste 138, frente a la Plaza Italia, Barrio Equipetrol, T03-339 4311, see www.sernap.gob.bo and www.biobol.org. There are also park offices in Samaipata and Buena Vista.

This vast (442,500 ha) protected area lies only three hours west of Santa Cruz. Amboró encompasses four distinct major ecosystems and 11 life zones and is home to thousands of animal, plant and insect species (it is reputed to contain more butterflies than anywhere else on earth). The park is home to over 850 species of bird, including the blue-horned curassow, quetzal and cock-of-the-rock, red and chestnut-fronted macaws, hoatzin and cuvier toucans, and 130 mammals, many native to Amazonia, such as capybaras, peccaries, tapirs, several species of monkey, and jungle cats like the jaguar, ocelot and margay, and the spectacled bear. There are also numerous waterfalls and cool, green swimming pools, moss-ridden caves and large tracts of virgin rainforest. The park itself is largely inaccessible, but there is good trekking in the surrounding 195,100-ha buffer zone which is where most tours operate. The best time of year to visit the park is during April to October. You cannot enter the park without a guide, either from a tour operator, or from a community-based project. Note that there are many biting insects so take repellent, long-sleeved shirts, long trousers and good boots. There are two places to base yourself: Samaipata (see above) to access the southern highland areas of the park, and Buena Vista (see below) for northern lowland sections.

Buena Vista

This sleepy little town is 100 km northwest of Santa Cruz by paved road (see www. buenavistabolivia.com). There's no ATM in town, but US dollars cash can be changed. There is an Amboró interpretation office one block from the plaza, T03-932 2055. Three kilometres from town is **Eco-Albergue Candelaria** ① T7668 7071, or contact in advance through Hacienda El Cafetal (see Where to stay, below), a community tourism project offering cabins in a pleasant setting, activities and tours. From Buena Vista there are five tourist sites for entering the national park.

Listings West of Santa Cruz map page 356.

Where to stay

Samaipata
Rooms may be hard to find at weekends in high season.

$$$$-$$ El Pueblito Resort
Camino a Valle Abajo, 20 mins' walk uphill from town, T03-944 6383, www.elpueblitoresort.com.
Fully equipped cabins and rooms, pool, restaurant and bar set around a mock colonial plaza, with shops and meditation chapel.

$$ Hostal Restaurant Nómada
C Bolívar next to the museum, T7782 8132.
Most rooms have private bath, electric shower, swimming pool, restaurant, meeting rooms for 70 people.

$$ La Víspera
1.2 km south of town, T03-944 6082, www.lavispera.org.

$$ Landhaus
C Murillo uphill from centre, T03-944 6033, www.samaipata-landhaus.com.
Cabins and rooms in nice ample grounds, small pool, hammocks, parking, sauna (extra), craft shop, good breakfast available. Older rooms are cheaper and good value.

Dutch-owned organic farm with accommodation in 5 cosy cabins with kitchen, camping US$6-7 pp, breakfast and lunch available in **Café-Jardín** (daily 0800-1500), book exchange, maps for sale. A peaceful slow-paced place; owners Margarita and Pieter are very knowledgeable. They also sell medicinal and seasoning herbs.

$ Andoriña
C Campero, 2½ blocks from plaza, T03-944 6333, www.andorinasamaipata.com.
Tastefully decorated hostel, cheaper without bath, good breakfast, kitchen, bar, good views, volunteer opportunities. Dutch/Bolivian-run, enthusiastic owners Andrés and Doriña are very knowledgeable, English spoken.

$ El Jardín
C Arenales, 2 blocks from market, T7311 9461, www.eljardinsamaipata.blogspot.com.
Cheaper with shared bath and in dorm, hot water, ample gardens, camping US$3 pp, kitchen facilities, nature-friendly.

$ Los Aventureros
C Murillo y Arteaga, T6505 5191, www.losaventureros.net.
Hostel with dorms and rooms with shared bath, hot water, kitchen, laundry facilities, bike rentals, good atmosphere.

$ Posada Guasu
C Terrazas 26, T7903 6460, http://posada-guasu-samaipata.com.
Rooms with private bath, small courtyard, includes breakfast, tranquil family atmosphere.

$ Residencial Paola
C Terrazas, diagonal to the plaza, T03-944 6093.
Simple rooms, cheaper without bath, electric shower, internet (extra), kitchen and laundry facilities.

Comarapa

$ El Paraíso
Av Comarapa 396 (main road to Cochabamba), T03-946 2045.
Pleasant economical hotel, electric shower, nice garden, parking, decent restaurant, popular.

Vallegrande and La Higuera

$ Hostal Juanita
M M Caballero 123, Vallegrande, T03-942 2231.
Cheaper without bath, electric shower, good value, Doña Juanita is kind.

$ La Casa del Telegrafista
La Higuera, T7493 7807/6773 3362, casadeltelegrafista@gmail.com.
Small, welcoming French-owned *posada*, rooms with shared bath, lovely garden, great views, meals on request, camping (US$2), horseback and mountain-bike tours, US$15, also bikes for hire.

$ Residencial Vallegrande
On the plaza, Vallegrande.
Basic accommodation.

Buena Vista

$$$-$$ Hacienda El Cafetal
5.5 km south of town (taxi from plaza US$3), T03-935 2067, www.haciendaelcafetal.com.
Comfortable suites for up to 5 people, double rooms, restaurant, bar, birdwatching platform, on a working coffee plantation (tours available), with shade forest.

$$ Buenavista
700 m out of town, T03-932 2104.
Pretty place with rooms, suites and cabins with kitchen, viewing platform, pool, sauna, very good restaurant, horse riding.

$ La Casona
Av 6 de Agosto at the corner of the plaza, T03-932 2083.

Small simple rooms with fan, shared bath, electric shower, courtyard in hammocks, plants and birds, good value.

$ Quimori
1 km east of Buena Vista, T03-932 2081.
Includes breakfast, other meals with advance notice, pool, nice grounds, tours in dry season, family-run.

$ Residencial Nadia
C M Saucedo Sevilla 186, T03-932 2049.
Cheaper without bath, simple, small, family-run.

Restaurants

Samaipata

$$ Latina Café
Bolívar, 3 blocks from plaza. Fri-Tue 1800-2200, Sat-Sun also 1200-1430.
Nice upmarket restaurant/bar with very good Bolivian and international food including vegetarian. French/Bolivian-run and recommended.

$$-$ Chakana
Terrazas on plaza. Daily 0800-2300.
Bar/restaurant/café serving *almuerzos*, good snacks, salads, cakes and ice cream, outside seating, book exchange, Dutch-owned.

$$-$ Tierra Libre
Sucre ½ block from plaza. Open 1130-2200, closed Tue.
Nice terrace with outdoor seating, good meat and vegetarian, pleasant atmosphere.

$ Café 1900
Sucre on plaza. Daily 0800-2300.
Good set lunch, sandwiches and crêpes.

$ El Nuevo Turista
Opposite the gas station on the highway.
Good local dishes.

$ La Bohème
Sucre y Terrazas, diagonal to plaza. Daily 1200-2400.
Trendy Australian-run bar for drinks and snacks.

$ La Cafette
C Terrazas on the plaza. Wed-Sun 0800-2000.
Café and bakery serving espresso, pannini, croissant and sweets.

$ La Cocina
Sucre y Terrazas by the plaza. Tue-Sun 1900-2200.
Middle Eastern and Mexican fast food with home-made breads.

Buena Vista

$$-$ La Plaza
On the plaza.
Elegant restaurant/bar with a terrace, wide range of international dishes, good service.

$ El Patujú
On the plaza.
The only café in town, serving excellent local coffee, teas, hot chocolate and a range of snacks. Also sells local produce and crafts.

What to do

Samaipata

Tour operators
Samaipata has many tour operators, more than we can list. Except as noted, all are on C Bolívar near the museum. Most day trips cost about US$20-25 pp in a group of 4.
Ben Verhoef Tours, *Campero 217, T03-944 6365.* Dutch-owned, English, German and Spanish also spoken. Offer tours along La Ruta del Che and throughout the area.
Jucumari Tours, *T944 6129, erwin-am@ hotmail.com.* Run by Edwin Acuña.
Michael Blendinger, *T03-944 6227, www. discoveringbolivia.com.* German guide raised in Argentina who speaks English, runs fully equipped 4WD tours, short and long treks, specialist in nature and archaeology.
Road Runners, *T944 6193/6294, www.hosteltrail. com/roadrunners.* Olaf and Frank speak English, German and Dutch, enthusiastic, lots of information and advice.
Tucandera Tours, *T7316 7735, tucandera.tours@ hotmail.com.* Saul Arias and Elva Villegas are biologists, excellent for nature tours and birdwatching, English spoken, competitive prices, off-the-beaten-path destinations including Parque Nacional Kaa-Iya. Recommended.

Wine tasting
2 bodegas located outside Samaipata are **Uvairenda** (www.uvairenda.com) and **Vargas** (www.vitivinicolavargas.com).

Buena Vista
Amboró Travel & Adventure, *C Celso Sandoval, ½ block from the plaza, T7663 2102, amborotravel@ hotmail.com.* Prices include transport to and from the park, guide and meals. Recommended.
Puertas del Amboró, *corner of the plaza, T03-932 2059.* They also offer full packages.

Transport

Samaipata
Bus From **Santa Cruz**, **Minibus El Fuerte**, C Arumá 90 y Av Grigotá (2ndo Anillo), Santa Cruz, T03-359 8958, Samaipata T03-944 6336; and **Taxis Expreso Samaipata**, Av Omar Chávez 1147 y Soliz de Holguín, Santa Cruz, T03-333 5067, Samaipata T03-944 6129; both companies leave when full Mon-Sat 0530-1900 (for Sun book in advance), US$4.50 per person shared; or US$22 in private vehicle, 2½ hrs. Returning to Santa Cruz, they pick you up from your hotel in Samaipata. Buses leaving Santa Cruz for **Sucre** and other towns pass through Samaipata between 1900 and 2200; tickets can be booked with 1 day's notice through **El Nuevo Turista** (see Restaurants, above). To get to **Samaipata** from **Sucre**, buses leave at night and arrive 0500-0600 (set your alarm in case the driver forgets to stop for you), stopping in Mataral or Mairana for breakfast, about ½ hr before Samaipata.

Comarapa
To/from **Santa Cruz** with **Turismo Caballero** (T03-350 9626) and **Trans Comarapa** (T7817 5576), both on Plazuela Oruro, Av Grigotá (3er Anillo), 3 daily each, US$4.50, 6 hrs. To **Cochabamba**, 2 buses a day pass through from Mairana.

Vallegrande and La Higuera
Bus **Flota Vallegrande** has 2 daily buses morning and afternoon from Santa Cruz to **Vallegrande** via **Samaipata** (at 1130 and 1630), 5 hrs, US$5. Best to book in advance. Samaipata–Vallegrande US$3.25. From Vallegrande market, a daily bus departs 0815 to **Pucará** (45 km, US$2.50), from where there is transport (12 km) to **La Higuera**.

Taxi Vallegrande–La Higuera US$30-35.

Buena Vista
Bus and taxi **Sindicato 10 de Febrero** in Santa Cruz at Izozog 668 y Av Irala, 1er Anillo behind ex-terminal, T03-334 8435, 0730-1830, US$3 pp (private vehicle US$15), 1¾ hrs. Also another shared taxi company nearby, micros from Av Banzer y 3er Anillo and 'Línea 102' buses from regional section of Terminal Bimodal, US$1.50, 3 hrs. From Buena Vista, the access to the Amboró park is by gravel road, 4WD jeep or similar recommended as rivers have to been crossed. All operators and community ecolodge coordinators offer transport.

a hot, friendly city en route to the borders

South of Santa Cruz a good paved road passes through Abapó, Camiri (Hotel Premier, Avenida Busch 60, T03-952 2204, is a decent place to stay), Boyuibe, Villamontes – access for the Trans-Chaco route to Paraguay – and Yacuiba, on the border with Argentina.

Villamontes *Colour map 3, C4.*

Villamontes, 500 km south of Santa Cruz, is renowned for fishing. It holds a **Fiesta del Pescado** in August. It is a hot, friendly, spread-out city on the north shore of the Río Pilcomayo, at the base of the Cordillera de Aguaragüe. The river cuts through this range (Parque Nacional Aguaragüe) forming **El Angosto**, a beautiful gorge. The road to Tarija, 280 km west, is cut in the cliffs along this gorge. At Plaza 6 de Agosto is the **Museo Héroes del Chaco** ⓘ *Tue-Sun 0800-1200, 1400-1800, US$0.30*, with photographs, maps, artefacts, and battle models of the 1932-1935 Chaco War. There are a couple of ATMs. **Prodem** and various *cambios* are on Avenida Méndez Arcos.

Border with Paraguay From Villamontes, the road to Paraguay, almost all paved, runs east to **Ibibobo** (70 km). Motorists and bus travellers should carry extra water and some food, as climatic conditions are harsh and there is little traffic in case of a breakdown. Bolivian exit stamps are given at Ibibobo. If travelling by bus, passports are collected by driver and returned on arrival at Mcal Estigarribia (Paraguay), with Bolivian exit stamp. Paraguayan immigration and thorough drugs searches take place in Mcal Estigarribia. There are Paraguayan consulates in Santa Cruz (Avenida San Martín, Equipetrol Norte, Calle H Este Casa 8, T03-344 8989, scruzcongralpar@mre. gov.py), and Villamontes (Avenida Ingavi entre Héroes del Chaco y Cochabamba, T4672 3648, villamontesconsulpar@mre.gov.py). See Santa Cruz Transport (page 355) for international bus services. From Ibibobo to the Bolivian frontier post at Picada Sucre is 75 km, then it's 15 km to the actual border and another 8 km to the Paraguayan frontier post at **Fortín Infante Rivarola**. There are customs posts, but no police, immigration nor any other services at the border.

Yacuiba and the border with Argentina *Colour map 3, C4.*

Yacuiba is a prosperous city (population 11,000) at the crossing to Pocitos in Argentina. Hotels include **Valentín**, San Martín 3271, T04-682 2645, www.valentinhotelbolivia.com, and **París**, Comercio 1175 y Campero, T04-682 2182 (both **\$\$**). The train service from Santa Cruz is slow and poor, road travel is a better option. In Yacuiba, there are ATMs on Campero. The Argentine consul is at Santa Cruz 1540, entre Sucre y Crevaux, T04-682 2062. Passengers leaving Bolivia must disembark at Yacuiba, take a taxi to Pocitos on the border (US$0.50, beware unscrupulous drivers) and walk across to Argentina.

Listings To Paraguay and Argentina

Where to stay

Villamontes

\$\$\$-\$\$ El Rancho Olivo
*Av Méndez Arcos opposite the train station,
15 blocks from the centre, T04-672 2059,
www.elranchoolivo.com.*
Lovely rooms, frigobar, nice grounds and pool, parking, excellent restaurant.

\$ Gran Hotel Avenida
Av Méndez Arcos 3 blocks east of Plaza 15 de Abril, T04-672 2828.
Helpful owner, parking.

\$ Residencial Raldes
Cap Manchego 171, 1½ blocks from Plaza 15 de Abril, T04-672 2088, fernandoarel@gmail.com.
Well maintained, family-run, electric shower, cheaper with shared bath and fan, nice courtyard, small pool, parking.

Transport

Villamontes
Bus To **Yacuiba**, **Coop El Chaco**, Av Méndez Arcos y Ismael Montes, hourly 0630-1830, US$1.35, 1½ hrs. Cars from Av Montenegro y Cap Manchego, hourly or when full, 0630-1830, US$2, 1½ hrs. Long-distance buses from terminal on

Av Méndez Arcos, 13 blocks east of Plaza 15 de Abril (taxi US$0.40 pp). To **Tarija** via Entre Ríos, mostly unpaved (sit on the right for best views), US$14.50, 10-11 hrs, several companies 1730-1930; for day travel, **Copacabana** may depart at 1030, 2-3 per week from the terminal; **Guadalupana**, Wed and Sat at 0930, from Coop El Chaco office. To **Santa Cruz**, several companies daily, US$5-8.50, some bus-cama, 7-8 hrs.

To **Asunción**, buses from Santa Cruz pass through 0200-0300, reserve a day earlier, US$35, about 15 hrs. 5 companies, offices all on Av Montenegro, either side of Av Méndez Arcos. Best are **Stel**, T04-672 3662, or Vicky Vides T7735 0934; **Yaciretá**, T04-672 2812, or Betty Borda, T7740 4111.

Yacuiba

Bus To **Santa Cruz**, about 20 companies, mostly at night, 14 hrs, US$8.50-13. To **Tarija**, daily morning and evening, US$5-7, vans US$14.50.

Eastern Bolivia

natural beauty, indigenous culture and Jesuit heritage

The vast and rapidly developing plains to the east of the Eastern Cordillera are Bolivia's richest area in terms of natural resources. For the visitor, the beautiful churches and traditions of the former Jesuit missions of Chiquitania are well worth a visit. Here too are some of the country's largest and wildest protected natural areas.

Essential Jesuit missions of Chiquitos

Getting around

Access to the mission area is by bus or train from **Santa Cruz**: a paved highway runs north to San Ramón (180 km) and on north to San Javier (40 km further), turning east here to Concepción (60 km), then to San Ignacio de Velasco (160 km, of which the first 30 are paved). A paved road runs south from San Ignacio either through San Miguel or Santa Ana to meet at San Rafael for the continuation south to San José de Chiquitos. Access is also possible by the paved Santa Cruz–Puerto Suárez highway, which goes via San José de Chiquitos. By rail, leave the Santa Cruz–Quijarro train at San José and from there travel north by bus. The most comfortable way to visit is by jeep, in about five days. The route is straightforward and fuel is available.

When to go

One of the best times to appreciate this region is at the bi-annual **Festival de Música Renacentista y Barroca Americana** (next in April/May 2018), but the living legacy of the missions can be appreciated year-round.

★Jesuit missions of Chiquitania

Nine Jesuit missions survive east of Santa Cruz six of which – San Javier, Concepción, San Rafael, Santa Ana, San Miguel and San José de Chiquitos – have churches which are UNESCO World Heritage Sites. Many of these were built by the Swiss Jesuit, Padre Martin Schmidt and his pupils.

Besides organizing *reducciones* and constructing churches, Padre Schmidt wrote music (some is still played today on traditional instruments) and he published a Spanish-Chiquitano dictionary based on his knowledge of all the dialects of the region. He worked in this part of the then-Viceroyalty of Peru until the expulsion of the Jesuits in 1767 by order of Charles III of Spain.

San Javier (San Xavier) The first Jesuit mission in Chiquitania (1691), San Javier's church was built by Padre Schmidt between 1749 and 1752. Some of the original wooden structure has survived more or less intact and restoration was undertaken between 1987 and 1993 by the Swiss Hans Roth, himself a former Jesuit. Subtle designs and floral patterns cover the ceiling walls and carved columns. One of the bas-relief paintings on the high altar depicts Martin Schmidt playing the piano for his indigenous choir. It is a fine 30-minute walk (best in the afternoon light) to **Mirador El Bibosi** and the small **Parque Piedra de Los Apóstoles**. There is also good walking or all-terrain cycling in the surrounding countryside (no maps, ask around) thermal swimming holes at **Aguas Calientes** and horse riding from several hotels. Patron saint's fiesta, 3 December, but 29 June, Feast of Saints Peter and Paul, is best for viewing traditional costumes, dances and music. Tourist guides' association has an office in the **Alcaldía** ① *T7761 7902, or 7763 3203 for a guide*. Information also from the **Casa de Cultura** ① *on the plaza, T963 5149*.

Concepción The lovely town is dominated by its magnificent **cathedral** ① *0700-2000, tours 1000, 1500, donation invited*, completed by Padre Schmidt and Johann Messner in 1755 and restored by Hans Roth (1975-1982). The interior of this beautiful church has an altar of laminated silver. In front of the church is a bell-cum-clock tower housing the original bells and behind it are well-restored cloisters. On the plaza, forming part of the Jesuit complex, is the **Museo Misional** ① *Mon-Sat 0800-1200, 1430-1830, Sun 1000-1230, US$3.50*, which has an *artesanía* shop. The ticket also gives entry to the **Hans Roth Museum**, dedicated to the restoration process. Visit also the **Museo Antropológico de la Chiquitania** ① *16 de Septiembre y Tte Capoblanco, 0800-1200, 1400-1800, free*, which explains the life of the indigenous peoples of the region. It has a café and guesthouse. The **municipal tourist office** ① *Lucas Caballero y Cabo Rodríguez, one block from plaza, T03-964 3057*, can arrange trips to nearby recreational areas, ranches and communities. An **Asociación de Guías Locales** ① *south side of plaza, contact Ysabel Supepi, T7604 7085; or Hilario Orellana, T7534 3734*, also offers tours to local communities many of which are developing grass-roots tourism projects: eg **Santa Rita**, **San Andrés** and **El Carmen**. With a week's advance notice, they can also organize private concerts with 30 to 40 musicians. There are various restaurants in town and many places sell wood carvings, traditional fabrics and clothing.

San Ignacio de Velasco This is the main commercial and transport hub of the region, with road links to Brazil. A lack of funds for restoration led to the demolition of San Ignacio's replacement Jesuit church in 1948, the original having burnt down in 1808. A modern replica contains the elaborate high altar, pulpit and paintings and statues of saints. Tourist information office at **Casa de la Cultura** ① *La Paz y Comercio, on the plaza, T03-962 2056 ext 122, culturayturismo.siv@gmail.com, Mon-Fri 0800-1200, 1430-1830*, can help organize guides and visits to local music schools. The **Centro Artesanal** ① *Santa Cruz entre Bolívar y Oruro, Mon-Sat 0800-1930, Sun 0800-1200*, sells lovely textile and wood crafts. There is community tourism in the villages of **San Juancito**, 18 km from San Ignacio, where organic coffee is grown, and **San Rafael de Sutuquiña**, 5 km; both have artisans. **Laguna Guapomó** reservoir on the edge of San Ignacio is good for swimming and fishing. There is only one ATM in town, best take some cash.

Santa Ana, San Rafael and San Miguel de Velasco These three small towns are less visited than some others along the missions circuit. Allow at least two days if travelling independently from San Ignacio: you can take a bus to Santa Ana in the afternoon, stay overnight, then continue to San Rafael the next afternoon and return to San Ignacio via San Miguel on Tuesday, Thursday or Sunday (see Transport, page 369). A day trip by taxi from San Ignacio costs about US$65 or an all-inclusive tour can be arranged by Parador Santa Ana (see Where to stay, page 366). Local guides are available, US$10.

The church in Santa Ana (town founded 1755, church constructed 1773-1780, after the expulsion of the Jesuits), is a lovely wooden building. It is the most authentic of all the Jesuit *templos* and Santa Ana is a particularly authentic little village. The tourist office on the plaza can provide guides. Simple accommodation is available (see page 367).

San Rafael's church was completed by Schmidt in 1749. It is one of the most beautifully restored, with mica-covered interior walls and frescoes in beige paint over the exterior. There are restaurants near the plaza. For the tourist information office, call T03-962 4022.

The frescoes on the façade of the church (1752-1759) at San Miguel depict St Peter and St Paul; designs in brown and yellow cover all the interior and the exterior side walls. The mission runs three schools and a workshop; the sisters are very welcoming and will gladly show tourists around. There is a **Museo Etnofolclórico**, off the Plaza at Calle Betania; next door is the Municipalidad/Casa de la Cultura, with a tourist information office, T03-962 4222. San Miguel has many workshops and rivals San Ignacio for the quality of its Jesuit-inspired art.

San José de Chiquitos *Colour map 3, B5.*
One complete side of the plaza is occupied by the imposing frontage of the Jesuit mission complex of four buildings and a bell tower, begun in the mid-1740s. Best light for photography is in the

afternoon. The stone buildings, in baroque style, are connected by a wall. They are the workshop (1754); the church (1747) with its undulating façade; the four-storey bell tower (1748) and the mortuary (*la bóveda* – 1750), with one central window but no entrance in its severe frontage. The complex and **Museo** ① *Mon-Fri 0800-1200, 1430-1800, Sat-Sun 0900-1200, 1500-1800, entry US$3*, are well worth visiting. Behind are the *colegio* and workshops, which house the **Escuela Municipal de Música**; visits to rehearsals and performances can be arranged by the tourist office. **InfoTur** ① *in the Municipio, C Velasco, ½ block from plaza, T03-972 2084, Mon-Fri 0800-1200, 1430-1830*, which has information and arranges various tours; there is internet upstairs. On Mondays, Mennonites bring their produce to San José and buy provisions. The colonies are 50 km west and the Mennonites, who speak English, German, Plattdeutsch and Spanish, are happy to talk about their way of life. There is only one ATM in town, best take some cash.

About 2 km south from San José is the 17,000 ha **Parque Nacional Histórico Santa Cruz la Vieja** ① *www.biobol.org*. It has a monument to the original site of Santa Cruz (founded 1561) and mirador with great views. The park's heavily forested hills contain much animal and bird life. There are various trails for hiking; guides can be organized by the tourist office in San José. It gets very hot so start early, allow over one hour to get there on foot (or hire a vehicle) and take plenty of water and insect repellent. There is also good walking with lovely views at **Cerro Turubó** and the **Serranía de San José**, both outside San José.

East of San José de Chiquitos

Paving of the highway from Santa Cruz east to Brazil opened up this once-isolated region of friendly villages surrounded by natural wonders. The village of **Chochís**, 90 km east of San José de Chiquitos, is known for its sanctuary of the Virgen Asunta built by Hans Roth in 1988 (one of his few major works not connected with restoring Jesuit missions). The large sanctuary is built at the foot of an impressive red sandstone outcrop called **La Torre**, 2 km from town. Along the rail line from Chochís toward La Torre is a signed trail leading to the **Velo de Novia** waterfall, a pleasant one- to two-hour walk. A much more challenging hike climbs 800 m to the flat top of **Cerro de Chochís**, where you can camp or return to town in a long day; guide required.

Chochís is at the western end of the **Serranía de Chiquitos**, a flat-topped mountain range running east–west, north of the highway and railroad. It is filled with rich vegetation, caves, petroglyphs, waterfalls, birds and butterflies. These hills are part of the 262,000-ha **Reserva Valle de Tucavaca** (www.biobol.org) which protects unique Chiquitano dry forest and offers great hiking opportunities.

Forty kilometers east of Chochís is **Roboré**, the regional centre and transport hub. The **Oficina de Turismo** ① *Av Ejército, Parque Urbano, T7761 8280*, has information about local excursions including **Los Helechos** and **Totaisales**, two lovely bathing spots in the forest, Chochís and Santiago de Chiquitos. Roboré was founded as a garrison town in 1916 and retains a strong military presence. The local fiesta is 25 October.

Seven kilometres east of Roboré, a paved road branches northeast and in 14 km reaches the particularly friendly village of **Santiago de Chiquitos**, within the Reserva Valle de Tucavaca. Founded in 1754, Santiago was one of the last missions built in Chiquitania. There are good accommodation and more good walking to a fine mirador, natural stone arches and caves with petroglyphs; guides are available in town. A poor road continues 150 km past Santiago to **Santo Corazón**, a still-isolated former Jesuit mission town (its church was built after the missionaries were expelled) inside **Area Natural de Manejo Integrado San Matías** ① *www.biobol.org*.

Aguas Calientes is 15 km east of Roboré along the rail line and highway to Brazil. The hot little village is unimpressive but nearby is a river of crystal-clear thermal water, teeming with little fish and bird life. There are several spots with facilities for bathing and camping, which is preferable to the basic accommodations in town. There are many tiny biting sand-flies, so your tent should have good netting. Soaking in the thermal water amid the sights and sounds of the surrounding forest at dawn or on a moonlit night is amazing.

☆Parque Nacional Noel Kempff Mercado

Park office in San Ignacio de Velasco, Bolívar 87 entre La Paz y Santa Cruz, T03-962 2747, turismonoelkempff@gmail.com, Mon-Fri 0830-1200, 1430-1800, lots of information, some in English; additional information from SERNAP (T03-335 2325 in Santa Cruz) and FAN, also in Santa Cruz (page 350).

also www.biobol.org. The park was reported closed in early 2017, confirm all details in advance with SERNAP and tour operators in Santa Cruz.

In the far northeast corner of Santa Cruz Department, Parque Nacional Noel Kempff Mercado (named after a Bolivian conservation pioneer who was killed while flying over the park), is one of the world's most diverse natural habitats. This World Heritage Site covers 1,523,446 ha and encompasses seven ecosystems, within which are 139 species of mammal (including black jaguars), 620 species of bird (including nine types of macaw), 74 species of reptile and 110 species of orchid. Highlights include the **Huanchaca** or **Caparú Plateau**, which with its 200- to 500-m sheer cliffs and tumbling waterfalls is a candidate for Sir Arthur Conan Doyle's *Lost World* (Colonel Percy Fawcett, who discovered the plateau in 1910, was a friend of Conan Doyle).

This outstanding natural area receives very few visitors. Organizing a trip requires time, money and flexibility; there is no infrastructure, visitors must be self-sufficient and take all equipment including a tent. The authorities sometimes restrict access, enquire in advance. Operators in Santa Cruz (see page 354) may be able to arrange all-inclusive tours. Otherwise, the best base is San Ignacio, which has some provisions but more specialized items should be brought from Santa Cruz. Note, though, that there is no direct access from San Ignacio. See Transport, page 369, for details.

The southwestern section of the park is reached from the village of **Florida**, where there is a ranger station and a community tourism project offering basic accommodation and guides (guide compulsory, US$25 per day). It is 65 km from Florida to the trailhead (pickup US$60 one way), which provides access to the 80-m-high **El Encanto** waterfall and the climb to the plateau; allow five to six days for the return excursion.

In the northeastern section of the park are the great **Arco Iris** and **Federico Ahlfeld** waterfalls, both on the Río Paucerna and accessible mid-December to May when water levels are sufficiently high. Access is either from the Bolivian village of **Piso Firme** or the Brazilian town of **Pimenteiras do Oeste**; in all cases you must be accompanied by a Bolivian boatman/guide, available in Piso Firme and organized by the park office in San Ignacio. It is six to seven hours by motorized canoe from Piso Firme to a shelter near the Ahlfeld waterfall, and a full day's walk from there to Arco Iris.

Parque Nacional Kaa-Iya del Gran Chaco
Park office in Santa Cruz, Av Irala 452, T03-337 0508, tluisfer@yahoo.com.

This enormous national park, in southeastern Santa Cruz Department, along the border with Paraguay, is, at 3,441,115 ha, the largest in the country and continent. It is very remote, difficult to access, and has only recently begun to open up to visitors. The majority of the park is uncharted and unknown except by local Guaraní peoples. Fauna is abundant, including jaguar and tapir. Access is from San José de Chiquitos and Roboré, both east of Santa Cruz. There are no services of any kind in the park and independent visits are not permitted. A handful of agencies, including **Tucandera Tours** in Samaipata (see page 360), visit the park; make arrangements well in advance.

To Brazil
There are four routes from Santa Cruz: by air to **Puerto Suárez**, by rail or road to **Quijarro** (fully paved), by road to **San Matías** (a busy border town reported unsafe due to drug smuggling), and via **San Ignacio de Velasco** to either Vila Bela or Pontes e Lacerda (both in Brazil). Puerto Suárez is near Quijarro and this route leads to Corumbá on the Brazilian side, from where there is access to the southern Pantanal. The San Matías and Vila Bela/Pontes roads both link to Cáceres, Cuiabá and the northern Pantanal in Brazil. There are immigration posts of both countries on all routes except Vila Bela/Pontes. If travelling this way, get your Bolivian exit stamp in San Ignacio (immigration office near **Jenecherú** bus station) and Brazilian entry stamp in Cáceres or Vilhena. There may be strict customs and drugs checks entering Brazil, no fresh food may be taken from Bolivia.

Quijarro and Puerto Suárez *Colour map 3, C6.*
The eastern terminus of the Bolivian road and railway is **Quijarro**. It is quite safe by day, but caution is recommended at night. The water supply is often unreliable. Prices are much lower than in neighbouring Brazil and there are some decent places to stay. ATMs and banks are at the border.

On the shores of Laguna Cáceres, 8 km west of Quijarro, is **Puerto Suárez**, with a shady main plaza. There is a nice view of the lake from the park at the north end of Avenida Bolívar.

Parque Nacional Otuquis, protecting the lake and extensive wetlands in the Bolivian Pantanal, is divided in two parts, both accessible from Puerto Suárez; **SERNAP** office: final Avenida Adolfo Rau, T03-976 3270, Puerto Suárez.

Border with Brazil The neighbourhood by the border is known as Arroyo Concepción. You need not have your passport stamped if you visit Corumbá for the day. Otherwise get your exit stamp at Bolivian immigration (see below), entry stamp at Brazilian border complex. A yellow fever vaccination may be required on either side of the border, best have it to hand. Bolivian immigration is at the border at Arroyo Concepción (0800-1200, 1400-1730 daily), or at Puerto Suárez airport, where Bolivian exit/entry stamps are also issued. There is one ATM at Arroyo Concepción, at the Hotel Pantanal. Money changers right at the border on the Bolivian side offer poor rates, better to ask around in the small shops away from the bridge; nowhere to change on the Brazilian side until Corumbá. There are Brazilian consulates in Arroyo Concepción (Calle Santa Cruz s/n, T03-978 2511, cg.pquijarro@itamaraty.gov.br) and Santa Cruz (Avenida Noel Kempff Mercado, Calle 9A Norte, casa 9, T03-344 7575, cg.santacruz@itamaraty.gov.br). See Transport, page 370, for taxis from the border.

Listings Eastern Bolivia

Where to stay

San Javier

$ Alojamiento Ame-Tauná
Across from the central plaza, T03-963 5095.
Perfect location in centre of town, quiet, rooms with bath, safe parking.

$ Alojamiento San Xavier
C Santa Cruz, T03-963 5038.
Cheaper without bath, electric shower, garden, nice sitting area. Recommended.

$ Residencial Chiquitana
Av Santa Cruz (Av José de Arce), ½ block from plaza, T03-963 5072.
Simple rooms, fan, large patio, good value.

Concepción

$$ Gran Hotel Concepción
On plaza, T03-964 3031, www. granhotelconcepcion.com.bo.
Excellent service, buffet breakfast, pool, gardens, bar, very comfortable. Highly recommended.

$$ Hotel Chiquitos
End of Av Killian, T03-964 3153, www.hotelchiquitos.com.
Colonial-style construction, ample rooms, frigobar, pool, gardens and sports fields, orchid nursery, parking. Tours available. Recommended.

$$-$ Hotel Balneario Oasis Chiquitano
S Saucedo 225, 1½ blocks from plaza, T7602 5442, www.facebook.com/ HotelYComplejoTuristicoOasisChiquitano.
Buffet breakfast, pool, nice patio with flowers.

$ Colonial
Ñuflo de Chávez 7, ½ block from plaza, T03-964 3050.
Economical place, hammocks on ample veranda, parking, breakfast available.

$ Residencial Westfalia
Saucedo 205, 2 blocks from plaza, T03-964 3040.
Cheaper without bath, German-owned, nice patio, good value.

San Ignacio de Velasco

$$$ La Misión
Libertad, on plaza, T03-962 2333, www.hotel-lamision.com.
Upmarket hotel, restaurant, meeting rooms, pool, parking, downstairs rooms have bath tubs.

$$$ Parador Santa Ana
Libertad entre Sucre y Cochabamba, T03-962 2075, www.paradorsantaana.blogspot.com.
Beautiful house with small patio, tastefully decorated, 5 comfortable rooms, good breakfast, knowledgeable owner arranges tours, credit cards accepted. Recommended.

$$ Apart Hotel San Ignacio
24 de Septiembre y Cochabamba, T03-962 2157, www.aparthotel-sanignacio.com.

Comfortable rooms, nice grounds, pool, hammocks, parking. Despite the name, no apartments or kitchenettes.

$$ San Ignacio Miguel Areiger
Plaza 31 de Julio, T03-962 2283.
In a beautifully restored former episcopal mansion, non-profit (run by diocese, funds support poor youth in the community), breakfast.

$ Residencial Bethania
Velasco y Cochabamba, T03-962 2307.
Simple rooms with shared bath, electric shower, small patio, economical and good value.

Santa Ana

Simple economical accommodation is available at **Comunidad Valenciana** (T03-980 2098).

San Rafael

$ Casa de Huéspedes
Belisario s/n, T03-962 4241.
Clean, shared bath, good for bus connections.

San Miguel de Velasco

$$-$ Alojamiento Altiplano
Av Santa Bárbara s/n (main road), T03-962 4018.
Near the plaza, best in town, very knowledgeable staff.

San José de Chiquitos

$$$-$$ Villa Chiquitana
C 9 de Abril, 6 blocks from plaza, T7315 5803, www.villachiquitana.com.
Charming hotel built in traditional style, restaurant open to public, frigobar, pool (US$3 for non-guests), garden, parking, craft shop, tour agency. French-run.

$ Turubó
Bolívar on the plaza, T03-972 2037, hotelturubo on Facebook.
With a/c or fan, electric shower, variety of different rooms, ask to see one before checking-in, good location.

East of San José de Chiquitos

Chochís

$ Ecoalbergue de Chochís
1 km west of town along the rail line, T7263 9467; Santa Cruz contact: Probioma, T03-343 1332, www.probioma.org.bo.
Simple community-run lodging in 2 cabins, shared bath, cold water, small kitchen, screened hammock area, camping US$3.50 pp, meals on advance request.

$ El Peregrino
On the plaza, T7313 1881.
Simple rooms in a family home, some with fan and fridge, shared bath, electric shower, ample yard, camping possible.

Roboré

$$ Anahí
Obispo Santiesteban 1½ blocks from plaza, T03-974 2362.
Comfortable rooms with electric shower, nice patio, parking, kitchen and washing facilities, owner runs tours.

$$ Choboreca
Av La Paz 710, T03-974 2566.
Nice hotel, rooms with a/c. Several other places to stay in town.

Santiago de Chiquitos

There are various *alojamientos familiares* around town, all simple to basic.

$$ Beula
On the plaza, T03-313 6274, http://hotelbeula.com.
Comfortable hotel in traditional style, good breakfast, frigobar. Unexpectedly upmarket for such a remote location.

$ El Convento
On plaza next to the church, T7890 2943.
Former convent with simple rooms, one has private bath, lovely garden, hot and no fan but clean and good value.

$ Panorama
1 km north of plaza, T03-313 6286.
Simple rooms with shared bath and a family farm, friendly owners Katherine and Milton Whittaker sell excellent home-made dairy products and jams, they are knowledgeable about the area and offer volunteer opportunities.

Aguas Calientes

$$ Cabañas Canaan
Across the road from Los Hervores baths, T7467 7316.
Simple wooden cabins, cold water, fan, restaurant, rather overpriced but better than the basic places in town.

$ Camping El Tucán
1 km from town on the road to Los Hervores baths, T7262 0168.
Lovely grounds with clean bathrooms, electric showers, barbecues, small pier by the river.

Quijarro

$$$-$$ Jardín del Bibosi
Luis Salazar 495, 4½ blocks east of train station, T978 2044, www.hotelbibosi.com.
Variety of rooms and prices, some with a/c, fridge, cheaper with fan and shared bath, breakfast, pool, patio, restaurant, upscale for Quijarro.

Willy Solís Cruz
Roboré 13, T7365 5587, wiland_54@hotmail.com.
For years Willy has helped store luggage and offered local information and assistance. His home is open to visitors who would like to rest, take a shower, do laundry, cook or check the internet while they wait for transport; a contribution in return is welcome. He speaks English, very helpful.

Puerto Suárez

$ Beby
Av Bolívar 111, T03-976 2700.
Private bath, a/c, cheaper with shared bath and fan, no frills, very basic.

$ Casa Real
Vanguardia 39, T03-976 3335.
A/c, frigobar, Wi-Fi and internet, parking, tours, a decent choice.

Restaurants

San Javier

$$ Ganadero
In Asociación de Ganaderos on plaza.
Excellent steaks. Other eateries around the plaza.

Concepción

$ El Buen Gusto
North side of plaza.
Set meals and regional specialities.

San Ignacio de Velasco

$$ Casa del Camba
24 de Septiembre y Av Santa Cruz.
Daily lunch and dinner.
Local fare as well as vegetarian, chicken dishes and mini pizzas.

$ Club Social
Comercio on the plaza. Daily 1130-1500.
Decent set lunch.

Mi Nonna
C Velasco y Cochabamba. Open 1700-2400, closed Tue.
Café serving cappuccino, sandwiches, salads and pasta.

San José de Chiquitos

$$ Pizzería Romanazzi
Bolívar 1 block north of plaza, T03-972 2349 (call ahead). Daily lunch and dinner except Sun.
Home-made pizza, and other Italian dishes. "Unquestionably the finest pizza in eastern Bolivia if not the country." Recommended.

$$ Sabor y Arte
Bolívar y Mons Santisteban, by the plaza. Tue-Sun 1800-2300.
International dishes, for innovation try their coca-leaf ravioli, nice ambience, French/Bolivian-run.

$$-$ Rancho Brasilero
By main road, 5 blocks from plaza. Daily 0900-1530.
Good Brazilian-style buffet, all you can eat grill on weekends.

East of San José de Chiquitos

Roboré
Several restaurants around the plaza, including:

$ Casino Militar
On the plaza. Daily for lunch and dinner.
Set meals and à la carte.

Santiago de Chiquitos

$ Churupa
½ block from plaza.
Set meals (go early or reserve your meal in advance) and à la carte. Best in town.

Festivals

The region celebrates the Festival de Música Renacentista y Barroca Americana every even year (next in 2018). Many towns have their own orchestras, which play Jesuit-era music on a regular basis. Semana Santa (Holy Week) celebrations are elaborate and interesting throughout the region.

Chiquitania
1 May Fiesta de San José, San José de Chiquitos, preceded by a week of folkloric and other events.
29 Jun Feast of St Peter and St Paul, San Javier, best for viewing traditional costumes, dances and music.

26 Jul **Fiesta de Santa Ana**, Santa Ana.
31 Jul **Patron saint's day**, San Ignacio
de Velasco, preceded by a cattle fair.
29 Sep **Patron saint's day**, San Miguel de Velasco.
2nd week Oct **Orchid festival**, Concepción.
24 Oct **Patron saint's day**, San Rafael,
with traditional dancing.
3 Dec **Patron saint's fiesta**, San Javier.
8 Dec **Fiesta de la Inmaculada Concepción**.

Transport

San Javier

Bus and trufi Línea 102, T03-346 3993, from
Santa Cruz Terminal Bimodal regional departures
area, 2 a day, 4 hrs, US$3, continue to **Concepción**.
Also **Flota 31 del Este** (poor buses, T03-334 9390,
same price) and **Jenecherú**, T03-348 8618, daily
at 2000, US$4.25, *bus-cama* US$5, continuing to
Concepción and, on Tue, Thu, Sat, **San Ignacio**.
Various taxi-*trufi* companies also operate from
regional departures area, US$5, 3½ hrs.

Concepción

Bus To/from **Santa Cruz**, companies as above,
US$3.55, 6½ hrs, and **Jenecherú**, as above, US$5-
5.75. To **San Ignacio de Velasco**, buses pass
though from Santa Cruz (many at night); **31 del
Este** leaves from C Germán Busch in Concepción.
Concepción to **San Javier**, 1 hr, US$1.50.

San Ignacio de Velasco

Bus and trufi From **Santa Cruz**, companies
as above, plus **Trans Bolivia** (daily, T03-336
3866), from Terminal Bimodal depart 1830-
2000, including **Jenecherú** (Tue, Thu, Sat, most
luxurious buses, see above), US$7, *bus-cama*
US$7.75, 10 hrs; returning 1800-1900. For daytime
services, *trufis* from regional departures area 0900
daily (with minimum 7 passengers), US$15, 8 hrs.
To **San José de Chiquitos**, see San José Transport,
below. To **San Rafael** (US$2, 2½ hrs) via **Santa
Ana** (US$1, 1 hr) **Expreso Baruc**, 24 de Septiembre
y Kennedy, daily at 1400; returning 0600. To **San
Miguel**, *trufis* leave when full from Mercado de
Comida, US$1.75, 40 mins, bus US$0.75. **Trans
Bolivia** and **Jenecherú** services also go to San
Miguel and San Rafael (US$6.50-7.75 from Santa
Cruz). To **San Matías** (for Cáceres, Brazil) several
daily passing through from Santa Cruz starting
0400, US$12, 8 hrs. To **Pontes e Lacerda** (Brazil),
Rápido Monte Cristo, from Club Social on the
plaza, Wed and Sat 0900, US$22, 8-9 hrs; returning
Tue and Fri, 0630. All roads to Brazil are poor. The
best option to Pontes e Lacerda is via Vila Bela
(Brazil), used by **Amanda Tours** (T7608 8476 in
Bolivia, T65-9926 8522 in Brazil), from **El Corralito**
restaurant by the market, Tue, Thu, Sun 0830,
US$28; returning Mon, Wed, Fri 0600.

San José de Chiquitos

Bus and trufi To **Santa Cruz** many companies
pass through starting 1700 daily, US$7-10.55. Also
trufis, leave when full, US$10, 3½ hrs. To **Puerto
Suárez**, buses pass through 1600-2300, US$10,
4 hrs. To **San Ignacio de Velasco** via San Rafael
and San Miguel, **Flota Universal** (poor buses,
terrible buses), Mon, Wed, Fri, Sat at 0700, US$5,
5 hrs, returning 1400; also **31 de Julio**, Tue, Thu,
Sun from San Ignacio at 0645, returning 1500.

Train Westbound, the **Ferrobús** passes through
San José Tue, Thu, Sat at 0150, arriving Santa
Cruz 0700; **Expreso Oriental**, Tue, Thu, Sun 2305,
arriving 0540. Eastbound, the **Ferrobús** passes
through San José Tue, Thu, Sun 2308, arriving
Quijarro 0700 next day; **Expreso Oriental** Mon,
Wed, Fri 1930, arriving 0602 next day. See Santa
Cruz, Transport (page 355) and www.fo.com.bo
for fares and additional information.

East of San José de Chiquitos

Bus and trufi To **Chochís** from San José de
Chiquitos, with **Perla del Oriente**, daily 0800 and
1500, US$3, 2 hrs; continuing to **Roboré**, US$1,
1 hr more; Roboré to San José via Chochís 0815
and 1430. Roboré bus terminal is by the highway,
a long walk from town, but some buses go by
the plaza before leaving; enquire locally. From
Santiago de Chiquitos to Roboré, Mon-Sat at
0700, US$1, 45 mins; returning 1000; taxi Roboré-
Santiago about US$15. Buses to/from Quijarro
stop at **Aguas Calientes**; taxi Roboré-Aguas
Calientes about US$22 return. From Roboré
to **Santa Cruz**, several companies, from US$7,
7-9 hrs; also *trufis* 0900, 1400, 1800, US$14.50,
5 hrs. From Roboré to **Quijarro** with **Perla del
Oriente**, 4 daily, US$4, 4 hrs; also *trufis* leave when
full, US$8, 3 hrs.

Train All trains stop in **Roboré** (see www.
fo.com.bo), but not in Chochís or Aguas Calientes.
Enquire in advance if they might stop to let you
off at these stations.

Parque Nacional Noel Kempff Mercado

Road/bus All overland journeys are long and
arduous, take supplies. The unpaved roads to
the park turn off the Concepción-San Ignacio
road at Santa Rosa de la Roca, 79 km before San

Ignacio (the better route, well signed, petrol at the turn-off), or Carmen Ruiz, 47 km before San Ignacio. Florida is 200 km northeast. Paso Firme is a further 129 km, via Porvenir, on an abysmal road. A bus runs **Santa Cruz–Piso Firme** (via Santa Rosa de la Roca, not San Ignacio), **Trans Bolivia**, C Melchor Pinto entre 2do y 3er Anillo, T03-336 3866, once a week (schedule changes often), US$24, 16 hrs minimum, very rough and exhausting. Otherwise the park can be reached by hired 4WD vehicle (US$100 a day) or on a tour. For **Pimenteiras do Oeste** (Brazil) see San Ignacio Transport (above) to Pontes e Lacerda and make connections there via Vilhena. This route is no easier than on the Bolivian side. Even hiring a 4WD vehicle to get to the park via Brazil is hard-going.

Quijarro and Puerto Suárez

Air Puerto Suárez airport is 6 km north of town, T03-976 2347; airport tax US$2. Flights to **Santa Cruz** with TAM, 3 times a week. Don't buy tickets for flights originating in Puerto Suárez in Corumbá, these cost more.

Bus Buses from Quijarro pick up passengers in Puerto Suárez (but not Arroyo Concepción) en route to **Santa Cruz**, many companies,

departures 1000-1130 and 1900-2030, *ejecutivo* US$14 and up, 8-10 hrs.

Taxi Quijarro to the border (**Arroyo Concepción**) US$1.40; to **Puerto Suárez** US$1 pp, more at night. Beware overcharging when arriving from Brazil. You will be approached by Bolivian taxi drivers who offer to hold your luggage while you clear immigration. These are the most expensive cabs (US$5 to Quijarro, US$15 to Puerto Suárez). Instead, keep your gear with you while your passport is stamped, then walk 200 m past the bridge to the **Preferida** bus office where other taxis wait (US$1.40 to Quijarro). *Colectivos* to Puerto Suárez leave Quijarro when full from Av Bolívar corner Av Luis de la Vega, US$1.

Train With paving of the highway from Santa Cruz train service is in less demand, but it remains a viable option. Ticket office in Quijarro station Mon-Sat 0730-1200, 1430-1800, Sun 0730-1100. Purchase tickets directly at the train station (passport required; do not buy train tickets for Bolivia in Brazil). The **Ferrobús** leaves Quijarro Mon, Wed, Fri 1800, arriving Santa Cruz 0700 next day; **Expreso Oriental**, Tue, Thu, Sun 1300, arriving 0540 next day. See Santa Cruz Transport (page 355) and www.fo.com.bo for fares and additional information.

Northern
lowlands

Bolivia's northern lowlands account for about 70% of national territory. Flat savannahs and dense tropical jungle stretch northwards from the great cordilleras, sparsely populated and mostly unvisited by tourists. Improved roads and frequent flights, particularly to Rurrenabaque and Trinidad, are opening up the area, and wildlife and rainforest expeditions are becoming increasingly popular. Most people head to Rurrenabaque, which gives access to two large and spectacularly diverse protected natural areas: Madidi National Park and the Pilón Lajas Biosphere Reserve. Here are several highly regarded and successful community tourism projects that allow visitors to experience life in the jungle and on the pampas.

Beni department has 53% of the country's birds and 50% of its mammals, but destruction of forest habitat by loggers and colonists is proceeding at an alarming rate, while the Bala Gorge near Rurrenabaque is threatened by a proposed large-scale hydroelectric project.

Madidi and Rurrenabaque

gateway to the jungle and the pampas

Caranavi to San Borja *Colour map 3, B3.*

From Caranavi (see page 294), a road runs north to Sapecho, where a bridge crosses the Río Beni. Beyond Sapecho (7 km from the bridge), the road passes through Palos Blancos (several cheap lodgings). The road between Sapecho and Yucumo, three hours from Sapecho tránsito, is a good all-weather gravel surface. There are basic *hospedajes* and restaurants in **Yucumo** where a road branches northwest, fording rivers several times on its way to Rurrenabaque. Taking the eastern branch from Yucumo it is 50 km (one to two hours) to **San Borja** (see page 376).

Rurrenabaque *Colour map 3, B3.*

The charming, picturesque jungle town of Rurre (as the locals call it), on the Río Beni, is the main jumping-off point for tours in the Bolivian Amazon and pampas, from two- to four-day trips through to full expeditions. Across the river is the smaller town of San Buenaventura (canoe US$0.15). Despite its growth as a trading, transport and ecotourism centre, Rurre is a pleasant town to walk around, although the climate is usually humid. Market day is Sunday. There are two ATMs, both on Comercio near the intersection with Aniceto, but don't rely on either of them.

> **Tip...**
> Fly from La Paz to Rurrenabaque (or vice versa) for outstanding views of the dramatic Cordillera Real.

Jungle tours There are two types of tours from Rurrenabaque: jungle and pampas tours. See below for the latter. Jungle tours normally involve travelling by boat on the Ríos Beni and Tuichi. Lodging is either in purpose-built camps on higher-end tours, or tents at the budget end. Tours are long enough

Best for
Jungle lodges ■ River trips ■ Wildlife

for most people to get a good feeling for life in the jungle and to experience community-run lodges. In the rainy season the jungle is very hot and humid with more biting insects and fewer animals to be seen. The best place for a one-day tour is ☆ **San Miguel del Bala**, in a beautiful setting, 3 km from the entrance to Madidi. They also have overnight programmes (see Where to stay, below). Other lodges are in the Parque Nacional Madidi, reached by boat a minimum of three hours' upstream.

★Parque Nacional Madidi *Colour map 3, B2.*

Headquarters in San Buenaventura, about 4 blocks upriver from the plaza, T03-892 2246. US$16 entry is collected near the dock in San Buenaventura. All visitors must disembark to have their permit checked on entry to the park, just past the Estrecho de Bala. Insect repellent and sun protection are essential. See www.sernap.gob.bo. See also http://identidadmadidi.org.

Parque Nacional Madidi is quite possibly the most bio-diverse of all protected areas on the planet. It is the variety of habitats, from the freezing Andean peaks of the Cordillera Apolobamba in the southwest (reaching nearly 6000 m), through cloud, elfin and dry forest to steaming tropical jungle and pampas (neotropical savannah) in the north and east, that account for the array of flora and fauna within the park's boundaries. In an area roughly the size of Wales or El Salvador (1,895,750 ha) are an estimated over 1100 bird species, 10 species of primate, five species of cat (with healthy populations of jaguar and puma), giant anteaters and many reptiles. Madidi is at the centre of a bi-national system of parks that spans the Bolivia–Peru border. The Heath river on Madidi's northwestern border forms the two countries' frontier and links with the Tambopata National Reserve in Peru. To the southwest the Area Protegida Apolobamba protects extensive mountain ecosystems. It is easiest to visit the lowland areas of Madidi through Rurrenabaque.

☆**Pampas tours** In the more open terrain of the pampas you will see a lot of wildlife: howler, squirrel and capuchin monkeys, caiman, capybara, pink dolphins and a huge variety of birds. These will be seen in the gallery forest as you travel on boat trips on the slow-moving river. To see anacondas, not very likely these days, you may have to wade through knee-deep water in the wide-open pampas; wear appropriate footwear (boots may be provided). Community tourism is being developed at ☆**Santa Rosa de Yacuma**, 100 km northeast of Rurre (for information contact FAN, page 385). There is a fee of US$18.75 to enter the Area Protegida Municipal. All pampas tours involve a four-hour jeep ride to El Puerto de Santa Rosa, 7 km beyond Santa Rosa on the Río Yacuma. There is an *albergue* at El Puerto and boats to other lodges depart from here.

Pilón Lajas Biosphere Reserve and Indigenous Territory *Colour map 3, B3.*

HQ at Campero y Germán Busch, Rurrenabaque, T03-892 2246, crtmpilonlajas@yahoo.com, www.sernap.gob.bo, entrance fee US$18.75.

Beyond the Beni River in the southeast runs the Pilón Lajas Biosphere Reserve and Indigenous Territory (400,000 ha), home to the Tsimane and Mosetene peoples. Together with Madidi, it constitutes approximately 60,000 sq km, one of the largest systems of protected land in the neotropics. Set up under the auspices of UNESCO, Pilón Lajas has one of the continent's most intact Amazonian rainforest ecosystems, as well as an incredible array of tropical forest animal life.

Listings Madidi and Rurrenabaque

Tourist information

Rurrenabaque

Infotur municipal tourist office
Abaroa y Vaca Díez. Mon-Fri 0800-1200, 1430-1830, Sat 0900-1100.
General information and information on tours, operators, hotels and restaurants in Spanish, English and French. Kiosks may open at the bus station and airport.

Regional tourist office
Abaroa casi Santa Cruz.
Mainly for statistics and records, but they can give general information.

Where to stay

Rurrenabaque

$$-$ Hostal Pahuichi
Comercio y Vaca Díez, T03-892 2558.
Some big rooms, cheaper with shared bath,
electric shower, fan, breakfast extra, rooftop
views, good.

$ Beni
Comercio y Arce, along the river, T03-892 2408.
Best rooms have a/c and TV, hot showers,
cheaper with fan and without bath, kitchen
facilities. Spacious, good service.

$ El Ambaibo
Santa Cruz entre Bolívar y Busch, T03-892 2107,
hotel_ambaibo@hotmail.com.
Includes breakfast and airport transfer, private
and shared rooms, large pool (US$2.50 for non-
guests), parking, also has dorms at **Tuky**, also on
Santa Cruz, T03-892 2686, Ambaibo Backpackers
Hotel on Facebook.

$ El Curichal
Comercio 1490, 7 blocks from plaza, T03-
892 2647, Facebook: ElCurichalhostel.
Nice courtyard, rooms with and without bath,
dorms, lockers, hammocks, laundry and small
kitchen facilities, pool, book exchange, games,
helpful staff. Popular economy option.

$ Hostal Lobo
Upstream end of Comercio, no fixed phone.
Cheap rooms in large breezy building overlooking
the river, shared bath, some double rooms, with
breakfast and Wi-Fi, laundry service, *parrillada*.

$ Los Tucanes de Rurrenabaque
Arce y Bolívar, T7153 4521,
www.hotel-tucanes.com.
Big place with thatched structures, hammocks
and an open communal area, rooms with and
without bath. Also has **$$ La Isla resort**, on the
outskirts between Av Bolívar and Av Amutari,
T03-892 2127, www.islatucanes.com.

$ Oriental
Pellicioli, on plaza, T03-892 2401.
Hot showers, fan, small breakfast included, quiet,
hammocks in peaceful garden, family-run, Wi-Fi
in public areas. A good option.

$ Santa Ana
Abaroa entre Vaca Díez y Campero, T03-892 2399.
A variety of rooms, all cheap and simple, laundry,
pleasant hammock area in garden, no breakfast.

Jungle trips

San Miguel del Bala
45-min boat trip upriver from Rurre (office
at C Comercio entre Vaca Díez y Santa Cruz),
T03-892 2394, www.sanmigueldelbala.com.
This award-winning community lodge gives
a good taste of the jungle, offers day trips,
well-laid-out trails and has en suite cabins
in a delightful setting, good restaurant with
typical dishes, including vegetarian, attentive
staff, bar and a pool fed by a waterfall. It is
owned and operated by the indigenous Tacana
community. They have a 2nd lodge in Madidi
with similar attention, walks, community visits.
3 days/2 nights cost US$240 pp. Advance
booking required. Highly recommended.

Parque Nacional Madidi
Berraco del Madidi is 6 hrs upriver from
Rurrenabaque (office Comercio y Vaca Díez,
T03-892 2966, www.berracodelmadidi.com).
This lodge is run by members of the San José de
Uchupiamonas community. Fully enclosed tents
with mosquito screens on covered platforms,
good mattresses, clean toilets, cold showers, good
kitchen with excellent food, well-run, professional,
plenty of activities, US$480 for 3 days/2 nights,
also longer programmes and specialist trips.
Chalalán Ecolodge is 5 hrs upriver from
Rurrenabaque, at San José de Uchupiamonas,
in Madidi National Park. La Paz office:
Sagárnaga 189, Edif Shopping Doryan, of 23,
T02-231 1451; in Rurrenabaque, C Comercio
entre Campero y Vaca Díez, T03-892 2419, www.
chalalan.com. This is Bolivia's top ecotourism
project, founded by the Quechua Tacana
community, Conservation International and the
Interamerican Development Bank, and now
has a well-deserved international reputation.
Accommodation in thatched cabins, and
activities include fantastic wildlife-spotting and
birdwatching, guided and self-guided trails, river
and lake activities, and relaxing in pristine jungle
surroundings. 3-day/2-night packages cost
US$410 pp (US$380 with shared bath).
Madidi Jungle Eco Lodge, also run by families
from the San José de Uchupiamonas community
3½ hrs from Rurre (office Av Comercio entre
Vaca Díez y Campero, T7128 2697, www.
madidijungle.com). Rooms around a central
garden, comfortable cabins in the forest, with
and without shower, hammocks, good regional
food, 11 trails to explore with expert guides, other
activities include tubing, handicraft-making,

piranha fishing. Programmes from 1 to 5 days, US$250-280 pp for 3 days, 2 nights, flexible, responsible and excellent service.

Pilón Lajas Biosphere Reserve and Indigenous Territory

Mapajo

Mapajo Ecoturismo Indígena, Santa Cruz entre Abaroa y Comercio, Rurrenabaque, T7113 8838, http://mapajo-ecoturismo-indigena.blogspot.co.uk.
A community-run ecolodge 3 hrs by boat from Rurrenabaque has 6 *cabañas* without electricity (take a torch), shared cold showers and a dining room serving traditional meals. You can visit the local community, walk in the forest, go birdwatching, etc. Take insect repellent, wear long trousers and strong footwear.

Restaurants

Rurrenabaque

$$ Casa del Campo
Comercio, opposite El Lobo. Daily 0730-1400, 1800-2130.
Restaurant in a thatched building with flowers around the terrace.

$$ Juliano's
Santa Cruz casi Bolívar. Daily 1200-1430, 1800-late.
French and Italian food, good presentation and service. Recommended.

$$ Paititi
Vaca Díez casi Bolívar.
Good Mediterranean-influenced dishes, friendly service.

$$-$ Funky Monkey
Comercio entre Santa Cruz y Vaca Díez. Open 0900-0100.
Big pizzas, imaginative pastas, vegetarian options, grilled meats and fish, bar, lively crowd.

$$-$ Luna Lounge
Abaroa entre Santa Cruz y Vaca Díez. Open 0800-2200.
International meals, pizza, snacks and drinks, also pool table and sports TV.

$$-$ The Angu's
Comercio entre Santa Cruz y Vaca Díez.
Pizzas, pastas, meat dishes, burgers soups and veggie options. Wi-Fi, music and sports, happy hour 1900-2200.

$ La Perla de Rurre
Bolívar y Vaca Díez. Daily 0730-2100.
Set lunch and à la carte, also breakfast and sandwiches in the morning, good food, eating outside under the mango trees.

Cafés

Café de la Jungla
Comercio y Vaca Díez. Mon-Sat 0800-1630.
Neat little café serving breakfasts, sandwiches, salads, snacks and juices, mostly local produce, Wi-Fi.

Moskkito Bar
Vaca Díez casi Abaroa. Evenings only.
Cool bar for tall jungle tales. Burgers, pizzas, rock music and pool tables.

Panadería París
Abaroa entre Vaca Díez y Santa Cruz. Mon-Sat 0600-1200.
Delicious croissants and *pain au chocolat*, get there early, also quiches and pizzas.

What to do

Rurrenabaque

Jungle and pampas tours cost about US$80 pp plus the park fee for a typical 3-day tour by a responsible operator. Prices and quality both vary but booking in Rurre is usually cheaper than in La Paz. Much effort is being put into ensuring that all companies adhere to codes of practice that do not permit hunting, feeding animals, especially monkeys, catching caiman or handling anaconda, but there are still a few that do so. If you do not want to encourage such activities, ask in advance what is offered on the tour. Before signing up for a tour, check the **Municipal Infotur** office for updates and try to talk to other travellers who have just come back. Guides who belong to **Agnatur** (**Asociación de Guías Naturalistas de Turismo Responsable**), from the same community as Chalalán, have pioneered respect for wildlife here, first in Madidi and recently in the pampas. Ask for a member, or for an operator who uses them.

Some operators pool customers, so you may not go with the company you booked with. There are many more agencies in town than those listed below. Shop around and choose carefully.

Tour operators

Bala Tours, *Av Santa Cruz y Comercio, T03-892 2527, www.balatours.com*. Arranges pampas and jungle tours, singly or combined, with their own lodge in each (with bath and solar power), also specialist programmes, visits to local communities and the Guanay-Rurrenabaque route. English-speaking guides. Award-winning, services and lodges recently upgraded, top-class service. Recommended.

Donato Tours, *Vaca Díez entre Abaroa y Comercio, T7126 0919, www.donatotours.com*. Regular tours plus the opportunity to stay in a community in Pilón Lajas for 1 to 20 days.

Lipiko Tours, *Av Santa Cruz entre Bolívar y Abaroa, T02-231 5408, http://lipiko.com*. Rurre office of a company offering tours throughout Bolivia.

Madidi Expeditions, *Comercio entre Vaca Díez y Campero, T7199 8372, www.madidiexpeditions.com*. Responsible tours to Madidi and the pampas, chief guide Norman is very experienced, knowledgeable and professional. Good staff. Recommended.

Madidi Travel, *Comercio y Vaca Díez, T03-892 2153, in La Paz, Linares 947, T02-231 8313, www.madidi-travel.com*. Specializes in tours to the private Serere Sanctuary in the Madidi Mosaic (details

on website), minimum 3 days/2 nights, good guiding. Recommended.

Mashaquipe Tours, *Abaroa entre Pando y Arce, T03-892 2704, www.mashaquipeecotours.com*. Jungle and pampas tours run by an organization which works with communities, with lodges in both locations. They offer combined jungle and pampas tours (eg 5 days US$390 pp), also short tours. Small groups, safe, most guides speak English, a popular company.

Transport

Caranavi to San Borja

Bus See page 296 for buses in Caranavi. **Yucumo** is on the La Paz–Caranavi–Rurrenabaque and San Borja bus routes. Rurrenabaque–La Paz bus passes through about 1800. If travelling to Rurrenabaque by bus take extra food in case there is a delay (anything from road blocks to flat tyres to high river levels). **Flota Yungueña** daily except Thu at 1300 from San Borja to **La Paz**, 19 hrs via Caranavi. Also San Borja to **Rurrenabaque**, **Santa Rosa**, **Riberalta**, **Guayaramerín** about 3 times a week. Minibuses and *camionetas* normally run daily between San Borja and **Trinidad** throughout

the year, US$15, about 7 hrs including 20 mins crossing of Río Mamoré on ferry barge (up to 14 hrs in wet season). Fuel available at Yolosa, Caranavi, Yucumo, San Borja and San Ignacio.

Rurrenabaque

Air Several daily flights to/from **La Paz** with **Amaszonas**, Comercio entre Santa Cruz y Vaca Díez, T03-892 2472, US$97; and 3 a week with **TAM**, Santa Cruz y Abaroa, T03-892 2398/7113 2500. Both also fly to **Trinidad**, but not daily. Book flights as early as possible and buy onward ticket on arrival. Check flight times in advance; they change frequently. Delays and cancellations are common. Airport taxes total US$2.75 (airport and municipal taxes). Airlines provide transport to/from town, US$1.25;

confirm flight 24 hrs in advance and be at airline office 2 hrs before departure.

Bus The bus terminal is near the airport. To/from **La Paz** via Caranavi with **Flota Yungueña, Totaí** and **Vaca Díez**; 18-20 hrs, US$10, daily at 1030 and Sat-Mon also at 1900. See under Sorata and Cocoico, Transport, for alternative routes to Rurre. Some La Paz buses continue to **Riberalta** (US$19, 13 hrs from Rurre), **Guayaramerín** (US$20, 15 hrs) or **Cobija** (US$35, 30 hrs). Rurrenabaque– **Riberalta** may take 6 days or more in the wet season. Take lots of food, torch and be prepared to work. To **Trinidad**, with **Trans Guaya** (buses) or **Trans Rurrenabaque** (minibuses) daily, **Flota Yungueña** Mon, Wed, via **Yucumo** and **San Borja**, US$20, check that the road is open.

San Borja to Trinidad

San Borja, a relatively wealthy cattle-raising centre (population 40,865) with simple hotels and restaurants clustered near the plaza, is 50 km east of Yucumo. The road east from San Borja to Trinidad passes through part of the Pilón Lajas Reserve (see page 372). There are five or six river crossings and, in the wetlands, a multitude of waterfowl. At times the road can be flooded out. Another route into Beni Department is from the lowland road between Cochabamba and Santa Cruz and then by river from Puerto Villarroel.

San Ignacio de Moxos *Colour map 3, B3.*

San Ignacio de Moxos, 90 km west of Trinidad, is known as the folklore capital of the Beni Department. It's a quiet town (population 22,165) with a mainly indigenous population; 60% are Macheteros, who speak their own language. San Ignacio still maintains the traditions of the Jesuit missions through big fiestas, especially during Holy Week and the ☆Fiesta del Santo Patrono de Moxos (see Festivals, below).

Trinidad *Colour map 3, C3.*

The hot and humid capital of the lowland Beni Department (population 106,420, altitude 327 m) is a dusty city in the dry season, with many streets unpaved. Primarily a service centre for the surrounding ranches and communities, most travellers find themselves in the area for boats up and down the ☆Río Mamoré. There are two ports, Almacén and Varador, check at which one your boat will be docked. **Puerto Varador** is 13 km from town on the Río Mamoré on the road between Trinidad and San Borja; cross the river over the main bridge by the market, walk down to the service station by the police checkpoint and take a truck, US$1.75. **Almacén** is 8 km from the city. The main mode of transport in Trinidad is the motorbike (even for taxis, US$0.50 in city), rental on plaza from US$2.50 per hour, US$10 per half day. There are several ATMs on or near the central Plaza Ballivián.

About 5 km from town is the **Laguna Suárez**, with plenty of wildlife; swimming is safe where the locals swim, near the café with the jetty (elsewhere there are stingrays and alligators). Motorbike taxi from Trinidad, US$1.50.

Tourist information

Trinidad

Beni department tourist offices
Prefectura building, Joaquín de Sierra y
La Paz, ground floor, T03-462 4831,
see TurismoBeniBolivia on Facebook.

Municipal tourism offices
Félix Pinto Saucedo y Nicolás Suárez,
T03-462 1322.

Where to stay

San Ignacio de Moxos
There are some cheap *alojamientos* on and
around the main plaza.

Trinidad

$$$ Campanario
6 de Agosto 80, T03-462 4733,
www.hotel-campanario.com.
Rooms with a/c and frigobar, meeting room,
restaurant, bar, pool.

$$ Jacaranda Suites
La Paz entre Pedro de la Rocha y 18 de Noviembre,
T462 2400.
Good services, restaurant, pool, meeting
rooms, internet.

$ Copacabana
Tomás M Villavicencio, 3 blocks from plaza,
T03-462 2811.
Good value, some beds uncomfortable,
cheaper with shared bath, helpful staff.

$ Monteverde
6 de Agosto 76, T03-462 2750.
With a/c (cheaper with fan), frigobar,
owner speaks English. Recommended.

$ Residencial 18 de Noviembre
Av 6 de Agosto 135, T03-462 1272.
With and without bath, welcoming,
laundry facilities.

Restaurants

Trinidad
There are several good fish restaurants in **Barrio
Pompeya**, south of the plaza across river.

$$ Club Social 18 de Noviembre
N Suárez y Vaca Díez on plaza.
Good-value lunch, lively, popular with locals.

$$ El Tábano
Villavicencio entre Mamoré y Néstor Suárez.
Good fish and local fare, relaxed atmosphere.

$$ La Estancia
Barrio Pompeya, on Ibare entre Muiba y Velarde.
A good choice for excellent steaks.

$ La Casona
Plaza Ballivián. Closed Tue.
Good pizzas and set lunch.

Heladería Oriental
On plaza.
Good coffee, ice cream, cakes, popular with locals.

Festivals

San Ignacio de Moxos
**Late Jul-early Aug Fiesta del Santo Patrono
de Moxos**, is the most important and colourful
fiesta in the Bolivian Amazon and features many
traditional elements of Beni culture, with sports,
food and drink and, above all, processions and
dances with feather headdresses, mask, wooden
machetes and huge wind instruments.

What to do

Trinidad
Most agents offer excursions to local estancias and
jungle tours. Most estancias can also be reached
independently in 1 hr by hiring a motorbike.
Flotel Reina de Enín, *Av Comunidad Europea 624,*
T7391 2965, http://amazoncruiser.com.bo. Cruises on
the Mamoré River in the Ibare-Mamoré Reserve.
Floating hotel with comfy berths with bath, US$455
pp for 3-day/2-night cruise includes: dolphin
watching, horse riding, visiting local communities,
jungle walks, swimming and piranha fishing.
La Ruta del Bufeo, *T7281 8317, laruta.delbufeo*
on Facebook. Specializes in river tours for
seeing dolphins.
Moxos, *6 de Agosto 114, T03-462 1141.* Multi-day river
and jungle tours with camping. Recommended.
Paraíso Travel, *6 de Agosto 138, T03-462 0692,*
paraiso@entelnet.bo. Offers excursions to
Laguna Suárez, Río Mamoré, camping and
birdwatching tours.

Transport

San Ignacio de Moxos

Bus The Trinidad to San Borja bus stops at the Donchanta restaurant for lunch, otherwise difficult to find transport to San Borja. Minibus to Trinidad daily at 0730 from plaza, also *camionetas*, check road conditions and times beforehand.

Trinidad

Air Flights with **TAM** (Bolívar 42, T02-268 1111) to **La Paz**, **Santa Cruz**, **Cochabamba**, **Riberalta**, **Guayaramerín** and other northern destinations. To **La Paz** and **Santa Cruz** with Ecojet (Av 6 de Agosto 146, T03-465 2617). **Amazonas** (18 de Noviembre 267, T03-462 2426) Mon, Wed, Fri to **Rurrenabaque**. Airport, T03-462 0678. Mototaxi to airport US$1.50.

Boat ☆Cargo boats down the Río Mamoré to **Guayaramerín** take passengers, 3-4 days, assuming no breakdowns, best organized from Puerto Varador (speak to the Port Captain). **Argos** is recommended as friendly, US$25 pp, take water, fresh fruit, toilet paper and ear-plugs; only for the hardy traveller.

Bus Bus station is on Rómulo Mendoza, between Beni and Pinto, 9 blocks east of main plaza. Motorbike taxis will take people with backpacks from bus station to centre for US$0.50. To **Santa Cruz** (10 hrs on a paved road, US$9-13, *bus-cama* US$20) and **Cochabamba** (US$14-20, 20 hrs), with **Copacabana**, **Mopar** and **Bolívar** mostly overnight (*bus-cama* available). To **Rurrenabaque**, US$20, 12-20 hrs. Enquire locally what services are running to San Borja and **La Paz**. Similarly to **Riberalta** and **Guayaramerín**.

Riberalta to Brazil

east via Guayaramerín or west via Cobija

Riberalta *Colour map 3, A3.*

At the confluence of the Madre de Dios and Beni rivers, Riberalta (population 97,982) is off the beaten track and a centre for brazil nut production. It's very laid back, but take care if your bus drops you in the middle of the night and everything is closed. There are places to eat on the plaza and near the airport. Change cash in shops and on street.

Guayaramerín and border with Brazil *Colour map 3, A3.*

Guayaramerín (population 39,010), 84 km from Riberalta by paved road, is a cheerful, prosperous little town on the bank of the Río Mamoré, opposite the Brazilian town of Guajará-Mirim. There are several restaurants and cafés around the town. It has an important Zona Libre. Passage between the two towns is unrestricted; boat trip US$1.75 (more at night).

Bolivian immigration Avenida Costanera near port; open 0800-1100, 1400-1800. Passports must be stamped here when leaving, or entering Bolivia. On entering Bolivia, passports must also be stamped at the Bolivian consulate in Guajará-Mirim. The Brazilian consulate is on 24 de Septiembre 28, Guayaramerín, T03-855 3766, open 0900-1300, 1400-1700; visas for entering Brazil are given here. To enter Brazil you must have a yellow fever certificate, or be inoculated at the health ministry (free). Exchange cash at the dock on the Bolivian side where rates are written up on blackboards, although there is an ATM at the Banco do Brasil in Guajará-Mirim; no facilities for cash.

Cobija *Colour map 3, A2.*

The capital of the lowland Department of Pando lies on the Río Acre which forms the frontier with Brazil. Cobija, a commercial city with few tourist attractions, is mostly of interest to Brazilian shoppers and travellers on route between the lowlands of Bolivia, Peru, and western Brazil. People are friendly and the atmosphere is relaxed. Bolivian time is one hour later than local Brazilian time.

Puente de la Amistad, a small suspension bridge, crosses the Río Acre to Brasiléia. The larger **Puente Internacional**, where Bolivian immigration is located (open 0800-1900 Bolivian time), spans Arroyo Bahía to reach Epitaciolândia, a larger Brazilian town. You can cross either bridge without passport stamps if visiting for a only few hours. **Policía Federal** for Brazilian immigration at Avenida Santos Dumont 926, Epitaciolândia, open 0700-2000 Brazilian time. Brazilian consulate in Cobija at Pizarro y Otto Felipe Braun, T03-842 2110, cgcobija@itamaraty.gov.br, Monday-Friday 0800-1200, 1400-1600 Bolivian time. Bolivian consulate in Epitaciolândia at Dom Julio Mattioli 84, near the church, Monday-Friday 0700-1100, 1300-1500 Brazilian time. There are *casas de cambio* on Avenida Internacional and Avenida Cornejo. Many shops will accept dollars or reais, and exchange money.

Where to stay

Riberalta
Ask for a fan and check the water supply.

$$ Colonial
Plácido Méndez 745, T03-852 3018.
Charming colonial *casona*, large, well-furnished rooms, no singles, nice gardens and courtyard, comfortable, good beds, helpful owners.

$$ Jomali
Av Nicolás Suárez, beside Banco Ganadero, T03-852 2398, www.hoteljomali.com.
Central, smart hotel with big rooms and suites, a/c, comfortable, central patio.

$ Alojamiento Comercial Lazo
NG Salvatierra 244, T03-852 2380.
With a/c, cheaper with fan, comfortable, laundry facilities, good value.

Guayaramerín

$$ San Carlos
6 de Agosto 347, 4 blocks from port, T03-855 3555.
With a/c, hot showers, changes dollars cash and reais, swimming pool, reasonable restaurant.

$ Santa Ana 25 de Mayo 611
Close to airstrip in town, T03-855 3900.
With bath, fan, cheap and recommended.

Cobija
Hotels are expensive by Bolivian standards. There is ample selection, however, as well as options in Brasiléia and Epitaciolândia in Brazil. A good popular restaurant is **$ La Pascana**, C Beni 61, Mon-Sat 1000-1500, 1900-2200, for set lunch and *à la carte*.

$$ Diana
Av 9 de Febrero 123, T7111 3832.
Rooms with a/c, buffet breakfast, pool, gym and shopping arcade. All-in-one place for Brazilian shoppers.

$$ Estrella del Norte
C Miguel Farah 48, Barrio Conavi, T03-842 2113, estrelladelnortecobijahotel@hotmail.com.
Comfortable rooms around a nice patio, a/c, pool, buffet breakfast, quiet area, good value.

$$ Nanijos
Av 9 de Febrero 147, T03-842 2230, hotelnanijos@hotmail.com.
Nice rooms with a/c, frigobar, buffet breakfast, *comedor* does good lunch, very helpful and attentive.

$ Triller
Av Internacional 640, T03-842 2024, josecondori480@gmail.com.
Some rooms with private bath and a/c, cheaper with shared bath and fan, restaurant. A bit run down but adequate economy option.

What to do

Riberalta
Riberalta Tours, *Av Sucre 634, T03-852 3475, www.riberaltatours.com.* Multi-day river and jungle tours, airline tickets, very helpful.

Transport

Riberalta
Air To **La Paz** and **Santa Cruz** with **Ecojet** (Av Bernardino Ochoa 966, T03-852 4837). **TAM** (Av Chuquisaca y Salvatierra, T03-852 2646) to **Trinidad**, **Santa Cruz**, **Cochabamba** and **La Paz**. Expect cancellations in the wet season. **Servicio Aereo Arial** (T03-852 3774, T7686 3880) has light aircraft serving regional destinations including **Cobija**.

Boat Cargo boats carry passengers along the **Río Madre de Dios**, but they are infrequent. There are no boats to Rurrenabaque.

Bus Roads to all destinations are appalling, even worse in the wet season. Several companies (including **Yungueña**) to **La Paz**, via **Rurrenabaque** and **Caranavi** daily, 35 hrs to 3 days or more, US$30. To **Trinidad** via Rurrenabaque and San Borja, 25-35 hrs. To **Guayaramerín** 7 daily, US$5, 1 hr, paved road. To **Cobija** several companies, none with daily service, 10-11 hrs.

Guayaramerín
Air Flights to **La Paz** with **Ecojet** (Sucre entre Beni y 16 de Julio, T03-855 9176). **TAM** has same services as for Riberalta. Airport is southwest of centre.

Boat Check the notice of vessels leaving port on the Port Captain's board, prominently displayed near the immigration post on the riverbank. Boats sailing up the Mamoré to **Trinidad** are not always willing to take passengers.

Bus Buses leave from General Federico Román. Same long-haul services as Riberalta, above. To **Riberalta** 1 hr, US$5, daily 0700-1730.

Cobija

Air To **La Paz** daily with **Boa** (Av Ernesto Nishicawa 50, Barrio Progreso, T03-842 4820) and **TAM** (Av 9 de Febrero 57, T03-542 2267), US$60-80. Boa also flies 2-3 times a week direct to **Santa Cruz**, US$75. **Ecojet** (Av Cornejo y Nicolás Suárez, T03-842 4141), 3 times a week to Trinidad, US$115. **Servicio Aereo Arial** (airport counter, T7621 0035) several daily to **Riberalta** in a 5-seater aircraft, 10 kg luggage allowance, US$72, 1 hr.

Bus Terminal Terrestre is 4 km from town, taxi US$3. **Flota Yungueña** (T7896 1101) and **Trans Pando** (T7291 7776) to **La Paz** via Rurrenabaque

(about half-way), 48 hrs in the dry season, a week or more in the wet, US$30-35. Roads are rough, buses are poor, and air travel is a recommended alternative. **Flota Cobija**, **Trans Pando** and **Vaca Díez** to **Riberalta**, good all-weather surface, 2 river crossings on pontoon rafts, US$20, 8-9 hrs; some continue to **Guayaramerín**, 2 hrs further.

Taxi Taxis charge US$1.50 in the centre, more beyond; moto-taxis are a cheaper option. Taxis from the Brazilian side of the border are at least twice as expensive. Beware overcharging by all drivers. Taxi from the airport: US$6 to town; US$12 to Bolivian immigration and Brazilian Polícia Federal in Epitaciolândia.

Border with Brazil

From the small Rodoviária in Brasiléia, **Trans Acreana** and **PetroAcre** have several buses a day to **Rio Branco**, and to **Assis Brasil** (the border with Peru).

Practicalities
Getting around

Air

All of the following offer internal air services: **Boliviana de Aviación (BoA)** ① *T901-105010, www.boa.bo*, also has a growing international network. **Amaszonas** ① *T901-105500, www.amaszonas.com*, flies to all main cities and La Paz-Rurrenabaque and La Paz-Uyuni; its international network is also increasing. **Ecojet** ① *T901-105055, www.ecojet.bo*, flies from Cochabamba, La Paz and Santa Cruz to the main lowland destinations, as well as Sucre and Tarija. **TAM** ① *T901-105510, www.tam.bo*, the civilian branch of the Bolivian Air Force, flies to smaller and more remote destinations. Many flights radiate from La Paz, Santa Cruz or Cochabamba. Make sure you have adequate baggage insurance.

Rail

The western highland railway is operated by **Ferroviaria Andina (FCA)** ① *T02-241 6545, www.fca.com.bo*. There are passenger trains to Villazón from Oruro, via Atocha, Tupiza and Uyuni. The eastern lowland line is run by **Ferroviaria Oriental** ① *www.fo.com.bo*, with services from Santa Cruz east to the Brazilian border and south to the Argentine border at Yacuiba.

Road

Bus
Buses ply most of the main roads. Inter-urban buses are called *flotas*, inter-urban minibuses are called minivans or *surubíes*; urban buses are *micros* or minibuses (vans); *trufis* are shared taxis. Larger bus companies run frequent services and offer air conditioning, TV and other mod cons. You can usually buy tickets with reserved seats a day or two in advance. Alternatively, savings may sometimes be obtained by bargaining for fares at the last minute, although not at peak travel times like national holidays. A small charge is made for use of bus terminals; payment is before departure.

In the wet season, bus travel is subject to long delays and detours, at extra cost, and cancellations are not uncommon. On all journeys, take some food, water and toilet paper. It is best to travel by day, not just to enjoy the scenery and avoid arriving at night, but also for better road safety (also see Road safety, page 386). Bus companies are responsible for any items packed in the luggage compartment or on the roof, but only if they give you a ticket for each bag.

Maps

Good maps of Bolivia are few and far between, and maps in general can be hard to find. Road maps can be downloaded from www.abc.gob.bo/mapas-de-la-red-vial-fundamental. The **Instituto Geográfico Militar** (IGM, see page 274) publishes a useful *Mapa Vial Turístico* (US$7). Their topographical maps, for climbing and trekking, date from the 1970s and accuracy is variable. For other maps try bookshops in La Paz. The **German Alpine Club (Deutscher Alpenverein)** ① *www.alpenverein.de*, produces maps of the Cordillera Real Norte (0/8) and Sur (0/9), generally unavailable in La Paz, order online.

Driving in Bolivia

A growing percentage of Bolivian roads is paved, the rest are gravel-surfaced or earth. Any road, whatever its surface, may be closed in the rainy season (December-March). The main paved road axis of Bolivia runs from the Peruvian border at Desaguadero (also Copacabana) via La Paz and Oruro to Cochabamba and Santa Cruz, continuing to the Brazilian border at Arroyo Concepción. Some sections, such as La Paz–Oruro, are dual carriageway; others are being dualled. Other paved roads connect the La Paz–Oruro highway with Tambo Quemado on the Chilean border, continuing paved to Arica. From Potosí there are paved roads to Uyuni, to Villazón (on the Argentine border) via Cotagaita and Tupiza and to Bermejo (also on the Argentine border) via Camargo and Tarija. The road from Cochabamba to Sucre via Vacas, Mizque and Aiquile is paved. North of La Paz the road to Cocoico and beyond is paved almost to Caranavi, while the road to Chulumani is also being paved. As well as the main route to Brazil mentioned above, paved routes from Santa Cruz go to Trinidad and to Yacuiba on the Argentine border. The Trans-Chaco highway, from Santa Cruz to Asunción (Paraguay) branches off the Yacuiba road at Villamontes; it is mostly paved. Road-improvement projects continue in many areas. Some older roads are notoriously narrow and tortuous in the highlands and prone to wash-outs in the lowlands.

Road tolls These vary from US$0.50 to US$2.45 for journeys up to 100 km. On toll roads you are given a receipt at the first toll; keep it at hand as it is asked for at subsequent toll posts. The Administradora Boliviana de Carreteras (ABC) maintains a useful website, www.abc.gob.bo, with daily updates of road conditions, including any roadblocks due to social unrest. ABC also has a toll-free phone for emergencies and to report road hazards, T800-107222.

Safety Always carry spare petrol/gas and supplies and camping equipment when driving in remote areas. Your car must be able to cope with high altitude and below-freezing temperatures. Take great care on the roads, especially at night. Too many truck drivers are reckless or drunk and many vehicles drive with faulty headlights. Stalled trucks without lights are a common cause of accidents.

Documents To bring a private vehicle into Bolivia you need an International Driving Permit, the vehicle's registration document (in your name, or with a notarized letter of authorization from the owner plus approval from the Bolivian consulate in the country of origin) and your passport. On entry you get temporary admission from customs (free of charge) and surrender the document on departure; maximum 90 days. Details are available at www.aduana.gob.bo. A carnet de passages en douane is required according to www.aduana.gob.bo and insurance is compulsory. It is called SOAT and can be bought locally. Generally the police are helpful to foreign motorists, but stop you often and ask to see your documents, a complete first-aid kit, triangle and fire extinguisher.

Note There are restrictions on which vehicles may drive in La Paz, depending on license plate number and day of the week.

Organizations Automóvil Club Boliviano, Calle 12 de Calacoto esq Inofuentes, La Paz, T02-279 1755, www.acbbolivia.com.bo.

Car hire The minimum age for hiring a car is 25. Rental companies may only require your licence from home, but police ask to see an international licence. Rental of a medium-sized car costs about US$370 per week; a small 4WD vehicle US$505-550 per week.

Fuel Especial, 85 octane, US$0.54 per litre (may cost more in remote areas). Diesel costs about the same. Higher-octane Premium, US$0.70 per litre, is rarely available. There may be fuel shortages, especially in border areas, so keep your tank full.

Where to stay

Hotels and hostales

Hotels must display prices by law, but often do not. The number of stars awarded each hotel is also regulated, but not always accurate. The following terms likewise reflect the size and quality of an establishment (from largest and best, to smallest and simplest): hotel, *hostal*, *residencial*, *alojamiento* and *casa de huéspedes*. A *pensión* is a simple restaurant and may double as a place to sleep in smaller towns. For a selection of boutique hotels and resorts, see **www.bolivianboutiquehotels.com**. See the Planning your trip chapter for our hotel price guide.

Camping

Camping is best suited to the wilderness areas of Bolivia, away from towns, and people. Organized campsites, car or trailer camping does not exist here. Because of the abundance of cheap hotels you should never have to camp in populated areas.

Youth hostels

Youth hostels or self-styled 'backpackers' are not necessarily cheaper than hotels. A number of mid-range residenciales are affiliated to Hostelling International (HI) ① *www.hihostels. com/destinations/bo/hostels*; some others just say they are. Another website listing hostels is **www.boliviahostels.com**, but they are not necessarily affiliated to HI.

Food & drink

Restaurants

Most restaurants do not open early but many hotels include breakfast, which is also served in markets (see below). In *pensiones* and cheaper restaurants a basic lunch (*almuerzo* – usually finished by 1300) and dinner (*cena*) are normally available. The *comida del día* is the best value in any class of restaurant. Breakfast and lunch can also be found in markets, but eat only what is cooked in front of you. Dishes cooked in the street are not safe. See the Planning your trip chapter for our restaurant price guide.

Food

Bolivian highland cooking is usually tasty and *picante* (spicy). Recommended local specialities include *empanadas* (cheese pasties) and *humintas* (maize pies); *pukacapas* are *picante* cheese pies. Recommended main dishes include *sajta de pollo* (hot spicy chicken with onion, fresh potatoes and *chuño* – dehydrated potatoes), *parrillada* (mixed grill), *fricase* (juicy pork with *chuño*), *silpancho* (very thin fried breaded meat with eggs, rice and bananas), and *ají de lengua*, ox-tongue with hot peppers, potatoes and *chuño* or *tunta* (another kind of dehydrated potato). *Pique macho* (roast meat, sausage, chips, onion and pepper) is especially popular with Bolivians and travellers alike. Near Lake Titicaca fish becomes an important part of the local diet and trout, though not native, is usually delicious. Bolivian soups are usually hearty and warming, including *chairo* made of meat, vegetables and *chuño*. *Salteñas* are very popular meat or chicken pasties eaten as a mid-morning snack, the trick is to avoid spilling the gravy all over yourself.

In the lowland Oriente region, the food usually comes with cooked banana, yucca and rice. This area also has good savoury snacks, such as *cuñapés* (cheese bread made with manioc flour). In the northern lowlands, many types of wild meat are served in tourist restaurants and on jungle tours. Bear in mind that the turtles whose eggs are eaten are endangered and that other species not yet endangered soon will be if they stay on the tourist menu.

Ají is hot pepper, frequently used in cooking. *Locoto* is an even hotter variety (with black seeds), sometimes served as a garnish and best avoided by the uninitiated. *Llajua* is a hot pepper sauce present on every Bolivian table. Its potency varies greatly so try a little bit before applying dollops to your food.

Bolivia's temperate and tropical fruits are excellent and abundant. Don't miss the luscious grapes and peaches in season (February-April). Brazil nuts, called *almendras* or *castañas*, are produced in the northern jungle department of Pando and sold throughout the country.

Drink

The several makes of local lager-type **beer** are recommendable; Paceña, Huari, Taquiña and Ducal are the best-known brands. There are also microbrews in La Paz. Singani, the national spirit, is distilled from grapes, and is cheap and strong. Chuflay is singani and a fizzy mixer, usually 7-Up. Good **wines** are produced by several vineyards near Tarija (tours are available, see page 332). *Chicha* is a fermented maize drink, popular in Cochabamba. The hot maize drink, *api* (with cloves, cinnamon, lemon and sugar), is good on cold mornings. **Bottled water** is readily available. Tap, stream and well water should never be drunk without first being purified.

Essentials A-Z

Accident and emergency

Contact the relevant emergency service and your embassy in La Paz. Make sure you obtain police/medical reports in order to file insurance claims.
  Ambulance: T165 nationwide, T161 in El Alto.
Police: T110 nationwide. **Fire**: T119 nationwide. Robberies should be reported to the **Policía Turística**, they will issue a report for insurance purposes but stolen goods are rarely recovered. In cities which do not have a Policía Turística report robberies to the **Fuerza Especial de Lucha Contra el Crimen** (FELCC), Departamento de Robos. In La Paz, see page 259.

Electricity

220 volts 50 cycles AC. Sockets usually accept both continental European (round) and US-type (flat) 2-pin plugs. Also some 110-volt sockets, when in doubt, ask.

Embassies and consulates

For all Bolivian embassies abroad and all foreign embassies and consulates in Bolivia, see http://embassy.goabroad.com.

Health

For hospitals, doctors and dentists, contact your consulate or the tourist office for advice.

La Paz

Laboratorios Illimani, Edif Alborada p 3, of 304, Loayza y Juan de la Riva, T02-231 7290, www.laboratoriosillimani.com. Open 0900-1230, 1430-1700. Fast, efficient, hygienic.

Ministerio de Desarollo Humano, Secretaría Nacional de Salud, Av Arce, near **Radisson Plaza**. Yellow fever shot and certificate, rabies and cholera shots, malaria pills, bring your own syringe.
Pharmacies Daily papers list pharmacies on duty (*de turno*).
Sumaya (Dr Orellana), Linares 339 esq Sagárnaga, T02-242 2342, or 7065 9743. Good English-speaking doctor; for more severe cases the same doctor runs the **Clínica Lausanne**, Av Los Sargentos, esq Costanera in Bajo LLojeta, close to upper side of Obrajes. Very helpful, recommended.

Santa Cruz

Clínica Foianini, Av Irala 468, T03-336 2211, www.clinicafoianini.com. Among the better-regarded and more expensive hospitals.
San Juan de Dios, Cuéllar y España.
The public hospital.

Sucre

Hospital Cristo de las Américas, Av Japón s/n, T04-643 7804. Private hospital.
Hospital Santa Bárbara, Ayacucho y R Moreno, Plazuela Libertad, T04-645 1900, Hospital-Santa-Barbara on Facebook. Public hospital.

Money

US$1 = Bs6.92; €1 = Bs7.80 (Jun 2017).
The currency is the boliviano (Bs), divided into 100 centavos. There are notes for 200, 100, 50, 20 and 10 bolivianos, and 5, 2 and 1 boliviano coins, as well as 50, 20 and (rare) 10 centavos. Bolivianos are often referred to as pesos; expensive items, including hotel rooms, may be quoted in dollars.

Many *casas de cambio* and street changers (but among banks only **Banco Nacional de Bolivia**, BNB, www.bnb.com.bo) accept cash euros as well as dollars. Large bills may be hard to use in small villages, always carry some 20s and 10s. ATMs (**Enlace** network T800-103060) are common in all departmental capitals and some other cities but not in all small towns, including several important tourist destinations. Sorata, for instance, has no ATM. Don't rely on ATMs in small towns with few machines, for example Rurrenabaque; they frequently run out of cash. **Banco Unión**, has most ATMs in small towns, see www.bancounion.com.bo for locations. ATMs are not always reliable and, in addition to plastic, you must always carry some cash. Some ATMs dispense both Bs and US$. Debit cards and Amex are generally less reliable than Visa/MC credit cards at ATMs. Note that Bolivian ATMs dispense cash first and only a few moments later return your card. In small towns without banks or ATMs, look for **Prodem**, which changes US$ cash at fair rates, and gives cash advances at tellers on Visa/MC credit – not debit – cards for about 5% commission. (Prodem ATMs do not accept international cards.) **Banco Fie** is also found throughout the country, changes US$ cash at all branches and gives cash advances at some locations. ATM scams are worst in La Paz, but may occur elsewhere. For lost Visa cards T800-100188, MasterCard T800-100172.

Cost of travelling Bolivia is cheaper to visit than most neighbouring countries. Budget travellers can get by on US$20-25 per person per day for 2 travelling together. A basic hotel in small towns costs about US$6-12 pp, breakfast US$1.50-2, and a simple set lunch (*almuerzo*) around US$2.50-3.50. For around US$35-40, though, you can find much better accommodation, more comfortable transport and a wider choice in food. Prices are higher in the city of La Paz; in the east, especially Santa Cruz and Tarija; and in Pando and the upper reaches of the Beni. The average cost of using the internet is US$0.50 per hr.

National parks

Servicio Nacional de Areas Protegidas (**SERNAP**), Francisco Bedregal 2904 y Victor Sanjinés, Sopocachi, T02-242 6268/6272, www.sernap.gob.bo. National parks administrative office with limited tourist information. Better are Sernap's regional offices, addresses given in the travelling text.

Involved NGOs include: **Fundación Amigos de la Naturaleza (FAN)** (Km 7.5 Vía a La Guardia, Santa Cruz, T03-355 6800, www.fan-bo.org); **Fundación para el Desarrollo del Sistema Nacional de Areas Protegidas** (Prolongación Cordero 127, across from US Embassy, La Paz, T02-211 3364/243 1875, www.fundesnap.org); **Probioma** (Calle 7 Este 29, Equipetrol, Santa Cruz, T03-343 1332, www.probioma.org.bo).

Useful websites
www.biobol.org A portal with information on Bolivia's protected areas.
www.ramsar.org Ramsar's worldwide site for protected wetlands.

Opening hours

Banks and offices: normally open Mon-Fri 0900-1600, Sat 0900-1300, but may close for lunch in small towns.
Shops: Mon-Fri 0830-1230, 1430-1830 and Sat 0900-1200. Opening and closing in the afternoon are later in lowland provinces.

Police and the law

You are required to carry your passport at all times, although this is seldom asked for outside border areas. In the event of a vehicle accident in which anyone is injured, all drivers involved are usually detained until blame has been established, which may take several weeks. Never offer to bribe a police officer. If an official suggests that a bribe must be paid before you can proceed on your way, be patient and they may relent. In general however, there are few hassles and most police are helpful to travellers. For La Paz **tourist police**, see page 259.

Post

The main branches of post offices in La Paz, Santa Cruz and Cochabamba are best for sending parcels. **DHL** and **FedEx** have offices in major cities.

Public holidays and festivals

Public holidays
Some dates may be moved to the nearest weekend. 1 Jan, New Year's Day; Carnaval Week, Mon, Shrove Tuesday, Ash Wednesday; Holy Week: Thu, Fri and Sat; 1 May, Labour Day; Corpus Christi (movable May/Jun); 16 Jul, La Paz Municipal Holiday; 5-7 Aug,

Independence; 24 Sep, Santa Cruz Municipal Holiday; 2 Nov, Day of the Dead; Christmas Day.

Festivals

2 Feb Virgen de la Candelaria, in Copacabana, Santa Cruz departments.

Feb/Mar Carnaval, especially famous in Oruro, is celebrated throughout the country. There are parades with floats and folkloric dances, parties, much drinking and water throwing even in the coldest weather and nobody is spared. Many related festivities take place around the time of Carnaval. 2 weeks beforehand is **Jueves de Compadres** followed by **Jueves de Comadres**. In the altiplano Shrove Tuesday is celebrated as **Martes de Challa**, when house owners make offerings to Pachamama and give drinks to passers-by. **Carnaval Campesino** usually begins in small towns on Ash Wednesday, when regular Carnaval ends, and lasts for 5 days, until **Domingo de Tentación**. Palm Sunday (**Domingo de Ramos**) sees parades to the church throughout Bolivia; the devout carry woven palm fronds, then hang them outside their houses.

Mar/Apr Semana Santa in the eastern Chiquitania features ancient processions, dances, and games not found outside the region.

3 May Fiesta de la Invención de la Santa Cruz, various places.

May/Jun Corpus Christi is another colourful festival.

2 Jun Santísima Trinidad in Beni Department.

24 Jun San Juan, bonfires throughout all Bolivia.

29 Jun San Pedro y San Pablo, at Tiquina, Tiwanaku and throughout Chiquitania.

25 Jul Fiesta de Santiago (St James), altiplano and lake region.

14-16 Aug Virgen de Urkupiña, Cochabamba, a multitudinous 3-day Catholic festivity mixed with Quechua rituals and parades with folkloric dances.

16 Aug San Roque, patron saint of dogs; the animals are adorned with ribbons and other decorations.

1 and 2 Nov All Saints and All Souls, any local cemetery.

Safety

Compared with some other parts of South America, Bolivia has less violent crime, but tricks and scams are common. The countryside and small towns are generally safe while the largest cities (Santa Cruz, El Alto, La Paz and Cochabamba) call for vigilance. Fake police, narcotics police and immigration officers – usually plain-clothed but carrying forged ID – have been known to take people to their 'office' and ask to see documents and money; they then rob them. Legitimate police do not ask people for documents in the street unless they are involved in an accident, fight, etc. If approached, walk away and seek assistance from as many bystanders as possible. Never get in a vehicle with the 'officer' nor follow them to their 'office'. Many robberies are very slick, involving taxis and various accomplices. It is safest to take radio taxis, identified by their dome lights and phone numbers. Always lock the doors, sit in the back and never allow other passengers to share your cab. If someone else gets in, get out at once. Also if smeared or spat on, walk away, don't let the good Samaritan clean you up, they will clean you out instead.

Civil disturbance is a sporadic part of Bolivian life. It can take the form of strikes, demonstrations in major cities and roadblocks (*bloqueos*), some lasting a few hours, others weeks. Try to be flexible in your plans and make the most of nearby attractions if transport is not running. You can often find transport to the site of a roadblock, walk across and get onward transport on the other side. Check with locals first to find out how tense the situation is.

Road safety

This should be an important concern for all visitors to Bolivia. Precarious roads, poorly maintained vehicles and frequently reckless drivers combine to cause many serious, at times fatal, accidents. Choose your transport judiciously and don't hesitate to pay a little more to travel with a better company. Look over the vehicle before you get on; if it doesn't feel right, look for another. If a driver is drunk or reckless, demand that he stop at the nearest village and let you off. Also note that smaller buses, although less comfortable, are often safer on narrow mountain roads.

Tax

Airport tax International departure tax (US$25) is included in tickets at La Paz, Cochabamba and Santa Cruz airports. Domestic tax is also included in tickets at these airports, but at all others an airport tax of US$1-2.50 is charged.

IVA/VAT 13%.

Telephone and Wi-Fi

Country code +591.
Equal tones with long pauses: ringing. Equal tones with equal pauses: engaged. IDD prefix: 00. Landlines have 7 digits and a 2-digit area code starting with '0'. Mobiles have 8 digits starting with '6' or '7'. When dialling a number from a landline, there is no need to include the 0 in an area code, unless calling from outside that area.

Mobile phone service is offered by 3 main companies, **Entel** (with the most extensive coverage), **Tigo** and **Viva**. They have shops everywhere and you can buy a SIM card (*un chip*) for your phone or tablet if you would prefer to use local services. Ask at a shop if a local SIM is compatible with your device and what the best package will be. There are call centres too to make calls on a phone or local mobile.

Wi-Fi coverage is best in major towns and cities and is standard in most hotels as well as many cafés and restaurants in tourist areas. In general, internet access is slow in smaller cities and towns.

Time

Official time is 4 hrs behind GMT all year.

Tipping

Up to 10% in restaurants is very generous, Bolivians seldom leave more than a few coins.

Tourist information

InfoTur offices are found in most departmental capitals (addresses given under each city), at international arrivals in El Alto airport (La Paz) and Viru Viru (Santa Cruz). In La Paz at Mariscal Santa Cruz y Colombia, Edif Cámara de Comercio, p11, T02-235 3713, Mon-Fri 0800-1200, 1400-1800. Also see La Paz listings. **Ministerio de Culturas y Turismo**, www.minculturas.gob.bo. **Viceministerio de Turismo**, C Mercado, Ed Ballivián, p 18, La Paz, T02-211 5380, www.bolivia.travel.

Useful websites

www.bolivia.com (Spanish) News, tourism, entertainment and information on regions.
www.bolivia-online.net (Spanish, English and German) Travel information about La Paz, Cochabamba, Potosí, Santa Cruz and Sucre.
www.boliviaentusmanos.com (Spanish) News, entertainment, hotel and restaurant guide, tourist information and more.

www.presidencia.gob.bo Presidential website.
www.noticiasbolivianas.com All the Bolivian daily news in one place.

Visas and immigration

A passport only, valid for 6 months beyond date of visit, is needed for citizens of Western European countries (except Romania), Japan, Canada, South American countries (except Guyana and Suriname), Mexico, Costa Rica, Panama, Australia and New Zealand. Most others require a visa issued in advance at a Bolivian consulate. US citizens need a visa which can be obtained in advance at consulates, or on arrival at international airports or land borders; US$160 cash fee plus various requirements including a return or onward ticket and yellow fever vaccination certificate. Israeli citizens need a visa which, in principle, must be issued at a consulate but exceptions may be made at the land borders at Kasani and Villazón; 648 bolivianos cash fee (US$93) and much paperwork. Always allow extra time to obtain a visa. Some nationalities must gain authorization from the Bolivian Ministry of Foreign Affairs, which can take 6 weeks. All regulations are subject to change and it is best to check current requirements before leaving home. Tourists are usually granted 90 days stay on entry by air, but 30 days on entry by land. This can be extended for free (*ampliación*) at immigration offices in all departmental capitals, up to a maximum stay of 90 days per calendar year (180 days for nationals of Andean nations). If you overstay, the current fine is Bs20, roughly US$3 per day. Be sure to keep the paper with entry stamp inside your passport, you will be asked for it when you leave. Information, including for student and work visas, from **Dirección General de Migración** in La Paz (see below).

Immigration offices

Dirección General de Migración, Camacho 1480, T02-211 0960, www.migracion.gob.bo. Mon-Fri 0730-1530, go early. Allow 48 hrs for visa extensions.

Weights and measures

Bolivia officially uses the metric system but some old Spanish measures, like the *quintal* (hundredweight), *arroba* (25 lbs) and *cuartilla* (6 lbs), are used for produce in markets.

This is
Brazil

There are few countries as beautiful and vibrant as Brazil with nature so exuberant and people so welcoming. Thousands of kilometres of pristine and deserted beaches line the coast, some pounded by superb surf, others lapped by gentle sea. They are backed by dunes the size of deserts or forests of coconut palms. Offshore, jewel-like islands offer some of the best snorkelling and diving in the South Atlantic. In the warm shallows humpback whales gather to calf and spinner dolphins cavort in the waves.

The tabletop mountains of the interior are covered in medicinal plants and drained by mineral-rich rivers that tumble through gorges and rush over tiered waterfalls. In the Amazon, virgin forest stretches unbroken for more than 2500 km in every direction and the earth is a tapestry of green broken by a filigree of rivers. There are islands here too: the largest bigger than Denmark, wilder and more forested than Borneo. The Pantanal, the world's biggest wetland, offers some of the best wildlife watching in the western hemisphere.

The cobble and whitewash gold-mining towns of Minas Gerais and Goiás contrast with the busy metropolises of São Paulo, Salvador and Recife, each of which has a thrilling urban culture. And then there is Rio de Janeiro, the jewel in the country's urban crown, with its bays and islands, boulder mountains, beaches and beautiful people.

Best of all, though, are the Brazilians themselves, in all their joyful diversity. Portugal, France, Ireland, Holland and Britain all laid claims here and left their cultures to mingle with the indigenous inhabitants. Brazil is now home to the greatest numbers of Africans, Arabs and Japanese in the Americas, and bierfests, sushi, bauhaus, rock music and rodeos are as much a part of the culture as bossa nova and football. As yet, the country is undiscovered beyond the clichés, but Brazil is becoming big news, with a burgeoning economy, the Football World Cup hosted in 2014 and the Olympics in 2016.

VENEZUELA
GUYANA
COLOMBIA
SURINAME
GUYANE
Boa Vista
Caracari
Al Içana
Xié
PN do Pico
da Neblima
Río Branco
Parque Indígena
Tumucumaque
Macapá
Óbidos
Amazonas
Ilha do
Marajó
Belém
Manaus
Santarém
Vitória
Alcântara
São
Luís
PN Lençóis
Maranhenses
Parnaíba
Fortaleza
Itaituba
Benjamin
Constant
Democracia
Estreito
Colinas
Teresina
Canoa
Quebrada
Japim
Humaitá
Alta
Floresta
Peixoto de
Azevedo
Miranorte
Balsas
Petrolina
Caruaru
Natal
João
Pessoa
Recife
Feijó
Porto Velho
Arapuaná
Juruena
Río
Branco
Cocoal
Juína
Sinop
São Félix
do Araguaia
Goiás
Velho
BRASÍLIA
Monte Santo
Chapada
Diamantina
Maceió
Aracaju
Salvador
Guajará-Mirim
Vilhena
PN da Chapada
dos Guimarães
Itaparica
PERU
BOLIVIA
Cáceres
Cuiabá
Goiânia
Anápolis
Ilhéus
PN do Pantanal
Matogrossense
Corumbá
Paraíso
Diamantina
Caravelas
Porto Seguro
Arraial de Ajuda
PN Marinho de Abrolhos
Bonito
Campo
Grande
S. José do
Río Preto
Belo Horizonte
Ouro Preto
Vitória
Ponta Porã
Petrópolis
Búzios
CHILE
PARAGUAY
Foz do
Iguaçu
São Paulo
Rio de
Janeiro
Curitiba
Iguape
Paranaguá
São
Joaquim
Florianópolis
Caxias
do Sul
Laguna
Torres
ARGENTINA
Porto Alegre
Río Grande
Curral Alto
URUGUAY
Chuy/Chuí

*Atlantic
Ocean*

N

300 km
300 miles

Footprint
picks

★ **Rio de Janeiro City**,
page 396
They say God made the world in
six days; the seventh he devoted
to Rio.

★ **Ouro Preto**, page 474
Surrounded by mountains, the streets of this 18th-century city are
lined with churches, mansions and fountains.

★ **Salvador de Bahia**, page 524
A heady mix of beautiful tropical beaches, African culture and
Portuguese colonial buildings with a vibrant music scene.

★ **Northeastern beaches**, pages 572 and 579
Brazil's most beautiful beaches, some backed by vertiginous dunes,
others party central.

★ **The Amazon**, page 596
Far more than just a river, this is a continent of forests, savannah and
mountains worthy of weeks of exploration.

★ **The Pantanal**, page 647
One of the world's great wildlife preserves, the wetlands are home
to South America's great predators and vast numbers of birds.

Route planner

Southeast

a tale of two cities, plus Brazil's literary heartland

The highlight of the southeast is **Rio de Janeiro**. No city on earth has a setting to compare: rainforest-covered mountains rise sheer from a bottle-green ocean around. And Rio clusters at them; its centre climbing over smaller hills and crowding behind crescent coves. The beaches and music are wonderful, and carnival – which takes place in a stadium, and not in the streets – is one of the world's great spectacles. Rio's ugly and far less courted big sister, **São Paulo**, lies a few hours' bus ride away. Its interminable labyrinths of concrete are unprepossessing at first, but those who find their way into the maze, preferably with a local guide, discover the best nightlife, restaurants and popular culture in South America. The land-locked state of **Minas Gerais** is Brazil's literary heartland. Its pastoral landscapes are broken by rocky mountains and dotted with tranquil colonial towns such as **Ouro Preto**, **Tirandentes** and **Diamantina**. Minas is infused with a nostalgic lyricism, which inspired Brazil's greatest writer (João Guimarães Rosa), its greatest poet (Carlos Drummond de Andrade), musician (Milton Nascimento) and footballer (Pelé).

Southern Brazil

high mountains, tropical islands, a German-Brazilian enclave

With its *maté*-sipping gauchos, beer festivals, squeeze-box tango and blonde-haired, blue-eyed supermodels, the three states of southern Brazil feel closer to Uruguay, or even Germany, than they do to the rest of Brazil. Most visitors come for the world's most famous waterfalls, **Iguaçu**, on the border with Argentina and Paraguay. But there are canyons and good hiking in the **Serra Gaúcha mountains** in Rio Grande do Sul and the **Serra Graciosa** in Paraná, and beautiful beaches around the laid-back city of **Florianópolis** in Santa Catarina and the tranquil sub-tropical island of **Ilha do Mel**. There's also the world's second-largest beer festival in the German-Brazilian enclave of **Blumenau**, every October.

Bahia and the northeast
sublime palm-fringed beaches and lively colonial cities

The most popular destination, **Bahia**, offers a string of palm-shaded silvery strands lining its coast and islands, and the largest colonial city in the Americas, **Salvador**. Bahia is the home of the martial art dance of capoeira and the African Brazilian Candomblé religion – which is related to voodoo. Salvador's street carnival is Brazil's most raucous. The state's arid backlands are broken by dramatic, waterfall-covered mountains in the **Chapada Diamantina**. **Recife**, capital of Pernambuco, and its twin city **Olinda**, are almost as pretty as Salvador and have an even livelier cultural scene, with some of the most exciting contemporary Brazilian music and the country's largest street carnival. Travelling to the north coast, there are hundreds of beaches to choose from, some highly developed, others less so. You can swim, surf or ride the dunes in buggies in **Jericoacoara** or **Genipabu**, or kitesurf in the neocolonial settlement of **Cumbuco**. Then there are the vast dune deserts of the **Lençóis Maranhenses** on the windswept Maranhão coast and the last major city before the mouth of the Amazon, **São Luís**, whose centre is covered in colonial tiles, and whose streets reverberate with some of Brazil's best nightlife.

Northern Brazil
the Amazon with settlements small and large

The north of the country is dominated by the **Amazon**. When the river is in full flood its tributaries link through the inundated forest to form what seems like an oceanic labyrinth of lakes. These are served by sea-going cargo boats that call in at river ports along its length. Some ports are little towns while others, like **Belém**, with its cutting-edge alternative music scene, and **Manaus**, with myriad forest lodges, are home to more than a million people. North of Manaus is the overland route through Boa Vista to Venezuela. The forest stretches north into Colombia at São Gabriel and Tabatinga, and into Venezuela and the Guianas near Boa Vista, and south to the central tablelands of Mato Grosso.

Centre west
expansive grass and wetlands, tabletop mountains and scrub forests

The **Cerrado** comprises South America's most acutely threatened biome, almost as rich in unique flora and fauna as the Amazon and, in the wilds of the Chapada dos Veadeiros or Jalapão, just as magnificent. The rivers, lakes and grasslands of the **Pantanal** are the best place to see wildlife in the Americas; at the end of the dry season, there are few places on earth where birds can be seen in such astonishing numbers. At the eastern end of the centre west is the country's capital, **Brasília**, carved from the Cerrado in the 1960s and now a World Heritage Site for its repository of striking modernist architecture.

Essential Brazil

Finding your feet

Flights into Brazil generally land in São Paulo, but Rio de Janeiro's international airport also has connections to the USA and Europe. Public transport in Brazil is very efficient, but distances are huge. You will either need to come for a long time, concentrate on a smaller area or be prepared to fly a lot.

Fact file

Location 15.7833° S, 47.8667° W
Capital Brasília
Time zone Brazil has 3 time zones: GMT -2, -3, -4 hrs
Telephone country code +55
Currency Brazilian real (BRL)

Getting around

Most visitors will find themselves travelling by buses and planes, except in the Amazon when a boat is often the only way to get around. Train routes are practically non-existent, car hire is expensive and hitchhiking not advisable. Taxis vary widely in quality and price but are easy to come by and safe when taken from a *posto de taxis* (taxi rank).

Best beaches

Ilha Grande, Rio, page 436
Ilha de Santa Catarina, Santa Catarina, page 501
Trancoso, Bahia, page 544
Fernando de Noronha, Pernambuco, page 563
Pipa, Rio Grande do Norte, page 574

Best Cultural World Heritage Sites

Ouro Preto, page 474
Historic Centre of Salvador de Bahia, page 524
São Francisco Square in São Cristóvão, page 568
Historic Centre of São Luís, page 587
Central Amazon Conservation Complex, page 614
Brasília, page 630

When to go

Brazil is a tropical country, but the further south you go the more temperate the winters. The heaviest rains fall at different times in different regions: November to March in the southeast, December to March in the centre west and April to August on the northeast coast. The rainy season in the north and Amazônia can begin in December and is heaviest March to May.

May to September is usually referred to as winter, but this is not to suggest that this is a bad time to visit. On the contrary, April to June and August to October are recommended times to go to most parts of the country. One major consideration is that carnival falls within the hottest, wettest time of year (in February). Also bear in mind that mid-December to February is the national holiday season, which means tourist facilities are busy and elsewhere businesses may be shut.

Weather Rio de Janeiro

	January	February	March	April	May	June
	32°C	32°C	32°C	31°C	28°C	27°C
	24°C	24°C	23°C	22°C	19°C	18°C
	7mm	14mm	3mm	3mm	2mm	1mm

	July	August	September	October	November	December
	27°C	28°C	28°C	29°C	30°C	32°C
	17°C	18°C	19°C	21°C	22°C	23°C
	2mm	5mm	10mm	12mm	12mm	10mm

Brazil is huge, with space inside its borders for Australia, France and the UK combined, and it has a continent's worth of things to see and do. It's important to be realistic about travel plans – you could spend a year in Brazil without exhausting the sights. At a push, three to four weeks is about enough to explore a decent amount of the northeast or the southern region.

Tip...

Brazilians dress casually. It's best to do likewise and blend in. Avoid flashy brands. You can always buy T-shirts on arrival; wearing local brands will make you less conspicuous and they are sold everywhere.

Best Natural World Heritage Sites
Atlantic Forest South-East Reserves,
Paranaguá, page 496
Iguaçu, page 518
Central Amazon Conservation Complex,
page 614
Pantanal Conservation Area, page 647
Chapada dos Veadeiros and Parque
Nacional Emas, page 639

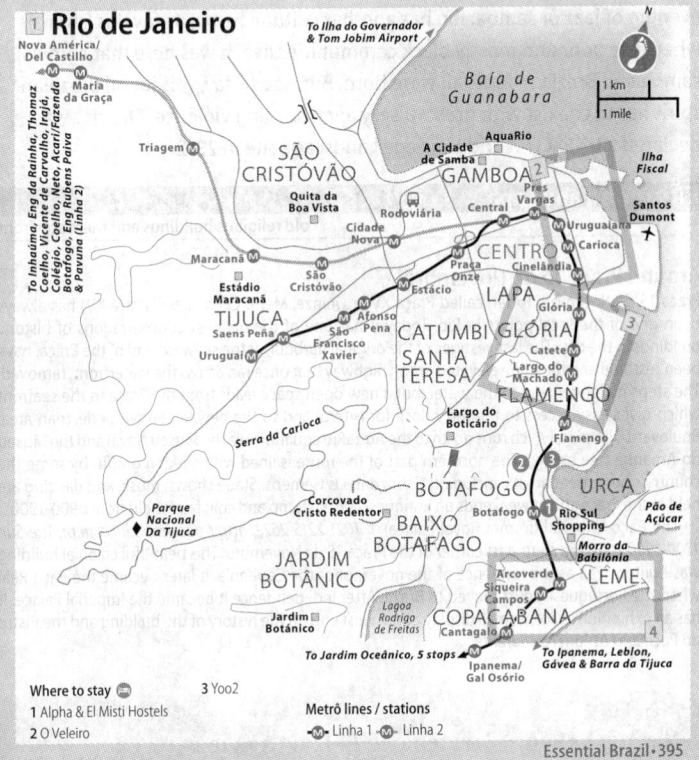

1 Rio de Janeiro

Where to stay
1 Alpha & El Misti Hostels
2 O Veleiro
3 Yoo2

Metrô lines / stations
Ⓜ Linha 1   Ⓜ Linha 2

Rio de Janeiro

★Brazilians say: God made the world in six days; the seventh he devoted to
Rio (pronounced 'Heeoo' by locals). Rio has a glorious theatrical backdrop of
tumbling wooded mountains, stark expanses of bare rock and a deep blue
sea studded with rocky islands. From the statue of Christ on the hunchbacked
peak of Corcovado, or from the conical Pão de Açúcar (Sugar Loaf), you
can experience the beauty of a bird's-eye view over the city which sweeps
along a narrow alluvial strip on the southwestern shore of the vast Baía
de Guanabara. Although best known for the curving Copacabana beach,
for Ipanema – home to the Girl and beautiful sunsets, and for its swirling,
reverberating, joyous Carnival, Rio also has a fine artistic, architectural and
cultural heritage from its time as capital of both imperial and republican
Brazil. But this is first and foremost a city dedicated to leisure: sport and
music rule and a day spent hang gliding or surfing is easily followed by an
evening of jazz or samba. Rio has another cultural heart, its favelas (slums),
where the poor and mostly black communities live. It was here that carnival,
samba and Brazilian football were born. But, sad to say, this joyful Brazilian
spirit has to coexist with great misery and shocking violence. The city was
declared a UNESCO World Heritage Landscape site in 2012.

City centre and Lapa *Colour map 7, B5.*

old religious buildings and the waterfront

Around Praça 15 de Novembro

Praça 15 de Novembro (often called Praça XV or Quinze, Metrô Carioca; VLT Praça XV) has always
been one of the focal points in Rio. Today it has one of the greatest concentrations of historic
buildings in the city. The last vestiges of the original harbour, at the seaward end of the Praça, have
been restored and the huge elevated urban highway that once ran across the waterfront, removed.
The steps no longer lead to the water, but a new open space leads from the Praça to the seafront
which gives easy access to the ferry dock for Niterói and to the new, extensive pedestrian area,
Boulevard Olímpico, which runs north to the **AquaRio** aquarium via the **Museu Naval** and the **Museu
do Amanhã** (see below). The northern part of the route is lined with striking graffiti by some the
country's best street artists, including Cobra and Os Gêmeos. Stage shows, music and dancing are
held in the Praça and at weekends an antiques, crafts, stamp and coin fair is held from 0900-1900.

The **Paço Imperial** (former Royal Palace) ① *T021-2215 2622, http://pacoimperial.com.br, Tue-Sun
1200-1900,* is on the southeast corner of the Praça 15 de Novembro. This beautiful colonial building
was built in 1743 as the residence of the governor of the Capitania. It later became the Paço Real
when the Portuguese court moved to Brazil. After Independence it became the Imperial Palace. It
has an exhibition space, a small display at the west end on the history of the building and the Bistro
do Paço and Atrium restaurants.

Best for
Nightlife ▪ People-watching ▪ Relaxing ▪ Views

Across the Rua da Assembléia is the neoclassical **Palácio Tiradentes** ① *T021-2588 1000, www. alerj.rj.gov.br, Mon-Sat 1000-1700, Sun and holidays 1200-1700, guided visits T021-2588 1251*, the state legislative assembly, built 1922-1926. It is named after the dentist Joaquim José da Silva Xavier, the symbolic father of Brazilian independence.

2 Rio de Janeiro centre

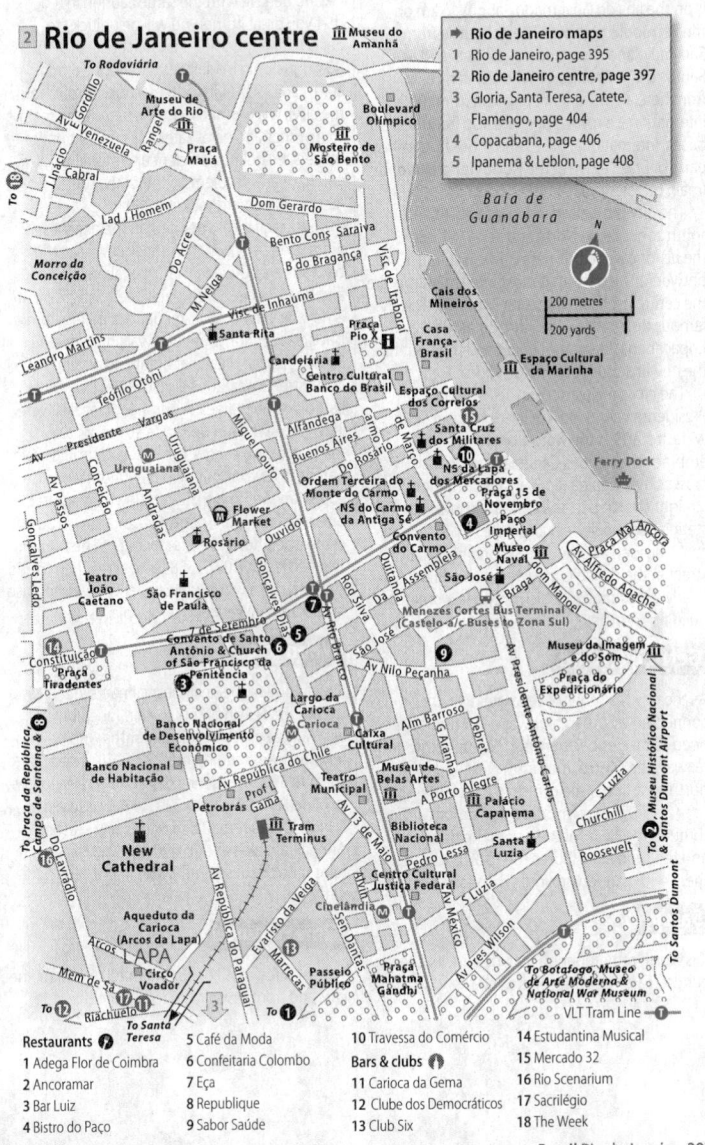

➡ **Rio de Janeiro maps**
1 Rio de Janeiro, page 395
2 Rio de Janeiro centre, page 397
3 Gloria, Santa Teresa, Catete, Flamengo, page 404
4 Copacabana, page 406
5 Ipanema & Leblon, page 408

Restaurants 🍴
1 Adega Flor de Coimbra
2 Ancoramar
3 Bar Luiz
4 Bistro do Paço
5 Café da Moda
6 Confeitaria Colombo
7 Eça
8 Republique
9 Sabor Saúde
10 Travessa do Comércio

Bars & clubs 🍷
11 Carioca da Gema
12 Clube dos Democráticos
13 Club Six
14 Estudantina Musical
15 Mercado 32
16 Rio Scenarium
17 Sacrilégio
18 The Week

Finding your feet

Aeroporto Internacional Tom Jobim (Galeão) is on the Ilha do Governador, about 16 km on the Petrópolis highway. The air shuttle from São Paulo and a few domestic flights end at Santos Dumont airport in the city centre. Taxis from here are much cheaper than from the international airport. There are also frequent buses. International buses and those from other parts of Brazil arrive at the **Rodoviária Novo Rio** (main bus station) near the docks.

The city is usually divided into north and south zones, Zona Norte and Zona Sul, with the historical and business centre, O Centro, in between. The parts that most interest visitors are the centre itself and the Zona Sul, which has the famous districts of Flamengo, Botafogo, Urca, Copacabana, Ipanema, Leblon and then out to the newer suburb of Barra de Tijuca.

The city's main artery is the Avenida Presidente Vargas, 4.5 km long and over 90 m wide. It starts at the waterfront, divides to embrace the famous Candelária church, then crosses the Avenida Rio Branco in a magnificent straight stretch past the Central do Brasil railway station until finally it incorporates a palm-lined, canal-divided avenue. The second principal street in the centre is the Avenida Rio Branco, nearly 2 km long, on which only a few ornate buildings remain.

Getting around

As the city is a series of separate districts connected by urban highways and tunnels, you need to take public transport. An underground railway, the **Metrô**, runs from west and northwest under the centre to the south. A tram network, VLT, runs from Santos Dumont airport through the heart of the city to the dock area and the rodoviária. Buses run to all parts, treat them with caution at night when taxis are better.

Safety

It is worth remembering that, despite its beach culture, carefree atmosphere and friendly people, Rio is one of the world's most densely populated cities. If you live in London, Paris, New York or LA and behave with the same caution in Rio that you do at home, you will be unlucky to encounter any crime. The tourist police, **BPTur**, Rua Figueiredo Magalhães 550, Copacabana, T021-2332 7937 (with other stations throughout the city), www.pmerj.rj.gov.br, patrols the main tourist sites and gives safety tips. Tourist police officers are helpful, efficient and multilingual. If you have any problems, contact the tourist police first, or ring emergency line 190.

Extra vigilance is needed on the beaches at night. Don't walk on the sand. Likewise in the back streets between the Copacabana Palace and Rua Figueiredo de Magalhães. Santa Teresa is now far safer and better policed than before, but great caution is needed walking between Santa Teresa and Lapa at night and around the small streets near the Largo das Neves and the Largo dos Guimarães. A number of favelas were 'pacified' in the run up to the 2014 and 2016 mega sporting events. Even so, you should never enter a favela on your own or without a person you know well and trust. A tour with a reputable operator (see Tours, page 424), or a stay in an established hostel (see for example **The Maze** in Tavares Bastos, T021-2558 5547, www.themazerio.com) can be a worthwhile experience. Otherwise favelas remain very dangerous places.

When to go

Rio has one of the healthiest climates in the tropics. Trade winds cool the air. June, July and August are the coolest months with temperatures ranging from 22°C (18° in a cold spell) to 32°C on a sunny day at noon. December to March is hotter, from 32°C to 42°C. Humidity is high. October to March is the rainy season. Annual rainfall is about 1120 mm and heavy rains tend to cause mud-slides in the early part of the year.

Time required

At least three days is recommended to explore the city, and from seven to 10 to explore the state.

On Rua 1 de Março, across from Praça 15 de Novembro, there are three buildings related to the Carmelite order. The convent of the **Ordem Terceira do Monte do Carmo**, started in 1611, is now used as the Faculdade Cândido Mendes. The order's present church, the **Igreja da Ordem Terceira do Carmo** ① *R Primeiro de Março, Mon-Fri 0800-1400, Sat 0800-1200*, is the other side of the old cathedral (see below) from the convent. It was started in 1755, consecrated in 1770 and its towers added in 1849-1850. It has strikingly beautiful portals by Mestre Valentim, the son of a Portuguese nobleman and a slave girl. He also created the main altar of fine moulded silver, the throne and its chair and much else.

Between the former convent and the Igreja da Ordem Terceira do Carmo is the old cathedral, the **Igreja de Nossa Senhora do Carmo da Antiga Sé**, separated from the Carmo Church by a closed passageway. It was the chapel of Convento do Carmo from 1590 until 1754 and has a beautiful baroque interior. A new church was built in 1761, which became the city's cathedral. In the crypt are the alleged remains of Pedro Alvares Cabral, the Portuguese explorer (though Santarém, Portugal, also claims to be his last resting place).

On the northwest side of Praça 15 de Novembro, you go through the Arco do Teles and the Travessa do Comércio to Rua do Ouvidor. The **Igreja Nossa Senhora da Lapa dos Mercadores** ① *R do Ouvidor 35, Mon-Fri 0800-1400*, was consecrated in 1750, remodelled 1869-1872 and has been fully restored. Across the street, with its entrance at Rua 1 de Março 36, is the church of **Santa Cruz dos Militares**, built 1770-1811. It is large, stately and beautiful and has the first neoclassical façade in Brazil; the altar is by Mestre Valentim.

The Church of **Nossa Senhora da Candelária** (1775-1810) ① *on Praça Pio X (Dez), at the city end of Av Pres Vargas where it meets R 1 de Março, VLT Candelária, Mon-Fri 0800-1600, Sat 0800-1200, Sun 0900-1300*, has beautiful ceiling decorations and romantic paintings. It has long been the church of 'society Rio'.

The **Centro Cultural Banco do Brasil (CCBB)** ① *entrances on Av Pres Vargas and R 1 de Março 66, Metrô Uruguaiana, VLT Candelária, T021-3808 2020, http://culturabancodobrasil.com.br, open 0900-2100, closed Tue*, is highly recommended for good exhibitions. It has a library, multimedia facilities, a cinema, concerts (prices vary) and a restaurant. Opposite is the **Centro Cultural Correios** ① *R Visconde de Itaboraí 20, T021-2253 1580, Tue-Sun 1200-1900*, which holds temporary exhibitions and a postage stamp fair on Saturdays. **Casa França-Brasil** ① *R Visconde de Itaboraí 78, T021-2332 5120, www.casafrancabrasil.rj.gov.br, Tue-Sun 1000-2000*, dates from the first French Artistic Mission to Brazil and it was the first neoclassical building in Rio. **Espaço Cultural da Marinha** ① *Av Alfredo Agache at Av Pres Kubitschek, VLT Parada dos Museus, T021-2532 5992, www1.mar.mil.br/dphdm/espaco-cultural-da-marinha, Tue-Sun 1200-1700 and every 3rd weekend of the month 1300-1500, US$3.50 (museum free, tickets for boarding vessels)*, was given to the navy to become a museum containing displays on underwater archaeology and navigation and the *Galeota*, the boat in which the royal family was rowed around the Baía de Guanabara. Moored outside are the tug *Laurindo Pitta* ① *1 hr 20 min trips Thu-Sun 1315 and 1515*, the warship *Bauru* and the submarine *Riachuelo* (both can be visited). Boats give access to **Ilha Fiscal** ① *T021-2233 9165, boats to Ilha Fiscal, Thu-Sun, 1300, 1430, 1600 Sep-Mar, 30 mins earlier Apr-Aug, US$5, in bad weather access is by minibus*, with its beautiful neo-Gothic palace. The **Museu Naval** ① *just south (off Praça XV, R Dom Manuel 15, Tue-Sun 1200-1700*, is good, with English summaries.

Praça Mauá (*VLT Parada dos Museus*), which lies north of Avenida Presidente Vargas, marks the end of Centro and the beginning of the port zone, which was revitalized for the 2016 Olympics. Empty warehouses have been replaced by galleries, a pedestrian boulevard and, north of the praça in Gamboa, the **AquaRio aquarium** ① *VLT Parada dos Navios, T021-4063 3003, www.aquariomarinhodorio.com.br, daily 1000-1800, last entry 1700, US$25*, showing mostly Brazilian aquatic life, and a shopping centre. The new museums include the **Museu de Arte do Rio (MAR)** ① *Praça Mauá, T021-3031 2741, www.museudeartedorio.org.br, Tue-Sun 1000-1700, US$6.30, half price under 21 and students, free for over 60s and for all on Tue, US$10.25 combined ticket with Museu do Amanhã*. The museum, which is housed in a beautifully converted building by celebrated architects Bernardes + Jacobsen, holds temporary exhibitions from historic, established and emerging artists (almost all from Rio) and focuses on their connections with the community. Immediately in front of MAR is the **Museu do Amanhã (Museum of Tomorrow)** ① *Praça Mauá, http://museudoamanha.org.br, Tue-Sun 1000-1800, ticket office closes 1700, US$6.30, half price under 21 and students, free for over 60s and for all on Tue, the museum is extremely popular so it is usually necessary to buy tickets online,*

BACKGROUND

Rio de Janeiro

The Portuguese navigator, Gonçalo Coelho, arrived at what is now Rio de Janeiro on 1 January 1502. Thinking that the Baía de Guanabara (the name the local *indígenas* used) was the mouth of a great river, they called the place the January River. Although the bay was almost as large and as safe a harbour as the Baía de Todos Os Santos to the north, the Portuguese did not take of advantage of it. In fact, it was first settled by the French, who, under the Huguenot Admiral Nicholas Durand de Villegagnon, occupied Lage Island on 10 November 1555, but later transferred to Sereigipe Island (now Villegagnon), where they built the fort of Coligny.

In early 1559-1560, Mem de Sá, third governor of Brazil, mounted an expedition from Salvador to attack the French. The Portuguese finally took control in 1567. Though constantly attacked by *indígenas*, the new city grew rapidly and when King Sebastião divided Brazil into two provinces, Rio was chosen capital of the southern captaincies. Salvador became sole capital again in 1576, but Rio again became the southern capital in 1608 and the seat of a bishopric.

Rio de Janeiro was by the 18th century becoming the leading city in Brazil. Not only was it the port out of which gold was shipped, but it was also the focus of the export/import trade of the surrounding agricultural lands. On 27 January 1763, it became the seat of the Viceroy. After independence, in 1834, it was declared capital of the Empire and remained so for 125 years.

a starship-shaped concrete wedge hovering over an artificial lake designed by Spanish neo-futurist Santiago Calatrava (of the Queen Sofía Palace of the Arts in Valencia). This is an environmental museum with exhibition halls devoted to how human beings are connected with, and how they are affecting and altering the planet.

Just north of Candelária, on a promontory overlooking the bay, is the **Mosteiro** (monastery) **de São Bento** ① *R Dom Gerardo 68, VLT São Bento, T021-2206 8100, www.osb.org.br, daily 0700-1800, free, guided tours Mon-Sat 0900-1600, shorts not allowed, no photography during mass.* Every Sunday at 1000, Mass is sung with plainsong,

> **Tip...**
> São Bento is reached either by a narrow road from Rua Dom Gerardo 68, or by a lift whose entrance is at Rua Dom Gerardo 40 (Metrô Uruguaiana or taxi from centre US$6).

which is free, but arrive an hour early to get a seat. On other days, Mass is at 0715. It contains some of the best 17th- and 18th-century rococo decoration in Brazil. The main body of the church is adorned in gold and red. The carving and gilding is remarkable, much of it by Frei Domingos da Conceição. The paintings, too, should be seen. The Chapels of the Immaculate Conception (Nossa Senhora da Conceição) and of the Most Holy Sacrament (Santíssimo Sacramento) are masterpieces of colonial art. The organ, dating from the end of the 18th century, is very interesting.

Southeast of Praça 15 de Novembro, by the Largo da Misericórdia, is the **Museu Histórico Nacional** ① *Praça Mcal Âncora, T021-2332 9068, www.museuhistoriconacional.com.br, Tue-Fri 1000-1730, Sat, Sun and holidays 1400-1800, US$4, free Sun,* has excellent displays on Brazil's history (starting with indigenous peoples), coins, a collection of beautiful carriages and temporary shows. It's a big complex, including a 16th-17th century fortress, the Caso de Trem (artillery store, 1760) and arsenal (1764). There are good English summaries and a restaurant. **Museu da Imagem e do Som (MIS)** ① *Praça Luis Souza Dantas, T021-2332 9068 and at R Visconde de Maranguape 15, Largo da Lapa, T021-2332 9509, www.mis.rj.gov.br, Mon-Fri 1100-1700 by appointment only, due to move to Copacabana in late 2018 – see below,* has photographs of Brazil and modern Brazilian paintings; also collections and recordings of Brazilian classical and popular music and a small cinema.

Around Largo da Carioca

The second oldest convent in the city is the **Convento de Santo Antônio** ① *T021-2262 0129, http://conventosantoantonio.org.br, Mon-Fri 0800-1800, Sat 0800-1100, free,* on a hill off the Largo da Carioca, built 1608-1615. Santo Antônio is an object of devotion for women looking for a husband and you will see them in the precincts. The church has a marvellous sacristy adorned with blue tiles and paintings illustrating the life of St Anthony. In the church itself, the baroque decoration is concentrated in the chancel, the main altar and the two lateral altars.

Separated from this church only by some iron railings is the beautiful church of the **Ordem Terceira** de **São Francisco da Penitência** ① *T021-2262 0197, Mon-Fri 0900-1200, 1300-1600, US$4.50, guided tours on Thu afternoon*. Its Baroque carving and gilding of walls and altar, much more than in its neighbour, is considered among the finest in Rio. Behind the church is a tranquil, catacomb-filled garden.

Across Ruas da Carioca and 7 de Setembro are the churches of **São Francisco de Paula** ① *upper end of R do Ouvidor, Mon-Fri 0900-1300*, containing some of Mestre Valentim's work, and **Nossa Senhora do Rosário e São Benedito dos Pretos** ① *R Uruguaiana 77 e Ouvidor, Mon-Fri 0700-1700, Sat 0700-1300*, the centre of African Christian culture in Rio, with a museum devoted to slavery. One long block behind the Largo da Carioca and São Francisco de Paula is the **Praça Tiradentes**, old and shady, with a statue to Dom Pedro I. At the northeast corner of the praça is the **Teatro João Caetano** ① *T021-2221 0305*, while the **Centro de Arte Hélio Oiticica** ① *R Luís de Camões 68, Mon-Fri 1000-1800*, a contermporary exhibition space, has a bookshop and air-conditioned café. Also on R Luís de Camões is the **Real Gabinete Português de Leitura** ① *No 30, T021-2221 3138, www. realgabinete.com.br, Mon-Fri 0900-1800, free*, an architectural gem with a magnificent reading hall and some 120,000 books. Shops nearby specialize in selling goods for umbanda, the Afro-Brazilian religion. Combine any of these with a drink at the Confeitaria Colombo, see Restaurants, page 415.

South of the Largo da Carioca are the modern buildings on Avenida República do Chile. The new cathedral here, the **Catedral Metropolitana** ① *www.catedral.com.br, 0700-1700, Mass Mon-Sat 1200, Sun 1000*, was dedicated in November 1976. It is an oblate concrete cone, whose most striking feature is four enormous 60-m-high stained-glass windows. Crossing Avenida República do Paraguai from the cathedral is the station, with museum, for the tram to Santa Teresa (see below).

> **Tip...**
> Some of Rio's better modern architecture is to be found along the Avenida República do Chile, such as the conical new Cathedral.

Avenida Rio Branco and Cinelândia

The area around Praça Floriano, Cinelândia, was the city's liveliest zone in the 1920s and 1930s. **Theatro Municipal** ① *Praça Floriano, T021-2332 9191, www.theatromunicipal.rj.gov.br, box office is open daily 1000-1800 (reduced hours in Jan), guided visits T021-2332 9220, US$6.30, 6 a day Tue-Fri, 3 a day Sat*. One of the most magnificent buildings in Brazil in the eclectic style, it was built in 1905-1909, in imitation of the Opéra in Paris. The decorative features inside and out represent many styles, all lavishly executed. Opera and orchestral performances are given here. The **Biblioteca Nacional** ① *Av Rio Branco 219, T021-3095 3879, www.bn.br, Mon-Fri 0900-2000, Sat 0900-1500, free*, dates from 1905-1910. The monumental staircase leads to a hall, off which lead the fine internal staircases of Carrara marble. It houses over nine million volumes and documents. The **Museu Nacional de Belas Artes** ① *Av Rio Branco 199, T021-3299 0600, mnba.gov.br, Tue-Fri 1000-1800, Sat, Sun and holidays 1200-1700, US$2.50*, was built between 1906 and 1908, in eclectic style. It has 800 original paintings and sculptures and 1000 direct reproductions. One gallery, dedicated to works by Brazilian artists from the 17th century onwards, includes paintings by Frans Janszoon Post (Dutch 1612-1680), who painted Brazilian landscapes in classical Dutch style, and Frenchmen Debret and Taunay. It has one of the best collections of Brazilian modernism in the country, with important works by artists like Cândido Portinári and Emiliano Di Cavalcanti. The **Centro Cultural Justiça Federal** (1905-1909) ① *Av Rio Branco 241, T021-3261 2550, www10.trf2.jus.br/ccjf, Tue-Sun 1200-1900*, in the former Supreme Court, has excellent eclectic architecture; you can see the court chamber and good temporary exhibitions and shows.

Just south of the Catedral Metropolitana is **Lapa**, an area rediscovering its belle époque, artistic past. After 40 years of neglect, streets with a reputation for extreme danger have revived; town houses have been renovated, antiques markets, cafés and music venues have opened and the area has become the main centre for weekend nightlife in Rio, with a wealth of bars and samba clubs. Despite this, you still need to be on the lookout for thieves here and be wary of walking on the quieter back streets, especially after dark.

West of the centre

About 3 km west of the public gardens of the Praça da República (beyond the Sambódromo – see box, Carnival, page 420) is the **Quinta da Boa Vista** ① *daily 0700-1800*, formerly the emperor's private park, from 1809 to 1889. If you are comfortable in crowds, a good time to visit is Saturday or Sunday afternoon. It is full of locals looking for fun and relaxation and therefore more police are on hand. **Note** Beware of thieves by the park entrance and in the park itself on weekdays.

In the **Museu Nacional** ① *Quinta da Boa Vista, T021-3938 1101, www.museunacional.ufrj.br, Tue-Sun 1000-1700 (but subject to frequent unannounced closures), US$2.10*, is the famous Bendegó meteorite, found in the State of Bahia in 1888; its original weight, before some of it was chipped, was 5360 kg. The museum also has important collections which are poorly displayed. The building was the principal palace of the Emperors of Brazil, but only the unfurnished Throne Room and ambassadorial reception room on the second floor reflect past glories. The museum contains collections of Brazilian indigenous weapons, costumes, utensils, etc, of minerals and of historical documents. There are also collections of birds, beasts, fishes and butterflies. Despite the need for conservation work, the museum is still worth visiting. The safest way to reach the museum is by taking a taxi to the main door. Having said that, it can be reached by Metrô to São Cristóvão, then cross the railway line and walk five minutes to the park. This is safer than taking a bus. Also in the park is the **Jardim Zoológico** ① *T021-3878 4200, www.rio.rj.gov.br/web/riozoo, Tue-Sun 0900-1630, US$2.10, young children free, students with ID pay half*, one of a tiny handful of places in the world where you can see Lear's Macaws with a captive breeding programme for many other endangered South American animals including golden lion tamarins.

Maracanã Stadium ① *T021-2334 1705, www.maracanaonline.com.br, daily 0900-1700*, is one of the largest sports centres in the world. Its original capacity of 200,000 was cut to about 80,000 in the complete and hugely expensive remodelling for the 2014 FIFA World Cup™ and the Olympics (the stadium hosted the opening ceremony). There is currently (2017) a dispute over ownership of the stadium and it is abandoned and falling into disrepair.

Santa Teresa *See map, page 404.*

known as the coolest part of Rio

☆This hilly inner suburb, southwest of the centre, boasts many colonial and 19th-century buildings, set in narrow, curving, tree-lined streets. Today the old houses are lived in by artists, intellectuals and makers of handicrafts. As Rio's up-and-coming place to stay, it has hostels, hotels and homestays (including the upper floor of the former home of Ronnie Biggs, the British, 1960s great train robber). At the end of the tram line (see below), Largo das Neves, you will be able to appreciate the small-town feel of the place.

There are several bars here. The essential stop is the Largo do Guimarães, which has some not-to-be-missed eating places (see Restaurants). Also here is **Chácara do Céu** ① *R Murtinho Nobre 93, T021-3970 1126, www.museuscastro maya.com.br, Wed-Mon 1200-1700, US$2*, take the Santa Teresa tram to Curvelo station, walk along R Dias de Barros, following the signposts to Parque das Ruínas. Also called Fundação Raymundo Ottoni de Castro Maia, it has a wide range of art objects and modern painters, including Brazilian; exhibitions change through the year. The **Chalé Murtinho** ① *R Murtinho 41, daily 1000-1700*, was in ruins until it was partially restored and turned into a cultural centre called **Parque das Ruínas**. There are exhibitions, a snack bar and superb views. Be vigilant in the streets leading up to the Parque, they are poorly policed

Santa Teresa is best visited on the traditional open-sided **tram**, the *bondinho*. ① *US$6.30 return, 2 routes: Largo da Carioca to Largo dos Guimarães, every 20 mins, and Largo da Carioca to R Francisco Muratori via Santa Teresa, every hour*. The route runs from Rua Profesor Lélio Gama, near the Largo da Carioca (Metrô to Carioca or Cinelândia), over the **Arcos da Lapa** aqueduct and then winds its way up to the district's historic streets. Buses number 434 and 464 run from Leblon (via Ipanema, Copacabana and the Guanabara Bay suburbs) to Avenida Riachuelo in Lapa, a few hundred metres north of the arches, from where minibus 014 Castelo (US$1.25) runs to the Largo do Guimarães. Taxis from Glória metro to Santa Teresa cost around US$8; at night, only take a taxi.

the world-renowned districts of Rio, Copacabana among them

The commercial district ends where Avenida Rio Branco meets Avenida Beira Mar. This avenue, with its royal palms and handsome buildings, coasting the Botafogo and Flamengo beaches, makes a splendid drive, Avenida Infante Dom Henrique, along the beach over reclaimed land (the Aterro), leading to Botafogo and through two tunnels to Copacabana.

Glória, Catete and Flamengo *See map, page 404.*

On the Glória and Flamengo waterfront, with a view of the Pão de Açúcar and Corcovado, is the **Parque do Flamengo**, designed by Burle Marx, opened in 1965 during the 400th anniversary of the city's founding and landscaped on 100 ha reclaimed from the bay. It is a popular recreation area. (**Note** Be careful after dark.) **Museu de Arte Moderna** ① *Av Infante Dom Henrique 85, city end of Parque Flamengo, T021-3883 5600, www.mamrio.com.br, Tue-Fri 1200-1800, 1100-1800 weekends and holidays, US$6.50.* This spectacular building houses works by many well-known Europeans and collections of Brazilian contemporary art, the best modern art in Brazil outside São Paulo.

The **Monumento aos Mortos da Segunda Guerra Mundial/National War Memorial** ① *Av Infante Dom Henrique 75, opposite Praça Paris, Glória, crypt and museum, T021-2240 1283, www.mnmsgm.ensino.eb.br, Tue-Sun 0900-1700, mausoleum Tue-Sun 1000-1600; free, beach clothes and rubber-thonged sandals not permitted,* to Brazil's dead in the Second World War. The Memorial is two slender columns supporting a slightly curved slab, representing two palms uplifted to heaven. In the crypt are the remains of Brazilian soldiers killed in Italy in 1944-1945 and on ships torpedoed by U-boats. The beautiful little church on the Glória Hill, overlooking the Parque do Flamengo, is **Nossa Senhora da Glória do Outeiro** ① *T021-2225 2869, Mon-Fri 0900-1200, 1300-1700, Sat-Sun 0900-1200, buses 119 from the centre and 571 from Copacabana.* It was the favourite church of the imperial family; Dom Pedro II was baptized here. The building is polygonal, with a single tower. It contains excellent examples of blue-faced Brazilian tiling. Its main wooden altar, was carved by Mestre Valentim. The adjacent museum of religious art keeps the same hours.

The charming **Parque do Catete** ① *0800-1800,* is a small park with birds and monkeys between Praia do Flamengo and the Palácio do Catete, which contains the fine **Museu da República** ① *R do Catete 153, T021-2127 0324, http://museudarepublica.museus.gov.br, Tue-Fri 1000-1700, Sat, Sun and holidays 1100-1800, US$2, take bus 571 from Copacabana, or the Metró to Catete station.* The palace was built in 1858-1866. In 1887 it was converted into the presidential seat, until the move to Brasília. The first floor is devoted to the history of the Brazilian republic.

Museu do Folclore Edison Carneiro ① *R do Catete 181, T021-2285 2545, www.cnfcp.gov.br, closed for refurbishment in 2017, signs in Portuguese, take bus 571 from Copacabana, or the Metró to Catete station.* This museum has an exhibit of small ceramic figures representing everyday life in Brazil, some very funny, some scenes animated by electric motors. There are fine Candomblé and Umbanda costumes, religious objects, ex-votos and sections on many of Brazil's festivals. It has a small, but excellent library, with helpful staff for finding books on Brazilian culture, history and anthropology.

The **Museu Carmen Miranda** ① *Rui Barbosa 560, Parque do Flamengo (in front of the Morro da Viúva), T021-2334 4293, Tue-Fri 1100-1700, Sat-Sun 1400-1700, US$1,* houses over 3000 items related to the famous Portuguese singer who emigrated to Brazil, then Hollywood, and is forever associated with Rio. These include her famous gowns, fruit-covered hats, jewellery and reviews, recordings and occasional showings of her films. This museum is due to move into the new Museu da Imagem e do Som in Copacabana in late 2018 (see page 407).

Botafogo

Museu Villa-Lobos ① *R Sorocaba 200, T021-2266 3845, www.museuvillalobos.org.br, closed for refurbishment in 2017.* Such was the fame and respect afforded to Latin America's most celebrated composer that Rio de Janeiro founded this museum only a year after his death in 1960. Inside the ▶

fine 19th-century building is the collection includes instruments, scores, books and recordings. The museum has occasional shows and concerts, and supports a number of classical music projects throughout Brazil. **Museu do Índio** ① *R das Palmeiras 55, T021-3214 8702, www.museudoindio.org.br, Tue-Fri 0900-1730, Sat and Sun 1300-1700, US$2, Sun free. It's a 10-min walk from Botafogo Metrô; from rodoviária, Bus 136 passes Rua São Clemente, also 172, 178, from Zona Sul 511, 512, 522 (to Botafogo Metrô).* The museum houses 12,000 objects from many Brazilian indigenous groups. There is also a small, well-displayed handicraft shop.

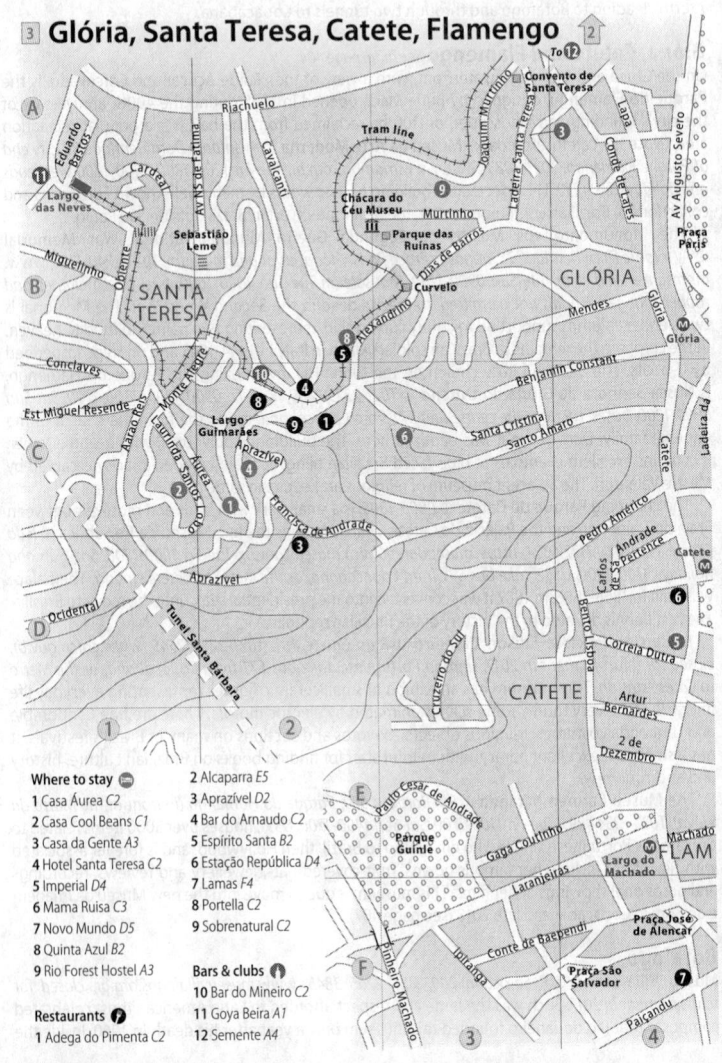

③ Glória, Santa Teresa, Catete, Flamengo

Where to stay
1 Casa Áurea *C2*
2 Casa Cool Beans *C1*
3 Casa da Gente *A3*
4 Hotel Santa Teresa *C2*
5 Imperial *D4*
6 Mama Ruisa *C3*
7 Novo Mundo *D5*
8 Quinta Azul *B2*
9 Rio Forest Hostel *A3*

2 Alcaparra *E5*
3 Aprazível *D2*
4 Bar do Arnaudo *C2*
5 Espírito Santa *B2*
6 Estação República *D4*
7 Lamas *F4*
8 Portella *C2*
9 Sobrenatural *C2*

Restaurants 🍴
1 Adega do Pimenta *C2*

Bars & clubs 🍸
10 Bar do Mineiro *C2*
11 Goya Beira *A1*
12 Semente *A4*

Pão de Açúcar (Sugar Loaf mountain)

The Pão de Açúcar, or Sugar Loaf, is a massive volcanic cone at the entrance to Guanabara Bay that soars to 396 m. Below it, halfway up the cable car ride, is the **Morro da Urca**, with the Abençoado restaurant (see page 415). You can get refreshments at the top. The sea-level cable car station is in a military area, so it is safe to visit. At Praia Vermelha, the beach to the south of the rock, is the Círculo Militar da Praia Vermelha restaurant. From here, the Pista Cláudio Coutinho runs part-way round the foot of the rock. It is a 1.2-km paved path for walking, jogging and access to climbing

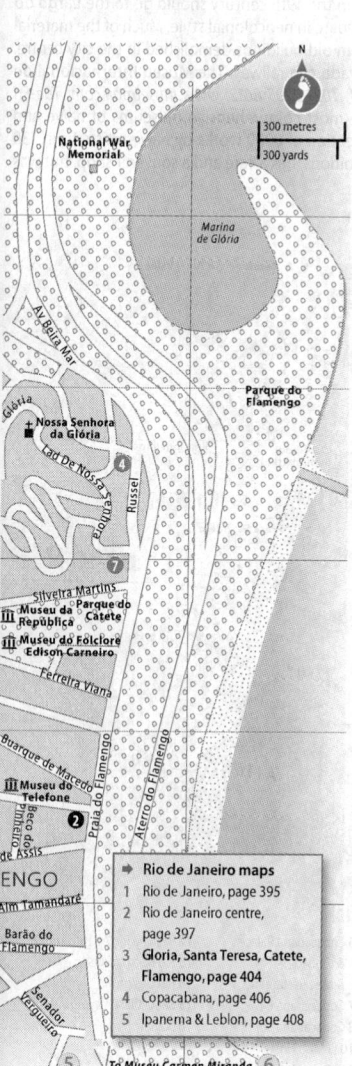

places. It is open 0700-1800. Here you have mountain, forest and sea side-by-side, right in the heart of the city. If you go early you may see marmosets and tanagers. You can also use the Pista Coutinho as a way of getting up the Pão de Açúcar more cheaply than the US$25 **cable car ride** ① *Av Pasteur 520, T021-2546 8400, www. bondinho.com.br, 0800-1950, last car down 2100, every 20 mins, ages 6-21 half price, under 6 free.* About 350 m from the path entrance is a track to the left, open 0800-1800, which leads though the forest (go left at the ridge) to Morro de Urca, from where the cable car can be taken (but tickets can only be bought at sea level). You can save money, but use more energy, by climbing the Caminho da Costa, the continuation of the Pista Coutinho, to the summit of the Pão de Açúcar. Only one stretch, of 10 m, requires climbing gear, but if you wait at the bottom of the path for a group going up, they will let you tag along. This way you can descend to Morro de Urca by cable car for free and walk down from there. See What to do, page 424, for climbing clubs; there is also a book on climbing routes. For getting there, see Transport, page 425.

☆Corcovado

Corcovado is a hunchbacked peak, 710 m high, surmounted by a 38-m-high statue of Christ the Redeemer, **O Cristo Redentor** ① *T021-2225 7036, https://cristoredentoroficial.com.br, daily 0800-1900,* which was completed in 1931. There is a superb view from the top (sometimes obscured by mist), to which there are a cog railway and road; taxis, official cooperative minivans and train put down their passengers behind the statue. Private cars are only allowed as far as Paineiras, from where you can catch train or cabs. See Transport, page 425, for full details of how to get there. The 3.8-km railway offers fine views. Average speed is 15 kph on

Tip...

There are 35 rock routes up the mountain, with various degrees of difficulty. The best months for climbing are April to August. Ask at the Tourist Office about permits to climb.

the way up and 12 kph on the way down. There is an exhibition of the history of the railway. From the upper terminus there is a system of escalators, one with a panoramic view, to the top, near which is a café (alternatively you can climb 220 steps up). To see the city by day and night ascend at 1500 or 1600 and descend on the last train, approximately 1815. Mass is held on Sunday in a small chapel in the statue pedestal. To reach the vast statue of Cristo Redentor at the summit of Corcovado, you have to go through Laranjeiras and Cosme Velho. The road through these districts heads west out of Catete.

Those who want to see what Rio was like early in the 19th century should go to the **Largo do Boticário** ① *R Cosme Velho 822*, a charming small square in neocolonial style. Much of the material used in creating the effect of the square came from old buildings demolished in the city centre. The square is close to the terminus for the Corcovado cog railway. The **Museu Internacional de Arte Naif do Brasil (MIAN)** ① *R Cosme Velho 561, T021-2205 8612, www.museunaif.com, Tue-Fri 1000-1800, Sat-Sun 1000-1700, US$5*, is one of the most comprehensive museums of naïve and folk paintings in the world with a permanent collection of 8000 works by naïve artists from 130 countries. The museum also hosts temporary exhibitions, has a café and a souvenir shop, but was closed owing to restricted funds in 2017.

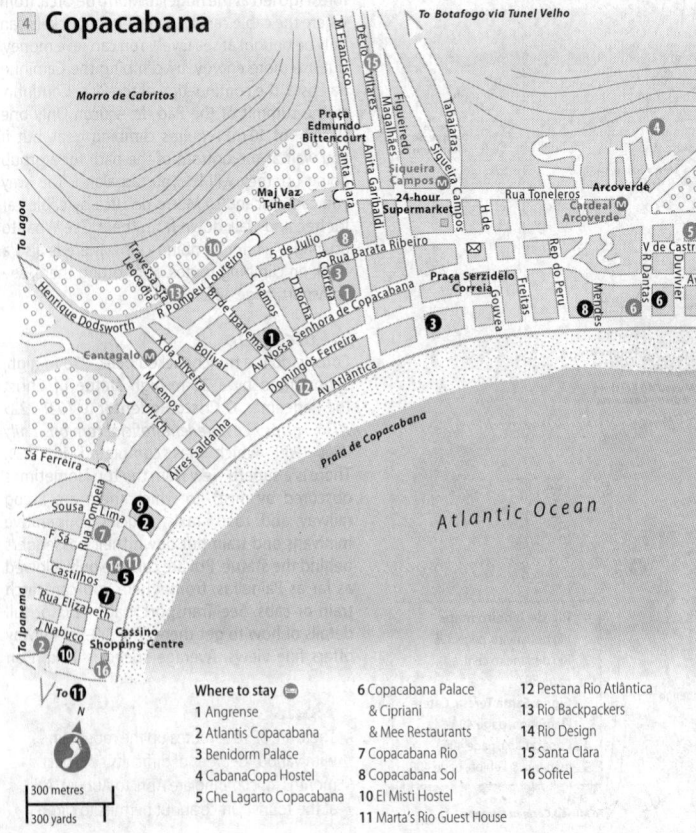

4 Copacabana

Where to stay
1 Angrense
2 Atlantis Copacabana
3 Benidorm Palace
4 CabanaCopa Hostel
5 Che Lagarto Copacabana
6 Copacabana Palace & Cipriani & Mee Restaurants
7 Copacabana Rio
8 Copacabana Sol
10 El Misti Hostel
11 Marta's Rio Guest House
12 Pestana Rio Atlântica
13 Rio Backpackers
14 Rio Design
15 Santa Clara
16 Sofitel

Copacabana

Tourist police patrol Copacabana beach until 1700.

Built on a narrow strip of land (only a little over 4 sq km) between mountain and sea, Copacabana has one of the highest population densities in the world: 62,000 per sq km, or 250,000 in all. Copacabana began to develop when the Túnel Velho (Old Tunnel) was built in 1891 and an electric tram service reached it. Weekend villas and bungalows sprang up; all have now gone. In the 1930s the **Copacabana Palace Hotel** was the only tall building; it is now one of the lowest on the beach. The opening of the Túnel Novo (New Tunnel) in the 1940s led to an explosion of population, which shows no sign of having spent its force. Unspoilt art deco blocks towards the Leme (city) end of Copacabana are now under preservation order.

After a brief period of decline, new beach cafés, paving and targeted policing have made the beach pleasant again and safer. While the water can be dirty when the currents wash shoreward, Copacabana and Leme are now as attractive places to relax in the sun as neighbouring Ipanema. And they're a good deal cheaper. The shops are mostly in Avenida Nossa Senhora de Copacabana and Rua Barata Ribeiro, but the more stylish shops remain in Ipanema, Leblon and in the various large shopping centres in the city. At the western (Arpoador) end of the beach, is **Museu Histórico do Exército e Forte de Copacabana** ① *Av Atlântica at Francisco Otaviano, T021-2521 1032, www.fortedecopacabana.com, Tue-Sun and bank holiday 1000-1800, US$1.90,* which charts the history of the army in Brazil. There are good views out over the beaches and a small restaurant. At the eastern (Leme) end of the beach is a fort offering superb views over the beach, **Forte Duque de Caxias** ① *Praça Almirante Julio de Noronha, T021-3223 5076, Tue-Sun 0930-1630, US$1.90.*

The world-famous beach is lined with modish little cafés where you can buy a fresh coconut, beer or coffee and is divided into numbered *postos*, where the lifeguards are based. They will advise on the water quality for swimming. Different sections attract different types of people, eg young people, artists and gays. See also Transport, page 425.

A striking new, state-of-the-art Music and Visual Arts museum, the **Museu da Imagem e do Som do Rio** ① *www.mis.rj.gov.br,* is due to open in Copacabana in late 2018. The building is by New York studio Diller Scofidio + Renfro who built the Boston ICA and the new MoMA expansion in New York and is a zig-zag of compressed and folded concrete platforms designed to echo the lines and waves of Copacabana's famous dragon's tooth pavements.

Ipanema and Leblon *See map, page 408.*

Beyond Copacabana are the seaside suburbs of Ipanema and Leblon. The two districts are divided by a canal from the Lagoa Rodrigo de Freitas to the sea, beside which is the Jardim de Alá. Ipanema and Leblon are a little less built-up than Copacabana, but they are more sophisticated. The sea is good for swimming. **Praia de Arpoadar** at the Copacabana end of

Restaurants ❼
1 Aipo and Aipim
2 Apetite Café
3 Cafeina
4 Cervantes
5 Chon Kou
6 Churrascaria Palace
7 Eclipse
8 La Tratoria
9 Nomangue
10 Siri Mole & Cia
11 TT Burgers

Ipanema is a peaceful spot to watch surfers, with the beautiful backdrop of Morro Dois Irmãos (on the slopes is **Vidigal favela**), which it's possible to climb, on a steep trail with **Jungle Me** (see page 424). A permanent cycle track runs all the way from the north end of Flamengo to Barra de Tijuca via Ipanema and Copacabana. The seaward lane of the road running beside the beach is closed to traffic until 1800 on Sundays and holidays; this makes it popular for rollerskating and cycling.

Lagoa, Jardim Botânico and Gávea

Backing Ipanema and Leblon are the residential districts of Lagoa and Jardim Botânico, beside the **Lagoa Rodrigo de Freitas**, a saltwater lagoon on which Rio's rowing and small-boat sailing clubs are active. The lake is too polluted for bathing, but parks and extensive leisure areas surround it. Avenida Epitácio Pessoa, on the eastern shore, leads to the Túnel Rebouças which runs beneath Corcovado and Cosme Velho.

Well worth a visit is the **Jardim Botânico** (Botanical Gardens) ① *T021-3874 1808, www.jbrj.gov.br, Mon 1200-1700, Tue-Sun 0800-1700, US$2.50*, 8 km from the centre (see Transport, page 425). These were founded in 1808. The most striking features are the transverse avenues of 30 m high royal palms. Among the more than 7000 varieties of plants from around the world are examples of the pau-brasil tree, now endangered, and many other threatened species. There is a herbarium, an aquarium, a library and a botanical museum. A new pavilion contains sculptures by Mestre Valentim transferred from the centre. Many improvements were carried out before the 1992 Earth Summit, including a new Orquidário and an enlarged bookshop.

The **Planetário** ① *Padre Leonel Franco 240, Gávea, T021-2274 0046, www.planetariodorio.com.br, office hours Mon-Fri 0900-1700, Sat-Sun 1430-1700; getting there: buses 176 and 178 from the centre,*

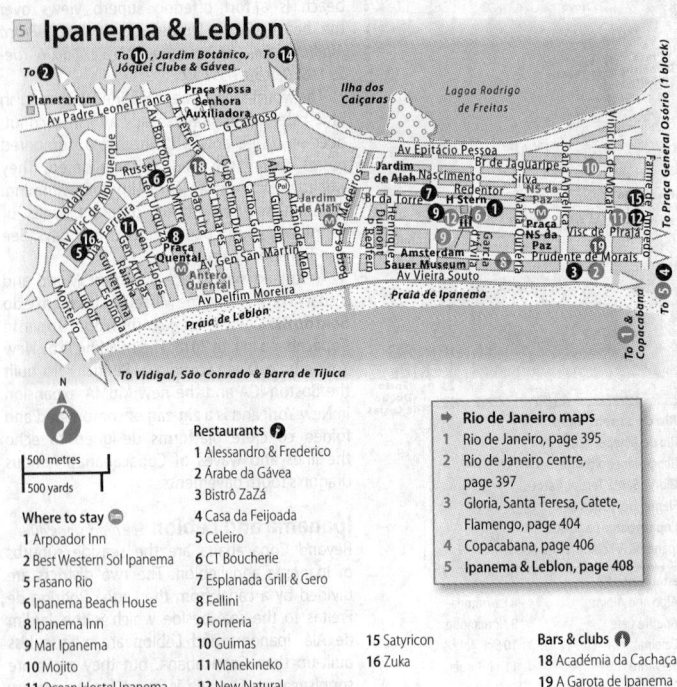

Ipanema & Leblon

Where to stay
1 Arpoador Inn
2 Best Western Sol Ipanema
5 Fasano Rio
6 Ipanema Beach House
8 Ipanema Inn
9 Mar Ipanema
10 Mojito
11 Ocean Hostel Ipanema
12 San Marco

Restaurants
1 Alessandro & Frederico
2 Árabe da Gávea
3 Bistrô ZaZá
4 Casa da Feijoada
5 Celeiro
6 CT Boucherie
7 Esplanada Grill & Gero
8 Fellini
9 Forneria
10 Guimas
11 Manekineko
12 New Natural
14 Roberta Sudbrack
15 Satyricon
16 Zuka

Bars & clubs
18 Académia da Cachaça
19 A Garota de Ipanema

➡ **Rio de Janeiro maps**
1 Rio de Janeiro, page 395
2 Rio de Janeiro centre, page 397
3 Gloria, Santa Teresa, Catete, Flamengo, page 404
4 Copacabana, page 406
5 Ipanema & Leblon, page 408

Flamengo, 591 and 592 from Copacabana. Inaugurated in 1979, the planetarium has a sculpture of the Earth and Moon by Mario Agostinelli. There are concerts and film shows.

The flat-topped **Pedra da Gávea** can be climbed or scrambled up for magnificent views (book with **Jungle Me** – see page 424), but beware of snakes. One part of the rock involves a short climb with a sheer drop below and is not suitable for those with a fear of heights. Behind the Pedra da Gávea is the Pedra Bonita. A road, the Estrada das Canoas, climbs up past these two rocks on its way to the Parque Nacional Tijuca. There is a spot on this road which is one of the chief hang-glider launch sites in the area (see page 423). On the slopes of the Pedra da Gávea is **Rocinha**, reportedly the largest favela in Rio. It was declared "pacified" in 2011, but there have been security problems since and the favela still faces health, sanitation and infrastructure problems. Tourism is one of many long-running initiatives here and property speculation is creeping in, although not at the rate of neighbouring Vidigal favela. The neighbourhood's website is www.rocinha.org. See also http://lifeinrocinha.blogspot.co.uk and for some tourist options, see Tour operators, page 424. See also Transport, page 425.

Southern suburbs

the parks provide a taster of what lies ahead

Leblon to São Conrado and Barra da Tijuca

From Leblon, two inland roads take traffic west to the outer seaside suburbs of São Conrado and Barra da Tijuca: the Auto Estrada Lagoa-Barra, which tunnels under Dois Irmãos, and the Rua Pacheco Leão, which goes through hills and forests of Tijuca national park (daytime only). A third route hugs the rocky coast on the spectacular Avenida Niemeyer, which passes the precipitously perched favela of Vidigal (and a small beach where the Sheraton is situated) and then reaches the upmarket, tranquil suburb of São Conrado and another magnificent ocean beach.

São Conrado

Metrô São Conrado Long an upmarket area, albeit backed by the giant **Rocinha** favela, São Conrado is now becoming an increasingly desirable alternative to Leblon and Ipanema as a beachside base. The metrô has made it easily accessible and Oscar Niemeyer's striking cylindrical **Hotel Nacional**, set in gardens by Burle Marx, reopened in late-2016.

Barra da Tijuca

Metrô Jardim Oceânico This rapidly developing residential area played host to the 2016 Olympics and is now one of the city's busiest suburbs and recreation areas, with 20-km of sandy beach and with good waves for surfing. At the westernmost end, towards the long stretch at Recreio dos Bandeirantes, Barra gets wilder with a series of beautiful surf beaches: Praia do Pontal, fronted by a small island, the Pedra do Pontal, Prainha, nesteld between two forested capes (with trails leading from behind the beach through a protected area to a spectacular viewpoint) and the long, wild beach at Grumari where the ocean can be very rough. The channels behind the Barra and Recreio are popular with jetskiers. It gets very busy on Sundays. There are innumerable bars and restaurants, clustered at both ends, campsites, motels and hotels: budget accommodation tends to be self-catering. The Metrô reaches Barra's northern end. Buses run further, to Receiro and Pontal. Reaching areas beyond is best by car. The **Museu Casa do Pontal** ① *Estrada do Pontal 3295, Recreio dos Bandeirantes, T021-2490 4013, www.museucasadopontal.com.br, Tue-Sun 0930-1700, US$4 (no photography),* with a collection of Brazilian folk art lies inland between Pontal and Prainha beaches. Recommended.

Parque Nacional da Tijuca

Entry US$12.50 (US$9 low season). Open 0800-1700, 1800 in summer. National park information, T021-2491 1700, www.parquedatijuca.com.br. See also www.amigosdoparque.org.br and Transport, page 425.

The Pico da Tijuca (1022 m) gives a good idea of the tropical vegetation of the interior and a fine view of the bay and its shipping. A two- to three-hour walk leads to the summit and back (easily done on a tour with Jungle Me – see page 424): on entering the park at Alto da Boa Vista

(0600-2100), follow the signposts (maps are displayed) to Bom Retiro, a good picnic place (1½ hours' walk). At Bom Retiro the road ends and there is another hour's walk up a fair footpath to the summit (take the path from the right of the Bom Retiro drinking fountain; not the more obvious steps from the left). The last part consists of steps carved out of the solid rock; look after children at the summit as there are several sheer drops, invisible because of bushes. The route is shady for almost its entire length. The main path to Bom Retiro passes the Cascatinha Taunay (a 30-m waterfall) and the Mayrink Chapel (built 1860). Beyond the Chapel is the restaurant Os Esquilos. Other places of interest not passed on the walk to the peak are the Paulo e Virginia Grotto, the Vista do Almirante and the Mesa do Imperador (viewpoints). Allow at least five to six hours for the excursion. Maps of the park are available; walking is safest at weekends and holidays. If hiking in the national park other than on the main paths, a guide may be useful if you do not want to get lost: a list of registered guides is available at the **Visitors Centre** ① *T021-2492 2252/2492 2253, open 0900-1700.*

Parque Estadual da Pedra Branca ① *Núcleo Camorim, Camorim, Jacarepaguá, T021-3417 3642, www.inea.rj.gov.br, Tue-Sun 0800-1700, website gives details of other entrances,* the largest urban forest in the world, is also in Rio, though few Cariocas are aware of it. Pedra Branca is the city's best kept natural secret, protecting an astounding 12,500 ha of pristine rainforest, lakes and mountains, which are home to over 500 animal species. A number are threatened or critically endangered. There are many trails in the park, including one leading to the highest peak in Rio de Janeiro, the Pedra Branca (1024 m), but they are very poorly maintained.

Listings Rio de Janeiro maps p395, p397, p404, p406 and p408

Tourist information

Riotur
Praça Pio X, 119, 9th floor, Centro, T021-2976 7301, visit.rioand www.rio.rj.gov.br/riotur.
The city's government tourist office. There are also booths or offices in **Copacabana** (Av Princesa Isabel 183, T021-2541 7522, Mon-Fri 0900-1800), and **Copacabana Quiosque 15** (Av Atlântica opposite R Hilário Gouveia, daily 0800-2000). The helpful staff speak English, French and German and have good city maps and a useful free brochure. There are information stands at the international airport, Terminals 1 and 2, and Novo Rio bus station. There is also a free telephone information service, *Alô Rio*, in Portuguese and English, T021-2542 8004 or T021-2542 8080.

The state tourism organization is **Turisrio** (R do Acre 30, Centro, T021-2334 6153, www. cidadesmaravilhosas.rj.gov.br, Mon-Fri 0900-1800). The private sector **Rio Convention and Visitors Bureau** (R Guilhermina Guinle 272, 6th floor, T021-2266 9750, www.rcvb.com.br), also offers information and assistance in English. *Trilhas do Rio*, by Pedro da Cunha e Menezes

(Editora Salamandra), US$30, describes walking trips around Rio. The guide *Restaurantes do Rio*, by Danusia Bárbara, published annually, is worth looking at for the latest ideas on where to eat in both the city and state of Rio. Many hotels provide guests with the quarterly *Guia do Rio*.

Student Travel Bureau
Av Nilo Peçanha 50, sala 3103, Centro, T021-3526 7700, and R Visconde de Pirajá 550, lj 201, Ipanema, T021-2512 8577, www.stb.com.br (offices throughout Brazil).
Has details of discounts and cultural exchanges for ISIC holders. See also Tours, page 424.

Where to stay

The best places to stay in Rio are Santa Teresa, for nightlife, culture and easy access to Lapa, the Sambódromo and carnival; Copacabana, Ipanema, Leblon, Sâo Conrado and the Arpoador for the beach. Ipanema is probably the safest area in the city. Backpackers are well catered for, with hostels opening all the time. Hostelling sites (www.hostels.com, www.hostelworld.com) list the latest options. Economy hotels, however, are usually dubious establishments in equally dubious areas. Guest houses and B&Bs are a better-value and better-run option, even for those on a medium budget. Self-catering apartments are available at all levels and are a popular form of accommodation; see below.

Tip...
Reserve well in advance at New Year and Carnaval because prices rise astronomically.

Homestays

$$$$-$$ Cama e Café
R Laurinda Santos Lobo 124, T021-2225 4366 (T021-99638 4850, 24 hrs), www.camaecafe.com.br.
One of the best accommodation options in Rio with a range of some 50 homestays in Santa Teresa, Cosme Velho and Ipanema from the simple to the luxurious. They provide the opportunity to get to know locals and see Rio from the inside. Rooms can be treated as impersonally as those in a hotel, or guests can fit in as part of the household; good value. Cama e Café work hard to match guests with hosts who share similar interests.

Santa Teresa
Santa Teresa is hilly and offers views out over Rio but is inconvenient for transport and is nothing like as safe as the beach neighbourhoods. Boutique hotels range from the $$$$ Hotel Santa Teresa (R Almte Alexandrino 660, T021-3380 0200, www.santa-teresa-hotel.com), French-owned, chic and exclusive 5-star, restaurant and spa behind high walls, and Mama Ruisa (R Santa Cristina 132, T021-2508 8142, www.mamaruisa.com), also French-run, simple, elegant.

$$$ Casa Áurea
R Áurea 80, Santa Teresa, T021-2242 5830, www.casaaurea.com.br.
Small hotel in a converted colonial house. Rooms are bright and airy and service attentive. Breakfast is served in a little garden visited by marmosets in the mornings.

$$$ Casa Cool Beans
R Laurinda Santos Lobo 136, T021-2262 0552, www.casacoolbeans.com, with another branch in Ipanema.
In a large Santa Teresa town house on a quiet back street, decorated with art and graffiti by local artists, with a small pool, spacious wood-floored rooms and a generous breakfast, American-run. No infants.

$$$-$$ Quinta Azul
R Almirante Alexandrino 256, T021-3253 1021, www.quintaazul.com.
Cosy little boutique hotel with sweeping views from the upper rooms, well situated, small pool.

$$ Casa da Gente
R Gonçalves Fontes 33, www.casadagente.com.
French/Brazilian-run, inspired by fair trade and sustainability principles, excellent accommodation, double and shared rooms

($$), helpful staff, convenient location, nice atmosphere, good value.

$$ Rio Forest Hostel
R Joaquim Murtinho 517, T021-3563 1020, www.rioforesthostel.com.br.
Bright, airy hostel with dorms and rooms with a view ($$ double). Decent showers, welcoming.

Glória, Catete and Flamengo
These are mainly residential areas between the centre and Copacabana. Catete, and Glória to the north and Flamengo to the south, lie next to a park landscaped by Burle Marx and a beautiful beach lapped by a filthy sea. They have good bus and Metrô links.

$$$ Novo Mundo
Praia Flamengo 20, Catete, T021-2105 7000, www.hotelnovomundo.com.br.
Renovated 4-star rooms with some 3-star fittings, suites with balcony views of the Sugar Loaf, a good business choice.

$$ Imperial
R do Catete 186, T021-2112 6000, Catete, www.imperialhotel.com.br.
One of the city's very first grand hotels (late 19th century). Rooms either in the grander main building, or the modern annexe (US motel-style), better equipped but overlooking the parking lot.

Botafogo
Another middle-class neighbourhood with a great beach lapped by dirty water. Convenient for public transport and mall shopping but care should be taken at night.

$$$ O Veleiro
R Mundo Novo 1440, Praia de Botafogo, T021-2554 8980, www.oveleiro.com.
B&B with a great breakfast, Canadian/Carioca-owned, transfers to/from airport or bus station, tours, guiding, helpful staff. Recommended.

$$$ Yoo2
R Praia de Botafogo 242, T021-3445 2000, www.yoo2.com.
Stylish boutique hotel with furniture by Philippe Starck, a beautiful rooftop bar and pool area and views of Pão de Azucar from the seafront rooms (choose floor 12 or above). Opened in 2016.

$$-$ pp Alpha Hostel
R Praia de Botafogo 462, casa 3, T021-2286 7799, www.alphahostel.com.
Hostel with private rooms and cheaper dorms, breakfast, tours, airport and bus terminal transfer.

$$-$ pp El Misti Hostel
R Praia de Botafogo 462, casa 9, T021-3269 4983,
www.elmistihostelrio.com.
Converted colonial house with dorms, shared
bath, private rooms with shared bath ($$),
capoeira classes, tour service. Popular with
party-goers. Convenient for public transport.
Free pick-up for all bookings. Has other branches
in Copacabana and around Brazil.

Copacabana

$$$$ Copacabana Palace
Av Atlântica 1702, T021-2548 7070,
www.belmond.com.
Justifiably world famous hotel with distinguished
guest list, dripping in 1920s elegance, superb
facilities and effortless service. Go for cocktails
and dinner if you can't afford to stay. **Cipriani**
and the new Michelin-starred Asian restaurant
Mee ($$$) are 2 of the best restaurants for formal
evening dining in Rio.

$$$$ Pestana Rio Atlântica
Av Atlântica 2964, T021-2548 6332,
www.pestana.com.
Part of the Portuguese Pestana group, an
excellent choice, spacious bright rooms and a
rooftop pool and terrace with sweeping views,
very high standards. Recommended.

$$$$ Rio Design
R Francisco Sá 17, T021-3222 8800,
www.riodesignhotel.com.
Comfortable mock-boutique suites in a great
location at the Arpoador end of Copacabana.
Decent breakfast with a view on the top floor,
small spa. Good service.

$$$$ Sofitel
Av Atlântica, 4240, T021-2525 1232,
www.sofitel.com.
One of the best beachfront options, at the safer
Arpoadoar end, an easy walk to Ipanema. Airy
rooms (best on the upper floors), sauna, pool and
Le Pré Catelan French restaurant, with one of the
best kitchens in the city.

$$$ Angrense
Travessa Angrense 25, T021-2548 0509,
www.angrensehotel.com.br.
Well-kept rooms in a little art deco block on a
quiet street, English-speaking staff, reliable tour
agency and good carnival rates.

$$$ Atlantis Copacabana
Av Bulhões de Carvalho 61, T021-2521 1142,
www.atlantishotel.com.br.
In a quiet, safe street close to the beach in
Arpoador. Small rooftop pool, sauna, good value.

$$$ Benidorm Palace
R Barata Ribeiro 547, T021-2548 8880,
www.benidorm.com.br.
Modern rooms decked out in light wood
in a tower, best and quietest at the back with
small marble bathrooms. Sauna and internet
in the lobby.

$$$ Copacabana Rio
Av N S de Copacabana 1256, T021-2267 9900,
www.copacabanariohotel.com.
Quiet, efficiently run 1970s tower with simple
but well-maintained 3-star rooms, small pool
and generous breakfasts. Safe area at Ipanema
end of beach, 1 block from the sand.

$$$ Copacabana Sol
R Santa Clara 141, T021-2549 4577,
www.copacabanasolhotel.com.br.
Safe, helpful, quiet, with good breakfast.

$$$ Marta's Rio Guest House
R Francisco Sá 5, T021-2521 8568,
www.martarioguesthouse.com.
Small, tidy rooms in a penthouse flat in a 1960s
Copacabana beach front apartment block. The
views from the shared living room are fabulous
and the warm and welcoming owner Marta is a
real Carioca character.

$$ Santa Clara
R Décio Vilares, 316, T021-2256 2650,
www.hotelsantaclara.com.br.
Quiet, central location, attentive service,
tours arranged.

$ pp Cabana Copa Hostel
Travessa Guimarães Natal 12, T021-3988 9912,
www.cabanacopa.com.br.
Dorms of various sizes, including one for
women only, a/c, also private rooms ($$),
tours, good reputation.

$ pp Che Lagarto Copacabana
R Barata Ribeiro 111, T021-3209 0348,
www.chelagarto.com.
Several dorms and doubles ($$). Helpful, young
party atmosphere, several languages spoken,
organizes tours, bar. 2 other Copacabana
branches and 1 nearby in Ipanema.

$ pp El Misti Hostel
Travessa Frederico Pamplona 20, T021-98485
5138, www.elmisti copacabana.com.
500 m from Copacabana beach, 200 m from
metro and buses. Dorms and doubles ($$$).

our services, open bar, meals. Free pick-up
or all bookings.

pp Rio Backpackers
*av Santa Leocádia 38 (just off
Rompeu Loureiro), T021-2236 3803,
www.riobackpackers.com.br.*
orms and private rooms (**$$**) with fan or a/c,
4-hr security, laundry, free bikes, tours and
ther services.

anema, Leblon and further west

$$$ Best Western Sol Ipanema
*v Vieira Souto 320, T021-2525 2020,
ww.bestwestern.com.*
uge breakfast, good member of
S chain, popular.

$$$ Fasano Rio
*v Vieira Souto 80, Ipanema, T021-3202 4000,
www.fasano.com.br.*
hillippe Starck-designed luxury hotel with
oftop terrace, fitness centre, etc, good bar
nd superior restaurant, **Fasano Al Mare**.

$$$ La Maison
*Sergio Porto 58, Gávea, T021-3205 3585,
www.lamaisonario.com.*
a period town house on a quiet backstreet.
ight spacious rooms tastefully decorated in
imary colours, wonderful views of Corcovado
om the open-sided breakfast area and the little
ool. The beach is a taxi ride away.

$$$ La Suite
*Jackson de Figueiredo 501, Joá, T021-3259 6123,
ww.lasuiterio.com.*
stinguished boutique hotel with 8 individually
emed rooms in a wealthy suburb between
blon and Barra da Tijuca. Fabulous location –
e pool sits eyrie-like over the exclusive beach
Joá with sweeping views out towards São
nrado. Every room has a terrace, view and a
arble bathroom.

$ Arpoador Inn
*ancisco Otaviano 177, T021-2529 1000,
ww.arpoadorinn.com.br.*
ell-maintained. Seafront restaurant **Azul
arinho**, off-season special offers are a good deal.

$ Ipanema Inn
*aria Quitéria 27, behind Caesar Park,
21-2529 1000, www.ipanemainn.com.br.*
opular package tour and small business
tel less than 100 m from beach. Good value
d location.

$$$ Mar Ipanema
*R Visconde de Pirajá 539, T021-3875 9191,
www.maripanema.com.*
1 block from the beach, simple, smart,
modern rooms.

$$ San Marco
*R Visconde de Pirajá 524, T021-2540 5032,
www.sanmarcohotelipanema.com.br.*
2-star hotel 2 blocks from beach, with simple
rooms and a free caipirinha for every internet
booking, very helpful. Recommended.

$$-$ Ipanema Beach House
*R Barão da Torre 485, T021-3202 2693,
www.ipanemahouse.com.*
Dorms (US$15) and doubles (**$$**) all with shared
baths. Great little hostel with rooms arranged
around a garden and small pool. Small bar,
kitchen, internet and tours, good service.

$$-$ Mojito
*R Barão de Jaguaripe 11, T021-3251 9194,
http://mojitohostels.com.*
One of several well-kept Mojito hostels in
Ipanema and Copacabana, in a building 2 blocks
from the Lagoa and 4 from the beach, a/c rooms
are pocket-sized and plain with little natural light,
includes breakfast.

$$-$ Ocean Hostel Ipanema
*R Barão da Torre 175, casa 15, T021-3796 0478,
http://oceanhostelipanema.com.*
Small, recently-renovated hostel with 2 private
rooms for up to 4 people and a very cheap 10-
bed dorm. Excellent location close to Ipanema
and Copacabana beaches, decent facilities and
24-hr reception.

São Conrado, Barra da Tijuca and beyond

$$$$ Nacional
*Av Niemeyer 769, São Conrado, T021-3094 4900,
www.melia.com.*
Newly opened in late 2016 this historic hotel in a
Niem eyer-designed cylinder sits over Burle Marx
gardens and the beach and offers the best-value
luxury rooms in the city. Stunning pool, excellent
restaurant, spa and 24-hr room service.

$$-$ Rio Surf n Stay
*R Raimundo Veras 1140, Recreio dos
Bandeirantes, T021-3418 1133,
www.riosurfnstay.com.*
Hostel and surf camp with dorms and private
rooms, camping, surf lessons, equipment rental.

Self-catering apartments

Renting a small flat, or sharing a larger one, can be much better value than a hotel room. All price levels are available. Copacabana, Ipanema and Leblon prices range from about US$25 a day for a simple studio (US$500-600 a month) up to US$2000 a month for a luxurious residence sleeping 4-6. Always get a written agreement when renting and check the building's (usually excellent) security arrangements.

See websites including www.alugue temporada.com.br, www.riotemporada.net and www.vivareal.com.br for more details. Also adverts in *Balcão*, twice weekly, *O Globo* or *Jornal do Brasil* (daily); under 'Apartamentos – Temporada'; advertisements are classified by district and size of apartment: *vagas e quartos* means shared accommodation; *conjugado* (or *conj*) is a studio with limited cooking facilities; *3 Quartos* is a 3-bedroom flat.

Copacabana Holiday
R Barata Ribeiro 90A, Copacabana, T021-2542 1525, www.copacabanaholiday.com.br.
Recommended, well-equipped apartments from studios to 4-bedroom and penthouses, studios from US$30 per day, 2-bedrooms from US$75, with a variety of prices and locations.

Fantastic Rio
Av Atlântica 974, Suite 501, Copacabana, T021-3507 7941, http://fantasticrio.br.tripod.com.
All types of furnished accommodation, studios from US$55 per day, 2-bedrooms from US$100, owned by Peter Corr, good service.

Restaurants

Expect to pay US$30-40+ pp in the better restaurants. You can eat well for an average US$5 pp, less if you choose the *prato feito* at lunchtime (US$2-7.50), or eat in a place that serves food by weight (about US$10 per kg).

Galetos are lunch counters specializing in chicken and grilled meat, very reasonable. In the shopping centres there is usually a variety of restaurants and snack bars grouped around a central plaza where you can shop around for a good meal. Rio lacks that almost ubiquitous Brazilian institution, the corner bakery, and a decent breakfast can be hard to find. But there are plenty of stand-up juice bars serving fruit juices made from as many as 25 different fruits, all of which are wonderful.

Tip...
The best of Rio's many restaurants are in Copacabana, Ipanema or Leblon.

City centre and Lapa

Many restaurants in the business district are open only for weekday lunch. Many *lanchonetes* in this area offer good, cheap meals. **Travessa do Comércio** has many informal street restaurant after 1800, especially on Fri. **R Miguel Couto** (opposite Santa Rita church) is called the **Beco das Sardinhas** because on Wed and Fri in particular it is full of people eating sardines and drinking beer. There are several Arab restaurants on Av Senhor dos Passos, which are also open Sat and Sun. In addition to those listed there are plenty of cafes, including a few new chic options on R Lavradio in Lapa, where the lively Sat antiques market is held.

$$$ Adega Flor de Coimbra
R Teotônio Regadas 34, Lapa, T021-2224 4582, adegaflordecoimbra.com.br.
Founded in 1938, Portuguese food and wines, speciality *bacalhau* (salt cod). Very good.

$$$ Ancoramar
Praça Marechal Âncora 184-6, T021-2240 8378, http://ancoramar.com.br. Open 1200-2200, Sun 1200-1700.
Popular, long-established fish and seafood, with lovely views of the bay. Formerly Albamar.

$$$ Eça
Av Rio Branco 128 (H Stern building), T021-2524 2300.
The best business lunch in the centre, classic French cooking with worldwide influences from chef Frédéric de Maeyer.

$$$ Republique
Praça da República 63 (2nd floor), T021-2532 9000.
Designed by architect Chicô Gouveia. Chef Paulo Carvalho cooks Portuguese, Italian and French dishes.

$$ Bar Luiz
R da Crioca 39, T021-2262 6900, http://barluiz.com.br.
A little bar in a colonial house in the centre, famous as much for its clientèle as its tapas and *chope* in the evening, good for a quiet snack lunch, too.

$ Café da Moda
Gonçalves Dias 49, 3rd floor, Centro,
021-2222 0610, www.folic.com.br.
n a/c café devoted to the narrow waistline,
cated in the **Folic** shop. Salads are named
ter famous models, or have more macho
ames for men. Light meals without hip names
so available.

$-$ Bistro do Paço
aça 15 de Novembro 48 (Paço Imperial),
2262 3613, www.bistro.com.br.
alads, sandwiches and light meals in a neat,
eaceful café in the former Imperial Palace.

$-$ Confeitaria Colombo
Gonçalves Dias 32, near Carioca Metrô station,
021-2505 1500, www.confeitariacolombo.
m.br. Open 0900-1800.
ecommended for atmosphere and the only one
its kind in Rio. Over 100 years old, it has the
iginal belle époque decor, no service charge
tip the excellent waiters. Has a branch in
opacabana fort, albeit witout the art deco décor.

Sabor Saúde
da Quitanda 21, T021-2157 0097,
tp://saborsaude.com.br.
eakfast and lunch only, vegetarian and
holefood dishes and sandwiches, also light
eals (not always vegetarian).

anta Teresa

$ Aprazível
Aprazível 62, T021-2508 9174,
tp://aprazivel.com.br.
cent but unspectacular Brazilian dishes and
afood with tables outdoors in a tropical garden
erlooking Guanabara Bay. This is a good Sun
nch spot when they have Choro and Samba
rformed by Rio's equivalent of the Buena Vista
cial Club.

Adega do Pimenta
lmte Alexandrino 296, T021-2224 7554,
p://adegadopimenta.com.br. Daily 1130-2200,
n 1100-1800, closed Sat, Tue.
ery small German restaurant in the Largo do
imarães with excellent sausages, sauerkraut
d cold beer.

Bar do Arnaudo
rgo do Guimarães, R Almte Alexandrino 316,
1-2252 7246.
modest-looking restaurant decorated with
adicrafts but serving generous portions of
nderful Northeast Brazilian cooking.

$$ Espírito Santa
R Almte Alexandrino 264, T021-2507 4840,
www.espiritosanta.com.br. Closed Mon,
lunch only Tue, Wed, Sun.
Upstairs is a chic Mediterranean restaurant with a
wonderful sweeping view of the city, downstairs
is a weekend basement club, good cocktails.

$$ Portella
R Paschoal Carlos Magno 139, Largo do Guimarães,
T021-2507 5181, www.portellabar.com.br.
São Paulo-style corner restaurant-bar with good
picanha steaks, award-winning *petiscos* (bar
snacks). Live music most weekends.

$$ Sobrenatural
R Almirante Alexandrino 432, T021-2224
1003, www.restaurantesobrenatural.com.br.
Open lunch and evening, closed Mon.
A charming rustic restaurant serving fish caught
daily on owner's boat. For a light lunch, order a
mix of excellent appetizers. Recommended.

Glória, Catete and Flamengo
There are many cheap and mid-range eating
places on R do Catete.

$$$ Alcaparra
Praia do Flamengo 144, Flamengo,
T021-2557 7236.
Elegant traditional Italian popular with politicians
and business people. Overlooking the sea.

$$ Lamas
Marquês de Abrantes 18A, Flamengo,
T021-2556 0799.
Steak, seafood and general Brazilian fare have
been served here for over 130 years. Excellent
value, great atmosphere, opens late, popular
with Brazilian arts/media people. Recommended.

$ Estação República
R do Catete 104, Catete, in the Palácio do Catete.
More than 40 dishes in this per kilo restaurant,
soups, sushi, salads and stews.

Botafogo
In Baixo Botafogo, those on a budget will find
a number of simple but good-value places on
R Praia Botafogo, including **Mate Mate** and
Catarina Lancheria (No 122).

$$$ Abençoado
On the summit of Morro de Urca, T021-2275 8925,
www.abencoadorio.com.br.
For Brazilian comfort snacks given a
gourmet twist, caipirinhas and *batidas*
and breathtaking views.

$$$ Cota 2000
Morro de Urca s/n, T021-2543 8200, www.cota200 restaurante.com.br. Daily and for evening Sun-Tue, booking essential.
This newly opened gourmet Brazilian restaurant is next to Abencoado, but specializes in dinner, with the same privileged view. Book for an early dinner with sunset cocktails; the restaurant closes at 2000 in time for the last cable car down at 2100.

$$$ Lasai
R Conde de Irajá 191, Botafogo, T021 3449 1834, http://lasai.com.br.
Michelin-starred cooking from newcomer Rafa Costa e Silva, who learnt his chops at Mugaritz in Spain. His inspired European-Brazilian fusion cooking is as beautifully presented as it is inventive. 2 degustation menus only, 1 short, 1 long. Reservations essential.

$$$ Miam Miam
Gen Goes Monteiro 34, T021-2244 0125, www.miammiam.com.br. Closed Mon.
Retro chic and highly fashionable, where the alternative fashion set go for cocktails and light Mediterranean food.

$$$ Oui Oui
R Conde de Irajá 85, Botafogo, T021-2527 3539, www.restauranteouioui.com.br.
Equally fashionable, for tapas-style *petiscos* and cocktails.

Copacabana, Ipanema and Leblon

$$$$ Esplanada Grill
R Barão de Torre 600, Ipanema, T021-2239 6028, www.esplanadagrill.com.br.
Formal atmosphere for the best steak and other cuts of meat in Rio.

$$$ Alessandro & Frederico
R Garcia D'Avila, 134 loja D, Ipanema, T021-2521 0828, www.alessandroefrederico.com.br.
Upmarket café with decent café latte and breakfasts.

$$$ Bistrô ZaZá
R Joana Angélica 40, Ipanema, www.zazabistro.com.br.
Hippy-chic, pseudo Moroccan/French restaurant, good fish dishes and cocktails and good fun. Evenings are best for intimate dining when the tables are lit by candles.

$$$ CT Boucherie
R Dias Ferreira 636, Leblon, T021-2543 1050, www.ctboucherie.com.br.

Elegant, unpretentious meat restaurant, with a focus on the superb cuts of meat, accompanied by sauces of choice and delectable side dishes.

$$$ Forneria
R Aníbal de Mendonça 112, Ipanema, T021-2540 8045, http://forneria.com.br.
Serves superior bar snacks and supreme burgers in pizza dough to the elegant, after-beach crow

$$$ Gero
R Aníbal de Mendonça 157, Ipanema, T021-2241 0050, www.fasano.com.br.
Light Italian fare and excellent fish in a beautiful, minimalist space.

$$$ Manekineko
R Dias Ferreira, 410, Leblon, T021-2540 7641, www.manekineko.com.br.
Exquisite Japanese and Japanese fusion cooking served in an intimately designed modern dining room.

$$$ Nomangue
R Sá Ferreira 25, lj B, Copacabana, T021-2521 32: www.nomangue.com.br.
Excellent northeast Brazilian and seafood.

$$$ Satyricon
R Barão da Torre 192, Ipanema, T021-2521 0627, www.satyricon.com.br.
The best seafood in Rio; especially the squid. Lively crowd in a large dining room. Avoid Sat when there is a seafood buffet.

$$$ Siri Mole & Cia
R Francisco Otaviano 90, T021-2267 0894, http://sirimole.com.br.
Good Bahian seafood and Italian coffee in elegant a/c. At the upper end of this price bracket.

$$$ Zuka
R Dias Ferreira 233, Leblon, T021-3205 7154, www.zuka.com.br.
One of the most fashionable restaurants in Rio with an eclectic fusion of everything – French and Japanese, American fast food and Italian.

$$$-$$ Churrascaria Palace
R Rodolfo Dantas 16B, Copacabana, T021-2541 5898, http://churrascariapalace.com.br.
20 different kinds of barbecued meat served on a spit at your table with buffet salads to accompany. One of the best churrascarias in the city. Good value.

$$-$$ TT Burgers
Francisco Otaviano 67, Arpoador,
021-2227 1192.
This hugely popular upmarket streetside burger
bar sitting behind the Arpoador in a modish row
of surf shops, bars (the best is Informalizinho) and
cafés is said to serve the best burgers in Rio. It is
owned and run by the son of Michelin-starred
chef Claude Troigros.

$ Casa da Feijoada
Prudente de Morais 10, Ipanema, T021-2247 2776.
Serves an excellent *feijoada* all week.
Generous portions.

$ Celeiro
Dias Ferreira 199, Leblon, T021-2274 7843,
http://celeiroculinaria.com.br.
Some of the best salads in the city, and light food
by weight.

$ Chon Kou
Av Atlântica 3880, T021-2287 3956.
A traditional Chinese restaurant which also offers
an extensive sushi menu, a/c; sit upstairs for good
views over Copacabana beach.

$ Fellini
General Urquiza 104, Leblon, T021-2511 3600,
http://fellini.com.br.
The best per kilo in the city with delicious buffet
options and plenty for vegetarians.

$ New Natural
Barão da Torre 173, T021-2287 0301.
One of Ipanema's most popular vegetarian and
wholefood restaurants, large range of hot dishes
and desserts served per kilo. Home delivery.
Natural products shop next door.

$-$ Aipo and Aipim
Av Nossa Senhora de Copacabana 391b and 920,
Copacabana, and R Visconde de Pirajá 145, Ipanema,
021-2267 8313, http://aipoeaipim.com.br.
Popular chain, plentiful tasty food sold by weight.

$-$ Eclipse
Av N S de Copacabana 1309, T021-2287 1788,
http://bareclipse.com.br.
Spruce, well-run and very popular 24-hr
restaurant offering good-value *prato feito* lunches
and a generous range of meats, pastas, snacks
and sandwiches served in the cool interior or on
streetside tables.

Apetite Café
Souza Lima 78, T021-2247 3319.

One of Copa's few bakery cafes. Offers a range of
breakfasts, respectable coffee, snacks, options for
kids and an a/c interior for when it gets too hot.

$ Cafeina
C Ramos 44, T021-2547 8651.
Very popular breakfast spot with good coffee,
tasty pastries and other snacks and ice cold juices

$ Cervantes
Barata Ribeiro 07-B e Prado Júnior 335B,
Copacabana, T021-2275 6147, http://
restaurantecervantes.com.br.
Stand-up bar or sit-down, a/c restaurant, open
all night, queues after 2200. Said to serve the
best sandwiches in town, a local institution.
Has 2 other branches.

$ La Tratoria
R Fernando Mendes 7A, Copacabana,
opposite Hotel Excelsior, T021-2255 3319,
http://latrattoriario.com.br.
Italian, good food and service, very reasonable.
Recommended.

Gávea, Lagoa and Jardim Botânico
Gávea is the heartland of trendy 20-something
Rio, while Jardim Botânico and Lagoa appear, at
first sight, to offer no end of exciting upmarket
dining opportunities. They're mostly all show
and poor value. Here are a few exceptions:

$$$ Roberta Sudbrack
Av Lineu de Paula Machado 916,
Jardim Botânico, T021-3874 0139,
http://robertasudbrack.com.br.
Celebrated for her European-Brazilian fusion
cooking, Roberta was the private chef for
President Henrique Cardoso.

$$ Árabe da Gávea
Gávea shopping mall, R Marquês de São Vicente
52, T021-2294 3538, www.oarabedagavea.com.
By far the best Arabic restaurant in Rio.

$$ Guimas
R José Roberto Macedo Soares 5,
Baixo Gávea, T021-2259 7996,
http://restauranteguimas.com.br.
One of the places where the under 30s come to
be seen, especially after 2200 towards the end
of the week and on Mon, before moving down
the street to the 2 tatty bars on the corner of the
street and Praça Santos Dumont. The restaurant
serves simple, traditional Portuguese food, at
only a handful of tables.

Bars and clubs

Rio nightlife caters for all ages – from dance clubs for young and vivacious to more sedentary Bossa Nova bars in Copacabana. The current hotspots are **Lapa** at weekends, with a string of clubs along Mem de Sá, Lavradio and the Beco do Rato, with dance steps from samba and *forró* to techno and hip hop. **Santa Teresa** is increasingly lively and is often used as a drinking spot before moving onto Lapa, or a night spot in its own. There is a cluster of bars around the Largo das Neves. Similarly busy, even on Sun and Mon is **Baixa Gávea**, where beautiful 20-somethings gather around Praça Santos Dumont. In **Ipanema/Leblon**, there is always activity in and around Av General San Martin and Rua Dias Ferreira.

Bars

Wherever you are, there's one near you. Beer costs around US$3.50 for a large bottle, but up to US$7 in the plusher bars; where you are often given an entrance card which includes 2 drinks and a token entrance fee. A cover charge of US$3-7 may be made for live music, or there might be a minimum consumption charge of around US$3, sometimes both. Snack food is always available. Copacabana, Ipanema and Leblon have many beach *barracas* (thatched bars), several open all night. The seafront bars on Av Atlântica are great for people-watching. The big hotels have good cocktail bars.

Centre, Lapa and Santa Teresa

Lapa is without doubt the centre of Rio nightlife and should not be missed if you are in Rio over a weekend. Ideally arrive early on Sat for the afternoon market and live street tango, eat and stay for a bar and club crawl. Always be wary of pickpockets around Lapa. See also Samba schools.

Bar do Mineiro
On the Largo dos Guimarães, R Paschoal Carlos Magno 99, T021-2221 9227, http://bardomineiro.net.
A very popular Santa Teresa bar.

Carioca da Gema
Av Mem de Sá 79, Centro, T021-2221 0043, www.barcariocadagema.com.br.
Great samba club café, 2nd only to **Rio Scenarium**, good food too.

Club Six
R das Marrecas 38, Lapa, T021-2510 3230, www.clubsix.com.br.

Huge pounding European/NYC dance club with everything from hip-hop to ambient house.

Clube dos Democráticos
R do Riachuelo 91, T021-2252 4611, www.clubedosdemocraticos.com.br.
An old dance hall where bands play *gafieira* or dance hall samba. If you're 20- or 30-something at heart and a samba lover it's the place to be.

Estudantina Musical
Praça Tiradentes 79, 3rd floor, T021-2232 1149, www.estudantinamusical.com.br. Closed Mon-Wed.
A famous old-school *gafieira* hall, busiest on Thu when hundreds gather to dance samba.

Goya Beira
Largo das Neves 13, Santa Teresa, T021-2232 5751
One of several restaurant bars on this pretty little square, attracts an arty crowd after 2100. Decent *petiscos* and a range of aromatic vintage *cachaças*.

Mercado 32
R do Mercado 32, Centro, T021-2221 2327, www.mercado32.com.br. Closed weekends.
In the heart of the centre in a converted 19th-century building, this little restaurant and bar offers live MPB on most nights during the week and live chorinho every Thu from 2030.

Rio Scenarium
R do Lavradio 20, Lapa, T021-3147 9005, www.rioscenarium.com.br.
3-storey samba club in a colonial house used as a movie prop warehouse. Overflowing with Brazilian exuberance and joie de vivre, with people dancing furiously, to the bizarre backdrop of a 19th-century apothecary's shop or a line of mannequins wearing 1920s outfits. This is Rio at its bohemian best. Buzzes with beautiful people of all ages on Fri. Arrive after 2300.

Sacrilégio
Av Mem de Sá 81, next to Carioca da Gema, Lapa, T021-3970 1461, www.sacrilegio.com.br.
Samba, *chorinho*, *pagode* and occasional theatre. Close to many other bars.

Semente
R Joaquim Silva 138, T021-2509 3591.
Popular for samba, choro and salsa from 2200 Mon-Sat, US$8 cover; minimum consumption US$7. Book a table at weekends. Great atmosphere both inside and in the streets outside. Recommended.

The Week
R Sacadura Cabral 154, Zona Portuária,
T021-2253 1020, www.theweek.com.br.
Heaving with a gay and straight crowd and with
state of the art spaces, DJs and sound systems.
But don't expect any Brazilian sounds, it's strictly
international dance here.

Glória, Flamengo and Botafogo
Look out for the frequent free live music
performances at the Marina da Glória and
along Flamengo beach during the summer.

Casa da Matriz
Av Mem de Sá, T021-2226 9691,
http://casadamatriz.com.br.
Great little grungy club with a bar, Atari
room, small cinema and 2 dance floors.
Full of Rio students.

Copacabana and Ipanema
There is frequent live music on the beaches
of Copacabana and Ipanema, and along
the Av Atlântica throughout the summer;
especially around New Year.

Garota de Ipanema
R Vinícius de Morais 49, Ipanema, T021-2522
340, www.bargarotadeipanema.com.
Where the song *Girl from Ipanema* was written.
Now packed with foreigners on the package
rio circuit listening to bossa. For the real thing
head up the street to Toca do Vinícius on Sun
afternoon (see below).

Acadêmia da Cachaça
R Conde de Bernadotte 26-G, Leblon; with
another branch at Av Armando Lombardi 800,
Barra da Tijuca, T021-2529 2680,
www.academiadacachaca.com.br.
The best *cachaças*, great caipirinhas and
traditional Brazilian dishes. Good on Fri.

Devassa
R Rainha Guilhermina 48, Leblon,
http://devassa.com.br.
2-floor pub/restaurant/bar which is always
heaving. Brews its own beer. Also at Av Visconde
de Pirajá 539, Ipanema.

Shenanigans
R Visconde de Pirajá 112, Ipanema, T021-
267 5860, www.shenanigans.com.br.
Obligatory mock-Irish bar with Guinness and
Newcastle Brown and sports on TV. Not a place
to meet the locals.

Vinícius
R Vinícius de Morais 39, Ipanema, 2nd floor,
http://viniciusbar.com.br.
Mirror image of the Garota de Ipanema with
slightly better acts and food.

Gávea, Jardim Botânico and Lagoa

Bar Lagoa
Av Epitácio Pessoa 1674, Lagoa, T021-2523 1135,
www.barlagoa.com.br.
Slightly older, arty crowd on weekday evenings.

Garota da Gávea
Praça Santos Dumont 148, T021-2274 2347.
Closed Mon-Wed.
Corner bar/restaurant, informal meeting place,
very popular for *petiscos* and a cold beer on Thu
and at weekends.

Barra da Tijuca

Pepê
At Posto 2, Barra da Tijuca beach.
Very popular with surfers.

Entertainment

Cinemas
There are cinemas serving subtitled Hollywood
films and major Brazilian releases on the top floor
of almost all the malls. The normal seat price is
US$10, discounts on Wed and Thu (students pay
half price any day of the week).
Centro Cultural Banco do Brasil, *see page 444,*
T021-3808 2020. One of Rio's better arts centres
with the best art films and exhibitions from fine
art to photography (Metro: Uruguaiana).
Cinemateca do MAM, *Infante Dom Henrique*
85, Aterro do Flamengo, T021-2210 2188. Cinema
classics, art films and roving art exhibitions and
a good café with live music. Views of Guanabara
Bay from the balconies.
Estação Ipanema, *R Visconde de Pirajá 605,*
Ipanema. European art cinema, less main-stream
US and Brazilian releases.

Live music
Many Cariocas congregate in Lapa from Thu-Sat
for live music. There are free concerts throughout
the summer, along the Copacabana and Ipanema
beaches, in Botafogo and at the parks: mostly
samba, reggae, rock and MPB (Brazilian pop):
there is no advance schedule, information
is given in the local press (see below). Rio's
famous jazz, in all its forms, is performed in lots

☆Carnival in Rio

Carnival in Rio is spectacular. On the Friday before Shrove Tuesday, the mayor of Rio hands the keys of the city to Rei Momo, the Lord of Misrule, signifying the start of a five-day party. Imagination runs riot, social barriers are broken and the main avenues, full of people and children wearing fancy dress, are colourfully lit. Areas throughout the city such as the Terreirão de Samba in Praça Onze are used for shows, music and dancing. *Bandas* and *blocos* (organized carnival groups) seem to be everywhere, dancing, drumming and singing.

There are numerous samba schools in Rio divided into two leagues, both of which parade in the Sambódromo. The Carnival parades are the culmination of months of intense activity by community groups, mostly in the city's poorest districts. Every school presents 2500-6000 participants divided into *alas* (wings) each with a different costume and 5-9 *carros alegóricos*, beautifully designed floats. Each school chooses an *enredo* (theme) and composes a *samba* (song) that is a poetic, rhythmic and catchy expression of the theme. The *enredo* is further developed through the design of the floats and costumes. A *bateria* (percussion wing) maintains a reverberating beat that must keep the entire school, and the audience, dancing throughout the parade. Each procession follows a set order with the first to appear being the *comissão de frente*, a choreographed group that presents the school and the theme to the public. Next comes the *abre alas*, a magnificent float usually bearing the name or symbol of the school. Schools are given between 65 and 80 minutes and lose points for failing to keep within this time. Judges award points to each school for components of their procession, such as costume, music and design, and make deductions for lack of energy, enthusiasm or discipline.

The Sambódromo is a permanent site at Rue Marquês de Sapucai, Cidade Nova, is 600 m long with seating for 43,000 people. Designed by Oscar Niemeyer and built in 1983-1984, it handles sporting events, conferences and concerts during the rest of the year. It was remodelled to hold some of the events at the 2016 Olympics. A Cidade de Samba (Samba City), Rivadávia Correia 60, Gamboa, T021-2213 2503, http://cidadedosambarj.globo.com, is a theme park bringing a number of the larger schools together in one location. There is a permanent carnival production centre of 14 workshops; visitors can watch floats and costumes being prepared, visit the gift shop or watch one of the year-round carnival-themed shows.

Rio's *bailes* (fancy-dress balls) range from the sophisticated to the wild. The majority of clubs and hotels host at least one. The Copacabana Palace hotel's is elegant and expensive whilst the Scala club has licentious parties. It is not necessary to wear fancy dress; just join in, although you will feel more comfortable if you wear a minimum of clothing to the clubs. The most famous are the Red & Black Ball (Friday) and the Gay Ball (Tuesday) which are both televised.

Bandas and *blocos* can be found in all neighbourhoods and some of the most popular and entertaining are Cordão do Bola Preta (www.cordaodabolapreta.com for programme), Simpatia é Quase Amor (meets at 1600 Sunday in Praça General Osório, Ipanema) and the Banda de Ipanema (meets in Praça General Osório, Ipanema; see Facebook: bandadeipanema). It is

of enjoyable venues, see the press. See www. samba-choro. com.br, for more information.
Circo Voador, *R dos Arcos s/n, Lapa, T021-2533 0354, www.circovoador.com.br*. Lapa's recuperation began with this little concert hall under the arches. Some of the city's best smaller acts still play here, including Seu Jorge who first found fame playing with Farofa Carioca at the Circo.

Praia Vermelha, *at Urca*. Residents bring musical instruments and chairs onto beach for an informal night of samba from 2130-2400, free. Bus No 511 from Copacabana.
Toca do Vinícius, *Vinícius de Moraes 129C, Ipanema, www.tocadovinicius.com.br*. Rio's leading bossa nova and choro record shop with live concerts from some of the finest past performers every Sun lunchtime.

necessary to join a *bloco* in advance to receive their distinctive T-shirts, but anyone can join in with the *bandas*.

Tickets The Sambódromo parades start with the Grupo de Acesso (Série A) schools on Friday and Saturday while Grupo Especial schools (the higher league) parade on Sunday and Monday. There are *cadeiras* (seats) at ground level closest to the parade, *arquibancadas* (terraces, prices vary according to sector), *frisas* (open boxes), *boxes especiais* (closed boxes), and *camarotes* (VIP boxes for 4-8 -- schedule and prices can be found on http://liesa.globo.com). The terraces, while uncomfortable, house the most fervent fans, tightly packed; this is where to soak up the atmosphere but not take pictures (too crowded). Tickets are sold at travel agencies as well as the Maracanã Stadium box office. Tickets are usually sold out well before Carnaval weekend. Samba schools have an allocation of tickets which members sometimes sell, if you are offered one of these check its date. Tickets for the champions' parade on the Saturday following Carnival are much cheaper. Taxis to the Sambódromo are negotiable and will find your gate. The nearest metrô is Praça Onze and this can be an enjoyable ride in the company of costumed samba school members. You can follow the participants to the *concentração*, the assembly and formation on Avenida Presidente Vargas, and mingle with them while they queue to enter the Sambódromo.

Sleeping and security Reserve accommodation well in advance. Virtually all hotels raise their prices during Carnival, although it is usually possible to find a room. Your property should be safe inside the Sambódromo, but the crowds outside can attract pickpockets; only take the money you need for fares and food.

Taking part Most samba schools accept a number of foreigners and you will be charged for your costume (the money helps fund poorer members of the school). You should be in Rio for at least two weeks before carnival. Attend fittings and rehearsals on time and show respect for your section leaders – enter into the competitive spirit of the event.

Rehearsals *Ensaios* are held at the schools' *quadras* from October on and are well worth seeing. (Go by taxi, as most schools are based in poorer districts.)

Samba Schools Acadêmicos de Salgueiro, R Silva Teles 104, Andaraí, T021-2238 9226, www.salgueiro.com.br. Beija Flor de Nilópolis, Pracinha Wallace Paes Leme 1025, Nilópolis, T021-2247 4800, www.beija-flor.com.br. Imperatriz Leopoldinense, R Prof. Lacê 235, Ramos, T021-2560 8037, www.imperatrizleopoldinense.com.br. Mocidade Independente de Padre Miguel, Av Brasil 31.146, Padre Miguel, T021-3332 5823, www.mocidadeindependente. com.br. Portela, R Clara Nunes 81, Oswaldo Cruz, T021-3217 1604, www.gresportela.com.br. Primeira Estação de Mangueira, R Visconde de Niterói 1702, Mangueira, T021-2567 3419, www.mangueira. com.br. Unidos da Tijuca, Av Francisco Bicalhao 47, Leopoldina, T021-2263 9679, http://unidosdatijuca.com.br. Vila Isabel, Boulevard 28 de Setembro 382, Vila Isabel, T021-2578 0077, www.unidosdevilaisabel.com.br.

Useful information Riotur's web pages, visit.rio and http://carnavalesamba.rio, and guide booklet give information on official and unofficial events (in English). The entertainment sections of newspapers and magazines such as *O Globo*, *Jornal do Brasil*, *Manchete* and *Veja Rio* are worth checking. Liga Independente das Escolas de Samba do Rio de Janeiro, T021-2233 8151, http://liesa. globo.com, for schools' addresses and rehearsal times, ticket prices and lots more information.

Festivals

Less hectic than Carnival, see box, above, but very atmospheric, is the festival of **Yemanjá** on the night of **31 Dec**, when devotees of the *orixá* of the sea dress in white and gather on Copacabana, Ipanema and Leblon beaches, singing and dancing around open fires and making offerings. The elected Queen of the Sea is rowed along the seashore. At midnight small boats are launched as offerings to Yemanjá. The religious event is dwarfed, however, by a massive New Year's Eve party, called **Reveillon** at Copacabana. The beach is packed as thousands of revellers enjoy free outdoor concerts by big-name pop stars, topped with a lavish midnight firework display. It is most crowded in front of Copacabana Palace Hotel. Another good place to see fireworks is in front of R Princesa Isabel, famous for its fireworks waterfall at about 10 mins past midnight.

Note Many followers of Yemanjá are now making their offerings on 29 or 30 Dec and at Barra da Tijuca or Recreio dos Bandeirantes to avoid the crowds and noise of Reveillon.

20 Jan The festival of **São Sebastião**, patron saint of Rio, is celebrated by an evening procession, leaving Capuchinhos Church, Tijuca, and arriving at the cathedral of São Sebastião. On the same evening, an **umbanda festival** is celebrated at the Caboclo Monument in Santa Teresa.

Feb Carnival 9-13 Feb 2018, 1-5 Mar 2019 (see box, page 420).

13 Jun Festas Juninas: Santo Antônio, whose main event is a mass, followed by celebrations at the Convento do Santo Antônio and the Largo da Carioca and dancing into the night at the **Feira do São Cristóvão**.

23-24 Jun Throughout the state of Rio, the festival of **São João** is a major event, marked by huge bonfires on the night of 23-24 Jun. It is traditional to dance the *quadrilha* and drink *quentão*, *cachaça* and sugar, spiced with ginger and cinnamon, served hot.

29 Jun The **Festas Juninas** close with the festival of **São Pedro**. Being the patron saint of fishermen, his feast is normally accompanied by processions of boats.

Oct The month of the feast of **Nossa Senhora da Penha**.

Shopping

Bookshops

Da Vinci, *Av Rio Branco 185, lojas 2, 3 and 9*. All types of foreign books.

Folha Seca, *R do Ouvidor 37, T021-2507 7175*. Next to NS de Lapa church, good range of Brazilian photography and art books difficult to find elsewhere. Ask here about **Samba do Ouvidor**, a samba show outside, or check http:// sambadaouvidor.blogspot.com for dates.

Livraria da Travessa, *R Visconde de Pirajá 572, Ipanema, T021-3205 9002*. Classy little bookshop, good choice of novels, magazines and guidebooks in English. Great café upstairs too.

Saraiva, *R do Ouvidor 98, T021-2507 9500*. A massive (megastore) bookshop which also includes a music and video shop and a café; other branches in **Shopping Iguatemi** and **Shopping Tijuca**.

Fashion

Fashion is one of the best buys in Brazil; with a wealth of Brazilian designers selling clothes of the same quality as European or US famous names at a fraction of the price. Rio is the best place in the world for buying high-fashion bikinis. The best shops in Ipanema are at the **Forum de Ipanema arcade** (R Visconde de Pirajá 351, Garcia D'Ávila and R Nascimento Silva), which runs off it, in Ipanema. This is where some of the best Brazilian designers, together with international big name stalwarts like Louis Vuitton and Cartier. Most of the international names, as well all the big Brazilian names like Lenny (Brazil's best bikinis), Alberta, Salinas, Club Chocolate and so on are also housed in the **Fashion Mall** in São Conrado.

Saara (www.saarario.com.br), is a multitude of little shops along R Alfândega, dos Andradas, Praça da República and Buenos Aires, where clothing bargains can be found (as well as costume jewellery, toys, perfume and other items). Little shops on Aires Saldanha, Copacabana (1 block back from beach), are good for bikinis and cheaper than in shopping centres.

Jewellery

There are several good jewellery shops at the Leme end of Av NS de Copacabana.

Amsterdam Sauer, *R Garcia D'Ávila 105, http:// amsterdamsauer.com.br*. With 10 shops in Rio and others throughout Brazil. They offer free taxi rides to their main shop.

Antônio Bernardo, *R Garcia d'Ávila 121, Ipanema, T021-2512 7204, and in the Fashion Mall, http://antoniobernardo.com.br*. Brazil's foremost jeweller who has been making beautifully understated jewellery with contemporary designs for 30 years. Internationally well known, but available only in Brazil.

H Stern, *next door to Amsterdam Sauer at R Visconde de Pirajá 490/R Garcia Dávila 113, Ipanema, www.hstern.com.br*. Has 10 outlets, plus branches in major hotels.

Markets

Northeastern market (at Campo de São Cristóvão, www.feiradesaocristovao.org.br, Tue-Thu 1000-1800, Fri-Sun 1000-2100, bus 472 or 474 from Copacabana or centre), with music and magic. A recommended shop for northeastern handi-crafts is **Pé de Boi** (R Ipiranga 55, Laranjeiras, www.pedeboi.com.br). Sat antiques market on the waterfront near Praça 15 de Novembro, 1000-1700. Also in Praça 15 de Novembro is **Feirarte II** (Thu-Fri 0800-

1800). **Feirarte I** (at Praça Gen Osório, Ipanema, www.feirahippieipanema.com, 0800-1800), is a Sun open-air handicrafts market (everyone calls it the Feira Hippy) with items from all over Brazil. **Babilônia Feira Hype** (held every other weekend at the Jockey Club, 1400-2300), selling clothes, crafts, massage, live music and dance, popular. A **stamp, coin and postcard market** (held in the Passeio Público on Sun 0800-1300). Markets on Wed 0700-1300 on R Domingos Ferreira and on Thu, same hrs, on Praça do Lido, both Copacabana (Praça do Lido also has a Feirarte on Sat-Sun 0800-1800). **Sunday market** (R da Glória), colourful, cheap fruit, vegetables and flowers; **early-morning food market** (R Min Viveiros de Castro, Ipanema, open 0600-1100). Excellent food and household goods markets at various places in the city and suburbs (see newspapers for times and places).

Music

Arlequim, Paço Imperial, Praça XV de Novembro 48, loja 1, www.arlequim.com.br. Mon-Fri 1000-2000, Sat 1000-1800. A good selection of music and film in the same space as the **Livraria Imperial**, which sells used books.
Bossa Nova & Companhia, R Duvivier 37a, Copacbana, www.bossanovacompanhia.com.br. Excellent selection of bossa nova, chorinho and jazz, small museum in the basement. See also Toca do Vinícius (under Live music, above).

Shopping malls

Rio Sul, at the Botafogo end of Túnel Novo, has almost everything the visitor may need. Some of the services in Rio Sul are: international phone office; Câmbio; post office at G2, a good branch of **Livraria Saraiva**, a gym and a cinema. A US$5 bus service runs as far as the Sheraton passing the main hotels, every 2 hrs between 1000 and 1800, then 2130.

Other shopping centres, which include a wide variety of services, include **Shopping Leblon** (Av Afrânio Melo Franco 290, www. shoppingleblon.com.br) and **The Fashion Mall** (in São Conrado, www.scfashionmall.com.br), see above, undoubtedly the most fashionable in the city. **Shopping Cidade Copacabana** (www.shoppingcidadedecopacabana.com.br), **Norte Shopping** (Todos os Santos), **Barra** and the mega **Shopping Village Mall** (Av das Américas 3900, www.shoppingvillagemall.com.br), in Barra da Tijuca (see page 409).

Boat trips

Several agencies offer trips to **Ilha de Paquetá** (www. ilhadepaqueta.com.br, to which there is also a US$1.75, 45-min ferry, see www.grupo ccr.com.br/barcas for times), and day cruises, including lunch, to Jaguanum Island (see under Itacuruçá) and a sundown cruise around Guanabara Bay.

Cycling

Mobilicidade Bike Rio, see www.mobilicidade. com.br or T4063 3999 for the city's bicycle hire scheme. There are dozens of cycle hire stations and bikes cost US$6, though you need to register with a Brazilian security card number. Bikes can be rented from **Velobike** (T021-3442 4315, R Francisco Otaviano 20C, Arpoador or R Gustavo Sampaio 802, Leme) in the Arpoador or Copacabana – around US$10 per hr.

There are some 140 km of cycle paths in Rio, over 6 km in Parque Nacional Tijuca (see www. ta.org.br/site2/index.htm for a map). Some hostels rent bicycles.

Dancing

Rio Samba Dancer, T021-98229 2843, http:// riosambadancer.com. Samba classes followed by samba night tours from US$35.

Football

See Maracanã stadium, page 402.

Helicopter rides

Helisight, R Visconde de Pirajá 580, loja 107, Térreo, Ipanema, T021-2511 2141, www.helisight.com.br. Prices from US$90 pp for 6/7-min overflights.

Horse racing and riding

Jockey Club Racecourse, by Jardím Botânico and Gávea. Meetings on Mon and Thu evenings and Sat and Sun 1400, US$1-2, long trousers required. Take any bus marked 'via Jóquei'.
Sociedade Hípico Brasileiro, Av Borges de Medeiros 2448, T021-2156 0156, www.shb.com.br, Jardim Botânico. For riding.

Language courses

Instituto Brasil-Estados Unidos, Av Copacabana 690, 5th floor, lots of branches and courses, www.ibeu.org.br. Good English library at Copacabana address.

Parapenting and hang-gliding

For the **Brazilian Association**, see www.abvl. com.br, the website of the Associação Brasileira de Vôo Livre, which oversees all national clubs and federations. Several offer tandem jumping; check that they are accredited with the Associação Brasileira de Vôo Livre. Ask for the **Parapente Rio Clube** at São Conrado launch site. Basic cost US$120 for a tandem flight. Many offer in-flight photos at about US$15-18 extra.

Barra Jumping, *Aeroporto de Jacarepaguá, Av Ayrton Senna 2541, T021-3151 3602, www.barra jumping.com.br.* Tandem jumping (Vôo duplo).

Delta Flight and **Rio by Jeep**, *T021-3322 5750/9693 8800, www.deltaflight.com.br.* Tandem flight tours above Rio from Pedra Bonita Mountain with instructors licensed by the Brazilian Hang-Gliding Association. Contact Ricardo Hamond.

Just Fly, *T021-2268 0565, T021-99985 7540, www.justfly.com.br.* Tandem flights with Paulo Celani (licensed by Brazilian Hang Gliding Association), pick-up and drop-off at hotel included, flights all year, best time of day 1000-1500 (5% discount for Footprint South American and Brazil Handbook readers on presentation of book at time of reservation).

Pedro Beltrão, *T021-97822 4206, pedrobeltrao@ gmail.com.* Highly regarded, experienced hang-gliding operator with flights from the Pedra Bonita. Some 20 years' flying experience. Excellent prices.

Rio Tandem Fly, *instructor Paulo Falcão T021-9966 3416, pilot Roni Falcão, T9963 6623, see Facebook.*

Rock climbing and hill walking

Clube Excursionista Carioca, *R Hilário Gouveia 71, room 206, T021-2255 1348, www.carioca. org.br.* Recommended for enthusiasts, meets Wed and Fri.

Jungle Me, *T021-4105 7533, www.jungleme. com.br.* Hikes in Rio off the beaten track including the 3 peaks in Tijuca national park (an 8-hr circuit), wild beaches and Pedra Bonita.

Rio Hiking, *T021-2552 9204/99721 0594, www. riohiking.com.br.* Hiking tours to the top of mountains in Rio city and state, friendly, fun, English spoken. Also offers many other activities including kayaking, cycling, birdwatching, surfing and horse riding.

Tours

Be A Local, *T021-99643 0366, http://bealocal. com.* Guided tours to football matches and recommended visits to favelas and baile funk parties.

Bravietour, *T021-98111 2073, www.bravietour. com.br.* Alternative carnival tours, cultural trips in Rio and throughout Brazil and excellent nightlife tours.

Brazil Expedition, *R Visconde Piraja 550 lj 201, Ipanema, T021-99998 2907, www.brazilexpedition. com.* Backpacker bus trips south to Paraty and Ilha Grande with stops along the Costa Verde. Day trips and Rio 'starter packs', accommodation advice. Recommended.

Cook in Rio, *T021-98761 3653, www.cookinrio.com.* Brazilian cooking, cocktail and drink-making classes in Copacabana. Great fun.

Favela Tour, *Estr das Canoas 722, Bl 2, apt 125, São Conrado, T021-3322 2727, T021-99989-0074, www.favelatour.com.br.* Safe, interesting guided tours of Rio's favelas in English, Spanish, Italian, German or French, 3 hrs. Ask Marcelo Armstrong, the owner, about ecotours and river rafting. For the best price call Marcelo direct rather than through a hotel. Recommended.

Jeep Tour, *T021-2108 5800, www.jeeptour.com.br.* Among their tours are escorted groups to favelas and trips to Tijuca national park.

Rio Adventures, *T021-96479 7414, http:// rioadventures.com.* All manner of adventure tours in and around Rio from rafting, zip-lining and canoeing to biking and rock climbing.

Rio Connexion Tours, *T021-99715 9794, http:// rioconnexiontours.com.* First-class driver-guided tours of Rio de Janeiro city and state, including less-visited areas like the southern beaches around Prainha and Grumari. Nightlife tours, music and general site seeing. Good English, personable company. Ask for Rodrigo.

Rio Cultural Secrets, *T021-2294 9469, www. rioculturalsecrets.com.* Day and half-day trips of Rio, including walking tours of the centre.

Rio EnCantos, *T021-98378 1895, www.rioencantos. com.* Excellent nightlife, music and walking tours of the city cenre and favela communities with Lapa local Kelly Tavares.

Rio Xtreme, *T021-8806 0235, www.rioxtreme.com.* Broad range of excursions from city tours, key sights and nightlife excursions to hikes to the Pedra da Gávea, Itatiaia National Park and Ilha Grande.

Trilhas e Cachoeiras, *www.trilhasecachoeiras. com.br.* Hikes, walks and climbs throughout Rio de Janeiro including to some little-visited locations around Barra da Tijuca, Itatiaia national park and Niterói.

Guides

Andre Albuquerque, *T021-97811 2737, andralbuquerque@yahoo.com.br, Facebook: Andre Luiz Souto Albuquerque.* Driver-guide tours of Rio including Sugar Loaf, Tijuca National Park, Niterói, beaches and Umbanda ceremonies. From US$170 including lunch.

Cultural Rio, *R Santa Clara 110/904, Copacabana, T021-3322 4872, T021-99911 3829, www.culturalrio. com.br*. Tours escorted personally by Professor Carlos Roquette, English/French spoken, almost 200 options available, entirely flexible to your interests.

Gilmar Lopes Walking tours, *T021-99369 2844, gilmar.lopes@talk21.com*. Fascinating walking and public transport tours of Rio telling the story of the city from the point of view of the communities rather than the wealthy aristocrats and churchmen, showing the places where everyday Cariocas love to shop, visit and drink a cold beer.

Luiz Amaral Tours, *R Visc de Pirajá 550, office 215, Ipanema, T021-2259 5532, T021-99637 2522, www. travelrio.com/tours.htm*. Good company offering personalized tours run by Luiz Felipe Amaral who speaks good English.

Rio EnCantos, *T021-98378 1895, www.rioencantos. com*. Excellent nightlife, music and walking tours of the city centre and favela communities with Lapa local Kelly Tavares.

Transport

Air

Rio has 2 airports, both of them recently renovated: **Tom Jobim International Airport** (*T021-3398 4527, www.aeroportogaleao.net*), previously called Galeão, and the **Santos Dumont** airport on Guanabara Bay (*T021-3814 7246, www.aeroportosantosdumont.net*), for domestic flights. Jobim international airport is situated on Governador Island some 16 km north of the centre of Rio. It is in 2 sections: international and domestic. There is a **Pousada Galeão** ($$$), comfortable, good value, and **Rio Aeroporto**, 3rd floor, Sector B, T021-3383 9800, www.rioaeroportohotel.com.br, if you need an early start, follow signs in airport. **Banco do Brasil** at the International Airport is open 0800-2200.

Taxis can be booked from within the airports or picked up at the stands outside the terminals. Standard taxis in daytime charge US$20 from Jobim to Copacabana, Ipanema and the city. **Aerotaxi** cabs (*T021-2467 1500*), available outside both terminals at Tom Jobim airport cost around US$33 Beware of pirate taxis, which are unlicensed. Fixed-price taxis leave from the 1st floor of both terminals and have clearly marked booths selling tickets.

The a/c **Real Auto** bus (*T0800-240850, www. realautoonibus.com.br*), runs frequently from the 1st floor of both terminals, 0500-2400, fares from US$5.30. There are 2 routes: Linha 2018 via Orla da Zona Sul, runs every 30 mins between 0530 and 2340 weekdays and 0540 and 2235 weekends and public holidays, to the Terminal Alvorada bus station in Barra da Tijuca and back again, stopping at the *rodoviária*, Av Rio Branco in the centre, Santos Dumont airport, Flamengo, Copacabana, Ipanema, São Conrado and Barra's Av das Américas. (This should not be confused with the Linha 2018 via Linha Vermelha, which runs a sporadic circular route via Barra and nowhere else of any use to foreign tourists.) Linha 2145 runs every 25 mins to Santos Dumont airport and back again between 0530 and 2230 weekdays, calling at Av Rio Branco along the way. Buses can be flagged down anywhere along their route and passengers can request to jump off at any time. There is also a standard Rio bus running along the 2018 line with similar frequency, US$1.50. Ordinary city buses also run from the airport to various locations in Rio, from the 1st floor of both terminals. These are far less secure and are not recommended.

There are *câmbios* in the airport departure hall. There is also a *câmbio* on the 1st floor of the international arrivals area, but it gives worse rates than the Banco do Brasil, 24-hr bank, 3rd floor, which has Visa ATMs (may not accept foreign cards) and gives cash advances against Visa. Duty-free shops are well stocked, but not cheap. Only US dollars or credit cards are accepted on the air-side of the departure lounge. There is a better choice of restaurants outside passport control. Left luggage only in Terminal 1.

The **Santos Dumont** airport on Guanabara Bay, right in the city, is used for Rio–São Paulo shuttle flights, other domestic routes, air taxis and private planes. The shuttle services operate every 30 mins from 0630 to 2230. Sit on the right-hand side for views to São Paulo, the other side coming back, book in advance. Taxi to the centre US$12, to Copacabana US$12, Ipanema US$18. Uber is far cheaper and many hotels and hostels will be willing to book a car for you (see Taxi below).

Metro

The Metrô, www.metrorio.com.br, provides good service, clean, a/c and fast; a better option to city buses. Line 1 runs between the inner suburb of Tijuca (station Uruguai) and Ipanema/General Osório; Line 2 from Pavuna in the city's northern suburbs, passing Engenho da Rainha and the

Maracanã stadium, to Botafogo. Line 2 joins Line 1 at Central and the two run together as far as Botafogo. Line 4 begins at General Osório and runs to Jardim Oceânico in Barra da Tijuca via Ipanema, Leblon and São Conrado. It links with an express bus service in Barra. The system operates 0500-2400 Mon-Sat, 0700-2300 Sun and holidays, 24 hrs during **Carnaval**. Stations often have a number of different access points, some close earlier than the main ones. On Mon-Fri 0600-0900 and 1700-2000, the last carriage of each train is for women only; it has a pink stripe. The fare is US$1.35 single and for the metro with the connecting *Metrô na superfície Gávea/Barra* express bus which passes through Ipanema and Leblon. Other integrated systems include *Integração Expressa* between certain stations (eg Estácio and *rodoviária*) and *Barra Expresso* from Ipanema/General Osório to Barra da Tijuca. There is also a pre-paid card, *Cartão Pré-Pago*, initial payment US$1.35.

Bus

Local There are good services, but buses are very crowded and not for the aged or infirm during rush hours; buses have turnstiles which are awkward if you are carrying luggage. Hang on tight, drivers live out Grand Prix fantasies. Buses run to all parts, but should be treated with caution at night, when taxis are a better bet. They are usually marked with the destination and any going south of the centre will call at Copacabana and generally Ipanema/Leblon. At busy times allow about 45 mins to get from Copacabana to the centre by bus, less if you take a bus on the *aterro* expressway on the reclaimed waterfront. The fare on standard buses is US$1.35; suburban bus fares are up to US$3 depending on the distance. Bus stops are often not marked. The route is usually written on the front of the bus. See www.rioonibus.com for all routes. Private companies operate a/c (*frescão*) buses which can be flagged down practically anywhere: **Real**, **Pegaso**, **Anatur**. They run from all points in Rio Sul to the city centre, *rodoviária* and the airports. Fares are from US$2 (US$3 for the international airport). **City Rio** is an a/c tourist bus service with security guards which runs between all the major parts of the city. Good maps show what sites of interest are close to each bus stop, marked by grey poles and found where there are concentrations of hotels. **Minivans** run from Av Rio Branco in the centre as far as Barra da Tijuca and have the destination written on the window. They are fast, frequent and by far

the cheapest way of getting along the beaches, fare US$1.10. These vans also run along the sea front from Leme to Rocinha and can be hailed from the kerb. **Note** Rio's public transport systems are being integrated by **Fetranspor**, www.fetranspor.com.br. A number of unified, pre-paid ticket options are available, for instance the rechargeable *Rio Card* and the *bilhete único*, US$1.80, which can be used on buses, Metrô, ferries, etc, under certain conditions (see www.cartaoriocard.com.br for the full range).

Long distance Rodoviária Novo Rio, Av Rodrigues Alves, corner with Av Francisco Bicalho, just past the docks, T021-3213 1800, www.novorio.com.br. Buses run from Rio to all parts of the country. It is advisable to book tickets in advance at the *rodoviária* or with one of the booking agencies listed below; timetables are on the web site. The *rodoviária* has a **Riotur** information centre, which is very helpful, T021-2263 4857. Left luggage costs US$3.50. There are ATMs and *câmbios* for cash only. A local bus terminal is just outside the *rodoviária*: turn right as you leave and run the gauntlet of taxi drivers – best ignored. The main bus station is reached by buses 326, Bancários/Castelo, from the centre and the airport; 136, *rodoviária*/Copacabana via Glória, Flamengo and Botafogo; 127, *rodoviária*/Copacabana via Túnel do Pasmado; 128, *rodoviária*/Leblon, via Copacabana and Ipanema; 170, *rodoviária*/Gávea, via Glória, Botafogo and Jardim Botânico; 172, *rodoviária*/Leblon, via Joquei and Jardim Botânico. The a/c Real bus (opposite the exit) goes to the airport and along the beach to São Conrado and will secure luggage. From the *rodoviária* it is best to take a taxi to your hotel or to the nearest metrô station (Estácio). Taxis can be booked at the booth on the ground floor, which ensures against overcharging. Fare to Flamengo US$7. Booking agencies include: **Dantur Passagens e Turismo**, Av Rio Branco 156, subsolo, loja 134, Metro Carioca, T021-2262 3624, www.dantur.com.br; **Guanatur**, R Dias da Rocha 16A, Copacabana, T021-2548 3275, www.guanaturturismo.com.br; **Paxtur Passagens**, R República do Líbano 61, loja L, Center, T021-3852 2277. They charge about US$2 for bookings.

International bus Asunción, 1511 km via Foz do Iguaçu, 30 hrs (**Pluma**, T0800-646 0300, www.pluma.com.br), US$85; **Buenos Aires** (Crucero del Norte, www.crucerodelnorte. com.ar), via Porto Alegre and Santa Fe, 48 hrs, US$225, book 2 days in advance.

Car

Service stations are closed in many places Sat and Sun. Road signs are notoriously misleading in Rio and you can easily end up in a favela. Take care if driving along the Estrada Gávea to São Conrado as it is possible to enter unwittingly Rocinha.

Car hire Many agencies on Av Princesa Isabel, Copacabana; **Telecar** (R Figueiredo Magalhães 701, Copacabana, T021-2548 6778, www.telecar. com.br). A credit card is essential for hiring a car.

Taxi

Official taxis are yellow with a blue stripe and have meters. Smaller ones are marked TAXI on the windscreen or roof. Only use taxis with an official identification sticker on the windscreen. Make sure meters are cleared and on tariff 1 (starting at R$4.20), except between 2100 and 0600 and on Sun and holidays, when tariff 2 applies (starting at R$5.65). The website www.tarifadetaxi.com/rio-de-janeiro has a map and allows you to calculate the approximate taxi price. Print the map and don't hesitate to argue if the route is too long or the fare too much. The fare between Copacabana and the centre is about US$8. It is safer to use taxis from *pontos* – taxi ranks or Radio Taxis, but the latter are more expensive, eg **Cootramo** (T021-3976 9944, www.cootramo. com.br), **Coopertramo** (T021-2209 9292, www. radio-taxi.com.br), **Central Táxi** (T021-2195 1000, www.centraltaxi.com.br), **Transcoopass** (T021-2209 1555, www.transcoopass.com.br). Uber is now widely used in Rio. Most hotels and hostels will book a cab for you using the app, which requires a Brazilian credit card to function in the country.

Tram

A VLT tram network operates in Rio's city centre connecting the rodoviária and dock area with Santos Dumont airport via the new AquaRio aquarium, Praça Mauá (for the new museums) and the heart of the centre along Av Rio Branco. Tickets cost US$1.35.

Pão de Açúcar

Bus Bus 107 (from the centre, Catete or Flamengo) and 511 from Copacabana (512 to return) take you to the cable-car station, Av Pasteur 520, at the foot.

Cable car T021-2546 8433, open 0800-1950 (last one down at 2040, quietest before 1000), US$25 return, free for children under 6, aged 6-21 half price, every 30 mins or when full.

There are 2 sections, Praia Vermelha to Morro de Urca and from Urca to Sugar Loaf. Termini are ample and efficient and the present Italian cable cars carry 75 passengers. Even on the most crowded days there is little queuing. See main text for walking options.

Corcovado

Bus The 206 bus does the very attractive run from Praça Tiradentes (or a 407 from Largo do Machado) to Silvestre (the railway has no stop here now), where the active walk of 9 km will take you to the top. For safety reasons go in company, or at weekends when more people are about. For more information contact T021-2225 7036, https://cristoredentoroficial.com.br.

Bus to the railway station Take a **Cosme Velho** bus to the cog railway station at R Cosme Velho 513: from the centre or Glória/Flamengo No 180, 422, 498, get off at Igreja São Jesus Tadeo; from Copacabana take No 583, 584, from Botafogo or Ipanema/Leblon No 583 or 584; from Santa Teresa Microônibus Santa Teresa. From Largo do Machado Metrô station take a Cosme Velho *integração* bus to the train station.

Foot, taxi and van If arriving on foot entrance costs US$13 (high season) or US$8.60 (low season), children under 11 are free. Cars are no longer permitted to drive to the entrance gate, only to the Paineiras car park from where you will have to walk or take a minivan. Entrance with a van (T021-2225 7036, www.paineirascorcovado. com.br, daily 0800-1600) costs US$12.70, US$8.60 low season (more than twice the price from Barra da Tijuca). Vans leave from Paineiras, from the Praça do Lido in Copacabana, the Largo do Machado near the cog railway in Cosme Velho and the beachfront in Barra. There is very little parking on the mountain. Some taxi drivers offer combination Corcovado and Dona Marta look-out tours (for views of the Sugar Loaf) from around US$30 plus entrance tickets, leaving from outside the Trem do Corcovado station. They cannot take you to the entrance gates.

Tours Most hotels and hostels can organize tours of Corcovado, often in combination with other sights. Time tends to be limited on these tours and they rarely involve a visit at the best times of day.

Train Cog railway trains leave from the Trem do Corcovado station in Cosme Velho R Cosme Velho 513, http://corcovado.com.br, daily 0800-1900, US$24, US$20 low season, ride takes 20 mins, over-60s half price, children aged 6-11 US$15, under-6s free). Tickets can be bought online though this involves a bureaucratic registration process. Go early to avoid long queues and ignore touts for tours who say that the train is not running. Climb the 220 steps or take the escalator to the top.

Copacabana
Bus/Metrô Cardeal Arcoverde, Siqueira Campos and Cantagalo Metrô stations are a few blocks inland from the beach. There are many buses to and from the city centre. Take numbers 119, 154, 413, 415, 455, 474 from Av Nossa Senhora de Copacabana. If you are going to the centre from Copacabana, look for 'Castelo', 'Praça 15', 'E Ferro' or 'Praça Mauá' on the sign by the front door. From the centre to Copacabana is easier as all buses in that direction are marked. 'Aterro' means the expressway between Botafogo and downtown Rio (closed Sun). The 'Aterro' bus does the journey in 15 mins.

Ipanema and Leblon
Bus/Metrô The Ipanema/General Osório Metrô station is at Praça General Osório, from where Line 4 goes to Barra da Tijuca via Leblon and São Conrado and 'Metrô do superfície' buses run to Gávea along Rua Visconde de Pirajá in Ipanema and Av Ataulfo de Paiva in Leblon. Many buses and minivans from the centre and/or Leme run to Ipanema and Leblon along the seafront roads.

Jardim Botânico
Bus Take bus No 170 from the centre, or any bus to Leblon, Gávea or São Conrado marked 'via Jóquei'; from Glória, Flamengo or Botafogo take No 571, or 172 from Flamengo, or the Metrô na Superfície from Botafogo or Ipanema/Gral Osório; from Copacabana, Ipanema or Leblon take No 572 (584 back to Copacabana).

Barra da Tijuca
Bus From the city centre to Barra, 1 hr, are Nos 175, 176; from Botafogo, Glória or Flamengo take No 179; Nos 591 or 592 from Leme; and from Copacabana via Leblon No 523 (45-60 mins). A taxi from the centre costs from US$15 (US$25 after 2400), from Ipanema US$12. A comfortable bus, Pegasus, goes along the coast from the Castelo bus terminal to Barra da Tijuca and continues to Campo Grande or Santa Cruz, or take the free 'Barra Shopping' bus. Bus 700 from Praça São Conrado (terminal of bus 553 from Copacabana) goes the full length of the beach to Recreio dos Bandeirantes. Metrô Line 4 runs from General Osório in Ipanema to Jardim Oceânico in Barra da Tijuca.

Parque Nacional Tijuca
Bus For the park entrance, take bus No 221 from Praça 15 de Novembro, No 233 'Barra da Tijuca' or 234 from the *rodoviária*, or No 454 from Copacabana to Alto da Boa Vista. There is no public transport within the park, best explore by trail, tour, bicycle or car.

East of Rio
chic resorts, surfing centres, forested hills

It is not only the state capital that is blessed with beautiful beaches, forests and mountains. East of Rio, there are chic resorts, surfing centres and emerald green coves, national parks in rainforest-clad hills and strange rocky mountains, and fine historical towns dating from both the colonial and imperial epochs. Within easy reach of Rio are the popular coastal resorts of Cabo Frio and Búzios and the imperial city of Petrópolis.

Niterói *Colour map 7, B5.*
This city is reached across Guanabara Bay by bridge and by ferries which carry some 200,000 commuters a day. Founded in 1573, Niterói has various churches and forts, plus buildings associated with the city's period as state capital (until 1960). Many of these are grouped around the Praça da República. The **Capela da Boa Viagem** (1663) stands on an island, attached by a footbridge to the mainland. **Museu de Arte Contemporânea-Niterói** ① *Mirante da Praia da Boa Viagem, T021-2620 2400, www.macniteroi.com.br, Tue-Sun 1000-1800, US$3.25, half price seniors, students with card, Wed free and if you arrive by bicycle, restaurant – www.bistromac.com.br – Tue-Fri 1000-1700, Sat-Sun 0900-1800,* is an Oscar Niemeyer project. It is best seen at night, especially when there is water in the pond beneath the building (which Niemeyer envisaged as a flower emerging from the water, but which is generally seen as a spaceship). There are other Niemeyer buildings near the port; when it's all done Niterói will be second to Brasília for Niemeyer buildings.

The most important historical monument is the **Fortaleza da Santa Cruz** ① *T021-2710 7840, daily 0900-1600, US$1.35, go with guide.* Dating from the 16th century and still a military establishment, it stands on a promontory which commands a fine view of the entrance to the bay. It is about 13 km from the centre of Niterói, on the Estrada Gen Eurico Gaspar Dutra, by Adão e Eva beach (taxi 30 minutes). The **Museu de Arqueologia de Itaipu** ① *20 km from the city, T021-2709 4079, Wed-Sun 1300-1800,* is in the ruins of the 18th-century Santa Teresa Convent and also covers the archaeological site of Duna Grande on Itaipu beach. **Tourist office:** Neltur ① *Estrada Leopoldo Fróes 773, São Francisco, T021-2710 2727, or T0800-282 7755, 5 km from ferry dock, www.niteroiturismo.com.br, Mon-Fri 0900-1700,* has a useful map. Office also at the Museu de Arte Contemporânea.

Local beaches Take bus No 33 from the dock, passing Icaraí and São Francisco, both with polluted water but good nightlife, plenty of eating places and superb sunset views, to the fishing village of Jurujuba, with simple bars at the water's edge. About 2 km further along a narrow road are the twin beaches of Adão and Eva just before the Fortaleza da Santa Cruz (see above). At weekends and holidays a tourist bus runs from the Praça Araribóia in the centre around the bay to Fortaleza da Santa Cruz at 1000, 1230, 1430, US$4. To get to the ocean beaches, take buses from the street directly ahead of the ferry entrance, at right angles to the coast road to Piratininga, Camboinhas (bus 39 for both), Itaipu (see the archaeology museum, above, buses 38 or 770D) and Itacoatiara (bus 38). These are fabulous stretches of sand, the best in the area, about 40 minutes' ride through picturesque countryside.

Lagos Fluminenses

To the east of Niterói lie a series of salt-water lagoons, the Lagos Fluminenses. The first major lakes, Maricá and Saquarema are muddy, but the waters are relatively unpolluted and wildlife abounds in the surrounding scrub and bush. An unmade road goes along the coast between Itacoatiara and Cabo Frio, giving access to the long, open beaches of Brazil's **Costa do Sol**.

In the holiday village of **Saquarema**, the little white church of Nossa Senhora de Nazaré (1675) is on a green promontory jutting into the ocean. Saquarema is a fishing town and one of the top spots for quality consistent pumping surf in Brazil.

The largest lake is **Araruama** (220 sq km), famous for its medicinal mud. The salinity is extremely high, the waters calm, and almost the entire lake is surrounded by sandy beaches, making it popular with families looking for safe, unpolluted bathing. The almost constant breeze makes the lake perfect for windsurfing and sailing. There are many hotels, youth hostels and campsites in the towns by the lakes and by the beaches. All around are saltpans and the wind pumps used to carry water into the pans. At the eastern end of the lake is **São Pedro de Aldeia**, which, despite intensive development, still retains some of its colonial charm.

Cabo Frio *Colour map 7, B5.*

Cabo Frio, 156 km from Rio, is a popular holiday and weekend haunt of Cariocas because of its cooler weather, white sand beaches, sailing, surfing and good underwater swimming. **Forte São Mateus** (1616) is now a ruin at the mouth of the Canal de Itajurú, which connects the Lagoa Araruama and the ocean. A small headland at its mouth protects the nearest beach to the town, Praia do Forte, which stretches south for about 7.5 km to Arraial do Cabo. The canal front, Avenida dos Pescadores, is pretty, lined with palm trees, restaurants and schooners tied up at the dock. It leads around to the bridge, which crosses to the Gamboa district. **Convento Nossa Senhora dos Anjos** (1696), Largo de Santo Antônio in the town centre, houses the **Museu de Arte Religiosa Tradicional** ① *Wed-Fri 1400-2000, Sat-Sun 1600-2000.* Above the Largo de Santo Antônio is the **Morro da Guia**, which has a look-out and an 18th-century chapel (access on foot only). The beaches of **Peró** and **Conchas** ① *'São Cristovão' (with 'Peró' on its notice board) or 'Peró' bus, US$0.80, 5-20 mins, has lots of condos, but not many places to stay,* are lovely (a headland, Ponta do Vigia, separates the two and you can walk from one to the other). **Tourist office** ① *Secretaria de Turismo, / Assunção s/n, Passagem, Terminal de Transatlânticos, T022-2646 7959, http://cabofrio.rj.gov.br/ rismo, open when cruise ships are in dock; there are 2 Centros de Atendimento, at the Rodoviária, daily 0800-1800, and on Boulevard Canal, daily 0900-1700.*

Búzios *Colour map 7, B5.*

Once considered a lost paradise in the tropics, this burgeoning cruise ship resort (population of the peninsula 70,278), 192 km from Rio, found fame in the 1964 when Brigite Bardot was photographed sauntering barefoot along the beach. The world's press descended on the sophisticated, yet informal resort, following the publicity. Originally a small fishing community, founded in 1740, Búzios remained virtually unknown until the 1950s when its natural beauty started to attract the Brazilian jet-set who turned the village into a fashionable summer resort. The city gets crowded at all main holidays and in cruise ship season, the price of food, accommodation and other services rises substantially and the traffic jams are long and stressful.

During the daytime, the best option is to head for one of the 25 beaches. The most visited are Geribá (many bars and restaurants), Ferradura (blue sea and calm waters), Ossos (the most famous and close to the centre), Tartaruga and João Fernandes. Schooner trips of two to three hours pass many of the beaches: many companies offer the trip from the pier in the centre, US$25. Watersports include diving, snorkelling, surfing on Geribá and Brava beaches, wind surfing, kite surfing, jet ski and stand-up paddleboarding. Some of the world's best sailing waters are found around the Búzios peninsula, which was one of the venues for the sailing competitions in the 2016 Olympics. On land there are **Radical Parque** ① *Estrada da Usina 1, www.radicalparque.com. br*, with karting, bowling, rock climbing walls and other adventure sports, and a first-class **golf course** ① *www.buziosgolf.com.br*. **Tourist office** ① *Pórtico de Búzios, Manguinhos, T022-2623 4254, daily 0900-2000*, with kiosks at *Estrada José Bento Ribeiro Dantas 100, Rasa, daily 0900-2000, and at Travessa dos Pescadores 111, by Praça Santo Dumont, T022-2623 2099, daily 0800-2000*. See also *www. buziosturismo.com* and *www.buziosonline.com.br*.

Petrópolis *Colour map 7, B5.*

A steep scenic mountain road from Rio leads to this summer resort, 68 km north of Rio, known for its floral beauty and hill scenery, coupled with adventure sports. Until 1962 Petrópolis was the 'summer capital' of Brazil. Now it combines manufacturing (particularly textiles) and tourism. Whitewater rafting, hiking, climbing, riding and cycling are possible in the vicinity. Petrópolis celebrates its foundation on 16 March. Patron saint's day, São Pedro de Alcântara, 29 June. **Tourist office**: Petrotur ① *Praça Liberdade, T0800-024 1516, Mon-Sun 0900-1700. See www.petropolis.rj.gov.b*

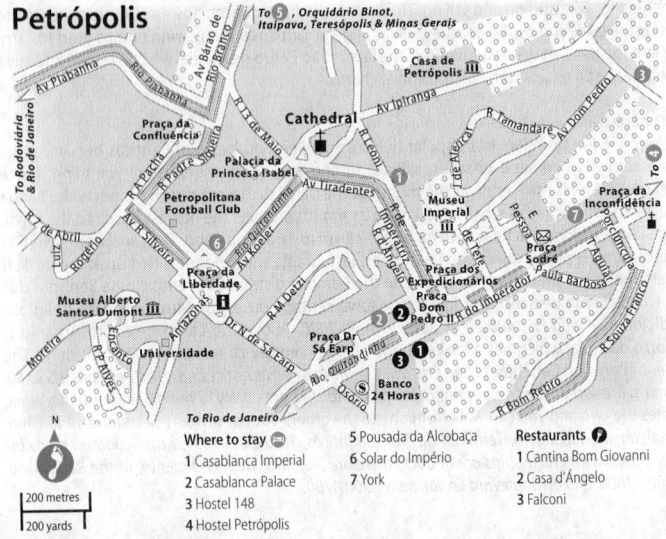

Petrópolis

Where to stay
1 Casablanca Imperial
2 Casablanca Palace
3 Hostel 148
4 Hostel Petrópolis
5 Pousada da Alcobaça
6 Solar do Império
7 York

Restaurants
1 Cantina Bom Giovanni
2 Casa d'Ângelo
3 Falconi

…nd http://destinopetropolis.com.br. Very helpful, good English; map not to scale. There are five other …iosks in and around the city, including Pórtico Quitandinha, 300 m from *rodoviária*.

The **Museu Imperial** (Imperial Palace) ① *R da Imperatriz 220, T024-2245 5550, http://museuimperial.* …gov.br, Tue-Sun 1100-1800, gardens Tue-Sun 0800-1800, US$3.20*, is Brazil's most visited museum. …t is an elegant building, neoclassical in style, fully furnished and equipped. It is so well kept you …might think the imperial family had left the day before, rather than in 1889. It's worth a visit just …o see the Crown Jewels of both Pedro I and Pedro II. In the palace gardens is a vehicle museum …nd a pretty French-style tearoom, the Petit Palais. The Neo-Gothic **Catedral de São Pedro de** …**lcântara** ① *Tue-Sat 0800-1200, 1400-1800, Sun 0800-1300, 1500-1930, Mon 0800-1200*, completed …n 1925, contains the tombs of the Emperor and Empress in the Imperial Chapel to the right of the …ntrance. The summer home of air pioneer **Alberto Santos Dumont** ① *R do Encanto 22, T024-2247* …*158, Tue-Sun 0930-1700, US$2.50*, is known as 'A Encantada' and is worth a visit. The interior of …he **Casa de Petrópolis** ① *R Ipiranga 716, T024-2231 6197, Fri-Tue 1300-1830*, is completely original …nd over-the-top, but has been lovingly restored. It holds art exhibitions and classical concerts. A …harming restaurant in the old stables is worth a stop for coffee, if not for lunch. **Orquidário Binot** ① *R Fernandes Vieira 390, T024-2248 5665, Mon-Fri 0800-1100, 1300-1600, Sat 0700-1100, take bus to* …*ila Isabel*, has a huge collection of orchids from all over Brazil (plants may be purchased).

Serra dos Órgãos

Open 0800-1700, entry US$12, best months for trekking Apr-Sep, US$17 for 1st day's trekking in the park, US$2 thereafter, but US$10 at weekends. For information from ICMBio, Av Rotariana s/n, Alto Teresópolis, …021-2152 1100, www.icmbio.gov.br.

…he Serra dos Órgãos, so called because their strange shapes are said to recall organ-pipes, is an …1,000-ha national park (created in 1939, the second oldest in the country). The main attraction …s the precipitous Dedo de Deus ('God's Finger') Peak (1692 m). The highest point is the 2263 m …edra do Sino ('Bell Rock'), up which winds a 14-km path, a climb of five to six hours (11 km). The …est face of this mountain is one of the hardest climbing pitches in Brazil. Another well-known …eak is the Pedra do Açu (2245 m) and many others have names evocative of their shape. Near …he Sub-Sede Guapimirim (Km 98.5, off BR-116, just outside the park) is the **Von Martius natural** …**istory museum** ① *0800-1700*. Near the headquarters (Sede) entrance is the Mirante do Soberbo, …vith views to the Baía de Guanabara. To climb the Pedra do Sino, you must sign a register (under 18s …nust be accompanied by an adult and have authorization from the park authorities). The Serra has …ery high bird biodiversity and is an excellent place for ornithology.

Further information on the area from the Teresópolis **tourism information centres** ① *Praça* …*límpica; and at entrance to town on road from Rio, Av Rotariano s/n*, or the **Secretaria de Turismo** ① *Av Rotariana s/n, Soberbo or Praça Olímpia Luís Camões, Várzea, T021-2742 5561, www.turistere.* …*logspot.com*. Check also the websites www.teresopolison.com and www.visiteteresopolis.com.br, …r phone for information T021-2742 9149, ext 4015.

Listings East of Rio *map p430*

Where to stay

Cabo Frio

$$ Pousada Água Marinha
Rui Barbosa 996b, Centro, T022-2643 8447, …*ww.pousadaaguamarinhacabofrio.com.br.*
…$ in low season, white rooms with comfortable …eds, a/c or fan, frigobar, breakfast, pool and …arking. About 4 blocks from Praia do Forte.

$$$-$$ Pousada Velas ao Vento
Av Júlia Kubitschek 5, T022-2645 3312, *eliascacarola@yahoo.com.br.*
Between *rodoviária* and centre. Cheaper in low season, comfortable, set back from the main road but still a bit of traffic noise. Hot water, a/c, helpful owner and staff.

$$ Marina dos Anjos
R Bernado Lens 145, Arraial do Cabo, T022-2622 4060, www.marinadosanjos.com.br.
Superior HI hostel with spruce dorms and doubles ($$$), facilities including a games

room, sun terrace and links to tour companies and dive shops.

$$ Pousada Suzy
Av Júlia Kubitschek 48, T022-2643 1742,
Facebook: Pousada-e-Restaurante-Suzy.
100 m from *rodoviária*, cheaper off season, with a/c, cheaper still with fan. Rooms for 8, $. Plain rooms but not spartan, pool, sauna, garage.

Peró

$$$ La Plage
R das Badejos 40, T022-2647 1746,
www.laplage.com.br.
Rates rise in high season when minimum stay of 7 days; fully equipped suites, those upstairs have sea view, excellent for families. Right on the beach, services include pool and bar, à la carte restaurant, hydro-massage, sauna, 24-hr cyber café, garage.

$$$ Pousada Espírito do Mar
R Anequim 122, T022-2644 3077,
www.espiritodomar.com.br.
$$ in low season. Orange building with central pool around which the rooms are built. Good, spacious but simple rooms, extra bed available. Frigobar, a/c, TV and fan. Cabo Frio bus passes outside.

Camping

Clube do Brasil
Av Wilson Mendes 700, 2 km from town,
T022-99861 5742.

Dunas do Peró
Estr do Guriri 1001, T022-2629 2323,
www.pousadadunasdopero.com.br.
Small *pousada* with a campsite on Praia do Peró.

Búzios
Reservations needed in summer, holidays such as Carnival and New Year's Eve, and weekends. For cheaper options and more availability, try Cabo Frio.

There are good, including luxury hotels on Praia da Ferradura and on Morro do Humaitá, superb views, 10 mins' walk from the town centre. Hire a buggy to get around town. Several private houses rent rooms, especially in summer and holidays. Look for the signs: 'Alugo Quartos'.

$$$$ Casas Brancas
Alto do Humaitá 8, T022-2623 1458,
www.casasbrancas.com.br.
A series of rooms perched on the hill in mock-Mykonos buildings with separate terraces for the pool and spa areas, wonderfully romantic at night when all is lit by candlelight. Very good. If you can't afford to stay go for dinner.

$$$$ El Cazar
Alto do Humaitá 6, T022-2623 1620,
www.buzioselcazar.com.
Next door to Casas Brancas and almost as luxurious; though a little darker inside. Beautiful artwork, tasteful and relaxing.

$$$$ Insólito
Rua E1 Lotes 3 e 4, Praia da Ferradura,
T022-2623 2172, www.insolitohotel.com.
Mediterranean-style boutique hotel with individually themed rooms each with a deck affording sea views, some have jacuzzis, very expensive. The restaurant offers a fusion of contemporary French and Brazilian cuisine, sea view and sophisticated atmosphere.

$$$$ Pousada Byblos
Alto do Humaitá 14, T022-2623 1162,
www.pousadabyblos.com.br.
Wonderful views over the bay, bright, light rooms with tiled floors and balconies.

$$$$ Pousada Pedra Da Laguna
Rua 6, lote 6, Praia da Ferradura, T022-2623 1965,
www.pedradalaguna.com.br.
Spacious rooms, the best with a view 150 m from the beach. Part of the Roteiros do Charme.

$$$$ Pousada Saint Germain
Alto do Humaitá 5, T022-2623 1044,
www.saintgermain-buzios.com.br.
Nice views, verandas, a/c, mosquito nets, pool, Brazilian/American-run.

$$$ Pousada Hibiscus Beach
R 1 No 22, Quadra C, Praia de João Fernandes,
T022-2623 6221, www.hibiscusbeach.com.
A peaceful spot, 15 pleasant bungalows, garden, pool, light meals available, help with car/buggy rentals and local excursions. One of the best beach hotels.

$$$ Pousada Santorini
R 9, Lote 28, Quadra C, Praia João
Fernandes, T022-2623 2802,
www.pousadasantorini.com.br.
Good service, lovely beach views, mock-Greek island design with spacious rooms and public areas, popular, book well ahead. Pool, restaurant bar and massage.

$$$-$ Nomad Hostel
R das Pedras 25, T022-2620 8085,
www.nomadbuzios.com.br.

Popular hostel with a/c, mixed and female dorms (US$19-24), private suites ($$$-$$), a beach bar, lockers and a travel desk.

$$-$ Hostel Ville Blanche
R Turibe de Farias 222, T022-2623 1644,
http://villeblanchebuzios.blogspot.co.uk.
Simple hostel, central, dorms for up to 10, and bright, tiled floor doubles with balcony.

Petrópolis

$$$$ Pousada da Alcobaça
R Agostinho Goulão 298, Correas, T024-2221 1240, www.pousadadaalcobaca.com.br.
Delightful, family-run country house in flower-filled gardens, pool and sauna. Worth stopping by for tea on the terrace, or dinner at the restaurant. Recommended.

$$$$ Solar do Império
Av Koeler 276, T024-2103 3000,
www.solardoimperio.com.br.
Converted neo-classical colonial mansion set in gardens on Petrópolis's grandest street. Fittings evoke the imperial era but modern facilities include a pool, sauna and ofuro hot tub.

$$$ Casablanca Imperial
R da Imperatriz 286, T024-2242 6662,
www.casablancahotel.com.br.
Most atmospheric in this chain, cheaper rooms in modern extension, good restaurant, pool. Also **$$$ Casablanca Palace** (R 16 de Março 123, T024-2242 0162).

$$$ York
R do Imperador 78, T024-2243 2662,
www.hotelyork.com.br.
Convenient, helpful, the fruit and milk at breakfast come from the owners' farm. Recommended.

$$-$ Hostel 148
R Alberto Torres 148, T024-2246 5848,
www.hostel148.com.br.
Dorms for 5-8, rooms for 3-7 with bath and a suite, lockers, kitchen for guests' use other than at breakfast time, tours and sports arranged.

$$-$ Hostel Petrópolis
R Santos Dumont 345, Centro, T024-2237 3811,
www.hostelpetropolisoficial.com.br.
Well-run hostel in a red town house, central. Double rooms and dorms are a little small, no breakfast. The owner has dogs.

Serra dos Órgãos/Teresópolis

ICMBio allows camping, US$3.50 pp. There is also lodging at the **Abrigo Quatro da Pedra do Sino** (T021-2152 1120).

$$$$ Reserva Ecológica Guapiaçu
(Guapi Assu Bird Lodge)
c/o Regua, Nicholas and Raquel Locke, Caixa Postal 98112, Cachoeiras de Macacu, T021-2745 3998, www.regua.co.uk.
Private rainforest reserve with very comfortable accommodation in a spacious wooden house and guided walks through pristine forest, price is full board. Families of South America's largest and rarest primate, the muriqui (woolly spider monkey) live here, excellent birding. Bookable in the UK through www.telltaletravel.com as part of a tour.

$$$$ Serra dos Tucanos
Caixa Postal 98125, Cachoeiras do Macacu, T021-2649 1557, www.serra dostucanos.com.br.
British-run lodge in the Parque Estadual Três Picos near Teresópolis, with some of the very best birdwatching, guiding and facilities in the Atlantic coast forest. Cabins around a spring-water swimming pool. Airport transfers.

$ Recanto do Lord
R Luiza Pereira Soares 109, Teresópolis, T021-2742 5586, www.teresopolishostel.com.br.
Big, well-equipped HI hostel, dorms and doubles, wonderful mountain views and 'adventure' trips in the Serra dos Órgãos.

Restaurants

Cabo Frio

There's a neat row of restaurants on Av dos Pescadores, mostly fish, local meats, or pasta. There is seating on the pavement under awnings, French-style. Upstairs are a number of bars/clubs.

$$$-$$ Picolino
R Mcal F Peixoto 319, T022-2647 6222,
www.restaurantepicolino.com.br.
In a nice old building, very smart, mixed menu but mostly local fish and seafood.

$$ Galeto do Zé
Av dos Pescadores e Trav Maçonica.
For seafood and snacks. Also **Do Zé** (Av dos Pescadores 100, T022-2643 4277), serving Brazilian specialities.

$$ Hippocampus
R Mcal F Peixoto 283, T022-2645 5757.

Mostly seafood, generally good, international and regional dishes.

$$ "In" Sônia
Av dos Pescadores 140 loja 04.
Good service and tasty fish, many dishes for 2.

$$ Tonto
Av dos Pescadores 140 loja 01, next to "In" Sônia.
Serves pizza and local dishes (T022-2645 1886 for delivery), has a bar too.

$$-$ Chico's
Av Teixeira e Souza 30, upstairs In Centro Comercial Victor Nunes da Rocha, T022-2647 2735.
Smart, does breakfast, self-service.

$ Branca
Praça Porto Rocha 15.
Lunches à kilo 1100-1700, also fast food, pizza after 1800, coffee, pastries and cakes, good, a big, popular place.

Búzios

There are many restaurants along Av José Bento Ribeiro Dantas/R das Pedras and Orla Bardot (too many to mention here); one of the charms of Búzios is browsing. In Manguinhos is the **Porto da Barra** gastronomic centre, with a collection of sophisticated and informal restaurants on the waterfront, as popular as the main drag. There are plenty of beachside *barracas* (thatched bars) on the peninsula (closed out of season) and cheaper places away from the sea front. A few places on Praça Santos Dumont off R das Pedras offer sandwiches and self-service food.

$$$ Bar do Zé
Orla Bardot 282.
Lovely spot for candlelit dinner. Go at sunset for a caipirinha and then follow with starlit al fresco dining and delicious seafood dishes.

$$$ Cigalon
*R das Pedras 199, T022-2623 0932,
www.cigalon.com.br.*
Good French and Italian restaurant in the Pousada do Sol, where Bardot once stayed. Extensive wine list.

$$$ Parvati
R das Pedras 144, T022-2623 1375.
Top class Italian restaurant, with a romantic air.

$$$ Satyricon
Av José Bento Ribeiro Dantas 500, Oral Bardot, T022-2623 2691.
Another illustrious Italian specializing in seafood. Decent wine list.

$$ O Barco
Av Jose Bento Ribeiro Dantas, Orla Bardot, T022-2629 8307.
Good value for fresh sea food from the owner's fishmonger. Very popular with locals. Hard to find a table in high season.

$ Bananaland
*R Manoel Turíbio de Farias 50, T022-2623 0855,
http://restaurantebananaland.com.br.*
Cheap and cheerful per kilo buffet.

$ Chez Michou
R das Pedras, 90, Centro, T022-2623 2169.
An open-air bar with videos, music and dozens of choices of pancakes accompanied by ice cold beer. Always crowded.

Petrópolis

$$ Falconi
R do Imperador 757.
Traditional Italian. Recommended.

$ Cantina Bom Giovanni
R do Imperador 729, upstairs.
Popular, Italian, lunch and dinner.

$ Casa d'Ângelo
R do Imperador 700, by Praça Dom Pedro II.
Traditional tea house with self service food that doubles as a bar at night.

Bars and clubs

Búzios

In season Búzios nightlife is young, beautiful and buzzing. Many of the bars and clubs are on R das Pedras. There are plenty of others including more upscale wine bar-style options.

Anexo
Av José Bento Ribeiro Dantas 392, Orla Bardot, T022-2623 4966. Daily from 2000.
Chill-out lounge with electronica. Open bar with tables on the streets overlooking Praia da Armação beach. Has another branch at Porto da Barra.

House of Rock and Roll
*R Maria Joaquina 01, loja 8, Centro,
http://thehouseofrockandroll.com.br.*
Daily live band plays music ranging from 70s Rock to Brazilian pop music.

Pátio Havana
R das Pedras 101, T022-2623 2169.
Has live jazz, blues and Brazilian music on

Fri and Sat, also a 5-star restaurant with international cuisine.

Privelège
Av José Bento Ribeiro Dantas 550, Orla Bardot. One of Brazil's best European-style dance clubs with pumping techno, house and hip hop and 5 rooms including a cavernous dance floor, sushi bar and lounge.

Transport

Niterói
Bus No 751-D Aeroporto–Galeão–Charitas, 761-D Galeão–Charitas, 740-D and 741 Copacabana–Charitas, US$1.75.

Car The toll on the Rio–Niterói bridge is US$1.50.

Ferry From the 'barcas' at Praça 15 de Novembro (ferry museum at the terminal), ferry boats and launches cross every 20 mins (30 mins Sat-Sun) to **Niterói** (15 mins, US$1.90). Catamarans (*aerobarcas*) leave every 10 mins Mon-Fri (US$3.50). They also go to **Charitas**, near São Francisco beach. Of the frequent ferry and catamaran services from Praça 15 de Novembro, Rio, ferries are slower, cheaper and give better views than catamarans.

Lagos Fluminenses: Saquarema
Bus Mil e Um (1001) Rio–Saquarema, every 2 hrs 0730-1800, 2 hrs, US$6.50.

Cabo Frio
Air Flights from **Belo Horizonte**, **Rio de Janeiro**, **São Paulo** and other cities.

Bus Urban Salineira and Montes Brancos run local services. US$1.75 to **Búzios**, **São Pedro da Aldeia**, **Saquarema**, **Araruama** and **Arraial do**

Cabo. The urban bus terminal is near Largo de Santo Antônio, opposite the BR petrol station.

Long distance The *rodoviária* is well within the city, but a 2-km walk from centre and beaches. City buses stop nearby. To **Belo Horizonte** US$43-71 (*leito*). To **Petrópolis** US$25. 1001 to **Rio de Janeiro**, **Niterói** US$14-20, to **São Paulo** US$35-60.

Búzios
Bus Mil e Um from Novo Rio, T021-2516 1001, US$16-20, 2½ hrs (be at the bus terminal 20 mins before departure). Departures every 2 hrs, 0700 to 1900 daily. You can also take any bus to **Cabo Frio** (many more during the day), from where it's 30 mins to Búzios. Buy return tickets well in advance in high season. At any other time buy return ticket 1 day in advance. Búzios' *rodoviária* is a few blocks' walk from centre. Some *pousadas* are within 10 mins on foot, while others need a local bus (US$1) or taxi. Buses from Cabo Frio run the length of the peninsula and pass several *pousadas*.

Car Via BR-106 takes about 2½ hrs from Rio.

Petrópolis
Bus New *rodoviária* 3 km north beyond Bingen by the highway; bus No 100 to centre, US$1. From **Rio** every 15 mins throughout the day (US$8) with **Única Fácil**, Sun every hr, 1½ hrs, sit on the left hand side for best views. Buses leave from the Novo Rio *rodoviária*; also a/c buses, hourly from 1100, from Av Nilo Peçanha, US$11. To **Teresópolis** for the Serra dos Órgãos, **Viação Teresópolis**, 8 a day, US$6.

Serra dos Órgãos
Bus Rio–Teresópolis: Viação Teresópolis buses leave hourly from the Novo Rio *rodoviária*. Rodoviária at R 1 de Maio 100. Fare US$10.

West of Rio

pretty colonial towns, rare birds and sublime beaches

One of the main attractions near the inland highway to São Paulo is the Itatiaia National Park, a good area for climbing, trekking and birdwatching. For a really beautiful route, though, take the Rio de Janeiro–Santos section of the BR101, which hugs the forested and hilly Costa Verde southwest of Rio.

Dutra Highway
The Dutra Motorway, BR-116 – Brazil's busiest, heads west from Rio towards São Paulo. It passes the steel town of **Volta Redonda** and some 30 km further west, the town of **Resende** near Itatiaia National Park. In this region, 175 km from Rio, is **Penedo** (five buses a day from Resende) which in the 1930s attracted Finnish settlers who brought the first saunas to Brazil. There is a Finnish museum, a cultural centre and Finnish dancing on Saturday. This popular weekend resort also provides horse

riding, and swimming in the Portinho River. There are plenty of mid-range and cheap hotels in town. For tourist information, T024-3351 1876.

☆Parque Nacional de Itatiaia

Entry per day is US$10.50 per person, half price for each succeeding day at weekends, 90% discount midweek. Open 0800-1700, 0700-1400 for the higher section (you can stay till 1700). Information can be obtained from ICMBio, Estrada Parque Km 8.5, T024-3352 1292 or T3352 2288, www.icmbio.gov.br/parnaitatiaia. Avoid weekends and holidays if you want to see wildlife.

This park, being so close to Rio and São Paulo, is a must for those with limited time who wish to see some of world's rarest birds and mammals in a whole range of different ecosystems. Trails from one hour to two days go through deep valleys shrouded in pristine rainforest, hiding icy waterfalls and clear-water rivers. The 30,000-ha mountainous park is Brazil's oldest, founded in 1937 to protect Atlantic Coast Rainforest in the Serra de Mantiqueira. It is divided into two parts, the lower, with the administration, reached from the town of Itatiaia (Km 316 on the Dutra Highway), and the upper section, reached from the Engenheiro Passos-Caxambu road (Circuito das Águas). Important species include jaguar, puma, brown capuchin and black-face titi monkeys. The park is particularly good for birds with a list of 350+, with scores of spectacular tanagers, hummingbirds, cotingas and manakins. The best trails head for Pedra de Taruga and Pedra de Maçã and the Poranga and Véu de Noiva waterfalls. The Pico das Agulhas Negras and the Serra das Prateleiras (up to 2540 m) offer decent rock climbing.

Information and maps can be obtained at the park office. The **Administração do Parque Nacional de Itatiaia** operates a refuge in the park, which acts as a starting point for climbs and treks. Although buses do run through the park calling at the hotels, hiring a car to visit Itatiaia is the best option.

Costa Verde (Emerald Coast)

The Rio de Janeiro-Santos section of the BR101 is one of the world's most beautiful highways, running along the aptly called Emerald Coast, which is littered with islands, beaches, colonial settlements and mountain fazendas. It is complete through to Bertioga (see page 461), which has good links with Santos and São Paulo. Buses run from Rio to Angra dos Reis, Paraty, Ubatuba, Caraguatatuba and São Sebastião, where you may have to change for Santos or São Paulo.

Mangaratiba, 116 km from Rio, has muddy beaches, but the surroundings are pleasant and better beaches can be found outside town. These include Ibicuí (2 km) and Brava to the east, Saco, Guiti and Cação at the head of the bay, and São Brás further west. Boats sail from Mangaratiba to Ilha Grande (see below).

Angra dos Reis *Colour map 7, B4.*

Said to have been founded on 6 January 1502 (O Dia dos Reis – The Day of Kings/Epiphany), this is a port, 151 km southwest of Rio, with an important fishing and shipbuilding industry. It has several small coves with good bathing within easy reach and is situated on an enormous bay full of islands. Of particular note are the church and convent of **Nossa Senhora do Carmo**, built in 1593 (Praça Gen Osório), the **Igreja Matriz de Nossa Senhora da Conceição** (1626) in the centre of town, and the church and convent of **São Bernardino de Sena** (1758-1763) on the Morro do Santo Antônio. On the Largo da Lapa is the church of **Nossa Senhora da Lapa da Boa Morte** (1752), with a sacred art museum ① *Thu-Sun 1000-1200, 1400-1800*. On the Península de Angra, just west of the town, is the **Praia do Bonfim**, a popular beach, and a little way offshore the island of the same name, on which is the hermitage of Senhor do Bonfim (1780). The **TurisAngra tourist office** is at ① *Av Júlio Maria 10, Sobrado, T024-3367 7866, with kiosks at Praia do Anil, Av Ayrton Senna 580, T024-3369 7704, open 0800-2000, Estação Santa Luiza, T024-3365 6421, and at the rodoviária, both open 0700-1900, www.angra.rj.gov.br; good information.*

☆Ilha Grande *Colour map 7, B5.*

Ilha Grande is a mountain ridge covered in tropical forest sticking out of an emerald sea and fringed by some of the world's most beautiful beaches. As there are no cars and no roads either, just trails through the forest, the island is still relatively undeveloped. Much of it forms part of a State Park and Biological Reserve, and cannot even be visited (INEA visitors centre, T3361 5553, Monday-Sunday 0900-1800). The island was a notorious pirate lair, then a landing port for slaves. By the 20th century it had become the site of an infamous prison for the country's most notorious criminals (closed in 1994 and now overgrown rubble). The weather is best from March to June and, like everywhere along the coast, the island is overrun during the Christmas, New Year and Carnaval period. There is a decent tourist booth at the ferry port on arrival, T024-3361 5760, 0700-1900. Information at www. ilhagrande.org; also www.ilhagrande.com.br.

The beach at **Vila do Abraão** may look beautiful to first arrivals but those further afield are far more spectacular. The two most famous are **Lopes Mendes**, two hours' walk from Abraão, and **Aventureiro**, six hours (book with Resamundi, see page 442). Good beaches closer to Abraão include the half moon bay at **Abraãoozinho** (15 minutes' walk) and **Grande das Palmas** which has a delightful tiny whitewashed chapel (one hour 20 minutes' walk), both east of town. Lagoa Azul, Freguesia de Santana and Saco do Céu are all boat trips. Good treks include over the mountains to Dois Rios, where the old jail was situated (13 km one way, about three hours), Pico do Papagaio (980 m) through forest, a stiff, three-hour climb, Pico da Pedra d'Água (1031 m) and the week-long walk around the island. State park accredited guides (Robson Alves is recommended – see page 442) are essential for all treks in the forest; people have gone off-trail and been lost for days.

☆Paraty *Colour map 7, B4.*

Paraty, 98 km from Angra dos Reis, is one of Brazil's prettiest colonial towns, whose centre has been declared a national historic monument in its entirety. It was the chief port for the export of gold in the 17th century and a coffee-exporting port in the 19th century. At the weekend Paraty buzzes with tourists who browse in the little boutiques and art galleries, or buy souvenirs from the indigenous Guaraní who sell their wares on the cobbles. Many of the numerous little bars and restaurants, like the *pousadas*, are owned by expat Europeans and Paulistanos, who are determined to preserve Paraty's charm. During the week, especially off season, the town is quiet and intimate. Much of the accommodation available is in colonial buildings, some sumptuously decorated, with flourishing gardens or courtyards. The town centre is out of bounds for motor vehicles; heavy chains are strung across the entrance to the streets. In spring the roads are flooded, while the houses are above the water level. **Centro de Informações Turísticas** ① *Av Roberto Silveira, near the entrance to the historical centre, T024-3371 1897, daily 0900-1600.* More information is available at http://infoparaty.com. There are two ATMs in town, one at Banco do Brasil, Av Roberto Silveira, not too far from the bus station.

There are four churches: **Santa Rita** (1722), built by the 'freed coloured men' in elegant Brazilian baroque, faces the bay and the port. It houses an interesting **Museum of Sacred Art** ① *Wed-Sun 0900-1200, 1300-1800, US$1.* **Nossa Senhora do Rosário e São Benedito** (1725, rebuilt 1757) ① *R do Comércio, Tue 0900-1200,* built by black slaves, is small and simple. **Nossa Senhora dos Remédios** (1787-1873) ① *Mon, Wed, Fri, Sat 0900-1200, Sun 0900-1500,* is the town's parish church, or Matriz, the biggest in Paraty. **Capela de Nossa Senhora das Dores** (1800) ① *Thu 0900-1200,* is a small chapel facing the sea that was used mainly by the wealthy whites in the 19th century. There is a great deal of distinguished Portuguese colonial architecture in delightful settings. **Rua do Comércio** is the main street in the historical centre. The **Casa da Cadeia**, close to Santa Rita church, is the former jail and is now a public library and art gallery. The **Casa da Cultura** ① *at the junction of R Samuel Costa and R Dona Geralda, Wed-Mon 1000-1930, winter to 1830, US$2.50,* houses an excellent multimedia history display (also in English, though this option can be hidden).

The town's environs are as beautiful as Paraty itself. Just a few kilometres away lie the forests of the Ponta do Juatinga peninsula (see below). At **Fazenda Murycana**, an old sugar estate and 17th-century *cachaça* distillery, you can taste and buy the different types of *cachaça*. It has an excellent restaurant. Mosquitoes can be a problem, take repellent and don't wear shorts. If short of time, the one must is a boat trip round the bay; some of its islands are home to rare animals. Boats also go to wonderful beaches like **Praia da Conçeicao**, **Praia Vermelha** and **Praia da Lula**, all of which have simple restaurants and are backed by forest and washed by gentle waves. Further south are **Saco da Velha**, protected by an island, and **Paraty Mirim** (17 km, also reached by bus, four a day, three on Sunday). The **Gold Trail**, hiking on a road dating from the 1800s, can be done on foot or horseback. Many other adventure sports are available.

Paraty Mirim and Trindade

The coast southwest of Paraty is particularly beautiful, winding around the Ponta da Juatinga peninsula which is swathed in primary rainforest (home to jaguars), cut with fjord-like inlets and fringed with lovely beaches. Access is from Paraty Mirim and Trindade, villages 15 and 27 km south of Paraty. Hikes can be taken from Paraty Mirim into the virgin forest of the Reserva Ecológica Juatinga, including the steep hike to the spectacular Pão de Açúcar (Sugar Loaf) boulder mountain (allow half a day from Paraty Mirim) for jaw-dropping views, and boat trips to remote beaches and the Saco de Mamanguá inlet. All are available through Rodrigo Oliveira (see page 442). Trindade is sandwiched between rainforested slopes and emerald sea. It has a long, broad beach and has long been a favourite for surf hippies from São Paulo and Rio who come in droves over Christmas and New Year. It is finding its place on the international backpacker circuit as the campsites, *pousadas* and restaurants are cheap and cheerful. See www.paratytrindade.com.br.

Note If travelling along the coast into São Paulo state as far as Guarujá, do not drive or go out alone after dark.

Listings West of Rio

Where to stay

Parque Nacional de Itatiaia

There is accommodation in hotels and cabins inside and outside the national park.

$$$$-$$$ Hotel Donati
T024-3352 1110, www.hoteldonati.com.br.
Delightful, mock-Swiss chalets and rooms, set in tropical gardens visited by animals every night and early morning. A series of trails lead off from the main building and the hotel can organize professional birding guides. Decent restaurant and 2 pools. Highly recommended.

$$$-$$ Aldeia dos Pássaros
Estrada do Parque Nacional, Km 6, T024-3352 1152, http://pousadaaldeiadospassaros.com.br.
Simple chalets in forest in park's lower reaches, with pool, riverside sauna, restaurant, organic garden and bar. Helpful staff, good breakfasts and reasonable off-season rates; good for birdwatchers.

$$ Pousada Esmeralda
Estrada do Parque, T024-3352 1643, www.pousadaesmeralda.com.br.
Comfortable chalets set around a lake in a lawned garden, wooden furnishings and log fires. Be sure to book a table for a candlelit dinner.

$$ Ypê Amarelo
R João Maurício Macedo Costa 352, Campo Alegre, T024-3352 1232, www.pousadaypeamarelo.com.br.
IYHA youth hostel with annexes set in an attractive garden visited by hummingbirds.

Angra dos Reis

$$ Caribe
R de Conceição 255, T024-3365 0033.
Central, in a 1970s tower, well-kept, a reasonable option.

Ilha Grande

There are many *pousadas* in Abraão and reservations are only necessary in peak season or on holiday weekends. Prices vary considerably from month to month. Ignore dockside hotel touts who lie about hotel closures and flash pictures of their lodgings to unsuspecting tourists.

Abraão

$$$ Aratinga Inn
Vila do Abraão, www.aratingailhagrande.com.br.
Simply furnished rooms, but lovely location in a tropical garden dotted with boulders right under the brow of Papagaio peak. Excellent service which includes Anglo-Australian afternoon tea.

$$$-$$ Ancoradouro
R da Praia 121, T024-3361 5153, www.pousadancoradouro.com.br.
Simple rooms with en suites in a beach front building, 10 mins' walk east of the jetty. The Pousada Caiçara next door is a good option if the hotel is full.

$$$-$$ Porto Girassol
R do Praia 65, T011-96228 7070, http://ilhagrande.org/portogirassol.
Simple rooms in a beach house 5 mins east of the jetty, best rooms have balconies, small garden.

$$ Pousada Sanhaço
R Santana 120, T024-3361 5102,
www.pousadasanhaco.com.
A range of a/c rooms, the best of which have
balconies with sea views and cosy en suites.
The *pousada* is decorated with paintings by
local artists, generous breakfast.

$$-$ Pousada Cachoeira
Rua do Bicão, T024-3361 9521, www.cachoeira.com.
Lovely little *pousada* with a dining room palapa
and living area, cabins and a terrace of rooms
nestled in a forest garden next to a fast-flowing
stream. Good breakfasts and boat tours. English
and German spoken. $$ in high season.

$ pp Albergue Holdandés
R Assembléia de Deus, T024-3361 5034,
www.holandeshostel.com.br.
Dormitories and four little chalets ($$) lost in
the forest, great atmosphere, be sure to reserve,
HI affiliated.

Paraty
Over 300 hotels and *pousadas*; in mid-week
look around and find a place that suits you best.
Browse through http://infoparaty.comfor yet
more options. During Carnival, New Year and FLIP

prices in *pousadas* escalate and many rooms are
available only in block bookings.

$$$$ Bromelias Pousada & Spa
*Rodovia Rio-Santos, Km 562, Graúna, T024-
3371 2791, www.pousadabromelias.com.br.*
Asian-inspired with its own aromatherapy
products and massage treatments, tastefully
decorated chalets in the Atlantic coastal forest.
Pool, sauna and restaurant.

$$$$ Casa Cairuçu
A 10- to 25-min boat ride from Paraty,
www.casa-cairucu.com.
Luxurious self-catering beach villa in a beautiful,
secluded location, 3 en suite double rooms, boat
transfer, maid service, internet and local phone
included. A professional chef and concierge are
available at extra cost, fridge can be pre-stocked.
Activities include kayaking and trekking.

$$$$ Pousada do Ouro
R Dr Pereira (or da Praia) 145, T024-3371 4300,
www.pousadaouro.com.br.
Near the eastern waterfront in the historic centre,
once a private home built from a gold fortune,
suites in the main building, plainer rooms in an
annexe, open-air poolside pavilion in a tropical
garden. Has had many famous guests.

$$$$ Pousada do Sandi
Largo do Rosário 1, T024-3371 2100,
www.pousadadosandi.com.br.
18th-century building with a grand lobby,
comfortable, adjoining restaurant and pool.

$$$$ Pousada Pardieiro
R do Comércio 74, T024-3371 1370,
www.pousadapardieiro.com.br.
Quiet, with a calm, sophisticated atmosphere, a
colonial building with lovely gardens, delightful
rooms facing internal patios and a small pool.
Always full at weekends, no children under 15.

$$$$ Pousada Picinguaba
T011-2495 1586, www.picinguaba.com.
Stylish French-owned hotel some 30 km from
Paraty; with superior service, an excellent
restaurant and simple, elegant (fan-cooled)
rooms. Marvellous views out over a bay of islands.
Booking ahead essential.

$$$$-$$$ Le Gite d'Indaitiba
Rodovia Rio-Santos (BR-101) Km 562, Graúna,
T024-3371 7174, www.legitedindaiatiba.com.br.
French-owned chalets set in gardens on a
hillsidewhich has views of the bay. French
restaurant in tropical surroundings.

$$$ Morro do Forte
R Orlando Carpinelli, T024-3371 1211,
www.pousadamorrodoforte.com.br.
Out of the centre, lovely garden, good breakfast,
pool, German owner Peter Kallert offers trips on
his yacht. Recommended.

$$$ Pousada Arte Colonial
R da Matriz 292, T024-3371 7347,
www.pousadaartecolonial.com.br.
Some rooms **$$$$** in high season. One of
the best deals in Paraty: colonial building in
the centre decorated with style and genuine
personal touch by its French owner. Helpful,
breakfast included. Highly recommended.

$$$ Pousada do Corsário
Beco do Lapeiro 26, T024-3371 1866,
www.pousadacorsario.com.br.
New building with a pool and its own gardens;
next to the river and 2 blocks from the centre,
simple but stylish rooms, most with hammocks
outside. Highly recommended. With branches in
Búzios and Santo André, Bahia.

$$$ Pousada Eclipse
R das Ingás 4, T024-3371 2168,
www.pousadaeclipse.com.br.
Just outside the old town, Good rooms,
comfortable, excellent service, good breakfast,
with pool, parking, bar.

$$$ Vivenda & Maris
R Beija Flor 9 and 11, Caboré, T024-3371 4272
and 3371 2116, www.vivendaparaty.com
and www.marisparaty.com.br.
Identical *pousadas* with lovely garden chalet
rooms around a pool, personal service, quiet,
intimate, 10-min walk from centre.

$$$-$ Chill Inn Hostel and Pousada
R Orlando Carpinelli 3, Praia do Pontal,
T024-3373 1302, www.chillinnhostel.com.
Beachfront accommodation, dorms (from US$11
pp), all with bathrooms and a/c. Breakfast at
beach bar, free taxi and internet.

$$$-$ Geko Hostel
R Orlando Carpinelli 5, Praia do Pontal,
T024-3371 7504, www.gekohostel.com.
Private rooms and dorms (US$11-16, all with a/c),
free pick-up from bus station, breakfast on the
beach, free internet café, free Wi-Fi.

$$ Solar dos Gerânios
Praça da Matriz, T024-3371 1550,
www.paraty.com.br/geranio.
Beautiful colonial family house on main square in
traditional rustic style, excellent value and English
spoken. Warmly recommended.

$$-$ Pousada do Careca
Praça Macedo Soares, T024-3371 1291,
www.pousadadocareca.com.
Very simple rooms in the historic centre,
those without street windows are musty.

$ pp Casa do Rio
R Antônio Vidal 120, T024-3371 2223,
www.casadoriohostel.com.br.
Peaceful little hostel with riverside courtyard
and hammock, HI discount, kitchen, breakfast
included, private rooms (**$$**). Offers jeep and
horse riding trips. Recommended.

Camping

Camping Beira-Rio
Just across the bridge, before the road to the fort,
T024-3371 1985.

Camping Club do Brasil
Av Orlando Carpinelli, Praia do Pontal,
T024-3371 1050.
Small, good, very crowded in Jan and Feb,
US$8 pp. Also at Praia Jabaquara, T024-3371 7364.

Paraty Mirim and Trindade

Paraty Mirim has a handful of very simple small *pousadas*.

\$\$\$ Garni Cruzeiro do Sul
R Principal, 1st on the right as you enter Trindade, T024-3371 5102, http://hotelgarnicruzeirodosul.com.br.
Smart little beachside *pousada* with duplex rooms, most of which have sea views, **\$\$\$\$** at highest season.

\$\$-\$ Ponta da Trindade Pousada & Camping
Trinidade, T024-3371 5113, www.trindade pousadas.com.br/pontadatrindade.html.
Simple rooms with fan, sand-floored campsite with cold water showers and no power.

\$\$-\$ Pousada Marimbá
R Principal, Trindade, T024-97404 4533, www.trindadepousadas.com.br/pousada-marimba.html.
Simple colourful rooms and a little breakfast area.

Restaurants

Ilha Grande

The number of good restaurants on the island is growing – look around.

\$\$\$ Lua e Mar
Abraão, on the waterfront, T024-3361 5113.
The best seafood restaurant in the town with a menu including *bobó do camarão*, fish fillets and various *moquecas*.

\$\$ Dom Mario
R da Praia, T024-3361 5349.
Good Franco-Brazilian dishes and seafood from a chef who trained at the Meridien in Rio. Try the fillet of fish in passionfruit sauce.

Paraty

The best restaurants in Paraty are in the historic part of town and are among the best in the southeast outside Rio or São Paulo. The less expensive restaurants, those offering *comida por kilo* (pay by weight) and the fast-food outlets are outside the historical centre, mainly on Av Roberto Silveira. Paraty has some plates unique to the region, like *peixe à Parati* – local fish cooked with herbs, green bananas and served with *pirão*, a mixture of manioc flour and the sauce that the fish was cooked in.

\$\$\$ Bartolomeu
R Samuel Costa 176, T024-3371 3052, www.bartholomeuparaty.com.
Brazilian-European fusion dishes, good atmosphere and cocktails. Has an associated *pousada* (see website).

\$\$\$ Caminho do Ouro
R Samuel Costa 236, T024-3371 1689.
Gourmet food using locally produced ingredients. The restaurant becomes a samba club on weekend nights.

\$\$\$ Punto Divino
R Mcal Deodoro 129, T024-3371 1348, http://puntodivino.com.
Wood-fired pizza (best in town) and calzoni served with live music and a good selection of wine.

\$\$\$ Thai Brasil
R do Comércio 308A, T024-3371 2760, www.thaibrasil.com.br.
Beautiful restaurant ornamented with handicrafts and hand-painted furniture, the cooking loosely resembles Thai, without spices.

\$\$ Café Paraty
R da Lapa and Comércio, T024-3371 0128. Open 1200-2300.
Sandwiches, appetizers, light meals, also bar with live music nightly (cover charge), a local landmark.

\$\$ Dona Ondina
R do Comércio 32, by the river, T024-3371 1584, www.donaondina.com.br. Closed Mon, Mar and Nov.
Family restaurant with well-prepared simple food, good value.

\$ Sabor da Terra
Av Roberto Silveira 180, T024-3371 2384. Closes 2200.
Reliable, if not bargain-priced, self service food.

Bars and clubs

Paraty

Armazem Paraty
R Samuel Costa 18, T024-3371 2082.
Arty shop by day, samba club by night.

Bar Dinho
Praça da Matriz at R da Matriz.
Good bar with live music at weekends, sometimes mid-week.

Coupé
Praça Matriz, T024-3371 6008,
www.casacoupe.com.br.
A popular hang-out, outside seating, good bar
snacks and breakfast.

Teatro Espaço
The Puppet Show, R Dona Geralda 327,
T024-3371 1575, www.ecparaty.org.br.
Wed, Sat 2100, US$12.
A silent puppet theatre for adults only which has
toured throughout the USA and Europe. Not to
be missed.

Festivals

Paraty
Feb/Mar Carnival, hundreds of people cover
their bodies in black mud and run through the
streets yelling like prehistoric creatures (anyone
can join in).
Mar/Apr Semana Santa, with religious
processions and folk songs.
Mid-Jul Semana de Santa Rita, traditional
foods, shows, exhibitions and dances.
Aug Festival da Pinga, the *cachaça* fair at which
local distilleries display their products and there
are plenty of opportunities to over-indulge.
Sep (around the 8th) **Semana da Nossa
Senhora dos Remédios**, processions and
religious events.
Sep/Oct Spring Festival of Music, concerts in
front of Santa Rita church. The city is decorated
with lights for Christmas.
31 Dec New year's, a huge party with open-air
concerts and fireworks (reserve accommodation
in advance). As well as the Dança dos Velhos,
another common dance in these parts is the
ciranda, in which everyone, young and old, dances
in a circle to songs accompanied by guitars.
　　The **Festa Literária Internacional de Paraty**
(FLIP, www.flip.org.br) occurs every Jun/Jul
and is one of the most important literary events
in Latin America. It is always attended by big
name writers.

What to do

Parque Nacional de Itatiaia
Information on treks can be obtained from **Clube
Excursionista Brasileira** (Av Almirante Barroso 2,
8th floor, Rio de Janeiro, T021-2220 3695).

Wildlife guides
Edson Endrigo, *T024-3742 8374, www.avesfoto.
com.br.* Birding trips in Itatiaia and throughout
Brazil. English spoken.
Ralph Salgueiro, *T024-3351 1823,
www.ecoralph.com.br.* Tours of Itatiaia
and throughout the region.

Angra dos Reis

Boat trips
Trips around the bay are available, some with
a stop for lunch on the island of Gipóia (5 hrs).
Several boats run tours from the Cais de Santa
Luzia and there are agencies for saveiros in town,
boats depart between 1030-1130 daily (during
Jan and Feb best to reserve in advance).

Ilha Grande

Boat trips
These are easy to organize on the quay in Abraão.

Hiking
Resamundi, *T021-2545 0036, http://resamundi.
com.br.* Tours and transfers around Ilha Grande
and Angra, by boat, trail and diving. Reliable,
good guides and equipment.
Robson Alves, *T024-99857 7725.* First-rate hiking
guide for Ilha Grande, including the climb to
Pico do Papagaio and the round-the-island hike.
Official state park guide.

Paraty
Angatu, *T011-3872 0945, www.angatu.com.*
Private tours and diving trips around the bay
in luxury yachts and motor cruisers. Also offers
entry to exclusive private parties and private villa
rental. Book well ahead.
Antígona, *Praça da Bandeira 2, Centro Histórico,
T024-3371 2199.* Daily schooner tours, 5 hrs, bar
and lunch on board. Recommended.
Paraty Tours, *Av Roberto Silveira 11, T024-3371
1327, www.paratytours.com.br.* Good range of
trips. English and Spanish spoken.

Paraty Mirim and Trindade
Rodrigo Oliveira, *through Danielle Migueletto,
WhatsApp T024-99952 8595, danimigueletto@
hotmail.com.* Excellent accredited guide offering
wildlife and hiking trips to the forests and
beaches around Paraty Mirim and Trindade.

Parque Nacional de Itatiaia

Bus Itatiaia lies just off the main São Paulo–Rio Dutra highway. There are connections to Itatiaia town or nearby Resende from both **Rio** and **São Paulo**. There is only one way into the park from Itatiaia town and one main road within it – which forks off to the various hotels, all of which are signposted. 4 times a day (variable hours), a bus marked '504 Circular' leaves Itatiaia town for the Park, calling at the hotels. Coming from Resende this may be caught at the crossroads before Itatiaia. Through tickets to São Paulo are sold at a booth in the large bar in the middle of Itatiaia main street.

Costa Verde: Mangaratiba

Bus From Rio Rodoviária with **Costa Verde**, several daily, US$12.50.

Angra dos Reis

Bus To **Angra** at least hourly from Rio's *rodoviária* with **Costa Verde**, www.costaverdetransportes. com.br, many direct, comfortable buses take the 'via litoral', sit on the left, US$18, 2½ hrs. From Angra to **São Paulo**, Reunidas, www.reunidas paulista.com.br, 4 buses daily (3 on Sat), US$27, 7 hrs. To **Paraty**, many buses leave from the local bus station on Largo da Lapa near the Ilha Grande jetty, then go to the *rodoviária*; **Colitur** every 30-40 mins (Sun, holidays hourly) US$5, 2 hrs.

Ilha Grande

Ferry Fishing boats and ferries (**Barcas SA**, T021-2533 7524) leave from **Mangaratiba**, **Conceição** de Jacareí and **Angra dos Reis** taking 20-90 mins to reach Vila do Abraão (quickest from **Conceição de Jacareí**). From Conceição de Jacareí there are 12 yacht and catamaran sailings daily between 0830 and 1815 (2100 on Fri), US$6-10. From Mangaratiba there is a ferry at 0800 and an extra ferry on Fri at 2200, US$5.35. From Angra there are 14 daily yachts sailings, US$8-16, and1 ferry, US$12.50, leaving between 0730 and 1800. Schedules change frequently and it's well worth checking for the latest on www.ilhagrande.com.br or www.ilhagrande. org, which detail the names and phone numbers of all boats currently sailing. All the towns are served by **Costa Verde** buses from the *rodoviária* in Rio. **Easy Transfer**, T021-99386 3919, www. easytransferbrazil.com, offer a van and boat service from Rio to Ilha Grande and on to Paraty; door to door from the city (US$30) and from the airport (add US$25 to transfer cost); and from Ilha Grande to Paraty (US$25), or Rio–Ilha Grande– Paraty–Rio (US$45).

Paraty

Bus *Rodoviária* at the corner of R Jango Padua and R da Floresta. 9 buses a day go to **Rio** (241 km), 5 hrs, US$25 with **Costa Verde**. More than 20 a day to **Angra dos Reis** (98 km), 1½ hrs, with **Colitur**, T024-3371 1238, who also go to Paraty Mirim, 4 a day, 3 on Sun and to Trindade, frequent service Mon-Fri, US$1.55. To **Ubatuba** (75 km), just over 1 hr, US$7, 3 a day. To **São Paulo**, 5 daily, **Reunidas** and **São José**, 5½ hrs, US$25, booked up quickly, very busy at weekends. To **São Sebastião**, change in Caraguatatuba. On holidays and in high season, the frequency of bus services increases.

São
Paulo

The city of São Paulo, with a population of around 20 million, is vast and can feel intimidating at first. But this is a city of separate neighbourhoods, only a few of which are interesting for visitors and, once you have your base, it is easy to negotiate. Those who don't flinch from the city's size and who are prepared to spend money and time here, and who get to know Paulistanos, are seldom disappointed. (The inhabitants of the city are called Paulistanos, to differentiate them from the inhabitants of the state, who are called Paulistas.) Nowhere in Brazil is better for concerts, clubs, theatre, ballet, classical music, all round nightlife, restaurants and beautifully designed hotels.

Centro Histórico *Colour map 7, B4.*

an area of museums, churches, monasteries

A focal point of the centre is the Parque Anhangabaú, an open space between the Triângulo and the streets which lead to Praça da República (Metrô Anhangabaú is at its southern end). Beneath Anhangabaú, north-south traffic is carried by a tunnel. Crossing it are two viaducts: Viaduto do Chá, which is open to traffic and links Rua Direita and Rua Barão de Itapetininga. The Viaduto Santa Ifigênia, an iron bridge for pedestrians only, connects Largo de São Bento with Largo de Santa Ifigênia.

On **Largo de São Bento** there is the **Igreja e Mosteiro de São Bento** ① *T011-3328 8799, www. mosteiro.org.br, Mon-Wed and Fri 0600-1800, closed 0800-1130 Thu, Sat-Sun 0600-1200, 1600-1800, see website for details of services, including Gregorian chant,* an early 20th-century building (1910-22) on the site of a 1598 chapel. Due south of São Bento is the **Martinelli building** ① *on R Líbero Badaró at Av São João, closed,* the city's first skyscraper (1922). It was surpassed by the **Edifício Banespa** (officially Altino Arantes, or Banespão, finished 1947) ① *R João Brícola 24, T011-2196 3730, closed for refurbishment in mid-2017,* with 360° views from the top, up to 40 km, smog permitting. South of these two buildings is the **Centro Cultural Banco do Brasil** ① *R Álvares Penteado 112, T011-3113 3651, http://culturabancodobrasil.com.br, Wed-Mon 0900-2100,* an art nouveau building with a diverse programme in its exhibition spaces, cultural centre, concert halls and galleries in the old vaults. The **Pateo do Collégio (Museu de Anchieta)** ① *Praça Pátio do Colégio, T011-3105 6899, www. pateodocollegio.com.br, Metrô Sé, with a café, Tue-Sun 0900-1630, US$3.15,* is an exact replica of the original Jesuit church and college, but dates from 1950s. Most of the buildings are occupied by the Museu de Anchieta, named after the Jesuit captain who led the first mission. This houses a 17th-century font that was used to baptize *indígenas*, a collection of Guaraní art and artefacts from the colonial era and a modernist painting of the priest, by Italian Albino Menghini.

A short distance southeast of the Pateo do Collégio is the **Solar da Marquesa de Santos**, an 18th-century residential building, which now contains the photographic record of São Paulo the **Museu da Cidade/Casa da Imagem** ① *R Roberto Simonsen 136B, T011-3106 5122, www museudacidade.sp.gov.br, Tue-Sun 0900-1700, free,* which has branches throughout the city (see website). The **Praça da Sé** is a huge open area south of the Pateo do Collégio, dominated

Best for
Culture ▪ Nightlife ▪ Restaurants

Essential São Paulo

Finding your feet

There are air services from all parts of Brazil, Europe, North and South America to the international **airport** at Guarulhos, also known as Cumbica, 30 km northeast of the city. The local airport of Congonhas, 14 km south of the city centre on Avenida Washington Luiz, is used for the Rio-São Paulo shuttle, and some flights to Belo Horizonte and Vitória. Some Azul flights arrive at São Paulo Viracopos aiport which is situated in the city of Campinas, 90 km from São Paulo. The **main rodoviária** is Tietê, which is very convenient and has its own Metrô station, as do the other three bus stations for inter-state bus services.

Orientation

The **Old Centre** (Praça da República, Sé, Santa Cecília) is a place to visit but not to stay. The central commercial district, containing banks, offices and shops, is known as the Triângulo, bounded by Ruas Direita, 15 (Quinze) de Novembro, São Bento and Praça Antônio Prado, but spreading as far as the Praça da República. **Jardins**, the city's most affluent inner neighbourhood, is a good place to stay and to visit. Elegant little streets hide hundreds of wonderful restaurants and accommodation ranges from the luxurious to the top end of the budget range. You are safe here at night. The northeastern section of Jardins abuts one of São Paulo's grandest modern avenues, **Paulista**, lined with skyscrapers, shops and a few churches and museums including **MASP (Museu de Arte de São Paulo)**. There are metro connections from here and a number of good hotels. Between Jardins and the centre, **Consolação**, with Rua Augusta at its heart, is undergoing a renaissance at the cutting edge of the city's underground live music and nightlife scene. **Ibirapuera Park and around**: the inner city's largest green space is home to a handful of museums, running tracks, a lake and frequent free live concerts on Sundays. The adjoining neighbourhoods of Moema, Itaim and Vila

Mariana have a few hotels, but **Moema, Itaim**, **Vila Olímpia** are among the nightlife centres of São Paulo with a wealth of streetside bars, designer restaurants and European-style dance clubs. Hotels tend to be expensive as they are near the new business centre on Avenidas Brigadeiro Faria Lima and Luis Carlos Berrini. **Pinheiros and Vila Madalena** are less chic, but equally lively at night and with the funkiest shops.

Getting around

Much of the city centre is pedestrianized, so walking is the only option if you wish to explore it. The best and cheapest way to get around São Paulo is on the integrated Metrô and CPTM urban light railway system, which is clean, safe, cheap and efficient, and being expanded. Bus routes can be confusing and slow due to frequent traffic jams, but buses are safe, clean and only crowded at peak hours. If travelling with luggage, take a taxi. See Transport, page 459.

Safety

Avoid the Centro after dark, especially the areas around Luz station and Praça da República and do not enter favelas.

When to go

São Paulo sits on a plateau at around 800 m and the weather is temperamental. Rainfall is ample and temperatures fluctuate greatly: summer averages 20-30°C (occasionally peaking into the high 30s), winter temperatures are 15-25°C (occasionally dropping to below 10° C). The winter months (April-October) are the driest, with minimal precipitation in June/July. January and February can be very wet. When there are thermal inversions, air pollution can be troublesome.

Time required

Stay two to three days for the city, preferably over a weekend for nightlife. To explore parts of the state as well, you will need five to seven days.

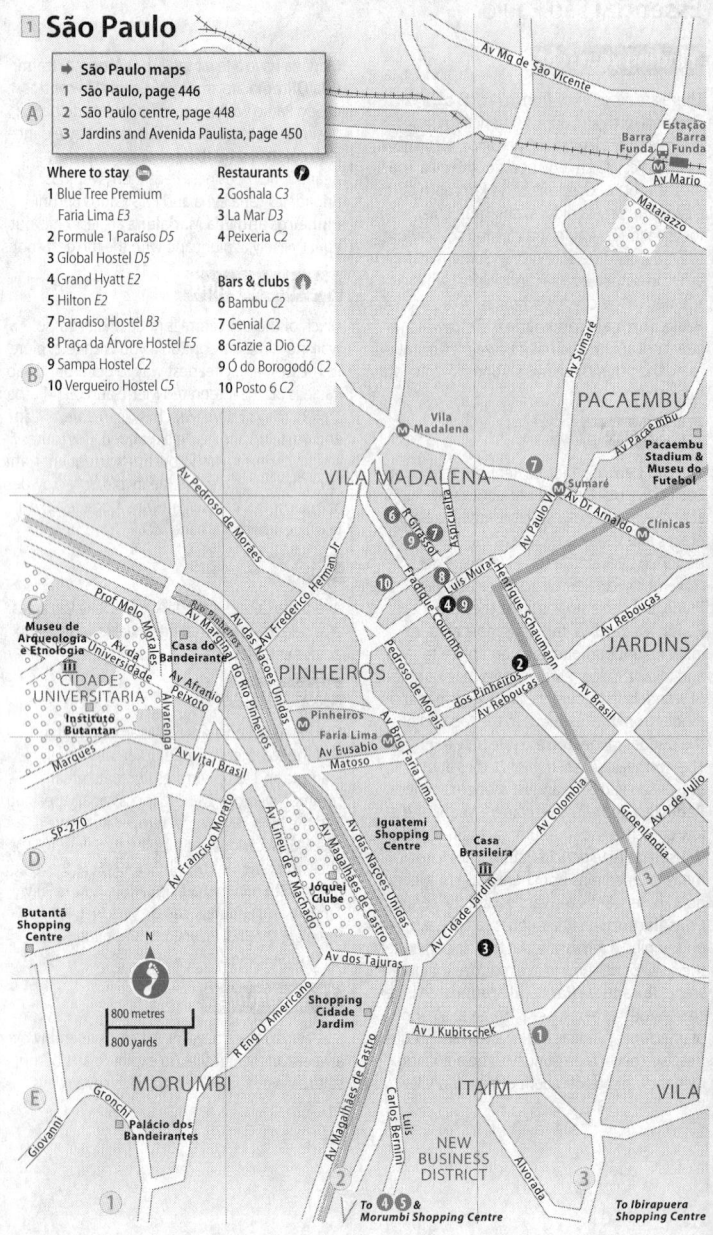

1 São Paulo

➡ **São Paulo maps**
1 São Paulo, page 446
2 São Paulo centre, page 448
3 Jardins and Avenida Paulista, page 450

Where to stay 🛏
1 Blue Tree Premium
 Faria Lima *E3*
2 Formule 1 Paraíso *D5*
3 Global Hostel *D5*
4 Grand Hyatt *E2*
5 Hilton *E2*
7 Paradiso Hostel *B3*
8 Praça da Árvore Hostel *E5*
9 Sampa Hostel *C2*
10 Vergueiro Hostel *C5*

Restaurants 🍴
2 Goshala *C3*
3 La Mar *D3*
4 Peixeria *C2*

Bars & clubs 🍸
6 Bambu *C2*
7 Genial *C2*
8 Grazie a Dio *C2*
9 Ó do Borogodó *C2*
10 Posto 6 *C2*

Av Mq de São Vicente

Estação
Barra
Funda

Av Mario

Matarazzo

PACAEMBU

Pacaembu
Stadium &
Museu do
Futebol

Vila
Madalena

Sumaré

VILA MADALENA

Clínicas

Prof Melo Morais

Museu de
Arqueologia
e Etnologia

Casa do
Bandeirante

JARDINS

CIDADE
UNIVERSITÁRIA

Instituto
Butantan

PINHEIROS

Pinheiros

Faria Lima

Av Vital Brasil

Av Eusabio
Matoso

Iguatemi
Shopping
Centre

Casa
Brasileira

Butantã
Shopping
Centre

N

Jóquei
Clube

800 metres

800 yards

Shopping
Cidade
Jardim

Av J Kubitschek

MORUMBI

Palácio dos
Bandeirantes

ITAIM

NEW
BUSINESS
DISTRICT

VILA

To 🍴🛏🛏 &
Morumbi Shopping Centre

To Ibirapuera
Shopping Centre

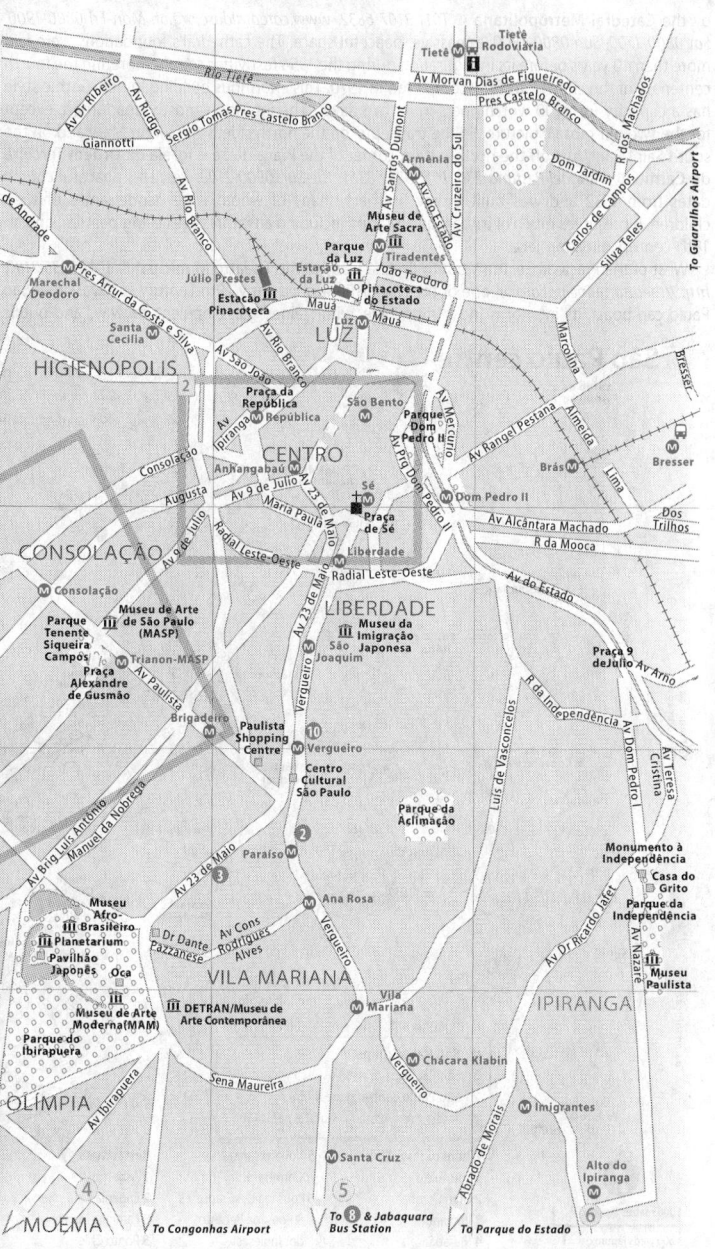

Tietê Rodoviária

Tietê

Av Morvan Dias de Figueiredo

Rio Tietê

Pres Castelo Branco

Av Dr Ribeiro

Giannotti

Av Rudge

Sergio Tomas

Pres Castelo Branco

Dom Jardim

de Andrade

Av Rio Branco

Carlos de Campos

Silva Teles

Marcolina

Bresser

To Guarulhos Airport

Museu de
Arte Sacra

Armênia

Av Santos Dumont

Av do Estado

Av Cruzeiro do Sul

Marechal
Deodoro

Pres Artur da Costa e Silva

Parque
da Luz

Tiradentes
João Teodoro

Júlio Prestes

Estação
da Luz

Estação
Pinacoteca

Pinacoteca
do Estado

Santa
Cecília

Av São João

Maná

Maná

LUZ

Luz

Av Rio Branco

HIGIENÓPOLIS

2

Praça da
República

São Bento

Av Mercúrio

Parque
Dom
Pedro II

Av Prg Pestana

Almeida

Bresser

República

Av Ipiranga

CENTRO

Consolação

Anhangabaú

Sé

Av Prg Dom Pedro II

Brás

Av Rangel Pestana

Lima

Dos
Trilhos

Augusta

Av 9 de Julho

Av 23 de Maio

Maria Paula

Praça
de Sé

Dom Pedro II

Av Alcântara Machado

CONSOLAÇÃO

Consolação

Liberdade

R da Mooca

Radial Leste-Oeste

Radial Leste-Oeste

Av do Estado

Parque
Tenente
Siqueira
Campos

Museu de Arte
de São Paulo
(MASP)

LIBERDADE

Museu da
Imigração
Japonesa

Praça 9
deJulio Av Arno

Trianon-MASP

Praça
Alexandre
de Gusmão

Av Paulista

São
Joaquim

Vergueiro

R da Independência

Av Dom Pedro I

Av Teresa
Cristina

Brigadeiro

Paulista
Shopping
Centre

10

Vergueiro

Av Brig Luiz Antônio

Manuel da Nóbrega

Centro
Cultural
São Paulo

Parque da
Aclimação

Luis de Vasconcelos

Monumento à
Independência

Casa do
Grito

2

Paraíso

Parque da
Independência

Museu
Afro-
Brasileiro

Av 23 de Maio

3

Ana Rosa

Av Nazaré

Av Dr Ricardo Jafet

Museu
Paulista

Planetarium

Pavilhão
Japonês

Oca

Dr Dante
Pazzanese

Av Cons
Rodrigues
Alves

Vergueiro

VILA MARIANA

IPIRANGA

Museu de Arte
Moderna (MAM)

DETRAN/Museu de
Arte Contemporânea

Vila
Mariana

Parque do
Ibirapuera

Sena Maureira

Vergueiro

Chácara Klabin

OLIMPIA

Av Ibirapuera

Imigrantes

Abração de Morais

Santa Cruz

Alto do
Ipiranga

4

MOEMA

To Congonhas Airport

5

To 8 & Jabaquara
Bus Station

To Parque do Estado

6

by the **Catedral Metropolitana** ① *T011-3107 6832, www.catedraldase.org.br, Mon-Fri 0800-1900, Sat 0800-1700, Sun 0800-1800*, a massive, peaceful space. The cathedral's foundations were laid more than 40 years before its inauguration during the 1954 festivities commemorating the fourth centenary of the city. It was fully completed in 1970. This enormous building in neo-Gothic style has a capacity for 8000 worshippers in its five naves. The interior is mostly unadorned, except for the two gilt mosaic pictures in the transepts: on the north side is the Virgin Mary and on the south Saint Paul. Just off the northeastern corner of the Praça da Sé is **Igreja da Ordem Terceira do Carmo** ① *R Rangel Pestana 230, T011-3242 8361, Tue-Sun 0900-2100, free*. This peaceful church dates from 1632 and was built by lay brothers, many of whom were bandeirantes or their children. It preserves much of its baroque interior, including an impressive ceiling painting and an 18th-century gilt altarpiece.

West of the Praça da Sé, the Viaduto do Chá leads to the **Theatro Municipal** ① *T011-3035 2100, http://theatromunicipal.org.br*, one of the few distinguished early 20th-century survivors that São Paulo can boast. Its interior is most impressive, with stained glass, opulent hallways and public

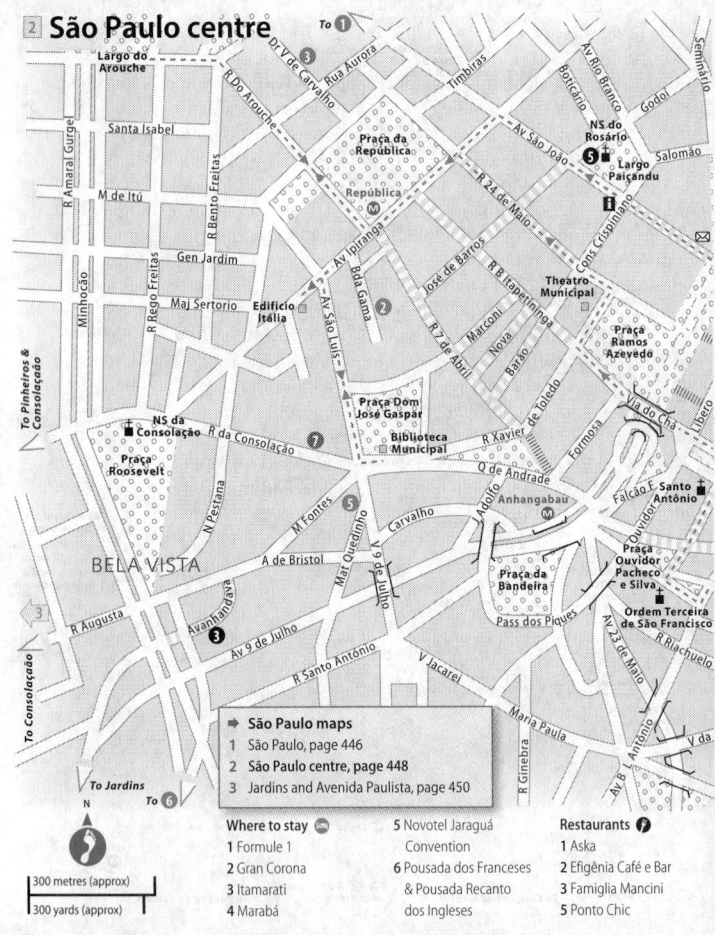

② São Paulo centre

⇒ São Paulo maps
1 São Paulo, page 446
2 São Paulo centre, page 448
3 Jardins and Avenida Paulista, page 450

Where to stay 🛏
1 Formule 1
2 Gran Corona
3 Itamarati
4 Marabá

5 Novotel Jaraguá Convention
6 Pousada dos Franceses & Pousada Recanto dos Ingleses

Restaurants 🍴
1 Aska
2 Efigênia Café e Bar
3 Famiglia Mancini
5 Ponto Chic

300 metres (approx)
300 yards (approx)

areas together with its stage and auditorium, thoroughly renovated and modernised and with an interesting and eclectic programme of classical music, ballet and performance.

Praça da República

In Praça da República the trees are tall and shady. Near the Praça is the city's tallest building, the **Edifício Itália** ① *Av Ipiranga 344, T011-2189 2929, terracoitalia.com.br*. There is a restaurant on top and a sightseeing balcony which was temporarily closed as this book went to press in 2017. If you walk up Avenida São Luís, which has many airline offices and travel agencies (especially found in the Galeria Metrópole), you arrive at Praça Dom José Gaspar, in which is the **Biblioteca Municipal Mário de Andrade**, surrounded by a pleasant shady garden.

North of the centre

About 10 minutes' walk from the centre is the old **Mercado Municipal** (see Shopping, page 458). **Parque da Luz** on Avenida Tiradentes (110,000 sq m) was formerly a botanical garden. It is next to the Luz railway station. There are two museums: in the park is the **Pinacoteca do Estado** (State Art Collection) ① *Praça da Luz 2, T011-3224 1000, www.pinacoteca.org.br, Tue-Wed 1000-1730, Thu 1000-2200, Fri-Sun 1000-1730, US$3.15, free on Sat (closes 1730)*. It and its neighbouring sister gallery, the **Estação Pinacoteca** ① *Largo General Osório 66, T011-3335 4990, Tue-Sun 1000-1730, US$3.15, Sat free*, preserve the best collection of modernist Brazilian art outside the Belas Artes in Rio, together with important works by Europeans like Picasso and Chagall. Both have good cafés, the Pinacoteca has a very good art bookshop. Nearby, the **Museu de Arte Sacra** ① *Av Tiradentes 676, T011-3326 3336, www.museuartesacra.org.br, Tue-Sun 1000-1700, US$2 (sat free)*, is modern and tasteful, housed in the serene **Mosteiro da Luz** (1774), still partially occupied. It has a priceless, beautifully presented collection including works by many of Brazil's most important Baroque masters. The convent is one of the few colonial buildings left in São Paulo; the chapel dates from 1579.

Liberdade

Directly south of the Praça da Sé, and one stop on the Metrô, is Liberdade, the central Japanese district, now also home to large numbers of Koreans and Chinese. The Metrô station is in Praça da Liberdade, in which there is an oriental market every Sunday (see Shopping). The Praça is one of the best places in the city for Japanese food. **Museu da Imigração Japonesa** ① *R São Joaquim 381, exhibition on 7th, 8th and 9th floors, T011-3209 5465, www.museubunkyo.org.br, Tue-Sun 1330-1730, US$2.10*, is excellent, with a roof garden; captions have English summaries.

6 Sushi Yassu

Bars & clubs 🎵
7 Royal Club   Historic buildings walk - ◄ -

Jardins and Avenida Paulista

Avenida Paulista has been transformed since the 1930s from the city's most fashionable promenade into six lanes of traffic lined with banks' and multinationals' headquarters, shopping centres and cafés. Its highlight is undoubtedly MASP, the common name for the ☆**Museu de Arte de São Paulo** ① *Av Paulista 1578 (above the 9 de Julho tunnel); T011-3149-5959, www.masp.art.br, Metrô Trianon-*

3 Jardins & Avenida Paulista

➡ **São Paulo maps**
1 São Paulo, page 446
2 São Paulo centre, page 448
3 Jardins and Avenida Paulista, page 450

Where to stay 🛏
1 Dona Zilah *A2*
2 Emiliano *B2*
3 Fasano hotel & restaurant *B2*
4 Guest Urban *A1*
5 Ibis São Paulo Paulista *A3*
6 Paulista Garden *C2*
7 Pousada dos Franceses & Pousada Recanto dos Ingleses *C3*
8 Renaissance *B3*
9 Tivoli Mofarrej *B3*
10 Unique *C2*

Restaurants 🍴
1 A Mineira *C3*
2 Buffet Charlô & Dalva e Dito *B2*
3 Cheiro Verde *B2*
4 DOM *B2*
5 Figueira Rubaiyat *B1*
6 Fran's Café *B2/C3*
7 Gero *B2*
8 Jun Sakamoto *A1*
9 Mani *B1*
10 MASP *B3*
11 Padaria Nova Charmosa *C3*
12 Sattva *A2*
13 Sujinho *A3*
14 Tavares *A2*
15 Tordesilhas *B2*
16 Vento Haragano *A2*

Bars & clubs 🍸
17 Bar Balcão *A2*
18 Beco 203 *B3*
20 Casa de Francisca *C3*
21 Finnegan's Pub *A1*
22 Kabul *A3*
23 Outs Club *A3*

MASP; open 1000-1800, except Thu 1000-2000, closed Mon, US$5. The museum has the finest collection of European masters in the southern hemisphere with works by artists like Raphael, Bellini, Bosch, Rembrandt, Turner, Constable, Monet, Manet and Renoir. Also some interesting work by Brazilian artists, including Portinari. Temporary exhibitions are also held and when a popular show is on, it can take up to an hour to get in. There is a very good art shop.

Opposite MASP is **Parque Tenente Siqueira Campos** ① *daily 0700-1830*, which covers two blocks on either side of Alameda Santos; a bridge links the two parts of the park. It is block of subtropical forest in the busiest part of the city. The **Museu da Imagem e do Som (MIS)** ① *Av Europa 158, T011-2117 4777, www.mis.sp.gov.br, Tue-Fri 1200-2100, Sat-Sun 1100-2000, free, exhibitions US$2*, has an arts cinema, sound labs, archives of Brazilian cinema and music, weekly club nights and a good restaurant. Next to MIS in a building by Pritzker prize-winning architect Paulo Mendes da Rocha is the **Museu Brasiliero da Escultura** (MuBE) ① *Av Europa 218, T011-2594 2601, http://mube.art.br, 1000-1900; free* to temporary exhibitions and recitals in the afternoons. Avenida Europa continues to Avenida Brigadeiro Faria Lima, on which is the **Casa Brasileira** ① *Av Faria Lima 2705, T011-3032 3727, www.mcb.org.br, Tue-Sun 1000-1800, US$2.50, Sun free*, a museum of Brazilian furniture. It also holds temporary exhibitions.

Cidade Universitária

The Cidade Universitária is on the west bank of the Rio Pinheiros, opposite the district of Pinheiros. The campus also contains the famous **Instituto Butantan (Butantan Snake Farm and Museums)** ① *Av Dr Vital Brasil 1500, T011-2627 9300, Tue-Sun 0900-1645, www.butantan.gov.br, US$1.90, children half price, under 7 free, Metrô Butanta.* The biological museum and vivarium (with live reptiles and arachnids) and a museum of microbiology are open to visitors. The **Museu de Arqueologia e Etnologia** (MAE) ① *Av Prof Almeida Prado 1466, T011-3091 4905, www.nptbr. mae.usp.br*, with Amazonian and ancient Mediterranean collections. Not far from the Butantan Institute, just inside Cidade Universitária, is the **Casa do Bandeirante** ① *Praça Monteiro Lobato, T011-3105 6118, www.museudacidade.sp.gov.br/casadobandeirante.php, Tue-Sun 0900-1700*, the reconstructed home of a 17th-century pioneer.

On the west bank of the Rio Pinheiros, just southeast of the Cidade Universitária, is the palatial **Jóquei Clube/Jockey Club** ① *Av Lineu de Paula Machado 1263, T011-2161 8300, www.jockeysp.com.br*, racecourse in the Cidade Jardim area. Take Butantã bus from República. Race meetings are held Monday and Thursday at 1930 and weekends at 1430. It has a **Museu do Turfe** ① *Tue-Sun, closed Sat-Sun mornings.*

South of the centre

green spaces and cultural events

☆Ibirapuera

The **Parque do Ibirapuera** ① *entrance on Av Pedro Álvares Cabral, www.parquedoibirapuera.com, daily 0500-2400 but unsafe after dark*, was designed by Oscar Niemeyer and landscape artist Roberto Burle Marx for the city's fourth centenary in 1954. Within its 160 ha are many public buildings and monuments. These include the state-of-the-art **Planetarium** ① *T011-5575 5206, Sat, Sun (4 sessions aimed squarely at young children 1100, 1200, 1500, 1700) and daily Dec-Feb and Jul, free*, the **Museu de Arte Moderna** (MAM) ① *T011-5085 1300, www.mam.org.br, Tue-Sun 1000-1800, US$2*, with temporary art exhibitions, a great café restaurant and art shop. The MAM overlooks a sculpture garden located between the **Oca** (Pavilhão Lucas Nogueira Garcez), a brilliant white dome which stages exhibitions, and the **Fundação Bienal**. Every even-numbered year the **Bienal Internacional de São Paulo** (São Paulo Biennial) has the most important show of modern art in Latin America, usually in September. Also in the park is **Museu Afro-Brasil** ① *T011-3320 8900, www.museuafrobrasil.org.br, Tue-Sun 1000-1800, US$2*, with temporary exhibitions, theatre, dance and cinema spaces, photographs and panels devoted to exploring African Brazil. **Pavilhão Japonês** ① *T011-5081 7296, http://bunkyo.org.br, Wed, Sat, Sun 1300-1700, free except for exhibitions*, exhibition space showing works from Japanese and Japanese-Brazilian artists, designed by Japanese and built exclusively with materials from Japan. It is set

BACKGROUND

Sleepy São Paulo

Until the 1870s São Paulo was a sleepy, shabby little town known as 'a cidade de barro' (the mud city), as most buildings were made of clay and packed mud. It was transformed in the late 19th century when wealthy landowners and Santos merchants began to invest. From 1885 to 1900 the coffee boom and arrival of large numbers of Europeans transformed the state. By the late 1930s São Paulo state had one million Italians, 500,000 each of Portuguese and immigrants from the rest of Brazil, 400,000 Spaniards and 200,000 Japanese. It is the world's largest Japanese community outside Japan. Nowadays, it covers more than 1500 sq km, three times the size of Paris.

in Japanese gardens and has a traditional tea house upstairs. Bicycles can be hired in the park, US$2 per hour. To get to Ibirapuera: Metrô Ana Rosa is a 15-minute walk and Metrô Brigadeiro a 35-minute walk, but Ibirapuera metro is under construction; bus 5164-21 every 30 minutes from Metrô Santa Cruz; any bus (eg 175T-10, 477U-10, 675N-10) to DETRAN, a Niemeyer building opposite the park which has reopened as the new headquarters of **Museu de Arte Contemporânea de São Paulo** ① *Av Pedro Álvares Cabral 1301, T011-2648 0254, www.mac.usp.br, Tue-Sun 1000-1800, free.* It has an important collection of Brazilian and European modern art. From DETRAN cross Av 23 de Maio by footbridge.

Parque da Independência

In the suburb of Ipiranga, 5.5 km southeast of the city centre, the Parque da Independência contains the **Monumento à Independência**. Beneath the monument is the **Imperial Chapel** ① *Tue-Sun 1300-1700*, with the tomb of the first emperor, Dom Pedro I, and Empress Leopoldina. **Casa do Grito** ① *Tue-Sun 0930-1700*, the little house in which Dom Pedro I spent the night before his famous cry of Ipiranga, 'Independence or Death', is preserved in the park (gardens open daily 0500-2300, free). The **Museu Paulista** ① *T011-2065 8001, www.mp.usp.br, closed for refurbishment in 2017*, contains old maps, traditional furniture, collections of old coins, religious art and *indígena* ethnology. Behind the Museum is the **Horto Botânico (Ipiranga Botanical Garden)** and the **Jardim Francês** ① *Tue-Sun 0900-1700, getting there: take bus 478-P (Ipiranga-Pompéia for return) from Ana Rosa, or take bus 4612 from Praça da República.*

Parque do Estado (Jardim Botânico)

This large park, a long way south of the centre, at **Água Funda** ① *Av Miguel Estefano 3031-3687, T011-5067 6000, http://botanica.sp.gov.br, Tue-Sun 0900-1700, US$1.50, getting there: take Metrô to São Judas on the Jabaquara line, then take bus 4742*, contains the Jardim Botânico, with lakes and trees and places for picnics, and a very fine orchid farm worth seeing during November-December (orchid exhibitions in April and November).

Paranapiacaba

a must for a train enthusiast

Paranapiacaba is a tiny 19th-century town in the cloudforest of the Serra do Mar, 50 km southeast of São Paulo. It was built by British railway workers. There is a small railway museum and a handful of *pousadas* and restaurants.

A frequent train runs on the Turquoise Line (Linha Turquesa, 10) from Luz station to Rio Grande da Serra, US$1.20, 55 minutes, from where bus No 424 runs to Paranapiacaba in the week, every 30 minutes at weekends, about one hour. A tourist train, the *Expresso Turístico*, runs from Luz at 0830 or Estação Prefeito Celso Daniel-Santo André at 0900 on Sundays direct to Paranapiacaba, returning 1630, 1½ hours, US$15. CPTM runs two other tourist trains, to Jundiaí northwest of the city, on the Linha Rubi (7), leaving Luz at 0830, returning 1630 on Saturdays, and to Mogi das Cruzes, east of the city, on the Linha Safira (12) on the second Satuday of each month from Luz at 0830, returning 1630, both 1½ hours, US$15. Details of all three on www.cptm.sp.gov.br.

Tourist information

There are tourist information booths with English speaking staff in international and domestic arrivals Guarulhos (Cumbica) airport, 0900-2200, and Congonhas airport, 0700-2200; and tourist booths in the Tietê bus station (0900-2200) and in the following locations throughout the city: **Olido** (Av São João 473, daily 0900-1800; at Praça da República, daily 0900-1800); at **Parque Prefeito Mário Covas** (Av Paulista 1853, daily 0900-1800); at the **Mercado Municipal** (R da Cantareira 306, Mon-Sat 0800-1700, Sun 0700-1600). An excellent map is available free at all these offices, as well as free maps and pamphlets in English. Visit **www.cidadedesaopaulo.com** (Portuguese, English and Spanish), also **www.guiadasemana.com.br/sao-paulo** and **http://vejasp.abril.com.br** for what's on and where to go.

Where to stay

The best area to stay is northeastern Jardins (also known as Cerqueria César), which is safe and well connected to the Metrô via Av Paulista.

Both **Novotel** (www.novotel.com) and **Accor** (www.accorhotels.com.br – **Formule 1** and **Ibis**) are well-represented in the Centro Histórico and Jardins and Avenida Paulista areas. There is a convenient Ibis at Congonhas, too, and other hotels just outside the airport. Useful if you have flight connections and most have shuttles to Congonhas airport. There are cheapies in the centre, but this is an undesirable area at night.

Centro Histórico

$$$ Gran Corona
Basílio da Gama 101, T011-3155 0053, www.grancorona.com.br.
In a small street. Comfortable if a bit dated, good services, good restaurant. Warmly recommended.

$$$ Marabá
Av Ipiranga 757, T011-2137 9500, www.hotelmaraba.com.br.
Good small hotel in the centre, colourful rooms, small bar, restaurant and gym.

$$$-$$ Itamarati
Av Dr Vieira de Carvalho 150, T011-3474 4133, www.hotelitamarati.com.br.

Good location, safe, cheaper at weekends, cheapest options have shared bathrooms. Highly recommended and very popular.

Jardins, Avenida Paulista and around

$$$$ Emiliano
R Oscar Freire 384, T011-3069 4369, www.emiliano.com.br.
Bright and beautifully designed, attention to every detail and the best suites in the city. No pool but a relaxing small spa. Excellent Italian restaurant, location and service.

$$$$ Fasano
R Vittorio Fasano 88, T011-3896 4077, www.fasano.com.br.
One of the world's great hotels with decor like a modernist gentleman's club designed by Armani, a fabulous pool and the best formal haute cuisine restaurant in Brazil. Excellently positioned in Jardins.

$$$$ Renaissance
Al Santos 2233 (at Haddock Lobo), T011-3069 2233, http://marriott.com.
The best business hotel off Av Paulista with standard business rooms, a good spa, gym, pool and 2 squash courts.

$$$$ Tivoli Mofarrej
R Alameda Santos 1437, Jardins, T011-3146 5900, www.tivolihotels.com.
Vies with the Emiliano and Fasano as the best hotel in the city with a selection of plush, modern carpeted suites and smaller rooms, the best of which are on the upper storeys and have superb city views. The hotel has the best spa in the city, run by the Anantara group.

$$$$ Unique
Av Brigadeiro Luis Antônio 4700, Jardim Paulista, T011-3055 4700, www.hotelunique.com.
The most ostentatious hotel in the country, an enormous half moon on concrete uprights with curving floors, circular windows and beautiful use of space and light. The bar on the top floor is São Paulo's answer to the **LA Sky Bar** with almost 360º views and is filled with tourists and the glamourous from dusk onwards as people watch the city lights come on, it opens 1200-1530, 1800-2330, restaurant open 1900, only hotel guests may reserve a table.

$$$ Dona Ziláh
*Al França 1621, Jardim Paulista, T011-3062 1444,
www.zilah.com.*
Little *pousada* in a renovated colonial house, well
maintained, decorated with a personal touch.
Excellent location, bike rental and generous
breakfast included.

$$$ Guest Urban
*R Lisboa 493, T011-3081 5030,
http://guesturbansp.com.br.*
A converted town house in a quiet back street in
the fashionable Pinheiros neighbourhood. Bright,
airy rooms have colourful scatter cushions, heavy
cotton, art photography prints. Sun deck lounge
and free bikes for guests.

$$ Paulista Garden
*Al Lorena 21, T011-3885 9062,
hotelpaulistagarden.com.br.*
Small, simple if dated rooms with small
workspaces and tiny bathrooms with electric
showers, quieter on upper floors, uninspiring
but good location close to Ibirapuera Park.

$$ Pousada Recanto dos Ingleses
*R dos Ingleses 267, Bela Vista, T011-3287 7822,
www.pousadarecantodosingleses.com.br.*
Descend from street level to reception, the
breakfast room and some of the rooms, with
more rooms further downstairs. Rooms with and
without bath, some quite small, good breakfast,
great service from Paulo and his team.

$$-$ Paradiso Hostel
*R Alegrete 44, near Metrô Sumaré, T011-97587
0747, www.paradisobnb.com.*
Penthouse and private rooms, dorms and a
campervan at a house dating from 1951, well-
kept, no breakfast. Other properties in the city
including in the historic Niemeyer-designed
Copan building.

$$-$ Pousada dos Franceses
*R dos Franceses 100, Bela Vista, T011-3288 1592,
www.pousadadosfranceses.com.br.*
Plain little *pousada* in a modern house 10 mins'
walk from Brigadeiro Metrô. Dorms, doubles and
singles, TV room.

$$-$ Sampa Hostel
*R Girassol 519, Vila Madalena, T011-3031 6779,
http://sampahostel.com.br.*
Dorms and private rooms which need booking
in advance, convenient, with fan, breakfast.

$$-$ Vergueiro Hostel
*R Vergueiro 434, Liberdade, T011-2649 1323,
www.hostelvergueiro.com.*
Simple rooms, some with balconies, studio
apartments and shared rooms for up to 6.

$ pp Global Hostel
*Eça de Queiroz 560, Vila Mariana, 5-min walk
from Paraíso Metro station, T011-2308 7401,
www.globalhostel.com.br.*
Near Parque Ibirapuera, 6- to 12-bed dorms with
fans and lockers which fit backpacks; kitchen and
laundry facilities. 2nd branch at R Pamplona 114,
Jardins, T011-3251 4680.

South of the centre
The area known as the New Centre, around
Av Brigadeiro Faria Lima and Av Luis Carlos
Berrini, has no sights of interest for the tourist,
however it has the plushest, most expensive
hotels, including **Grand Hyatt** (www.saopaulo.
hyatt.com), and the **Hilton** (www.hilton.com),
both as good as you would expect.

$$$ Blue Tree Premium Faria Lima
*Av Brigadeiro Faria Lima 3989, Vila Olímpia,
T011-3896 7544, www.bluetree.com.br.*
Modern business hotel with excellent service,
ideally positioned for Faria Lima, Vila Olímpia
and Itaim, pool, massage, gym, sauna and
business centre. There are several other **Blue
Trees** around the city.

$$-$ Praça da Árvore Hostel
*R Pageú 266, Saúde, T011-5071 5148,
www.spalbergue.com.br.*
Well-kept *pousada* in a quiet street, cheaper for H
members, helpful, 2 mins from Praça do Árvore
metro, private rooms with shared bath and
dorms for 4 to 8, kitchen, laundry.

Associação Paulista de Albergues
da Juventude
*R 7 de Abril 404, 12th floor, Conj 124, T011-3258
0388, www.alberguesp.com.br.*

Restaurants

Centro Histórico
There are plenty of restaurants and cafés in the
centre, most open lunchtime only. There are
many per kg options and *padarias*.

$$$-$$ Famiglia Mancini
*R Avanhandava, Bela Vista,
www.famigliamancini.com.br.*

group of Italian restaurants and delicatessens, most owned by the same family, on a pretty pedestrianized street in Bela Vista, can be very busy.

$-$ Café da Pinacoteca
Pinacoteca Museum, Praça da Luz 2, 011-3326 0350.
Portuguese-style café with marble floors and mahogany balconies. Great coffee, sandwiches and cakes.

$-$ Efigênia Café e Bar
Largo São Bento s/n, T011-3311 8800.
A perfect pit stop while exploring the city centre. Tables under the Viaduto Santa Ifigênia and good-value buffet of hot and cold plates of Brazilian standards.

$-$ Ponto Chic
Largo do Paiçandu 27, T011-3222 6528, http://pontochic.com.br.
A corner café where the *bauru* sandwich (cheese, salad and roast beef) was born. An unpretentious place, very popular.

Liberdade

$ Aska
R Galvã Bueno 466, Liberdade, T011-3277 9682, facebook: Aska Restaurante. Closed Mon.
Traditional Japanese restaurant with a bar overlooking an open kitchen serving lunchtime noodle dishes.

$ Sushi Yassu
Tomás Gonzaga 98, T011-3209 6622, http://sushiyassu.com.br.
The best of Liberdade's traditional Japanese restaurants. Excellent sushi/sashimi combinations.

Jardins, Avenida Paulista and around

Those on a budget can eat to their stomach's content in per kg places or, cheaper still, bakeries (*padarias*) There's one on almost every corner and they serve sandwiches, delicious Brazilian burgers made from decent meat and served with ham, egg, cheese or salad. They always have good coffee, juices, cakes and set lunches (*almoços*) for a very economical price. Most have a designated sitting area – either at the *padaria* bar or in an adjacent room. Juices are made from mineral or filtered water. Bela Vista, while not that close to the metro (nearest are Trianon MASP and Brigadeiro – 10 mins), but within walking distance of Avs Paulista and Brigadeiro Luis Antonio, it has got lots of little bars and

restaurants, especially at the Conselheiro Carrão e 13 de Maio junction which is the heart of an Italian district.

$$$ Buffet Charlô
R Barão de Capanema 440, T011-3087 4444, http://charlo.com.br.
One of the premier VIP and old family haunts in the city run by a scion of one of the city's establishment families. Decked out in tribute to a Paris brasserie and with food to match.

$$$ Dalva e Dito
R Padre João Manoel 1115, T011-3068 4444, http://dalvaedito.com.br.
Brazilian home cooking with a gourmet twist from chef Alex Atala. The soaring dining room is split by a long open kitchen.

$$$ D.O.M
R Barão de Capanema 549, T011-3088 0761, http://domrestaurante.com.br.
Jardins' evening restaurant of the moment. Alex Atala's groundbreaking restaurant is the only in Brazil to have 2 Michelin stars and is listed at No 16 on the World's 50 best restaurants 2017. Contemporary food, fusing Brazilian ingredients, particularly from the Amazon, with French and Italian styles and served in a large modernist dining room.

$$$ Figueira Rubaiyat
R Haddock Lobo 1738, T011-3087 1399, http://rubaiyat.com.br.
The most interesting of the Rubaiyat restaurant group. Very lively for Sun lunch, light and airy and under a huge tropical fig tree.

$$$ Gero
R Haddock Lobo 1629, T011-3064 0005, www.fasano.com.br.
Fasano's version of a French Bistrô a Côté, but serving pasta and light Italian. Ever so casual design; be prepared for a long wait at the bar alongside people who are there principally to be seen. Reservations are not accepted.

$$$ Jun Sakamoto
R Lisboa 55, Pinheiros, T011-3088 6019.
Japanese with a touch of French; superb fresh ingredients (some of it flown in especially from Asia and the USA).

$$$ Mani
R Joaquim Antunes 210, Pinheiros, T011-3085 4148, http://manimanioca.com.br.
A menu of light Mediterranean dishes using Brazilian ingredients, by the European-trained

Helena Rizzo. Consistently appears in the Top 50 in the World's Best Restaurants awards (www.theworlds50best.com).

$$$ Vento Haragano
Av Rebouças 1001, T011-3083 4265, www.ventoharagano.com.br.
One of the best *rodízios* in the city.

$$$-$$ Tordesilhas
Al Tietê 489, Consolação, T011-3107 7444, www.tordesilhas.com.
Informal, with shady plants, polished floor tiles and plenty of natural light, serving Brazilian home comfort fare, with a contemporary touch.

$$ A Mineira
Al Joaquim Eugénio de Lima 697, T011-3283 2349, www.grupoamineira.com.br.
Self-service Minas food by the kilo. Lots of choice. *Cachaça* and pudding included.

$$ Fran's Café
Av Paulista 358, T011-3283 5306, and throughout the city. Open 24 hrs.
Excellent coffee and light meals.

$$ Goshala
R dos Pinheiros 267, Pinheiros, T011-3063 0367, http://goshala.com.br.
100% vegetarian, Brazilian food with an Indian face, plenty of choice and variety.

$$ Padaria Nova Charmosa
R Joaquim Eugénio de Lima 19, Bela Vista, T011-3266 2983, www.novacharmosacasadepaes.com.br.
Bakery, restaurant serving good buffet lunch, snacks and small shop, convenient if staying in this area. With branches in Perdizes.

$$ Peixeria
R Inácio Pereira da Rocha 112, T011-2859 3963. Closed Mon.
This rustic-chic fish restaurant with raw brick walls, wood tables, culinders for lampshades and a giant model tarpon suspended from the ceiling draws a fashionable crowd sick of the inflated prices of gourmet São Paulo and seduced by the ultra-fresh fish, seafood *petiscos* and modest bills.

$$ Sattva
Alameda Itu 1564, T011-3083 6237, www.sattvanatural.com.br.
Vegetarian dishes, pizzas and pastas, all made with organic ingredients, good value lunchtime dish of the day, often has live music at night.

$$ Sujinho
R da Consolação 2068, Consolação, T011-3154 5207, http://sujinho.com.br.
South American beef in large portions, other carnivorous options also available.

$$ Tavares
R da Consolação 3212, T011-3064 0970.
Good-value breakfasts and *prato feito* lunches and an à la carte menu ranging from pasta and pizzas to steaks and *bacalhau* (salt cod).

$ Cheiro Verde
R Peixoto Gomide 1078, T011-3262 2640, http://cheiroverderestaurante.com.br. Lunch only.
Hearty veggie food, like vegetable crumble in gorgonzola sauce and pasta with buffalo mozarella and sun-dried tomato.

South of the centre

Vila Olímpia and Itaim

Restaurants here are ultra, ultra trendy; full of the beautiful posing in beautiful surroundings. We include only a handful of the best.

$$$ Kosushi
R Viradouro 139, Itaim Bibi, T011-3167 7272, http://kosushi.com.br.
The 1st of São Paulo's chic Japanese restaurants which began life in Liberdade and is now housed in a beautifully designed Asian modernist space. Great sushi combinations. Also in Cidade Jardim Shopping.

$$$ La Mar
R Tapabuã 1410, Itaim, T011-3073 1213, www.lamarcebicheria.com.br.
Peruvian seafood dishes adapted for the Brazilian palate, also Japanese fusion.

$$$ Parigi
R Amauri 275, Itaim, T011-3167 1575, www.fasano.com.br.
One of the city's premier evening places to be seen; Franco-Italian dining in a beautiful dining room.

Bars and clubs

The best places for nightlife are Itaim, Moema and Vila Olímpia, Consolação (for a grungy alternative, student scene) and Vila Madalena/Pinheiros. Jardins' best bars are in the top hotels. Vila Olímpia, Itaim and Moema have a series of funky, smart bars overflowing onto the street, filled with an eclectic mix of after-workers, clubbers, singles and couples;

all united by being under 40 and having money. These sit alongside imitation US and European club/lounge bars playing techno, hip hop and the like. The busiest streets for a bar wander are R Atílio Inocenti near the junction of Av Juscelino Kubitschek and Av Brigadeiro Faria Lima, Av Hélio Pellegrino and R Araguari, which runs behind it. Vila Madalena is younger still, more hippy-chic, but is the best part of town to hear live, Brazilian music and uniquely Brazilian close dances like *forró*, as opposed to international club sounds. The liveliest streets are Aspicuelta and Girassol.

West of the centre

Consolação

Beco 203
R Augusta 609, T011-2339 0351,
www.beco203.com.br.
Cutting edge alternative rockers from Brazil and the world over play here.

Kabul
R Pedro Taques 124, T011-2503 2810,
www.kabul.com.br.
Live misic ranging from Brazilian jazz to samba, rock and alternative acts.

Outs Club
R Augusta 486, T011-3237 4940,
www.clubeouts.com.br.
One of the bastions of alternative, rock and hard rock, from UK indie to Brazilian metal.

Royal Club
R Consolação 222, T011-3129 9804,
www.royalclub.com.br.
Highly fashionable funk and rare groove club playing non-Brazilian music.

Jardins

Bar Balcão
R Dr Melo Alves 150, T011-3063 6091.
After work meeting place, very popular with young professionals and media types who gather on either side of the long low wooden bar which winds its way around the room like a giant snake.

Casa de Francisca
R José Maria Lisboa 190, T011-3493 5717,
www.casadefrancisca.art.br.
Intimate bar/restaurant with refined live music.

Finnegan's Pub
R Cristiano Viana 358, Pinheiros,
www.finnegan.com.br.

One of São Paulo's various Irish bars, this one actually run by an Irishman, popular with ex-pats.

Vila Madalena/Pinheiros

Bambu
R Purpurina 272, T011-3031 2331,
www.bambubrasilbar.com.br.
For dancing *forró* and other northeastern styles and drinking *caipirinhas*.

Genial
R Girassol 374, T011-3812 7442,
www.bargenial.com.br.
Music-themed bar which serves good *petiscos* and a popular *feijoada* on Sun.

Grazie a Dio
R Girassol 67, T011-3031 6568,
Facebook: GrazieADioSP.
The best bar in Vila Madalena for live music, different band every night. Great for dancing, always packed.

Ó do Borogodó
R Horácio Lane 21, T011-3814 4087,
Facebook: odoborogodob ar.
An intimate club, hard to find as it is unmarked (next to a hairdresser), open Wed-Sat for samba, choro and *forró*.

Posto 6
R Aspicuelta 644, Vila Madalena, T011-3812 7831,
www.barposto6.com.br.
An imitation Rio de Janeiro *boteco* with an attractive crowd and a backdrop of *bossa nova* and MPB. Busy from 2100 onwards.

South of the centre

Itaim, Moema and Vila Olímpia

The area just south of Ibirapuera and north of the new centre is packed with lively bars, each with its own atmosphere. The busiest streets are Atilio Inocenti, near the junction of Av Kubitschek and Av Brig Faria Lima, Av Hélio Pellegrino and Araguari, which runs behind it.

Bourbon Street Music Club
R dos Chanés 127, Moema, T011-5095 6100,
www.bourbon street.com.br.
Great little club with emerging local acts and international stars, too.

Entertainment

See www.guiasp.com.br, the 'Guia da Folha' section of *Folha de São Paulo* and *Veja São Paulo* of the weekly news magazine *Veja* for listings.

Cinema

Entrance is usually half price on Wed; normal seat price is US$7.50. Cine clubs: **Cine SESC** (R Augusta 2075), and cinemas at: **Museu da Imagem e do Som**, **Centro Cultural Itaú** and **Centro Cultural São Paulo**.

Theatre

The **Theatre Municipal** (see page 448) is used by visiting theatrical and operatic groups, as well as the City Ballet Company and the Municipal Symphony Orchestra who give regular performances. There are several other 1st-class theatres: **Aliança Francesa** (R General Jardim 182, Vila Buarque, T011-3017 5699, www.aliancafrancesa.com.br). **Paiol** (R Amaral Gurgel 164, Vila Buarque, T011-3337 4517, www.teatropaiolcultural.com); among others. Free concerts at **Teatro Popular do Sesi** (Av Paulista 1313, T011-3284 9787, Mon-Sat), at midday, under MASP. **Centro Cultural São Paulo** (R Vergueiro 1000, T011-3397 4002, www.centrocultural.sp.gov.br). Arts centre and concert halls with regular classical music and ballet, library, theatres and exhibition spaces.

Festivals

25 Jan Foundation of the City.
Feb Carnival (most attractions and businesses are closed). This includes the parades of the *escolas de samba* in the Anhembi sambódromo – the São Paulo special group parades on the Fri and Sat and the Rio group on the Sun and Mon to maximize TV coverage.
Jun Festas Juninas and the **Festa de São Vito**, the patron saint of the Italian immigrants.
Sep Festa da Primavera.
Dec Christmas and **New Year** festivities.
All year, there are countless anniversaries, religious feasts, international fairs and exhibitions, look in the press or the monthly tourist magazines to see what is on while you are in town. See page 451 for the **São Paulo Biennial**.

Shopping

Handicrafts

Casa dos Amazonas, Al dos Jurupis 460, Moema, T011-4178 9946, www.arteindigena.com.br. Huge variety from all over Brazil.
Galeria Arte Brasileira, Al Lorena 2163. Good value, stock from all over Brazil.
Sutaco, R Boa Vista 170, Edif Cidade I, 3rd floor, Centro, T011-3241 7333. Handicrafts from São Paulo state.

Jewellery

There are many shops selling Brazilian stones, including branches of **H Stern**.

Markets

Antiques market, *below the Museu de Arte de São Paulo. Sun, 1000-1700.*
Ceasa flower market, *Pavilhão Mercado Livre do Produtor (MLP), or Praça da Batata, both at Doutor Gastão Vidigal 1946, Jaguaré. Tue and Fri 0000-0900, Mon and Thu 0200-1400, www.ceagesp.gov.br.* Between 800 and 1000 tons plants and flowers on sale weekly; should not be missed.
Flea markets, *in Praça Benedito Calixto in Pinheiros, www.pracabeneditocalixto.com.br, on Sat (with chorinho music 1430-1830), and in the main square of the Bixiga district (Praça Don Orione) on Sun.* There is a Sun market in the Praça da República in the city centre.
Mercado Municipal, R da Cantareira 306, T011-3326 3401, www.oportaldomercadao.com.br. In an art deco building, with foodstalls below and restaurants on the upper gallery.
'Oriental' fair, *Praça de Liberdade. Sun 1000-1900.* Good for Japanese snacks, plants and some handicrafts, very picturesque, with remedies on sale, tightrope walking, gypsy fortune tellers, etc.

What to do

City tours, drivers and guides

Around SP, T011-99391 2302, www.aroundsp.com. Excellent tours in and around São Paulo, including city tours, hiking in the forests of the Serra da Cantareira, scenic flights and trips to the coast.
Francisco Fransa, T011-97155 4701 (and WhatsApp), ffranssa@yahoo.com.br. Airport pick-ups and driver services throughout the city. Safe (the driver is a former police officer), reliable and excellent value (better value than the equivalent rate by taxi). Give at least 2 days' notice.
SPin Brazil Tours, T011-5904 2269/99185 2623, www.spintours.com.br. Tailor-made services and private tours of São Paulo city and state with options on destinations further afield. These include bilingual 3- and 4-hr tours of the city of São Paulo, bilingual tours tailored to visitor interest and coordinated visits to football matches, the Brazilian Grand Prix and so on.

Football

The most popular local teams are Corinthians, Palmeiras and São Paulo who play in the Morumbi and Pacaembu stadiums. The latter has a **Museu do Futebol** (Praça Charles Miller,

T011-3664 3848, www.museudofutebol. org.br, Tue-Sun 0900-1700, US$3.50).

Language courses
Universidade de São Paulo (USP) in the Cidade Universitária has courses available to foreigners, including a popular Portuguese course, registry is through the **Comissão de Cooperação Internacional** (R do Anfiteatro 181, Bloco das Colméias 05508, Cidade Universitária).

Tour operators
Pure Brazil by Venturas, *R Minerva 268, Perdizes, T011-3872 0362, www.purebrasil.net*. Customized itineraries to well-known and remote destinations throughout Brazil, specialists in wildlife and adventure tourism.

Transport

Air From the international airport **Guarulhos** (Cumbica), Av Monteiro Lobato 1985, T011-2445 2945, www.aeroportoguarulhos.net, taxis charge US$35-45. The lower price is for standard white cabs, higher for those on a ticket system (the taxi offices are outside Customs, 300 m down on the left; go to get your ticket then take your bags right back to the end of the taxi queue). Fares from the city to the airport are slightly less and vary from cab to cab, US$30-35. The best service between the airport and city is on the fast, a/c **Airport Bus Service** (www.airportbusservice. com.br) leaving from outside Terminal 4 (where it has its ticket office just outside the entrance; from other terminals you may get one of their buses to drop you at Terminal 4, otherwise get an inter-terminal shuttle. There are numerous routes, almost all of them costing US$16, delineated with prices on the website and including: Tietê bus terminal (40 mins), Praça da República (1 hr), Av Paulista (1¼ hrs – but may take more as it calls at hotels), Brooklin Novo – World Trade Center (1 hr 10 mins), Barra Funda rodoviária (1 hr 20 mins), Aeroporto Congonhas (1 hr 10 mins). Buses leave around twice an hour, 0530-2300 and every 90 mins thereafter throughout the night to the Tietê terminal and Congonhas and until around 2300 to other destinations. If you have a flight connection to Congonhas, your airline will provide a courtesy bus. Allow plenty of time for getting to the airport and for checking in. In rush hour transfer times can double and the airport is often overcrowded. A new, fast road between airport and city is due to open in 2019 and the Jade line of the Metrô will also have a line to the airport (partially built; completion date

unknown). If looking for a hotel near the airport, **$$$ Monreale**, www.monrealehotels.com, has been recommended. From **Congonhas airport**, T011-5090 9000, there are about 400 flights a week to Rio. To get to Congonhas, take a bus or Metrô and bus (see www.sptrans.com.br), or a taxi, about US$9-13 from the centre, Vila Madalena or Jardins.

Airport information Money exchanges, in the arrivals hall of the new international terminal, Guarulhos, 0800-2200 daily. See Tourist information, above, for the tourist office.

Connecting to other Brazilian cities through Guarulhos Flight arrivals in Brazil at São Paulo (with connections to other destinations) are usually required to pass through immigration and bag collection before going through customs in Guarulhos' international terminal. Connecting flights then usually leave from the neighbouring domestic terminal. Allow at least an hour for the process. Signage is poor.

The **Azul** airline advertises some flights from São Paulo, which in fact leave from Viracopos airport in Campinas, 1 hr 40 mins north of the city. Azul has a free bus service for ticket holders from Congonhas, Tietê and other points (see Azul's website), but not from Guarulhos. If you arrive at Guarulhos, take the **Airport Bus Service** or a taxi to one of Azul's departure points and change. Viracopos is an efficient airport with a helpful information desk, a Campinas tourist office (not always manned), food outlets, shops, ATMs and a bank upstairs, car hire and 2 taxi offices. **VB** and **Lira** have frequent buses to **Tietê** for US$6.50 and **VB** to **Campinas**, US$3.60; their joint office is in the car hire section. Lira from Campinas rodoviária to Guarulhos US$12.25, 2 hrs (taxi Viracopos-Campinas rodoviária US$25). The nearest hotels are about 7 km away: **Golden Park Viracopos**, T19-3725 1600, www.goldenparkviracopos.com.br, and **Ibis Indaiatuba**, T19-3801 2400, www.ibis.com. Campinas doesn't appear to have much to offer other than the Dom Pedro Mall, said to be the biggest in South America.

Bus City buses are run by SP Trans, www. sptrans.com.br. You can work out your route on the planner on the bus company's website and on Google maps, which mark bus stops. These maps, plus those on the Metrô and CPTM websites (see below) will give you a good coverage of the city. Even if you do not speak Portuguese they are fairly self-explanatory. Local transport maps are also available at stations and depots. Some city bus routes are run by trolley buses. City bus fare is US$1.20 using the *bilhete único*, which integrates bus, metro and light railway in a single, rechargeable plastic swipe card available from thousands of authorized outlets, including SP Trans' own shops (eg Praça da Sé 188, R Augusta 449), metro stations, newsstands, lottery shops, *padarias*, etc.

The main *rodoviária* for long-distance buses is Tietê, T011-2223 7152, which handles buses to the interior of São Paulo state, all state capitals (but see also under Barra Funda and Bresser below) and international buses. Taxis at the arrivals level can be paid for up-front at a desk, or by meter. There are 2 companies: **Taxi Comum** and **Taxi Especial**; fares to/from the Jardins area are US$11-15. The left luggage charges US$4 per day per item.

Buses from Tietê: To **Rio**, 6 hrs, every 30 mins, US$32-36 (*leito* 64), special section for this route in the *rodoviária*, ask how to take the coastal route via Santos ('via litoral') unless you wish to go the direct route. To **Florianópolis**, 11 hrs, US$32-45 (*leito* 70). **Porto Alegre**, 18 hrs, US$55-70. **Curitiba**, 6 hrs, US$15-35. **Salvador**, 30 hrs, US$85. **Recife**, 40 hrs, US$125. **Cuiabá**, 24 hrs, US$70. **Brasília**, 16 hrs, US$40-65. **Foz do Iguaçu**, 16 hrs, US$30-55. **São Sebastião**, 4 hrs US$20-35 (say 'via Bertioga' if you want to go by the coast road, beautiful journey but few buses take this route).

Tip...
Low-cost airlines offer fares that can either be as cheap as, or only a few dollars more than travelling by bus on long journeys (when booked through the internet). Compare airline websites with bus price websites.

International buses from Tietê: to **Montevideo**, via Porto Alegre, with **TTL**, once a week, US$197-248, plenty of meal stops, bus stops for border formalities, passengers disembark only to collect passport and tourist card on the Uruguayan side. To **Buenos Aires**, **Pluma**, 36 hrs, US$143. To **Asunción** (1044 km), US$45-68, 18 hrs with **Pluma**, stopping at Ciudad del Este. **Cometa del Amambay**, T011-6221 1485, runs to **Pedro Juan Caballero** and **Concepción**.

There are 3 other bus stations: **Barra Funda**, T011-3666 4682, with Metrô station, for buses

from cities in southern São Paulo state and many places in Paraná. **Bresser**, T011-6692 5191, on the Metrô, is for destinations in Minas Gerais, eg **Cometa** (T011-4004 9600, www.viacaocometa.com.br) or **Gontijo** (T011-3392 6890, www.gontijo.com.br) go to Minas Gerais: **Belo Horizonte**, 9 hrs, US$33.50. (Note that Util's service to São João del Rei uses Tietê, US$30.) Buses from **Santos** and the southern coast of São Paulo state arrive at **Jabaquara**, T011-5012 2256, at the southern end of the Metrô. Buses leave here for Santos every 10-30 mins, taking about 70 mins, last bus at midnight, US$8.15.

Car The *rodízio*, restriction on car use by licence plate number, to curb traffic pollution, may be extended beyond the winter months. Check.

Metrô The best and cheapest way to get around São Paulo is on the excellent Metrô system, daily 0500-2400, www.metro.sp.gov.br, with a clear journey planner and information in Portuguese and English. It is clean, safe, cheap and efficient and has 5 main lines. It is integrated with the overground **CPTM** (Companhia Paulista de Trens Metropolitanos), www.cptm.sp.gov.br, an urban light railway which extends the metrô along the margins of the Tietê and Pinheiros rivers and to the outer city suburbs. There are 6 lines, numbers 7 to 12, which are colour-coded like the Metrô. Information T0800-055 0121. Basic fare US$1.20 with the *bilhete único* (see above); backpacks are allowed.

Taxi Taxis display cards of actual tariffs in the window (starting price R$1.30). From 2000-0600 fares rise by 75 cents per km. There are ordinary taxis, which are hailed on the street, or at taxi stations such as Praça da República, radio taxis and deluxe taxis. For **Radio Taxis**, which are more expensive but involve fewer hassles, **Central Radio Táxi**, T011-3035 0404, www.centralradiotaxi.com; **São Paulo Rádio Táxi**, T011-5073 2814; **Vermelho e Branco**, T011-3146 4000, www.radiotaxivermelhoebranco.com.br; visit **www.taxisp.com.br** for a list, or look in the phone book; calls are not accepted from public phones.

Train São Paulo has 2 stations: 1) **Estação da Luz** the hub for three CPTM suburban lines which operate at Metrô frequencies and with free transfers to the Metrô; 2) **Júlio Prestes station**, for services to the west.

On the coast there are fine beaches, although pollution is sometimes a problem. The further you go from the port of Santos, the more unspoilt the beaches become, with some areas of special natural interest.

Santos *Colour map 7, C4.*

Santos, on an island about 5 km from the open sea, is the most important Brazilian port. Over 40% by value of all Brazilian imports and about half the total exports pass through it. Santos is also a holiday resort with magnificent beaches and views. The scenery on the routes crossing the Serra do Mar is superb. The roadway includes many bridges and tunnels. From Rio the direct highway, the Linha Verde is also wonderful for scenery. The port is approached by the winding Santos Channel; at its mouth is an old fort (1709).

Tip...

The best way get around the centre of Santos is by the restored Victorian trams which leave on guided tours from in front of the Prefeitura Municipal on Praça Visconde de Mauá (US$1.75). The tram passes in front of most of the interesting sights, including the *azulejo*-covered houses on Rua do Comércio.

The centre of the city is on the north side of the island. Due south, on the Baía de Santos, is **Gonzaga**, where hotels and bars line the beachfront. Between these two areas, the eastern end of the island curves round within the Santos Channel. **Tourist offices** ① *at the rodoviária; Orquidário Municipal; Aquário Municipal; Praça Mauá; Bonde de Gonzaga (tram car); Praça das Bandeiras; and the cruise ship terminal; information by phone T0800-173887. Head office: Estação do Valongo, Largo Marquês de Monte Alegre s/n, T013-3201 8000, www.turismosantos.com.br.*

Sights The streets around **Praça Mauá** are very busy in the daytime. **Museu do Café** ① *R 15 de Novembro 95, T013-3213 1750, www.museudocafe.com.br, Tue-Sat 0900-1700, Sun 1000-1700, US$3.15.* The old Bolsa Oficial de Café was closed to all but rich men up until the mid-20th century, but is now a delightful museum, with large wall paintings by Benedito Calixto and a very impressive art deco stained-glass ceiling. Upstairs is a small but very well-presented collection of displays. The lobby café serves some of the best coffee in Brazil. The only colonial church regularly open to the public in the centre is the 17th-century restored **Santo Antônio do Valongo** ① *T013-3219 1481, www.portalvalongo.com, Tue-Sun 0800-1700,* which is by the railway station on Largo Marquês de Monte Alegre. Nearby is the new **Museu Pelé** ① *Largo Marquês de Monte Alegre 2, T013-3257 1700, Tue-Sun 1000-1700, US$5.50,* in a fully restored 19th-century building with trophies, shirts and other items from the great footballer's career. **Fundação Pinacoteca** ① *Av Bartolomeu de Gusmão 15, T013-3288 2260, www.pinacotecadesantos.org.br, Tue-Sun 0900-1800, free,* features a large collection of ecclesiastical paintings and landscapes from Brazil's most distinguished early 19th-century artists. At **Santos Football Stadium and Museum** ① *Princesa Isabel 77, Vila Belmiro, T013-3257 4099, www.santosfc.com.br, Tue-Sun 0900-1900, tours US$2.50-8,* the ground floor houses a collection of trophies and photographs chronicling the history of Pelé's club, including several cabinets devoted to him and containing his shirts, boots and other memorabilia. **Monte Serrat**, just south of the city centre, has at its summit a semaphore station and look-out post which reports the arrival of all ships in Santos harbour. There is also a church, dedicated to Nossa Senhora da Monte Serrat. The top can be reached on foot or by funicular (every 30 minutes, US$12 return). In the western district of José Menino is the **Orquidário Municipal** ① *daily 0800-1700, bird enclosure 0800-1800, US$1.35,* the municipal orchid gardens, in the **Praça Washington**. The flowers bloom October to February; the orchid show is in November.

The **Ilha Porchat**, a small island reached by a bridge at the far end of Santos/São Vicente bay, has beautiful views of the high seas on one side and of the city and bay on the other. The lookout was designed by Oscar Niemeyer and, in summer, there is lively nightlife here.

São Sebastião *Colour map 7, B4.*
East of Santos, a vehicle ferry (free for pedestrians) crosses from Ponta da Praia to **Guarujá**, from where a road (SP-061) runs to **Bertioga** (US$10 by bus from São Paulo). The coastal road beyond

Bertioga is paved, and the Rio-Santos highway, 1-2 km inland, provides a good link to São Sebastião. Beyond Praia Boracéia are a number of beaches, including **Camburi**, surrounded by the Mata Atlântica, into which you can walk on the Estrada do Piavu (bathing in the streams is permitted, but use of shampoo is forbidden). There are several good hotels and restaurants in Camburi and at Praia de Boracéia. The road carries on from Camburi, past the clean beach of **Maresias**, a fashionable place for surfers.

From Maresias it is 21 km to São Sebastião. There are 21 good beaches and an adequate, but not overdeveloped, tourist infrastructure. The natural attractions of the area include many small islands offshore and a large portion of the **Parque Estadual da Serra do Mar** on the mainland, with other areas protected for their ecosystems (http://www.ambiente.sp.gov.br/parque-serra-do-mar-nucleo-picinguaba/). There are forest trails and old sugar plantations. In the colonial centre is **Museu de Arte Sacra** ① *R Sebastião Neves 90*, in the 17th-century chapel of São Gonçalo. The town's parish church on Praça Major João Fernandes dates from the early 17th century and rebuilt in 1819. The **tourist office** ① *Av Dr Altino Arantes 174, T012-3892 2620*, is in the historic **Casa Esperança**.

The beaches within 2-3 km of São Sebastião harbour are polluted; others to the south and north are clean. Ilhabela is expensive in season, when it is cheaper to stay in São Sebastião.

Ilhabela

The island of São Sebastião, known popularly as Ilhabela, is of volcanic origin, roughly 390 sq km in area. The four highest peaks are Morro de São Sebastião, 1379 m, Morro do Papagaio, 1309 m, Ramalho, 1205 m, and Pico Baepi, 1025 m. All are often obscured by mist. Rainfall on the island is heavy, about 3000 mm a year. The slopes are densely wooded and 80% of the forest is protected by the Parque Estadual de Ilhabela. The only settled district lies on the coastal strip facing the mainland, the Atlantic side being practically uninhabited except by a few fisherfolk. The island abounds with tropical plants, flowers, and wild fruits, whose juice mixed with *cachaça* and sugar makes a delicious cocktail. The terraced **Cachoeira da Toca** ① *US$5, includes insect repellent*, waterfalls amid dense jungle close to the foot of the Baepi peak give cool freshwater bathing; lots of butterflies. You can walk on a signed path, or go by car; it's a few kilometres from the ferry dock. The locals claim there are over 300 waterfalls on the island, but only a few can be reached on foot. There is a small hospital (helpful) by the church in town. **Secretaria Municipal de Turismo** ① *Praça José Leite dos Passos 14, Barra Velha, T012-3896 9200, www.ilhabela.sp.gov.br. Also www.ilhabela.com.br.*

No alterations are allowed to the frontage of the main township, Ilhabela. It is very popular during summer weekends, when it is difficult to find space for a car on the ferry. It is, however, a nice place to relax on the beach, with good food and some good value accommodation.

Visit the old **Feiticeira** plantation, with underground dungeons. The road is along the coast, sometimes high above the sea, towards the south of the island (11 km from the town). You can go by bus, taxi, or horse and buggy. A trail leads down from the fazenda to the beautiful beach of the same name. Another old fazenda is **Engenho d'Água**, which is nearer to the town, which gives its name to one of the busiest beaches (the fazenda is not open to the public).

There are some three dozen beaches around Ilhabela, but only about 12 of them away from the coast facing the mainland. **Praia dos Castelhanos**, reached by the rough road over the island to the Atlantic side (no buses), is recommended. Several of the ocean beaches can only be reached by boat. The island is considered the **Capital da Vela** (of sailing) because its 150 km of coastline offers all types of conditions. There is also plenty of adventure for divers. On the mainland side the beaches 3 to 4 km either side of the town are polluted: look out for oil, sandflies and jellyfish on the sand and in the water.

> **Warning...**
>
> In all shady places, especially away from the sea, there thrives a species of midge known locally as *borrachudo*. Those allergic to insect bites should remain on the inhabited coastal strip.

Ubatuba *Colour map 7, B4.*

This is one of the most beautiful stretches of the São Paulo coast with a whole range of watersports on offer. In all, there are 72 beaches, some large, some small, some in coves, some on islands. They are spread out over a wide area, so if you are staying in Ubatuba town, you need to use the buses

Rodeo Romeos

Some 422 km northwest of São Paulo and 115 km northwest of the city of Ribeirão Preto, is **Barretos**, where, in the third week in August, the **Festa do Peão Boiadeiro** is held. This is the biggest annual rodeo in the world. The town is taken over as 600,000 fans come to watch the horsemanship, enjoy the concerts, eat, drink and shop in what has become the epitome of Brazilian cowboy culture. See www.osindependentes.com.br/festadopeao/.

which go to most of them. The commercial centre of Ubatuba is at the northern end of the bay. Here are shops, banks, services, lots of restaurants (most serving pizza and fish), but few hotels. These are on the beaches north and south and can be reached from the Costamar bus terminal. The **tourist office** ① *Av Iperoig 214, T012-3833 9123, www.ubatuba.sp.gov.br; also www.ubatuba.com.br*, is very helpful.

Saco da Ribeira, 13 km south, is a natural harbour which has been made into a yacht marina. Schooners leave from here for excursions to **Ilha Anchieta** (or dos Porcos), a popular four-hour trip. On the island are beaches, trails and a prison, which was in commission from 1908-1952. Agencies run schooner trips to Ilha Anchieta and elsewhere. Trips leave Saco da Ribeira at about 1100, returning around 1700, four-hour journey with Mykonos ① *T012-3842 0329, www.mykonos.com.br, US$17 pp*. A six-hour trip can be made from Praia Itaguá, but in winter there is a cold wind off the sea in the afternoon, same price. The Costamar bus from Ubatuba to Saco da Ribeira (every 20 minutes, 30 minutes, US$1.30) drops you at the turn-off by the Restaurante Pizzaria Malibu.

Straddling the border of São Paulo and Rio de Janeiro states is the **Parque Nacional Serra da Bocaina** ① *visit in advance ICMBio, T012-3117 2143, in São José do Barreiro, the nearest town, www.icmbio.gov.br/parnaserradabocaina/*. It rises from the coast to its highest point at Pico do Tira (or Chapéu) at 2200 m, encompassing three strata of vegetation. Just outside the park is the coastal town of Itamambuca, a popular place for visiting the forested mountains and beaches and, above all, surfing and SUP. There are several restaurants and hotels, eg **$$-$ Bamboo Groove** (R Carlos E Oliveira Correa, Casa 1, Itamambuca, T012-99646 3008, www.bamboogroove.com.br), good value for private rooms and droms, close to the beach.

Southwest from Santos

Itanhaém, 61 km from Santos, has a pretty colonial church of Sant'Ana (1761), Praça Narciso de Andrade, and the Convento da Nossa Senhora da Conceição (1699-1713, originally founded 1554), on a small hill. There are several good seafood restaurants along the beach, hotels and camping. There are more beaches 31 km south of Itanhaém at **Peruíbe**, where the climate is said to be unusually healthy owing to a high concentration of ozone in the air. Local rivers have water and black mud which has been proven to contain medicinal properties. There are plenty of places to stay and to eat in Peruíbe (none close to the bus station, some close out-of-season). Peruíbe marks the northernmost point of the **Estação Ecológico Juréia-Itatins** ① *contact the Instituto Florestal, Estrada do Guaraú 4164, CEP 11750-000, Peruíbe, T013-3457 9243, for permission to visit the ecological station, www.ambiente.sp.gov.br/e-e-jureia-itatins/*. The station was founded in 1986 and protects 820 sq km of Mata Atlântica, "as it was when the Portuguese arrived in Brazil". The four main ecosystems are restinga, mangrove, Mata Atlântica and the vegetation at 900 m on the Juréia mountain range.

Iguape Colour map 7, C3.

At the southern end of Juréia-Itatins is the town of Iguape founded in 1538. Typical of Portuguese architecture, the small **Museu Histórico e Arqueológico** ① *R das Neves 45, Tue-Sun 0900-1730*, is housed in the 17th-century Casa da Oficina Real de Fundição. There is also a **Museu de Arte Sacra** ① *Sat-Sun 0900-1200, 1330-1700*, in the former Igreja do Rosário, Praça Rotary. **Tourist office** ① *9 de Julho 63, T013-3841 3012, www.iguape.sp.gov.br*.

Opposite Iguape is the northern end of the **Ilha Comprida** with 86 km of beaches (some dirty and disappointing). This **Área de Proteção Ambiental** ① *the ICMBio office of the Area de Proteção Ambiental Cananéia-Iguape-Peruíbe is at R da Saúde 350, Canto do Morro, Iguape, T013-3841 2692,* *www.icmbio.gov.br/apacip*, is not much higher than sea level and is divided from the mainland by the Canal do Mar Pequeno. The northern end is the busiest and on the island there are good restaurants, hotels, supermarkets -- fresh fish is excellent. There is also accommodation.

Cananéia and Ilha do Cardoso *Colour map 7, C3.*

At the southern end of Ilha Comprida, across the channel, is Cananéia, 270 km from São Paulo. The colonial centre, around Praça Martim Afonso de Souza and neighbouring streets, contains the 17th-century church of **São João Batista** and the **Museu Municipal**. To the south are good beaches. For guides, contact Manoel Barroso, Avenida Independencia 65, T013-3851 1273, Portuguese only. Recommended. Cananéia has several hotels, starting in price range **$$**.

For the densely wooded Ilha do Cardoso, a protected area, take a ferry from the dock at Cananéia, four hours, three daily (T013-3851 1268/3841 1122, www.dersa.sp.gov.br, **Travessias** page). Or drive 70 km along an unpaved road, impassable when wet, to **Ariri**, 10 minutes by boat to the island. The tiny village of **Marujá**, no electricity, has rustic *pousadas* and restaurants. There is camping and idyllic beaches; best for surfing is Moretinho.

Listings São Paulo coast

Where to stay

Santos

Many beachfront hotels on Av Pres Wilson, cheap hotels are near the Orquidário Municipal (Praça Washington), 1-2 blocks from the beach.

$$$$ Ville Atlântico
No 1, T013-3289 4500, www.atlantico-hotel. com.br.
Good, on the seafront, sauna, restaurant, bar.

$$$ Hotel Natal
Av Marechal Floriano Peixoto 104, T013-3284 2732, www.hotelnatalsantos.com.br.
Safe, comfortable, cheaper with shared bath, fridge, full breakfast.

Ilhabela

Several in the **$$$$-$$$** range and some in the **$$$-$$** range, mostly on the road to the left of the ferry.

$$$ Bonns Ventos
R Benedito Serafim Sampaio 371, Perequê, T012-3896 5676, http://pousadabonnsventos.com.br.
Well-kept and well-run simple hotel with basic dorms and spacious doubles with and without bath, prices rise at weekends and high season, garden, pool.

$$$ Ilhabela
Av Pedro Paulo de Morais 151, T012-3896 1083, www.hotelilhabela.com.br.
Family-oriented, gym, pool, good breakfast. Recommended.

$$$ Pousada dos Hibiscos
Av Pedro Paulo de Morais 714, T012-3896 1375, www.pousadadoshibiscos.com.br.
Good atmosphere, swimming pool. Recommended.

$$$ Vila das Pedras
R Antenor Custódio da Silva 46, Cocaia, T012-3896 2433, www.viladaspedras.com.br.
11 chalets in a forest garden, tastefully decorated, nice pool.

$ Granola Hostel
R Antônio de Carvalho 314, T012-3896 1561, http://granolahostel.com.br.
Good value hostel with 4 dorms for 4-6 people (1 for women only, 1 without bath), short walk from town centre, good breakfast, nice verandah, kitchen, helpful owners. New in 2016.

Camping

Pedras do Sino
Perequê, near ferry dock, www.camping pedradosino.com.br, and at Praia Grande, 11 km south, www.cantogrande.com.br.

Ubatuba

At all holiday times it is expensive. On many of the beaches there are hotels and *pousadas*, ranging from luxury resorts to more humble establishments.

$$$$-$$$ Saveiros
R Lucian Strass 65, Praia do Lázaro, 14 km from town, T012-3842 0172, www.hotelsaveiros.com.br.
Pretty *pousada* with pool, restaurant, English spoken.

$$$ Coquille
R Praia Grande 405, T012-3835 1611,
www.hotelcoquille.com.
On the edge of the forest and 250 m from the beach, pool, bike rental and surfing lessons.

$$$ São Nicolau
R Conceição 213, T012-3832 5007,
www.hotelsaonicolau.com.br.
Good, fridge, good breakfast.

$$$ Xaréu
R Jordão Homem da Costa 413, T012-3832 1525,
www.hotelxareubatuba.com.br.
Pleasant, quiet. Recommended.

$$ São Charbel
Praça Nóbrega 280, T012-3832 1090,
www.saocharbel.com.br.
Helpful, comfortable, restaurant, bar, swimming pool, etc, holiday packages available.

$$-$ Tribo Hostel
R Amoreira 71, Praia do Lázaro,
14 km from Ubatuba, T012-3842 0585,
www.ubatubahostel.com.
On a very pretty beach, great value, dorms (price depends on season) with fan and shared bath, also suites, pool, restaurant, party atmosphere at weekends, quiet in the week.

Camping
There are about 10 sites in the vicinity, including 2 **Camping Clube do Brasil** sites at Lagoinha (25 km from town) and Praia Perequê–Açu, 2 km north. Robbery at campsites occurs at weekends.

Southwest from Santos

Peruíbe

$$$ Waldhaus Ecopousada
R Gaivota 1201, Praia do Guaraú,
T013-3457 9170, www.jureiaeco
adventure.com.br.
In lovely gardens with views acorss the beach to Juréia, comfortable, plain rooms, with breakfast (other meal available in Guaraú), offers trips on foot, by jeep or canoe.

Iguape

$$ Solar Colonial Pousada
Praça da Basílica 30, T013-3841 1591,
Facebook: Solar-Colonial-Pousada.
A range of rooms in a converted 19th-century house.

Camping
At Praia da Barra da Ribeira, 20 km north. Wild camping is possible at Praia de Juréia, the gateway to the ecological station.

Transport

Santos
Bus In Santos US$1; to **São Vicente**, US$1.60. To **São Paulo** (50 mins, US$8.15) every 15 mins, from the *rodoviária* near the city centre, José Menino or Ponta da Praia (opposite the ferry to Guarujá). (The 2 highways between São Paulo and Santos can get very crowded, especially at rush hours and weekends.) To **Guarulhos/Cumbica airport**, 11 daily, US$10.30, allow plenty of time as the bus goes through Guarulhos, 2-3 hrs. To **Rio**, many daily, 8 hrs, US$25-42; to **São Sebastião**, US$17.40, 6 daily, to **Caraguatatuba**, US$20, 3 daily, change here for Ubatuba and Paraty.

Taxi All taxis have meters. The fare from Gonzaga to the bus station is about US$15.

São Sebastião
Bus 2 buses a day from **Rio** (more on Fri and Sun), heavily booked in advance, US$23-34; from **Santos**, see above; 11 buses a day also from **São Paulo**, US$20-35, which run inland via São José dos Campos, unless you ask for the service via Bertioga, only 2 a day.

Ilhabela
Bus A bus runs along the coast. **Litorânea** from **São Paulo** connects with a service right through to Ilhabela; office in Ilhabela at R Dr Carvalho 136.

Ferry At weekends and holidays the 15- to 20-min ferry between São Sebastião and Perequê runs non-stop day and night. Free for foot passengers; cars US$4.50 weekdays, US$6.75 at weekends. Schedules and fares are given at www.dersa.sp.gov.br.

Ubatuba
Bus There are 3 bus terminals: 1) Rodoviária Costamar, R Hans Staden e R Conceição, serves all local destinations; 2) Rodoviária at R Profesor Thomaz Galhardo 513 for buses to **Paraty**, US$5; services to **Rio**, US$25-30, and **São Paulo**, 8-12 daily, US$22; 3) Rodoviária Litorânea, the main bus station: go up **Conceição** for 8 blocks from Praça 13 de Maio, turn right on R Rio Grande do Sul, then left into R Dra Maria V Jean.

Taxi In town are very expensive.

Iguape

Bus To Iguape: from **São Paulo**, **Santos**, or **Curitiba**, changing at Registro.

Ferry A continuous ferry service runs from Iguape to **Ilha Comprida** (free but small charge for cars); buses run until 1900 from the ferry stop to the beaches. From Iguape it is possible to take a boat trip down the coast to **Cananéia** and **Ariri**. Tickets and information from **Dpto Hidroviário do Estado**, R Major Moutinho 198, Iguape. It is a beautiful trip, passing between the island and the mainland. **Intersul** (T013-3851 1715) runs 2-3 buses a day between **Cananéia** and **São Paulo Barra Funda**. Information on ferries from Iguape to **Juréia** and from Cananéia to Ilha Comprida at www.dersa.sp.gov.br (Travessias page).

Minas Gerais &
Espírito Santo

Minas Gerais was once described as having a heart of gold and a breast of iron. Half the mineral production of Brazil comes from the state, including most of the iron ore. Minas Gerais also produces 95% of all Brazil's gemstones. All this mineral wealth has left the state a legacy of sumptuous colonial cities built on gold and diamond mining. Streets of whitewashed 18th-century houses with deep blue or yellow window frames line steep and winding streets leading to lavishly decorated churches with rich gilt interiors. The colonial gold mining towns of Minas Gerais are the highlights of any visit. There are also other attractions: rugged national parks, which are great for trekking, lots of festivals and a famous cuisine, the *comida mineira*. The state of Minas Gerais, larger than France, is mountainous in the south, rising to the 2787 m peak of Agulhas Negras in the Mantiqueira range, and in the east, where there is the Parque Nacional Caparaó containing the Pico da Bandeira (2890 m). The capital, Belo Horizonte is culturally very active. From Belo Horizonte north are undulating grazing lands, the richest of which are in the extreme west: a broad wedge of country between Goiás in the north and São Paulo in the south, known as the Triângulo Mineiro. The coastal state of Espírito Santo is where Mineiros head to for their seaside holidays. The most popular beaches are south of Vitória, the state capital, while north of the city are several turtle-nesting beaches. Inland are immigrant towns.

Belo Horizonte   *Colour map 7, B5.*

a big city with a cultural bent

Belo Horizonte is surrounded by mountains and enjoys an excellent climate except for the rainy season (December-March). It was founded on 12 December 1897 and is one of Brazil's fastest growing cities, now suffering from atmospheric pollution. The third largest city in Brazil, with a population 4.8 million, is hilly, with streets that rise and fall and trees lining many of the central avenues.

The large **Parque Municipal** is an oasis of green in the heart of downtown; closed at night and on Monday, except for a small section in the southwest corner (the Parque Municipal is not too safe, so it's best not to go alone). The main commercial district is around Avenida Afonso Pena; at night the movimento shifts to Savassi, southwest of the centre, where all the good eating places are.

Sights

The principal building in the Parque Municipal is the **Palácio das Artes** ① *Afonso Pena 1537, T031-3236 7400, 1000-2200, Sun 1400-2200*, which contains the **Centro de Artesanato Mineiro** (with craft shop), exhibitions, cinema and theatres. See http://fcs.mg.gov.br for the programme of classical performances and dance. On the stretch of Avenida Afonso Pena outside the Parque Municipal an open-air market operates each Sunday (0800-1430). The avenue is transformed by thousands of coloured awnings covering stalls selling every conceivable type of local handicraft. Six blocks up Avenida João Pinheiro from Avenida Afonso Pena is the **Praça da Liberdade**, which is very attractive, with trees, flowers and fountains which are lit at night. It is surrounded by fine public buildings, some in eclectic, fin-de-siècle-style, others more recent. Some house museums, others cultural centres and they form part of the **Circuito Cultural Praça da Liberdade** (T031-3239 2000, see http:// circuitoculturalliberdade.com.br). The Palácio da Liberdade itself was temporarily closed in mid-2017. Museums, which open from Tuesday, include the Museu das Minas e do Metal and Memorial Minas Gerais Vale; the Espaço do Conhecimento UFMG includes a planetarium. Only the Centro Cultural Banco do Brasil is open on Monday, till 2100 (but it's closed on Tuesday), with temporary exhibitions and a branch of Café com Letras. There is an information desk in the **Prédio Verde** (former Secretaria da Viação at the corner of the Praça and R Gonçalves Dias), but this will move when the building is converted into another museum. The **Museu Mineiro** ① Av João Pinheiro 342, T031-3269 1169, website

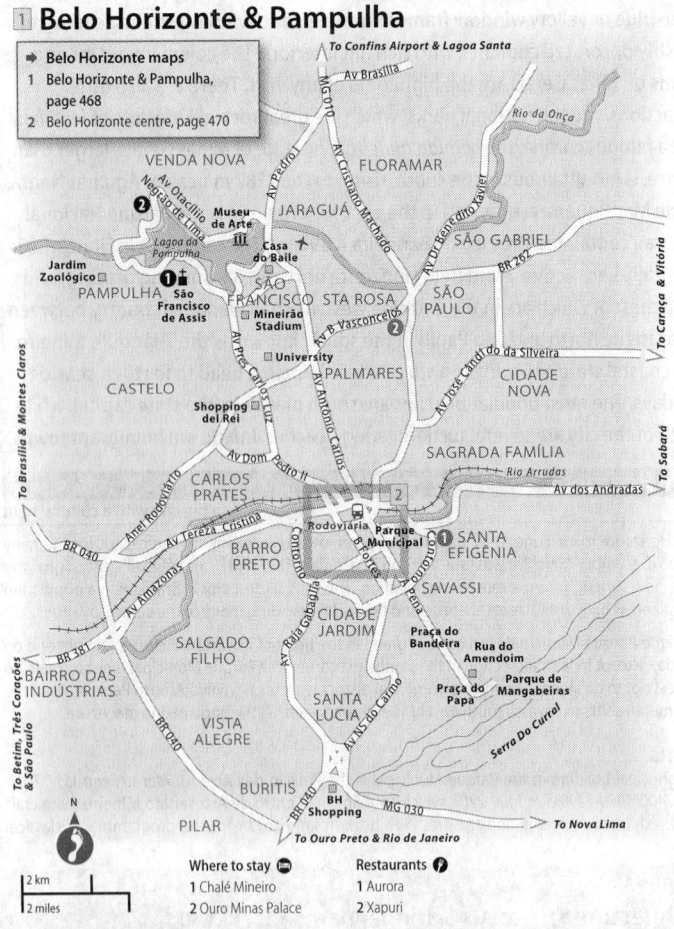

Belo Horizonte & Pampulha

➡ Belo Horizonte maps
1 Belo Horizonte & Pampulha, page 468
2 Belo Horizonte centre, page 470

Where to stay
1 Chalé Mineiro
2 Ouro Minas Palace

Restaurants
1 Aurora
2 Xapuri

as above, Tue, Wed, Fri 1000-1900,Thu 1200-2100, Sat-Sun 1200-1900, free, houses religious and other art and is part of of the Circuito Cultural, even though it is not on the Praça.

The **railway station** is part of a complex that includes buildings dating from the 1920s around the **Praça da Estação** (also called Praça Rui Barbosa). Here is the **Museu de Artes e Ofícios** ① *Praça Rui Barbosa s/n, T031-3248 8600, www.mao.org.br, open 1200, at 1100 Sat, Sun, closed Mon*, telling the story of various public and private professions in Minas.

Museu Histórico Abílio Barreto ① *Av Prudente de Morais 202, Cidade Jardim, T031-3342 1268, www.amigosdomhab.com.br, bus 2902 from Av Afonso Pena*, in an old fazenda, is the last reminder of Belo Horizonte's predecessor, the village of **Arraial do Curral d'el Rey**. It has historical exhibits.

About 8 km northwest from the centre is the picturesque suburb of **Pampulha**, famous for its modern buildings and the artificial lake, created in the 1930s by Brasilia architect Oscar Niemeyer and landscaped by Roberto Burle Marx. The **Igreja São Francisco de Assis** ① *Av Otacílio Negrão de Lima Km 12, T031-3427 1644, Tue-Sat 0900-1700, Sun 1200-1700, US$1.35*, was inaugurated in 1943. The painter Cândido Portinari installed beautiful blue and white tiles depicting Saint Francis' life on the exterior. On the wall behind the altar is a powerful composition also by Portinari. On the opposite shore is the glass and marble **Museu de Arte de Pampulha (MAP)** ① *Av Octacílio Negrão de Lima 16585, T031-3443 4533, Tue-Sun 0900-1900, free*. It has a fine collection of modern art from Minas Gerais. The **Casa do Baile** ① *Av Octacílio Negrão de Lima 751, T031-3277 7433, Tue-Sun 0900-1900, free*, is a perfect example of Niemeyer's fascination with the curved line. Just south of the lake is the **Mineirão** football stadium, about 750 m away. This is the second largest stadium in Brazil after the Maracanã stadium in Rio.

Inhotim ① *Rua B, 20, Inhotim, Brumadinho, T031-3571 9700, www.inhotim.org.br, Tue-Fri 0930-1630, Sat-Sun 0930-1730, US$12.25, free on Wed (except holidays), 2 expensive but good restaurants and several cheaper snack bars dotted about the site. There are lots of drinking fountains and toilets on site. Electric buggies take visitors to far-flung galleries, US$8.55 for unlimited use (free for disabled visitors and under 5s), but you must pay at the entrance, otherwise you can walk everywhere. You are given a map on arrival. It can get very crowded on Sat and at long weekends.* This is a captivating contemporary art complex set in 97 ha of beautiful tropical gardens with lakes and 1500 palm species from around the world. It contains 22 purpose-built galleries showing the work of Brazilian and international artists, mostly permanent but also temporary exhibitions. There are also works in the open air. Some galleries are interactive, including swimming. Allow a day, or better still two, for a full visit, which can be organized through a tour operator, or hire a car. There is one bus a day with Saritur from the rodoviária at 0815 (0830 Thursday and Saturday), return 1630 (1730 weekends), 1½ hours with 48 speed bumps once you leave the motorway, US$12.50. There are places to stay in or near Brumadinho, eg **Empório Fazendinha** ① *MG-40, Km 48, T031-3571 2415, www.emporiofazendinha.com*, about 5 km before Inhotim, with restaurant, café and shop.

Tourist information

The municipal information is **Belotur** (R da Bahia 888, 7th floor, T156 in Belo Horizonte or 031-3426 0297, www.belohorizonte.mg.gov.br or https:// prefeitura.pbh.gov.br). Very helpful, with lots of useful information and maps. The monthly *Guia Turístico* for events, opening times, etc, is freely available. See www.guiabh.com.br. Belotur has offices at Tancredo Neves/Confins and Pampulha airports, at the *rodoviária* (particularly polyglot, one at the main entrance, another, less helpful office on the arrivals floor), at the Mercado Central, the **Mercado das Flores** (Av Afonso Pena 1055), at Praça da Liberdade and at Veveco, Av Otacílio Negrão de Lima 855, Pampulha.

SETUR (Rodovia Papa João Paulo II 4001, Prédio Gerais, 11th floor, Bairro Serra Verde, T031-3915 9454, www.turismo.mg.gov.br or www. minasgerais.com.br, Mon-Fri 0800-1800), the tourism authority for the state of Minas Gerais, is helpful.

Where to stay

There are many chain hotels in the city, some mentioned below. Others include **Holiday Inn**, **Ramada**, **Royal** (www.royalhoteis.com.br) and **Promenade**, of which a good example is **Promenade Toscanini** (R Arturo Toscanini 61, Santo Antônio, T031-3064 2200, www. promenade.com.br/toscanini/), with 5 others in Savassi.

$$$$-$$$ Othon Palace
*Av Afonso Pena 1050, T031-2126 0000,
www.hoteis-othon.com.br.*
1980s hotel, glass-fronted, excellent, safe, good
restaurant, pool, helpful staff, lower floors can
be noisy.

$$$$-$$$ Ouro Minas Palace
*Av Cristiano Machado 4001, T031-3429 4001 (toll
free T0800-314000), www.ourominas.com.br.*
The most luxurious hotel in the city with palatial
suites, including several for women-only on the

top floors, excellent service, pool, sauna, gym,
excellent business facilities, not central but within
easy reach of the centre and airports.

$$$ Quality Hotel Afonso Pena
*Av Afonso Pena 3761, T031-2111 8900,
www.atlanticahotels.com.br.*
Good business hotel with spacious, practical
modern rooms and, on the upper floor, city
views, decent business facilities, helpful staff,
generous breakfast, a pool and a pocket-sized
gym. Has an equally good sister hotel at Av Pres

2 **Belo Horizonte centre**

➡ **Belo Horizonte maps**
1 Belo Horizonte &
  Pampulha, page 468
2 Belo Horizonte centre, page 470

	4 Quality Hotel Afonso Pena	6 Manjericão	12 Vinnil
		7 Taste Vin	
		8 Três Corações	**Museums** 🏛
		9 Vecchio Sogno	1 Memorial Minas Gerais
	Restaurants 🍴		Vale
500 metres	1 Café com Letras	**Bars & clubs** 🍸	2 Museu das Minas
500 yards	2 Cantina do Lucas		do Metal
	3 Dona Derna	10 A Obra	3 Espaço do Conhecimento
Where to stay 🛏	4 Dona Lucinha	11 Bar do Museu Clube	UFMG
1 Chalé Mineiro	5 Eddie Fine Burger	da Esquina	
2 Dayrell Minas			
3 Othon Palace			

Antônio Carlos 7456, São Luís/Pampulha,
T031-3505 9200, same website.

$$ Dayrell Minas
*R Espírito Santo 901, T031-3248 1000,
www.dayrell.com.br.*
One of the best business hotels in the centre,
full business facilities, 4 standards of room,
Asian restaurant, café, rooftop pool.

$ pp Chalé Mineiro
*R Santa Luzia 288, Santa Efigênia, T031-3467
1576, www.chalemineirohostel.com.br.*
Attractive, with a small pool, dorms (US$11.50
pp) and private rooms (**$$** with bath, **$** without),
a shared kitchen, TV lounge and telephones.
Towels and, breakfast are extra, Wi-Fi is free.

Restaurants

Mineiros love their food and drink and Belo
Horizonte has a lively café, dining and bar scene.
Savassi and Lourdes districts overflow with street
cafés, bars and restaurants. There is a lively, cheap
food market on R Tomé de Souza, between
Pernambuco and Alagoas, in Savassi every Thu
night between 1900 and 2300. Pampulha has
the best of the fine dining restaurants; which
are well worth the taxi ride. There are plenty of
cheap per kilo restaurants and *padarias* near the
budget hotels in the city centre and the Mercado
Central is a good place for lunch or a snack.

$$$ Aurora
*R Expedicionário Mário Alves de Oliveira 421,
São Luís, T031-3498 7567. Closed Mon-Tue.*
One of the best restaurants in town, garden
setting next to Lago da Pampulha. Imaginative
menu fusing Mineira and Italian techniques and
making use of unusual Brazilian fruits.

$$$ Taste Vin
R Curitiba 2105, Lourdes, T031-3292 5423.
Excellent French, soufflés and provençale
seafood. The wine list includes decent Brazilian
options. Recommended.

$$$ Vecchio Sogno
*R Martim de Carvalho 75 and R Dias Adorno,
Santo Agostinho, under the Assembléia
Legislativo, T031-3292 5251. Lunch only on Sun.*
The best Italian in the city with an inventive
menu fusing Italian and French cuisine with
Brazilian ingredients, excellent fish.

$$$ Xapuri
*R Mandacaru 260, Pampulha, T031-3496 6198.
Closed Mon.*

Great atmosphere, live music, very good food,
a bit out of the way but recommended.

$$$-$$ Cantina do Luca
*Av Augusto de Lima 233, loj 18, Ed Maletta,
www.cantinadolucas.com.br.*
Long-established, with a wide-ranging menu
of meat dishes, fish, local specialities, pastas,
with bar.

$$$-$$ Dona Lucinha
*R Sergipe 811, Funcionários, near Praça da
Liberdade, T031-3261 5930, www.donalucinha.
com.br. Lunch and dinner.*
One of the best-known restaurants serving
mineiro buffet food, with other branches in the
city and in São Paulo.

$$ Dona Derna
R Tomé de Souza 1380, Savassi, T031-3223 6954.
A range of restaurants in one. Upstairs is
Italian fine dining with excellent dishes and a
respectable wine list. Downstairs on weekdays
is traditional Italian home cooking and by night
a chic pizzeria called **Memmo**.

$$-$ Café com Letras
*R Antônio de Albuquerque 781, Savassi,
T031-2555 1610, www.cafecomletras.com.br.*
Arty little a/c café bar and bookshop with
live music on Mon and Sun; varied menu of
healthy, well-prepared *petiscos*, sandwiches,
salads and light lunches.

$$-$ Eddie Fine Burger
*4 branches including R da Bahia 2652,
Lourdes, Pátio Savassi, BH Shopping,
www.eddieburger.com.br.*
US-style diner serving North American
and Brazilian burgers, all made with prime
Brazilian beef.

$$-$ Três Corações
R Antônio de Albuquerque 480, Savassi.
Bar and café with outdoor seating on the edge
of Praça Savassi, for daily lunch specials and early
evening beer and snacks.

$ Mala e Cuia
*R Gonçalves Dias 874, Savassi, T031-3261 3059,
Av Antônio Carlos 8305, Pampulha, T031-3441
2993, Av Raja Gabaglia 1617, São Bento.*
A chain of restaurants serving good
comida mineira.

$ Manjericão
Av Pasteur 116. Lunch only, Mon-Fri.
Pay-by-weight, good salads and hot dishes,
self-service. Also has a Japanese selection.

Bars and clubs

Rua Tomé de Souza in Savassi has umpteen lively bars, particularly between Paraíba and Sergipe. The beer and caipirinhas are cheap and plentiful. Also try Santa Teresa neighbourhood for lively nightlife.

A Obra
R Rio Grande do Norte 1168, Savassi, T031-3215 8077, www.aobra.com.br.
The leading alternative music venue in the city. Great for DJs and new Minas acts.

Bar do Museu Clube da Esquina
Rua Paraisópolis 738, Santa Tereza, T031-2512 5050, http://bardomuseuclubedaesquina.com. Mon-Sat 1900-0100.
Recalling the famous club frequented by musicians such as Milton Nascimento, Lô Borges and Beto Guedes, with live music and poetry and restaurant.

Vinnil
R dos Inconfidentes 1068, Savassi, T031-3657 4760, vinnil.wixsite.com/vinnil. Thu, Fri, Sat and for special events.
Funky retro club bar in a 1940s building decorated with art and hosting great live acts.

Festivals

Mar/Apr Maundy Thu.
May/Jun Corpus Christi.
15 Aug Assunção (Assumption).
8 Dec Conceição (Immaculate Conception).

Shopping

Markets
See above for the Sun **handicraft fair** (Av Afonso Pena).
Mercado Central, *Av Augusto de Lima 744. Daily.* "A temple to Minas produce", with a handicrafts corridor upstairs, cheeses, fruit, vegetables, artisanal beers and other produce. Visit Tupiguá, Loja 49, T031-8476 1991, for *cachaça* tasting and Botequim Santo Antônio, near the information desk, for a beer after you have done your shopping.

What to do

Minas Golden Tours, *R da Bahia 1345, T031-3023 1451, www.minasgoldentours.com.br.* Offers a broad range of tours throughout the state (and connections with Rio, São Paulo, Brasília and

Bahia) and around Belo Horizonte, including to Inhotim, Caraça and the colonial towns. Recommended.

Transport

Air The international airport, **Tancredo Neves**, is near Lagoa Santa, at Confins, 39 km from Belo Horizonte, T031-3689 2700, www.aeroporto confins.net. Taxi to centre about US$40, *comum* and *executivo* both have fixed rates to different parts of the city. Airport bus, Unir (T031-3689 2415, www.conexaoaeroporto.com.br, kiosk by baggage reclaim), US$3-13.75, go to/from the *rodoviária*, 55 mins (desk #10 at bus station), Pampulha airport, 40 mins, and other parts of the city.

Closer to the city is the national airport, **Carlos Drummond de Andrade**, at Pampulha, which has shuttle services from Rio, São Paulo and Salvador, T031-3490 2001. Urban transportation to/from this airport is cheaper than from Confins. From Pampulha airport to town, take blue bus 1202, 25 mins, US$1, passing the *rodoviária* and the cheaper hotel district.

Bus The city has a good public transport system (www.bhtrans.pbh.gov.br), with express routes, circular routes around the Contorno and diagonal routes. All charge US$1.25 except yellow Circular routes, US$0.90. There are also buses which integrate with the regional, overground Metrô, which is part of the BRTrapid transit bus and metro system, **Move**, www.bhtrans.pbh.gov.br/move, which has 3 corridors linking outer districts to the centre, also US$1.25 per journey. The city has a programme to promote sustainable transport, with new pedestrian streets and cycle ways in the city.

The *rodoviária* is by Praça Rio Branco at the northwest end of Av Afonso Pena, T031-3271 3000/8933. The bus station has toilets, post office, phones, left-luggage lockers (US$3.35, open 0700-2200), shops and is clean and efficient. Buses leave from the rather gloomy platforms beneath the ticket hall. Taxi to centre US$6.

To **Rio** at least 6 a day, 6-7 hrs, US$30-37 (*semi-leito*), US$43 (*leito*). To **Vitória** many daily, 8½ hrs, US$33-45. To **Brasília**, 3 every night, 12 hrs, US$39-52. To **São Paulo** at least once an hour, 9-10 hrs, US$33.50. All major destinations served. For buses in Minas Gerais, see under destination.

Train To **Vitória**, see page 484. Ticket office, R Aarão Reis 423, Praça da Estação, is open daily 0600-1730; closes 1530 Sat and 1200 Sun.

charming colonial stop offs, some en route to/from Rio

Most of the colonial cities lie southeast and south of Belo Horizonte and many people choose to visit them on the way to or from Rio as they make for the most charming and restful of stopping places. Ouro Preto is the most famous and a much more pleasant place to stay than the state capital. Mariana is a good day trip from Ouro Preto. Further south are Congonhas, with its remarkable statuary, São João del Rei, with some beautiful colonial architecture, and Tiradentes, the most heavily visited of the Minas colonial towns after Ouro Preto.

Sabará *Colour map 7, B5.*

East of the state capital by 23 km is the colonial gold-mining (and steel-making) town of Sabará, strung along the narrow steep valleys of the Rio das Velhas and Rio Sabará. Secretaria de Turismo ① *R Pedro II 223, T031-3672 7690, www.sabara.org.br.*

Rua Dom Pedro II is lined with beautiful 18th-century buildings. Among them is the **Solar do Padre Correa** (1773) at No 200, now the **Prefeitura**; the **Casa Azul** (also 1773), No 215, closed on weekends; and the **Teatro Municipal**, former Opera House (1770 – the second oldest in Brazil, open 0800-1200, 1400-1730 daily). At the top of Rua Dom Pedro II is the Praça Melo Viana, in the middle of which is **Nossa Senhora do Rosário dos Pretos** ① *church and museum Tue-Sun 0900-1200, 1400-1730*. The church was left unfinished at the time of the slaves' emancipation. There is a museum of religious art in the church. To the right of the church as you face it is the **Chafariz do Rosário** (the Rosário fountain). In Rua da Intendência is the museum of 18th-century gold mining in the **Museu do Ouro** ① *Tue-Sun 1200-1730, US$0.50*. It contains exhibits on gold extraction, plus religious items and colonial furniture. Another fine example is the **Casa Borba Gato** ① *R Borba Gato 71, Tue-Fri 1200-1700*; the building currently belongs to the Museu do Ouro.

The church of **Nossa Senhora do Carmo** (1763-1774) ① *US$0.50 (includes a leaflet about the town)*, with doorway, pulpits and choirloft by Aleijadinho (see box, page 474) and paintings by Athayde, is on Rua do Carmo. **Nossa Senhora da Conceição** ① *Praça Getúlio Vargas, Tue-Sun 0900-1200, 1400-1730, US$0.50*, built 1701-1720, has much visible woodwork and a beautiful floor. The carvings have much gilding, there are painted panels and paintings by 23 Chinese artists brought from Macau. The clearest Chinese work is on the two red doors to the right and left of the chancel. **Nossa Senhora do Ó**, built in 1717 and showing Chinese influence, is 2 km from the centre of the town at the Largo Nossa Senhora do Ó (take local bus marked 'Esplanada' or 'Boca Grande').

If you walk up the Morra da Cruz hill from the Hotel do Ouro to a small chapel, the Capela da Cruz or Senhor Bom Jesus, you can get a wonderful view of the whole area.

Caeté *Colour map 7, B5.*

A further 25 km is Caeté, which has several historical buildings and churches. On the Praça João Pinheiro are the **Prefeitura** and **Pelourinho** (both 1722), the **Igreja Matriz Nossa Senhora do Bom Sucesso** (1756 rebuilt 1790) ① *daily 1300-1800*, and the **Chafariz da Matriz**. Also on the Praça is the tourist information office in the Casa da Cultura (T6511855). Other churches are **Nossa Senhora do Rosário** (1750-1768), with a ceiling attributed to Mestre Athayde, and **São Francisco de Assis**. The **Museu Regional** ① *R Israel Pinheiro 176, Tue-Sun 1200-1700*, in the house of the Barão de Catas Altas, or Casa Setecentista, contains 18th- and 19th-century religious art and furniture.

Parque Natural de Caraça
The entrance is 11 km from the seminary, www.santuariodocaraca.com.br, 0800-1700, last entry 1530, US$3 pp; if staying overnight you cannot leave after 2000 (see Where to stay, page 478).

The Parque Natural de Caraça is a remarkable reserve about 120 km east of Belo Horizonte. It has been preserved so well because the land belongs to a seminary, part of which has been converted into a hotel. The rarest mammal in the park is the maned wolf; the monks feed them on the seminary steps in the evening. Also endangered is the southern masked titi monkey. Other primates include the common marmoset and the brown capuchin monkey. Some of the bird species at Caraça are

ON THE ROAD

O Aleijadinho

Antônio Francisco Lisboa (1738-1814), the son of a Portuguese architect and a black slave woman, was known as O Aleijadinho (the little cripple) because in later life he developed a maiming disease (possibly leprosy) which compelled him to work in a kneeling (and ultimately a recumbent) position with his hammer and chisel strapped to his wrists. His finest work, which shows a strength not usually associated with the sculpture in the 18th century, is probably the set of statues in the gardens and sanctuary of the great Bom Jesus church in Congonhas do Campo, but the main body of his work is in Ouro Preto, with some important pieces in Sabará, São João del Rei and Mariana.

endemic, others rare and endangered. The trails for viewing the different landscapes and the wildlife are marked at their beginning and are quite easy to follow.

★Ouro Preto Colour map 7, B5.

Founded in 1711, this famous former state capital has cobbled streets that wind up and down steep hills, crowned with 13 churches. Mansions, fountains, terraced gardens, ruins, towers shining with coloured tiles, all blend together to maintain a delightful 18th-century atmosphere. October-February is the wettest time, but the warmest month of the year is February (average 30°C). The coldest months are June-August, with the lowest temperatures in July (10°C).

Tourist offices ① *Praça Tiradentes 41, T031-3559 3269, and R Cláudio Manoel 61, T031-3559 3287, www.ouropreto.org.br,* Portuguese only spoken, very helpful; also has a desk at the *rodoviária,* Monday-Friday 0700-1300. The R Cláudio Manoel 61 office is in the Centro Cultural e Turístico mini-mall, with the town's best exhibition space, as well as shops and cafés. An accredited local guide, **Associação de Guias de Turismo (AGTOP)**, can be obtained through the tourist office, or at the *rodoviária,* T031-3559 3252. Do not use unaccredited guides. See also www.ouropreto. com.br (in Portuguese) and www.ouropreto.mg.gov.br.

Sights In the central **Praça Tiradentes** is a statue of the leader of the **Inconfidentes,** Joaquim José da Silva Xavier. Another Inconfidente, the poet Tomás Antônio Gonzaga lived at Rua Cláudio Manoel 61, close to São Francisco de Assis church. On the north side of the praça (at No 20) is a famous **Escola de Minas** (School of Mining), founded in 1876, in the fortress-like

Tip...

Churches in Ouro Preto are all closed Mondays. Bags and cameras are stowed in lockers (visitors keep the key).

Palácio dos Governadores (1741-1748); it has the interesting **Museu de Ciencia e Técnica** ① *Tue-Sun 1200-1700, US$1.55,* with a fine display of rocks, minerals, semi-precious and precious stones. On the south side of the Praça, No 139, is the **Museu da Inconfidência** ① *T031-3551 4977, Tue-Sun 1200-1730, US$2,* a fine historical and art museum in the former **Casa de Câmara e Cadeia,** which has some drawings by Aleijadinho and the studio of Manoel da Costa (Mestre) Athayde, in an annex. In the Casa Capitular de NS do Carmo is **Museu do Oratório** ① *T031-3551 5369, daily 0930-1730,* a collection of beautiful 18th- and 19th-century prayer icons and oratories including many made of egg and sea shell. **Casa dos Contos** ① *R São José 12, T031-3551 1444, Mon 1400-1800, Tue-Sat 1000-1800, Sun and holidays 1000-1600.* Built between 1782-1784, it is the Centro de Estudos do Ciclo de Ouro (Centre for Gold Cycle Studies) and a museum of money and finance. The **Casa Guignard** ① *R Conde de Bobadela 110, T031-3551 5155, Tue-Fri 1200-1800, Sat-Sun 1000-1500, free,* displays the paintings of Alberto da Veiga Guignard. The **Teatro Municipal** ① *in R Brigadeiro Musqueiro, Mon-Fri 1200-1700,* is the oldest functioning theatre in Latin America. It was built in 1769.

São Francisco de Assis (1766-1796) ① *Largo de Coimbra, T031-3551 3282, Tue-Sun 0830-1200, 1330-1700, US$3;* the ticket also permits entry to NS da Conceição (keep your ticket for admission to the museum). This church is considered to be one of the masterpieces of Brazilian baroque. Aleijadinho worked on the general design and the sculpture of the façade, the pulpits and many other features. Mestre Athayde (1732-1827) was responsible for the painted ceiling. **Nossa Senhora da Conceição**

(1722) ① *Tue-Sun 0800-1200, 1330-1700, US$3 – ticket shared with NS das Mercês e Perdões*, is heavily gilded and contains Aleijadinho's tomb. It has a museum devoted to him. **Nossa Senhora das Mercês e Perdões** (1740-1772) ① *R das Mercês, 1000-1400, US$3*, was rebuilt in the 19th century. Some sculpture by Aleijadinho can be seen in the main chapel. **Santa Efigênia** (1720-1785) ① *Ladeira Santa Efigênia e Padre Faria, Tue-Sun 0800-1630, US$1.50 (entry shared with Capela do Padre Faria)*; Manuel Francisco Lisboa (Aleijadinho's father) oversaw the construction and much of the carving is by Francisco Xavier de Brito (Aleijadinho's mentor). It has wonderful panoramic views of the city. **Nossa Senhora do Carmo** (1766-1772) ① *R Brigadeiro Mosqueira, Tue-Sun 0900-1100, 1300-1645, US$1*, has a museum of sacred art with Aleijadinho sculptures. **Nossa Senhora do Pilar** (1733) ① *Praça Mons Castilho Barbosa, Tue-Sun 0900-1045, 1200-1645, US$3*, also contains a religious art museum. Entry is shared with São Francisco de Paula, Ladeira de São José (1804). **Nossa Senhora do Rosário** ① *Largo do Rosário, Tue-Sun 1200-1645*, dated from 1785, has a curved façade. The interior is much simpler than the exterior, but there are interesting side altars.

The **Mina do Chico Rei** ① *R Dom Silvério, 0800-1700, US$4*, is not as impressive as some other mines in the area, but is fun to descend on the pulley, crawl through the narrow tunnels and learn how the gold was mined. Between Ouro Preto and Mariana is the **Minas de Passagem** ① *T031-3557 5000, www.minasdapassagem.com.br, Mon-Tue 0900-1700, Wed-Sun 0900-1730, US$8.40*, gold mine, dating from 1719. It's an exciting place to visit with a thrilling descent on an old mining cart followed by a guided wander through gloomy passages and large artificial caverns to a dark crystal-clear lake. Much of the machinery dates from the early 18th century.

☆Mariana *Colour map 7, B5.*

Streets are lined with beautiful, two-storey 18th-century houses in this old mining city, which is much less hilly than Ouro Preto. Mariana's historical centre slopes gently uphill from the river and the Praça Tancredo Neves, where buses drive from Ouro Preto stop. **Tourist office:** Secretaria de Cultura e Turismo de Mariana ① *R Direita 93, T031-3558 2315, www.mariana.mg.gov.br. See also www.marianatur.com.br and http://mariana.org.br.* The tourist office will help with guides and tours and offers a map and other informative publications.

Sights The first street parallel with the Praça Tancredo Neves is Rua Direita, and is home to the 300-year-old houses. At No 54 is the **Casa do Barão de Pontal** ① *Tue 1400-1700*, whose balconies are carved from soapstone, unique in Minas Gerais. The ground floor of the building is a museum of furniture. At No 35 is the **Museu-Casa Afonso Guimarães** (or Alphonsus de Guimaraens) ① *T031-3557 3259, Mon-Fri 1200-1800*, the former home of a symbolist poet: photographs and letters. At No 7 is the **Casa Setecentista**, which now belongs to the Patrimônio Histórico e Artístico Nacional.

Rua Direita leads to the Praça da Sé, on which stands the **Cathedral** ① *Basílica de Nossa Senhora da Assunção, Tue-Sun 0800-1700, US$0.65, organ concerts are given on Fri at 1100 and Sun at 1200*. The portal and the lavabo in the sacristy are by Aleijadinho. The painting in the beautiful interior and side altars is by Manoel Rebello de Sousa. Also in the cathedral is a wooden German organ (1701), a gift to the first diocese of the Capitania de Minas do Ouro in 1747. The **Museu Arquidiocesano** ① *R Frei Durão 49, Tue-Sun 0900-1200, 1300-1700, US$1*, has fine church furniture, a gold and silver collection, Aleijadinho statues and an ivory cross. Opposite holds the **Casa da Intendência/Casa de Cultura** ① *R Frei Durão 22, 0800-1130, 1330-1700*, which holds exhibitions and has a museum of music. On the south side of Praça Gomes Freire is the **Palácio Arquiepiscopal**, while on the north side is the **Casa do Conde de Assumar**, who was governor of the Capitania from 1717 to 1720.

From Praça Gomes Freire, Travessa São Francisco leads to Praça Minas Gerais and one of the finest groups of colonial buildings in Brazil. In the middle of the Praça is the **Pelourinho**, the stone monument to Justice, at which slaves used to be beaten. On one side of the square is the fine **São Francisco church** (1762-1794) ① *daily 0800-1700*, with pulpits designed by Aleijadinho, paintings by Mestre Athayde, who is buried in tomb No 94, a fine sacristy and one side-altar by Aleijadinho. At right angles to São Francisco is **Nossa Senhora do Carmo** (1784) ① *daily 1400-1700*, with steatite carvings, Athayde paintings, and chinoiserie panelling. Across Rua Dom Silvério is the **Casa da Cámara e Cadéia** (1768), at one time the Prefeitura Municipal. On Largo de São Pedro is **São Pedro dos Clérigos** (begun in 1753), one of the few elliptical churches in Minas Gerais. Restoration is under way.

Capela de Santo Antônio, on Rua Rosário Velho, is wonderfully simple and the oldest in town. It is some distance from the centre. Overlooking the city from the north, with a good viewpoint, is the church of **Nossa Senhora do Rosário**, Rua do Rosário (1752), with work by Athayde and showing Moorish influence.

Parque Nacional Caparaó

US$7.75 (Brazilians half price), open 0700-1800. Contact R Vale Verde s/n, Alto do Caparaó, CEP 36979-000, T032-3747 2086, www.icmbio.gov.br/parnacaparao.

This is one of the most popular parks in Minas (on the Espírito Santo border), with good walking through stands of Atlantic rainforest, páramo and to the summits of three of Brazil's highest peaks: Pico da Bandeira (2890 m), Pico do Cruzeiro (2861 m) and Pico do Cristal (2798 m). The park, surrounded by coffee farms, features rare Atlantic rainforest in its lower altitudes and Brazilian alpine on top. Loss of forest and floral biodiversity has adversely affected wildlife, but there are nonetheless a number of Atlantic coast primates, like the brown capuchins, together with a recovering bird population. From the park entrance it is 6 km on a good unpaved road to the car park at the base of the waterfall. From the hotel (see page 479) jeeps run to the car park at 1970 m (2½ hours' walk), then it's a three to four hour walk to the summit of the Pico da Bandeira, marked by yellow arrows; plenty of camping possibilities, the highest being at Terreirão (2370 m). This is good walking country. It is best to visit during the dry season (April-October). It can be quite crowded in July and during Carnival. See Transport, page 483, for how to get there.

Congonhas *Colour map 7, B5.*

This hill town is connected by a paved 3.5 km road with the Rio-Belo Horizonte highway. Most visitors spend little time in the town, but go straight to **O Santuário de Bom Jesus de Matosinhos** ① *Tue-Sun 0700-1900, there are public toilets on the Alameda das Palmeiras, the information desk at the bus station will guard luggage and you can visit the sanctuary between bus changes*, which dominates Congonhas. The great pilgrimage church was finished in 1771; below it are six linked chapels, or pasos (1802-1818), showing scenes with life-size Passion figures carved by Aleijadinho and his pupils in cedar wood. These lead up to a terrace and courtyard. On this terrace (designed in 1777) stand 12 prophets, sculpted by Aleijadinho between 1800 and 1805. Carved in soapstone with dramatic sense of movement, they constitute one of the finest works of art of their period in the world. Inside the church, there are paintings by Athayde and the heads of four sainted popes (Gregory, Jerome, Ambrose and Augustine) sculpted by Aleijadinho for the reliquaries on the high altar. To the left of the church, as you face it, the third door in the building alongside the church is the Room of Miracles, which contains photographs and thanks for miracles performed.

On the hill are souvenir shops, the Colonial Hotel and Cova do Daniel restaurant (both are good). From the hotel the Alameda das Palmeiras sweeps round to the **Romarias**, which contains the Espaço Cultural, the headquarters of the local tourist office, workshops, the museums of mineralogy and religious art and the Memória da Cidade. Between the Sanctuary and the Romarias is the new **Museu de Congonhas** ① *Alameda Cidade Matozinhos de Portugal, Basílica, T031-3731 3056, Tue-Sun 0900-1700, Wed 1300-2100, US$2.75, sponsored by UNESCO*, with a permanent collection on the history of the Sanctuary and Aleijadinho's work, library and café. To get there take bus marked 'Basílica' which runs every 30 minutes from the centre of the *rodoviária* to Bom Jesus, 5 km, US$1. A taxi from the *rodoviária* costs US$6, US$12.50 return including the wait while you visit the sanctuary. In town, the bus stops in Praça JK. You can walk up from Praça JK via Praça Dr Mário Rodrigues Pereira, cross the little bridge, then go up Ruas Bom Jesus and Aleijadinho to the Praça da Basílica. **Tourist office**: Diretoria de Turismo ① *Alameda Cidade Matozinhos de Portugal 153, Basílica, T031-3731 2077, with a help point at Av Júlia Kubistchek 2039, T031-3731 7394, both open daily, www.congonhas.org.br.*

São João del Rei *Colour map 7, B5.*

This colonial city is at the foot of the Serra do Lenheiro. A good view of the town and surroundings is from Alto da Boa Vista, where there is a Statue of Christ (Senhor dos Montes). São João del Rei is very lively at weekends, but feels far less of a tourist museum piece than nearby Tiradentes (see below). Through the centre of town runs the Corrego do Lenheiro (sadly a winding stream no more); across it are two fine stone bridges, A Ponte da Cadeia (1798) and A Ponte do Rosário (1800). **Tourist office**: Secretaria da Cultura e Turismo ① *Av Tiradentes 136, T032-3372 7338, 0900-1700, free map, www.guiadelrei.com.br.*

There are five 18th-century churches in the town, three of which are splendid examples of Brazilian colonial building. **São Francisco de Assis** (1774) ① *Praça Frei Orlando, 0800-1700, Sun 0800-1600, US$1.35.* The façade, with circular towers, the doorway intricately carved and the greenish stone framing the white paint to beautiful effect was designed by Francisco de Lima Cerqueira and his disciple Aniceto de Souza López. Inside are two sculptures by the same artists, about whom nothing is known beyond their names in the church's records and that they carried out the work in 1774. The six side altars are in wood; restoration has removed the plaster from the altars, revealing fine carving in sucupira wood.

Basílica de Nossa Senhora do Pilar (the Cathedral) ① *R Getúlio Vargas (formerly R Direita), Tue-Sun 0900-1100, 1330-1700,* built 1721, has a 19th-century façade which replaced the 18th-century original. It has rich altars and a brightly painted ceiling. In the sacristy are portraits of the Evangelists. **Nossa Senhora do Carmo** ① *Praça Dr Augusto Viegas (Largo do Carmo), Mon 0600-1200, 1300-1700, Tue-Sun 0900-1100, 1330-1700, US$0.30 in afternoon,* very well restored, is all in white and gold. Construction commenced in 1733. Almost opposite São Francisco is the house of **Bárbara Heliodora** which contains the **Museu Municipal Tomé Portes del Rei**, with historical objects and curios, and, downstairs. The **Museu Ferroviário** (railway museum) ① *Av Hermílio Alves 366, T032-3371 8485, Wed-Sat 0900-1300, 1400-1700, Sun 0900-1300, ticket office Wed-Thu 0900-1100, 1200-1745, Fri-Sat 0900-1300, 1400-1700, US$2.50 (included in the train ticket to Tiradentes, see below),* is well worth exploring. The museum traces the history of railways in general and in Brazil in brief. You can walk along the tracks to the round house, in which are several working engines in superb condition, an engine shed and a steam-operated machine shop, still working. It is here that the engines get up steam before going to couple with the coaches for the run to Tiradentes. On days when the trains are running, you can get a good, close-up view of operations even if not taking the trip; highly recommended.

☆Tiradentes
This charming little town (population about 7000), 15 km from São João, with its nine carefully restored, baroque churches, is at the foot of the green Serra de São José. Neat whitewashed cottages trimmed in yellow, maroon and blue hide art galleries, restaurants, souvenir shops and *pousadas*, all busy with tourists even during the week. It is especially busy during Carnival, Holy Week, when there are numerous religious processions, July, August, Christmas and New Year and during its many festivals (see below). It was founded as São José del Rei on 14 January 1718. After the ousting of the emperor in 1889 the town was renamed in honour of the martyr of the Inconfidência. **Tourist office** ① *R Resende Costa 71, T032-3355 1212, www.tiradentes.mg.gov.br and www.tiradentes.net, daily 0900-1700,* is in the Prefeitura on the main square, Largo das Forras. There is also a useful app: **Achou Tiradentes**.

Sights The **Igreja Matriz de Santo Antônio** (1710-1736) ① *at the top of R da Câmara, daily 0900-1700, US$1.35, no photos,* contains some of the finest gilded wood carvings in the country. The church has a small but fine organ brought from Porto in the 1790s (concerts every Friday 2000, T032-3355 1238). The upper part of the reconstructed façade is said to follow a design by Aleijadinho. In front of the church are also a cross and a sundial by him. **Santuário da Santíssima Trindade**, on the road which leads up behind the Igreja Matriz de Santo Antônio, is 18th century, while the room of miracles associated with the annual Trinity Sunday pilgrimage is modern. Just below Santo Antônio and the former Casa da Câmara is the new **Museo da Liturgia** ① *R Jogo de Bola 15, T032-3355 1552, www.museudaliturgia.com.br, Thu-Mon 1000-1700 (till 1500 on Sun),* dedicated to sacred texts. At the junction of Rua da Câmara and Rua Direita is the **Sobrado Ramalho**, said to be the oldest building in Tiradentes. It has been beautifully restored as a cultural centre.

The charming **Nossa Senhora do Rosário** church (1727) ① *set back from R Direita, Wed-Mon 0900-1600, US$0.65,* has fine statuary and ornate gilded altars. Near NS do Rosário is the Antiga Cadeia (old prison) which houses the **Museu de Sant'Ana** ① *R Direita 93, entrance on R Cadeia, T032-3355 2798, http://museudesantana.org.br, Wed-Sun 1000-1900, US$1.35,* well-presented, with onscreen descriptions and presentations, some in English, devoted entirely to images of Sant'Ana, the mother of the Virgin Mary. Also sells Cambraia coffee in the smart entrance lobby. **São João Evangelista** ① *Largo do Sol, Wed-Mon 0800-1700, free*, is in a lovely open space. It is a simple church, built by the Irmandade dos Homens Pardos (mulattos). Beside Igreja São João Evangelista is the **Museu Padre Toledo** ① *T032-3355 1549, Tue-Fri 1000-1700, Sat 1000-1630, Sun 0900-1500, no ticket sales 30 mins before closing time, US$2.65*, the house of one of the leaders of the Inconfidência Mineira. It exhibits some handsome colonial furniture and a painted roof depicting the Five Senses. **Nossa Senhora das Mercês** (18th century) ① *Largo das Mercês, Sun 0800-1700*, has an interesting painted ceiling and a notable statue of the Virgin. The magnificent **Chafariz de São José** (public fountain, 1749) is still used for drinking, clothes washing and watering animals. You can follow the watercourse into the forest of the Serra de São José (monkeys and birds can be seen); you must take a guide, see What to do, below.

The Maria Fumaça **steam train** ① *ticket office T032-3355 2789, Wed-Thu 0900-1100, 1200-1745, Fri-Sat 0900-1300, 1400-1700, Sun 0900-1400 or at Museu Ferroviário in São João del Rei (above), runs on Fri, Sat, 1000 and 1500 from São João del Rei, returning from Tiradentes at 1300 and 1700, Sun and holidays 1000 and 1300 from São João del Rei, 1100 and 1400 from Tiradentes, US$15 return*, on the line between São João del Rei and Tiradentes (13 km) has been in continuous operation since 1881, using the same locomotives and rolling stock, running on 76 cm gauge track, all lovingly cared for. The maximum speed is 20 kph.

Listings East and south of Belo Horizonte

Where to stay

Parque Natural de Caraça

$$$ Pousada do Caraça
The seminary hotel, for reservations T031-98978 3180/99617 3533. Mon-Fri 0800-1700, or pousadadocaraca@gmail.com.
It has pleasant rooms in a variety of wings and individual houses; room rates vary, price is full board. There is a restaurant serving good food which comes from farms within the seminary's lands. Lunch is served 1200-1400, US$6.15. Lodging also available at the **$$ Pousada Fazenda do Engenho** (T031-3809 4004, faz. engenho@gmail.com, on a farm 11 km from the seminary), breakfast available at the fazenda, other meals at the seminary, all included in the price, Wi-Fi available but no mobile phone reception. Details for both places on www. santuariodocaraca.com.br.

Ouro Preto
Prices indicated here are for high season; many hotels offer, or will negotiate, lower prices outside holiday times or when things are quiet.

Ask at the tourist office for accommodation in *casas de família*, reasonably priced. Avoid touts who greet you off buses and charge higher prices than those advertised in hotels; it is difficult to get hotel rooms at weekends and holiday periods.

$$$$ Pousada do Mondego
Largo de Coimbra 38, T031-3551 2040, www.mondego.com.br.
Beautifully kept colonial house in a fine location by São Francisco church, room rates vary according to view, small restaurant, Scotch bar, popular with groups. A recommended **Roteiro de Charme** hotel, see page 670. The hotel runs a jardineira bus tour of the city, 2 hrs, minimum 10 passengers, US$10 for non-guests.

$$$$ Pousada Solar de NS do Rosário
Av Getúlio Vargas 270, T031-3551 5040, www.hotelsolardorosario.com.br.
Fully restored historic building with a highly recommended restaurant, bar, sauna, pool; all facilities in rooms.

$$$ Pousada Casa Grande
R Conselheiro Quintiliano, 96, T031-3551 4314, www.hotelpousadacasagrande.com.br.
In a large colonial town house, smart, safe, good views. Recommended.

$$$-$$ Colonial
Trav Padre Camilo Veloso 26, close to Praça Tiradentes, T031-3551 3133, www.hotelcolonial.com.br.
With new rooms and refurbished older rooms, but check for size, pleasant.

$$$-$$ Pousada Mirante do Café
Fazenda Alto das Rubiáceas, Santo Antônio do Leite, 25 km west of Ouro Preto, T031-3335 8478, www.mirantedocafe.com.br.

Price varies with season and weekend. Coffee farm with full board available, visits allowed during coffee harvest, pool, trails, horse riding and other leisure activities.

$$$-$$ Pouso Chico Rey
R Brig Musqueira 90, T031-3551 1274, www.pousodochicorei.com.br.
Fascinating old house with Portuguese colonial furnishings, very small and utterly delightful (but plumbing unreliable), book in advance.

$$ Pousada Nello Nuno
R Camilo de Brito 59, T031-3551 3375, www.pousadanellonuno.com.br.
Cheaper rooms have no bath, friendly owner speaks some French. Highly recommended.

$$ Pousada São Francisco de Paula
Padre JM Pen 201, next to the São Francisco de Paula church, 100 m from rodoviária, T031-3551 3456, www.pousadasaofranciscodepaula.com.br.
One of the best views of any in the city. Rooms with and without bath or breakfast, dormitory, use of a kitchen, multilingual staff, excursions. Snacks are available. Check in after 1200. Recommended.

$$ Pousada Tiradentes
Praça Tiradentes 70, T031-3551 2619, www.pousadatiradentesop.com.br.
Spartan rooms, but well kept and moderately comfortable, fridge, conveniently located.

$ Brumas
R Antônio Pereira 43 (next to the Museu da Inconfidência), T031-3551 2944, www.brumashostel.com.br.
Small well-kept double rooms (**$$**) and dorms with parquet floors, cheaper for HI members, those on the upper corridor have mountain views. Excellent location in the heart of the colonial town overlooking São Francisco church.

$ Ouro Preto Hostel
Trav das Lajes 32, Antônio Dias, T031-3551 6011, www.ouropretohostel.com.
Also HI-affiliated, dorms, also suites (**$$**), some with balcony, near Mina do Chico Rei.

Camping

Camping Clube do Brasil
Rodovia dos Inconfidentes Km 91, 2 km north, T031-3551 1799.
Expensive but good.

Students

Students may be able to stay, during holidays and weekends, at the self-governing student hostels,
known as *repúblicas* (very welcoming, 'best if you like heavy metal music' and 'are prepared to enter into the spirit of the places'). The Prefeitura has a list of over 50 repúblicas with phone numbers, available at the Secretaria de Turismo. Many are closed Christmas to Carnival.

Mariana

$$$ Pousada do Chafariz
R Cônego Rego 149, T031-3557 1492, www.pousadado chafariz.com.br.
Converted colonial building, fridge, parking.

$$$ Pousada Solar dos Corrêa
R Josefá Macedo 70 and R Direita, T031-3557 2080.
Central, restored 18th-century town house with spacious a/c rooms, with fridge, parking.

$$$ Pouso da Typographia
Praça Gomes Freire 220, T031-3557 1311.
Much the best in town with fan-cooled rooms in an attractive colonial house which once was a printing works.

$$ Faísca
R Antônio Olinto 48, T031-3557 1206, www.hotelfaisca.com.br.
Up the street from the tourist office, rooms with fan and fridge, breakfast room.

$$ Providência
R Dom Silvério 233, T031-3557 1444, www.hotelprovidencia.com.br.
Along the road that leads up to the Basílica; has use of the neighbouring school's pool when classes finish at noon, small rooms, quiet.

Parque Nacional Caparaó

$$$ Caparaó Parque
2 km from the park entrance, T032-3747 2559, http://caparaoparquehotel.com.br.
15 mins' walk from the town of Alto Caparaó, nice. Ask where camping is permitted.

$$ São Luiz
In Manhumirim.
Good value, but **Cids Bar**, next door, Travessa 16 do Março, has better food.

São João del Rei

$$$ Beco do Bispo
Beco do Bispo 93, 2 mins west of São Francisco de Assis, T032-3371 8844, www.becodobispo.com.br.
The best in town, bright rooms with firm mattresses, hot showers, pool, convenient, very

helpful English speaking staff. Organizes tours. Highly recommended.

$$$ Lenheiros Palace
Av Pres Tancredo Neves 257, T032-3371 8155, www.hotellenheiros.com.br.
A modern hotel with good facilities, parking, **Lenheiros Casa de Chá** tea house, breakfast, no restaurant.

$$$ Ponte Real
Av Eduardo Magalhães 254, T032-3371 7000, www.hotelpontereal.com.br.
Modern, comfortable, sizeable rooms, good restaurant.

$$ Pousada Casarão
Opposite São Francisco church, Ribeiro Bastos 94, T032-3371 7447, www.pousadacasarao.com.
In a delightful converted mansion house, firm beds, fridge, swimming pool, games room.

Tiradentes
There are over 200 *pousadas* in and around town; below is a brief selection. Many are located on the main road and on the Estrada Real to São João del Rei and in the new condominiums on the edge of town. Most charge one rate for Mon-Thu and a higher rate for Fri-Sun. During festivals and high season, only packages for several nights are sold. Afternoon tea is often included in the price, as well as breakfast.

$$$$ Pequena Tiradentes
Av Gov Israel Pinheiro 670, T032-3355 1262, www.pequenatiradentes.com.br (on the road out of town).
Remarkable hotel, like a small town with streets between buildings which house luxurious suites, all named after famous Brazilian women, gardens, 2 pools, spa and fitness centre and a huge, contemporary lobby. Anything you like you can buy; it also has a vast shop selling furniture and household decorations. Its restaurant, Mandolin, has a good reputation.

$$$$ Pousada Araújo Bazilio,
R das Jacarandas 106, Condomínio Cuiabá (about 20 mins' walk from centre), T032-3355 2304, www.pousadaaraujobazilio.com.br.
Rooms descend on several floors from street-level lobby and breakfast room. Colonial style but modern decor and fittings, comfortable, good service, pool.

$$$$ Solar da Ponte
Praça das Mercês, T032-3355 1255, www.solardaponte.com.br.
Country house atmosphere, 18 rooms, fresh flowers in rooms, bar, sauna, lovely gardens, swimming pool, light meals for residents only, restaurants nearby (it is in the **Roteiros de Charme** group, see page 670). Recommended.

$$$$-$$$ Pouso de Bartolomeu
R Herculano dos S 377, Alto da Torre (outside the centre on a hillside), T032-3355 2142, www.pousodebartolomeo.com.br.
Pleasant rooms with 4-poster beds and good views, on different levels in a garden, swimming pool, no restaurant.

$$$ Pousada do Largo
Largo das Forras 18, T032-3355 1166, www.pousadadolargo.com.br.
Bright if small rooms, attractive public areas decorated with artsy Minas furniture and paintings, tiny pool, sauna, great location on the Praça. In same group as Pequena Tiradentes.

$$$ Pousada Mãe D'Água
Largo das Forras 50, T032-3355 1206, www.pousadamaedagua.com.br.
Including breakfast but not tax, very nice, large hotel with indoor pool, sauna and hydromassage at the back.

$$$ Pousada Três Portas
R Direita 280A, T032-3355 1444, www.pousadatresportas.com.br.
Charming, central, in restored town house, has sauna, thermal pool, hydromassage, heating, all food served is home-produced. Recommended.

$$ Pousada Coração Inconfidente
R dos Inconfidentes 120, T032-3355 2464, www.pousadacoracaoinconfidente.com.br.
Rooms along an outside passage leading to pool, simple, with fan, possibly the cheapest near the centre during the week (at weekends and festivals no different from others in this category).

$$ Santa Edwiges
R Joaquim Ramalho 435, Bairro Cuiabá, T032-3355 1415, www.santaedwigespousada.com.
Some distance from centre, not far from the Posto de Gasolina, nice clean tiled rooms, good breakfast with home-made ingredients, welcoming.

Restaurants

Ouro Preto
Try the local liquor *de jaboticaba*.

$$ Adega
R Teixeira Amaral 24, T031-3551 4171.

Vegetarian smorgasbord, all you can eat, 1130-1530. Highly recommended.

$$ Casa do Ouvidor
R Conde de Bobadela 42, T031-3551 2141, www.casadeouvidor.com.br.
Traditional Minas fare served in a lovely old mansion 2 mins' walk from the Praça Tiradentes, very good.

$$ Forno de Barro
Praça Tiradentes 54.
Decent Mineira cooking.

$$ O Sotão
R São José 201.
Great value pancake and crepe restaurant with some 40 different flavours, lively at weekends. Also in Mariana on Praça Gomes Freire.

$$ Taverna do Chafariz
R São José 167, T031-3551 2828.
Good local food. Recommended.

$ Beijinho Doce
R Direita 134A.
Delicious pastries and cakes, try the truffles.

$ Café & Cia
R São José 187, T031-3551 0711. Closes 2300.
Very popular, *comida por kilo* at lunchtime, good salads, juices.

$ Pasteleria Lampião
Praça Tiradentes.
Best at lunchtime; good views at the back.

Mariana

$$ Bistrô
R Salomão Ibrahim da Silva 61, T031-3557 4138. Open at night.
Comida mineira, decent steaks, pasta, pizza and *petiscos*, German-Brazilian beers.

$$ Lua Cheia
Dom Viçoso.58, T031-3557 3232.
Good-value lunchtime buffet with Minas food, pasta, salads and juices.

$$ Rancho da Praça
Praça Gomes Freire 108, T031-3557 3444.
Buffet of well-prepared Minas dishes served in traditional iron pots and pans.

São João del Rei

$$$ Churrascaria Ramón
Praça Severiano de Resende 52.
One of the better *churrascarias* with generous portions and plenty of side dishes.

$$$ Quinto do Ouro
Praça Severiano de Rezende 04, T032-3371 7577.
Tasty and well-prepared regional food. Said to be the best Mineira cooking in town.

$ Restaurant 611
R Tome Portes del Rei 511, Vila Santo Antônio, T032-3371 5590.
Very cheap but great Mineira cooking. Lots of choice, popular. Also **611 Centro** (R Getulio Vargas 145, Centro).

Tiradentes

There are many restaurants, snack bars and *lanchonetes* in town and it is a small enough place to wander around and see what takes your fancy. Many restaurants are closed on Tue, especially in low season, others open only Fri, Sat and Sun.

$$$ Estalagem do Sabor
R Ministro G Passos 280, T032-3355 1144.
Excellent and generous traditional Mineira meat dishes.

$$$ Sabor Rural
Estrada da Caixa Dágua Km 4 (a dirt road that turns off by the train station), T032-9934 4005.
Excellent Mineira food, all made to order, has its own still for *cachaça* to make caipirinhas which is served in teapots, beer served in buckets full of ice. There are other places along this road.

$$$ Theatro da Vila
R Padre Toledo 157, T032-3355 1275, www.theatro davilla.com.br. Mon-Sat from 1930, phone after 1730 to reserve, or at 1300 on 032-8456 0606.
Inventive and delicious Franco-Brazilian fusion cooking served in intimate rustic-chic dining room. Views over the Serra across the garden, small theatre that holds performances in summer.

$$$ Virados do Largo, da Beth
R do Moinho 11, T032-3355 1111, www.viradas dolargo.com.br. Wed-Mon 1200-2200.
Good à la carte Mineira food and service. Walk past the Chafariz de São José, then turn right.

$$$-$$ Padre Toledo
R Direita 250, www.padretoledo.com.br.
Good Mineira food, popular, also has a pousada. Behind it, on Largo do Sol, is **Panificação Padre Toledo**, which is open earlier than most in the centre for breakfast, bread, juices, etc.

$$$-$$ Sapore d'Italia
Largo das Forras 54, T032-3355 1250.
Popular Italian/Brazilian restaurant with tables on the Praça, some artisanal beers.

Ouro Preto

Feb/Mar Attracting many Brazilians, **Carnival** here is also memorable.

Mar/Ap Ouro Preto is famous for its **Holy Week** processions, beginning on the Thu before Palm Sun and continuing (but not every day) until Easter Sun. The most famous is that commemorating Christ's removal from the Cross, late on Good Friday. Many shops close then, and on winter weekends.

Jun **Corpus Christi** and the **Festas Juninas** are celebrated.

Jul **Festival do Inverno da Universidade Federal de Minas Gerais (UFMG)**, the **Winter Festival**, about 3 weeks of arts, courses, shows, concerts and exhibitions. Also in Jul, on the 8th, is the **anniversary of the city**.

15 Aug **Nossa Senhora do Pilar**, patron saint of Ouro Preto.

12-18 Nov **Semana de Aleijadinho**, a week-long arts festival.

Congonhas

Mar/Ap Congonhas is famous for **Holy Week** processions at Bom Jesus church. The most celebrated ceremonies are the **meeting of Christ and the Virgin Mary** on the Tue, and the dramatized **Deposition from the Cross** late on Good Fri.

Sep The pilgrimage season, 1st half of Sep, draws thousands.

8 Dec **Nossa Senhora da Conceição**.

São João del Rei

Mar **Semana Santa**.

15-21 Apr **Semana da Inconfidência**.

May/Jun **Corpus Christi**.

Jul FUNREI, the university (R Padre José Maria Xavier), holds **Inverno Cultural**.

1st 2 weeks of Aug **Nossa Senhora da Boa Morte**, with baroque music (*novena barroca*).

12 Oct **Nossa Senhora do Pilar**, patron saint of the city.

8 Dec **Founding of the city**.

Tiradentes

There are festivals throughought the year, at which times prices rise and the town can be full.

Late Jan **Mostra de Cinema**, www.mostra tiradentes.com.br, festival of Brazilian cinema.

Mar **Festival de Fotografia**, www.fotoempauta.com.br.

Late Apr **Homage to Tiradentes**, the leader of the Inconfidência.

Early May **Theatre festival**.

26-29 May **Corpus Christi**, processions with floral carpets.

Mid-Jun **Vinho e Jazz**.

Jul Lots of events during the school holidays and another jazz festival.

2nd half of Aug **Festival de Gastronomia**, www.farturagastronomia.com.br, one of Tiradentes' most popular events.

Ouro Preto

Gems are not much cheaper from sellers in Praça Tiradentes than from the shops, and in the shops, the same quality of stone is offered at the same price. If buying on the street, ask for the seller's credentials. Buy soapstone carvings at roadside stalls and bus stops rather than in cities; they are much cheaper. Many artisans sell jewellery and semi-precious stones in Largo de Coimbra in front of São Francisco de Assis church. Recommended is **Gemas de Minas**, Conde de Bobadela 63.

Tiradentes

Shopping for household items, furniture, antiques and gifts is one of the town's attractions. There are many shops selling such goods and pewter ware.

One posh gallery is **Oscar Araripe** on R da Câmara, but there are many others. More chic and more expensive than Tiradentes is the village of Bichinho, 6 km away, selling much the same stuff (a reasonable walk along the Estrada Real). Santa Cruz de Minas, on the outskirts of São João del Rei, specializes in furniture made from reclaimed wood. For the best value go to Resende Costa, some 50 km from Tiradentes, 14 km off the BR-040 (bus from São João del Rei), whose main street is entirely given over to shops and manufacturers of blankets, cushions, place settings and handicrafts.

Tiradentes

Agencies offer local excursions and can provide guides for walking on local trails and in the Serra de São José (also ask at Tourist Office). These include **Uai Trip** (R Henrique Diniz 119, T032-3355 1161, www.uaitrip.com.br), and **Viva Minas**

(R Custódio Gomes 13, T032-3355 1811, Facebook: AgenciaVivaMinas). Horse-drawn buggies do trips around town for US$18.75 for 40-60 mins.

Transport

Sabará

Bus Viação Cisne from separate part of **Belo Horizonte** *rodoviária*, US$2, 30 mins.

Parque Natural de Caraça

Turn off the BR-262 (towards Vitória) at Km 73 and go via Barão de Cocais to Caraça (120 km). There is no public transport to the seminary. **Buses** go as far as **Santa Bárbara** (Util, 1800, 3 hrs, US$15), or Barão de Cocais, then take a taxi, about US$30 one way. You must book the **taxi** to return for you, or else **hitch** (not easy). The park entrance is 10 km before the seminary. Or hire a **car**, or take a tour from Belo Horizonte, which will work out cheaper than going under your own steam if you can join a tour.

Ouro Preto

Bus Don't walk from the *rodoviária* to town at night; robberies have occurred. The *rodoviária* is at R Padre Rolim 661, near São Francisco de Paula church, T031-3559 3252. A 'Circular' bus runs from the *rodoviária* to Praça Tiradentes, US$1. Taxi US$6 at least. Hourly buses 0600-2300 from Belo Horizonte 2 hrs, US$7.75. Day trips are run. Book your return journey to **Belo Horizonte** early if returning in the evening; buses get crowded. Bus to/from **Rio**, 4 a day, US$26-35, 8 hrs. To **Congonhas** you will need to change bus in **Ouro Branco**: 3 daily to Ouro Branco from Ouro Preto, 1st at 0715 (US$2, 1 hr), 7 daily from Ouro Branco to Congonhas (US$4, 90 mins). Take the 1615 bus from Congonhas to Ouro Branco for the last bus back to Ouro Preto. Direct buses to **São Paulo**, 1 at night, 10 hrs, US$45.

Train The **Maria Fumaça Trem da Vale** is now a diesel train, not a steam locomotive, Praça Cesário Alvim, s/n, T031-3551 7310, www.tremdavale.org. It leaves Fri-Sun at 1000 and 1530, returning from Mariana at 0830 and 1400, US$15/US$20 return. For the best views for 18-km, 40-min journey, sit on the right side and in the back carriages.

Mariana

Bus Mariana is only 12 km from Ouro Preto and can easily be visited as a side trip. Buses run between the Escola de Minas near Praça Tiradentes in **Ouro Preto** and the Secretaria de Cultura e Turismo de Mariana, Praça Tancredo Neves, every 30 mins, US$2.

Parque Nacional Caparaó

Bus The park is 49 km by paved road from Manhuaçu (about 190 km south of Governador Valadares) on the Belo Horizonte-Vitória road (BR-262). There are buses from **Belo Horizonte** (twice daily), Ouro Preto or Vitória to **Manhumirim**, 15 km south of Manhuaçu. From Manhumirim, take a **Rio Doce** bus direct to Alto Caparaó, 7 a day, US$2. From Alto Caparaó walk 4 km to the park, or hire a jeep. By **car** from the BR-262, go through Manhumirim, Alto Jaquitibá and Alto Caparaó, then 1 km to Hotel Caparaó Parque.

Congonhas

Bus The *rodoviária* is 1.5 km outside town, Av Júlia Kubitschek 1982, T031-3731 3886; bus to town centre US$1; for 'Basílica', see above. To **Belo Horizonte**, 1½ hrs, US$7, 3 buses direct (5 on Sun) with **Sandra**, T031-3731 1386, otherwise go to the main road where many more pass. To **São João del Rei**, 2½ hrs, US$8, direct Sat and Sun only, otherwise flag down bus on main BR-040 road, 7 daily, or go to **Conselheiro Lafaiete**, 20 mins, US$2, from where 7 buses a day go to São João del Rei. Bus to **Ouro Preto**: see above.

São João del Rei

Bus *Rodoviária* is 2 km west of the centre; platform tax US$1.20; has ATM and information desk. To **São Paulo**, 8 hrs, 3-4 a day with Util, US$30. **Belo Horizonte**, 7 daily with **Sandra**, 4 hrs, US$14.25. To **Tiradentes**, 19 a day from 0550-1900, 9 on Sun and holidays from 0700, US$0.90. **Viação Real** goes to Tiradentes along the cobbled Estrada Real, 0530-2210 (from 0610 On Sun), leaving from Tejuco.

Tiradentes

Bus Last bus back to **São João del Rei** is 1940. A taxi to Tiradentes' *rodoviária* costs US$4, while a taxi to São João del Rei *rodoviária* starts at US$10.75.

The coastal state of Espírito Santo is where Mineiros head to for their seaside holidays. The most popular beaches are south of Vitória, the state capital, while north of the city are several turtle-nesting beaches. Inland are immigrant towns.

Vitória and around *Colour map 7, B6.*

Five bridges connect the island on which Vitória stands with the mainland. The state capital is beautifully set, its entrance second only to Rio's, its beaches quite as attractive, but smaller, and the climate is less humid. Port installations at Vitória and nearby Ponta do Tubarão have led to some beach and air pollution at places nearby. It is largely a modern city. The upper, older part of town, reached by steep streets and steps, is less hectic than the lower harbour area, but both are full of cars. The car-parking boys have their work cut out to find spaces. **Tourist offices**: in the *rodoviária* (open daily from 0600, closed Saturday afternoon and Sunday), at the airport, T027-3235 6350 (open daily, helpful, with map and leaflets) and near Kiosk 2, Praia de Camburi (open daily 0900-1700). **Fala Vitória** ① *T156, www.vitoria.es.gov.br.* For the state see www.descubraoespiritosanto.es.gov.br.

On Avenida República is the large **Parque Moscoso**, an oasis of quiet, with a lake and playground. Of the few colonial buildings still to be seen in the upper city, the **Capela de Santa Luzia** (1551) ① *R José Marcelino, Mon-Fri 0800-1800* has a painted altar, otherwise a small open space. In the **Palácio Anchieta**, or **do Governo** ① *Praça João Climaco (upper city)*, is the tomb of Padre Anchieta, one of the founders of São Paulo. Praça João Climaco has some restored buildings around it, including the Casa do Cidadão. The **Teatro Carlos Gomes** ① *Praça Costa Pereira*, often presents plays, also jazz and folk festivals.

Urban beaches such as **Camburi** can be affected by pollution, but it is pleasant, with a fair surf. Several buses run from the centre to Camburi, look for one with Av Beira Mar on the destination board. Buses pass Praia do Canto, a smart district with good restaurants and shops, then cross A Ponte de Camburi.

Vila Velha, reached by A Terceira Ponte (the Third Bridge) across the bay, is a separate municipality from Vitória. The Third Bridge, a toll road, is a sweeping structure and one of the symbols of the city. It has an excellent series of beaches: Praia da Costa is the main one, with others, including Itaparica, heading south. The second main symbol of Vila Velha is the monastery of **Nossa Senhora da Penha** (1558) ① *daily 0515-1645, http://conventodapenha.org.br*, on a high hill with superb views of the bay, bridge and both cities. The Dutch attacked it in 1625 and 1640. Minibuses take the infirm and not-so-devout up the hill for US$1 return, 0630-1715 (you have to use the phone in the upper car park if you want a ride down). A museum in the convent costs US$0.50. From here you will see that Vila Velha is neither old, nor a small town. It's a built up beachfront city, noisy at times, but the sea suffers less from pollution than Camburi. Vila Velha is the place of origin of Garoto chocolates, whose factory can be visited on weekdays (T027-3320 1709 for times). **Tourist information** ① *T027-3149 7287, or 0800-283 9059, www.vilavelha.es.gov.br.*

Some 14 km south of Vila Velha is **Barra do Jucu**, which has bigger waves, and the **Reserva de Jacarenema**, which preserves coastal ecosystems.

Inland from Vitória

Santa Leopoldina or **Domingos Martins**, both around 45 km from Vitória, are less than an hour by bus (Pretti to Santa Leopoldina five a day, four on Sunday; Aguia Branca to Domingos Martins, Friday 1700 only). Both villages preserve the architecture and customs of the first German and Swiss settlers who arrived in the 1840s. Domingos Martins (also known as Campinho) has a Casa de Cultura with some items of German settlement. Santa Leopoldina has an interesting **museum** ① *Tue-Sun 0900-1100, 1300-1800*, which covers the settlers' first years in the area. Domingos Martins is on the route of a tourist train that runs on Saturday and Sunday from the town of Viana, outside Vitória, to Domingos Martins, Marechal Floriano and Araguaya. The railcar of the **Trem das Montañas Capixabas** ① *US$31 one way, return trip special offers available, http://serraverdeexpress.com.br, ticket office in Vitória: R Gelu Vervloet 500, sala 603, T027-3237 1789*, leaves at 0900, getting back to Viana at 1440. The line climbs over 500 m from the coastal plain into Mata Atlântica.

Along the BR-262 west towards Minas Gerais, most of the hills are intensely worked, with very few patches of Mata Atlântica remaining. A significant landmark is the **Pedra Azul**, a huge granite outcrop, with a sheer face (a bit like a massive tombstone). From the side you can see a spur which looks like a finger pointing to the summit. It's a Parque Estadual, whose entrance is on the BR-262. The Pedra Azul bus stop is at the turn-off to the town of Alonso Cláudio ('region of waterfalls'). There are many *pousadas* here. The next town, **Venda Nova do Imigrante**, some 10 km, is a pretty place to stop, with well-tended flower beds along the main street, plenty of eating places, handicrafts and local Italian produce and at least one hotel.

Santa Teresa is a charming hill town two hours, 78 km by bus from Vitória. A brochure from the Prefeitura lists local sites of interest including waterfalls, valley views and some history. It also lists where to stay and eat. Fazendas also offer accommodation, days out and rural pursuits. See Santa Teresa's website, www.santateresa-es.com.br. In the Galeria de Arte, just past the *rodoviária*, shops sell handicrafts and honey, jams, liqueurs, sweet wines and biscuits. Stalls on the side of the main road also sell local products. There is a museum, botanical garden and small zoo for study of Mata Atlântica wildlife at the **Museu Mello Leitão** ① *Av José Ruschi 4, T027-3259 1192, 0800-1200, 1300-1700 (closed Mon morning), US$1.* Its library includes the works of the hummingbird and orchid scientist, Augusto Ruschi. Hummingbird feeders are hung outside the admin building.

Guarapari and beaches south of Vitória *Colour map 7, B6.*

South of Vitória (54 km) is Guarapari, whose beaches are the closest to Minas Gerais, so they get very crowded at holiday times. The beaches also attract many people seeking cures for rheumatism, neuritis and other complaints, from the radioactive monazitic sands. Information about the sands can be found at **Setuc** ① *in the Casa de Cultura, Praça Jerônimo Monteiro, T027-3261 3058,* and at the **Antiga Matriz** church on the hill in the town centre, built in 1585.

Further south (28 km) is **Anchieta** with nearby beaches at Praia de Castelhanos (5 km east, on a peninsula) and Iriri. The next spot down the coast, 5 km, is **Piúma**, a calm place, renowned for its craftwork in shells. About 3 km north of the village is Pau Grande beach, where you can surf. The resort town of **Marataízes**, with good beaches, hotels and camping, is 30 km south of Piúma. It is just north of the Rio state border. Planeta buses go to Mataraízes and Piúma from Vitória.

Turtle beaches

The **Reserva Biológica Comboios** ① *open 0800-1200, 1300-1700, for information, contact Projeto Tamar, Regência, T027-3274 1905, www.projetotamar.org.br,* 104 km north of Vitória via Santa Cruz, is designed to protect the marine turtles which frequent this coast. **Regência**, at the mouth of the Rio Doce, 65 km north of Santa Cruz, is part of the reserve and has a regional base for Tamar, the national marine turtle protection project.

Linhares, 143 km north of Vitória on the Rio Doce, has good hotels and restaurants. It is a convenient starting place for the turtle beaches. If you cannot visit Tamar's turtle project here, there is another visitor centre further north at **Guriri** ① *T027-3761 2104, www.projetotamar.org.br,* 12 km from São Mateus, which is 220 km north of Vitória, or contact **Tamar** ① *T027-3225 3787, tamarvitoria@tamar.org.br, Tue-Sun 0830-1700,* in Vitória.

Itaúnas and around *Colour map 7, B6.*

The most attractive beaches in the state are around **Conceição da Barra**. Corpus Christi (early June) is celebrated with an evening procession for which the road is decorated with coloured wood chips.

Itaúnas, 27 km north by road, or 14 km up the coast, has been swamped by sand dunes, 30 m high. From time to time, winds shift the sand dunes enough to reveal the buried church tower. Itaúnas has been moved to the opposite river bank. The coast here is a protected turtle breeding ground. There are a few *pousadas* and a small campsite at Itaúnas and other hotels 3 km further north at Guaxindiba. Take a bus from the bakery in Conceição da Barra at 0700; it returns at 1700.

Where to stay

Vitória

Many hotels belonging to chains such as **Bristol** (www.alliahotels.com.br) and **Accor** (www.accorhotels.com). Adequate hotels can be found opposite the *rodoviária* and a couple in the city centre.

$$$ Slaviero Slim Alice Vitória
R Cnel Vicente Peixoto 95, Praça Getúlio Vargas, T027-3331 1144, www.gruponeffa.com.br.
In the busy lower city, good rooms with comfy beds, typical business hotel. With 2 restaurants.

$$ Vitória
R Cais de São Francisco 85, T027-3223 0222, hotelsolemar-es@hotmail.com.br.
Near Parque Moscoso. Comfortable rooms, some with round beds, rambling building, good restaurant Mar e Sol.

Camburi

$$$ Aeroporto
R Ary Ferreira Chagas 30, T027-2127 3100, www.hotelaeroportovitoria.com.br.
Large rooms, well-furnished, good breakfast, on way to airport from Camburi beach.

$$$-$$ Minuano
Av Dante Michelini 337, T027-2121 7877, www.hotelminuano.com.br.
Hotel and churrascaria at the Canal end of Camburi, 3 standards of room.

Vila Velha

$$$ Itaparica Praia
R Itapemirim 30, Coqueiral de Itaparica, Vila Velha, T027-3320 4000, www.hotelitaparica.com.br.
More pricey in high season, rooms with sea view cost a bit more. Huge rooms, pool, garage, quiet, safe and good.

Inland from Vitória: Santa Teresa

$$$-$$ Pierazzo
Av Getúlio Vargas 115, T027-3259 1233, www.hotelpierazzo.com.br.
Central, nice rooms with frigobar, comfortable, helpful, small pool, sauna. Recommended.

Itaúnus and around: Conceição da Barra

$$$-$$ Porto Márlin
Praia Guaxindiba, T027-3762 1800, www.redemarlin.com.br.
With a/c, fridge, seaview, waterpark, restaurant and bar.

$$ Pousada Mirante
Av Atlântica 566, T027-3762 1633, http://pousadamirante.com.br.
With a/c, spotless, English spoken.

Camping

Camping Clube do Brasil
Rodovia Adolfo Serra, Km 16, T3762 1346.
Full facilities.

Restaurants

Vitória

A local speciality is *moqueca capixaba*, a seafood dish served in an earthenware pot. It is a variant of the *moqueca* which is typical of Bahia. Note that it's big enough for 2 people, but you can get half portions. It is served with rice and *siri desfiado*, crab and shrimp in a thick sauce, very tasty. Several places on R Joaquim Lírio, Praia do Canto, from breads to pastas to seafood. Lots of *lanches*, etc, on R G Neves at Praça Costa Pereira, in the city centre, and pizzas and others on R 7 de Setembro.

$$$ Pirão
R Joaquim Lírio 753, Praia do Canto.
Closed evenings.
Specializes in *moqueca*, also fish, seafood and a couple of meat dishes. Well-established and rightly highly regarded. Ask for a bib to keep your front clean.

$ Restaurante Expresso
G Neves 22, T027-3223 1091.
A better class of self-service for lunch, good choice and puddings, a/c, clean, popular.

Cafés/padarias

Cheiro Verde
R Prof Baltazar, next to Pão Gostoso.
Churrascaria and *comida caseira*, self-service.

Expressa
As above, next door and open later in afternoon, on G Neves.
For good breads, cakes, savouries and cold stuffs.

Pão Gostoso
R Prof Baltazar.
Also selling breads, cakes, savouries and cold stuffs.

Bars and clubs

Vitória
The junction of Joaquim Lírio and João da Cruz in Praia do Canto is known as O Triângulo. 2 bars at the junction, **Bilac** and **Búfalo Branco** are very popular Fri and Sat with young crowd. Another bar is **Apertura** (J Lírio 811), quieter. All serve food. Many other places in the area. From centre take any bus going to Camburi and get out opposite São José supermarket just before Ponte de Camburi.

Transport

Vitória
Air Eurico Salles airport is at Goiaberas, 11 km from the city, T027-3235 6300. Several buses go there eg Nos 162, 163, 122, 212. Taxi from centre US$15.

Bus City buses are mostly green, US$1. No 212 is a good route, from *rodoviária* to airport, marked Aeroporto; make sure it says Via Av Beira Mar: it goes right along the waterfront, past the docks (ask to be let off for Av Princesa Isabel in centre), **Shopping Vitória** opposite the State Legislative Assembly, by the Third Bridge, São José supermarket just before Ponte de Camburi, all along Camburi beach, then turns left to airport.

To **Vila Velha**: from Vitória take a yellow 500 bus marked 'Vilha Velha' from Praça Getúlio Vargas, or a 514 from Av Mal Mascarenhas de Moraes. No 508 connects Camburi and Vila Velha. Buses back to Vitória leave from the *rodoviária*, or a stop on Champagnat, almost opposite Carone supermarket, fare US$1. For NS da Penha, ask to be let off the yellow bus into Vila Velha on Av Henrique Moscoso at or near R Antônio Ataíde, which you go down (right from direction of bus) to R Vasco Coutinho then turn right.

The *rodoviária* is a 15-min walk west of the centre at Av Alexandre Buaiz 350, T027-3203 3666; many buses go there and there is a city bus stop just outside. It has good lanches, sweet shops and toilets. **Rio**, 8 hrs, US$27-34. **Belo Horizonte**, see above. **Ouro Preto**, US$23.25, 7 hrs. **São Paulo**, US$40-56, 16 hrs. **Alvorada** bus from Vitória to **Guarapari**, 1½ hrs, several daily, US$4.

Train Daily passenger service to **Belo Horizonte**, departs 0700, arrives Belo Horizonte at 2010, returns 0730, arrives 2030; US$32 *executivo* (very comfortable), US$22.35 *econômico*. Tickets online or from various outlets, including stations, up to 30 mins before departure, T0800-285 7000 for information, www.vale.com/tremdepassage irosefvm. The station is called Pedro Nolasco, Cariacica, Km 1 BR-262, T027-3333 2444: take a yellow bus saying 'Ferroviária', best is No 515 going to Campo Grande; to the city (cross the main road outside the station), Praia do Canto and Camburi, take a 'T Laranjeiras via Beira Mar' bus.

Inland from Vitória: Santa Teresa
Bus Several buses daily from **Vitória** *rodoviária* with Lirio dos Vales, US$7.50, most go via Fundão on the BR-101 going north, all paved. Fewer via Santa Leopoldina, not all paved, a beautiful journey.

North of Belo Horizonte
remote colonial towns and rocky terrain

Diamantina, the most remote of the colonial cities to the north of the State capital is reached from Belo Horizonte by taking the paved road to Brasília (BR-040). Turn northeast to Curvelo, beyond which the road passes through the impressive rocky country of the Serra do Espinhaço. Equally remote is the town of Serro, while in the Serra do Espinhaço itself is the Cipó national park, protecting high mountain grassland and rare species.

☆Diamantina *Colour map 7, A5.*
This centre of a once-active diamond industry Diamantina has excellent colonial buildings. Its churches are not as grand as those of Ouro Preto, but it is the least spoiled of all the colonial mining cities, with carved overhanging roofs and brackets. This very friendly, beautiful town is in the deep interior, amid barren mountains. It is lively at weekends. **President Juscelino Kubitschek**, the founder of Brasília, was born here. His **house** ⓘ *R São Francisco 241, Tue-Sat 0800-1700, Sun 0800-1300, US$1.35*, is now a museum, with a modern annexe at the back and a café below the old house. Banco do Brasil, beside the Prefeitura, behind the Cathedral, has ATMs. **Santiago Câmbio** ⓘ *R da Quitanda, prédio 8, sala 9, T038-3532 2356, santiagocambio.com.br, Mon-Fri 0900-1200, 1300-1800, Sat 0900-1200*, changes cash at decent rates.

Sights The oldest church in Diamantina is **Nossa Senhora do Rosário** ① *Largo Dom Joaquim, open to the public from 1400*, built by slaves in 1728. **Nossa Senhora do Carmo** ① *R do Carmo, also open at 1400*, dates from 1760-1765 and was built for the Carmelite Third Order. It is the richest church in the town, with fine decorations and paintings and a pipe organ, covered in gold leaf, made locally.

São Francisco de Assis ① *R São Francisco, just off Praça JK, only open for Mass*, was built between 1766 and the turn of the 19th century. It is notable for its paintings. Other colonial churches are the small, blue and white **Capela Imperial do Amparo** (1758-1776) ① *R do Amparo, open 0900-1120, US$0.50*, **Nossa Senhora das Mercês** (1778-1784) and **Nossa Senhora da Luz** (early 19th century), both open for services only. The **Catedral Metropolitana de Santo Antônio**, on Praça Guerra (or da Catedral), was built in the 1930s in neocolonial style to replace the original cathedral.

After repeated thefts, the diamonds of the **Museu do Diamante** ① *R Direita 14, Tue-Sat 1000-1700, Sun 0900-1300, free*, are now kept in the Banco do Brasil. The museum houses an important collection of materials used in the diamond industry, plus oratories, slave shackles, weapons, furniture and parts of statues (heads, hands, feet), and has toilets. **Casa de Chica da Silva** ① *Praça Lobo Mesquita 266, T038-3531 2491, Tue-Sat 1200-1730, Sun 0830-1200, free*. Chica da Silva was a slave in the house of the father of Padre Rolim (one of the Inconfidentes). She became the mistress of João Fernandes de Oliveira, a diamond contractor. Chica, who died 15 February 1796, has become a folk-heroine among Brazilian blacks.

The 18th-century building which now houses the **Prefeitura Municipal** (originally the diamonds administration building, Praça Conselheiro Matta 11) is behind the Cathedral. To the east and below is the blue **Mercado Municipal** or **Mercado dos Tropeiros** (muleteers) ① *Praça Barão de Guaicuí*. The **Casa da Glória** ① *R da Glória 297, Tue-Sun 1300-1700*, is two houses on either side of the street connected by an enclosed bridge, also painted blue. It is some distance from the centre and contains the Instituto Eschwege de Geologia.

Walk along the 20-km **Caminho dos Escravos**, the old paved road built by slaves between the mining area on Rio Jequitinhonha and Diamantina. A guide is essential (ask ASGITUR or at the Secretaria de Turismo), and beware of snakes and thunderstorms. Along the river bank it is 12 km on a dirt road to **Biribiri**, a pretty village with a well-preserved church and an abandoned textile factory. It also has a few bars and at weekends it is a popular, noisy place. About halfway, there are swimming pools in the river; opposite them, on a cliff face, are animal paintings in red. The age and origin are unknown. The plant life along the river is interesting and there are beautiful mountain views. There is no public transport to Biribiri; take a taxi or contact ASGITUR (see below).

Gruta do Salitre ① *9 km from Diamantina in the Curalinho district, T038-3531 2197, grutadosalitre@biotropicos.org.br to arrange a visit*, is an area of strange rock formations, once a quarry for saltpetre, now popular for activities such as trekking and bouldering. Because of its acoustic properties concerts are often held here,

The sleepy little town of **São Gonçalo do Rio Preto**, which sits next to a beautiful mountain river, is famous for its traditional festivals. It lies some 60 km from Diamantina. 15 km away is the **Parque Estadual de São Gonçalo do Rio Preto**, an area of pristine *cerrado* filled with flowering trees and particularly rich in birdlife. There are *pousadas* in São Gonçalo and cabins in the park (accessible by taxi). Guides are also available.

Serro *Colour map 7, B5.*

From Diamantina, 92 km by paved road and reached by bus from there or from Belo Horizonte, is this unspoiled colonial town on the Rio Jequitinhonha. It has six fine baroque churches, a museum and many beautiful squares. It makes queijo serrano, one of Brazil's best cheeses, being in the centre of a prosperous cattle region. The most conspicuous church is **Santa Rita** on a hill in the centre of town, reached by a long line of steps. On the main Praça João Pinheiro, by the bottom of the steps, is **Nossa Senhora do Carmo**, arcaded, with original paintings on the ceiling and in the choir. The town has two large mansions: those of the **Barão de Diamantina** ① *Praça Presidente Vargas*, now in ruins, and of the **Barão do Serro** ① *across the river on R da Fundição, Tue-Sat 1200-1700, Sun 0900-1200*, beautifully restored and used as the town hall and Casa de Cultura. The **Museu Regional Casa dos Ottoni** ① *Praça Cristiano Ottoni 72*, is an 18th-century house with furniture and objects from the region. There are hotels in town.

At **São Gonçalo do Rio das Pedras** and **Milho Verde** (35 and 42 km south of Diamantina on an unsealed road, or paved road as far as Milho Verde from Serro), there are trails for hiking and riding, waterfalls and some colonial buildings in the towns. Simple lodging is available.

Parque Nacional da Serra do Cipó
Open 0800-1700, headquarters in Jaboticatubas, T031-3718 7475, www.icmbio.gov.br/parnaserrado cipo/; www.guiaserradocipo.com.br.

About 105 km northeast of Belo Horizonte, Parque Nacional da Serra do Cipó, 33,400 sq km of the Serra do Espinhaço, covers important *cerrado* and gallery forest habitats, which provide a home for rare bird species like the Cipó Canastero and Grey-backed Tachuri, as well as endangered mammals such as maned wolf and monkeys such as the masked titi and brown capuchin. There are a number of carnivorous plants. The predominant habitat is high mountain grassland, with rocky outcroppings. As infrastructure in the park is not fully developed, ICMBio recommend employing a local guide.

Listings North of Belo Horizonte

Tourist information

Secretaria de Cultura, Turismo e Patrimônio (Praça Antônio Eulálio 53, T038-3531 9532, http:// diamantina.mg.gov.br), has an information office at street level, Mon-Sat 0900-1800, Sun and holidays 0900-1300; pamphlets, reliable map, friendly and helpful. Signposts on the streets give a suggested walking tour. **ASGITUR** (the guides' association, contact through the Secretaria de Turismo, at pousadas, or on T038-3531 3197, 9-8811 7515 or 9-881 2119 (Aguinaldo Clemente)), offers city tours and a Passeio Ecológico to the Cruzeiro da Serra for views of the city, the Caminho dos Escravos, waterfalls, Biribiri (for lunch) for US$39; add the Gruta do Salitre for an extra US$13. For the region see also http:// circuitodosdiamantes.com.br.

Where to stay

Diamantina
All are within 10 mins' walking distance of the centre unless otherwise stated. Many hotels have higher prices and often only 2- or 4-day packages for Vesperatas and Carnaval.

$$$ Pousada do Garimpo
Av da Saudade 265, T038-3532 1040, www.pousadadogarimpo.com.br.
Plain, well-kept rooms in a smart hotel on the outskirts, pool, sauna, restaurant serving some of the city's best Minas cooking.

$$$-$$ Relíquias do Tempo
R Macau de Baixo 104, T038-3531 1627, www.pousadareliquiasdotempo.com.br.
Cosy rooms in a pretty 19th-century house just off Praça JK, decorated like a colonial family home, generous breakfasts, swimming pool. Also has a handicrafts shop, **Relíquias do Vale** (R Macau do Meio 401, T038-3531 1353).

$$ Montanhas de Minas
R da Roman 264, T038-3531 3240, www. grupomontanhasde minas.com.br.
Spacious rooms with stone floors, some with balconies, decent breakfasts.

$$ Pousada Capistrana
R Campos Carvalho 35, T038-3531 6560, www.pousadacapistrana.com.br.
Very central pousada in a converted building, smart, public areas painted ochre yellow.

$$ Pousada Ouro de Minas
R do Amparo 90A, T038-3531 2306, www.grupomontanhasdeminas.com.br.
Simple well-kept rooms with tiny bathrooms in a converted colonial house.

$$ Pousada Sempre Viva
R Augusto Nelson 117, T038-3531 1043, www.pousadasempreviva.tur.br.
Comfortable rooms with tiny bathrooms, good, well-presented breakfast, helpful staff, laundry service, but rooms are above a busy street junction.

$$ Tijuco
R Macau do Melo 211, T038-3531 1022, www.hoteltijuco.com.br.
A deliciously dated Niemeyer building with tastefully renovated plush wood interior and rooms which retain their 60s feel, great views.

$$-$ Santiago
Largo Dom João 127, T038-3531 3407,
http://santiagohotel.com.br.
Next to municipal bus station, plain, small
but tidy rooms, reasonable breakfast.

Parque Nacional da Serra do Cipó

$$$ Cipó Veraneio
*Rodovia MG-10, Km 95, Jaboticatubas, T031-3718
7018, www.cipoveraneiohotel.com.br.*
Comfortable a/c rooms with cable TV, fridge, in
terraces of stone cabins, pool, sauna, very good
tour operator and a *cachaça* distillery just up the
road which produces some of Minas's finest.

Restaurants

Diamantina

$$ Caipirão
R Campos Carvalho 15, T038-3531 1526.
Minas cooking with buffet lunch cooked over
a traditional wood-fired clay oven, evening
simple à la carte or *caldos* (hearty broths) and
other dishes on the oven.

$$ Recanto do Antônio
Beco da Tecla 39, T038-3531 1147.
Minas food and decent steaks, chic rustic dining
room in a colonial house.

$ Sisisi
Beco da Mota 89, T038-3531 3071.
Pasta, Minas cooking and good value *prato feito*
at lunchtime.

Cafés

Café Mineiro
*R Beco da Tecla, at the top end. Mon-Fri 0730-
2000, Sat 0800-2000, Sun 1000-1400.*
A good, limited menu of freshly made *tortas* and
pastéis, pão do queijo, sweets, coffee and drinks.

Espaço B
R Beco da Tecla 31.
A bookshop/café serving coffees, drinks and a
limited choice of meals, Wi-Fi.

Bars and clubs

Diamantina

Apocalipse Point
Praça Barão de Guaicuí 78, T038-3531 9296.
Sertaneja and Axe music. Lively.

Café a Baiuca
R da Quitanda.
Coffee bar by day, funky bar by night with music
DVDs and a crowd spilling out into the street.

Gringo's Bar
R Direita 68, on the Praça, T038-3531 2639.
Popular little bar with a wide selection
of beers from around the world, other
drinks and meals.

Festivals

Diamantina
Feb/Mar Carnaval.
12 Sep O Dia das Serestas, the Day of the
Serenades, for which the town is famous; this is
also the anniversary of Kubitschek's birth. A full
timetable of the town's festivals, including
the **Vesperatas,** when musicians and singers
serenade from balconies along the colonial
streets and drum troupes and bands parade
is given on www.vivadiamantina.com.br.

Transport

Diamantina
Bus The Rodoviária is east of the centre, not far
to walk but tricky if you have heavy or wheeled
luggage; taxi US$4-5.20. To **São Gonçalo do
Rio Preto, Pássaro Verde** (T038-3531 1471)
at 1200 and 1500, US$4. Bus to **São Gonçalo
do Rio das Pedras** Mon-Sat 1500, Sun 1730,
return 0600, 1330 on Sun, otherwise go from
Serro. To **Serro,** Mon-Fri 0700, 1520, Sat 0900,
1520, Sun 1000, 1430, US$6.55. 6 buses a day
to **Belo Horizonte,** via Curvelo, with **Pássaro
Verde:** 2½ hrs to **Curvelo,** US$13.50, to **Belo
Horizonte,** US$23, 5 hrs. To **Bahia,** Gontijo buses
to **Araçuaí** pass through Diamantina at 0225
and 1355, US$24.50 (about 6 hrs); from here
combis and buses run to **Itaobim** from where
there are connections to Porto Seguro and other
destinations in Bahia. For **Brasília:** connect in
Curvelo to **Montes Claros** (2 a day, US$13.50),
then make connections onwards.

Parque Nacional da Serra do Cipó
Bus Take bus to **Serro** (2 daily) for Santa Ana
do Riacho and the Serra do Cipó. Bus Belo
Horizonte–Serro with **Serro** (www.serro.com.br),
3-4 a day, US$18.55, or US$25.15 via paved road.

Southern
Brazil

Southern Brazil comprises three states: Paraná, Santa Catarina and Rio Grande do Sul. Paraná has one of the premier tourist sites in South America, the Iguaçu Falls, described in its own section (see page 518). The Paraná coastline, albeit short, has a large area of coastal rainforest and little beach-fringed islands, like Ilha do Mel. Its main port, Paranaguá, is connected with the capital, Curitiba, by one of the most impressive railways in South America. It is the coast, however, from which Santa Catarina gains most of its reputation, with highly regarded surfing beaches and a growing interest in whale watching. Inland, the state has a distinctive European feel, including frosty and snowy winters in the highest parts. The culture of the region has been heavily influenced by large immigrant communities from Japan, Germany, Poland, Italy, Syria and Ukraine. In Rio Grande do Sul this can be seen (and tasted) in the Italian communities, well known for their wines. The southernmost state, as well as having yet more beaches, has some beautiful national parks, the remnants of Jesuit missions and the south's largest industrial centre, Porto Alegre. But above all, this is the land of the gaucho, the Brazilian cowboy.

Curitiba and around *Colour map 7, C2.*

a relaxed city and a geological wonder

Situated in the Serra do Mar, Curitiba is regarded as one of Brazil's model cities for quality of life. It has something of a European feel, with leafy squares and a street that is open 24 hours. It makes a pleasant base for exploring the coast and the surrounding mountains, and is the start of one of the world's most spectacular railway journeys.

Sights

One of the cleanest cities in Latin America, the capital of Paraná state has extensive open spaces and some exceptionally attractive modern architecture. The commercial centre is the busy Rua 15 de Novembro, part of which is a pedestrian area called **Rua das Flores**. The **Boca Maldita** is a particularly lively part where local artists exhibit. On Praça Tiradentes is the **Cathedral** ① *R Barão do Serro Azul 31, T041-3324 5136*, built in neo-Gothic style and inaugurated in 1893 (restored in 1993). Behind the cathedral, near Largo da Ordem, is a pedestrian area with a flower clock and old buildings, very beautiful in the evening when the old lamps are lit, nightlife is concentrated here. The oldest church in Curitiba is the **Igreja de Ordem Terceira da São Francisco das Chagas**, built in 1737 in Largo da Ordem. Its most recent renovation was in 1978-1980. In its annex is the **Museu de Arte Sacra** ① *T041-3321 3265*. The **Igreja de Nossa Senhora do Rosário de São Benedito** was built in the Praça Garibáldi in 1737 by slaves and was the Igreja dos Pretos de São Benedito. It was demolished in 1931 and a new church was inaugurated in 1946. A mass for tourists, Missa do Turista, is held on Sunday at 0800.

Best for
Islands ▪ Surfing ▪ Whale watching ▪ Wine

Museu Paranaense ① *in the Palácio São Francisco, R Kellers 289, T041-3304 3300, www. museuparanaense.pr.gov.br, Tue-Fri 0900-1800, Sat-Sun 1000-1600, US$1*, holds permanent and temporary exhibitions, including documents, manuscripts, ethnological and historical material, stamps, works of art, photographs and archaeological pieces. **Museu de Arte Contemporânea** ① *R Desembargador Westphalen 16, Praça Zacarias, T041-3222 5172, Tue-Fri 1000-1900, Sat-Sun 1000-1600*, displays Brazilian contemporary art in its many forms, with an emphasis on artists from Paraná.

North of the centre, the **Solar do Barão** ① *R Presidente Carlos Cavalcanti 53, T041-3321 3240*, built in 1880-1883, is used for concerts in the auditorium and exhibitions. The **Passeio Público**, in the heart of the city (closed Monday), inaugurated in 1886. It has three lakes, each with an island, and playground. The **Centro Cívico** is at the end of Avenida Dr Cândido de Abreu, 2 km from the centre: a monumental group of buildings dominated by the **Palácio Iguaçu**, headquarters of the state and municipal governments. In a patio behind it is a relief map to scale of Paraná. The **Bosque de João Paulo II** behind the Civic Centre on Rua Mateus Leme, was created in December 1980 after the Pope's visit to Curitiba. It also contains the **Memorial da Imigração Polonesa no Paraná** (Polish immigrants memorial). The **Museu Oscar Niemeyer (MON)** ① *R Mal Hermes 999, T041-3350 4400, www.museuoscarniemeyer.org.br, Tue-Sun 1000-1800, US$3.20* was designed by, and is devoted to the famous Brazilian modernist architect who designed Brasília and was a disciple of Le Corbusier (he died in 2012), together with other Paranense artists. The stunning principal building is shaped like a giant eye. An underground passage, lined with exhibits and photographs, links it to a sculpture garden.

Curitiba

100 metres
100 yards

Where to stay 🛏
1 Bourbon Batel Express
2 Bourbon Curitiba
4 Del Rey
6 Estação Tour
7 Hostel Roma
9 O'Hara

Restaurants 🍴
1 Bar do Victor
2 Durski
3 Jardins Grill

Close to the *rodoferroviária* is the market, where there are a couple of *lanchonetes*. **Shopping Estação** ① *Av 7 de Setembro 2775*, in the old railway station, has a railway museum and exhibitions on perfume and Brazil's natural environments, as well as shops and restaurants, etc. About 4 km east of the *rodoferroviário*, the **Jardim Botânico Fanchette Rischbieter** has a fine glass house, inspired by Crystal Palace in London. The gardens are in the French style and there is also a **Museu Botânico** ① *R Ostoja Roguski (Primeira Perimetral dos Bairros), T041-3362 1800 (museum), 0600-2000.* Take the orange Expreso buses from Praça Rui Barbosa.

Parque Estadual Vila Velha *Colour map 7, C2.*
The park office (phone, toilets, lanchonete, tourist information) is 300 m from the highway and the park a further 1.5 km (entrance US$7.75 for all 3 sites, 0830-1530, closed Tue). Allow all day if visiting all 3 sites (unless you hitch, or can time the buses well, it's a lot of walking). www.pontagrossa.pr.gov.br/parque-estadual-vila-velha.

....

West of Curitiba on the road to Ponta Grossa is the **Museu Histórico do Mate** ① *T041-3555 1939, BR 277 at Km 17, www.museuparanaense.pr.gov.br, temporarily closed in 2017,* an old water-driven mill where mate was prepared. On the same road is Vila Velha, 91 km from Curitiba: the sandstone rocks (Arenitos, US$4.65) have been weathered into most fantastic shapes. About 4 km away are the **Furnas** ① *US$3 Furnas and Lagoa Dourada,* three water holes, the deepest of which has a lift (US$0.75 – not always working) which descends almost to water level. Also in the park is the **Lagoa Dourada** (surrounded by forest) whose water level is the same as that in the Furnas.

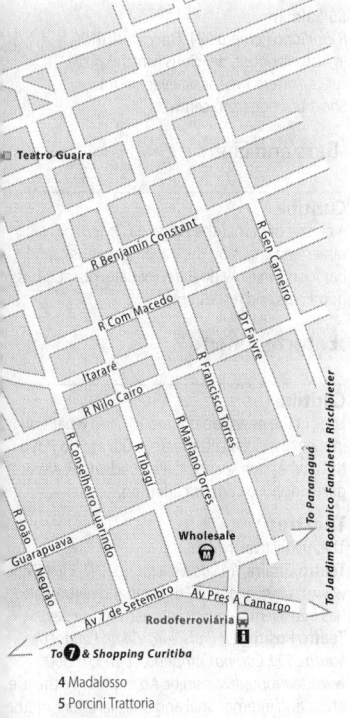

4 Madalosso
5 Porcini Trattoria
6 Salmão
7 Trattoria Barolo

Listings Curitiba and around

Tourist information

Setu (R Dr Murici 950, T041-3254 1516, www.turismo.pr.gov.br). **Municipal office:** Instituto Municipal de Turismo/Curitiba Turismo, R da Glória 362, 1st floor, T041-3250 7728. Mon-Fri 0800-1200 and 1400-1800. Also at R 24 Horas, T041-3225 4336, open 0900-1800. See Transport, below, for the city's integrated transport system.

Where to stay

Curitiba
There are good hotels southeast of the centre in the vicinity of the Rodoferroviária, but the cheaper ones are close to the wholesale market, which operates noisily through the night.

$$$$ Bourbon Curitiba
R Cândido Lopes 102, T041-3337 9200, www.bourbon.com.br.
Good modern hotel in the centre with a mock old-fashioned charm, rooms have jacuzzis, business centre.

$$$ Bourbon Batel Express
Av Visconde de Guarapuava 4889, T041-3337 9200, www.bourbon.com.br.
Modern and comfortable, good breakfast, Wi-Fi in rooms US$3 per day, attentive service, good value.

$$$ Del Rey
R Ermelino de Leão 18, T041-2106 0099,
www.hoteldelrey.com.br.
Central, upmarket yet relaxed, large rooms, good restaurant, gym, good value. Recommended.

$$ O'Hara
R 15 de Novembro 770, T041-3778 6044,
www.hotelohara.com.br.
Good location, fan, excellent breakfast, parking.

$$ Estação Tour
R Des Westphalen 122, T041-3322 9840,
http://hotelestacaotour.com.br.
Excellent for price, 24-hr room service, rather stark but immaculate. Recommended.

$ pp Hostel Roma
R Barão do Rio Branco 805, T041-3224 2117,
www.hostelroma.com.br.
Smart HI hostel with single-sex dorms, also family rooms ($$), TV room, members' kitchen.

Camping

Camping Clube do Brasil
BR-116, Km 84, 16 km towards São Paulo,
T358 6634.

Restaurants

Curitiba
The shopping malls have good food courts, eg include **Shopping Crystal Plaza** (R Com Araújo, Batel), **Shopping Curitiba** (R Brig Franco at Praça Osvaldo Cruz), and largest of all, **Barigüi** (R Prof Pedro Viriato Parigot de Souza 600, Ecoville). Hot sweet wine sold on the streets in winter helps keep out the cold.

$$$ Bar do Victor
R Lívio Moreira 284, São Lourenço,
T041-3353 1920. Tue-Sat 1200-1430,
1830-2330, Sun 1130-1430.
Excellent fish restaurant.

$$$ Durski
R Jaime Reis 254, T041-3225 7893. Open 1930-2300, closed Tue, Sat 1200-1600, 1930-2300, Sun 1200-1600.
Good variety of Eastern European cuisine, with top quality.

$$$ Jardins Grill
Av Silva Jardim 1477 e Lamenha Lins, Rebouças, T041-3232 4717, www.jardinsgrill.com.br.
Very good for, meats, salad and sushi buffets and pastas.

$$$ Madalosso
Av Manoel Ribas 5875, Santa Felicidade, T041-3372 2121. Closed Sun evening.
The largest Italian *rodízio* in Brazil, 4600 seats!

$$$ Porcini Trattoria
R Buenos Aires 277, Batel, T041-3022 5115, www.porcini.com.br. Daily for lunch and dinner, except Mon lunch.
Mainly Italian food, good salads and vegetables, superb quality, fantastic wine list. Recommended.

$$$ Terra Madre Ristorante
R Des Otávio do Amaral 515, Bigorrilho, T041-3335 6070, www.terramadreristorante.com.br.
Superb Italian cuisine at better prices than others in its category. Also run a wine store.

$$$ Trattoria Barolo
Av Silva Jardim 2487, Água Verde, T041-3243 3430. Closed Sun evening.
Excellent Italian for fish and meat dishes and pizza, huge wine list, good prices.

$$ Salmão
R Emiliano Perneta 924. Open until 0100.
In historic house, delicious fish and pizza, special offers, live music every night.
Short taxi ride from centre.

Bars and clubs

Curitiba
A cluster of bars at the Largo da Ordem have tables and chairs on the pavement, music, and bar food, while Av do Batel (or Batel district) has good bars and restaurants.

Entertainment

Curitiba
Look in the newspaper for music and what's on in the bars, clubs and theatres; **Gazeta do Povo** has a what's on section called *Caderno G*, www.gazetadopovo.com.br/cadernog.

Theatres
Theatre festival in Mar.
Teatro Guaíra, *R 15 de Novembro, T041-3304 7999, www.tguaira.pr.gov.br.* For plays and revues (also has free events – get tickets early in the day).
Teatro Positivo, *R Prof Pedro Viriato Parigot de Souza 5300, Campo Comprido, T041-3317 3000, www.teatropositivo.com.br.* An impressive theatre attracting international and Brazilian stars, on the magnificent campus of the Universidade Positivo.

www.up.edu.br. Good exhibitions are held here, too (bus lines Linha Expresso Centenário and Linha Ligeirinho Pinhais from centre).

Shopping

Curitiba

Handicrafts
Feira de Arte e Artesanato, *Praça Garibáldi. Sun 0900-1400.*
Lojas de Artesanato, *Casa de Artesanato Centro, R Mateus Leme 22, T041-3352 4021.*

What to do

Curitiba
Gondwana, *Av República Argentina 369, sala 804, Água Verde, T041-3566 6339, http://gondwanabrasil. com.br.* Specialists in ecotourism in Paraná, but also offers tours elsewhere in southern Brazil and to national parks further afield. Small groups, experienced and professional.

Transport

Curitiba
Air Afonso Pena (21 km away) for international and national flights, T041-3381 1515, www. aeroportocuritiba.net; good services: ATMs, left luggage, hotel booking desk, and cafés. Daily flights from Rio, São Paulo, Buenos Aires, Asunción, and cities in the interior of Paraná state. 2 types of bus run from the Rodoferroviária to the airport, making several stops: **Aeroporto Executivo**, www.aeroportoexecutivo.com.br, daily 0510-2400 (fewer on Sun), 25-45 mins, US$4.60; regular city bus No 208, 40 mins, US$1.50.

Bus There are several route types on the integrated transport system (RIT) and you are advised to pick up a map with details; see www.urbs.curitiba.pr.gov.br/transporte/ rede-integrada-de-transporte. **Express** are red and connect the transfer terminals to the city centre, pre-paid access through the silver 'tubo' bus stops; conventional orange **Feeder**

buses connect the terminals to the surrounding neighbourhoods; **Interdistrict** green buses run on circular routes connecting transfer terminals and city districts without passing through the centre; **Direct or speedy** silver grey buses use the 'tubo' stations to link the main districts and connect the surrounding municipalities with Curitiba; **Conventional** yellow buses operate on the normal road network between the surrounding municipalities, the Integration Terminals and the city centre; white Circular Centro mini busescircle the major transport terminals and points of interest in the traditional city centre area. Lime green **Linha Turismo** buses go to the main sites of interest, every 30 mins from Praça Tiradentes, 0900-1730, except on Mon. 5 stops allowed. The basic fare on the integrated system is US$1.30 (multi-ticket booklets available).

Long distance International and interstate buses use the combined bus and railway station, the **rodoferroviária**, Av Pres Affonso Camargo 330, Jardim Botânico, T041-3320 3000, where there are restaurants, banks, shops, phones, a post office, pharmacy, tourist office and other public services. Frequent buses to **São Paulo**, US$15-35, 6 hrs, and **Rio de Janeiro**, US$52, 12 hrs. To **Foz do Iguaçu**, 10 a day, US$456-760, 10 hrs; **Porto Alegre**, US$43-47; 10 hrs; **Florianópolis**, every 2 hrs, US$19-29, 4½-6 hrs.

Train Rodoferroviária, as above. See next section for trains to Morretes.

Parque Nacional Vila Velha
Bus Take a bus from **Curitiba** to the park, not to the town of Ponta Grossa 26 km away. **Princesa dos Campos** bus from Curitiba 0745, 1700, 2 hrs, US$10. One bus from Vila Velha between 1530-1600, US$1, 4.5 km to turn-off to Furnas (another 15 mins' walk) and Lagoa Dourada. Bus Mon-Sat 1330 to **Furnas** – Ponta Grossa that passes the car park at the top of the park. On Sun, 1200, 1620, 1800. It may be advisable to go to Ponta Grossa and return to Curitiba from there, 114 km, many buses a day, US$12.25, **Princesa dos Campos**, www.princesadoscampos.com.br.

The railway to the coast winds its way around the slopes of the Marumbi mountain range, across rushing rivers and through the forest to the sea. There are pretty colonial towns en route. The coast itself only has a few beaches, but in compensation has some of the richest biodiversity in Brazil.

Curitiba to Paranaguá

Two roads and a railway run from Curitiba to Paranaguá. The railway journey is the most spectacular in Brazil. There are 13 tunnels and sudden views of deep gorges and high peaks and waterfalls as the train rumbles over dizzy bridges and viaducts. Near Banhado station (Km 66) is the waterfall of Véu da Noiva; from the station at Km 59, the mountain range of **Marumbi** can be reached. See Transport, below, for schedules and fares. Of the roads, the older, cobbled Estrada da Graçiosa, with numerous viewpoints and tourist kiosks along the way, is much more scenic than the paved BR277.

Parque Nacional Marumbi

Marumbi Park is a large area of preserved Atlantic rainforest and is a UNESCO World Heritage Site and Biosphere Reserve. The forest in the 2343-ha park is covered in banana trees, palmito and orchids. There are rivers and waterfalls and among the fauna are monkeys, snakes and toucans. A climbing trail reaches 625 m to Rochedinho (two hours). Hands need to be free to grasp trees, especially during the rainy season (December to March), when trails are muddy. The last five minutes of the trail is a dangerous walk along a narrow rock trail. At the park entrance, notify administration of your arrival and departure. There is a small museum, video, left luggage and the base for a search and rescue unit at weekends. Volunteer guides are available at weekends. Wooden houses can be rented for about US$50 a night; take torch. Camping is free. To get there take the train from Curitiba at 0815, arriving Marumbi at 1035. Return at 1540 to Curitiba. If continuing the next day to Morretes your Curitiba-Marumbi ticket is valid for the onward journey.

☆Morretes *Colour map 7, C3.*

Morretes, founded in 1721, is one of the prettiest colonial towns in southern Brazil. Whitewashed colonial buildings with painted window frames straddle the pebbly river and church spires stick up from a sea of red tiled roofs against the backdrop of forested hills. The Estrada da Graciosa road passes through Morretes and the train journey ends here. Most of the numerous restaurants serve the local speciality, *barreado*, a meat stew cooked in a clay pot – originally a day in advance of Carnaval in order to allow women to escape from their domestic chores and enjoy the party. There are a handful of *pousadas* too and a series of walks into the mountains. **Antonina**, 14 km from Morretes is as picturesque, less touristy, and sits on the Baía do Paranaguá. It can be reached by local bus from Morretes.

Paranaguá *Colour map 7, C3.*

In the centre of Paranaguá colonial buildings decay in the heat and humidity; some are just façades encrusted with bromeliads. The **Museu de Arqueologia e Etnologia** ① *R 15 Novembro 575, T041-3721 1200, www.proec.ufpr.br, Tue-Fri 0900-1200, 1330-1800, Sat-Sun 1200-1800, US$1*, is housed in a formidable 18th-century Jesuit convent. Other attractions are a 17th-century fountain, the church of **São Benedito**, and the shrine of **Nossa Senhora do Rocio**, 2 km from town. **Tourist information** ① *Fumtur, next to rodoviária, T041-3420 2785, www.paranagua.pr.gov.br*. Boat schedules, toilet, and left luggage available.

The Paranaguá region was an important centre of indigenous life. Colossal shell middens, called ☆**Sambaquis**, some as high as a two-storey building, protecting regally adorned corpses, have been found on the surrounding estuaries. They date from between 7000 (possibly earlier) and 2000 years ago, built by the ancestors of the Tupinguin and Carijo people who encountered the first Europeans to arrive here. The Spanish and Portuguese disputed the bay and islands when gold was found in the late 16th century. More important is the area's claim to be one of Latin America's biodiversity hotspots and the best place on the Brazilian coast to see rare rainforest flora and fauna. Mangrove and lowland subtropical forests, islands, rivers and rivulets here form the largest stretch of **Atlantic coast rainforest** in the country and protect critically endangered species (see below). Most of the bay is protected by a series of national and state parks, but it is possible to visit on an organized tour from Paranaguá. The **Barcopar** cooperative ① *R General Carneiro s/n, access from Praça 29 de Julho (Palco Tutóia), T041-3425 6173*, offers a range of excellent trips in large and small vessels ranging from two hours to two days, US$20 per person to US$100.

At the mouth of the Baía de Guaratuba are two towns connected by ferry, **Caiobá** on the north shore (50 km from Paranaguá) and **Guaratuba** on the south. A few km north of Caiobá is **Matinhos**, a popular beach resort, especially in October when Paraná's surf championships are held here. A recommended restaurant here is **La Bodeguita**, Avenida Paranaguá, Betaras, T041-3452 6606, mainly fish, huge helpings.

Ilha do Mel
Limit of 5000 visitors a day. An entrance fee is included in the boat fare (see Transport, below); foreigners must show passport and fill in a form before boarding the boat.

Ilha do Mel sits in the mouth of the Baía de Paranaguá and was of strategic use in the 18th century. On this popular weekend escape and holiday island there are no roads, no vehicles, limited electricity, no banks or ATMs, and no chemists. Outside of Carnaval and New Year it is a laid back little place. Bars play Bob Marley and Maranhão reggae; surfers lounge around in hammocks and barefooted couples dance *forró* on the wooden floors of simple beachside shacks. Much of the island is forested, its coastline is fringed with broad beaches, broken in the south by rocky headlands.

The rugged eastern half, where most of the facilities are to be found is fringed with curving beaches and capped with a lighthouse, Farol das Conchas, built in 1872 to guide shipping into the bay. The flat, scrub forest-covered western half is predominantly an ecological protection area, its northern side watched over by the Fortaleza Nossa Senhora dos Prazeres, built in 1767 on the orders of King José I of Portugal, to defend what was one of the principal ports in the country. The best surf beaches are Praia Grande and Praia de Fora. Both are about 20 minutes' walk from the Nova Brasilia jetty. Fortaleza and Ponta do Bicho on the north shore are more tranquil and are safe for swimming. They are about 45 minutes' walk from the jetty or five minutes by boat. Farol and Encantadas are the liveliest and have the bulk of the accommodation, restaurants and nightlife. A series of well-signposted trails, from 20 minutes to three hours, cover the island and its coast. It is also possible to take a long day walking around the entire island, but the stretch along the southern shore between Encantadas and Nova Brasília has to be done by boat. For information see www.ilhadomel.net.

Superagüi National Park
The island of Superagüi and its neighbour, Peças, are the focus for the Guaraqueçaba Environmental Protection Area. They also form a national park and UNESCO World Heritage Site (the Atlantic Forest South-East Reserves). Access to the park and accommodation can be arranged through the village on Superagüi beach, just north of Ilha do Mel. Many endangered endemic plants and animals live in the park, including hundreds of endemic orchids, Atlantic rainforest specific animals like brown howler monkeys and large colonies of red-tailed Amazons (a parrot on the red list of critically endangered species and which can be seen nowhere else). There are also jaguarundi, puma and jaguar. The indígenous village is one of several Guarani villages in the area; other inhabitants are mostly of European descent, living off fishing. Contact **ICMBio** ① *R Paula de Miranda s/n, Guaraqueçaba, T041-3482 7146, www.icmbio.gov.br*, for information.

Tip...
There is superb swimming from deserted beaches, but watch out for stinging jelly fish.

Where to stay

Morretes

$$$$-$$$ Santuário Nhundiaquara
T041-3462 1938, www.nhundiaquara.com.br.
A range of chalets set around a tinkling stream in 400 ha of private rainforest under the Pico do Marumbi. They range from super-luxurious mock-Alpine *malocas* with plunging roofs to simpler rooms in annexes. Kids are welcome and there's a lovely, if chilly, spring-water swimming pool.

$$$ Pousada Graciosa
Estrada da Graciosa, Km 8 (Porto da Cima village), T041-3462 1807, www.pousadagraciosa.com.
Simple but comfortable wooden chalets set in rainforest some 10 km north of Morretes. Very peaceful and green but no children under 12 allowed.

$$$-$$ Hakuna Matata
Reta Porto de Cima s/n, Km 2.5, T041-3462 2388, www.pousadahakunamatata.com.br.
Stylish *pousada* set in beautiful grounds 15 km from Antonina with luxury apartments and chalets equipped with a/c, frigobar and TV. Also has pool and great restaurant. Perfect for nature lovers reluctant to abandon creature comforts.

$$-$ Hotel Nhundiaquara
R General Carneiro 13, Morretes, T041-3462 1228, www.nundiaquara.com.br.
A smart whitewashed building beautifully set on the river whose exterior appearance and excellent restaurant belie the hotel's small, plain whitewashed rooms. With breakfast.

Paranaguá

$$$ Camboa
R João Estevão (Ponta do Caju), T041-3420 5200, www.hotelcamboa.com.br.
Full- or half-board available. Family resort, tennis courts, large pool, saunas, trampolines, restaurant, out of town near the port. Book ahead. Also has **$$$ Camboa Capela**, in an 18th-century house in Antonina, T041-3432 3267, same website.

$$$ San Rafael
R Julia Costa 185, T041-3423 2123, www.sanrafaelhotel.com.br.
Business hotel with plain rooms, restaurants, pool and jacuzzis.

$$ Ponderosa
R Pricilenco Corea 68 at 15 Novembro, T041-3423 2464.
A block east and north of the boat dock, some rooms with a view, basic.

$$ Pousada Itiberê
R Princesa Isabel 24, T041-3423 2485, www.ilhadomelpreserve.net/itibere.htm.
Very smart spartan rooms, some with sea views, helpful service, shared bath, 3 blocks east of the boat dock.

Ilha do Mel
All rooms are fan cooled unless otherwise stated.

$$$$-$$$ Astral da Ilha
Praia da Fora, T041-3426 8916, www.astraldailha.com.br.
Themed suites and chalets (some suites **$$$** in low season) 30 m from beach, with a/c, mezzanine, solar-heated water, gardens, restaurant, excursions by boat and bike.

$$$$-$$$ Pôr do Sol
Nova Brasilia, T041-3426 8009, www.pousadapordosol.com.br.
Simple, elegant rooms around a shady garden, large deck with cabins and hammocks by the beach.

$$$ Enseada das Conchas
Farol, T041-3426 8040, www.pousadaenseada.com.br.
4 en suite rooms with TVs and fridge, charmingly decorated. Lots of rescued cats.

$$$-$$ Aconchego
Nova Brasilia, T041-3426 8030, www.pousadadaconchego.com.br.
Very clean, beachside deck with hammocks, TV and breakfast area, charming. Includes breakfast.

$$$-$$ D'Lua
Farol, T041-3426 8031.
Another feline-friendly place, basic and hippy with a helpful owner, Maria José (cheaper in low season).

$$$-$$ Plancton
Farol at Fora, T041-3426 8061, www.pousadaplancton.com.br.
A range of wooden buildings in a hummingbird-filled garden, cheaper with shared bath, fresh atmosphere, Italian food in high season.

\$\$\$-\$\$ Recanto do Frances
Encantadas, T041-3426 9105,
www.recantofrances.com.br.
Full of character, with each chalet built in a
different style to represent a different French city.
5 mins from Prainha or Encantadas. Good crêpe
restaurant. Recommended.

\$\$ Recanto da Fortaleza
Ponta do Bicho, T041-3426 8000,
www.pousadarecantodafortaleza.com.br.
The best of the 2 next to the Fort, basic cabins,
free pick-up by boat from Nova Brasilia (ring
ahead), bike rental. Price includes breakfast
and dinner.

Camping
There are mini campsites with facilities at
Encantadas, Farol and Brasília. Camping is
possible on the more deserted beaches (good
for surfing). If camping, watch out for the tide,
watch possessions and beware of the *bicho de pé*
which burrows into feet (remove with a needle
and alcohol) and the *borrachudos* (discourage
with repellent).

Restaurants

Morretes

\$\$\$ Armazém Romanus
R Visc Do Rio Branco 141.
Family-run restaurant with the best menu and
wine list in the region, dishes from home-grown
ingredients, including *barreado* and desserts.

\$\$ Terra Nossa
R 15 de Novembro 109.
Barreado, pasta, pizzas and fish,
generous portions.

\$ Madalozo
*R Alm Frederico de Oliveira 16, overlooking
the river.*
Good *barreado*, generous salads.

Ilha do Mel
Many *pousadas* serve food, some only in season
(Christmas-Carnaval). Many have live music or
dancing (especially in high season) after 2200.

\$\$ Fim da trilha
Prainha (Fora de Encantadas), T041-3426 9017.
Spanish seafood restaurant, one of the best on
the island. Also has a *pousada*.

\$ Colmeia
Farol.

Seafood, snacks, crêpes, juices and good
cakes and puddings. Also has a *pousada*,
www.pousadacolmeia.com.br.

\$ Mar e Sol
Farol.
Huge portions of fish, chicken with chips and rice
and a small selection of more adventurous dishes.

\$ Toca do Abutre
Farol.
Live music and huge plates of fish or chicken with
rice, beans and chips.

Transport

Curitiba to Paranaguá

Train From the **Rodoferroviária** in Curitiba
there are 2 trains running on the line to **Morretes**:
the *Litorina*, a modern a/c railcar with on-board
service with bilingual staff which stops at the
viewpoint at Santuário da Nossa Senhora do
Cadeado; hand luggage only; weekends only,
tickets can be bought 2 days in advance; departs
0915, returns 1430, US$80 to Morretes, 3 hrs. Also
the **Serra Verde Express**, which runs daily to
Morretes, with a stop at Marumbi, buy tickets
2 days in advance, departs daily 0815, returns 1500:
turístico, US$28 (US$24 back), *executivo* US$45
(US$32 back). Schedules change frequently; check
times in advance; delays to be expected. For
information and reservations, **Serra Verde Express**,
T041-3888 3488, www.serraverde express.com.br.
Tickets sold at the **Rodoferroviária**, Portão 8, 0900-
1700 (till 1200 on Sun). Sit on the left-hand side
on journey from Curitiba. On cloudy days there's
little to see on the higher parts. The train is usually
crowded on Sat and Sun. **Serra Verde Express** also
gives information about trips by car on the Estrada
de Graciosa and sells various packages to the coast.

Ilha do Mel
Ferry There are 2 main routes. From Paranaguá,
large ferries leave from Rua General Carneiro
(Rua da Praia) in front of the tourist information
kiosk and run to **Encantadas**, twice daily, 0930,
1530, Sat-Sun 1000, 1600, 1½ hrs, US$8 return.
Alternatively, there are regular buses from
Paranaguá to **Pontal do Sul**, from where a small
boat runs to the island Mon-Thu 0600-1700
(hourly), and one boat at 1730, Fri, Sat 0800-1800
hourly, Sun 0800-1700, US$2.50. There are
souvenir and handicraft stalls at the ferry point.
The last bus back to Paranaguá leaves at 2200. For
further information contact www.ilhadomel.net.

Superagüi National Park

Ferry To/from **Paranaguá** Mon-Sat leaving **Superagüi** 0700, returning from Paranaguá 1430, more frequent at holiday times, Sun only 1400 Superagüi to Paranaguá, 2½-3½ hrs, US$12 one way, T041-3482 7150, 3482 7152 or 3482 7131. Boats sail daily Paranaguá–Guaraqueçaba, 2½-3 hrs, then take another boat to Superagüi on Mon, Thu or Fri, 1400, 2½-3 hrs. The road Paranaguá–Guaraqueçaba is unmade.

Santa Catarina

surfing, rafting, beer festivals and the coldest places in Brazil

Famous for its beaches and popular with Argentine and Paraguayan holidaymakers in high summer, this is one of the best stretches of Brazilian coast for surfing, attracting 1½ million visitors to the 170 beaches just in the summer months of January and February. For the rest of the year they are pleasant and uncrowded. Immigrant communities, such as the German, give a unique personality to many towns and districts with the familiar European pattern of mixed farming. Rural tourism is important and the highlands, which are 100 km from the coast, are among the coldest in Brazil, giving winter landscapes reminiscent of Europe, or Brazil's southern neighbours.

Florianópolis *Colour map 7, C3.*

Halfway along the coast of Santa Catarina is the state capital and port of Florianópolis, founded in 1726 on the Ilha de Santa Catarina. The island is joined to the mainland by two bridges, one of which is Ponte Hercílio Luz, the longest steel suspension bridge in Brazil (closed for repairs). The newer Colombo Machado Salles bridge has a pedestrian and cycle way beneath the roadway. The natural beauty of the island, beaches and bays make Florianópolis a magnet for holidaymakers in summer. The southern beaches are usually good for swimming, the east for surfing, but be careful of the undertow. **Tourist offices: SETUR** ① *R Tenente Silveira 60, Centro, T048-3952 7000, www.pmf. sc.gov.br/entidades/turismo/, Mon-Fri 0700-2400.* There are also SETUR booths in the **rodoviária** ① *T048-3228 1095,* and at the **airport** ① *daily 0700-2400.* The airport also has a general information desk ① *daily 1200-1800.* All have maps and some pamphlet information in English. Useful websites include www.guiafloripa.com.br, www.floripa-guide.com (English) and www.visitefloripa.com.br.

In the 1960s Florianópolis port was closed and the aspect of the city's southern shoreline was fundamentally changed, with land reclaimed from the bay. The two main remnants of the old port area are the late 19th-century **Alfândega** and **Mercado Público**, both on Rua Conselheiro Mafra, fully restored and painted ochre. In the Alfândega is a **handicraft market** ① *Mon-Fri 0900-1900, Sat 0900-1200.* The market is divided into boxes, some are bars and restaurants, while others are **shops** ① *T041-3224 0189, Mon-Fri 0600-1830, Sat 0600-1300,* a few fish stalls open on Sunday. The **Catedral Metropolitana** ① *Praça 15 de Novembro T048-3224 3357, www.catedralflorianopolis.org.br, Mon-Fri 0615-2000, Sat 0800-1200, 1400-2000, Sun 0700-1200, 1600-2100, holidays 0615-1200, 16000-2000,* was built in 1773 on the site of the first chapel erected by the founder of the city, Francisco Dias Velho. Inside is a life-size sculpture in wood of the Flight into Egypt, originally from the Austrian Tyrol.

The **Forte Sant'Ana** (1763) houses the **Museu de Armas Major Lara Ribas** ① *beneath the Ponte Hercílio Luz, R Osvaldo Rodrigues Cabral 525, T048-3229 6263, Tue-Sun 0900-1700, free,* with a collection of guns and other items, mostly post Second World War. The **Museu Histórico de Santa Catarina** ① *Praça 15 de Novembro, T048-3665 6363, www.mhsc.sc.gov.br, Tue-Fri 1000-1800, Sat, Sun and holidays 1000-1600, US$1.45,* in the 18th-century Palácio Cruz e Souza, has a lavish interior with highly decorated ceilings and contains furniture, documents and objects belonging to governors of the state. The **Museu de Antropólogia** ① *T048-3721 9325, Mon-Fri 0900-1200, 1300-1700,* at the Universidade Federal de Santa Catarina Campus, has a dusty collection of stone and other archaeological remains from the indigenous cultures of the coast. It is also possible to visit the former home of Imperial Brazil's foremost propaganda painter, **A Casa Victor Meirelles** ① *R Victor Meirelles 59, T048-3222 0692, Tue-Fri 1000-1800, Sat 1000-1400, free (donation).* The Catarinense painter depicted various apotheoses of colonization, such as Primeira Missa no Brasil (the First Mass in Brazil) and the war against the Dutch in Pernambuco, A Batalha de Guararapes.

There is a lookout point at Morro da Cruz; take the Transol bus from the city centre bus station, US$0.85, which waits for 15 minutes then returns; or walk back.

☆Ilha de Santa Catarina *Colour map 7, C3.*

There are 42 beaches around the island. All have their own characteristics and attractions and are popular, especially in high season. Surfing is very popular but is prohibited 30 April-30 June because it is the breeding season of the tainha (flathead mullet), a popular table fish. Besides the sand and surf, there are watersports on the Lagoa de Conceição, walking in the forest reserves, hang gliding or paragliding from the Morro da Lagoa and sandboarding. See Transport, page 508, for bus services around the island.

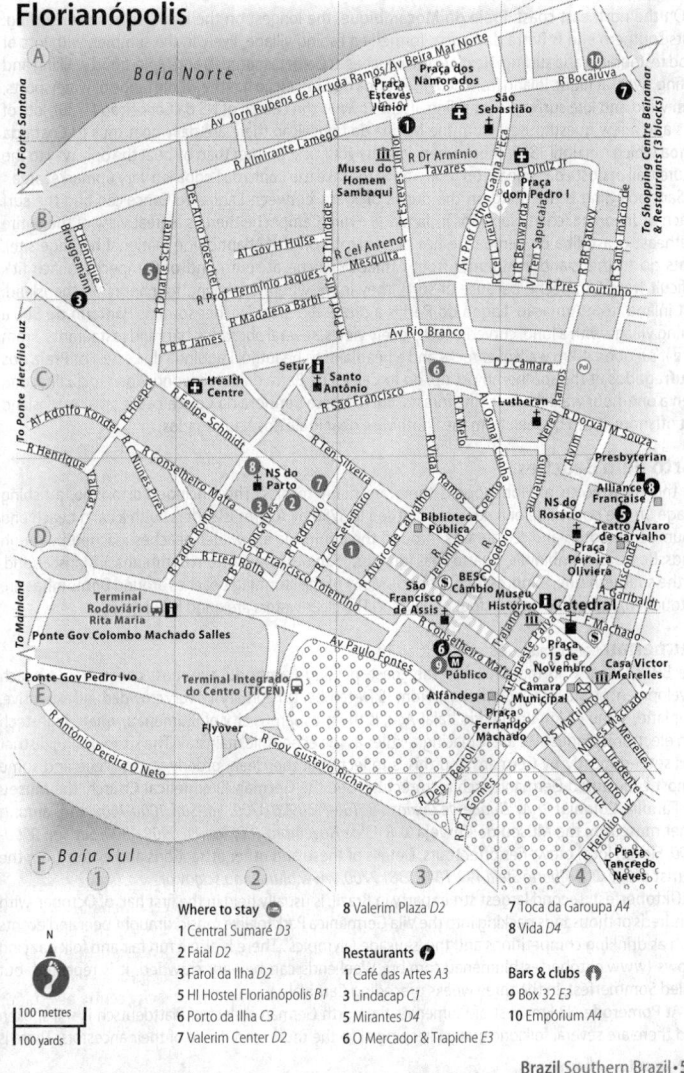

Florianópolis

Where to stay
1 Central Sumaré *D3*
2 Faial *D2*
3 Farol da Ilha *D2*
5 HI Hostel Florianópolis *B1*
6 Porto da Ilha *C3*
7 Valerim Center *D2*

8 Valerim Plaza *D2*

Restaurants
1 Café das Artes *A3*
3 Lindacap *C1*
5 Mirantes *D4*
6 O Mercador & Trapiche *E3*

7 Toca da Garoupa *A4*
8 Vida *D4*

Bars & clubs
9 Box 32 *E3*
10 Empórium *A4*

N

100 metres
100 yards

The island, from north to south: northern beaches tend to have calmer waters, eg Daniela, Jurerê and Canasvieiras. Near Jurerê **Forte São José da Ponta Grossa** is beautifully restored with a small **museum** ① US$1. Jurerê Internacional is the favourite haunt of the very wealthy. There is a pleasant fishing village at **Ponta das Canas**, 1 km from which is Praia Brava for good surfing. Also in the north of the island is Praia dos Ingleses, very built up, but popular with families.

On the northeast coast, **Praia do Moçambique**, the longest on the island, is good for surfing. At its southern end is **Barra da Lagoa**, formerly a fishing village, lively in the summer, with lots of good restaurants and surfing. Next are the beaches at Galheta (naturist) and Mole, good walking and surfing, lively at night. Inland from here **Lagoa da Conceição** has the whole range of watersports, from wind and kite surfing to jet skiing. In the town is the church of NS da Conceição (1730), lots of bars and a few guesthouses. From the Marina da Conceição there are daily boat trips to **Costa da Lagoa** which run until 1830, check when you buy your ticket. Other than by boat the only way to the nature trail of Costa da Lagoa is on foot. Above the lake the Canto da Lagoa is a very upmarket area.

Sandboarding is the thing on the dunes of Joaca between Lagoa de Conceição and the surf beach of Joaquina (championships in January). From Campeche there is a great view of the entire southeast coast. Ilha de Campeche has petroglyphs on the Atlantic side (national heritage site). Boats go to the island in summer from Armação village at south end of Campeche beach (it's difficult from Campeche because of surf); they leave when full, giving four hours on the island. Just inland from Armação, **Lagoa do Peri** is a protected area. Further south is **Pântano do Sul**, a fishing village with a long, curved beach, lovely views, several *pousadas*, bars and restaurants. From here it's a good 4-km walk over rocks and a headland to beautiful Lagoinha do Leste. For **Praia dos Naufragados** at the southernmost tip, go to Caieira da Barra do Sul (beyond Ribeirão da Ilha) and then a one-hour walk through fine forests. **Forte Nossa Senhora da Conceição** is on a small island just offshore. It can be seen from the lighthouse near Praia dos Naufragados.

Porto Belo Beaches

On the coast north of Florianópolis there are many resorts. They include Porto Belo, a fishing village on the north side of a peninsula settled in 1750 by Azores islanders, with a calm beach and a number of hotels and restaurants. Around the peninsula are wilder beaches reached by rough roads: Bombas, Bombinhas, Quatro Ilhas (quieter, 15 minutes' walk from Bombinhas) and, on the southern side, Zimbros (or Cantinho). Many of the stunning beaches around **Bombinhas** are untouched, accessible only on foot or by boat. The clear waters are good for diving.

Blumenau *Colour map 7, C3.*

The BR-101 heads north, parallel to the coast, passing **Camboriú**, the most concentrated beach development on Brazil's southern coast. From 15 December to February it is very crowded and expensive.

Inland, some 47 km up the Rio Itajaí-Açu, is the prosperous city of Blumenau, where high-tech and electronics industries are replacing textiles as the economic mainstay. The surrounding district was settled mostly by Germans and this is reflected in the clean, orderly street scene and some almost caricatured Germanic architecturecture. See the **German Evangelical Church**, the **Museu da Família Colonial** ① *Av Duque de Caxias 78, Tue-Fri 0900-1700, Sat-Sun 1000-1600* and, among other museums, the **Museu da Cerveja** ① *R 15 de Novembro 160, Tue-Fri 0900-1800, Sat-Sun 0900-1700*. Eleven local breweries offer tours. Details of these and other attractions and events from the **tourist office** ① *R Alberto Stein 199, T047-3381 7700, www.blumenau.sc.gov.br.*

Oktoberfest, second largest street party in Brazil, is usually held in the first half of October, with hundreds of thousands packing into the Vila Germânica Park for live music, draught beer and events such as drinking competitions and the 'sausage Olympics'. There is also a fun fair and folk dancing shows (www.oktoberfestblumenau.com.br). Weekends can be very crowded. It is repeated, but called Sommerfest, in the three weeks preceding Carnival.

At **Pomerode**, 33 km west of Blumenau, the north German dialect of Plattdeutsch is still spoken and there are several folkloric groups keeping alive the music and dance of their ancestors. There is an excellent **zoo** ① *R Herman Weege 180, daily 0800-1800, US$5.* Next door, **Cevejaria Schornstein** ① *R Herman Weege 60*, serves beers from its own onsite microbrewery, with German-influenced snacks and main meals, huge portions, high quality ingredients. The **Museu Pomerano** ① *Rodovia SC 418, Km 3*, tells the story of the colonial family. **Festa do Pomerania** is in January, www.pomerode.sc.gov.br.

São Francisco do Sul and Joinville *Colour map 7, C3.*

Some 80 km up the coast at the mouth of the Baía de Babitonga, São Francisco do Sul is the port for the town of Joinville, 45 km inland at the head of the Rio Cachoeira. There is an interesting **Museu Nacional do Mar** reflecting Brazil's seafaring history. The centre has over 150 historical sites and has been protected since 1987. There are some excellent **beaches** nearby.

Joinville itself is the state's largest city. It lies 2 km from the main coastal highway, BR-101, by which Curitiba and Florianópolis are less than three hours away. The industry does not spoil the considerable charm of the city. The **Alameda Brustlein**, better known as the **Rua das Palmeiras**, is an impressive avenue of palm trees leading to the **Palácio dos Príncipes**. The trees have been protected since 1982. The futuristic **cathedral** ① *on Av Juscelino Kubitscheck with R do Príncipe*, has spectacular windows recounting the story of man. The **Casa da Cultura** (Galeria Municipal de Artes 'Victor Kursancew') ① *R Dona Fransisca 800, Mon-Fri 0900-1800, Sat 0900-1300*, also contains the School of Art 'Fritz Alt', the School of Music 'Vila Lobos' and the Municipal School of Ballet (not to be confused with the Bolshoi Ballet School, Av José Vieira 3185). A number of museums and exhibition centres reflect the history of the area and the city's artistic achievements. In July, Joinville hosts the largest dance festival in the world, attracting around 4000 dancers over 12 days. Styles include jazz, folklore and classical ballet. There is also a large **Festa das Flores** (flower festival) in November. There are many good restaurants and good air and road links to other parts of Brazil. **Tourist office** at the **Fundação Turística** ① *Pórtico, R 15 de Novembro s/n, T047-3433 5007; the airport T047-3427 4409; Casa Krüger, Rodovia SC418, T047-3427 5623; and R Ottakar Doerffel s/n, T047-3453 0177, all open daily. Head office: R 15 de Novembro 4315, T047-3453 2663, information line 0800-643 5015, https://fundacaoturistica.joinville.sc.gov.br.*

Southern Santa Catarina

At **Praia do Rosa**, 101 km south of Florianópolis, is the headquarters of the **Right Whale Institute** ① *Instituto Baleia Franca. The institute has two bases: Praia do Rosa, Imbituba, Santa Catarina, CEP 88780-000, T048-3355 6111, and R Manoel Álvaro de Araújo 186, Garopaba, T048-3254 4198, http://institutobaleiafranca.blogspot.com.br.* The southern right whales come to the bays to calve from July to November. Boat trips have been suspended, but there are viewing points on the shore to see whales and dolphins. The **$$$$-$$$ Vida, Sol e Mar** eco-resort and beach village ① *T048-3355 6111, www.vidasolemar.com.br*, is the Praia do Rosa HQ of the institute and offers land-based whale-watching tours for US$17, children half price. It has villas and suites, pool, good restaurant, horse riding, snorkelling, surf school and other activities under **Turismo Vida, Sol e Mar**. There are many other *pousadas* in the town (eg the tasteful, luxury Quinta do Bucanero, Praia do Rosa, T048-3355 6056, www.bucanero.com.br), and a good youth hostel ① *Albergue de Juventude Dinda Rosa, Estrada Geral do Rosa s/n, T048-3355 6614.* The hostel has its own (expensive) convenience store. Praia do Rosa is listed as one of the 29 most beautiful bays in the world by the French-based organization Les Plus Belles Baies du Monde. The town is confusing to walk around, with few signs and poor access to the beach blocking the way (even though they shouldn't). If lodging is hard to find, try 14 km north in **Garopaba** (www.garopaba.sc.gov.br), where there are other beaches to visit and many more places to stay, eg Pousada do Morro (T048-3254 0098, http://pousadadomorro.com.br, same owners as Casa da Lagoa, see below).

Laguna *Colour map 7, C3.*

Some 27 km from Tubarão is the fishing port of Laguna. The town, founded in 1676, was the capital of the Juliana Republic in 1839, a short-lived separatist movement led by Italian idealist Guiseppe Garibáldi. In the centre of historic Laguna is an Azorean church (1696), **Santo Antônio dos Anjos**, light blue and white inside, with features picked out in gold. Across the street is birthplace of Garibáldi's wife, Anita, a simple house, now a small museum (US$2.75), with pieces from the period of her life. Behind, in a similar house, is a handicraft shop. There is also a Museu Anita Garibáldi on the Praça da República Juliana and a number of other colonial buildings, mostly around the main square and neighbouring streets. The **Fonte do Carioca** is still the spring from which people collect drinking water. Beside it is a tiled building, **Pinto D'Ulysséu**, with a private collection on Garibáldi.

Some 5 km from the centre of town, beyond the town's main beach resort, **Mar Grosso** (Laguna Internacional – many hotels abd *pousadas*), is the Molhes da Barra channel to Santo Antônio lagoon on which Laguna stands. Here you can watch fishermen with cast nets fishing with bottle-nosed dolphins. You can see dolphins at almost any time, but most frequently in May-July, the red mullet season. They are more active in the mornings. A little ferry crosses to Ponta da Barra which has several restaurants, the best being **Boião**, T048-3644 5065. (Taxis at the Rodoviária Municipal will go to Molhes da Barra.)

Serra Catarinense *Colour map 7, C2.*

From Florianópolis to the southern highlands BR-282 first passes **Termas de Imperatriz**, a popular rafting area. The road climbs to the **Costa da Serra** (about 800 m), which has *mata atlântica* and several community tourism farms. Some 700 m higher still is the **Serra Geral**. The university town and regional centre of **Lages** (229 km) has no tourist attractions but has pioneered rural tourism. It has some two-star hotels. Outside town is the **Fazenda Boqueirão** ① *Rodovia BR 282, Km 228, T049-3289 0700, www.fazendaboqueirao.com.br,* a working cattle farm since 1896 now offering accommodation ($$$$-$$$, cheaper midweek when it's quieter), gaucho entertainment and food, good riding, outdoor sports, very busy at weekends. 74 km south of Lages is **São Joaquim** (population 22,836, altitude 1360 m), the *Capital Nacional da Maçã* (apples). For information contact **Secretaria de Turismo de São Joaquim** ① *T049-3233 2790, www.serracatarinense.com.* It claims to be the coldest place in Brazil, but that honour goes to **Urubici**, 60 km away. Surrounded by natural beauty spots and with an excellent tourist infrastructure, this is the place to go for adventure: trekking and riding, homestays and guesthouses in town. From the coast the road up the Serro do Corvo Branco goes to Urubici. It separates a proposed new national park, Campo dos Padres from the **Parque Nacional de São Joaquim** (33,500 ha, T049-3278 4002), which has canyons containing sub-tropical vegetation, araucaria forest at higher levels and puma, ocelot, wild cat and wild dog. From São Joaquim to the coast SC-438 passes **Bom Jardim da Serra** (43 km) then descends the **Serra do Rio do Rastro**. The first 12 bends, about 5 km, are very sharp. There are plenty of stopping places for the view and street lamps for night driving. At the top viewpoint are coatis – don't feed them, they attack. Once out of the cloudforest (and the ceiling of clouds) the jagged mountains can be appreciated, with the plain to the Costa da Serra stretching away below. Continue to Lauro Müller, the junction with the Corvo Branco road and Gravatal, before rejoining the BR-101 at the coalfield town of Tubarão (27 km from Laguna).

Listings Santa Catarina *map p501*

Where to stay

Florianópolis

$$$ Faial
R Felipe Schmidt 603, T048-3203 2766, www.hotelfaial.com.br.
Comfortable and traditional hotel with good restaurant. Also owns the **Farol da Ilha** (R Bento Gonçalves 163, T3203 2760, www.hotelfaroldailha.com.br), which is good too, convenient for the bus station.

$$$ Porto da Ilha
R Dom Jaime Câmara 43, T048-3229 3000, www.portodailha.com.br.

Central, comfortable, cheaper at weekends. Recommended.

$$$ Valerim Plaza
R Felipe Schmidt 705, T048-2106 0200, www.hotelvalerim.com.br.
More modern than Valerim Center, buffet restaurant open till 2300.

$$$-$$ Valerim Center
R Felipe Schmidt 554, T048-3225 1100, www.hotelvalerim.com.br
Large rooms, hot water, hard beds.

$$-$ Central Sumaré
R Felipe Schmidt 423, T048-3222 5359, www.hotelcentralsumare.com.br.

With breakfast, simple rooms, cheaper with shared bath, central.

$ pp HI Hostel Florianópolis
R Duarte Schutel 227, T048-3225 3781, www.floripahostel.com.br.
HI, good breakfast included, cooking facilities, some traffic noise, luggage store. Prices rise in Dec-Feb; more expensive for non-members, private rooms **$$**.

Camping

Camping Clube do Brasil
São João do Rio Vermelho, north of Lagoa da Conceição, 21 km out of town.
Also at Barra da Lagoa, Lagoa da Conceição, Praia da Armação, Praia dos Ingleses, Praia Canasvieiras.

Ilha de Santa Catarina

There are many *pousadas* and apartments to rent on the island, also many resorts and top-end hotels. Prices rise steeply for Reveillon/New Year and Carnaval. Agencies have offices in Florianópolis *rodoviária*, where you can shop around.

Lagoinha

$$$ Pousada da Vigia
R Cônego Walmor Castro 291, T048-3284 1789, www.pousadavigia.com.br.
A Roteiros do Charme hotel at the northern tip of the island, above a calm bay, suites and rooms with sea or garden view, terrace restaurant, very good.

Canasvieiras

$ pp HI Floripa Hostel Canasvieiras
R Dr João de Oliveira 517, esq Av das Nações, T048-3266 2036, www.floripahostel.com.br. Mid-Dec to mid-Mar.
2 blocks from the sea with well-kept dorms and doubles (**$$**), cheaper for HI members.

Praia dos Ingleses

$$$-$$ Companhia Inglesa
R Dom João Becker 276, T048-3269 1350, www.hotelciainglesa.com.br.
Little beach hotel with pool and helpful staff. Recommended for families.

Barra da Lagoa

$$$-$$ Pousada 32
R Angelina Joaquim dos Santos 300, by beach, T048-3232 1886, www.pousada32.com.br.

Apartments for 4 to 8 with kitchen and fan, double rooms without kitchen, comfortable, trips arranged, surf school, diving.

$ pp The Backpackers Sharehouse
Estr Geral, across hanging bridge (and to the left), T048-3232 7606.
Good hostel, free surfboard hire, English spoken. Recommended.

$ Banana Beach
Servidão da Prainha 20 (across hanging bridge at bus station, take bus 320 or 330 from TICEN terminal, then change to no 360), T048-3232 3193, florianopolis.hostel on Facebook.
Book in advance, female and mixed dorms and doubles, shared bath, kitchen, tours by boat and car on island. Recommended.

$ pp HI Hostel Barra da Lagoa
R Inelzyr Bauer Bertolli s/n, T048-3232 4491, www.floripahostel.com.br.
Modern hostel with kitchen, rooms with fan, private rooms **$$**.

Camping

Fortaleza da Barra
Estr Geral 3317, T048-3232 4235.
Basic facilities, helpful owner. Looks after valuables.

Lagoa da Conceição

$$$ Casa da Lagoa
Servidão Palmeiras Nativas 500, T048-3269 9569, http://casalagoa.com.br.
Close to the lake and the centre of town, rooms for 2-4 with a/c, frigobar, safe, breakfast included, garden, a good choice.

$$$-$$ Pousada Pau de Canela
R Pau de Canela 606, Rio Tavares, T048-3233 4989, www.pousadadecanela.com.br.
Pleasant *pousada* between Lagoa da Conceição and Campeche. Restaurant, bar and swimming pool.

Joaquina

$$$-$$ Joaquina Beach
R A Garibaldi Santiago, T048-3232 5059, www.joaquinabeachhotel.com.br.
Pleasant hotel with 3 standards of room, those with sea views, safe and a/c are more expensive, buffet breakfast, pool.

$ Pousada Dona Zilma
R Geral da Praia da Joaquina 279, T048-3232 5161, Facebook: PousadaDZilma.
Quiet, safe. Recommended.

Praia do Campeche

$$$$-$$$ Pousada Vila Tamarindo
Av Campeche 1836, T048-3237 3464,
www.tamarindo.com.br.
Tranquil setting with lovely views, gardens,
helpful staff, good buffet breakfast.

$$$ Pousada Natur Campeche
Servidão Família Nunes 59, T048-3237 4011,
http://naturcampeche.com.
Lovely *pousada* with tasteful rooms, some with
jacuzzi, gardens, quiet, pool, close to the beach.

$$ São Sebastião da Praia
Av Campeche 1373, T048-3338 2020,
www.hotelsaosebastiao.com.br.
Resort hotel on splendid beach, chalets, rooms,
suites, a/c, buffet breakfast, restaurant, good value.

Near Pântano do Sul

$$$ Pousada Sítio dos Tucanos
Estrada Geral da Costa de Dentro 2776, T048-3237 5084, http://pousadasitiodostucanos.com.
Prices rise in high season. English, German,
Spanish spoken, suites and 1 chalet in garden
setting, excellent organic food, transport to
beach. Highly recommended. Take bus 410 from
TICEN to Rio Tavares, phone the *pousada* then
change to 563 Costa do Dentro bus and await
pick-up at end of line.

$ Albergue do Pirata
Estrada Geral da Costa de Dentro, 4973,
near Pântano do Sul, T048-3389 2727.
Dorms with and without bath, and doubles
($$$-$$), with breakfast, in natural surroundings
with lots of trails. Also has camping, US$8.75 pp
without breakfast.

Blumenau

Reservations are essential during Oktoberfest.

$$$-$$ Glória
R 7 de Setembro 954, T047-3326 1988,
www.hotelgloria.com.br.
German-run, modern, excellent coffee shop.

$$ Hermann
Floriano Peixoto 213, T047-3322 4370,
www.hotelhermann.com.br.
One of the oldest houses in Blumenau, cheaper
rooms with shared bath, excellent big breakfast,
German spoken.

Pomerode

There are a couple of good mid-range hotels in the
$$$-$$ range: **Pousada Max**, R 15 de Novembro

257, T048-3387 3070, www.pousada max.com.br,
and **Schroeder**, R 15 de Novembro 514, T048-3387
0933, www.hotelschroeder.com.br.

São Francisco do Sul

$$$-$$ Zibamba
R Fernandes Dias 27, T047-3444 2020,
www.hotelzibamba.com.br.
Central, good, restaurant.

Joinville

$$$ Germânia
Ministro Calógeras 612, T047-3433 9886,
www.hotelgermania.com.br.
Colourful modern building with pretty garden,
pool, fitness centre, reading room.

$$$ Tannenhof
Visconde de Taunay 340, T047-3145 6700,
www.tannenhof.com.br.
4-star, pool, gym, traffic noise, excellent
breakfast, restaurant.

$$ Mattes
15 de Novembro 801, T047-3422 3582,
www.hotelmattes.com.br.
Good facilities, big breakfast, German spoken.
Recommended.

$$-$ Pousada Flor do Brasil
R Paraíba 919, T047-3027 2152.
Opposite bus station, clean rooms with fan,
private bath.

Serra Catarinense

In the **Lages** area there are a number of farms
which take guests, as well as the **Fazenda do
Boqueirão** mentioned above. Likewise in the
São Joaquim, **Urubici** and other areas, there
are many Turismo Rural and more conventional
places to stay, with too many *pousadas* to list
here: see www.serracatarinense.com. 2 upmarket
options are:

$$$$-$$$ Rio do Rastro Eco Resort
*Rodavia SC-438, Km 130, near Bom Jardim da
Serra, T048-99931 6100, http://www.roteiros
decharme.com.br/riodorastroecoresort
(a Roteiros do Charme hotel).*
Built around lakes that feed into one another,
nice cabins with good facilities, TV, some
with jacuzzi. Good restaurant, games room,
outdoor jacuzzi, sauna, pool, gym. Views of
valley and escarpments, trails (not signed –
guides are provided).

$$ Urubici Park
Av Adolfo Konder 2278, T048-3278 5300, Urubici,
http://urubiciparkhotel.com.br.
Cosy and attractive mountain lodge hotel with
pool and excellent breakfast, helpful staff, good
value. Highly recommended.

Restaurants

Florianópolis
On Rua Bocaiúva, east of R Almte Lamego, there
are several Italian restaurants and BBQ places.

$$ Lindacap
R Felipe Schmidt 1162. Closed Mon, Sun lunch only.
Recommended for its varied range of dishes,
good buffet.

$$ Toca da Garoupa
R Alves de Brito 178.
A very good seafood restaurant in a rustic,
wood slat house.

$$ O Mercador
Box 33/4 in the Mercado Público.
Excellent self-service specializing in seafood.

$$ Trapiche
Box 31 in the Mercado Público.
Self-service fish and seafood (see Bars and
clubs, below).

$$ Vida
R Visc de Ouro Preto 298, next to Alliance Française.
Decent value vegetarian lunches served in an
attractive colonial building.

$ Café das Artes
R Esteves Junior 734 at north end.
Nice café with excellent cakes.

$ Mirantes
R Alvaro de Carvalho 246, Centro.
Self-service, good value. Other branches in
the city.

Ilha de Santa Catarina

Barra da Lagoa
On R Altimiro Barcelos Dutra are several
snackbars selling excellent wholemeal pastries
stuffed with tasty, fresh ingredients. Good
vegetarian options.

$$ Ponta das Caranhas
Estr Geral da Barra da Lagoa 2377,
T048-3232 3076.
Excellent seafood, lovely location on the lake.

Pântano do Sul

$$ Bar do Vadinho
Praia do Pántano do Sul, Facebook: Bar-do-
Vadinho. Daily in summer, weekends only in winter.
Set lunch of the day's fish catch, with rice, chips,
salad, pirão and beans, set price US$11 for all you
can eat. Recommended.

Bars and clubs

Florianópolis
To find out about events and theme nights
check the Beiramar centre for notices in shop
windows, or ask in surf shops. The Mercado
Público in the centre, which is alive with fish
sellers and stalls during the day, has a different
atmosphere at night; the stall, Box 32, serves
good, if expensive, seafood, and at night
becomes a busy bar specializing in cachaça,
including its own brand.

Empórium
Bocaiúva 79, T048-3224 1670,
www.emporiumbocaiuva.com.br.
A delicatessen by day (Mon-Fri 0930-2200, Sat
1030-2030) and popular bar at night (Mon-Fri
1700-0200, Sat – May-Nov only – 1200-1800).

Ilha de Santa Catarina
Throughout high summer the beaches open their
bars day and night. The beach huts of Praia Mole
invite people to party all night (bring a blanket).
Any bars are worth visiting in the Lagoa area,
especially the Confraria Chopp da Ilha, packed at
weekends, good for watching football matches,
or The Black Swan pub.

Festivals

Florianópolis
Dec/Jan The whole island dances to the
sound of the Boi-de-Mamão, a dance which
incorporates the puppets of Bernunça, Maricota
(the Goddess of Love, a puppet with long arms to
embrace everyone) and Tião, the monkey.
Mar/Apr Around Easter is the Festival of the
Bull, Farra de Boi. It is only in the south that,
controversially nowadays, the bull is killed on
Easter Sun. The festival arouses fierce local pride.

What to do

Florianópolis
Brazil Ecojourneys, *Estrada Rozália Paulina Ferreira, 1132 Armação*, T048-3389 5619, http://brazilecojourneys.com. Small group guided tours in Southern Brazil covering many interests: adventure, wildlife, farm stays, community-based tourism, gay and lesbian tourism and volunteering, English spoken, very professional. Warmly recommended.

Serra Catarinense
In July there is a long horse ride between Santa Catarina and Rio Grande do Sul, the direction changes each year. Thousands of riders participate; it's open to anyone, camp on the way.
Caminhos da Serra, *Av Adolfo Konder 2628, Urubici*, T049-3278 4273, acaminhosdaserra@yahoo.com.brr. Trekking, riding, information and reservations for places to stay.
Gaúcho do Brasil, T047-99789 8001, www.gauchodobrasil.com. Paul Coudenys, Belgian-owned company offering 6-day rides in the Serra from fazenda to fazenda, "be a *gaúcho* for a week". Operates out of Lages. The riding season is Oct-May.
Tribo da Serra, *Praça João Ribeiro 204, sala 1, São Joaquim*, T049-99101 2451, www.tribodaserraeco.com.br. Trekking, horse riding and 4WD trips.

Transport

Florianópolis
Air International and domestic flights arrive at Hercílio Luz airport, Av Deomício Freitas, 12 km south of town, on the island. Take 'Corredor Sudoeste' bus No 183 or 186 from TICEN. Flights to **São Paulo** (Congonhas), **Rio de Janeiro**, **Porto Alegre**, **Foz de Iguaçu** and **Curitiba** with **TAM**, **Gol** and **Azul**.

Bus Regular buses from the city to destinations on the island leave from the Terminal Integrado do Centro (TICEN), Av Paulo Fontes, immediately east of the *rodoviária* Rita Maia. For most destinations, buses go from TICEN to another Terminal Integrado (eg TICAN – Canasvieiras; TILAG – Lagoa de Conceição), where you change to another bus for the final point. You do not have to pay for the onward bus as long as you don't leave the platform. For instance, from Florianópolis to Jurerê, take a bus from TICEN to

TICAN, then change buses. Yellow micro buses (Transporte Ejecutivo), starting from the south end of Praça 15 de Novembro and other stops, charge US$1.75. International and buses from other Brazilian cities arrive at the *rodoviária* Rita Maia, at the east (island) end of the Ponte Colombo Machado Salles.

Several buses daily with **Catarinense** to **Porto Alegre** (US$29-38, 7 hrs, road being made into a dual carriageway), **São Paulo**, 10 hrs (US$32-45), to **Foz do Iguaçu** (US$56-62, leito US$90), to **Curitiba** US$19-29.

International buses Buenos Aires, US$140, **JBL**, buses very full in summer, book 1 week in advance. **Asunción**, US$71 (**Catarinense**). To **Ciudad del Este**, Catarinense, 1720, arrive 0930, US$52.

Car hire There are many car hire companies on the island; see www.guiafloripa.com.br for listings. Promotional rates are about US$45 a day.

Porto Belo Beaches
Bus **Florianópolis** to Porto Belo, several daily with **Rainha**, fewer at weekends, more frequent buses to **Tijuca**, **Itapema** and **Itajaí**, all on the BR-101 with connections. Buses from Porto Belo to the beaches on the peninsula.

Blumenau
Bus *Rodoviária* is 7 km from town (get off at the bridge over the river and walk 1 km to centre). Bus to the *rodoviária* from Av Presidente Castelo–Branco (Beira Rio). There are connections in all directions from Blumenau. To **Florianópolis** US$13, 3 hrs. To **Curitiba**, US$13, 4 hrs, frequent. To **Pomerode Coletivos Volkmann** (T3395 1400) daily US$2, 1 hr; and others; check schedules at tourist offices.

São Francisco do Sul
Bus Terminal is 1.5 km from centre. 2 buses daily with **Catarinense** to **Curitiba**, US$10, 3½ hrs.

Laguna
Bus To/from **Porto Alegre**, 5½ hrs, US$18.75, with **Eucatur** and **Santo Anjo**; **Florianópolis**, 2 hrs, US$11, 6 daily.

Serra Catarinense
Bus **Florianópolis** to/from **Lages**, 3½ hrs, US$20-29, 4-5 a day. **São Joaquim** to/from **Florianópolis** 2 a day with **Reunidos**, 5½ hrs, US$20.

gaucho country with vineyards and beaches to boot

Rio Grande do Sul is gaucho country and also Brazil's chief wine producer. The capital, Porto Alegre, is the most industrialized city in the south, but in the surroundings are good beaches, interesting coastal national parks and the fine scenery of the Serra Gaúcha. On the border with Santa Catarina is the remarkable Aparados da Serra National Park. In the far west are the remains of Jesuit missions. In southern Rio Grande do Sul there are great grasslands stretching as far as Uruguay to the south and Argentina to the west.

In this distinctive land of the gaucho, or cowboy (pronounced ga-oo-shoo in Brazil), people feel closer to Uruguay and Argentina than Brazil (except where football is concerned). The gaucho culture has developed a sense of distance from the African-influenced society of further north. This separatist strain was most marked in the 1820s and 1830s when the Farroupilha movement, led by Bento Gonçalves, proclaimed the República Riograndense in 1835.

Porto Alegre *Colour map 7, inset.*

The capital of Rio Grande do Sul (population 1,476,867) is where cowboy culture meets the bright lights. It lies at the confluence of five rivers (called Rio Guaíba, although it is not a river in its own right) and thence into the great freshwater lagoon, the Lagoa dos Patos, which runs into the sea. The freshwater port is one of the most up-to-date in the country and Porto Alegre is the biggest commercial centre south of São Paulo. It is also one of the richest and best-educated parts of Brazil and held the first three World Social Forums (2001-2003), putting the city in a global spotlight. Standing on a series of hills and valleys on the banks of the Guaíba, it has a temperate climate through most of the year, though the temperature at the height of summer can often exceed 40°C and drop below 10°C in winter. The city has a good tourist infrastructure, interesting cultural centres and lively nightlife. Football is also a great source of local pride, with Porto Alegre's two major sides, Grêmio and Internacional, both making the spurious claim to be 'world champions'.

The older residential part of the town is on a promontory, dominated previously by the **Palácio Piratini** (Governor's Palace) and the imposing **cathedral** (1921-45 and 1972, but very neoclassical) on the **Praça Marechal Deodoro** (or da Matriz). Also on, or near this square, are the neoclassical **Theatro São Pedro** (1858), the **Solar dos Câmara** (1818, now a historical and cultural centre), the **Biblioteca Pública** – all dwarfed by the skyscraper of the **Assembléia Legislativa** – and the **Museu Júlio de Castilhos** ⓘ *Duque de Caxias 1231, T051-3221 3959, http://museujuliodecastilhos.blogspot. co.uk, Tue-Sun 1000-1800,* which has an interesting collection on the history of the state. Down Rua General Câmara from Praça Marechal Deodoro is the **Praça da Alfândega**, with the old customs house and the Museu de Arte de Rio Grande do Sul (see below). A short walk east of this group, up Rua 7 de Setembro, is Praça 15 de Novembro, on which is the neoclassical **Mercado Público**, selling everything from religious artefacts to spices and meat. There are some good cafés and bars here and the Chalé da Praça XV, which has a large restaurant serving local food. For art from the state, visit the **Museu de Arte do Rio Grande do Sul** ⓘ *Praça Senador Florêncio (Praça da Alfândega), T051-3227 2311, www.margs.rs.gov.br, Tue-Sun 1000-1900, free.* **Museu de Comunicação Social** ⓘ *R dos Andradas 959, T051-3224 4252, Mon-Fri 0900-1800, Sat 0900-1200, free,* in the former A Federação newspaper building (1922), deals with the development of the media in Brazil since the 1920s.

A large part of **Rua dos Andradas** (Rua da Praia) has been pedestrianised and gets very busy in the afternoons. Going west along Rua dos Andradas, you pass the wide stairway that leads up to the two high white towers of the church of **Nossa Senhora das Dores**, the oldest in the city. At the end of the promontory, the **Usina do Gasômetro** has been converted from a thermoelectric station into a cultural centre and good café. Its enormous chimney is a city landmark and there is a stunning view of sunset from the balcony. In the **Cidade Baixa** quarter are the colonial **Travessa dos Venezianos** (between Ruas Lopo Gonçalves and Joaquim Nabuco) and the **house of Lopo Gonçalves**, which houses the **Museu de Porto Alegre Joaquim José Felizardo** ⓘ *R João Alfredo 582, T051-3289 8096, http://museudeportoalegre. com.br, Tue-Sun 0900-1200, 1330-1800, free,* a collection on the history of the city.

The central **Parque Farroupilha** (called Parque Redenção) has many attractions and on Sundays there is an antiques and handicrafts fair at the José Bonifácio end.

Around Porto Alegre

The main beach resorts of the area are to the east and north of the city. Heading east along the BR-290, 112 km from Porto Alegre is **Osório**, a pleasant lakeside town with a few hotels. From here it is 18 km southeast to the rather polluted and crowded beach resort of **Tramandaí** (daily buses from Porto Alegre). The beaches here are very popular, with lots of hotels, bars, restaurants, and other standard seaside amenities. Extensive dunes and lakes in the region provide an interesting variety of wildlife and sporting opportunities. The beach resorts become less polluted the further north you travel, and the water is clean by the time you reach the well-developed resort of **Torres**. Dolphins visit Praia dos Molhes, north of town, year round; whales can occasionally be seen in July.

There is a paved road running south from Tramandaí along the coast to **Quintão**, giving access to many beaches, including **Cidreira**. Bus from Porto Alegre US$8.

Serra Gaúcha

The Serra Gaúcha boasts stunningly beautiful scenery, some of the best being around the towns of Gramado and Canela, about 130 km north of Porto Alegre. There is a distinctly Swiss/Bavarian flavour to many of the buildings in both towns. In December the Christmas displays are genuinely impressive, and in winter it can snow. This is excellent walking and climbing country among hills,

Porto Alegre

Rio Guaíba

Trensurb Station

Cisne Branco Boat Trips

Mercado Público

Praça 15 de Nov

Siqueira

Prefeitura

Praça 15 de Novembro

Alfândega

Museu de Arte de Rio Grande do Sul

Praça Senador Florência

Gen Gal Andr Neves

Shopping Rua da Praia

Riachuelo

Museu da Comunicação Social

São Pedro Theatre

Jerônimo Coelho

Casa de Cultura Mário Quintana

Solar dos Câmara

Praça Mal Deodoro

Barco Porto Alegre 10 & Noiva do Caí Boat Trips

Nossa Senhora das Dores

Duque de Caxias

Palácio Piratini

Museo Júlio de Castilhos

To Praia de Belas

Cathedral

Cel Fernando Machado

Centro Cultural Usina do Gasômetro

Demetrio Ribeiro

To

Washington Luiz

N

200 metres

200 yards

Where to stay 🛏
2 Blue Tree Towers
   Millenium Flats
3 Comfort

4 Continental
5 Elevado
6 Erechim
7 Ritter

Restaurants 🍴
1 Atelier de Massas
2 Café do Cofre &
   Santander Cultural

woods, lakes and waterfalls. For canoeists, the Rio Paranhana at Três Coroas is renowned, especially for slalom ($$-$ pp Refúgio do Pomar, Estrada do Laticínio 1330, Rodeio Bonito, T051-99880 6282, http://pousada-refugiodopomar.blog spot.com, is recommended for peace and quiet, also has chalet, Buddhist temple nearby, good food and rafting and walking options, HI affiliated). Local crafts include knitted woollens, leather, wickerwork, and chocolate.

Gramado, at 850 m on the edge of a plateau with views, provides a summer escape from the 40°C heat of the plains. It lives almost entirely by tourism and the main street, Avenida Borges de Medeiros, is full of kitsch artisan shops and fashion boutiques. In December the Christmas displays draw hordes of visitors and throughout the summer, thousands of hydrangeas (*hortênsias*) bloom. For a good walk/bike ride into the valley, take the dirt road Turismo Rural 28, Um Mergulho no Vale (A Dive into the Valley), which starts at Avenida das Hortênsias immediately before Prawer. **Tourist office** ① *Av das Hortênsias 2029, T054-3286 0200, see www.portalgramado.com.br or www.gramadosite.com.br.*

A few kilometres along the plateau rim, **Canela** is less tourism and shopping-oriented than its neighbour (frequent bus service from Gramado, 10 minutes). **Tourist office** ① *R Largo da Fama 77, T054-3282 1287, turismo@canela.rs.gov.br, see also www.canelaturismo.com.br.* The **Mundo a Vapor museum** ① *RS 235 Rodovia Canela-Gramado, T054-3282 1125, www.mundoavapor.com.br, 0845-1700, closed Wed except Jan Jul, Dec when open every day, US$6.25, children half price,* is an interesting

To Guaíba Bridge
Footbridge

To Museu de Porto Alegre Joaquim José Felizardo

3 Café Dos Cataventos
4 Chopp Stübel
5 Nova Vida

museum dedicated to steam power. The main attraction is the dramatic reconstruction of the famous 1895 rail disaster in Montparnasse, Paris. Kids and adults clamour to have their picture taken alongside a giant steam train that appears to have burst through the front of the building.

About 7 km away is the **Parque Estadual do Caracol** ① *T054-3278 3035, 0830-1800, US$5.65,* with a spectacular 130-m-high waterfall where the Rio Caracol tumbles out of thick forest. A 927-step metal staircase leads to the plunge pool. There is an 18-km circular bike route continuing on to **Parque Ferradura** (US$2.50), with good views into the canyon of the Rio Cai. From the Ferradura junction, take the right to continue to the **Floresta Nacional** ① *T054-3282 0037, flonacanela.rs@icmbio.gov.br, 0800-1700.* From here, the dirt road continues round to Canela. Another good hike or bike option is the 4-km track southeast of Canela past Parque das Sequóias to **Morro Pelado**. At over 600 m, there are spectacular views from the rim edge.

Parque Nacional de Aparados da Serra *Colour map 7, inset.*

Tue-Sun 0800-1700 (open also on bank holiday Mon), US$5.20 plus US$4.60 per car, T054-3251 1277/1262, www.icmbio.gov.br/parnaaparadosdaserra.

The major attraction at the Parque Nacional de Aparados da Serra is a canyon, 7.8 km long and 720 m deep, known locally as the Itaimbezinho. Here, two waterfalls cascade 350 m into a stone circle at the bottom. For experienced hikers (and with a guide) there is a difficult path to the bottom of Itaimbezinho. One can then hike 20 km to Praia Grande in Santa Catarina state. The park is 80 km from São Francisco de Paula (18 km east of Canela, 117 km north of Porto Alegre). With similar scenery but no tourist infrastructure is the neighbouring **Parque Nacional da Serra Geral** ① *open daily 0800-1700 (1800 in summer), same phone as above, free.*

Tourist excursions, mostly at weekends, from **São Francisco de Paula** (a few hotels and *pousadas*; tourist information at southern entrance to town, T054-3244 1602). At other times, take a bus to Cambará do Sul (0945, 1700, 1¼ hours, US$5): several *pousadas* (see www.cambaraonline.com.br for a list). Also near Cambará is **Campofora** ① *T054-3244 2993, www.campofora.com.br,* for riding expeditions in national park.

Caxias do Sul and around *Colour map 7, inset.*

This expanding modern city's population is principally of Italian descent and it is the centre of the Brazilian wine industry. The church of **São Pelegrino** has paintings by Aldo Locatelli and 5 m-high bronze doors sculptured by Augusto Murer. There is a good **Museu Municipal** ① *R Visconde de Pelotas 586, T054-3221 2423, Tue-Sat 0830-1130, 1330-1700, Sun 1400-1700,* with displays of artefacts of the Italian immigration. Italian roots are again on display in the **Parque de Exposições Centenário**, 5 km out on Rua Ludovico Cavinato. January-February is the best time to visit. There is a tourist information kiosk in Praça Rui Barbosa and another at the **rodoviária** ① *R Ernesto Alves 1341, T054-3218 3000,* a 15-minute walk from the main *praça* (but many buses pass through the centre). **Tourist office** ① *R Ludovico Cavinatto, 1431, T054-3222 1875, 0800-541 1875, www.caxias.tur.br.*

Caxias do Sul's festival of grapes is held February to March. Good tour and tasting at Adega Granja União, R Os 18 de Forte 2346. Visit also the neighbouring towns and sample their wines: **Farroupilha** 20 km from Caxias do Sul. **Nova Milano,** 6 km away (bus to Farroupilha, then change – day trip). **Bento Gonçalves,** 40 km from Caxias do Sul, www.bentogoncalves.rs.gov.br. **Garibáldi,** which has a dry ski slope and toboggan slope. A restored steam train leaves Bento Gonçalves for a two-hour trip to **Carlos Barbosa;** called 'a rota do vinho' (the wine run), it goes through vineyards in the hills. US$27 (US$28 July), including wines, with live band; reserve in advance through Giordani Turismo ① *railway station, R Duque de Caxias, Bento Gonçalves, T054-3455 2788, www.giordaniturismo.com.br.* Another worthwhile trip is to **Antônio Prado,** 1½ hours by Caxiense Bus. The town is now a World Heritage Site because of the large number of original buildings built by immigrants in the Italian style.

Jesuit Missions *Colour map 7, C1.*

West of **Passo Fundo**, 'the most gaucho city in Rio Grande do Sul', are the **Sete Povos das Missões Orientais**. The only considerable Jesuit remains in Brazilian territory are at **São Miguel das Missões**, some 50 km from **Santo Ângelo**. At São Miguel, now a World Heritage Site, there is a church, 1735-1745, and small **museum** ① *0900-1800, US$2.* The ruins are not well signposted, it is best to ask for directions at the *rodoviária*. A son et lumière show in Portuguese is held daily, in winter at 2000, and later in summer, although times depend on how many people there are. The show ends too late to return to Santo Ângelo but is worth sticking around for; book a room at the lovely hostel next to the ruins. Gaucho festivals are held on some Sunday afternoons, in a field near the Mission.

Border with Argentina *Colour map 7, C1.*

From Santo Ângelo it is a four-hour bus ride to the border town of **Porto Xavier** and an easy crossing (short ferry ride across the Río Uruguay) into Argentina. For exit and entry stamps, visit the federal police at the ferry stations on either side. The five-minute crossing (US$3) takes passengers to San Javier, from where there are regular buses, via Posadas, to Iguazú. From the Argentine ferry station it is a short bus or taxi ride to the town centre, with cashpoints, shops, and the bus station.

South of Porto Alegre *Colour map 7, inset.*

The Rio Guaíaba enters the Lagoa dos Patos, which is protected from the Atlantic by a long peninsula. About midway along, 208 km from Porto Alegr, is the charming town of **Mostardas** (www.mostardas.rs.gov.br, with a list of hotels and *pousadas*), a good base for visiting the national park **Lagoa do Peixe** ① *information: Praça Luís Martins 30, Mostardas, T051-3673 2435, free,* park has no infrastructure. This is one of South America's top spots for migrating birds. The main lake (which has highest bird concentration) is about 20 km from Mostardas and the town of **Tavares**. The park is, however, under threat from invasive planting of trees. The poor road along the peninsula continues 152 km to São José do Norte, opposite Rio Grande (see below).

On the landward side of the Lagoa dos Patos, **São Lourenço** is a good place to enjoy the lake, the beaches, fish restaurants and watersports. The town hosts a popular four-day festival in March. On the BR-116, **Pelotas** is the second largest city in the State of Rio Grande do Sul, 271 km south of Porto Alegre, on the Rio São Gonçalo which connects the Lagoa dos Patos with the Lagoa Mirim. There are many good hotels and transport links to all of the state and the Uruguay border at Chuí.

Some 59 km south of Pelotas, at the entrance to the Lagoa dos Patos, is the city **Rio Grande**. It is the distribution centre for the southern part of Rio Grande do Sul, with significant cattle and meat industries. During the latter half of the 19th century Rio Grande was an important centre, but today it is a rather poor town, notable for the charm of its old buildings. The tourist kiosk is at junction of Rua Duque de Caxias and Rua General Becaleron and the municipal tourist secretariat at Avenida Buarque de MAcedo s/n, T053-3232 4521. **Cassino**, a popular seaside town on the ocean, is 24 km away over a good road. There are more beaches further south, all with surf. Across the inlet from Rio Grande is the settlement of **São José do Norte**, founded in 1725. There are frequent passenger ferries and fewer car ferries.

Border with Uruguay: coastal route *Colour map 7, inset.*

South of Pelotas the BR-471 passes the **Taim water reserve** ① *T053-3503 3151, Estação Ecológica do Taim, BR-471, Km 492, a permit from ICMBio is needed to visit,* between the Lagoa Mirim and the ocean. Many protected species, including black swans and the quero-quero (the Brazilian lapwing). There are trails outside the reserve. The main road continues to the Brazilian border town of **Chuí**. The highway skirts the town and carries straight through to Uruguay, where it becomes Ruta 9. The main street crossing west to east, Avenida Internacional (Avenida Uruguaí on the Brazilian side, Avenida Brasil in Uruguay) is lined with clothes and household shops in Brazil, duty free shops and a casino in Uruguay. São Miguel fort, built by the Portuguese in 1737, now reconstructed with period artefacts, is worth a visit. A lighthouse 10 km west marks the Barro do Chuí inlet, which has uncrowded beaches and is visited by sea lions. Brazilian immigration is about 2.5 km from the border, on BR-471. Make sure that your bus will stop at customs and immigration on both sides of the border. If you not get your passport stamped, you will have trouble leaving either country later on. International buses make the crossing straightforward: the company holds passports; hand over your visitor's card on leaving Brazil and get a Uruguayan one on entry. Have luggage available for inspection. **Uruguayan consulate** ① *Av Venezuela 311, T053-3265 1151.*

Entering Brazil From Uruguay, on the Uruguayan side, the bus will stop if asked, and wait while you get your exit stamp (with bus conductor's help); on the Brazilian side, the appropriate form is completed by the *rodoviária* staff when you purchase your ticket into Brazil. The bus stops at Polícia Federal (BR-471) and the conductor completes formalities while you sit on the bus.

Border with Uruguay: inland routes *Colour map 8, A6.*

At **Aceguá**, 60 km south of Bagé, where Brazilian immigration is located, there is a crossing to the Uruguayan town of Melo, and further east, **Jaguarão** with the Uruguayan town of **Rio Branco**, linked by the 1.5 km long Mauá bridge and approach road across the Rio Jaguarão. **Uruguayan consulate** ① *R 27 de Janeiro 701, Jaguarão, T053-3261 1411.*

Entering Uruguay Before crossing into Uruguay, you must visit Brazilian Polícia Federal in Bagé (R Barão de Triunfo 1572) to get an exit stamp; if not, the Uruguayan authorities will send you back. The crossing furthest west is **Barra do Quaraí** to Bella Unión, via the Barra del Cuaraim bridge. This is near the confluence of the Rios Uruguai and Quaraí. Thirty kilometres east is another crossing from **Quaraí** to **Artigas** in a cattle-raising and agricultural area. **Uruguayan consulate** ① *R Francisco Carlos Reverbel 348, Quaraí, T055-3423 1802.*

The southern interior of the state is the region of the real gaúcho. Principal towns of this area include **Santana do Livramento**. Its twin Uruguayan city is Rivera. All one need do is cross the main street to Rivera, but by public transport this is not a straightforward border. The town has hotels and a youth hostel. **Uruguayan consulate** ① *Av Tamandaré 2101, 4th floor, T055-3242 1416.*

Tourist information

Porto Alegre Turismo
*Travessa do Carmo 84, Cidade Baixa, T051-3289
6700. Tue-Sun 0830-1800, Mon 0830-1200,
1330-1800. Also at airport 0800-2030, Mercado
Público, Mon-Sat 0800-1800, Casa de Cultura
Mário Quintana, R dos Andradas 736 an d Galeria
Chaves, Loja 16, R dos Andradas 1444, Mon-Fri
0900-1900, Sat 0900-1300.*
Information on city culture and museums
can be found on www.cultura.rs.gov.br.

Prefeitura de Porto Alegre
*T0800-517686 or 156, www2.portoalegre.rs.
gov.br/turismo, or www.portoalegre.travel.*

SETUR
*Av Borges de Medeiros 1501, 10th floor,
T051-3288 5400, www.turismo.rs.gov.br.*
For the state. The market area in Praça 15 de
Novembro and the bus terminal are dangerous at
night. Thefts have been reported in Voluntários
da Pátria and Praça Parção.

Where to stay

Porto Alegre
Hotels in the area around R Garibáldi and
Voluntários da Patria between Av Farrapos and
rodoviária are overpriced and used for short stays.
A full list of accommodation is givevn on www.
portoalegre.travel. There is only one HI-affiliated
hostel, **Porto Alegre Hostel Boutique** (R São
Carlos 545, T051-3228 3802, www.hostel.tur.br).

$$$ Blue Tree Towers Millenium Flats
*Av Borges de Medeiros 3120, Praia de Belas,
T051-3026 2200, www.bluetree.com.br.*
Smart mini-apartments with microwave, study
and breakfast bar. The rooftop pool, gym and bar
have stunning sunset views. Recommended.

$$$ Ritter
*Lg Vespasiano Júlio Veppo 55, opposite rodoviária,
T051-3228 4044, www.ritter hoteis.com.br.*
4-star and 3-star wings, English, French, German
spoken, bar, small pool, sauna.

$$$-$$ Comfort
*R Loureiro da Silva 1670, Cidade Baixa, T051-
2117 9000, www.atlanticahotels.com.br.*

Good value 3-star with gym, breakfast.
Handy for Cidade Baixa nightlife.

$$$-$$ Continental
*Lg Vespasiano Júlio Veppo 77, T051-3061 1900,
www.hoteiscontinental.com.br.*
High standards, cheaper at weekends, pool, gym.

$$ Erechim
*Av Júlio de Castilhos 341, near rodoviária,
T051-3225 1090, www.hotelerechim.
com.br.* A good option among several cheap
places in this area, 2 standards of room.

$ Elevado
*Av Farrapos 65, T051-3224 5250,
www.hotelelevado.com.br.*
Big rooms, microwave and coffee, good value.

Serra Gaúcha

Gramado
Plenty of hotels and restaurants (mostly pricey).

$$$ Chalets do Vale
*R Arthur Reinheimer 161 (off Av das
Hortênsias at about 4700), T054-3286 4151,
www.chaletsdovale.com.br.*
3 homely chalets in lovely setting, kitchen,
good deal for groups of 4 or families.

$ pp Albergue Internacional de Gramado
*Av das Hortênsias 3880, T054-3295 1020,
www.gramadohostel.com.br.*
Cosy, dorms, doubles, cheaper for HI members.

Canela

$$$ Serra Nevada
*Av Osvaldo Aranha 610, T054-3278 9700,
http://hotelserranevada.com.br.*
Thermal pools, sauna, massage, parking,
very good.

$$$ Vila Suzana Parque
*R Col Theobaldo Fleck 15, T054-3282 2020,
www.hotelvilasuzana.com.br.*
Tiled cabins in a sub-tropical garden, heated
pool, welcoming.

$ pp Hostel Viajante
*R Ernesto Urbani 132, T054-3282 2017,
www.pousadadoviajante.com.br.*
Central, opposite the rodoviária, dormitories
and private rooms (**$$**), cheaper without bath,
discounts for HI members.

Camping

Camping Clube do Brasil
1 km from waterfall in Parque do Caracol, 1 km off main road, signposted (8 km from Canela), T054-3282 4321.
Sells excellent honey and chocolate.

Sesi
R Francisco Bertolucci 504, 2.5 km outside Canela, T054-3282 1311.
Camping or cabins. Lovely parkland setting, good facilities. Recommended.

Caxias do Sul

$$$-$$ Somensi
R Siba Paes 367, Bento Gonçalves, T054-3453 3111, www.hotelsomensi.com.br.
Near the Pipa Pórtico and Cristo Rei church in the upper town. Rooms with a/c or fan, breakfast, garage.

$$-$ Pousada Casa Mia
Trav Niterói 71, Bento Gonçalves, T054-3451 1215, www.pousadacasamia.com.br.
HI youth hostel with 2 branches (Av Osvaldo Aranha 381, T3454 4936).

Jesuit Missions

São Miguel
There is a pizza restaurant next to the *rodoviária* and several snack bars selling decent burgers.

$$ HI Pousada das Missões
São Nicolau 601, next to the ruins, T055-3381 1202, www.pousadadasmissoes.com.br.
Private rooms with or without a/c and TV, youth hostel (**$**), lovely site with swimming pool, cheaper for HI members. Highly recommended.

$$ Hotel Barichello
Av Borges do Canto 1567, T055-3381 1272.
Nice and quiet, restaurant with *churrasco* for lunch.

Santo Ângelo

$$ Turis
R Antônio Manoel 726, T055-3313 5255.
Good value rooms with a/c and fridge, good breakfast, internet.

$$-$ Hotel Nova Esperança
R Sete Povos 463, T055-3312 1173, www.hotelnovaesperanca.com.br.
Simple hotel behind bus station.

Rio Grande

$$$ Atlântico Rio Grande
R Duque de Caxias 55, T053-3231 3833, www.hoteisatlantico.com.br.
Reasonable value, restaurant and all services.

Border with Uruguay: coastal route

Chuí

$$$ Bertelli Chuí
BR-471, Km 648, 2 km from town, T053-3265 1266, www.bertellichuihotel.com.br.
Comfortable, with pool.

$$ Rivero
Colômbia 163-A, T053-3265 1271.
With bath, without breakfast.

$$ San Francisco
Av Colombia e R Chile.
Shower, restaurant.

Restaurants

Porto Alegre
The Central Market along the Praça is lined with *lancherias*. As well as restaurants serving gaucho cooking, there are many German, Italian and Japanese places. Vegetarians might try some of the *campeiro* soups and casseroles or visit one of the many health food lunch buffet spots.

$$$ Al Dente
R Mata Bacelar 210, Auxiliadora, T051-3342 8534. Closed Sun, reservations needed Fri-Sat.
Good, if expensive northern Italian cuisine.

$$$ Chopp Stübel
R Quintino Bocaiúva 940, Moinhos de Vento, T051-3332 8895, http://choppstubel.com.br. Mon-Sat 1800-0030.
German food and beers. Recommended.

$$ Atelier de Massas
R Riachuelo 1482, T051-3225 1125. Closed Sun.
Lunch and dinner, Italian, fantastic pastas and steaks, excellent value.

$$ Komka
Av Bahia 1275, San Geraldo, T051-3222 1881. Open 1130-1430, 1930-2300, closed Sun, for churrasco.
Recommended.

$$ Nova Vida
R Demétrio Ribeiro 1182, T051-3226 8876, Facebook: novavidarestaurantenatural. Mon-Sat 1100-1500.
Vegetarian, good lasagne.

Cafés

The café in **Usina do Gasômetro** is good for sandwiches and speciality coffee.

Café do Cofre
7 de Setembro 1028 (below Santander Cultural), T051-3227 8322. Lunch only.
Good light meals, including salads and sushi.

Café Dos Cataventos
In Casa de Cultura Mário Quintana, R dos Andrades 736, in courtyard. Open 1200-2300.
Also **Restaurant Majestic** on roof, T051-3226 0153. Both serve good drinks, snacks and meals. Fantastic rooftop sunsets.

Bars and clubs

Porto Alegre

Bars
On weekend nights, thousands head for the Cidade Baixa and spill out of the bars and clubs along Rua da República and José do Patrimônio.

Bar do Goethe
R 24 de Outubro 112, Moinhos de Vento, T051-98404 9356, www.bardogoethe.com.br. Mon-Fri 1400-2200, Sat 0900-1500.
Excellent range of artisan beers and German snacks, Wi-Fi.

Entertainment

Porto Alegre

Exhibitions and theatres
Casa de Cultura Mário Quintana, *R dos Andrades 736, T051-3221 7147. Sat-Sun 0900-2100, 1200-2100.* A lively centre for the arts, with exhibitions, theatre, pleasant bar.
Santander Cultural, *R 7 de Setembro 1028, T051-3287 5718. Mon-Fri 1000-1900, Sat-Sun 1100-1900.* Cultural centre with a beautiful interior (a former bank), good value art house cinema and a café, holds some interesting exhibitions.
Theatro São Pedro, *Praça Mal Deodoro, T051-3227 5100.* Free noon and late afternoon concerts Sat, Sun, art gallery, café.

Festivals

Porto Alegre
2 Feb A local holiday, **Nossa Senhora dos Navegantes** (Iemanjá), whose image is taken by boat from the central quay in the port to the industrial district of Navegantes.
Feb/Mar Carnival parade takes place in Av A do Carvalho, renamed Av Carlos Alberto Barcelos (or Roxo) for these 3 days only, after a famous Carnival designer.
Sep Semana Farroupilha celebrates gaucho traditions with parades in traditional style, its main day being 20 Sep.
Oct-Nov Feira do Livro in Praça da Alfândega.

Shopping

Porto Alegre

Markets
Street market (leather goods, basketware, etc) in area around the central Post Office. Good leather goods are sold on the streets. Sun morning handicraft and bric-a-brac market (plus sideshows) Av José Bonifácio (next to Parque Farroupilha). There is a very good food market.

What to do

Porto Alegre
Ask at the tourist office, Travessa do Carmo 84, Cidade Baixa, about tours of the city, on foot, or by open-top bus, twice a day Tue-Sun. See also FreeWalkPOA, http://freewalkpoa.com.
Several boats trips around islands in estuary:
Barco Porto Alegre 10, *from the Usina do Gasômetro, T051-3109 2312, www.barcoportoalegre 10.com.br.* Daily trips at 1630, 1700 in summer, 2-3 at weekends (no sailings on Mon), US$8.
Cisne Branco, *from Cais do Porto, near Museu de Arte de Rio Grande do Sul, T051-3224 5222, www. barcocisnebranco.com.br.* 4 sailings daily, Tue-Sun, 1 hr, US$9. Also has a Happy Hour cruise, 1½ hrs, with bar, Oct-Mar.
Melannie Kaminski, *T051-9722 4331, http:// melguiadeturismo.wixsite.com/melguiadeturismo.* Authorised tour guide for individuals and groups in Porto Alegre and Rio Grande do Sul.
Noiva do Caí, *from the Usina do Gasômetro, T051-3211 7662.* Several on Sun, fewer mid-week, 1 hr, US$8 (check winter schedules).

Transport

Porto Alegre
Air The international airport is on Av dos Estados, 8 km from the city, T051-3358 2000.

Bus The city's integrated transport system (*Tri*, www.tripoa.net.br) operates with pre-paid cards. There are normal buses and 1st-class minibuses (*Lotação*), painted in a distinctive red, blue and white pattern. 1 journey costs US$1.25. There is also a Linha Turismo with 2 routes, hop-on, hop-off service from tourist office at Travessa do Carmo 84, Tue-Sun, US$7.65, US$9.35 at weekends: Centro Histórico departures through the day 0900-1600, 1¾ hrs; Zona Sul at 1000 and 1500, 1 hr 35 mins.

International and interstate buses arrive at the *rodoviária* at Largo Vespasiano Júlio Veppo, on Av Mauá with Garibáldi, T051-3210 0101, www.rodoviaria-poa.com.br. There are 2 sections to the terminal; the ticket offices for interstate and international destinations are together in 1 block, beside the municipal tourist office (very helpful). The intermunicipal (state) ticket offices are in another block; for travel information within the state, ask at the very helpful booth near the station concourse.

To **Rio**, US$97, 26 hrs; **São Paulo**, US$55-70, 18 hrs; **Florianópolis**, US$29-38, 7 hrs (take an *executivo* rather than a *convencional*, which is much slower); **Curitiba**, from US$43-47, coastal and Serra routes, 11 hrs. **Foz do Iguaçu**, US$56-64, 13 hrs. To **Uruguaiana**, US$15, 8 hrs. Many other destinations.

International buses Note Take your passport and tourist card when purchasing international bus tickets. To **Montevideo**, with TTL (www.ttl.com.br), US$74 (leito 110), or take an ordinary bus to border town of Chuí, 7 hrs, US$35-54, walk or taxi across the border, then bus to Montevideo. There are services to **Buenos Aires**, 19 hrs with JBL, http://jblturismo.com.br, 1730 daily, US$102, route is Uruguaiana, Paso de los Libres, Entre Ríos and Zárate.

Metrô The Trensurb urban light railway, T051-129 8477, www.trensurb.com.br, single journey US$0.50, runs from the southern terminal at Mercado (station beside the market), as far north as the city of Novo Hamburgo, 40 km, stopping at the *rodoviária*, airport and Canoas along with other locations. Trains run every 10-15 mins.

Road Good roads radiate from Porto Alegre, and Highway BR-116 is paved to Curitiba (746 km). To the south it is paved (mostly in good condition), to Chuí on the Uruguayan border,

512 km, and to Rio Branco, also on the border. In summer visibility can be very poor at night owing to mist; unfenced cows are a further hazard. The paved coastal road to Curitiba via Itajaí (BR-101), the 1st 100 km is the 4-lane Estrada General Osório highway, is being dualled to Florianópolis, so a rough ride while work progresses. Nevertherless it's a better journey than the BR-116 via Caxias and Lajes. The road to Uruguaiana is entirely paved but bumpy.

Jesuit Missions
Bus From **Porto Alegre** to **São Miguel das Missões** Sat at 0645 with **Ouro e Prata**, 9½ hrs, US$39. Same company runs many more buses a day to **Santo Ângelo**, 6½-8 hrs, US$38-46. Buses between São Miguel and Santo Ângelo with **Antonello**, 4 a day.

South of Porto Alegre: Lagoa do Peixe
Bus **Porto Alegre–Mostardas**, 4½ hrs, US$15 with **Palmares**. From Mostardas you can hop off the 1045 bus which passes through the northern end of the park on its way to the beach (basic hotels and restaurants). 3 buses a week between Mostardas/Tavares and São José do Norte (130 km, terrible in the wet), via Bojuru, US$15, 5 hrs in theory.

São Lourenço do Sul
Bus From **Porto Alegre**, US$15, several daily.

Rio Grande
Bus Frequent daily to and from **Pelotas** (56 km), 1 hr, US$5 and **Porto Alegre** (8 a day, US$25, 4½ hrs). Road to Uruguayan border at **Chuí** is paved, but the surface is poor (5 hrs by bus, at 0700 and 1430).

Border with Uruguay: coastal route

Chuí
Bus *Rodoviária* on R Venezuela. Buses run from Chuí to **Pelotas** (6-7 daily, US$16, 4 hrs), **Rio Grande** (0700, 1400, 5 hrs, US$15) and **Porto Alegre** (1200, 2330, 7¾ hrs, US$35-54).

Border with Uruguay: inland routes

Santana do Livramento
Bus *Rodoviária* at Gen Salgado Filho e general Vasco Alves. Bus to **Porto Alegre**, 4 daily, 7 hrs, US$30-45.

★ The magnitude of the Iguaçu Falls, and the volume of water that thunders over the edge has to be seen to be believed. They are 28 km from the city of Foz do Iguaçu. For a description of the falls, maps and an account of road links between Argentina, Brazil and Paraguay, see the Argentina chapter.

Parque Nacional Foz do Iguaçu *Colour map 7, C1.*

T045-3521 4400, www.cataratasdoiguacu.com.br, US$19.75, payable in reais, Argentine pesos (only pesos accepted in Argentina), euros, dollars or credit card, or online by credit card, includes obligatory transport within the park (discounts for Mercosur, Brazilian, local residents and over-60s; children 2-11, US$3); 2-day tickets are available with a 50% discount at weekends and 90% on weekdays for the 2nd day. The park is open daily, 0900-1700.

The Brazilian national park was founded in 1939 and the area was designated a World Heritage Site by UNESCO in 1986. Fauna most frequently encountered are little and red brocket deer, South American coati, white-eared opossum and a sub-species of the brown capuchin monkey. The endangered tegu lizard is common. Over 100 species of butterflies have been identified, among them the electric blue Morpho, the poisonous red and black heliconius and species of Papilionidae and Pieridae. The bird life is rewarding for birdwatchers; five members of the toucan family can be seen.

Take a bus or taxi to the park's entrance, Km 21 from Foz. There's a smart modern **visitor centre** here, with toilets, ATMs, a small café, a large souvenir shop and a Banco Itaú *câmbio* (1000-1500). An **Exposição Ecológica** has information about the natural history of the falls and surrounding park (included in entry fee; English texts poor). Nature lovers are advised to visit first thing in the morning or late in the afternoon, preferably in low season, as crowds can significantly detract from the experience of the falls and surrounding park (at peak times like Semana Santa up to 10,000 visitors a day arrive). From the entrance, shuttle buses leave every 10-15 minutes, stopping first at Park Administration. Next is the start of the **Poço Preto** trail (9 km through the forest to the river, walking or by bicycle), then the **Bananeiras** trail and **Macuco Safari** (see page 522). After 10 km the bus stops at the start of the Cascadas Trail and the Hotel das Cataratas, and finally at the end of the road, Porta Canoas. There are Portuguese, Spanish and English announcements of the five stops. The 1.5-km paved Cascadas Trail is an easy walk, taking you high above the Rio Iguaçu, giving splendid views of all the falls on the Argentine side from a series of galleries. At the end of the path is Espaço Naipi, a three-level viewing platform at the foot of the Floriano Falls which gives a dramatic view of the canyon and the Floriano Falls. From Espaço Naipi there is a boardwalk to the Garganta do Diabo. From Naipi, there are 150 steps up to the **Porto Canoas** complex (there are lifts for those who find stairs difficult); you can also return the way you came, and walk a little further along the road. The complex consists of a big souvenir shop, toilets, a smart buffet **restaurant**, a café and *lanchonete*, all with good view of the river above the falls. Return to the visitor centre and entrance by free shuttle bus. The whole visit will take around two hours, plus time for lunch.

Never feed wild animals and keep your distance when taking photos; coatis have been known to attack visitors with food.

Essential Foz do Iguaçu

There are good communications by air and road with the main cities of southern Brazil, plus frequent cross-border links to Argentina and Paraguay, see Transport, below. It is difficult to change money on Sunday, but quite possible in Paraguay where US dollars can be obtained on credit cards. There are plenty of banks with ATMs, *câmbios* and travel agents on Avenida Brasil.

Foz do Iguaçu and around

A small, modern city, 28 km from the falls, Foz has a wide range of accommodation. The **Parque das Aves bird zoo** ① *Rodovia das Cataratas Km 17.1, 100 m before the entrance to the falls, T045-3529 8282, www.parquedasaves. com.br, 0830-1700, US$12.25,* has received frequent good reports. It contains Brazilian and foreign birds, many species of parrot and beautiful toucans, in huge aviaries through which you can walk, with the birds flying and hopping around you. There are other birds in cages and a butterfly and hummingbird house.

The **Itaipu dam** ① on the Río Paraná 12 km north, *a short film is shown at the visitor centre 10 mins before each guided visit, there are bus tours every 30 mins 0800-1700, 2 hrs, US$11, full tours including the interior of the dam: 8 departures daily between 0800 and 1600, 2½ hrs, US$24, and night views, Fri-Sat 2000 (2100 in summer), US$5.50, children and seniors half price for all visits, check times with tourist office, take passport and wear long trousers and sensible shoes, best light for photography in the morning, T045-3529 8282, www.itaipu.gov.br, www.turismoitaipu.com.br,* was the site of the largest single power station in the world, built jointly by Brazil and Paraguay. Although China's Three Gorges Dam is a larger construction, Itaipu generates more electricity each year. This massive scheme began in 1975 and it became operational in 1984. The main dam is 8 km long, creating a lake which covers 1400 sq km. The 20 turbines have an installed capacity of 14,000 Mw. Only 18 run at any one time and produce about 100 mn Mwh a year, providing up to 80% of Paraguay's electricity and 17% of Brazil's. The Paraguayan side may be visited from Ciudad del Este. Several beaches can be visited around the lake. A large reforestation project is underway and six biological refuges have been created on the lakeshore in both countries. There is also the **Ecomuseu de Itaipu** ① *Av Tancredo Neves, Km 11, Tue-Sun 0800-1730, US$3.65,* and **Refúgio Bela Vista** ① *Tue-Sun 6 visits a*

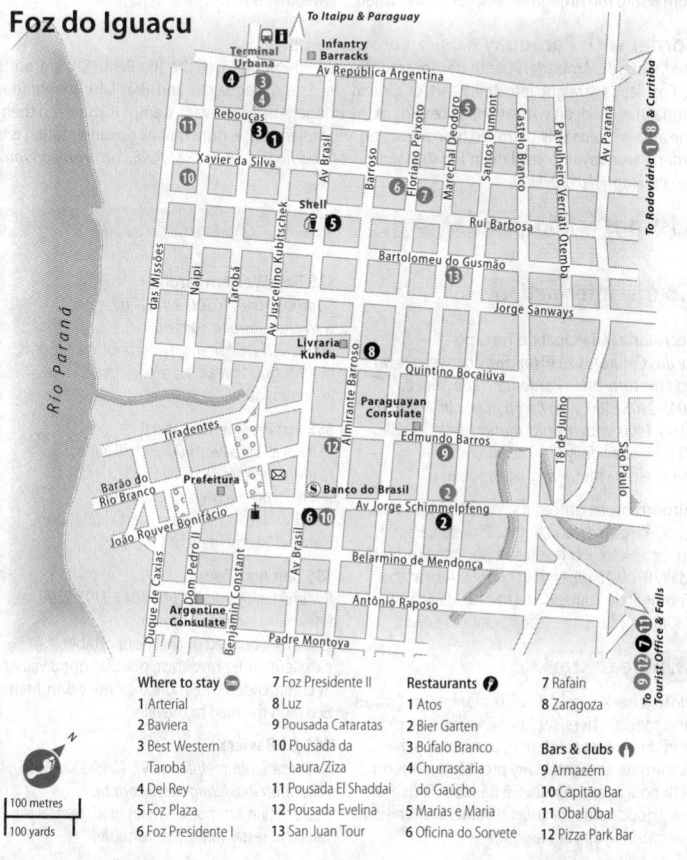

Foz do Iguaçu

Where to stay 🛏
1 Arterial
2 Baviera
3 Best Western Tarobá
4 Del Rey
5 Foz Plaza
6 Foz Presidente I
7 Foz Presidente II
8 Luz
9 Pousada Cataratas
10 Pousada da Laura/Ziza
11 Pousada El Shaddai
12 Pousada Evelina
13 San Juan Tour

Restaurants 🍴
1 Atos
2 Bier Garten
3 Búfalo Branco
4 Churrascaria do Gaúcho
5 Marias e Maria
6 Oficina do Sorvete
7 Rafain
8 Zaragoza

Bars & clubs 🍸
9 Armazém
10 Capitão Bar
11 Oba! Oba!
12 Pizza Park Bar

100 metres
100 yards

day 0830 to 1530 from the visitor centre, 2-km trail, 2½ hrs, US$7.35, animal rescue centre and home to the fauna displaced by the dam, both geared to educate about the preservation of the local culture and environment, or that part which isn't underwater. Recommended. In addition there is the **Polo Astronômico** ① *T045-3576 7203, Tue-Sun at 1000 and 1600, Fri-Sat also 1830 (1930 in summer), 2½ hrs, US$7.35,* a planetarium and astronomical observatory.

Border with Argentina

All foreigners must get exit and entry stamps both in Brazil and Argentina every time they cross the border, even if it is only for the day. It is your responsibility to get the stamps; if riding a taxi make sure it stops at both border posts. City buses only stop and wait for exit stamps at immigration of the country being left. They do not stop for entry stamps in the country you are entering. You have to get off the bus with your bags, get an entry stamp and wait for the next bus. Tickets are not interchangeable between companies, but you can pay for a new ticket. If you don't want to pay twice, ask the bus driver for a transfer ticket, get off at the border post for an entry stamp and get on the next bus of the same company without paying again. **Argentine consulate in Foz** ① *Travessa Eduardo Bianchi 26, T045-3574 2969, Mon-Fri 1000-1500.*

Between October-February Brazil is one hour ahead of Argentina. It takes about two hours to get from Foz to the Argentine falls, very tiring when the weather is hot.

Border with Paraguay *Brazil is 1 hr ahead of Paraguay.*

The Ponte de Amizade/Puente de Amistad (Friendship Bridge) over the Río Paraná, 6 km north of Foz, leads straight into the heart of Ciudad del Este. Paraguayan and Brazilian immigration formalities are dealt with at opposite ends of the bridge. Ask for relevant stamps if you need them. The area is intensively patrolled for contraband and stolen cars; ensure that all documentation is in order. **Paraguayan consulate in Foz** ① *R Marechal Deodoro 901, T045-3523 2898, fozconsulpar@mre. gov.py, Mon-Fri 0900-1700.*

Listings Foz do Iguaçu *map p519*

Tourist information

Secretaria Municipal de Turismo
Av das Cataratas 2330 (midway between town and the turn-off to Ponte Tancredo Neves), T045-2105 8100, www.pmfi.pr.gov.br. Mon-Fri 0800-1400, with an information desk, T0800-451516, open daily 0700-2300.
Very helpful, many languages spoken.

Airport tourist office (open 0800-2200), is also good, gives map and bus information, English spoken. Helpful office, free map, at the **rodoviária** (daily 0700-1800), English spoken. Also at the **Terminal de Transporte Urbano** (daily 0730-1800), helpful, English and Spanish spoken.

Where to stay

Note Check hotels' websites for internet prices and special offers. Av Juscelino Kubitschek and the streets south of it, towards the river, are unsafe at night. Many prostitutes around R Rebouças and Almirante Barroso. Taxis are only good value for short distances when you are carrying all your luggage.

$$$ Best Western Tarobá
R Tarobá 1048, T0300-2102 7700, www.hoteltaroba.com.br.
Bright and welcoming, small pool, nice rooms, helpful, good breakfast (extra), good value. Recommended.

$$$ Foz Presidente I and II
(I) R Xavier da Silva 1000 and (II) R Mcal Floriano Peixoto 1851, T045-3572 4450, www.fozpresidentehoteis.com.br.
Good value, decent rooms, restaurant, pool, Number 1 is convenient for buses.

$$$ San Juan Tour
R Marechal Deodoro 1349, T045-2105 9200, www.sanjuanhoteis.com.br.
Cheaper if booked online. Comfortable, excellent buffet breakfast, popular, good value. Recommended. The more expensive **San Juan Eco** is on the road to the falls.

$$$-$$ Baviera
Av Jorge Schimmelpfeng 697, T045-3523 5995, www.hotelbavieraiguassu.com.br.
Chalet-style exterior, on main road, central for bars and restaurants, comfortable.

$$$-$$ Del Rey
R Tarobá 1020, T045-2105 7500,
www.hoteldelreyfoz.com.br.
Nothing fancy, but perennially popular, little pool,
great breakfasts. Recommended.

$$$-$$ Foz Plaza
R Marechal Deodoro 1819, T045-3521 5500,
www.fozplazahotel.com.br.
Serene and very nice, restaurant, pool. Also has
a new annex.

$$$-$$ Luz
Av Gustavo Dobrandino da Silva 145,
near rodoviária, T045-4053 9434,
www.luzhotel.com.br.
Offers lots of packages, tours and promotional
offers. Buffet restaurant, pool. Recommended.

$$ Pousada Cataratas
R Parigot de Sousa 180, T045-3523 7841,
www.pousadacataratas.com.br.
Well-maintained modern rooms with decent
hot showers, small pool, good value with regular
discounts and promotions through the website.
Can organize tours and transfers to and from the
airport and *rodoviária*.

$$ Pousada da Laura/Ziza
R Naipi 671, T045-3572 3374,
www.pousadalauraziza.com.
$ pp in shared dorm with good breakfast. Secure,
kitchen, laundry facilities, a popular place to meet
other travellers.

$$-$ Arterial
Av José Maria de Brito 2661, T045-3573 1859,
http://hotelarterial.com.br.
Near *rodoviária*. Good value, huge breakfast,
opposite is a 24-hr buffet restaurant.

$$-$ Pousada El Shaddai
R Rebouças 306, near Terminal Urbana, T045-
3025 4490, http://pousadaelshaddai.com.br.
Fully equipped rooms, use of kitchen, English
and Spanish spoken, pool.

$$-$ Pousada Evelina
R Irlan Kalichewski 171, Vila Yolanda, T045-9135
4346, http://pousadaevelinafoz.com.br.
Lots of tourist information, English, French,
Italian, Polish and Spanish spoken, good
breakfast and location, near Muffato
Supermarket, near Av Cataratas on the
way to the falls. Warmly recommended.

Camping

Camping is not permitted by the Hotel das
Cataratas and falls.

Camping e Pousada Internacional
R Manêncio Martins 21, 1.5 km from town, T045-
3529 8183, www.campinginternacional.com.br.
For vehicles and tents, half price with
International Camping Card, also basic cabins
($), helpful staff, English, German and Spanish
spoken, pool, restaurant.

Outside Foz do Iguaçu

On the road to the falls (Rodovia das Cataratas)
are several expensive modern hotels with good
facilities (eg **Bourbon**, www.bourbon.com.br,
Bristol Viale Cataratas, www.vialecataratas.
com.br, **Carimã**, www.hotelcarima.com.br,
San Martin, www.hotelsanmartin.com.br).

$$$$ Hotel das Cataratas
Directly overlooking the falls, Km 32 from Foz,
T045-2102 7000, www.belmond.com/hotel-
das-cataratas-iguassu-falls.
Generally recommended, caters for lots of
groups, attractive colonial-style building with
pleasant gardens (where wildlife can be seen
at night and early morning) and pool. Non-
residents can eat here, midday and evening
buffets; also à-la-carte dishes and dinner with
show. An environmental fee of about US$10 is
added to the room rate.

$$-$ Paudimar Campestre
Av das Cataratas Km 12.5, Remanso Grande, near
airport, T045-3529 6061, www.paudimar.com.br.
In high season HI members only. From airport or
town take Parque Nacional bus (0525-0040) and
get out at Remanso Grande bus stop, by **Hotel
San Juan Eco**, then take the free *alimentador*
shuttle (0700-1900) to the hostel, or 1.2 km walk
from main road. Camping as well (US$8), pool,
soccer pitch, quiet, kitchen and communal meals,
breakfast. Highly recommended. Tours run to
either side of the falls (good value). **Paudimar**
desk at *rodoviária*.

$ Hostel Natura
Rodovia das Cataratas Km 12.5, Remanso Grande,
T045-3529 6949, www.hostelnatura.com (near
the Paudimar).
Rustic hostel with a small pool set in fields.
Rooms with fan, also male and female dorms
(US$11), camping (US$7.75), pool table, TV lounge,
small kitchen, arrange visits to the falls; website
has detailed instructions for how to reach them.

Restaurants

$$$ Búfalo Branco
R Rebouças 530, T045-3523 9744,
http://bufalobranco.com.br.
Superb all you can eat *churrasco*, includes filet mignon, bull's testicles, salad bar and desert. Sophisticated surroundings and attentive service. Highly recommended.

$$$ Rafain
Av das Cataratas 1749, T045-3523 1177, www. rafainchurrascaria.com.br. Closed Sun evening.
Out of town, take a taxi or arrange with travel agency. Set price for excellent buffet with folkloric music and dancing (2100-2300), touristy but very entertaining. Recommended.

$$$ Zaragoza
R Quintino Bocaiúva 882, T045-3028 8084,
http://restaurantezaragoza.com.br.
Large and upmarket, for Spanish dishes and seafood. Recommended.

$$ Atos
Av Juscelino Kubitschek 865, T045-3572 2785.
Lunch only.
Per kilo buffet with various meats, salads, sushi and puddings.

$$ Bier Garten
Av Jorge Schimmelpfeng 550, T045-3523 3700,
Facebook: Bier Garten.
Bustling pizzeria, *churrascaria* and *choperia*.

$$ Churrascaria do Gaúcho
Tarobá 632 esq Rep Argentina, T045-3029 1303, www.churrascariadogaucho.com.br, and other branches.
Price includes everything except drinks, good value *churrascaria* with the usual supply of meats and salad bar, close TTU bus station.

Cafés

Marias e Maria
Av Brasil 505, T045-3523 5472,
http://mariasemaria.com.br.
Established *confeitaria* with good savouries and sweets.

Oficina do Sorvete
Av Jorge Schimmelpfeng 244. Daily 1100-0100.
Excellent ice creams, a popular local hang-out.

Bars and clubs

Bars, all doubling as restaurants, concentrated on Av Jorge Schimmelpfeng for 2 blocks from Av Brasil to R Mal Floriano Peixoto. Wed to Sun are best nights; crowd tends to be young.

Armazém
R Edmundo de Barros 458, T045-3572 0007,
www.armazemrestaurante.com.br.
Intimate and sophisticated, attracts discerning locals, good atmosphere, mellow live music. Recommended.

Capitão Bar
Av Jorge Schimmelpfeng 288 and Almte Barroso, T045-3572 1512, http://capitaobar.com.
Large, loud and popular, nightclub attached.

Oba! Oba!
Av Mercosul 400, T045-3529 9070, www.obaoba sambashow.com.br. At Churrascaria Bottega. Daily 1200-1530 for lunch, Mon-Sat 2000-2200.
With live samba show at 2200.

Pizza Park Bar
R Almirante Barroso 993.
Specializes in vodka and whisky brands. Wi-Fi zone.

What to do

Tours

There are many travel agents on Av Brasil. Lots of companies on both sides organize conventional tours to the falls, useful more for convenience rather than information, since they collect you from your hotel. Confirm whether all entrance fees are included. Beware of overcharging by touts at the bus terminal.

Parque Nacional Foz do Iguaçu

Tours

Guayi Travel, *Av Nacional 611, T045-3027 0043, www.guayitravel.com.* Some of the best tours to both sides of the falls, Ciudad del Este, Itaipu and around, including options for birders and wildlife enthusiasts. Excellent English and Spanish.
Macuco Safari, *Rodovia das Cataratas, Km 20, Parque Nacional do Iguaçu, T045-3574 4244, www. macucosafari.com.br.* Involves a ride down a 3-km path through the forest in open trailers, then a 600-m walk, followed by a fast motorboat trip close to the falls themselves, US$66 (half price without the boat trip). Portuguese, English and Spanish spoken, take insect repellent and waterproof camera bag. There is also

Macuco Eco Aventura (T045-3529 9665, www.
macucoecoaventura.com.br). Various trips
involving walking in the forest or riding in electric
vehicles, boat trips on the upper and lower river,
either motorized or floating in inflatibles, from
20 mins to 4 hrs, prices from US$19-66, also
intensive birdwatching tours for US$158.
STTC Turismo, Av das Morenitas 2250, Jardim das
Flores, T045-3529 6161, www.sttcturismo.com.br.
Standard packages to the Brazilian and
Argentine side of the falls to Ciudad del
Este, Itaipu and with trips on the river.
Also in Bourbon Hotel, changes money.

Transport

Parque Nacional Foz do Iguaçu

Bus **Linha 120** leaves from the Terminal
Urbana in Foz, Av Juscelino Kubitschek and
República Argentina, every 30 mins or so from
0520-1930, with fewer departures till midnight,
and is clearly marked 'Parque Nacional', 40 mins,
US$1.10 one way, payable in reais or pesos (bus
route ends at the park entrance where you
purchase entry tickets and change to a park bus).

Foz do Iguaçu

Air Aeroporto Internacional de Cataratas,
BR 469, Km 16.5, 13 km east of the centre and
12 km from the falls, T045-3521 4200. In Arrivals
are ATMs and **Caribe Tours e Câmbio**, car rental
offices, tourist office and an official taxi stand,
US$17.50 to town centre. All buses marked
Parque Nacional (No 120) pass the airport in
each direction, US$1.10, 0525-0040, does not
permit large amounts of luggage but backpacks
OK. Many hotels run minibus services for a small
charge. Daily flights to **Rio**, **São Paulo**, **Curitiba**
and other Brazilian cities.

Bus For transport to the falls see above under
Parque Nacional Foz do Iguaçu. Local buses leave
from the **Terminal de Transporte Urbano, TTU**
on Av Juscelino Kubitscheck and passengers
can buy pre-paid cards, US$1.10 per journey
(you can pay in cash). Rodoviária long distance
terminal, Av Costa e Silva, 4 km from centre on
road to Curitiba, T045-522 3590; bus to centre
from next to the taxis, US$1.10, Nos 105 and 115
go to TTU. Taxi US$10. Book departures as soon

as possible. As well as the tourist office, there is
Guarda Municipal (police), Visa ATM, and luggage
store. To **Curitiba**, 9-10 hrs, paved road, US$56-76.
To **Florianópolis**, US$56-62, 14 hrs. **Unesul** to
Porto Alegre, US$56-64. To **São Paulo**, 16 hrs,
US$30-55. To **Campo Grande**, US$48, 20 hrs, for
the Pantanal.

Foz do Iguaçu and around: Itaipu dam

Bus Take bus lines 101, 102 or 104 from Foz do
Iguaçu Terminal de Transporte Urbano, US$1.10.

Border with Argentina: Foz do Iguaçu/
Puerto Iguazú

Bus Marked 'Puerto Iguazú' run every 30 mins
Mon-Sat, hourly on Sun, from the street next to
the Terminal Urbana, crossing the border bridge;
30 mins' journey, 3 companies, US$1.25. See
above for procedures regarding entry stamps.
Note Be sure you know when the last bus
departs from Puerto Iguazú for Foz (usually 1830);
last bus from Foz 1930. If visiting the Brazilian
side for a day, get off the bus at the Hotel
Bourbon, cross the road and catch the bus to the
Falls, rather than going into Foz and out again.
Alternatively, take Río Uruguay's direct Puerto
Iguazú-Brazil Cataratas bus which stops and waits
at both border posts for US$5 return (marginally
more than taking separate buses).

Border with Paraguay: Foz do Iguaçu/
Ciudad del Este

Bus (Marked Cidade–Ponte, Nos 10, 35, 103, 107,
360, 380) leave from the Terminal Urbana for
the Ponte de Amizade (Friendship Bridge),
US$1.10, then walk across. To go direct to
Ciudad del Este over the bridge, take one of the
buses (4 companies) from opposite the TTU
on Av Kubitschek, frequent 0700-1830, US$2.
To **Asunción**, **Nuestra Señora de la Asunción**
(0005, 1830) from rodoviária, about US$18
(more options from Ciudad del Este).

Car If crossing by private vehicle and only
intending to visit the national parks, this presents
no problems. Another crossing to Paraguay is at
Guaíra, at the northern end of the Itaipu lake.
It is 5 hrs north of Iguaçu by road and can be
reached by bus from Campo Grande and São
Paulo. Ferries cross to Saltos del Guaira on the
Paraguayan side.

Salvador
de Bahia

★Salvador, the third largest city in Brazil, is capital of the state of Bahia, dubbed 'Africa in exile' for its mixture of the African and the European. Often referred to as Bahia, rather than Salvador, the city is home to a heady mix of colonial buildings, beautiful beaches, African culture and pulsating musical rhythms. It stands on the magnificent Baía de Todos os Santos, a sparkling bay dotted with 38 islands. The bay is the largest on the Brazilian coast covering an area of 1100 sq km. Rising above the bay on its eastern side is a cliff which dominates the landscape and, perched on top, 71 m above sea level, are the older districts with buildings dating back to the 17th and 18th centuries. Beyond the state capital are many fine beaches, particularly in the south around Porto Seguro, while inland is the harsh Sertão, traversed by the Rio São Francisco.

Sights   Colour map 5, C5.

pastel-painted historic buildings and lively suburbs

From Praça Municipal to the Carmo area 2 km north along the cliff is the Centro Histórico (Historical Centre), now a national monument and also protected by UNESCO. It was in this area that the Portuguese built their fortified city and where today stand some of the most important examples of colonial architecture in the Americas. This area is undergoing a massive restoration programme funded by the Bahian state government and UNESCO.

Colonial houses have been painted in pastel colours. Many of the bars have live music which spills out onto the street on every corner. Patios have been created in the open areas behind the houses with open air cafés and bars. Artist ateliers, antique and handicraft stores have brought new artistic blood to what was once the bohemian part of

> **Tip...**
> There is much more of interest in the Upper City than in the Lower City.

the city. Many popular traditional restaurants and bars from other parts of Salvador have opened branches here. Its transformation has also attracted many tourist shops and the area can get crowded.

Praça Municipal, Praça de Sé and Terreiro de Jesus

Dominating the Praça Municipal is the old Casa de Câmara e Cadeia or **Paço Municipal** (Council Chamber – 1660), while alongside is the **Palácio Rio Branco** (1918), once the Governor's Palace. Leaving it with its panoramic view of the bay, Rua da Misericórdia goes north passing the **Santa Casa Misericórdia** ① *Rua da Misericórdia 6, T071-3322 7666, Mon-Fri 1000-1730, Sun 1300-1700*, (1695 – see the high altar and painted tiles), to Praça da Sé. This *praça* with its mimosa and flamboyant trees leads into Terreiro de Jesus, a picturesque *praça* named after the church which dominates it. Built in 1692, the **church of the Jesuits** became the property of the Holy See in 1759 when the Jesuits were expelled from all Portuguese territories. The façade is one of the earliest examples of baroque in Brazil, an architectural style which was to dominate the churches built in the 17th and

Essential Salvador

Finding your feet

Luis Eduardo Magalhães airport is 32 km from city centre. The **Rodoviária** is 5 km from the city with regular bus services to the centre and Campo Grande; the journey can take up to one hour especially at peak periods.

The broad peninsula on which the city is built is at the mouth of the Baía de Todos Os Santos. On the opposite side of the bay's entrance is the Ilha de Itaparica. The commercial district of the city and its port are on the sheltered, western side of the peninsula; residential districts and beaches are on the open Atlantic side. The point of the peninsula is called Barra, which is itself an important area. The centre of the city is divided into two levels, the Upper City (or Cidade Alta) where the Historical Centre lies, and the Lower City (Cidade Baixa) which is the commercial and docks district.

Most visitors limit themselves to the Pelourinho and historical centre, Barra, the Atlantic suburbs (notably Rio Vermelho which has lively nightlife) and the Itapagipe peninsula, which is north of the centre.

Getting around

The two levels of the city are connected by a series of steep hills called *ladeiras*. The easiest way to go from one level to the other is by the 74-m-high **Lacerda** lift which connects Praça Cairu in the lower city with Praça Municipal in the upper, US$0.05. There is also the **Plano Inclinado Gonçalves**, a funicular railway which leaves from behind the Cathedral going down to Comércio, the commercial district (US$0.05, closes 1300 on Saturday and all Sunday).

The roads and avenues between the areas most frequented by the visitor (see above) are straightforward to follow and well served by public transport. Other parts of the city are not as easy to get around, but have less of a tourist interest. If going to these areas a taxi may be advisable until you know your way around. See Transport, page 538.

Safety

As in all large cities, use your common sense and be careful of your possessions at all times and in all districts. The authorities have made efforts to police the old part of the city and Barra, which are now well lit at night. The civil police are reported to be very sympathetic and helpful. Police are little in evidence after 2300, however, and at night you should leave valuables securely in your hotel. Also at night, the areas around and in the lifts and buses are unsafe. Do not walk down any of the links between the old and new city, especially the Ladeira de Misericórdia, which links the Belvedere, near the Lacerda Lifts, with the lower city. Nor should you walk around the forts in Porto da Barra at night. Don't change money on the street especially in the Upper City where higher rates are usually offered. Avoid using communal washrooms in popular venues on show nights since thieves target such places; use a restaurant loo instead. Should a local join you on the street or at your table for a chat, leave at once if drugs are mentioned.

When to go

Temperatures range from 25°C to 32°C, never falling below 19°C in winter. Humidity can be high, which may make the heat oppressive. It rains somewhat all the year but the main rainy season is between May and September.

Time required

Two to three days are needed for Salvador, five days for Salvador and the beaches, and seven to 10 days for Salvador, the Chapada Diamantina and beaches.

18th centuries. Inside, the vast vaulted ceiling and 12 side altars in baroque and rococo frame the main altar completely leafed in gold. The tiles in blue, white and yellow in a tapestry pattern are also from Portugal. The church is now the **Catedral Basílica** ① *T071-3321 4573, 0900-1200, 1400-1800*. On the eastern side of the square is the church of **São Pedro dos Clérigos** ① *Mon-Fri 0900-1200, 1400-1800*, which is beautifully renovated, while close by, on the south-side, is the church of the **Ordem Terceira de São Domingos** (Dominican Third Order) ① *T071-3242 4185, Mon-Fri, 0900-1200, 1400-1700*, which has a beautiful painted wooden ceiling and fine tiles. Nearby is **Museu Afro-Brasileiro (MAfro)** ① *in the former Faculty of Medicine building, Terreiro de Jesus, T071-3283 5540, www.mafro. ceao.ufba.br, Mon-Fri 0900-1700, US$2, joint ticket with MAE*, compares African and Bahian *orixás* (deities) celebrations, beautiful murals and carvings, all in Portuguese. **Museu Arqueológico e Etnográfico (MAE)** ① *in the basement of the same building, same hours and ticket as MAfro*, houses archaeological discoveries from Bahia (stone tools, clay urns, etc), an exhibition on *indígenas* from the Alto Rio Xingu area (artefacts, tools, photos).

Facing Terreiro de Jesus is Praça Anchieta and the church of **São Francisco** ① *T071-3322 6430, Mon-Sat 0800-1700, Sun 0800-1600, US$1.50*. Its simple façade belies the treasure inside. The entrance leads

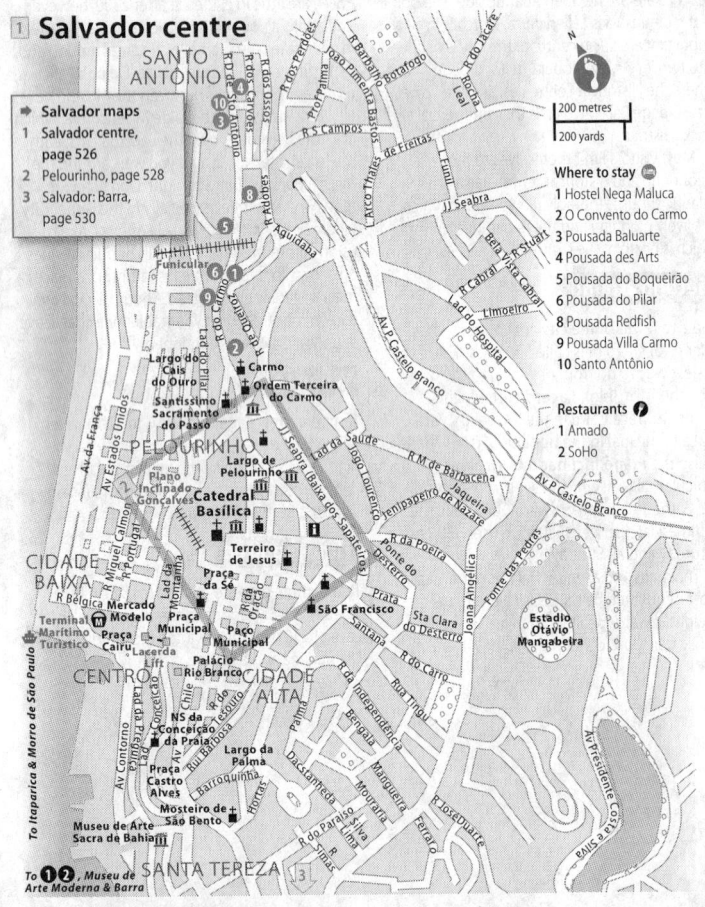

Salvador centre

Salvador maps
1 Salvador centre, page 526
2 Pelourinho, page 528
3 Salvador: Barra, page 530

Where to stay 🛏
1 Hostel Nega Maluca
2 O Convento do Carmo
3 Pousada Baluarte
4 Pousada des Arts
5 Pousada do Boqueirão
6 Pousada do Pilar
8 Pousada Redfish
9 Pousada Villa Carmo
10 Santo Antônio

Restaurants 🍴
1 Amado
2 SoHo

BACKGROUND

Salvador

On 1 November 1501, All Saints' Day, the navigator Amérigo Vespucci sailed into the bay. As the first European to see it, he named it after the day of his arrival. The first Governor General, Tomé de Sousa, arrived on 23 March 1549 to build a fortified city to protect Portugal's interest from constant threats of Dutch and French invasion. Salvador was formally founded on 1 November 1549 and remained the capital of Brazil until 1763. By the 18th century, it was the most important city in the Portuguese Empire after Lisbon, ideally situated in a safe, sheltered harbour along the trade routes of the 'New World'.

The city's first wealth came from the cultivation of sugar cane and tobacco, the plantations' workforce coming from the West coast of Africa. For three centuries Salvador was the site of a thriving slave trade. Even today, Salvador is described as the most African city in the Western Hemisphere and the University of Bahia boasts the only chair in the Yoruba language in the Americas. The influence permeates the city: food sold on the street is the same as in Senegal and Nigeria, Bahian music is fused with pulsating African polyrhythms, men and women nonchalantly carry enormous loads on their heads, fishermen paddle dug-out canoes in the bay, the pace of life is a little slower than elsewhere. The pulse of the city is Candomblé, an Afro-Brazilian religion in which the African deities of Nature, the Goddess of the sea and the God of creation are worshipped. These deities (or *orixás*) are worshipped in temples (*terreiros*), which can be elaborate, decorated halls, or simply someone's front room with tiny altars to the *orixá*. Candomblé ceremonies may be seen by tourists – but not photographed – on Sunday and religious holidays. Contact the tourist office, Bahiatursa, or see their twice-monthly calendar of events. Salvador today is a city of 15 forts, 166 Catholic churches, 1000 Candomblé temples and a fascinating mixture of old and modern, rich and poor, African and European, religious and profane. It has a population of around 3 million and is still a major port exporting tropical fruit, cocoa, sisal, soya beans and petrochemical products. Its most important industry, though, is tourism. Local government has done much to improve the fortunes of this once run-down, poor and dirty city and most visitors feel that the richness of its culture is compensation enough for any problems they may encounter. The Bahianas (black women who dress in traditional 18th-century costumes) are street vendors who sit behind their trays of delicacies, savoury and seasoned, made from the great variety of local fish, vegetables and fruits. Their street food is one of the musts for visitors.

to a sanctuary with a spectacular painting on the wooden ceiling, by local artist José Joaquim da Rocha (1777). The main body of the church is the most exuberant example of baroque in the country. The cedar wood carving and later gold leaf was completed after 28 years in 1748. The cloisters of the monastery are surrounded by a series of blue and white tiles from Portugal. Next door is the church of the **Ordem Terceira de São Francisco** (Franciscan Third Order – 1703) ① *T071-3321 6968, Mon-Sat 0800-1700 (Sun to 1600), US$1.50.* It has a façade intricately carved in sandstone. Inside is a quite remarkable Chapter House with striking images of the Order's most celebrated saints.

Largo do Pelourinho

Leading off the Terreiro de Jesus is Rua Portas do Carmo (formerly Alfredo Brito), a charming, narrow cobbled street lined with fine colonial houses painted in different pastel shades. This street leads into the Largo do Pelourinho (Praça José Alencar). Considered the finest complex of colonial architecture in Latin America, it was once the site of the whipping post at which slaves were auctioned and punished and of a pillory where unscrupulous tradesmen were publicly punished and ridiculed. The area is now full of galleries, boutiques, small hotels and restaurants and at night the Largo is lively, especially on Tuesday (see Bars and clubs, page 534). **Nosso Senhor Do Rosário Dos Pretos church** ① *T071-3241 5781, Mon-Fri 0830-1800 (Sat-Sun to 1500), free,* dominates the square. It was built by former slaves over a period of 100 years. The side altars honour black saints. The painted ceiling is very impressive, the overall effect being one of tranquillity in contrast to the complexity of the Cathedral and São Francisco. Afro-Brazilian Mass is held every Tuesday at 1800.

At the corner of Portas do Carmo and Largo do Pelourinho is a small museum to the work of Jorge Amado, who died in 2002, **Fundação Casa Jorge Amado** ① *T071-3321 0070, www.jorgeamado.org.br, Mon-Fri 1000-1800, Sat 1000-1600, free.* Information is in Portuguese only, but the café walls are covered with colourful copies of his book jackets. The Carmo Hill is at the top of the street leading out of Largo do Pelourinho. **Museu Abelardo Rodrigues** ① *Solar Ferrão, Pelourinho, R Gregório de Mattos 45, T071-3117 6440, www.ipac.ba.gov.br, Tue-Fri 1200-1800, Sat-Sun 1200-1700, US$2,* is a religious art museum, with objects from the 17th, 18th and 19th centuries, mainly from Bahia,

2 Pelourinho

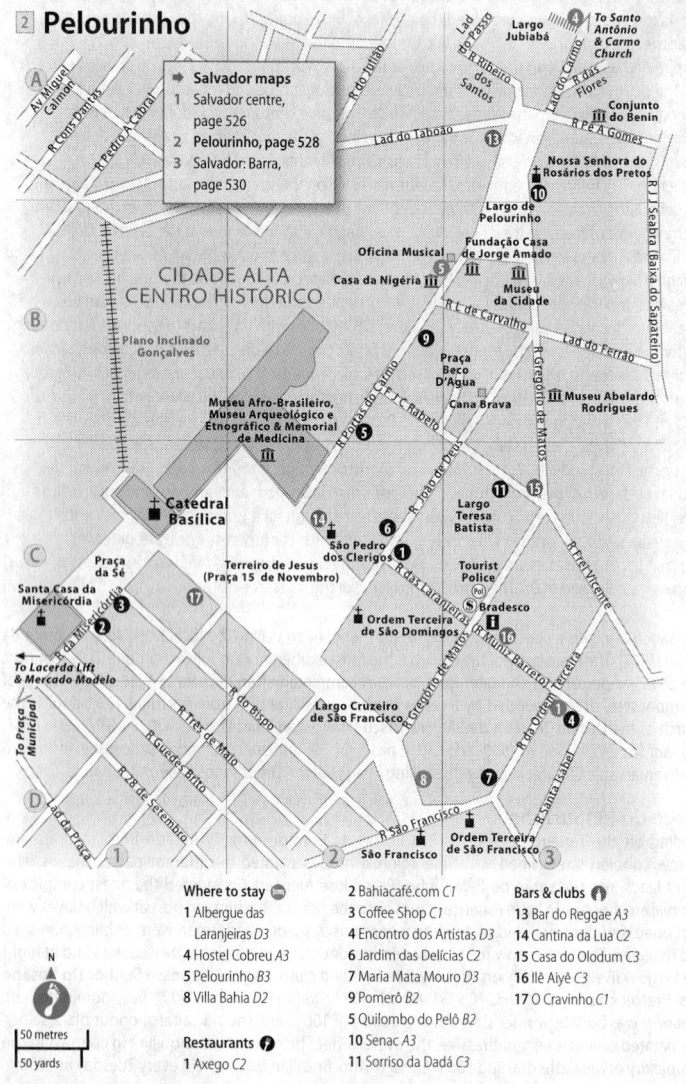

Where to stay 🛏
1 Albergue das Laranjeiras *D3*
4 Hostel Cobreu *A3*
5 Pelourinho *B3*
8 Villa Bahia *D2*

Restaurants 🍴
1 Axego *C2*
2 Bahiacafé.com *C1*
3 Coffee Shop *C1*
4 Encontro dos Artistas *D3*
5 Jardim das Delícias *C2*
7 Maria Mata Mouro *D3*
9 Pomerô *B2*
5 Quilombo do Pelô *B2*
10 Senac *A3*
11 Sorriso da Dadá *C3*

Bars & clubs 🎵
13 Bar do Reggae *A3*
14 Cantina da Lua *C2*
15 Casa do Olodum *C3*
16 Ilé Aiyê *C3*
17 O Cravinho *C1*

➡ Salvador maps
1 Salvador centre, page 526
2 Pelourinho, page 528
3 Salvador: Barra, page 530

50 metres
50 yards

Pernambuco and Maranhão. **Museu da Cidade** ① *Largo do Pelourinho 3, T071-3321 1967, Tue-Fri 0900-1830, Sat 1300-1700, Sun 0900-1300*, has exhibitions of arts and crafts and old photographs. From the higher floors of the museum you can get a good view of the Pelourinho. The **Conjunto do Benin** ① *R Padre Agostinho Gomes 17, Pelourinho, T071-3241 5679, Mon-Fri 1200-1800, below NS do Rosario dos Pretos*, has diverse exhibitions and shows African crafts, photos and videos on Benin and Angola. The **Casa da Nigéria** ① *R Portas do Carmo 26, Pelourinho, T071-3328 3782, www. casadanigeria.blogspot.co.uk*, offers a similar programme orientated more to Yoruba culture and has showcases of African and African Brazilian arts and crafts, photographs and a library.

The **Igreja da Ordem Terceira do Carmo** (1709) ① *Mon-Sat 0800-1130, 1330-1730, Sun 1000-1200, US$1*, houses one of the sacred art treasures of the city, a sculpture of Christ made in 1730 by a slave who had no formal training, Francisco Xavier das Chagas, known as O Cabra. One of the features of the piece is the blood made from whale oil, ox blood, banana resin and 2,000 rubies to represent the drops of blood. The **Igreja do Carmo** ① *Morro do Carmo, Mon-Sat 0800-1200, 1400-1800, Sun 0800-1200, US$1*, has a beautiful ceiling painted by the freed slave José Teófilo de Jesus.

South of the Praça Municipal

Avenida Chile leads to **Praça Castro Alves**, with its monument to Castro Alves, who started the campaign which finally led to the Abolition of Slavery in 1888. Two streets lead out of this square, Avenida 7 de Setembro, busy with shops and street vendors selling everything imaginable, and, parallel to it, Rua Carlos Gomes. **Museu de Arte Sacra** ① *R do Sodré 276 (off R Carlos Gomes), T071-3283 5591, Facebook: Museu de Arte Sacra da UFBA, Mon-Fri 1130-1730, US$2*, is in the 17th-century convent and church of Santa Teresa, at the bottom of the steep Ladeira de Santa Teresa. Many of the 400 carvings are from Europe, but some are local. Among the reliquaries of silver and gold is one of gilded wood by Aleijadinho (see box, page 474). **Mosteiro São Bento** ① *Av 7 de Setembro, Mon-Fri 0900-1200, 1300-1600, US$3*, dates from 1582, but was rebuilt after Dutch occupation in 1624. It houses a religious art musuem.

Both streets eventually come to **Campo Grande** (also known as Praça Dois de Julho). In the centre of the *praça* is the monument to Bahian Independence, 2 July 1823. Avenida 7 de Setembro continues out of the square towards the Vitória area. There are some fine 19th-century homes along this stretch, known as Corredor da Vitória. The **Museu de Arte Moderna** ① *Solar do Unhão, off Av Contorno, T071-3117 6139, www.bahiamam.org, Tue-Fri 1300-1900, Sat-Sun 1400-1900, US$2*, converted from an old sugar estate house and outbuildings, has a fine collection of works by some of Brazil's foremost artists and holds special exhibitions. It also has an arts cinema and a bar/café with live jazz on Saturday from 1830. The buildings are worth seeing for themselves (best to take a taxi as access can be dangerous). **Museu de Arte da Bahia** ① *Av 7 de Setembro 2340, Vitória, T071-3117 6902, Facebook: museudeartedabahia, Tue-Fri 1400-1900, Sat-Sun 1430-1900, US$2*, has interesting paintings of Brazilian artists from the 18th to the early 20th century. **Museu Costa Pinto** ① *Av 7 de Setembro 2490, T071-3336 6081, www.museucostapinto.com.br/acervo.asp, Tue-Sun 1430-1900, US$1.50*, is a modern house with collections of crystal, porcelain, silver, furniture, etc. It also has the only collection of *balangandãs* (slave charms and jewellery). It also has a garden and pleasant café. The **Palacete das Artes Rodin Bahia** ① *R da Graça 289, Graça, T071-3117 6987, www.palacetedasartes. ba.gov.br*, is a museum and cultural centre based around work by Auguste Rodin. Many works are on loan from Paris. The museum also holds temporary exhibitions, has a café/bar and gardens.

Barra

From Praça Vitória, the avenue continues down Ladeira da Barra (Barra Hill) to Porto da Barra. The best city beaches are in this area. Also in this district are the best bars, restaurants and nightlife. The Barra section of town has received a facelift with a new lighting system. The pavements fill with people day and night and many sidewalk restaurants and bars are open along the strip from Porto da Barra as far as the Cristo at the end of the Farol da Barra beach. Great attention to security is given. A little further along is the **Forte de Santo Antônio da Barra** and **lighthouse**, 1580, built on the spot where Amérigo Vespucci landed in 1501. It is right at the mouth of the bay where Baía de Todos Os Santos and the South Atlantic Ocean meet and is the site of the first lighthouse built in the Americas. The interesting **Museu Hidrográfico** ① *Tue-Sat 1300-1800, US$2*, which has a good café for watching the sunset, is housed in the upper section of the Forte de Santo Antônio; fine views of the bay and coast, recommended.

Atlantic beach suburbs

The promenade leading away from the fort and its famous lighthouse is called Avenida Oceânica, which follows the coast to the beach suburbs of **Ondina**, Amaralina and Pituba. The road is also called Avenida Presidente Vargas and, confusingly, has different numbering. Beyond Pituba are the best ocean beaches at **Jaguaripe**, **Piatã** and **Itapoã**. En route the bus passes fishing colonies and surf centres at Amaralina and Pituba where *jangadas* can be seen. A *jangada* is a small raft peculiar to the northeastern region of Brazil used extensively as well as dug-out canoes. Near Itapoã is the **Lagoa do Abaeté**, surrounded by brilliant, white sands. This is a deep, freshwater lake where local women traditionally come to wash their clothes and then lay them out to dry in the sun. The road leading up from the lake offers a panoramic view of the city in the distance, the coast, and the contrast of the white sands and fresh water less than 1 km from the sea and its golden beaches. (Do not go there alone.) Beyond the lighthouse at **Itapoã** are the magnificent ocean beaches of Stella Maris and Flamengo, both quiet during the week but very busy at the weekends. Beware of strong undertow at these beaches.

Bonfim and Itapagipe

See also the famous church of **Nosso Senhor do Bonfim** ① *Largo do Bonfim, T071-3316 2196, http://santuariosenhordobonfim.com*, on the Itapagipe peninsula in the suburbs north of the centre, whose construction began in 1745. It draws endless suppliants (particularly on Friday and Sunday) offering favours to the image of the Crucified Lord set over the high altar; the number and variety of ex-voto offerings is extraordinary. The processions over the water to the church on the third Sunday in January are particularly interesting. Also on the Itapagipe peninsula is a colonial fort on **Monte Serrat** point, and at Ribeira the church of **Nossa Senhora da Penha** (1743). The beach here has many restaurants, but the sea is polluted.

Itaparica

Across the bay from Salvador lies the island of Itaparica, 29 km long and 12 km wide. The town of Itaparica has many fine residential buildings from the 19th century, plus the church of **São Lourenço**, one of the oldest in Brazil. During the summer months the streets are ablaze with the blossoms of

Salvador: Barra

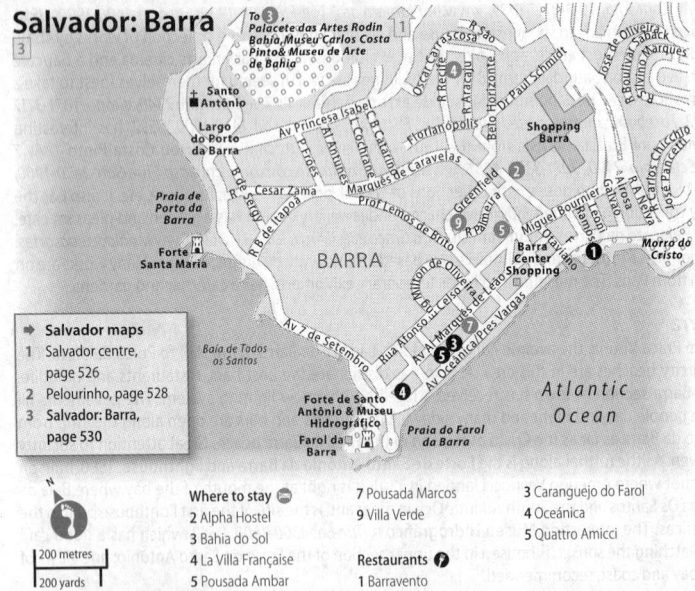

➡ **Salvador maps**
1 Salvador centre, page 526
2 Pelourinho, page 528
3 Salvador: Barra, page 530

200 metres
200 yards

Where to stay 🛏
2 Alpha Hostel
3 Bahia do Sol
4 La Villa Française
5 Pousada Ambar

7 Pousada Marcos
9 Villa Verde

Restaurants 🍴
1 Barravento

3 Caranguejo do Farol
4 Oceánica
5 Quattro Amicci

the beautiful flamboyant trees. Take a bus or kombi by the coast road (Beira Mar) which passes through the villages of Manguinhos, Amoureiras and Ponta de Areia, which has one of the best beaches on the island with many *barracas*.

The beaches at **Mar Grande** are fair but can be dirty at times. There are many *pousadas* in Mar Grande and at Penha, to the south. The further south you go, the better the beaches.

From Bom Despacho there are many buses, combis and taxis to all parts of the island. Combis and taxis can be rented for trips but be prepared to bargain, US$30-40 for half a day. There are also buses to other towns such as Nazaré das Farinhas, Valença (see page 549) and also **Jaguaribe**, a small, picturesque colonial port. Both of these towns are on the mainland connected by a bridge on the southwest side of the island, turn off between Mar Grande and Cacha Pregos (bus company, **Viazul**). There are good beaches across the bay on the mainland, but a boat is needed to reach these (US$12).

Listings Salvador de Bahia *maps p526, p528 and p530*

Tourist information

Bahiatursa
Palácio Rio Branco, Praça Thomé de Souza s/n, Centro, T071-31166814, www.bahiatursa.ba.gov.br.
Its offices for the public are at: **Pelourinho** (R das Laranjeiras 02, T071-3321 2133, daily 0830-2100), English and German spoken; **Rodoviária** (T071-3450 3871, daily 0730-2100), good, English spoken; and **airport** (T071-3204 1244, daily 0730-2300). 2 4-hr tourist hotline, T071-3103 3103. See also www.bahia.com.br (has lists of where to stay and eat and services) and www.setur.ba.gov.br.

Policia Federal
Av O Pontes 339, Aterro de Água de Meninos, Lower City, T071-3319 6000. Open 1000-1600.
For immigration, extensions of entry permits. Show an outward ticket or sufficient funds for your stay.

Tourist Police (Beptur)
Av Simon Bolívar s/n, Jardim Armação, Centro de Convenções da Bahia, T071-3117 3280. Delegacia de Proteção ao Turista, T071-3116 6817

Where to stay

The Centro Histórico is the ideal place to stay; the Pelourinho if you're on a tight budget and Santo Antônio if you are looking for reasonably priced hotels with real charm and character. Barra also has some reasonable options.

Business visitors will find the best hotels in Rio Vermelho, a 10-min taxi ride from the centre.

Centro Histórico

$$$$ O Convento do Carmo
R do Carmo 1, T071-3327 8400, www.pestana.com.
Outstanding historical hotel in the centre with a range of suites in a beautifully converted baroque convent, excellent restaurant, spa, small pool, business services.

$$$$ Villa Bahia
Largo do Cruzeiro de São Francisco 16-18, T071-3322 4271, www.lavillabahia.com.
Boutique hotel in a renovated 18th-century town house, themed rooms, the airiest and brightest of which is the Goa room. Small pool, hot tub on the roof.

$$$-$$ Pelourinho
R das Portas do Carmo 20, T071-3322 3982, www.hotelpelourinho.com.
Refurbished 1960s hotel with bright decorations, some rooms with great views over the bay, some special offers.

$ pp Albergue das Laranjeiras
R Inácio Acciolli 13, Pelourinho, T3321 1366, www.laranjeirashostel.com.br.
In beautiful colonial building in heart of the historical district, can be noisy, café and crêperie downstairs, English spoken. **$$** double, cheaper with shared bath, for HI members and in low season. Good for meeting other travellers. Warmly recommended.

$ pp Hostel Cobreu
Ladeira do Carmo 22, T3117 1401, www.hostelcobreu.com.
Good value, US-run, convenient for Pelourinho nightlife, simple but attractive dorms and rooms (**$$**).

Santo Antônio

$$$$-$$$ Pousada des Arts
R Direita de Santo Antônio 442, near Santo Antônio fort, T071-3012 5964, http://pousadadesarts.com.br.
Brazilian/French owners, excellent breakfast, beautiful old house.

$$$$-$$$ Santo Antônio
R Direita de Santo Antônio 130, T071-3326 1270,
www.hotel-santoantonio.com.
Bright and comfortable converted colonial house,
best rooms with views over the bay, all rooms
different, good service.

$$$ Pousada do Pilar
R Direita do Santo Antônio 24, T071-3241 2033,
www.pousadadopilar.
com. Same owners as Morro do São Paulo's **Vila
Guaiamu**, verandas with excellent bay views,
good breakfast, helpful manager, pleasant roof
terrace bar.

$$$ Pousada Redfish
Ladeira do Boqueirão 1, T071-3241 0639,
www.hotelredfish.com.
English-owned stylish little boutique with
plain, large rooms, some with terraces and
open-air showers.

$$$-$$ Pousada Baluarte
Lad Baluarte 13, T071-3327 0367,
www.pousadabaluarte.com.
Bohemian household, lovely owners, 5 rooms,
cheaper without bath, excellent breakfasts.

$$$-$$ Pousada do Boqueirão
R Direita do Santo Antônio 48, T071-3241 2262,
www.pousadaboqueirao.com.br.
Family-run, beautiful remodelled house
overlooking bay, relaxed atmosphere, most
European languages spoken, great food, first
class in all respects. Highly recommended.

$$$-$$ Pousada Villa Carmo
R do Carmo 58, T071-3241 3924,
www.pousadavillacarmo.com.br.
Italian/Brazilian-owned, many European
languages spoken, very comfortable, rooms
with fan or a/c.

$ pp Hostel Nega Maluca
R dos Marchantes 15, T071-3242 9249,
www.negamaluca.com.
Popular party hostel, good dorms and private
rooms ($$), well-equipped, good breakfast.

Campo Grande/Vitória
Upmarket residential area, between Barra and
city centre, convenient for museums.

$$$ Bahia do Sol
Av 7 de Setembro 2009, T071-3338 8800,
www.bahiadosol.com.br.
Comfortable, safe and frigobar in room, family-
run, good restaurant, bureau de change. Ask for
a room on the upper floors.

Barra

$$$ Villa Verde
R da Palmeira 190, T071-98854 6601,
www.pousadavillaverde.com.
A/c studios with kitchen and double room with
fan, garden, terrace, hammocks, safe, very good.
Recommended.

$$ Pousada Ambar
R Afonso Celso 485, T071-3264 6956,
www.ambarpousada.com.br.
Also has *albergue* at $. Good service, breakfast,
convenient, French owner also speaks English.

$ pp Alpha Hostel
R Eduardo Diniz Gonçalves 128, T071-3237 6282,
www.alphahostel.com.
Barra branch of the Rio hostel, bright, colourful
dorms and rooms with fan, helpful staff,
hammocks in public areas. The backstreets in the
area should be treated with caution at night.

$ La Villa Francaise
R Recife 222, Jardim Brasil, T071-3245 6008,
www.lavilafrancaise.com.
Small guesthouse behind Shopping Barra,
bright, colourful, well run, quieter than many
others, helpful French-Brazilian owners,
sumptuous breakfast.

$ Pousada Marcos
Av Oceânica 281, T071-3264 5117,
www.pousadamarcos.com.br.
Youth hostel-style, great location near the
lighthouse, very busy, notices in Hebrew for
potential travelling companions, efficient.

Atlantic beach suburbs

$$$ Catharina Paraguaçu
R João Gomes 128, Rio Vermelho, T071-3334 0089,
www.hotelcatharinaparaguacu.com.br.
Charming, small, colonial-style,
tastefully decorated.

$$$ Ibis
R Fonte do Boi 215, T071-3330 8300,
www.accorhotels.com.br.
Large hotel in this budget business chain, safe,
sea views from the upper floors. Great value.

Camping
Note that sea bathing is dangerous off shore near
the campsites.

Camping Clube do Brasil
R Visconde do Rosário 409, Rosário,
T071-3242 0482.

Ecológica
R Alameda da Praia, near the lighthouse at Itapoã,
take bus from Praça da Sé direct to Itapoã, or to
Campo Grande or Barra, change there for Itapoã,
about 1 hr, then 30 mins' walk, T071-3374 3506.
Bar, restaurant, hot showers. Highly recommended.

Itaparica

$$$-$$ Sonho do Verão
R São Bento 2, opposite Pousada Arco
Iris, Mar Grande, T071-3633 1316,
http://hotelsonhodeverao.com.br.
Chalets and apartments, cooking facilities,
French and English spoken, jazz club and art
gallery. Like other pousadas they rent bicycles;
they also rent horses.

$$ Pousada Zimbo Tropical
Estrada de Cacha Pregos, Km 3, Rua Yemanjá,
Aratuba, T071-3638 1148, www.zimbo-tropical.com.
French/Brazilian-run, bungalows in tropical
gardens, good breakfast, evening meals and
tours available. Recommended.

Restaurants

Local specialities
The main dish is moqueca, seafood cooked in a
sauce made from coconut milk, tomatoes, red
and green peppers, fresh coriander and dendê
(palm oil). It is traditionally cooked in a wok-like
earthenware dish and served piping hot at the
table. Served with moqueca is farofa (manioc
flour) and a hot pepper sauce which you add at
your discretion, it's usually extremely hot so try
a few drops before venturing further. The dendê
is somewhat heavy and those with delicate
stomachs are advised to try the ensopado, a sauce
with the same ingredients as the moqueca, but
without the palm oil.

Nearly every street corner has a Bahiana
selling a wide variety of local snacks, the most
famous of which is the acarajé, a kidney bean
dumpling fried in palm oil which has its origins
in West Africa. To this the Bahiana adds vatapá,
a dried shrimp and coconut milk pâté (also
delicious on its own), fresh salad and hot sauce
(pimenta). For those who prefer not to eat the
palm oil, the abará is a good substitute. Abará is
steamed, wrapped in banana leaves. Seek local
advice on which are most hygienic stalls to eat
from. Two good Bahianas are Chica, at Ondina
beach (on the street to the left of Mar A Vista
Hotel) and Dinha in Rio Vermelho (who serves
acarajé until midnight, extremely popular), and

Regina at Largo da Santana (very lively in the late
afternoon). Bahians usually eat acarajé or abará
with a chilled beer on the way home from work
or on the beach at sunset. Another popular dish
with African origins is xin-xin de galinha, chicken
on the bone cooked in dendê, with dried shrimp,
garlic and squash.

Centro Histórico

$$$ Maria Mata Mouro
R da Ordem Terceira 8, Pelourinho, T071-
3321 3929, www.mariamatamouro.com.br.
Closed Sun night.
International menu, good service,
relaxing ambience.

$$$ Sorriso da Dadá
R Frei Vicente 5, T071-3321 9642,
www.dada.com.br.
Bahia's most famous chef has had many
illustrious clients, but Dadá herself is not always
in attendance.

$$$-$$ Axego
R João de Deus1, T071-3242 7481.
Celebrated for its seafood, feijoada at Sun lunch.

$$$-$$ Encontro dos Artistas
R das Laranjeiras 15, T071-3321 1721.
Very good seafood and moquecas served in a
little street-side restaurant.

$$$-$$ Jardim das Delícias
R João de Deus 12, Pelourinho, T071-3321 1449.
Elegant restaurant and antiques shop with
tropical garden, very reasonable for its setting,
classical or live music.

$$ Quilombo do Pelô
R das Portas do Carmo 13, T071-3322 4371.
Daily from 1100
Rustic Jamaican restaurant, good food with
relaxed, if erratic service, vegetarian options.
Also has hotel.

$$ Senac
Praça José Alencar 13-15, Largo do Pelourinho,
T071-3324 4557.
State-run catering school, with typical Bahian
cooking upstairs and per kilo lunches downstairs,
both a/c. Upstairs is better but lots of choice,
including vegetarian, downstairs.

$$-$ Pomerô
R Portas do Carmo 33, Pelourinho, T071-3321
5556, www.pomero.com.br. Closed Mon.
Good value, simple grilled meats, fish steaks,
bar snacks, moquecas, popular.

$ Bahiacafé.com
Praça da Sé 20, T071-3322 1266.
Smart, Belgian-run internet café, good breakfasts, excellent food, English spoken.

$ Coffee Shop
Praça da Sé 5, T071-3322 7817.
Cuban-style café serving sandwiches; main attraction is excellent coffee, and tea served in china cups, doubles as cigar shop.

Between Historical Centre and Barra

$$$ Amado
Av Lafayete Coutinho 660, Comércio, Campo Grande, T071-3322 3520, www.amadobahia.com.br.
The best of Salvador's top-end restaurants, set on a deck overlooking the bay.
The menu is strong on seafood.

$$$ SoHo
Av Contorno 1010, Píer D, Bahia Marina, T071-3322 4554, http://sohorestaurante.com.br.
One of the city's most fashionable restaurants. Excellent Japanese food. Great cocktails and sea views, dinner only. Bus connections poor, go by taxi.

Barra

$$$ Barravento
Av Oceânica 814, T071-3245 5916, www.restaurantebarravento.com.br.
Popular, upmarket beach bar restaurant, seafood, steaks, cocktails and *chope*.

$$ Oceánica
Pres Vargas 1, T071-3264 3561.
Long-established, popular seafood restaurant, open late.

$$ Quatro Amicci
R Dom Marcos Teixeira 35.
Excellent pizzas from wood-fired oven, bright, lively at weekends.

$ Caranguejo do Farol
Av Oceânica 235, above the road, T071-3264 7061.
Specializing in crab, extremely busy, also a buzzing bar.

Many medium-priced a/c restaurants in **Shopping Barra** and **Barra Center Shopping**.

Itaparica

There are many Bahianas selling *acarajé* in the late afternoon and early evening in the main *praça* by the pier at Mar Grande.

$$$ Philippe's Bar and Restaurant
Largo de São Bento, Mar Grande.
French and local cuisine, information in English and French.

$$ Volta ao Mundo
Largo de São Bento 165, Mar Grande.
Good value, buffet lunches, all-you-can-eat.

Bars and clubs

Nightlife is concentrated on and around the Pelourinho where there is always a free live street band on Tue and at weekends. The Pelourinho area is also good for a bar browse; though be wary after 2300. There are many bars on the Largo de Quincas Berro d'Água, especially along R Portas do Carmo. R João de Deus and its environs are dotted with simple pavement bars with plastic tables. The most famous Salvador musicians are the *maracatú* drum orchestras like **Olodum** and **Ilê Aiyê** (see below). There is live music all year round but the best time to hear the most frenetic performers, particularly the *axê* stars, is during Carnaval.

Largo do Pelourinho

Bar do Reggae and Praça do Reggae
Ladeiro do Pelourinho, by Nossa Senhora dos Rosarios dos Pretos.
Live reggae bands every Tue and more frequently closer to carnival.

Cantina da Lua
Praça 15 de Novembro 2, Terreiro de Jesus, T071-3322 4041, www.cantinadalua.com.br. Daily.
Popular, good place to meet, outdoor seating, but the food isn't great.

O Cravinho
Praça 15 de Novembro 3, T071-3322 6759.
Dark little bar with occasional live music, *cachaça* made on the premises and bar food.

Barra

Most Barra nightlife happens at the Farol da Barra (lighthouse). R Marquês de Leão is very busy, with lots of bars with tables on the pavement. Like the Pelourinho, the whole area is good for a browse, but be wary of pickpockets.

Habeas Copos
R Marquês de Leão 172.
Famous and traditional street side bar, very popular.

Atlantic beach suburbs

Once the bohemian section of town the nightlife in **Rio Vermelho** rivals the Pelourinho. There are a number of lively bars around the Largo de Santana, a block west of the Hotel Catharina Paraguaçu.

Entertainment

Salvador de Bahia

The **Fundação Cultural do Estado da Bahia** edits *Bahia Cultural*, a monthly brochure listing monthly cultural events. These can be found in most hotels and Bahiatursa information centres. Local newspapers *A Tarde* and *Correio da Bahia* have good cultural sections listing all events in the city.

Cinema

The main shopping malls at Barra, Iguatemi, Itaigara and Brotas, and **Cineart** in Politeama (Centro), run more mainstream movies. See www.saladearte.art.br for film shows in various cinemas and other locations. The impressive Casa do Comércio building near Iguatemi houses the **Teatro do SESC** with a mixed programme of theatre, cinema and music Wed-Sun.

Music

During the winter (Jul-Sep) ring the *blocos* to confirm that free rehearsals will take place.
Ara Ketu, *T071-3264 8800*. Hails from the sprawling Peripe[?]ri suburb in the Lower City. Once a purely percussion band Ara Ketu has travelled widely and borrowed on various musical forms (samba, Candomblé, *soukous*, etc) to become a major carnival attraction and one of the most successful bands in Bahia. Rehearsals take place on Thu nights at 1930 on Trapiche Barnabé, Comércio. As these get very full, buy tickets in advance from Pida kiosks, the Central do Carnaval, Ticketmix and at the *bloco's* HQ, R Afonso Celso, 161, Barra.
Banda Olodum, *R Gregório de Mattos 22, T071-3321 4154, www.olodum.com.br*. Olodum's headquarters where the drumming troupe made famous by their innovative power-house percussion and involvement with Paul Simon, Michael Jackson and Branford Marsalis perform live every Tue and Sun at 1930 to packed crowds.
Didá, Neguinho do Samba was the musical director of Olodum until he founded Didá, an all-woman drumming group based along similar lines to Olodum. They rehearse on Fri nights in the Praça Teresa Batista, Pelourinho. Starts 2000, US$10.
Filhos de Gandhi, the original and largest African drumming group, formed by striking stevedores during the 1949 carnival. The hypnotic shuffling

cadence of Filhos de Gandhi's afoxé rhythm is one of the most emotive of Bahia's carnival.
Ilê Aiyê, *R do Curuzu 197, Liberdade, T071-3256 8800, www.ileaiye.com.br*. Established in the largest suburb of the city, Ilê Aiyê is a thriving cultural group dedicated to preserving African traditions which under the guidance of its president Vovô is deeply committed to the fight against racism. Rehearsals take place mid-week at Boca do Rio and on Sat nights in front of their headquarters (address above, details of live performances throughout Salvador are published here).
Timbalada, *T071-3355 0680, www.timbalada.com*. Carlinhos Brown is a local hero. He has become one of the most influential musical composers in Brazil today, mixing great lyrics, innovative rhythms and a powerful stage presence. He played percussion with many Bahian musicians, until he formed his own percussion group, Timbalada. He has invested heavily in his native Candeal neighbourhood: the Candy All Square, a centre for popular culture, is where the Timbalada rehearsals take place every Sun night, 1830, from Sep to Mar. Not to be missed. Brown opened the **Museu du Ritmo** (R Torquato Bahia 84, Edif Mercado do Ouro, T071-3353 4333, www.carlinhosbrown.com.br/universo/museu-du-ritmo), and the **International Centre for Black Music**, a complex built around a 1000-sq-m concert arena in a giant courtyard formed from the walls of a former colonial mansion house which once was home to the gold exchange.

Artists and bands using electronic instruments and who tend to play in the *trios eléctricos* draw heavily on the rich rhythms of the drumming groups creating a musical genre known as **Axé**. The most popular of such acts are **Chiclete com Banana** (www.chicletecombanana.com.br), and **Ivete Sangalo**. Also look out for the internationally famous **Daniela Mercury**. **Gerónimo** was one of the first singer/songwriters to use the wealth of rhythms of the Candomblé in his music and his song *E d'Oxum* is something of an anthem for the city. **Mariene de Castro** is Bahia's most exciting new artist and one of the few singing traditional Bahian samba.

All the above have albums released and you can find their records easily in most record stores. See Shopping in the Pelourinho. Also try **Flashpoint** in Shopping Iguatemi.

Theatre

Castro Alves, *at Campo Grande (Largo 2 de Julho), T071-3339 8000, www.tca.ba.gov.br*. Seats 1400 and is considered one of the best in Latin

America. It also has its own repertory theatre, the **Sala de Coro**, for more experimental productions. The theatre's Concha Acústica is an open-air venue used frequently in the summer, attracting the big names in Brazilian music.

Teatro Gregório de Matos, *in Praça Castro Alves, T071-3322 2646.* Offers space to new productions and writers.

Theatro XVIII, *R Frei Vicente, T071-3332 0018.* An experimental theatre in the Pelourinho.

Vila Velha, *Passéio Público, Gamboa da Cima, T071-3336 1384.* A historically important venue where many of the *tropicalistas* first played. Nowadays it has an eclectic programme of modern dance, theatre and live music.

Festivals

Salvador de Bahia
6 Jan Epiphany.
Jan/Feb Festa do Nosso Senhor do Bonfim. 2nd Sun after Epiphany, but the washing or *lavagem* of the Bonfim church, with its colourful parade, takes place on the preceding Thu (usually mid-Jan). The Festa da Ribeirav is on the following Mon.
2 Feb Fishermen of Rio Vermelho on **2 Feb**; gifts for Yemanjá, Goddess of the Sea, are taken to sea in a procession of sailing boats to an accompaniment of Candomblé instruments.
Feb/Mar For Carnival, see box, opposite.
Mar/Apr Ash Wed and Maundy Thu, half-days.
Mar/Apr Holy Week processions among the old churches of the upper city are also interesting.
2 Jul Independence of Bahia.
Dec Christmas Eve, half-day.

Shopping

Largo do Pelourinho
Handicrafts
Artesanato Santa Bárbara, *R Portas do Carmo 7.* Excellent handmade lace products.

Atelier Portal da Cor, *Ladeira do Carmo 31.* Run by a co-operative of local artists, Totonho, Calixto, Raimundo Santos, Jô, good prices. Recommended.

Instituto Mauá, *R Gregório de Matos 27. Tue-Sat 0900-1800, Sun 1000-1600.* Good-quality Bahian handicrafts at fair prices, better value and quality for crafts than the Mercado Modelo.

Loja de Artesanato do SESC, *Largo Pelourinho. Mon-Fri 0900-1800 (closed for lunch), Sat 0900-1300.* Similar store to Instituto Mauá.

Jewellery
In the Pelourinho are:
Casa Moreira, *Ladeira da Praça, just south of Praça da Sé.* Exquisite jewellery and antiques, most very expensive, but some affordable charms.

Scala, *Praça da Sé.* Handmade jewellery using locally mined gems (eg acquamarine, amethyst and emerald), workshop at back.

Markets
Mercado Modelo, *at Praça Cairu, lower city.* Offers many tourist items such as wood carvings, silver-plated fruit, leather goods, local musical instruments. Lace items for sale are often not handmade (despite labels), are heavily marked up and are much better bought at their place of origin (for example Ilha de Maré, Pontal da Barra and Marechal Deodoro). Bands and dancing, especially Sat (but for money from tourists taking photos), closed at 1200 Sun. The largest and most authentic market is the **Feira de São Joaquim** (5 km from Mercado Modelo along the sea front): trucks, donkeys, horses, boats, people, mud, very smelly, every day (Sun till 1200 only), busiest on Sat morning; interesting African-style pottery and basketwork; very cheap. (The car ferry terminal for Itaparica is nearby.) Every Wed from 1700-2100 is a **handicrafts fair** in the 17th-century fort of Santa Maria at opposite end of Porto da Barra beach.

Music in the Pelourinho
The major carnival *afro blocos* have boutiques selling T-shirts, etc: **Boutique Olodum** (Praça José Alencar), **Ilê Aiyê** (R Francisco Muniz Barreto 16). **Cana Brava** (R João de Deus 22, T071-3321 0536). CD shop with knowledgeable American owner. **Oficina de Investigação Musical** (R das Portas do Carmo 24, T071-3322 2386). Handmade traditional percussion instruments (and lessons, US$15 per hr), Mon-Fri 0800-1200 and 1300-1600. Best place to buy berimbaus in Bahia.

What to do

Salvador de Bahia
Boat and bus tours
Available from several companies. All-day boat trip on Baía de Todos Os Santos last from 0800-1700 including a visit to Ilha dos Frades, lunch on Itaparica (not included). There are also city tours.

Capoeira
A martial art, often said to have developed from the traditional foot-fighting technique introduced from Angola by African slaves, but

Carnival in Bahia

Carnival officially starts on Thursday night at 2000 when the keys of the city are given to the Carnival King 'Rei Momo'. The unofficial opening though is on Wednesday with the Lavagem do Porto da Barra, when throngs of people dance on the beach. Later on in the evening is the Baile dos Atrizes, starting at around 2300 and going on until dawn, very bohemian, good fun. Check with Bahiatursa for details on venue, time, etc (carnival dates in 2018 8-13 February, in 2019 1-5 March); see also http://home.centraldocarnaval.com.br and www.carnaval.bahia.com.br.

Carnival in Bahia is the largest in the world and it encourages active participation. It is said that there are 1½ million people dancing on the streets at any one time.

There are two distinct musical formats. The *afro blocos* are large drum-based troupes (some with up to 200 drummers) who play on the streets accompanied by singers atop mobile sound trucks. The first of these groups was the Filhos de Gandhy (founded in 1949), whose participation is one of the highlights of Carnival. Their 6000 members dance through the streets on the Sunday and Tuesday of Carnival dressed in their traditional costumes, a river of white and blue in an ocean of multicoloured carnival revellers. The best known of the recent *afro blocos* are Ilê Aiye, Olodum, Muzenza and Malê Debalê. They all operate throughout the year in cultural, social and political areas. Not all of them are receptive to foreigners among their numbers for Carnival. The basis of the rhythm is the enormous *surdo* (deaf) drum with its bumbum bumbum bum anchor-beat, while the smaller *repique*, played with light twigs, provides a crack-like overlay. Ilê Aiye take to the streets around 2100 on Saturday night and their departure from their headquarters at Ladeira do Curuzu in the Liberdade district is not to be missed. The best way to get there is to take a taxi to Curuzu via Largo do Tanque thereby avoiding traffic jams. The ride is a little longer in distance but much quicker in time. A good landmark is the Paes Mendonça supermarket on the corner of the street from where the *bloco* leaves. From there it's a short walk to the departure point.

The enormous *trios eléctricos* 12-m sound trucks, with powerful sound systems that defy most decibel counters, are the second format. These trucks, each with its own band of up to 10 musicians, play songs influenced by the *afro blocos* and move at a snail's pace through the streets, drawing huge crowds. Each *afro bloco* and *bloco de trio* has its own costume and its own security personnel who cordon off the area around the sound truck. The *bloco* members can thus dance in comfort and safety.

There are three official Carnival routes. The oldest is Osmar, from Campo Grande to Praça Castro Alves near the old town. The *blocos* go along Avenue 7 de Setembro and return to Campo Grande via the parallel R Carlos Gomes. The best night at Praça Castro Alves is Tuesday (the last night of Carnival) when the famous '*Encontro dos trios*' (Meeting of the Trios) takes place. Trios jostle for position in the square and play in rotation until dawn (or later!) on Ash Wednesday. It is not uncommon for major stars from the Bahian (and Brazilian) music world to make surprise appearances.

The second route is Dodô, from Farol da Barra to Ondina. The *blocos alternativos* ply this route. These are nearly always *trios eléctricos* connected with the more traditional *blocos* who have expanded to this now popular district. The third and newest route is Batatinha, in the historic centre and the streets of Pelourinho. No *trios eléctricos* take part on this route, but marching bands, folkloric groups and fancy-dress parades.

Day tickets for these are available the week leading up to Carnival. Check with Bahiatursa on where the tickets are sold for the stands. (Also available online at centraldocarnaval.com.br) There is little or no shade from the sun so bring a hat and lots of water. Best days are Sunday to Tuesday. Or just go it alone; find a *barraca* in the shade and watch the *blocos* go by.

latterly claimed to be have originated with the indigenous people of Brazil and then modified by slaves. The music is by drum, tambourine and berimbau; there are several different kinds of the sport. If you want to attempt capoeira, the best school is **Mestre Bimba** (R das Laranjeiras, T071-3322 0639, www.capoeiramestre bimba.com.br). It has male and female teachers. Exhibitions take place in the Largo do Pelourinho every Friday evening around 2000. You can also see capoeiristas in public spaces like the Pelourinho, outside the Mercado Modelo and at Campo Grande. Genuine capoeiristas do not expect a contribution, but if you wish to take pictures ask first. At the Casa da Cultura at **Forte de Santo Antônio Alem do Carmo**, there are several capoeira schools, usually giving classes in the evening.

Language classes

Diálogo, *R Dr João Pondé 240, Barra, T071-3264 0053, www.dialogo-brazilstudy.com.* Accommodation with host families, optional dance, capoeira and cookery classes.

Tour operators and guides

Ben Paris, *T071-98812 4576, bt_paris@yahoo.com.* A US resident in Salvador who can take you around the sights. Good access to musicians, Candomblé *terreiros* and fascinating spots in the Recôncavo. **Tatur Turismo**, *Av Tancredo Neves 274, Centro Empresarial Iguatemi, Sala 222-224, bloco B, T071-3114 7900, www.tatur.com.br.* Run by Irishman, Conor O'Sullivan. English spoken. Specializes in Bahia, arranges private guided tours and can make any travel, hotel and accommodation arrangements. Highly recommended.

Transport

Salvador de Bahia

Air An a/c bus service every 30-40 mins between Luis Eduardo Magalhães Airport (across the street from the terminal) and Praça da Sé in the centre, a distance of 32 km, costs US$1.35, 0600-2130. It takes the coast road to the city, stopping at hotels en route. 'Special' taxis to both Barra and centre (buy ticket at the airport desk next to tourist information booth), US$45; normal taxis (from outside airport), US$30-40. Allow plenty of time for travel to the airport and for check-in. ATMs are in a special area to the extreme right as you arrive, a good place to get money. **Banco do Brasil** is to the extreme left, open Mon-Fri 0900-1500. **Jacarandá** exchange house is in front of international arrivals, open 24 hrs a day, but poor rates and only good for changing a small amount (count your money carefully). Tourist information booth, English spoken, has list of hotels and useful map. Daily flights to all the main cities.

Bus Local buses US$1.35-2.50, *executivos*, a/c. On buses and at the ticket-sellers' booths, watch your change and beware pickpockets. To get from the old city to the ocean beaches, take a 'Barra' bus from Praça da Sé to the Barra point and walk to the nearer ones; the Aeroporto executivo leaves Praça da Sé, passing Barra, Ondina, Rio Vermelho, Amaralina, Pituba, Costa Azul, Armação, Boca do Rio, Jaguaripe, Patamares, Piatã and Itapoã, before turning inland to the airport. The glass-sided Jardineira bus goes to Flamengo beach (30 km from the city) following the coastal route; it passes all the best beaches; sit on the right hand side for best views. It leaves from the Praça da Sé daily 0730-1930, every 40 mins, US$2.50. For beaches beyond Itapoã, take the executivo to Stella Maris and Flamengo beaches. These follow the same route as the Jardineira.

Long distance buses leave from the *rodoviária*, near Shopping Iguatemi, T071-3460 8300. Bus RI or RII, 'Centro–Rodoviária–Circular'; in the centre, get on in the Lower City at the foot of the Lacerda lift; buses also go to **Campo Grande** (US$1.35). A quicker executive bus from Praça da Sé or Praça da Inglaterra (in front of McDonald's), Comércio, run to Iguatemi Shopping Centre, US$2, weekdays only, from where there is a walkway to the *rodoviária* (take care in the dark, or a taxi, US$13-19). To **Recife**, Penha, US$49. To **Fortaleza**, 19 hrs, US$73.25 at 2000. To **Rio**, 27 hrs, US$93, Itapemirim, T071-3350 5644, www.itapemirim.com.br good stops, clean toilets, US$100 *leito* with Aguia Branca. **São Paulo**, 30 hrs, US$85, with São Geraldo, www.saogeraldo.com.br and **Gontijo**, T071-3358 7448, www.gontijo.com.br. There are daily bus services to **Brasília** along the fully paved BR-242, via Barreiras, 23 hrs, US$61-86. **Ilhéus**, 7 hrs, Aguia Branca, US$36.50. **Porto Seguro**, Aguia Branca, overnight at 2000, US$56. To **Lençóis** 4 a day, 6½ hrs, US$22 with **Rápido Federal**, quickest and safest is early morning bus. Frequent services to the majority of destinations; a large panel in the main hall lists destinations and the relevant ticket office.

Taxi Taxi meters start at US$1.35 for the 'flagdown' and US$0.70 per 100 m. They charge US$30 per hr within city limits, and 'agreed' rates outside. Taxi Barra–Centro US$10 daytime; US$15 at night. Watch the meter, especially at night; the night-time charge should be 30% higher than daytime charges.

Itaparica

Ferry The main passenger ferry leaves for **Bom Despacho** from São Joaquim (buses for Calçada, Ribeira stop across the road from the ferry terminal; the 'Sabino Silva – Ribeira' bus passes in front of the Shopping Barra). 1st ferry from Salvador at 0540 and, depending on demand, at intervals of 45 mins thereafter; last ferry from Salvador at 2320. Returning to **Salvador** the 1st ferry is at 0515 and the last at 2300. In summer ferries are much more frequent. Information from **COMAB/Ferry Fácil**, open 0700-2300 at terminal. A one way ticket for foot passengers Mon-Fri is US$1.25, Sat-Sun US$1.65. Catamarans depart for **Bom Despacho** twice daily, US$2.50 (US$3.25 at weekends). **Mar Grande** can be reached by a smaller ferry (**Lancha**) from the Terminal Marítimo in front of the Mercado Modelo in Salvador. The ferries leave every 45 mins and the crossing takes 50 mins, US$3 return.

Inland from Salvador

ideal trekking country

There are strong historical associations inland from Salvador, seen in the colonial exploitation of sugar and diamonds. Lençóis, famous for the latter, also has some beautiful countryside, which is ideal for trekking.

The Recôncavo

The area around Salvador, known as the Recôncavo Baiano, was one of the chief centres of sugar and tobacco cultivation in the 16th century. Some 73 km from Salvador is **Santo Amaro da Purificação**, an old sugar centre sadly decaying, noted for its churches (often closed because of robberies), municipal palace (1769), fine main *praça*, birthplace of the singers Caetano Veloso and his sister Maria Bethânia and ruined mansions including Araújo Pinto, former residence of the Barão de Cotegipe. Other attractions include the splendid beaches of the bay, the falls of Vitória and the grotto of Bom Jesus dos Pobres. The festivals of Santo Amaro, 24 January-2 February, and Nossa Senhora da Purificação on 2 February itself are interesting. There is also the Bembé do Mercado festival on 13 May. Craftwork is sold on the town's main bridge. There are no good hotels or restaurants.

Cachoeira and São Félix

At 116 km from Salvador and only 4 km from the BR-101 coastal road are the towns of **Cachoeira** (Bahia's 'Ouro Preto', population 30,416) and **São Félix** (population 13,699), on either side of the Rio Paraguaçu below the Cachoeira dam. Cachoeira was twice capital of Bahia: once in 1624-1625 during the Dutch invasion, and once in 1822-1823 while Salvador was still held by the Portuguese. There are beautiful views from above São Félix.

Cachoeira's main buildings are the **Casa da Câmara e Cadeia** (1698-1712), the **Santa Casa de Misericórdia** (1734 – the hospital, someone may let you see the church), the 16th-century **Ajuda** chapel (now containing a fine collection of vestments), and the Convent of the **Ordem Terceira do Carmo**, whose church has a heavily gilded interior. Other churches are the **Matriz** with 5-m-high *azulejos*, and **Nossa Senhora da Conceição do Monte**. There are beautiful lace cloths on the church altars. The **Museu Hansen Bahia** ① *R Ana Néri*, houses fine engravings by the German artist who made the Recôncavo his home in the 1950s. There is a great wood-carving tradition in Cachoeira. The artists can be seen at work in their studios. A 300 m railway bridge built by the British in the 19th century spans the Rio Paraguaçu to São Felix where the Danneman cigar factory can be visited to see hand-rolling. **Tourist office** ① *R Ana Néri 4, Cachoeira, T075-3425 1123.*

Lençóis *Colour map 5, C4.*

This historical monument and colonial gem was founded in 1844 to exploit the diamonds in the region. While there are still some *garimpeiros* (gold prospectors), it is not precious metals that draw most visitors, but the climate, which is cooler than the coast, the relaxed atmosphere and the wonderful trekking and horse riding in the hills of the Chapada Diamantina. A few of the options are given below under What to do, and *pousadas* and tour operators offer guiding services. This is also a good place for buying handicrafts. **Tourist office** ① *Praça Otaviano Alves 01, Antiga Prefeitura, T075-3334 1380, daily 0800-1200, 1700-2100.* There is a **Bradesco ATM** on the main square.

☆Parque Nacional da Chapada Diamantina *Colour map 5, C4.*

Palmeiras, 50 km from Lençóis, is the headquarters of the Parque Nacional da Chapada Diamantina (founded 1985), which contains 1500 sq km of mountainous country. There is an abundance of endemic plants, waterfalls, large caves (almost all of which can only be visited with a guide), rivers with natural swimming pools and good walking tours. Parque Nacional da Chapada Diamantina information, ICMBio ① *R Barão do Rio Branco 25, Palmeiras, T075-3332 2310, entry US$2.75.* See also www.parnachapadadiamantina.blogspot.co.uk and www.infochapada.com.

Excursions near Lençóis and in the Chapada Diamantina

There are more than 24 tour operators in Lençóis and visiting even the most distant sights on a tour (or an extended hike) is straightforward. Most tours tend to be car-based and rather sedentary as these are more profitable. The most impressive sights in the Chapada are included in the standard packages. Most have an entrance fee. These include the extensive **Gruta do Lapa Doce**, US$3.50, and **Pratinha** caves, US$3.50 (the latter are cut through by glassy blue water). The tabletop mountains at the **Morro de Pai Inácio**, US$1.50, 30 km from Lençóis, offer the best view of the Chapada, especially at sunset. The 384-m-high **Cachoeira da Fumaça** (Smoke Waterfall, also called **Glass**) is the second highest in Brazil and lies deeper within the park, 2½ hours hike from the village of **Capão**. The view is astonishing; the updraft of the air currents often makes the water flow back up creating the 'smoke' effect. The **Rio Marimbus** flows through an area of semi-swamp reminiscent of the Pantanal and very rich in birdlife while the **Rio Mucugezinho** plunges over the blood-red **Cachoeira do Diabo** in an extensive area of *cerrado* just below the craggy **Roncador** (snorer) waterfall. Near Lençóis, visit the **Serrano** with its wonderful natural pools in the river bed, which give a great hydromassage, or the **Salão de Areia**, where the coloured sands for the bottle paintings come from. **Ribeirão do Meio** is a 45-minute walk from town; here locals slide down a long natural water chute into a big pool (it is best to be shown the way it is done and to take something to slide in). Also near Lençóis are two very pretty waterfalls, the **Cachoeira da Primavera** and the **Cachoeira Sossego**, a 'picture postcard' cascade plunging into a swimming pool.

Listings Inland from Salvador

Where to stay

Lençóis

$$$$-$$$ Canto das Águas
Av Senhor dos Passos, T075-3334 1154,
www.lencois.com.br.
Riverside hotel with a/c or fan, pool, efficient, best rooms are in the new wing. A Roteiro de Charme hotel.

$$$ Casa da Geleia
R Gen Viveiros 187, T075-3334 1151,
www.casadageleia.com.br/.
6 smart chalets in a huge garden at the entrance to the town, English spoken, good breakfast, home-made jam, information on birdwatching and hikes.

$$$ Hotel de Lençóis
R Altinha Alves 747, T075-3334 1102,
www.hoteldelencois.com.br.
Rooms organized in terraces set in a grassy garden on the edge of the park. Good breakfast, pool and restaurant.

$$$ Pousada Vila Serrano
R Alto do Bonfim 8, T075-3334 1486,
www.vilaserrano.com.br.
Great little mock-colonial *pousada* in a small garden 5 mins from town centre. Excellent service, welcoming, excursions organized.

$$$-$$ Estalagem de Alcino
R Gen Viveiros 139, T075-3334 1171,
www.alcinoestalagem.com.
An enchanting, beautifully restored house furnished with 19th-century antiques. Most have shared bathrooms. Superb breakfast served in hummingbird-filled garden. Highly recommended.

$$ Casa de Hélia
R da Muritiba 3, T075-3334 1143,
www.casadehelia.com.br.
Attractive little guesthouse, English and some Hebrew spoken, good facilities, legendary breakfast. Recommended.

$$-$ Pousada dos Duendes
R do Pires, T075-3334 1229,
www.pousadadosduendes.com.

English-run *pousada*, shared hot showers, breakfast and other meals (vegetarians and vegans catered for), welcoming, comfortable. Their tour agency (**H2O Expeditions**) arranges tours and treks from 1-11 days and more, Olivia Taylor is very helpful.

$ pp Hostel Lençóis
R Urbano Duarte 121, T075-3334 1497,
www.hostelchapada.com.br.
A large, well-run hostel with an adventure sports agency in one of the town's grand old houses. Singles, en suite doubles (**$$**) and single-sex 4- to 6-room dorms; shared kitchen and a large garden with hammocks.

Camping

Camping Lumiar
Near Rosário church in centre, T075-9984 1300,
http://pousadaecampinglumiar.com.br.
With popular restaurant. Recommended.

Restaurants

Cachoeira

$ Café com Arte Sebo Ana Néri
R 13 de Maio 16.
Petiscos, good coffee, beer and art from local and international artists.

$ Casa Comercial NS Rosário o Recanto do Misticismo
Praça da Aclamação s/n.
Typically 'Cachoeira', pizza café and restaurant with 2 Candomblé-inspired shrines, live music.

$ Pouso da Palavra
Praça da Aclamação s/n.
Arty little café in a cosy period house, owned by poet Damário Da Cruz, exhibitions of local artists' work, CDs, souvenirs and beautiful mandala candle shades for sale.

Lençóis

$$$ Cozinha Aberta
Rui Barbosa 42, T075-3334 1321,
www.cozinhaaberta.com.br.
The best in town with organic and slow food from Paulistana chef Deborah Doitschinoff. Just east of main *praça*.

$$ Neco's
Praça Maestro Clarindo Pachêco 15, T075-3334 1179.
Neco and his wife offer a set meal of local dishes of the kind eaten by the *garimpeiros*.

Bars and clubs

Lençóis

Fazendinha e Tal
Rua das Pedras 125.
Very popular bar with rustic *garimpeiro* decoration serving hundreds of different *cachaças* and with occasional live music.

Festivals

Cachoeira

24 Jun São João, 'Carnival of the Interior' celebrations include dangerous games with fireworks.
Early Aug Nossa Sehora da Boa Morte is also a major festival.
4 Dec A famous Candomblé ceremony at the Fonte de Santa Bárbara.

Shopping

Lençóis

The Mon morning market is recommended. There is a local craft market just off the main *praça* every night.
Instrumentos, *R das Pedras 78, T075-3334 1334.* Unusual faux-Brazilian and African musical instruments by quirky ex-pat Argentine Jorge Fernando.
Zambumbeira, *R das Pedras at Tamandare, T075-3334 1207.* Beautiful ceramics by renowned artisans like Zé Caboclo, jewellery, walking sticks and arty bric-a-brac.

What to do

Lençóis

Body and soul
The Chapada is a centre for alternative treatments and there are many practitioners. Ask on arrival for recommendations.

Guides
Each *pousada* generally has a guide attached to it to take residents on tours, about US$20-30. The following are recommended:
Edmilson (known locally as Mil), *R Domingos B Souza 70, T075-3334 1319.* Knows the region extremely well, knowledgeable and reliable.
Roy Funch, *T075-3334 1305, funchroy@yahoo.com.* The ex-director of the Chapada Diamantina

National Park is an excellent guide and has written a visitor guide to the park in English. (Recommended as the best information on history, geography and trails of the Chapada.) Highly recommended. He can be booked through www.elabrasil.com from the USA or UK.
Luiz Krug, *contact via Vila Serrano, T075-3334 1102*. An independent, English-speaking guide specializing in geology and caving.
Trajano, *contact via Vila Serrano or Casa da Hélia, T075-3334 1143*. Speaks English and some Hebrew and is a good-humoured guide for treks to the bottom of the Cachoeira da Fumaça.
Zé Carlos, *T075-3334 1151, through Casa da Geleia or Vila Serrano*. The best guide for birding.

Tour operators
Chapada Adventure, *Av 7 de Setembro 7, T075-3334 2037, www.chapadaadventure.com.br*. A small operator offering good value car-based tours, cycling, riding, canoeing and light hiking throughout the Chapada.
Fora da Trilha, *R das Pedras 202, www.forada trilha.com.br*. Longer hikes and light adventures, from canyoning to rapelling.

Venturas e Aventuras, *Praça Horácio de Matos 20, T075-3334 1428*. Excellent trekking expeditions, up to 6 days.

Transport

Cachoeira
Bus From **Salvador** (Camurjipe) every hr or so from 0530; **Feira Santana**, 2 hrs, US$5.

Lençóis
Air Airport, Km 209, BR-242, 20 km from town T075-3625 8100. (Azul, www.voeazul.com.br) fly from **Salvador** twice weekly, otherwise air taxi.

Bus Terminal, T075-3334 1112. **Rápido Federal** from **Salvador** 4 a day, US$22, *convencional* via Feira de Santana. Book in advance, especially at weekends and holidays. For the rest of Bahia state change at Feira de Santana; it is not necessary to go via Salvador. Buses also from **Recife**, **Ibotirama**, **Barreiras** or **Palmas** (for Jalapão), **Chapada dos Veadeiros** and **Brasília**, 16 hrs (all with transfer in Seabra, several buses daily).

idyllic beaches, tourist resorts and a marine reserve

On the coast south of Salvador is a whole string of popular resorts. It was on this part of what is now Brazil that the Portuguese first made landfall. Bahia's north coast runs from the Coconut Highway onto the Green Line, to give of an idea of how the shore looks, and don't forget the beaches there.

Tinharé, Morro de São Paulo and Boipeba *Colour map 7, A6.*
Valença, a town 271 km south of Salvador, is at the mouth of the Rio Una, which enters an enormous region of mangrove swamps. The river estuary and the swamps separate Tinharé, 1½ hours south of Valença by boat, from the mainland and it is hard to tell which is land and which is water. Some say that Tinharé is a mini archipelago rather than a large island. The most popular beaches are at Morro de São Paulo, a tourism hotspot. Immediately south is the island of **Boipeba**, separated from Tinharé by the Rio do Inferno. Accommodation is split between Velha Boipeba, the little town where the riverboat ferry arrives, the adjacent beach, Boca da Barra, which is more idyllic and the fishing village Moreré. This is a two-hour walk or half an hour's boat ride south, US$25 minimum (high tide only). Boipeba's community tourism association is at www.ilhaboipeba.org.br.
   Morro de São Paulo is on the headland at the northernmost tip of Tinharé, lush with ferns, palms and birds of paradise. The village is dominated by the lighthouse and the ruins of a colonial fort (1630), built as a defence against European raiders. It has a landing place on the sheltered landward side, dominated by the old gateway of the fortress. From the lighthouse a path leads to a ruined look out with cannon, which has panoramic views. The fort is a good point to watch the sunset from. Dolphins can be seen in August. Fonte de Ceu waterfall is reached by walking along the beach to **Gamboa** then inland. Watch the tide; it's best to take a guide, or take a boat back to Morro (US$8-12). The beaches, numbered Primeira to Quinta (First to Fifth) are progressively quieter the further south you go. From town to Quarta Praia is 40 minutes on foot, but VW buses, motorbikes and buggies run to the beaches and there is a service to Boipeba. On 7 September there's a big festival with live music on the beach. **Tourist office** ① *Praça Aureliano Lima, T075-3652 1083, see http://morrodesaopaulo.com.br.* **Note** There is a port tax of US$3.50 payable at the prefeitura on arrival, and US$1 on leaving the island.

☆Itacaré

This picturesque fishing village sits in the midst of remnant Atlantic Coast rainforest at the mouth of the Rio de Contas. Some of Bahia's best beaches stretch north and south. A few are calm and crystal clear, the majority are great for surfing. There are plenty of beaches within walking distance of town. Itacaré is a surf resort for Paulistanos and is very busy with Brazilian tourists in high season. Much of the accommodation here is tasteful, blending in with the natural landscape and there are many excellent restaurants and lively if still low key nightlife. *Pousadas* are concentrated in town and around the Praias da Coroinha and Concha, the first beaches to the north and south of the town centre. Besides surfing, operators are now offering trekking and mountain biking trips in the Mata Atlântica, off-roading, rafting, waterfall-climbing and other adrenalin activities. North of Itacaré is the **Peninsula de Maraú**, fringed with beautiful beaches to its tip at **Barra Grande**. To explore the area fully you will need a car or to take a tour. **Secretaria Municipal de Turismo de Itacaré** ① *R Lodônio Almeida 160 s 4, T073-3251 3922, sec.turismo@ itacare.ba.gov.br; see www.itacare.com.br.*

Ilhéus *Colour map 7, A6.*

At the mouth of the Rio Cachoeira, 462 km south of Salvador, the port serves a district which produces 65% of all Brazilian cocoa. A bridge links the north bank of the river with Pontal, where the airport is located. Ilhéus is the birthplace of Jorge Amado (1912-2002) and the setting of one of his most famous novels, *Gabriela, cravo e canela* (Gabriela, Clove and Cinnamon). The church of **São Jorge** (1556), the city's oldest, is on the Praça Rui Barbosa; it has a small museum. **Secretária de Turismo** ① *on the beach opposite Praça Castro Alves; see www.brasilheus.com.br.*

North of Ilhéus, two good beaches are Marciano, with reefs offshore and good surfing, and Barra, 1 km further north at the mouth of the Rio Almada. South of the river, Pontal beaches can be reached by 'Barreira' bus; alight just after Hotel Jardim Atlântico. Between Ilhéus and **Olivença** are more fine beaches. At nearby **Una** there is an important wildlife sanctuary and ecopark devoted to protecting the golden-faced tamarin, the **Reserva Biológica de Una**. Further south, 52 km, is **Canavieiras**, a former cocoa port, now a fishing port with a colonial centre and restaurants at the harbour. Its beach, Ilha de Atalaia, with *barracas* (thatched bars), surfing and kite-surfing is getting onto the tourist map. There are *pousadas* in town and a five-star resort some 40 km away.

Porto Seguro and the Discovery Coast *Colour map 7, A6.*

About 400 km south of Ilhéus on the coast is the old town of Porto Seguro. In 1500, Pedro Álvares Cabral sighted land at Monte Pascoal south of Porto Seguro. As the sea here was too open, he sailed north in search of a secure protected harbour, entering the mouth of the Rio Burnahém to find the harbour he later called Porto Seguro (safe port). Where the first mass was celebrated, a cross marks the spot on the road between Porto Seguro and Santa Cruz Cabrália. A rather uncoordinated tourist village, **Coroa Vermelha**, has sprouted at the site of Cabral's first landfall, 20 minutes by bus to the north of Porto Seguro.

Porto Seguro itself is Bahia's second most popular tourist destination, with charter flights from Rio and São Paulo and plenty of hustle and bustle. Contact the **Secretária de Turismo de Porto Seguro** ① *Praça dos Pataxós, T073-3288 3708.* Information desk at Praça Manoel Ribeiro Coelho 10.

To its historical quarter, **Cidade Histórica**, take a wide, steep, unmarked path uphill from the roundabout at the entrance to town. Three churches (Nossa Senhora da Misericórdia (1530), Nossa Senhora do Rosário (1534), and Nossa Senhora da Pena (1718), the former jail, Casa de Câmara e Cadêia (now a sacred art museum) and the monument marking the landfall of Gonçalo Coelho comprise a small, peaceful place with lovely gardens and panoramic views.

Only 10 minutes north of Coroa Vermelha, **Santa Cruz Cabrália** is a delightful small town at the mouth of the Rio João de Tiba, with a splendid beach, river port, and a 450-year-old church with a fine view. A good trip from here is to Coroa Alta, a reef 50 minutes away by boat, passing along the tranquil river to the reef and its crystal waters and good snorkelling. A 15-minute river crossing by ferry to a new road opposite gives access to the deserted beaches of **Santo André** and **Santo Antônio**.

☆Arraial da Ajuda *Colour map 7, A6.*

Immediately across the Rio Buranhém south from Porto Seguro is the village of Arraial da Ajuda, the gateway to the idyllic beaches of the south coast. Set high on a cliff, there are great views of the coastline from behind the church of Nossa Senhora da Ajuda in the main *praça*. Each August there is a pilgrimage to the shrine of Nossa Senhora da Ajuda. Ajuda has become more popular than Porto Seguro with younger tourists and independent travellers and there are many *pousadas*, restaurants, bars and small shops. In high season there are frequent parties on the road to the beach. At Brazilian holiday times it is very crowded. The town has a famous capoeira school (with classes for foreigners).

The **beaches**, several protected by a coral reef, are splendid. During daylight hours those closest to town (take 'R da Praia' out of town to the south) are extremely busy; excellent *barracas* sell good seafood, drinks, and play music. The best beaches are Mucugê, Pitinga and Taípé.

☆Trancoso

Some 15 km from Ajuda, 25 km south of Porto Seguro by paved road, is Trancoso. This pretty, peaceful town, with its beautiful beaches (Praia dos Nativos is the most famous), has become very chic, with the rich and famous from home and abroad buying properties and shopping in the little boutiques. In summer it can get packed. Trancoso has a historic church, **São João Batista** (1656). From the end of Praça São João there is a fine coastal panorama.

Caraíva and around

This atmospheric, peaceful fishing village on the banks of the Rio Caraíva, 65 km south of Porto Seguro, has marvellous beaches and is a real escape from the more developed Trancoso and Porto Seguro. Despite the difficulty of getting there, it is becoming increasingly popular. Good walks are north to Praia do Satu and, across a headland, Praia Espelho (9 km), or 6 km south to a Pataxó village, Barra Velha (watch the tides). The high season is December-February and July; the wettest months are April-June and November. Use flip-flops for walking the sand streets and take a torch. There are no medical facilities and only rudimentary policing. There are a series of super-luxurious isolated resorts 10 km south of Caraíva at the Ponta do Corumbau.

Parque Nacional de Monte Pascoal *Colour map 7, A6.*
Office: R do Mamoeiro 25, Taperapuã, Porto Seguro, T073-3288 1633, parquemontepascoal@icmbio.gov.br.

Caraíva is the northern entrance to the Parque Nacional de Monte Pascoal, set up in 1961 to preserve the flora and fauna of the coastal area in which Europeans made landfall in Brazil. Another 14 km paved access road leaves the BR-101 at Km 796. There are three trails which cost US$13-16 to walk; guides US$2 per person. Visits can be organized through **Mata N'ativa** in Trancoso (see page 548).

Caravelas and around *Colour map 7, A6.*

Further south still, 107 km from Itamaraju, is this charming town, rapidly developing for tourism, a major trading town in 17th and 18th centuries. Its in the mangroves; the beaches are 10 km away at Barra de Caravelas (hourly buses), a fishing village. There are food shops, restaurants and bars.

The **Parque Nacional Marinho dos Abrolhos** is 70 km east of Caravelas. Day trips leave from Caravelas and take about 2½ hours to reach the archipelago. Humpback whales are invariably seen between July and November. Abrolhos is an abbreviation of *Abre os olhos*: 'Open your eyes' from Amérigo Vespucci's exclamation when he first sighted the reef in 1503. Established in 1983, the park consists of five small islands (Redonda, Siriba, Guarita, Sueste, Santa Bárbara), which are volcanic in origin, and several coral reefs. The warm current and shallow waters (8-15 m deep) make for a rich undersea life (about 160 species of fish) and good snorkelling. The park is best visited in October-March, entry is US$7.50 (half price for Brazilians). Diving is best December to February. Permission from **Parque Nacional Marinho dos Abrolhos** ① *Praia do Kitongo s/n, Caravelas, Bahia 45900, T073-3297 2258, www.icmbio.gov.br/parnaabrolhos*. Visitors can't stay on the islands, but may stay overnight on schooners. Visits and permits can be organized through **Portomondo** in Porto Seguro, **Mata N'ativa** in Trancoso, or in Caravelas (see page 548).

Where to stay

Tinharé, Morro de São Paulo and Boipeba

Morro de São Paulo

There are many cheap *pousadas* and rooms to rent near the fountain (Fonte Grande) but this part of town is very hot at night. The beaches are backed by hotels for about 20 km south of town.

$$$$-$$$ Pousada Farol do Morro
Primeira Praia, T075-3652 1036,
www.faroldomorro.com.br.
Little huts running up the hill all with a sea view and served by a private funicular railway, pool.

$$$ Pousada Vista Bela
R da Biquinha 15, T075-3652 1001,
www.vistabelapousada.com.
Owner Petruska is extremely welcoming, good rooms, those to the front have good views and are cooler, all have fans, hammocks. Price depends on season and type of room.

$$$-$$ Pousada Colibri
R do Porto de Cima 5, T075-3652 1056,
www.pousada-colibri.com.
6 apartments up some steep steps. Cool, always a breeze blowing, excellent views, Helmut, the owner, speaks English and German.

$$ Pousada Ilha do Sol
Primeira Praia, T075-3652 1457,
www.minhapousadailhadosol.com.br.
Modest but scrupulously clean, good views.

Terceira Praia (3rd beach)

$$$ Fazenda Vila Guaiamú
T075-3652 1035, www.vilaguaiamu.com.br.
7 tastefully decorated chalets set in tropical gardens visited by marmosets, tanagers and rare cotingas, excellent food. The hotel has a spa and the Italian photographer-owner runs an eco-tourism project protecting a rare species of crab which lives in the fazenda's river. Guided walks available. Highly recommended.

$$$ Pousada Fazenda Caeira
T075-3652 1310, www.fazendacaeira.com.br.
Spacious, airy chalets in a coconut grove overlooking the sea, good breakfasts, library, games room.

$$$-$$ Village do Dendê
Gamboa, T075-3653 7104, http://
villagedodendechales.yolasite.com.

Close to centre, dock and beach, self-contained 2-room chalets (prices are higher according to season, breakfast and cleaning extra), gardens, restaurant.

Boipeba

$$$ Santa Clara
Boca da Barra, T075-3653 6085,
www.santaclaraboipeba.com.
Californian-owned, with the island's best restaurant, large, tasteful cabins and a good-value room for 4 at $ pp. Therapeutic massages available.

$$$-$$ Pousada Tassimirim
½-hr walk south of town, T075-3653 6030
(R Com Madureira 40, 45400-000 Valença),
http://tassimirim.com.br.
Bungalows, bar, restaurant, including breakfast and dinner.

$$ Horizonte Azul
Boca da Barra, T075-3653 6080,
www.pousadahorizonteazul.com.
Next to Santa Clara, a range of chalets in a hillside garden visited by hundreds of rare birds. Owners speak English and French. Lunch available.

$$ Pousada do Canto
Moreré, T075-3653 6131, http://cantodomorere.
tumblr.com.
A variety of rooms and cabins, some thatched, prices rise in high season, lovely surroundings.

Itacaré

$$$-$$ Art Jungle
T073-99975 0007, http://artjungle.com.br.
8 tree houses and cabins on stilts in a modern sculpture garden in the middle of forest, great views. Relatively unpretentious, with spa.

$ pp Itacaré Hostel
Praça Santos Dumont 2, T073-3251 2402,
www.itacarehostel.com.br.
Pleasant little HI hostel with small doubles $$-$ and dorms (US$11-16 pp, price depends on season and a/c) in an annexe, small pool, internet and TV area.

Ilhéus

Plenty of cheap hotels near the municipal *rodoviária* in centre and *pousadas* along the coast to Olivença. Official list on www.ilheus.ba.gov.br.

$$ Britânia
R Jorge Amado 16, T073-3634 1722.

Reasonable value in the town centre with large rooms in an early 20th-century wooden hotel just west of the Cathedral square.

Porto Seguro

Prices rise steeply Dec-Feb and Jul. Off-season rates can drop by 50%, for stays of more than 3 nights negotiate.

$$$ Estalagem Porto Seguro
R Marechal Deodoro 66, T073-3288 2095,
www.hotelestalagem.com.br.
In an old colonial house, relaxing atmosphere, pool, good breakfast. Highly recommended.

$$ Pousada dos Navegantes
Av 22 de Abril 212, T073-3288 2390.
A/c, pool, conveniently located.

Camping

Camping Mundaí Praia
T073-3679 2287, www.campingmundai.com.br.
Good value.

Santa Cruz Cabrália

$$$-$$ Terra Morena
Vila de Santo André, T073-3671 4060,
www.pousadaterramorena.com.br.
Delightful small pousada set in gardens by the river in sleepy Santo André village. Cosy cabins, great macrobiotic food, massage and excursions to beaches and islands.

Arraial da Ajuda

At busy times, don't expect to find much under US$20 pp in a shared room for a minimum stay of 5-7 days. Camping is best at these times.

$$$$ Pousada Pitinga
Praia Pitinga, T073-3575 1067,
www.pousadapitinga.com.br.
Bold architecture amid Atlantic forest, a hideaway, great food and pool, a Roteiros de Charme hotel.

$$$ Pousada Erva Doce
Estrada do Mucugê 200, T073-3575 1113,
www.ervadoce.com.br.
Good restaurant, well-appointed chalets (more expensive in high season).

$$ Pousada do Roballo
T073-3575 1053, www.pousadadoroballo.com.br.
Welcoming with a tiny pool and rooms with little verandas in gardens.

$$ Pousada Flamboyant
Estrada do Mucugê 89, T073-3575 1025,
www.flamboyant.tur.br.
Pleasant courtyard, pool, good breakfast.

$ pp Hostel Arraial
R do Campo 94, T073-3575 1192,
www.arraialdajudahostel.com.br.
Backpacker hostel with HI discounts, more expensive in Jan, private rooms **$$**, with breakfast, snack bar, pool, good location at the top of town.

Trancoso

$$$$ Etnia
Estrada Velha do Arraial (just west of the Quadrado), T073-3668 1137,
www.etniabrasil.com.br.
Very chic, well-run and beautifully kept *pousada* set in shady, hilly lawned gardens. Fashionable.

$$$$-$$$ Mata N'ativa
Estrada Velha do Arraial (next to the river on the way to the beach), T073-3668 1830,
www.matanativapousada.com.br.
The best in town, a series of elegant cabins in a lovingly maintained garden by the riverside, cheaper in low season. Owners Daniel and Daniela are very hospitable and run one of the few hotels to adopt environmental best practice. Good English, Spanish and Italian. Tours throughout the region, Recommended. Small tour agency runs high quality boat, cycle trips and excursions along the southern Bahian coast.

$$$ Capim Santo
T073-3668 1122, to the left of the main praça,
www.capimsanto.com.br.
With breakfast and the best restaurant in Trancoso. Recommended.

$ pp Café Esmeralda
On the Quadrado (main praça), T073-3668 1527,
Facebook: Café-Esmeralda-Albergue-Pousada.
Small rooms with fan at a locally owned café which serves good breakfast and lunch.

Caraíva

$$$$ Le Paxa
Rua da Praia s/n, T073-99926 6621.
2 rustic chic raw wood cabins set in a garden in front of the beach, luxuriously decked out with a huge bed draped in Egyptian cotton, bric-a-brac collected over a lifetime of travelling by the Franco-Brazilian owners and cooled by gorgeous wood shutters letting the breeze in right off the

sea. 80% of the money from the pousada goes to supporting local community projects. One of the best places in Bahia.

$$$ Vila do Mar
R 12 de Outubro s/n, T073-99942 3877 www.pousadaviladomar.com.br.
The plushest hotel in town, with spacious, stylish airy, wooden *cabanas* overlooking the beach set on a lawn around an adult and children's pool.

$$$-$$ Pousada San Antonio
Praia de Caraíva, T073-99999 9552, www.pousadasanantonio.com.br.
Pleasant, simple, colourful rooms in a garden, by the beach, breezy public areas, with breakfast. Has 2 properties.

Caravelas

$$$ Pousada Liberdade
Av Ministro Adalicio Nogueira 1551, T073-3297 2415, www.pousadaliberdade.com.br.
Spacious chalets in a large garden, just outside town centre. Diving excursions to Abrolhos arranged.

$$ Pousada Caravelense
Praça Teófilo Otoni 2, T073-3297 1182.
TV, fridge, good breakfast, excellent restaurant. Recommended.

Restaurants

Tinharé, Morro de São Paulo and Boipeba
There are plenty of restaurants in Morro de São Paulo town and on the 2nd and 3rd beaches. Most are OK though somewhat overpriced. For cheap eats stay in a *pousada* which includes breakfast, stock up at the supermarket and buy seafood snacks at the *barracas* on the 2nd beach.

$$ Belladonna
On the main street. Evenings only.
Good Italian restaurant with great music, a good meeting point, owner Guido speaks Italian, English and French.

$$ Chez Max
3rd beach.
Simple but decent seafood in a pretty restaurant overlooking the sea.

$ Comida Natural
On the main street.
Good breakfasts, *comida a kilo*, good juices.

Itacaré
There are lots of restaurants in Itacaré, mostly on R Lodônio Almeida. Menus here are increasingly chic and often include a respectable wine list.

$$$ Casa Sapucaia
R Lodônio Almeida, T073-3251 3091.
Sophisticated Bahian food with an international twist.

$$ Boca de Forno
R Lodônio Almeida 134, T073-3251 2174.
The busiest restaurant in Itacaré, serving good wood-fired pizzas in tasteful surroundings.

$ Casa Martins
R Pedro Longo 150, T073-3251 2446.
One of the few restaurants with a *prato feto*, and a mixed seafood menu.

Porto Seguro
Several restaurants on the town's streets and many snack bars along the waterfront and river.

$$ da Japonêsa
Praça Pataxós 38. Open 0800-2300.
Excellent value with varied menu. Recommended.

$$-$ Portinha
R Saldanha Marinho 33, T073-3288 2743.
Lively little self-service restaurant in a square near the river. Good variety and great puddings.

Arraial da Ajuda
Recommended *barracas* are **Tem Q Dá** and **Agito** on Mucugê beach and **Barraca de Pitinga** and **Barraca do Genésio** on Pitinga.

$$$ Don Fabrizio
Estrada do Mucugê 402, T073-3575 1123.
The best Italian in town, in an upmarket open air restaurant with live music and reasonable wine.

$$$ Manguti
Estrada do Mucugê, T073-3575 2270, www.manguti.com.br.
Reputed by some to be the best in town, meat, pasta, fish alongside other Brazilian dishes. Very popular and informal.

$$ Pizzaria do Arraial
Praça São Bras 28.
Basic pizzeria and pay by weight restaurant.

$ Mineirissima
Estrada do Mucugê, T073-3575 3790. Opens until late but menu service only after 1800.
Good value pay by weight with very filling Minas Gerais food and *moquecas*.

$ Paulinho Pescador
Praça São Bras 116. Open 1200-2200, closed Mon.
Excellent seafood, also chicken and meat, one price, English spoken, good service, popular, there are often queues for tables.

Trancoso

Food in Trancoso is expensive. Those on a tight budget should shop at the supermarket between the main square and the new part of town. There are numerous fish restaurants in the *barracas* on the beach. None is cheap.

$$$ Cacau
Praça São João, Quadrado, T073-3668 1266,
http://ocacautrancoso.com.br.
One of the best in town with a varied international and Brazilian menu. Pleasant surrounds.

$$$ Capim Santo
Praça São João, Quadrado, T073-3668 1122,
http://capimsanto.com.br.
Wonderful Brazilian-European fusion cooking in intimate garden surroundings. Great caipirinhas.

$ Portinha
Praça do Quadrado s/n, T073-3668 1054,
http://portinha.com.br
The only place serving food at a reasonable price. Excellent pay by weight options and good if overpriced juices.

Caraíva

There is *forró* dancing 0100-0600 at **Pelé** and **Ouriços** on alternate nights in season.

$$ Boteco do Pará
T073-9959 1276, http://botecodoparacaraiva.
com.br. By the river, just east of the 'port'.
Serves the best fish in the village. Also has simple lodging, **Pousada da Canoa**.

Bars and clubs

Tinharé, Morro de São Paulo and Boipeba

Morro de São Paulo

There is always plenty going on in Morro. The liveliest bars are **87** and **Jamaica**, both on the 2nd beach. These tend to get going after 2300 when the restaurants in town empty.

Itacaré

There is frequent extemporaneous *forró* and other live music all over the city and most restaurants and bars have some kind of music between Oct and Apr.

Porto Seguro

Porto Seguro is famous for the lambada. There are lots of bars and street cafés on Av Portugal.

Porto Prego
R Pedro Álvares Cabral.
A good bar for live music, small cover charge.

Arraial da Ajuda

Many top Brazilian bands play at the beach clubs at Praia do Parracho during the summer, entry is about US$15. Entry to other beach parties is about US$8. There is also a capoeira institute: R da Capoeira 57, T073-3575 2981, www.capoeirasuldabahia.com.br.

Festivals

Ilhéus

17-20 Jan Festa de São Sebastião.
Feb/Mar Carnival.
23 Apr Festa de São Jorge.
28 Jun Foundation day.
Oct Festa do Cacau throughout the month.

What to do

Trancoso

Mata N'ativa Travel, *T073-8804 6830,*
matanativapousada.com.br. Whale-watching, trips to the southern beaches, wildlife visits to Estação Veracel, mountain biking and canoeing.
Pataxo Turismo, *Shopping Rio Mar, loja 3, Passarela do Alcool, T073-3288 1256, www.pataxo turismo.com.br.* An excellent little tour operator offering light adventure trips throughout the region including to Pataxó communities, Monte Pascoal, whale watching and diving around the Abrolhos and to the Jequitinonha delta.
Portomondo, *Trancoso, T073-3668 1373, www. portomondo.com.* Tours from around Arraial, Trancoso, Caraíva and Corumbau to Jaqueira, Veracel, Monte Pascoal and Abrolhos. Excellent diving and ecotourism itineraries and car or helicopter transfers to hotels in Trancoso and further south.

Transport

Tinharé, Morro de São Paulo and Boipeba
Air Air taxi from Salvador airport US$135 1-way, 20 mins, **Addey** T073-3377 1393, www.addey. com.br, and **Aerostar** T073-3377 4406, www. aerostar.com.br.

Ferry From Salvador, several companies operate a speed boat and catamaran (1½ hrs) service from the Terminal Marítimo in front of the Mercado Modelo to Morro de São Paulo, US$27-32. 4 boats daily (last about 1400). Times vary according to the weather and season. **Catamara Gamboa do Morro**, T075-99975 6395. Part of the trip is on the open sea, which can be rough. Boats leave every day from **Valença** for Gamboa (1½ hrs) and Morro de São Paulo (1½ hrs) from the main bridge in Valença 5 times a day (signalled by a loud whistle). The fare is US$5. A *lancha rápida* taking 25 mins travels the route between Valença and Morro, US$15. Only boats between 0530-1100 from Salvador to Valença (5 hrs, US$14) connect with ferries. For the shortest route to Valença, take the ferry from São Joaquim to Bom Despacho on Itaparica island, from where it is 130 km to Valença via Nazaré das Farinhas by Camarujipe bus, 2 hrs, US$5. If not stopping in Valença, get the bus by the main bridge in town (the *rodoviária* is a long way from the ferry). Private boat hire can be arranged if you miss the ferry schedule. There is a regular boat from Valença to Boipeba Mon-Sat 1230 (check tide), return 1500-1700, 4 hrs, US$7; speedboats charge US$18. The Salvador–Morro catamaran at 0900 connects with a boat to Boipeba at 1200, US$77 total fare. Also, Mon-Sat bus Valença–Torrinha at 1100 (plus 1400 in summer) connects with a boat to Boipeba, 2½ hrs.

Itacaré

Bus The *rodoviária* is a few mins' walk from town. Porters are on hand with barrows to help with luggage. Frequent buses 0700-1900 to **Ilhéus** (the nearest town with an airport), 45 mins, US$4 along the paved road. To **Salvador**, change at **Ubaitaba** (3 hrs, US$4) or Ilhéus; Ubaitaba–Salvador, 6 hrs, US$22, several daily.

Ilhéus

Air Daily flights to **Salvador** in high season with **Gol** and others.

Bus *Rodoviária* is 4 km from the centre on Itabuna road. Several daily to **Salvador**, 8 hrs, US$36.50, **Aguia Branca**. To **Eunápolis**, 4 hrs, US$13-18. Local buses leave from Praça Cairu.

Porto Seguro

Air Airport T073-3288 1880. Regular flights from **Rio**, **São Paulo**, **Salvador** and **Belo Horizonte**. Taxi airport–Porto Seguro, US$5. Also buses.

Bus From Porto Seguro: **Salvador Aguia Branca**, once daily, 12 hrs, US$56. **Eunápolis**, 1 hr, US$5. For **Rio** direct bus (**São Geraldo**), leaving at 1700, US$68, 19 hrs, from Rio direct at 2100, or take bus for Ilhéus and change at Eunápolis. Other services go via Eunápolis (bus to/from Salvador 10-11 hrs, US$35-40) or Itabuna (5 hrs, US$14-18). Buses for **Caraíva** via Trancoso leave from the town centre ferry dock (0700, 1130 and 1530, 3-4 hrs) with an additional service via Eunápolis and Itabela. There are services every 30 mins or so from the other side of the ferry dock in Arraial d'Ajuda to Trancoso. Buses for **Santa Cruz Cabrália** go via Eunápolis (6 daily, 1 hr from Eunápolis).

The *rodoviária* has reliable luggage store and lounge on the 3rd floor, on the road to Eunápolis, 2 km from the centre, regular bus service (30 mins) through the city to the old *rodoviária* near the port. Local buses US$0.50. Taxis charge US$5 from the *rodoviária* to the town.

Bicycle hire Oficina de Bicicleta, Av Getúlio Vargas e R São Pedro, about US$12 for 24 hrs. Also at Praça de Bandeira and at 2 de Julho 242.

Car hire Several companies at the airport.

Arraial da Ajuda

Ferry Across the Rio Buranhém from Porto Seguro take 15 mins to the south bank, US$0.75 for foot passengers, US$6 for cars, every 30 mins day and night. It's a further 5 km to Arraial da Ajuda, bus US$1; combi US$1.35 pp; taxi US$8.

Trancoso

Bus Buses run regularly on the paved road between Porto Seguro, Ajuda and Trancoso, at least every hour in high season: US$4 Porto Seguro–Trancoso, US$2.50 Ajuda–Trancoso. Arriving from the south, change buses at Eunápolis from where the Linha Verde road runs, several buses daily.

Caraíva and around

Caraíva can only be reached by canoe across the river, US$2.50 return. Access roads are poor and almost impossible after heavy rain. For buses from Porto Seguro via Trancoso, see above.

Parque Nacional de Monte Pascoal

From Caraíva there is a river crossing by boats which are always on hand. Buses run from **Itamaraju** 16 km to the south, at 0600 Fri-Mon.

Caravelas

Bus To **Texeira de Freitas** (on the BR-101, 4 a day), **Eunápolis** and **Prado**. Also twice weekly to/from **Porto Seguro**.

Parque Nacional Marinho dos Abrolhos

The journey to the islands takes about 3-4 hrs depending on the sea conditions. Between Jul and early Dec humpback whale sightings are almost guaranteed. Boats leave at 0700 from the Marina Porto Abrolhos just north of Caravelas town centre (around US$50 depending on numbers) and they return at dusk. It is possible to dive or snorkel at Abrolhos. If you are coming from Porto Seguro everything including transfers can be arranged by **Portomondo**, **Pataxó** or **Mata N'ativa** (see page 548). Trips will only run with a minimum number of people so book ahead. From Caravelas, book with **Horizonte Aberto**, Av das Palmeiras 313, T073-3297 1474, www.horizonteaberto.com.br, or **Catamarã Sanuk**, T073-3297 1344, T073-98871 6634, http://abrolhos.net. Both companies can organize multi-day live aboard dive trips.

beautiful beaches and remote villages

The paved BA-099 coast road from near Salvador airport is known as the Estrada do Côco (Coconut Highway), because of the many plantations and for 50 km passes some beautiful beaches.

☆Beaches

The best known from south to north are **Ipitanga** (with its reefs), **Buraquinho**, **Jauá** (with reefs, surfing, pools at low tide, clean water), **Arembepe** (famous hippy village in 1960s with a Tamar turtle protection project, T071-3624 3694, cv.arembepe@tamar.org.br), **Guarajuba**, **Itacimirim**, **Castelo Garcia D'Ávila** (with its 16th-century fort) and **Forte**. Regular buses serve most of these destinations.

Praia do Forte

The former fishing village, 80 km north of Salvador, takes its name from the castle built by a Portuguese settler, Garcia D'Ávila, in 1556 to warn the city to the south of enemy invasion. Praia do Forte is now a pleasant resort town with lovely beaches and all but one of the streets of sand. Inland from the coast is a restinga forest, which grows on sandy soil with a very delicate ecosystem. Near the village is a small *pantanal* (marshy area), which is host to a large number of birds, caimans and other animals. Birdwatching trips on the Pantanal are rewarding. The **Tamar Project** ① *Av Farol Garcia D'Ávila s/n, T071-3676 0321, www.projetotamar.org.br,* preserves the sea turtles which lay their eggs in the area. Praia do Forte is now the headquarters of the national turtle preservation programme and is funded by the Worldwide Fund for Nature. Praia do Forte is ideal for windsurfing and sailing owing to constant fresh Atlantic breezes.

The coast road north

The Linha Verde (the extension of the Estrada do Coco) runs for 142 km to the border of Sergipe, the next state north; the road is more scenic than the BR-101, especially near Conde. There are very few hotels or *pousadas* in the more remote villages. The most picturesque are **Imbassaí**, **Subaúma**, **Baixio** (very beautiful, where the Rio Inhambupe meets the sea) and **Conde**. Sítio do Conde on the coast, 6 km from Conde, has many *pousadas*, but the beaches are not very good. Sítio do Conde is an ideal base to explore other beaches at Barra do Itariri, 12 km south, at the mouth of a river (fine sunsets). The last stop on the Linha Verde is **Mangue Seco**. A steep hill rising behind the village to tall white sand dunes offers superb view of the coastline. There are plenty of small cheap places to stay along the seafront from the jetty and simple restaurants around the main square next to the church. The beach has a handful of *barracas* serving cheap fish. Access from Sergipe is by boat on the Rio Real from Pontal (10-minute crossing). Buses run between Pontal and Estância twice a day. The ferry across the river usually leaves before 1000 in the morning. There are private launches as well; it is usually possible to find someone to share the ride.

Where to stay

North of Salvador: Jauá

$$$-$$ Lagoa e Mar
Praia de Jauá, T071-3672 1573,
www.hotellagoaemar.com.br.
Very good breakfast, spacious bungalows,
swimming pool, 350 m to beach, restaurant,
helpful, transport to airport, 10% discount to
Footprint owners.

Praia do Forte

The town's main street had its name changed
from Alameda do Sol to Av ACM (no street
numbers marked, so you just walk along to find
the place you want). Prices rise steeply in the
summer season. It may be difficult to find cheap
places to stay.

$$$$ Tivoli Eco-Resort
Av do Farol, T071-3676 4000,
www. tivolihotels.com.
A luxurious family resort owned by the high-end
Tivoli group with a fabulous spa, large pool and
boxy but beautfully appointed rooms set in long
annexes in tropical gardens by the beach at the
entrance to town. Full programme of activities.

$$$ Aloha Brasil Pousada
R da Aurora, T071-3676 0279,
www.pousadaalohabrasil.com.br.
Relaxing tropical garden and pool, charming
rooms with king size beds and verandas.

$$$ Ogum Marinho
Av ACM, T071-3676 1165,
www.ogummarinho.com.br.
A/c, cheaper with fan, nice little courtyard
garden, good restaurant and service. It has
an art gallery with work by Brazilian artists.

$$$ Pousada Tatuapara
Praça dos Artistas 1, T071-3676 1466,
www.tatuapara.com.br.
Spacious and well-maintained, fan, fridge, good
breakfast, pool.

$$$ Sobrado da Vila
Av ACM, T071-3676 1088,
www.sobradodavila.com.br.
Best in the village itself. Rooms with
balconies and a good-value restaurant;
convenient for restaurants.

$$$-$$ Pousada Casa de Praia
Praça dos Artistas 08-09, T071-3676 1362,
www.casadepraia.tur.br.
Good value and location rooms, with and
without a/c, popular.

$$ Pousada João Sol
R da Corvina, T071-3676 1054,
www.pousadajoaosol.com.br.
6 well-appointed chalets. The owner speaks
English, Spanish and German. Great breakfast.

$ pp Albergue da Juventude
Praia do Forte, R da Aurora 3, T071-3676 1094,
www.albergue.com.br.
Smart youth hostel with decent shared rooms
and rooms with en suites ($$), a large breakfast,
fan, kitchen and shop, cheaper for HI members.

Restaurants

Praia do Forte

$$ Bar Do Souza
Av ACM, on the right as you enter the village.
Daily.
Best seafood in town, live music at weekends.
Recommended.

$$ O Europeu
Av ACM, T071-3676 0232.
Anglo/Brazilian-owned, with adventurous menu
well-prepared dishes. Recommended.

$ Cafe Tango
Av ACM, T071-3676 1637.
Pleasant open-air tea and coffee bar with great
pastries and cakes.

$ Casa da Nati
Av ACM, T071-3676 1239.
Per kilo and Bahian food.

$ Point do Ivan
Av ACM, T071-99997 1711.
Bahian food, good *moque, cabobo de camarão*
and cheap *prato feito*.

Transport

Praia do Forte
Bus To **Salvador** (US$3-5): **Linha Verde** from
0530 to 1800 daily, 1½ hrs.

Recife &
the northeast coast

The eight states north of Bahia are historically and culturally rich, but generally poor economically. Recife, Olinda and São Luís are steeped in history, and cultural heritage abounds (eg *forró* and other musical styles, many good museums, lacework, ceramics). There is a multitude of beaches: if established resorts aren't your thing, you don't have to travel far for somewhere more peaceful, while off the beaten track are some which have hardly been discovered.

Pernambuco was the seat of Dutch Brazil in the 17th century. Its capital, Recife, and close neighbour, Olinda, have the most creative music scene in the northeast and their famous wild carnival draws thousands of visitors.

Recife *Colour map 5, B6.*

a busy city with a vibrant culture and varied past

The capital of Pernambuco State, 285 km north of Maceió and 839 km north of Salvador, was founded on reclaimed land by the Dutch prince Maurice of Nassau in 1637 after his troops had burnt Olinda, the original capital. The city centre consists of three portions, always very busy by day; the crowds and the narrow streets, especially in the Santo Antônio district, can make it a confusing city to walk around. Recife has the main dock area, with commercial buildings associated with it. South of the centre is the residential and beach district of Boa Viagem, reached by bridge across the Bacia do Pina. Olinda, the old capital, is 7 km to the north but now absorbed by the conurbation (see page 561).

Sights

Recife Antigo is the 2-km-long island between the ocean and the Rio Beberibe, the heart of old Recife and recently rehabilitated as the spiritual heart of the city, with great nightlife at weekends. **Marco Zero** on Praça Rio Branco is the official centre and focal point for Recife's carnival. Just north is the **Kahal Zur Israel synagogue and museum** (Centro Cultural Judaico) ① *R de Bom Jesus 197, T081-3224 8351, www.kahalzurisrael.com, Tue-Fri 0900-1630, Sun 1400-1700, US$3*, on the old R dos Judeus, has been redeveloped with a museum telling the story of the Jewish presence in Dutch-held Recife in 16th century until Portuguese persecution. On the Praça do Arsenal da Marinha is the **Torre da Malakoff** ① *Praça do Arsenal da Marinha, T081-3184 3182, Tue-Fri 1000-1800, Sat 1500-1800, Sun 1500-1900 free*, the venue works as a cultural centre hosting occasional art exhibitions, music performances and theatre plays, with a good view of the city from the observatory (Sun 1600-2000, free). Continuing north, the church of **Nossa Senhora do Pilar** ① *R de São Jorge*, which has been in the process of refurbishment. **Forte do Brum** ① *Praça Comunidade Lusa Brasileira, T081-3224 7559, Tue-Fri 0900-1630, Sat-Sun 1400-1700, US$0.70* (built by the Dutch in 1629) is an army museum.

> **Fact...**
> Hours of opening of museums, art galleries, churches, etc are published in the *Diário de Pernambuco* and *Jornal do Comércio*. The former's website has lots of tourist information, www.diariodepernambuco.com.br.

Best for
Carnival ▪ Craft ▪ Music

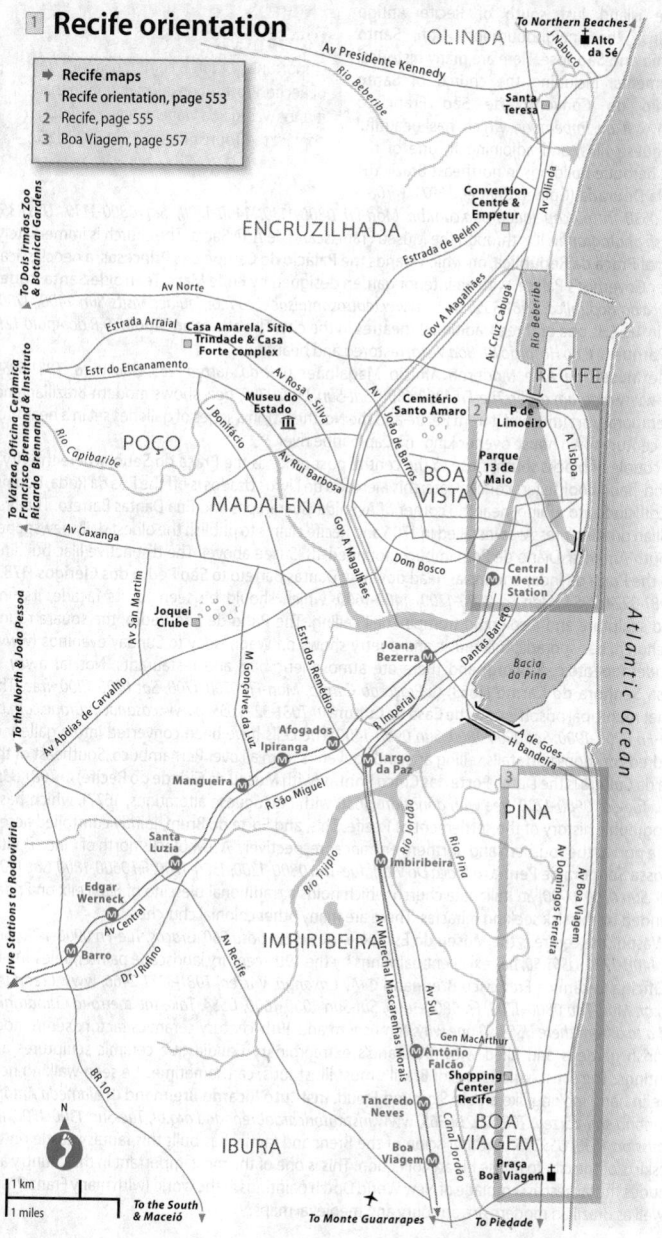

① Recife orientation

➡ **Recife maps**
1 Recife orientation, page 553
2 Recife, page 555
3 Boa Viagem, page 557

OLINDA

Av Presidente Kennedy

Rio Beberibe

To Northern Beaches
J. Nabuco
Alto da Sé

Santa Teresa

Av Cruz Cabugá

Convention Centre & Empetur

ENCRUZILHADA

Estrada de Belem

Gov A Magalhães

Rio Beberibe

RECIFE

To Dois Irmãos Zoo & Botanical Gardens

Av Norte

Estrada Arraial

Casa Amarela, Sítio Trindade & Casa Forte complex

Av Rosa e Silva

Museu do Estado 🏛

Cemitério Santo Amaro

P de Limoeiro

A. Lisboa

To Várzea, Oficina Cerâmica Francisco Brennand & Instituto Ricardo Brennand

Bonifácio

Av de Barros

Parque 13 de Maio

POÇO

Rio Capibaribe

Av Rui Barbosa

BOA VISTA

MADALENA

Gov A Magalhães

Av Caxanga

Dom Bosco

Central Metrô Station

Av San Martim

Joquei Clube

Estr dos Remedios

Joana Bezerra

Dantas Barreto

Bacia do Pina

To the North & João Pessoa

Av Abdias de Carvalho

M Gonçalves da Luz

R Imperial

A de Góes
H Bandeira

PINA

Afogados

Ipiranga

Largo da Paz

Mangueira

R São Miguel

Rio Capibaribe

Atlantic Ocean

Av Domingos Ferreira

Santa Luzia

Rio Tijipio

Imbiribeira

Av Boa Viagem

Five Stations to Rodoviária

Edgar Werneck

Av Central

IMBIRIBEIRA

Av Marechal Mascarenhas Morais

Barro

Dr J Rufino

Av Recife

Av Sul

Canal Jordão

BR 101

Gen MacArthur

Antônio Falcão

Shopping Center Recife

Tancredo Neves

BOA VIAGEM

IBURA

Boa Viagem

Praça Boa Viagem

N

1 km
1 miles

To the South & Maceió

To Monte Guararapes

To Piedade

The island just south of Recife Antigo contains the neighbourhoods of **Santo Antônio and São José**. Here are many historical monuments, including the church of **Santo Antônio do Convento de São Francisco** (1606) ① *R do Imperador*, which has beautiful Portuguese tiles, and adjoining it, one of the finest baroque buildings in northeast Brazil, the **Capela Dourada** (Golden Chapel, 1697) ① *T081-*

3224 0530, http://capeladourada.com.br, Mon-Fri 0800-1130, 1400-1700, Sat 0800-1130, US$1.35, no flash photography. It is through the Museu Franciscano de Arte Sacra. The church is immediately south of **Praça da República**, on which stands the **Palácio do Campo das Princesas**, a neoclassical former Governor's Palace, with an interior garden designed by Burle Marx. **Teatro de Santa Isabel** ① *Praça da República, T081-3355 3323, www.teatrosantaisabel.com.br, guided visits Sun 1400, 1700*, built in 1851, is one of three traditional theatres in the city. The others are **Apolo** ① *R do Apolo 121*, and **Parque** ① *R do Hospício 81, Boa Vista*, restored and beautiful.

The **Museu de Arte Moderna Aloisio Magalhães** ① *R da Aurora, 265, Boa Vista, T081-3355 6870, www.mamam.art.br, Tue-Fri 1200-1800, Sat-Sun 1300-1700, free*, shows modern Brazilian and contemporary art (much of it from Recife and the Northeast), in a series of galleries set in a beautiful 19th-century town house overlooking the Capibaribe river.

A couple of blocks south, close to the central post office, is the **Praça do Sebo**, where the city's second-hand booksellers concentrate; this Mercado de Livros Usados is off the Rua da Roda, behind the **Edifício Santo Albino**, near the corner of Avenida Guararapes and Rua Dantas Barreto. The first Brazilian printing press was installed in 1706 and Recife claims to publish the oldest daily newspaper in South America, Diário de Pernambuco, founded 1825 (see above). The distinctive lilac building is on the Praça da Independência. Head down Av Dantas Barreto to **São Pedro dos Clérigos** (1782) ① *T081-3224 2954, Mon-Fri 0800-1200, 1400-1600*, which should be seen for its façade, its fine wood sculpture and a splendid trompe-l'oeil ceiling. The **Pátio de São Pedro**, the square round the church, has sporadic folk music and poetry shows on Wednesday to Sunday evenings (www.patiodesaopedro.ceci-br.org) and there are atmospheric bars and restaurants. Not far away, is **Nossa Senhora do Carmo** (1663) ① *Praça do Carmo, Mon-Fri 0700-1700, Sat 0700-1200, free*. The former municipal prison is now the **Casa da Cultura** ① *T081-3224 0557, www.casadaculturape.com.br, Mon-Fri 0900-1900, Sat 0900-1800, Sun 0900-1400*. The cells have been converted into a gallery of hundreds of shops and stalls selling arts and souvenirs from all over Pernambuco. Southeast of the Casa da Cultura is the Dutch **Forte das Cinco Pontas** (with **Museu da Cidade do Recife**) ① *T081-3355 3106, Tue-Sat 0900-1700, free with donation* (1630 with Portuguese alterations, 1677), which has a cartographic history of the settlement of Recife. This, and Forte do Brum, jointly controlled access to the port at the southern and northern entrances respectively. A few blocks north of Cinco Pontas is **Nossa Senhora de Penha** ① *Praça Do Vital, Tue-Thu 0800-1200, 1500-1700, Fri 0600-1800, Sat 1500-1700, Sun 0700-0900*, an Italianate church which holds a traditional blessing of São Felix on Friday attended by the sick seeking miracles. There are many other colonial churches.

West of the centre is the **Museu do Estado** ① *Av Rui Barbosa 960, Graças, Tue-Fri 0900-1700, Sat-Sun 1400-1700, US$1.50*, has excellent paintings by the 19th-century landscape painter, Teles Júnior.

Oficina Cerâmica Francisco Brennand ① *Av Caxangá, Várzea, T081-3271 2466, www.brennand.com.br, Mon-Thu 0800-1700, Fri 0800-1600, Sat-Sun 1000-1600, US$4. Take the metrô to Camaragibe and a taxi from there US$4.50 one way.* A museum and 19th-century ceramics factory set in mock Moorish gardens and filled with Brennand's extraordinary Gaudiesque ceramic sculptures and paintings. The artist, who is one of Brazil's most illustrious, can sometimes be seen walking here cane in hand looking like an old Sigmund Freud. **Instituto Ricardo Brennand** ① *Alameda Antônio Brennand s/n, Várzea, T081-2121 0365, www.institutoricardobrennand.org.br, Tue-Sun 1300-1700, las admission 1630, US$7.75.* Another scion of the Brennand family has built this fantasy castle on the outskirts of the city to house his art collection. This is one of the most important in the country and includes the largest assemblage of New World Dutch paintings in the world (with many Franz Posts as well as Brazilian modern art, armoury and medieval maps.

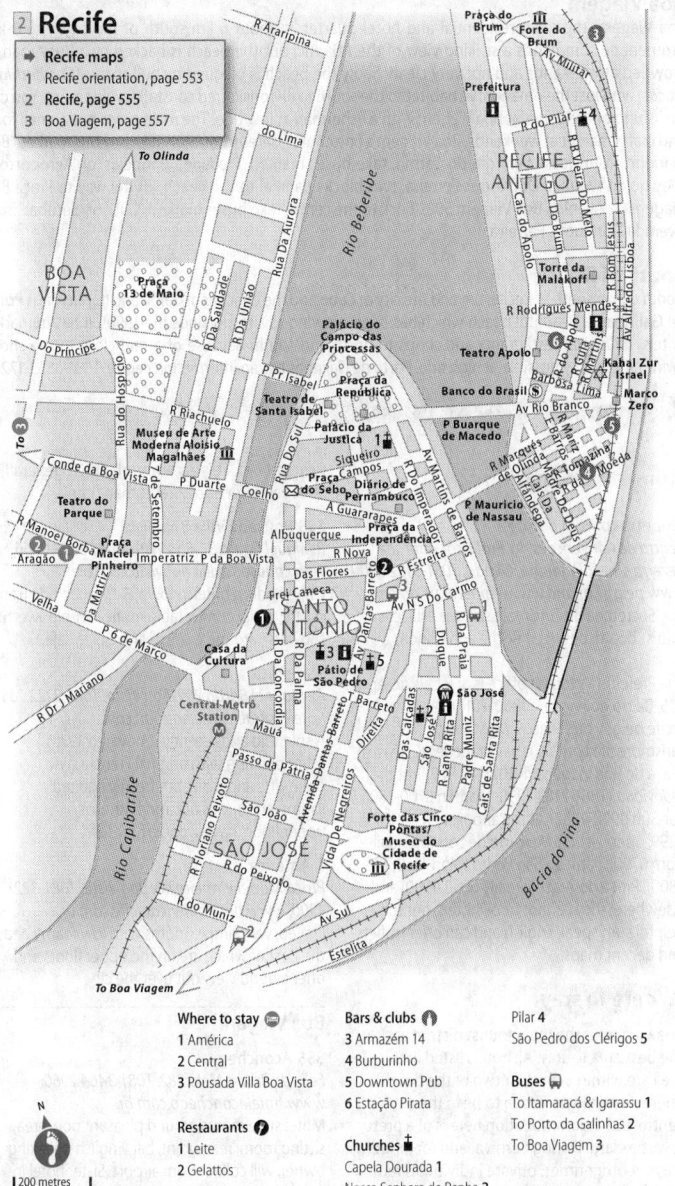

2 Recife

➡ **Recife maps**
1 Recife orientation, page 553
2 Recife, page 555
3 Boa Viagem, page 557

BOA VISTA

RECIFE ANTIGO

SANTO ANTÓNIO

SÃO JOSÉ

To Olinda

To Boa Viagem

Rio Beberibe

Rio Capibaribe

Bacia do Pina

Praça do Brum
Forte do Brum

Prefeitura

Praça 13 de Maio

Palácio do Campo das Princesas

Praça da República

Teatro de Santa Isabel

Museu de Arte Moderna Aloísio Magalhães

Teatro do Parque

Praça Maciel Pinheiro

Casa da Cultura

Central Metrô Station

Forte das Cinco Pontas/ Museu da Cidade de Recife

Torre da Malakoff

Teatro Apolo

Banco do Brasil

Kahal Zur Israel

Marco Zero

Palácio da Justiça

Diário de Pernambuco

P Mauricio de Nassau

Pátio de São Pedro

São José

200 metres
200 yards

N

Brazil Recife & the northeast coast • 555

Where to stay
1 América
2 Central
3 Pousada Villa Boa Vista

Restaurants
1 Leite
2 Gelattos

Bars & clubs
3 Armazém 14
4 Burburinho
5 Downtown Pub
6 Estação Pirata

Churches
Capela Dourada 1
Nossa Senhora de Penha 2
Nossa Senhora do Carmo 3

Pilar 4
São Pedro dos Clérigos 5

Buses
To Itamaracá & Igarassu 1
To Porto da Galinhas 2
To Boa Viagem 3

Boa Viagem

Boa Viagem, the main residential and hotel quarter, is about 6 km south of the city. The 8-km promenade commands a striking view of the Atlantic, but the beach is backed by a busy road, is crowded at weekends and not very clean. Sadly the beach is plagued by bull sharks (*Carcharhinus leucas*) who lost their mangrove habitat to the south to ill-considered coastal development. You can go fishing on *jangadas* at Boa Viagem with a fisherman at low tide. The main *praça* has a small food and crafts market at weekends. Boa Viagem's fine church dates from 1707. Take any bus marked 'Boa Viagem'; from Nossa Senhora do Carmo, take buses marked 'Piedade', 'Candeias' or 'Aeroporto' – they go on Avenida Domingos Ferreira, two blocks parallel to the beach, all the way to Praça Boa Viagem (at Avenida Boa Viagem 500). Back to the centre take buses marked 'CDU' or 'Setubal' from Avenida Domingos Ferreira.

South of Recife

About 60 km south of Recife, beyond the city of Cabo and the beaches of Gaibu and Itapuama, is **Porto de Galinhas**, a beautiful beach which has been growing as a resort since the 1990s. It has upmarket hotels, *pousadas*, restaurants and shops to north and south. Because of a reef close to the shore, swimming is only possible at high tide. Porto de Galinhas has an information centre, T081-3552 1728.

Listings Recife maps p553, p555 and p557.

Tourist information

Empetur (part of Seturel)
Centro de Convenções, Av Professor Andrade Bezerra s/n, Salgadinho, Olinda, T081-3182 8300, www.pe.gov.br and www.empetur.pe.gov.br.
The Secretaria de Turismo, Esportes e Lazer's tourist board, between Recife and Olinda.

The Prefeitura's tourist office is at R Cais do Apolo 925, Bairro do Recife, T0800-281 0040, www2. recife.pe.gov.br/servicos/turista and www. turismorecife.com.br. It has branches (CATs) in Praça de Boa Viagem (T081-3182 8297), at the *rodoviária* (T081-3182 8298, Mon-Fri 0700-1800, Sat-Sun 0900-1500), at the airport (T081-3182 8299, open 24 hrs), Mercado de São José (daily from 0700), Pátio de São Pedro (Mon-Fri 0800-1800), Praça do Arsenal (daily 0800-1900) and elsewhere; they cannot book hotels, but the helpful staff speak English and can offer leaflets and decent maps.

Where to stay

Boa Viagem is the main tourist district and the best area to stay. All hotels listed in this area are within a block or two of the beach. There is not much reason to be in the city centre and accommodation here is of a pretty low standard. During Carnival and for longer stays at other times, private individuals rent rooms and houses in Recife and Olinda; listings can be found in the classified ads in *Diário de*

Pernambuco. This accommodation is generally cheaper, safer and quieter than hotels.

$$$ Pousada Villa Boa Vista
R Miguel Couto 81, Boa Vista, T081-3223 0666, www.pousadavilla boavista.com.br.
Only modern hotel in town, 5-min cab ride from centre, plain, comfortable rooms (with powerful showers), around a courtyard. Quiet, safe.

$$ Central
Av Manoel Borba 209, Boa Vista, T081-3222 2353, hotelcentralrecife@hotmail.com.
A splendid and recently renovated 1920s listed building with original French-style open-lifts and plain, but freshly painted rooms, enormous old iron bathtubs, upper floors have wonderful views.

$ América
Praça Maciel Pinheiro 48, Boa Vista, T081-3221 1300, www.hotelamericarecife.com.br.
Frayed, very simple rooms with low foamy beds, the best of which are on the upper floors and offer a good view out over the city.

Boa Viagem

$$$ Aconchego
Félix de Brito e Melo 382, T081-3464 2960, www.hotelaconchego.com.br.
Motel style rooms around pleasant pool area, sitting room, restaurant, bar, English-speaking owner, will collect from airport. Sister hotel in Porto de Galinhas.

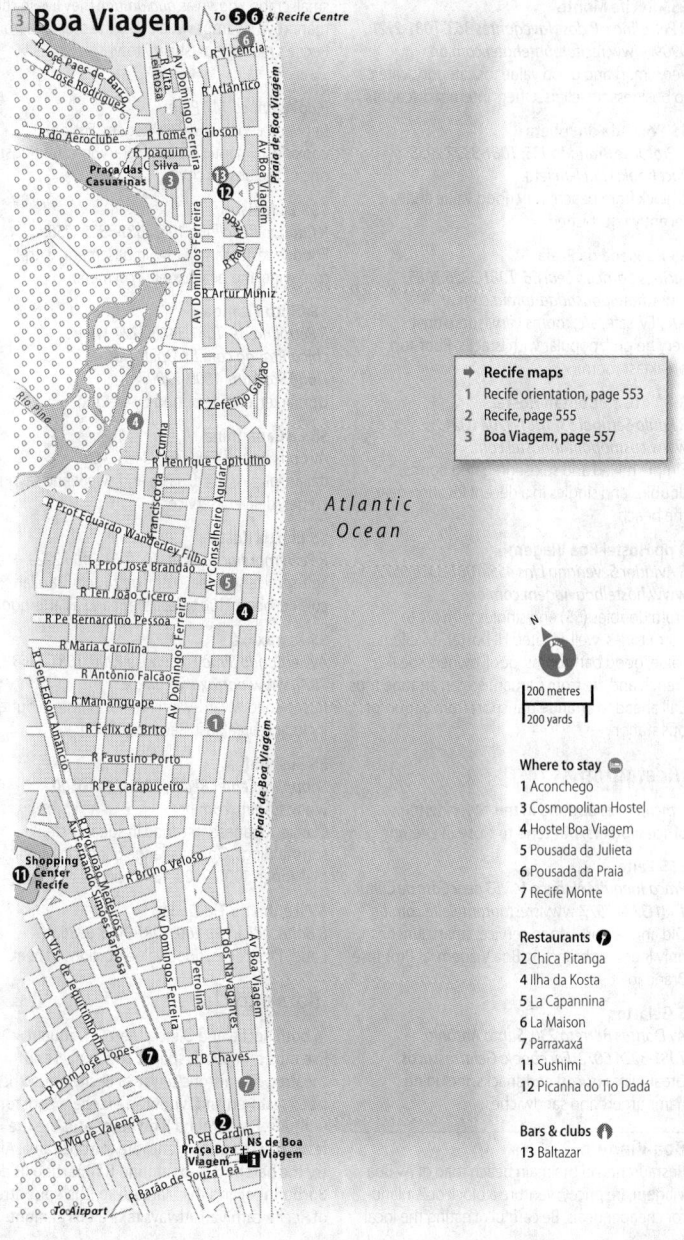

Atlantic Ocean

➡ **Recife maps**
1 Recife orientation, page 553
2 Recife, page 555
3 Boa Viagem, page 557

200 metres
200 yards

Where to stay
1 Aconchego
3 Cosmopolitan Hostel
4 Hostel Boa Viagem
5 Pousada da Julieta
6 Pousada da Praia
7 Recife Monte

Restaurants
2 Chica Pitanga
4 Ilha da Kosta
5 La Capannina
6 La Maison
7 Parraxaxá
11 Sushimi
12 Picanha do Tio Dadá

Bars & clubs
13 Baltazar

$$$ Recife Monte
R Petrolina e R dos Navegantes 363, T081-2121 0909, www.recifemontehotel.com.br.
Very smart and good value for category, caters to business travellers. Offers internet discounts.

$$ Pousada da Julieta
R Prof Jose Brandão 135, T081-3327 2958, Facebook: Hotel-Julieta.
1 block from beach, very good value and recently refurbished.

$$ Pousada da Praia
Alcides Carneiro Leal 66, T081-3326 7085, www.hotelpousadadapraia.com.br
A/c, TV, safe, a/c, rooms vary (some tiny), very helpful, popular with Israelis. Roof-top breakfast room.

$$-$ Cosmopolitan Hostel
R Paulo Setubal 53, T081-3204 0321, www.cosmopolitanhostel.com.
Simple mixed and sex-segregated dorms, doubles and singles in a decent location near the beach.

$ pp Hostel Boa Viagem
R Aviador Severiano Lins 455, T081-3326 9572, www.hostelboaviagem.com.br.
From doubles ($$) and singles with a/c to dormitories, well-located HI hostel, excellent value, good bathrooms, pool, owners speak French and are from Caruaru so can arrange trips. Call ahead to arrange transport from airport or bus station.

Restaurants

Lanchonetes abound in the city, catering to office workers, but tend to close in evening.

$$$ Leite
Praça Joaquim Nabuco 147/53 near Casa de Cultura, T081-3224 7977, www.restauranteleite.com.br.
Old and famous, good service, smart, lunches only (another branch in Boa Viagem, at Prof José Brandão 409).

$ Gelattos
Av Dantas Barreto 230, Santo Antônio, T081-3224 6072, Facebook: Gelattossucos.
Great juices (*sucos*) and snacks, including hamburgers and sandwiches.

Boa Viagem
Restaurants on the main beach road of Av Boa Viagem are pricey; venture a block or 2 inland for cheaper deals. Be careful of eating the local small crabs, known as *guaiamum*; they live in the mangrove swamps which take the drainage from Recife's *mocambos* (shanty towns).

$$$ É
R do Atlântico 147, Pina.
Between centre and Boa Viagem. Fusion-cooking, romantic contemporary surroundings, one of the best in city.

$$$ La Maison
R Capitão Rebelinho 106, T081-3325 1158.
Fondue restaurant in low-lit basement, with rosé wine and peach melba on menu.

$$ Chica Pitanga
R Petrolina, 19, T081-3465 2224, www.chicapitanga.com.br. Open 1130-1530 (1600 Sat-Sun), 1800-2200.
Upmarket, excellent food by weight.

$$ La Capannina
Av Cons Aguiar 538, T081-3465 9420.
Italian, pizzas, salad, pasta and sweet and savoury crêpes, delivery service.

$$ Ilha da Kosta
R Pe Bernardino Pessoa, 50, T081-3466 2222.
Self-service seafood, sushi, pizza and Brazilian cuisine, open 1100 to last client and all afternoon.

$$ Parraxaxá
Av Fernando Simões Barbosa 1200, T081-3463 7874, www.parraxaxa.com.br.
Rustic-style, award-winning, northeastern buffet, including breakfast. Recommended.

$$ Sushimi
Shopping Center Recife, T081-3463 6500, www.sushimi.com.br.
Classic, Japanese fast-food in suitably sterile surroundings. One of a range of options in this Mall (open 1000-2200, T3464 6000).

$ Picanho do Tio Dadá
R Baltazar Pereira 100, T081-3465 0986.
Loud, TV screens, good value portions of beef.

Bars and clubs

In both Recife and Olinda there is frequent live music, in public spaces and in bars and theatres. The historic centre of Recife Antigo has been restored and is now an excellent spot for nightlife. Bars around R do Bom Jesus are the result of a scheme to renovate the dock area. Also try the bars and clubs around R Tomazino (R do Burburinho) and the Marco Zero (the epicentre of Recife carnival). Always take a taxi at night.

Others include **Armazém 14** (Av Alfredo Lisboa s/n, Cais do Porto), for big name acts; **Burburinho** (R Tomazina 106, T3224 5854), a live music and comedy club, good starting place for the bars on this street; and **Estação Pirata** (R do Apolo), good live bands. Try to visit a northeastern *forró* where couples dance to typical music, very lively especially Fri and Sat, several good ones at Candeias.

The most popular nightclub () is **Downtown Pub** (R Vigário Tenório 105, T081-3424 6317, www. downtownpub.com.br), live international and Brazilian rock music and dance club, huge, 2300 to dawn, US$10.

Boa Viagem

Baltazar
R Baltazar Pereira 130, T081-3327 0475.
Open 1600 to early hours.
Live music nightly, bar snacks, large and popular.

Festivals

☆See https://confiramais.com.br/recife-pernambuco/ for a weekly calendar of events.
1 Jan Universal Brotherhood. Carnival in Recife features a *pre-carnavalesca* week of shows, processions and balls, before the Galo da Madrugada, with up to a million participants officially opens Carnaval on the Sat morning. The festival continues until Tue with *trios elétricos*, samba and the distinctive local *maracatu* and *frevo* dances and rhythms.
12-15 Mar Parades to mark the city's foundation.
Mid-Apr Pro-Rock Festival, a week-long celebration of rock, hip-hop and manguebeat at Centro de Convenções, Complexo de Salgadinho and other venues. Check *Diário de Pernambuco* or *Jornal do Comércio* for details.
Jun Festas Juninas. The days of **Santo Antônio** (13 Jun), **São João** (24 Jun), **São Pedro** and **São Paulo** (29 Jun), form the nuclei of a month-long celebration whose roots go back to the Portuguese colony. Intermingled with the Catholic tradition are Indian and African elements. The annual cycle begins on **São José's day** (19 Mar), historically the 1st day of planting maize; the harvest in Jun then forms a central part of the Festas Juninas. During the festivals the *forró* is danced. This dance, now popular throughout the Northeast, is believed to have originated when the British builders of the local railways held parties that were 'for all'.
11-16 Jul Nossa Senhora do Carmo, patron saint of the city.

Aug Mes do Folclore.
1-8 Dec Festival of Iemanjá, with typical foods and drinks, celebrations and offerings to the goddess; also 8 Dec, **Nossa Senhora da Conceição**.

Shopping

Handicrafts
Casa da Cultura, *R Floriano Peixoto, Santo Antônio, T081-3224 0557, www.casadaculturape. com.br (see above).* Some 150 arts and crafts shops selling contemporary and antique figurines, prints and art work. Prices for ceramic figurines are lower than Caruaru.
Centro do Artesanato de Pernambuco, *Av Alfredo Lisboa, Armazém 11, Recife Antigo, T081-3181 3450, www.artesanatodepernambuco. pe.gov.br.* A big complex of small shops and stalls selling typical Pernambuco art, including ceramic figurines, knitwear and clothing.

Markets
Cais de Alfândega, *Bairro do Recife.* Market of local work, 1st weekend of every month.
Domingo na Rua, *Bairro do Recife.* Sun market, with stalls of local artesanato and performances.
Feira do Recife Antigo, *Altura do Centro Judaico. Every Sun 1400-2000.* Arts and crafts, foodstuffs and miscellany.
Hippy fair, *Praça Boa Viagem, on the sea front.* Wooden statues of saints, weekend only.
Mercado São José (1875) for local products and handicrafts.
Sítio Trindade, *Casa Amarela.* Sat craft fair. On 23 Apr, here and in the Pátio de São Pedro, you can see the *xangô* dance.

What to do

Diving
Offshore are some 20 wrecks, including the remains of Portuguese galleons, with diverse marine life.
Seagate, *Av Herculano Bandeira 287, Boa Viagem, T081-98798 2109, www.seagaterecife.com.br.* Daily departures and night dives.

Transport

Air The **Gilberto Freyre international airport**, T081-3464 4188, www.aeroportorecife.com, 12 km from the city in Boa Viagem, is one of the best and most modern in Brazil; with plenty of places for coffees and magazines and boutiques of elegant little tourist shops. There is a bank desk before customs which gives much the same rate for US$ as the moneychangers in the lobby. Internal flights to all major cities and international flights to Portugal and the US. Airport taxis cost US$3.30 to the seafront and US$15.40 to Olinda (about 22 km). Special taxis that work as minicabs at a prearranged price about U$60 leave from south wing arrivals at Recife airport. Some hotels offer transfers, about U$40 per car, for up to 4 people in a taxi sent by the hotel, they will have your name on a placard. The journey now takes about 40 mins since the inauguration of the expressway Rota do Atlântico in 2014. The Aeroporto metrô station (on Rua Dez de Junho in front of Praça Ministro Salgado Filho, just outside the airport terminal) connects to Shopping Recife and Recife Central station in the city centre via the blue Linha Sul line. You can change for a metrô to the rodoviária (on the Camaragibe branch of the Linha Centro) at Joana Bezerra or Central. The a/c bus No 42 runs (Mon-Fri 0530-1920, Sat 0615-1850, no bus Sun, US$1) from the airport to Shopping Recife, then along the entire length of Avs Cons Aguiar and Domingos Ferreira, Boa Viagem, to Recife Antigo, returning to the airport through Boa Vista. The non a/c bus 33 takes a similar route (daily 0400-2310, US$1). To Olinda, take bus 42 or 33 to Boa Viagem and change to bus 910 (daily 0330-2225, US$1.30) which runs from both Praça Nossa Senhora da Boa Viagem and Av Boa Viagem to Praça do Varadouro in Olinda, the closest bus stop to the colonial centre. Bus 370 (TIP/TI Aeroporto, US$1, daily 0400-2250) connects the airport and the rodoviária.

Bus City buses cost US$0.50-1; they are clearly marked and run frequently until about 2300 weekdays, 0100 weekends. Many central bus stops have boards showing routes. See www. granderecife.pe.gov.br for details. On buses, especially at night, look out for landmarks as street names are written small and are hard to

see. Integrated bus-metrô (see Train, below) routes and tickets (US$1.35) are available. Urban transport information, T158. See below for buses to Olinda and other destinations outside the city. Taxis are plentiful; fares double on Sun, after 2100 and on holidays; number shown on meter is the fare; don't take the taxi if a driver tells you it is km. **Porto de Galinhas** can be reached by frequent buses and minivans from Av Dantas Barreto and R do Peixoto and from outside the rodoviária, US$3.75. Buses leave for **Igarassu** from Av Martins de Barros, in front of Grande Hotel, Recife, 45 mins, US$1.65.

The rodoviária, mainly for long-distance buses, is 20 km outside the city at Jaboatão dos Guararapes (it is called Terminal Integrado dos Passageiros, or TIP). T081-3452 1999/2824. There is a 30-min metrô connection to the central railway station, opposite the Casa da Cultura. From Boa Viagem a taxi all the way costs US$15, or go to Central or Joanna Bezerra metrô stations and change there. To Olinda from the rodoviária, take the metrô to Recife Central and then bus No 983 (Rio Doce/Princesa Isabel, daily 0400-2250) to Largo do Varadouro.

To **Salvador**, 17 hrs, US$49. To **Rio**, 2 daily, 44 hrs, US$126. To **São Paulo**, 2 daily, 50 hrs, US$125. To **João Pessoa**, every 20-30 mins, 2 hrs, US$6.55-9. To **Caruaru**, see below. Buses to Olinda, see below; to beaches beyond Olinda from Av Dantas behind the post office. To **Cabo** (every 20 mins) and beaches south of Recife from Cais de Santa Rita.

Train Commuter services, known as the Metrô (overground light rail), leave from the central station. It has 2 lines: Linha Centro (which has 2 branches, one of which, the Camaragibe branch connects to the rodoviária) and the Linha Sul which runs to Shopping Recife, Tancredo Neves and the airport, all of which stations are close to Boa Viagem. Basic fare US$0.50.

Around Recife

a colonial capital, fine figurines and distant islands

'Around Recife' is a bit of literary licence because this section deals with not only fine colonial towns not far from the state capital, but also the Fernando de Noronha archipelago, way out in the Atlantic. Of the former, Olinda is one of the best examples in Brazil and only minutes from Recife. In the drier interior is Caruaru, a fascinating market town. Fernando de Noronha, best reached from Recife (hence its inclusion here), has a wonderful marine environment and is ideal for those who are seeking a remote destination.

☆Olinda *Colour map 5, B6.*

The old capital of Brazil founded in 1537 and named a World Heritage Site by UNESCO in 1982 is about 7 km north of Recife. A programme of restoration, partly financed by the Netherlands government, was initiated in order to comply with the recently conferred title of National Monument, but many of the buildings are still in

Warning...
Opportunistic theft is still common in Olinda, especially on the streets up to Alto da Sé. Take care of your belongings.

need of repair. The compact network of cobbled streets is steeped in history and invites wandering. This is a charming spot to spend a few relaxing days and a much more appealing base than Recife.

Many of the historic buildings have irregular opening hours, but can be viewed from the outside. The **tourist office** ① *Praça do Carmo, Av Liberdade 98, T081-3429 0244, daily 0900-2100 (Cass de Turista also at R Prudente de Moraes 472, Quatro Can tos, T081-3305 1060), www.olindaturismo. com.br*, provides a complete list of all historic sites with a useful map, Sítio Histórico. Guides with identification cards wait in Praça do Carmo. Some are former street children and half the fee for a full tour of the city (about US$20) goes to a home for street children.

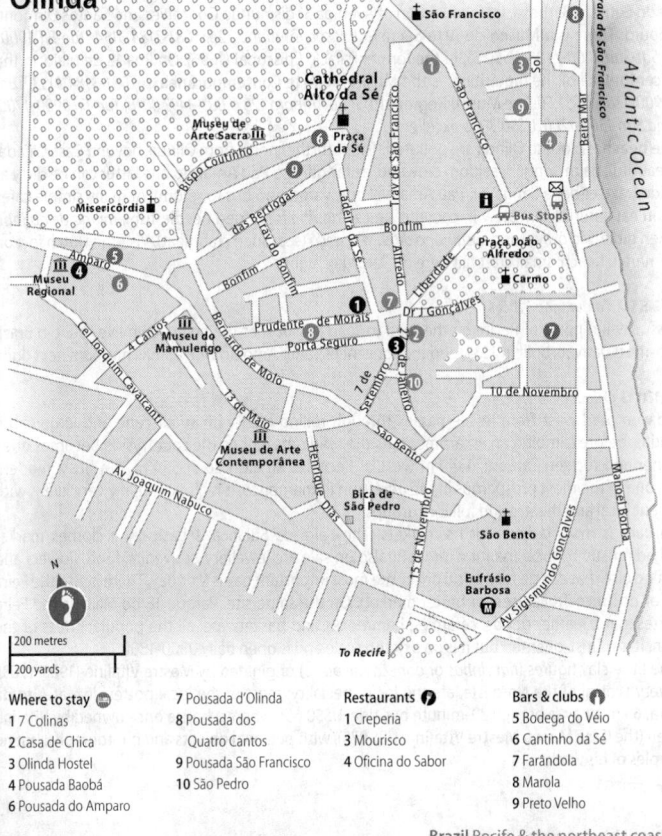

Where to stay 🛏
1 7 Colinas
2 Casa de Chica
3 Olinda Hostel
4 Pousada Baobá
6 Pousada do Amparo
7 Pousada d'Olinda
8 Pousada dos Quatro Cantos
9 Pousada São Francisco
10 São Pedro

Restaurants 🍴
1 Creperia
3 Mourisco
4 Oficina do Sabor

Bars & clubs 🍸
5 Bodega do Véio
6 Cantinho da Sé
7 Farândola
8 Marola
9 Preto Velho

The **Basílica e Mosterio de São Bento** ① *R São Bento, T081-3316 3290, daily 0530-1145, 1400-1830, Mass daily at 0630, Sun at 1000,* with Gregorian chant. Monastery closed except with written permission. Founded 1582 by the Benedictine monks, burnt by the Dutch in 1631 and restored in 1761, this is the site of Brazil's first law school and the first abolition of slavery. The magnificent gold altar is one of the finest pieces of baroque carving in the Americas. Despite its weathered exterior, the **Convento de Franciscano de NS das Neves** (1585) ① *T081-3429 0517, Mon-Sat 0900-1230, 1400-1730, Sun 0900-1200, US$1,* has splendid woodcarving and paintings, superb gilded stucco, and azulejos showing scenes from the life of St Francis and from Lisbon before the 1755 earthquake. The Capela de São Roque within the church of **Nossa Senhora das Neves** has a glorious painted ceiling. Make the short, but very steep, climb up to the **Alto da Sé** for memorable views of the city and the coastline stretching all the way to Recife. Here, the simple **Igreja da Sé** (1537) ① *Tue-Sun 0900-1700,* a cathedral since 1677, was the first church to be built in the city. Nearby, the **Igreja da Misericórdia** (1540) ① *R Bispo Coutinho, daily 1145-1230, 1800-1830,* has fine tiling and gold work. On a small hill overlooking Praça do Carmo, the **Igreja do Carmo** church (1581) is also impressive.

There are some houses of the 17th century with latticed balconies, heavy doors and brightly painted stucco walls. The local colony of artists means excellent examples of regional art, mainly woodcarving and terracotta figurines, may be bought in the Alto da Sé, or in the handicraft shops at the **Mercado da Ribeira** ① *R Bernardo Vieira de Melo* (Vieira de Melo gave the first recorded call for independence from Portugal, in Olinda in 1710). Handicrafts are also sold at good prices in the Mercado Eufrásio Barbosa, by the junction of Avenida Segismundo Gonçalves and Santos Dumont, Varadouro. There is a **Museo de Arte Sacra** ① *R Bispo Coutinho 726, T081-3184 3154, Tue-Fri 1000-1600, Sat-Sun 1000-1400, US$0.65,* in the former Palacío Episcopal (1696). On Rua 13 de Maio, in the 18th-century jail of the Inquisition, is the **Museu de Arte Contemporânea** ① *T081-3184 3153, Tue-Sun 0900-1700, US$1.50.* The **Museu Regional** ① *R do Amparo 128, T 081-3493 0018, Tue-Fri 0900-1700, Sat and Sun 1300-1700, US$0.30,* is excellent.

The **beaches** close to Olinda are polluted. Those further north from Olinda, beyond Casa Caiada, are beautiful, palm-fringed, seldom crowded; at **Janga,** and **Pau Amarelo,** the latter can be dirty at low tide (take either a 'Janga' or 'Pau Amarela' bus, Varodouro bus to return). At many simple cafés you can eat sururu (clam stew in coconut sauce), *agulha frita* (fried needle-fish), *miúdo de galinha* (chicken giblets in gravy) and *casquinha de carangueijo* (seasoned crabmeat). Visit the Dutch fort on Pau Amarelo beach; small craft fair here on Saturday nights.

Igarassu *Colour map 5, B6.*

Igarassu, 39 km north of Recife on the road to João Pessoa, has the first church ever built in Brazil (SS Cosme e Damião, built in 1535) and the convent of Santo Antônio with a small museum next door.

Caruaru *Colour map 5, C6.*

The paved road west from Recife passes through rolling hills, with sugar cane and large cattle fazendas, before climbing an escarpment. As the road gets higher, the countryside becomes drier, browner and rockier. Caruaru, 134 km west of Recife at an altitude of 554 m, is a busy, modern town, one of the most prosperous in the *agreste* in Pernambuco. It is also culturally very lively, with excellent local and theatre and folklore groups.

Caruaru is most famous for its markets. The Feira da Sulanca is basically a clothes market supplied mostly by local manufacture, but also on sale are jewellery, souvenirs, food, flowers and anything else that can go for a good price. The most important day is Monday. There is also the Feira Livre or do Troca-Troca (free, or barter market). On the same site, Parque 18 de Maio, is the Feira do Artesanato, leather goods, ceramics, hammocks and basketware, all the popular crafts of the region. It is tourist-oriented but it is on a grand scale and is open daily 0800-1800.

The little clay figures (*figurinhas* or *bonecas de barro*) originated by Mestre Vitalino (1909-1963), and very typical of the Nordeste, are the local speciality; most of the local potters live at **Alto da Moura,** 6 km away (a bumpy 30-minute bus ride, US$0.65), where a house once owned by Vitalino is open (the **Casa Museu Mestre Vitalino,** US$1.75), with personal objects and photographs, but no examples of his work.

☆Fernando de Noronha

This small archipelago 345 km off the northeast coast was declared a Marine National Park in 1988. There are many unspoilt beaches and interesting wildlife and excellent scuba-diving and snorkelling. Only one island is inhabited and is dominated by a 321-m peak. It is part of the state of Pernambuco administered from Recife. It is one hour ahead of Brazilian Standard Time.

The islands were discovered in 1503 by Amérigo Vespucci and were for a time a pirate lair. In 1738 the Portuguese built the Forte dos Remédios (begun by the Dutch), later used as a prison in this century, and a church to strengthen their claim to the islands. Remains of the early fortifications still exist.

Vila dos Remédios, near the north coast, is where most people live and socialize. At Baía dos Golfinhos is a lookout point for watching the spinner dolphins in the bay. On the south side there are fewer beaches, higher cliffs and the coastline and islands are part of the marine park.

All development is rigorously controlled by ICMBio, to prevent damage to the nature reserve. Many locals are dependent on tourism and most food is brought from the mainland; prices are about double. Entry to the island is limited to two plane-loads per day. There is a national park fee of US$60 (Brazilians half price) valid for 10 days (available on www.parnanoronha.com.br) and a daily tax of US$21, to be paid on arrival. An additional tax of US$4 is payable for walking the trails. There are ATMs in the airport and at the Post Office in Vila dos Remédios. Cash can be exchanged at the Santander bank. For information, contact the national park office and **Tamar information centre** ① *Al do Boldró s/n, Fernando de Noronho, T081-3619 1171, infonoronha@tamar.org.br, open 0900-2200.* See also www.noronha.pe.gov.br or www.ilhadenoronha.com.br. The rains are from February-July; the island turns green and the sea water becomes lovely and clear. The dry season is August-March, but the sun shines all year round.

Listings Around Recife *map p561*

Where to stay

Olinda

Prices at least triple during Carnival when 5-night packages are sold. Rooms at regular prices can often be found in Boa Viagem during this time. If you can afford it, staying in a beautiful converted mansion (*pousada*) is the ideal way to absorb the colonial charm of Olinda.

$$$ 7 Colinas
Ladeira de São Francisco 307, T081-3493 7766, www.hotel7colinas.com.br.
Spacious hotel with delightful, light rooms in beautiful private gated grounds with a large swimming pool, restaurant and bar. Helpful staff.

$$$ Pousada Baobá
R do Sol 147, T081-3429 0459, www.pousadabaobadeolinda.com.br.
Modestly sized and simply decorated rooms, with or without en suite bathrooms. Public areas are bright and colourful, staff attentive, small pool.

$$$ Pousada do Amparo
R do Amparo 199, T081-3429 6889, www.pousadoamparo.com.br.
Olinda's best hotel is a gorgeous, 18th-century house, full of antiques and atmosphere in the Roteiros do Charme group. Rooms have 4-poster beds and each is decorated differently. The public areas include a spacious, art-filled foyer, a pool and sauna area surrounded by a little garden and an excellent, delightfully romantic restaurant.

$$ Casa de Chica
R 27 de Janeiro 43, T081-3494 3232, www.casadechica.com.br.
Boxy but well-kept rooms in a bright little *pousada* next to São Pedro church. Attractive public areas.

$$ Olinda Hostel
R do Sol 233, T081-3429 1592, www.alberguedeolinda.com.br.
HI hostel, 8-bed rooms with fan and shared bath, tropical garden, TV room, hammocks, small pool.

$$ Pousada d'Olinda
P Prudente de Moraes 178, T081-3494 2559, www.pousadadolinda.com.br.
Basic but well-kept dorms and doubles around a pool, garden, communal breakfast area, good breakfast, lunchtime restaurant, 10% off for owners of Footprint Handbooks in low season, English, French, German, Arabic and Spanish spoken.

$$ Pousada dos Quatro Cantos
R Prudente de Morais 441, T081-3429 0220, www.pousada4cantos.com.br.

A large converted town house with a little walled garden and terraces, bright rooms and suites decorated with Pernambuco arts and crafts, furnished mostly with antiques, welcoming and full of character.

$$ Pousada São Francisco
R do Sol 127, T081-3429 2109,
www.pousadasaofrancisco.com.br.
Well-kept and airy rooms with terraces and pokey bathrooms. Pool and bar in pleasant gardens visited by hummingbirds in the early morning, restaurant, parking. Within walking distance of the historic centre.

$$ São Pedro
R 27 de Janeiro 95, T081-3439 9546,
www.pousadapedro.com.
Quiet, walled garden, small shaded pool, delightful breakfast area and lobby decorated with art and antiques. Rustic rooms are tiny, especially on the lower floors.

Caruaru
Cheap *hospedarias* are around the central Praça Getúlio Vargas. Lots of cheap lunch restaurants.

$$$ Grande Hotel São Vicente de Paulo
Av Rio Branco 365, T081-3721 5011,
www.grandehotelcaruaru.com.br.
Good, a/c, central, laundry, garage, bar, restaurant, pool, TV.

$$ Center Plaza
7 de Setembro 84, T081-3041 3989, Facebook: Center-Plaza-Hotel-216923638319990.
Also suites, good breakfast, pool, central, can be noisy, otherwise recommended.

$$ Central
R Vigário Freire 71, T081-3721 5880,
http://citihoteis.com.br.
Suites or rooms, all with a/c, TV, good breakfast, in the centre. Same group has 2 other hotels in town. Recommended.

Fernando de Noronha

$$$$ Pousada do Vale
T081-3619 1293, www.pousadadovale.com.
Well-run *pousada*, comfortable rooms, best are the duplex wooden bungalows. 300 m from Vila dos Remedios town centre.

$$$$ Solar dos Ventos
T081-3619 1347, www.pousada solardosventos.com.br.

Spectacular view, 2 standards of well-appointed bungalows, restaurant, veg and salads from own garden, no pool.

$$$$ Zé Maria
R Eunice Cordeiro 1, T081-3619 1258,
www.pousadazemaria.com.br.
Spacious bungalows with generous beds, verandas with hammocks and views to the Morro do Pico, small deep-blue half-moon pool.

$$$ Pousada Recanto dos Corais
Residencial Floresta Nova, Quadra "D" Casa 07, T081-3619 1147, www.pousadacorais.com.br.
10 small, plain a/c rooms around a little pool. Good breakfast.

$$ Verde Livre
Vila Remédios, T081-3619 1312.
With a/c, TV, fridge and breakfast, simple but good.

Restaurants

Olinda
Several *lanchonetes* and fast-food options along the seafront. The traditional Olinda drinks, **Pau do Índio** (contains 32 herbs) and **Retetel**, are both made on the R do Amparo. Also try tapioca, a manioc pancake stuffed with cheese, fruit or syrup.

$$$ Oficina do Sabor
R do Amparo 355, T081-3429 3331,
www.oficinadosabor.com.
Consistently wins awards, pleasant terrace overlooking city, food served in hollowed-out pumpkins and lots of vegetarian options.

$$ Creperia
R Prudente de Morais 168, T081-3429 2935.
Savoury and sweep crêpes, pizzas and *petiscos* (bar snacks) served in an open-plan dining area.

$ Mourisco
Praça João Alfredo 7.
Excellent, good value food by weight in lovely, part-covered, garden, delicious deserts. Warmly recommended.

Fernando de Noronha

$$$ Mergulhão
Porto Santo Antonio, T081-3619 0215,
www.mergulhaonoronha.com.br.
Modern Bahian food served outdoors, best time is late afternoon, when the sun is lower. Lovely sunset view. At lunch time take a hat to shield yourself from the hot sun. Busy, especially in high

season. When making a reservation ask for a table with a view.

$$$ Porto Marlin
Porto de Santo Antônio, T081-3619 1452.
Good Japanese food à la carte with an all you can eat buffet on Thu and Sat from 1800.

$ Açai e Raizes
BR363, Floresta Velha, T081-3619 0058.
Roadside sandwich bar with good snacks, puddings and delicious cream of *cupuaçu* and *açai*.

$ Cia da Lua
Bosque dos Flamboyantes, T081-3619 1631.
Decent coffee, snacks, sandwiches, internet access and car and buggy rental.

$ Jacaré
Praça Pres Eurico Dutra (next to the Banco Real), T081-3619 1947.
Best value on the island with lunchtime seafood and general Brazilian buffet.

Bars and clubs

Olinda
Every Fri night bands of wandering musicians walk the streets serenading passers-by. Each Sun from 1 Jan to Carnival there is a mini Carnival in the streets.
  Beginning at dusk, but best after 2100, the Alto da Sé becomes the scene of a street fair, with arts, crafts, makeshift bars and barbecue stands, and impromptu traditional music; even more animated at Carnival. Plenty of funky bars on R do Sol.

Bodega do Véio
R do Amparo 212, T081-3429 0185.
An Olinda institution, live music Thu-Sun. Great *petiscos* and caipirinhas, vibrant crowd.

Cantinho da Sé
Ladeira da Sé 305.
Lively, good view of Recife, food served.

Farândola
R Dom Pedro Roeser 190, behind Carmo church.
Mellow bar with festival theme and 'big-top' style roof. Warmly recommended.

Marola
Trav Dantas Barreto 66.
Funky wooden *barraca* on rocky shoreline specializing in seafood, great *caiprifrutas* (frozen fruit drink with vodka – try the cashew), can get crowded. Recommended.

Preto Velho
Alto da Sé.
Live samba at weekends, most lively on Sat.

Fernando de Noronha
Vila dos Remédios town has several bars; including a pizzeria with lively weekend *forró* from 2200 on weekends, and a bar with live reggae nightly in high season.

Festivals

Olinda
Feb At Olinda's **carnival** thousands of people dance through the narrow streets of the old city to the sound of the frevo, the brash energetic music which normally accompanies a lively dance performed with umbrellas. The local people decorate them with streamers and straw dolls, and form themselves into costumed groups to parade down the R do Amparo; **Pitombeira** and **Elefantes** are the best known of these groups.
12-15 Mar Foundation Day is celebrated with 3 days of music and dancing, night time only.

Caruaru
17 Dec-2 Jan Festas Natalinas; Semana Santa, Holy Week, with folklore and handicraft events.
18-22 May City's anniversary.
13 and 24 Jun 13 Jun **Santo Antônio** and 24 Jun **São João**, the latter a huge *forró* festival, are part of Caruaru's **Festas Juninas**.
Sep Micaru, a street carnival; also in Sep, **Vaquejada** (a Brazilian cross between rodeo and bull fighting), biggest in the northeast.

What to do

Fernando de Noronha
There are good hiking, horse riding and mountain biking possibilities, but you must either go with a guide or ranger in many parts.

Boat trips and jeep tours
These are available; it is also possible to hire a beach buggy. You can hitch everywhere as everyone stops.

Diving
Diving is organized by **Atlantis Divers** (T081-3619 1371, www.atlantisdivers.com.br), **Águas Claras** (T081-3619 1225, www.aguasclaras-fn.com.br), and **Noronha Divers** (T081-3619 1112, www.noronhadivers.com.br). Diving costs about US$95

for 2 tanks. This is the diving mecca for Brazilian divers with a great variety of sites and fish.
Trip Noronha, *T019-3808 5265, www.tripnoronha. com.br.* Offers tours around the island, attractive *pousada* packages and dive trips, good.

Olinda

Bus See Recife Transport, page 560, for buses from airport and *rodoviária* to Olinda. From Recife take a Rio Doce (Princesa Isabel) bus, No 981, which runs from Recife Central metrô (useful for connections to Boa Viagem, the airport and the *rodoviária*); or Jardim Atlântico No 974 (0430-2330), which leaves from the R do Sol and Ponte Duarte Coelho in Recife. From Boa Viagem take bus No 910 (Piedade/Rio Doce, daily 0330-

2225), which runs through Recife to the Praça do Varadouro, the closest stop to the historical centre of Olinda. All fares US$1. Taxi drivers between Olinda and Recife try to put meters onto *bandeira* (rate) 2 – only meant for Sun, holidays, after 2100 and when an Olinda taxi is operating in Recife or vice versa – but should change it back to 1 if queried (taxi to Boa Viagem US$20, US$23 at night).

Caruaru

Bus The *rodoviária* is 4 km from town; buses from Recife stop in the centre. Bus from centre, at the same place as Recife bus stop, to *rodoviária*, US$1. Many buses from TIP in **Recife**, 2 hrs, US$6.25.

Fernando de Noronha

Air Daily flights from **Recife**, 1 hr 20 mins, about US$250 return. From **Natal**, 1 hr, US$300 return.

South of Recife

beautiful beaches and fine colonial buildings

Two small states, Alagoas and Sergipe, are wedged between Pernambuco and Bahia. For no good reason, most people pass through, but there are some good examples of colonial architecture and, like the entire northeast coast, some fine beaches.

South to Alagoas

There are many interesting stopping points along the coast between Recife and Maceió. The main highway, BR-101, heads a little inland from the coast, crossing the state border near Palmares. It then continues to Maceió. On the coast the Pernambuco–Alagoas border is by São José da Coroa Grande, after which a coastal road, unpaved in parts, runs to Barra do Camaragibe. Mid-way between Recife and Maceió is **Maragogi** ① *www.maragogionline.com.br* (with a list of places to stay). Although it is becoming increasingly popular and crowded in high season, this little beach town has preserved something of its local character. The beach is glorious and some 6 km offshore, a reef reveals a series of deep swimming pools at low tide. Trips out there are easy to organize (expect to pay around US$13.50). Real Alagoas buses run daily from both Recife and Maceió, three hours from either; there are also combis from Maceió.

Near the mouth of the Rio Camaragibe, 38 km south of Maragogi, is **São Miguel dos Milagres**, a tiny colonial town with a crumbling Portuguese church, close to some of the best beaches in northeastern Brazil. Some, such as Praias do Patacho, do Toque and do Riacho, are becoming popular with the São Paulo jet set and 'boutique' *pousadas* are springing up. The Tatuamunha river near São Miguel is the best place in the world to see West Indian manatees. The **Santuário do Peixe Boi** ① *Projeto Aribama, R Luiz Ferreira Dorta, s/n, Porto de Pedras, T082-3298 6247, daily 1000-1600, US$13.50,* on the river is devoted to the rehabilitation of the mammals, which are subsequently released into the estuary. *Pousadas* can organize visits. They can also arrange transfers from Maceió or Recife (US$40 or US$60 respectively); alternatively take a combi from Maceió's *rodoviária* or a taxi from Maragogi (US$25).

Maceió and around *Colour map 5, C6.*

The capital of Alagoas state is mainly a sugar port, but for tourism it's friendly, safe and good value. Two of its old buildings, the **Palácio do Governo**, which also houses the **Fundação Pierre Chalita** (Alagoan painting and religious art) and the church of **Bom Jesus dos Mártires** (1870, covered in tiles), are particularly interesting. Both are on the Praça dos Martírios (or Floriano Peixoto). The **cathedral**, Nossa Senhora dos Prazeres (1840), is on Praça Dom Pedro II. The helpful **tourist** office is at **Sedetur** ① *Av da Paz 1108, Jaraguá, T082-3315 1713, http://turismoalagoas.com and www. sedetur.al.gov.br (also at airport, T082-3214 4125, and rodoviária, T082 3223 5404).* The municipal tourist authority is **Maceió Turismo** ① *R Firmino de Vasconcelos 685, Pajuçara, T082-3327 7711, www. maceioturismo.com.br;* information post on Pajuçara beach, by Sete Coqueiros artisan centre. Also visit www.turismomaceio.com.br.

Lagoa do Mundaú, a lagoon whose entrance is 2 km south at **Pontal da Barra**, limits the city to the south and west: excellent shrimp and fish are sold at its small restaurants and handicraft stalls; a nice place for a drink at sundown. Boats make excursions in the lagoon's channels. Beyond the city's main dock the beachfront districts begin; within the city, the beaches are smarter the further from the centre you go. The first, going north, is **Pajuçara** where there is a nightly craft market. At weekends there are wandering musicians and entertainers. Further out, **Jatiúca**, **Cruz das Almas** and **Jacarecica** (9 km from centre) are all good for surfing. The beaches, some of the finest and most popular in Brazil, have a protecting coral reef a kilometre or so out. Bathing is much better three days before and after full or new moon, because tides are higher and the water is more spectacular. *Jangadas* (traditional fishing boats) take passengers to a natural swimming pool 2 km off Pajuçara beach (**Piscina Natural de Pajuçara**), at low tide you can stand on the sand and rock reef (beware of sunburn). You must check the tides, there is no point going at high tide. *Jangadas* cost US$16 per person per day (about US$30 to have the *jangada* to yourself). On Sunday or local holidays in the high season it is overcrowded (at weekends lots of jangadas anchor at the reef selling food and drink).

By bus (22 km south), past Praia do Francês, the attractive colonial town and former capital of Alagoas, **Marechal Deodoro**, overlooks the Lagoa Manguaba. The 17th-century **Convento de São Francisco**, Praça João XXIII, has a fine church (Santa Maria Magdalena) with a superb baroque wooden altarpiece, badly damaged by termites. You can climb the church's tower for views. Adjoining it is the **Museu de Arte Sacra** ① *Mon-Fri 0900-1300, US$1.35, guided tours available, payment at your discretion.* Also open to visitors is the **Igreja Matriz de Nossa Senhora da Conceição** (1783). The town is the birthplace of Marechal Deodoro da Fonseca, founder of the Republic; the modest **house** ① *Mon-Sat 0800-1700, Sun 0800-1200, free,* where he was born is on the Rua Marechal Deodoro, close to the waterfront. On a day's excursion, it is easy to visit the town, then spend some time at beautiful **Praia do Francês**. The northern half of the beach is protected by a reef, the southern half is open to the surf. Along the beach there are many *barracas* and bars selling drinks and seafood; also several *pousadas*.

Penedo *Colour map 5, C6.*

This charming town, some 35 km from the mouth of the Rio São Francisco, with a nice waterfront park, Praça 12 de Abril, was originally the site of the Dutch Fort Maurits (built 1637, razed to the ground by the Portuguese). The colonial town stands on a promontory above the river. Among the colonial architecture, modern buildings on Av Floriano Peixoto do not sit easily. On the Praça Barão de Penedo is the neoclassical **Igreja Matriz** (closed to visitors) and the 18th-century **Casa da Aposentadoria** (1782). East and a little below this square is the Praça Rui Barbosa, on which are the **Convento de São Francisco** (1783 and later) and the church of **Santa Maria dos Anjos** (1660). As you enter, the altar on the right depicts God's eyes on the world, surrounded by the three races, one indigenous, two black and the whites at the bottom. The church has fine trompe-l'oeil ceilings (1784). The convent is still in use. Guided tours are free. The church of **Rosário dos Pretos** (1775-1816), on Praça Marechal Deodoro, is open to visitors. **Nossa Senhora da Corrente** (1764), on Praça 12 de Abril, and **São Gonçalo Garcia** (1758-1770) ① *Av Floriano Peixoto, Mon-Fri 0800-1200, 1400-1700.* Also on Avenida Floriano Peixoto is the pink **Teatro 7 de Setembro** (No 81) of 1884. The **Casa de Penedo** ① *R João Pessoa 126 (signs point the way up the hill from F Peixoto), Tue-Sun 0800-1800,* displays photographs and books on, or by, local figures. **Tourist information** at Praça Barão de Penedo 2, T082-3551 3907.

An interesting crossing into Sergipe can be made by frequent ferry (car and foot passengers, US$5 and US$1 respectively) from Penedo to **Neópolis**.

The canyons and beaches of the **Rio São Francisco** make a good excursion. The river courses its way through the hills of Minas Gerais and the desert backlands of Bahia before cutting through a series of dramatic gorges near the Xingó dam and subsequently through windswept dunes before entering the Atlantic in northern Sergipe. A number of tour operators in Atalaia (see below) run day-trips to the river mouth stopping at deserted beaches along the way; US$50-60 per person, depending on numbers.

Aracaju *Colour map 5, C5.*

Capital of Sergipe founded 1855, it stands on the south bank of the Rio Sergipe, about 10 km from its mouth, 327 km north of Salvador. In the centre is a group of linked, beautiful parks: **Praça Olímpio Campos**, in which stands the cathedral, **Praça Almirante Barroso**, with the Palácio do Governo, **Praça Fausto Cardoso**, with the **Palácio Museum Olímpio Campos** ① *Tue-Fri 1000-1700, Sat 0900-1300, Facebook: palaciomuseu.olimpiocampos* (also holds concerts), and **Praça Camerino**. Across Avenida Rio Branco from these two is the river. There is a handicraft centre, the **Centro do Turismo** ① *in the restored Escola Normal, on Praça Olímpio Campos, Rua 24 Horas, 0900-1300, 1400-1900*; the stalls are arranged by type (wood, leather, etc). The city's beaches are at **Atalaia**, 16-km by road (taxi US$22), and the 30-km-long **Nova Atalaia**, on Ilha de Santa Luzia across the river. It is easily reached by boat from the Hidroviária (ferry station), which is across Avenida Rio Branco from Praça Gen Valadão. See www.visitearacaju.com.br.

☆ **São Cristóvão** is the old state capital, 17 km southwest of Aracaju on the road to Salvador; bus US$3.50 from *rodoviária* and the old bus station at Praça João XXIII (taxi US$35-40 round trip from Aracaju). It was founded in 1590 by Cristóvão de Barros. It is the fourth oldest town in Brazil. Built on top of a hill, its colonial centre is unspoiled: the **Museu de Arte Sacra e Histórico de Sergipe** contains religious and other objects from the 17th to the 19th centuries; it is in the **Convento de São Francisco** ① *Tue-Fri 1000-1700, Sat-Sun 1300-1700, US$2.* Also worth visiting (and keeping the same hours) is the **Museu de Sergipe** in the former **Palácio do Governo** both are on Praça de São Francisco. Also on this square are the churches of **Misericórdia** (1627) and the **Orfanato Imaculada Conceição** (1646, permission to visit required from the Sisters). On Praça Senhor dos Passos are the churches **Senhor dos Passos** and **Terceira Ordem do Carmo** (both 1739), while on the Praça Getúlio Vargas (formerly Praça Matriz) is the 17th-century **Igreja Matriz Nossa Senhora da Vitória** ① *Tue-Fri 1000-1700, Sat-Sun 1500-1700.*

Estância *Colour map 5, C5.*

On the BR-101, almost midway between Aracaju and the Sergipe-Bahia border, and 247 km north of Salvador, is Estância, one of the oldest towns in Brazil. Its colonial buildings are decorated with Portuguese tiles. The month-long festival of **São João** in June is a major event. There are pleasant hotels, but most buses stop at the *rodoviária*, which is on the main road (four hours from Salvador).

Listings South of Recife

Where to stay

Maceió

It can be hard to find a room during the Dec-Mar holiday season, when prices go up. There are many hotels on Praia Pajuçara, mostly along Av Dr Antônio Gouveia and R Jangadeiros Alagoanos.

$$$$-$$ Ponta Verde Praia
Av Alvaro Otacílio 2933, Ponta Verde, T082-2121 0990, www.hotel pontaverde.com.br.
The best option on the beach, convenient for clubs, restaurants and Pajuçara, comfortable, good buffet breakfast.

$$$ Coqueiros Express
R Deportista H Guimarães 830, Ponta Verde, T082-4009 4700, www.coqueirosexpress.com.br.

Smart, well-run, best rooms on upper floors, small pool, good breakfast.

$$$ Pousada Estalagem
R Eng D Sarmento Barroca 70, T082-3327 0088, www.pousadaestalagem.com.br.
Flats for up to 6, with little cookers in a quiet backstreet above a photo shop.

$$$ Ritz Praia
R Eng Mário de Gusmão 1300, Laranjeiras, T082-2121 4600, www.ritzpraia.com.br.
1 block from beach, sun deck and tiny pool on top floor, bright and airy rooms.

$$$-$$ Gogá da Ema
R Laranjeiras 97, T082-3327 0329, www.hotelgogodaema.com.br.
Close to beach on a quiet backstreet, good breakfast, simple rooms.

Penedo

$$$ São Francisco
Av Floriano Peixoto 237, T082-3551 2273,
www.hotelsaofrancisco.tur.br.
Standard rooms have no a/c, fridge.
Recommended except for poor restaurant.

$$ Pousada Colonial
Praça 12 de Abril 21, T082-3551 2355,
pousada-colonial@hotmail.com.
Luxo and suite have phone, TV and fridge, suites
have a/c, spacious, good cheap restaurant, front
rooms with view of the river.

$$ Pousada Estylos I
Praça Jacome Calheiros 79, T082-3551 2465. Also
Estylos II, R Damaso do Monte 86, T082-3551 2429.
Modest, modern, rooms with a/c or fan, quiet,
river views, nice, not always open out of season.

Aracaju
The centre is best avoided at night. Stay at Atalaia
beach, just 10 mins from the city.

$$$-$$ San Manuel Praia
R Niceu Dantas 75, Orla Aracaju, T079-3218 5200,
www.sanmanuelpraiahotel.com.br.
Pleasant, modern, business facilities, best rooms
have sea view.

$$ Raio de Sol
R François Hoald 89, Atalaia, T079-3212 8600,
Facebook: pousadaraiodesolaju.
Well-kept, bright rooms in a block 50 m back
from the beach, quieter than on the sea front.
Courteous, efficient staff.

Restaurants

Maceió
Local specialities include oysters, *pitu*, a crayfish
(now becoming scarce), and *sururu*, a kind of
cockle. Local ice cream, Shups, recommended.
The best restaurants, bars and clubs are on
and around R Egenheiro Paulo B Nogueira on
Jatiúca beach. Many others in Pajuçara, eg on
Av Antônio Gouveia. The beaches for 5 km from
the beginning of Pajuçara to Cruz das Almas in
the north are lined with *barracas* (thatched bars),
providing music, snacks and meals until 2400
(later at weekends). Vendors on the beach sell
beer and food during the day: clean and safe.
There are many other bars and *barracas* at Ponto
da Barra, on the lagoon side of the city.

$$$ Divina Gula
R Eng Paulo B Nogueira 85, Jatiúca, T082-3235
1016. Closed Mon.
Wide-ranging menu, lively atmosphere and busy,
large portions.

$$ Barrica's
Av Álvaro Calheiros 354, Ponta Verde.
Lively waterfront bar with a menu that includes
pasta, pizza, grilled meat and fish and some
vegetarian options.

Festivals

Maceió
27 Aug Nossa Senhora dos Prazeres.
16 Sep Freedom of Alagoas.
8 Dec Nossa Senhora da Conceição.
15 Dec Maceiofest, 'a great street party with
trios elêctricos.

Transport

Maceió
Air 20 km from centre, T082-3036 5200, taxi
US$17. **Transporte Tropical Bus** from airport to
Ponta Verde/Pajuçara, every 30 mins 0630-2100,
US$1; allow 45 mins.

Bus Taxis from town go to all the northern
beaches, but buses run as far as Ipioca (23 km).
The Jangadeiras bus marked 'Jacarecica–Center,
via Praias' runs past all the beaches as far as
Jacarecica. From there you can change to 'Riacho
Doce–Trapiche', 'Ipioca' or 'Mirante' buses for
Riacho Doce and Ipioca. To return take any of
these options, or take a bus marked 'Shopping
Center' and change there for 'Jardim Vaticana'
bus, which goes through Pajuçara. Combis to
Marechal Deodoro, Praia do Francês and Barra de
São Miguel leave from opposite the Hospital Santa
Casa in front of the Texaco station. Combi US$2
to Marechal Deodoro, 30 mins, calling at Praia do
Francês in each direction. Last bus back from Praia
do Francês to Maceió at 1800. Taxi US$17.
   The *rodoviária* is 5 km from centre, on a hill
with good views. Taxi, US$8 to Pajuçara. To **Ponte
Verde/Pajuçara** take buses No 711 or 715, or
buses marked Ouro Preto p/Centro; they run
every few mins. To the *rodoviária*, Ponte Verde/
Jacintinho bus runs via Pajuçara from the centre,
also take 'Circular' bus (25 mins Pajuçara to bus
station). Bus to **Recife**, 10 a day, 3½ hrs express
(more scenic coastal route, 5 hrs) US$11-19.

Maceió–Aracaju, 5 hrs, US$15. **To Salvador**, 10 hrs, 4 a day, US$34-44.

Penedo

Bus To **Aracaju**, 2 a day, US$6, 4½ hrs, book in advance. It is quicker to take the ferry to **Neópolis**, then a minibus to Aracaju from there, 3½ hrs, US$5.50. 115 km from **Maceió**, 4 buses a day, US$9, 3-4 hrs. *Rodoviária*: Av Beira Rio, near service station.

Aracaju

Air The airport is 12 km from the centre. Flights to **Brasília**, **Maceió**, **Rio de Janeiro**, **Salvador**, **São Paulo** and **Recife**.

Bus Interstate *rodoviária* is 4 km from centre, linked by local buses from adjacent terminal, US$1 (buy a ticket before going on the platform), T079-3259 2848. To **Salvador**, 6-7 hrs, several daily, US$17-26.

João Pessoa *Colour map 5, B6.*

baroque treasures, miles of beach, exquisite crafts

It is a bus ride of two hours through sugar plantations over a good road from Recife (126 km) to João Pessoa, capital of the State of Paraíba on the Rio Paraíba. It's a pleasant, historical town with a rich cultural heritage and a population of around 600,000. The beaches, beside the turquoise waters of the Atlantic, are wonderful. At Ponta do Seixas is the most easterly point in Brazil; near here the Transamazônica highway begins its immense, if not controversial, route west into the heart of the country.

Sights

João Pessoa is a capital that retains a small town atmosphere. In the **Centro Histórico** is the **São Francisco Cultural Centre** ① *Praça São Francisco 221, T083-3218 4505 www.igrejadesaofrancisco pb.org, Mon-Fri 0830-1700 and Sat-Sun 0900-1400, US$1.20*, one of the most important baroque structures in Brazil, with the beautiful church of **São Francisco** which houses the **Museu Sacro e de Arte Popular** ① *Tue-Sun 0800-1200, 1400-1700*. Other tourist points include the **Casa da Pólvora**, now the **Museu Fotográfico Walfredo Rodríguez** (Ladeira de São Francisco) ① *Tue-Sun 0800-1200, 1400-1700*. Also the **Teatro Santa Roza** (1886) ① *Praça Pedro Américo, Varadouro, 1400-1700*. **Casa do Artesão** ① *Praça da Independência 56, Centro, Tue-Fri 0900-1 700, Sat-Sun 1000-1800*, where popular artists exhibit their work, with more than a thousand items on display, has been nominated as the best popular museum in Brazil.

João Pessoa's parks include the 17-ha **Parque Arruda Câmara**, north of the centre, and **Parque Solon de Lucena** or **Lagoa**, a lake surrounded by impressive palms in the centre of town, the city's main avenues and bus lines go around it.

The beachfront stretches for some 30 km from Ponta do Seixas (south) to the port of **Cabedelo** (north), on a peninsula between the Rio Paraíba and the Atlantic Ocean. This is Km 0 of the Transamazônica highway. The ocean is turquoise green and there is a backdrop of lush coastal vegetation. About 7 km from the city centre, following Avenida Presidente Epitáceo Pessoa is the beach of **Tambaú** (take bus No 510 'Tambaú' from outside the *rodoviária* or the city centre, alight at Hotel Tropical Tambaú), which has many hotels and restaurants. A taxi from Tambaú to Cabedelo costs US$17.50. Regional crafts, including lace-work, embroidery and ceramics are available at Mercado de Artesanato, Centro de Turismo, Almte Tamandaré 100. The town's main attractions are its beaches, where most tourists stay. About 14 km south of the centre is the Cabo Branco lighthouse at Ponta do Seixas, the most easterly point of continental Brazil and South America; there is a panoramic view from the cliff top. **Cabo Branco** is much better for swimming than **Tambaú**. Take bus 507 'Cabo Branco' from outside the *rodoviária* to the end of the line; hike up to the lighthouse.

The best known beach of the state is **Tambaba**, the only official nudist beach of the Northeast, 49 km south of João Pessoa in a lovely setting. Two coves make up this famous beach: in the first bathing-suits are optional, while the second one is only for nudists. Strict rules of conduct are enforced. Between Jacumã (many hotels, restaurants) and Tambaba are several nice beaches such as **Tabatinga** which has summer homes on the cliffs and **Coqueirinho**, surrounded by coconut palms, good for bathing, surfing and exploring caves.

Tourist information

The city tourist office is **SETUR** (Av Odon Bezerra 367, Tambaú, T083-3218 9850, www.joaopessoa. pb.gov.br/secretarias/setur), with information offices (Mon-Fri 0800-1400) at São Francisco church (Mon-Fri 0900-1900, Sat-Sun 0900-1400, Estação Cabo Branco (Tue-Fri 0900-1800, Sat-Sun 1000-1900) and at PBTur's **Centro Turístico** (Av Almte Tamandaré 100, Tambaú, T083-3247 7848, http://www.destinoparaiba.pb.gov.br, daily 0800-1800), also at the **airport**, T083-3041 4200, and *rodoviária*. The **Centro de Turismo** has internet, phones and, behind it, a post office. Tourist police, **Delegacia de policia ao turista** (Centro de Turismo, Tambaú, T083-3214 8022, open 0800-1800).

Where to stay

All those listed are at Tambaú, unless indicated otherwise:

$$$$-$$$ Tropical Tambaú
Av Alm Tamandaré 229, T083-3247 1070,
www.tropicaltambau.com.br.
An enormous round building on the seafront which looks like a military bunker and has motel-style rooms around its perimeter. Comfortable and with good service. Recommended.

$$$ Caiçara
Av Olinda 235, T083-2106 1000,
www.hotelcaicara.com.
A slick, business orientated place (Best Western) with a pleasant restaurant attached.

$$$ Nobile Inn Royal
Coração de Jesus, T083-2106 3000,
www.royalhotel.com.br.
Comfortable rooms with fridges around a pool.

$$$-$$ Xênius
Av Cabo Branco 1262, T083-3015 3535,
www.xeniushotel.com.br.
Popular standard 4-star with a pool, good restaurant and well-kept but standard rooms (low-season reductions).

$$ Solar Filipéia
Rua Isidro Gomes 44, Tambaú, T083-3219 3744,
www.hotelfilipeia.com.br.
Very smart hotel with large, bright rooms with bathrooms in tile and black marble and excellent service.

$$ Teiú Hotel Pousada
R Carlos Alverga 36, T083-3247 5475,
www.teiupraia.webnode.pt.
Centrally located and 1 block from the beach. Intimate, with balconies and sea view.

$ Hostel Manaíra
R Major Ciraulo 380, Manaíra, T083-3247 1962,
www.manairahostel.com.br.
Friendly, brand new hostel close to the beach, with a pool, barbecue, cable TV and breakfast, good value.

Restaurants

There are few options in the centre, other than the stalls in Parque Solon de Lucena next to the lake, beside which are some simple restaurants. Every evening on the beachfront, stalls are set up selling all kinds of snacks and barbecued meats. At Cabo Branco there are many straw huts on the beach serving cheap eats and seafood.

$$$ Adega do Alfredo
Coração de Jesus s/n, T083-3226 4346,
www.adegadoalfredo.com.br.
Very popular traditional Portuguese restaurant in the heart of the club and bar area.

$$$ Gulliver
Av Olinda 590, Tambaú, T083-3226 2504,
www.restaurantegulliver.com.br.
Fashionable French/Brazilian restaurant frequented by João Pessoa's upper middle classes.

$$ Cheiro Verde
R Carlos Alverga 43, Manaíra, T083-3226 2700.
Self service, well established, regional food.

$$ Mangaí
Av General Édson Ramalho 696, Manaíra,
T083-3226 1615, www.mangai.com.
This is one of the best restaurants in the north-east to sample the region's cooking, with almost 100 hot dishes to choose from, sitting in copper tureens over a traditional wood-fired stove some 20 m long. Has branches in Brasília and Natal.

$$ Sapore d'Italia
Av Cabo Branco 1584, T083-3247 3322,
www.saporeonline.com.
Standard Italian fare including pizza.

$$ Toca do Caju
Av N S dos Navegantes 750, T083-2107 8700,
www.pousadadocaju.com.br.

Self service, price by kilo, good value. international food and barbecue. Has an adjoining *pousada*.

Bars and clubs

There are many open bars on and across from the beach in Tambaú and Cabo Branco. The area known as Feirinha de Tambaú, on Av Tamandaré by the **Tambaú Hotel**, is very lively, with R Coração do Jesus being the centre. There are numerous little bars and *forró* places here.

Festivals

Feb Pre-carnival celebrations are renowned: the *bloco* Acorde Miramar opens the celebrations the Tue before Carnival and on Wed, known as **Quarta Feira de Fogo**, thousands join the Muriçocas de Miramar.
5 Aug Celebrations for the patroness of the city, **Nossa Senhora das Neves**, take place for 10 days at the beginning of Aug.

Shopping

Mercado Central, *Centro. Bus 513, 511.* Basic, big, dirty, but interesting. All fruit and spices of the region are sold there.
O Canto do Galeto, *Av Ruy Carneiro 183.* Minimarket next to fruit market, serves take-away grilled chicken.

Supermercado Pão de Açúcar, *Av Epitácio Pessoa. Open 1200-1400.* Also good value lunches.

What to do

City tours and trips to beaches are available. For night-time folklore dances, ask at **Tropical Tambaú** for details. Buggy tours go to places where buses do not go. English-speaking driver **Orlando** (T083-99984 8010), has car for sightseeing, very helpful, takes 3.

Transport

Air Aeroporto Presidente Castro Pinto, Bayeux 11 km from centre, T083-3232 1200; national flights Taxi to centre costs US$12, to Tambaú US$32.

Bus Most city buses stop at the *rodoviária* and go by the Lagoa (Parque Solon de Lucena). Take No 510 for Tambaú, No 507 for Cabo Branco.
Rodoviária is at R Francisco Londres, Varadouro, 10 mins from the centre, T083-3222 6567; luggage store; PBTUR (see above) information booth is helpful. Taxi to the centre US$4, to Tambaú US$7.50. To **Recife**, every 30 mins, US$6.55-9, 2 hrs To **Natal** with **Nordeste**, every 2 hrs, US$12.50, 3 hrs. To **Fortaleza** with **Nordeste**, 2 a day, 12 hrs, US$30. To **Salvador**, US$42, 14 hrs.

Natal *Colour map 5, B6.*

an attractive city blessed with good beaches and clean air

★Natal, capital of Rio Grande do Norte, located on a peninsula between the Rio Potengi and the Atlantic Ocean, is one of the most attractive cities of Brazil's northeast coast, as well as a popular destination for those seeking sun and good beaches. The air is said by NASA to be the second purest in the world, after Antarctica. The inventors of the beach-buggy must have had Rio Grande do Norte in mind as the dunes and strand that surround the city are ideal for daredevil stunts and whizzing along the open sands.

Sights

The oldest part is the **Ribeira** along the renovated riverfront. The **Cidade Alta**, or Centro, is the main centre and Avenida Rio Branco its principal artery. The main square is made up by the adjoining **praças: João Maria, André de Albuquerque, João Tibúrcio** and **7 de Setembro**. At Praça André de Albuquerque is the old cathedral (inaugurated 1599, restored 1996). The small church of **Santo Antônio** ① *R Santo Antônio 683, Cidade Alta, Tue-Fri 0800-1700, Sat 0800-1400,* dates from 1766. It has a blue and white façade, a fine, carved wooden altar and a sacred art museum.

On a hill overlooking Ribeira is the **Centro do Turismo** ① *R Aderbal de Figueiredo 980, off R Gen Gustavo C Farias,* Petrópolis (see Bars and clubs, and Shopping, page 577). A converted prison with a wide variety of handicraft shops, art gallery, antique shop and tourist information booth, it offers good view of the Rio Potengi and the sea. At Praia do Forte, the tip of Natal's peninsula, is the **Forte dos Reis Magos** ① *T084-3221 0342, daily 0800-1630 except Christmas Day, New Year and Carnaval, US$3.* The star-shaped fort was begun in 1598 and is now the city's main historical monument. Its blinding white walls contrast with the blue of sea and sky. You can wander round the interior rooms, mostly empty although the former military prison now houses a *lanchonete*, and there are guides

The easiest way to get there is by taxi or on a tour; no buses go to the entrance, from where you have to walk along a causeway to the fort. Between it and the city is a military installation.

The **Museu Câmara Cascudo** ① *Av Hermes de Fonseca 1398, Tirol, T084-3342 4903, Facebook: museucamaracascudoufrn, Tue-Fri 0900-1700, Sat300-1700, US$0.75*, has exhibits on archaeological digs, Umbanda rituals and the sugar, leather and petroleum industries.

A large ecological zone, the **Parque das Dunas**, separates the commercial centre from Ponta Negra, 12.5 km away, the beach and nightlife spot where most visitors stay.

Beaches

Natal has excellent beaches, some of which are also the scene of the city's nightlife. East of the centre, from north to south are: **Praia do Forte, do Meio, dos Artistas de Areia Preta** and **Mãe Luzia**. The first two have reefs offshore, therefore little surf, and are appropriate for windsurfing. The others are urban beaches and local enquiries regarding pollution are recommended before bathing. Mãe Luzia marks the start of the **Via Costeira**, which runs south along the ocean beneath the towering sand dunes of **Parque das Dunas** (access restricted to protect the 9 km of dunes), joining the city to the neighbourhood and popular beach of Ponta Negra. A cycle path parallels this road and provides great views of the coastline. Lining Mãe Luzia and Barreira d'Água (the beach across from Parque das Dunas) are the city's four and five-star hotels.

Furthest south is vibrant and pretty **Ponta Negra**, justifiably the most popular beach. The seafront, Avenida Erivan França, is a car-free promenade for much of its length; the remainder is the busiest part of town. It has many hotels, from *albergues* up to three- and four-star, restaurants and bars. The northern end of the beach is good for surfing, while the southern end is calmer and suitable for swimming. At the south end of the beach is **Morro do Careca**, a 120-m-high protected dune surrounded by vegetation. Although no longer used for sand-skiing, it remains one of the 'postcards' of the city.

Ponta Negra

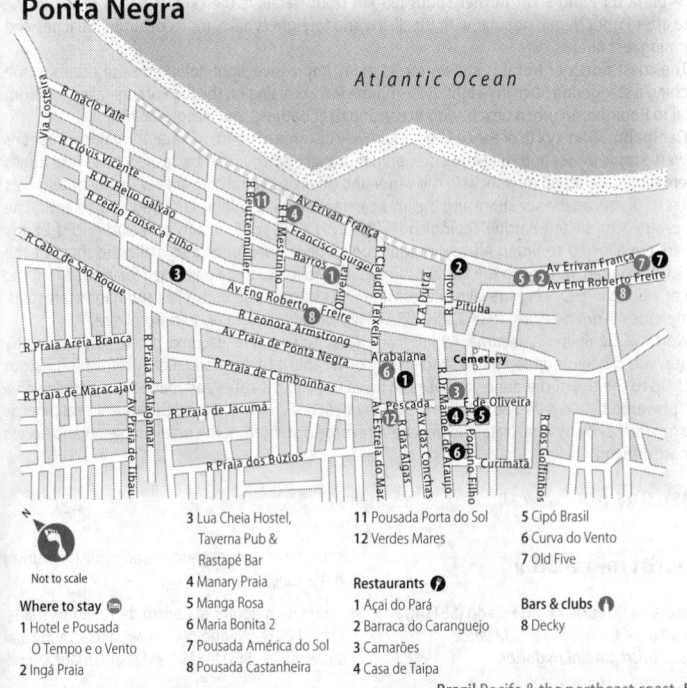

Not to scale

Where to stay 🛌
1 Hotel e Pousada O Tempo e o Vento
2 Ingá Praia
3 Lua Cheia Hostel, Taverna Pub & Rastapé Bar
4 Manary Praia
5 Manga Rosa
6 Maria Bonita 2
7 Pousada América do Sol
8 Pousada Castanheira
11 Pousada Porta do Sol
12 Verdes Mares

Restaurants 🍴
1 Açaí do Pará
2 Barraca do Caranguejo
3 Camarões
4 Casa de Taipa
5 Cipó Brasil
6 Curva do Vento
7 Old Five

Bars & clubs 🍸
8 Decky

Around Natal

The coast south of the city is referred to as **Litoral Sul**, to the north as **Litoral Norte**. While there are buses south (leaving from the *rodoviária* in Natal), notably to Tibau and Pipa along the coastal road, agencies in Ponta Negra also offer dune buggy day trips along the beaches (see page 578).

Pirangi do Norte, 25 km from Natal, has calm waters, is popular for watersports and offshore bathing (500 m out) when natural pools form between the reefs. In the town is the world's largest cashew-nut tree (*maior cajueiro do mundo*, entry US$1.50); branches springing from a single trunk cover an area of some 8400 sq m, a whole city block. A guide on site offers a brief explanation and there is a look-out for seeing the tree from above. Outside are handicraft stalls, tourist information and musicians.

Beyond Barreta is the long, pristine beach of **Malembar**, access on foot or by a five-minute boat ride across the mouth of the **Lagoa Guaraíra** from Tibau do Sul at the south end. The ferries to/from Tibau do Sul costs US$8 return; buggy drivers should not add this fee to a day tour. Crossings are determined by the state of the tide (times are critical and you should follow the buggy driver's instructions regarding departure times). Around **Tibau do Sul** the lovely beaches circled by high cliffs, the lagoons, Atlantic forest and the dolphins are some of the attractions that make this one of the most visited stretches of the southern coast (it can get crowded during holiday periods and weekends). South of town there are fine, wide, white-sand beaches, separated by rocky headlands, set against high cliffs and coconut groves.

At Praia do Madeiro and neighbouring **Baía dos Golfinhos**, the ocean is calm and clear and dolphins can often be seen (ask locally for the best time and swim from Madeiro beach to see them, rather than take an expensive tour from Pipa). Between Praia do Madeiro and Pipa, on a 70-m high dune, is the **Santuário Ecológico de Pipa** ① *0800-1600, US$3*. This 60-ha park was created in 1986 to conserve the Mata Atlântica forest; there are 17 trails and lookouts over the cliffs which afford an excellent view of the ocean and dolphins.

☆**Praia da Pipa**, 3 km further south (85 km from Natal), is the busiest beach resort in the state after Ponta Negra, popular with Brazilians and foreigners alike, for its beautiful beaches and charming restaurants.

The coast **north of Natal** is known for its many impressive, light-coloured sand dunes, some reaching a staggering 50 m in height. A 25-minute ferry crossing on the Rio Potengi takes you from Natal to **Redinha**, an urban beach, with ocean and river bathing, and buggies to hire.

Genipabu, 30 km north of the city, has effectively become a suburb of Natal. Its major attractions are very scenic dunes and the Lagoa de Genipabu, a lake surrounded by cashew trees and dunes where tables are set up on a shoal in the water and drinks served. There are also many hotels, bars and restaurants on the sea shore and the area can feel overwhelmingly crowded at weekends. The dunes are a protected **Parque Ecológico** ① *T084-3211 0574, US$3.15*, and only authorized buggy drivers are allowed to enter. All buggy tours go through the dunes and make the most of the vehicles' manoeuvrability on the fantastic slopes and hollows: prepare yourself for '*emoção*'. At the top of a dune overlooking the lake and coast are lots of colourful umbrellas and handicraft stalls. Camel rides ① *dromedários, T084-3225 2053, www.dromedunas.com.br*, start from here.

North of Genipabu is **Jacumã**, 49 km from Natal. At Lagoa de Jacumã, a lake surrounded by dunes, you can aerobunda, sit in a sling and fly on a cable into the water. Really refreshing. To get back up to the top of the dune you take the fusca funicular, a 'cable car' made from a trolley on a rail, powered by a wheel-less VW Beetle. Lovely beaches continue along the state's coastline; as you get further away from Natal the beaches are more distant from the main highways and access is more difficult.

Listings Natal *map p573*

Tourist information

Secretaria de Turismo do Estado (SETUR)
R Jundiaí 644, Tirol, T084-3232 9065,
http://turismo.natal.rn.gov.br.

Is the government agency responsible for tourism in the state.

Information booths at **Centro de Turismo** (T084-3211 6149, see Shopping, below), at the municipal tourist office, **SETUR** (Av Sen Dinarte Mariz s/n,

Ponta Negra, T084-3232 2486, http://natalbrasil.
tur.br, Mon-Fri 0800-1400), on Erivan Franca in
Ponta Negra, *rodoviária* (T084-3232 7310), and
airport (T084-3644 1170).

For information T0800-841516, or, for the
Polícia Federal (T194), and for the **Tourist Police**
(Av Engenheiro Roberto Freire 8790, Ponta Negra,
T084-3232 7404, Delegacia do Turista).

Where to stay

The **Via Costeira** is a strip of enormous,
upmarket beachfront hotels, which are very
isolated, with no restaurants or shops within
easy walking distance. **Ponta Negra** is the ideal
place to stay, with its attractive beach and
concentration of restaurants. Economical hotels
are easier to find in the city proper but there is
otherwise not much reason to stay there (no
nightlife and a long way from the action). Prices
of beach hotels below are for the high season
(Dec-Feb and Jul), unless otherwise stated.

In the centre

$$$ Golden Tulip Interâtlantico
*Av Getúlio Vargas 788, Petrópolis, T084-3087
4800, www.goldentulipinteratlantico.com.*
Business hotel in the city centre, restaurant,
gym and pool.

$$$ Maine
*Av Salgado Filho 1791, Lagoa Nova, T084-4005
5774, www.hotelmaine.com.br.*
On the principal avenue leading from the centre
to Ponta Negra. Full service in this 4-star hotel,
restaurant with panoramic views.

Beaches

Praia do Meio, Praia dos Artistas and Praia de Areia Preta

The distinction between these 1st 2 beaches
is often blurred. Most hotels here are on the
beachfront Av Pres Café Filho, the numbering of
which is illogical. Many *pousadas* open for just
1 season, then close for good. There are better
budget options in Ponta Negra.

$$$ Bruma
*Av Pres Café Filho 1176, Praia dos Artistas,
T084-3202 4303, www.hotelbruma.com.br.*
Slick, intimate, 2 rooms per floor beachfront
balconies, also has more expensive suites, tiny
pool, terrace. Recommended.

Ponta Negra

Here, too, the street numbering is pretty chaotic.

$$$$-$$$ Manary Praia
*R Francisco Gurgel 9067, T084-3204 2900,
www.manary.com.br.*
Price depends on view from room; phone in
advance as prices vary greatly according to
month. This is a very stylish hotel on a quiet
corner, some rooms overlook the pool/terrace
and beach, all are very comfortable, 'neocolonial'
design using local materials, spa, member of
the Roteiros de Charme group, see page 670.
Recommended.

$$$ Hotel e Pousada O Tempo e o Vento
*R Elias Barros 66, T084-3219 2526,
www.otempoeovento.com.br.*
$$ in low season, fridge, safe in room, pool and
wet bar, luxo rooms are very comfortable, good
breakfast. Recommended.

$$$ Ingá Praia
*Av Erivan França 17, T084-3219 3436,
www.ingapraiahotel.com.br.*
$$ without sea view, cheaper in low season
(service tax not included). Very comfortable,
cosy, rooms have all the expected facilities.
Recommended.

$$$ Manga Rosa
*Av Erivan França 240, T084-3219 0508,
www.mangarosanatal.com.br.*
Well-appointed small rooms with attractive
wooden fittings, colourful bedspreads and
sea views.

$$$-$$ Pousada Castanheira
*Rua da Praia 221, T084-3219 0168,
www.pousadacastanheira.com.br.*
English/Brazilian owners, **$$** in low season,
comfortable spacious rooms with fridge and
safe, small pool, breakfast room with sea
view, room service, parking, very helpful staff.
Recommended.

$$ Maria Bonita 2
*Estrela do Mar 2143, Arabaiana, T084-3236 2941,
www.mariabonita2.com.br.*
With a/c, cheaper with fan, not as close to
the beach as most, but near the Broadway
and its nightlife.

$$ Pousada Porta do Sol
*R Francisco Gurgel 9057, T084-3236 2555,
www.pousadaportadosol.com.br.*
Clean and tidy, good seafront location, fridge,
a/c except in rooms with sea breeze, some fans,

good mattresses, excellent breakfast, pool, good value, English and French spoken (ask for Patrick or Suerda). Recommended.

$ pp Lua Cheia
R Dr Manoel Augusto Bezerra de Araújo 500, T084-3236 3696, www.tavernapub.com.br.
Purpose-built HI hostel in 'castle' with 'medieval' **Taverna Pub** in basement (see Bars and clubs, below). Dorms and private rooms (**$$**), discounts for HI members, holds cultural events and parties. Highly recommended.

$ Pousada América do Sol
R Erivan França 35, T084-3219 2245.
Price per person in albergue-style rooms with bath, hot water, lockers, cheaper without a/c, popular, simple, use of kitchen. Also has *pousada* rooms at **$$** (half-price in low season), a/c, frigobar, parking.

$ pp Verdes Mares
R das Algas 2166, Conj Algamar, T084-3236 2872, albergue@hostelverdesmares.com.br.
HI hostel, **$$** in nicely decorated doubles, discount in low season, quiet, comfortable, pool. Recommended.

Around Natal: Praia da Pipa
In Pipa more than 30 *pousadas* and many private homes offer accommodation. See www.pipa.com.br for some listings.

$$$$ Toca da Coruja
Av Baía dos Golfinhos, T084-3246 2226, www.tocadacoruja.com.br.
Comfortable chalets and cheaper suites in a separate block, with all facilities including safe in room, in gardens with lots of trees, 2 spring-water swimming pools, bar, quiet, member of the Roteiros de Charme group, see page 670.

$$$ Ponta do Madeiro
Rota do Sol, Km 3, Tibaú do Sul, T084-3246 4220, www.pontadomadeiro.com.br.
Beautifully set in Mata Atlântica, views of and access to Madeiro beach, between Pipa and Tibaú, 3 types of chalet in gardens, pool, restaurant, trips on land and sea and hourly transfers to Pipa, US$4.

$$$ Sombra e Água Fresca
R Praia do Amor 1000, T084-3246 2258, www.sombraeaguafresca.com.br.
A/c, fridge, pools, restaurant with beautiful view especially at sunset. Cheaper in low season, rooms of varying size and standard.

$$$ Tartaruga
Av Baía dos Golfinhos 508, T084-3246 2385, www.pousadatartaruga.com.br.
Rooms around a pretty little pool, nicely decorated, shady bar and restaurant area.

$$ Pousada Aconchego
R do Ceu s/n, Praia da Pipa, T084-3246 2439, www.pousada-aconchego.com.
Family-run *pousada* with simple chalets, in a garden filled with cashew and palm trees, tranquil, central, good breakfast.

$$ Pousada Pomar da Pipa
R da Mata, T084-3246 2696, www.pomardapipa.com.
150 m from *praça*, quiet, beautiful garden, hammocks, very helpful, good value.

$$-$ Pousada da Pipa
R do Cruzeiro s/n, T084-3246 2271.
Small rooms decorated with a personal touch. The best are upstairs and have a large shared terrace with glazed terracotta tiles, sitting areas and hammocks.

Restaurants

Prawns feature heavily on menus here as Natal is the largest exporter in Brazil. The city centre area of Petrópolis is well known locally for having the best restaurants in the state.

$$ Mangaí
Av Amintos Barros 3300, Lagoa Nova, www.mangai.com.br. Open 0600-2200, closed Mon.
Very good regional food (*carne do sol*, tapioca and many other *sertaneja* dishes) in rustic atmosphere. Recommended.

$ A Macrobiótica
Princesa Isabel 524.
Vegetarian, shop, lunch only. Next door is **Neide** (at No 530), for coffee and sweets.

Beaches

Ponta Negra

$$ Barraca do Caranguejo
Av Erivan França 1180.
Live music nightly from 2100. 12 different types of prawn dish, *rodízio* style.

$$ Camarões
Av Eng Roberto Freire 2610.
Also at Natal Shopping Centre. Touristy, but very good seafood.

$$ Cipó Brasil
Av Erivan França 3 and Rua Aristides Porpino Filho 3111.
Jungle theme, 4 levels, sand floors, lantern-lit, dishes and rinks well-presented. Serves pizzas and crêpes (house speciality), good for cocktails, live music nightly after 2100. In the same group is **Casa de Taipa** (R Dr Manoel A B de Araújo 130A), by Taverna Pub (see below), serving tapioca, salads, juices and coffee.

$$ Curva do Vento
R Dr Manoel A B de Araújo 396, T084-2010 4749.
Some of the best pizzas in Ponta Negra, together with all manner of rosti (stuffed with curry, lobster or stroganoff) and a broad selection of ice-cold beers. Lively.

$$ Old Five
Av Erivan França 230, T084-3236 2505.
Romantic and rustic chic beach bar/restaurant, next to the dunes with outdoor candles, low-light, decent cocktails and a menu of seafood, fish and chicken standards and bar snacks.

$$-$ Açai do Pará
R das Algas 2151, T084-3219 3024.
Pará dishes including delicious *takaka*, *frango no tucupi* and *maniçoba*, snacks and a superb selection of juices including *camu camu* and *açai*.

Bars and clubs

Natal's nightlife hot spot lies in the streets around Dr Manoel A B de Araújo (behind Ponta Negra beach on the other side of Av Eng Roberto Freire).

Centro de Turismo
See Shopping, below.
Has *Forró com Turista*, a chance for visitors to learn this fun dance, Thu at 2200; many other enjoyable venues where visitors are encouraged to join in.

Decky
Av Roberto Freire 9100, Ponta Negra, T084-3219 2471.
Models of Mick Jagger and John Lennon greet you at the entrance of this al fresco rock bar, where live bands play to a buzzing crowd at weekends. Also serves food.

Rastapé
R Aristides Porpino 2198, Ponta Negra, T084-3219 0181, www.rastapenatal.com.br.
Lively faux-rustic *forró* bar with 3 live bands a night and areas for eating, chatting and dancing. Very popular.

Taverna Pub
R Dr Manoel A B de Araújo 500, Ponta Negra, T084-3236 3696, www.tavernapub.com.br.
Medieval-style pub in youth hostel basement. Eclectic (rock, Brazilian pop, jazz, etc.) live music Tue-Sun from 2200, best night Wed, singles night Mon. Recommended. This street and the one that joins it by Taverna/Lua Cheia is known as 'Broadway', with lots of bars and cafés.

Festivals

Jan Festa de Nossa Senhora dos Navegantes, when numerous vessels go to sea from Praia da Redinha, north of town.
Dec Carnatal, the Salvador-style out of season carnival, a lively 4-day music festival in the first week of the month, with dancing in the streets.

Shopping

Handicrafts
Centro Municipal de Artesanato, *Av Pres Café Filho, Praia do Meio. Daily 1000-2200.* Sand-in-bottle pictures are very common in Natal.
Centro de Turismo, *R Aderbal de Figueiredo, 980, off R Gen Gustavo C Farias, Petrópolis.* A converted prison with a wide variety of handicraft shops, art gallery, antique shop, café, restaurant and tourist information booth, offers good view of the Rio Potengi and the sea, daily 0900-1900, Thu at 2200 is *Forró com Turista* (see Bars and clubs, above).

Shopping centres
Natal Shopping, *Av Senador Salgado Filho 2234, Candelária, between Ponta Negra and the centre.* Large mall with restaurants, ATMs, cinemas and 140 shops. Free shuttle bus service to major hotels.
Praia Shopping, *Av Eng Roberto Freire 8790, Ponta Negra.* Smart shops, food hall. There are more restaurants outside, mostly fast food, on R Praia de Genipabu. It also has exchange and the **Central do Cidadão**. This facility has a post office, federal police office and **Banco do Brasil** with ATM; Tue-Fri 1000-2200, Sat 1000-1800.

What to do

Boat tours
To natural swimming pools at Pirangi do Norte, 25 km south of Natal, and to the nearby beaches of the Litoral Sul are available from **Marina Badauê** (Pirangi do Norte, T084-3238 2066, www.marinabadaue.com.br). A 2-hr tour includes hotel pick-up, a snack (or breakfast if you take an early tour), and allows time for a swim, US$19 pp.

Departures depend on the tide. The company has a restaurant and bar at the seashore.

Tour operators

Buggy tours are by far the most popular, around US$55-80 for a dune buggy trip. If you book direct with the buggy owner, rather than through a hotel or agency, there will be a discount. The price should include all commissions and ferry crossings, but not entrance to Parque Ecológico. Buggy drivers (*bugueiros*) have an association (**APCBA**, *Av Beria Mar 405, Praia de Genipabu, T084-3225 2077, www.genipabudebuggy.com.br*) and all members must be approved by Setur and Detran. Look for the sign 'Autorizado Setur' plus a number on the buggy.

Cariri Ecotours, *R Francisco Gurgel 9067, Ponta Negra, T084-99993 0027, www.caririecotours. com.br*. Mainly 4WD tours throughout Rio Grande do Norte, Ceará, the Sertão, Paraíba and Pernambuco, beach safaris along the coast to Fortaleza or Paraíba, to natural monuments, national parks and archaeological sites, with a strong ecological emphasis. Trustworthy, excellent guides. Good English, will also begin/end tours in Recife or Fortaleza.

Around Natal: Praia da Pipa

Several agencies run buggy trips, offer boat trips for dolphin watching or lunch/dinner cruises, kayaking, surfing and kitesurfing. There is also horse riding and walking in the Santuário Ecológico.

Transport

Air Aeroporto Governador Aluízio Alves, at São Gonçalo do Amarante 40 km from Natal,

T084-3334 6060, www.natal.aero. The airport has a tourist office, Global Câmbio, ATMs, car hire, restaurants and shops. **Trampolim da Vitória** micro-buses route R (www.trampolimdavitoria. com) from airport to the city centre (Midway Mall), US$1, from where there are connections to other parts of the city. Also Coopcon Taxis, T084-3343 6429, www.coopcon.com.br.

Bus *Rodoviária*, Av Capitão Mor Gouveia 1237, Cidade da Esperança, T084-3205 2931. Regional tickets are sold on street level, interstate on the 2nd floor. To **Recife**, 9 daily, convencional and more comfortable executive both US$21, 4 hrs. With **Nordeste** to **Mossoró**, US$14.35-16.25, 4 hrs. To **Aracati**, US$21, 5½ hrs. To **Fortaleza**, US$29, 7½ hrs. To **João Pessoa**, see page 570. To **Teresina**, US$53 convencional, 17-20 hrs.

Car hire There are many rental agencies on Av Eng Roberto Freire for cars and buggies. Buggy rental about US$50 a day, price depends on make.

Taxi Taxis are expensive compared to other cities; US$10 for 10-min journey. Standard US$20 fare from airport or *rodoviária* to centre, US$12-17 to Ponta Negra.

Around Natal

Pirangi do Norte

Bus From Natal, new *rodoviária*, many daily, US$3 to Pirangi, 1 hr.

Tibau do Sul and Pipa

Bus From Natal 12 a day (6 at weekends) to Tibau do Sul and on to Pipa, US$4, 2½ hrs. Combis go to **Goianinha**, US$3, from where buses run south to João Pessoa.

Fortaleza &
the north coast

★The state of Ceará has been dubbed A Terra da Luz, Land of Light. It has some of the finest beaches in Brazil, scenic dunes and almost constant sunshine. The sophisticated capital, Fortaleza, is still home to *jangadas* (traditional fishing boats), while its nightlife is famous throughout the country. As well as the mysterious Parque Nacional de Sete Cidades, Piauí shares with Maranhão the remarkable Parnaíba delta, which is beginning to be recognized as a major ecological site with great tourist potential. The Parque Nacional Lençóis Maranhenses, across the delta, is a landscape of fabulous sand dunes and crystal lakes. Maranhão's capital, São Luís, is one of Brazil's UNESCO sites of worldwide cultural importance, because of its colonial centre.

Fortaleza *Colour map 5, B5.*
a buzzing metropolis with miles of beaches and busy bars

Fortaleza, the fourth largest city in Brazil with a population of 2.1 million, is a busy metropolis with many highrise buildings, an important clothes manufacturing industry, many hotels and restaurants and a lively nightlife. Fishermen's *jangadas* still dot the turquoise ocean across from the beach and transatlantic cruise ships call in for refuelling. The midday sun is oppressive, tempered somewhat by a constant breeze; evening temperatures can be more pleasant, especially by the sea. The wettest months are March to July.

Sights

Praça do Ferreira, from which pedestrian walkways radiate, is the heart of the commercial centre. The whole area is dotted with shady squares. **Fortaleza Nossa Senhora da Assunção** ① *Av Alberto Nepomuceno, daily 0800-1100, 1400-1700*, originally built in 1649 by the Dutch, gave the city its name. Near the fort, on Rua Dr João Moreira, is the 19th-century **Passeio Público** or Praça dos Mártires, a park with old trees and statues of Greek deities.

West of here, a neoclassical former prison (1866) houses the **Centro de Turismo do Estado** ① *Av Senador Pompeu 350, near the waterfront, T085-3101 5508, http://emcetur.com.br, Mon-Sat 0800-1700, Sun 0800-1200*, with museums, theatre and high-quality craft shops (bargaining expected). It houses the **Museu de Arte e Cultura Populares** and the **Museu de Minerais**. Further west along Rua Dr João Moreira, at **Praça Castro Carreira** (commonly known as Praça da Estação), is the nicely refurbished train station **Estação João Felipe** (1880).

> ### Warning...
> Avoid the Serviluz favela between the old lighthouse (Avenida Vicente de Castro), the favela behind the railway station, the Passeio Público at night, Avenida Abolição at its eastern (Nossa Senhora da Saúde church) and western ends. Also be careful at Mucuripe and Praia do Futuro. Generally, though, the city is safe for visitors.

Best for
Architecture ▪ Beaches ▪ Nightlife ▪ Wildlife

The **Teatro José de Alencar** ① *on praça of the same name, T085-3101 2583, Facebook: theatro josedealencar, Mon-Fri 0800-1700, hourly tours, English speaking guides, US$1.35, Wed free*, was inaugurated in 1910. This magnificent iron structure was imported from Scotland and is decorated in neo-classical and art nouveau styles. It also houses a library and art gallery. The new **cathedral**, completed in 1978, in gothic style but concrete, stands beside the new, **Mercado Central** with beautiful stained glass windows. Both are on Praça da Sé, at Avenida Alberto Nepomuceno. The **Museu do Maracatu** ① *Rufino de Alencar 231, at Teatro São José*, houses costumes of this ritual dance of African origin.

The **Centro Dragão do Mar de Arte e Cultura** ① *R Dragão do Mar 81, Praia de Iracema*, hosts music concerts, dance, and art and photography exhibitions. It has various entrances, from Ruas Almirante Barroso, Boris and from junction of Monsenhor Tabosa, Dom Manuel and Castelo Branco. This last one leads directly to three museums: on street level, the **Memorial da Cultura Cearense**, with changing exhibitions; on the next floor down is an art and cultural exhibit; in the basement is an excellent audio-visual museum of **El Vaqueiro**. Also at street level is the Livraria Livro Técnico. There is a planetarium with a whispering gallery underneath. The centre also houses a contemporary art museum **Museu de Arte Contemporânea do Ceará** ① *T085-3488 8600, www.dragaodomar.org.br, Mon-Thu 0800-2200, Fri-Sun 0800-2300, free*. This area is very lively at night.

Fortaleza has 25 km of beaches, many of which are the scene of the city's nightlife; those between **Barra do Ceará** (west) and **Ponta do Mucuripe** (east) are polluted. **Praia de Iracema** is

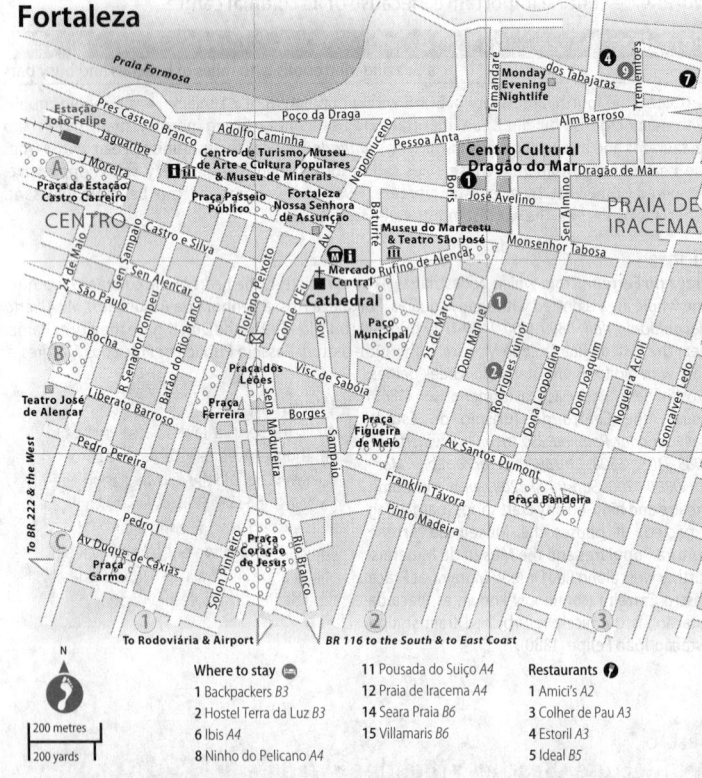

Fortaleza

Where to stay
1 Backpackers *B3*
2 Hostel Terra da Luz *B3*
6 Ibis *A4*
8 Ninho do Pelicano *A4*
11 Pousada do Suíço *A4*
12 Praia de Iracema *A4*
14 Seara Praia *B6*
15 Villamaris *B6*

Restaurants
1 Amici's *A2*
3 Colher de Pau *A3*
4 Estoril *A3*
5 Ideal *B5*

one of the older beach suburbs with some original turn-of-the-century houses. East of Iracema, the **Avenida Beira Mar** (Avenida Presidente Kennedy) connects **Praia do Meireles** with Volta da Jurema and **Praia do Mucuripe**, 5 km from the centre. Fortaleza's main fishing centre, *jangadas*, bring in the catch here. **Praia do Futuro**, 8 km southeast of the centre, is the most popular bathing beach, 8 km long, unpolluted, with strong waves, sand dunes and fresh-water showers, but no natural shade; there are many vendors and *barracas* serving local dishes. Thursday night, Saturday and Sunday are very busy. A city bus marked 'P Futuro' from Praça Castro Carreira, 'Praia Circular', does a circular route to Praia do Futuro; a bus marked 'Caça e Pesca' passes all southeast beaches on its route. About 29 km southeast of the centre is **Praia Porto das Dunas**, popular for watersports including surfing.

Northwest of the centre is **Praia Barra do Ceará**, 8 km, where the Rio Ceará flows into the sea. Here are the ruins of the 1603 Forte de Nossa Senhora dos Prazeres, the first Portuguese settlement in the area. The beaches west of the Rio Ceará are cleaner, lined with palms and have strong waves. A new bridge across this river gives better access to this area, for example, **Praia de Icaraí**, 22 km, and **Tabuba**, 5 km further north. Beyond Tabuba, 37 km from Fortaleza, is **Cumbuco**, renowned as the kitesurf capital of Brazil, with a lively beach, which can be dirty in high season. There are also chaotic bars, palm trees, horse riding and dunes which you can sandboard down into a rainwater lake.

6 La Fiorentina *B6*
7 La Habanera *A3*

Bars & clubs 🎵
9 Pirata *A3*

Tourist information

Setfor (Municipal Tourist Office)
Rua Leonardo Mota 2700, T085-3105 1600,
Facebook: secretariadeturismodefortaleza.
Mon-Fri 0800-1700. Also at Mercado Central
(Mon-Fri 0900-1700, Sat 0900-1200) and
Praça do Ferreira (same hours).

Setur
Av Washington Soares 999, Centro de Eventos,
Pavilhão Leste, 2 Mezanino, T085-3195 0200,
www.setur.ce.gov.br.
State tourism agency, information booths
at airport (0600-2300) and the Centro de
Turismo (Mon-Fri 0800-1800, Sat 0800-1600,
Sun 0800-1200).

Where to stay

Almost all hotels offer reduced prices in the low
season. There are many *pousadas* in the Iracema/
Meireles area, but they change frequently.

Centre

$ Backpackers
R Dom Manuel 89, T085-8411 8997,
www.backpackersce.com.br.
Lively central hostel with basic rooms, dorms and
private, no breakfast, but use of kitchen, helpful,
English spoken, bike and car parking, information.

By the beach

There are several business-oriented hotels on
Av Beira Mar, all of a similar standard.

$$$$-$$$ Seara Praia
Av Beira Mar 3080, Meireles, T085-4011 2222,
www.hotelseara.com.br.
30% cheaper in low season, smart, comfortable
hotel with pool, gym, cyber café, French cuisine.

$$$ Ibis
Atualpa Barbosa de Lima 660, Iracema,
T085-3052 2450, www.accorhotels.com.br.
Breakfast extra, in Accor style, with usual
facilities, pool.

$$ Hostel Terra da Luz
R Rodrigues Júnior 278, Iracema, T085-3082 2260,
www.hostelterradaluz.com.
Good quality backpacker hostel with dorms and
private rooms (**$$-$**), good facilities and garden,
very helpful staff.

$$ Ninho do Pelicano
Av Beira Mar 934, Iracema, T085-3219 0871.
Rooms with fan, great value for location,
convenient for everything, French owner.

$$ Pousada do Suiço
R Antônia Augusto 133, Iracema, T085-3219 3873,
www.pousadadosuico.com.br.
Must reserve mid-Oct to Feb. Very private, no
sign, quiet street, variety of rooms, some with
kitchens, small pool, fridge, Swiss-run, changes
cash. Recommended.

$$ Pousada Salinas
Av Zezé Diogo 3300, Praia do Futuro, T085-
3234 3626, www.pousadasalinas.com.br.
$ in low season, popular, fridge, parking, just
across from sea, some English spoken.

$$ Praia de Iracema
Raimundo Girão 430, Iracema, T085-3219 2299,
www.hotelpraiadeiracema.com.
20% discount in low season, fridge, safe in
room, coffee shop, pool, brightly coloured
bed covers, on corner so traffic outside, but
OK for value and comfort.

$$ Villamaris
Av Abolição 2026, Meireles, T085-3032 5599,
www.hotelvillamaris.com.br.
Cheaper in low season, cosy, security guard,
fridge, small rooftop pool, 1 block from beach.

Restaurants

Iracema and Dragão do Mar

2 good areas for places to eat, with plenty
of variety. There are many eating places of
various styles at the junction of Tabajaras and
Tremembés, mostly smart.

$$ Amici's
R Dragão do Mar 80.
Pasta, pizza and lively atmosphere in music-filled
street, evenings only. Some say it's the best at the
cultural centre.

$$ Colher de Pau
Ana Bilhar 1178, Meireles, T085-3267 6680.
Opens daily at 1830.
Sertaneja food, seafood, very pleasant.

$$ Estoril
R dos Tabajaras 397, Iracema.
Varied food in this landmark restaurant, which is
also a restaurant school.

Urban beaches

Several good fish restaurants at Praia de Mucuripe, where the boats come ashore between 1300 and 1500. **R J Ibiapina** (at the Mucuripe end of Meireles, 1 block behind beach), has pizzerias, fast food restaurants and sushi bars.

$$$-$$ La Fiorentina
Osvaldo Cruz 8, corner of Av Beira Mar, Meireles.
Some seafood expensive, but fish, meats, pasta, unpretentious, attentive waiters, good food, frequented by tourists and locals alike.

$$-$ Ideal
Av Abolição e José Vilar, Meireles.
Open 0530-2030.
Bakery serving lunches, small supermarket and deli, good, handy.

$ La Habanera
Praça da Igreja in Iracema,
Av Beira Mar e Ararius 6.
Café, wicker chairs, marble tables, old photos of Fidel, Che, et al, coffee and cigars.

Bars and clubs

Fortaleza is renowned for its nightlife and prides itself with having the liveliest Mon night in the country. *Forró* is the most popular dance and there is a tradition to visit certain establishments on specific nights.

Mon *Forró* is danced at the **Pirata Bar**, Iracema, US$15, open-air theme bar, from 2300, and other establishments along R dos Tabajaras and its surroundings. **Tue** Live golden oldies at **Boate Oásis**, Av Santos Dumont 6061, Aldeota. **Wed** Regional music and samba-reggae at **Clube do Vaqueiro**, city bypass, Km 14, by BR-116 south and E-020, at 2230. **Thu** Live music, shows and crab specialities at the beach shacks in Praia do Futuro. **Fri** Singers and bands play regional music at **Parque do Vaqueiro**, BR-020, Km 10, past city bypass. **Sat** *Forró* at **Parque Valeu Boi**, R Trezópolis, Cajueiro Torto, **Forró Três Amores**, Estrado Tapuio, Eusêbio and **Cantinho do Céu**, CE-04, Km 8. **Sun** *Forró* and *música sertaneja* at **Cajueiro Drinks**, BR-116, Km 20, Eusêbio.

The streets around Centro Cultural Dragão do Mar on R Dragão do Mar are lively every night of the week. Brightly painted, historic buildings house restaurants where musicians play to customers and the pavements are dotted with cocktail carts.

Caros Amigos
R Dragão do Mar, 22.
Live music at 2030: Tue, Brazilian instrumental; Wed, jazz; Thu, samba; Sun, Beatles covers, US$1 (also shows music on the big screen).

Restaurant e Crêperie Café Crème
R Dragão do Mar 92.
Live music on Tue.

Festivals

6 Jan Epiphany; Ash Wed.
19 Mar São José.
Jun The **Festas Juninas** in Ceará are much livelier than carnival.
Last Sun in Jul The **Regata Dragão do Mar**, Praia de Mucuripe: the traditional *jangada* (raft) races take place. Also during the last week of Jul, the out-of-season Salvador-style carnival, **Fortal**, takes place along Avs Almte Barroso, Raimundo Giro and Beira Mar.
15 Aug The local Umbanda *terreiros* (churches) celebrate the **Festival of Iemanjá** on Praia do Futuro, taking over the entire beach from noon till dusk, when offerings are cast into the surf. Well worth attending (members of the public may 'pegar um passo' – enter into an inspired religious trance – at the hands of a pai-de-santo).
Mid-Oct **Ceará Music**, a 4-day festival of Brazilian music, rock and pop held at Marina Park.

Shopping

Handicrafts

Fortaleza has an excellent selection of locally manufactured textiles, which are among the cheapest in Brazil, and a wide selection of regional handicrafts. The local craft specialities are lace and embroidered textile goods; also hammocks (US$15 to over US$100), fine alto-relievo wood carvings of northeast scenes, basket ware, leatherwork and clay figures (*bonecas de barro*). Bargaining is OK at the **Mercado Central** (Av Alberto Nepomuceno, closed Sun), and the **Centro de Turismo** (in the old prison, see above). Crafts also available in shops near the market, while shops on R Dr João Moreira 400 block sell clothes. Every night (1800-2300) there are stalls along the beach at Praia Meireles. Crafts also available in the commercial area along Av Monsenhor Tabosa.

Surfing

Surfing is popular on a number of Ceará beaches.

Tour operators

Many operators offer city and beach tours. Others offer adventure trips further afield, most common being off-road trips along beaches from Natal in the east to the Lençóis Maranhenses in the west.

Windsurfing

A number of Ceará beaches are excellent for windsurfing and kitesurfing. Equipment can be rented in some of the popular beaches such as Porto das Dunas and in the city. Cumbuco is a premier kitesurfing destination. Winds are most reliable Aug-Dec. Many clubs and *pousadas* cater for kitesurfers with all levels of experience. See www.portalcumbuco.com.br, but there are many other websites to explore.

Air Aeroporto Pinto Martins, Praça Eduardo Gomes, 6 km south of centre, T085-3392 1030, www.infraero.gov.br. Airport has a tourist office, car hire, food hall upstairs, Banco do Brasil. Direct flights to major cities. Bus 404 (Aeroporto/ Benfica/Rodoviária) from airport to Praça José de Alencar in the centre and the *rodoviária*, US$1. Taxis charge US$10-15 to centre, Av Beira Mar or Praia do Futuro, US$23 at night. Use Cooperativa Taxi Comum or Taxi Especial Credenciado.

Bus *Rodoviária* at Av Borges de Melo 1630, Fátima, 6 km south from centre, T085-3256 2100. For city transport information look up www. fortaleza. ce.gov.br/etufor/ and www.fortalbus. com. Many city buses to the centre (US$0.75); if in doubt the tourist kiosk will point you in the right direction. Taxi to Praia de Iracema, or Av Abolição US$8. There is a luggage store. Opposite the *rodoviária* is Hotel Amuarama, which has a bar and restaurant; there's also a *lanchonete*.

To **Mossoró**, 6 a day, US$13.25, **Natal**, 8 daily, US$29, 7½ hrs. **João Pessoa**, 2 daily, US$30, 10 hrs. **Guanabara**, to **Recife**, 5 daily, US$24, 12 hrs. **Guanabara**, to **Teresina**, several daily, US$25 (leito US$34), 10 hrs; to **Parnaíba** US$16-22 (leito US$32.50); to **Belém**, 3 daily, US$61-65, 23 hrs. **Piripiri**, for **Parque Nacional de Sete Cidades**, US$15.50-19, 9 hrs, a good stop en route to Belém, with **Guanabara**, who go to **São Luís**, 2 daily, US$35-48, 24 hrs at least, also Itapemirim.

In **Ceará**: Guanabara to **Sobral** US$8, to **Ubajara** twice a day, 6 hrs, US$15. **Fretcar**, T085-3402 2244, www.fretcar.com.br, to the west of the state, including **Camocim** US$11.75-14.75.

Car hire Many car hire places on Av Monsenhor Taboso, and at its junction with Ildefonso Albano. **Brasil Rent a Car**, Av Abolição 2300, T085-3242 0868. There are also many buggy rental shops. **Note** When driving outside the city, have a good map and be prepared to ask directions frequently as road signs are non-existent, or placed after junctions.

The coast east of Fortaleza

a coastline of fishing villages, coloured cliffs and sands

Aquiraz and beaches

Aquiraz, 31 km east of Fortaleza, first capital of Ceará which conserves several colonial buildings and has a religious art museum, is the access point for the following beaches: **Prainha**, 6 km east, a fishing village and 10 km long beach with dunes, clean and largely empty. You can see jangadas coming in daily in the late afternoon. The village is known for its lacework: you can see the women using the bilro and labirinto techniques at the **Centro de Rendeiras**. Some 18 km southeast of Aquiraz is **Praia Iguape**, another fishing and lacework village, 3 km south of which is **Praia Barro Preto**, wide, tranquil, with sand dunes, palms and lagoons. All these beaches have accommodation.

Cascavel and beaches

Cascavel, 62 km southeast of Fortaleza (Saturday crafts fair), is the access point for the beaches of **Caponga** and **Águas Belas**, where traditional fishing villages coexist with fancy weekend homes and hotels.

Morro Branco and around

Some 4 km from **Beberibe**, 78 km from Fortaleza, is Morro Branco, with a spectacular beach, coloured craggy cliffs and beautiful views. *Jangadas* (traditional fishing boats) leave the beach at

0500, returning at 1400-1500, lobster is the main catch in this area. The coloured sands of the dunes are bottled into beautiful designs and sold along with other crafts such as lacework, embroidery and straw goods. *Jangadas* may be hired for sailing (one hour for up to six people US$60). Beach buggies are also for hire. There are *pousadas*, or you can rent fishermen's houses. Meals can also be arranged at beachfront bars. South of Morro Branco and 6 km from Beberibe is **Praia das Fontes**, which also has coloured cliffs with sweet-water springs; there is a fishing village and a lagoon. South of Praia das Fontes are several less developed beaches including **Praia Uruaú** or **Marambaia**. The beach is at the base of coloured dunes, there is a fishing village with some accommodation. Just inland is Lagoa do Uruaú, the largest in the state and a popular place for watersports. Buggy from Morro Branco US$50 for four.

Canoa Quebrada and around *Colour map 5, B5.*

On the shores of the Rio Jaguaribe, **Aracati** is the access point to the southeastern-most beaches of Ceará; it is along the main BR-304. The city is best known for its Carnival and for its colonial architecture.

About 10 km from Aracati is Canoa Quebrada on a sand dune, famous for its labirinto lacework and coloured sand sculpture, for sand-skiing on the dunes, for the sunsets, and for the beaches. There are many bars, restaurants and *forró* establishments. To avoid biting insects (bicho do pé), wear shoes. In the second half of July the Canoarte Festival takes place, it includes a *jangada* regatta and music festival.

South of Canoa Quebrada and 13 km from Aracati is **Majorlândia**, an attractive village, with many-coloured sand dunes and a wide beach with strong waves, good for surfing; the arrival of the fishing fleet in the evening is an important daily event; lobster is the main catch. It is a popular weekend destination with beach homes for rent and Carnaval here is lively.

☆Prainha do Canto Verde

Getting there: To get to Prainha do Canto Verde, take a São Benedito bus to Aracati or Canoa Quebrada, buy a ticket to Quatro Bocas and ask to be let off at Lagoa da Poeira, 2 hrs from Fortaleza. If you haven't booked a transfer in advance, Márcio at the Pantanal restaurant at the bus stop will take you, US$4. A truck from the village goes to Aracati for US$5 return.

Some 120 km east of Fortaleza, in the district of Beberibe, is Prainha do Canto Verde, a small fishing village on the vast beach with an award-winning community tourism project. There are guesthouses (eg $ **Dona Mirtes**, with breakfast, will negotiate other meals), houses for rent (**Casa Cangulo**, or **Chalé Marésia**), restaurants (good food at **Sol e Mar**), a handicraft cooperative, *jangada* and catamaran cruises, fishing and walking trails. Each November there is a Regata Ecológica, with *jangadas* from up and down the coast competing. (For the regatta, Christmas and Semana Santa, add 30% to prices.) This is a simple place, which lives by artesanal fishing (ie no big boats or industrial techniques) and has built up its tourism infrastructure without any help from outside investors (they have been fighting the speculators since 1979). It's a very friendly place and foreigners are welcome to get to know how the fisher folk live; knowledge of Portuguese is essential.

Ponta Grossa and Redonda

Ponta Grossa is near Icapuí, the last municipality before Rio Grande do Norte (access from Mossoró), from where you then head to Redonda. Ponta Grossa is down a sand road just before Redonda. Both Ponta Grossa and Redonda are very pretty places, nestled at the foot of the cliffs, but Ponta Grossa has its own community tourism development. One of the main attractions of Ponta Grossa is that, offshore, is one of the few places where manatees (*peixe boi marinho*) visit. There's a good lookout from the cliffs and a delightful walkway extending over the ocean into an area of pristine mangrove forest. Beach trips go from Canoa Quebrada to Ponta Grossa for lunch, but if you want to stay here, contact Tucum, Rede Cearense de Turismo Comunitário ① *R Pinho Pessoa 86, Joaquim Távora, Fortaleza, T085-3226 2476, Facebook: RedeTucumTurismoComunitario*, who can give information on all community tourism and the preservation of traditional ways of life in Ceará.

Where to stay

Canoa Quebrada

There are many *pousadas* in town, see
www.portalcanoaquebrada.com.br.

$$$-$$ Pousada Califôrnia
R Nascer do Sol 136, T088-3421 7039,
www.californiacanoa.com.
Prices vary according to room and season, a/c,
TV, pool, bar, internet, buggy tours, horse riding,
kite surfing, book exchange, several languages
spoken, use of kitchen.

$$$-$$ Pousada Via Láctea
R Descida da Praia e Av Beira Mar, T088-3241
7103, www.pousadavialactea.com.
Rooms and chalets, good views, 50 m from
the sea, pool, English spoken, tours organized.
Recommended.

$$ Hostel Ibiza
R Dragão do Mar (Broadway) 360, T088-3421
7262, www.hostelpousada ibiza.com.
Tiny, boxy but cheap and fairly spruce doubles
and dorms in a bright, hostel decorated with

dozens of international flags, party atmosphere,
200 m from the beach.

$$ Pousada Alternativa
R Francisco Caraço, T088-3421 7278,
www.pousada-alternativa.com.br.
Rooms with a/c and bath, cheaper with fan
and without fridge, central, safe.

$$ Pousada Oasis do Rei
R Nascer do Sol 110, T088-3421 7081,
www.pousadaoasisdorei.com.br.
Simple rooms with a/c, safe, around a pool
in a small garden, some with sea view.

Transport

Bus For the eastern beaches near Fortaleza
(**Prainha**, **Iguape**, **Barro Preto**) and towns such as
Aquiraz or **Aracati**, take São Benedito buses from
the *rodoviária*. To **Beberibe**, 10 a day US$8. To
Morro Branco 4 daily US$10. To **Canoa Quebrada**
4 daily, US$12, 3 hrs, more via Aracati (eg with
Guanabara or Nordeste). There are regular buses
to the western beaches near Fortaleza, including
Cumbuco, from the *rodoviária*.

The coast west of Fortaleza

sleepy fishing villages and famous beaches

Paracuru

Paracuru, a fishing port which has the most important Carnaval on the northwest coast, is
two hours by bus from Fortaleza ($$ **Villa Verde**, near the main square, is a good place to stay). West
of Paracuru, about 120 km from Fortaleza and 12 km from the town of Paraipaba, is **Lagoinha**, a
very scenic beach, with cliffs, dunes and palms by the shore; a fishing village is on one of the hills.

Almofala

Some seven hours by bus and 230 km from Fortaleza is the sleepy fishing village of Almofala,
home of the Tremembés people who live off the sea and some agriculture. There is electricity, but
no hotels or restaurants, although locals rent hammock space and cook meals. Bathing is better
elsewhere, but the area is surrounded by dunes and is excellent for hiking along the coast to explore
beaches and lobster-fishing communities. In Almofala, the church with much of the town was
covered by shifting sands and remained covered for 50 years, reappearing in the 1940s; it has since
been restored. There is also a highly praised turtle project.

Jijoca de Jericoacoara

Jijoca de Jericoacoara (Gijoca) is near the south shore of scenic Lagoa Paraíso (or Lagoa Jijoca), the
second largest in the state. There are *pousadas* on its shore. It is excellent for windsurfing as it has
a 'comfortable' wind, very good for beginners and those gaining experience (Jericoacoara is for
'professionals'). There is also good for kite surfing. **Note** The low season, August to November, is
the windy season.

Jericoacoara

Jijoca is one of the access points for 'Jeri'. One of the most famous beaches of Ceará and all Brazil (if not the world), it has towering sand dunes, deserted beaches with little shade, cactus-covered cliffs rising from the sea and interesting rock formations. The most famous is the **Pedra Furada**, a rock arch by the sea. Its atmosphere has made it popular with Brazilian and international travellers and developers, with crowds at weekends mid-December to mid-February, in July and during Brazilian holidays. Many places are full in low season, too. Jericoacoara is part of an environmental protection area which includes a large coconut grove, lakes, dunes and hills covered in caatinga vegetation. ICMBio ① *R Praia da Malhada s/n, Jericoacoara, T088-3669 2140, https://sites.google.com/site/parquenacionaldejericoacoara/*. The village east of Jeri, **Preá**, is much quieter, with simple fish restaurants.

Parnaíba *Colour map 5, A4.*

Parnaíba makes a good break in the journey north or south. It's a relaxed, friendly place, with a pretty colonial centre by the river and connections to Jericoacoarara and Tutóia (and onward to São Luís and the Lençóis Maranhenses). Tours into the Delta do Parnaíba can be arranged from here (see page 592). They leave from Porto das Barcas (Tatus), a pleasant shopping and entertainment complex, with several good restaurants and a large open-air bar on the riverside. Buses between Parnaíba and Porto das Barcas leave every hour and take 10 minutes. There is a tourist office, **Piemtur** ① *Terminal Turístico Porto das Barcas and at R Dr Oscar Clark 575, T086-3321 1532.*

Delta do Parnaíba and the Parque Nacional Lençóis Maranhenses

These twin parks comprise two of Brazil's most extraordinary landscapes. The **Delta do Parnaíba** is one of the largest river deltas in the world, a labyrinth of mangroves, rivers and unspoilt tropical islands with largely unstudied wildlife and traditional Caiçara fishing communities. The adjacent **Lençóis Maranhenses** (ICMBio contact T098-3349 1267, pnlm@icmbio.gov.br) is a 155,000-ha coastal desert of vast shifting dunes and isolated communities cut by broad rivers and, in the rainy season (June-September), pocked with lakes, whose clear reflective waters are a vivid sky blue against brilliant white sand. Crossing the Parnaíba delta, which separates Piauí from Maranhão, can only be done by chartered boat for up to 12 people from either **Tutóia** or Porto das Barcas (see page 593). Trips into the Lençóis Maranhenses all the way from São Luís to Jericoacoara are easy to organize from São Luís or **Barreirinhas** with Eco Dunas (see page 592). As well as Barreirinhas – the main centre – there is accommodation in the little beach towns of Caburé, Atins (with a superb beach for kite surfing) and Vassouras up the Rio Preguiças. Rural Maranhão and Piauí have a big problem with wind- and ocean-borne plastic waste.

☆São Luís *Colour map 5, A3.*

The capital of Maranhão state, 1070 km west of Fortaleza, founded in 1612 by the French and named after St Louis of France, is in a region of heavy tropical rains, but the surrounding deep forest has been cut down to be replaced by babaçu palms. It stands upon São Luís island between the bays of São Marcos and São José. The urban area extends to São Francisco island, connected with São Luís by three bridges. An old slaving port, the city has a large black population, and has retained much African culture with, these days, lots of music including good reggae. São Luís tourist offices, municipal tourist office ① *R da Palma 53, T098-3212 6215*, state tourist office ① *R Portugal 165, T098-3231 4696*, and at Lagoa da Jansen (Ponta d'Areia), the airport and *rodoviária*. Also see www.saoluis.ma.gov.br.

The old part, on very hilly ground with many steep streets, is full of colonial and art deco buildings which have been very badly neglected over the last decade. The damp climate stimulated the use of ceramic tiles for exterior walls, and until they were stripped off the houses in the last few years (and some say sold off), São Luís had a greater variety of such tiles than anywhere else in Brazil, in Portuguese, French and Dutch styles. Today only a handful of the historic buildings retain them. The commercial quarter (R Portugal, also called Rua Trapiche) is still much as it was in the 17th century. One house on this street has been renovated as the **Casa do Maranhão** ① *Tue-Fri 0900-1900, Sat-Sun 0900-1800, free*, a showcase for the Bumba-Meu-Boi festival and the music of the state, with displays of costumes and video presentations. The progress of the renewal of the historical centre can be seen in the 19th-century **Solar dos Vasconcelos** ① *R da Estrela 462, T098-3231 9075, Tue-Sun 0900-1900, free.*

The **Palácio dos Leões** (Governor's Palace) ① *Av Dom Pedro II, T098-3214 8638, Mon, Wed, Fri 1500-1800, US$3,* has beautiful floors of dark wood (jacarandá) and light (cerejeira), European furniture and great views from terrace. The **Centro de Cultura Popular Domingos Vieira Filho (Casa da Festa)** ① *R do Giz 225, T098-3218 9924,* has exhibitions on the Festa do Divino, the African-Brazilian Tambor-de-Mina spirit religion (similar to Candomblé) and Christmas festivities.

The best colonial churches are the **Cathedral** (1629), on Praça Dom Pedro II, and the churches of **Carmo** (1627), Praça João Lisboa, **São João Batista** (1665), Largo São João, **Nossa Senhora do Rosário** (1717), on Rua do Egito, and the 18th-century **Santana**, Rua de Santana. On Largo do Desterro is the church of **São José do Desterro**, finished in 1863, but with some much older parts.

The **Cafua das Mercês** ① *R Jacinto Maia 43, Mon-Fri 0800-1900,* is a museum of Afro-Brazilian culture housed in the old slave market. **Museu de Artes Visuais** ① *R Portugal 293, Praia Grande, T098-3231 6766, Tue-Fri 0900-1900, Sat-Sun 0900-1800, free,* has a collection of tiles, rare photographs, Marahnese artists and holds temporary exhibitions. **Casa de Nhozinho** ① *R Portugal 185, T098-3218 9951, Tue-Sun 0900-1900, free* is a fine, tiled colonial building with exhibitions devoted to Maranhão *caboclo* life. The **Casa das Minas** ① *R São Pantaleão 857, T098-3218 9920, T098-3221 6856, open sporadically and during festivals,* is one of the oldest sacred spaces in Brazil for African-Brazilian religions and is an important centre of black culture in São Luís.

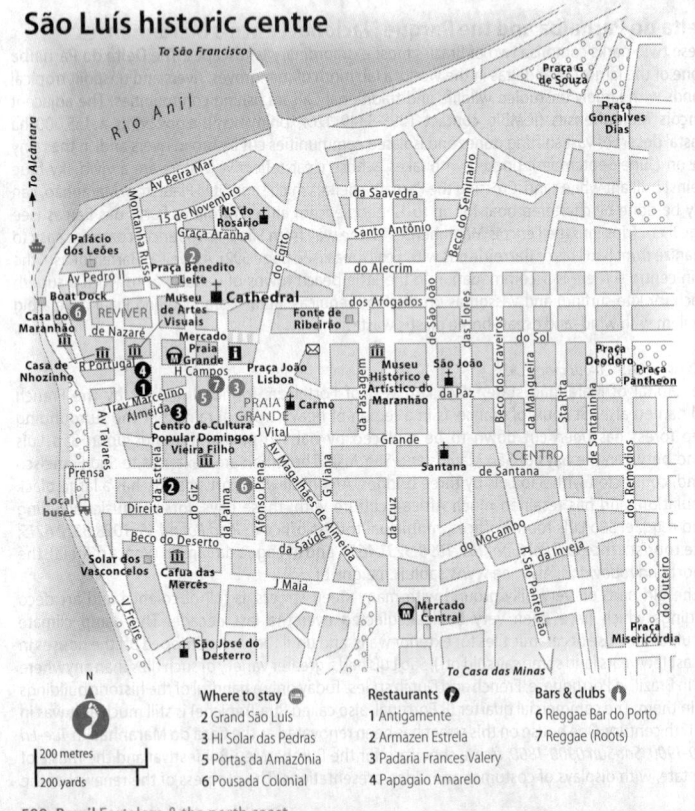

São Luís historic centre

Where to stay 🛏
2 Grand São Luís
3 HI Solar das Pedras
5 Portas da Amazônia
6 Pousada Colonial

Restaurants 🍽
1 Antigamente
2 Armazen Estrela
3 Padaria Frances Valery
4 Papagaio Amarelo

Bars & clubs 🎵
6 Reggae Bar do Porto
7 Reggae (Roots)

The **Museu Histórico e Artístico do Maranhão** ① *R do Sol 302, T098-3221 4537, Tue-Sun 0900-1530, US$1*, in a 19th-century mansion, has displays of costumes, a theatre and exhibition space.

Alcântara *Colour map 5, A3.*

Some 22 km away by boat is Alcântara the former state capital, on the mainland bay of São Marcos. Construction of the city began in the early 17th century and it is now a historical monument. There are many old churches, such as the ruined **Matriz de São Matias** – 1648, and colonial mansions (see the **Casa**, and **Segunda Casa, do Imperador**, also the old cotton barons' mansions with their blue Portuguese-tiled façades). On the grassy **Praça da Matriz**, which retains a pillory at its centre, is the **Museu Histórico** ① *daily 0900-1400,* with fine tiles and colonial miscellanea. The **Casa Histórica** ① *Praça da Matriz, Mon-Fri 1000-1600,* has some 18th-century English furniture and porcelain imported by the Alcântara aristocracy. Canoe trips go to **Ilha do Livramento**, good beaches, good walking around the coast (can be muddy after rain), mosquitoes after dark.

Listings The coast west of Fortaleza *map p588*

Where to stay

Jijoca de Jericoacoara

$$$ Pousada do Paulo
Córrego do Urubu s/n, T088-3669 1181.
Has a windsurf school. It's also a good place to stay (prices depends on season and cabin, lovely location with lake views, garden, beach, hammocks and various sizes of cabin, all very nice, some with TV and a/c; excellent restaurant, bar.

Jericoacoara

4-5-day packages for Reveillon are available, but prices rise steeply. Many *pousadas* can be found on www.portaljericoacoara.com. Ask around for families who take in guests.

$$$$-$$$ Recanto do Barão
R do Forró 433, T088-3669 2149,
www.recantodobarao.com.
21 rooms mostly for 3 to 5 (ie families, groups), nicely decorated with hibiscus theme, lots of hammocks, fridge, hot shower, big rooms, upper balcony for sunset, pool, Land Rover tours. Good reputation.

$$$-$$ Casa Nostra
R das Dunas, T088-3669 2035,
http://casanostra.tur.br.
Nice rooms, good breakfast, money exchange, Italian spoken. Recommended.

$$$-$$ Pousada da Renata
T088-99919 3011, www.pousadadarenata.com.
Owned by the sister of Fernanda at **Pousada do Paulo** at Jijoca. Patio with hammocks, breakfast, English, Italian and German spoken. See also

Pousada do Serrote (R da Igerja, T088-3669 2061, www.pousadadoserrote.com.br). With 4 chalets.

$$$-$ Pôr do Sol
R das Dunas 50, T088-3669 2099,
www.pousadapordosoljeri.com.br.
Family atmosphere, lovely place to stay, with a/c or fan, buggy trips arranged. Recommended.

$$ Calanda
R das Dunas (across from Casa do Turismo, by setting sun dune), T088-3669 2285,
www.pousadacalanda.com.
With solar energy, good rooms, good breakfast, restaurant with varied menu, good views, helpful, German, English and Spanish spoken, full moon party every month. Warmly recommended.

$$ Chalé dos Ventos
R São Francisco 51, T088-3669 2023,
www.portaljericoacoara.com/en/pousada_chale_dos_ventos_jericoacoara.htm.
Price depends on room, chalet on 2 floors, good views, great breakfast, nice atmosphere.

$$-$ Pousada Tirol
R São Francisco 202, T088-3669 2006,
http://jericoacoarahostel.com.br.
HI-affiliated, non-members pay more, has dorms and double rooms, with breakfast, hot water, safe, helpful, great fun. Recommended.

Parnaíba

$$$-$$ Pousada dos Ventos
Av São Sebastião 2586, Universidade, T086-3323 2555, www.pousadadosventos.com.br.
The best business hotel in town, 10 mins' taxi ride from the centre, spacious, simple rooms and an attractive breakfast area next to the pool.

$$ Pousada Chalé Suíço
Av Padre R J Vieira 448, Fátima, T086-3321 3026,
www.chalesuico.com.br.
Cheaper without a/c or breakfast, bar,
laundry, pool, tours arranged, wind-surfing,
sandboarding, buggies and bikes.

$ Residencial
R Almirante Gervásio Sampaio 375, T086-3322
2931, www.residencialpousada.com.br.
Very plain, simple doubles, dorms and plusher en
suites with cold water showers gathered around
a plant-filled courtyard. There are many other
basic hotels nearby.

Delta do Parnaíba and Parque Nacional Lençóis Maranhenses

Delta do Parnaíba

$ pp Ilha das Canarias
Morro do Meio Caiçara Comunidade, www.
deltadorioparnaiba.com.br/ilhadascanarias.htm.
Bring a hammock and ask at **Raimundo Aires**
restaurant (good for fish), idyllic beaches nearby.
Simple, no showers, just the river.

Barreirinhas
Most hotels can organize tours.

$$ Belo Horizonte
R Joaquim Soeiro de Carvalho 245, T098-3499
0054, www.bhmirante.com.br.
Near the central square, well-kept tiled and
whitewash rooms, quietest at the front,
welcoming owner, pleasant rooftop breakfast
area. Also owns **Pousada do Mirante** in Caburé,
with restaurant.

$$ Pousada Igarapé
R Coronel Godinho 320, Centro, T098-3349 0641.
Small, boxy rooms, a/c or fan, opposite the
Assembleia de Deus church (noisy hellfire
sermons at weekends).

$ Tia Cota
R Coronel Godinho 204, T098-3349 1237.
Simple rooms, fan or a/c, decent beds and
mattresses, ranging from phone box-sized with
shared baths to more spacious en suite doubles.

Caburé, Vassouras, Mandacaru and Atins
It is possible to rent hammock space in the
restaurant shacks in Vassouras or Mandacaru for
around US$12 per day with food included. All the
towns are so tiny it's impossible to get lost. None
has more than 3 streets.

$$$ Cajueiro
R Principal, Atins, T098-99204 0222,
www.pcatins.com.br.
9 simple suites with hammock-slung balconies
and a palm-thatch public restaurant area. Tours
and kite-surfing can be organized through the
pousada. Decent food, friendly service.

$$$ Rancho do Buna
R Principal s/n, Atins, T098-3349 5005,
http://ranchodobuna.com.br.
Attractive pousada set on the river at the back of
town. Small rooms are situated in a brick annexe
in front of a fish-filled lake, there's a pool and
pleasant, airy public areas. Excellent food and
tours available to the Lençóis and the beaches.

$ Pousada do Paulo (aka Pousada Lençóis de Areia)
Praia do Caburé, T098-9143 4668.
Well kept rooms for up to 4. The owner was the
1st to settle here and named the town after a
local bird. Best food in the village. Watch out for
glass on the vast, sweeping Atlantic beach. There
are other options in town and rooms are always
available outside peak season.

São Luís
Many cheap hotels can be found in R da Palma,
very central, and R Formosa.

$$$ Grand São Luís
Praça Dom Pedro II 299, T098-2109 3500,
www.grandsaoluis.com.br.
1960s 'grand dame' with plainly decorated
rooms, the best of which have sweeping sea
views. Business facilities, pool and gym.

$$$ Portas da Amazônia
R do Giz 129, T098-3222 9937,
www.portasdaamazonia.com.br.
Tastefully converted rooms in a colonial building
in the heart of the centre. Smart and well run.

$$$ Pousada Colonial
R Afonso Pena 112, T098-3232 2834.
Well kept rooms in a beautiful restored, tiled
house, a/c, comfortable, quiet. Recommended.

$ pp HI Solar das Pedras
R da Palma 127, T098-3232 6694,
http://ajsolardaspedras.com.br/site/.
By far the best backpacker option in town. Well-
run with a range of tidy 4- to 6-person dorms and
doubles ($$), internet, large lockers and a little
garden out back.

Alcântara

$$$ Pousada dos Guarás
Praia da Baronesa, T098-3337 1339.
A beach front *pousada* with bungalows, good restaurant, canoe hire and advice on excursions around the town.

$$ Pousada Bela Vista
Vila Jerico s/n, Cema, T098-3337 1569,
daniloalcantara80@gmail.com.
Cabins and pretty suites with breathtaking views over the bay and forest; good restaurant. Excellent tours in the environs of Alcântara: a real adventure.

$ Pousada da Josefa
Direita, T098-3337 1109.
A family-run restaurant and *pousada* right in the centre with a range of very simple, plain rooms. Look at several.

$ Sítio Tijupá
R de Baixo s/n at the Post Office, T098-3337 1291.
Tiny simple *pousada* with small but well-kept rooms, with fan.

Restaurants

Jericoacoara
There are several restaurants serving vegetarian and fish dishes.

$$ Bistrogonoff
Beco do Guaxelo 60.
Fish and meat combinations, stroganoffs and a healthy selection of pastas. Convivial atmosphere, very popular in the evenings.

$ Carcará
R do Forró.
Restaurant and bar, northeastern specialities, seafood and pastas, said to be "o mais fino" in town.

$$ Do Sapão
R São Francisco s/n.
Good-value *prato feito*, set meals including vegetarian pizzas and pastas. Live music. Named in homage to the giant toads that appear everywhere in Jeri after dark.

$$ Espaço Aberto
R Principal.
Meat dishes, delicious seafood, salads, pleasant atmosphere.

$ Na Casa Dela
R Principal.

Northeastern Brazilian and Bahian cooking in an intimate setting.

$$ Naturalmente
On the beach.
Nice atmosphere, wonderful crêpes.

$$ Pizzaria Dellacasa
R Principal, next to phone office.
Good variety of pizza, pasta, salads, art gallery.

$$ Taverna
R Principal.
Cantina and restaurant, lovely pasta and pizza, crêpes, expresso coffee. Drinks.

$$ Tudo na Brasa
R Principal.
Particularly recommended for the *churrascaria*.

São Luís
R da Estrela has many eating places with good food and outdoor terraces, eg **Antigamente** (No 220, T098-3232 3964), which has live music Thu-Sat, and adjacent **Papagaio Amarelo** (No 210), both of which have live music. Good food also in the Mercado Praia Grande. R dos Afogados has many places for lunch. There is further choice in the São Francisco district, just across bridge. The centre is very lively on Fri and Sat. On Sun it is largely closed and most people go to Praia Calhau to eat and relax.

$$ Armazen Estrela
R da Estrela 401, T098-3254 1274.
Fine dining upstairs and a great little *botequin* downstairs, in a cool room with Romanesque brick arches. Good food and live music at weekends.

$ Padaria Frances Valery
Rua do Giz 164.
Delicious cakes, quiches and good coffee.

Bars and clubs

Jericoacoara
Forró nightly in high season at R do Forró, Wed and Sat in low season, 2200. Action moves to bars when *forró* has stopped about 0200. There are also frequent parties to which visitors are welcome. Once a week in high season there is a folk dance show which includes capoeira. **Sky** (R Principal on the beach). A popular sunset bar and evening chill-out space with tables under the stars.

São Luís

There is *cacuriá* dancing, drum parades and buzzing nightlife every Fri and Sat along the north end of **R do Giz** and along **R João Gualberto**. For cultural events see www.cultura.ma.gov.br.

Reggae Bar do Porto
R do Portugal 49, T098-3232 1115.
One of the best reggae bars in the city with a broad range of live acts and DJs.

Reggae (Roots) Bar
R da Palma 86, T098-3221 7580.
Live reggae and Maranhão roots music most nights. Especially lively at weekends.

Festivals

São Luís

24 Jun (São João) **Bumba-Meu-Boi.** For several days before the festival street bands parade, particularly in front of the São João and São Benedito churches. There are dances somewhere in the city almost every night in Jun.
Aug **São Benedito**, at the Rosário church.

Alcântara

May/Jun **Festa do Divino**, at **Pentecost** (Whitsun).
29 Jun **São Pedro.**
Early Aug **São Benedito.**

What to do

Jericoacoara

Clube dos Ventos, *R das Dunas, T088-3669 2288, www.clubedosventos.com.* With restaurant and bar, windsurf equipment hire; windsurf and kitesurf courses. Kite surfing at Preá and Lagoa Jijoca.
Jeri Off Road, *T088-3669 2268, T99958 5457, www.jeri.tur.br.* Adventure trips in the area, transfers, buggy rides and kitesurf. Recommended, but popular.

Buggy tours
Associação de Bugueiros, *ABJ, R Principal.*
Run buggy to all the local sites.

Delta do Parnaíba and Parque Nacional Lençóis Maranhenses

Eco Dunas, *R Inácio Lins 164, Barreirinhas, T098-3349 0545, also at São Luís airport, www.ecodunas.com.br.* The best option for tours of Lençóis Maranhenses, the Delta and options all the way from São Luís to Jericoacoara, also

the beautiful, remote Parque Nacional de Sete Cidades (see page 594). Excellent guides, infrastructure and organization. Some English spoken and flights arranged.

Transport

Paracuru and Lagoinha

Bus from **Fortaleza**, Fretcar (www.fretcar.com.br) to Paracuru, 2 hrs, US$3. To **Lagoinha**, 3 hrs, US$5.

Almofala

Bus From **Fortaleza** to Almofala **Fretcar**, US$10.

Jijoca and Jericoacoara

Bus Fretcar buses, see above, run from Fortaleza to destinations throughout western Ceará, including **Jijoca** (T088-3669 1143), may daily, US$12, and **Jericoacoara** (T088-9900 2109), 6 a day, US$16-21.50. The journey takes 6-7 hrs all told. A *jardineira* (open-sided 4WD truck) meets the bus from Fortaleza at Jijoca, US$4, 20 mins. There are also faster a/c combis which can be booked through hotels and *pousadas* in Jeri.

If coming from Belém or other points north and west, go via Sobral (from Belém US$47, 20 hrs), where you change for Cruz, 40 km east of Jijoca, a small pleasant town with basic hotels (there is only 1 bus a day Sobral–Cruz, US$12, 3-4 hrs, but **Fretcar** runs to **Cruz** from Fortaleza 4 times a day, US$8-12. Either continue to Jijoca the next day (Cruz–Jijoca, daily, US$2, meets *jardineira* for Jeri) or take an horário pick-up Cruz–Jijoca.

An alternative from the west, especially if going through Parnaíba, is by buggy or *jardineira* from **Camocim** (a pleasant town at the mouth of the Rio Coreaú separating Piauí and Ceará, facing the dunes on the eastern shore), which is 1½-2 hrs by road from Parnaíba, 0715, US$8, with **Guanabara**. It has several hotels and eating places. You take a ferry across the river, US$1 per passenger, then the vehicle at 1100 to Jericoacoara (2 hrs, US$8). You can break the journey from Camocim to Jericoacoara at villages such as **Nova Tatajuba** (on the west margin of the outflow of Lagoa Grande; the beach is wide, dunes follow the shore, the ocean is clear and calm and there is a fishing village with a few basic *pousadas*), or **Guriú** where hammock space can be found. There is good bird watching here. Walk 4 hrs, or take a boat across the bay to Jericoacoara. The journey along the beach has beautiful scenery. In Jericoacoara ask around for buggy or *jardineira* rides to Camocim, about US$16 pp.

Parnaíba

Bus *Rodoviária* is 5 km south of the centre on BR-343. Taxi from centre US$5. To **Fortaleza**, 10 hrs, US$15.50-21 (33 leito); **São Luís**, 10 hrs, US$25.50; **Teresina**, 6 hrs, US$18.50-27.

Delta do Parnaíba and Lençóis Maranhenses

Bus Parnaíba–Tutóia: bus, 2½ hrs, US$6, with **Nazaré** at 0700, 1200 and 1400. Tutóia–**Barreirinhas** by Toyota pick-up, leave when full from the dock area for **Paulinho Neves** (1 hr, US$5); pick-ups leave from here to Barreirinhas (2 hrs, US$8). Frequent buses from Tutóia to São Luís. **São Luís–Barreirinhas**, with **Cisne Branco**, 3-3½ hrs on a new road, US$16, 4 a day. Hotels in São Luís can book minivan trips, same price as bus.

Ferry Up the Parnaíba delta to the crab-fishing village of **Morro do Meio** on Ilha das Canarias, boats on Mon at high tide (usually in the small hours) from Porto das Barcas (Tatus), 12 km from Parnaíba. It is sometimes possible to hitch a lift from Ilha das Canarias to Tutóia with a crab fisherman. Charter boat to Tutóia from Parnaíba, Porto das Barcas, for 12 people for about US$160 (eg **Capitão Báu**, T086-3323 0145, 8831 9581), or contact **Clip Turismo** (Av Presidente Vargas, Porto das Barcas, T086-99978 5358, http://clipecoturismo.tur.br) for boat trips, minimum 4 people. To **Caburé**, **Mandacuru** (with a lighthouse offering sweeping views) and

Atins: daily boat service from end of the Orla in Barreirinhas (3-4 hrs). There is accommodation in Caburé and Atins and in the tiny riverside dune community at Vassouras (bring hammock).

São Luís

Air Flights with **Gol** and **LATAM** from most state capitals via Fortaleza or Belém, also from Parnaíba and Teresina. Airport 13 km from centre, T098-3217 6100; buses ('São Cristovão') to city until midnight, US$1. Minivans every 40 mins until 2200 stop at Praça Deodoro (1 hr), US$1.35. Taxi US$17.

Bus *Rodoviária* is 12 km from the centre on the airport road, 'Rodoviária via Alemanha' bus to centre (Praça João Lisboa), US$1. Bus to **Fortaleza**, US$35-48, 3 a day, 18 hrs. To **Belém**, 14 hrs, US$37-48. Also to **Recife**, 26 hrs, US$76, and all other major cities and local towns.

Alcântara

Ferry Ferries cross the bay daily, leaving São Luís dock (Terminal Hidroviário Campos Melo, west end of R Portugal, T098-3222 8431): check time and buy the ticket the day before as departure depends on the tides. The journey takes 60 mins, US$4 on foot, US$22 for car. The sea can be rough between Sep and Dec. Sometimes catamaran tours can be booked through tour operators in São Luís, meals are not included.

West of Fortaleza

caves and rock formations are the highlights

Western Ceará and Piauí

At 340 km from Fortaleza and at 840 m is **Ubajara** ① *T088-3634 1300 ext 231 for information; www.portalubajara.com.br*, with an interesting Sunday morning market selling produce of the Sertão.

About 3 km from town is **Parque Nacional Ubajara** ① *the ICMBio office is at the park entrance, 5 km from the caves, T088-3634 1388, www.icmbio.gov.br/parnaubajara/, Tue-Sun 0800-1700, cave open 0900-1500, US$1.55, and each trail, from 300 m to 7 km, has a compulsory guide, for which you pay US$1.55-4.65; there is bar by the entrance serving juices, snacks, soft drinks, etc, with 563 ha of native highland and caatinga brush.* The park's main attraction is the Ubajara cave on the side of an escarpment. Fifteen chambers totalling 1120 m have been mapped, of which 360 are open to visitors. Access is along a 7-km footpath and steps (two to three hours, take water) or with a **cable car** ① *T088-3634 1219, Tue-Sun 0900-1430, last up at 1500, US$2.45 each way for descent and ascent (in mid 2017 the cable car was not running)*, which descends the cliff to the cave entrance. Lighting has been installed in nine caverns of the complex. A guide leads visitors in the cave, which is completely dry and home to 14 types of bat. At one point the lights are turned out to appreciate total blackness. Several rock formations look like animals: horse's head, jacaré, snake. The views of the Sertão from the upper cable car platform are superb. In the national park there is a 1.5 km trail, Samambaia, through the woods with stunning views at the end. Another trail leads off Samambaia to some waterfalls, including Cafundo where you can swim.

Teresina *Colour map 5, B4.*

About 435 km up the Rio Parnaíba is the state capital. The city is reputed to be the hottest after Cuiabá (temperatures rise to 42°C). **Praça Pedro II** lies at the heart of the city and is the hub of Teresina life. See the **Museu do Piauí** ① *Praça Marechal Deodoro, Tue-Fri 0800-1730, Sat-Sun 0800-1200, US$1.35.* The **Casa da Cultura** ① *Praça Saraiva, Centro, T086-3215 7815, www.fcmc.pi.gov.br, Mon-Fri 0800-1800, Sat 0900-1300,* is devoted to the history of the city and to the lives of famous ex-residents. The website has lots of cultural information. The **Central do Artesanato** ① *Praça Dom Pedro II, T086-3222 5772, Mon-Fri 0800-2200,* is a handicraft market and cultural centre. Local handicrafts include carved wood, leather and hammocks. There is an interesting **open market** by the Praça Marechal Deodoro and the river is picturesque. Every morning along the river bank there is the **troca-troca** where people buy, sell and swap. Most of the year the river is low, leaving sandbanks known as coroas (crowns). **Tourist office:** municipal tourist office Turismo Teresina ① *SEMDEC at the Prefeitura Municipal, Av Campos Sales 1292, T086-3215 7470, http://semdec.teresina pi.gov.br/turismo/.* The state tourist office, SETUR, is at ① *Av Antônio Freire 1473, 2nd floor, T086-3216 2199, www.turismo.pi.gov.br.* Sindicato dos Guias de Turismo do Piauí ① *R Eliseu Martins 2029 at Magalhães Filho, T086-3226 1622, singtur-pi@bol.com.br.*

Parque Nacional de Sete Cidades *Colour map 5, B4.*
Open 0800-1700, T086-3343 1342, www.icmbio.gov.br, US$4, with a fee for a compulsory guide, price depends on whether visiting by car, bicycle or on foot.

Unusual eroded rock formations decorated with mysterious inscriptions are to be found in the Parque Nacional de Sete Cidades, 12 km from Piracuruca, 190 km northeast of Teresina. The rock structures are just off the Fortaleza-Teresina road. From the ground it looks like a medley of weird monuments. The inscriptions on some of the rocks have never been deciphered; one theory suggests links with the Phoenicians, and the Argentine Professor Jacques de Mahieu considers them to be Nordic runes left by the Vikings. There is plenty of birdlife, and iguanas, descending from their trees in the afternoon. There are places to stay near the park including **$$ Hotel Fazenda Sete Cidades**, BR-222, Km 63, T086-3276 2222, http://hotelfazendasetecidades.com.br, with pool hammocks, restaurant and information on the park. **Piripiri** is a cheap place to break the Belém-Fortaleza journey; several good hotels.

Listings West of Fortaleza

Where to stay

Western Ceará: Ubajara

$$ Gruta de Ubajara
50 m from the park entrance, T088-3634 1375, grutadeubajara@hotmail.com.
Rooms in chalets of various sizes, restaurant, owner makes his own *cachaça*.

$$ Sítio do Alemão
Take Estrada do Teleférico 2 km from town, after the Pousada da Neblina turn right, signposted, 1 km to Sítio Santana, in the coffee plantation of Herbert Klein, T088-99961 4645, www.sitio-do-alemao.20fr.com.
Here, down a path, there are 3 small chalets, with full facilities, and 2 older ones with shared bath, $, view from breakfast/hammock area to Sertão,

excursions, bicycle hire offered, if chalets are full Mr Klein may accommodate visitors at the house (Caixa Postal 33, Ubajara, CE, CEP 62350-000). No meals other than breakfast but Casa das Delícias in Ubajara will send lasagne if necessary. Warmly recommended. **Note** Camping not allowed in the national park.

Teresina
Many cheap hotels and dormitórios around Praça Saraiva. Many other cheap ones in R São Pedro and in R Alvaro Mendes.

$$$ Formula Flat Europa
R José Olímpio de Melo 3330, Ilhotas, T086-3223 7100, www.formulaflateuropa.com.br.
Bright, modern and well-appointed flats with microwaves, kitchenettes and living areas. Space for up to 3 people making this an $ option pp.

\$\$\$ Real Palace
R Areolino de Abreu 1217, T086-2107 2700,
www.realpalacehotel.com.br.
Business oriented hotel with a range of no-frills
rooms and suites and a small business centre.

\$\$\$ Sambaíba
R Gabriel Ferreira 230-N, T086-3222 6712,
hotelsambaiba@bol.com.br.
2-star, central, good.

\$ Teresinha
Av Deputado Paulo Ferraz 2885,
opposite rodoviária, T086-3211 0919,
www.hotelteresinha.com.br.
A/c, cheaper with fan, helpful.

Restaurants

Teresina
Many places for all pockets around Praça Dom
Pedro II; diners are frequently serenaded by
violeiros (itinerant musicians).

\$\$ Camarão do Elias
Av Pedro Almeida 457, T086-3232 5025.
Good seafood.

\$\$ Pesqueirinho
R Domingos Jorge Velho 6889, in Poty Velho
district, T086-3225 2268.
For fish dishes, by the river.

Festivals

Teresina
Feb/Mar Teresina is proud of its **Carnival**,
which is then followed by **Micarina**, a local
carnival in Mar.
Jul and Aug Much music and dancing at
the **Bumba-meu-Boi**, the Teresina dance

festival, **Festidanças**, and a convention of
itinerant guitarists.

Transport

Western Ceará: Ubajara
Bus Guanabara bus from **Fortaleza**, 0800,
1800, return 0800, 1600, 6 hrs, US\$15.

Teresina
Air Senador Petrônio Portela airport is 5 km
from the centre, T086-3133 6270. Flights to
Brasília, **Campinas**, **São Paulo**, **São Luís**, **Recife**.
Buses from outside the airport run straight to
town and to the *rodoviária*.

Bus *Rodoviária*, 4 km from the centre, T086-3229
9047. The bus trip from **Fortaleza** is scenic and
takes 9 hrs (US\$25, leito US\$34). There are direct
buses to **Belém** (13 hrs, US\$37-45), **Recife** (16 hrs,
US\$54) and to **São Luís** (6 hrs, US\$21-26) and
Salvador (18 hrs, US\$60).

Parque Nacional de Sete Cidades and Piripiri
Bus ICMBio staff bus leaves the Praça da
Bandeira in Piripiri (26 km away, *rodoviária*
T086-3276 2333), at 0700, ask for a lift. It passes
Hotel Fazenda Sete Cidades at 0800, reaching
the park 10 mins later. If you miss the bus, take
a mototaxi. Return at 1630, or hitchhike (to
walk takes all day, very hot, start early). Taxi
from Piripiri, US\$30 or from Piracuruca, US\$40.
Bus **Teresina**–Piripiri and return, throughout
the day 2½ hrs, US\$8. Bus **São Luís**–Piripiri, 3 a
day, 10 hrs, US\$31. Several daily buses Piripiri–
Fortaleza, 9 hrs, US\$15-21. Bus Piripiri–**Ubajara**,
marked 'São Benedito', or 'Crateús', 2½ hrs; US\$8,
1st at 0700 (a beautiful trip).

The Amazon

★The area is drained by the mighty Amazon, which in size, volume of water – 12 times that of the Mississippi – and number of tributaries has no equal in the world. At the base of the Andes, far to the west, the Amazonian plain is 1300 km wide, but east of the confluences of the Madeira and Negro rivers with the Amazon, the highlands close in upon it until there is no more than 80 km of floodplain between them. Towards the river's mouth – about 320 km wide – the plain widens once more and extends along the coast southeastwards into the state of Maranhão and northwards into the Guianas.

Brazilian Amazônia, much of it still covered with tropical forest, is 56% of the national area. Its jungle is the world's largest and densest rainforest, with more diverse plants and animals than any other jungle in the world. It has only 8% of Brazil's population, and most of this is concentrated around Belém (in Pará), and in Manaus, 1600 km up the river. The population is sparse because other areas are easier to develop.

This section covers the states of Pará, Amazonas, Amapá and Roraima. The states of Rondônia and Acre are dealt with under Amazon frontiers, see page 620.

Travel up the Amazon River

tips and information relating to boat trips

Riverboat travel is no substitute for visiting the jungle. Except for a few birds and the occasional dolphin, little wildlife is seen. However, it does offer an insight into the vastness of Amazônia and a chance to meet some of its people. Extensive local inquiry and some flexibility in one's schedule are indispensable for river travel.

Rivers are the arteries of Amazônia for the transport of both passengers and merchandise. The two great ports of the region are Belém, at the mouth of the Amazon, and Manaus at the confluence of the Rio Negro and Rio Solimões. Manaus is the hub of river transport, with regular shipping services east to Santarém and Belém along the lower Amazon, south to Porto Velho along the Rio Madeira, west to Tabatinga (border with Colombia and Peru) along the Rio Solimões and northwest to São Gabriel da Cachoeira along the Rio Negro. There is also a regular service connecting Belém and Macapá, on the northern shore of the Amazon Delta, and Santarém and Macapá.

The size and quality of vessels varies greatly, with the largest and most comfortable ships generally operating on the Manaus–Belém route. Hygiene, food and service are reasonable on most vessels but **overcrowding** is a common problem. Many of the larger ships offer air-conditioned berths with bunkbeds and, for a higher price, 'suites', with a private bathroom (in some cases, this may also mean a double bed instead of the standard bunkbed). The cheapest way to travel is 'hammock class'; on some routes first class (upper deck) and second class (lower deck) hammock space is available, but on many routes this distinction does not apply. Some new boats have air-conditioned hammock space. Although the idea of swinging in a hammock may sound romantic, the reality is you will probably be squeezed in with other passengers, possibly next to the toilets, and have difficulty sleeping because of **noise** and an aching back.

Best for
Culture ▪ River trips ▪ Wildlife

Agencies on shore can inform you of the arrival and departure dates for several different ships, as well as the official (highest) prices for each, and they are sometimes amenable to bargaining. Whenever possible, see the vessel yourself (it may mean a journey out of town) and have a chat with the captain or business manager to confirm departure time, length of voyage, ports of call, price, etc. Inspect cleanliness in the kitchen, toilets and showers. All boats are cleaned up when in port, but if a vessel is reasonably clean upon arrival then chances are that it has been kept that way throughout the voyage. You can generally arrange to sleep on board a day or two before departure and after arrival, but be sure to secure carefully your belongings when in port. If you take a berth, lock it and keep the key even if you will not be moving in right away. If you are travelling hammock class, board ship at least six to eight hours before sailing in order to secure a good spot (away from the toilets, tables where people eat and the engine and check for leaks in the deck above you). Be firm but considerate of your neighbours as they will be your intimate companions for the duration of the voyage. Always keep your gear locked and, if possible, don't leave it unattended. Take some light warm clothing, it can get very chilly at night.

Compare fares for different ships and remember that prices may fluctuate with supply and demand. Most ships sail in the evening and the first night's supper is not provided. Payment is usually in advance. Insist on a signed ticket indicating date, vessel, class of passage and berth number if applicable.

All ships carry cargo as well as passengers and the amount of cargo will affect the length of the voyage because of weight (especially when travelling upstream) and loading/unloading at intermediate ports.

Belém and around

from a fine city to life on the Amazon

From Belém, the great city near the mouth of the Amazon, to Parintins, site of a renowned annual festival, on the border with Amazonas state, it is 60 hours by boat. This section deals with the first few stops on the river, plus the route through Amapá state to the frontier with French Guiane.

Belém *Colour map 5, A1.*

Belém (do Pará) is the great port of the Amazon. It is hot (mean temperature, 26°C), but frequent showers freshen the streets. There are fine squares and restored historic buildings set along broad avenues. Belém used to be called the 'City of Mango Trees' and there are many such trees remaining.

Sights The largest square is the **Praça da República** where there are free afternoon concerts; the main business and shopping area is along the wide Av Presidente Vargas leading to the river and the narrow streets which parallel it. The neoclassical **Theatro da Paz** (1868-1874) ① *Tue-Fri 0900-1800, Sat 0900-1200, Sun 0900-1100, tours US$2*, is one of the largest theatres in the country. It has its own orchestra and stages performances by national and international stars and also gives free concert and theatre shows. An opera festival is staged, usually each August or September. Visit the **Cathedral** (1748) ① *Mon 1500-1800, Tue-Fri 0800-1100, 1530-1800*, another neoclassical building which contains several remarkable paintings. It stands on Praça Frei Caetano Brandão, opposite the 18th-century **Santo Aleixandre** church, which is noted for its wood carving. The 17th-century **Mercês** church (1640), near the market, is the oldest church in Belém; it forms part of an architectural group known as the Mercedário, the rest of which was heavily damaged by fire in 1978 and is being restored.

The **Basílica of Nossa Senhora de Nazaré** (1909) ① *Praça Julho Chermont on Av Magalhães Barata, Mon-Sat 0500-1130, 1400-2000, Sun 0545-1130, 1430-2000*, built from rubber wealth in romanesque style, is an absolute must for its stained-glass windows and beautiful marble. A museum at the basílica describes the Círio de Nazaré religious festival. The **Palácio Lauro Sodré** or **Museu do Estado do Pará** ① *Praça Dom Pedro II, T091-3225 3853, Mon-Fri 0900-1800, Sat-Sun 1900-1200*, a gracious 18th-century Italianate building, contains Brazil's largest framed painting, 'The Conquest of Amazônia', by Domenico de Angelis. The **Palácio Antônio Lemos**, **Museu da Cidade** ① *Tue-Fri 0900-1200, 1400-1800, Sat-Sun 0900-1300*, which houses the **Museu de Arte de Belém**

Fact...

A yellow-fever inoculation is compulsory: **Clínica de Medicina Preventiva**, Avenida Bras de Aguiar 410 (T091-3181 1644), will give injections.

Essential Amazon

Getting around

This is mainly possible using internal flights and boats; there are some buses, but very few passable roads. The following boat services are the major shipping routes in Amazônia. All fares shown are one-way only and include all meals unless otherwise stated.

Belém–Manaus Via Santarém, Óbidos and Parintins on the lower Amazon. Five to six days upriver, four days downriver, including 18-hour stop in Santarém: hammock space US$92-100 (up to US$145 with a/c); a bunk costs US$307 and a private suite about US$370, downriver fares. For upriver fares add about US$30-35. Vehicles are also carried. The Belém–Manaus route is very busy. Try to get a cabin.

Belém–Santarém 2½ days upriver, 1½ days downriver, berth US$123, suite US$138, hammock space US$46 up, US$37 downriver. All vessels sailing Belém–Manaus will call in Santarém.

Santarém–Manaus Same intermediate stops as above. Two days upriver, 1½ days downriver, US$154-185 cabin, US$42-49 hammock. All vessels sailing Belém–Manaus will call in Santarém and there are many others operating only the Santarém–Manaus route. Speedboats (*lanchas*) on this route take 11 hours sitting, US$95 (US$66, nine hours, to Parintins).

Belém–Macapá (Porto Santana) Non-stop, 24 hours on large ships, double berth US$138, hammock space US$46 pp, meals not included but can be purchased onboard (expensive). Also non-stop fast catamaran *Atlântica*, eight hours, three a week, US$38. Same voyage, 36-48 hours on smaller riverboats, hammock space US$32 per person including meals. See page 602.

Macapá (Porto Santana)–Santarém Via Boca do Jari, Prainha, and Monte Alegre on the lower Amazon, two days upriver, 1½ days downriver, berth US$160, hammock US$48.

Manaus–Porto Velho Via Humaitá on the Rio Madeira (US$62, from where there are buses to Porto Velho, saving about 24 hours). Tuesday and Saturday, five days upriver, 3½ days downriver (up to seven days when the river is low), US$220, hammock space US$77.

Manaus–Tefé 36 hours, US$125 double berth, US$46 hammock space. Jet boats US$65, daily 0600-0700 except Sunday, 13 hours, continuing to Tabatinga (flights Manaus–Tefé–Tabatinga). Speedboats Tefé-Tabatinga Wednesday, Friday evening, take 24 hours; Tabatinga-Tefé Sunday, Friday morning, 20 hours. Slow boats between Tabatinga and Tefé do not sail from Tefé, but from Alvarães, two boat rides away, change in Nogueira.

Manaus–Tabatinga (see page 620) Via Fonte Boa (three days), Tonantins (four days), São Paulo de Olivença (five days) and Benjamin Constant along the Rio Solimões. Six days upriver (depending on cargo), three to four days downriver, US$118 upriver, US$100 downriver (hammock, US$320 berth for two, negotiable). The better boats on this run include: *M Monteiro*, *Oliveira V* and the *Voyager* fleet from number *III* up. Jet boat, *Puma*, Tuesday 0700, 38 hours, US$225.

Manaus–São Gabriel da Cachoeira Leaving from Porto Raimundo in Manaus not the main boat port, three days by slow boat, 24 hours by fast boat, along the Rio Negro (see page 621).

When to go

The rainfall is heavy, but varies throughout the region; close to the Andes, up to 4000 mm annually, under 2000 at Manaus. Rains occur throughout the year but the wettest season is between December and May, the driest month is October. The humidity can be extremely high and the temperature averages 26°C. There can be cold snaps in December in the western reaches of the Amazon basin. The soil, as in all tropical forest, is poor.

What to take

A hammock is essential on all but the most expensive boats; it is often too hot to lie down in a cabin during day. Light cotton hammocks seem to be the best solution. Buy a wide one on which you can lie diagonally; lying straight along it leaves you hump-backed. A climbing carabiner clip is useful for fastening hammocks to runner bars of boats. It is also useful for securing baggage, making it harder to steal.

Health

There is a risk of malaria and other mosquito-borne diseases in Amazônia. Many pharmacies in towns and cities do not sell medications for malaria prophylaxis – bring an adequate supply from home. Mosquito nets are not required when in motion as boats travel away from the banks and too fast for mosquitoes to settle, though repellent is a boon for night stops. A yellow-fever inoculation is strongly advised; it is compulsory in some areas, and may be administered on the spot with a pressurized needle gun. It is best to get a yellow fever vaccination at home (always have your certificate handy) and avoid the risk of recycled needles. The larger ships must have an infirmary and carry a health officer. Drinking water is generally taken on in port (ie city tap water), but taking your own mineral water is a good idea.

Money

You can exchange dollars but, outside of Manaus and Belém, rates can be poor.

Time required

As a guide, take three days for Manaus or Belém, two to three days for Cristalino Jungle Lodge or Mamirauá and ten days to travel between Manaus. To get off the beaten track, two to four weeks.

Food

In Amazônia, inevitably fish dishes are very common, including many fish with indigenous names, eg matrinchã, jaraqui, pacu, tucunaré, and tambaqui, which are worth trying. Pirarucu is another delicacy of Amazonian cuisine, but because of overfishing it is in danger of becoming extinct. Also shrimp and crab dishes (more expensive). Specialities of Pará include duck, often served in a yellow soup made from the juice of the root of the manioc (*tucupi*) with a green vegetable (*jambu*), the famous *pato no tucupi*. Also *tacaca* (shrimps served in tucupi), *vatapá* (shrimps served in a thick sauce, highly filling, simpler than the variety found in Salvador), *maniçoba* (made with the poisonous leaves of the bitter cassava, simmered for eight days to render it safe – tasty). *Caldeirada*, a fish and vegetable soup, served with *pirão* (manioc puree) is a speciality of Amazonas. There is also an enormous variety of tropical and jungle fruits, many unique to the region. Try them fresh, or in ice creams or juices. Avoid food from street vendors.

Food on the boats is ample but monotonous, better food is sometimes available to cabin passengers. Meal times can be chaotic. Fresh fruit is a welcome addition; also take plain biscuits, tea bags, seasonings, sauces and jam. Non-meat eaters should take vegetables and tinned fish. Fresh coffee is available. Most boats have some sort of rooftop bar serving expensive drinks and snacks. Plates and cutlery may not be provided. Bring your own plastic mug as drinks are served in plastic beakers which are jettisoned into the river.

and is now the **Prefeitura**, was originally built as the Palácio Municipal between 1868 and 1883. In the downstairs rooms there are old views of Belém; upstairs the historic rooms, beautifully renovated, contain furniture, paintings etc, all well explained.

The Belém market, known as '**Ver-o-Peso**' was the Portuguese Posto Fiscal, where goods were weighed to gauge taxes due (hence the name: 'see the weight'). It now has lots of gift shops selling charms for the local African-derived religion, umbanda; the medicinal herb and natural perfume stalls are also interesting. It is one of the most varied and colourful markets in South America; you can see giant river fish being unloaded around 0530, with frenzied wholesale buying for the next hour. Immediately opposite Ver-o-Peso inland is the 19th century, wrought-iron meat market, the Mercado Municipal de Carnes Francisco Bolonha, beautifully restored in 2015, hosting galleries of little shops and with a viewing platform reached by a winding stairway.

> **Warning...**
> The area around the market swarms with people, including many armed thieves and pickpockets. All over the city, take sensible precautions especially at night.

In the old town, too, is the **Forte do Castelo** ① *Praça Frei Caetano Brandão 117, T091-4009 8828, Tue-Fri 1000-1800, Sat-Sun 1000-1400*. The fort overlooks the confluence of the Rio Guamá and the Baía de Guajara and was where the Portuguese first set up their defences. It was rebuilt in 1878. The excellent museum (Museu do Forte do Presépio) has interesting displays on indigenous archaeology and some artefacts. The site also contains the Boteca Onze restaurant (entry US$2; drinks and *salgadinhos* served on the ramparts from 1800 to watch the sunset). At the square on the waterfront below the fort the açaí berries are landed nightly at 2300, after picking in the jungle (açaí berries ground up with sugar and mixed with manioc are a staple food in the region). At the square on the waterfront below the fort, açaí berries are landed in the early morning before dawn after being picked in the jungle, to be sold in a lively market. Açaí berries, ground up with sugar and mixed with manioc, are a staple food in the region. Opposite the fort across the square is the

Belém

Where to stay
1 Amazônia Hostel
2 Grão Pará
3 Itaoca Belém
4 Le Massilia
5 Machado's Plaza
6 Novo Avenida
8 Unidos
9 Vila Rica

Restaurants 🍴
1 Açaí at Hilton Hotel
3 Cantina Italiana
4 Churrascaria Rodeio
6 Doces Bárbaros
7 Govinda
8 Lá em Casa
9 Mãe Natureza
10 Remanso do Bosque

11 Sabor Paraense

Bars & clubs 🍸
12 A Pororó & Carousel
13 Café Com Arte
14 do Gilson
15 Mormoço
16 São Mateus

Espaço Cultural Casa das Onze Janelas ① *Praça Dom Pedro II s/n, T091-4009 8825, Tue-Fri 1000-1800, Sat-Sun, 1000-1400, US$1.50, Tue free*, in a stately 18th-century mansion, with galleries devoted to temporary exhibitions, usually of Amazonian art and photography.

At the **Estação das Docas**, the abandoned warehouses of the port have been restored into a complex with an air-conditioned interior and restaurants outside. The **Terminal Marítimo** has an office of **Valverde Tours**, which offers sunset and night-time boat trips. The Boulevard das Artes contains the **Cervejaria Amazon** brewery, with good beer and simple meals, an archaeological museum and arts and crafts shops. The Boulevard de Gastronomia has smart restaurants and the five-star Cairu ice cream parlour (try açaí or the Pavê de Capuaçu). Also in the complex are ATMs, internet café, phones and good toilets.

Belém's brand new boat terminal, **Terminal Hidroviário**, for boats to Marajó island and other destinations (see page 606) is immediately north of the Estação das Docas.

The **Mangal das Garças** ① *end of Av Tamandaré, on the waterfront, 10 mins' walk east of cathedral*, is a good park with flora of the state, including mangroves, a butterfly and hummingbird house, colourful birds, a museum, viewing tower and the **Manjar das Garças** restaurant (good for all-you-can-eat meals).

The **Bosque Rodrigues Alves** ① *Av Almte Barroso 2305, T091-3226 2308, 0900-1700, closed Mon*, is a 16-ha public garden (really a preserved area of original flora), with a small animal collection; yellow bus marked 'Souza' or 'Cidade Nova' (any number) 30 minutes from 'Ver-o-Peso' market, also the bus from the Cathedral. The **Museu Emílio Goeldi** ① *Av Magalhães Barata 376, T091-3182 3200, www. museu-goeldi.br, Tue-Thu 0900-1200, 1400-1700, Fri 0900-1200, Sat-Sun 0900-1700, US$1, additional charges for specialist area*, takes up a city block and consists of the museum proper (with a fine collection of Marajó indigenous pottery, an excellent exhibition of the lifestyle of the Mebengokre people) and botanical exhibits including Victoria Régia lilies. Take a bus from the Cathedral.

A return trip on the ferry from Ver-o-Peso to **Icaoraci** provides a good view of the river. Several restaurants here serve excellent seafood; you can eat shrimp and drink coconut water and appreciate the breeze coming off the river. Icaoraci is 20 km east of the city and is well-known as a centre of ceramic production. The pottery is in Marajoara and Tapajonica style. Take the bus from Av Presidente Vargas to Icaoraci (one hr). Open all week but best on Tuesday to Friday. Artisans are friendly and helpful, will accept commissions and send purchases overseas.

The nearest beach is at **Outeiro** (35 km) on an island near Icaoraci, about an hour by bus and ferry (the bus may be caught near the *maloca*, an indigenous-style hut near the docks which serves as a nightclub). A bus from Icaoraci to Outeiro takes 30 minutes. Further north is the island of **Mosqueiro** (86 km) ① *buses Belém-Mosqueiro every hour from rodoviária, US$2, 80 mins*, accessible by an excellent highway. It has many beautiful sandy beaches and jungle inland. It is popular at weekends when traffic can be heavy (also July) and the beaches can get crowded and polluted. Many hotels and weekend villas are at the villages of Mosqueiro and Vila; recommended (may be full weekends and July). Camping is easy and there are plenty of good places to eat.

Ilha do Marajó *Colour map 5, A1.*

At almost 50,000 sq km, the world's largest island formed by fluvial processes is flooded in rainy December to June and provides a suitable habitat for water buffalo, introduced from India in the late 19th century. They are now farmed in large numbers (try the cheese and milk). It is also home to many birds, crocodiles and other wildlife, and has several good beaches. It is crowded at weekends and in the July holiday season. The island was the site of the pre-Columbian Marajoaras culture.

Ponta de Pedras

Boats leave Belém (near Porto do Sal, five hours) most days for Ponta de Pedras (\$\$ Hotel Ponta de Pedras, good meals, buses for Soure or Salvaterra meet the boat). Bicycles for hire to explore beaches and the interior of the island. Fishing boats make the eight-hour trip to Cachoeira do Arari (one *pousada*, \$\$-\$) where there is a Marajó museum. A 10-hour boat trip from Ponta de Pedras goes to the Arari lake where there are two villages, Jenipapo built on stilts, *forró* dancing at weekends, and Santa Cruz which is less primitive, but less interesting (a hammock and a mosquito net are essential). There is a direct boat service to Belém twice a week.

Soure *Colour map 5, A1.*

The 'capital' of the island has fine beaches: Araruna (2 km – take supplies and supplement with coconuts and crabs, beautiful walks along the shore), do Pesqueiro (bus from Praça da Matriz, 1030, returns 1600, eat at the *maloca*, good, cheap, big, deserted beach, 13 km away) and Caju-Una (15 km). Small craft await passengers from the river boats, for **Salvaterra**

Tip...
When in Soure, make sure you have plenty of insect repellent.

village (good beaches and bars: seafood), 10 minutes, or trips are bookable in Belém from Mururé, T3241 0891. There are also 17th-century Jesuit ruins at **Joanes** as well as a virgin beach.

Macapá *Colour map 2, C6.*

The capital of Amapá State is situated on the northern channel of the Amazon Delta and is linked to Belém by boat and daily flights. Along with Porto Santana it was declared a Zona Franca in 1993 and visitors flock to buy cheap imported electrical and other goods. Each brick of the **Fortaleza de São José do Macapá**, built between 1764 and 1782, was brought from Portugal as ballast; 50 iron cannons remain. Today it is used for concerts, exhibits, and colourful festivities on the anniversary of the city's founding, 4 February. In the handicraft complex, **Casa do Artesão** ① *Av Azárias Neto, Mon-Sat 0800-1900*, craftsmen produce their wares onsite. A feature is pottery decorated with local manganese ore, also woodcarvings, leatherwork and indigenous crafts. **São José Cathedral**, inaugurated by the Jesuits in 1761, is the city's oldest landmark.

The riverfront is a very pleasant place for an evening stroll. The **Complexo Beira-Rio** has food and drink kiosks, and a nice lively atmosphere. The pier (*trapiche*) has been rebuilt and is a lovely spot for savouring the cool of the evening breeze, or watching sunrise over the Amazon. There is a monument to the equator, **Marco Zero** (take Fazendinha bus). The equator also divides the nearby enormous football stadium in half, aptly named O Zerão. South of here, at Km 12 on Rodovia Juscelinho Kubitschek, are the **botanical gardens**. **Fazendinha** (16 km from the centre) is a popular local beach, very busy on Sunday. **Curiarú**, 8 km from Macapá, was founded by escaped slaves, and is popular at weekends for dancing and swimming.

Tourist offices: Setur ① *R Bingo Uchôa 29, Centro, T096-4009 9751, Facebook: Secretaria-de-Estado-do-Turismo-do-Amapá, open 0800-1800.*

Border with Guyane *Colour map 2, B6.*

The main road crosses the Rio Caciporé and continues to the border with Guyane at **Oiapoque**, on the river of the same name. It is 90 km inland from the Parque Nacional Cabo Orange (ICMBio contact T096-3521 2706), Brazil's northernmost point on the Atlantic coast. About 7 km to the west is Clevelândia do Norte, a military outpost and the end of the road in Brazil. Oiapoque is remote, with its share of contraband and prostitution. It is also the gateway to gold fields in the interior of both Brazil and Guyane. Prices here are high, but lower than in neighbouring Guyane. The **Cachoeira Grande Roche** rapids can be visited, upstream along the Oiapoque River, where it is possible to swim, US$25 per motor boat. Paving of the entire road north to the Guyane border (BR-156) was due for completion in 2014, but was still incomplete as this book went to press. It is advisable to carry extra fuel, food and water from Macapá onwards. Immigration officers will stamp you out the day before if you want to make an early start to Guyane. Polícia Federal, for Brazilian exit and entry stamps, is at Avenida Rio Branco 500, T096-3521 1380. For the French honorary consul,

Fact...
It is possible to exchange US dollars and reais to euros, but dollar rates are low. It's best to buy euros in Belém, or abroad. Banco do Brasil and Bradesco have Visa facilities to withdraw reais which can be changed into euros if necessary.

ask at **Pousada Ekinox** (see below), visas for Guyane have to be obtained from Brasília which can take a while. A bridge linking Guyane and Amapá was completed in 2011, but was still not open to traffic in 2017. The road is asphalted all the way to Cayenne. As combis to Cayenne leave before lunch it is best to get to St-Georges before 1000. There is already much deforestation along the Brazilian side of the road and many Brazilian *garimpeiros* and hunter are causing havoc in Guyane.

Tourist information

Belém Paratur
Praça Maestro Waldemar Henrique s/n, T091-3110 5000, www.paraturismo.pa.gov.br.
Helpful, some staff speak English.

Banks

Money can only be changed at banks during the week. At weekends hotels will only exchange for their guests, while restaurants may change money, but at poor rates. Exchange rates are generally the best in the north of the country.

Consulates

Venezuela
Ferreira Cantão 331, T091-3222 6396, see Facebook.
Check website before arriving if you need a Venezuelan visa for entering overland; it takes 3 hrs and costs US$30.

Where to stay

Belém

There are now a few decent mid-range hotels in the city and a few clean, well-kept bargains in the upper budget category. The cheapest rooms are still very scruffy in Belém: consider an upgrade, this is a place where US$3-4 can make an enormous difference.

$$$ Itaoca Belém
Av Pres Vargas 132, T091-4009 2400, www.hotelitaoca.com.br.
Well kept, bright rooms, the best are on the upper floors away from the street noise, and with river views. Decent breakfast.

$$$ Machado's Plaza
R Henrique Gurjão 200, T091-3347 9800, www.machadosplazahotel.com.br.
Bright hotel with smart and tastefully decorated rooms, a small business centre, plunge pool and a pleasant a/c breakfast area. Good value.

$$$-$$ Le Massilia
R Henrique Gurjão 236, T091-3222 2834, www.massilia.com.br.
Intimate, French owned boutique hotel with chic little duplexes and more ordinary doubles. Excellent French restaurant (**$$$**) and a tasty French breakfast.

$$$-$$ Vila Rica
Av Júlio César 1777, T091-3210 2000, www. hotelvilarica.com.br/hotel_belem.htm.
5 mins from airport, taxi US$6.25, helpful with transfers, very good. In front of it is the Ibis Aeroporto hotel, which is OK.

$$ Grão Pará
Av Pres Vargas 718, T091-3321 2121, www.hotelgraopara.com.br.
Contemporary fittings, smart, hot water, the best have superb river views, excellent breakfast, great value.

$$ Unidos
Ó de Almeida 545, T091-3252 1411, http://hotelunidos.com.
Simple, spacious rooms with clean en suites.

$$-$ Novo Avenida
Av Pres.Vargas 404, T091-3242 9953, www.hotelnovoavenida.com.br.
Slightly frayed but spruce rooms with decent breakfast. Groups of can sleep in large rooms for **$** pp. Very good value.

$ pp Amazônia Hostel
Av Gov José Malcher 592, Nazaré (between Quintino Bocaiúva and Rui Barbosa), T091-98195 8571, www.amazoniahostel.com.br.
Good hostel with shared rooms and lockers, kitchen and laundry. (Don't confuse with **Amazônia**, R Ó de Almeida 548, which is not recommended.)

Soure

$$$ Canto do Frances
6 Rua, Trav 8, Soure, T091-3741 1298, www.ocantodofrances.blogspot.com.
French/Brazilian-owned *pousada* 20 mins' walk from the centre, well-kept but simple rooms in a pretty bungalow surrounded by a garden filled with flowers and fruit trees. Breakfast is generous and the owners organize horse riding, canoe and bike trips around Soure. Book ahead to be met at the ferry port.

$$$ Casarão da Amazônia
4Rua No 646, Soure, T091-3741 1988, www.casaraoamazonia.com.br.
Far and away the best hotel on the island and the only boutique hotel in the Pará Amazon, lovingly restored and run by Neapolitan Nello Gentile and his wife Camila. In a fabulous, sky-blue belle époque rubber boom mansion in Soure village, in its own tropical garden next to a pool

and restaurant. Rooms are comfortable, well appointed and cool. Good Italian-Amazonian food (with crispy pizzas). Wonderful horseback and boat tours around Marajó. Stay for several days.

$$$ Pousada dos Guarás
Av Beira Mar, Salvaterra, T091-4005 5656, www.pousadadosguaras.com.br.
Well-equipped little resort hotel on the beach with an extensive tour programme.

$$ Paracaury Eco Pousada
Rio Paracaury, Soure, T091-2121 2600, www.paracauary.com.br.
A/c rooms with en suites in mock-colonial chalets around a pool 3 km from Soure, on the banks of the Rio Paracaury.

$$ Ventania
Praia de Joanes, T091-3646 2067, www.pousadaventania.com.
Pretty little cliff-top *pousada* in a lawned garden, a stroll from the beach, arranges tours on horseback or canoe. Lovely breakfast areas with beach views. Each apartment has room for 2 couples. Bike rental, French, Dutch, English and Spanish spoken. Ask about their social integration projects with locals.

Macapá

$$$ Atalanta
Av Coracy Nunes 1148, T096-3223 1612, www.atalantahotel.com.br. 10 mins' walk from the river.
The best business-style hotel in town with a rooftop pool and comfortable, modern rooms, includes generous breakfast.

$$$ Ceta Ecotel
R do Matodouro 640, Fazendinha, T096-3227 3396, www.ecotel.com.br. 20 mins from town centre by taxi.
All furniture made on site, sports facilities, gardens with sloths and monkeys, ecological trails. Highly recommended.

$$ Pousada Ekinox
R Jovino Dinoá 1693, T086-3223 0086, http://ekinoxmacapa.com.
Nice atmosphere, book and video library, excellent meals and service, riverboat tours available. Recommended.

$$-$ Santo Antônio
Av Coriolano Jucá 485, T096-3222 0226, 1 block south and half a block east of Praça da Bandeira.
Best rooms are on upper floors, cheaper with fan, good breakfast extra; in dorm.

Border with Guyane: Oiapoque
Plenty of cheap, poorly maintained hotels along the waterfront.

Restaurants

Belém
All the major hotels have good restaurants. Good snack bars ($) serving *vatapá* (Bahian dish), tapioca rolls, etc, are on Assis de Vasconcelos on the eastern side of the Praça da Republica.

$$$ Remanso do Bosque
R 25 de Setembro 2350, Marco, T091-3347 2829, Facebook: RemansoDoBosque.
One of the finest restaurants in Latin America serving gourmet *paraense* cooking made by celebrity chef Thiago Castanho.

$$$ Açaí
Hilton Hotel, Av Pres Vargas 882, T091-3242 6500.
Recommended for regional dishes and others, Sun brunch or daily lunch and dinner.

$$$ Churrascaria Rodeio
Trav Padre Eutíquio 1308 and Rodovia Augusto Montenegro Km 4, T091-3248 2004.
A choice of 20 cuts of meat and 30 buffet dishes for a set price. Well worth the short taxi ride to eat all you can.

$$$ Lá em Casa
Av Governador José Malcher 247 (also in Estação das Docas).
Good *paraense* cooking, including *tacaca* and *pato no tucupi*.

$$ Cantina Italiana
Trav Benjamin Constant 1401.
Very good Italian, also delivers.

$$ Mãe Natureza
Manoel Barata 889, T091-3212 8032.
Vegetarian and wholefood dishes in a bright clean dining room. Lunch only.

$$ Sabor Paraense
R Sen Manoel Barata 897, T091-3241 4391.
A variety of fish and meat dishes served in a bright, light dining room.

$ Doces Bárbaros
Benjamin Constant 1658, T091-3224 0576. Lunch only.
Cakes, snacks, sandwiches and decent coffee.

$ Govinda
Ó de Almeida 198. Lunch only.
Basic but tasty vegetarian food.

Macapá

$$$ Chalé
Av Pres Vargas 499.
Nice atmosphere and good food.

$$ Cantinho Baiano
Av Beira-Rio 1, Santa Inês.
Good seafood. 10 mins' walk south of the fort.
Many other restaurants along this stretch about
1.5 km beyond the Cantino Baiano.

$$ Martinho's Peixaria
Av Beira-Rio 810.
Another good fish restaurant.

$ Bom Paladar Kilo's
Av Pres Vargas 456.
Good pay-by-weight buffet.

$ Sorveteria Macapá
R São José 1676, close to centre.
Excellent ice cream made from local fruit.

Bars and clubs

Belém
Belém has some of the best and most distinctive
live music and nightlife in northern Brazil.

A Pororó
Vast warehouse jam packed with techno *brega*
acts playing a kind of up tempo disco driven 2/4
dance to thousands of people every Fri and Sat.

Bar do Gilson
Travessa Padre Eutíquio 3172, T091-3272 1306.
A covered courtyard decorated with black
and white photography, live samba and
choro at weekends.

Café com Arte
Av Rui Barbosa 1436.
Good after 2300. A colonial house with 3 floors
devoted to live rock and DJs.

Carousel
Av Almte Barroso at Antônio Baena. Every Fri.
Live *aparelhagem* – a kind of up-tempo techno
with twanging guitars played by DJs on a sound
stage that looks like the flight control gallery for a
1970s starship. Has to be seen to be believed.

Mormoço
Praça do Arsenal s/n, Mangal das Garças.
A warehouse-sized building on the waterfront,
some of the best live bands in Belém at
weekends, playing local rhythms like *carimbó*
and Brazilianized reggae and rock.

São Mateus
Travessa Padre Eutíquio 606.
A mock Carioca *boteco* street bar, Belém rock and
Brazilian soul most nights.

Festivals

Belém
Oct Círio (Festival of Candles), is based on the
legend of the Nossa Senhora de Nazaré, whose
image was found on the site of her Basílica
around 1700. On the 2nd Sun in Oct, a procession
carries a copy of the Virgin's image from the
Basílica to the cathedral. On the Mon, 2 weeks
later, the image is returned to its usual place.
There is a Círio museum in the Basílica crypt,
enter at the right side of the church; free. (Hotels
are fully booked during Círio.)

Macapá
Marabaixo is the traditional music and dance of
the state of Amapá; a festival held 40 days after
Easter. The **Sambódromo**, near Marco Zero, is
used by Escolas de Samba during Carnaval and
by Quadrilhas during the São João festivities.

Shopping

Belém
A good place to buy hammocks is the street
parallel to the river, 1 block inland from Ver-o-
Peso, starting at US$5-7.50.
Arts and crafts market, *Praça da República.*
Every weekend. Seed and bead jewellery, whicker,
hammocks and raw cotton weave work, toys and
knic-knacs. Mostly predictable but the odd gem.
Complexo São Brás, *Praça Lauro Sodré.*
Handicraft market and folkloric shows in a
building dating from 1911.
Parfumaria Orion, *Trav Frutuoso Guimarães 268.*
Sells a variety of perfumes from Amazonian
plants, much cheaper than tourist shops.

What to do

Belém
Larger hotels organize city and 1-day boat tours.
Amazon Star, *R Henrique Gurjão 210, T091-3241
8624, www.amazonstar.com.br.* City and river
tours, Ilha de Marajó hotel bookings and tours,
very professional, good guides, jungle tours. Also
scheduled sailings to Manaus and Santarém and
flight bookings. Repeatedly recommended.

Amazônia Sport & Ação, *Av 25 de Setembro 2345, T091-3226 8442*. Extreme sports, diving and climbing.

Marola Stand-up, *T091-98162 7473, Facebook: MarolaStandUp*. Stand-up paddle boarding on the Amazon rivers. Full instruction and all equipment provided.

Rumo Norte Expedições, *T091-3225 5915, http://rumonorte.tur.br*. The only company offering a comprehensive menu of adventure, safari and general activities in the eastern Amazon including Belém city tours, boat trips around Belém and Santarém, visits to indigenous people near Alter do Chão and expeditions and light adventure on Marajó, Algodoal and the other islands in the mouth of the Amazon. Reliable and good value.

Transport

Belém

Air Val-de-Cans international airport, Av Júlio César s/n, 12 km from the city, T091-3210 6000, receives flights from Lisbon (with TAP), Suriname and Guyane and the major Brazilian capitals. The terminal has car rentals, 2 tour operators, a hotel booking service, ATMs, a food court, a chemist and a very helpful tourist office booth (daily 1000-1700).

A/c 'VIP' airport bus (daily 0730-1700, every 75 mins, US$0.70) leaves from outside the terminal. Buses 638 (Pratinha–Pte Vargas), 637 (Pratinha–Ver-o-Peso) and 634 (Estação Marex–Arsenal) also make the journey, leaving every 15 mins, US$0.70. A taxi costs US$14; there are cooperative taxi desks at the exit.

Bus The *rodoviária* is at the end of Av Governador José Malcher 5 km from the centre (T091-3246 8178). Take Aeroclube, Cidade Novo, No 20 bus, or Arsenal or Canudos buses, US$1, or taxi, US$8 (day), US$10 (night) (at *rodoviária* you are given a ticket with the taxi's number on it, threaten to go to the authorities if the driver tries to overcharge). Good snack bar, showers (US$0.10) and 2 agencies with information and tickets for riverboats. Regular bus services to all major cities. To **Santarém**, via Marabá (on the Trans-amazônica) once a week (US$109, can take longer than boat, goes only in dry season). 3 companies go to **Marabá**, 9 hrs, US$23-33. To **São Luís**, 4 a day, US$37-48, 14 hrs, interesting journey through marshlands. To **Fortaleza**, US$61-65 (at least 24 hrs), 3 companies.

Boats To **Ilha do Marajó** see below. All larger ships berth at Portobrás/Docas do Pará (the main commercial port) at Armazém (warehouse)

No 10 (entrance on Av Marechal Hermes, corner of Av Visconde de Souza Franco). The guards will sometimes ask to see your ticket before letting you into the port area, but tell them you are going to speak with a ship's captain. Ignore the touts who approach you. **Macamazónia**, R Castilho Franca, sells tickets for most boats, open Sun. There are 2 desks selling tickets for private boats in the *rodoviária*; some hotels recommend agents for tickets. Purchase tickets from offices 2 days in advance. Smaller vessels (sometimes cheaper, usually not as clean, comfortable or safe) sail from small docks along Estrada Nova (not a safe part of town). Take a Cremação bus from Ver-o-Peso.

To **Macapá (Porto Santana)**, the quickest (12 hrs) are the catamaran *Atlântico I* or the launches *Lívia Marília* and *Atlântico II* (slightly slower), all leaving at 0700 on alternate days. Other boats take 24 hrs: *Silja e Souza* (Wed) of Souzamar, Trav Dom Romualdo Seixas corner R Jerônimo Pimentel, T091-3222 0719, and *Almirante Solon* (Sat) of Sanave (Serviço Amapaense de Navegação, Castilho Franca 234, opposite Ver-o-Peso, T091-3222 7810), slightly cheaper, crowded, not as nice. Via **Breves**, **ENAL**, T091-3224 5210 (see Getting around, page 598). Smaller boats to **Macapá** also sail from Estrada Nova.

Buy boat tickets for destinations through **Rumo Norte Expedições** (see above), or Macamazon, Av Castilho França 716, T091-3031 5899, www.macamazon.com.br.

Ilha do Marajó

Ferry Boats leave from the Terminal Hidroviário (see page 601) to Porto de Camará near Salvaterra on **Ilha do Marajó**, Mon-Sat 0630, 1430, Sun 1000, 3 hrs, US$5. A fast catamaran service to **Soure** takes 2 hrs, US$15.25, Mon-Sat 0900, return same days 0600. Car ferries to Marajó (with space for passengers) run from the port at Icoaraci (20 km north of Belém, 30 mins by bus from the *rodoviária* or from the Ver-o-Peso market, taxi US$25), Mon-Fri 0630, 0730, Sat 1600, 1700, Sun 1600, 1700 and 1800.

Macapá

Air Flights to **Belém**, **Belo Horizonte**, **Brasília** and **São Paulo** with Azul, GOL and LATAM.

Bus *Rodoviária* on BR-156, north of Macapá. To **Amapá**, **Calçoene** and **Oiapoque** (15-17 hrs, US$36), at least 2 daily. The road is from Amapá to the border is due to be paved; before then you may have to get out and walk up hills, bus has no a/c.

Ferry Ships dock at Porto Santana, 30 km from Macapá (frequent buses US$2, or share a taxi US$24). To **Belém**, *Silja e Souza* of Souzamar, Cláudio Lúcio Monteiro 1375, Santana, and *Almirante Solon* of Sanave, Av Mendonça Furtado 1766. See under Belém, Ferry, for other boats. Purchase tickets from offices 2 days in advance. Also smaller and cheaper boats. The faster (12 hrs) catamaran *Atlântico I* or launches leave for Belém most days. *São Francisco de Paula I* sails to **Santarém** and **Manaus**, not going via Belém.

Border with Guyane: Oiapoque

Bus At least 2 a day for **Macapá**, 12-15 hrs (dry season), 14-24 hrs (wet season), US$36. Also shared jeeps, cheaper in the back than in the cabin. You may be asked to show your Polícia Federal entry stamp and Yellow Fever vaccination certificate either when buying a ticket from the offices on the waterfront or at the bus station when boarding for Macapá.

Ferry Crossing to Guyane: motorized canoes cross to St-Georges de L'Oyapock, 10 mins downstream, US$4 pp, bargain for return fare. A vehicle ferry will operate until the bridge is completed.

Belém to Manaus

islands as far as the eye can see

A few hours up the broad river from Belém, the region of the thousand islands is entered. The passage through this maze of islets is known as The Narrows and is perhaps the nicest part of the journey. The ship winds through 150 km of lanes of yellow flood with equatorial forest within 20 m or 30 m on both sides. On one of the curious flat-topped hills after the Narrows stands the little stucco town of Monte Alegre, an oasis in mid-forest (airport; some simple hotels, $$-$). There are lagoon cruises to see lilies, birds and pink dolphins; also village visits (US$40 per day).

Santarém *Colour map 4, A5.*

The third largest city on the Brazilian Amazon, at its confluence with the 20-km wide Rio Tapajós, sits halfway (two or three days by boat) between Belém and Manaus. It was founded in 1661 as the Jesuit mission of Tapajós; the name was changed to Santarém in 1758. There was once a fort here and attractive colonial squares overlooking the waterfront remain. Modern Santarém is a business and agricultural centre with little of interest to other visitors, most of whom head 40 minutes' south to the delightful village of Alter do Chão. **Tourist office**: Semtur ① *Av Adriano Pimentel 170, T093-3523 2434, www.santarem.pa.gov.br*, has good information available in English. See also www.paraturismo.pa.gov.br.

The yellow Amazon water swirls alongside the green-blue Tapajós; the **meeting of the waters**, in front of the market square, is nearly as impressive as that of the Negro and Solimões near Manaus. A small **Museu dos Tapajós** in the old city hall on the waterfront, now the **Centro Cultural João Fona** ① *open 0900, closed weekend, free*, downriver from where the boats dock, has a collection of ancient Tapajós ceramics, as well as various 19th-century artefacts. The unloading of the fish catch between 0500 and 0700 on the waterfront is interesting. There are good beaches nearby on the Rio Tapajós.

Alter do Chão and Floresta Nacional do Tapajós

Alter do Chão is a small, relaxed, welcoming village. It is made-up of Caboclo river people, Borari people, who come from a conglomeration of different tribal nations, and a community of ex-pat southeastern Brazilians, many of whom have a spirituality influenced by a mixture of Amazonian traditions based around the taking of Ayahuasca. It sits on the Tapajós river, 30 km west of Santarém. In the dry season (July-January) the town is surrounded by tens of kilometres of broad, white-pepper fine sandy beaches, which form a lagoon (Lago Verde) immediately in front of the town. A long spit (cheesily known as Love Island by hoteliers), extends to a small hill (O Morro), from where there are spectacular views over the river, the *cerrado* forests around Alter do Chão and the vast Amazon rainforests which stretch along the other side of the river.

The 545,000-ha **Floresta Nacional do Tapajós** ① *office at Av Tapajós 2201, Laguinho, Santarém, T093-3522 0564, www.icmbio.gov.br/flonatapajos, Mon-Fri 0800-1200, 1400-1800, park open daily 0800-1800, entry permits from this office, unless going on a tour – see below*, on the eastern banks of the Tapajós south of Alter do Chão, is home to 26 riverine communities who eke a living from harvesting Brazil nuts, rubber and from fishing. The protected area forms part of a larger reserve spanning both banks of the river. On the less accessible west shore is the 648,000-ha **Reserva Extrativista Tapajós Arapiuns**, created to allow local people to extract rubber and nuts and hunt on a small scale. Both areas are open to tourism and agencies in Alter do Chão offer trips which include Amazon homestays with riverine communities. The forests and rivers themselves are not as wild as those in similar reserves in Acre or Amazonas, but the area is stunningly beautiful, with white-sand beaches, pink river dolphins and the forest itself with its many towering kapok and Brazil nut trees.

Óbidos and around

At 110 km up-river from Santarém (five hours by boat), Óbidos is located at the narrowest and deepest point on the river. It is a picturesque and clean city with many beautiful, tiled buildings and some nice parks. Worth seeing are the **Prefeitura Municipal** ① *T093-3547 1194*, the *cuartel* and the **Museu Integrado de Óbidos** ① *R Justo Chermont 607, Mon-Fri 0700-1100, 1330-1730*. There is also a **Museu Contextual**, a system of plaques with detailed explanations of historical buildings throughout town. The airport has flights to Manaus, Santarém and Parintins.

Just across the Pará-Amazonas border, between Santarém and Manaus, is **Parintins**, 15 hours by boat upriver from Óbidos. Here, on the last three days of June each year, the **Festa do Boi** draws over 50,000 visitors. Since the town has only two small hotels, everyone sleeps in hammocks on the boats that bring them to the festival from Manaus and Santarém. The festival consists of lots of folkloric dancing, but its main element is the competition between two rival groups, the Caprichoso and the Garantido, in the Bumbódromo, built in 1988 to hold 35,000 spectators.

Listings Belém to Manaus

Where to stay

Santarém
The city has a limited choice of hotels.

$$$ Barruda Tropical
Av Mendonça Furtado 4120, T093-3222 2200, http://barrudadatropicalhotel.com.br.
Large 1970s concrete hotel, 4 km from the centre, with boxy rooms, a pool and restaurant. Best in town but nothing special.

$$ Tapajós Center
Av Tapajós 1827, T093-3522 5353, http://tapajoscenterhotel.com.br.
A big concrete block well situated in the city centre. Simple, plain rooms with few furnishings, some have no window. The best, on the top floor, have balconies with great river views. No lift.

Alter do Chão

$$$ Beloalter
R Pedro Teixeira 500, T093-3527 1230, http://beloalter.com.br.
Beautifully situated, a stroll from the beach and lagoon and 15 mins' walk from the centre, with a pool, pleasant open-sided public areas and a garden visited by monkeys in the early morning and afternoon. Best in town, despite plain, uninspiring rooms with ugly windows and noisy a/c.

$$ Agualinda Hotel
R Dr Macedo Costa 777, T093-3527 1314, www.agualindahotel.com.br.
Brick floor and cream rooms, with little more than a bed, some suites for families, in a pleasant, airy *pousada* in the town centre.

$$ Belas Praias Pousada
R da Praia 507, at the praça, T093-3527 1365, www.pousadabelaspraias.com.br.
Very simple rooms in a town house, balconies on the upper floor give pleasant river views, central, 10 m from the beach.

$$ Terramor
On Carauari hill, R Everaldo Martins Km 27, Facebook: TerrAmor, book through Arkus Rodrigues, see Sabiá Tour, below.
A retreat community and private ecological reserve on a forested hill overlooking the town. Chalets, or hammocks in a *maloca* in the community, stays are for a minimum of a few days. Meditation, movement, music and Ayahuasca sessions can be included.

$ Albergue Pousada da Floresta
T093-9921 6566, http://alberguedafloresta-alterdochao.blogspot.co.uk.
A simple but colourful backpacker hostel with basic cabins and a cheap open-space for slinging hammocks. Facilities include kitchen, tour booking, canoe and bike rental. Just south of the village, surrounded by forest. Gets booked well ahead.

$ Pousada do Tapajós
R Laura Soudre 100, T093-9210 2166,
http://pousadadotapajos.com.br.
HI hostel with very spartan tiled rooms and
dorms, attentive staff who can organize tours.

$ Pousada Ecológica
Trav Pedro Teixeira 66, Carauri, T093-99186 9849,
http://pousadadojohnlennon.blogspot.co.uk.
Simple wooden huts in a forested garden
10 mins' walk from beach, decent breakfast.
Helpful staff include owner and guide Antônio
'John Lennon' Augusto.

Óbidos

$$ Braz Bello
R Corrêia Pinto, on top of the hill.
Shared bath, full board available.

Restaurants

Santarém

$$ Mascote
Praça do Pescador 10. Open 1000-2330.
Restaurant, bar and ice cream parlour.

$$ Mascotinho
Praça Manoel de Jesus Moraes, on riverfront.
Bar/pizzeria, popular, outside seating, good view.

$ Lucy
Praça do Pescador.
Good juices and pastries. Recommended.

Alter do Chão

Lago Verde
Praça 7 de Setembro.
Good fresh fish, huge portions.

Festivals

Santarém

29 Jun São Pedro, with processions of boats on
the river and *boi-bumbá* dance dramas.

Alter do Chão

2nd week in Sep Festa do Çairé, one of Pará's
biggest festivals, with costumed processions
in the sandy streets and a pageant depicting
the seduction of a river dolphin by a beautiful
Cabocla girl.

What to do

Santarém

Amazon Dream, *www.amazon-dream.com*. For
5, 6 and 10-day cruises out of Santarém, on a
traditional-style river boat.
Gil Serique, *80 R Adriano Pimentel, T093-99115
8111, www.gilserique.com*. Enthusiastic, larger-
than-life, English-speaking tour guide who visits
the creeks, flooded forest, primary forests and
savannahs around Alter do Chão, including the
Tapajós National Park and Maica wetlands. Good
on conservation.
Santarém Tur, *in Amazon Park, and at R Adriano
Pimental 44, T093-3522 4847, www.santaremtur.
com.br*. Owned by Perpétua and Jean-Pierre
Schwarz (speaks French), friendly, helpful, also
group tours from 1 to 7 days. Recommended.

Alter do Chão

Sabiá Tour, *T093-99173 2071, arkusrodrigues@
hotmail.com*. Local artist Arkus Rodrigues and
partner Anamaria Freitas operate some of the
best low-key boat tours in the region and can
organize homestays in Alter do Chão, along the
Tapajós and the Arapiuns and in their own home
which is decorated with Arkus' paintings. Trips are
excellent value and if you are lucky or ask ahead
include a beach barbecue at sunset.
Vento em Popa, *T093-99154 2120, receptivo.vento
empopa@gmail.com*. Boat trips around Alter do
Chão in converted wooden Amazon river boats
run by Idelfonso Taketomi, half-Japanese, half-
indigenous Amazonian, with many fascinating
stories to tell.

Transport

Santarém

Air 15 km from town, T093-3522 4328. Internal
flights only. Buses run to the centre or waterfront.
From the centre the bus leaves in front of the
cinema in Rui Barbosa every 80 mins from 0550
to 1910, or taxis (US$13.50 to waterfront).

Bus *Rodoviária* is on the outskirts, take
'Rodagem' bus from the waterfront near the
market, US$0.50. Santarém to **Marabá** on
the Rio Tocantins with **Transbrasiliana**. From
Marabá there are buses east and west on the
Transamazônica. Enquire at the *rodoviária* for
other destinations. Road travel during rainy
season is always difficult, often impossible.

Ferry To **Manaus**, **Belém**, **Macapá**, **Itaituba**, and intermediate ports (see Getting around, page 598). Boats to Belém and Manaus dock at the Cais do Porto, 1 km west, take 'Floresta–Prainha', 'Circular' or 'Circular Externo' bus; taxi US$5. Boats to other destinations, including Macapá, dock by the waterfront by the centre of town. Local service, www.expressotapajos.com.br, to **Óbidos**, US$17.50, 3 hrs, **Oriximiná** US$25, 4 hrs, and **Alenquer**, US$14, 2½ hrs.

Alter do Chão
Bus Tickets and information from the bus company kiosk opposite Pousada

Tupaiulândia. From **Santarém**: bus stop on Av São Sebastião, in front of Colégio Santa Clara, US$1.50, about 1 hr.

Óbidos and around: Parintins
Air There is a small airport with flights to **Manaus** and **Óbidos**; taxi to town US$8.

Ferry Apart from boats that call on the **Belém–Manaus** route, there are irregular sailings from **Óbidos** (ask at the port). Journey times are about 12-15 hrs from **Manaus** (US$35-43) and 20 hrs from **Santarém**. Boat Manaus–Parintins, US$31.

Manaus *Colour map 4, A3.*

an expanding metropolis from which jungle tours begin

The next city upriver is Manaus, capital of Amazonas State – the largest state in Brazil. Once an isolated urban island in the jungle, it now sprawls over a series of eroded and gently sloping hills divided by numerous creeks (*igarapés*). The city is growing fast and 20-storey modern buildings are rising above the traditional flat, red-tiled roofs. An initiative in 2001 saw the start of a restoration programme in which historic buildings have been given a new lease of life and theatres, cultural spaces and libraries created.

Further expansion is bound to come now that a new 3.5-km road bridge has been built over the Rio Negro connecting Manaus with Iranduba. More development has resulted from Manaus being a 2014 FIFA World Cup™ venue, for instance a new airport. Manaus is an excellent port of entry for visiting the Amazon. Less than

Fact...
Manaus is one hour behind Brazilian standard time and two hours October-February (Brazil's summer time).

a day away are river islands and tranquil waterways. The opportunities for trekking in the forest, canoeing and meeting local people should not be missed and, once you are out of reach of the urban influence, there are plenty of animals to see. There is superb swimming in the natural pools and under falls of clear water in the little streams which rush through the woods, but take locals' advice on swimming in the river (both for nature's animal hazards and man's pollution).

Sights
Dominating the centre is a **Cathedral** built in simple Jesuit style on a hillock; very plain inside or out. Nearby is the main shopping and business area, the tree-lined Avenida Eduardo Ribeiro; crossing it is Avenida 7 de Setembro, bordered by ficus trees. **Teatro Amazonas** ① *Largo de São Sebastião, T092-3232 1768 for information on programmes, Mon-Sat 0900-1700, compulsory guided tour US$3, students and over-60s half price, tours in languages other than Portuguese on demand (you may see a rehearsal). Recommended.* This opulent theatre was completed in 1896 during the great rubber boom following 15 years of construction. It has been restored four times and should not be missed. There are ballet, theatre and opera performances several times a week, many of them free. The opera season is April-May. **Igreja São Sebastião** (1888), on the same *praça*, has an unusual altar of two giant ivory hands holding a water lily of Brazil wood. Largo de São Sebastião is surrounded by shady trees, several galleries and eating places. At night there is usually music, some live, some recorded.

Tip...
The city centre is easily explored on foot, although bear in mind an average temperature of 27°C.

Museu Casa de Eduardo Ribeiro ① *R José Clemente e Joaquim Saremtno, T092-3631 2938, Tue-Sat 0900-1700 (Thu to 2000), Sun 1600-2100* was the house of the state governor from 1890 to 1900. Inside are old maps of Manaus, a modest collection of period furniture and Ribeiro's bedroom, lovingly re-created. On Thursdays actors dressed in belle époque costumes guide visitors through the museum and re-enact moments from a typical day in the life of the house during the rubber boom. It has a pretty garden.

On the waterfront in the heart of the docks, the **Mercado Adolfo Lisboa** ① *Rua dos Barés 46*, was built in 1902 as a miniature copy of the now demolished Parisian Les Halles. The wrought ironwork which forms much of the structure was imported from Europe and is said to have been designed by Eiffel. It was restored

in 2013. Just to the east of it are the fish and banana and fruit markets. A short distance to the west the remarkable **Floating Harbour installations**, completed in 1902, were designed and built by a Scottish engineer to cope with the up to 14 m annual rise and fall of the Rio Negro. The large passenger ship floating dock is connected to street level by a 150 m-long floating ramp, at the end of which, on the harbour wall, can be seen the high water mark for each year since it was built. When the water is high, the roadway floats on a series of large iron tanks measuring 2½ m in diameter. The

Manaus

To ⑤

To Airport, Rodoviária & ⑬

Where to stay
1 10 de Julho & Restaurant Marlene
4 Casa Teatro & Restaurant Himawari
5 Go Inn
6 Hostel Amazonas
7 Hostel Manaus
9 Lider
10 Manaós
11 Manaus Hostel Trip Tour
12 Taj Mahal Continental
13 Tropical

Restaurants 🍴
1 Africa House & Casa do Pensador
2 Alemã Gourmet
3 Bar do Armando
4 Búfalo
5 Canto da Peixada
6 Fiorentina
7 Pizzaria Scarola
8 Senac
9 Skina dos Sucos
10 Sorveteria Glacial

200 metres
200 yards

ON THE ROAD

Tours from Manaus

There are two types of tours: those based at **jungle lodges** and **river boat trips**. Most tours, whether luxury or budget, combine river outings on motorized canoes with piranha fishing, caiman spotting, visiting local families and short treks in the jungle. Flights over the jungle give a spectacular impression of the extent of the forest. Specialist tours include fishing trips and those aimed specifically at seeing how the people in the jungle, Caboclos, live. Booking in advance on the internet is likely to secure you a good guide (who usually works for several companies and may get booked up). Be sure to ascertain in advance the exact itinerary of the tour, what the price includes (are drink and tips extra?), that guides are knowledgeable and will accompany you themselves and that there will be no killing or capture of anything. Ensure that others in your party share your expectations and are going for the same length of time. Choose a guide who speaks a language you understand. A shorter tour may be better than a long, poor one. Packaged tours, booked overseas, are usually of the same price and quality as those negotiated locally.

Note

There are many hustlers on the street, even at the hotels. Freelance guides not permitted to operate at the airport. Check for official and ABAV (Brazilian Association of Travel Agents) credentials personally and don't go with the first friendly face you meet. Investigate a few operators and make enquiries at your own pace. **Secretaria de Estado da Cultura e Turismo** is not allowed by law to recommend guides, but can provide you with a list of legally registered companies. Unfortunately, disreputable operations are rarely dealt with in any satisfactory manner and most continue to operate. When you are satisfied that you have found a reputable company, book direct with the company itself and ask for a detailed, written contract if you have any doubts. The tourist police (**Politur**) is at Rua Monsenhor Coutino in the centre, 24-hour bilingual attention, T092-98842 1786 or 190.

Areas

Bill Potter, resident in Manaus, writes: "opposite Manaus, near the junction of the Rio Negro and the Rio Solimões, lies the **Lago de Janauri**, a small nature reserve. This is where all the day or half-day trippers are taken, usually combined with a visit to the 'meeting of the waters'. Although many people express disappointment with this area because so little is seen and/or there are so many 'tourist-trash' shops, for those with only a short time it is worth a visit. You will see some birds and with luck dolphins. In the shops and bars there are often captive parrots and snakes. The area is set up to receive large numbers of tourists, which ecologists agree relieves pressure on other parts of the river. Boats for day trippers leave the harbour constantly

large beige **Alfândega** (Customs House) ① *R Marquês de Santa Cruz, Mon-Sat 0800-1200*, is at the entrance to the city if your boat arrives to dock at the passenger port. It was entirely prefabricated in England, and the tower once acted as lighthouse. The entire **Conjunto Arquitetônico do Porto de Manaus** was declared a national heritage site in 1987.

The **Biblioteca Pública Estadual** (Public Library) ① *R Barroso 57, Mon-Fri 0730-1730*, inaugurated in 1871, features an ornate European cast iron staircase. It is well stocked with 19th-century newspapers, rare books and old photographs, and worth a visit. The **Palacete Provincial** ① *Praça Heliodoro Balbi (also called Praça da Polícia), T092-3635 5832, Tue-Thu 0900-1900, Fri-Sat 0900-2000, free*, is a stately, late 19th-century civic palace, housing six small museums: **Museu de Numismática** (Brazilian and international coins and notes), **Museu Tiradentes** (history of the Amazon police and Brazilian military campaigns), **Museu da Imagem e do Som** (with free internet, cinema showings and a DVD library), **Museu de Arqueologia** (preserving a few Amazon relics), a **restoration atelier** and the **Pinacoteca do Estado**, one of the best art galleries in northern Brazil. There are guides in every room. It has a decent air-conditioned café, **Café do Pina**, which also has a stand in the nicely laid out park outside.

throughout the day, but are best booked at one of the larger operators." If you take a tour in a canoe early in the morning away from the main lake area, you will see a lot of birds. Remember, though, that here as elsewhere throughout the region there is a great difference between high water (June) and low water (November). Water level falls between these two months and channels are increasingly difficult to navigate. The rainy season starts in December.

Those with more time can take the longer cruises and will see various ecological environments. To see virgin rainforest, a five-day trip by boat is needed. Most tour operators operate on both the Rio Solimões and the Rio Negro. The Rio Negro is considered easier to navigate, generally calmer and with fewer biting insects, but as it is a black water river with forest growing on poor soil and the tannin-filled waters are acidic, there are fewer frutiferous trees and fish and therefore fewer animals. The tributaries of the Solimões have higher concentrations of wildlife; including biting insects. Currently most Solimões tours go to the Rio Mamori and Rio Juma areas via the Port Velho highway. There is plenty of deforestation along the initial stages of Rio Mamori. The best lodges for wildlife are the furthest from Manaus but don't expect to see lots of animals. This is difficult anywhere in the Amazon, but you should see caiman, macaws, boa constrictors and river dolphins. It is the immensity of the forest and rivers and the seemingly limitless horizons, as well as a glimpse of the extraordinary way of life of the Amazon people, which make these tours exciting. For the best wildlife options in the Brazilian Amazon head for Alta Floresta, the Mamirauá reserve near Tefé (see above), or the little visited forests of northern Roraima.

Generally, between April and September excursions are only by boat; in the period October to March the Victoria Regia lilies virtually disappear.

Price

Prices vary, but usually include lodging, guide, transport, meals and activities. The recommended companies charge approximately the following (per person, per day): up to US$60 for hammock accommodation; US$50-75 in a shared room; US$80-90 in a private room. All transport, meals and English-speaking guides are included. Longer, specialized, or more luxurious excursions will cost significantly more. Most river trips incorporate the meeting of the waters on the first day, so there is no need to make a separate excursion. For Lodges, see under Where to stay, below.

What to take

Leave luggage with your tour operator or hotel in Manaus and only take what is necessary for your trip. Long sleeves, long trousers, shoes and insect repellent are advisable for treks where insects are voracious. Take a mosquito net (and a hammock mosquito net if going on a cheaper tour) for trips in February-June. A hat offers protection from the sun on boat trips. Bottled water and other drinks are expensive in the jungle, so you may want to take your own supplies.

The **Instituto Geográfico e Histórico do Amazonas** ⓘ *R Frei José dos Inocentes 132 (near Prefeitura), T092-3622 1260, Mon-Fri 0900-1200, 1300-1600, US$1.35,* located in a fascinating older district of central Manaus, houses a museum and library of over 10,000 books which thoroughly document Amazonian life through the ages. The **Centro Cultural dos Povos da Amazônia** ⓘ *Praça Francisco Pereira da Silva s/n, Bola da Suframa, T092-2125 5300, Mon-Fri 0900-1700,* is a large cultural complex devoted to Amazonian indigenous peoples, with a large, well-curated museum whose artefacts including splendid headdresses, ritual clothing and weapons; explanatory displays in Portuguese and passable English. There are also play areas for the kids, a library and internet.

The botanic gardens, **Instituto Nacional de Pesquisas Amazonas** (INPA) ⓘ *Estrada do Aleixo, at Km 3, not far from the Museu de Ciências Naturais da Amazônia, T092-3643 3377, www.inpa.gov.br, Tue-Fri 0900-1200, 1400-1600, Sat-Sun 0900-1600, US$1.50, take any bus to Aleixo,* is at the centre for scientific research in the Amazon. Its labs (not open to the public) investigate farming, medicines and tropical diseases in the area. There is a small museum and restaurant, lots of birds, named trees and manatees (best seen Wednesday and Friday mornings when the water is changed), caimans and giant otters; worth a visit. INPA also manages what is probably the largest urban rainforest reserves in the world, on the northeastern edge of Manaus. The **zoo** ① *Estrada Ponta Negra 750 (look for the life-size model jaguar), T092-2125 6400, Tue-Sun 0900-1700, US$0.65, plus US$1 for trail, getting there: take bus 120 or 207, 'Ponta Negra', from R Tamandaré, US$1,* is run by CIGS, the army jungle-survival unit. It has been expanded and improved and has a 800-m trail which leads into the zoo itself.

There is a curious little church, **Igreja do Pobre Diabo** ① *at the corner of Av Borba and Av Ipixuna in the suburb of Cachoeirinha;* it is only 4 m wide by 5 m long, and was built by a tradesman, the 'poor devil' of the name. Take Circular 7 Cachoeirinha bus from the cathedral to Hospital Militar.

Around Manaus
About 15 km from Manaus is the confluence of the yellow-brown Solimões (Amazon) and the blue-black Rio Negro, which is itself some 8 km wide, commonly known as the **'meeting of the waters'**. The two rivers run side by side for many kilometres without their waters mingling. You can see this natural phenomenon in a range of ways depending on time and budget. Tourist agencies' day trips, including a boat trip to this spot, cost US$50-60 including lunch. The simplest route is to take a taxi or No 713 'Vila Buriti' bus to the CEASA ferry dock, and take the car ferry across. The ferry (very basic, with no shelter on deck and no cabins) runs all day until 1800 (approximately). Passenger ferries commute the crossing and you'll skim over the meeting of the waters for US$1.50 each way. Small private launches cross, 40 minutes' journey, about US$15 per seat, ask for the engine to be shut off at the confluence, you should see dolphins especially in the early morning. Alternatively, hire a motor boat from near the market (US$13.50 per person, US$75 per boat, up to eight people), or take a boat from **Fontur Ponta Negra** ① *T092-3658 3052, www.fontur.com.br,* at the **Hotel Tropical**; allow three to four hours to experience the meeting properly. A 2-km walk along the Porto Velho road from the CEASA ferry terminal will lead to a point from which Victoria Regia water lilies can be seen in April/May-September in ponds, some way from the road. Agencies can arrange tours.

Museu do Seringal ① *Igarapé São João, 15 km north of Manaus up the Rio Negro, Tue-Sun 0800-1600, T092-3633 2850, US$2, US$17 round trip on a private launch from the Hotel Tropical/ParkSuites, access only by boat,* is a full-scale reproduction of an early 20th-century rubber-tapping mansion house, serf quarters, factory and shop complete with authentic products. A guided tour, especially from one of the former rubber tappers, brings home the full horror of the system of debt peonage which enslaved Brazilians up until the 1970s. The museum can be visited with **Amazon Eco Adventure** or **Amazon Gero Tours**.

The small town of **Presidente Figueiredo** is set in forest and savannah rich in waterfalls and cut by many clear-water rivers. Numerous threatened and endangered bird species live here, including Guianan Cock of the Rock. Presidente Figueiredo is 117 km north and can easily be visited in a day trip from Manaus (bus US$20; tour for two people US$70).

★**Arquipélago de Anavilhanas**, the largest archipelago in a river in the world, is in the Rio Negro, from about 80 km upstream from Manaus, near the town of Novo Airão, nine hours by public boat, US$10.75, four hours by bus, US$12.25 (park office in Novo Airão, T092-3365 1345, see www.icmbio.gov.br/parnaanavilhanas/ for full details). There are hundreds of islands, covered in thick vegetation. Tour companies arrange day visits to the archipelago starting at US$150 per person (see page 618). Most Rio Negro lodges and Rio Negro safari cruises visit the archipelago.

Mamirauá ① *Packages of 3-7 nights, all inclusive (highly recommended). Reservations through T097-3343 9700 (Tefé) or 092-3584 4475 (Manaus), www.mamiraua.org.br. Book well in advance. All profits go to local projects and research. Daily flights Manaus-Tefé, then 1½ hrs by boat to lodge.* This sustainable development reserve, at the confluence of the Rios Solimões, Japurá and Auti-Paraná, is one of the best places to see the Amazon. It protects flooded forest (*várzea*) and is listed under the Ramsar Convention as an internationally important wetland. Like Anavilhanas, it is part of the UNESCO-recognized **Central Amazon Conservation Complex**. In the reserve Uakari (www.johnsonfung. com/uakari/) is a floating lodge with 10 suites. Lots of mammals and birds to see, including cayman, dolphin and harpy eagles, also the endangered pirarucu fish. Visitors are accompanied by guides the whole time. If you wish to stop off in Tefé, contact the **Pousada, Café e Turismo Regional Multicultura** ① *R 15 de Junho 136, Bairro Jurúa, T097-3343 6632 or 097-98117 0615, www. pousadamulticultura.com,* family guesthouse, many languages spoken, lots of local information.

Tourist information

AmazonasTur (state tourism office, Av Djalma Batista 200-B, Chapada, T092-2123 3838, Facebook: visitamazonas, Mon-Fri 0800-1700). Office at the **airport** (T092-3182 9850, daily 24 hrs). **Manaustur Fundação Municipal de Turismo** (Av 7 de Setembro 157, Centro, T092-3622 4948, Mon-Fri 0800-1800. See www.manaus online.com). Weekend editions of *A Crítica*, newspaper, list local entertainment and events.

Where to stay

10% tax and service must be added to bills. Hotel booking service at airport (see Transport, below, on taxi drivers' ruses). The best option is the area around the Teatro Amazonas, where the Italianate colonial houses and cobbled squares have been refurbished. Av Joaquim Nabuco and R dos Andradas have many cheap hotels, most of which charge by the hour and all of which are in an area which is undesirable after dark. Similarly risky at night is the Zona Franca around the docks.

$$$$ Tropical
Av Coronel Teixeira 1320, Ponta Negra, T092-3659 5000, www.tropicalhotel.com.br.
A lavish though increasingly frayed 5-star hotel 20 km outside the city in semi-forested parkland next to the river. The hotel has a private beach, tennis court and a large pool with wave machine. There are several restaurants including a decent *churrascaria*. The river dock is a departure point for many river cruises.

$$$$-$$$ Taj Mahal Continental
Av Getúlio Vargas 741, T092-3627 3737, www.grupotajmahal.com.br.
Large, impressive central hotel, popular, tour agency for flights, revolving restaurant, massage and high level of service.

$$$ Casa Teatro
10 de Julho 632, T092-3633 8381, www.casateatro.com.br.
A self-styled boutique hotel in the historic zone, nicely decorated rooms, café for breakfast, but no restaurant, a good central choice.

$$$ Lider
Av 7 de Setembro 827, T092-3621 9700, http://liderhotelmanaus.wix.com/lider.

Small, modern rooms with little breakfast tables. The best are at the front on the upper floors. Very well kept.

$$$-$$ Go Inn
R Mons Coutinho 560, T092-3306 2600, www.atlanticahotels.com.br.
Modern, central, no-nonsense style, café, Wi-Fi extra, disabled facilities, gym.

$$ Manaós
Av Eduardo Ribeiro 881, T092-3633 6148, www.hotelmanaos.com.br.
Smart rooms with marble floors, decent breakfast, close to Teatro Amazonas.

$$-$ 10 de Julho
R 10 de Julho 679, T092-3232 6280, www.hosteltrail.com/hoteldezdejulho.
Near opera house, a good cheap option, English speaking, simple rooms (some with a/c and hot water), also has hostel accommodation ($), efficient, laundry, tour operators in the lobby which also assist with boat transport arrangements.

$ Hostel Amazonas
R Ramos Ferreira 922, T092-98145 0223, www.hostelamazonas.com.br.
Shared rooms US$8-9 (cheaper for HI members), also triples, double ($), and family apartments. Towels are not included.

$ pp Hostel Manaus
R Lauro Cavalcante 231, Centro, T092-3233 4545, www.hostelmanaus.com.
"The original", Australian-owned. Cheaper for HI members. Fine restored old house, with excellent value dorms (US$11-12.50 pp) and private rooms ($$-$), best to confirm bookings, kitchen, laundry, airport pick-up. Good location 1 block from Museu do Homem do Norte, reasonably central and quiet. (Not to be confused with another hostel using a similar name.) Also here is **Amazon Antônio Jungle Tours** (www.antonio-jungletours.com). Ask here about the Rio Negro route to São Gabriel da Cachoeira, where **Pousada Pico da Neblina** has accommodation and tours; see page 621.

$ pp Manaus Hostel Trip Tour
R Costa Azevedo 63, T092-3231 2139, www.hosteltrail.com/hostels/manaushosteltriptour.
Not to be confused with the above. All rooms with shared bath, private doubles have a/c, dorms with fan and with a/c.

Lodges near Manaus

There are several lodges within a few hrs boat or car journey from Manaus. Most emphasize comfort (although electricity and hot water is limited) rather than a real jungle experience, but they are good if your time is limited and you want to have a brief taste of the Amazon rainforest. It is not possible just to turn up at a jungle lodge, you will need the lodge to take you there through its own designated transport, or to arrive with a tour company. Agencies for reservations are also listed. Very few of the lodges are locally owned and only a small percentage of labour is drawn from local communities. For Homestays in the jungle, see **Amazon Gero Tours**, page 618.

$$$$ Amazon Ecopark Lodge
Igarapé do Tarumã, 20 km from Manaus, 15 mins by boat, jungle trails; 60 apartments with shower, bar, restaurant, T092-99146 0594 (021-3005 5536 Mon-Fri), www.amazonecopark.com.br.
Comfortable lodge with 60 apartments and a decent restaurant. 1- to 4-day packages. Pleasant guided walks but poor for wildlife.

$$$$ Anavilhanas Jungle Lodge
Edif Manaus Shopping Center, Av Eduardo Ribeiro 520, sala 304, T092-3622 8996, www.anavilhanaslodge.com.
Small, elegant lodge on the Anavilhanas Archipelago, 3- to 6-day packages, comfortable, trips to see river dolphins included. In the Roteiros do Charme group.

$$$$ Ariaú Amazon Towers
Rio Ariaú, 2 km from Archipélago de Anavilhanas, Manaus office at R Leonardo Malcher 699, T092-2121 5000, www.ariautowers.com.br.
60 km and 2 hrs by boat from Manaus on a side channel of the Rio Negro. Complex of towers connected by walkways, beach (Sep-Mar), trips to the Anavilhanas islands in groups of 10-20. Highly recommended.

$$$$ Juma Lodge
T092-3232 2707, www.jumalodge.com.
Small lodge on the Rio Juma, idyllic location near the Rio Mamori, 2½ hrs south of Manaus by road and boat, all-inclusive 3- to 6-day packages. One of best options for wildlife and birdwatching.

$$$$ Malocas Lodge
160 km northeast of Manaus on the Rio Preto (80 km by road then canoe, 3 hrs total), T3648 0119, www.malocas.com.

Simple rooms with bath plus 1 suite, includes good food and activities, 1- to 7-day packages, French/Brazilian-run.

$$$ Amazon Antônio's Lodge
Through Amazon Antônio Tours, www.antonio-jungletours.com (see below).
A thatched roof wooden lodge, rooms with fan, 6 new chalets, observation tower. In a beautiful location overlooking a broad curve in the river Urubu some 200 km from Manaus.

$$$ Amazon Eco Adventures
Rio Urubu, book through Amazon Eco Adventures (see page 618).
Lovely little floating lodge with palm-thatched walls and an attractive deck. The lodge is set on a bend in the Urubu river close to where it meets the main stream of the Amazon. The area is rich in wildlife with few mosquitoes.

$$$ Ararinha Lodge
Exclusively through Amazon Gero Tours, www.amazongerotours.com.
One of the more comfortable lodges in Paraná do Araça on the Lago Mamori. Smart wooden chalets with suites of individual rooms, beds with mosquito nets. One of the best areas for wildlife in the Mamori region.

Restaurants

Many restaurants close on Sun nights and Mon. City authorities grade restaurants for cleanliness: look for A and B.

$$$ Himawari
R 10 de Julho 618, T092-3233 2208.
Swish, sushi and Japanese food, attentive service, opposite Teatro Amazonas, open Sun night, when many restaurants close. Recommended.

$$ Búfalo
Churrascaria, Av Joaquim Nabuco 628.
Best in town, all-you-can-eat Brazilian barbecue with a vast choice of meat.

$$ Canto da Peixada
R Emílio Moreira 1677 (Praça 14 de Janeiro).
Superb fish dishes, lively atmosphere, unpretentious, close to centre, take a taxi.

$$ Fiorentina
R José Paranaguá 44, Praça Heliodoro Balbi.
Fan-cooled, traditional Italian, including vegetarian dishes, average food but one of best options in centre, dishes served with mugs of wine! Great *feijoada* on Sat, half-price on Sun.
Bob's Shakes is in the same building.

$$ Marlene
10 de Julho 625, Tue-Sun 1100-2300.
Good Brazilian food per kg at lunch, also grill and desserts at night when prices are higher, a/c inside, plus sidewalk seating, popular.

$$ Pizzaria Scarola
R 10 de Julho 739, corner with Av Getúlio Vargas.
Standard Brazilian menu, pizza delivery, popular.

$ Alemã Gourmet
R José Paranaguá, Praça Heliodoro Balbi.
Food by weight, good for lunch, great pastries, hamburgers, juices, sandwiches.

$ Casa do Pensador
J Clemente 632. Open 1600-2300.
For drinks and good, reasonably priced food, at night has tables on the street. **Africa House**, next door, serves mainly juices.

$ Senac
R Saldanha Marinho 644. Daily, lunch only.
Cookery school, self-service.
Highly recommended.

$ Skina dos Sucos
Eduardo Ribeiro e 24 de Maio.
Regional fruit juices and snacks.

$ Sorveteria Glacial
Av Getúlio Vargas 161 and other locations.
Recommended for ice cream.

Bars and clubs

Manaus has a lively and constantly changing night-life. Clubs and bars are often far from the centre.

Bar do Armando
10 de Julho e Tapajós, near the Teatro.
Good place for drinking outside.

Djalma Oliveira
R 10 de Julho 679, T092-99185 4303, djalmatour@hotmail.com.
Nightlife tours throughout Manaus and private car hire. Djalma is far better value for a night out than a taxi. He also offers day tours and transfers.

Entertainment

Performing arts
For **Teatro Amazonas**, see page 610.
Teatro da Instalação, *R Frei José dos Inocentes, T092-3622 2840. Mon-Fri May-Dec at 1800. Charge for performances Sat and Sun.* Performance space in recently restored historic buildings with free music and dance (everything from ballet to jazz).

Festivals

Feb Carnival. 5 days culminating in the parade of the Samba Schools.
3rd week in Apr Week of the Indians, indigenous handicraft.
Jun Festival do Amazonas; a celebration of all the cultural aspects of Amazonas life, indigenous, Portuguese and from the northeast, especially dancing.
29 Jun São Pedro, boat processions on the Rio Negro.
Sep Festival da Bondade, last week, stalls from neighbouring states and countries offering food, handicrafts, music and dancing, SESI, Estrada do Aleixo Km 5.
Oct Festival Universitário de Música – FUM, the most traditional festival of music in Amazonas, organized by the university students, on the University Campus.
8 Dec Procissão de Nossa Senhora da Conceicão, from the Igreja Matriz through the city centre and returning to Igreja Matriz for a solemn mass.

Shopping

Since Manaus is a free port, the whole area a few blocks off the river front is full of electronics shops. All shops close at 1400 on Sat and all day Sun.

Handicrafts
There are many handicrafts shops in the area around the Teatro Amazonas.
Central de Artesanato Branco e Silva, *R Recife 1999, T092-3236 1241.* A gallery of arts and crafts shops and artists studios selling everything from indigenous art to wooden carvings by renowned Manaus sculptor Joe Alcantara.
Eco Shop, *R 10 de Julho 509, T092-3633 3569.* Indigenous arts and crafts from all over the Amazon, including Yanomami and Tikuna baskets, Wai Wai necklaces and Baniwa palm work. The souvenir shop at the INPA has some interesting Amazonian products on sale. For hammocks go to R dos Andradas, many shops.
Galeria Amazônica, *R Costa Azevedo 272, Largo do Teatro, T092-3233 4521, www.galeriamazonica.org.br.* A large, modern space filled with Waimiri Atroari indigenous arts and crafts, one of the best places for buying indigenous art in Brazil. In the Praça do Congresso, Av E Ribeiro, there is a very good Sun craftmarket.

What to do

Swimming

For swimming, go to Ponta Negra beach by Soltur bus, US$1, though the beach virtually disappears beneath the water in Apr-Aug; popular by day and at night with outdoor concerts and samba in the summer season. Boats to nearby beaches from **Hotel Tropical** cost US$2 pp. Every Sun, boats leave from the port in front of the market to beaches along Rio Negro, US$2.25, leaving when full and returning at end of the day. This is a real locals' day out, with loud music and foodstalls on the sand. Good swimming at waterfalls on the Rio Tarumã, lunch is available, shade, crowded at weekends. Take Tarumã bus from R Tamandaré or R Frei J dos Inocentes, 30 mins, US$1 (very few on weekdays), getting off at the police checkpoint on the road to Itacoatiara.

Tour operators

Check agencies' licences from tourist office and **ABAV** (www.abavam.com.br). If in the least doubt, use only a registered company.

Amazing Tours Agency, *R Praia Canoa Quebrada 262, Campos Salles, close to the International Airport Eduardo Gomes, T092-8165 1118, (UK: T07726 115298), www.manaus jungletours.com*. Leonardo Mendes is a local guide who grew up in the jungle and has a good knowledge of flora and fauna. English spoken, and some Dutch. Also trips to Jau National Park.

Amazon Antônio Tours, *Hostel Manaus, R Lauro Cavalcante 231, T092-3234 1294, www.antonio-jungletours.com*. Jungle tours on the Rio Urubu, a black water river 200 km northeast of Manaus. Good prices for backpackers.

Amazon Clipper Cruises, *T092-3656 1246, www.amazonclipper.com.br*. Informed guides, well-planned activities, comfortable cabins and good food on comfortable small boats, traditional and premium classes.

Amazon Eco Adventures, *R 10 de Julho 695, T092-98831 1011/99175 8464, www. amazonecoadventures.com*. Some of the best 1-day boat tours of the Solimões and Rio Negro available in Manaus, with options for water sports and fishing. The agency also runs spectacular ultra-light flights over the forest. Good value, excellent guiding.

Amazon Gero Tours, *R 10 de Julho 679, sala 2 (outside Hotel 10 de Julho), T092-99983 6273, www. amazongerotours.com*. Backpacker-oriented tours south of the Solimões and bookings made for lodges everywhere. Tours throughout the region are frequently recommended. Gero, the

owner is very friendly and dedicated. Operates **Ararinha Lodge** (see above). He can also arrange homestays in a riverine community in the heart of the Amazon, a fascinating, immersive alternative to a jungle lodge offering a real glimpse of the realities of Amazon life. Take a Portuguese phrasebook, your own mosquito net, toiletries, torch (flashlight) and insect repellent.

Amazon Nature Tours, *Av 7 de Setembro 188, Manaus, www.amazon-nature-tours.com (in USA T401-423 3377)*. Excellent expedition cruises on the live-aboard motor yacht *Tucano*, all cabins with a/c and bath, solar-powered, small groups, experienced guides for trips into the forest, 5 or 8 days on the rivers Negro and Amazon.

Amazon Riders, *R 10 de Julho 679 (inside Hotel 10 de Julho), T092-98807 2730/99298 0109, www. amazonriders.com*. Extended tours in the jungle, wildlife tours, meeting tribes on the Yavari river, 2 days from Manaus, and more.

Amazon Tours Brazil, *T092-99156 7185, www. amazontoursbrazil.com*. Carlos Jorge Damasceno, multilingual, many years experience, deep jungle exploration and visits to remote settlements, also arranges boat trips on typical Amazonian craft and on luxury boats. Families, individuals, small and large groups catered for.

Iguana Tour, *R 10 de Julho 663, T092-3633 6507, or 092-99105 5659, www.amazon brasil.com.br*. Short and long tours, plenty of activities, many languages spoken.

MV Desafio, *T092-99601 9645 (or 021-3539 5400), www.mvdesafio.com.br*. Schooner offering 4-day, 3-night river cruises, 12 cabins, restaurant and bar, refurbished to a high standard.

Tucunaré Turismo, *Av Djalma Batista 1719, loja 1B Ed Atlantic Tower, São Geraldo, T092-3186 8309, www.tucunareturismo.com.br*. Branch at the airport and a few blocks east of the docks. Good for internal flights and short tours.

Viverde, *R das Guariúbas 47, Parque Acarquara, T092-3248 9988, www.viverde.com.br*. Family-run agency acting as a broker for a wide range of Amazon cruises and lodges and running their own city tours and excursions.

Guides Guides are licensed to work through tour agencies, so it is safest to book guides through approved agencies. They do sometimes work individually. Advance notice and a minimum of 3 people for all trips offered by these guides:
Cristina de Assis, *T092-99114 2556, amazonflower@bol.com.br*. Offers tours telling the story of the city and the rubber boom with visits to historic buildings and the Museu Seringal,

trips to the Rio Negro, to Presidente Figueiredo, the Boi Bumba party in Parintins and the forest. Cristina speaks good English.

Transport

Boats dock in Manaus at different locations depending on where they have come from. The docks are quite central. The airport is 18 km from the centre, the bus terminal 9 km. Both are served by local buses and taxis. All city bus routes start below the cathedral in front of the port entrance; just ask someone for the destination you want.

Air Airport T092-3652 1212, www.infraero. gov.br. International flights to **Miami**, **Panama City** and **Lisbon** (via Belém with TAP). Internal flights to many Amazonian and northern Brazilian destinations; for other cities change in Brasília or São Paulo. The taxi fare to or from the airport is US$20, taxi syndicate price; arrange to be met and, when returning to the airport, ask your hotel for their recommended cheapest option. Bus to town leaves from stop outside terminal on the right. Bus No 306 'Aeroporto Internacional' (or from Praça da Matriz restaurant to the cathedral), US$1.10, 0500-2300. Many tour agencies offer free transfers without obligation. Check all connections on arrival. **Note** Check in time is 2 hrs in advance. Allow plenty of time at Manaus airport, formalities are slow especially if you have purchased duty-free goods. Many flights depart in the middle of the night and while there are many snack bars there is nowhere to rest. In the terminal there are also shops, internet, **Banco do Brasil**, **Confidence câmbio** and a tourist office.

Bus Manaus *rodoviária* is 9 km out of town at the intersection of Av Constantino Nery and R Recife, T092-3642 5808. Take a local bus from centre, US$1.10, marked 'Aeroporto Internacional' or 'Cidade Nova' (or taxi, US$20) and ask the driver to tell you where to get off. Services and fares are given under destinations.

Ferry There are 3 main docks: the westernmost floating docks are for large cargo vessels. The next floating docks, at the end of Av Eduardo Ribeiro below the Praça da Matriz, belonging to the Estação Hidroviária (R Taqueirinha 25, T092-123 4350, www.portodemanaus.com.br), have a large plaque showing the levels of the Rio Negro. Vessels for major destinations, **Santarém**, **Belém**, **Porto Velho**, **Tabatinga** (for Colombia and Peru), and intermediate ports, sail from here. There is a small Porto Ajato, just downstream from the Estação Hidroviária, where the fast boats sail,

eg to **Tabatinga**, **Tefé** and **Santarém**; ticket sales are right on this pier, Mon-Fri 0800-1700, Sat 0800-1200. See also Boat services, page 598.

Further downstream along the shore, behind the markets, are various other piers where riverboats sail to smaller destinations such as Tefé. In this area are many agents under umbrellas identified with photo IDs. They claim to sell tickets for all boats. There is another cluster of these agents outside the Estação Hidroviária, between it and the Alfândega. In principle, tickets for major destinations must be purchased from official booths inside the Estação Hidroviária, but these have the highest prices and they are not negotiable. Alternatively, you can buy tickets from one of the agents outside, who may be amenable to discounts (about 10-20%), but shop around and beware tricks and scams. A third option is to approach boat owners directly and try to negotiate the fare with them, but if you have not purchased your ticket at the Estação Hidroviária, you will not be allowed onto their dock to visit boats or embark. Small motorboats provide water taxi service from near the Porto Ajato to the Estação Hidroviária dock (US$2.50 pp, beware overcharging), circumventing this restriction. Another workaround is to take a taxi (car) to the Estação Hidroviária dock; you will not be asked to show your ticket, but will have to pay a toll of US$6; go very early in the morning to avoid traffic and long queues at the port entrance. This plus the taxi fare may be substantially less than the savings for purchasing tickets outside the Estação Hidroviária. **Note** Be careful of people who wander around boats after they've arrived at a port: they are almost certainly looking for something to steal. Also beware of overcharging and theft by porters at all docks.

Immigration For those arriving by boat who have not already had their passports stamped (eg from Leticia), the immigration office is at **Polícia Federal** (Av Domingos Jorge Velho 40, Bairro Dom Pedro II, Planalto, T092-3655-1515/1517).

Road The Catire Highway (BR 319) from Manaus to Porto Velho (868 km), has been officially closed since 1990. For over 200 km at each end of the road (Manaus to Careiro–Castanho; Humaitá to Porto Velho), driving is no problem, but the paving of the middle 400 km or so is subject to study and controversy. Enquire locally if the road is passable for light vehicles; some bridges are flimsy. The alternative for drivers is to ship a car down river on a barge, others have to travel by boat.

Amazon frontiers

To get to the border with Colombia and Peru, a river boat is the only alternative to flying and this, of course, is the true way to experience the Amazon. On the route to Venezuela, buses and trucks have almost entirely replaced river traffic to Boa Vista, from where roads go to Santa Elena de Uairén and Lethem in Guyana.

Rondônia and Acre mark not just the political boundaries between Brazil and Peru and Bolivia, but also developmental frontiers between the forest and colonization. Much of Rondônia has been deforested. Acre is still frontier country with great expanses of forest in danger of destruction.

Manaus to Colombia, Peru, Venezuela and Guyana

routes out of Brazil

Benjamin Constant and up the Rio Javari *Colour map 3, A5.*
At the confluence of the Rios Solimões and Javari is the friendly pleasant town of Benjamin Constant. Some boats between Tabatinga and Manaus call here. The **Museu Magüta** ① *Av Castelo Branco 396,* www.museumaguta.com.br, *Sun-Fri 0800-1600, Sat 0800-1400*, displays photographs, costumes, traditional art and music of native indigenous groups. The Rio Javari is the border between Brazil and Peru, upriver on the Peruvian side is the town of **Islandia**. Further upriver is the Brazilian town of **Atalaia do Norte**, 26 km by paved road from Benjamin Constant. Further still are the Território Indígena do Vale do Javari and privately owned nature reserves, with accommodation and facilities for birdwatching, dolphin and caiman spotting. We list two below.

Border with Colombia and Peru
The busy Brazilian port of Tabatinga is upstream and on the opposite shore from Benjamin Constant, along the Rio Solimões. Tabatinga is also on the land border with **Leticia** (Colombia), a pleasant city with the best infrastructure in the area. There is no separation between the two and Avenida da Amizade in Tabatinga becomes Avenida Internacional in Leticia. On an island across from Tabatinga and Leticia is the small Peruvian town of **Santa Rosa**, which is prone to severe flooding in the rainy season. All three towns have accommodation and restaurants and people move freely between them with no border formalities. If you are visiting any of the towns for the day, there is no need to get stamped-in, but keep your passport with you. There is drug smuggling throughout the area and Tabatinga is particularly unsafe; do not go out here at night. Reais and pesos colombianos are accepted in all three towns; soles are seldom used. There are ATMs in Tabatinga and Leticia, and the latter is the best place to change cash. Leticia and Santa Rosa are one hour behind Tabatinga.

Tabatinga
Tabatinga has several ports. There are about five boats a week to Manaus, *Voyager* boats use their private docks near Rua Santos Dumont. The docks for local boats to Santa Rosa and Benjamin Constant are behind the market by Rua Pedro Teixeira. There are **tourist offices** ① *at the land border and on Av da Amizade, 4 blocks from the border, Mon-Sat 0800-1700.*

Immigration Once you get an exit stamp from one country, you must get the entry stamp at your next destination within 24 hours, there are fines if you are late. Yellow fever vaccination certificate may be requested to enter any of the three countries.

Brazil Entry and exit stamps at **Policia Federal** ① *Av da Amizade 26, about 1 km from the border, Tabatinga, T097-3412 2180, open daily 0800-1200, 1400-1800.* Proof of US$500 or an onward ticket may be asked for. Taxi to port US$7.25, to Leticia $10. There are no immigration facilities in Benjamin Constant. **Brazilian Consulate** ① *Cra 10, No 10-10, Leticia, T8-592 7530, Mon-Fri 0800-1300; onward ticket, 5x7 photo and yellow fever vaccination certificate needed for visa; allow 36 hrs,* is efficient and helpful. There is also a consulate in Iquitos, Peru.

Colombia Entry and exit stamps at **Migración Colombia** ① *C 9 No 9-62, Centro, T8-592 5930, open 0800-1200, 1400-1700.* Go there for extensions or fines. The **Colombian Consulate** ① *R Gral Sampaio 623 (1 block from Av da Amizade, behind Canto da Peixada Restaurant, about 10 blocks from the border), Tabatinga, T097-3412 2104, http://tabatinga.consulado.gov.co, Mon-Fri 0700-1300,* issues visas.

Peru Entry and exit stamps at **Migración Peruana** ① *Santa Rosa, 0730-1700.* You may be asked to show your boat ticket in order to get the entry stamp; if taking an early morning *rápido* to Iquitos, get your entry stamp the day before. **Peruvian Consulate** ① *Cra 11 5-32, Leticia, T8-592 7755, Mon-Fri 0800-1200, 1400-1600;* it is a lengthy (one week minimum), involved process to get a visa here. Best get a visa in your home country.

Up the Rio Negro to Colombia or Venezuela Boats go from Manaus to **São Gabriel da Cachoeira** (population 40,000), from where you can continue to Colombia via San Felipe (fortnightly flights from here to Villavicencio) or to Venezuela via San Felipe or Cucuí. This route goes to Puerto Ayacucho via the Canal de Casaquiare, which links the Amazon and Orinoco river systems. São Gabriel da Cachoeira has the largest indigenous population of any municipality in Brazil. The neighbouring Parque Nacional do Pico da Neblina is closed to visitors. All information and tours at **Pousada Pico da Neblina** ① *R Cap Euclides 322, Bairro da Praia, T097-9168 0047, www.pousadapicodaneblina.com (same owner as Hostel Manaus, see page 615), $ in a/c double rooms, or in dorms,* a big yellow house behind Comercial Carneiro. Four-day guided tours including visits to villages, climbing Bella Adormecida mountain, camping in the jungle and river trips cost US$85 per person per day. Between Manaus and São Gabriel is the town of **Barcelos**, which has **Hotel Barcelos**.

Boats for São Gabriel da Cachoeira (see page 596) go from the Porto Beira Mar de São Raimundo, upriver from the main port. Take bus 101 'São Raimundo', or 112 'Santo Antônio', 40 minutes. Two companies go to São Gabriel: **Tanaka** ① *in Manaus T092-99239 8024, in São Gabriel opposite Maraska internet, T097-3471 1730, Fri 1800 from Manaus, returns Fri 0800, 3 days, US$120, and fast boat, 24 hrs, Tue and Fri 1500, return Tue and Fri 0800, US$135 (take a mattress for the express boat).* **Genesis** ① *in Manaus T092-98119 8591, in São Gabriel at Hotel Roraima II, T Manuel Felício Braga 3500, T097-3471 1771,* quicker boats than Tanaka, but smaller and rowdier. No scheduled boats travel beyond São Gabriel, so you have to wait until there are enough passengers and cargo to leave.

Manaus to Venezuela and Guyana

The road which connects Manaus and Boa Vista (BR-174 to Novo Paraíso, then the Perimetral, BR-210, rejoining the BR174 after crossing the Rio Branco at Caracaraí) can get badly potholed. There are service stations with toilets, camping, etc, every 150-180 km, but all petrol is low octane. Drivers should take a tow cable and spares, and bus passengers should prepare for delays in the rainy season. At Km 100 is Presidente Figueiredo, described above. About 100 km further on is a service station at the entrance to the **Uaimiri Atroari Indian Reserve**, which straddles the road for about 120 km. Private cars and trucks are not allowed to enter the Indian Reserve between sunset and sunrise, but buses are exempt from this regulation. Nobody is allowed to stop within the reserve at any time. At the northern entrance to the reserve there are toilets and a spot to hang your hammock (usually crowded with truckers overnight). At Km 327 is the village of Vila Colina with **Restaurante Paulista**, good food, clean, you can use the shower and hang your hammock. At Km 359 there is a monument to mark the **equator**. At Km 434 is the pleasant **Restaurant Goaio**, and south of Km 500 **Bar Restaurante D'Jonas**, where you can camp or sling a hammock. Beyond here, large tracts of forest have been destroyed for settlement already many homes have been abandoned.

At **Caracaraí**, a busy port with modern installations, a bridge crosses the Rio Branco for traffic on the Manaus-Boa Vista road. It has hotels in our $$-$ range. Boa Vista has road connections with the Venezuelan frontier at Santa Elena de Uairén (237 km, paved, the only gasoline 110 km south of Santa Elena) and Bonfim for the Guyanese border at Lethem. Both roads are open all year.

Boa Vista *Colour map 2, B2.*

The capital of the extreme northern state of Roraima, 785 km north of Manaus, is a pleasant, clean, laid-back city (population 400,000) on the Rio Branco. Tourism is beginning here and a few interesting destinations are opening up, including the Tepequém plateau, Serra Grande mountains, Rio Uraricoera and the mushroom-shaped Pedra Pintada (with rock art) in the São Marcos indigenous reserve, offering a chance to explore far wilder and fauna-rich country than that around Manaus. The landscape is more diverse, too, with a mix of tropical forest, savannah and highlands dotted with waterfalls. The area immediately around the city has been heavily deforested. The city has an interesting modern cathedral, Cristo Redentor, whose design, by Mário Fiameni, suggests a harp, a ship and a maloca (long house). It is by the Praça do Centro Cívico on which stand the Palácio da Cultura and the Palácio Senador Hélio Campos and from which all the central streets radiate. Nighttime city tours take in the city's monuments, the Praça das Águas on Av Ene Garcez which runs to the airport and the Orla Taumanan, see Bars and clubs, below. **Tourist office:** Detur ① *R Coronel Pinto 267, T095-3623 2365, www.turismo.rr.gov.br, Mon-Fri 0730-1330 (go right inside the building to a back office, helpful once you find it).* Information is available at the *rodoviária*, T095-3623 1238; see also www.rr.gov.br. The city centre is quite safe, but don't wander into outlying suburbs.

US dollars, euros and stirling can be changed in Boa Vista, but not (officially) Guyanese dollars or bolívares (get rid of these two currencies at the border). ATMs at banks including **Banco do Brasil** ① *Av Glaycon de Paiva 74, by the Praça do Centro Cívico.* Cambios at ParCam ① *Av Getúlio Vargas 6091, T095-3623 2579,* next to **Hiper DB** supermarket, and **Top Viagens** ① *A Filho 229.*

Border with Venezuela

Border searches are thorough and frequent at this border crossing, known as Pacaraima. If entering Brazil, ensure in advance that you have the right papers, including yellow fever certificate, before arriving at this border. Officials may give only two months' stay and car drivers may be asked to purchase an unnecessary permit. Ask to see the legal documentation. Everyone who crosses this border to Venezuela must also have a yellow fever certificate. Check requirements for visas beforehand (some nationalities need one, but not, for example, Western Europeans). There is another Venezuelan consulate in Manaus (see above). On the Brazilian side there is a basic hotel, **Pacaraima Palace**, a guesthouse, camping and a bank. **Venezuelan consulate** ① *Av Benjamin Constant 968, Boa Vista T095-3623 9285, Mon-Fri 0830-1300.* Visas available, relaxed service, allow 24-48 hours.

Border with Guyana *Colour map 2, B2.*

The main border crossing between Brazil and Guyana is from **Bonfim**, 125 km (all paved) northeast of Boa Vista, to Lethem. The towns are separated by the Rio Takutu, which is crossed by a bridge 2.5 km from Bonfim, 1.6 km north of Lethem. After the bridge one lane of the road crosses the other so that traffic is on the correct side of the road in the neighbouring country. Formalities are strict on both sides of the border: it is essential to have a yellow fever vaccination both to leave Brazil and to enter Guyana. **Brazilian Immigration (Polícia Federal)** where you receive your exit stamp is just before the bridge. Taxis cross the bridge to the **Guyana Immigration** office. The border is open 0800-1200, 1400-1800. Entering Brazil there is an Agropecuária check a few kilometres out of Bonfim. There is no Guyanese consul in Boa Vista, so if you need a visa for Guyana, you must get it in Rio de Janeiro or Brasília. Reais can be changed into Guyanese dollars in Lethem; taxi drivers may help, rates are poor. See Transport, below.

Listings Manaus to Colombia, Peru, Venezuela and Guyana

Where to stay

Benjamin Constant and up the Rio Javari
There are a number of very cheap, simple *pousadas* in town.

$$-$ Benjamin Constant
R Getulio Vargas 36, near port and market, T097-3415 5310.

Has a variety of rooms with a/c, bath, cold water, helpful owner. Recommended.

$ Amazonas
R Getúlio Vargas 181, T097-3415 5902.
Wooden building with nice porch, a/c, cheaper with fan, bath, cold water, frigobar.

Atalaia do Norte

\$\$ Itacoaí
Av Pedro Teixeira, T097-3417 1123.
Nice clean rooms with a/c, electric shower, no breakfast, same owner runs hotel next door.

Up the Rio Javari

\$\$\$\$ Heliconia
T+57-311-508 5666 (Leticia),
www.amazonheliconia.com.
Price, based on 2 people, includes transport from Leticia and all food and activities (except canopy and massage treatments). Up a small tributary of the Javari, 3 hrs by boat from Leticia, isolated, comfortable cabins (with bathrooms open to the forest behind) set around a jungle garden. Night-time caiman-spotting excursions as well as trips to visit local indigenous communities, excellent walks, birdwatching and fishing tours.

\$\$\$\$ Palmarí
T+57-1-610 3514 (Bogotá), www.palmari.org.
Includes meals, drinks, guiding and all activities (except canopy). The reserve is on terra firme forest, walkable year-round, with both other types of Amazon forest nearby. Various types of accommodation and prices, starting at US\$130 pp per night plus transport from Leticia, Tabatinga or Santa Rosa. The reserve has Wi-Fi and cell phone access, attentive service. German owner Axel Antoine-Feill has set up the **Instituto de Desenvolvimento Socioambiental do Vale do Javarí** (www.idsavj.org), to work with local indigenous communities.

Tabatinga

Tabatinga is dangerous at night, do not leave your your hotel after dark. Apart from those listed, there are various other hotels on the streets leading from the port to Av da Amizade.

\$\$\$-\$\$ Takana
R Osvaldo Cruz, 970, T097-3412 3557,
www.takanahotel.com.br.
Comfortable and clean, hot water, frigobar. Upmarket for Tabatinga.

\$\$\$-\$\$ Tarumã
R da Pátria 70, near Igreja da Matriz, T097-3412 3889, hoteltaruma@hotmail.com.
Rooms/suites with electric shower, frigobar, nice.

\$\$ Vitoria Regia
R da Patria, 820, T097-3412 2083, www.portaltabatinga.com.br/hotelvitoriaregia.htm.
Quiet area near Igreja da Matriz, ample rooms, cold water, frigobar.

\$ International Bagpacker
R Santos Dumont 2, upstairs, T+57-313-219 5121 (Colombian cell phone), amazonasdiscover@hotmail.com, Facebook: TabatingaBackpackers.
Basic rooms with bath, fan, cold water, cheaper still in dorm or hang your hammock on the porch, basic kitchen facilities, no breakfast. Right at the port; convenient for night-time arrivals/departures.

\$ Pajé
R Pedro Teixeira 367, T097-3412 2774, hotelpaje@gmail.com.
Small rooms, cheaper with fan, bath, cold water, very basic but friendly.

Boa Vista

\$\$\$ Aipana Plaza
Praça do Centro Cívico 974, T095-3212 0800, www.aipanaplaza.com.br.
Best in town with plain rooms, hot water, attractive pool area with a shady little bar.

\$\$\$ Barrudada
R Araújo Filho 228, T095-2121 1700, www.hotelbarrudada.tur.br.
Unpretentious, plain white rooms in a modern tower block very close to the centre. The best on the upper floors have views of the river. Breakfast included, helpful staff, pool.

\$\$\$-\$\$ Euzêbio's
R Cecília Brasil 1107, T095-2121 0300, www.hoteleuzebios.com.br.
Spruce, modest rooms with cold water showers. The best are airy and on the upper floors. Pleasant pool and a laundry service. Has a good a/c restaurant (\$\$) and a generous breakfast.

\$\$ Uiramutam Palace
Av Capt Ene Garcez 427, T095-3198 0000, www.uiramutam.com.br.
Business hotel with modest rooms and large bathrooms. Decent pool.

\$\$-\$ Ideal
R Araújo Filho 481, T095-3224 6342, Hotel-Ideal88@hotm ail.com (WhatsApp 045-99967 5645).
Simple well-kept rooms, some have a/c and TV, generous breakfast and convenient for the centre. Opposite **La Pérgola** Italian restaurant and pizzeria.

Tabatinga

\$\$\$ Te Contei?
Av da Amizade 1813. Closed Tue.

International and regional dishes à la carte, excellent pizza.

$$$ Tres Fronteras Do Amazonas
R Rui Barbosa, Bairro San Francisco.
Excellent mix of Brazilian, Peruvian and Colombian dishes.

$$-$ Tapioquinha e Taco
Av da Amizade near Marechal Mallet, 4 blocks from border. Daily 0800-2200.
Brazilan, Peruvian and Mexican food, economical *prato feito*.

Boa Vista

$$-$ La Gôndola
Benjamin Constant 35/W, Centro, close to Praça do Centro Cívico, T095-3224 9547. Daily 1100-1500.
Self service, by kg restaurant with good food, good value, popular.

$ Hola!
Ben jamin Constant e Bitencourt, near Praça do Centro Cívico. Mon 1200-1800, Tue-Sun 1200-2300. Also at airport.
For Mexican snacks and ice creams.

$ Ponto do Café
S Botelho 537, T095-99177 41 91.
Mon-Fri 0700-1900, Sat-Sun 0700-1200.
Clean modern café selling coffee, teas, juices, sandwiches, omelettes, tapioca, and sweets.

Hiper DB supermarket
Av Getúlio Vargas at Av S Botelho. Daily till 2200.
For everything you may need.

Border with Guyana: Bonfim

There is a café by the CoopBom office (see below) and at the *rodoviária*.

Bars and clubs

Boa Vista

R Floriano Peixoto is lively after dark at weekends when there is live music in and around the **Orla Taumanan**, a complex of little bars/restaurants.

What to do

Boa Vista

Makunaima Expedições, *F Peixoto 136, T095-3624 6004, www.makunaima.com.* Short and long tours, boat trips, kayaking, cycling, city tours.
Roraima Adventures, *R Coronel Pinto 97, T095-3624 9611, www.roraimabrasil.com.br.* A range of interesting trips to little-known and little-visited

parts of Roraima. Pre-formed groups get the best prices, which are competitive with Manaus. Helpful with visas for Venezuela.

Transport

Benjamin Constant and up the Rio Javari

Shared taxis run all day between Benjamin Constant and **Atalaia do Norte**, US$8, 30 mins. There is no public river transport up the Rio Javari.

Border with Colombia and Peru

Tabatinga

Air There are separate airports at Tabatinga and Leticia. From Tabatinga, Azul fly daily to **Manaus**.

River About 5 sailings a week to **Manaus** and intermediate ports (see page 596). Buy tickets directly from docked riverboats or at **Transtur** (see below). Expect long queues and thorough drug searches when boarding vessels, have your passport at hand and never accept bags from other passengers. All boats for **Iquitos** leave from Santa Rosa. Tickets for *rápidos* (fast boats) to Iquitos are sold in Tabatinga: **Transtur**, R Marechal Mallet 290, T097-8113 5239, departures Wed, Fri, Sun; **Golfinho**, office next door, T097-3412 3186, www.transportegolfinho.com, Tue, Thu, Sat. Both leave at 0400 Peruvian time, US$70 including breakfast and lunch, 10-12 hrs. Buy tickets and get your exit and entry stamps the day before, and be at the dock in Santa Rosa at 0300. Canoes cross from Tabatinga to Santa Rosa, US$1.50 during the day, US$3 starting 0230 (Peruvian time) to reach the *rápido*. Take a taxi to the dock in Tabatinga, do not walk; or spend the night in Santa Rosa. There are also *lanchas* (large riverboats) sailing most evenings from Santa Rosa to Iquitos, US$25 in hammock, 3-4 days, tickets sold onboard, conditions vary and may be crowded and dirty. Small ferries run from Tabatinga to Benjamin Constant throughout the day, US$8, 30 mins.

Taxi Charge US$10 to most destinations in Tabatinga or Leticia, payable in reais or pesos colombianos, beware overcharging and negotiate.

Boa Vista

Air Flights to **São Paulo**, **Rio de Janeiro**, **Belém**, etc. At the airport (4 km from the centre, T095-3198 0100), there are ATMs, a few shops and food outlets, car rental and an information desk open from 1000 for arriving flights. Bus 'Aeroporto' from the centre is US$1. Taxi to *rodoviária*, US$12, to centre US$13, 5-10 mins; taxi desk at exit, T095-3198 0116.

Bus *Rodoviária* is 3 km at the end of Av Ville Roy, T095-3623 3233; taxi to centre, US$12, bus US$1, 10 mins (marked '13 de Setembro' or 'Joquey Clube' to centre). The local bus terminal is on Av Amazonas, by R Cecília Brasil, near central praça. It is difficult to get a taxi or bus to the *rodoviária* in time for early morning departures; as it's a 25-min walk, book a taxi the previous evening. To **Manaus**, US$28-46, with **Eucatur** (www.eucatur.com.br), **Amatur** (www.amatur.com.br), **Asatur** (www.asaturturismo.com) and others, 12 hrs, several daily. Buses between Boa Vista and **Caracaraí** take 8 hrs.

Border with Venezuela

Bus Amatur bus goes from Boa Vista *rodoviária* to **Santa Elena de Uairén**, stopping at all checkpoints, US$16, 4 hrs, take water; to Pacaraima, 3½ hrs, US$9.25 with Asatur or Rival. Shared taxis, US$14.50 to Santa Elena, go from the terminal in Caimbé district at the northwest end of Av Mário de Melo (take a taxi from Banco do Brasil and ask).

Border with Guyana: Bonfim

Bus Boa Vista–Bonfim 6 a day US$8.25, 2½ hrs, or US$8.75 with **CoopBom** shared taxis, T095-3623 0644/3552 1357. Bonfim *rodoviária* is on Av São Sebastião, about 4 blocks off the main border-to-Boa Vista highway, 3.5 km from the bridge. **CoopBom** is 1 long block closer to town, past Hotel Tacutu, at Av Tuxuá de Farias, opposite Assambléia de Deus, US$3 from immigration by taxi. The bus may go to **Brazilian immigration**; otherwise take a car from the rodoviária. Taxis then take you across the bridge to **Guyana immigration**, wait for formalities, then in to Lethem, US$10.

Brazil's frontiers with Bolivia and Peru

Porto Velho *Colour map 4, B1.*

This city stands on a high bluff overlooking a curve of the Rio Madeira. It first prospered during the local gold and timber rush and now is booming as the result of the Madeira Hydroelectric Complex, which comprises four dams, the first two of which, Santo Antônio and Jirau, are nearing completion. The other two, on the Bolivian border and in Bolivia, plus an associated international shipping canal are under study and are being contested by environmental and other lobby groups. Buildings in the city centre are being renovated and a large riverside park is being developed. But it is less of a tourist city than Rio Branco, a far more interesting access point to Brazil from Peru or Bolivia.

At the top of the hill, on Praça João Nicoletti, is the **Cathedral**, built in 1930, with beautiful stained-glass windows; the **Prefeitura** is across the street. The principal commercial street Avenida 7 de Setembro, runs from the railway station and market hall to the upper level of the city, near the *rodoviária*. The new **Museu Palácio da Memória Rondoniense** ① *R Dom Pedro II 608*, in the former government palace, brings together archaeological, ethnographic, historical and zoological collections and will house the geological collection which was in the Praça Madeira-Mamoré. The centre is hot, noisy and sprawls from the river to the bus station (1.5 km). In the old railway yards known as Praça Madeira-Mamoré is the **Museu Ferroviário** (see below) and a promenade with bars by the river, a wonderful place to watch the sunset. Boat trips from here cost US$2.75. There are several viewpoints over the river and railway yards: **Mirante I** (with restaurant) is at the end of Rua Carlos Gomes; **Mirante II** (with a bar and ice cream parlour), at the end of Rua Dom Pedro II, is the best place to watch the sunset over the river. There is a fruit and vegetable market at the corner of Rua Henrique Dias and Avenida Farquhar and a dry goods market three blocks to the south, near the port. **Tourist office:** Semdestur ① *Av Brasília 2512 entre Duque de Caxias e Carlos Gomes, Liberdade, T069-3901 3180.* See also www.portovelho.ro.gov.br and www.turismoderondonia.com. Tourist office at the airport opens when flights arrive; ask here where to change money. Banks open in the morning only. Exchange is difficult elsewhere in Rondônia. Marco Aurélio Câmbio ① *R José de Alencar 3353, Porto Velho, T069-3221 4922, Mon-Fri 0900-1500*, offers good rates. Malaria is common in the area.

The Madeira–Mamoré Railway

Porto Velho was the terminus of the Madeira-Mamoré railway. It was supposed to go as far as Riberalta, on the Río Beni, above that river's rapids, but stopped short at Guajará Mirim. Over 6000 workers died during its construction (1872-1913). The BR-364 took over many of the railway bridges, leaving what remained of the track to enthusiasts to salvage what they could. The **museum**

Ⓘ *Praça Madeira-Mamoré, T069-3901 3186,* was one of the railway facilities that was flooded, like much of Porto Velho, in early 2015. The historical objects were removed for safekeeping and cleaning. It is hoped that the railway will reopen to run some 10 km through Porto Velho and its suburbs, and that it will be listed as a World Heritage Site by UNESCO. At the time of research (mid-2017) the railway facilities were abandoned. See http://efmm100anos.wordpress.com.

The BR-364

The Marechal Rondon Highway, BR-364, is fully paved to Cuiabá, 1550 km. A result of the paving of BR-364 is the development of farms and towns along it. **Note** At the Mato Grosso state border, proof of yellow-fever inoculation is required: if no proof is presented, a new shot is given.

Parque Nacional Pacaás Novos

The Parque Nacional Pacaás Novos lies west of the BR-364; it is a transitional zone between open plain and Amazonian forest and covers an area of 765,800 ha. The majority of its surface is covered with *cerrado* vegetation and the fauna includes jaguar, brocket deer, puma, tapir and peccary. The average annual temperature is 23°C, but this can fall as low as 5°C when the cold front known as the *friagem* blows up from the South Pole. Details from **ICMBio** Ⓘ *Av Tancredo Neves 2106, Porto Velho, T069-3239 2203.*

Guajará Mirim *Colour map 4, B1.*

From Porto Velho, the paved BR-364 continues 220 km southwest to Abunã (hotels $), where the BR-425 branches south to Guajará Mirim. The BR-425 is a fair road, partly paved, which uses the former rail bridges (poor condition). It may be closed March-May. Across the Mamoré from Guajará Mirim is the Bolivian town of Guayaramerín, which is connected by road to Riberalta, from where there are air services to other Bolivian cities. Guajará Mirim is a charming town. The **Museu Municipal** Ⓘ *T069-3541 3362, 0500-1200, 1400-1800,* is at the old Guajará Mirim railway station beside the ferry landing; highly recommended. Banco do Brasil only changes money in the morning.

Border with Bolivia

Get Brazilian exit and entry stamps from **Polícia Federal** Ⓘ *Av Presidente Dutra 180, T069-3541 2437.* Visas are given at the **Bolivian consulate** Ⓘ *Av Beira Rio 505, 1st floor, T069-3541 8622, Guajará Mirim, ivillabernal@hotmail.com.*

Rio Branco *Colour map 3, B6.*

The BR-364 runs west from Porto Velho to Abunã (239 km), then in excellent condition, 315 km to Rio Branco the capital of the State of Acre. This intriguing state is rich in natural beauty, history and the seringueiro culture. During the rubber boom of the late 19th century, many Nordestinos migrated to the western frontier in search of fortune. As a result, the unpopulated Bolivian territory of Acre was gradually taken over by Brazil and formally annexed in the first decade of the 20th century. In compensation, Bolivia received the Madeira–Mamoré railroad, as described above. The chief industries are rubber and *castanha-de-pará* (Brazil nut) extraction and, now that ranching has slowed down, ecotourism. While Rondônia has lost well over 50% of its forest, Acre retains 82% primary forest. It has some of the most exciting ethno-tourism projects in South America.

Rio Branco is clean, well maintained and orderly with the highest percentage of cycle ways of any city in Brazil. There are attractive green spaces and a lively waterfront promenade, the **Mercado Velho**, which buzzes with bar life in the evenings, especially at weekends. The Rio Acre, navigable upstream as far as the Peru and Bolivia borders, divides the city into two districts, Primeiro (west) and Segundo (east), on either side of the river. In the central, Primeiro district are **Praça Plácido de Castro**, the shady main square; the **Cathedral**, Nossa Senhora de Nazaré, along Avenida Brasil; the neo-classical **Palácio Rio Branco** on Rua Benjamin Constant, across from Praça Eurico Gaspar Dutra. Two bridges link the districts. In the Segundo district is the **Calçadão da Gameleira**, a pleasant promenade along the shore, with plaques and an old tree marking the location of the original settlement. The **Horto Forestal**, in Vila Ivonete (1° distrito), 3 km north of the centre ('Conjunto Procon' or 'Vila Ivonete' city-buses), has native Amazonian trees, a small lake, paths and picnic areas.

Museu da Borracha (Rubber Museum) Ⓘ *Av Ceará 1144, T068-3223 1202, Tue-Fri 0800-1800, Sat-Sun 1600-2100,* in a lovely old house with a tiled façade, has information about the rubber boom, archaeological artefacts, a section about the Acreano people, memorabilia from the annexation and a display about the Santo Daime doctrine. Recommended. **Casa Povos da Floresta** ① *Parque da Maternidade, Centro, T068-3224 5667, Wed-Fri 0800-1800, Sat-Sun 1600-2100, free* has displays and artefacts devoted to the forest people of Acre, including various of the indigenous peoples and the *seringueiro* rubber tappers who colonised the state. **Tourist office**: For Acre: Secretária de Turismo e Lazer ① *at the Estádio, Av Chico Mendes, T068-3901 3024, www.ac.gov.br*. **Polícia Federal** ① *R Floriano Peixoto 874, Centro, T3212 1228,* Acre state HQ for immigration matters.

Xapuri *Colour map 3, B5.*

Xapuri is where **Chico Mendes** lived and worked. Mendes, leader of the rubber tappers and opponent of deforestation, was murdered by landowners in 1988. His legacy is increased awareness of sustainability in the state and his colleague, Marina Silva, was appointed Environment Minister by President Lula da Silva. Both the rubber-tappers' community and fragments of the forest Mendes sought to protect survive. The area has interesting birds and mammals, towering Brazil nut trees which remain the mainstay of the local encomy, and an excellent Pousada Ecológica (30 km away – see Where to stay); one or two nights here is a magical and worthwhile experience. Xapuri has a small **museum** ① *R Coronel Brandão, Mon-Sat 0800-1800, free*, featuring local history and the life of Chico Mendes.

Border with Bolivia and Peru

The BR-317 from Rio Branco heads south and later southwest, parallel to the Rio Acre; it runs to Epitaciolândia and **Brasiléia**, opposite the Bolivian city of Cobija. Brasiléia is quaint and tranquil, with a few places to stay and eat (**$$$-$$ Brasiléia Palace Hotel**, Rua Hilário Mireles 180, T068-3546 3829, nelio701@live.com). Epitaciolândia has more services: several hotels (**$$ Vale das Orquídeas**, Avenida Internacional 249, T068-3546 3763, valedasorquideas@hotmail.com), **Polícia Federal** office for passport stamps (Avenida Santos Dumont 926, 0700-2000), **Bolivian consulate** (Dom Julio Mattioli 84, near the church, Monday-Friday 0700-1100, 1300-1500), and banks with ATMs. Change cash in Cobija. There are two bridges to Cobija: the small **Ponte da Amizade** from Brasiléia and the larger **Ponte Internacional** (with Bolivian immigration) from Epitaciolândia. You can cross either bridge without passport stamps if visiting for only a few hours. See Cobija, in the Bolivia chapter, for onward connections.

The road continues to Assis Brasil (120 km) where it crosses the Rio Acre to Iñapari, to Peru. **Assis Brasil** has a couple of simple hotels (**$$-$ Pousada Renascer**, Valero Magalhães, T068-3546 1006), *churrascarias* and shops. Entry/exit stamps are given by **Polícia Federal** (open 0700-1900) just outside town on the BR. **Peruvian immigration** (same hours) is 1 km from the centre of Iñapari on the road to Puerto Maldonado. Taxi or mototaxi between immigration offices, US$3. See Iñapari, in the Peru chapter, for money exchange and onward transport. Also across the Rio Acre from Assis Brasil is the Bolivian village of **Bolpebra**, but there is no official border crossing here and no road connections with Cobija or other points in Bolivia.

Listings Southern Amazônia

Where to stay

Porto Velho

Cheap rooms are hard to come by as many are taken by migrant workers on the twin dams project. There are hotels by the *rodoviária*, or take bus No 301 'Presidente Roosevelt' (outside Hotel Pontes), which goes to railway station at riverside, then along Av 7 de Setembro as far as Av Marechal Deodoro. It passes several hotels.

$$$ Vila Rica
Av Carlos Gomes 1616, T069-3224 3433, www.hotelvilarica.com.br.
Tower block with restaurant, pool and sauna.

$$$-$$ Central
Tenreiro Aranha 2472, T069-2181 2500, www.hotelcentral-ro.com.br.
A reliable, central place, business-style with all services, parking. Recommended.

$$ Por do Sol
R Carlos Gomes 3168, behind the rodoviária to the northeast, T069-3222 9161, hotelpordosol@yahoo.com.br.
A/c rooms off a corridor, the best are in the middle.

$$ Samauma
R Dom Pedro II 1038, T069-3224 5300, hotelsamauma@hotmail.com.

Best mid-range option in the centre, comfortable rooms, popular restaurant, breakfast, welcoming staff.

$$-$ Tía Carmen
Av Campos Sales 2995, T069-3221 7910.
Very good, honest, good cakes in lanchonette in front of hotel. Recommended.

Guajará Mirim

$$$ Pakaas Palafitas Lodge
Estrada do Palheta Km 18, T069-3541 3058, www.pakaas.com.br.
28 bungalows in a beautiful natural setting, price is per person per day.

$$ Jamaica and $$ Lima Palace
Av Leopoldo de Mato 755, T069-3541 3721 and Av 15 de Novembro 1613, T069-3541 3421.
Both have a/c, fridge, parking.

$ Mamoré
R M Moraes, T069-3541 5500.
Clean, friendly and popular.

Rio Branco

There are hotels and restaurants by the *rodoviária*.

$$$ Imperador Galvez
R Santa Inés 401, T068-3223 7027.
Comfortable, quiet, modern rooms, large pool, huge breakfasts.

$$$ Inácio Palace
R Rui Barbosa 69, and Pinheiro Palace, No 450, T068-3214 7100, www.irmaospinheiro.com.br.
Bright, spacious rooms, pool, generous breakfast, some English-speaking staff. In the same groupis a restaurant, a fast-food place and a tour agency.

$$$-$$ Terra Verde
R Marechal Deodoro 221, T068-3213 6000, www.hotelterraverdeac.com.br.
One of the best in the city, well appointed rooms and more luxurious suites, pool, good breakfast.

$$ Afa
R Franco Ribeiro 109, T068-3224 1396.
Simple rooms, quiet and well-kept but small windows, good breakfast. Also has a bistro.

$$ Papai
R Floriano Peixoto 849, T068-3223 2044.
Central, simple but garish pink and lime green rooms, best on the upper floors. Also has restaurant.

$ Ouro Verde
R Uirapuru 326, next to rodoviária, T068-3223 2378.

No frills option, rooms only a little larger than the beds they contain, but with bath, tidy, on a sunny terrace.

Xapuri

$$ Pousada Chapurys
R Sadala Kury, T068-3542 2253, pousada_chapurys@hotmail.com.
Charming place and owner, rooms with a/c, nice garden, includes a generous breakfast.

$$ Pousada Ecológica Seringal Cachoeira
Ramal do Cachoeira (16 km from signed turn-off at Km 214 of BR-317; 30 km from Xapuri, taxi US$35), T068-3901 3020/068-99947 8399, Facebo k:pousadaecologicaseringalcachoeira.
Comfortable wooden *cabanas*, with a/c, cheaper in dorms, camping possible, lovely open-sided dining and lounge area, meals ($$) with advance notice, overlooking a small river. Chico Mendes' cousins work as a guides, Nilson Teixeira (T068-99965 8513, nilsonteixieramendes73@gmail.com) is recommended for birdwatching. Trail use fee US$32 per visit, plus guiding which is charged separately.

Restaurants

Porto Velho

$$$ Caravela do Madeira
R José Camacho 104, T069-3221 6641.
The city's business lunch venue, a/c, international menu.

$$ Café Madeira
Majo Amarantes at Carlos Gomes on the riverfront, T069-3229 1193.
Overlooking the Madeira, *petisco* bar snack, a favourite spot for a sunset beer.

$$ Emporium
Av Presidente Dutra 3366, T069-3221 2665. Open 1800-2400.
Nice atmosphere, good meats and salads, expensive drinks. The street behind Emporium is known as the **Calçada da Fama** and is replete with bars and restaurants. It's very busy at weekends.

Guajará Mirim

Oasis
Av 15 de Novembro 460. Closed Mon.
The best place to eat. Recommended.

Rio Branco

Local specialities

Tacacá; a soup served piping hot in a gourd (*cuia*) combines manioc starch (*goma*), cooked jambu leaves which numb mouth and tongue, shrimp, spices and hot pepper sauce. Also a delicious Amazonian take on Espírito Santo or Bahia's *moqueca*, rich coconut sauce flavoured with an Amazon leaf, *xicoria*, and fresh coriander and accompanied with rice, *pirão*, *farofa* and delicious chilli and tucupi sauce.

\$\$ Afa
R Franco Ribeiro 108, T068-3224 1396.
The best-value per kilo restaurant in the city, with a wide choice of dishes. Plenty of veggie options.

\$\$ Elcio
Av Ceará 2513.
Superb fish *moquecas*. Serves 2-3 people.

Shopping

Porto Velho

Indigenous handicrafts

Artesanato Indígena Karitiana, *R Rui Barbosa 1407 between José Camacho and Calama, T069-3229 7591.* Daily 0800-1200, 1400-1700. An indigenous-run cooperative selling art including beads, earrings and necklaces, ritual items and weapons.

Transport

Porto Velho

Air Airport 8 km west of town. Take bus marked 'Aeroporto' (last one between 2400-0100). Daily flights to many Brazilian cities.

Bus *Rodoviária* is on Jorge Teixeira between Carlos Gomes and Dom Pedro II. It has restaurants, snack bars and 24-hr ATM. From town take bus No 407 'Norte Azul', or any 'Esperança da Comunidade' or 'Presidente Roosevelt' bus from the cathedral in the centre to the *rodoviária*, 1.5 km. Health and other controls at the Rondônia–Mato Grosso border are strict. To break up a long trip is much more expensive than doing it all in one stretch.

To **Cuiabá**, 24 hrs, US\$74-89. To **Guajará–Mirim**, see below. To **Rio Branco**, Eucatur, 2 daily, 8-10 hrs, US\$31. To **Campo Grande**, 27 hrs, US\$123. To **Cáceres** for the Pantanal, 18 hrs, US\$56-66.

Ferry See Getting around, page 598. Passenger service from **Porto Cai N'Água** (which means 'fall in the water', watch out or you might!), for best prices buy directly at the boat, avoid touts on the shore. Boat tickets for Manaus are also sold in the *rodoviária*. The Rio Madeira is fairly narrow so the banks can be seen and there are several 'meetings of waters'.

Road Road journeys are best done in the dry season, the 2nd half of the year.

Guajará Mirim

Bus From **Porto Velho** to Guajará Mirim, 5-6 hrs, 6 daily from 0630, fastest at midday, US\$18.

Guajará Mirim/Guayaramerín

Boat Speedboat across the Rio Mamoré (border with Bolivia), US\$2 (more at night), 5-min crossing, operates all day, tickets at the waterside; ferry crossing for vehicles, T069-3541 3811, Mon-Sat 0800-1200, Mon-Fri 1400-1600, 20-min crossing.

Rio Branco

Air Plácido de Castro, BR-364, Km 18 Sena Madureira, T068-3211 1003; taxi to centre US\$23, or take any bus marked 'Custódio Freire' (US\$1) to the urban bus terminal in the city centre. Buses also run to the *rodoviária*. **GOL** and **LATAM** fly to Rio Branco: daily flights to **Brasília**, **Cruzeiro do Sul** and **Porto Velho**.

Bus *Rodoviária* on Av Uirapuru, Cidade Nova, 2° distrito (east bank), T068-3224 6984, 5 km from centre; city bus 'Norte–Sul' to the centre. Taxi drivers will change money, poor rates. To **Porto Velho**, Eucatur, see above. To **Guajará Mirim**, daily with **Rondônia** at 1130 and 2200, 5-6 hrs, US\$16; or take Inácio's Tur shopping trip, 3 per week. From Rio Branco the BR-364 continues west (in principle) to Cruzeiro do Sul and Japim, with a view to reaching the Peruvian frontier further west when completed.

Car Prices for car rentals with the nationwide agencies are higher in Acre than in other states.

Border with Bolivia and Peru

From Rio Branco to Assis Brasil, 3 daily buses with **PetroAcre** and **Trans Acreana**, US\$16.50, 4-5 hrs; also *taxi lotação* (shared taxis) from Calçadão da Gameleira, Segundo district, Rio Branco, US\$22 pp. All go via **Epitaciolândia** (convenient for Polícia Federal and the Ponte Internacional) and **Brasiléia** (*rodoviária* is far from town and border posts), US\$13, 2 hrs; some buses also go via **Xapuri**. Bus between Epitaciolândia/Brasiléia and Assis Brasil US\$5.50, 2½ hrs; *taxi lotação* US\$14 pp.

Brasília, Goiás
& Tocantins

This area is the frontier where the Amazon meets the central plateau. It is also Brazil's frontier with its Spanish American neighbours. Lastly, it contains the border between the expansion of agriculture and the untouched forests and savannahs. On this region's eastern edge is Brasília, the symbol of the nation's commitment to its empty centre. Although not generally viewed as a tourist attraction, Brasília is interesting as a city of pure invention along the lines of Australia's Canberra and Washington in the United States. Its central position makes it a natural crossroads for visiting the north and interior of Brazil and, when passing through, it is well worth undertaking a city tour to view its innovative modern design.

Goiás is quite a mixture: colonial mining towns, a modern state capital, and centres which owe their existence to rapidly expanding agro-industry. There are two fine national parks, Emas and Chapada dos Veadeiros. Pirenópolis is a beautifully restored colonial town surrounded by natural attractions and lively with weekenders from Brasília. An interesting festival, with processions on horseback, is held here during May/June. The former state capital, Cidade de Goiás, has fine plazas, churches and museums. See also www.cidadeshistoricasgoias.com.br.

In Tocantins, Brazil's newest state, the incomprehensibly planned capital of Palmas provides access to the fantastic hinterland of Jalapão, fast becoming popular with Brazilians but as yet little visited by foreigners. Information from www.turismo.to.gov.br.

Brasília   *Colour map 7, A3.*

a planned city of radical design and pioneering architecture

☆Brasília (altitude 1171 m) is an unusual city not just for its position and town planning, but also because only light industry is allowed in the city and its population was limited to 500,000. This has now been exceeded and more people live in a number of shanty towns, with minimal services, located well away from the main city. The main city is a UNESCO World Heritage Site.

Sights

At the tip of the arrow is the **Praça dos Três Poderes**, with the Congress buildings, the Palácio do Planalto (the President's office), the Supremo Tribunal Federal opposite it and the Ministério da Justiça and Palácio Itamaraty respectively below them. Nineteen tall Ministry buildings line the Esplanada dos Ministérios, west of the Praça, culminating in two towers linked by a walkway to

Best for
Architecture ▪ National parks

ON THE ROAD

Asa Sul and Asa Norte

The Eixo Monumental divides the city into Asa Sul and Asa Norte (north and south wings) and the Eixo Rodoviário divides it east and west. Buildings are numbered according to their relation to them. For example, 116 Sul and 116 Norte are at the extreme opposite ends of the city. The 100s and 300s lie west of the Eixo and the 200s and 400s to the east; Quadras 302, 102, 202 and 402 are nearest the centre and 316, 116, 216 and 416 mark the end of the Plano Piloto. Residential areas are made up of six-storey apartment blocks, called 'Super-Quadras'. All Quadras are separated by feeder roads, along which are the local shops. There are also schools, parks and cinemas in the spaces between the Quadras (especially in Asa Sul). The main shopping areas, with more cinemas, restaurants, etc, are situated on either side of the city bus station (*rodoviária*). The private residential areas are west of the Super-Quadras, and on the other side of the lake. At right angles to these residential areas is the 'arrow', the 8-km-long, 250-m-wide **Eixo Monumental**. The main north–south road (Eixo Rodoviário), in which fast-moving traffic is segregated, follows the curve of the bow; the radial road is along the line of the arrow – intersections are avoided by means of underpasses and cloverleaves. Motor and pedestrian traffic is segregated in residential areas. A Metrô has been built from the centre to the southwestern suburbs. The Park Shopping station serves the new interstate *rodoviária*. It is worth telephoning addresses away from the centre to ask how to get there.

form the letter H, representing Humanity. They are 28 storeys high: no taller buildings are allowed in Brasília. Where the bow and arrow intersect is the city bus terminal (Rodoviária Municipal, or do Plano Piloto), with the cultural and recreational centres and commercial and financial areas on either side. There is a sequence of zones westward along the shaft of the arrow; a hotel centre, a radio city, an area for fairs and circuses, a centre for sports, the **Praça Municipal** (with the municipal offices in the Palácio do Buriti) and, lastly (where the nock of the arrow would be), the old combined bus and railway station (*rodoferroviária* – now closed) with the industrial area nearby. Other than the Santuário Dom Bosco and the JK bridge, the most impressive buildings are all by Oscar Niemeyer.

The **Palácio da Alvorada**, the President's official residence (not open to visitors), is on the lakeshore. The 80-km drive along the road round the lake to the dam is attractive. There are spectacular falls below the dam in the rainy season. Between the Praça dos Três Poderes and the lake are sites for various recreations, including golf, fishing and yacht clubs, and an acoustic shell for shows in the open air. The airport is at the eastern end of the lake. Some 395 ha between the lake and the northern residential area (Asa Norte) are reserved for the Universidade de Brasília, founded in 1961. South of the university area, the Avenida das Nações runs from the Palácio da Alvorada along the lake to join the road from the airport to the centre. Along it are found all the principal embassies. Also in this area is the attractive vice-presidential residence, the **Palácio do Jaburu** (not open to visitors). This area is very scenic.

A fine initial view of the city may be had from the **television tower** ① *West Eixo Monumental, Mon 1400-2000, Tue-Sun 0800-2000*, which has a free observation platform at 75 m; also bar and souvenir shop. If the TV tower is closed, the nearby Alvorada hotel has a panoramic terrace on the 12th floor (lift to 11th only): ask at reception. A good and cheap way of seeing Brasília is by taking a bus from the municipal *rodoviária* at the centre: the destinations are clearly marked. The circular bus routes 106, 108 and 131 go round the city's perimeter. If you go around the lake by bus, you must change at the Paranoá dam; to or from Paranoá Norte take bus 101, 'Rodoviária', and to and from Sul, bus 100, bypassing the airport. Tours 1300-1700, start from the downtown hotel area and municipal *rodoviária* (US$9.50-16). Many hotels arrange city tours (see also Tour operators). Some buildings are open 1000-1400 Saturday-Sunday, with guided tours in English, well worth it.

Praça dos Três Poderes: **Congress** ① *Mon-Fri 0930-1200, 1430-1630 (take your passport), guides*

Tip...
Low humidity and a warm climate make this a pleasant city for sightseeing on foot. Summer downpours do occur though.

free of charge (in English 1400-1700), www.congressonacional.leg.br. Visitors may attend debates when Congress is in session (Friday morning). Excellent city views from the 10th floor in Annex 3. The **Palácio do Planalto** ① *Sun 0930-1330, 30-min tours, www2.planalto.gov.br,* may also be visited. The guard is changed ceremonially at the Palácio do Planalto on Friday at 1730. Opposite the Planalto is the Supreme Court building, **Supremo Tribunal Federal**. **Espaço Lúcio Costa** ① *Tue-Sun 0900-1800, free,* contains a model of Plano Piloto, sketches and autographs of the designer's concepts and gives the ideological background to the planning of Brasília. (Town clothes (not shorts or minis) should be worn when visiting all these buildings.) The **Museu Histórico de Brasília** ① *Tue-Sun and holidays 0900-1800,* is really a hollow monument, with tablets, photos and videos telling the story of the city. The sculpture 'Os Candangos' in front of the Planalto is a symbol of the city. By Bruno Giorgi, it pays homage to the *candangos,* or pioneer workers who built Brasília on empty ground. The marvellous building of the Ministry of Foreign Affairs, the **Itamarati** ① *guided visits must be booked in advance, visita@itamaraty.gov.br, or T061-2030 8051, 7 a day from 0900-1700 Mon-Fri, in Portugues, English and French,* has modern paintings and furniture and beautiful water gardens. Opposite the Itamarati is the **Palácio da Justiça** ① *Mon-Fri 0900-1200, 1500-1700,* with artificial cascades between its concrete columns. The **Panteão Tancredo Neves** is a 'temple of freedom and democracy', built 1985-1986 by Niemeyer. It includes an impressive homage to Tiradentes, the precursor of Brazilian independence.

Niemeyer's **Procuradaria Geral da República,** comprising two glass cylinders, one suspended from a concrete cog, opened in 2002. The **Museu Nacional de Brasília** ① *T061-3325 5220, www.cultura.df.gov.br, Tue-Sun 0900-1830,* on the Conjunto Cultural da República (next to the cathedral) and the adjacent **Biblioteca Nacional** ① *www.bnb.df.gov.br,* are the last grand projects Niemeyer designed for the capital. The former is particularly impressive, a huge dome of white concrete, blank but for a door halfway up, sitting in a shallow pool of water which reflects like a mirror. This door is reached by a long sinuous ramp. Inside is a 700-seat auditorium and state-of-the-art galleries.

The **Catedral Metropolitana** ① *0800-1930, T061-3224 4073, http://catedral.org.br,* on the Esplanada dos Ministérios, is a spectacular circular building in the shape of the crown of thorns. Three aluminium angels, suspended from the airy, domed, stained-glass ceiling, are by the sculptor

Brasília: Plano Piloto

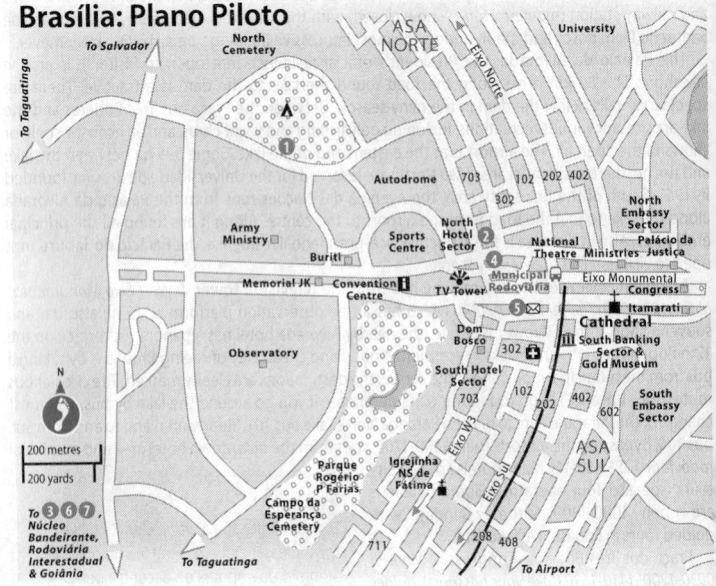

A city in the making

The purpose-built federal capital of Brazil succeeded Rio de Janeiro (as required by the Constitution) on 21 April 1960. The creation of an inland capital had been urged since the beginning of the 19th century, but it was finally brought into being after President Kubitschek came to power in 1956, when a competition for the best general plan was won by Professor Lúcio Costa, who laid out the city in the shape of a bent bow and arrow. (It is also described as an aeroplane, or a bird in flight.) Brasília is on undulating ground in the unpopulated uplands of Goiás, in the heart of the undeveloped Sertão. The official name for central Brasília is the Plano Piloto.

Alfredo Ceschiatti, who also made the five life-sized bronze apostles outside. The baptistery, a concrete representation of the Host beside the cathedral, is connected to the main building by a tunnel (open Sundays only). The outdoor carillon was a gift from the Spanish government: the bells are named after Columbus's ships.

South of the TV tower on Avenida W3 Sul, at Quadra 702, is the Sanctuary of **Dom Bosco** ① *T061-3223 6542, 0800-1800*, a modernist cube with tall gothic arches filled with stained glass that shades light to dark blue and indigo as it ascends. It is especially striking in late afternoon when shafts of light penetrate the building.

The **Templo da Boa Vontade** ① *Setor Garagem Sul 915, lotes 75/76, T061-3114 1070, www.tbv. com.br, 24 hrs, getting there: take bus 151 from outside the Centro do Convenções or on Eixo Sul to Centro Médico*, is a seven-faced pyramid topped by one of the world's largest crystals, a peaceful place dedicated to all philosophies and religions.

A permanent memorial to Juscelino Kubitschek, the '**Memorial JK**' ① *daily 0900-1800, US$1.35*, contains his tomb and his car, together with a lecture hall and exhibits. It has toilets and a *lanchonete*. The **Monumental Parade Stand** has unique and mysterious acoustic characteristics (the complex is north of the Eixo Monumental, between the 'Memorial JK' and the *rodoferroviária*). There are remarkable stained glass panels, each representing a state of the Federation, on the ground floor of the Caixa Econômica Federal.

Some 15 km out along the Belo Horizonte road is the small wooden house, known as '**O Catetinho**', in which President Kubitschek stayed in the late 1950s during his visits to the city when it was under construction; it is open to visitors and most interesting. Northwest of Brasília, but only 15 minutes by car from the centre, is the 30,000-ha **Parque Nacional de Brasília** ① *entrance at Rodovia BR 450 Via EPIA; contact the park's office, Rodovia DF 003, Km 8.5, T061-3233 6897, www.icmbio.gov.br, US$8 (Brazilians half price), open 0800-1700 (last entry 1600)*. Founded in 1961 to conserve the flora and fauna of the Federal Capital, only a portion of the park is open to the public without a permit. There is a swimming pool fed by clear river water, a snack bar and a series of trails through gallery forest (popular with joggers in the early morning and at weekends). The rest of the park is grassland, gallery forest and *cerrado* vegetation. Large mammals include tapir, maned wolf and pampas deer; birdwatching is good.

Lago Do Paranoá

⑧ Palácio da Alvorada

Palácio do Jaburu

Palácio do Planalto

Praça dos Três Poderes

Avenida das Nações

Núcleo

Where to stay
1 Albergue da Juventude de Brasília
2 Aristus, Bittar Inn, Casablanca & El Pilar
3 El Salvador
4 Kubitschek Plaza
5 Nacional
6 Olinda
7 Potiguar
8 Royal Tulip Alvorada

Metrô lines
— Current

Tourist information

Tourist offices

Setur
SDC Eixo Monumental, Lote 05, Centro de Convenções, Ala Sul 1st floor, T061-3214 2744/2764, www.setur.df.gov.br.
Mon-Fri 0800-1200, 1400-1800.
Helpful, English-speaking staff, good map of the city. There are branches at Praça dos Três Poderes, daily 0800-1800, and the airport, international arrivals daily 0800-1800, national arrivals Mon-Fri 0800-1800; they have maps of the city and information on tourist sites and routes.

For national tourism entities, see Tourist information in Essentials A-Z, page 674. See also www.aboutbrasilia.com.

Maps

Detailed street maps of the city are impossible to find. Newsagents and the airport sell a map showing the Quadras. Otherwise, see **Setur**'s map.

Where to stay

The best area is the northern hotel zone which has shops and restaurants nearby. Weekend discounts of 30% are often available but must be requested. Most cheap accommodation is in Núcleo Bandeirante, reasonably close to both the Rodoviária Interestadual and the Airport. It can be reached by city bus from either (see Transport, below). The area is reported safe and has a number of economical hotels along Av Central, with more upmarket options on 3ra Av. The tourist office (see above) has a list of places to stay.

Asa Norte

$$$$-$$$ Kubitschek Plaza
Qd 2, bloco E, T3319 3543,
www.kubitschek.com.br.
Popular business hotel with modern rooms and excellent facilties; pool, sauna and gym. Sister hotel, the **Manhattan Plaza** (same website) next door is very similar.

$$$$-$$$ Royal Tulip Alvorada
Trecho 1, Lt 1-B, Bl C (Lagoa Norte), T061-3424 7000, www.royaltulipbrasiliaalvorada.com.
The city's newest, most luxurious business hotel, with rooms in a giant red horseshoe overlooking the lake, an enormous pool and excellent, comprehensive business facilities.

$$$ Aristus
Qd 2, bloco O, T061-3328 8675,
www.aristushotel.com.br.
Delightfully dated but smart 70s block with simple rooms and breakfast.

$$$ Bittar Inn
Qd 2, bloco N, T061-3704 3010,
www.hoteisbittar.com.br.
Simple rooms, a bit cramped, at the cheaper end of this chain's hotels, good value for the area.

$$$ Casablanca
Qd 3, bloco A, T061-3328 8586,
www.casablancabrasilia.com.br.
Another 1970s delight; more intimate than most in the area, but some noisy rooms.

$$$ El Pilar
Qd 3, bloco F, T061-3533 5900,
www.elpilar.com.br.
Plain, freshly painted, with fan. Avoid rooms below street level as they collect car fumes.

$$-$ Albergue da Juventude de Brasília
Setor Recreativo Parque Norte (SRPN), Qd 02, Lt 02, T061-3343 0531, www.brasiliahostel.com.br.
Cheaper for HI members, dorms and double rooms ($$), also cheaper Jan-Feb. Kitchen, laundry, cyber-café, in same grounds as **Camping de Brasília**. Take bus 143 from municipal *rodoviária*.

Asa Sul

$$$$-$$$ Nacional
Qd 1, bloco A, T061-3321 7575,
www.hotelnacional.com.br.
Cavernous, frayed old-fashioned and a city landmark with many tour agencies outside.

Núcleo Bandeirante

$$$ Potiguar
3ra Av, Bl 518, Lt 566, T061-3552 3032,
hotelpotiguar.com.br.
Ample rooms, cheaper without a/c, frigobar, good breakfast, helpful owner.

$$ El Salvador
Av Central, Lt 605, next to Banco do Brasil, T061-3386 0021, www.hotelelsalvador.com.br.
Functional rooms, cheaper without a/c, breakfast.

$$ Olinda

Av Central, Lts 380/510, above supermarket, Núcleo Bandeirante, T061-3552 4115.
Simple, basic rooms, cheaper without a/c, frigobar, breakfast, run-down but still the best economy option in the area.

Restaurants

At weekends, few restaurants in central Brasília are open. Plenty of choice of restaurants in all brackets in the Pier 21 entertainment mall on the lake shore. Other cheaper options along R 405/406. Snack bars can be found all over the city. Places serving *prato feito* or *comercial can* be found all over the city, especially on Av W3 and in the Setor Comercial Sul. Other good bets are the **Conjunto Nacional** and the **Conjunto Venâncio**, 2 shopping/office complexes on either side of the municipal *rodoviária*, and **Shopping Brasília**, below the southern hotel zone, and Patio Brasília, below the northern. Both have a wide range of boutiques and fast food restaurants. Tropical fruit flavour ice cream can be found in various parlours, eg Av W3 Norte 302. Freshly made fruit juices in all bars.

Asa Norte

All of the large hotels in this area have upmarket restaurants, most catering to business visitors.

The municipal *rodoviária* sells the best coffee and pastries in town (bottom departure level).

$$$ Trattoria da Rosario

SHIS QI 17, bloco H, Loja 215, Lago Sul, Fashion Park, T061-3248 1672. Closed Mon, lunch only on Sun.
Northern Italian food and excellent Uruguayan lamb.

$$$ Universal Diner

SCLS 210, bloco B, loja 30, T061-3443 2089, Facebook: restauranteuniversaldiner. Lunch only on Sun.
One of the city's best contemporary restaurants with strong Asian influences.

$$ Boa Saúde

Av W3 Norte, Qd 702, Edif Brasília Rádio Center. Sun-Fri 0800-2000.
Respectable vegetarian with a range of salads, quiches and pies.

$$ Bom Demais

Av W3 Norte, Qd 706.
Comfortable, serving fish, beef and rice, etc, live music at weekends.

Asa Sul

There are many cheap places on Av W3 Sul, eg at *blocos* 502 and 506. Good mid-range options around Av Anhaguera between Tocantins and Goiás and especially around Praça Tamandaré and Av República Líbano.

$$$ La Chaumière

Av W3 Sul, Qd 408, bloco A, loja 13, T061-3242 7599, www.lachaumiere.com.br. Lunch only Sun.
The city's favourite French cooking in classical surroundings.

$$$ Le Français

Av W3 Sul, Qd 404, bloco B, loja 27, T061-3225 4583.
French food served in bistro atmosphere, classic and modern dishes.

$$$ O Convento

SHIS, QI 9, conjunto 9, casa 4, T061-3248 1211.
The best for regional and Brazilian cuisine in a mock farmhouse dining room decorated with antiques and arts and crafts.

$$$ Piantella

SCLS 202, bloco A, loja 34, T061-3224 9408, www.piantella.com.br.
A favourite of senior politicians, vast menu combining *feijoada*, Italian food, steaks and seafood, good wines, too.

$$ Oca da Tribo

SCES Trecho 2 m opposite Agenpol, T061-3226 9880.
Wholefood restaurant with vegetarian options and others, good buffet lunch.

$$ Vercelli

SCLS 410, bloco D, loja 34, T061-3443 0100. Lunch only.
Pizzas, pastas and a great deal more on a huge menu.

$ Naturama

SCLS 102, bloco B, loja 9, T061-3225 5125.
Vegetarian and wholefood dishes, lunchtime.

Bars and clubs

Arena Café

CA 7, bloco F1, loja 33, T061-3468 1141.
Popular gay bar with DJs from Thu to Sat.

Bier Fass

SHIS Q 5, bloco E, loja 52/53, T061-3248 1519.
Cavernous bar/restaurant with live music Tue-Sun and 20/30s crowd. Happy hour from 1800.

Café Cancun
Shopping Liberty Mall, SCN, Qd 3,
bloco D, loja 52, T061-3327 1566.
Tacky Mexican restaurant by day and teen and
20-something beautiful people club after dark.

Clube de Choro
SDC, Qd 3, bloco G, T061-3224 0599,
www.clubedochoro.com.br. Wed-Sat.
One of the best clubs in the country devoted to
the music which gave rise to samba. Top names
from all over Brazil as well as the city itself. Great
atmosphere. Tickets sold 9 days in advance.

UK Music Hall Pub
SCLS 411, bloco B, loja 28, T061-3257 1993,
www.ukmusichall.com.
Some of the best live bands in the city play here.
Guinness, sandwiches, all ages.

Entertainment

Information about entertainment, etc is available
in 2 daily papers, *Jornal de Brasília* and *Correio
Brasiliense*. Any student card (provided it has
a photograph) will get you into the cinema/
theatre/concert hall for half price.

Cinema
Pier 21, *SCSS, Trecho 2, Cj 32/33*. An enormous
complex with 13 cinema screens, nightclubs,
restaurants, video bars and children's theme park.

Theatre
There are 3 auditoria of the **Teatro Nacional**
(Setor Cultural Norte, Via N 2, next to the bus
station, T061-3325 6109, foyer open 0900-2000,
box office open at 1400), the building is in the
shape of an Aztec pyramid. The Federal District
authorities have 2 theatres, the **Galpão** and
Galpãozinho (between Quadra 308 Sul and
Av W3 Sul). There are several other concert halls.

Shopping

Handicrafts
Artíndia, *SRTVS, Qd 702, also in the rodoviária
and at the airport*. For Amerindian handicrafts.
Feira hippy, *at the base of the TV tower. Sat, Sun
and holidays*. Leather goods, wood carvings,
jewellery, bronzes.
Galeria dos Estados, *which runs underneath the
eixo from Setor Comercial Sul to Setor Bancário Sul,
10 mins' walk from municipal rodoviária, south
along Eixo Rodoviário Sul*. For handicrafts from
all the Brazilian states.

What to do

Many tour operators have their offices in the
shopping arcade of the Hotel Nacional.
    City tours (3-4 hrs) with English commentary
can also be booked at the airport by arriving air
passengers – a convenient way of getting to
your hotel if you have heavy baggage. Some
tours have been criticized as too short, others
that the guides speak poor English, and for night-
time tours, the flood lighting is inadequate on
many buildings.
Presmic Turismo, *SIA trecho 03, lotes 625/695,
Shopping SIA, sala 208C, T061-3233 0115, www.
presmic.com.br*. Full-, half-day and night-time
city tours (0845, 1400 and 1930 respectively).

Transport

Air Airport, 12 km from centre, T061-3364 9000,
www.bsb.aero/br/. Frequent daily flights to **Rio**
and **São Paulo** (1½ hrs in both cases) and to main
cities. From the airport, take **Ônibus Executivo
113** to Esplanada dos Ministérios, Rodoviária
do Plano Piloto (not the Interestadual), Setores
Hoteleiros Norte e Sul, and back to airport every
20 mins 0630-2400, US$2.75, T061-3344 2769,
www.tcb.df.gov.br. To **Núcleo Bandeirante**, take
bus Nos 129 or 73.1 (small bus) to Candanga, then
change to No 80.1, total fare US$1.50, about 1 hr
but allow plenty of extra time; to **Rodoviária
Interestadual**, to Candanga (as above) then
take any bus to Park Shopping, or take bus 011 to
Metrô station 114 S, then train to Park Shopping
station. **Taxis**: US$14 to Núcleo Bandeirante or
Rodoviária Interestadual, US$16 to Rodoviária
Municipal, US$18 to hotel sectors.

Bus The terminal, **Rodoviária Interestadual**
(or Nova) is southwest of the city opposite
Park Shopping. The **Rodoviária Municipal
do Plano Piloto** in the centre serves regional
destinations in DF and some parts of Goiás;
many city buses also stop here. Both rodoviárias
are on the Metrô, fare between them US$0.75,
station for Rodoviária Interestadual is called "Park
Shopping". Rodoviária Interestadual to Núcleo
Bandeirante: walk first to the Metrô station, then
over the large pedestrian overpass toward Park
Shopping, then down to the main road where
buses stop, No 092 (runs on 3a Av in Núcleo
Bandeirante), fare US$1, about 30 min but allow
plenty of extra time. Taxi fare US$8. From Núcleo
Bandeirante to the Rodoviária Municipal, take bus
No 160, which runs on Av Central. If travelling by

city us always allow plenty of time as traffic can cause long delays.

To **Rio**: 17 hrs, US$60-78. To **São Paulo**, 16 hrs, US$40-65. To **Belo Horizonte**: 12 hrs, US$39-52. To **Belém** 36 hrs, with **Rápido Marajó**, US$92. To **Salvador**: 24 hrs, 3 daily, US$61-86. To **Cuiabá** 17½ hrs, US$57-61 daily with **Eucatur** and **São Luís**. To **Campo Grande**, 21 hrs, US$80 with **Motta** or **São Luís**. All major destinations served. Bus tickets for major companies sold at the city *rodoviária*.

Car hire All large companies at the airport and the Car Rental Sector. Multinational agencies and **Interlocadora**, airport, T0800-138000. **Unidas**, T061-2365 2266 at airport, Mon-Fri 0800-1800.

Metro The Metrô, www.metro.df.gov.br, runs from the Central station to the southwest suburbs of Ceilândia (green line) and Samambaia (orange line). A single ticket is US$0.75, but multiple-use smart cards are available. Trains run 0600-2330, 0700-1900 on Sun and holidays. The network was due to be extended to the airport by 2014, but this never happened as funds went missing in a corruption scheme. It is not clear when the network will be completed.

Goiás

some star attractions in a little-visited area

Goiânia *Colour map 7, A3.*

This once friendly and safe state capital has become increasingly violent over the last five years. It has few attractions of its own but provides access to several outstanding areas in the state of Goiás.

Sights It is a spacious city, founded in 1933, which conserves many art-deco buildings from that decade. Main avenues radiate out from the central **Praça Cívica**, on which stands the Government Palace. The city has more parks and gardens than any other of Brazil's large cities and many are filled with forest and *cerrado* plants, as well as marmosets and large numbers of birds. **Bosque dos Buritis** ① *3 blocks east of the Praça Cívica, daily 0700-2000*, is pleasant for a stroll, and contains the **Museu de Artes de Goiânia** ① *R 6 605, T062-3524 1190, Tue-Sun 1000-1200, 1300-1700, free*. **Tourist office**: There are Centros de Atendimento ao Turista (CAT) at the rodoviária ① *near food court, T062-3524 7261, Mon-Sat 1000-2130, Sun 1100-1900*, and airport ① *T062-3524 5060, daily 0700-2300*. The Prefeitura's website is www.goiania.go.gov.br.

The **Memorial do Cerrado Museum** ① *Campus II da Universidade Católica de Goiás, Parque Atheneu, T062-3946 1723, US$5, Mon-Sat 0700-1930, Sun 0800-1200, 1300-1700*, just outside the city, provides an interesting introduction to Cerrado life, with reconstructions of indigenous villages, *quilombos* and colonial streets as well as planted *cerrado* vegetation. The **Museu Zoroastro Artiaga** ① *Praça Cívica 13, T062-3201 4676, Mon-Fri 0800-1800, Sat-Sun 0900-1500, free*, has a small but interesting collection of objects from indigenous and early settler life, fossils and religious items. **Museu Antropológico da UFG** ① *Praça Universitária, 1 km east of Praça Cívica, T062-3209 6010, Tue-Fri 0900-1700, free*, houses wide-ranging ethnographic displays on the *indígenas* of the Centre West.

☆Cidade de Goiás *Colour map 7, A2.*

This delightful town, nestled amid *cerrado*-covered ridges, is one of Central Brazil's hidden gems. Its cobbled streets lined with Portuguese whitewash and brilliant yellow and blue façades and elegantly simple baroque churches have been awarded UNESCO World Heritage status. The town was founded in 1727 as Araial de Santana, later renamed Vila Boa de Goyaz, then Cidade de Goiás. Like its Minas counterparts it became rich on gold, before becoming the capital of Goiás state, which it remained until just before the Second World War. The **tourist office** ① *R Moretti Foggia near the river, T062-3371 7714, catcidadedegoias@hotmail.com, Mon-Fri 0800-1800, Sat-Sun 0900-1730, Portuguese only*, has knowledgeable, helpful staff. Most churches are closed on Monday.

The most interesting streets in the colonial part of town spread out from the two principal plazas, Praça Brasil Caiado and, immediately below it towards the river, Praça do Coreto. The former is dominated by a lavish baroque fountain which once supplied all the town's water, while on the latter is the imposing **Catedral de Santana** (or Igreja Matriz) ① *Mon-Sat 0700-1100, 1300-1700, free*, built in 1743. The church of **São Francisco de Paula** (1763) ① *Praça Zacheu Alves de Castro, Mon-Fri 1300-1700, Sat-Sun 0900-1200*, sits on a platform overlooking the market and the Rio Vermelho. It has a beautiful 19th-century painted ceiling by André Antônio da Conceição, depicting the life of

St Francis. **Nossa Senhora da Abadia** ① *R Abadia s/n, Tue-Sun 0900-1300*, has a similarly understated but impressive painted ceiling, whilst the other 18th-century churches like **Nossa Senhora do Carmo** ① *R do Carmo, on the riverside, Tue-Fri 1300-1700, Sat-Sun morning only*, and **Santa Bárbara** ① *R Passo da Pátria, open only during festa in early Dec*, are even simpler. The latter sits on a hill a kilometre or so east of the town affords wonderful sunset views. The **Museu das Bandeiras** ① *Praça Brasil Caiado/Largo do Chafariz, T062-3371 1087, Tue-Sat 0900-1700, Sun 0900-1400, US$1.75*, was once the centre of local government. Its rooms, furnished with period pieces, sit over a small but forbidding dungeon. Also on Praça Brasil Caiado is the **Museu Quartel do Vinte** ① *US$1.25, Mon-Fri 0800-1800*, a beautiful 18th-century former barracks. The old governor's palace, the **Palacio Conde dos Arcos** ① *Praça do Coreto, T062-3371 1200, Tue-Sat 0800-1700, Sun 0900-1300, US$1.25*, has a display of 19th-century furniture and plaques describing the town's life in colonial times. The **Museu de Artes Sacras** ① *Igreja da Boa Morte, Praça do Coreto, T062-3371 1207, Tue-Fri 0800-1700, Sat-Sun 0900-1300, US$1.25*, houses some 18th-century church silverware and a series of painted wooden statues by one of Brazil's most important religious sculptors, José Joaquim da Veiga Valle. A stroll from the Praça do Coreto, downhill and across the river will bring you to the **Museu Casa de Cora Coralina** ① *R do Cândido 20, T062-3371 1990, Tue-Sat 0900-1645, Sun 0900-1500, US$2, no photography allowed*, the former home of Goiás's most respected writer, with a collection of her belongings. The staff here are extremely helpful and knowledgeable about the city, though they speak only Portuguese. The 18th-century **Mercado Municipal**, next to the old *rodoviária*, 500 m west of the central Praça do Coreto, is a wonderful spot for cheap lunches, breakfasts and photography. Little artisan shops are springing up all over the town.

Pirenópolis *Colour map 7, A3.*

This lovely colonial silver mining town, 150 km due west of Brasília at an altitude of 770 m), has a well-preserved centre. It's almost as pretty as Cidade de Goiás and is a National Heritage Site. It's also a favourite weekend haunt for the capital's middle classes who congregate in the

Tip...

Pirenópolis is the nation's unofficial silver capital and is a good place to stock up on presents.

lively restaurants and bars which line the northern end of Rua do Rosário. One of Brazil's most unusual and vibrant festivals takes place here every May/June (see page 643) and at weekends the Praça Central fills with country folk in stetsons and spurs, blasting out Sertanejo music from their souped-up cars. **Tourist office**: Centro de Atendimento ao Turista ① *R do Bonfim s/n, Centro Histórico, T062-3331 2633, daily 0800-1800, Portuguese only, www.pirenopolis.go.gov.br*.

The **Igreja Matriz Nossa Senhora do Rosário** ① *Wed-Sun 0800-1900, US$1*, which has been restored after being gutted by a fire in 2002, is the oldest church in the state (1728), but its lavish interior is sadly no more. **Nossa Senhora do Carmo** ① *Wed-Sun 1400-1800*, serves as a museum of religious art. **Museu Família Pompeu** ① *R Nova 33, T062-3331 1102, US$1, by appointment only*, displays the best collection of pictures and documents devoted to the history of the city (in Portuguese only). The tiny, private **Museu das Cavalhadas** ① *R Direita 37, daily 0800-1100, 1300-1700, US$1*, has a collection of masks and costumes from the Festa do Divino.

The walks and adventure activities in state parks, private reserves and fazendas in the Cerrado and hills are as much as a draw as the colonial architecture. The landscape is rugged, with many waterfalls and canyons, birding is good and there is a reasonably healthy population of maned wolf and the various South American cats. **Santuário de Vida Silvestre Vagafogo** ① *6 km from town, T062-3335 8515, www.vagafogo.com.br, daily 0900-1700, US$5.75; Sat-Sun for brunch (US$13.50) and adventure sports (US$40 for all activities, US$14 for 1)*; 17 ha private reserve of Evandro Engel and family, bathing in the lovely Rio Vagafogo, good birding (200 species), many interesting animals, excellent nature library, local fruits and nuts for sale. Evandro is very knowledgeable, helpful and speaks good English; "a special place". **Mosteiro Buddhista** ① *T062-99643 0452, US$12 plus guide (required)*, a simple Zen monastery near eight beautiful cascades on a 3-km path in the heart of pristine *cerrado* forest. Day visits with light walks or longer term retreats. Particularly magical at sunset. **Parque Estadual Serra dos Pireneus** ① *20 km from town, guide required*, a 2833-ha wilderness area reaching up to 1385 m elevation, offers great views (especially at sunset), walking and climbing, waterfalls and natural pools.

☆Chapada dos Veadeiros

This spectacular natural area, about 250 km northeast of Brasília, has eroded mountains drained by countless fast-flowing rivers which rush through deep gorges and plummet over spectacular waterfalls. It was designated a UNESCO World Heritage Site in 2001. The Chapada is covered in *cerrado* forest, rich in biological diversity. Rare mammals include jaguar, maned wolf, puma, tapir, ocelot and giant anteater; birds feature red shouldered macaw, coal crested finch, helmeted manakin and many king vultures. A 600,000 ha Tombador-Veadeiros biological corridor is being assembled here, encompassing the existing Parque Nacional Chapada dos Veadeiros (65,514 ha), various private reserves including Serra do Tombador (9000 ha), and the **Kalunga ethnic reserve** (262,000 ha), home to several Quilombo communities – the descendants of African slaves wholed to the hinterlands in colonial times.

The main access towns are **Alto Paraíso de Goiás** (altitude 1250 m), closest to Brasília and an alternative lifestyles centre; **São Jorge** (1000 m), a resort village on the park boundary, 36 km west of Alto Paraíso; and **Cavalcante** (825 m), a quiet little place with access to Kalunga, good facilities north of the park and less visited than the others. The most popular attractions are waterfalls, found both inside and outside the national park. The area has a pleasant climate and gets busy at weekends, crowded at major holidays including July. **National park headquarters** ① *1 km outside São Jorge, T062-3445 1114, www.icmbio.gov.br/parnachapadadosveadeiros/, Tue-Sun 0800-1200 for entry, trails close 1800, in Jan and Jul park is open every day, only day-visits permitted*. There are two national park trails, a waterfall circuit (daily limit 250 visitors) and a canyon circuit (limit 200 visitors), entry free but guide required. Guides wait at park headquarters where groups form, they charge US$59 for up to 10 visitors. Guides are not required for most sites outside the park, which are on private land and charge US$6-9 entry per person. A vehicle is an asset but hitching is easy at busy times and some attractions can be reached on foot. Tours throughout the region are offered by operators in Alto Paraíso.

☆Parque Nacional Emas

US$4.25. Permission is needed to take photographs, but not to visit, as long as you have a voucher and are accompanied by an authorized guide; apply at least a week in advance. Information from ICMBio, Rod GO 206 Km 27, Caixa postal 115, Chapadão do Céu, GO – CEP75828-000, T064-3929 6000, www.icmbio.gov.br. Tourist office in Mineiros, T064-3661 0006. Day trips are not recommended, but longer visits to the Park can be arranged through agencies (eg Trekking Turismo, Mineiros, T064-99611 5259, Facebook: trekkingmineiros, 4WD, biking and trekking tours in the park and to other attractions, rafting and watersports).

In the far southwest of the state, covering the watershed of the Araguaia, Taquari and Formoso rivers, is the small Parque Nacional Emas. Access is from Mineiros, 89 km northeast, Chapadão do Céu, 27 km southeast of the park, and Costa Rica in Mato Grosso do Sul (see page 660). Almost 132,868 ha of undulating grasslands and *cerrado* contain the world's largest concentration of termite mounds. Pampas deer, giant anteater, greater rhea, or 'ema' in Portuguese, and maned wolf are frequently seen roaming the grasses. The park holds the greatest concentration of blue-and-yellow macaws outside Amazônia, and blue-winged, red-shouldered and red-bellied macaws can also be seen. (There are many other animals and birds.) Along with the grasslands, the park supports a vast marsh on one side and rich gallery forests on the other. As many of the interesting mammals are nocturnal, a spotlight is a must.

Where to stay

Goiânia

The city is well supplied with hotels, including chains, the best being 1 km from the centre in the Setor Oeste.

$$$ Address
Av República do Líbano 2526, T062-3257 1000, www.goldentulipaddress.com.
Well-equipped business hotel, best in the city, modern rooms with separate living areas, gym, pool, restaurant, bar, good views from the upper floors.

$$$ Oeste Plaza
389 Rua 2, Setor Oeste, T062-3224 5012, www.oesteplaza.com.br.
Well-maintained, modern, small rooms, those on higher floors have good views, small pool and gym.

$$$-$$ Papillon
Av República do Libano 1824, T062-3608 1500, www.papillonhotel.com.br.
Modern rooms and suites, pool, gym, sauna, business facilities, very popular, book ahead.

$$ Goiânia Palace
Av Anhangüera 5195, T062-3224 4874, www.goianiapalace.com.br.
Nicely refurbished art deco building with plenty of character. Good breakfast, French-run, English also spoken, good location and value. Recommended.

$ Hostel 7
Av T-2, Q 107 Lote 04, Setor Bueno, T062-3877 6077, http://hostel7.com.br.
Mixed and women-only dorms (US$15-17 pp), 2 private rooms with shared bath, with all hostel facilities and swimming pool, breakfast. See website for bus routes. Has another branch in Brasília.

Cidade de Goiás

$$$ Casa da Ponte
R Moretti Foggia s/n, T062-3371 4467, casadapontehotel_@hotmail.com.
Art deco building next to bridge across Rio Vermelho, the best rooms overlook the river (cheaper without a/c), nice terrace, parking, mid-week discounts are good value.

$$$ Pousada Goyá
R Sta Barbara 38, T062-3371 4423.
Colonial house set in a little garden with views over the river and Serra, frigobar, good breakfast.

$$$ Vila Boa
Morro Chapéu do Padre s/n, 1 km southeast of the centre, T062-3371 1000, www.hotelvilaboa.com.br.
The best in town, though inconvenient for the centre, pool, bar, restaurant and good views.

$$ Pousada do Sol
R Americano do Brasil, T062-3371 1717.
Well maintained, fans, central.

$$-$ Pousada Vovó Dú
R 15 Novembro 22, T062-3372 1224.
Simple rooms, some very small (cheaper without a/c), electric shower, basic breakfast, good economy option.

Camping

Cachoeira Grande campground
7 km along the BR-070 to Jussara (near the tiny airport, hard to find).
Attractive, well-run, with bathing place and snack bar.

Pirenópolis

Plenty of places to stay but they fill quickly at holidays. Weekday discounts are usually available. At **Festa do Divino** (see page 643) it's essential to book ahead or visit from Brasília. **Central de Reservas** (T062-3331 3323, www.pirenopolis.com.br), is a hotel booking service.

$$$ Arvoredo
Av Abercio final da R Direita, T062-3331 3479, www.arvoredo.tur.br.
Peaceful, small pool, views over the town. Simple rooms with large beds, hammocks, excellent special rates Sun-Thu.

$$$ Casa Grande
R Aurora 41, T062-3331 1758, http://casaraovilladoimperio.com.br
Chalets and rooms in a tropical garden with a pool set around a large colonial house, Wi-Fi in common areas.

$$$ Pousada O Casarão
R Direita 79, T062-3331 2662, www.ocasaraopirenopolis.com.br.

A converted 1896 town house decorated with antiques, mosquito nets, great breakfast, nice gardens, rooms with a/c, fan and frigobar, lovely place, attentive service, must stay 2 nights at weekends. Recommended.

$$$ Pouso do Sô Vigario
R Nova 25, T062-3331 1206, http://pirenopolis.org.
Rooms with a/c and fan, pleasant public areas, good location, decent breakfast in a little garden next to the pool. Same owner runs **Pouso do Frade** (R do Bonfim 37, T3331 1046), same price and facilities.

$$ Recanto da Vila
A 5, across from rodoviária, T062-3331 3162, lulu.siqueira2@hotmail.com.
Simple rooms in private home, with fan, electric shower, no breakfast but great *pão de queijo* courtesy of friendly owner, good value.

$$ Rex
Praça da Matriz, T062-331 1121, http://rexhotelpirenopolis.com.br.
In what was the first hotel in town, lots of character, electric shower, parking. Good breakfast and location, helpful owner.

Camping

AABB
R Pireneus near Hospital Público, T062-3331 1106, www.aabbpirenopolis.com.
Lawns for tents, toilets, showers and grills, US$15 pp, includes use of pool and sports facilities.

Chapada dos Veadeiros

Alto Paraíso
Pousadas are scattered around town. Several expensive restaurants on Av Ary Ribeiro Veladão with vegetarian options and organic foods.

$$$ Recanto da Grande Paz
R 2 (de João-de-barro) 322, T062-3446 1452, www.recantodagrande paz.com.br.
Small comfortable chalets with porch and hammocks, frigobar, pool, breakfast and cafeteria, massage available.

$$$-$$ Casa Rosa
R Gumercindo Barbosa 233, T062-3446 1319, www.pousadacasarosa.com.br.
Good rooms, the best in chalets near the pool, nice grounds, discounts mid-week and for long stays.

$$ Novo Portal da Chapada
9 km along the road to São Jorge, T062-99911 3337, www.novoportaldachapada.com.br.
The best choice for birdwatchers, with cabins in the Cerrado. Comfortable. Also camping, US$15, and day visits US$5.

$$ Pousada do Sol
R Gumercindo Barbosa 911, T062-3446 1201, http://pousadadosolaltoparaiso.blogspot.co.uk.
Small and simple, with a range of rooms, the best with balconies and fridges, nice grounds with fruit trees, good breakfast, good value.

São Jorge
There are some 45 *pousadas* and various campsites in this little village but advance booking is indispensable at holidays. Hotel prices often go up 30% at weekends and food is expensive at all times.

$$$$-$$$ Baguá
Up the hill on the road to national park, T062-3455 1046, www.baguapousada.com.br.
Gorgeous bungalows, each with its own porch and outdoor jacuzzi, hammocks, fans, lovely ample grounds, all very tasetefully done, a real gem.

$$$$-$$$ Casa das Flores
T062-3455 1055, www.pousada casadasflores.com.br.
Elegant, tastefully decorated rooms (candle-lit), a/c and fan, hammocks, massage and therapies, sauna, pool, restaurant, great breakfast.

$$$ Bambu
T062-3455 1004, www.bambu brasil.com.br.
Roooms with fan and hammocks, nice grounds, breakfast, restaurant, attentive service.

$$$-$$ Áquas de Março
T062-99962 2082, www.chapada dosveadeiros.com.br.
A range of rooms and prices, older smaller ones are good value, decorations by local artists, pleasant garden, saunas, good breakfast, helpful. Recommended.

$$ Casa Grande
T062-3446 1388, www.pousada casagrande.com.br.
Simple but well looked after, electric shower, fan, breakfast.

$$ Trilha Violeta
T062-3455 1088, www.trilhavioleta.com.br.
Fan, frigobar, rooms around a bougainvillea filled garden, hammocks, includes breakfast.

Cavalcante

$$$-$$ Sol da Chapada
R Borba Gato, 100 m from tourist office at
lower end of town, T062-3494 1372, www.
soldachapada.com.br.
Comfortable chalets with fan, nice grounds,
breakfast and excellent organic restaurant (daily
1300-2000), attentive owner. Recommended.

$$ Aruana
Uphill from Praça da Bíblia, T062-3494 1562,
www.aruanacavalcante.com.br.
Includes breakfast, rooms with fan and solar
hot water, nice common areas, ample grounds,
therapies arranged, long-stay discounts.

$$ Pioneiro
At the petrol station on Praça Diogo Cavalcante,
T062-3494 1125.
Rooms with a/c, electric shower, helpful, good
value but no breakfast.

Parque Nacional Emas

Mineiros

$$$ Pilões Palace
Praça Alves de Assis, T064-3661 1547.
Restaurant, comfortable, a/c, fridge.

Other hotels: $$$ Dallas (www.dallashotel.com.
br), and $$-$ América (R 18, Q 4, Bairra Santa
Isabel, T064-3661 5089). Dorm accommodation at
the park headquarters; kitchen and cook available
but bring own food.

Restaurants

Goiânia
Goiânian specialities include dishes made with
pequí (a local fruit, careful not to bite the seed
which has spines), guariroba (a type of palm
heart), peixe na telha, and emapadão (a savoury
pie, best at Alberto's and other stalls in the
Mercado Central, R 3 No 322). The city has a
good range of restaurants and bars, many in
the upscale setores Marista and Bueno (see
www.curtamais.com.br). Economy options
include the Mercado Central, and several
places near R 55 corner R 68.

$$$ Celsin & Cia
R 22 No 475 e R 15, http://celsinecia.com.br.
Evenings only except at weekends.
Very popular Goiás and Mineira meat restaurant
with a good cold buffet.

$$$ Chão Nativo
Av Rep Líbano 1809, also at Av T11 e T4, Setor
Bueno, www.restaurantechaonativo.com.br.
The city's most famous Goiânian restaurant also
serving local and Mineira food. Lively after 2000
and lunchtime on weekends.

$$$ Piquiras
R 146 No 464, Setor Marista, several other
locations, www.piquiras.com.
Fine dining with a wide range of Brazilian dishes.

$$$ Walmor
R 3 1062 at R 25-B, www.churrascariado
walmor.com.br.
Large portions of some of Brazil's best steaks,
attractive open-air dining area, best after 2000.

$$$-$$ Pizzaria Cento e Dez
R 3 No 1000, T062-3225 5070, http://centoedez.
com.br. Daily 1100-1400, 1800-2400.
Traditional pizzeria and Italian dishes,
home delivery.

$$ Bendita Tapioca
Alameda dos Buritis 88,
www.benditatapioca.com.br.
Per kilo lunch and à la carte at night.

Cidade de Goiás

$$$ Dali
R 13 de Maio 26, T062-3372 1640.
Tue-Sun 1200-1330.
Riverside restaurant offering a broad range of
international and local dishes.

$$$ Flor do Ipê
Praça da Boa Vista 32, T062-3372 1133.
Tue-Sun 1100-1430, 1900-late.
The best Goiânian food, enormous variety, buffet
lunch and à la carte at night, lovely
garden setting. Highly recommended.

$$ O Braseiro
Praça Brasil Caiado 03.
In a colonial house, good Goiânian specialities,
buffet served on a wood stove.

$$-$ Espaço Ouro Fino
Praça do Coreto. Lunch only, closed Tue-Wed.
Good value for varied Brazilian food.

Pirenópolis
There are plenty of upmarket options along
R do Rosário, serving a surprising range of
international food. Many have live music at night
(and an undisclosed cover charge – be sure to
ask), lively at weekends. For economy, try the

cafeteria upstairs in **Casa Melo** supermarket
(Av Sizenando Jayme 30, Mon-Sat 1100-1430).

$$$-$$ Deli-Deli
Ruia Barbosa 11. Daily 1230-1700,
open later on weekends.
Meat and vegetarian options, organic ingredients,
international dishes, German/Brazilian-run.

$$ Tilapa
R Direita, across from Igreja da Matriz.
Open 1200-1600, closed Wed.
Very good buffet with fish specialities,
nice fruit juices. Recommended.

Pireneus Café
Praça do Coreto. Mon-Thu 1500-2300,
Fri-Sun 0900-0100.
Café in a traditional home, also sidewalk seating,
pleasant place to watch the world go by.

Sorvetes Naturais
R Nova 16. Daily 0800-2100.
Good locally made ice cream.

Festivals

Goiânia
Events are listed in www.emgoiania.com.
The following are alternative rock festivals
with some international participation.
May Bananada.
Nov-Dec Goiania Noise, www.goianianoise
festival.com.br.

Cidade de Goiás
Many festivals here and a very lively arts scene.
Feb/Mar Carnaval is a good deal more joyous
and still little known to outsiders.
Mar/Apr 3 weeks of religious events precede
Easter. The streets blaze with torches during the
solemn **Fogaréu** procession on the Wed of Holy
Week, when hooded figures re-enact Christ's
descent from the cross and burial.

Pirenópolis
May/Jun Festa do Divino Espírito Santo,
50 days after Easter (Pentecost), is one of Brazil's
most famous and extraordinary folkloric/
religious celebrations. It lasts 3 days, with
medieval costumes, tournaments, dances and
mock battles between Moors and Christians,
a tradition held annually since 1819. The whole
city throbs with life.

Shopping

Goiânia
Crafts at the **Centro do Artesanato** (R 1 near
Praça Cívica); and **Mercado Central** (R 3 No 322).

Cidade de Goiás
Local ceramics are sold at the tourist information
office and next to Igreja do Rosário. Candied fruit
is a regional speciality.

Pirenópolis
There are many jewellers on, R do Rosário.
Craft fair by Praça do Coreto, Sat evening
and Sun daytime. **Municipal craft shop** on
R do Bomfim. Many craft shops on R do Rosário
and on R Rui Barbosa.

What to do

Goiânia
Travel agents in town can arrange day tours.
Ararauna Turismo, *R C-143 esq T-63, Ed Janaína*
No 876, Jardim América, T062-3932-2277, www.
ararauna.tur.br. For city and regional tours.

Cidade de Goiás
Serra Dourada Aventura, *no fixed office,*
reachable on T062-3371 2277 or T062-99238 5195.
Hiking in the Serra Dourada and bespoke trips to
the wilds of the Rio Araguaia (with notice). Very
good value.

Pirenópolis
Morro Alto, *R Direita 71, T062-3331 3348,*
www.morroalto.tur.br. Run by Mauro Cruz.

Chapada dos Veadeiros
Most tour operators are in Alto Paraíso, but
guides also available in São Jorge, Cavalcante and
Engenho II (in the Kalunga Reserve). Prices vary
according to season and group number.
Alternativas Ecoturismo, *uphill Av Ary Ribeiro*
Veladão, T062-3446 1000, www.alternativas.tur.br.
Light adventure activities and treks, run by locals,
excellent and really go out of the way to help.
English-speaking guides available.
EcoRotas, *R das Nascentes 129, T062-3446 1820,*
www.ecorotas.com.br. Van-based tours to the
principal sights. Suitable for all ages.
Transchapada Ecoturismo, *R dos Cristais,*
T062-3446 1345, www.transchapada.com.br.
Light adventure and visits to the major sights.

Travessia, *Av Ary Ribeiro Veladão, T062-3446 1595, www.travessia.tur.br*. Short or long treks, plus adventure sports from one of the country's most respected instructors, Ion David. Little English.

Transport

Goiânia

Air Santa Genoveva, 6 km northeast off Rua 57, T062-3265 1500. Flights to many state capitals. Taxi to centre US$13.50, to *rodoviária* US$10; bus to centre, Linha 258, US$1, 30 mins. Note that Setor Aeroporto is a central district nowhere near the airport.

Bus *Rodoviária* in Araguaia Shopping, Setor Norte Ferroviário, 40-min walk from Praça Cívica (T062-3240 0000). Taxi to centre US$5; many buses to centre (US$1) including Linha 002 and 003 along Av Goiás. If arriving from the west, you can get off at the small Rodoviária de Campinas and take the Eixão rapid transit line (US$0.50) to the centre, easier with luggage than a bus from the main *rodoviária*.

To **Brasília**, 207 km, at least 15 departures a day, 2½ hrs, US$11-16, and **São Paulo**, 900 km via Barretos, US$51-70, 14½ hrs. To **Cidade de Goiás**, 136 km, hourly 0600-1600 with **Moreira**, direct 1200, 1800, 2000, 2-3 hrs, US$12. **Pirenópolis** with **Goianésia**, see below. To **Campo Grande**, US$31-69. To **Porto Velho**, US$80, 36-38 hrs. To **Belo Horizonte**, US$48-55, 13 hrs.

Cidade de Goiás

Bus The *rodoviária* is 1 km out of town. Regular services to **Goiânia** (2½ hrs), **Aruanã**, **Barra do Garças** and **Jussara**. Some buses stop at the old bus station by the market. Ask to get out here. For Pirenópolis, change in Goiânia.

Pirenópolis

Bus To/from **Brasília** with **Goianésia**, 4 a day, US$10-50, 3 hrs. Same company to **Goiânia** 0915 daily, US$7.25, 3 hrs, return 1700; or change in Anápolis, frequent service, US$2.50.

Chapada dos Veadeiros

Alto Paraíso: to **Brasília** buses pass through around 0740 (to Rodoviária do Plano Piloto), 1330 (to Interestadual), 1600 (to Plano Piloto), US$17, 3-4 hrs, but often delayed. From Brasília some buses (eg **Santo Antônio**, see São Jorge and Cavalcante below) leave from Rodoviária do Plano Piloto, others from Rodoviária Interestadual. Private shared taxis to Brasília from bakery behind *rodoviária* leave when full daily 0630-0830, US$20 to either *rodoviária*, and to other destinations such as the airport. To **São Jorge**, Santo Antônio passes Alto Paraíso around 1630, US$2, 1 hr. To **Cavalcante**, Santo Antônio passes around 1100, US$12, 1½ hrs. To **Palmas** with **Real Expresso**, 1 daily. **São Jorge**: To **Brasília** (Rodoviária do Plano Piloto) via Alto Paraíso, **Santo Antônio** passes around 0700, US$20, 6-7 hrs; from Brasília at 1230. **Cavalcante**: To **Brasília** (Rodoviária do Plano Piloto) via Alto Paraíso, at 1500, US$20, 6-7 hrs; from Brasília at 0700 daily.

Parque Nacional Emas

Bus Twice weekly from **Mineiros**. From **Campo Grande**, take a bus to Costa Rica (6½ hrs) and arrange transport from there (see page 660).

Tocantins

a state with stunning scenery

To the north of Goiás, and extracted from that state in 1988, is Tocantins, dominated by vast rivers, *cerrado* forests and, increasingly, soya plantations. Early attempts at regional autonomy date from colonial times, but creation of the new state was largely the work of José Wilson Siqueira Campos, who became its first governor. He is prominently featured in many of the state capital's grandiose monuments. Although new to tourism Tocantins has some stunning scenery and is the only state in the country to have Amazonian forest, Pantanal, *cerrado* forest and sertão

Jalapão

The greatest draw is Jalapão, a Brazilian Outback of vast *cerrado*-covered plains with massive table-top mountains cut by fast-flowing, clear-water rivers and thundering waterfalls. Wind-sculpted dunes form at the base of crumbling sandstone cliffs and plentiful wildlife includes maned wolf, puma, Brazilian merganser, hyacinth- and Spix's-macaw. Here too is the Afro-Brazilian village of Mombuca, whose residents produce unique crafts from *capim dourado*, the golden-sheened flower stalk of an endemic plant. As yet little known outside Brazil, Jalapão is among the great natural wonders of South America but it is not easy to visit. The closest towns are **Ponte Alta do Tocantins** and **Mateiros**, both have hotels and limited public transport but distances to and between attractions can be over 100 km with no public transport. You must have your own vehicle (carry spare fuel, water and all supplies), or take an excursion from Palmas (see What to do, below) which start around US$410-510 per person for three to five days. The area receives a growing number of Brazilian tourists and visitor sites get crowded at major holidays.

Natividade

In the southeast of Tocantins, 200 km from Palmas along the road to Brasília, is the colonial town of Natividade, nestled at the base of the eponymous 500-m-high serra. The town has restored churches and brightly coloured houses set around neat little plazas, a small **Museu Histórico** and a relaxed, authentic atmosphere.

Ilha do Bananal

Along the western border of the state is Ilha do Bananal, the world's largest river island (20,000 sq km), bounded by the Rios Araguaia and Javaé. The island contains an indigenous reserve in the south and two parks in the north (**Parque Nacional Araguaia** and **Parque Estadual do Cantão**) all very rich in birds and other fauna. There are several permanent lakes, marshland areas and seasonally flooded habitats similar to those of the Pantanal. Tours are offered by agencies in Palmas, or you can travel to **Lagoa da Confusão** or **Formoso do Araguaia** and hire guides there (eg Sra Raimunda, Lagoa da Confusão, T063-99265 7341; US$275 for an all-inclusive tour). CC Trekking ① T063-3379 1016/8405 5011, www.cctrekking.com.br, based in Caseara, specializes in trips to **Parque Estadual do Cantão** and the meeting of the Cerrado, Amazon and Pantanal biomes, from one-day trips to six-day expeditions.

Palmas

The capital of Tocantins is Palmas, a planned city laid out in an utterly incomprehensible mathematical plan on the edge of the dammed and flooded Tocantins river. Brazil's newest state capital can be hot, humid and hard on pedestrians, but sunsets are gorgeous and people very friendly. There are beaches on the Rio Tocantins, 4 km from the centre, and many waterfalls in the Serra de Lajeado reached from Taquaruçu, 32 km from Palmas and busy at weekends, www.taquarussu.com. **Tourist offices:** CATUR ① at airport, T063-3219 3760/2111 2773, daily 1000-1730; and on Av JK e 103 Norte Av NS 01, T063-2111 0213, Mon-Fri 0800-1800, turismo.palmas@gmail.com. Also at Taquaruçu.

Listings Tocantins

Where to stay

Natividade

$$ Pousada dos Sertões
Av Justino Camelo Rocha 100, 1 km from centre on the road to Dianópolis, T063-3372 1182.
Rooms with bath and a/c, cheaper with fan, parking.

$$-$ Pousada do César
Av Filadélfia Nunes, Q 52 lote 19, downhill from the colonial centre, T063-3372 1353.
Clean simple rooms with bath and a/c, cheaper with fan, breakfast, parking, family-run, also has a *churrascaría* nearby.

Palmas

Palmas is well supplied with hotels but cheaper places (many around Quadras 103 Norte and Sul) are often full.

$$$ Pousada das Artes
103 Sul, Av LO-1 No 78, T063-3219 1500, www.arteshotel.com.br.
Very comfortable rooms with marble and mosaic bathrooms, frigobar, small pool, sauna, gym, bar, tasteful decor, good breakfast, other meals available, cash discounts.

$$$ Pousada dos Girassóis
103 Sul, Av NS 1, T063-3212 0202, www.pousadadosgirassois.com.br.
Comfortable rooms, pool, good breakfast, more expensive ones have balconies. 2nd location 3 blocks away, T3212 0200, more modern and expensive, also with pool, gym and restaurant.

$$ Graciosa Palace
103 Norte, NO-1 No 19, T063-3225 8688, www.hotelgraciosa.com.br.

Rooms around a small courtyard, breakfast, simple and pleasant.

$$-$ Alfredu's
Av JK 103 Sul, Qd 101, lotes 23/24, T063-3215 3036.
Simple rooms around a garden courtyard, cheaper with fan, breakfast, helpful, good value. Trips arranged.

Restaurants

Palmas
Fish specialities are served at river beaches on weekends. For economy options in the centre try kiosks around Av JK corner Theotônio Segurado.

$$ Paço do Pão
103 Sul, Av JK, T063-3215 5665.
Open 1900-2400, closed Tue.
Wood-oven pizza with home delivery.

Açaí.com
604 Sul, Av Lo 15, 24, T063-3214 1234.
Daily 1700-2300.
Açaí palm fruit in various forms, sidewalk seating, cool and refreshing in the tropical heat.

What to do

Palmas
Most Palmas agencies do not have storefronts, contact in advance by email or phone.
40 Graus no Cerrado (T063-3215 8313, www.40grausnocerrado.com.br), Diego Sommer, English and Spanish spoken. Jalapão trips cover a great deal of distance and involve much driving, minimum 4 days recommended.
Korubo Expedicoes, *São Paulo T011-4063 1502, or 98222 5028, www.korubo.com.br.* Excellent tours to Jalapão staying in their luxurious purpose-built safari camp, modelled on those in Botswana; whitewater kayaking, trekking, jeep trips and wildlife tours included in the price. Professional, reliable.

Transport

Air Airport is 23 km from the centre, taxi US$28 or take 'Eixão' bus from centre and transfer to Linha 46 which runs hourly, US$2 total. Flights to **Brasília**, **Goiânia**, **São Paulo**, **Belo Horizonte** and **Belém**.

Bus *Rodoviária* is very far from centre, taxi US$24, or 'Eixão' and transfer to Linha 23, allow 1-2 hrs. Bus services to Goiânia (Transbrasiliana and Catedral), US$26-48, São Paulo, Salvador and Belém. Several vans run daily to Natividade. **Tranbrasiliana** passes through Natividade en route to **Goiânia** around 1900, US$36, 12 hrs. Palmas to **Lagoa da Confusão** (for Ilha do Bananal) with **Tocantinense** at 0600 and 1530, US$12, 4 hrs, poor road; also van service daily at 0900, T063-3215 2111, will pick up from hotel.

The Pantanal

★This vast wetland, which covers a staggering 21,000 sq km (the size of Belgium, Portugal, Switzerland and Holland combined), between Cuiabá, Campo Grande and the Bolivian frontier, is one of the world's great wildlife preserves. Parts spill over into Bolivia, Paraguay and Argentina to form an area totalling some 100,000 sq km. Partly flooded in the rainy season (see below), the Pantanal is a mecca for wildlife tourism or fishing. Whether land or river-based, seasonal variations make a great difference to the practicalities of getting there and what you will experience. A road runs across Mato Grosso do Sul via Campo Grande to Porto Esperança and Corumbá, both on the Rio Paraguai; much of the road is across the wetland, offering many sights of birds and other wildlife.

The ecosystem

a vast tropical wetland

The Pantanal plain slopes some 1 cm in every kilometre north to south and west to east to the basin of the Rio Paraguai and is rimmed by low mountains. One hundred and seventy five rivers flow from these into the Pantanal and after the heavy summer rains they burst their banks, as does the Paraguai itself; to create vast shallow lakes broken by patches of high ground and stands of *cerrado* forest. Plankton then swarm to form a biological soup that contains as many as 500 million microalgae per litre. Millions of amphibians and fish spawn or migrate to consume them. And these in turn are preyed upon by waterbirds and reptiles. Herbivorous mammals graze on the stands of water hyacinth, sedge and savanna grass and at the top of the food chain lie South America's great predators – the jaguar, ocelot, maned wolf and yellow anaconda.

In June after the wet season, when the sheets of water have reduced to small lakes or canals wildlife concentrates and then there is nowhere on earth where you will see such vast quantities of birds or such enormous numbers of crocodilians. Only the plains of Africa can compete for mammals and your chances of seeing a jaguar or one of Brazil's seven other species of wild cat are greater here than anywhere else on the continent.

There are over 700 resident and migratory bird species in the Pantanal and birding along the Transpantaneira road in the north or in one of the fazendas in the south can yield as many as 100 species a day; especially between late June and early October. Many species overlap with the Amazon region, the Cerrado and Chaco and the area is particularly rich in waterbirds.

Although the Pantanal is often described as an ecosystem in its own right, it is in reality made up of many distinct habitats which in turn have their own, often distinct biological communities. Botanically it is a mosaic, a mixture of elements from the Amazon region including *várzea* and gallery forests (*mata ciliar*) and tropical savanna, the *cerrado* of central Brazil and the dry *chaco* of Paraguay.

Best for
Fishing ▪ Horse riding ▪ Wildlife

Essential The Pantanal

Finding your feet

Only one area is officially a national park, the Parque Nacional do Pantanal Matogrossense in the municipality of Poconé, 135,000 ha of land and water, only accessible by air or river. Obtain permission to visit the park at **ICMBio**, Caixa Postal 8005, Cuiabá, CEP 78048-970, T061-3341 9710, parnapantanal@icmbio.gov.br. Hunting in any form is strictly forbidden throughout the Pantanal and is punishable by four years imprisonment. Fishing is allowed with a licence (enquire at travel agents for latest details); it is not permitted in the spawning season or piracema (1 October-1 February in Mato Grosso do Sul, 1 November-1 March in Mato Grosso).

Getting there

There are three options for visiting the Pantanal: by tour, through a working ranch (fazenda) or by self-drive. Entry into the northern Pantanal comes either via the Transpantaneira road in the north, reached from the city of Cuiabá, which cuts through the wetland and is lined with fazendas, or the town of Barão do Melgaço which is surrounded by large lakes and rivers and is not as good for wildlife. Coxim on the Rio Taquari is the best entry point in the central Pantanal. In the south the main access points are Campo Grande, for arranging tours, Aquidauana and Miranda, which offers access to many of the fazendas. Fazendas in the northern or southern Pantanal can also be booked directly; most now have websites and a tour of them can be taken with a hire car.

When to go

The Pantanal is good for seeing wildlife year-round. The dry season between July and October is the ideal time as animals and birds congregate at the few remaining areas of water. During these months you are very likely to see jaguars. This is the nesting and breeding season, when birds form vast nesting areas, with thousands crowding the trees, creating an almost insupportable cacophony of sounds. The white sand river beaches are exposed, caiman bask in the sun, and capybaras frolic amid the grass. July sees lots of Brazilian visitors who tend to be noisy, decreasing the chances of sightings. From the end of November to the end of March (wettest in February), most of the area, which is crossed by many rivers, floods. At this time mosquitoes abound and cattle crowd on to the few islands remaining above water. In the southern part, many wild animals leave the area, but in the north, which is slightly higher, the animals do not leave. As the wet season coincides with the piracema (see above) there are no fishing boats on the rivers, which makes for peaceful boat tours as well as good wildlife watching. Note that seasons are becoming less predictable. A good tour operator will adapt trips according to the weather.

Types of tour

Tourist facilities in the Pantanal currently cater to four main categories of visitors. Sport fishermen usually stay at one of the numerous speciality lodges scattered throughout the region, which provide guides, boats, bait, ice and other related amenities. Bookings can be made locally or in any of Brazil's major cities.

All-inclusive tours combining air and ground transportation, accommodation at the most elaborate fazendas, meals, guided river and land tours, can be arranged from abroad or through Brazilian travel agencies. This is the most expensive option.

Moderately priced tours using private guides, camping or staying at more modest fazendas can be arranged in Cuiabá (where guides await arrivals at the airport) for the northern Pantanal, and Campo Grande, for budget tours, or Miranda for the southern Pantanal. Corumbá, once the region's backpacker capital, has now reverted to its status as a border town, but many boat tour operators are based there. For those with the minimum of funds, a glimpse of the Pantanal and its wildlife can be had on the bus ride from Campo Grande to Corumbá, by lodging or camping near the Porto Esperança crossing over the Rio Paraguai, or by staying in Poconé and day-walking or hitching south along the Transpantaneira.

Choosing a tour

Most tours combine 'safari' jeep trips, river-boat trips, piranha fishing and horse riding with accommodation in lodges. Excursions often take place at sunset and sunrise as these are the best times for spotting bird and wildlife. Choose an agency or fazenda with care. Not all act responsibly or professionally. Be aware that cut price operators tend to cut corners and pay their staff very low wages. We list the best operators and consider those in Cuiabá (for the north) and Miranda (for the south) to be best. Many operators offer an increasingly interesting range of trips, including hard-core camping safaris, photo workshops and indigenous culture exchanges.

The Pantanal faces many threats to its integrity, such as illegal hunting, poaching, overfishing, land clearance and pollution from agrochemicals and goldminers' mercury from the neighbouring planalto. Visitors can make an important contribution to protecting the area by acting responsibly and choosing guides accordingly. Take your rubbish away with you, don't fish out of season, don't let guides kill or disturb fauna, don't buy products made from threatened or endangered species (including macaw-feather jewellery), don't buy live birds or monkeys and report any violation to the authorities. The practice of catching caiman, even though they may then be released, is traumatic for the animals and has potentially disruptive long-term effects.

What to take

Most tours arrange for you to leave your baggage in town, so you need only bring what is necessary for the duration of the tour. In winter (June-August), temperatures fall to 10° C, warm clothing and covers or sleeping bag are needed at night. It's very hot and humid during summer and a hat and sun protection, SPF 30 or above, is vital. Wear long sleeves and long trousers and spray clothes as well as skin with insect repellent. Insects are less of a problem July-August. Take insect repellent from home as mosquitoes, especially in the North Pantanal, are becoming immune to local brands. Yellow and dengue fevers are both present in Mato Grosso do Sul. Get your yellow fever immunization at home. Drinks are not included in the price of packages and tend to be overpriced, so if you are on a tight budget take your own. Most importantly, make sure you take a pair of binoculars.

Campo Grande *Colour map 7, B1.*

Capital of the State of Mato Grosso do Sul. It was founded in 1899. It is a pleasant, modern city. Because of the terra roxa (red earth), it is called the 'Cidade Morena'. In the centre is a shady park, the **Praça República**, commonly called the Praça do Rádio after the Rádio Clube on one of its corners. Three blocks west is **Praça Ary Coelho**. Linking the two squares, and running through the city east to west, is Avenida Afonso Pena; much of its central reservation is planted with yellow and pink ypé trees. Their blossom covers the avenue, and much of the city besides, in spring. The other main east-west artery is Avenida Mato Grosso.

The municipal tourist secretariat is Sectur ① *R Brasil 464, Monte Castelo, T067-3314 3227, www.pmcg.ms.gov.br,* which has **Centros de Atendimento ao Turista (CAT)** throughout the city, including: **airport** ① *T067-3363 3116, daily 0700-2300,* and **rodoviária** ① *T067-3382 2350, Mon-Fri 0600-2200, Sat-Sun 0630-2130;* in the historic building and exhibition centre **Morada dos Baís** ① *Av Noroeste 5140, T067-3314 9968, Tue-Sat 0800-1800, Sun 0900-1200;* at the **Feira Central market** ① *R 14 de Julho 3351, Wed-Sun 1800-2200* (see Restaurants, page 655); **Shopping Campo Grande;** and others. **Fundtur** ① *Av Afonso Pena 7000, Portal Guarani, T067-3318 7600, www.turismo.ms.gov.br,* the state tourist office, is in the **Parque das Nações Indígenas**.

Some distance from the centre is the large **Parque dos Poderes**, which contains the Palácio do Governo and other secretariats, paths and lovely trees. Even larger, and closer to the centre, is the 119-ha **Parque das Nações Indígenas**. It is largely covered with grassy areas and ornamental trees and is a pleasant place for a stroll or quiet read and has good birdlife. In the park is the **Museu de Arte Contemporânea (MARCO)** ① *R Antônio Maria Coelho 6000, T067-3326 7449, https://marcovirtual.wordpress.com, Tue-Fri 1200-1800, Sat-Sun 1400-1800, free.* This preserves the largest collection of modern art in the state; permanent and temporary exhibitions. **Museu Dom Bosco (Indian Museum)** ① *Av Afonso Pena 7000, Parque das Nações Indígenas, T067-3326 9788, www.mcdb.org.br, Tue-Sun 0800-1630, US$2.65,* contains relics from the various tribes who were the recipients of the

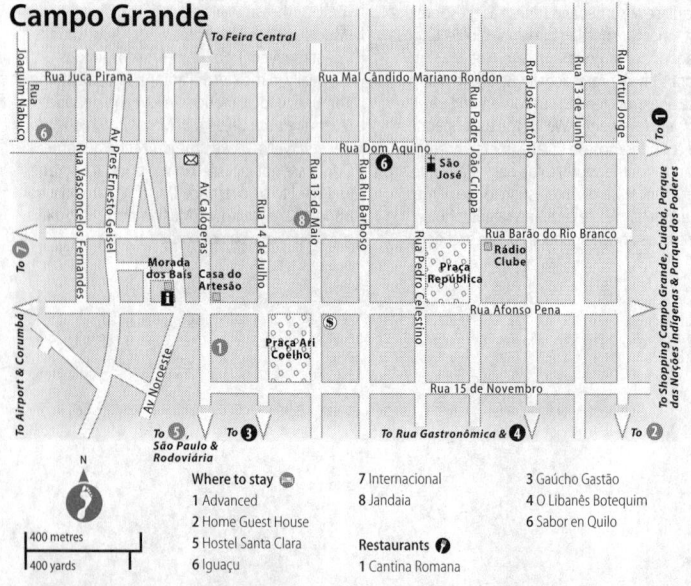

Campo Grande

Where to stay
1 Advanced
2 Home Guest House
5 Hostel Santa Clara
6 Iguaçu
7 Internacional
8 Jandaia

Restaurants
1 Cantina Romana
3 Gaúcho Gastão
4 O Libanès Botequim
6 Sabor en Quilo

Salesians aggressive missionary tactics in the early and mid-20th century. The largest collections are from the Tukano and Bororo people from the Upper Rio Negro and Mato Grosso respectively, both of whose cultures the Salesians were responsible for almost completely wiping out. It also holds temporary exhibitions.

Bonito *Colour map 6, B6.*

The municipality of Bonito, 248 km from Campo Grande, is in the Serra do Bodoquena. It is surrounded by beautiful *cerrado* forest by clear-water rivers rich with fish and dotted with plunging waterfalls and deep caves. It has become Brazil's foremost ecotourism destination; which, in Brazilian terms, means that families come here to romp around in Nature: from light adventure activities like caving to gentle rafting and snorkelling, all with proper safety measures and great even for small children. Despite the heavy influx of visitors plenty of wildlife appears around the trails when it's quiet. The wet season is January to February; December to February is hottest, July to August the coolest. High seasons, when prices rise and pre-booking is essential, are January, Carnaval, Easter, 1-3 May, July, 4-7 September, 10-13 October, 19-31 December. **Tourist office:** Comtur/Sectur ① *R Cel Pilad Rebud 1780, T067-3255 1351, www.turismo.bonito.ms.gov.br (no English spoken), Mon-Fri 0730-1130, 1330-1700. See also www.portalbonito.com.br.* There are ATMs at **Banco do Brasil** ① *Av Coronel Pilad Rebuá 1900 block, by R Sen F Muller,* on the Praça and **Bradesco.**

Bonito is expensive for those on a budget. All the attractions in the area can only be visited with prior purchase of a voucher at a travel agent (of which there are over 50). The sites are nearly all on private land and must by visited with a guide. Owners also enforce limits on the number of daily visitors. Wetsuits are provided for snorkelling and diving activities, when you are not allowed to use sunscreen or insect repellent. Some of the sites are in Bodoquena, others in Jardim, but all are sold as tours from Bonito. As taxis are exorbitant, it is best to book with one of the agencies that offers tours and transport, or check with Terratransportes and Vanzella (see Transport, page 657).

There are about 40 sites and agencies have a full list with prices. Some 26 km from Bonito is **Lago Azul.** The cave is named after a lake 50 m long and 110 m wide, 75 m below ground level. The water, 20°C, is a jewel-like blue as light from the opening is refracted through limestone and magnesium. Prehistoric animal bones have been found in the lake. The light is at its best January-February, 0700-0900, but is fine at other times. A 25-ha park surrounds the cave. Entry costs US$12 (16 high season), half day. Other caves to visit are **Abismo Anhumas** ① *Fazenda Anhumas, Estrada para Campo dos Indios s/n, T067-3255 3313, http://abismoanhumas.com.br, only 20 visitors per day,* with a glassy pool. The ticket, US$168, permits abseiling into the cave, followed by three to four hours snorkelling or scuba diving. And **Grutas de São Miguel** ① *Estrada para Campo dos Indios 16 km (12 km from the centre), US$12,* a dry cave with numerous bats, albino owls and impressive cave formations entered along a vertiginous hanging bridge.

The **Balneário Municipal** ① *7 km on road to Jardim, US$6-8,* on the Rio Formoso, with changing rooms, toilets, camping, swimming in clear water, plenty of fish to see (strenuous efforts are made to keep the water and shore clean). At the **Parque Ecológico Rio Formoso:** there are various activities, including kayaks, SUP, snorkelling, rafting and riding; prices from US$19-23 per activity. The **Aquário Natural** ① *8 km on road to Jardim, open 0900-1800, US$46-51 half day,* is one of the springs of the Rio Formoso. You can swim and snorkel with five types of fish. A similar excursion is to the Rio da Prata in Jardim (a friendly town, with similar attractions to Bonito, www.jardim. ms.gov.br), a full day trip with a 40-minute walk to the source of the Rio Olho D'Agua where you snorkel for about 2000 m, followed by 600 m on the **Rio da Prata** ① *50 km from Bonito, US$38-47, lunch US$11 if not on voucher.* Also in Jardim is the **Buraco das Araras** ① *54 km from Bonito, US$15.50, guided tour 1 hr 20 mins, hats provided, shop, helpful staff,* a 120-m deep, 500-m circumference sink hole in a patch of Cerrado forest which is home to many pairs of red and green macaws and other birds. Other tours are: from the springs of the Rio Sucuri to its meeting with the Formoso (US$42-49, lunch extra), about 2 km of crystal-clear water, with swimming or snorkelling, birdwatching, very peaceful; horse riding; canyoning and waterfalls; and scuba diving.

Ponta Porã *Colour map 7, B1.*

There is a paved road from Campo Grande to the Paraguayan border to Ponta Porã, separated from Pedro Juan Caballero in Paraguay only by a broad avenue. With paved streets, good public transport and smart shops, Ponta Porã is more prosperous than its neighbour, although Brazilians cross the border to play the casino and visit the shops. In addition to the free movement of people and goods, the blending of cultures here is impressive. There are many Brasiguayos with one parent of each nationality and Portoñol is the common tongue. There are many banks on Avenida Brasil (one block back from the border) with ATMs but no exchange facilities; many *cambios* on the Paraguayan side.

Border with Paraguay There are no border posts between the two towns. The **Brazilian Polícia Federal** ① *Av Pres Vargas 70, ½ block back from the border street, T067-3437 0500, Mon-Fri 0730-1130, 1330-1730*, is closed weekends but officers on duty might provide an entry stamp if you are on a bus that is passing through. The **Paraguayan consulate** ① *Av Pres Vargas 277, Ponta Porã, T067-3431 6312, pontaporaconsulpar@mre.gov.py*, does not issue visas, the nearest ones that do are in São Paulo, Curitiba and Foz do Iguaçu. Check requirements carefully, and ensure your documents are in order: without the proper stamps you will inevitably be sent back somewhere later on in your travels. Taking a taxi between offices can speed things up if pressed for time; drivers know border crossing requirements; US$10.

There are two more border crossings to Paraguay west of Ponta Porã, Bela Vista and Porto Murtinho. They are best reached from Jardim, 1½ hours by bus to the former (www.cruzeirodosulms. com.br), three hours minimum to the latter. Neither has Brazilian immigration facilities so if you wish to use these crossings you must get stamps etc in Ponta Porã, Campo Grande or Corumbá. Both Bela Vista, opposite Bela Vista, and Capitán Carmelo Peralta, across the river from Porto Murtinho, have Paraguayan customs and immigration. See the Paraguay chapter for details.

Campo Grande to Corumbá

BR-262 is paved from Campo Grande to Corumbá and the Bolivian border. The scenery is marvellous. Some 200 km west of Campo Grande is **Miranda**, where a road heads south to Bodoquena and Bonito. As a gateway to the Pantanal and Bonito, it is far closer to both than either Corumbá or Campo Grande. The best of the southern Pantanal tour operators are here and there are good *fazendas* within easy reach. There is a cultural and arts centre of the local Terena communities opposite Zero Hora restaurant, by the main roundabout on BR-262, open daily, free.

To the southern Pantanal

Many tours out of Campo Grande and Miranda take a dirt road running off the BR-262 Campo Grande–Corumbá highway called the **Estrada Parque**. It begins halfway between Miranda and Corumbá at a turn off called **Buraco das Piranhas** (Piranha hole). Here there is a police post and a bar and information centre run by a man called Barba. He has been helping travellers for 15 years and can find accommodation at lodges if you have no reservation, has all transport details (see below) and knows all there is to know. The road heads north into the Pantanal and then, after 51 km, turns west to Corumbá at a point called the **Curva do Leque** (with Bar do Que Qué). This is the overland access point to **Nhecolândia**, a region rich in wildlife. There is a ferry across the Rio Paraguai at Porto da Manga: 0700-1700 daily, US$9.50 for a car. The Estrada rejoins the BR-262 at Lampião Aceso, south of Corumbá. There are several good *fazendas* off the Estrada Parque road.

Where to stay

Campo Grande

$$$$-$$$ Jandaia
R Barão do Rio Branco 1271, T067-3316 7700, www.jandaia.com.br.
The city's best hotel, aimed at a business market. Modern well-appointed rooms in a tower, pool, gym and some English spoken.

$$$ Advanced
Av Calógeras 1909, T067-3321 5000, www.hoteladvanced.com.br.
Spacious if spartan rooms with hot showers, in an 80s block, very small pool, cheaper with fan.

$$$ Internacional
Allan Kardec 223, T067-3384 4677, www.hotelintermetro.com.br.
Modern, on a quiet street, comfortable rooms with a/c or fan, some suites, small pool, restaurant.

\$\$ Iguaçu
R Dom Aquino 761, T067-3322 4621,
www.hoteliguacu.com.br.
\$ with fan. Very popular well-kept hotel with
smart, simple a/c rooms. Good breakfast.

\$\$-\$ Hostel Santa Clara
R Vítor Meirelles 125, T067-3384 3011,
www.pantanalsantaclara.com.br.
A pleasant hostel in a converted town house with
a/c doubles and dorms, a large garden 5 mins
from the *rodoviária*. Free airport pick-up, kitchen,
tour agency.

\$ Home Guest House
Travessa Alecrim 21, Centro, T067-99846 5373,
homereservas@gmail.com.
New guesthouse (2017) with private rooms for up
to 3 people, with bath, a/c and fridge, convenient
location; reserve in advance.

Bonito

\$\$\$ Pousada Muito Bonito
Pilad Rebuá 1444, T067-3255 3077,
www.pousadamuitobonito.com.br.
Well-appointed, bright white rooms, a/c, nice
patio, excellent, helpful owners, also with tour
company, staff speak English and Spanish).
Recommended.

\$\$\$ Pousada Olho d'Água
Rod Três Morros, Km 1, T067-3255 1430,
www.pousadaolhodagua.com.br.
Comfortable cabins with fan, some with kitchette
and veranda, set in a garden next to a small lake.
Solar-powered hot water and great food from
the vegetable garden. Recommended.

\$\$\$-\$\$ Gira Sol
R Pérsio Schamann 710, T067-3255 2677,
www.girasolbonito.com.br.
An attractive *pousada* with a small pool in a
garden 5 mins' walk from the centre. Bright,
spacious rooms with balconies, decent breakfast.

\$\$\$-\$\$ Pousada Rancho Jarinu
R 24 de Fevereiro 1895, T067-3255 2094,
www.pousadaranchojarinu.com.br.
Comfortable brick-lined rooms built around
a courtyard with plants and a fishpond,
good bathrooms, comfortable, parking.
Recommended.

\$\$\$-\$\$ Tapera
Rod Guia Lopes, Km 1, on hill above
Shell station on road to Jardim, T067-
3255 1700, www.taperahotel.com.br.

Fine views, cool breezes, peaceful, a/c, very
comfortable, roomsin newer block have balcony,
no restaurant, own transport an advantage, taxi
from town US\$4 or 20 mins' walk.

\$\$ Che Lagarto
R Antônio Alle 77 (opposite petrol station
and drive to Tapera), T067-3255 1559,
www.chelagarto.com.
Member of the South American group, private
doubles and en suite dorms (US\$13.25 pp), a/c,
modern, with pool, bar, kitchen and parking.

\$\$-\$ Pousada São Jorge
Av Col Pilad Rebuá 1605, T067-3255 4046,
www.pousadasaojorge.com.br.
Fully refurbished, 12 en suites and 2 shared rooms
(US\$10.25-13.25 pp), pleasant public dining area,
owner Felipe is very enthusiastic, speaks English,
also has travel agency, an urban camping site and
a glass-recycling project.

\$ Bonito Hostel
R Lúcio Borralho 716, T067-3255 1022,
www.ajbonito.com.br.
US\$10-12.25 pp in dorm, \$\$ doubles, HI-affiliated
hostel, cheaper for members, English spoken,
pool, laundry facilities, hot showers, secure
parking, rents bicycles, camping, tour agency
for Bonito and Pantanal trips. Sister hostel to the
Oka Brasil in Campo Grande.

Camping
There are several campsites in the vicinity,
including **Camping Rio Formoso** (Rodovia
Bonito/Guia Lopes Km 6, T067-9284 5994,
www.campingrioformoso.com.br), as well
as **Bonito Hostel** and **São Jorge**, above.

Ponta Porã

\$\$\$-\$\$ Barcelona
R Guia Lopes 45, T067-3437 2500,
www.hotelbarcelona.com.br.
Rooms with a/c or fan in a tower, bar and sauna.

\$\$ Guarujá
R Guia Lopes 63, T067-3431 9515.
With a/c and fridge, cheaper with fan, parking,
faded but functional.

\$\$ Pousada do Bosque
Av Pres Vargas 1151, T067-3437 7200,
www.hotelpousadadobosque.com.br.
'Fazenda style' with lovely grounds and pool,
sports fields, restaurant, parking, comfortable
rooms, midweek discounts.

Campo Grande to Corumbá: Miranda

$$$ Nativos
R Manoel R da Costa 59, T067-3242 1427,
pousadanativos@outlook.com.
Contemporary cabins with bedroom upstairs,
some with kitchenette, backpacker rooms,
distinctive decorations, away from centre
but not for from *rodoviária*, parking.

$$$ Pantanal
Av Barão do Rio Branco 609, T067-3242 1068.
Well-maintained, large a/c rooms with en suites,
a/c, swimming pools, regarded as best in town.

$$$-$$ Águas do Pantanal
Av Afonso Pena 367, T067-3242 1242,
www.aguasdopantanal.com.br.
In the town itself, with comfortable a/c rooms
and shared rooms for up to 6, good breakfast,
laundry service, attractive pool surrounded by
tropical flowers. Usually have a rep waiting at
the *rodoviária*.

$$ Diogo
Av Barão do Rio Branco 08, T067-3242 1468.
Simple but well-kept rooms on outside corridor,
ask for newer rooms, a/c, budget option.

$$ Karaguata Bed & Breakfast
R São Benedito 99, T067-99831 3038,
www.pantanalwilderness.com.
1 comfortable double room with a/c and ensuite,
kitchen, pool and garden, hammocks, use of
bicycles, welcoming, spacious. Tours can be
arranged with **Pantanal Wilderness** (see below),
several languages spoken.

To the southern Pantanal
Fazendas are located in 2 different zones, those in
the wetlands, reached from Aquidauana, Miranda
and the Estrada Parque, and those on the higher
ground near Miranda. The latter usually offer
tours to the rivers and wetlands at extra cost.

$$$$ Chácara Anis
Rodoviária Cerá 10, 79200-000 Aquidauana,
T067-3241 8312, www.brasil-pantanal.ch.
Working cattle ranch, Swiss-owned (Anne-Lyse
and Caspar Burn), lovely *pousada* offering up
to 7-night stays, several European languages
spoken, horse riding expeditions, wildlife
watching, tours arranged, swimming pool.

Near Miranda

$$$$ Refúgio Ecológico Caiman
36 km from Miranda, T067-3242 1450, T011-3706
1800 (São Paulo), www.caiman.com.br.

The most comfortable, stylish accommodation
in the Pantanal. Excellent tours and guiding.
Has 2 small lodges, Baiazinha and Cordilheira
(latter open in high season only or for private
groups). Check website for opening times and
contact details. It is headquarters of Onçafari,
jaguar habituation and research project, www.
projetooncafari.org, which allows guests to see
jaguars in an African safari-type environment.
The Arara Azul conservation project is also
based here.

$$$ Fazenda 23 de Março
T067-3321 4737, www.fazenda23demarco.com.br.
Charming working fazenda on the uplands,
swimming pool, restaurant, 6 rooms. Visitors
can turn their hand to cowboy activities (book
in advance), riding, walking trails for wildlife
spotting, birdwatching, day and night safaris.

$$$ Fazenda Baia Grande
Estr La Lima Km 19, T067-9984 6658,
www.fazendabaiagrande.com.br,
22 km from Miranda.
Very comfortable, 5 a/c rooms around a pool in a
garden, price is all-inclusive, all food produced on
the farm, bar, no TV. The fazenda is surrounded
by savanna and stands of *cerrado* for photo
safaris, guided birdwatching, riding. The owner,
Alex is very eager to please and enthusiastic,
English spoken.

$$$ Fazenda San Francisco
Turn off BR-262 30 km west of Miranda, T067-
3242 3333, www.fazendasanfrancisco.tur.br.
Simple rustic a/c cabins around a pool in a
garden filled with rheas. Food and guides
are excellent, but can be crowded with tour
groups. Several scientific projects take place
here, including GadOnça, for the study of wild
cats. Birdwatching is also excellent.

$$$ Rancho Meia Lua
BR-262 Km 547, east of Miranda, T067-9686 9064,
www.pantanalranchmeialua.com
Completely refurbished, 8 rooms set in gardens,
with pool, lunch and dinner extra, excursions
include riding, free bikes, night walks, fishing
in lake.

Núcleo Salvar a Vida
BR-262 Km 554, T067-99223714, https://
nucleoserviravida.com, 3 km from Miranda,
contact Miriam and Wagner.
A project based on sustainable principles with
recycling of all water, organic vegetables and
fruit, composting toilets, etc. Work with the

rehabilitation of former addicts. Guests can volunteer to work and can pay what they feel is appropriate. Bicycles to borrow to ride to town on a back road.

Estrada Parque

$$$$ Fazenda Xaraés
Estrada Parque, T067-99906 9272,
www.xaraes.com.br.
One of the most luxurious fazendas, with a pool, tennis court, sauna, air strip and surprisingly plain but well-appointed a/c rooms. The immediate environs have been extensively cleared, but there are some wild areas of savanna and *cerrado* nearby and there are giant otter in the neighbouring Rio Abobral.

$$$ Pantanal Jungle Lodge
7 km from Buraca das Piranhas by the bridge over Rio Miranda, T067-3242 1488,
reserve@pantanaljunglelodge.com.br.
New lodge with 12 rooms, 5 dorms and 1 room with disabled access, all a/c, fridge, all-inclusive, but meals can be paid for separately, TV room, bar, pool, laundry service, all guides speak English, 1-night packages include 5 activities, longer stays include 9-10 activities (canoeing, safaris day and night, on land and on water, fishing, swimming).

$$$ Passo do Lontra Parque Hotel
1.5 km from Estrada Parque, turn off just after Rio Miranda bridge, T067-3245 2407,
www.passodolontra.com.br.
Cabin blocks on stilts, also 4 dorm rooms, dining room with Wi-Fi, good food, all meals included, packages of 2 or more nights, day use also available, offers boat trips, but no walks. Walking and riding can be done at the same group's **$$$ Fazenda São João**, further along the Estrada Parque, which also has lodging and dining room.

$$$ Santa Clara
Estrada Parque Km 22, T067-9665 1394,
www.pantanalsantaclara.com.br.
A budget option for staying in a ranch house in the Southern Pantanal, on the banks of the Rio Abobral (where there's a community of giant otters), and with a pool, games areas, internet, double rooms and dorms, camping, full transfers from Campo Grande (where they have an office in the *rodoviária*, T067-3384 0583), full board and tours included.

Restaurants

Campo Grande
Local specialities
Caldo de piranha (soup), *chipa* (Paraguayan cheese bread), sold on streets, delicious when hot, and local liqueur, *pequi com caju*, which contains *cachaça*. The **Feira Central** (R 14 de Julho 3351, in the old railway station, www.feiracentralcg.com.br, Wed-Fri from 1600, Sat-Sun from 1200), has lots of foods to try, but the main dish is *sobá*, an Asian bowl of broth, noodles, onion and meat – there is even a statue of it outside – one of the don't misses of the city. There is also local produce on sale and goods imported from Bolivia and Paraguay. Av Bom Pastor, in Bairro Vilas Boas, is known as Rua Gastronômica with restaurants, pizzerias, bars and markets. There are many eating places in a/c surroundings in the **Shopping Campo Grande** mall (R Afonso Pena 4909) and the latest fashion is for "food trucks" selling self-styled gourmet food on the street.

$$$ Gaúcho Gastão
R Doutor Zerbini 3875, opposite
Shopping Campo Grande, T067-3028
4326, www.gauchogastao.com.br.
The best *churrascaria* in a town, famous for its beef, also has daily specials pay by weight, comfortable, a/c, lunch only.

$$$-$$ O Libanês Botequim
R Spipe Calarge 550, Vilas Boas, T067-9144 8913,
Facebook: O-Libanês-Botequim.
Good Arabic food, sometimes has live music and dance.

$$ Cantina Romana
R da Paz 237, T067-3324 9777,
www.cantinaromana.com.br.
Over 20 years serving Italian dishes, salads and a lunchtime buffet, good atmosphere.

$$-$ Sabor en Quilo
R Dom Aquino 1786, T067-3325 5102.
Self-service per kilo restaurant with plenty of choice including sushi on Sat, lunchtime only.

Bonito
On the Praça there are lots of cabins and small restaurants for drinks and snacks in the evening. Rua Cel Pilad Rebuá has many places to choose from in all price ranges. Cheaper beer and snacks at *convivências* (convenience stores).

$$$-$$ Casa do João
R Nelson F dos Santos 664A (behind Banco do Brasil), T067-3255 1212, www.casadojoao.com.br. Tue-Sun 1100-1530, 1800-2300.
Large, all wooden building serving fish, meat and local dishes, salads and soupls, very good.

$$$-$$ Taboa
R Cel Pilad Rebuá 1837,T067-3255 1862, www.taboa.com.br.
A lively bar that also sells food and sandwiches, wide range of drinks, occasional live music. Also has a shop and its own brand of *cachaça*.

$$$-$$ Tapera
R Cel Pilad Rebuá 480, T067-3255 1110. Opens 1900 for evening meal.
Good, home-grown vegetables, breakfast, lunch, pizzas, meat and fish dishes.

$$-$ Da Vovó
R Sen F Muller 570, T067-3255 2723.
A great per kilo serving Minas and local food all cooked in a traditional wood-burning stove. Plenty of vegetables and salads and lots of philosophy on the walls. Recommended.

$ Mercado da Praça
R Cel Pilad Rebuá, on the Praça next to Petrobras, T067-3255 2317. Open 0600-2400.
A snack bar and bakery in a minimarket, offering sandwiches, juices, etc.

Vício da Gula
R Cel Pilad Rebuá e 29 de Maio.
Café for drinks, coffee, cakes and snacks, popular.

Campo Grande to Corumbá: Miranda
There are food trucks with tables and chairs along Afonso Pena; Joel's Lanches is good (opposite R Barão do Rio Branco), also has a *lanchonete* and ice cream parlour on the Praça. Also on the Praça is **Val Lanches** (opposite Bradesco).

$$ Bento's
R Floriano Peixoto e Afonso Pena, next to Farmacia.
Good restaurant serving local food.

$$-$ Querência Pantaneira
BR-262, Km 558, T067-3242 3119, www. querenciapantaneira.com.br. 24 hrs.
Big restaurant on main road serving lunch buffet and à la carte in the evening, good value.

$$-$ Zero Hora
Av Barão do Rio Branco at theroundabout on BR-262, T067-3242 4200.
24-hr snack bar, provision shop and restaurant, with its own private waterfall.

Campo Grande

Arts and crafts
Local native crafts, including ceramics, tapestry and jewellery, are good quality. A local speciality is Os Bugres da Conceição, squat wooden statues covered in moulded wax.
Casa do Artesão, *Av Calógeras 2050, on corner with Av Afonso Pena. Mon-Fri 0800-2000, Sat 0800-1200.* Housed in a historic building.

Campo Grande
Be wary of the lower-end operators in the Pantanal. Many cut corners to save money and services are not always reliable.
Clube de Observadores de Aves de Campo Grande, *www.facebook.com/COACGR.* The city's active birdwatching club has produced a guide to birds in Campo Grande's urban parks, *Guia de aves de Campo Grande, áreas verdes urbanas.*

Bonito
There is very little to choose between agencies in Bonito, who offer the same packages for the same price, so shop around to see which you like the feel of best. English speakers are hard to come by.
Sucuri, *R Cel Pilad Rebuá 1890, T067-3255 s994, www.agenciasucuri.com.br.* As well as selling tours, also has car hire from US$32 per day, not including insurance, with extra for car wash afterwards; you can leave the car elsewhere if required.
Ygarapé, *R Cel Pilad Rebuá 1853, T067-3255 1733, http://agenciaygarape.com.br.* English-speaking staff, offers transport to the sights. Also PDSE accredited cave diving.

Campo Grande to Corumbá: Miranda
Águas do Pantanal, *Av Afonso Pena 367, T067-3242 1242, www.aguasdopantanal.com.br, at hotel, above.* Tours to the Pantanal and Serra do Bodoquena, associated with many hotels, helpful.
Pantanal Wilderness…Beyond Imagination, *R São Benedito 99, Miranda, T067-99831 3038, www. pantanalwilderness.com.* A good tour agency with a broad range of standard and more adventurous bespoke tours, including treks into the heart of the wetlands which include camping. Run by Marcelo Yndio and Ekta Shah. Several languages

spoken. Great for small groups who want to get off the beaten track with indigenous guides from the Kadiweu and Terena tribes, Marcelo Yndio and Luiz Marcelo respectively. Recommended.

Transport

Campo Grande

Air Daily flights to most major cities. **Airport**, T067-3368 6000. Take city bus No 158, or the designated a/c 015 airport bus which runs from the centre via Av Afonso Pena, R 26 de Agosto, Rui Barbosa, Cândido Mariano, Via Parque and Mato Grosso and costs US$3. Taxi to airport, US$6.50. Airport has car rental offices.

Bus The new *rodoviária* is at Av Gury Marques 1215, about 15 km south of the city on the road to São Paulo (BR-163), T067-3026 6789, www.transportal.com.br/rodoviaria-campo-grande/ (bus 087 leaves every 20 mins form Praça Ary Coelho in the centre, US$1.35, shuttle bus to the airport US$4, taxi to the centre US$8.50, to the airport US$7.50). The terminal has a tourist office opposite platforms 5/6, cafés, internet, a handful of shops and left luggage. Most Pantanal tour operators will meet clients off the bus and organize transfers to destinations further afield.

To **Miranda** and **Bonito**, see below. **São Paulo**, US$66, 13-19 hrs, Motta 3 a day, and others. **Cuiabá**, US$37-46, 13-14 hrs, 18 buses daily. To **Goiânia**, with **São Luís** 5 a day, US$31-69, 13-21 hrs, fastest at night. Direct to **Brasília** with Motta or **São Luís**, 21 hrs, US$ 80. **Corumbá**, with **Andorinha**, T067-3382 3710, www.andorinha. com, 8 daily from 0715, 6-7 hrs, US$37-43. Campo Grande–Corumbá buses connect with those from Rio and São Paulo, similarly those from Corumbá through to Rio and São Paulo. To **Foz do Iguaçu**, 20 hrs at 1720, US$48 with **Nova Integração**, or change at **Cascavel**, US$27-40. To **Ponta Porã** for Paraguay, see below.

Car hire Agencies on Av Afonso Pena and at airport.

Bonito

Bus The airport, for weekend flights from São Paulo, is south of town on the road to Jardim/Porto Murtinho. *Rodoviária* is on the edge of town, a short walk from R Cel Pilad Rebuá. From **Campo Grande**, US$18-21, 6 hrs, 4 daily with **Cruzeiro do Sul**, T067-3255 1606 (T067-3312 9700 Campo Grande), www.cruzeirodosulms.com.br. Buses go via Jardim, Nioaque and Sidrolândia. See under Corumbá for Cruzeiro do Sul's Corumbá–Ponta Porã service. **Terratransportes**, R Olívio Flores 600, T067-3255 1601, www.terratransportes.com.br, and **Vanzella**, T067-3255 3005 (067-3391 1029 Campo Grande), www.vanzellatransportes.com.br, run door-to-door services to Campo Grande and its airport daily (3 and 4 times respectively) and go to different local sites every day. There are other similar companies.

Ponta Porã

Bus The *rodoviária* is 3 km out on the Dourados road (Brazilian city buses from the centre to Rodoviaria, 20 mins, US$1.35; taxi US$8). To/from **Campo Grande**, 4 hrs, US$25. From Ponta Porã to **Bonito**, either change at **Jardim** (US$17.50, 4 hrs; Jardim–Bonito 4 a day, 1½ hrs, US$5.35), or take **Cruzeiro do Sul's** Corumbá–Ponta Porã service (see Corumbá Transport, below).

Campo Grande to Corumbá: Miranda

Bus *Rodoviária* is on R 7 de Setembro. **Campo Grande**–Miranda, 8 a day with **Andorinha**, 4 hrs, US$18.50. **Expreso Miranda**, T067-9937 7782, runs a daily car service to/from Campo Grande, US$120 per car. To **Corumbá**; 9 daily, 4 hrs, US$18.50-22. From Buraco das Piranhas, Catarino runs a daily door-to-door service to **Bonito**, 191 km, at 1400, 5 hrs, US$18.75 pp; **Prainha**, leaves for Campo Grande also at 1400, 5 hrs. Ask Barba (see page 652) to book either in advance. See under Corumbá Transport, below, for **Cruzeiro do Sul's** Corumbá–Ponta Porã service (Miranda T067-3266 1060, open 0730-1030, 1330-1430).

Corumbá

a hot and humid river town

Situated on the south bank by a broad bend in the Rio Paraguai, 15 minutes from the Bolivian border, Corumbá offers beautiful views of the river, especially at sunset. It is hot and humid (70%); cooler in June to July, and very hot from September to January. It also has millions of mosquitoes December to February.

There is a spacious shady **Praça da Independência** and Avenida Gen Rondon between Frei Mariano and 7 de September has a pleasant palm lined promenade which comes to life in the evenings.

From Gen Rondon streets drop steeply to the waterfront, which has a row of colourful colonial buildings, a park and the convention centre, with cinema and cultural events. Also on the waterfront is the **Museu de História do Pantanal** ① *R Manoel Cavassa 275, T67-3232 0303, Tue-Sat 1300-1800, free*, which is a good place to learn about the Pantanal, especially if arriving from Bolivia. The **Forte Junqueira** ① *R Cáceres 425, T067-3231 5296*, the city's most historic building, was built in 1772. It may be visited accompanied by a soldier from the base in which it is situated, but you must apply in advance. For tourtist information, **Fundação de Turismo do Pantanal** ① *Ladeira Cunha e Cruz 37, by the port, T067-3231 2886, Mon-Fri 0730-1330*, see the informative www.corumba.travel (also at the *rodoviária*, 0700-1800, and the Mirante Cristo Rei do Pantanal, daily 0700-1900).

Border with Bolivia

Over the border from Corumbá are Arroyo Concepción, Puerto Quijarro and Puerto Suárez. From Puerto Quijarro a 650-km railway and paved road run to Santa Cruz de la Sierra. There are flights to Santa Cruz from Puerto Suárez.

Brazilian immigration Brazilian **Polícia Federal** and **immigration** are at the border complex right at the frontier (open daily 0800-1730); there may be queues for entry stamps but it's much quicker for exit. If leaving Brazil merely to obtain a new visa, exit and entry must not be on the same day. Money changers (usually women sitting at tables) on the Bolivian side and in Quijarro (there is none on the Brazilian side) offer the same rates as in Corumbá. **Bolivian consulate** ① *R 7 de Setembro 47 between Delamare and Av Gen Rondon, Corumbá, T067-3231 5605, consuladoboliviacorumba@gmail. com, Mon-Fri 0800-1230, 1400-1730*. A fee is charged to citizens of those countries which require a visa. A yellow fever vaccination certificate is not required to enter Brazil, but regulations change, so enquire at a consulate before arriving at the border. A tourist office on the Brazilian side is open Monday-Saturday 0730-1330.

Listings Corumbá

Where to stay

For a full list of hotels see
www.corumba.travel.

$$$-$$ Nacional Palace
*R América 936, T067-3234 6000,
www.hnacional.com.br.*
Smart, modern a/c rooms, a decent pool
and parking.

$$ El Dorado
*R Porto Carreiro 554 esq Tiradentes, T067-3231
6677, hotel_eldorado@top.com.br.*
Close to rodoviária, 46 rooms with electric
shower, no frills but OK.

There are 2 Cama e café options: **Casa da Mama**
(R Firmo de Mattos 1400, T067-3232 4240,
elmamonaco@gmail.com), with 1 double room
and 1 twin, shared bath, a/c, parking, convenient
location, and **Casa Marela** (R Dom Aquino 597,
T067-3233 4578, iaramarela@hotmail.com),
1 room with bath, fan. In both you share facilities
with the family, both $ pp.

Restaurants

Local specialities

These include *peixadas corumbaenses*, a variety
of fish dishes prepared with the catch of the day;
as well as ice cream, liquor and sweets made of
bocaiúva, a small yellow palm fruit, in season
Sep-Feb. There are several good restaurants in
R Frei Mariano.

$$ Glória Grill
*R Cabral 1628, T067-3231 4441.
Open 1100-1430, 1800-2330*
Smart, clean restaurant serving buffet at
lunchtime, self-service or per kg, and à la carte in
the evening, specializing in *espeto* (spit roast).

$$ Laço de Ouro
*R Frei Mariano 556, T067-3232 5555,
lacodeourocorumba@hotmail.com.
Open 1100-2330.*
Popular fish and meat restaurant with a
lively atmosphere and tables spilling out
onto the street.

$$ Rodeio do Pantanal
*R 13 de Junho 760, T067-3231 6477, www.rodeio
dopantanal.com.br. Daily 1100-1500, 1800-2300.*

Good restaurant for lunchtime buffet or per kg, local food.

$ Panela Velha
R 15 de Novembro 156, T067-3232 5650.
Mon-Sat 1100-1500.
Popular lunchtime restaurant with a decent, cheap all-you-can-eat buffet.

$ Verde Frutti
R Delamare 1164, T067-3231 3032.
A snack bar with a wide variety of juices and great, ice-cold *acai na tigela*.

Dolce Café
Frei Mariano 572, T067-3232 7333,
dolcecafecorumba@gmail.com.
New bakery, bar and restaurant.

Festivals

2 Feb Festa de Nossa Senhora da Candelária, Corumbá's patron saint, all offices and shops are closed.
Feb/Mar Carnaval, the largest in Brazil's centre-west, with samba schools and processions.
23-25 Jun Festa do Arraial do Banho de São João, fireworks, parades, traditional food stands, processions and the main event, the bathing of the image of the saint in the Rio Paraguai.
21 Sep Corumbá's anniversary, includes a Pantanal fishing festival held on the eve.
Early to mid-Oct Festival Pantanal das Águas, with street parades featuring giant puppets, dancing in the street and occasional water fights.

What to do

Most tour operators for the southern part of the Pantanal are in Campo Grande or Miranda, but a few agencies keep offices here and there are a number of upmarket cruise companies along the water front. There is a list on www.corumba. travel; companies include **Joice Pesca & Tur** (T067-3232 4048, or 9912 0265, www.joicetur. com.br), with good boats, crew and service, and **Pérola do Pantanal** (T067-3231 1460, www. peroladopantanal.com.br), with its boat *Kalypso*.

Mutum Turismo, *R Frei Mariano 17, T067-3231 1818, www.mutumturismo.com.br*. Cruises and upmarket tours (mostly aimed at the Brazilian market) and airline, train and bus reservations.

Transport

Air Airport, R Santos Dumont, 3 km. Flights to **Campinas** on Mon, Wed, Fri, Sun with **Azul**. Infrequent bus from airport to town, so take a taxi, US$5. Car hire at the airport.

Bus The local bus station is 6 blocks from the *rodoviária* at 13 de Junho e Tiradentes; there is another stand at Delamare e Antônio Maria Coelho by the Praça da República. The *rodoviária* is on R Porto Carreiro at the south end of R Tiradentes, 10 mins walk from the centre. City bus to *rodoviária* from Praça da República, US$1.35; taxis are expensive but mototaxis charge US$1. **Andorinha**, T067-3231 2033, services to all points east. To **Campo Grande**, 7 hrs, US$37-43, 8 buses daily, from 0700-2359, connections from Campo Grande to all parts of Brazil. **Cruzeiro do Sul**, T067-3231 9318, www.cruzeirodosulms. com.br, office open 0600-1000, 1300-1630, has a daily service except Sun to Ponta Porã via Miranda, Bodoquena, Bonito, Jardim and Bela Vista, in a 20-seater bus towing a trailer for luggage, leaving at 0630, arriving **Miranda** 0930, US$18.50, **Bonito** 1130, US$29(US$10.50 Miranda–Bonito) and **Ponta Porã** at 1800, US$51. It returns from Ponta Porã at 0600, passing Bonito at 1130 and Miranda at 1400.

Border with Bolivia: Corumbá/Arroyo Concepción

Bus Leaving Brazil, take city bus marked Fronteira from either of the stops given above to the Bolivian border (15 mins, US$1.35), walk over the bridge to Bolivian immigration, then take a *colectivo* to Quijarro or Puerto Suárez. Taxi from Corumbá *rodoviária* to the border US$8. Brazilian taxis are not allowed to cross into Bolivia, but it is only a short walk between the 2 frontier posts. For onward travel, always buy train or bus tickets once in Bolivia.

When travelling from Quijarro, take a taxi to the Bolivian border to go through formalities. On the left, 50 m from the border is the stop for taxis to Corumbá and a little further on, the bus stop; don't believe taxi drivers who say there is no bus.

Train Timetables for trains from Puerto Quijarro to Santa Cruz change frequently, so check on www.fo.com.bo or on arrival in Corumbá. If you haven't booked a ticket via the website, it may be best to stay in Quijarro to get tickets.

Costa Rica

The BR-163, the highway from Paraná to Cuiabá, heads north out of Campo Grande towards Rondonópolis. Several sections are being dualled, but many stretches are slow because of the heavy traffic. At Km 74 BR-060 turns east through Camapuã to **Costa Rica** (population: 23,000) a prosperous, neat town at the heart of a thriving agricultural zone. The town has a list of 47 tourist attractions and is well set up for visitors. The **Secretaria de Turismo** ① *R Ambrosina Paes Coelho 228, T067-3247 7070, www.costarica.ms.gov.br*, can organize all excursions, which must be accompanied by a guide. Contact AMAS, **Associação de Monitores Ambientais Sucuriú** ① *Victor Renato, T067-9614 2977, victor.renato.de.freitas@gmail.com*, who offer guiding services. All tourist sites are on private land; a full-day tour costs US$40. Just out of town is the **Parque Natural Municipal Salto do Sucuriú** ① *MS-316 Km 1, Paraíso das Águas, T067-3247 7074, Tue-Sun 0800-1700, US$2.65, with extra costs for activities such as canopy walkways, rafting, abseiling*, which has an impressive 70-m waterfall and smaller falls. It takes over an hour to walk to the foot of the big falls and back. For US$8 and a quicker view take the two zip-lines which cross the gorge. A third, short zip-line plunges into the swimming pool in the shape of the letters CR below the restaurant.

Costa Rica is a good access point for the **Parque Nacional Emas** (see page 639), which is only 45 km away (15 unpaved). Bike hire in the park costs US$13 a day, US$4 per hour; snorkelling US$13; inner-tube rafting US$10.50.

There are hotels near the *rodoviária* (Avenue Kendi Nakai 847), the best of which is $$$-$$ Ives (Avenue Kendi Nakai 101, T067-3247 3005, reservas@iveshotel.com.br). Three daily buses to/from Campo Grande (São Luís, Itamarati and Van Costa Rica), 6½ hours, US$24.

The BR-359 goes to Coxim on the BR-163. At Km 31 is the entrance to the **Parque Estadual Nascente do Rio Taquari**, where six dramatic canyons meet at the westernmost edge of the central Brazilian plateau. There are great views, especially at sunset, walking trails and *urubu* nesting sites; you must go with a guide. The road to the canyons' edge passes through the vast fields of the Fazenda Planalto and you can arrange visits to learn about agroindustry. Some 40 km from Alcinópolis, midway between Costa Rica and Coxim, is the **Parque Natural Municipal Templo dos Pilares**, an important archaeological sites, with 2000 cave paintings and etchings in the sandstone cliffs up to 12,000 years old. There is also an area of naturally sculpted rock pillars.

Coxim

Coxim (population: 33,000) is on the banks of the Rio Taquari, at its junction with the Rio Coxim. Historically, the town and the Taquari were an important part of the route between the gold mines of Cuiabá and São Paulo, but by the late 20th century Coxim had become a huge draw for fishing tourism (compared with the town's 42 hotels there are 412 fishing ranches). In recent years fishing has been replaced by ecotourism and birdwatching and the boatmen are turning to guiding on the Rios Taquari and Coxim. The Rio Taquari flows into the Pantanal and there are numerous *baias* of still water to pull into, with thick vegetation and lots of wildlife. Trips may also stop at fishing communities or rustic ranches to cook a meal and rest in the heat of the day. Land-based tours enter fazendas to see jacaré, capybara in great numbers, armadillos, anteaters, deer, other mammals and many birds. You eat at roadside pantaneira restaurants for passing truckers and farmers. No fazendas offer lodging, but you do see the wildlife co-existing with the cattle farms.

All tourism is community-based, be it on water or land. The **tourist office** ① *Centro de Atendimento ao Turista, R Antônio Albuquerque 100, T067-3291 1143, turismo.coxim@gmail.com, Mon-Fri 0700-1100, 1300-1700*, has all information and can put visitors in touch with boatmen, *Toyoteros* (pick-up drivers) and local families. Normally tours are full-day, 0700-1700, and cost US$40 pp in a boat for a group of four, US$65 per person in a 4WD for four. November-February is a good time to find a boat tour as fishing is prohibited at this time. Heaviest rains start in late December; May-September is best for flowering plants; July-August is when water is lowest and thousands of birds can be seen fishing. There are very few bilingual guides, although Ariel Albrecht of the tourist office speaks English and is most helpful. Ask here about the community tourism project at **Jauru** (60 km away), where diamond-mining families show visitors their traditional methods. You can also visit **Rio Verde de Mato Grosso**, 50 km south, whose **Área de Proteção Ambiental Sete Quedas** has bathing spots and a selection of places to stay (eg Pousada Paraíso, www.pousadaparaisorv.com. br; Balneário Quedas d'Água; more details on www.rioverde.ms.gov.br).

The town centre has all services, a **Casa do Artesão** ① *R Antônio Albuquerque 100, Mon-Fri 0700-1700*, and a small **Museu Arqueológico e Histórico** ① *R João Pesso 210, T067-3291 2304, Mon-Fri 0700-1100, 1300-1700*. On the BR-163 there are several hotels (including **$$ Piracema** (BR-163, Km 658, T067-3291 1610, htlpiracema@yahoo.com.br) the oldest in town, comfortable rooms, pleasant and helpful) and restaurants, which are 3 km from the centre of town where there are more of each. The tourist office has a full list. **Andorinha, Eucatur** and **Motta** buses all charge US$15.50-17 from Campo Grande to Coxim, 4½ hours, and US$18.50-23 Coxim-Cuiabá, 7½ hours.

Cuiabá and around

wildlife opportunities and one of the oldest plateaux on earth

Cuiabá

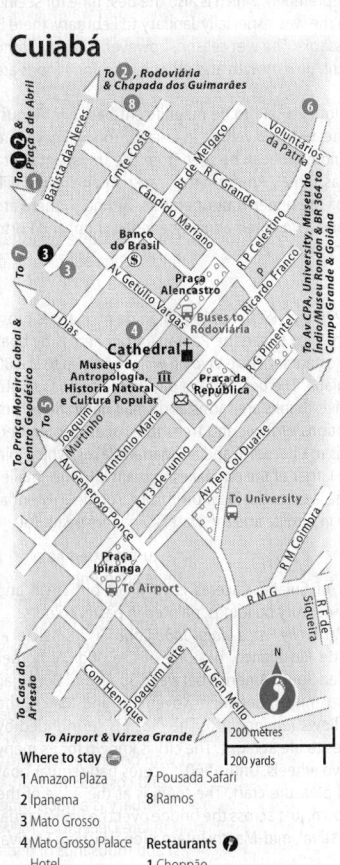

Where to stay 🛏
1 Amazon Plaza
2 Ipanema
3 Mato Grosso
4 Mato Grosso Palace Hotel
5 Portal do Pantanal
6 Pousada Ecoverde
7 Pousada Safari
8 Ramos

Restaurants 🍴
1 Choppão
2 Getúlio
3 Miranda's

Cuiabá *Colour map 6, A6.*
The capital of Mato Grosso state on the Rio Cuiabá, an upper tributary of the Rio Paraguai, is in fact two cities: Cuiabá on the east bank of the river and Várzea Grande, where the airport is, on the west. It is very hot; coolest months for a visit are June, July and August, in the dry season. Cuiabá was the smallest host city for the 2014 FIFA World Cup™ and went through a construction frenzy before the event. Many works, however, were left unfinished.

The city has an imposing government palace and other fine buildings round the green **Praça da República**. On the square is the **cathedral**, with a plain, imposing exterior, two clock-towers and, inside, coloured-glass mosaic windows and doors. Behind the altar is a huge mosaic of Christ in majesty, with smaller mosaics in side chapels. Beside the cathedral is the leafy **Praça Alencastro**. On **Praça Ipiranga**, at the junction of Avenidas Isaac Póvoas and Tenente Col Duarte, a few blocks southwest of the central squares, there are market stalls and an iron bandstand from Huddersfield, UK. In front of the Assembléia Legislativa, Praça Moreira Cabral, is a point marking the **Geogedesic Centre of South America** (see also under Chapada dos Guimarães). **Museus de Antropologia, História Natural e Cultura Popular** ① *in the Fundação Cultural de Mato Grosso, Praça da República 151, Mon-Fri 0800-1730, US$0.50*, displays historical photos, a contemporary art gallery, stuffed Pantanal fauna, indigenous, archaeological finds and pottery. At the entrance to Universidade de Mato Grosso, 10 minutes by bus from the centre (by pool), is the small **Museu do Índio/ Museu Rondon** ① *T065-3615 8489, Tue-Sun 0800-1100, 1330-1700, US$1*, with artefacts from tribes mostly from the state of Mato Grosso. Particularly beautiful are the Bororo and Rikbaktsa headdresses made from macaw and currasow feathers and also the Kadiwéu pottery. Bus Nos 501 or 505 ('Universidade') to the university museums leave from Av Tenente Col Duarte by Praça Bispo Dom José, a triangular park just east of Praça Ipiranga. **Tourist information** at Sedtur, Secretaria de Desenvolvimento do Turismo ① *in the rodoviária, Av Jules Rimet; in the city centre, Praça Rachid Jaudy; in Museu da Caixa d'Água Velha, R Nossa Senhora de Santana 1-105; small office at R Ricardo Franca at Voluntários da Pátria 118, T065-3613 9300, Mon-Fri 0800-1200, 1300-1700, www.sedtur.mt.gov.br*, provides maps and general information on hotels and car hire and has a website in English. Staff are friendly and speak English and Spanish. They are very helpful in settling disputes with local tour companies.

Cuiabá to Pantanal *Colour map 6, A6.*

A paved route turns south off the main Cuiabá–Cáceres road to **Poconé** (102 km from Cuiabá, hotels, 24-hour gas station – closed Sunday). From here, the Transpantaneira runs 146 km south to Porto Jofre. The road is of earth, in poor condition, with ruts, holes and many bridges that need care in crossing. Easiest access is in the dry season (July-September), which is also the best time for seeing birds and, in September, the trees are in bloom. In the wet, especially January to February, there is no guarantee that the Transpantaneira will be passable. The wet season, however, is a good time to see many of the shyer animals because more fruit, new growth and other high calorie foods are available, and there are fewer people.

Campos de Jofre, about 20 km north of Porto Jofre, is said to be magnificent between August and October. In Poconé one can hitch to Porto Jofre, or hire a vehicle in Cuiabá. You will get more out of this part of the Pantanal by going with a guide; a lot can be seen from the Transpantaneira in a hired car, but guides can take you into fazendas some 7 km from the Transpantaneira and will point out wildlife. Recommended guides in Cuiabá are under Tour operators. Although there are gas stations in **Pixaim** (a bridge across the Rio Pixaim, two hotels and a tyre repair shop) and Porto Jofre, they are not always well stocked, best to carry extra fuel.

Barão de Melgaço *Colour map 7, A1.*

On Rio Cuiabá, 130 km from Cuiabá (TUT bus at 0730 and 1500, US$10), Barão de Melgaço is most easily reachable via Santo Antônio do Leverger. The way to see the Pantanal from here is by boat down the Rio Cuiabá. Boat hire, for example from Restaurant Peixe Vivo on waterfront, up to US$80 for a full day; or enquire with travel agencies in Cuiabá. The best time of day would be sunset, but this may mean returning after dark. Initially the river banks are farms and small habitations, but they become more forested, with lovely combinations of flowering trees (best seen September-October). After a while, a small river to the left leads to Chacororé and Sia Mariana lakes, which join each other via an artificial canal which has led the larger of the two lakes to drain into the smaller and begin to dry out. Boats can continue beyond the lakes to the Rio Mutum, but a guide is essential because there are many dead ends. The area is rich in birdlife and the waterscapes are beautiful.

Cáceres *Colour map 6, A6.*

On the banks of the Rio Paraguai, 200 km west of Cuiabá, Cáceres is very hot but clean and hospitable. It has a number of well-preserved 19th-century buildings, painted in pastel colours.

The **Museu Histórico de Cáceres** ① *R Antônio Maria by Praça Major João Carlos*, is a small local history museum. The main square, Praça Barão de Rio Branco, has one of the original border markers from the Treaty of Tordesillas, which divided South America between Spain and Portugal; it is pleasant and shady during the day. In the evenings, between November and March, the trees are packed with thousands of chirping swallows (*andorinhas*). The *praça* is surrounded by bars, restaurants and ice cream parlours and comes to life at night. The city is known for its many bicycles as most people seem to get around on two wheels. Until 1960, Cáceres had regular boat traffic, today it is limited to a few tour boats and pleasure craft. The town is at the edge of the Pantanal. Vitória Regia lilies can be seen north of town, just across the bridge over the Rio Paraguai along the BR-174. Local festivals are the Piranha Festival, mid-March; International Fishing Festival in mid-September; annual cattle fair.

Border with Bolivia

An unpaved road runs from Cáceres to the Bolivian border at San Matías. Alternatively, go some 300 km north of Cáceres to **Pontes e Lacerda**, from where you can cross to San Ignacio de Velasco. When crossing at San Matías or travelling to/from San Igancio de Velasco, there are thorough drugs and customs searches at all border points but passports are not stamped. Stamps are given at the **Polícia Federal** in either **Cáceres** ① *Av Getúlio Vargas 2125, Bairro COC, 20-min walk from rodoviária in the centre, T065-3211 6307, daily 0800-1200, 1400-1800*) or perhaps **Vilhena** ① *Av 15 de Novembro 3485*. Do not go directly to Polícia Federal in Cuiabá, you will be sent back to Cáceres. There are Bolivian immigration offices in San Matías and San Ignacio de Velasco. **Bolivian consulate in Cuiabá** ① *R Paramaribo 174, Qd 08, lote 06, Jardim das Américas, T065-3627 4937, colivian-cuiaba@brturbo.com*.

Along one route to San Ignacio de Velasco is the delightfully friendly and authentic little town of **Vila Bela da Santíssima Trindade** on the shores of the Rio Guaporé. Once the capital of Mato Grosso state, Vila Bela has a huge crumbling old cathedral and an interesting **Museu Histórico** ① *R Pouso Alegre 668, Mon-Fri 0800-1100, 1300-1700, free*. Dolphins and many birds may be seen by the river and there is bathing by the beautiful 60-m-high Cascata waterfall, 14 km from town in Parque Estadual Ricardo Franco (taxi US$15 each way, or walk and hitch).

☆Chapada dos Guimarães and Nobres *Colour map 4, C5.*

Some 68 km northeast of Cuiabá lies one of the oldest plateaux on earth. It is one of the most scenic areas of Brazil and visitors describe it as an energizing place. The pleasant town of Chapada dos Guimarães, the main centre, is a base for many beautiful excursions in this area; it has the oldest church in the Mato Grosso, **Nossa Senhora de Santana** (1779), a bizarre blending of Portuguese and French baroque styles, and a huge spring-water public swimming pool (on Rua Dr Pem Gomes, behind the town). Formerly the centre of an important diamond prospecting region, today Chapada is a very popular destination for Cuiabanos to escape the heat of the city at weekends and on holidays. It is a full day excursion from Cuiabá through lovely scenery with many birds, butterflies and flora. There is a post office at Rua Fernando Corrêa 848. The Festival de Inverno is held in last week of July, and Carnival is very busy. Accommodation is scarce and expensive at these times.

The Chapada is an immense geological formation rising to 700 m, with rich forests, curiously eroded rocks and many lovely grottoes, peaks and waterfalls. A **national park** (park office ① *Rodovia Emanuel Pinheiro (MT251), Km 50, T065-3301 1133, www.icmbio.gov.br/parnaguimaraes/*, provides a useful map of the region and organizes tours, open all year, free) has been established in the area just west of the town, where the **Salgadeira** tourist centre offers bathing, camping and a restaurant close to the Salgadeira waterfall.

The beautiful 85 m **Véu da Noiva** waterfall (Bridal Veil), 12 km before the town near Buriti (well signposted, ask bus from Cuiabá to let you off), is reached by a short route, or a long route through forest. Other sights include the **Mutuca** beauty spot, **Rio Claro**, the viewpoint over the breathtaking 80-m-deep **Portão do Inferno** (Hell's Gate), and the falls of **Cachoeirinha** (small restaurant) and **Andorinhas**.

About 8 km east of town is the **Mirante do Ponto Geodésico**, a monument officially marking the Geodesic Centre of South America, which overlooks a great canyon with views of the surrounding plains, the Pantanal and Cuiabá's skyline on the horizon; to reach it take Rua Fernando Corrêa east. Continuing east, the road goes through agricultural land and later by interesting rock formations including a stone bridge and stone cross. Some 45 km from Chapada you reach the access for **Caverna Arroe-Jari** ('the dwelling of the souls' in the Bororo language), a sandstone cave over 1 km long, the second largest in Brazil; it is a 1-km walk to the cave, in it is Lagoa Azul, a lake with crystalline blue water. Take your own torch/flashlight (guides' lamps are sometimes weak); daily 0800-1300, US$5, allow three to four hours for the walk to and from the cave. A guide is necessary to get through fazenda property to the cave, but not really needed thereafter.

Some 100 km north of the Chapada is **Nobres** (www.nobres.mt.gov.br), a little town surrounded by caves and clear rivers full of fish. The village of **Bom Jardim** has two-*pousadas*-in-one (Pousada Bom Jardim, www.pousadabomjardim.com, $$$-$$) and a restaurant. At Lago das Araras, 2 km away, hundreds of blue and yellow macaws roost in the buriti palms and create a raucous dawn chorus. Other attractions such as good snorkelling at the Reino Encantado ① *US$45 per day, $$ for overnight stay*, the Recanto Ecológico Lagoa Azul ① *US$20 entry* and the Rio Triste, both of which offer floating downstream to see the fish. If swimming, beware the sting rays. Buses run Cuiabá-Nobres, with onward buses to Bom Jardim (direct from Cuiabá once a day). Pousada Bom Jardim has a taxi service and agencies in Cuiabá run tours.

Listings Cuiabá and around *map p661*

Where to stay

Cuiabá

$$$ Amazon Plaza
Av Getúlio Vargas 600, T065-2121 2000,
www.hotelamazon.com.br.
By far the best in the centre with very smart modern rooms, good views over the city, shady pool area, excellent services.

$$$-$$ Mato Grosso Palace Hotel
Joaquim Murtinho 170, T065-3614 7000,
www.hotelmt.com.br.
Conveniently located behind the Praça República, standard 3-star rooms with fridge, hot showers.

$$ Ipanema
Jules Rimet 12, T065-3621 3069.
Opposite the front of the *rodoviária*, well-kept rooms, a/c or fan, huge lobby TV for films or football. Many other options in this area.

$$ Mato Grosso
R Comandante Costa 252, T065-3614 7777,
www.hotelmt.com.br.
The best value mid-range option in the centre with renovated a/c or fan-cooled rooms, the brightest of which are on the 2nd floor or above, good breakfast, very helpful. Recommended.

$$ Pousada Ecoverde
R Pedro Celestino 391, T065-3624 1386,
http://ecoverdetours.com.
The best value, if idiosyncratic option, rooms with spacious bathrooms in a converted town house. Facilities include excellent tour agency, laundry service and free airport/bus station pick-up (with 12 hrs' notice). See Joel Souza under Guides, below.

$$-$ pp Portal do Pantanal
Av Isaac Povoas 655, T065-3624 8999,
www.portaldopantanal.com.br.
HI hostel, with breakfast, cheaper with fan, internet access US$3 per hr, laundry, use of kitchen.

$$-$ Pousada Safari
R 24 de Outubro 111, Centro, T065-3359 2344/99992 2126, Facebook:
HostelPousadaSafari.

Rooms with shared bath, electric shower, fan, breakfast, laundry facilities, library and book exchange. Owner Laercio Sá is an experienced guide who runs good Pantanal tours.

$$-$ Ramos
R Campo Grande 487, T067-3624 7472,
hotelramos@hotmail.com.
A variety of simple a/c and fan-cooled rooms, also has dorms, laundry service. **Pantanal Nature** travel agency is in reception.

Cuiabá to Pantanal

$$$$ Araras Eco Lodge
Km 32, T065-3682 2800, www.araraslodge.com.
br. Book direct or through Pantanal Explorer.
One of the most comfortable with 14 a/c rooms; pool, excellent tours and food, home-made *cachaça* and a walkway over a private patch of wetland filled with capybara and cayman. Very popular with small tour groups from Europe. Book ahead.

$$$$ Pousada Rio Clarinho
Km 42, book through Pantanal Nature.
Charming budget option on the Rio Clarinho which makes up in wildlife what it lacks in infrastructure. The river has rare water birds, as well as river and giant otters and occasionally tapir.

$$$$ Pousada Rio Claro
Km 42. Book through Natureco.
Comfortable fazenda with a pool and simple a/c rooms on the banks of the Rio Claro which has a resident colony of giant otters.

$$$$-$$$ Fazenda Piuval
Km 10, T065-3345 1338,
www.pousadapiuval.com.br.
The first fazenda on the Transpantaneira and one of the most touristy, with scores of day visitors at weekends. Rustic farmhouse accommodation, pool, excellent horse and walking trails and boat trips on their vast lake.

$$$$-$$$ Pouso Alegre
Km 33, T065-3626 1545, www.pousalegre.com.br.
Rustic *pousada*, simple accommodation, a/c or fan. One of the largest fazendas and overflowing with wildlife and particularly good for birds

(especially on the morning horseriding trail). Many species not yet seen elsewhere in the northern Pantanal have been catalogued here. Their remote oxbow lake is particularly good for water birds. Birding guides provided with advance notice. Best at weekends when the very knowledgeable owner Luís Vicente is there.

$$$-$$ Caranda Fundo
Transpantaneira Km 43, book through Pantanal Nature, T065-3322 0203.
One of the best options for budget travellers. Visitors sleep in hammocks in a large room (bring a hammock mosquito net). Tours include horse rides, treks and night safaris; hyacinth macaws nest on the fazenda and there are many mammals, including howler monkeys, peccaries and huge herds of capybara.

Barão de Melgaço

$$$$-$$$ Mutum Pantanal Ecolodge
T065-3052 7022, www.pousadamutum.com.br. Book through Pantanal Nature, or agencies in Cuiabá.
Comfortable roundhouses and cabins set on a lawn around a lovely pool. Arranges horse riding, jeep and boat tours.

Cáceres

$$$-$$ Caiçaras
R dos Operários 745, corner R Gen Osório, T065-3223 2234.
Modern, with a/c rooms and cheaper options without a fridge.

$$$-$$ Riviera Pantanal
R Gen Osório 540, T065-3223 1177.
Simple town hotel with a/c rooms, a pool and a restaurant.

$$ La Barca
R Gen Osório s/n, T065-3223 5047.
Basic town hotel, single, double and triple rooms. With a/c and pool.

$$ Porto Bello
Av São Luís 1188, T065-3224 1437, www.hotelportobello.amawebs.com.
Basic standard rooms, with a/c, tv and private bathrooms.

$ União
R 7 de Setembro 340, T065-3223-4240.
Fan-cooled rooms, cheaper with shared bath, basic but good value.

Border with Bolivia: Vila Bela da Santíssima Trindade

$$ Cascata
R Conde Azambuja 493, T065-3259 1154, hotel.cascata@terra.com.br.
Rooms with breakfast, a/c, some have frigobar, ample grounds, parking.

$$-$ Guaporé
R Pouso Alegre 607, T065-3259 1030.
Simple rooms with a/c and frigobar, cheaper and more basic with fan, breakfast, restaurant, internet, very helpful owner, good value.

Chapada dos Guimarães

$$$ Casa da Quineira
R Frei Osvaldo 191, T065-3301 3301, www.casadaquineira.com.br.
Very close to the city centre, this homely *pousada* has comfortable, modern rooms and pool.

$$$ Pousada Vento Sul
Av Rio da Casca 850, T065-3301 2706, www.pousadaventosul.tur.br.
1.5 km from town centre, spacious rooms with hammock on veranda, very nice, English spoken, birdwatching guide available.

$$$ Turismo
R Fernando Corrêa 1065, a block from rodoviária, T065-3301 1176, www.hotel turismo.com.br.
Rooms are cheaper without a/c, restaurant, breakfast and lunch excellent, very popular, German-run; Ralf Goebel, the owner, is very helpful in arranging excursions.

$$ Rio's Hotel
R Tiradentes 333, T065-3301 1126, www.chapadadosguimaraes.com.br.
Rooms are cheaper without a/c and with shared bath, good breakfast.

$$-$ São José
R Vereador José de Souza 50, T065-3301 3013/1574.
Fan, cheaper with shared bath and no fan, hot showers, basic, no breakfast, good, owner Mário sometimes runs excursions.

Camping

Oásis
1 block from main praça, T065-3301 2444, www.campingoasis.com.br.
Central, in garden with fruit trees, separate bathrooms for men and women, cooking facilities, car park.

Restaurants

Cuiabá

City centre restaurants only open for lunch. On Av CPA are many restaurants, snack bars, bars and clubs.

$$$ Getúlio
Av Getúlio Vargas 1147, T065-3264 9992.
An a/c haven from the heat with black tie waiters, excellent food, with meat specialities, pizza, good buffet lunch on Sun. Live music upstairs on Fri and Sat from significant cult Brazilian acts.

$$$-$$ Choppão
Praça 8 de Abril, T065-3623 9101.
A local institution, buzzing at any time of the day or night. Go for huge portions of delicious food or just for *chopp* served by fatherly waiters. The house dish of chicken soup promises to give diners drinking strength in the early hours and is a meal in itself. Warmly recommended.

$$-$ Miranda's
R Cmdte Costa 716.
Decent self-service per kilo lunchtime restaurant with good value specials.

Cáceres

$ Gulla's
R Cel José Dulce 250.
Buffet by kilo, good variety. Recommended.

Shopping

Cuiabá

Handicrafts in wood, straw, netting, leather, skins, Pequi liquor, crystallized caju fruit, compressed guaraná fruit (for making the drink), indigenous objects on sale at the airport, *rodoviária*, craft shops in centre, and daily market, Praça da República, interesting. Fish and vegetable market, picturesque, at the riverside.
Casa de Artesão, *Praça do Expedicionário 315, T065-3321 0603.* Sells all types of local crafts in a restored building. Recommended.

What to do

Cuiabá

You should expect to pay about US$160-250 per person per day for tours in the Pantanal. All these agencies arrange trips to the Pantanal. Budget trips are marginally more expensive than those

in the Southern Pantanal, but accommodation based in fazendas is more comfortable. For longer or special programmes, book in advance. Tour operators also handle flight and bus tickets.
Natureco, *R Benedito Leite 570, T065-3321 1001, www.natureco.com.br.* Tours to remote fazendas in the Pantanal as well as regular trips to north and south Pantanal, to Nobres and Chapada dos Guimarães. Longer 6-night "3-Biome" tours to the Amazon, Pantanal and savannahs. Specialist birding and wildlife tours and trips throughout Brazil. English spoken. Professional and well run.
Pantanal Explorer, *R Gov Ponce de Arruda 670, Várzea Grande, T065-3682 2800, www.pantanalexplorer.com.br.* Offers tours to the Pantanal, Amazon, Cerrado and Chapada dos Guimarães, with various packages including birdwatching and riding. Low-impact and responsible, running its own lodge, **Araras Eco Lodge** (see above) and with connections to others.

Wildlife guides for the Pantanal and Mato Grosso

Recommended birding and wildlife guides for the northern Pantanal and Mato Grosso are listed below. All guides work freelance for other companies as well as employing other guides for trips when busy. Most guides await incoming flights at the airport; compare prices and services in town if you don't wish to commit yourself at the airport. The tourist office recommends guides; this is not normal practice and their advice is not necessarily impartial.
Boute Expeditions, *R Getúlio Vargas 64, Várzea Grande, near airport, T079-3223 1791, www.bouteexpeditions.com.* Paulo Boute, one of the most experienced birding guides in the Pantanal; works from home and speaks good English and French.
Fabricio Dorileo, *fabriciodorileo18@yahoo.com.br or through Eduardo Falcão, rejaguar@bol.com.br.* Excellent birding guide with good equipment, good English and many years' experience in the Pantanal and Chapada dos Guimarães.
Giuliano Bernardon, *T065-98115 6189, giubernardon@gmail.com.* Birding guide and photographer with a good depth of knowledge and experience in the Chapada, Pantanal, Mato Grosso Amazon and Atlantic coastal forest.
Joel Souza, *Ecoverde Tours, owner of Pousada Ecoverde, see Where to stay, above, T065-99638 1614, http://ecoverdetours.com.br.* Speaks English, French, German and Spanish, knowledgeable and very helpful, checklists for flora and fauna provided, will arrange all transport,

accommodation and activities, tends to employ guides rather than guiding himself.

Ocelot Natur, *R Agua Boa 14a, T065-9647 3514.* Good value guided hikes in the Chapada dos Guimarães, visits to Nobres and Pantanal safaris with local guide Alex Gomes.

Pantanal Bird Club, *www.pantanalbirdclub.org.* Good for even the most exacting birders, PBC are the most illustrious birders in Brazil with many years of experience, owner Braulio Carlos. Tours throughout the area and to various parts of Brazil.

Pantanal Eco Safari, *see Pousada Safari, above.*

Pantanal Nature Tours, *R Campo Grande 487, T065-3322 0203, or T065-99994 2265, www.pantanalnature.com.br.* Embratur licensed guide, Ailton Lara, expert wildlife and birding knowledge, frequent jaguar sitings, works with small groups and will customize tours, well organized agency. He also goes to the Chapada dos Guimarães, Nobres (with crystal clear rivers filled with dourado) and Jardim da Amazônia in the north of Mato Grosso. Speaks English. Recommended.

Chapada dos Guimarães

Chapada Pantanal, *Av Fernando Correa da Costa 1022, T065-3301 2757, www.chapadapantanal.tur.br.* Tours to all the principal sights in the Chapada and trips further afield to Nobres.

Ecoturismo Cultural, *Av Cipriano Curvo 655, T065-3301 1393, www.chapadadosguimaraes.com.br/ecoturis.htm.* Recommended tours, with bilingual guides who know the area well; tours from 1 to 8 days.

Transport

Cuiabá

Air Marechal Rondon international airport is 10 km from the city; taxi US$10, or take bus No 24 from Av Tenente Coronel Duarte to the city centre, US$1. There are also *aeroporto* buses from and to the *rodoviária*, No 007. The VLT (Veículo Leve sobre Trilhos) urban light rail system running between the airport, the city centre and the Arena Pantanal stadium is one

of the World Cup projects left unfinished. It is due to be completed by 2019.

Bus Many bus routes have stops in the vicinity of Praça Ipiranga. *Rodoviária* is on R Jules Rimet, Bairro Alvorada, north of the centre, T065-3621 3629 (Bradesco ATM, cafés and restaurants); town buses stop at the entrance. Bus No 329 from R Joaquim Murtinho by the cathedral, 20 mins. Taxi from the centre, US$5. Comfortable buses (toilets) to **Campo Grande**, 10 hrs, US$37-46, several daily. Direct to **Brasília**, 24 hrs, US$57-61. To **Porto Velho**, 9 buses a day, US$74-89, 26 hrs. Connections to all major cities.

Cáceres

Bus *Rodoviária*, Terminal da Japonesa. **Verde** (http://verdetransportes.com.br) or **Juina** buses Cuiabá–Cáceres, US$18, 5 daily (book in advance), 3½ hrs.

Ferry For information on sailings, ask at the **Capitânia dos Portos**, on the corner of the main square at waterfront.

Border with Bolivia

Bus The bus fare Cáceres–San Matías is US$20 with **Transical–Velásquez**, Mon-Sat at 0630 and 1500, Sun 1500 only (return at same times), 3 hrs. Bus from **Pontes e Lacerda** to **San Ignacio de Velasco** (Bolivia) with **Rápido Monte Cristo**, Tue and Fri 0630, US$17, 8-9 hrs, much longer in rainy season when roads may be impassable; and **Amanda Tours** via Vila Bela, Mon, Wed, Fri 0600, US$22, on slightly better roads. From **Vila Bela** to Cuiabá via Pontes e Lacerda and Cáceres, daily at 0800 and 1930, US$36, 7-8 hrs.

Chapada dos Guimarães

Bus 7 daily to and from **Cuiabá** (Rubi 0700-1900, last back to Cuiabá 1800), 1½ hrs, US$5.50.

Car Hiring a car in Cuiabá is the most convenient way to see many of the scattered attractions, although access to several of them is via rough dirt roads which may deteriorate in the rainy season; drive carefully as the area is prone to dense fog. Agencies at the airport.

Practicalities
Getting around

Air

Because of the great distances, flying is often the most practical option. All state capitals and larger cities are linked several times a day and all national airlines offer excellent service. Low-cost airlines offer fares that can either be as cheap as, or only a few dollars more than travelling by bus on long journeys (when booked through the internet). Compare airline websites with the bus price websites given below. Paying with an international credit card is not always possible online, but it is usually possible to buy an online ticket through a hotel, agency or willing friend without surcharge. Most airlines' websites provide full information, including a booking service, although not all are in English. The dominant airlines are GOL ① T0300-115 2121, www.voegol.com.br, LATAM ① T0300-570 5700/011-4002 5700 (in São Paulo), www.latam.com, and Azul ① T4003-1118, or T0800-887 1118 outside main cities, www.voeazul.com.br. Many other airlines operate, some regional, others nationwide. Avianca ① T4004 4040/T0300-789 8160, www.avianca.com.br, have extensive routes. Small scheduled domestic airlines fly to virtually every city and town with any semblance of an airstrip. Internal flights often have many stops and can be quite slow. Most airports have left-luggage lockers. Seats are often unallocated on internal flights; board in good time.

GOL has a 90-day **airpass**, from four to nine coupons, starting at US$505 (plus tax), which must be bought outside Brazil. It is available to passengers entering Brazil on GOL or a GOL partner airline. If you have to change planes on a route, this counts as one coupon if the stop-over is less than four hours. A maximum of two connections may be made in the same city. Dates may be changed, but routes cannot once the ticket has been bought.

Avianca has a similar 90-day airpass, with similar conditions, from four to eight coupons, costing US$500-967.

Azul has a 21-day airpass, www.azulairpass.com, starting at US$399 for four coupons (US$499 if arriving in Brazil on a carrier other than Azul, United or TAP) and a 10-day airpass costing US$299.

Road

Bus

There are three standards of **bus**: *comum* or *convencional*, which are quite slow, not very comfortable and fill up quickly; *executivo* (executive), which are a few reais more expensive, comfortable, but don't stop to pick up passengers en route and are therefore safer; and *semi-leito* or *leito* (literally, bed), which run at night between the main centres, offering reclining seats with foot and leg rests, toilets, and sometimes refreshments, with a higher ticket price. For journeys over 100 km, most buses have chemical toilets. A/c can make *leito* buses cold at night, so take a blanket or sweater (and toilet paper); on some services blankets are supplied. Some companies have hostess service. Ask for a window seat (*janela*) if you want the view.

Buses stop frequently (every two to four hours) for snacks at *postos*. Bus stations for interstate services and other long-distance routes are called *rodoviárias*. They are normally outside the city centres and offer snack bars, lavatories, left-luggage (*guarda volume*), local bus services and information centres. The bus companies themselves are the best source of reliable information, at *rodoviárias* or online (most take credit and Visa debit cards). See www.buscaonibus.com.br or https://rodoviariaonline.com.br for one-stop sources of services and fares between major cities in Portuguese and English. Buses usually arrive and depart in good time, although loading luggage, ID checks and, in some cities such as São Paulo, metal detector checks can slow things up.

TRAVEL TIP

Driving in Brazil

Road Around 13% of roads are paved and many more all-weather. The best highways are concentrated in the southeast; those serving the interior are being improved to all-weather status and many are paved. Some main roads are narrow and dangerous; many are in poor condition.

Safety Try never to leave your car unattended except in a locked garage or guarded parking area.

Documents To drive in Brazil you need an international licence. A national driving licence is acceptable as long as your home country is a signatory to the 1968 Vienna and 1949 Geneva conventions on road traffic. There are agreements between Brazil and all South American countries (but check in the case of Bolivia) whereby a car can be taken into Brazil (or a Brazilian car out of Brazil) for a period of 90 days without any special documents. For cars registered in other countries, you need proof of ownership and/or registration in the home country and valid driving licence (as above). A 90-day permit is given by customs and procedure is very straightforward. Make sure you keep **all** the papers you are given when you enter, to produce when you leave.

Car hire Renting a car in Brazil is expensive: the cheapest rate for unlimited mileage for a small car is about US$30-50 per day. Minimum age for renting a car is 21 and it is essential to have a credit card. Companies operate under the terms *aluguel de automóveis* or *autolocadores*.

Fuel Fuel prices vary from week to week and according to region (average prices given, http://anp.gov.br). *Gasolina comum* costs about US$1.10 per litre with *gasolina maxi* and *maxigold* a little more. *Etanol comum* costs about US$0.80. Diesel costs US$0.95. There is no unleaded fuel. Fuel is only 85 octane. It is virtually impossible to buy premium grades of petrol anywhere.

Car share

Bla Bla Car ① *www.blablacar.com.br, or sign up on Facebook*, the long-distance car-sharing service, operates in Brazil. Prices are lower than buses and are indicated on www.buscaonibus.com.br but Bla Bla Car's website is more detailed.

Taxi

Taxi meters measure distance/cost in reais. At the outset, make sure the meter is cleared and shows tariff '1', except Sunday 2300-0600, and in December when '2' is permitted. Check the meter works, if not, fix price in advance. Designated airport and radio taxi services cost about 30-50% more but cheating is less likely. Taxis outside larger hotels usually cost more than ordinary taxis. If you are seriously cheated, note the taxi number and insist on a signed bill, threatening to go to the police; it can work.

Note Be wary of mototaxis; many are unlicensed and a number of robberies have been reported.

Rail

There are 30,379 km of railway track; almost all run goods trains only. Brazil has two gauges and there is little transfer between them. Two more gauges exist for the isolated Amapá Railway and the tourist-only São João del Rei and Ouro Preto-Mariana lines. The other main tourist service runs from Curitiba to the Paraná coast. There are suburban passenger services in Rio de Janeiro, São Paulo and other cities and a long-distance service between Belo Horizonte and Vitória.

River

The only area where boat travel is practical (and often necessary) is the Amazon region, see Getting around, page 598.

Maps and guides

Editora Abril publishes the magazines *Quatro Rodas* and *Viagem e Turismo*, as well as a wide range of other publications. All are available at news stands and bookshops all over the country and online: http://quatrorodas.abril.com.br. For the group's travel blog, see http://viajeaqui.abril.com.br.

Where to stay

Hotels

Usually hotel prices include breakfast of rolls, ham, eggs, cheese, cakes and fruit. There is no reduction if you don't eat it. Normally an *apartamento* is a room with sleeping and living areas and sometimes cooking facilities. A *quarto* is a standard room: *com banheiro* is en suite, *sem banheiro* is with shared bathroom. A *pousada* is either the equivalent of bed-and-breakfast, often small and family-run, or a sophisticated and often charming small hotel. A *hotel* is the same as anywhere in the world. The star rating system (five-star hotels are not price-controlled) is not the standard used in North America or Europe. Many of the older hotels can be cheaper than hostels. Business visitors are strongly recommended to book in advance. It is also a good idea to book in advance in small towns that are popular at weekends with city dwellers (eg near São Paulo and Rio de Janeiro) and it is essential to book at peak times. If staying more than three nights in a place in low season, ask for a discount. A *motel* is specifically intended for guests who are not intending to sleep: there is no stigma attached and they usually offer good value (the rate for a full night is called the *pernoite*), though the decor can be a little garish. See the Planning your trip chapter for our hotel price guide.

Private associations

Roteiros de Charme ⓘ www.roteirosdecharme.com.br, and Circuito Elegante ⓘ www.circuito elegante.com.br, are private associations of hotels and *pousadas* which aim to give a high standard of accommodation in establishments typical of the town they are in. They are equivalent to international hotel associations such as Small Luxury Hotels of the World ⓘ www.slh.com, Leading Hotels of the World ⓘ www.lhw.com, and Relais et Chateaux ⓘ www.relaischateaux.com, all of which have members in Brazil. There are, however, many fine hotels and *pousadas* to suit all budgets listed in our text that are not included in these associations.

Youth hostels

For information contact Federação Brasileira de Albergues da Juventude ⓘ R São Carlos 545, Bairro Floresta, Porto Alegre, CEP 90220-121, T051-3228 3802, www.albergues.com.br. Its annual book and website provide a full list of good-value accommodation. Also see the *Internet Guide to Hostelling*, which has list of Brazilian youth hostels: www.hostels.com/brazil.

Camping

Members of the Camping Clube do Brasil or those with an international campers' card pay only half the rate of a non-member. The club has 43 sites around the country. See Camping Clube do Brasil ⓘ R Sen Dantas 75, 17th floor, sala 1708, Rio de Janeiro, T021-2532 0203, www.campingclube. com.br. It may be difficult to get into some Clube campsites during the high season (January/February). Private campsites charge about US$10-15 per person for non-club members. For those on a very low budget and in isolated areas where there is no camp site, service stations can be used as camping sites; they have shower facilities, watchmen and food; some have dormitories; truck drivers are a mine of information. There are also various municipal sites. Campsites often tend to be some distance from public transport routes and are better suited to those with their own transport. Never camp at the side of a road; wild camping is generally not possible. Good camping equipment may be purchased in Brazil and there are several rental companies. Camping gas cartridges are easy to buy in sizeable towns in the south. Most sizeable towns have laundromats with self service. *Lavanderias* do the washing for you but are expensive.

Food & drink

Food

The main meal is usually taken in the middle of the day; cheap restaurants tend not to be open in the evening. The most common dish is *bife* (or *frango*) *com arroz e feijão*, steak (or chicken) with rice and the excellent Brazilian black beans. The most famous dish with beans is the *feijoada completa*: several meat ingredients (jerked beef, smoked sausage, smoked tongue, salt pork) along with spices, herbs and vegetables, are cooked with the beans. Manioc flour is sprinkled over it, and it is eaten with kale (*couve*) and slices of orange, and accompanied by glasses of *cachaça* (see below). Almost all restaurants serve the *feijoada completa* for Saturday lunch (until about 1630).

Throughout Brazil, a mixed grill, including steak, served with roasted manioc flour (*farofa*; raw manioc flour is known as *farinha*) goes under the name of *churrasco* (originally from the cattlemen of Rio Grande do Sul), served in specialized restaurants known as churrascarias or *rodízios*; good places for large appetites.

Brazil's best cooking is regional. For instance, Bahia has some excellent fish dishes (see local specialities on page 533); some restaurants in most of the big cities specialize in them. Minas Gerais has two splendid special dishes involving pork, black beans, farofa and kale; they are *tutu á mineira* and *feijão tropeiro*. A white hard cheese (*queijo prata*) or a slightly softer one (*queijo Minas*) is often served for dessert with bananas, or guava or quince paste. *Comida mineira* is quite distinctive and very wholesome and you can often find restaurants serving this type of food in other parts of Brazil.

Meals are extremely large by European standards; portions are usually for two and come with two plates. Likewise beer is brought with two glasses. If you are on your own and in a position to do so tactfully, you may choose to offer what you can't eat to a person with no food. Alternatively you could ask for an *embalagem* (doggy bag) or get a take away called *a marmita* or *quentinha*, most restaurants have this service but it is not always on the menu. Many restaurants serve *comida por kilo*, usually at lunchtime, where you serve yourself and pay for the weight of food on your plate: good for vegetarians. Unless you specify to the contrary many restaurants will lay a *coberto opcional*, olives, carrots, etc, costing US$2-4. **Warning** Avoid mussels, marsh crabs and other shellfish caught near large cities: they are likely to have lived in a highly polluted environment. In a restaurant, always ask the price of a dish before ordering.

For **vegetarians**, there is a growing network of restaurants in the main cities. In smaller places where food may be monotonous try vegetarian for greater variety. Most also serve fish. Alternatives in smaller towns are the Arab and Chinese restaurants. And don't forget that there are myriad unusual, delicious fruits from all over Brazil, especially the Amazon and the Cerrado.

Lanchonetes are cheap eating places where you generally sit on a stool at the counter to eat. *Salgados* (savoury pastries, also *pastel* – plural *pasteis*), *coxinha* (a pyramid of manioc filled with meat or fish and deep fried), *kibe* (deep-fried or baked mince with onion, mint and flour), *esfiha* (spicey hamburger inside an onion-bread envelope), *empadão* (a filling – eg chicken – in sauce in a pastry case), *empadas* and *empadinhas* (smaller fritters of the same type), are the usual fare. In Minas Gerais, *pão de queijo* is a hot roll made with cheese. A *bauru* is a toasted sandwich which, in Porto Alegre, is filled with steak, while further north it has tomato, ham and cheese filling. *Cocada* is a coconut and sugar biscuit. See the Planning your trip chapter for our restaurant price guide.

Drink

The national alcoholic drink is *cachaça* (also known as *pinga*), which is made from sugar-cane, and ranging from cheap fire-water, to boutique distillery and connoisseur labels from the interior of Minas Gerais. Mixed with fruit juice, sugar and crushed ice, *cachaça* becomes the principal element in a *batida*, a refreshing but deceptively powerful drink. Served with pulped lime or other fruit, mountains of sugar and smashed ice it becomes caipirinha. A less potent caipirinha made with vodka is called a *caipiroska* and with sake a *saikirinha* or *caipisake*.

Some genuine Scotch whisky brands are bottled in Brazil; they are cheaper even than duty free. Teacher's is the best. Locally made gin, vermouth and campari are good. Wine is becoming increasingly popular, with good-value Portuguese and Argentinean bottles and some reasonable national table wines. The wine industry is mainly concentrated in the south of the country where the conditions are most suitable, with over 90% of wine produced in Rio Grande do Sul. There are also vineyards in Pernambuco.

Brazilian beer is generally lager, served ice-cold. Draught beer is called *chope* or *chopp* (after the German Schoppen, and pronounced 'shoppi'). There are various national brands of bottled beers, which include Brahma, Skol, Cerpa, Antartica and the best Itaipava and Bohemia. There are black beers too, notably Xingu. They tend to be sweet. The best beer is from the German breweries in Rio Grande do Sul and is available only there.

Brazil's fruits are used to make fruit juices or *sucos*, which come in a delicious variety. *Açai, acerola, caju* (cashew), *pitanga, goiaba* (guava), *genipapo, graviola (soursop) and cherimoya, maracujá* (passion fruit), *sapoti, umbu* and *tamarindo* are a few of the best. *Vitaminas* are thick fruit or vegetable drinks with milk. *Caldo de cana* is sugar-cane juice, sometimes mixed with ice. *Água de côco* or *côco verde* is coconut water served straight from a chilled, fresh, green coconut. The best known of many local soft drinks is *guaraná*, which is a very popular carbonated fruit drink, completely unrelated to the Amazon nut. The best variety is *guaraná Antarctica*. Coffee is ubiquitous and good tea entirely absent.

Essentials A-Z

Accident and emergency

Ambulance: T192. **Directory enquiries**: T102.
Fire service: T193. **Police**: T190.

Electricity

Generally 110 V 60 cycles AV, but in some areas 220 V 60 cycles. Sockets also vary, often combination sockets for twin flat and twin round pin.

Embassies and consulates

For Brazilian embassies abroad and for all foreign embassies and consulates in Brazil, see http://embassy.goabroad.com.

Health

For hospitals, doctors and dentists, contact your consulate or the tourist office for advice.

Rio de Janeiro

The **Prefeitura do Rio de Janeiro** website, http://prefeitura.rio/web/sms/principal, lists all the health facilities in the city.
Hospital Municipal Rocha Maia, R Gen Severiano 91, Botafogo, T021-2295 2295/2121, near Rio Sul Shopping Centre. A good public hospital for minor injuries and ailments. Free, but there may be queues.
Hospital Miguel Couto, Mário Ribeiro 117, Gávea, T021-3111 3720. Has a free casualty ward.

São Paulo

Hospital Samaritano, R Conselheiro Brotero 1486, Higienópolis, T011-3821 5300, http://samaritano.com.br. Recommended.

Money

US$1 = R$3.31; €1 = R$3.70 (Jun 2017).
The unit of currency is the real, R$ (plural reais). It floats freely against the dollar. Any amount of foreign currency and 'a reasonable sum' in reais can be taken in; residents may only take out the equivalent of US$4000. Notes in circulation are: 100, 50, 10, 5 and 1 real; coins 1 real, 50, 25, 10, 5 and 1 centavo.

Credit cards Credit or debit cards are the most convenient way of withdrawing money. ATMs are common and frequently offer the best rate of exchange. Note, though, that **Banco 24 Horas** ATMs give a long list of cards that they accept, but often do not take international cards. The same is true of **Banco do Brasil**. In some places you may have to hunt long and hard for an ATM that will accept a foreign card. During banking hours you should be able to withdraw cash against a credit card, eg at branches of **Banco do Brasil** and **Bradesco**. Credit cards will be charged interest, debit cards should not, but machines that take debit cards are harder to find. The lobbies in which machines are placed usually close 2130-0400. **Bradesco** is the best for ATM service. Some **BBV** branches have Visa and MasterCard ATMs.

Emergency phone numbers: MasterCard T0800-891 3294; Visa T0800-891-3680.

Banks In major cities banks will change cash. If you keep the exchange slips, you may convert back into foreign currency up to 50% of the amount you exchanged. Take US dollars in cash, or euros. In larger cities and tourist destinations, most large hotels and reputable travel agencies will change currency. In smaller places it can be difficult to change dollars cash and in some exchange houses US$1 notes are not accepted.

Cost of travelling A bed in a hostel costs on average US$10-18 pp. Budget hotels have rooms with few frills for US$20-30, but you can find a good double room for under US$55 in any part of the country. Hostels can be a good choice when travelling alone. For 2 or more people, however, a room in a simple hotel may cost less than several dorm beds in a hostel. Hotels and even restaurants in resort areas may offer discounts mid-week, be sure to ask. Conversely, prices rise during holidays and festivals. Eating out in higher class restaurants can be costly; you should expect to pay around US$20-30 a head and, in larger cities, up to US$50 for a 2-course meal with non-alcoholic drinks. There are many more moderately priced restaurant options at lunchtime than in the evening. If travelling on a tight budget, ask for the *refeição* (buffet), or *prato feito* (single serving), both money-saving options. The *prato comercial* is similar but rather better and a bit more expensive. Bakeries always offer cheap snacks and sandwiches. Vegetarians should ask the price without meat, it may be lower. Flying may be less expensive than bus travel when airfares are booked online at least 21 to 28 days in advance. Hourly rate for use of internet, US$1-2, though most hotels and hostels now have free Wi-Fi.

Opening hours

Banks: 1000-1600, but closed on Sat.
Businesses: Mon-Fri 0900-1800, closing for lunch some time between 1130 and 1400.
Government offices: Mon-Fri 1100-1800.
Shops: open on Sat until 1230 or 1300.

Post

Postal services are handled by **Correios do Brasil**, whose website lists all agencies and services offered (in Portuguese), www.correios.com.br. It offers services for traditional letters, fax and transmission of documents by internet. Poste Restante is available nationwide; there is a charge of US$0.40 for letters addressed to Poste Restante. **Federal Express** and other courier services operate within Brazil.

Public holidays and festivals

See also Carnival box, page 420. National holidays are **1 Jan** (New Year); **Feb** 3 days up to and including Ash Wed (Carnival); **21** (Tiradentes); **1 May** (Labour Day); **Corpus Christi** (Jun); **7 Sep** (Independence Day); **12 Oct** (Nossa Senhora Aparecida); **2** (All Souls' Day); **15 Nov** (Day of the Republic); and **25 Dec** (Christmas). Local holidays in the main cities are given in the text.

Safety

Although Brazil's big cities suffer high rates of violent crime, this is mostly confined to the favelas (slums), which should be avoided unless accompanied by a tour leader or NGO. If the worst does happen and you are threatened, try not to panic, but hand over your valuables. Do not resist, but report the crime to the local tourist police, who should be your 1st port of call in case of difficulty. The situation is much more secure in smaller towns and in the country. Also steer well clear of areas of drug cultivation and red-light districts. In the latter drinks are often spiked with a drug called 'Goodnight Cinderella'.

Police There are several types of police: **Polícia Federal**, civilian dressed, who handle all federal law duties, including immigration. A subdivision is the **Polícia Federal Rodoviária**, uniformed, who are the traffic police. **Polícia Militar** are the uniformed, street police force, under the control of the state governor, handling all state laws. They are not the same as the Armed Forces' internal police. **Polícia Civil**, also state-controlled, handle local laws; usually in civilian dress, unless in the traffic division. In cities, the Prefeitura controls the **Guarda Municipal**, who handle security. **Tourist police** operate in places with a strong tourist presence.

Identification You must always carry ID when in Brazil; it is a good idea to take a photocopy of the personal details in your passport, plus that with your Brazilian immigration stamp, and leave your passport in the hotel safe deposit. See the Safety section in the Practicalities chapter at the back of the book for general advice.

Tax

Airport tax The international departure tax is usually included in the ticket price. If not, you will have to pay on leaving Brazil. Most domestic airport tax is included in domestic tickets.
VAT Rate varies from 7 to 25% and varies from state to state; the average is 17-18%. It is known as **ICMS, Imposto sobre Circulação de Mercadorias e Prestação de Serviços**, www.tabelaicms.com.

Telephone and Wi-Fi

International phone code +55.
Ringing: equal tones with long pauses. Engaged: equal tones, equal pauses. Dialling: it is necessary to dial a 2-digit telephone company code before the area code for all calls. Phone numbers are now printed: 0XX21, where the XX stands for the company code (we do not show the XX in the text of this chapter). To dial internationally dial 00 + company code without the zero, then the country code and number. **Operating company codes**: Embratel/Claro, 21 (nationwide); **Vivo/Telefônica**, 15; **Oi**, 31 and 14; **Algar**, 12; TIM, 41.

Telephone booths, or *orelhões* (big ears) are easy to find and normally take phone cards, which can be bought at newsstands, post offices and some chemists/pharmacies. They cost from US$4 for 30 units. International phone cards, *cartões telefônicas internacionais*, are also available in tourist areas and are often sold at hostels. Local calls from private phones are often free. International calls may be made from telephone company offices.

Mobile phones These are widespread and coverage is excellent even in remote areas, but prices are among the highest in the world and users pay to receive calls outside the metropolitan area where their phone is registered. SIM cards can be hard to buy as users officially require a Brazilian social security number (CPF), though most hire shops will have a way of getting round this and hostels and hotels are usually helpful. While fixed lines have 8 digits, mobile phone numbers have 9 digits beginning with 9, generally starting 97, 98 or 99. When using a mobile phone you do not drop the zero from the area code as you have to when dialling from a fixed line.

Public internet access is available everywhere. Cyber-cafés are plentiful and are usually called **Lan house** or **ciber-café**. Some cities have free Wi-Fi in public areas. More and more hotels offer internet, often in-room Wi-Fi; usually free but sometimes at exorbitant rates.

Time

Official time Brazil has several time zones: Brasília standard time, which is GMT -3. States in this zone are divided into 2 groups: those with daylight saving (GMT -2, 3rd Sun in Oct to 3rd Sun in Feb), which are Brasília (Federal District), Espírito Santo, Goiás, Minas Gerais, Paraná, Rio de Janeiro, Rio Grande do Sul, Santa Catarina, São Paulo and Tocantins; and those without daylight saving, Alagoas, Amapá, Bahia, Ceará, Maranhão, Pará, Paraíba, Pernambuco, Piauí, Rio Grande do Norte, Sergipe. Amazon standard time (GMT -4) is used in most of Amazonas, Rondônia, and Roraima, while Mato Grosso and Mato Grosso do Sul use Amazon time, plus daylight saving (as above, GMT -3). Acre and the southwest part of Amazonas are GMT -5. Fernando do Noronha is GMT -2.

Tipping

Tipping is not usual, but is always appreciated. Restaurants, 10% of bill if no service charge but small tip if there is; taxi drivers, none; cloakroom attendants, small tip; hairdressers, 10-15%; porters, fixed charges but tips as well; unofficial car parkers on city streets should be tipped 2 reais.

Tourist information

Ministério do Turismo, Esplanada dos Ministérios, bloco U, 2nd and 3rd floors, Brasília, www.turismo.gov.br (in many languages). **Embratur**, the Brazilian Institute of Tourism, SCN Quadra 02 bloco G, Ed Embratur, Brasília, is in charge of promoting tourism abroad, www.embratur.gov.br. Tourist information bureaux are not usually helpful with information on cheap hotels and it is difficult to get information on neighbouring states. Expensive hotels provide tourist magazines for their guests. Telephone directories (not Rio) contain good street maps.

National parks are run by the **Instituto Chico Mendes de Conservação da Biodiversidade**, **ICMBio**, EQSW 103/104, bloco C, Complexo Administrativo, Setor Sudoeste, Brasília, DF, www.icmbio.gov.br. National parks are open to visitors, usually with a permit issued by ICMBio. See also the **Ministério do Meio Ambiente** website, www.mma.gov.br.

Useful websites

See tourist office sites under individual cities.

http://abeta.tur.br The Brazilian Association of Adventure Tourism Companies' website, with a list of members by state and types of activity available (in Portuguese); Abeta, R Minerva 156, Perdizes, São Paulo, T011-2371 5336.

http://washington.itamaraty.gov.br (USA).

http://londres.itamaraty.gov.br (UK).

www.gringo-rio.com Guide to all things about Rio, city and state, by a gringo, for gringos, also apartment rentals.

www.ipanema.com Insider's guide to Rio in English.

www.angloinfo.com/sao-paulo Information in English on São Paulo life for ex-pats.

www.socioambiental.org Accurate information on environmental and indigenous issues.

www.survivalinternational.org The world's leading campaign organization for indigenous peoples with excellent info on various Brazilian indigenous groups.

www.wwf.org.br World Wide Fund in Brazil.

Visas and immigration

Consular visas are not required for stays of up to 90 days by tourists from EU countries, Israel, Norway, South Africa, Switzerland, South and Central American countries and some Caribbean, Asian and African countries. At the port of disembarkation these tourists will need: a passport valid for at least 6 months; and a return or onward ticket, or adequate proof that you can purchase your return fare. Visas are required by US and Canadian citizens, Japanese, Australians and people of other nationalities in advance who cannot meet the requirements above. Visas are valid from date of issue. Visa fees vary from country to country, so apply to the Brazilian consulate, in the country of residence of the applicant. The consular fee is generally US$80, but is US$120 for Australians and US$160 for US citizens (processing fee, the visa itself is free). Do not lose the emigration permit given to you when you enter Brazil. If you leave the country

without it, you may have to pay a fine. Brazilian consulates will advise on regulations and costs for student and business visas; these vary according to nationality and proposed length of stay.

Foreign tourists may stay a maximum of 180 days in any one year. 90-day renewals (*pedido de prorrogação de prazo de estada*) are easily obtainable, but only at least 30 days before the expiry of your first 90-day permit, from and at the discretion of the Polícia Federal. You will have to obtain a copy of form 154 online at www.pf.gov. br; go to "servicos", then "estrangeiro" page for the procedure (in Portuguese). Since 2015, the necessary documents must be presented at one time and the Polícia Federal should deal with the request in a set period. The total cost of an extension is US$34 in cash. Regulations state that you must show a return ticket, a bank statement or a credit card to demonstrate that you have sufficient funds for your next 90 days, your passport and the entry card you received when you arrived in Brazil. Some points of entry, such as the Colombian border, refuse entry for longer than 30 days, renewals are then for the same period, insist if you want 90 days. For longer stays you must leave the country and return (not the same day) to get a new 90-day permit. If your visa has expired, getting a new visa can be costly and may take up to 45 days. If you overstay your visa you will be fined a minimum of US$2.55, maximum US$255. After paying the fine, you will be issued with an exit visa and must leave within 8 days. **Note** Officially, if you leave Brazil within the 90-day permission to stay and then re-enter the country, you should only be allowed to stay until the 90-day permit expires. If, however, you are given another 90-day permit, this may lead to charges of overstaying if you apply for an extension. For UK citizens a joint agreement allows visits for business or tourism of up to 6 months a year from the date of first entry.

Weights and measures

Metric.

This is Chile

Chile is a ribbon of land squashed between the Pacific and the Andes. Its landscape embraces glacial wilderness and moonscapes, lakes and volcanoes, beaches and salt flats. The north is characterized by the burnt colours of the driest desert in the world. Should rain fall in this barren land, flower seeds that have lain in wait seize the moment to bloom, bringing brilliant colours where no life seemed possible. Snow-capped volcanoes in the Lauca National Park appear close enough to touch in the rarefied air. In one day it is possible to scale a mountain with ice axe and crampons, soak off the exhaustion in a thermal bath and rest beneath the stars of the Southern Cross. Real stargazers will want to visit the astronomical observatories near La Serena, while lovers of mystery will head south for the folklore of Chiloé, Land of Seagulls. The Chilean Lake District is the homeland of the Mapuche, the people who resisted the Spaniards and who proudly maintain their culture and traditions. The lakes themselves are beautiful, set in farmland, overlooked by yet more snow-capped volcanoes. Before the road peters out, blocked by fjords and icefields, the Carretera Austral reveals ancient woodlands, hot springs beside the sea, mountains like castles and raging, emerald rivers – a paradise for fishing and cycling. To reach the ultimate goal of trekkers and birdwatchers, the fabulous granite towers and spires of the Torres del Paine National Park, you have to take a boat, or fly, or make the long haul through Argentina. There are seaports of every size, with their fishing boats, pelicans and sea lions. The most romantic is Valparaíso, described by one observer as "a Venice waiting to be discovered", with its warren of streets and brightly painted houses, its singular lifts up to the clifftops and its old bars.

PERU

Visviri
PN Lauca
Arica   Putre   Tambo Quemado
Pisagua
BOLIVIA
Iquique

Quillagua   Ollagüe
Tocopilla   Chuquicamata
Calama   El Tatio
San Pedro de Atacama
Salar de   Toconao
Atacama
Antofagasta   Socompa
Desert of
Atacama
Taltal
Parque Nacional
Pan de Azúcar
Chañaral   Potrerilleros
Caldera
Copiapó

PARAGUAY

Vallenar

Pacific
Ocean

La Serena
Coquimbo
Ovalle

ARGENTINA

Viña
del Mar   Los Andes
Valparaíso
SANTIAGO
Rancagua

URUGUAY

Talca
Área de
Protección Vilches
Chillán   Paso Pehuenche
Concepción
Los Angeles
Cañete   Angol
Temuco   Curacautín
Villarrica   Pucón
Valdivia   Panguipulli
Lago Ranco
Osorno
Frutillar
Ancud   Puerto Montt
Castro
Chiloé   Chaitén
Quellón

Puyuguapi
Puerto Cisnes
Puerto   Coyhaique
Aisén

Atlantic
Ocean

Cochrane
Villa O'Higgins

PN Torres
del Paine
PN Bernardo
O'Higgins   Puerto Natales

Punta   Porvenir   Tierra
Arenas   del Fuego
Puerto Williams

N

200 km
200 miles

Footprint picks

★ **Valparaíso**, page 706

This UNESCO World Heritage Site
is one of South America's most
captivating cities with its
labyrinthine hills and vibrant culture.

★ **Parque Nacional Lauca**, page 755

One of several high-altitude parks in the far north,
set against a backdrop of snow-capped volcanoes.

★ **Central Valley**, page 761

Chile's finest vintages come from the valleys south of Santiago.

★ **Lake District**, page 772

Green forests, blue waters and lofty volcanoes characterize
this delightful region, ideal for trekking and water sports.

★ **Chiloé**, page 810

A magical island of distinctive architecture, fishing, forests and
mythical creatures.

★ **Carretera Austral**, page 820

Cycle, hike, hitch or take a minibus through the spectacular
scenery between Puerto Montt and Villa O'Higgins.

★ **Torres del Paine**, page 851

Quite simply one of the world's greatest national parks.

Route planner

Chile is hemmed in by the Pacific Ocean, the Atacama Desert and the Andes. When combined with the country's shape, these geographical barriers rule out circular routes within the country – the choice therefore comes down to whether to go north or south. If you don't mind flying, you could combine elements from the two-week itineraries to create a month-long trip that takes in the best of both.

Northern Chile

cities, deserts, stars and volcanoes

Two weeks

On a two-week trip your first stop should be beguiling **Valparaíso**. From there, catch a bus north to **La Serena**, enjoying the beauties of the mountainous semi-desert en route. Spend perhaps three days exploring the area around La Serena, visiting the **Elqui Valley** and its observatories, the **Parque Nacional Fray Jorge**, the sea life at **Isla Damas**, or the cave paintings at the **Valle del Encanto**. Continue to **Chañaral** to see the spectacular **Parque Nacional Pan de Azúcar**, before moving on to **San Pedro de Atacama**. Spend three days visiting the geysers, altiplano lakes, salt flats and the Valley of the Moon. Then, take an overnight bus to **Arica**, and spend two days visiting the spectacular **Parque Nacional Lauca** and the world's highest lake, **Chungará**, before flying back to the capital for some last-minute shopping and culture.

One month

A month would allow you to add some fascinating destinations to your itinerary. On the journey north from Valparaíso, for example, spend two or three days exploring the **Limarí Valley** and the **Monumental Natural Pichasca**, which has much to interest the geologist and archaeologist in the form of petrified trees and ancient rock art. Heading north from Chañaral, break your journey at the attractive coastal town of **Taltal** and then visit **Chuquicamata**, the largest open-cast copper mine on earth. With two extra days at San Pedro, you could tour the beautiful altiplano villages, before travelling to Arica to get to know the city itself and take a four-day altiplano tour, visiting **Lauca**, **Surire** and **Isluga** parks. Finish in **Iquique** where you can relax on the beach for a couple of days, do a tandem paraglide over the city, or visit the thermal baths at **Pica**.

Southern Chile

vineyards, lakes, glaciers and more volcanoes

Two weeks

After arriving in Santiago, visit Valparaíso before heading south by bus to spend a few days in the **Central Valley**. Explore the high mountains around **Vilches**, or the **Parque Nacional Siete Tazas**. Sample some of Chile's best wines, or go surfing at **Pichilemu**. Move on to **Lago Villarrica** to climb the volcano or trek in the Araucaria forests of Huerquehue or Cañi. You could also spend a day whitewater rafting or relaxing in natural thermal springs. Continue south to **Lago Llanquihue**, where the Osorno volcano provides a spectacular backdrop to the lake. The impressive **Petrohué waterfalls** are an hour to the east. Alternatively, head to Valdivia, on the river of the same name, with its lively culture, German heritage and colonial fortifications near the ocean. From Puerto Montt, visit the beautiful island of **Chiloé**, where there are penguins, Jesuit churches, rich mythology and close-knit communities. Then fly from Puerto Montt to **Puerto Natales** and spend a few days visiting the mountains and eerie blue glaciers of **Torres del Paine**, one of the world's greatest national parks, before flying back to Santiago.

One month

Spend a further two or three days on Chiloé, visiting the **Parque Nacional Chiloé** and **Castro**. Then catch a boat to Chaitén and spend eight or nine days travelling along the fabulous **Carretera Austral**. See giant alerce forests in the **Parque Pumalín**, experience some of the world's best whitewater rafting around **Futaleufú** and hike around **Cerro Castillo**. If money is no object, you could also head for Puerto Chacabuco and take a cruise to the **Laguna San Rafael** glacier. Fly down from Coyhaique to **Punta Arenas** and visit the nearby penguin colonies or splash out on a whale-watching trip before making your way on to **Torres del Paine**. Add the pioneering little town of Porvenir and the wilds of **Tierra del Fuego** to complete your southern odyssey.

Essential Chile

Finding your feet

Much of northern Chile is desert, except for an occasional oasis, and there are often large distances between places of interest. Unlike the south, it is pleasant to visit during the colder months of the year (May to September). Highlights include the peaceful Elqui Valley, for pisco-tasting and star-gazing, and the oasis of San Pedro de Atacama, surrounded by archaeological sites and awesome natural phenomena. At the northern tip of Chile the desert rises up to meet the lush green of the altiplano, home to a dozen volcanoes and a wide variety of wildlife.

The Central Valley is the heart of the country and is where most Chileans live. Santiago has a couple of world-class museums and is close to the country's best ski resorts, while Valparaíso on the coast has a bohemian atmosphere unlike anywhere else in Chile. Beach lovers can head to the nearby resort of Viña del Mar or to any number of quiet fishing villages. Stretching south from Santiago are Chile's prime wine valleys.

Southern Chile is filled with forests, fjords, rivers, lakes and snow-capped volcanoes, overlooked by the Andes to the east. In the Lake District adventure tourism is easy, especially around Pucón or Puerto Varas. The remote Carretera Austral runs south through Chilean Patagonia, with access to wonderful landscapes and adventure opportunities. South of vast Lago General Carrera are Patagonia s enormous ice fields and Torres del Paine national park, whose glaciers and granite towers are the jewel in the crown of Chilean Patagonia.

Getting around

Internal transport is usually straightforward. There are domestic flights with LATAM (and, to a lesser extent, Sky) from Santiago to most cities, allowing you to move between the north and south of the country relatively easily; in some cases the fares may be cheaper than a long-distance bus ticket. Most of Chile is linked by one road, the paved Pan-American Highway (or Panamericana), marked on maps as Ruta 5, which runs from the Peruvian border south to Puerto Montt and the island of Chiloé. However, some of the most popular destinations in Chile lie to the south of Puerto Montt, and travelling to this part of the country requires careful planning. Though much of this area can be reached by the Carretera Austral, a gravel road marked on maps as Ruta 7, bus services here are far less reliable than elsewhere in the country. Furthermore, the Carretera Austral is punctuated by three ferry crossings, with a further crossing at Villa O'Higgins for those on the direct overland route to the far south of Argentina (summer only). Alternatives are to travel by sea and air from Puerto Montt. Ferries provide vital links in this region: notably from Chiloé to both Puerto Montt and Chaitén for the Carretera Austral; from Puerto Montt to Puerto Chacabuco (for Coyhaique, midway down the Carretera Austral); and from Puerto Montt to Puerto Natales in the far south.

Weather Santiago

January ☀ 30°C / 12°C / 0mm	**February** ☀ 30°C / 11°C / 0mm	**March** ⛅ 27°C / 10°C / 3mm
April ☁ 23°C / 7°C / 10mm	**May** 🌧 18°C / 5°C / 50mm	**June** 🌧 15°C / 4°C / 70mm
July 🌧 15°C / 2°C / 70mm	**August** 🌧 16°C / 4°C / 50mm	**September** 🌧 18°C / 5°C / 20mm
October ☁ 22°C / 7°C / 10mm	**November** ⛅ 22°C / 7°C / 3mm	**December** ☀ 22°C / 8°C / 1mm

When to go

The best times to visit vary according to geographical location. For the heartland, any time between October and April is good, but the most pleasant seasons are spring (September to November) and autumn (March to April). In Santiago itself, summers (December to February) are roasting hot and winters (June to August) polluted. The heat of the north is less intense from June to September. In the south December to March, summer, is the best time to visit. Along the Carretera Austral this is the only realistic time to travel because at other times ferry schedules are restricted and in mid-winter many transport services do not run at all. Further south, there is more leeway. The Torres del Paine park is open year round, though snow, fewer hours of daylight and reduced accommodation mean that only day hikes are feasible in winter. Also bear in mind

Fact file
Location 33.4330° S, 70.6670° W
Capital Santiago
Time zone GMT -4 hrs
(-3 hrs mid-Sep/Oct-Mar)
Telephone country code +56
Currency Chilean peso ($)

that January to February in the Lake District and further south are the busiest months, with raised prices, hotels and buses full, lots of backpackers on the road and advance booking often essential.

Time required

Two weeks is the minimum for a meaningful trip. Four weeks will allow you to explore either the north or the south of the country in more depth; see also Route planner, page 680.

Santiago
& around

Santiago, the political, economic and financial capital of Chile, is one of the most beautifully set of any city, standing in a wide plain with the magnificent chain of the Andes in full view – rain and pollution permitting. Nearly 40 percent of Chileans live in and around Santiago, the sixth largest city in South America, with a population of over seven million. It's a modern industrial capital, full of skyscrapers, bustle, noise and traffic, and smog is a problem especially between April and September. Santiago is within easy reach of vineyards, beaches and Andean ski resorts.

Sights Colour map 8, B1.

parks, museums, shops and hectic nightlife

Around the Plaza de Armas

On the eastern and southern sides of the Plaza de Armas there are arcades with shops; on the northern side the post office and the Municipalidad; and on the western side the Cathedral and the archbishop's palace. The **Cathedral**, much rebuilt, contains a recumbent

> **Tip...**
> Almost all museums are closed on Mondays and all day on 1 November.

statue in wood of San Francisco Javier and the chandelier which lit the first meetings of Congress after independence. In the Palacio de la Real Audiencia is the **Museo Histórico Nacional** ① T2-2411 7010, www.museohistoriconacional.cl, Tue-Sun 1000-1800, free, signs in Spanish, covering the period from the Conquest until 1925.

Just west of the Plaza is the ☆**Museo Chileno de Arte Precolombino** ① in the former Real Aduana, Bandera 361, T2-2928 1500, www.precolombino.cl, Tue-Sun 1000-1800, US$7, free 1st Sun of month, children free, displays in English, for guided tours write to reservas@museoprecolombiano.cl. Its well-presented collection of high-quality objects from the pre-Columbian cultures of Central America and the Andean region is highly recommended. At Calle Merced 860, is the **Casa Colorada** (1769), home of the Governor in colonial days and then of Mateo de Toro, first president of Chile. It is now the **Museo de Santiago** ① T2-2386 7400, www.santiagocultura.cl/casa-colorada, Tue-Fri 1000-1800, Sat 1000-1700, Sun and holidays 1100-1400, US$1, students free, only part of the museum is open during a renovation project. It covers the history of Santiago from the Conquest to modern times, with excellent displays and models, some signs in English, guided tours. Paseo Ahumada, a pedestrianized street lined with cafés, runs south from the Plaza to the Alameda four blocks away, crossing Huérfanos.

Four blocks north of the Plaza de Armas is the interesting ☆**Mercado Central** ① 21 de Mayo y San Pablo, the best place in Santiago for seafood. The building faces the Parque Venezuela, on which is the Cal y Canto metro station and, at its western end, the **Centro Cultural Estación Mapocho** ① www.estacionmapocho.cl, in the old Mapocho station. East of the Mercado Central is the Parque Forestal (see below), through which you come to Plaza Italia.

Essential Santiago

Finding your feet

The centre of the old city lies between the Mapocho and the Avenida O'Higgins, which is usually known as the Alameda. From the Plaza Baquedano (usually called Plaza Italia), in the east of the city's central area, the Mapocho flows to the northwest and the Alameda runs to the southwest. From Plaza Italia Calle Merced runs due west to the Plaza de Armas, the heart of the city, five blocks south of the Mapocho. An urban motorway runs the length of Santiago from east to west under the course of the Río Mapocho. The airport is 26 km northwest of the centre. The railway station, Estación Central, which only serves the south of the country, is on the Alameda, as are the four main bus terminals.

Getting around

The metro (underground railway) has five lines: Line 1 runs west-east, linking the bus and train stations, the centre, Providencia and beyond. City buses are operated under the Transantiago system; details under Transport, page 701. Taxis are abundant, but Radio Taxis, called in advance, tend to be safer.

Safety

Like all large cities, Santiago has problems of theft. Pickpockets and bag-snatchers, who are often well-dressed, operate especially on the metro and around the Plaza de Armas. Avoid the *poblaciones* (shanty towns), notably Pudahuel and parts of the north (such as Conchalí), especially if you are travelling alone or have only recently arrived. Avoid street money changers (particularly common on Ahumada, Bandera, Moneda and Agustinas): they pull any number of tricks, or might ask you to accompany them to somewhere obscure. The passing of forged notes and muggings has been reported.

Tip...

Smog forecasts are published in the daily papers, during television weather forecasts and inside underground stations.

When to go

There is rain during the winter (May-August), but the summers are dry. On the coast at Viña del Mar rainfall is 483 mm a year, but there is less inland. Temperatures, on the other hand, are higher inland than on the coast. There is frost now and then, but very little snow. Temperatures are highest in January, falling to single digits at night in July. Days are usually hot, the nights cool. There is usually less wind in winter, making smog a more serious problem.

Along the Alameda

The Alameda runs through the heart of the city for over 3 km. It is 100 m wide, and ornamented with gardens and statuary: the most notable are the equestrian statues of Generals O'Higgins and San Martín; the statue of the Chilean historian Benjamín Vicuña MacKenna who, as mayor of Santiago, beautified Cerro Santa Lucía (see page 689); and the great monument in honour of the battle of Concepción in 1879.

At Plaza Italia, there is a statue of General Baquedano and the Tomb of the Unknown Soldier; from here the Alameda skirts, on the right, Cerro Santa Lucía, and on the left, the Catholic University. Beyond the hill the Alameda passes the neoclassical **Biblioteca Nacional** ① *Av O'Higgins 651, T2-2360 5400, Santa Lucía metro, www.bibliotecanacional.cl, Mon-Thu 0900-1800, Fri 0900-1700 in Jan-Feb (Mon-Fri 0900-1900, Sat 0910-1400 Mar-Dec), free,* good concerts, temporary exhibitions. Beyond, on the left, between calles San Francisco and Londres, is the oldest church in Santiago: the red-walled church and monastery of **San Francisco** (1618). Inside is the small statue of the Virgin that Valdivia carried on his saddlebow when he rode from Peru to Chile. The **Museo Colonial San Francisco** ① *by Iglesia San Francisco, Londres 4, T2-2639 8737, www.museosanfrancisco.com, Mon-Fri 0930-1330, 1500-1800, Sat-Sun 1000-1400, US$1.50, discounts for students and children,* houses religious art, including 54 paintings of the life of St Francis; in the cloisters is a room containing poet Gabriela Mistral's Nobel medal. South of San Francisco is the Barrio París-Londres, built 1923-1929, now restored. Two blocks north of the Alameda is **Teatro Municipal** ① *C Agustinas 794, T2-2463 1000, www.municipal.cl, guided visits Mon, Wed, Fri 1200, 1630, US$9.25, in Spanish and English,* which has a full programme of opera, ballet, concerts and other events.

A little further west along the Alameda, is the Universidad de Chile; the **Club de la Unión** (www.clubdelaunion.cl), a National Monument, is almost opposite. Nearby, on Calle Nueva York is the **Bolsa de Comercio**; the public may view the trading floor, passport required. One block further west is the Plaza de la Libertad. North of the plaza, hemmed in by the skyscrapers of the Centro Cívico, is the **Palacio de la Moneda** ① *T2-2690 4000, visitas@presidencia.cl or http://visitasguiadas. presidencia.cl/ to book a guided tour of the palace; courtyards are open to the public (access from north side) Mon-Fri 1000-1800 unless important state business is being carried out,* the **Presidential Palace** (1805) containing historic relics, paintings and sculpture, and the elaborate 'Salón Rojo' used for official receptions. Although the Moneda was damaged by air attacks during the military coup of 11 September 1973 it has been fully restored. Ceremonial changing of the guard takes place every other day at 1000. The large **Centro Cultural Palacio La Moneda** ① *T2-2355 6500, www.ccplm.cl, 0900-2030, US$ for foreigners, US$4 for foreign students,* houses temporary exhibitions as well as an arts cinema and an interesting gallery of Chilean handicrafts (both closed Monday).

West of the centre

Barrios Brasil and Yungay Barrio Brasil (Metro República) is one of the earliest parts of the city. It has Plaza Brasil at its heart and the Basílica del Salvador two blocks from the plaza. There are some fine old buildings, especially around Calle Concha y Toro, but now it's a bohemian, student-centric area with lots of places to stay, and

Santiago orientation

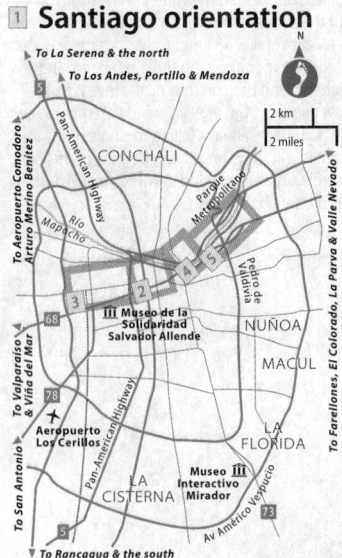

To La Serena & the north
To Los Andes, Portillo & Mendoza
2 km
2 miles
CONCHALI
Pan-American Highway
Río Mapocho
To Aeropuerto Comodoro Arturo Merino Benítez
Parque Metropolitano
Pedro de Valdivia
To Valparaíso & Viña del Mar
III Museo de la Solidaridad Salvador Allende
NUÑOA
MACUL
To Farellones, El Colorado, La Parva & Valle Nevado
To San Antonio
Pan-American Highway
Aeropuerto Los Cerillos
LA FLORIDA
Museo III Interactivo Mirador
LA CISTERNA
Av Américo Vespucio
To Rancagua & the south

well as numerous bars, clubs, cafés and lively restaurants. The next barrio west, Yungay, is in much the same vein, with many once-elegant buildings, a leafy plaza and, today, a lot of street art. See the historic Peluquería Francesa ① Compañía y Libertad, www.boulevardlavaud.cl, which houses a barber's shop dating from 1868, a restaurant, deli and antiques.

Parque Quinta Normal and around You can walk from Brasil through Yungay to this popular park (at Avenida D Portales), founded as a botanical garden in 1830. Near the park is **Museo Artequín** ① Av Portales 3530, T2-2681 8656, www.artequin.cl, Tue-Fri 0900-1700, Sat-Sun 1100-1800, closed Feb, US$2.50. Housed in the Chilean pavilion built for the 1889 Paris International Exhibition, it contains prints of famous paintings and activities and explanations of the techniques of the great masters. 200 m from the Quinta Normal metro station is the Biblioteca de Santiago (public library, www. bibliotecasantiago.cl), in front of which is **Centro Cultural Matucana 100** (www.m100.cl), with

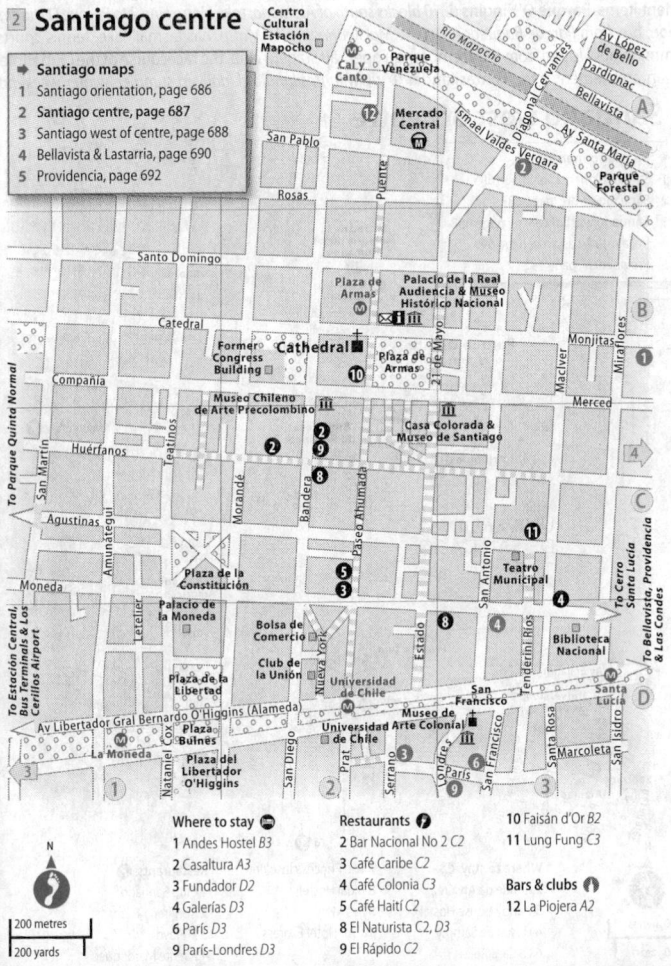

2 Santiago centre

➡ **Santiago maps**
1 Santiago orientation, page 686
2 Santiago centre, page 687
3 Santiago west of centre, page 688
4 Bellavista & Lastarria, page 690
5 Providencia, page 692

Where to stay
1 Andes Hostel B3
2 Casaltura A3
3 Fundador D2
4 Galerías D3
6 París D3
9 París-Londres D3

Restaurants
2 Bar Nacional No 2 C2
3 Café Caribe C2
4 Café Colonia C3
5 Café Haití C2
8 El Naturista C2, D3
9 El Rápido C2

10 Faisán d'Or B2
11 Lung Fung C3

Bars & clubs
12 La Piojera A2

several exhibition halls and a theatre. Across Avenida Matucana from Quinta Normal metro station is the **Museo de la Memoria y los Derechos Humanos** ⓘ *Av Matucana 501, T2-2597 9600, www. museodelamemoria.cl, Tue-Sun 1000-1800, free, audio guide for non-Spanish speakers*, a huge block covered in oxidized copper mesh suspended above an open space. On three floors it concentrates on the events and aftermath of 11 September 1973, with videos, testimonies, documents and other items. It also has information on human rights struggles worldwide and temporary exhibits, a gift shop and café. Avenida Matucana, runs south of here to join the Alameda at the railway station (Estación Central or Alameda). Opposite is the **Planetarium** ⓘ *Alameda 3349, T2-2718 2900, www. planetariochile.cl, US$7, discount for students*.

South of the Alameda Five blocks south of the Alameda is the **Palacio Cousiño** ⓘ *C Dieciocho 438, T2-2386 7450, Metro Toesca, closed due to earthquake damage; until it reopens in 2017 you can tour the grounds*. This large mansion in French rococo style has a superb Italian marble staircase and other opulent items. **Parque O'Higgins** ⓘ *10 blocks south of Alameda; take Metro Line 2 to Parque O'Higgins station, bus from Parque Baquedano via Av MacKenna and Av Matta*, has a small lake, tennis courts, swimming pool (open from 5 December), an open-air stage, a club, the racecourse of the Club Hípico and an amusement park, **Fantasilandia** ⓘ *www.fantasilandia.cl, daily in summer, winter weekends*.

③ Santiago west of centre

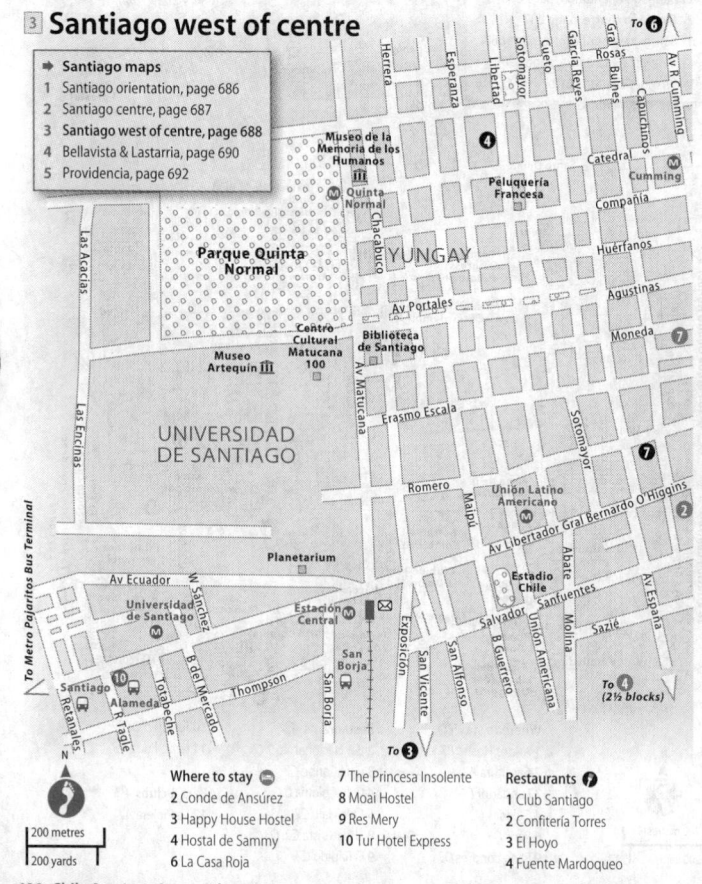

➡ **Santiago maps**
1 Santiago orientation, page 686
2 Santiago centre, page 687
3 **Santiago west of centre, page 688**
4 Bellavista & Lastarria, page 690
5 Providencia, page 692

Where to stay 🛏
2 Conde de Ansúrez
3 Happy House Hostel
4 Hostal de Sammy
6 La Casa Roja

7 The Princesa Insolente
8 Moai Hostel
9 Res Mery
10 Tur Hotel Express

Restaurants 🍴
1 Club Santiago
2 Confitería Torres
3 El Hoyo
4 Fuente Mardoqueo

only times vary but mostly from 1100 or 1200 to early evening, closed early Nov to Christmas, US$20, US$11 children and seniors, unlimited rides. The **Museo de la Solidaridad Salvador Allende** ① *Av República 475, T2-2689 8761, www.mssa.cl, Tue-Sun 1000-1800 (until 1900 Dec-Jan), closed Feb and Mar, US$1.50, Sun free,* houses a highly regarded collection of 20th-century works donated by Chilean and other artists (Picasso, Miró, Matta and many more) who sympathized with the Allende government, plus some personal items of the president himself. The contents were hidden during the Pinochet years.

East of the centre

Cerro Santa Lucía ① *closes at 2100,* bounded by Calle Merced to the north, Alameda to the south, and calles Santa Lucía and Subercaseaux to the west and east, is a cone of rock rising steeply to a height of 70 m (reached by stairs and a lift from the Alameda). It can be climbed from the Caupolicán esplanade, on which stands a statue of that Mapuche leader, but the ascent from the northern side, with a statue of Diego de Almagro, is easier. There are striking views of the city from the top, where there is a fortress, the Batería Hidalgo (no public access). It is best to descend the eastern side, to see the small Plaza Pedro Valdivia with its waterfalls and statue of Valdivia. The area is not safe after dark. At the foot of the hill to the west, the Hotel Magnolia ($$$$ Huérfanos 539, www. hotelmagnolia.cl) is a brand new conversion of a 1920s mansion, opened in 2016.

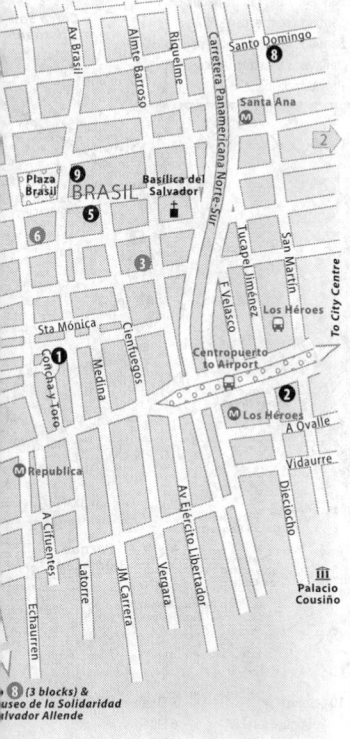

Parque Forestal lies due north of Santa Lucía hill and immediately south of the Mapocho. In the park is the **Museo Nacional de Bellas Artes** ① *T2-2499 1600, www.mnba.cl (Spanish only), Tue-Sun 1000-1845, free, café,* an extraordinary example of neoclassical architecture. It has a large display of Chilean and foreign painting and sculpture; contemporary art exhibitions are held several times a year. In the west wing is the **Museo de Arte Contemporáneo** ① *www.mac.uchile.cl.* Further east, beyond Plaza Italia, **is Parque Balmaceda** (Parque Gran Bretaña), perhaps the most beautiful in Santiago.

Lastarria Between the Parque Forestal, Plaza Italia and the Alameda is the Lastarria neighbourhood (Universidad Católica Metro). Calle José Victorino Lastarria itself has a number of popular, smart restaurants, while the **Plaza Mulato Gil de Castro** ① *C Lastarria 307,* has a mural by Roberto Matta and the **Museo Arqueológico de Santiago** and the **Museo de Artes Visuales** ① *T2-2664 9337, www.mavi.cl, Tue-Sun 1100-1900, US$1.50 for both, free on Sun.* The former exhibits Chilean archaeology, anthropology and pre-Columbian art, and the latter, modern art.

Bellavista The Bellavista district, on the north bank of the Mapocho from Plaza Italia at the foot of Cerro San Cristóbal, is one of the main eating and nightlife districts in the old city. On its streets are restaurants and cafés, theatres, galleries and craft shops (most selling lapis lazuli on C Bellavista itself). You can cross the Mapocho by bridges from Baquedano or Salvador metro stations, or by a pedestrian bridge between the two which is adorned with hundreds of lovers' eternity padlocks. **La Chascona** ① *F Márquez*

5 Las Vacas Gordas
6 Los Buenos Muchachos
7 Los Chinos Ricos
8 Majestic
9 Ostras Azócar

de la Plata 0192, Bellavista, T2-2777 8741, www.fundacionneruda.org, Tue-Sun 1000-1800 (till 1900 Jan-Feb), US$11 with audio tour, was the house that the poet Pablo Neruda built for Matilde Urrutia, with whom he lived from 1955. It was wrecked during the 1973 coup, but Matilde restored it and lived there till her death in 1985 (see also page 718).

☆**Cerro San Cristóbal** ① www.parquemet.cl. Daily 0830-2000 (1900 in winter). Taxi-colectivos run to the summit, US$4.50, and, in summer, to the swimming pools (see What to do, page 700). Vehicles have to pay to enter. The sharp, conical hill of **San Cristóbal**, to the northeast of the city, forms the **Parque Metropolitano**, the largest and most interesting of the city's parks. The main entrance is at Plaza Caupolicán at the northern end of Calle Pío Nono in Bellavista, from where a **funicular** ① Tue-Sun 1000-1945, Mon 1300-1945, US$3.10 return (US$4 at weekends), runs to near the summit; on the way up only, you can get out at the zoo half way up. Souvenirs and snacks are sold at the top of the funicular. Further east is an entrance from Pedro de Valdivia Norte, from where a teleférico runs (Tue-Sun 1000-1900, to 2000 in summer, US$4 return, US$4.70 at weekends). On the summit (300 m) stands a colossal statue of the Virgin, which is floodlit at night; beside it is the astronomical observatory

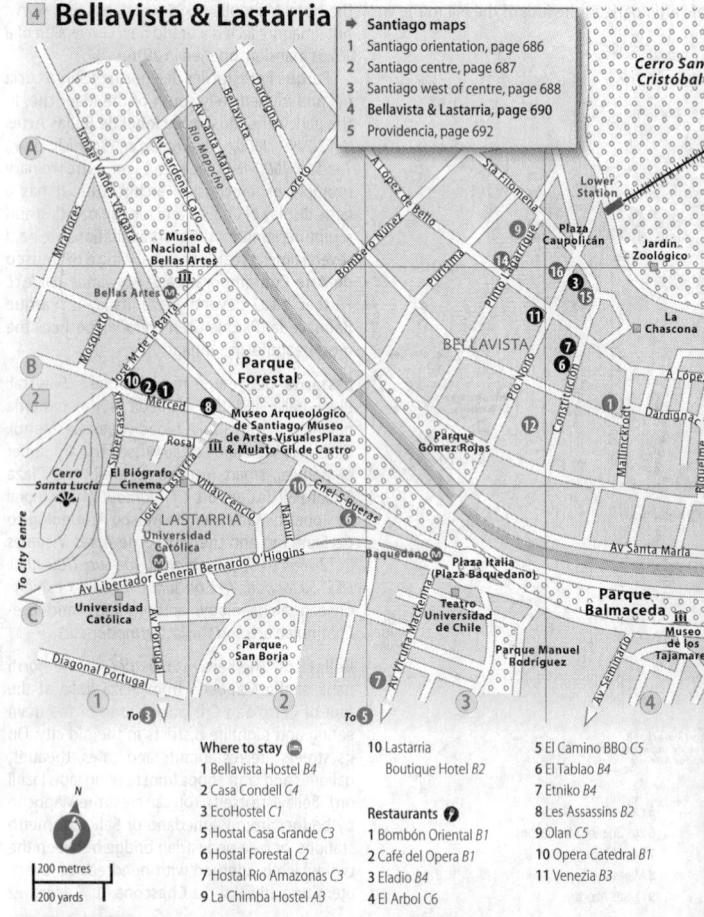

4 **Bellavista & Lastarria**

➡ **Santiago maps**
1 Santiago orientation, page 686
2 Santiago centre, page 687
3 Santiago west of centre, page 688
4 Bellavista & Lastarria, page 690
5 Providencia, page 692

Where to stay 🛏
1 Bellavista Hostel B4
2 Casa Condell C4
3 EcoHostel C1
5 Hostal Casa Grande C3
6 Hostal Forestal C2
7 Hostal Río Amazonas C3
9 La Chimba Hostel A3
10 Lastarria Boutique Hotel B2

Restaurants 🍴
1 Bombón Oriental B1
2 Café del Opera B1
3 Eladio B4
4 El Arbol C6
5 El Camino BBQ C5
6 El Tablao B4
7 Etniko B4
8 Les Assassins B2
9 Olan C5
10 Opera Catedral B1
11 Venezia B3

200 metres
200 yards

of the Catholic University which can be visited on application to the observatory's director. Further east in the Tupahue sector (about 1 km from Pedro de Valdivia metro station), there are terraces, gardens, and paths; nearby is the **Casa de la Cultura Anahuac** which has art exhibitions and free concerts at midday on Sunday. There are two good swimming pools at Tupahue and Antilén. East of Tupahue are the **Botanical Gardens** ① Mon-Thu 0930-1200, 1430-1630, Fri 0930-1200, Sat-Sun 1100-1700, guided tours available, with a collection of Chilean native plants.

Providencia and Las Condes East of Plaza Italia, the main east–west axis of the city becomes **Avenida Providencia** which heads out towards the residential areas, such as **Las Condes**, at the eastern and upper levels of the city. It passes through the neighbourhood of Providencia, a modern area of shops, offices, bars and restaurants around Pedro de Valdivia and Los Leones metro stations, which also contains the offices of Sernatur, the national tourist board. At Metro Tobalaba it becomes Avenida Apoquindo. Here, in **El Bosque Norte**, there are lots more good, mid-range and expensive restaurants.

Museo Ralli ① Sotomayor 4110, Vitacura, T2-2206 4224 (further east still), www.museoralli.cl, Tue-Sun 1030-1700, Jan weekends only, closed Feb, free, has an excellent collection of works by modern European and Latin American artists, including Dali, Chagall, Bacon and Miró. Also in this district is **Museo de la Moda** ① Vitacura 4562, Metro Escuela Militar, T2-2219 3623, www.museodelamoda.cl, closed for remodelling in 2017, El Garage café Mon-Fri 0900-1900.

Other sights

In the barrio of Recoleta, just north of the city centre, the **Cemeterio General** ① www.cementeriogeneral.cl, to get there take any Recoleta bus from C Miraflores, or go to Cementerio General metro station, contains the mausoleums of most of the great figures in Chilean history and the arts, including Violeta Parra, Víctor Jara and Salvador Allende. There is also an impressive monument to the victims, known as the 'desaparecidos' (disappeared) of the 1973-1990 military government.

Another memorial to the troubled Pinochet era is in the southeastern suburb of Peñalolén, the **Parque por la Paz** ① Av Arrieta 8401, www.villagrimaldi.cl; from Tobalaba Metro take any bus marked Peñalolén heading south down Tobalaba, get off at Tobalaba y José Arrieta and catch a bus, or walk 15-20 mins, up Arrieta towards the mountains. It stands on the site of **Villa Grimaldi**, the most notorious torture centre. Audioguides are available in English (leave passport at reception).

Also southeast of the centre, in La Florida district, is the excellent **Museo Interactivo Mirador** (MIM) ① Punta Arenas 6711, Mirador Metro (Line 5), T2-2828 8000, www.mim.cl, Tue-Sun 0930-1830, US$6, discounts for children and seniors, a fun, interactive science and technology museum, perfect for a family outing. There is also an **aquarium** in the grounds.

Statue of the Virgin

Upper Station (Funicular)

Parque Metropolitano

Bellavista

Av Andrés Bello

Av Providencia

Salvador

To ❹ & Providencia & Las Condes

To ❷❺❾ & Ñuñoa

Bars & clubs 🍸
11 Patio Bellavista with
    Backstage Life,
    La Casa en el Aire
    & many more B4
14 Jammin' Club A3
15 La Bodeguita de Julio B4
16 La Otra Puerta B3

Tourist information

Municipal Tourist Board
North side of Plaza de Armas, T2-2713 6745, Mon-Fri 0900-1800, Sat-Sun 1000-1600; at Terminal Santiago, Tue-Fri 0700-2200, Sat, Mon 0900-2000, Sun 0900-1900; and at Cerro Santa Lucía, T2-2386 7186, Mon-Thu 0900-1800, Fri 0900-1700, www.santiagocapital.cl; see also www.ciudad.cl.
Free walking tours most days of the week.

Servicio Nacional de Turismo Sernatur
Av Providencia 1550, between metros Manuel Montt and Pedro de Valdivia, T2-2731 8310, info@sernatur.cl. Mon-Fri 0900-1800, Sat 0900-1400.
Maps, brochures. Good notice board and free Wi-Fi. **Information office** also at the airport daily 0800-1900, T2-2601 9320.

Where to stay

Check if breakfast and 19% tax are included in the price quoted. Hostels have double rooms with private or shared bath, **$$**, and dorms for US$13-18pp, **$**.

Santiago centre

$$$$-$$$ Fundador
Paseo Serrano 34, T2-2387 1200, www.hotelfundador.cl.
Helpful, charming, stylish, good location, pool, spa, bar, restaurant.

$$$$-$$$ Galerías
San Antonio 65, T2-2470 7400, www.hotelgalerias.cl.
Excellent, large rooms, generous breakfast, good location, welcoming.

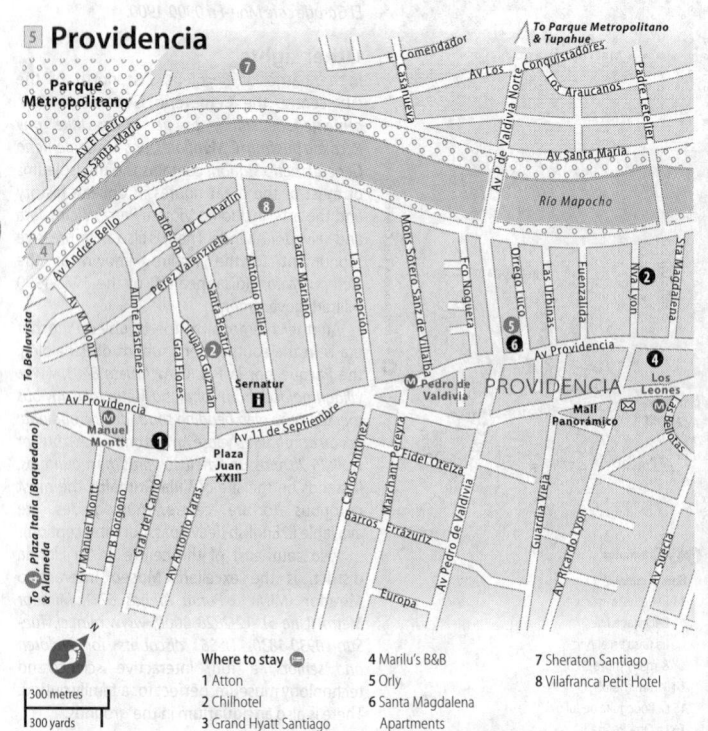

5 Providencia

300 metres
300 yards

Where to stay
1 Atton
2 Chilhotel
3 Grand Hyatt Santiago
4 Marilu's B&B
5 Orly
6 Santa Magdalena Apartments
7 Sheraton Santiago
8 Vilafranca Petit Hotel

$$$-$$ París-Londres

Londres 54, T2-2638 2215, www.londres.cl.
1920s mansion with original features in perfect location near San Francisco church, pleasant common rooms, laundry service, usually full, advance bookings in high season.

$$$-$ Andes Hostel

Monjitas 506, T2-2632 9990,
www.andeshostel.com.
In Bellas Artes neighbourhood, dorms, rooms or apartments, bar downstairs with pool table, barbecue nights on roof terrace, well run.

$$$-$ Casaltura

San Antonio 811, T2-2633 5076,
www.casaltura.com.
'Boutique hostel', up a long wooden staircase in a renovated house, roof terrace, comfortable and convenient, private rooms and dorms, nice staff.

$$ París

París 813, T2-2664 0921,
www.hotelparis813.com.

Great location, good meeting place, 3 standards of room, breakfast extra, Wi-Fi available in some parts. Phone in advance in summer.

West of the centre

$$-$ Happy House Hostel

Moneda 1829, T2-2688 4849,
www.happyhousehostel.cl.
In a restored mansion with all mod cons. One of the best hostels in the city, spacious kitchen and common areas, pool table, bar, spa, free tea and real coffee all day, book exchange, English and French spoken, lots of information.

$$-$ La Casa Roja

Agustinas 2113, Barrio Brasil, T2-2695 0600,
www.lacasaroja.cl.
Huge, renovated mansion, dorms and private rooms, no breakfast, pool party on Sat, guests can be chef for the night, live music, 2 bars, cricket net, lots of activities and tours, Spanish classes, lively. Shares services with **The Princesa Insolente**, below.

$$$ Conde de Ansúrez

Av República 25, T2-2696 0807, República metro,
www.ansurez.cl.
Convenient for airport bus, central station and bus terminals, helpful, safe.

$$$ Tur Hotel Express

O'Higgins 3750, p 3, in the Turbus Terminal, T2-2685 0100, www.turbus.cl (under "turismo" heading).
Comfortable business standard. Useful if you need to take an early flight as buses leave for the airport from here. There is an Ibis hotel here, too.

$$ Residencial Mery

Pasaje República 36, off 0-100 block of República,
T2-2699 4982, www.residencialmery.cl.
Big green art deco building down an alley, most rooms without bath, all with single beds, quiet, breakfast extra.

$$-$ Moai Hostel

Toesca 2335, 5 blocks from República metro,
T2-2689 0977, www.moaiviajerohostel.cl.
Airport transfer, book exchange, film library, Spanish classes arranged, gay-friendly, popular.

$ The Princesa Insolente

Moneda 2350, T2-2671 6551,
www.princesainsolentehostel.cl.
4, 6, 8, 11-bed dorms and 3 private rooms ($$) and 2 apartments across the street ($$$), organic café, mountain bike rental, travel information, maps, activities almost every night of the week,

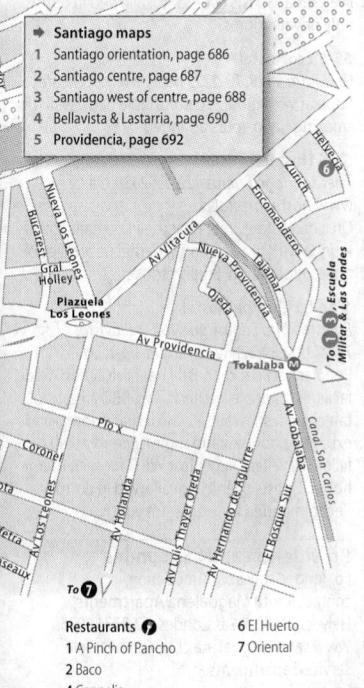

➡ **Santiago maps**
1 Santiago orientation, page 686
2 Santiago centre, page 687
3 Santiago west of centre, page 688
4 Bellavista & Lastarria, page 690
5 Providencia, page 692

Restaurants ❼
1 A Pinch of Pancho
2 Baco
4 Coppelia
6 El Huerto
7 Oriental

great courtyard and bar, good meeting place. Breakfast only included in private rooms. Might have the most comfortable dorm beds in the entire country. Also has hostels in Pichilemu and Pucón. Near bus terminals and Estación Central. Highly recommended.

South of the Alameda

$ Hostal de Sammy
Toesca 2335, T2-2689 8772,
www.hostaldesammy.com.
Good-value US-run hostel with decent common areas, table tennis, pool table, big-screen TV with hundreds of films. Good info, helpful.

East of the centre

$$$$ Lastarria Boutique Hotel
Cnel Santiago Bueras 188, T2-2840 3700,
www.lastarriahotel.com.
In a converted 1927 building, beautifully decorated, spacious rooms, with personalized service. Lounge for breakfast and light meals, cocktails and wines, garden, swimming pool.

$$$-$$ Hostal Casa Grande
Vicuña MacKenna 90, T2-2222 7347, metro
Baquedano, www.hostalcasagrande.cl.
Labyrinthine, old high-ceilinged building, colourful, pleasant patio garden, quiet.

$$$-$$ Hostal Río Amazonas
Plaza Italia, Vicuña Mackenna 47, T2-2635 1631,
www.hostalrioamazonas.cl.
In a restored mansion, good value, helpful, lots of information, parking.

$$ Casa Condell
Condell 114, T2-2209 2343, Salvador metro,
www.casa-condell.cl.
Pleasant old house, central, quiet, nice roof-terrace, free local phone calls, English spoken, good but baths shared between rooms can be a problem.

$$-$ Bellavista Hostel
Dardignac 0184, Bellavista, T2-2899 7145,
www.bellavista.hostel.com.
European-style, sheets provided but make your own bed, good fun hostel in the heart of this lively area. Guests over 35 not allowed in dorms, only private rooms.

$$-$ EcoHostel
Gral Jofré 349B, T2-2222 6833, www.ecohostel.cl.
Popular with groups, comfortable beds, well run, smoking patio, tours arranged.

$$-$ Hostal Forestal
Cnel Santiago Bueras 122, T2-2638 1347,
www.hostalforestal.cl.
On a quiet side street near the Plaza Italia. Comfy lounge with big-screen TV, barbecue area, pool table, information, English spoken.

$ pp La Chimba Hostel
Ernesto Pinto Lagarrigue 262, Bellavista,
T2-2732 9184, www.lachimba-hostel.cl.
Popular backpacker hostel near the action. Good facilities, multiple kitchens, TVs, BBQ area, pool table, great showers, etc, with many dorms and expansive doubles and triples. Friendly staff of fellow travellers, super fast Wi-Fi for such a large hostel. Guests over 35 not allowed in dorms. Recommended for exuberant youth.

Providencia and Las Condes

For longer-stay accommodation, contact **Santa Magdalena Apartments**, Helvecia 240 L3, Las Condes, T2-2374 6875, www.santamagdalena.cl, which has well-serviced apartments.

$$$$ Grand Hyatt Santiago
Av Kennedy 4601, Las Condes, T2-2950 1234,
www.santiago.grand.hyatt.com.
Superb, beautifully decorated, large outdoor
pool, gym, 3 restaurants.

$$$$ Sheraton Santiago
Santa María 1742, T2-2233 5000,
www.starwoodhotels.com/sheraton.
One of the best, good restaurant with
international menu, good buffet lunch,
and all facilities.

$$$$-$$$ Atton
Alonso de Córdova 5199, Las Condes,
T2-2422 7900, www.atton.cl.
Comfortable, very helpful, full disabled access.
Has several other branches.

$$$ Chilhotel
Cirujano Guzmán 103, T2-2264 0643,
metro Manuel Montt, www.chilhotel.cl.
Small, comfortable, family-run, airport transfer.

$$$ Orly
Pedro de Valdivia 027, Metro Pedro de Valdivia,
T2-2630 3000, www.orlyhotel.com.
Small, comfortable, convenient, **Cafetto** café
attached with good value meals.

$$$ Vilafranca Petit Hotel
Pérez Valenzuela 1650, metro Manuel Montt,
T2-2235 1413, www.vilafranca.cl.
High end B&B, small but impeccable rooms,
quiet, cosy, pleasant garden, English spoken.

$$ Marilú's Bed and Breakfast
Rafael Cañas 246, p 1, Metro Salvador,
T2-2235 5302, www.bedandbreakfast.cl.
Comfortable, quiet, convenient, some rooms
with shared bath with 1 other room, good
beds, English and French spoken, secure, very
helpful and welcoming, lots of information.
Recommended.

Restaurants

For good seafood restaurants go to the
Mercado Central (by Cal y Canto Metro, www.
mercadocentral.cl, lunches only), including
Donde Augusto, www.dondeaugusto.cl,
El Galeón, www.elgaleon.cl, and others; or
the **Vega Central** market, www.lavegacentral.
com, on the opposite bank of the Mapocho,
or Av Cumming and C Reyes in Barrio Brasil. It
is difficult to eat cheaply in the evening apart
from fast food, so if you're on a tight budget,
make the lunchtime *almuerzo* your main meal.

Santiago centre

$$$-$$ Lung Fung
Agustinas 715 (downstairs), T2-2639 6550,
http://lungfung.cl.
Delicious oriental food, the oldest Chinese
restaurant in Santiago.

$$ Faisán d'Or
Plaza de Armas.
Good *pastel de choclo*, pleasant place to watch
the world go by.

$ Bar Nacional No 2
Bandera 317.
Popular, local specialities, big portions; also at
Huérfanos 1151 (No 1) and at Matías Cousiño
(no 3, www.barnacional3.cl).

$ El Naturista
Moneda 846 and Huérfanos 1046,
www.elnaturista.cl.
Excellent vegetarian, "healthy portions", wide-
ranging menu, as well as juices, beer and wine,
closes 2100 during the week.

$ El Rápido
Bandera 347, next to Bar Nacional No 2.
Specializes in *empanadas* and *completos*.
Good food.

Cafés

Café Caribe and Café Haití
Both on Paseo Ahumada and elsewhere in
centre and Providencia (www.cafecaribe.cl
and www.cafehaiti.cl respectively).
Good coffee, institutions for the Santiago
business community.

Café Colonia
MacIver 133 and 161, www.cafecolonia.cl.
Splendid variety of cakes, pastries and pies,
fashionable and pricey.

West of the centre

$$$-$$ Las Vacas Gordas
Cienfuegos 280, Barrio Brasil, T2-2697 1066,
see Facebook.
Good-value grilled steaks, nice wine selection,
very popular, book in advance.

$$$-$$ Majestic
Santo Domingo 1562, T2-2694 9400,
www.majestic.cl, in hotel of same name
($$$, www.hotelmajestic.cl).
Excellent Indian restaurant, with a good range of
vegetarian dishes.

$$ Club Santiago
*Erasmo Escala 2120, T 2-2673 4700,
www.clubsantiago.cl. Open till 0300
at weekends, happy hour 1700-2200.*
Historic restaurant/bar in Concha y Toro district,
lunches, snacks, cocktails.

$$ El Hoyo
San Vicente 375, T2-2689 0339. Closed Sun.
Celebrated 100-yr-old *chichería* serving hearty
Chilean fare.

$$ Fuente Mardoqueo
*Libertad 551, www.fuentemardoqueo.cl.
Daily 1200-2300.*
Simply sandwiches, with a limited choice of
fillings, and beer, a wide range, popular.

$$ Los Buenos Muchachos
*Cumming 1031, T2-2566 4660,
www.losbuenosmuchachos.cl.*
Cavernous hall seating over 400 serving plentiful
traditional Chilean food, traditional Chilean dance
shows at night. Very popular.

$$ Los Chinos Ricos
*Brasil 373, T2-2696 3778, www.loschinosricos.com.
Open until 2300 during week, 0100 Fri-Sat.*
Good Chinese, popular with families on
Sun lunchtime.

$$ Ostras Azócar
*Gral Bulnes 37, T2-2682 2203,
www.ostrasazocar.cl.*
Good prices for oysters. Other seafood places
in same street.

$ Confitería Torres
*Alameda 1570, T 2-2688 0751,
www.confiteriatorres.cl.*
Traditional bar/restaurant, good ambience,
live music Fri-Sat.

East of the centre
On C Lastarria are many smart eateries, several in
the precinct at Lastarria 70: also **Sur Patagónico**,
Don Victorino, **El Bocanariz** (www.bocanariz.cl),
El Observatorio and **Zabo** (www.zabo.cl).
Bellavista is full of restaurants, cafés and bars too,
particularly C Dardignac and Patio Bellavista, the
block between Dardignac, Pío Nono, Bellavista
and Constitución.

$$$ Les Assassins
Merced 297, T2-2638 4280, see Facebook.
Good French cuisine in small, family-run bistro,
with decent wine list; good-value set lunches.

$$$-$$ El Camino BBQ
*Italia 1034, T2-2986 0765,
www.elcaminobbq.com.*
The owner spent time in Texas learning the
finer points of North American BBQ. The effort
is seen and felt in the top-notch ribs and brisket
as well as the general ambience, which features
communal patio dining and giant beers.

$$$-$$ Etniko
*Constitución 172, Bellavista, T2-2732 0119,
www.etniko.cl.*
Fusion restaurant with oriental influences and
seafood, also tapas bar/*cevichería* and dance
floor under transparent roof for night sky, live DJs
at weekends.

$$$-$$ Los Adobes del Argomedo
*Argomedo 411 y Lira, 10 blocks south
of the Alameda, T2-2222 2104,
www.losadobesdeargomedo.cl.*
Long-established traditional restaurant.
Good Chilean food, floor show (Tue-Sat)
includes *cueca* dancing, salsa and folk.

$$$-$$ Opera Catedral
*Jose Miguel de la Barra 407, Bellas Artes metro,
T2-2664 3048, www.operacatedral.cl.*
Very good, if expensive, French restaurant on
the ground floor. Upstairs is a minimalist pub-
restaurant, usually packed at night, serving fusion
food at reasonable prices.

$$ El Tablao
Constitución 110, T2-2737 8648, see Facebook.
Traditional Spanish restaurant. The food is
reasonable but the main attraction is the live
flamenco show on Fri-Sat nights.

$$ Eladio
Pío Nono 251, T2-2777 5083, www.eladio.cl.
Good steaks, Argentine cuisine, excellent value.
Also locations in Providencia and Plaza Vespuccio.

$$ Venezia
Pío Nono, corner of López de Bello.
Huge servings of traditional Chilean home-
cooked fare (allegedly one of Neruda's favourite
haunts), good value.

Bombón Oriental
Merced 353, Lastarria, T2-2639 1069.
Serves Middle Eastern food, Turkish coffee,
Arabic snacks and sweets.

Café del Opera
Merced 391.
For breakfasts, sandwiches, salads, ice creams
and breads.

Providencia

$$$-$$ A Pinch of Pancho
Gral del Canto 45, T2-2235 1700.
Very good seafood on a wide-ranging menu.

$$$-$$ Baco
Nueva de Lyon 113, Metro Los Leones,
T2-2231 4444.
Sophisticated French restaurant, good food,
extensive wine list with many quality wines
available by the glass.

$$$-$$ Oriental
Holanda 1927, T2-2223 2272,
www.restaurantoriental.cl.
Excellent Chinese, one of the best in Santiago.
Also has a branch at Av Ossa at 1881.

$$ El Huerto
Orrego Luco 054, Providencia, T2-2233 2690,
www.elhuerto.cl. Daily.
Vegetarian, varied menu, very good.

$$-$ El Arbol
Huelén 74, T2-2235 0822.
Vegetarian and vegan café. Cheese used in vegan
dishes is made from coconut oil. Also cocktails
and snacks.

$$-$ Olan
Condell 200, www.restaurantolan.com.
Excellent value, tasty Peruvian food in
unpretentious surroundings.

Cafés

For snacks and ice cream there are several good
places on Av Providencia including **Coppelia**
(No 2111, www.coppelia.cl), **Bravissimo**
(No 1406, www.bravissimo.cl). Lots of cafés
and some restaurants on the passageways at
Metro Los Leones and streets nearby, including
Café di Roma, **The Coffee Factory**, **Sebastián**
(Fuenzalida 26, www.heladeriasebastian.cl), very
good, **Tavelli** (Fuenzalida 36, www.tavelli.cl).

Las Condes

This area has many first-class restaurants,
including grills, serving Chilean (often with
music), French and Chinese cuisine. They tend
to be more expensive than central restaurants.
Many are located on El Bosque Norte, near
Tobalaba metro stop.

$$$-$$ Miguel Torres
Isidora Goyenechea 2874, T2-2245 7332,
www.migueltorres.cl.
Tapas bar owned by the well-known
Spanish winery.

$$$-$$ Puerto Marisko
Isidora Goyenechea 2918, T2-2233 2096,
www.restaurantmariscos.cl.
Renowned for seafood but also serves pasta and
meat dishes, over 20 years of experience.

Bars and clubs

For all entertainments, nightclubs, cinemas,
theatres, restaurants, concerts, *El Mercurio
Online* website has all listings and a good
search feature, www.emol.com. Listings are
also given in weekend newspapers, particularly
El Mercurio and *La Tercera*. For an organized
night out, contact **Santiago Pub Crawl**, Santa
Filomena 22, Recoleta, T9-8299 4086, Facebook:
pubcrawlsantiagochile, 2200, Fri and Sat, US$15.

Santiago centre

La Piojera
Aillavilú 1030 (metro Cal y Canto), T2-2698 1682,
www.lapiojera.cl.
A Santiago institution long held to be the
birthplace of the famous *terremoto* cocktail
(although local taxistas dispute this claim). This
is a seedy dive bar in a seedy area, appropriate
only for those looking to have a rollicking
good time. It's got a nice mix of locals and
backpackers, plus a menu of hearty Chilean fare
like *pernil* (leg of pork) to help line the stomach.
Take a taxi when leaving.

West of the centre

Barrio Brasil has a number of bars and restaurants
dotted around the Plaza Brasil and on Avs Brasil
and Cumming. Popular with Chilean students
(Metro República).

East of the centre

Bellavista has a good selection of varied
restaurants, bars and clubs (Metro Baquedano).

Bellavista

Backstage Life
Patio Bellavista.
Good-quality live jazz and blues.

Jammin' Club
Antonia López de Bello 49, see Facebook.
Reggae.

La Bodeguita de Julio
Constitución 256, see Facebook.
Cuban staff and Cuban cocktails, excellent live
music and dancing possible, very popular, very
good value.

La Casa en el Aire
Patio Bellavista, www.lacasaenelaire.cl.
Pleasant atmosphere, live music.

La Otra Puerta
Pío Nono 348, www.laotrapuerta.cl.
Lively salsoteca with live music.

Providencia and Las Condes

There is a collection of bars and eateries on the 1st couple of blocks of Román Díaz (between metros Salvador and Manuel Montt), eg **Kleine Kneipe** (No 21, also in Ñuñoa, www.kleinekneipe.cl), and **Santo Remedio** (No 152, www.santoremedio.cl). In Providencia, Av Suecia and Av Gral Holley are popular and largely pedestrianized. From Av Providencia, Condell leads to the middle class suburb of Ñuñoa, 18 blocks, passing various small bars and restaurants on the way, eg at junctions with Rancagua and Santa Isabel, or take metro to Irrarrázaval. Plaza Ñuñoa itself has a number of good bars. El Bosque Norte has chic bars and expensive restaurants for the Chilean jetset (Metro Tobalaba). There are also many smart places in Las Condes.

Ilé Habana
Bucarest 95, www.ilehabana.cl.
Bar with salsa music, often live, and a good dance floor.

Entertainment

Cinemas

There's a good guide to cinema in the free newspaper *publimetro*, given out at metro stations on weekday mornings. 'Ciné Arte' (quality foreign films) is popular. Many multiplex cinemas across the city show mainstream releases, nearly always in the original English with subtitles. Seats cost US$6-8 with reductions on Wed (elsewhere in the country the day varies). Some cinemas offer discounts to students and over 60s (proof required).

Theatre and classical music

There are a great number of theatres that stage plays in Spanish.
Teatro Municipal, *Agustinas y San Antonio, www.municipal.cl.* Stages international opera, concerts by the Orquesta Filarmónica de Santiago, and

Tip...

Free classical concerts are sometimes given in **San Francisco** church in summer; arrive early for a seat.

the Ballet de Santiago, throughout the year. The full range of events and ticket prices is given on the website (but it is generally expensive). Some cheap seats are often sold on the day of concerts.
Teatro Municipal de Ñuñoa, *Av Irarrázaval 1564, T2-2277 7903, www.ccn.cl.* Dance, art exhibitions, cinema, children's theatre.
Teatro Universidad de Chile, *Plazaltalia, T2-2978 2480, www.ceacuchile.com.* Home of the Orquesta y Coro Sinfónica de Chile and the Ballet Nacional de Chile (cheaper than Teatro Municipal).

Festivals

Mar/Apr Semana Santa. Religious rituals and ceremonies continue throughout Holy Week, when a priest washes the feet of 12 men.
16 Jul Virgen del Carmen (patron of the Armed Forces). The image of the Virgen is carried through the streets by cadets.
18 Sep Independence Day. Many families get together or celebrate in *fondas* (small temporary constructions made of wood and straw where people eat traditional dishes, drink *chicha* and dance *cueca*).
Nov Art fair. This free fair in the Parque Forestal on the banks of the Río Mapocho lasts a fortnight

Shopping

Bookshops

Book prices are high compared with neighbouring countries and Europe. There are several bookshops in and around the Drugstore precinct off Av Providencia 2124 between La Urbinas and Fuenzalida, including **Feria Chilena del Libro** (www.feriachilenadellibro.cl), with many other branches, good for travel books and maps. For foreign language books: **Le Comptoir** (www.comptoir.cl), **Librería Albers** (www.texto.cl), **Librería Inglesa** (www.libreriainglesa.cl).
LOM Ediciones, *Concha y Toro 23, www.lom.cl.* Large stock from its own publishing house (literature, history, sociology, art, politics), also bar and reading room with recent Chilean papers and magazines.

Camping and outdoor equipment

There are a number of 'hunting' shops on Bulnes 1-2 blocks south of the Alameda, with a basic range of outdoor equipment.
Andes Gear, *Helvecia 210, Las Condes, T2-2245 7076, www.andesgear.cl.* Good range of quality clothes and equipment. Imported camping goods from **Club Andino** and **Federación de Andinismo** (see below).

La Cumbre, *Av Apoquindo 5220, T2-2220 9907, www.lacumbreonline.cl. Mon-Fri 1100-2000, at 1100-1600*. Dutch-run, very helpful, good climbing and trekking equipment.
Lippi, *www.lippioutdoor.com*. With several branches. Chile's premier outdoor equipment maker. Excellent-quality clothes, boots, tents, etc.
Parafernalia, *Plaza Pedro de Valdivia 1783, Providencia, www.parafernaliaoutdoor.com*. New and second-hand gear.
Peregrin, *del Arzobispo 0607, Bellavista, T2-2735 587, Salvador metro, www.peregrin.cl*. Decent-quality locally made outdoor clothes.
Tatoo Adventure Gear, *Av Los Leones 81, Providencia, and MallSport, Las Condes 13.451, www.tatoo.ws*. Has all the best brands of outdoor gear.

Crafts

For good-quality crafts go to Pomaire (see page 702), where items from all over Chile are for sale at competitive prices. The gemstone, lapis lazuli, can be found in a few expensive shops in Bellavista but is cheaper in the **Feria Artesanal** at Diagonal Oriente between Alameda y Portugal, on the 600 to 800 blocks of Santo Domingo and at Pío Nono y Av Santa María in Bellavista.
Centro Artesanal Los Dominicos, *Apoquindo 9085, Las Condes, Metro Los Dominicos, www.culturallascondes.cl*. The best upmarket craft fair in Chile. A good range of modern and traditional Chilean crafts from ceramics to textiles, a pleasant central piazza, places where the artisans can be seen working on wood, silver, glass and so on, cafés, toilets, information.
Centro Artesanal Santa Lucía, *Santa Lucía metro, south exit*. Generic *artesanía*. Lapis lazuli can be bought.
La Aldea, *Luis Pasteur 6420, loc 5, Vitacura, www.laaldea.net*. Open 1000-2100, Sun 1100-1500. Crafts, wines, delicatessen.

Markets

For food: **Mercado Central**, between Puente y 21 de Mayo by the Río Mapocho (Cal y Canto metro) is excellent for fish and seafood. There is a cheaper market, the **Vega Central**, on the opposite bank of the river. The **Bío Bío** flea market on C Bío Bío, Metro Franklin (follow crowds), on Sat and Sun morning is huge and sells everything under the sun, lots of it having fallen off the back of a lorry.

Wine

El Mundo del Vino, *Isidora Goyenechea 3000, T2-2584 1173, www.elmundodelvino.cl*. For all types of Chilean wines, good selection across the price range; also in the Alto Las Condes, Parque Arauco and Costanera Center malls.
La Vinoteca, *Manuel Montt 1452, Providencia, T2-2829 2200, www.lavinoteca.cl*. Extensive collection of wine and spirits. Online ordering available.

What to do

Cricket

There is a burgeoning cricket league based around Santiago, see www.cricketchile.cl for more information. **La Casa Roja** hostel, see page 693, has a cricket net on its premises.

Cycling

For parts and repairs go to C San Diego, south of the Alameda. The 800 and 900 blocks have scores of bike shops with spare parts, new models and repairs.

Football

Main teams include: Colo Colo who play at the **Estadio Monumental** (reached by any bus to Puente Alto, or metro to Pedreros); **Universidad de Chile**, who play at Estadio Nacional, Av Grecia 2001, Ñuñoa, Ñuble metro, Line 5, and **Universidad Católica**, who play at San Carlos de Apoquindo, reached by bus from Metro Escuela Militar. Tickets can be bought at the grounds on match day, or throughwww.puntoticket.com/deportes, T600-462 6000.

Language schools

Bellavista, *C del Arzobispado 0605, Providencia, T2-2732 3443, www.escuelabellavista.cl*. Group and individual classes, lodging with families, free activities.
Instituto Norteamericano Santiago, *Moneda 1467, T2-2677 7167. www.norteamericano.cl*. Institute run through the US embassy with many branches. One of the best options.
Isabel Correa, *T9-6360 3533, isabelcorreaparker@gmail.com*. Teaches Spanish, French and English. Also does translations in 3 languages and offers walking tours/lessons in the city and customized VIP tours.
Natanislang Language Centre, *Arturo Bürhle 047, Metro Baquedano, Providencia, T2-2222 8685, www.natalislang.com*. Also has a branch in Valparaíso: Plaza Justicia 45, of 602, T32-225 4849.
Tandem (Escuela de Idiomas Violeta Parra), *Triana 853, Providencia, T2-2236 4241, www.tandemsantiago.cl*. Courses aimed at budget travellers, information programme on social issues, arranges accommodation and visits to local organizations and national parks.

Skiing and climbing
Club Alemán Andino, *El Arrayán 2735,*
T2-2232 4338, www.dav.cl. Mon-Fri 1900-2200.
Club Andino de Chile, *Av Lib O'Higgins 108,*
clubandino@ski lagunillas.cl.
Federación de Andinismo de Chile, *Almte*
Simpson 77 (T2-2222 0888, www.feach.cl). Daily
(frequently closed Jan/Feb). Has the addresses of
all the mountaineering clubs in the country and
runs a mountaineering school.
Skitotal, *Apoquindo 4900, of 40-46, T2-2246 0156,*
www.skitotal.cl. For 1-day excursions and good
value ski hire. Equipment hire is much cheaper in
Santiago than in ski resorts. For ski resorts in the
Santiago area, see below.

Swimming
In Parque Metropolitano, Cerro San Cristóbal:
Antilén (open in summer Tue-Sun 1000-1830,
US$11), fine views, and **Tupahue** (same hours), large
pool with cafés, entry US$9.35-11.70 but worth it
(check if they are open in winter, one usually is).
   There is an Olympic pool in **Parque O'Higgins**
(www.piscinatemperadasantiago.cl, Mon-Fri
0700-2100, US$11 per hr).

Tours
A number of agencies offer walking tours of the city,
others day trips from Santiago. Typical excursions
are to the wine valleys, from US$40-60 (by bike
if you wish), Isla Negra (Pablo Neruda's seaside
villa with wine) US$75, visits to nearby haciendas
and adventure tours, such as whitewater rafting,
rock climbing or trekking in the Cajón del Maipo,
southeast of the city. Many agencies advertise in
the **Sernatur** tourist office (see page 692).

Adventure tours and trekking
Altue, *Coyancura 2270, Of 801, Providencia, T2-*
2333 1390, www.altue.com. For wilderness trips
including tour of Patagonia.
Azimut 360, *Eliodoro Yañez 1437, Providencia,*
T2-2235 1519 , www.azimut360.com. Adventure
and ecotourism including tour of Patagonia.
Cascada Expediciones, *Don Carlos 3227C,*
Las Condes, T2-2923 5950, www.cascada.travel.
Specialize in activity tours in remote areas.
Chile Excepción, *T2-2951 5476, www.chile-*
excepcion.com. French/Argentine agency offering
tailor-made, upper end tours, fly-drives, themed
trips and other services.
Chile Off Track, *T9-9436 9235, www.chileofftrack.*
com. Customized and tailor-made tours around
Santiago and in Patagonia, 6 languages spoken,
features include horse riding, mountain
excursions, wine tours, visits to hot springs.

Travel Art, *Europa 2081, Providencia, T2-2437 5660,*
www.chile-reise.com. Biking, hiking and multi-
active tours throughout Chile. German-run.
Upscape, *T2-2244 2750, www.upscapetravel.com.*
US-run, offering adventure day tours, wine tours,
city tours, skiing and Patagonia.

City tours La Bicicleta Verde, *Loreto 6 esq*
Santa María, T2-25709939 , http://labicicletaverde.
com. Sightseeing tours around the capital and of
vineyards by bike. Also rents bicycles.
Spicy Chile, *www.spicychile.cl.* 3 walking tours
of the city, Mon-Sat, pay by tip, good reputation.
Tours4Tips, *T2-25709939, www.tours4tips.com.*
2 daily walking tours, pay by tip, also in
Valparaíso, popular.
Turistik, *T2-2820 1000, www.turistik.cl.* Hop-on,
hop-off bus tours of the city, US$29, also offers
tours outside the city and tour, dinner and show.

Transport

Air
International and domestic flights leave from
Arturo Merino Benítez Airport at Pudahuel, 26 km
northwest of Santiago, off Ruta 68, the motorway
to Viña del Mar and Valparaíso. The terminal has
most facilities, including Afex *cambio*, ATMs,
tourist offices which will book accommodation
and a fast-food plaza. Left luggage US$10 per bag
per day. Airport information T2-2690 1752, www.
nuevopudahuel.cl.
   Airport taxi: drivers offer rides to the city
outside Arrivals, but the official taxi service,
T2-2601 9880, www.taxioficial.cl, is more reliable,
if a little more expensive: US$20 to Pajaritos or
Quinta Normal, US$25 to the centre, US$30-35 to
Providencia, up to US$35 to Las Condes. Frequent
bus services to/from city centre by 2 companies:
Tur-Bus (T2-2822 7500, from Terminal Alameda),
0615-2300, US$2.65, every 30 mins; and **Centro
Puerto** (T2-2601 9883, www.centropuerto.cl, from
Metro Los Héroes), US$2.65, 0640-2330, every
15 mins. Buses leave from outside airport terminal
and, in Santiago, call at Metro Pajaritos (from
0500), Estación Central, Terminal Santiago and
most other regular bus stops. From airport you
can take Tur-Bus to Pajaritos, US$2.50, and take
metro from there. Companies that run a good
shuttle service are: **Delfos** (T2-2913 8800, www.
transferdelfos.cl) and **Transvip** (T2-2677 3000,
www.transvip.cl), US$12-14 shared vehicle, US$34-
44 exclusive, depending on zone. Otherwise, to go
to the airport, book a day ahead. They pick you up
from your hotel and, before reaching the terminal,
stop at their airport depot where you pay.

Bus

Local The Transantiago (www.transantiago.cl) system is designed to reduce congestion and pollution, but has not entirely succeeded. The city is divided into 10 zones lettered A to J. Within each zone, buses (known as *micros*) are the same colour as that given to the zone (eg white for zone A: central Santiago). Zones are linked by trunk lines, run by white *micros* with a green stripe. The system integrates with the metro. Buses display the number and direction of the route within the system. Payment is by prepaid *bip!* card only. A card costs US$2.25, to which you add however much you want to pay in advance. They are most conveniently bought at metro stations. For a few days it's probably not worth investing in a *bip!* card (just use the metro), but for more than 3 days it's good value. Long-term visitors can buy personalized cards to prevent theft, etc. There are also *colectivos* (collective taxis) on fixed routes to the suburbs. Routes are displayed with route numbers. Fares vary, depending on the length of the journey, but are usually between US$1.50-2.50 (higher fares at night).

Long distance There are frequent, and good, interurban buses to all parts of Chile. Take a look at the buses before buying the tickets (there are big differences in quality among bus companies); ask about the on-board services, many companies offer drinks for sale, or free, and luxury buses have meals, videos, headphones. Reclining seats are standard and there are also *salón cama* sleeper buses. Fares from/to the capital are given in the text.

There are 5 bus terminals: 1. **Terminal Alameda**, which has a modern extension called Mall Parque Estación with good left luggage (0600-2400, US$3-5per day), ATMs and internet, O'Higgins 3712, Metro Universidad de Santiago, T2-2776 2424. All **Pullman-Bus** and **Tur-Bus** services go from here, reaching almost every destination in Chile, good quality but prices a little higher than others. **Tur-Bus** also has booking offices at Universidad de Chile and Tobalaba metro stations, at Cal y Canto, at Av Apoquindo 6421, T2-2212 6435, and in the Parque Arauco and Alto Las Condes malls for those beginning their journeys in Las Condes. 2. **Terminal Santiago**, O'Higgins 3850, 1 block west of Terminal Alameda, T2-2376 1750, www.terminaldebusessantiago.cl, Metro Universidad de Santiago. Services to all parts of southern Chile, including service to Punta Arenas (48 hrs). Also international departures. Has a Redbanc

Tip...
On Friday evening, when night departures are getting ready to go, the bus terminals can be chaotic.

ATM. **3**. **Terminal San Borja**, O'Higgins y San Borja, 1 block west of Estación Central, 3 blocks east of Terminal Alameda, Metro Estación Central (entrance is, inconveniently, via a busy shopping centre, Mall Arauco Estación), T2-2776 0645. Mainly departures to the Central Valley area, but also to northern Chile. Booking offices and departures organized according to destination. **4**. **Terminal Los Héroes**, on Tucapel Jiménez, just north of the Alameda, Metro Los Héroes, T2-2420 0099. A smaller terminal with booking offices of 8 companies, to the north, the south and Lake District and some international services (Lima, Asunción, Montevideo, Buenos Aires, Bariloche, Mendoza). **5**. **Metro Pajaritos** (Metro Línea 1), to Valparaíso, Viña del Mar and places on the central coast; airport shuttle buses call here. It can be more convenient to take a bus from here than from the central terminals. Some long-distance buses call at Las Torres de Tajamar, Providencia 1108, which is more convenient if you are planning to stay in Providencia. **Note** See the note under Taxis about not taking expensive taxis parked outside bus terminals, but bear in mind that official **Tur-Bus** taxis (see opposite) are good and reliable. Also check if student rates are available (even for non-students), or reductions for travelling same day as purchase of ticket; it is worth bargaining over prices, especially shortly before departure and out of summer season.

International buses Most services leave from **Terminal Santiago**, though there are also departures from **Terminal Los Héroes**. There are frequent bus and minibus services from Terminal Santiago through the Cristo Redentor tunnel to **Mendoza** in Argentina, 6-7 hrs, US$35-47, many companies, departures start around 0745 with last departure around 2200, touts approach you in Terminal Santiago. Minibuses have shorter waiting time at customs. Many of these services continue to **Buenos Aires**, 24 hrs, and many companies in Terminal Santiago have connections to other Argentine cities. For destinations like **Bariloche** or **Neuquén**, it is better make connections in Temuco or Osorno. To **Lima**, Andesmar (Terminal Santiago), thrice weekly at 1000, 51½ hrs, about US$140. It is cheaper to take a bus to Arica, a *colectivo* to Tacna, then bus to Lima.

Car

Car hire Prices vary a lot so shop around first. Tax of 19% is charged, usually included in price quoted. If possible book a car in advance. Information boards full of flyers from companies at airport and tourist office. A credit card is usually asked for when renting a vehicle. Many companies will not hire a car to holders of drivers licences in left hand drive countries unless they have an international licence. Remember that in the capital driving is restricted according to licence plate numbers; look for notices in the street and newspapers. Main international agencies and others are available at the airport. **Automóvil Club de Chile** car rental from head office (see Driving in Chile box, page 872), discount for members and members of associated motoring organizations. **Alameda**, Av Bernardo O'Higgins 4709, T2-2779 0609, www.alamedarentacar.cl, San Alberto Hurtado metro, Line 1, also in the airport, good value. **Rosselot**, call centre T600-582 9988, www.rosselot.cl. Reputable Chilean firm with national coverage. **Verschae**, T600 5000 700, www.verschae.com. Good value, branches throughout country.

Ferry and cruise operators

Navimag, Naviera Magallanes SA, www.navimag.com. For services from **Puerto Montt** to **Puerto Chacabuco and Puerto Natales**. M/n **Skorpios**: Augusto Leguía Norte 118, Las Condes, T2-2477 1900, www.skorpios.cl. For luxury cruise out of Puerto Montt to **Laguna San Rafael** and adventure strips from Puerto Natales to Puerto Edén and the Campo Hielo del Sur.

Metro

See www.metrosantiago.cl. Line 1 runs west–east between **San Pablo** and **Los Dominicos**, under the Alameda; Line 2 runs north-south from **Vesupcio Norte** to **La Cisterna**; Line 4 runs from **Tobalaba** on Line 1 south to **Plaza de Puente Alto**, with a branch (4a) from **V Mackenna** to **La Cisterna**; Line 5 runs north, east and southeast from **Plaza de Maipú** via **Baquedano** to **Vicente Valdés** on Line 4. The trains are modern, fast, quiet, and very full at peak times. The first train is at 0600 (Mon-Fri), 0630

on Sat and 0800 Sun and holidays, the last about 2300 (2330 on Fri-Sat, 2230 on Sun). Fares vary according to time of journey; there are 3 charging periods, according to demand: the peak rate is US$1.25, the general rate US$1.10 and there is a cheaper rate at unsociable hours, US$1. The simplest solution is to buy a *tarjeta bip!* (see Local buses, above), the charge card from which the appropriate fare is deducted. Transantiago bus services link with the metro.

Taxi

Taxis (black with yellow roofs) are abundant and fairly cheap: minimum charge of US$0.40, plus US$0.20 per 200 m. In every type of taxi always double check the fare (see www.taximetro.cl). Drivers are permitted to charge more at night, but in the daytime check that the meter is set to day rates. At bus terminals, drivers will charge more – best to walk a block and flag down a cruising taxi. Avoid taxis with more than one person in them especially at night. Various Radio Taxi services operate (eg **Radio Taxis Andes Pacífico**, T2-2912 6000, www.andespacifico.cl); rates are above those of city taxis but they should be more reliable.

Train

Trenes Metropolitanos, T600-585 5000, www.trencentral.cl has details of services. All trains leave from **Estación Central (Alameda)** at O'Higgins 3170. **TerraSur** south to **Chillán** with 10 intermediate stops; **Metrotren** suburban route to **San Fernando**; **Expreso Maule** to **Talca**; **Buscarril** links **Talca**, **Maule**, **Pencahue** and **Constitución**. **Expreso del Recuerdo** is a tourist train to **San Antonio**, T2-2585 5991, www.trendelrecuerdo.cl, www.tren.cl or www.efe.cl, 4 standards of coach, runs on special occasions in summer only. **Booking offices** Alameda O'Higgins 3170, daily 0900-1830; Universidad de Chile metro, loc 10, Mon-Fri 0900-2000, Sat 0900-1300 and others. Left luggage office at Estación Central, open 0600-2400, US$3-5. **Note** Schedules change with the seasons, so check timetables in advance. Summer services are booked up a week in advance.

Around Santiago

crafts, vines, thermal springs and ski resorts

Pomaire

In this little town 65 km west of Santiago, good-quality handicrafts from all over Chile are for sale at prices cheaper than those in Santiago. The area is rich in clay and pottery can be bought and the artists can sometimes be seen at work. The town is famous for its *chicha de uva* and for its Chilean dishes.

ON THE ROAD

Vineyards around Santiago

Several vineyards in the Santiago area offer quality tours in English or Spanish, followed by wine tastings (US$14-25). The following are easily accessible. Tours need booking in advance.

Aquitania Avenida Consistorial 5090, Peñalolén, T2-2791 4500, www.aquitania.cl, bus D17 or taxi from Metro Quilín.

Concha y Toro Avenida Nueva Tajamar 481, Torre Norte, piso 15, Las Condes, T2-2476 5000, www.conchaytoro.cl, metro to Las Mercedes, then taxi or *colectivo*.

Cousiño-Macul Avenida Quilín 7100, on the eastern outskirts of the city, T2-2351 4100, www.cousinomacul.cl, US$22, Metro Quilín.

De Martino Manuel Rodríguez 229, Isla de Maipo, 40 km southwest of Santiago, T2-2577 8800, www.demartino.cl.

Undurraga Santa Ana, 34 km southwest of Santiago, T2-2372 2900, www.undurraga.cl.

Viña Santa Rita Padre Hurtado 0695, Alto Jahuel, Buin, 45 km south of Santiago on the Camino a Padre Hurtado, T2-2362 2590, www.santarita.cl.

☆Maipo Valley

The Maipo Valley is considered by many experts to be the best wine-producing area in Chile. Several vineyards in the area can be visited and there are tours from Santiago (see box, above, and What to do, page 715). Beyond, a road runs through the rugged, green valley of the **Cajón del Maipo**, past Centros Vacacionales, with a variety of activities, and through many villages to the main town of San José de Maipo. Its historic centre has a walking route to visit the old station, the church and other sites. There are places to eat, banks and other services; **tourist office** ① *T2-2678 4900, www. sanjosedemaipo.cl, Mon-Thu 0830-1730, Fri 0830-1630,* in the Municipalidad on the Plaza. Some 11 km further is San Alfonso, near which is the Cascada de Ánimas waterfall (entry through a lodge and vacation centre, 60-90 minutes' walk to falls, entry US$18 high season, US$9 low season). Next is San Gabriel (11 km) with a few places selling drinks and snacks and, 2 km further, the bridge over the Río Yeso, a scruffy picnic spot with two eating places in dramatic scenery At **El Volcán** (1400 m), 21 km beyond San Alfonso, there are astounding views, but little else. From El Volcán the road (very poor condition) runs 14 km east to Lo Valdés and the nearby warm natural baths at **Baños Morales** ① *Tue-Sun 1000-1800, US$5.75.* About 12 km further east up the mountain are **Baños Colina** ① *US$12.50,* hot thermal springs (horses for hire). This area is popular at weekends and holiday times, but is otherwise deserted. If visiting this area or continuing further up the mountain, be prepared for military checks. There are no shops, so take food (local goat's cheese may be sold at the roadside, or at farmhouses). North of Baños Morales, **Monumento Natural El Morado** ① *T2-8901 9775, mn.elmorado@yahoo.es, or www.conaf.cl, Oct-Apr 0830-1800, May-Sep 0830-1700, US$8, administration near the entrance, check with Conaf which parts of the park are open,* covers 3000 ha including several high peaks, an exceptionally secluded and beautiful place with wonderful views.

Ski resorts

There are six main ski resorts near Santiago, four of them around the village of **Farellones**. Situated on the slopes of Cerro Colorado at 2470 m, only 32 km from the capital and reached by road in under 90 minutes, this was the first ski resort built in Chile. Now it is a service centre for the three other resorts, popular at weekends. It provides accommodation and several large restaurants and has a good beginners' area with basic equipment for hire. It is connected by lift to El Colorado and offers beautiful views for 30 km across 10 Andean peaks and incredible sunsets. One-day return shuttles are available from Santiago; enquire at **Ski Club Chile** ① *Goyenechea Candelaria 4750, Vitacura (north of Los Leones Golf Club),* T2-2211 7341.

El Colorado ① *www.elcolorado.cl,* is 8 km further up Cerro Colorado and has a large ski lodge at the base, offering all facilities, and a restaurant higher up. There are 16 lifts giving access to a large intermediate ski area with some steeper slopes. **La Parva** ① *www.laparva.cl,* nearby at 2816 m, is the upper-class Santiago weekend resort with 30 pistes and 14 lifts. Accommodation is in a chalet village and there are some good bars in high season. Good intermediate to advanced skiing, not suitable for beginners.

☆**Valle Nevado** ① *T2-2477 7705, www.vallenevado.com*, is 16 km from Farellones. It offers the most modern ski facilities in Chile with 34 runs, 40 km of slopes and 41 lifts. The runs are well prepared and are suitable for intermediate level and beginners. There is a ski school and heli-skiing. In summer, this is a good walking area, but altitude sickness can be a problem.

Portillo ① *www.skiportillo.cl*, 2855 m, is 145 km north of Santiago and 62 km east of Los Andes near the customs post on the route to Argentina. One of Chile's best-known resorts, Portillo is on the Laguna del Inca, 5.5 km long and 1.5 km wide; this lake, at an altitude of 2835 m, is frozen over in winter and its depth is not known. It is surrounded on three sides by accessible mountain slopes. The 23 runs are varied and well prepared, connected by 12 lifts, two of which open up the off-piste areas. This is an excellent family resort, with a highly regarded ski school. Cheap packages can be arranged at the beginning of and out of season, when there are boats for fishing in the lake (afternoon winds can make the homeward pull much longer than the outward pull) and good walking, but get detailed maps before setting out.

Lagunillas ① *www.skilagunillas.cl*, is 67 km southeast of Santiago in the Cajón del Maipo. Accommodation is in the lodges of the **Club Andino de Chile** (see Skiing, page 700). It is more basic than the other ski centres in the region, with less infrastructure, but the skiing is good. Being lower than the other resorts, its season is shorter, but it is also cheaper.

Santiago to Argentina

The route across the Andes via the Cristo Redentor tunnel is one of the major crossings to Argentina. Before travelling check on weather and road conditions beyond Los Andes. See International buses, page 701. Some 77 km north of Santiago is the farming town of **Los Andes**. There is a monument to the Clark brothers, who built the Transandine Railway to Mendoza (now disused). The town has several hotels. The road to Argentina follows the Aconcagua valley for 34 km until it reaches the village of **Río Blanco** (1370 m). East of Río Blanco the road climbs until Juncal where it zig-zags steeply through a series of 29 hairpin bends at the top of which is the ski resort of Portillo (see above).

Border with Argentina Los Libertadores The old pass, with the statue of Christ the Redeemer (**Cristo Redentor**), is above the tunnel on the Argentine side. On the far side of the Andes the road descends 203 km to Mendoza. The 4-km-long tunnel is open 24 hours September to May, 0800-2000 (Chilean time) June to August, toll US$2.50. Note that this pass is closed after heavy snowfall, when travellers may be trapped at the customs complex on either side of the border. The Chilean border post of Los Libertadores is at Portillo, 2 km west of the tunnel. Bus and car passengers are dealt with separately. Bicycles must be taken through on a pick-up. There may be long delays during searches for fruit, meat and vegetables, which may not be imported into Chile. A *casa de cambio* is in the customs building in Portillo.

Listings Around Santiago

Where to stay

Maipo Valley

$$$-$$ Cabañas Corre Caminos
Alto Cajón del Maipo, Baños Morales,
T2-9269 2283, www.loscorrecaminos.cl.
Cabins sleeping 2-5 people, open all year. Food available, activities including horse riding.

$$ Residencial Los Chicos Malos
Baños Morales, T9-9323 6424,
www.banosmorales.cl.

Comfortable, fresh bread, good meals included in price. There are also *cabañas*, horse riding, open in winter for hot drinks.

Camping

Comunidad Cascada de las Animas
500 m off the main road, San Alfonso, T2-28611303, www.cascadadelasanimas.cl.
Has camping packages starting at US$16 per site in high season (up to 4 people). Also cabins with hot water, cooking equipment, etc, sauna and horse riding. There are a dozen or so other campsites throughout the valley.

Ski resorts

Farellones

$$$$ Posada de Farellones
Los Cóndores 225, T2-2201 3704,
www.skifarellones.com.
Cosy and warm, Swiss style, transport service to
slopes, decent restaurant. Price for half board.
Also **Farellones**, www.hotelfarellones.cl, and
La Cornisa, www.lacornisa.cl.

$$$$-$$ Lodge Andes
Camino La Capilla 662, www.lodgeandes.cl.
Shared rooms with shared bathrooms or private
double rooms, rate includes half board. English
spoken. Good value.

$$ pp Refugio Universidad de Chile
Los Cóndores 879, T2-2321 1595, www.uchile.cl
(enter 'refugio' in the search box).
Shared rooms half board. Standard *refugio*, often
fills up with university students at weekends.

El Colorado and Valle Nevado

Apartments for daily or weekly rental in
El Colorado. Also apartment and resort hotel
facilities in **Valle Nevado**, where the 5-star
resort has boutique shops, gourmet dining, and
backpacker facilities, www.vallenevado.com.

La Parva

$$$$ Condominio Nueva La Parva
Reservations in Santiago, Luis Carrera 1263,
no 402, T2-2964 2118, www.laparva.cl.
Good hotel with swimming pool and many
services, including babysitting.

Portillo

$$$$-$$$ Hotel Portillo
Renato Sánchez 4270, Las Condes, T2-2263 0606,
www.skiportillo.com.
On the shore of Laguna del Inca. From lakeside
suites with full board and fabulous views, to bunk
rooms without bath. Self-service lunch, open
all year, minibus to Santiago. Cinema, nightclub,
pool, sauna and medical service.

Lagunillas

$$$ Refugio Club Andino
www.skilagunillas.cl.
Cabins sleep 2-5, shared bathrooms, room only,
B&B or full board.

Santiago to Argentina

$$$$ Baños El Corazón
At San Esteban, 2 km north of Los Andes,
T2-2236 3636, www.termaselcorazon.cl.
Full board, with use of pool; also day passes for
thermal baths, spa, meals and combinations.
Take bus San Esteban/El Cariño.

Transport

Pomaire

Bus From Santiago take the Melipilla bus from
Terminal San Borja, every few mins, US$1.50
each way, 1 hr; alight at side road to Pomaire,
2-3 km from town, *colectivos* every 10-15 mins.
It's easier to visit on a tour, often combined with
Isla Negra, see page 718, or by car.

Maipo Valley

Take line 5 metro to **Bellavista La Florida**,
change to Metrobus 72 to the Plaza in San José
de Maipo, or take line 4 to Las Mercedes and
take bus No 72, to **San José**, 40 mins, US$1-3, or
a *colectivo* which can go as far as San Gabriel.
Colectivo fares: Las Mercedes to San José US$2,
to San Alfonso US$3, to San Gabriel, US$4.20. San
José to San Alfonso US$1, to San Gabriel, US$3.
San Alfonso-San Gabriel US$2. There is a bus
every 30 mins from San José to San Alfonso, US$1,
every hr to San Gabriel and from Bellavista La
Florida at 1230 and 1830 to El Volcán. In summer
only 1 bus at 0730 to Baños Morales, US$13.

Ski resorts

Bus Centro de Ski El Colorado y Farellones
buses leave from CC Omnium, Av Apoquindo
4900 (Escuela Militar Metro) in Santiago daily
0730-1100 with minimum of 6 passengers,
return 1600-1800, essential to book in advance,
T2-2363 0559, US$25 return. Note that the road
to Farellones and El Colorado is one way 1 Jun-
30 Sep: up 0800-1330; down 1530-2000. **Ski
Total**, T2-2246 0156, www.skitotal.cl, and **Ski
Van**, T2-2219 2672, www.skivan.cl, offer transport to
ski resorts. Reserve in advance; also for hotel or
airport pick-up and minibuses to Portillo. It is
easy to hitch from the junction of Av Las Condes/
El Camino Farellones (**YPF** petrol station in the
middle), reached by a Barnechea bus. **Portillo**
is easily reached by any bus from Los Héroes
terminal, Santiago, or Los Andes to **Mendoza**.
You may have to hitch back.

Valparaíso
& around

★Sprawling over a crescent of 42 hills (*cerros*) that rear up from the sea, Valparaíso, the capital of V Región, is unlike any other Chilean city. The main residential areas obey little order in their layout and the *cerros* have a bohemian, slightly anarchic atmosphere. Here you will find mansions mingling with some of Chile's worst slums and many legends of ghosts and spirits. It is an important naval base and, with the Congress building, it is also the seat of the Chilean parliament. Pacific beaches close to the capital include the international resort of Viña del Mar, Reñaca, Concón and several others. On the same stretch of coast is the port of San Antonio. This coastline enjoys a Mediterranean climate; the cold sea currents and coastal winds produce much more moderate temperatures than in Santiago and the central valley. Rainfall is moderate in winter and the summers are dry and sunny.

Sights Colour map 8, B1.

street art and poetry in the most beguiling city in Chile

El Plan is the business centre, with once fine office buildings on narrow streets strung along the edge of the bay. Above, covering the hills (*cerros*), is a fantastic, multicoloured agglomeration of fine mansions, tattered houses and shacks, scrambled in oriental confusion along the narrow back streets and affording superb views over the bay. The lower and upper cities are connected by steep winding roads, flights of steps and 16 *ascensores* or funicular railways dating from 1883-1914. For several years there have been problems keeping them running and some operate irregularly for lack of funding for repairs and maintenance.

Plaza Sotomayor and El Puerto

The old heart of the city is the **Plaza Sotomayor**, dominated by the former Intendencia (Government House), now used as the seat of the admiralty. Opposite is a fine monument to the 'Heroes of Iquique'. Bronze plaques on the Plaza illustrate the movement of the shoreline over the centuries. The passenger quay is one block away (with poor quality, expensive handicraft shops). Nearby is the remodelled Merval railway station and shopping mall for trains to Viña del Mar and Limache.

The streets of El Puerto run to the northwest of Plaza Sotomayor. Calle Serrano runs for two blocks to Plaza Echaurren, the oldest plaza in Valparaíso, once the height of elegance, today the home of sleeping drunks. Nearby stands the stucco church of **La Matriz**, built in 1842 on the site of the first church in the city. Remnants of the old colonial city can be found in the area around La Matriz. **Museo del Mar Almirante Cochrane** ① *Merlet 195, Tue-Sun 1000-1800, free*, has temporary exhibitions and has good views over the port. To get there, take Ascensor Cordillera from Calle Serrano, off Plaza Sotomayor, to Cerro Cordillera; otherwise there's a long, steep flight of stairs next to the *ascensor*. At the top, on Plazuela Eleuterio Ramírez, take Calle Merlet to the left (not a safe area).

West of the centre

Further northwest, along Bustamante, lies the Plaza Aduana from where Ascensor Artillería (open 0700-2200) rises to **Cerro Artillería**, which is crowned by the huge Naval Academy and the **Museo Naval** ① *www.museonaval.cl, Tue-Sun 1000-1800, US$1.50*. It has displays on naval history 1810-1880, with labels in good English, and exhibitions on Chile's two naval heroes, Lord Cochrane and Arturo Prat, as well as one of the phoenix capsules used to rescue the 33 trapped miners in 2010. Great views are to be had from the Paseo 21 de Mayo at the upper station of the *ascensor*.

Avenida Altamirano runs along the coast at the foot of Cerro Playa Ancha to **Las Torpederas**, a small bathing beach. The **Faro de Punta Angeles** ① *T9-8621 8728, contacto@ farosdechile.com, contact for an appointment to visit the lighthouse and attached museum*, on a promontory just beyond Las Torpederas, was the first lighthouse on the west coast (15 minutes' walk from Cerro Artillería).

El Plan

Southeast of Plaza Sotomayor Calles Prat, Cochrane and Esmeralda run through the old banking and commercial centre to Plaza Aníbal Pinto, around which are several of the city's oldest bars and cafés. On Esmeralda, just past the Turri Clock Tower and Ascensor Concepción is the building of **El Mercurio de Valparaíso**, the world's oldest Spanish-language newspaper still in publication, first published in 1827. Furthest east, on Plaza Victoria, is the Cathedral, with the **Museo de Historia Natural** ① *Condell 1546, T32-254 4840, www.mhnv.cl, Tue-Sat 1000-1800, Sun 1000-1400, free*, nearby. It's housed in the 19th-century Palacio Lyon, which has been redesigned with a library and café.

☆Cerros Alegre and Concepción

Both **Cerro Concepción** and **Cerro Alegre** have fine architecture and scenic beauty as well as a thriving street art scene. Artists and students have long lived there, lending them a slightly bohemian feel, and the *cerros* are becoming deservedly very popular with visitors. A 2-km walk starts at the top of Ascensor Concepción, leading to Paseo Mirador Gervasoni and

Essential Valparaíso

Getting around

The lower city along the waterfront is called El Plan and is connected to the upper city in the *cerros* by steep winding roads, flights of steps and *ascensores* or funicular railways. In 2017 eight were working. Taxis, *colectivos* and buses also run between El Plan and the *cerros*. Buses are frequent in El Plan, which is also served by a trolley bus, which takes a circular route from the Congress to the port (US$0.40, also accepts Metrobus cards). This is one of the best ways to see the lower city; some of the cars, imported from Switzerland and the US, date from the 1930s. Another good viewpoint is from the top of Ascensor Barón, near the bus terminal. Pudahuel international airport is 108 km away and can be reached by bus with one change. The long-distance bus terminal is on Pedro Montt 2800 block (one of the main streets running east from the Cathedral), corner of Rawson, opposite the Congreso Nacional.

Tip...

Sadly, the unusual **Ascensor Polanco** (entrance from Calle Simpson, off Avenida Argentina, a few blocks from the bus station), with its 160-m horizontal tunnel through the rock, then a vertical lift to the summit, is not safe to visit: you have to walk down through a very dangerous area.

Safety

Robbery is a problem in El Puerto and La Matriz and also around the *ascensores* on Avenida Argentina. The upper outskirts of town, while offering amazing views, are not the safest places, particularly after dark. The poorer and rougher districts tend to be those furthest from the centre. Also, be aware that Calle Chacabuco (on which some hotels are located) is the pick-up point for local rent-boys.

Calle Pupudo through a labyrinth of narrow streets and stairs. There are two worthwhile museums on these hills: **Museo Municipal de Bellas Artes** ① *Paseo Yugoslavo 176, Cerro Alegre, T32-225 2332, www.museobaburizza.cl, Tue-Sun 1030-1900, US$6.20, concessions US$1; take Ascensor El Peral from Plaza de la Justicia, off Plaza Sotomayor*, is housed in the impressive Palacio Baburizza and displays Chilean landscapes and seascapes and some modern paintings. Opposite is the 1920s mansion,

Palacio Astoreca, restored as a luxury hotel (Montealegre 149, www.hotelpalacioastoreca.com). **Casa de Lukas** ① *Paseo Mirador Gervasoni 448, Cerro Concepción, www.lukas.cl, US$2.35, free Sat, Sun, Tue-Sun 1100-1800*, is a beautiful villa dedicated to the work of one of Chile's most famous caricaturists. It has a café.

The *cerro* east of Concepción is Panteón, on which are the cemeteries, founded in the 19th century: one for Catholic families (Cementerio No 1) and one for non-Catholic (Cementerio de Disidentes). Both can be visited. Further up Cumming is the Parque Cultural ex-Cárcel de Valparaíso on Cerro Cárcel. The prison has been renovated to hold art exhibitions, theatre, workshops and other events.

Cerro Bellavista and the eastern cerros

Above Plaza Victoria on Cerro Bellavista is the **Museo al Cielo Abierto**, a collection of 20 street murals on the exteriors of buildings, designed by 17 of Chile's most distinguished contemporary artists. It is reached by the Ascensor Espíritu Santo at the end of Calle Huito, by walking up Huito to Rudolph, or Edwards to Ferrari, or by walking downhill from Casa 'La Sebastiana', former house of **Pablo Neruda** ① *Ferrari 692, Av Alemania, Altura 6900 on Cerro Florida, T32-225 6606, www. fundacionneruda.org, Tue-Sun 1010-1800, Jan-Feb 1000-1900, US$11 including audioguide in several*

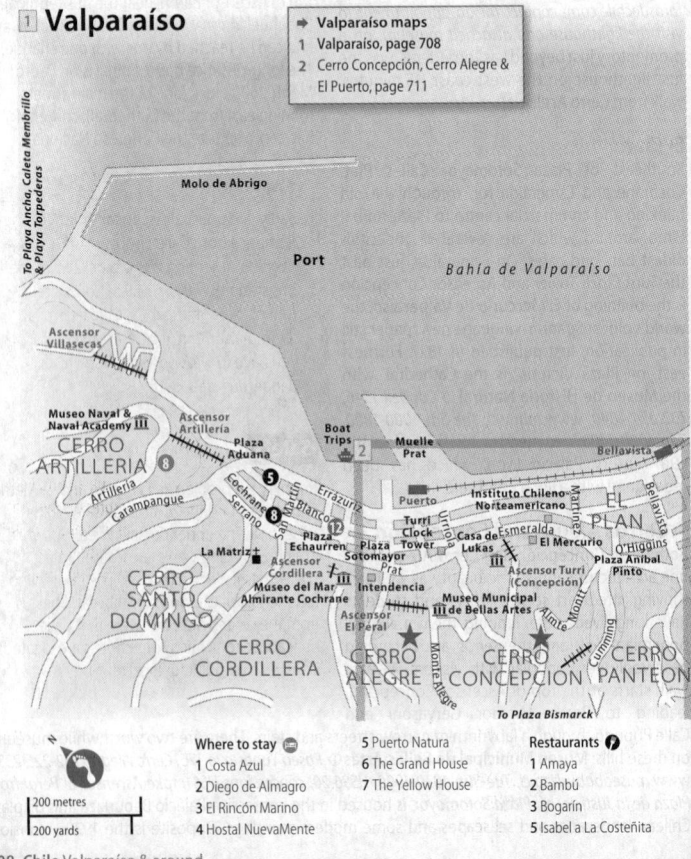

1 Valparaíso

➡ Valparaíso maps
1 Valparaíso, page 708
2 Cerro Concepción, Cerro Alegre & El Puerto, page 711

Where to stay 🛏
1 Costa Azul
2 Diego de Almagro
3 El Rincón Marino
4 Hostal NuevaMente
5 Puerto Natura
6 The Grand House
7 The Yellow House

Restaurants 🍴
1 Amaya
2 Bambú
3 Bogarín
5 Isabel a La Costeñita

This has interesting displays, wonderful views and is worth a visit (see also his house at Isla Negra, page 718). It has an art gallery, gardens and a small café.

Plaza O'Higgins and Muelle Barón

East of Plaza Victoria, reached by following Calle Pedro Montt, is Plaza O'Higgins, which is dominated by the huge square arch of the imposing Congreso Nacional. Opposite is the bus terminal, while four blocks north on Errázuriz is the Barón train station and the **Muelle Barón**, near which is the terminal for cruise ships. The end of this pier gives a good view of Valparaíso's amphitheatre-like setting. Just off the pier is a small colony of sea-lions, and at the base kayaks and sailing boats can be hired and lessons taken (www.puertodeportivo.cl). A coastal walkway runs northeast from here past several small beaches as far as **Caleta Portales**, a small fishing harbour with several seafood restaurants almost at the edge of Viña del Mar.

> **Tip...**
>
> As in Santiago, there is artistic activity all over the city: people practising dance moves, demonstrating circus skills or decorating walls with murals and graffiti; for a study of this art form see *Street Art Chile* by Rod Palmer (8 Books).

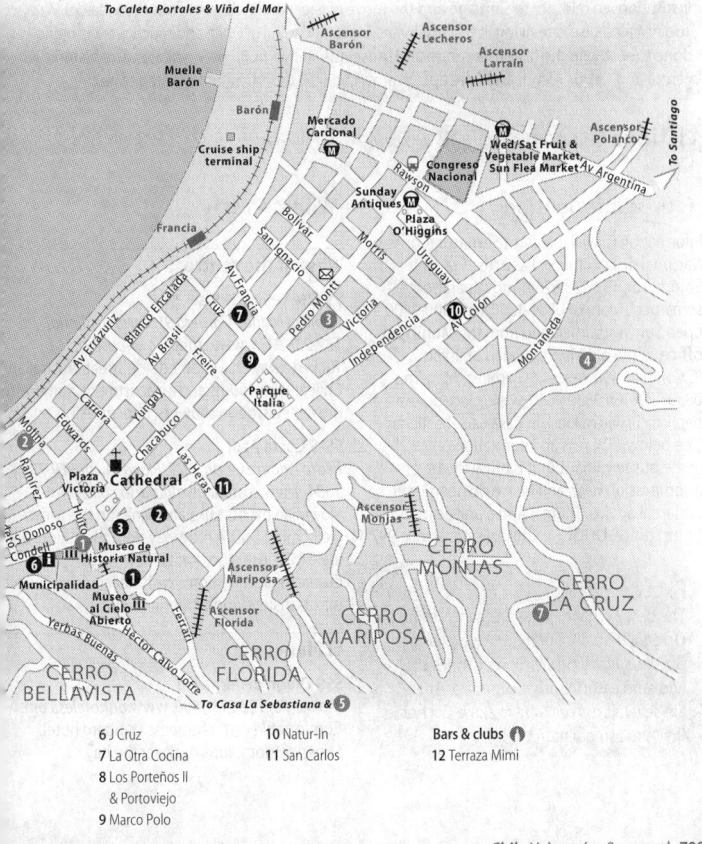

6 J Cruz	10 Natur-In	**Bars & clubs** (●)
7 La Otra Cocina	11 San Carlos	12 Terraza Mimi
8 Los Porteños II		
& Portoviejo		
9 Marco Polo		

BACKGROUND

Valparaíso

First settled in 1542 (but not officially 'founded' until the beginning of the 21st century), Valparaíso became a small port used for trade with Peru. It was raided by corsairs, including Sir Francis Drake, at least seven times. Little of the city's colonial past survived the pirates, tempests, fires and earthquakes of the period, but the city prospered from independence more than any other Chilean town. It was used in the 19th century by commercial agents from Europe and the US as their trading base in the southern Pacific and became a major international banking centre as well as the key port for US shipping between the east coast and California (especially during the gold rush). Most of the principal buildings date from after the devastating earthquake of 1906 (further serious earthquakes occurred in 1971, 1985 and 2010), though some impressions of the city's 19th-century glory can be gained from the banking area of El Plan. Its decline was the result of the opening of the trans-continental railway in the United States and then the Panama Canal in 1914, a decrease in mining activity leading to reduced bank profits, followed by the 1929-1930 Depression, after which British business left. It then declined further owing to the development of a container port in San Antonio, tax breaks encouraging financial institutions to relocate to Santiago and the move of the middle-classes to nearby Viña del Mar. Today, Valparaíso is reviving. It is officially the Cultural Capital of Chile and much work is being done to renovate the historical centre and museums, and to build new galleries. The historic centre and Cerros Alegre and Concepción are a UNESCO World Cultural Heritage Site.

Listings Valparaíso map p706 and p709

Tourist information

Information is available from **Sernatur** (Consejo Nacional de la Cultura y Las Artes, Prat y Sotomayor, T32-223 6264, infovalparaiso@ sernatur.cl, Mon-Fri 0830-1800, Sat 1000-1400, open Sun in summer) and from the **Municipal office**, in the old Municipalidad building (C Condell 1490, opposite Ramírez, Mon-Thu 0830-1730, Fri 0830-1630, www.ciudaddeval paraiso.cl), with a kiosk in Casa La Sebastiana (see below). There is an information office in the bus terminal, but it is privately run on a commission basis and hence do not give impartial advice. There is also a university-run tourist office, **DUOC**, in Edif Cousiño, Blanco 997.

Fact...

The best exchange rates are from **Marín Orrego**, third floor of the stock exchange building, Prat y Urriola, only changes US\$ and euro cash; for other currencies, there are several *casas de cambio* along Cochrane, Prat and Esmeralda.

Where to stay

West of the centre

\$\$ The Yellow House
Capitán Muñoz Gamero 91, Cerro Artillería, T32-233 9435, www.theyellowhouse.cl.
Tucked away on a cobbled side street. Australian/ Chilean-run, rooms and an apartment, some with great views, good showers, non-smoking.

\$\$-\$ Costa Azul
Pedro Aguirre Cerda 1079, Playa Ancha, T9-7973 1684, www.costaazulvalparaiso.com.
Slovenian expats Luka and Nina run this most welcoming B&B. A little way from the action, but ideal for those who don't fancy the party vibe. Colourful private rooms with stellar views, tourist info, transfers, good meeting point.

El Plan

\$\$\$ Diego de Almagro
Molina 76, T32-213 3600, www.dahoteles.com.
Comfortable 4-star business standard hotel. Superior rooms look out over the bay.

Cerros Alegre and Concepción

Cerros Alegre, Concepción and, to a lesser extent, Bellavista have many *hostales*, more than we can list. For a selection, see www.hhyr.cl.

$$$$ Acontraluz
San Enrique 473, Cerro Alegre, T32-211 1320, www.hotelacontraluz.cl.
Probably the best of the boutique hotels here. Rooms facing the sea have balconies with tremendous views. Bright, Victorian house

with attention to detail and no expense spared. English, French, Russian spoken, most hospitable, 24-hr café, solar power, recycling, TV on demand only.

$$$$ Casa Higueras
Higuera 133, Cerro Alegre, T32-249 7900, www.hotelcasahigueras.cl.
Small, elegant hotel on 5 levels, variety of rooms, good views, fine restaurant, spa, sauna, pool and gardens.

Cerro Concepción, Cerro Alegre & El Puerto

N	
400 metres	
400 yards	

Where to stay 🛏
1 Acontraluz *C2*
3 Casa Aventura *B2*
4 Casa Higueras *B1*
6 Catalejo House *B2*
7 Hostal Casa
  Verde Limón *B3*
8 La Bicyclette *B2*
9 La Nona *C2*
10 La Valija Hostel
  & Colour Café *B2*
12 Luna Sonrisa
  & El Nidito *C2*
13 Manoir Atkinson *B2*
14 Pata Pata *B2*
15 Somerscales Boutique *C2*
16 Ultramar *B3*

Restaurants 🍴
1 Allegretto *B2*
2 Bar Inglés *A2*
3 Bote Salvavidas *A1*
4 Café con Letras *B2*
5 Café Vinilo *B2*
8 Delicias Express *B1*
9 El Desayunador *B2*
10 E l Dominó *B3*
11 Fauna *B2*
12 La Cocó *C2*
13 La Colombina *B1*
14 La Concepción *B2*
15 La Rotonda *B1*
16 Le Filou de Montpellier *B2*
17 Malandrino *C2*
18 Mastodonte *A2*
19 Pan de Magia *C2*
20 Pasta e Vino *B2*
21 Pimentón *B3*
22 Turri *B2*
23 Zamba & Canuta *A2*

Bars & clubs 🍸
24 Altamira *B3*
25 Cinzano *B3*
26 El Huevo *A3*
27 El Irlandés *A3*
28 El Viaje *B3*
29 La Piedra Feliz *A2*
30 La Playa *B1*

➡ Valparaíso maps
1 Valparaíso, page 708
2 Cerro Concepción,
  Cerro Alegre & El Puerto,
  page 711

$$$$ Manoir Atkinson
Paseo Atkinson 165, T32-327 5425,
www.hotelatkinson.cl.
A boutique hotel, 7 comfortable rooms, terraces with views of the city and bay, English and French spoken, meals, tours arranged.

$$$$-$$$ Somerscales Boutique
San Enrique 446, Cerro Alegre, T32-233 1006,
www.hotelsomerscales.cl.
Spacious rooms in former home of English painter, period furniture. Basic English spoken, top-floor rooms have lovely views.

$$$-$$ La Nona
Galos 660/662, Cerro Alegre, T32-238 0108,
9-6618 6186, www.bblanona.com.
Comfortable, welcoming, family-run B&B, plenty of information, maps and activities like historical tours and wine tastings, delicious breakfast, laundry service, English spoken. Warmly recommended.

$$-$ Casa Aventura
Pasaje Gálvez 11, off C Urriola, Cerro Concepción,
T32-275 5963, www.casaventura.cl.
One of Valparaíso's longest established backpackers' hostels, with rooms and dorms in a traditional house, German and English spoken, tours, helpful, deservedly popular, informative.

$$-$ Hostal Casa Verde Limón
Subida Cumming 196, Plaza El Descanso, Cerro Cárcel, T32-212 1699, www.casaverdelimon.com.
Double, single rooms, dorm and loft, shared bath, breakfast extra, laundry, good budget choice.

$$-$ La Bicyclette
Almte Montt 213, Cerro Alegre, T32-222 2415,
www.bicyclette.cl.
Basic, bright rooms, dorm, shared bath, book exchange, lovely patio, French-run, rents bicycles.

$$-$ La Valija Hostel
Papudo 526, Cerro Concepción, T32-317 1395,
lavalijahostel.cl.
This 2-storey tumbledown hostel with winding stairs and open-air courtyard captures Valparaíso perfectly, as does the adjacent **Color Café**. Comfy beds and friendly staff make this a good budget choice. Great location.

$$-$ Luna Sonrisa
Templeman 833, Cerro Alegre, T32-273 4117,
www.lunasonrisa.cl.
Room for 16 guests in doubles, singles or dorm with shared or en suite bath. Bright, comfortable, lots of information, excellent breakfast including

wholemeal bread and real coffee, tours arranged, English and French spoken, helpful. Also **El Nidito** (www.elnidito.cl), 1 classically elegant apartment with 3 en suite bedrooms, large living/dining room with upright piano and spacious balcony, parking. Also 1 smaller apartment, sleeps 2-4.

$$-$ Pata Pata
Templeman 657, Cerro Alegre, T32-317 3153,
www.patapatahostel.com.
Family-run, doubles and big dorms ($), shared facilities, lots of movies, good choice.

Cerro Bellavista and the eastern cerros

$$$ The Grand House
Federico Varela 27, Cerro La Cruz, T32-221 2376,
www.thegrandhouse.cl.
Charming house, almost Victorian decor, excellent breakfast, "a true gem".

$$$ Puerto Natura
Héctor Calvo 850, Cerro Bellavista, T32-211 2730,
www.puertonatura.cl.
Large grounds with fruit trees and small pool, café, excellent views. There is also a holistic centre with sauna, massages, reiki, reflexology and meditation.

$$$ Ultramar
Pérez 173, Cerro Cárcel, T32-221 0000,
www.hotelultramar.com.
Italianate building (1907), modern design, buffet breakfast, café, attentive staff. Rooms are spacious with great views but may get stuffy in summer.

$$-$ Catalejo House
Bernardo Vero 870, Cerro San Juan de Dios,
T32-225 9150, www.catalejohouse.com.
Rooms with shared bath, good view, good reports.

$$-$ Hostal NuevaMente
Pocuro 1088, T32-317 0184, hostalnuevamente.
valparaiso on Facebook.
Beautiful old hostel with big, light rooms, about 15 mins' walk from centre. Run by a helpful young couple, good local information, some English spoken, movies, tours, bike hire.

Plaza O'Higgins and Muelle Barón

$ El Rincón Marino
San Ignacio 454, T 9-7497 1909 ,
www.rinconmarino.cl.
Uninspiring location, but good-value *hostal*.

Restaurants

Plaza Sotomayor and El Puerto

$$$-$$ Bote Salvavidas
By Muelle Prat, T32-225 1477,
www.restaurantbotesalvavidas.cl.
Elegant fish restaurant overlooking the port.

$$ Isabel a La Costeñita
Blanco 86.
Good seafood, with incredibly kitsch decor.

$$ Los Porteños II
Cochrane y Valdivia.
A seafood favourite, terse service
but good food.

$$ Porto Viejo
Cochrane y Valdivia.
Good-value set lunch fish dishes, good service.
Recommended.

West of the centre
At Caleta Membrillo, 2 km northwest of
Plaza Sotomayor (take any Playa Ancha bus),
there are several good fish restaurants such as
El Membrillo.

El Plan

$$$ Zamba & Canuta
Blanco 1065, T32-218 3331, see Facebook.
Elegant, modern cuisine, wide range
of dishes. Excellent views across the bay,
also holds events.

$$$-$$ Marco Polo
Pedro Montt 2199, www.marco-polo.cl.
Traditional restaurant, *pastelería* and *salón de té*,
since 1955, good-value set lunches, plus mostly
Italian dishes.

$$ Bar Inglés
Cochrane 851 (entrance also on
Blanco Encalada), T32-221 4625.
Historic bar dating from the early 1900s,
a chart shows the ships due in port.
Good food and drink.

$$ La Otra Cocina
Yungay 2250, near Francia.
Good seafood, cosy, good service.

$ Bambú
Independencia 1790, p 2, T32-223 4216,
see Facebook. Closed Sun.
Vegetarian lunches only.

$ J Cruz
Condell 1466, T32-221 1225, www.jcruz.cl.
Valparaíso's most traditional restaurant/museum,
famous for its *chorillanas*, open all night, very
popular, queues at lunchtime.

$ Mastodonte
Esmeralda 1139, T32-225 1205,
www.mastodonte.cl.
No nonsense, very good value, traditional food in
incredibly kitsch surroundings. Excellent service
and cheap locally brewed draft beer.

$ Pimentón
Ecuador 27, see Facebook.
Homecooked traditional Chilean dishes.
Menu changes daily, good value.

$ San Carlos
Las Heras y Independencia.
Traditional family-run restaurant with lots of
character that hasn't changed in years. Lunch
only. Good food guaranteed, always full of locals.
Recommended.

Cafés

Bogarín
Plaza Victoria 1670.
Great juices, ice cream and snacks.

La Rotonda
Prat 701.
One of Valparaíso's more traditional cafés,
good coffee and breakfast.

Cerros Alegre and Concepción
These *cerros* have a great many places to eat,
again more than we can list; wander around to
see what takes your fancy.

$$$ La Concepción
Papudo 541, Cerro Concepción, T32-249 8192.
Creative food, beautifully presented and well
served, magnificent views. Next door is a
charming art gallery and café, **La Belle Epoque**.

$$$-$$ Café Vinilo
Almte Montt 448, T32-223 0665.
Inventive lunchtime menus with gourmet
interpretations of traditional Chilean dishes.
Also a lively bar at night.

$$$-$$ Fauna
Dimalow 166, T32-212 1408.
Varied menu, mostly seafood and fish, Chilean,
desserts, large wine list, eat inside or on terrace.
One of the best views in the city. Also has a hotel,
www.faunahotel.cl.

$$$-$$ La Colombina
Paseo Yugoeslavo 15, Cerro Alegre, T32-223 6254.
The most traditional of the area's restaurants.
Good food, wide range of wines, fine views,
especially from the top floor.

$$$-$$ Le Filou de Montpellier
Almte Montt 382, T32-222 4663, see Facebook.
French-run, set lunch menu deservedly popular,
also open weekday evenings.

$$$-$$ Pasta e Vino
*Papudo 427, Cerro Concepción, T32-249 6187,
www.pastaevinoristorante.cl. Closed Mon.*
Wonderfully inventive, tasty pasta dishes,
haughty service. Advance booking essential.

$$$-$$ Turri
*Templeman 147, Cerro Concepción,
T32-225 2091, www.turri.cl.*
Reasonable food, good range of fish dishes,
wonderful views, a bit of a tourist trap.

$$ Allegretto
*Pilcomayo 529, Cerro Concepción, T32-296 8839,
www.allegretto.cl. Sun-Thu until 2300, Sat-Sun
until 0100.*
Lively British-owned pizzería, exotic but very
tasty toppings, can get busy.

$$ Malandrino
*Almirante Montt 532, Cerro Alegre, www.
malandrino.cl. Wed-Thu until 2300, Fri-Sat
until 2400, Sun 1300-1700.*
Traditional pizzas baked in a clay oven using
mostly organic ingredients. Cosy atmosphere.
Popular with locals as well as tourists.

$ El Dominó
Cumming 67. Open till 0330.
Traditional, serves *empanadas*, *chorillanas*,
calagas de pescado (fish nuggets).

Cafés

Café con Letras
*Almte Montt 316, Cerro Concepción
(also on Plaza Sotomayor), see Facebook.*
Intimate café serving good coffee and snacks,
soup in winter, lots of reading material.

Color Café
Papudo 526, Cerro Concepción, see Facebook.
Cosy arty café serving tea and real coffee, fresh
juice, good cakes, snacks and all-day breakfasts,
regular live music, art exhibits, local art and
craft for sale. Upstairs is **La Valija Hostel** (see
page 712).

Delicias Express
Urriola, near Prat.
A whole range of fried *empanadas*, good for a
quick snack.

El Desayunador
*Almte Montt 399, Cerro Alegre, T32-275 5735,
http://eldesayunador.wixsite.com/inicio.*
Breakfast bar open early. Wide range of teas,
real coffee, cakes, also vegetarian lunches.

La Cocó
Monte Alegre 546, Cerro Alegre, see Facebook.
A good selection of sandwiches, including
vegetarian, tapas, desserts, teas, coffees and
drinks. Live flamenco once a month.

Pan de Magia
*Almte Montt 738 y Templeman, Cerro Alegre,
see Facebook.*
Cakes, cookies, fantastic *empanadas* and by far
the best wholemeal bread in town, all take away.

Cerro Bellavista and the eastern cerros

$$ Amaya
*Rudolf 112, Cerro Bellavista, T9-6835 9702.
Fri-Sun.*
At the top of the *ascensor* Espíritu Santo. Peruvian
food, mostly seafood-based, friendly service,
good views from terrace.

Plaza O'Higgins and Muelle Barón
There are good cheap seafood lunches upstairs
at Mercado Cardonal behind the bus terminal.

$ Natur-In
Colón 2634, see Facebook. Lunch only.
Tasty home-made, mostly vegetarian food. Menu
changes daily, excellent value, fills up quickly.

Bars and clubs

The area around El Puerto can be dangerous at
night. There are many bars on Subida Ecuador,
but be careful which ones you go into, as in some
of them you risk being eaten alive. **El Coyote
Quemado** is a good option. Calle Blanco, near
Plaza Sotomayor, is ground zero for Valparaíso's
hottest nightspots, with some of the best being:

El Huevo
Blanco 1386, www.elhuevo.cl.
One of Valparaíso's most popular nightspots with
3 levels of dancing and drinking.

El Irlandés
*Blanco 1279, see Facebook. Open from early
evening to at least 0300 at weekends.*

Decent and good fun Irish-run Irish bar with bitter on tap and a good selection of beer, live music at weekends.

La Piedra Feliz
Errázuriz 1054, www.lapiedrafeliz.cl.
Wed-Sat from 2000.
Every type of music depending on the evening, large pub, live music area and dance floor, clientele of all ages, entrance US$7.50.

La Playa
Serrano 567 through to Cochrane 558.
Old English-style bar, live music, attracts a student crowd.

Terraza Mimi
Blanco 375, see Facebook.
Dance hall with 2 large rooms, one of which hosts popular international DJs and live touring bands. Revellers light on cash can bring their own alcohol. Gets full around 0200 and lasts until the wee hours of the morning. Entrance US$4.50-7.50 depending on night.

Other areas

Altamira
Elias 126, across from Ascensor Reina Victoria, T32-319 3619, www.cerveceraaltamira.cl.
Specializes in craft beers, live music, great atmosphere.

Cinzano
Plaza Aníbal Pinto 1182, T32-221 3043, www.barcinzano.cl.
Oldest bar in Valparaíso, also serves food. Flamboyant live music at weekends, noted for tango (no dancing by guests allowed).

El Viaje
Cumming 93, just above Plaza Aníbal Pinto.
Popular with travellers, great live music (everything from samba to jazz) and nice *mojitos* and *terremotos*, too. Recommended.

Festivals

31 Dec New Year is celebrated by a spectacular, 40-min firework display launched from the harbour and naval ships, which is best seen from the *cerros*. The display is televised nationally and about a million visitors come to the city. Book well in advance; accommodation doubles or trebles in price at this time, but it's well worth it.

Markets
Large antiques market on Plaza O'Higgins every Sat and Sun. Very good selection, especially old shipping items. Along Av Argentina there is a huge, colourful fruit and vegetable market on Wed and Sat and a crowded flea market on Sun. Good locally made handicrafts on Cerros Alegre and Concepción.

Boat trips
Small boats make 45-min and 1-hr tours of the harbour from Muelle Prat, near Plaza Sotomayor, offering a pleasant view of the city, especially if it's sunny: US$5-7 pp plus tip for the commentator; wait for the boat to fill up. Boats run till 1930. There are also night trips at 2000 (only in summer).

City tours
Free Tour, *T9-9236 8789, www.freetourvalparaiso.cl.* 3-hr walking tour starting from Plaza Aníbal Pinto, daily 1000 and 1500. Payment by tips.
La Porteña, *orianapp@gmail.com.* Tours on foot or by bike.

Cooking classes
Chilean Cuisine, *T9-6621 4626, www.cooking classeschile.cl.* Fun introduction to Chilean food with English-speaking chef/teacher, can include wine tour, wine tastings.

Wine tours
Wine Tours Valparaíso, *T9-8428 3502, www.winetoursvalparaiso.cl.* Small-group tours to the Casablanca Valley with an English-speaking guide.

Air To reach Valparaíso from the international airport at Pudahuel: take a bus to Pajaritos, US$3, cross the platform and take a bus to Valparaíso, US$5. Return to the airport via the same route. Alternatively, a taxi from Pajaritos costs US$5-7 (about 7 mins' ride). Only take a taxi with an official Airport Taxi sticker (pirates overcharge).

Ascensores Municipal *ascensores* run daily 0700-2200, some till 2300 (US$0.15-0.50). Sometimes you pay on entrance, sometimes on exit.

Bus US$0.55 within El Plan, US$0.75 to *cerros*, US$0.95 to Viña del Mar from Av Errázuriz. Bus 612, known as the 'O', from Av Argentina near the bus terminal to Plaza Aduana gives fine panoramic views of the city and bay.

Long-distance terminal is on Pedro Montt 2800 block, corner of Rawson, 1 block from Av Argentina, T32-293 9695; plenty of buses between terminal and Plaza Sotomayor.

To **Santiago**, 1¾ hrs, US$5, frequent (book return in advance on long weekends and public holidays). Fares are much the same as from Santiago to places such as **Chillán**, 7 hrs, **Concepción**, 8 hrs, **Pucón**, 12 hrs, **Puerto Varas** and **Puerto Montt**, 14 hrs; to **La Serena**, 7 hrs, **Antofagasta**, 17 hrs, **San Pedro de Atacama**, 24 hrs. To **Mendoza** (Argentina) 5 companies, 8 hrs, early morning.

Taxi More expensive than Santiago: a short run under 1 km costs US$2 and a journey across town about US$8-10. Taxi *colectivos*, slightly more expensive than buses, carry sign on roof indicating route, very convenient.

Train Regular service every 10 mins on **Metro Valparaíso** (Merval), T32-252 7633, www.metro-valparaiso.cl, between Valparaíso, **Viña del Mar**, **Quilpué** and **Limache**, with a bus service to **Olmué**. Operates on a similar card system to Santiago: cards cost US$2.50; fare depends on time of day and distance travelled, lowest fare about US$0.50, to **Viña del Mar** US$0.75.

Around Valparaíso

sand, sea and the home of a poet

Avenida España runs northeast from Valparaíso along a narrow belt between the shore and precipitous cliffs to one of South America's leading beach resorts, Viña del Mar. There are a mixture of fashionable seaside destinations and fishing communities along the coast to the north, while, south of Valparaíso, are more popular resorts at the mouth of the Río Maipo. Pablo Neruda's famous seaside home at Isla Negra is also found here. For a change from the sea, visit La Campana national park with its native woodlands, panoramic views and Darwinian associations.

☆Viña del Mar *Colour map 8, B1.*

The older part of Viña del Mar is situated on the banks of an estuary, the Marga Marga, which is crossed by bridges. Around Plaza Vergara and the smaller Plaza Sucre to its south are the **Teatro Municipal** (1930) and the exclusive **Club de Viña**, built in 1910. The municipally owned

> **Warning...**
> For safety's sake, don't change money on the street, there are plenty of ATMs and *casas de cambio* on Arlegui and Valparaíso.

Quinta Vergara, formerly the residence of the shipping entrepreneur Francisco Alvarez, lies two blocks south. The **Palacio Vergara**, in the gardens, housed the **Museo de Bellas Artes** and the **Academia de Bellas Artes**. It is in poor shape and closed to the public (2017; T32-218 5720). Part of the grounds is a playground, and there is a modern outdoor auditorium where concerts and events are held throughout the year and, in February, a huge international music festival.

Calle Libertad runs north from the plaza, lined with banks, offices and shops. At the junction with 4 Norte is the **Palacio Carrasco** and **Museo Fonck** ① *4 Norte 784, www.museofonck.cl, Mon 1000-1400, 1500-1800, Tue-Sat 1000-1800, Sun 1000-1400, US$4,* an archaeological and natural history museum, with objects from Easter Island and the Chilean mainland, including Mapuche silver.

On a headland overlooking the sea is **Cerro Castillo**, the summer palace of the President of the Republic. Just north, on the other side of the lagoon is the Casino, built in the 1930s and set in beautiful gardens, US$5 (open all year). **Museo de la Cultura del Mar** ① *in the Castillo Wulff, on the coast near Cerro Castillo, T32-218 5751, closed in 2017,* contains a collection on the life and work of the novelist and maritime historian, Salvador Reyes. The main beaches, Acapulco and Mirasol are located to the north, but south of Cerro Castillo is Caleta Abarca, also popular and the best beach for swimming. The coastal route north to Reñaca provides lovely views over the sea.

Formerly the estate of the nitrate baron Pascual Baburizza and covering 405 ha, **Jardín Botánico Nacional** ① *8 km southeast of the city, www.jardin-botanico.cl, open 0900-1900, US$3.25, getting there: take bus No 203 from C Alvarez, or Av Errázuriz in Valparaíso, and get off at the puente El Olivar, cross the bridge and walk 15 mins,* contains over 3000 species from all over the world and a collection of Chilean cacti, but the species are not labelled. It's a good place for a picnic; there's a canopy adventure trail, with zip-lines, and occasional concerts in the summer.

Resorts north of Viña del Mar

North of Viña del Mar the coast road runs through **Las Salinas**, a popular beach between two towering crags, **Reñaca** (long beach, upmarket, good restaurants) and **Cochoa**, where there is a sealion colony 100 m offshore, to **Concón** (18 km). Famous for its restaurants, Concón has six beaches stretching along the bay between Caleta Higuerilla in the west end and, in the east, La Boca (the largest of the six, excellent for beach sports, horses and kayaks for hire). **Quintero**, 23 km north of Concón, is a slightly dilapidated fishing town on a rocky peninsula with lots of small beaches (hotels and *residenciales*).

☆ **Horcón** is set back in a cove surrounded by cliffs. It's a pleasant small village, mainly of wooden houses, and, though it's packed out in January-February, it is a charming place the rest of the year, populated by fishermen, artists and hippies, with a tumbledown feel unlike the more well-to-do resorts to north and south. Horses still drag the small fishing boats out of the sea. Vegetation is tropical with many cacti on the cliff tops. There are lots of *cabañas*; shop around, especially off season.

Further north is **Maitencillo** with a wonderful long beach, heaving in high summer but a ghost town off season. Some 14 km beyond is **Zapallar**, an expensive resort with a lovely beach. A hint of its former glory is given by a number of fine mansions along Avenida Zapallar. At **Cachagua**, 3 km south, a colony of penguins on an offshore island may be viewed from the northern end of the beach; take binoculars.

Papudo, 10 km further north, was the site of a naval battle in November 1865 in which the Chilean vessel Esmeralda captured the Spanish ship Covadonga. Following the arrival of the railway Papudo rivalled Viña del Mar as a fashionable resort in the 1920s but it has long since declined. With its lovely beach and fishing port, it is an idyllic spot (except in high summer).

Viña del Mar

Where to stay
1 Agora
2 Cap Ducal
3 Hotel del Mar
4 Offenbacher Hof

Restaurants
1 Alster
2 Bogarín
3 Café Journal
4 Cevasco
5 Ciboulette
6 Enjoy Viña del Mar
7 Fellini
8 Jerusalem
9 La Flor de Chile
10 Las Delicias del Mar
11 Samoiedo
13 Wok and Roll

Cartagena and around

Cartagena, 8 km north of **San Antonio**, is the most popular resort on the coast south of Valparaíso. The centre is around the hilltop Plaza de Armas. To the south is the picturesque Playa Chica, overlooked by many of the older hotels and restaurants; to the north is the Playa Larga. Between the two a promenade runs below the

Tip...

This stretch of coast is known as the Litoral de los Poetas, since many famous Chilean poets found inspiration here.

cliffs; high above hang old houses, offering spectacular views. Cartagena is packed in summer, when it can have quite an edgy feel, but out of season it is a good centre for visiting nearby resorts of Las Cruces, El Tabo and El Quisco.

☆**Museo-Casa Pablo Neruda** ① *T35-246 1284, www.fundacionneruda.org, US$11, students US$4, audio guides in several languages, Jan-Feb Tue-Sun 1000-1900, rest of year Tue-Sun 1000-1800*. North of Cartagena in the village of **Isla Negra** is the beautifully restored home that Neruda bought in 1939. The house, overlooking the sea, was constantly added to over time and served as a writing retreat in his later years. It contains artefacts gathered by Neruda from all over the world. Neruda and his last wife, Matilde, are buried here; the touching gravestone is beside the house. The house has a good café specializing in Neruda's own recipes.

East of Valparaíso

At **Limache**, on the Merval railway, is the **Quinta Escondida** ① *Cra 13, T9-8418 0531, www.quintaescondida.com*, a late-19th century house with fruit orchards which offers B&B, self-catering, day visits, access to local sites and activities. On site is also Rosa Puga's healing centre. The Limache Valley is renowned for its alternative medicine and spiritual retreats, as well as its fruit and vegetable production.

☆**Parque Nacional La Campana** ① *T33-244 1342, www.conaf.cl, daily 0900-1730, US$6 for foreigners*. From Limache, there is access to this 8000-ha park, which includes Cerro La Campana (1828 m), which Darwin climbed in 1834, and Cerro El Roble (2200 m). Some of the best views in Chile can be seen from the top. There are three entrances: Granizo (from which the hill is climbed) is reached by paved road east from Limache, via Olmué; Cajón Grande (with natural bathing pools, camping) is reached by unpaved road which turns off the Olmué–Granizo road, and Palmar de Ocoa to the north, reached by unpaved road (10 km; camping) leading off the Pan-American Highway at Km 100 between Hijuelas and Llaillay. Near Ocoa there are areas of Chilean palms (*kankán*), which give edible, walnut-sized coconuts in March and April. The tree is now found in its natural state in only two locations in Chile.

Listings Around Valparaíso *map p715*

Tourist information

For tourist information in Viña del Mar contact **Sernatur** (8 Norte 580 y 2 Poniente, T32-288 2285, infovalparaiso@sernatur.cl, Mon-Fri 0830-1730). There's also a **municipal office** (near Plaza Vergara on Arlegui, by Hotel O'Higgins, and at the bus station, daily 0900-1300, 1500-1800). See also www.vinadelmarchile.cl and www. vinadelmar.cl. **Concón tourist office** (Rotonda de Concón s/n, Mon-Fri 0800-1715, Sat 1000-1715, www.concon.cl).

Where to stay

Viña del Mar

There are lots of places to stay, mostly **$$$**, although many are in the business district and not convenient for the beaches. Out of season agencies rent furnished apartments. In season it's cheaper to stay in Valparaíso.

$$$$ Hotel Del Mar
San Martín 199, T600-700 6000, www.enjoy.cl/enjoy-vina-del-mar.
Viña's top hotel, in spacious grounds above the casino overlooking the bay. Gym, spa and several good restaurants.

$$$$-$$$ Cap Ducal
Marina 51, T32-262 6655.
Old mansion charm – a ship-shaped building literally overhanging the ocean, with an elegant restaurant, serving good seafood.

$$$ Agora
5½ Poniente 253, T32-269 4669,
www.hotelagora.cl.
On a quiet side street, brightly coloured rooms, most with full-size bathtub, English spoken, helpful staff (on 4 floors but no lift).

$$$-$$ Offenbacher Hof
Balmaceda 102, T32-262 1483,
www.offenbacher-hof.cl.
Large wooden house in a quiet residential street overlooking the city centre, peaceful, helpful.

Restaurants

Viña del Mar
Many good bars and restaurants on and around San Martín between 2 and 8 Norte; cuisine including Austrian, Mexican, Chinese and Italian. Cheap bars and restaurants around C Valparaíso and Von Schroeders. Not too safe at night.

$$$ Ciboulette
1 Norte 191, T32-269 0084.
Intimate Belgian-owned and run bistro serving traditional French cuisine. Good wine list.

$$$$-$$ Enjoy Viña del Mar
San Martín 199.
Modern restaurant serving everything from gourmet dishes to barbecues and fast food, all on an open terrace on the seafront.

$$$-$$ Fellini
3 Norte y 6 Poniente in front of the Casino, T32-297 5742, www.fellini.cl.
Wide range of fresh pasta dishes in delicious sauces, good.

$$$-$$ Las Delicias del Mar
San Martín 459, T32-290 1837.
Traditional Basque seafood restaurant.

$$ La Flor de Chile
8 Norte 601, T32-268 9554, www.laflordechile.cl.
Consistently good, typical Chilean food.

$$ Wok and Roll
5 Norte 476, T32-212 3480, www.wokandroll.cl.
One of the better sushi restaurants in town. Free delivery service.

$$-$ Cevasco
Av Valparaíso 700, T32-271 4256,
see www.cevasco.cl for 3 other locations.
Freshly prepared Chilean fast food. Famous for its oversized hamburgers.

$ Café Journal
Agua Santa y Alvarez, T32-262 0482,
see Facebook.
Excellent-value set lunch.

$ Jerusalem
Quinta 259, T32-247 4704, see Facebook.
Authentic Middle Eastern fare, including falafel, shawarma and stuffed vine leaves.

Cafés

Alster
Valparaíso 225.
Elegant but pricey.

Bogarín
In a mall on Valparaíso between Quinta and Etchevers.
For juices and ice cream. Several other fast food places in the mall.

Samoiedo
Valparaíso 639, see Facebook.
A large modern *confitería*, ice cream, coffee, popular.

Bars and clubs

Viña del Mar
There are dozens of bars and clubs in the triangle formed by San Martín, 5 Poniente and 2 Norte. They tend to change name and style every other year. **Ovo** in the casino, is one of the most popular discos in Viña.

What to do

Viña del Mar

Cycling
Bicitours, *San Martín 448, T9-9409 4506, www.bicitours.cl.* 8 cycling tours based in Viña, from 2 to 5 hrs, city tours, to resorts, to Valparaíso, from US$16; also bicycle hire, US$4 per hr, US$31 per day.

Resorts north of Viña del Mar

Horse riding
Ritoque Expediciones, *north of Concón, T9-6785 5092, www.ritoqueexpediciones.cl.*

Excellent day trips over a variety of terrain. Galloping encouraged. Full moon rides. Pick-up service from Valparaíso and Viña del Mar.

Transport

Viña del Mar

Bus **Terminal** 2 blocks east of Plaza Vergara at Av Valparaíso y Quilpué, T32-275 2000. To **Santiago**, US$3-6, 1¾ hrs, frequent, same companies as for Valparaíso from Pajaritos in Santiago, book in advance for travel on Sun afternoons. Long-distance services: prices and itineraries similar to Valparaíso.

Train Services on the Metro Valparaíso line stop at Viña (see under Valparaíso).

Resorts north of Viña del Mar

Bus From Valparaíso and Viña del Mar: to **Concón**, bus 601, US$0.60, frequent; to **Quintero** and **Horcón**, **Sol del Pacífico**, every 30 mins, US$2.50, 2 hrs; to **Papudo**, **Sol del Pacífico**, US$3.75. All from Av Libertad in Viña, or Errázuriz in Valparaíso.

Cartagena and around

Regular bus services to **Isla Negra** from Santiago (**Pullman Bus**) and **Valparaíso** (**Pullman Lago Peñuelas**), 1½ hrs, US$2. Many tours go here, too. From Santiago to Cartagena, US$10.

East of Valparaíso: Parque Nacional La Campana

The entrances to the national park at **Granizo** (paradero 45) and **Cajón Grande** (paradero 41) are reached by local bus/colectivo from outside Limache train station. No public transport to Ocoa; get a bus to La Calera and bargain with a taxi or colectivo driver; expect to pay around US$20-25.

North of Santiago

Along the coast is a mixture of fishing villages, deserted beaches and popular resorts, while inland the scenery is wonderfully dramatic but little visited. The land becomes less fertile as you go further north. Ovalle is a good centre for trips to see petroglyphs and the coastal forests at the Parque Nacional Fray Jorge. The largest resort is La Serena, from where access can be made to the Elqui Valley, one of Chile's major pisco-producing regions and one of the world's major astronomical centres.

From the Río Aconcagua to the Río Elqui is a transitional zone between the fertile heartland and the northern deserts. The first stretch of the Pan-American Highway from Santiago is inland through green valleys with rich blue clover and wild artichokes. North of La Ligua, the highway mainly follows the coastline, passing many beautiful coves, alternately rocky and sandy, with good surf, though the water is very cold. The valleys of the main rivers, the Choapa, Limarí and Elqui, are intensively farmed using irrigation to produce fruit and vegetables. There is a striking contrast between these lush valley floors and the arid mountains with their dry scrub and cactus. In some areas, condensation off the sea provides sufficient moisture for woods to grow. Rainfall is rare and occurs only in winter. On the coast the average temperature is 15°C in winter, 23°C in summer; the interior is dry, with temperatures reaching 33°C in summer, but it is cooler in winter and very cold at night.

Ovalle and around

petroglyphs and coastal forests

Ovalle Colour map 8, A1.

This town lies inland, 412 km north of Santiago, in the valley of the Río Limarí, a fruit-growing and mining district. Market days are Monday, Wednesday, Friday and Saturday, till 1600; the market (*feria modelo*) is off Benavente (east of the centre). The town is famous for its *talabarterías* (saddleries), products made of locally mined lapis lazuli, goat cheese and dried fruits. Wine is produced in the Limarí Valley and tours are available to *bodegas* such as **Tamaya** (www.tamaya.cl) and **Tabalí** (www.tabali. cl). **Museo del Limarí** ① *in the old railway station, Covarrubias y Antofagasta, www.museolimari.cl, Mon-Fri 1000-1800, Sat-Sun 1000-1400, free,* has displays of petroglyphs and a good collection of Diaguita ceramics and other artefacts. There's an unofficial tourist information kiosk on the Plaza de Armas.

Around Ovalle

About 22 km southwest of Ovalle is an important archaeological site known as the **Monumento Nacional Valle del Encanto** ① *www.ovallito.cl/encanto, daily 0830-2000 (to 1830 in winter), US$1, getting there: no local bus service; you must take a southbound long-distance bus and ask to be dropped off – 5-km walk to the valley; flag down a bus to return; alternatively, use a tour operator.* Artefacts from

Best for

Petroglyphs ■ Pisco ■ Star-gazing ■ Surfing

hunting peoples from over 2000 years ago have been found here, but the most visible remains date from the Molle culture (AD 700). There are over 30 petroglyphs as well as great boulders, distributed in six sites. There are camping facilities.

Beyond are the **Termas de Socos** ① *35 km southwest of Ovalle on the Pan-American Highway, www.termasocos.cl, visits starting at US$7*, where there's a swimming pool and individual tubs fed by thermal springs, as well as sauna, jacuzzi and water massage (very popular). It also boasts a reasonable hotel and a campsite.

☆**Parque Nacional Fray Jorge** ① *90 km west of Ovalle and 110 km south of La Serena at the mouth of the Río Limarí, T9-9346 2706, parque.frayjorge@conaf.cl, open 0900-1600 Dec-Mar, rest of year Thu-Sun only, 0900-1600, cars must leave by 1730, US$9.30; no public transport, take a tour.* Visits closely controlled owing to risk of fire. The park is reached by a dirt road leading off the Pan-American Highway. It contains original forests which contrast with the otherwise barren surroundings. Receiving less than 113 mm of rain a year, the forests survive because of the almost constant covering of fog. Waterproof clothing is essential when you visit.

Along the Río Limarí

From Ovalle a road leads 77 km northeast, following the course of the river, to the village of Hurtado. About 42 km from the city, an unpaved and largely winding road turns off to the **Monumento Natural Pichasca** ① *daily 0900-1630 (Apr-Nov, open Wed-Sun only), last entry at 1630, US$9.30, getting there: daily buses run from Ovalle towards Hurtado, from the turn-off it is 3 km to the park and about 2 km more to sites of interest,* which contains petrified tree trunks, archaeological remains, including a vast cave with vestiges of ancient rock paintings, and views of rock formations on the surrounding mountains.

Beyond the village of Pichasca it is 32 km to Hurtado. The road winds along the side of the valley, with the Andes easily visible at its head. The road continues to **Hurtado** village at 1300 m, near which are the only petroglyphs in Chile depicting the sun, hinting at possible links to the Incas, **Cerro Gigante** (2825 m) and a Diaguita cemetery. From Hurtado a road runs north to Vicuña in the Elqui Valley (see page 726) only 46 km away. This is a desolate but beautiful road, very poor in places with very little traffic and no public transport. Pickups can be hired in Hurtado for US$35-40.

Andacollo

The good inland road between Ovalle and La Serena makes an interesting contrast to Ruta 5 (Panamericana), with a fine pass and occasional views of the Andes across cacti-covered plains and semi-desert mountain ranges. North of Ovalle 61 km a side road runs 44 km southeast (last 20 km very bad) to Andacollo (altitude 1050 m). This old town, in an area of alluvial gold washing and manganese and copper mining, is one of the great pilgrimage sites in Chile. In the enormous **Basilica** (1893), 45 m high and with a capacity of 10,000, is the Virgen del Rosario de Andacollo, celebrated around Christmas time (see Festivals, below). The tourist office on the Plaza arranges tours to the Basilica and to mining operations.

Listings Ovalle and around

Where to stay

Ovalle

$$$ Plaza Turismo
Victoria 295, T53-262 1970, www.plazaturismo.cl.
Spacious rooms, some overlooking the plaza.

$$ Gran Hotel
Vicuña Mackenna 210 (entrance through Galería Yagnam), T53-262 1084, www.granhotelovalle.cl.
Decent rooms, good value and service.

$$ Roxy
Libertad 155, T53-262 0080.
Big basic rooms, large colonial-style patio covered in vines in summer, a bit run down, but a good choice.

Around Ovalle

$$$ Hacienda Juntas
*Near Monte Patria,
Km 38, T53-271 1290,
www.haciendajuntas.cl.*

In 90 ha of vineyards, with gardens, spectacular views and pool. Restaurant open in high season.

$$$ Termas de Socos
Panamericana Norte Km 370, 35 km southwest of Ovalle, T53-2198 2505, www.termasocos.cl.
Reasonable hotel offering full board and access to thermal pools.

Camping

$ pp Camping y Piscina Los Pumas del Encanto
10 mins' walk from Valle del Encanto, T53-262 3667, see Facebook.
Nice place with lots of trees and plants, owner Adrián Tello is very knowledgeable.

Along the Río Limarí

$$$-$ Hacienda Los Andes
Vado Morillos, T53-269 1822, www.haciendalosandes.com.
German/Austrian management at this highly regarded colonial-style hacienda, all meals use organic local produce, camping (US$7.75), expert horse riding tours.

Restaurants

Ovalle
There are many cheap eateries at the entrance to the Feria Modelo.

$$ Club Social Arabe
Arauco 255.
Spacious glass-domed premises, limited selection of Arab dishes.

$$ El Relajo
Antonio Tirado 177.
Popular restaurant serving Mexican and Peruvian dishes.

$ El Quijote
Arauco 294.
Intimate bar, old-timers' haunt full of socialist posters and memorabilia.

Festivals

Andacollo
23-27 Dec Fiesta Grande attracts 200,000 pilgrims. The ritual dances date from a pre-Spanish past. *Colectivos* run to the festival from Benavente, near Colocolo, in La Serena, but 'purists' walk (torch and good walking shoes essential). There is also a smaller festival, the **Fiesta Chica** on the 1st Sun of Oct.

Transport

Ovalle and around
Bus Most of the many rural buses leave from either of 2 terminals outside the Feria Modelo. The main bus terminal is the Terminal Media Luna (by the rodeo ring on Ariztía Oriente) just south of the city centre. Buses to **Santiago**, several, 6½ hrs, US$19-29; to **Valparaíso**, 6 hrs, US$18; to **Antofagasta**, 14 hrs, US$35-61; to **La Serena**, 1½ hrs, US$4.50. To **Hurtado**, buses leave from the Feria Modelo from 1030 to 1900 (2030 on Sun), US$4.To **Andacollo**, *colectivo* US$4, bus US$3.

La Serena and around *Colour map 8, A1.*

go star-gazing in the fertile Elquí Valley

La Serena, built on a hillside 2 km inland from Bahía de Coquimbo (473 km north of Santiago), is an attractive city and tourist centre and is the capital of IV Región (Coquimbo). The city was founded by Juan de Bohón, aide to Pedro de Valdivia, in 1544, destroyed by the Diaguita in 1546 and rebuilt by Francisco de Aguirre in 1549, before being sacked by the English pirate Sharpe in 1680. In the colonial period La Serena was the main staging-post on the route north to Peru. In the 19th century the city grew prosperous from copper-mining. Although it retains its colonial architecture and churches, the present-day layout and style have their origins in the 'Plan Serena' drawn up in 1948 on the orders of President Gabriel González Videla, a native of the city. East of the city, the valley of the Río Elqui is one of the most attractive oases in this part of northern Chile, with orchards, orange groves, vineyards and mines set against the imposing, arid mountains.

Sights
Around the attractive Plaza de Armas are most of the official buildings, including the post office, the **Cathedral** (built in 1844 and featuring a carillon which plays every hour) and the **Museo Histórico Regional** ⓘ *Casa González Videla, Matta 495, T51-221 7189, www. museohistoricolaserena.cl, Mon-Fri 1000-1800, Sat 1000-1300, free,*

Fact...
There are plenty of ATMs and *casas de cambio*.

which includes several rooms dedicated to Videla's life. **Museo Arqueológico** ① *Cordovez y Cienfuegos, T51-267 2210, www.museoarqueologicolaserena.cl, Tue-Fri 0930-1750, Sat 1000-1300, 1600-1900, Sun 1000-1300, free,* has an outstanding collection of Diaguita and Molle exhibits, especially of attractively decorated pottery, also Easter Island exhibits. There are 29 churches, several of which have unusual towers. **La Recova**, the craft market, at Cienfuegos y Cantournet, includes a large display of handicrafts (some imported) and, upstairs, has several good restaurants. One block west of the Plaza de Armas is the **Parque Pedro de Valdivia** ① *daily 0900-1800.* One block south is the delightful **Parque Japonés**.

Avenida Francisco de Aguirre, a pleasant boulevard lined with statues and known as the Alameda, runs from the centre to the coast, terminating at the **Faro Monumental**, a small, neo-colonial mock-castle and lighthouse, now a pub. A series of beaches stretch from here to Coquimbo, 11 km south, linked by the Avenida del Mar. Many apartment blocks, hotels, *cabañas* and restaurants line this part of the bay. The sectors between 4 Esquinas and Peñuelas are probably the best bet for sunbathing or dipping a toe in the water.

Coquimbo and the coast
On the same bay as La Serena is this important port, with one of the best harbours on the coast and major fish-processing plants. The city is strung along the north shore of a peninsula. On the south shore lies the suburb of Guayacán, with an iron-ore loading port, a steel church designed by Eiffel,

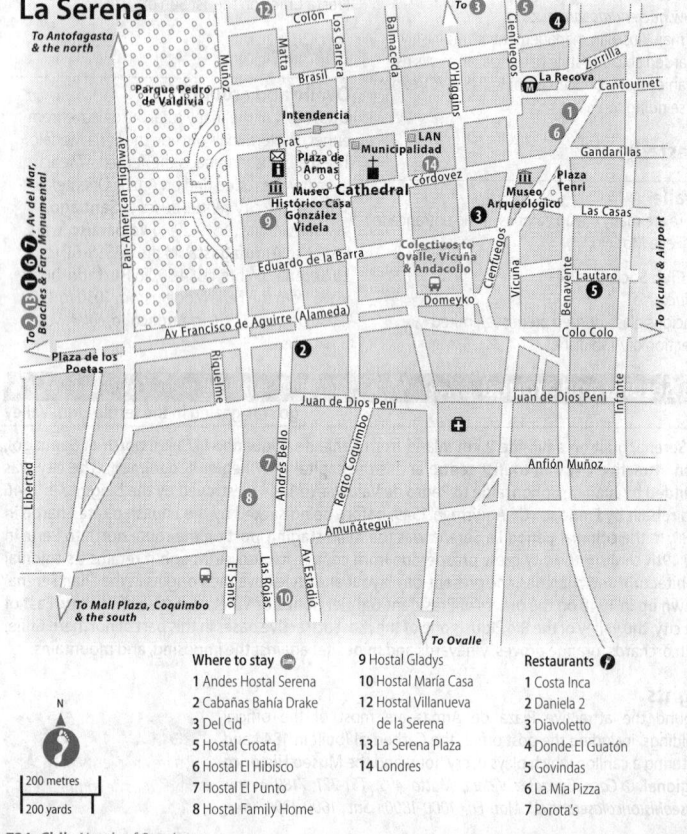

La Serena

Where to stay 🛏
1 Andes Hostal Serena
2 Cabañas Bahía Drake
3 Del Cid
5 Hostal Croata
6 Hostal El Hibisco
7 Hostal El Punto
8 Hostal Family Home
9 Hostal Gladys
10 Hostal María Casa
12 Hostal Villanueva de la Serena
13 La Serena Plaza
14 Londres

Restaurants 🍴
1 Costa Inca
2 Daniela 2
3 Diavoletto
4 Donde El Guatón
5 Govindas
6 La Mía Pizza
7 Porota's

an English cemetery and a 83-m-high cross to mark the Millennium (US$3 to climb it). In 1981 heavy rain uncovered an ancient burial site where 39 sacrificed humans and llamas were found; they are exhibited in a small **Museo del Sitio** ① *Plaza Gabriela Mistral, open Jan-Feb only, Mon-Fri 0900-1415, 1500-1715, free, tourist information*. Summer boat trips of the harbour and nearby Punta Lobos cost US$3.75. Nearby is **La Herradura**, 2.5 km from Coquimbo, slightly more upmarket and with the best beaches. Resorts further south, **Totoralillo** (12 km), **Guanaqueros** (37 km) and **Tongoy** (50 km), have good beaches and can be reached by rural buses or *colectivos*.

☆Observatories around La Serena

Permits (free) for El Tololo are available on written application to ctio@noao.edu, or T51-220 5200; pick your permit up from the AURA observatory office, Colina El Pino, La Serena before 1200 the day before your visit; transport to/from the observatory is not included. The office will insist that you have private transport; you can hire a taxi, US$132 for the whole day, but you will require the registration number when you book. Personal applications can be made for La Silla, see below. Tour operators in La Serena and Coquimbo arrange tours to the smaller municipal observatories near Vicuña.

The Elqui Valley is one of the main astronomical centres of the world, with three important observatories and two smaller ones. **El Tololo** ① *89 km southeast of La Serena in the Elqui Valley, 51 km south of Vicuña, www.ctio.noao.edu, visitors by permit only every Sat 0900 and 1300*, belongs to Aura, an association of US and Chilean universities. It is located at 2200 m and possesses one of the largest telescopes in the southern hemisphere (4-m diameter), six others and a radio telescope. **La Silla** ① *150 km northeast of La Serena, www.ls.eso.org, registration in advance with online visitor form for free tour Sep-Jun Sat 1400*, belongs to ESO (European Southern Observatory) and comprises 14 telescopes at 2240 m. From La Serena it is 120 km north along Route 5 to the turn-off, then another 36 km. If without private transport, take any bus towards Vallenar (two hours, US$4), get out at the junction (*desvío*) and hitch from there. **Las Campanas**, 162 km northeast of La Serena, 30 km north of La Silla, belongs to the Carnegie Institute, has four telescopes and is a smaller facility than the other two at 2510 m. It is closed to the public, but occasionally open for large groups (contact rbermudez@lco.cl for details).

There are two observatories near Vicuña, which give the public the chance to see the stars: **Observatorio Comunal Cerro Mamalluca** ① *Gabriela Mistral 260, Vicuña, T51-267 0330, mamalluca@munivicuna.cl, night time tours 2030-0030, US$6.50 per person, guides in Spanish and English for groups of 5 or more, book in advance, collect tickets 30 mins before tour, transfer to observatory US$4.50 return*, is located on Cerro Mamalluca, 6 km north of Vicuña, 1500 m above sea level; **Observatorio del Pangue** ① *bookings through agencies in La Serena as part of a tour or directly from San Martín 233, Vicuña, T51-241 2584, www.observatoriodelpangue.blogspot.com, various tours, starting at US$36 including transport*, is 16 km south of Vicuña on the road to Hurtado. Groups are limited to 12 people; tours are informative and in good English and French as well as Spanish, and the telescopes are more powerful than those at Mamalluca. Always book in advance.

☆Elqui Valley

The Elqui Valley is the centre of pisco production with nine distilleries. It is also well-known as a centre of mystical energy and star-gazing (see above). **Vicuña**, the valley's capital, is a small, friendly town, 66 km east of La Serena. It was founded in 1821. On the west side of the plaza are the municipal chambers, built in 1826 and topped in 1905 by a medieval-German-style tower, the Torre Bauer, imported by the German-born mayor of the time. The tourist office is on Plaza de Armas. There is an ATM. There are good views from Cerro La Virgen, north of town. **Museo Gabriela Mistral** ① *Gabriela Mistral 759, www.mgmistral.cl, Tue-Fri 1000-1745, Sat 1030-1800, Sun 1000-1300, free*, contains manuscripts, books, awards and many other details of the poet's life. Next door is the house where the poet was born. Near town is the **Capel Pisco distillery** ① *1.5 km east of Vicuña, to the right of the main road, T51-255 4300, www.cooperativacapel.cl, guided tours (in Spanish) are offered Dec-May daily 1000-1800, starting at US$3.75, no booking required*, the largest in the valley.

> **Tip...**
> At night, there is no better place on earth to star gaze. When the moon is new, or below the horizon, the stars seem to be hanging in the air; spectacular shooting stars can be seen every couple of seconds, as can satellites crossing the night sky.

From Vicuña the road runs through Paihuano (camping) to **Monte Grande**, where the schoolhouse where Gabriela Mistral lived and was educated by her sister is now a **museum** ① *C Principal s/n, T51-241 5015, Tue-Sun 1000-1300, 1500-1800 (till 1900 in Jan and Feb), US$0.75*. The poet's tomb is at the edge of town, opposite the Artesanos de Cochiguaz pisco distillery, which is open to the public. (Buses from the plaza in Vicuña.) Here the road forks, one branch leading to the Cochiguaz valley (no public transport). Along this road are several new age settlements – it is said that the valley is an important energy centre –and several campsites.

Back on the main road, just south of Monte Grande, is the **Cavas del Valle** organic winery with free tastings. The other branch road leads to **Pisco Elqui**, an attractive village with the newly restored church of Nuestra Señora del Rosario on a shady plaza. It's also famous for its night skies and beautiful scenery. At the Hotel Elqui, the **Astropub** has telescopes for stargazing. Horses can be hired, with or without guide (Ramón Luis is recommended, ask around for him). Its new-age attractions include alternative therapies and massages. More traditional is the **Tres Erres pisco plant** ① *open daily, guided tours in Spanish, US$1.50*. Beyond Pisco Elqui, the road up the valley is unpaved. Some 4 km further on at **Los Nichos** is a small pisco distillery open for visits (closed lunchtime), which sells dried fruit and other local products.

Border with Argentina: Paso Agua Negra
Paso Agua Negra (4775 m) is reached by a partly paved road from Guanta, 30 km past Rivadavia. The Chilean immigration and customs is at Juntas, 84 km west of the border and 88 km east of Vicuña. The border is open 0700-1700 November to May, weather permitting (check for the rest of year). There is no public transport beyond Rivadavia. Tell officials if you intend to camp between border posts. For information see www.pasodeaguanegra.org.

> **Tip…**
> If you're heading for Argentina, there is basic, clean accommodation at Guanta (Huanta on many maps), 46 km from Vicuña.

Listings La Serena and around *map p724*

Tourist information

La Serena

Sernatur
Matta 461, of 108, in Edif de Servicios Públicos (next to post office on the Plaza de Armas), T51-222 5138, infocoquimbo@sernatur.cl. Jan-Feb daily 0900-2000, rest of year 0900-1900 Mon-Fri, Sat 1000-1400.
See also www.laserena.cl.

Coquimbo and the coast
The **municipal tourist office** is at Trigo 485 (T51-233 5300, www.municoquimbo.cl).

Where to stay

Route 5 from La Serena to Coquimbo is lined with cheap accommodation; as is also Av del Mar, 500 m off the highway (buses run along Route 5, not Av del Mar). Generally accommodation is cheaper in Coquimbo than in La Serena. There are also several hotels in La Herradura. The tourist office in La Serena bus terminal is helpful. Do not be bullied by touts at the bus station into choosing rooms. Similarly, do not be pressured

to buy tours in hotels: established agencies may give better service and deals.

La Serena

$$$ Cabañas Bahía Drake
Av del Mar 1600, T44-890 9220, http://cabanasbahiadrake.redhotelera.cl.
Pleasant, fully equipped units for 2 to 6, on the seafront, with swimming pool.

$$$ Del Cid
O'Higgins 138, T51-221 2692, www.hoteldelcid.cl.
Characterful, central, with smallish but spotless rooms around a courtyard. Parking available, English spoken.

$$$ La Serena Plaza
Francisco de Aguirre 0660, T51-222 5745, www.hotelserenaplaza.cl.
Upmarket hotel by the beach with spacious rooms, swimming pool, gym and restaurant.

$$$-$$ Hostal Villanueva de La Serena
Matta 269, T51-255 0268, www.hostalvillanueva.cl.
Large rooms sleeping up to 5, with private or shared bath in colonial house dating from 1800.

$$$-$$ Londres
Cordovez 550, T51-221 9066, www.hotellondres.cl.
Simple, bright rooms with good beds,
decent bathrooms.

$$ Andes Hostal Serena
Vicuña 431, T51-252 9581,
www.andeshostalserena.cl
Newish hostel with private rooms, family run,
convenient location.

$$ Hostal Croata
Cienfuegos 248, T51-222 4997, see Facebook.
Small rooms, double or dorms, patio, hospitable.

$$ Hostal El Hibisco
Vicuña 455, T51-221 1407,
mauricioberrios2002@yahoo.es.
Delightful hosts, welcome drink, lots of information.

$$-$ Hostal El Punto
Andrés Bello 979, T51-222 8474,
www.hostalelpunto.cl.
Dorms and rooms with shared or private bath,
tasteful, comfortable, good facilities, café,
laundry, parking, book exchange, English and
German spoken, tours to Elqui Valley.

$$-$ Hostal Family Home
Av Santo 1056, T51-221 2099,
www.familyhome.cl.
Private or shared bath, thin walls, but it has a
24-hr reception and is close to the bus terminal
so useful if you are arriving at night.

$$-$ Hostal Gladys
Gregorio Cordovez 247 (by the Plaza de Armas),
T51-222 0324.
Shared bath, laundry service, helpful.

$$-$ Hostal María Casa
Las Rojas 18, T9-7466 7433,
www.hostalmariacasa.cl.
Very welcoming and helpful, near bus terminal,
laundry facilities, garden, private rooms and
dorm, book in advance, excellent value.

Elqui Valley

Vicuña

$$$ Hostería Vicuña
Sgto Aldea 101, T51-241 1301,
www.hosteriavicuna.cl.
In spacious grounds, pool, tennis court, poor
restaurant, parking. Has seen better days.

$$$-$$ ElquiTerra
Callejón Cuatro Esquinas Norte 31, El Durazno,
T9-9699 5573, www.elquiterra.com.

B&B 5 mins by *colectivo* outside Vicuña, rooms
with and without bath, also shared rooms (**$**),
comfortable beds, rustic design, kitchen, pool,
bike rental and excursions. First-class attention
from owners. Recommended.

$$ Halley
Gabriela Mistral 542, T51-241 2070,
www.turismohalley.cl.
Pleasantly old-fashioned hotel with high-
ceilinged rooms, colonial-style courtyard,
and a pleasant pool.

$$ Hospedaje Sundari
C Principal 3, San Isidro (15 mins walk from
Vicuña), T9-9884 5702, see Facebook.
Delightful bungalows, with breakfast, spotless,
bicycles, pool in lovely gardens, aloe and other
herbal therapies.

$$ Sol del Valle
Gabriela Mistral 739, T9-7456 6130.
Swimming pool, vineyard, restaurant.

$$-$ Donde Rita
Condell 443, T51-241 9611, www.hostaldonderita.cl.
Impeccably kept B&B. Excellent breakfast,
pleasant garden with pool, helpful, German
and some English spoken.

$$-$ La Elquina
O'Higgins 65, T51-241 1317, www.laelquina.cl.
Relaxed, quiet, lovely garden, private or
shared bath.

$$-$ Valle Hermoso
Gabriela Mistral 706, T51-241 1206,
www.hostalvallehermoso.com.
Comfortable, parking.

Camping

Camping y Piscina Las Tinajas
East end of Chacabuco.
Swimming pool, restaurant.

Pisco Elqui
Prices are much lower outside Jan and Feb;
cabañas include **$$$$-$$$ Los Misterios de
Elqui** (A Prat, T51-245 1126, see Facebook).

$$$$ Elqui Domos
Sector los Nichos s/n, T9-7709 2879,
www.elquidomos.cl.
Accommodation in geodesic tent domes or
observatory cabins with windows and roofs that
open for a direct view of the sky, English spoken.

$$$-$$ El Tesoro del Elqui
Artura Prat s/n, T51-245 1069, www.tesoro-elqui.cl.

Cabañas for up to 4, shared room for up to 4 with shared bath ($), café, pool, pleasant gardens, German and English spoken.

$ Hostal Triskel
Callejón Baquedano, T9-9419 8680,
www.hostaltriskel.cl.
Single, double, twin, dorm rooms, attractive, bike rental, activities and tours arranged, therapies.

$ Hotel Restaurante Elqui
O'Higgins s/n by the plaza, T51-245 1130,
www.hotelelqui.cl.
Hot shower, central, good restaurant and bar.

Camping

$ Campsite behind **Camping El Olivo.** Excellent facilities, cold water, lots of trees by river, helpful owner, laundry facilities, very nice.

Restaurants

Most restaurants close off season on Sun; generally more expensive here than in Coquimbo. The best place for seafood is the Sector de Pescadores (**$$**) at *Peñuelas*, on the coast halfway between La Serena and Coquimbo. Take any bus to Coquimbo and get out at the junction with Los Pescadores; walk 300 m to the coast.

La Serena

$$$-$$ Donde El Guatón
Brasil 750, see Facebook.
Parrillada, also good seafood, one of the better places in the town centre.

$$$-$$ Porota's
Av del Mar 900-B, Sector El Faro, T51-9-8289 4875, see Facebook.
Wide variety of well-presented dishes (fish, meat and pasta), decent portions and attentive service.

$$ Costa Inca
Av del Mar 2500, T51-212802.
Good value and a range of delicious Peruvian dishes.

$$ La Mía Pizza
Av del Mar 2100, T51-221 2232, see Facebook.
Italian, good-value pizzas and also fish dishes, good wine list.

$ Daniela 2
F de Aguirre 335.
Good-quality Chilean home cooking.

$ Govindas
Lautaro 841, T51-222 4289, see Facebook.
Mon-Fri lunchtime.

Cheap vegetarian and vegan food served in a Hari Krishna yoga centre.

Cafés

Diavoletto
O'Higgins 560.
Fast food and ice cream, popular. Other cafés on Prat 500 block and Balmaceda 400 block.

Elqui Valley

Vicuña

$$ Club Social de Elqui
Gabriela Mistral 445.
Attractive patio, good value *almuerzo*, real coffee.

$$ Halley
Gabriela Mistral 404.
Good meat, with local specialities, goat (huge portion) and rabbit.

$ Michel
Gabriela Mistral 180.
Popular, good-value *almuerzo*.

$ Yo Y Soledad
Carrera 320.
Inexpensive, hearty Chilean food, good value.

Bars and clubs

La Serena

Most clubs are on Av del Mar and in Peñuelas, such as youth-oriented **Club Oxígeno** (see Facebook). Also in the same area, the disco in **Casino Enjoy**, www.enjoy.cl, is a popular nightspot. In town you could try **El Nuevo Peregrino** (Peni y Andrés Bello; see Facebook), an intimate bar with live music at weekends.

Festivals

Coquimbo and the coast

Mid-Sep Coquimbo hosts **La Pampilla**, by far the biggest independence day celebrations in Chile. Between 200,000 and 300,000 people come from all over the country for the fiesta, which lasts for a week. It costs a nominal US$1.50 to enter the main dancing area (*peñas* cost extra); plenty of typical Chilean food and drink.

What to do

Responsible operators will not run tours to Mamalluca or Las Damas in bad weather.

La Serena

Delfines, *Matta 655, T51-222 3624, www.turismo delfines.com*. Traditional and adventure tours, bike rental, birdwatching and full tourist service.

Elqui Total, *Parcela 17, El Arrayan at Km 27 along the road from La Serena to Vicuña, T9-6191 0497, www.mundocaballo.cl*. Principally equine tourism, day and night rides, courses, also birdwatching.

Jeep Tour La Serena, *T9-9454 6000, www.jeep tour-laserena.cl*. Private and small group tours (max 6 people) of the area led by Swiss guide Daniel Russ. Apart from the usual tours he also offers trips to the Paso Agua Negra and also a transfer service to San Juan in Argentina (summer only).

Talinay Adventure Expeditions, *Prat 470, in the courtyard, T9-8360 6464, www.talinaychile.com*. Offers local tours, also trekking and climbing.

Transport

La Serena

Air Aeropuerto La Florida, 5 km east of the city, T51-227 0236, www.aeropuertodela serena.cl (*colectivo* US$0.90, taxi US$10). To **Santiago** andAntofagasta, with **LATAM** and **Sky**.

Bus City buses US$0.90. Bus terminal, El Santo y Amunátegui (about 8 blocks south of the centre). **Tur-Bus** office, Balmaceda 1475 entre Prat y

Cordovez, T51-222 1104. Buses daily to **Santiago**, a few companies, 7-8 hrs, US$16-36; to **Valparaíso**, 7 hrs, US$22-40. To **Caldera**, 6 hrs, US$27. To **Calama**, US$41, 16 hrs. To **Antofagasta**, 12-13 hrs, several companies, US$30-57, and to **Iquique**, 17 hrs, US$41-50, and **Arica**, 20 hrs, US$47-69. To **Vicuña** and **Pisco Elqui**, see below. To **Coquimbo**, bus No 8 from Av Aguirre y Cienfuegos, US$1, every few mins.

Car hire AM, De la Fragata 50, Av del Mar, T9-9468 1564, contacto@amrentacar.cl (also Facebook). Economic choice with good service. **Theo Car**, Balmaceda 4310, T51-224 3770, www. theocar.cl. Also transfers to/from airport. **West Rent a Car**, www.westrentacar.cl, in airport.

Taxi charge about US$0.25 per every 200 m. *Colectivos* with fixed rates, destination on roof; also to Coquimbo from Aguirre y Balmaceda.

Coquimbo

Bus Terminal at Varela y Garriga. To **La Serena**, US$1.

Elqui Valley

Bus From Vicuña to **La Serena**, many daily, most by **Via Elqui/Solo de Elqui/Elqui Bus**, US$3, *colectivo* from bus terminal US$4.50. To **Pisco Elqui**, US$3. Buses from Pisco Elqui to La Serena go via Vicuña, US$4.50.

North of La Serena

witness the flowering of the desert

☆North of the Río Elqui, the transitional zone continues to the mining and agro-industrial centre of Copiapó. Thereafter begins the desert, which is of little interest, except after rain. Then it is covered with a succession of flowers, insects and frogs, in one of the world's most spectacular wildlife events, known as the *desierto florido*. It is particularly worth seeing around Vallenar: as the brief spring unfolds, the colours change and new species push through to replace others. Rain, however, is rare: there is none in summer; in winter it is light and lasts only a short time. The worst flash flood to hit Chile in 80 years occurred in 2015, affecting areas between Coquimbo and Antofagasta. Dozens of people were killed and scores of homes and buildings destroyed. Chañaral was one of the places hardest hit.

☆Reserva Nacional Pingüino de Humboldt

Some 72 km north of La Serena, a road branches west off the Panamericana to **Punta de Choros** (CONAF in Punta de Choros, T9-544 3052). This is the departure point for the Humboldt Penguin Natural Reserve, on Islas Chañaral, Choros and Damas. Besides penguins, there are seals, sea lions, a great variety of seabirds, and offshore, a colony of grey dolphin. Isla Damas has interesting flora, too. To visit the reserve, tours are available from La Serena and Vallenar or you can hire a boat with local fishermen (around US$15-18 per person). Isla Damas is the only island at which it is possible to disembark (entrance US$9.50 for foreigners). Neither camping nor swimming is allowed; there is a toilet but no drinking water.

Vallenar and the Huasco valley *Colour map 8, A1.*

This is the chief town of the Huasco valley, 194 km north of La Serena. It has a pleasant Plaza de Armas, with marble benches. About seven blocks southeast is the **Museo del Huasco** ① *Ramírez1001, Tue-Fri 1500-1800, entry by donation*. It contains historic photos and artefacts from the valley. At the mouth of the river, 56 km west, is the pleasant port of Huasco (cheap seafood restaurants near the harbour). There is a tourist kiosk on the plaza in summer. Inland, the Huasco valley is an oasis of olive groves and vineyards. It is rugged and spectacular, dividing at Alto del Carmen, 30 km east of Vallenar, into the Carmen and Tránsito valleys. There are pisco distilleries at Alto del Carmen and San Félix. A sweet wine, *pajarete*, is also produced.

Copiapó *Colour map 6, C2.*

The valley of the Río Copiapó, generally regarded as the southern limit of the Atacama desert, is an oasis of farms, vineyards and orchards about 150 km long. The Río Copiapó overflowed in 2015, causing severe damage. Copiapó is an important mining centre. Founded in 1744, Copiapó became a prosperous town after the discovery in 1832 of the third largest silver deposits in South America at Chañarcillo (the mine was closed in 1875). The discoverer, Juan Godoy, a mule-driver, is commemorated at Matta y O'Higgins. Opposite is the **Museo Regional de Atacama** ① *Tue-Fri 0930-1800, Sat 1000-1300, 1500-1800, Sun 1030-1300, free*, with collections on local history, especially the Huentelauquén people, thought to have flourished 10,000 years ago. **Museo Mineralógico** ① *Colipí y Rodríguez, 1 block east from Plaza Prat, due to reopen in 2017 after 2015 flooding*, is the best museum of its type in Chile, with a collection of weird and wonderful minerals and fossils from Chile and around the world. Many ores shown are found only in the Atacama Desert. The Museo Ferroviario at the old railway station on Calle Martínez opens irregularly, but the Norris Brothers steam locomotive and carriages used in the inaugural journey between Copiapó and Caldera in 1851 (the first railway in South America) can be seen at the Universidad de Atacama about 2 km north of the centre on Avenida R Freire. Tour agencies offer visits to San José, the site of the 2010 incident that trapped 33 iiners underground for 69 days. Or you can visit for free by driving to the location (Friday-Sunday 1000-1800). One of the miners, Jorge, even gives one-hour tours. Tipping is encouraged.

Warning...
Drivers must beware of high winds and blowing sand north of Copiapó.

Border with Argentina: Paso San Francisco Paso San Francisco is reached either by the Camino Internacional northeast from Copiapó, or by an unpaved road southeast from El Salvador: both routes join near the Salar de Maricunga in the **Parque Nacional Tres Cruces**, 96 km west of Paso San Francisco. Here are Chilean immigration and customs, open 0900-1900 (24 hours in summer); US$1.50 per vehicle charge for crossing Saturday, Sunday and holidays. The road then passes Laguna Verde before entering Argentina, where a paved road continues to Tinogasta. The Argentine border post is at Fiambalá, 210 km beyond the border, open 0700-1900, but there is also a police post at La Gruta, 24 km beyond the border. This crossing is liable to closure after snow: for information contact the **Copiapó provincial government** ① *T52-221 3131, and see www.pasosfronterizos.gov.cl/cf_sanfco.html*. Always take spare fuel.

Caldera

From Copiapó the road heads northwest 73 km to the coast at Caldera, a port and terminal for the loading of iron ore. **Iglesia de San Vicente de Paul** (1862) on the Plaza de Armas was built by English carpenters working for the railway company. The train station, restored to its former glory, houses a cultural centre. **Bahía Inglesa**, 6 km south of Caldera, named after the visit in 1687 of the English *corsario*, Edward Davis, is popular for its beautiful white sandy beaches and unpolluted sea. Staying in Caldera is cheaper in summer than in Bahía Inglesa, where there are lots of *cabañas* by the beach (see http://bahiainglesachile.com or www.portaldebahiainglesa.com for listings). A frequent bus service runs between the two in January-February, while *colectivos* run all year (US$1.50).

Chañaral and around

Just over 90 km north of Caldera, at the mouth of the Río Salado, is **Chañaral**, a town with old wooden houses perched on the hillside and a base for visits to beaches and the Parque Nacional Pan de Azúcar. There are several *residenciales* and *hostales* in town, some offering tours of the area. Tourist office in the Municipalidad, Latorre 700, T52-254 3305. Inland, the valley of the Río Salado, 130 km in length, is less fertile or prosperous than the Copiapó or Huasco valleys and is the last oasis south of Antofagasta. From here to Antofagasta is 420 km and the only town along the way is **Taltal**, where there are simple hotels and restaurants (bus from Chañaral US$8, two hours; to Antofagasta four hours, US$12).

☆Parque Nacional Pan de Azúcar

US$9.50 (US$4.70 for Chileans). CONAF office in Caleta Pan de Azúcar, 0830-1230, 1400-1800 daily, maps available. There are heavy fines for driving in 'restricted areas' of the park.

The park, north of Chañaral, consists of the Isla Pan de Azúcar on which Humboldt penguins and other seabirds live, and some 43,769 ha of coastal hills rising to 800 m. There are fine beaches (popular at weekends in summer). Fishermen near the CONAF office offer boat trips round Isla Pan de Azúcar to see the penguins, about US$10 per person. Alternatively, a 2½-hour walk goes from the office to a mirador with extensive views over the south of the park. Vegetation is mainly cacti, of which there are 26 species, nourished by frequent sea mists (*camanchaca*). The park is home to 103 species of birds as well as guanaco and foxes. Pollution from nearby copper mining is a threat. There are two entrances: north by good secondary road from Chañaral for 28 km to Caleta Pan de Azúcar; or from the Pan-American Highway 45 km north of Chañaral, along a side road for 20 km.

Listings North of La Serena

Tourist information

Copiapó

Tourist office
Los Carrera 691, north side of Plaza Prat, T52-221 2838, infoatacama@sernatur.cl. Mon-Fri 0830-2100, Sat 1000-1400; out of season Mon-Fri 0830-1800 only).
Helpful.

Where to stay

Reserva Nacional Pingüino de Humboldt

$$ Cabañas Los Delfines
Pilpilén s/n, sitio 33, Punta de Choros, T9-9639 6878.
Cabins for up to 6. There are other sleeping and eating options in the area.

Vallenar

$$$ Puerto de Vega
Ramírez 201, T51-261 8534, www.puertodevega.cl.
Probably the best in town, 12 individually decorated rooms, pleasant patio and pool.

$$ Camino del Rey
Merced 943, T51-261 3184, see Facebook.
Good value, private or shared bath.

$$ Hostal Santa Elvira
Prat 494, T9-7476 5464.
More hotel than *hostal*, this is central and has a good restaurant and Wi-Fi.

Copiapó

$$$ Chagall
O'Higgins 760, T52-221 1459, www.chagall.cl.

Executive hotel, central, some rooms with king-size beds and desk, modern fittings, spacious lounge and bar open to public.

$$$ La Casona
O'Higgins 150, T52-221 7277, www.lacasonahotel.cl.
More like a home than a hostel, good beds, pleasant garden, restaurant, bar, English spoken.

$$ Montecatini
Infante 766, T52-221 1363, and at Atacama 374, T52-221 1516, www.hotelmontecatini.cl.
Helpful, best value in this price bracket. Rooms sleep 1-4, simple but OK for a night or 2.

$$ Palace
Atacama 741, T52-233 6427, www.hotelpalacecopiapo.cl.
Comfy, parking, central, nice patio. Good value.

$ Residencial Benbow
Rodríguez 541, T52-221 7634.
Basic rooms, some with bath, best value *residenciale* on this part of Rodríguez. Usually full of mine workers. Excellent value full-board deals.

$ Residencial Eli
Maipú 739, T52-221 9588.
Singles cheaper. Simple rooms, good beds, decent choice.

$ Residencial Rocío
Yerbas Buenas 581, T52-221 5360.
Singles cheaper. Some rooms with bath and cable TV, patio. Good budget option.

Caldera

$ Residencial Millaray
Cousiño 331, main plaza, Caldera, T52-231 5528.
Welcoming, good value, basic, price per person.

Parque Nacional Pan de Azúcar

$$$-$$ Gran Atacama offers camping (**$**) and *cabañas* (www.pandeazucarlodge.cl). Reservations and advance payment are essential in high season. Contact their office in Copiapó (0900-1900) for booking, T9-9280 2483, granatacama@gmail.com. The *cabañas* are perfectly placed on a deserted beach behind the *caleta*, sleep 2 or 6.

Some fishermen let out basic rooms. There are also 3 **campsites** in the park, one in the Caleta, run by the fishermen, and **Camping El Piquero** and **El Soldado** (US$11) run by **Gran Atacama** in Copiapó (see above).

Restaurants

Vallenar

Cheap eating places along south end of Av Brasil.

$$ Bavaria
Serrano800, www.bavaria.cl.
Chain restaurant, good.

$$ Pizza Il Boccato
Plaza O'Higgins y Prat.
Good coffee, good food, popular.

$ La Pica
Brasil y Faez.
Good cheap meals, seafood, cocktails.

Copiapó

$$ A-Chau
Chañarcillo 991.
Good Chinese with long-standing reputation.

$$ Bavaria
Chacabuco 487 (Plaza Prat), www.bavaria.cl.
Good variety, restaurant and café.

$$-$ Pizza Piero
Gana 451, esq O'Higgins, www.pizzapiero.cl.
Ultra-thin and crispy pizzas.

$ Don Elias
Los Carrera e Yerbas Buenas.
Excellent seafood, popular.

Festivals

Copiapó

1st Sun in Feb Fiesta de la Candelaria, for 9 days. Up to 50,000 pilgrims and 3000 dancers congregate at the Santuario de la Candelaria from all over the north of Chile.

What to do

Vallenar

If it rains (Sep-Oct), a tour of the desert in flower can be done with **Roberto Alegría**, no phone. Ask at the tourist kiosk in Vallenar (if it's open).

Transport

Vallenar

Bus The main terminal is at Prat 137, a few blocks northwest of the centre, but **Tur-Bus** is at Prat 32, T51-261 1738; **Pullman**, Serrano 551, T51-261 2461 (the most frequent buses going north). Also **Libac**, www.buseslibac.cl. To **La Serena**, 2 hrs, US$9-15. To **Copiapó**, 2 hrs, US$8. To **Santiago**, 10 hrs, US$30-57.

Copiapó

Air Desierto de Atacama Airport is 45 km northwest of Copiapó and 15 km east of Caldera. **LATAM**, Colipí 484, T600-526500, and **Sky**, Colipí 526, T52-221 4640. For airport transfer: Buses Casther, T52 2231 8413.

Bicycle repairs Biman, Los Carrera 998A, T52-221 7391, excellent.

Bus Long-distance terminal 2 blocks from centre on Chañarcillo y Chacabuco. **TurBus** terminal is opposite and **Pullman** is 1 block away on Colipí. To **Santiago** US$37-67, 12 hrs. To **La Serena** US$11, 5 hrs. To **Antofagasta**, 7 hrs, US$21-48. To **Caldera**, US$8 (5 return), 1 hr, cheapest services on **Buses Casther** from the street 1 block west of the main bus terminal.

Caldera

Bus Buses on the Panamericana do not go into Caldera, but stop at Cruce Caldera, outside town. To **Copiapó** and **Santiago**, US$41-60, several daily. To **Antofagasta**, US$18, 7 hrs. To travel north, it may be better to take a bus, US$3, to **Chañaral** (no main terminal), then change: same fare to Antofagasta, US$25 to San Pedro, US$39 to Iquique.

Parque Nacional Pan de Azúcar

There is no bus service. A **taxi** costs US$20-30 from Chañaral, or hitch a lift from fishermen at sunrise.

Far north

Antofagasta, capital of the Second Region, is a major port for the export of copper from La Escondida and Chuquicamata. It is also a major commercial centre and home of two universities. The coast north of Antofagasta is much more picturesque than the aridity surrounding much of the Panamerican Highway. Two possible stops are the fishing port of Mejillones and Tocopilla, beneath towering cliffs. Despite this being the driest region, the climate is delightful. Temperature varies from 16°C in June and July to 24°C in January and February, never falling below 10°C at night.

From the mining service centre of Calama, the route heads up to the altiplano with its saltflats and lunar landscapes. In an oasis on the Río San Pedro is the historic town of San Pedro de Atacama. This has become a popular destination for visitors seeking high altitudes, clear skies, steaming geysers and volcanic horizons. It is also, increasingly, a staging post on the route between Bolivia's Salar de Uyuni and the Pacific Ocean. The Atacama Desert extends over most of the far north to the Peruvian border. The main cities are Iquique and Arica; between them are old mineral workings and geoglyphs. Large areas of the Andean highland have been set aside as national parks; the most visited is Lauca with its volcanoes and lakes.

Antofagasta and around *Colour map 6, C2.*

urban gateway to the north coast and the altiplano

The largest city in northern Chile, Antofagasta, 1367 km north of Santiago, is not especially attractive in itself, but its setting beside the ocean and in view of tall mountains is dramatic.

Sights

In the main square, **Plaza Colón** is a clocktower donated by the British community in 1910 to commemorate 100 years of Chilean independence. It is a replica of Big Ben in London. Calle A Prat, which runs southeast from Plaza Colón, is the main shopping street. Two blocks north of Plaza Colón, at the old port, is the former Aduana, built as the Bolivian customs house in Mejillones and moved to its current site after the War of the Pacific. It houses the **Museo Histórico Regional** ⓘ *Balmaceda y Bolívar, www.museodeantofagasta.cl, Tue-Fri 0900-1700, Sat, Sun, holidays 1100-1400, free,* which has fascinating visual displays (explanations in Spanish only) on life on land and in the oceans, the development of civilization in South America, minerals and human artefacts.

East of the port are the buildings of the Antofagasta and Bolivia Railway Company (FCAB) dating from the 1890s and beautifully restored, but still in use and difficult to visit. **Museo del Ferrocarril a Bolivia** ⓘ *Bolívar 280, T55-220 6592, www.fcab.cl, free,* has an interesting museum of the history of the Antofagasta–Bolivia railway, with photographs, maps, instruments and furniture. **Museo Geológico** ⓘ *Av Angamos 0610, inside the university campus, gchong@ucn.cl, Mon, Tue, Thu 0930-1300, Mon-Fri 1530-1800, free, colectivo 114 or 333 from town centre,* is the mineral museum of the

Best for
Adventurous journeys ▪ Desert landscapes ▪ National parks ▪ Volcanoes

Universidad Católica del Norte. Tours of the port by boat leave from **La Cabaña de Mario** ① *C Aníbal Pinto s/n between the Museo Regional and the Terminal de Pescadores, 30 mins, US$4.50.*

On a hill to the south of town (bus No 102 or 103) are the imposing ruins of **Huanchaca**, a Bolivian silver refinery built after 1868 and closed in 1903. From below, the ruins resemble a fortress. Its museum ① *www.ruinasdehuanchaca.cl, Tue-Sun 1000-1300, 1430-1900, US$3,* features archaeological and mineral exhibits. There is a casino and hotel opposite.

Around Antofagasta

☆The fantastic cliff formations and natural arch at **La Portada** are 16 km north and reached by minibus for Mejillones from Latorre, between Sucre and Bolívar (US$4.50 return), or on Condell,

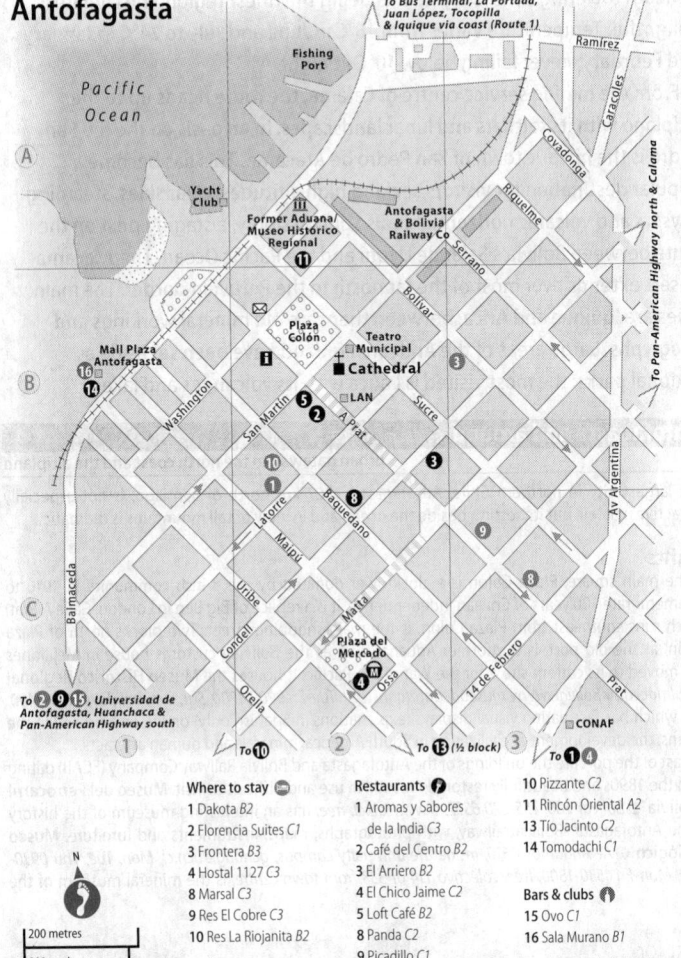

Antofagasta

Pacific Ocean

To Bus Terminal, La Portada, Juan López, Tocopilla & Iquique via coast (Route 1)

To Pan-American Highway north of Calama

Fishing Port

Yacht Club

Former Aduana/ Museo Histórico Regional ⑪

Antofagasta & Bolivia Railway Co

Mall Plaza Antofagasta ⑯ ⑭

Plaza Colón

Teatro Municipal

✚ **Cathedral**

LAN

⑤ ②

⑩

①

⑧

⑨

⑧

Plaza del Mercado

④

To ② ⑨ ⑮, Universidad de Antofagasta, Huanchaca & Pan-American Highway south

CONAF

To ⑩   *To ②*   *To ⑬ (½ block)*   *To ① ④*

Washington · San Martín · A Prat · Sucre · Bolívar · Serrano · Riquelme · Covadonga · Caracoles · Ramírez · Av Argentina · Prat · Baquedano · Maipú · Matta · Ossa · 14 de Febrero · Latorre · Uribe · Condell · Orella · Balmaceda

200 metres / 200 yards

Where to stay 🛏
1 Dakota *B2*
2 Florencia Suites *C1*
3 Frontera *B3*
4 Hostal 1127 *C3*
8 Marsal *C3*
9 Res El Cobre *C3*
10 Res La Riojanita *B2*

Restaurants 🍴
1 Aromas y Sabores de la India *C3*
2 Café del Centro *B2*
3 El Arriero *B2*
4 El Chico Jaime *C2*
5 Loft Café *B2*
8 Panda *C2*
9 Picadillo *C1*

10 Pizzante *C2*
11 Rincón Oriental *A2*
13 Tío Jacinto *C2*
14 Tomodachi *C1*

Bars & clubs 🍸
15 Ovo *C1*
16 Sala Murano *B1*

between Sucre and Bolívar. They drop you 2 km from La Portada. Take a hat. (The arch is used as the symbol of the Second Region.) Buses to Juan López will drop you much closer to La Portada but run at weekends in the summer only. Taxis charge US$25-30 (for a small extra fee, taxis from the airport will drive past La Portada). Hitching is easy. From the main road it is 2 km to the beach which, though beautiful, is too dangerous for swimming; there is a seafood restaurant (La Portada) and café (open lunch-time only). A number of bathing beaches are also within easy reach.

Juan López, 38 km northwest of Antofagasta, is a windsurfers' paradise. The sea is alive with birds, including Humboldt penguins, especially opposite Isla Santa María. For those with their own transport, follow the road out of Juan López to the beautiful cove at Conchilla. Keep on the track to the end at Bolsico.

Mejillones

This port town 60 km north of Antofagasta, stands on a good natural harbour protected from westerly gales by high hills. Until 1948 it was a major terminal for the export of tin and other metals from Bolivia. Remnants of that past include a number of fine wooden buildings: the Intendencia Municipal, the Casa Cultural (built in 1866) and the church (1906), as well as the Capitanía del Puerto. The town has been transformed in recent years by the building of the largest port in South America, to be completed by 2030, which links Argentina, southern Brazil and Paraguay with the lucrative markets of the Asian Pacific Rim.

Listings Antofagasta and around *map p733*

Tourist information

Tourist office
Prat 384, p 1, T55-245 1818, infoantofagasta@ sernatur.cl. Mon-Fri 0830-1800, Sat 1000-1400, summer Mon-Fri till 1900, Sat till 1500.
Several ATMs around the plaza and in the rest of the centre; *casas de cambio* are mainly on Baquedano.

Where to stay

There are several international chain hotels, such as **Holiday Inn**, **Ibis** and **Radisson**, and others designed for the business market.

$$$$-$$$ Florencia Suites
Croacia 0126, T55-279 8221, www.florenciasuites.cl.
Luxury suites on the coast south of the city centre with lovely sea views, restaurant and pool.

$$$-$$ Marsal
Prat 867, T55-226 8063, www.hotelmarsal.cl.
Modern, very comfortable, bright and spacious rooms, Catalan owner.

$$ Dakota
Latorre 2425, T55-225 1749, Dakota_hotel@hotmail.com.
Popular, good value.

$$ Hostal 1127
Coquimbo 1127, T55-284 1497, www.hostal1127.com.
Ensuite rooms with all services, in a residential neighbourhood, quiet, helpful.

$$-$ Frontera
Bolívar 558, T55-228 1219.
Basic but with good hot showers and decent beds, convenient for Tur-Bus and Pullman.

$$-$ Residencial El Cobre
Prat 749, T55-222 5162.
Private or shared bath, set around a central courtyard, bright but tatty, helpful staff.

$ Residencial La Riojanita
Baquedano 464, T55-276 8407.
Basic, very helpful, older rooms have high ceilings but are run-down, newer rooms with bath are smaller. Not a bad budget option.

Camping
To the south on the road to Coloso are:
Las Garumas (Km 6, T55-263 7395), **$$** per site (ask for lower price out of season), **$$** for cabins, cold showers and beach (reservations Av Angamos 601, Av Jaime Guzman s/n, or see http://www.uantof.cl/universidad/bienestar).

Restaurants

Many bars and restaurants are closed on Sun. Above the market are a few good places selling cheap seafood *almuerzos* and super-cheap set lunches, including **El Mariscal** and **Toledo**. Good fish restaurants in Terminal Pesquero Centro and at Caleta Coloso, which is 18 km south.

$$$-$$ Picadillo
Av Grecia 1000, T55-224 7503.
Lively atmosphere, serves a wide range of dishes. Good music.

$$$-$$ Tomodachi
Balmaceda 2355, Local 21R, Mall Plaza, T55-253 3300, www.tomodachi.cl.
The best of the city's sushi restaurants.

$$ Aromas y Sabores de la India
Argentina 1294, T9-9514 4944.
Indian restaurant and takeaway, the only one of its kind in northern Chile.

$$ El Arriero
Condell 2644, T55-226 4371, www.arrieroafta.cl/restaurant.
Grills and traditional hearty criollo food. Good service, cheap set lunch, popular, live music.

$$ Panda
Condell 2505, T55-225 4827.
Self-service, Chinese and Chilean, eat all you can for set price.

$$ Pizzante
Carrera 1857, T55-222 3344, www.pizzante.cl.
Good pasta, seafood and vegetarian options.

$$ Rincón Oriental
Washington 2743, T55-222 6869, see Facebook.
Excellent Cantonese, 'over the top' decor.

$$-$ El Chico Jaime
Mercado Central 2nd floor, local 115, T55-222 7401.
Best of the restaurants in the central market, good food and friendly service.

$ Tío Jacinto
Uribe 922, T55-222 8486, www.tiojacinto.cl. Closed Mon.
Friendly atmosphere, serves good seafood.

Cafés

Loft Café
Prat 470, see Facebook. Open from 0815 on weekdays, 0900 on Sat.
Trendy café with real coffee.

Café del Centro
Galería, Prat 482.
Real coffee.

Bars and clubs

Thanks to Antofagasta's student population, the city's nightlife is buzzing. The most popular bars and clubs are 16 km south of the town in Balneario El Huáscar. Take micro 103 from C Matta to get there. There is also a wide choice on O'Higgins.

Ovo
In Casino Enjoy, Av Angamos 01455, T9-9919 9435, www.enjoy.cl, see Facebook: Casino-Enjoy-Antofagasta for promotions.
One of the most popular nightclubs in the city.

Sala Murano
In Mall Plaza Antofagasta (see below).
Another popular club.

Entertainment

Teatro Municipal, *Sucre y San Martín, T55-259 1732, www.culturaantofagasta.cl.* Modern, state-of-the art theatre.
Teatro Pedro de la Barra, *Condell 2495.* Theatre run by University of Antofagasta, regular programme of plays, reviews, concerts, etc, high standard, details in press.

Festivals

29 Jun San Pedro, the image of the patron saint of the fishermen is taken out by launch to the breakwater to bless the first catch of the day.
Last weekend of Oct The city's immigrant communities put on a joint festival on the seafront, with national foods, dancing and music.

Shopping

The **Mall Plaza Antofagasta** (Balmaceda y Maipú) has a wide variety of shops and a pleasant promenade on the roof, with colourful flowers and views out to the ocean.

Feria Modelo O'Higgins, *next to fish market on Av Pinto.* Excellent fruit and veg, also restaurants. Municipal market at Matta y Uribe.

What to do

Many tour companies offer packages to the Atacama, but the tourt office recommends booking tours in San Pedro de Atacama, as it is far cheaper. See **Escuela de Surf Antofagasta** (Facebook: escueladesurf.antofagasta) for information on surfing in the area.

Buceo Magallanes, *Balmaceda 2705, T9-9232 7932, www.buceomagallanes.cl*. Regular diving trips and courses.

Transport

Air **Cerro Moreno Airport**, 22 km north. Taxi to airport US$20-30, but cheaper if ordered from hotel. For airport transfers, **Transfer Antofagasta**, T55-225 3411, US$10-12. LATAM and Sky fly daily to **Santiago**. Sky also daily to **La Serena**.

Bus The bus terminal is at Aguirre Cerda 5750, on the northern edge of the city. Bus company phone numbers: **Flota Barrios**, T55-2243 4626; **Romani**, T55-256 1021; **Pullman Bus**, T600-320 3200; **Tur-Bus**, T600-660 6600. To **Santiago**, many companies: 19hrs, US$44-77; book in advance in high season. If all seats to the capital are booked, catch a bus to **La Serena** (12 hrs, US$30-57), or **Ovalle**, 14 hrs, and re-book. To **Valparaíso**, US$56. To **Copiapó**, 7 hrs, US$21-48. Frequent buses to **Iquique**, US$16-28, 6 hrs. To **Arica**, from US$18-42, 11 hrs. To **Calama**, several companies, US$8, 3 hrs; to **San Pedro de Atacama**, many daily with **Tur-Bus** and others, 5 hrs, US$13-21, or via Calama. Buses for **Mejillones**, 1 hr, US$3, from Corsal terminal, Condell y Sucre; also minibuses Latorre 2730. To **Juan López**, bus 129 from Condell y Sucre. To **Tocopilla**, 2½ hrs, US$8, many daily.

Car hire **First**, Bolívar 623, T55-222 5777. Plus international agencies like Avis, Baquedano 364, www.avis.cl.

North of Antofagasta

routes north along the coast or northeast towards Bolivia

Pan-American Highway to Iquique

Two routes go north towards Iquique: the Pan-American Highway and the coastal route. From **Carmen Alto** at Km 101 (98 km north of Antofagasta), where there is petrol and food, a paved road leads northeast to Calama (see below). North of here, to the west of the Highway, are the remains of several nitrate towns. Some 107 km north of Carmen Alto is the crossroads, leading west to Tocopilla (72 km) and east to Chuquicamata. Travel a further 81 km north to reach **Quillagua**, officially the driest place in the world. There's a customs post here, where all southbound vehicles and buses are searched. The first of three sections of the **Reserva Nacional del Tamarugal** is reached 111 km beyond Quillagua (see page 748).

Coastal route to Iquique

The coastal route is more picturesque than the Pan-American Highway. On this road, 187 km north of Antofagasta, is **Tocopilla**, a useful place to stop with a few *hostales ($$)*. It has one of the most dramatic settings of any Chilean town, sheltering at the foot of 500-m mountains that loom inland. The town is dominated by a thermal power station and the port facilities used to unload coal and to export nitrates and iodine from María Elena and Pedro de Valdivia. There are some interesting early 20th-century buildings with wooden balustrades and façades, but it was heavily damaged by an earthquake on 14 November 2007, and it's generally a run-down, slightly menacing place. There are two good beaches, however: Punta Blanca (12 km south) and Caleta Covadonga, 3 km south with a pool.

The coast road from Tocopilla north to Iquique is paved, 244 km, with fantastic views of the rugged coastline and tiny fishing communities. The customs post at **Chipana-Río Loa** (90 km north) searches all southbound vehicles for duty-free goods; 30 minutes' delay. Basic accommodation is available at **San Marcos**, a fishing village, 131 km north. At **Chanaballita**, 184 km north there is a hotel, *cabañas*, camping, restaurant, shops. There are also campsites at **Guanillos**, Km 126, **Playa Peruana**, Km 129 and **Playa El Aguila**, Km 160.

Calama *Colour map 6, B2.*

Calama lies in the oasis of the Río Loa, 202 km north of Antofagasta. Initially a staging post on the silver route between Potosí and Cobija, it is now an expensive, unprepossessing modern city, serving the nearby mines of Chuquicamata and Radomiro Tomic. Calama can be reached from the south by the paved road from Carmen Alto (see above), or from the north by Route 24 via Chuquicamata. The road passes many abandoned nitrate mines, *oficinas*.

Two kilometres from the centre on Avenida B O'Higgins is the **Parque El Loa** ① *daily 1000-1800, till 1900 in summer*, which contains a reconstruction of a typical colonial village built around a reduced-scale reproduction of Chiu Chiu church. In the first two weeks of March a festival, Feploa, celebrating the heritage of surrounding areas is held here. The **Museo de Historia Natural** ① *museocalama@vtr.net, Tue-Sun 1000-1300, 1500-1800, US$0.30*, has an interesting collection on the *oficinas* and on the region's ecology and palaeontology.

☆Chuquicamata *Colour map 6, B2.*

Located 16 km north of Calama, this is the site of the world's largest open-cast copper mine, employing around 6000 workers and operated by Codelco (the state copper corporation). The visual spectacle of the site makes for a memorable visit. Everything about Chuquicamata is huge: the pit from which the ore is extracted is 4 km long, 2 km wide and 730 m deep; the giant trucks, with wheels over 3.5 m high, carry 310 ton loads and work 24 hours a day; in other parts of the plant 60,000 tonnes of low-grade ore are processed a day to produce refined copper of 99.99% purity. Output is around 345,000 tonnes of fine copper a year. Guided tours, by bus, in Spanish (although guides usually speak reasonable English) leave from the Codelco office ① *Av Central Sur y Av Granaderos, Villa Ayquina, Calama, T55-232 2122, visitas@codelco.cl, Mon-Fri 1 in 300, make reservation in advance; either call the office in Calama or ask at the tourist office; passport number essential.* Wear covered shoes, long trousers and long sleeves; filming is permitted in certain areas. Tours may be cancelled without notice if there are high winds.

☆Chui Chui and around

From Calama it is 273 km north to Ollagüe on the Bolivian border. The road follows the Río Loa, passing Chiu Chiu (33 km), one of the earliest Spanish settlements in the area. Just beyond this oasis, a small turning branches off the main road to the hamlet of **Lasana**, 8 km north of Chiu Chiu; petroglyphs are clearly visible on the right-hand side of the road. There are striking ruins here of a pre-Inca *pukará* (a national monument); drinks are on sale. If arranged in advance, Línea 80 *colectivos* will continue to Lasana for an extra charge; pre-book the return trip, or walk back to Chiu Chiu. At **Conchi**, 25 km north of Lasana, the road crosses back over the Río Loa via a bridge dating from 1890; it's a military zone, so no photographs of the view are allowed.

East of Chiu Chiu, towards El Tatio (see below), **Caspana** is beautifully set among hills at 3305 m. It has a tiny church dating from 1641 and the **Museo Arqueológico y Etnográfico de Caspana** ① *Tue-Sun 1000-1300, 1500-1800, US$0.75*, with interesting displays on Atacameño culture. Basic accommodation is available (the nearest to El Tatio). A poor road runs north and east from here, through valleys of pampas grass with llama herds, to **Toconce**, which has extensive prehispanic terraces set among interesting rock formations. There are archaeological sites nearby and the area is ideal for hiking. Further information is available from the tourist office in Calama, who may also help with arranging transport.

Ollagüe *Colour map 6, B2.*

Beyond Chiu Chiu the road to Ollagüe deteriorates, with deep potholes, but north of Ascotán (*carabinero* checkpoint at 3900 m), it improves as it crosses the salares de Ascotán and de Carcote. There are many llama and vicuña herds along this road and flamingos on the *salares*. Ollagüe, on the dry floor of the Salar de Ollagüe at 3690 m, is surrounded by a dozen volcanic peaks of over 5000 m. The **border with Bolivia** is open 0800-2000; US$2 charge to enter Bolivia (see Bolivia chapter, Practicalities, for reciprocity fees payable by some nationalities). When entering Chile here, customs inspection is strict and officious; expect several hours delay. See www.pasosfronterizos.gov.cl/cf_ollague.html for information. There is a municipal hostel and food and drink is available in town. At this altitude the days are warm and sunny, nights cold (minimum -20° C). There are only 50 mm of rain a year, and water is very scarce.

Listings North of Antafagasta

Tourist information

Calama

Tourist office
Granaderos 1690 (but may return to its original location at Latorre 1689 in 2017), T55-253 1707, www.calamacultural.cl (the head office of the Corporación de Cuyltura y Turismo is at Av O'Higgins s/n, Sector El Loa, T55-271 1150). Mon-Fri 0800-1300, 1400-1800.
Map, tours, helpful staff, English spoken.

Where to stay

Coastal route to Iquique

$ Emilia
Merino 1205, Tocopilla, T55-281 3135, www.hotelemiliatocopilla.com.
Expansive, brightly coloured hotel, rooms with bath, Wi-Fi, parking.

Calama

$$$ Hostería Calama
Latorre 1521, T55-234 1511, www.hosteriacalama.cl.
Comfortable heated rooms, good service; gym and small pool. Airport transfer.

$$$ L&S
Vicuña MacKenna 1819, T55-236 1113, www.lyshotel.cl.
Business hotel, upstairs rooms more spacious. Often full Mon-Wed with mining engineers. A good choice.

$$$ Park
Alcalde José Lira 1392, T55-271 5800, www.parkcalama.cl.
On the edge of town by the airport. First class, pool, bar and restaurant, excursions to the salar.

$$ Hotel Jatata
Sotomayor 1822, T55-236 1640, jatataexpress.hoteles@gmail.com.

Decent rooms with bath, most face onto a corridor, but those with windows onto the street are much better and good value.

$$-$ Hospedaje Urkupiña Arce
Ramírez 1825, T9-6245 6461, hospedaje.arce@gmail.com.
Single, double and triple rooms, private or shared bath, well maintained, family atmosphere, Wi-Fi, often crowded with miners, safe, central location. Meals extra.

$$-$ Hostal El Arriero
Ramírez 2262, T55-231 5556, www.hostalelarriero.cl.
Family run, spacious doubles and triples (with thin walls) situated around a narrow courtyard, shared bath, Wi-Fi functional most of the time, good value.

Restaurants

Calama

On pedestrian part of C Eleuterio Ramírez are several cafés, juice bars, *heladerías* and fast food places.

$$ Bavaria
Sotomayor 2093.
Good restaurant with cafetería downstairs, real coffee, breakfast 0830-1200 Mon-Sat, very popular, not quiet, also cheaper café at Latorre 1935, upstairs.

$$ Mariscal JP
Félix Hoyos 2127, T55-231 2559. Closed Mon.
Best seafood in town, worth that bit extra.

$$ Mexicano
Vivar 2037.
So-called Mexican cuisine, live music at weekends.

$$-$ Pasión Peruana
Abaroa 1694, T9-5733 8750, see Facebook.
Peruvian-run restaurant featuring authentic dishes such as *lomo saltado*, giant ceviches, *aji de gallina* and more; delicious set lunch specials, but small portions.

Shopping

Calama

Craft stalls
On Latorre 1600 block.

Market
Feria El Loa and Feria Modelo are on Antofagasta between Latorre and Vivar, selling fruit juices and crafts.

What to do

Calama
Several agencies run 1-day and longer tours to the Atacama region, including San Pedro; these are usually more expensive than tours from San Pedro and require a minimum number for the tour to go ahead. Be wary of agencies with poorly maintained vehicles and poor guides; standards here not generally very high. Operators with positive recommendations include: **Sol del Desierto** (Caur 3486, Villa Lomas Huasi, T55-267 5163, www.soldeldesierto.cl), who offer a variety of day tours around Chiu Chiu and San Pedro. For other options, see under San Pedro de Atacama, below.

Transport

Coastal route to Iquique
In Tocopilla, bus companies' offices are on 21 de Mayo. To **Antofagasta** many daily, US$12, 2½ hrs. To **Iquique**, along coastal road, 3 hrs, US$22, frequent. To **Calama**, Tur-Bus 6 a day, 3 hrs, US$20.

Calama
Air Airport is modern and efficient with Redbanc ATM, restaurant upstairs, shop with internet. **LATAM**, daily, to **Santiago**, via **Antofagasta**; also **Sky**. LAN also flies direct to **La Serena** twice a week. Transfer services from the airport are offered by **Transfer City Express**, T9-9816 2091 (see Facebook), US$10; taxi fare US$10-12.

Bus Local Public transport runs on a *colectivo* system, black cabs with a number on the roof.

Just ask which number goes where you want to and flag it down. US$1 by day, US$1.50 after 2400.

Long distance Main terminal, Granaderos 3048, T55-231 3727, many companies: **Tur-Bus**, **Pullman**, **Flota Barrios**, **Géminis**, **Kenny Bus**. To **Santiago** 21 hrs, US$56-73. To **La Serena**, usually with delay in Antofagasta, 16 hrs, US$41-62. To **Antofagasta**, 3 hrs, several companies, US$8. To **Iquique**, 6 hrs, via Tocopilla, US$14-21, 3 daily with **Tur-Bus**. To **Arica**, usually overnight, US$18-27, 9 hrs, or change in Antofagasta. To **San Pedro de Atacama**, Tur-Bus, Frontera del Norte (Antofagasta 2046, http://busesfrontera delnorte.cl) and Atacama 2000 have several daily, 1½ hrs, US$4. Some continue to Toconao an d Peine. Minibus to **Chiu Chiu**, Turismo Alto Loa, T9-9616 5657 beforehand to be picked up in front of the Tur-Bus office, US$3. To **Uyuni**, for Bolivia via Ollagüe: Cruz del Norte (Ramírez 1931, T9-7241 5772, good vehicles, recommended) direct at 0630 daily, US$21.50, 7-8 hrs; also with **Frontera del Norte**, 5 a week at 0545, and **Atacama 2000**, Mon, Wed, Thu, Sun 0750, these two cost US$12 and change buses at **Ollagüe**. To **Salta**, Argentina, 12 hrs, Géminis (Tue, Fri, Sun), **Pullman Bus** (Sun, Wed, Fri) and **Andesmar** (Sun, Wed), US$42-60 (check in advance as days change).

> ### Warning...
> If intending to drive in the border area, visit the police in San Pedro to get maps of which areas may have landmines.

Car hire A hired car shared between several people is an economical alternative for visiting the Atacama region. A 4WD jeep (necessary for the desert) costs US$120 a day, a car US$55-65. Hire companies in the centre include **Alamo**, Hoyos 2177, T55-255 6802 (good), **First**, Antofagasta 2268, T55-231 5453, **EconoRent**, Latorre 2507, T55-234 1076; in the airport **Hertz**, T55-234 0018, and **Avis**, T55-256 3151. Airport offices only open when flights arrive.

Taxi Basic fare US$5.

San Pedro de Atacama, 103 km southeast of Calama (paved, no fuel, food or water along the way), is a small town, more Spanish-looking than is usual in Chile. Long before the arrival of the Spanish, the area was the centre of the Atacameño culture. There is a tangible sense of history in the shady streets and the crumbling ancient walls, which drift away from the town into the fields, and then into the dust. Owing to the clear atmosphere and isolation, there are wonderful views of the night sky. Now famous among visitors as the centre for excursions in this part of the Atacama, San Pedro can be overrun with visitors during holidays and the main tourist season from October to the end of February, resulting in high prices and pressure on resources.

Sights

The **Iglesia de San Pedro**, dating from the 17th century, is supposedly the second oldest church in the country. It has been heavily restored (the tower was added in 1964). The roof is made of cactus. Nearby, on the Plaza, is the **Casa Incaica**, the oldest building in San Pedro. **Museo Arqueológico** ① *due to reopen in 2018 after complete rebuilding,* will still house the collection of Padre Gustave Paige, a Belgian missionary who lived in San Pedro between 1955 and 1980. It is under the care of the Universidad Católica del Norte. It is a fascinating and well-organized repository of artefacts, tracing the development of prehispanic Atacameño society.

Fact...

There are BCI ATMs inside the pharmacies on Calle Caracol, as well as BCI bank itself. Don't use the ATM in Banco Estado, as it has been known to eat cards. If coming from inside Chile stock up on pesos before arriving. Dollars, Argentine pesos and bolivianos can be exchanged at bad rates and most companies accept credit cards, but with high charges. The tourist office recommends always changing money at banks; however, Casa de Cambios Mazzetti, on Toconao, daily 1000-2200, is reputable and changes dollars and euros (also at bus terminal daily 0800-2000). Some other places change euros; ask around.

Around San Pedro de Atacama

☆ **Valle de la Luna** ① *12 km west of San Pedro, US$4.50,* is a nature reserve with fantastic landscapes caused by the erosion of salt mountains. It is crossed by the old San Pedro–Calama road. Although buses on the new Calama–San Pedro road will stop to let you off where the old road branches off, 13 km northwest of San Pedro (signposted to Peine), it is far better to travel from San Pedro on the old road, either by bicycle (but difficult after sunset) or by car (a 20-km round trip is possible). The Valle is best seen at sunset (if the sky is clear), although this is also the most crowded time. Take water, hat, camera and torch. Camping is forbidden.

The **Pukará de Quitor** ① *3 km north of San Pedro along the river, US$8,* is a pre-Inca fortress restored in 1981. The fortress, which stands on the west bank, was stormed by the Spanish under Pedro de Valdivia. A further 4 km up the river there are Inca ruins at Catarpe.

Tip...

Do not leave any rubbish behind on desert excursions; the dry climate preserves it perfectly.

At **Tulor** ① *12 km southwest of San Pedro, US$8,* there is an archaeological site where parts of a stone-age village (dated 800 BC-AD 500) have been excavated; it can be visited on foot, or take a tour that includes Quitor, US$37. Nearby are the ruins of a 17th-century village, abandoned in the 18th century because of lack of water.

☆**El Tatio** ① *Altitude: 4321 m; entry US$8.* The geysers are a popular attraction, reached by a maintained road which runs northeast past the thermal pools at **Puritama** (28 km, US$17 – discount after 1400 on weekdays, worth a visit). The geysers are at their best 1100-1500, though the spectacle varies: locals say the performance is best when weather conditions are stable. Following recent accidents a series of stone walls and wooden walkways has been built around the geysers, which some say has taken away from the spectacle. A swimming pool has been built nearby (take costume and towel). There is no public transport to the geysers and hitching is impossible. If going in a hired car, make sure the engine is suitable for very high altitudes and is protected with antifreeze. If driving in the dark it is almost impossible to find your way: the sign for El Tatio is north of the turn off (follow a tour bus). Tours are arranged by agencies in San Pedro and Calama. The nearest *hospedaje* is in Caspana (see page 738).

Border with Argentina The ride from San Pedro de Atacama to Salta (Argentina) on a fully paved road through the 4400-m **Paso de Jama** is spectacular. It stays high on the puna, going by snow-capped peaks, lakes and salt pans, before reaching the border, 160 km from San Pedro. There are no money-changing facilities, nor any other services here. Be prepared for cold. The road continues paved on the Argentine side to Susques and Jujuy. This is much more popular than the **Paso Sico** route further south (see below).

Fact...
When crossing by private vehicle, check the road conditions before setting out as Paso de Jama can be closed by heavy rain in summer and blocked by snow in winter.

There is a large modern border complex at Paso de Jama shared by officials of both countries, open 0800-2300 (Argentine time; see Time in Practicalities). Formalities are relatively efficient but still need 1-2 hours for buses. There are no services, money exchange or ATMs at the border. There's an Argentine consulate in Antofagasta (Blanco Encalada 1933, T55-222 0440).

Tip...
At all border crossings, incoming vehicles and passengers are searched for fruit, vegetables, dairy produce and coca leaves, which may not be brought into Chile.

Border with Bolivia Hito Cajón (4480 m) for the border with Bolivia is reached by road 47 km east of San Pedro. The first 35 km is on the paved road to Paso de Jama (see above), then it's 12 km to Hito Cajón, which may be blocked by snow in

San Pedro de Atacama

Where to stay
1 Altiplánico
2 Awasi
3 Don Raul
4 Elim
6 Hostal Mamatierra
8 Hostal Miskanty
10 Hostal Sonchek
11 Hostelling International
13 Kimal
14 La Casa de Don Tomás
15 Res Chiloé
16 Res Vilacoyo
17 San Pedro
18 Takha-Takha

Restaurants
1 Adobe & Casa Piedra
2 Bendito Desierto
3 Café Etnico
4 Café Tierra Todo Natural
6 El Huerto
7 Estrella Negra
8 La Casona
9 La Estaka
10 Lola

winter. From the border it is 7 km north to Laguna Verde. Since 2014, there have been no buses from San Pedro to the border at Hito Cájon, except tour buses. Those who wish to take public transport to the border must do so from Calama. Do not be tempted to hitch to the border and beyond as you risk being stranded without water or shelter at sub-zero temperatures. Chilean immigration and customs at Hito Cajón are open 0800-2000. See www.pasosfronterizos.gov.cl/cf_hitocajon.html. There are Bolivian consulates in Calama (León Gallo 1985A, T55-234 1976, coliviancalama@yahoo. com, open Monday-Friday 0900-1230, helpful but not always open) and Antofagasta (Washington 2675, p 13, T55-279 4369, colivian.afta@vtr.net).

Toconao and south

The village, with simple places to stay and eat (\$\$ Hostal Altos del Láscar, Av Norte 92, T9-8458 6603, www.altoslascar.cl, with its own vineyards), is located 37 km south of San Pedro on the eastern shore of the Salar de Atacama. The 18th-century church and bell tower and all houses are built of bricks of white volcanic stone, known as *liparita*. The quarry where the *liparita* is worked can be visited, about 1.5 km east (the stones sound like bells when struck). Also east of the village is a beautifully green gorge called the Quebrada de Jere, filled with fruit trees (entry US\$2.50). Worth visiting are the vineyards which produce a sweet wine. About half-way to Toconao a side road heads east to the Atacama Large Millimeter/submillimeter Array (**ALMA**), the largest astronomical project on Earth (www.almaobservatory.org); it is open to the public by appointment, but it is incredibly popular, so try to book at least two months in advance.

South of Toconao is one of the main entrances to the **Salar de Atacama** ① *entry is controlled by CONAF in Toconao, US\$4.* This vast 300,000-ha salt lake (the third largest expanse of salt flats in the world) is home to three of the world's five species of flamingo – the Andean, Chilean and James – and other birds (although some can only be seen when lakes form in winter). The air is so dry that you can usually see right across the Salar. A huge lake half a metre below the surface contributes to a slight haze in the air. The area is also rich in minerals. Three areas of the Salar form part of the **Reserva Nacional de los Flamencos**, which is in seven sectors totalling 73,986 ha and administered by CONAF in San Pedro (Ayllú de Solcor), T55-285 1608.

From Toconao, a road runs 67 km along the eastern edge of the Salar de Atacama to the attractive village of **Peine**, with offices of the lithium extraction company, whose access road may be used with permission to visit the Salar's spectacular salt formations. Nearby are some prehistoric cave paintings. Guides in the village offer tours. There is also a thermal pool where you can swim. To the east of the village lies a group of beautifully coloured hills, more vibrant at sunset, with good views over the Salar.

From Toconao another road heads south through scenic villages to the mine at Laco (one poor stretch below the mine), before proceeding to Laguna Sico (4079 m) and **Paso Sico** to Argentina. This crossing is hardly used by any public or heavy traffic. It is paved as far as Socaire on the Chilean side and about 40% paved in Argentina to San Antonio de los Cobres (slow going on the unpaved parts).

Listings San Pedro de Atacama *map p741*

Tourist information

Tourist office
Toconao y Gustavo Le Paige, on the plaza, T55-285 1420, sanpedrodeatacama@sernatur.cl. Mon-Sun 0900-2100.
Staff are helpful staff but besieged. Has a useful suggestions book, with feedback from other visitors about agencies' tours. See also www. sanpedrochile.com, www.sanpedroatacama.com and www.sanpedrodeatacama.net.

Where to stay

There is electricity, but take a torch (flashlight) for walking at night. Rooms are scarce in Jan/Feb, and pricey all year round. There are unregistered hostels, usually \$ pp, but security is often lax.

\$\$\$\$ Altiplánico
Atienza 282, reservations T2-3224 4237, www.altiplanico.com.
Comfortable boutique hotel on the edge of town (20-min walk), adobe huts, well designed and spacious.

$$$$ Alto Atacama
Camino Pucara Suchor, T2-2912 3945 (reservations), www.altoatacama.com.
In the Catarpe valley, spacious rooms, all with terrace, spa, observatory, packages and excursions offered.

$$$$ Awasi
Tocopilla 4, reservations T2-2233 9641, www.awasi.cl.
All-inclusive packages. Just 8 luxury cabins, all built with traditional materials, fine food, excellent customer service, professional tours included.

$$$$ Explora
Atienza y Ayllú de Larache, T2-2395 2800 (head office Av Américo Vespucio Sur 80, 5 piso, Santiago), www.explora.com.
Luxury full board and excursion programme, solar-heated pool, sauna, jacuzzi, massages, the only lodge with its own stables and horses.

$$$$ Kimal
Atienza 452 y Caracoles, T55-285 1152, www.kimal.cl.
Small, intimate, near the centre, room size varies, pool with jacuzzi and spa. Good restaurant (open to the public). Opposite is **Poblado Kimal**, under same ownership.

$$$$ San Pedro
Toconao 460, T55-285 1011, www.dahotelessanpedro.com.
The town's oldest luxury hotel. Pool (residents only), petrol station, cabins, some rooms with satellite TV, quite comfortable.

$$$$ Tierra Atacama
Camino Séquitor s/n, T2-2207 8861 (or 1-800-829 5325 USA), www.tierraatacama.com.
Modern design, elegant and minimalist, somewhat removed from the village itself. Very good reports, including fine dining, spa, excursions, birdwatching.

$$$ Don Raul
Caracoles 130-B, T55-285 1138, www.donraul.cl.
Pleasant, simple rooms, good value, some with kitchenette, one for the disabled.

$$$ La Casa de Don Tomás
Tocopilla s/n, T55-285 1055, www.dontomas.cl.
Good rooms, bright and spacious lounge, quiet, swimming pool. Late check out/and check in. Decent value.

$$$-$$ Elim
Palpana 6, T55-285 1567, www.hostalelim.cl.

Rooms sleep 1-3, nice hot showers, garden, hammock area, bicycle rental, laundry service.

$$$-$$ Takha-Takha
Caracoles 151-A, T55-285 1038, www.takhatakha.cl.
Pretty, lovely garden and shady patio rooms with bath are nicer than those without. Also camping under trees, with hot showers.

$$$-$ Hostelling International
Caracoles 360, T55-256 4683, www.hostellingsanpedro.cl.
Lively hostel, cramped shared rooms with lockers, also private rooms. Bicycle rental, tours, sandboarding school.

$$ Haramaksi
Coya, near Tulor, 7 km southwest of San Pedro, T9-9595 7567.
Simple accommodation in traditional Atacameño surroundings away from the hubbub of San Pedro. Free transfer from bus station.

$$ Hostal Mamatierra
Pachamama 615, T55-285 1418, www.hostalmamatierra.cl.
5 mins' walk from the centre, will pick you up from the bus terminals. Some rooms with bath, kitchen facilities, peaceful.

$$$ Hostal Miskanty
Pasaje Mutulera 141, T55-285 1430, see Facebook.
Simple but pleasant rooms with bath, laundry service.

$$ Hostal Sonchek
Le Paige 198, T55-285 1112, www.hostalsonchek.cl.
Decent-value eco hostel, some rooms with bath, café Delicias de Carmen, breakfast extra, English and French spoken, central, quiet, not a party *hostal*. Wi-Fi in central courtyard. Solar-powered showers offer hot water 24/7 in summer, only in daytime in winter. Recommended.

$$ Residencial Chiloé
Atienza 404, T55-285 1017, www.residencialchiloe.supersitio.net.
Rooms with bath much nicer than those without, good clean bathrooms, good beds, breakfast extra. Sunny veranda, laundry facilities, luggage store, parking.

$$-$ Residencial Vilacoyo
Tocopilla 387, T55-285 1006.
Shared bath, good kitchen facilities, hammock in courtyard, laundry service. One of few good budget options in the centre.

Camping

No camping is allowed outside town. **Camping Los Perales**, Tocopilla 481, and Camping Los Abuelos, Atienza 294-B, has swimming pool.

Restaurants

Few places are open before 1000. Drink bottled water as the local supply has a high mineral content, which may not agree with some.

$$$-$$ Bendito Desierto
Atienza 426, see Facebook.
Inventive food served in a kind of grotto.

$$$-$$ La Estaka
Caracoles 259, T55-285 1164, www.laestaka.cl.
Wood fire, cane roof, jazz music, good pizzería and other dishes, bar and book exchange, lively after 2300, favoured spot of the local New Age crowd.

$$ Adobe
Caracoles 211.
Open fire, internet, good atmosphere, loud music. Described as "like Greenwich Village/Islington in the Atacama".

$$ Casa Piedra
Caracoles 225, T9-7984 4148,
www.restaurantcasadepiedra.com.
Open fire, also has a cheap menu, waiters sometimes play live folk music, good food and cocktails.

$$ La Casona
Caracoles, T56-285 1164,
www.lacasonadeatacama.cl.
Good food, vegetarian options, cheap *almuerzo*, large portions. Interesting Cubist-style desert paintings. Check bill with care.

$$ Lola
Toconao 441, T9-9611 2135,
lola.spa.chile@gmail.com.
The place to be at night (especially weekends). Extensive menu of pizzas, pastas, vegetarian plates and the speciality, the giant *empanada*. Also cocktails, beers on tap and DJ. Popular with tourists and locals. Karaoke every night. Closes at 0100 on weeknights, 0200 at weekends.

$$-$ Café Etnico
Tocopilla 423, T55-285 1377.
Good food, juices and sandwiches, cosy, book exchange, internet (free for diners).

$ Café Tierra Todo Natural
Caracoles 271 T55-285 1585,
www.tierratodonatural.cl.
Excellent fruit juices, "the best bread in the Atacama", real coffee, yoghurt, best for breakfast, opens earliest.

$ El Huerto
Le Paige 230.
It may not look like much from the outside, but there's a wonderful patio area in which to enjoy good-value set lunches.

$ Estrella Negra
Caracoles 362, in patio de comidas.
Good cheap vegetarian and some vegan food.

Shopping

Handicrafts

There are a couple of craft markets, one on the plaza, and the other in the **Galería el Peral** (Caracoles 317). Very little *artesanía* is produced in San Pedro itself, most comes from Bolivia.

What to do

Mountain biking

Bicycles for hire all over town, by the hour or full day: 'professional' model or cheaper 'amateur'. Tracks in the desert can be really rough, so check the bike's condition and carry a torch if riding after dark.

Swimming pools

Piscina Oasis, *at Pozo Tres, 3 km southeast but walking there is tough and not recommended. Open all year daily (except Mon) 0900-1800. US$7.50, discounts for children.* Good showers and picnic facilities, very popular Sat-Sun.

Tour operators

Usual tours include: to Valle de la Luna (from US$15), the Salar de Atacama (US$16-24), altiplano lakes (including Toconao and Salar de Atacama – US$35 for half day), El Tatio (begin at 0400 – US$40 including breakfast) with trekking (take swimming costume and warm clothing). Beware of tours to Valle de la Luna leaving too late to catch sunset – leave around 1500, 1600 at the latest. Most agencies in San Pedro pool their clients, so you cannot be sure that the company that you booked with will be the one that takes you on the tour. Always get a receipt. Report any complaints to the municipality or Sernatur. There are about 25 agencies, but some are temporary and/or open for only part of the year. Some operators will offer a reduction if you book a series of tours with them.

Atacama Horse Adventure (La Herradura), Tocopilla 406, T55-285 1956, www.atacama horseadventure.com. Horse-riding tours with good local guides, mountain bike hire.

Atacama Mística, Caracoles 238, T55-285 1956, www.atacamamistica.cl. Chilean-Bolivian company, daily tours with transfer to San Pedro de Atacama, also transfers between San Pedro and Uyuni, good service.

Azimut 360º, T56-235 3085, www.azimut360. cl. Santiago-based company offers excursions, trekking, private tours with English, German and French-speaking guides.

Cordillera Traveller, Tocopilla 429, T9-7617 6347, www.cordilleratraveller.com. Specializes in tours to Salar de Uyuni.

Cosmo Andino Expediciones, Caracoles y Tocopilla, T55-285 1069, www.cosmoandino.cl. Very professional and experienced, English, French, German, Dutch spoken, good vehicles, drivers and guides, owner Martin Beeris (Martín El Holandés).

Desert Adventure, Caracoles y Tocopilla, T55-285 1067, www.desertadventure.cl. Good guides and range of trips, English spoken, modern fleet of vehicles, mostly good reports.

Rancho Cactus, Toconao 568, T55-285 1506, www. rancho-cactus.cl. Offers horse riding with good guides to Valle de la Luna and other sites (Farolo and Valerie – speaks French and English), suits inexperienced riders.

Space, Caracoles 166, T55-256 6278/9-9817 8354, www.spaceobs.com. Run by French astronomer Alain, who speaks 3 languages and has set up a small observatory in the village of Solor, south of San Pedro; gives tours 2100 in summer, 1900 in winter, to study the night sky, hot drink included but wear all your warmest clothes.

Vulcano, Caracoles 317, T55-285 1023, www. vulcanochile.cl. Mountain climbs, sandboarding and other adventure tours, mountain bike hire, English-speaking guides.

Transport

Bus Most buses leave from Tumiza y Láscar, modern terminal with ticket offices of tour companies. **Tur-Bus** terminal on Atienza, north of the centre, office Licancábur 294, T55-285 1549. To **Calama**: US$5, many daily, 1½ hrs, also to **Antofagasta**. Companies include **Atacama 2000, Ciktur, Frontera** and **Tur-Bus**. Frequencies vary with more departures in Jan-Feb and some weekends. Book in advance to return from San Pedro on Sun afternoon. **Tur-Bus** to **Arica**, 2000, 2130, US$30. **Tur-Bus** to **Santiago**, several daily, 23 hrs, US$69-97. To **Toconao**, Atacama 2000 at 0930, 1530, 1930, returning 0700, 1220, 1815, US$1.50, 45 mins.

To **Salta (Argentina)** US$30-50, 10-12 hrs depending on border delays; **Géminis**, Tue, Fri, Sun 0900; **Andesmar** Sun, Wed 0830; **Pullman** Sun, Wed, Fri 0930. Reserve in advance as buses fill early (fewer buses and lower prices in low season).

Car Expensive fuel is available in the grounds of Hotel San Pedro. If planning to cross the border to Bolivia, remember that octane ratings are different in the 2 countries, but diesel cars can safely be used.

geoglyphs, nitrate towns and thermal springs

The capital of I Región (Tarapacá), Iquique takes its name from the Aymara word ique-ique, meaning place of 'rest and tranquillity'. The city, 492 km north of Antofagasta and 47 km west of the Pan-American Highway, is situated on a rocky peninsula, sheltered by the headlands of Punta Gruesa and Cavancha. Around it the desert pampa stretches north, south and east to the mountains.

Inland, the central depression at 1000-1200 m is arid pampa, punctuated by salt flats south of Iquique. Between Iquique and Arica it is crossed from east to west by four gorges. Several oases have strong historical associations, either in the form of geoglyphs, the last evidence of peoples long vanished, or the ghost towns of nitrate operations. Mamiña and Pica are thermal resorts within easy reach of Iquique; both are beautiful, tranquil places.

East of the pampa lies the sierra, the western branch of the Andes, beyond which is a high plateau, the altiplano (3500-4500 m) from which rise volcanic peaks. The coastal strip and the pampa are rainless; on the coast temperatures are moderated by the Pacific, but in the pampa variations of temperature between day and night are extreme, ranging from 30°C to 0°C. The altiplano is much colder.

Sights

Iquique is an attractive port and city with well-preserved historical buildings. It was partly destroyed by earthquake in 1877, but became the centre of the nitrate trade after its transfer from Peru to Chile at the end of the War of the Pacific. In the centre of the old town is the **Plaza Prat**. On the northeast corner of the Plaza is the Centro Español, built in extravagant Moorish style by the local Spanish community in 1904; the ground floor is a restaurant, on the upper floors are paintings of scenes from Don Quijote and from Spanish history. Three blocks north of the Plaza is the old Aduana (customs house) built in 1871; in 1891 it was the scene of an important battle in the Civil War between supporters of President Balmaceda and congressional forces. Part of it housed the **Museo Naval**, focusing on the Battle of Iquique, 1879. A fire in 2015 nearly destroyed the building and the collection is temporarily in the Museo Militar ⓘ *Baquedano 1396*. Along Calle Baquedano, which runs south from Plaza Prat, are the attractive former mansions of the 'nitrate barons', dating from between 1880 and 1903. The finest of these is the **Palacio Astoreca** ⓘ *O'Higgins 350, Mon-Fri*

Iquique

Pacific Ocean

To Zofri

Av Centenario

Souper

Covadonga

Former Aduana/ Museo Naval

Solomayor

Tur-Bus

Esmeralda

To Bolivia

✝ Cathedral

Bolívar

San Martín

Lagos

Anibal Pinto

Patricio Lynch

Obispo Labbé

Ramirez

Vivar

Barros Arana

Amunátegui

Juan Martínez

Thompson

Gorostiaga

Plaza Prat

Teatro Municipal

Plaza Condell

Municipalidad

Serrano

Tarapacá

Wilson

Thompson

Latorre

Sargento Aldea

Grumete Bolados

Museo Regional

Palacio Astoreca

Zegers

O'Higgins

Buines

To ❺❶❶ (1 block)

To ❸ ❻❼ (2½ blocks), Playa Cavancha, Tocopilla & Antofagasta via Route 1

To ❻ (4 blocks)

To ❾

To Route 5 (Pan-American Highway)

N

200 metres

200 yards

Where to stay 🛏
1 Arturo Prat
3 Backpacker's Hostel Iquique
4 Cano
5 Hostal Cuneo
6 Hostal La Casona 1920
7 Hostal Li Ming
8 YMCA

Restaurants 🍴
3 Casino Español
4 Cioccolata
5 Doña Filomena
6 El Rincón del Cachuperto
7 El Tercer Ojito
8 El Viejo Wagon
9 Kiru
10 La Picada Curicana
11 Muselina
12 Nan King
13 Peña mi Perú
14 Sumapuriwa

1000-1800, Sat 1100-1300. Built in 1903, it was subsequently the Intendencia and now a museum of fine late 19th-century furniture and shells. The **Museo Regional** ① *Tue-Sat 0900-1730, Sun 0930-1800, free,* contains an archaeological section tracing the development of prehispanic civilizations in the region; an ethnographical collection of the Isluga culture of the altiplano (AD 400), and of contemporary Aymara culture; also a section devoted to the nitrate era which includes a model of a nitrate office and the collection of the nitrate entrepreneur, Santiago Humberstone. Sea lions and pelicans can be seen from the harbour. There are **cruises** ① *US$4.50, 45 mins, minimum 10 people,* from the passenger pier.

The **beaches** at Cavancha just south of the town centre are good; those at Huaiquique are reasonable November-March. There are restaurants at Cavancha. For surfers the better bet is the pounding surf of Playa Brava, further south. Cerro Dragón, the large sand dune behind Iquique, is good for sandboarding with great views, too. There are several hills for paragliding, good for beginners.

A short distance north of town is the **Free Zone (Zofri)** ① *www.zofri.cl, Mon-Sun 1100-2100, limit on tax free purchases US$1300 for foreigners; getting there: colectivo from the centre US$1.* It is worth visiting this giant shopping centre, which sells all manner of imported items, including electronic goods. It is much better value than its equivalent in Punta Arenas. The *casas de cambio* here have the best rates for cash.

☆Nitrate towns

Humberstone ① *T57-276 0626, daily 0900-1800, US$4.50, leaflets available; colectivo from Iquique US$4.65; phone near site for booking return,* is a large, abandoned nitrate town at the junction of the Pan-American Highway and the road to Iquique. Though closed since 1961, you can still see the church, theatre, *pulpería* (company stores) and the pool (built of metal plating from ships' hulls). Granted World Heritage status by UNESCO in 2005, the town is being slowly restored by former residents who are happy to reminisce with visitors. Nearby are the ruins of other mining towns, including Santa Laura. Local tours to the area, include a visit to **Pozo Almonte**, 52 km east, which was the chief service provider of the nitrate companies until their closure in 1960. The **Museo Histórico Salitrero** ① *on the tree-shaded plaza, www.museodelsalitre.cl, daily 1000-1900,* displays artefacts and photos of the nitrate era.

☆Cerro Pintados

The **Reserva Nacional del Tamarugal** protects three areas of geoglyphs, south, east and north of Iquique. To the south is Cerro Pintados (111 km north of Quillagua), where some 400 figures (humans, animals, geometric shapes) can be seen on the hillside, 3 km west of the Pan-American Highway; to get there take any bus south, US$3, and ask the drive to let you off at the entrance, from where it is a 10- to 20-minute walk. Or you could take a taxi from Pozo Almonte to the geoglyphs, US$4.50. The second part of Tamarugal is near La Tirana; the third is 60 km north of Pozo Almonte, near Huara (see below).

Mamiña

From Pozo Almonte it is 74 km (paved) to **Mamiña** at 2750 m, which has abundant thermal springs and a mud spring, **Baño Los Chinos** ① *0900-1600, US$4.50.* The therapeutic properties of the waters and mud are Mamiña's main claim to fame. Mineral water from the spring is sold throughout northern Chile. There are ruins of a prehispanic *pukará* (fortress) and a church, built in 1632, the only colonial Andean church in Chile with two towers. An Aymara cultural centre, Kaspi-kala, has an *artesanía* workshop and outlet. It is very difficult to find lodging in Mamiña as hotels have exclusive contracts with the ever-expanding mine nearby.

☆La Tirana and Pica

La Tirana, 10 km east of the Pan-American Highway (70 km east of Iquique), is famous for a religious festival to the **Virgen del Carmen**, held from 12 to 18 July, which attracts up to 250,000 pilgrims. Over 100 groups dance night and day, decked out in spectacular colourful masks, starting on 12 July. All the dances take place in the main plaza in front of the church; no alcohol is served. Accommodation is impossible to find, other than in organized campsites (take tent), which have basic toilets and showers. To get there, turn off the Pan-American Highway 9 km south of Pozo Almonte.

Pica, 42 km from La Tirana, was the most important centre of early Spanish settlement in the area, although most of its older buildings date from the nitrate period when it became a popular resort. The town is famous for its pleasant climate, citrus groves and two natural springs, the best of which is **Cocha Resbaladero** ① *daily 0830-2000, US$3*, which has a snack bar, changing rooms, beautiful pool and a tourist office opposite.

Tip...
Many sites around Iquique, including the Gigante del Atacama (see below) and places to see fossilized dinosaur footprints, are difficult to visit without a car, although tours are available from Pica.

From Iquique to the Bolivian border

☆ At **Huara**, 33 km north of Pozo Almonte, a paved road turns off the Pan-American Highway to the border at **Colchane**. Thirteen kilometres east of Huara are the huge geoglyphs of **Cerro Unitas**, with the giant humanoid figure of the Gigante del Atacama (86 m tall) and a sun with 24 rays, on the sides of two hills (best seen from a distance). The geoglyphs are difficult to visit without a car, although some buses from Iquique to La Paz and Oruro pass through, or La Paloma at 2300 from Esmeralda y Juan Martínez.

The village of **Isluga**, 6 km northwest of Colchane, has an 18th-century Andean walled church and bell tower. Nearby is the entrance to the **Parque Nacional Volcán Isluga** ① *administration at Enquelga, 10 km north of the entrance, but guardaparques are seldom there; contact tarapaca.oirs@ conaf.cl for details of hospedaje at the guardería.* The park covers 174,744 ha at altitudes above 2100 m and has some of the best volcanic scenery in northern Chile. Wildlife varies according to altitude but includes guanacos, vicuñas, llamas, alpacas, vizcachas, condors and flamingos.

Border with Bolivia Colchane is 173 km northeast of Huara. The border is open daily 0730-1930. On the Bolivian side the road is paved from Pisiga for about 100 km to Huachacalla and from Toledo to Oruro, 32 km northeast. The remaining 170 km are scheduled to be paved. There's a Bolivian consulate in Iquique (Gorostiaga 215, p 3, Departamento E, T57-252 7472, colivianiquique@ gmail.com, Monday-Friday 0930-1200).

North of Iquique

The Cordillera de la Costa slowly loses height north of Iquique, terminating at the Morro at Arica (see page 752): from Iquique north it drops directly to the sea and, as a result, there are few beaches along this coast. The Pan-American Highway runs across the Atacama Desert at an altitude of around 1000 m, with several steep hills which are best tackled in daylight; at night, the sea mist (*camanchaca*) can reduce visibility.

At **Zapiga**, 80 km north of Pozo Almonte, there is a crossroads. Head east for 67 km on a poor road to reach Camiña, a picturesque village in an oasis, whence mountain roads lead across the Parque Nacional Volcán Isluga to Colchane (see above). The westerly branch runs 41 km to **Pisagua**, formerly an important nitrate port, now a small fishing village, with several old wooden buildings that are National Monuments. The fish restaurants make a pleasant stop for a meal. Mass graves dating from just after the 1973 military coup were discovered near here in 1990.

At Km 57 north of Huara there is a British cemetery at Tiliviche dating from 1825. The Geoglyphs of Tiliviche representing a group of llamas (signposted to the left and easily accessible) can be seen from the highway at Km 127.

Tourist information

Iquique

Sernatur
Aníbal Pinto 436, T57-241 9241, infoiquige@
sernatur.cl. Mon-Fri, 0900-1800, Sat 1000-1400.
There is also an administrative office a block
away at Serrano 145, of 401, T57-242 7686.
Mon-Fri 0830-1730.
Masses of information, including a full list of tour
operators. Very helpful. See also www.iquique.cl.

Where to stay

Iquique

Accommodation is scarce in July and also in
high summer. There's no campsite in Iquique
and wild camping is forbidden on Playa Brava
and Playa Cavancha.

\$\$\$ Arturo Prat
Aníbal Pinto 695, Plaza Prat, T57-236 6401,
www.terrado.cl.
Member of the Terrado group, good location
if a bit noisy, good standard, nice pool.

\$\$\$-\$\$ Cano
Ramírez 996, T57-247 0277, www.hotelcano.cl.
Mostly big rooms, but also some small interior
rooms to be avoided. nice atmosphere, brightly
coloured, modern decor, parking.

\$\$ Hostal Cuneo
Baquedano 1175, T57-242 8654,
hostalcuneo@hotmail.com.
Long-established hostel, helpful, piano in the
living room, good value.

\$\$-\$ Hostal La Casona 1920
Barros Arana 1585, T57-241 3000, see Facebook.
Fun, in a quiet area of town not far from the
beach, English spoken.

\$\$-\$ Hostal Li Ming
Barros Arana 705, T57-242 1912, www.hostal.cl.
Simple, good value, small rooms, also beachfront
apartments to rent.

\$ Backpacker's Hostel Iquique
Amunateguí 2075 esq Hernán Fuenzalida,
T57-232 0223, www.hosteliquique.cl.
Seafront location at Cavancha, all the usual
backpacker's services plus surfboard and wetsuit
rental, surf classes, sand duning, paragliding,
bicycles, roof terrace with ocean view, young
party vibe. Recommended.

\$ YMCA
Baquedano 964, T57-241 5551,
www.ymcaiquique.org.
Impressive façade, modern interior, most rooms
are dorm-style with their own bathroom. Basic,
but clean and central.

La Tirana and Pica

Hotels fill up at weekends, holiday times and
during La Tirana's festival 12-18 Jul: book ahead.

\$\$ Camino del Inca
Esmeralda 14, Pica, T57-274 2054.
Shady patio, table football, good value.

\$\$ Hostal Los Emilios
Cochrane 213, Pica, T57-274 1126.
Interesting old building, nice lounge and patio.

\$\$-\$ O'Higgins
Balmaceda 6, Pica, T57-274 1524,
hohiggins@123mail.com.
Modern, well furnished.

\$ San Andrés
Balmaceda 197, Pica, T57-274 1319.
Basic, excellent restaurant, serves good-value
4-course *almuerzos*. Safe parking.

Restaurants

Iquique

The restaurants on the wharf on the opposite
side of Av Costanera from the bus terminal
are poor value. There are several good, cheap
seafood restaurants on the 2nd floor of the
central market, Barros Arana y Latorre. There are
also many restaurants on the Península Cavancha.

\$\$\$-\$\$ Casino Español
Plaza Prat, T57-233 3911, see Facebook.
Good meals well served in beautiful Moorish-
style 1904 building.

\$\$\$-\$\$ El Tercer Ojito
P Lynch 1420, T57-241 3847,
www.eltercerojito.cl.
Well-presented fish, sushi, pasta and vegetarian
options with a Peruvian twist, served in a
pleasant courtyard, deservedly popular.

$$$-$$ El Viejo Wagon
Thompson 85.
Fish and seafood cooked to traditional northern recipes. Regarded as the best eatery in the centre.

$$$-$$ Kiru
Amunátegui 1912, Cavancha, T57-276 0795, www.kiru.cl. Mon-Sat 1300-1600, 2000-0030, Sun 1300-1600.
Half elegant restaurant, half sports bar, Peruvian influenced food, fish and good pasta. Huge *pisco sours*.

$$$-$$ Sumapuriwa
Prat 1062, T57-241 7121 (see Facebook: restaurantesumapuriwa.sumapuriwa). Tue-Sun for lunch and dinner.
Probably the most authentic altiplano food in the city. Staples like lamb, rabbit, llama and fish are lovingly prepared and presented with just a bit of flash.

$$ La Picada Curicana
Pinto y Zegers 204, T57-276 5830, www.lapicadacuricana.cl.
Good hearty Central Chilean country cooking (such as oven-roasted game, served in clay pots), large portions, good value *menú de la casa*.

$$ Nan King
Amunátegui 533, T57-242 0434.
Large portions, good value, renowned as best Chinese in town.

$ Doña Filomena
Valenzuela 298, on the peninsula (also Filomena Express at Martínez 2060), T57-231 1235, see Facebook.
The other local eatery purported to have the best *empanadas* in the city. Also good pizzas and ceviches.

$ El Rincón del Cachuperto
Valenzuela 125, Península Cavancha.
Famed as having possibly the best seafood *empanadas* in Iquique.

$ Peña mi Perú
Bolívar 711. Open 24 hrs.
Cheap Chilean and Peruvian staples, good value *menú* on weekdays.

Cafés

Cioccolata
Pinto 487, T57-253 2290 (another branch in the Zofri), www.cioccolata.cl.
Very good coffee and cakes.

Muselina
Baquedano 1406, see Facebook. Mon-Fri 0900-1300, 1700-1900, Sun 1800-2100 (closes for 1 month each year for vacation).
Café/bistro with good coffee, delicious cakes and smoothies.

La Tirana and Pica

In Pica, try the local *alfajores*, delicious cakes filled with cream and mango honey.

$$ El Pomelo
Simón Bolívar s/n, Pica.
Good for local staples like rabbit and llama, as well as delicious fruit and ice cream. One of the most popular restaurants in town.

$ La Mía Pappa
Balmaceda 118, near plaza, Pica.
Good selection of meat and juices, attractive location.

$ La Viña
Ibáñez 70, by Cocha de Resbaladero, Pica.
Good cheap *almuerzo*.

$ Yacaré
Blanco Encalada s/n, Pica.
Fast and cheap.

Bars and clubs

Iquique
Most discos are out of town on the road south to the airport.

Ronnie Tequila
Baquedano y Zegers, see Facebook.
Popular food spot with drink specials and happy hour at night.

Siddharta Lounge
On the peninsula, see Facebook.
Sushi.

What to do

Iquique

Language schools
Academia de Idiomas del Norte, *Ramírez 1345, T57-241 1827, www.languages.cl.* Swiss-run, Spanish classes and accommodation for students.

Paragliding
Iquique is a good place for **paragliding**: several agencies offer 30- to 40-min tandem flights from around US$60.

Altazor, *Flight Park, Vía 6, manzana A, sitio 3, Bajo Molle, T57-238 0110, www.altazor.cl.* Parapenting; will pick you up from wherever you are staying. Also offers week-long courses including accommodation, as do many other operators.

Surfing

Iquique offers some of the best surfing in Chile with numerous reef breaks on Playa Brava, south of the city. Surfboard rental and surf classes are available from a number of agencies.

Tour operators

Avitours, *Baquedano 977, T57-241 3334, www.avitours.cl.* Tour to Pintados, La Tirana, Humberstone, Pica, etc, some bilingual guides, day tours start at US$30.

Desierto Verde, *Allende 450, of 808, T57-276 2291, www.dsvexpediciones.cl.* Tours to the altiplano and desert. Also boat tours of Iquique's bay.

Turismo Iquique, *Baquedano 1054, T57-276 7460, www.turismoiquiqueagencia.cl.* A large assortment of tours, including desert attractions, city tour, and thermal pools.

Transport

Iquique

Air Diego Aracena international airport, 35 km south at Chucumata. Taxi US$27; airport transfer, T57-231 0800, US$6.75 for 3 or more passengers, unreliable. **LATAM** and **Sky** fly to **Arica**, **Antofagasta** and **Santiago**.

Bus Terminal at north end of Patricio Lynch (not all buses leave from here); bus company offices are near the market on Sgto Aldea and

B Arana. **Tur-Bus**, Esmeralda 594, T57-273 6656, with Redbanc ATM and luggage store. **Pullman**, in terminal T57-242 9852. Southbound buses are searched for duty-free goods, at Quillagua on the Pan-American Highway and at Chipana on the coastal Route 1. To **Arica**, buses and *colectivos*, US$11-18, 4½ hrs. Many buses to and from Arica (even Tur-Bus) don't use a/c; be sure to books a seat in the middle of the bus under one of the emergency hatches. To **Antofagasta**, US$16-28, 6 hrs. To **Calama**, 6 hrs, US$17-24, Frontera del Norte at 2200. To **Tocopilla** along the coastal road, buses and minibuses, several companies, 3 hrs, US$22. To **La Serena**, 18 hrs, US$41-50. To **Santiago**, 25 hrs, several companies, US$49-83.

International buses To La Paz, **Bolivia**, **Litoral**, 0530 and 1300 daily except Sat, US$27. Other companies in Terminal Rodoviario, Patricio Lyunch 50, T57-241 6315.

Car hire **Econorent**, Fuenzalida 1058, T57-242 3723, www.econorent.cl, weekend specials; **IQSA**, Labbé 1089, T57-241 7068. **Procar**, Serrano 796, T57-241 3470.

Mamiña

Minibuses leave at 0800 from the central market, US$6.

La Tirana and Pica

Minibus from **Iquique** to Pica, US$4.50 one-way, 2 hrs, with **San Andrés** (Terminal Rodoviario, PLynch 50, www.busessanandres.cl) daily; **Pullman Chacón** (Barros Arana y Latorre), many daily, or **Santa Rosa** (Salvador Allende 2360, www.pullmansantarosa.cl), daily.

Arica and the altiplano *Colour map 6, A1.*

volcanoes, salt lakes and vicuñas

Arica, Chile's northernmost city and capital of the new Arica-Parinacota Region (Región XV), lies 20 km south of the Peruvian border. It is built at the foot of the Morro headland and is fringed by sand dunes. The Andes can be clearly seen from the anchorage. As well as providing easy access to Peru, Arica is also an important staging post for travellers going overland to Bolivia. The road route to La Paz via Tambo Colorado is now paved, making the city a popular seaside destination for landlocked Bolivians, as well as Chileans. East of Arica on the altiplano, Parque Nacional Lauca is the most northerly national park in Chile and has some of the country's most stunning scenery: high lakes, snow-capped volcanoes, lava fields and varied bird life. Small Andean villages near the park retain their Aymara culture. South of Lauca are two more wildlife reserves; all three combined are designated a World Biosphere Reserve.

Sights

El Morro de Arica, with a good view from the park on the top, was the scene of a great victory by Chile over Peru in the War of the Pacific on 7 June 1880. To get there, walk to the southernmost end of Calle Colón, past the small **Museo** ① *Colón 10, Tue-Sun 1000-1800*, displaying a number of

Chinchorro mummies, and then follow the pedestrian walkway up to the summit of the hill. Here there is the **Museo Histórico y de Armas** ① *Mon-Fri 0800-1900, Sat 0900-1900, US$2*, which contains weapons and uniforms from the War of the Pacific.

At the foot of the Morro is the **Plaza Colón** with the cathedral of San Marcos, built in iron by Eiffel. Though small, it is beautifully proportioned and attractively painted. It was brought to Arica from Ilo (Peru) in the 19th century, before Peru lost Arica to Chile, as an emergency measure after a

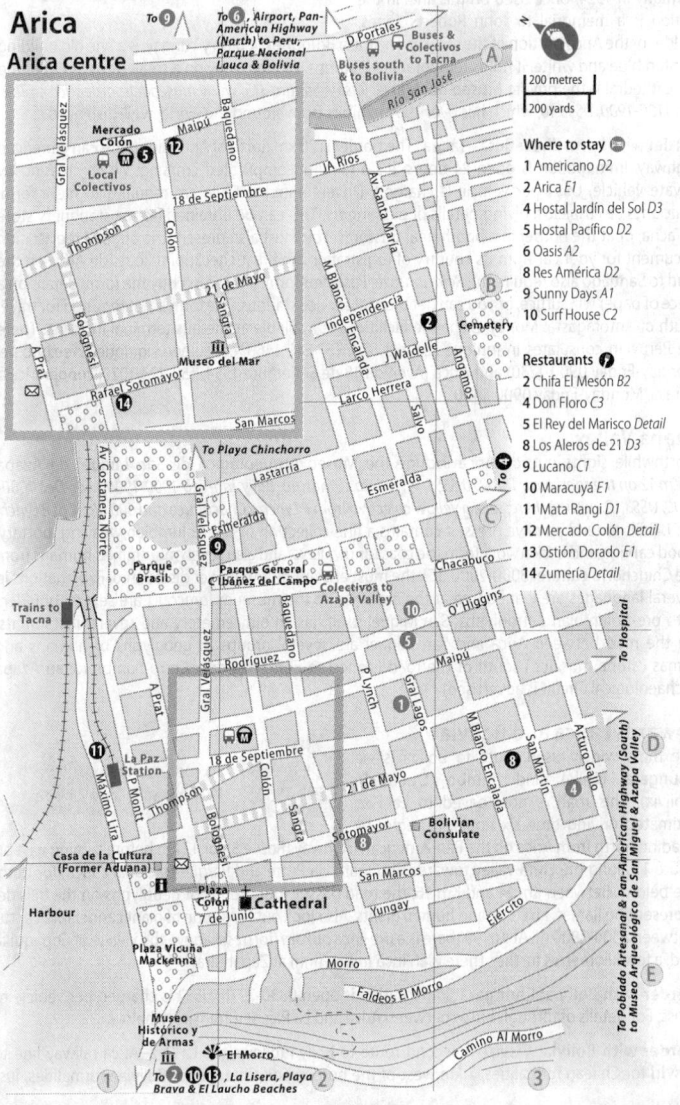

Arica

Arica centre

To Airport, Pan-American Highway (North) to Peru, Parque Nacional Lauca & Bolivia

Buses & Colectivos to Tacna

Buses south & to Bolivia

Río San José

D Portales

200 metres
200 yards

Mercado Colón
Local Colectivos

Maipú
Baquedano
Gral Velásquez
JA Ríos
Av Santa María
18 de Septiembre
Colón
Thompson
Sangra
Bolognesi
A Prat
21 de Mayo
M Blanco Encalada
Independencia
Waidelle
Salto
Angamos
Cemetery
Larco Herrera
Museo del Mar
Rafael Sotomayor
San Marcos

To Playa Chinchorro
Lastarria
Esmeralda
Esmeralda
Av Costanera Norte
Gral Velásquez
Parque Brasil
Parque General Ibáñez del Campo
Chacabuco
Colectivos to Azapa Valley
O'Higgins
To Hospital
Trains to Tacna
A Prat
Baquedano (Tarapacá)
Rodríguez
Maipú
P Lynch
Gral Lagos
La Paz Station
Máximo Lira
S P Montt
Thompson
Colón
18 de Septiembre
21 de Mayo
Sotomayor
Sangra
Bolognesi
Bolivian Consulate
M Blanco Encalada
San Martín
Arturo Gallo
To Poblado Artesanal & Pan-American Highway (South) to Museo Arqueológico de San Miguel & Azapa Valley
Casa de la Cultura (Former Aduana)
Plaza Colón
Cathedral
7 de Junio
San Marcos
Yungay
Ejército
Harbour
Plaza Vicuña Mackenna
Morro
Faldeos El Morro
Museo Histórico y de Armas
El Morro
Camino Al Morro
To La Lisera, Playa Brava & El Laucho Beaches

Where to stay
1 Americano *D2*
2 Arica *E1*
4 Hostal Jardín del Sol *D3*
5 Hostal Pacífico *D2*
6 Oasis *A2*
8 Res América *D2*
9 Sunny Days *A1*
10 Surf House *C2*

Restaurants
2 Chifa El Mesón *B2*
4 Don Floro *C3*
5 El Rey del Marisco *Detail*
8 Los Aleros de 21 *D3*
9 Lucano *C1*
10 Maracuyá *E1*
11 Mata Rangi *D1*
12 Mercado Colón *Detail*
13 Ostión Dorado *E1*
14 Zumería *Detail*

tidal wave swept over Arica and destroyed all its churches. Eiffel also designed the nearby Aduana (customs house) which is now the **Casa de la Cultura** ① *closed for renovation in 2017*. Just north of the Aduana is the La Paz railway station; outside is an old steam locomotive (made in Germany in 1924) once used on this line. In the station is a memorial to John Roberts Jones,

Tip...

Just north of the city, the estuary of the Río Lluta is an important stopping place for migrating birds and has been designated a wildlife sanctuary.

builder of the Arica portion of the railway. The **Casa Bolognesi**, Colón y Yungay, is a fine old building painted blue and white. It holds temporary exhibitions. Hidden away on a small side street behind the cathedral is the private **Museo del Mar** ① *Pasaje Sangra 315, www.museodelmardearica.cl, Tue-Sun 1100-1900, US$3.10*, which has over 1000 exhibits from around the world, well-displayed.

Border with Peru: Chacalluta–Tacna The border is 20 km north of Arica along the Pan-American Highway. Immigration is open 24 hours; it's a fairly uncomplicated crossing. When crossing by private vehicle, US$2 per vehicle is charged. Drivers entering Chile are required to file a form, *Relaciones de Pasajeros*, giving details of passengers. This can be obtained from a stationery store in Tacna, or at the border in a booth near Customs. You must also present the original registration document for your car from its country of registration. The first checkpoints outside Arica on the road to Santiago also require the *Relaciones de Pasajeros* form. If you can't buy the form, details on a piece of paper will suffice, or you can get them at service stations. The form is not required for travel south of Antofagasta. Money exchange facilities are available at the bus terminal in Tacna. There are Peruvian consulates in Iquique (Zegers 570, T57-241 1466, consulperu-iquique@rree.gob.pe, Monday-Friday 0900-1230) and Arica (Avenida 18 de Setiembre 1554, T58-223 1020, conperarica@ terra.cl, Monday-Friday 0900-1400).

Azapa Valley

Worthwhile sights outside Arica include the **Museo Arqueológico de San Miguel de Azapa** ① *Km 12 on the road east, T58-220 5555, www.uta.cl/masma, daily Jan-Feb 1000-1900, Mar-Dec 1000-1800, US$3.10, getting there: take a yellow colectivo from P Lynch y Chacabuco and 600 block of P Lynch, US$1*. Built around an olive press, it contains a fine collection of pre-Columbian weaving, pottery, wood carving and basketwork from the coast and valleys, and also seven mummified humans from the Chinchorro culture (8000-2000 BC), the most ancient mummies yet discovered. Explanations in several languages are loaned free at the entrance. In the museum forecourt are several boulders with pre-Columbian petroglyphs. San Miguel itself has an old cemetery and several restaurants. On the road between Arica and San Miguel are several groups of geoglyphs of humans and llamas ('stone mosaics') south of the road (signed to Cerro Sagrado, Cerro Sombrero; an Azapa Archaeological Circuit is advertised).

Towards Lauca and Bolivia

The most widely used route to Boliva is via **Chungará** (Chile) and **Tambo Quemado** (Bolivia). This road is now paved to La Paz, estimated driving time six hours. It begins by

Tip...

There's a Bolivian consulate in Arica (P Lynch 298, T58-258 3390, colivian_arica@yahoo.es).

heading north from Arica on the Pan-American Highway (Route 5) for 12 km before turning east on Route 11 along the Lluta valley towards Chungará via Putre and Parque Nacional Lauca (for both, see below). Between Km 14 and Km 16, the road passes four groups of geoglyphs on the hillside, representing llamas, an eagle and human giants. Also look out for a zone of giant candelabra cactus between 2300-2800 m. At Km 90 there is a pre-Inca *pukará* (fortress) above the village of Copaquilla and, a few kilometres further, there is an Inca *tambo* (inn) at Zapahuira.

Border with Bolivia: Chungará Immigration is open 0830-2030; US$2 is charged per vehicle to cross. For details of through buses between Arica and La Paz, see Transport, below.

Border with Bolivia: Visviri A second route to Boliva follows the La Paz–Arica railway line to **Visviri** for Chilean formalities, 7 km west of the border, and **Charaña** for Bolivian formalities, just over the border (local barter market every other Friday). This route should not be attempted in wet weather. Immigration is open 0800-2000. Private vehicles are charged US$2. If travelling by public transport to Visviri, take a jeep across the border to Charaña. A motorized rail car usually runs from Charaña to Viacha Tuesday and Friday 1200, 4 hours, US$4.30; take a bus Viacha-La Paz.

Putre

This scenic village on the Arica–La Paz road, 15 km west of the park entrance, is a good base for exploring Lauca national park and for acclimatization (altitude 3500 m). It has a church dating from 1670 and is surrounded by terracing dating from pre-Inca times, now used for cultivating alfalfa and oregano. From here paths provide easy walking and great views. East of the village are the **Termas de Jurasi** ① *look for sign just after Km 130 on Route 11, US$3*, rustic thermal baths, with mud baths and a small swimming pool.

Tip...

Coming from Arica, it is best to ascend to the altiplano in stages, spending a night in Putre before going on to Lago Chungará; one-day tours are not recommended.

Fact...

The bank in Putre changes dollars. The ATM does not take international cards.

★Parque Nacional Lauca

The Parque Nacional Lauca, stretching to the border with Bolivia, is one of the most spectacular national parks in Chile. It is 176 km east of Arica and access is easy as the main Arica–La Paz road runs through the park and is paved (see above). The park covers 137,883 ha and includes numerous snowy volcanoes three of which are over 6000 m. The altitude of the park varies from 3200 m to 6340 m, so beware of *soroche* unless you are coming from Bolivia. The park contains over 120 species of bird, resident or migrant, as well as camelids, vizcacha and puma.

Exploring the park **Parinacota** (4392 m), a small village of whitewashed adobe houses, lies 26 km into the park and 41 km from Putre, at the foot of Volcán Parinacota and its twin, Pomerape (known

Essential Parque Nacional Lauca

Getting there

One-day tours are offered by most tour operators and some hotels in Arica, daily in season, according to demand at other times, but bear in mind that you will spend all day in a cramped and dusty minibus (0730-2030) and you will almost certainly suffer from *soroche*. You can leave the tour and continue another day as long as you ensure that the company will collect you when you want (tour companies try to charge double for this). Much better are three-day, two-night tours, such as with Latinorizons (http://latinorizons.com), which include a stop on the ascent at the Aymara village of Socoroma and two nights in Putre. For five or more, the most economical proposition is to hire a vehicle. However, note that during the rainy season (January-February), roads in the park may be impassable; check in advance with CONAF in Arica (see below). A map of the park is available from Sernatur in Arica or from the Instituto Geográfico Militar in Santiago. If driving off the main road, 4WD is necessary.

When to go

The rainy season is in January and February, but it can be foggy as well as wet until March. August-November is the best season for mountain climbing. Permits are needed for summits near borders; either go to the governor's office in Putre, or contact **Dirección Nacional de Fronteras y Límites del Estado** (DIFROL) Teatinos, p 7, Santiago, T2-2827 5900, also in Putre (best to get permission in Santiago), www.difrol.cl, in advance, listing the mountains you wish to climb. Snowfall can limit travel and activities in August.

What to take

Buy all food for the park in Putre. Other than a small shop with limited supplies in Parinacota, no food is available inside the park. Take drinking water with you as water in the park is not safe. If driving, make sure you have spare fuel and antifreeze.

collectively in Bolivia as Payachatas). From the village an unpaved road runs north to the Bolivian border at Visviri (see above). There is an interesting 17th-century church in Parinacota, rebuilt in 1789, with 18th-century frescoes and the skulls of past priests (ask at the stalls outside the church for Señor Hugo Morales who holds the key, donations appreciated). The stalls sell local weavings of wildlife scenes and alpaca sweaters. The **CONAF** office, which administers the national park, has a visitor centre here (open 0830-1735). Ask at the office about ascents of Guane Guane (5097 m), which can be done in two to three hours from Parinacota. Another walk of about one hour leads from the village to the Lagunas de Cotacotani, a series of lakes among a jumble of rocks, with black lava flows visible above. **Lago Chungará** (7 km by 3 km) is 20 km southeast of Parinacota. This is the largest lake in the Chilean altiplano and is one of the highest in the world at 4517 m. It is a must for its views of the Parinacota, Sajama and Guallatire volcanoes and for its varied wildlife. At the far end of the lake is the Chile–Bolivia border (see above).

☆South of Lauca

South of Lauca is the beautiful **Reserva Nacional Las Vicuñas** ① *administration at Guallatiri, T58-258 5704, luis.araya@conaf.cl, www.conaf.cl/parques/reserva-nacional-las-vicunas; turn off the Arica–La Paz road onto the A147, 2 km after Las Cuevas.* The reserve covers 209,131 ha of altiplano at altitudes of 4300-6060 m. Many beautiful vicuñas can be seen, as well as condors, rheas and other birds. The road to the CONAF administration at Guallatire continues south into the **Monumento Natural Salar de Surire**. The *salar*, also at 4300 m, is a drying salt lake of 17,500 ha. It has a year-round population of 12,000-15,000 flamingos (Chilean, Andean and James). Administration is in **Surire**, 48 km south of Guallatiri and 129 km south of Putre. A normal car can reach Surire in the dry season, but a high-clearance vehicle is essential for all other roads and, in the summer wet season (January to March, also August) a 4WD vehicle is required: take extra fuel. In the wet, roads may be impassable. There is no public transport to these wildlife reserves, but tours can be arranged in Putre or Arica. See Footprint's *Chile Handbook*, or ask tour operators such as **Latinorizons** about routes through these parks from Arica to San Pedro de Atacama. Also check with CONAF in Arica about road conditions and whether the parks are closed at any time.

Listings Arica and the altiplano *map p752*

Tourist information

Arica

CONAF
Av Vicuña MacKenna 820, T58-220 1225, aricayparinacota.oirs@conaf.cl. Mon-Thu 0830-1735, Fri 0830-1610 (take Colectivo 1, 4, 7, 8). There are also CONAF offices in Putre and Parinacota.

Sernatur
San Marcos 101, T58-223 3993, infoarica@sernatur.cl. Mon-Fri 0900-1800, Sat 1000-1400. Very helpful, English spoken, list of accommodation and restaurants. Municipal office at Chacabuco 320, Ed Parque Colón, of 52, T58-238 6527, www.arica.travel; see also www.muniarica.cl.

Putre

The **tourist office** on the main plaza is helpful, some English spoken, organizes tours, Mon-Thu 0830-1300, 1400-1745, Fri 0800-1300, 1400-1545. Also in town is the **CONAF** subadministration office (Teniente del Campo 301, T58-258 5704, Mon-Thu 0830-1735, Fri 0830-1610).

Where to stay

Arica

For apartment rental on the beach, see local newspapers.

$$$$ Arica
San Martín 599, about 2 km along shore (frequent micros and colectivos), T58-225 4540, www.panamericanahoteles.cl. 4-star, best, price depends on season, decent restaurant, tennis court, pool, lava beach (not safe for swimming).

$$$ Americano
General Lagos 571, T58-225 7752, www.hotelamericano.cl.

Airy, spacious rooms, pleasant patio, rooms on upper floor have views to the Morro. Gym and sauna (extra charge).

$$ Hostal Jardín del Sol
Sotomayor 848, T58-223 2795,
www.hostaljardindelsol.cl.
Comfortable, beds with duvets, good value, bike hire. Large kitchen area (US$1 charge).

$$ Oasis
Av Las Du nas esq Ponderosa, lote 1, T9-5113 4631 or 9-9363 7213, www.oasisarica.cl.
North of town, 300 m from Río Lluta bird sanctuary, close to the beach, minimum 2 nights' stay, comfortable, spacious rooms, good for weekly or longer stays, ideal for RV campers, kitchen and laundry facilities, Wi-Fi.

$$ Sunny Days
Tomás Aravena 161 (a little over halfway along P de Valdivia, 800 m from bus terminal, transport to hotel), T58-224 1038,
www.sunny-days-arica.cl.
Run by a New Zealander and his Chilean wife. Rooms with shared or private bath, English spoken, cosy atmosphere, lots of info, book exchange, bike rental. Convenient for the beach. One of the best hostels in the north of Chile.

$$-$ Residencial América
Sotomayor 430, T58-225 4148,
www.residencialamerica.com.
Variety of room sizes, shared or private bath, hospitable, good value.

$$-$ Surf House
O'Higgins 661, T58-231 2213, see Facebook.
Surfers' hostel (the owner also runs a surf school), decent beds and showers, large common areas. Bike rental and tours, also good café. Recommended.

$ Hostal Pacífico
Gen Lagos 672, T58-225 1616,
hostalpacificos672@hotmail.com.
Good option in the city centre, singles with private or shared bath.

Putre

$$ Kukulí
Baquedano 301 y Canto, T9-9161 4709,
www.translapaloma.cl.
10 decent rooms with bath, in town.

$$ La Chakana
Cochrane s/n, T9-9745 9519,
www.la-chakana.com.

Cabins on the edge of town sleep up to 4, private bath, with pleasant views, good breakfast, lots of hiking and mountaineering info, tours, involved with social projects, Aymara museum on site. A good choice.

$$ Terrace Lodge & Tours
Circunvalación 25, T58-258 4275,
www.terracelodge.com.
Small lodge with café, 5 rooms, heating, Wi-Fi, comfortable, helpful owner, Flavio, runs excellent tours by car, pick-up from Arica can be arranged, accepts credit cards.

$$-$ Hostal Cali
Baquedano 399, T9-8536 1242.
Private or shared bath, pleasant, no heating, warm water, good restaurant, supermarket.

$$-$ Parinacota Trek
Baquedano 501, T9-9282 6195,
www.parinacotatrek.cl.
Hostel rooms and dorm, private or shared bath, washing machine, parking, open all year, near La Paloma and Gutiérrez buses. Also has travel agency for tours and treks throughout the region.

$$-$ Residencial La Paloma
O'Higgins 353, T9-9197 9319,
www.translapaloma.cl.
Some rooms with bath, hot showers after 0800 unless requested, no heating but lots of blankets, good food in large, warm restaurant, indoor parking; supermarket opposite. Also runs buses – see Transport, below.

Parque Nacional Lauca
You can camp behind the CONAF office in Parinacota for free, great site, or accommodation is available with various families; ask at food and *artesanía* stands.

$ Hostal Uta Kala
Parinacota, T9 8895 3373,
leonel_parinacota@hotmail.com.
Private rooms, bar, Wi-Fi, hot water and food.

South of Lauca
Neither of the park administration offices in Guallatiri (see above), or Surire have lodging. They may be able to offer help in an emergency.

$ Sra Olga Sánchez Calle
Guallatiri, T9-8784 4017,
olgasanchezcalle@gmail.com.
Overnight accommodation in 6 rooms. Food available.

Restaurants

Arica

Many good places on 21 de Mayo offering meals, drinks, real coffee, juices and outdoor seating.

$$$ Don Floro
V MacKenna 847, T58-223 1481.
Good seafood, steaks and Peruvian specialities, good service, popular, cosy little place.

$$$ Los Aleros de 21
21 de Mayo 736, T58-225 4641, see Facebook.
One of the city's longest-established restaurants, specializing in southern Chilean cuisine, large portions, lots of pork dishes.

$$$ Maracuyá
San Martín 321, at the northern end of Playa El Laucho south of the centre, T58-222 7600, see Facebook.
Arica's premier restaurant specializing in fish and seafood. Expensive, but worth it. Has a sports bar on the top floor.

$$ Chifa El Mesón
Santa María 1364.
One of several good-value Chinese restaurants in the area. Generous portions and clean kitchen.

$$ El Rey del Marisco
Colón 565, p 2, T58-222 9232, see Facebook.
Seafood specialities. A timeless sort of place, in business for over 30 years, very good.

$$ Lucano
Velásquez 992, T58-247 5233, www.pizzerialucano.cl.
Pizzas, pastas, calzones and salads.

$$ Mata Rangi
On the pier.
Good food in fishy environment, good-value *menú de casa*.

$$-$ Ostión Dorado
Playa Corazones, see Facebook.
A small shack selling fabulous *empanadas* and other super-fresh seafood.

$ Mercado Colón
Maipú y Colón.
Several stalls offering tasty good-value lunches and fresh juices.

$ Zumería
Sotomayor 193, T58-225 1587, see Facebook.
Juice bar and vegetarian café specializing in soups and wraps.

Putre

$ Kuchu Marka
Baquedano 351 between La Paloma supermarket and Hostal Cali.
Popular, good value, specializes in local dishes, including alpaca, as well as vegetarian options.

Bars and clubs

Arica

Mojito
Playa Chinchorro, T58-221 3055, www.mojito.cl.
Popular bar/restaurant specializing in cocktails of the same name. Also does sushi.

Soho
Buenos Aires 209, Playa Chinchorro, T9-8905 1806, www.discosoho.com.
A collection of popular bars and nightclubs all under one banner. Discos open Thu-Sun starting at 2200. Foam parties and all that. See Facebook for specials.

Entertainment

Arica

Teatro Municipal de Arica, *Baquedano 234.*
Wide variety of theatrical and musical events, as well as exhibitions.

Festivals

Arica

End Jan/Feb Con la Fuerza del Sol, a festival of Andean dance and music, a slightly more debauched version of the festival at La Tirana, see Facebook.
Jun Festival of Arica and the national *cueca* dance championships.
7 Jun Anniversary of the Chilean victory in the **Battle of the Morro**, with parties and fireworks.
21 Jun Machaq Mara, 1-night celebration kicking of the beginning of winter.
29 Jun San Pedro, religious service at fishing wharf and boat parades.
1st weekend of Oct Virgen de las Peñas, pilgrimage to the site of the Virgin, some 90 km inland near Livilcar.

Putre

Feb Carnaval, smaller, more intimate version of the classic party, lots of dancing and festivities.

Shopping

Arica

Calle 21 de Mayo is pedestrianized, with many shops, restaurants and internet cafés. There is a small fruit and veg market, with food stalls, on Colón between 18 de Septiembre and Maipú.
Feria Turística Dominical, *Sun market, along Chacabuco between Valásquez and Mackenna.* Mostly bric a brac.
Poblado Artesanal, *Plaza Las Gredas, Hualles 2825 (take bus 2, 3 or 7).* Expensive crafts but especially good for musical instruments, open Tue-Sun 0930-1330, 1530-2000; not always open out of season.

Putre

Buy all food for the park in Putre, which has markets where bottled water, fresh bread, vegetables, meat, cheese and canned foods can be obtained. Fuel (both petrol and diesel) is available from the **Cali** and **Paloma** supermarkets; expect to pay a premium. **Sra Daria Condori's** shop on O'Higgins sells locally made *artesanía* and naturally coloured alpaca wool.

What to do

Arica

Language classes
North Light, *21 de Mayo 483, p 3, T9-8360 0049, see Facebook.* Canadian-run school.

Surfing
There's good surfing at Playa Las Machas (good waves, relatively few people) and Playa Chinchorro, north of the city (good for beginners), and at La Ex Isla Alacrán.
Magic Chile Surf School, *T9-8790 6124, www.surfschool.cl.* For surfing lessons and equipment rental, English spoken, best to call the night before or before 0800.

Swimming
Olympic pool in **Parque Centenario**, usually only allows accredited athletes, but will allow ordinary mortals in summer. Take No 5A bus from 18 de Septiembre. The best beach for swimming is Playa Chinchorro, north of town (bus 24). Buses 7 and 8 run to beaches south of town – the first 2 beaches, La Lisera and El Laucho, are both small and mainly for sunbathing. Playa Brava is popular for sunbathing but not swimming (dangerous currents).

Tour operators
Latinorizons, *Colón 9, T58-225 0007, http://latinorizons.com.* Specializes in tours to Parque Nacional Lauca and the altiplano, small groups in 4WD; also tourist train rides from Arica, bike rental, not cheap, but good. Also run hostel, **Le Petit Clos** (www.lepetitclos.cl).
Parinacota Expeditions, *Héroes del Morro 632, T58-223 3305, www.parinacotaexpediciones.cl.* One of the oldest operators in Arica for altiplano tours.
Raices Andinas, *Héroes del Morro 632, T9-5111 7797, www.raicesandinas.com.* Specializes in altiplano trips, English spoken.
Suma Inti, *Gonzalo Cerda 1366, T058-222 5685, www.sumainti.cl.* Tours to the altiplano.

Putre
Parinacota Trek, *see Where to stay, above.*
Tour Andino, *C Baquedano 340, T9-9011 0702, www.tourandino.com.* Comfortable 4WD tours from 1 to 4 days with Justino Jirón (owner) to Lauca and other areas, excellent, knowledgeable, flexible.

Transport

Arica
Air Airport 18 km north of city at Chacalluta, T58-221 1116. Taxi to town US$18, *colectivo* US$7.50 per person, minibus transfer US$6. Flights to **Santiago**, LATAM and Sky (daily) direct or via Iquique and, less frequently, **Antofagasta**. To **Lima**, LATAM Perúand others from Tacna (Peru), enquire at travel agencies in Arica.

Bus Local buses run from Maipú, US$0.60. Long distance buses leave from 2 adjacent terminals, both northeast of the centre at Av Portales y Santa María, T58-220 2522, many buses and *colectivos* (eg Nos 8, 18, 28) pass (US$0.75), taxi US$3.75; terminal tax US$0.30. All luggage is carefully searched for fruit 30 mins prior to boarding and at 2 stops heading south. Bus company offices at bus terminal: **Pullman**, T58-222 3837; **Tur-Bus**, T58-222 5202.

To **Iquique**, frequent, US$11-18, 5hrs, also collective taxis, several companies, all in the terminal. To **Antofagasta**, US$18-42, 11 hrs. To **Calama**, 8-10 hrs, US$27, Pullman, Tur-Bus and many others throughout the day from 0950 to 2230. To **San Pedro de Atacama**, Tur-Bus 2100 and 2200, 11½ hrs, US$40. To **La Serena**, 23 hrs, US$47-69. To **Santiago**, 30 hrs, a number of companies, from US$63 (most serve meals of a kind, somewhat better on the more expensive services; student discounts available). To **Viña del Mar** and **Valparaíso**, 29 hrs, from US$60.

To Bolivia There are daily buses between Arica and **La Paz**, via the border towns of **Chungará** (Chile) and **Tambo Quemado** (Bolivia), 8-10 hrs: **Norte Bus** at 0930, US$17; **Pullman** at 1000, US$22. If you are going to Putre, these will drop you off 3 km away. **To Peru** *Colectivos* run from the international bus terminal on Diego Portales to **Tacna**, US$25 pp, 1½ hrs. There are many companies and you will be besieged by drivers. For quickest service take a Peruvian *colectivo* heading back to Peru. Give your passport to the *colectivo* office where your papers will be filled; after that, drivers take care of all the paperwork. Also buses from the same terminal, US$2, 2½ hrs. For Arequipa it is best to go to Tacna and catch an onward bus there.

Car hire Europcar, Chacabuco 602, T58-257 8500. Hertz, Baquedano 999, T58-223 1487, and at airport, www.hertz.cl, good service. Several others and at Chacalluta airport.

Taxi Taxis are black and yellow and are scarce; hire a *colectivo* instead, US$4.50. These run on fixed routes within the city limit; they line up on Maipú entre Velásquez y Colón (all are numbered).

Train Station at Máximo Lira, by the port. Daily at 0800, 1830, US$5.50, 1½ hrs. Also tourist train to Poconchile in the Valle de Lluta twice monthly.

Putre and Parque Nacional Lauca

Bus La Paloma (Germán Riesco 2071, T58-222 2710, www.translapaloma.cl; bus U from centre) leave Arica for **Putre** daily at 0700, 3-4 hrs, US$6, returning from La Paloma supermarket 1400 (book in advance – beware overcharging, overworked drivers); also Gutiérrez (Esteban Ríos 2140, Arica, T58-222 9338), Mon, Wed, Fri 0700, return same days. If you take an Arica–La Paz bus for Putre, it is a 3-km walk from the crossroads to the town at some 4000 m, tough if you've come straight up from sea level. Hostal Cali runs buses to Bolivia. Bus to **La Paz** from Putre crossroads or Lago Chungará can be arranged in Arica (same fare as from Arica).

Hitchhiking Trucks from Arica to La Paz sometimes give lifts, a good place to try is at the Poconchile control point, 37 km from Arica, but to get to this point can cost more than taking a direct bus from the terminal. Hitching back to Arica is not difficult, with lots of *carabineros* coming and going; you may also be able to bargain your way on to one of the tour buses.

Central Valley

★One of the world's most fecund and beautiful landscapes, with the snow-clad peaks of the Andes to the east and the Cordillera de la Costa to the west, the Central Valley contains most of Chile's population. A region of small towns, farms and vineyards, it has several protected areas of natural beauty. Five major rivers cross the Central Valley, cutting through the Coastal Range to the Pacific: from north to south these are the Rapel, Mataquito, Maule, Itata and Biobío. Some of the river valleys provide ideal conditions for growing grapes and making wine. As this is the heart of Chilean cowboy country, you can see displays of horsemanship at rural shows. It is also a region plagued by earthquakes, most recently in 2010.

Rancagua to Chillán

vineyards and rodeos, trekking and thermal springs

Rancagua *Colour map 8, B1.*

The capital of VI Región (Libertador Gen Bernardo O'Higgins) lies on the Río Cachapoal, 82 km south of Santiago. Founded in 1743, it is a service and market centre. At the heart of the city are an attractive tree-lined plaza, the Plaza de los Héroes, and several streets of single-storey colonial-style houses. In the centre of the plaza is an equestrian statue of O'Higgins. The main commercial area lies along Avenida Independencia, which runs west from the plaza towards the bus and rail terminals. The **Museo Regional** ① *Estado 685, T72-222 1524, www.museorancagua.cl, Tue-Thu 1000-1800, Fri 1000-1700, Sat-Sun 0900-1300, free,* has collections on regional history and culture and temporary exhibitions. The **National Rodeo Championships** are held at the end of March in the Complejo Deportivo, north of the centre (plenty of opportunities for purchasing cowboy items).

☆Wineries near Rancagua

The Cachapoal wine-producing zone lies just south of Rancagua, with most wineries east of the highway. Continue on the highway to **San Fernando** (51 km south of Rancagua), from where a road heads west into the Colchagua Valley, another very successful wine-producing zone centred around Santa Cruz. For details of vineyards, hotels, tours and festivals, visit the Santa Cruz office of the **Ruta del Vino** ① *Plaza de Armas 298, T72-282 3199, www.rutadelvino.cl.* Also in town is a **Museo de Colchagua** ① *Av Errázuriz 145, T72-282 1050, www.museocolchagua.cl, daily 1000-1800 (till 1900 in summer), US$11.* See also Curicó, below.

☆Pichilemu

On the coast, 126 km west of San Fernando, is Pichilemu (TranSantin buses from Santiago US$12). The town is on two levels, one at sea level and the main town above. In summer it is a popular destination for Chileans; for the rest of the year, there is a steady flow of foreigners who come to enjoy some of the best surf in South America. Nightlife is good, too. There is a small museum, the **Museo del Niño Rural de Ciruelos**, a few kilometres south of town, with three rooms of interesting exhibits from the pre-Hispanic cultures of the region. The former train station, made of wood in 1925, is a national monument and now home to the **tourist office** ① *T72-284 2700, monicacornejoturismo@gmail.com; there is another tourism office in the municipal building, Angel 365 p 1, Mon-Fri 0800-1300,*

Best for
Rodeos ■ Trekking ■ Wine

1400-1720. The tourism pages of the online newspaper www.pichilemunews.cl are informative; see also www.pichilemu.cl and www.depichilemu.cl for lodgings.

Curicó *Colour map 8, B1.*

Between the Río Lontué and Río Teno, 192 km from Santiago, Curicó is the only town of any size in the Mataquito Valley. It was founded in 1744. Most of the historic centre was destroyed in the 2010 earthquake, but has been restored. Overlooking the city, the surrounding countryside and with views to the distant Andean peaks is Cerro Condell (100 m); it is an easy climb to the summit from where there are a number of walks. Close to Curicó is one of the largest bodegas in Chile, **Miguel Torres** ① *5 km south of the city, T75-256 4121, www.migueltorres.cl, daily 1000-1700, tours in English and Spanish Mon-Fri only; getting there: take a bus for Molina from the local terminal or outside the railway station and get off at Km 195 on the Pan-American Highway.* For information on the vineyards of Curicó, see the **Ruta del Vino del Valle de Curicó** ① *Prat 301-A, Curicó, T75-232 8972, www.rutadelvinocurico.cl, Mon-Fri 0900-1400, 1530-1930.* In mid-March is the **Fiesta de la Vendimia** with displays on traditional wine-making.

Parque Nacional Radal Siete Tazas
Entry US$11.

The park is in two parts, one at Radal, 65 km east of Curicó, the other at Parque Inglés, 9 km further east. At Radal, the Río Claro flows through a series of seven rock cups (*siete tazas*) each with a pool emptying into the next by a waterfall. The river goes through a canyon, 15 m deep but only 1.5 m wide, ending abruptly in a cliff and a beautiful waterfall. There is excellent trekking in the park, through beautiful woods and scenery, similar to what can be found further south, but with a better climate.

Talca *Colour map 8, B1.*

At 56 km south of Curicó (258 km from Santiago), this is the most important city between Santiago and Concepción. It is a major manufacturing centre and the capital of VII Región (Maule), another wine-producing region; for information contact the **Ruta del Vino** ① *T9-9744 5058, www.valledelmaule.cl.* Founded in 1692, Talca was destroyed by earthquakes in 1742 and 1928 and was again heavily damaged in February 2010. The colonial mansion in which Bernardo O'Higgins lived as a child, **Museo O'Higginiano** ① *1 Norte 875, T71-261 5884, www.museodetalca.cl, closed for restoration in 2017,* was later the headquarters of O'Higgins' Patriot Government in 1813-1814, before his defeat at Rancagua. In 1818 O'Higgins signed the declaration of Chilean independence here. **Paseo peatonal** ① *C 1 Sur entre 3 y 6 Oriente,* is a nice place for a stroll, with handicrafts, cafés, bookstalls and shops.

Constitución

A daily train makes the lovely 3¼-hour journey beside the Río Maule from Talca to Constitución on the coast, with halts at villages. (By road, the town is 89 km west of San Javier, a town on the Pan-American Highway south of Talca.) Constitución is an important port and seaside resort. The town and coast were almost completely destroyed in 2010, but the seafront has since been remodelled with restaurants open all year. Boats trips can be taken on the Río Maule, five blocks from the Plaza.

☆Reserva Nacional Altos deLircay
Entrance 2 km from Alto Vilches bus stop, www.vilchesalto.weebly.com (for tourism and accommodation information), park entry US$11.

This reserve covers 12,163 ha and includes the volcanoes **Quizapú** (3050 m) and **Descabezado** (3850 m), both of which can be climbed from **Vilches**, southeast of Talca. There are well-signed trails and horses can be hired in Alto Vilches. Near the entrance is CONAF administration with full information on trails and activities. Two stand-out treks are to Enladrillado (10 km), a mysterious 800 m by 60 m rock platform, subject to many theories including UFO landings, with fabulous views of Descabezado and Cerro Azul. A further 1.5 km is Laguna del Alto; allow eight to 10 hours to the lake and back. A second walk goes to Mirador del Venado from where you can descend to the river and the lovely Valle del Venado. From here you can continue to Descabezado Grande and Quizapú (five to six days overall).

Southeast to the border

From Talca, the international route to the border goes through San Clemente and up the broad valley of the Río Maule to reach the Argentine border at Paso Pehuenche (2553 m). Off this road, beyond the turning to Vilches (see above) and the town of Armerillo, is the private **Parque Natural y Refugio Tricahue** ① *see Facebook, US$3; bus Talca–Armerillo, US$2, 6 daily*. A Belgian/Chilean enterprise, the park is open all year for trekking, with snowshoes in winter, cycling and fishing. The beautiful **refugio** ($$-$, www.refugio-tricahue.cl) has cabins, sauna, pool, bicycle hire and kitchen (take your own food – no meals, or walk 500 m to El Fosforito).

An alternative route, south of Talca, is paved for the first 65 km, running southeast from the Panamericana along **Lago Colbún**. At the western end of the lake is the town of Colbún, from where a road goes back to Linares on the Panamericana. There are thermal springs 5 km south of Colbún at Panimávida and 12 km south

> **Tip...**
> While in Panimávida, try the local *bebida Panimávida*, made from spring water, sparkling or still, flavoured with lemon or raspberry.

at Quinamávida. The road southeast from Lago Colbún to the border is poor and unpaved.

Border with Argentina: Paso Pehuenche Chilean customs is at La Mina, 106 km from Talca, 60 km from the border. On the Argentine side the road continues to Malargüe and San Rafael. The border is open 0900-1900 for those heading into Argentina and until 2000 for those entering Chile.

Chillán *Colour map 8, B1.*

Chillán, 150 km south of Talca, is capital of Ñuble province. Following an earthquake in 1833, the site was moved slightly to the northwest, though the older site, Chillán Viejo, is still occupied. Further earthquakes in 1939, 1960 and 2010, ensured that few old buildings have survived. Chillán was the birthplace of Bernardo O'Higgins and of the world-famous pianist Claudio Arrau who is remembered at an interactive **museum** ① *Arrau 558, T42-243 3490, www.museoarrau.cl, Tue-Fri 0830-1330, 1500-1930, Sat 1000-1300, 1600-1900, Sun 1000-1300, free*. The centre of the city is **Plaza O'Higgins**, on which stands the modern **Cathedral** designed to resist earthquakes. **San Francisco** church, three blocks northeast, has a museum of religious and historical artefacts (museum closed indefinitely, but the church is open). Above the main entrance is a mural by Luis Guzmán Molina, a local artist, an interpretation of the life of San Francisco in a Chilean context. Northwest of Plaza O'Higgins, on the Plaza Héroes de Iquique, is the **Escuela México** ① *Mon-Fri 0830-1800*. It was donated to the city after the 1939 earthquake. In its library are murals by the great Mexican artists David Alvaro Siqueiros and Xavier Guerrero which present allegories of Chilean and Mexican history. The **Mercado y Feria Municipal** (covered and open markets) at Riquelme y Maipón sell regional arts and crafts, including from the nearby village of Quinchamalí. They also have many cheap, good restaurants, serving regional dishes; open daily, Sunday until 1300. Three blocks further south is the **Museo Naval El Chinchorro** ① *Collin y I Riquelme, Mon-Fri 0930-1200*, containing naval artefacts and models of Chilean vessels. In Chillán Viejo (southwest of the centre) there is a monument, art gallery and park at **O'Higgins' birthplace**.

☆Termas de Chillán
Ruta N-55 Km 80, www.nevadosdechillan.com, US$15.60.

East of Chillán a good road (paved for the first 50 km) runs for 82 km into the Cordillera. At 1850 m are thermal baths and, above, the largest ski resort in southern Chile. There are two open-air thermal pools, a hotel (T42-220 6124) and a health spa (T42-220 6127) with jacuzzis, sauna, mud baths, etc. Summer activities include horse riding, trekking, canyoning, canopy zip-lines, golf and mountain biking. Suitable for families and beginners and cheaper than centres nearer Santiago, the ski resort has 32 runs (the longest is 13 km), 11 lifts, snowboarding and other activities.

Tourist information

Rancagua

Tourist office (Germán Riesco 350, T72-222 7261, inforancagua@sernatur.cl, Mon-Thu 0900-1400, 1500-1800, Fri 0900-1300, 1400-1700, some English spoken).

Talca

Tourist office (C 1 Oriente 1150 p 1, T71-223 3669, infomaule@sernatur.cl, Mon-Thu 0830-1730, Fri 0830-1630, Sat 1000-1300 in summer). See also www.talca.cl. **CONAF** (C4 Norte 1673, T71-220 9517, maule.oirs@conaf.cl).

Curicó

Municipal tourist office (Velasco 449, Mon-Fri 0700-1700), and a helpful tourist kiosk on the Plaza de Armas, Mon-Fri 1000-1700.

Chillán

Sernatur (18 de Septiembre 455, T42-222 3272, Mon-Fri 0830-1800, Sat 1000-1400. See www. municipalidadchillan.cl). The **Fiesta de la Vendimia** is an annual wine festival held in the 3rd week in March.

Where to stay

Rancagua

$$$ Aguila Real
Brasil 1045, T72-222 2047, www. hotelaguilareal.jimdo.com.
Modern 3-star, with restaurant.
Some English spoken.

$$$ Mar Andino
Bulnes 370, T72-264 5400, www.hotelmarandino.cl.
Modern, comfortable, decent restaurant, business centre, pool.

$$ Hostal El Parrón
San Martín 135, T9-9703 6907, www.hostalelparron.cl.
2-storey art-deco-style house in the centre, singles, doubles, triples, parking, patio.

$ Alojamientos Angélica
Ibieta 281, T9 9477 6498, see Facebook.
Angélica gives a warm welcome in this old colonial home, central, best budget choice.

Wineries near Rancagua

$$$$ Hacienda Los Lingues
Panamericana Sur, Km 124.5, 22 km north of San Fernando (1 hr 25 mins from Santiago), T72-297 7080, www.loslingues.com.
This hacienda, with its roots in the colonial period and a national historic site, offers luxury accommodation, fine dining, its own line of wines, an organic garden, horse breeding and outdoor activities such as riding and mountain biking; swimming pool Nov-Mar. Day tours (US$75) and other excursions can be arranged.

Pichilemu

There are dozens of places to stay and several campsites, starting at US$7 per pitch.

$$$$ Alaia
Camino a Punta de Lobos 681, T9-5701 5971, www.hotelalaia.com.
Boutique surfers' lodge, with single, double and triple rooms, surf classes, SUP, mountain biking and other activities, hot tub, restaurant.

$$$-$$ Asthur
Ortúzar 540, T9-9599 7991, www.hotelasthur.cl.
Traditional hotel dating from the 1930s but redesigned since then. Small comfortable rooms, the best of which back on to the terrace with extensive views to the north. There is a pleasant bar/breakfast area where meals are served in summer and an unheated pool outside. Recommended.

$$-$ The Sirena Insolente
Camino Punta de Lobos 169, T9-5856 5784, www.sirenainsolentehostel.cl.
In same group as **The Princessa Insolente** in Santiago and Pucón, private and shared rooms, surf and wetsuit rental, lessons, bike rental, Spanish classes at **Pichilemu Institute of Language Studies** (Aníbal Pinto 21, T72-284 2449), BBQ area and all-you-can-eat pizza on Thu, fast Wi-Fi, 5 mins from beach. Recommended.

$$$-$ Surf Hostal
Eugenio Díaz Lira 167, Playa Infernillo, T907-492 6848, www.surfhostal.com.
Cheaper on weekdays and in low season (Apr-Nov), $ per person in shared rooms, comfortable rooms, some with sea view. Dutch-owned. Good surfing information.

Curicó

$$ Residencia Vichuquén
Merced 575, T75 231 6648,
www.residenciavichuquen.cl
Colonial home in the centre, beautiful
courtyard and a/c in rooms. Full board available.
Recommended.

$$-$ Residencial Colonial
Rodríguez 461, T75-231 4103.
Welcoming, some rooms with bath, patio.
Full board available. Good value.

Parque Nacional Radal Siete Tazas

$$ Hostería Flor de la Canela
Parque Inglés, Km 9 al interior de El Radal,
T75-249 1613. Open all year.
Breakfast extra, good food, good value.

Camping

$$$-$ Valle de las Catas
Camino Radal-Parque Inglés (Fundo Frutillar),
T9-9168 7820.
Cabins for 4-6 people or camping, hot showers,
good service, convenient.

$ Los Robles
Parque Inglés, Km 7 al interior de El Radal,
T75-222 8029. Open all year.
Toilets, hot showers, tables and benches, good.

Talca

$$$ Terrabella
1 Sur 641, T71-222 6555.
Good service, cafetería and swimming pool.

$$$-$ Casa Chueca
Camino Las Rastras, 4 km from Talca by the
Río Lircay, T71-197 0096, T9-9419 0625,
www.trekkingchile.com. Closed Jun-Aug.
Phone *hostal* from bus terminal for directions
on how to get there. From suites to rooms with
shared bath. Vegetarian restaurant, Austrian and
German owners, many languages spoken, lovely
setting, pool, mountain bikes, good trekking,
riding and climbing tours.

$$ Hostal del Puente
1 Sur 407, T71-222 0930, www.hostaldelpuente.cl.
Family-owned, parking in central courtyard,
lovely gardens, English spoken, pleasant
atmosphere and surroundings.

$$ Hostal del Río
1 Sur 411, T71-251 0218, www.hostaldelrio.cl.
Rival to **Del Puente** next door, a bit cheaper, good.

Constitución

$$$ Casa Pucllana
Los Hibiscos 1855, Villa Copihue, T71-267 3393,
www.casapucllana.com.
Sea view, perched above the Piedra de la Iglesia,
modern rooms, parking.

$$$ Las Azucenas
Enrique Donn 910, T71-267 1933,
www.lasazucenashotel.com.
Colonial style, 6 well-equipped and spacious
rooms. Local cuisine and wines offered.

Reserva Altos de Lircay

$$ Refugio Galo
Vilches Altos, T71-251 9553,
Facebook: Refugio-de-Galo.
Open all year for food and lodging, warm
welcome, good service, can organize horse riding.

$$-$ pp Refugio Biotamaule
T9-9609 3644, www.biotamaule.blogspot.co.uk.
Summer only.
Meals available.

Camping

Antahuaras
500 m from the reserve administration, at 1300 m.
Hot showers, water, good services, light at each
site, beautiful location, US$17 for up to 4 people.

Chillán

$$$ Gran Hotel Isabel Riquelme
Arauco 600 y Constitución, T42-243 4400,
www.hotelisabelriquelme.cl.
Central business hotel, with restaurant, parking.

$$$-$$ Libertador
Libertad 85, T42-222 3255, www.hlbo.cl.
Quite spacious rooms, parking.

$$$-$$ Ventura
O'Higgins 638, T42-222 7588,
www.hotelventura.cl.
3 star, pleasant garden, good home cooked food
in restaurant.

$ Residencial Sonia
Itata 288, T42-221 4879,
soniaitata288@yahoo.com.
Hospedaje in a pleasant multi-storey home. Full
board available. Great value, friendly owners.

Termas de Chillán
There are many *cabañas* in Las Trancas, usually
$$$ pp for up to 6, see www.vallelastrancas.cl.

\$\$\$ Cabañas La Piedra
Los Coigües 1143, Km 48 on road to
Termas de Chillán, Recinto, T9-9673 4250,
www.cabanaslapiedra.cl.
5 cabañas sleep 2, 4, 8 or 10, nestled in forest, "tranquil and rejuvenating", pool, hiking trips to the mountains, music performances outdoors around the pool under stars, good restaurants close by. Manager Jacqueline van Nunen speaks English, German, Dutch, Spanish.

\$\$\$ Robledal
At Las Trancas on the road to the Termas, Km 72 from Chillán, T42-2835235, www.hotelrobledal.cl.
Pleasant rooms, bar, restaurant, sauna and jacuzzi, tours offered.

\$\$\$-\$\$ MI Lodge
T9-9321 7567, www.misnowchile.com.
Small lodge with fine views, hot tub and good restaurant. Price depends on season.

Restaurants

Rancagua

\$\$-\$ Schopdog
Independencia 529, www.schopdog.cl.
Chilean burger-and-beer chain. Nothing exceptional, but it's central and open later than most restaurants.

Curicó

Tortas Montero
Prat 659, www.tortasmontero.cl.
Salón de té, restaurant and manufacturer of traditional *tortas de manjar* and *dulce de alcayotas*.

Talca
There are cheap local restaurants and fresh food on sale at the **Mercado Municipal**, entrance on C 1 Norte.

\$ Casino de Bomberos
2 Sur y 5 Oriente.
Good value, open every day. It has the **Museo Bomberil Benito Riquelme** attached.

Transport

Rancagua
Bus The terminal for regional buses is at Doctor Salinas 1165, T72-223 6938, just north of the market. Frequent services to **Santiago** from **Tur-Bus** terminal at O'Carroll 1175, T72-224 1117,

US\$2.75, 2 hrs. Main terminal for long-distance buses is at Av O'Higgins 0480, T72-222 5425.

Train Metrotren station on Av Plaza La Marina, T600-585 5000 for tickets. To **Santiago**, US\$3.50, 1¼ hrs.

Curicó
Bus Terminal is on Prat, opposite the train station. Local and long-distance services leave from here. **Tur-Bus** stop and office, M de Velasco, 1 block south, T75-231 2115. **Pullman del Sur** terminal, Henríquez y Carmen. Many southbound buses bypass Curicó, but can be caught by waiting outside town. To **Santiago** US\$8, 2½ hrs, several companies, frequent. To **Talca** every 15 mins, US\$4, 1 hr. To **Temuco**, Alsa and Tur-Bus, US\$35-55, 7 hrs.

Train Station is at the west end of Prat, 4 blocks west of Plaza de Armas, tickets from Maipú 657, T600-585 5000. To/from **Santiago**, daily, 2 hrs 20 mins, US\$8-17.

Parque Nacional Radal Siete Tazas
Access by car is best as the road through the park is paved, but if this is not possible, take a minibus from Curicó Terminal to **Molina**, 26 km south, US\$1; from Molina there's a bus at 1630, return 0630, to **Radal** village, 3 hrs, US\$2, **Buses Hernández**. It's a further 2 km to La Vela de la Novia and 4 km to Siete Tazas. It's 9 km from Radal to Parque Inglés, US\$2.

Talca
Bus Terminal at 12 Oriente and 2 Sur. From **Santiago**, US\$11. To **Chillán**, frequent, US\$8. To **Temuco**, US\$25, 6 hrs. To **Puerto Montt**, US\$51, 8-10½ hrs with Tur-Bus. To **Alto Vilches** (for Altos del Lircay), bus from platform 22, US\$4, at 1030 daily with Interbus.

Train Station is at Av 2 Sur y 11 Oriente, T600-585 5000. Daily to/from **Santiago**, 3 hrs, US\$8-38. Talca-**Constitución** daily 0730, return 1630, 3½ hrs, US\$3.30 one way, preference given to local residents.

Constitución
Bus To **Santiago**, Pullman del Sur, US\$18 (US\$11.50 Mon-Thu).

Chillán
Bus 2 long-distance terminals: Central, Brasil y Constitución (**Tur-Bus, Línea Azul**); Northern, Ecuador y O'Higgins for other companies.

Local buses leave from Maipón y Sgto Aldea. To **Santiago**, 5½ hrs, US$15. To **Concepción**, every 30 mins, 1½ hrs, US$4-6. To **Temuco**, 3½ hrs, US$15.

Train Station, 5 blocks west of Plaza de Armas on Brasil, T600-585 5000. To/from **Santiago**, daily, 5 hrs, US$15-38, www.trencentral.cl. No trains run south of Chillán.

Termas de Chillán

Bus service daily 0750, 1320, with **Rem Bus**, Maipón 890, of 15, T42-222 9377, return 0930, 1620, US$6 return, book in advance. Direct bus from **Santiago** with **Nilahue** (Porto Seguro 4420, Santiago, T2-2776 1139, www.busesnilahue.cl, in Chillán T42-270569), daily at 1450, returns from Chillán at 0900. At busy periods hitching may be possible from Chillán Ski Centre.

Concepción and around   *Colour map 8, B1.*

industrial centre at the mouth of the Biobío river

The third biggest city in Chile, with a population of nearly 250,000, Concepción, 516 km from Santiago, is capital of VIII Región (Biobío) and is the most important city and industrial centre in southern Chile. Founded in 1550, Concepción became a frontier stronghold in the war against the Mapuche after 1600. Destroyed by an earthquake in 1751, it was moved to its present site on the river Biobío in 1764. It was severely damaged again by the 2010 earthquake. The climate is very agreeable in summer, but from April to September the rains are heavy; the annual average rainfall, nearly all of which falls in those six months, is from 1250 mm to 1500 mm.

Sights

In the centre of the city is the attractive **Plaza de Armas**, or de la Independencia, location of the **Intendencia** and the **Cathedral**. It was here that Bernardo O'Higgins proclaimed the independence of Chile on 1 January 1818. **Cerro Caracol** can easily be reached on foot starting from the statue of Don Juan Martínez de Rozas in the Parque Ecuador, arriving at the Mirador Chileno after 15 minutes. From here it is another 20 minutes' climb to **Cerro Alemán**. The **Río Biobío** and its valley running down to the sea lie below.

The **Galería de la Historia** ① *Lincoyán y V Lamas by Parque Ecuador, T41-285 3756, www.gh concepcion.cl*, is a depiction of the history of Concepción and the region; upstairs is a collection of Chilean painting. The **Casa del Arte Pinacoteca** ① *Chacabuco y Paicaví, near Plaza Perú, T41-220 3835 (Facebook: Pinacoteca UdeC), Tue-Fri 1000-1800, Sat 1100-1700, Sun 1100-1400, free,* contains the University art collection; the entrance hall is dominated by La Presencia de América Latina, by the Mexican Jorge González Camerena (1965), a mural depicting Latin American history. Free explanations are given by University art students.

The **Parque Museo Pedro del Río Zañartu** ① *16 km from Concepción on the Hualpen peninsula, T41-241 7386, www.parquepedrodelrio.cl, US$5 per car, Tue-Sun 0900-1700, Sat-Sun 1000-1700 in summer, 0900-1700 in winter,* is a house built around 1885 (a National Monument) and its gardens. It contains beautiful pieces from all over the world. The park, a nature sanctuary, also contains Playa Rocoto, at the mouth of the Río Biobío. Take a city bus to Hualpencillo from Freire; ask the driver to let you out then walk 40 minutes, or hitch. Go along Avenida Las Golondrinas to the Enap oil refinery, turn left, then right (it is signed).

Talcahuano

At the neck of Península de Tumbes, Talcahuano has the best harbour in Chile. In the naval base you can visit the great ship **Huáscar** ① *Tue-Sun 0930-1200, 1400-1630, US$1.50 www.huascar.cl,* a relic of the War of the Pacific which miraculously survived the 2010 earthquake. Photography is permitted, but passports must be handed in at the main gate. Along the peninsula is **Parque Tumbes** ① *T41-223 916, free,* with paths leading along the coast. At Caleta Tumbes, 5 km from Talcahuano (take the 10T bus labelled 'Tumbes' from San Martín), the seafood stalls along the waterfront of this lovely fishing village have some of the freshest, best and cheapest mariscos and crab in the country.

Costa del Carbón

South of the Biobío is the Costa del Carbón, until recently the main coal-producing area of Chile, linked with Concepción by road and two bridges over the Biobío. **Lota**, 42 km south of the city, was, until its closure in 1997, the site of the most important **coal mine** in Chile. The **Parque de Lota Isidora Cousiño**, covering 14 ha on a promontory to the west of the town, was the life's work of Isidora Goyenechea de Cousiño, whose family owned the mine, and is now a national monument. Laid out by an English landscape architect in 1862-1872, it contains plants from all over the world, ornaments imported from Europe, romantic paths and shady nooks overlooking the sea, and peafowl and pheasants roaming freely. South of Lota the road runs past the seaside resort of **Laraquete** where there are miles of golden sand, very popular in summer.

Cañete to Contulmo *Colour map 8, C1.*

Cañete, 130 km south of Concepción, is on the site of Fort Tucapel where Pedro de Valdivia and 50 of his men were killed by Mapuche warriors in 1553. **Museo Mapuche Juan Antonio Ríos** ① *1 km south on the road to Contulmo, T41-261 1093, www.museomapuchecanete.cl, Jan-Feb Mon-Fri 0930-1730, Sat 1100-1730, Sun 1300-1730, rest of year Tue-Fri 0930-1730, Sat-Sun 1300-1730, free,* is housed in a modern building inspired by the traditional Mapuche *ruca*; the displays include Mapuche ceramics and textiles.

A road runs south from Cañete along the north side of **Lago Lanalhue** to Contulmo, a sleepy village at the foot of the Cordillera. It hosts a **Semana Musical** (music week) in January. The wooden Grollmus house and mill are 3 km northwest along the south side of the lake. The house, dating from 1918, has a fine collection of every colour of *copihue* (the national flower) in a splendid garden. The mill, built in 1928, contains the original wooden machinery. From here the track runs a further 9 km north to the **Posada Campesina Alemana**, an old German-style hotel in a fantastic spot at the water's edge. The **Monumento Natural Contulmo** ① *administered by CONAF: Av Pdte Frei 288, Cañete, T41-261 1241, 8 km south, covers 82 ha of native forest.*

Los Angeles and around *Colour map 8, C1.*

On the Pan-American Highway, Los Angeles is 110 km south of Chillán. It is the capital of Biobío province. Founded in 1739 as a fort, it was destroyed several times by the Mapuche. Here, too, severe damage was recorded in February 2010. It has a large Plaza de Armas and a good daily market. Some 25 km north of Los Angeles is the spectacular **Salto El Laja** where the Río Laja plunges 47 m over the rocks. Numerous tour groups stop here and the place is filled with tourist kiosks.

Parque Nacional Laguna de Laja

East of Los Angeles a 93-km road runs past the impressive rapids of the Río Laja to this national park, dominated by the active Antuco volcano (2985 m) and the glacier-covered Sierra Velluda. The Laguna is surrounded by stark scenery of scrub and lava. There are 46 species of birds, including condors and the rare Andean gull. There are several trails. Nearby is the **Club de Esquí de Los Angeles** ① *T43-232 2651, www.skiantuco.cl, season May-Aug,* with two ski-lifts, giving a combined run of 4 km on the Antuco volcano.

Angol *Colour map 8, C1.*

Capital of the Province of Malleco, Angol is reached from Collipulli and Los Angeles. Founded by Valdivia in 1552, it was seven times destroyed by the *indígenas* and rebuilt. The church and convent of **San Beneventura**, northwest of the attractive Plaza de Armas, built in 1863, became the centre for missionary work among the **Mapuche. El Vergel** ① *5 km southeast of Angol, T45-271 2103, www.fundoelvergel.cl, daily 0900-1300, 1430-1800, US$1.50,* founded in 1880 as an experimental fruit-growing nursery, now includes an attractive park and the **Museo Dillman Bullock** ① *Tue-Fri 0900-1300, 1400-1900, Sat-Sun 1300-1900, US$1, 5 km from town, colectivo No 2,* with pre-Columbian indigenous artefacts.

Parque Nacional Nahuelbuta

Visitor centre at Pehuenco, 5 km from the entrance, www.conaf.cl, Spring and summer daily 0800-1300, 1400-2000, US$8 for foreigners (Apr-Oct US$4).

Situated in the coastal mountain range at an altitude of 800-1550 m, this beautiful park covers 6832 ha of forest and offers views over both the sea and the Andes. Although the forest includes many species of trees, the monkey puzzle (araucaria) trees are most striking; some are over 2000 years old, 50 m high and 3 m in diameter. There are also 16 species of orchids as well as pudu deer, Chiloé foxes, pumas, black woodpeckers and parrots. There is a camping near the Visitor Centre (US$17) and many other campsites along the road from El Cruce to the entrance, at Km 20 and Km 21.

Listings Concepción and around

Tourist information

Concepción

Sernatur (Aníbal Pinto 460, T41-274 1337, infobiobio@sernatur.cl, Sun-Mon 0900-1800, Tue-at 0900-1900 in summer, Mon-Fri 0900-1900, at 1000-1400 in winter); **CONAF** (Rengo 345, p 2, T41-262 4062, biobio.oirs@conaf.cl).

Los Angeles and around

Tourist office (Plaza de Armas, T43-220 1500); **CONAF** (J Mansode Velasco 275, T43-232 1086, Mon-Fri 1000-1900, Sat 1000-1800).

Angol

Tourist office (Plaza de Armas, T45-299 0840, www.angolturismo.es.tl, Mon-Fri 0830-1400, 1500-1900, Sat-Sun in summer only 1000-1400, 1600-2000); **CONAF** (Prat 191, p 2, T45-271 1870).

Where to stay

Concepción

$$ Alborada
Barros Arana 457, T41-291 1121,
www.hotelalborada.cl.
Good 4-star with all mod cons,
disabled-friendly, tours offered.

$$ El Dorado
Barros Arana 348, T41-222 9400,
www.hoteleldorado.cl.
Comfortable, spacious rooms,
central, bar, cafeteria, parking.

$$ Hostal Buró
Freire 1565, T41-295 0700.
More of a hotel than hostel, comfortable
rooms with all mod-cons. Great location.
Breakfast extra.

$ Concepción
Serrano 512, T41-262 9000,
www.hotelconcepcion.cl.
Central, comfortable, heating, English spoken.

$$ Hostal Bianca
Salas 643-C, T41-225 2103,
www.hostalbianca.cl.
Private or shared bath, food available, parking.

$$ Maquehue
Barros Arana 786, p 7, T41-221 0261,
www.hotelmaquehue.cl.
Good services, with restaurant, laundry.

$ El Tata
Collao 480, T9-94514496.
Across from the football stadium and a block
from the bus terminal. Run by a lovely and
pious family. Many rooms, clean bathrooms.

Cañete to Contulmo

$$$ Hostal Licahue
4 km north of Contulmo towards Cañete,
T9-8209 4403, www.licahue.cl.
Hotel rooms and cabins, attractively set
overlooking lake, pool.

$$ Nahuelbuta
Villagrán 644, Cañete, T41-261 1593,
www.hotelnahuelbuta.cl.
Private or shared without bath,
pleasant, parking.

$$-$ Héctor Gajardo Lavín
7° de la Línea 817 (1 block from plaza), Cañete.
Shared bath, old fashioned, pleasant rooms.

Camping
Playa Blanca, 10 km north
of Contulmo.

Los Angeles and around

$$$ Salto del Laja
Salto El Laja, T43-232 1706, www.saltodellaja.cl.
Good rooms, fine restaurant, 2 pools, on an island
overlooking the falls.

$$$-$$ El Rincón
Panamericana Sur Km 494 (18 km north of
Los Angeles), exit Perales/El Olivo, 2 km east,
T9-9441 5019, www.elrinconchile.cl.

English/German owners, rooms with private or shared bath. Beautiful, beside a small river, restful, fresh food from organic garden, good base for excursions, English, French, German and Spanish spoken, cash only.

$$$-$$ Muso
Valdivia 222 on the plaza, T43-254 6100, www.hotelmuso.cl
Fun hotel that fancies itself as grand. All rooms have TV and mini-refrigerator. Wi-Fi in lobby only. Central, good value.

$$$-$ Complejo Turístico Los Manantiales
Salto El Laja, T43-231 4275, www.losmanantiales.saltosdellaja.com.
Hotel rooms, cabins and camping. Private or shared bathrooms, even for tents.

Parque Nacional Laguna de Laja

$$-$ Cabañas Lagunillas
T41-232 1086, 2 km from park entrance.
Open all year.
Cabins sleep 6, lovely spot close to the river among pine woods, restaurant, also camping.

There are 2 other *refugios* ($): **Digeder**, 11 km from the park entrance, and **Universidad de Concepción**, both on slopes of Volcán Antuco. For both T41-222 9054, office O'Higgins 740.

Restaurants

Concepción

$$ Casona del Cinzano Penquista
Castellón 881, T9-9572 6140, www.casonadelcinzano.com.
Characterful restaurant, decorated with movie memorabilia and old photos, Chilean food, jazz and blues music.

$ Quick Biss
O'Higgins entre Tucapel y Castellón, T41-222 6458.
Salads, real coffee, good lunches and service.

Shopping

Concepción
The main shopping area, Paseo Peatonal, is north of Plaza de Armas. For **handicrafts**, try **Casa Fiero** (Alessandri L-74).

What to do

Concepción
Hello Chile, *T9-8433 0101, www.hello-chile.com.* For tours of the Biobío region and further afield, Austrian/Chilean-run, Spanish courses, car hire arranged, lots of information.

Transport

Concepción
Air Airport north of the city, off the main road to Talcahuano. In summer flights daily to and from **Santiago** (**LATAM** and **Sky**), fewer in winter connections to **Temuco**, **Puerto Montt** and **Punta Arenas**.

Bus Terminal Collao, www.terminalcollao.cl, for long-distance services (also for **Lota**, **Cañete** and **Contulmo**), is 2 km east, at Tagualda 860, T41-274 9000, next to football and athletics stadium. (Several buses to city centre, US$0.65, taxi US$7-8.) **Tur-Bus, Línea Azul** and **Buses Bío Bío** services leave from Terminal Camilo Henríquez, 2 km northeast of main terminal on J M García, reached by buses from Av Maipú in centre, via Terminal Collao. To **Santiago**, 6½ hrs, US$18-40. To Lota, 1½ hrs, US$2 (many buses bypass the centre; catch them from the main road). To **Los Angeles**, US$4.50-6. To **Loncoche**, 5½ hrs, US$16. To Temuco, US$24, 4 hrs. To **Pucón**, direct in summer only, 7 hrs, US$31. To **Valdivia**, 7 hrs, US$21-41. To **Puerto Montt** several companies, US$36-47, about 9 hrs. Best direct bus to **Chillán** is Línea Azul, 2 hrs, US$6.

Train Station at Prat y Barros Arana, **Bío Tren** ticket office, Av Padre Hurtado 570, T41-286 8015, www.biotren.cl, for suburban services in rush hour.

Cañete to Contulmo
Buses leave from 2 different terminals in Cañete: **J Ewert** and **Inter Sur** from Riquelme y 7° de la Línea; **Jeldres**, **Erbuc** and other companies from the Terminal Municipal, Serrano y Villagrán. To **Santiago**, 9 hrs, US$32-44. To **Concepción**, 3 hrs US$7. To **Angol**, US$7. To Contulmo, frequent, US$3. To **Temuco**, **Erbuc**, US$7.

Los Angeles
Long-distance bus terminal on northeast outskirts of town; local terminal at Villagrán y Rengo in centre, by market. To **Salto de Laja**, every 30 mins with **Pullman**, US$3 To **Santiago**, 6½ hrs,

US$22-41. To **Viña del Mar** and **Valparaíso**, 8 hrs, US$31-52. Every 30 mins to **Concepción**, US$4.50-6, 2 hrs. To **Temuco**, US$8, hourly. To Victoria, where you can change for **Curacautín**, US$8.

Parque Nacional Laguna de Laja
Expreso Volcán Bus from Los Angeles to **Abanico**, 20 km past Antuco (hourly 0630-2100, US$3), then 2 hrs/4 km walk to park entrance (hitching possible). Or bus to **Antuco**, 2 hrs, daily, US$3, then hitch last 24 km. Details from CONAF in Los Angeles.

Angol
Bus to **Santiago** US$28-50, **Los Angeles**, US$4. To **Temuco**, Trans Bío-Bío, frequent, US$8.

Parque Nacional Nahuelbuta
Bus From **Angol** to **Vegas Blancas** (27 km west of Angol) Mon, Wed, Fri (Dec-Mar only) 0700 and 1700, 1½ hrs, US$3, get off at El Cruce, from where it is a steep 7 km walk to park entrance. Transporte Rivant, T9-9940 6423, offers direct services (summer only) US$30 (includes park entrance fee).

Lake District

★The Lake District, stretching southwards from Temuco to Puerto Montt, is one of Chile's most beautiful regions. There are some 12 great lakes of varying sizes, as well as imposing waterfalls and snow-capped volcanoes. There are a number of good bases for exploring. Out of season many facilities are closed; in season (from mid-December to mid-March), prices are higher and it is best to book well in advance, particularly for transport. About 20,000 Mapuches live in the area, particularly around Temuco, and there are possibly 100,000 more Chileans of mixed descent who speak the native tongue, Mapudungun, although nearly all of them are bilingual.

Temuco and around *Colour map 8, C1. See map, page 774.*

vibrant city in the Mapuche heartland

Although at first sight rather grey and imposing, Temuco is a lively university city, 677 km south of Santiago, and is one of the fastest-growing commercial centres in the south. Founded in 1881 after the final treaty with the Mapuches and the arrival of the railway, this city is the capital of IX Región (Araucanía). Temuco is proud of its Mapuche heritage and it is this that gives it a distinctive character, especially around the outdoor market. North and east of the city are five national parks and reserves, notably Conguillío with its araucaria forests, and flora and fauna found nowhere else. It is great for hiking, or touring by car or even mountain bike. There are also various skiing opportunities.

Sights

The centre is the Plaza Aníbal Pinto, around which are the main public buildings including the cathedral and the Municipalidad. Very little of the old city remains; practically every wooden building burned down following the 1960 earthquake.

Tip...
For information on visits to Mapuche settlements, such as Chol Chol, go to the main Sernatur office.

Temuco is the Mapuches' market town and you may see some women in their traditional costumes in the huge produce market, the ☆ **Feria** ① *Lautaro y Pinto*, which is one of the most fascinating markets in Chile. Mapuche textiles, pottery, woodcarving, jewellery and more are also sold inside and around the **municipal market** ① *Aldunate y Diego Portales*, along with fish, meat and dairy produce. **Agrupación de Mujeres Artesanas** ① *Claro Solar 1005 y Aldunate, T45-7790 3676, wanglenzomo@gmail.com, Mon-Fri 1000-1800*, sells many crafts, including textiles made by a Mapuche weavers' co-operative, all with traditional designs. It also offers design classes for traditional dresses.

A couple of kilometres northwest of the centre is the **Museo Regional de la Araucanía** ① *Alemania 084, www.museoregionalaraucania.cl, Tue-Fri 0930-1730, Sat 1100-1700, Sun 1100-1400, free, take bus 1 from the centre*. It is devoted to the history and traditions of the Mapuche nation, with a section on German settlement.

There are views of Temuco from **Cerro Ñielol** ① *T45-229 8222, 0830-2045, US$3*. This park has a fine collection of native plants in their natural state, including the national flower, the *copihue rojo*. This is a good spot for a picnic, with an excellent visitors' centre run by CONAF. A tree marks the spot where peace was made with the Mapuche. Bicycles are only allowed in before 1100. At the top of the hill is a restaurant, which also has dancing (not always open).

Best for
Adventure tourism ■ Scenery ■ Thermal springs ■ Trekking

Lake District

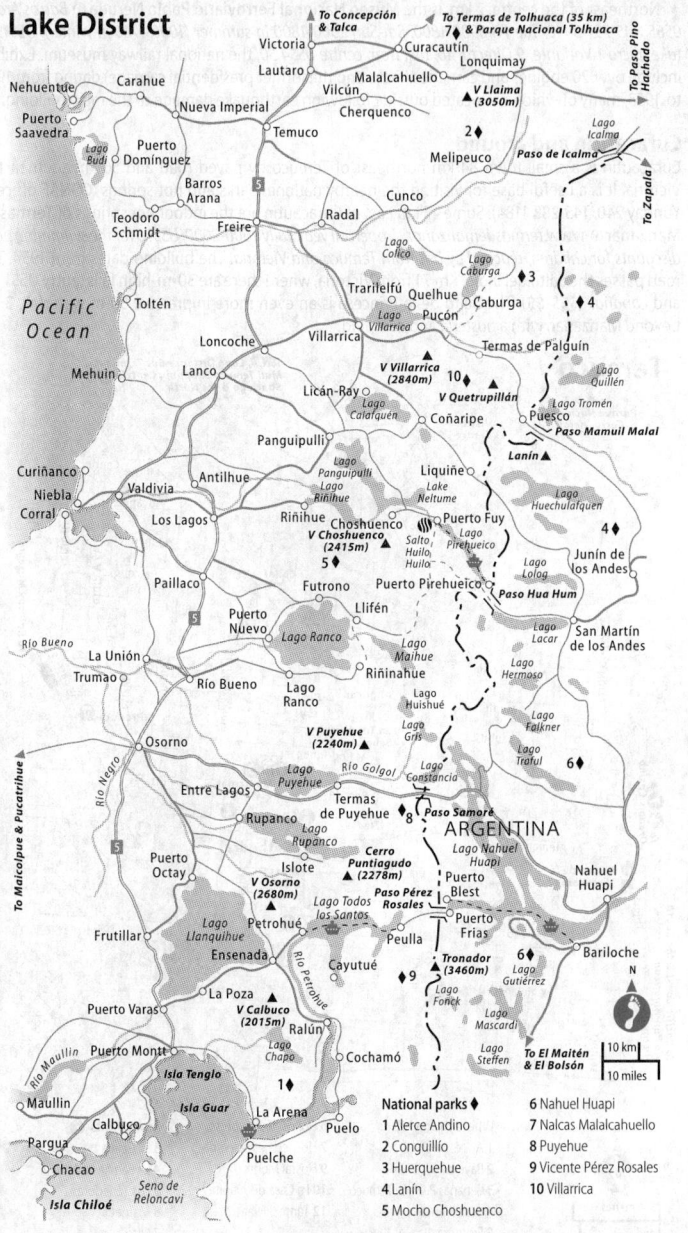

To Concepción & Talca
To Termas de Tolhuaca (35 km) & Parque Nacional Tolhuaca
To Paso Pino Hachado

Victoria
Lautaro
Malalcahuello
Curacautín
Lonquimay

Nehuentue
Carahue
Vilcún
Cherquenco
V Llaima (3050m)
Lago Icalma
To Zapala

Nueva Imperial
Temuco
2♦
Melipeuco
Paso de Icalma

Puerto Saavedra
Lago Budi
Puerto Domínguez
Barros Arana
Teodoro Schmidt
Freire
Radal
Cunco
Lago Colico
Lago Caburga
♦3
♦4

Pacific Ocean

Toltén
Loncoche
Lanco
Villarrica
Trarilelfú
Quelhue
Pucón
Caburga
Lago Villarrica
Termas de Palguín
Lago Quillén

Mehuin
Lican-Ray
Lago Calafquén
Coñaripe
V Villarrica (2840m)
10♦
V Quetrupillán
Lago Tromén
Puesco
Paso Mamuil Malal

Curiñanco
Niebla
Corral
Valdivia
Antilhue
Panguipulli
Lago Panguipulli
Liquiñe
Lake Neltume
Lanín ▲
Lago Huechulafquén
4♦

Los Lagos
Riñihue
Choshuenco
V Choshuenco (2415m)
5♦
Puerto Fuy
Salto Huilo Huilo
Lago Pirehueico
Junín de los Andes

Paillaco
Futrono
Puerto Pirehueico
Lago Lolog
Paso Hua Hum

Puerto Nuevo
Llifén
Lago Maihue
San Martín de los Andes
Lago Lacar

Río Bueno
La Unión
Trumao
Río Bueno
Lago Ranco
Riñinahue
Lago Huishué
Lago Hermoso
Lago Falkner

Osorno
Lago Grís
Lago Traful
6♦

V Puyehue (2240m) ▲
Río Golgol
Lago Constancia

To Maicolpue & Pucatrihue
Río Negro
Entre Lagos
Lago Puyehue
Termas de Puyehue ♦8
Paso Samoré
ARGENTINA
Lago Nahuel Huapi

Rupanco
Lago Rupanco
Puerto Blest

Puerto Octay
Islote
Cerro Puntiagudo (2278m) ▲
Paso Pérez Rosales
Puerto Frias
Nahuel Huapi

Frutillar
V Osorno (2680m) ▲
Lago Todos los Santos
Petrohué
Peulla
Bariloche

Puerto Varas
Ensenada
Río Petrohue
Cayutué
Tronador (3460m)
♦9
Lago Gutiérrez
6♦

La Poza
V Calbuco (2015m) ▲
Ralún
Lago Fonck

Puerto Montt
Lago Llanquihue
Lago Chapo
Cochamó
Lago Mascardi

Maullín
Isla Tenglo
Puerto Varas
La Arena
Lago Steffen
To El Maitén & El Bolsón

Pargua
Calbuco
Isla Guar
Puelo
Puelche

Chacao
Isla Chiloé
Seno de Reloncaví
1♦

National parks ♦
1 Alerce Andino
2 Conguillío
3 Huerquehue
4 Lanín
5 Mocho Choshuenco
6 Nahuel Huapi
7 Nalcas Malalcahuello
8 Puyehue
9 Vicente Pérez Rosales
10 Villarrica

10 km
10 miles
N

Northeast of the centre, 2 km, is the **Museo Nacional Ferroviario Pablo Neruda** ① *Barros Aran[a] 0565, T45-297 3940, Tue-Fri 0900-1800, Sat-Sun 1000-1800 in summer (1000-1700 in winter), US$1.5[0] take micro 1 Variante, 9 Directo, 4b, taxi from centre US$4.50*, the national railway museum. Exhibit[s] include over 20 engines and carriages (including the former presidential carriage) dating from 190[4] to 1953, many of which are located outside following earthquake damage to the main building.

Curacautín and around

Curacautín is a small town 84 km northeast of Temuco by paved road and 56 km southeast o[f] Victoria. It is a useful base for visiting the nearby national parks and hot springs (CONAF office a[t] Yungay 240, T45-288 1184). Some 17 km east of Curacautín are the indoor hot springs of **Termas d[e] Manzanar** ① *www.termasdemanzanar.cl, open all year daily 1000-2000, US$20 for the swimming poo[l] discounts for children, reached by bus from Temuco and Victoria*. The building dates from 1954. Th[e] road passes the Salto del Indio, Km 71 from Victoria, where there are 30-m-high falls (entry US$1.5[0] and *cabañas* ($$$-$$). The Salto de la Princesa is an even more impressive 50-m waterfall, 3 km beyond Manzanar, with a *hostería* and camping.

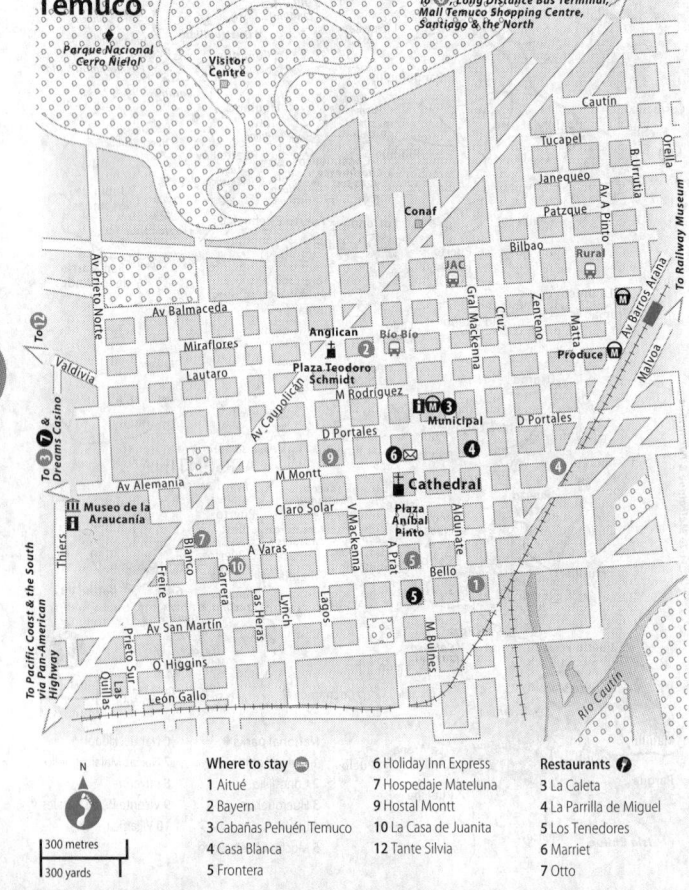

Where to stay		6 Holiday Inn Express	Restaurants
1 Aitué		7 Hospedaje Mateluna	3 La Caleta
2 Bayern		9 Hostal Montt	4 La Parrilla de Miguel
3 Cabañas Pehuén Temuco		10 La Casa de Juanita	5 Los Tenedores
4 Casa Blanca		12 Tante Silvia	6 Marriet
5 Frontera			7 Otto

N

300 metres
300 yards

The beautiful pine-surrounded **Termas Malleco** ① *formerly Tolhuaca, www.termasmalleco.cl, all year, US$19, US$27 with lunch, taxi from Curacautín US$40-50*, are 35 km northeast of Curacautín by unpaved road, or 82 km by rough, unpaved road from just north of Victoria (high clearance 4WD vehicle essential). Just 2 km north of the Termas is the **Parque Nacional Tolhuaca** ① *Dec-Apr, US$5, taxi from Curacautín US$35-40*, including waterfalls, two lakes, superb scenery and good views of volcanoes from Cerro Amarillo. Park administration is near Laguna Malleco, with a campsite nearby. Much of the park, together with the neighbouring Reserva Nacional Malleco, was severely damaged by forest fires in early 2002 and will take several decades fully to recover, but some half-day trails are open.

Reserva Nacional Nalcas Malalcahuello

Northeast of Curacautín, this 31,305 ha park is on the slopes of the **Lonquimay** volcano (2865 m; entry US$3). It is much less crowded than nearby Parque Nacional Conguillío and is one of the best areas for seeing unspoilt araucaria forest. The volcano began erupting on Christmas Day 1988, resulting in a new crater called Navidad. Access to the crater is from Malalcahuello, 15 km south and halfway between Curacautín and Lonquimay town. There is a municipal *refugio* at the foot of the volcano. CONAF has opened several marked trails in the park, from one hour to two days in length. From Malalcahuello it is a one-day hike to the Sierra Nevada mountain, or a two-day hike to Conguillío national park (with equipment and experience, otherwise use a guide). The CONAF office on the main road in Malalcahuello gives information, as does **La Suizandina** hotel, which gives good access to treks and the ascent of the volcano. In winter, the main route from Malalcahuello to Lonquimay town goes through the ex-railway tunnel of **Las Raíces** ① *toll US$0.60*, which was, until recently, the longest tunnel in South America at 4.8 km. Now it's in poor condition, unlit and has constant filtration. It's unwise to go through by bicycle; try to hitch a ride in a pick-up.

Corralco ① *T2-2206 0741, http://corralco.com, season Jun-Oct*, on the southeast side of Volcán Lonquimay, is a high-end resort with four lifts servicing 18 runs that are suitable for beginner, intermediate and advanced skiers. **Centro de Ski Los Arenales** ① *access from Lonquimay town, T45-289 1071, see Facebook, season Jun-Sep*, is at Las Raíces Pass on the road from Malalcahuello to Lonquimay town. It is a pleasant, small resort with a nice restaurant and four lifts that go up to 2500 m with great views.

Border with Argentina: Paso Pino Hachado Paso Pino Hachado (1884 m) can be reached either by paved road, 73 km southeast from Lonquimay, or by unpaved road 129 km east from Melipeuco (see below). On the Argentine side this road continues to Zapala. **Chilean immigration** and customs are in Liucura, 22 km west of the border, open September to mid-May 0800-2000, winter 0800-1900 (www.pasosfronterizos.gov.cl/cf_pinohachado.html). Very thorough searches and two- to three-hour delays reported, especially when entering Chile. Buses from Temuco to Zapala and Neuquén use this crossing (see Transport, page 779).

☆Parque Nacional Conguillío

US$9 in high season, US$4 in low season, discounts for children, visitor centre at the park administration by Lago Conguillío, Mon-Sun 0900-2300, www.conaf.cl.

East of Temuco by 80 km, this is one of the most popular parks in Chile. In the centre is the active 3125-m **Llaima volcano** (eruptions may cause partial closure of the park). There are two large lakes, **Laguna Verde** and **Laguna Conguillío**, and two smaller ones, **Laguna Arco Iris** and **Laguna Captrén**. North of Laguna Conguillío rises the snow-covered **Sierra Nevada**, the highest peak of which

Tip...
Buy supplies in Temuco, Curacautín or Melipeuco, where they are much cheaper than at the shop in the park.

reaches 2554 m. This is one of the best places in Chile to see araucaria forest, which used to cover an extensive area in this part of the country. Other trees include cypresses, lenga and winter's bark (*canelo*). Birdlife includes the condor and the black woodpecker, and there are foxes and pumas.

There are three entrances: from **Curacautín**, north of the park (see Transport, page 779); from **Melipeuco**, 13 km south of the southern entrance at Truful-Truful (open all year); and from

Cherquenco to the west. Cherquenco is near the pretty **Araucarias ski resort** ① *T45-227 4141, www.ski araucarias.cl, US$39*, which has four ski lifts, a café, restaurant, bar, *refugio* and equipment rental, US$22.

Crampons and ice-axe are essential for climbing Llaima; the ascent should only be made by experienced climbers; the less-experienced are strongly encouraged to hire a guide. Information on the climb is available from **Guardería Captrén**, where the climb begins, heading south. Allow five hours to ascend, two hours to descend. There is also a range of walking trails in the park, from 1 km to 22 km in length. One is a two- or three-day hike around Volcán Llaima to Laguna Conguillío, which is dusty, but with beautiful views of Laguna Quepe, then on to the Laguna Captrén *guardería*. Information on access and trails from **CONAF** in Temuco or administration by Lago Conguillío. The nearest ATMs are in Cunco and Vicún.

Border with Argentina: Paso de Icalma Paso de Icalma (1298 m) is reached by unpaved road, 53 km from Melipeuco, a good crossing for those with their own transport, although it may be impassable in winter; phone the police post, 3 km from the border, T45-246 6554 to check conditions, www.pasosfronterizos.gov.cl/cf_icalma.html. Chilean immigration is open mid-October to mid-March 0800-2000, winter 0800-1900.

Listings Temuco and around *map p773*

Tourist information

Temuco
For information on the national parks, contact **CONAF** (Bilbao 931, p 2, T45-2298114, temuco. oirs@conaf.cl); for fishing permits, contact **Sernap** (Vicuña Mackenna 51, T45-223 8390).

Sernatur
Bulnes 590, p 1, T45-2406205, infoaraucania@ sernatur.cl. Mon-Fri 0900-1800.
Has good leaflets in English. Also in the municipal market, T45-297 3116, and Plaza Aníbal Pinto, T45-297 3628, daily in summer 0900-1900. See also www.temucochile.com.

Where to stay

Temuco
Accommodation in private houses, category $, can be arranged by tourist office.

$$$ Aitué
A Varas 1048, T45-221 2512, www.hotelaitue.cl.
Business standard, central, bar, English spoken, comfortable.

$$$ Bayern
Prat 146, T45-227 6000, www.hotelbayern.cl.
Standard 3-star. Small rooms, helpful staff, buffet breakfast, cafetería/restaurant, parking.

$$$ Frontera
Bulnes 733-726, T45-220 0400, www.hotelfrontera.cl.
Good business standard, comfortable rooms.

$$$ Holiday Inn Express
Av R Ortega 01800, T45-222 3300, www.holidayinnexpress.cl.
A member of the Chileanized version of this chain, good value, gym, pool, out of town but convenient for the bus terminal, worth considering if driving.

$$ Hostal Montt
M Montt 637, T45-298 2488.
Comfortable if overpriced, some rooms with bath, parking, gym.

$$-$ La Casa de Juanita
Carrera 735, T45-221 3203, www.lacasadejuanita.co.cl.
Private or shared bath, quiet, good bathrooms, parking, lots of information.

$$-$ Cabañas Pehuén Temuco
Recreo 209, off Av Alemania, T45-240 9804, www.pehuentemuco.cl.
Small rooms, helpful, nice atmosphere.
Also has a good-value *cabaña* sleeping 4.

$$-$ Casa Blanca
Montt 1306 y Zenteno, T45-227 2677, hostalcasablancatemuco@gmail.com.
Slightly run down, but good value for rooms with bath.

$$-$ Hospedaje Mateluna
Blanco 730, T45-273 0699.
Lovely home on several floors run by welcoming husband and wife, central, comfy, good value.

$$-$ Tante Silvia
Pinto Puelma 259, T45-248 4442.
Rooms or dorms, meals available, for students and groups.

Curacautín and around

$$ Hostal Las Espigas
Prat 710, T45-288 1138,
rivaseugenia@hotmail.com.
Good rooms, dinner available on request.

$$-$ Plaza
Yungay 157 (main plaza), T45-288 1256,
www.rotondadelcautin.cl.
With **La Cabaña** restaurant, pricey. Also has
Hostería La Rotunda del Cautín, Termas de
Manzanar, T45-2881569. Rooms and good
mid-range restaurant.

$ Turismo
Tarapacá 140, T45-288 1116.
Good food, hot shower, comfortable,
good value if old-fashioned.

Termas de Manzanar

$$$-$$ Andenrose
Carr Int Km 68.5, 5 km west of Manzanar,
Curacautín, T9-9869 1700, www.andenrose.com.
Cosy rooms and cabins, restaurant serving
international and Bavarian food, bike, horse,
kayak rental, jeep tours arranged, German/
Chilean-run.

$$$-$$ Termas de Manzanar
T45-288 1200, www.termasdemanzanar.cl.
Overpriced rooms, also has suites with
thermal jacuzzi.

$ Hostería Abarzúa
Km 18, T45-287 0011.
Simple, cheaper rooms without bath, full board
available (good food), also campsite.

Termas de Malleco

$$$$-$$ Termas Malleco
Km 33 T45-2323800, www.termasmalleco.cl.
With breakfast or full board, including use
of baths and horse riding, very good; jacuzzi
and massage. Camping (**$**), good facilities and
unlimited use of pools.

Reserva Nacional Nalcas Malalcahuello

$$$-$ La Suizandina
Km 83 Ctra Internacional a Argentina, 3 km
before Malalcahuello (Erbuc bus from Temuco
2½ hrs), T45-2197 3725 or T9-9884 9541,
www.suizandina.com.
Hostel with a range of rooms in main house,
guesthouse, dorm, cabin or camping. Large Swiss
breakfast with home-baked bread, half board
available, credit cards accepted, laundry, book

exchange, bike and ski rental, horse riding, hot
springs, travel and trekking information, German
and English spoken. "Like being in Switzerland".

$$ La Casita de Nahuelcura
Balmaceda 320, Malalcahuello, T9-7432 1192,
www.hosteriamalalcahuello.cl.
Hostería, lodge and *cabañas*.

Parque Nacional Conguillío
There are other *hostales* and restaurants
in Melipeuco.

$$$ La Baita
In the park, 3 km south of Laguna Verde, Km 18,
T45-258 1073, www.labaitaconguillio.cl.
Cabins with electricity, hot water, kitchen and
wood stoves, charming, lots of information,
Italian/Chilean-owned.

$$$-$$ Cabañas Vista Hermosa
10 km from the southern entrance, T9-9444 1630,
www.vistahermosaconguillio.cl.
Clean but spartan wooden cabins, each with a
wood stove and fantastic views to the volcano.
Solar-powered electricity in afternoon only. Run
by a horse-riding guide (former champion rider).
Good food.

$$-$ Adela y Helmut
Faja 16000, Km 5 Norte, Cunco (on the way
to Melipeuco, 16 km from Cunco, website has
directions, phone for pick-up from bus stop;
Nar-Bus, Cruzmar and Inter-Sur buses from
Santiago and Temuco pass the Faja and will drop
passengers who phone the guesthouse for pick-
up), T9-8258 2230, www.adelayhelmut.com.
Guesthouse and restaurant on a Mapuche/
German owned farm, English spoken, room for
families and for backpackers in 6-bed dorm,
breakfast and dinner available, kitchens, hot
showers, solar heating, mountain bike rental,
good reports. Pick-up from Temuco US$42 for
up to 4 people. They run year-round tours to
Conguillío, visiting lakes, waterfalls, with hikes
adapted to physical ability. They can also arrange
fly-fishing packages.

$ Hospedaje Icalma
Aguirre Cerda 729, Melipeuco, T9-9280 8210,
www.melipeucohospedaje.cl.
Spacious, basic rooms.

Camping

Cabañas y Camping Sendas Conguillío
Administered by SENDAS, T2-2882 1632,
www.sendasconguillio.cl. Nov-Apr.

Restaurants

Temuco

Many good restaurants around Av Alemania and Mall Mirage, about 10 blocks west of centre. Make for the Mercado Municipal on Aldunate y Portales, or the rural bus terminal, where there are countless restaurants serving very cheap set meals at lunch.

$$ La Caleta
Mercado Municipal, Aldunate y Portales, T45-221 3002.
One of the better choices in the covered market serving fish and seafood.

$$ La Parrilla de Miguel
Montt 1095, T45-227 5182.
Good for meat, large portions, and wine; one of the better restaurants.

$$ Otto
Alemania 360.
Popular for sandwiches.

$ Los Tenedores
San Martín 827.
Good-value lunch.

Cafés

Marriet
Prat 451, loc 9, www.marriet.cl.
Excellent coffee.

Entertainment

Temuco

Dreams, *Av Alemania 945, www.mundodreams. com.* Casino and hotel holds concerts by local and international artists.

Shopping

Temuco

Crafts

Best choice in the indoor municipal market at Aldunate y Portales, and in the **Agrupación de Mujeres Artesanas** (see page 772).
Fundación Chol-Chol, *Sector Rengalil, Camino Temuco–Nueva Imperial Km 16, T45-261 4007, http://es.cholchol.org.* This non-profit organization sells traditional Mapuche textiles, naturally dyed and hand woven by local women. Book in advance to sample some traditional, freshly made Mapuche fare.

Market

Temuco Feria, *Lautaro y Aníbal Pinto.* This is one of the most fascinating markets in Chile, with people bringing excellent fruit and vegetables from the surrounding countryside, including spices, fish, grains, cheese and honey. Sells dried fruit, useful for climbing/trekking. Also many cheap bars and restaurants nearby.

What to do

Most companies in Temuco offer tours to **Parque Nacional Conguillío**, 1 day, US$90 (minimum 2 people); to **Puerto Saavedra** on the coast and **Villarrica volcano**, US$120 (minimum 2 people), but unless you are in a hurry it is better and cheaper to book a tour closer to the destination. Some also offer skiing and snowboarding.

Anay Tour, *Estébanez 580, T9-8448 8633, www. anaytour.com.* Wide range of tours in the Araucanía region, including Lago Budi and Conguillío and Nahuelbuta national parks.

Transport

Temuco

Air Manquehue Airport 6 km southwest of the city. There is an airport transfer service to the city, **Transfer Temuco**, T45-233 4033, www. transfertemuco.cl, US$9 (book 24 hrs in advance). Also goes to hotels in Villarrica and Pucón, US$14.50 (may not run out of season). There is no public bus; taxis charge US$20-25. **LATAM** daily to **Santiago**.

Bus Buses to neighbouring towns leave from Terminal Rural, Pinto y Balmaceda, or from bus company offices nearby. To **Coñaripe**, 3 hrs, US$6, and **Licán Ray**, 2 hrs, US$7 with **JAC**. To **Panguipulli**, Regional Sur 3 hrs, US$6. **JAC** to **Loncoche**, US$2.50, **Los Lagos**, US$6.50, **Mehuin** in summer only. To **Curacautín** via Lautaro, **Erbuc**, US$2, 3 daily, 2½ hrs. To **Contulmo**, US$5.50, and **Cañete**, US$7, with **Igi Llaima**.

Long-distance bus terminal (Rodoviária) north of city at Pérez Rosales y Caupolicán, city bus 2, 7 or 10; *colectivo* 11P; taxi US$4.50. **JAC** has its own efficient terminal at Balmaceda y Aldunate, T45-246 5463, www.jac.cl, 7 blocks north of the Plaza, which also serves neighbouring towns. **NarBus** and **Igi-Llaima** are opposite. Buses to **Santiago**, many overnight, 8-9 hrs, US$37-65. To **Concepción**, **Bío Bío**, **Tur-Bus** and others, US$24, 4 hrs. To **Chillán**, 3½ hrs, US$15. **Cruz del Sur**, 10 a day to **Castro**, US$23, many daily to **Puerto**

Montt, US$12-23, 5-6 hrs. To **Valdivia**, JAC, Narbus/Igi Llaima, Tur-Bus, several daily, US$7, 2½ hrs. To **Osorno**, from US$8, 4¼ hrs. To **Villarrica** and **Pucón**, JAC, many between 0705 and 2045, 1½ hrs, and 2 hrs, US$7.

To Argentina El Valle and **Caraza** to **Zapala** and **Neuquén**, US$29-36, via Paso Pino Hachado. To **Bariloche** change in Osorno, or Andesmar has direct services at 0730 on Thu and Sat US$40-50.

Car hire Ace, Encalada 838 (also in airport), T(877) 822 3872. **Automóvil Club de Chile**, San Martín 278, T45-299 5755. **Avis**, San Martín 755, T45-245 6280 (also in airport).

Train Occasional tourist trains run between Santiago and Temuco; details from Tren Central, Av Barros Arana 791, T45-223 3416, www. trencentral.cl, US$37 *salón*, US$59 *preferente*.

Curacautín and around
Bus terminal on the main road, by the plaza. Buses to/from **Temuco**, **Los Angeles** and **Santiago**.

Reserva Nacional Nalcas Malalcahuello
Buses Bio Bio, www.busesbiobio.cl, has daily services from Temuco via Lautaro and Curacautín to **Malalcahuello**, 3 hrs, US$7, and **Lonquimay** town, 3½ hrs (or 4 hrs via Victoria), US$8.

Parque Nacional Conguillío
For touring, hire a 4WD vehicle in Temuco (essential in wet weather). See also **Adela y Helmut**, under Where to stay, above. To the northern entrance, poor *ripio* road: **taxi** from Curacautín to Laguna Captrén, US$40-50 one way. To **Melipeuco** (paved road, stops at **Hospedaje Icalma**), buses every hour from 0800-1800 from Balmaceda bus terminal, **Temuco** (or flag down at Mackenna y Varas), 2½ hrs, US$3, and once a day to **Icalma** when no snow on road. From May to end-Dec the only access is via Melipeuco. Transport can be arranged from Melipeuco into the park (ask in grocery stores and *hospedajes*, US$40-50 one way). To **Cunco**, every 20 mins from same terminal. To the western entrance: daily **buses** from Temuco to Cherquenco, from where there is no public transport to the park. Private transport or taking a tour are the best ways to see the area.

Lagos Villarrica, Calafquén and Panguipulli
picture-perfect scenery and a holiday getaway

Wooded Lago Villarrica, 21 km long and about 7 km wide, is one of the most beautiful in the region, with the active, snow-capped Villarrica volcano (2840 m) to the southeast. Villarrica and Pucón, resorts at the lake's southwest and southeast corners, are among the more expensive in the Lake District, but are definitely worth a visit. South of Lago Villarrica is a necklace of six lakes with snowy peaks behind. Calafquén and Panguipulli are the most visited, but there are also hot springs and national parks.

Villarrica Colour map 8, C1.
The quiet town of Villarrica, pleasantly set at the extreme southwest corner of Lago Villarrica, can be reached by a 63 km paved road southeast from Freire (24 km south of Temuco on the Pan-American Highway), or from Loncoche, 54 km south of Freire, also paved. Founded in 1552, the town was besieged by the Mapuche in the uprising of 1599; after three years the surviving Spanish settlers, 11 men and 13 women, surrendered. The town was refounded in 1882; the **Museo Leandro Penchulef** ⓘ *O'Higgins 501, T45-241 1667, Mon-Fri 0930-1230, 1400-1730, free*, in the striking Universidad Católica, focuses on this event. The **Muestra Cultural Mapuche** ⓘ *Pedro de Valdivia y Zegers, opens 1000 all year*, features a Mapuche *ruca* and has stalls selling good handicrafts. Next door is a small **Museo Histórico** ⓘ *T45-241 5706, Mon-Fri 0900-1300, 1500-1830, Sat 1000-1300, 1500-1800*.

☆Pucón Colour map 8, C1.
Pucón, on the southeastern shore of Lago Villarrica, 26 km east of Villarrica, is the major tourist centre on the lake. The black sand beach is very popular for swimming and watersports. From New Year to the end of February it is very crowded and expensive; off season it is far more pleasant. Apart from the lake, other attractions nearby include whitewater rafting, winter sports and several canopy sites; see What to do, below. There are also 14 thermal springs in the area, ranging from the upmarket to the natural; transport is provided by tour operators.

There is a pleasant *paseo*, the **Costanera Otto Gudenschwager**, which starts at the lake end of Ansorena (beside Gran Hotel Pucón) and goes along the shore. Walk 2 km north along the beach to the mouth of the Río Trancura (also called Río Pucón), with views of the volcanoes Villarrica, Quetrupillán and Lanín. To cross the Río Pucón: head east out of Pucón along the main road, then turn north on an unmade road leading to a new bridge; from here

there are pleasant walks along the north shore of the lake to Quelhue and Trarilelfú, or northeast towards Caburga (see below), or up into the hills through farms and agricultural land, with views of three volcanoes and, higher up, of the lake.

Boat trips ① *5 a day, 4 in winter, 1 hr, US$7*, on the lake leave from the landing stage at La Poza at the western end of O'Higgins. Or take a **boat** ① *summer only, US$57 for up to 8 people*, to the mouth of the river from near the **Gran Hotel**.

Parque Nacional Villarrica
Park office Lincoyán 336, Pucón, T45-244 3781, parque.villarrica@conaf.cl, entry US$4 (Apr-Oct), US$8 (Nov-Mar).

The park has three sectors: **Volcán Villarrica**, **Volcán Quetrupillán** (see below) and the **Puesco sector,** which includes the slopes of the Volcán Lanín on the Argentine border. Each sector has its own entrance and ranger station.

The **Villarrica volcano** ① *there is an ascent fee of US$150 pp, which includes 2 guides, ski and ice equipment and bags; food is not included; if you wish to rent crampons or ice axe, operators charge US$14*, 2840 m, 8 km south of Pucón, can be climbed up and down in a one-day trip: good boots, ice axe and crampons, sunglasses, plenty of water, chocolate and sun block are essential. Villarrica has earned the reputation of one of the most active volcanoes in South America. Beware of sulphur fumes at the top – occasionally agencies provide gas masks, otherwise take a cloth mask moistened with lemon juice – but on good days you can see into the crater with lava bubbling at 1250°C. On the descent you toboggan down the snow rather than walk, good fun. Entry to Volcán Villarrica is permitted only to groups with a guide and to individuals who can show proof of membership of a mountaineering club in their own country (consult the CONAF office). Several agencies take excursions. Entry is refused if the weather is poor. There are many independent guides, all with equipment; ask for recommendations at the tourist office. Take the ski lift for the first part of the ascent as it saves 400 m climbing on scree (winter only, US$11.50). A campsite with drinking water and toilets is below the refuge, 4 km inside the park.

Pucón ski resort ① *T45-244 1901, www.skipucon.cl. Ski season is Jul-Sep, occasionally longer. Information on snow and ski-lifts (and, perhaps, transport) from tourist office or Gran Hotel Pucón.* The **Pucón ski resort**, owned by the **Gran Hotel Pucón**, is on the eastern slopes of the volcano, reached by a track, 35 minutes. The centre offers equipment rental, ski instruction, first aid, restaurant and bar as well as wonderful views from the terrace. The centre is good for beginners; more advanced skiers can try the steeper areas.

Lago Caburga
Lago Caburga (spelt locally Caburgua) is a glassy, tranquil lake in a wild setting 25 km northeast of Pucón. It is unusual for its beautiful white-sand beach and supposedly has the warmest water of all the lakes here. The north shore can be reached by a road from Cunco (east of Freire) via the north shore of Lago Colico, a more remote lake north of Lago Villarrica. The village of Caburga, at the southern end is reached by a turning off the main road 8 km east of Pucón. The southern end of the lake around Caburga is lined with campsites. Rowing boats may be hired. Just off the road from Pucón, Km 15, are the Ojos de Caburga, beautiful pools fed from underground, particularly attractive after rain (entry US$1; ask bus driver to let you off). Alternatively, take a mountain bike from Pucón via the Puente Quelhue–a perfect day trip.

Parque Nacional Huerquehue

Entrance is 7 km from Paillaco, reached by an all-weather road which turns off 3 km before Caburga. Daily 0830-2000 (1800 in winter; may be closed after heavy snow). US$8; free parking 1.5 km along the track.

East of Lago Caburga, this park includes steep hills and at least 20 lakes, some of them very small. Entrance and administration are near Lago Tinquilco, the largest lake, on the western edge of the park. From the entrance there is a well-signed track north to three beautiful lakes, Lagos Verde, Chico and Toro. The track zig-zags up 5 km to Lago Chico, then splits left to Verde, right to Toro. From Toro you can continue to Lago Huerquehue and Laguna los Patos (camping). People in the park rent horses and boats. There is a restaurant at Tinquilco or take your own food.

South of Huerquehue

South of Parque Nacional Huerquehue, and reached by turning off the Pucón–Caburga road, are three sets of thermal baths. **Termas de Quimey-Co** ① *T9-8775 2113, www.termasquimeyco.com, US$25 in high season*, about 29 km from Pucón, have a campsite, cabins and hotel. A little further east are the **Termas de Huife Hostería** ① *Pucón, Km 33, T45-244 1222, www.termashuife.cl, US$23 Dec-Mar*, and beyond Huife are the basic but popular Termas **Los Pozones** ① *Km 35, www.termaslospozones.cl, US$12.50 per day, US$15.50 at night (1830-2400)*, set in natural rock pools. The road there is rough.

Cañi Forest Sanctuary ① *US$6, with self-guided trail, transport extra; for tours with English-speaking guides, contact the reserve, www.santuariocani.cl, or Cañi Guides Program at www.ecole.cl*, is also south of the park and covers 500 ha. It was the first private forest reserve established in Chile, owned by the non-proft Fundación Lahuén. It contains 12 small lakes and is covered by ancient native forests of coihue, lenga and some of the oldest araucaria trees in the country. From its highest peak, **El Mirador**, five volcanoes can be seen.

Towards Argentina

From Pucón a road runs southeast via Currarehue to the Argentine border. At Km 18 there is a turning south to the **Termas de Palguín** ① *T45-244 1968, US$14.50*, with a hotel. There are many beautiful waterfalls within hiking distance: **Salto China** ① *entry US$3.50*, with restaurant and camping; **Salto del Puma and Salto del León** *800 m from the Termas*. From Pucón bus terminal take a Vipo Ray bus to Currarehue and ask the driver to let you off at the entrance (10 km from Termas); first bus from Pucón at 0730; last bus from junction to Pucón at 2030. Taxi from Pucón, about US$40.

Near Palguín is the entrance to the Quetrupillán section of the Parque Nacional Villarrica. A high-clearance vehicle is necessary in this area of the park; horses are best. There's free camping, with wonderful views over Villarrica and six other peaks. Ask rangers for the route to the other entrance.

The road from Pucón to Argentina passes turnings north at Km 23 to **Termas de San Luis** ① *T45-241 2880, www.termasdesanluis.cl, US$23*, and **Termas Trancura** ① *T45-244 1189, http://trancura.cl, US$14 or US$22 including transport from Pucón*, at Km 35 to **Termas de Pangui** ① *15 km from main road, US$28*, which has accommodation ($$$). It continues to Currarehue, from where it turns south to Puesco and climbs to **Lago Quellelhue**, a tiny gem set between mountains at 1196 m. Beyond is the border at Paso **Mamuil Malal**. To the south of the pass rises the graceful cone of Lanín volcano. On the Argentine side the road runs south to Junín de los Andes, San Martín de los Andes and Bariloche.

Border with Argentina: Paso Mamuil Malal Chilean immigration and customs at Puesco, open 0800-1900 mid-March to mid-October, until 2000 rest of year. The border may be closed during heavy rain or snow (to check phone Cautín provincial government, T45-296 8126; see www.pasosfronterizos.gov.cl/cf_puesco.html). There are free CONAF campsites with no facilities at Puesco and 5 km from the border near Lago Tromén. Daily bus from Pucón, two hours, US$3. It's a hard road for cyclists, but not impossible.

Lago Calafquén *Colour map 8, C1.*

Dotted with small islands, Lago Calafquén is a popular tourist destination. **Licán Ray**, 30 km south of Villarrica on a peninsula on the north shore, is the major resort on the lake. There are two fine beaches each side of the rocky peninsula. Kayaks can be hired for US$5 per hour and there are catamaran trips, US$4.75. Although it's very crowded in season, most facilities close by the end of March and, out of season, Licán Ray feels like a ghost town.

Coñaripe (population 1253), 21 km southeast of Licán Ray at the eastern end of Lago Calafquén, is another popular tourist spot. Its setting, with a 3 km black sand beach surrounded by mountains, is very beautiful. From here a road (mostly *ripio*) around the lake's southern shore leads to Lago Panguipulli (see below) and offers superb views over Villarrica volcano, which can be climbed from here. Most services are on the Calle Principal.

Northeast of Coñaripe a steep *ripio* road towards Palguín reaches **Termas Vergara** after 14 km. There are nice open-air pools here. **Termas Geométricas** ① *3 km beyond Termas Vergara, T2-2795 1606, www.termasgeometricas.cl, US$39 from 1200-2000, cheaper in morning,* has 17 pools, geometrically shaped and linked by wooden walkways. There is a small café.

From Coñaripe a road runs southeast over the steep **Cuesta Los Añiques** offering views of tiny Lago Pellaifa. The **Termas de Coñaripe** ① *T45-232 4800, www.termasconaripe.cl, US$24,* are at Km 16. Further south at Km 32 are the **Termas de Liquiñe.** Opposite Liquiñe are the **Termas Río de Liquiñe** ① *T9-8197 3546, termasrioliquine@gmail.com (also on Facebook), US$13, with 8 different thermal centres.* There is a road north to Pucón through Villarrica national park, high-clearance and 4WD vehicle essential.

Border with Argentina: Paso Carirriñe The border with Argentina at **Paso Carirriñe** is reached by unpaved road from Termas de Liquiñe. It is open 15 October-31 August. On the Argentine side the road continues to San Martín de los Andes.

Lago Panguipulli and around *Colour map 8, C1.*
The lake is reached by paved roads from Lanco and Los Lagos on the Pan-American Highway or unpaved roads from Lago Calafquén. A road leads along the beautiful north shore, wooded with sandy beaches and cliffs. Most of the south shore is inaccessible by road. **Panguipulli**, at the northwest edge of the lake in a beautiful setting, is the largest town in the area. The Iglesia San Sebastián is in Swiss style, with twin towers; its belltower contains three bells from Germany. In summer, catamaran trips are offered on the lake and trips can be made to Lagos Calafquén, Neltume, Pirehueico and to the northern tip of Lago Riñihue.

Choshuenco lies 45 km east of Panguipulli at the southeastern tip of the lake. To the south is the Reserva Nacional Mocho Choshuenco (7536 ha) which includes two volcanoes: Choshuenco (2415 m) and Mocho (2422 m). On the slopes of Choshuenco the **Club Andino de Valdivia** has ski-slopes and three *refugios*. These can be reached by a turning from the road which goes south from Choshuenco to Enco at the east end of Lago Riñihue. East of Choshuenco a road leads to Lago Pirehueico, via the impressive waterfalls of Huilo Huilo, where the river channels its way through volcanic rock before thundering down into a natural basin. The falls are three hours' walk from Choshuenco, or take the Puerto Fuy bus and get off at the Nothofagus Hotel (see Where to stay, below), from where it is a five-minute walk to the falls. At Huilo Huilo is a biological reserve, lots of outdoor activities and a variety of lodgings in the trees; see www.huilohuilo.com/en.

Lago Pirehueico
East of Choshuenco is Lago Pirehueico, a long, narrow and deep lake, surrounded by virgin lingüe forest. It is largely unspoilt, although there are plans to build a huge tourist complex in Puerto Pirehueico. There are no roads along the shores of the lake, but there are two ports connected by a ferry. **Puerto Fuy** (population 300) is at the north end, 21 km from Choshuenco and 7 km from Neltume. **Puerto Pirehueico** is at the south end, from where a road runs to the Argentine border crossing at Paso Hua Hum.

Border with Argentina: Paso Hua Hum Paso Hua Hum (659 m) is 11 km from Puerto Pirehueico (very hard for cyclists with steep climbs, no public transport to border). On the Argentine side the road leads alongside Lago Lacar to San Martín de los Andes and Junín de los Andes. Chilean immigration is open all year 0800-2000, see www.pasosfronterizos.gov.cl/cf_huahum.html.

Tourist information

Villarrica

The **tourist office** (Valdivia 1070, T45-220 6619, daily in summer 0800-2300, off season 1000-1800) has information and maps.

Pucón

The **tourist office** (in the municipal building, O'Higgins 483, T45-229 3001, ofturismo@ municipalidadpucon.cl, daily 0830-2100 summer, to 1900 in winter), sells fishing licences (Mon-Fri). There is also the private **Chamber of Tourism** (Brasil 315, T45-244 1671, www.puconturismo.cl, daily 0900-2000 in summer, 1100-1800 in winter).

Lago Calafquén

There is a **tourist office** on the plaza in both Licán Ray (0815-2245 daily in summer, Mon-Fri 0900-1600 off season) and Coñaripe (T63-231 7378, daily 0900-1100 in summer, till 1800 in winter).

Lago Panguipulli

Panguipulli **tourist office** is by the plaza (T63-231 0436, www.sietelagos.cl, also www. municipalidadpanguipulli.cl, daily Dec-Feb 0830-2100, otherwise Mon-Fri 0830-1800).

Where to stay

Villarrica

Lodging in private homes in our **$$-$** range can be found on Muñoz blocks 400 and 500, Koerner 300 and O'Higgins 700 and 800. More upmarket accommodation is on the lakefront.

$$$$-$$$ Villarrica Park Lake
Km 13 on the road to Pucón, T44-222 8400, www.hotelvillarricaparklake.com.
5-star, all rooms with balconies overlooking the lake, spa with pools, sauna, solarium, fishing trips.

$$$ Hostería de la Colina
Las Colinas 115, overlooking town, T45-241 1503, www.hosteriadelacolina.com.
Large gardens, good restaurant (the owners make their own fresh ice cream), fine views, very attentive service. Fishing, horse riding and dog sledding can be organized from the *hostería* as well.

$$$ Hotel y Cabañas El Parque
Camino Villarrica, Km 2.5, T45-241 1120, www.hotelelparque.cl.

Lakeside with beach, tennis courts, good restaurant set meals.

$$$ Parque Natural Dos Ríos
13 km west of Villarrica, Putue Alto s/n, Casilla 535, T9-9419 8064, www.dosrios.de.
B&B rooms or self-catering cabins. Tranquil 40-ha nature park on the banks of the Río Tolén (white-sand beach), birdwatching, child-friendly, German and English spoken.

$$$$-$$ Bungalowlandia
Prat 749, T45-241 1635, www.bungalowlandia.cl.
Cabañas, dining room, good facilities, pool.

$$$-$$ El Ciervo
Koerner 241, T45-241 1215, www.hotelelciervo.cl.
Comfortable rooms, pleasant grounds, German-style breakfasts, German and some English spoken, pool, terrace.

$$ Hostal Don Juan
Korner 770, T9-94432070, www.hostaldonjuan.cl.
Reputable choice close to the centre, 23 spotless rooms on sprawling property with lush gardens, *parrilla*, large dining room. Breakfast optional. Best option for the price. Recommended.

$$ Hostería Bilbao
Henríquez 43, T45-241 1186, see Facebook.
Small rooms, pretty patio, good restaurant.

$$-$ Hospedaje Nicolás
Anfion Muñoz 477, T45-241 2637.
Simple rooms with bath. Good value, but thin walls.

$$-$ La Torre Suiza
Bilbao 969, T45-241 1213, www.torresuiza.com.
Rooms and dorms, camping, cycle rental, book exchange, lots of info, reserve in advance. German and English spoken.

$ Chito Fuentes
Vicente Reyes 665, T45-241 1595.
Basic rooms above a restaurant.

$ Mapu Hostal
Urrutia 302, T45-241 2098, www.mapuhostel.cl.
Legitimate *hostal* at the entrance to Villarrica. Dorms for 8, 6 and 4 and doubles (**$$**). Laundry service, breakfast included, Wi-Fi.

Camping

Many sites east of town on Pucón road, open in season only and expensive.

Pucón

In summer (Dec-Feb) rooms may be hard to find. Plenty of alternatives (usually cheaper) in Villarrica. Prices below are Jan-Feb. Off-season rates are 20-40% lower and it is often possible to negotiate. Many families offer rooms, look for the signs or ask in bars/restaurants. Touts offer rooms to new arrivals; check that they are not way out of town.

$$$$ Antumalal
2 km west of Pucón, T45-244 1011,
www.antumalal.com.
Small, luxury, picturesque chalet-type boutique hotel, magnificent views of the lake (breakfast and lunch on terrace), 12 acres of gardens, with meals, open year round, indoor pool, hot tub, sauna, spa, jacuzzis and private beaches.

$$$ Cabañas Rucamalal
O'Higgins 770, T45-244 2297, www.rucamalal.cl.
Lovely cabins (with satellite TV) in a pretty garden, spacious, well equipped and decorated, various sizes, pool.

$$$-$$ Hostal Gerónimo
Alderete 665, T45-244 3762, www.geronimo.cl.
Open all year.
Quiet, smart, multilingual staff, bar, restaurant.

$$$-$$ Interlaken
Caupolicán 720, T45-244 2709,
www.hotelinterlaken.cl.
Chalets with full facilities, water skiing, pool, no restaurant.

$$$-$$ La Tetera
Urrutia 580, T45-246 4126, www.tetera.cl.
6 rooms, some with bath, English spoken, book swap, information centre, good Spanish classes, car rental, book in advance. Nearby bar music is audible on weekends.

$$ El Refugio
Palguín 540, T45-244 1596,
www.hostalelrefugio.cl.
Dorm or double room, shared bath, small, convenient, cosy, Dutch/Chilean-owned. Trips sold, but shop around.

$$ Hostal Backpackers
Palguín 695, T45-244 1417, see Facebook.
With or without bath, quiet, next to JAC buses, lots of activities, **Navimag** reservations, tourist information.

$$-$ Donde Germán
Las Rosas 590, T45-244 2444,
www.dondegerman.cl.

Single, double or triple rooms with private or shared bath. Fun, organizes tours, book in advance.

$$-$ Etnico Hostel and Adventures
Colo Colo 36, T9-8527 5940,
www.etnico.hostel.com.
Owner is mountain guide. Double rooms and mixed dorms, car and bike parking, lots of activities and keen on recycling.

$$-$ Hospedaje Irma Torres
Lincoyán 545, T45-244 2226, http://hirma.cl.
Private or shared bath, tourist information, bicycle hire.

$$-$ Hospedaje Víctor
Palguín 705, T45-244 3525, www.hostalvictor.cl.
Rooms sleep 2-4 with private or shared bath, laundry. A decent choice.

$$-$ Hostería ¡école!
General Urrutia 592, T45-244 1675, www.ecole.cl.
Rooms and dorms, shop, vegetarian and fish restaurant, forest treks (departure for Lahuén Foundation's Cani Forest Sanctuary), rafting and biking, information, language classes, massage.

$$-$ La Bicicleta
Palguín 361, T45-244 4679.
Cosy budget hostel offering excursions and bike tours. Owner José can help with all the details.

Camping

There are many camping and cabin establishments. Those close to Pucón include **La Poza** (Costanera Geis 769, T45-244 4982, campinglapoza@hotmail.com – see Facebook), hot showers, good kitchen. Several sites en route to volcano, including: **L'Etoile** (Km 2, T45-244 2188, www.letoilepucon.com, US$7 per night), in attractive forest.

Lago Caburga

$$$-$$ Landhaus San Sebastián
Camino Pucón a Caburga, Pucón 2222,
T9-9443 1786, www.landhaus.cl.
With bath and breakfast, good meals, laundry facilities, English and German spoken, Spanish classes, good base for nearby walks.

Parque Nacional Huerquehue

$$$-$ Puerto Parque Tinquilco
Parque Huerquehue, Km 37, T9-8538 7716,
www.parquehuerquehue.cl.
Hotel, cabins, camping and motorhome parking, restaurant, kayaks, boats for hire.

$$$-$ Refugio Tinquilco
2 km from park entrance, where forest trail leads to lakes Verde and Toro, T2-2278 9831, T9-9539 2728, www.tinquilco.cl.
Range of cabins, bunk beds or doubles, cheapest without sheets, bring sleeping bag, private or shared bath, meals available, heating, 24-hr electricity, sauna.

Camping

Camping at the park entrance, 2 sites.

$ Camping Olga
T45-244 1938, www.campingolga.com.
Nov to mid-Apr.
Camping in the park, 2 km from park entrance, with hot water.

Towards Argentina

$$-$ Kila Leufu/Ruka Rayen
23 km east on road to Curarrehue, T9-9876 4576,
www.kilaleufu.cl.
2 adjacent guesthouses run by the same Austrian/Mapuche owners. **Kila Leufu** offers rooms on the Martínez family farm, contact Irma or Margot at **Ruka Rayen** in advance, home-grown food, boat tours. **Ruka Rayen** is on the banks of the Río Palguín, 15 mins' walk from the main road (regular buses to Pucón). Some rooms with bath, English-speaking hosts (Margot's parents own **Kila Leufu**), mountain-bike hire. Both serve meals, offer horse-riding, trekking information and camping. The perfect choice if you want to avoid the hustle and bustle of Pucón.

$ Rancho de Caballos
Palguín Aito Km 32, T9-8346 1764 (limited signal),
www.rancho-de-caballos.com.
Restaurant with vegetarian dishes; also *cabañas* and camping, self-guided trails, horse-riding trips ½-6 days, English and German spoken.

Lago Calafquén and around

Licán Ray

$$ Cabañas Los Nietos
Manquel 125, Playa Chica, T9-5639 3585,
see Facebook.
Self-catering cabins.

$ Residencial Temuco
G Mistral 517, T45-243 1130.
Shared bath, with breakfast, good.

Camping

$ Las Gaviotas
Km 5 Camino Licán Ray, T9-9030 1153,
see Facebook.
Beach camping with many amenities, such as
hot showers, mini market and volleyball area.

Coñaripe

$$-$ Hospedaje Chumay
Las Tepas 201, on Plaza, T9-9744 8835,
www.turismochumay.cl.
With restaurant, tours, some English spoken, good.

Camping

Sites on beach charge US$28, but if you walk 0.5-
0.75 km from town you can camp on the beach
free. Cold municipal showers on beach, US$0.25.

Isla Llancahue
5 km east, T9-9562 0437.
Campsite with *cabañas* on an island in
Río Llancahue.

Termas de Coñaripe

$$$$-$$$ Termas de Coñaripe
T45-232 4800, www.termasconaripe.cl.
Excellent hotel with 4 pools, good restaurant,
spa with a variety of treatments, cycles and
horses for hire. Full board available.

Termas de Liquiñe

$$$ Termas de Liquiñe
T9-8197 3546.
Full board, cabins, restaurant, hot pool, small
native forest.

$$ Hospedaje Catemu
Camino Internacional, T63-2197 1629,
neldatrafipan@yahoo.es.
Known as much for its restaurant as its cosy,
wood-paneled cabins, this option can arrange
excursions to the Termas.

Lago Panguipulli
See www.sietelagos.cl for list of lodgings.

$$ La Casita del Centro
J M Carerra 674, Panguipulli, T9-6495 5040.
B&B, refurbished, safe, with restaurant, parking.

$ pp Hostal Orillas del Lago
M de Rosas 265, Panguipulli, T63-231 1710
(or T63-231 2499 if no reply, friends have key).
From plaza walk towards lake, last house
on left, 8 blocks from terminal. Good views,
backpacker place.

Camping

El Bosque
P Sigifredo 241, Panguipulli, T63-231 1489.
Small, good, but not suitable for vehicle
camping, hot water.

Also 3 sites at Chauquén, 6 km southeast
on lakeside.

Choshuenco

$$$$ Nothofagus Hotel
Carretera Internacional Km 55 (to arrive, take a
bus from Panguiplli to Puerto Fuy and tell the
driver to let you off at Huilo Huilo), T2-2887 3535,
www.huilohuilo.com.
Probably the most famous hotel in the country,
the Nothofagus boasts seven sites clustered
around the reserve's 100,000 ha. The main hotel
is built to resemble a treehouse, with wooden
walkways spiralling 5 floors up the trunk. Besides
the main building, there are lodges, refuges
cabañas and camping ($). Included in the price
are a buffet meal, welcome drink and entrance
to the Sendero Huilo Huilo, home to wild boars
and *huemules* (deer). The Nothofagus offers over
30 different seasonal activities and excursions,
from rafting to skiing to zip-lining, that make full
use of the surroundings. There is an outdoor/
indoor swimming area and hydromassage
therapy rooms. They even have their own
craft brewery. 90% of the staff come from the
surrounding towns and villages.

$$$-$$ Cabañas Peumayén
Los Cipreses 27, 6 km from Puerto Fuy, T9-9438
8191, www.turismopeumayen.cl.
Fully equipped *cabañas*, Wi-Fi, DirecTV, laundry
service, breakfast included. 5-min drive from the
Saltos del Huilo Huilo.

$$$-$$ Hostería Ruca Pillán
San Martín 85, T63-231 8220, www.rucapillan.cl.
Family-run hotel rooms and cabins overlooking
the lake, restaurant, English spoken, tours.

$$ Cabañas Choshuenco
Bernabé 391, T63-231 8316,
www.choshuencochile.cl.
Cabañas, fully equipped, self-contained,
for 6-8 people.

Lago Pirehueico

$$$-$$ Hospedaje y Cabañas Don Aníbal
Puerto Fuy, T9-8725 0827,
www.cabañaspuertofuy.cl.
Hot water, good food in restaurant.

$ pp Restaurant San Giovani
Puerto Fuy, T63-2197 1562.
Family atmosphere, good rooms.

Camping

On the beach (take own food).

Restaurants

Villarrica

$$$ El Tabor
S Epulef 1187, T45-241 1901.
Fish and seafood specialities, excellent but pricey.

$$-$ La Taquería Azteca
Bilbao 581, T45-241 0272, see Facebook.
The Tex-Mex tastes good, the vibe is fun and the cocktails are strong. Recommended if you are not a strict *comida mexicana* originalist.

$$-$ Pizzería Los Sicilianos
Muñoz 415, T45-260 9189.
Owner Fabrizzio tosses pies, flirts and sings along to Calabreze music, all while delivering the most authentically Italian pizzas in the city.

$$ The Travellers Resto Bar
Letelier 753, T45-241 3617, see Facebook.
Varied menu including vegetarian and Asian food, bar, English spoken.

$ El Marítimo
Alderete 769, T45-241 9755.
Generally first-rate, unpretentious, serving traditional fish and seafood.

Café 2001
Henríquez 379, T45-241 1470, www.cafebar2001.cl.
Best coffee in town. Also good cakes and friendly service at a reasonable price. For ice cream, try the stall next door.

Pucón

See Where to stay, for other recommendations.
There are many upscale and mid-range restaurants on Fresia between O'Higgins and Valdivia.

$$$ Puerto Pucón
Fresia 246, T45-244 1592.
One of Pucón's older restaurants, Spanish, stylish.

$$$-$$ La Maga
Alderete 276 y Fresia, T45-244 4277, www.lamagapucon.cl.
Uruguayan *parrillada* serving excellent steak. So good that several imitations have opened up nearby to take the overspill.

$$$-$$ Senzo
Fresia 284, T45-244 9005, see Facebook.
Fresh pasta and risotto prepared by a Swiss chef.

$$ Arabian
Fresia 354-B, T45-244 3469.
Arab specialities, including stuffed vine leaves, falafel, etc.

$$ ¡école!
In Hostería of same name, General Urrutia 592, T45-244 1675.
Good vegetarian restaurant.

$$ Mora Sushi
Fresia 236, T45-244 4857, www.morasushibar.cl.
Decent sushi and a solid happy hour featuring great mojitos. A nice change of pace from steaks and fried fish.

$ Rap Hamburguesa
O'Higgins 625. Open late.
Freshly made hamburgers, chips and Chilean fast food.

Cafés

Abuela Goye
Fresia y Urrutia, T9-8760 1580, see Facebook.
Argentine chain specializing in artesenal chocolates, ice cream and gourmet coffee. Also menu featuring pizzas, sandwiches and *tablas*. Plays good music; great for people-watching.

Café de la P
O'Higgins y Lincoyán, T45-244 3577, www.cafedelap.cl.
Real coffee, also at the airport.

Café Lounge Brasil
Colo Colo 485, T45-244 4035, www.cafeloungebrasil.com.
Gourmet cafeteria which also has a 'boutique' hostel. Meals include vegetarian options, Jamaican coffee.

Cassis
Fresia 223, T45-244 9088, www.chocolatescassis.com.
Chocolates, ice creams, pancakes and snacks as well as coffee.

Lago Calafquén: Licán Ray

$$ Cábala
Urrutia 201.
Nice central location, good pizzas and pastas.

$$-$ The Ñaños
Urrutia 105.

Good café and restaurant, reasonable prices, helpful owner. Service can be patchy.

Lago Panguipulli: Panguipulli
Several cheap restaurants on O'Higgins 700 block.

$$-$ El Chapulín
M de Rosas 639, see Facebook.
Good food and value.

$$-$ Gardylafquen
M de Rosas 722.
Typical Chilean fare, popular with locals and tourists.

$ El Pollo Cotoco
On the plaza opposite the church, T9-9587 2728, see Facebook.
Fast food specializing in chicken, good for on the go.

Festivals

Villarrica
Jan-Feb Villarrica has the **Feria Costumbrista** with many cultural and sporting events (www. villarrica.org).

Lago Panguipulli
Last week of Jan **Semana de Rosas** in Panguipulli, with dancing and sports competitions.

Shopping

Pucón

Camping equipment
Eltit supermarket, *O'Higgins y Fresia.*
Outdoors & Travel, *Lincoyán 36.* Clothing, equipment, maps.

Handicrafts market
Just south of O'Higgins on Ansorena; local specialities are painted wooden flowers.

What to do

Villarrica
Claudio Rodríguez, *T7-794 1228.* Private guide, offers river and fly-fishing trips, speaks English.
Novena Región, *Parque Ecológico 3 Esteros, 20 km from Villarrica towards Panguipulli, T9-8901 4518, info@auroraaustral.com, see Facebook.* Mushing and husky trekking on the winter snow and in summer with Siberian huskies. Unique in Chile.
Ríos Family, *T45-241 2408.* Birdwatching and fishing trips.

Villarrica Extremo, *Valdivia 910, T45-241 0900, www.villarricaextremo.com.* Good excursions featuring the usual suspects like volcano tours, rafting, thermal pools and paintball.

Pucón

Climbing
See page 780 for official ascent fees for climbing Volcán Villarrica.
Sierra Nevada, *O'Higgins 524-A, T9-5733 5037, see Facebook.* Offers tours to Volcán Villarrica.

Fishing
Pucón and Villarrica are celebrated as centres for fishing on Lake Villarrica and in the beautiful Lincura, Trancura and Toltén rivers. Local tourist office will supply details on licenses and open seasons, etc. 2 fishing specialists are **Mario's Fishing Zone** (O'Higgins 580, T9-9760 7280, www.flyfishingpucon.com), expensive but good, and **Off Limits** (O'Higgins 560, T9-9949 2481, www.offlimits.cl), English and Italian spoken.

Horse riding
Centro de Turismo Ecuestre Huepilmalal, *Camino a Termas de Huife, Km 25, T9-9643 2673, www.huepilmalal.cl.*
Rancho de Caballos, *see Where to stay, Towards Argentina, page 785.* Average hire costs about US$28 for ½ day, US$72 full day (transfer from Pucón extra).

Mountain biking
Bike hire from US$14 per day for cross-country excursions with guide. Available from several travel agencies on O'Higgins.

Water sports
Waterskiing, sailing, rowing boats and windsurfing at Playa Grande beach by Gran Hotel and La Poza beach end of O'Higgins (more expensive than Playa Grande, not recommended).

Whitewater rafting and kayaking
Very popular on the Río Trancura. Many agencies offer trips (see below), **Trancura Bajo** (grade III), US$22; **Trancura Alto** (grades 3 and 4), US$29. Many agencies offer trips, including **Kayak Chile** (O'Higgins, T9-8452 1693, www. raftingkayakchile.com); **Pucón Kayak Hostel** (10 km from town on road to Caburga, T9-4247 2676, www.puconkayakhostel.com).

Zip-lining/canopy
(Sliding from platform to platform along a metal cord). Several agencies can arrange this. The best (and most safety conscious) is **Bosque**

Aventura (Arauca 611 y O'Higgins, T9-9325 4795, www.canopypucon.cl).

Tour operators

Tour operators arrange trips to thermal baths, trekking to volcanoes, whitewater rafting, etc. For falls, lakes and termas, it's cheaper in a group to flag down a taxi and bargain. Many agencies, so shop around: prices vary at times, quality of guides and equipment variable. In high season, when lots of groups go together, individual attention may be lacking.

Aguaventura, *Palguín 336, T45-244 4246, www.aguaventura.com*. French-run, in summer kayaking and rafting specialities, in winter 'snowshop' for ski and snowboard rental, volcano climbing, trekking.

Elementos, *Pasaje Las Rosas 640, T45-244 1750, www.elementos-chile.com*. Provider covering the entire country and specializing in sustainable tourism. Has its own **EcoHostel**. Good option for volcano treks.

Mountain Life Adventure, *T9-7472 3665, mountainlifeadventure@hotmail.com*. Villarrica hike plus treks and climbs up other volcanoes in the region, Chilean/Swiss owned (ask here about Hostel One Way).

Politur, *O'Higgins 635, T45-244 1373, www.politur. com*. Well-established and responsible, good for volcano trek and rafting; a little pricier than others.

Travel Aid, *Ansorena 425, loc 4, T45-244 4040, www.travelaid.cl*. Helpful general travel agency, sells trekking maps, guidebooks, lots of information, agents for **Navimag** and other boat trips, English and German spoken.

Volcán Villarrica, *O'Higgins 555, T45-244 1577, volcan.villarica@hotmail.com*. Specializes in group excursions to Volcán Villarrica as well as a number of other activities, including rafting, canyoning and paintball. English spoken, good equipment.

Towards Argentina

Escape, *in Curarrehue, T9-9678 5380, www. patagonia-escape.com*. Owned by John 'LJ' Groth, specializing in SUP, private kayak guiding trips and rafting on some beautiful sections of the Río Trancura and around. Safe, responsible, environmentally aware and different.

Transport

Villarrica

Bus Terminal at Pedro de Valdivia y Muñoz. JAC at Bilbao 610, T45-246 7777, and opposite for Pucón and Licán Ray. Terminal Rural for other local services at Matta y Vicente Reyes. To **Santiago**, 10 hrs, US$45-80, several companies. To **Pucón**, with **Vipu-Ray** (main terminal) and **JAC**, in summer every 15 mins, 40 mins' journey, US$1.50; same companies to **Licán Ray**, US$1.50. To **Valdivia**, **JAC**, US$8, many daily, 2½ hrs. To **Coñaripe** (US$3.50) and **Liquiñe** 5 a day, 2 on Sun, US$5. To **Temuco**, JAC, US$7. To **Loncoche** (Ruta 5 junction for hitching), US$2. To **Panguipulli**, go via Licán Ray, occasional direct buses. Buses to Argentina: buses from Valdivia to **San Martín de los Andes** pass through Villarrica, US$23, **Igi Llaima**, T45-241 2733, book in advance. Note that if the Mamuil Malal pass is blocked by snow buses go via Panguipulli instead of Villarrica and Pucón.

Pucón

Air Airport 2 km on Caburga road. Check with airlines for summer flights from **Santiago** via Temuco. There are usually very few.

Bus No municipal terminal: each company has its own terminal: **JAC**, Uruguay y Palguín; **Tur-Bus**, O'Higgins 910, east of town; **Igi Llaima** and **Cóndor**, Colo Colo y O'Higgins. JAC to **Villarrica** (very frequent, US$1.50) and **Valdivia** (US$8.50, 3 hrs). **Tur-Bus** direct to **Valdivia**, **Osorno** (US$17) and **Puerto Montt**, 6 hrs, US$18, daily. To **Santiago**, 10 hrs, US$57-86, many companies, early morning and late evening. Buses to Argentina: Buses from Valdivia to **San Martín** pass through Pucón.

Car hire Hire prices start at US$30 per day; **Hertz**, Alderete 324, T45-244 1664; **Kilómetro Libre**, Alderete 480, T45-244 4399, www.rentacar kilometrolibre.com; **Pucón Rent A Car**, Valdivia 636, T 9-8998 0294 , www.puconrentacar.cl.

Lago Caburga

Buses Caburgua run minibuses every 30 mins from Pucón to **Caburga**, US$1.50. If walking or cycling, turn left 3 km east of Pucón (sign to Puente Quelhue) and follow the track (very rough) for 18 km through beautiful scenery.

Parque Nacional Huerquehue

Buses Caburgua from **Pucón**, 4 daily, 3 in winter, 1½ hrs, US$3.

Lago Calafquén and around

Licán Ray

Bus Leave from offices around plaza. To **Villarrica**, 1 hr, US$1.50, JAC frequent in summer. In summer, there are direct buses from **Santiago** (Tur-Bus US$50-80, 10 hrs) and **Temuco** (2½ hrs, US$6). To **Panguipulli**, every hour until 1930, US$2, to **Coñaripe** US$1.50.

Coñaripe
Bus To **Panguipulli**, 5 a day, US$2 and regular services to **Villarrica**, US$3.50 with JAC and Buses Coñaripe. Nightly bus direct to **Santiago**, Tur-Bus and JAC, 11½ hrs, US$60-90. To **Temuco** US$8.

Lago Panguipulli
Bus Terminal at Gabriela Mistral y Portales in Panguipulli. To **Santiago** daily, US$40-75. To **Valdivia**, every 30 mins, several companies, 2 hrs, US$6. To **Temuco** frequent, **Regional Sur**, US$6, 3 hrs. To **Puerto Montt**, US$13. To **Choshuenco**, **Neltume** and **Puerto Fuy**, 3 daily, 3 hrs, US$3. To **Coñaripe** (with connections for Licán Ray and Villarrica), 5 daily, 1½ hrs, US$2.

Lago Pirehueico
Bus Daily Puerto Fuy to **Panguipulli**, 5 daily, fewer at weekends, 3 hrs, US$3.50.

Ferry The Hua Hum sails from **Puerto Fuy** to Puerto Pirehueico at Mon-Thu 0800, 1300, 1800 and 0700, 1100, 1500, 1900 Fri-Sun, returns 2 hrs later (Dec-Mar), 1300 daily (return 1600) except Fri when it sails 1200, 1600 (rest of year), foot passengers US$1.50, cars US$27, motorbikes US$8.50. A beautiful crossing, comparable to the lakes crossing from Puerto Montt to Bariloche, but at a fraction of the price (to take vehicles reserve in advance on T9-4277 3450, see https://barcazahuahum.com for fares and schedules). Buses to **San Martín de los Andes, Argentina**, 50 km, are run by **Ko Ko** in San Martín (T02972-427422) usually all year.

boat trips and fortifications around a lively city

Valdivia, 839 km south of Santiago, is a very pleasant city at the confluence of the Ríos Calle Calle and Cruces, which form the Río Valdivia. It is set in rich agricultural land receiving some 2300 mm of rain a year. To the northwest of the city is a large island, Isla Teja, where the Universidad Austral de Chile is situated. The student population adds zest to the nightlife which takes place mostly in Barrio Esmeralda any night of the week. At the mouth of the Río Valdivia are a group of historic forts which make a good day's outing from the city. The two main centres are Niebla on the north bank and Corral opposite on the south bank.

Valdivia was one of the most important centres of Spanish colonial control over Chile. Founded in 1552 by Pedro de Valdivia, it was abandoned as a result of the Mapuche insurrection of 1599 and the area was briefly occupied by Dutch pirates. In 1645 it was refounded as a walled city, the only Spanish mainland settlement south of the Río Biobío. The coastal fortifications at the mouth of the river also date from the 17th century. They were greatly strengthened after 1760 owing to fears that Valdivia might be seized by the British, but were of little avail during the Wars of Independence: overnight on 2 February 1820 the Chilean naval squadron under Lord Cochrane seized San Carlos, Amargos and Corral and turned their guns on Niebla and Mancera, which surrendered the following morning. From Independence until the 1880s Valdivia was an outpost of Chilean rule, reached only by sea or by a coastal route through Mapuche territory. From 1849 to 1875 Valdivia was a centre for German colonization of the Lake District. In 2007 it became capital of the newly created Región XIV, Los Ríos.

Sights
The city centre is the tree-lined, shady **Plaza de la República**. A pleasant walk is along **Avenida Prat** (or **Costanera**), which follows the bend in the river, from the bus station to the bridge to **Isla Teja**, the **Muelle Fluvial** (boat dock) and the riverside market. The modern **Hotel y Casino Valdivia** overlooks the Puente Pedro de Valdivia and the grassy area below it is popular on sunny days. Boats can be hired per hour at the bend. Sealions lounge around the dock. On Isla Teja, near the library in the University, are a **botanic garden** and **arboretum** with trees from all over the world. West of the botanical gardens is the 30-ha **Parque Saval**, with areas of native forest, as well as the **Lago de los Lotos** (beautiful blooms in spring) ⓘ *all open during daylight hours in summer, 1000-1800 in winter, US$0.75*. On boat trips round the island you can see lots of waterfowl. Also on Isla Teja is the **Museo Histórico y Antropológico** ⓘ *T63-221 2872, http://museosregiondelosrios.cl, Mar-Dec Tue-Sun 1000-1300, 1400-1800, Jan and Feb daily 1000-2000, US$2.35, discount for seniors and children*. Run by the University, it contains exhibits on archaeology, ethnography and the history of German settlement, beautifully housed in the former mansion of Carlos Anwandter, a prominent German immigrant.

Next door is the **Museo de Arte Contemporáneo** ① *T63-222 1968, www.macvaldivia.cl, Tue-Sun 1000-1300, 1400-1800 in winter, 1000-2000 in summer, US$2.35, free for students and children, times change according to the exhibition.*

Around Valdivia

The surrounding district has lovely countryside of woods, beaches, lakes and rivers. The various rivers are navigable and there are pleasant journeys by rented motor boat on the **Ríos Futa** and **Tornagaleanes** around the **Isla del Rey**. Boat tours go to the **Santuario de la Naturaleza Carlos Anwandter**① *Embarcaciones Bahía, T9-9316 5728, www.embarcacionesbahia.cl, on the riverfront near the fish market, offers daily tours leaving at 1600 and returning at 1945, US$21.50 pp.* The refuge is an area on the Río Cruces which flooded as result of the 1960 tidal wave; lots of bird species are visible.

 Parque Oncol ① *27 km northwest of Valdivia, T800-370 222, www.parqueoncol.cl, park entry US$5.50, camping US$13.50 for up to 5 people, tour bus to/from park in Jan-Feb US$22,* covers 754 ha of Valdivian native forest, with several trails and lookouts, **zip-line (canopy)** ① *US$21.50, weekends only 1100-1800,* picnic area, café and campsite.

 Every Sunday during January and February there is a special **steam train service**① *T9-91004726, leaves at 1130, returns from Antilhue at 1600, US$11 return, advance booking essential,* from the train station on Equador to **Antilhue**, 20 km to the east. The train is met by locals selling all sorts of culinary specialities. The engine dates from 1913. Special additional trips are often made on public holidays; check departure times before travelling.

Coastal forts near Valdivia

At the mouth of the Río Valdivia are attractive villages which can be visited by land or river boat. **Niebla**, 18 km from Valdivia, is a spread-out resort with seafood restaurants and accommodation (also plenty of *cabañas* and campsites on the road from Valdivia). To the west of the resort is the **Fuerte de la Pura y Limpia Concepción de Monfort de Lemus**① *open daily, free,* on a promontory. It

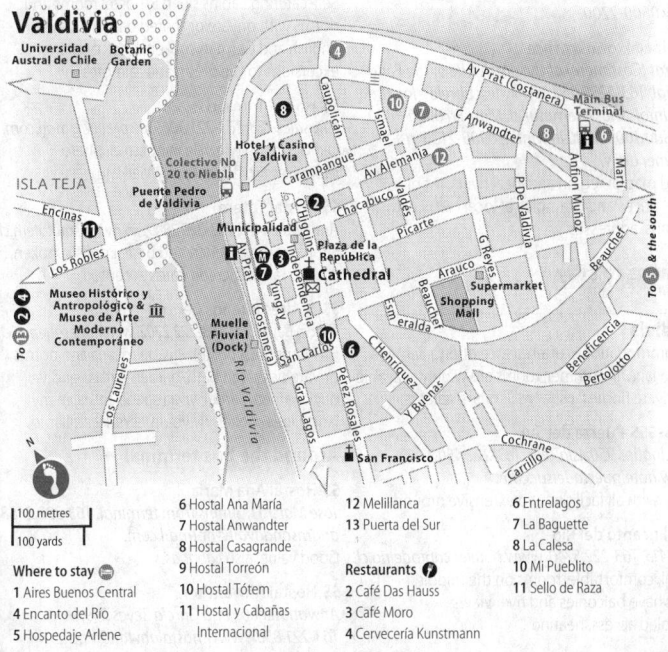

Valdivia

Universidad Austral de Chile
Botanic Garden

Av Prat (Costanera)

Main Bus Terminal

Caupolicán
Ismael
C Anwandter

ISLA TEJA

Encinas

Hotel y Casino Valdivia

Colectivo No 20 to Niebla
Puente Pedro de Valdivia

Carampangue
O'Higgins
Chacabuco

Av Alemania
Valdés
Picarte

P De Valdivia
Antfon Muñoz
Maíti
Beauchef

To ⑤ & the south

Municipalidad

Plaza de la República
Cathedral

Arauco
G Reyes
Beauchef
Esmeralda

Supermarket
Shopping Mall

Benavente

Los Robles

Museo Histórico y Antropológico y Museo de Arte Moderno Contemporáneo

Independencia
Yungay
Muelle Fluvial (Dock)
San Carlos
(Costanera)

C Henríquez
Y Bueras

Gral Lagos
Pérez Rosales

Benedicencia

Bertolotto

Cochrane

■ San Francisco

Carrillo

| 100 metres | | |
| 100 yards | | |

N

Where to stay 🛏
1 Aires Buenos Central
4 Encanto del Río
5 Hospedaje Arlene

6 Hostal Ana María
7 Hostal Anwandter
8 Hostal Casagrande
9 Hostal Torreón
10 Hostal Tótem
11 Hostal y Cabañas Internacional

12 Melillanca
13 Puerta del Sur

Restaurants 🍴
2 Café Das Hauss
3 Café Moro
4 Cervecería Kunstmann

6 Entrelagos
8 La Baguette
8 La Calesa
10 Mi Pueblito
11 Sello de Raza

has an interesting **museum** ① *Tue-Sun 1000-1900,* on Chilean naval history, and a **tourist kiosk** ① *daily 1000-2100.*

Corral, quieter than Niebla, is a fishing port with several good restaurants, 62 km from Valdivia by road (unsuitable for cars without four-wheel drive or high clearance). The dilapidated but atmospheric **Castillo de San Sebastián** ① *entry US$2.50, US$2 off season, open 0830-2000 summer, to 1900 in winter,* with 3-m-wide walls, was defended by a battery of 21 guns. It has a museum and offers a view upriver. In summer there are daily re-enactments of the 1820 storming of the Spanish fort by the Chileans (15 December-15 March, 1615, 1730, 1815). North along the coast are the remains of Castillo San Luis de Alba de Amargos (3 km) and Castillo de San Carlos, with pleasant beaches (4 km). The coastal walks west and south of Corral are splendid. The helpful tourist office on Corral's pier can provide some trekking tips.

In midstream, between Niebla and Corral is **Isla Mancera** a small island, fortified by the Castillo de San Pedro de Alcántara, which has the most standing buildings. The island is a pleasant place to stop, but it can get crowded when an excursion boat arrives.

Listings Valdivia and around *map p790*

Tourist information

Valdivia

CONAF office
Los Castaños 100, Isla Teja, T65-224 5200.

Municipal tourist office
Upstairs in the bus terminal and other locations. Daily 0800-2200.

Provincial tourist office
Av Prat (Costanera) at the north side of the Feria Fluvial, T63-2239 060, www.descubreloslrios.cl, also infoloslrios@sernatur.cl. Mon-Fri 0900-1800, Sat-Sun 1000-1600 in winter, 0900-2100 in summer daily.
Good map of region and local rivers, list of hotel prices and examples of local crafts with artisans' addresses.

Where to stay

Valdivia
Accommodation is often scarce during Semana Valdiviana. In summer, rooms are widely available in private homes, usually **$$**, or **$** singles.

$$$$-$$$ Puerta del Sur
Los Lingües 950, Isla Teja, T63-222 4500, www.hotelpuertadelsur.com.
4star, with all facilities and extensive grounds.

$$$ Encanto del Río
Prat 415, T63-222 5740, www.hotelencantodelrio.cl.
Small, comfortable, rooms on the middle floor have balconies and river views, disabled access, heating.

$$$ Melillanca
Alemania 675, T63-221 2509, www.hotelmelillanca.cl.
4-star, decent business standard, with restaurant, sauna.

$$ Hostal y Cabañas Internacional
García Reyes 660, T63-221 2015, www.hostalinternacional.cl.
Self-catering cabins sleep 5, hostel rooms and dorms with private or shared bath, helpful, English and German spoken, book exchange, excursions to the ocean and rainforest.

$$ Hostal Torreón
P Rosales 783, T63-221 3069, mrprelle@gmail.com.
Old German-style villa, nice atmosphere, rooms on top floor are airy, parking.

$$ Hostal Tótem
Anwandter 425, T63-229 2849, www.turismototem.cl.
Simple rooms, French and basic English spoken, tours arranged, credit cards accepted.

$$-$ Aires Buenos Central
García Reyes 550, T63-222 2202, www.airesbuenos.cl.
Eco-conscious hostel. Private rooms and dorms, private or shared bath, garden with friendly duck named Gardel, yoga space, tours, many languages spoken by volunteers, HI affiliated.

Around the bus terminal

$$ Hostal Ana María
José Martí 11, 3 mins from terminal, T63-222 2468, anamsandovalf@hotmail.com.
Good value, also *cabañas.*

$$ Hostal Anwandter
Anwandter 601 and García Reyes 249, T63-221 8587, www.hostalanwandter.cl.

Rooms sleep 1-4, private or shared bathroom, meals available, usual hostel facilities.

$$ Hostal Casagrande
Anwandter 880, T63-220 2035, www.hotelcasagrande.cl.
Heated but small rooms, some gloomy, in attractive house, convenient, great views from breakfast room.

$ Hospedaje Arlene
Picarte 1397, T9-7984 5597, arlene_ola@hotmail.com.
The original charming tumbledown mansion was lost to a fire in 2015. But the owners moved their operation and still offer the same hospitality and welcoming family vibe in a large house, albeit far from the main plaza. Still a great budget option during the high season. Doubles and singles, Wi-Fi, use of kitchen, free laundry service once a week, some English spoken. Recommended.

Camping

Camping Isla Teja
Los Cipreses 1125, T63-222 5855, www.islateja.com/camping.
25 sites on Isla Teja. Also hostel, *cabañas*.

Camping Orilla Verde
Pasaje Eusebio Lillo 23, T63-243 3902, www.campingvaldivia.jimdo.com.
Camping on the river for US$7.50 per night. Also *cabañas*. Services include Wi-Fi and kayak rental. Open year round.

Coastal resorts near Valdivia

$$$ El Castillo
Antonio Duce 750, Niebla, T63-228 2061, www.hotelycabanaselcastillo.com.
Typical Germanic 1920 mansion, lots of character. Rooms and apartments. Parking, playground, pool.

$$ Cabañas Fischer
Del Castillo 1115, Niebla, T63-228 2007, www.cabanasfischer.cl.
Cabins and 2 campsites. Worth bargaining out of season.

Restaurants

Valdivia

$$$-$$ Sello de Raza
Las Encinas 171, Isla de Teja, T63-222 6262.
Steakhouse and traditional food, warm atmosphere.

$$ Cervecería Kunstmann
Ruta T350, No 950, T63-229 2969, www.cerveza-kunstmann.cl.
On road to Niebla. German/Chilean food, brewery with 5 types of beer, beautiful interior, museum. Open from 1200 for visits; take the orange No 20 bus to Niebla.

$$ La Calesa
O'Higgins 160, T63-222 5467.
Elegant, intimate, Peruvian and international cuisine. Good *pisco sours*.

Cafés

Café Das Hauss
O'Higgins 394, T63-221 3878, see Facebook.
A Valdivia institution (originally Café Haussmann) Good tea, cakes and *crudos*.

Café Moro
Independencia y Libertad, T63-223 9084, see Facebook.
Airy café with a mezzanine art gallery. Good for breakfast, good value lunches, popular bar at night.

Entrelagos
Pérez Rosales 622, T63-221 2047, www.entrelagos.cl/valdivia.
Ice cream and chocolates.

La Baguette
Yungay 518, T63-221 2345.
Panadería with French-style cakes, brown bread.

Mi Pueblito
San Carlos 190, T63-224 5050, www.mipueblito.cl.
Wholemeal bread and vegetarian snacks to take away.

Coastal resorts near Valdivia

$$-$ Entre Costa
Duce 806, Niebla, T63-228 2678.
Popular corner restaurant serving Chilean specialities and seafood.

$$-$ Ona
Duce 875, T63-220 3969.
New, modern restaurant with a great view and food that is good value for the price. Specializes in seafood and ceviches.

Festivals

Valdivia
Last week of Jan Cervecería Kuntsmann holds a **Bierfest** in Parque Saval with music, games, food and beer.

Oct Film festival. Also in Oct there is **Oktoberfest** in Parque Saval with beer and live oompah bands.

Dec to end-Feb Semana Valdiviana, culminates in **Noche Valdiviana** on the last Sat of Feb with a procession of elaborately decorated boats that sail past the Muelle Fluvial. Accommodation is scarce during festival.

Shopping

Valdivia

Markets

Colourful riverside market with livestock, fish, etc. The separate **municipal market** building has been restored and is occupied mainly by *artesanía* stalls. On the riverside of the market building several fish restaurants serve cheap, tasty food and have nice atmosphere.

What to do

Valdivia

Boat trips

To Corral and Niebla and other destinations along the river; many kiosks along the Muelle Fluvial. Boats will only leave with a minimum of 10 passengers, so off-season organizein advance. Full list of operators in tourist information office.

Sea kayaking

Pueblito Expediciones, *San Carlos 188, T63-224 5055, www.pueblitoexpediciones.cl*. Offer classes and trips in sea kayaks in the waters around Valdivia.

Tour operator

Bahía II, *Costanera s/n, in kiosk next ro Feria Fluvial, T63-234 8727*. Offers a range of trips. Highly recommended.

Transport

Valdivia

Air Sky to/from **Santiago** 6 days a week.

Bus Well-organized terminal at Muñoz y Prat, by the river. To **Santiago**: several companies, 10 hrs, most services overnight, US$58-84; ½-hourly buses to/from **Osorno**, 2 hrs, several companies, US$6.50. To **Panguipulli**, **Empresa Pirehueico**, and others, about every 30 mins, US$6. Many daily to **Puerto Montt**, US$11, 3 hrs. To **Puerto Varas**, 3 hrs, US$11. To **Frutillar**, US$7.50, 2½ hrs. To **Villarrica**, by **JAC**, 2½ hrs, US$8, continuing to **Pucón**, US$8.50, 3 hrs. Frequent daily service to **Riñihue** via Paillaco and Los Lagos with **Buses Runisur**, US$4. To **Bariloche** (Argentina) via Osorno, 8 hrs, **Andesmar**, US$38-46.

Coastal resorts near Valdivia

Tourist boats offer a guided 5-hr tour (US$29-46, most with meals) to **Isla Mancera** and **Corral** from the Muelle Fluvial or the Marqués de Mancera (behind the tourist office on Av Prat). The river trip is beautiful, but you can also take a **bus** (No 20) to Niebla from outside bus station or along Calles Andwandter and Carampangue in Valdivia, regular service between 0630 and 1130, 30 mins, US$0.85 (bus continues to Los Molinos), then cross to Corral by **Somarco** vehicle ferry, every 20 mins, US$1.50.

Osorno and around *Colour map 8, C1.*

head east for thermal springs and volcanoes

Osorno is not a tourist city, but it is a base for visiting the attractive southern lakes or for heading east to Argentina. Founded in 1553, abandoned in 1604 and refounded in 1796, Osorno later became one of the centres of German immigration in the Lake District.

Sights

On the large Plaza de Armas stands the modern cathedral, while to the east of the plaza along MacKenna are a number of late 19th-century mansions built by German immigrants, now National Monuments. **Museo Histórico Municipal** ① *Matta 809, entrance in Casa de Cultura, Mon-Thu 0930-1730, Fri until 1700, Sat from 1400-1800, free*, includes displays on natural history, Mapuche culture, the refounding of the city and German colonization. The **Museo Interactivo de Osorno** (MIO) ① *in the former train station, Portales 901, 3 blocks southwest of the plaza, T64-221 2996, Mon-Thu 0900-1300, 1430-1730, Fri closes 1700, Sat 1430-1800 (closes 30 mins-1 hr earlier in winter), free*, is an interactive science museum designed for both children and adults.

Lago Puyehue and the national park *Colour map 8, C1.*

About 47 km east of Osorno, **Lago Puyehue** is surrounded by relatively flat countryside. At the western end is **Entre Lagos**; the all-inclusive **Termas de Puyehue** ① *www.puyehue.cl, day passes (1000-1900) or night passes (1800-0100) from US$88*, is at the eastern end. The main road east of Termas de Puyehue continues to the border at Paso Samoré (formerly Puyehue; see below).

At Aguas Calientes, 4 km south of the Termas de Puyehue, are more indoor and open-air **thermal pools** ① *www.termasaguascalientes.cl, day passes US$38-43 depending on day of week and season, daily 0830-1900,* plus camping, cabins, massages and other therapies. Also here is the administration for the **Parque Nacional Puyehue**, which stretches from east of Lago Puyehue to the Argentine border, with several lakes and two volcanic peaks: **Volcán Puyehue** (2240 m) in the north (access via private track US$13 belonging to **El Caulle** restaurant, with camping, www.elcaulle.com) and **Volcán Casablanca** (also called Antillanca, 1900 m). There is a ranger station at Anticura. Leaflets on attractions are available.

From Aguas Calientes the road into the park continues 18 km southeast to **Antillanca** on the slopes of **Volcán Casablanca**, past three small lakes and through forests. This is particularly beautiful, especially at sunrise, with the snow-clad cones of Osorno, Puntiagudo and Puyehue forming a semicircle. The tree-line on Casablanca is one of the few in the world made up of deciduous trees (*nothofagus* or southern beech). From Antillanca it is possible to climb Casablanca for even better views of the surrounding volcanoes and lakes (no path, seven hours return journey, information from Club Andino in Osorno). Attached to the Hotel Antillanca is one of the smallest ski resorts in Chile; there are three lifts, ski instruction and first aid available. Skiing quality depends on the weather: rain is common.

Border with Argentina: Paso Samoré The border is normally open 0800-1900 (from 0900 in winter). The Chilean border post is at Pajaritos, 4 km east of **Anticura**, which is 22 km west of the border, T64-231 1563, www.pasosfronterizos. gov.cl/cf_cardenalsamore.html. For vehicles entering Chile, formalities are quick (about 15 minutes), but includes the spraying of tyres, and shoes have to be wiped on a mat. This route is liable to closure after snow. Cyclists should know that there are no supplies between Entre Lagos and La Angostura (Argentina).

> **Tip...**
> Several bus companies run daily services from Puerto Montt via Osorno to Bariloche along this route (see under Puerto Montt for details). Although less scenic than the ferry journey across Lake Todos Los Santos and Laguna Verde (see page 775), this crossing is far cheaper, more reliable and still a beautiful trip (best views from the right-hand side of the bus).

Listings Osorno and around

Tourist information

Osorno
Sernatur is in provincial government office (Plaza de Armas, O'Higgins 667, p 1, Mon-Thu 0830-1730, till 1630 on Fri, T64-223 7575, infosorno@sernatur.cl). The **municipal office** is in the bus terminal, the Mercado Municipal and in a **kiosk** on the Plaza de Armas, 0900-1900 (www.municipalidadosorno.cl).

Where to stay

Osorno
There are plenty of cheap options near the bus terminal, none of them ideal.

$$$ Sonesta
Ejército 395 Rahue, T64-255 5000, www.sonesta.com.
First-class hotel overlooking river, all amenities, **El Olivillo** restaurant, attached to Plaza de los Lagos mall and casino.

$$$ Waeger
Cochrane 816, T64-223 3721, www.hotelwaeger.cl.
4-star, restaurant, comfortable but room sizes vary greatly.

\$\$\$-\$\$ Eduviges
Eduviges 856, T64-223 5023, www.hoteleduviges.cl.
Spacious, quiet, attractive, gardens, also *cabañas*.

\$\$ Residencial Riga
Amthauer 1058, T64-223 2945, resiriga@surnet.cl.
Pleasant, good value, quiet area, parking, heavily
booked in season.

\$ Hostal Hein's
Errázuriz 1757, T64-223 4116.
Private or shared bath, old-fashioned, spacious,
family atmosphere.

Lago Puyehue and the national park

\$\$\$\$ Hotel Termas de Puyehue
*At the Termas de Puyehue, T64-233 1400,
www.puyehue.cl.*
All inclusive: meals, drinks, use of thermal pools
and all activities (spa extra), well maintained,
in beautiful scenery, heavily booked Jan-Feb,
cheaper May to mid-Dec.

\$\$\$-\$\$ Hostal y Cabañas Miraflores
*Ramírez 480, Entre Lagos, T64-237 1275,
www.hostal-miraflores.cl.*
Pleasant rooms and cabins.

\$\$\$-\$\$ Hotel Antillanca
Antillanca, T64-261 2070, www.antillanca.cl.
Full board. Located at the foot of Volcán Casablanca
and offering skiing and snowboarding in the
winter, outdoor sports in summer: hiking, caving,
climbing and rappelling. Has swimming pool.

\$\$ Hospedaje Millaray
Ramírez 333, Entre Lagos, T9-9761 6625.
Very good place to stay.

Camping

Camping Los Copihues
*On south shore of Lake Puyehue, Km 58, T9-
9344 8830, www.campingloscopihues.cl.*
Restaurant, spa, camping (US\$13) and *cabañas*.

Camping No Me Olvides
*Ruta 215, Km 56, on south shore of Lake Puyehue,
T9-7452 3327, www.nomeolvides.cl.*
Tent site and *cabañas*.

Refugio at Volcán Puyehue
Basic *refugio* for US\$15. Check whether it is
open with CONAF in Anticura, T64-197 4572,
carlos.hernandez@conaf.cl.

Los Derrumbes
1 km from Aguas Calientes.
No electricity.

Restaurants

Osorno
Good cheap restaurants in the municipal market.

\$\$\$ Atelier
Freire 468.
Fresh pasta and other Italian delights, good.

\$\$ Dino's
Ramírez 898, on the plaza.
Restaurant upstairs, bar/cafeteria downstairs, good.

\$\$ Wufehr
Ramírez 1015, T64-222 6999.
Local raw meat specialities (*crudos*) and
sandwiches. Popular with locals.

\$\$-\$ Club de Artesanos
MacKenna 634.
Decent and hearty traditional Chilean fare.

\$ Café Literario Hojas del Sur
MacKenna 1011 y Cochrane.
More like a living room than a café, cosy, Wi-Fi.

\$ Jano's
Ramírez 977, T64-221 1828.
Bakery with fresh juices and lunch/dinner options.
Many vegetarian options as well. Has another
branch in the shopping mall at C Freire 542.

\$ La Cabaña
Ramírez 774, T64-227 2479.
Wide variety of cheap lunches ranging from
Chinese to home-cooked Chilean. Excellent value.

Lago Puyehue and the national park

\$\$\$-\$\$ Jardín del Turista
*Ruta 215, Km 46, Entre Lagos, T64-437 1214,
www.interpatagonia.com/jardindelturista.*
Very good; also has *cabañas* and suites.

Transport

Osorno
Air LATAM, 1 flight daily Osorno–**Santiago**.

Bus Local buses to **Entre Lagos** and **Aguas
Calientes**, from the Mercado Municipal terminal,
see below. Main terminal 4 blocks from Plaza
de Armas at Errázuriz 1400. Left luggage open
0730-2230, US\$1.50. Bus from centre, US\$0.60.
To **Santiago**, frequent, US\$66-93, 11 hrs. To
Concepción, US\$35. To **Temuco**, from US\$8. To
Pucón, US\$17, and **Villarrica**, US\$13, frequent.
To **Frutillar**, US\$3, **Llanquihue**, **Puerto Varas**

(US$4) and **Puerto Montt** (US$3.50) services every 30 mins. To **Puerto Octay**, US$3, every 30 mins. To **Bariloche** (Argentina), several companies, US$28.

Lago Puyehue and the national park
Bus To **Entre Lagos** from Osorno, hourly in summer 0640-2100, **Expreso Lago Puyehue** and **Buses Barria**, 1 hr, US$3, reduced service off-

season. Some buses by both companies continue to **Aguas Calientes** (off-season according to demand) 2 hrs, US$7. Buses that continue to Aguas Calientes do not stop at the lake (unless you want to get off at Hotel Termas de Puyehue and clamber down). There's no public transport from Aguas Calientes to Antillanca; try hitching – always difficult, but it is not a hard walk.

<h1>Lago Llanquihue and around</h1>

stunning scenery and a memorable route to Argentina

☆This is one of the most beautiful areas in a part of Chile which already has plenty to boast about. Lago Llanquihue, with its views to volcanoes and German-influenced towns, adjoins Parque Nacional Vicente Pérez Rosales, the oldest national park in the country. It contains another beautiful lake, Todos los Santos, three major volcanoes and several waterfalls. The region ends at the Seno de Reloncaví, a peaceful glacial inlet, often shrouded in soft rain.

Lago Llanquihue, covering 56,000 ha, is the second-largest in Chile. Across the great blue sheet of water can be seen two snow-capped volcanoes: the perfect cone of Osorno (2680 m) and the shattered cone of Calbuco (2015 m – which erupted in April 2015). When the air is clear, distant Tronador (3460 m) is also visible. The largest towns, Puerto Varas, Llanquihue and Frutillar, are on the western shore, linked by the Pan-American Highway. There are roads around the rest of the lake; the route from Puerto Octay east to Ensenada is very beautiful, but is narrow with lots of blind corners, necessitating speeds of 20-30 kph at best in places (see below).

Tip...
Wild camping and barbecues are forbidden on the lakeshore.

Puerto Octay *Colour map 8, C1.*
Tourist office: Puerto Montt 378, T64-239 1860.

A sleepy, picturesque small town at the northern tip of the lake with a backdrop of rolling hills, Puerto Octay was founded by German settlers in 1852. The town enjoyed a boom in the late 19th century when it was the northern port for steamships on the lake. The church and the enormous German-style former convent survive from that period. **Museo el Colono** ① *Independencia 591, T64-239 1523, www.museoelcolono.jimdo.com, daily 1000-1300, 1500-1900, US$1.60*, has displays on German colonization. Another part of the museum, housing agricultural tools and machinery for making *chicha*, is just outside town on the road to Centinela.

Some 3 km south along an unpaved road is the Peninsula of Centinela, a beautiful spot with a launch dock and watersports. From the headland are fine views of the volcanoes and the cordillera of the Andes; it's a very popular spot in good weather, good for picnics (taxi US$3 one way). Rowing boats and *pedalos* can be hired.

Frutillar Bajo *Colour map 8, C1.*
About halfway along the west side of the lake, Frutillar is divided into Frutillar Alto, just off the main highway, and Frutillar Bajo, beautifully situated on the lake, 4 km away. (*Colectivos* run between the two towns, five minutes, US$1.) Frutillar Bajo is possibly the most attractive – and expensive – town on the lake. At the north end of the town is the **Reserva Forestal Edmundo Winckler**, run by the Universidad de Chile, 33 ha, with a guided trail through native woods. **Museo Colonial Alemán** ① *Pérez Rosales s/n, T65-242 1142, www.museosaustral.cl, daily 0900-1930 in high season, daily 0900-1730, 1400-1800 in winter, US$4*, includes a watermill, replicas of two German colonial houses with furnishings and utensils of the period, a *campanario* (circular barn with agricultural machinery inside) and gardens. There is a state-of-the-art concert hall on the lakefront, **Teatro del Lago** (www.teatrodellago.cl). Accommodation must be booked well in advance.

Puerto Varas and around *Colour map 8, C1.*

This beauty spot was the southern port for shipping on the lake in the 19th century. It is infinitely preferable as a centre for visiting the southern lakes to Puerto Montt, 20 km to the south. The Catholic church, built by German Jesuits in 1918, is a copy of the church in Marieenkirche in the Black Forest. North and east of the **Gran Hotel Puerto Varas** (1934) are German-style mansions dating from the early 20th century. **Parque Philippi**, on top of the hill, is pleasant; walk up to **Hotel Cabañas del Lago** on Klenner, cross the railway and the gate is on the right. Just past the village of Nueva Braunau, 9 km west of Puerto Varas, is the remarkable **Museo Antonio Felmer** ① T9-9449 8130, https://museoaleman.cl, Tue-Sun 1100-2000, IUS$4.70, a huge private collection of machinery, tools and household items used by the first Austrian immigrants to the area, some with English descriptions. On quiet days staff may give demonstrations of the more ingenious objects.

Puerto Varas is a good base for trips around the lake. On the south shore two of the best beaches are **Playa Hermosa** (Km 7) and **Playa Niklitschek** (Km 8, US$9 high season, US$10 weekends). **La Poza**, at Km 16, is a little lake to the south of Lago Llanquihue reached through narrow channels overhung with vegetation. **Isla Loreley**, an island on La Poza, is very beautiful (frequent boat trips, US$3.50); a concealed channel leads to yet another lake, the Laguna Encantada. East of Puerto Varas by 47 km, **Ensenada** is at the southeast corner of the lake. Much of the town was smothered in ash by the eruption of Volcán Calbuco in 2015, but it has been cleaned up and rebuilt (2017). Minibuses run from Puerto Varas, frequent in summer (see Transport, page 805).

Volcán Osorno

Volcán Osorno can be reached from Ensenada, or from a road branching off the Puerto Octay–Ensenada road at Puerto Klocker, 20 km southeast of Puerto Octay. Guided ascents (organized by agencies in Puerto Varas) set out from the *refugio* at **La Burbuja** where there is a small **ski centre** ① T9-9158 7337, usually open Jun-Sep in winter, www.volcanosorno.com, ski ticket US$41, equipment rental US$32, and pleasant short walks with great views in summer. From here it is six hours to the summit. The volcano can also be climbed from the north (La Picada); this route is easier and may be attempted without a guide, although only experienced climbers should climb right to the top as ice-climbing equipment is essential and there are many craters hidden below thin crusts of ice. Note that Refugio La Picada, marked on many maps, burned down several years ago.

Parque Nacional Vicente Pérez Rosales
Daily 0900-1800 (1730 in winter), US$6.25. There is a guardaparque office in Puella.

The national park is centred around **Lago Todos los Santos**, the most beautiful of all the lakes in this part of Chile. The long, irregularly shaped sheet of emerald-green water has deeply wooded shores and several small islands rising from its surface. In the waters are reflected the slopes of Volcán Osorno. Beyond the hilly shores to the east are several graceful snow-capped mountains, with the mighty Tronador in the distance. To the north is the sharp point of Cerro Puntiagudo and, at the northeastern end, Cerro Techado rises cliff-like out of the water.

At the western end of the lake, the port of Petrohué, 16 km northwest of Ensenada, is a good base for walking and for trout and salmon fishing. CONAF has an office here with a visitors' centre, small museum and 3D model of the park. Nearby is the **Salto de Petrohué** ① 6 km southwest of Petrohué (unpaved, dusty, lots of traffic, bus US$1.50), or 10 km (paved) from Ensenada, entry US$6.25, with a snackbar and two short trails, the Senderos de los Enamorados and Carileufú. **Peulla**, at the eastern end of the lake, is a good starting point for hikes in the mountains. The Cascadas Los Novios, signposted above the Hotel Peulla, are stunning. Petrohué and Peulla are connected by the **Cruce Andino** service with connections to Bariloche (Argentina). There are no roads round the lake, but private launches can be hired for trips, including to Cayetué on the lake's southern shore (US$17 per person, minimum three people) from where it is a five- to six-hour hike to Ralún (see below).

Fact...
The park is infested by horseflies in December and January: cover up as much as possible with light-coloured clothes which may help a bit.

☆To Argentina via Lago Todos Los Santos

This popular route to Bariloche, involving ferries across Lago Todos Los Santos, Lago Frías and Lago Nahuel Huapi, is outstandingly beautiful whatever the season, though the mountains are often obscured by rain and heavy cloud. The route is via Puerto Varas, Ensenada and Petrohué Falls (20 minutes stop) to Petrohué, where it connects with a catamaran service across Lago Todos Los Santos to Peulla. There's a two-hour stop in Peulla for lunch and Chilean customs, followed by a two-hour bus ride through the Paso Pérez Rosales to Argentine customs in Puerto Frías. Then it's a 20-minute boat trip across Lago Frías to Puerto Alegre and a 15-minute bus trip from Puerto Alegre to Puerto Blest. From Puerto Blest it is a beautiful one hour catamaran trip along Lago Nahuel Huapi to Puerto Pañuelo (Llao Llao), from where it's a 30-minute bus journey to Bariloche (bus drops passengers at hotels, campsites or centre). The route is operated by **Cruce Andino**, see Transport, page 805.

Border with Argentina: Paso Pérez Rosales Chilean immigration is in Peulla, 30 km west of the border, open daily, summer 0800-2100. There is an Argentine consulate in Puerto Montt: Pedro Montt 160, piso 6, T65-228 2878, www.cpmon.cancilleria.gov.ar, quick visa service.

Seno de Reloncaví and Cochamó

The Reloncaví estuary, the northernmost of Chile's glacial inlets, is recommended for its local colour, its wildlife (including sealions and dolphins) and its peace, although the salmon farming boom of the last decade has left its mark in the shape of hundreds of cages and multicoloured buoys dotted about the fjord. **Ralún**, a small village at the northern end of the estuary, with a village shop and post office, is 31 km southeast from Ensenada by a mostly paved road along the wooded lower Petrohué valley. Just outside the village are thermal springs with **baths** ① *US$1.70, reached by boat across Río Petrohué, US$3.75 pp (see Facebook).* Roads continue, unpaved, along the east side of the estuary to Cochamó and Puelo and on the west side to Canutillar.

Cochamó and the Gaucho Trail Cochamó, 17 km south of Ralún on the east shore of the estuary, is a pretty village, with a fine wooden church similar to those on Chiloé, in a striking setting, with the estuary and volcano behind. Four kilometres south of the village a road branches inland for about 3 km, following the course of the Río Cochamó. At the end of the road is the trailhead up the valley (taxi to start of trail US$12, or ask at your *hostal*). It is a five-hour hike up to **La Junta**, described as Chile's Yosemite for its imposing granite peaks and now becoming a popular centre for many outdoor activities in and around the *alerce* forests (trekking, climbing, kayaking, riding, birdwatching and fishing). For more information call T65-235 0271, or see www. cochamo.com. To visit the valley in summer you must reserve campsites and other services in advance; see www.reservasvallecochamo.cl.

The **Gaucho Trail** east from Cochamó to **Paso León** on the Argentine border dates from the colonial period and runs along Río Cochamó to La Junta (see above), then along the north side of Lago Vidal, passing waterfalls and the oldest surviving *alerce* trees in Chile at El Arco. The route takes three to four days by horse, or five to six days on foot, depending on conditions, which are best December to March. From Paso León it is a three-hour walk to the main road to Bariloche.

Puelo to Argentina South of Cochamó, on the south bank of the Río Puelo, **Puelo** is a most peaceful place, with expensive fly fishing lodges nearby. Here the road forks. One branch (very rough) continues to Puelche on the Carretera Austral, while the other heads southeast, past **Lago Tagua Tagua** ① *ferry 0730, 0900, 1300, return 0815, 1200, 1630, US$1.50 single, US$10.50 for vehicles,* to the peaceful village of Llanada Grande, nestled in the Andes, with basic accommodation. The road continues to the village of Primer Corral from where it is a two-day trek to the Argentine village of Puelo and on to El Bolsón.

An alternative route to Argentina starts with a 45-minute walk to Lago Azul from the road between Llanada Grande and Primer Corral. A 25-minute boat trip across Lago Azul leads to a 45-minute hike through pristine forest to Lago Las Rocas, where another 25-minute boat ride ends at the Carabineros de Chile post on Lago Inferior. Go through immigration, then navigate Lagos Inferior and Puelo to the pier at Lago Puelo.

Tourist information

Frutillar Bajo

The **tourist office** on the Costanera (Filippi 754, T65-246 7450, www.munifrutillar.cl and www. frutillar.com, daily 0900-2000 in high season, till 1800 in low season) is helpful.

Puerto Varas

There's a **municipal tourist office** (Del Salvador 320, T65-236 1194, gonzalo@ptovaras.cl, see www.ptovaras.cl). The **information office** on the pier belongs to the chamber of tourism and does not give wholly impartial advice. There is a helpful **Informatur** office near the Costanera at San José y Santa Rosa, T65-223 7773. Many places close in the off-season.

Where to stay

Puerto Octay

$$$-$$ Zapato Amarillo
Km 35, 35 mins' walk north of town,
T64-221 0787, http://zapatoamarillo.cl.
$ pp in dorms. Book in advance in high season, private or shared bath, home-made bread, meals, German/English spoken, mountain bikes, sailboats, tours, house has a grass roof.

$$ Hostería La Baja
Centinela, T9-8218 6897, www.hosterialabaja.cl.
Beautifully situated at the neck of the peninsula. Good value.

Camping

$$-$ Camping Doña Irma
1 km south of Las Cascadas, T64-239 6227.
Beach camping, hot water.

El Molino
Beside lake east of Puerto Octay, T64-239 1375,
see Facebook.

Frutillar Bajo

There are several good-value places to stay in Frutillar Alto, along Carlos Richter (main street).

$$$$ Ayacara
Av Philippi 1215, T65-242 1550,
www.hotelayacara.cl.
Beautiful rooms with lake view, welcoming, have a *pisco sour* in the library in the evening.

$$$$-$$$ Salzburg
Camino Playa Maqui, north of town,
T65-242 1589, www.salzburg.cl.
Excellent, spa, sauna, restaurant, mountain bikes, arranges tours and fishing.

$$$ Hotel am See
Av Philippi 539, T65-242 1539, see Facebook.
Good breakfast, café has German specialities.

$$$ Lagune Club
3 km north of Frutillar Bajo, T65-233 0033,
www.laguneclub.com.
In an old country house in 16 ha of land, private beach, fishing trips, free pickup from terminal. Disabled-visitor friendly, discounts for the over-65s. Also *cabañas*. Good value in dollars.

$$$ Winkler
Av Philippi 1155, T65-242 1388,
hosteriawinkler@gmail.com.
Much cheaper ($) in low season. Also sells cakes from the garage, **Kuchen Laden**.

$$$-$$ Casa Ko'
Camino Playa Maqui s/n km 1.5, T9-8210 8306,
www.casako.com.
Traditional house, helpful owners, lovely surroundings and views, good meals. Plenty of outdoor activities.

$$ Hospedaje Tía Clarita
Pérez Rosales 658, T65-242 1806, canfrut@live.com.
Kitchen facilities, very welcoming, good value.

$$ Hostería Trayén
Av Philippi 963, T65-242 1346,
tttrayen33@hotmail.com.
Nice rooms with bath.

Camping

La Gruta
2 km from Frutillar Bajo on 21 de Mayo s/n,
T9-7696 1237, see Facebook.
Offers most services.

Playa Maqui
6 km north of Frutillar, T9-7175 1377,
see Facebook.
Fancy, expensive.

Puerto Varas and around

$$$$ Cabañas del Lago
Luis Welmann 195, T65-220 0100,
www.cabanasdellago.cl.

On hill overlooking lake, upper floor rooms have the best view in town. Service not up to much. Also self-catering cabins sleeping 5, heating, sauna, swimming pools and games room. Often full with package groups.

$$$$ Cumbres
Imperial 0561, T65-222 2000,
www.cumbrespuertovaras.com.
Best hotel in town. All rooms look out over the lake, attentive staff, good restaurant. Spa and small pool with great views.

$$$$-$$$ Bellavista
Pérez Rosales 060, T65-223 2011,
www.hotelbellavista.cl.
4-star hotel, king-size beds; cheerful, restaurant and bar, overlooking lake and main road, sauna, parking.

$$$ Casa Kalfu
Tronador 1134, T65-275 1261, www.casakalfu.cl.
Characterful blue wooden building remodelled in traditional style. Helpful owners, English spoken, good value.

$$$ Weisserhaus
San Pedro 252, T65-234 6479,
www.weisserhaus.cl.
Central, cosy, family-run, German-style breakfast, good facilities, very helpful, central heating, very pleasant.

$$$-$$ Amancay
Walker Martínez 564, T65-223 2201,
www.cabanahostalamancay.cl.
Nice *cabañas* with log-burning stoves or hostel rooms, good, German spoken.

$$ Casa Margouya
Santa Rosa 318, T65-223 7640, www.margouya.com.
Bright, colourful hostel, lots of information, French-run, English spoken.

$$ Hostería Outsider
San Bernardo 318, T65-223 1056, www.turout.com.
Rooms sleep 1-3, private bath, comfortable, heating, helpful, restaurant, travel agency, English and German spoken, book in advance.

$$-$ Canales del Sur
Pérez Rosales 1631A, 1km east of town,
T65-223 0909, www.canalesdelsur.cl.
Pleasantly set on the lakeside. Very helpful, family-run, tours arranged, garden, car hire.

$$-$ Casa Azul
Manzanal 66 y Rosario, T65-223 2904,
www.casaazul.net.

Wooden building, variety of rooms and dorms, heating, beautiful Japanese garden, book exchange, German and English spoken, excursions offered. Reserve in advance in high season.

$$-$ Compass del Sur
Klenner 467, T65-223 2044,
www.compassdelsur.cl.
Chilean/Swedish-run hostel, rooms with shared or private bath, dorms, comfy lounge, helpful, German, English, Swedish spoken, excursions offered. Also camping. Reserve in advance in high season.

$$-$ Hospedaje Don Raúl
Salvador 928, T65-231 0897.
Shared rooms and bath, hostel facilities, spotless, helpful, camping.

Camping

Casa Tronador
Tronador y Manzanal,
campingtronador@gmail.com.
Expensive but central.

Playa Hermosa
Km 7, T65-233 8283, www.
campingplayahermosa.com.
Fancy, negotiate off season, take own supplies.

Playa Niklitschek
Km 8, T9-4166 0330, www.playanik.cl.
Full facilities.

Ensenada

$$$$ Hotel Ensenada
Km 45, T65-221 2028, www.hotelensenada.cl.
Olde-worlde, half-board, good food, good view of lake and Osorno Volcano, mountain bikes and tennis for guests.

$$$ Cabañas Brisas del Lago
Km 42, T65-221 2012, www.brisasdellago.cl.
Chalets for up to 6 and rooms for up to 3 on beach, good restaurant nearby, supermarket next door.

$$ Hospedaje Ensenada
Km 43, T65-221 2050, www.hospedajensenada.cl.
Typical old house, rooms sleep 1-4, private or shared bath, beach, parking.

Camping

Montaña
Central Ensenada, T9-7306 3545.
Fully equipped, nice beach sites, also has a good local restaurant ($). Also at Playa Larga, 1 km further east, and at Puerto Oscuro, 2 km north.

Trauco
4 km west, T65-223 6262, see Facebook.
Large site with shops, fully equipped.

Volcán Osorno

There are 2 *refugios* ($ pp), both of them south
of the summit and reached from the southern
access road: **La Burbuja**, the former ski-club
centre, 14 km north of Ensenada at 1250 m (T65-
222 5380, marco.carrillo@conaf.cl), and **Refugio
Teski Ski Club** (T9-6238 3799, www.teski.cl), just
below the snowline, with café.

CONAF campsite
*Km 49, site at Puerto Oscuro, beneath road
to Volcán Osorno.*
Very good.

Parque Nacional Vicente Pérez Rosales

Petrohué

$$$$ Hotel Petrohué
*Ruta 225, Km 64, T65-221 2025,
www.petrohue.com.*
Excellent views, half-board available, also has
cabins, cosy, restaurant, log fires, sauna and
heated pool; hiking, fishing and other activities.

Peulla

$$$$ Natura Patagonia
T65-297 2289, www.hotelnatura.cl.
Rooms and suites, disabled facilities, lots of
activities offered, restaurant.

$$$$ Hotel Peulla
T65-297 2288, www.hotelpeulla.cl.
Half-board. Beautiful setting by the lake and
mountains, restaurant and bar, cold in winter,
often full of tour groups (older partner of **Natura**).

Camping

Camping wild and picnicking within the national
park is forbidden. There's a basic site with
no services and cold showers at Petrohué
beside the lake; locals around the site sell fresh
bread (local fishermen will ferry you across).
There's also a good campsite 1½ hrs' walk east
of Peulla, but you'll need to take your own food.
A small shop in Peulla sells basic goods, including
fruit and veg. The CONAF office can help find
cheap accommodation.

Seno de Reloncaví

Ralún

Lodging is available with families.

Cochamó and the Gaucho Trail

There are also *cabañas* and campsites; see
www.cochamo.com. Also a few eating places.

$$$ Cochamó Aventura
*San Bernadino 318, Puerto Varas, T9-9289 4314,
www.campoaventura.cl.*
4 km south of Cochamó in Valle Rio Cochamó,
full board available (great breakfast), local food,
and very fresh milk from their own cow. Also a
renovated mountain house at their other base in
the valley of La Junta. Camping ($) available at
both locales. They specialize in horse riding and
trekking between the Reloncaví Estuary and the
Argentine border, 2-10 days.

$$ Hostal Cochamó
*Av Aeródromo s/n T9-6135 2163,
www.hostalcochamo.com. Price pp.*
Private rooms and shared dorms, local meals
available, activities arranged as well as transport.

$$-$ Edicar
*Prat y Sgto Aldea, T9-7445 9230, on seafront by
the dock/ramp.*
With breakfast, hot shower, good value.

$$-$ Refugio Cochamó
*La Junta, Cochamó valley, www.cochamo.com.
Oct-Apr.*
The perfect base for outdoor activities in the
Cochamó valley, only accessible on foot (4-6 hrs)
or horseback. Private rooms have bed linen, bring
sleeping bag for dorm beds.

$ Hostal Maura
*JJ Molina 12, T9-9334 9213,
www.experienciapatagonia.cl.*
Beautiful location overlooking the estuary,
rooms with shared bath, meals served, kayaks,
horse riding, good information, sauna and hot
tub (at extra cost).

Puelo

Basic lodging is available with families.

$$$$-$$$ Mítico Puelo Lodge
*At the southern end of Lago Tagua Tagua,
T9-7806 1565, www.miticopuelo.com;
office Walker Martín ez 807, Puerto Varas,
T65-223 4892.*
Lodge with 2 standards of room, lake or
mountain views, heating, full board or all-
inclusive packages available, activities include
cycling, horse riding, trekking, kayking and
fishing, experienced guides.

$$$ Posada Martín Pescador
Lago Totoral, 2 km from Llanada Grande on road to Primer Corral, www.posadamartinpescador.cl.
With bath, hot water, meals, BBQs, horse riding, trekking, fishing, canoeing and rafting.

Restaurants

Puerto Octay

$$ El Rancho del Espantapájaros
6 km south on the road to Frutillar, T65-233 0049, www.espantapajaros.cl.
In a converted barn with wonderful views over the lake, serves spit-roasted meat. All-you-can-eat, with salad bar and drinks included.

$$ Fogón de Anita
1 km out of town, T65-239 1276, www.fogondeanita.blogspot.co.uk.
Mid-priced grill. Also German cakes and pastries.

$ Restaurante Baviera
Germán Wulf 582, T65-239 1460, see Facebook.
Cheap and good, salmon and *cazuelas*.

Frutillar Bajo

$$ Andes
Philippi 1057.
Good set menus and à la carte.

$$ Trattoria
Philippi 1000, downstairs from the theatre, see Facebook.
Italian chef Alessando Guarneri brings an eclectic mix of dishes from his homeland, home-made pastas and pizzas. Recommended.

Cafés

Many German-style cafés and tea-rooms on C Philippi (the lakefront).

Di Parma
Carlos Richter y Winkler, Frutillar Alto, T9-8928 6146, see Facebook.
Specializes in strudel (the strawberry is highly recommended). Cheaper option than cafés in Frutillar Bajo.

Duendes del Lago
Philippi y O'Higgins, T9-8583 9040, see Facebook.
Corner café with an extensive menu of coffees, hot chocolate, salads, sandwiches and delicious kuchens. Fun decor; gnomes.

Puerto Varas and around

$$$-$$ Mediterráneo
Santa Rosa 068, T65-223 7268, see Facebook.
On the lakefront, international and local food, interesting varied menu, often full.

$$$-$$ Xic Dalí
Purísima 690, T65-223 4424.
Intimate Catalan bistro. Inventive menu, top quality preparation and service, good wine list.

$$ Bravo Cabrera
Pérez Rosales 1071, 1 km east of centre, T65-223 3441, www.bravocabrera.cl.
Popular bar/restaurant opposite the lake, big portions, good value, varied menu, lively bar.

$$ Di Carusso
San Bernardo 318.
Italian trattoria, good fresh pasta dishes on Fri.

$$ Donde El Gordito
San Bernardo 560, T65-223 3425, downstairs in market.
Good range of meat dishes, no set menu.

$$ La Chamaca Inn
Del Salvador y San Bernard, T65-223 2876.
Good choice for traditional Chilean seafood. Larger than life owner.

$$ La Olla
Ruta 225, 4 km east of town towards Ensenada, T65-223 4605.
Good, popular for seafood, fish and meat, traditional Chilean cuisine.

$ There are a couple of little snack bars along the coast on Santa Rosa at the foot of Cerro Philippi, serving, among other things, tasty vegetarian burgers.

Cafés

Café Danés
Del Salvador 441.
Coffee and cakes.

Cassis
San Juan41, local A, www.chocolatescassis.com.
Very sweet cakes, great ice creams and brownies.

El Barista
Walker Martínez 211A, T65-223 3130, www.elbarista.cl.
Probably the best place for a coffee. Good value set lunches and bar.

Ensenada

Most eating places close off season. There are a few pricey shops. Take your own provisions.

$$$ Latitude 42
Yan Kee Way Resort, T65-221 2030.
Expensive, excellent and varied cuisine, very good quality wine list. Lake views.

$$$-$$ Don Salmón
Km 42.4, T65-220 2108, www.donsalmon.cl.
Expansive restaurant with a magnificent view of the lake. Specializes in everything salmon, lunchtime buffet of fish, *mariscos* and ceviches. Also *parrilla* serving *picanha* BBQ.

Bars and clubs

Puerto Varas and around

Club Orquídea
San Pedro 537, T65-223 3024, see Facebook. Mon-Sat from 1900.
Popular club with tables dotted around several small rooms and alcoves. Occasional live music, huge pizzas.

Frutillar Bajo

O'clock
Pérez Rosales 690.
Many microbrews on offer; great for a pitcher or a pint.

Festivals

Frutillar Bajo
27 Jan-5 Feb A highly regarded classical music festival (Semanas Musicales) at the **Teatro del Lago**.

What to do

Puerto Varas and around

Horse riding
See **Cochamó Aventura**, below.

Kayak
Al Sur, *Aconcagua e Imperial, T65-223 2300, www. alsurexpeditions.com.* Sea-kayak, rafting and trekking tours, good camping equipment, English spoken, official tour operators to Parque Pumalín.
Inside Nature Expeditions, *T9-7872 7672, lactorisfernandeziana@hotmail.com.* Based out of Puerto Varas, owner Carlos gives private

4x4 tours all throughout the Lake District. Also rafting and kayaking.
Ko'kayak, *San Pedro 311 and Ruta 225, Km 40, T65-223 3004, www.kokayak.cl.* Kayaking and rafting trips, good equipment and after-trip lunch, French/Chilean-run.
Miralejos, *Independencia 50, of 7, T65-223 4892, www.miralejos.cl.* Kayaking in northern Patagonia, also trekking, horse riding and mountaineering. Associated is **Trekking Cochamó**, same address, www.trekkingcochamo.cl, which concentrates on adventure sports in Cochamó. Both are part of the **www.secretpatagonia.com** group of operators who specialize in the area.
Yak Expediciones, *owner Juan Federico Zuazo (Juanfe), T9-8332 0574, www.yakexpediciones.cl.* Experienced and safe kayaking trips on lakes and sea, in the fjords of Pumalín, enthusiastic and excellent, small groups, also runs courses. Repeatedly recommended.

Zip-lining (canopy)
Offered by several operators, including:
Canopy Pro, *Santa Rosa 132, T65-223 5120, www.canopypro.com.*

Seno de Reloncaví
In **Puelo**, fly fishing guides generally charge around US$30 per hr, boat included.
Cabalgatas Cochamó, *Cra Principal, Cochamó, T9-7764 5289, www.cabalgatascochamo.wix.com/ chile.* On a farm by the water, riding trips from 1 to 8 days, also boat trips, climbing and fishing.
Cochamó Aventura Travel Agency, *Cochamó, T9-9289 4318, www.campo-aventura.com.* Specializes in tailor-made tours and excursions in Chile, including 1-, 3- and 10-day trips on horseback (see above under Cochamó, Where to stay).

Transport

Puerto Octay
Bus Terminal is at C Esperanza 433, T64-239 1189, open daily 0620-2130. To **Osorno** every 20-30 mins, US$3; last bus at 2015; to **Frutillar** (2 hrs, US$2, last at 2000), **Puerto Varas** (2 hrs) and **Puerto Montt** (US$3.50 last at 1800) with **Thaebus**. Around the east shore: to **Las Cascadas** (34 km), Mon-Fri 0800, 1700, returns next day 0830, 1700, US$3.

Frutillar Bajo
Bus Most leave from the small bus terminal at Alessandri y Richter in Frutillar Alto. To **Puerto Varas** (US$2) and **Puerto Montt** (US$3), frequent

Thaebus. To **Osorno**, Cruz del Sur 1½ hrs, US$3. To **Puerto Octay**, Thaebus, 6 a day, US$2.

Puerto Varas and around
Bus Pullman and ETM are the only long-distance bus companies to have terminals in the town centre (Diego Portales). Other companies have ticket offices dotted around the centre but buses leave from the outskirts of town (**Turbus**, **Jac** and **Cóndor** from Del Salvador 1093 and **Cruz del Sur** from San Fransisco y García Moreno). To **Santiago**, US$66-93, several companies, 12 hrs. To **Osorno** hourly, US$4, 1 hr. To **Valdivia** US$11, 3 hrs. Minibuses to the following destinations leave from San Bernardo y Walker Martínez: **Puerto Montt**, Thaebus, **Suyai, Expreso Puerto Varas Express** and others every 5 mins, US$2.50, 30 mins, last at 2200. Every 15 mins to **Frutillar** (US$2, 30 mins). To **Ensenada** every 45 mins, last at 2000.

Ferry Cruce Andino (Del Salvador 72, www.cruceandino.com) operates the bus and ferry crossing from Puerto Varas 0800 to Bariloche, US$280 one way (US$230 in low season, 2017).

From 1 May to 30 Aug this trip is done over 2 days with overnight stay in Peulla at **Hotel Peulla** or **Hotel Natura**. You may break the journey at any point and continue next day.

Parque Nacional Vicente Pérez Rosales
Minibuses Every 30 mins to **Petrohué** from Puerto Montt and Puerto Varas in summer (US$5, 1¼ hrs from Puerto Varas), much less frequent off season. Last bus to **Ensenada** at 1800, US$4.

Seno de Reloncaví
Boat In summer boats sail up the estuary from Angelmó (Puerto Montt). The **Sernatur** office in Puerto Montt (see below) has details of trips.

Bus From Puerto Montt to **Ralún, Cochamó** and **Puelo**, 3 a day via Puerto Varas and Ensenada, 2 on Sun, with **Transhar** (T65-225 4187) and **Buses Río Puelo** (T9-9123 0838): US$5 to Ralún, US$6 to Cochamó (2½ hrs) and US$8 to Puelo (3 a day Mon-Sat, 2 on Sun). Minibus services from Puerto Montt airport cost between US$18 and US$140-200 depending on size of vehicle (see www.cochamo.com).

gateway to Chiloé and the far south

Just 20 minutes south of Puerto Varas, and 1016 km south of Santiago, Puerto Montt is a rapidly growing, disordered modern city, developing in line with a boom in salmon fishing. The capital of X Región (Los Lagos), it was founded in 1853 as part of the German colonization of the area. The port is used by fishing boats and coastal vessels, and is the departure point for journeys south to Chaitén, Puerto Chacabuco, Laguna San Rafael and for the long haul to Puerto Natales (if operating – see below). A dual carriageway runs 55 km southwest to Pargua, where there is a ferry service to the unique island of Chiloé.

Sights
Good views over the city and bay are offered from outside the Intendencia Regional on Avenida X Region. The **Iglesia de los Jesuitas** on Gallardo, dating from 1872, has a fine blue-domed ceiling; behind it on a hill is the *campanario* (clock tower). **Museo Regional Juan Pablo II** ① *Portales 997 near the bus terminal, Mon-Fri 1000-1300, 1430-1800, free but may charge in the future*, documents local history and has a fine collection of historic photos of the city; there's also memorabilia of Pope John Paul II's visit in 1988. The **Casa Pauly** ① *Rancagua 210, T65-248 2611, Mon-Fri 1000-1700*, is one of the city's historic mansions, now in a poor state, which holds temporary exhibitions. Near the plaza, the **Casa del Arte Diego Rivera** ① *Varas y Quillota, www.corporacionculturalpuertomontt.cl*, has a theatre and holds regular exhibitions.

☆The fishing port of **Angelmó** ① *2 km west, reached by Costanera bus along Portales and by colectivos Nos 2, 3, 4, 22, 33 from the centre, US$0.80*, has become a tourist centre with seafood restaurants and handicraft shops. The wooded **Isla Tenglo**, reached by launch from Angelmó (US$0.65 each way), is a favourite place for picnics. There are magnificent views from the summit. The island is famous for its *curantos* (seafood stews), served by restaurants in summer. Boat trips round the island from Angelmó last 30 minutes, US$4.25.

Parque Provincial Lahuen Ñadi ① *T65-248 6101/6400, US$2*, contains 200 ha of native forest including probably the most accessible ancient alerce forest in Chile. Take the main road to the airport, which leads off Ruta 5; after 5 km, turn right (north) and follow the signs.

Sea routes south of Puerto Montt

To Puerto Natales Navimag ferries make the dramatic 1460-km journey south. It is quicker and cheaper to fly or even go by bus via Argentina, but the voyage by boat is spectacular given a little luck with the weather. The route goes first through Seno Reloncaví and Canal Moraleda, before heading west through the Canal Chacabuco to Bahía Anna Pink. From here, there is a 12- to 17-hour sea journey, usually rough, across the infamous Golfo de Penas to Bahía Tarn. The journey continues through Canal Messier, Angostura Inglesa and the Concepción, Sarmiento and White channels, taking just under four days. If weather conditions permit, the ferry stops at Puerto Edén (population 180) on **Isla Wellington** (one hour south of Angostura Inglesa), a fishing village with *hospedaje* (20 beds, open intermittently), some shops, scant provisions and a café. It is the drop-off point for exploring Isla Wellington, which is largely untouched, with stunning mountains. If stopping, take food; maps (not very accurate) are available in Santiago.

The vessels are functional but comfortable passenger and freight (including live animals) roll-on, roll-off ferries. On board is a book exchange, bingo is played, video films are shown, bilingual guides give talks on fauna, botany, glaciation and history. Food is good and plentiful and includes vegetarian options at lunch and dinner. Passengers tend to take their own alcohol and extra food. Standards of service and comfort vary, depending on the number of passengers and weather conditions. Take sea-sickness tablets, or buy them on board (you'll be advised when to take them!). For details of schedules and fares, and for Navimag ferries to Puerto Chacabuco, see Transport, below.

To Laguna San Rafael M/N Skorpios 2, run by **Skorpios Cruises** ① *Augusto Leguía Norte 118, Santiago, T2-2477 1900, www.skorpios.cl,* leaves Puerto Montt for a six-day, five-night luxury cruise to San Rafael, via Chiloé and Puerto Aguirre. The fare varies according to season, type of cabin and number of occupants: double cabin from US$2000 per person. Generally service is excellent, the food superb, and, at the glacier, you can chip ice off the face for your whisky. After the visit to San Rafael the ship visits Quitralco Fjord where there are thermal pools and boat trips on the fjord, and Chiloé. See also page 826.

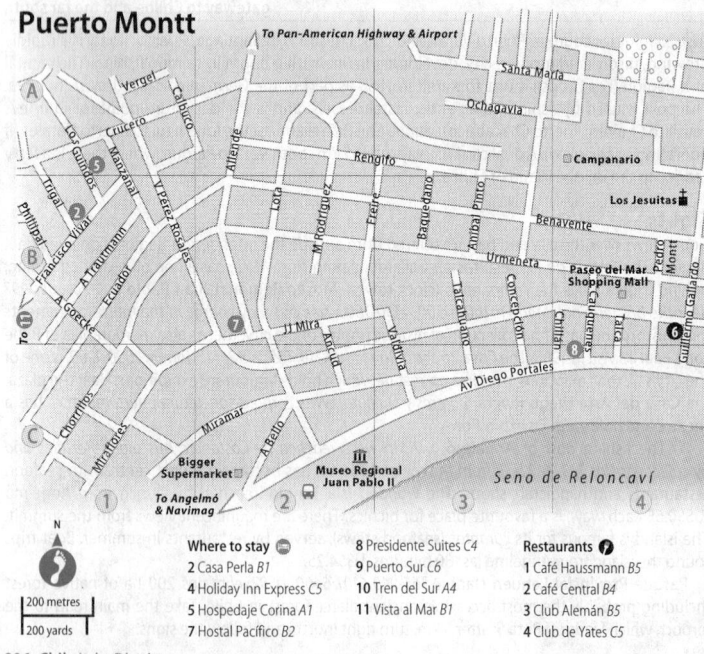

Puerto Montt

N
200 metres
200 yards

Where to stay
2 Casa Perla *B1*
4 Holiday Inn Express *C5*
5 Hospedaje Corina *A1*
7 Hostal Pacífico *B2*
8 Presidente Suites *C4*
9 Puerto Sur *C6*
10 Tren del Sur *A4*
11 Vista al Mar *B1*

Restaurants
1 Café Haussmann *B5*
2 Café Central *B4*
3 Club Alemán *B5*
4 Club de Yates *C5*

Tourist information

CONAF
*Ochogavía 458, T65-248 6102,
loslagos.oirs@conaf.cl.*

Sernatur
*Just southwest of the Plaza de Armas, Antonio
Varas 415 y San Martín, T65-222 3016,
turismopuertomontt@gmail.com, www.puerto
monttchile.cl. High season daily 0900-2100,
low season Mon-Fri 0830-1300, 1500-1730.*
Information and town maps. There are also
information desks at the airport and the bus
station (daily 0830-1600).

Where to stay

Accommodation is often much cheaper
off season. Check with the tourist office.

$$$$ Presidente Suites
*Av Portales 664, T2-2480 3000,
www.hotelespresidente.com.*
4-star, very comfortable, rooms, suites,
some with sea view. Often full Mon-Fri
with business travellers.

$$$ Holiday Inn Express
*Mall Paseo Costanera, T65-256 6000,
www.holidayinn.cl.*
Good business standard. Spacious rooms
with desks and great views, some with
balcony. Slightly pokey bathrooms but
the best in its category.

$$$ Puerto Sur
Huasco 143, T65-235 1212, www.hotelpuertosur.cl.
Small business-oriented hotel in a quiet part of
town. 4 floors, no lifts or views but otherwise
good value, parking.

$$$ Tren del Sur
*Santa Teresa 643, T65-234 3939,
www.trendelsur.cl.*
'Boutique' *hostal* with pleasant public areas,
objects recycled from the old railway, some
rooms without windows, café, heating, helpful
English-speaking owner.

$$$-$$ Hostal Pacífico
*J J Mira 1088, T65-225 6229,
www.hostalpacifico.cl.*
Comfortable, some rooms a bit cramped.
Parking, transfers.

$$ Vista al Mar
*Vivar 1337, T65-225 5625,
www.hospedajevistaalmar.cl.*
Impeccable small guesthouse, good breakfast,
peaceful, great view from the double en suite.

$$-$ Casa Perla
Trigal 312, T65-226 2104, www.casaperla.com.
French, English spoken, helpful, use of kitchen,
pleasant garden, good meeting place.
Recommended.

$$-$ Hospedaje Corina
*Los Guindos 329, T65-227 3948,
www.hospedajecorina.cl.*
Pleasant doubles and triple in a charming
house, breakfast included.

Camping

Camping Los Alamos
*Chinquihue Km 15, T65-226 4666,
www.complejolosalamos.com.*
Also has *cabañas*. Others on this road.

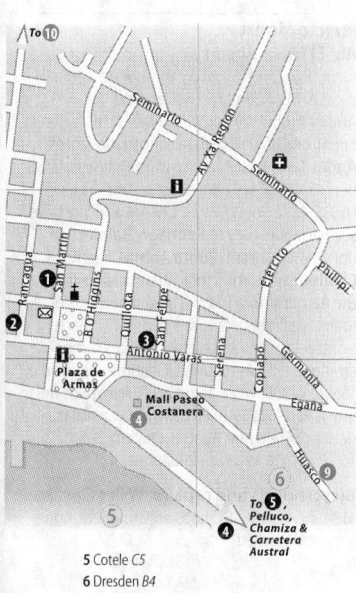

5 Cotele *C5*
6 Dresden *B4*

5
6

To Pelluco,
Chamiza &
Carretera
Austral

Restaurants

Local specialities include *picoroco al vapor*, a giant barnacle whose flesh looks and tastes like crab, and *curanto*. In Angelmó, there are several dozen small, seafood restaurants in the old fishing port, past the fish market, very popular, open till late in Jan-Feb. Other seafood restaurants in Chinquihue, west of Angelmó.

$$$ Club Alemán
Varas 264, T65-229 7000, www.elclubaleman.cl.
Old fashioned, good food and wine.

$$$ Club de Yates
Juna Soler200, Costanera east of centre, T65-228 2810, www.clubdeyates.wix.com/bannercdy.
Excellent seafood, fine views from a pier.

$$$-$$ Cotele
Juan Soler 1661, Pelluco, 4 km east, T65-227 8000, www.cotele.cl. Closed Sun.
Only serves beef, but serves it as well as anywhere in southern Chile. Reservations advised.

$$ Café Haussmann
San Martín 185, T65-229 3390, www.cafehaussmann.cl.
German cakes, beer and *crudos*.

$$-$ Dresden
Varas 500, T65-225 0000, Facebook: Café-Dresden-1477322962583160
Corner café in the centre with an extensive menu of breakfast, lunch and dinner options. Great coffee; fast Wi-Fi.

$ Café Central
Rancagua 117.
Spartan decor, generous portions (sandwiches and *pichangas* – savoury salad snack). Giant TV screen.

Shopping

Woollen goods and Mapuche-designed rugs can be bought at roadside stalls in Angelmó and on Portales opposite the bus terminal. Prices much the same as on Chiloé, but quality often lower.

Supermarkets
Bigger (opposite bus terminal, daily 0900-2200). Also in the **Paseo del Mar** shopping mall (Talca y A Varas). **Paseo Costanera**, is a big mall on the seafront opposite the Sernatur office.

What to do

Diving
Ecosub, *Panamericana 510, T65-226 3939, www.ecosub.cl.* Scuba-diving excursions.

Sailing
Club de Deportes Náuticas Reloncaví, *Camino a Chinquihue Km 7, T65-225 5022, www.nauticoreloncavi.com.* Marina, sailing lessons.
Marina del Sur (MDS), *Camino a Chinquihue Km 4.5, T65-225 1958, www.marinadelsur.cl.*
All facilities, restaurant, yacht charters, notice board for crew (*tripulante*) requests, specialists in cruising the Patagonian channels.

Tour operators
There are many tour operators. Some companies offer 2-day excursions along the Carretera Austral to Hornopirén, including food and accommodation. Most offer 1-day excursions to Chiloé and to Puerto Varas, Isla Loreley, Laguna Verde, and the Petrohué falls: both are much cheaper from bus company kiosks inside the bus terminal.

Transport

Puerto Montt
Air El Tepual Airport is 13 km northwest of town, T65-229 4161, www.aeropuertoeltepual.cl. It has ATMs, a Sernatur desk and car hire desks. **Andes Tur** bus to/from terminal, 1½ hrs before departure, US$5; also meets incoming flights. **Andes Tur** minibus service to/from hotels, US$8 per person, US$10 pp to Puerto Varas. Taxi US$19, US$35-45 to Puerto Varas. **LATAM** and **Sky** have several flights daily to **Santiago**, **Balmaceda** (for Coyhaique) and **Punta Arenas**. Flights to **Chaitén** (or nearby Santa Bárbara) leave from the Aerodromo la Paloma on the outskirts of town. For flight details, see page 823. Charters, sightseeing trips and air taxi services can be arranged with **Aerocord**, La Paloma aerodrome, T65-226 2300, www.aerocord.cl; **Aerotaxis del Sur**, A Varas 70, T9-9583 8374, www.aerotaxis delsur.cl; **Cielo Mar Austral**, Quillota 245 loc 1, T65-226 4010, www.cielomaraustral.cl.

Bicycle parts and repairs **Willer**, Chorillos 1184, T65-226 8640. Shops on Urmeneta, none very well stocked.

Bus Terminal is on seafront at Portales y Lota with rural buses leaving from one side and long distance buses from the other. There are also telephones, restaurants, ATMs, *casa de cambio* (left luggage 0700-2245, US$2-3.15 per bag for 24 hrs); see www.terminalpm.cl. There is an official taxi rank on level 1.

To **Puerto Varas** (US$2.50), **with Expreso Puerto Varas, Thaebus** and **Buses JM** several daily (with transfers to Llanquihue, Ensenada, Puerto Octay, etc). To **Cochamó** US$6, 2½ hrs. To **Hornopirén**, 5 hrs, US$8, **Kémel** (which also runs daily to **Chaitén**, US$10). To **Osorno** US$3, 2 hrs, to **Valdivia**, US$11, 3½ hrs. To **Pucón**, US$18, 6 hrs. To **Temuco** US$12-23. **Concepción**, US$36-47. To **Valparaíso**, 14 hrs, US$69-91, same fare to Viña del Mar. To **Santiago**, 12 hrs, US$62-97, several companies including **Tur-Bus**. To **Punta Arenas**, Cruz del Sur-Turibus, Pullman, 3 a week, 1100 (bus goes through Argentina via Bariloche, take US$ cash for Argentina expenses en route), 32-38 hrs, US$88.

Also take plenty of food for this "nightmare" trip. Book well in advance in Jan-Feb and check if you need a multiple-entry Chilean visa. Also book any return journey before setting out. For services to **Chiloé**, see page 811.

Buses to Argentina via Osorno and the Samoré pass Daily services to Bariloche on this route via Osorno, 7 hrs, are run by **Vía Bariloche** and others, US$42. Out of season, services are reduced. Buy tickets for international buses from the bus terminal. Book well in advance in Jan and Feb; ask for a seat on the right hand side for the best views.

Car hire **Autovald**, Sector Cardenal, Pasaje San Andrés 50, T65-221 5366, www.autovald.cl. Cheap rates. **Full-Car**, O'Higgins 525, T56-223 3055, www.full-car.cl. **Hunter**, T65-225 1524 or 9-9920 6888, office is in Puerto Varas, San José 130, T65-223 7950, www.interpatagonia.com/ hunter. Good service. **Salfa Sur**, Pilpilco 800, also at the airport, T600-600 4004, or T65-229 0201, www.salfasur.cl. Good value, several regional offices.

Ferry For services to Chiloé, see page 811.

To **Puerto Natales** **Navimag** (Naviera Magallanes SA, Terminal Transbordadores, Angelmó 1735, T65-243 2360 or T2-2869 9900, www.navimag.com) throughout the year, leaving Puerto Montt usually on Mon at 2000 (check in 0900-1300, board 1700), arriving Thu. Return is on Sat, arriving Puerto Montt Tue morning. In Puerto Natales check-in is Fri 0900-1830, board 2100, depart Sat 0600; dinner is not included. Always confirm times and booking well in advance. In winter especially days and vessels may change. The fare, including meals, ranges from US$350 pp for a bunk in a shared cabin on the Amadeo in low season, to US$2100 for 2 people in AAA double cabin. First class is recommended, but hardly luxurious. Check the website for discounts and special offers. Mid-size cars are carried for US$450 (SUVs for US$475), motorcycles for US$137. Payment by credit card or foreign currency is accepted in all **Navimag** offices. Tickets can be booked through many travel agencies, **Navimag** offices throughout the country, or direct from www.navimag.com. Book well in advance for departures between mid-Dec and mid-Mar. It is well worth going to the port on the day of departure if you have no ticket. Departures are frequently delayed by weather conditions.

To **Puerto Chacabuco** **Navimag**'s ferry sails twice a week (usually Thu and Sun) to Puerto Chacabuco (80 km west of Coyhaique). The cruise to Puerto Chacabuco lasts about 24 hrs. Cabins sleep 4 or 6 (private bath, window, bed linen and towel) with a berth costing US$80-170 in high season. Cars, motorcycles and bicycles are also carried. There is a canteen; long queues if the boat is full. Meals are included, but extra food is expensive so take your own.

To **Chaitén** via Ayacara, with **Naviera Austral** (Angelmó 1673, T65-227 0430, www. navieraustral.cl), also Hornopirén–Ayacara, but check with the company for schedules.

Chiloé

★The island of Chiloé is 250 km long, 50 km wide and covers 9613 sq km. Thick forests cover most of its western side. The hillsides in summer are a patchwork quilt of wheat fields and dark green plots of potatoes. The population is 170,000 and most live on the sheltered eastern side. The west coast, exposed to strong Pacific winds, is wet for most of the year. The east coast and the offshore islands are drier, though frequently cloudy.

The culture of Chiloé has been strongly influenced by isolation from Spanish colonial currents, the mixture of early Spanish settlers and indigenous people and a dependence on the sea. Religious and secular architecture, customs and crafts, combined with delightful landscapes, all contribute to Chiloé's uniqueness. The island is famous for its traditional handicrafts, notably woollens, basketware and wood, which can be bought in the main towns and on some of the off-shore islands, as well as in Puerto Montt. The frequent *fiestas costumbistas* are good events at which to capture the spirit of the place.

Ancud and around *Colour map 9, A1.*

Ancud lies on the north coast of Chiloé 34 km west of the Straits of Chacao at the mouth of a great bay, the Golfo de Quetalmahue. Founded in 1767 to guard the shipping route around Cape Horn, it was defended by two fortresses, the Fuerte San Antonio and Fuerte Ahui on the opposite side of the bay. **Fuerte San Antonio** ① *open daily 0800-2100, 0900-2000 at weekends, free,* built in 1770, was the site of the Spanish surrender of Chiloé to Chilean troops in 1826. It has a few cannon and surrounding wall. Close to it are the ruins of the **Polvorín del Fuerte**. A lovely 1-km walk north of the fort leads to **Arena Gruesa** beach, where public concerts are held in summer. Two kilometres east is a **mirador** offering good views of the island and across to the mainland, even to the Andes on a clear day. By the Plaza de Armas is the **Museo Regional** ① *Libertad 370, T65-262 2413, www.museoancud.cl, Mar-Dec Tue-Fri 1000-1730, Sat-Sun 1030-1330, Jan-Feb Tue-Fri 1000-1700, Sat-Sun 1030-1530, free.* As well as an interesting collection on the early history of Chiloé, it has a replica of the sailing boat that was used on the expedition to take the Straits of Magellan. Beside it is the Centro Cultural, with details of events and handicrafts outside. The modern cathedral stands on the plaza, built anew after the 1960 tsunami. **Fundación Amigos de las Iglesias de Chiloé** ① *Errázuriz 227, T65-262 1046, www.iglesiasdechiloe.cl, open daily, suggested donation US$1,* in a precinct off the street, has an exhibition of various churches and styles of construction and a shop.

West of Ancud

Faro Corona, the lighthouse on Punta Corona, is 34 km west along the beach and offers good views with birdlife and dolphins. The best time of day to see birds is early morning or late afternoon/ evening; there are two to three buses daily, though none is at the right time for seeing birds. The duty officer may give a tour.

☆Near **Pumillahue**, 27 km southwest, there is a Humboldt and Magellanic penguin colony from October to late March; the birds are seen early morning or late afternoon. There are two to three buses daily or you can take a tour (US$30 per person, twice a day, 3½ hours including short boat trip, several agencies), taxi or hitch.

Best for
Architecture ■ Crafts ■ Traditional culture ■ Wildlife

Chepu ① *38 km southwest of Ancud, bus Mon, Wed, Fri at 0630, 1600 US$3, taxi US$30-35* (population 230), at the mouth of the Río Anguay is famed for its sea-fishing and for the Valley of Dead Trees, a drowned forest devastated by the tsunami in 1960. There is a wide range of birdlife and good opportunities for horseriding and boat trips. The **Mirador de Chepu/Chepu Adventures information centre** ① *T9-6336 9040, www.chepu.cl*, gives views of the wetlands and information about the flora, fauna and tourist options. It has a café, (electric) kayaks for hire and accommodation in cabins or dorms ($$$-$ – no children under 14). Chepu is also the northern entry for the Parque Nacional Chiloé, see page 814.

Ancud to Castro

There are two routes south to Castro: direct along Route 5, the Pan-American Highway, crossing rolling hills, forest and agricultural land, or via the east coast, passing through small farming and fishing communities. This road is paved to Huillinco, a few km before Linao, then is *ripio* to Quemchi. A paved road also branches off Route 5 at Degán to **Quemchi** (population 2000), which has a small **tourist office** ① *in the plaza open 0830-1300 summer only, www. muniquemchi.cl*, and a wooden church; the bridge to Isla Aucar (botanical park) is also made of wood. Every summer cultural events are held and kayaks are available.

South of Quemchi is the village of **Tenaún**, whose church with three towers, like 15 other Chilote churches, is a UNESCO World Heritage Site. Offshore is Isla Mechuque (http://turismoislamechuque.blogspot.co.uk) in the Chauques archipelago. It has two small museums of island life and *palafito* houses in the town. Boats go from Tenaún (45 minutes), Quicaví and Dalcahue (not daily), but the easiest way to get there is on a tour from Castro, with **Turismo Pehuén** (see below) or **Turismo Mi Tierra** (San Martín 487, Castro, T9-7793 4685, www.turismomitierra.cl), which includes a meal of *curanto al hoyo* and a visit to waterfalls at Tocoihue on main island.

Dalcahue (population 4600), 74 km south of Ancud, is more easily reached from Castro, 30 km further south. The wooden church on the main plaza dates from the 19th century. There is a large *artesanía* market on the waterside, near which are several restaurants. A good Sunday market is held nearby, 0700-1300. There's a tourist kiosk in season, plus various hotels ($ per person and up). Between Dalcahue and Castro is the **Rilán Peninsula**, with several traditional villages but also a growing number of upmarket hotels, golf and agrotourism.

☆**Quinchao Island** A 10-minute ferry crosses the strait between Dalcahue and Quinchao island. The main settlements on this island are Curaco de Vélez (handicrafts sold on the plaza in summer) and **Achao**, a quiet, pretty fishing village with a market. Its wooden church, built in 1730 and saved by a change of wind from a fire which destroyed much of the town in 1784, is a fine example of Chilote Jesuit architecture with a decorated ceiling. It has a small museum, US$1. The **tourist office** at Serrano y Progreso is open between December and March only. There are various hotels ($$-$) and restaurants. See www.islaquinchao.cl.

Getting there

Ferries cross the straits between Pargua, 55 km southwest of Puerto Montt on the mainland, and Chacao on Chiloé, 30-minute crossing. Sea lions, penguins, birds and occasionally dolphins can be seen. There are regular crossings from 0630 to 2400 daily, operated by several companies including **Transmarchilay** (www.transmarchilay.cl) and **Cruz del Sur**; all ferries carry buses, private vehicles (cars US$19 one way, motorcycles US$13, bicycles US$4) and foot passengers (US$1). There are frequent buses from Puerto Montt to Pargua (US$4, one hour), although most services continue via the ferry to Ancud (3½ to four hours) and Castro. Transport to the island is dominated by **Cruz del Sur** (Puerto Montt terminal, Panamericano 500, at end of Avenida Salvador Allende, T65-243 6410, www.buscescruzdelsur.cl), who also own **Trans Chiloé** and have their own ferries; their fares are highest but they are faster because their buses have priority over cars on Cruz del Sur ferries. They run frequent buses from Puerto Montt to Ancud (US$7) and Castro (US$10.50), also six buses a day to Chonchi (US$12) and Quellón (US$14). A bridge to the island across the Chacao channel was approved in 2014; it is scheduled to be finished by 2019. There is an airport near Castro. For further details, see Transport, page 818.

Castro *Colour map 9, A1.*

The sprawling capital of Chiloé lies on a fjord on the east coast, 88 km south of Ancud. Founded in 1567, the centre is situated on a promontory, from which there is a steep drop to the port. It is far livelier and more commercial than other towns on the island. On the Plaza de Armas is the large **Cathedral**, strikingly decorated in lilac and yellow, with a splendid wood-panelled interior, built by the Italian architect, Eduardo Provosoli in 1906. It contains models of other churches on the

Chiloé

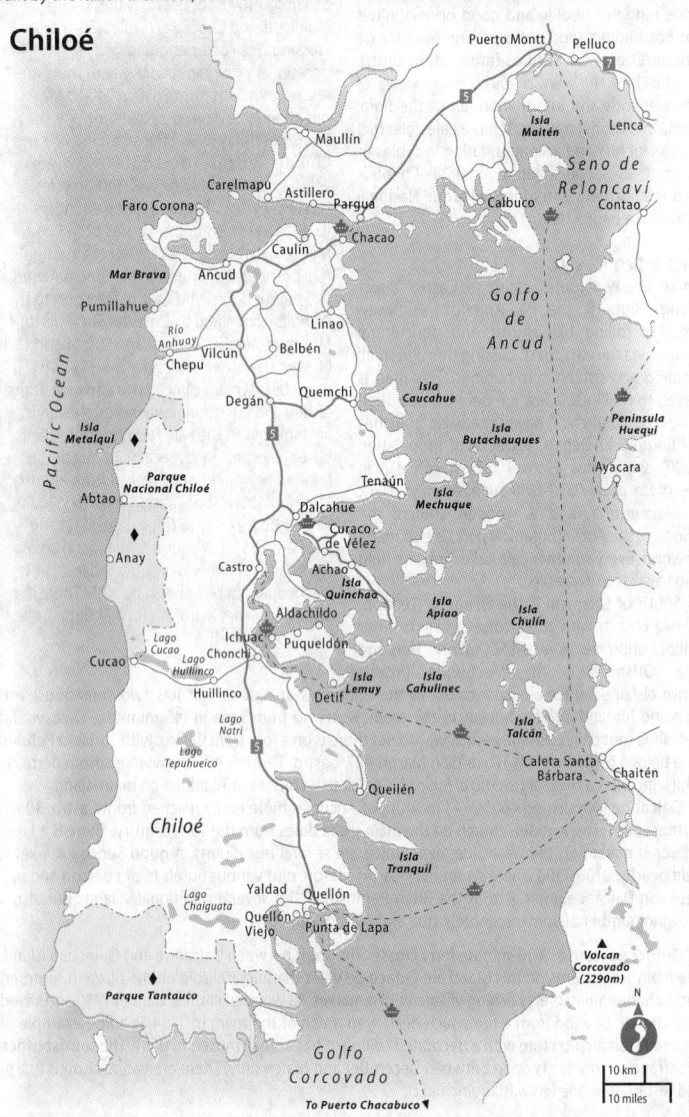

BACKGROUND

Chiloé

The original inhabitants of Chiloé were the Chonos, who were pushed south by the Huilliches invading from the north. The first Spanish sighting was by Francisco de Ulloa in 1553, and in 1567 Martín Ruiz de Gamboa took possession of the islands on behalf of Spain. The small Spanish settler population divided the indigenous population and their lands between them. The 1598 Mapuche victory during the Arauco Wars which drove the Spanish out of the mainland south of the Río Biobío, left the Spanish community on Chiloé (some 200 settlers in 1600) isolated. During the 17th century, it was served by a single annual ship from Lima. The islanders were the last supporters of the Spanish Crown in South America. When Chile rebelled, the last of the Spanish Governors fled to the island and, in despair, offered it to Britain; Canning, the British Foreign Secretary, turned the offer down. The island finally surrendered in 1826.

The availability of wood and the lack of metals have left their mark on the island. Some of the earliest churches were built entirely of wood, using wooden pegs instead of nails. These early churches often displayed some German influence as a result of the missionary work of Bavarian Jesuits. Two features of local architecture often thought to be traditional are in fact late 19th century in origin: the replacement of thatch with thin tiles (*tejuelas*) of several distinctive patterns made from alerce (larch) wood that are nailed to the frame and roof, and *palafitos* or wooden houses built on stilts over the water.

Although the traditional mainstays of the economy, fishing and agriculture, are still important, salmon farming has become a major source of employment. Seaweed is harvested for export to Japan. Tourism provides a seasonal income for a growing number of people. Also see www.chiloe.cl.

islands. South of the Plaza on the waterfront is the **Feria**, or Mercado Municipal de Artesanía, where excellent local woollen articles (hats, sweaters, gloves) can be found. Behind it are four traditional restaurants. *Palafitos* can be seen on the northern side of town and by the bridge over the Río Gamboa (Calle Riquelme, with a number of *hostales*, cafés and handicraft shops). There are good views of the city from **Mirador La Virgen** on Millantuy hill above the cemetery. **Museo Municipal** ① *on Esmeralda, T65-263 5967, Mon-Fri 0900-1300, 1500-1900,* has displays on the history, folklore, handicrafts and mythology of Chiloé and photos of the 1960 earthquake. **Museo de Arte Moderno** ① *near the Río Gamboa, in the Parque Municipal, over 3 km northwest of the centre, T65-263 5454, www.mamchiloe.cl, 1000-1700, donations,* is reached by following Calle Galvarino Riveros up the hill west of town; take bus marked 'Al Parque'. There are good views from the hill. On the southern outskirts of town is Nercón, whose UNESCO-recognized church is signed off Ruta 5. From the ceiling of the nave hang models of sailing boats. The community holds its **Fiesta Costumbrista** at the end of January.

Chonchi *Colour map 9, A1.*

Chonchi is a picturesque fishing village 25 km south of Castro. The wooden **church** ① *Mon-Sat 0900-2000, Sun 1000-2000,* on the plaza was built in 1754 and remodelled in neoclassical style in 1859 and 1897. The nave ceiling is painted blue and dotted with stars. (There is another undecorated 18th-century church at Vilupulli, 5 km north, signed off Ruta 5, along a *ripio* road; the woman with the tiny handicraft stall behind the church, Sra Teresa Velásquez, T9-9395 5635, holds the key, visiting hours Tuesday-Sunday 1000-1330, 1430-1830.) From Chonchi's plaza Calle Centenario, with several attractive but sadly neglected wooden mansions, drops steeply to the waterfront at Avenida Irarrázabal. Fishing boats bring in the catch which is carried straight into the modern market at the opposite end of Av Irarrázabal from the pier. The small **Museo de Tradiciones Chonchinas** ① *Centenario 116, T65-263 2802, Mon-Fri 0930-1330, 1430-1800, Sat 0930-1330, US$1,* is housed in a former residence, laid out to give an idea of domestic life in the first decade of the 20th century when Chonchi was the most important port in Chiloé. It shows videos on the churches of Chiloé. The tiny **Museo del Acordeón Sergio Colivoro Barria** ① *Andrade next to Restaurant La Quila, daily 1100-1900,* has some 50 instruments on display. A **tourist information kiosk** ① *T65-267 1522, 0830-1230, 1330-1700 in summer,* is at the crossroads one block uphill from the main plaza.

Excursions from Chonchi

☆A pleasant excursion is to the **Isla Lemuy** ① *ferry 4 km south at Huicha on road to Quellén every 10 mins 0700-0100, cars US$5, foot passengers free (micro from Castro)*. **Parque Yayanes** ① *Puqueldón, T9-8861 6462, www.parqueyayanes.cl*, is a small private park on the island which offers a 30-minute walk across a hanging bridge and through mixed forest. It also has lodging in cabins and serves traditional food.

At Queilén, a fishing village on a peninsula 46 km southeast of Chonchi, is **Museo Refugio de Navegantes** ① *Pres Alessandri s/n, T65-236 7149, Jan and Feb 1100-2000, free*. Also here are places to stay and several restaurants, including **Restaurant Melinka** (Alessandri 126, www.restaurantmelinka.blogspot.cl), for good food.

☆Cucao

From Chonchi a paved road leads west to Cucao, 40 km, one of two settlements on the west coast of Chiloé. At Km 12 is **Huillinco**, a charming village on Lago Huillinco, with *cabañas* and cafés: **Café de Lago** (50 m off the road on the lakeshore by Camping Huillinco) for teas, coffees, cakes, sandwiches, open January to mid-March and weekends to Semana Santa, and **Los Coihues** (above the village), for more substantial fare.

Cucao is divided by a creek. The landward side is beside the lake and has the small church, a helpful tourist information desk and a couple of traditional restaurants, plus places to stay. Cross the bridge to the newer sector, with *hostales*, eating places, adventure sports agencies (horse riding, trekking, kayaks, SUP) and the road to the national park. Beyond the park entrance the rough road continues to Canquín, where there is another bridge shaped like a boat. Over this bridge, on the left, is a track through private property to an immense 20-km beach with thundering Pacific surf and dangerous undercurrents (US$1.50 to park car). It's about 30 minutes' walk from bridge to bridge.

☆Parque Nacional Chiloé

T65-297 0724, contacto@parquechiloe.cl. US$6.25. Open all year 0900-1700.

The park is divided into three sections. Much of its 43,057 ha is covered by evergreen forest. The northern sector, covering 7800 ha, is reached by a path which runs south from **Chepu** (see page 811). The second section is a small island, **Metalqui**, off the coast of the north sector. The

> **Tip...**
> Wear light-coloured clothing because the horseflies are bad in summer.

southern sector, 35,207 ha, is entered 1 km north of Cucao, where there is an administration centre, small museum, restaurant Fogón and *cabañas* ($$$ for five to six people) and camping ($ per person). There are six trails from 108 m to 1700 m: four are along the lakeside, two lead to the dunes and beach. Ask at the administration centre or horse riding agencies about excursions further into the park.

Quellón and around *Colour map 9, A1.*

The main settlement in the south of the island, Quellón is 92 km south of Castro and has amazing views of the mainland on a clear day. The Golfo de Corcovado between southern Chiloé and the mainland is visited by blue whales from December to April. There are pleasant beaches nearby at Quellón Viejo (with an old wooden church), Punta de Lapa and Yaldad. Boat trips go to Isla Cailín in summer from the pier, US$30 for a full day (www.turismochiloe.cl). A trip can also be made to Chaiguao, 11 km east, where there is a small Sunday morning market. Horses can be hired, also kayaks with a guide. **Museo Municipal Amador Cárdenas** ① *García Gómez s/n, T65-268 3543, Mon-Fri 0830-1300, 1430-1745*, has an odd collection of antique typewriters and sewing machines.

From Quellón you can go to **Parque Tantauco** ① *information from Ruta 5 Sur 1826, Club Aero Gamboa, Castro, T65-263 3805, www.parquetantauco.cl, US$5.50, children US$0.80*, which covers 120,000 ha of woods and wetlands at the southernmost part of the island, with many endangered endemic species of mammal. Access is by road or by plane from Quellón to Inio (US$375) with the air club next to the administration office. Reservations can be made online through Parque Tantauco. It's a private park, with campsites (no electricity, $), *casa de huéspedes* ($$$) and a *refugio* ($). There are 120 km of trails, taking from three hours to five days.

> **Fact...**
> The street-numbering system in Quellón is unfathomable.

Tourist information

Ancud

CONAF
*Errázuriz 317. Mon-Wed 0900-1250, 1430-1730,
Fri till 1630.*

Sernatur
*Libertad 665, on the plaza, T65-262 2800,
infochiloe@sernatur.cl. Mon-Thu 0830-1730,
Fri 0830-1630.*
Ask here about the *agroturismo* programme,
staying with farming families. There is another
tourist office in the Feria Municipal.

Castro

CONAF
Gamboa 424, Mon-Fri 0900-1300, 1400-1730.

Tourist information kiosk
*Plaza de Armas, Gamboa 300, opposite
the cathedral. Daily 1000-2100 high season,
1000-1900 low season.*
Has a list of accommodation, prices, models of
the area's churches and other information.

Quellón

The tourist office on Vargas y García is often
closed, even in summer. Try also the municipality,
www.muniquellon.cl.

Where to stay

Ancud

$$$ Don Lucas
*Salvador Allende (Costanera) 906, T65-262 0950,
www.hoteldonlucas.cl.*
Nice rooms, some with sea view, disabled access,
restaurant. A good choice.

$$$ Galeón Azul
*Libertad 751, T65-262 2567,
www.hotelgaleonazul.cl.*
Small heated rooms, rather basic for the price but
excellent views. Bright restaurant.

$$$ Panamericana
*San Antonio 30, T65-262 2340,
www.panamericanahoteles.cl.*
Nice views of the bay, attractive, very comfortable,
helpful, restaurant, tours offered, English spoken.

$$$-$ Mundo Nuevo
*Salvador Allende (Costanera) 748, T65-262 8383,
www.backpackerschile.com.*
Comfortable hostel, dorms, rooms with and
without bath, 1 room has a boat-bed, great views
over the bay, lots of info, heating, good showers,
car and bicycle hire, English and German spoken.

$$ Balai
Pudeto 169, T65-262 2541, www.hotelbalai.cl.
With heating, parking, restaurant, interesting
local paintings, models and artefacts on display.
Tours arranged.

$$ Hostal Lluhay
*Cochrane 458, T65-262 2656,
www.hostal-lluhay.cl.*
Attentive, sea views, heating, meals, nice lounge,
kayak and bicycle rental, tours with Ancud Mágico.

$$ Hostal Vista al Mar
*Salvador Allende (Costanera) 918, T65-262 2617,
www.vistaalmar.cl.*
Close to **Cruz del Sur** buses, cabins for 2-5, also
private rooms with or without bath. Views over
the bay, safe, heating, parking.

$$-$ 13 Lunas
*Los Carrera 855, T65-262 2106, www.13lunas.cl.
Opposite Cruz del Sur bus terminal.*
Single-sex and mixed dorms, private rooms,
wheelchair accessible, very helpful, *asados* and
ping pong in the basement, parking, great
penguin tour and other activities.

$ pp Hospedaje Austral
*A Pinto 1318, T65-262 4847,
www.ancudchiloechile.com.*
Cosy wooden house, near long-distance bus
station, with small breakfast, lots of bathrooms,
double room (**$$**), family of Mirta Ruiz, very
welcoming and caring, lots of information.

$ pp Hostal Altos de Bellavista
*Bellavista 449, T65-262 2384,
cecilia2791@gmail.com.*
Rooms for 1-5, with or without bath, family
atmosphere, long stay available, tatty outside
but welcoming inside. Several other places to
stay on Bellavista.

Camping

Hostal y Cabañas Arena Gruesa
*Av Costanera Norte 290, T65-262 3428,
www.hotelarenagruesa.cl.*

US$11 for campsite, also mobile homes, with light, water and services, also cabins for 2-10 and hotel.

Ancud to Castro: Quemchi

There are a few places to eat, such as **Restaurante Barloventos** (barloventos. quemchi@gmail.com), which also offers kayak trips, and basic places to stay, including **Camping La Casona** (T9-9909 9015).

Castro

$$$$ Cabañas Trayen
Nercón, 5 km south of Castro, T65-263 3633, www.trayenchiloe.cl.
Lovely views, cabins for 4 to 6.

$$$$-$$$ Hostería de Castro
Chacabuco 202, T65-263 2301, www.hosteriadecastro.cl.
The newer section is spacious and comfortable, with wonderful views and nice suites. Spa, pool. Good restaurant and bar.

$$$ Unicornio Azul
Pedro Montt 228, T65-263 2359, www.hotelunicornioazul.cl.
Striking pink and blue building climbing the hillside from the waterfront, good views over bay, comfortable, restaurant.

$$$-$$ Palafito Hostel
Riquelme 1210, T9-9229 0576.
In a restored traditional *palafito* building on stilts over the water, downhill from centre and across bridge. Helpful staff, good breakfast, tours arranged. (On same street are places with similar names: **Palafito Azul**, No 1242, www.palafitoazul.cl, and **Palafito 1326**, No 1326, www.palafito1326.cl.)

$$ Casita Española
Los Carrera 359, T65-263 5186, www.hosteriadecastro.cl.
Heating, parking, good, in same group as **Hostería de Castro**.

$$ Hostal Don Camilo
Ramírez 566, T65-263 2180, hostaldoncamilo@gmail.com.
Pleasant accommodation in functional rooms with all services, good value restaurant, secure parking.

$$-$ Hospedaje El Mirador
Barros Arana 127, T65-263 3795, www.hostalelmiradorcastro.cl.

Private or shared bath, rooms a bit small, cosy, relaxing, kitchen (shared with family).

$ pp Hospedaje América
Chacabuco 215, T65-263 4364, hosameri@telsur.cl.
Good location, family welcome, shared bath, comfortable. They offer an evening meal service: you buy, they cook, everyone shares.

Camping

Camping Pudú
Ruta 5, 10 km north of Castro.
Cabins, showers with hot water, sites with light, water, kids' games.

Several sites on road to Chonchi, including **Llicaldad** (6 km south of Castro, T9-9100 1361, apachecocornejo@gmail.com), also has *cabañas*.

Chonchi

$$$ Cabañas Treng Treng
José Pinto Pérez 420, T65-267 2532, www.trengtreng.cl.
Impeccable fully furnished cabins sleeping 2-7. Splendid views, some English spoken.

$$ Hostal Emarley
Irarrázabal 191, T65-267 1202.
Near market, cheaper rooms with shared bath.

$$ Hostal La Tortuga
Pedro Montt 241, T9-9098 2925.
In a historic house on the main plaza, comfortable rooms, cafeteria, laundry.

$$ Huildín
Centenario 102, T65-267 1388, www.hotelhuildin.com.
Old fashioned, decent rooms with good beds but windows are onto interior passages, also *cabañas*, garden with superb views.

Cucao

Most lodgings and restaurants open Jan-Mar, but you can camp all year.

$$$-$$ Hostal Palafito Cucao
T65-297 1164, www.hostelpalafitocucao.cl. Open all year.
300 m from park entrance, built from native timber overlooking Lake Cucao. Large windows for great views. Transfers and excursions arranged Private rooms and a 6-bed dorm (**$**), comfortable, good breakfast and kitchen, meals available.

$$ La Paloma
Behind the church on lakeshore.
Cabañas and camping (US$6.50 pp) open all year.

Camping

Campsites, some with restaurants and shops on the road to the national park, others on the road east of Cucao. There are minimarkets on the little street behind Jostel and another before the tourist office.

Quellón

$$ El Chico Leo
P Montt 325, T65-268 1567.
Private or shared bath, heating, games room, restaurant.

There are several other places to stay including *cabañas* and campsites: see www.turismochiloe.cl.

Restaurants

Ancud

$$ La Pincoya
Prat 61, near the dock entrance, T65-262 2511.
Good seafood, service and views.

$$ Quetalmahue
12 km west of Ancud on the road to Faro Corona and Fuerte Ahui, T9-9033 3930, www.restaurantequetalmahue.es.tl.
The best place for traditional *curantos al hoyo* (stew cooked in the ground, daily in summer).

$ El Cangrejo
Dieciocho 171.
Has a good reputation for its seafood.

$ El Embrujo
Maipú 650.
Café serving teas, coffees, sandwiches, cakes, beers and *tragos*.

Above the handicrafts in the Mercado Municipal are 2 restaurants, **Los Artesanos**, loc 71, and **Rincón Sureño**, loc 53, both serving *comida típica*. Walking up Dieciocho towards the Feria Municipal there are many eating places behind the Mercado, including **La Ñaña**, which is cheap and good. All serve much the same local fare. In an alley from Dieciocho to Prat is a row of even cheaper lunch spots, including **El Pingüinito**, decent lunches, but more basic than others. In the Feria Municipal there are 4 restaurants upstairs, all much the same with lunch specials at US$4-7.

Castro

Breakfast before 0900 is difficult to find. There are several eating places and bars on the south side of the Plaza, on Portales and Balmaceda. By the market many places offer set lunch, usually fish dishes. In the market, try *milcaos*, fried potato cakes with meat stuffing. Also *licor de oro* like Galliano.

$$$-$ Donde Eladio
Lillo 97.
Meat and seafood specialities on offer.

$$$-$ La Playa
Lillo 41.
Good seafood, also meat dishes.

$$ Don Octavio
Pedro Montt 261.
Good food and nice views over bay, specializes in seafood.

$$ Palafito restaurants
Near the Feria Artesanía on the waterfront.
Offer good food and good value: **Brisas del Mar**, **El Caleuche** (see Facebook), **El Curanto** and **La Pincoya**.

$$-$ Descarriada
Esmeralda y Blanco Encalada, corner of the Plaza.
Good local dishes, meat and fish, nice atmosphere, also desserts, tea and coffee, ice cream cart outside.

$$-$ Sacho
Thompson 213. Tue-Sat 1205-1530, 2000-2330, Sun 1205-1530.
Good sea views and good food.

Cafés

Café Blanco
Blanco 268.
Busy little place for coffee, teas, juices, sandwiches, cakes, piscos, beers and wine. Similar, at No 264, is **Ristretto Caffe**.

Café del Puente
Riquelme 1180-B, T65-263 4878.
Tue-Sun 0900-2100.
Smart café over the water serving breakfast, lunches, afternoon tea (30 varieties of tea), coffee, sandwiches, cakes, juices and ice cream.

La Brújula del Cuerpo
O'Higgins 302, Plaza de Armas, see Facebook.
Fast food, grill, snacks, drinks and coffee.

Chonchi

There are a few places to eat on Av Irarrázabal. Most places close on Sun, even in summer. **Supermercado Economar**, Irarrázabal 49, far end of Costanera from Mercado, has a café. Next door is **Chocolatería Pastelería Alejandra**.

\$\$-\$ Tres Pisos
Pedro Andrade 296 y Esmeralda, near the market.
Serves good food.

\$ Café Sueños de la Pincoya
P J Andrade 135. All day Sun, until 2100 on weekdays and until 0100 at weekends.
For sweet *empanadas*, cakes, teas and coffee.

Quellón

\$\$ Tierra del Fuego
P Montt 445, T65-268 2079.
For fish, seafood and other local dishes. In hotel of same name.

\$ Fogón Onde Agüero
La Paz 307, T65-268 3653.
Good cheap traditional food. Popular at lunchtime.

Shopping

Ancud

Handicrafts
Mercado Municipal, at Libertad between Dieciocho and Prat. The Feria Municipal (or Rural) is at Pedro Montt y Pratt, selling local produce, fish and handicrafts on the 2nd floor. Also has a tourist office. Opposite is a huge **Unimarc** supermarket.

Castro

Handicrafts
Mercado Artesanal, *Lillo on the wharf.*
Good value woollens at reasonable prices.

Market
The municipal market is on Yumbel, off Ulloa, uphill northwest of town: fish and veg.

Supermarket
Unimarc, *O'Higgins y Aldea.* Bakes good bread.

Chonchi

Handicrafts
From **Feria artesanal**, on the waterfront – woollens, jams, liqueurs, and from the *parroquia*, next to the church (Oct-Mar only).

What to do

Ancud

Aki Turismo, *patio of Mercado Municipal, T65-262 0868, www.akiturismochiloe.cl.* Good-value trips to the penguin colony and other tours.

Austral Adventures, *Salvador Allende (Costanera) 904, T65-262 5977, www.austral-adventures.com.*
Small-group tours of the archipelago and northern Patagonia (including Parque Pumalín) on land and sea. Good English-speaking guides, lots of interesting choices; director Britt Lewis.
Mistyk's, *Los Carrera 823, T9-9644 3767.* For local tours and diving.
Viajes Nativa, *in Cruz del Sur bus terminal, T65-262 2303, www.viajesnativa.cl, or T65-254 6390, www.chiloetour.com.* Tours to the penguin colony.

West of Ancud
Boat trips around Chepu are offered by **Javier Silva** (at Puente Anhuay, T9-9527 8719, turismo_riochepu@hotmail.com).

Castro
Boat trips with **Mar y Magia**, cabin on the dockside or at Blanco 60, T9-9642 5222, www.marymagia.cl. Fjord trips US\$9 pp, longer trips in summer.
Chiloé Natural, *P Montt next to Unicornio Azul, T9-6319 7388, www.chiloenatural.org.* Offers lots of activities, trips to islands and boat trips.
Turismo Pehuén, *Chacabuco 498, T65-263 5254, www.turismopehuen.cl.* **Naviera Austral** agency, kayak and boat trips, trips to national park, penguin colony, around the island and car hire.

Transport

Ancud
Bus Terminal on the east outskirts at Av Prat y Marcos Vera, reached by bus 1, or Pudeto *colectivos.* **Cruz del Sur** has its own station in centre, Los Carrera 850, T65-262 2249. To **Castro**, US\$2.65, frequent (see below), 1½ hrs. To **Puerto Montt**, frequent services, see Essential Chiloé box, page 811. To **Quemchi**, most via Degán, 2 hrs, US\$2.50; to **Dalcahue** US\$2.65. Terminal Rural for local services is on **Colo Colo**, up a ramp behind Unimarc supermarket. Timetables are posted on the door to the admin office and toilet. *Colectivos* around town have destinations signed on the roof, US\$0.60, US\$1 after 2100.

Ancud to Castro
Ferry From **Dalcahue** to Quinchao Island, 10 mins, frequent, in summer it runs till 0100, cars US\$5, free for pedestrians. San Cristóbal buses from **Ancud** and **Castro** (many daily, fewer at weekends, US\$2.65).

Castro

Air There is an airport outside Castro; flights from Santiago with **LATAM**, via Puerto Montt.

Bus There are 2 bus terminals: the crowded Terminal Municipal, San Martín 667, from which all buses and micros to island and long-distance destinations leave; and Cruz del Sur terminal, San Martín 486, T65-263 5152. **Trans Chiloé's** office is in Terminal Municipal. Frequent services to **Ancud**, **Chonchi** and **Puerto Montt** by Cruz del Sur, Queilén Bus and others. Cruz del Sur goes as far as Santiago, US$51, and all cities in between. Isla de Chiloé and **Ojeda** both run to **Cucao**, almost hourly in summer, 2-3 a day in winter, 1½ hrs, US$2.50. Buses to Cucao go via **Chonchi** and **Huillinco**. To **Dalcahue** frequent services, US$2.50. To **Achao** via Dalcahue and Curaco de Vélez, see above. To **Puqueldón** on the island of Lemuy, **Gallardo**, Llamaca, many daily Mon-Fri fewer Sat-Sun, US$3.50. To **Quemchi**, daily with Queilén Bus, 1½ hrs, US$2.50. To **Queilén**, Queilén Bus and others, US$2.80.

Ferry Naviera Austral (Chacabuco 492, T65-263 5254) services to **Chaitén** Jan/Feb only. Other ferries leave from Castro when Quellón's port is out of commission (see below). Check with the company for schedules and fares for 2017-2018.

Chonchi

Buses and taxis to **Castro**, frequent, US$1.50, from main plaza. Services to **Quellón** (US$1.75), **Cucao** and **Queilén** from Castro and Puerto Montt also call here.

Quellón

Bus To **Castro**, 2 hrs, frequent, **Quellón Expreso**, and **Cruz del Sur** (Pedro Aguirre Cerda 052, T65-268 1284), US$3; also to **Ancud**, US$7, and **Puerto Montt**.

Ferries Naviera Austral (Pedro Montt 457, Quellón, T65-268 2207, www.navieraustral.cl) runs ferries from Quellón to **Chaitén** once a week (more in high season), 5 hrs, seat US$20, US$17 bicycle, US$28 motorbike, US$115 car. To **Puerto Chacabuco**, via Melinka, Raúl Marín Balmaceda, Santo Domingo, Melimoyu, Puerto Gala (Isla Toto), Puerto Cisnes, Puerto Gaviota and Puerto Aguirre twice weekly, 28 hrs, reclining seat US$27, cars US$217. All services leave from Castro when Quellón's port is out of commission and schedules are subject to last-minute changes due to inclement weather. Check with the company for schedules and fares for 2017-2018.

Carretera
Austral

★A third of Chile lies to the south of Puerto Montt, but until recently its inaccessibility and rainy climate meant that it was only sparsely populated and unvisited by tourism. The Carretera Austral, or Southern Highway, has now been extended south from Puerto Montt to Villa O'Higgins, giving access to the spectacular virgin landscapes of this wet and wild region, with its mountains, fjords and islands, hitherto isolated communities and picturesque ports. Ships, which were once the only means of access, remain important for exporting timber and bringing in visitors.

The only settlement of any size is Coyhaique; nearby, the airport at Balmaceda and the port at Puerto Chacabuco are the principal entry points. Coyhaique is a good starting point for exploring the Carretera, north to the thermal springs at Puyuhuapi and the unspoilt national park of Queulat, for trekking expeditions and for fishing. Coyhaique is also a good place for booking glacier trips to Parque Nacional Laguna San Rafael, for which boats leave from Puerto Chacabuco.

The Carretera extends 575 km from Coyhaique to Villa O'Higgins, beyond which the southern icefields and their glaciers bring the roadway to a halt. This southernmost section of the Carretera is the wildest and most dramatic, with beautiful unspoilt landscapes around Lago General Carrera. The fairy-tale peaks of Cerro Castillo offer challenging trekking, and there's world class fishing in the turquoise waters of Río Baker. A road runs off to Puerto Ibáñez for lake crossings to Chile Chico, a convenient border crossing to Argentina, while a more adventurous cross-border route involves road, lake and foot or horseback travel to El Chaltén, Argentina.

Puerto Montt to Chaitén

don't miss Parque Pumalí

This section of the Carretera Austral, 205 km, should include two ferry crossings. Before setting out, it is imperative to check which ferries are running and when. If driving, make a reservation in Puerto Montt (not Santiago), on the website of Transportes Austral, www.taustral.cl, which is a consortium of the three ferry companies that operate the routes, or at the offices of the ferry companies listed in Transport, page 823. An alternative route to Chaitén is by direct ferry from Puerto Montt or Quellón/Castro.

Best for
Cycling ▪ Fishing ▪ Road trips ▪ Trekking

Essential Carretera Austral

Getting around

Ruta 7 can be divided into three major sections: **Puerto Montt–Chaitén**, **Chaitén–Coyhaique**, and **Coyhaique–Villa O'Higgins**. The road is paved south of Chaitén to 32 km beyond Villa Santa Lucía, most of the way from La Junta to Coyhaique and south of there to Villa Cerro Castillo and Puerto Ibáñez. Currently, the rest is ripio (loose stones) and many sections are extremely rough and difficult after rain. In the summer, the highway can be closed for several hours each day for roadworks; check www.recorreaysen.cl/estados-de-caminos. The Carretera is very popular with cyclists, even though they can't expect to make fast progress. Motorists need to carry sufficient fuel and spares, especially if intending to detour along any of the highway's many side roads, and protect windscreens and headlamps from stones. Unleaded fuel is available all the way to Villa O'Higgins. There is a road between Puerto El Vagabundo and Caleta Tortel, and the Carretera Austral is connected by a free ferry between Puerto Yungay and Río Bravo, where it continues to Villa O'Higgins. There is little infrastructure for transport or accommodation among the rural hamlets, so allow plenty of time for bus connections, and be sure to take enough cash. There are Cirrus and MasterCard ATMs in Chaitén, Puerto Aysén and Cochrane and Visa is being accepted in more and more places. Coyhaique also has Visa ATMs. There are no banking services at all after Cochrane. Camping will give you more freedom for accommodation and there are many beautiful sites. Many of the buses that ply the Carretera Austral are minibuses operated by small companies, often driven by their owners. Services are less reliable than elsewhere in Chile and timetables change frequently; rains can affect service on the unpaved section. Having your own transport here is definitely preferable. If you intend to hitchhike, note that it is essential to take up to three days' worth of supplies as you can be stuck for that long, especially in the far south. At the same time (for campers too), food supplies are limited and tend to be expensive.

When to go

The landscape throughout the region is lushly green because there is no real dry season. On the offshore islands and the western side of the Andes annual rainfall is over 2000 mm, though inland on the steppe the climate is drier and colder. Westerly winds are strong, especially in summer, but there's plenty of sunshine too. Lago General Carrera in particular (described in the Southern section) has a warm microclimate. January and February are the best months. Snowfall in winter months can be so heavy as to close sections of the highway and isolate towns.

Parque Nacional Alerce Andino

Northern entrance 2.5 km from Correntoso, 35 km east of Puerto Montt (with ranger station and campsite). Southern entrance 7 km east of Lenca (40 km south of Puerto Montt), T65-248 6115, loslagos. oirs@conaf.cl, US$6.25, daily 0900-1800. Ranger station at the northern entrance; there's a private campsite near the Lencaentrance (with showers).

The road (Ruta 7) heads east out of Puerto Montt, through Pelluco, and follows the shore of the beautiful Seno Reloncaví. It passes the southern entrance of the Parque Nacional Alerce Andino, which contains one of the best surviving areas of alerce trees, some over 1000 years old (the oldest is estimated at 4200 years old). Wildlife includes pudú, pumas, vizcachas, condors and black woodpeckers. There are ranger posts at the two entrances, as well as at Río Chaicas, Lago Chapo and Sargazo; these have little information, but a map is available from CONAF in Puerto Montt.

La Arena to Caleta Gonzalo

The first ferry, 46 km from Puerto Montt (allow one hour), crosses the Reloncaví Estuary from **La Arena** to **Puelche**. For details, see Transport, in Listings, below. From Puelche the road continues 54 km south to **Hornopirén** (formerly **Río Negro**) at the northern end of a fjord below Volcán Hornopirén. At the mouth of the fjord is the small **Isla Llancahué** ① *boat 25 mins, US$17one-way, minimum 4 passengers*, with a hotel and thermal springs (www.termasdellancahue.cl). There's good hiking in the forests amid beautiful scenery, and dolphins and fur seals can be seen from the boat.

A second ferry sails from Hornopirén to Leptepu, from where a road runs to Fiordo Largo, where another ferry goes to Caleta Gonzalo.

☆Parque Pumalín

Information: Klenner 299, Puerto Varas, T65-225 0079; in USA T415-229 9339, www.parquepumalin.cl (Spanish and English). Open all year, free.

Caleta Gonzalo is the entry point for Parque Pumalín for visitors from the north. The park, created by the US billionaire Douglas Tompkins who died in 2015, was a private reserve of 700,000 ha in two sections which now has Nature Sanctuary status and was handed to the Chilean state in 2017. Covering large areas of the western Andes, with virgin temperate rainforest, the park is spectacularly beautiful, and is seen by many as one of the most important conservation projects in the world. The government is to create more national parks adjoining Pumalín. There are campsites and cabins throughout the park, a number of hot springs and hiking trails.

South of Caleta Gonzalo the Carretera Austral winds through the park's beautiful unspoilt scenery, and there is a steep climb on the *ripio* road to two lakes, Lago Río Blanco and Lago Río Negro, with panoramic views.

Chaitén

After the 2008 eruption of Volcán Chaitén and consequent river flooding, the government decided to abandon Chaitén, cutting off utilities and moving the seat of provincial government to Futaleufú. They started to rebuild the town 10 km north at Santa Bárbara. Chaitén, however, survived with running water, generators and fuel, and, in 2011, the government reversed its decision. The town, once more the provincial capital, is being reestablished in the northern part of the old town, where there are shops, *hospedajes*, *cabañas* and all transport links: ferries to Puerto Montt and Chiloé, flights and buses. See www.municipalidadchaiten.cl.

Listings Puerto Montt to Chaitén

Where to stay

Parque Nacional Alerce Andino

$$$$ Alerce Mountain Lodge
Km 36 Carretera Austral, T65-225 3044, www.mountainlodge.cl.
In Los Alerces de Lenca private reserve, beside Parque Nacional Alerce Andino, remote lodge, rooms and cabins, all-inclusive 2- to 4-night packages, with hiking, guides speak English, good food.

La Arena to Caleta Gonzalo

$$$$ Hotel Termas de Llancahué
Isla Llancahué, T9-9642 4857, www.termasdellancahue.cl.
Full board (excellent food), hot spring at the hotel, excursions by boat, fishing, kayaking.

$$ Hornopirén
Carrera Pinto 388, Hornopirén, T65-221 7256, h.hornopiren@gmail.com.
Rooms with shared bath, also *cabañas* and restaurant at the water's edge.

$$ Hostería Catalina
Ingenieros Militares s/n, Hornopirén, T65-221 7359, www.hosteriacatalina.cl.
Comfortable rooms and *cabañas*, meals, excursions, a good place to stay.

Chaitén

There are many *hospedajes* and hostels in the centre and along the waterfront.

$$$-$$ Hotel Schilling
Corcovado 230, T65-273 1295, hotelschilling@hotmail.com.
Probably the most upscale hotel in town. Rooms have ocean views.

$ El Quijote
O'Higgins 42, T65-273 1204, relquijotechaiten@live.cl.
Hostel opposite the bus station, welcoming, also has restaurant. Dorms from US$11.50 per night.

$ Hostería Llanos
Corcovado 378, T65-273 1332.
Pleasant, family-run B&B on the waterfront. Good breakfast.

What to do

Chaitén

Chaitur, *O'Higgins 67, T9-7468 5608, www.chaitur. com*. Nicolás La Penna runs this agency making bus, boat, plane and hotel reservations, transfers, tours to Parque Pumalín, Volcán Chaitén, hot springs, glaciers, Santa Bárbara beach, bike rentals, Carretera Austral, photography trips. Still *the* best place for local information. English and French spoken, helpful, book exchange, internet.

Transport

Parque Nacional Alerce Andino
Bus To the north entrance: take a **Fierro** bus to **Correntoso** (or **Lago Chapo** bus which passes through Correntoso), several daily except Sun, then walk. To the south entrance: take any bus marked "La Arena/Chaicas" towards Lenca, US$2. Tell the driver to let you off in Lenca at the road leading to the park entrance, then walk (signposted).

La Arena to Caleta Gonzalo
Ferry See www.taustral.cl. **Naviera Puelche** (Av Italia 2326, Parque San Andrés, Puerto Montt, T65-227 0761, www.navierapuelche.cl), and **Naviera Paredes** (T65-227 6490, www.naviera paredes.cl) run 2 ferries across the Reloncaví Estuary from La Arena, 30 mins, every 45 mins, 0600-0030 daily (0600-0045 from Puelche), US$15 for a car, US$11 for motorcycle, US$4.25 for bicycle, US$1 for foot passengers. Arrive at least 30 mins early to guarantee a place; buses have priority. Roll-on roll-off type operating all year. **Hornopirén** to **Chaitén** via Leptepu and Fiordo Largo-Caleta Gonzalo: check on www. taustral.cl, or with **Naviera Puelche**, as above for schedules, normally once a day each way to/from

Leptepu, twice a day in high season; 2 a day to/ from **Caleta Gonzalo**, 4 in high season. If driving your own car, it is essential to reserve a place: cars US$52, motorbikes US$13, bicycles US$8.75, passengers in addition to driver US$8.75, bus passengers US$8. 1 fare covers both ferries.

Bus **Kémel** (T65-225 3530) has daily services between **Puerto Montt** and Hornopirén, US$7.

Chaitén
Air Flights on Mon-Sat at 0930 from **Puerto Montt** to Santa Bárbara with **Aerocord** (19 passengers), US$87.

Bus Terminal at **Chaitur**, O'Higgins 67. **Kémel** (as above) have a daily bus/ferry service from Puerto Montt, 0700, US$22, 10 hrs, return from Chaitén 1200, 12 hrs. To **Coyhaique**, Sun, Mon with **Becker** (www.busesbecker.com), 1130, also **Terraustral**, with an overnight stay in La Junta, 12 hrs, Mon, Fri at 1700, Tue, Thu, Sat at 1200. Connections to Puyuhuapi and Coyhaique next day, 0500. **Terraustral** direct to Coyhaique Mon and Sat 0700. Minibuses usually travel full, so can't pick up passengers en route. Buses to **Futaleufú**, daily 1200 and 1700; change here for buses to the **Argentine border**, Mon, Fri (Mon, Wed, Fri in summer) and **Palena** daily 1200, 1700.

Ferry The ferry port is about 1 km north of town. Schedules change frequently and ferries are infrequent off season. **Naviera Austral** (Corcovado 466, T65-273 1011, www. navieraustral.cl) operates ferry services. Check www.taustral.cl for all future sailings. To **Quellón** or **Castro** (Jan-Feb only), once a week, Tue, more in summer (Dec-Mar); fares given under Quellón, above. To **Puerto Montt**, Mon, Thu, Fri via Ayacara, 10 hrs, passengers (seat/*butaca*) US$27, car US$146, motorbike US$32.50, bicycle US$16.

Chaitén to Coyhaique

thermal pools, trekking routes and a boat trip to a glacier

This section of the Carretera Austral, runs 422 km through breathtaking and varied scenery, passing tiny villages, most notably the idyllic Puyuhuapi.

Lago Yelcho and around
Puerto Cárdenas, 44 km south of Chaitén, is on the northern tip of **Lago Yelcho**, a beautiful lake on Río Futaleufú surrounded by hills, much loved by anglers for its salmon and trout. (There are no shops or restaurants in Puerto Cárdenas, but Viola, T9-9884 2946, bungalow opposite yellow house next to old *carabinero* post, offers half board ($$) and excellent food). Further south at Km 60, a path leads to **Ventisquero Yelcho** (two hours' walk there), a dramatic glacier with high waterfalls.

At **Villa Santa Lucía**, an uninspiring modern settlement 76 km south of Chaitén, with basic food and accommodation, a road branches east to the Argentine border. The road divides at **Puerto**

Ramírez, past the southern end of Lago Yelcho, 24 km east of Santa Lucía: the north branch runs along the valley of the Río Futaleufú to Futaleufú and the border at Paso Futaleufú; the southern branch goes to another border crossing at Paso Palena. The scenery is spectacular, but the road is hard going: single track *ripio*, climbing steeply in places (tough for bikes; allow plenty of time).

☆Futaleufú and around *Colour map 9, A1.*

Eight kilometres west of the border, Futaleufú nestles in a bowl amid steep mountains on the Río Espolón. Its houses are neatly slatted with alerce wood and the wide streets are lined with shrubs and roses. Access to challenging whitewater rafting on the Río Futaleufú has made it into one of the southern hemisphere's prime centres for the sport, and with kayaking, riding, trekking, mountain biking and canyoning on offer too, Futaleufú now calls itself the capital of adventure tourism. **Lago Espolón**, west of Futaleufú, reached by a turning 41 km northeast of Villa Santa Lucía, is a beautiful lake with a warm microclimate: 30°C in the day in summer, 5°C at night, with excellent fishing at the lake's mouth. The lake is even warm enough for a quick dip, but beware of the currents.

Border with Argentina: Paso Futaleufú and Paso Palena Chilean immigration is at the border, 8 km east of Futaleufú; see www.pasosfronterizos.gov.cl/cf_futaleufu.html. The border is just west of the bridge over the Río Grande: straightforward crossing, open 0800-2000. For Argentinian immigration, see Argentina chapter. Change money in Futaleufú; nowhere to change at the border but you can pay the bus fare to Esquel (Argentina) in US dollars. Alternatively, cross into Argentina further south near **Palena**, which is 8 km west of the border and has a Chilean immigration office. Check conditions locally before crossing at this border. **Note** If entering from Argentina, no fresh produce may be brought into Chile.

La Junta and around

La Junta in the XI (eleventh) Region is a village 151 km south of Chaitén. It has a service station, where there's a minimarket. From the village you can visit **Lago Rosselot**, surrounded by forest in the **Reserva Nacional Lago Rosselot**, 9 km east. The same road continues east, 74 km, to the unofficial border crossing at Lago Verde: open 0800-2000 in summer only. In the other direction, a road leads northwest, with a ferry crossing over the Río Palena (runs 0830-1800), to the fishing village of **Puerto Raúl Marín Balmaceda** on the coast (hostels and camping). Different species of dolphin can be seen offshore. Raúl Marín forms one apex of the blue whale triangle: the giant cetacean may be sighted on the ferry to Quellón in the summer. On clear days there are superb views of Volcán Melimoyu from the beach.

Puyuhuapi and around

With the most idyllic setting along the whole Carretera Austral, Puyuhuapi (also spelled Puyuguapi) lies in a tranquil bay at the northern end of the Puyuhuapi fjord, 46 km south of La Junta. The village was founded by four German-speaking Sudeten families in 1935. Handwoven carpets are made here to world renown at **Alfombras de Puyuhuapi** ① *T67-232 5131, www.puyuhuapi.com, daily in summer.* **Puyuhuapi** is the best stopping point between Chaitén and Coyhaique, with phone, fuel, shops, but no banks: hotels may change dollars. Close to the village are the thermal pools at **Termas del Ventisquero** ① *6 km south of Puyuhuapi beside the Carretera overlooking the fjord, T9-7966 6862, www.termasventisqueropuyuhuapi.cl, daily 1000-2100, until 2000 in low season, entry US$24.50, US$14.50 children under 10.* South of Puyuhuapi, 24 km, is the 154,093-ha **Parque Nacional Queulat** ① *CONAF, La Junta, T67-221 2225,aysen.oirs@conaf.cl, US$8, reductions for Chileans and children, daily Dec-Mar 0830-2100, rest of year 0830-1830.* It is most visited for the spectacular hanging glacier, **Ventisquero Colgante**. There are parking spaces and camping areas 2.5 km off the road passing the *guardaparque's* house. Three walks begin from here: a short stroll through the woodland to a viewpoint of the Ventisquero, or cross the river where the path begins to Laguna Tempanos, where boats cross the lake in summer. The third trail, 3.25 km, takes 2½ hours to climb to a panoramic viewpoint of the Ventisquero, where you can watch the ice fall into huge waterfalls like sifted sugar.

At 59 km south of Puyuhuapi, a winding road branches west and follows the Río Cisnes 33 km to Puerto Cisnes (www.municipalidadcisnes.cl), a fishing village and salmon-farming centre at the mouth of the river on Puyuhuapi fjord, set amongst steep mountains. The Río Cisnes, 160 km in length, is recommended for rafting or canoeing, with grand scenery and modest rapids except for the horrendous drop at Piedra del Gato. There's good camping in the forest, and fuel is available in the village.

Continuing on the Carretera Austral, at 89 km south of Puyuhuapi is **Villa Amengual** and, at km 92, a road branches east, 104 km to La Tapera and the Argentine border. Chilean immigration is 12 km west of the border, open summer 0800-2200, winter 0800-2000. On the Argentine side the road joins the Ruta 40, a section with few services for fuel or food.

Coyhaique and around *Colour map 9, A1.*

A growing centre for tourism, Coyhaique, 420 km south of Chaitén, is a busy small town perched on a hill between the Ríos Simpson and Coyhaique. It has a cinema and all main services, including stores selling hiking gear and warm clothes. The brand new **Museo Regional de Aysén** is set to open at the end of 2017 in the restored Estancia Coyhaique (a historical monument). It will house the collections of the old Museo Regional de la Patagonia Central, which has been replaced by the new Centro Cultural de Coyhaique at Lillo 23. While the new museum is being built, collections can be seen in the regional library ① *Cochrane 233, T67-2211621, www.museoregionalaysen.cl, Mon-Fri*

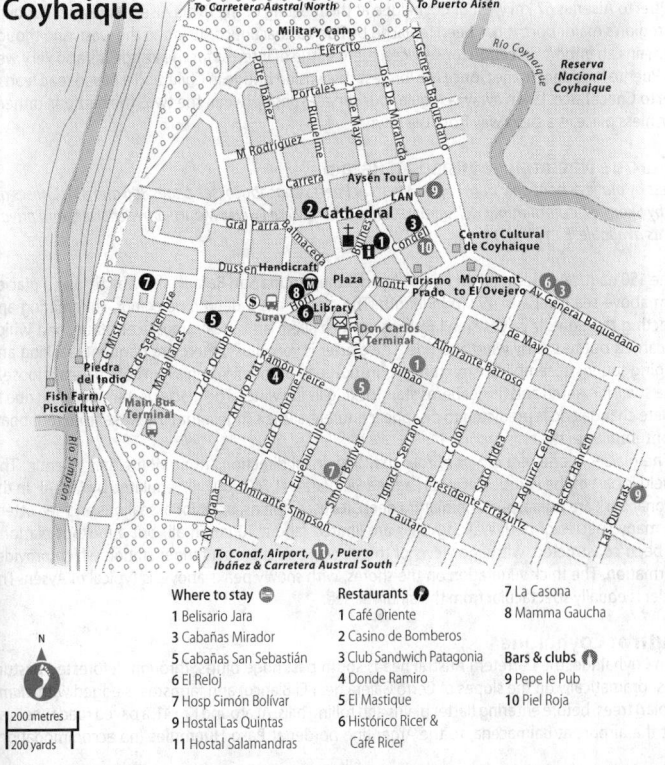

Coyhaique

Where to stay	Restaurants	7 La Casona
1 Belisario Jara	1 Café Oriente	8 Mamma Gaucha
3 Cabañas Mirador	2 Casino de Bomberos	
5 Cabañas San Sebastián	3 Club Sandwich Patagonia	**Bars & clubs**
6 El Reloj	4 Donde Ramiro	9 Pepe le Pub
7 Hosp Simón Bolívar	5 El Mastique	10 Piel Roja
9 Hostal Las Quintas	6 Histórico Ricer &	
11 Hostal Salamandras	Café Ricer	

0900-1750. From the bridge over the Río Simpson, look for the **Piedra del Indio**, a rock outcrop which looks like a face in profile.

Just outside the town, the **Reserva Nacional Coyhaique** ① *0830-1730, US$4.75, information from CONAF*, has some trails for walking or biking, with picnic grounds and campsites (US$6.75). To reach the trailheads, follow Baquedano to the end; go over the bridge and past the *guardaparque's* hut. There are well-marked walks of between 20 minutes and five hours, including a satisfying walk up to Cerro Cinchao, and a path to Laguna Verde and Laguna Venus, particularly recommended for its great views.

Ski centre **El Fraile** ① *29 km from Coyhaique, www.chileanski.com/eng/el-fraile, season May-Sep,* 1000-people capacity, is 1599 m above sea level, with five pistes and powder snow, surrounded by *ñire* (Antarctic beech) and *lenga* forests.

Border with Argentina: Coyhaique Alto A 43-km road runs east to this crossing. On the Argentine side the road leads through Río Mayo and Sarmiento to Comodoro Rivadavia. **Chilean immigration** is at Coyhaique Alto, 6 km west of the border, open summer 0800-2200, winter 0800-2000, www. pasosfronterizos.gov.cl/cf_coyhaiquealto.html.

Puerto Aisén and Puerto Chacabuco *Colour map 9, A1.*
The paved road west between Coyhaique and Puerto Aisén passes through **Reserva Nacional Río Simpson** ① *administration/museum at the entrance, 32 km west of Coyhaique, US$4.75,* with beautiful waterfalls, lovely views of the river and excellent fly-fishing. There are no marked trails; campsite opposite turning to Santuario San Sebastián, US$10.

Puerto Aisén is 67 km west of Coyhaique at the meeting of the rivers Aisén and Palos. Formerly the region's major port, it has been replaced by Puerto Chacabuco, 15 km to the west, and though it remains an important centre for services, there's little of interest for the visitor. It's also very wet. The Puente President Ibáñez, once the longest suspension bridge in Chile, and a paved road lead to **Puerto Chacabuco** 15 km away; a regular bus service runs between the two. The harbour, rather charmless place, is a short way from the town.

☆Parque Nacional Laguna San Rafael
Access by plane of boat only from Puerto Montt or Puerto Chacabuco (see pages 806 and 831). Cruises are run by Skorpios, Catamaranes del Sur and Compañía Naviera Puerto Montt; other charters and private yachts available. Entry US$11.

Some 150 nautical miles south of Puerto Aisén is the **Laguna San Rafael**, into which flows a glacier 30 m above sea level and 45 km in length. The glacier has a deep blue colour, shimmering and reflecting the light. It calves small icebergs, which seem an unreal, translucent blue, and which are carried out to sea by wind and tide. The glacier is very noisy; there are frequent cracking and banging sounds, resembling a mixture of gunshots and thunder. When a hunk of ice breaks loose, a huge swell is created and the icebergs start rocking in the water. The glacier is disintegrating due to climate change and is predicted to disappear entirely; some suggest that the wake from tour boats is contributing to the erosion.

The glacier is one of a group of four that flow in all directions from Monte San Valentín. This icefield is part of the Parque Nacional Laguna San Rafael (1,740,000 ha), regulated by CONAF. In the national park are puma, *pudú* (miniature deer), foxes, dolphins, occasional sealions and sea otters, and many species of bird. Walking trails are limited (about 10 km in all) but a lookout platform has been constructed, with fine views of the glacier, and there's a ranger station which provides information. The thick vegetation on the shores, with snowy peaks above, is typical of Aysén. The glacier is equally spectacular from the air or the sea.

South of Coyhaique
From Coyhaique, the Carretera Austral heads south past huge bluffs, through deforested pasture (most dramatically on the slopes of Cerro Galera near El Blanco) and farmsteads edged with *alamo* (poplar) trees, before entering flatter plains and rolling hills. At around Km 41, a paved road runs east past the airport at Balmaceda, to the Argentine border at **Paso Huemules** (no accommodation,

Chilean immigration is open winter 0800-2000, summer 0800-2200, www.pasosfronterizos.gov.cl/f_balmaceda.html. The Carretera Austral, meanwhile, starts to climb again, past the entrance to the Reserva Nacional Cerro Castillo (see below). It winds up through the attractive narrow gorge of Río Horqueta, to a pass between Cerro Castillo and its neighbours, before dropping down a 6-km slalom into the breathtaking valley of Río Ibáñez. (This is currently the most southerly paved section and the road is safe and wide here.) Here the road forks east to Puerto Ibáñez, a further 31 km away, or the ferry crossing of vast Lago General Carrera (see page 832).

Listings Chaitén to Coyhaique *map p825*

Tourist information

Futaleufú

Tourist office
In the plaza at O'Higgins 596, T65-272 1241, www.futaleufu.cl. Oct-Apr 0930-2200 (1030-1330, 1500-1900 low season).
For accommodation, maps and fishing licences.

Puyuhuapi

Tourist office
By the Municipalidad, main street. Oct-May Mon-Sat, 0900-1200, 1500-1830.
Helpful.

Coyhaique

CONAF
Av Ogana 1060, T67-221 2109, aysen.oirs@conaf.cl. Mon-Fri 0830-1730.

Sernatur
Bulnes 35, T67-224 0290, infoaysen@sernatur.cl. Mon-Fri 0900-2100, Sat 0900-1800.
Very helpful, English spoken. There is also an information kiosk on the plaza.

Puerto Aisén and Puerto Chacabuco

Puerto Aisén tourist office
Tourism Cerro Mirador, Carrera y O'Higgins. Daily in summer 0815-1930, in winter Mon-Thu 0815-1730-1730, Fri 0815-1630.
For information on shipping movements, www.chacabucoport.cl.

Where to stay

Lago Yelcho and around: Villa Santa Lucía
pp Several places on main street: ask at **Nachito**, the café where the bus stops, which serves good breakfasts.

Futaleufú

$$$$ El Barranco
O'Higgins 172, T65-272 1314, www.elbarrancochile.cl.
Elegant rustic rooms, luxurious, pool, sauna, good restaurant, and expert fishing guides, horses and bikes for hire.

$$$ Cabañas Río Espolón
Follow Cerda to the end, T65-272 1423, www.patagoniafutaleufu.cl.
Cosy *cabañas* in secluded riverside setting, restaurant overlooking Río Espolón, *parrilla*, bar. Popular with river-rafting groups, book ahead.

$$$-$$ Río Grande
O'Higgins 397 y Aldea, T65-272 1320, www.pachile.com.
Also upmarket, spacious attractive rooms, international restaurant, popular with rafting groups.

$$-$ Adolfo B&B
O'Higgins 302, T65-272 1256.
Best value in this range, comfortable rooms in family home, shared hot showers.

$ pp Continental
Balmaceda 595, T65-272 1222.
Oldest in town, no breakfast, basic, but clean and welcoming.

Camping
There are several other campsites.

Aldea Puerto Espolón
Sector La Puntilla, 400 m from town, T9-5324 0305, www.aldeapuertoespolon.blogspot.com.
Teepees, dome-tents or your own tent, take sleeping bag, hot showers.

La Junta and around

$$$$-$$$ Espacio y Tiempo
Carretera Austral 399, T67-231 4141, www.espacioytiempo.cl.

Spacious rooms, warm and cosy atmosphere, restaurant, attractive gardens, fishing expeditions.

$$ Hostal Casa Museo Copihue
Varas 611, T67-231 4184.
Some rooms with bath, good meals.

$$-$ Hostería Valdera
Varas s/n, T67-231 4105.
Private bath, meals served. Excellent value.

Puyuhuapi

$$$$ Puyuhuapi Lodge and Spa
Bahía Dorita, Reservations: on the website, or Santiago, T2-2225 6489, www.puyuhuapilodge.com.
Splendidly isolated on a nook in the sea fjord, the hotel owns the thermal baths: outdoors by the fjord, or indoor spa complex. Good packages for de-stressing with riding, fishing, kayaking, trekking, mountain biking, yoga and the thermals included.

$$$$-$$$ El Pangue
18 km north, Km 240 at end of Lago Risopatrón, Parque Nacional Queulat, T67-252 6906, www.elpangue.com.
Rooms and luxurious *cabañas* for 4 to 7 in splendid rural setting, fishing, horseriding, trekking, mountain bikes, pool, sauna, hot tubs, great views, restful.

$$$-$$ Casa Ludwig
Otto Uebel 202, T67-232 5220, www.casaludwig.cl. Oct-Mar; enquire in advance at other times.
Cheaper with shared bath. In a beautiful 4-storey house built by first German settlers, wonderful views, a range of rooms, good breakfast, comfortable; charming owner Luisa is knowledgeable about the area, speaks German and English.

$$$-$$ Hostería Alemana
Otto Uebel 450, T67-232 5118, www.hosteriaalemana.cl.
A large traditional wooden house on the main road by the water, very comfortable, lovely lake views and garden.

$$ Aonikenk
Hamburgo 16, T67-232 5208, aonikenkturismo@yahoo.com.
Pleasant heated rooms or *cabañas* (not sound-proofed), good beds, meals, helpful, informative, bike hire.

Camping
Campsite behind the general store.

South of Puyuhuapi
Puerto Cisnes also has various *cabañas* and *residenciales*.

$$$-$$ Cabañas Río Cisnes
Prat 101, Puerto Cisnes, T67-234 6404.
Cabins sleep 4 to 8. Owner, Juan Suazo, offers sea fishing trips in his boat.

$$ Hostería El Gaucho
Holmberg 140, Puerto Cisnes, T67-234 6514.
With bath and breakfast, dinner available.

$ pp Hospedaje El Encanto
Pasaje Plaza 3, Villa Amengual, T9-9144 8662.
With restaurant and café, one of several cheap options in town.

Coyhaique
There are many more *hospedajes* and private houses with rooms; ask tourist office for a list.

$$$$-$$$ El Reloj
Baquedano 828, T67-223 1108, www.elrelojhotel.cl.
Tasteful, in a former sawmill, with a good restaurant, charming, comfortable wood panelled rooms, some with wonderful views, nice lounge, the best in town.

$$$ Belisario Jara
Bilbao 662, T67-223 4150, www.belisariojara.cl.
Most distinctive and delightful, an elegant and welcoming small place.

$$$ Cabañas Mirador
Baquedano 848, T67-223 3191.
Attractive, well-equipped *cabañas*, also rooms, in lovely gardens with panoramic views of the Reserva Forestal, and Río Coyhaique below.

$$$ Cabañas San Sebastián
Freire 554, T67-223 1762, see Facebook.
Central, very good.

$$ Hostal Las Quintas
Bilbao 1208, T67-223 1173, nolfapatagonia@hotmail.com.
Spartan, but clean and very spacious rooms (some in very bizarre design) with bath.

$$-$ Hospedaje Simón Bolívar
Simón Bolívar 616, T9-9761 6918.
This family-run hostel is a welcoming change of pace from the party *hostales* in the area. Dorms starting at US$15, also doubles. Wi-Fi, breakfast and refreshing rainwater showers.

$$-$ Hostal Salamandras
Sector Los Pinos, 2 km south in attractive forest,
T67-221 1865, www.hostalsalamandras.com.
Variety of rooms, dorms cabin and camping,
kitchen facilities, trekking and other sports
and tours.

Camping

Tourist office on plaza or Sernatur in Coyhaique
has a full list of all sites in XI Región. There are
many camping sites in Coyhaique and on the
road between Coyhaique and Puerto Aisén,
eg **Camping Alborada** (at Km 2, T67-223 8868),
hot shower.

Puerto Aisén and Puerto Chacabuco

Accommodation is hard to find, most is taken up
by fishing companies in both ports. There are
several places to eat along Tte Merino and Aldea
in Puerto Aisén.

$$$$ Loberías del Sur
José Miguel Carrera 50, Puerto Chacabuco,
T67-235 1112, www.loberiasdelsur.cl.
5-star hotel, whose restaurant serves the best
food in the area (handy for meal or a drink
before boarding ferry – climb up steps direct
from port). Same owner as **Catamaranes del Sur**
(see Shipping, below), which also has a nearby
nature reserve, Parque Aikén del Sur.

$$$ Patagonia Green
400 m from bridge (on Pto Chacabuco side),
T67-233 6796, www.patagoniagreen.cl.
Nice rooms or cabins for up to 5, kitchen, heating,
gardens, arranges tours to Laguna San Rafael,
fishing, mountain biking, riding, trekking, etc,
English spoken.

$$$-$$ Caicahues
Michimalonco 660, Puerto Aisén, T67-233 6623,
hcaicahues@puertoaysen.cl.
Popular business hotel, with heating,
book ahead.

Restaurants

Futaleufú

$$ Futaleufú
Cerda 407, T65-272 1295.
Serves typical Chilean meat dishes and
local foods.

$$ Martín Pescador
Balmaceda y Rodríguez, T65-272 1279.
For fish and meat dishes, rustic.

$$-$ Sur Andes
Cerda 308, T65-272 1405.
Café serving cakes, sweets, light meals and real
coffee. Also sells handicrafts.

Puyuhuapi

$$ Café Rossbach
Costanera.
Run by the descendants of the original German
settlers, an attractive place by the water for
delicious salmon, tea and *küchen*.

$$ Lluvia Marina
Next to Casa Ludwig.
The best café, also selling handicrafts. Superb
food in relaxed atmosphere, a great place to just
hang out, owner Veronica is very helpful.

Coyhaique

$$$ Histórico Ricer
Horn 48 y 40, p 2, T67-223 2920, see Facebook.
Central, warm and cosy, serving breakfast
to dinner, regional specialities, with good
vegetarian options, historical exhibits. Also
has **Café Ricer** at No 48, serving light food.

$$ La Casona
Obispo Vielmo 77, T67-223 8894.
Justly reputed as best in town, charming family
restaurant serves excellent fish, *congrío* especially,
but best known for grilled lamb.

$$-$ Casino de Bomberos
Next to the fire station, Gral Parra 365,
T67-223 1437.
For great atmosphere and a filling lunch,
can be slow when serving groups.

$$-$ Donde Ramiro
Freire 319.
Good set lunches, big screen TV.

$$-$ Mamma Gaucha
Horn 47, T67-221 0721.
Pizzas and big salads. Also rumoured to
have the best locally brewed beer in Chile.

$ Club Sandwich Patagonia
Moraleda 433, T67-224 4664.
24-hr fast food and huge Chilean sandwiches,
a local institution.

$ El Mastique
Bilbao 141, T67-282 4067.
Cheap but good pasta and Chilean food.

Cafés

Café Oriente
Condell 201.
Serves a good lunch and tasty cakes.

Coyhaique

Pepe le Pub
Parra 72, see Facebook.
Good cocktails and snacks, relaxed, live music at weekends, karaoke.

Piel Roja
Moraleda y Condell, www.pielroja.cl.
Good music, laid back, dancing, happy hour 1900-2100.

Shopping

Coyhaique

Handicrafts
Artesanía Manos Azules, *Riquelme 435.*
Sells fine handicrafts.
Feria de Artesanía, *on the plaza.*

What to do

Futaleufú

Tour operators arrange whitewater rafting trips, prices starting from US$75 pp. Local fishing guides can also be found in the village.
Expediciones Chile, *Mistral 296, T65-272 1386 (in US T1-208-629 5032), www.exchile.com.*
Whitewater rafting, kayaking, etc. Offers the best multi-day trips, book in advance. Day trips can be booked at office.
Futaleufú Explore, *O'Higgins 772, T9-7433 4455, www.futaleufuexplore.com.* A respected rafting company.
Rancho Las Ruedas, *Pilota Carmona 337, T9-7735 0989, guide.stallion@gmail.com.* The best horse riding in the area.

Coyhaique

Cycling
Austral Biker, *Av Norte Sur 1228, T9-7618 3588, see Facebook.* For tours and bike rentals.

Fishing
The surrounding area is famous for trout fishing with several *estancias* offering luxury accommodation and bilingual guides. Most tour operators also offer specialist fishing trips.
Expediciones Coyhaique, *Portales 195, T67-223 1783, www.coyhaiqueflyfishing.com.*
Fly-fishing experts.

Language schools
Baquedano International Language School, *Baquedano 20, T67-223 2520, www.balasch.cl.*
US$600 per week course including lodging and all meals, or US$40 for 3 classes a day one-to-one tuition, other lodging options and activities can be arranged.

Tour operators
Many tours operate Sep to Apr, some Dec-Mar only.
Andes Patagónicos, *Casilla 241, T67-221 6711, www.ap.cl.* Trips to local lakes, Tortel, and historically based tours all year round. Good, but not cheap.
Aysén Tour, *Pasaje Río Backer 2646, T67-223 7070, www.aysentour.cl.* Tours along the Carretera Austral, also car rental.
Camello Patagón, *Condell 149, T67-224 4327, www.camellopatagon.cl.* Daily trips to Cavernas de Marmol in Río Tranquilo, among others, also car rental and other services.
Casa del Turismo Rural, *Odeón Plaza de Armas, T67-221 4031, www.casaturismorural.cl.*
An association of 40 families, mostly in the countryside, who offer activities such as horseriding and fishing. Many do not have telephones or internet, make reservations free.
Geo Turismo, *21 de Mayo 398, T67-258 3173, www.geoturismopatagonia.cl.* Offers wide range of tours, English spoken, professional.
Turismo Prado, *21 de Mayo 417, T67-223 1271, www.turismoprado.cl.* Tours of local lakes and other sights, Laguna San Rafael trips and historical tours.

Transport

Futaleufú
Bus Bus to **Chaitén** 6 days a week, information from **Chaitur** in **Chaitén**. From west side of plaza in Futaleufú, a **Jacobsen** bus (www.transportejacobsen.com.ar) runs to the Argentine border, 3 times a week, and Mon-Fri in Jan-Feb, US$2.50, 30 mins, connecting with services to Trevelin and Esquel. Buses also run between Futaleufú and Palena, US$2.

La Junta

Bus To **Chaitén** 4 a week, information from **Chaitur** on **Chaitur**. To **Coyhaique**, with **Daniela** (T9-9512 3500), **Becker** (T9-8554 7774), and **Aguilas Patagónicas** (T67-252 3730, www. aguilaspatagonicas.cl), 7 hrs, US$21.

Puyuhuapi

Bus Daily to **Coyhaique**, US$12, 6 hrs, plus 2 weekly to **Lago Verde**.

South of Puyuhuapi

Aguilas Patagónicas run daily between Puerto Cisnes and Coyhaique (on Sun only to Coyhaique), US$10-12.

Coyhaique

Air Most flights are from Balmaceda, 56 km east of Coyhaique, including daily flights to **Santiago** with **LATAM**, mostly via **Puerto Montt**, and **Sky**, which sometimes makes several stops. Landing can be dramatic owing to strong winds. **LATAM** also flies to **Punta Arenas**, twice a week, once via Puerto Montt, the other via Santiago. Buses run between Balmaceda and Coyhaique, while minibuses go to/from hotels in Coyhaique (US$9); companies sell tickets at baggage carousel. Taxi from airport to **Coyhaique**, 1 hr, US$40. There are also buses to Puerto Aisén (US$10-13). Car rental agencies at the airport; very expensive, closed Sun. Coyhaique also has its own airport, Tte Vidal, about 5 km southwest of town. **Aerocord**, T67-224 6300, www.aerocord.cl, has services from Coyhaique to various towns, such as Puerto Montt, Chaitén and Puyuhuapi.

Bus Full list of buses from tourist information. Terminal at Lautaro y Magallanes, T67-223 2067, but most buses leave from their own offices.

To **Puerto Aisén**, minibuses run every 45 mins, 1 hr, **Alí** (Dussen 283, T67-223 2788, in Puerto Aysén Aldea 1143, T67-233 3335, www.busesali.cl), **Suray** (A Prat 265, T67-223 4085, in Puerto Aysén, T67-223 8387), US$4. Change here for **Puerto Chacabuco**, 20 mins, US$1. To **Puerto Ibáñez** on Lago Gral Carrera, several minibus companies (connect with ferry to Chile Chico) pick up

Tip…
Book buses on the Carretera Austral as they are usually full. Bikes can be taken by arrangement.

0530-0600 from your hotel, 1½ hrs, book the day before. North towards **Chaitén**: twice a week direct with **Becker** (Parra 335, T67-223 2167, www. busesbecker.com), US$37, otherwise change in La Junta; in winter these stop overnight in La Junta. To **Futaleufú**, with **Becker**, 2 a week, US$37. To **Puerto Cisnes**, **Aguilas Patagónicas** (Lautaro 109, T67-221 1288, www.aguilaspatagonicas.cl), US$10-12. South to **Cochrane** daily in summer with **Don Carlos** (Subteniente Cruz 63, T67-223 1981), **Aguilas Patagónicas** or **Acuario 13** (at terminal, T67-252 2143), US$23. All buses stop at **Cerro Castillo** (US$8), **Bahía Murta** (US$13), **Puerto Tranquilo** (US$14) and **Puerto Bertrand** (US$19).Bus to Puerto Natales with Becker (US$93 passenger, US$31 bicycle).

Car hire If renting a car, a high 4WD vehicle is recommended for Carretera Austral. Buy fuel in Coyhaique, several stations. There are several rental agencies in town, charging at least US$100 a day, including insurance, for 4WD or pick-up. Add another US$50 for paperwork to take a vehicle into Argentina.

Ferry office Navimag, Eusebio Lillo 91, T67-223 3306, www.navimag.com. **Naviera Austral**, Horn 40, of 101, T67-221 0727, www.navieraustral.cl.

Tip…
It is best to make ferry reservations in the companies' offices in Puerto Montt or Coyhaique.

Taxi US$6 to Tte Vidal airport. Fares in town US$2. Taxi *colectivos* (shared taxis) congregate at Prat y Bilbao, average fare US$0.75.

Puerto Aisén and Puerto Chacabuco

Bus See under Coyhaique, above.

Ferry Navimag (Terminal de Transbordadores, Puerto Chacabuco, T67-235 1111, www.navimag. com) sails twice a week from Puerto Chacabuco to **Puerto Montt**, taking about 24 hrs (for details, see Ferry, page 809). **Catamaranes del Sur** (J M Carrera 50, T67-235 1112, www. loberiasdelsur.cl) have sailings to Laguna San Rafael. Other operators include **Agemar** (Terminal Aysén, T67-235 1151, Puerto Aisén) and **Naviera Austral** (Terminal de Transbordadores, T67-235 1493, www.navieraustral.cl).

Lago General Carrera (Lago Buenos Aires in Argentina) straddles the border and, at 2240 sq km, is the second largest lake in South America. It's an area of outstanding beauty. Sheltered from the icy west winds by the Campo de Hielo Norte, the region also has the best climate in southern Chile, with little rain, some 300 days of sunshine and a microclimate at Chile Chico that allows the cultivation of the same crops and fruit as in the Central Valley. Ferries cross the lake from Puerto Ibáñez, but it is worth taking time to follow the Carretera Austral around the lake's western and southern shores.

Puerto Ibáñez

Puerto Ibáñez (population 828) is the principal port on the Chilean section of the lake. As such you'll probably just pass through to reach the ferry. It is, however, a centre for distinctive pottery, leather production and vegetable growing (you can buy salad from greenhouses and visit potters). Local archaeology includes rock art and the largest Tehuelche cemetery in Patagonia. There are various hotels, but no other services. Fuel (sold in five-litre containers) is available at Luis A Bolados 461 (house with five laburnum trees outside). Most shops and restaurants are closed Sunday. There are some fine waterfalls, including the Salto Río Ibáñez, 6 km north.

Villa Cerro Castillo and around

Beyond the turning to Puerto Ibáñez the Carretera Austral goes through Villa Cerro Castillo (Km 8), a quiet village in a spectacular setting beneath the striking, jagged peaks of **Cerro Castillo**, overlooking the broad valley below. There's a petrol station, public phone, several food shops and a tiny tourist information kiosk by the road side (January and February only), with details of guides offering trekking and horse rides.

The village is a good place to stop for a few days. There are truly spectacular treks from one to four or five days in the 179,550-ha **Reserva Nacional Cerro Castillo** ① *entrance 64 km south of Coyhaique, US$4.65*. One goes around the fairytale castle peaks of Cerro Castillo, starting at Las Horquetas Grandes, a bend in the river Río Ibáñez, 8 km south of the park entrance, where any bus driver will let you off. It follows Río La Lima to the gorgeous Laguna Cerro Castillo, then animal trails around the peak itself, returning to the village (accommodation or bus back to Coyhaique). Another equally spectacular five-day trek goes around Lago Monreal. These are challenging walks: attempt only if fit and, ideally, take a guide, as trails are poorly marked (IGM map essential, purchase in advance in Coyhaique).The *guardería* is on the Senda Ibáñez, 50 m to the left of the main road (as you head south), opposite Laguna Chinguay to the right, with access to walks and a **campsite** ① *T67-221 2225, US$7.75*, no amenities or firewood in 2016; take all equipment. There are no *refugios* in the reserve. The picnic ground is open summer 0830-1930, winter to 1730. Ask in Villa Cerro Castillo for details.

A few kilometres south of the village is the **Monumento Nacional Alero Las Manos de Cerro Castillo** ① *open all year 1000-1700, US$1.50*. In a shallow cave, a few handprints have been made on the side of vertical rocks high above the Río Ibáñez. There's no clue to their significance, but they're in a beautiful place with panoramic views. This makes a delightful two-hour walk. The site is accessible all year, signposted clearly from the road. There is also a small local **museum** ① *Dec-Mar 0900-1200*, 2 km south of Villa Cerro Castillo.

Southwest of Villa Cerro Castillo, the Carretera continues to afford stunning views, for instance minty-green Lago Verde and the meandering Río Manso, with swampy vegetation punctuated by the silver stumps of thousands of burnt trees, huge mountains behind.

Western shore of Lago General Carrera

Bahía Murta (Km 198; population 586), 5 km off the Camino, lies at the northern tip of the central 'arm' of the lake. Petrol is available from a house with a sign just before Puerto Murta. There's a public phone in the village.

Back on the Carretera Austral, **Puerto Río Tranquilo**, Km 223, is a slightly larger hamlet where the buses stop for lunch: there is a petrol station for fuel. Capilla y Catedral del Marmol, in fact a limestone peninsula resembling sculpted caves, is reached by a wonderful boat ride; tour operators run group trips (two hours, US$12, best to go in the early morning when the lake is calmer).

El Maitén, Km 277 south of Coyhaique, an idyllic spot at the southwest tip of Lago General Carrera, is where a road branches off east along the south shore of the lake towards Chile Chico, while the Carretera Austral continues south becoming steeper and more winding (in winter this stretch, all the way to Cochrane, is icy and dangerous). At Km 294, is the hamlet of **Puerto Bertrand**, lying by the dazzling turquoise waters of Río Baker. This is a good place for fishing and the best base in the region for whitewater rafting and kayaking. Day hikes are possible along decent trails. There is no tourist office, but a tour operator can be reached on T9-8817 7525.

☆ Towards Chile Chico

At **Puerto Guadal**, 13 km east of El Maitén, there are shops, accommodation, restaurants, a post office, petrol and a lovely stretch of lakeside beach. Further east is the village of Mallín Grande (Km 40); **Paso de las Llaves**, a 30-km stretch carved out of the rock face on the edge of the lake, and **Fachinal** (turn off at Km 74). A further 5 km east is the **Garganta del Diablo**, a narrow gorge of 120 m with a fast-flowing stream below.

> **Tip...**
> It's best to change money in Coyhaique, but Martín Pescador, O'Higgins 497, changes money and the ATM in the middle of O'Higgins accepts Visa.

Chile Chico (population 4500) is a quiet town in a fruit-growing region, 125 km east of El Maitén. It has an annual fruit festival at the end of January and a small **Casa de la Cultura** ① *0800-1300, 1400-1700*. There are fine views from Cerro de las Banderas. It's 7 km from here to Los Antiguos, Argentina, where food and accommodation are preferable.

Laguna Jeinimeni ① *52 km south of Chile Chico, entry US$4.75, may be inaccessible Apr-Oct*, is a beautiful place with camping (US$15.50) and excellent fishing, where you can also see flamingos and black-necked swans. For more on this region and the projected new Patagonia National Park, see www.patagoniapark.org.

Border with Argentina: Chile Chico–Los Antiguos **Chilean immigration** is 2 km east of Chile Chico. Open December-May 0800-2200, April-November 0800-2000, www.pasosfronterizos.gov.cl/cf_chilechico.html. Argentine side is open 0900-2100. Remember that you can't take fresh food across in either direction, and you'll need ownership papers if crossing with a car. If entering Argentina here you will not have to fill in an immigration form (ask if you need entry papers).

Cochrane and around

From Puerto Bertand heading south, the road climbs up to high moorland, passing the confluence of the Ríos Neff and Baker (there is a mirador here), before winding into Cochrane, 343 km south of Coyhaique. The scenery is splendid all the way; the road is generally rough but not treacherous. Watch out for cattle on the road and take blind corners slowly. Sitting in a hollow on the Río Cochrane, Cochrane is a simple place, sunny in summer, good for walking and fishing. The **Reserva Nacional Lago Cochrane**, 12 km east, surrounds Lago Cochrane. There's a campsite at Playa Vidal. Boat tours on the lake cost US$28 for up to six people.

Reserva Nacional Tamango ① *Access 9 km northeast of Cochrane, along Río Cochrane Dec-Mar 0830-2100, Apr-Nov 0830-1830. US$7.75, plus guided visits to see the huemules, Tue, Thu, Sat, US$14 pp for up to 6 people. Camping US$5.50 per night. Ask in the CONAF office (Río Neff 417, T67-252 2164, claudio.manzur@conaf.cl) about visiting because some access is through private land and tourist facilities are rudimentary*. Northeast of Cochrane is this beautiful reserve, which has *lenga* forest, a few surviving *huemul* deer as well as guanaco, foxes and lots of birds including woodpeckers and hummingbirds. There are marked paths for walks between 45 minutes and five hours, up to Cerro Tamango (1722 m) and Cerro Temanguito (1485 m). Take water and food, and windproof clothing if climbing the Cerros. The views from the reserve are superb, over the town, the nearby lakes and to the Campo de Hielo Norte to the west. It is inaccessible in the four winter months.

Caleta Tortel

The Carretera Austral runs south of Cochrane and, after 105 km, at the rather bleak looking Puerto Vagabundo, the road branches west to Caleta Tortel (population 448). This quiet village at the mouth of the river was, until very recently, accessible only by water and has no streets, only 7 km of walkways of cypress wood. Surrounded by mountainous land with abundant vegetation, it has a cool, rainy climate, and its main trade is logging, though this is declining as the town looks towards tourism. Located between the Northern and Southern Ice Fields, Tortel is within reach of two glaciers: **Glaciar Steffens** is to the north, a 2½-hour boat journey and three-hour walk, crossing a glacial river in a rowing boat. A boat for 8-10 people costs between US$56 per person, includes snack and whisky with glacier ice. **Glaciar Jorge Montt** is a five-hour round trip by boat through landscapes of pure ice and water. Another boat trip is to the **Isla de los Muertos**, which has an interesting history, US$70 for 10 people.

Cochrane to Villa O'Higgins

The Carretera Austral runs to Puerto Yungay (122 km from Cochrane), then another 110 km to **Villa O'Higgins** on Lago O'Higgins. There is one free ferry (*Padre Antonio Ronchi*) crossing between Yungay (military base) and **Río Bravo** ① *www.barcazas.cl, 1000, 1200, 1700, return to Yungay 1 hr later; 45 mins, capacity 4-5 cars*. The road beyond Río Bravo is very beautiful, but often closed by bad weather (take food – no shops or fuel on the entire route, few people and few vehicles for hitching). In Villa O'Higgins there is a tiny **Museo de la Patagonia Padre Antonio Ronchi** ① *Mon-Fri 0900-1230, 1430-1700*, on the plaza, as well as a **tourist information kiosk** ① *Mon-Fri 0900-1230, 1430-1700; shorter hours in winter*, which can provide trekking guides.

Villa O'Higgins to El Chaltén (Argentina)

Route open November to April. Full details available from **Villa O'Higgins Expeditions** ① *T67-243 1821, www.villaohiggins.com*, who also own the **Robinson Crusoe Lodge** in town, can arrange boat trips, treks, expeditions and rents bicycles (US$4.50 for two hours, US$13.50 per day), www.robinsoncrusoe.com, or www.hielosur.com.

With the opening of this route, it is possible to travel the Carretera Austral and go on to Argentina's Parque Nacional Los Glaciares and Chile's Torres del Paine without doubling back on yourself.

From Villa O'Higgins the road heads 7 km south to Bahía Bahamóndez on Lago O'Higgins (bus US$4), from where a boat leaves for **Candelario Mancilla** ① *2¾ hrs, US$65; departures vary each year, but usually 2 a week in Nov, 3 a week in Dec, 4 a week in Jan, Feb, 3 in total in Mar, check exact dates in advance*. Sailings may be cancelled if the weather is bad. Camping and beds are available in Candelario Mancilla at the home of Tito and Ricardo, two brothers who offer 4WD and horses to the Argentine border. Their mother cooks meals. Chilean immigration is 1 km from Candelario Mancillo, open November to April 24 hours daily. Then it's 14 km to the Argentine border on foot, on horseback, or by 4WD service (US$35 for two to four passengers and luggage, or US$15.50 luggage only). The next 5 km is a demanding hike to Argentine immigration at Punta Norte on **Lago del Desierto**, or you can take a horse for US$47 for the whole 19 km, with an extra horse to carry bags (Ricardo is great horseman with an excellent sense of humour). The route descends sharply towards Lago de Desierto, and bridges are sometimes washed away; make sure to wear good boots for crossing wet land. Panoramas on the descent are breathtaking, including of Cerro Fitz Roy. A short detour to Laguna Larga (on the right as you walk from the border) is worth it if you have the energy. The boat crossing of Lago de Desierto passes glaciers and ice fields (daily 1000, 1700, 40 minutes, US$43), on your right. Several companies, including **Transporte Las Lengas** and **JR Turismo**, await the boat for the final hour by bus or minivan on a gravel road to El Chaltén (37 km; US$33). There is no food available on the Argentine side of the lake, but Argentine immigration officers at Punta Norte are friendly and, if you are cold, may offer you coffee, food and shelter. Note that there are no banking or exchange facilities between Cochrane and El Chaltén.

> **Tip...**
> The best combination is to take 4WD from Candelario Mancilla to the border and then continue on horseback. This ensures that the trip can be done in a day, departing Villa O'Higgins 0800, arriving El Chaltén 2115. Allow for delays, though, especially if horses aren't available for hire. It's a good option to pay for each portion of the route separately.

Tourist information

Chile Chico
Tourist office (O'Higgins s/n, T67-241 1303, infochilechico@sernatur.cl; it's fairly helpful but usually closed). An unofficial **purple tourist kiosk**, on the quay where the ferry arrives, sells bus tickets for Ruta 40 (Argentina) and has some accommodation information. See also www.chilechico.cl.

Cochrane
Tourist kiosk (on corner of plaza on Dr Steffen, T67-252 2115, www.cochranepatagonia.cl, summer only Tue-Sun 0900-1400, 1500-1800). The ATM in town is for MasterCard and Visa; this is the last banking service on the Carretera Austral.

Caleta Tortel
At the entrance to the village is a small tourist information office with details of lodgings and a useful map, open 0900-2300 in high season, closed in low season. Medical centre near the tourist information office offers emergency care. For **CONAF**, call T67-294 1980.

Where to stay

Puerto Ibáñez

$$ Cabañas Shehen Aike
Luis Risopatrón 55, T67-242 3284.
Swiss/Chilean-owned, large cabins, lots of ideas for trips, bike rental, organizes tours, fine food, welcoming, English spoken, best to phone in advance.

$ pp Hospedaje Don Francisco
San Salvador y Lautaro, T9-8503 3626.
Very hospitable, lunch or dinner extra, good food round the clock, camping US$7, tents and free bike hire.

$ Vientos del Sur
Bertrán Dixon 282, T9-8972 6519.
Good, nice family, dorms, cheap meals (restaurant open till late); also arranges adventure activities.

Villa Cerro Castillo

$ Residencial Villarrica
O'Higgins 592, next to Supermercado Villarrica, T9-6656 0173, hospedajevillarrica@gmail.com.

Welcoming, basic, hot showers, and restaurant, kind owners can arrange trekking guides and horse riding. There are other *residenciales* in town.

Western shore

$$$$ Hacienda Tres Lagos
Carretera Austral Km 274, just west of cruce Maitén, T2-2333 4122 (Santiago), www.haciendatreslagos.com.
Small, boutique resort on the lakeshore with bungalows, suites and cabins; good restaurant. Temporarily closed in 2017, but also has **$$$ Parador Austral**, at Km 273, T67-257 3417, same website. English spoken.

$$$$ Mallín Colorado Ecolodge
Carretera Austral Km 273, 2 km west of El Maitén, T9-7137 6242, www.mallincolorado.cl. Oct-Apr.
Comfortable *cabañas* in sweeping gardens, complete tranquility, charming owners, packages available, including transfers from Balmaceda, horseriding, estancia trip, superb meals.

$$$ Hostal El Puesto
Pedro Lagos 258, Puerto Río Tranquilo, T9-6207 3794, www.elpuesto.cl.
No doubt the most comfortable place in Río Tranquilo, with breakfast, also organizes tours.

$$$ Hostal Los Pinos
Godoy 51, Puerto Río Tranquilo, T67-241 1572, lospinos_hosteriasuite@outlook.com.
Family-run, well maintained, and café with good mid-price meals.

$$ Campo Alacaluf
Km 44 on the Río Tranquilo-Bahía Exploradores side road, T67-241 9500, campoalacaluf@yahoo.de.
Wonderful guesthouse hidden away from civilization. Run by very friendly German family.

$$ Hostal Carretera Austral
Carretera Austral 373, Río Tranquilo, T67-241 9500.
Also serves meals (**$$-$**).

$$ Hostería Puerto Bertrand
Puerto Bertrand, T9-9219 1532, www.casaturismorural.cl (this website includes other places to stay, eat and find services).
With breakfast, other meals available, also *cabañas*, activities.

$ Hospedaje/Camping Bellavista
Población Esperanza s/n, T9-7619 5125,
transportebellavista@hotmail.com.
Budget option with camping for US$14 per night.

Towards Chile Chico

$$$$-$$ Terra Luna Lodge
On lakeside, 2 km from Puerto Guadal,
T9-8449 1092, http://terraluna.cl.
Welcoming well-run place with lodge,
bungalows and camping huts, also has
restaurant, sauna, cinema, private disco,
climbing wall, many activities offered.

$$$ El Mirador Playa Guadal
2 km from Puerto Guadal towards Chile Chico,
T9-9234 9130, www.elmiradordeguadal.com.
Cabañas near beach, excursions and activities
with or without guide, walks to nearby
waterfalls, restaurant.

$$$-$$ Eco Hostal Un Destino No Turístico
Camino Laguna La Manga, off road to Chile Chico
1.5 km from Puerto Guadal, T9-8756 7545,
www.destino-noturistico.com. Closed Apr-Sep.
2 rooms, 1 private room, 1 shared dorm
(US$38 pp), dedicated to eco initiatives and slow
travel, with workshops, tours and information;
no TV or internet. Website gives all transport
details; will pick guests up at Cruce El Maitén on
Carretera Austral for US$7.7 5 with prior notice
(free if staying 3 nights or more).

$$ Hospedaje Brisas del Lago
Manuel Rodríguez 443, Chile Chico,
T9-8462 6289, brisasdellago@gmail.com.
Simple rooms with shared bath and *cabañas*,
with Wi-Fi and breakfast, good value.

$$ Hostal La Victoria
O'Higgins 210 (corner of the plaza), Chile Chico,
T67-241 1344, lavictoria@outlook.com.
Pricey *hostal* with private rooms, which are
spotless with TVs, breakfast included, good
kitchen and communal area with plush sofa.
Helpful owner has maps galore.

$$ La Perla del Lago
Los Notros s/n, Puerto Guadal, T9-5722 1356,
tarcila-fica2007@hotmail.com.
Delightful, English-speaking owner has comfy
beds in well-furnished doubles and triples (also
a *cabaña* $$$). Has information about tours,
laundry service, breakfast included and great
home-cooked meals.

$ El Gringo
Los Lidios 510, on the corner of the plaza,
Puerto Guadal, T9-7394 0396. Open all year.
Very helpful owner, 2 private rooms, good value
(breakfast extra). No Wi-Fi. Also restaurant
serving good pizzas and great juices.

$ Hospedaje Jerafita
Carerra 150, Chile Chico, T9-762 76497,
hospedaje.jerafita@gmail.com.
No-frills lodging with unkempt rooms with very
thin walls, but it is one of the cheapest options
in town.

$ Hospedaje Ventisqueros
35 km from Guadal on the road to Coyhaique,
T9-7805 4165, elidadaguirre@hotmail.com.
Quaint *hospedaje* on the Río León. Organizes
tours, horse riding and has a *parrilla*. Breakfast
included and the owner prepares homemade
lunches and dinners. Also camping for US$4.25.

Camping
Free site at Bahía Jara, 5 km west of Chile Chico,
then turn north for 12 km.

Camping Cerro Color
3 km from Guadal on the road to Cochrane
T9-5663 1830.
Owner Filomena offers campsites from
US$7 per night. Also sells marmalade and
vegetables in summer.

Camping El Parque
Km 1 on road to Chile Chico.

Cochrane
In summer it is best to book rooms in advance.

$$$ Wellmann
Las Golondrinas 565, T67-252 2171,
hotelwellmann@gmail.com.
Comfortable, warm, hot water, good meals.

$$$-$$ Cabañas Rogeri
Río Maitén 80, T9-8827 1342, rogeri3@hotmail.com.
Cabañas with kitchen for 4.

$$ Residencial Sur Austral
Prat 334, T67-252 2150.
Private or shared bath, hot water and *cabañas*
$$$, very posh.

$ Hospedadje La Catita
Prat 536, T67-252 2201,
gonzalezvasquezanamaria@gmail.com.
Run by a welcoming couple, with breakfast
and Wi-Fi, best budget option.

Caleta Tortel

All prices are cheaper in the low season.

$$$ Entre Hielos Lodge
Sector centro, Tortel, T9-9599 5730,
www.entrehielostortel.cl.
Upmarket place in town, excursions, boat trips.

$$ Estilo
Sector Centro, Tortel, T9-8255 8487.
Warm and comfortable, good food.
Entertaining, talkative host (Spanish).

$$-$ Hospedaje Don Adán
Sector Rincón, T9-8135 6931.
Cosy, warm, well-kept, run by Norma, rooms
with and without bath, breakfast optional,
amazing view of the bay, Wi-Fi, a good choice.
Recommended. Also runs **Comedor Venus** at
the entrance to town.

Camping

There is camping at sector Junquillo at the far
end of town.

Villa O'Higgins

$$$$-$$$ Robinson Crusoe
Carretera Austral Km 1240, T67-243 1909,
www.robinsoncrusoe.com.
Newer hotel that stands out as the nicest
lodging in town. Wi-Fi; breakfast included.
Has an expedition kiosk next door that arranges
trips to nearby glaciers and El Chaltén.

$$-$ El Mosco
At the northern entrance to the town, T67-243
1819, patagoniaelmosco@yahoo.es.
Rooms, dorms, camping (US$7.50) and *cabañas*
($$$). Spanish-run hostel, with breakfast. English
spoken, trekking maps and information. Nothing
else competes in terms of infrastructure.

$$-$ Hostería Patagonia
Río Pagua 195, in front of plaza.
Family-run, rooms with and without bath,
breakfast included, serves lunch and dinner.
A good choice for small groups.

Camping

Los Ñires
Adjacent to Robinson Crusoe office.
Camping US$6, shared *cabaña* US$10.50.

Chile Chico

Café Elizabeth y Loly
PA González 25, on Plaza.
Good for coffee, as well as delicious cakes.
Offers Middle Eastern food on Wed.

Restaurant Turístico J&D
O'Higgins 455.
Decent food including lake-caught trout. Same
owner as **Hotel Austral** (O'Higgins 501, T67-241
1815, $$) and the supermarket next door.

Cochrane

Ada's
Merino 374, T9-8399 5889,
adascaferestaurant@gmail.com.
Fancy family-run restaurant with an extensive menu
featuring grilled meats and many other items.

Caleta Tortel

Bella Vista
Costanera s/n, Sector Rincón, T9-6211 7430.
Good for salmon, lamb and beef.

Villa O'Higgins

$$ Entre Patagones
At the northern entrance to the town,
T9-9498 0460, www.entrepatagones.cl.
The only restaurant in town with any sort of style.
Great fish and meat dishes; a fine choice after
a long journey to the end of the road. Owner
Alfonso Díaz can arrange fishing trips.

What to do

Lago General Carrera and south

Patagonia Adventure Expeditions, *T9-8182*
0608, www.adventurepatagonia.com. Professional
outfit running exclusive fully supported treks to
the Campo de Hielo Norte and the eastern side
of Parque Nacional Laguna San Rafael. Expensive
but a unique experience. Also rafting on the Río
Baker and general help organizing tours, treks
and expeditions.

Transport

Puerto Ibáñez

Bus Minibus to **Coyhaique**, 1½ hrs, US$8.50. There is a road to **Perito Moreno**, Argentina, but no public transport.

Ferry The *Tehuelche* sails between Puerto Ibáñez and **Chile Chico** daily. It takes passengers and vehicles, fares US$3.40 per adult, US$2.35 for bicycles, US$6 for motorbikes, cars US$29.65, beautiful 2-hr crossing. It's a new vessel with indoor seating, café and heating. Passports required, reservations essential: in Coyhaique, Baquedano 1198, T67-223 7958; in Puerto Ibáñez, Gral Carrera 202, T67-252 6992, in Chile Chico T67-241 1003, online at http://sotramin.cl. At the quay, Café El Refugio has toilets and sells sandwiches and snacks. Minibuses meet the ferry in Puerto Ibáñez for Coyhaique.

Villa Cerro Castillo

Bus 6 a week in summer to both **Coyhaique**, US$8, and **Cochrane**, companies as above, under Coyhaique. To **Río Tranquilo**, US$8.

Chile Chico

Bus Minibuses on Mon, Wed, Fri at 0800 to **Cochrane**, US$20, 5 hrs. See above for ferry to Puerto Ibáñez and connecting minibus to Coyhaique. In summer, frequent minibuses from Chile Chico to Los Antiguos on the Argentine side, US$8 (in Chilean pesos), ½-1 hr including formalities: purchase at Martín Pescador,

B O'Higgins 497, T67-241 1033, daily 0800-2200. Ferry and minibus tickets from Martín Pescador and Miguel Acuña, Sector Muelle, T9-8900 4590. To/from **Coyhaique**, via **Puerto Guadal**, ECA (T67-243 1224 or T67-252 8577) on Tue and Fri.

Cochrane

Bus Company agencies: **Don Carlos**, Prat 334, T67-252 2150; **Buses Aldea**, Las Golondrinas 399, T67-252 2448; **Aguilas Patagónicas**, Río Maitén y Dr Steffens, T67-252 3730, www.aguilaspatagonicas.cl; **Acuario 13**, Río Baker 349, T67-252 2143. There are buses every day between Coyhaique and Cochrane, check with companies for current timetables, US$23. To **Río Tranquilo**, US$12. To **Villa O'Higgins**, Katalina (T67-252 2333), Wed, Sat 0800, return Mon, Fri 1000, 6-7 hrs, US$23. To **Tortel**, Buses Aldea, Tue, Thu, Fri, Sun, 0930, return 1500, US$12. Minibuses on Mon, Wed, Fri to **Chile Chico**, US$20. Petrol is available at the **Esso** and **Copec** servicentros.

Caleta Tortel

Bus From **Cochrane**, see above. From Tortel to **Villa O'Higgins**, Tue, Fri, Sun at 1530, 4 hrs, US$23, T9-8180 1962. To return, the owner of Hostería Patagonia in Villa O'Higgins has a bus service Mon, Fri 0800, T9-7376 5288.

Villa O'Higgins

Air Aerocord, T67-224 6300, www.aerocord.cl, air taxi flies to Villa O'Higgins from **Coyhaique**, twice a week, weather permitting. Priority is given to locals.

Southern Patagonia

This wild and wind-blown area, covering the glacial regions of southern Patagonia and Chilean Tierra del Fuego, is beautiful and bleak, with stark mountains and open steppe. Little vegetation survives here and few people; though it represents 17.5% of Chile's total area, it is inhabited by under 1% of the population. The southernmost city of Punta Arenas and the attractive port of Puerto Natales are the two main centres, the latter being the gateway to the Torres del Paine and Bernardo O'Higgins national parks. In summer it is a wonderful region for climbing, hiking, boat trips and the southernmost crossings to Argentina.

Summers are sunny and very variable, with highs of 15°C. In winter snow covers the country, except those parts near the sea, making many roads more or less impassable, except on horseback. Cold, piercing winds blow year-round, but are particularly fierce in late spring, when they may exceed 100 kph. Despite chilly temperatures, protection against the sun's ultraviolet rays is essential here all year round and windproof clothing is a must.

Punta Arenas and around *Colour map 9, C2.*

this attractive city serves as the hub for southern adventures

About 2140 km south of Santiago, Punta Arenas (population 160,000) lies on the eastern shore of the Brunswick Peninsula facing the Straits of Magellan at almost equal distance from the Pacific and Atlantic oceans. Founded in 1843, it has grand neoclassical buildings and an opulent cemetery, testimony to its wealthy past as a major port and centre for exporting wool. In the late 19th century, Salesian Missions were established to control the indigenous population so sheep farming could flourish. The city's fortunes slumped when the Panama Canal opened in 1914, but it remains a pleasant place, with attractive, painted wooden buildings away from the centre and good fish and seafood restaurants. Paved roads connect the city with Puerto Natales, 247 km north, and with Río Gallegos in Argentina.

Sights

In the centre of the **Plaza Muñoz Gamero** is a striking statue of Magellan with a mermaid and two indigenous Fuegians at his feet. Around the plaza are a number of impressive neoclassical buildings, the former mansions of the great sheep ranching families of the late 19th century. **Palacio Sara Braun** ① *Mon 1000-1300, Tue-Sat, 1000-1300, 1600-1930, closed Sun, US$1.50,* (built between 1894 and 1905), part of which now houses the Hotel José Nogueira, has several elegant rooms which are open to the public. The fascinating **Museo Regional de Magallanes** ① *Palacio Braun Menéndez, Magallanes 949, T61-224 2049, www.museodemagallanes.cl, Wed-Mon 1030-1700 (May-Sep closes 1400), free, guided tours in Spanish, information sheet in poor English*, was once the mansion of Mauricio Braun, built in 1905. It has fabulously decorated rooms, with ornate furniture, paintings and marble and crystal imported from Europe. Further north, is the impressive **cemetery (Cementerio Municipal Sara Braun)** ① *Av Bulnes 29, daily, 0730-2000 in summer, 0800-1800 in winter, US$5*, charting a history of European immigration and shipping disasters through the huge mausoleums, divided by avenues of imposing sculpted cypress trees.

Best for

Boat trips ▪ Glaciers ▪ Hiking ▪ Isolation

☆The perfect complement to this is **Museo Regional Salesiano Maggiorino Borgatell** ① *in the Colegio Salesiano, Av Bulnes 336 (the entrance is next to church), T61-222 1001, see Facebook Tue-Sun 1000-1230, 1500-1730, US$3.75.* It covers the fascinating history of the indigenous people and their education by the Salesian missions, beside an array of stuffed birds and gas extraction machinery. The Italian priest, Alberto D'Agostini, who arrived in 1909 and presided over the mission, took wonderful photographs of the region and his 70-minute film can be seen on video (ask).

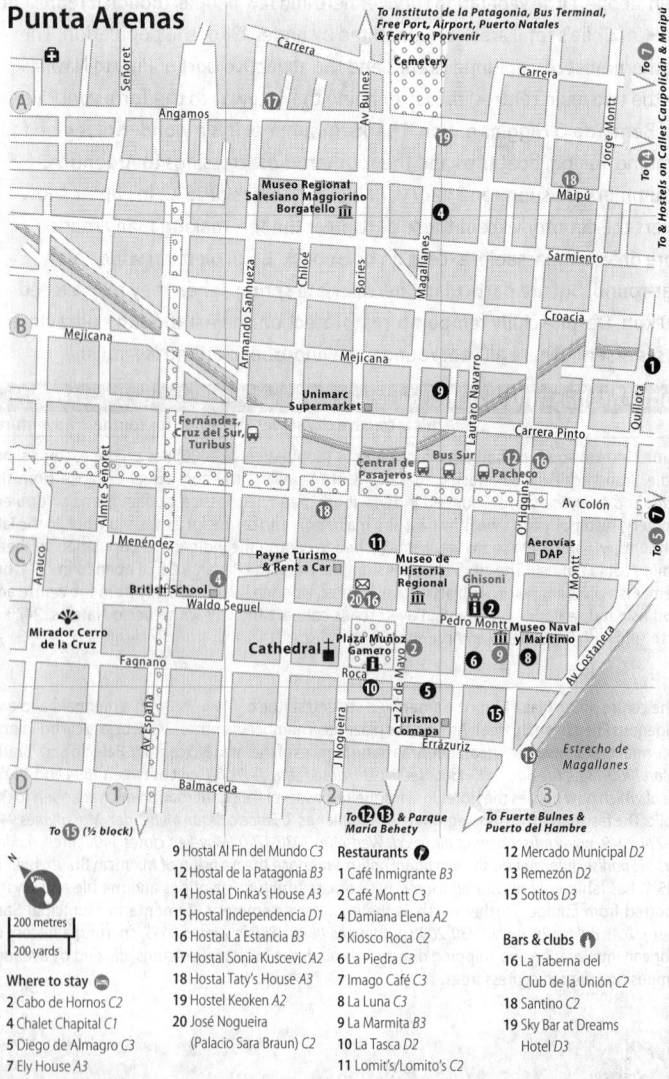

Punta Arenas

To Instituto de la Patagonia, Bus Terminal, Free Port, Airport, Puerto Natales & Ferry to Porvenir

To Hostels on Calles Caupolicán & Maipú

Museo Regional Salesiano Maggiorino Borgatello

Unimarc Supermarket

Fernández, Cruz del Sur, Turibus

Central de Pasajeros

Payne Turismo & Rent a Car

Museo de Historia Regional

Aerovías DAP

Ghisoni

British School

Mirador Cerro de la Cruz

Cathedral

Plaza Muñoz Gamero

Museo Naval y Marítimo

Turismo Comapa

Estrecho de Magallanes

To Fuerte Bulnes & Puerto del Hambre

To ⑮ & Parque Maria Behety

To ⑮ (½ block)

200 metres
200 yards

Where to stay
2 Cabo de Hornos *C2*
4 Chalet Chapital *C1*
5 Diego de Almagro *C3*
7 Ely House *A3*
9 Hostal Al Fin del Mundo *C3*
12 Hostal de la Patagonia *B3*
14 Hostal Dinka's House *A3*
15 Hostal Independencia *D1*
16 Hostal La Estancia *B3*
17 Hostal Sonia Kuscevic *A2*
18 Hostal Taty's House *A3*
19 Hostel Keoken *A2*
20 José Nogueira (Palacio Sara Braun) *C2*

Restaurants 🍴
1 Café Inmigrante *B3*
2 Café Montt *C3*
3 Damiana Elena *A2*
4 Kiosco Roca *C2*
5 La Piedra *C3*
6 Imago Café *C3*
7 La Luna *C3*
8 La Marmita *B3*
9 La Tasca *D2*
10 Lomit's/Lomito's *C2*
11
12 Mercado Municipal *D2*
13 Remezón *D2*
15 Sotitos *D3*

Bars & clubs 🍸
16 La Taberna del Club de la Unión *C2*
18 Santino *C2*
19 Sky Bar at Dreams Hotel *D3*

Museo del Recuerdo/Museum of Memory at the Instituto de la Patagonia ① *Av Bulnes 01890, Km 4 northeast (opposite the University), T61-220 7051, outdoor exhibits Mon-Sat 0830-1700, US$2.75*, has an open-air museum with 3000 artefacts used by the early settlers, pioneer homes, research library and botanical gardens. Museo Naval y Marítimo ① *Pedro Montt 981, T61-224 5987, www. museonaval.cl, Tue-Sat, 0930-1230, 1400-1700, US$1.50*, has shipping instruments, maps, photos and relics from the Chilean navy and famous navigators. West of the Plaza Muñoz Gamero on Calle Fagnano is the Mirador Cerro de La Cruz offering a view over the city and the Magellan Straits. The Parque María Behety, south of town along 21 de Mayo, features a scale model of Fuerte Bulnes, popular for Sunday picnics; ice rink here in winter.

The city's waterfront has been given an extensive face-lift, with public boardwalks and outdoor spaces under special shelters giving protection from the sun's strong ultraviolet rays.

Around Punta Arenas

West of town (9 km) is the Reserva Nacional Magallanes ① *US$6.25, taxi US$5.50*, with nature trails, from 45 minutes to two days, and picnic areas. A recommended walk is a four-hour circuit up to a lookout with beautiful views over town and the surroundings and back down along the Río Minas to Punta Arenas. Nearby is the Club Andino (see under Skiing, page 844).

Some 56 km south, Fuerte Bulnes (US$17, children US$8.50), is a replica of the wooden fort erected in 1843 by the crew of the Chilean vessel *Ancud* to secure Chile's southernmost territories after Independence. An interesting story, but there's not that much to see. Nearby is Puerto de Hambre, a beautiful, panoramic spot where there are ruins of the church built in 1584 by Sarmiento de Gamboa's colonists. Tours are run by several agencies.

North of Punta Arenas

Isla Magdalena, US$11, US$5.50 children, a small island 35 km northeast, is the location of the Monumento Natural Los Pingüinos, a spectacular colony of 80,000 pairs of Magellanic penguins, who come here to breed between November and January (also skuas, kelp gulls and other marine wildlife). A small lighthouse on the island gives the best views of the surroundings and the half-hour walk up there gets you close to the all the penguin action. Tread carefully and don't get too close to the nests: protective parent penguins sometimes get a bit fierce. Magdalena is one of a group of three islands (the others are Marta and Isabel), visited by Drake, whose men killed 3000 penguins for food. Boat trips to the island are run by Comapa and Solo Expediciones, while the Australis cruise ships also call here (see What to do, page 844).

☆Less spectacular but more easily accessible (70 km north of Punta Arenas by road), Otway Sound ① *Oct to mid-Mar, US$10.50*, has a colony of thousands of Magellanic penguins, viewed from walkways and bird hides, best seen in the morning. Rheas can also be seen. It is becoming a popular area for sea-kayaking and other adventure sports.

Some 210 km to the northeast on Ruta 255, towards Argentina, is Parque Nacional Pali Aike ① *US$4.65, childrenUS$2.35*, near Punta Delgada, one of the oldest archaeological sites in Patagonia (Pali Aike means 'desolate place of bad spirits' in Tehuelche). There's evidence of aborigines from 10,000 to 12,000 years ago, in an extraordinary volcanic landscape pockmarked with countless tiny craters, rocks of different colours and several caves. Tour operators offer full day trips, US$47; for more details, ask at CONAF, who manage the park.

Listings Punta Arenas and around *map p840*

Tourist information

CONAF
Av Bulnes 0309, p 4, T61-223 8554, magallanes.oirs@conaf.cl.

Municipal tourist information kiosk
In the Plaza de Armas, opposite Centro Español, T61-220 0610, www.puntaarenas.cl. High season Mon-Fri 0800-1900, Sat-Sun 0900-1700, low season Mon-Fri 0800-1700.
Experienced staff, good town map with all hotels marked, English spoken, can book hotels.

Sernatur

Lautaro Navarro 999 y Pedro Montt, T61-222 5385, infomagallanes@sernatur.cl. High season Mon-Fri 0830-2000, Sat-Sun 1000-1800; low season Mon-Fri 0830-1800, Sat-Sun 1000-1600. See also www.patagonia-chile.com.

Where to stay

Hotel prices are lower during winter months (Apr-Sep). A few streets, in particular Caupolicán and Maipú, some 10-15 mins' walk from the centre have become a "hotbed of hostels", most of them with similar facilities and similar prices (**$$**). These include **Ely House**, **Maipú Street** and **Hostal Dinka's House**, the latter painted bright-red and run by the indomitable Dinka herself. The area is also full of car repair places, which can make it noisy day-time and occasionally at night. For accommodation in private houses, usually **$** pp, ask at the tourist office. No campsites in or near the city, except at certain hostels.

$$$$-$$$ Cabo de Hornos
Plaza Muñoz Gamero 1039, T61-271 5000, www.hoteles-australis.com.
4-star, comfy, bright and spacious rooms, with good views from 4th floor up.

$$$$-$$$ Diego de Almagro
Av Colón 1290, T61-220 8800, www.dahotelespuntaarenas.com.
Very modern, good international standard, on waterfront, many rooms with view, heated pool, sauna, small gym, big bright rooms, good value.

$$$$-$$$ José Nogueira
Plaza de Armas, Bories 967 y P Montt, in former Palacio Sara Braun, T61-271 1000, www.hotelnogueira.com.
Best in town, stylish rooms, warm atmosphere, excellent service. Smart restaurant in the beautiful loggia. A few original rooms now a 'small museum'.

$$$ Chalet Chapital
Sanhueza 974, T61-273 0100, www.hotelchaletchapital.cl.
Small well-run hotel, smallish rooms, helpful staff, a good choice in this price range.

$$$ Hostal de la Patagonia
O'Higgins 730, T61-224 9970, www.ecotourpatagonia.com.
Rooms with heating, good services, dining room, 10 mins' walk from centre. Organizes a variety of tours, including fly fishing.

$$$-$$ Hostel Keoken
Magallanes 209, T61-224 4086/6376, www.hostelkeoken.cl.
Light, wooden, spacious building on 3 floors each with its own entrance up rickety outside staircases. Some rooms with small bath. Good value, some info. Top floor rooms with shared bathroom have paper thin walls. Recently expanded into an even bigger, rambling place.

$$ Hostal La Estancia
O'Higgins 765, T61-224 9130, www.hosteltrail.com/hostels/hostallaestancia.
Simple but comfortable rooms, some with bath. **$** pp in dorms. English spoken, small shop attached, music and games room.

$$ Hostal Sonia Kuscevic
Pasaje Darwin 175, T61-224 8543, www.hostalsk.cl.
One of the city's oldest guesthouses, with heating and parking. Better value for longer stays, good discount if you have a Hostelling International card. (Hostel may be for sale.)

$$ Hostal Taty's House
Maipu 1070, T61-224 1525, www.hostaltatyshouse.cl.
Nice rooms with good beds, decent choice in this price bracket, basic English spoken.

$$-$ Hostal Al Fin del Mundo
O'Higgins 1026, T61-271 0185, www.alfindelmundo.hostel.com.
Rooms and dorms, bright, cosy, shared baths, central, helpful, pool table, English spoken.

$ Hostal Independencia
Independencia 374, T61-222 7572, www.hostalindependencia.es.tl.
Private rooms, dorms (3 or 4 beds) and camping with use of kitchen and bathroom. Trekking equipment rental, parking, fishing and other tours, lots of information; very knowledgeable owners. Discount without breakfast. Recommended.

Restaurants

Many eating places close on Sun.

$$$ Remezón
21 de Mayo 1469, T61-224 1029, see Facebook.
Regional specialities such as krill. Very good, but should be, given the prices.

$$$-$$ Damiana Elena
Magallanes 341, T61-222 2818, see Facebook. Mon-Sat from 2000-2400.

Stylish restaurant serving Mediterranean food with a Patagonian touch, popular with locals, book ahead at weekends.

$$$-$$ La Tasca
Plaza Muñoz Gamero 771.
Large helpings, limited selection, decent set lunch, views over the plaza.

$$$-$$ Sotitos
O'Higgins 1138, T61-224 3565, see Facebook.
Daily lunch and dinner (Sun 1200-1500 only).
An institution, famous for seafood in elegant surroundings, excellent. Book ahead in season. 2nd floor serving local specialities and Italian food.

$$ La Luna
O'Higgins 1017, T61-222 8555, www.laluna.cl.
Fish, shellfish and local specialities, huge *pisco* sours, popular, reasonable. Quirky decor, friendly staff. Recommended.

$$ La Marmita
Plaza Sampaio 678, T61-222 2056, www.
marmitamaga.cl. Mon-Thu 1230-1500,
1900-2300, Fri-Sat 1230-1530, 1900-2400.
Regional dishes with international twist, vegetarian options, good sized portions, prettily presented, chatty owner, generally very good.

$$-$ La Piedra
Lautaro Navarro 1087, T9-665 1439.
Mon-Sat 1200-2300.
Meat dishes, fish, soups, salads, good burgers and sandwiches, daily lunch specials, housed over 2 floors.

$ Kiosco Roca
Roca 875. Mon-Fri 0700-1900, Sat 0800-1300.
Unassuming sandwich bar, voted best in Punta Arenas. Takeaway or a few seats available at the counter. Always packed, also serves breakfast and brunch.

$ Lomit's/Lomito's
Menéndez 722.
A fast-food institution with bar attached, cheap snacks and drinks (local beers are good), open when the others are closed, good food.

$ Mercado Municipal
21 de Mayo 1465. Daily 1000-2000.
Wide range of *cocinerías* offering cheap *empanadas* and seafood on the upper floor of the municipal market.

Cafés

Café Inmigrante
Quillota 599 (esq Mejicana), T61-222 2205, www.
inmigrante.cl. Daily afternoons and evenings.
Hugely popular cafe run by 3rd generation Croatian expats. Beautifully prepared sandwiches, daily changing cake menu, huge portions, family history on menus. Quirky and popular. Book in advance if possible. Highly recommended.

Café Montt
Pedro Montt 976, T61-222 0381, www.cafemontt.cl.
Coffees, teas, cakes, pastries and snacks, Wi-Fi. Cosy, friendly. Recommended.

Imago Café
Costanera y Colón.
Tiny, laid-back café hidden away in a beachfront bunker overlooking the straits. Live music occasionally.

Bars and clubs

La Taberna del Club de la Unión
In the Sara Braun mansion.
Atmospheric bar, good for evening drinks.

Santino
Colón 657, T61-271 0882, www.santino.cl.
Open 1800-0300.
Also serves pizzas and other snacks, large bar, good service, live music Sat.

Sky Bar
O'Higgins 1235.
Bar with panoramic views on the top floor of the luxury **Dreams** hotel and spa.

Shopping

Punta Arenas has certain free-port facilities; Zona Franca, 4 km north of the centre, opposite Museo del Recuerdo, Instituto de la Patagonia, is cheaper than elsewhere. The complex now has over 100 shops and is open daily 1000-2100 (www.zonaustral.cl), take bus 8 or take *colectivo* 15 or 20; taxi US$5.

Handicrafts

Chile Típico
Cra Pinto 1015, T61-222 5827. Mon-Sat 0900-2130, Sun 1000-2000.
Beautiful knitwear and woollen ponchos.

Mercado Municipal
See Restaurants, above.
Excellent handicrafts and souvenirs on the lower floors.

What to do

Skiing
Cerro Mirador, *only 8 km west of Punta Arenas in the Reserva Nacional Magallanes*. One of the few places in the world where you can ski with a sea view. Taxi US$7. Equipment rental available. Midway lodge with food, drink and equipment. Season Jun-Sep, weather and snow permitting. In summer there is a good 2-hr walk on the hill, with labelled flora. Contact **Club Andino** (T61-224 1479, www.clubandino.cl).

Tour operators
Most tour operators organize trips to Torres del Paine, Fuerte Bulnes, the *pingüineras* on Isla Magdalena and Otway Sound and Tierra del Fuego; shop around.
Adventure Network International, *T+1-801 266 4876, www.adventure-network.com*. Antarctic experiences of a lifetime, operating out of Punta Arenas, flying to the interior of the Antarctic Continent. Flights to the South Pole, guided mountain climbing and fully guided skiing expeditions. Camping with emperor penguins in Nov.
Arka Patagonia, *Manuel Señoret 1597, T61-224 8167, www.arkapatagonia.com*. All types of tours, whale-watching, trekking, Cabo de Hornos, etc.
Australis Expedition Cruises, *at Comapa, address below, check-in O'Higgins 1385 at the port, (in Santiago: Av El Bosque Norte 0440, of 1103, T2-2840 0100)*. Runs expedition cruises on the *Stella Australis*, with a new, similar sized vessel, *Ventus Australis*, to be added in 2017-18, between Punta Arenas and Ushuaia, through the Magellan Straits and the 'avenue of glaciers', with stops at Cape Horn and Isla Navarino, glaciers and Isla Magdalena (the itinerary varies according to route). There

are plenty of opportunities to disembark and see wildlife. Round trips 3-7 nights, one-ways 3-4 nights, service from Sep-Apr, check website for promotions. Very safe and comfortable, first-class service, fine dining, daily lectures, an unforgettable experience. Advance booking is essential. Highly recommended.
Go Patagonia, *Lautaro Navarro 1013, T61-237 1074, www.gopatagoniachile.com*. Full range of local tours, also Torres del Paine and Cordillera Darwin on Tierra del Fuego, car rental, transport and transfers.
Solo Expediciones, *Nogueira 1255, T61-271 0219, www.soloexpediciones.cl*. Operate their own service to **Monumento Natural Los Pingüinos** on a faster, smaller boat, also passing by Isla Marta, half-day tour, mornings only.
Turismo Aventour, *Soto 2876, T9-7827 9479, www.aventourpatagonia.cl*. Specialize in fishing trips, organize tours to Tierra del Fuego, helpful, English spoken.
Turismo Comapa, *Lautaro Navarro 1112, T61-220 0200, www.comapa.com*. Tours to Torres del Paine (responsible, well-informed guides), Tierra del Fuego and to see penguins at Isla Magdalena. Agents for **Australis Expedition Cruises** (see above).
Turismo Laguna Azul, *21 de Mayo 1011, T61-222 5200, www.turismolagunaazul.com*. Full-day trips to a colony of King Penguins on Tierra del Fuego. Trips run all year round. Also city tours, trips to glaciers and others.
Turismo Yamana, *T61-222 2061, www.yamana.cl (no storefront)*. Conventional and deluxe tours, trekking in Torres del Paine, kayaking the fjords of Parque Nacional Alberto de Agostini (Tierra del Fuego), multilingual guides.
Whale Sound, *Lautaro Navarro 1191, T9-9887 9814, www.whalesound.com*. Whale-watching trips in the Magellan Straits.

Transport

Most transport is heavily booked from Christmas to Mar: advance booking strongly advised.

Air **Carlos Ibáñez del Campo Airport**, 20 km north of town. Minibus service by **Transfer Austral**, Colón y Magallanes, T61-224 5811, www.transferaustral.com, US$4. Taxi US$11 to city. Note that in most taxis much of the luggage space is taken up by natural gas fuel tanks. To **Santiago**, **LATAM** and **Sky** direct, many daily. To **Porvenir**, **Aerovías DAP** (O'Higgins 891, T61-261 6100, www.aeroviasdap.cl) 3 times daily Mon-Fri, 2 on Sat, 9 passengers, 12 mins.

To **Puerto Williams**, daily except Sun, 1¼ hrs (book a week in advance for Porvenir, 2 in advance for Puerto Williams). To Balmaceda (Coyhaique) weekly. **To Argentina** To Ushuaia, twice weekly with DAP. Take passport when booking tickets to Argentina.

Bus The bus terminal is at the northern edge of town by the Zona Franca. At the time of writing bus companies were maintaining their own offices in the city centre. **Cruz del Sur**, **Fernández**, and **Turibus**, Sanhueza 745, T61-224 2313/222 1429, www.busesfernandez.com. **Pacheco**, Colón 900, T61-224 2174, www.busespacheco.com; **Pullman**, Colón 568, T61-222 3359, www.pullman.cl, tickets for all Chile. **Central de Pasajeros**, Colón y Magallanes, T61-224 5811, office for booking all tickets, also cambio and tour operator. **Bus Sur**, Colón 842, T61-261 4224, www.bussur.com. **Ghisoni** and **Tecni Austral**, Lautaro Navarro 975, T61-261 3422, www.turismoghisoni.com. Bus services: To **Puerto Natales**, 3-3½ hrs, **Bus Sur, Ghisoni, Pullman, Pacheco** and **Tecni Austral**, up to 8 daily, last departure 2100, US$11, look out for special offers and connections to Torres del Paine. Buses may pick up at the airport with advance booking and payment. To **Puerto Montt** with Queilen, **Bus Sur** and **Pullman**, Mon, Wed, Fri, 0800 US$88, 34 hrs, also **Osorno** US$88, 30 hrs.

To **Río Grande** and **Ushuaia** via **Punta Delgada** (route is described in Argentina, Arriving in Tierra del Fuego; no buses via Porvenir) **Ghisoni, Pacheco, Sur, Tecni-Austral** and others, 8-10 hrs, US$25-33, heavily booked; US$38-52 to Ushuaia, 11-12 hrs. Some services have to change in Río Grande for Ushuaia, others direct. Check companies for frequencies. Book well in advance in Jan-Feb. To **Río Gallegos**, Argentina, via Punta Delgada, **Ghisoni**, Mon, Wed, Thu, Fri, Sat, 1100; Pingüino, daily 1200. Fares US$23, 6-8 hrs, depending on customs, 15 mins on Chilean side, up to 2 hrs on Argentine side.

To **Otway Sound**: bus with **Fernández** 1500, return 1900, US$11. Tours by several agencies, US$18, entry extra, taxi US$80 return.

Car hire EMSA, Kuzma Slavic 706, T61-261 4378, www.emsarentacar.cl. **Payne**, Menéndez 631, T61-224 0852, www.payne.cl, also tours, treks, birdwatching, etc. Also multinational companies. **Note** You need a hire company's authorization to take a car into Argentina. This takes 24 hrs (not Sat or Sun) and involves mandatory international insurance at US$100 per week, plus notary fees.

Ferry Shipping offices: **Navimag** (Lautaro Navarro 1225, p 1, T61-220 0200, www.navimag.com) for up to date information on Navimag ferries between Puerto Montt and Puerto Natales; details under Puerto Montt, Transport. For **Australis Expedition Cruises** to Cape Horn and Ushuaia, see above.

To Tierra del Fuego The *Crux Australis* sails from Tres Puentes, 5 km north of Punta Arenas (bus A or E from Av Magallanes, or *colectivo* 15, US$1; taxi US$5) at 0900 or 1500-1600 Tue-Sun; less frequent sailings off season. Book through **Tabsa/Transboradora Austral Broom** (Bulnes 5075, Tres Puentes, T61-272 8100, www.tabsa.cl) or through **Turismo Comapa**, see Tour operators, above. The 2½-hr crossing can be rough and cold, watch for dolphins, US$10 pp, US$17.50 motorcycle, US$62 per vehicle. Boat disembarks at Bahía Chilota, 5 km from Porvenir, bus US$2; bus drops you where you want to go in town. Timetable dependent on tides and subject to change; check in advance. **Tabsa** website gives monthly schedules. Reservations for cars essential, especially in summer.

The other crossing is the Primera Angostura from **Punta Delgada** (170 km northeast of Punta Arenas) to **Punta Espora** on Bahía Azul (80 km north of Porvenir). There are 3 boats working continuously. On board is a café, lounge, toilets and decks for getting splashed. Boats run 0830-2400, 20 mins' crossing, US$23 per vehicle, US$7 motorcycle, foot passengers US$2.65, www.tabsa.cl. The ferries takes about 4 trucks and 20 cars; before 1000 most space is taken by trucks, and buses can wait up to 90 mins to board.

To Antarctica Most cruise ships leave from Ushuaia, but a few operators are based in Punta Arenas. See above, **Adventure Network International**, or try **Antarctica XXI**, O'Higgins 1170, T61-261 4100, www.antarcticaxxi.com, flight/cruise packages. See under Santiago Tour operators, page 700. Otherwise, another possibility is with the Chilean Navy, enquire at the **Tercera Zona Naval**, Lautaro Navarro 1150, T61-220 5599, www.armada.cl. The Navy does not encourage passengers, so you must approach the captain direct. Present yourself as a professional or student as opposed to a tourist. Spanish is essential. 2 vessels, *Galvarino* and *Lautaro*, sail regularly (no schedule, about US$50, 1 month).

Taxi Ordinary taxis have yellow roofs. *Colectivos* (all black) run on fixed routes, pick up from taxi stands around town, US$0.50, US$0.60 at night.

Beautifully situated on the calm waters of Canal Señoret fjord, an arm of the Ultima Esperanza Sound, edged with spectacular mountains, Puerto Natales (population 20,500), 247 km north of Punta Arenas, is a quiet town of brightly painted corrugated tin houses. It's the base for exploring the magnificent O'Higgins and Torres del Paine national parks, and even when inundated with visitors in the summer, it retains an unhurried feel.

Sights

Museo Histórico Municipal ① *Bulnes 285, T61-241 1263, Nov-Apr, Mon-Fri 0800-1900, May-Oct, 0800-1700, Sat-Sun 1000-1300, 1500-1900, US$2*, has displays and photos of early colonizers, as well as a small collection of archaeological and natural history exhibits. There are lovely walks along the waterfront or up to Cerro Dorotea, which dominates the town, with superb views (watch out for high winds). Take any bus going east and alight at the road for summit (Km 9.5). There is a US$7 charge to use the trail.

Some 25 km north of town is the **Monumento Natural Cueva Milodón** ① *in high season daily 0800-1900 (0830-1800 in low season), www.cuevadelmilodon.cl, US$7.75 (US$3.10 in low season), getting there: regular bus from Prat 297, T61-241 5891 (Huellas del Milodón), leaves 0900 and 1500,*

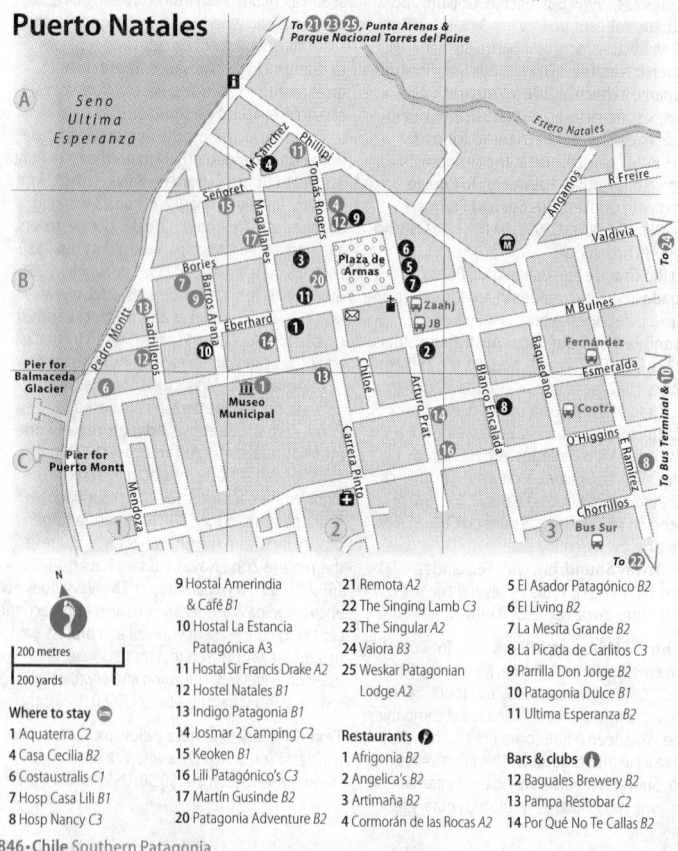

Puerto Natales

Where to stay 🛏
1 Aquaterra *C2*
4 Casa Cecilia *B2*
6 Costaustralis *C1*
7 Hosp Casa Lili *B1*
8 Hosp Nancy *C3*
9 Hostal Amerindia & Café *B1*
10 Hostal La Estancia Patagónica *A3*
11 Hostal Sir Francis Drake *A2*
12 Hostel Natales *B1*
13 Indigo Patagonia *B1*
14 Josmar 2 Camping *C2*
15 Keoken *B1*
16 Lili Patagónico's *C3*
17 Martín Gusinde *B2*
20 Patagonia Adventure *B2*
21 Remota *A2*
22 The Singing Lamb *C3*
23 The Singular *A2*
24 Vaiora *B3*
25 Weskar Patagonian Lodge *A2*

Restaurants 🍴
1 Afrigonia *B2*
2 Angelica's *B2*
3 Artimaña *B2*
4 Cormorán de las Rocas *A2*
5 El Asador Patagónico *B2*
6 El Living *B2*
7 La Mesita Grande *B2*
8 La Picada de Carlitos *C3*
9 Parrilla Don Jorge *B2*
10 Patagonia Dulce *B1*
11 Ultima Esperanza *B2*

Bars & clubs 🍸
12 Baguales Brewery *B2*
13 Pampa Restobar *C2*
14 Por Qué No Te Callas *B2*

returns 1300 and 1900. US$21, includes guide; taxi US$27 return, 20 mins each way, driver waits 1 hr. The cave (70 m wide, 30 m high and 220 m deep) was formed by ice-age glacial lakes. Remains were found of a prehistoric ground-sloth, together with evidence of occupation by early Patagonian humans some 11,000 years ago. There is a small, well-presented visitor centre, shop and toilets.

Parque Nacional Bernardo O'Higgins
Access by boat from Puerto Natales only; all agencies can arrange trips. Summer daily 0800, returning 1730; winter Sun only, US$100-130 (minimum 10 passengers), heavily booked in high season. Park fee US$11. Take warm clothes, hat and gloves.

Also referred to as the **Parque Nacional Monte Balmaceda**, the park is at the north end of Ultima Esperanza Sound. After a three-hour journey up the Sound, the boat passes the Balmaceda Glacier which drops steeply from the eastern slopes of Monte Balmaceda (2035 m). The glacier is retreating; in 1986 its foot was at sea level. The boat docks further north at Puerto Toro, from where it's a 1-km walk to the base of Serrano Glacier on the north slope of Monte Balmaceda. Kayaking is popular here. On the trip dolphins, sea lions (in season), black-necked swans, flightless steamer ducks and cormorants can be seen. The boat then returns to Puerto Natales. There is a route from Puerto Toro on the eastern side of the Río Serrano for 35 km to the Torres del Paine administration centre; guided tours are available on foot or on horseback. It is also possible to go along the river by boat or zodiac. It's best going towards Torres del Paine this way, as the view suddenly opens up and then just gets better and better.

Border with Argentina
There's an **Argentine consulate** in Punta Arenas ① *21 de Mayo 1878, T61-226 1532, caren@mrecic.gov.ar, Mon-Fri 0900-1800;* visas take 24 hours. There are three crossing points east of Puerto Natales. See also www.pasosfronterizos.gov.cl and the Argentina chapter.

> **Fact...**
> Border crossings can take up to several hours in peak season.

Dorotea 16 km east of Puerto Natales. On the Argentine side the road continues to a junction, with alternatives to Río Turbio and north to La Esperanza and Río Gallegos. Chilean immigration is open all year 0800-2200.

Paso Casas Viejas/Laurita 16 km northeast of Puerto Natales. On the Argentine side this joins the Río Turbio–La Esperanza road. Chilean immigration is open 0800-2200 (winter 0700-2100).

Río Don Guillermo/Cerro Castillo 65 km north of Puerto Natales on the road to Torres del Paine. Immigration is 7 km from the border, open 0800-2200 (winter 0700-2100). Cerro Castillo is well-equipped with café, toilets, ATM, tourist information and souvenir shop; the small settlement has several hospedajes and cafeterías. There's sheep shearing in December, and a rodeo and rural festival third weekend in January. On the Argentine side, Paso Río Don Guillermo (Cancha Carrera, 14 km) has few facilities. The road leads to La Esperanza and Río Gallegos. All buses between Puerto Natales and El Calafate go via Cerro Castillo, making it the most convenient route for visiting the Parque Nacional Los Glaciares from Chile, or for visiting Torres del Paine from Argentina.

Listings Puerto Natales and around *map p845*

Tourist information

For further information, consult the **municipal tourist office** at the bus station (Av España 1455, open 0600-1200 all year) and **CONAF** (Baquedano 847, T61-241 1438,juan.romero@conaf.cl).

Sernatur
On the waterfront, Av Pedro Montt 19, T61-241 2125, infonatales@sernatur.cl. Oct-Mar Mon-Fri 0830-2000, Sat-Sun 0900-1300,1500-1800, Apr-Sep, Mon-Fri 0830-1800, Sat 1000-1600. Good leaflets on Puerto Natales and Torres del Paine in English, and bus and boat information for the park.

Where to stay

In season cheaper accommodation fills up quickly. Hotels in the countryside open only in summer months; dates vary. Good deals in upper range hotels may be available; out of season especially and prices may be 50% lower.

$$$$ Costaustralis
Pedro Montt 262, T61-241 2000,
www.hoteles-australis.com.
Very comfortable, tranquil, lovely views (but not from inland-facing rooms), lift, English spoken, waterfront restaurant Paine serves international and local seafood.

$$$$ Indigo Patagonia
Ladrilleros 105, T 61-274 0670, 2-2432 6800,
www.indigopatagonia.cl.
Relaxed atmosphere, on the water front, great views, a boutique hotel with roof-top spa, rooms and suites, café/restaurant serves good seafood and vegetarian dishes. Tours organized.

$$$$ Remota
Ruta 9 Norte, Km 1.5, Huerto 279,
T61-241 4040, www.remota.cl.
Modernist design with big windows, lots of trips, activities and treks offered, spa, all-inclusive packages, good food, first-class.

$$$$ The Singular
Km 5 Norte, Puerto Bories, T61-272 2030,
www.thesingular.com.
In converted warehouses, outside the town centre, in a scenic spot overlooking the Ultima Esperanza Sound. Spa, gourmet restaurant and varied excursions offered.

$$$$-$$$ Martín Gusinde
Bories 278, T61-271 2100,
www.hotelmartingusinde.com.
Modern 3-star standard, smart, parking, laundry service, excursions organized.

$$$$-$$$ Weskar Patagonian Lodge
Ruta 9, Km 05, Huerto 274-B, T61-241 0839 ,
www.weskar.cl.
Quiet lodge overlooking the fjord, standard or deluxe rooms with good views, 3-course dinners served, lunch boxes prepared for excursions, many activities offered, helpful.

$$$ Aquaterra
Bulnes 299, T61-241 2239,
www.aquaterrapatagonia.com.
Good restaurant with vegetarian options, 'resto-bar' downstairs, spa, warm and comfortable but not cheap, very helpful staff. Excursions and tours.

$$$ Hostal Sir Francis Drake
Phillipi 383, T61-241 1553,
www.hostalfrancisdrake.com.
Calm and welcoming, tastefully decorated, smallish rooms, good views.

$$$ Keoken
Señoret 267, T61-241 3670,
www.keokenpatagonia.com.
Cosy, upmarket B&B, spacious living room, some rooms with views. All rooms have bathroom but not all are en suite, English spoken, helpful staff, tours.

$$$-$ Hostel Amerindia
Arana 135, T61-241 1945, www.hostelamerindia.com.
Central, near restaurants and the plaza. Dorms and private rooms. Breakfast included and served in the popular café (see below).

$$ Casa Cecilia
Tomás Rogers 60, T61-241 2698,
www.casaceciliahostal.com.
Welcoming, popular, with small simple rooms, private or shared bath. English, French and German spoken, rents camping and trekking gear, tour agency and information for Torres del Paine.

$$ Hospedaje Nancy
Ramírez 540, T61-241 0022, www.nataleslodge.cl.
Private rooms and dorm (*albergue*), warm and hospitable, information, tours, equipment rental.

$$ Lili Patagónico's
Prat 479, T61-241 4063, www.lilipatagonicos.com.
$ pp in dorms. Small but pleasant heated rooms, helpful staff. Lots of information, good quality equipment rented. Tours offered. Indoor climbing wall.

$$ Patagonia Adventure
Tomás Rogers 179, T61-241 1028,
www.apatagonia.com.
Lovely old house, bohemian feel, shared bath, $ pp in dorms, equipment hire, bike and kayak tours and tour arrangements for Torres del Paine.

$$-$ Hostel Natales
Ladrilleros 209, T61-241 4731, www.hostelnatales.cl.
Private rooms or dorms in this high-end hostel, comfortable, minibar and safety boxes.

$$-$ pp The Singing Lamb
Arauco 779, T61-241 0958,
www.thesinginglamb.com.
Very hospitable New Zealand-run backpackers, dorm accommodation only but no bunks. Home-from-home feel. Good information.

$ Hospedaje Casa Lili
Bories 153, T61-241 4039,
lilipatagonia@gmail.com.
Dorms or private rooms, small, family-run, rents
equipment and can arrange tickets to Paine,
free luggage store.

$ Hostal La Estancia Patagónica
Juan MacLean 567, T9-9224 8601,
hostallaestanciapatagonica@gmail.com.
Family-run *hostal* near the bus terminal. 4-bed
dorms and private rooms (**$$**). Breakfast included.
Thin walls, great showers.

Camping

Josmar 2
McLean 367, T61-241 1685, www.josmar.cl.
Family-run, convenient, hot showers, parking,
barbecues, electricity, café, tent site, US$9.50,
or shared room, US$9.50.

Vaiora
Kruger 233, T61 241 1737, see Facebook.
Camping and *hospedaje* in centre,
US$11 per night.

Border with Argentina

$ pp Hospedaje Mate Amargo
Santiago Bueras s/n, Cerro Castillo, T9-536 1966.
Rooms for 4, with bath, Wi-Fi and luggage store.

Restaurants

$$$ Afrigonia
Eberhard 343, T61-241 2877.
An unexpected mixture of Patagonia meets
East Africa in this Kenyan/Chilean-owned fusion
restaurant, considered by many to be the best,
and certainly the most innovative, in town.

$$$ Angelica's
Bulnes 501, T61-241 0007.
Elegant Mediterranean style, well-prepared
pricey food with quality ingredients.

$$$-$$ Cormorán de las Rocas
Miguel Sánchez 72, T61-261 5131-2,
www.cormorandelasrocas.com.
Patagonian specialities with an innovative
twist, wide variety of well-prepared dishes,
pisco sours, good service and attention to detail,
incomparable views.

$$$-$$ El Asador Patagónico
Prat 158 on the Plaza, T61-241 3553.
Spit-roast lamb, salads, home-made puddings.

$$$-$$ Parrilla Don Jorge
Bories 430, on Plaza, T61-241 0999,
reservas@parrilladonjorge.cl.
Also specializes in spit-roast lamb, but serves fish
too, good service.

$$ La Mesita Grande
Prat 196 on the Plaza, T61-241 1571,
www.mesitagrande.cl.
Fresh pizzas from the wood-burning oven, also
pasta and desserts. Poor service but good food,
wildly popular.

$$ Ultima Esperanza
Eberhard 354, T61-241 1391, www.
restaurantuesperanza.galeon.com.
One of the town's classic seafood restaurants.

$$-$ El Living
Prat 156, Plaza de Armas, www.el-living.com.
Mon-Sat in high season.
Comfy sofas, good tea, magazines in all languages,
book exchange, good music, delicious vegetarian
food, British-run, popular. Wi-Fi. Recommended.

$$-$ La Picada de Carlitos
Blanco Encalada y Esmeralda, T61-241 4885.
Good, cheap traditional Chilean food, popular with
locals at lunchtime, when service can be slow.

$ Artimaña
Bories 349, T61-241 4856, see Facebook.
Newish café/restaurant offering fresh salads,
sandwiches, juices and desserts. Bright, intimate
surroundings; Wi-Fi.

Cafés

Amerindia
Barros Arana 135, T61-241 1945, www.
hostalamerindia.com (see Where to stay).
Recommended for coffee and hot chocolate. Fun
vibe; also sells artisan sundry and baked goods.

Patagonia Dulce
Barros Arana 233, T61-241 5285.
Tue-Sun 1400-2100.
For the best hot chocolate in town, good coffee
and chocolates.

Bars and clubs

Baguales Brewery
Bories 430, on the plaza, www.cervezabaguales.cl.
Sep-Mar Mon-Sat 1300-0230.
Pub with microbrewery attached. Also
serves hamburgers and other snacks
and great lunch specials.

Pampa Resto Bar
Bulnes 371, T9-532 2361, see Facebook.
Fun, live music on Tue night. Good spot for meeting travellers and locals. In high season expect to pay premium prices for bar food.

Por Qué No Te Callas
Magallanes 247, T61-241 4942.
Neighbourhood bar with beer, pizza and Chilean favourites like *chorillana* on the menu. Live music various nights.

Shopping

Camping equipment
Check all camping equipment and prices carefully. (Deposits required.) Camping gas is widely available in hardware stores. See under Where to stay and What to do for places that hire equipment, eg **Casa Cecilia**, **Lili Patagónico's**, **Sendero Aventura**, **Erratic Rock**. Always check exactly what the price covers.

Supermarkets
Several in town. The town markets are also good.

What to do

Many agencies along Arturo Prat. It is better to book tours direct with operators in Puerto Natales than through agents in Punta Arenas or Santiago. Several agencies offer tours to the Perito Moreno glacier in Argentina, 1 day, US$70-80, 14-hr trip, 2 hrs at the glacier, without food or park entry fee. You can then leave the tour in Calafate to continue into Argentina.

Baguales Group, *Encalada 353, T9-5168 8447, www.baguulesgroup.com.* Specialists in the route from the park back to Puerto Natales. Tailor made multi-activity tours that can incorporate zodiacs, horse riding, kayaking and trekking, mostly off the beaten track.
Blue Green Adventures, *Galvarino 618, T61-241 1800, www.bluegreenadventures.com.* Adventure tour specialist and travel agent, with trekking, riding, kayaking, fishing and multi-activity options, estancia, whalewatching, wine and yoga programmes. Also caters for families.
Comapa, *Bulnes 541, T61-241 4300, www.comapa.com.* Large regional operator offering decent day tours to Torres del Paine.
Erratic Rock, *Baquedano 719 and Zamora 732, T61-241 4317, www.erraticrock.com.* Trekking experts offering interesting expeditions from half a day to 2 weeks. Also hostel (walk-ins only), good-quality equipment hire, daily trekking seminar at 1500.

Estancia Travel, *Casa 13-b, Puerto Bories, T61-241 2221, www.estanciatravel.com.* Based at the Estancia Puerto Consuelo, 5 km north of Puerto Natales, offers horse-riding trips from 1 to 12 days around southern Patagonia and Torres del Paine, with accommodation at traditional estancias. Also kayaking trips, British/Chilean run, bilingual, professional guides, at the top end of the price range.
Kayak in Patagonia, *Bories 327 (but no storefront – contact by email), T9-9480 7381, www.kayakenpatagonia.com.* Specializes in half-day, full-day and multi-day kayaking trips around Cisne Bay and the Serrano and Gray rivers.
Punta Alta, *Blanco Encalada 244, T61-241 0115, www.puntaalta.cl.* Fast boat to the Balmaceda glacier in Bernardo O'Higgins and the possibility to continue by zodiac to Pueblito Serrano at the southern edge of Torres del Paine national park (from US$180 one way). Also has an option to return to Natales on the same day by minibus along the southern access road, thus avoiding Torres del Paine entry fees.
Sendero Aventura, *T9-6171 3080, www.senderoaventura.com.* Adventure tours by land rover, bike or kayak; virtual office only
Skorpios, *www.skorpios.cl.* 2- to 3-day cruises up the southern fjords to Puerto Edén and the Pío XI Glacier. No office in Puerto Natales; book online or through an agency. Their terminal is at Puerto Bories.
Turismo 21 de Mayo, *Eberhard 560, T61-261 4420, www.turismo21demayo.com.* Sailings to the Balmaceda glacier in Bernardo O'Higgins and the possibility to continue by zodiac to Pueblito Serrano at the southern edge of Torres del Paine national park (from US$144 one way, includes lunch).

Transport

Air Aerodromo Teniente Julio Gallardo, 7 km north of town. **LATAM** and **Sky** airline operate direct services in summer only from Santiago. Also charter services from **Punta Arenas** and onward connections to Argentina with **Aerovías DAP**.

Bicycle repairs El Rey de la Bicicleta, Galvarino 544, T61-241 1905. Good, helpful.

Bus In summer book ahead. All buses leave from the new bus terminal 20 mins outside town at Av España 1455, but tickets can be bought at the individual company offices in town. *Colectivos* leave regularly from the centre US$0.55 (US$0.65 at night and Sun), taxi US$1.75 flat fee (US$2 at night and Sun) throughout Puerto Natales. **Bus Fernández**, E Ramírez 399, T61-241 1111, www.busesfernandez.com. **Pacheco**, only at terminal, T61-241 4800, www.busespacheco.com. **Bus Sur**, Baquedano 668, T61-241 0784, www.bussur.com. **Zaahj**, Prat 236 and in terminal, T61-249 1631, www.turismozaahj.co.cl.

To **Punta Arenas**, several daily, 3-3½ hrs, US$11, **Fernández**, **Pacheco**, **Bus Sur** and others. In theory buses from Punta Arenas to Puerto Natales will also pick passengers up at Punta Arenas airport (US$12) as long as reservations and payment have been made in advance through Buses Pacheco. To **Argentina**: to **Río Gallegos**, **Bus Sur**, Mon, Wed, Fri 0730, 8 hrs via Punta Arenas, US$30, returns direct from Río Gallegos 1630, same days, US$16, 5 hrs. Hourly to **Río Turbio**, Cootra, Pacheco and others, US$12, 2 hrs (depending on Customs – change bus at border). To **El Calafate**, US$36, Cootra, daily 0830, 1800, 4 hrs; **Zaahj**, 5 hrs via Cerro Castillo, daily 0700, 1630; **Bus Sur**, Tue, Thu, Sat 0745, 1430, US$18, 5 hrs (bus at 0700 or 1000 from Punta Arenas connects with 1430 service, US$29 from Punta Arenas, 8 hrs). Otherwise travel

agencies run several times a week depending on demand; they do not include Perito Moreno glacier entry fee (12-hr trip), shop around, reserve 1 day ahead. **Bus Sur** runs to **Ushuaia** Oct-Apr on Mon, Wed, Fri 0730, 14 hrs, US$50; **Pacheco** to **Ushuaia**, Tue, Thu, Sun 0730, 15 hrs, US$63. See Essential Torres del Paine box (opposite) for buses from Puerto Natales into the park.

Car hire EMSA, Arana 118, T61-261 4388, www.emsarentacar.com. **Punta Alta**, Blanco Encalada 244, T61-241 0115, www.puntaalta.cl. Hire agents can arrange permission to drive into Argentina, takes 24 hrs to arrange, extra insurance is required.

Ferry Details of the *Navimag* ferries between Puerto Montt and Puerto Natales are given under Puerto Montt, Transport. Contact **Navimag** (in bus terminal, T61-241 1421, www.navimag.com) for up-to-date information.

The *Skorpios 3* sails from Puerto Natales to Glaciar Amalia and Fiordo Calvo in the Campo de Hielo Sur, 4 days, fares from US$1690 pp, double cabin. An optional first day includes a visit to Torres del Paine or the Cueva del Milodón.

Parque Nacional Torres del Paine *Colour map 9, B1.*

towers of rock and sheets of ice to take your breath away

★Nothing prepares you for the spectacular beauty of Parque Nacional Torres del Paine. World renowned for its challenging trekking, the park's 242,242 ha contain 15 peaks above 2000 m. At its centre is the glacier-topped granite massif Macizo Paine, from which rise the vertical pink granite Torres (Towers) del Paine and, below them, the Cuernos (Horns) del Paine, swooping buttresses of lighter granite under caps of darker sedimentary rock. From the vast Campo de Hielo Sur ice cap on its western edge, four main glaciers (*ventisqueros*), Grey, Dickson, Zapata and Tyndall, drop into vividly coloured lakes formed by their meltwater: turquoise, ultramarine and pistachio expanses, some filled with wind-sculpted royal blue icebergs. Wherever you explore, there are constantly changing views of dramatic peaks and ice fields. The park enjoys a micro-climate especially favourable to wildlife and plants: there are 105 species of birds including condors, ibis, flamingos and austral parakeets, and 25 species of mammals including guanaco, hares, foxes, pumas and skunks.

The park is administered by CONAF ① *T61-236 0496, magallanes.oirs@conaf.cl, www.parque torresdelpaine.cl*, whose administration centre is in the south of the park at the northwest end of Lago Toro; phone the administration centre for information (in Spanish) on weather conditions. It also has videos and exhibitions with summaries in English of flora and fauna. There are 13 ranger stations (*guarderías*) staffed by rangers, who give help and advice. The impact of huge numbers of visitors to the park, over 100,000 a year, is often visible in litter around the *refugios* and camping areas. Take all your rubbish out of the park including toilet paper. For the 2016-2017 season the park authorities applied various restrictions in order to limit the environmental damage caused by such intense tourism and, in mid-2017, added the requirement that hikers must be accompanied by a registered guide in the winter months. See www.parquetorresdelpaine.cl for the most recent information.

Hikes

There are about 250 km of well-marked trails, and walkers must keep to the paths: cross-country trekking is not permitted. The times indicated should be treated with caution: allow for personal fitness and weather conditions.

Essential Torres del Paine

Getting there

The park administration is 147 km northwest of Puerto Natales via the old road, which is used by public buses (4½ hours). A shorter road, 85 km, goes to the south side of the park (1½ hours). The most practical way to get to Torres del Paine is with one of the many bus or tour companies that leave Puerto Natales daily. After mid-March there is little public transport and trucks are irregular.

Admission

There are entrances at Laguna Amarga, Lago Sarmiento, Laguna Azul and Río Serrano, open daily 0830-2000 in summer (Río Serrano, 0700-2200) and 0830-2000 at other times (Río Serrano, until 1815). Entry for foreigners is US$32.50 October-April (low season, May-September, US$17), payable in Chilean pesos, dollars or euros; Chilean pesos only in low season. You are required to register and show your passport when entering the park. If you are based outside the park and plan on entering and leaving several times, request a multiple-entry stamp valid for three consecutive days. Reservations must be made for all lodging on treks in the park; printed copies of the reservation will need to be shown to access the El Circuito and the W hiking circuits. Climbing the peaks requires two permits, first from **DIFROL** (can be obtained free online, www.difrol.cl; it takes two weeks to receive the permit), then from **CONAF** in the park itself (take passports, DIFROL permit, insurance and route plan).

Getting around

The park is well set up for tourism, with frequent bus services running from Puerto Natales through the park. However, other than these routes, getting around the park without your own transport is difficult and expensive. For details, see Transport, below.

Safety warning

Be aware of the severity and unpredictability of the weather here (which can change in a few minutes). Also do not underestimate the arduousness of some of the stretches on the long hikes. Rain and snowfall are heavier the further west you go and bad weather sweeps off the Campo de Hielo Sur without warning. The only means of rescue are on horseback or by boat; the nearest helicopter is in Punta Arenas and high winds usually prevent its operation in the park. An Argentine visitor disappeared in 2013 and was not found, despite extensive searches. It is vital to take adequate equipment/clothing and report your route to staff. Mobile phone coverage is erratic.

Forest fires are also a serious hazard in summer. Make sure you follow all regulations. Recent unauthorized campfires have led to the destruction of vast areas; open fires are now banned throughout the park. Only camp stoves may be used in designated areas.

Equipment and maps

A strong, streamlined, waterproof tent gives you more freedom than crowded *refugios* and is essential if doing the complete circuit. Also essential at all times of year are protective clothing against cold, wind and rain, strong waterproof footwear, hat, a compass, a good sleeping bag, sleeping mat, camping stove and cooking equipment. Most *refugios* will hire camping equipment for a single night. Sun-screen and sunglasses are also necessary, and you'll want shorts in summer. Take your own food: the small shops at the *refugios* and at **Posada Río Serrano** are expensive and limited. The entry fee includes a reasonable trail map to take with you (not waterproof), also available in the CONAF office. Other maps (US$8), published by Mattassi and (more accurate) Cartografía Digital and Patagonia Interactiva, are in shops in Punta Arenas or Puerto Natales. All have a few mistakes, however.

When to go

The park is open all year round, although snow may prevent access in the winter. The warmest time is December to March, but these months are also the most unstable: strong winds often blow off the glaciers, and rainfall can be heavy. The park is most crowded in the summer holiday season, January to mid-February, less so in December or March. October and November are recommended for wild flowers. In winter there can be good, stable conditions and well-equipped hikers can do some good walking, but some treks may be closed and boats may not be running.

Time required

A day tour from Puerto Natales will give a broad overview of the park, but seven to 10 days are needed to see it all properly.

El Circuito (Allow at least seven days) The park's emblematic hike is a circuit round the Torres and Cuernos del Paine: it is usually done anticlockwise starting from the Laguna Amarga *guardería*. (Under new regulations in the 2016-2017 season, the Amarga-Serón trail is closed; the trek now begins at Las Torres hotel/campsite. Also, the Coirón to Paso leg may only be done anticlockwise.) From Laguna Amarga the route is north along the west side of the Río Paine to Lago Paine, before turning west to

follow the Río Paine to the south end of Lago Dickson. From here the path runs along the wooded valley of the Río de los Perros before climbing steeply to Paso John Gardner (1241 m, the highest point on the route), then dropping to follow the Grey Glacier southeast to Lago Grey, continuing to Lago Pehoé and before joining up with the 'W' (see below) back to the Hostería Las Torres or Laguna Amarga. There are superb views, particularly from the top of Paso John Gardner.

Camping gear must be carried, and printed proof of camping reservations must be shown (www.parquetorresdelpaine.cl has a page dedicated to this). The circuit is often closed in winter because of snow. Walking times between campsites is four to six hours. The most difficult section is the steep slippery slope between Paso John Gardner and Campamento Paso, a poorly signed section exposed to strong westerly winds. The major rivers are crossed by footbridges, which are occasionally washed away.

The 'W' (Allow four to five days) A more popular alternative to El Circuito, it can be completed without camping equipment by staying in *refugios*, and can be done only anticlockwise. It combines several of the hikes described separately below. From Laguna Amarga the first stage runs west via Hotel Las Torres and up the valley of the Río Ascensio via Refugio Chileno to the base of the Torres del Paine (see below). From here return to the Hotel Las Torres and then walk along the northern shore of Lago Nordenskjold via Refugio Los Cuernos to Campamento Italiano. From here climb the Valley of the Río del Francés (see below) before continuing to Lodge Paine Grande. From here you can complete the third part of the 'W' by walking west along the northern shore of Lago Grey to Refugio Grey and Glaciar Grey before returning to Lodge Paine Grande. To do the hike from west to east, either take the scheduled catamaran service across Lago Pehoé to Lodge Paine Grande and start from there, or take the trail to Paine Grande from the administration centre (during the high season, this trail is closed in the Las Carretas-Administración direction). This precursor to the main hike passes Campamento Las Carretas (permanently closed) and for all but the last hour is easy, with views of what you will be undertaking on the 'W'. Printed proof of camping reservations must be shown.

The Valley of the Río del Francés (Allow five hours each way) From Lodge Paine Grande this route leads northeast across undulating country along the west edge of Lago Skottberg to Campamento Italiano and then follows the valley of the Río del Francés, which climbs between (to the west) Cerro Paine Grande and the Ventisquero del Francés, and (to the east) the Cuernos del Paine to Campamento Británico. Allow 2½ hours from Lodge Paine Grande to Campamento Italiano, 2½ hours further to Campamento Británico. The views from the mirador, 20 minutes above Campamento Británico, are superb.

To the base of the Torres del Paine (Allow five to six hours each way) From Laguna Amarga the route follows the road west to Hotel Las Torres before climbing along the west side of the Río Ascensio via Campamento Chileno to Campamento Las Torres, close to the base of the Torres and near a small lake. Allow 1½ hours to Hotel Las Torres, then two hours to Campamento Chileno, two hours further to Campamento Torres where there is a fork: the path to the base of the Torres is well-marked, but these last 30 minutes are up the moraine (the last bit involves a hard scramble over rocks at a near-vertical gradient); to see the towers lit by sunrise (spectacular, but you must have good weather), it's well worth humping camping gear up to Campamento Torres and spending the night (no *refugio*). One hour beyond Campamento Torres is the good site at Campamento Japonés (for climbers only; non-climbers need to arrive with a guide).

Up the Río Pingo valley (Allow five hours each way; only to be undertaken with a certified private guide. Check with CONAF for available guides.) From Guardería Grey (18 km west by road from the Administration Centre) follow the Río Pingo, via Refugio Pingo and Refugio Zapata (four hours), with views south over Ventisquero Zapata (plenty of wildlife, icebergs in the lake). It is not possible to reach Lago Pingo as a bridge – marked on many maps – has been washed away. Ventisquero Pingo can be seen 3 km away over the lake.

Parque Nacional Torres del Paine

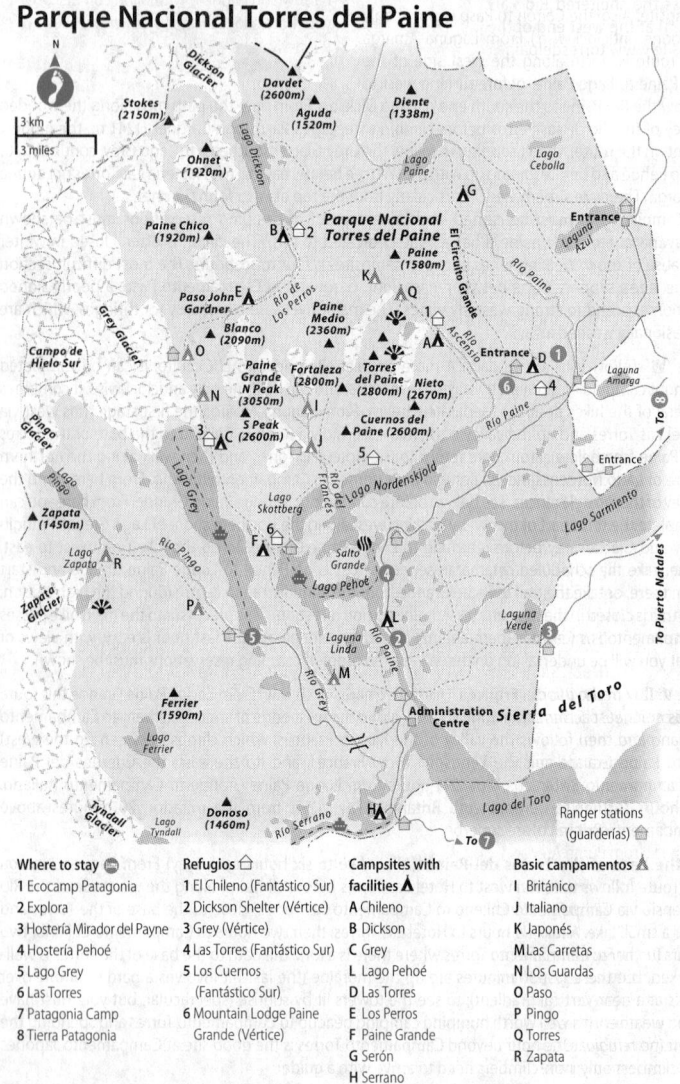

Where to stay 🏨
1 Ecocamp Patagonia
2 Explora
3 Hostería Mirador del Payne
4 Hostería Pehoé
5 Lago Grey
6 Las Torres
7 Patagonia Camp
8 Tierra Patagonia

Refugios 🏠
1 El Chileno (Fantástico Sur)
2 Dickson Shelter (Vértice)
3 Grey (Vértice)
4 Las Torres (Fantástico Sur)
5 Los Cuernos (Fantástico Sur)
6 Mountain Lodge Paine Grande (Vértice)

Campsites with facilities ⛺
A Chileno
B Dickson
C Grey
L Lago Pehoé
D Las Torres
E Los Perros
F Paine Grande
G Serón
H Serrano

Basic campamentos ⛺
I Británico
J Italiano
K Japonés
M Las Carretas
N Los Guardas
O Paso
P Pingo
Q Torres
R Zapata

To Laguna Verde (Allow four hours each way) From the administration centre follow the road north 2 km, before taking the path east over the Sierra del Toro and then along the south side of Laguna Verde to the Guardería Laguna Verde. This is one of the easiest walks in the park and may be a good first hike.

To Laguna Azul and Lago Paine (Allow 8½ hours each way) This route runs north from Laguna Amarga to the west tip of Laguna Azul (following the road for 7 km), from where it continues across the sheltered Río Paine valley past Laguna Cebolla to the Refugio Lago Paine (now closed) at the west end of the lake. There are also plenty of shorter walks in the park, see park website www.torresdelpaine.com.

Listings Parque Nacional Torres del Paine *map p852*

Where to stay

Accommodation is available in 4 categories: there are hotels (expensive, over US$300 for a double room per night), privately run *refugios* (well equipped, staffed, offering meals and free hot water for tea, soup, etc), campsites with amenities and basic *campamentos*. All options fill up quickly in peak summer months, Jan and Feb, so plan your trip and book hotels, *refugios* and campsites in advance. Pay in dollars to avoid IVA (VAT). Agencies in Puerto Natales offer accommodation and transfers or car hire.

$$$$ Ecocamp Patagonia
www.ecocamp.travel (reservations: Don Carlos 3227C, Las Condes, Santiago, T2-2923 5950).
Indigenous Kaweskar-influenced domes, luxurious, all-inclusive, powered by renewable energy, the only ISO14001, environmental sustainability-certified hotel in Chile. Offers 4- to 10-day hiking, wildlife-watching and multi-sports trips, meals included.

$$$$ Explora (Hotel Salto Chico Lodge)
T61-241 1247 (reservations: Av Américo Vespucci Sur 80, p 5, Santiago, T2-2395 2800, www.explora.com).
The park's priciest and most exclusive place is nestled into a nook at Salto Chico on edge of Lago Pehoé, superb views. It's all included: pool, gym, horse riding, boat trips, tours. Arrange packages from Punta Arenas.

$$$$ Hostería Mirador del Payne
Estancia Lazo, 52 km from Sarmiento entrance, T9-9640 2490 , www.miradordelpayne.cl (reservations: Fagnano 585, Punta Arenas).
Lovely location on Laguna Verde on east edge of the park. Comfortable, meals extra, but inconvenient for park itself, riding, hiking, birdwatching. Private transport essential, or hike there from the park.

$$$$ Hostería Pehoé
5 km south of Pehoé ranger station, 11 km north of park administration, T61-261 7727, www.hosteriapehoe.cl (reservations: José Menéndez 647-A, Punta Arenas, T61-272 2853)
Beautifully situated on an island with spectacular view across Lago Pehoé, restaurant.

$$$$ Hotel Lago Grey
T61-236 0280, www.turismolagogrey.com (reservations:Lautaro Navarro 1077, Punta Arenas, T61-271 2100).
Great views over Lago Grey, superior rooms worth the extra, glacier walks.

$$$$ Hotel Las Torres
T61-261 7450, www.lastorres.com.
Comfortable rooms, beautiful lounge with wood fire and great views of the Macizo, good service, horse riding, transport from Laguna Amarga ranger station, spa, disabled access. Visitor centre and *confitería* open to non-residents.

$$$$ Patagonia Camp at Lago Toro
www.patagoniacamp.com (reservations: Eberhard 230, Puerto Natales, T61-241 5149).
Luxury yurts outside the park, 15 km south of Administration.

$$$$ Tierra Patagonia
T2-2207 8861, www.tierrapatagonia.com.
Excellent, environmentally sensitive luxury hotel with spa, pool and outdoor jacuzzi on the edge of the national park overlooking Lago Sarmiento. Full- and half-day guided trips by minibus, on foot or on horseback. Gourmet dining in panorama restaurant overlooking the lake and mountains. Highly recommended.

Refugios

2 companies run the *refugios* in the park, comfortable dormitory or *cabaña* accommodation (bring your own sleeping bag, or hire sheets for US$11-13 per night).

Prices start from US$48 pp bed only and go up to US$245pp in a *cabaña* with full board. Meals can be bought individually (**$$**); restaurants are open to non-residents. *Refugios* have good hot showers and space for camping, **$** (book in advance for **Vértice Refugios** as they have very few tents available). Kitchen facilities are available in some **Vértice Refugios**. **Fantástico Sur** will not let you prepare your own hot food unless you are camping. Most close in winter, although 1 or 2 may stay open, depending on the weather. Advance booking essential.

Fantástico Sur Book through agencies in Puerto Natales or direct at Esmeralda 661, Puerto Natales, T61-261 4184, or via www.fantasticosur.com: **Refugio El Chileno**, in the Valley of Río Ascencio, at the foot of the Torres; **Refugio Las Torres (Torre Central, Torre Norte)**, 2 *refugios* next to the **Hotel Las Torres** (see above), good facilities, especially in the newer **Torre Central**; **Refugio Los Cuernos**, on the northern shore of Lago Nordenskjold, also has 8 cabins (**$$$$**).

Vértice Refugios book through agencies in Puerto Natales, or at Bulnes 100, Puerto Natales, T61-241 2742, or via www.verticepatagonia.com: **Mountain Lodges Paine Grande**, on the northwest tip of Lago Pehoé (kitchen facilities, internet); **Vértice Grey**, and the basic **Vértice Dickson Shelter**.

Camping

Free camping is permitted in 9 locations in the park; these sites are known as campamentos and are generally extremely basic. Reservations for these campsites must be made (online) in advance. The *guardaparques* expect people to have a stove if camping; these may be used only in authorized areas. Equipment hire is available in Puerto Natales (see page 850). Fires are prohibited. The wind tends to rise in the evening so pitch tent early.

There are 4 campsites run by Vértice Patagonia: **Camping Los Perros, Paine Grande, Dickson** and **Grey** (from US$10 pp). **Fantástico Sur** (see above) runs **Camping Serón, Las Torres** (by the Refugio Las Torres), **Central** and **El Francés**, US$15, hot showers; and **Los Cuernos** and **El Chileno** campsites from US$77, full board. Alternatives are **Camping Lago Pehoé** (www.campingpehoe.com, US$16 pp, tent rental US$19

for 2 including sleeping mat), also pre-pitched dome tents, hot showers, shop and restaurant, and **Camping Río Serrano** (just outside the park's southern entrance on a working estancia), also has horse rides and hikes.

What to do

See under Puerto Natales, What to do, page 850, for recommended operators. Before booking a tour, check details carefully and get them in writing.

Experience Chile, T2-2570 9436, www.torres delpaine.org, www.experiencechile.org. Specializes in tailor-made itineraries for individuals, couples and small groups.

Boat trips

From Refugio Lago Pehoé to Refugio Pudeto, US$28 one way with 1 backpack (US$7 for extra backpacks), US$44 return, from Pudeto 0900, 1100, 1400, 1615, 1800, from Paine Grande 0930, 1130, 1430, 1700, 1830, 30 mins in high season, reserve in advance at the *refugios* at either end or at **Catamarán Hielos Patagónicos** (Los Arrieros 1517, Puerto Natales, T61-241 1133, info@hielospatagonicos.com, also in bus terminal, 2nd floor). Reduced service off season (also Christmas Day and New Year's Day), 1200 only from Pudeto, 1230 from Lago Paine Grande, 1 Apr-15 Nov. At all times check in advance that boats are running. See Parque Nacional Bernardo O'Higgins, see page 847, for entry by 3-hr zodiac trip up the Río Serrano from Balmaceda glacier. Boat to face of glacier from **Hostería Grey**, 2-4 times daily, 3½ hrs, US$109 return. A one-way trip can be made via the glacier face to/from the *hostería* to the **Refugio Grey** for US$93. Book through **Hotel Martín Gusinde**.

Transport

Bus There are several companies running daily services into the park, leaving Puerto Natales in high season between 0630 and 0800, and again at 1430, using the old road, with a 15-min stop at Cerro Castillo (3 cafés and some shops), to Laguna Amarga, 3 hrs to Guardería Pudeto and 4 hrs the administration centre (US$16 one way, US$26 open return; return tickets are not interchangeable between different companies). Buses will stop anywhere en route, but all stop at Laguna Amarga entrance, Salto Grande del Paine and the administration centre. Return buses to Puerto Natales stop at Laguna Amarga from 1430 to 2000. In high season the buses

> **Tip...**
> Keep food off the ground because mice can be a problem around camping sites.

fill quickly. Depending on route, for the return trip to Puerto Natales it's best to catch the bus at Laguna Amarga if you are coming from Mirador Los Torres; take a bus at Pudeto if you are coming from Glaciar Grey; or take a bus from Administration if you don't have a boat pass. All buses wait at Refugio Pudeto until the 1200 boat from Refugio Paine Grande arrives. Services are provided by **Bus Gómez** (in terminal, T61-241 5700); **JB** (Prat 258, T61-241 0242) and **Trans Vía Paine** (in terminal, T61-241 1927).

In season there are frequent minibus connections within the park: eg from Laguna Amarga to **Hotel Las Torres**, US$7, and from the administration centre to **Hostería Lago Grey**, US$23. Other than these routes getting around

the park without your own transport is difficult and expensive.

From Torres del Paine to **El Calafate** (Argentina): take services from Puerto Natales (see above); alternatively take a bus from the park to Cerro Castillo (106 km south of administration centre) then catch a direct service to Calafate (see Puerto Natales Buses). Zaahj (address above) has a very comfortable **Super Pullman** service, US$30, Cerro Castillo–El Calafate.

Car hire Hiring a pick-up in Punta Arenas is an economical proposition for a group (up to 9 people): US$400-450 for 4 days. A more economical car can cope with the roads if you go carefully; ask the rental agency's advice.

Tierra del Fuego

desolate and dramatic scenery for adventurous travellers

The western side of this, the largest island off the extreme south of South America, belongs to Chile and the eastern to Argentina. Here the Andes cordillera runs from west to east, so that the north of the island is flat, covered with vast sheep farms, while the south has mountains, glaciers, lakes and forests. The major population centres, Ushuaia and Río Grande, are on the Argentine side, but Chile has the most southerly town in the world, Puerto Williams, on the island of Isla Navarino below Tierra del Fuego. See Argentine Tierra del Fuego for background information.

Porvenir and around Colour map 9, C2.

Porvenir is the only significant settlement on the Chilean side of the island. Founded in 1894 in the gold boom, when many people from Croatia and Chiloé came seeking fortunes, it's a quiet, pleasant place with painted tin houses and neatly trimmed yew trees lining the main avenue. There is a small museum, the **Museo Provincial Fernando Cordero Rusque** ① Zavattaro 402, T61-258 1800, Mon-Thu 0800-1730, Fri 0900-1600, Sat-Sun 1030-1330, 1500-1700, US$1, with archaeological and photographic displays on the Selk'nam (Onas), plus displays on natural history and the early colonizers. **Mirador de la Ciudad** is a walkable excursion round the bay from Porvenir and uphill to the radio aerials. North of Porvenir, 6 km, is the **Monumento Natural Laguna de los Cisnes**, free. Access is across private land; the owner will give permission.

> **Tip...**
> There is no car hire on the island and no public transport to Argentina. All roads are good *ripio* except paved from Bahía Chilota to Porvenir and in Porvenir itself.

Beyond Porvenir

Porvenir is the base for exploring the wonderfully wild virgin territory of Chilean Tierra del Fuego. In the north, there is fuel and lodging at **Cerro Sombrero**, 46 km south of Primera Angostura, a village built to administrate oil drilling in the area, and a *hostal* and a place to eat in San Sebastián. Trips in the more interesting, southern portion of the island, however, must be totally self-sufficient: there are no hotels, shops, petrol stations or public transport.

Wildfowl, including black-necked swans gather from December at **Laguna Santa María**, not far from Porvenir on road to **Bahía Inútil**, a wonderful windswept bay. Cabo Boquerón, the headland at the start of Bahía Inútil, has great views on a clear day, as far as Cabo Froward, Isla Dawson and the distant Cordillera Darwin's snow peaks. Driving east along the bay you pass Los Canelos, with trees, a rare sight, and then the junction for the Cordón Baquedano, on the **Circuito de Oro**. This is a recommended tour, on which you can see gold panning using the same techniques since mining began in 1881; it's a four-hour, 115-km round trip. The main road goes to **Onaisin**, 99 km east of Porvenir, and the Argentine border at San Sebastián (see below). A road south at Onaisin passes Caleta Josefina, a handsome ex-estancia built in 1833, where some old buildings remain. The only town in the south is Cameron, on the southern shore of Bahía Inútil. To reach the most southerly point by road, Estancia Lago Fagnano, and the most southerly habitation at Río Azopardo is four hours. The government is hoping, by 2020, to complete the road south to **Yendegaia** with a view to having a summer route, including ferry, to Puerto Navarino on Isla Navarino. This road would traverse **Parque Nacional Yendegaia** (created December 2013), which adjoins the Parque Nacional Tierra del Fuego in Argentina.

Other options are sailing from Porvenir to **Río Cóndor** across Bahía Inútil, south of Cameron, with trekking or riding from Cameron to **Seno Almirantazgo**, a beautiful, wild and treeless place, where mountains sink into blue fjords with icebergs. A large part of the peninsula between Bahía Inútil and Seno Almirantazgo is the **Karukinka** nature reserve; visit the Wildlife Conservation Society at www. wcs.org to learn more. You can also sail to the **Marinelli glacier**, where you can sail, kayak and dive.

Border with Argentina The only legal border crossing between the Chilean and Argentine parts of Tierra del Fuego is 142 km east of Porvenir at **San Sebastián**; open 0800-2200. There are two settlements called San Sebastián, on each side of the border but they are 14 km apart and taxis are not allowed to cross. On the Argentine side the road continues to Río Grande. **Note** No fruit, vegetables, dairy produce or meat permitted on entry to Chile. Argentine time is one hour ahead of Chilean time, March to October. For entry to Argentina, see Argentina chapter.

☆Isla Navarino

Isla Navarino lies south of the Beagle Channel and is totally unspoilt and beautiful, offering great geographical diversity. The **Dientes de Navarino** mountain range has peaks over 1000 m, covered with southern beech forest up to 500 m. South of that are great plains covered in peat bogs, with many lagoons and abundant in flora. The island was the centre of the indigenous Yaganes culture and has 500 archaeological sites, with the oldest dating from around 3000 years ago.

Tip...
The flight from Punto Arenas to Puerto Williams is beautiful; sit on right from Punta Arenas for superb views of Tierra del Fuego, the Cordillera Darwin, the Beagle Channel, and the islands stretching south to Cape Horn.

Puerto Williams is a small, friendly and remote naval base on the island, about 50 km southeast of Ushuaia (Argentina) at 54° 55′ 41″ south, 67° 37′ 58″ west. The town is a mixture of neat naval housing and the more haphazard civilian building with some impressive, modern municipal and school buildings. On an inlet at the western edge is the Micalvi, an old naval vessel which is now HQ of the yacht club. **Museo Martín Gusinde** ① *Aragay 1, T61-262 1043, www.museomartingusinde. cl, Nov-Mar Tue-Fri 0930-1300, 1500-1800, Sat-Sun 1430-1830, Apr-Oct same hours but closed Sun, free*, is full of information about vanished tribes, local wildlife and voyages, including Charles Darwin and Fitzroy of the *Beagle*, a must. Businesses in town accept US dollars; facilities include a Centro Comercial, minimarkets and a hospital.

For superb views, climb **Cerro Bandera** (three to four hours' round trip, steep, take warm clothes). **Villa Ukika**, 2 km east of town, is where the last descendants of the Yaganes people live, relocated from their original homes at Caleta Mejillone; an old, overgrown cemetery marks the spot on the road to Puerto Navarino.

There is excellent trekking around the **Dientes de Navarino**, the southernmost trail in the world, through impressive mountain landscapes, with superb views of Beagle Channel. The whole trail is a challenging 53 km in five days and is only open November to March, snowfall permitting; good level of fitness needed. One highlight is hiking to Lago Windhond. In the guestbook at the entrance to the reserve you'll find routes suggested by earlier trekkers, some of which lead to Windhond Bay, which offers views of Cape Horn.

Omora Ethnobotanical Park, an NGO dedicated to conservation and biological

Tip...
There is no trekking equipment rental on the island. Ask for information in the tourist office at Puerto Williams, but it's best to go with an organized expedition from Punta Arenas.

research in the Cape Horn Region, has three circuit tours of one to two hours each, entrance US$50 (with guide) and can be booked through Lakutaia Lodge (see Where to stay).

Cape Horn

It may be possible to catch a boat south from Isla Navarino to Cape Horn (the most southerly piece of land on earth apart from Antarctica); enquire at the yacht club. There is one pebbly beach on the north side of the island; boats anchor in the bay and passengers are taken ashore by motorized dinghy. A stairway climbs the cliff above the beach, up to the building where a naval officer and his family run the lighthouse and naval post. A path leads from here to the impressive monument of an albatross overlooking the wild, churning waters of the Drake Passage below.

> ### Tip...
>
> **Australis Expedition Cruises** (Avenida El Bosque Norte 0440, oficina 1103, Las Condes, Santiago, T2-2840 0100, www.australis.com; see page 844), call at Wulaia Bay on the west side of Isla Navarino after visiting Cape Horn; you can disembark to visit the information centre and take a short trek.

Listings Tierra del Fuego

Tourist information

Porvenir

The best information is available from the museum. There are tourist notice boards outside the Municipalidad, on the seafront and elsewhere. A handicrafts stall in a kiosk on the seafront also gives tourist information (opposite Comercial Tuto, No 588).

Isla Navarino

Tourist information is available from the **Municipalidad de Cabos de Hornos** in Puerto Williams (Arturo Prat y Piloto Pardo, T61-262 1018 ext 25, www.ptowilliams.cl/Turismo.html, Mon-Thu 0800-1300, 1430-1700, Fri 0800-1300, 1400-1600, closed in winter). They may have maps and details on hiking. There's also a **CONAF** post in town (Carabinero M Leal 106, T61-262 1303, miguel.gallardo@conaf.cl).

Where to stay

Porvenir

$$$ Hostería Yendegaia
Croacia 702, T61-258 1919.
Comfortable, family-run inn with good facilities and helpful staff. English-speaking owner runs birdwatching tours and to the king penguins.

$$ Central
Phillipi 298, T61-258 0077, opposite Rosas.
All rooms with bath.

$$ España
Croacia 698, T61-258 0540, www.hotelespana.cl.
Comfortable, well equipped, light and spacious rooms, helpful and friendly. Good restaurant with food all day.

$$ Rosas
Phillippi 269, T61-258 0077.
Heating, restaurant and bar.

$ pp Hostal Kawi
Pedro Silva 144, T61-258 1570.
Comfortable, rooms for 3, meals available, offers fly-fishing trips.

Beyond Porvenir

$$$-$$ Hostería Tunkelen
Arturo Prat Chacón 101, Cerro Sombrero, T61-221 2757, www.hosteriatunkelen.cl.
3 buildings with rooms of different standards: with private bathrooms, shared bathrooms or backpacker dorms. Restaurant. Good for groups.

$$-$ Hostería de la Frontera
San Sebastián, T61-269 6004.
At the border where some buses stop for meals and cakes. Cosy, with bath (the annex is much more basic), good food.

Isla Navarino

$$$$ Lakutaia
2 km west of Puerto Williams, T61-262 1721 (Santiago: T9-6226 8448), www.lakutaia.cl.
A 'base camp' for a range of activities and packages (horse riding, trekking, birdwatching, boating, kayaking, flight tours – book 48 hrs

in advance), 24 double rooms in simple but attractive style, lovely views from spacious public areas, free bike rental, 3 golf 'holes' – most southerly in world!

$$$-$$ Errante Ecolodge
5.5 km west of Puerto Williams, T9-9368 9723, www.errantecolodge.com.
Well away from town, backed by forest, overlooking the channel, lodge has 1 private suite and 2 shared rooms for dorm or family use, wooden construction, self-sufficient and sustainable, good food, very helpful.

$$$-$$ Hostal Beagle
Presidente Ibáñez 147, Puerto Williams, T9-7765 9554.
Pleasant self-service *hostal*, no dorms, but plenty of doubles and triples.

$$ Hostal Akainij
Austral 22, Puerto Williams, T61-262 1173, www.turismoakainij.cl.
Comfortable rooms, very helpful, excellent, filling meals, basic English spoken, adventure tours and transfers.

$$ Hostal Cabo de Ornos
Maragaño 146, Puerto Williams, T61-262 1849.
Good central option above Plaza O'Higgins. Above the *hostal* itself is a good restaurant run by the same owners (see Restaurants).

$$ Hostal Coirón
Maragaño 168, Puerto Williams, T61-262 1227.
Double rooms or dorms, shared or private bath, helpful, good food, relaxed, quite basic, but OK.

$$ Hostal Miramar
Muñoz 155, Puerto Williams, T61-262 1372.
Small, family-run *hostal*, comfortable living areas, good food upon request.

$$ Hostal Pusaki
Piloto Pardo 222, Puerto Williams, T61-262 1116, pattypusaki@yahoo.es.
Double room or dorms, good meals available, owner Patty is helpful and fun.

$$ Refugio El Padrino
Costanera 276, Puerto Williams, T61-262 1136, T9-8438 0843, ceciliamancillao@yahoo.com.ar.
The vivacious Cecilia Mancilla is great fun, good food, musical instruments on hand. Also has camping. Recommended.

Restaurants

Porvenir

$$ Club Croata
Señoret entre Phillippi y Muñoz Gamero, next to the bus stop on the waterfront.
A lively place with good food.

$$-$ El Chispa
Señoret 202, T61-258 0054.
Good restaurant for seafood and other Chilean dishes.

Isla Navarino

$$-$ Resto del Sur
Maragaño 146, Puerto Williams, T61-262 1849.
Above **Hostal Cabo de Ornos**, this restaurant has more food options than other places, including all-you-can-eat pizza on Fri nights.

$ Los Dientes de Navarino
Centro Comercial Sur, Puerto Williams.
Open until 0400 at weekends.
Colombian owner Yamilla incorporated much of her native flavour into this popular eatery, down to the Caldas rum on the shelves and Romeo Santos playing on the TV. Good, wholesome fare, set menu.

Cafés

Panaderías and minimarkets: **Simón & Simón** and **Temuco** are opposite each other on Piloto Pardo, junction Condell. The former seems to be centre of reference in town.

Puerto Luisa
Costanera 317, Puerto Williams, T9-9934 0849, see Facebook.
Espressos, hot chocolate, teas and home-made cakes and pastries.

What to do

Porvenir

For adventure tourism and trekking activities contact tour operators in Punta Arenas (see What to do, page 844). Fly fishing is world-renowned. The area is rich in brown trout, sea-run brook trout and steelheads, weighing 2-14 kg.

Isla Navarino

Boat trips

No tour companies in Puerto Williams go to Cape Horn. It's possible to ask at the yacht club about boat hire, but it all depends on the owner.

Navarino Travel, *Centro Comercial (in the Fio Fio souvenir shop), Puerto Williams, T9-6629 9201, navarinotravel@gmail.com*. Knowledgeable owner Maurice offers boat trips to different destinations around the island, including glaciers.

Wulaia Expeditions, *Yelcho 224, Puerto Williams, T9-9832 6412, wulaiaexpediciones@gmail.com*. Runs all-day boat tours and fishing trips from Puerto Williams to Wulaia Cove, lunch included. About US$800 per trip, better value with parties of 4-6.

Estancias

Estancia Santa Rosa, *Piloto Pardo s/n, T9-8464 2053, fcofilgueira29@gmail.com*. Day tours to the oldest estancia on the island. Activities include kayaking in Bahía Santa, horse riding, trekking and a traditional Chilean BBQ. US$100 for the day.

Tour operators

Akainij, *see Where to stay.*
Navarino Beaver, *T9-9548 7365, barberjorge@gmail.com*. Hunters Miguel and Jorge run beaver-watching tours (including trips to a tannery), beaver hunting, beaver meat sampling. Pretty much everything beaver.
Shila, *O'Higgins 322, Puerto Williams (a hut at entrance to Centro Comercial), T9-7897 2005, www.turismoshila.cl*. Luis Tiznado Gonzáles is an adventure expert, trekking and fishing, equipment hire (bikes, tents, sleeping bags, stoves, and more). Lots of trekking information, sells maps.

Trekking

You must register first with **Carabineros** in Puerto Williams (C Piloto Pardo, near Brito). Tell them when you get back, too. Sometimes they will not allow lone trekking.

There are 2 ferry crossings to Chilean Tierra del Fuego, plus flights to Porvenir and Puerto Williams. The ferry companies accept no responsibility for damage to vehicles.

Porvenir

Air To/from Punta Arenas (weather and bookings permitting), with **Aerovías DAP** (*Señoret s/n, T61-258 0089, Porvenir, www.aeroviasdap.cl*), details under Punta Arenas, Transport. Heavily booked so make sure you have your return reservation confirmed.

Bus The only public transport on Chilean Tierra del Fuego is Jorge Bastian's minibus Porvenir–Cerro Sombrero, T61-234 5406/

9-8503 3662, jorgebastian@hotmail.com, or the driver axelvig20@hotmail.com. Mon, Wed, Fri, leaves Sombrero at 0830, returns from Porvenir Municipalidad, 2 hrs, US$5.

Ferry Crux Australis, sails from Bahía Chilota, 5 km from Porvenir (bus US$2) to Tres Puentes, 5 km north of Punta Arenas at varying times Tue-Sun mostly 1400-2000; less frequent sailings off season. Book through **Tabsa** (*Señoret, seafront in Porvenir, T61-258 0089, Mon-Fri 0900-1200, 1400-1830, www.tabsa.cl*) or through **Comapa** in Punta Arenas. For further details, see page 845.

Beyond Porvenir

Ferry There are 3 boats working continuously daily 0830-2400 on the 20-min crossing from Punta Espora on Bahía Azul (80 km north of Porvenir) to **Punta Delgada**, 170 km northeast of Punta Arenas. For further details, see page 845. There is no bus service to or from this crossing, but if hitching, this route is preferable as there is more traffic.

Puerto Williams

Air To/from Punta Arenas with DAP (details under Punta Arenas). Book well in advance; long waiting lists (be persistent). Also army flights available (they are cheaper), but the ticket has to be bought through DAP. Also from the Aeroclub in Ushuaia (see Ushuaia, Transport). Airport is in town.

Boat Yaghan ferry of Broom, www.tabsa.cl, to/from **Punta Arenas** once a week, 65 passengers, US$164 for Pullman seat, US$230 for sofa-bed seat, 30-34-hr trip through beautiful channels. To/from **Ushuaia** with **Ushuaia Boating**, www.ushuaiaboating.com, US$125 each way, which includes a 30-90 min crossing in a semi-rigid boat to Puerto Navarino, to Puerto Williams, where there's a jetty, the Alcaldía del Mar and 4 more houses, plus a few horses and cows. Ushuaia Boating deals with documents when you buy the ticket, but there is a bit of a wait at Puerto Navarino. The setting is nice and they sometimes offer coffee and pastries for impatient passengers. Then it's a 1-hr ride in a combi on a lovely, *ripio* road past inlets and forests, river outflows, Bahía Mejillones and birdlife to Williams. For return make sure you are clear about transport arrangements. Also **Fernández Campbell** (www.fernandezcampbell.com) has a 1½-hr crossing to/from **Ushuaia**, Fri, Sat, Sun 1000, return 1500, US$125 for foreigners, tickets sold at **Naviera RFC** in Puerto Williams.

Chilean
Pacific Islands

Chile has two national parks in the Pacific: Juan Fernández Islands, a little easier to reach (and leave) now than in Alexander Selkirk's time, and the remarkable Easter Island. In 2007, a constitutional reform gave Easter Island and Juan Fernández the status of special territories.

Juan Fernández Islands

become a castaway in the Pacific

This group of small volcanic islands, with a population of 850, is administered by CONAF and is situated 667 km west of Valparaíso. Declared a UN World Biosphere Reserve in 1977, the islands enjoy a mild climate and the vegetation is rich and varied. Fauna includes wild goats, hummingbirds and seals. The islands are named after Juan Fernández, the first European to visit in 1574. There are three islands: Robinson Crusoe, the largest, Alejandro Selkirk and Santa Clara, the smallest. The islands are famous for langosta de Juan Fernández (a pincerless lobster), which is sent to restaurants on the mainland. Park entry is US$7.75, children US$4.

Robinson Crusoe Island

The island has long been the target for treasure seekers who claim that looted gold from Inca times is buried there. Scot Alexander Selkirk (the original of Defoe's Robinson Crusoe) was put ashore on this island from *HMS Cinque Ports* in 1704 and was taken off four years and four months later by a privateer, the *Duke*. The island has the only settlement in the group, **San Juan Bautista**, a fishing village of wooden frame houses, located on Bahía Cumberland on the north coast: many facilities close to the shore were destroyed by the February 2010 tsunami. The remains of the **Fuerte Santa Bárbara**, the largest of the Spanish fortresses, overlook San Juan Bautista. Near Santa Bárbara are the **Cuevas de los Patriotas**, home to the Chilean independence leaders, deported by the Spanish after the Battle of Rancagua. South of the village is the **Mirador de Selkirk**, a hill on which Selkirk lit his signal fires. A plaque was set in the rock at the look-out point by British naval officers from *HMS Topaze* in 1868; nearby is a more recent plaque placed by his descendants. Selkirk's cave, about 4 km northwest of the village, can be visited on a boat trip. The Mirador is the only easy pass between the north and south sides of the island. Further south is the anvil-shaped **El Yunque**, 915 m, the highest peak on the island, where Hugo Weber, a survivor from the *Dresden*, lived as a hermit for 12 years. (The *Dresden* was a German cruiser, cornered by two British destroyers in Bahía Cumberland in 1915; the scuttled *Dresden* still lies on the seabed and a monument on the shore commemorates the event.) The only sandy beach on Robinson Crusoe is **Playa Arenal**, in the extreme southwest corner, two hours by boat from San Juan Bautista.

Tip...
The best time to visit the Juan Fernández Islands is between October to March; take insect repellent.

Fact...
There are no exchange facilities. Only pesos and US dollars cash are accepted; no credit cards.

Best for
Getting away from it all ▪ Historical mysteries ▪ Seascapes

Tourist information

CONAF
Vicente González 130, San Juan Bautista, T32-268
0381, parquenjfernandez@yahoo.com. Mon-Thu
0800-1250, 1400-1800, Fri 1400-1750.
Information on flora, fauna and services.

Where to stay

Juan Fernández Islands
See www.comunajuanfernandez.cl, www.
sernatur.cl and www.experiencerobinson.com
for other accommodation options.

$$$$ Crusoe Island Lodge
T2-2946 1636 ext 209, 9-7307 8297,
www.crusoeislandlodge.com.
An ecolodge which offers many packages and
activities, as well as therapies in its spa. It also
has a gourmet restaurant.

$$$$ Más a Tierra Ecolodge
Subida el Castillo 128, T9-5379 1915.
Bed-and-breakfast or half-board available, 4 rooms
with bath and terrace, price includes welcome
drink, internet, use of kayaks, tours arranged.

Transport

Juan Fernández Islands
Air Aerolíneas ATA, Av Diego Barros Ortiz
2012B, **Aeropuerto Arturo Merino Benítez**,
T2-2611 3672 (on Robinson Crusoe T9-7389 1826),
www.aerolineasata.cl, and **LASSA**, Av Larraín
7941, **Tobalaba**, T2-2322 3300, lassa@tie.cl,
fly the year round (subject to demand) from
Santiago, 2½ hrs (US$820 round trip). Planes
leave from Aeródromo Tobalaba in La Reina
(eastern outskirts of city) and land on an airstrip
in the west of the island; passengers are taken
by boat to **San Juan Bautista** (1½ hrs, US$2.50
one way). Travelling by sea isn't recommended,
as conditions can be extreme. Still, it's possible
to attempt the journey with a cargo ship, such as
Naviera Iorana (see Facebook) and **Transmarko**,
www.transmarko.cl, US$300 return. **Transmarko**
leaves in the 1st and 3rd weeks of the month.
Pre-booking is essential.

Rapa Nui/Easter Island

mysterious moai in the vast Pacific

Known as the navel of the world by the original inhabitants, this is one of the remotest places on
earth. Isla de Pascua (Rapa Nui) is officially part of V Región of Chile (Valparaíso) but it lies just
south of the Tropic of Capricorn, 3790 km west of Chile and 4050 km from the Great Polynesian
Archipelago (at Tahiti). Its nearest neighbour is Pitcairn Island, some 2081 km away. The island is
triangular in shape, 24 km across, with an extinct volcano at each corner. About half the island,
of low round hills with groves of eucalyptus, is used for horses and cattle, and over a third
constitutes a national park.

Here are some of the most impressive and mysterious sites on earth. The cultural and archeological
treasures of Easter Island were the first of any Pacific island nation to be registered by UNESCO on
its World Heritage list. Whereas other Pacific islands can claim an impressive intangible heritage
(story-telling, music and dance), but little in
terms of structures and artwork, Easter Island
has both tangible and intangible heritage of
epic proportions, including statues, historic
dwellings and petroglyphs that far exceed those
in Polynesia, Melanesia and Micronesia. The
most potent symbols of its past are the 800 or
so *moai*, huge stone figures up to 9 m tall and
broad in proportion that appear trance-like in a
stunning landscape, their gaze fixed on a distant
horizon on the Pacific.

Tip...
Phone calls are expensive. The cheapest way
to call home or mainland Chile is over the
internet. **Omotohi Cybercafé** (Avenida Te
Pito o te Henua, daily 0830-2200 (from 0930
at weekends), offers fast and reliable internet
at US$2 per hour.

Essential Easter Island

Arriving

National Park entry is US$80, children US$40 (Chileans adults pay less); this is payable at the airport when flights arrive, or at the CONAF office (Mataveri Otai s/n, T32-210 0236, hotu.pate@conaf.cl, daily 0830-1700).
Set your watches: Easter Island is always two hours behind the Chilean mainland.

Getting around

In theory, a tour of the main part of the island can be done on foot. This would need at least two days, returning to Hanga Roa in the evening and setting out again the next day, as camping is not permitted in the park (see page 867). You would also need to be in great shape and bear in mind that once you leave Hanga Roa services (including lodging and food) are scarce. If you're walking, take plenty of food and water and inform your hotel or park rangers of your exact route. Good free bilingual tourist maps are available from Sernatur, hotels and tour agencies. More detailed maps (recommended for driving or bicycling) are sold on Avenida Policarpo Toro for about US$18, or at the ranger station at Orongo for US$10. To see more, hire a bicycle, a horse or a vehicle. Sample distances and times: Hanga Roa to Anakena Beach, 17 km, 4½ hours on foot, 1¾ hours by bike; Hanga Roa to Jau-Orongo, 4 km, one hour on foot, 30 minutes by bike; Hanga Roa to Rano Raraku, 25 km, 6½ hours on foot, three hours by bike. Even with a car you will need at least two nights and one long day; a basic loop around the island is 50 to 80 km, depending whether you go off road or not. For driving advice, see page 872. For details of tours, see What to do, page 869.

When to visit

Average monthly temperatures vary between 15-17°C in August and 24°C in February, the hottest month. Average annual rainfall is 1100 mm. There is some rain throughout the year, but the rainy season is March to October (wettest in May). The tourist season is from September to April.

History of Easter Island

It is now generally accepted that the original islanders were of Polynesian origin (see box for the historical and cultural contexts). They called the island *Te Pito o te Henua*, the navel of the world. Over 1000 years of isolation ended in 1722 with the visit of the Dutch admiral, Jacob Roggeven, on Easter Sunday 1722. A Spanish captain, Don Felipe González, arrived in 1770 and claimed the island for the King of Spain, but no Spanish ship came to make it official. British Captain James Cook stopped briefly in 1774, and a French admiral and explorer, le Comte de La Pérouse, spent 11 hours on the island in 1786. Early visitors spent very little time on the island because of the lack of wood and drinking water, but first encounters led to tragic consequences, first with the introduction of diseases, principally venereal, by whalers in the 1800s.

In 1862 eight Peruvian ships kidnapped one third of the population of the island, including the King. Most were sold for use as hard labour on plantations or as domestic servants. Many died, and international outcry forced Peru to repatriate the islanders. Even this task was handled with utmost neglect, so that, out of 1407 Rapa Nui originally taken, only 15 made it back to their homeland. Further indignities ensued. In 1864, the religious order, Société de Picpus, brought new diseases in its mission to christianize the eastern Pacific. They were followed by French sea captain Jean-Baptiste Onéxime Dutroux-Bornier, who was charged with transporting missionaries to the island and instead decided to become its sole ruler. Dutroux-Bornier and the missionaries clashed as each shipped islanders out, the former to plantations in Tahiti, the latter to missions elsewhere. The Frenchman was eventually murdered, but by this time only 175 islanders were left and, historians believe, the culture and traditions of Rapa Nui had been irreversibly destroyed.

In 1888 Captain Policarpo Toro Hurtado took formal possession of the island, and the chiefs ceded sovereignty to Chile 'forever'. In fact, a single wool company became the new ruler, and, yet again, treatment of the islanders was so appalling that in desperation, the Rapa Nui petitioned the Chilean government to allow them to emigrate en masse to Tahiti. A rebellion erupted in 1914 and the Chilean navy was sent to restore order. In 1953 the Chilean government took over the administration of the island, but it was not until 1967, the year of the first regular

ON THE ROAD

The cultural development of Easter Island

Among the prominent 20th-century theories concerning the colonization of Easter Island, those of the late Thor Heyerdahl, as expressed in *Aku-Aku, The Art of Easter Island* (1975), based on South American influence, became less widely accepted at the turn of the century, as the theory of Polynesian origin gained ascendency. According to the latter theory, the islanders came from possibly the Marquesas Islands or Mangareva, between about AD 400-600, and that by AD 1000 the island's society was established.

The very precise stone fitting of some of the *ahu*, and the tall gaunt *moai* with elongated faces and ears for which Easter Island is best known came quite late in the development of island culture. The *moai* were sculpted at the Rano Raraku quarry and transported on wooden rollers over more or less flat paths to their final locations; their red topknots were sculpted at and brought from the inland quarry of Puna Pau; and the rounded pebbles, laid out checkerboard fashion at the *ahu*, all came from the same beach at Vinapu.

The theory held that with the growth in sophistication of Easter Island society, almost all the island's trees were felled. The wood was used for building fishing vessels and most probably for transporting and supporting statues. Deforestation led to soil erosion, the extinction of up to half the native plants, loss of nesting sites for birds and no means of making fishing boats. Rapa Nui, according to Jared Diamond in *Collapse: How Societies Choose to Fail or Succeed* (2005), was "the clearest example of a society that destroyed itself by overexploiting its own resources". What followed were brutal wars between the clans that erupted by the end of 17th century.

After the islanders had lost their clan territoriality and were concentrated at Hanga Roa, inter-clan rivalry was stimulated by the birdman cult at Orongo. The central feature was an annual ceremony in which the heads of the lineages, or their representatives, raced to the islets of Motu Nui, Motu Iti and Motu Kao to obtain the first egg of the sooty tern (known as the Manatara). The winning chief was named Bird Man, Tangata Manu, for the following year. It appears that the egg represented fertility to the cult, although it is less clear what the status of the Tangata Manu actually was.

The "ecocide" theory and almost everything to do with it was questioned by Carl Lipo and Terry Hunt in *The Statues that Walked* (2011). They claim that Polynesians arrived in about AD 1200; that the rats that arrived with them caused far greater destruction of the palm forests, by eating the tree roots, than the humans; that the statues were "walked", not rolled to their ceremonial sites (much as Heyerdahl demonstrated); and that the population, after rapid growth, was stable until the arrival of Europeans. The environment was damaged, but as other research has proposed, the people learnt how to prevent soil erosion by "sowing" stones on their fields and supplemented their diet with rat meat. Serious decline was precipitated by the arrival of European diseases, not before.

commercial flight, that relaxation of colonial rules took place and interests of the islanders were taken into consideration.

Modern Easter Island Although administratively the island belongs to the Valparaíso Region of Chile, Easter Island is run (at least in theory) by an independent Council of Chiefs and elected local officials. It is the only commune of the Provincia de Isla de Pascua. According to officials, it has about 6000 residents, of whom some 60% are descendants of the aboriginal Rapa Nui. Most live in the village of **Hanga Roa**. Rapa Nui and Spanish are the official languages; some people speak English and/or French. Rapa Nui has its own script recorded on tablets. Although it is not widely used, it is being studied and may be implemented again. The islanders have preserved their indigenous songs and dances, and are extremely hospitable. Chile provides good education and health care for all and the local diet is much healthier than on many Pacific islands. The range of services includes a modern mobile phone network, reliable internet, a television station, stadium, gymnasiums, a modern bank and excellent running water and electricity. Foreigners and Chileans from the mainland cannot own land on Easter Island, even if they live and work there, or are married to a local. Nevertheless, islanders own very little land outside Hanga Roa; the national park covers more than a third of the island, but negotiations for other land to be returned to the islanders are in progress. Easter Islanders do not pay taxes and they refuse entry to insurance companies, junk food outlets, public buses and other concepts they find hostile to their traditional culture. The flag of Easter Island is white charged with a red reimiro, a wooden pectoral ornament once worn by the women of the island. It was adopted on 9 May 2006.

Hanga Roa and around

There is one village on the island, Hanga Roa, where most of the population live. In front of the football field is Ahu Tautira. Next to it is a swimming area marked out with concrete walls and a breakwater (cold water). There is a cultural centre next to the football field, with an exhibition hall and souvenir stall. To the east is an interesting modern church with locally stylized religious art and carvings, mixing Catholic themes with elements of the cult of the Bird Man. Services are held on Sundays with hymns sung in Rapa Nui.

The **Museo Antropológico Sebastián Englert** ① *2 km north of town, very near Ahu Tahai, T32-255 1020, www.museorapanui.cl, Tue-Fri 0930-1730, Sat and Sun 0930-1230, closed for some public hols, free*, has good descriptions of island life, although most of the objects are reproductions since the originals were removed from the island. Free guided visits are available with advance notice. In the same complex is the excellent **William Molloy Library** ① *Tue-Fri 0930-1230, 1430-1730*, where only locals are allowed to borrow books.

A 15-minute walk from town is Ahu Tahai (a *moai* with eyes and topknot, plus a cave house). It's a great place for watching the sunset and is the start of a six-hour walk along the west coast. Two caves can be reached north from here: the one inland appears to be a ceremonial centre, while the other (nearer the sea) has two 'windows' (take a strong flashlight and be careful). Further north is Ahu Te Peu, with a broken *moai* and ruined houses. Beyond here you can join the path to Hanga o Teo (see below), or turn right, inland to Te Pahu cave and the seven *moai* at Akivi. Either return to Hanga Roa or continue to the Puna Pau crater (two hours), where the *moai's* distinctive red topknots were carved.

South of Hanga Roa is Rano Kau, the extinct volcano where the curious Orongo ruins can be seen. The road south from Hanga Roa passes the two caves of Ana Kai Tangata, one of which has paintings, and continues southeast. If, however, you're on foot, take the path just past the CONAF sign for a much shorter route to the impressive Rano Kau crater. A lake with many reed islands lies 200 m below the rim of the crater. Locals occasionally scramble down to collect medicinal herbs. On the seaward side of the volcano is Orongo, one of the most important sites on the island, with many ruined buildings and petroglyphs, where the bird man cult flourished. Out to sea are the 'bird islets', Motu Nui, Motu Iti and Motu Kao. It is very windy at the summit, with good views at sunset or under a full moon. It is easy to follow the road back to Hanga Roa in the dark.

Rest of the island

From Hanga Roa, take the road going southeast past the airport; at the oil tanks turn right to Vinapu, where there are two *ahu* and a wall whose stones are joined with Inca-like precision. Head back northeast along the south coast to reach first Vaihu (an *ahu* with eight broken *moai* and a small harbor), then Akahanga (an *ahu* with toppled *moai*) and Hanga Tetenga (a toppled *moai* and an *ahu*, with bones visible inside). Beyond is Ahu Tongariki, the largest platform on the island with a row of 15 *moai*, which was damaged by a tidal wave in 1960 and later restored with Japanese aid. Turn left here to Rano Raraku (2 km), the volcano where the *moai* were originally carved and where many statues can still be seen, some of them buried to the neck, a breathtaking sight. In the crater is a small lake surrounded by reeds; swimming is possible beyond the reeds. The road heads north past 'the trench of the long ears'; an excursion can be made from here east to Poike headland to see the open-mouthed statue that is particularly popular with local carvers. Ask the farmer for permission to cross his land. At the northeast end of the headland is the cave where a virgin was kept before marriage to the victor of ceremonies during the time of the bird man cult; ask someone for directions. The road along the north coast passes Ahu Te Pito Kura, the 10-m-tall *moai* is one of the largest ever brought to a platform. The road continues to Ovahe where there is a very attractive beach with pink sand and some rather recently carved faces and a cave.

From Ovahe, you can return direct to Hanga Roa or continue to the palm-fringed, white-sand beach at Anakena, the site of the village of the island's first king, Hotu Matua and the spot where Thor Heyerdahl landed in 1955; his visit is commemorated with a plaque. The moai here has been restored to its probable original state. There is a picnic area and stalls selling meat and tuna *empanadas* (US$4.50). From Anakena a coastal path of variable quality runs west, passing beautiful cliff scenery and interesting remains. The path skirts the island's highest point, the extinct volcano of Terevaka (507 m), to which you can trek for a view of the ocean on all sides. At Hanga o Teo, there appears to be a large village complex, with several round houses, while further on is a burial place, built like a long ramp with several ditches containing bones. From Hanga o Teo the path goes west then south, inland from the coast, to meet the road north of Hanga Roa.

Listings Rapa Nui/Easter Island

Tourist information

Anyone wishing to spend time exploring the island would be well-advised to speak to **CONAF** first (Mataveri Otai s/n, T32-210 0236, hotu.pate@conaf.cl, open 0830-1700); they also give good advice on special interests (biology, archaeology, handicrafts, etc). Also try **Sernatur** (C Policarpo Toro s/n, T32-210 0255, ipascua@sernatur.cl, Mon-Thu 0830-1700, Fri 0830-1630) and the following useful websites: **www. islandheritage.org** (Easter Island Foundation,

in English) and **www.rapanui.co.cl** (the Easter Island newspaper). The book, *A Companion to Easter Island*, by James Grant Peterkin (the British Consul, c/o Easter Island Spirit, Tu'u Koihu s/n, T9-8741 5166), in English is on sale on the island and in Santiago airport.

The **post office** is half a long block up from Caleta Hanga Roa on Av Te Pito o te Henua. It sells Easter Island stamps, post cards and will put a souvenir stamp in your passport on request, Mon-Fri 0900-1300, 1430-1800, Sat. 0900-1230.

Tip...
ATMs can dispense 200,000 pesos daily. Cash can be exchanged in shops, hotels, etc, at about 5% less than Santiago. Credit cards are widely accepted for purchases, but some places add a surcharge. US dollars may be accepted, at poor rates. **Banco del Estado** (Avenida Pont, T32-210 0221, Monday-Friday 0800-1300), has an ATM that accepts MasterCard and Cirrus, offers cash advances on Visa and reasonable rates for dollars or euros. **Banco Santander** (Policarpo Toro on the waterfront, T32-251 8007, Monday-Friday 0800-1300) has an ATM that accepts Visa and MasterCard. It also has an ATM in the airport departure area. There is another reliable ATM at the gas station shop on Avenida Hotu Matua.

Where to stay

Unless it is a particularly busy season, there is no need to book in advance; mainland agencies make exorbitant booking charges. The airport information desk has an accommodation list. Flights are met by large numbers of hotel and residencial representatives with whom you can negotiate. Alternatively, take a taxi to the centre of Hanga Roa, drop your things in a café and look around. Many places offer accommodation and tours (rates ranging from US$25 to US$150 pp, includes meals). Rates, especially in residenciales, can be cheaper out of season and if you do not take full board.

$$$$ Explora En Rapa Nui
reserve in Santiago T2-2395 2800, in US T1-866 750 6699, or through www.explora.com.
All-inclusive hotel, easily one of the poshest in the South Pacific. Intentionally hard to find (take

Cross Island road, turn right about 6 km from town on the wider unpaved road), transport provided for guests, as are all food, drinks and tours. Views of the ocean are tremendous and each room has a jacuzzi.

$$$$ Gomero
Av Tu'u Koihu, T32-210 0313,
www.hotelgomero.com.
Comfortable place near the beach, spotless, cosy rooms. Restaurant, pool.

$$$$ Hanga Roa
Av Pont, T2-29570141, www.hotelhangaroa.cl.
The largest hotel in town, within walking distance of centre. Full board, excellent ocean views, spa and pool.

$$$$ Iorana
Ana Magaro s/n, outside Hanga Roa, opposite airport, 30 mins' walk from town, T32-210 0312 (Santiago T2-2695 2058), www.ioranahotel.cl.
3-star, hot water morning and evening, comfortable, small pool, good views.

$$$$ O'Tai
Te Pito o Te Henua s/n, T32-210 0250,
www.hotelotai.com.
Great location, pool, lovely gardens, restaurants, best rooms with terrace, family-run.

$$$$ Taha Tai
Api Na Nui s/n, T32-255 1192,
www.hoteltahatai.cl.
Well-kept bright hotel with rooms or cabins, sea view, small swimming pool, tours organized.

$$$$-$$$ Chez Cecilia
Policarpo Toro y Atamu Tekema, near Tahai Moai, T32-210 0499, see Facebook.
Packages with tours offered, excellent food. Rooms, *cabañas* or camping ($), quiet, free airport transfer.

$$$$-$$$ Taura'a
C Principal s/n, T32-210 0463,
www.tauraahotel.cl.
Upmarket B&B, very comfy, good beds, spacious bathrooms, nice garden, good service. **Taura'a Tours** is also good.

$$$ Cabañas Sunset
Near Ahu Tahai site and old cemetery, T32-255 2171.
Spotless *cabañas* overlooking the sea, discounts for Handbook users, ask for the owner, Ms 'China' Pakarati. She also arranges full day tours for groups of 1-4.

$$$ HI Kona Tau
Avareipua, T32-210 0321, https:// konatauhostelling.com.
HI hostel, $ pp in dorms, all rooms with bath

$$$ Inaki Uhi
Atamu Tekena s/n, T32-210 0231,
www.inakiuhi.com.
Clean hostel and a central, good option. 15 rooms (triples available). Also arranges a wide range of tours.

$$$ Mana Nui Inn
Tahai s/n, opp cemetery, T32-210 0811,
www.mananui.cl.
Pleasant cabins and rooms on north edge of town, airport transfers, tours run.

$$$ Orongo
Atamu Tekena s/n, T32-210 0572,
www.hotel-orongo.com.
Half-board available (excellent restaurant), good service, nice garden.

$$$ Residencial Tadeo y Lili
Apina Ichi s/n, T32-210 0422,
tadeolili@entelchile.net.
Simple but clean, French-Rapa Nui run, all rooms with sea view and terrace, tours.

$$-$ Mihinoa
Av Pont s/n, T32-255 1593,
www.camping-mihinoa.com.
Campsite, which hires out camping equipment, with dorms, a few rooms and cabin. Huge kitchen for campers, airport transfers, welcoming, exceptional value.

Camping
Camping is not allowed anywhere in the national park. Many people offer campsites in their gardens, check availability of water first. Some families can also provide food.

Restaurants

Some *residenciales* offer full board. Vegetarians will have no problems on the island; locally produced fruit and vegetables are plentiful and cheaper than meat and other foodstuffs, which are imported from mainland. Locally caught fish is also good value. Wine and beer are expensive by Chilean standards because of freight charges.

Another local favourite, **Los Carritos**, is in a group of a few cheap eateries near the football field. Try tuna *empanadas* and delicious fruit juices at **Carrito Hitu**, Tuu Maheke s/n (near corner of Apina), which also has a good *menú del día*. On Av Te Pito o te Henua near Av Atamu Tekena is **Donde el Gordo**, the best place for *completo* (besides wraps, huge *empanadas*, fruit juices etc, at very affordable prices).

$$$ La Kaleta, Hanga Roa
T32-255 2244, www.lakaletarestaurant.com.
Superb ocean views and great seafood. Try the tuna steak or ceviche, arguably the best on the island. Tucked away behind the diving schools.

$$$ Te Moana
Hanga Roa.
Lovely outdoors terrace with ocean views, good steaks, fresh seafood, creative cuisine. Live music at weekends.

$$ Haka Honu
Av Policarpo Toro s/n .
Popular seafood restaurant, excellent tuna carpaccio, great (and huge) salads. Also good for a cocktail in the evening. Friendly staff, sea views.

$$ Tataku Vave
Caleta Hanga Piko s/n, T32-255 1544, see Facebook.
Worth the detour, this ocean front restaurant offers great pastas and salads, as well as seafood dishes. One-way taxi fare to the restaurant included if you book in advance.

$ Ariki o Te Pana (also known as Tia Berta)
Av Atamu Tekena s/n, T32-210 0171.
Mon-Sat lunch and dinner.
For inexpensive local and Chilean food. Aunt Berta makes delicious *empanadas*, filled with tuna and cheese, meat, cheese, veggies etc. Great value at US$4.50 per huge *empanada*.

$ Toromiro Café
Av Atamu Tekena s/n.
Excellent Jamaican coffee and great value for money breakfast and lunch.

Bars and clubs

Several places in town offer music and entertainment; one of the best is **Kari Kari** at Hotel Hanga Roa, T32-210 0595, 3 times a week, US$15. Late-night clubs get going after 0100. Drinks are expensive: **Piriti** (near airport, Thu-Sat); **Toroko** (Caleta Hanga Roa, near harbour, daily), slightly "rougher" ambience; **Topa Tangi** (Atamu Tekena, Thu and Sat 2300-0300), popular pub, with free shows and dancers on Thu.

Festivals

End Jan/early Feb Tapati, or **Semana Rapa Nui**, 10 days of dancing competitions, singing, sports (horse racing, swimming, modified decathlon), body-painting, typical foods (lots of small booths by the football field), necklace-making, etc. Everyone gets involved, many tourists too. Only essential activities continue outside the festival.

Shopping

All shops and rental offices close 1400-1700.

On Av Atamu Tekena, the main street, there are lots of small shops and market stalls (which may close during rain) and a couple of supermarkets. Wood carvings and stone *moais* are available throughout Hanga Roa. The expensive Mercado Artesanal, left of church, will give you a good view of what is available – authentic, no compunction to buy. Good pieces cost from US$50 to US$200. Souvenirs at dozens of decent places on Atamu Tekena.

What to do

Diving
Mike Rapu, *Caleta Hanga Roa Otai s/n, T32-255 1055, www.mikerapu.cl.* Diving courses, expeditions, fishing trips and kayaks.
Orca, *Caleta Hanga Roa, T32-255 0877, www.orcadivingcenter.cl.* Run by Michel and Henri García, very experienced (Henri is a member of the **Cousteau Society**), PADI courses, with dive shop and surf equipment rental. Both have similar prices: introductory dive US$60; single dive for experienced diver US$45-66; also night dives and boat trips with snorkeling (from US$22). Both at the harbour, all equipment provided.

Horse riding
The best way to see the island, provided you are fit, is on horseback: horses, US$55 for a day, including guide. **Cabañas Pikera Uri** (T32-210 0577, www.pikerauri.com), offers several riding tours, as well as *cabañas* for overnight stays.

Tour operators
Many agencies, residenciales and locals arrange excursions around the island. The English of other tour guides is improving. Half- and full-day tours of the island by minibus cost US$50-100 pp, including guide, without lunch. For the best light go early or late in the day.
Aku-Aku Tours, *Tu'u Koihu s/n, T32-210 0770, www.akuakuturismo.cl.* Wide range of tours.

Easter Island Travel, *T32-210 0510, www. easterisland.travel.* Offers a wide range of tours, good reports.

Haumaka Archeological Guide Services, *Av Atamu Tekena y Hotu Matua, T32-210 0274.* English spoken.

Rapa Nui Travel, *Tu'u Koihu s/n, T32-210 0548, www.rapanuitravel.com.* Recommended agency with years of experience. Ask for Terangi Pakarati, a well-informed and super friendly local guide, who speaks English, Spanish and Rapa Nui.

Transport

The airport runway has been improved to provide emergency landing for US space shuttles.

Air Airport terminal is tiny but it has several reasonably priced souvenir shops and a café. No internet, but good mobile phone signal. For those in transit, in the garden at the departure lounge stands one lonely *moai*. Taxi to town centre US$3. **LATAM** (Av Atamu Tekena s/n, near Av Pont, T600-526 2000, Mon-Fri 0900-1630, Sat 0900-1230) fly daily in high season, less often in low season, 5-5½ hrs going east, 3½-4 hrs going west (most flights continue to **Papeete**, **Tahiti**). The cheapest return fare from **Santiago**, booked well in advance, is about US$600, with occasional special deals available through travel agents. Under 24s and over 65s are often eligible for a 28% discount on some fares. If you fly between Papeete and Santiago or vice versa, you will be considered in transit and will not be allowed to exit the airport. So, if flying to or from Tahiti, check if you can stay over till another flight.

Car hire Many vehicle hire agencies on the main street. US$ 65-200 per day for a small 4WD with manual transmission (usually). In theory, a Chilean or international driving licence is necessary, but your national licence will usually do. If a rental company makes a fuss, go next door.

There is no insurance available, drive at your own risk; be careful at night, since deep potholes and wild horses are not uncommon. Speeding, drunk driving and poor driving skills are also a problem on the island. If you are hit, demand that the person who dented your car and the rental car agency settle the bill. If you hit something or someone, you will be expected to pay, cash only. The speed limit in Hanga Roa is under 30 kph. Check oil and water before setting out. There is only 1 petrol station, near the airport. **Oceanic Rent-A-Car**, Atamu Tekena s/n, T32-210 0986, www.rentacaroceanic.com. The biggest rental car agency on the island. **Insular**, Atamu Tekena s/n, T32-210 0480, www. rentainsular.cl. Jeeps from US$66 and motorbikes from US$45. You can also rent scooters (US$50 for 24 hrs), bicycles (from US$12 from your *residencial*) and quadbikes.

Taxi Taxis cost a flat US$3 within Hanga Roa. Longer trips can be negotiated, with the cost depending mainly on the time. For example, a round-trip to the beach at Anakena costs about US$25 (per taxi); be sure to arrange for the taxi driver to pick you up at a predetermined time. For touring the island, it is cheaper to hire a car or take a tour if there are more than 3 people sharing.

Practicalities
Getting around

Air

LATAM ① www.latam.com (formerly LAN) has a modern fleet and good service between Santiago and major towns and cities, but allow plenty of time when checking in. If you didn't print your boarding pass from the internet, there are machines to do so at the airport before you get to the counter to drop luggage. Sky ① www.skyairline.cl, has a less extensive network than LATAM. On long routes with stops, check if it is cheaper to buy each sector separately. Confirm domestic flights at least 24 hours before your departure.

Tip...
Try to sit on the left flying south, on the right flying north to get the best views of the Andes.

Rail

There are passenger services from Santiago to Chillán; regional train lines in the Valparaíso and Concepción areas; a scenic line from Talca along the valley of the Río Maule to Constitución. In the far north, the line from Arica to Tacna (Peru) carries passengers, if it is running. Plans to revive the Arica–La Paz line are still under discussion, but a tourist train now runs as far as Poconchile in the Valle de Lluta. Trains in Chile are moderately priced. See Santiago, transport, page 702, for rail company offices.

Road

Bus
Buses are frequent and on the whole good. Apart from holiday times, there is little problem getting a seat on a long-distance bus. *Salón-cama* services run between main cities on overnight services. Tur-Bus ① www.turbus.cl, and Pullman ① www.pullman.cl, each covering the whole country as far south as Puerto Montt, are among the best companies. Standards on routes vary. *Prémium* buses have six fully reclining seats. *Salón-cama* means 25 seats, *semi-cama* means 41 and *salón-ejecutivo* or *clásico* means 45 seats. Stops are infrequent. Many bus itineraries can be checked online but often a Chilean ID card number is needed for buying tickets online. Since there is lots of competition between bus companies, fares may be bargained lower with smaller operators, particularly just before departure. Prices are highest between December and March, and during the Independence celebrations in September. Students with ISIC cards may get discounts, except in high season; discounts are also often available for return journeys. Most bus companies will carry bicycles, but may ask for payment.

Pachamama by Bus ① Agustinas 2113, Santiago, T2-2688 8018, www.pachamamabybus.com, is a backpackers' hop-on, hop-off bus service running from Santiago to the north and south weekly, taking scenic routes with frequent stops, with camping where hostel accommodation is not available. English-speaking guides.

Hitchhiking
Hitchhiking is generally easy and safe throughout Chile, although you may find that in some regions traffic is sparse, so you are less likely to catch a lift (drivers will sometimes make hand signals if they are only going a short distance beyond – this is not a rude gesture!).

Taxi
Taxis have meters, but agree beforehand on fares for long journeys out of city centres or special excursions. In some places a surcharge is applied late at night. Taxi drivers may not know the location of streets away from the centre. There is no need to tip unless some extra service, like the carrying

TRAVEL TIP

Driving in Chile

Road Most roads are in good condition and about a quarter are paved. The main road is the Panamericana (Ruta 5) from Arica to Chiloé. It is motorway from La Serena to Puerto Montt. A coastal route running much of the length of Chile is being paved. Motorways tolls are very expensive, but the charge includes towing to the next city and free ambulance in case of accident.

Safety In the south (particularly on the Carretera Austral), and in the desert north, always top up your fuel tank and carry spare fuel (you may have to buy a can if renting a car). *Carabineros* (national police) are strict about speed limits (100-120 kph on motorways): *Chiletur Copec* maps mark police posts. Car drivers should have all their papers in order and to hand as there are occasional checks. In suburban areas, headlights should be switched on, day and night.

Documents For drivers of private vehicles entering Chile from Argentina, there is a special *salida y admisión temporal de vehículos* form. From Peru or Bolivia, customs type out a *título de importación temporal de vehículos* (temporary admission), valid for the length of stay granted by immigration. Your immigration entry/exit card is stamped '*entrada con vehículo*' so you must leave the country with your vehicle (so you cannot go to Bariloche, for example, without your car). Foreigners must have an international driving licence. Insurance is obligatory and can be bought at borders. A *carnet de passages* is not officially required for foreign-owned motorcycles: a temporary import paper is given at the border.

Organizations Automóvil Club de Chile, Avenida Andrés Bello 1863, Providencia, Santiago, T600-464 4040, www.automovilclub.cl. It has a countrywide network and a car hire agency (with discounts for members or affiliates).

Car hire Shop around as there is a lot of competition. Reputable Chilean companies offer much better value than the well-known international ones, although rates may not always include insurance or 19% VAT. The daily rate for the smallest car starts at US$30 in the north of the country, which rises to about US$50 in Santiago; a saloon car starts at US$55 and a small jeep US$85. The legal age for renting a car is 22. In northern Chile, where mountain roads are bad, check rental vehicles very carefully before setting out. Hire companies charge a large premium to collect the car from another city, so unless making a round-trip it makes economic sense to travel by public transport, then rent a car locally. If intending to leave the country in a hired car, you must obtain authorization from the hire company.

Fuel Gasoline (*bencina*) becomes more expensive the further north and further south you go. Unleaded fuel, 93, 95 and 97 octane, US$1-1.50, is available in all main cities. Diesel is widely available, US$1-1.25 a litre. Larger service stations usually accept credit cards, but check before filling up.

of luggage, is given, but rounding up the change is appreciated. Black *colectivos* (collective taxis) in urban areas operate on fixed routes identified by numbers and destinations. They have fixed charges, often little more expensive than buses, which increase at night and which are usually advertised in the front windscreen. They are flagged down on the street corner (in some cities such as Puerto Montt there are signs). Take small change as the driver takes money and offers change while driving. Yellow *colectivos* also operate on some inter-urban routes, leaving from a set point when full.

Maps

The **Instituto Geográfico Militar** ① *Dieciocho 369, Santiago, T2-2410 9363, www.igm.cl, Mon-Thu 0830-1300, 1400-1700, Fri 0830-1300, 1400-1600*, has detailed geophysical and topographical maps of the whole of Chile, useful for climbing; expensive, but the **Biblioteca Nacional** ① *Alameda 651, Santiago, T2-2360 5200*, will allow you to photocopy. *Matassi* maps (JLM Mapas), available from www.travelaid.cl, from US$7.75, usually with a red cover, are good value but often contain errors. The *Chiletur Copec* guides (see Tourist information, page 877) are useful for roads and towns, but not all distances are exact. Good road maps are also published by Tur-Bus.

Where to stay

Chile has its share of international chains and some 'historic' establishments. Boutique hotels and characterful B&Bs are becoming more common and in most parts of Chile accommodation is plentiful across the budget ranges. In popular tourist destinations, especially in the south in high season, many families offer rooms: these are advertised by a sign in the window. People often meet buses to offer rooms, which vary greatly in quality and cleanliness; have a look before committing. In summer especially, single rooms can be hard to find.

On hotel bills IVA (VAT) is charged at 19%. The government waives VAT on hotel bills paid in dollars or euros at authorized hotels only. As a result, larger hotels (but few other establishments) can offer you much lower tariffs if you pay in dollars or euros than those advertised in pesos. But check the exchange rate: it may be so poor that you end up paying more in dollars than in pesos. Establish clearly in advance what is included in the room price. See Planning your trip for our hotel price guide.

Camping

Campsites often charge US$15-20 for up to five people, but if a site is not full, owners may give a pitch to a single camper for US$7-10. A few hostels allow camping in their garden and offer good value rates. Cheap gas stoves can be bought in camping shops in Santiago and popular trekking areas and green replaceable cylinders are available. Campsites are very busy in January and February.

Wild camping is easy and safe in remote areas of the far south and in the cordillera north of Santiago. In Mapuche and Aymará communities it is courteous and advisable to go to the primary school or some other focal point to meet prominent members of the community first. Camping wild in the north is difficult, because of the lack of water. In much of central and central-southern Chile the land is fenced off and as it is officially illegal to camp on private land without permission, it may be necessary to ask first. Also note that in the Lake District and Chiloé, between mid-December and mid-January, huge horseflies (*tábanos*) can be a real problem when camping, hiking and fishing: do not wear dark clothing.

Youth hostels

www.backpackerschile.com focuses on hostels charging around US$15-25 per person of a good standard. There are youth hostels (*albergues*) throughout Chile; average cost about US$10-24 per person. Although some hostels are open only from January to the end of February, many operate all year round. The IH card is usually readily accepted, but YHA affiliated hostels are not necessarily the best. A Hostelling International card costs US$22. These can be obtained from **Asociación Chilena de Albergues Turísticos Juveniles** ① *Hernando de Aguirre 201, of 401, Providencia, Santiago, T2-2411 2050*. In summer there are makeshift hostels in many Chilean towns, usually in the main schools; they charge up to US$7 per person and are good meeting places. Don't expect much sleep or privacy, though.

Food & drink

Eating out

Breakfast is usually instant coffee or tea with bread, butter and jam. Lunch, served from 1300 to 1530, tends to be the main meal of the day and many restaurants serve a cheaper fixed-price meal at lunch time. When this consists of a single dish it is known as *la colación*, when there is more than one course it is called *el menú*. In more expensive places, this may not be referred to on the menu. Dinner is between 2000 and 2230. *Las onces* (literally elevenses) is the name given to a snack usually including tea, bread, cheese, etc, eaten by many Chileans as their evening meal. The cheapest restaurants in urban areas tend to be by the transport terminals and markets or, in coastal areas, by the port. Also try the *casinos de bomberos* (firemen's canteens) in most towns. See Planning your trip for our restaurant price guide.

Food

A very typical Chilean dish is *cazuela de ave* (or *de vacuno*), a nutritious stew containing large pieces of chicken (or beef), pumpkin, potatoes, rice, and maybe onions, and green peppers. *Valdiviano* is another stew, common in the south, consisting of beef, onion, sliced potatoes and eggs. *Empanadas de pino* are turnovers filled with meat, onions, raisins, olives and egg chopped up together. *Pastel de choclo* is a casserole of meat and onions with olives, topped with a maize-meal mash, baked in an earthenware bowl. *Humitas* are mashed sweetcorn mixed with butter and spices and baked in sweetcorn leaves. *Prieta* is a blood sausage stuffed with cabbage leaves. A normal *parrillada* or *asado* is a giant mixed grill served from a charcoal brazier. *Bife/lomo a lo pobre* (a poor man's steak) can be just the opposite: it is a steak topped by two fried eggs, chips and fried onions. The Valparaíso speciality is the *chorrillana*, chips topped with fried sliced steak, fried onions and scrambled eggs, while in Chiloé you can enjoy a *curanto*, a meat, shellfish and potato stew traditionally cooked in a hole in the ground. Many dishes in Mapuche districts are flavoured with *merkén*, a spice blend of smoked red goat's horn pepper, toasted coriander seed and salt. Ready-made packets are sold.

What gives Chilean food its personality is the **seafood**. The delicious congrio fish is a national dish, and *caldillo de congrio* (a soup served with a massive piece ofred or pink cusk-eel, onions and potatoes) is excellent. A *paila* can take many forms (the *paila* is simply a kind of dish), but the commonest are made of eggs or seafood. *Paila chonchi* is a kind of bouillabaisse, but has more flavour, more body, more ingredients. *Parrillada de mariscos* is a dish of grilled mixed seafood, brought to the table piping hot on a charcoal brazier. Other excellent local fish are the *cojinova*, the *albacora* (swordfish) and the *corvina* (bass). A range of mussels (*choritos/cholgas*) is available, as are abalone (*locos*), clams (*almejas*) and razor clams (*machas*). Some bivalve shellfish may be periodically banned because they carry the disease **marea roja** (which is fatal in humans). *Cochayuyo* is seaweed, bound into bundles, described as 'hard, leathery thongs'. The *erizo*, or sea-urchin, is also commonly eaten as are *picorocos* (sea barnacles) and the strong flavoured *piure*. *Luche* is dried seaweed, sold as a black cake, like 'flakey bread pudding' to be added to soups and stews. **Avocado** pears (*paltas*) are excellent, and play an important role in recipes. Make sure that vegetables are included in the price for the main dish; menus often don't make this clear. Note for vegetarians: the "vegetarian menu" in restaurants usually includes fish, or only vegetables (with no rice or beans). Local **fast food** is excellent. *Completos* are hot dogs with a huge variety of fillings. A *barros jarpa* is a grilled cheese and ham sandwich and a *barras luco* is a grilled cheese and beef sandwich. *Sopaipillas* are cakes made of a mixture including pumpkin, served in syrup. Ice cream is very good; try *lúcuma* and *chirimoya* (custard apple) flavours.

Drink

Tap **water** is safe to drink in main cities but bottled water is safer for the north. The local **wines** are very good; the best are from the central areas. The bottled wines cost from US$3 upwards; the very best wines will cost about US$50 in a smart restaurant. **Beer** is quite good and cheap. Draught lager is known as Schop. Chilean brewed beers include Cristal, Escudo and Royal Guard, Austral (good in the far south), Báltica, Brahma and Heineken. Malta, a brown ale, is recommended for those wanting a British-type beer. There are good local breweries in Valparaíso, the Elqui valley (Guayacán), Punta Arenas and Llanquihue near Puerto Varas and an increasing number of microbreweries around the country. Bars in the capital give as much prominence to craft and other beers as to wine.

Pisco, made from grapes, is the most famous spirit. It is best drunk as a *pisco sour* with lime or lemon juice and sugar. Two popular drinks are **vaina**, a mixture of brandy, egg and sugar and **cola de mono**, a mixture of aguardiente, coffee, milk and vanilla served very cold at Christmas. **Chicha** is any form of alcoholic drink made from fruit, usually grapes. **Cider** (*chicha de manzana*) is popular in the south. **Mote con huesillo**, made from wheat hominy and dried peaches, is a soft drink, refreshing in summer. A *vitamina* is a 100% pure fruit juice drink.

Coffee is generally instant except in espresso bars in major cities. Elsewhere specify *café-café* or *expresso*. A *cortado* is an espresso with hot frothed milk served in a glass. Tea is widely available. If you order *café*, or *té*, *con leche*, it will come with all milk; if you want just a little milk, you must specify that. After a meal, try an *agüita* (infusion) – hot water in which herbs such as mint or aromatics such as lemon peel have been steeped. There is a wide variety, very refreshing.

Essentials A-Z

Accident and emergency

Air rescue service: T138. For earthquake updates and other information see the **Ministerio del Interior y Seguridad Pública** website, www. onemi.cl, and www.reddeemergencia.cl. **Ambulance** (*ambulancia*): T131. **Fire brigade** (*bomberos*): T132, www.bomberos.cl. **Forest fires** (*incendios forestales*): T130. **Police** (*carabineros*): T133; (detectives, *investigaciones*) T134. **Policía Internacional** (E Ramírez 852, Santiago, T2-2708 1043, www.policia.cl, Mon-Fri 0800-1400), handle immigration, lost tourist cards.

Electricity

220 volts AC, 50 cycles. Sockets are 3 round pins in a line, which accept 2-pin plugs.

Embassies and consulates

For all Chilean embassies and consulates abroad and for all foreign embassies and consulates in Chile, see http://embassy.goabroad.com.

Health

Medical services
Santiago Emergency hospital at Marcoleta 377, T2-2633 2051 (emergency), T2-2770 9500 (general enquiries). **Hospital del Salvador**, Av Salvador 334 or J M Infante 551, T2-2575 4000, open 24 hrs, reception Mon-Fri 0800-1700, Sat 0800-1300, 1400-1700. **Vacunatoria Internacional**, Marcoleta 350, T2-2235 4534. Hospital Luis Calvo MacKenna, Antonio Varas 360, T2-2575 5800, www. calvomackenna.cl. **Clínica Central**, San Isidro 231-243, Santa Lucía metro, T2-2402 4200 (call centre), open 24 hrs. Instituto Norteamericano Santiago, Moneda 1467, T2-2677 7167, www. norteamericano.cl. Institute run through the US embassy with many branches, one of the best options. **Emergency pharmacy**, Portugal 125, Universidad Católica metro, T2-2631 3005. Consult www.farmaciasahumada.cl for other emergency pharmacies.
Punta Arenas Clínico Magallanes "Dr Lautaro Navarro Avaria", Av Los Flamencos 01364, T61-229 3000, www.hospitalclinicomagallanes.cl. Public hospital; for emergency room ask for La Posta, also has good dentists. **Clínica Magallanes**, Bulnes 01448, T61-220 7200, www.clinicamagallanes.cl, private clinic.

Note If you need to get to a hospital, it is better to take a taxi than wait for an ambulance. Hospitals are public facilities, while clinics are private. Those with adequate insurance who find themselves in a medical emergency should request a *clínica* instead of a hospital to avoid long queues.

Money

US$1= 667 pesos; €1= 749 pesos (Jun 2017).
The unit of currency is the peso, its sign is $. Notes are for 1000, 2000, 5000, 10,000 and 20,000 pesos and coins for 1, 5, 10, 50, 100 and 500 pesos. Small shops and bus drivers do not like large notes, especially in the morning and in rural areas.

ATMs and credit cards
The easiest way to obtain cash is by using ATMs which operate under the sign Redbanc (www.redbanc.cl, for a full list); they take Cirrus (MasterCard), Maestro and Plus (Visa) and permit transactions up to 200,000 pesos chilenos per day. Instructions are available in English. Note that ATMs in Chile charge 3500-5000 pesos commission for each transaction. At some Banco Estado ATMs, if you choose the Spanish option, you can opt not to have a receipt and save yourself a further US$2 in charges; in English you don't get this choice. For credit card transactions, Visa and MasterCard are common in Chile; American Express and Diner's Club are less useful.

Currency exchange
The best exchange rates offered are in Santiago; you'll find *casas de cambio* (exchange houses) in the centre, mainly on Paseo Ahumada and Huérfanos (metro Universidad de Chile or Plaza de Armas), and in Providencia on Av Pedro de Valdivia. US dollars cash and euros can be exchanged but even slightly damaged or marked foreign notes may be rejected. *Casas de cambio* are open longer hours and often give slightly better rates than banks. It is always worth shopping around. Rates get worse as you go north from Santiago. Official rates are quoted in daily newspapers.

Cost of travelling
The average cost for a traveller on an economical budget is about US$40-45 per day for food, accommodation and land transportation (more for flights, tours, car hire, etc). Breakfast in hotels,

if not included, is US$2.50-4. A basic lunch costs US$4-5. *Alojamiento* in private houses and hostels (bed, breakfast and often use of kitchen) starts at about US$10. Internet costs US$0.60-1 per hr. Southern Chile is much more expensive between 15 Dec and 15 Mar. Santiago tends to be more expensive for food and accommodation than other parts of Chile.

Opening hours

Banks: 0900-1400, closed Sat. **Government offices**: 1000-1230 (the public is admitted for a few hours only). **Other offices**: Mon-Fri 0830-1230, 1400-1800. **Shops** (Santiago): 1030-1930, Sat 0930-1330.

Post

The post office is **Correos Chile**, www.correos.cl. Its branches are usually open Mon-Fri 0900-1800. The main office in the capital is on the Plaza de Armas. Poste restante is well organized (though only kept for 30 days), passport essential to collect letters and parcels; a list of those received in the hall of the central post office (one list for men, another for women, indicate Sr or Sra/Srta on envelope). The central post office also has philatelic section, 0900-1630, and small stamp museum (ask to see it). If sending a parcel, the contents must first be checked at the post office.

Public holidays and festivals

1 Jan, New Year's Day; Semana Santa (Fri and Sat); 1 May, Labour Day; 21 May, Glorias Navales/Navy Day; 29 Jun, San Pedro y San Pablo; 16 Jul, Virgen del Carmen; 15 Aug, Asunción de la Virgen; 18, 19 Sep, Independence Days; 12 Oct, Día de la Raza; 31 Oct, Día Nacional de las Iglesias Evangélicas y Protestantes; 1 Nov, Todos los Santos; 8 Dec, Inmaculada Concepción; 25 Dec, Christmas.

Safety

Chile is one of the safest countries in South America for the visitor. Like all major cities around the world, though, Santiago and Valparaíso do have crime problems. Law enforcement officers are *carabineros* (green military uniforms), who handle all tasks except immigration. *Investigaciones*, in civilian dress, are detective police who deal with everything except traffic.

Tax

Airport tax US$30 for international flights; US$11.80 for international flights under 500 km and domestic flights over 270 km; US$4.65 for domestic flights under 270 km. All taxes included in ticket price.
VAT/IVA 19%.

Telephone and Wi-Fi

Country code T+56.
Ringing: a single ring (as in the US). Engaged: equal tones with equal pauses. *Centros de llamadas* (phone centres) are abundant and are the easiest places to make a call. They are much cheaper than main company offices. They have private booths where you can talk as long as you like and pay afterwards. They often have internet, photocopying and fax, too. For international calls use a *centro de llamadas* or a pre-paid phone scratch card, available from *kioskos*.

International roaming is becoming more common, but buying a local pay-as-you-go may be cheaper. Major airports and hotels often have rental desks, can advise on local outlets and how to use mobiles. All Chilean phone numbers have 9 digits. Landlines start with a 2-digit area code followed by a 7-digit number (in Santiago it is 2, followed by an 8-digit number). For mobile numbers 9 precedes an 8 digit number. Area and mobile codes do not start with zero.

Travellers should have no problem accessing the internet either through Wi-Fi or in internet cafés in Chile. Many companies provide service, for instance **Entel** (www.entel.cl), **Movistar** (www.movistar.cl) and **VTR** (http://vtr.com). Their websites give details of mobile packages, but note that you have to be a resident to take out a contract.

Time

Official time is 4 hrs behind GMT, but in 2016-17 Chile was using daylight saving, 3 hrs behind, all year.

Tipping

10% in restaurants, if service is not included; tip about 100 pesos in bars. Porters: US$1 or US$0.15 a piece of luggage. Taxi drivers are not tipped, but rounding up the changes is common.

Tourist information

The national secretariat of tourism, **Sernatur**, www.sernatur.cl, has offices throughout the country (addresses given in the text). The official online guide is www.chile.travel. Look on the website for establishments with the official *Sellos de Calidad Turística and Sustentabilidad*. City offices provide town maps and other information. Copec publishes a 5-part guide to the country, *Norte, Centro, Sur*, a national route map and a camping guide with road map, with information and a wealth of maps including neighbouring tourist centres in Argentina, in Spanish only, found in bookshops, Copec filling stations and news stands in most city centres.

CODEFF (**Comité Nacional Pro-Defensa de la Fauna y Flora**), Padre Alonso Ovalle 612, of 1, Santiago, T2-2777 2534, www.codeff.cl, can also provide information on environmental questions. For regulations on sport fishing, see http://pescarecreativa.sernapesca.cl.

CONAF (the **Corporacíon Nacional Forestal**), Presidente Bulnes 285, Santiago, T2-2663 0000, www.conaf.cl, publishes a number of leaflets (in Spanish and English) and has documents and maps about the national park system.

Useful websites

www.dibam.cl Official site for museums, libraries and galleries.

www.pasosfronterizos.gov.cl Details on the border posts between Chile and Argentina.

www.senderodechile.cl About the project for a country-long trekking/mountain biking path.

www.trekkingchile.com Hiking, trekking, mountaineering, culture and travelling in Chile.

www.welcomechile.com Interpatagonia's Chile site with tourist information, in Spanish and English.

Visas and immigration

Citizens of Kuwait, Egypt, Saudi Arabia and UAE, most African and Asian countries, Guyana, Cuba and former Soviet bloc countries not now in the EU require visas for entry to Chile. Other foreigners require a passport (valid for at least 6 months) and tourist card only. It is imperative to check tourist card and visa requirements before travel. National identity cards are sufficient for entry by citizens of all South American countries. Tourist cards are valid in most cases for 90 days, but some are for 60 and others 30 days. Tourist cards can be obtained from immigration offices at major land borders and Chilean airports; you must surrender your tourist card on departure (if you lose it ask immigration for a replacement). If you wish to stay longer than 90 days (as a tourist), you must buy a 90-day extension from the Departamento de Extranjería (head office San Antonio 580, Santiago, T600-486 3000, www.extranjeria. gob.cl, Mon-Fri 0900-1600), or any local *gobernación* office. It costs US$140. To avoid the long queue and long-winded bureaucracy, make a day trip to Argentina, Bolivia or Peru and return with a new tourist card (the authorities don't like it if you do this more than 3-4 times). An onward ticket is required. Tourist card holders may change their status to enable them to stay on in employment if they have a contract; they need to contact the Extranjería in whichever province they will be working. On arrival you will be asked where you are staying in Chile. For some nationalities a visa will be granted within 24 hrs upon production of an onward ticket, for others, authorization must be obtained from Chile. For other nationalities who need a visa, a charge is made. To travel overland to or from Tierra del Fuego a multiple entry visa is essential since the Argentine-Chilean border is crossed more than once (it is advisable to get a multiple entry visa before arriving, rather than trying to change a single entry visa once in Chile). On arrival by air, Australian citizens will be charged an administration fee of US$117 and Mexicans US$23 (this is a reciprocal tax; rates are posted at arrivals). This tax is not charged at land borders.

Note Chile has strict laws (*regulaciones fitosanitarias*) governing the import of animal and plant products into the country. At all entry points visitors are asked to declare any food or other products which may risk introducing disease. This covers all fresh produce and many prepared products as well. The web page http://chile.gob.cl/en/consulados/tramites/para-extranjeros/tramites-aduaneros-sag/ lists items that are allowed in, but these must still be declared and inspected by the Agricultural and Livestock Service (SAG).

Weights and measures

The metric system is obligatory.

This is
Colombia

The adventurous will love this land of sun and emeralds, with its excellent opportunities for climbing, trekking and diving. The gold museum in Bogotá, the Lost City of the Tayrona and San Agustín all have superb examples of cultures long gone. Among several fine colonial cities, the jewel is Cartagena, whose history of slavery and pirates can be seen in the massive fortifications. Today, pelicans share the beach with holidaymakers. Colombia's Caribbean, from Venezuela to the Panamanian isthmus, was the inspiration for Gabriel García Márquez's world of magical realism and is the land of accordion-led *vallenato* music. Of the country's many snow-capped mountain ranges, the Sierra Nevada de Santa Marta, with its secretive *indígenas*, is the most remarkable, rising straight out of the Caribbean. Also not to be missed is the cathedral inside a salt mine at Zipaquirá. There are mud volcanoes to bathe in, acres of flowers, coffee farms to visit and a digital library's worth of music festivals. In fact, dancing is practically a national pastime and having a good time is taken very seriously: as García Márquez once said, "five Colombians in a room invariably turns into a party". Colombia has impressively rebuilt a prominent position on the South American tourist circuit, despite the lingering effects of the drugs trade and dwindling guerrilla violence.

Caribbean Sea

Península de
la Guajira

To San Andrés y Providencia

PANAMA

VENEZUELA

Pacific
Ocean

ECUADOR

PERU

BRAZIL

N

100 km
100 miles

Footprint picks

★ **Museo del Oro,**
page 889
The Gold Museum in Bogotá possesses a dazzling collection of pre-Columbian art.

★ **Zipaquirá**, page 899
Visit the imposing cathedral carved inside an ancient salt mine for an unforgettable day trip from the capital.

★ **Cartagena**, page 918
Cartagena is colonial Spain's finest legacy in the Americas. Spend several days exploring the fortified historical centre, then laze on the city's beautiful beaches.

★ **Ciudad Perdida**, page 944
Trek through the rainforest to the Lost City of the Tayrona tribe.

★ **La Zona Cafetera**, page 973
Stay on a coffee finca to learn about Colombia's 'black gold'.

★ **Tierradentro and San Agustín**, pages 989 and 994
Admire pre-Columbian burial tombs and mysterious megaliths in the south of the country.

Route planner

putting it all together

Two to three weeks

the northern loop

Start by exploring **Bogotá** and its colonial sector, **La Candelaria**. A visit to the **Gold Museum** is a must. It's a short bus ride to Villa de Leiva, with the magnificent **Zipaquirá** salt cathedral as a stopover. Soak up the colonial atmosphere in **Villa de Leiva** before heading up to **San Gil** for rafting, kayaking and hiking. **Barichara** has colonial architecture. Make your way up to **Santa Marta** and the beaches of **Tayrona National Park**. Along the coast is **Cartagena**. Spend a few days exploring before relaxing on **Playa Blanca** or the coral **Islas del Rosario**. It's worth stopping at the colonial town of **Mompós** before **Medellín**. After taking in the Antioquian capital, spend a few days in traditional villages, such as **Santa Fe de Antioquia** or Guatapé, then travel overland to Bogotá, via the **Río Claro Nature Reserve**.

Alternatively, omit the Villa de Leiva-San Gil-Barichara route and replace it, after Medellín, with the 'coffee zone' and Los Nevados (see below).

Four weeks or more

the figure of eight

Start by following the northern loop described above and then from Bogotá, take a bus south, stopping off at the **Tatacoa desert**. From nearby **Neiva** it's a hard day's slog (but a worthwhile one) to **Tierradentro**. Spend a few days exploring the tombs before heading down to **San Agustín** for more pre-Columbian archaeology. Then make the spectacular drive to the dazzling white city of **Popayán**, with the nearby market at **Silvia**. From here, head to the salsa-mad city of **Cali**. Next, head to the 'coffee zone' for a stay on a finca. The village of **Salento**, the **Valle de Cocora** and the snowy peaks of **Los Nevados National Park** are highlights. From here it's a nine-hour bus journey or a short flight back to Bogotá.

Another option, especially suitable if heading to Ecuador, is to follow the northern loop and, after Medellín, head south to Los Nevados and the 'coffee zone'. From there continue to Cali and Popayán, from where you can make the lengthy detour to Tierradentro and San Agustín before turning south to Pasto and Ipiales.

Essential Colombia

Finding your feet

Bogotá is the capital and the hub for international flights, although there are also some flights to Cartagena and Barranquilla (for the Caribbean coast), Medellín (for the west of the country) and Cali (for the south). In Colombia the Andes split into three distinct cordilleras: Occidental, Central and Oriental. The main population centres (and sights) lie in the western third of the country, along the north–south valleys and plateaus created by these ranges. A vast area east of the Cordillera Oriental is taken up by the sparsely populated *llanos* (plains) in the north and by the tropical forest of the Amazon Basin in the south.

Fact file

Location 3.9976° N, 73.2780° W
Capital Bogotá
Time zone GMT -5 hrs
Telephone country code +57
Currency Peso (COP$)

Getting around

A country as large and varied as Colombia has a great many sights worth visiting. A comprehensive tour will require a good deal of planning. If you have limited time and want to see as much as possible, you could consider air travel; cheap fares can be found through most local carriers. If you have more time, there are good long-distance bus services and minibuses.

When to go

Climate in Colombia is a matter of altitude: there are no real seasons, though some periods are wetter than others. Generally, around 2000 m

Best national parks
Sierra Nevada de Santa Marta, page 944
Macuira, page 953
Old Providence, page 957
Los Nevados, page 974
Puracé, page 993

is 'temperate'; anywhere higher will require warm clothing in the early mornings and evenings. December to February are generally the driest months, but many local people are on holiday at this time. It gets especially busy and crowded at Christmas, from early to mid-January and at Easter, when many hotels put up their rates and transport can be overloaded. In most of Colombia the rainy season is from April to November, but the *cordilleras* tend to have a short dry season in July to August. Intermittent heavy rain can fall at any time, however. The Pacific coast is wet the year round.

Colombians will use almost anything as a pretext for a celebration; there are more festivals, parties and carnivals than days in the year. Every city, town and village has at least three or four annual events in which local products and traditions are celebrated with music, dancing and raucous revelry. These are given throughout the chapter and may help you to plan your visit. Public holidays are listed in Practicalities on page 1012.

Time required

Two weeks is just enough time to make a quick tour of Colombia's northern highlights; add another week if you want to relax on a beach and explore in more depth. A month would allow you to cover most of the country's sights, both north and south. See also Route planner, opposite.

Weather Bogotá

January	February	March	April	May	June
18°C 6°C 40mm	18°C 7°C 50mm	19°C 8°C 80mm	18°C 8°C 110mm	18°C 8°C 100mm	17°C 8°C 60mm

July	August	September	October	November	December
17°C 8°C 40mm	17°C 7°C 40mm	18°C 7°C 50mm	18°C 8°C 140mm	18°C 8°C 110mm	18°C 7°C 60mm

Bogotá

Bogotá, the fifth-largest city in Latin America, is a vast sprawling metropolis where, despite its modernity, it is not uncommon to see the horse and cart still in use on the streets. It is the cultural centre of the country with cosmopolitan restaurants and a vibrant nightlife. Predictably, there are staggering extremes of wealth and poverty, with the city segregated between the rich north and the poorer south. The capital has advanced in leaps and bounds since the mid-1990s, winning awards for its environmental efforts, libraries and transport systems, as well as improving quality of life.

Emerald sellers do deals on street corners, but for a safer view of all that glitters, visit the Gold Museum, one of the most stunning collections of pre-Columbian treasures in the Americas. The old centre, La Candelaria, has countless well-preserved colonial buildings and important museums along cobbled, hilly streets.

La Candelaria

the historical and cultural heart of the city

☆ When the *conquistadores* first arrived in the 16th century, the area was inhabited by the Chibcha people. The district, named after Nuestra Señora de la Candelaria, is where the conquistador Gonzalo Jiménez de Quesada founded Santafé (later renamed Bogotá) in 1538. Events in 1810 made La Candelaria synonymous with the Independence movement (see below), while the Franciscans and Jesuits founded schools and monasteries giving La Candelaria a reputation as a centre of learning. Among the oldest educational establishments is the Colegio Nacional de San Bartolomé on Calle 10, No 6-57, founded 1573, now a prestigious school. The narrow cobbled streets and mansions of the Barrio La Candelaria cluster around Plaza Bolívar. There is some modern infill but many of the houses are well-preserved in colonial style, one or two storeys high with tiled roofs, projecting eaves, wrought ironwork and carved balconies.

Plaza Bolívar

The heart of the city and government is Plaza Bolívar, a good starting point for exploring the colonial district. It is claimed that the first ever statue of South America's liberator, Simón Bolívar, stands here. On the northern side of the Plaza is the **Corte Suprema de Justicia** (the supreme court of justice) destroyed by fire in 1985 after the now defunct M-19 guerrilla group stormed in. The court was wrecked and the present building was completed in 1999. On the west side of the plaza is the **Alcaldía Mayor de Bogotá** (the office of Bogotá's influential mayor and City Hall). On the south side is the **Capitolio Nacional** (congress), an imposing classical style structure with fine colonnades (1847-1925).

The **Catedral** ① *Tue-Sun 0900-1700*, was rebuilt 1807-1823 in classical style. It has a notable choir loft of carved walnut and wrought silver on the altar of the Chapel of El Topo. The banner brought by Jiménez de Quesada to Bogotá is now in the sacristy and there is a monument to Jiménez inside the Cathedral. Gregorio Vásquez de Arce y Ceballos (1638-1711), the most famous painter in colonial Colombia, is buried in one of the chapels and many of his paintings can be seen in the Cathedral. Next door is the beautiful **Capilla del Sagrario** ① *Mon-Fri 0730-1200, 1300-1800, Sun 1500-1800, US$2.20*, built in the late 17th century, with several paintings by Vásquez de Arce.

Best for
Churches ■ Museums ■ Nightlife

Essential Bogotá

Tip...

As Bogotá is Latin America's third-highest city at 2640 m, it gets chilly at night and warm clothes are needed. Visitors should also be careful with food and alcoholic drinks for the first day or so.

Finding your feet

To the east of the city are the mountains of the eastern cordillera, a useful landmark for getting your bearings. Most of the interesting parts of the city follow the foot of the cordillera in a south-north line. **La Candelaria**, full of character, occupies the area bounded by Avenida Jiménez de Quesada, C 6, Cra 3 and Cra 10. The main colonial churches, palaces and museums are concentrated around and above the Plaza Bolívar. Some hotels are found in this part, more along the margins. Cra 7 is pedestrian-only from C 11 (Plaza Bolívar) to C 24, 0800-1800. **Downtown Bogotá** runs in a band northeast along Cra 7 from Av Jiménez de Quesada to C 26. It is a thorough mix of styles including modern towers and run-down colonial and later buildings, together with a few notable exceptions. From C 50 to C 68 is **El Chapinero**, once the outskirts of the city and now a commercial district with a sprinkling of old, large mansions. Also known as 'Chapigay', it doubles up as the epicentre of Bogotá's gay scene, with many bars and clubs. Next to the National Park, along La Séptima (Cra 7) is **La Merced**, a cluster of English country-style houses. A few blocks further south, along Cra 4 between C 25 and C 27, is the Bohemian area of **La Macarena** (Zona M), which was formerly inhabited by struggling artists, now fashionable with many good restaurants and bars. Beyond C 60, the main city continues to **North Bogotá**, which is split into various points of interest. Most of the best hotels, restaurants and embassies are in this area. El Dorado **airport** is 15 km west of the centre. The long-distance **bus terminal**, Terminal de Transportes, is in the same direction as the airport, but not as far out. Some buses leave passengers at termini in the north and south of the city.

Tip...

On Sundays, 0700-1400, the city's main streets are closed to traffic for the benefit of cyclists, joggers and rollerbladers.

Getting around

Even though pavements can be congested, walking in the Downtown area and in La Candelaria by day is recommended, as distances are short and traffic is heavy on those streets that are not pedestrianized. North Bogotá is more spacious so buses and taxis are more convenient. Several types of **bus** cover urban routes. All stop when flagged down. There are also **TransMilenio** buses on dedicated lanes. **Taxis** are relatively cheap and easy to come by. Radio taxis are especially recommended at night; keep the doors locked.

Addresses

The following address system is used throughout Colombia. The Calles (abbreviated 'C', or 'Cll') run at right angles across the Carreras ('Cra' or 'K'). The address Calle 10, No 12-45 would be the building on Calle 10 between Carreras 12 and 13 at 45 paces from Carrera 12; however transversals (Tra) and diagonals (Diag) can complicate the system. The Avenidas (Av), broad and important streets, may be either Calles (like 26) or Carreras (like 14). The Calles in the south of the city are marked 'Sur' or 'S'; this is an integral part of the address and must be quoted.

Tip...

Most museums and tourist attractions are open Tuesday to Sunday, 0900-1700, but may be closed for a period in the middle of the day. Times change often. Very little is open on Mondays. The best time to visit the churches is before or after Mass (not during). Mass times are 0700, 1200 and 1800.

Safety

La Candelaria is relatively safe by day, but there continue to be reports of muggings and robberies by night. Even though street cameras have been installed, you must take care after dark. Anyone approaching you with questions, offering to sell something or making demands, may well be a thief or a con-artist. They may be well-dressed and plausible, may pose as plain-clothes officials, and often work in pairs. They are frequently active in and near the Plaza Bolívar.

Also on the east side of the plaza, visit the **Casa del Florero** or **Museo de la Independencia** ① *Cra 7, No 11-28, T1-334 4150, museoindependencia@mincultura.gov.co, Tue-Fri, 0900-1700, Sat-Sun 1000-1600, US$1, Sun free, seniors and children under 5 free, guided tours Tue-Fri 1100, 1500, Sat 1100, 1400, Wed 1500 in English.* It was here that the first rumblings of independence began and it houses the famous flower vase that featured in the 1810 revolution. Its 10 rooms display the history of Colombia's independence campaigns and their heroes. It still has original early 17th-century Spanish-Moorish balconies.

East of Plaza Bolívar

At the southeastern corner of the plaza is the **Palacio Arzobispal**, with splendid bronze doors. In the block behind it is the colonial **Plazuela de Rufino Cuervo**. Located here is the house of Manuela Sáenz, who was the mistress of Simon Bolívar. Inside is the **Museo de Trajes Regionales** ① *C 10,*

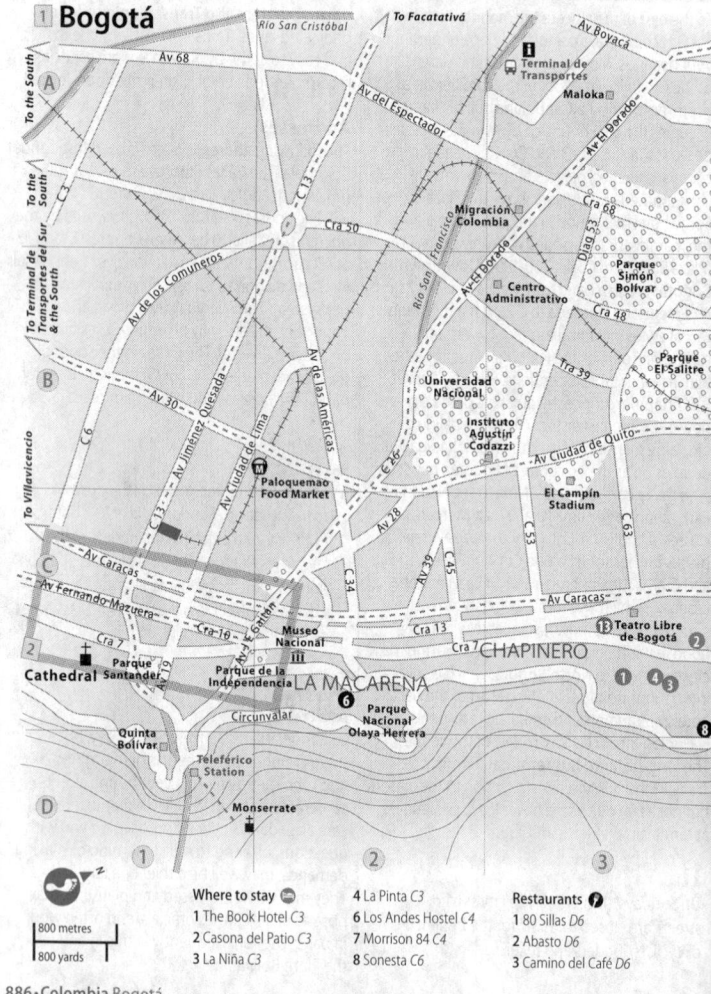

Bogotá

Where to stay 🛏
1 The Book Hotel *C3*
2 Casona del Patio *C3*
3 La Niña *C3*
4 La Pinta *C3*
6 Los Andes Hostel *C4*
7 Morrison 84 *C4*
8 Sonesta *C6*

Restaurants 🍴
1 80 Sillas *D6*
2 Abasto *D6*
3 Camino del Café *D6*

800 metres
800 yards

No 6-18, http://museodetrajesregionales.com, Mon-Fri 0900-1600, Sat 0900-1400, US$1, reductions for seniors, children and on Sat, a small collection of traditional costumes from indigenous groups of Colombia. Beside it is the house in which Antonio Nariño printed in 1794 his translation of Thomas Paine's 'The Rights of Man' which had a profound influence on the movement for independence. You can read an extract of the text in Spanish on the wall of the building. Across from Plazuela de Rufino Cuervo is **San Ignacio**, a Jesuit church built in 1605. Emeralds from the Muzo mines in Boyacá were used in the monstrance and it has more paintings by Gregorio Vásquez de Arce. The **Museo de Arte Colonial** ① *Cra 6, No 9-77, www.museocolonial.gov.co, Tue-Fri 0900-1700, Sat-Sun 1000-1600, US$1, reductions for students and children, seniors free*, is a fine colonial brick building. It belonged originally to the Society of Jesus, and was once the seat of the oldest University in Colombia and of the National Library. It has a splendid collection of colonial art and paintings by Gregorio Vásquez de

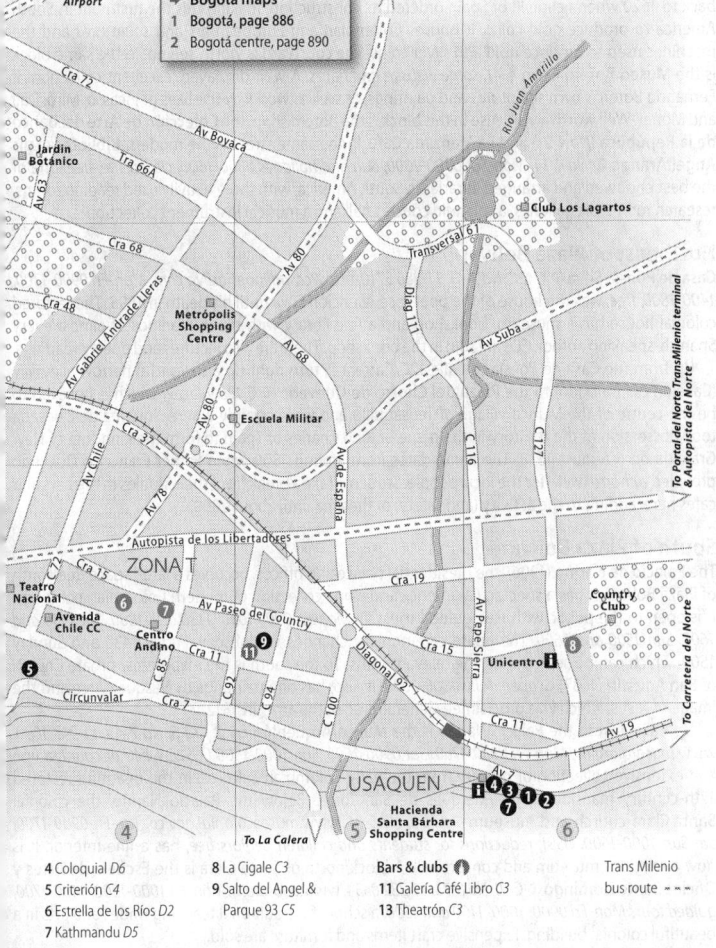

Arce, all kinds of utensils, and two charming patios. Across Cra 6 is the **Palacio de San Carlos** ① *C 10, No 5-51, T1-381 4000 (restricted access, book appointment, www.cancilleria.gov.co)*, where Bolívar lived, which now houses the Foreign Ministry. Bolívar is said to have planted the huge walnut tree in the courtyard. On 25 September 1828, there was an attempt on his life. His mistress, Manuela, thrust him out of the window and he hid for two hours under the stone arches of the bridge across the Río San Agustín (now Calle 7). Santander, suspected of complicity, was arrested and banished.

Almost opposite the Palacio de San Carlos is the **Teatro Colón** ① *C 10, No 5-32, T1-381 6380, http://teatrocolon.gov.co*. It is considered Colombia's most prestigious theatre. Its opulent style is typical of late 19th-century Italian architecture. South of the Palacio de San Carlos is the **Iglesia de María del Carmen** ① *Cra 5, No 8-36*, the most striking church building in Bogotá, in neo-Gothic style, with excellent stained glass and walls in bands of red and white.

One block northeast of here is the **Casa de la Moneda** (Mint) ① *C 11, No 4-93, www.banrep cultural.org, Mon-Sat 0900-1900, Sun and holidays, 1000-1700, closed Tue, free*. The building dates back to 1620 when Felipe III of Spain ordered its construction, making this the first mint in South America to produce gold coins. It houses Colombian and European art and sculptures and the machines used to produce gold and silver coins. The courtyard is worth seeing. In the same block is the **Museo Botero** ① *No 4-41, same website and hours*. A well-displayed, excellent collection of Fernando Botero's own sculptures and paintings, as well as works by the likes of Picasso, Miró, Dalí and Monet. Well worth a visit. Also in this block is the Botero shop, the **Colección de Arte del Banco de la República** (*No 4-21*) and La Manzana Café. In the same street is the modern **Biblioteca Luis Angel Arango** ① *No 4-14, Mon-Sat 0800-2000, Sun and holidays 0800-1600, closed Tue, free*, one of the best endowed and arranged libraries in South America, with three heavily used reading rooms, research rooms, art galleries, a splendid concert hall and a musical instrument collection.

Northeast of Plaza Bolívar

Casa de Poesía Silva ① *C 12C, No 3-41, T1-286 5710, http://casadepoesiasilva.com, Mon-Fri 0900-1300, 1400-1800, free*, was the house of the poet José Asunción Silva until his death in 1895. The restored colonial house has a museum, bookshop and a fine library with taped readings of almost every Spanish-speaking author. CDs are sold in the bookshop. There are also lectures and poetry readings.

Up from the Casa de Poesía to Calle 12C/Carrera 2, turn right up a delightful narrow alleyway (Callejón del Embudo) to the **Plaza del Chorro de Quevedo** ① *C 12B y Cra 2*, which is believed to be the centre of the Muisca village of Teusaquillo and was certainly where Jiménez de Quesada took possession of the territory in the name of King Charles of Spain to form the kingdom of New Granada on 6 August 1538. The name dates from around 1800 when Father Francisco Quevedo provided a *chorro* (well) for the local people. Students take a break from their studies in the bars and cafés here, adding to the activity (and safety) of the area until about 2000.

South of Plaza Bolívar

The **Palacio de Nariño** (1906), the presidential palace and offices, occupies a large space due south of Plaza Bolívar. It has a spectacular interior and a fine collection of modern Colombian paintings. It is open to the public with *free guided tours* ① *Mon-Fri 0900,1030, 1430 and 1800, Sat 1430 and 1600, Sun 1500 and 1600*. The guard ceremonially changes Wednesday, Friday 1430 and Sunday 1500, which can be seen during the relevant tours. To the south is the elaborately ornate Church of **San Agustín** (1637) ① *open daily 0800-2000*. It, too, has fine paintings by Vásquez Arce and the Image of Jesus, which was proclaimed Generalísimo of the army in 1812.

Up Calle 7 from the Palacio Nariño is the **Museo Arqueológico** ① *Cra 6, No 7-43, T1-243 1690, www.musarq.org.co, Mon-Fri 0830-1700, Sat 0900-1600, Sun 1000-1600 US$1.35, ISIC discount*, a fine and extensive collection of pottery from the early Colombian cultures, in the beautiful restored 17th-century mansion of the Marqués de San Jorge. Below the Palacio Nariño, the colonial **Santa Clara church and museum** ① *Cra 8, No 8-91, www.museocolonial.gov.co, Tue-Fri 0900-1700, Sat-Sun 1000-1600, US$1, reductions for students and children, seniors free*, is the best preserved church in the city. It is now a religious museum and concert hall. A block north of Santa Clara is the **Escuela de Artes y Oficios Santo Domingo** ① *C 10, No 8-73, T1-282 0534, www.eaosd.org, Mon-Fri 1000-1300, 1400-1700, guided tours Mon-Fri 0900, 1000, 1100 and 1500*, a school for traditional teaching trades and arts in a beautiful colonial building. Expensive craft items and furniture are sold.

colonial meets modern and an unmissable museum

Avenida Jiménez de Quesada marks the La Candelaria and Downtown boundary. This is one of Bogotá's best-known streets and owes its lack of straightness to having been built over a river bed; a water feature now runs along it called Eje Ambiental. At the junction of Cra 7 is the Plazoleta del Rosario with, on its southern side, the Colegio Mayo de Nuestra Señora del Rosario (1651), a beautiful colonial building, now a university.

Around Parque Santander

Across Avenida Jiménez de Quesada is the **Banco de la República** and the **Parque Santander**, with a bronze statue of Santander, who helped Bolívar to free Colombia and was later its president. There is a handicraft market most days. Around the park are three of the city's finest churches.

San Francisco ① *C 6, No 7-35, www.templodesanfrancisco.com, open daily for mass 0700-1800, Sun 0800-1900, holidays 0900-1200,* dates from the mid-16th century, with paintings of famous Franciscans, choir stalls, an ornate gold high altar (1622), and a fine Lady Chapel with blue and gold ornamentation. The remarkable ceiling is in *mudéjar* style. Try to visit when it is fully illuminated.

The church of **La Veracruz was** first built five years after the founding of Bogotá, rebuilt in 1631, and again after the 1827 earthquake. José de Caldas, the famous scientist, was buried along with many other victims of the 'Reign of Terror' under the church. It has a bright white and red interior and a fine ceiling.

La Tercera Orden is a colonial church famous for its carved woodwork along the nave and a high balcony, massive wooden altar reredos, and confessionals, built by the Third Franciscan Order in the 17th century.

★Museo del Oro (Gold Museum)

Parque Santander, C 16, No 5-41, T1-343 2222, www.banrepcultural.org/museo-del-oro, Tue-Sat 0900-1800 (leave by 1900), Sun and holidays 1000-1600 (leave by 1700), closed every Mon, 1 Jan, Good Fri, 1 May, 20 Jul, 24, 25, 31 Dec, US$1, free on Sun, audioguides in Spanish, English and French, also guided tours in Spanish and English.

This unique collection is a must and a poignant reminder of why the *conquistadores* found Colombia and the rest of the continent so appealing. There are more than 35,000 pieces of pre-Columbian gold work in the total collection, most of which is held here. The rest are in other Museos de Oro sponsored by the Banco de la República throughout Colombia. The ancient gold objects discovered in Colombia were not made by primitive hammering alone, but show the use of virtually every technique known to modern goldsmiths. A tasteful light show in the Salón Dorado (Gold Room) highlights some 8000 pieces and should not be missed. Opposite the Gold Museum is **Galería Artesanal de Colombia** ① *C 16, block 5, Mon-Sun 0900-1900,* an arts and crafts market.

Parque de la Independencia and around

Continuing north along Carrera 7, at Calle 26 you reach **Parque de la Independencia**, adorned with wax palms. In the park is the **Planetarium /Museo del Espacio** ① *C 26 B, No 5-93, T1-281 4150, www.planetariodebogota.gov.co, Tue-Sun 1000-1700, US$13.30 including dome and museum, reductions for students, children and seniors.* Behind is the impressive Moorish-style brick bullring, **La Santamaria**, see under What to do.

Also at this junction (Carrera 7 and Calle 26) are the church and monastery of San Diego, a picturesque, restored building. The Franciscan monastery with fine *mudéjar* ceiling was built in 1560 and the church in 1607 as its chapel. Local craft items are sold in the old monastery. Across the street is the Tequendama Hotel, one of the city's finest. Near the park is the **Biblioteca Nacional** ① *entrance at Calle 24, No 5-60, www.bibliotecanacional.gov.co, Mon-Fri 0800-1800, Sat 0900-1600.* On the corner is the **Museo de Arte Moderno** (Mambo) ① *C 24, No 6-00, www.mambogota.com, Tue-Sat 1000-1800, Sun-holidays 1200-1630, US$1.30, students and seniors half price,* with a well-displayed collection of Colombia's modern artists and foreign artists including Picasso, Dalí and Ernst. There is also a good shop. **Museo Nacional** ① *Cra 7, No 28-66, T1-381 6470, www.museonacional.gov.co,*

Tue-Sat 1000-1800, Sun 1000-1700, permanent collections free, various tours available (in English by request), is in a converted old prison, founded by Santander in 1823. There is an excellent archaeological collection. Its top floor houses a fine art section, comprising national paintings and sculptures. Allow at least two hours to look round. There is a gourmet restaurant, El Panóptico.

Beyond the centre

shopping, eating, nightlife – and a great view

El Chapinero and around

In the link between Central and North Bogotá is Colombia's main state university, **Universidad Nacional**, housed in the Ciudad Universitaria. Be aware that the university's main entrance on Carrera 30 is periodically the focal point of protests (sometimes violent) between students and riot police. Avoid the area during these times. Instead, escape to the ☆**Jardín Botánico José Celestino Mutis** ① *Av 63, No 68-95, T1-437 7060, www.jbb.gov.co, Mon-Fri 0800-1700, Sat-Sun and holidays 0900-1700, US$, US$1, children US$50 guided tours at weekends*, which is interesting, peaceful and well-organized. It has a large collection of orchids, plus roses, gladioli and trees from all over the country.

Maloka ① *Cra 68D, No 24A-51, near the bus terminal, www.maloka.org, Tue-Fri 0800-1700, weekends and holidays 0900-1800, US$10 including everything*, is a complex of science and technology exhibits, multi-screen cinema including 3-D, ice rink, all under a dome. Entry is cheaper without cinema ticket

② Bogotá centre

200 metres
200 yards

Where to stay 🛌
1 Abadia Colonial *C3*
2 Alegría's Hostel *C2*
3 Casa Platypus *C4*
4 Hostal Fátima *C3*
5 Hostal Martinik *C3*
6 Hostal Sue Candelaria *C3*
7 Hotel de la Opera *B2*
8 Iku Hostel Backpackers *C4*
9 Masaya *C3*
11 Swiss Hostal Martinik *C3*
12 Tequendama *B5*
13 The Cranky Croc *C3*

Restaurants 🍴
2 Artesano *C6*
3 Asadero Capachos *B4*
4 Boulevard Sésamo *C3*
5 La Paella *B2*
6 La Puerta Falsa *B3*
9 La Totuma Corrida & Rosita *C3*
10 Moros y Cristianos *C2*
11 Panadería Pastelería La Vieja Suiza *C3*
12 Tábula *C6*

Bars & clubs 🍸
14 Bogotá Beer Company *C3*
15 Quiebra Canto *B4*

☆Monserrate

T1-284 5700 (answer service in English too), www.cerromonserrate.com. The main site is open Mon-Sat 0630-2400; Sun 0630-2100; closed the week after Semana Santa and with shorter opening times during other religious holidays. Funicular every 15 mins Mon-Fri 0630-1145, 1730-2100, Sat-Sun 0630-2100; US$3.10 one way Mon-Sat, US$1.75 on Sun, US$6.60 return at night, reductions for over-62s on all fares. The cable car runs Mon-Sat 1200-2400, Sun 1030-1830; fares are the same as the funicular. Times and fares change frequently.

There is a very good view of the city from the top of Monserrate (3152 m), the lower of the two peaks rising sharply to the east. It is reached by a funicular railway, a cable car and a path. The new convent at the top is a popular shrine and pilgrimage site. At the summit, near the church, a platform gives a bird's-eye view of the city's tiled roofs, modern suburbs and of the plains beyond stretching to the rim of the Sabana. Sunrise and sunset can be spectacular. There are two upmarket touristy restaurants at the top, **Casa Santa Clara**, which also has a café, and **Casa San Isidro** (closed Sunday). The bottom station and path entrance are not far from the top end of Avenida Jiménez de Quesada and Las Aguas terminus of the TransMilenio; you can walk there in daylight with the same precautions you would take anywhere else in the city. If you prefer, you can take a taxi to or from the entrance. There is a health centre at the top if you need it.

The path (operated by Instituto Distrital de Recreación y Departe, www.idrd.gov.co) is dressed stone and comfortably graded all the way up, but as of 2016 was closed indefinitely. No indication has been given when (if) it will reopen. The walk up to **Guadalupe**, the higher peak opposite Monserrate, is not recommended.

At the foot of Monserrate is the **Quinta de Bolívar** ① *C 21, No 4A-31 Este, T1-336 6410, www.quintadebolivar.gov.co, Tue-Fri 0900-1700, Sat-Sun 1000-1600, US$1, reductions for students and children, free on Sun, guided tours 1100 and 1400, in English on Wed 1100.* This is a fine colonial mansion, with splendid gardens and lawns. There are several cannons captured at the battle of Boyacá. The elegant house, once Bolívar's home, is now a museum showing some of his personal possessions and paintings of events in his career.

North Bogotá

North of Calle 68 are expanding wealthy suburbs, shopping malls and classy restaurants, an area regarded as having the best hotels. Between Cra 4 and Cra 5 and Calle 68 and Calle 71 is the **Zona G** (for 'gourmet'), home to some of Bogotá's best (and most expensive) restaurants. The T-shaped pedestrianized area made up by Calle 83 and Cra 13 is Bogotá's **Zona Rosa** (also known as the Zona T) with many fashionable bars, clubs and restaurants. Further north the streets around Parque 93 have more expensive bars and restaurants, while at the very limits of the city, off Carratera 7 between Calle 117 and Calle 119, is **Usaquén**, formerly a satellite town with a pleasant plaza, a popular evening and weekend excursion for Bogotanos wishing to escape the metropolis.

Churches ✝
1 Catedral *B2*
2 Capilla del Sagrario & Palacio Arzobispal *B2*
3 La Tercera Orden *B4*
4 La Veracruz *B3*
5 Mária del Carmen *C2*
6 San Agustín *B2*
7 San Diego *B5*
8 San Francisco *B3*
9 San Ignacio *B2*
10 Santa Clara *B2*

Trans Milenio
bus route - - - - -

North Bogotá is also noted for its huge, lavish shopping malls, which are worth a visit even if the prices don't grab you. One of the largest, the **Hacienda Santa Bárbara** ① *Cra 7 115-60, T1-6120388*, has some 350 shopping outlets within a large country mansion, and parts of the colonial architecture, even some of the old gardens have been retained.

Listings Bogotá *maps pages 886 and 890.*

Tourist information

Instituto Distrital de Turismo (Cra 24, No 40-66, La Soledad, T1-217 0711, www.bogotaturismo. gov.co, open 0700-1630, in Spanish and English) has 12 detailed tourist routes and 7 permanent tourist-information kiosks dotted around the city. They are: **La Candelaria** (Cra 8, No 9-83, T1-555 7627/8, Mon-Sat 0800-1800, Sun and holidays0800-1600), 2-hr tourist walks leave from here daily 1000 and 1400 (Tue and Thu in English); **El Dorado airport** (at international arrivals, T1-746 9636, daily0700-2200); **bus station** (Módulo 5, local 127, T1-410 0929, daily 24 hrs); southern bus terminal (Calle 57 Q Sur 65F-68, T1-555 7696/7, daily 0700-1300); western bus terminal (Diagonal 23 No. 69-60, Modulo 5, Local 127, T1-555 7692/3); **Parque de la Independencia** (Quiosco de la Luz, Cra 7, No 26-07, T1-555 7700/1 Mon-Sat 0900-1700); **Unicentro shopping centre** (Entrada Principal, T1-555 7694/5, Mon-Sat 1100-1900, Sun1100-1600); **Centro Internacional** (Cra 13, No 26-62, T1-555 7700/1, Mon-Sat 0900-1700. There is also a **Cundinamarca tourist office** (C 26, No 51-53, T1-749 1844, www.cundinamarca. gov.co; Mon-Fri 0830-1600).

Guía del Ocio (known as GO, www. goguiadelocio.com.co, also for Cartagena) and Vive.in (www.vive.in) have listings on events, restaurants and clubs in Spanish.

Where to stay

IVA tax of 16% is charged by mid-range and more expensive hotels in Bogotá. It is additional to the bill but included in our price classification. Always insist that taxi drivers at the airport or bus station take you to the address we quote. There are many small, cheap, unregistered hotels and *hostales* in parts of the city which may be unsafe for tourists and are far from the sights.

La Candelaria

Several hostels and hotels are members of the **Asociación de Alojamiento de la Candelaria** (ASACAN), T311-530 2677, asacan on Facebook.

$$$ Abadia Colonial
C 11, No 2-32, T1-341 1884,
www.abadiacolonial.com.
Fine colonial building in the heart of this area. Comfortable rooms if a bit small, ask for a street-facing room, safe, Italian and Colombian dishes in restaurant. Recommended.

$$$ Hotel de la Opera
C 10, No 5-72, T1-336 2066, www.hotelopera.com.co.
Once the residence of Simón Bolívar's personal guard. Opulent, exquisite rooms in colonial, republican and deco style, 2 rooftop restaurants with superb views, spa facilities.

$$ Casa Platypus
Cra 3, No 12F-28, T1-281 1801,
www.casaplatypusbogota.com.
Beautiful colonial building overlooking the Parque de los Periodistas, excellent rooms with extra-large beds and duvets, also has dorms (US$12.25), kitchen, dining room, roof terrace with views of Monserrate. Very helpful. Highly recommended.

$$-$ The Cranky Croc
C 12D, No 3-46, T1-342 2438, www.crankycroc.com.
Aussie-run hostel in a beautiful 300-year-old building, carefully restored to retain many of the original features, lounge with a fireplace. Several private rooms with and without bath and dorms with bunks, US$12-15 pp.

$$-$ Masaya
Cra 2, No 12-48, T1-747 1848,
www.masaya-experience.com.
French-owned hostel with dorms for 4 to 6 (US$12-13.30), also private rooms with breakfast ($$), tapas bar, games, excursions and cultural events. Has other branches in Santa Marta and Medellín ($$-$).

$$-$ Swiss Hostal Martinik
Cra 4, No 11-88, T1-283 3180,
www.hostalbogota.com.
Swiss management, good location, from US$10 pp in 4- to 10-bed dorms, also private rooms, good facilities, information and activities.

$ Alegría's Hostel
C9, No 2-13, T1-282 3168, http://alegriashostel.com.

In the heart of La Candelaria, set around a pleasant patio. Private room and 4- to 10-bed dorms (US$9-10) available.

$ Hostal Fátima
C 12C, No 2-24, T1-281 6389,
www.hostalfatima.com.
A maze of brightly coloured rooms and sunny patios with lots of stained-glass windows and potted plants. Sauna, jacuzzi, weekly programme of events and its own travel agency. Several private rooms with and without bath as well as dorms with bunks (US$8). Long stays available. Also has another branch, **Fátima Suites**, in La Candelaria.

$ Hostal Sue Candelaria
Cra 3, No 12C-18, T1-341 2647,
www.suecandelaria.com.
Excellent facilities, including hot water and places to relax in hammocks. Attracts a young crowd, with a party atmosphere. Dorms with bunks (from US$10).

$ Iku Hostel Backpackers
C 12F, No 2-55, T1-334 8894, http://ikuhostel.com.
Arranges activities from dance to gastronomy, has a tour company, good for students and groups.

Downtown and El Chapinero

$$$ Tequendama
Cra 10, No 26-21, T1-382 0300, www. hotelestequendama.com/nuestros-hoteles/.
One of Bogotá's traditional grand hotels, witness to some of Colombia's most important political events since its inauguration in 1953. With 4 restaurants, a spa, pool and large rooms it is well equipped for the conferences it hosts.

$$ The Book Hotel
Cra 5, No 57-79, Chapinero Alto, T1-745 9988, www.thebookhotel.co.
In an 'English-like' house, quiet, well appointed, with restaurant and café, good reports, also has a bookshop on the premises, **La Madriguera del Conejo**.

$ La Pinta
C 65, No 5-67, T1-211 9526, www.lapinta.com.co, and La Niña, C 66, No 4a-07, T1-704 4323, www.lanina.com.co.
2 popular, welcoming hostels with private rooms, with and without bath, and dorms (US$7.50-11.25), Colombian-run, with gardens, tours and Spanish classes offered, lots of activities. Also has hostels and apartments on the Caribbean coast and in Cali.

North Bogotá
Many international hotel chains are well represented here, such as **Sonesta**, www. sonesta.com (opposite Unicentro), as are local groups such as **Estelar**, www.hotelesestelar.com.

$$$$-$$$ Morrison 84
C 84 Bis, No 13-54, T1-622 3111,
www.hotelmorrison.com.
Handily located near the Zona T, contemporary British design, large rooms with thermo-acoustic windows. It looks out onto the beautiful Parque León de Greiff.

$$ Casona del Patio
Cra 8, No 69-24, T1-212 8805,
http://casonadelpatio.com.
With 24 immaculate rooms set around a sunny patio and well situated near the Zona G, this is one of the best mid-range options. Recommended.

$$-$ Los Andes Hostel
Cra 13A, No 79-07, El Lago, T1-482 9554,
www.losandeshostel.com.
1 block from Zona T and its nightlife, with and without bath, safe, quiet, laundry facilities, airport pick-up, Spanish and salsa classes arranged.

Restaurants

The more exotic and fashionable places to eat are in North Bogotá, but Candelaria has its bistros and good value, typical Colombian food. Take local advice if you want to eat really cheaply in markets or from street stalls.

Throughout the city there are a number of chains with several outlets. Don't miss **Crepes & Waffles** (www.crepesywaffles.com, see website for branches in Colombia and elsewhere), serving very good salads, pittas, crêpes, soups, vegetarian choices, plus lots of desserts, and **Wok** (www.wok.com.co), for Asian cuisine. Also **El Corral** (www.elcorral.com), for hamburgers, pizzas, etc, with regular and **Gourmet** branches; **La Hamburguesería** (www.lahamburgueseria.com), for more than just burgers. Also the popular coffee shop chains **Juan Váldez** (www.juanvaldezcafe.com); and **Oma** (www.cafeoma.com/).

La Candelaria

$$ La Paella
C 11, No 5-1, T1-609 9956.
Close to the Centro Cultural García Márquez, serves Spanish food and specializes in paellas, as well as steaks, fish and gluten-free dishes.

$$ Moros y Cristianos
C 7, No 5-30, T1-342 6273, Facebook: Restaurante-Moros-y-Cristianos-Cocina-Cubana. Mon-Fri 1200-1600, Sat-Sun 1200-1800.
Cuban restaurant with Colombian and other touches. Live music Fri-Sat nights and Sun.

$$ Rosita
C12B 1A-26, T1-283 6737.
On Plazoleta Chorro de Quevedo, this is an excellent little breakfast and lunchtime spot.

$$-$ La Totuma Corrida
Cra 2, No 12B-90, T1-284 9462, Facebook: La-Totuma-Corrida.
On C del Embudo, economic sushi and other Japanese and Colombian fusion dishes. Colourful surroundings.

$ Boulevard Sésamo
Av Jiménez de Quesada 4-64.
Busy vegetarian lunch spot; pay first and find a table; give ticket to waitress; extensive menu includes veggie burgers, vegan empanadas and mixed fruit smoothies.

$ Panadería Pastelería La Vieja Suiza
Cra 3 at C 12C 3-07. Closed Sun.
Tiny place selling coffee, *pasteles*, vegetables, breads and cakes. Has hotel above.

Downtown Bogotá
Many restaurants and cafes along Cra 4A in Barrio La Macarena (behind the Bull Ring), as well as Zona G nearby.

$$$ Criterión
C 69A, No 5-75, T1-310 1377, www.criterion.com.co.
Minimalist decor, expensive French-influenced menu, with shellfish and steak, large wine list; also has booming chain of gastro restaurants, with branches around Bogotá and the rest of the country.

$$$ Estrella de los Ríos
C 26D, No 4-50, La Macarena, T1-334 0502, www.estrelladelosrios.com.
Estrella, the author of several cookbooks, calls her small place an 'anti-restaurant', with no menu. Her food is Colombian and Caribbean. You must book 8 days in advance for a 7-course meal costing US$55, excluding alcohol; cash only.

$$$-$$ Artesano
Cra 4A, No 27-12, T1-337 6853, www.artesanogourmet.com.
Specializes in 'woodfire cooking': fish and meat dishes, as well as pizzas, plus pastas, sandwiches, etc. Also has a high-class *pastelería*.

$$$-$$ La Cigale
C 69A, No 4-93, T1-249 6839, www.lacigale.com.co.
French restaurant, run by Belgian-born François Cornelis, serving a variety of Gallic specialities.

$$$-$$ Tábula
C 29 bis, No 5-90, T1-287 7228, http://elorigendelacomida.co/tabula.
Daily 1200-1600, also Thu-Sat 1900-2300.
Gourmet international menu in stylish surroundings a couple of blocks from La Macarena; also has large chain of gastro-sandwich bars, Sr Ostia, dotted around the city.

$$ Asadero Capachos
C 18, No 4-68, T1-243 4607, www.asaderocapachos.com. Closed Mon.
Not for vegetarians, meat from the Llanos, simple menu, good food, live music Fri-Sun, busy; diners eat in a huge barn-like building with thatch-roofed cubicles to complete the rustic vibe.

$$-$ La Puerta Falsa
C 11, No 6-50, T1-286 5091.
One of Bogotá's oldest, long-standing restaurants, serving excellent value traditional dishes and Spanish-style tapas in a lively, bustling setting.

North Bogotá
North of C 76 there are 3 popular areas for eating and drinking: Zona T, also known as the Zona Rosa, C 83 and Cra 13; further north is Parque 93, surrounded by eating places, most of which have queues at lunchtime; and C 117 with Cra 6A and Cra 7 in Usaquén.

$$$ Abasto
Cra 6, No 119b-52, Usaquén, T1-215 1286, http://abasto.com.co. From 0700 Mon-Fri, 0900 Sat-Sun (closes Sun 1700).
Decribed as "honest" food with the best organic local ingredients, breakfast and market, gourmet coffees and teas. Many good reports.

$$$ Kathmandu
Cra 6, No 117-26, T1-213 3276, http://kathmandusite.com.
Excellent Asian restaurant in Usaquén, with cocktails, events and a shop.

$$$-$$ 80 Sillas
C 118, No 6A-05, Usaquén, T1-644 7766, www.80sillas.com. Daily from 1200 (closed Sun 1800).
All kinds of ceviches and other seafood served in wooden elevated patios with encroaching ferns.

$$$-$$ Coloquial
Cra 6A, No 116-17 in Usaquén, T1-853 8385.
Tue-Sat 1600-0300.
Traditional Colombian cuisine with imaginative twists, plus rich desserts and local cheese, in a stylish modern setting.

$$$-$$ Salto del Angel
Cra 13, No 93A-45, T1-654 5455,
Facebook: Salto-del-Angel-Bogota.
This huge restaurant on Parque 93 has a large, varied menu including steaks, ceviches and international options including fish and chips. On Sat-Sun, after dinner, the tables are cleared and it becomes a popular upmarket disco, plus occasional live music.

$$ Camino del Café
Cra 6A, No 117-26, Usaquén, T1-637 5152,
Facebook: Camino-Del-Café.
Pleasant café with outdoor terrace and Wi-Fi. Good coffees, sandwiches, ice creams and cocktails.

Bars and clubs

La Candelaria
There are any number of bars and cafés around Plaza Chorro de Quevedo and along Cra 3 which come alive in the early evening.

Bogotá Beer Company
C 12D, No 4-02, www.bogotabeercompany.com.
The La Candelaria branch of this expanding chain of good pubs (throughout Bogotá, also in Medellín and on the Caribbean coast), belonging to a microbrewery with 11 types of beer, plus snacks and pizzas.

Quiebra Canto
Cra 5, No 17-76, T1-243 1630,
www.quiebracanto.com.
In colonial house, world music, funk, reggae, soul and salsa, best nights Wed, Thu, friendly crowd.

Downtown to North Bogotá
Most bars and clubs are concentrated in the Cra 11-13, C 80-86 region, known as the Zona Rosa. Some of these have live entertainment. Further south along Cra 7, from C 32 up to C 59 draws an edgier crowd of filmmakers, artists and students.

Galería Café Libro
Cra 11A, No 93-42, T1-218 3435, www.
galeriacafelibro.com.co. Tue-Sat.
Restaurant, bar and dancing, with 2 other branches in Palermo, Tr 15B, No 46-38, and

Salón Café Bohemia, Tr 15B, No 46-32, and 1 in Parque 93, C 11A 93-42

Theatrón
C 58, No 10-32, T1-235 6879, www.portal
theatron.co. Fri-Sat 2100-0500, or later.
In old large theatre, claiming to be the biggest nightclub in Latin America; gay and mixed crowd, attracts international DJs, good atmosphere with 10 different zones, from low-lit bars to heaving dance floors. Be careful leaving the club at night, use a taxi.

Entertainment

Cinema
Consult *El Espectador*, or www.vive.in for programmes. There are cinema complexes in the principal shopping centres; see for instance CineColombia, www.cinecolombia. com. Foreign films, old and new, are shown on weekend mornings in some commercial cinemas and there are many small screening rooms running features.
Cine Paraíso, *C 120A, No 5-69, Usaquén, T1-213 3756, www.cinemaparaiso.com.co.* Foreign art films and independent mainstream productions.
Cinemanía, *Cra 14, No 93A-85, T1-621 0122, www. cinemania.com.co.* Mainstream and foreign art films.
There's an international film festival in mid-Oct (**Festival de Cine de Bogotá**, www.bogocine.com), founded in 1984, and a European film festival (**Eurocine**, www.festivaleurocine.com) in Apr/May.

Dance classes
Punta y Taco, *Salón de Baile, C 85, No 19A-25, of 201B, T300-218 7199, www.puntaytaco.com.* Tango and salsa classes Mon-Fri 0700-2200, Sat 0800-1800, Sun 0800-1200. Lessons, workshops and shows. Flexible class times, professional.

Theatre
Many of the theatres are in the Candelaria area. For **Teatro Colón** (see details on page 888). Bogotá hosts the biennial **Ibero American Theatre Festival** (next in Mar 2018; www.festival deteatro.com.co). The **Temporadas de Opera** and **de Zarzuela** are held annually, the former in Sep, the latter in May-Jun, with international artists (http://www.primerafila.com.co, www.operade colombia.com). In the city centre, **Centro Cultural Gabriel García Márquez** (C 11, entre Cras 5 y 6, T1-283 2200, www.fce.com.co/CCGGM), has activities, concerts, dance classes and exhibitions; it also has a large **FCE** bookshop, **El Corral Gourmet** restaurant and **Banco de Bogotá**.

Festivals

There are many local religious festivals and parades at Easter and Christmas.

Jan Fiesta de Reyes Magos (Three Kings) in the suburb of Egipto (up the hill to the east of Candelaria) with traditional processions is one of the best.

Apr/May Feria Internacional del Libro (book fair) is held in **Corferias** (see below), www.feriadellibro.com.

Jun/Jul Rock al Parque, the biggest annual rock festival in Latin America (www.rockalparque.gov.co).

Sep Festival Internacional de Jazz (www.teatrolibre.com).

Dec Expoartesanía fair, at Corferias, www.expoartesanias.com, an excellent selection of arts and crafts and regional food from across Colombia. Highly recommended.

There are events throughout the year at **Corferias** (Cra 37, No 24-67, www.corferias.com), a vast modern exhibition and entertainment complex.

Shopping

In Barrio Gaitán, Cra 30 y C 65, are rows of leather shops. This is an excellent area to buy made-to-measure leather jackets, good value; not safe at night, go during the day.

Camping equipment

Monodedo, *Cra 16, No 82-22, T1-616 3467, www.monodedo.com.* Good selection of camping and climbing equipment. Enquire here for information about climbing in Colombia.

Tatoo, *C 122, No 18-30, T1-629 9949, and Cra 14A, No 82-56, T1-300 2140, https://tatoo.ws.* Complete outdoor gear suppliers.

Handicrafts

See also markets, below.

Artesanías de Colombia, *Claustro de Las Aguas, next to the Iglesia de las Aguas, Cra 2, No 18-58, see http://artesaniasdecolombia.com.co for other outlets.* Beautiful but expensive designer crafts.

Centro Colombiano de Artesanos, *Cra 7, No 22-66,* and **Colombia Linda**, *Cra 7, No 23-49,* are 2 central craft galleries.

Galería Cano, *Ed Bavaria, Cra 13, No 27-98 (Torre B, Int 119), also at Unicentro, Airport and elsewhere, www.galeriacano.com.co.* Sell textiles, pottery, and gold and gold-plated replicas of some of the jewellery on display in the Gold Museum.

Pasaje Rivas, *C10 y Cra 10.* Persian-style bazaar. Hammocks, basketware, ceramics, cheap.

Jewellery

The pavements and cafés along Av Jiménez, below Cra 7, and on Plazoleta del Rosario are used on weekdays (especially Fri) by emerald dealers. Rows of jewellers and emerald shops also along C 12 with Cra 6. Great expertise is needed in buying: bargains, but synthetics and forgeries abound.

Emerald Trade Centre, *Av Jiménez, No 5-43, p 1 y 2.* Has a collection of outlets in one place.

GMC Galería Minas de Colombia, *Diag 20A, No 0-12, T1-281 6523, www.galeriaminasdecolombia.com, at foot of Monserrate diagonal from Quinta de Bolívar.* Great choice of gold and emerald jewellery at good prices.

Markets

Mercado de Pulgas (fleamarket) *on Cra 7/C 24, on Sun morning and holidays.* A better fleamarket can be found at the Usaquén market around the plaza, Cra 6 y C 119B, on Sun, also a good arts and crafts market at the top of the hill in Usaquén.

Paloquemao food market, *C19, No 25-04, www.plazadepaloquemao.com. Mon-Sat 0430-1630, Sun 0500-1430.* Bogotá's huge central market, good to visit just to see the sheer abundance of Colombia's tropical fruits and flowers. Cheap stalls serving *comida corriente.* Safe.

San Andresito de la 38, *Cra 38 entre C 8 y C12.* Popular market, cheap alcohol, designer sports labels, electrical goods, football shirts.

What to do

Bullfighting

A ban on bullfighting in 2012 was overturned in 2014. Nevertheless, since then the debate has rumbled on which makes trying to predict future legality of the sport a dubious proposition. When bullfighting is allowed, there are *corridas* on Sat and Sun during the season (Jan-Feb), and occasionally for the rest of the year, at the municipally owned **Plaza de Toros de Santamaría** (Cra 6, No 26-50, T1-334 1482, near Parque Independencia). Local bullfight museum at bullring, door No 6.

Cycling

The *Ciclovía* is a set of streets leading from Cra 7 to the west, closed to motor traffic every Sun and bank holidays, 0700-1400 for cyclists, joggers, rollerskaters etc. There are also the extensive *Cicloruta* paths.

Bogotá Bike Tours, *Cra 3, No 12-72, La Candelaria, T1-281 9924, T312-502 0554, www.bogotabiketours.com.* Bike tours (US$12pp) at 1030, 1330, rentals

(US$6.50 half-day), walking tours, cooking classes and more besides.

Bogotravel Tours, *C 12F, No 2-52, T1-282 6313, T313-308 0441, www.bogotraveltours.com.* Bike tours (US$20) and rentals, emeralds tours, walking tours, party bus tour, Zipaquirá and Guatavita, and other tours in Bogotá and beyond; Spanish classes; enthusiastic, local guides.

Football

Tickets for matches at El Campín stadium can be bought in advance at **Federación Colombiana de Futbol** (Cra 45A, No 94-06, http://fcf.com.co) or from online ticketing agencies such as Tuboleta (www.vivetuboleta.com). It is not normally necessary to book in advance, except for the local Santa Fe-Millonarios derby, and internationals. Take a cushion, matches Sun at 1545, Wed at 2000. Big matches can be rowdy and sometimes violent.

Horse riding

Cabalgatas San Francisco, *47 km from the city near La Vega, T310-265 2706, Facebook: Cabalgatas-San-Francisco.* Daily rides around coffee farms, in the mountains, by rivers and lakes, from US$16 per hr.
Riding Colombia, *www.ridingcolombia.com.* Small ecotourism company offering day-long and multi-day horse rides.

Language courses

You need a student visa, not a tourist visa, to study. Some of the best Spanish courses are in the **Universidad Nacional** (see map, page 886, T1-316 5000, www.unal.edu.co, about US$586 for intensive courses, group discount available, or at the **Universidad de los Andes** (T1-339 4949, www.uniandes.edu.co, summer/semester courses US$700, 45/90 hrs), and **Pontificia Universidad Javeriana** (T1-320 8320 ext 4563, www.javeriana.edu.co). Good-value Spanish courses at the **Universidad Pedagógica** (C 79, No 16-32, T1-610 8000 ext 211, http://spanishcourse.pedagogica.edu.co). Good reports. Language exchanges with students wishing to learn English are also popular. **Spanish World Institute** (Cra 4A, No 56-56, T1-248 3399, www.spanishworld institute.com). Personalized courses from beginner to advanced, activities and events organized, 30 hrs US$290.

Trekking

Camina por Colombia, *Cra 7, No 22-31, of 226, T1-286 7487, www.caminaporcolombia.com.* Walks in different parts of Colombia. There are several other groups and operators.

Caminantes del Retorno, *T1-457 0716, or 315-249 0090, www.caminantesdelretorno.com.* A group of guides with 25 years' experience of treks in out-of-the-way places in the country.
Corporación Clorofila Urbana, *Cra 49B, No 91-41, T1-616 8711, Facebook: Corporación Clorofila Urbana.* Offers walking opportunities with an emphasis on environmental awareness.
Sal Si Puedes, *Cra 7, No 17-01, of 640, T1-283 3765, www.salsipuedes.org. Mon-Fri 0800-1700.* Hiking group arranges walks every weekend and sometimes midweek on trails in Cundinamarca, and further afield at national holiday periods; very friendly, welcomes visitors. Hikes are graded for every ability, from 6 km to 4-day excursions of 70 km or more, camping overnight. Groups are often big (30-60), but it's possible to stray from the main group. Reservations should be made and paid for a week or so in advance at.

Tour operators

Aventure Colombia, *Av Jiménez No 4-49, Of 204, T1-702 7069, http://aventurecolombia.com.* Specialize in classic (Caribbean coast, coffee region, the Andes) and alternative (Guajira, Sierra Nevada, Cocuy, Amazon) tours and expeditions across Colombia, focusing on trekking, eco and rural tourism. Head office is in Cartagena. Highly recommended.
Aventureros, *Cra 15, No 79-70, of 403, T1-467 3837, www.aventureros.co. Mon-Fri 0900-1700, Sat 0900-1300.* Arranges a variety of tours and adventure sports throughout the country.
Colombia Oculta, *Cra 29, No 74-19, T1-301 0213, www.colombiaoculta.org.* Adventure tours throughout Colombia, ecotourism, programmed or personalized tours.
De Una Colombia Tours, *Cra 24 (Parkway), No 39b-25, of 501, La Soledad, T1-368 1915, www.deunacolombia.com.* Dutch-run tour agency with tailor-made trips throughout Colombia and an emphasis on introducing tourists to the country's people as well as its landscapes.
Eco-Guías, *Cra 7, No 57-39, of 501, T1-347 5736 or T1-212 1423, www.ecoguias.com.* Colombian/English team specializes in tailor-made trips, ecotourism, adventure sports, trekking, riding and tourism on coffee fincas, efficient, knowledgeable and well organized. Highly recommended.
Universal Tourism, *T313-352 9355, http://universaltourismcolo.wix.com/mbia/inicio.* Individual and small-group tours with bilingual guides (several languages), focus on Colombia from a local's perspective.

Transport

Air

El Dorado airport, on Av El Dorado, has 2 terminals: Terminal 1 for all international and most domestic flights. Some **Avianca** domestic flights and smaller airlines use Puente Aéreo (Terminal 2). T1-266 2000 for the airport call centre, or visit http://eldorado. aero/ for information in Spanish, Portuguese, French and English. Allow at least 2 hrs for checking in and security for all flights. The terminals have *casas de cambio* and ATMs which accept international credit cards. Use only uniformed porters. There are tourist offices in international arrivals and in domestic arrivals, see Tourist information, above. An expansion programme is under way and an additional airport, El Dorado II, is planned for 2021, in the east of Bogotá.

The taxi fare from airport to city is roughly US$10. Only take a yellow, registered taxi by getting a ticket from the official booth at international, or domestic arrivals. There are *colectivos* (US$1-1.50 plus luggage pp) from airport to centre. A *bus satélite* connects the terminals and the bus stop for the city, 0500-2300. The **TransMilenio** extends almost to the airport on a route starting at C 100 on Cra 7, then taking Calle 26. A feeder bus links the airport with the TransMilenio terminus, Portal Eldorado. It is usually too crowded for luggage.

For internal flights, which serve all parts of the country, see page 1005. Reconfirmation is not necessary if booking online. Otherwise reconfirm all flights 48 hrs before departure.

Bus

Local Fares start at US$0.60, depending on length of route and time of day. Most buses have day/night tariff advertised in the window. **Busetas** (green) charge a little more and can be dirty. Fares are a little higher on Sun and holidays. The **TransMilenio** (www.transmilenio.gov.co), an articulated bus system running on dedicated lanes connects North, Central and South Bogotá. **Corriente** services stop at all principal road intersections, *expresos* limited stops only. Journeys cost US$0.60-0.80; charge cards are available for frequent use. Using the **TransMilenio** is a good way of getting around, but it can be crowded and confusing; make sure you know which bus stops at your destination. Taking luggage onto the **TransMilenio** is not recommended.

Long distance The main **Terminal de Transportes** is at Diagonal 23, No 69-60, near Av Boyacá (Cra 72) between El Dorado (Av 26) and Av Centenario (C 13), sometimes referred to as Terminal El Salitre, T1-423 3630, www. terminaldetransporte.gov.co. There is also access from Cra 68. It is divided in 5 modules; modules 1-3 have several bus companies serving similar destinations, with luggage deposits at the entrance to each module. Module 4 is for interdepartmental taxis and has a first aid centre beside it (open 24 hrs) and module 5 is for arrivals. If possible, buy tickets at the ticket office before travelling to avoid overcharging and to guarantee a seat, especially during bank holidays. Fares and journey times are given under destinations below. If you are travelling to or from the north or northwest, you can significantly cut down on the journey time by taking the **TransMilenio** to Portal del Norte, or Portal de la 80 on C 80, thus avoiding an arduous journey through Bogotá's traffic. If you are travelling to or from the south, many buses use the **Terminal de Transportes del Sur**, C 57 Q Sur, No 75F-82, by Autopista Sur, near the Portal del Sur **TransMilenio** terminus. This is as convenient for the centre of the city as the main terminal if you don't have large bags. To get to the main terminal take a bus marked '**Terminal terrestre**' from the centre or a *buseta* on Cra 10. A taxi costs around US$5 from or to the centre, with a surcharge at night. Give your desired address at the kiosk in module 5, which will print out a slip with the address and price. At airport and bus terminals, unofficial taxis are dangerous and should be avoided. To get into town from the terminal take buses marked 'Centro' or 'Germania'; ask the driver where to get off (the 'Germania' bus goes up to the centre). To get to North Bogotá from the terminal, take a bus heading in that direction on Cra 68.

International Ormeño, bus terminal modelo 2, T1-410 7522, has a service Lima-Caracas 3 days a week via Cúcuta; there is also a Bogotá-Lima service weekly. International tickets with Ormeño can only be bought at the bus terminal. Much better (and cheaper) is to do the trip in stages and enjoy the countries you are travelling through.

Tip...

If going to towns in Boyacá or Cundinamarca for a long weekend, leave Bogotá before Friday 1200 as it can take 1½ hours to get from the terminal to outskirts. Try to return before 1300, or ask to be set down in North Bogotá and take a **TransMilenio** bus to centre (see above regarding luggage).

Car hire

There are lots of agencies at the airport.
Colombiana Rent a Car, Av Boyacá, No 63-12,
T1-473 8694, www.colombianarentacar.com.

Taxi

See Taxi, page 1006. Taxis are relatively cheap,
with fares priced in units, starting at 25. The
minimum fare is about US$1.30. Average fare
from North Bogotá to the centre US$6. Check for
additional charges above what the meter states
eg: night charge and rides to the airport. At busy
times, empty taxis flagged down on the street
may refuse to take you to less popular places.
If you are going to an address out of the city
centre, it is helpful to know the neighbourhood
(barrio) you are going to as well as the street
address, eg Chicó, Chapinero (ask at your hotel).
Radio taxis are recommended for safety and
reliability; when you call, the dispatcher gives
you a cab number, confirm this when it arrives.
Try these numbers and websites: T434 2000,
www.autotaxiejecutivo.com; T250 3670, or www.
coopteletaxi.com. Also the taxi apps such as
http://tappsi.co and www.easytaxi.com/co/.

Around Bogotá

a wealth of weekend escapes

The basin on which Bogotá stands, with high ranges of the Cordillera to the east, is known as
La Sabana de Bogotá and is the centre of Colombia's important cut-flower industry. Around
La Sabana are many places of interest in nearby towns for weekend excursions out of the city,
including the salt cathedral at Zipaquirá and the Laguna de Guatavita, perhaps the nearest place
the Spaniards came to finding their El Dorado.

★Zipaquirá *Colour map 1, B3.*

Zipaquirá's famous rock salt mine is still producing salt after centuries. Within the mines, the
Salt Cathedral ⓘ *www.catedraldesal.gov.co, daily 0900-1740 (last entry 1640), various ticket
combinations available starting at US$11.30; discounts for children and seniors,* is one of the major
attractions of Colombia. The entrance is in hills about 20 minutes' walk west of the town from
Parque Villaveces. At the site, there is an information centre and the **Museo de la Salmuera (Brine)**
ⓘ *US$1,* which explains how salt is produced. The original underground cathedral was dedicated
in 1954 to Nuestra Señora del Rosario (patron saint of miners). Continuing deterioration made the
whole cave unsafe and it was closed.

A remarkable, new salt cathedral, minimalist in style, was opened on 16 December 1995. Inside,
near the entrance, are the 14 Stations of the Cross, each sculpted by a different artist. Other sections
of the cathedral follow to the Nave, 180 m below the surface, with huge pillars 'growing' out of the
salt. All is discreetly illuminated and gives an austere impression.

Zipaquirá has a pleasant colonial plaza, which is dominated by a brick cathedral (see www.
zipaquira-cundinamarca.gov.co). Tuesday is market day. In the town is the **Museo Quevedo
Zornoza** ⓘ *C 3, No 7-69, Mon-Fri 0830-1200, 1400-1700, Sat-Sun 0900-1600, US$1,* which displays
musical instruments and paraphernalia including the piano of General Santander. The **Museo
Arqueológico** ⓘ *C 1, No 6-21, T1-852 3499, next to the Parque Villaveces entrance, Tue-Sun 1000-1800,
US$1.60,* houses more than 1500 pieces of pre-Columbian pottery at the station ⓘ *C 4, No 11-01,
T1-593 9150 ext 138.*

Around Zipaquirá

Nemocón, 15 km northeast of Zipaquirá, has **salt mines** ⓘ *C 2, No 0-05, T1-854 4120, www.minadesal.
gov.co, daily 0900-1700, US$7.10, children US$4.60, 10 mins' walk from centre,* colourfully lit, with a
small museum, and a church with original 17th-century frescos. (ATM on main plaza.) **Tourist office**
ⓘ *Cra 6, No 6-11, T1-854 4123.* A side road connects with the Bogotá–Cúcuta highway. Some 8 km
beyond Nemocón, with its own access to the main Tunja road, is **Suesca,** a centre of rock climbing
on sandstone cliffs overlooking the Río Bogotá. **Tourist office** ⓘ *Cra 4, No 2-20, T1-856 3565.*

Guatavita

The modern town of Guatavita Nueva, 75 km from Bogotá at 2650 m, is a popular haunt for
Bogotanos. It was rebuilt in replica colonial style when the old town of Guatavita was submerged
by the Embalse de Tominé. There is a small bullring, cathedral and two small museums, one devoted

ON THE ROAD

The Gilded Man

The basis of the El Dorado (Gilded Man) story is established fact. It was the custom of the Chibcha king to be coated annually with resin, on which gold dust was stuck, and then to be taken out on Laguna de Guatavita on a ceremonial raft. He then plunged into the lake and emerged with the resin and gold dust washed off. The lake was also the repository of precious objects thrown in as offerings; there have been several attempts to drain it (the first, by the Spaniards in colonial times, caused the sharp cut in the crater rim) and many items have been recovered over the years. The factual basis of the El Dorado story was confirmed by the discovery of a miniature raft with ceremonial figures on it, made from gold wire, which is now one of the most prized treasures of the Museo del Oro in Bogotá. Part of the raft is missing; the story is that the gold from it ended up in one of the finder's teeth! (Read John Hemming's *The Search for El Dorado* on the subject.)

to the Muisca people and the other to relics of the old Guatavita church. There many artisan shops, which sell *ruanas*. Market day is Sunday. The tourist information booth can find accommodation.

Laguna de Guatavita, a sacred lake of the Muisca, is where the legend of El Dorado (see box, above) originated. Access to the Laguna del Cacique Guatavita y Cuchilla de Peñas Blancas park is only allowed with a permit from the **Corporación Autónoma Regional de Cundinamarca** (CAR) ① *Cra 7, No 36-45, Bogotá, T1-320 9000, lake open Tue-Sun 0900-1600 (closed Tue when Mon is a holiday) but you can stay in the park till 1800, US$5 for foreigners, children and locals pay less*. The lake is a quiet, beautiful place; you can walk right round it, 1½ hours, or climb to the rim of the crater. From the park entrance there are guided walks and interpreted trails; guides speak English and Spanish. Opinions differ on whether the crater is volcanic or a meteorite impact, but from the rim at 3100 m there are extensive views over the countryside.

Southwest of Bogotá

The picturesque Simón Bolívar Highway runs 132 km from Bogotá to **Girardot**, the former main river port for Bogotá. About 20 km along this road from the centre of Bogotá is Soacha, the end of the built-up area. A right fork here leads to the **Chicaque Parque Natural** ① *in Bogotá, Tr 26B, No 41-51, La Soledad, T1-368 3114, www.chicaque.com, park open daily 0800-1500, US$5.15, with separate prices for lodging, guides, riding*, a privately owned 300 ha park, principally cloudforest between 2100 m and 2700 m on the edge of the Sabana de Bogotá. It is a popular spot for walkers and riders at weekends with good facilities for day visitors and a Swiss-style *refugio*, cabins, camping and restaurant, about 45 minutes down the trail from the entrance (full board price from US$70 double, camping from US$21).

Towards Honda

The Sabana de Bogotá is dotted with farms and groves of eucalyptus. Two routes go to Honda (see Transport, page 903). The older road passes through the small towns of Fontibón, Madrid and **Facatativá**, 40 km from Bogotá. Some 3 km from Facatativá, on the road to the west, is the park of Piedras de Tunja, a natural rock amphitheatre with enormous stones, numerous indigenous pictographs and an artificial lake. The roads meet at **Villeta**, 71 km from Facatativá, a popular weekend resort. The road continues to the interesting historical town of **Guaduas**. In the main plaza is a statue of the heroine of independence (Policarpa Salavarrieta), the cathedral and one of several museums in the town; also the **tourist office** ① *C3, No3-45, T1-846 6052, Mon-Fri 0800-1200/1400-1700, Sat 0800-1200*. Sunday market. Nearby La Piedra Capira offers great views of Río Magdalena. From here, a bus to Honda is US$1.75, one hour.

Honda and beyond

On the west bank of the Río Magdalena, Honda was founded in 1539. Until the rise of first rail, then road transport, it was a major port for cargo and passengers from the centre of the country to the Caribbean. It is well known for its many bridges spanning the Ríos Magdalena and Guali, at whose junction the town lies. The historic centre has narrow, picturesque streets and the lively indoor market in a grand, early 20th-century building. There are two museums: **Museo del Río Magdalena**

① at end of C del Retiro, irregular opening hours, and **Casa Museo Alfonso López Pumarejo** ① C13, No 11-75, Plaza América, Tue-Sat 0800-1200, 1400-1800, Sun 0900-1300, free, dedicated to the ex-president (1934-38, 1942-45). El Salto de Honda (the rapids which separate the Lower from the Upper Magdalena) is just below the town. In February the Magdalena rises and fishing is unusually good.

Beyond Honda the road passes cattle fincas and eroded outcrops on its way to La Dorada and, across the river, Puerto Salgar with a huge military base. The highway to Medellín leaves the south–north road to Santa Marta just before Puerto Triunfo. The other main road from Honda heads west to Manizales (see page 973).

Villavicencio and Los Llanos *Colour map 1, B3.*

Through Colombia's longest tunnel, the impressive Buenavista, and along an 85-km road running southeast from Bogotá lies **Villavicencio**, capital of Meta Department. For information visit, **Instituto de Turismo de Villavicencio** ① C 33A, No 39-43, p 2, Centro, T8-683 3681 or 8-673 3681, www.turismovillavicencio.gov.co, Mon-Sat 0900-1200, 1400-1800, with offices at the airport and bus terminal. See also **Instituto de Turismo del Meta** ① Km 3, Vía Camino Ganadero, Parque Las Malocas, T8-683-0848 or 314-405 0407, www.turismometa.gov.co, Mon-Fri 0730-1600.

Villavicencio (known as 'Villavo') is a modern town and is a good base for visiting Los Llanos (the plains), which stretch more than 800 km east from the foot of the Eastern Cordillera as far as Puerto Carreño, on the Orinoco in Venezuela. Los Llanos is cowboy country and the never-ending expanse of fertile plains makes it ideal for cattle raising, the area's main industry. The area is also rich in oil and the flames from distant oil refineries can be seen flickering on the horizon. Some ranches welcome visitors and tour operators are beginning to offer trips to destinations such as San José de Guaviare, southeast of Villavicencio, the Ecolodge Juan Solito (www.juansolito.com) in Casanare, Parque Nacional Tuparro, reached from Puerto Carreño, and Los Cerros de Mavecure, reached from Puerto Inírida (both near the Venezuelan border). Consult tour operators such as De Una, Colombia Oculta and Aventure Colombia in Bogotá (see page 897).

Serranía de la Macarena

Caño Cristales is a river in which Macarenia clavigera plants bloom deep red for a brief period and, together with other natural colours – red, blue, green and black – make an amazing spectacle. It is often called "the most beautiful river in the world". The river, in the south of the Serranía de la Macarena, is reached from the town of La Macarena, to which there are three weekly flights from Bogotá from June to December with **Satena** and local air taxi flights from Villavicencio. You must check in advance when the phenomenon is occurring as it can happen anytime between June and November. The site is closed January-May. The area is protected and policed, but you cannot camp there or go independently. Several agencies run tours and there are two- to five-day packages available, all controlled by **Cormacarena** ① www.cormacarena.gov.co. At bank holidays and weekends it is usually packed. Two websites give a wealth of information: www.cano-cristales.com (Calle 5, No 7-35, La Macarena, T321-842 2728) and the private portal of local photographer Mario Carvajal, www.canocristales.co. As of this writing, the area of La Macarena near Río Caño is safe to visit, but don't venture outside the organized tour routes and check with local authorities before embarking anywhere else in La Macarena.

Listings Around Bogotá

Where to stay

Zipaquirá

$$ Cacique Real
Cra 6, No 2-36, T1-851 0209 or 311-532 1251, www.hotelcaciquereal.com.
Declared a Patrimonio Cultural, fine little, colonial-style hotel, lovely courtyard with hanging baskets, good rooms, car park.

$$-$ Casa Virrey
C 3, No 6-21, T1-852 3720, casavirreyorani@hotmail.com.
Housed in a new building with comfortable rooms.

$ Torre Real
C 8, No 5-92, T1-851 1901, hoteltorrereal@yahoo.es.
Light and airy rooms with large beds.

Around Zipaquirá: Suesca

$$$ La Esperanza
Cra 71C, No 98A-44, Vereda Cuaya, Km 1along railway from Suesca, T1-637 3753 (Bogotá), 320-277 0011 (Suesca), www.hotellaesperanza.com.co.
With restaurant, conference centre, sauna, camping at Campamento Zhay, or rent a house or room sleeping 3-5, good for groups.

$ Caminos de Suesca
Vereda Cacicazgo, Entrada a las Rocas, T310-341 8941, http://caminosdesuesca.wix.com/hostal.
Hostal and restaurant offering packages that include adventure sports or just B&B, very helpful. Rooms are cheaper midweek and without bath, also has dorm accommodation. Arranges all sorts of outdoor sports, climbing, riding, rafting, parapenting, in various combinations. Recommended.

Honda

$$$ Posada Las Trampas
Cra 10A, No 11-05, T310-343 5151, www.posadalastrampas.com.
Boutique hotel in a converted mansion on C Las Trampas, suites and standard rooms, pool on the terrace, bar and business centre.

$$$-$$ Casa Belle Epoque
C 12, No 12A-21, Cuesta de San Francisco, T8-251 1176/310-481 4090, www.casabelleepoque.com.
A lovely old house overlooking the market, with spacious rooms, all with fan or a/c, 1 small dorm ($ pp), beautiful roof terrace with jacuzzi, pool and period touches. British/Colombian-run, very helpful, advance booking preferred. Arranges horse riding, boat and fishing trips. Recommended.

$$-$ Riviera Plaza
C 14, No 12-19, T312-745 1446, hotelrivieraplaza@hotmail.com.
Cheaper with fan, rooms around a large pool, which is open till 2200. End rooms have views over the Río Gualí and the colonial part of town. All meals extra, in restaurant 0700-2100.

$ Calle Real
Cra 11, No 14-40, T8-251 7737, opposite Teatro Honda.
Central, safe, cheaper with fan, parking, restaurant, small rooftop pool.

$ Tolima Plaza
Cra 11, No 15-75, T8-251 7216.
Large, rambling hotel, pool, large car park. Rooms are a bit spartan but OK, with fan, cheaper in shared room. Helpful management.

Villavicencio and Los Llanos

$$$ Hotel del Llano
Cra 30, No 49-77, T311-562 5040, www.hoteldelllano.com.
Tucked under the forested hills of the Cordillera Oriental, a smart modern option with good rooms, spa, sauna, pool, restaurant, tour agency.

$$$-$$ María Gloria
Cra 38, No 20-26, T8-672 0197, www.hotelmariagloria.com.
Large rooms in a featureless building, with a good pool area with sauna and Turkish bath.

$$ Savoy
C 41, No 31-02, T8-662 2666.
Simple rooms with a/c. Vegetarian restaurant downstairs.

$ Mochilero's Hostel
C 18, No 39-08-10, Barrio Balatá, T8-667 6723/320-488 5046, Facebook: mochileroshostelvillavicencio.
Hostel with private rooms and dorms, restaurant, also offers salsa and yoga classes, adventure tours.

Restaurants

Zipaquirá
There are several eating places near the plaza and there is a **Plazoleta de Comidas** in town.

$$$ Andrés Carne de Res
C 3, No 11-56, Chía, T1-863 7880, www. andrescarnederes.com. Thu-Sun 1200 till late.
On the route north to Zipaquirá, this arty, rustic restaurant and bar has become a tourist institution with typical food, highly original decor, 'performers' to liven things up and free arts and crafts workshops for children. Opposite is an **Andrés Exprés** take-away stand, which is open daily. Now also has 2 branches in North Bogotá, but this is the original.

Honda
C Centenario is the Zona Rosa, with restaurants, burger bars, discos, supermarkets, etc. It is buzzing at weekends. **Alejo Parrilla** (C Centenario, only Fri-Sun evenings), is best for meat. **Arepas La 21** (street stall at corner of Cra 21 y C Centenario, opposite restaurant **Sazón y Son**), sells *pinchos* (kebabs), *empanadas* and *torta de chócolo* (maize).

There is an economical fish restaurant by Río Magdalena a short walk from town, serving fresh catch of the day: **KZ (Donde Marta)**, at Av Pacho María, Bahía 3.

Festivals

Honda

Feb **Subienda Festival**. People come from all over the country for the festival, which marks the end of the fishing season.

Mar/Apr **Semana Santa**. Celebrations are good.

Villavicencio and Los Llanos

Jun-Jul **Torneo Internacional del Joropo**, involving parades, singers and over 3000 couples dancing the *joropo* in the street.

Mid-Oct **Encuentro Mundial de Coleo**. Similar to rodeo in which cowboys tumble young calves by grabbing their tails and twisting them until they lose their balance.

Dec **Festival Llanero**, www.turismovillavicencio. gov.co, with *joropo* and other music, *coleo* and other cowboy skills and gastronomy from the Llanos.

What to do

Around Zipaquirá

Rock climbing

For information call **Monodedo** climbing centre, T311-577 6008, www.monodedo.com (shop open at weekends). In Suesca turn right at the entrance to Las Rocas, past Rica Pizza restaurant. **Ricardo Cortés**, the owner of Rica Pizza, also arranges climbing trips and local accommodation. See also **Caminos de Suesca**, Where to stay.

Transport

Zipaquirá

Bus The Zipaquirá bus station is 15 mins' walk from the mines and cathedral. Many buses from **Bogotá**: from the Terminal de Transporte, take a bus from Módulo 3, otherwise from the Intermunicipio terminal at the Portal del Norte terminus of the **TransMilenio** in North Bogotá, US$1.50 each way on either route, 1½ hrs from Terminal de Transport, 45 mins from Portal Norte. Zipaquirá can also be reached from Tunja (see page 904), by taking a Bogotá-bound bus and getting off at La Caro for connection to Zipaquirá, US$2.50. Note when arriving to C174 terminus from Zipaquirá you need to buy a **TransMilenio** bus ticket to leave the station. To avoid this, ask the driver to drop you off before the bus station.

Train La Sabana station at C 13, No 18-24, Bogotá. A slow tourist steam train runs on Sat, Sun and holidays at 0815, calling at **Usaquén** in the north of Bogotá, going north to **Zipaquirá** (1105) and **Cajicá**, back in Bogotá, **La Sabana** at 1730. In 2016 trains left from Usaquén at 0915, arriving back at 1630. Cost: adult US$17.30, child up to 12, US$12.70. Tickets should be bought in advance at La Sabana station, T1-316 1300, or Usaquén station, Trv 10, No 100-08, Mon-Fri 0830-1730, Sat 0800-1700, www.turistren.com.co, or from travel agents.

Guatavita

Bus Bogotá–Guatavita Nueva via Autopista del Norte and Sesquilé, from Portal del Norte on the **TransMilenio**, US$2.75, 2 hrs, several departures morning; last return bus at 1730. A 2nd route goes from C 72 y Cra 13 opposite Universidad Pedagógica via La Calera, Tres Esquinas, Guasca and Guatavita Nueva, US$2.30. The routes meet at the entrance to the park, but from Guatavita Nueva it's a 1½-hr walk to the park entrance, or you can share vehicle, about US$5 pp.

Southwest of Bogotá

To reach the **Chicaque Parque Natural**, take the **Transmilenio** from Bogotá to Terreros/Hospital in Soacha. At weekends the park runs transport from there for US$2 each way at set times. See www.chicaque.com for details of how to arrive on weekdays and how to get there by car.

Honda

Bus terminal is on the outskirts, where Diagonal 17 meets the main road heading north to La Dorada. Buses to **Bogotá** take 2 routes, via Facatativá ('Faca') which is slower but has cheaper tolls and is used by most companies, and via La Vega and C 80 to the north. The roads diverge at Villeta. Several companies go to Bogotá via Faca, from US$9.30, 4-5 hrs; **Cundinamarca** go via La Vega, 3 a day, US$10 (also to **Zipaquirá**, US$12), also **Tax La Feria** *camioneta*, 9 a day on Manizales-Bogotá route, 3½ hrs, US$13 (for La Feria, T1-263 8678, or 320-696 6016). To **Manizales**, US$14. Several daily buses to **Medellín**, Bolivariano, Flota Magdalena, US$15-18, 6 hrs.

Villavicencio and Los Llanos

Air Avianca, LATAM and Satena to **Bogotá** daily (it is much more convenient to go by bus to Villavicencio than by plane). Satena flies to **Puerto Carreño** and to destinations in the Llanos.

Bus Station outside town, taxi US$1.50. To/from **Bogotá**, Flota Magdalena, Bolivariano mini vans and others leave frequently, US$7.15, 1½ hrs.

Bogotá to the
Venezuelan border

The main road route from Bogotá to Venezuela has some beautiful stretches and passes through, or near, several colonial towns. In Cundinamarca and Boyacá it gives access to historical battle sites and the Sierra Nevada del Cocuy, excellent climbing and hiking country. The principal towns, both with a strong colonial heritage, are Tunja and charming Villa de Leiva.

The highway crosses Santander and Norte de Santander Departments on its way to Cúcuta. That this was an important route for the Spaniards can be seen in the colonial villages, like Barichara, and the more important centres like Bucaramanga and Pamplona. There is also some grand scenery in the Chicamocha canyon and the eastern cordillera, with possibilities for adventure sports.

Bogotá to Villa de Leiva
colonial towns with historic and prehistoric sites nearby

Tunja *Colour map 1, B3.*

Tunja, capital of Boyacá Department and 137 km from Bogotá, has some of the finest and best-preserved colonial churches in Colombia. When the Spaniards arrived in what is now Boyacá, Tunja was already an indigenous city, the seat of the Zipa, one of the two Chibcha kings. It was refounded as a Spanish city by Gonzalo Suárez Rendón in 1539. The **Cathedral** and five other churches are all worth visiting, particularly for their colonial woodwork and lavish decoration.

The **Casa del Fundador Suárez Rendón** ① *Plaza de Bolívar (Cra 9, No 19-56, next door to the cathedral), daily 0830-1230, 1400-1800, US$1*, is one of Colombia's few mansions of a Spanish conquistador (1539-1543) and has a peaceful courtyard with fine views of the valley; see the unique series of plateresque paintings on the ceilings. The **municipal tourist office** is at ① *Cra 9, No 9-95, T8-740 5770, www.tunja-boyaca.gov.co/turismo.shtml.*

The market, near Plaza de Toros on the outskirts of town, is open every day (good for *ruanas* and blankets). Friday is main market day. During the week before Christmas (16-22 December), there is a lively festival with local music, traditional dancing and fireworks.

The battle of Boyacá was fought about 16 km south of Tunja, on the road to Bogotá. Overlooking the bridge at Boyacá is a large **monument to Bolívar** ① *daily 0800-1800, entrance free.* There are several other monuments, an exhibition hall and restaurant at the site. Bus from Tunja, US$1, ask for 'El Puente'. Bolívar took Tunja on 6 August 1819, and next day his troops, fortified by a British Legion, the only professional soldiers among them, fought the Spaniards on the banks of the swollen Río Teatinos. With the loss of only 13 killed and 53 wounded they captured 1600 men and 39 officers. Only 50 men escaped, and when these told their tale in Bogotá the Viceroy Samao fled in such haste that he left half a million pesos of the royal funds.

☆Villa de Leiva *Colour map 1, B4.*

About 40 km west is the beautiful and unmissable colonial town of **Villa de Leiva** (also spelt Leyva), which has one of the largest plazas in the Americas. It is surrounded by cobbled streets, a charming

Best for
Adventure sports ■ Colonial heritage ■ Independence history

peaceful place. The town dates back to the early days of Spanish rule (1572), but unlike Tunja, it has been declared a national monument so will not be modernized. The first president of Nueva Granada, Andrés Días Venero de Leiva, lived in the town. Many of the **colonial houses** are now hotels, others are museums, such as the restored birthplace of the independence hero, **Casa de Antonio Ricaurte** ① *Cra 8 y C 15, Wed-Fri 0900-1200, 1400-1700, Sat-Sun 0900-1300, 1400-1800, free.* Ricaurte was born in Villa de Leiva and died in 1814 at San Mateo, Venezuela, fighting with Bolívar's army. The house has a nice courtyard and garden. **Casa de Nariño** ① *Cra 9, No 10-25, daily except Wed 0900-1700, free,* displays documents from the Independence period. The **Casa del Primer Congreso** ① *Cra 9, No 13-25, on the corner of the Plaza Mayor, daily 0800-1200, 1400-1700, free,* in which the first Convention of the United Provinces of New Granada was held, is worth a visit if the local authority is not in session. On the Plaza Mayor the **Casa-Museo Luis Alberto Acuña** ① *http:// casamuseoacuna8.wix.com/casamuseoacuna, US$2, daily 1000-1200, 1400-1800, guided tours at weekends,* houses fascinating examples of Acuña's work.

The **Monasterio de las Carmelitas Descalzas** ① *C 14 y Cra 10, Sat, Sun and holidays 1000-1300, 1400-1700, US$0.75,* has one of the best museums of religious art in Colombia. Part of the monastery is the **Iglesia del Carmen** and the **Convento**, all worth a visit. The shops in the plaza and adjoining streets have a great selection of Colombian handicrafts.

Some colonial houses close Monday to Friday out of season, but the trip is worthwhile for the views and for long, peaceful walks in the hills. Many places, particularly restaurants, are closed Monday and Tuesday. Market day is Saturday, held in the Plaza de Mercado 0400-1300. During weekends and public holidays, the town is very crowded with Bogotanos. The helpful **tourist office** ① *Cra 9, No 13-11 just off the plaza, T8-732 0232, http://villadeleyva-boyaca.gov.co, Tue-Fri 0800-1230, 1400-1800, Sat 0800-*

Villa de Leiva

To ③ ② & Museo Paleontológico

N

200 metres
200 yards

To Santa Sofía, Ecce-Homo & El Fósil

Av Circunvalar

Monasterio de las Carmelitas Descalzas

Plazuela de San Agustín

Casa de Antonio Ricaurte

Alcaldía

Museo Luis Alberto Acuña

Casa del Primer Congreso

Plaza Mayor

Iglesia Parroquial

Casa de Antonio Nariño

Parque Nariño

Plaza de Mercado

San Francisco

To Bogotá, via Tunja or Chiquinquirá

Where to stay ⊜
1 Candelaria
2 Casa Viena
3 Colombian Highlands & Hostal Renacer
5 El Marqués de San Jorge
6 El Molino la Mesopotamia
7 Hostal Sinduly
8 Plaza Mayor
9 Posada de los Angeles
10 Posada Don Blas

Restaurants ❼
1 Casa Blanca
2 Casa Quintero (La Cocina de la Gata, Savia, Zarina)
3 Olivas & Especias and Carnes & Olivas

1500, has local maps, gives advice on cheaper accommodation and bus schedules. Useful websites include www.envilladeleyva.com, and www.villaleyvanos.com. There is an ATM on the Plaza Mayor.

Around Villa de Leiva

The wide valley to the west of Villa de Leiva abounds in fossils. A **palaeontological museum** ① *15 mins' walk north of the town, Cra 9, No 11-42, US$1.10, Tue-Sat 0900-1200, 1400-1700, Sun 0900-1500*, part of the Universidad Nacional de Colombia, this museum has some 440 well-displayed exhibits. Some 5 km along the road to Santa Sofía is the fossil of a dinosaur (possibly a Kronosaurus) found in 1977, now with a museum built around it. A second fossil found in 2000 nearby has been put alongside. Look for road signs to **El Fósil** ① *daily 0800-1800, US$2*. About 2 km from El Fósil along this road is the turning for (1 km) the archaeological site of **Parque Arqueológico de Monquirá** or **El Infiernito** ① *Tue-Sun 0900-1200, 1400-1700, US$1.75 with guide*, where there are several carved stones believed to be giant phalli and a solar calendar. About 1 km beyond El Infiernito is the **Fibas Jardín del Desierto** ① *T311-222 2399, US$5, Wed-Sun 0830-1730, Mon and Tue with forewarning*, which sells cactus and desert plants. It features two mazes, based on indigenous designs, in which meditation exercises are held.

Some 6 km after the Infiernito turning is the **Monasterio del Santo Ecce-Homo** (founded 1620) ① *museum open Mon-Fri 0900-1700, US$1.50*; note the fossils on the floor at the entrance. It was built by the Dominicans between 1650 and 1695. It was reclaimed from the military in 1920, since when it has been repeatedly robbed; some of the religious art is now in the Chiquinquirá museum. What can be seen of the monastery is impressive, but the fabric and roof are in a poor state. There are buses from Villa de Leiva (0800-1745) to Santa Sofía, US$2.20-; it is 30 minutes to the crossing, then a 1-km walk to the monastery. About 12 km north of Villa de Leiva is a right turn for the **Santuario de Fauna y Flora de Iguaque** ① *www.parquesnacionales.gov.co, or Naturar Iguaque, T312-585 9892, http://naturariguaquesp.weebly.com, the Laguna Sagrada section is open (2016), but other parts are closed, 0800-1000 for access to the 4.6 km trail, US$14 (US$5.30 for Colombians)*. The 6750-ha park is mainly high cloudforest of oak, fig and other temperate trees, many covered with epiphytes, lichens and bromeliads. There is also *páramo* (moorland) and a series of lakes at over 3400 m, and the mountains rise to 3800 m. At the Furachiogua visitor centre, there is accommodation in lodge dorms and camping, restaurant, entry 0800-1700.

Ráquira

In the Chibcha language, **Ráquira** means 'city of pots' and with over 100 *artesanía* shops selling earthenware pottery in a village of just a dozen blocks, it is rightly considered the capital of Colombian handicrafts (see http://raquira.turismo.co). In recent years, however, there has been an influx of cheap products from Ecuador, somewhat diluting its appeal. The village itself, 25 km from Villa de Leiva, has been painted in an array of primary colours and has a picturesque plaza embellished with terracotta statues. Accommodation ($$-$) and places to eat on or near the plaza.

About 7 km along a very rough road, which winds up above Ráquira affording spectacular views, is the beautiful 16th-century **Monasterio Desierto de La Candelaria** ① *daily 0900-1200, 1300-1700, US$2.50 includes Hermit's Cave*. On the altar of the fine church is the painting of the Virgen de La Candelaria, dating from 1597, by Francisco del Pozo de Tunja. The painting's anniversary is celebrated on 1 February and 28 August, the saint's day of San Agustín. The convent has two beautiful cloisters, one with a 170-year-old dwarf orange tree, the other virtually untouched since the 17th century. They are lined with anonymous 17th-century paintings of the life of San Agustín.

Chiquinquirá *Colour map 1, B3.*

On the west side of the valley of the Río Suárez, 134 km from Bogotá and 80 km from Tunja, this is a busy market town for this large coffee and cattle region. In December thousands of pilgrims honour a painting of the Virgin whose fading colours were restored by the prayers of a woman, María Ramos. The picture is housed in the imposing **Basílica**, but the miracle took place in what is now the **Iglesia de la Renovación** ① *Parque Julio Flores*. In 1816, when the town had enjoyed six years of independence and was besieged by the Royalists, this painting was carried through the streets by Dominican priests from the famous monastery, to rally the people. The town fell, all the same. There are special celebrations at Easter and on 26 December, the anniversary of the miracle. The town is known for making toys and musical instruments. See http://chiquinquira-boyaca.gov.co.

Where to stay

Tunja

$$$ Hunza
C 21A, No 10-66, T8-742 4111,
www.hotelhunza.com.
One of several smart hotels in the **$$$-$$** ranges.

$$ Alicante
Cra 8, No 19-15, T310-852 1636,
www.hotelalicantetunja.com.
Minimalist design, sunny patio fringed by
varieties of cactus, bright rooms, great value.

$$ Casa Real
C 19, No 7-65, T310-852 1636,
www.hotelcasarealtunja.com.
Sister hotel to **Alicante**. A real bargain,
comfortable rooms in a lovely colonial
building with varnished wooden
floorboards. Highly recommended.

$$ Posada San Agustín
C 23, No 8-63, T8-742 2986,
www.posadadesanagustin.co.
Beautiful colonial building on the Parque Pinzón,
balustraded courtyard, antiques and old photos
of Tunja, comfortable rooms, "a bit of a gem".

$ Conquistador de América
C 20, No 8-92, T8-742 3534.
Lovely foyer with a bright skylight, rooms are
small but comfortable.

Villa de Leiva

The town tends to be full of visitors at weekends
and holidays when booking is advisable. Book
in advance for the Festival of Light; see What to
do, below.

$$$ Candelaria
C del Silencio (Cra 18), No 8-12, T8-732 0534,
hotelcandelaria@hotmail.com.
Refurbished colonial building with 9 rooms
of "monastic simplicity", in delightful location.

$$$ El Marqués de San Jorge
C 14, No 9-20, T8-732 0480, www.
hospederiaelmarquesdesanjorge.com.
Simple little place with rooms around
a courtyard, cheaper Mon-Thu.

$$$ El Molino la Mesopotamia
Cra 8, 15A-265, T8-732 0235,
www.lamesopotamia.com.
A beautifully restored colonial mill filled with
antiques, excellent home cooking, beautiful
gardens, freshwater pool (US$2.50 for non-
guests), memorable. Recommended.

$$$ Plaza Mayor
Cra 10, No 12-31, T8-732 0425,
www.hotelplazamayor.com.co.
On the plaza, delightful octagonal courtyard
with lemon trees, comfortable rooms and a
good restaurant.

$$ Posada Don Blas
C 12, No 10-61, T8-732 0406,
posada.donblas@hotmail.com.
Sweet, simple little place 1 block from the plaza,
with just 10 rooms.

**$$-$ Colombian Highlands and
Hostal Renacer**
Cra 10, No 21-Finca Renacer, T8-732 1201, or
T311-308 3739, www.colombianhighlands.com.
15-min walk from town, this hostel, belonging
to English-speaking biologist Oscar Gilède, has
very comfortable dorm rooms, highly rated.
Extensive gardens, wood-fired pizza oven,
hammocks, bike hire, tour agency. Camping
US$6-8.25, also tent rental.

$$-$ Posada de los Angeles
Cra 10, No 13-94, T8-732 0562.
Attractive, clean rooms in a fine building
2 blocks from the plaza, restaurant, ask for
a room overlooking the Iglesia del Carmen.

$ Casa Viena
Cra 10, No 19-114, T8-732 0711,
http://hostel-villadeleyva.com.
Austrian/Colombian-run, 10 mins from plaza,
small, comfortable homestay with 4 rooms,
kitchen and communal area, long-stays
welcome. Also has Finca Puente Piedra outside
Villa de Leiva, which takes working guests,
minimum stay 20 days.

$ Hostal Sinduly
Cra 11, No 11-77, T8-732 0325,
www.hostalsinduly.com.
Run by Austrian Manfred, 2 private rooms (1 with
bath) and 2 dorms in a colonial house 1 block
from the plaza. English and German spoken.

Chiquinquirá

$$ El Gran
C 16, No 7A-55, T1-726 3700,
www.elgranhotel.amawebs.com.
Central, secure, comfortable, good restaurant.

$$ Sarabita
C 16, No 8-12, T316-330 8701,
Facebook: HOTEL-Sarabita.
In a national monument, with pool and restaurant.

Restaurants

Tunja

$ El Balcón
Pasaje Vargas C 19A, No 10-16, T8-743 3954.
Expansive café overlooking the main plaza.
Lovely wood interior, friendly service, free
Wi-Fi, and a long list of excellent coffees.

$ El Maizal
Cra 9, No 20-30, T8-742 5876.
Good varied menu of local specialities.

$ La Cascada
Pasaje Vargas (C32), No 5-60, T8-744 5750.
Popular at lunchtime, good value for lunches and
breakfasts. There are other places on this street.

Villa de Leiva

Villa de Leiva has dozens of good restaurants
with international and local menus. Most are
concentrated in the town's upmarket food courts,
Casa Quintero (on the plaza) and **La Guaca** (on
C Caliente). Some are closed Mon-Wed.

$$ La Cocina de la Gata
Casa Quintero.
Pleasantly decorated fondue restaurant,
which also serves chicken and steak.

$$ Olivas & Especias
Cra 10, No 11-99.
On the corner of the plaza, pizzas and pastas
in homely surroundings. Next door's **Carnes &
Olivas ($$$)** is also worth a try.

$$ Savia
Cra 9, No 11-75 (Casa Quintero).
Great range of organic starters and interesting
mains, including some tasty veggie dishes.

$$ Zarina
Cra 9, No 11-75 (Casa Quintero).
Good Arabic, Mediterranean and vegetarian
cuisine, as well as the usual chicken and steak.

$ Casa Blanca
C 13, No 7-06.
A simple little place, popular with locals, for
regional specialities, plus *ajiaco* and other classics.

Festivals

Villa de Leiva

Jan-Feb Astronomical festival, telescopes are
set up in the Plaza for public use.
Apr Encuentro de Música Antigua celebrates
historic music from all over the world (Facebook:
Encuentro de Música Antigua en Villa de Leyva).
12 Jun Anniversary of founding of town, with
fireworks, market, music and other arts events.
13-17 Jul Virgen del Carmen, with street
market, agricultural fair, music and entertainment
based in and around the main plaza.
Mid-Aug International kite festival is held in
the Plaza Mayor (see www.villadeleyva-boyaca.
gov.co), for 3 days usually over the 2nd weekend.
Early Dec Festival of Light is held every year, for
the Immaculate Conception, with balconies and
streets decorated with candles and lanterns.

What to do

Villa de Leiva

Horse riding
Raul Oswaldo, *T310-757 5327*. Offers horse
riding trips, group discounts when booking
with Colombian Highlands.

Tour operators
Alpine Colombia, *5 km outside town, http://alpine
colombia.weebly.com*. Hiking trip for individuals
and small groups, also homestay in our **$$-$**
range, owner Christian speaks German and English.
Colombian Highlands, *see Where to stay,
above*. Tours of the local area and throughout
Colombia, specifically geared towards botanists,
ornithologists and enthusiasts of adventure sports.
Zebra Trips, *C Caliente, Cra 9 No 14-80, T 098-732
0016/311-870 1749, www.zebratrip.com*. With its
zebra-striped fleet of Land Rovers, this company
provides a fun way to explore the desert area
outside Villa de Leiva. A variety of different tours
starting at US$15, including a gourmet outing.

Transport

Tunja
Bus Bus station is 400 m steeply down from
city centre. From **Bogotá** several companies,
3-3½ hrs, 4½-5 hrs weekends and holidays,

S$8. To **Villa de Leiva**, *colectivos* every 15 mins 0600-1900, US$3, 45-60 mins. To **Bucaramanga**, equent services, 7 hrs, US$20.

Villa de Leiva

Bus The bus station is on Cra 9 between C 11 and C 12. Advisable to book the return journey on arrival at weekends. Buses to/from **Tunja**, 45-50 mins, US$3, every 15 mins from 0600 to 1800. To **Bogotá**, either go via Tunja, or 5 direct buses a day, 3½-4 hrs with **Valle Flota de Tenza**, at main bus terminal, T1-428 1008 (T320-337 6585 in Villa de Leiva), www.flotavalledetenza.com, US$8, or

2 a day with **Libertadores**. To/from **Chiquinquirá**, 1½ hrs, US$3, 6 a day. To **Ráquira** see below.

Ráquira

Buses from **Villa de Leiva** 4 a day, 0600-1730, 30 mins, US$2. For the return, check if you have to change at Ramal. There are also buses to **Tunja** (3 a day) and **Bogotá**, US$7.50.

Chiquinquirá

Bus To **Tunja**, 3 hrs, US$7. To **Zipaquirá**, US$5.50. To **Bogotá**, 2½ hrs, US$4.

Tunja to El Cocuy

a must-visit national park for high-altitude climbing and trekking

Leaving Tunja

A road runs northeast of Tunja to **Paipa** (41 km; bus from Bogotá US$8), noted for the Aguas Termales complex, 3 km to the southeast, T321-209 5655, www.termalespaipa.co, Mon-Fri 1000-1900, Sat 1000-2030, entrance US$4.50, with a range of massage and mud therapies at extra cost, hydrotherapy US$22, and on for 15 km to Duitama. From here it is 85 km to Soatá, one of the junctions for reaching the Parque Nacional Natural El Cocuy. The other route to the park is 20 km further north, by the bridge over the Río Chicamocha at Capitanejo.

☆Parque Nacional Natural El Cocuy

Entrance fee, US$18 for foreigners, payable at the park offices (C 5, No 4-22, T098-789 0359, El Cocuy, Transversal 4A, No 6-60, T098-789 7280, Güicán, both open 0700-1145, 1300-1645), where you must also obtain rescue insurance, which costs US$2.50 per day, and a walking map. It is obligatory to visit a park office, here, in Bucaramanga (Av Quebrada Seca, No 30-12, T7-645 4868), Tame (Cra 22, No 15-04, T097-888 6054), or in Bogotá (www.parquesnacionales.gov.co), to get a permit to enter the park and to receive the rules of conduct within the park. Guiding association Aseguicoc, T311-236 4275, aseguicoc@gmail.com. Note: at the time of research the entire park was closed to tourists. The U'wa people and campesinos blockaded all entrances to protest against a perceived threat from tourism to the park's fragile environment and against the disrespectful actions of some visitors at U'wa sacred sites.

The breathtaking **Sierra Nevada del Cocuy** in the Eastern Cordillera is the best range in Colombia for mountaineering and rock climbing. The Sierra consists of two parallel north–south ranges about 30 km long, offering peaks of rare beauty (more than 22 are snow covered), lakes and waterfalls. The flora is particularly interesting, notably the thousands of *frailejones*.

The park is accessible from the small towns of **El Cocuy** or, further north, **Güicán**. Either town is a perfect start or end point for hiking or climbing in the park. On the central plaza of El Cocuy is a model of the mountain area. One of the most spectacular hikes is from south to north (or vice versa), during which you will see a great part of what the park has to offer. It might appear an easy marked trail, but it is highly recommended to go with a guide as sudden changes in weather can cause visibility to drop to less than 10 m. You need to know where to camp and to get drinking water.

There is no accommodation on the longer treks in the park, so you must take all equipment. Basic food supplies can be bought in El Cocuy or Güicán, otherwise you should buy your food in Bogotá or Bucaramanga. There is no need to take ice axe or crampons, unless you are climbing Pan de Azúcar. Temperatures can drop below 0°C at night as most campsites are around 4000 m. The peak holiday periods (the last week in December, the first two weeks of January and Easter week) can get very busy. The best season for trekking is December to March but even in those months it can rain or be very foggy.

Exploring the park La Laguna de La Plaza is probably the most beautiful lake in the Sierra Nevada del Cocuy, surrounded by the snow tops of **Pan de Azúcar** and **Toti** in the west and Picos **Negro** and

Blanco to the east. Just below Pan de Azúcar is **Cerro El Diamante**. At sunrise, this rock can change from grey to yellow, gold, red and orange if you are lucky with the weather. **Laguna Grande de l Sierra** is surrounded by the Pan de Azúcar, Toti, Portales, Concavo and Concavito peaks and is perfect base camp for climbing one of these. **El Púlpito de Diablo** is an enormous, altar-shape rock at 5000 m. From El Púlpito you can continue to climb up to the top of **Pan de Azúcar** (5100 m overlooking Laguna de la Plaza on one side and Laguna Grande de la Sierra on the other. **Valle d los Cojines** is an enormous valley surrounded by snow peaks, filled with *cojines* (pillow plants **Ritacuba Blanco** is the highest mountain of all (5322 m) and is not too difficult to climb. The view at the top over the Valle de Cojines and many other parts of the park are stunning.

Listings Tunja to El Cocuy

Where to stay

Sierra Nevada del Cocuy
There are places to stay in El Cocuy and Güicán and *cabañas* on some of the trails into the park.

$$ Hotel Pinares del Carrizalito
2.45 km from El Cocuy, T300 776 7529,
Facebook: Pinares del Carrizalito
Country lodge B&B in leafy grounds, friendly hosts will pick up and drop off guests at bus station.

$ Casa Muñoz
Cra 5, No 7-28, El Cocuy, on the main plaza,
T098-789 0328, T313-829 1073, https://sites.
google.com/site/hotelcasamunoz/Home.
With private and shared rooms, *comedor*.

$ La Posada del Molino
Cra 3, No 7-51, El Cocuy, T8-789 0377, 312-352
9121, http://elcocuycasamuseo.blogspot.co.uk.
In a historic building, with private rooms, restaurant and information on tours to the national park, highly recommended.

Cabañas

Cabaña Guaicany
At the entrance to Valle de Lagunillas,
T310-566-7554, guaicany@hotmail.com.

Shared bath, great views of Ritacuba Blanco and other peaks, also possible to camp and to hire horses and/or guide.

Cabañas Kanwara
At the foot of Ritacuba Blanca, T311-231 6004.
The perfect starting point to climb the mountain or to walk to Laguna Grande de los Verdes, shared bath.

Hacienda La Esperanza
T310-209 9812/200 4214,
Facebook: HdaLaEsperanza.
Convenient for the walk to Laguna Grande de la Sierra, simple rooms with shared bath, good, horse riding.

Transport

Sierra Nevada del Cocuy
Bus El Cocuy and Güicán can be reached by direct bus (0650 departure) from **Bogotá**, 10-12 hrs, US$17; buses also from **Tunja**. Around 0600 a milk truck leaves the main plaza of El Cocuy, taking you to **Cabañas Guaicany** (the southern park entrance), **Finca la Esperanza** (for Laguna Grande de la Sierra) or to **Hacienda Ritacuba**, from where it's a 1-hr walk to **Cabañas Kanwarra**. Or take an *expreso* (private transport), US$28, from El Cocuy main plaza.

Tunja to Bucaramanga and Cúcuta
visit San Gil for thrills, then recover your composure in beautiful Barichar

Socorro *Colour map 1, B3.*
The main road from Tunja heads northeast and then roughly follows the Río Suáraz to Socorro with steep streets and single-storey houses set among graceful palms. It has a singularly larg stone cathedral. The **Casa de Cultura** museum (opening hours vary) covers the local history an the interesting part played by Socorro in the fight for Independence. It is well worth a visit. Ther is a daily market.

☆San Gil Colour map 1, B3.

About 21 km beyond Socorro, northeast on the main road to Bucaramanga, is San Gil, an attractive colonial town with a good climate. It's a friendly, relaxed place and its main square is lively at night. San Gil is a centre for adventure sports (rafting, kayaking, parapenting, paragliding and caving) and is also a good place for biking, horse riding and walking. See What to do, page 916.

Parque Gallineral ① www.gallineral.sangil.com.co, daily 0800-1700, US$2, guides, some English speaking, tip them as they are not paid, a delightful riverside park, covers 4 ha where the Quebrada Curití runs through a delta to the Río Fonce. It has a superb freshwater swimming pool and beautiful trees covered with moss-like tillandsia. Good view from **La Gruta**, the shrine overlooking the town (look for the cross). Visit **Juan Curi** waterfalls for abseiling or hiking (take a bus, US$2.75 return, towards Charalá and ask to be dropped off. There are two approaches, passing through private fincas. You may have to pay a small fee for access, about US$3. A return taxi fare is US$17).

☆Barichara and around Colour map 1, B3.

From San Gil a paved road leads 22 km to Barichara, a beautiful, quiet colonial town founded in 1741 and designated as a national monument. Among Barichara's places of historical interest are the Cathedral and three churches, the cemetery and the house of the former president **Aquileo Parra Gómez** ① Cra 2 y C 6, daily 0900-1700, free. There is a superb wide-ranging view from the mirador at the top of Carrera 10 across the Río Suárez to the Cordillera de los Cobardes, the last section of the Cordillera Oriental before the valley of the Magdalena. Tourist office ① Cra 5 y C 9, www.barichara-santander.gov.co, daily 0730-1200, 1400-1800.

An interesting excursion is to **Guane**, 9 km away by road (bus US$1), or two hours' delightful walk by camino real (historic trail), where there are many colonial houses and an archaeological museum in the **Parroquia San Isidro** ① daily 0800-1200, 1300-1800 (but times can be erratic), US$1. It has an enormous collection of fossils found in the local area (which is constantly being added to), as well as Guane textiles and a mummified woman. Three good restaurants on the plaza serve regional food.

☆Chicamocha canyon

Between San Gil and Bucaramanga is the spectacular Río Chicamocha canyon, with the best views to the right of the road. The **Parque Nacional** ① www.parquenacionaldelchicamocha.com, Mon-Fri 0900-1800, Sat, Sun and holidays 0800-1900, US$8.30, US$23.50, including cable car and Aqua Park, children under 2 free, has a visitor centre with panoramic views, activities, parking, snack bars and toilets and a 6.3-km cable car across the canyon. Another way to experience the canyon is on a three-day walk from San Gil to the villages of Barichara, Guane, Villanueva, Los Santos, and the ghost town of Jordán. The walk involves a spectacular descent of the canyon. Speak to the staff at the Macondo Hostal in San Gil for more details of hostales and eating places on the way.

Bucaramanga Colour map 1, B3.

The capital of Santander Department, 420 km from Bogotá, was founded in 1622 but was little more than a village until the latter half of the 19th century. The metropolitan area of this modern, commercial city has grown rapidly because of the success of coffee, tobacco and staple crops, but the city's great problem is space for expansion. Erosion on the lower, western side topples buildings over the edge after heavy rain, leaving behind spectacular deep ravines.

Bucaramanga is known as the 'city of parks' for its fine green spaces, such as Mejoras Públicas, de los Niños, San Pío and Las Palmas, but some areas, particularly Parque Centenario, are not very safe even in daylight. The **Parque Santander** is the heart of the modern city, while the **Parque García Rovira** is the centre of the colonial area. On it stands the city's oldest church, **Capilla de Los Dolores** ① C 35/Cra 10, a national monument. Just off Parque García Rovira is the **Casa de Cultura** ① C 37, No 12-46, T7-642 0163, Mon-Fri 0800-1200, 1400-1800, in a fine colonial building with exhibitions, flms and an artesanía display. The **Casa de Bolívar** ① C 37, No 12-15, T7-630 4258, Mon-Fri 0800-1800, at 0800-1200, US$1, where Bolívar stayed in 1828. It is interesting for its connections with Bolívar's campaign in 1813. The **tourist office** ① Instituto Municipal de Cultura, C 30, No 26-117, T7-634 1132, Mon-Fri 0800-1200, 1400-1900, is friendly and knowledgeable. The departmental **Cultura y Turismo, Secretaría de Desarrollo** is at ① C 37, No 10-30, T7-633 9666, www.imcut.gov.co. **Migración Colombia** at ① Cra 11, No 41-13, T7-633 9426, Mon-Fri 0800-1200, 1400-1700.

Around Bucaramanga

In **Floridablanca**, 8 km southwest, is the **Jardín Botánico Eloy Valenzuela** ①, *T7-634 6100, daily 0800-1600, US$1.70, take a Florida Villabel bus from Cra 33, US$1, or Florida Autopista to the plaza and walk 1 km; taxi from centre, US$4,* belonging to the national tobacco agency.

Girón a tobacco centre 9 km southwest of Bucaramanga on the Río de Oro, is a quiet and attractive colonial town. Its white buildings, beautiful church, bridges and cobbled streets are well preserved and the historic part of town unspoilt by modernization. Girón can be easily reached from Bucaramanga and makes a good day trip. By the river are *tejo* courts and open-air restaurants with cumbia and salsa bands. *Bus from Cra 15 or 22 in Bucaramanga, US$1, taxi US$4.*

Piedecuesta is 18 km southeast of Bucaramanga. Here you can see cigars being handmade, furniture carving and jute weaving. Cheap, hand-decorated *fique* rugs can be bought. There are frequent buses to all the surrounding towns; taxi costs US$8. Corpus Christi processions in these towns in June are interesting. *Bus from Cra 22, 45 minutes.*

Berlín to Pamplona

The road (paved but narrow) runs east to Berlín, and then northeast (a very scenic run over the Eastern Cordillera) to Pamplona, about 130 km from Bucaramanga. Berlín is an ideal place to appreciate the grandeur of the Eastern Cordillera and the hardiness of the people who live on the *páramo*. The village lies in a valley at 3100 m, the peaks surrounding it rise to 4350 m and the temperature is constantly around 10°C, although on the infrequent sunny days it may seem much warmer. There is a tourist complex with cabins and there are several basic eating places.

Pamplona *Colour map 1, B4.*

Founded in 1548 in the mountains, Pamplona became important as a mining town but is now better known for its university. It is renowned for its Easter celebrations. The climate is chilly at this altitude: 2342 m. Pamplona is a good place to buy *ruanas* and has a good indoor market. The **Cathedral** in the spacious central plaza is the most attractive feature of this otherwise unprepossessing city. The **Iglesia del Humilladero**, adjoining the cemetery, is very picturesque and allows a fine view of the city. Museums include the **Casa Colonial** ① *C 6, No 2-56, T7-568 2043, Mon-Fri 0800-1200, 1400-1800,* archaeological museum, a little gem, and the **Museo de Arte Moderno** ① *C 5, No 5-75, Tue-Sun 0900-1200, 1400-1700, US$0.50.* Tourist office ① *Instituto de Cultura y Turismo in the Casa Colonial, same phone and hours as above, www.ictpamplona.gov.co.* Very helpful, organizes tours and guides.

Cúcuta *Colour map 1, B4.*

Some 72 km from Pamplona is the city of Cúcuta, capital of the Department of Norte de Santander 16 km from the Venezuelan border at San Antonio. Founded in 1733, destroyed by earthquake 1875, and then rebuilt, its tree-lined streets offer welcome respite from the searing heat, as does the **cathedral**, on Avenida 5 between Calles 10 and 11. The **Casa de Cultura** (also known as Torre de Reloj) ① *C13, No 3-67,* houses art exhibitions and the **Museo de la Ciudad** which covers the city's history and its part in the Independence Movement. For a border town, it is a surprisingly pleasant place to visit, with plenty of green spaces and a busy but non-threatening centre, but see Warning page 917. The **Corporación Mixta de Promoción de Norte de Santander** ① *C 10, No 0-30, T7-57 8981,* is helpful. Tourist police at the bus station and airport. The international bridge between Colombia and Venezuela is southeast of the city.

Border with Venezuela

If you do not obtain an exit stamp, you will be turned back by Venezuelan officials and the next time you enter Colombia, you will be fined. At the time of writing, the border was closed to vehicle traffic, but people on foot were allowed to cross from time to time. Check in advance if the crossing is open. At root is the problem of smuggling, especially of gasoline, between the two countries.

Tip...
Venezuela is 30 minutes ahead of Colombia.

Colombian immigration ① *Migración Colombia (CFSM), Av 1, No 28-57, T7-573 5210, Mon-F 0800-1200, 1400-1700.* Take a bus from the city centre to Barrio San Rafael, south towards the road to Pamplona. Shared taxi from border is US$6, then US$1.50 to bus station. Exit and entry formalities are also handled at the Migración Colombia office the white building on the lefthand side of road just before the international border bridge (Puesto Terrestre CENAF Villa del Rosario, Puente Internacional Simón Bolívar). See Venezuela chapter for Venezuelan immigration. There is no authorized charge at the border. For exchange, see page 1010.

Venezuelan consulate ① *Av Aeropuerto Camilo Daza y C 17, Zona Industrial, T7-579 1954, http://cucuta.consulado.gob.ve, near airport, Mon-Thu 0800-1000, 1400-1500, Fri 0800-1000.* Nationals not requiring a visa are issued an automatic free tourist card by the Venezuelan immigration officers at the border. Overland visitors requiring a visa to Venezuela can get one here, or at the Venezuelan Embassy in Bogotá, although they may send you to Cúcuta. As requirements change frequently, it is recommended that all overland visitors check with a Venezuelan consulate in advance. Apply for visa at 0800 to get it by 1400. If you know when you will arrive at the border, get your visa in your home country.

Leaving and entering Colombia by private vehicle Passports must be stamped with an exit stamp at the white Migración Colombia building before the crossing. If not you will have to return later. Expect very long queues. Car papers must be stamped at the SENIAT office in Venezuela, see Venezuela chapter. With all the right papers, the border crossing is easy and traffic flows smoothly (but see above – the border is closed to vehicles, 2017).

Exchange For the best exchange rates, it is recommended to change pesos to bolívares in Cúcuta and not in Venezuela. Exchange rates fluctuate throughout the day. There is an ATM tucked away on the left side of the international bridge in Venezuela. Good rates of exchange at the airport, or on the border. It is difficult to change pesos beyond San Antonio in Venezuela; likewise, bolívares are rarely accepted elsewhere in Colombia. Money changers on the street all around the main plaza and many shops advertise bolívares exchange. There are also plenty of *casas de cambio*, and new ones were opened in San Antonio in 2017.

Listings Tunja to Bucaramanga and Cúcuta

Where to stay

San Gil

$$ Abril
C 8, No 9-63, T7-724 8795,
Facebook: hotelabrilcomco.
Strangely laid out, but rooms have comfortable antique beds, fan.

$$-$ La Posada Familiar
Cra 10, No 8-55, T7-724 8136.
Small, 6 rooms set around a sunny courtyard.
Recommended.

$$-$ Sam's VIP Hostel
Cr 10, No 12-33, p 2, main plaza,
T7-724 2746/249 7400.
Good reports on value and services, dorms and private rooms, rooftop pool, adventure activities, bar, sauna, English spoken. Recommended.

$ Macondo Hostel
Cra 8, No 10-35, T7-724 8001,
www.macondohostel.com.
Australian Shaun Clohesy has created more of a home-from-home than a hostel. Social area decked out with hammocks, garden, jacuzzi,

board games, free coffee and Wi-Fi, regular BBQs and other events, comfortable dorms (US$7.25-9), and a wealth of information on local activities. Recommended.

$ Santander Alemán
C 10, No 15-07, T7-724 0329,
www.hostelsantanderaleman.com.
Private and shared rooms, nice common areas including a roof terrace, hammocks, book exchange, bicycle hire, and adventure sports arranged.

Barichara

$$$ Hicasua
C 7, No 3-85, T7-726 7700, www.hicasua.com.
If you have the cash to splash this is the place to stay. Located at the edge of town, Hicasua offers tastefully decorated rooms with fans and flatscreen TVs. There is a restaurant and a stunning swimming pool on the courtyard, as well as a spa and sauna.

$$$-$$ Coratá
Cra 7, No 4-08, T7-726 7110, www.hotelcoratabarichara.inf.travel.
Delightful colonial building with a fine courtyard, no fan or a/c but high ceilings keep you cool.

$$$-$$ Hostel Color de Hormiga
*C 6, No 5-35, T7-726 7156/312-558 1256,
Facebook: ColordeHormigaHostel*
Good budget option in a charming colonial
building just off the plaza. Offers dorms and
privates with ensuite bath, but no hot water
or fan. Hammock-filled, grapevine-covered
courtyard. In the future they plan to offer
breakfast and lunch. With same owner is
Color de Hormiga Reserva Natural (T315-297
1621/314-455 8268), a finca 1 km outside town.
Immense rooms with high ceilings, owner Jorge
often cooks dinner for guests in the large, open-
air kitchen. Tours of the grounds include visiting
ant colonies, turtles and natural fish farms.

$$ La Mansión de Virginia
*C 8, No 7-26, T7-726 7170,
www.lamansiondevirginia.com.*
Impeccable colonial house with rooms around
a lovely courtyard, comfortable beds, hot water.
Recommended.

$$-$ Barichara Tinto Hostel
Cra 4, No 5-39, T7-726 7725, www.tintohostel.com.
Probably the best hostel in town; sits on a hill
with nice views of the surrounding countryside.
There are 4 and 6-bed dorms, as well as large
private rooms.

$$-$ La Posada de Pablo 2
C 3, No 7-30, T7-726 7719.
One of several places belonging to Pablo. This
one is next to the Iglesia de Jesús Resucitado and
a gorgeous park. Good beds, rooms 10 and 11
have fine views.

Camping
In Barichara, at Baralomas campsites (T311-
828 0062, Facebook: Camping-Baraloma-en-
Barichara-430335113813259/), ask for Rodrigo.
On the road to San Gil is **La Chorrera** (T318-832
7327, US$2 to camp), a natural swimming pool,
meals by arrangement, clean, attractive.

Guane

$$-$ Hotel Santa Lucia de Mucuruva
Cra 5 y C 7, T7-724 2761, 318-459 2474.
1 block off the plaza, this option offers rooms at
affordable rates.

$ Posada Mi Tierra Guane
*Cra 7, No 7-45, Parque Principal, opposite
museum, T311-566 0402.*
Same owner as the *artesanía* shop on the plaza,
comfortable and charming small hostel with a

pleasant courtyard. Some rooms have bunk beds.
Recommended.

Bucaramanga

$$$$-$$$ Dann Carlton
*C 47, No 28-83, T7-697 3266,
www.hotelesdann.com.*
Part of the **Dann** hotel chain, top of the range,
business class, in city centre, with rooftop bar,
gym and usual 5-star service.

$$$ El Pilar
*C 34, No 24-09, T7-634 7207,
www.hotelelpilar.com.co.*
Business-style hotel with good rooms and
lots of extras, parking, restaurant, close to
Parque Santander.

$$$ Guane
C 34, No 22-72, T7-634 7014, www.hotelguane.com
Smart hotel with large rooms, pool, gym and spa.

$$ Colonial Plaza
*C 33, No 20-46, T7-645 4125,
www.hotelcolonialplaza.inf.travel.*
It's not colonial but rooms are good,
cheaper with fan. Restaurant.

$$-$ Kasa Guane
*C 11, No 26-506, T7-657 6960, Facebook:
kasaguanehostelbucaramanga.*
The best budget option in town. Owned
by paragliding instructor Richi of Colombia
Paragliding and British expats Milo and Tim,
it's decorated with Guane culture artefacts, has
private rooms and dorms (US$10), pool table,
kitchen, lively bar, dance classes and good local
information. Also runs volunteer programmes.

Around Bucaramanga

$$$ Girón Chill Out
*Cra 25, No 32-06, Girón, T7-646 1119/315-475
3001, www.gironchillout.com.*
Suites and studios in a colonial house, boutique
style, with restaurant.

$$ Las Nieves
C 30, No 25-71, Girón, T7-681 2951.
Characterful colonial building on the main plaza,
large rooms. Street-facing rooms have balconies,
good value restaurant. Much cheaper with fan.

Pamplona

$$$-$$ 1549 Hostal
*C 8B, No 5-84, T7-568 0451 or 317-699 6578,
http://1549hostal.com.*

nother lovingly restored colonial building.
ooms are light and airy and decorated with
reat taste. Coffee bar and *panadería* in a large
ourtyard. Highly recommended.

$$-$$ El Solar
5, No 8-10, T7-568 2010, www.elsolarhotel.com.
eautifully restored colonial building. Rooms
pstairs are enormous and have kitchen and
alconies. Rooms downstairs, without kitchen, are
heaper. Also has by far the best restaurant in town.

úcuta

$$-$$ Arizona Suites
v 0, No 7-62, T7-572 6020,
ww.hotelarizonasuites.com.
entral, all mod cons including safety boxes,
estaurant serving Mediterranean and
nternational food, pool, gym and sauna.

$ Casa Blanca
v 6, No 14-55, T7-582 1600,
www.hotelcasablanca.com.co.
Modern block, business-style, with large pool,
estaurant serving regional and international food.

$ Hotel de la Paz
6, No 3-48, T7-571 8002.
asic rooms, but has a pool. 10% discount for
ays longer than 5 days.

$ Zaraya
11, No 2-46, T7-571 0829, www.hotelzaraya.com.
entral, with restaurant, pool and sauna.

$-$ Lady Di
v 7, No 13-76, T7-583 1922.
huge photo of Princess Di above the doorway
nd more photos throughout. Rooms are clean
ut basic.

Restaurants

an Gil
ew places open in the evening. The **market**
Cra 11 entre C13/14), is good for breakfast, fruit
alads and juices.

$-$ Gringo Mike's Sandwiches
12, No 8-35, T7-724 1695, www.gringomikes.net.
pen 0800-2300.
S/British-run restaurant and bar, with West
oast specialities and lovely Mexican influences,
xcellent sandwiches. Friendly staff, good nosh
nd cocktails. Recommended.

7 Tigres Pizza
12, No 8-40.

Facebook: 7-Tigres-Pizza-1374818486121483.
Basic place but serves delicious pizzas and good
veggie dishes.

$ Doña Rogelia
Cra 10, No 8-09, T7-724 0823.
Good for lunch, local specialities, *menú
ejecutivo*, also has home delivery service.

$ Donde Betty
Cra 9 y C 12, Parque Principal.
Good for breakfast, *arepas*, scrambled eggs,
fruit juices and people-watching.

$ El Maná
C 10, No 9-12, www.elmanasangil.inf.travel.
Tue-Sun lunchtime and evenings.
Filling set menus with local food for under US$5.

$ Torino's Pizzeria
C 9, No 11-68, loc 210, T7-724 7496,
Centro Comercial Camino Real. Open evenings.
Popular pizzeria with a brick oven. Home delivery.

Barichara

$$ Al Cuoco
Cra 4, No 3B-15, T312-527 3628.
Across from Parque Cemeterio, in a cosy dining
room and large patio. Owner Máximo serves
handmade pastas with recipes that have been
passed down through generations in Rome.

$$ Las Cruces
Cra 5, No 4-26, San Antonio, T7-726 7577,
http://tallerdeoficiosbarichara.com. Fri 1900-
2130, Sat-Sun 1200-1600, 1900-2130, holidays
1200-1600, open every day in high season.
Café Mon-Fri 1200-2100, weekends 0900-2130.
In the Escuela Taller, with a plant and tree-filled
courtyard, offers cooking and ceramics classes as
well as an upscale restaurant. Those who want to
try a local speciality should ask for the roast goat
in ant sauce (yes, those ants.)

$ El Compá
C 5, No 4-48, T7-726 7492.
Family-run restaurant serving regional dishes,
including *sobre barriga* and *arepa santandereana*.

Bucaramanga
Try the *hormigas culonas* (a large, winged ant
often eaten as a deep-fried, crunchy snack), a
local delicacy available Mar-May (mostly sold
in shops, not restaurants).

$$$ La Carreta
Cra 27, No 42-27, T7-643 6680,
www.lacarreta.com.co.

Established by football legend Roberto Pablo Janiot, tastefully restored, swish colonial building, meat-based international food, *parrillas* and seafood.

$$$ Mercagán
Cra 33 y C42, T7-632 4949.
Steaks and hamburgers in a parrilla restaurant near the beautiful Parque San Pío. Several other locations in the city.

$$ Di Marco
C 28, No 54-21, T7-643 2626, www.dimarco parrilla.com. Tue-Sat lunch and dinner, Sun-Mon 1100-1600.
Argentine-style *parrilla*, excellent meat, since the 1960s.

$$ El Viejo Chiflas
Cra 33, No 34-10, T7-632 0640, www. elviejochiflasrestaurante.inf.travel/
Well-established, since 1957, good, typical food from the region, generous portions. Recommended.

$$ La 22
Cra 22, No 45-18, www.restaurantela22.com.
This local canteen is so popular that at weekends (when they serve *mute* – regional speciality) you will struggle to be seated.

$$ Los Tejaditos
C 34, No 27-82, T7-634 6028, www.restaurantelostejaditos.com.
Popular for its varied menu of meat, seafood, pastas and salads.

$$ Tony
Cra 33A, No 33-67, http://desayunostony.com. Daily 24 hrs.
Typical food, popular. Good *tamales* and *arepas*, breakfasts their speciality.

$ Típico Llanero
C 31, No 25-07, T7-634 5586.
Just off Parque Los Niños, corner restaurant serving regional food hot off a coal-fired grill, popular, set-price *almuerzos* and refreshing iced juices for US$4.

Pamplona

Pamplona is famous for its bread. Particularly well known *panaderías* are **Chávez** (Cra 6, No 7-30), and **Araque** (Cra 5, No 8B-15). Try *pastel de horno, queso de hoja, pan de agua* or *cuca*, a kind of black ginger biscuit often topped with cheese. Pamplona even has a *cuca* festival in Sep/Oct of each year.

$$ La Casona
C 6, No 7-58, T7-568 3555.
Local favourite serving meats and seafood.

$$-$ Delicias del Mar
C 6, No 7-60, T7-568 4558.
Popular lunchtime venue specializing in fish.

Cúcuta

Lots of fast food outlets on the 3rd level of **Centro Comercial Ventura Plaza** (C 10 y 11 Diagonal Santander), also cinema and shops.

$$ Rodizio
Av Libertadores, No 10-121, Malecón II Etapa, T7-575 0095, www.rodiziocucuta.com.
Elegant, good service, big choice of meat dishes, seafood, salad bar.

$ Venezia
C 13, No 6AE-46, Edif La Riviera, loc 5, T7-575 0006.
Oven-fired pizzas and other Italian specialities.

Festivals

San Gil
Nov Festival San Gil, during the 1st weekend of the month the town celebrates with dancers, music, local gastronomy, horse parades and even bullfighting.

Bucaramanga
Sep Feria Bucaramanga, 2 weeks of music, dancing, food, theatre and every type of vendor.

What to do

San Gil
Activities include **abseiling** (rappel) at Juan Curí waterfall (US$20); a 3-day beginner's **kayaking** course on Río Fonce (US$150, minimum 2 persons); **parapenting** over the Chicamocha canyon (US$65 for 30-60 mins). For rafting, the Río Fonce is best for beginners, US$13.50; Río Suárez, for more advanced, 1-2 hrs from US$47. The area also offers bungee jumping (US$14), caving (US$12), mountain biking, hiking, horse riding (said to be better in Barichara) and swimming.
Aventura Total, *C 7, No 10-27, T7-723 8888, www.aventuratotal.com.co.* Biggest tour company in town, specializes in parapenting, rafting, abseiling and caving.
Colombia Rafting Expeditions, *Cra 10, No 7-83, T311-283 8647, www.colombiarafting.com.*
The best for rafting, with International Rafting Federation-qualified guides. Also hydrospeed.

Páramo Santander Extremo, *Parque Principal, Cra 4, No 4-57, Páramo, T7-725 8944, www.paramo santanderextremo.com*. Based in nearby Páramo, this company is best for abseiling and canyoning. But it also has caving, rafting and horse riding.

Bucaramanga

Parapenting At Mesa del Ruitoque and Cañón de Chicamocha. Good schools are **Las Aguilas** (Km 2 vía Mesa de Ruitoque, Floridablanca, T300-762 2662, www.voladerolasaguilas.com), and **Colombia Paragliding** (T312-432 6266, www.colombiaparagliding.com).

Transport

San Gil

Bus Station 5 mins out of town by taxi on road to Tunja. To **Bogotá**, US$13, 7-8 hrs; **Bucaramanga**, US$7, 2½ hrs, sit on right for lovely views of the Chicamocha Canyon; **Barichara** from C 12, US$2, 45 mins, every 30 mins.

Bucaramanga

Air Palonegro, on 3 flattened hilltops south of city. Taxi US$10.50, *colectivo* US$3.50. Spectacular views on take-off and landing. Daily flights to **Bogotá**, **Cúcuta**, **Medellín**, **Cartagena** and **Barranquilla**.

Bus Local buses cost US$0.65. The long-distance terminal is on the Girón road, T7-637 1000, with cafés, shops and showers. Taxi to centre, US$3; bus US$0.65. To **Bogotá**, 9 hrs, US$20-27 with **Berlinas del Fonce** (C 53, No 20-40, T7-630 4468, www.berlinasdelfonce.com, or at bus terminal), and Cotranal, 9½-10½ hrs, US$17-27. To **Cartagena**, Copetran, US$30-43, 12-14 hrs. **Barranquilla**, 13 hrs, US$23-37, Copetran, **Berlinas** or Brasilia. **Santa Marta**, Copetran, 11-13 hrs, US$20-33. To **Valledupar**, 9 hrs, US$25-28 with Copetran. To/from **Pamplona**, US$7-11, 4-5 hrs. To/from **Cúcuta**, 6-8 hrs, US$11-15. The trip to Cúcuta is spectacular and passes through cloudforests and *páramos*. Best to start the journey early morning as thick fog usually covers the mountains by afternoon. To **Medellín**, US$17-30, 8 hrs. **Barrancabermeja**, 2½ hrs, US$7, paved road, scenic journey. To **El Banco** on the Río Magdalena, US$13-20, 9 hrs, several companies, direct or change at Aguachica. Hourly buses to **San Gil**, see above. Other companies with local services to nearby villages on back roads, eg the folk-art buses of **Flota Cáchira** (C 32, Cra 33-34).

Taxi Most have meters, minimum fare US$1.75.

Pamplona

Bus To **Bogotá**, **Berlinas del Fonce** and Copetran, US$30-35, 13 hrs. To **Cúcuta**, US$7, 2½ hrs. *Colectivos* or shared taxis to **Bucaramanga** (US$12-18) and **Cúcuta** (US$6.50) usually cut the journey by 1 hr, with door-to-door pick-up and delivery. To **Berlín**, US$5. Buses leave from Cra 5 y C 4, minibuses to Cúcuta from Cra 5 y C 5.

Cúcuta

Air The airport is 5 km north of the town centre, T7-587 9797, 15 mins by taxi in normal traffic from the town and border, US$2, US$7 to border. Daily flights to **Bogotá**, **Bucaramanga** and **Medellín**. It's cheaper to buy tickets in Colombia for these than in advance in Venezuela.

Bus Bus station: Av 7, No 1-50 (a really rough area). Taxi from bus station to town centre, US$1.75. **Copetran**'s private terminal is at Av 7, No 16N-33, Zona Industrial, T7-587 4205 (also at municipal terminal); taxi to town centre, US$3. The **Berlinas de Fonce** terminal is at Av 7, No 0-05, opposite the airport, T7-587 5105 (also at the main terminal). To **Bogotá**, 14½ hrs, US$26-28, frequent with **Berlinas del Fonce** and Copetran. To **Cartagena**, 16-19 hrs, Copetran and **Berlinas del Fonce**, US$45-60. Reliable taxi service at the bus terminal, Cotranol, T7-572 6139, 314-413 2316 (Sr Orlando).

Warning...

To avoid theft at Cúcuta bus terminal, go straight to the **Berlinas del Fonce** and **Copetran** terminals. Otherwise, on the first floor of the main terminal there is a tourist office for help and information and a café/snack bar where you can wait in comparative safety. Do not allow anyone to divert you from the service you want and don't let your belongings out of your sight. Report any theft to the police, or Migración Colombia.

Border with Venezuela

Bus **San Cristóbal**, US$2 (**Bolivariano**), *colectivo* US$3; **San Antonio**, taxi US$12, bus and *colectivo* from C 7, Av 4/5, US$1 to Migración Colombia, then US$0.75 to SAIME in San Antonio. From Cúcuta to **Mérida** or beyond, go to San Antonio or (better) San Cristóbal and change. Make sure that the driver knows that you need to stop to obtain exit/entry stamps etc. You will have to alight and flag down a later *colectivo*.

Caribbean
Colombia

Reaching Colombia's Caribbean coast is like entering another world, quite different in spirit from the highlands. Steamy, colourful and lively, the entire area pulses to the seductive rhythms of *vallenato*, heard at festivals throughout the region. Cartagena, the emerald in the crown of Colombia, is a stunning colonial city positively bursting with colour and history, and with various sparkling coral islands within easy reach. South of Cartagena the shoreline stretches towards the virgin jungles of the Darién Gap. To the east, Santa Marta is the gateway to the spectacular Tayrona and Sierra Nevada de Santa Marta National Parks. The latter conceals the Ciudad Perdida, the culmination of an unforgettable trek. Further east is the arid Guajira Peninsula.

Cartagena *Colour map 1, A2.*

colonial splendour meets Caribbean spirit

★Cartagena should not be missed. Besides being Colombia's top tourist destination and a World Heritage Site, it is one of the most vibrant and beautiful cities in South America. It's an eclectic mix of Caribbean, African and Spanish tastes and sounds. During the high season the city becomes a playground for the rich and famous, while cruise liners dock at its port.

The colonial heart of Cartagena lies within 12 km of ramparts. Inside the walled city, El Centro is a labyrinth of colourful squares, churches, mansions of former nobles and pastel-coloured houses along narrow cobbled streets. Most of the upmarket hotels and restaurants are found here. The San Diego quarter, once home to the middle classes, and Plaza Santo Domingo, next to the city's oldest church, perhaps best capture the lure of colonial Cartagena; don't miss a drink at night in the cafés here. Less touristy and developed is the poorer Getsemaní neighbourhood, where colonial buildings of former artisans are being rapidly restored. Here are most of the budget hotels. Immediately adjoining Getsemaní is the downtown sector known as La Matuna, where vendors and fruit-juice sellers crowd the pavements and alleys between the modern commercial buildings and banks.

Cartagena is also a popular beach resort and along Bocagrande and El Laguito are modern high-rise hotels on the seafront. Beyond Crespo on the road to Barranquilla is a fast-growing beach resort lined with luxury apartments.

☆The ramparts

The city walls (www.patrimoniodecartagena.com/es/fortificaciones) make a great walk and are an excellent way to visit many of the attractions inside the old city (see below). A good place to start is the **Baluarte San Francisco Javier** from where, with a few ups and downs, the circuit is continuous to **La India Catalina**. From this point, there are two further sections along the lagoons to the **Puente Román** and then a final section along the Calle del Arsenal. The entire walk takes about 1½ hours. It is spectacular in the morning around 0600 and equally at sunset.

Historic centre: Outer city

The **Puente Román** leads from the island of Manga into Getsemaní. North of the bridge, in an interesting plaza, is the church of **Santísima Trinidad**, built 1643 but not consecrated until 1839. North of the church, at Calle Guerrero 10 lived Pedro Romero, who set the revolution of 1811 going with his cry of "Long Live Liberty". The chapel of **San Roque** (early 17th century), near the hospital of Espíritu Santo, is by the junction of Calles Media Luna and Espíritu Santo.

If you take Calle Larga from Puente Román, you come to the two churches and monastery of **San Francisco**. The oldest church (now a cinema) was built in 1590 after the pirate Martin Côte had destroyed an earlier church built in 1559. The first Inquisitors lodged at the monastery. From its courtyard a crowd surged into the streets claiming independence from Spain on 11 November 1811. The monastery is now used by the Corporación Universitaria Rafael Núñez. Originally part of the Franciscan complex, the **Iglesia de la Tercera Orden** on the corner of Calle Larga is worth a visit.

Past the San Francisco complex is **Plaza de la Independencia**, with the landscaped **Parque del Centenario** beyond. Alongside the Plaza, by the water, runs the **Paseo de los Mártires**, flanked by the busts of nine patriots executed in the square on 24 February 1816 by the royalist Morillo when he retook the city. At its western end, the **Torre del Reloj** (clocktower) is one of Cartagena's most prominent landmarks and the main entrance to the inner walled city.

Historic centre: inner city

Slaves from Africa were brought under the arches of the clocktower to the **Plaza de los Coches**, which served as a slave market. Around almost all the plazas of Cartagena arcades offer refuge from the tropical sun. On the west side of this plaza is the **Portal de los Dulces**, a favourite meeting place, where sweets are still sold. At night, the area becomes a popular place for an evening drink.

The **Plaza de la Aduana**, which has a statue of Columbus, is flanked by the **Palacio Municipal** and the old Customs House. The **Museo de Arte Moderno** ① *www.mamcartagena.org, Mon-Fri 0900-1200, 1500-1900, Sat, Sun 1600-2100, US$2.60, free Wed*, exhibits modern Colombian artists and has a shop. Continue southwest to the **Church of San Pedro Claver and Monastery** ① *Mon-Fri 0800-1730, Sat-Sun 0800-1630, US$3.50*. Built by Jesuits in 1603, it was later dedicated to San Pedro Claver, a monk in the monastery, who was canonized 235 years after his death in 1654. Known as the Slave of the Slaves (El Apóstol de los Negros), he used to beg from door to door for money to give to the black slaves brought to the city. His body is in a glass coffin on the high altar and his cell and the balcony from which he sighted slave ships are shown to visitors. The monastery has a pleasant courtyard filled with flowers and trees in which Pedro Claver baptised slaves.

Essential Cartagena

Finding your feet

Rafael Núñez **airport** is 1.5 km east of the city in the Crespo district and the **bus terminal** is at least 35 minutes from town on the road to Barranquilla. The old walled city lies at the north end of the Bahía de Cartagena, with the Caribbean Sea to the west.

Getting around

The colonial centre should be explored on foot, but public transport and boats are needed for the beach areas. See Transport, page 931.

Safety

Carry your passport, or a photocopy, at all times. Failure to present it on police request can result in imprisonment and fines. There is a police station in Matuna (Central Comercial La Plazoleta), another in Barrio Manga. In Bocagrande there is a police station on Parque Flanaga. Never change money on the street under any circumstances. There are many ATMs, the most convenient are in the Plaza de la Aduana, the banks in La Matuna (across from Parque del Centenario) and the **Exito** supermarket, Escallón y Boquete. In Bocagrande a number of banks can be found around Avenida San Martín y C 8. There are *cambios* in the arcade at Torre Reloj and adjoining streets (Carretas, Manuel Román y Pico, Colegio).

When to go

The weather is warm year-round, although trade winds from December to February provide relief from the heat. The city is very crowded around Christmas, Easter and at festival time.

Cartagena historic centre

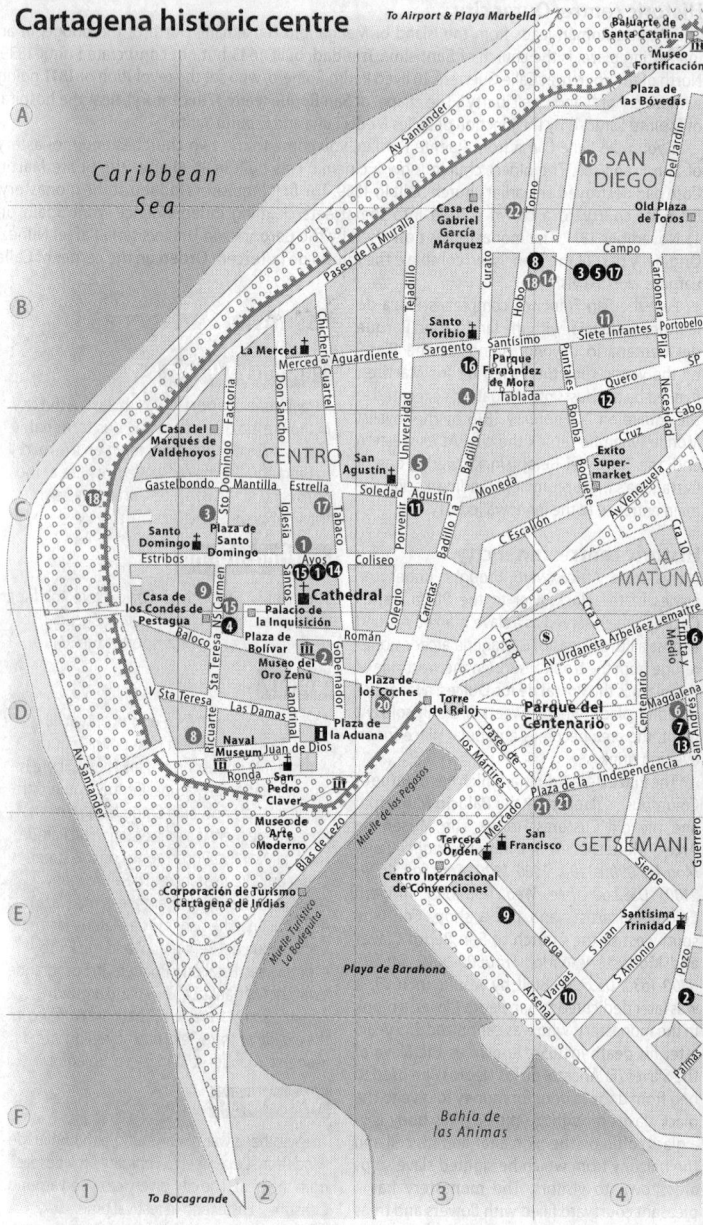

To Airport & Playa Marbella

Baluarte de Santa Catalina
Museo Fortificación
Plaza de las Bóvedas

Caribbean Sea

SAN DIEGO

Old Plaza de Toros

Casa de Gabriel García Márquez

Campo

La Merced

Santo Toribio

Parque Fernández de Mora

Siete Infantes

Casa del Marqués de Valdehoyos

CENTRO

San Agustín

Éxito Supermarket

Santo Domingo
Plaza de Santo Domingo

LA MATUNA

Casa de los Condes de Pestagua

Cathedral

Palacio de la Inquisición

Plaza de Bolívar

Museo del Oro Zenú

Plaza de los Coches

Parque del Centenario

Naval Museum

Torre del Reloj

Plaza de la Aduana

San Pedro Claver

Plaza de la Independencia

Museo de Arte Moderno

Tercera Orden

San Francisco

GETSEMANI

Corporación de Turismo Cartagena de Indias

Centro Internacional de Convenciones

Santísima Trinidad

Playa de Barahona

Bahía de las Animas

To Bocagrande

Where to stay

1 Agua C2
2 Cartagena de Indias D2
3 Casa de Pestagua C2
4 Casa La Fe B3
5 Casa San Agustín C3
6 Casa Viena D4
7 Casa Villa Colonial D5
8 Charleston Santa Teresa D2
9 El Marqués C2
10 El Viajero Hostel B4
11 Familiar D4
12 Familiar D4
13 Hostal Casa Baluarte D5
14 Hostal Casa Nativa B4
15 Hostal Santo Domingo C2
16 Kartaxa LifeStyle A4
17 La Passion C2
18 Las Tres Banderas B3
19 Mamallena D5
20 Marlin D5
21 Monterrey D4
22 Santa Clara B3
23 Villa Colonial D5

Restaurants

1 Bistro C2
2 Café Creperie
   Le Petit Versailles E4
3 Café Zebra B4
4 Donde Olano D2
5 El Balcón B4
6 El Coroncoro D4
7 Este es el Punto D4
8 Juan del Mar B4
9 La Casa de Socorro E3
10 La Cocina de Pepina E4
11 La Esquina del
   Pan de Bono C3
12 La Mulata B4
13 Lunarossa D4
14 Oh Là Là Café Bistrot C2
15 Perú Fusión C2
16 Pizza en el Parque B3
17 Teriyaki B4

Bars & clubs

18 Café del Mar C1
19 Café Havana D4
20 Donde Fidel &
   Tu Candela D3
21 Quiebra Canto D4

100 metres
100 yards

The church and convent of **Santa Teresa** on the corner of C Ricaurte, was founded in 1609. It is now a hotel, renamed the **Charleston Santa Teresa** (Carrera 3, No 31-23, www.hotelcharleston santateresa.com). Opposite is the **Museo Naval del Caribe** ⓘ *C San Juan de Dios No 3-62, T5-664 2440, www.museonavaldelcaribe.com, daily 1000-1730, US$2.75, discount for children,* displaying the detailed naval history of Cartagena and the Caribbean.

The **Plaza de Bolívar** (the old Plaza Inquisición) has a statue of Bolívar. On its west side is the **Palacio de la Inquisición** ⓘ *www. muhca.gov.co, Mon-Sat 0900-1800, Sun 1000-1600, US$6.* It was first established in 1610 and the present building dates from 1706. The stone entrance with its coats of arms and ornate wooden door is well preserved. The whole building, with its balconies, cloisters and patios, is a fine example of colonial baroque. It has been restored with air-conditioned rooms. The small museum contains photographs of Cartagena from the 20th century, paintings of historical figures, models of colonial houses and a torture chamber (with reproductions of actual instruments). On the opposite side of the Plaza de Bolívar is the **Museo del Oro Zenú** ⓘ *T5-660 0778, www.banrepcultural.org/Cartagena, Tue-Sat 0900-1700, Sun 1000-1500, free.* It has well displayed pre-Columbian gold and pottery.

The **Cathedral**, in the northeast corner of Plaza de Bolívar, was begun in 1575 and partially destroyed by Francis Drake. Reconstruction was finished by 1610. Great alterations were made between 1912 and 1923. It has a severe exterior, with a fine doorway and a simply decorated interior. See the gilded 18th-century altar, the Carrara marble pulpit, and the elegant arcades which sustain the central nave.

The church and monastery of **Santo Domingo** ⓘ *Santo Domingo y Estribos,* was built 1570 to 1579 and is now a seminary. Inside, a miracle-making image of Christ, carved towards the end of the 16th century, is set on a baroque 19th-century altar. There is also a statue of the Virgin with a crown of gold and emeralds. Opposite the church is a fine bronze sculpture by Fernando Botero, the *Gertrudis,* presenting an interesting juxtaposition between the colonial and the modern.

Plaza Santo Domingo and Calle Santo Domingo have lots of pavement cafés, restaurants and wandering musicians, an excellent place to go in the evening. In Calle Santo Domingo, No 33-29, is one of the

BACKGROUND

Fortifying Cartagena

The full name of Cartagena is Cartagena de Indias, a reminder that the early Spanish navigators believed they had reached the Far East. The city was founded by Pedro de Heredia on 13 January 1533 and was built by the Spaniards on an island separated from the mainland by marshes and lagoons, close to a prominent hill. It was near to the mouth of the Río Magdalena, the route to the interior of the continent, and thus became one of the most important depots for merchandise arriving from Spain and for treasure collected from the Americas to be sent back. The Bahía de Cartagena, which is 15 km long and 5 km wide, was protected by several low, sandy islands, which formed natural sea defences. There were originally just two approaches to the bay -- Bocagrande, at the northern end of Tierrabomba island, and Bocachica, a narrow channel to the south -- thus making it a perfect place for a harbour and, more importantly at the time, easy to defend against attack. The city's wealth made it a prize target for French and English privateers operating in the Caribbean, including Sir Francis Drake who took the city in 1586. In response, a series of forts were built to protect Cartagena from raids from the sea, and formidable walls were constructed around the city, making it almost impregnable.

The harbour was protected by fortifications on Tierrabomba, Barú, Bocagrande and on the mainland, while the Puente Román, which connected the old city with Manga island to the southeast, was defended by three forts: **San Sebastián del Pastelillo**, built between 1558 and 1567 (now occupied by the Club de Pesca), **San Lorenzo** and the very powerful **Castillo San Felipe de Barajas inland** to the east. Yet another fort, **La Tenaza**, protected the northern point of the walled city from a direct attack from the open sea. In 1650, the Spaniards built the 145-km long **Canal del Dique** connecting the city to the Río Magdalena and allowing free access for ships from the upriver ports. The city suffered a devastating raid by the French, led by Baron de Pointis and Jean Baptiste Ducasse, in 1697, but returned to prosperity during the 18th century as one of the most important cities in the newly formed Viceroyalty of New Granada. Following an unsuccessful but sustained attack by Admiral Edward Vernon in 1741, Bocagrande was blocked by an underwater wall, thus leaving only one entrance to the harbour.

The huge walls that encircle the old city were started early in the 17th century and finished by 1735. They were on average 12 m high and 17 m thick, with six gates. Besides barracks, they contained a water reservoir. The old city was in two sections, outer and inner, divided by a wall. The artisan classes lived in one-storey houses in the outer city, in an area known as **Getsemaní** where many colonial buildings survive. The **inner** city, or **El Centro**, was originally occupied by the high officials and nobility, with the clerks, merchants, priests and military living in **San Diego** at the northern end.

Cartagena declared its Independence from Spain in 1811. A year later Bolívar used the city as a jumping-off point for his Magdalena campaign. After heroic resistance, Cartagena was retaken by the royalists under General Pablo Morillo in 1815. It was finally freed by the patriots in 1821.

---

great patrician houses of Cartagena, the **Casa de los Condes de Pestagua** (now restored with great care as a hotel, www.casapestagua.com). North of Santo Domingo is the magnificent **Casa del Marqués de Valdehoyos** ① *C de la Factoria 36-57*, home of some of the best woodcarving in Cartagena and used for cultural events and conferences.

The monastery of **San Agustín** (1580) is now the Universidad de Cartagena (at Universidad y La Soledad). From its chapel the pirate Baron de Pointis stole a 500-pound silver sepulchre. It was returned by the King of France, but the citizens melted it down to pay their troops during the siege by Morillo in 1815. (The luxury hotel Casa San Agustín is at Calle de la Universidad No 36-44, www.hotelcasasanagustin.com.) The church and convent of **La Merced** ① *Merced y Chichería*, was founded 1618. The convent was a prison during Morillos reign of terror and its church is now the Teatro Heredia, beautifully restored. Building of the church of **Santo Toribio** ① *Badillo y Sargento*, open for mass only Mon-Fri 0630, 1200 and 1815, Sat 0630, 1200 and 1800, Sun 0800, 1000, 1800 and

1900, *closed at other times*, began in 1729. In 1741, during Admiral Vernon's siege, a cannon ball fell into the church during Mass and lodged in one of the central columns; the ball is now in a recess in the west wall. The font of Carrara marble in the Sacristy is a masterpiece. There is a beautiful carved ceiling (mudéjar style) above the main altar. The church and monastery of **Santa Clara de Assisi**, built 1617-1621, have been converted into a fine hotel (Santa Clara, Calle del Torno, No 39-29, www. sofitel.com). Near the hotel is the orange **Casa de Gabriel García Márquez**, for former Cartagena home of Colombia's most famous author, on the corner of Calle del Curato.

North of Santa Clara is the **Plaza de las Bóvedas**. The walls of Las Bóvedas, built 1799, are some 12 m high and 15 to 18 m thick. From the rampart there is a grand view. At the base of the wall are 23 dungeons, now containing tourist shops. Both a lighted underground passage and a drawbridge lead from Las Bóvedas to the fortress of La Tenaza at the water's edge (see above). In the neighbouring Baluarte de Santa Catalina is the **Museo Fortificación de Santa Catalina** ① *www. fortificacionesdecartagena.com, daily 0800-1700, US$2.50, children US$1.35*, inside the city walls.

Casa de Núñez ① *just outside the walls of La Tenaza in El Cabrero district opposite the Ermita de El Cabrero, C del Coliseo, Tue-Fri 0900-1700, Sat-Sun 1000-1600, free*, was the home of Rafael Núñez, president (four times) and poet (he wrote Colombia's national anthem). His grandiose marble tomb is in the adjoining church.

East of the centre

Castillo San Felipe de Barajas ① *daily 0800-1800, US$8, guides available*, is located 41 m above sea level on San Lázaro hill across the **Puente Heredia** from the old city. It is the largest Spanish fort built in the Americas. Under the huge structure is a network of tunnels cut into the rock, lined with living rooms and offices. Visitors pass through these and on to the top of the fortress. Good footwear is advisable in the damp sloping tunnels, and although some are open and illuminated, a flashlight is handy in the others. In the **Almacén de Pólvora** (Gunpowder store), there is a reproduction of Admiral Vernon's map, dating from his abortive attempt to take the city in 1741. A statue of Don Blas de Lezo below the fortress has a plaque displaying the medal prematurely struck celebrating Vernon's 'victory'.

At **Convento La Popa** ① *daily 0830-1730, US$1.50, children and students US$1*, on La Popa hill (named after its imagined likeness to a ship's poop) is the church and monastery of **Santa Cruz** and the restored ruins of the convent dating from 1608. The only reason to visit is for good views of the harbour and the city from this height (nearly 150 m). In the church is the beautiful little image of the Virgin of La Candelaria, reputed to be a deliverer from plague and a protector against pirates. Every year, nine days before 2 February, thousands of pilgrims go up the hill and on the day itself carry lighted candles in her honour. It can be unsafe to walk up on your own; seek local advice first. There are guided tours, or take a public bus to Teatro Miramar at the foot of the hill (US$0.75), then negotiate with a taxi up; they charge about US$20 with waiting time. If driving, take Carretera 21 off Avenida Pedro de Heredia and follow the winding road to the top.

Beaches

Bocagrande Take a bus south from the Torre del Reloj (10 minutes), taxi US$2.50, or walk to Bocagrande, a spit of land crowded with hotels and apartment blocks. Sand and sea can be dirty and you will be hassled by vendors. But do not ignore the *palenqueras*, the black women who majestically carry bowls of fruits on their heads, serving excellent fruit salads on the beach. The **Hilton** hotel beach (www.cartagena.hilton.com, excellent hotel), at the end of the peninsula, is cleaner and has fewer vendors.

Marbella and the northern beaches Northeast of the city is Marbella, just north of Las Bóvedas. The city continues beyond Marbella, with beaches along a spit of land between the sea and the Ciénaga de la Virgen. During the week, they are quiet and are decent for swimming, though sometimes there are dangerous currents. The promontory beyond the airport is built up with high rises, including many well-known hotels which have their own access to the beach. City buses run to Los Morros and Las Américas conference centre, carrying on towards La Boquilla and Manzanillo, which is a sparsely populated stretch of beach still close to the city. There are upscale dining options (including a gourmet supermarket) at the turnoff to Manzanillo.

Bocachica The Bocachica beach, on Tierrabomba island, is also none too clean. Boats leave from Muelle Turístico. The round trip can take up to two hours each way and costs about US$5 with regular services. *Ferry Dancing*, about half the price of the faster, luxury boats, carries dancing passengers. Boats taking in Bocachica and the San Fernando fortress include *Alcatraz*, which runs a daily trip from the Muelle Turístico. Recommended.

Playa Blanca Boats to the Islas del Rosario (see below) may stop at the San Fernando fortress and Playa Blanca on the Isla Barú for two to 2½ hours. Many consider this to be the best beach in the region, with stretches of white sand and shady palm groves. Take food and water since these are expensive on the island. Playa Blanca is crowded in the morning, with armies of hawkers, but the tour boats leave at 1400. If snorkelling, beware drunken jetski drivers. There are several fish restaurants on the beach, a growing number of upmarket places to stay and a few hammock and camping places (take repellent against sandflies if sleeping in a tent or *cabaña*). You can arrange to be left and collected later, or you can try to catch an earlier boat on to Islas del Rosario or back to Cartagena with a boat that has dropped off people at the beach.

☆Islas del Rosario

The **Parque Nacional Corales del Rosario** embraces the Rosario archipelago (a group of 30 low-lying, densely vegetated coral islets 45 km southwest of the Bay of Cartagena, with narrow strips of fine sand beaches and mangroves) and the Islas de San Bernardo, a

> **Tip...**
> When taking boat trips be certain that you and the operator understand what you are paying for.

further 50 km south (see page 932). **Isla Grande** and some of the smaller islets are easily accessible by day trippers. Other visitors who may need permits (US$2.55 entrance fee, park open 0800-1700) should contact the National Parks office in Bogotá or Ecohotel La Cocotera (T314-514 4067, Facebook: hotellacocoteracartagena). **Rosario** (the best conserved) and **Tesoro** both have small lakes, some of which connect to the sea. There is an incredible profusion of aquatic and birdlife. The **San Martín de Pajarales Aquarium** ⓘ *US$9, not included in boat fares (check that it's open before setting out)*, is an open sea aquarium; there are guides, but also shark and dolphin shows (Footprint does not endorse dolphins in captivity, see www.wdcs.org/captivity). Many of the smaller islets are privately owned. Apart from fish and coconuts, everything is imported from the mainland, fresh water included. Enquire in Bocagrande for other places to stay on the islands. Diving permits are organized by diving companies and are included in the tour price.

North of Cartagena

A good road continues beyond La Boquilla. On the coast, 50 km northeast, is **Galerazamba**, no accommodation but good local food. Nearby are the clay baths of **Volcán del Totumo** ⓘ *US$3.50, a bathe will cost you US$3.50, masseurs available for a small extra fee*, in beautiful surroundings. The crater is about 20 m high and the mud lake, at a comfortable temperature, 10 m across, is reputed to be over 500 m deep.

Tourist information

Useful websites include www.ticartagena. com, www.cartagenaturismo.es/ and www. cartagenacaribe.com.

Corporación Turismo Cartagena de Indias (Corpoturismo)
Casa del Marqués del Premio Real, Pl de la Aduana, T5-660 1583, www.cartagena deindias.travel. Daily Mon-Sat 0900-1200, 1300-1800, Sun and holidays 0900-1700.

This is the main tourist office and has very helpful and knowledgeable staff.

There are also kiosks in Plaza de la Paz (same hours as above), at the airport (daily 0700-2300, reduced hours on Sun), Bocagrande, Av del Malecón, opposite Parque Flanagan (Mon-Sat 0800-1200, 1300-1700, Sun 0900-1700) and at the Sociedad Portuaria Regional de Cartagena (open for cruise ship arrivals).

Instituto Agustín Codazzi
C 34, No 3A-31, Edif Inurbe, T5-664 4171, www.igac.gov.co. Mon-Fri 0800-1200, 1300-1700. Contact for maps.

Instituto de Patrimonio y Cultura de Cartagena
C Larga No 9A-37, T5-664 9443, www.ipcc.gov.co. Mon-Fri 0800-1200, 1400-1800.
May also provide information.

Where to stay

Hotel prices rise for the high seasons, Nov-Mar and Jun-Jul. From 15 Dec to 31 Jan they can increase by as much as 50% (dates are not fixed and vary at each hotel). Hotels tend to be heavily booked right through to Mar. Bargain in low season.

Historic centre

There is a growing number of attractive boutique hotels in Cartagena. Most budget hostels are in Getsemaní. This area is very popular with travellers and has been smartened up, with many places to stay, eat and drink (lots of happy hour offers). Do not, however, walk alone late at night.

See the description of the Historic centre for descriptions and websites of colonial buildings converted to luxury hotels: **Charleston Santa Teresa** (see page 921), **Casa de los Condes de Pestagua** (see page 922), **Casa San Agustín** (see page 922) and **Santa Clara** (see page 923) are all special places to stay.

$$$$ Agua
C de Ayos, No 4-29, T5-664 9479, www.hotelagua.com.co.
Exclusive, pricey, small boutique hotel, colonial, quiet, pleasant patio.

$$$$ Cartagena de Indias
C Vélez Daníes 33, No 4-39, T5-660 0133, www.movichhotels.com.
Small hotel in a colonial building, comfortable, luxury accommodation with pool and terrace with great view of the city.

$$$$ El Marqués
C Nuestra Señora del Carmen, No 33-41, T5-664 4438, www.elmarqueshotelboutique.com.
A house belonging to the Pestagua family, famous in the 1970s for its celebrity guests. The central courtyard has giant birdcages, hanging bells and large palm trees. The rooms are crisp and white. Peruvian restaurant, wine cellar and a spa. Exquisite.

$$$$ La Passion
C Estanco del Tabaco, No 35-81, T5-664 8605, www.lapassionhotel.com.
Moroccan-style chic, elegant and discreet comfort, helpful staff, breakfast served by the roof top pool, very pleasant. Some rooms have balconies. Massage treatments and boat trips to Islas del Rosario organized. Highly recommended.

$$$$-$$$ Casa La Fe
Parque Fernández de Madrid, C 2a de Badillo, No 36-125, T5-664 0306, http://kalihotels.com.
Discreet sign (pink building), run by British/Colombian team. Very pleasant converted colonial house, quiet, jacuzzi on roof, free bicycle use. Recommended. Also has new sister hotel, **$$$** Posada la Fe, in Getsemaní district (same website).

$$$ Hostal Casa Baluarte
C Media Luna, No 10-86, Getsemaní, T5-664 2208, www.hostalcasabaluarte.com.
Small rooms in colonial house, family-run, fan, laundry service. Offers massage and can arrange tours to the Islas del Rosario.

$$$ Kartaxa LifeStyle
C de las Bóvedas, No 39-120, T5-645 5300, http://hotelkartaxacartagena.com.
Near the delightful Plaza San Diego, this colonial building has modern rooms with an art and literature theme, courtyard, **La Comunión** restaurant.

$$$ Las Tres Banderas
C Cochera de Hobo, No 38-66, T5-660 0160, www.hotel3banderas.com.
Off Plaza San Diego, popular, helpful owner, very pleasant, safe, quiet, good beds, spacious rooms, massage treatments, small patio. Price depends on standard of room and season. Free ferry transport to sister hotel on Isla de la Bomba, has another hotel in Manzanillo.

$$$ Monterrey
Paseo de los Mártires Cra 8B, No 25-103, T5-650 3030, www.hotelmonterrey.com.co.
Colonial style, nice terrace with jacuzzi, pool, business centre, comfortable rooms.

$$ Hostal Santo Domingo
C Santo Domingo, No 33-46, T5-664 2268, hsantodomingopiret@yahoo.es.
Prime location, rooms are simple and open onto a sunny patio. Gate is usually locked, so security is good.

$$-$ Mamallena

C de la Media Luna, No 10-47,
T5-670 0499, www.hostel
mamallenacartagena.com.
Rooms and dorms (US$12, some a/c), in same group as Mamallena hostels in Panama, www.mamallena.com. Thorough info on boat travel to Panama and on local activities and day tours. There's a small kitchen, café, breakfast, tea and coffee included.

$$-$ Marlin

C de la Media Luna, No 10-35, T5-664 3507,
Facebook: HOTELMARLIN.
Aquatic-themed hostel run by a friendly Colombian. Private rooms and dorms (US$10 pp). Has a fine balcony overlooking the busy C de la Media Luna, free coffee, laundry service, lockers, tours and bus tickets organized. Recommended.

$$-$ Villa Colonial

C de las Maravillas, No 30-60, Getsemaní,
T5-664 5421, www.hotelvillacolonial.com.
Safe, well-kept hostel run by friendly family, English spoken, cheaper with fan, tours to Islas del Rosario. Its sister hotels, **Casa Villa Colonial**, C de la Media Luna No 10-89, and Casa Mara, C del Espíritu No 29-139, same phone, www.casavillacolonial.com, are more upmarket ($$$-$$) and are also recommended.

$ Casa Viena

C San Andrés, No 30-53 Getsemaní, T5-668 5048,
T320-538 3619, www.casaviena.com.
Popular traveller hostel with very helpful staff who provide lots of information and sell tours and Brasilia bus tickets. Cooking facilities, washing machine, TV room, range of dorms (US$10-13) and rooms: more expensive with private bath and a/c. Enquire here for information about boats to Panama.

$ El Viajero Hostel Cartagena

C Siete Infantes, No 9-45, T318-257 5354,
www.hostelcartagena.com.
Member of the South American chain of hostels, with a/c in rooms and dorms (average dorm bed price US$13-15 pp), busy and popular party hostel with bar, daily activities including dance lessons.

$ Familiar

C El Guerrero, No 29-66, Getsemaní, T5-664 2464.
Fresh and bright, family-run hotel with 15 rooms set around a colonnaded patio. Has a good noticeboard full of information. Recommended.

$ Hostal Casa Nativa

C Tumbamuertos, No 38-68, T5-645 6064,
Facebook: Nativa-Cartagena-179423822136658.
No-frills *hostal* ideally located in the centre. Dorms for 4 to 8 people, no private rooms. A decent budget option.

Bocagrande

$$$$ Capilla del Mar

Cra 1, No 8-12, T5-650 1500,
www.capilladelmar.com.
Resort hotel across the road from the beach, with swimming pool on the top floor and 2 restaurants featuring regional cuisine.

$$$$-$$$ Hotel Caribe by Faranda

Cra 1, No 2-87, T5-650 1160, www.hotelcaribe.com.
Enormous Caribbean-style hotel, the first to be built in Cartagena, retaining some splendour of bygone years, with 2 newer annexes, a/c, beautiful grounds and a swimming pool. Expensive restaurant, has several bars overlooking the sea, various tour agencies and a dive shop.

$$$$-$$$ Playa Club

Av San Martín, No 4-87, T5-665 0552,
www.hotelplayaclubcartagena.com.
Good rooms, inviting pool and direct access to the beach. TV, a/c and breakfast included. Restaurant on premises.

$$$ Bahía

Cra 4 with C 4, T5-665 0316,
www.hotelbahiacartagena.com.
Retains the feel of a 1950s hotel – it was opened in 1958 – but with mod cons such as Wi-Fi and safes in rooms. Discreet and quiet, with 2 fine pools, children's play area and 3 restaurants.

$$$-$$ Cartagena Millennium

Av San Martín, No 7-135, T5-665 8711,
www.hotelcartagenamillennium.com.
A range of different suites and spacious rooms at various prices. Chic and trendy, with minimalist decor, a small pool, restaurant serving typical and international food, a terrace bar and a lobby bar, good service.

$$$-$$ Charlotte

Av San Martín, No 7-126, T5-665 9365,
www.hotelescharlotte.com.
Comfortable rooms stylishly designed in cool whites. Has a small pool, and Wi-Fi by the pool. Smart restaurant serving regional food. Recommended.

$$ Mary
Cra 3, No 6-53, T5-665 2833,
Basic rooms but pleasant and friendly. A/c or fan.

Marbella and the northern beaches

$$$ Hotel Kohsamui
Anillo Vial, Entrada Km 9.7 a Manzanillo del Mar,
T317-648 9303, www.kohsamuicartagena.com.
Situated 20 km north of Cartagena, this is an ideal
beachside spot for relaxation and rejuvenation.
Owner María Fernanda runs the hotel and has
information on mangrove tours, excursions and
trips to Islas del Rosario and Volcán del Totumo.
Amenities include a/c and fans, security box, Wi-
Fi, minibar, restaurant, spa with massage, and a
2nd-floor terrace with hammocks. 10% discount
for paying in advance. Highly recommended.

Isla Barú

$$$ Playa Manglares
Km 12, Isla Barú Ararca, T311-403 9391,
www.playamanglares.com.
Ecolodge, with pool and private beachfront,
restaurant, evening cocktails, attentive
service, delightful.

$$ Hostal Restaurante Mama Ruth
Isla Barú, T300-710 2444, Mamaruthbaru@
gmail.com, see Facebook.
Thatched cabins right on the beach and a
popular restaurant. Recommended.

Islas del Rosario

$$$$ San Pedro de Majagua
Isla Grande; book at C del Torno, No 39-29,
Cartagena, T5-693 0987, www.hotelmajagua.com.
Everything from a 'pillow menu' to Egyptian
cotton bed sheets, this is a lovely, luxurious
place for utter relaxation.

$$$$-$$$ Isla del Pirata
C 6, No 2-26, local 2, Edif Granada, Bocagrande,
T5-665 2952, www.hotelislapirata.com.
Simple, comfortable *cabañas*, activities include
diving, snorkelling, canoeing and pétanque,
good Caribbean restaurant. Prices include
transport to the island from Cartagena, food and
non-guided activities. Highly recommended.

$$$ Ecohotel La Cocotera
Comunidad de Orika, Isla Grande,
T376 474 0781, see Facebook.
Rooms with bath and solar power, also
has camping and hammocks, restaurant,
diving school.

Restaurants

There is a wide range of excellent restaurants.
Reservations are recommended during high
season. At cafés try *patacón*, a round flat 'cake'
made of green banana, mashed and baked; it's
also available from street stalls in Parque del
Centenario in the early morning. At restaurants
ask for *sancocho*, the local soup of the day made
from vegetables and fish or meat. Stands serving
tasty shrimp cocktails can be found just outside
of El Centro. Also try *obleas* for a snack: biscuits
with jam, cream cheese or caramel fudge
(*arequipe*); and *buñuelos*, deep-fried cheese
dough balls. Fruit juices are fresh, tasty and
cheap in Cartagena: a good place is on the Paseo
de los Pegasos (Av Blas de Lezo) from the many
stalls alongside the boats. **Crepes y Waffles**,
Jeno's Pizza and **Juan Valdez** have outlets in
the centre, Bocagrande and elsewhere.

Historic centre

$$$-$$ Donde Olano
C Santo Domingo, No 33-81, T5-664 7099,
www.dondeolano.com.
Tucked away, Art Deco style, intimate atmosphere,
great seafood with French and Creole influences.

$$ Bistro
C de los Ayos, No 4-46, T5-660 2065,
www.el-bistro.com. Closed Sun.
German-run restaurant with a relaxed
atmosphere. Sofas, music, Colombian and
European menu at reasonable prices, German
bakery. Recommended.

$$ Café Creperie Le Petit Versailles
Cra 10-B, No 27-34, T5-660 2115, Getsemaní,
see Facebook.
Excellent French-style crepes and coffee. Highly
recommended, especially for breakfasts.

$$ Café Zebra
Plaza San Diego, No 8-34.
Café with a wide selection of coffees,
hot sandwiches and African dishes.

$$ El Balcón
C de Tumbamuertos, No 38-85,
p 2 (above Zebra), T5-643 4393.
Small restaurant with a nice balcony overlooking
the Plaza de San Diego. Good atmosphere and
good views.

$$ Juan del Mar
Plaza San Diego, No 8-21, T5-664 2782,
www.juandelmar.com.

Two restaurants in one: inside for expensive seafood, outside for fine, thin-crust pizzas, though you are likely to be harassed by street hawkers, as with any place on the street here.

$$ Lunarossa
C Media Luna No 9-91 y San Andrés.
Italian place, with pastas, thin-crust pizzas and other dishes, also has a cocktail bar and open-air terrace at the back.

$$ Oh Là Là Café Bistrot
C de los Ayos, No 4-48, T5-660 1757, see Facebook.
Café/restaurant serving very good French and Colombian food. Next door is **Jugoso** juice bar and **El Gallinero** for ice creams, yoghurts and snacks.

$$ Perú Fusión
C de los Ayos, No 4-36, T5-660 5243, see Facebook.
Good value Peruvian-style food, including ceviches.

$$ Teriyaki
Plaza San Diego, No 8-28, T5-664 8651, www.teriyaki.com.co.
Serves sushi and Thai food in smart surroundings; part of the chain with outlets in Bogota and Barranquilla.

$$-$ La Casa de Socorro
C Larga, No 8B-112, Getsemaní, T315-718 6666.
Busy at lunchtime, serves seafood and Caribbean dishes. There are 2 restaurants of the same name on the street and this is the original.

$$-$ La Cocina de Pepina
C Vargas, No 9A-6, T5-664 2944.
Serving Colombian-Caribbean fare, established by the late chef and cookbook author María Josefina Yances Guerra.

$ El Coroncoro
C Tripita y Media, No 31-22.
Typical local restaurant which is popular at lunchtime and serves good, inexpensive food.

$ Este es el Punto
C San Andrés, No 30-35.
Another popular restaurant, *comida corriente* at lunchtime, big portions, also serves breakfast.

$ La Esquina del Pan de Bono
San Agustín Chiquito, No 35-78, opposite Plazoleta San Agustín. Daily from 0600.
Breads, *empanadas, pasteles* and juices, popular for a quick snack.

$ La Mulata
C Quero, No 9-58.

A popular lunchtime venue with locals, you get a selection of set menu dishes. Try the excellent seafood casserole and coconut lemonade. Wi-Fi.

$ Pizza en el Parque
C 2a de Badillo, No 36-153.
This small restaurant serves delicious pizzas with some interesting flavours (pear and apple) which you can enjoy in the delightful atmosphere of Parque Fernández de Madrid.

East of the historic centre

$$$ Club de Pesca
San Sebastián de Pastelillo fort, Manga island, T5-651 7400, www.clubdepesca.com.
Wonderful setting, excellent fish and seafood. Recommended.

Bocagrande

$$$ Ranchería's
Av 1A, No 8-86. T5-665 6163
Serves mainly parrilla-style meats in thatched huts just off the beach.

$$$-$$ Arabe
Cra 3A, No 8-83, T5-665 4365, www. restaurantearabeinternacional.com.
Upmarket Arab restaurant serving tagines, etc. A/c, indoor seating or pleasant outdoor garden.

$$$-$$ Carbón de Palo
Av San Martín, No 6-40, T5-665 6004.
Steak heaven (and other dishes), cooked on an outdoor *parrilla*.

$ La Fonda Antioqueña
Cra 2, No 6-164, T5-665 5805.
Traditional Colombian food from Antioquia served in a pleasant atmosphere.

Marbella and the northern beaches
There are good fish dishes in La Boquilla and upscale dining options (including a gourmet supermarket) at the turn-off to Manzanillo.

$$ Archie's Trattoria
Km 9 via Manzanillo, Local 601, T5-643 7070, www.archies.com.
Chain Italian restaurant serving delicious thin-crust pizzas and a large selection of pastas.

$$ Hotel Kohsamui
Trans 2, No 3-51, Manzanillo, T317-648 9303.
Chef Elbert runs the restaurant in the hotel, serving up a variety of seafood dishes, including fresh ceviches, *arroz con mariscos* and fried fish. Probably the best seafood on the beach.

Bars and clubs

Most night life is found in the historic centre. Many of the hotels have evening entertainment and can arrange *chiva* tours, usually with free drinks and live music on the bus.

Most places don't get going until after 2400, though the Cuban bars **Donde Fidel** (Portal de los Dulces), and **Café Havana** (see below) start a bit earlier and are recommended for Cuban salsa. The former is open daytime, with good atmosphere. Many clubs are on C del Arsenal. Most bars play crossover music.

Historic centre

Café del Mar
Baluarte de Santo Domingo, El Centro.
The place to go for a drink at sundown.

Café Havana
C de la Media Luna y C del Guerrero, T314-556 3905, www.cafehavanacartagena.com. Wed-Sat 2030-0400.
A fantastic Cuban bar/restaurant, which feels like it has been transported from Havana brick by brick. The walls are festooned with black-and-white portraits of Cuban salsa stars and live bands play most nights. No credit cards. Highly recommended.

Quiebra Canto
Cra 8B, No 25-119 al Parque Centenario, next to Hotel Monterrey and above Café Bar Caponero, Getsemaní, www.quiebracanto.com.
Good for salsa, nice atmosphere, free admission.

Tu Candela
Portal de los Dulces, No 32-25, www.tucandela.co.
Where you can dance to 'crossover' in the vaults, open 2000-0400.

Bocagrande

There are good local nightclubs in Bocagrande eg Club Cartagena, opposite Hotel Bahía on C 4, with other places nearby, including spontaneous musical groups on or near the beach most evenings.

Entertainment

Cinema

There are many cinemas in Cartagena. In Bocagrande there is one in the **Centro Comercial Bocagrande** (Cra 2, No 8-142, T5-665 5024). Others are in the **Centro Comercial Paseo de la Castellana** (C 30, No 30-31, www.paseodela castellana.com), and in **Centro Comercial**

La Plazuela (Diag 31, No 71-130, www. multicentrolaplazuela.com).

Dance

El Colegio del Cuerpo, *Campus Universidad Jorge Tadeo Lozano, Módulo 6, Km 15-200, Anillo Vial Zona Norte, T5-665 4081, www.elcolegiodelcuerpo. org.* A classical dance studio that works with children from Cartagena's slums. They perform internationally and occasionally in Cartagena.

Festivals

Mid-Jan **Festival Internacional de Música**, www.cartagenamusicfestival.com. Classical music festival with associated education programme for young musicians.
End-Jan **Hay Festival Cartagena**, www.hay festival.com. Franchise of the famous UK literary festival, with internationally renowned writers.
Jan-Feb **La Candelaria**, religious processions and horse parades (see La Popa, page 923).
Early Mar **International Film Festival**, www. ficcifestival.com. The longest running festival of its kind in Latin America. Although mainly Spanish American films are featured, the US, Canada and European countries are represented in the week-long showings.
1 Jun **Foundation of Cartagena**, celebrations to commemorate the founding of the city, in 1533.
2nd week of Nov **Independence celebrations**: masked people in fancy dress dance to the sound of *maracas* and drums. There are beauty contests, battles of flowers and general mayhem.

Shopping

Pricey antiques can be bought in C Santo Domingo and there are a number of jewellery shops near Plaza de Bolívar in Centro, which specialize in emeralds. The handicraft shops in the Plaza de las Bóvedas (see page 923) have the best selection in town but tend to be expensive – cruise ship passengers are brought here. Woollen *blusas* are good value; try the **Tropicano** in Pierino Gallo building in Bocagrande. Also in this building are reputable jewellery shops.

Abaco, *C de la Iglesia with C Mantilla, No 3-86, T5-664 8338, www.abacolibros.com.* A bookshop and popular hangout for local writers and poets. Delightful atmosphere and a café serving juices and snacks.
Centro Comercial Getsemaní, *C Larga between San Juan and Plaza de la Independencia.* A large shopping centre. Good *artesanías* in the grounds of the convent.

El Centavo Menos, *C Román, No 5-08, Plaza de la Proclamación*. Good selection of Colombian handicrafts.

Exito, *Escallón y del Boquete*. A supermarket, with a/c and cafeteria.

Galería Cano, *Plaza Bolívar No 33-20, www.lacano.co (and at the airport and Hotel Santa Clara)*. Has excellent reproductions of pre-Columbian designs.

Librería Nacional, *C 2 de Badillo, No 36-27, T5-664 1448, www.librerianacional.com*. A good bookshop with large stock.

Upalema, *C San Juan de Dios, No 3-99*. A good selection of handicrafts.

Markets

The main market is to the southeast of the old city near La Popa off Av Pedro de Heredia (**Mercado Bazurto**, open daily). Good bargains in the **La Matuna** market, also open daily.

What to do

City tours

Many agencies, hotels and hostels offer city tours, US$15-25, depending on length of tour and what's included etc. There are also hop-on, hop-off city sightseeing bus tours, www.citysightseeing.com.co and www.colombiatrolley.com. A party tour on a *chiva* bus costs US$20. **Horse-drawn carriages** can be hired for a trip around the walled city from Puerta del Reloj, about US$15-20 for up to 4 people. Or from opposite Hotel El Dorado, Av San Martín, in Bocagrande, to ride into town at night (romantic but a rather short ride). You can also rent **bicycles** for riding the city streets from several places in the historic centre.

Diving

Discounts are sometimes available if you book via the hotels. There is a recompression chamber at the naval hospital in Bocagrande.

Club Isla del Pirata, *Islas del Rosario, T5-665 5622, www.hotelislapirata.com*. Has the best boats and is near the top end of the price range.

Diving Planet, *C Estanco del Aguardiente, No 5-09, T300-603 7284 (English), www.divingplanet.org*. PADI training courses, PADI e-learning, snorkelling trips and various tours of the coral reefs and mangroves. English spoken.

Hotel Caribe, *Bocagrande (see Where to stay)*. Scuba lessons in its pool and diving at its resort on Isla Grande, US$320 for 3- to 5-day PADI course.

La Tortuga Dive Shop, *Edif Marina del Rey, C 1, No 2-23, loc 4, Av del Retorno, El Laguito, Bocagrande, T5-665 6994, www.tortugadive.com*. Fast boat, which allows for trips to Isla Barú as well as Salmedina and Los Rosarios.

Football

Estadio Jaime Morón León, *Villa Olímpica, south of the city*. Games are infrequent.

Language schools

Nueva Lengua School, *T315-855 9551, www.nuevalengua.com*. Offers courses ranging from ½-day schedules to a scheme that arranges volunteer jobs. There are even Spanish courses combined with dance, music, adventure, kitesurfing or diving.

Tour operators

Aventure Colombia, *C de la Factoría, No 36-04, T5-660 9721, www.aventurecolombia.com*. Also with branches in Bogotá and Santa Marta. The only tour organizer of its kind in Cartagena, French/Colombian-run, offering alternative tours across Colombia, local and national activities and expeditions, working (wherever possible) with local and indigenous groups. The focus is on ecotourism and trekking, also organizes boat trips. Highly recommended.

Ocean & Land, *Cra 2, No 4-15, Edif Antillas, Bocagrande, T5-665 7772, 727, oceanlandtours_cartagena@hotmail.com*. Organizes city tours, rumbas in *chivas* (brightly coloured local buses) and other local activities.

Yachting

Club Isla del Pirata, *T5-665 5622, www.hotelislapirata.com*. Has the best boats and is near the top end of the price range; or enquire at the quay.

Club Náutico, *Av Miramar No 19-50, Isla Manga (across the Puente Román), T5-660 4863, www.clubnauticocartagena.com*. Good for opportunities to charter, crew or for finding a lift to other parts of the Caribbean.

Yates Alcatraz, *T5-665 9339 www.yatesalcatraz.com*. An economical outfit offering day cruises at US$12 pp.

> **Tip…**
> A horse-drawn carriage can be hired for US$16, opposite Hotel El Dorado, Avenida San Martín, in Bocagrande, to ride into town at night (short ride). Also, a trip around the walled city, up to four people, US$16, from Torre del Reloj.

Transport

Air

Rafael Núñez Airport (www.sacsa.co) is 1.5 km from the city in the Crespo district and can be reached by local buses from Blas de Lezo, in the southwest corner of El Centro. A bus from the airport to Pl San Francisco costs US$0.70; a taxi to San Diego or the centre is US$4 and to Bocagrande, US$7, but drivers may charge more. City buses can be very crowded so if you have a lot of luggage, a taxi is recommended. There is a *casa de cambio* (daily 0830-2000) at the airport, but rates are better in town. Travel agents have offices on the upper level. There are also a number of fast-food outlets.

There are direct flights daily to/from major Colombian cities, **San Andrés** and smaller places in the north of the country, as well as direct international flights to/from Fort **Lauderdale**, **Miami**, **New York** and **Panama**. From Dec to Mar flights can be overbooked, so arrive at the airport early. Airline servicing the airport include **Avianca**, C del Arzobispado, No 34-52, T5-664 7376, Mon-Fri 0800-1200, 1400-1800, Sat 0800-1300; Av Venezuela 33, No 8B-05, Edif City Bank, loc B2, T5-664 7822; also in Bocagrande, C 7, No 7-17, L 7, T5-665 0287 and at the airport, T5-666 1175. **Copa**, at the airport, Mon-Fri 0800-1800, Sat-Sun 0800-1700. **EasyFly**, T5-693 0400. **LATAM**, Cra 3, No 4-21 local 1, T1-800 094 9490. **Viva Colombia**, T5-693 7777.

Bus

The bus terminal, known as the '**Terminal de Transportes**' (www.terminaldecartagena.com) is at least 35 mins away from town on the road to Barranquilla. A Metrocar city bus to the terminal from the centre costs US$0.75, or a taxi, US$6-8; agree your taxi fare before you get in.

Several bus companies run to **Barranquilla**, every 15 mins, 2-3 hrs, US$5-6; there's also a **Berlinastur** (www.berlinastur.com) minibus service from C 46C, no 3-80, Marbella, T5 693 0006 318-724 2424, and *colectivos* from C 70, Crespo, every 2 hrs (centre-to-centre service). To **Santa Marta**, hourly, US$14, 4 hrs. Few buses go direct to Santa Marta from Cartagena, most stop in Barranquilla. To/from **Bogotá** via Barranquilla and Bucaramanga, daily, 21-28 hrs (depending on number of checkpoints), US$36-38, several companies. To **Medellín** 665 km, US$45-50, more or less hourly from 0530, 13-16 hrs; book early (2 days in advance at holiday times); the road is paved but in poor condition. To **Magangué** on

the Río Magdalena (for connections to Mompós) with **Brasilia/Unitransco**, US$14-16, 4 hrs (www.expresobrasilia.com). For transport to **Mompós**, see below (page 936). To **Riohacha**, US$21, with Expreso **Brasilia**. To **Maicao** on Venezuelan border, in the evening, 8 hrs, US$24, with **Expreso Brasilia**.

Car hire

Several of the bigger hotels have car rental offices in their foyers, such as S&M Rent a Car at the **Hotel Cartagena Plaza**, Cra 1, N 6-154, T5-665 9047. There are also car rental companies in Edif Torremolinos, Av San Martín, including **International Car Rentals**, T5-665 5399, and **National**, T5-655 1215; and on Av San Martín: **Budget**, No 13-37 L-3, T5-664 1293; **Trans**, No 11-67, Edif Tulipana L-5, T5-665 2427. Multiple companies at the airport.

Sea

For boat services to Cartagena's beaches and islands, see pages 923-924. Boats also go from Cartagena to the **San Blas Islands** (Panama); the journey takes 5 days in total, 2 sailing to the archipelago and 3 touring the San Blas islands. Trips usually end at Porvenir on the mainland, from where you can continue to Colón and thence to Panama City. The fare, about US$550, includes food, water and snorkelling gear. Some boats are cheaper, but you get what you pay for, so take your time before choosing a boat. Some captains are irresponsible and unreliable. The journey is cramped so it's best to get on with the captain. There are many notices in hostels in Getsemaní advertising this trip, for example in **Casa Viena** and **Mamallena**. Also **Sailing Koala**, T312-670 7863, www.sailingkoala.com, which offers a trip to San Blas and Panama. If entering Panama by boat, tourists pay a US$105 immigration fee, although this isn't consistently applied.

Note On the street, do not be tempted by offers of jobs or passages on board a ship. Jobs should have full documentation from the Seamen's Union office and passages should only be bought at a recognized shipping agency.

Taxi

There are no meters; journeys are calculated by zones and fixed by the Alcaldía with fares ranging from US$2-3. It is quite common to ask other people waiting if they would like to share, but, in any case, always agree the fare with the driver before getting in. By arrangement, taxis will wait for you if visiting more remote places. Fares go up at night.

Towards Mompós

The highway south towards Medellín goes through **Turbaco**, 24 km (Botanical Garden, 1.5 km before village on the left, www.jbgp.org.co, Tue-Sun 0800-1600), **Malagana**, 60 km, San Jacinto, known for its cumbia music using *gaitas* and local craft work (handwoven hammocks) and **El Carmen de Bolívar**, 125 km. A road runs east from the highway at El Bongo to **Magangué** on the western loop of the Río Magdalena. It is the port for the savannas of Bolívar. From here boats go to La Bodega where you pick up the road again for the small town of **Mompós**.

☆ **Mompós** *Colour map 1, A3.*

Also spelt Mompox, this town is a UNESCO World Heritage Site on the eastern arm of the river. Alfonso de Heredia (brother of the founder of Cartagena) founded the town in 1540, but due to the silting up of the Río Magdalena here, little has changed in this sweltering, humid town since the early 20th century. Simón Bolívar stayed here frequently and wrote, "If I owe my life to Caracas, I owe my glory to Mompós" (a monument outside the Alcaldía proclaims this).

Today, Mompós is one of Colombia's most beautiful colonial towns. Facing the river, on the Albarrada, is the old customs house and the mansions of Spanish merchants for whom this was an important stopping-off point on the Cartagena trade route. Rows of well-preserved buildings, some with balconies, have served as a backdrop in many Colombian films. Of its six churches, **Santa Bárbara**, **La Concepción** and **San Francisco** stand out. In the **Claustro de San Agustín** is a workshop where youngsters are taught local skills. The cemetery is of considerable historical interest. Mompós is packed during Easter week when visitors flock to see its ornate traditional processions. There is also a popular jazz festival at the end of October (http://mompoxcolombia. blogspot.co.uk/p/eventos.html), with national and international artists, concerts and street music. The town is known for its handworked silver jewellery and its wicker rocking chairs. There are ATMs on Calle 18 by the junction with Calle del Medio. The town is safe and peaceful. Guided tours of the city on foot or motortaxi cost US$5-7 per hour (guides approach you on the street). Boat trips can be taken along the Río Magdalena and into the surrounding wetlands, which provide excellent opportunities for birdwatching: three to four hours, US$10-15. In the early morning or at dusk, you can walk along the river bank to look for birds, or in the afternoon, cross the river on the small ferry from beyond the Parque Santander, US$0.50, for a stroll on the opposite bank where birds can also be seen. Ferocious mosquitoes and the odd bat are a nuisance after dusk; take insect repellent and wear long sleeves.

Tolú and around

On the coast, 35 km northwest of Sincelejo (the capital of Sucre Department) is **Tolú**, a fast developing holiday town popular for its mud volcanoes, offshore islands and diving. Along the *malecón* (promenade), there are plenty of bars and restaurants and many lodges are opening. There are several banks with ATMs on the Parque Principal. Bicycle rickshaws armed with loud sound systems blast out *vallenato*, salsa and reggaeton. There are two mud volcanoes to visit. The nearer is in San Antero, 30 minutes' drive from Tolú, and farther is in San Bernando del Viento, 1¼ hours (turn off the main road at Lorica). Both make good day trips; a six-hour trip to San Antero, including lunch and visits to other sights, costs US$55.

From Tolú, another good trip is by boat three hours to Isla Múcura or Titipán in the **Islas de San Bernardo**. With all tour boats converging on the island at the same time, it gets very crowded, attracting plenty of beach vendors. There is a charge for everything, including sitting at a table. To enjoy the islands at your leisure, it is better to stay overnight. If camping, take your own supplies. Trips to the mangrove lagoons also recommended. Tolú and the islands are easy to combine with Cartagena; the road goes via Malagana, San Onofre and Toluviejo, 2½ to 3 hours by bus. Toluviejo is 20 km north of Sincelejo.

There are good beaches at **Coveñas**, 20 km further southwest (several *cabañas* on the beach and hotels). This is the terminal of the oil pipeline from the oilfields in the Venezuelan border area. Buses and *colectivos* from Tolú.

The main road south from Tolú passes **Montería**, the capital of Córdoba Department, on the east bank of the Río Sinú. It can be reached from Cartagena by air, by boat, or from the main highway to Medellín (US$48, nine hours).

☆Arboletes

Southwest of Tolú is the unremarkable town of Arboletes, near which is the largest mud volcano in the area. Dipping into this swimming pool-sized mud bath is a surreal experience – like bathing in treacle. It´s very good for your skin. You can wash the mud off with a dip in the sea by walking down to the beach 100 m below. Arboletes is also a convenient stopover on the way to Turbo and the Darién coast. The **Volcán de Lodo** is a 15-minute walk from town on the road to Montería or a two-minute taxi ride (US$7 return – the driver will wait for you while you bathe). A mototaxi costs US$2. There is a small restaurant and changing rooms (US$ 0.50), plus a locker room (US$1 per bag) and showers (US$0.50).

Turbo and the Darién Gap

On the Gulf of Urabá is the port of Turbo, an important centre of banana cultivation. It is a rough place, so it's best to move on quickly. There are various routes from Turbo involving sea and land crossings around or through the Darién Gap, which still lacks a road connection linking the Panamanian Isthmus and South America.

The trek across the Darién is held in high regard by adventurers but we strongly advise against it, not simply because it is easy and fatal to get lost, but also because it has a heavy guerrilla and drug-trafficking presence; it is virtually deserted by police and the military, and indigenous communities do not welcome tourists. The Caribbean coastline, however, heavily patrolled by Colombian and Panamanian forces, is safe.

Acandí

Acandí is a small fishing village on the Caribbean side of the Darién (population about 7000). It has a spectacular, forest-fringed bay with turquoise waters. To the south are other bays and villages, such as **San Francisco**. In March-June, thousands of leatherback turtles come here to lay their eggs. There are several *residencias* in Acandí.

Capurganá Colour map 1, A2.

For many years, Capurganá and neighbouring Sapzurro have been one of the best-kept secrets in Colombia: a glistening, untouched shore of crystal waters, coral reefs and quiet villages. Capurganá has developed into a resort popular with Colombians, increasingly visited by foreigners. There are no banks, ATMs or cars. Taxi rides are provided by horse and cart. The village has two beaches, La Caleta at the northern end, with golden sand, and Playa de los Pescadores, south of the village, fringed by palm and almond trees but with grey sand and pebbles. Ask the fishermen about fishing trips from here.

> **Tip...**
> There are flights from Medellín to Capurganá and some Cartagena–Panama boat trips stop at the beautiful beaches here, but if going by road, check the latest information on security.

Several half- and full-day trips can be made by launch to neighbouring beaches, for example Aguacate, near which is a natural jacuzzi known as La Piscina, and Playa Soledad, perhaps the most attractive beach in the area. You can also walk to Aguacate, 1½ hours along the coast, though not to Playa Soledad. Note that it can be difficult to obtain a return by launch if you walk. There are also boat trips to the San Blas Islands (Panama) for about US$70 per person; ask at lodges, hostales and tour operators.

A delightful half-day excursion is to **El Cielo**, a small waterfall in the jungle (open 0600-1700, entry US$2; 40-minute walk, take flip flops or waterproof boots for crossing a stream several times). Take the path to the left of the airport and keep asking for directions. Just before the waterfall a small restaurant serves *patacones* and drinks. Alternatively, you can hire horses to take you there. Another horse ride is to El Valle de Los Ríos. The primary forest in this area is rich in wildlife, but you should take a guide. The trip includes lunch at a *ranchería*.

Sapzurro and the Panamanian border

Another trip is to **Sapzurro**, a few kilometres north and the last outpost before Panama and Central America. The houses of this tiny village are linked by intersecting paths bursting with tropical flowers. It is set in a shallow horseshoe bay dotted with coral reefs, excellent for snorkelling, with a couple of underwater caves to explore. A day's walking trip (there are no cars here) is to the village of **La Miel**, on a gorgeous white-sand beach in Panama. This could qualify as the most relaxed border crossing in the world. The Colombian and Panamanian immigration officers share a hut and copy each other's notes. Be sure to take your passport; if only going to La Miel they won't stamp it but they will take your details. There are breathtaking views of Panama and back into Sapzurro at the frontier on the brow of the hill. You can arrange for a launch to pick you up and take you back to Sapzurro or Capurganá.

Colombian immigration Ask Migración Colombia in Cartagena, Medellín or Montería (Calle 28, No 2-27, T4-781 0841, cf.monteria@migracioncolombia.gov.co, Monday-Friday 0800-1200, 1400-1700) whether the immigration office in Capurganá is open.

Entering Panama Panamanian immigration at Puerto Obaldía will check all baggage for drugs. Requirements for entry are proof of US$500 in the bank and a yellow fever certificate. There is a **Panamanian consul** in Capurganá opposite the main square: T310-303 5285, nayi051991@hotmail.com. Check with the consul in Cartagena, Medellín, or the embassy in Bogotá (Calle 92, No 7A-40, T01-257 5067, www.panamaenelexterior.gob.pa/bogota) before setting out.

> **Fact…**
> Colombian pesos are impossible to change at fair rates in Panama.

Listings South from Cartagena

Where to stay

Mompós

It is essential to book in advance for Semana Santa, the jazz festival in Oct and other holiday periods, when prices go up.

$$$-$$ Bioma
C Real del Medio (Cra 2), No 18-59, T5-685 6733, www.bioma.co.
Boutique style, cool and fresh, courtyard garden with running water, jacuzzi on roof terrace and a small pool. Rooms are large, family rooms have 2 floors. There's a restaurant but reserve in advance.

$$$-$$ La Casa Amarilla
Cra 1, No 13-59, T5-685 6326, www.lacasaamarillamompos.com.
A block up from the Iglesia Santa Bárbara near the riverfront. Master suites, suites and cheaper 'colonial' rooms, all beautifully decorated. All rooms open onto a cloister-style colonial garden. English owner Richard McColl is an excellent source of information on Colombia. Laundry, book exchange, use of kitchen, roof terrace, bicycle hire, tours arranged to silver filigree workshops and to wetlands for birdwatching and swimming (US$10 pp). Recommended.

$$$-$$ Portal de la Marquesa
Cra 1, No 15-27, on the Albarrada, T5-664 3163, www.portaldelamarquesa.com.
Hotel in a converted colonial mansion, fronting the river, with gardens and patios, suites and standard rooms with modern facilities, can arrange local guides and boat trips.

$$ Casa de España
C Real del Medio (Cra 2), No 17A-52, T5-685 5373, www.hotelcasaespanamompox.com.
Some family rooms, a/c or fan, TV and Wi-Fi. Snacks and drinks available.

$ Casa Hotel La Casona
C Real del Medio (Cra 2), No 18-58, T5-685 5307, www.hotelmompos.com.
Fine colonial building with delightful courtyards and plants, pool and outdoor terrace.

$ Casa Hotel Villa de Mompox
Cra 2, No 14-108, 500 m east of Parque Bolívar, T5-685 5208, http://hotelvillademompox.blogspot.co.uk/.
Charming, family-run, decorated with antique bric-a-brac. Also arranges rooms for families during festivals.

Tolú and around

$$$-$$ Soleira
Cra 11, No 4-12, T5-288 2288,
http://hotelsoleira.com.
Colourfully decorated modern hotel a couple of kms out of town, with pool, terrace, and spacious rooms.

$$ Alcira
Av La Playa, No 21-151, T5-288 5016,
www.hotelalcira.amawebs.com.
Modern, on the promenade, with restaurant and parking.

$ Villa Babilla
C 20, No 3-40, Barrio el Cangrejo, T312-677 1325,
www.villababillahostel.com.
Run by a Colombian/German team. 3 blocks from the beach, well organized, dorms and private rooms, good restaurant, horse-riding, bike hire, good information on diving and island tours. Recommended travellers' hostel.

Islas de San Bernardo

$$$$ Punta Faro
Isla Múcura, T317-435 9583, www.puntafaro.com.
Low-key luxury resort with 45 rooms in a gorgeous setting by the sea, inside Corales del Rosario National Park. Price includes all meals (buffet-style) and happy hour cocktails. Return boat transfer from Cartagena costs US$53 plus US$4.20 port tax (boats leave once a day), some boats also leave from Tolú. Massage treatments, hammocks on the beach, eco walks around the island and a good sustainability policy. Highly recommended.

Turbo

$$ Castilla de Oro
C 100, No 14-07, T4-827 2185,
hotelcastilladeoro@hotmail.com.
The best option in town has a/c, safety box, minibar, a good restaurant and a swimming pool. Modern building with reliable water and electricity. Friendly staff.

$$ Simona del Mar
Km 13 Vía Turbo, T4-842 3729,
www.simonadelmar.com.
Turbo is not a safe place to walk around at night, so this option a few kilometres outside town is a safer choice. It has a number of *cabañas* in a tranquil setting near the beach. Good restaurant. A taxi to and from Turbo is US$10. You can also ask *colectivos* to drop you there.

Capurganá

Accommodation and food are generally more expensive than in other parts of Colombia. Upmarket options include **Tacarcuna Lodge** (www.hotelesdecostaacosta.com/capurgana).

$$$-$$$ Bahía Lodge
Playa Aguacate, T314-812 2727,
www.bahia-lodge.com.
Price is for 2 people on a 2-night, 3-day package in cabins with fan a d bath, includes breakfast and dinner, lunch extra, excursions available. Very good.

$$ Cabaña Darius
T310-397 7768, see Facebook.
In the grounds of Playa de Capurganá, excellent value, simple, comfortable rooms in tropical gardens, fan, breakfast included.

$$ Marlin Hostal
Playa de los Pescadores, T310 593 6409,
http://hostalmarlin.com/.
The best mid-range option in town, good rooms, also bunks ($), restaurant serving excellent fish.

$ Hostal Capurganá
C del Comercio, T316-482 3665,
www.hostalcapurgana.net.
Comfortable, pleasant patio, well situated. Has a restaurant and offers tours. Price is per person for a 2-night, all-inclusive package, 3- and 4-nights also available; transfers from Turbo and Medellín can be included. Recommended.

$ Posada del Gecko
C del Comercio 2, T314-525 6037,
www.posadadelgecko.com.
Small place, 5 rooms with bath and 3 cabins, gardens, popular café/bar that serves good Italian food. Also tours to San Blas Islands.

Sapzurro and the Panamanian border

$$ Paraíso Sapzurro
T313-685 9862, www.hosteltrail.com/hostels/elchilenoresortparaiso.
Cabañas on the beach at the southern end of the village, Chilean-run (ask for El Chileno), higher price includes half-board. Also has dorms ($) and space for camping.

$ Zingara Cabañas
Camino La Miel, T313-673 3291,
www.hospedajesapzurrozingara.com.
Almost the last building in Colombia, 2 lovely *cabañas* overlooking the bay. The owners have a vegetable and herb

garden and sell home-made chutneys. This also doubles up as the village pharmacy.

Restaurants

Mompós

Every night stallholders sell freshly cooked food and fresh juices in Plaza Santo Domingo.

$$$-$$ El Fuerte
Parque Santander, T314-564 0566, www.fuertemompox.com.
Serves gourmet pizza in a restored colonial building. It is the art gallery of Walter Maria Gurth and displays his wooden furniture. Contact in advance.

$$-$ Comedor Costeño
On the riverfront between C 18 and C 19.
Good local food, popular for lunch.

$ Islandés
On the riverfront between C 18 and C 19.
In same vein as **Comedor Costeño** and almost next door, same owner as **Hotel San Andrés** (www.hotelsanandresmompox.com), which also offers river tours.

Capurganá

$$ Donde Josefina
Playa La Caleta.
Josefina cooks exquisite seafood, served to you under a shady tree on the beach. Try the lobster cooked in garlic and coconut sauce.

Shopping

Mompós

Mompós is famous for its filigree gold and silver jewellery and its wicker rocking chairs. Several jewellers can be found on C del Medio (Cra 2). You can visit the workshops.

Jewellery

Filimompox, *C 23, No 3-23, T5-685 6604.*
Joyería Sam, *C 23 No 3-04, T311-403 5492.* Fine selection of beautifully worked gold and silver earrings, bracelets and brooches.
Santa Cruz, *Cra 2, No 201 132, T310-656 5568, tallersantacruz@yahoo.com.*

What to do

Capurganá

Dive and Green, *near the jetty, T311-578 4021, www.diveandgreen.com.* Dive centre offering

PADI and NAUI, lots of courses, snorkelling and excursions to San Blas. English spoken.

Transport

Mompós

Cars are rare here: the main ways to get around are bicycle, moped, auto-rickshaw or walking.

Air The closest airport is **Corozal** (near Sincelejo), which has regular connections with **Medellín** and **Bogotá**. It's 1 hr by *colectivo* from Corozal Airport to Magangué, or 15 mins from Corozal to Sincelejo; then take a *colectivo* to Magangué, as below.

Bus Buses from Cartagena and Barranquilla travel to Mompós either via Magangue for the river crossing (see below), or they take the new route El Carmen de Bolívar-Plato-La Gloria (on the road to Bosconia), then the new paved road to Santa Ana, where a bridge now crosses the Magdalena to Talaigua Nueva; transport from Santa Marta and Valledupar goes to Bosconia, then to La Gloria and Santa Ana. Buses from central Colombia travel via El Banco. **Note** Prices for public transport rise Dec-Jan and at Easter.

Direct services to/from **Cartagena** are run by Brasilia/**Unitransco**, 6½ hrs, US$17.65. **Toto Express**, T310-707 0838, totoexpress2@hotmail.com, runs a door-to-door *colectivo*, 6 hrs, US$30. There are additional services between Cartagena and Magangué. **For transport** between Mompós and **Santa Marta** and **Valledupar**, see the respective transport sections, below. From **Medellín**, Copetran runs an overnight service from Medellín to Mompós, or catch the overnight **Rápido Ochoa or Brasilia** bus to Magangué, 12 hrs, US$45-50, or travel to Magangué by *colectivo* from **Sincelejo**, US$9.50, 1½ hrs. From **Bogotá**, Copetran have a direct service at 1700, US$55, 14-15 hrs, otherwise **Copetran** and **Omega** have services to **El Banco** at 1700, 14 hrs, US$47, then take a 4WD to Mompós, US$10 (US$12 a/c), 1 hr.

Ferry To get to Mompós from Magangué you have to travel to **La Bodega**, either by fast *chalupa* (motorized canoe, 20 mins, US$2.50, life jacket provided), or on the vehicle ferry (from 0600, 1 hr, food and drink on board), which leaves from Yati, about 2 km outside town. From La Bodega you continue by *colectivo* to Mompós (1¼ hrs, US$6).

Tolú

Bus Rápido Ochoa and others from **Cartagena** from about 0615, 3 hrs, US$13. 7 a day to **Medellín** with Brasilia and Rápido Ochoa, US$43, via Montería except at night.

Turbo and the Darién Gap

Bus To **Medellín**, buses every 90 mins, 8-10 hrs, US$20-24. To **Montería**, Rápido Ochoa, 4-5 hrs, US$12. Fewer to **Cartagena**. Check safety carefully before travelling by road to/from Turbo.

Sea Turbo's port is known as El Waffe. Launches for **Capurganá**, T312-701 9839, leave daily at 0700-0900, 3 hrs, US$19. It's a spectacular journey that hugs the Caribbean shoreline of Darién. Rush for a seat at the back as the journey is bumpy and can be painful in seats at the front. There is a 10-kg limit on baggage (US$0.20 per extra kilo). Make sure that all your belongings, especially

valuables, are in watertight bags and be prepared to get wet. From mid-Dec to end Feb the sea is very choppy and dangerous. We advise you not to make the journey at this time.

Capurganá

Sea Launches to **Turbo**, T312-701 9839, daily 0800-0900, US$20, 10 kg limit on baggage (US$0.25 per extra kg); we advise you not to make this journey from mid-Dec to end Feb. To **Acandí**, T314-614 0704, daily 1300, US$7. To **Sapzurro**, US$6, 30 mins. There are also launches to **Puerto Obaldía** in Panama, US$20. From here it's possible to catch an **Air Panamá** flight to **Panama City**, daily, cost US$110, www. flyairpanama.com. Essential to book in advance.

Sapzurro

Sea Launch to **Capurganá**, US$6, 30 mins; to **Puerto Obaldía**, 45 mins, US$15.

Barranquilla *Colour map 1, A3.*

carnival city and an important port

Barranquilla (population 1,120,000) lies on the western bank of the Río Magdalena, about 18 km from its mouth. The deepening of the river and the clearing of silted sandbars has made the city a seaport as well as a river port, although its commercial and industrial importance has declined in recent years. Few colonial buildings remain, but its historic centre is being revived. In the northwest of the city are pleasant leafy residential areas and parks. Many people stay a night in Barranquilla because they can find better flight deals than to Cartagena or Santa Marta. It is worth a short stay as it is growing as a cultural centre; safety has improved; there are several things to do and see, and handicrafts, the same as can be found elsewhere, are cheaper.

Sights

The **Catedral Metropolitana** ① *Cra 45, No 53-140, opposite Plaza de la Paz*, has an impressive statue of Christ inside by the Colombian sculptor, Arenas Betancur. The church of **San Nicolás**, formerly the Cathedral, stands on Plaza San Nicolás, the central square, and before it is a small statue of Columbus. The commercial and shopping districts are round Paseo Bolívar, the main boulevard, a few blocks north of the old Cathedral, and in Avenida Murillo (Calle 45). A cultural centre, **Parque Cultural del Caribe**, is on the Paseo Bolívar end of Avenida Olaya Herrera (Carretera 46). It contains the **Museo del Caribe** ① *C36, No 46-66, T5-372 0581, www.culturacaribe.org, Mon-Fri 0800-1700, Sat-Sun 0900-1800, ticket office closes 1600 (1700 weekends), US$4.50*, an excellent introduction to the region, in Spanish only, but guided tours in English are available. Visits start on the top floor, at the Sala García Márquez, which has audiovisual displays and a library, then work your way down through floors dedicated to nature, indigenous people and cultures, languages, to a video musical presentation at the end. Outside is a large open space for theatre and children's games, and the Cocina del Museo restaurant. Not far away is the restored **Antiguo Edificio de la Aduana**, customs house (1919) ① *Vía 40 y C 36*, which has historical archives. The **Museo Romántico** ① *Cra 54, No 59-199, Mon-Fri 0900-1200, 1430-1700, US$2.50*, covers the city's history with an interesting section on Carnival.

Barranquilla also attracts visitors because the most important national and international football matches are held here in Colombia's largest stadium, **Estadio Metropolitano** ① *Av Murillo, south of the city*. The atmosphere is considered the best in the country. There is a good-value handicrafts market near the old stadium, which is at Carretera 46 y Calle 74 (at the end of Transmetro).

Around Barranquilla

Regular buses run from Paseo Bolívar and the church at Calle 33 y Carrera 41 to the attractive bathing resort of **Puerto Colombia**, 20 minutes, www.puertocolombia-atlantico.gov.co. February to May is the best time to learn surfing here; the biggest waves are seen from November to January.

Heading south along the Magdalena, 5 km from Barranquilla, is **Soledad**; around its cathedral are narrow, colonial streets. **Parque Nacional Natural Isla de Salamanca** ① *T312-577 7111, www.parqueisladesalamanca.org, open 0800-1600, US$14 (US$5.30 for Colombians)*, is a national park across the Río Magdalena from the city, comprising the Magdalena delta and the narrow area of beaches, mangroves and woods that separate the Ciénaga Grande de Santa Marta (see page 942) from the Caribbean. Its purpose is to restore the mangroves and other habitats lost when the highway to Santa Marta blocked off the channels that connect the fresh- and saltwater systems. There is lots of wildlife and there is an interpretation centre and guided walking trails (US$7-9) and canoe trips with guides (US$50-130 for groups of 10).

Listings Barranquilla

Tourist information

La Casa de Carnaval
Cra 54, No 49B-39, T5-319 7616,
www.carnavaldebarranquilla.org.
The official carnival office and best place for carnival information.

Secretaría de Cultura
Patrimonio y Turismo, C 34, No 43-31, p 4, T5-339 9450, www.barranquilla.gov.co/cultura.
The main tourist office. Information is also available at the main hotels.

Tourist police
Plaza de San Nicolás. Open 0800-1200, 1500-1700.

Where to stay

Hotel prices rise significantly during carnival; it's essential to book well in advance. Most people stay in the north zone, beyond the Catedral Metropolitano, C 50. There are also a few hotels in the business zone, Cra 43-45, C 42-45.

$$$ Barranquilla Plaza
Cra 51B, No 79-246, T5-361 0333, www.hbp.com.co.
This deluxe hotel, popular with Colombian businessmen, is worth visiting just for the 360° view of the city from its 26th-floor restaurant. It has all the other amenities you would expect of a hotel of this standard, including gym, spa, sauna and Wi-Fi.

$$$ El Prado
Cra 54, No 70-10, T5-330 1530/40,
www.hotelelpradosa.com.
A landmark in Barranquilla, this enormous hotel with 200 rooms has been around since 1930 and still retains some of its old-fashioned service.

Fantastic pool shaded by palm trees, various restaurants, tennis courts and a gym.

$$$ Majestic
Cra 53, No 54-41, T5-349 1010, www.hotelmajesticbarranquilla.com.
An oasis of calm in the city, with large, fresh rooms. It has a fine pool and a restaurant serving the usual fish and meat dishes and sandwiches.

$$$ Sonesta
C 106, No 50-11, T5-385 6060, www.sonesta.com.
Overlooking the Caribbean, a 1st-class business hotel with fitness facilities and restaurant to match. There is a shopping centre and nightclub nearby.

$$ Girasol
C 44, No 44-103, T5-379 3191.
Safe, central with a helpful manager, it has a restaurant.

$$ San Francisco
C 43, No 43-128, T5-351 5532,
http://www.sfcol.com/barranquilla.html
Bright rooms, courtyard full of songbirds, a good, safe bet, with restaurant.

$ Cayenas
C 43, No 44-136, T5-370 6912.
A simpler option, welcoming, rooms are cheaper with fan.

$ Meeting Point
Cra 61, No 68-100, El Prado, T5-318 2599,
www.themeetingpoint.hostel.com.
Very helpful and congenial Italian/Colombian-owned hostel – the best choice for budget travellers. Mixed dorms or women only, US$10-1 cheaper with fan and shared bath, also has

ON THE ROAD

Carnival in Barranquilla

The main reason people visit the city is for its famous annual **Carnival**, held 40 days before Easter week, end-February/beginning of March. It's one of the oldest in Latin America and less commercial and touristy than the Rio Carnival. It is a UNESCO "masterpiece of the oral and intangible heritage of humanity". Pre-carnival parades and dances last through January until an edict that everyone **must** party is read out. Carnival itself lasts from Saturday, with the Batalla de las Flores, through the Gran Parada on Sunday, to the funeral of Joselito Carnaval on Tuesday. The same families going back generations participate, keeping the traditions of the costumes and dances intact. Prepare for four days of intense revelry and dancing with friendly and enthusiastic crowds, spectacular float processions, parades and beauty queens. Tickets for the spectator stands are sold in major restaurants and bars. **La Casa de Carnaval**, Carretera 54, No 49B-39, T5-319 7616, www.carnavaldebarranquilla.org, is the official office and the best place for information.

…private rooms. Eating places and cultural centres nearby. Warmly recommended.

Restaurants

In Barranquilla you'll find places to suit all tastes and budgets. Many upmarket restaurants can be found along Cras 52-54 from C 70 to 93. There are numerous good Middle Eastern restaurants, especially Lebanese, in Barranquilla, due to waves of immigration in the 20th century; also Chinese restaurants and pizzerias.

$$$-$$ Arabe Gourmet
Cra 49C, No 76-181, T5-360 5930/358 3805, http://arabegourmetrestaurante.co.
More formal and expensive than other Arabic restaurants. There are others in the same chain.

$$$-$$ La Cueva
Cra 43, No 59-03, T5-379 0342/340 9813, www.fundacionlacueva.org. Closed Sun.
This cultural centre was formerly a high-class brothel and a favourite haunt of Gabriel García Márquez and his literati friends during the 1950s. Its bohemian charm may have gone, but its bar/restaurant is recommended for a visit. Good typical food, live music and other events.

$$$-$$ La Parrilla Libanesa
Cra 61, No 68-02, near Meeting Point, T5-360 6664, http://parrillalibanesa.amawebs.com.
Well-regarded Lebanese place, colourful, indoor and terrace seating.

$ Arabe Internacional
C 93, No 47-73, T5-378 4700.
Good Arab cuisine in an informal setting.

$$ Firenze Pizza
C 68, No 62-12, El Prado, near Meeting Point, T5-344 1067, www.firenzepizza.com.co.
Open 1500-2300.
Pizza to eat in or take away.

$$-$ Los Helechos de Carlos
Cra 52, No 70-70, T5-345 1739, http://restauranteshowloshelechos.com.
Daily from 1000 (closes 1700 on Sun).
Offers comida antioqueña in a good atmosphere.

Bars and clubs

Carrera 8 is a popular nightlife area, but you'll need to take a taxi there and back.

Frogg Club
C 93, No 43-122, T5-304 8973, www.frogg.co.
Popular bar, good atmosphere.

Guararé
Cra 8 at C 35. T300-503 3303, Facebook: GuarareSalsaDisco. Open until 0400.
A good spot for salsa dancing.

Henry's Café
C 80, No 53-18, CC Washington, T5-345 6431.
See Facebook: Henryscafebaq, Daily from 1600.
Popular US-style bar and restaurant.

Entertainment

Teatro Amira de la Rosa, Cra 54, No 52-258, T5-371 6690 ext 5153, www.banrepcultural.org/amira-de-la-rosa. This modern theatre offers a full range of stage presentations, concerts, ballets, art exhibitions and more throughout the year.

Festivals

Jan/Mar Carnaval. Carnaval is a long-standing tradition in Barranquilla and is comparable to the carnivals in Rio de Janeiro and Trinidad. Pre-carnival parades and dances throughout Jan until an edict that everyone must party is read out. Carnaval itself lasts from Sat, with the Batalla de las Flores, through the Gran Parada on Sun, to the funeral of Joselito Carnaval on Tue. For more information, contact **La Casa de Carnaval**, www.carnavaldebarranquilla.org. See box, page 939. Take special care of your valuables.

Shopping

There is a good-value handicrafts market near the old stadium, which is at Cra 46 y C 74 (at the end of Transmetro). **Portal del Prado**, C 53, No 46-92, www.portaldelprado.com, is one of the larger and more popular shopping complexes in the city.

Transport

Air Ernesto Cortissoz Airport, www.aerocivil. gov.co, is 10 km from the city. The airport has an ATM outside the terminal entrance, a *casa de cambio* in the hall (closed after 1900) and a tourist information desk. A city bus from the airport to town costs US$0.95 (more on Sun). Only take buses marked 'centro'; you can catch them 200 m from the airport on the right. Taxis are booked at the central taxi kiosk; tell them your destination and you will be given a ticket with the price to pay the driver at end of ride. A taxi to the centre costs US$10 and takes about 30 mins. From town, the bus to the airport (marked Malambo) leaves from Cra 44, travels up C 32 to Cra 38, then along C 30 to the airport.

There are daily flights to **Bogotá**, **Cali** and **Medellín**. International flights go to **Miami**, **Curaçao** and **Panama City**. Airlines include; **Avianca**, C 53, No 46-38, T5-351 8344, and Cra 56, No75-155, local 102, T5-353 4989, at airport T5-334 8396; **Copa**, C 72, No 54-49, loc 1 y 2; **LATAM**, C 75 No 52-56 local 3; **EasyFly**, T5-385 0676; and **Viva Colombia**, T5-319 7989.

Bus Local Within the city, the **Transmetro**, www.transmetro.gov.co, is a dedicated bus service with 2 routes: *Troncal Murillo* and *Troncal Olaya Herrera*. It takes prepaid cards; single journey US$0.95 (a little more on Sun and holidays). Taxis for trips within town should cost US$2-4.

Long distance The main long-distance bus terminal, Km 1.5 Prolongación Murillo, www.ttbaq.com.co, is south of the city near the Circunvalación.

To **Santa Marta** with **Brasilia**, US$5, 2 hrs. To **Valledupar**, Copetran, 5-6 hrs, US$15. To **Bogotá**, 24 hrs, frequent, US$55-60, direct. To **Maicao**, US$15-20, 6 hrs (with **Brasilia** and others, frequent). To **Cartagena**, 2½-3 hrs, US$5-7, several companies. **Brasilia Van Tours** (Cra 35, No 44-63, T5-371 5226, as well as at the bus terminal) and **Berlinastur** (Cra 43, No 74-133, T318-396 9696, and other offices) have minibus services to **Cartagena** and **Santa Marta** (US$8).

Santa Marta and around   *Colour map 1, A3.*

this lively city is a gateway to stunning beaches and mountains

Santa Marta (population 454,860) is Colombia's third-largest Caribbean port and capital of Magdalena Department. It lies on a deep bay at the mouth of the Río Manzanares, with high shelving cliffs to the north and south. The snow-clad peaks of the Sierra Nevada de Santa Marta are occasionally visible less than 50 km to the east. Nearby is the Tayrona National Park, with pre-Columbian remains. Santa Marta is the base for treks to La Ciudad Perdida.

Sights

The main promenade (Carrera 1) along the seafront is lined with hotels, restaurants and bars; the beach stretches as far as the port, although much more attractive beaches are to be found around Taganga and Parque Nacional Tayrona. There has been much investment in new business, such as bars and restaurants on Carrera 3, the hub of nightlife in the centre. Much of Carrera 3 and Calle 19 are pedestrianized and Carrera 5 has many kerbside stalls. In the city

Fact...

There are banks with ATMs in Plaza Bolívar and Plaza San Francisco. *Casas de cambio* on Calle 13 entre Carreteras 5 y 6, and Calle 14 entre Carreteras 4 y 5. **Exito** supermarket, in the block bounded by C 19 y 20, Cra 5 y 6, also has an ATM and a *cambio*.

centre, well-preserved colonial buildings and early churches still remain and more are currently being restored. On **Plaza de la Catedral** is the impressive white **cathedral** ① *Cra 4, C 16/17, open for Mass Mon-Fri at 1200 and 1800 (Sun 0800, 1000, 1700, 1800, 1900)*, on the site of what is claimed to be Colombia's oldest church and one of the oldest in Latin America. **Casa de la Aduana/Museo del Oro Tairona** ① *C 14, No 2-07 on Parque Bolívar, T5-421 0251, http://proyectos.banrepcultural.org/museo-del-oro-tairona, Tue-Sat 0900-1700, Sun 1000-1500, free*, has an excellent archaeological collection, Tayrona culture exhibits and pre-Columbian gold artefacts; a visit is recommended before going to Ciudad Perdida. The **Convento de Santo Domingo** ① *Cra 2, No 16-44, open to the public Mon-Fri*

Santa Marta

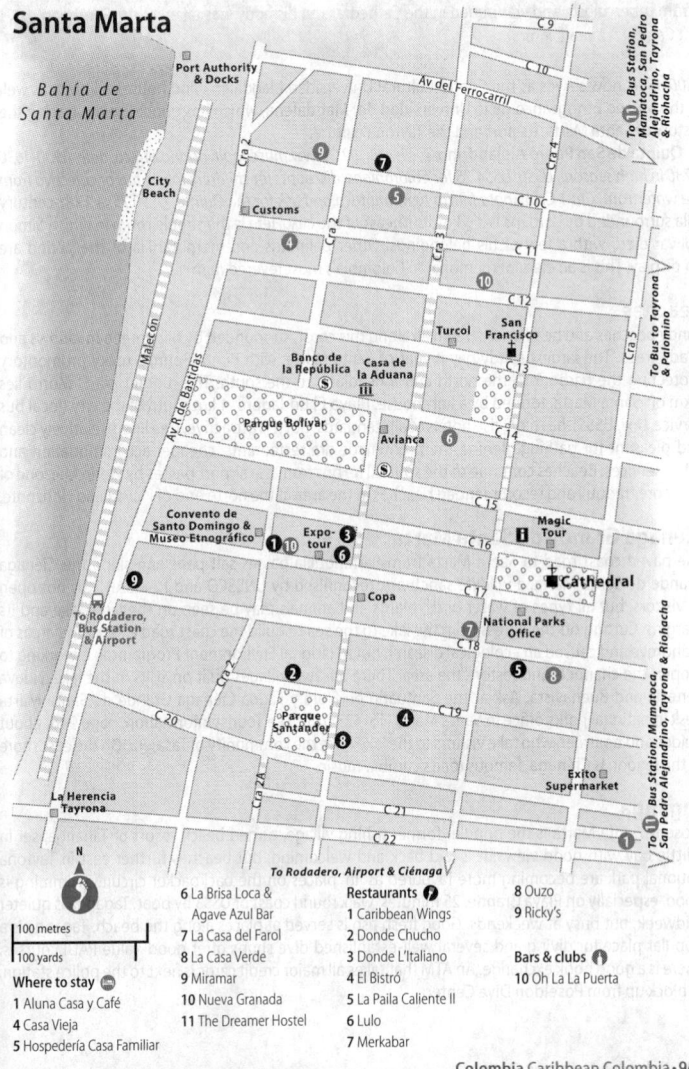

Where to stay 🛏
1 Aluna Casa y Café
4 Casa Vieja
5 Hospedería Casa Familiar
6 La Brisa Loca & Agave Azul Bar
7 La Casa del Farol
8 La Casa Verde
9 Miramar
10 Nueva Granada
11 The Dreamer Hostel

Restaurants 🍴
1 Caribbean Wings
2 Donde Chucho
3 Donde L'Italiano
4 El Bistró
5 La Paila Caliente II
6 Lulo
7 Merkabar
8 Ouzo
9 Ricky's

Bars & clubs 🍸
10 Oh La La Puerta

BACKGROUND

Santa Marta

Santa Marta has strong historical associations. It was the first town founded by the *conquistadores* in Colombia, in 1525 by Rodrigo de Bastidas. Most of the famous sea-dogs – the brothers Côte, Drake and Hawkins – sacked the city despite the forts on the mainland. It was here that Simón Bolívar, his dream of Gran Colombia shattered, came to die. Almost penniless, he stayed at San Pedro Alejandrino *hacienda*, see below. He died, aged 47, on 17 December 1830, apparently from tuberculosis, and was buried in the Cathedral, but his body was taken to the Pantheon at Caracas 12 years later.

0800-1800, now serves as the Centro Cultural Universidad Magdalena and houses a library as well as the **Museo Etnográfico de la Universidad del Magdalena**, which has good displays tracing the history of Santa Marta, its port and the Tayrona culture.

   Quinta de San Pedro Alejandrino ① *T5-433 1021, www.museobolivariano.org.co, daily 0900-1630 (1730 in high season), US$6, US$4.25 for Colombians, discounts for children; take a bus or colectivo from the waterfront, Cra 1 C, in Santa Marta to Mamatoca and ask for the Quinta, US$0.75,* a 17th-century villa surrounded by gardens lies 5 km southeast of the city. Here is the simple room in which Simón Bolívar died, with a few of his belongings. Other paintings and memorabilia of the period are on display. This is an elegant memorial to Colombia's most revered man.

Beaches

Sandy beaches and headlands stretch all along this coast, surrounded by hills, green meadows and shady trees. The largest sandy bay is that of Santa Marta, with Punta Betín, a rocky promontory protecting the harbour to the north and a headland to the south. The rugged Isla El Morro lies 3 km off Santa Marta, topped by a lighthouse. **Playa El Rodadero**, 4 km south of the city (local bus service, taxi, US$5), has high-rise hotels of all standards, but it is attractive, tree lined, relatively clean and pleasant for bathing. Behind the promenade are restaurants, cheaper accommodation and other services. Beaches continue to the south. The bus from the airport passes by Pleno Mar, one of the more tranquil and recommended beaches in the area at the north end of Playa Bello Horizonte.

Ciénaga Grande de Santa Marta

The paved coast road to Santa Marta from Barranquilla passes salt pans and skirts the Ciénaga Grande de Santa Marta, a wildlife sanctuary, recognised by UNESCO and RAMSAR. It is not open to visitors, but all types of water birds, plants and animals may be seen on the large lake and its margins. Cutting off the egress from the lake to the sea to build the coast road killed large areas of mangrove and caused an ecological disaster, but a National Environment Programme is working to reopen the channels and restore the area. There are two villages built on stilts in the lake, Nueva Venecia and Buenavista. Ask at the Santuario de Flora y Fauna Ciénaga Grande de Santa Marta desk in national parks office in Santa Marta (T5-423 0752, see Tourist information, page 946) about guides and boatmen who take visitors to the lake from the community of Tasajera. On the east shore of the lagoon is **Ciénaga**, famous for its cumbia music.

Taganga

Close to Santa Marta is the popular former fishing village, turned beach resort of Taganga, set in a little bay with good views. It is laid back and welcoming, but beaches further east in Tayrona national park are becoming more favoured as 'in' places on the backpacker circuit. Swimming is good, especially on Playa Grande, 25 minutes' walk round coast or US$3 by boat. Taganga is quieter midweek, but busy at weekends. Good fresh fish is served at places along the beach. Taganga is a popular place for diving and several well-established dive shops offer good-value PADI courses. There is a good book exchange. An ATM that takes all major credit cards is next to the police station, ½ block up from **Poseidon Dive Center**.

Parque Nacional Tayrona

www.parquesnacionales.gov.co, daily 0800-1700, US$14 foreigners, US$5.30 Colombians, US$3 children, parking extra. For the address of the national parks office in Santa Marta, see page 946.

Stretching north of Taganga for some 85 km is the beautiful and mostly unspoilt coastline of Tayrona National Park, where the densely forested northern slopes of the Sierra Nevada fall into the Caribbean. Small, secluded bays with beaches of golden sand are guarded by giant boulders and islets. In the lush jungle vegetation and in the mangroves, you can see monkeys, iguanas, birds and maybe snakes. Of its 15,000 ha, 3000 are marine. There is accommodation at the eastern end, where the beaches and the accessible remnants of the Tayrona culture can only be reached on foot or horseback.

Arriving at the park The park has three entrances: Palangana for day visits to Neguanje, Gayraca and Playa Cristal; Calabazo for Pueblito and Cabo San Juan de Guía, and El Zaino, at the eastern end of the park, 35 km from Santa Marta, for Cañaveral and Arrecifes; this last is the most commonly used entrance. At El Zaino you sign in and buy a ticket. From the gate *colectivos*

Fact...

During high season, the park is very crowded. Sometimes it closes temporarily for a variety of reasons, but never for long. It's best to arrive early.

make a 10-minute ride to **Cañaveral**, US$2, where there is a gift shop, a car park, a museum (closed) and the trail of Nueve Piedras, to a mirador (about 30 minutes there and back). A few metres from the car park is a juice bar, campsite, the road to the Ecohabs Minca (see Where to stay, page 948) and horse hire at the start of the trail to Arrecifes (see below). It costs US$9 to ride to Arrecifes, US$14.50 to La Piscina, US$18 to Cabo San Juan, one way. See also Transport, page 951, for how to get to the park.

Exploring the park It is a one-hour walk through the forest from Cañaveral to **Arrecifes**. The trail is mostly level, apart from a couple of short, steep sections. At Arrecifes, beyond the cabins, campsites and eating places, is a long beach backed by mangroves. On no account be tempted to swim here as the tides and surf are treacherous. Every year, people drown because they do not heed the warnings. Walk on from Arrecifes to **La Piscina**, 40 minutes further, passing a little beach, La Arenilla, two-thirds of the way along, with a *cevichería* and juice stall. La Piscina also has a couple of places selling drinks and food. The beach is narrow, but the swimming after the walk is divine; excellent snorkelling, too. From La Piscina you can walk on to **Cabo San Juan de Guía**, 45 minutes, which also has excellent bathing, places to eat and a popular campsite/hammock place. From Cabo San Juan you can return the way you came, take the boat to Taganga (see Transport, page 952), or walk 1½ hours on a clear path up to the archaeological site of **Pueblito**. A guided tour around the site is free, every Saturday or as arranged with a park guard. Other Tayrona relics abound. At Pueblito there are indigenous people; do not photograph them. From Pueblito you can continue for a pleasant two-hour walk up to Calabazo on the Santa Marta–Riohacha road. A circuit Santa Marta, Cañaveral, Arrecifes, Pueblito, Calabazo, Santa Marta in one day needs a 0700 start at the latest. It is easier to do the circuit in reverse, although the first two hours from Calabazo is uphill (start walking before 0700); ask to be dropped at Calabazo. Tours can be arranged at several hotels and agencies in Santa Marta.

It is advisable to inform park guards when walking in the park. Wear hiking boots and beware of bloodsucking insects. Take food, water and only necessary valuables. If you are staying overnight in one of the campsites or hammock places, remember to take all supplies with you as there is only a small store in the park.

East of the national park

Beyond Cañaveral on the Santa Marta–Riohacha road is **Los Angeles**, with access to fine empty beaches, excellent for surfing. Ten minutes west of Los Angeles is the mouth of the Río Piedras, the border of Tayrona Park, where you can bathe and enjoy sights to rival those in the park. At **Quebrada Valencia**, several natural swimming pools amid waterfalls, with good views. From the marked roadside entrance, it is a pleasant 20 minutes' walk along a clear path, or horse ride, to the waterfalls. It can get overcrowded during high season. Drinks and snacks are available along the way. The paved coastal road continues from Tayrona and crosses into Guajira Department at **Palomino**, 80 km from Santa Marta, which has a fine beach, a river running into the sea and fine views of the Sierra Nevada, including snow-capped Pico Bolívar. There are hotels, hostels and *cabañas*, with more under construction.

☆Parque Nacional Natural Sierra Nevada de Santa Marta
Entry US$8, US$3.30 for Colombians, US$1.50 children. For the latest information check with national parks offices in Santa Marta (page 946) and Bogotá (page 1011) and the Fundación Pro Sierra Nevada, C 17, No 3-83, Santa Marta, T5-431 5589, www.prosierra.org.

The Sierra Nevada, covering a triangular area of 16,000 sq km, rises abruptly from the Caribbean to 5800 m snow peaks in about 45 km, a gradient comparable with the south face of the Himalaya, and unequalled along the world's coasts. Pico Colón is the highest point in the country. Here can be found the most spectacular scenery and most interesting of Colombia's indigenous communities. The area has been a drugs-growing, processing and transporting region. For this reason, plus the presence of guerrilla and paramilitary groups, some local *indígenas* have been reluctant to welcome visitors. But the situation is improving and limited activities are now possible, such as the trek to Ciudad Perdida.

★Ciudad Perdida *Colour map 1, A3.*
Trips of 4-6 days are organized by 4 authorized agencies in Santa Marta (see What to do, page 950). Going on your own is not allowed.

The Ciudad Perdida (Lost City) was called Teyuna by the Tayrona, meaning Mother Nature. The city covers 400 ha in the Sierra Nevada de Santa Marta and was built around AD 700. It was the political and trading centre of the Tayrona. The circular and oval stone terraces were once the living quarters for some 1400-3000 people. The city was also an important religious and burial site. The Tayrona built sophisticated irrigation systems and walls to prevent erosion. By around 1600, the Tayrona had been almost wiped out by the conquistadors and the few who survived were forced to flee. For the next four centuries, the city disappeared under the forest growth. In 1973, tomb looters searching for gold known to exist in burial urns and graves, rediscovered the city by chance. By 1975, the city was officially re-found, attracting local and international anthropologists and archaeologists who started to excavate, leading to the first tourist groups in 1984. Today the area is a protected indigenous reserve, where three main indigenous groups, the Koguis, Arhuacos and Arsarios (Wiwa), continue to live. For archaeological information, see **ICANH** ① *C 12, No 2-41, Bogotá, T1-444 0544, www.icanh.gov.co.*

Trekking to the Ciudad Perdida The 20-km trek to the Lost City is, at times, gruelling and challenging. It is not a leisurely walk, but is well worth the effort for a rewarding and memorable experience. The trek is perhaps more spectacular than the archeological site itself. Depending on the length of tour, it starts and ends at Machete Pelao or El Mamey. Along with lush tropical humid and dry forests, abundant flora and fauna, there are crystal-clear rivers, waterfalls and natural swimming pools. There are some 1200 steep slippery steps to climb to the summit of the site; the nearest campsite is below these steps. Watch out for snakes. Along the way, you will pass friendly Kogui villages. All tours include transport to the start of the trail and back, sleeping in hammocks with mosquito nets, food, insurance, guides and entrance fees. The companies (see What to do, page 951) list the clothes and equipment you should take, such as sleeping bag, insect repellent, water bottle, etc. Accommodation is in organized camping or cabin sites. Tours run all year; be prepared for heavy rain. Don't forget that Ciudad Perdida is in a national park: it is strictly forbidden to damage trees and collect flowers or insects. Leave no rubbish behind and encourage the guides to ensure no one else does.

Minca and around
There are places to visit in the foothills of the Sierra Nevada, such as **Minca**, 20 km from Santa Marta ① *bus from C 11 entre Cra 11 y 12 in Santa Marta, 30 mins, US$3, taxi US$18-20.* This village is

surrounded by coffee fincas and begonia plantations, with several charming places to stay. Horse riding, birdwatching and tours further into the Sierra Nevada can be arranged from here. About 45 minutes' walk beyond the village is **El Pozo Azul**, a local swimming spot under a waterfall, which is popular at weekends but almost always empty during the week. Beyond Minca, the partly paved road rises steeply to San Lorenzo which is surrounded by a forest of palm trees. On the way to San Lorenzo is **La Victoria**, a large coffee finca which offers tours to demonstrate the coffee-making process. You can stay in *cabañas* run by the park authorities near San Lorenzo.

Aracataca

Aracataca, 60 km south of Ciénaga (see page 942) and 7 km before Fundación, is the birthplace of **Gabriel García Márquez**, fictionalized as Macondo in some of his stories (notably *100 Years of Solitude*). His home is now a **Casa Museo** ① *take Cra 5 away from plaza at corner with Panadería Delipán, museum is next to La Hojarasca café, open Tue-Sat 0800-1300, 1400-1700, Sun 0800-1400.* Different rooms have objects and quotations from his work in Spanish and English to provide an overview of his family life. You can also visit the **Casa del Telegrafista**, which houses a few dusty items. **Finca Macondo** (named after a type of tree) is 30 minutes from town. You can visit it in the afternoon, or take a tour in and around Macondo and to some outlying towns, such as Sevilla. Tour takes 8-9 hours and can be arranged through Expotur ① *T5-420 7739, US$32*. Other sites related to the stories are the river, where you can swim, and the railway station, through which coal trains pass.

Valledupar *Colour map 1, A3.*

South of Aracataca and Fundación is the important road junction of **Bosconia** (80 km). The main road continues to Bucaramanga; a road west heads to the Río Magdalena (with a turning at La Gloria towards Mompós – see Mompós Transport, above), while a road east goes towards Maicao, Valledupar (after 89 km) and **Cuestecitas**, where you can turn north to Riohacha, or carry on to Maicao on the Venezuelan border.

Valledupar, capital of César Department, lies on the plain between the Sierra Nevada de Santa Marta and the Sierra de Perijá. It is the home of *vallenato* music and culture (a UNESCO intangible cultural heritage). On the main Plaza Alfonso López Pumarejo, with a dramatic statue of La Revolución en Marcha, is the cultural centre **Fundación Festival de la Leyenda Vallenata: Compai Chipuco** ① *C 16, No 6-05, T5-738 393, www.festivalvallenato.com,* a good place for information. It sells handicrafts, books and music and has a bar, restaurant and photographic exhibition of La Cacica, Consuelo Araujonoguera, one of the founders of El **Festival de la Leyenda Vallenata**, which draws thousands of visitors each April (last week of the month). Also of interest are **La Academia de Música Vallenata Andrés Turco Gil** ① *C 31, No 4-265,* http://static.losninosvallenatos.com, with photos of events and famous personalities, and **Casa Beto Murgas/Museo del Acordeón** ① *Cra 17, No 9A-18, T5-573 7376, www.museodelacordeon.com, Mon-Fri 0900-1200, 1400-1700, Sat 0900-1200, US$7,* with a nice collection of photographs, indigenous instruments and accordions. Palenke Cultura Bar ① *Cra 5, No 13C-52,* is a good spot offering dance classes, free cinema nights and other cultural events. There are other cultural events throughout September. At the **Centro Artesanal Calle Grande** ① *C 16, block 7,* lots of stalls sell hats, bags, jewellery, hammocks and some musical instruments. (The **Exito** supermarket, Carreteras 6 y 7, Calle 16 y 17, has ATMs.)

Around Valledupar

The Río Guatapurí runs cold and clear from the Sierra Nevada past the city. The **Balneario Hurtado** is a popular bathing spot, especially at weekends, with food, drink and music (the water is muddy after heavy rain). It is by the bridge just past the Parque de la Leyenda, the headquarters of the Vallenato Festival. From the centre take Carrera 9, the main commercial avenue, or, if cycling, the quieter Carrera 4. Across the bridge is **Ecoparque Los Besotes** (9 km), a dry forest wildlife reserve, good for birdwatching.

From Valledupar, it is possible to enter the **Sierra Nevada de Santa Marta**, with permission from community leaders. The **Casa Indígena** (Avenida Simón Bolívar, just past the accordion statue at end of Carrera 9) is where the *indígenas* from the Sierra gather; go here if you need permission to go to remote places. A full-day tour from the city is to **La Mina** (20 km), a natural swimming pool by magnificent rocks, also popular at weekends. The Arhuaco community of **Nabusímake** is one of the most important centres of indigenous culture in the Sierra. It may be possible to visit, but tourism is sometimes not allowed by the Arhaucos (this was the case in 2016). The nearest town is Pueblo Bello, 1½ hours by regular bus from Valledupar (from Carrera 7A, where it splits from Carrera 7, beyond 5 Esquinas, 0600). A jeep runs to Nabusímake (not daily), 2½ to three hours and comes straight back; as there are no hotels you cannot stay overnight, so ask at the Casa Indígena or at reputable tour operators about visits.

Listings Santa Marta and around *map page 941.*

Tourist information

Santa Marta

National parks office
C 17, No 4-06, Plaza de la Catedral, T5-423 0752, www.parquesnacionales.gov.co.
Has information for each of the 4 local parks.

Tourist office
On Plaza de la Catedral, C 16, No 4-15, T5-420 9600, www.santamarta.gov.co. Mon-Fri 0800-1200, 1400-1800.
The main tourist office.

Parque Nacional Tayrona

See above for the address of the national parks office in Santa Marta. Information can also be found at www.colombia.travel and www.parquesnacionales.gov.co.

Where to stay

Santa Marta

Do not stay at the north end of town near the port and beyond the old railway station. It's essential to book ahead during high season, particularly weekends, when some hotels increase their prices by 50%.

$$$ La Casa del Farol
C 18, No 3-115, T5-423 1572, www.lacasadelfarol.com.
A luxury boutique hotel with 6 rooms, each with its own style, all modern conveniences, laundry service, beauty salon with massages and roof terrace with pool. Price includes breakfast.

$$$ La Casa Verde
C 18, No 4-70, T5-431 4122, www.casaverdesantamarta.com.
Only 5 suites, 'boutique' style, safe, small jacuzzi pool and juice bar. A *desayuno típico* is available.

$$ Aluna Casa y Café
C 21, No 5-72, T5-432 4916, www.alunahotel.com.
Pleasant and large Irish-run hostel in a converted 1920s villa, central and convenient. It has private rooms and dorms (US$10-12 pp), with roof terrace. Breakfast is extra. There's a café, extensive book exchange, and a good noticeboard. Recommended. Under same ownership is **Finca Entre Ríos**, www.fincaentrerios.com, 15 km from Santa Marta, a working farm with private and dorm rooms, full board **$$** pp.

$$ Nueva Granada
C 12, No 3-17, T5-421 1337.
This charming old building in the historic quarter has rooms round a pleasant courtyard, quiet. Shared rooms with fan are cheaper (**$**). Safety deposit boxes in rooms, small pool with jacuzzi, includes breakfast and welcome drink. Reductions in low season. Recommended.

$$-$ Casa Vieja
C 12, No 1C-58, T5-431 1606, www.hotelcasavieja.com.
Has a Spanish feel about it with white tiling and simple, clean rooms and a/c. Cheaper with fan, welcoming.

$$-$ La Brisa Loca
C 14, No 3-58, T5-431 6121, www.labrisaloca.com.
US-owned lively hostel, with or a/c private rooms, all with shared bath. Meals extra. Also bar, swimming pool and billiard room.

$$-$ pp The Dreamer Hostel
Cra 51, No 26D-161 Diagonal, Los Trupillos, Mamatoco, T5-433 3264, or T300-251 6534, www.thedreamerhostel.com.
Travellers' hostel in a residential district 15 mins from the centre, on the way to Tayrona, 5 mins by taxi from the bus station. All rooms are set around a sunny garden and pool, dorms for 4-10 people and private rooms with and without bath, fan or a/c, bar, good Italian restaurant, tour information and activities, good atmosphere.

All services close at hand, including a huge shopping mall, San Pedro Alejandrino and the bus stop for Tayrona.

$ Hospedería Casa Familiar
C 10C, No 2-14, T5-421 1697, Facebook: casafamiliarSantaMarta.
Run by an extremely helpful family, rooms with fan, roof terrace, and laundry service. Has information on diving and other activities, and organizes trips to Tayrona, Sierra Nevada and Ciudad Perdida.

$ Miramar
2 blocks from Malecón, C 10C, No 1C-59, T316-745 8947, www.hotelmiramar.com.co.
Very knowledgeable and helpful staff at this backpacker favourite. Can be crowded. Simple dorms and some nicer more expensive private rooms (US$15), motorbike parking, cheap restaurant. Often full. Reservations via the internet are held until 1500 on the day of arrival. Tours to the Ciudad Perdida, Tayrona, Guajira and local sites are available with the in-house operator. Airline tickets also sold here.

Taganga

$$$-$$ Bahía Taganga
C 8, No 1B-35, T5-421 0653, www.bahiataganga.com.
Up on a hill at the north end of the bay with an unmissable sign on the cliff face. It has commanding views over the village and is tastefully decorated with clean rooms. Breakfast is served on a lovely terrace, hospitable, a/c, more expensive in the new building.

$$ La Ballena Azul
Cra 1, No 18-01, T5-421 9009, www.hotelballenaazul.com.
Attractive hotel with a French Riviera touch, decorated in cool blues and whites. Comfortable, spacious rooms with sea views, cheaper with fan. Also runs boat tours to secluded beaches, horses for hire. Nice restaurant on the beach, crêperie, terrace bar.

$$-$ Hostal Moramar
2 blocks uphill from beach opposite football pitch, Cra 4, No-17B-83, T5-421 9098.
Bright, airy patio area, Wi-Fi, breakfast and laundry extra, attentive owners, welcoming.

$$-$ La Casa de Felipe
Cra 5A, No 19-13, 500 m from beach behind football pitch, T316-318 9158 (mob), T5-421 9101, www.lacasadefelipe.com.
Cosy traveller place run by knowledgeable French team of Jean-Phillipe and Sandra Gibelin. Good kitchen facilities, excellent restaurant, hospitable, relaxing hammock and expansive roof with terrace with sea views, studio apartments, dorms (US$8-10.50) and rooms. Good information on trips to Tayrona (maps provided), English spoken.

$$-$ Techos Azules
Sector Dunkarinca, Cabaña 1-100, T5-421 9141, www.techosazules.com.
Off the road leading into town, *cabañas* with good views over the bay, private rooms and dorm US$8 pp (low season prices), free coffee, laundry service.

$ Bayview
Cra 4, No 17B-57, T5-421 9560, www.hosteltrail.com/bayview.
With a technicolour façade, pleasant rooms, cheaper dorms (US$7 pp), kitchen, barbecue area, lounges with DVD player.

$ Casa Blanca
Cra 1, No 18-161, T5-421 9232, at the southern end of the beach, Facebook: Hospedaje-Casa-Blanca.
Characterful. Each room has its own balcony with hammock, also has dorms. The roof terrace is a fine place to pass the evening, drinking beer with fellow guests. Also has a tour desk.

$ pp Divanga B&B
C 12, No 4-07, T5-421 9092, also Republica Divanga, C 11, No 3-05, T5-421 9217, www.divanga.com.
French-owned hostel, private rooms with or without bath or dorms (US$11-17), includes great breakfast in the B&B, breakfast not included at Republika, but rooms are cheaper, comfortable, 5 mins' walk from beach, nice views, attentive service, lovely atmosphere, good pool (at B&B). Also has Diva Expe tour operator and dive shop. Recommended.

$ Pelikan Hostal
Cra 2, No 17-04, T5-421 9057, www.hosteltrail.com/hostalpelikan.
Rooms with fan for 2-7 people, apartments, kitchen, laundry service, restaurant.

Parque Nacional Tayrona

Cañaveral and Arrecifes
Comfortable cabins ($) with thatched roofs (*ecohabs*) for 1-4 people can be booked at Cañaveral, Arrecifes and other locations in or near the park, T311-600 1614, www.ecohabsantamarta.com. They offer privacy,

great views over sea and jungle; they have decent restaurants.

Also at Arrecifes are various places to stay with double tents with mattress, US$5 pp (cheaper with own tent) and hammocks. These include **Bukaru**, T310-691 3626; and Don Pedro, T322-550 3933.

Cabo de San Juan de Guía
Centro Eco-turístico del Cabo de San Juan de Guía, www.cecabosanjuandelguia.com.co. A beautifully located campsite on a headland inside the park, with restaurant, hammocks for hire (US$10-12.50) and 2 *cabañas* (US$60). Pitching your own tent costs US$10; double tent hire, US$25.

East of Tayrona
There is an ecohostel called **Yuluka** about 2 km from El Zaino entrance on the main road.

$$$ Cabañas Los Angeles
Los Angeles, T321-522 1292, www. cabanasantamartalosangeles.com.
Beachside apartments next to Tayrona National Park, with gorgeous sea views. Facilities include free breakfast, hammocks, large communal area and a restaurant. Choose from 4 different *cabañas*. The owner is Nohemi Ramos who also offers tours and hires out surfboards.

Minca
There are many more places to stay in Minca.

$$$ Ecohabs Minca
T311-600 1614, www.ecohabsantamarta.com.
Wood and thatch cabins for 2-8 people, with restaurant, bar, spa, activities and events organized, a good place for relaxation and birdwatching, transfers and packages can be arranged.

$$ Finca Carpe Diem
Paso del Mango, Bonda, 50 mins from Santa Marta, T5-420 9610, www.fincacarpediem.com.
Belgian-owned hostel on a farm and nature reserve, with private and dormitory accommodation (US$12-13.50), camping, home-produced vegetables, coffee and honey, activities include treks, swimming and local visits. See website for how to get there.

$$ Minca-La Casona
On the hill to the right as you enter, T315-519 3679, www.hotelminca.com.
Converted convent with views of the valley below, fully remodelled, with breakfast, bath,

fan, hot water, restaurant and bar, various activities including birdwatching.

$$ Sans Souci
Minca, T313-590 9213, sanssouciminca@yahoo.com.
Rambling house in beautiful garden, German-owned, rooms in the house or separate apartments, pool, kitchen, discount in exchange for gardening. Stunning views.

$$ Sierra's Sound
C Principal, Minca, T321-522 1292, www.mincahotelsierrasound.com.
Italian owned, overlooking a rocky river, hot water, home-made pasta, organized tours into the Sierra Nevada.

Aracataca
Most people visiting the town stay in neighbouring Fundación. **Restaurant El Patio Mágico de Gabo y Leo Matiz** occasionally organizes rooms.

$$-$ Hotel Milán
C 7 No 8-24, Fundación, T301-707 9070.
Comfortable if functional hotel, clean rooms with a/c and fridge.

Valledupar

$$$ Sonesta
Diag 10, No 6N-15, T5-574 8686, www.sonesta.com.
Business-class hotel, next to CC Guatapurí Plaza, it has all the usual amenities including a pool and restaurant.

$$ Casa de Los Santos Reyes
C 13, No 4A-90, T5-580 1782, www. hotelboutiquevalledupar.com.
Centrally located, this restored colonial home has been turned into a boutique hotel. Its 2 spacious rooms and a suite have all mod cons and there's a small pool. Run by the same people as **Hostal Provincia**.

$$ Hostal Provincia
C 16A, No 5-25, T5-580 0558, www.provinciavalledupar.com.
Private rooms and cheaper dorms for 6. A very good choice, with a nice atmosphere. Bike rental, Wi-Fi throughout, hammocks, barbecue and bar, lots of information, helpful staff can organize tours and excursions to local indigenous communities. Warmly recommended.

\$\$ Vajamar
Cra 7, No 16A-30, T5-573 2010,
www.hotelvajamar.com.
Smart city centre hotel with pool and an
expensive restaurant. Rooms are cheaper
at weekends.

\$ Aqua Hostal
Cra 7 No 13A-42, T5-570 0439,
www.aquahostalvalledupar.com.
Hostel with private rooms as well as
12-bed dorms. Wi-Fi throughout.

Restaurants

Santa Marta

\$\$\$-\$\$ El Bistró
C 19, No 3-68, T5-421 8080. Daily 1100-2300,
happy hour 1730-1930.
Meat dishes, pastas, salads, burgers,
sandwiches and set lunches, not a
large place and the menu is limited, wine
list, Argentine influence throughout.

\$\$ Donde Chucho
C 19, No 2-17, T5-421 0861.
A little expensive but well situated in the corner
of Parque Santander. Serves mostly seafood.

\$\$ Donde L'Italiano
Cra 3, No 16-26, T316-429 1131. Mon-Sat 1130-
1430, 1800-2230.
Tasty Italian fare at reasonable prices,
generous portions.

\$\$ La Paila Caliente II
C 18, No 4-60, T5-421 4954.
Delightful restaurant with good Colombian/
Caribbean food, à la carte at night, excellent
value lunch.

\$\$ Ouzo
Cra 3, No 19-29, T5-423 0658, www.
ouzosantamarta.com. Closed Sun.
Mediterranean, Italian, Greek restaurant
and bar with seating on the street, popular.

\$\$ Ricky's
Cra 1a, No 17-05, T300-712 9163.
Beachside restaurant serving international food,
including Chinese. Reasonably priced.

\$\$-\$ Caribbean Wings
C 17, No 2-53, T574-306 055.
Small *parrilla* near the water with a sports-bar
vibe. Popular for American-style chicken wings.
Great option on a budget.

\$\$-\$ Lulo
Cra 3, No 16-34, www.lulocafebar.com.
Café and bar serving *arepas*, wraps, paninis,
fresh juices, coffee and cocktails.

\$ Merkabar
C 10C, No 2-11. Opens early for breakfast.
Pastas, great pancakes, good juices and seafood.
Family-run, good value and provides tourist
information. Recommended.

Taganga
Fresh fish is available along the beach and good
pancakes can be found at the crêperie at the
Hotel La Ballena Azul.

\$\$ Babaganoush
Cra 1C 18-22, 3rd floor next to the Tayrona
Dive Center.
Serves up international dishes. Great steaks and a
generous half-off happy hour from 1700-2200.

\$\$ Bitácora
Cra 1, No17-13.
Seafood, pastas, burgers, steaks and salads, has a
good reputation.

Parque Nacional Tayrona
There are decent restaurants at both Cañaveral
and Arrecifes, as well as smaller eateries at many
of the beaches.

Aracataca

\$\$ El Patio Mágico de Gabo y Leo Matiz
C 7 No 4-57.
Central option offers Italian and local dishes in an
open-air courtyard. Also has vegetarian options.

\$ La Hojarasca
Next to the Casa Museo. Daily 1800-2200.
Juices, snacks and drinks, clean and pleasant.

Valledupar
There are some cafés on the Plaza Alfonso López,
but all types of restaurants on Cra 9 from C 15
down, heading towards Plaza del Acordeón.

\$\$ Varadero
C12 N0 6-56, T5-570 6175.
Simply put: the best seafood in town.

\$ Café de Las Madres
Pl de las Madres, Cra 9, No 15-19.
A nice shady place, with a limited selection:
coffee, beer, ices.

Bars and clubs

Santa Marta

Santa Marta is a party town; new clubs, discos and bars open every week. In the evening wander along Cra 3 and C 17 and 18 either side of it to see what's going on.

Agave Azul
C 14, No 3-74, Facebook: agaveazul.santamarta. In the same building as **La Brisa Loca**. This Mexican bar is run by 2 brothers from San Francisco. It offers tasty food and good cocktails at affordable prices.

Oh La La Puerta
C 17, No 2-29. Excellent bar and atmosphere in a colonial house. Recommended.

Taganga

Mirador
C 1, No 18A-107, T301-638 8500, Facebook: Mirador-de-Taganga. Rooftop bar and disco that strikes a nice balance between in- and outdoor fun. Also has a hostel.

Sensation
C 14, No 1-04, T300-668 9144, Facebook: SensationTaganga. Dance club that's open till 0300 at weekends.

Entertainment

Valledupar
Palenke Cultura Bar, *Cra 5 No 13C 52, T315-235 4378.* A good spot offering dance classes, free cinema nights and other cultural events.

Festivals

Santa Marta
Jul Festival Patronal de Santa Marta. Celebrates the founding of the city with parades and musical performances.
Jul Fiestas del Mar. Aquatic events and a beauty contest.

Valledupar
6 Jan The anniversary of the founding of Valledupar. There's dancing and accordion music in the streets.
Last week of Apr Festival de la Leyenda Vallenata. The festival celebrating *vallenato* music and culture draws thousands of visitors. It is focused around Parque de la Leyenda. Contact the cultural centre (C 16, No 6-05, T5-580 8710, www.festivalvallenato.com) for information.
Sep There are other cultural events throughout Sep.

Shopping

Santa Marta
Craft shops
The **market** is at C 11/Cra 11, just off Av del Ferrocarril and has stalls with excellent selections of hammocks. There are several good handicraft shops on Parque Bolívar. Also try **Artesanías Sisa** (Cra 4, No 16-42 on the Plaza Catedral, T5-421 4510), which sells local handicrafts including clothes, bags, hammocks and sombreros.

Valledupar
Centro Artesanal Calle Grande, *C 16, block 7.* Lots of stalls selling handicrafts and local artwork, including distinctive hats (US$15-US$150), indigenous bags, jewellery, hammocks and some musical instruments.
   Compai Chipuco, on the plaza. Sells books and music CDs of the region.
   La Casa de la Música, Cra 9, No 18-85. Books, music and CDs.

What to do

Santa Marta
For trips to Ciudad Perdida and the Sierra Nevada, see under the relevant destination, below.

Tour operators
Aventure Colombia, *C 14, No 4-80, T5-430 5185, http://aventurecolombia.com.* Branch of the recommended Cartagena agency specializing in classic and alternative tours and expeditions across Colombia, focusing on trekking, eco and rural tourism.
New Frontiers Adventures, *C 27, No 1C-74, close to Playa Los Cocos, T318-736 1565/317-648 6786, www.colombia.newfrontiersadventures.com.* Trekking to Ciudad Perdida, birdwatching, diving and other adventures and ecotours, with English-speaking guides.
Turcol, *C 13, No 3-13, CC San Francisco Plaza loc 115, T5-421 2256, http://turcoltravel.com.* Arranges trips to Ciudad Perdida, Tayrona, Pueblito, Guajira and provides a guide service.

Taganga

Adventure tours

Elemento, C 18. No 3-31, T5-421 0870. Mountain biking, hiking and other tours in the Sierra Nevada, Minca and Tayrona.

Vergel Tours, T304-571 1425, www.vergeltours. com. The Vergel family organizes a number of excursions from Taganga, including trips to Ciudad Perdida, scuba outings, snorkelling and cliff jumping.

Diving

There are several dive shops in Taganga.
Oceano Scuba, Cra 2, No 17-46, T5-421 9004, www.oceanoscuba.com.co. PADI, NAUI, TDI and other courses, 2, 3 and 4 days.

Poseidon Dive Center, C 18, No 1-69, T5-421 9224, www.poseidondivecenter.com. PADI courses at all levels and the only place on the Colombian Caribbean coast to offer an instructor course. German owner, several European languages spoken. Own pool for beginners. Wi-Fi.

Ciudad Perdida

Trips of 4-6 days are organized by 4 authorized agencies in Santa Marta: **Turcol** (see above), **Magic Tour** (C 16, No 4-41, Santa Marta, T5-421 5820, and C 14, No 1b-50, T5-421 9429, Taganga, www.magictourcolombia.com), **Expotur** (Cra 3, No 17-27, T5-420 7739, www.expotur-eco.com) and **Wiwa Tour** (Cra 3, No 18-49, T5-420 3413, www.wiwatour.com). Other tour operators and hotels in Santa Marta or Taganga can make arrangements. The cost starts at about US$260 pp and includes park permits. Under no circumstances should you deal with unauthorized guides; check with the tourist office if in doubt.

Minca

Semilla Tours, Minca, T313-872 2434, www.hosteltrail.com/tour_companies/semillatours. Community tourism company offering tours in the region and elsewhere in Colombia. Also has volunteering opportunities.

Aracataca

Expotur, Cra 3, No 17-27, Edif Rex, Loc 3, T5-420 7739, http://expotur-eco.com/. Arranges 8- to 9-hr tours of the town and surroundings, US$37.

Valledupar

Paseo Vallenato Tour, Diagonal 21, No 18-2 a 18-136, T313-571 9025, www.paseovallenato.com. Offers cultural tours in and around Valledupar

as well excursions to the river and indigenous communities. Recommended.

Transport

Santa Marta

Air **Simón Bolívar Airport** is 20 km south of the city. A bus to town costs US$0.80; a taxi is US$15-20, less to Rodadero; beware of taxi drivers taking you to a hotel of their choice, not yours.

There are daily flights to **Bogotá**, **Bucaramanga**, **Cali** and **Medellín** for connections to other cities. During the tourist season, get to the airport early and book well ahead (the same goes for bus reservations). Airlines include **Avianca**, Cra 2A No 14-17, Edif de los Bancos, loc 105, T5-421 4958, T5-432 0106 at airport; **Copa**, CC Rex, Cra 3, No 17-27, loc 2; **EasyFly**; T5-435 1777; and **LATAM**, C 23, No 6-18, loc 2.

Bus The **bus terminal** is southeast of the city, towards Rodadero. A minibus to the centre of Santa Marta costs US$0.80; taxi to the centre US$3-4, or US$5 to Rodadero.

Local To **Aracataca**, US$5 with **Berlinas**. Buses to **Taganga** can be picked up on Cra 5; buses to **Rodadero** leave from the waterfront. Buses to **Tayrona** leave from the corner of C 11/Cra 11 in the market area, every 15 mins, US$3.

Long distance To **Bogotá**, 7 daily, 16 hrs, US$35-52, **Brasilia** or **Berlinas del Fonce**. **Berlinas** and **Brasilia** to **Bucaramanga** about 9 hrs, US$33-37, frequent departures 0700-2200. Buses to **Barranquilla**, frequent, 2 hrs, US$5-6. To **Cartagena**, 5 hrs, US$14-16, with **Brasilia**. To **Riohacha**, 3 hrs, US$10-12. Frequent buses to **Maicao**, 4-5 hrs, US$15 a/c, cheaper non a/c. **Asotranstax** runs a door-to-door *colectivo* service to **Mompós**, via Bosconia, which leaves Santa Marta 0300 and 1100, 6 hrs, US$25.50.

Taganga

Minibus from **Santa Marta**, US$0.75 (frequent, 0600-2130).

Taxi US$5, 15-20 mins.

Parque Nacional Tayrona

The beaches of Bahía Concha, Neguanje and Playa Cristal (a 10-min boat ride from Neguanje) can be reached from Santa Marta by tours (eg from hostels), or in the case of Neguanje by *colectivos* from the market at 0700, return 1600.

To get to the park entrance in El Zaino, take a **Cootrans Oriente** 'La Guajira' bus from the market in Santa Marta, Cra 11 y C 11 outside the general store, or from in front of the **Buenavista** shopping centre in Mamatoco, near San Pedro Alejandrino and **The Dreamer**, US$2.25, every 15 mins from 0700, 1 hr, last back 1800-1830 (check on the day with the bus driver).

To return to Santa Marta (unless going to Pueblito and Calabazo, or taking the Taganga boat; see below), walk from Arrecifes to the car park and take the *colectivo* to the main road. At the car park there may be taxis waiting: US$25 per car, US$20 for 1 person to Santa Marta, or you may get lucky and find a cheaper ride back to Santa Marta.

Hotels and hostels arrange tours, but there is no need to take guides (who charge US$20 or more pp for a day trip).

There is a **boat** service from **Taganga** at 1000-1100 to **Cabo San Juan**, 1 hr journey, US$25 pp one way (and you have to pay park entry); returns to Taganga 1500-1600.

Aracataca

Bus To **Santa Marta**, US$4-5. To **Barranquilla**, US$6. To **Valledupar**, 3 hrs 45 mins, US$7-9 with **Cootracosta**. There may be a long stop in Fundación, but you don't have to change bus. To go to **Bucaramanga** (US$25) or **Bogotá** (US$35), you have to catch a bus coming from Santa Marta at the toll station (*peaje*) outside town 1½ hrs

after the bus has left Santa Marta. Be at the toll 30 mins early. For information on all buses, go to the **Berlinas** office. Bicycle taxi from bus stop to centre US$0.65.

Valledupar

Air The airport is 3 km southeast of the town, close to the bus station (taxi, US$5).

Flights to **Barranquilla** (30 mins) and **Bogotá** (1½ hrs) with **Avianca** (T01-8000-953434) and **LATAM** (Av Hurtado Diag 10N-6N, 15, CC Guatapuri, p 1, Plazoleta Juan Valdez). **Easyfly** (www.easyfly.com.co) also has flights from here.

Bus The bus terminal is near the airport (taxi, US$3.55).

To **Aracataca**, US$7-9. To **Santa Marta**, 4 hrs, US$10-12. To **Barranquilla**, 5-6 hrs, US$13-15. To **Cartagena**, 7-8 hrs, US$17-21. To **Mompós** (via Bosconia) door-to-door service with local taxi/minibus driver Lalo Castro, T312-673 5226, US$22; if he isn't going, **CotraNorte**, **Cotracol** or **Cootracegua** buses leave every morning, or minibus from outside bus terminal to Santa Ana on the Río Magdalena, via Bosconia and La Gloria, US$27, then cross the Río Magdalena by bridge to Talaigua Nueva (if the bus isn't going to Mompós, take motorbike taxi to Mompós, US$6-9). There are also door-to-door services to **Riohacha**, US$15, and **Bucaramanga**, 8 hrs, US$25-28.

To Venezuela

visit the other-worldly Guajira Peninsula on the way to the border

Roads head for the insalubrious border town of Maicao, but on the way is plenty of interest: lagoons where flamingos feed and the arid, empty Guajira Peninsula with its wildlife and special Wayúu culture.

Riohacha *Colour map 1, A4.*

The port of Riohacha, 160 km east of Santa Marta and capital of La Guajira Department, comes alive at the weekend, when it fills with party-goers and music (almost always *vallenato*). It was founded in 1545 by Nicolás Federmann, and in early years its pearling industry was large enough to tempt Drake to sack it (1596). Pearling almost ceased during the 18th century and the town was all but abandoned. Today, there is a pleasant stretch of beach with shady palms and a long wooden pier in the centre. A promenade along the beachfront (Calle 1) is lined with banks, hotels, restaurants and tour agencies. It is common to see Wayúus selling their wares and beautiful handmade *mochilas* (bags) along the seafront.

Riohacha is a useful base for exploring the semi-desert landscape of La Guajira. The **Dirección de Turismo de la Guajira** ① *C 1, Av de La Marina No 4-42, T5-727 1015*, has little information about the region, so it's better to ask tour operators and visit the University of the Guajira, which has an excellent resource centre related to the region and the Wayuú culture (ID is necessary to get in). The provincial website is www.laguajira.gov.co (T892-115 0151), and the municipal site is www. riohacha-laguajira.gov.co.

Santuario Los Flamencos
95 km east of Santa Marta and 25 km short of Riohacha.

There are several small and two large saline lagoons (Laguna Grande and Laguna de Navío Quebrado), separated from the Caribbean by sand bars. The latter is near Camarones (*colectivo* from Riohacha, roundabout between water tower and bus station, US$3) which is just off the main road. About 3 km beyond Camarones is 'La Playa', a popular beach to which some *colectivos* continue at weekends. Flamingos normally visit the large lagoons between October and December, during the wet season, though some birds are there all year. They are believed to migrate to and from the Dutch Antilles, Venezuela and Florida. Across Laguna de Navío Quebrado is a community-run visitor centre called **Los Mangles**, with accommodation in *cabañas*, in hammocks ($), or camping. Meals are also available and the centre arranges birdwatching trips on foot or by boat (US$3 per person). For travel packages see http://ecoturismosantuario.weebly.com (T301-675 3862) and www.parquesnacionales.gov.co. There are several bars and two stores on the beach.

☆Guajira Peninsula
Beyond Riohacha to the east is the arid and sparsely inhabited Guajira Peninsula. You'll see fields of cactii and fine views of flamingos and other brightly coloured birds. The sunsets and barren landscapes of the Guajira are magnificent. The indigenous Wayúu (or Guajiros) here collect dividivi (the curved pods of trees used in tanning and dyeing), tend goats and go fishing. Of special interest are the coloured robes worn by the women. Their language is Wayuunaiki; beyond Cabo de Vela little Spanish is spoken.

Manaure is known for its salt flats southwest of the town. If you walk along the beach past the salt works, there are several lagoons where flamingos congregate year round (take binoculars). Local children hire out bicycles to travel to the lagoons and salt flats. Take plenty of sunblock and water and a torch/flashlight for returning in the evening. Around 14 km from Manaure in this direction is **Musichi**, an important haunt of the flamingos, sometimes out of the wet season, with the **Area Natural Protegida de los Flamencos Rosados**. From Manaure there are *busetas* to **Uribia** (US$4-5, 30 minutes), which has a Wayúu festival in June (no other reason to stop here), and thence to Maicao. You can get *busetas* from Uribia to Puerto Bolívar (from where coal from El Cerrejón mine is exported) and from there transport to **Cabo de Vela**, where the lagoons seasonally shelter vast flocks of flamingos, herons and sandpipers. It costs about US$7-11 from Uribia to Cabo de Vela, busetas run until 1400, few on Sunday, all transport leaves from the market and the journey is slow. There are fine beaches, but very strong currents offshore. Good walks through desert scrubland, eg to Pan de Azúcar hill (one hour from beach) and El Faro, with superb views of the coastline and desert. To enjoy deserted beaches, avoid Christmas and Easter when the *cabañas* and beaches are crowded and full of cars.

> **Warning...**
> The Guajira Peninsula is not a place to travel alone; if not taking an organized tour, parties of three or more are recommended. If going in your own transport, check on safety before setting out. Also remember it is hot, easy to get lost, and there is little cover and very little water. Locals, including police, are very helpful in giving lifts. Stock up with provisions and water in Riohacha or Maicao. Elsewhere, what little there is, is expensive.

Parque Nacional Macuira ① *For information, C 8, No 5-73, T5-728 2636 in Riohacha. Mon-Fri 0800-1200, 1400-1600, entry US$11.25, Colombians US$3.75, children US$2.40, registration and 30-min compulsory induction at Nazareth park office, open Mon-Fri 0700-1200, 1400-1700, guides US$20.* Towards the northeast tip of the Guajira peninsula is the Serranía de Macuira, a range of hills over 500 m which creates an oasis of tropical forest in the semi-desert. Moisture comes mainly from clouds that form in the evening and disperse in the early morning. Its remoteness gives it interesting flora and fauna and indigenous settlements little affected by outsiders. To reach the area, travel northeast from Uribia either round the coast past Bahía Portete, or direct across the semi-desert, to the Wayúu village of **Nazareth** on the east side of the park. Someone may let you stay the night in a hammock in Nazareth. Otherwise, there is camping beside the park office. Macuira can be seen on two-day trips from Nazareth. Beyond Cabo de la Vela take a tour, as there is no public transport.

Another worthwhile, but arduous trip is the journey to **Punta Gallinas**, the northernmost tip of the South American continent. It takes up to eight hours on unpaved roads, followed by a boat journey (three hours, shorter in dry season) that's not for the fainthearted, but the magic of the place makes it all worth it. Few people make it this far north, adding to the isolated feel and special atmosphere. The nearby sand dunes of Taroa are also spectacular.

Maicao *Colour map 1, A4.*

The paved highway runs from Riohacha to Maicao, 12 km from the Venezuelan border. It is hot, dusty and has a strong Arab presence, with several mosques and restaurants selling Arabic food. Clothing and white goods make up much of the business, but the city has a reputation for black-market activities. Most commercial premises close early and after dark the streets are unsafe.

Border with Venezuela

Colombian immigration is at the border. Migración Colombia ① *C 16, No 3-28, Maicao, open 0800-1200, 1400-1700 (in Riohacha at C 5, No 4-48, same hours).* With all the right papers, the border crossing is easy and there are few traffic delays. Make sure your bus or *por puesto* driver stops for you to get exit and entry stamps at both country's immigration posts. There are plenty of money changers hanging around at the border crossing. The border is closed to traffic between 1800 and 0500 and from 2100 for pedestrians (opening hours prone to change, see below).

There is no Venezuelan consul in Maicao. If you need a visa, get it in Barranquilla (Edificio Concasa, Carretera 52, No 69-96, piso 3, T5-368 2207, http://barranquilla.consulado.gob.ve, Monday-Thursday 0800-1200, 1330-1600, Friday 0800-1300), Cartagena (Carretera 3, Edificio Centro Ejecutivo, piso 14, Bocagrande, T5-665 0382, http://cartagena.consulado.gob.ve) or Riohacha (Carretera 7, No 3-08, piso 2, T5-727 4076, http://riohacha.consulado.gob.ve, Monday-Thursday 0800-1200, Friday 0800-1300). If you need a visa, you should check all requirements for your nationality before arriving at any of these consulates. It is easiest to get a Venezuelan visa in Barranquilla or Cartagena where visa is issued on the same day, but you must be there before 0900 with all documents and US$30 cash (onward ticket may be requested). Entering Venezuela, a transit visa will only do if you have a confirmed ticket to a third country within three days. See 'Entering Venezuela', Venezuela chapter. **Note** At the time of writing, the border between Venezuela and Colombia was closed to vehicles. At root is the problem of smuggling, especially of gasoline, between the two countries. Seek local advice about crossing.

Listings To Venezuela

Where to stay

Riohacha

$ Almirante Padilla
Cra 6, No 3-29, T5-727 3612/2328, hotel_almirante_padilla@yahoo.es.
Crumbling but with character. Has an inviting patio and a restaurant with cheap *almuerzo*. It's clean, friendly, large and very central. Some rooms with a/c.

$ Happiness Hostel
Av Los Estudiantes, Cra 15, No 14-51, T5-7273828, http://happinesshostelcol.wix.com/hostel.
With private rooms ($$) and dorms with bath (US$11.25 pp), bar, kitchen, patio, can arrange tours.

$ Internacional
Cra 7, No 13-37, T5-727 3483, hriohachainternacional@gmail.com.
A friendly option down an alleyway off the old market, with a pleasant restaurant on the patio. Free iced water. Recommended.

$ Yalconia del Mar
Cra 7, No 11-26, T5-727 3487, hotelyalconiadelmar@hotmail.com.
Rooms with bath, cheaper with fan, clean, safe, friendly, helpful, halfway between the beach and the bus station.

Guajira Peninsula

Manaure

$$ Palaaima
Cr 6, No 7-25, T5-717 8455, T314-581 6789, irisfaep@hotmail.com.

The best in town. Comfortable, cool rooms, helpful. There are always Wayúu locals hanging around the hotel who are eager to talk about their culture and traditions.

Uribia
Basic *hostales* (\$, no running water); most transport stops in Uribia.

\$\$ Juyasirain
Diag 2A, No 2B-04, T5-717 7284, juyasirain2009@hotmail.com.
The only more upmarket accommodation in town. Large, light and airy, with a pleasant patio restaurant.

Cabo de Vela
This area becomes very crowded during high season, but there are 60 hostels to choose from, mostly basic with hammocks, but some have TV, a/c. There is a telecom centre. Most places have hammock space on the beach, US\$5-10. Fish meals cost US\$4-6, including a large breakfast.

Maicao

\$\$\$-\$\$ Hotel Maicao Internacional
C 12, No 10-90, T5-726 8186, hotelmaicao2009@telecom.com.co.
Good rooms with a/c, rooftop pool and bar. A good option in Maicao, attentive staff.

\$\$ Maicao Plaza
C 10, No 10-28, T5-726 0310, maicaoplazahotel@hotmail.com.
Modern, central, with spacious rooms.

Restaurants

Riohacha
Many ice cream and juice bars, and small *asados*, serving large, cheap selections of barbecued meat at the western end of the seafront. Western end also has a lovely row of brightly painted huts selling fresh seafood and ceviche. The eastern end has more restaurants for sit-down meals.

\$\$ La Tinaja
C 1, No 4-59.
Lovely seafood in light, breezy setting. Recommended, though usually quiet on Sun.

\$\$ Malecón
C 1A, No 3-47.
Good selection of seafood and meat served in a palm-thatched barn looking out to sea, music and dancing in the evening.

Shopping

Riohacha
Market 2 km from town on Valledupar road; hammocks and bags woven by the Wayúu of the Guajira are sold.

What to do

Guajira Peninsula
Trips to the Guajira Peninsula are best arranged in Riohacha where there are several operators, but can also be taken with national operators and others in Cartagena and Santa Marta. Tours to Cabo de la Vela, 1-2 days usually include Manaure (salt mines), Uribia, Pilón de Azucar and El Faro. All organize tours to Wayúu *rancherías* in the afternoon (includes typical goat lunch).

Uribia
Kaí Eco Travel, *Diagonal 1B, No 8-68, T5-717 7173, or 311-436 2830, also at Hotel Castillo del Mar, C 9A, No 15-352 and at Av 1-A No 4-49, T05-727 0728, in Riohacha and in Hotel Juyasirain, www.kaiecotravel.com.* Run by a network of Wayúu families. Organizes tours to Cabo de la Vela (for 2 days, US\$130 pp for 2 people, discounts for larger groups), Parque Natural Nacional Macuira (for 5 days US\$600 pp for 2 people), Punta Gallinas (for 3 days US\$390 pp for 2 people), up to US\$980 for a 8-day full circuit, including transport, accommodation and food. Highly recommended.
Kaishi, *Plaza Principal, T 311-429 6315, www.kaishitravel.com.* Andrés Delgado; organizes jeep tours around La Guajira, with lodging.

Transport

Riohacha
Air Daily flights to **Bogotá**, 1 hr 35 mins.

Bus Main terminal is on C 15 (El Progreso). **Coopcaribe Taxis** travel throughout the region and can be picked up almost anywhere in town, especially close to the old market area near the Hotel Internacional: daily to **Uribia**, US\$11, 1½ hrs, **Manaure** US\$12, 1¾ hrs. Leave when full (4 people), be prepared to pay slightly more if there are no travellers. Early morning best for travel, transport is scarce in the afternoon. No buses leave from Riohacha direct to Cabo de la Vela: travel to Uribia and wait for a jeep (leaves when full, irregular service) to Cabo de La Vela, long and uncomfortable, unpaved road. Take plenty of water with you. It is much easier and recommended to take a tour from Riohacha to Cabo de La Vela. To **Santa Marta**, US$10-12, 3 hrs, and **Cartagena**, US$23, 8 hrs, every 30 mins.

Maicao
Bus Buses to/from **Riohacha**, US$4.50, frequent, 1-1½ hr. **Santa Marta** 3 hrs, US$14.50. **Barranquilla**, US$19-21. **Cartagena**, US$20-24. Trucks leave regularly for **Cabo de Vela**, 2½-3 hrs, US$10 (can be uncomfortably crowded). Take water. **Fleta** is the local name for the faster taxis. *Colectivos* (*por puestos* in Venezuela), Maicao–**Maracaibo**, US$15, or microbus, US$10, very few buses to Venezuela after midday. Buses leave from the bus terminal where you can change money. Taxis from Maicao to Maracaibo stop at both immigration posts and take you to your hotel.

San Andrés and Providencia

coral reefs and white-sand bays in the sea of seven colours

Colombia's Caribbean islands of the San Andrés and Providencia archipelago are 480 km north of the South American coast, 400 km southwest of Jamaica and 180 km east of Nicaragua. This proximity has led Nicaragua to claim them from Colombia in the past. In 2000, the Archipelago of San Andrés, Old Providence and Santa Catalina was declared a World Natural Heritage Site called the Seaflower Biosphere Reserve. San Andrés is larger and more developed than Providencia and has lost much of its colonial Caribbean feel. Both are very expensive by South American standards. Nevertheless, their surrounding islets and cays, good diving, white sand beaches and spectacular turquoise waters make them popular holiday resorts with Colombians and North Americans looking for winter sun. The original inhabitants, mostly descendants of Jamaican slaves, speak English, but the population has swollen with unrestricted immigration from Colombia. There are also Chinese and Middle Eastern communities.

San Andrés
The 11-km-long San Andrés island is made of coral and rises at its highest to 104 m. The town, commercial centre, resort hotel sector and airport are at the northern end. A picturesque road circles the island. The island's beaches are located in town and on the east coast, of which the best are at San Luis and Bahía Sonora/Sound Bay. Places to see include the Hoyo Soplador, at the south end of the island, a geyser-like hole through which the sea spouts into the air when the wind is in the right direction. The west side is less developed, but there are no beaches. Instead there is **The Cove**, the island's deepest anchorage, and **Morgan's Cave** (Cueva de Morgan), reputed hiding

Essential San Andrés and Providencia

Finding your feet

A cheap way to visit San Andrés is by taking a charter flight from Bogotá or other major cities, with accommodation and food included; see supplements in the local Colombian press. On arrival in San Andrés, you must buy a tourist card, US$33. It is also valid for Providencia. Do not lose it. You must also have an onward or return ticket. There are onward flights and boat services from San Andrés to Providencia. ATMs are available in San Andrés town and at the airport. Some shops and most hotels will change US$ cash. On Providencia, an ATM is tucked away just before the Lover's Bridge, on the road to Santa Catalina. San Andrés is very crowded with Colombian shoppers looking for foreign-made, duty-free bargains, but international shoppers will find few bargains, and essentials and eating out are expensive.

When to go

The rainiest months are October and November, while the driest are January to April, but this season attracts the largest crowds. Between April and May, Providencia is awash with migrating black crabs.

Useful numbers

Civil defence: T144 or T8-512 5608. **Fire**: T119. **Police**: T123 (Providencia T8-514 8000). **Red Cross**: T8-512 7333/5788.

place for the pirate's treasure, which is penetrated by the sea through an underwater passage. Next to Cueva de Morgan is a **museum** ① *US$5*, with exhibitions telling the history of the coconut, paraphernalia from wrecks around the island and a replica pirate ship.

About 1 km south from Cueva de Morgan is **West View** ① *daily 0900-1830, small restaurant opposite entrance*, an excellent place to see marine life as the sea is very clear. At The Cove, a road crosses up to the centre of the island and back to town over La Loma, on which is a Baptist Church, built in 1847.

Cays Boats leave from San Andrés in the morning for El Acuario (Rose Cay) and Haynes Cay, and continue to Johnny Cay in the afternoon, which has a white beach and parties all day Sunday (US$10 return). **El Acuario** has crystalline water and is a good place to snorkel. You can wade across to **Haynes Cay** where there is good food and a reggae bar at Bibi's Place (open daily 0930-1530, T313-831 9039, also organizes full moon parties and civil and rasta weddings). If you want to avoid the crowds, hire a private boat and do the tour in reverse (US$150 for the day). Boats for the cays leave from Tonino's Marina between 0930 and 1100, US$10, returning at 1530, or from Muelle Casa de la Cultura on Avenida Newell.

Parque Nacional Natural Old Providence McBean Lagoon

Located 80 km north-northeast of San Andrés, and commonly called **Old Providence**, Providencia is a mountainous island of volcanic origin. The barrier reef that surrounds it, the third largest in the world, is called Old Providence McBean Lagoon; it is easily visited (entry US$5.50). The official languages of its 5500 inhabitants are Spanish and Caribbean English. Musical influences are the mento from the Antilles, calypso from Trinidad and reggae from Jamaica. There are no high-rises, apartment blocks or shopping malls on Providencia and its quieter atmosphere than San Andrés attracts more European visitors.

Superb views can be had by climbing from Casabaja/Bottom House or Aguamansa/Smooth Water to the peak (about one hour, US$15 with a guide). There are relics of the fortifications built on the island during its disputed ownership. Horse riding is available, and boat trips can be made to Santa Catalina and to Crab Cay (good snorkelling – see What to do, below) to the northeast.

Santa Catalina (an old pirate lair) is separated from Providencia by a channel cut to improve defence of the island. This is crossed by the wooden Lover's Bridge (Malecón de los Enamorados). Go left after crossing this bridge (right is a dead end) and walk for about 500 m. Climb stairs to the Virgin statue for excellent views of Providencia. If you continue past the Virgin and go down the flight of stairs you will arrive at a very small beach (nice snorkelling). On the west side is a rock formation called Morgan's Head; from the side it looks like a profile.

Of the three main beaches, Manzanillo is the best preserved and wildest. Not much space for lying out, but pleasant for walking. Roland's Roots Bar has excellent live, traditional island music on weekends. South West Bay/Suroeste has stunning beaches and is the best for hanging out. There is access at each end. Agua Dulce is where most hotels and restaurants are.

Listings San Andrés and Providencia

Tourist information

Centro Administrativo Aury (T8-514 8054), provides information on Providencia. **San Andrés Tourist office** (Av Newball, opposite Restaurante La Regatta, T8-512 5058, securismosai@yahoo. com, Mon-Fri 0800-1200, 1400-1800), is helpful, English spoken, maps and hotel lists. There is also a kiosk at the end of Av 20 de Julio, across from the sea, daily 0800-2000.

Where to stay

Hotels quote rates per person, but we list prices for double rooms. Prices include half board, but most can be booked without meals. Most raise prices by 20-30% on 15 Dec.

San Andrés
The Decameron group has 5 hotels on San Andrés, www.decameron.com.

$$$$ Casa Harb
C 11, No 10-83, T8-512 6348, www.casaharb.com.
Just outside town, this boutique hotel takes
its inspiration from the Far East and is the
most stylish on the island. Each room is
individually decorated with antique furniture,
enormous granite baths, infinity pool and
home-cooked meals.

$$$$ Portobelo
*Av Colombia, No 5A-69, T8-512 7008,
www.portobelohotel.com.*
In a couple of buildings at the western
end of the *malecón*, large beds.

$$$$ Sunset Hotel
*Cra Circunvalar Km 13, T318-523 2286,
http://sunsethotelspa.com.*
On the western side of the island, ideal for diving
or for getting away from the crowds. Bright, fresh
rooms set around a salt-water swimming pool.
Restaurant with international and regional food
in a typical clapboard house, dive shop next door.

$$$-$ pp El Viajero Hostel
*Av 20 de Julio No 3A-122, T8-512 7497,
www.elviajerohostels.com.*
A member of the South American El Viajero
hostel chain. It has private rooms and dorms
(US$19 per bed) all with ensuite bath, a/c and
safe boxes. Breakfast included in the price,
bicycles can be hired, rooftop bar and scuba
certification courses. There's a tourist office at
reception that books all tours and excursions.
Like its sister hostel in Cartagena, El Viajero is
for the party crowd.

$$ Hernando Henry
*Av Las Américas, No 4-84, T8-512 3416,
www.hotelhernandohenry.com.*
At the back of town, shoddy but passable rooms,
cheaper with fan, laundry service.

$$ La Posada de Lulú
Av Antioquia, No 2-28, T8-512 2919/523 6308.
Brightly coloured hostel, comfortable rooms
and 2 apartments to rent for longer stays,
excellent restaurant. Recommended.

$$ Posada Doña Rosa
*Av Las Américas con Aeropuerto, T8-512 3649,
http://posadarosa.blogspot.co.uk.*
A 2-min walk from the airport, this is a reasonable
an economical option, use of kitchen, TV room, a
short walk from the beach. Also has 2 apartments
to rent.

Providencia
Rooms can be rented at affordable prices in local
houses or *posadas nativas*. Hotels in Agua Dulce
are 10 mins by motor taxi (US$1) from centre or
1-hr walk. Suroeste is a 20-min walk from Agua
Dulce. The **Decameron** group (www.decameron.
co), represents 5 properties on the island,
including **Cabañas Miss Elma** (T8-514 8229), and
Cabañas Miss Mary (T8-514 8454), at Aguadulce.

$$$ Posada del Mar
Aguadulce, T8-514 8168, www.decameron.co.
Pink and purple clapboard house with
comfortable rooms, each with a terrace
and hammock, hot water.

$$$ Sol Caribe Providencia
Agua Dulce, www.solarhoteles.com.
Chain hotel with 2-5 night deals, pool, sea views,
a/c, TV, fridge, bright.

$$$-$$ Sirius
Suroeste, T8-514 8213, www.siriushotel.net.
Large, colourful house set back from the beach.
Large, light rooms, some with balconies, on the
beach. Also dive centre, kayaks, wakeboarding,
horse riding, massage. The owner speaks
German, Italian and English. Half-board and
diving packages available.

$$ Old Providence
*Diagonal Alcaldía Municipal, Santa Isabel (centre),
T318-788 0099, Facebook: Hotel-Old-Providence.*
Above supermarket **Erika**, rooms are basic
but clean.

Restaurants

San Andrés
Good fish and seafood meals at San Luis beach.

$$$-$$ La Regatta
Av Newball, next to Club Náutico, T8-512 0437.
Seafood restaurant on a pier, fine reputation.

$$$-$$ Margherita e Carbonara
Av Colombia, No 1-93, T8-512 1050.
Good Italian, pizzas and coffee.

$$ Niko's
Av Colombia, No 1-93, T8-512 7535.
Bills itself as a seafood restaurant though its
steaks are actually better. Lovely setting by
the water.

Providencia

Typical dish is *rondón*, a mix of fish, conch, yucca and dumplings, cooked in coconut milk. Fish and crab are most common. Corn ice cream is also popular – it tastes a little like vanilla but a little sweeter.

As well as hotels, good places include: **Café Studio**, between Agua Dulce and Suroeste. Great pies and spaghetti.

$$ Caribbean Place (Donde Martín)
Aguadulce, T311-287 7238.
Bogoteño chef Martín Quintero uses local ingredients.

$$ Roland's Roots bar
Playa Manzanillo, T8-514 8417,
rolandsbeach@hotmail.com.
Parties at Roland's bar-restaurant are legendary. The menu is mainly seafood. He also hires tents ($).

$ Arturo Newbell
On Suroeste beach, next to Miss Mary.
Palm-thatched shack right on the beach, highly recommended for its fish soup, lobster and other seafood.

Entertainment

San Andrés
San Andrés is famous in Colombia for its different styles of music, including the local form of calypso, soca, reggae and church music. Concerts are held at the **Old Coliseum** (every Sat at 2100 in the high season).

Festivals

San Andrés
Jun Jardín del Caribe. A folkloric festival.
20 Jul Independence celebrations on San Andrés with various events.
Late Nov 10 days of music, parades and cultural events for San Andrés de Apóstol, patron saint of the island.
Dec Rainbow Festival. Reggae and calypso music.

Providencia
The island holds its **carnival** in **Jun**.

What to do

San Andrés

Canopying
Canopy La Loma, *Vía La Loma-Barrack, T314-447 9868*. Site at the top of the hill in San Andrés. 3 'flights' over the trees at 450 m, 300 m and 200 m all with spectacular views out to sea. Safety precautions and equipment are good.

Diving
Diving off San Andrés is good; depth varies from 3 to 30 m, visibility from 10 to 30 m. There are 3 types of site: walls of seaweed and minor coral reefs, different types of coral, and underwater plateaux with much marine life. It is possible to dive in 70% of the insular platform. Diving trips to the reef:
Banda Dive Shop, *Hotel Lord Pierre, Local 104, T8-513 1080, www.bandadiveshop.com*. PADI qualified, various courses. Fast boat and good equipment.
Sharky Dive Shop, *Cra Circunvalar Km 13, T8-512 0651, www.sharkydiveshop.com*. Good equipment and excellent, English-speaking guides. PADI qualifications and a beginner's course held in the Sunset Hotel's saltwater pool.

Watersports and boat trips
Cooperativa Lancheros, *on the beach in San Andrés town*. Can arrange fishing trips, wind-surfing, jet skiing and kite surfing. Snorkelling equipment can be hired for US$5.
Galeon Morgan, *Centro Comercial New Point Plaza, T8-512 8787*. Boat tours to El Acuario.

Providencia

Diving
Recommended diving spots on the Old McBean Lagoon reef are Manta's Place, a good place to see manta rays; Felipe's Place where there is a submerged figure of Christ; and Stairway to Heaven, which has a large wall of coral and big fish.
Felipe Diving, *South West Bay, T8-851 8775, www.felipediving.com*. Mini and full courses, also rents snorkel equipment, can arrange lodging. Owner Felipe Cabeza even has a diving spot on the reef named after him. Warmly recommended. See also **Hotel Sirius**, above. PADI qualifications, mini courses.

Snorkelling and boat trips
Recommended snorkelling sites include the waters around Santa Catalina, where there

are many caves to explore as well as Morgan's Head and lots of starfish; Hippie's Place, which has a little bit of everything; and El Faro (The Lighthouse), the end of the reef before it drops into deep sea.

Tour operators

Body Contact, *Aguadulce, T8-514 8160, http:// cabanasaguadulce.com.* Owner Jennifer Archbold organizes excursions, fishing and hiking trips, currency exchange, accommodation, and more.

Walking

A good 1.5-km walk over Manchineel Hill, between Bottom House (Casa Baja) and South West Bay, through tropical forest, fine views, many types of bird, iguanas and blue lizards.

Transport

San Andrés

Air Regular flights from **Bogotá**, **Cartagena**, **Cali** and **Medellín**. **Copa** once daily to **Panama City**. Sun flights are always heavily booked, similarly Jul-Aug, Dec-Jan. The airport at San Andrés is 15 mins' walk to town centre; buses to centre and San Luis leave from opposite the airport.

Bus Buses run every 15 mins on the eastern side of the island, US$1, and more often at night and during the holidays.

Taxi Taxis around the island cost US$15-20, but in town fares double after 2200. To airport US$7-9 (*colectivo* US$1). Motorbikes are easy to hire, US$40, as are golf buggies, US$50 a day. Cars can also be hired for 2 hrs or for a day. Passport may be required as deposit; you must have a driver's license. Bikes are easy to hire, but they may be in poor condition.

Providencia

Air **Satena** and **Searca** fly from San Andrés twice a day. Bookable only in San Andrés. Essential to confirm flights to guarantee a seat. Schedules change frequently. Taxi from airport to centre, US$10 (fixed).

Boat Catamaran Sensation, www.catamaran sanandresyprovidencia.com, sails Mon, Wed, Thu, Fri, Sun 0800, returning at 1430, US$53 one way, US$100 return, 4 hrs. Cargo boat trips leave from San Andrés, taking 4 uncomfortable hrs, 3 times a week, US$65 return. They usually leave at 0600-0700. *Miss Isabel*, *Doña Olga* and *Raziman* make the trip regularly, about US$18 one way. Speak directly to the captain at the port in San Andrés, or enquire at the Port Authority (Capitanía del Puerto) in San Luis.

Motoped hire US$30-40 per day from many hotels. No licence or deposit needed. Golf buggies are also available for US$40-50 per day.

Northwest
Colombia

Encompassing the cordilleras Central and Occidental, Antioquia is the largest of the western departments. It is full of diversity and is an important agricultural and commercial region, with the rejuvenated city of Medellín as its urban hub. The people of Antioquia are called 'paisas'. To the west, between the Cordillera Occidental and the Pacific Coast, from Panamá to Valle del Cauca, Chocó is one of Colombia's least developed and most beautiful departments.

Medellín *Colour map 1, B2.*

modern art, tango clubs and cable cars

☆Medellín (population 2,700,000), capital of Antioquia, is considered by many to be the engine of Colombia; *paisas* are known for their canny business sense as well as their hospitality. Previously the home and headquarters of notorious narco-trafficker Pablo Escobar, Medellín has, since his death, shaken off its association with drugs and violence in what is one of the most remarkable turnarounds in Latin America. It is now a fresh, vibrant, prosperous city known for its progressive social politics and culture. In the centre, few colonial buildings remain, but many large new buildings incorporate modern works of art. Music, arts and gastronomy festivals attract many visitors, and the flower festival, the Desfile de Silleteros, in August, is the most spectacular parade in Colombia.

Central Medellín

Plaza Botero (or de las Esculturas) is dotted with 23 bronze sculptures by **Fernando Botero**, who is Colombia's leading contemporary artist, born in Medellín in 1932. One side of the plaza has **El Palacio de la Cultura Rafael Uribe**, formerly the governor's office, which is now a cultural centre and art gallery (free entry). Across the square is the **Museo de Antioquia** ① *Cra 52,*

> **Tip...**
> Don't miss a ride on the cable car to Santo Domingo Savio to gain a bird's eye view of the city and to witness the regeneration of one the city's most deprived barrios.

No 52-43, T4-251 3636, www.museodeantioquia.co, Mon-Sat 1000-1730, Sun and holidays, 1000-1630, US$6, metro stop: Parque Berrío, which has well-displayed works by contemporary Colombian artists, including a large collection by Botero. More works by Botero can be seen in **Parque San Antonio** ① *between C 44/46 and Cra 46,* including the 'Torso Masculino' (which complements the female version in Parque Berrío), and the 'Bird of Peace' which was severely damaged by a guerrilla bomb in 1996. At Botero's request, it has been left unrepaired as a symbol of the futility of violence, with a new sculpture placed alongside. Parque Berrío has the church of Señora de la Candelaria on one side, formerly the city's cathedral. It was succeeded by the **Catedral Metropolitana on Parque de Bolívar**. Built between 1875 and 1931, this is claimed to be the third-largest brick building in the world. Parque Bolívar has flowering trees and a fountain display. The **Mercado San Alejo** is held here on the first Saturday of every month (except January), selling handicrafts at good prices. Of the colonial churches near the centre, white **La Veracruz** ① *C 51, No 52-58, T4-512 5095, Mon-Sat 0730-1800, Sun Mass 0830-1000, 1200-1600,* is a national historical monument.

Best for
Adventures ■ Urban regeneration ■ Wildlife

Essential Medellín

Finding your feet

The city is based around the old and the new cathedrals, the former on Parque Berrío and the latter overlooking Parque de Bolívar. The main commercial area is three blocks away on Carrera 46. In the south, El Poblado is an upmarket commercial and residential area. This is where many hotels, hostels and restaurants can be found. The area around Parque Lleras, known as the Zona Rosa, is where most of the bars and nightclubs are situated. West of the centre, Carrera 70 and Calle 44 are busy commercial and entertainment sectors with many hotels, shopping centres and the huge **Atanasio Girardot** sports stadium nearby. Many central streets are named as well as numbered. Particularly important are: Carrera 46, part of the inner ring road, which is known popularly as 'Avenida Oriental'; Carrera 80/Carrera 81/Diagonal 79, the outer ring road to the west, which is called 'La Ochenta' throughout; Calle 51/52, east of the centre is 'La Playa'; and Calle 33, which crosses the Río Medellín to become Calle 37, is called 'La Treinta y Tres'. The International airport (José María Córdova, also called Rionegro) is 28 km from Medellín and 9 km from the town of Rionegro. The city airport, Enrique Olaya Herrera, has regional flights to some destinations in Colombia.

Getting around

City buses are comfortable and plentiful, but the overground Metro is the quickest way to get around. In the centre, Pasaje Junín (Carrera 49) is closed to traffic from Parque de Bolívar to Parque San Antonio (Calle 46), as is the central part of Carrera 52, which makes walking in this area a pleasure. The terminal for long-distance buses going north and east is **Terminal del Norte**, about 3 km north of the centre, close to Caribe Metro station. For buses going south, **Terminal del Sur** is alongside the domestic Olaya Herrera airport, a 1.5-km taxi ride from Poblado Metro station. See also Transport, page 967.

When to go

Known as 'The City of Eternal Spring', Medellín has a pleasant, temperate climate year-round; warm during the day and cool in the evening. Visitors flock to the flower festival in August.

North of the centre

To the north, near the University of Antioquia campus, are **Joaquín Antonio Uribe botanical gardens** ① C 73, No 51D-14, T4-444 5500, www.botanicomedellin.org, daily 0900-1630, free, metro Universidad, with 5500 species of plants, orchids and trees. There are two restaurants, one more economical than the other, a café and facilities for children. Opposite the botanical gardens is the **Parque Explora** ① Cra 52, No 73-75, T4-516 8300, www.parque explora.org, Tue-Fri 0830-1730 (ticket office closes 1600), Sat, Sun and holiday Mondays, 1000-1830 (ticket office closes 1700), US$8, a science and technology museum plus associated aquarium, planetarium (entry US$5, www.planetariomedellin.org) and other spaces. With more than 300 interactive scientific puzzles and games, this is fun for adults and heaven for kids. Nearby is **Museo Casa Gardeliana** ① Cra 45, No 76-50, T4-444 2633, Mon-Sat 0900-1700, shows last Fri of month 1800-2200 (free entry, donations welcome), commemorating the tango legend Carlos Gardel, who died in a plane crash in Medellín in 1935.

West of the centre

Museo de Arte Moderno ① Cra 44N, No 19A-100, T4-444 2622, www.elmamm.org, Tue-Fri 0900-1800, Sat 1000-1800, Sun 1000-1700, US$3.50, children, students with card and seniors US$2.50, has a small collection, shows films, has a variety of special visits and holds many events at other locations. **Biblioteca Pública Piloto para América Latina** ① Cra 64, No 50-32, T4-460 0590, entrance at Cra 64 y C 52, www.bibliotecapiloto.gov.co, Mon-Sat 0830-1730, is one of the best public libraries in the country with art and photo exhibitions, readings and films. **Puntocero** ① at the C 67 river bridge is an elegant steel double arch with a pendulum marking the centre of the city.

In Alpujarra district, southwest of the centre is **El Edificio Inteligente** ① Cra 58, No 42-125, a highly energy-efficient building used jointly by Medellín's public services. Nearby is the **Parque de Los Pies Descalzos** (The Barefoot Park), a relaxing space with cafés, sand pits, Zen garden and fountains. Also here is the interactive **Museo del Agua EPM** ① Cra 57, No 42-139, T4-380 6960, www.epm.com.co, Tue-Fri 0830-1730, Sat-Sun 1030-1830, US$2.50.

As you ride the metro you will notice two prominent hills in the Aburrá valley. **Cerro Nutibara** ① C 30A y Cra 55, T4-235 8370, in the southwest, has good views over the city. The is a stage for open air concerts, a sculpture park, a miniature Antioquian village (known as Pueblito Paisa), souvenir and crafts shops and restaurants. **Cerro El Volador** (seen as the Metro turns between Universidad and Caribe stations) is tree-covered and the site of an important indigenous burial ground.

Listings Medellín *maps below and pages 964 and 967.*

Tourist information

Information booth
Plaza Botero, Cra 51, No 52A-48, T4-511 1309,
http://infolocal.comfenalcoantioquia.com.
Mon-Sat 0900-1700.
English, French and Spanish spoken,
very helpful staff.

Oficina de Turismo de Medellín
C 41, No 55-80, of 306, in the Centro de
Convenciones, T4-261 7277, www.medellin.travel.
For information on the city. Helpful staff, English
spoken. Has kiosks (PITs) at both airports, both
bus terminals, at the Pueblito Paisa at the top
of Cerro Nutibara, open daily, the Arví cablecar
station (El Tambo) and in the main hall of Plaza
Mayor (less regular hours).

Other sources of information include the
Subsecretaría de Turismo, C 53A, No 42-101,

p 11, Ala B, T4-385 6966; www.guiaturisticade
medellin.com; and the **national parks office**
(C 49, No 78A-67, T4-422 0883). The **tourist police**
can be contacted on T4-265 5907 or, 4-437 6125.

Where to stay

Most of the city's better accommodation
options are around Cra 70 and in El Poblado.

Central Medellín
Many of the cheaper hostels in this part of
town are now *acostaderos* or pay-by-the-hour
brothels with questionable security that we
advise you to avoid.

$$$ Nutibara
C 52A, No 50-46, T4-511 5111,
www.hotelnutibara.com).
This grand old lady of Medellín was the city's first
major hotel, built in 1945. Its best days may be
behind it, but it retains a certain art deco charm,

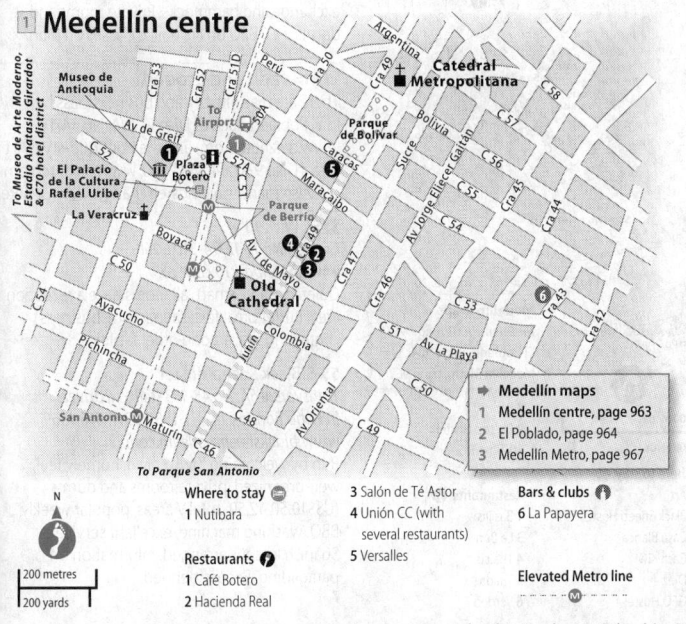

① Medellín centre

N

200 metres
200 yards

Where to stay 🛏
1 Nutibara

Restaurants 🍴
1 Café Botero
2 Hacienda Real

3 Salón de Té Astor
4 Unión CC (with
  several restaurants)
5 Versalles

→ **Medellín maps**
1 Medellín centre, page 963
2 El Poblado, page 964
3 Medellín Metro, page 967

Bars & clubs 🍸
6 La Papayera

Elevated Metro line
- - - - -Ⓜ- - - -

has all modern amenities, including a pool, sauna, Turkish bath, a food court with banks and Wi-Fi zone on the first floor and a wine bar in the tunnel that connected with the old Residencias Nutibara.

West of the centre

Cra 70 (metro Estadio) is full of hotels in roughly the same price range. Although standards can vary they are good value. There are plenty of eateries, bars and discos as well.

$$$-$$ Florida Inn
Cra 70, No 44B-38, T4-260 4900,
www.hotelfloridamedellin.com.
A bit more upmarket than others, car park and restaurant.

$$ Lukas
Cra 70, No 44A-28, T4-260 1761,
www.lukashotel.com.

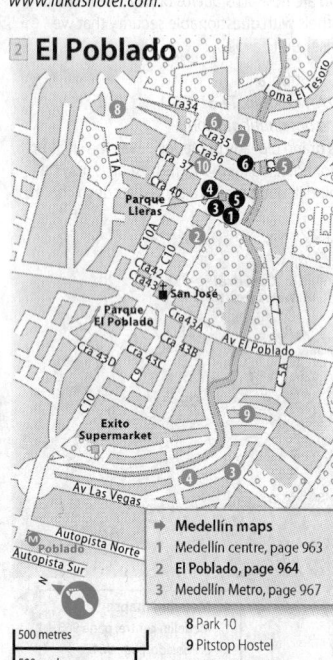

El Poblado

⮕ **Medellín maps**
1 Medellín centre, page 963
2 El Poblado, page 964
3 Medellín Metro, page 967

500 metres
500 yards

Where to stay 🛏
2 Art
3 Black Sheep Hostel
4 Casa Blanca
5 Casa Kiwi
6 Diez
7 GEO Hostel
8 Park 10
9 Pitstop Hostel
10 Tiger Hostel

Restaurants 🍴
1 Basílica
3 Le Bon
4 Thaico
5 Triada
6 Verdeo

Crisp rooms with safe and all facilities, weekend and long-stay rates available.

$$ Plaza 70
Cra 70, No 45E-117, T4-412 3266,
www.hotelplaza70.com.co.
This functional hotel has clean, prettily decorated rooms, breakfast not included, meals at nearby restaurant arranged.

$$ Villa Real
Cra 70, No 45E-153, T4-414 4905,
www.hotelvillarealmedellin.co.
Comfortable, modern hotel, cheaper without street view or a/c, parking.

$ Hostal Medellín
C 44B, No 69-13, T4-260 0660,
www.hostalmedellin.com.
Spacious hostel, private rooms and dorms (US$8.50), German/Colombian run, popular with bikers. Garden with a hammock, pool table, organizes tours, close to Estadio Metro. Recommended.

$ Palm Tree Hostal
Cra 67, No 48D-63, T4-444 7256, www.hostalenmedellin.com. (Metro Suramericana, behind Exito supermarket on C 50).
Good backpackers' hostel, bike hire, book exchange and hammocks. Private rooms and dorms, free BBQ on Fri, dance classes on Mon.

El Poblado and around

There are many luxury and business class hotels in El Poblado, such as **Diez** (C 10A, No 34-11, www.diezhotel.com) and the boutique-style **Art** (Cra 41, No 9-31, T4-369 7900, www.arthotel.com. co). Also many more hostels than we can list here.

$$$$ Park 10
Cra 36B No 11-12, T4-310 6060,
www.hotelpark10.com.co.
Quiet location, smart, all rooms have a reception area. Buffet breakfast, sauna, gym, business centre and spa, among other facilities.

$$-$ Black Sheep Hostel
Transversal 5A, No 45-133 (tell taxi drivers it's in Patio Bonito), T4-311 1589, T317-518 1369, www.blacksheepmedellin.com.
Run by welcoming Kiwi, Kelvin, homely feel, well-organized, private rooms and dorms (US$10.50-12.50 pp), TV areas, popular weekly BBQ, washing machine, excellent service, Spanish lessons arranged. Information on paragliding. Recommended.

$$-$ Casa Blanca
Transversal 5A, No 45-256 (Patio Bonito),
T4-586 5149, www.casablancamedellin.com.
Large hostel with dorms (US$8-10) and
private rooms, quiet location, parking for
cars or motorbikes, pool table, table tennis.

$$-$ Pitstop Hostel
Cra 43E, No5-110, T4-352 1176,
www.pitstophostel.com.
A big hostel with party atmosphere, swimming
pool, Irish bar, steam room, gym, pool table and
a huge outdoor area. Dorms US$9-11 pp, private
rooms with and without bath for up to 4 people.
Tours and events organized.

$ Casa Kiwi
Cra 36, No 7-10, T4-268 2668,
www.casakiwihostel.com.
Private rooms and dorms, US$10 pp. Good
travellers' hostel, hammock terrace, roof-top
pool, bar and TV room with theatre seating.
Near Parque Lleras, welcoming, paragliding
arranged. Recommended.

$ GEO Hostel
Cra 35, No 8A-58, T4-311 7150, www.geohostel.com.
Smart, modern mid-range option, close to the
Zona Rosa, private rooms and 8-bed dorms
(US$10 pp including breakfast).

$ Tiger Hostel
Cra 36, No 10-49, T4-311 6079,
www.tigerpawmedellin.com.
A variety of rooms, some with bath, dorms US$8-
9, remodelled in 2016, tourist packages, sports
bar with micro brews and lots of activities.

Restaurants

Central Medellín

$$ Café Botero
Cra 52, No 52-43.
Excellent lunchtime venue in the Museo
de Antioquia building. Fish, fine steaks
and delicious puddings.

$$ Hacienda Real
Cra 49, No 52-98 (next door to Salón de Té Astor).
Pleasant restaurant with balcony seating,
overlooking Pasaje Junín/Cra 49.

$$ Versalles
Pasaje Junín, No 53-59, T4-511-9146,
http://versallesmedellin.com.
Famous Argentine-run *pastelería* and restaurant,
parrillas and *empanadas*, good-value set

lunches. Lovely coffees and breakfasts too.
Highly recommended.

$$-$ Salón de Té Astor
Cra 49, No 52-84.
Delightful traditional tea and pastry house,
famous for its chocolate delicacies and ice cream.

$$-$ Unión CC
Cra 49 (Junín), No 52-107, www.
elunioncentrocomercial.com.
Many eateries on the Balcón de Comidas of this
shopping mall, including **San Miguel Cazuelas**,
for typical dishes; **Malibú Gourmet Parrilla**,
crêpes, pastas, salads; **Latin Coffee**, combos,
crêpes, sandwiches; all do breakfasts.

West of the centre
Several eateries on Cra 70, No 45E block,
all serving *bandeja paisa* (**$$$**) and other
cheaper lunches.

$$ La Margarita No 2
Cra 70, No 45E-11.
Antioquian dishes in a lively, friendly atmosphere.

$$-$ Pomo d'Oro
C 42, No 71-24, T4-412 3404,
www.restaurantepomodoro.com.
Wide variety of pastas and sauces at
reasonable prices.

$ Opera Pizza
C 42, No 70-22, T4-413 1920,
http://operapizza.jimdo.com.
Paisas swear these are the best pizzas in town.

$ ¡Orale!
C 41, No 70-138.
Excellent little Mexican cantina with tables
on the street. Another branch at Cra 43B,
10A-49, El Poblado, does Mexican and pizza.
Recommended.

El Poblado and around
In Parque Lleras/Zona Rosa, there are so many
places that it is impossible to mention them all.
Those we do list have been found to be good,
but recommendations change as places become
fashionable. Just wander around and see what
takes your fancy, but at weekends especially,
don't leave it too late as places get very busy,
with queues for tables.

$$$ Basílica
Cra 38, No 8A-42, T4-311 7366.
Steaks, sushi and Peruvian specialities
on an open terrace on Parque Lleras.

$$$ Triada
Cra 38, No 8 (Vía Primavera)-03, T4-311 5781.
Enormous restaurant/bar/club in the heart of
the Zona Rosa, steaks, sushi, salads and Tex Mex,
good atmosphere. Packed at weekends.

$$$-$$ Thaico
C 9A, No 37A-40, T4-352 2166.
Good Thai food, popular spot for watching
televized sports. 3-for-1 happy hour cocktails
until 1900.

$$$-$$ Verdeo
Parque Explora, Cra 35, No 8A-3, T4-444 0934,
www.ricoverdeo.com.
Excellent vegetarian on a pedestrian alley, open
from 1200 daily (closes 1600 on Mon and holidays).

$$ Le Bon
C 9, No 39-09, T57-266 7790.
French café with lovely atmosphere.
Often has jazz in the evening.

Bars and clubs

In El Poblado, the best bars and clubs are in
the Zona Rosa, around Parque Lleras; there
are plenty of them. If the prices of the Zona
Rosa get too much, an alternative after-hours
location is Sabaneta (www.sabaneta.gov.co),
11 km from the centre, with an attractive plaza.
It's popular with young and old alike. There are
several excellent bars and restaurants with lots
of local history. Take the metro to Sabaneta or
La Estrella or a taxi from El Poblado, US$10-
15. Also check out Medellín's local brewery,
Tres Cordilleras (www.3cordilleras.com).

El Viejo John
Cra 45, No 70 Sur-42, Sabaneta, T4-288 7022.
A popular local spot with strings of chorizo hanging
from the ceiling. Also serves typical dishes.

Fonda Sitio Viejo
C 70 Sur, No 44-25, Sabaneta, T4-288 1170.
Another bar full of character. This one has
photographs of every church in Medellín.

La Herrería
Cra 45, No 70 Sur-24, Sabaneta, T4-288 1385.
Packed to the ceiling with pictures of local
characters, Mexican sombreros, saddles
and bananas.

La Papayera
C 53, No 42-55, Centro, T4-239 3400.
A local institution for salsa, popular with
foreigners. Live salsa on Tue and Thu nights.

Cinema
Check the press for movies, music, theatre and
other cultural events.
Centro Colombo Americano, *Cra 45, No 53-24,*
T4-204 0404, www.colomboworld.com.
Shows foreign art films, also holds cultural
events, has a café and bookshop. The main
malls have multiplexes.

Tango
Medellín is famous in Colombia for its love
of tango. There are popular tango bars in
El Envigado.
La Boa, *C 53, No 43-59, T4-239 3580.* This bar
has been around for more than 40 years and
is famous for its tango and jazz, open nightly
until 0300.
Salón Málaga, *Cra 51, No 45-80, T4-231 2658,*
www.salonmalaga.com. One of Medellín's oldest
tango bars.

Theatre
Teatro Metropolitano, *C 41, No 57-30,*
T4-232 2858, www.teatrometropolitano.com.
Major artistic presentations, from classical
concerts to modern dance.

Mar/Apr Semana Santa (Holy Week) is
celebrated with religious parades.
Jun Festival Internacional de Tango.
Jul International Poetry Festival, see
www.festivaldepoesiade medellin.org.
1st week of Aug Flower fair (Feria de las
Flores/Desfile de Silleteros) (www.feriadelas
floresmedellin.gov.co) is held annually with
spectacular parades and music, one of the finest
shows in Colombia.
End Aug Otro Sabor gastronomy festival.
Sep-Nov International Jazz and World Music
Festival, www.festivalmedejazz.com.

Expoartesano, held in the Plaza Mayor exhibition
centre, is an annual handicrafts exhibition, http://
artesaniasdecolombia.com.co; its date changes
each year. There are many other music and
cultural festivals throughout the year.

Dance classes
Academia Dance, *Cra 46, No 10 Sur-36, T4-444*
8583, www.danceas.com. Offers many dance
lessons, including salsa, merengue and rumba.

Language classes

Eafit University, *Cra 49, No 7 Sur 50, Av Las Vegas*, *T4-261 9500*, www.eafit.edu.co. Popular, well-organized Spanish courses.

Pablo Escobar tours

A number of operators offer tours of the most significant places from the life and times of this notorious leader of the Medellín drugs cartel. Contact **Paisa Road** (T317-489 2629, www.paisaroad.com), or via hostels.

Sports complex

Estadio Atanasio Girardot, *Cras 70-73, C 48-50, T304-375 7149*. Football, baseball, velodrome, swimming, next to the *Estadio* Metro station. Just outside the station is **EnCicla** bicycle hire (www.encicla.gov.co).

Tour operators

Destino Colombia, *C 50, No 65-42, CC Contemporáneo, loc 225, T4-260 6868*, www.destinocolombia.com. Tours to nearby attractions in Antioquia and nationwide. Very well-informed English-speaking guides. Can also arrange flights. Recommended.

Real City Tours, www.realcitytours.com. Pablo Alvarez-Correa and his team lead tours from Alpujarra metro station Mon-Fri 0900 and 1445, Sat 1000, about 4 hrs, in English, excellent, enthusiastic, pay by tip. Also has an Exotic Fruits Tour. Essential to book in advance on the website.

Transport

Air **José María Córdova international airport** (T4-444 2818, www.airplan.aero, also called Rionegro) is 28 km, 40 mins, from Medellín by road and 9 km from the town of Rionegro. Taxi to town from US$20-22. *Buseta* to centre, US$4, frequent service from 0330-1800, taking about 1 hr to the San Diego terminal on the small road (Cra 50A/C 53) behind **Hotel Nutibara**. To Rionegro from the airport US$2 bus, US$8 taxi. The airport has good shops and services, but no left luggage. Frequent services to **Bogotá**, **Cartagena**, and all major Colombian cities.

Municipal airport: **Enrique Olaya Herrera**, airport information T4-365 6100, www.aeropuertoolayaherrera.gov.co, 10 mins by taxi from the centre, US$5.50, or you can take the metro to Poblado for all but the last 1.5 km. Taxi to/from Rionegro airport US$18. National flights only including to **Quibdó** (change here for **Nuquí**), **Acandí**, **Capurganá** and major cities.

The terminal for long-distance buses going north and east is **Terminal del Norte** at Cra 64

(Autopista del Norte) y Transversal 78 (Cra 64C, No 78-58), T4-444 8020, about 3 km north of the centre, with shops, cafés, left luggage, ATMs and other facilities. It is well policed. Walkway from Metro stop Caribe. Taxi to/from the centre US$7. To/from **Bogotá**, 9-12 hrs, US$18-21, frequent with many companies. To **Cartagena**, 15 hrs, US$41 (take food with you, the stops tend to be at expensive restaurants). Same fare to **Barranquilla**, 18 hrs, and to **Santa Marta**.

3 **Medellín Metro**

Medellín maps	
1	Medellín centre, page 963
2	El Poblado, page 964
3	Medellín Metro, page 967

Niquía
Bello
Madera
Acevedo
Andalucía
Santo Domingo
Arví
Popular
Tricentenario
Terminal del Norte
Caribe
Universidad
(Service Link)
Hospital
La Aurora
Prado
Vallejuelos
Parque Berrío (see map detail)
Juan XXIII
Santa Lucía
San Javier
Estadio
San Antonio
Floresta
Cisneros
Alpujarra
Suramericana
Exposiciones
Industriales
Olaya Herrera Airport
Terminal del Sur
Poblado (see map detail)
Aguacatala
Ayurá
Envigado
To Sabaneta & La Estrella

Línea A
Línea B
Línea J
Línea K
Línea L

N
Not to scale

To **Turbo**, US$18-21 with **Gómez Hernández** (the best), 10 hrs. To **Magangué** (for Mompós), US$41, with **Rápido Ochoa**.

Bus City buses charge US$0.65. Busetas charge US$0.70. For buses going south, **Terminal del Sur**, Cra 65, No 8B-91, T444 80 20, or T361 1499, alongside the Olaya Herrera airport. Similar services to Terminal del Norte plus a shopping centre. Take No 143 bus marked 'Terminal del Sur' from C 47 (in front of Edificio del Café) along Cra 46, or metro to Poblado, then a taxi for the remaining 1.5 km to the bus station, US$4 (US$6 to centre). To **Quibdó**, 7-8 hrs, US$17-21, with **Rápido Ochoa**. Frequent buses to **Manizales**, 4-7 hrs US$12-17, including **Empresa Arauca**. To **Pereira**, 6-8 hrs, US$14-21. Frequent buses for **Cali**, **Flota Magdalena** among others, US$19-24, 7-8 hrs. To **Popayán**, US$30-35, 12 hrs, **Flota Magadalena**. To **Ipiales**, US$50, 20 hrs.

Metro and cable car The city's integrated transport system (metro, cable car, tram and bus detailed here – www.metromedellin.gov.co) operates Mon-Sat 0430-2300, Sun and hols 0500-2200. A single journey (anywhere on the system) is US$0.65. There are 2 metro lines: A from Niquía in the east to La Estrella in the south, B from San Javier to San Antonio, where they intersect. A tramway continues from San Antonio to Oriente and two rapid-transit bus lines link Parque Aranjuez and Universidad de Medellín, taking different routes around the centre. There are also three connecting cable cars, known as Metro Cable: J from San Javier to La Aurora; K serving the areas on the mountain slopes up to Santo Domingo Savio, and L from Santo Domingo further up the mountains to Arví (0900-1800, closed Mon, or Tue if Mon is a holiday); change at Acevedo on line A for this cable car. 2 additional cable cars, from Miraflores to Trece de Noviembre (M) and Oriente to Villa Sierra (H), both connecting with the tramway, are under construction.

Taxi Meters are used; minimum charge US$2.50. **Radio taxis:** Cootransmede, T4-265 6565, www.cootransmede.com, Tax Andaluz, T4-444 5555, http://taxandaluz.co. Many others. For airport service for up to 8 people, try **Iván Agudelo Gómez**, T313-744 0667, T315-509 9035.

Around Medellín

paisa villages and a very large rock

Southeast from Medellín

Five kilometres from Medellín airport is **Rionegro** in a delightful valley of gardens and orchards. The **Casa de Convención** and the **cathedral** are worth a visit. There are colourful processions in Easter Week. There are various hotels and many places to eat in and near the plaza.

On the Medellín–Bogotá highway is **Marinilla**, 46 km from Medellín. A road north goes 25 km to ☆ **El Peñol** ① US$5, a precipitous, bullet-shaped rock which towers above the surrounding hills and the Embalse del Peñol reservoir. It has been eroded deeply, but a spiral staircase has been built into a crack from the base to the summit (649 steps). The views from the top are spectacular. At the entrance and summit are snack bars. The rock and the nearby town of **Guatapé** are a popular excursion, especially at weekends. Ask the bus driver to drop you off at the small road leading to El Peñol, from where it's a 10-minute walk uphill to the entrance. Guatapé is 3 km further along the main road. All the houses are cheerfully painted, each with a distinctive frieze. The *malecón* is lined with restaurants and pleasure boats offering tours (US$15-25). There is also a zip-line.

Another popular trip is to **Reserva Natural Cañón del Río Claro** ① *T313-671 4459, www.rioclaroelrefugio.com, daily 0800-2000, free*, clearly signed on the Medellín-Bogotá highway, three hours from either Medellín or Honda. The crystal-clean Claro river is lined with limestone cliffs and is a beautiful, tranquil place to relax and take leisurely walks along its banks. The reserve is noted for its incredible biodiversity with over 50 new species of plants discovered and more than 370 different species of bird identified since its foundation. Oilbirds live in the caves. Take an early bus, spend a day and a night at the reserve and continue to Honda the next day (or vice versa).

Santa Fe de Antioquia *Colour map 1, B2.*

Santa Fe de Antioquia (usually called Santa Fe) is 78 km from Medellín, just west of the Río Cauca, surrounded by mountainous green countryside. It is a safe, peaceful, well-preserved colonial town from where it is best to explore on horseback or bicycle. It is a popular weekend haunt with Antioquians.

Santa Fe was founded as a gold mining town by the Spaniards in 1541 and became famous for its gold jewellery. Today, most of the gold mines have been abandoned but there is still some gold mining in the Río Cauca. In 1813, Santa Fe was declared the capital of the short-lived independent state of Antioquia, but in 1826, its status had collapsed and political control was lost to Medellín.

The lively main plaza is dominated by a fine old Cathedral. There are several other churches worth seeing, notably Santa Bárbara. Next door is a **Museo de Arte Religioso/Museo Juan del Corral** ⓘ *C 11, No 9-77, Mon-Fri 0900-1200, 1400-1730, Sat-Sun 1000-1700, closed Wed*, which has a collection of items from colonial and more recent times. Opposite the Plaza Santa Bárbara is the site of a former slave market. Major local festivals at Easter, Christmas and New Year. **Tourist office** ⓘ *Cra 9 y C 9, T4-853 4139, municipal website http://santafedeantioquia-antioquia.gov.co; see also http://santafedeantioquia.net, Mon-Fri 0800-1200, 1400-1800, Sat 0800-1200.*

South from Medellín

Santa Bárbara lies 57 km south of Medellín on the main road via the town of Caldas, with stunning views in every direction of coffee, banana and sugar plantations, orange-tiled roofs and folds of hills. A further 26 km is **La Pintada**. Here the main road crosses the Río Cauca and continues via Marmato to Manizales. A left turn after La Pintada takes an alternative and particularly attractive route to Manizales through Aguadas, Pácora and Salamina, all perched on mountain ridges. Salamina is a national monument with colonial houses with balconies overlooking pretty streets in a landscape of coffee fincas and wax palms. Its famous Noche de Fuego (7 December) is at the end of the week-long festivities for La Inmaculada Concepción. There are several places to stay and direct transport from Manizales bus terminal (road paved, 2½-three hours, US$6.25). A right turn from La Pintada, meanwhile, heads northwest to some beautiful country on the west side of the Río Cauca.

This region can also be reached shortly after Caldas, by a road to the west which descends through Amagá to cross the Cauca at Bolombolo. From here, several attractive towns can be visited. **Jericó**, is an interesting Antioquian town with a large cathedral, several other churches, two museums and a good view from **Morro El Salvador. Andes** is a busy coffee-buying centre, with several places to stay and to eat. **Jardín** is 16 km southeast of Andes. This pretty Antioquian village is surrounded by cultivated hills, passionfruit farms, trout farms and good horse riding. The plaza is full of flowering shrubs and trees. There is a delightful Fiesta de las Rosas in January. The **Templo Parroquial de la Inmaculada Concepción** is a National Monument and the small museum in the Casa Cultura has paintings and local artifacts. Jardín, like Salamina above, is one of the Pueblos Patrimonio de Colombia (www.pueblospatrimoniodecolombia.co).

Listings Around Medellín

Where to stay

Southeast from Medellín

$$$-$$ Refugio Río Claro
Reservations in Medellín, T4-268 8855, T311-354 0119, www.rioclaroelrefugio.com.
Tranquil spot, good value, delightful wooden lodges with great views of river (hotel, hostel and cabin accommodation). Includes 3 meals, restaurant service. Book ahead. Rafting trips, zip-lines over canyon and hiking trips are extra. Recommended.

$$-$ Lake View Hostel
Over the bridge at the end of the Malecón, Guatapé, T4-861 0023, or T310-378 8743, www.lakeviewhostel.com.

Private rooms and dorms (US$7-9 pp). Activities include boat tours, kayaking, mountain biking, hikes, riding, Spanish classes and fishing.

$ Mi Casa Guatapé
4 mins' before Guatapé at foot of El Peñol, behind Restaurante La Mona, T4-861 0632, www.micasaguatape.com.
Smart, bright rooms, private and shared (US$10 pp), good views, meals extra, plenty of activities can be arranged, Colombian/English owners.

Santa Fe de Antioquia

It's best to book in advance at weekends and public holidays. Rates can be 40% more in high season and bank holiday weekends. Most hotels organize horse rides and town tours and offer weekend packages.

$$$-$$ Caserón Plaza
C 9, No 9-41, T4-853 2040,
www.hotelcaseronplaza.com.co.
Large colonial building, comfortable rooms,
some with balconies looking onto pool, cheaper
Mon-Fri. Sun deck has fantastic views, bike hire.

$$$-$$ Hostal Tenerife
Cra 8, No 9-50, T4-539 1965,
www.hotelcasatenerife.com.co.
Beautifully decorated colonial house. Free use of
house bikes, pool. Recommended.

$$$-$$ Mariscal Robledo
Cra 10, No 9-70, T4-853 1111, http://santafede
antioquia.net/hotelmariscalrobledo.html.
Stylish colonial hotel. Nice pool area with palms.
Good weekend lunch buffet. Recommended.

$$ Las Carnes del Tío
C 10, No 7-22, T4-853 3385,
lascarnesdeltio@gmail.com. Facebook:
lascarnesdeltio.santafedeantioquia.
A restaurant that also offers good rooms with
huge bathrooms. Also dorms with shared bath.

$$-$ Hostal Plaza Mayor
Cra 9, No 9-59, Parque Principal, T4-853 3448,
hostalplazamayor2011@hotmail.com.
Popular with backpackers. There are hammocks,
a small pool and a small *cabaña* with bunk beds.

$ Alejo
C 9, No 10-56, T4-853 1091.
1 block from the Parque Principal, small, basic
rooms, restaurant serves cheap food.

South from Medellín

$$$ El Despertar
T312-326 1134, Jericó, http://eldespertarhotel.com.
Nice rooms and lovely views, good breakfast,
tours arranged, Spanish owner speaks English.

$$$-$$ Hacienda Balandú
Vía Jardín Río Sucio, 800 m from Jardín, T4-444
7110, www.comfenalcoantioquia.com.
Comfortable rooms, pool, gardens, lake, spa, sports,
used by birdwatching groups, good restaurant.

$$$-$$ La Casa de Lola García
C 6 No 7-54, Salamina, T6-859 5919,
www.lacasdelolagarcia.com.
Good central hotel with restaurant, garden,
informative and helpful staff, tours arranged.

Several other residencias and restaurants
by the plaza in Jardín. **Dulces del Jardín**
(C 13 No 5-47, Facebook: dulcesdeljardin),
is a very good sweetshop.

Restaurants

Santa Fe de Antioquia

$$ Las Carnes del Tío
See above.

$ La Comedia
C 11, No 8-03, T4-853 1243. 301-596 3032.
Café/bar/restaurant with music and art
exhibitions, Colombian and international
art house films.

Transport

Southeast from Medellín

Bus From Terminal del Norte in Medellín,
desk 14, many buses to **El Peñol**, US$4, and
Guatapé, US$5 with Sotransvicente, T4-861
0595, 1½ hrs. From **Guatapé** to Rionegro, take
Sotransvicente to Marinilla, US$3. To **Río Claro**,
take a Bogotá-bound bus and tell the driver you
want to get off at Río Claro, 3 hrs.

Santa Fe de Antioquia

Bus The station is on the road to Turbo
at the north end of Cras 9 and 10 (5 mins' walk
to main plaza). To **Medellín** US$3 (numerous
companies), 1 hr. To **Turbo**, US$15-18, 8-9 hrs,
every 2 hrs or so.

South from Medellín

Bus Medellín–Santa Bárbara, US$2.50.
Medellín–**Andes**, US$6. From Medellín (Terminal
Sur), **Trans Suroeste Antioqueño** and **Rápido
Ochoa** to Jardín, US$6.50-8, several daily, 3-4 hrs.

Department of Chocó
see humpback whales and other migratory species on the unspoiled Pacific coast

Situated in the heavy rainbelt along Colombia's northwest coast, Chocó is one of the rainiest and most
biodiverse regions in the world, densely forested and sparsely inhabited. In the northern part of the
department, the mountain ranges rise directly from the ocean to reach a height of about 500 m. Chocó
is home to a number of indigenous groups, including the Embera, whose communities are based on
hunting, fishing and subsistence farming. The coastline is also dotted with poor Afro-Colombian
fishing communities. Tourism centres on the coastal towns of Nuquí and Bahía Solano.

Quibdó *Colour map 1, B2.*

Quibdó is on the eastern bank of the Río Atrato. There is little to detain the visitor here apart from the unstoppable partying during the city's fiestas. The San Pacho festival (September-October, www.sanpachobendito.org), for instance, has parades and a San Francisco de Asís procession. There is an interesting mural in the cathedral. Hordes of birds fly in to roost at dusk and there are magnificent sunsets, which locals watch from the waterfront promenade, El Malecón. There are ATMs in town, but it is best to buy pesos before arriving.

Nuquí to El Valle

On the Gulf of Tribugá, surrounded by estuaries, mangroves and virgin beaches, the Afro-Colombian town of **Nuquí** gives access to the beaches and ecolodges up and down the Pacific coast. Visitors have to pay a US$2.50 tourism tax. To the south lies the wide curve of Playa Olímpica. To the north is another splendid beach. Various communities, including Jobí, Coquí, Termales and Jurubidá, welcome visitors.

About 50 km north of Nuquí along the coast, **El Valle** has the best bathing and surfing beaches in the area. Between Nuquí and El Valle is **Parque Nacional Ensenada de Utría** ① *entry US$14, see Where to stay, below,* home to many aquatic species and birds. The surrounding hillsides are covered with pristine rainforest and there are mangroves and several magnificent beaches. Activities include diving over the coral reefs, swimming, trekking (national park guides obligatory, US$13-30 per day) and whale watching in season. Most hotels organize day trips to the Park, or you can hire a boat with a group from El Valle, takes 1 hour, or from Nuquí, minimum 1½ hours. Isla Playa Blanca is recommended as part of the trip. Boat prices start at US$150 and vary considerably, depending on time and number of passengers. Ask at hotels and Mano Cambiada (see below) for information. Insist on a life jacket and, on all boat trips, be prepared to get soaked – keep all valuables in watertight bags.

Bahía Solano

The town lies on a large bay set against jungle-covered hills. As a resort, it gets busy during holiday periods (the whale season and the fishing season, March to Easter), otherwise it's a functional fishing town. Good bathing beaches may be reached by launch or by walking about 1½ hours at low tide (for example Playa Mecana; be sure to return before the tide rises or you will be stranded). Tourist information is available from the **Alcaldía** ① *T4-682 7418, www.bahia solano-choco.gov.co.* There are no ATMs in the town.

Listings Department of Chocó

Tourist information

Nuquí to El Valle
The best place for information is the **NGO Mano Cambiada**, whose office is opposite

Nuquí airport (T310-348 6055/T313-7596270, corporacionmanocambiada@yahoo.es, or on Facebook: ManoCambiada, http://manocambiada.org).

Where to stay

It is possible to stay in Nuquí and Bahía Solano cheaply if you rent a basic room in a family house. Ask locals or look for rent signs on windows. Negotiate prices during low season.

Quibdó

There are few decent places to stay, but centrally located and safe is the **Malecón** (Cra 1, No 26A-60, p 2, T4-671 2725).

Nuquí to El Valle

Along the beach at the north end of Nuquí are several tourist hotels usually fully booked during the holiday period; it's best to make arrangements through travel agents in Medellín or Bogotá. At El Valle, try the **$ Humpback Turtle Lodge/La Tortuga Jorobada** (on Playa Almejal, T314-766 8708 or 312-756 3439, www.humpbackturtle.com), which offers surfing, surf kayaking, camping, dorms and private rooms, restaurant and bar, use of kitchen.

The following are environmentally aware, award-winning and design-oriented options:

Cabañas El Almejal
El Valle, T4-412 5050, www.almejal.com.co.
Cabins with private bath, full board, price depends on the package. In private reserve, turtle conservation programme, educational programmes, lots of wildlife-watching opportunities.

Cabañas Pijiba
Near Nuquí, T4-474 5221or 311-762 3763, www.pijibalodge.com.
Award-winning ecotourism development with full board. Comfortable wooden lodges with thatched roofs. Arranges guided trips, diving, forest walks, airport pick-up (45-min boat ride to hotel), from US$250 pp double for 3 nights, longer packages available.

El Cantil
T4-448 0767, www.elcantil.com.
35 mins south of Nuquí, several packages from about US$360 pp double for a 2-night package, full board, transfers, 2 whale-watching boat trips, and a trail walk included. Wooden cabins with sea view, bath, mosquito nets. Also surfing courses, hot springs trips, diving, whale watching in season.

Jaibaná (Ensenada de Utría visitors centre)
Run by Mano Cambiada (address above) on a beautiful inlet in the national park.
Comfortable cabins with bath, cold water, mosquito nets, no electricity (but solar power in the main building), good simple fresh food, wonderful staff. Guiding is included in packages.

Lodge Piedra Piedra
45 mins south of Nuquí, T315-874 1773, 315-510 8216, www.piedrapiedra.com.
Prices from US$240 double for 3-night package, full board (bed only, US$110). Also all-inclusive, whale-watching and fishing packages, 3-7 days. Organizes local tours, wood and thatched lodges, camping US$20, use of kitchen and kayak rental.

Bahía Solano

$$$$ Mapara Crab
T314-700 8424, www.maparacrab.com.
Run by Nancy and Enrique Ramírez, small, comfortable cabins on a private beach, 30 mins by boat from Bahía Solano. Enrique is a master sports fisherman and diving enthusiast. Several packages available. There are also hotels in Bahía Solano itself.

Transport

Quibdó

Air Flights daily to Medellín, Bogotá and nearby towns with LATAM, Satena, ADA and EasyFly.

Bus Flota Occidental (T4-361 1312, or T4-671 1865 in Quibdó) and Rápido Ochoa from Medellín, daily, 7-8 hrs, US$15-20.

Nuquí to El Valle

Air Satena and ADA fly to Nuquí from Medellín, Bogotá and Quibdó (daily).

Bahía Solano

There are flights from Medellín, Bogotá, Cali and Quidbo to Bahía Solano with Satena and ADA. **Pickups** run from Bahía Solano to El Valle throughout the day, 18 km (6 km paved). Check also with Pacifico Tours, http://pacificotours.com.

La Zona
Cafetera

★Modern and colonial cities line the fertile western slopes of the Cordillera Central which is the centre of Colombia's coffee production. The three departments of Caldas, Quindío and Risaralda are generally known as the 'Zona Cafetera'. Much of the land here is between the critical altitudes for coffee of 800-1800 m, and has the right balance of rain and sunshine. The area has beautiful rolling countryside of coffee plantations, interspersed with bamboo, plantain and banana trees. The best way to enjoy the Zona Cafetera is to stay on a coffee farm, where you can tour the plantations and see how coffee is produced at harvest time. And of course, there is excellent, fresh, coffee all year round. In recent years, the Zona Cafetera has been building a reputation as an adventure sports destination, including rafting, kayaking and canopying (whizzing across ravines on steel cables). The region is overlooked by the high peaks of Los Nevados national park to the east. Earthquakes and volcanoes remain a feature of this volatile region.

Manizales and around *Colour map 1, B2.*

gateway to coffee country and Los Nevados

Manizales, 309 km from Bogotá, is overlooked by the Nevado del Ruiz volcano, which erupted catastrophically in November 1985. The town sits at 2150 m on a mountain saddle, which falls away sharply from the centre into the adjacent valleys. Rich in coffee and flowers, Manizales is one of the principal starting points for excursions to the Parque Nacional Los Nevados.

The city's climate is humid (average temperature is 17°C and annual rainfall is 3560 mm), encouraging prodigious growth in the flowers that line the highways to the suburbs north and south. Frequently the city is covered in cloud. The best months of the year are from mid-December to early March. The city looks down on the small town of Villa María, "the village of flowers", now almost a suburb.

Sights

Several earthquakes and fires have destroyed parts of the city over the years, so the architecture is predominantly modern with high-rise office and apartment blocks. Traditional styles are still seen in the suburbs and the older sections of the city. The centre is dominated by the enormous concrete Cathedral. Opposite is the departmental **Gobernación** building in the Parque de Bolívar, an imposing example of neocolonial architecture and a national monument. Inside is a local arts and crafts shop. The **bullring** ① *Av Centenario, T6-883 8124, www.cormanizales.com*, is an impressive copy of the traditional Moorish style. Along Avenida 12 de Octubre to the suburb of Chipre is a park, providing a great view to the west and paragliding opportunities (well visited on Sunday); El Tanque, on the Avenida, is a popular landmark and viewpoint. The **Centro de Museos** ① *part of Caldas University, Cra 23, No 58-65, T6-885 1374, www.ucaldas.edu.co/portal/tag/centro-de-museos/,*

Best for
Coffee ■ Landscapes ■ Wildlife

Mon-Fri 1000-1800, take a 'Fátima' bus to the University, has an art gallery, natural history museum and exhibitions on geology and archaeology. The area known as El Cable, east of the centre, is the Zona Rosa, with good restaurants and bars.

Reserva Forestal Protectora Río Blanco

Owned by Aguas de Manizales, T6-887 9770, ext 72187, send an email before visiting to reservarioblanco@ aguasdemanizales.com.co, or socampo@aguasdemanizales.com.co (Sergio Ocampo, technical director); US$7 entry, and a guide is compulsory, US$10-30 for half or full day, depending on size of group. Tour operators and hostels can arrange visits. The earlier you go (tours start at 0700), the better the birdwatching.

About 8 km from Manizales is the **Río Blanco reserve**, a 4343-ha protected cloudforest, considered by the World Wildlife Fund the best place for birdwatching in Colombia. To date, 372 species of bird have been identified, including 33 species of hummingbird. There are also 40 types of orchid, 180 species of daytime butterfly and 61 species of mammal, including spectacled bear, ocelot and the white-tailed deer. There are several hikes of between 30 minutes and three hours as well as a rangers' hut where 22 species of hummingbird come to feed. Trails and other facilities are operated by **Fundación Ecológica Gabriel Arango Restrepo** (FUNDEGAR).

☆Parque Nacional Los Nevados

Oficina del Parque de Los Nevados, C 69, No 24-69, Barrio La Camelia, Manizales, T6-887 1611/2273, Mon-Fri 0800-1800, for information and entrance fees, north sector: US$13 for non-Colombians, US$7 for Colombians (children US$5.50), including compulsory guide.

The park has all the wild beauty of the high Cordillera, towering mountains (snowcapped above 4850 m), mostly dormant volcanoes, hot springs and recent memories of tragic eruptions. The park comprises 58,000 ha and straddles the departments of Caldas, Quindío, Risaralda, and Tolima. Visitors should come prepared for cold, damp weather, and remember to give themselves time to acclimatize to the altitude.

The northern sector of the park is reached from Manizales along the main highway to Bogotá via a turn-off at La Esperanza. Volcanic activity on **Nevado del Ruiz** (5400 m) has restricted access to Parque de los Nevados in recent years. While the southern section was open in 2016 (0930-1500, US$8, access from Salento, Pereira and Ibagué), the northern section (access from Manizales and Brisas and Murillo in Tolima department) was open only as far as Valle de las Tumbas, from 0800 to 1400; all visitors must leave by 1530. If you wish to enter the northern part of the park or intend to do some serious mountain climbing and or mountain biking, apply to the above office in advance. The tourist office in Manizales can give advice on which parts of the park are open and can put you in touch with agencies who organize day trips to Nevado del Ruiz. Hotels and hostels offer trips to the park. Guides can be arranged and trips extended to include Nevado del Tolima (see page 978). **Mountain Hostels**, see below, has information on trips and provides maps, which are also available at the **Instituto Geográfico** ① *Cra 24, No 25-15, Manizales, T6-884 5864, Mon-Fri 0700-1200, 1400-1800.*

Armero

The main road from Manizales to Bogotá goes east to Honda (see page 900). It passes through **Mariquita**, capital of a fruit-growing region (21 km before Honda). From Mariquita a road turns south to (32 km) Armero, which was devastated by the eruption of the Nevado del Ruiz volcano in November 1985. Over 25,000 people were killed as 10% of the ice core melted, causing landslides and mudflows. Armero can be reached by *colectivo* from Honda; the road heads south to Ibagué via **Lérida**, 12 km south.

Tourist information

Manizales
There is a tourist information point at **Parque Benjamín López**, Cra 22 y C 31, T6-873 3901. The **Instituto de Cultura y Turismo** is at Av Alberto Mendoza Hoyos, Km 2 Vía al Magdalena, T6-874 9712, www.ctm.gov.co, Mon-Fri 0700-1200, 1400-1800.

Where to stay

When planning a trip here, take into account price rises during the popular Feria de Manizales in Jan.

$$$ Tinamu
30 mins from centre in Vereda San Peligrino, T314-771 1557, www.hoteltinamu.com.
Former coffee plantation turned nature reserve just outside the city with a firm focus on wildlife watching, especially birds (over 180 native species, plus migrants). 4 private rooms with Wi-Fi, price includes guiding. Meals other than breakfast extra.

$$ Escorial
C 21, No 21-11, T6-884 7696, www.hotelesmanizales.com.
Nicely decorated, central, parking, restaurant.

$$ Varuna
C 62, No 23C-18, T6-881 1122, http://varunahotel.com.
Slick, minimal look, good restaurant, **Tabil**. Rooms are large and comfortable, hydro massage showers. Recommended.

$ Mountain Hostels Manizales
C 66, No 23B-91, Barrio Palermo, T6-887 4736, or 300-439 7387, http://manizaleshostel.com.
Popular travellers' hostel, has all the expected facilities, hammocks, TV room, book exchange, bike rental, hot showers, free coffee, restaurant. Dorms and rooms with bath. Excellent information about trips to Los Nevados and coffee farms. Recommended.

$ The Secret Garden
Km 3 Vía a Llanitos, Vereda La Floresta, sector La Alqueria, Villa María, T321-770 3020, http://thesecretgardenmanizales.com.
Hostel and bistro with 3 rooms (1 shared) 30 mins from central Manizales, all meals extra, local produce and coffee, airport and bus terminal transfer, rural setting.

Restaurants

Apart from the hotels, the best restaurants are on or near Cra 23 in El Cable (La Zona Rosa) and Barrio Milán, a taxi ride from Cable Plaza, in the east of the city.

$$$-$$ Bologninis
C 77, No 21-116L 2.
Italo-Argentine restaurant with good pasta, steak and wines.

$ Don Juaco Snacks
C 65A, No 23A-44.
Sandwiches, burgers and typical dishes.

$ Il Forno
Cra 23, No 73-86.
Italian, pleasant, pastas, pizzas and salads. Good vegetarian dishes.

$ Pollos Asados Mario
C 23 esq Cra 22.
Traditional Colombian *asadero* with the best rotisserie chicken in downtown. Also burgers and steaks.

Entertainment

Cinema and theatre
Centro Cultural y Convenciones los Fundadores, *Cra 22 y C 33, T6-878 2530, www.ccclosfundadores.com.* Has interesting wood-carved murals by Guillermo Botero, who also has murals in the **Club Manizales** and **Hotel Las Colinas**. Many events held here.

Festivals

Early Jan Feria de Manizales includes a coffee festival, bullfights, beauty parades and folk dancing as well as general partying.
Sep Festival Internacional de Teatro, www.festivaldemanizales.com.

What to do

Tour operators
Colombia57, *T6-886 8050, www.colombia57.com.* Ex-pats Simon Locke, Russell Coleman, Brendan Rayment and team organize tailor-made trips for individuals or groups around the coffee zone and the rest of Colombia. Well organized, thoroughly

researched with a commitment to sustainability and quality. Highly recommended.

Colombia Eco Travel, *at The Secret Garden, see Where to stay, above, T311-319 3195, www.colombiaecotravel.com.* Aims to provide responsible tours throughout Colombia, from day trips to longer tours.

Transport

Air Airport 7 km east; flights are often delayed by fog. Buses to the centre US$1, taxi US$4. There are frequent flights of **Bogotá** and **Medellín**.

Bus Terminal at Cra 43, No 65-100, T6-878 7858, with a direct cable car system from the station up to the area of El Cable (US$0.75 per journey); taxi to El Cable US$3-4, to centre US$2.50. To **Medellín**, many daily, 5-6 hrs, US$12-17, many companies, including mini vans (eg **Tax La Feria**, T6-878 7001, http://taxlaferia.com), 4½ hrs, which also run to **Cali**, 4½ hrs, and **Pereira**, 1½ hrs. Many buses to **Bogotá**, **Bolivariano**, US$21-23, 9 hrs. To **Honda**, US$9, also **Tax La Feria** to Honda and Bogotá. **Cali**, hourly, 6 hrs, US$12-14, 4½ hrs, many companies. **Pereira**, every 30 mins, 2 hrs, excellent road, beautiful scenery, US$4. **Armenia**, 3 hrs, US$7, hourly 0600-1800.

Pereira to Ibagué

the heart of the coffee zone

Still in the shadow of the Nevados, this is a region of modern cities (in several cases rebuilt after earthquakes), delightful scenery and botanical parks and gardens. Coffee is still by far the most important agricultural product of the area.

☆Chinchiná and the coffee fincas

Midway between Manizales and Pereira is Chinchiná, one of the main coffee-producing towns. The surrounding hills are carpeted with coffee bushes and on roasting days the smell of coffee hangs in the air. Many local fincas have diversified into other crops and opened up to tourism, from day visits to overnight stays, highly recommended. No two fincas are the same; they range from beautiful historic country mansions to more modest properties.

Pereira *Colour map 1, B2.*

Capital of Risaralda Department and 56 km southwest of Manizales, Pereira stands within sight of the Nevados of the Cordillera Central. It is a pleasant modern city, founded in 1863, its past chequered by earthquake damage. The central **Plaza de Bolívar** is noted for the striking sculpture of a nude Bolívar on horseback, by Rodrigo Arenas Betancur. There are other fine works of his in the city. The **Área Cultural Banco de la República** ① *C 18 bis 9-37, Mon-Fri 0830-1800, Sat 0900-1300, free,* features a library, art exhibitions and an auditorium with a programme of classical music. The **botanical garden** ① *on the campus of Universidad Tecnológica de Pereria, T6-313 7500, www.utp.edu.co/jardin, US$7, Mon-Fri, 0800-1600, Sat-Sun 0900-1400, guided visits weekends and holidays at 1100, US$6,* is good for birdwatching and has bamboo forests and two-hour nature walks.

Around Pereira

Fifteen kilometres north of Pereira is **Santa Rosa de Cabal**, from where several thermal pools can be reached. A 9-km unpaved road from Santa Rosa leads to the **Termales de Santa Rosa de Cabal** ① *T6-365 5237, http://termales.com.co, daily 0900-2300, US$12 (US$7.50 midweek and in low season), early morning chiva or taxi, US$8 to entrance.* The hot baths are surrounded by forests, with waterfalls and nature walks. It's packed at the weekend, quiet during the week. It also has a hotel.

Northwest of Pereira, 30 km towards the Río Cauca, is **Marsella**, and the **Alexander von Humboldt Gardens** ① *T314-623 4941, Tue-Sun 0800-1700,* a carefully maintained botanical display with cobbled paths and bamboo bridges. Just outside the town is the **Ecohotel Los Lagos** ① *T6-368 5298, www.ecohotelloslagos.com.co,* previously a gold mine, then a coffee hacienda, and now restored as a hotel ($$) and nature park with lakes.

Cartago, 25 km southwest of Pereira, is at the northern end of the rich Cauca Valley. Founded in 1540 and noted for its embroidered textiles, Cartago has some colonial buildings, like the fine **Casa del Virrey**, Calle 13, No 4-29, and the **cathedral**. From here, the Panamericana goes south along the Cauca Valley, stretching south for 240 km but no more than 30 km wide, to Cali and Popayán.

Parque Ucumarí

Park office, T6-325 4781, www.colparques.net/UCUMARI, daily for information, if visiting for the day and not staying overnight, entrance is free. A chiva leaves from C12, No 9-40 in Pereira daily at 0700, 0900, 1500 (plus 1200 at weekends and more frequently during high season) with Transporte Florida (T6-334-2721) to the village of El Cedral, approximately 2 hrs. The 0700 chiva Mon-Fri only goes to La Suiza for the Otún Quimbaya sanctuary.

From Pereira it is possible to visit the beautiful Parque Ucumarí, one of the few places where the Andean spectacled bear survives. From El Cedral it is a two- to 2½-hour walk to **La Pastora**, the park visitors' centre and refuge. There is excellent camping, or lodging at a refuge ($), meals extra. From La Pastora it is a steep, rocky one- to two-day hike to Laguna de Otún through beautiful scenery of changing vegetation. According to the national parks office, this sector was open in 2016, but check locally for the current situation. The **Otún Quimbaya flora and fauna sanctuary** ① *T314-674 9248, www.parquesnacionales.gov.co and www.yarumoblanco.co, 0800-1700, US$2, transport with La Florida, as above, 3 a day, 4 on Sat-Sun*, forms a biological corridor between Ucumari and Los Nevados to the east, as well as protecting the last remaining area of Andean tropical forest in Risaralda. There are marked paths and Yarumo Blanco community has **Montaña Hostal-Restaurante** at La Florida with *cabañas* ($) and meals.

Salento

A 44 km road runs through the heart of the Zona Cafetera. A turn off at the *Posada Alemana* goes east for 9 km to Salento, well into the foothills of the Cordillera. This small town is brightly painted with an attractive plaza surrounded by traditional houses. Up Carrera 6 (continuation of the north side of the plaza), now lined with attractive craft shops and restaurants, is a 250-step climb. The 14 stations of the cross measure your progress to an outstanding viewpoint, overlooking the upper reaches of the Quindío and Cárdenas rivers known as the Cocora valley, possibly one of the finest views in Colombia. It is a popular weekend resort for Colombians for walking, riding and trekking but is quieter during the week. More places to eat and to stay are opening up constantly, but try to make arrangements early in the day, particularly at the weekend. Fiesta is in the first week of January and every Sunday night after mass the plaza is taken over by food, drink and craft stalls, with a lively atmosphere. **Tourist information** is provided by the **Alcaldía de Salento** ① *Parque Principal, C 6, No 6-30, T6-759 3252, http://salento-quindio.gov.co, Mon-Fri 0800-1200, 1400-1800, Sat 0800-1200*. There are ATMs in the main plaza.

Valle de Cocora and the Acaime Natural Reserve

The centre of the Cocora valley is 12 km beyond Salento along a road with some unpaved sections; it's a picturesque two-hour walk, or 35 minutes by jeep (six departures Monday-Friday 0610-1700; 10 departures Saturday and Sunday, last return 1800, US$2). Some 5 km beyond Cocora at 2770 m is the **Acaime Natural Reserve** with visitor centre, ponies for hire, beds for 20 and a small restaurant. There are hummingbirds, cloudforest and the most important area of wax palm in the country. (The wax palm is the national tree and one of the tallest trees in the world; the Wax Palm Festival is celebrated in January.) The reserve borders **Parque Nacional Los Nevados**, and there are many trails into the high mountains above Acaime. Experienced climbers can also make the three-day ascent of Nevado del Tolima (5125 m) from here (see also page 978).

Armenia and around *Colour map 1, B2.*

The capital of Quindío Department was founded in 1889. In January 1999, an earthquake flattened much of the city. Impressive reconstruction continues and Armenia is as busy as ever. The fine example of Rodrigo Arenas Betancur's work, the **Monumento al Esfuerzo**, in the Plaza de Bolívar, poignantly portrays the spirit of the local people. The **Museo del Oro Quimbaya** ① *Av Bolívar, C 40 norte-80, T6-749 8169 ext 6070, www.banrepcultural.org/armenia, Tue-Sat 0900-1700*, is worth a visit, free entry. **Parque de la Vida**, north of the city, has bamboo structures, waterfalls and a lakeside theatre.

Near Calarcá, 6 km from Armenia, is **Jardín Botánico y Mariposario del Quindío** ① *T6-742 7254 ext 105, www.jardinbotanicoquindio.org, daily 0900-1600, US$6*, featuring a huge covered butterfly house, with some 50 species of butterflies. There is also an insect zoo and forest walks. Twenty minutes south of Calarcá or Armenia is **Recuca** ① T310-830 3780, www.recuca.com, daily 0900-1500, US$7 for day visit, US$5.50 for lunch, reserve in advance, US$5 coffee tasting lesson, take bus Armenia-Barcelona, a coffee farm with tours featuring all aspects of coffee-growing, also tastings.

Montenegro and around

Some 12 km northwest of Armenia is Montenegro, near which is the **Parque del Café** ① 1 km from Pueblo Tapao, T6-741 7417, www.parquedelcafe.co, high season daily 0900-1800, low season Wed-Sun and public holidays 1000-1800, general entrance US$9, or US$15-20 for additional activities and rides, parking US$2; take a bus or colectivo (US$2.50) from Armenia to Montenegro. There are restaurants, a coffee shop, a botanical garden, ecological walks, a Quimbaya cemetery, a tower with a fine view and an interesting museum which covers all aspects of coffee. A cableway links to a children's theme park (roller coasters, water rides etc). Beyond Montenegro is **Quimbaya**, known for its **Fiesta de Velas y Faroles** in December each year. About 7 km away is the **Parque Nacional de la Cultura Agropecuaria** (Panaca) ① T01-800 012 3999, www.panaca. com.co, Tue-Sun 0900-1800, US$10-28, an educational theme park with many varieties of horses (and a very good show/display), cattle and other animals. A good family outing.

Ibagué and around *Colour map 1, B2.*

The **Quindío Pass**, 3350 m, is on the Armenia to Ibagué road (105 km) across the Cordillera Central. On the east side of the Pass is **Cajamarca**, in a beautiful setting at 1900 m with an interesting market on Sunday.

Tip...
Try the local alcoholic drink called *mistela*.

Ibagué, capital of Tolima Department, lies at the foot of the Quindío mountains at 1248 m. Visit the Colegio de San Simón and the market for good tamales. The Parque Centenario is pleasant, and there is a famous music conservatory.

Warning...
Because of volcanic activity, it is safest to visit Nevado del Tolima from Ibagué or Salento, not Manizales.

Just outside town, on the Armenia road, a dirt road leads up the Río Combeima to El Silencio and the slopes of **Nevado del Tolima** (5215 m), the southernmost *nevado* in the **Parque Nacional Los Nevados** and the toughest to climb. The ascent takes two to three days, camping at least one night over 4000 m; ice equipment is necessary. Entry to the park costs US$9. A milk truck (*lechero*) leaves Ibagué marketplace for El Silencio between 0630 and 0730, US$2-3, two hours.

Listings Pereira to Ibagué

Tourist information

Pereira
Centro Cultural Lucy Tejada (Cra 10, No 16-60, T6-311 6544, Mon-Fri 0800-1200, 1400-1830, http://pereiraculturayturismo.gov.co); also at the airport, daily 0900-1730. **Corporación Autónomo Regional de Risaralda** (Carder; Av de las Américas and C 46, No 46-40, T6-311 6511, www.carder.gov.co), also has information.

Armenia
Secretaría de Turismo (C 20, No 13-22, T6-741 7700 ext 202, www.turismocafeyquindio.com) and **Corporación de Cultura y Turismo** (Cra 19A entre C 26 y 29, Edif Republicano, p 2, T6-731

4531, www.armeniaculturayturismo.gov.co, Mon-Fri 0800-1200, 1400-1800), with information booths at Centro Comercial Portal del Quindío and the bus terminal.

Ibagué
Tourist office (Cra 3 entre C 10 y 11, p 2, T8-261 1111, www.desarrolloeconomicotolima.gov.co).

Where to stay

Chinchiná and the coffee fincas
There are far too many coffee farms in the Pereira region to list here. They range from huge traditional haciendas to smaller, more modern farms. See www.clubhaciendasdelcafe.com, T6-741 3698, for a good selection.

$$$ Finca Guayabal
Near Chinchiná, T314-772 4856,
www.haciendaguayabal.com.
A hacienda that takes day and overnight visitors.
Nature trail, swimming pool. Tours include full
explanations of the coffee-growing process and
lunch. Full board is offered in private bedrooms
and dorms.

$$$-$$ Hacienda Venecia
Vereda El Rosario, 3.5 km off the
Chinchiná autopista, T320-636 5719,
www.haciendavenecia.com.
Delightful 4th-generation working coffee finca
in a beautiful location with 2 different types
of accommodation: hostel with private and
dorm beds (US$8-9 pp), or the main hacienda;
both include breakfast, and other meals can be
arranged. Attentive, English-speaking hosts.
Swimming pools on site as well as riding, coffee
and other tours. Highly recommended.

$$ pp Finca Villa María
12 km from Pereira, via Marsella, follow the signs,
turning before La Bodega, unpaved 3-km road,
25 mins by taxi from Pereira, US$12, T312-722
3006, fincavillamaria@hotmail.com.
Charming typical coffee hacienda set in beautiful
countryside. Large rooms, peaceful, full board.
Coffee plantations tours. Recommended.

Pereira

$$$$ Hacienda San José
Entrada 16 cadena El Tigre, Km 4
Vía Pereira–Cerritos, T6-313 2612,
www.haciendahotelsanjose.com.
One of the oldest houses in the region, almost
all of its features have been preserved. Breakfast
included. Activities include horse riding and
visits to one of the largest bamboo reserves in
the region.

$$$$-$$$ Sazagua
Km 7 vía Cerritos, T6-337 9895, www.sazagua.com.
This boutique hotel just outside of town is
one of Pereira's oldest and swankiest options.
Amenities include a spa and massage services
and there is a restaurant serving upscale takes
on regional dishes.

$$$ Soratama
Cra 7, No 19-20, T6-335 8650,
www.hotelsoratama.com.
On the Plaza Bolívar with helpful staff and lots
of services available, 11th-floor Sky Lounge

restaurant and bar with panoramic views.
Discounts available Sat-Sun.

$$-$ Cataluña
C 19, No 8-61, T6-335 4527,
www.hotelcatalunapereira.com.
2 floors up, airy rooms, popular restaurant,
good value.

$ Kolibri Hostel
C 4, No 16-35, T6-331 3955,
www.kolibrihostel.com.
Close to the centre, with dorms (US$6.55-7.50 pp),
private rooms with bath and an apartment for
up to 8 people. Organizes bike tours through
Retrociclas (see What to do).

$ Sweet Home
C 42, No 10-37, T6-345 4453,
www.sweethomehostel.com.
Slightly out of town, but this backpackers'
hostel is worth the trek. 3 dorms, 1 private
room, breakfast. Handy for the airport.

Around Pereira

$$ Hotel Termales de Santa Rosa de Cabal
Comfortable, chalet style, with restaurant
(see above).

Salento

$$$-$$ La Posada del Café
Cra 6, No 3-08, T6-759 3012,
www.laposadadelcafe.webs.com.
This traditional house has rooms set around a
beautiful garden brimming with flowers. The
rooms are nicely decorated and there is a larger
family room for 5. Friendly, English-speaking
owner. Recommended.

$$ Hostal Ciudad de Segorbe
C 5, No 4-06, T6-759 3794,
www.hostalciudaddesegorbe.com.
Splendid old *hostal* not far from the main
square. Rooms all have private bath, including
the spacious dorm (US$11.50 pp). Music, TV and
reading room and 1 room with disability access.
Recommended.

$$-$ Tralala Hostel
Cra 7, No 6-45, T314-850 5543,
www.hosteltralalasalento.com.
Dutch-run hostel with a dorm (US$6.50 pp),
private rooms and a studio in the garden, cosy
DVD/reading room, great views, Wellington boot
hire. Recommended.

$ Camping Monteroca
Vereda Boquío, 5 mins before Salento, before the bridge on the Río Quindío, T310-422 3720, www.campingmonteroca.com.
Beside the Río Quindío. Owner Jorge knows the area, its history and wildlife well. Well-maintained campsite with clean showers, communal cooking area, TV lounge. Fantastic themed cabins, from tree house to "Hippie Hilton", all with hot showers, one has a jacuzzi. Museum of fossils and meteorites, a room dedicated to Simón Bolívar and a serpentarium.

$ pp La Casona de Lili
*C 6, No 3-45, T314-625 1151,
Facebook: hostallacasadelilisalento.*
Good beds, tasteful decor, excellent breakfast, Lili is an enthusiastic hostess.

$ Las Palmas
*C 6, No 3-02, T6-759 3065, or 311-540 3828,
www.hosteltrail.com/hostels/laspalmas.*
Small, traditional hostel, comfortable rooms and dorms, good value.

$ Plantation House
*Alto de Coronel, C 7, No 1-04, T316-285 2603,
www.theplantationhousesalento.com.*
Popular backpackers' hostel in 2 houses, with private rooms and dorms, outdoor seating area. Gorgeous views, bike hire. English/Colombian owned, the best local information, also offer tours of their coffee finca nearby. It's possible to stay the night on the top floor of the finca ($). Email reservations only. Highly recommended.

Valle de Cocora

$$ Las Palmas de Cocora
*Km 10 Valle de Cocora, T310-455 5400,
http://laspalmas decocora.com.*
Comfortable rooms with beds and bunks. Restaurant serving trout ($$). Horses for hire (US$6 per hr, guide available at extra cost), also guided walks.

$$-$ Bosques de Cocora
*Km 11 Vía Cocora, T6-746 3515,
www.bosquesdecocora.com.*
Restaurant, with finca accommodation or tent hire with mattresses and bedding. Shower facilities and free coffee and hot chocolate.

Armenia

$$$$-$$$ Hacienda Bambusa
*vía El Caimo– Portugalito Km 93,
T301-639 8727, 301-230 2418 in English,
www.haciendabambusa.com.*
Not strictly a coffee finca, this enchanting traditional hacienda sits amid banana plantations in 160 ha. Very much a place to relax, but also plenty of activities, including canopying in a bamboo forest, horse riding, or birdwatching. Has cable TV, swimming pool, restaurant and free pick up from airport or bus station.

$$$ Centenario
*C 21, No 18-20, T6-744 3143,
www.hotelcentenario.com.*
Bright rooms, attentive staff, gym, sauna, parking.

$$ Café Plaza
*Cra 18, No 18-09, T6-741 1500,
hotelcafeplaza@hotmail.com.*
Near the Plaza Bolívar, a little noisy but simple, clean rooms with bath and TV, breakfast included.

$$ Zuldemayda
*C 20, No 15-38, T6-741 0580,
http://hotelzuldemayda.co.*
A popular central hotel in minimalist style, with restaurant, offers weekend packages.

Montenegro and around

$$$ El Delirio
*Km 6 vía Montenegro-Parque del Café,
T6-745 0405, casadelirio@hotmail.com.*
Beautiful, traditional finca restored with immaculate taste, a "perfect place to unwind", pool, large gardens, delicious food.

$$ El Carriel
*Km 1 vía Quimbaya-Filandia, T315-404 2235,
http://elcarrielagroturismo.com.*
An excellent option if you are looking for an economic stay on a working coffee finca. Simple but comfortable rooms, hot water, restaurant. The coffee tour takes you through the whole coffee-making process.

Ibagué

$$$ Ambalá
*C 11, No 2-60, T8-261 4444,
www.hotelambala.com.*
Breakfast, TV, pool, sauna, parking, restaurant.

$ San Remo
C 16, No 2-88, T8-261 3339.
Rooms with fan and TV.

Restaurants

Pereira

$$ Mediterráneo
*Av Circunvalar, No 4-47, T6-331 0398,
see Facebook.*
Steaks, seafood, fondus and crêpes in a
relaxed atmosphere.

$$-$ Pasaje de la Alcaldía
In a narrow alleyway next to the Alcaldía.
A number of cheap eating options including
French, Italian, Colombian and a few cafés.

Salento

$$-$ Balcones del Ayer
*C 6, No.5-40, T6-759 3273,
www.balconesdelayer.com.*
Serving trout, the local speciality, as well as good
quality meat dishes. Efficient and recommended.
Also has rooms to let ($).

$ Café Jesús Martín
Cra 6, No 6-14.
Excellent little café with its own coffee from
Señor Bedoya's father's finca. (see also What to
do, below); has 2 coffee shops in Salento and
1 in Armenia.

$ El Rincón de Lucy
Cra 6, No 4-02.
Excellent breakfasts, lunches and dinners,
limited menu, but great value, tasty local food.
Recommended.

$ Galería Café-Libro Salento
C 3, No 3-25 (Salida a Cocora).
Art gallery and bookshop with vegetarian food
and coffee, family-run; also has a room for rent.

Armenia

$$ Café Quindío
*Cra 19, No 33N-41, T6-745 4478,
www.cafequindio.com.co.*
Gourmet coffee shop and restaurant next
to Parque de la Vida, serving recipes such as
chicken or steak in coffee sauce as well as
international dishes. Also sells coffee products
from its own farm.

$$ Keizaki
*Oasis de Laureles loc 10, Cra 15, No 22N-59,
T6-731 2234, www.keizaki.com.*
Sushi and other Asian dishes. There are several
other good restaurants on the same block,
and 2 other Keizaki outlets in Pereira.

$$ La Fogata
Cra 13, No 14N-39.
One of Armenia's most popular restaurants,
serving steaks, pork chops and typical dishes.

$ La Puerta Quindiana
C 17, No 15-40.
This restaurant serves cheap *comida corriente*,
with dishes such as *sancocho* a speciality, as well
as good fruit juices.

$ Natural Food Plaza
*Cra 14, No 4-51, T6-745 1597, www.natural
foodplaza.fundacionlasdelicias.org.*
Vegetarian, varied menu and fruit juices.
Also has a wholefood shop.

Festivals

Ibagué

Jun-Jul National Folklore Festival, www.
festivalfolclorico.com. Tolima Department
commemorate **San Juan** (24 Jun) and SS Pedro
y Pablo (29 Jun) with fireworks, and music.

What to do

Pereira

Living Trips, *Entrada 16 via Cerritos, T6-312 8671,
www.livingtrips.com.* Offers a number of multiple-
day excursions, such as rafting and coffee tours,
in the region.
Retro Ciclas, *C 4, No 16-36 (at Kolibrí Hostel), T310-
540 7327, www.retrociclas.co.* Bike tour agency that
runs city tours as well as adventure trips through
the surrounding areas.

Salento

Aldea del Artesano, *C 12A, No 5-148,
book through Alejandro, T320-782 9128,
aldeadelartesano@gmail.com.* Craftworkers
community project with handicraft courses
and a shop.
Café Jesús Martín, *Cra 6, No 6-14 (coffee shop),
T6-759 3282, www.cafejesusmartin.com.* 2-hr
tours of local coffee-roasting factory, fun and
informative. Also 3- to 4-hr tours visiting a
coffee finca in Quimbaya, plantation tour with
explanation of coffee-making and coffee and a
brownie in the Salento coffee shop, minimum
3 participants. There are outlets in Armenia and
Valle de Cocora. Recommended.
The Colombian Way, *http://thecolombian
way.co.* Jeep tours of Salento and Cocora valley,
from US$9 pp.

Armenia

Balsaje Los Remansos, *C 16, No 16-34, Quimbaya, T314-775 4231, see Facebook. Balsaje* excursions (punting on bamboo rafts) on the Río La Vieja.

Transport

Pereira

Air Matecaña airport is 5 km to the south, bus, US$0.40. Daily flights to **Medellín**, **Bogotá**, **Cali** and **Ibagué**; less frequent to other cities.

Bus Local taxi and bus services, including the **Megabús**, www.megabus.gov.co, are good. Terminal is at C 17, No 23-157, 1.5 km south of city centre, T6-315 2323, www.terminalpereira.com. Bus to **Armenia**, 1 hr, US$2-3, a beautiful trip. To **Salento**, 1 hr, US$2, frequent, from 0630-1830. To **Cartago**, US$1.50, 45 mins, **Arauca** *buseta* every 10 mins. To **Cali**, US$7-10, 4½-5 hrs, *colectivo* by day, bus by night. To **Medellín**, 6-8 hrs, US$15-22. To/from **Bogotá**, US$18-21, 7 hrs (route is via Girardot, Ibagué – both cities bypassed – and Armenia).

Salento

Bus To **Armenia** every 20 mins, US$2, 1 hr. To **Pereira**, 4 a day, hourly from 0730 to 1830 at weekends, US$2.50, 1 hr.

Armenia

Air El Edén, 13 km from city. Daily to **Bogotá** and **Medellín**. Fog can delay flights.

Bus Terminal at C 35, No 20-68, T6-747 3355, www.terminalarmenia.com. Bus to **Salento**, 1 hr, US$2, frequent, from 0520-2000. To **Ibagué**, US$6-8, 3 hrs. **Bogotá**, hourly, 7-9 hrs, US$12-18. **Cali**, US$7-9, 3 hrs, frequent.

Ibagué

Air Daily flights to **Bogotá**, **Cali** and **Medellín**, also to **Pereira**.

Bus Terminal is between Cra 2, No 20-89, www. terminalibague.com. Tourist police at terminal helpful. Frequent services to **Bogotá**, US$11.50, 4 hrs. To **Cali** US$15-21, 6-7 hrs; **Neiva**, US$12-14, 4 hrs, and many other places.

Southern
Colombia

The sensual city of Cali has branded itself as the capital of salsa music and sits in the tropical, sugar cane-rich plains of the Valle del Cauca. To the west lies the port of Buenaventura. The Pan-American Highway continues south to the city of Popayán, known for its dazzling white colonial buildings and its solemn Easter processions, second in size only to Seville in Spain. Hidden in the mountains east of Popayán are the mysterious archaeological sites of Tierradentro and San Agustín, while next to the Magdalena river lies the geographical anomaly that is the Tatacoa Desert.

Further south, the Cordillera Occidental reaches ever higher, rising up to the highland towns of Pasto and Ipiales on the border with Ecuador. To the west is Colombia's most southerly stretch of Pacific coast, while far to the east is Leticia, the country's toehold on the Amazon and a gateway to Brazil and Peru.

Cali and Valle de Cauca   Colour map 1, B2.

a city besotted with salsa

☆The hot, rich agricultural land of the Valle de Cauca is flanked on either side by the slender fingers of two mountain ranges, the Cordillera Occidental and the Cordillera Central. Capital of the department, Cali (population 2,732,000) is Colombia's third city and the country's self-declared salsa capital. If you're looking to join swinging salsa couples on the dance floor, Cali should not to be missed. Sensuous, tropical rhythms are ubiquitous, seeming to seep from every part of the city's being. Cali was founded in 1536, and until 1900 it was a leisurely colonial town. Then the railway came and Cali is now a rapidly expanding industrial complex serving the whole of southern Colombia.

Sights

The city's centre is the **Plaza de Caicedo**, with a statue of one of the independence leaders, Joaquín Caicedo y Cuero. Facing the plaza is the elegant **Palacio Nacional** and the **Cathedral**, seat of the influential Archbishop of Cali. Nearby is the renovated church and 18th-century monastery of **San Francisco** ① *Cra 6, C 9/10*, with a splendidly proportioned domed belltower. Cali's oldest church, **La Merced** ① *C 7, between Cras 3 and 4*, has been restored by the Banco Popular. The adjoining convent houses two museums: **Museo de Arte Colonial** (which includes the church), a collection of 16th- and 17th-century paintings, and the **Museo Arqueológico** ① *Cra 4, No 6-59, T2-885 5309, Mon-Sat 0900-1800, Sun 1000-1600, US$3* with pre-Columbian pottery. **Museo del Oro Calima** ① *C 7, No 4-69, T2-684 7751, www.banrepcultural.org/cali/museo-del-oro-calima, Tue-Fri 0900-1700, Sat 1000-1700, free*, has pre-Columbian goldwork and pottery.

The **Museo La Tertulia** ① *Av Colombia, No 5-105 Oeste, T2-893 2939 ext 101, www.museolatertulia. com, Tue-Sat 1000-1800, Sun 1400-1800, US$3.50, Sun free*, exhibits South American, including local, modern art and shows unusual films (US$1.50). The neighbourhood of **San Antonio** (behind the Intercontinental Hotel) is the city's oldest area, where Cali's colonial past can still be felt. The area

Best for
Archaeology ▪ Festivals ▪ Volcanoes

·983

has a relaxed, bohemian atmosphere, especially at weekends when it's livelier. There are good views of the city from the 18th-century church of San Antonio.

West of Buga

From the colonial city of **Buga**, 74 km north of Cali on the Panamericana (1¼ hours by bus, US$3-4), the road to Buenaventura on the coast passes the **Laguna de Sonso** reserve, good for birdwatching, before crossing the Río Cauca. Beyond the river, near the crest of the Cordillera, is another park, **Reserva Natural Bosque de Yotoco**, noted for orchids. The road continues to the man-made **Lago Calima**. Many treasures of the Calima culture are said to have been flooded by the lake, when the dam was built. This is an important centre for watersports, riding and other activities. The northern route round the lake goes through **Darién** at 1500 m with an **archaeological museum** ① *Tue-Fri 0800-1200, 1300-1700, Sat-Sun 1000-1800*, with good displays of Calima and other cultures. There are hotels in the village, and cabins at a Centro Náutico on the lakeside. Camping is possible near the village. There are direct buses to Darién from Cali, US$6, 2½ hours.

☆San Cipriano

A popular excursion from Cali is to San Cipriano, 30 km west on the railway line to Buenaventura. The line is now freight-only, so to get to the village, you must get off the bus at Córdoba, from where ingeniously adapted rail cars (man-powered or motorbike-powered) descend to the village through beautiful scenery (US$3, only pay for the return leg when returning). There are crystal-clear rivers

Cali

BARRIO
GRANADA

Where to stay 🛏
1 Apartahotel Colombia
2 Aparta Hotel Del Río
3 Casa Republicana
4 Colombian Home Hostel
5 El Viajero Hostel
7 Hotel Boutique
  San Antonio
8 Iguana
9 Intercontinental &
  La Terraza Restaurant
11 La Casa Café
12 La Pinta Boogaloo
13 Pelican Larry
14 Posada de San Antonio
15 Tostaky

Restaurants 🍴
1 Carambolo
2 D'Toluca
3 Faro El Solar
4 La Tartine
5 Ojo de Perro Azul
6 Pampero
7 Tortelli

Bars & clubs 🍸
8 Tin Tin Deo
9 Zaperoco

and waterfalls and inner tubes can be rented for US$2 for floating downstream. The village and its surroundings are a national reserve of 8564 ha, entry US$0.75. Take insect repellent.

Buenaventura and the islands

The port of Buenaventura is not safe to visit, for this reason it is not included in this edition. **Isla Gorgona**, the former prison island now a national park, is partially open. Entrance fee is US$14 for foreigners, but entry is allowed only for day visits, research or dive boats. There are no facilities for overnight stays and no reservation system. **Isla Malpelo**, 506 km west of Buenaventura, was declared a UNESCO site in 2006. It is an acclaimed birdwatching haven with great diving opportunities. The island is considered to be one of the world's best places to observe hammerhead sharks in great numbers. It can only be reached by boat from Buenaventura, a 36-hour bumpy voyage. There are no places to stay on the island and camping is not allowed. If you wish to visit Gorgona or Malpelo contact the national parks office in Bogotá, T1-353 2400, www.parquesnacionales. gov.co, or the parks office in Cali. For information on dive boats contact **Embarcaciones Asturias** ① *Harold Botero, T2-242 4620, or 313-7672864, barcoasturias@yahoo.com.*

Essential Cali

Getting around

Alfonso Bonilla Aragón (Palmaseca) airport is 20 km from city. The **bus terminal** is at Calle 30N, No 2AN-29, 25 minutes' walk from the centre. For getting around the city there is the **MIO** metro system, with north–south and west–east trunk routes and some pre-trunk routes. On Sunday, 0700-1400, Calle 9 is closed from north to south to allow people to cycle, run and exercise on the roadway. See also Transport, page 987.

Safety

Although the atmosphere in Cali is quite relaxed, carry your passport (or photocopy) at all times. Cali has some rough parts, particularly east or south of Carretera 10 and Calle 15, and caution is needed when walking around the city, especially at night. Do not change money on the street under any circumstances and avoid all people who approach, offering to sell.

Listings Cali and Valle de Cauca *map page 984.*

Tourist information

Punto de Información Turística (PIT), Cra 4 C 6 esq, Mon-Fri 0800-1700, Sat 1000-1400, housed inside the large red-brick **Cultural Centre**, has pamphlets but otherwise isn't much help. The centre also has free exhibitions in the hallways. The **Secretaría de Cultura y Turismo**, Cra 5, No 6-05, sala 102, T2-885 4777 ext 102, www.cali. gov.co, also has a PIT in reception, open same hours. The **National Parks Office**, C 29N, No 6N-43, Santa Mónica, T2-667 6041, is very helpful.

Where to stay

$$$$-$$$ Intercontinental
Av Colombia, No 2-72, T2-882 3225,
www.intercontinental.com.
On the edge of San Antonio, the most expensive hotel in town. Spa, outdoor pool and elegant restaurant, **La Terraza**, along with 4 others. Cheaper Sat-Sun.

$$$ Casa Republicana
C 7, No 6-74, T2-896 0949, reservas@
hotelcasarepublicana.com.
Lovely plant-filled courtyard, good rooms (cheaper with fan) and a fine restaurant, welcoming. Recommended.

$$$ Hotel Boutique San Antonio
Cra 6, No 2-51, T2-524 6364,
www.hotelboutiquesanantonio.com.
Charming hotel with 10 sound-proofed rooms, own security system, cheaper at weekends.

$$$ Posada de San Antonio
Cra 5, No 3-37, T2-893 7413,
www.posadadesanantonio.com.
Rooms set around a couple of patios, decorated with Calima artefacts, good value. 10% discount for Footprint readers.

$$ Aparta Hotel Del Río
Av 2N, No 10N-30, T2-660 2713,
www.apartahoteldelrio.com.

Comfortable suites and rooms with good facilities (gym, sauna, pool, laundry), safe, good restaurant, parking.

$$ Apartahotel Colombia
C 31 Norte, No 2 Bis-48, T2-660 8081,
www.apartahotelcolombia.com.
1 block from bus terminal and close to Barrio Granada, steam room, restaurant, secure, English spoken.

$$-$ El Viajero Hostel Cali & Salsa School
Cra 5 No 4-56, San Antonio, T2-893 8342,
www.elviajerohostels.com.
Doubles (cheaper with shared bath) with TV, dorms (US$9-10 pp), salsa school, pool, open-air bar, cinema room and a stage for shows. Breakfast, internet and Wi-Fi included.

$$-$ La Pinta Boogaloo
Cra 3 Oeste, No 11-49, Bellavista, T2-892 2448,
www.lapinta.com.co.
In a mansion in a quiet neighbourhood, private rooms (cheaper with shared bath), dorms (US$7-10) and camping, restaurant, bar, pool, garden, cinema room, kitchen available, salsa classes arranged.

$ Colombian Home Hostel
C 3bis, No 35A-70, San Fernando Viejo, T320-629 7879/315-705 2343, colombianhostecolombian@ hotmail.com. See Facebook.
Colombian-owned hostel, dorms with and without bath and a private room, cold water, welcoming and helpful.

$ Iguana
Av 9 Norte, No 22N-22, T2-382 5364,
or 313-768 6024, www.iguana.com.co.
In 2 suburban houses on the edge of fashionable Barrio Granada, dorm US$9 pp, popular backpackers' hostel so there can be a lot of *movimiento*. Private rooms, some with bath, garden, TV room with DVDs, Spanish and free salsa classes and good local information.

$ La Casa Café
Cra 6, No 2-13, T316-521 7388,
www.lacasacafecali.blogspot.com.
Nice backpackers' hostel and café. Simple rooms with high ceilings, wooden floor-boards and shared baths, bed in dorm US$7.50. Next door they have rooms with bath; café hosts cultural and music evenings.

$ Pelican Larry
C 20 Norte, No 6AN-44, Barrio Granada,
T2-382 7226, www.hostelpelicanlarry.com.

Rooms with and without bath, also has dorms. Close to Zona Rosa restaurants and bars, 15 mins' walk from bus terminal and centre, hot water, laundry and internet extra, Sun night BBQ, Spanish lessons and free salsa classes arranged, TV room, helpful staff. Recommended.

$ Tostaky
Cra 10, No 1-76, T2-893 0651, www.tostakycali.com.
At the bottom of San Antonio park, good backpackers' hostel, French/Colombian-run, airy rooms and dorms (US$8) above a café open only to guests, hot water, shared bath, breakfast extra. There is also a studio with private bath. Recommended.

Restaurants

In the centre, Parque de Peñón, just north of San Antonio, has an excellent selection of restaurants serving all types of international food, while San Antonio itself has many good restaurants and cafés. In the north, Barrio Granada has an enormous number of eating places to choose from.

$$$ Carambolo
C 14, No 9N-18/28, T2-667 5656,
http://carambolo.com.co.
Excellent themed friendly restaurant with Latin and Mediterranean dishes. Recommended.

$$$ Faro El Solar
C 15 Norte, No 9N-62, Barrio Granada, T318-348 9327.
Great atmosphere and a varied international menu, popular.

$$$ La Tartine
C 3 Oeste, No 1-74, T2-893 6617.
Classic French-owned restaurant in an eccentric setting.

$$$ Tortelli
C 3 Oeste, No 3-15, T2-893 3227,
www.restaurantetortelli.com.
Little Italian restaurant serving great home-made pasta. 3 more branches in the city.

$$$-$$ Pampero
C 21N, No 9-17, Barrio Granada, T2-661 3117.
Argentine steaks on pleasant terrace with good service. Recommended.

$$-$ D'Toluca
C 17N, No 8N-46, Barrio Granada, T2-668 9372,
www.dtoluca.com. Mon-Fri from 1200 and Sat-Sun from 1730 until late.
Good little Mexican restaurant serving fajitas, tacos and burritos at reasonable prices;

another branch in the Ciudad Jardín district, with similar hours.

$ Ojo de Perro Azul
Cra 9, No 1-27. Wed-Sun 1600-0100.
Bright bohemian hangout with games, mixed drinks, *picadas*, *tostadas* and traditional Colombian dishes.

Bars and clubs

Cali's nightlife is legendary, especially the *salsatecas* – salsa-playing discos. The most popular with *caleños* can be found on Av 6 Norte where there are dozens to choose from. Barrios Juanchito and Menga also have a range of salsa bars and huge, hi-tech *salsatecas*. It is worth visiting just to watch couples dancing salsa and to join in, if you dare! Go with locals and couples; groups of foreign male tourists might have a hard time getting in. If heading to Juanchito or Menga, it's advisable to take a registered radio taxi there and back (15 mins), across the bridge over the Río Cauca.

Blues Brothers
Av 6AN, No 21-40, T2-661 3412, www.caliblues.net.
Jazz and live rock bands, happy hour Tue-Sat 1800-2000.

Club Living
Cra 40 No 11-83, Barrio Menga, Facebook: livingclubcali.
Lively salsa in a raging nightclub.

Talberts Pub
C 17N, No 8N-60, T2-660 5080/8371, and Bourbon St, Facebook: bourbonstcol, Av 9N, No 15AN-27, T2-381 6398, Barrio Granada, opens 1700.
English- and American-themed bars, with same owner. English music generally, good live bands on Fri and good atmosphere in general.

Tin Tin Deo
C 5, No 38-71, T2-514 1537, www.tintindeo.com.
Attracts students and teachers and is more forgiving of salsa beginners.

Zaperoco
Av 5N, No 16-46,T313-751 3266, Facebook: zaperoco.
The place for salsa purists.

Entertainment

Theatre
Teatro Experimental, *C 7, No 8-63, T2-884 3820, www.enriquebuenaventura.org.* Weekend theatre productions by the resident company.

Teatro Jorge Isaacs, *Cra 3, No 12-28, T2-889 9322, www.teatrojorgeisaacs.com.co.* Neoclassical 1930s building declared a National Monument in 1984. Hosts jazz and pop music events as well as comedy nights.
Teatro La Máscara, *Cra 10, No 3-40, T2-893 6640, Facebook: Teatro-La-Mascara.* Principally a women's theatre ensemble that stages alternative productions.
Teatro Municipal, *Cra 5, No 6-64, T2-881 3131, www.teatromunicipal.gov.co.* Since 1918, opera, ballet and weekly classical concerts, also home to the Cali Symphony Orchestra.

Festivals

Aug/Sep Festival Petronio Alvarez, Facebook: FestivalPetronioAlvarez, celebrating Afro-Latino and Pacific music.
Sep AjazzGo festival, www.ajazzgofestival.com, with international artists.
25-31 Dec Feria de Cali (www.feriadecali.com) is the biggest salsa festival in Latin America, bullfights at the Canaveralejo bullring, carnival in streets, horse parades, masquerade balls, sporting contests and general heavy partying.

Shopping

Best shopping districts are Av 6N, from Río Cali to C 30 Norte, and Cra 5 in the south with several new shopping malls including **Chipichape**, at the end of Av 6N, which has cinemas and a good choice of restaurants and shops.

Handicrafts
Artesanías Pacandé, *Av 6N, No 17A-53, Facebook: artesaniaspacande.* Typical regional handicrafts, Mon-Sat 0800-1830.
La Caleñita, *Cr 24, No 8-53, www.lacalenita.com.* Good selection of typical handicrafts.
Parque Artesanal Loma de la Cruz, *C 5, Cras 14/16. Daily 0900-2200.* Permanent handicraft market in a pleasant, safe neighbourhood, with cafés around the park, best in the mornings.
Platería Ramírez, *5 outlets including CC Unicentro, T2-660 5460, www.plateriaramirez.com.* Good selection of jewellery, lessons offered in jewellery making.

Transport

Air Alfonso Bonilla Aragón (Palmaseca) airport, 20 km from city. Minibus from airport, from far end of pick-up road outside arrivals, to bus terminal (ground floor), every 15 mins from 0430 up to 2020, approximately 30 mins, US$1.50-

2; taxis from here to city centre US$2-3. Minibuses to airport from 2nd floor of bus terminal till 2020. Taxi to city US$15-25, 20 mins. Frequent services to **Bogotá**, **Medellín**, **Cartagena**, **Ipiales** and other Colombian cities. International flights to **Miami**, **New York**, and **Panama**.

Bus Urban MIO metro buses US$0.75 a ride, single tickets sold at the stations; for multiple journeys and to use pre-trunk routes you need a MIO smart card, which you pre-charge (minimum US$1), www.metrocali.gov.co.

Long distance Terminal is at C 30N, No 2AN-29, T2-668 3655, www.terminalcali.com, 25 mins' walk from the centre (leave terminal by the taxi stands, take 1st right, go under railway and follow river to centre, or go through tunnel,

marked *túnel*, from the terminal itself). Left luggage (US$1), ATMs, showers and good food outlets. Buses between the bus station and the centre, US$0.75. Taxi from bus station to centre as above. To **Popayán**, many buses, US$7-9, 3 hrs. To **Pasto**, US$18-22, 8-9 hrs. To **Ipiales** (direct), US$24-27, 10-11 hrs; to **San Agustín**, 9 hrs, US$16-20. To **Cartago**, US$9-11, 3-4 hrs. To **Armenia**, US$8-12, 3-4 hrs. To **Manizales**, US$13-16, 4-6 hrs. To **Medellín**, US$21-24, 8-10 hrs. To **Bogotá**, 9-11 hrs, 4 companies, US$22-26. *Busetas* charge more than buses but save time; taxi-*colectivos* charge even more and are even quicker.

Taxi Ensure that taxi meters are used. Prices, posted in the window, minimum fare US$2. Extra charge on holidays, Sun and at night.

Popayán to Tierradentro

colonial architecture and pre-Columbian archaeology

The Pan-American Highway climbs out of the valley to Popayán, a historic city that gives access to the *páramo* of Puracé in the Cordillera Central and serves as a good base for visiting some of Colombia's most intriguing sights, including the burial caves of Tierradentro and the archaeological site of San Agustín. The Cauca valley has strong indigenous cultures, notably the Páez people.

Popayán *Colour map 1, C2.*

Founded by Sebastián de Belalcázar, Francisco Pizarro's lieutenant, in 1536, Popayán became the regional seat of government, subject until 1717 to the Audiencia of Quito and, later, to the Audiencia of Bogotá. It is now the capital of the Department of Cauca. The city lies in the Pubenza valley, a peaceful landscape of palm, bamboo, and the sharp-leaved agave. The early settlers, after setting up their sugar estates in the hot, damp Cauca valley, retreated to Popayán to live, for the city is high enough to give it a delightful climate. To the north, south, and east the broken green plain is bounded by mountains. The cone of the volcano Puracé (4646 m) rises to the southeast.

Sights Popayán has retained its colonial character, even though it had to be fully restored after the March 1983 earthquake. The streets of two-storey buildings are in rococo Andalucian style, with beautiful old monasteries and cloisters of pure Spanish classic architecture. **The Cathedral** (C 5, Cra 6) has been beautifully restored and has a fine marble Madonna sculpture behind the altar by Buenaventura Malagón and the unusual statue of Christ kneeling on the globe. Among the other churches are **San Agustín** (C 7, Cra 6), note the gilt altar piece; **Santo Domingo** (C 4, Cra 5), used by the Universidad del Cauca; and **La Encarnación** (C 5, Cra 5), also used for religious music festivals. Walk to **Belén** chapel (C4, Cra 0), seeing the statues en route, and then continue to **El Cerro de las Tres Cruces** if you have the energy, and on to the equestrian statue of Belalcázar on the **Morrode Tulcán** which overlooks the city; this hill is the site of a pre-Columbian pyramid. A fine arcaded bridge, **Puente del Humilladero**, crosses the Río Molino at Carrera 6. Public concerts and events are given in the gardens below. **Museo Negret y Museo Iberoamericano de Arte** (MIAMP) ① *C 5, No 10-23, T2-824 4546, http://museonegret.wordpress.com, Wed-Mon 0800-1200, 1400-1800, Sat-Sun 0900-1200, 1400-1700, closed Tues free*, has works, photographs and furniture of Negret and exhibitions of contemporary art. **Casa Mosquera** ① *C 3, No 5-14, www.unicauca.edu.co/museos/museomosq/info.html, Tue-Sun 0800-1200, 1400-1800, US$0.75*, has collections of colonial religious art and historical objects in the house of four-times president

Fact...
There are several ATMs on the main plaza. Best exchange rates are offered at **Titan** (Carretera 7, No 6-40, T824 4659, inside CC Luis Martínez, Monday-Friday 0800-1200, 1400-1700, Saturday 0830-1200).

Tomás Cipriano de Mosquera. **Museo de Historia Natural** ⓘ *Cra 2, No 1A-25, www.unicauca.edu.co/ museonatural, daily 0900-1100, 1400-1600, US$1*, has good displays of archaeological and geological items with sections on insects (particularly good on butterflies), reptiles, mammals and birds.

East from Popayán *Colour map 1, C2.*

The road from Popayán to **Tierradentro** is difficult and narrow, but with beautiful scenery. At Totoró there is a turning to **Silvia** in a high valley at 2520 m, 59 km northeast of Popayán. The town is best known for its Tuesday market when the friendly local Guambianos come to town in their distinctive blue and fuchsia clothes. The market (also full of Otavalo from Ecuador) is at its best between 0600 and 0830 and is very colourful. Information is available at the **Municipio** ⓘ *C 9, No 2-49, on the plaza, T2-825 1168, http://silvia-cauca.gov.co, 0800-1200, 1400-1800.* For horse riding enquire at the tourist office or hotels.

Inzá is 67 km east of Totoró and has several stone statues in its new plaza. Some 9 km beyond Inzá is the Cruce de Pisimbalá (or Cruce de San Andrés or just El Cruce), where a road turns off to **San Andrés de Pisimbalá** (4 km) and the archeological park (see below).

★Parque Arqueológico Tierradentro *Colour map 1, C2.*
Park and museum daily 0800-1600, US$7, under-7s and over-60s free, students half price, children 7-14 US$2, www.icanh.gov.co. When walking between the sites, take a hat and plenty of water. It gets crowded at Easter.

Popayán To Bus Station, Airport & Pasto / To ❶ ❷ & Cali

Where to stay ⬤	Restaurants ❼	9 Viña Parrilla *B2*
1 Auberge Campobello *A2*	1 Balcón de Los Santos *B2*	10 Wipala *B3*
2 Caracol *B3*	2 Capriccio *B2*	
3 Casa Familiar Turística *B2*	3 Casa Mosquera *B2*	**Bars & clubs** 🍸
4 Dann Monasterio *B1*	4 Italiano *B2*	11 El Sotareño *B2*
5 HostelTrail Guesthouse *B1*	5 Jengibre Especias y Sabores *B2*	12 La Iguana Café Bar *B1*
6 La Plazuela *B2*	6 Madeira Café *B3*	
7 Los Balcones *B2*	7 Salud y Vida *C2*	
10 Pass Home *B1*	8 Tequila's *B1*	

N

200 metres
200 yards

Tierradentro is one of Colombia's great pre-Columbian attractions and a World Heritage Site. Scattered throughout the area are man-made burial caves dating from the sixth to the 10th centuries AD. The tombs are decorated with red, black and white geometric patterns; some are shallow, others up to 8 m deep.

The **Tierradentro Museum** has exhibits on indigenous culture and very good local information. The second floor is dedicated to the work of the Páez, not to be missed. At the archway opposite the museum or at Pisimbalá village you can hire horses (US$3 an hour US$24 per day with guide; make sure they are in good condition) to explore the site, or you can walk. There are four cave sites: Segovia, El Duende, Alto de San Andrés and El Aguacate. The main caves are lit, but a torch is advisable. At **Segovia** (15 minutes' walk up behind the museum across the river), the guards are very informative (Spanish only) and turn lights on in the main tombs. Segovia has about 30 tombs, five of which can be lit. Fifteen minutes up the hill beyond Segovia is **El Duende** (two of four tombs are very good, faint paintings can be seen but take torch/flashlight). From El Duende continue directly up to a rough road descending to **Pisimbalá** (40 minutes). **El Tablón**, with eight stone statues, is just off the road 20-30 minutes' walk down. **El Alto de San Andrés** is 20 minutes from Pisimbalá. From the back of El Alto it is 1½ hours up and down hill, with a long climb to **El Aguacate** (superb views). Only one tomb is maintained although there may be 30 more. Guides are available.

The village of **San Andrés de Pisimbalá** lies at the far end of the Tierradentro Park (2 km from the museum). It has a unique and beautiful colonial church with a thatched roof; for the key ask behind the church. The surrounding scenery is spectacular, with small indigenous mountain villages to explore (get exact directions before setting out). The Páez people in the Tierradentro region can be seen on market days at Inzá (Saturday) and Belalcázar (Saturday); both start at 0600. The area is also good for birdwatching.

Listings Popayán and Tierradentro *map page 989.*

Tourist information

Popayán

The **tourist office** (Cra 5, No 4-68, T2-824 2251) has a good selection of maps and brochures. The **Alcaldía** (Cra 6 No 4-21), has set up 10 interactive information posts at strategic sites in the city. Its website is www.popayanmas.co. There is also a **Punto de Información Turística** (known as PIT), next door to the Cámara de Comercio de Cauca, **Cultura y Turismo** (Cra 7, No 4-36, T2-824 3625, www.cccauca.org.co, daily 0800-1200, 1400-2000). Ask the **tourist police** (T2-822 0916) which areas of the city are unsafe.

Where to stay

Popayán

Prices can rise by 100% for Holy Week and festivals, eg 5-6 Jan, when it's essential to book in advance. It is not safe walking alone at night outside the central area.

$$$ Dann Monasterio
C 4, No 10-14, T2-824 2191, www. hoteldannmonasteriopopayan.com.
In what was the monastery of San Francisco, lovely grounds, pool, spa, gym, very good.

$$$-$$ La Plazuela
C 5, No 8-13, T2-824 1084, www.hotellaplazuela.com.co.
Opposite Iglesia San José, beautiful colonial building, good-sized rooms with antique furniture set around a courtyard.

$$ Auberge Campobello
C 33AN, No 14A-14, T315-482 0265, www.hostalcampobello.com.
Off the Pan-American Highway, 300 m down road opposite **Torremolino** restaurant. Swiss/Colombian owners speak French, English, Spanish and Italian, safe, family atmosphere, nicely decorated, terrace, laundry service. Near bus station. Recommended.

$$ Los Balcones
Cra 7, No 2-75, T2-824 2030, www. hotellosbalconespopayan.com.
Huge and small rooms, antique furniture but up-to-date services.

$$-$ Pass Home
C 5, No 10-114, T2-824 3725/320-735 5088, hotelpasshome@gmail.com.
Relaxing atmosphere, welcoming, free laundry service if staying 3 days. Recommended.

$ Caracol
C 4, No 2-21, T2-820 7335/311-626 8840,
www.hostelcaracol.com.
Private rooms and a dorm (US$9 pp), shared bath,
café, book exchange, laundry service, kitchen,
bike hire and tours.

$ Casa Familiar Turística
Cra 5, No 2-07, T2-824 4853,
casafamiliarturistica@hotmail.com.
Popular, simple rooms with high ceilings and
thin walls, good notice boards for information
and messages from other travellers.

$ Hostel Trail Guesthouse
Cra 11, No 4-16, T2-831 7871/314-696 0805,
www.hosteltrailpopayan.com.
This excellent, efficient backpackers' hostel is run
by Scottish couple Tony and Kim. The rooms are
comfortable (cheaper with shared bath), cheaper
dorms (US$9 pp), good communal areas, DVD
room, bike hire, book shop and lockers. Extensive
knowledge of the local area. Bike tours to nearby
thermal springs. Recommended.

Tierradentro

$$ Albergue El Refugio
T321-811 2395.
Upscale cottages situated around a large pool.
Offers private bathrooms and hot water.

$ Hospedaje La María
San Andrés de Pisimbalá, T312-803 8947.
A family home in the village. Moto pick-ups are
available on request.

$ Hospedaje Lucerna
Next to the museum, T312-764 7333.
Run by a lovely couple, this little place has
clean, basic rooms and good showers (with
30 mins' notice).

$ Hospedaje Ricabet
Near the museum, T312-795 4636.
Flower-filled courtyard, clean rooms with bath
and hot water. Rooms with a shared bath are a
little cheaper.

$ La Portada
San Andrés de Pisimbalá, T311-601 7884.
Bamboo building at jeep/bus stop in
village. Rooms with bath and hot water.
Kind owners. Restaurant with excellent
menú del día, fresh soups.

Restaurants

There is a good selection of typical food from
the Cauca region in Popayán.

$$ Balcón de Los Santos
Cra 7, No 5-06, T2-832 0050,
www.balcondelossantos.com.
On the 2nd floor, on the corner of the plaza
with good views, serves traditional dishes.

$$ Rancho Grande
Autopista Norte 32N-50, T2-820 5219. Open Sun.
A short taxi ride from the city on the road to
Cali. 2 thatched restaurants, delicious *chuzos*
(barbecued beef), credit cards accepted.

$$ Viña Parrilla
C 4, No 7-07. Open 24 hrs.
Parrillada, huge selection of steaks and salads.

$$-$ Italiano
C 4, No 8-83, T2-824 0607.
Swiss-run, excellent selection of pastas, pizzas,
crêpes and fondues. Recommended.

$$-$ Salud y Vida
C 8, No 7-19, T2-822 1118.
Popular vegetarian place which also has cheap
lunches for about US$2.50.

$$-$ Tequila's
C 5, No 9-25.
Mexican-run cantina with decent Mexican food,
reasonably priced. Good cocktails. Recommended.

$ Jengibre Especias y Sabores
Cra 7, No 2-38, T2-820 5456.
Good for breakfast venue, *almuerzos* as well
as à la carte options.

Cafés
Popayán has a thriving café culture, with many in
colonial buildings.

Capriccio
Centro Comercial Campanario, Local 25,
Av Panamericana No 24 AN-21
Popular with the locals, in shopping mall out
of town beyond the airport, serving excellent
frappes, brownies and ice creams.

Madeira Café
C 3 y Cra 5.
Good selection of coffee, milkshakes, brownies,
juices and cheesecakes.

Wipala
Cra 2, No 2-38, see Facebook.
Art, local handicrafts and café in lovely
surroundings, with occasional live music.

Bars and clubs

Popayán

El Sotareño
C 6, No 8-05.
This eccentric bar plays old tango LPs from the 1940s and '50s as well as *bolero* and *ranchero* music. The owner has a huge collection of vinyl records.

La Iguana Café Bar
C 4, No 9-67.
Good music, jazz, salsa, loud and lively, friendly owner.

Festivals

Popayán

Jan **Fiestas de Pubenza**, with plenty of local music, incorporating **Día de los Negros** on 5 Jan and **Día de los Blancos** on 6 Jan as at Pasto but less violent; drenching with water is not very common. **Mar/Apr** **Semana Santa**, spectacular processions take place every night until Good Fri; at the same time there is an **International Religious Music Festival** and local handicraft fairs. The city is very crowded. The children's processions in the following week are easier to see.
Sep **Congreso Gastronómico de Popayán** (www.gastronomicopopayan.org), food stalls offer examples of the traditional cuisine of the area.

Shopping

Popayán

During the week, the open markets are interesting. **Mercado Bolívar** (C 1N, Cra 5) is best in the early morning for local foods such as *pipián*, *tamales* and *empanadas*. Another, better market, is **Mercado Esmeralda** on C 5 and Autopista.

Transport

Popayán

Air The airport is 20 mins' walk from the centre, T2-823 1671. Service twice daily to **Bogotá**. All passengers need a Migración Colombia stamp on their boarding pass from the Migración Colombia office (see page 1000), a quick formality.

Bus The bus terminal is opposite the airport, T2-823 1817, 15 mins' walk from the centre (Ruta 2-Centro bus, terminal to centre, US$0.50, or taxi, US$2 in the day, US$2.50 at night), www.terminalpopayan.com. Luggage can be stored safely (receipt given). From the bus station, walk up Cra 11 and take a left at C 4 to reach the centre. Take care if you cross any of the bridges over the river going north, especially at night. To **Bogotá**, **Continental**, US$33, 12-16 hrs, also **Expreso Bolivariano**. To **Cali**, US$7-9, 2½-3 hrs, *colectivos* leave from the main plaza. To **Pasto**, US$12-15, 4-6 hrs, spectacular scenery (sit on right – night buses are not safe). To **Ipiales**, **Expreso Bolivariano**, **Cootranar** and **Transipiales**, US$14-20, 6-8 hrs, frequent services, but some buses arrive full from Cali, book in advance. To **San Agustín**: several companies go to **Pitalito**, US$9-11, 7 hrs (eg **Cootranshuila**) from where you can catch a taxi *colectivo*, US$2. Via Isnos **Cootranshuila**, US$10-13, and others, several a day mainly mid-morning to afternoon, 5-7 hrs. Sit on the left for the best views. To **Puracé**, **Cootranshuila** US$5, 2½ hrs, hourly. To **Silvia**, daily **Coomotorista** and **Belalcázar**, several *busetas* in the morning, US$2.50.

Taxi No meters; normal price within city is US$2.

Tierradentro

Bus From Popayán, 4-5 daily 0430-1330, US$7-9, 4-6 hrs to **Cruce Pisimbalá**. Best to take early buses, as afternoon buses will leave you at the Cruce in the dark. Walk uphill (about 2 km, 30 mins) to the museum and on, 20 mins, to the village. If you want to go to **Silvia**, take this bus route and change to a *colectivo* (US$1) at Totoró. Returning to Popayán, there are 4 daily buses from Pisimbalá, but services are erratic. Otherwise, you must go to El Cruce. Buses and *camionetas* also go from El Cruce south to **La Plata** (en route to San Agustín, see below), US$3, 4-5 hrs or more frequent *colectivo* jeeps, US$4.50. If you cannot get a direct Cruce–La Plata bus, take one going to Páez (Belalcázar) (US$1), alight at Guadualejo, 17 km east of Inzá, from where there is a more frequent service to La Plata. The roads from Totoró and La Plata to Inzá are being paved.

Routes to San Agustín

don't miss the mysterious megaliths

There are two routes from Popayán to San Agustín, both of which go through the highlands of the Puracé National Park, with its volcanoes, hot springs and the sources of four great rivers. One route goes east to join the main highway from Bogotá, while the other, less secure road heads due south. The goal of the journey is one of South America's most mysterious archaeological sites, which is also one of Colombia's main tourist destinations.

☆Parque Nacional Puracé

At the time of writing the park was closed because of tensions between the park and its indigenous population. For information contact Parque Nacional Puracé office in Popayán, Sr Diomar Castro, T8-521 2578, or 313-424 6563, purace@parquesnacionales.gov.co, or the Parques Nacionales headquarters in Bogotá.

The national park contains Volcán Puracé (4640 m), Pan de Azúcar (4670 m), with its permanent snow summit, and the line of nine craters known as the Volcanes los Coconucos. The park also encompasses the sources of four of Colombia's greatest rivers: the Magdalena, Cauca, Caquetá and Patía. Virtually all the park is over 3000 m. The Andean condor is being reintroduced to the wild here from Californian zoos. There are many other birds to be seen and fauna includes the spectacled bear and mountain tapir. Pilimbalá is a good base from which to explore the northern end of the park.

Before climbing or hiking in the national park get advice on which areas are safe and, preferably, hire a guide. The terrain can be difficult, or dangerous from volcanic fumes. Although the best weather is reported to be December-March and July-August, this massif makes its own climate, and high winds, rain and sub-zero temperatures can come in quickly at any time. Some military areas are mined.

Puracé to La Plata

Some 30 km from Popayán is the small town of Puracé, at Km 12, which has several old buildings. Behind the school a 500-m-long path leads to Chorrera de las Monjas waterfalls on the Río Vinagre, which is notable for the milky white water due to concentrations of sulphur and other minerals. At Km 22, look for the spectacular San Francisco waterfall on the opposite side of the valley. At Km 23 is the turning right to Puracé sulphur mines (6 km) which can be visited by applying to the Popayán tourist office. About 1 km along this road is a turning left leading in 1.5 km to **Pilimbalá** in the **Parque Nacional Puracé** at 3350 m. Ordinary cars will struggle up this last stretch, but it's an easy walk from Km 23. Here there is a park office, seven sulphur baths (cold, no bathing), a restaurant and lodging (see Where to stay, page 996).

Continuing on the main road to La Plata, there is a viewpoint for Laguna Rafael at Km 31, the **Cascada de Bedón** (also chemically charged water) at Km 35, and another entrance to the most northerly part of the Parque Nacional Puracé at Km 37. Here you'll find a visitor centre, a **geology/ethnology museum** ① US$1, and the very interesting **Termales de San Juan** ① *700 m from the road, US$0.50,* where 112 hot sulphur springs combine with icy mountain creeks to produce spectacular arrays of multicoloured mosses, algae and lichens, a must if you are in the area (bathing strictly prohibited; there is a restaurant).

In the central plaza in **La Plata** is an enormous ceiba tree, planted in 1901. La Plata is an important road junction in the region, with transport north to El Cruce for Tierradentro (see above). Another road goes 41 km east to join the main Bogotá–Neiva–Pitalito highway, some 60 km south of Neiva (see page 995), while a southerly road through Pital joins the same highway some 42 km before Pitalito.

Pitalito and Parque Nacional Cueva de los Guácharos

Permission to visit the park must be obtained from the National Parks Office, Cra 4, No 9-25, Acevedo, T8-831 7487/313-258 0268, guacharos@parquesnacionales.gov.co, or in Bogotá.

Pitalito has little to offer the tourist, save convenient access to the **Parque Nacional Cueva de los Guácharos**, which lies to the south. Between December and June swarms of oilbirds (*guácharos*) may be seen; they are nocturnal, with a unique radar-location system. The reserve also contains many of the unusual and spectacular cocks-of-the-rock and the limestone caves are among the most interesting in Colombia. The rangers are particularly friendly, providing tours and basic accommodation.

Popayán to San Agustín direct

South of Puracé towards San Agustín is **Coconuco** (altitude 2460 m; bus from Popayán US$1.50). Coconuco's baths, **Agua Hirviendo** ① T321-934 1746, http://aguahirviendo1.wixsite.com/coconuco, 1.5 km beyond the Hostería Coconuco (see Where to stay, page 996), on a paved road (mostly), US$3, US$2, children 5-8 years, have one major and many individual pools with an initial temperature of at least 80°C. There is one pool where you can boil an egg in five minutes. There are cabins for overnight stays. A track from town is quicker than the road. It gets crowded at weekends, but during the week it is a fine area for walking and relaxing in

Warning...

Heavy rain has weakened the road from Paletará to Isnos, 25 km of which are impassable to light vehicles and very tedious for buses and trucks. No efforts are being made currently to improve this road. There have also been reports of theft on the buses between Popayán and San Agustín; do not trust 'helpful' locals and do not put bags on the luggage rack. For all these reasons, avoid travelling by night on this route. Cyclists should avoid this route entirely.

the waters. About 6 km beyond Coconuco, near the road, are **Aguas Tibias** ① T310-543 7172, www.termalesaguatibias.com US$6, children US$3, warm rather than hot, with various pools, including one of mud, waterslide, zip-line, restaurant and accommodation ($$).

South of Coconuco by 24 km is **Paletará** with high grassland on a grand scale with the Puracé/Pan de Azúcar volcanoes in the background. Below the village (roadside restaurant and national park post) flows the infant Río Cauca. Ten kilometres south of Paletará, the road enters the **Parque Nacional Puracé** and there is a track northeast to Laguna del Buey. The road then enters a long stretch of virgin cloud forest. Some 62 km from Paletará at the end of the cloudforest is San José de Isnos (see opposite), followed by a steep drop to a dramatic bridge over the Río Magdalena and shortly to the main road between Pitalito and San Agustín.

★San Agustín Colour map 1, C2.

The little town of San Agustín, near the source of the Río Magdalena, is a peaceful place with a few colonial houses and cobbled streets still intact. It is on every travellers' itinerary because of its proximity to the 'Valley of the Statues', where hundreds of large rough-hewn stone figures of men, animals and gods can be found, dating from roughly 3300 BC to just before the Spanish conquest.

Little is known of the culture which produced them or what exactly the stone sculptures represent. One theory suggests that this culture came from the Amazon region. The sculptures also display indigenous and Asian influences. No evidence of writing has been discovered, but traces of small circular bamboo straw-thatched houses have been found. The sites were burial and ceremonial sites where it is thought sacrifices, including of children, were made to the gods. Some sites were also residential areas. Various sculptures found here are exhibited in the National Museum at Bogotá. Only about 30% of the burial mounds in the area have been excavated and many of those that have been opened were previously ransacked by grave diggers, who had looted their precious statues. There are about 20 well-kept sites.

The area offers excellent opportunities for hiking, although some trails to remote sites are not well marked, and other adventure sports. The rainy season is April-June/July, but it rains almost all year – hence the beautiful green landscape; the driest months are November-March. The whole area leaves an unforgettable impression: the strength and strangeness of the statues set against the great beauty of the rolling countryside.

Parque Arqueológico ① Daily 0800-1700. US$7 including museum, Parque Arqueológico and Fuente de Lavapatas, students half price, 7 to 14-year olds US$2, under 7s and over 60s free; if, at the end of the day, you wish to visit the following day for free, enquire first at the ticket office. It is recommended to hire a guide to gain a better understanding of the statues and what they represent. Guidebook in Spanish/English US$4 (available online for free at www.icanh.gov.co). The nearest archaeological sites are in the Parque Arqueológico, 3 km from San Agustín. At the entrance is the **Museo Arqueológico**, which displays pottery and information about San Agustín culture (Spanish only). The 130 statues and graves in the Parque are in situ, though those in the Bosque (a little wood) have been moved and rearranged, and linked by gravel footpaths. Originally, the statues were found lying down and covered in the graves. Those excavated have been placed upright next to the graves and fenced in. Beyond the central area are the carved rocks in and around the stream at the **Fuente de Lavapatas** in the park, where the water runs through carved channels. The **Alto de Lavapatas**, above the Fuente, has an extensive view. You can get a good idea of the Parque, the Bosque and the museum in the course of three hours' walking, or add in El Tablón and La Chaquira (see below) for a full day.

Tip...
Enquire about safety before walking to the more distant monuments. Beware of 'guides' and touts who approach you in the street. Have nothing to do with anyone offering drugs, pre-Columbian objects, gold, emeralds or other precious minerals for sale.

Other sites around San Agustín El Tablón is reached up Carrera 14, over the brow of the hill and 250 m to a marked track to the right. El Tablón (five sculptures brought together under a bamboo roof) is shortly down to the left. Continue down the path, muddy in wet weather, ford a stream and follow signs to the Río Magdalena canyon. **La Chaquira** (figures carved on rocks) is dramatically set half way down to the river. To walk to and from San Agustín is two hours.

At **La Pelota**, two painted statues were found in 1984 (three-hour return trip, six hours if you include El Tablón and La Chaquira, 15 km in all). Discoveries from 1984/1986 include some unique polychromed sculptures at **El Purutal** near La Pelota and a series of at least 30 stones carved with animals and other designs in high relief. These are known as **Los Petroglifos** and can be found on the right bank of the Río Magdalena, near the **Estrecho** (narrows) to which jeeps run.

Alto de los Idolos ① *10 km from San Agustín, daily 0800-1630, US$5, discounts for Colombians, those over 62 and 7-15*, can be reached by horse or on foot, a lovely (if strenuous) walk, steep in places, via **Puente de la Chaquira**. Here on a levelled hill overlooking San Agustín are 13 uncovered tombs and statues dating from 100 BC-AD 600. These statues, known as *vigilantes*, each guard a burial mound. One is an unusual rat totem; stone crocodiles are believed by some to have strong links with the Amazon region. The few excavated have disclosed large stone sarcophagi. It is not certain whether the vigilantes bear a sculpted resemblance to the inmate.

San José de Isnos and around
Alto de los Idolos can also be reached from **San José de Isnos**, 5 km northeast or 27 km by road from San Agustín. The road passes the **Salto del Mortiño**, a 170 m fall 7 km before Isnos, 500 m off the road. The main plaza in **Isnos** has restaurants and cafés and a **Cootranshuila** bus office. Isnos' market day is Saturday (bus 0500, US$2, return 1100, 1300, otherwise bus from Cruce on Pitalito road, or hitch).

About 6 km north of Isnos is **Alto de las Piedras** (included on same ticket as Alto de los Idolos), which have seven interesting tombs and monoliths, including the famous 'Doble Yo' and the tombs of two children. There are still over 90 tombs to be excavated. Only less remarkable than the statues are the orchids growing nearby. Some 8 km further is Bordones; turn left at end of the village and there is (500 m) parking for the **Salto de Bordones** falls, which are good for birdwatching.

Bogotá to San Agustín
The route south from Bogotá to San Agustín passes through **Neiva**, the capital of Huila Department. Neiva is a modern city on the east bank of the Río Magdalena, surrounded by rich coffee plantations, with a large and colourful daily market. **Villavieja**, 45 km north of Neiva, provides access to the ☆**Desierto de Tatacoa**, a small area (300 sq km) of scrub and arid eroded red soil with large cacti, isolated mesas and unusual wildlife. Four- or five-hour guided walks through the desert cost US$12 per person per day. There is also a **museum** ① *in the Casa de la Cultura on the main plaza, daily 0800-1800, US$2*, showing prehistoric finds in the area. On top of a small incline some 15 minutes' drive from Villavieja is the **Observatorio Astronómico de la Tatacoa** ① *T310-465 6765, www.tatacoa-astronomia.com*, run by Javier Fernando Rua who gives an excellent talk every evening at 1830, US$10 per person. There are also daytime observances of solar flares and eruptions, US$2.

Tourist information

San Agustín

For impartial advice visit the **Oficina Municipal de Turismo** (Plaza Cívica, C 3 y Cra 12, T8-837 3062 ext 15, www.sanagustin-huila.gov.co) or the tourist police at **Oficina de Policía de Turismo** (C 3, No 11-86). There are also 4 tour agencies calling themselves 'tourist offices'. They give out useful advice, but they also hold contracts with hotels and other operators. There are 2 banks with ATMs, but don't arrive short of cash.

Where to stay

Puracé to La Plata

In Pilimbalá there are picnic shelters, restaurant, lodging in room with bath ($ pp) and camping (tents and sleeping bags can be hired). Firewood is provided. Sleeping bags or warm clothing recommended to supplement bedding.

Other basic places to stay in La Plata are **Berlín** (C 4, No 4-76 on the Plaza, T8-837 0229), and **El Portal de Valencia** (C 6, No 3-58, T8-837 6304).

$ Cambis
C 4, No 4-28, La Plata, T8-837 1891.
Helpful, near bus station. Recommended.

$ Residencias Cubina
Puracé.
Safe, cold showers, secure parking.

Pitalito

$$ Hotel Calamó Plaza
Cra 5, No 5-45, T8-836 0603,
www.hotelcalamoplaza.com.
Hot water, pool, cafetería, parking.

$$-$ Hotel Yorytania Boutique
C 7, No 3-31, T8-836 6368.
Helpful, laundry service, café.

Popayán to San Agustín direct

$$$-$$ Hostería Coconuco
500 m south of Coconuco, T2-827 1014, or 313-652 6179, www.comfandi.com.co, 10 mins' drive to the baths, transport arranged.
The best, comfortable, hot water, price is full board, colonial-style hotel, restful atmosphere, activities arranged. There are several other modest hotels and restaurants in town.

San Agustín

Some hotels increase prices during Easter and Christmas by around 10-20%.

$$$ Yalconia
Vía al Parque Arqueológico, T8-837 3013,
hotelyalconia@hotmail.com.
By municipal pool, the only mid-range hotel in town, modern building, pool.

$$ Hacienda Anacaona
Vía al Estrecho del Magdalena, 2 km from town, T311-231 7128, www.anacaona-colombia.com.
Elegant traditional finca, attractive, beautiful views and garden, hammocks, restaurant, quiet. Camping allowed on grounds. Good.

$$ Hostal Huaka-Yo
200 m from entrance to San Agustín. T571-489 9269, www.huakayo.com.
Large rooms in wooden terraced buildings in spacious manicured grounds, popular with school groups.

$$-$ Casa de Nelly
Km 2 Vía Parque Archeológico, T310-215 9067, www.hosteltrail.com/hostels/hotelcasadenelly.
On top of the hill on the road to the archeological park, colourful rooms and *cabañas* set in a gorgeous garden, home-cooked pastas and pizzas, hammocks.

$$-$ El Jardín
Cra 11, No 4-10, T8-837 3455,
www.hosteltrail.com/hostels/eljardin.
In town, colonial house with a colourful patio, simple rooms, dorms, restaurant with fixed-menu lunches.

$$-$ pp Finca El Maco
1 km from town, 400 m past Piscina Las Moyas, T8-837 3437, www.elmaco.ch.
Swiss owned, working organic farm with colourful gardens, rustic, peaceful, cosy cabins for 1-6 (US$7-47 pp), also teepee, welcoming, laundry service, very good restaurant (reserve ahead), great local information; see **Chaska Tours** below.

$ pp Finca El Cielo
3 km from San Agustín, Vía El Estrecho/Obando, T313-493 7446, Facebook: fincaelcielosanagustin.
Guesthouse and organic farm, overlooking Río Magdalena, restaurant, camping, swimming pool, tours organized in the area and beyond, also live music, dance and riding classes.

$ La Casa de François
T8-837 3847, T314-358 2930, 200 m via El Tablón,
www.lacasadefrancois.com.
Just outside town, French-run, private rooms,
dorms (US$8.50-10) and camping set in 2 ha
of gardens, good breakfast, meals, crêpes and
home-baked bread available, bike and horse hire.

$ Posada Campesina
Cra 14, Camino al Estrecho (on the route to
El Tablón), 1 km from town, T312-562 0826,
posadacampesinasanagustin@gmail.com.
A recommended farmhouse, owned by Doña
Silvina Patiño, who makes good pizza and cheese
bread, meals with family, simple working farm,
shared bath, use of kitchen, camping possible,
good walks nearby.

Camping

Camping San Agustín
1 km from town towards Parque Arqueológico,
opposite clean public swimming pool,
Las Moyas, T8-837 3804/311-846 7555.
US$7, plus charge pp with own tent, US$6 pp to
hire tent, clean, pleasant, safe (guards), showers,
toilets, lights, laundry service, horse hire.

Bogotá to San Agustín

Neiva

$$$ Neiva Plaza
C 7, No 4-62, T8-871 0806,
www.hotelneivaplaza.com.
Neiva's traditional smart hotel for some
60 years, good, comfortable rooms,
restaurant, gym and pool.

$$-$ Andino
C 9, No 5-82, T8-871 0184, hotelandinoycolina@
hotmail.com.
Central, rooms are a little small and dark but clean.

Villavieja and Desierto de Tatacoa

Camping is permitted at the observatory
(US$3.50 to hire tent) or accommodation is
available in Villavieja (**$**). There are also several
posadas nativas, run by local families, enquire
at the **Asociación de Operadores Turísticos**
(on the Parque Principal, T313-804 9580, www.
villavieja-huila.gov.co).

Restaurants

San Agustín

Tap water in San Agustín is not safe to drink.

$$ Donde Richard
C 5, No 23-45, T312-432 6399.
On the outskirts of town. Good steaks,
chicken and fish, soups and salads, agreeable
surroundings. Recommended.

$$-$ Pepe Nero
C 5, No 18-287, T319-258 4556.
Red-checkered tablecloths and Italian fare in a
pleasant environment, has a good wine selection.

$ Brahama
C 5, No 15-21, T310-750 5934.
This small restaurant serves Colombian fare and
some good vegetarian options.

$ El Fogón
C 5, No 14-30.
Family run, good *comida* and juices, fresh salads.
Recommended.

$ Surabhi
C 5, No 14-09, T314-294 5368.
Tasty regional specialities and set lunches.

Festivals

San Agustín

24 Jun **San Juan**, horse races and dances.
29 Jun **San Pedro**, horse races, dances,
fancy dress and more.
Mid-Jul **Santa María del Carmen**.
1st week of Oct **La Semana Cultural
Integrada** at the Casa de Cultura, with folklore
performances from all parts of the country.

Bogotá to San Agustín

Neiva

Late Jun/early Jul **Festival Nacional del
Reinado del Bambuco**, incorporating San Juan
and San Pedro: dancing competitions, parades
on the river and through the streets.

What to do

San Agustín

Guides

There are countless guides in town offering
tours of the various sites. Some give a better
service than others. Enquire at your hotel or at
the tourist office for advice. Some recommended
names are **Marino Bravo** (T311-835 6736), takes
walking, riding and minibus tours, authorized,
professional, speaks English, French and Italian;
Gloria Amparo Palacios (T311-459 5753), and
Carlos Bolaños (T311-459 5753); **Fabio Burbano**

(T8-837 3592, 311-867 5665), professional, reliable and knowledgeable; **Luis Alfredo Salazar** (T8-837 3426), speaks English, French, Italian. They charge US$15 for a half day, US$30 for a full day.

Horse riding

You are strongly advised to hire horses for trips around San Agustín through hotels. These cost about US$6 per hr, per rider, or US$25 per day with guide. **Pacho** (T311-827 7972, pachitocampesinito@yahoo.es, also does tours to Lago Magdalena, the source of the Río Magdalena, US$27 for guidance plus US$20 pp), is recommended and is contactable through **La Casa de Nelly**.

Rafting

Magdelana Rafting, *C 5, No 16-04, T311-271 5333, www.magdalenarafting.com*. Run by experienced Frenchman Amid Bouselahane, offers various rafting, kayaking and caving tours.

Tours

Jeeps may be hired for 4-5 people. Prices vary according to the number of sites to be visited, but the rate is about US$20 pp per day with a minimum of 4 people.

Chaska Tours, *T8-837 3437, 311-271 4802, www.chaskatours.net*. Run by Swiss René Suter (who also owns **Finca El Maco**), organizes tours around San Agustín, Tierradentro and throughout Colombia. English and German spoken. Recommended.

Theft is common at all bus stations in this region.

Puracé to La Plata

Several buses daily to Puracé from Popayán, last returning 1700. Bus stops 3.5 km from Pilimbalá. All the places beyond Puracé village can be reached by bus from **Popayán** to La Plata. The bus service can be erratic so check time of last daylight bus to Popayán and be prepared to spend a cold night at 3000 m. The rangers will allow you to stay in the centre.

From La Plata there are buses to **Bogotá**, via Neiva, **Coomotor**, 9 hrs, in the evening, **Cootranshuila**, 5 a day, US$21-25. To **Popayán** 0500 and others, US$12.50, 5½ hrs. To **San Agustín**, direct US$10 or take a *colectivo* to Pitalito and change. For **Tierradentro** take a bus towards Popayán (leaves 0600-0630) and alight at the Cruce US$3. Private jeep hire La Plata–Tierradentro US$50, cheaper if you pick up other passengers. To **Pitalito**, 3½ hrs, US$7.50-10.

Pitalito

Plenty of buses and *colectivos* to **San Agustín**, US$3-4. Bus to **La Plata**, 3½ hrs, US$7.50-10. Bus to **Bogotá**, 9-10 hrs, US$25-28. Bus to **Mocoa** (in the Putumayo), US$8, 3-4 hrs. To **Tierradentro**, catch a *colectivo* jeep to La Plata, US$9, 3½ hrs, from where you can usually get a *chiva*, bus or *colectivo*, 2-3 hrs to San Andrés de Pisimbalá the same day. To **Parque Nacional Cueva de los Guácharos**, take a bus/*chiva* to Palestina, US$2, 1 hr, then a 40-min *chiva* to Mensura. From there, 8-km walk or horse ride to visitor centre.

San Agustín

Bus To Bogotá by *colectivo* with **Taxis Verdes** (C 3, No 11-27, T8-837 3068, or C 17, No 68D-54, T1-411 1152 in Bogotá, www.taxisverdes.net) daily, direct or change at Neiva, US$19-22, 9-11 hrs (go early); or by bus with **Coomotor** (C 3, No 10-71), 4 a day, US$22-26, 10-12 hrs. Most services going to Bogotá will also stop at Neiva, 6 hrs, US$10-15. From **Bogotá**, **Taxis Verdes** will pick up at hotels (extra charge); alternatively, travel to Pitalito (30 mins, see above), then change. To **Tierradentro**, check first if any of the tourist offices is running a jeep, otherwise travel via Pitalito. Do not take a night bus to Tierradentro. There are several daily buses from San Agustín to **Popayán** via Isnos with **Cootranshuila** (office on C 3, No 10-81) and others, along the slow, unpaved road, 6-8 hrs, US$10-12. Do not travel between San Agustín and Popayán at night; the road is isolated and dangerous. Some Popayán-San Agustín buses drop passengers outside San Agustín. It's best to book seats the day before.

Bogotá to San Agustin

Neiva

Air La Marguita, 1.5 km from city. Daily flights to/from **Bogotá** and principal cities. Taxi to bus terminal US$4.

Bus Station out of town, www.elterminalneiva.com; bus from the centre leaves from the old terminal (Cra 2, Cs 5 y 6). To **Bogotá**, 6 hrs, US$15-19. To **San Agustín**, US$10-12, 6 hrs. To **Pitalito**, US$10-12, 3 hrs. To **La Plata**, for Tierradentro, US$7.50-10, 2 hrs, frequent services (especially early morning, 0400, 0500). To **Popayán**, US$14-17, 8-11 hrs, poor road in parts. All services with Coomotor. To **Villavieja**, daily with **Flotahuila** and **Coomotor** from Neiva bus terminal, 1 hr, US$3-5.

Villavieja

From Villavieja hire a taxi to **Tatacoa desert**, US$12 return. You can cross the Magdalena by motorized canoe near Villavieja for US$1, then it's 1.5 km to Aipe for buses on the Neiva–Bogotá road.

South to Ecuador

dramatic journeys through the cordillera

From Popayán to Ecuador is scenic highland country, much of it open *páramo* intersected here and there by spectacular deep ravines. From Popayán to Pasto is 285 km (five hours' driving). The road drops to 700 m in the valley of the Río Patía before climbing to Pasto with big temperature changes. To the west is the long slope down to the Pacific. To the east is the continental divide of the Cordillera Oriental and the beginning of the great Amazonian basin.

Pasto *Colour map 1, C2.*

Pasto, 88 km from Ecuador, is in a very attractive setting, overlooked from the west by Volcán Galeras and to the east by green hills not yet suburbanized by the city. It was founded in the early days of the conquest and retains some of its colonial character. During the wars of independence, it was a stronghold of the Royalists and the last town to fall into the hands of the patriots after a bitter struggle. The people of Nariño Department, of which Pasto is capital, wanted to join Ecuador when that country split off from Gran Colombia in 1830, but were prevented by Colombian troops.

There are several churches worth visiting: ornate **San Juan Bautista** and **La Merced** ① *C 18A, No 25-11*, **Cristo Rey** ① *C 20, No 24-64* and **Santiago** ① *Cra 23 y C 13*, which has good views over the city to the mountains. The **Museo de Oro del Banco de la República** ① *C 19, No 21-27, T2-721 3001, www.banrepcultural.org/pasto, Tue-Sat 1000-1700, free*, has a small well-displayed collection of pre-Columbian pieces from the cultures of southern Colombia. **Museo Zambrano** ① *C 20, No 29-78, Mon-Sat 0800-1200, 1400-1600, free*, houses indigenous and colonial period arts, especially *quiteño* (from Quito). The **tourist office** ① *just off the main plaza, C 18, No 25-25, p 2, T2-723 4962, http://turismo.narino.gov.co, Mon-Fri 0800-1200, 1400-1800*, is friendly and helpful. See also the state tourist information website: www.culturapasto.gov.co, which is quite useful.

> **Tip…**
> Every Sunday paddle ball is played on the edge of the town (bus marked 'San Lorenzo'), similar to the game played in Ibarra, Ecuador.

Around Pasto

Volcán Galeras (4276 m) has been erupting frequently since 1989. Check at the tourist office whether it is safe to climb on the mountain and whether you need a permit ① *open 0800-1400, information as for Isla de La Corota below, entry US$1*. A road climbs up the mountain to a ranger station and police post at 3700 m, beyond which you are not permitted.

On the north side of the volcano lies the village of **Sandoná** ① *frequent buses and colectivos daily, US$3, 1½-2 hrs from Pasto*, where panama hats are made; they can be seen lying in the streets in the process of being finished. Sandoná market day is Saturday.

The Putumayo

About 25 km east of Pasto, on the road to Mocoa is **Laguna La Cocha**, the largest lake in south Colombia (sometimes called Lago Guamuez). In the lake is the **Isla de La Corota** nature reserve ① *open 0800-1600, 10 mins by boat from the Hotel Sindanamoy, information T2-732 0493, corota@parquesnacionales.gov.co, or from the national parks office in Bogotá, US$1*, with interesting trees; camping is possible.

A steep climb over the Sierra leads to a large statue of the Virgin marking the entry into the Putumayo. The road then descends steeply to Sibundoy and Mocoa, in the transitional zone between Andes and Amazon. Beyond are the lowlands and the river towns of Puerto Asís and San Miguel (a crossing to Lago Agrio in Ecuador). For many years this was guerrilla territory, but it is opening up for ecotourism with lots of potential for visiting rivers and waterfalls and nature-watching. Seek local advice before heading to Ecuador this way.

Ipiales and Las Lajas *Colour map 1, C2.*

Passing through deep valleys and a spectacular gorge, buses on the paved Pan-American Highway cover the 84 km from Pasto to Ipiales in 1½-2 hours. The road crosses the spectacular gorge of the Río Guáitara at 1750 m, near El Pedregal, where *choclo* (corn) is cooked in many forms by the roadside. **Ipiales**, 'the city of the three volcanoes', is famous for its colourful Friday morning indigenous market but the main attraction is the ☆ **Sanctuary of the Virgin of Las Lajas**, about 7 km to the east. Seen from the approach road, looking down into the canyon, the Sanctuary is a magnificent architectural conception, set on a bridge over the Río Guáitara: close up, it is very heavily ornamented in the gothic style. The altar is set into the rock face of the canyon, which forms one end of the sanctuary with the façade facing a wide plaza that completes the bridge over the canyon. There are walks to nearby shrines in dramatic scenery. It is 10-15 minutes' walk down to the sanctuary from the village. There are great pilgrimages to it from Colombia and Ecuador (very crowded at Easter) and the Sanctuary must be second only to Lourdes in the number of miracles claimed for it.

Border with Ecuador

Ipiales is 2 km from the Rumichaca bridge across the Río Carchi into Ecuador. The border post stands on a concrete bridge, beside a natural bridge, where customs and passport examinations take place 24 hours. All Colombian offices are in one modern complex: **Migración Colombia** (immigration, exit stamp given here), customs, **INTRA** (Dept of Transportation, car papers stamped here; if leaving Colombia you must show your vehicle entry permit)

> **Fact...**
> There is a *casa de cambio* on the plaza. Money changers on the street, in the plaza and at the border may take advantage of you if the banks are closed.

and **ICA** (Department of Agriculture for plant and animal quarantine). There is also a restaurant, Telecom, clean bathrooms (US$0.10) and ample parking. See Ecuador chapter for the Ecuadorean side. The **Ecuadorean consulate** ① *Cra 7, No 14-10, p2, T2-773 2292/4801, cecuipiales@mmrree.gob.ec, weekdays 0830-1700,* is in the Migración Colombia complex. There are many money changers near the bridge on both sides. There are better rates on the Colombian side but check all calculations.

Listings South to Ecuador

Where to stay

Pasto

$$$-$$ Galerías
Cra 26, No 18-71, p 3, T2-723 7390, www.hotel-galerias.com.
In the town's main shopping centre, good-sized rooms, parking, with a good restaurant.

$$$-$$ Loft Hotel
C 18, No 22-33, T2-722 6737, www.lofthotelpasto.com.
Comfortable, with minimalist decor, spa, gym. 20% discount if you show a copy of a Footprint guide.

$$ Fernando Plaza
C 20, No 21B-16, T2-729 1432, www.hotelfernandoplaza.com.
Smart, lots of good details such as orthopaedic mattresses, restaurant.

$ Koala Inn
C 18, No 22-37, T2-722 1101, www.hosteltrail.com/hostels/koalainn.
The best backpackers' option in town. Large, antiquated rooms, some with bath, laundry, cable TV, good local information. There is a small café serving decent breakfasts (US$2-3).

The Putamayo

There are hotels on the plaza in Mocoa and the Belgian-owned **$ Hostal Casa del Río**, Vereda Caliyaco, T8-420 4004, T314-304 5050, www.hosteltrail.com/hostels/casadelrio, dorms from US$6pp.

Ipiales and Las Lajas

Several basic hotels and a small number of restaurants at Las Lajas. The following are in Ipiales:

$$-$ Santa Isabel 2
Cra 7, No 14-27, T2-773 4172.
Smart, central, good services, parking, restaurant.

$ Belmonte
Cra 4, No 12-111, T2-773 2771.
Basic but clean, shared bath.

$ Emperador
Cra 5, No 14-43, T2-773 2311.
Central, best budget option, good rooms, hot water, parking.

Restaurants

Pasto

$ Asadero Inca Cuy
C 29, No 13-65, T2-723 8050.
Down a narrow corridor behind the Plaza de Bombona, specializes in fried guinea pig (*cuy*); book ahead as it takes an hour to prepare.

$ Guadalquivir Café
C 19, No 24-84, T2-723 9504,
See Facebook: GuadalquivirCafeSAS/.
A Pasto stalwart with more than 35 years' experience, this atmospheric café serves home-made snacks such as *tamales, empanadas de añejo* and *envueltos de choclo*.

$ Picantería Ipiales
C 19, No 23-37, T2-723 0393,
www.picanteriaipiales.com.
Typical food from Nariño, specifically pork-based dishes, and *almuerzos*.

Festivals

Pasto

5 Jan New Year festivities include **Día de los Negros** and **Día de los Blancos** the next day. On 'black day' people smear each others' faces in black grease. On 'white day' they throw talc or flour at each other. Local people wear their oldest clothes.

5 Feb and 28 Dec Fiesta de las Aguas, when anything that moves gets drenched with water from balconies and even from fire engines' hoses. All towns in the region are involved in this legalized water war!

31 Dec Concurso de Años Viejos, in Pasto and Ipiales huge dolls are burnt; they represent the old year and sometimes lampoon local people.

Shopping

Pasto

Handicrafts

Pasto varnish (*barniz*) is mixed locally, to embellish the colourful local wooden bowls. Leather goods shops are on C 17 and C 18. Try the municipal market for handicrafts.

Transport

Pasto

Air Daily flights to **Bogotá and Cali**, 3 a week to **Puerto Asís**. The airport is at Cano, 40 km from Pasto; by *colectivo* (beautiful drive), 45 mins, US$3 or US$18 by taxi.

Bus Bus terminal at Cra 6, No 16D-50, T2-732 4935, 4 km from centre, taxi, US$2. **Bogotá**, 18-23 hrs, US$47. **Ipiales**, 2 hrs, US$5-9, sit on the left for the views. **Popayán**, US$11-15. **Cali**, US$15-23, 8½-10 hrs. To La Cocha, take a taxi, a *colectivo* from C 20 y Cra 20, or a bus to **El Encano** and walk 20 mins from bus stop direct to lake shore.

Ipiales and Las Lajas

Air San Luis airport is 6.5 km out of town. Flights to **Cali** and **Puerto Asís**. Taxi to Ipiales centre, US$6.

Bus Companies have individual departure points: *busetas/colectivos* mostly leave from main plaza. *Colectivo* taxis go direct to Las Lajas, 10 mins, US$1 one way, or US$5 return by taxi. To **Popayán**, **Expreso Bolivariano**, **Transipiales**, US$15-19, 7½-8 hrs, hourly 0800-2000; also *colectivo* taxis, US$25. **Expreso Bolivariano** to **Cali**, US$20-27, 10-12 hrs. To **Pasto** US$8-10, 2-3 hrs. Frequent buses to **Bogotá** every 2 hrs, 20-24 hrs, US$47-52 (check if you have to change buses in Cali).

Border with Ecuador

It is easiest to take a taxi from Ipiales to the border, about US$7, although there are also *colectivos* from C 14 y Cra 11 to the border, US$1.50, and from the border to Tulcán, US$1.50.

Car If entering Colombia by car, the vehicle should be fumigated against diseases that affect coffee trees, at the ICA office. The certificate must be presented in El Pedregal, 40 km beyond Ipiales on the road to Pasto. (This fumigation process is not always carried out.) You can buy insurance for your car in Colombia at Banco Agrario, in the plaza.

Leticia, Colombia's port on the Amazon, is on the southern tip of a spur of territory which gives Colombia access to the great river, 3200 km upstream from the Atlantic. At the east edge of town is the land border with Brazil; the Brazilian port of Tabatinga starts directly at the border and the two cities function as one unit, although Leticia is safer and has better tourist services than Tabatinga; it's more expensive too. Across the river and downstream is a more relaxed and pleasant Brazilian town, Benjamin Constant, at the confluence of the Amazon and the Rio Javari (see Brazil chapter). On an island across from Leticia and Tabatinga is the small Peruvian town of Santa Rosa, which is prone to severe flooding in the rainy season. The best time to visit the area is in July or August, during the early months of the dry season. For the border between Brazil, Colombia and Peru see the Brazil chapter, where all procedures are detailed in one section.

Leticia *Colour map 3, A5.*

Capital of Amazonas Department, the city is clean and modern. Changes in the height of the river sometimes mean that the water is quite a distance from town and port facilities. Parque Santander y Orellana is pleasant and is a popular meeting place. Leticia is a good place to buy typical products made by the Amazon *indígenas*, which are sold at Museo Artesanal Uirapurú (C 8, 10-35). Housed in the beautiful Biblioteca del Banco de la República is the **Museo Etnográfico** ① *Cra 11 9-43, T8-592 7213 ext 8053, www.banrepcultural.org/leticia/museo, Tue-Sat 0900-1700, free,* which has displays on local ethnography and archaeology. There is a well-equipped hospital.

Tip...
Brazilian reais and Colombian pesos are accepted in all three towns, Peruvian soles are seldom used.

Tip...
For entry and exit stamps go to Leticia airport (T8-592 4535, Monday-Friday 0800-1700, Saturday-Sunday 0800-1500).

Jungle trips from Leticia

Full-day trips (eg to Puerto Nariño and Lago de Tarapoto) cost about US$75 per person. Colombian operators also run tours to several jungle reserves and lodges in Colombian, Brazilian and Peruvian territory; see What to do, below.

Reserva Natural Isla de los Micos ① *Entry US$10; Decameron has the concession for the restaurant here.* Upriver from Leticia, this island has few monkeys now, and those left are semi-tame. Native communities can be visited in the area: Huacarí of the Yagua people, opposite the island; Santa Sofía, upriver from the island, and Nazareth downriver, the latter two of the Ticuna people.

Parque Nacional Amacayacu ① *Partly open again since flood damage caused its closure in 2016. For the latest information write to amacayacu@parquesnacionales.gov.co, or contact the national parks office in Bogotá, www.parquesnacionales.gov.co.* The national park is located 60 km upstream, at the mouth of the Matamata Creek, two hours from Leticia. There is a jungle walk to a lookout and a rope bridge over the forest canopy, with wonderful views over the surrounding jungle. There are various other guided day treks through the jungle.

☆**Puerto Nariño** This is a small, attractive settlement on the Río Loretoyacu, a tributary of the Amazon, beyond the Parque Nacional Amacayacu, 75 km from Leticia. Where the two rivers meet is a popular place to watch dolphins. Tours include Lago de Tarapoto to see pink and grey river dolphin – the latter when the water level is high (US$70 per person by motorized canoe) and walks to indigenous communities. **Fundación Natütama** ① *T313-456 8657, http://natutama.org, daily except Tue 0800-1230, 1400-1700, US$6,* works to preserve the marine life of this part of the Amazon by organizing educational programmes with local communities. They have an informative visitor centre with an elaborate display of underwater life. Internet and international calls (expensive) can be made next to the school.

Tourist information

The tourist office is at **Secretaría de Turismo y Cultura** (C 8, No 9-75, T2-592 7569, Mon-Fri 0700-1200, 1400-1700, see www.amazonas. gov.co). There is also an office at the airport. There are several banks with ATMs in Leticia, and this is the best place to change money in the border area (cash only): good rates for US$ and reais, poor rates for Peruvian soles. Many street changers and *cambios* on C 8, near the market and port; beware of tricks. Tourist police (Policía de Turismo del Amazonas), T99-592 7569.

Where to stay

Leticia

$$$ Malokamazonas
C 8, No 5-49, T8-592 6642, www. hotelmalokamazonas.es.tl.
Family run, close to the border, a variety of rooms in thatched cabins, welcome drink, meals apart from breakfast extra, jacuzzi, laundry, cable TV, garden.

$$$-$$ Yurupary
C 8, No 7-26, T8-592 4743, www.hotelyurupary.com.
Good, large rooms, pool fringed with tropical plants, dinner available. Also arranges tours into the Amazon through **Yurupary Amazonas Tours** and runs **Aldea Yurupary** in Puerto Nariño.

$$ Fernando Real
Cra 9, No 8-80, T8-592 7362.
Intimate atmosphere, $ with fan, rooms open onto a flower-filled patio, minibar, good value.

$$-$ Divino Niño
Cra 6, No 7-23, T8-592 5594, www.divinoninohotel.com.
Not central but good value, simple, cheaper with fan, welcoming, dorm US$7 pp.

$ Mahatu Hostel
Cra 7, No 1-40, T311-539 1265, see Facebook: Mahatu-Hostel-568839959808864.
Far from the centre, a couple of private rooms with bath and dorms with fan (US$7-12 pp), kitchen, bar, nice ample grounds with ponds, small pool, hammocks, quiet location. Owner

speaks English, Flemish, French and Portuguese and organizes alternative tours of the Amazon.

Puerto Nariño

Increasingly travellers are choosing to stay in Puerto Nariño. Several options are available, see www.puertonarino-amazonas.gov.co, T321-454 7752.

$$$-$$ Casa Selva
Cra 6, No 6-78, T311-201 2153.
Comfortable, airy, spotless rooms, with breakfast. Tours to Lago de Tarapoto and other destinations through their operator **AT Amazonas Turismo Ecológico**.

$$-$ Maloca Napu
C 4, No 5-72, 2 blocks from river, T315-607 4044, www.malocanapu.com.
Simple private wooden rooms, dorms (US$7), quiet and relaxing. Breakfast provided.

$ Hospedaje Manguaré
C 4, No 5-52, T311-276 4873, claudia_alzate81@hotmail.com.
Comfortable cabin-style rooms with fans and bath, also has bunks in dorms. It doubles up as the town chemist.

Restaurants

Leticia

Several popular sidewalk restaurants near the corner of Cra 9 and C 8 serve good value set lunches (*comida corriente*) and à la carte in the evening.

$$ El Cielo
C 7, No 6-50.
Leticia's only 'gourmet fusion' restaurant, doing interesting things with local ingredients.

$$-$ Tierras Amazónicas
Cra 8, No 7-50, T8-592 4748.
Has an a/c dining room, faux jungle decor, but most of all great fresh fish (including crunchy piranha).

$ El Maná
Cra 8 No 10-24. Mon-Thu 0700-1900, Fri 0700-1600.
Good vegetarian set lunches, fruit juices, fruit salad, breakfast.

What to do

Leticia

Tour operators
Isaac Rodríguez, *Cra 6N, No 7-91 apto 117, T312-314 0311, isaacdrc@gmail.com*. Ministry of Tourism-registered guide.
Reserva Natural Palmarí, *Cra 10, No 93-72, Bogotá, T01-610 3514, www.palmari.org*. They operate a reserve on the Río Javarí (see Manaus to Colombia Where to stay, in the Brazil chapter).
SelvAventura, *Cra 9, No6-85, T8-592 3977, 311-287 1307, www.selvaventura.org*. Jungle tours and expeditions to natural reserves and indigenous territories, activities such as kayaking, trekking and canopying. English and several other languages spoken. Also run **Casa del Kurupira** hostel.
Turismo Verde, *no storefront, Leticia, T311-508 5666, www.amazonheliconia.com*. Run **Kurupira** floating hotel on the Colombian Amazon and **Heliconia Lodge** on the Río Javarí (see Brazil chapter).

Puerto Nariño

Tour guides
Ever Sinarahua (a boatman), **Clarindo López** and **Milciades Peña** are recommended for their local knowledge of flora and fauna and indigenous customs; they work with tour operators. Also, **Pedro Nel Cuello**, enquire through **Fundación Natutama** (see page 1002), also recommended.

Transport

Leticia
Air Airport is 1.5 km north of the city; small terminal, few facilities, T8-592 8133. Expect

> #### Fact...
> There is an obligatory US$7 environment tax payable upon arrival by plane in Leticia. You may also be asked for a yellow fever inoculation certificate on arrival; if you do not have this, an inoculation will be administered on the spot (not recommended).

to be searched before leaving Leticia airport, and on arrival in Bogotá from Leticia. Daily flights from **Bogotá**.

Boat Different docks are used at different times depending on water levels; ask around. Motorboat to **Santa Rosa**, Peru, daily 0700-1800, US$2 pp; to cross at night arrange ahead with a boatman, US$6.50 pp, beware overcharging and negotiate. If crossing to Santa Rosa in the early morning to catch the *rápido* to Iquitos, better to take a taxi to Tabatinga docks (it is not safe to walk) where a motorboat shuttles passengers starting 0230 (Colombia/Peru time), US$3 pp. Speedboats to **Puerto Nariño**, daily 0800, 1100 and 1500, return 0730, 1100 and 1600 (check times as they often change), 2 hrs, US$14-18. These will take passengers to the **Parque Nacional Amacayacu**, US$16 one way; let them know when you wish to return; 2 companies on alternate days, make sure that your operator travels the day you want to return.

Taxi Airport to the centre US$3.50; Leticia (including airport) to **Tabatinga** (including Brazilian immigration and ports) US$14 during the day, US$18 at night, mototaxi US$2.70; mototaxi (1 passenger only) within Leticia US$1.

Practicalities
Getting around

Avianca ⊕ www.avianca.com, is the national carrier. Other airlines are **LATAM Colombia** ⊕ www.latam.com, **Copa Airlines Colombia** ⊕ www.copaair.com, **Satena** ⊕ www.satena.com (government-owned, but linked with Avianca on some flights), **Easyfly** ⊕ www4.easyfly.com.co (a budget airline serving Bogotá, Medellín, Cartagena, Cúcuta, Bucaramanga, Neiva, Popayán, Valledupar and other smaller cities), **Viva Colombia** ⊕ www.vivacolombia.co (a budget airline serving Barranquilla, Bogotá, Bucaramanga, Cali, Cartagena, Medellín, Montería, Pereira, San Andrés, Santa Marta, other Colombian towns, Lima, Miami and Panama) and **Aerolínea de Antioquia, ADA** ⊕ www.ada-aero.com (based in Medellín, 19- to 32-seater planes serving most of the country). You cannot buy tickets with an international credit card online, but you can pay over the phone. Domestic airports vary in the services they offer and tourist facilities tend to close early on weekdays, and all Sunday. Local airport taxes are included in the price. Security checks can be thorough, watch your luggage. For information on airport taxes, see page 1013.

Always allow plenty of time if making international connections. The low-cost carriers are not always on time and bad weather can affect any domestic flight. Bus transport can also be delayed for a variety of reasons.

Bus

Travelling by bus in Colombia is exciting. The scenery is generally worth seeing, so travel by day; it is also safer and you can keep a better eye on your valuables. Almost all the main routes are paved, but the state of the roads, usually single-lane, varies considerably between departments. On main routes you usually have choice of company and type of bus. The cheapest (*corriente*) are basically local buses, stopping frequently, uncomfortable and slow, but offering plenty of local colour. Try to keep your luggage with you. *Pullman* (each company has a different name for the service) are long-distance buses usually with a/c, toilets, hostess service, DVDs. Sit near the back with your iPod to avoid the movie and the need to keep the blinds down. Luggage is normally carried in a locked compartment against receipt. The following bus company websites have further information: **Berlinas del Fonce** ⊕ www.berlinasdelfonce.com, **Bolivariano** ⊕ www.bolivariano.com.co, **Coomotor** ⊕ www.coomotor.com.co, **Copetran** ⊕ www.copetran.com.co, **Expreso Brasilia** ⊕ www.expresobrasilia.com, **Expreso Palmira** ⊕ www.expresopalmira.com.co, **Flota Magdalena** ⊕ www.flotamagdalena.com, **Velotax** ⊕ www.velotax.com.co and other *busetas* are slightly quicker and more expensive than ordinary buses to long-distance destinations. They may be called *colectivos*, or *vans* and are usually 12-20 seat vehicles, sometimes seven-seater cars or pick-up trucks. It is also possible to order a *puerta-a-puerta* (door-to-door) service at a reasonable price. When taxis provide this service they are *por puestos* (pay by seat) and do not leave till full. Fares shown in the text are middle of the range, where there is a choice, and are no more than a guide.

Note that meal stops can be few and far between, and short; take your own food. Be prepared for climatic changes on longer routes and for the vagaries of a/c on buses, sometimes fierce, sometimes none. If you entrust your luggage to the bus companies' luggage rooms, remember to load it on to the bus yourself; it will not be done automatically. There are few interdepartmental bus services on holidays. During holidays and high season, arrive at the bus terminal at least an hour before the departure time to guarantee a seat, even if you have bought a ticket in advance. If you are joining a bus at popular or holiday times, not at the starting point, you may be left behind even though you have a ticket and reservation. Always take your passport (or photocopy) with you: identity

Driving in Colombia

Road Signposting is poor and roads may be in poor condition. There are toll stations every 60-100 km on major roads: tolls are about US$2-3. Motorcycles don't have to pay. For excellent information in Spanish and English, including all the toll costs, see www.viajaporcolombia.com.

Safety Lorry and bus drivers tend to be reckless, and stray animals are often encountered. Always check safety information for your route before setting out. Police and military checks are frequent in troubled areas, keep your documents handy. In town, only leave your car in an attended car park (*parqueadero*). Only park in the street if there is someone on guard, tip US$0.50.

Documents International driving licences are advised, especially if you have your own car. To be accepted, a national driving licence must be accompanied by an official translation if the original is in a language other than Spanish. To bring a car into Colombia, you must also have documents proving ownership of the vehicle, and a tourist card/transit visa. These are normally valid for 90 days and must be applied for at the Colombian consulate in the country which you will be leaving for Colombia. A *carnet de passages* is recommended when entering with a European registered vehicle. Only third-party insurance issued by a Colombian company is valid; there are agencies in all ports. You will frequently be asked for this document while driving. Carry driving documents with you at all times.

Car hire In addition to passport and driver's licence, a credit card may be asked for as additional proof of identity and to secure a returnable deposit to cover any liability not covered by the insurance. If renting a Colombian car, note that major cities have the *pico y placa* system which means cars are not allowed entry in the city during morning and afternoon rush hour depending on the day and car number plate (does not apply during the weekends and public holidays); see www.picoyplaca.info for information.

Fuel 'Corriente' 86 octane, US$2.80 per gallon. More expensive 'Extra 94' octane, US$3.25, is only available in large cities. Diesel (known as ACPM) US$2.50.

and luggage checks on buses are frequent and on rare occasions you may be body-searched at army roadblocks.

Cycling

Cycling is a popular sport. There are good shops for spares in all big cities. Around Calle 13 with Cra 20 in front of La Sabana train station in Bogotá are a few repair and accessory shops.

Hitchhiking

Hitchhiking (*autostop*) is inadvisable and not common. In safe areas, try enlisting the cooperation of the highway police checkpoints outside each town and toll booths. Truck drivers are often very friendly, but be careful of private cars with more than one person inside. Travelling on your own is not recommended.

Taxi

Whenever possible, take an official taxi with a meter and ensure that it is switched on. If there is no meter, fix a price at the start of the journey. Official taxis should display the driver's ID with photo and additional legal tariffs that may be charged after 2000, on Sunday and fiestas. In some cities, fares are registered in units on the meter, which the driver converts to pesos with a fare table. This should be shown to the passenger. It is safest to call a radio taxi, particularly at night, rather than hailing one on the street. Bars, hotels and restaurants will order taxis for customers. The dispatcher will give you the cab's number which should be noted in case of irregularities. The last two digits of the number from where the call was made is *el clave*, the security code. Remember it as taxi drivers will ask for the code before setting off. Never get into a taxi if there are already passengers in it. If the taxi 'breaks down', take your luggage and find another taxi immediately. Taxis in some cities, such as Cali, have helpful Spanish phrases with English translation on display.

Where to stay

Hotels

The more expensive hotels charge VAT (IVA) – see Tax, below. Some hotels add a small insurance charge. From 15 December to mid-January, Easter and 15 June to 31 August and bank holidays (*puentes*), hotels in holiday centres may increase prices by up to 50%. Prices are normally displayed at reception, but in quiet periods it is always worth negotiating. See www.colfincas.com for a list of rural properties that can be rented. In the Zona Cafetera, try to stay at least one night on a coffee finca. See the Planning your trip chapter for our hotel price guide.

Camping

Sites are given in the text but also check locally very carefully before deciding to camp. Local tourist offices have lists of official sites, but they are seldom signposted on main roads. Permission to camp with tent, camper van or car is usually granted by landowners in less populated areas. Many haciendas have armed guards protecting their property: this can add to your safety. Vehicles may camp at truck drivers' restaurants, *balnearios campestres* with armed guards, or ask if you may overnight beside police or army posts.

Youth hostels

Federación Colombiana de Albergues Juveniles ① *Cra 7, No 6-10 Torre B, Bogotá, T1-280 3041, hostelling@fcaj.org.co*, is the national body. See **Hostelling International** ① *www.hihostels.com*, for affiliated hostels. **Colombian Hostels** ① *www.colombianhostels.com.co*, has a good network of 37 members around the country; **Hostel Trail** ① *www.hosteltrail.com/colombia*, also lists dozens of hostels countrywide (including many in these pages), and covers all of Latin America.

Food & drink

Restaurants

Most major cities have restaurants with non-local Colombian food and some international cuisine. Small towns do not often cater for vegetarians, but this is changing. Restaurants in smaller towns often close on Sunday, and early on weekday evenings, but you will probably find something to eat near the bus station. The filling three-course *menú del día*, also known as *menú ejecutivo* (daily set lunch), is excellent value. See the Planning your trip chapter for our restaurant price guide.

Food

Colombia's food is regionally varied. Some of the standard items on the menu are: *sancocho*, a meat stock (may be fish on the coast) with potato, corn (on the cob), yucca, sweet potato and plantain. *Arroz con pollo* (chicken and rice), a common Latin American dish, is excellent in Colombia. *Carne asada* (grilled beefsteak), usually an inexpensive cut, is served with *papas fritas* (chips) or rice and you can ask for a vegetable of the day. *Sobrebarriga* (belly of beef) is served with varieties of potato in a tomato and onion sauce. *Huevos pericos*, eggs scrambled with onions and tomatoes, are a popular, cheap and nourishing snack available almost anywhere, especially for breakfast. *Tamales* are meat pies made by folding a maize dough round chopped pork mixed with potato, rice, peas, onions and eggs wrapped in banana leaves (which you don't eat) and steamed. Other ingredients may be added such as olives, garlic, cloves and paprika. Colombians eat *tamales* for breakfast with hot chocolate. *Empanadas* are another popular snack; these are made with chicken or other meats, or vegetarian filling, inside a maize dough and deep-fried in oil. *Patacones* are cakes of mashed and baked *plátano* (large green banana). *Arepas* are standard Colombian fare; these are flat maize griddle cakes served instead of bread or as an alternative. *Pan de bono* is cheese flavoured bread, best enjoyed hot. *Almojábanas*, a kind of sour milk/cheese bread roll, great for breakfast when freshly made. *Buñuelos* are 4- to 6-cm balls of wheat flour and eggs mixed and deep-fried, also best when still warm. *Arequipe* is a sugar-based caramel syrup used with desserts and in confectionery, universally savoured by Colombians.

Bogotá and Cundimarca specialities *Ajiaco de pollo* is a delicious chicken stew with maize, manioc (yuca), three types of potato, herbs and sometimes other vegetables, served with cream and capers, and pieces of avocado. *Chunchullo* (tripe) and *morcilla* (blood sausage) are popular dishes. *Cuajada con melado* (or *melao*) is a dessert of fresh cheese served with cane syrup, or *natas* (based on the skin of boiled milk).

Boyacá specialities *Mazamorra* is a meat and vegetable soup with broad and black beans, peas, varieties of potato and cornflour. *Puchero* is a stew based on chicken with potatoes, yuca, cabbage, turnips, corn (on the cob) and herbs. *Cuchuco*, another soup with pork and sweet potato. *Masato* is a slightly fermented rice beverage. *Longaniza* (long pork sausage) is also very popular.

Santander and Norte de Santander specialities *Hormigas culonas* (large-bottomed black ants) are the most famous culinary delight of this area, served toasted, and particularly popular in Bucaramanga at Easter time. *Mute* is a soup of various cereals including corn. *Hallacas* are cornmeal turnovers with different meats, and whatever else is to hand, inside. *Carne oreada* is salted dried meat marinated in a *panela* (unrefined sugarcane) and pineapple sauce with the consistency of beef jerky. *Bocadillo veleño* is similar to quince jelly but made from guava.

Caribbean Colombia specialities Fish is naturally a speciality the coastal regions. In *Arroz con coco*, rice here is often prepared with coconut. *Cazuela de mariscos*, a soup/stew of shellfish and white fish, maybe including octopus and squid, is especially good. *Sancocho de pescado* is a fish stew with vegetables, usually simpler and cheaper than *cazuela*. *Chipichipi*, a small clam found along the coast in Barranquilla and Santa Marta, is a standard local dish served with rice. *Empanada* (or *arepa*) *de huevo* is deep fried with eggs in the middle. *Canasta de coco* is a pastry containing coconut custard flavoured with wine and topped by meringue.

Northwest Colombia specialities *Lechona*, suckling pig with herbs is a speciality of Ibagué. *Bandeja paisa* consists of various types of grilled meats, usually pork, *chorizo* (sausage), *chicharrón* (pork crackling), sometimes an egg, served with rice, beans, potato, manioc and a green salad; this is a paisa dish that has now been adopted in other parts of the country. *Natilla*, a sponge cake made from cornflour and *salpicón*, a tropical fruit sala, are popular desserts.

Southern Colombia specialities The emphasis here is on corn, plantain, rice and avocado with the usual pork and chicken dishes. *Manjar blanco*, made from milk and sugar or molasses, served with biscuit is a favourite dessert. *Cuy, curí* or *conejillo de Indias* (guinea pig) is typical of the southern department of Nariño. *Mazorcas* (baked corn-on-the-cob) are typical of roadside stalls in the south.

Drink

Tinto, the national small cup of black coffee, is taken at all hours and is usually sweetened. Apart from at the coffee fincas, Colombian coffee is always mild. Coffee with milk is called *café perico*; *café con leche* is a mug of milk with coffee added. To make sure you get cold milk with your coffee, ask for it separately at an additional cost. *Agua de panela* is a common beverage (hot water with unrefined sugar), also made with limes, served with cheese. *Care* is a milk and maize drink, known as *mazamorro* in Antioquia and as *peto* in Cundinamarca. *Kumis* is a type of liquid yoghurt. Another drink you must try is *champús*, a corn base, with fruit and spices. Many decent brands of beer are brewed, including Costeña, Aguila, Club Colombia and Poker. The **Bogotá Beer Company (BBC)** has its own small brewery in the capital and several bars serving its own delicious British- and German-style beers. Its bottled ales are becoming available around the country. The local rum is good and cheap; ask for *ron* eg **Ron Viejo de Caldas** and **Ron de Medellín**. *Aguardiente* is a 'rougher' cane-based spirit distilled with or without aniseed (*aguardiente anisado*). Try *canelazo*, cold or hot *aguardiente* with water, sugar, lime and cinnamon, common in Bogotá. Local table wines include Isabella; none is very good. Wine is very expensive, US$15 in restaurants for an average Chilean or Argentine wine, more for European and other wines.

Fruit and juices

As well as fruits familiar in northern and Mediterranean climates, Colombia has a huge variety of local fruits: *chirimoyas* (a green fruit, white inside with pips); *curuba* (banana passion fruit); *feijoa* (a green fruit with white flesh, high in vitamin C); *guayaba* (guava); *guanábana* (soursop); *lulo* (a small orange fruit); *maracuyá* (passion fruit); *mora* (literally 'black berry' but dark red more like a loganberry); *papaya*; the delicious *pitahaya* (taken either as an appetizer or dessert); *sandía* (watermelon); *tomate de árbol* (tree tomato, several varieties normally used as a fruit); and many more. All can be served as juices, either with milk or water. Fruit yoghurts are nourishing and cheap; **Alpina** brand is good; *crema* style is best.

Essentials A-Z

Accident and emergency

General line for all emergencies: T123; Policía Nacional: T112; **Fire**: T119; **Red Cross emergency**: T132; **CAI Police**: T156. If you have problems with theft or other forms of crime, contact a **Centro de Atención Inmediata (CAI)** office for assistance. CAI has many offices in Bogotá, including C 62 No 42C-07, La Candelaria, T1-715 1934; C 60 y Cra 9, Chapinero, T1-217 7472.

Electricity

110 volts AC, alternating at 60 cycles per second. Most sockets accept both continental European (round) and North American (flat) 2-pin plugs.

Embassies and consulates

For all Colombian embassies and consulates abroad and for all foreign embassies and consulates in Colombia, see http://embassy.goabroad.com.

Health

Medical facilities

Bogotá 24-hr emergency health service, T123. **Cruz Roja Nacional**, Cra 68, No 68B-31, T1-746 0909, www.cruzrojabogota.org.co, has 9 vaccination centres in **Bogotá** as well as emergency (T132) and other services. **Santa Fe de Bogotá** (Cra 7, No 117-15, T1-603 0303, www.fsfb.org.co), and **El Bosque** (C 134, No 7B-41, T1-649 9300, www.clinicaelbosque.com.co) are both modern, private hospitals, with good service. **Medellín** **Hospital San Vicente de Paul**, C 64, No Cra 51D-154, T4-444 1333, http://hospitaluniversitario.sanvicentefundacion.com, one of the best. **Clínica Soma**, C 51, No 45-93, T4-576 8400, good doctor and general services. There is an emergency health clinic in the Rionegro airport building.

ID

Always carry a photocopy of your passport with you, as you may be asked for identification. This is a valid substitute for most purposes though not, for example, for cashing TCs or drawing cash across a bank counter. Generally acceptable for identification (eg to enter government buildings) is a driving licence, provided it is plastic, of credit card size and has a photograph. For more information, check with your consulate.

Maps

Maps of Colombia are sold at the **Instituto Geográfico Agustín Codazzi**, Carrera 30, No 48-51, Bogotá, T1-369 4000, www.igac.gov.co, Mon-Fri 0730-1545, or from their offices in other large cities; see the website. They have a wide range of official, country-wide and departmental maps and atlases, but many are a few years old. Maps are US$2.25-4.50 and you pay at the bank next door. Many maps are available on the website. There is a library and refreshments are available at lunchtime.

A guide with detailed road maps is the annual *Guía de Rutas de Colombia* available at toll booths and some bookshops. Town maps are usually available from local tourist offices.

Money

US$1 = COP$3057; €1 = COP$3413 (Jun 2017). The currency is the peso colombiano ($). There are coins of 50, 100, 200, 500 and 1000 pesos in circulation; there are notes of 1000, 2000, 5000, 10,000, 20,000 and 50,000 pesos (the last can be difficult to change). Change is in short supply, especially in small towns, and in the morning. Watch out for forged notes. The 50,000-peso note should smudge colour if it is real, if not, refuse to accept it. There is a limit of US$10,000 on the import of foreign exchange in cash, with export limited to the equivalent of the amount brought in.

Currency exchange

Cash can in theory be exchanged in any bank, except the **Banco de la República**; go early to banks in smaller places to change these. In most sizeable towns there are *casas de cambio* (exchange shops), which are quicker to use than banks but sometimes charge higher commission. It's best to use euros and, even better, dollars. It can sometimes be difficult to buy and sell large amounts of sterling, even in Bogotá. Hotels may give very poor rates of exchange. Hotels are not allowed to accept dollars as payment by law. Some may open a credit card account and give you cash on that. It is dangerous to change money on the streets and you may well be given counterfeit pesos, or robbed. Also in circulation are counterfeit US$ bills. You must present your original passport when changing money (it will be photocopied and you may be fingerprinted, too). Take US$ cash with you for emergencies.

Credit/debit cards

As it is unwise to carry large quantities of cash, credit cards are widely used, especially MasterCard and Visa; Diners Club is also accepted. American Express is only accepted in expensive places in Bogotá. Many banks accept Visa (Visaplus and ATH logos) or Cirrus/MasterCard (Maestro and Multicolor logos) to advance pesos against the card, or through ATMs. There are ATMs for Visa and MasterCard everywhere but you may have to try several machines. All Exito supermarkets have ATMs. Credit card loss or theft: Visa call collect to T01-800-912 5713, MasterCard T01-800-912 1303.

ATMs do not retain cards – follow the instructions on screen. If your card is not given back immediately, do not proceed with the transaction and do not type in your pin number. There are reports of money being stolen from accounts when cards have been retained. ATMs dispense a frustratingly small amount of cash at a time. The maximum withdrawal is often 300,000 pesos, which can accrue heavy bank charges over a period of time. For larger amounts try **Davivienda** (occasionally 500,000, or more, per visit) and **Bancolombia** (400,000 per visit).

Only use ATMs in supermarkets, malls or where a security guard is present. Don't ask a taxi driver to wait while you use an ATM. Be particularly vigilant around Christmas time when thieves may be on the prowl.

Changing money in Bogotá

Some bank head offices are grouped around the Avianca building and the San Francisco church, others in North Bogotá on or near C 72. The best way to obtain pesos in Bogotá is to use ATMs. Any other method will require your passport and, often, queues. Since it will probably require at least 2 or 3 attempts, either go downtown or in the north, where there are many banks. Several *cambios* on Av Jiménez de Quesada, between Cras 6 and 11, and in the north of the city. On Sun exchange is virtually impossible except at the airport. CC Hacienda Santa Bárbara has several *cambios*. **Orotur**, in the Hotel Tequendama building, is quick and efficient, cash only, including sterling. **Cambios**

New York Money, in CC Andino, loc 3-48, CC Unicentro locs 1-118 and 2-247, and other shopping malls, www.newyorkmoney.com.co, accepts sterling, efficient.

Cost of travelling

Prices are a little lower than Europe and North America for services and locally produced items, but more expensive for imported and luxury goods. Modest, basic accommodation will cost about US$15-25 pp per night in Bogotá, Cartagena, Santa Marta and colonial cities like Villa de Leiva, Popayán or Santa Fe de Antioquia, but a few dollars less elsewhere. A bed in a dormitory will cost US$8-12 in the main tourist cities, less elsewhere. A *menú ejecutivo* (set lunch) costs about US$2-4 and breakfast US$1.5-2.50. A la carte meals are usually good value and fierce competition for transport keeps prices low. The typical cost of internet is US$1 per hr.

National parks

The national parks service is at the **Ministerio del Medio Ambiente**, Vivienda y Desarrollo Territorial (Ministry of the Environment, www. minambiente.gov.co), **Ecotourism office**, C 74, No 11-81, Bogotá, T1-353 2400, www.parques nacionales.gov.co, Mon-Fri 0800-1700. It has a list of regional offices. Staff can provide information about facilities and accommodation, and have maps. If you intend to visit the parks, this is a good place to start and ask for up-to-date details and to obtain a permit. There is a library and research unit (Centro de Documentación) for more information. Some parks and protected areas require permits to visit; enquire here where these must be obtained before going to the park. Do not go directly to the parks themselves. Some prices vary according to high and low seasons. High season includes: weekends, Jun-Jul, Dec-Jan, public holidays and Semana Santa. Foreigners over 18 can participate on the voluntary park ranger programme; details from the Ecotourism office in Bogotá. You will have to provide photocopies of ID documents and Colombian entry stamp in your passport. A good level of Spanish is required.

The **Asociación Red Colombiana de Reservas Naturales de la Sociedad Civil**, Cra 39, No 16-39, Teusaquillo, Bogotá, www.resnatur.org.co, is a network of privately owned nature reserves that works with local people to build a sustainable model of environmentally friendly tourism.

Other conservation websites

www.colparques.net Promotes the national parks network, with useful background info (in Spanish only).

www.humboldt.org.co Site of Institute Von Humboldt, probably the most important environment research organization in Colombia. An excellent site describing different ecosystems and projects with ethnic communities (in Spanish).

www.natura.org.co Fundación Natura, excellent conservation information.

www.proaves.org Fundación ProAves, an NGO for the study and conservation of birds and their habitats; publishes a good *Field Guide to the Birds of Colombia*.

Opening hours

Business hours depend a lot on where you are, so enquire locally. Generally offices are open Mon-Fri 0800-1700, but in hotter zones may close for lunch, 1200-1400, closing 1830 or 1900. **Banks**: Mon-Thu 0900-1500, 1530 on Fri. **Shops**: open 0700 or 0800 till 2000 and on Sat, but may close for lunch; supermarkets have longer hours and are open on Sat and Sun, usually 0900-1900. Most businesses such as banks and airline offices close for official holidays while supermarkets and street markets may stay open.

Post

The name of the Colombian postal service is **4-72**, www.4-72.com.co. It offers a range of services from normal and express post to electronic mail, but its reputation for reliability and value is poor. Private couriers, such as **Servientrega** (www.servientrega. com), **Deprisa** (www.deprisa.com – a branch of Avianca, related to UPS) and international brands, are commonly used to send letters and packages, but they are not cheap either.

Public holidays and festivals

There are some 18 public holidays. The most important are:

1 Jan New Year's Day; 6 Jan Epiphany*; 19 Mar St Joseph*; Maundy Thu; Good Fri; 1 May Labour Day; Ascension Day*; Corpus Christi*; 15 Jun Sacred Heart*; 29 Jun SS Peter and Paul*; 20 Jul Independence Day; 7 Aug Battle of Boyacá; 15 Aug Assumption*; 12 Oct Columbus' arrival in America* (Día de la Raza); 1 Nov All Saints' Day*; 11 Nov Independence of Cartagena*; 8 Dec Immaculate Conception; 25 Dec Christmas Day.

When those marked with an asterisk (*) do not fall on a Mon, they will be moved to the following Mon. Public holidays are known as *puentes* (bridges).

Safety

Travellers confirm that the vast majority of Colombians are polite, honest and will go out of their way to help visitors and make them feel welcome. In general, anti-gringo sentiments are rare. However, in addition to the general advice given in the Practicalities chapter, the following local conditions should be noted. Colombia is part of a major drug-smuggling route. Police and customs activities have greatly intensified and smugglers may try to use innocent carriers. Do not carry packages for other people. Be very polite if approached by policemen in uniform, or if your hotel room is raided by police looking for drugs. Colombians who offer you drugs could be setting you up for the police, who are very active in Cali, on the north coast, San Andrés island and other tourist resorts.

There have been reports of travellers and Colombians being victims of *burundanga (scopolamine)*, a drug obtained from a white flower, native to Colombia. At present, the use of this drug appears to be confined to major cities. It is very nasty, almost impossible to see or smell. It leaves the victim helpless and at the will of the culprit. Usually, the victim is taken to ATMs to draw out money. Be wary of accepting cigarettes, food and drink from strangers at sports events and in buses. In bars watch your drinks very carefully.

At the time of writing (2017), Colombia features highly on many surveys of up-and-coming places to visit. This assessment is based in part on the improvement in the security situation as the internal armed conflict becomes less of a threat. For instance, a ceasefire between FARC and government is in place and negotiations, albeit sporadic, between the government and ELN are under way. Nevertheless, in some areas fighting between the armed forces and guerrilla groups continues and, where the influence of FARC and ELN has declined, paramilitary-style criminal groups are vying for control. Travellers should bear in mind that the situation is almost impossible to predict and for this reason, it is essential to consult regularly with locals for up-to-date information. Taxi and bus drivers, local journalists, soldiers at checkpoints, hotel owners and Colombians who actually travel around their country are usually good sources of reliable information. Travelling overland between towns, especially during the holiday season and bank holiday weekends, is in general safe owing to increased military and police presence along main roads. Do not travel between towns by road at night. As a loose rule, places to avoid are coca-growing areas, oil-producing regions and along Colombia's borders. The following areas, known as *zonas calientes* (hot zones), have been the focus of significant unrest: the rural areas down the eastern part of the country from **Arauca** and **Casanare** to **Meta**, including the entire border with Venezuela (but see below); some parts of **Putumayo** and **Nariño**; **Norte de Santander**; much of **Cauca**; from **Urabá** near the border with **Panamá** into northwestern **Antioquia** and most of **Chocó** (Bahía Solano and Nuquí are reported safe to visit); the ports of **Buenaventura** and **Tumaco** on the Pacific coast. If venturing into rural areas and hot zones ask first at your embassy. Unrest usually increases in the run up to local and national elections. Incidents in cities, including **Bogotá**, may also occur. It is essential to follow this up with detailed enquiries at your chosen destination. If arriving overland, go to the nearest hotel favoured by travellers (given in the text) and make enquiries. **Note** that rural hot zones are often littered with land mines.

Amazonas and, to a lesser extent, **Los Llanos**, have always been difficult to visit because of their remoteness, the lack of facilities and the huge distances involved. Our text is limited to **Villavicencio** and **Caño Cristales** and the **Leticia** region, but tour operators are beginning to offer trips to remote destinations in the Llanos. Remoteness is also a factor in visiting **La Guajira** in the north, but many tours go there.

Tax

Airport tax

The airport departure tax is about US$37, payable in dollars or pesos; see http://eldorado.aero. It may be included in the ticket price. Travellers changing planes in Colombia and leaving the same day are exempt from this tax. When you arrive, ensure that all necessary documentation bears a stamp for your date of arrival. There is also an airport tax on internal flights, about US$4 (varies according to airport), usually included in the ticket price.

VAT

19% as from Jan 2017. You can ask for an official receipt. Some hotels and restaurants add IVA (VAT) onto bills, but foreigners do not officially have to pay.

Telephone and Wi-Fi *Country code T+57.*

Ringing: equal tones with long pauses. Engaged: short tones with short pauses. To call a landline in Colombia from outside the area, dial the 1-digit area code, followed by the 7-digit number. To make an international call from Colombia, dial the IDD code of the carrier – Orbitel 005; ETB 007; Telecom 009 – followed by the country code. National and international calls can be made from public phone offices in all major cities and rural towns. You are assigned a cabin, place your calls, and pay on the way out. There is usually a screen to show you how much you are spending. You can also make calls from street vendors who hire out mobile phones (usually signposted '*minutos*'). For phone boxes for local calls, phone cards are the best option. It is relatively inexpensive to buy a pay-as-you go SIM card for your mobile phone. Mobile phone numbers start with a 3-digit prefix beginning with 3.

Public internet access is available in most areas of Colombia, although the cost and speed of access varies. Small towns and villages may not have connectivity, or it may be slow; the best service is generally available in the largest cities. Most hotels and major airports now have free Wi-Fi, as do cafés, bars, restaurants and some public spaces, but connectivity can be erratic. Keep your wits about you if using Wi-Fi spots outdoors; not all are safe. Likewise, cyber cafés sometimes get crowded and noisy, so keep an eye on your belongings.

Time

Official time is 5 hrs behind GMT.

Tipping

A voluntary charge is added to most bills, but you can have it removed if you are not happy with the service. Otherwise, 10% is customary. The bill will state the tipping policy. Porters, cloakroom attendants and hairdressers expect US$0.05-0.25. It is not customary to tip taxi drivers, but it is appreciated.

National tourism is handled by the **Ministry of Commerce, Industry and Tourism**, C 28, No 13A-15, Bogotá, www.mincit.gov.co, with its portal, **ProColombia**, at the same address, piso 36, www.colombia.travel. Departmental and city entities have their own offices responsible for tourist information: see the text for local details. These offices should be visited as early as possible for information on accommodation and transport, but also for details on areas that are dangerous to visit. Regional tourist offices are better sources of information on safety than the Bogotá offices; otherwise contact Colombia's representation overseas. See also Useful websites, below.

Useful websites
www.experienciacolombia.com A good tourism website.
http://off2colombia.com A tourism portal with loads of information.
es.presidencia.gov.co The government website.
http://fontur.com.co A government tourism website, with useful listings of all local tourist offices: PIT (Puntos de Información Turísticos).
www.pueblospatrimoniodecolombia.co Under the auspices of the Fondo Nacional de Turismo, 17 towns of the greastest national cultural interest.

Tourists are allowed to stay a maximum of 180 days in a calendar year. Make sure that, on entry, you are granted enough days for your visit. On entry you are given 90 days. If you wish to extend your permission to stay in Colombia, for a further 90 days, apply 2-3 days before your permit expires at a **Centro Facilitador de Servicios Migratorios** (**CFSM**) of Migración Colombia (www.migracioncolombia.gov.co gives a full list); it costs about US$28 in cash (US$32 by credit card). Take 2 copies of your passport details, the original entry stamp, 2 passport photos and a copy of your ticket out of Colombia. This does not apply to visas. If you overstay an entry permit or visa, a *salvoconducto* can be applied for at a CFSM. The *salvoconducto* is only issued once for a period of 30 days and is usually processed within 24 hrs; it costs about US$22. Take 2 recent photos and copies of your passport. The **Migración Colombia** head office in Bogotá is, C 26, No 59-51, Edif Argos Torre 3

p 4, T018000-510454, www.migracioncolombia. gov.co (see main text for addresses in other cities). Arrive early in the morning, expect long queues and a painfully slow bureaucratic process. **Note** Migración Colombia accepts credit and debit cards, but does not accept cash payments; these are made at the branches of authorized local banks with special payments slips (the CFSMs will indicate which bank). An onward ticket may be asked for at land borders or Bogotá international airport. You may be asked to prove that you have sufficient funds for your stay.

Visas
To visit Colombia as a tourist, nationals of countries of the Middle East (except Israel and UAE), Asian countries (except Japan, South Korea, Phillipines, Indonesia and Singapore), Cuba, Haiti, Nicaragua, Serbia, Bosnia and Herzegovina, Kosovo, Macedonia, Montenegro and all African countries (except South Africa) need a **visa**. Always check for changes in regulations before leaving your home country. Visas are issued only by Colombian consulates. When a visa is required you must present a valid passport, 2 photos on a white background, the application form (in duplicate), US$80, onward tickets, and a photocopy of all the documents (allow 2 weeks maximum). A non-refundable charge of US$52 is made for any study made by the Colombian authorities prior to a visa being issued. Canadian citizens have to pay a fee of COP$160,000 (about US$53) to enter Colombia.

If you are going to take a Spanish course for an academic term or longer, you must have a student visa which costs US$51, with an additional US$16 administration fee, valid for 5 years. You may not study on a tourist visa. A **student visa** can be obtained while in Colombia on a tourist visa. Proof of sufficient funds is necessary. You must be first enrolled in a course from a bona fide university to apply for a student visa. Various business and other temporary visas are needed for foreigners who have to reside in Colombia for a length of time. The **Ministerio de Relaciones Exteriores**, C 10, No 5-51, T1-381 4000, www.cancilleria.gov.co, Mon-Fri 0800-1700, processes student and some work visas. In general, Colombian work visas can only be obtained outside Colombia at the appropriate consulate and or embassy. You must register work and student visas at a Migración Colombia office within 15 days of obtaining them, otherwise you will be liable to pay a hefty fine.

Visas must be used within 3 months. Supporting documentary requirements for visas change frequently. Check with the appropriate consulate in good time before your trip.

Entering Colombia

When entering the country, you will be given the copy of your DIAN (Customs) luggage declaration. Keep it; you may be asked for it when you leave. If you receive an entry card when flying in and lose it while in Colombia, apply to any Migración Colombia office who should issue one and restamp your passport for free. Normally passports are scanned by a computer and no landing card is issued, but passports still must be stamped on entry. Note that to leave Colombia you must get an exit stamp from the Migración Colombia. They often do not have offices at the small border towns, so try to get your stamp in a main city.

Note It is highly recommended that you photocopy your passport details, including entry stamps which, for added insurance, you can have witnessed by a notary. Migración will not authorize photocopies of passports; look in Yellow Pages for notaries.

Selected Migración Colombia offices

Barranquilla Cra 42, No 54-77, T5-351 3401.

Bogotá C 100, No 11B-27, T1-511 1150, www.migracioncolombia.gov.co, Mon-Fri 0800-1600. For extending entry permits.
Calí Av 3 N, No 50N-20, T2-397 3510, Mon-Fri 0800-1200, 1400-1700.
Cartagena Cra 20B, No 29-18, T5-670 0555, Mon-Fri 0800-1200, 1400-1700.
Manizales Cra 53, No 25A-35, T6-885 0350, Mon-Fri, 0080-1200, 1400-1700.
Leticia C 9, No 9-62, T8-592 6001, Mon-Fri 0800-1200, 1400-1700. Go to the airport for entry and exit stamps.
Medellín C 19, No 80A-40, Belén, T4-345 5500, Mon-Fri 0800-1600.
Pasto C 17, No 29-70, T2-722 9393, Mon-Fri 0800-1200, 1400-1700. Will give exit stamps if you are going on to Ecuador.
Popayán C 4N, No 10B-66, T2-839 1051, Mon-Fri 0700-1200, 1400-1800. Opposite bus terminal next to fire station, go early to extend visas.
San Andrés Cra 10, No 3-92, T8-512 1818, Mon-Fri 0800-1200, 1400-1700.
Santa Marta C 22, No 13A-88, T5-421 7817. Mon-Fri 0800-1200, 1400-1700.

Weights and measures

Generally metric, but US gallons for petrol.

This is
Ecuador

Tucked in between Peru and Colombia, this country is small enough for you to have breakfast with scarlet macaws in the jungle, lunch in the lee of a snow-capped peak and, at tea time, be eyeballed by an iguana whose patch of Pacific beach you have just borrowed.

A multitude of national parks and conservation areas emphasise the incredible variety of Ecuador. They include mangroves; an avenue of volcanoes – many of them active – striding across the equator; forests growing on the dry Pacific coast, in the clouds and under the Amazonian rains; not forgetting all the animals and birds which flourish in these habitats. In fact, as Ecuador is one of the richest places in the world for birds, with some of the planet's most beautiful species, the country is a prime birdwatching destination.

The capital, Quito, and the southern highland city of Cuenca, are two of the gringo centres of South America, bursting at the seams with language schools, tour operators and restaurants. The smaller towns and villages of Ecuador offer the most authentic experience. Indulge your senses at one of their many markets, with dizzying arrays of textiles, ceramics, carvings and other crafts, not to mention the cornucopia of fresh produce.

The exotic wildlife of the Galápagos Islands will also keep you enthralled, whether it's watching an albatross take off on its flight path, swimming with marine iguanas, sea lions and penguins, or admiring the sexual paraphernalia of the magnificent frigatebird. If the Galápagos are beyond your budget, then Isla de la Plata, in Parque Nacional Machalilla, is a more accessible alternative for seeing marine life.

N

50 km
50 miles

Pacific Ocean

COLOMBIA

San Lorenzo
Limones
La Tola
Mataje
Rioverde
Maldonado
Atacames
Rocafuerte
Tonchigue
Esmeraldas
Lita
Tulcán
Punta Galeras
Viche
La Libertad
Muisne
San Gabriel
Bolívar
Quinindé
Apuela
Ibarra
Bolívar
Cojimíes
PV Maldonado
Cotacachi
La Bonita
El Conejo
Pedernales
Otavalo
Cayambe
Lago Agrio
Santo Domingo
Mindo
Calderón
Lumbaquí
Cuyabeno
de los Tsáchilas
Reventador
Reserve
Tarapoa
Jama
San Isidro
QUITO
Shushufindi
Canoa
Sangolquí
Baeza
Coca
Aguarico
Cuyabeno
Bahía de
San Vicente
Machachi
Pañacocha
Caráquez
Chone
Chugchilán
Lasso
Vol
Loreto
Napo
Nuevo
Crucita
Quevedo
Zumbahua
Cotopaxi NP
Archidona
Tiputini
Rocafuerte
Manta
Pujilí
Cotopaxi
Latacunga
Tena
Misahuallí
Yasuní NP
Portoviejo
Sucre
Balzar
Ambato
Baños
Puyo
Shiripuno
Jipijapa
Chugchilán
Guaranda
El Altar
Villano
Curaray
Nashino
Isla de
la Plata
Riobamba
(5319m)
Sarayacu
Cononaco
Puerto López
Babahoyo
Guamote
Vol Sangay
Conambo
Curaray
Montañita
Palmira
(5230m)
Pintuyaco
Manglaralto
Durán
Bucay
Alausí
Macas
Montalvo
Conambo
Valdivia
Salinas
Guayaquil
Huigra
Sucúa
Cañar
Ingapirca
Chanduy
Puná
Azogues
Paute
Méndez
San José de
Playas
Gualaceo
Morona
Posorja
I Puná
Cuenca
Santiago
Golfo de
Girón
Plan de
Machala
Guayaquil
Sigsig
Milagro
I Sta Clara
Oña
Gualaquiza
Huaquillas
Santa Rosa
El Pangui
Arenillas
Piñas
Saraguro
Puyango
Zaruma
Yantzaza
Alamor
Loja
Zamora
Catacocha
Podocarpus NP
Cariamanga
Vilcabamba
Zapotillo
Macará
Valladolid
Amaluza
Zumba
La Balsa

To The Galápagos Islands

PERU

Footprint
picks

1 Quito, page 1023
2 Otavalo, page 1060
3 Cuenca, page 1104
4 Vilcabamba, page 1120
5 Northern Oriente, page 1155
6 Galápagos Islands, page 1172

Footprint
picks

★ **Quito**, page 1023

In a valley at the foot of a
volcano, with a colonial centre
of steep cobbled streets and
fading façades, it isn't any wonder that it was the first
city to be declared a UNESCO World Heritage Site.

★ **Otavalo**, page 1060

The enormous Saturday market blisters with colour as the Otavaleños
gather to sell textiles and crafts.

★ **Cuenca**, page 1104

The well-preserved colonial centre of Ecuador's third city overflows
with flowering plazas and pastel-coloured buildings.

★ **Vilcabamba**, page 1120

A favourite of expats and travellers alike, this once isolated village has
nature reserves on its doorstep and wonderful places to stay and eat.

★ **Northern Oriente**, page 1155

Visitors can stay deep in the rainforest in jungle lodges and
experience contact with life in the tropical lowlands.

★ **Galápagos Islands**, page 1172

An extraordinary collection of islands that have to be seen to
be believed.

Route planner

putting it all together

Quito and around

a city of two halves

The capital, Quito, boasts some of the best-preserved colonial architecture in South America in its 'colonial city', while 'modern Quito' is where you'll find most accommodation, restaurants, tour operators and language schools. From the capital many of the country's attractions are accessible by paved road in only a few hours. Day trips include nature reserves, hot springs, and, of course, the equator. There is also good mountaineering and whitewater rafting nearby.

North of Quito

handicrafts and hiking in the highlands

North of Quito is **Otavalo** with its outstanding handicrafts market, a regular one-day tour, but equally popular as a base for exploring nearby craft villages, lakes, more nature reserves and hiking or cycling routes. Carrying on towards the Colombian border is **Ibarra**, another good centre for visiting the north.

Central Sierra

volcano climbing, village explorations and a famous train ride

South of Quito, in the Central Sierra, is the active **Cotopaxi** volcano and surrounding national park. Further south is the **Quilotoa Circuit**, a 200-km loop through small villages and beautiful landscapes, with lots of possibilities for trekking, cycling and riding. The starting point is **Latacunga** on the Pan-American Highway. On one of the main routes from the Sierra to the eastern jungle is **Baños**, a popular spa town with hiking, biking, adrenaline sports, horse riding and more opportunities to see an active volcano (Tungurahua) close at hand. The heart of the central highlands is **Riobamba**, beneath Chimborazo, Ecuador's highest mountain. This is another good base for climbing, biking and trekking, as well as a starting point for the famous railway ride over **La Nariz del Diablo** (The Devil's Nose).

Southern Sierra

historic sightseeing and national parks

The archaeological site of **Ingapirca** is between **Riobamba** and **Cuenca**, a lovely colonial city in the Southern Sierra, especially popular with visitors and expats. Nearby is **Cajas National Park**. En route from Cuenca towards Peru are the provincial capital of **Loja**, close to **Podocarpus National Park**, and **Vilcabamba**, with a delightful climate and another favourite with travellers and expats alike. Several border crossings to Peru are accessible from Loja.

Coastal Ecuador

resorts, whale watching, beach and birdlife

Ecuador's Pacific capital is **Guayaquil**, 45 minutes by air from Quito (eight hours by bus) and only four hours by bus south to the Peruvian border via Machala. Key areas of the city have been renewed, such as its historic riverfront. To the north stretch the Pacific lowlands with beaches, pre-Columbian archaeological sites and small seaside resorts such as **Puerto López**, **Montañita**, **Canoa** and **Mompiche**, as well as a few more developed ones like **Salinas**, **Bahía de Caráquez** and **Atacames**. Near Puerto López, **Parque Nacional Machalilla** contains dry tropical forest, offshore islands and marine ecosystems. It is a good place for riding, diving, whale watching, birdwatching and relaxing on the beautiful **Los Frailes beach**.

East of the Andes

jungle towns and birdwatching heaven

The **Oriente** (eastern lowlands) offers good opportunities for nature tourism, with a number of specially designed jungle lodges, mainly in the north. A stay in one of these places is best booked in Quito or from home, but you can head for jungle towns such as **Coca**, **Tena**, **Puyo** or **Misahuallí** to arrange a tour with a local agency. The **southern Oriente** is less developed for tourism, but interest is growing, with **Macas** or **Zamora** as the places to aim for. Here, as on the other side of the Andes, there are some great birdwatching opportunities in a wide variety of protected areas.

Galápagos Islands

very close encounters with nature

The nature destination par excellence is the Galápagos Islands, 970 km west of the mainland. Tours, which are usually arranged in advance from Quito, Guayaquil or from home, traditionally involve cruising from island to island to see new species with each landfall, but island-based activities are growing in popularity.

Essential Ecuador

Finding your feet

Ecuador's two international airports are in Quito (UIO) and Guayaquil (GYE). The latter is good if visiting only the coast or Galápagos.

Getting around

If you are short of time, it's well to opt for a few flights. Most destinations, however, have frequent bus services and bus travel is generally convenient except for the location of Quito's terminals very far from the city centre. Shared taxis and vans are another option for getting around.

When to go

Ecuador is a year-round destination. The climate is unpredictable. In the Sierra there is little variation. It varies from 6-10°C, to 19-23°C, though it can get hotter in the lower basins. Rainfall depends on distance from eastern or western slopes of the Andes. To the west, June to September are dry and October to May are wet (with a dry spell in December or January). To the east, October to February are dry and March to September are wet. The southern highlands are drier.

Along the Pacific coast, rainfall also decreases from north to south, so that it can rain throughout the year in northern Esmeraldas and seldom at all near the Peruvian border. The coast, however,

can be enjoyed year-round, although it's cool from June to November, when mornings are often grey with the *garúa* mists. January to May is the hottest and rainiest time of the year. Like the coast the Galápagos may receive *garúa* from May to December; from January to April the islands are hottest and brief but heavy showers can fall. In the Oriente, heavy rain can fall at any time, but it is usually wettest from March to September.

Ecuador's high season is from June to early September, the best time for climbing and trekking.

National parks

Ecuador has an outstanding array of protected natural areas including a system of 51 national parks and reserves administered by the **Ministerio del Ambiente**, T02-398 7600, www.ambiente.gob.ec. Entry to all national protected areas is currently free except for Parque Nacional Galápagos. Some parks can only be visited with authorized guides. Contact park offices in the cities nearest the parks, they have more information than the ministry in Quito.

Time required

Two to five weeks can easily be filled.

Tip...
At major fiestas, such as Carnival, Semana Santa (Easter), Finados (2 November) and over New Year, accommodation can be hard to find. Hotels will be full in individual towns during their particular festivals and resorts may be busy on weekends year-round.

Fact file

Location 0.1500° S, 78.3500° W
Capital Quito
Time zone GMT -5 hrs, Galápagos -6 hrs
Telephone country code +593
Currency United States dollar (US$)

Weather Ecuador

January	February	March	April	May	June
18°C 10°C 110mm	18°C 10°C 120mm	18°C 10°C 150mm	18°C 10°C 170mm	18°C 10°C 120mm	19°C 9°C 20mm

July	August	September	October	November	December
19°C 9°C 20mm	19°C 9°C 20mm	19°C 9°C 70mm	19°C 9°C 120mm	19°C 9°C 100mm	18°C 10°C 100mm

Quito

★Few cities have a setting to match that of Quito (2850 m), the second highest capital in Latin America after La Paz. The city is set in a hollow at the foot of the volcano Pichincha (4794 m). The city's charm lies in its colonial centre – the Centro Histórico as it's known – a UNESCO World Heritage Site, where cobbled streets are steep and narrow, dipping to deep ravines. From the top of Cerro Panecillo, 183 m above the city level, there is a fine view of the city below and the encircling cones of volcanoes.

North of the colonial centre is modern Quito with broad avenues lined with contemporary office buildings, fine private residences, parks, embassies and villas. Here you'll find Quito's main nightlife and restaurant area in the district known as La Mariscal, bordered by Avenidas Amazonas, Patria, 12 de Octubre and Orellana.

Sights *Colour map 1, A4.*

a capital city not to be missed

Colonial Quito

Plaza de la Independencia (Plaza Grande) Quito's revitalized colonial district is a pleasant place to stroll and admire the architecture, monuments and art. At night, the illuminated plazas and churches are very beautiful. The heart of the old city is Plaza de la Independencia or Plaza Grande, whose pink-flowered arupo trees bloom in September. It is dominated by a somewhat grim **Cathedral** ① *entry through museum, Venezuela N3-117 or off Plaza Grande, T02-257 0371, www.catedraldequito.org, Mon-Sat 0930-1700, no visits during Mass 0600-0900, US$3 for the museum, US$6 including cupolas, night visits to church on request,* built 1550-1562, with grey stone porticos and green tile cupolas. On its outer walls are plaques listing the names of the founding fathers of Quito, and inside are the tomb of Sucre and a famous Descent from the Cross by the indigenous painter Caspicara. There are many other 17th- and 18th-century paintings; the interior decoration shows Moorish influence. Facing the Cathedral is the **Palacio Arzobispal**, part of which now houses shops. Next to it, in the northwest corner, is the **Hotel Plaza Grande** (1930), with a baroque façade, the first building in the old city with more than two storeys. On the northeast side is the concrete **Municipio**, which fits in quite well. The low colonial Palacio de Gobierno or **Palacio de Carondelet**, silhouetted against the flank of Pichincha, is on the northwest side of the Plaza. On the first floor is a gigantic mosaic mural of Orellana navigating the Amazon. The ironwork on the balconies looking over the main plaza is from the Tuilleries in Paris. Visitors can take tours ① *T02-382 7700, www.presidencia. gob.ec, Mon 1500-1845, Tue-Fri 0900-1845, Sat 0900-2200, Sun 0900-1600, take passport or copy.* The Municipal Band plays in Plaza de la Independencia every Wednesday at 1100.

South to El Panecillo From Plaza de la Independencia two main streets, Venezuela and García Moreno, lead straight towards El Panecillo. Parallel with Venezuela is Calle Guayaquil, the main shopping street. These streets all run south from the main plaza to meet Calle Morales, better known as **La Ronda**, one of the oldest streets in the city. This narrow cobbled pedestrian way and its colonial homes with wrought iron balconies have been refurbished and house hotels, restaurants, bars, artisans' workshops, cultural centres, galleries and shops. It is a quaint corner of

Best for
Colonial architecture ▪ Eating out ▪ Museums ▪ Views

Essential Quito

Finding your feet

Most places of historical interest are in colonial Quito, while the majority of the hotels, restaurants, tour operators and facilities for visitors are in the modern city to the north. Quito is a long city stretching from north to south, with Pichincha rising to the west. Its main arteries run the length of the city and traffic congestion along them is a serious problem.

The street numbering system is based on N (Norte), E (Este), S (Sur), Oe (Oeste), plus a number for each street and a number for each building. An older system is also still in use, however.

Getting around

Both colonial Quito and La Mariscal in modern Quito can be explored on foot, but getting between the two requires some form of public transport. Using taxis is the best option. There are vehicular restrictions on weekdays 0700-0930 and 1600-1930, based on the last digit of the license plate, seniors are exempt. Colonial Quito is closed to vehicles Sunday 0900-1600 and main avenues across the city close Sunday 0800-1400 for the *ciclopaseo* (page 1042).

There are five parallel public transit lines running north to south on dedicated lanes: the *Trole*, *Ecovía*, *Metrobus*, *Corredor Sur* and *Universidades*, as well as city buses. Avenida Occidental or Mariscal Sucre is a somewhat more expedite road to the west of the city. The Corredor Periférico Oriental or Simón Bolívar is a bypass to the east of the city running 44 km between Santa Rosa in the south and Calderón in the north. Roads through the eastern suburbs in the Valle de los Chillos and Tumbaco can be taken to avoid the city proper.

Safety

For all emergencies T911. Public safety in Quito appears to have improved in 2014-2015 relative to previous years, but it is still not a safe city. For further details see page 1193. In colonial Quito, the main plazas and nearby streets as well as La Ronda are patrolled by officers from the Policía Metropolitana and Policía de Turismo, who speak some English and are very helpful. The top of El Panecillo is patrolled by neighbourhood brigades (see page 1025), but

Tip...
Tip...
Because of the altitude, visitors may initially feel some discomfort and should slow their pace for the first 48 hours. The city also has a serious air pollution problem.

walking up the stairs is not recommended. In modern Quito increased police presence has brought some improvement, but La Carolina and La Mariscal districts still call for vigilance at all hours. Plaza Foch (Calle Foch y Reina Victoria) in La Mariscal is one of the patrolled areas, but do not stray outside its perimeter at night. There have been occasional reports of 'express kidnappings', choose your taxi judiciously, see page 1049. Do not walk through any city parks in the evening or even in daylight at quiet times. There have been reports of scams on long distance buses leaving Quito, especially to Baños; do not give your hand luggage to anyone and always keep your things on your lap, not in the overhead storage rack nor on the floor.

Servicio de Seguridad Turística (Tourist Police) offers information and is the place to obtain a police report in case of theft. HQ at Reina Victoria N21-208 y Roca, La Mariscal, T02-254 3983, ssturistica98@gmail.com, open 24 hours; offices at: Plaza de la Independencia, Casa de los Alcaldes, Chile Oe4-66 y García Moreno, T02-295 5785, open Sunday-Wednesday 0900-2400, Thursday-Saturday 0900-0400; La Ronda, Casa de las Artes, Morales y Guayaquil, T02-295 6010, Sunday-Tuesday 0800-2300, Wednesday-Saturday 0800-0400; airport, T02-394 5000, ext 3023, Monday-Friday 0600-2400, Saturday-Sunday 0600-1800; Terminal Quitumbe, Monday-Friday 0800-0030, Saturday-Sunday 0800-1730; and Mitad del Mundo, daily 0800-1800, offers information. There is also a regular police station at Reina Victoria y Baquerizo Moreno, in La Mariscal. A report on a robbery can be filed on line at www.gestiondefiscalias.gob.ec/rtourist.

When to go

Quito is within 25 km of the equator, but it stands high enough to make its climate much like that of spring in England, the days pleasantly warm (average high 22°C) and the nights cool (average low 8°C). The rainy season is October to May with a lull in December and the heaviest rainfall in April. Rain usually falls in the afternoon. The length of days (sunrise to sunset) is almost constant throughout the year.

BACKGROUND

An ancient city

Archaeological finds suggest that the valley of Quito and surrounding areas have been occupied for some 10,000 years. The city gets its name from the Quitus, who lived here during the period AD 500-1500. By the end of the 15th century, the northern highlands of Ecuador were conquered by the Incas and Quito became the capital of the northern half of their empire under the rule of Huayna Capac and later his son Atahualpa. As the Spanish conquest approached, Rumiñahui, Atahualpa's general, razed the city, to prevent it from falling into the invaders' hands.

The colonial city of Quito was founded by Sebastián de Benalcázar, Pizarro's lieutenant, on 6 December 1534. It was built at the foot of El Panecillo on the ruins of the ancient city, using the rubble as construction material. Examples of Inca stonework can be seen in the façades and floors of some colonial buildings such as the Cathedral and the church of San Francisco. Following the conquest, Quito became the seat of government of the Real Audiencia de Quito, the crown colony, which governed current-day Ecuador as well as parts of southern Colombia and northern Peru. Beautifully refurbished, colonial Quito, is today the city's most attractive district. In 1978, Quito was the first city to be declared a UNESCO World Heritage Site.

The 20th century saw the expansion of the city to the north and south, and later to the valleys to the east. The commercial, banking and government centres moved north of the colonial centre and residential and industrial neighbourhoods sprawled in the periphery. These make up the Distrito Metropolitano, which stretches for almost 50 km from north to south.

the city growing in popularity for a night out or an afternoon stroll (best Wednesday to Sunday). On García Moreno N3-94 is the beautiful **El Sagrario** ① *Mon-Fri, 0800-1800, Sat-Sun 1000-1400, no entry during Mass, free*, church with a gilded door. The **Centro Cultural Metropolitano** is at the corner of Espejo, housing the municipal library, a museum for the visually impaired, temporary art exhibits and the **Museo Alberto Mena Caamaño** ① *entry on C Espejo, T02-395 2300, ext 15535, Tue-Sat 0900-1730, Sun 1000-1600, US$1.50*. This wax museum depicts scenes of Ecuadorean colonial history. The scene of the execution of the revolutionaries of 1809 in the original cell is particularly vivid. The fine Jesuit church of **La Compañía** ① *García Moreno N3-117 y Sucre, T02-258 1895, Mon-Thu 0930-1830, Fri 0930-1730, Sat and holidays 0930-1600, Sun 1200-1600, US$4, students US$2, visits including cupolas and nighttime visits US$6*, has the most ornate and richly sculptured façade and interior. Diagonally opposite is the **Casa Museo María Augusta Urrutia** ① *García Moreno N2-60 y Sucre, T02-258 0103, Tue-Fri 1000-1800, Sat-Sun 0930-1730, US$2*, the home of a Quiteña who devoted her life to charity, showing the lifestyle of 20th-century aristocracy.

Housed in the fine restored, 16th-century Hospital San Juan de Dios, is the **Museo de la Ciudad** ① *García Moreno S1-47 y Rocafuerte, T02-228 3883, www.museociudadquito.gob.ec, Tue-Sun 0930-1730 (last group 1630), US$3, free entry on the last Sat of each month, non-Spanish guide service US$4 per group (request ahead)*. A very good museum which takes you through Quito's history from prehispanic times to the 19th century, with imaginative displays; café by the entrance overlooking a Ronda. Almost opposite on García Moreno are the convent and museum of **El Carmen Alto** ① *T02-295 5817, Wed-Sun 0930-1630, US$3, request ahead for guiding in English, small shop sells sweets and wine made in the convent*. In 2013, this beautifully refurbished cloister opened its doors to the public for the first time since 1652.

On **Cerro Panecillo** ① *Mon-Thu 0900-1700, Fri-Sun 0900-2100, US$1 per vehicle or US$0.25 pp if walking (not recommended), for the neighbourhood brigade; entry to the interior of the monument US$2*, there is a statue of the Virgen de Quito and a good view from the observation platform. Although the neighbourhood patrols the area, it is safer to take a taxi (US$6 return from the colonial city, US$10 from La Mariscal, with a short wait). There is a museum of the monastery of **San Diego** ① *Calicuchima 117 y Farfán, entrance to the right of the church, T02-317 3185, Tue-Sat 1000-1300, 1400-1700, Sun 1000-1400, US$2 (by the cemetery of the same name, just west of El Panecillo)*. Guided tours (Spanish only) take you to the cupolas and around four colonial patios where sculpture and painting are shown. Of special interest are the gilded pulpit by Juan Bautista

Menacho and the Last Supper painting in the refectory, in which a *cuy* and *humitas* have taken the place of the paschal lamb.

West of Plaza de la Independencia Plaza de San Francisco (or Bolívar) is west of Plaza de la Independencia; here are the great church and monastery of the patron saint of Quito, **San Francisco** ① *daily 0800-1200, 1500-1800*. The church was constructed by the Spanish in 1553 and is rich in art treasures. A modest statue of the founder, Fray Jodoco Ricke, the Flemish Fransiscan who sowed the first wheat in Ecuador, stands nearby. See the fine wood-carvings in the choir, a high altar of gold and an exquisite carved ceiling. There are some paintings in the aisles by Miguel de Santiago, the colonial *mestizo* painter. The **Museo Franciscano Fray Pedro Gocial** ① *in the church cloisters to the right of the main entrance, T02-295 2911, Mon-Sat 0900-1730, Sun 0900-1300, US$2*, has a collection of religious art. Also adjoining San Francisco is the **Cantuña Chapel** ① *Cuenca y Bolívar, T02-295 2911, Tue and Thu 0800-0900, Sun 0900-1000, free*, with sculptures. Not far to the south along Calle Cuenca is the excellent archaeological museum, **Museo Casa del Alabado** ① *Cuenca 335 y Rocafuerte, T02-228 0940, daily 0900-1730, US$4, guides extra*, with an excellent art shop. An impressive display of pre-Columbian art from all regions of Ecuador, among the best in the city. North of San Francisco is the church of **La Merced** ① *Chile y Cuenca, 0630-1200, 1300-1800, free*, with many splendidly elaborate styles. Nearby is the **Museo de Arte Colonial** ① *Cuenca N6-15 y Mejía, T02-228 2297, Tue-Sat 0900-1630, US$2, free concerts on the last Wed of each month at 1100*, housed in a 17th-century mansion. It has a collection of colonial sculpture and painting and temporary exhibits (free).

Southeast of Plaza de la Independencia At Plaza de Santo Domingo (or Sucre), southeast of Plaza de la Independencia, is the church and monastery of **Santo Domingo** ① *daily 0700-1300, 1700-1845*, with its rich wood-carvings and a remarkable Chapel of the Rosary to the right of the main altar. In the monastery is the **Museo Dominicano Fray Pedro Bedón** ① *T02-228 0518, Mon-Sat 0915-1330, 1500-1700, US$2, English speaking guides available*, with another fine collection of religious art. In the centre of the plaza is a statue of Sucre, facing the slopes of Pichincha where he won his battle against the Royalists. Just south of Santo Domingo, in the old bus station, is **Parque Qmandá** ① *Tue-Sun 0900-1300, 1500-1800, busy on weekends*, with a pool, sport fields, climbing wall, gym and activities. **Museo Monacal Santa Catalina** ① *Espejo 779 y Flores, T02-228 4000, Mon-Fri 0900-1700, Sat 0900-1200, US$2.50*, said to have been built on the ruins of the Inca House of the Virgins, depicts the history of cloistered life. Many of the heroes of Ecuador's struggle for independence are buried in the monastery of **San Agustín** ① *Chile y Guayaquil, Tue-Fri 0730-1200, 1500-1700, Sat-Sun 0800-1200*, which has beautifully painted cloisters on three sides where the first act of independence from Spain was signed on 10 August 1809. Here is the **Museo Miguel de Santiago** ① *Chile 924 y Guayaquil, T02-295 1001, Mon-Fri 0900-1230, 1400-1700, Sat 0900-1230, US$2*, with religious art.

Northeast of Plaza de la Independencia To the northeast of Plaza de la Independencia is Plaza del Teatro with the lovely neoclassical 19th-century Teatro Sucre ① *Manabí N8-131 y Guayaquil*. Further north, on Parque García Moreno, the **Basílica** ① *Carchi 122 y Venezuela, T02-228 9428, visit 0600-1900 daily, US$2, mass at 0700, 1200 and 1800 (please be respectful); clock tower open 0900-1630 daily, US$2*, is very large, has many gargoyles (some in the shape of Ecuadorean fauna), stained glass windows and fine, bas relief bronze doors (begun in 1926; some final details remain unfinished due to lack of funding). The **Centro de Arte Contemporáneo** ① *Luis Dávila y Venezuela, San Juan, T02-398 8800, Tue-Sun 0900-1700, free*, in the beautifully restored Antiguo Hospital Militar, built in the early 1900s, has rotating art exhibits. To the west of the city, the **Yaku Museo del Agua** ① *El Placer Oe11-271, T02-251 1100, www.yakumuseoagua.gob.ec, Tue-Sun 0900-1730, US$3, take a taxi to main entrance or enter through the parking lot at the top of C Bolívar and take the lift up*, has lovely views. This interactive museum is great for kids of all ages. Its main themes are water and climate, also a self-guided trail: *eco-ruta*. Another must for children, south of the colonial city, is the **Museo Interactivo de Ciencia** ① *Sincholagua y Maldonado, Chimbacalle, T02-266 6061, www.museo-ciencia.gob.ec, Wed-Sun 0900-1730, US$3, children US$1*. East of the colonial city is **Parque Itchimbía** ① *T02-228 2017, park open daily 0600-1800, exhibits 0900-1630*; a natural look-out over

Tip...

Climb above the coffee shop in the Basílica to the top of the clock tower for stunning views.

Quito orientation

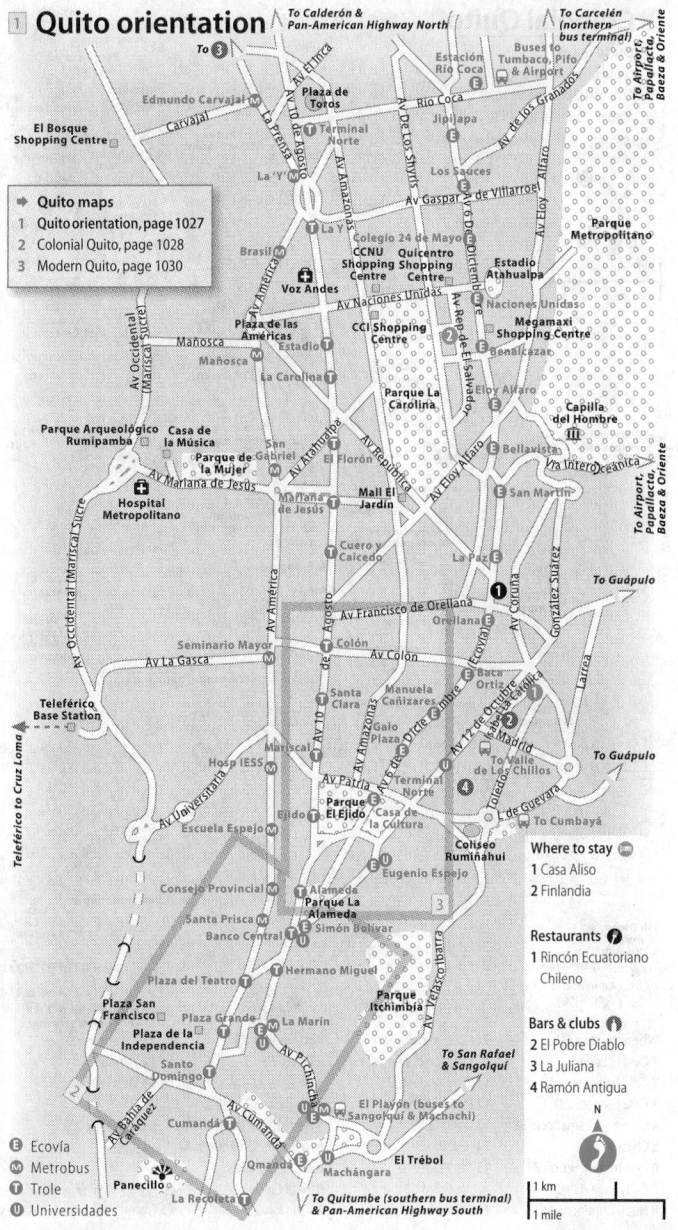

Quito maps
1. Quito orientation, page 1027
2. Colonial Quito, page 1028
3. Modern Quito, page 1030

To Calderón & Pan-American Highway North

To Carcelén (northern bus terminal)

To ③

El Bosque Shopping Centre

Edmundo Carvajal

Carvajal

Av El Inca

Av La Prensa

Av de Agosto

Plaza de Toros

Terminal Norte

Río Coca

Estación Río Coca

Buses to Tumbaco, Pifo & Airport

To Airport, Papallacta, Baeza & Oriente

La 'Y'

Brasil

Av América

Av Occidental (Mariscal Sucre)

Voz Andes

Mañosca

Mañosca

Plaza de las Américas

Estadio

La Carolina

Parque Arqueológico Rumipamba

Casa de la Música

Parque de la Mujer

San Gabriel

Av Mariana de Jesús

Hospital Metropolitano

Jipijapa

Los Sauces

Av Gaspar de Villarroel

Av de los Granados

Av Eloy Alfaro

Parque Metropolitano

Colegio 24 de Mayo

CCNU Shopping Centre

Quicentro Shopping Centre

Estadio Atahualpa

Av Naciones Unidas

Naciones Unidas

Megamaxi Shopping Centre

CCI Shopping Centre

Benalcázar

Eloy Alfaro

Parque La Carolina

Capilla del Hombre

Av República

El Florón

Av Atahualpa

Mariana de Jesús

Mall El Jardín

Bellavista

San Martín

Vía Interoceánica

To Airport, Papallacta, Baeza & Oriente

Cuero y Caicedo

La Paz

Av Francisco de Orellana

Orellana

González Suárez

To Guápulo

Seminario Mayor

Av La Gasca

Colón

Av Colón

Av América

Av de Agosto

Ecovía

Baca Ortiz

Av Coruña

Santa Clara

Manuela Cañizares

Av 12 de Octubre

Isabel La Católica

Madrid

To Valle de Los Chillos

To Guápulo

Teleférico Base Station

Teleférico to Cruz Loma

Hosp IESS

Mariscal

Av Amazonas

Av 10 de Dicre mbre

Galo Plaza Lasso

Av Patria

Terminal Norte

Casa de la Cultura

Coliseo Rumiñahui

Eugenio Espejo

Toledo

L de Guevara

To Cumbayá

Escuela Espejo

Av Universitaria

Eloy Alfaro

Parque El Ejido

Consejo Provincial

Alameda

Parque La Alameda

Santa Prisca

Banco Central

Simón Bolívar

Parque Itchimbía

Plaza del Teatro

Hermano Miguel

Plaza San Francisco

Plaza Grande

La Marín

Av Pichincha

To San Rafael & Sangolquí

Plaza de la Independencia

Santo Domingo

Av Bahía de Caráquez

Cumandá

Av Cumandá

Qmandá

El Playón (buses to Sangolquí & Machachi)

Machángara

Panecillo

La Recoleta

El Trébol

To Quitumbe (southern bus terminal) & Pan-American Highway South

Where to stay 🛏
1. Casa Aliso
2. Finlandia

Restaurants 🍴
1. Rincón Ecuatoriano Chileno

Bars & clubs 🍸
2. El Pobre Diablo
3. La Juliana
4. Ramón Antigua

N

0   1 km
0   1 mile

E Ecovía
M Metrobus
T Trole
U Universidades

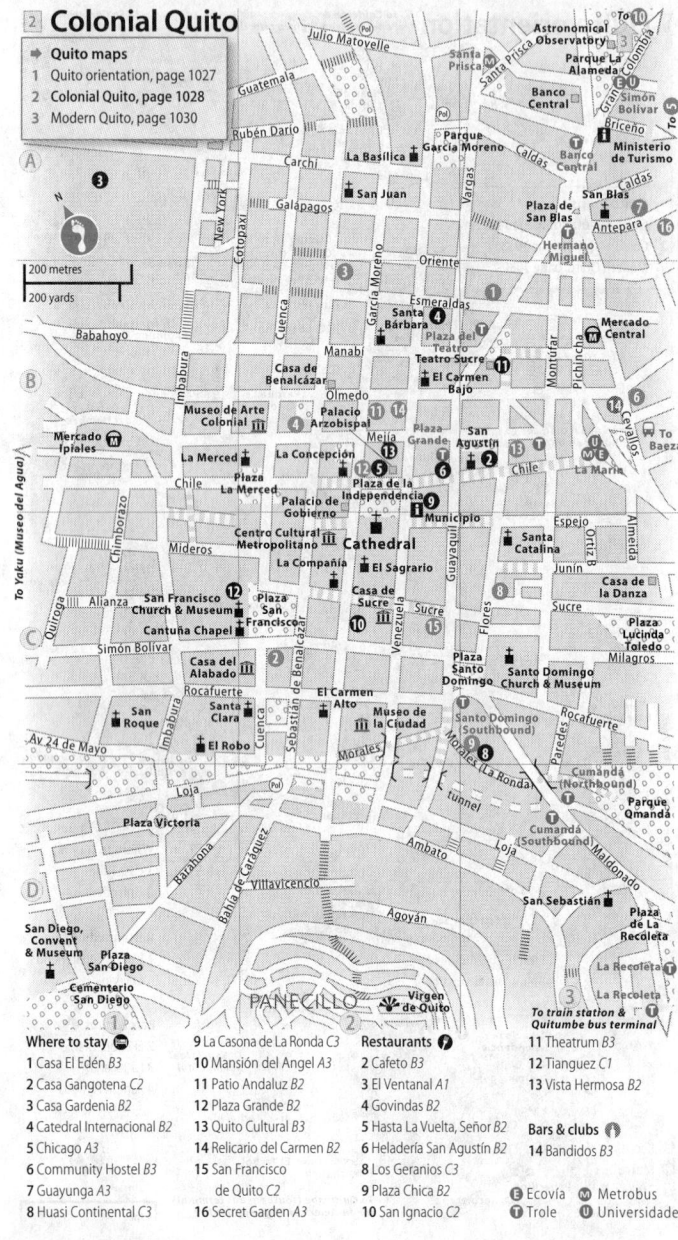

2 Colonial Quito

➡ **Quito maps**
1 Quito orientation, page 1027
2 Colonial Quito, page 1028
3 Modern Quito, page 1030

200 metres
200 yards

Where to stay
1 Casa El Edén *B3*
2 Casa Gangotena *C2*
3 Casa Gardenia *B2*
4 Catedral Internacional *B2*
5 Chicago *A3*
6 Community Hostel *B3*
7 Guayunga *A3*
8 Huasi Continental *C3*
9 La Casona de La Ronda *C3*
10 Mansión del Angel *A3*
11 Patio Andaluz *B2*
12 Plaza Grande *B2*
13 Quito Cultural *B3*
14 Relicario del Carmen *B2*
15 San Francisco
de Quito *C2*
16 Secret Garden *A3*

Restaurants
2 Cafeto *B3*
3 El Ventanal *A1*
4 Govindas *B2*
5 Hasta La Vuelta, Señor *B2*
6 Heladería San Agustín *B2*
7 Los Geranios *C3*
9 Plaza Chica *B2*
10 San Ignacio *C2*
11 Theatrum *B3*
12 Tianguez *C1*
13 Vista Hermosa *B2*

Bars & clubs
14 Bandidos *B3*

🄴 Ecovía 🄼 Metrobus
🄣 Trole 🅄 Universidades

the city with walking and cycle trails and a cultural centre housed in a 19th-century 'crystal palace' which came from Europe, once housed the original Santa Clara market.

Modern Quito

Parque La Alameda has the oldest **astronomical observatory** ① T02-257 0765, ext 100, http://oaq. epn.edu.ec, museum Mon-Sat 0900-1300, 1400-1700, US$2, night observations Tue-Thu 11900-2030 weather permitting, US$3, in South America dating to 1873 (native people had observatories long before the arrival of the Europeans). There is also a splendid monument to Simón Bolívar, lakes, and in the northwest corner a spiral lookout tower with a good view.

A short distance north of Parque La Alameda, opposite Parque El Ejido and bound by 6 de Diciembre, Patria, 12 de Octubre and Parque El Arbolito, is the **Casa de la Cultura**, a large cultural and museum complex. If you have time to visit only one museum in Quito, it should be the **Museo Nacional** ① entrance on Patria, T02-222 3258, closed for renovation in 2017, housed in the north side of the Casa de la Cultura. The **Sala de Arqueología** is particularly impressive with beautiful pre-Columbian ceramics, the **Sala de Oro** has a nice collection of prehispanic gold objects, and the **Sala de Arte Colonial** with religious art from the Quito School. On the east side of the complex are the museums administered by the **Casa de la Cultura** ① entrance on 12 de Octubre, T02-222 0967, www.casadelacultura.gob.ec, Tue-Sat 0900-1300, 1400-1645, US$2: **Museo de Arte Moderno**, paintings and sculpture since 1830 also rotating exhibits and **Museo de Instrumentos Musicales**, an impressive collection of musical instruments, said to be the second in importance in the world. Also on the east side are an art gallery for temporary exhibits and the **Agora**, a large open space used for concerts. On the west side are halls for temporary art exhibits, in the original old building, and the entrance to the **Teatro Nacional**, with free evening performances. On the south side are the **Teatro Demetrio Aguilera Malta** and other areas devoted to dance and theatre. Near the Casa de la Cultura, in the Catholic University's **cultural centre** ① 12 de Octubre y Roca, www.centroculturalpuce. org, is the superb **Museo Jijón y Caamaño** ① T02-299 1710, Mon-Fri 0900-1600, free, with a private collection of archaeological objects, historical documents and art. The interactive displays and narration in Spanish are excellent. Here too are temporary exhibits and the **Museo Weilbauer** ① T02-299 1710, www.museoweilbauer.org, Mon-Fri 0900-1700, free, with archaeological and photo collections and a sala táctil where the visually impaired can touch replicas of ceramics.

A focal point in La Mariscal, north of Parque El Ejido, is **Plaza Foch** (Reina Victoria y Foch), also called **Plaza del Quinde**, a popular meeting place surrounded by cafés and restaurants. At the corner of Reina Victoria and La Niña, is the excellent **Museo Mindalae** ① T02-223 0609 ext 101, www.mindalae.com.ec, Mon-Sat 0900-1730, US$3, which exhibits Ecuadorean crafts and places them in their historical and cultural context, as well as temporary exhibits and a good fair-trade, non-profit shop. (For another handicrafts museum and shop, see Folklore, page 1041.)

North of La Mariscal is the large **Parque La Carolina**, a favourite recreational spot at weekends. Around it is the banking district, several shopping malls, hotels and restaurants. In the park is the **Jardín Botánico** ① T02-333 2516, http://jardinbotanicoquito.com, Mon-Fri 0800-1645, Sat-Sun 0900-1645, US$3.50, which has a good cross section of Andean flora. Also the **Vivarium** ① T02-227 1799, www.vivarium.org.ec, Tue-Sun 0930-1300, 1330-1730, US$3.25, dedicated to protect endangered snakes, reptiles and amphibians, and the **Museo de Ciencias Naturales** ① T02-244 9824, Mon-Fri 0800-1300,1345-1630, US$2. Beyond La Carolina, on the grounds of Quito's former airport, is **Parque Bicentenario** ① daily 0430-1800, with sports fields and a great cycling track, right on the old tarmac.

Quito suburbs

East Built by indigenous slaves in 1693, the **Santuario de Guápulo** ① Mass Mon-Fri 1900, Sat 0700, Sun 0700-1200, 1600-1700, perched on the edge of a ravine east of the city, is well worth seeing for its many paintings, gilded altars, stone carvings and the marvellously carved pulpit. The **Museo Fray Antonio Rodríguez** ① Plaza de Guápulo N27-138, T02-256 5652, Mon-Fri 0800-1200, 1400-1800, US$1.50, has religious art and furniture, from the 16th to the 20th centuries. Guided tours (Spanish only) include a visit to the beautiful Santuario.

Overlooking the city from the northeast is the grandiose **Capilla del Hombre** ① Lorenzo Chávez E18-94 y Mariano Calvache, Bellavista, T02-244 6455, www.guayasamin.org, daily 1000-1700, except holidays, US$8, take a taxi or Jesús del Gran Poder-Bellavista bus, a monument to Latin America

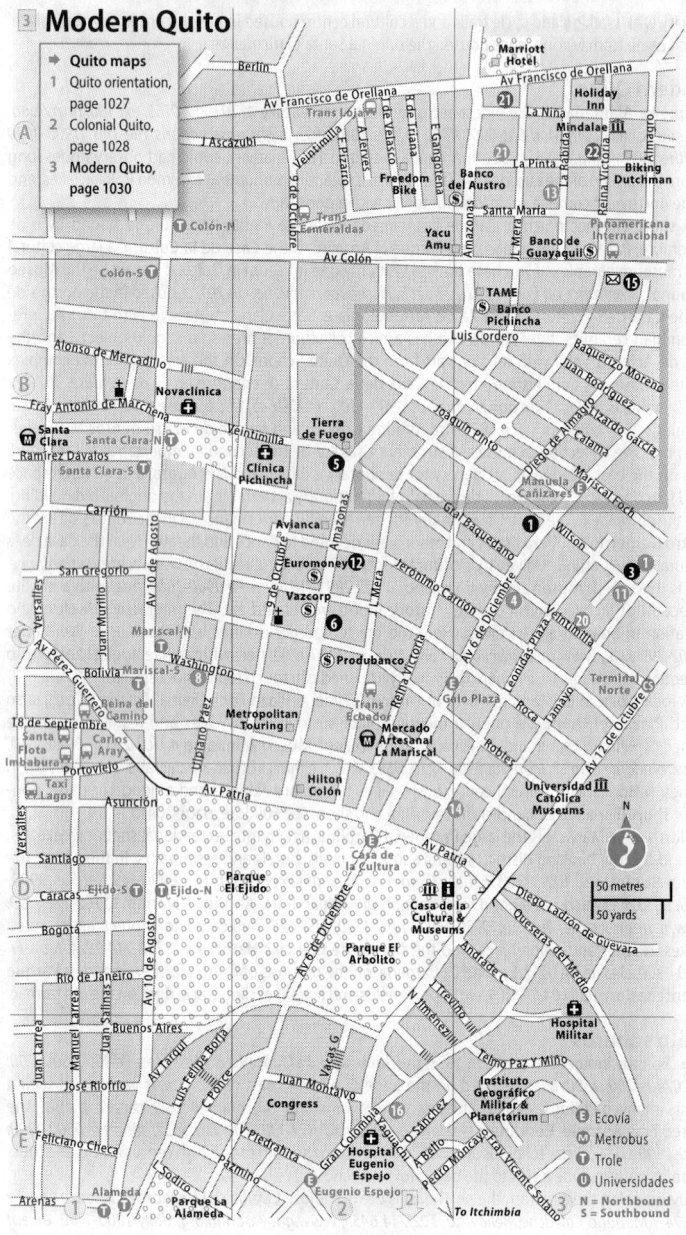

Modern Quito

Quito maps
1. Quito orientation, page 1027
2. Colonial Quito, page 1028
3. Modern Quito, page 1030

Berlín

Marriott Hotel

Av Francisco de Orellana

Holiday Inn

Av Francisco de Orellana

Trans Loja

La Niña

Freedom Bike

Banco del Austro

Mindalae

Biking Dutchman

Yacu Amu

Santa María

Banco de Guayaquil

Pañamericana Internacional

Av Colón

TAME

Banco Pichincha

Luis Cordero

Baquerizo Moreno

Juan Rodríguez

Alfonso de Mercadillo

Novaclínica

Joaquín Pinto

Tierra de Fuego

Diego de Almagro

Manuela Cañizares

Mariscal Foch

Santa Clara

Clínica Pichincha

Carrión

Avianca

Euromoney

Jerónimo Carrión

Vazcorp

San Gregorio

Produbanco

Washington

Mariscal

Leonidas Plaza

Terminal Norte

Golo Plaza

Roca

Metropolitan Touring

Trans Esmeraldas

Mercado Artesanal La Mariscal

Robles

Universidad Católica Museums

Hilton Colón

Asunción

Av Patria

Santiago

Casa de la Cultura

Av Patria

Diego Ladrón de Guevara

50 metres

50 yards

Caracas

Ejido-S

Ejido-N

Casa de la Cultura & Museums

Queseras del Medio

Bogotá

Parque El Ejido

Parque El Arbolito

Río de Janeiro

Andrade C

Buenos Aires

Hospital Militar

José Riofrío

Congress

Instituto Geográfico Militar & Planetarium

Feliciano Checa

Hospital Eugenio Espejo

Ecovía

Metrobus

Alameda

Parque La Alameda

Eugenio Espejo

To Itchimbia

Trole

Universidades

N = Northbound
S = Southbound

La Mariscal detail

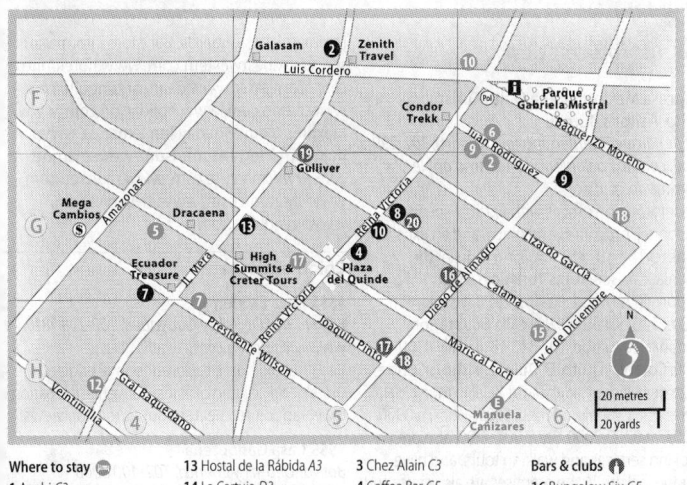

Where to stay
1 Anahi *C3*
2 Backpackers Inn *G6*
3 Cayman *F6*
4 Casa Helbling *C3*
5 Casa Joaquín *G4*
6 Cayman *F6*
7 City Art Hotel Silberstein *G4*
8 Cultura Manor *C1*
9 El Arupo *F6*
10 El Cafecito *F6*
11 Fuente de Piedra I *C3*
12 Fuente de Piedra II *H4*
13 Hostal de la Rábida *A3*
14 La Cartuja *D3*
15 La Casa Sol *H6*
16 L'Auberge Inn *E2*
17 Nü House *G5*
18 Posada del Maple *G6*
20 Sierra Madre *G4*
21 Travellers Inn *A3*

Restaurants
1 Baalbek *C3*
2 Chandani Tandoori *F5*
3 Chez Alain *C3*
4 Coffee Bar *G5*
5 El Hornero *B2*
6 Ethnic Coffee *C2*
7 Kallari *G4*
8 La Boca del Lobo *G5*
9 La Petite Mariscal *G6*
10 Mama Clorinda *G5*
12 Sakti *C2*
13 The Magic Bean *G5*
15 Yu Su *B3*

Bars & clubs
16 Bungalow Six *G5*
17 Cherusker *H5*
18 Finn McCool's *H5*
19 No Bar *F5*
20 Selfie *G5*
21 Turtle's Head *A3*
22 Varadero *A3*

conceived by the internationally famous Ecuadorean artist Oswaldo Guayasamín (1919-1999) and completed after his death. This highly recommended museum includes a collection of murals depicting the fate of Latin America from pre-Columbian to modern times and, in Guayasamín's home and studio, his works, as well as pre-Columbian, colonial and contemporary art collections. Works of art, jewellery and clothing decorated with Guayasamín's art are for sale.

West For spectacular views ride the **Teleférico** ① *Av Occidental above La Gasca, T02-222 2996, Mon-Fri 0900-1800, Sat-Sun 0900-2000, US$8.50, children and seniors US$6.50, the area below is not safe, best take a taxi (US$1.50 from América y Colón)*. The cable car is part of a complex with an amusement park, shops and food courts. It climbs to 4050 m on the flanks of Pichincha, where there are walking trails, including one to the summit of Rucu Pichincha, and horse riding just past the fence.

Parque Arqueológico y Ecológico Rumipamba ① *east side of Av Occidental just north of Mariana de Jesús, Wed-Sun 0830-1600, free, some English speaking guides*, is a 32-ha park on the slopes of Pichincha, where vestiges of human occupation of several pre-Inca periods, dating from 1500 BC to AD 1500, have been found. There are walking trails in some pockets of native vegetation. Northwest of Rumipamba, in the neighbourhood of San Vicente de la Florida is **Museo de Sitio La Florida** ① *C Antonio Costas y Villacrés, T02-380 3043, Wed-Sun 0800-1600, free, some English speaking guides, at north end of El Ejido-San Vicente bus line*. At this necropolis of the Quitus people, 10 17-m deep burial chambers, dating to AD 220-640, have been excavated. The elaborate dress and jewellery found in the tombs suggests most were prominent citizens.

Tourist information

**Empresa Metropolitana Quito Turismo/
Quito Visitor's Bureau**
*HQ at Parque Bicentenario (old airport), T02-299
3300, comunicacion@quito-turismo.gob.ec,
www.quito.com.ec.*
Has information offices with English-speaking
personnel, brochures and maps, and an excellent
website. They also run walking tours of the
colonial city, see **Rutas Turísticas**, page 1042.
Airport, in Arrivals area, T02-281 8363, Mon-Fri
0600-2200, Sat-Sun 0700-1900. **Bus station**,
Terminal Quitumbe, T02-382 4815, daily 0800-
1800. **Colonial Quito**, **El Quinde Visitors Centre**,
Plaza de la Independencia, at Palacio Municipal,
Venezuela y Espejo, T02-295 5785, Mon-Fri 0900-
1800, Sat 0900-2000, Sun 1000-1700; also offer
booking services and walking tours, and have
storage lockers. In the premises are also crafts and
chocolate shops, tour operators and sale points
for double-decker bus tours, see page 1041,
Mitad del Mundo, train tours and travel insurance.
La Mariscal, at Ecuador Gourmet, Reina Victoria
N24-263 y Lizardo García, T02-223 9469, Mon-Sat
0900-1730. General information about Quito is
found in www.in-quito.com. To file a complaint
about services contact the **Quito Visitor's Bureau**
headquarters (see above).

Ministerio de Turismo
*Av Gran Colombia y Briceño, T02-399 9333
or T1-800-887476, www.ecuador.travel,
www.turismo.gob.ec. Mon-Fri 0815-1700.*
Offers information at their reception desk.

Sistema de Museos y Centros Culturales Quito
*Calle el Placer Oe11-271, Yaku Museo del Agua,
T02-251 1 100 ext 101, www.museosquito.gob.ec.*
Offers useful information about museums and
cultural centres throughout Quito. Good website.

Where to stay

For lodgings near the airport, see Quito
suburbs, below. Near the Quitumbe bus
terminal are a few simple establishments
catering to short stay customers and there
is one simple *hostal* (**$ Madrid**) opposite the
Carcelén bus terminal, along busy Avenida
Eloy Alfaro. Large international chain hotels
are represented in the city and meet their

international standards. For more information
see: www.bestwestern.com, www.hotelquito.
com (**Compass**), www.danncarltonquito.com,
www.hilton.com, www.holidayinn.com, www.
hiexpress.com (**Holiday Inn Express**), www.
hojo.com (**Howard Johnson**), www.marriott.
com, www.mercure.com, www.radisson.com,
www.sheraton.com, www.swissotel.com,
www.wyndham.com.

Colonial Quito

$$$$ Casa El Edén
*Esmeraldas Oe 3-30 y Guayaquil, T02-228 1810,
www.casaeleden.com.*
Beautiful old home restored to save original
murals and painted ceilings, convenient location,
6 well-appointed heated rooms, rooftop views.

$$$$ Casa Gangotena
*Bolívar Oe6-41 y Cuenca, T02-400 8000,
www.casagangotena.com.*
Superb location by Plaza San Francisco, luxury
accommodation in beautifully refurbished
classic family home with 31 rooms and suites,
fine restaurant.

$$$$ La Casona de La Ronda
*Morales Oe1-160 y Guayaquil, T02-228 7501,
www.lacasonadelaronda.com.*
Tastefully refurbished colonial house in the
heart of La Ronda, comfortable rooms and
suite, includes buffet breakfast, restaurant
serves Ecuadorean specialities and some
international dishes.

$$$$ Patio Andaluz
*García Moreno N6-52 y Olmedo, T02-228 0830,
www.hotelpatioandaluz.com.*
Beautifully reconstructed 16th-century mansion
with large arches, balconies and patios, breakfast
extra, exclusive restaurant with Ecuadorean and
Spanish cuisine, library, gift shop.

$$$$ Plaza Grande
*García Moreno N5-16, Plaza de la Independencia,
T02-251 0777, www.plazagrandequito.com.*
Exclusive top-of-the-line hotel with an
exceptional location, 15 suites including a
presidential suite for US$2000, jacuzzi in all
rooms, climate control, 2 restaurants, including
La Belle Epoque, gourmet French cuisine and
a wine cellar, mini-spa.

$$$ Casa Gardenia
Benalcázar N9-42 y Oriente, T02-295 7936,
www.hotelcasagardenia.com.
Nice 9-room B&B in a quiet location, buffet
breakfast, lovely views from the terrace.

$$$ Relicario del Carmen
Venezuela N6-43 y Olmedo, T02-228 9120,
www.hotelrelicariodelcarmen.com.
Beautifully refurbished colonial house, good
restaurant, cafeteria, good rooms and service,
no smoking.

$$ Catedral Internacional
Mejía Oe6-36 y Cuenca, T02-295 5438,
www.hotelcatedral.ec.
Well-restored colonial house with
15 carpeted rooms, heaters, small
patio, popular restaurant, spa.

$$ Quito Cultural
Flores N4-160 y Chile, T02-228 8084,
Facebook: hostalquitocultural
Nicely refurbished colonial house, bright,
rooftop terrace with nice views, patio with
plants, a bit pricey.

$$ San Francisco de Quito
Sucre Oe3-17 y Guayaquil, T02-295 1241,
www.sanfranciscodequito.com.ec.
Converted colonial building, breakfast served
in attractive patio or underground cloisters,
restaurant, suites are particularly good value,
well run by owners.

$$-$ Community Hostel
Cevallos N6-78 y Olmedo, T09-5904 9658,
www.communityhostel.com.
Popular hostel with 2 double rooms and dorms
for 4-6 (US$10-12.50 pp), comfy beds, shared
bath (may have to wait for toilet in the morning),
good showers, very clean and efficient, nice
sitting area, breakfast extra, kitchen facilities,
helpful staff.

$$-$ Huasi Continental
Flores N3-08 y Sucre, T02-295 7327,
www.hotelhuasi.com.
Colonial house, a bit dark, restaurant serves
good breakfast and lunch (both extra), private or
shared bath, parking, good service and value.

In between the colonial and modern cities

$$$$ Mansión del Angel
Los Ríos N13-134 y Pasaje Gándara, T02-255 7721,
www.mansiondelangel.com.ec.

Luxurious hotel decorated with antiques in a
beautifully renovated mansion, 14 ample rooms
and a palatial suite, dinner available, nice gardens,
lovely atmosphere, spa.

$$-$ Guayunga
Antepara E4-27 y Los Ríos, T02-228 8544,
http://guayunga.com.
Attractive hostel with a few double rooms with
and without bath and dorms for 3-9 (US$14 pp),
breakfast extra, interior patio, rooftop terrace
with great views, parking.

$$-$ L'Auberge Inn
*Gran Colombia N15-200 y Yaguachi, T02-255
2912, www.auberge-inn-hostal.com.*
Nice spacious rooms, duvets, private or shared
bath, excellent hot water, buffet breakfast and
dinner available, grill next door for lunch, spa,
cooking facilities, parking, lovely garden, terrace
and communal area, helpful, good atmosphere.
Highly recommended.

$$-$ Secret Garden
Antepara E4-60 y Los Ríos, T02-295 6704,
www.secretgardenquito.com.
Well-decorated house, some rooms small and
dark, lovely rooftop terrace restaurant, private
or shared bath, US$10-12 pp in dorm, breakfast
extra, pleasant atmosphere, very popular
meeting place. Ecuadorean/Australian-owned,
also run a rustic lodge between Pasochoa and
Cotopaxi, www.secretgardencotopaxi.com.

$ Chicago
Los Ríos N11-142 y Briceño, T02-228 1695,
www.chicagohostalecuador.com.
Popular family-run hostel, small rooms,
US$10 pp in dorm, cooking facilities, a good
economy option.

Modern Quito

$$$$ Cultura Manor
Jorge Washington E2-43 y Páez, T02-222 4271,
www.culturamanor.com.
Brand new luxury hotel to replace old favourite
Café Cultura, incorporating historic Quito
architecture and Renaissance style, high-end
suites and restaurant, bar, terrace, spa, wood-
panelled library with fireplace, garden and
infinity pool, attentive service. Opened 2017.

$$$$ Le Parc
República de El Salvador N34-349 e Irlanda,
T02-227 6800, www.leparc.com.ec.

Modern hotel with 30 executive suites, full luxury facilities and service, restaurant, spa, gym, parking.

$$$$ Nü House
Foch E6-12 y Reina Victoria, T02-255 7845, www.nuhousehotels.com.
Modern luxury hotel with minimalist decor, restaurant, some suites with jacuzzi, parking, all furnishings and works of art are for sale.

$$$ Anahi
Tamayo N23-95 y Wilson, T02-250 1421, www.anahihotelquito.com.
Very nice tastefully decorated suites, each one is different, ample bathrooms, buffet breakfast, safety box, fridge, terrace with nice views, good value.

$$$ Casa Aliso
F Salazar E12-137 y Toledo, La Floresta, T02-252 8062, www.casaliso.com.
Small "boutique" hotel in a converted residential house, stylish, helpful staff, convenient for restaurants in this quiet district, with restaurant and bar, gardens.

$$$ Casa Joaquín
Pinto E4-376 y JL Mera, T02-222 4791, www.hotelcasajoaquin.com.
Nicely refurbished hotel in the heart of La Mariscal, covered patio makes it warm, good service, Belgian-run.

$$$ City Art Hotel Silberstein
Wilson E5-29 y JL Mera, T02-515 1651, www.cityartsilberstein.com.
10 comfortable rooms and suites in an attractively refurbished building, includes buffet breakfast.

$$$ Finlandia
Finlandia N35-129 y Suecia, north of centre, T02-382 0860, www.hotelfinlandia.com.ec.
Pleasant hotel in residential area, buffet breakfast, restaurant, spacious rooms, sitting room with fireplace, small garden, parking, helpful staff.

$$$ Fuente de Piedra I & II
Wilson E9-80 y Tamayo, T02-255 9775 and JL Mera N23-21 y Baquedano, T02-290 0323, www.ecuahotel.com.
Well-decorated modern hotels, comfortable, some rooms are small, nice sitting areas, pleasant.

$$$ Hostal de la Rábida
La Rábida 227 y Santa María, T02-222 2169, www.hostalrabida.com.

Lovely converted home, bright comfortable rooms, good restaurant for breakfast and dinner (both extra), parking, Ecuadorean/Italian-run. Recommended.

$$$ La Cartuja
Plaza N20-08 y 18 de Septiembre, T02-252 3577, www.hotelacartuja.com.
In the former British Embassy, beautifully decorated, spacious comfortable rooms, cafeteria, parking, lovely garden, very helpful and hospitable. Highly recommended.

$$$ Sierra Madre
Veintimilla E9-33 y Tamayo, T02-250 5687, www.hotelsierramadre.com.
Fully renovated villa, comfortable rooms, includes buffet breakfast, restaurant, nice sun roof, English spoken.

$$$-$$ La Casa Sol
Calama 127 y 6 de Diciembre, T02-223 0798, www.lacasasol.com.
Attractive small hotel with courtyard, very helpful, English and French spoken, also run **Casa Sol** in Otavalo. Recommended.

$$ El Arupo
Rodríguez E7-22 y Reina Victoria, T02-255 7543, www.hostalelarupo.com.
Good hotel, cooking facilities, English and French spoken. Recommended.

$$ Cayman
Rodríguez E7-29 y Reina Victoria, T02-256 7616, www.hotelcaymanquito.com.
Pleasant hotel, lovely dining room, cafeteria, rooms a bit small, sitting room with fireplace, parking, garden, very good.

$$ Travellers Inn
La Pinta E4-435 y Amazonas, T02-255 6985, www.travellersecuador.com.
In a nicely converted home, includes good breakfast, private or shared bath, parking, nice common area, bike rentals. Recommended.

$$-$ Casa Helbling
Veintimilla E8-152 y 6 de Diciembre, T02-256 5740, www.casahelbling.de.
Very good, popular hostel, spotless, breakfast extra, private or shared bath, also 6-bed dorm, laundry and cooking facilities, English and German spoken, pleasant atmosphere, reliable information, luggage storage, parking. Highly recommended.

$$-$ Posada del Maple
Rodríguez E8-49 y 6 de Diciembre, T02-254 4507,
www.posadadelmaple.com.
Popular hostel, private or shared bath, also 8-bed
dorm (US$8.50 pp), cooking facilities, warm
atmosphere, free tea and coffee.

$ Backpackers Inn
Rodríguez E7-48 y Reina Victoria, T02-250 9669,
www.backpackersinn.net.
Popular hostel, breakfast extra, private or shared
bath, adequate dorms (US$8 pp), laundry and
cooking facilities.

$ Casona de Mario
Andalucía N24-115 y Galicia (La Floresta),
T02-254 4036, www.casonademario.com.
Popular hostel, shared bath, laundry facilities,
no breakfast, well equipped kitchen, parking,
sitting room, nice garden, book exchange,
long stay discounts, Argentine owner.
Repeatedly recommended.

$ El Cafecito
Cordero E6-43 y Reina Victoria, T02-223 0922,
www.cafecito.net.
Popular with backpackers, breakfast extra, good
café including vegetarian and vegan, cheaper
in dorm (US$10), 1 room with bath ($$), relaxed
atmosphere but can get noisy until 2200,
Canadian-owned.

Quito suburbs

$$$$ Hacienda Rumiloma
Obispo Díaz de La Madrid, T02-254 8206,
www.rumiloma.com.
Luxurious hotel in a 40-ha hacienda on
the slopes of Pichincha. Sumptuous suites
with lots of attention to detail, lounges
with antiques, good but pricey restaurant,
bar with fireplace, nice views, personalized
attention from owners, ideal for a luxurious
escape not far from the city.

$$$ Hostería San Jorge
Km 4 via antigua Quito-Nono, to the
west of Av Mariscal Sucre, T02-339 0403,
www.eco-lodgesanjorge.com.
Converted 18th-century hacienda on a 80-ha
private reserve on the slopes of Pichincha, full
board available, good pricey restaurant, heating,
pool, sauna and jacuzzi, horse riding and
birdwatching. Operates 6 nature reserves.

Quito airport
The **Wyndham Quito Airport** (www.wyndham.
com) luxury hotel is 500 m from the airport
terminal. A short distance further away a **Holiday
Inn** (www.holidayinn.com) and a **Eurobuilding**
(www.hoteleuro.com) were due to open in 2017.
Towns near the airport with accommodation
include Tababela, off highway E-35, 10 mins from
the airport towards Quito (airport taxi US$10).
Nearby, by the junction of E-35 and the Vía
Interoceánica, is Pifo, also about 10 mins from
the airport (taxi US$10). From Pifo you can go
northwest to Quito, southwest to Sangolquí and
points south or east to Papallacta and Oriente.
Puembo, northwest of Pifo, is 20 mins from
the airport (taxi US$15-20) and closer to Quito.
Oyambarillo, southeast of the airport off E-35,
is 10 mins away (taxi US$10). On E-35 north of
Oyambarillo are Checa, about 15 mins away
(taxi US$12-15), and El Quinche, about 20 mins
from the airport (taxi US$15-20). The last 2 are
convenient if going to Otavalo and points north,
without going to Quito. Taxi drivers may not be
familiar with the hotels in these towns, so it is
worth printing the hotel's map before travelling.
Some hotels are in rural settings where there
are no restaurants, but there are places to eat in
Tababela and Puembo and a food court in the
shopping area opposite the airport.

$$$$-$$$ Hostal Su Merced
Julio Tobar Donoso, Puembo, T02-389 5351,
www.sumerced.com.
Nicely refurbished 18th-century hacienda house,
well-appointed rooms with bathtubs, includes
traditional breakfast, restaurant, sauna, gardens,
airport transfers US$15 per vehicle.

$$$ Posada Mirolindo
Vía Oyambarillo, T02-215 0363,
www.posadamirolindo.com.
Pleasant rooms and cottages, includes transfers
to and from the airport, breakfast provided,
other meals on request.

$$ Hostería San Carlos
Justo Cuello y Maldonado, Tababela, T02-
359 9057, http://hosteriasancarlos.com.
Hacienda-style inn with ample grounds,
restaurant, pool, jacuzzi, airport transfers US$5 pp.

$$ Quito Airport Suites
Alfonso Tobar 971 y Tulio Guzmán, Tababela,
1 block from the plaza, T02-359 9110 or
T09-8889 9774, airporthotelquito.com.
Room price includes breakfast which can be
a box breakfast in case of an early departure,

dinner extra, English spoken; rooms available for day use between flights ($); luggage storage US$1 per case, per day, available to non-guests US$2; long-term parking; airport transfers US$5-8 per vehicle.

$$-$ Hostal Colibrí
Pje Tobías Trujillo, 3 blocks downhill from the Tababela park, T09-9547 0312, www.hostalcolibriaeropuerto.com.
Hacienda-style hotel with private rooms and dorm for 12 (US$15 pp), include breakfast, dinner extra, garden with pool and jacuzzi, plenty of information, also arrange excursions; airport transfers US$8 for 2 passengers. Recommended.

Restaurants

Eating out in Quito is excellent, varied, upmarket and increasingly cosmopolitan. There are many elegant restaurants offering Ecuadorean and international food, as well as small simple places serving set meals for US$2.50-5, the latter close by early evening and on Sun.

Colonial Quito
Many restaurants serving economical *almuerzos* (set lunches) post their daily menu at the entrance; look for them along Calles Benalcázar, García Moreno, Guayaquil and Espejo.

$$$ El Ventanal
Carchi y Nicaragua, west of the Basílica, in Parque San Juan, take a taxi to the parking area and a staff member will accompany you along a footpath to the restaurant, T02-257 2232, www.elventanal.ec. Tue-Sat 1300-1500, 1800-2230, Sun 1200-1600.
International nouvelle cuisine with a varied menu including a number of seafood dishes, fantastic views over the city.

$$$ Los Geranios
Morales Oe1-134, T02-295 6035. Mon-Thu 0900-0000, Fri-Sat 0900-0200, Sun 1000-2200.
Upscale *comida típica*, in a nicely restored La Ronda house.

$$$ Theatrum
Plaza del Teatro, 2nd floor of Teatro Sucre, T02-228 9669, www.theatrum.com.ec. Mon-Fri 1230-1500, 1900-2200, Sat-Sun 1900-2200.
Good traditional Ecuadorean cuisine in the city's most important theatre, excellent service, free transport.

$$$-$$ Hasta la Vuelta Señor
Pasaje Arzobispal, 3rd floor, T02-258 0887, https://hastalavuelta.com. Mon-Sat 1100-2300, Sun 1100-2100.
A *fonda quiteña* perched on an indoor balcony with *comida típica* and snacks, try *empanadas* (pasties) or a *seco de chivo* (goat stew).

$$ Tianguez
Plaza de San Francisco under the portico of the church, T02-295 0233, see Facebook. Sun-Wed 0730-1900, Thu 0730-2200, Fri-Sat 0730-2400.
International and local dishes, good coffee, snacks, sandwiches, popular, also craft shop (closes 1830), run by Fundación Sinchi Sacha.

$$ Vista Hermosa
Mejía 453 y García Moreno, T02-295 1401, http://vistahermosa.ec. Mon-Sat 1300-2400.
Good meals, drinks, pizza, live music on weekends, lovely terrace-top views of the colonial centre.

$$-$ San Ignacio
García Moreno N2-60, at Museo María Agusta Urrutia, T02-258 4173, see Facebook. Mon-Tue 0800-2100, Wed-Sat 0800-2200, Sun 0800-1600.
Good popular set lunch (US$4.50) with a choice of dishes and buffet salad bar; à la carte in the evening.

$ Govindas
Esmeraldas Oe3-115 y Venezuela, T02-295 7849, see Facebook. Mon-Sat 0800-1800.
Vegetarian dishes, good-value economical set lunch and à la carte snacks, also breakfast and yoga centre.

$ Plaza Chica
Between Venezuela and Guayaquil, on an interior patio behind the Municipio, T02-228 6434, see Facebook. Mon-Fri 0830-1600.
Very good elegant set lunch with a choice of dishes (US$5), also coffee and pastries. Very popular, so be prepared to wait.

Cafés

Cafeto
Chile 930 y Flores. Mon-Sat 0800-2000, Sun 0800-1600, T 02-257 2921, Facebook: cafetoquito.
Variety of coffees, snacks, sandwiches, sweets.

Heladería San Agustín
Guayaquil N5-59 y Chile. Mon-Fri 1000-1730, Sat-Sun 1030-1600.
Coffee, traditional home-made cakes, ices and lunch, a Quito tradition since 1858.

Modern Quito

There are at least 25 restaurants (**$$$-$$**) and cafés within a block of Plaza Foch. There are many restaurants serving good economical set lunches along both Pinto and Foch, between Amazonas and Cordero. A number of restaurants in La Floresta, east of La Mariscal, near Parque La Carolina and along Av Eloy Alfaro, fall outside the scope of our map.

$$$ Carmine
Catalina Aldaz N34-208 y Portugal, T02-333 2829, www.carministorante.com. Mon-Sat 1200-2300, Sun 1200-1800.
Creative international and Italian cuisine.

$$$ Chez Jérôme
Whymper N30-96 y Coruña, T02-223 4067, www.chezjeromerestaurante.com. Mon-Fri 1230-1500, 1930-2300.
Excellent traditional and modern French cuisine, with local ingredients, good ambiance and service.

$$$ Il Risotto
Eloy Alfaro N34-447 y Portugal, T02-224 6850 and República de El Salvador N35-79 y Portugal, T02-224 8487. Mon-Fri 1130-1530, 1830-2300, Sat 1130-2300, Sun 1130-2200 (Eloy Alfaro); Mon-Sat 1200-2300, Sun 1200-2200 (Rep ES).
Very popular and very good Italian cooking, prices on Eloy Alfaro are somewhat higher. A Quito tradition.

$$$ La Boca del Lobo
Calama 284 y Reina Victoria, T02-223 4083, wwwlabocadellobo.com.ec. Sun-Wed 1700-2330, Thu-Sat 1700-0100.
Stylish bar-restaurant with eclectic food, drink, decor, and atmosphere, good food and cocktails, popular, good meeting place.

$$$ La Briciola
Isabel la Católica y Salazar esquina, T254 5157, www.labriciola.com.ec. Daily 1200-2400.
Extensive Italian menu, excellent food, very good personal service.

$$$ La Choza
12 de Octubre N24-551 y Cordero, T02-223 0839. Mon-Sat 1200-1600, 1800-2130, Sun 1200-1600.
Traditional Ecuadorean cuisine, good music and decor.

$$$ La Gloria
Valladolid N24-519 y Salazar, La Floresta, T02-252 7855, www.lagloria.com.ec. Daily 1200-1530, 1900-2200.

Very innovative Peruvian and international cuisine, excellent food and service. Same ownership as Theatrum, see Colonial Quito Restaurants, above.

$$$ La Petite Mariscal
Almagro N24-304 y Rodríguez, T02-604 3303, www.lapetitemariscal.com. Tue-Fri 1200-1500, 1800-2200, Sat 1800-2200.
Upmarket European cuisine with an Ecuadorean touch, also a good set lunch.

$$$ San Telmo
Portugal 440 y Casanova, T02-225 6946, Facebook: santelmouio. Daily 1200-2300.
Good Argentine grill, seafood, pasta, pleasant atmosphere, great service.

$$$ Zazu
Mariano Aguilera 331 y La Pradera, T254 3559, www.zazuquito.com. Mon-Fri 1230-1500, 1900-2300, Sat 1900-2300.
Very elegant and exclusive dinning. International and Peruvian specialities, extensive wine list, attentive service, reservations required.

$$$-$$ Baalbek
6 de Diciembre N23-103 y Wilson, T02-255 2766, http://restaurantbaalbek.com. Sun-Tue 1200-1700, Wed-Sat 1200-2230.
Authentic Lebanese cuisine, great food and atmosphere, friendly service.

$$ Chez Alain
Wilson E9-68 y Tamayo, T02-222 5889, see Facebook. Mon an d Sat 1200-1530, Tue-Fri 1200-1600.
Choice of good 4-course set lunches, pleasant relaxed atmosphere, monthly dinner/show specials. Recommended.

$$ The Magic Bean
Foch E5-08 y JL Mera, daily 0800-2200, and Portugal y El Salvador, daily 0800-1730, T02-256 6181, http://magicbeanquito.com.
Fine coffees and natural food, more than 20 varieties of pancakes, good salads, large portions, outdoor seating.

$$ Mama Clorinda
Reina Victoria N24-150 (11-44) y Calama, T02-254 4362, www.restaurantemamaclorinda.com. Daily 1100-2345.
Ecuadorean cuisine à la carte and set meals, filling, good value.

$$ Mr Bagel
Portugal E10-95 y 6 de Diciembre, see Facebook. Mon-Fri 0700-1500, Sat-Sun 0730-1500.

Very popular breakfast and lunch restaurant, 17 varieties of bagels and many spreads, sandwiches, soups, salads, desserts, also take out, Wi-Fi and book exchange.

$$ Pekín
Whymper N28-42 y Orellana, T02-223 5273, www.restaurante-pekin.com. Mon-Sat 1200-1530, 1800-2230, Sun 1200-2000.
Excellent Chinese food, very nice atmosphere.

$$-$ El Hornero
Veintimilla 1149 y Amazonas, República de El Salvador N36-149 y Naciones Unidas, González Suárez 1070 y Bejarano and other branches, www.pizzeriaelhornero.com.ec. Daily 1200-2300.
Very good wood oven pizzas, try one with *choclo* (fresh corn). Recommended.

$$-$ Las Palmeras
Japón N36-87 y Naciones Unidas, opposite Parque la Carolina, and 9 other branches, www.laspalmeras.com.ec. Daily 0900-1700.
Very good *comida Esmeraldeña*, try their hearty *viche de pescado* soup, outdoor tables, popular, good value. Recommended.

$$-$ Rincón Ecuatoriano Chileno
6 de Diciembre N28-30 y Belo Horizonte, T02-250 9462, see Facebook. Mon 1200-1800, Tue-Sat 1200-2000, Sun 1200-1700.
Good tasty home-cooking, Chilean specialities including *empanadas*, large portions, efficient service, some tables in back garden.

$$-$ Sakti
Carrión E4-144 y Amazonas, T02-252 0466, http://sakti-quito.com. Mon-Fri 0830-1730.
Good-quality vegetarian food, tasty healthy breakfast, daily specials, fruit juices, great desserts (also rooms around a small garden, $$-$). Recommended.

$ Chandani Tandoori
JL Mera 1312 y Cordero. Mon-Sat 1200-2130, Sun 1200-1530.
Good authentic Indian cuisine, economical set meals, popular, good value. Recommended.

$ Yu Su
Colón E7-60 y Almagro, edif Torres de Almagro, T02-223 5001, see Facebook. Mon-Sat 1200-1600, 1800-2100.
Very good sushi bar, pleasant, Korean-run, takeaway service.

Cafés

Coffee Bar
Foch E6-12 y Reina Victoria, Facebook: Coffeebarfoch. Daily 1100-2400, t ill 0300 Fri-Sat.
Popular café serving a variety of snacks, pasta, burgers, coffee, Wi-Fi. Very similar are **Yasuní Café**, Amazonas y Washington, and **Coffee Tov**, next to Museo Mindalae, La Niña y Reina Victoria.

Ethnic Coffee
Amazonas entre Robles y Roca, Edif Hotel Mercure, local 3, www.ethniccollection.com. Mon-Fri 0930-2100.
Nice popular café with gourmet coffee as well as a wide range of desserts, meals (**$$**) and drinks.

Kallari
Wilson E4-266 y JL Mera, T02-223 6009. Mon-Fri 0900-1830, Sat 0900-1400.
Fairtrade café, breakfast, snacks, salad and sandwich set lunches, organic coffee and chocolate, crafts, run by an association of farmers and artisans from the Province of Napo working on rainforest and cultural conservation.

Bars and clubs

Colonial Quito

In the old city, much of the nightlife is concentrated along La Ronda.

Bandidos
Olmedo E1-136 y Cevallos, T02-228 6504, http://bandidobrewing.com. Mon-Fri 1600-2300, Sat 1400-2300.
Very popular pub, partly housed in an old chapel, serves a choice of excellent microbrews and snacks.

Modern Quito

Bungalow Six
Almagro N24-139 y Calama. Tue-Sat 1900-0200, Sun 1200-1900.
US-style sports bar and club. Popular place to hang out and watch a game or a film, dancing later on, varied music, cover US$5 (Thu free), ladies' night on Wed, happy hour 2000-2200.

Cherusker
Pinto E7-85 y Diego de Almagro, T02-601 2142, http://cherusker.com. Mon 1600-2400, Tue-Wed 1500-2400, Thu-Sat 1200-0200.
Various microbrews and German food.

El Pobre Diablo
Isabel La Católica N24-224 y Galavis, La Floresta, www.elpobrediablo.com. Mon-Sat 1230-0200.
Relaxed atmosphere, friendly, jazz, sandwiches, snacks and nice meals and set lunches, live music Wed, Thu and Sat, a popular place to hang out and chill.

Finn McCool's
Almagro N24-64 y Pinto, T02-252 1780, www.irishpubquito.com. Daily 1100-0300.
Irish-run pub, Irish and international food, darts, pool, table football, sports on TV, Wi-Fi, popular meeting place.

La Juliana
Av 12 de Octubre N24-722 y Coruña, T02-604 1569, www.lajuliana.com.ec. Fri-Sat 2100-0300.
Popular club, live 1990s Latin music.

No Bar
Calama E5-01 y JL Mera, T02-254 5145, Facebook: nobarquito. Tue-Sat 2000-0300.
Good mix of Latin and Euro dance music, busy at weekends. Nightly specials on drinks, free drinks for women some evenings, see Facebook.

Ramón Antigua
Mena Caamaño E12-86 e Isabel la Católica, T09-9519 5748. Open 2100-0200.
Live music Fri-Sat, cover US$5-10 depending on band. Great for salsa and other hip tropical music, popular with locals.

Selfie
Calama E7-35 y Reina Victoria. Wed-Thu 1500-2400, Fri 1200-0200, Sat 1200-2400.
Popular disco attracting a young crowd, entry US$3.

Turtle's Head
La Niña E4-451 y JL Mera, T02-256 5544, see Facebook. Mon-Wed 1600-2345, Thu-Sat 1600-0200.
Microbrews, fish and chips, curry, pool table, darts, fun atmosphere.

Varadero
Reina Victoria N26-105 y La Pinta, T02-254 2476. Fri-Sat 2000-0300.
Bar-restaurant, live Cuban music, attached to **La Bodeguita de Cuba** restaurant (see Facebook), mixed crowd.

Entertainment

There are always many cultural events taking place in Quito, often free of charge. Films are listed daily in *El Comercio*, www.elcomercio.com.

Cinema
There are several multiplexes, eg **Cinemark**, www.cinemark.com.ec and **Multicines**, www.multicines.com.ec.
Casa de la Cultura, *Patria y 6 de Diciembre, T02-290 2272, www.casadelacultura.gob.ec (click on Manifestaciones Culturales for programme).* Shows foreign films, often has documentaries, film festivals, free.
Ocho y Medio, *Valladolid N24-353 y Guipuzcoa, La Floresta, T02-290 4720, www.ochoymedio.net.* Cinema and café, good for art films, programme available at *Libri Mundi* and elsewhere.

Dance
Casa de la Danza, *Junín E2-186 y Javier Gutiérrez, Parque San Marcos in colonial city, T02-295 5445, www.casadeladanza.org.* Run by the well-known Ecuadorean dancer Susana Reyes, is the venue for dance festivals and events. Also has **Museo del Danzante**, an exhibit about Ecuadorean folk dance and hosts other exhibits and folk dance presentations on Thu or Sat night. Enquire ahead.

Dance schools 1-to-1 or group lessons are offered for US$4-6 per hr.
Ritmo Tropical, *Amazonas N24-155 y Calama, T02-255 7094, www.ritmotropicalsalsa.com.* Salsa, capoeira, merengue, tango and more.
Salsa y Merengue School, *Foch E4-256 y Amazonas, T02-222 0427,* also cumbia.

Ecuadorean folk ballet Ballet Andino **Humanizarte** (Casa 707, Morales 707, La Ronda, T09-8750 0595, see Facebook, Fri-Sat 2130, US$5), plays and comedies are also often in their repertoire, restaurant on the premises. **Jacchigua** (at **Teatro Demetrio Aguilera Malta**, Casa de la Cultura, 6 de Diciembre y Patria, T02-295 2025, www.jacchigua.org. Wed at 1930). Entertaining, colourful and touristy, reserve ahead, US$35, see website for offers, dinner and transfers. Other dance groups highlighting Ecuadorean traditions and folklore are **Saruymanda** (T09-8414 3747, www.saruymanda.com) and **Danzando Tierra** (at Casona del Centro de Desarrollo Comunitario de San Marcos, T09-8393 7813, see Facebook).

Music
Classical The Orquesta Sinfónica Nacional (T02-250 2815), performs at **Teatro Sucre**, **Casa de la Música, Teatro Escuela Politécnica Nacional, Teatro México**, in the colonial churches and regionally. **Casa de la Música** (Valderrama N32-307 y Mariana de Jesús, T02-226 7093, www.casadelamusica.ec), concerts by the Orquesta Sinfónica Nacional, Orquesta Filarmónica del

Ecuador, Orquesta de Instrumentos Andinos and invited performers. Excellent acoustics.

Folk Folk music is popular in *peñas* which come alive after 2230:
Noches de Quito, *Washington E5-29 y JL Mera, T02-223 2388. Thu-Sat 2000-0300, show starts 2130.* Varied music, entry US$6.
Ñucanchi, *Av Universitaria Oe5-188 y Armero, T02-254 0967, www.nucanchipeniaecuador.com. Fri-Sat 1945-0245.* Ecuadorean and other music, including Latin dance later in the night, entry US$7.50-15.

Theatre
Agora (open-air theatre), **Teatro Nacional** (large) and **Prometeo** (informal), all at Casa de la Cultura, stage plays and concerts. For upcoming events, see website listed under Cinema.
Teatro Bolívar, *Espejo 847 y Guayaquil, T02-258 2486, www.teatrobolivar.org.* Despite restoration work you can have a tour.
Teatro Sucre, *at Plaza del Teatro, T02-295 1661, www.teatrosucre.org (includes programme).* Beautifully restored 19th-century building, the city's classical theatre.

New Year Años Viejos: life-size puppets satirize politicians and others. At midnight on 31 Dec a will is read, the legacy of the outgoing year, and the puppets are burnt; good at Av Amazonas, where a competition is held, very entertaining and good humoured. On New Year's day everything is shut.
6 Jan (may be moved to the weekend) Colourful **Inocentes** procesion from Plaza de Santo Domingo at 1700.
8 Mar International Women's Day, marks the start of **Mujeres en la Danza**, a week long international dance festival organized by Casa de la Danza, www.casadeladanza.org.
Mar-Apr Música Sacra, a 10-day religious music festival is held before and during Easter week.
Palm Sunday, colourful procession from the Basílica, 0800-1000. The solemn **Good Friday** processions are most impressive.
24 May Independence, commemorating the Battle of Pichincha in 1822 with early morning cannon-fire and parades, everything closes.
Aug Agosto Arte y Cultura, organized by the municipality, cultural events, dance and music in different places throughout the city.
1-6 Dec Día de Quito. The city's main festival celebrated, commemorates the foundation of the city with elaborate parades, bullfights,

performances and music in the streets, very lively. Hotels charge extra, everything except a few restaurants shuts on 6 Dec.
25 Dec Foremost among **Christmas** celebrations is the **Misa del Gallo**, midnight Mass. Nativity scenes can be admired in many public places.

Shopping

Shops open generally 0900-1900 on weekdays, some close at midday and most shut Sat afternoon and Sun. Shopping centres are open at weekends. In modern Quito much of the shopping is done in malls. Be aware that over Christmas, Quito is crowded and the streets are packed with vendors and shoppers. For purchasing maps see Practicalities, page 1190.

Bookshops
The following have a selection of books in English:
Confederate Books, *Amazonas N24-155 y Calama.* Used books.
Libri Mundi, *at Quicentro Shopping, other malls and the airport, www.librimundi.com.*
Mr Books, *Mall El Jardín, p3 and Scala and El Condado shopping centres, www.mrbooks.com.*
The English Bookshop, *Calama 217 y Almagro.* Used books sales and exchange.

Camping
Camping gas is available in many of the shops listed below, white gas is not.
Aventura Sport, *Quicentro Shopping, 2nd level.* Tents, good selection of glacier sunglasses, Ecuadorean and imported outdoor clothing and gear. The following two shops stock the same products.
Camping Sports, *Colón E6-39 y Reina Victoria.*
Equipos Cotopaxi, *6 de Diciembre N20-36 y Patria.*
Explorer, *Plaza Foch and all main shopping centres in the city.* Clothing and equipment for adventure sports.
Mono Dedo, *Rafael León Larrea N24-36 y Coruña, La Floresta, www.monodedoecuador.com.* Climbing equipment. Part of a rock climbing club, lessons.
Tatoo, *Av de los Granados y 6 de Diciembre and CC Scala in Cumbayá, www.tatoo.ws.* Quality backpacks and outdoor clothing.

Chocolate
Ecuador has exported its fine cacao to the most prestigious chocolatiers around the world for over 100 years. Today, quality chocolate is on offer in specialized shops and food stores.

Cacao & Cacao, *JL Mera N21-241 y Roca, T02-222 4951, plus 3 shops, http://cacaoshopcacao.com.* Shop and café featuring many brands of Ecuadorean chocolate and coffee.

Galería Ecuador, *Reina Victoria N24-263 y García, http://galeriaecuador.com.* Shop and café featuring Ecuadorean gourmet organic coffee and chocolate as well as some crafts.

Pacari, *Zaldumbide N24-676 y Miravalle, www. pacarichocolate.com.* Factory outlet for one of the most highly regarded manufacturers. They have won more international chocolate awards than any other company in the world. Also have an organic products market on Tue.

República del Cacao, *Reina Victoria y Pinto, Plaza Foch; Morales Oe1-166, La Ronda, El Jardín and Scala malls and at the airport, www.republicadelcacao.com.* Chocolate boutique and café, also sell Panama hats.

Handicrafts

There are controls on export of arts and crafts: unless they are obviously new handicrafts, you may have to get a permit from the **Instituto Nacional de Patrimonio Cultural** (Colón Oe1-93 y 10 de Agosto, T02-254 3527, offices also in other cities), before you can mail or take things home; permits cost US$5 and take time.

A wide selection can be found at the following craft markets: **Mercado Artesanal La Mariscal**, Jorge Washington, between Reina Victoria and JL Mera, daily 1000-1800, interesting and worthwhile; **El Indio**, Roca E4-35 y Amazonas, daily 0900-1900; and **Centro de Artesanías CEFA**, 12 de Octubre 1738 y Madrid, Mon-Sat 0930-1830.

On weekends, crafts are sold in stalls at **Parque El Ejido** and along the Av Patria side of this park, artists sell their paintings. There are crafts and art shops along La Ronda and souvenir shops on García Moreno in front of the Palacio Presidencial.

Recommended shops with an ample selection are:

Camari, *Marchena 260 y Versalles.* Fair Trade shop run by an artisan organization.

EBD Carmal, *Amazonas N24-126 y Foch, ebdcarmal.com.* Panama and fedora hats.

Ethnic Collection, *Amazonas y Roca, Edif Hotel Mercure, www.ethniccollection.com.* Wide variety of clothing, leather, bags, jewellery and ceramic items. Also café 2 doors south.

Folklore, *Colón E10-53 y Caamaño, http:// olgafisch.com.* The store of the late Olga Fisch, who for decades encouraged craftspeople to excel. Attractive selection of top quality, pricey handicrafts and rugs. Small museum upstairs includes a very good collection of pre-Columbian ceramics.

Galería Latina, *JL Mera 823 y Veintimilla. Daily.* Fine selection of alpaca and other handicrafts from Ecuador, Peru and Bolivia, visiting artists sometimes demonstrate their work.

Hilana, *6 de Diciembre N23-10 y Veintimilla.* Beautiful unique 100% wool blankets, ponchos and clothing with Ecuadorean motifs, also cotton garnments, excellent quality.

Kallari, crafts from Oriente at café, page 1038.

K Dorfzaun, fine Panama hats are sold at the **República del Cacao** shops, see under Chocolate, above.

La Bodega, *JL Mera 614 y Carrión.* Recommended for antiques and handicrafts.

Mindalae, nice crafts at museum, page 1029.

Productos Andinos, *Urbina 111 y Cordero.* Artisan's co-op, good selection, unusual items.

Saucisa, *Amazonas N22-18 y Veintimilla, and a couple other locations in La Mariscal.* Very good place to buy Andean music and instruments.

Jewellery

Argentum, *JL Mera 614.* Excellent selection, reasonably priced.

Ari Gallery, *Bolívar Oe6-23, Plaza San Francisco.* Fine silver with ancestral motifs.

Taller Guayasamín, at the **Capilla del Hombre**, see page 1029. Jewellery with native designs.

What to do

Birdwatching and nature

The following are specialized operators: **Andean Birding**, www.andeanbirding.com; **Birdsexplore**, www.exploraves.com; **Ecuador Experience**, www.ecuador-experience.com (in French); **Mindo Bird Tours**, www.mindobirdtours.com; **Neblina Forest**, www.neblinaforest.com; **Real Nature**, www.realnaturetravel.com. Local birding guides are also available in Mindo.

City tours

Quito Tour Bus, *T02-245 8010, www.quitotour bus.com.* Tours on double-decker bus, stops at 11 places of interest, it starts and ends at Av Naciones Unidas, south side. You can start at any stop along the route and can alight at a site and continue later on another bus. Hourly, 0900-1600, 3-hr ride, US$15, children and seniors US$7.50, ticket valid all day. Night tour Fri, Sat and holidays at 1900, US$15, with a 1½-hr stop at La Ronda. Mitad del Mundo and Pululahua tour, Sat and Sun at 1100, US$30, children and seniors US$20, includes museum entrance fees, 7 hrs.

They also offer weekly tours to Mindo, Otavalo, Cotopaxi, Papallacta and Quilotoa (US$60-70). Reservations required; see website for details.

Rutas Turísticas, walking tours of the colonial city led by English- or French-speaking officers of the Policía Metropolitana start at the Plaza de la Independencia El Quinde Visitors Centre, Venezuela y Espejo, T02-257 2445. Advanced reservation and a minimum of 2 passengers required. 2 choices: **Ruta Patrimonial**, Tue-Sat at 0900, 1000 and 1400, Sun at 1100, 2½ hrs, US$15, children and seniors US$7.70, includes museum entrance fees for La Compañía, San Francisco and Museo de la Ciudad; and **Fachadas**, a daily historic buildings walking tour, at the same times, 1½ hrs, US$8; also an evening tour at 1800, US$10. **Quito Eterno** (www.quitoeterno.org) a programme rescuing the city's identity, offers tours in which Quito's legendary characters guide you through their city, most on Sat 1900-2000, US$8-10.

Climbing, trekking and walking

The following Quito operators specialize in this area, most also offer conventional tours and sell Galápagos and jungle tours. Note that no one may climb without a licensed guide employed by an authorized agency. Independent climbers and guides are refused entry to national parks, but exceptions may be made for internationally (UIAA) certified guides and members of Ecuadorian climbing clubs. The Asociación Ecuatoriana de Guías de Montaña (ASEGUIM) is at Pinto E4-385 y JL Mera, T02-254 1563, www.aseguim.nicotinamedia.com.

Campus Adventures, T02-234 0601, www.campus-trekking.com. Good-value trekking, climbing and cultural tours, 8- to 15-day biking trips, tailor made itineraries. Also run **Hostería Pantaví** near Ibarra, 8 languages spoken.

Climbing Tours, Amazonas N21-221 y Roca, T02-254 4358, www.climbingtour.com. Climbing, trekking and other adventure sports, also tours to regional attractions, jungle tours and Galápagos. Well-established operator.

Compañía de Guías, Valladolid N24-70 y Madrid, T02-290 1551, www.companiadeguias.com. Climbing and trekking specialists. Speak English, German, French and Italian.

Condor Trekk, Reina Victoria N24-295 y Cordero, T02-222 6004, www.condortrekkexpeditions.com. Climbing, trekking and fishing trips, 4WD transport, equipment rentals and sales.

Cotopaxi Cara Sur, contact Eduardo Agama, T09-9800 2681, eagamaz@gmail.com. Offers climbing and trekking tours, runs Albergue Cara Sur on Cotopaxi.

Gulliver, Foch y Reina Victoria, T02-252 9297, www.gulliver.com.ec. Climbing and trekking and a wide range of economical adventure and traditional tours. Operate **Hosterías PapaGayo** at Cotopaxi, Cayambe and in Quito.

High Summits, Pinto E5-29 y JL Mera, p2, T02-254 9358, www.climbing-ecuador.com. Climbing specialists for over 40 years, Swiss/Ecuadorean-run.

Latitud 0°, Mallorca N24-500 y Coruña, La Floresta, T02-254 7921, www.latitud0.com. Climbing specialists, French spoken.

Original Ecuador, T09-9554 5821, www.originalecuador.com. Runs 1- to 7-day highland tours which involve walking several hours daily, also custom-made itineraries.

TribuTrek, T09-9282 5404, http://tributrek.com. Hiking and trekking, cultural and budget tours.

Cycling and mountain biking

Quito has many bike paths and bike lanes on city streets, but mind the traffic and aggressive drivers. The city organizes a ciclopaseo, a cycle day, every Sun 0800-1400. Key avenues are closed to vehicular traffic and thousands of cyclists cross the city in 29 km from north to south. This and other cycle events are run by **Fundación Ciclópolis** (G Córdova N23-53 y Wilson, T02-604 1433, www.ciclopolis.ec); they also hire bikes, US$5.60 per ciclopaseo (must book Mon-Fri), US$11.20 per day on other days. Rentals also from **La Casa del Ciclista** (República 770 y Eloy Alfaro, near the ciclopaseo route, T02-254 2852, Facebook: Lacasdelciclistaecuador, US$3 per hr, US$12 per day). If staying a long time in the city, sign up with **BiciQ**, to use their bikes stationed throughout town. **Biciaccion**, www.biciaccion.org, has information about routes in the city and organizes trips outside Quito.

Mountain bike tours Many operators offer bike tours, the following are specialists:

Aries, T09-9981 6603, www.ariesbikecompany.com. 1- to 3-day tours, all equipment provided.

Biking Dutchman, La Pinta E-731 y Reina Victoria, T02-256 8323, after hours T09-9420 5349, www.bikingdutchman.com. 1- and several-day tours, great fun, good food, very well organized, English, German and Dutch spoken, pioneers in mountain biking in Ecuador.

Horse riding

Horse riding tours are offered on Pichincha above the gate of the teleférico (see page 1031).

Language schools

Quito is one of the most important centres for Spanish language study in Latin America with over 80 schools operating. There are also schools in Baños, Cuenca, Manta, Canoa and other cities. There is a great variety to choose from. Identify your budget and goals for the course: rigorous grammatical and technical training, fluent conversation skills, getting to know Ecuadoreans or just enough basic Spanish to get you through your trip.

Visit a few places to get a feel for what they charge and offer. Prices vary greatly, from US$5 to US$22 per hour. There is also tremendous variation in teacher qualifications, infrastructure and resource materials. Schools usually offer courses of four or seven hours tuition per day. Many readers suggest that four is enough. Some schools offer packages which combine teaching in the morning and touring in the afternoon, others combine teaching with travel to various attractions throughout the country. A great deal of emphasis has traditionally been placed on one-to-one teaching, but remember that a well-structured small classroom setting is also recommended.

The quality of homestays likewise varies, the cost including half board runs from US$16 to US$20 per day (more for full board). Try to book just one week at first to see how a place suits you. For language courses as well as homestays, deal directly with the people who will provide services to you, avoid intermediaries and always get a detailed receipt.

If you are short on time then it can be a good idea to make your arrangements from home, either directly with one of the schools or through an agency, who can offer you a wide variety of options. If you have more time and less money, then it may be more economical to organize your own studies after you arrive. **South American Explorers** provides a list (free to members) of recommended schools and these may give club members discounts.

See What to do, Language courses, for schools in Quito and other cities. We list those for which we have received positive recommendations, but there are other good schools as well.

Green Horse Ranch, see page 1055.
Ride Andes, T09-9973 8221, www.rideandes.com. Private and set date tours in the highlands including stays in haciendas, also in other South American countries.

Language courses
Andean Global Studies, www.andeanglobalstudies.org.
Beraca, www.beracaspanishschool.com.
Cristóbal Colón, www.colonspanishschool.com.
Equinox, www.ecuadorspanish.com.
Instituto Superior, www.superiorspanishschool.com.

La Lengua, http://la-lengua.com.
Sintaxis, www.sintaxis.net.
South American, www.southamerican.edu.ec.
Universidad Católica, T02-299 1700 ext 1388, idiomas@puce.edu.ec. Group lessons.
Vida Verde, www.vidaverde.com.

Motorbiking
Freedom Bike Rental, Finlandia N35-06 y Suecia, T02-600 4459, www.freedombikerental.com. Motorcycle rentals US$95-225 per day, scooter US$25, good equipment including mountain bikes, GPS, route planning, also tours.

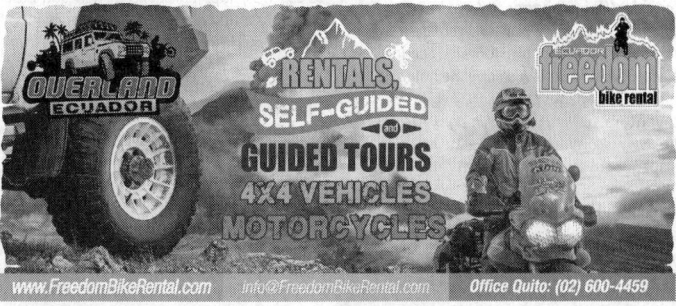

Paragliding

Escuela Pichincha de Vuelo Libre, *Carlos Endara Oe3-60 y Amazonas, T02-225 6592 (office hours), T09-9993 1206, parapent@uio.satnet.net.* Offers complete courses for US$450 and tandem flights for US$65-US$105 (Pichincha).

Tour operators

Most operators also sell Galápagos cruises and jungle tours.

Advantage Travel, *Gaspar de Villarroel N40-143, T02-336 0887, https://advantage-travel-ecuador. com.* Tours on the **Manatee** floating hotel on Río Napo and to Machalilla.

Andando Tours – Angermeyer Cruises, *Moreno Bellido E6-167 y Amazonas, T02-323 7330, www.visitgalapagos.travel.* Operate the *Mary Anne* sailing vessel, *Anahi* catamaran, *Passion* motor yacht and others, as well as LGBT cruises and tours.

Andean Travel Company, *Guipuzcoa E13-117 y Lugo, La Floresta, T02-222 8385, www.andeantc. com.* Dutch/Ecuadorean-owned operator, wide range of tours including trekking and cruises on the *Nemo I* catamaran and *San José* and *Odyssey* motor yachts and *Treasure of the Galápagos* catamaran.

Andes Overland, *Santa Fe N43-106 y Río Coca, T02-512 3358, www.andesoverland.com.* A 72-day tour through Bolivia, Peru, Ecuador and Colombia, offered with 2 levels of comfort, which you can join or leave at any point. Part of an international group, which guarantees departure.

Creter Tours, *Pinto E5-29 y JL Mera, T02-254 5491, www.cretertours.com.ec.* Offers cruises on several mid- and upper-class yachts and catamarans in the Galápagos, also a wide range tours on Ecuador mainland and in South America.

Dracaena, *Pinto E4-375 y Amazonas, T02-290 6644, www.amazondracaena.com.* Runs good budget jungle tours to **Nicky Lodge** in Cuyabeno and trekking trips, popular.

EcoAndes/Unigalapagos, *JL Mera N23-36 y Baquedano, T02-222 0892, www.ecoandestravel. com.* Classic and adventure tours in Ecuador, Bolivia, Chile and Peru. Also operate hotels in Quito and Galápagos cruises.

Ecoventura, *La Niña E8-52 y Almagro, T02-323 7393, www.ecoventura.com.* Operate first-class Galápagos cruises on the *Eric*, *Letty* and *Origin* motor yachts and *Galápagos Sky* dive boat, and sell mainland tours and Peru.

Ecuador Expat Journeys, *T02-603 5548, www.ecuadorexpatjourneys.com.* Adventure tours to off-the-beaten-path destinations, day tours, treks to volcanoes, tours to expat hotspots.

Ecuador Galapagos Travels (EGT), *Veintimilla E10-78 y 12 de Octubre, Edif El Girón, Torre E, of 104, T02-254 7286, www.galapagos-cruises.ec, www.ecuadortravels.ec.* Wide range of traditional and adventure tours throughout Ecuador; tailor-made itineraries.

Ecuador Nature, *Jiménez de la Espada N32-156 y González Suárez, T02-222 2341, www. ecuadornature.com.* Offers a variety of mainland and Galápagos tours, can arrange kosher food.

Ecuador Treasure, *Wilson E4-266 y JL Mera, T02-255 9919, http://ecuadortreasure.com.* Daily tours, climbing, hiking, biking, trekking, horse riding and transport including a shuttle service to Lago Agrio, see page 1157. Run **Chuquiragua Lodge**, near Reserva Los Ilinizas.

Enchanted Expeditions, *de las Alondras N45-102 y de los Lirios, T02-334 0525, www.enchanted expeditions.com.* Operate the *Cachalote* and *Beluga* Galápagos vessels, sell jungle trips to Cuyabeno and highland tours. Very experienced.

Equateur Voyages Passion, *Gran Colombia N15-220 y Yaguachi, next to L'Auberge Inn, T02-322 7605, www.magical-ecuador.com.* Full range of adventure tours, run in highlands, coast and jungle. Also custom-made itineraries.

Galacruises Expeditions, *9 de Octubre N22-118 y Veintimilla, pb, T02-252 3324, www.islasgalapagos. travel.* Galápagos cruises on the *Archipel I and II* vessels and diving tours on the *Pingüino Explorer*. Also island hopping and land tours on Isabela, mainland and South America packages.

Galasam, *Cordero N24-214 y Amazonas, T02-290 3909, www.galasam.net.* Has a fleet of boats in different categories for Galápagos cruises, including the *Humboldt Explorer* diving yacht. City tours, full range of highland tours and jungle trips to **Siona Lodge** in Cuyabeno.

Galextur, *De los Motilones E14-58 y Charapa, T02-292 1739, http://galextur.com.* Run land-based Galápagos tours with daily sailings and island hopping. Sell live aboard and diving tours from the Silberstein Dive Center. Operate **Hotel Silberstein** in Puerto Ayora and **City Art Hotel Silberstein** in Quito. Good service.

Geo Reisen, *República del Salvador N36-24 y Suecia, T02-292 0583, www.georeisen-ecuador.com.* Specializing in cultural, adventure and nature tours adapted for individuals, groups or families.

Happy Gringo, *Catalina Aldaz N34-155 y Portugal, Edif Catalina Plaza, of 207, T02-512 3486, www.happygringo.com.* Tailor-made tours throughout Ecuador, Quito city tours, Otavalo, sell Galápagos, jungle and other destinations, good service. Recommended.

Klein Tours, *Eloy Alfaro N34-111 y Catina Aldaz, T02-226 7000, www.gogalapagos.com.* Operate the *Galapagos Legend* and *Coral I* and *II* cruise ships. Also run community-based tours in Imbabura and highland tours with tailor-made itineraries, English, French and German spoken.

Latin Trails, *T02-286 7832, www.latintrails.com.* Run cruises in various Galápagos vessels including the *Seaman Journey* and *Sea Star Journey*; offer a variety of land trips in several countries and operate **Hakuna Matata Lodge** in Archidona.

Metropolitan Touring, *Av de las Palmeras N45-74 y de las Orquídeas, T1800-115115, T02-298 8312, www.metropolitan-touring.com.* A large organization operating in Ecuador, Peru and Colombia. Run 3 luxury Galápagos vessels (see page 1180, the **Finch Bay Hotel** in Puerto Ayora, **Casa Gangotena** in Quito and **Mashpi Lodge** west of Quito. Also adventure, cultural and gastronomy tours.

Positiv Turismo, *Jorge Juan N33-38 y Atahualpa, T02-252 7305, www.positivturismo.com.* Cultural trips, Cuyabeno, trekking and special interest tours, Swiss-run.

Pure! Ecuador, *Muros N27-94 y González Suárez, T02-512 3358, www.pure-ecuador.com.* A Dutch-Ecuadorean operator offering tours throughout Ecuador and the Galápagos, trips to **Cotococha Amazon Lodge**, **Polylepis Lodge** (El Angel), and tailor-made tours.

Quasar Expeditions, *Ponce Carrasco E8-06 y Almagro, T02-382 5680, T1-800 247 2925 (USA), www.quasarex.com.* Offer 7-day naturalist and diving Galápagos cruises on yachts *Evolution* and *Grace*; also mainland extensions.

Rolf Wittmer Turismo/Tip Top Travel, *Foch E7-81 y Almagro, T02-2563181, www.rwittmer.com.* Run first class yachts: *Tip Top II*, *III* and *IV*. Also tailor-made tours throughout Ecuador.

South America for All, *T02-237 7430, www.southamericaforall.com.* Specialized tours to all regions of Ecuador for the mobility and hearing-impaired traveller, also chocolate tours. Also operate in Peru.

Surtrek, *San Ignacio E10-114 y Caamaño, T02-250 0660, T1-866-978 7398 in the US, www.surtrek.com.* Wide range of tours in all regions, helicopter and ballon flights, birdwatching, rafting, horse riding, mountain biking and jungle tours, arrange last

minute Galápagos tours, also sell domestic flights and run **Las Cascadas Lodge**.

Tierra de Fuego, *Amazonas N23-23 y Veintimilla, T02-250 1418, www.ecuadortierradefuego.com*. Provide transport and tours throughout the country, book domestic flight tickets and make Galápagos bookings.

Tropic Ecuador, *Pasaje Sánchez Melo Oe1-37 y Av Galo Plaza, T02-240 8741, http://destination ecuador.com and www.tropiceco.com*. Environmental and cultural tours, Quito, coast and highland tours, lodge-to-lodge mountain treks (Chilcabamba Mountain Lodge and Villa Rumilahua near Cotopaxi), Amazon lodges and Galápagos land-based tours (Floreana, Isabela and Santa Cruz –Magic Galápagos safari camp). Community-based tourism working with and donating a percentage of all profits to **Conservation in Action**. Winner of awards for responsible tourism.

Yacu Amu Experiences, *Amazonas N25-23 y Colón, Edif España, of 58, T02-255 0558, www.yacuamu.com*. Tailor-made adventure, nature and cultural trips for active couples, families and small groups.

Zenith Travel, *JL Mera N24-264 y Cordero, T02-252 9993, www.zenithecuador.com*. Good-value Galápagos cruises as well as various land tours in Ecuador and Peru. All-gay Galápagos cruises available. Multilingual service, knowledgeable helpful staff, good value.

Train rides

The lovely refurbished train station, **Estación Eloy Alfaro (Chimbacalle)**, with a railway museum and working concert hall, is 2 km south of the colonial city at Maldonado y Sincholagua, T1-800-873637, T02-265 0421, www.trenecuador. com, Mon-Fri 0800-1630. *Tren Crucero*, a luxury tourist train, runs about twice per month in either direction between Quito and Durán, outside Guayaquil, part of the route is run with a historic steam locomotive. The complete route takes 4 days and costs US$1650 one way; you can also take it for segments 1-3 days. The tour includes visits to places of interest and accommodation in luxury inns. See http://trenecuador.com/es/tren-crucero/ for details. Tourist trains run Thu-Sun and holidays from Quito to **Machachi** and **El Boliche** (0800, US$41-53 includes lunch), combined transport by train one way and by bus the other. A farm is visited in Machachi. At El Boliche station is **Restaurante Nuna**, and nearby, **Area Nacional de Recreación El Boliche**, a protected area bordering Parque Nacional Cotopaxi, where the tour includes a walk. There are lovely views of Cotopaxi and Los Ilinizas. Purchase tickets in advance by phone, internet, at the station or **El Quinde Visitors Centre**, Palacio Municipal, Venezuela y Espejo. You need each passenger's passport number and age to purchase tickets. Boarding 30 mins before departure, you can visit the railway museum before boarding.

Whitewater rafting

Río Blanco/Toachi tours cost US$87.

Ríos Ecuador, *T02-260 5828 in Quito, www.riosecuador.com*. Rafting and kayaking trips of 1-6 days, also have an office in Tena and run trips in Oriente.

Transport

Air

Details of internal air service are given under the respective destinations. Quito's **Mariscal Sucre Airport** (T02-395 4200, www.quitoairport.aero for information about current arrival and departures, airport services and airlines) is in Tababela, off Highway E-35, about 30 km northeast of the city, at 2134 m above sea level. There are ATMs and a *casa de cambio* for exchange in the arrivals level and banks and ATMs in the shopping mall across the street. Luggage storage and lockers downstairs at arrivals, www.bagparkingquito.com, US$8-15 per case per day; see also **Quito Airport Suites** hotel, page 1035. The information office (arrivals level, T02-395 4200, ext 2008, open 24 hrs), will assist with hotel bookings. The airport taxi cooperative, T02-281 8008, www.taxienquitoecuador.com, has set rates to different zones of the city; these are posted by arrivals (US$25 to La Mariscal, US$26 to colonial Quito, US$33 to Quitumbe bus station, US$26.50 to Carcelén station); taxi rates from the city to the airport are about 10% cheaper. **Aero Servicios** express bus, T02-604 3500, T1-800-237673, www.aeroservicios. ec, runs almost 24 hrs per day, between the new airport and the old airport in northern Quito (Parque Bicentenario), US$8-13.50. From Tababela, departures are hourly from 2400 to 0600 and every 30 mins the rest of the day; from Quito, departures are hourly from 1800 to 0300 and every 30 mins the rest of the day. They also offer transfers between the old airport and other locations in the city. Taking a transfer service or a taxi from the old airport to your hotel is recommended. Regional buses with limited stops, run every 15 mins, 0530-2200, between the airport and Terminal Río Coca in the north and 0530-1700 to Terminal Quitumbe in the south, US$2. Private van services are good value for groups, but require advanced arrangements: **Trans-Rabbit**, T02-290 2690, www.transrabbit. com.ec, US$30 for 2 passengers, US$5 per additional person.

Note It takes at least 45 mins to reach the airport from Quito, but with traffic it can be much longer, allow enough time. There are 3 access roads to the airport: the most direct from the city centre is the Ruta Viva which starts on Av Simón Bolívar; the Vía Interoceánica originates in Plaza Argentina, northeast of La Mariscal, and goes through the suburbs of Cumbaya, Tumbaco and Puembo; and the Vía Collas, starts in Oyacoto, past the toll booth along the Panamericana, north of the city. If going to the airport from other cities, take a bus that bypasses Quito along highway E-35 (available from Baños, Ambato and Ibarra), get off at the airport roundabout and take the regional bus 4.5 km from there. If coming from the east (Papallacta, Baeza or Oriente), go as far as Pifo and transfer to the regional bus there.

Bus

Local Quito has 5 parallel mass transit lines running from north to south mostly on exclusive lanes, covering almost the length of the city. There are several transfer stations where you can switch from one line to another without cost. At rush hour there are express buses with limited stops. Feeder bus lines (*alimentadores*) go from the terminals to outer suburbs. Within the city the fare is US$0.25; the combined fare to some suburbs is US$0.40. Public transit is not designed for carrying heavy luggage and is often crowded. **Trole** (T02-266 5016, Mon-Fri 0500-2345, weekends and holidays 0600-2145, plus hourly overnight service with limited stops) is a system of trolley buses which runs along Av 10 de Agosto in the north of the city, C Guayaquil (southbound) and C Flores (northbound) in colonial Quito, and mainly along Av Maldonado and Av Teniente Ortiz in the south. The northern terminus is north of 'La Y', the junction of 10 de Agosto, Av América and Av de la Prensa; south of the colonial city are important transfer stations at El Recreo and Morán Valverde; the southern terminus is at the Quitumbe bus station. Trolleys do not necessarily run the full length of the line, the destination is marked in front of the vehicle. Trolleys have a special entrance for wheelchairs. **Ecovía** (T02-243 0726, Mon-Sat 0500-2200, Sun and holidays 0600-2200), articulated buses, runs along Av 6 de Diciembre from Estación Río Coca, at C Río Coca east of 6 de Diciembre, in the north, to La Marín transfer station and on to Cumandá, east of colonial Quito. **Metrobus** (T02-346 5149, Mon-Fri 0530-2230, weekends and holidays 0600-2100) also runs articulated buses along Av de la Prensa and Av América from Terminal La Ofelia in the north to La Marín in the south. **Corredor Sur** buses run from the Seminario Mayor interchange (Av América y Colón) in the north, along Av América, Av Universitaria and Av Occidental to Terminal Quitumbe in the south; interchanges on this route are at Av Universitaria and the El Tejar and San Roque tunnels on Av Occidental; several routes branch out from Hospital del IESS station in the north. **Universidades** articulated buses run from 12 de Octubre y Veintimilla in the north to Quitumbe bus terminal. There are also 2 types of **city buses**: *Selectivos* are red, and *Bus Tipo* are royal blue, both cost US$0.25. Many bus lines go through La Marín and El Playón Ecovía/Metrobus stations. Extra caution is advised here: pickpockets abound and it is best avoided at night.

Regional Outer suburbs are served by green *Interparroquial* buses. Those running east to the valleys of Cumbayá, Tumbaco and the airport leave from the Estación Río Coca (see Ecovía, above). Buses southeast to Valle de los Chillos leave from El Playón Ecovía/Metrobus station, from Isabel la Católica y Mena Caamaño, behind Universidad Católica and from Alonso de Mercadillo by the Universidad Central. Buses going north (ie Calderón, Mitad del Mundo) leave from La Ofelia Metrobus station. Regional destinations to the north (ie Cayambe) and northwest (ie Mindo) leave from a regional station adjacent to La Ofelia Metrobus station. Buses west to Nono from the Plaza de Cotocollao, to Lloa from C Angamarca in Mena 2 neighbourhood. Buses south to Machachi from El Playón, La Villaflora and Quitumbe. Buses to **Papallacta**, **Baeza** and **El Chaco** leave from Chile E3-22 y Pedro Fermín Cevallos, near La Marín.

Long distance Quito has 2 main bus terminals: **Terminal Quitumbe** in the southwest of the city, T02-398 8200, serves destinations south, the coast via Santo Domingo, Oriente and Tulcán (in the north). It is served by the Trole (line 4: El Ejido–Quitumbe, best taken at El Ejido) and the Corredor Sur and Universidades buses, however it is advisable to take a taxi, about US$6, 30-45 mins to the colonial city, US$8-10, 45 mins-1 hr to La Mariscal. Arrivals and tourist information are on the ground floor. Ticket counters (destinations grouped and colour coded by region), and departures in the upper level. Left luggage (US$0.90 per day) and food stalls are at the adjoining shopping area. The terminal is large, allow extra time to reach your bus. Terminal use fee US$0.20. Watch your belongings at all times. On holiday weekends it is advisable to reserve the day before. The smaller **Terminal Carcelén**, Av Eloy Alfaro, where it meets the Panamericana Norte, serves destinations to the north (including Otavalo) and the coast via the Calacalí–La Independencia road. It is served by feeder bus lines from the northern terminals of the Trole, Ecovía and Metrobus, a taxi costs about US$5, 30-45 mins to La Mariscal, US$7, 45 mins-1 hr to colonial Quito. Ticket counters are organized by destination. See under destinations for fares and schedules; these are also listed in http://andestransit.com and www.multipasajes.com, where you can also purchase tickets online for buses departing Quito. A convenient way to travel between Quitumbe and Carcelén is to take a bus bound for Tulcán, **Trans Vencedores** or **Unión del Carchi** (Booth 12), every 30 mins during the day, hourly at night, US$1, 1 hr; from Carcelén to Quitumbe, wait for a through bus arriving from the north; taxi between terminals, US$15.

All long distance buses depart from either Quitumbe or Carcelén, the following companies also have ticket sales points in modern Quito: **Flota Imbabura**, Larrea 1211 y Portoviejo, T02-256 9628, http://flota-imbabura.com, for **Cuenca**, **Guayaquil** and **Manta**; **Transportes Ecuador**, JL Mera N21-44 y Washington, T02-222 5315 (terminal Quitumbe T02-382 4851), www.transportesecuador.com.ec, hourly to **Guayaquil**; **Trans Esmeraldas**, Santa María y 9 de Octubre, T02-250 5099, www.transesmeraldas.com, for **Esmeraldas**, **Atacames**, **Coca**, **Lago Agrio**, **Manta** and **Huaquillas**. **Reina del Camino**, Larrea y 18 de Septiembre, T02-321 6633, for **Bahía**, **Puerto López** and **Manta**; **Carlos Aray**, Larrea y Portoviejo, T02-256 4406, for **Manta** and **Puerto López**; **Transportes Loja**, Orellana y Juan de Velasco, T02-222 4306, http://cooperativaloja.com.ec, for **Loja** and **Lago Agrio**, they offer transport from their office to Quitumbe for US$2.50 pp (minimum of 4 passengers); **Transportes Baños**, Santa María E5-37 y JL Mera, T02-223 2752, www.cooperativabanos.com.ec, for **Baños** and **Oriente** destinations. **Panamericana Internacional**, Colón E7-31 y Reina Victoria, T02-255 7133, ext 127 for national routes, ext 125

Tip...
The Metro de Quito, a single line from Quitumbe to El Labrador, is under construction and expected to be in operation in 2019. Works may cause traffic disruption at certain times.

for international, www.panamericana.ec, for **Huaquillas**, **Machala**, **Cuenca**, **Loja**, **Manta**, **Guayaquil** and **Esmeraldas**.

International Buses depart from private stations; prices vary according to demand (higher in Jul-Aug and Dec); reserve ahead. **Ormeño Internacional**, of Perú, Shyris N35-52 y Portugal, of 3B, T02-245 6632, passes through Quito (and Guayaquil) on its once or twice weekly services between Lima and Colombia (Cali, Bogotá, Medellín, Cartagena and Santa Marta) and Caracas; from Lima there are connections to other countries. **Panamericana Internacional**, see above, to **Caracas**, on Mon; does not go into Colombian cities, but will let passengers off by the roadside (eg Popayán, Palmira for Cali, or Ibagué for Bogotá); Rutas del Sur, at Trans Esmeraldas office (see above), Sat at 1100 to Lima, with connections beyond. The route to **Peru** via Loja and Macará takes much longer than the Huaquillas route, but is more relaxed. Don't buy Peruvian (or any other country's) bus tickets here, they're cheaper outside Ecuador.

Car hire
All the main international car rental companies are at the airport. For rental procedures see Getting around, page 1189. A local company is: **Simon Car Rental**, Los Shyris 2930 e Isla Floreana, T02-243 1019, www.simoncarrental.com, good rates and service. **Achupallas Tours**, T02-255 1614, www.achupallastour.amawebs.com, and **Trans-Rabbit**, see above, rent vans for 8-14 passengers, with driver, for trips in Quito and out of town.

Long-distance taxis and vans
Shared taxis and vans offer door-to-door service to some cities and avoid the hassle of reaching Quito's bus terminals. Some companies have set departures, others travel according to demand; on weekends there are fewer departures. Reserve at least 2 days ahead. There is service between Quito and Otavalo, Ibarra, Latacunga, Ambato, Riobamba, Cuenca, Baños, Puyo, Lago Agrio, Santo Domingo and Esmeraldas. For details, see Transport under the corresponding destination.

Taxi

Taxis are a cheap and efficient way to get around the city, but for safety it is important to know how to select a cab. Authorized taxis have orange license plates or white plates with an orange stripe on the upper edge; they display stickers with a unit number on the windshield, the front doors and back side-windows; the name of the company should be displayed on the back doors, the driver's photograph in the interior and they should have a working meter. Taxis with a red and blue 'Transporte Seguro' sticker on the windshield and back doors should have cameras and red panic buttons linked to the 911 emergency system. At night it is safer to use a radio taxi (*taxi ejecutivo*), ie: **American Taxi**, T02-254 8355, www.americantaxi.com.ec; **Fast Line**, T02-222 2222; **Llamada Fácil**, T02-266 6666, http://taxillamadafacil.com. Make sure

they give you the taxi number and description so that you get the correct vehicle, some radio taxis are unmarked. All taxis should use a meter, negotiate the price ahead if they refuse to use it. The minimum daytime fare is US$1.45, US$1.75 after 1900. Note the registration and the license plate numbers if you feel you have been seriously overcharged or mistreated. You may then complain to the municipal police or tourist office. To hire a taxi by the hour costs from US$8 in the city, more out of town. For trips outside Quito, agree the fare beforehand: US$70-85 a day. Outside luxury hotels cooperative taxi drivers have a list of agreed excursion prices and most drivers are knowledgeable.

Train

There is no regular passenger service. For tourist rides, see Train rides, page 1046.

Around Quito

equatorial line, thermal pools, cloudforest and nature reserves

Mitad del Mundo

The location of the equatorial line here (23 km north of central Quito) was determined by Charles-Marie de la Condamine and his French expedition in 1736, and agrees to within 150 m with modern GPS measurements. The monument forms the focal point of **Ciudad Mitad del Mundo** ⓘ *T02-239 4803, 0900-1800 daily (very crowded on Sun), entry to complex and 5 pavilions US$3.50, all the facilities US$7.50, all facilities plus a bar of chocolate US$10*, a leisure park built as a typical colonial town, with restaurants, a Plaza de Cacao, gift shops, post office and travel agency. In the interior of the equatorial monument is the very interesting Museo Etnográfico, with displays about Ecuador's indigenous cultures. Each of the nations which participated in the 18th-century expedition has a pavilion with exhibits which include an interesting **model of old Quito**, about 10 m sq, with artificial day and night and an **insectarium**. The **Museo Inti-Ñan** ⓘ *200 m north of the monument, T02-239 5122, www.museointinan.com.ec, daily 0930-1700, US$4,* is eclectic, very interesting, has lots of fun activities and gives equator certificates for visitors. Research about the equator and its importance to prehistoric cultures is carried out near Cayambe, by an organization called **Quitsa-to** ⓘ *www.quitsato.org, daily 0800-1700, US$2.* Beyond Mitad del Mundo is Pululahua, see below.

> **Tip…**
> On weekends, **Quito Tour Bus**, see page 1041, offers bus tours to Mitad del Mundo and Pululahua.

Papallacta

This small village high in the hills (3200 m), 64 km east of Quito, has thermal pools and walking opportunities. During the holidays and at weekends the hotels can get very busy. It is conveniently placed, 30 km east of the airport, so it is feasible to relax at the baths and go directly to the airport, without returning to the city (taxis can be arranged at the village).

☆At the **Termas de Papallacta** ⓘ *2 km from the town of Papallacta, T02-250 4787 (Quito), www.termaspapallacta.com,* the best developed hot springs in the country, are eight thermal pools, three large enough for swimming, and four cold plunge pools. There are two public complexes of springs: the regular **pools** ⓘ *daily 0600-2100, US$8.50,* and the **spa centre** ⓘ *Mon-Fri 1000-1800, Sat-Sun 0900-1800, US$22 (massage and other special treatments extra).* There are additional pools at the Termas' hotel and cabins (see Where to stay, page 1052) for the exclusive use of their guests. The complex is tastefully done and recommended.

In addition to the Termas there are nice municipal pools in the village of Papallacta: **Santa Catalina** ① *daily 0800-1800, US$3* and several more economical places to stay (some with pools) on the road to the Termas and in the village. The view, on a clear day, of Antisana while enjoying the thermal waters is superb. Along the highway to Quito, are several additional thermal pools. There are several walking paths in the **Rancho del Cañón private reserve** ① *behind the Termas, US$2 for use of a short trail, to go on longer walks you are required to take a guide for US$8 pp.* To the north of this private reserve is Reserva Cayambe-Coca ① *T02-211 0370, werner.barrera@ambiente.gob.ec.* A scenic road starts by the Termas information centre, crosses both reserves and leads in 45 km to Oyacachi. A permit from Cayambe-Coca headquarters is required to travel this road even on foot, write ahead. It is a lovely two-day walk, there is a ranger's station and camping area 1½ hours from Papallacta. Reserva Cayambe-Coca is also accessed from La Virgen, the pass on the road to Quito, where there is a ranger's station. Ríos Ecuador, see Whitewater rafting, page 1046, offer a hiking tour here which can be combined with rafting.

Refugio de Vida Silvestre Pasochoa
45 mins southeast of Quito by car, busy at weekends; park office at El Ejido de Amaguaña, T09-9894 5704.

This natural park is set in humid Andean forest between 2700 and 4200 m. The reserve has more than 120 species of birds (unfortunately some of the fauna has been frightened away by the noise of the visitors) and 50 species of trees. There are walks of 30 minutes to eight hours. There are picnic and camping areas. Take a good sleeping bag, food and water.

☆Western slopes of Pichincha
Despite their proximity to the capital (two hours from Quito), the western slopes of Volcán Pichincha and its surroundings are surprisingly wild, with fine opportunities for walking and birdwatching (the altitude ranges from 1200-2800 m). This scenic area known as **El Noroccidente** has lovely cloudforests and many nature reserves. The main tourist town in this region is Mindo. To the west of Mindo is a warm subtropical area of clear rivers and waterfalls, with a number of reserves, resorts and lodges.

Ecoruta Two roads go from Quito over the western Cordillera before dropping into the northwestern lowlands. The old route via **Nono** (the only town of any size along this route) and **Tandayapa**, is dubbed the Ecoruta or **Paseo del Quinde** (Route of the Hummingbird). It begins towards the northern end of Avenida Mariscal Sucre (Occidental), Quito's western ring road, at the intersection with Calle Machala. With increased awareness of the need to conserve the cloudforests of the northwest slopes of Pichincha and of their potential for tourism, the number of reserves here is steadily growing. Keen birdwatchers are no longer the only visitors and the region has much to offer all nature lovers. Infrastructure at reserves varies considerably. Some have comfortable upmarket lodges offering accommodation, meals, guides and transport. Others may require taking your own camping gear, food, and obtaining a permit. There are too many reserves and lodges to mention here.

Above Tandayapa along the Ecoruta is **Bellavista Cloud Forest Reserve** ① *T02-211 6232 (lodge), 09-9416 5868 (cell phone), www.bellavistacloudforest.com,* a 700-ha private reserve rich in botany and fauna, including the olinguito (*Bassaricyon neblina*), a mammal new to science, first identified in 2013 (you can see it near the lodge most evenings). Excellent birdwatching and guides, lovely scenery including waterfalls. There are 10 km of well-maintained trails ranging from wheelchair accessible to slippery/suicidal. Day-visits including transport from Quito, two meals and guided walks arranged, restaurant open to non-guests. For lodge information, see Where to stay, below.

The new route From the Mitad del Mundo monument the road goes past **Calacalí**, also on the equator, whose plaza has an older monument to the Mitad del Mundo. Beyond Calacalí at Km 15 a road turns south to Nono and north to Yunguilla, with a community tourism project (www.yunguilla.org.ec). Another road at Km 52 goes to Tandayapa and Bellavista. The main road, with heavy traffic at weekends, continues to Nanegalito (Km 56), Miraflores (Km 62) where another road goes to the Ecoruta, the turn-off for a third road to the Ecoruta at Km 77 and the turn-off for Mindo at Km 79. For places beyond here, see West of Mindo, below.

Pululahua ① *park office by the rim lookout, T02-239 6543, 0800-1700,* is a geobotanical reserve in an inhabited, farmed volcanic caldera. A few kilometres beyond Mitad del Mundo, off the road to Calacalí, Mirador Ventanillas, a lookout on the rim of Pululahua gives a great view, but go in the morning, as the cloud usually descends around 1300. You can go down to the reserve and experience the rich vegetation and warm micro-climate inside. From the mirador: walk down 30 minutes to the agricultural zone then turn left. There are picnic and camping areas. A longer road allows you to drive into the crater via Moraspungo. To walk out this way, starting at the mirador, continue past the village in the crater, turn left and follow the unimproved road up to the rim and back to the main road, a 15- to 20-km round trip.

At **Nanegalito**, the transport hub for this area, is the turn-off to Nanegal and the cloudforest in the 18,500-ha **Maquipucuna Biological Reserve** ① *www.maqui.org, knowledgeable guides: US$25 (Spanish), US$100 (English) per day for a group of 9,* which contains a tremendous diversity of flora and fauna, including spectacled bear, which can be seen when the *aguacatillo* trees are in fruit (around January) and about 350 species of birds. The reserve has 40 km of trails (US$10 per person) and a lodge (see below).

Next to Maquipucuna is **Santa Lucía** ① *T02-215 7242, www.santaluciaecuador.com.* Access to this reserve is 30 minutes by car from Nanegal and a walk from there. Day tours combining Pululahua, Yunguilla and Santa Lucía are available. Bosque Nublado Santa Lucía is a community-based conservation and ecotourism project protecting a beautiful 650-ha tract of cloudforest. The area is very rich in birds (there is a cock-of-the-rock lek) and other wildlife. There are waterfalls and walking trails and a lodge (see below).

At Armenia (Km 60), a few kilometres beyond Nanegalito, a road heads northwest through Santa Clara, with a handicrafts market on Sunday, to the village and archaeological site of **Tulipe** (14 km; 1450 m). The site consists of several man-made 'pools' linked by water channels. A path leads beside the Río Tulipe in about 15 minutes to a circular pool amid trees. The site **museum** ① *T02-285 0635, www.museodesitiotulipe.com, US$3, Wed-Sun 0900-1600, guided tours (arrange ahead for English),* has exhibits in Spanish on the Yumbos culture and the *colonos* (contemporary settlers). There is also an orchid garden. For reserves and tours in the area, see www.tulipecloudforest.org and www.cloudforestecuador.com.

The Yumbos were traders who linked the Quitus with coastal and jungle peoples between AD 800-1600. Their trails are called *culuncos*, 1 m wide and 3 m deep, covered in vegetation for coolness. Several treks in the area follow them. Also to be seen are *tolas*, raised earth platforms; there are some 1500 around Tulipe. Turismo Comunitario Las Tolas ① *6 km from Tulipe, T02-286 9488,* offers lodging, food, craft workshops and guides to *tolas* and *culuncos*.

To the northwest of Tulipe are Gualea and **Pacto**, beyond which is the secluded, luxurious **$$$$ Mashpi Lodge**, www.mashpilodge.com, at the heart of a 3000-ha private Reserve which protects both rain- and cloud forest. Back along the main road, by Miraflores, is **Tucanopy** (turn north at Km 63.5, closed Wednesday), www.tucanopy.com, a reserve with lodging, trails, canopy zip-lines and conservation volunteer opportunities. At Km 79 is the turn-off for Mindo.

Mindo Mindo, a small town surrounded by dairy farms and lush cloudforest climbing the western slopes of Pichincha, is the main access for the 19,500-ha Bosque Protector Mindo-Nambillo. The reserve, which ranges in altitude from 1400 m to 4780 m, features beautiful flora (many orchids and bromeliads), fauna (butterflies, frogs, about 450 species of birds including the cock-of-the-rock, golden-headed quetzal and toucan-barbet) and spectacular cloudforest, rivers and waterfalls. The region's rich diversity is threatened by proposed mining in the area. **Amigos de la Naturaleza de Mindo** ① *9 de Octubre opposite El Quetzal Café, T02-217 0086, luisnolbertoj@yahoo.com, Tue-Sat 0900-1200, 1330-1700, entry US$2, US$40 per group for guided walk,* runs the **Centro de Educación Ambiental (CEA)** 4 km from town, a 17-ha reserve, with a shelter for 30 people. Lodging: US$25 per person full board including excursion. Arrangements have to be made in advance. During the rainy season (October to May), access to the reserve can be rough. There are also several private reserves with lodges bordering the Bosque Protector. The area has many rivers and waterfalls. Mindo also has orchid gardens, butterfly farms, a climbing wall (www.mindopuravida.com) and a microbrewery and chocolate factory. Activities include visits to waterfalls, canopy zip-lines, canyoning and tubing regattas in the rivers. The town gets very crowded with Quiteños at weekends and holidays.

West of Mindo The road continues west beyond the turn-off to Mindo, descending to the subtropical zone north of Santo Domingo de los Tsáchilas. It goes via San Miguel de los Bancos, Pedro Vicente (PV) Maldonado and Puerto Quito (on the lovely Río Caoni) to La Independencia on the Santo Domingo–Esmeraldas road. From San Miguel de Los Bancos two side-roads also go to Santo Domingo. The entire area is good for birdwatching, swimming in rivers and natural pools, walking, kayaking, or simply relaxing in pleasant natural surroundings. There are many reserves, resorts, lodgings and places to visit along the route, of particular interest to birdwatchers. There are tours from Quito, see Birdwatching, page 1041, and What to do, page 1044. See Where to stay, below, for resorts.

Listings Around Quito

Tourist Information

Municipal Tourist Information
Quito y 9 de Octubre, next to the bus station, Mindo, turismo.municipiosmb@gmail.com. Tue-Fri and Sun 0730-1300, 1430-1700.
Plenty of local information and pamphlets, map, some English spoken, very helpful.

Where to stay

Papallacta

$$$$ Guango Lodge
Near Cuyuja, 9 km east of Papallacta, T02-289 1880 (Quito), www.guangolodge.com.
In a 350 ha temperate forest reserve along the Río Papallacta. Includes 3 good meals, nice facilities, excellent birdwatching. Day visits US$5. Reserve ahead. Taxi from Papallacta US$10.

$$$$ Hotel Termas Papallacta
At the Termas complex, T06-289 5060.
Comfortable heated rooms and suites, good expensive restaurant, thermal pools set in a lovely garden, nice lounge with fireplace, some rooms with private jacuzzi, also cabins for up to 6, transport from Quito extra. Guests have access to all areas in the complex and get discounts at the spa. For weekends and holidays book 1 month in advance. Recommended.

$$$-$$ Hostería Pampallacta
On the road to Termas, T06-289 5022, www.pampallactatermales.com.
A variety of rooms with bathtubs, pools for exclusive use for guests, higher prices on the weekend, restaurant.

$$$-$$ La Choza de Don Wilson
At turn-off for Termas, T06-289 5027, www.hosteriachozapapallacta.com.
Rooms with nice views of the valley, fancier rooms have hot tubs and heaters,

cheaper rooms are small and heaters extra, good popular restaurant, pools (US$5 for non-residents), attentive.

$$ Coturpa
Next to the Santa Catalina baths in Papallacta town, T06-289 5040, www.hostalcoturpa.com.
A variety of rooms, some with hot tubs, heaters, restaurant.

$$-$ El Leñador
By entrance to Termas, T06-289 5003.
Simple rooms with electric shower, skylights make it bright and warm, restaurant, breakfast extra.

Western slopes of Pichincha

Ecoruta

$$$$ Tandayapa Bird Lodge
T02-244 7520 (Quito), www.tandayapa.com.
Designed and owned by birders. Full board, comfortable rooms, some have a canopy platform for observation, large common area; packages including guide and transport from Quito. Not always staffed, must reserve ahead.

$$$$-$$ Bellavista Cloud Forest
T02-361 3447 (lodge), in Quito T02-223 2313, www.bellavistacloudforest.com.
A dramatic lodge perched in beautiful cloudforest, includes unique geodesic dome. A variety of comfortable rooms with great views ranging from large superior rooms to rooms with shared bath, all can include 3 excellent meals (with vegetarian options), heaters, 1 wheelchair-accessible room. Camping US$9 pp. Bilingual guide service included in packages. Good research station with dorms and kitchen facilities (US$21 pp). Package tours with guide and transport from Quito. Guided tours to Mindo and other reserves in the area. Restaurant open to non-guests for breakfast and lunch. Best booked in advance. Very good service. Recommended.

$$$ San Jorge
T02-339 0403, www.eco-lodgesanjorge.com.
A series of reserves with lodges in bird-rich
areas. One is 4 km from Quito (see **Hostería San
Jorge**, page 1035), 1 in Tandayapa at 1500 m and
another in Milpe, off the new road, at 900 m.
Advanced reservations required.

The new route

$$$$ Santa Lucía
T02-215 7242, www.santaluciaecuador.com.
The lodge with panoramic views is a 1½-hr walk
from the access to the reserve. Price includes
full board with good food and guiding. There
are cabins with private bath, rooms with shared
composting toilets and hot showers and dorms
($ pp including food but not guiding).

$$$$-$$$ Maquipucuna Lodge
T02-250 7200, 09-9237 1945, www.maqui.org.
Comfortable rustic lodge, includes full board with
good meals using ingredients from own organic
garden (vegetarian and vegan available). Rooms
range from shared to rooms with bath, hot water,
electricity. Campsite is 20 mins' walk from main
lodge, under US$6 pp (food extra), cooking
lessons, chocolate massages.

$$$ Hostería Sumak Pakari
*Tulipe, 200 m from the village, T02-286 4716,
www.hosteriasumakpakari.com.*
Cabins with suites with jacuzzi and rooms set
in gardens, includes breakfast and museum
fee, terraces with hammocks, pools, restaurant,
sports fields.

$ Posada del Yumbo
Tulipe, T02-286 0121.
Up a side street off the main road. Cabins in large
property with river view, also simple rooms,

electric shower, pool, horse riding. Also run
Restaurant **La Aldea**, by the archaeological site.

Mindo

$$$$ Casa Divina
*1.2 km on the road to Cascada de Nambillo,
T09-9172 5874, www.mindocasadivina.com.*
Comfortable cabins, lovely location
surrounded by 2.7 forested ha, includes
breakfast and dinner, bathtubs, guiding
extra, US/Ecuadorean-run.

$$$$ El Monte
*2 km from town on road to CEA, then opposite
Mariposas de Mindo, cross river on tarabita
(rustic cable car), T02-217 0102, T09-9308 4675,
www.ecuadorcloudforest.com.*
Beautifully constructed lodge in 44-ha property,
newer cabins are spacious and very comfortable,
includes 3 meals, some (but not all) excursions
with a *guía nativo* and tubing, other adventure
sports and horse riding are extra, no electricity,
reserve in advance. Recommended.

$$$ Séptimo Paraíso
*2 km from Calacalí–La Independencia road
along Mindo access road, then 500 m right on
a small side road, well signed, T09-9368 4417,
www.septimoparaiso.com.*
All wood lodge in a 420-ha reserve, comfortable,
restaurant with good choice of set meals
including vegetarian, warm and spring-fed
pools and jaccuzi, parking, lovely grounds,
great birdwatching, walking trails open to
non-guests for US$10. Recommended.

$$ Caskaffesu
*Sixto Durán Ballén (the street leading
to the stadium) y Av Quito, T02-217 0100,
www.caskaffesu.net.*

Pleasant *hostal* with nice courtyard, no breakfast, good coffee at café/bar, live music Wed-Sat, US/Ecuadorean-run.

$$ Dragonfly Inn
On Av Quito (main street), 1st block after bridge, T02-217 0319, www.mindo.biz.
Popular hotel, restaurant and café, comfortable rooms, also run popular apiary tours (www.thebeehivemindo.com), arrange well in advance, US$25 pp. Visa and MasterCard accepted.

$$ Hacienda San Vicente (Yellow House)
500 m south of the park, T02-217 0124, www.ecuadormindobirds.com.
Family-run lodge set in 200 ha of very rich forest, includes excellent breakfast, nice rooms, good walking trails open to non-guests for US$6, reservations required, good value. Highly recommended for nature lovers.

$$ Mindo Real
Vía al Cinto (extension Av Sixto Durán) 500 m from town, T02-217 0120, www.mindoreal.com.
Cabins and rooms on ample gardens on the shores of the Río Mindo, camping US$5 pp, pool, trails.

$$-$ El Descanso
C Colibríes (1st right after Río Canchupi bridge at entrance to town), 5 blocks from Av Quito, T02-217 0213/390 0443.
Nice house with comfortable rooms, cheaper in loft with shared bath, ample parking. Recommended. Good birdwatching in garden, open to non-guests for US$3, cafeteria open to the public for breakfast.

$$-$ Jardín de los Pájaros
C Colibríes 415, T09-7977 5923, www.hostaljardindelospajaros.com.
Family-run hostel, several types of rooms, includes good breakfast, small pool, parking, large covered terrace with hammocks, good value. Recommended.

$ Charito
C Colibríes, 2 blocks from Av Quito, T02-217 0093, http://hostalcharitodemindo.com.
Family-run hostel in a wooden house, nice rooms, newer ones in back overlook the Río Canchupi, good value.

$ Rubby
5 blocks past the park along C Quito, T09-9193 1853, Facebook: hostalrubby.
Family-run *hostal* on the outskirts of town, nice rooms, kitchen and laundry facilities,

good value. English spoken, owner Marcelo Arias is a birding guide.

West of Mindo

$$$$ Arashá
4 km west of PV Maldonado, Km 121, T02-390 0007, Quito T02-244 9881 for reservations, www.arasharesort.com.
Resort and spa with pools, waterfalls (artificial and natural) and hiking trails. Comfortable thatched cabins, price includes all meals (world-class chef), use of the facilities (spa extra) and tours, can arrange transport from Quito, attentive staff, popular with families, elegant and very upmarket.

$$$ Selva Virgen
At Km 132, east of Puerto Quito, T02-362 9626, Quito office T02-331 7986, www.ute.edu.ec. Wed-Sun, Mon-Tue with advanced booking only.
Nice *hostería* in a 100-ha property owned by the Universidad Técnica Equinoccial (UTE). Staffed by students. Restaurant, rooms with ceiling fan and spacious comfortable cabins for 4 with fan, fridge, jacuzzi and nice porch, 3 pools, lovely grounds, part of the property is forested and has trails, facilities also open to restaurant patrons.

$$ Mirador Río Blanco
Av 17 de Julio L20 y El Cisne, SanMiguel de los Bancos, at the east end of town, T02-277 0307, www.miradorrioblanco.com.
Popular hotel/restaurant serving tropical dishes (**$$**), vegetarian options, good coffee, rooms in *cabañas* overlooking the river, breakfast extra, parking, terrace with bird feeders (many hummingbirds and tanagers) and magnificent views of the river.

Western slopes of Pichincha

Mindo

$$$-$$ El Quetzal
9 de Octubre, 3 blocks from the park, T02-217 0034, www.elquetzaldemindo.com. Daily 0800-2000.
Nice restaurant serving international food with vegetarian options, microbrews, local chocolate and other sweets for sale. Hourly chocolate tours 1000-1700 daily, US$10.

$$ Fuera de Babilonia
9 de Octubre y Los Ríos, 2 blocks from the park, no sign. Daily 0800-2100.

A la carte international dishes, trout, pizza, pasta, good food and nice atmosphere.

$ La Sazón de Marcelo
Av Quito past the park, opposite children's playground. Daily 0830-2100.
Set meals and à la carte including vegetarian dishes; *bandeja mindeña* a dish for 2 with trout and tilapia is one of their specialities. Very popular.

What to do

Mitad del Mundo
Calimatours, *30 m east of monument, Mitad del Mundo, T02-239 4796, www. mitaddelmundotour.com.* Tours to Pululahua and other sites in the vicinity.

Western slopes of Pichincha

Pululahua
The Green Horse Ranch, Astrid Müller, T09-8612 5433, www.horseranch.de. 1- to 9-day rides, among the options is a 3-day ride to Bellavista.

Mindo
Endemic Tours, *Av Quito y Gallo de la Peña, T09-9888 5801, romelly85@hotmail.com.* Bicycle rentals US$10/half day, US$15 per full day, hiking, regattas and other adventure activities.
Julia Patiño, *T09-8616 2816, juliaguideofbirds@gmail.com.* Is an English-speaking birding guide.
Mindo Xtreme Birds, *Sector Saguambi, just out of town on the road to CEA, T02-217 0188, www. mindoxtreme.com.* Birdwatching, regattas, cycling, hiking, waterfalls, horse riding, English spoken, very helpful.
Vinicio Pérez, *T09-947 6867, www.birdwatchers house.com.* Is a recommended birding guide, he speaks some English.

Transport

Mitad del Mundo and around
Bus From Quito take a 'Mitad del Mundo' feeder bus from La Ofelia station on the Metrobus (transfer ticket US$0.15), or from the corner of Bolivia y Av América (US$0.40). Some buses continue to the turn-off for Pululahua or Calacalí beyond. An excursion by **taxi** to Mitad del Mundo (with 1 hr wait) is US$25, or US$30 to include Pululahua. Just a ride from La Mariscal costs about US$15.

Papallacta
Bus From **Quito**, buses bound for Tena or Lago Agrio from Terminal Quitumbe, or buses to Baeza from near La Marín (see page 1047), 2 hrs, US$2.50. The bus and taxi stop is at El Triángulo, east of (below) the village, at the junction of the main highway and the old road through town. A taxi to Termas costs US$1 pp shared or US$2.50 private. The access to the Termas is uphill from the village, off the old road. The complex is a 40-min walk from town. To return to Quito, most buses pass in the afternoon, travelling back at night is not recommended. Taxi to Quito starts at US$50, to the airport US$40. **Transporte Santa Catalina** taxis in Papallacta, T09-8510 2556.

Refugio de Vida Silvestre Pasochoa
Bus From Quito buses run from El Playón to Amaguaña US$0.50 (ask the driver to let you off at the 'Ejido de Amaguaña'); from there follow the signs. It's about 8-km walk, with not much traffic except at weekends, or book a pick-up from Amaguaña, **Cooperativa Pacheco Jr**, T02-287 7047, about US$6.

Western slopes of Pichincha

Pululahua
Bus Take a 'Mitad del Mundo' bus from La Ofelia Metrobus terminal. When boarding, ask if it goes as far as the Pululahua turn-off (some end their route at Mitad del Mundo, others at the Pululahua Mirador turn-off, others continue to Calacalí). It is a 30-min walk from the turn to the rim.

Tulipe
Bus From **Quito**, Estación La Ofelia, from 0615, US$1.90, 1¾ hrs: **Transportes Otavalo**, 7 daily, continue to Pacto (US$2.50, 2 hrs) and **Transportes Minas** 5 daily, continue to Chontal (US$3.15, 3 hrs). To **Las Tolas**, **Transportes Minas**, daily at 1730, US$2.50, 2½ hrs or take pick-up from Tulipe, US$5.

Mindo
Bus From **Quito**, Estación La Ofelia, **Coop Flor del Valle**, T02-217 0171, Mon-Fri 0800, 0900, 1100, 1300, 1600, Sat and Sun 0740, 0820, 0920, 1100, 1300, 1400, 1600 (last one on Sun at 1700 instead of 1600); Mindo–Quito: Mon-Fri 0630, 1100, 1345, 1500, Sat and Sun 0630, 1100 and hourly 1300-1700; US$3.10, 2 hrs; weekend buses fill quickly, buy ahead. You can also take any bus bound for Esmeraldas or San Miguel de los Bancos (see below) and get off at the

turn-off for Mindo from where there are taxis until 1930, US$0.50 pp or US$3 without sharing. **Cooperativa Kennedy** to/from **Santo Domingo** 5 daily, US$5, 3½ hrs.

West of Mindo

From **Quito**, Terminal Carcelén, departures every 30 mins (**Coop Kennedy** and associates) to Santo Domingo via: **Nanegalito** (US$1.90, 1½ hrs), **San Miguel de los Bancos** (US$3.15, 2½ hrs), **Pedro Vicente Maldonado** (US$3.75, 3 hrs) and **Puerto Quito** (US$4.70, 3½ hrs). **Trans Esmeraldas** frequent departures from Terminal Carcelén also serve these destinations along the Quito-Esmeraldas route.

Northern
highlands

The area north of Quito to the Colombian border is outstandingly beautiful. The landscape is mountainous, with views of the Cotacachi, Imbabura, and Chiles volcanoes, as well as the glacier-covered Cayambe, interspersed with lakes. The region is also renowned for its *artesanía*.

Quito to Otavalo

a few places worth stopping at en route

On the way from the capital to the main tourist centre in northern Ecuador, the landscape is dominated by the Cayambe volcano.

Quito to Cayambe

At **Calderón** ① *getting there: take a bus at La Ofelia Metrobus terminal*, 32 km north of the centre of Quito, you can see the famous bread figurines being made. Prices are lower than in Quito. On 1-2 November, the graves in the cemetery are decorated with flowers, drinks and food for the dead. The Corpus Christi processions are very colourful.

The Pan-American Highway goes to **Guayllabamba**, home of the Quito zoo (www.quitozoo.org), where it branches, one road going through Cayambe and the second through Tabacundo before rejoining at Cajas. At 10 km past Guayllabamba on the road to Tabacundo, just north of the toll booth, a cobbled road to the left (signed Pirámides de Cochasquí) leads to Tocachi and further on to the **Parque Arqueológico Cochasquí** ① *T09-9822 0686, Quito T02-399 4405, www.pichincha.gob. ec/visita-cochasqui, 0800-1600, US$3, entry only with a 1½-hr guided tour, getting there: from Terminal Carcelén, be sure to take a bus that goes on the Tabacundo road and ask to be let off at the turn-off. From there it's a pleasant 8-km uphill walk. Alternatively, from Terminal La Ofelia, take a bus to Malchinguí (hourly, US$1.50, 2 hrs) and a pickup to Cochasquí (US$3, 15 mins) or a taxi (US$6). There are also buses between Malchinguí and Cayambe which go by Cochasquí.* The protected area contains 15 truncated clay pyramids (*tolas*), nine with long ramps, built between AD 950 and 1550 by the Cara or Cayambi-Caranqui people. Festivals with dancing at the equinoxes and solstices. There is a site museum and views from the pyramids, south to Quito, are marvellous.

Opposite the park entrance is **Camping Cochasquí** ① *T09-9491 9008, US$3 pp for camping, US$10 pp in cabins, meals available.*

On the other road, 8 km before Cayambe, a globe carved out of rock by the Pan-American Highway is at the spot where the French expedition marked the equator (small shops sell drinks and snacks). A few metres north is **Quitsato** ① *T02-361 0908, www.quitsato.org, US$2,* where studies about the equator and its importance to ancient cultures are carried out. There is a sun dial, 54 m in diameter, and a solar culture exhibit, with information about indigenous cultures and archaeological sites along the equator; here too there are special events for the solstices and equinoxes.

Cayambe Colour map 1, A4.

Cayambe, on the eastern (right-hand) branch of the highway, 25 km northeast of Guayllabamba, is overshadowed by the snow-capped volcano of the same name. The surrounding countryside consists of a few dairy farms and many flower plantations. The area is noted for its *bizcochos* (biscuits) served with *queso de hoja* (string cheese). At the Centro Cultural Espinoza-Jarrín, is the

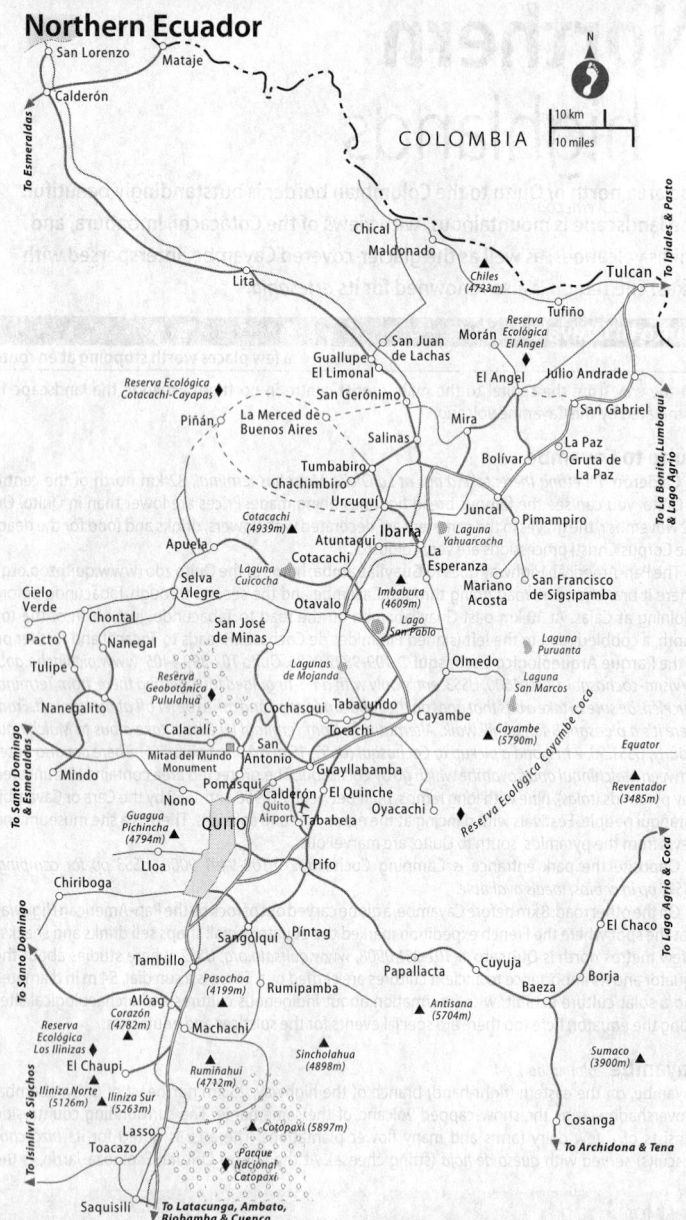

Northern Ecuador

Museo de la Ciudad ① *Rocafuerte y Bolívar, Wed-Sun 0800-1700, free*, with displays about the Cayambi culture and ceramics found at Puntiachil, an important but poorly preserved archaeological site at the edge of town. There is a fiesta in March for the equinox with plenty of local music; also Inti Raymi solstice and San Pedro celebrations in June. Market day is Sunday. A community tourism project, **Camino del Cóndor** ① *Terán S0-54 y Sucre, T02-212 9022, https://caminodelcondorec.jimdo.com*, is based in town, which provides lodging, food, cultural events and trekking, riding and mountain biking in the highlands of the Cayambe Coca reserve at Paquiestancia.

Reserva Ecológica Cayambe Coca
T02-211 0370, werner.barrera@ambiente.gob.ec.
....

Cayambe is a good place to access the western side of Reserva Ecológica Cayambe-Coca, a large park which spans the Cordillera Oriental and extends down to the eastern lowlands. **Volcán Cayambe**, Ecuador's third highest peak, at 5790 m, lies within the reserve. It is the highest point in the world to lie so close to the equator (3.75 km north). The equator goes over the mountain's flanks. About 1 km south of the town of Cayambe is an unmarked cobbled road heading east via Juan Montalvo, leading in 26 km to the **Ruales-Oleas-Berge refuge** ① *T09-5955 9765, rooms for 4-10 passengers take sleeping bag, US$14 pp with use of kitchen or US$30 with dinner and breakfast*, at 4600 m. The standard climbing route, from the west, uses the refuge as a base. There is a crevasse near the summit which can be very difficult to cross if there isn't enough snow, ask the refuge keeper about conditions. There are nice acclimatization hikes around the refuge. Otavalo and Quito operators offer tours here.

To the southeast of Cayambe, also within the reserve and surrounded by cloudforest at 3200 m is **Oyacachi** ① *T06-299 1842, oyacachi@gmail.com*, a traditional village of farmers and woodcarvers, with thermal baths (US$3). Accommodation at (\$\$-\$) **Cabañas Oyacachi**, T06-299 1846, www.cabanasoyacachi.com, and in family *hospedajes*. There is good walking in the area, including a two-day walk to Papallacta and a three-day walk to El Chaco in the lowlands; these require a permit from the reserve, write ahead.

Listings Quito to Otavalo

Where to stay

Cayambe

\$\$\$ Hacienda Guachalá
South of Cayambe on the road to Cangahua, T02-361 0908, www.guachala.com.
The first hacienda in Ecuador, nicely restored, the chapel (1580) is built on top of a pre-Inca structure. Simple but comfortable rooms in older section and fancier ones in newer area, fireplaces, delicious meals, covered swimming pool, parking, attentive service, good walking, horses for rent, excursions to nearby ruins, small museum.

\$\$\$ Jatun Huasi
Panamericana Norte Km 1.5, T02-236 3777, www.hosteriajatunhuasi.com.
US motel style, cabins with a sitting room with fireplace and frigo-bar and rooms, restaurant, indoor pool, spa, parking.

\$\$ Shungu Huasi
Camino a Granobles, 1 km northwest of town, T02-236 1847, www.shunguhuasi.com.
Comfortable cabins in a 6.5-ha ranch, excellent Italian restaurant with advanced reservation, heaters on request, nice setting, attentive service, offers horse riding excursions. Recommended.

\$ La Gran Colombia
Panamericana y Calderón, T02-236 1238.
Modern multi-storey building, restaurant, parking, traffic noise in front rooms.

Restaurants

Cayambe

\$\$\$ Casa de Fernando
Panamericana Norte 1.5. Closed Mon.
Varied menu, good international food.

\$\$-\$ Aroma
Bolívar 404 y Ascázubi. Closed Wed.
Large choice of set lunches and à la carte, variety of desserts, very good.

Transport

Cayambe

Bus Flor del Valle, from La Ofelia, **Quito**, every 7 mins 0530-2100, US$1.50, 1½ hrs. Their Cayambe station is at Montalvo y Junín. To **Otavalo**, from traffic circle at Bolívar y Av N Jarrín, every 15 mins, US$0.95, 45 mins.

Reserva Ecológica Cayambe Coca

Road To **Volcán Cayambe**, most vehicles can go as far as the **Hacienda Piemonte El Hato** (at about 3500 m) from where it is a 3- to 4-hr walk,

longer if heavily laden or if it is windy, but it is a beautiful walk. Regular pick-ups can often make it to 'la Z', a sharp curve on the road 30-mins' walk to the *refugio*. 4WDs can often make it to the *refugio*. Pick-ups can be hired by the market in Cayambe, Junín y Ascázubi, US$45, 1½-2 hrs. Arrange ahead for return transport. A milk truck runs from Cayambe's hospital to the hacienda at 0600, returning between 1700-1900. To **Oyacachi**, from the north side of Cayambe, near the Mercado Mayorista, Mon, Wed, Sat at 1500, Sun at 0800, US$2.50, 1½ hrs; return to Cayambe Wed, Fri, Sat at 0400, Sun at 1400.

Otavalo and around *Colour map 1, A4.*

a beautiful area of mountains and lakes

★Otavalo, only a short distance from the capital, is a must on any tourist itinerary in Ecuador. The Tabacundo and Cayambe roads join at Cajas, then cross the *páramo* and suddenly descend into the land of the Otavaleños, a thriving, prosperous group, famous for their prodigious production of woollens. The town itself, consisting of rather functional modern buildings, is one of South America's most important centres of ethno-tourism and its enormous Saturday market, featuring a dazzling array of textiles and crafts, is second to none and not to be missed. Set in beautiful countryside, the area is worth exploring for three or four days.

Otavalo

Men here wear their hair long and plaited under a broad-brimmed hat and wear white, calf-length trousers and blue ponchos. The women's colourful costumes consist of embroidered blouses, shoulder wraps and many coloured beads. Indigenous families speak Quichua at home, although it is losing some ground to Spanish with the younger generation.

The **Saturday market** comprises four different markets in various parts of the town with the central streets filled with vendors. The *artesanías* market is held 0700-1800, based around the Plaza de Ponchos (Plaza Centenario). The livestock section begins at 0500 until 0900, outside the centre, west of the Panamericana; go west on Calderón from the town centre. The

Tip...

Indigenous people in the market respond better to photography if you buy something first, then ask politely.

produce market, Mercado 24 de Mayo, at the old stadium, west of the centre, lasts from 0700 till 1400. The *artesanías* industry is so big that the Plaza de Ponchos is filled with vendors every day of the week. The selection is better on Saturday but prices are a little higher than other days when the atmosphere is more relaxed. Wednesday is also an important market day with more movement than other weekdays. Polite bargaining is appropriate in the market and shops. Otavaleños not only sell goods they weave and sew themselves, but they bring crafts from throughout Ecuador and from Peru and Bolivia.

The **Museo Viviente Otavalango** ① *Vía Antigua a Quiroga 1230, antigua Fábrica San Pedro, T06-292-4034, www.otavalango.org, Fri-Sun 0900-1700, call ahead at other times, US$5*, displays on all cultural aspects of Otavaleño life; live presentations of local traditions for groups. The **Museo de Tejidos El Obraje** ① *Sucre 6-08 y Olmedo, T06-292 0261, US$2, must call ahead*, shows the process of traditional Otavalo weaving from shearing to final products. There are good views of town from **Centro de Exposiciones El Colibrí** ① *C Morales past the railway line*.

Around Otavalo

Otavalo weavers come from dozens of communities. Many families weave and visitors should shop around as the less known weavers often have better prices and some of the most famous ones only sell from their homes, especially in Agato and Peguche. The easiest villages to visit are **Ilumán** (there are also many felt hatmakers in town and *yachacs*, or shamen, mostly north of the plaza – look for signs); **Agato**; **Carabuela** (many homes sell crafts including wool sweaters); **Peguche**. These villages are only 15-30 minutes away and have good bus service; buses leave from the Terminal and stop at Plaza Copacabana (Atahualpa y Montalvo). You can also take a taxi (US$2).

To reach the lovely **Cascada de Peguche**, from Peguche's plaza, facing the church, head right and continue straight until the road forks. Take the lower fork to the right, but not the road that heads downhill. There is a small campsite at the falls. From the top (left side, excellent views) you can continue the walk to Lago San Pablo. The **Pawkar Raymi** festival is held in Peguche before carnival. At the falls there is a small information centre (contributions are appreciated).

The **Ciclovía** is a bicycle path which runs along the old rail line 21 km between Eugenio Espejo de Cajas and Otavalo. Because of the slope, starting in Cajas is recommended. You can take a tour or hire a bike and take a bus bound for Quito to the bike path. There is a network of old roads and

Otavalo

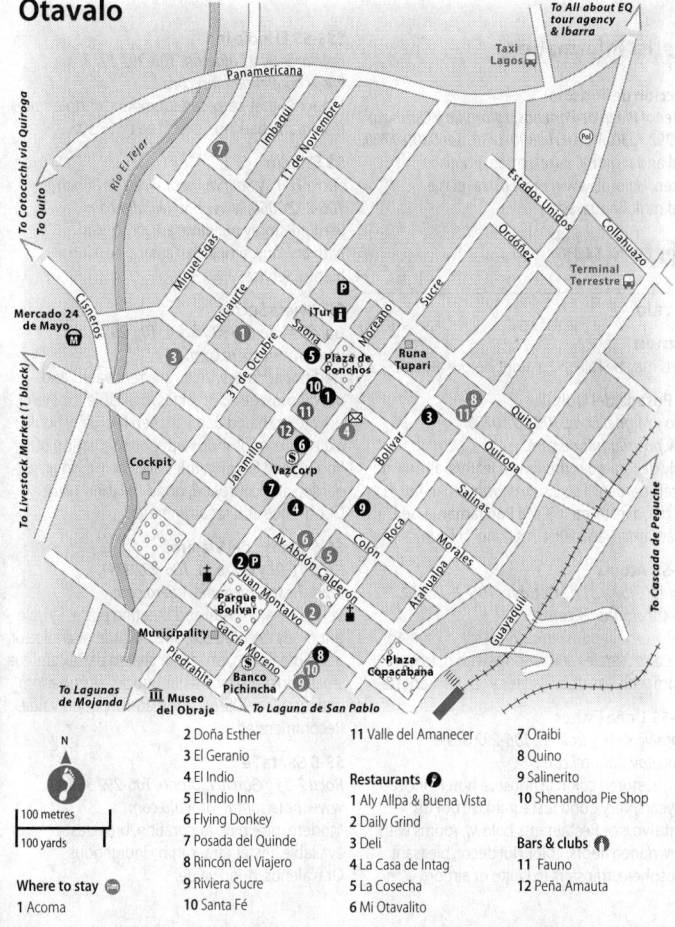

N

100 metres
100 yards

Where to stay 🛏
1 Acoma

2 Doña Esther
3 El Geranio
4 El Indio
5 El Indio Inn
6 Flying Donkey
7 Posada del Quinde
8 Rincón del Viajero
9 Riviera Sucre
10 Santa Fé

11 Valle del Amanecer

Restaurants 🍴
1 Aly Allpa & Buena Vista
2 Daily Grind
3 Deli
4 La Casa de Intag
5 La Cosecha
6 Mi Otavalito

7 Oraibi
8 Quino
9 Salinerito
10 Shenandoa Pie Shop

Bars & clubs 🍸
11 Fauno
12 Peña Amauta

trails between Otavalo and **Lago San Pablo**, none of which takes more than two hours to explore. It is worth walking either to or back from the lake for the views. Going in a group is recommended for safety. A good half-day excursion is via Cascada de Peguche, **Parque Cóndor** ① *on a hill called Curiloma, near the community of Pucará Alto, T06-304 9399, www.parquecondor.org, Wed-Sun 0930-1700, raptor flight demonstrations at 1130 and 1530, US$4.75, crowded on weekends*, a reserve and birds of prey rehabilitation centre, and back via **El Lechero**, a lookout by a tree considered sacred among indigenous people.

From **San Pablo del Lago** it is possible to climb **Imbabura** volcano (4630 m, a serious climb and frequently under cloud), allow at least six hours to reach the summit and four hours for the descent. An alternative access is from La Esperanza or San Clemente (see page 1067). Easier, and no less impressive, is the nearby Cerro Huarmi Imbabura, 3845 m, it is not signed but several paths lead there. Take a good map, food and warm clothing.

Listings Otavalo and around *map page 1061.*

Tourist information

Dirección de Turismo
Corner of Plaza de Ponchos, Jaramillo y Quiroga, T06-292 7230. Mon-Fri 0800-1730, Sat 0800-1700.
Local and regional information, English spoken, helpful; www.otavalo.travel is a good multilingual site.

Where to stay

Otavalo
In town
Hotels may be full on Fri night before market.

$$$ Posada del Quinde
Quito y Miguel Egas, T06-292 0750, www.posadaquinde.com.
Nicely decorated rooms with heaters, all around a lovely garden, also 2 suites with kitchenettes, very good restaurant (**Café Pachamama**, see Restaurants, page 1064), parking, US-run.

$$$-$$ Acoma
Salinas 07-57 y 31 de Octubre, T06-292 6570, www.acomahotel.com.
Lovely re-built home in colonial style, parking, nice comfortable rooms, some with balcony, 1 room with bathtub, 2 suites with kitchenette.

$$$-$$ Doña Esther
Montalvo 4-44 y Bolívar, T06-292 0739, www.otavalohotel.com.
Nicely restored colonial house, a hotel for over 100 years, very good restaurant (**Arbol de Montalvo**, see Restaurants below), rooms with nice wooden floors, colourful decor, pleasant atmosphere, transfers to Quito or airport.

$$$-$$ El Indio Inn
Bolívar 9-04 y Calderón, T06-292 2922, www.hotelelindioinn.com.
Modern hotel, carpeted rooms and simple suites, restaurant, parking, use of spa US$6.50.

$$ El Indio
Sucre 12-14 y Salinas, near Plaza de Ponchos, T06-292 0060, www.hotelelindio.com.
In multi-storey building, ask for a room with balcony, simple restaurant, parking, helpful service.

$$ Riviera Sucre
García Moreno 380 y Roca, T06-292 0241, www.rivierasucre.com.
Traditional hotel with ample renovated and new rooms, good breakfast available, cafetería, private or shared bath, kitchen facilities, book exchange, bookshop with good selection of English and German titles, nice common areas, garden and courtyard, good meeting place. Good value and recommended.

$$-$ Rincón del Viajero
Roca 11-07 y Quiroga, T06-292 1741, www.hostalrincondelviajero.com.
Very pleasant hostel and meeting place. Simple but nicely decorated rooms, includes a choice of good breakfasts, private or shared bath, cafetería, small parking, rooftop hammocks, sitting room with fireplace, US/Ecuadorean-run, good value. Recommended.

$$-$ Santa Fé
Roca 7-34 y García Moreno, T06-292 3640, www.hotelsantafeotavalo.com.
Modern, nice pine decoration, breakfast available, restaurant, run by indigenous Otavaleños, good value.

\$\$-\$ Valle del Amanecer
Roca y Quiroga, T06-292 0990.
Small rustic rooms with thin walls, nice courtyard,
hammocks, private or shared bath, popular.

\$ El Geranio
Ricaurte y Morales, T06-292 0185,
www.hostalelgeranio.com.
2 types of rooms, smaller ones with electric
shower and no TV are cheaper, laundry facilities
and use of kitchen to prepare cold foods, parking,
quiet, family-run, popular, runs trips, good value.
Recommended.

\$ Flying Donkey
Abdón Calderón 510 y Bolívar, T06-292 8122,
www.flyingdonkeyotavalo.com.
Popular backpacker's hostel, rooms with
private bath, US\$10 pp in dorm, kitchen
facilities and terrace.

Out of town

\$\$\$\$ Ali Shungu Mountaintop Lodge
5 km west of Otavalo by the village
of Yambiro, T09-8950 9945, www.
alishungumountaintoplodge.com.
Rental homes in the countryside on a 16-ha
private reserve. 3 comfortable nicely decorated
guesthouses for 2 or 4, each with living room,
woodstove and kitchenette. Includes welcome food
basket, Wi-Fi and TV, 4 nights minimum; US-run.

\$\$\$\$ Casa Mojanda
Vía a Mojanda Km 3.5, T09-8033 5108,
www.casamojanda.com.
Comfortable cabins set in a beautiful hillside.
Includes breakfast prepared with ingredients
from own organic garden and short guided hike
to waterfall; each room is decorated with its own
elegant touch, outdoor hot tub with great views,
quiet, good library, horse riding. Recommended.

\$\$\$ Hacienda Pinsaquí
Panamericana Norte Km 5, 300 m north of
the turn-off for Cotacachi, T06-294 6116,
www.haciendapinsaqui.com.
Converted hacienda dating to 1790, with 30 suites,
1 with jacuzzi, restaurant with lovely dining room,
lounge with fireplace, beautiful antiques, colonial
ambience, gardens, horse riding.

\$\$\$ Las Palmeras Inn
Outside Quichinche, 15 mins by bus from Otavalo,
T06-266 8067, www.laspalmerasinn.com.
Cabins with terrace and fireplace in a rural
setting, restaurant, parking, nice grounds and
views, pool table and ping-pong, British-owned.

\$\$ La Casa de Hacienda
Vía Ilumán, entrance at Panamericana Norte
Km 3, then 300 m east, T06-269 0245,
Facebook: hosterialacasadehacienda.
Tasteful cabins with fireplace, restaurant, parking,
horse riding.

\$\$ La Luna
On a side-road going south off the Mojanda road
at Km 4, T09-9315 6082, www.lalunaecuador.info.
Pleasant hostel in nice surroundings, some rooms
with fireplace, heater and private bath, others
with shared bath, US\$14 pp in dorm, camping
US\$8 pp, terrace with hammocks, pleasant
dining room-lounge, transport information on
hostel's website, excursions arranged, popular.
Recommended.

Around Otavalo

Peguche

\$\$\$ La Casa Sol
Near the Cascada de Peguche, T06-269 0500,
www.lacasasol.com.
Comfortable rustic lodge set on a hillside. Bright
cosy rooms and suites with balcony, some with
fireplace, lovely attention to detail, restaurant
and conference room.

\$\$ Aya Huma
On the railway line in Peguche, T06-269 0164,
www.ayahuma.com.
In a country setting between the railway tracks
and the river. Quiet, pleasant atmosphere,
kitchen facilities, restaurant for breakfast and
dinner, camping (US\$4 pp), organizes ancestral
ceremonies, Dutch/Ecuadorean-run, popular.
Recommended.

Lago San Pablo

\$\$\$\$ Sacha Ji
Vía del Condor y Angel Vaca, San Pablo,
T06-304 9245, www.mysachaji.com.
A wellness and yoga retreat on a hilltop
overlooking Lago San Pablo and Imbabura
volcano. Spacious rooms with heating, organic
gardens, restaurant, outdoor hot tub, yoga
classes, horse therapy.

\$\$\$\$-\$\$\$ Hacienda Cusín
By the village of San Pablo del Lago to
the southeast of the lake, T06-291 8013,
www.haciendacusin.com.
A converted 17th-century hacienda with lovely
courtyard and garden, fine expensive restaurant,
rooms with fireplace, sports facilities (horses,

bikes, squash court, games room), library, book in advance, British-run.

$$ Green House

C 24 de Junio, Comunidad Araque, by the east shore of the lake, northwest of San Pablo del Lago, T06-291 9298, www.araquebyb.hostel.com.
Family-run *hostal*, some rooms with bath, others with detached bath, dinner on request, sitting room with fireplace, rooftop terrace with views, Quito airport pickup (US$55).

Restaurants

Otavalo

$$$-$$ Arbol de Montalvo

Montalvo 4-44 y Bolívar, in Hotel Doña Esther, T06-292 0739, www.otavalohotel.com. Tue-Thu 1800-2100, Fri-Sat 0715-2100, Sun 0715-2100.
Wide variety of dishes including excellent wood-oven pizzas.

$$$-$$ Café Pachamama

Quito y Miguel Egas, in Posada del Quinde, T06-292 0750, www.posadaquinde.com. Daily 0730-2030, reservations advised for groups over 6 people.
Pleasant relaxed setting, tasty meals with plenty of vegetarian options, good reviews.

$$$-$$ Quino

Roca 7-40 y Juan Montalvo. Mon-Sat 1000-2200.
Traditional coastal cooking, good seafood and some meat dishes, pleasant seating around patio, popular.

$$ Aly Allpa

Salinas 509 at Plaza de Ponchos. Daily 0730-2030.
Good-value set meals, breakfast and à la carte including trout, vegetarian, meat. Recommended.

$$ Buena Vista

Salinas entre Sucre y Jaramillo, p2, www.buena vistaotavalo.com. Sun-Mon 1300-2200, Wed-Thu 1000-2200, Fri 1100-2300, Sat 0900-2300.
Bistro with balcony overlooking Plaza de Ponchos. Good international food, sandwiches, salads, vegetarian options, trout, good coffee, Wi-Fi.

$$ Mi Otavalito

Sucre y Morales. Daily 1200-2100
Good for set lunch and international food à la carte. Popular with tour groups.

$$ Oraibi

Sucre y Colón. Wed-Sat 0800-2000.
Vegetarian food in nice patio setting, pizza, salads, pasta, Mexican, breakfast, Swiss-owned. Live music Fri and Sat night.

$$-$ Deli

Quiroga 12-18 y Bolívar. Daily 1130-2100.
Economical set lunch, plus good Mexican food, international and pizza à la carte, nice desserts, pleasant atmosphere, family-run, good value.

Cafés

Daily Grind

Juan Montalvo esquina Sucre, Parque Bolívar. Daily 0900-1900.
Small outdoor café with very good coffee, muffins and other treats.

La Casa de Intag

Colón 465 y Sucre. Mon-Sat 0800-1800.
Fairtrade cafeteria/shop run by Intag coffee growers and artisans associations. Good organic coffee, breakfast, pancakes, sisal crafts, fruit pulp and more.

La Cosecha

Jaramillo y Salinas, upstairs. Daily 0900-2000.
Great modern café and bakery overlooking Plaza de Ponchos. Excellent coffee, sandwiches and bagels. Recommended.

Salinerito

Bolívar 10-08 y Morales. Mon-Sat 0800-2200.
Café/deli run by the Salinas de Guaranda coop. Good sandwiches, breakfast, pizza, coffee and juices. A good place to buy supplies such as cheese, coldcuts and chocolate.

Shenandoa Pie Shop

Salinas y Jaramillo. Open 1100-2100, Sat from 0900.
Good fruit pies, milk shakes and ice cream, popular meeting place, an Otavalo tradition.

Bars and clubs

Otavalo

Otavalo is generally safe but avoid deserted areas at night. Nightlife is concentrated at Morales y Jaramillo and C 31 de Octubre. *Peñas* are open Fri-Sat from 1930, entrance US$3.

Fauno

Morales y Jaramillo.
Café/bar, variety of cocktails, snacks.

Peña Amauta

Morales 5-11 y Jaramillo.
Good local bands, welcoming, mainly foreigners.

Festivals

Otavalo

End of Jun Inti Raymi combines celebrations of the summer solstice (21 Jun), with the **Fiesta de San Juan** (24 Jun) and the **Fiesta de San Pedro y San Pablo** (29 Jun). These combined festivities are known as **Los San Juanes** and participants are mostly indigenous. They take place in the smaller communities surrounding Otavalo, each one celebrates separately on different dates, some for a full week. The celebration begins with a ritual bath, the Peguche waterfall is used by Otavalo residents (a personal spiritual activity, best carried out without visitors and certainly without cameras). In Otavalo, indigenous families have costume parties, which at times spill over onto the streets. In the San Juan neighbourhood, near the Yanayacu baths, there is a week-long celebration with food, drink and music.

1st 2 weeks of Sep Fiesta del Yamor and **Colla Raymi**, feature local dishes, amusement parks, bands in the plaza and sporting events.

Oct Mes de la cultura, cultural events throughout the month.

Last weekend of Oct Mojanda Arriba is an annual full-day hike from Malchinguí over Mojanda to reach Otavalo for the foundation celebrations.

What to do

Otavalo

Horse riding

Several operators offer riding tours. Half-day trips to nearby attractions cost US$40-50. Full-day trips such as Cuicocha or Mojanda run US$40-50.

Language schools

Instituto Superior de Español, *Jaramillo 6-23 y Morales, T06-292 7354, www.instituto-superior.net*. **Mundo Andino Internacional**, *Bolívar 816 y Abdón Calderón, p3, T06-292 1864, www.mandino spanishschool.com*. Cooking classes and other activities included.

Otavalo Spanish Institute, *31 de Octubre 476 y Salinas, p 3, T06-293 0275, www.otavalospanish. com*. Also offers Quichua lessons.

Mountain bikes

Several tour operators rent bikes and offer cycling tours for US$35-70 a day trip. See also **Ciclovía**, page 1061. Rentals cost US$10-12 per day. **Taller Ciclo Primaxi**, Ricaurte y Morales and in Peguche.

Tour operators

Most tours are to indigenous communities, Cuicocha and Mojanda, US$25-35 pp.

All about EQ, *Los Corazas 433 y Albarracín, at the north end of town, T06-292 3633, www.all-about-ecuador.com*. Interesting itineraries, trekking and horse riding tours, climbing, cycling, trips to Intag, Piñán, Cayambe, Oyacachi, volunteering on organic farms. English and French spoken. Recommended.

Ecomontes, *Sucre y Morales, T06-292 6244, www.ecomontestour.com*. A branch of a Quito operator, trekking, climbing, rafting, also sell tours to Cuyabeno and Galápagos.

Runa Tupari, *Sucre y Quito, T06-292 2320, www.runatupari.com*. Arranges indigenous homestays in the Cotacachi area, also the usual tours, trekking, horse riding and cycling trips and transport.

Train rides

Beautifully restored historic train station at Calderón y J Montalvo, T1-800-873637, www. trenecuador.com, Wed-Sat 0800-1300, 1400-1700, Sun 0800-1300. Train ride to **Salinas** (57 km away) and back, **El Tren de la Libertad**, US$53. Departures Fri-Sun 0800, returning 1750; on Sun return from Ibarra to Otavalo is by bus. Includes stops at San Roque, Andrade Marín (with **Museo Textil**) and San Antonio de Ibarra. You can continue by bus from Salinas to **San Lorenzo**, see page 1151.

Transport

Otavalo

Bus Terminal at Atahualpa y Ordóñez (no departures after 1930). The Ibarra Terminal offers many more destinations. To **Quito** 2 hrs, US$2.50, every 10 mins; all depart from Terminal Carcelén in Quito, **Coop Otavalo** and **Coop Los Lagos** go into Otavalo, buses bound for Ibarra or Tulcán drop you off at the highway, this is inconvenient and not safe at night. From **Quito** or airport by taxi takes 1½ hrs, US$60 one way; shared taxis with **Taxis Lagos/Serviquito**, in Quito, Asunción Oe2-146 y Versalles, T02-256 5992; in Otavalo,

Tip...

Never leave anything in your car or taxi in the street. There are public car parks at Juan Montalvo y Sucre, by Parque Bolívar, and on Quito between 31 de Octubre and Jaramillo.

Av Los Sarances y Panamericana, T06-292 3203, who run a hotel to hotel service (to/from modern Quito only) and will divert to resorts just off the highway; Mon-Sat hourly, 6 departures on Sun, 1½ hrs, US$15 pp, buy ticket at least 1 day ahead; they also go from Quito to Ibarra. Tour operators also offer transfers. Bus to **Ibarra**, every 4 mins, US$0.55, 40 mins. To **Peguche**, city bus on Av Atahualpa, every 10 mins, bus stops in front of the terminal and at Plaza Copacabana, US$0.35; taxi US$2. To **Apuela** in the Intag region, daily at 0730, 1000 and 1400, US$2.50, 2 hrs. To **Ambato** bypassing Quito, US$5.65, see Ibarra Transport (page 1074), **CITA** buses from Ibarra stop along the Panamericana, enquire locally where to wait for them, and note that this is not safe after dark.

Around Otavalo

Bus From Otavalo to **San Pablo del Lago** every 25 mins, more often on Sat, US$0.25, 30 mins; taxi US$4. Also buses to many nearby communities.

Otavalo to the Colombian border

an area of diverse attractions and scenery

Northwest of Otavalo is Cotacachi from where a road goes west to the Cotacachi-Cayapas reserve and the subtropical Intag region. The main highway goes north to the city of Ibarra and beyond into the hot Chota Valley from where a branch road goes west to the subtropical valley of the Río Mira and the coastal town of San Lorenzo. The Panamericana reaches the border at the busy town of Tulcán, with its fantastic cemetery topiary.

Cotacachi

West of the road between Otavalo and Ibarra is Cotacachi. There is also access along a secondary road from Otavalo through Quiroga. Cotacachi, home to a growing expatriate community, produces and sells many leather goods.

The **Casa de las Culturas** ① *Bolívar 1334 y 9 de Octubre*, a beautifully refurbished 19th-century building, is a monument to peace. It houses the post office, a library, gallery and radio station. The **Museo de las Culturas** ① *García Moreno 13-41y Bolívar, T06-255 4155, Mon-Fri 0800-1300, 1400-1700, Sat-Sun 0930-1400, free*, has good displays of early Ecuadorean history and regional crafts and traditions.

Local festivals include **Inti Raymi/San Juan** in June and **Jora** during the September equinox.

☆Laguna Cuicocha

15 km from Cotacachi, visitor centre has good natural history and cultural displays, daily 0800-1700.

This crater lake (altitude 3070 m) is part of the **Reserva Ecológica Cotacachi-Cayapas**, which extends from Cotacachi volcano to the tropical lowlands on the Río Cayapas in Esmeraldas. It is a crater lake with two islands, which are closed to the public to protect the native species. There is a well-marked 8-km path around the lake, which takes four to five hours and provides spectacular views of the Cotacachi, Imbabura and, occasionally, Cayambe peaks. The best views are in the morning, when condors can sometimes be seen. There is a lookout at 3 km, two hours from the start. Take water and a waterproof jacket. There is a shorter trail which takes 40 minutes. Motor boat rides around the islands, US$3.25 per person for minimum eight persons.

To the northwest of Otavalo lies the lush subtropical region of **Intag**, reached along a road that follows the southern edge of Cuicocha and continues to the town of **Apuela**. The region's primary cloudforest is threatened by a proposed large-scale copper mine, vigorously opposed by local communities. See **Defensa y Conservación Ecológica de Intag** ① *www.decoin.org*, for local conservation and community development projects.

The area's rivers will also be affected by an irrigation and hydroelectric scheme in the Piñán area, see Northwest of Ibarra, below. The **Asociación Agroartesanal de Café Río Intag (AACRI)** ① *on the main street, T06-264 8489, www. aacri.com*, a Fairtrade organic coffee grower's association, offers tours of coffee, sisal and sugar cane plantations and processing plants, also lodging and volunteer

Tip...

Beware! Some of the berries, which grow near the lake, are poisonous: do not eat them. The path around the lake is not for vertigo sufferers.

opportunities. Beyond are pleasant thermal baths at **Nangulví**. The area is rich in cloudforest and has several nature reserves. On the southwest boundary of the Cotacachi-Cayapas reserve is **Los Cedros Research Station** ① *2 hrs walk from the road, T06-361 2546, T09-9277 8878, www.reservaloscedros. org*, 6400 ha of pristine cloudforest, with abundant orchids and bird life. Full board in $$$ range. **Cloud Forest Adventure** (T06-301 7543, www.cloudforestadventure.com) offers accommodation, tours and volunteer opportunities in the Intag region.

Ibarra and around *Colour map 1, A4.*

Ibarra, the provincial capital, is the main commercial centre and transport hub of the northern highlands. The city has an interesting ethnic mix, with blacks from the Chota valley and Esmeraldas alongside Otavaleños and other highland *indígenas*, mestizos and Colombian immigrants.

On **Parque Pedro Moncayo** stand the Cathedral, the Municipio and Gobernación. One block away, at Flores y Olmedo, is the smaller Parque 9 de Octubre or **Parque de la Merced** after its church. Beyond the railway station, to the south and west of the centre, is a busy commercial area with several markets beyond which is the bus terminal. At the Centro Cultural Ibarra, the **Museo Regional Sierra Norte** ① *Sucre 7-21 y Oviedo, T06-260 2093, Tue-Fri, 0900-1630, Sat-Sun and holidays 1000-1600,* has interesting archaeological displays about cultures of northern Ecuador, colonial and contemporary art and temporary exhibits. **Bosque Protector Guayabillas** ① *Urbanización La Victoria, on the eastern outskirts of town, Tue-Sun 0900-1700,* is a 54-ha park on a hill overlooking the city which offers great views. There are trails amid the eucalyptus forest. **Virgen del Carmen** festival is on 16 July and **Fiesta de los Lagos** is in the last weekend of September.

Off the main road between Otavalo and Ibarra is **San Antonio de Ibarra**, well known for its wood carvings. It is worth seeing the range of styles and techniques and shopping around in the galleries and workshops. Further west is the town of **Atuntaqui**. On the opposite side of the Panamericana and along the rail line is Andrade Marín, home of the **Museo Fábrica Textil Imbabura** ① *T06-253 0240, Wed-Sun 0900-1600, US$3, knowledgeable guides,* a good display of machinery of the most important producer and employer in the area between1926 and1966; included in train tours.

About 8 km from Ibarra on the road to Olmedo is **La Esperanza**, a pretty village in beautiful surroundings. Some 15 km further along, by Angochagua is the community of **Zuleta**. The region is known for its fine embroidery. West of La Esperanza, along a road that starts at Avenida Atahualpa, and also 8 km from Ibarra, is the community of **San Clemente**, which has a very good grassroots tourism project, **Pukyu Pamba**, see Where to stay, page 1071. From either La Esperanza or San Clemente you can climb **Cubilche** volcano and **Imbabura**, more easily than from San Pablo del Lago. From the top you can walk down to Lago San Pablo (see page 1062). *Guías nativos* are available for these climbs.

Ibarra to the coast The spectacular train ride from Ibarra to San Lorenzo on the Pacific coast no longer operates. A tourist train runs on a small section of this route, see pages 1065 and 1073.

Some 24 km north of Ibarra is the turn-off west for **Salinas**, a mainly Afro-Ecuadorean village with a Museo de la Sal, an ethnographic cultural centre and a restaurant offering local cuisine, and the very scenic road beside the Río Mira down to San Lorenzo. At 41 km from the turn-off are the villages of **Guallupe**, **El Limonal** (see Where to stay, page 1071), and **San Juan de Lachas**, in a lush subtropical area. Ceramic masks and figurines are produced at the latter. In **Lita**, 33 km from Guallupe, there is nice swimming in the river. Beyond is the Río Chuchubi with waterfalls and swimming holes; here is **Las Siete Cascadas resort** ① *entry US$10, guide US$10 per group* (see Where to stay, page 1071). It is 66 km from Lita to **Calderón**, where this road meets the coastal highway coming from Esmeraldas. Two kilometres before the junction, on the Río Tululbí, is **Tunda Loma** (see Where to stay, page 1152). About 7 km beyond is San Lorenzo (see page 1151).

Northwest of Ibarra Along a secondary road to the northwest of Ibarra is the town of **Urcuquí** with a basic hotel. Nearby is **Yachay**, a university and national research and technology centre, in a beautiful historic hacienda. From just south of Urcuquí, a road leads via Irunguicho towards the **Piñán lakes**, a beautiful, remote, high *páramo* region, part of the Reserva Ecológica Cotacachi-Cayapas. The local community of Piñán (3112 m) has a tourism programme (www.pinantrek.com), with a well-equipped refuge (US$12 per person, meals available), *guías nativos* (US$15 per day) and muleteers (US$12 per day, per horse). Another access to the hamlet of Piñán is via La Merced de

Buenos Aires, a village reached from either Tumbabiro (see below) or San Gerónimo, near Guallupe (on the road to the coast). Along the Tumbabiro access is the community of Sachapamba, where muleteers and mules can be found. The nicest lakes, Donoso and Caricocha, are one-hour walk from the community. They can also be reached walking from either Chachimbiro (see below), Irubí or Cuellaje in the Intag area. Otavalo agencies and hotels in Chachibiro and Tumababiro also offer trekking tours to Piñán. Note that a proposed irrigation and hydroelectric scheme will affect this beautiful area.

Beyond Urcuquí is the friendly town of **Tumbabiro**, with a mild climate, a good base from which to explore this region; it can also be reached from Salinas on the road to the coast. Some 8 km from Tumbabiro along a side road, set on the slopes of an extinct volcano, is **Chachimbiro**, a good area for walking and horse riding, with several resorts with thermal baths. The largest one, run by the provincial government, is **Santa Agua Chachimbiro** ① T06-264 8308, www.santagua.com.ec, 0700-2000, entry to recreational pools US$5, to medicinal pools and spa US$10, with several hot mineral pools, lodging, restaurants, zip-line and horses for riding; weekends can be crowded.

North to Colombia

From Ibarra the Pan-American highway goes past Laguna Yahuarcocha (with a few hotels, a campground, see Where to stay, Ibarra, and many food stalls, busy on weekends) and then descends to the hot dry Chota valley, a centre of Afro-Ecuadorean culture. Beyond the turn-off for Salinas and San Lorenzo, 30 km from Ibarra, the highway divides. The western branch follows an older route through Mira and El Angel to Tulcán on the Colombian border, the eastern route, the Pan-American Highway, goes to Tulcán via Bolívar, San Gabriel and Huaca. A paved road between El Angel and Bolívar connects the two branches. From El Angel a beautiful paved road west connects with the road between Ibarra and the coast.

Western route to Tulcán At **Mascarilla**, 1 km after the roads divide, ceramic masks are made. The women's crafts association here runs a hostel ($ El Patio de mi Casa, T09-9316 1621, meals available). Beyond by 16 km is **Mira** (2400 m), where fine woollens are made. This road is paved and in good condition as far as **El Angel** (3000 m), where the main plaza retains a few trees sculpted by José Franco (see Tulcán Cemetery, opposite); market day is Monday. The road north beyond El Angel goes through beautiful *páramo*. It is poor requiring a 4WD and is a great mountain bike route.

The **Reserva Ecológica El Angel** ① T06-297 7597, office in El Angel near the Municipio; best time to visit May to Aug, nearby protects 15,715 ha of *páramo* ranging in altitude from 3400 m to 4768 m. The reserve contains large stands of the velvet-leaved *frailejón* plant, also found in the Andes of Colombia and Venezuela. Also of interest are the spiny *achupallas*, *bromeliads* with giant compound flowers. The fauna includes *curiquingues* (caracara), deer, foxes, and a few condors. From El Angel follow the poor road north towards Tulcán for 16 km to **El Voladero** ranger station/shelter, where a self-guided trail climbs over a low ridge (30 minutes' walk) to two crystal-clear lakes. Pickups or taxis from the main plaza of El Angel charge US$25 return with one-hour wait for a day trip to El Voladero. A longer route to another area follows an equally poor road to Cerro Socabones, beginning at **La Libertad**, 3.5 km north of El Angel (transport El Angel–Cerro Socabones, US$30 return). It climbs gradually to reach the high *páramo* at the centre of the reserve and, in 40 minutes, the **El Salado** ranger station. From Socabones the road descends to the village of **Morán** (lodging and guides, transport with Sr Calderón, T09-9128 4022), the start of a nice three-day walk down to Guallupe, on the Ibarra–San Lorenzo road.

Eastern route to Tulcán From Mascarilla, the Panamericana normally runs east through the warm Chota valley to El Juncal, before turning northeast to **Bolívar**, a neat little town where the houses and the interior of its church are painted in lively pastel colours; there is also a huge mural by the roadside. At the **Museo Paleontológico** ① by the north entrance to town, US$2, remains of a mammoth, found nearby, can be seen. There is a Friday market.

Some 16 km north of Bolívar is **San Gabriel**, an important commercial centre. The 60-m-high **Paluz** waterfall is 4 km north of town, beyond a smaller waterfall. To the southeast, 11 km from town on the road to Piartal is **Bosque de Arrayanes**, a 16-ha mature forest with a predominance of myrtle trees, some reaching 20 m, taxi US$5.

East of San Gabriel by 20 km is the tiny community of **Mariscal Sucre** also known as Colonia Huaqueña, the gateway to the **Guandera Reserve and Biological Station** ① *the reserve is part of Fundación Jatun Sacha. Reservations should be made at the Quito office, T02-331 7163, www. jatunsacha.org.* You can see bromeliads, orchids, toucans and other wildlife in temperate forest and *frailejón páramo*. From San Gabriel, take a taxi beyond Mariscal Sucre, one hour, then walk 30 minutes to the reserve, or make arrangements with Jatun Sacha.

Between San Gabriel and Tulcán are the towns of Huaca, site of a pre-Inca settlement and Julio Andrade, with $$-$ **Hotel Naderik**, T06-220 5433, and a Saturday market (good for horses and other large animals) and, afterwards, paddleball games. This is the beginning of the road east to La Bonita, Lumbaqui and Lago Agrio. The road follows the frontier for much of the route. Make enquiries about safety before taking this beautiful route.

Tulcán *Colour map 1, A4.*

The chilly city of Tulcán (altitude 2960 m) is the busy capital of the province of Carchi. There is a great deal of informal trade here with Colombia, a textile and dry goods fair takes place on Thursday and Sunday. The eastern and western roads from the south join at Las Juntas, 2 km south of the city. In the **cemetery** ① *daily 0800-1800*, two blocks from Parque Ayora, the art of topiary is taken to beautiful extremes.

> **Tip...**
> Tulcán is a generally safe city, but the area around the bus terminal requires caution, especially at night. Do not travel outside town (except along the Panamericana) without advance local enquiry.

Cypress bushes are trimmed into archways, fantastic figures and geometric shapes in *haut* and *bas* relief. To see the stages of this art form, go to the back of the cemetery where young bushes are being pruned. The artistry, started in 1936, is that of the late Sr José Franco, born in El Angel (see above), now buried among the splendour he created. The tradition is carried on by his sons. Around the cemetery is a promenade with fountains, souvenir and flower stalls and the **tourist office**, Unidad de Turismo ① *entrance to the cemetery, T06-298 5760, daily 0800-1800, turismo@gmtulcan.gob.ec, helpful.* Write in advance to request a guided tour of the cemetery. Two blocks south is the **Museo de la Casa de la Cultura** ① *Mon-Fri 0730-1300, 1500-1800*, with a collection of pre-Inca ceramics.

Border with Colombia: Tulcán–Ipiales

The border is at **Rumichaca** (stone bridge), 5 km from Tulcán. Border posts with immigration, customs and agriculture control are on either side of a concrete bridge over the Río Carchi, to the east of the natural stone bridge. This well organized border is open 24 hours. On the Ecuadorean side, next to immigration (T06-298 6169), is a tourist information office. **Colombian consulate in Tulcán** ① *Bolívar entre Ayacucho y Junín, T06-298 0559, Tue-Thu 0800-1300.* Visas require three days.

> **Tip...**
> Banks in Tulcán can be found on de Agosto y Sucre. Few places accept credit cards. Pesos Colombianos can easily be changed on Parque La Independencia, the bus terminal and the border. There are money changers on both sides of the bridge, check all calculations.

Listings Otavalo to the Colombian border

Tourist information

Cotacachi

iTur Turec
Centro de Convenciones El Convento, García Moreno 13-66 y Sucre, T06-255 4122, Facebook:

tureturismocotacachi for upcoming events. Mon-Fri 0900-1700, Sat 0900-1500.
Run by an association of disabled people. It provides maps, regional information, tours, rides on horse-drawn carriages and chivas (both with advanced reservations); also rents camping equipment and bicycles (US$2 per hr). On the

same premises are a restaurant and cafeteria. Additional tourist information in Spanish and a city map are found in www.cotacachi.gob.ec.

Ibarra

Dirección de Turismo del Municipio
Sucre y Oviedo, T06-260 8489, www.touribarra. gob.ec. Mon-Fri 0800-1230, 1400-1730, holidays 0900-1500.
City map, pamphlets, English spoken, free Wi-Fi.

Where to stay

Cotacachi

$$$$ La Mirage
500 m west of town, T06-291 5237, www.mirage.com.ec.
Luxurious converted hacienda with elegant suites and common areas, includes breakfast and dinner, excellent restaurant, pool, gym and spa (treatments extra), beautiful gardens, tours arranged.

$$$-$$ Land of Sun
García Moreno 1376 y Sucre, T06-291 6009.
Refurbished colonial house in the heart of town, rooms with balcony, internal ones are cheaper, breakfast served in lovely patio, local specialities in restaurant, request dinner in advance, sauna, parking. Recommended.

$$ Runa Tupari
A system of homestays in nearby villages.
Visitors experience life with a indigenous family by taking part in daily activities. The comfortable rooms have space for 3, fireplace, bathroom and hot shower, and cost US$35 pp including breakfast, dinner and transport from Otavalo. Arrange with **Runa Tupari** (www.runatupari. com), or other Otavalo tour operators.

$$-$ La Cuadra
Peñaherrera 11-46 y González Suárez, T06-291 6015, www.lacuadra-hostal.com.
Modern comfortable rooms, good matresses, private or shared bath, no breakfast, kitchen facilities.

$ Bachita
Sucre 16-82 y Peñaherrera, T06-291 5063.
Simple place, private or shared bath, no breakfast, quiet.

Laguna Cuicocha

$$$ Hostería Cuicocha
Laguna Cuicocha, by the pier, T06-301 7218, www.cuicocha.org.
Rooms overlooking the lake, internal ones are cheaper, includes breakfast and dinner, restaurant, no overnight staff.

$$-$ Cabañas Mirador
On a lookout above the pier, follow the trail or by car follow the road to the left of the park entrance, T09-9055 8367, miradordecuicocha@yahoo.com.
Rustic cabins with fireplace and modern rooms overlooking the lake, good economical restaurant, trout is the speciality, parking, transport provided to Quiroga (US$5), Cotacachi (US$5), or Otavalo (US$10); owner Ernesto Cevillano is knowledgeable about the area and arranges trips.

Ibarra

$$$$ Hacienda Pimán
9 km northeast of town, Quito T02-256 6090, www.haciendapiman.com.
Luxuriously restored 18th-century hacienda, price includes breakfast and dinner. All inclusive 2- and 3-day packages with a train ride and visit to El Angel Reserve.

$$$ Hacienda Chorlaví
Panamericana Sur Km 4, T06-293 2222, www.haciendachorlavi.com.
In a historical hacienda dating to 1620, comfortable rooms, very good expensive restaurant, excellent *parrillada*, pool and spa, parking, busy on weekends, folk music and crafts on Sat.

$$$ La Estelita
Km 5 Vía a Yuracrucito, T09-9811 6058.
Modern hotel 5 km from the city, high on a hill overlooking town and Laguna Yahuarcocha. Rooms and suites with lovely views, good restaurant, pool, spa, can arrange paragliding.

$$ Montecarlo
Av Jaime Rivadeneira 5-61 y Oviedo, near the obelisk, T06-295 8266, www.hotelmontecarloibarra.ec.
Nice comfortable rooms, buffet breakfast, restaurant, heated pool open on weekends, parking.

\$\$ Royal Ruiz
Olmedo 9-40 y P Moncayo, T06-264 4653,
www.hotelroyalruiz.com.
Modern, comfortable carpeted rooms, restaurant, solar-heated water, parking, long-stay discounts.

\$\$-\$ Finca Sommerwind
Autopista Yahuarcocha Km 8, T09-3937 1177,
www.finca-sommerwind.info.
A 12-ha ranch by Laguna Yahuarcocha with cabins and campground, US\$3 pp in tent, US\$5 pp for camper vans, electricity, hot shower, laundry facilities.

\$ Fran's Hostal
Gral Julio Andrade 1-58 y Rafael Larrea,
near bus terminal, T06-260 9995.
Multi-storey hotel, bright functional rooms, no breakfast, parking.

\$ Las Garzas
Flores 3-13 y Salinas, T06-295 0985.
Simple comfortable rooms, no breakfast, sitting room.

Around Ibarra

\$\$\$\$ Hacienda Zuleta
By Angochahua, along the Ibarra-Cayambe road,
T06-266 2232, www.haciendazuleta.com.
A 2000-ha working historic hacienda, among the nicest in the country. Superb accommodation and food, 15 rooms with fireplace, price includes all meals (prepared with organic vegetables, trout and dairy produced on the farm) and excursions, advance reservations required.

\$\$\$ Pukyu Pamba
In San Clemente, T06-266-0045, 09-9916 1095,
www.sanclementetours.com.
Part of a community-run programme. Nicely built cottages with hot water on family properties, cheaper in more humble family homes, price includes 3 tasty meals and a guided tour. Opportunities to participate in daily activities in the field and kitchen and learn about local traditions and celebrations. Options for hiking, horse riding and climbing Imbabura volcano.

\$\$ Casa Aída
In La Esperanza village, T06-266 0221.
Simple rooms with good beds, includes dinner and breakfast, restaurant, shared bath, hot water, patios, some English spoken, meeting place for climbing Imbabura.

Ibarra to the coast

\$\$\$\$ Hacienda Primavera
North of Guallupe on the road to Chical, T09-9370 8571, www.haciendaprimavera.com.
8 rooms in a beautiful forest setting, pool, includes full board, guided hiking and horse riding.

\$\$\$ Las Siete Cascadas
Km 111, 15 km past Lita, T09-8261 1195,
lily_tarupi@hotmail.com.
A-frame cabins with balconies in a 204-ha reserve, price includes full board and excursions to waterfalls and the forest, reserve well ahead.

\$\$-\$ Parque Bambú
In El Limonal, about 600 m uphill from the main square, T06-301 6606, www.bospas.org.
Family-run farm with splendid views of the valley and many birds. Private rooms with terrace, US\$14 pp in dorm, good breakfast, tasty meals available, camping U\$3 pp, trekking. Run by Belgian Piet Sabbe, a permaculture landscape designer, and his daughters; Piet will share his knowledge and experience in landscape restoration and welcomes volunteers with a green thumb (arrange ahead). Recommended.

Northwest of Ibarra

\$\$\$ Aguasavia
In Chachimbiro,15-min walk from Santa Agua complex, T06-304 8347, www.aguasavia.com.
Community-run modern hotel in a beautiful setting in the crater of La Viuda Volcano, includes 3 meals, rooms on ground floor with jacuzzi, thermal pools, trips.

\$\$\$ Hacienda San Francisco
In the community of San Francisco, 5 km past Tumbabiro on the road to Chachimbiro, T06-304 8232, www.hosteriasanfrancisco.com.
Intimate family-run inn in tastefully converted hacienda stables, includes breakfast, expensive restaurant, full board packages available, small thermal pool, nice grounds, good walking, horse riding, tennis court, excursions to Piñán, best Thu to Sun when owners are in.

\$\$\$ Santa Agua Chachimbiro
Part of the recreational complex, T06-264 8063, in Ibarra T06-261 0250, www.santagua.com.ec.
Rooms and cabins (some with jacuzzi), includes 3 meals and access to spa and pools, restaurant, busy on weekends, reserve ahead.

$$$-$$ Hostería Spa Pantaví
7 km from Salinas, at the entrance to Tumbabiro,
T06-293 4185, Quito reservations T02-234 0601,
www.hosteriapantavi.com.
Stylish inn in a tastefully restored hacienda. Very
comfortable rooms, decorated with the owner's
original works of art, includes nice breakfast,
good restaurant, pool, spa, jacuzzi, nice gardens,
attentive service, bikes and horses for rent, tours.

$ Tío Lauro
1 block from plaza, Tumbabiro, T06-293 4148.
Nice *residencial*, simple rooms, meals on request,
parking, friendly owner.

North to Colombia
El Angel

$$$$ Polylepis Lodge
Abutting the reserve, 14 km from El Angel
along the road to Socabones, T06-263 1819,
www.polylepislodgeec.com.
Rustic cabins with fireplace by a lovely 12-ha
forest, includes 3 meals (vegetarian on request)
and 3 guided walks, jacuzzi.

$$ Las Orquídeas
In the village of Morán, T09-8641 6936,
castro503@yahoo.com.
Mountain cabin with bunk beds, shared bath,
includes 3 meals, horse riding and guide,
run by Carlos Castro, a local guide and
conservation pioneer.

$ Blas Angel
C Espejo, facing the roundabout by the entrance
to town, T06-297 7346.
Private or shared bath, parking, a good
economical option.

Eastern route to Tulcán
San Gabriel

$$ Gabrielita
Mejía y Los Andes, above the agricultural supply
shop, T06-229 1832.
Modern hostel, includes breakfast, parking, best
in town.

Tulcán

$$$ Palacio Imperial
Sucre y Pichincha, T06-298 0638,
www.hotelpalacioimperial.com.

Modern hotel with ample rooms with wood
floors, suites with jacuzzi, warm blankets, includes
buffet breakfast, very popular Chinese restaurant
Chifa Pak Choy, rooftop spa, gym, parking.

$$ Grand Hotel Comfort
Colón y Chimborazo, T06-298 1452,
www.grandhotelcomfort.com.
Modern high-rise hotel with rooms and suites
with jacuzzi, fridge, safety box, with breakfast,
restaurant with set lunch and à la carte (closed
Sat-Sun evening), parking.

$$-$ Los Alpes
JR Arellanoy Centenario, next to bus station, T06-
298 2235, www.hoteleslosalpesyalejandra.com.
Best option near the bus terminal, breakfast extra,
restaurant, good value.

$$-$ Sara Espíndola
Sucre y Ayacucho, on plaza, T06-298 2464, http://
hotelsaraespindiol.wixsite.com/hotelespindola.
Comfortable rooms, with breakfast, spa,
parking, helpful.

$$-$ Torres de Oro
Sucre y Rocafuerte, T06-298 4660,
www.hoteltorresdeoro.com.
Modern, nice, restaurant, parking.

$ Florida
Sucre y Ayacucho, T06-298 3849.
Simple, clean, shared bath, no breakfast,
a good economy option.

Restaurants

Cotacachi
A local speciality is *carne colorada* (spiced pork).

$$ D'Anita
10 de Agosto, y Moncayo. Daily 0800-2100.
Good set meal of the day, local and international
dishes à la carte, popular, English spoken,
good value.

$$-$ La Vaca Gorda
10 de Agosto entre Rocafuerte y Pedro Moncay.
Open 1200-2200.
Grilled meats, burgers, wings, fries and beer,
popular with expats.

Café Río Intag
On Plaza San Francis. Mon-Fri 0800-2000,
Sat 1000-2200, Sun 1000-1800.
The best coffee, snacks, meeting place.

Ibarra

$$ Caribou
*Pérez Guerrero 537 y Sucre and in Yacucalle south
of the bus terminal, T06-260 5137. Mon 1700-
2300, Tue-Thu 1300-2300, Fri-Sat 1300-0030.*
Excellent meat specialities, including burgers,
salads, bar, Canadian-owned. Recommended.

$$ El Argentino
*Sucre y P Moncayo, at Plazoleta Francisco
Calderón. Tue-Sun.*
Good mixed grill and salads, small, pleasant,
outdoor seating.

$$-$ La Cassona
Bolívar 6-47 y Oviedo. Daily.
In a nice colonial patio, international, seafood and
local dishes, also set lunch.

$ Casa Blanca
Bolívar 7-83. Closed Sun.
Family-run, in colonial house with patio, good set
lunches and snacks. Recommended.

Cafés and heladerías

Café Arte
Salinas 5-43 y Oviedo. Daily from 1700.
Café-bar with character, drinks, Mexican snacks,
sandwiches, live music Fri-Sat night.

Café Pushkin
Olmedo y Oviedo. Open 0700-1700.
For breakfast, snacks, coffee. An Ibarra classic,
very popular.

El Quinde Café
Sucre 562 y Flores.
A good place for breakfast, coffee, cake, snacks.

Heladería Rosalía Suárez
Oviedo y Olmedo.
Excellent homemade *helados de paila* (fruit
sherbets made in large copper basins), an Ibarra
tradition since 1896. Highly recommended.

Olor a Café
Flores y Bolívar.
Café/bar/cultural centre in a historic home,
music, library.

Tulcán

$$-$ Dubai
Chimborazo. Open 1030-2200.
Set lunch, à la carte and *comida típica*, popular.

$ Bocattos
Bolívar y Panamá on Parque Ayora.

Tip...
Economical meals and juices at the
attractively renovated and clean Mercado
Central, entrances on Boyacá, Bolívar and
Sucre in Tulcán, open 0700-1700.

Set lunch and à la carte, Italian and
Ecuadorean specialities.

$ Café Tulcán
Sucre 52-029 y Ayacucho. Open 0800-1800.
Café, snacks, desserts, juices, set lunches.
A Tulcán classic.

Bars and clubs

Ibarra
Plazoleta Francisco Calderón on Sucre y Pedro
Moncayo has several café-bars with outdoor
seating and a pleasant atmosphere.

Rincón de Ayer
Olmedo 9-59.
A bar with lots of character, attractively restored.

Sambuca
Oviedo 636 y Sucre.
Bar/club, the in-place among Ibarreño youth.

What to do

Ibarra
A unique form of paddle ball, *pelota nacional*, is
played in the afternoon at Yacucalle, south of the
bus station. Players have huge studded paddles
for striking the 1-kg ball.

Paragliding
Fly Ecuador, *T06-295 3297 or T09-8487 5577,
www.flyecuador.com.ec.* Tandem flight US$67-90,
course US$448, arrange ahead.

Tour operators
EcuaHorizons, *Bolívar 4-67 y García Moreno, T06-
295 9904.* Bilingual guides for regional tours.
Intipungo, *Rocafuerte 6-08 y Flores, T06-295 7766.*
Regional tours.

Train rides
A tourist train runs from Ibarra to **Salinas**,
29 km away, Thu-Sun and holidays at 1125,
returning 1640, US$30 one way. When there
is high demand, there is also *ferrochiva* (open
sided motorized railcar) service at 1030, US$15
one way, US$20 return. Purchase tickets in

advance. Ibarra station at Acosta y Colón, daily 0800-1700 or through T1-800-873637; you need each passenger's passport number and date of birth to purchase tickets. The ride takes 2 hrs with stops. You can continue by bus from Salinas to **San Lorenzo**, see page 1151.

see page 1151

Transport

Cotacachi
Bus Terminal at 10 de Agosto y Salinas by the market. Every 10 mins to/from Otavalo terminal, US$0.25, 25 mins; service alternates between the Panamericana and the Quiroga roads. To **Ibarra**, every 15 mins, US$0.50, 40 mins; service alternates between the Panamericana and Imantag roads.

Laguna Cuicocha
Pick-ups From **Otavalo** US$10. From **Cotacachi**, US$5 one way, US$10 return with short wait. From **Quiroga** US$5. Return service from the lake available from **Cabañas El Mirador**, same rates.

Los Cedros Research Station
Bus From Estación La Ofelia in Quito, **Trans Minas**, daily at 0615, 1000, 1530, 1800 to **Magdalena Alto**, US$4.50, 3½ hrs; then a 2-hr **walk**; arrange with the station for mules to carry luggage up. If the road is passable, 2 daily buses from Otavalo, pass **Chontal** on route to Cielo Verde. Take a pickup from Chontal to Magdalena Alto or it is a 5-hr walk from Chontal to Los Cedros.

Ibarra
Bus Terminal is at Av Teodoro Gómez y Av Eugenio Espejo, southwest of the centre, T06-264 4676. Most inter-city transport runs from here. There are no ticket counters for regional destinations, such as Otavalo, proceed directly to the platforms. City buses go from the terminal to the centre or you can walk in 15 mins. To/from **Quito**, Terminal Carcelén, every 10 mins, US$3, 2½ hrs. Shared taxis with **Taxis Lagos/Serviquito** (Quito address under Otavalo Transport, page 1065, in Ibarra at Flores 924 y Sánchez y Cifuentes, near Parque La Merced, T06-260 6858), buy ticket at least 1 day ahead, US$15 pp, 2½ hrs. To **Tulcán**, with **Expreso Turismo**, 9 daily, US$3, 2½ hrs. To **Otavalo**, platform 12, every 4 mins, US$0.50, 40 mins. To **Cotacachi**, platform 15, every 15 mins, US$0.50, 40 mins, some continue to **Quiroga**. To the coast, several companies,

some go all the way to **San Lorenzo** US$7, 4 hrs, others only as far as **Lita**, US$4.50, 2 hrs. To **Ambato**, CITA goes via El Quinche and the Quito airport roundabout and bypasses Quito, 10 daily, US$6.50, 5 hrs. To **Baños**, **Expreso Baños**, also by the airport and bypasses Quito, at 0500 and 1430, US$7.50, 6 hrs. To **Lago Agrio**, Valle de Chota, at 0900, US$11.25, via La Bonita. To **Tumbabiro** via Urcuquí, **Coop Urcuquí**, hourly, US$1, 1 hr. To **Chachimbiro**, Coop Urcuquí, at 0700, 0730 and 1200, returning Mon-Fri at 1215 (Sat-Sun at 1300), 1530 and 1630, US$1.60, 1½ hrs, taxi US$40 return. Buses to La Esperanza, Zuleta and San Clemete leave from **Parque Germán Grijalva** (east of the Terminal Terrestre, follow C Sánchez y Cifuentes, south from the centre). To **La Esperanza**, every 20 mins, US$0.30, 30 mins. To **Zuleta**, hourly, US$0.60, 1 hr. To **San Clemente**, frequent, weekdays 0650-1840, Sat-Sun 0720-1500, US$0.30, 30 mins. For nearby destinations such as **San Antonio de Ibarra**, city buses run along Pérez Guerrero.

North to Colombia

Western route to Tulcán
Bus from **Ibarra** Terminal Terrestre to **Mira**, every 30 mins, US$1.25, 1 hr; to **El Angel**, hourly, US$1.75, 1½ hrs. El Angel to **Mira**, every 30 mins, US$.50, 20 mins. El Angel to **Tulcán**, US$1.75, 1½ hrs. El Angel to **Quito**, US$5, 4 hrs.

Eastern route to Tulcán
Bus From **San Gabriel** to **Tulcán**, vans and jeeps US$0.70, shared taxis US$0.95, 30 mins, all from the main plaza. From San Gabriel to **Ibarra**, buses, US$2, 2 hrs. From San Gabriel to **Quito**, buses, US$4.50, 3½ hrs. See Note, under Tulcán, below.

Tulcán
Air There is an airport, but no commercial flights were operating in early 2017.

Bus The bus terminal is 1.5 km uphill from centre; best to take a taxi, US$1.25. To **Quito**, US$5, 5 hrs, every 15 mins, service to Terminal Carcelén, some continue to Quitumbe; from Quito, service from both terminals. To **Ibarra**, 2½ hrs, US$3. **Otavalo**, US$3.75, 3 hrs (they don't go in to the Otavalo Terminal, alight at the highway turn-off where taxis are available or transfer in Ibarra). To **Guayaquil**, 20 a day, 13 hrs, US$16. To **Lago Agrio via La Bonita**, 3 a day with **Putumayo** and 2 daily with **Coop Petrolera**, US$8.75, 7 hrs, spectacular.

Border with Colombia

Bus Minivans and shared taxis (US$1 pp) leave when full from Parque Ayora (near the cemetery); private taxi US$3.50. Taxi from the bus terminal to the border US$3, shared US$1.25 pp. **Note** These vehicles cross the international bridge and drop you off on the Colombian side, where onward transport waits. Remember to cross back over the bridge for Ecuadorean immigration. *Colectivo* border–Ipiales, US$1, taxi US$6-8.

Cotopaxi,
Latacunga
& Quilotoa

An impressive roll call of towering peaks lines the route south of Quito, appropriately called the Avenue of the Volcanoes. This area obviously attracts its fair share of trekkers and climbers, while the less active tourist can browse through the many colourful indigenous markets and colonial towns that nestle among the high volcanic cones. The Pan-American Highway's six lanes head south from Quito towards the central highlands' hub of Ambato. The perfect cone of Cotopaxi volcano is ever-present and is one of the country's main tourist attractions. Machachi and Latacunga are good bases from which to explore the region and provide access to the beautiful Quilotoa Circuit of small villages and vast expanses of open countryside.

Best for
Markets ▪ Trekking ▪ Vistas ▪ Wildlife

Machachi

In a valley between the summits of Pasochoa, Rumiñahui and Corazón, lies the town of **Machachi**, famous for its horsemen (*chagras*), horse riding trips, mineral water springs and crystal clear swimming pools. The water, 'Agua Güitig' or 'Tesalia', is bottled in a plant 4 km from the town, where there is also a sports/recreation complex with one warm and two cold pools, entry US$5. Annual highland 'rodeo', El Chagra, third week in July; tourist information office on the plaza. Just north of Machachi is Alóag, where an important road goes west to Santo Domingo and the coast.

Reserva Ecológica Los Ilinizas

Machachi is a good starting point for a visit to the northern section of the **Reserva Ecológica Los Ilinizas**. Below the saddle between the two peaks, at 4740 m, is the **Refugio Nuevos Horizontes** ① T09-8133 3483, office and café in El Chaupi, T02-367 4125, www.ilinizas-refuge.webs.com, US$15 per night, US$30 with dinner and breakfast, reserve ahead, take sleeping bag, a shelter with capacity for 25. **Iliniza Norte** (5105 m) although not a technical climb, should not be underestimated, a few exposed, rocky sections require utmost caution. Some climbers suggest using a rope and a helmet is recommended if other parties are there because of falling rock; allow two to four hours for the ascent from the refuge. **Iliniza Sur** (5245 m) involves ice climbing despite the deglaciation: full climbing gear and experience are absolutely necessary. All visitors must register and be accompanied by an authorized mountain guide for both ascents; maximum three climbers per guide on Iliniza Norte, two per guide on Iliniza Sur.

Access to the reserve is through a turn-off west of the Panamericana 6 km south of Machachi, then it's 7 km to the village of El Chaupi, which is a good base for day-walks and climbing **Corazón** (4782 m, not trivial). A dirt road continues from El Chaupi 9 km to 'La Virgen' (statue), pickup US$15. Nearby are woods where you can camp. El Chaupi hotels arrange for horses with muleteer (US$25 per animal, one way).

★Parque Nacional Cotopaxi *Colour map, 1, B4.*

Visitors to the park must register at the entrance. Park gates are open 0800-1500, although you can stay until 1700. Visitors arriving with guides not authorized by the park are turned back at the gate. The park administration, a small museum (open daily 0800-1530) and snack bar, are 10 km from the park gates. La Rinconada shelter and camping area are 5 km beyond, just before lake Limpio Pungo. (See also Transport section, page 1082.) The museum has a 3D model of the park, information about the volcano and stuffed animals.

Cotopaxi Volcano (5897 m) is at the heart of a much-visited national park. This scenic snow-covered perfect cone is the second highest peak in Ecuador. Cotopaxi, one of the highest active volcanoes in the world, resumed activity in 2015, see box, page 1091. Volcanic material from former eruptions can be seen strewn about the *páramo* surrounding Cotopaxi. The northwest flank is most often visited. Here is a high plateau with a small lake (Laguna Limpio Pungo), a lovely area for walking and admiring the delicate flora, and fauna including wild horses and native bird species such as the Andean lapwing and the Chimborazo hillstar hummingbird. The lower slopes are clad in planted pine forests, where llamas may be seen. The southwest flank, or Cara Sur, has not received as much impact as the west side. Here too, there is good walking, and you can climb Morurco (4881 m) as an acclimatization hike; condors may sometimes be seen. Just north of Cotopaxi are the peaks of Rumiñahui (4722 m), Sincholagua (4873 m) and Pasochoa (4225 m). To the southeast, beyond the park boundary, are Quilindaña (4890 m) and an area of rugged *páramos* and mountains dropping down to the jungle. The area has several large haciendas which form the Fundación Páramo (www.fundacionparamo.org), a private reserve with restricted access.

The **main entrance** to Parque Nacional Cotopaxi is approached from Chasqui, 25 km south of Machachi, 6 km north of Lasso. Once through the national park gates, go past Laguna Limpio Pungo to a fork, where the right branch climbs steeply to a parking lot (4600 m). From here it's a 30-minute to one-hour walk to the José Ribas refuge, at 4800 m; beware of altitude sickness. Walking from the highway to the refuge takes an entire day or more. The **El Pedregal entrance**, from the northwest, is accessed from Machachi via Santa Ana del Pedregal (21 km from the Panamericana), or from Sangolquí via Rumipamba and the Río Pita Valley. From Pedregal to the refuge car park is 14 km. There are infrequent buses to Pedregal (two a day) then the hike in is shorter but still a couple of hours. The **Ticatilín access** leads to the southwest flank. Just north of Lasso, a road goes east to the village of San Ramón and on to Ticatilín (a contribution of US$2 per vehicle may be requested at the barrier here, be sure to close all gates) and Rancho María. From the south, San Ramón is accessed from Mulaló. Beyond Rancho María is the private Albergue Cotopaxi Cara Sur (4000 m, see Where to stay, below). Walking four hours from here you reach Campo Alto (4760 m), a climbers' tent camp. Note Cotopaxi was closed to climbers in 2017 owing to volcanic activity.

Lasso

Some 30 km south of Machachi is the small town of Lasso, on the railway line and off the Panamericana. In the surrounding countryside are several *hosterías*, converted country estates, offering accommodation and meals. Intercity buses bypass Lasso.

Latacunga *Colour map, 1, B3.*

The capital of Cotopaxi Province is a place where the abundance of light grey pumice has been artfully employed. Volcán Cotopaxi is much in evidence, though it is 29 km away. Provided they are not hidden by clouds, which unfortunately is all too often, as many as nine volcanic cones can be seen from Latacunga; try early in the morning. The colonial character of the town has been well preserved. The central plaza, **Parque Vicente León**, is a beautifully maintained garden (locked at night). There are several other gardens in the town including **Parque San Francisco** and **Lago Flores** (better known as 'La Laguna'). **Casa de los Marqueses de Miraflores** ① *Sánchez de Orellana y Abel Echeverría, T02-281 1382, Mon-Fri 0800-1700, Sat 0900-1300, free*, in a restored colonial mansion has a modest museum, with exhibits on Mama Negra (see Festivals, page 1081), colonial art, archaeology, numismatics, a library and the Jefatura de Turismo, see below.

Where to stay	Restaurants
1 Central	1 Café Abuela
2 Endamo	2 Chifa China
3 Rodelú	3 Chifa Dragón
4 Rosim	4 Cunani
5 Tiana & Tovar Expediciones	5 Gamber Rosso
6 Villa de Tacunga	6 Guadalajara Grill
	7 Parrilladas La Española

Casa de la Cultura ① *Antonia Vela 3-49 y Padre Salcedo T03-281 3247, Tue-Fri 0800-1200, 1400-1800, Sat 0800-1500, US$1,* built around the remains of a Jesuit Monastery and the old Monserrat watermill, houses a fine museum with pre-Columbian ceramics, weavings, costumes and festival masks; also gallery, library and theatre. It has week-long festivals with exhibits and concerts. There is a Saturday **market** on the Plaza de San Sebastián (at Juan Abel Echeverría). Goods for sale include *shigras* (fine stitched, colourful straw bags) and homespun wool and cotton yarn. The produce market, El Salto, has daily trading and larger fairs on Tuesday, Friday and Saturday.

Listings Cotopaxi and Latacunga *map p1078.*

Tourist information

Latacunga

Cámara de Turismo de Cotopaxi
Quito 14-38 y General Maldonado, Latacunga, T03-280 1112, www.capturcotopaxi.com/fest.htm. Mon-Fri 0900-1300, 1400-1700.
Local and regional information, Spanish only.

Jefatura de Turismo
Casa de los Marqueses, T03-280 8494. Mon-Fri 0800-1700.
Local and regional information and maps.

Where to stay

Machachi

$$$ La Estación y Granja
3 km west of the Panamericana, by railway station outside the village of Aloasí, T02-230 9246.
Rooms in a lovely old home and newer section, also cabins, fireplaces, meals available (produce from own garden), parking, family-run, hiking access to Volcán Corazón (guides arranged), reserve ahead.

$$$ Papagayo
In Hacienda Bolívia, west of the Panamericana, take a taxi fom Machachi, T02-231 0002, www.hosteria-papagayo.com.
Nicely refurbished hacienda, pleasant communal areas with fireplace and library, restaurant, jacuzzi, parking, central heating, homey atmosphere, horse riding, biking, tours, popular.

$$$ Puerta al Corazón
500 m south of the train station, T02-230 9858.
Cosy lodge, located near the rail line with good views of the mountains, small restaurant, price includes dinner and breakfast. A good base for mountain trips.

$$ Chiguac
Los Caras y Colón, 4 blocks east of the main park, T02-231 0396, amsincholagua@gmail.com.

Nice family-run hostel, comfortable rooms, good breakfast, other meals available, shared bath.

Reserva Ecológica Los Ilinizas

$$$-$$ Chuquiragua Lodge
500 m before El Chaupi, then 200 m on a cobbled road, T02-367 4046, Quito T02-603 5590, www.chuquiragualodgeandspa.com.
Inn with lovely views, a variety of rooms and prices, restaurant with roaring fireplace. US$18 pp in dorm, camping US$10 pp with hot shower (bring your own tent). Spa, horse riding, trekking, climbing, bike tours, and transport from Quito available, advance booking advised.

$$-$ La Llovizna
100 m behind the church, on the way to the mountain, T02-367 4076.
Pleasant hostel, sitting room with fireplace, includes breakfast and dinner, cheaper without meals and includes use of kitchen, private or shared bath, ping pong, horse, bike and gear rentals, helpful owner, guiding, transport to Ilinizas, book in advance.

$$-$ Nina Rumy
Near the bus stop in El Chaupi, T02-367 4088.
Includes breakfast and supper, cheaper without meals, simple rooms, private or shared bath, hot water, family-run and very friendly.

Parque Nacional Cotopaxi

All these inns are good for acclimatization at altitudes between 3100 m and 3800 m.

$$$-$$ Tambopaxi
3 km south of the El Pedregal access (1 hr drive from Machachi) or 4 km north of the turn-off for the climbing shelter, T02-600 0365 (Quito), www.tambopaxi.com.
Comfortable straw-bale mountain shelter at 3750 m. 3 double rooms and several dorms (US$25 pp), duvets, camping US$7.50 pp, restaurant, excellent horse riding with advance notice.

$$ Albergue Cotopaxi Cara Sur

At the southwestern end of the park,
at the end of the Ticatilín road,
T09-9800 2681, eagamaz@gmail.com.
Very nice mountain shelter at 4000 m, day
use US$1. Includes breakfast and dinner, use
of kitchen, some cabins with private bath, hot
shower, transport from Quito and climbing tours
available, equipment rental. **Campo Alto** is a very
basic tent camp (4780 m, US$8 pp), 4 hrs' walk
from the shelter, horse to take gear to Campo
Alto US$15, muleteer US$15.

Outside the park

$$$$ Hacienda San Agustín de Callo

2 access roads from the Panamericana, 1 just
north of the main park access (6.2 km); the
second, just north of Lasso (4.3 km), T03-271 9160,
Quito T02-290 6157, www.incahacienda.com.
Exclusive hacienda, the only place in Ecuador
where you can sleep and dine in an Inca building,
the northernmost imperial-style Inca structure
still standing. Rooms and suites with fireplace
and bathtub, includes breakfast and dinner, horse
rides, treks, bicycles and fishing. Restaurant ($$$)
and buildings open to non-guests (US$5-10).

$$$$ Hacienda Santa Ana

10 mins from north entrance to Cotopaxi National
Park, T02-222 4950, www.santaanacotopaxi.com.
17th-century former Jesuit hacienda in beautiful
surroundings. 7 comfortable rooms with
fireplaces, central heating, great views, horse
riding, hiking, trekking, climbing. Also run
Hotel Sierra Madre in Quito.

$$$$ Hacienda Yanahurco

On access road to Quilindaña, 2 hrs from
Machachi, T09-9612 7759, Quito T02-244 5248,
www.haciendayanahurco.com.
Large hacienda in wild area, rooms with fireplace
or heater, includes meals, 2-4 day programmes,
all-inclusive.

$$$ Secret Garden

T09-9357 2714, www.secretgardencotopaxi.com.
Rooms and dorms (US$35 pp), includes 3 meals,
hot drinks, good common areas with fireplace,
indoor jacuzzi with views of Cotopaxi. Offer
hiking tours, horse riding and transport (US$5
from Quito). Good value for where it is. Popular.

$$$-$$ Chilcabamba

Loreto del Pedregal, by the northern access to
the National Park, T09-9946 0406, T02-237 7098,
www.chilcabamba.com.

Cabins and rooms, US$30.50 pp in dorm,
magnificent views.

$$$-$$ Cuello de Luna

2 km northwest of the park's main access on a dirt
road, T09-9970 0330, www.cuellodeluna.com.
Comfortable rooms with fireplace, includes
breakfast, other meals available, US$22 pp in
dorm (a very low loft). Can arrange tours.

$$$-$$ Tierra del Volcán

T09-9498 0115/0121, Quito T02-600 9533,
www.tierradelvolcan.com.
3 haciendas: **Hacienda El Porvenir**, a working
ranch by Rumiñahui, between El Pedregal and
the northern access to the park, 3 types of rooms,
includes breakfast, set meals available, horses and
mountain bikes for hire, camping, zip-line; **Hacienda
Santa Rita**, by the Río Pita, on the Sangolquí-El
Pedregal road, with zip-lines, entry US$6, camping
US$5 pp; and the more remote, rustic **Hacienda
El Tambo** by Quilindaña (limited access during
volcanic activity), southeast of the park. Also
offers many adventure activities in the park.

$$ Huagra Corral

200 m east of Panamericana along the
park's main access road, T09-9771 9729,
Quito T02-380 8427, www.huagracorral.com.
Nicely decorated, restaurant, private or shared
bath, heaters, convenient location, helpful,
reserve ahead.

Lasso

$$$$ Hacienda Hato Verde

Panamericana Sur Km 55, by entry to
Mulaló, southeast of Lasso, T03-271 9348,
www.haciendahatoverde.com.
Lovely old hacienda and working dairy farm near
the south flank of Cotopaxi, tastefully restored.
10 rooms with wood-burning stoves, includes
breakfast, other meals available; horse riding (for
experienced riders), trekking, trip up Cotopaxi
Cara Sur, charming hosts.

$$$ Hostería La Ciénega

2 km south of Lasso, T03-271 9052,
www.haciendalacienega.com.
A historic hacienda with nice gardens, rooms with
heater or fireplace, good expensive restaurant.

$ Cabañas Los Volcanes

At the south end of Lasso, T03-271 9524,
maexpediciones@yahoo.com.
Small hostel, nice rooms, private or shared bath.
Tours to Cotopaxi.

Latacunga

$$$ Villa de Tacunga
Sánchez de Orellana y Guayaquil, T03-281 2352.
Well-restored colonial house built of Cotopaxi pumice stone. Comfortable rooms and suites with fireplace.

$$ Endamo
2 de Mayo 438 y Tarqui, T03-280 2678.
Modern hotel with nice rooms and a small restaurant, good value.

$$ Rodelú
Quito 16-31, T03-280 0956, www.rodelu.com.ec.
Popular hotel, restaurant, suites and rooms (some are very small, look before taking a room), breakfast included starting the 2nd day.

$$-$ Rosim
Quito 16-49 y Padre Salcedo, T03-280 2172, www.hotelrosim.com.
Centrally located, breakfast available, some carpeted rooms, quiet and comfortable. Discounts in low season.

$$-$ Tiana
Luis F Vivero N1-31 y Sánchez de Orellana, T03-281 0147, www.hostaltiana.com.
Includes breakfast, drinks and snacks available, private or shared bath, US$10 pp in dorm, nice patio, kitchen facilities, luggage store, popular backpackers' meeting place. Tour agency **Tovar Expediciones** (see What to do, below), good source of information for Quilotoa Loop.

$ Central
Sánchez de Orellana y Padre Salcedo, T03-280 2912.
A multi-storey hotel in the centre of town, breakfast available, simple adequate rooms, a bit faded but very helpful.

Restaurants

Machachi
Not much to choose from in town.

$$$-$$ Café de la Vaca
4 km south of town on the Panamericana. Daily 0800-1730.
Very good meals using produce from their own farm, popular.

$$-$ Pizzeria Di Ragazzo
Av Pablo Guarderas N7-107, north of centre.
Is reported good.

Latacunga
Few places are open on Sun. Many along the Panamericana specialize in *chugchucaras*, a traditional pork dish. *Allullas* biscuits and string cheese are sold by the road.

$$ Chifa China
Antonia Vela 6-85 y 5 de Junio. Daily 1030-2200.
Good Chinese food, large portions.

$$ Chifa Dragón
Amazonas y Pastaza. Daily 1100-2300.
Chinese food, large portions, popular.

$$ Gamber Rosso
Quito y Padre Salcedo, T03-281 3394. Mon-Sat 1600-2200.
Good pizzas, antipasto and lasagne.

$$ Parrilladas La Española
2 de Mayo 7-175. Mon-Sat 1230-2100.
Good grill, popular with locals.

$$-$ Guadalajara Grill
Quijano y Ordóñez y Vivero.
Economical set lunch Mon-Fri 1200-1500, good Mexican food 1800-2200.

Café Abuela
Guayaquil 6-07 y Quito, by Santo Domingo church. Closed Sun.
Pleasant cosy café/bar, nicely decorated, drinks, sweets and sandwiches, popular with university students.

Cunani
Vivero y Sanchez de Orellana. Mon-Fri 1300-2100.
Cosy café/restaurant serving home-made ravioli, *humitas* and excellent hot chocolate. Also a handicraft store.

Festivals

Latacunga
23-24 Sep La Mama Negra, in homage to the Virgen de las Mercedes. There are 5 main characters in the parade and hundreds of dancers, some representing black slaves, others the whites. Mama Negra herself (portrayed by a man) is a slave who dared to ask for freedom in colonial times. The colourful costumes are called La Santísima Trajería. **1st or 2nd Sat in Nov** (but not 2 Nov, Día de los Muertos) The civic festival of **Mama Negra**, with a similar parade, is on. It is part of the **Fiestas de Latacunga**, 11 Nov.

Shopping

Latacunga
Artesanía Otavalo, *Guayaquil 5-50 y Quito*.
A variety of souvenirs from Otavalo.

What to do

Latacunga
All operators offer day trips to **Cotopaxi** and
Quilotoa (US$50 pp, includes lunch and a visit
to a market town if on Thu or Sat, minimum
2 people). Trekking trips US$80 pp per day.
Note Many agencies require passport as deposit
when renting gear.
Greivag, *Guayaquil y Sánchez de Orellana,
Plaza Santo Domingo, L5, T03-281 0510,
www.greivagturismo.com*. Day trips.
Neiges, *Guayaquil 6-25, Plaza Santo Domingo,
T03-281 1199, neigestours@hotmail.com*. Day trips
and climbing.
Tovar Expediciones, *at Hostal Tiana,
T03-281 1333*. Climbing and trekking.

Transport

Machachi
Bus To **Quito**, from El Playón behind the
stadium, every 15 mins to Terminal Quitumbe,
every 30 mins to Villa Flora and El Trebol, all US$1,
1½ hrs. To **Latacunga**, from the monument to
El Chagra at the Panamericana, US$0.75, 1 hr.

Reserva Ecológica Los Ilinizas
Bus From El Playón in Machachi, to **El Chaupi**
(every 20 mins, US$0.50, ½ hr), from where you
can walk to the *refugio* in 7-8 hrs. A pick-up
from El Chaupi to 'La Virgen' costs US$15, from
Machachi US$30. It takes 3 hrs to walk with a full
pack from 'La Virgen' to the *refugio*.

Parque Nacional Cotopaxi
Main park entrance and Refugio Ribas, take
a Latacunga bus from Quito and get off at
the main access point, where there is a large
overpass. Do not take an express bus as you
can't get off before Latacunga. At the overpass
there are usually pickup trucks which go to the

park, US$20 to Laguna Limpio Pungo for up to
4 passengers, or US$3 to the main park entrance
where other vehicles offer half-day guided tours
for US$60. From **Machachi**, pick-ups go via the
cobbled road to El Pedregal and on to Limpio
Pungo and the *refugio* parking lot, US$40. From
Lasso, full day trip to the park, US$50 return, with
Cabañas los Volcanes. From **Latacunga**, see
Tour operators.
To **Cara Sur** from Quito, **Cotopaxi Cara Sur**
offer transport to the **Albergue Cara Sur**, US$60
per vehicle up to 5 passengers. Alternatively take
a Latacunga bound bus and get off at **Pastocalle**,
and take a pick-up from there, US$15 per vehicle.
All prices subject to considerable variation, ask
around and negotiate politely.

Latacunga
Air The airport is north of the centre. 1 flight a
day to **Guayaquil** with **TAME**, Mon-Fri.

Bus Buses leave from the terminal just south
of 5 de Junio. At night (1900-0700) they enter
the city to pick up passengers if they have space
available. **Transportes Santa** has its own terminal
at Eloy Alfaro y Vargas Torres, T03-281 1659,
serving **Cuenca**, US$11; **Loja**, US$15; **Machala**,
US$11; **Guayaquil**, US$9.50; 4 daily to each. Other
companies from main terminal: to **Quito**, every
15 mins, 2 hrs, US$2.50; also shared taxis with
Servicio Express, T03-242 6828 (Ambato) or
T09-9924 2795, US$10. To **Ambato**, 1 hr, US$1.25.
To **Guayaquil**, US$8.75, 7 hrs. To **Saquisilí**, every
20 mins (see below). Through buses, which
are more frequent, do not stop at Latacunga
Terminal. During the day they stay on the 'Paso
Lateral', the city bypass of the Panamericana,
and stop at the roundabout at the road to Pujilí,
taxi from town US$3. For long-haul service
southbound, it may be easiest to take a local bus
to Ambato and transfer there. To **Otavalo** and
Ibarra, bypassing Quito, **Cita Express**, T03-280
9264, 12 daily from the Paso Lateral, US$5; also
with **Expreso Baños**. To **Baños**, US$2.25, 2 hrs,
every 20 mins from the Paso Lateral. Buses on the
Zumbahua, Quilotoa, Chugchilán, Sigchos circuit
are given below. **Note** On Thu most buses to
nearby communities leave from Saquisilí market
instead of Latacunga.

☆The popular and recommended 200-km round trip from Latacunga to Pujilí, Zumbahua, Quilotoa crater, Chugchilán, Sigchos, Isinliví, Toacazo, Saquisilí, and back to Latacunga, can be done in two to three days by bus. It is also a great route for biking and only a few sections of the loop are cobbled or rough. Hiking from one town to another can be challenging, especially when the fog rolls in. For these longer walks hiring a guide might not be unreasonable if you don't have a proper map or enough experience.

Latacunga to Zumbahua

A fine paved road leads west from Latacunga to **Pujilí** ① *15 km, bus US$0.35*, which has a beautiful church. There is a good market on Sunday, a smaller one on Wednesday, and the Corpus Christi celebrations are colourful. Beyond Pujilí, many interesting crafts are practised by the *indígenas* in the **Tigua valley**: paintings on leather, hand-carved wooden masks and baskets. **Chimbacucho**, also known as Tigua, is home to the Toaquiza family, most famous of the Tigua artists. The road goes on to Zumbahua, then over the Western Cordillera to La Maná and Quevedo. This is a great paved downhill bike route. It carries very little traffic and is extremely twisty in parts but is one of the most beautiful routes connecting the highlands with the coast. Beyond Zumbahua are the pretty towns of **Pilaló** (two restaurants, small *hostal* and petrol pumps), **Esperanza de El Tingo** (two restaurants and lodging at **Carmita's**, T03-281 4657) and **La Maná** (two hotels).

Zumbahua *Colour map 1, B3.*

Zumbahua lies 800 m from the main road, 62 km from Pujilí. It has an interesting Saturday market (starts at 0600) for local produce, and some tourist items. Just below the plaza is a shop selling dairy products and cold drinks. Friday nights involve dancing and drinking. Take a fleece, as it can be windy, cold and dusty. There is a good hospital in town, Italian-funded and run. The Saturday trip to Zumbahua market and the Quilotoa crater makes an excellent excursion.

Quilotoa

Zumbahua is the point to turn off for a visit to Quilotoa, a volcanic crater filled by a beautiful emerald lake. From the rim of the crater (3850 m) several snowcapped volcanoes can be seen in the distance. The crater is reached by a paved road which runs north from Zumbahua (about 12 km, three- to five-hours' walk). There's a 300-m drop down from the crater rim to the water. The hike down takes about 30 minutes (an hour or more to climb back up, mind the altitude). The trail starts at the village of Quilotoa, up the slope from the parking area, then, down a steep canyon-like cut. You can hire a mule to ride up from the bottom of the crater (US$10), best arrange before heading down. There is a basic hostel by the lake and kayaks for rent (US$5 per hour). Everyone at the crater tries to sell the famous naïve Tigua pictures and carved wooden masks, so expect to be besieged (also by begging children). To the southeast of the crater is the village of **Macapungo**, which runs the **Complejo Shalalá**, see Where to stay, below. The Mirador Shalalá platform offers great views of the lake. To hike around the crater rim takes 4½ to six hours in clear weather. Be prepared for sudden changes in the weather, it gets very cold at night and can be foggy. Never deviate from the trail. For a shorter loop (three to four hours), start on the regular circuit going right when you reach the rim by Quilotoa village and follow it to Mirador Shalalá, a great place for a picnic; then backtrack for about five minutes and take the path down to the lake. To return, follow a path near the lake until you reach the large trail which takes you back up to Quilotoa village. If you are tired, you can hire a horse to take you up.

Chugchilán, Sigchos and Isinliví

Chugchilán, a lovely scenic village, is 16 km by paved road from Quilotoa. An alternative to the road is a five- to six-hour walk around part of the Quilotoa crater rim, then down to Guayama, and across the canyon (Río Sigüí) to Chugchilán, 11 km. Outside town is a cheese factory and nearby, at Chinaló, a woodcarving shop. The area has good walking.

Continuing from Chugchilán the road runs to **Sigchos**, the starting point for the Toachi Valley walk, via Asache to San Francisco de las Pampas (0900 bus daily to Latacunga). There is also a vehicle road to Las Pampas, with two buses from Sigchos. Southeast of Sigchos is **Isinliví**, on the old route to Toacazo and Latacunga. It has a fine woodcarving shop and a pre-Inca *pucará*. Trek to the village of Guantualó, which has a fascinating market on Monday. You can hike to or from Chugchilán (five hours), or from Quilotoa to Isinliví in seven to nine hours.

From Sigchos, a paved road leads to **Toacazo** ($$ **La Quinta Colorada**, T03-271 6122, www.quintacolorada.com, price includes breakfast and dinner) and on to Saquisilí.

Saquisilí

Some 16 km southwest of Lasso and 4 km west of the Panamericana is the small but very important market town of Saquisilí. Its Thursday market (0500-1400) is famous throughout Ecuador for the way in which its seven plazas and some streets become jam-packed with people, the great majority of them local *indígenas* with red ponchos and narrow-brimmed felt hats. The best time to visit the market is 0900-1200 (before 0800 for the animal market). Be sure to bargain, as there is a lot of competition. This area has colourful Corpus Christi processions.

Listings Quilotoa Circuit

Where to stay

Latacunga to Zumbahua

$$ La Posada de Tigua
3 km east of Tigua-Chimbacucho,
400 m north of the road, T03-305 6103,
posadadetigua@yahoo.com.
On a working dairy ranch, 6 rooms, wood-burning stove, includes tasty home-cooked breakfast and dinner, pleasant family atmosphere, horse riding, trails, nice views.

Zumbahua

$ Cóndor Matzi
Overlooking the market area, T09-8906 1572
or T03-281 2953 to leave message.
Basic but best in town, shared bath, hot water, dining room with wood stove, kitchen facilities, try to reserve ahead, if closed ask at **Restaurante Zumbahua** on the plaza.

$ Richard
Opposite the market on the road in to town,
T09-9015 5996.
Basic shared rooms and 1 shower with hot water, cooking facilities, parking.

Quilotoa

$$ Complejo Shalalá
In Macapungo, T09-6917 3990, on Facebook.
Community-run lodge in a lovely 35-ha cloudforest reserve. Nice cabins, 1 with wheelchair access, includes breakfast and dinner, restaurant, trails.

> **Tip…**
> Quilotoa hotels are all expensive for what they offer, and polite bargaining is appropriate.

$$ Quilotoa Crater Lake Lodge
On the main road facing the access to Quilotoa, T03-305 5816, http://quilotacraterlodge.hlsecuador.com.
Somewhat faded hacienda-style lodge, includes breakfast and dinner, dining room, views.

Humberto Latacunga, a good painter who also organizes treks, runs 3 good hostels, T09-9212 5962, all include breakfast and dinner:
$$ Hostería Alpaca, www.alpakaquilotoa.com, the most upmarket, rooms with wood stoves;
$$ Cabañas Quilotoa, *on the access road to the crater*, private or shared bath, wood stoves;
$$ Hostal Pachamama, *at the top of the hill by the rim of the crater*, private bath.

Chugchilán

$$$$-$$$ Black Sheep Inn
Below the village on the way to Sigchos, T03-270-8077, www.blacksheepinn.com.
A lovely eco-friendly resort which has received international awards. Includes 3 excellent vegetarian meals, private and shared bath, US$35 pp in dorms, spa, water slide, zip-line, arrange excursions.

$$ El Vaquero
Just outside town on the road to Quilotoa, T03-270 8003, www.hostalelvaquero.com.
Variety of rooms with bath, great views, heaters in common areas, includes generous dinner and

breakfast, helpful owners, transport to Quilotoa available (US$20).

$$ Hostal Cloudforest
At the entrance to town, T03-270 8016, www.cloudforesthostal.com.
Simple popular family-run hostel, sitting room with wood stove, includes dinner and great breakfast, restaurant open to public for lunch, private or shared bath, also dorm, parking, very helpful, great value.

$$ Hostal Mama Hilda
On the road in to town, T03-270 8015, www.mamahilda.com.
Pleasant family-run hostel, warm atmosphere, large rooms some with wood stoves, includes good dinner and breakfast, private or shared bath, camping, parking, arrange trips.

Sigchos

$$ Hostería San José de Sigchos
1.5 km south of town, Quito T02-240 19 68, www.sanjosedesigchos.com.
Comfortable rooms on a 150 ha working hacienda with heated pool, spa, restaurant, karaoke, horse riding, day visit US$8.

$ Jardín de los Andes
Ilinizas y Tungurahua, T03-271 2114.
Basic but quite clean and friendly.

Isinliví

$$$ Llullu Llama
T09-9258 0562, www.llullullama.com.
Farmhouse with cosy sitting room with wood stove, tastefully decorated rooms, cheaper in dorm, shared ecological bath. Also cottages with bath, fireplace and balcony. All include good hearty dinner and breakfast. Warm and relaxing atmosphere, a lovely spot. Recommended.

$ Taita Cristóbal
T09-9137 6542, taitacristobal@gmail.com.
Simple economy hostel with rooms and dorms, includes dinner and breakfast.

Saquisilí

$$ Gilocarmelo
By the cemetery, 800 m from town on the road north to Guaytacama, T09-9966 9734, T02-340 0924.
Restored hacienda house in a 4 ha property. Plain rooms with fireplace, restaurant, pool, sauna, jacuzzi, nice garden.

$ San Carlos
Bolívar opposite the Parque Central.
A multi-storey building, electric shower, parking, good value, but watch your valuables. Will hold luggage for US$1 while you visit the market.

Transport

Zumbahua
Bus Many daily on the Latacunga–Quevedo road (0500-1900, US$1.50, 1½ hrs). Buses on Sat are full, get your ticket on Fri. A pick-up truck can be hired from Zumbahua to **Quilotoa** for US$5-10 depending on number of passengers; also to **Chugchilán** for around US$30. On Sat mornings there are many trucks leaving the Zumbahua market for Chugchilán which pass Quilotoa. Pick-up Quilotoa–Chugchilán US$25.

Taxi Day-trip by taxi to Zumbahua, Quilotoa, and return to **Latacunga** is about US$60.

Quilotoa
Bus From the terminal terrestre in Latacunga **Trans Vivero** daily at 1000, 1130, 1230 and 1330, US$2.50, 2 hrs. Note that this leaves from Latacunga, not Saquisilí market, even on Thu. Return bus direct to Latacunga at 1300. Buses returning at 1400 and 1500 go only as far as Zumbahua, from where you can catch a Latacunga bound bus at the highway. Also, buses going through Zumbahua bound for Chugchilán will drop you at the turn-off, 5 mins from the crater, where you can also pick them up on their way to Zumbahua and Latacunga. Taxi from Latacunga, US$40 one way. For **Shalalá**, **Trans Ilinizas** from Latacunga to **Macapungo** at 1300, US$2, or go to Zumbahua and take a pick-up from there, US$5. From Macapungo it is a 30-min walk to the cabins.

> ### Tip...
> Note that throughout this region, buses leave when full, sometimes ahead of schedule.

Chugchilán
Bus From **Latacunga**, daily at 1130 (except Thu) via Sigchos, another bus, also at 1130, goes via Zumbahua; on Thu from **Saquisilí market** via Sigchos around 1130, US$3.25, 3 hrs. Buses return to Latacunga at 0330 via Sigchos, at 0400 via Zumbahua. On Sun there are extra buses to Latacunga leaving 0600, 0900, 1100 and 1200.

There are extra buses going to Zumbahua Wed 0600, Fri 0600 and Sun between 0900-1000; these continue towards the coast. Milk truck to Sigchos around 0900. On Sat also pick-ups going to/ from market in Zumbahua and Latacunga. From **Sigchos**, through buses as above, US$0.75, 1 hr. Pick-up hire to Sigchos US$20, up to 5 people, US$5 additional person. Pick-up to **Quilotoa** US$25, up to 5 people, US$5 additional person. Taxi from Latacunga US$50; to **Isinliví**, taxi US$30.

Sigchos

Bus From **Latacunga** almost every hour, 0930-1600; returning to Latacunga most buses leave Sigchos before 0700, then at 1430 (more service on weekends); US$2, 2 hrs. From **Quito** direct service Mon-Sat at 1400 (more frequent Sun) with **Reina de Sigchos**; also Fri 1700 with **Illinizas**; US$3.75, 3 hrs. To **La Maná** on the road to Quevedo, via Chugchilán, Quilotoa and Zumbahua, Fri at 0500 and Sun at 0830, US$4.50, 6 hrs (returns Sat at 0730 and Sun at 1530). To **Las Pampas**, at 0330 and 1400, US$3.25, 3 hrs. From Las Pampas to **Santo Domingo**, at 0300 and 0600, US$3.25, 3 hrs.

Isinliví

From **Latacunga** daily (except Thu), via Sigchos at 1215 (**14 de Octubre**) and direct at 1300 (**Trans Vivero**), on Thu both leave from Saquisilí market around 1100, on Sat the direct bus leaves at 1100 instead of 1300, US$2.25, 2½ hrs. Both return to Latacunga 0300-0330, except Wed at 0700 direct, Sun 1245 direct and Mon 1500 via Sigchos. Buses fill quickly, be early. Connections to Chugchilán, Quilotoa and Zumbahua can be made in Sigchos. Bus schedules are posted on www.llullullama.com.

Saquisilí

Bus Frequent service between **Latacunga** and Saquisilí, US$0.50, 20 mins; many buses daily to/ from **Quito** (Quitumbe), 0530-1300, US$2.50, 2 hrs. Buses and trucks to many outlying villages leave from 1000 onwards. Bus tours from Quito cost US$45 pp, taxis charge US$80, with 2 hrs wait at market.

Ambato *Colour map 1, B3.*

service and transport hub of the area

Almost completely destroyed in the great 1949 earthquake, Ambato lacks the colonial charm of other Andean cities, though its location in the heart of fertile orchard-country has earned it the nickname of 'the city of fruits and flowers'. It is also a transport hub and the principal commercial city of the central highlands, with a large Monday market and smaller ones Wednesday and Friday.

Sights

The modern cathedral faces **Parque Montalvo**, where there is a statue of the writer Juan Montalvo (1832-1889), whose house ⓘ *Bolívar y Montalvo, T03-282 4248, US$1, Mon-Fri 0800-1200, 1400-1800,* can be visited. The **Museo de la Provincia** in the Casa del Portal (built 1900), facing Parque Montalvo, has a photo collection.

Northeast of Ambato is the colonial town of **Píllaro**, gateway to **Parque Nacional Los Llanganates**, a beautiful rugged area (for tours see Sachayacu Explorer, page 1095). The town is known for its colourful festivals: a *diablada* (devils' parade) 1-6 January and Corpus Christi.

Ambato to Baños

To the east of Ambato, an important road leads to **Salasaca**, where the *indígenas* sell their weavings; they wear distinctive black ponchos with white trousers and broad white hats. Further east, 5 km, is **Pelileo**, the blue jean manufacturing capital of Ecuador with good views of Tungurahua. There are opportunities for cultural tourism, walking and paragliding in the area (contact Patricio Cisnero at **Blue Land Adventures** ⓘ *T03-283 0236, bluelandsalasaca@yahoo.com.ar*). From Pelileo, the road descends to Las Juntas, where the Patate and Chambo rivers meet to form the Río Pastaza. About 1 km east of Las Juntas bridge, the junction with the road to Riobamba is marked by a large sculpture of a macaw and a toucan (locally known as Los Pájaros – the lower bird was destroyed by the volcano). It is a favourite volcano watching site. The road to Baños then continues along the lower slopes of the volcano.

Eight kilometres northeast of Pelileo on a paved side-road is **Patate**, centre of the warm, fruit growing Patate valley. There are excellent views of Volcán Tungurahua from town. The fiesta of

Nuestro Señor del Terremoto is held on the weekend leading up to 4 February, featuring a parade with floats made with fruit and flowers.

Ambato to Riobamba and Guaranda

After Ambato, the Pan-American Highway runs south to Riobamba (see page 1096). About half way is **Mocha**, where guinea pigs (*cuy*) are bred for the table. You can sample roast *cuy* and other typical dishes at stalls and restaurants by the roadside, **Mariadiocelina** is recommended. The highway climbs steeply south of Mocha and at the pass at **Urbina** there are fine views in the dry season of Chimborazo and Carihuayrazo.

To the west of Ambato, a paved road climbs through tilled fields, past the *páramos* of Carihuayrazo and Chimborazo to the great Arenal (a high desert at the base of the mountain), and down through the Chimbo valley to Guaranda (see page 1097). This spectacular journey reaches a height of 4380 m and vicuñas can be seen.

Listings Ambato

Tourist information

Ministerio de Turismo
Guayaquil y Rocafuerte, Ambato, T03-282 1800.
Mon-Fri 0800-1700.

Where to stay

$$$ Florida
Av Miraflores 1131, T03-242 2007,
www.hotelflorida.com.ec.
Pleasant hotel in a nice setting, restaurant with good set meals, weekend discounts.

$$$ Mary Carmen
Av Ceballos y Martínez, T03-242 0908,
www.hotelboutiquemc.com.
Very nice boutique hotel with gym,
spa and parking.

$$$ Roka Plaza
Bolívar 20-62 y Guayaquil, T03-242 3845,
www.hotelrokaplaza.com.
Small stylish hotel in a refurbished colonial house in the heart of the city, sushi restaurant.

$$-$ Colony
12 de Noviembre 124 y Av El Rey, near the bus terminal, T03-282 5789.
A modern hotel with large rooms,
parking, spotless.

SS-$ Pirámide Inn
Cevallos y Mariano Egüez, T03-242 1920.
Comfortable hotel, cafeteria, English spoken.

Ambato to Baños

Salasaca and Pelileo

$$ Runa Huasi
In Salasaca, 1 km north off main highway,
T09-9984 0125, www.hostalrunahuasi.com.
Simple hostel, includes breakfast and fruit, other meals on request, cooking facilities, nice views, guided walks.

$ Hostal Pelileo
Eloy Alfaro 641, T03-287 1390.
Shared bath, hot water, simple.

Patate

$$$$-$$$ Hacienda Manteles
In the Leito valley on the road to El Triunfo,
T09-9213 5309, Quito T02-603 9415, www.
haciendamanteles.com.
Converted hacienda with views of Tungurahua and Chimborazo, includes breakfast, dinner, snacks, walk to waterfalls, hiking and horse riding. Reserve ahead.

$$$ Hacienda Leito
On the road to El Triunfo, T03-306 3196,
www.haciendaleito.com.
Classy hacienda with spacious rooms and great views of Tungurahua.

$$$ Hostería Viña del Río
3 km from town on the old road to Baños,
T03-287 0314, www.hosteriavinadelrio.com.
Cabins on a 22-ha ranch, restaurant, pool, spa and mini golf, US$7 for day use of facilities.

$ Hostal Casa del Valle
Juan Montalvo y Ambato, 2 blocks from plaza,
T09-8150 1062.
A good simple place right in town.

Restaurants

$$$-$$ Ali's Parrillada y Pizzeria
*Bolívar entre JL Mera y Martínez, also in Ficoa
neighbourhood and opposite Mall de los Andes.
Open 1030-2230.*
Good pizzas and international meat dishes.

$$$-$$ La Fornace
Cevallos 1728 y Montalvo. Open 1100-2200.
Wood oven pizza. Opposite is **Heladería
La Fornace**, Cevallos y Castillo. Snacks,
sandwiches, ice cream, very popular.

$$ El Alamo Chalet
*Cevallos 1719 y Montalvo.
Open 0800-2300 (2200 Sun).*
Ecuadorean and international food. Set meals
and à la carte, Swiss-owned, good quality.

$$-$ Govinda's
*Cuenca y Quito. Mon-Sat 0800-2030,
Sun 0800-1600.*
Vegetarian set meals and à la carte, also a
meditation centre (T03-282 3182).

$ Roho Wine
Quito 924 y Bolívar. Mon-Sat 1200-1530.
Good set meals.

Cafés

Crème Brulée
Juan B Vela 08-38 y Montalvo. Daily 0900-2100.
Very good coffee and pastries.

Pasterlería Quito
JL Mera y Cevallos. Daily 0700-2100.
Coffee, pastries, good for breakfast.

Festivals

Feb/Mar Ambato has a famous festival, the
Fiesta de frutas y flores, during carnival when
there are 4 days of festivities and parades (best
Sun morning and Mon night). Must book ahead
to get a hotel room.

Shopping

Ambato is a centre for leather: shoe shops on
Bolívar; jackets, bags, belts on Vela between
Lalama and Montalvo. Take a bus up to the
leather town of Quisapincha for the best deals,
every day, but big market on Sat.

What to do

Train rides

An *autoferro* runs from Ambato to **Urbina** and
back via **Cevallos**, Fri-Sat at 0800, US$22. The
train station is at Av Gran Colombia y Chile, near
the Terminal Terrestre, T03-252 2623; Mon-Thu
0800-1630, Fri-Sun 0800-1600.

Transport

Bus The main bus station is on Av Colombia y
Paraguay, 2 km north of the centre. City buses
go there from Plaza Cevallos in the centre,
US$0.25. Buses to **Quito**, 3 hrs, US$3.25; also
door to door shared taxis, US$12, with **Servicio
Express**, T03-242 6828 or T09-9924 2795 and
Delux, T09-3920 9827or 09-8343 0275. Buses
to **Cuenca**, US$10, 6½ hrs. To **Guayaquil**,
6 hrs, US$7.50. To **Riobamba**, US$1.50, 1 hr.
To **Guaranda**, US$2.50, 3 hrs. To **Ibarra**, via
the Quito airport and bypassing Quito, **CITA**,
8 daily, 5 hrs, US$6.25. To **Santo Domingo de
los Tsáchilas**, 4 hrs, US$5. To **Tena**, US$6.25,
4½ hrs. To **Puyo**, US$3.75, 2½ hrs. To **Macas**,
US$8.75, 5½ hrs. To **Esmeraldas**, US$10, 8 hrs.
Note Buses to **Baños** leave from the Mercado
Mayorista and then stop at the edge of town,
1 hr, US$1.10. Through buses do not go into the
terminal, they take the Paso Lateral bypass road.

Baños
& Riobamba

Baños and Riobamba are both good bases for exploring the Sierra and their close proximity to high peaks gives great opportunities for climbing, cycling and trekking (but check about Tungurahua's volcanic activity before you set out). The thermal springs at Baños are an added lure and the road east is a great way to get to the jungle lowlands. Riobamba and Alausí offer the opportunity to ride the train on the famous section of the line from the Andes to Guayaquil, around the Devil's Nose.

Baños and around   *Colour map 1, B4. See map, page 1090.*

a busy place popular with tourists from near and far

Baños is nestled between the Río Pastaza and the Tungurahua volcano, only 8 km from its crater. Baños bursts at the seams with hotels, *residenciales*, restaurants and tour agencies. Ecuadoreans flock here on weekends and holidays for the hot springs, to visit the Basílica and enjoy the local *melcochas* (toffees), while escaping the Andean chill in a sub-tropical climate (wettest in July and August). Foreign visitors are also frequent; using Baños as a base for trekking, organizing a visit to the jungle, making local day trips or just plain hanging out.

Sights

The **Manto de la Virgen** waterfall at the southeast end of town is a symbol of Baños. The **Basílica** attracts many pilgrims. The paintings of miracles performed by Nuestra Señora del Agua Santa are worth seeing. There are various thermal baths in town, all charge US$2 unless otherwise noted. The **Baños de la Virgen** ① *0430-1700*, are by the waterfall. They get busy so best visit very early morning. Two small hot pools open evenings only (1800-2200, US$3). The **Piscinas Modernas** ① *Fri-Sun and holidays 0900-1700*, with a water slide, are next door. **El Salado baths** ① *daily 0500-1600, weekends also 1800-2100, US$3*, several hot pools, plus icy cold river water, repeatedly destroyed by volcanic debris (not safe when activity is high), 1.5 km out of town off the Ambato road. The **Santa Ana baths** ① *Fri-Sun and holidays 0900-1700*, have hot and cold pools in a pleasant setting, just east of town on the road to Puyo. All the baths can be very crowded at weekends and holidays; the brown colour of the water is due to its high mineral content. The **Santa Clara baths** ① *C Velasco Ibarra behind Parque Montalvo, Mon-Fri 1400-2100, Sat-Sun 1000-2100, US$4*, are not natural springs but have clean heated pools as well as a nice large cold pool for swimming laps.

As well as the medicinal baths, there are various spas, in hotels, as independent centres and massage therapists. These offer a combination of sauna, steam bath (Turkish or box), jacuzzi, clay and other types of baths, a variety of massage techniques (Shiatsu, Reiki, Scandinavian) and more.

Around Baños

There are many interesting **walks** in the Baños area. The **San Martín shrine** is a 45-minute easy walk from town and overlooks a deep rocky canyon with the Río Pastaza thundering below. Beyond the shrine, crossing to the north side of the Pastaza, is the **Ecozoológico San Martín** ① *T03-274 0552, 0800-1700, US$2.50*, with the **Serpentario San Martín** ① *daily 0900-1700, US$2*, opposite. Some 50 m beyond is a path to the **Inés María waterfall**, cascading down, but polluted. Further, a *tarabita* (cable

Best for
Hot springs ■ Relaxing ■ Spas ■ Trekking

car) and zip-lines span the entrance to the canyon. You can also cross the Pastaza by the **Puente San Francisco** road bridge, behind the kiosks across the main road from the bus station. From here a series of trails fans out into the hills, offering excellent views of Tungurahua from the ridge-tops in clear weather. A total of six bridges span the Pastaza near Baños, so you can make a round trip.

On the hillside behind Baños are a series of interconnecting trails with nice views. It is a pleasant 45-minute hike to the **statue of the Virgin**; go to the south end of Calle JL Mera, before the street ends, take the last street to the right (Misioneros Dominicanos) at the end of which are stairs leading to the trail. A steep narrow path continues along the ridge, past the statue. Another trail also begins at the south end of JL Mera and leads to the **Hotel Luna Runtún**, continuing on to the village of Runtún (five- to six-hour round-trip). Yet another trail starts at the south end of Calle Maldonado and leads in 45 minutes to the **Bellavista cross**, from where you can also continue to Runtún.

The scenic road to **Puyo** (58 km) has many waterfalls tumbling down into the Pastaza. Many *tarabitas* (cable cars) and zip-lines span the canyon offering good views. By the Agoyán dam and bridge, 5 km from town, is **Parque de la Familia** ① *0900-1700, entry free, parking US$1*, with orchards, gardens, paths and domestic animals. Beyond, the paved road goes through seven tunnels between Agoyán and Río Negro. The older gravel road runs parallel to the paved road, directly above the Río Pastaza, and is the preferred route for cyclists who, coming from Baños, should only go through one

Where to stay

1 Alisamay *B1*
2 Apart-Hotel Napolitano *A4*
3 Casa del Molino Blanco *C1*
4 El Belén *B2*
5 El Oro *B1*
6 Finca Chamanapamba *A4*
7 Hostal Ilé *C3*
8 Isla de Baños *C2*
9 La Casa Verde *A4*
10 La Chimenea *C4*
11 La Floresta *C2*
12 La Petite Auberge *C3*
13 Los Pinos *B4*
14 Luna Runtún *A3*
15 Plantas y Blanco *C3*
16 Posada del Arte *C4*
17 Princesa María *B1*
18 Puerta del Sol *B4*
19 Samari *A4*
20 Sangay *C2*
21 Santa Cruz *C3*
22 Transilvania *B3*
23 Villa Santa Clara *C4*
24 Volcano *C4*

Restaurants 🍴

1 Ali Cumba *C3*
2 Café Blah Blah *B2*
3 Café Honey *B2*
4 Café Hood *C4*
5 Casa Hood *C4*
6 El Castillo *C4*
7 Jota Jota *C3*
8 Mariane *C2*
9 Pancho's *C2*
10 Rico Pan *B2*
11 Sativa *C3*
12 Swiss Bistro *C3*
13 Taberna Armenia *C2*

Bars & clubs 🍸

14 Buena Vista *B3*
15 Ferchos *B3*
16 Jack Rock *B3*
17 Leprechaun *B3*
18 Peña Ananitay *B3*

ON THE ROAD

Tungurahua and Cotopaxi volcanoes: active again

In 1999, after over 80 years of dormancy, Tungurahua became active again and remains so. The level of activity is variable; the volcano can be quiet for weeks or months between bursts of energy. Baños continues to be a safe and popular destination unless and until the level of volcanic activity greatly increases. The volcano is closed to climbers but all else is normal. In 2015, after 135 years of tranquility, it was Cotopaxi's turn and this volcano also remains active. Although the level of activity diminished in early 2016, some restrictions remain in force. Day visits to the José Rivas refuge at 4800 m and the entrance of the glacier at 5000 m are permitted, as well as camping at the La Rinconada area. Overnight stays in the refuge and ascents are still not allowed. You should be prepared to leave immediately in the event of an alarm. This very beautiful mountain and its surroundings can still be enjoyed, keeping the above in mind. Also under surveillance is Cayambe, which showed signs of increased activity in 2016. Since the level of volcanic activity can change, you should enquire locally before visiting any of these mountains and surrounding areas. Reports from the National Geophysical Institute are posted daily on www.igepn.edu.ec.

tunnel at Agoyán and then stay to the right avoiding the other tunnels. Between tunnels there is only the paved road, cyclists must be very careful as there are many buses and lorries. The area has excellent opportunities for walking and nature observation.

At the junction of the Verde and Pastaza rivers, 17 km from Baños is the town of **Río Verde** with snack bars, restaurants and a few places to stay. The Río Verde has crystalline green water and is cold but nice for bathing. The paved highway runs to the north of town, between it and the old road, the river has been dammed forming a small lake where rubber rafts are rented for paddling. Near the paved road is **Orquideario** ① *0900-1700, closed Wed, US$1.50*, with nice regional orchids. Before joining the Pastaza the Río Verde tumbles down several falls, the most spectacular of which is **El Pailón del Diablo** (the Devil's Cauldron). Cross the Río Verde on the old road and take the path to the right after the church, then follow the trail down towards the suspension bridge over the Pastaza, for about 20 minutes. Just before the bridge take a side trail to the right (signposted) which leads you to **Paradero del Pailón**, a nice restaurant, and viewing platforms above the falls (US$1.50). The **San Miguel Falls**, smaller but also nice, are some five minutes' walk from the town along a different trail. Cross the old bridge and take the first path to the right, here is **Falls Garden** (US$1.50), with lookout platforms over both sets of falls. Cyclists can leave the bikes at one of the snack bars while visiting the falls and return to Baños by bus.

Listings Baños and around *map page 1090.*

Tourist information

iTur
Oficina Municipal de Turismo, at the Municipio, Halflants y Rocafuerte, opposite Parque Central, Baños, T03-274 0483. Mon-Fri 0800-1230, 1400-1730.

Where to stay

Baños has plenty of accommodation but can fill during holiday weekends.

$$$$ Luna Runtún
Caserío Runtún Km 6, T03-274 0882, www.lunaruntun.com.

A classy hotel in a beautiful setting overlooking along Baños. Includes dinner, breakfast and use of pools (spa extra), very comfortable rooms with balconies and superb views, lovely gardens. Good service, English, French and German spoken, tours, nanny service.

$$$$ Samari
Vía a Puyo Km 1, T03-274 1855, www.samarispa.com.
Upmarket resort opposite the Santa Ana baths, nice grounds, tastefully decorated hacienda-style rooms and suites, pool and spa (US$24.50 for non-residents, daily 0800-2000), fine upmarket restaurant.

$$$$-$$$ Sangay
*Plazoleta Isidro Ayora 100, next to
waterfall and thermal baths, T03-274 0490,
www.sangayspahotel.com.*
Traditional Baños hotel with spa, buffet breakfast,
good restaurant specializes in Ecuadorean food,
pool and spa open to non-residents 1600-2100
(US$10), parking, tennis and squash courts,
games room, car hire, disco, attentive service,
mid-week discounts, British/Ecuadorean-run.
Recommended.

$$$ Apart-Hotel Napolitano
*C Oriente 470 y Suárez, T03-274 2464,
napolitano-apart-hotel@hotmail.com.*
Large comfortable apartments with kitchen,
fireplace, pool and spa, garden, parking. A bit
pricey, daily rentals or US$600 per month.

$$$ Finca Chamanapamba
*On the east shore of the Río Ulba, a short
ride from the road to Puyo, T03-274 2671,
www.chamanapamba.com.*
2 nicely finished wooden cabins in a spectacular
location overlooking the Río Ulba and just next to
the Chamanapamba waterfalls, very good café-
restaurant serves German food.

$$$ La Floresta
*Halflants y Montalvo, T03-274 1824,
www.laflorestahotel.com.*
Nice hotel with large comfortable rooms
set around a lovely garden, excellent buffet
breakfast, wheelchair accessible, craft
and book shop, parking, attentive service.
Warmly recommended.

$$$ Posada del Arte
*Pasaje Velasco Ibarra y Montalvo, T03-274 0083,
www.posadadelarte.com.*
Cosy inn, restaurant with vegetarian options,
pleasant sitting room, more expensive rooms
have fireplace, terrace, US-run.

$$$ Volcano
*Rafael Vieira y Montalvo, T03-274 2140,
www.volcano.com.ec.*
Spacious modern hotel, large rooms with
fridge, some with views of the waterfall, buffet
breakfast, restaurant, heated pool, massage,
nice garden.

$$$-$$ Isla de Baños
*Halflants 1-31 y Montalvo, T03-274 0609,
www.isladebanios.com.*
Well-decorated comfortable hotel, includes
European breakfast and steam bath, spa operates
when there are enough people, pleasant garden.

$$ Alisamay
*Espejo y JL Mera, T03-2741391,
www.hotelalisamay.com.*
Rustic hotel, nice cosy rooms with balconies,
includes breakfast and use of spa, gardens
with pools.

$$ Casa del Molino Blanco
*Misioneros Dominicanos y JL Mera, T03-274 1138,
www.casamolinoblanco.com.*
Located in a quiet area, with bath, US$11 pp in
dorm, spotlessly clean, includes buffet breakfast,
German spoken.

$$ Hostal Ilé
*12 de Noviembre y Montalvo, T03-274 2699,
www.facebook.com/hostalile.*
Rustic feel with lots of wood, ample comfortable
rooms, Mexican restaurant.

$$ La Casa Verde
*In Santa Ana, 1.5 km from town on Camino Real,
a road parallell and north of the road to Puyo,
T03-274 2671, www.lacasaverde.com.ec.*
Spacious hotel decorated in pine, the largest
rooms in Baños, laundry and cooking facilities,
very quiet, New Zealand-run.

$$-$ El Belén
*Reyes y Ambato, T03-274 1024,
www.hotelelbelen.com.*
Nice hostel, cooking facilities, spa, parking,
helpful staff.

$$-$ La Petite Auberge
*16 de Diciembre y Montalvo, T03-274 0936,
www.lepetit.banios.com.*
Rooms around a patio, some with fireplace,
good French restaurant, parking, quiet.

$$-$ Los Pinos
Ricardo Zurita y C Ambato, T03-274 1825.
Large hostel with double rooms and dorms
(US$9-10 pp), includes breakfast (and dinner
Mon-Wed), spa, kitchen and laundry facilities,
pool table Argentine-run, great value.

$$-$ Puerta del Sol
*Ambato y Arrayanes (east end of C Ambato),
T03-274 2265.*
Modern hotel, better than it looks on the outside,
large well-appointed rooms, includes breakfast,
pleasant dining area, laundry facilities, parking.

$ El Oro
Ambato y JL Mera, T03-274 0736.
With bath, laundry and cooking facilities,
good value, popular. Recommended.

$ La Chimenea
Martínez y Rafael Vieira, T03-274 2725,
www.hostalchimenea.com.
Nice hostel with terrace café, breakfast available, private or shared bath, US$8 pp in dorm, small pool, jacuzzi extra, parking for small cars, quiet, helpful and good value. Recommended.

$ Plantas y Blanco
12 de Noviembre y Martínez, T03-274 0044,
www.plantasyblanco.com.
Pleasant popular hostel decorated with plants, private or shared bath, US$9-10 pp in dorm, excellent breakfast available, rooftop cafetería, steam bath, classic films, good restaurant (open 1700-0100), bakery, French-owned, good value. Recommended.

$ Princesa María
Rocafuerte y Mera, T03-274 1035.
Spacious rooms, US$8 pp in dorm, laundry and cooking facilities, parking, popular budget travellers' meeting place, helpful and good value.

$ Santa Cruz
16 de Diciembre y Martínez, T03-274 3527,
www.santacruzbackpackers.com.
Large rooms, US$10.50 pp in dorm, fireplace in lounge, small garden with hammocks, kitchen facilities, mini pool on roof.

$ Transilvania
16 de Diciembre y Oriente, T03-274 2281,
www.hostal-transilvania.com.
Multi-storey building with simple rooms, includes breakfast, US$8.50 pp in dorm, Middle Eastern restaurant, nice views from balconies, large TV and movies in sitting room, pool table, popular meeting place.

$ Villa Santa Clara
12 de Noviembre y Velasco Ibarra, T03-274 0349,
www.hotelvillasantaclara.com.
Nice cabins in a quiet location, breakfast available, laundry facilities, wheelchair accessible, garden, spa, parking.

Around Baños

$$$ Miramelindo
Río Verde, just north of the paved road, T03-249 3004, www.miramelindo.banios.com.
Lovely hotel and spa, well-decorated rooms, good restaurant, pleasant gardens include an orchid collection with over 1000 plants.

$$ Hostería Río Verde
Between the paved road and town, T03-249 3007 (Ambato), www.hosteriarioverde.com.
Simple cabins in a rural setting, includes breakfast and use of spa, large pool, restaurant specializes in trout and tilapia.

Restaurants

$$$ Mariane
On a small lane by Montalvo y Halflants.
Mon-Sat 1300-2200.
Excellent authentic Provençal cuisine, generous portions, lovely setting, popular, slow service. Highly recommended. **Hotel Mariane ($$)** at the same location, very clean and pleasant.

$$$ Swiss Bistro
Martínez y Alfaro. Daily 1200-2230.
International dishes and Swiss specialities, Swiss-run.

$$$ Taberna Armenia
Pastaza y Montalvo. Fri-Mon 1600-2400.
Upmarket restaurant serving mostly meat dishes, including llama. Russian owner, very friendly, professional and good quality.

$$ Café Hood
Montalvo y Vieira. Thu-Tue 1200-2200.
Mainly vegetarian but also some meat dishes, excellent food, English spoken, always busy. Also rents rooms.

$$ Casa Hood
Martínez between Halflants and Alfaro.
Open 1200-2200.
Largely vegetarian, juices, milkshakes, varied menu including Indonesian and Thai, good set lunch and desserts. Travel books and maps sold, book exchange, cinema, cultural events, nice atmosphere. Popular and recommended.

$$ Sativa
Martínez y Eloy Alfaro. Open 1100-2200.
Wholesome food, some organic ingredients from their own garden.

$ El Castillo
Martínez y Rafael Vieira, in hostel.
Open 0800-1000, 1200-1330.
A favourite for a good filling set lunch.

Cafés

Ali Cumba
12 de Noviembre y Martínez. Daily 0800-2000.
Excellent breakfasts, salads, good coffee (filtered, espresso), muffins, cakes, home-made bread,

large sandwiches, book exchange. Danish/
Ecuadorean-run.

Café Blah Blah
Halflants y Martínez. Daily 0800-2000.
Cosy, popular café serving very good breakfasts,
coffee, cakes, snacks and juices.

Café Honey
*Maldonado y Rocafuerte at the Parque Central.
Daily 0900-2100.*
Fine modern café with all kinds of coffees, teas
and pastries, very good.

Jota Jota
Martínez y Halflants. Tue-Sun to 1000-2200.
Great choice of coffees and cocktails, book
exchange. German-run.

Pancho's
*Rocafuerte y Maldonado at Parque Central.
Daily 1530-2200.*
Hamburgers, snacks, sandwiches, coffee,
large-screen TV for sports and other events.

Rico Pan
*Ambato y Maldonado at Parque Central.
Mon-Sat 0700-1900, Sun 0700-1300.*
Good breakfasts, hot bread (including whole
wheat), fruit salads and pizzas, also meals.

Bars and clubs

Eloy Alfaro, between Ambato and Oriente has
many bars including:

Buena Vista
Alfaro y Oriente.
A good place for salsa and other Latin music.

Ferchos
Alfaro y Oriente. Tue-Sun 1600-2400.
Café-bar, modern decor, snacks, cakes,
good varied music, German-run.

Jack Rock
Alfaro y Ambato.
A favourite traveller hangout.

Leprechaun
Alfaro y Oriente.
Popular for dancing, bonfire on weekends,
occasional live music.

Entertainment

Chivas, open-sided buses, cruise town playing
music, they take you to different night spots and
to a volcano lookout when Tungurahua is active.

Peña Ananitay, *16 de Diciembre y Espejo.* Bar,
good live music and dancing on weekends,
no cover.

Festivals

During Carnival and Holy Week hotels are full
and prices rise.

Oct Nuestra Señora de Agua Santa. Daily
processions, bands, fireworks, sporting events
and partying through the month.
15 Dec Verbenas. A night-time celebration
when each barrio hires a band and parties.
16 Dec The town's anniversary, with parades,
fairs, sports, cultural events leading up to this date.

Shopping

Look out for jaw-aching toffee (*melcocha*)
made in ropes in shop doorways, or the less
sticky *alfeñique*.

Handicrafts
Crafts stalls at Pasaje Ermita de la Vírgen, off
C Ambato, by the market. Tagua (vegetable ivory
made from palm nuts) crafts on Maldonado y
Martínez. Leather shops on Rocafuerte between
Halflants and 16 de Diciembre.
Centro Naturista, *Eloy Alfaro y Oriente*. Health
foods and alternative medicine.
Latino Shop, *Ambato y Alfaro and 4 other
locations*. For T-shirts.
Librería Vieira – Arte Ilusion, *Halflants y
Martínez*. Bookstore with a café, Wi-Fi, nice
meeting place.

What to do

Adventure sports are popular in Baños, including
mountaineering, white water rafting, canyoning,
canopying and bridge jumps. Safety standards
vary greatly. There is seldom any recourse in the
event of a mishap so these activities are at your
own risk.

Bus tours
The *chivas* (see Entertainment) and a **double-
decker bus** (C Ambato y Halflants, T03-274 0596,
US$6) visit waterfalls and other attractions.
Check destinations if you have a specific interest
such as El Pailón falls.

Canopying or zip-line
Involves hanging from a harness and sliding on
a steel cable. Prices vary according to length,
US$10-20. Cable car, US$1.50.

Canyoning

Many agencies offer this sport, rates US$30 half day, US$50 full day.

Climbing and trekking

There are countless possibilities for walking and nature observation near Baños and to the east. Tungurahua has been officially closed to climbers since 1999. Operators offer trekking tours for about US$45 per day.

Cycling

Many places rent bikes, quality varies, US$5-10 per day; check brakes and tyres, find out who has to pay for repairs, and insist on a helmet, puncture repair kit and pump. The following have good equipment:

Carrillo Hermanos, *16 de Diciembre y Martínez*. Rents mountain bikes and motorcycles (reliable machines with helmets, US10 per hr).
Hotel Isla de Baños, rentals, US$10 per day.

Horse riding

There are many places, but check their horses as not all are well cared for. Rates around US$8-10 per hr (minimum 2 hrs), US$40 per day. The following have been recommended: **Antonio Banderas** (Montalvo y Halflants, T03-274 2532). **Hotel Isla de Baños** (see above), 3½ hrs with a guide and jeep transport costs US$35 pp, English and German spoken. **José & Two Dogs** (Maldonado y Martínez, T03-274 0746), flexible hours.

Language schools

Spanish schools charge US$7-9 per hr, many also offer homestays. **Baños Spanish Center** (www.spanishcenter.banios.com). **Home Stay Baños** (T03-274 0453). **Mayra's** (www.mayraspanishschool.com). **Raíces** (www.spanishlessons.org).

Paragliding

See www.aeropasion.net; US$60 per day.

Puenting

Many operators offer this bungee-jumping-like activity from the bridges around Baños, US$10-20 per jump, heights and styles vary.

Tour operators

There are many tour agencies in town, some with several offices, as well as 'independent' guides who seek out tourists on the street (the latter are generally not recommended). Quality varies considerably; to obtain a qualified guide and avoid unscrupulous operators, it is best to seek advice from other travellers who have recently returned from a tour. We have received some critical reports of tours out of Baños, but there are also highly respected and qualified operators here. Most agencies and guides offer trips to the jungle (US$50-70 per day pp). There are also volcano-watching, trekking and horse tours, in addition to the day-trips and sports mentioned above. Several companies run tours aboard a *chiva* (open-sided bus). The following agencies and guides have received positive recommendations but the list is not exhaustive and there are certainly others.

Expediciones Amazónicas, *Oriente 11-68 y Halflants, T03-274 0506.*
Geotours, *Ambato y Halflants, next to Banco Pichincha, T03-274 1344, www.geotoursbanios.com.* Offer good rafting trips and paragliding for US$60.
Imagine Ecuador, *16 de Diciembre y Montalvo, T03-274 3472, www.imagineecuador.com.*
Natural Magic, *Martínez y 16 de Diciembre, T095-879 6043, www.naturalmagic.travel.*
Sachayacu Explorer, *Bolívar 229 y Urbina, in Píllaro, T03-287 5316 or T09-8740 3376, www.treasureoftheincas.com.* Trekking in the Llanganates, jungle tours in Huaorani territory, Yasuní and as far as Peru, English spoken.
Wonderful Ecuador, *Maldonado y Oriente, T03-274 1580, www.wonderfulecuador.org.* Good for whitewater rafting.

Whitewater rafting

Fatal accidents have occurred, but not with the agencies listed above. Rates US$30 for half-day, US$70 for full-day. The Chambo, Patate and Pastaza rivers are all polluted.

Transport

Bus City buses run from Alfaro y Martínez east to Agoyán and from Rocafuerte by the market, west to El Salado and the zoo. The long distance bus station is on the Ambato–Puyo road (Av Amazonas). It gets very busy on weekends and holidays, buy tickets in advance. To **Rio Verde** take any Puyo-bound bus, through buses don't go in the station, 20 mins, US$0.65. To **Quito**, US$4.25, 3 hrs, frequent service; going to Quito sit on the right for views of Cotopaxi; also shared taxis US$20, with **Autovip**, T02-600 2582 (Quito) or 09-9629 5406 and **Delux**, T09-3920 9827 or 09-8343 0275. To **Ambato**, 1 hr, US$1.10. To **Riobamba**, some buses take the direct Baños–Riobamba

> **Tip...**
> There have been reports of thefts targeting tourists on Quito-Baños buses, take extra care of your hand luggage.

road but most go via Mocha, 1½ hrs, US$2.50. To **Latacunga**, 2 hrs, US$2.25. To **Otavalo** and **Ibarra** direct, bypassing Quito, **Expreso Baños**, at 0400 and 1440, US$6, 5½ hrs. To **Guayaquil**, 1 bus per day and 1 overnight, US$10, 6-7 hrs; or change in

Riobamba. To **Puyo**, 1½ hrs, US$2.40. Sit on the right. You can cycle to Puyo and take the bus back (passport check on the way). To **Tena**, 3½ hrs, US$6. To **Misahuallí**, change at Tena. To **Macas**, 4½ hrs, US$9 (sit on the right).

Riobamba and around

colourful markets and mountains to climb

☆Guaranda and Riobamba are good bases for exploring the Sierra. Riobamba is the bigger of the two and is on the famous railway line from Quito to Guayaquil. Many indigenous people from the surrounding countryside can be seen in both cities on market days. Because of their central location Riobamba and the surrounding province are known as 'Corazón de la Patria' – the heartland of Ecuador – and the city boasts the nickname 'La Sultana de Los Andes' in honour of lofty Mount Chimborazo.

Riobamba *Colour map 1, B3.*

The capital of Chimborazo Province has broad streets and many ageing but impressive buildings. The main square is **Parque Maldonado** around which are the **Cathedral**, the **Municipality** and several colonial buildings with arcades. The **Cathedral** has a beautiful colonial stone façade and an incongruously modern interior. Four blocks northeast of the railway station is the **Parque 21 de Abril**, named after the Batalla de Tapi, 21 April 1822, the city's independence from Spain. The park, better known as **La Loma de Quito**, affords an unobstructed view of Riobamba and Chimborazo, Carihuairazo, Tungurahua, El Altar and occasionally Sangay. It also has a colourful tile tableau of the history of Ecuador; ask about safety before visiting. **Convento de la Concepción**① *Orozco y España, entrance at Argentinos y J Larrea, T03-296 5212, Tue-Sat, 0900-1230, 1500-1730, US$5,* has a religious art museum. **Museo de la Ciudad**① *Primera Constituyente y Espejo, at Parque Maldonado, T03-294 4420, Mon-Fri 0800-1230, 1430-1800, free,* in a beautifully restored colonial building, has an interesting historical photograph exhibit and temporary displays.

Riobamba is an important **market centre** where people from many communities congregate. Saturday is the main day when the city fills with colourfully dressed *indígenas* from all over

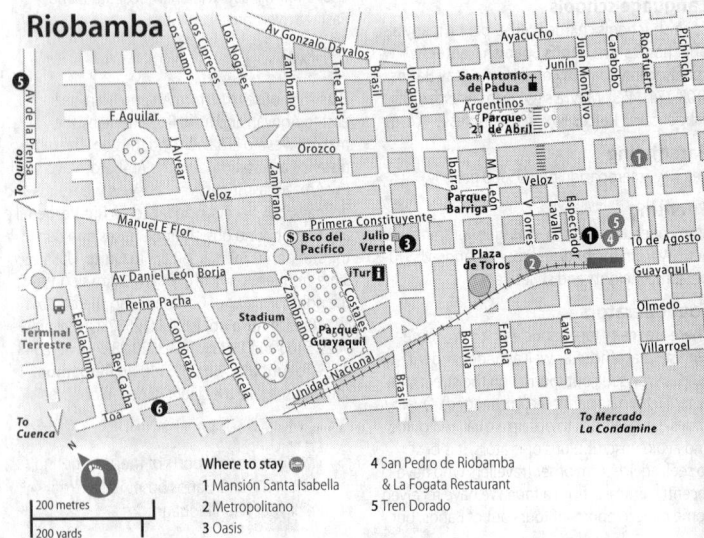

Riobamba

Where to stay 🛏
1 Mansión Santa Isabella
2 Metropolitano
3 Oasis
4 San Pedro de Riobamba
 & La Fogata Restaurant
5 Tren Dorado

200 metres
200 yards

Chimborazo, each wearing their distinctive costume; trading overflows the markets and buying and selling go on all over town. Wednesday is a smaller market day. The 'tourist' market is in the small **Plaza de la Concepción or Plaza Roja** ① *Orozco y Colón, Sat and Wed only, 0800-1500*, is a good place to buy local handicrafts and authentic *indígena* clothing. The main produce market is **San Alfonso**, Argentinos y 5 de Junio, and also sells clothing, ceramics, baskets and hats. Other markets in the colonial centre are **La Condamine** ① *Carabobo y Colombia, daily*, largest market on Fridays, **San Francisco** and **La Merced**, near the churches of the same name.

Guano ① *getting there: buses leave from the Mercado Dávalos, García Moreno y New York, every 15 mins, US$0.30, last bus back at 1900, taxi US$5*, is a carpet-weaving, sisal and leather working town, 8 km north of Riobamba. Many shops sell rugs and you can arrange to have these woven to your own design.

Guaranda *Colour map 1, B3.*

This quaint town, capital of Bolívar Province, proudly calls itself 'the Rome of Ecuador' because it is built on seven hills. There are fine views of the mountains all around and a colourful market. Locals traditionally take an evening stroll in the palm-fringed main plaza, **Parque Libertador Simón Bolívar**, around which are the Municipal buildings and a large stone **Cathedral**. Towering over the city, on one of the hills, is an impressive statue of **El Indio Guaranga**; museum (free) and art gallery. There is also a small local museum at the **Casa de la Cultura** ① *Sucre entre Manuela Cañizares y Selva Alegre.*

> **Tip...**
> Although not on the tourist trail, there are many sights worth visiting in the province, for which Guaranda is the ideal base. Of particular interest is the highland town of Salinas, with its community development projects (accommodations and tours available, see Where to stay, below), as well as the *subtrópico* region, the lowlands stretching west towards the coast.

Market days are Friday (till 1200) and Saturday (larger), when many indigenous people in typical dress trade at the market complex at the east end of Calle Azuay, by Plaza 15 de Mayo (9 de Abril y Maldonado), and at Plaza Roja (Avenida Gen Enríquez). Carnival in Guaranda is among the best known in the country. **Tourist office:** Oficina Municipal de Turismo ① *García Moreno entre 7 de Mayo y Convención de 1884, T03-298 0321, www.guaranda.gob.ec (in Spanish), Mon-Fri 0800-1200, 1400-1800.* Provides information in Spanish and maps.

Restaurants ⑦
1 Café París
2 Helados de Paila
3 Jamones La Andaluza & Naranjo's
5 Mónaco Pizzería
6 Zen Wei

Reserva Faunística Chimborazo

Information from Ministerio del Ambiente, Avenida 9 de Octubre y Duchicela, Quinta Macají, Riobamba, T03-261 0029, ext110, Mon-Fri 0800-1300, 1400-1700. Ranger station T03-302 7358, daily 0800-1700.

The most outstanding features of this reserve, created to protect the camelids (vicuñas, alpacas and llamas) which were re-introduced here, are the beautiful snow-capped volcanos of **Chimborazo** and its neighbour **Carihuayrazo**. Chimborazo, inactive, is the highest peak in Ecuador (6310 m), while Carihuayrazo, 5020 m, is dwarfed by its neighbour. Day visitors can enjoy lovely views, a glimpse of the handsome vicuñas and the rarefied air above 4800 m. There are great opportunities for trekking on the eastern slopes, accessed from **Urbina**, west of the Ambato–Riobamba road, and of course climbing Ecuador's highest peak. Horse riding and trekking tours are offered along the Mocha Valley between the two peaks and downhill cycling from Chimborazo is popular.

To the west of the reserve runs the Vía del Arenal which joins San Juan, along the Riobamba–Guaranda road, with Cruce del Arenal on the Ambato–Guaranda road. A turn-off from this road leads to the main park entrance and beyond to the **Refugio Hermanos Carrel**, a shelter at 4800 m, from where it is a 45-minute walk to Refugio **Whymper** at 5000 m. The Carrel shelter has 32 dorm beds, shared bath, no shower, US$30 pp including dinner and breakfast, lunch available (US$6), no cooking facilities. The Whymper refuge normally opens only 0900-1600; book in advance if you want to spend the night, prices as above for a minimum of four people, with meals in the Carrel refuge. Contact T09-7908 4401, refugioschimborazo@gmail.com.

The access from Riobamba (51 km, paved to the park entrance) is very beautiful. Along the Vía del Arenal past San Juan are a couple of small indigenous communities which grow a few crops and raise llamas and alpacas. They offer lodging and *guías nativos*, the area is good for acclimatization The *arenal* is a large sandy plateau at about 4400 m, to the west of Chimborazo, just below the main park entrance. It can be a harsh, windy place, but it is also very beautiful; take the time to admire the tiny flowers which grow here. This is the best place to see vicuñas, which hang around either in family groups, one male and its harem, or lone males which have been expelled from the group.

Climbing Chimborazo At 6310 m, this is a difficult climb owing to the altitude. Climbers must go with a certified guide working for an operator who has a special permit (*patente*). Rope, ice-axe, helmet and crampons must be used. It is essential to have at least one week's acclimatization above 3500 m. Chimborazo can be climbed all year round but the weather is unpredictable. It is best to avoid late July and August, when it can be very windy and the risk of rock fall increases. Deglaciation is making the climb more difficult and ice pinnacles, *penitentes*, sometimes prevent climbers reaching the main, Whymper summit.

Tip...
Climbers arriving at the Chimborazo park entrance without a guide and tour operator or with services not authorized by the ministry are turned back at the gate; exceptions are made for members of alpine clubs. Apply for an entry permit at the Ministerio del Ambiente in Riobamba.

The Devil's Nose Train
This spectacular ride is popular with Ecuadorean and foreign tourists alike. Tourist trains run between Alausí and Sibambe, the most scenic part of the trip including the **Devil's Nose**, as well as Riobamba-Alausí and Riobamba-Colta. For details see What to do, page 1103.

Alausí *Colour map 1, B3.*
This picturesque town perched on a hillside is where many passengers join the train for the amazing descent over *La Nariz de Diablo* to Sibambe. There is good walking, a Sunday market and a **Fiesta de San Pedro** on 29 June.

Parque Nacional Sangay
Riobamba provides access to the central highland region of **Sangay National Park** ① *information from Ministerio del Ambiente, see Reserva Chimborazo, above*, a beautiful wilderness area with excellent opportunities for trekking and climbing. A spectacular road, good for downhill biking, runs from Riobamba to Macas in the Oriente, cutting through the park. Near Cebadas (with a good cheese factory) a branch road joins from **Guamote**, a quiet, mainly indigenous town on the Pan-American highway, which comes to life during its colourful Thursday market. At **Atillo**, south of Cebadas, an area of lovely *páramo* dotted with lakes, there is lodging (US$7 per person) and restaurant at **Cabaña Saskines** (T03-301 4383, atillosaskines@hotmail.com). **Sangay** (5230 m) is an active volcano, access to the mountain takes at least three days and is only for those who can endure long, hard days of walking and severe weather. Climbing Sangay can be dangerous even when volcanic activity seems low and a helmet to protect against falling stones is vital, November to January is a good time to climb it. Agencies in Quito and Riobamba offer tours or you can

organize an expedition independently. A guide is essential; porters can be hired in the access towns of **Alao** and **Guargualá**. The latter has a **community tourism project** ① T03-302 6688, T09-9121 3205, accommodation in Guargualá Chico US$15 pp, US$23.50 pp with dinner and breakfast (reserve in advance), kitchen facilities US$5 per group. Guías nativos, US$40 per day plus US$110 for ascent; porters and horses US$20 per day. Also in Sangay National Park is the beautiful **El Altar** volcano (5315 m), whose crater is surrounded by nine summits. The most popular climbing and trekking routes begin beyond Candelaria at **Hacienda Releche** (see Hostal Capac Urcu, Where to stay).

Listings Riobamba and around *map page 1096.*

Tourist information

iTur
Av Daniel León Borja y Brasil, Riobamba, T03-296 3159. Mon-Fri 0830-1230, 1430-1800.
Municipal information office, English spoken.

Where to stay

Riobamba

$$$$-$$$ Abraspungo
Km 3 on the road to Guano, T03-236 4275, www.haciendaabraspungo.com.
Nice country hotel, comfortable rooms, includes buffet breakfast, excellent restaurant, parking, attentive service. Recommended.

$$$$-$$$ La Andaluza
16 km north of Riobamba along the Panamericana, T03-294 0002, www.hosteriaandaluza.com.
An old hacienda, rooms with heaters and roaring fireplaces, includes buffet breakfast, good restaurant, lovely views, good walking.

$$$ Mansión Santa Isabella
Veloz 28-48 y Carabobo, T03-296 2947, www.mansionsantaisabella.com.
Lovely restored house with pleasant patio, comfortable rooms most with bathtub, duvets, includes buffet breakfast, restaurant serves set lunches and à la carte, bar in stone basement, parking, attentive service, British/Ecuadorean-run. Recommended.

$$$ San Pedro de Riobamba
Daniel L Borja 29-50 y Montalvo, opposite the train station, T03-294 0586.
Elegant hotel in a beautifully restored house in the centre of town, ample comfortable rooms, bathtubs, cafeteria, parking, covered patio, reservations required. Recommended.

$$ Rincón Alemán
Remigio Romero y Alfredo Pareja, Ciudadela Arupos del Norte, T03-260 3540, www.rinconalemanla.com.
Family-run hotel in a quiet residential area north of the centre, laundry and cooking facilities, parking, fireplace, sauna, gym, garden, terrace, good views, German spoken.

$$ Tren Dorado
Carabobo 22-35 y 10 de Agosto, near station, T03-296 4890, www.hoteltrendorado.com.
Modern hotel with nice large rooms, buffet breakfast available (starting 0730, open to non-guests), restaurant, reliable hot water, good value. Recommended.

$$-$ Oasis
Veloz 15-32 y Almagro, T03-296 1210, www.oasishostelriobamba.com.
Small, quiet, family-run hostel, laundry facilities, some rooms with kitchen and fridge, shared kitchen for the others, parking, nice garden, Wi-Fi US$1 per day, popular with backpackers. Recommended.

$ Metropolitano
Daniel L Borja y Lavalle, near the train station, T03-296 1714.
One of the oldest hotels in Riobamba, built in 1912 and nicely restored. Ample rooms, convenient location, no breakfast.

Guaranda

$$$ La Colina
Av Guayaquil 117, on the road to Ambato, T03-298 0666, www.complejolacolina.com.
Nicely situated on a quiet hillside overlooking the city. Bright spacious rooms, nice views, gardens, parking, tours available.

$$-$ Bolívar
Sucre 704 y Rocafuerte, T03-298 0547, http://hotelbolivar.wordpress.com.
Pleasant hotel with courtyard, small modern rooms, best quality in the centre of town.

Restaurant next door open Mon-Fri for economical breakfasts and lunches.

$ El Marquez
10 de Agosto y Eloy Alfaro, T03-298 1053.
Pleasant hotel with family atmosphere, newer rooms with private bath are clean and modern, older ones with shared bath are cheaper, parking.

$ La Casa de las Flores
Pichincha 402 y Rocafuerte, T03-298 5795.
Renovated colonial house with covered courtyard and flowers, private bath, hot water, simple economical rooms.

$ Oasis
Gen Enriquez y Garcia Moreno, T03-298 3762.
Modern multi-storey building with large, bright and clean rooms.

Salinas

$$ Hotel Refugio Salinas
45 min from Guaranda, T03-221 0044, www.salinerito.com.
Pleasant community-run hotel, economical meals on request, private or shared bath, dining/sitting area with fireplace, visits to community projects, walking and horse riding tours, packages available, advance booking advised.

$$-$ La Minga
By the main plaza, T09-9218 8880, www.laminga.ec.
Simple rooms with bath and dorms, meals on request, offer full board packages including tour.

Reserva Faunística Chimborazo
The following are all good for acclimatization; those in Urbina can be reached by *autoferro* from either Riobamba or Ambato.

$$$ Chimborazo Lodge
Operated by Expediciones Andinas, see tour operators below.
Comfortable cabins in a beautiful location on the south flank of Chimborazo, includes dinner and breakfast, advance booking required.

$ Casa Cóndor
In Pulinguí San Pablo, Vía del Arenal, T03-301 3124, T09-8650 8152.
Basic community-run hotel, dinner and breakfast available, use of cooking facilities extra, tours in the area.

$ Posada de la Estación
Opposite Urbina train station, T09-9969 4867.

Comfortable rooms with heaters, shared bath, meals available or cooking facilities (US$5 per group), wood stoves, magnificent views, trips and equipment arranged, tagua workshop, helpful. Also run **$ Urcu Huasi**, cabins at 4150 m, 10 km (2½ hrs walking) from Urbina, in an area being reforested with polylepis trees.

Alausí

$$$ El Molino
Sucre N141 y Bolívar, T03-293 1659, http://hotelelmolino.com.ec/.
Comfortable rooms in a restored historical home, one block from station, pleasant common areas, includes buffet breakfast.

$$$ La Quinta
Eloy Alfaro 121 y M Muñoz, T03-293 0247, www.hosteria-la-quinta.com.
Well-restored old house along the rail line to Riobamba. Pleasant atmosphere, restaurant, gardens, excellent views, not always open, reserve ahead.

$$$ Posada de las Nubes
On the north side of the Río Chanchán, 7 or 11 km from Alausí depending on the route, best with 4WD, pick-up from Alausí US$7, T03-302 9362 or T09-9315 0847, www.posadadelasnubes.com.
Rustic hacienda house in cloudforest at 2600 m. Rooms are simple to basic for the price, some with bath, includes dinner and breakfast, hiking and horse riding, advance booking required.

$$ Gampala
5 de Junio 122 y Loza, T03-293 0138, www.hotelgampala.com.
Nicely refurbished modern rooms and 1 suite with jacuzzi (**$$$**), restaurant and bar with pool table.

$$ La Posada del Tren
5 de Junio y Orozco, T03-293 1293.
Nice, modern, with parking.

$$-$ San Pedro
5 de Junio y 9 de Octubre, T03-293 0196, hostalsanpedro@hotmail.com.
Simple comfortable rooms, a few cheaper rooms in older section, restaurant downstairs, parking, nice owner.

Parque Nacional Sangay

$ Hostal Capac Urcu
At Hacienda Releche, near the village of Candelaria, T03-301 4067.

Basic rooms in small working hacienda. Use of kitchen (US$10 per group) or meals prepared on request, rents horses for the trek to Collanes, US$40 per horse, plus US$40 per muleteer, round trip. Also runs the *refugio* at Collanes (same price), by the crater of El Altar: thatched-roof rustic shelters with solar hot water. The *refugio* is cold, take a warm sleeping bag. Rubber boots are indispensable for the muddy trail.

Guamote

$$ Inti Sisa
Vargas Torres y García Moreno, T03-291 6529, www.intisisa.org.
Basic but pleasant guesthouse, part of a community development project, most rooms with bath, US$23.75 pp in dorm, includes breakfast, other meals available, dining room and communal area with fireplace, horse riding and cultural tours to highland villages, reservations necessary.

Restaurants

Riobamba
Many places close after 2100 and on Sun.

$$ Mónaco Pizzería
Av de la Prensa y Francisco Aguilar.
Mon-Fri 1500-2200, Sat-Sun 1200-2200.
Delicious pizza and pasta, nice salads, good food, service and value. Recommended.

$ La Fogata
Daniel L Borja y Carabobo, opposite the train station. Wed-Mon 0730-2115, Tue 0730-1500.
Simple but good local food, economical set meals and breakfast.

$ Naranjo's
Daniel L Borja 36-20 y Uruguay. Tue-Sun 1200-1500.
Excellent set lunch, friendly service, popular.

$ Zen Wei
Princesa Toa 43-29 y Calicuchima.
Mon-Sat 1200-1500.
Oriental restaurant serving economical vegetarian and vegan set meals.

Cafés and bakeries

Café París
Daniel L Borja y Juan Montalvo.
Mon-Sat 0800-2200.
Small popular meeting place serving excellent coffees and snacks.

Helados de Paila
Espejo y 10 de Agosto. Daily 0900-1900.
Excellent home-made ice cream, coffee, sweets, popular.

Jamones La Andaluza
Daniel L Borja y Uruguay. Daily 0830-2300.
Indoor and outdoor seating, good set lunches, coffee, sandwiches, salads, variety of cold-cuts and cheeses, tapas.

La Abuela Rosa
Brasil y Esmeraldas. Mon-Sat 1600-2100.
Cafetería in grandmother's house serving typical Ecuadorean snacks. Nice atmosphere and good service.

Guaranda
Most places close on Sun.

$$$-$$ Pizza Buon Giorno
Sucre at Parque Bolívar. Tue-Sun 1100-2200.
Pizza and salads.

$$ La Bohemia
Convención de 1884 y 10 de Agosto.
Mon-Sat 0800-2100.
Very good economical set meals and pricier international dishes à la carte, nice decor and ambiance, very popular. Recommended.

$$ La Estancia
García Moreno y Sucre. Mon 1200-1500,
Tue-Sat 1200-2100.
Excellent buffet lunch for quality, variety and value, à la carte in the evening, nicely decorated, pleasant atmosphere, popular.

$$-$ Chifa Gran Cangrejo Rojo
10 de Agosto y Convención de 1884.
Open 1100-2200.
Good Chinese food.

Cafés

Cafetería 7 Santos
Convención de 1884 y Olmedo.
Mon-Sat 1000-2200.
Pleasant café and bar with open courtyard. Good coffee and snacks, fireplace, live music Fri and Sat, popular.

Salinerito
Plaza Roja. Daily 0800-1300, 1430-1900.
Salinas cheese shop also serves coffee, sandwiches and pizza.

Alausí

$$ Bukardia
Guatemala 107. Open 1300-2200, closed Wed.
Meat specialities, snacks and drinks.

$$ El Mesón del Tren
Ricaurte y Eloy Alfaro. Tue-Sun 0700-0930, 1200-1430.
Good restaurant, popular with tour groups, breakfast, set lunch and à la carte.

$ Flamingo
Antonio Mora y 9 de Octubre. Open 0700-2000, closed Sat.
Good economical set meals. Also run **Ventura Hostal ($$-$)**, simple.

Bars and clubs

Riobamba

La Rayuela
Daniel L Borja 36-30 y Uruguay. Mon-Sat 1200-2200, Sun 1200-1600.
Trendy bar/restaurant, sometimes live music on Fri, sandwiches, coffee, salads, pasta.

San Valentín
Daniel L Borja y Vargas Torres. Mon-Thu 1800-2400, Fri-Sat 1800-0200.
Very popular bar, good pizzas and Mexican dishes.

Entertainment

Riobamba

Casa de la Cultura, *10 de Agosto y Rocafuerte*, T03-296 0219. Cultural events, cinema on Tue.
Super Cines, at El Paseo Shopping, Vía a Guano. 12 screens, some with 3-D.

Festivals

Riobamba

Dec-Jan Fiesta del Niño Rey de Reyes, street parades, music and dancing, starts in Dec and culminates on 6 Jan.
Apr Independence celebrations around 21 Apr lasting several days, hotel prices rise.
29 Jun Fiestas Patronales in honour of San Pedro.
11 Nov Festival to celebrate the 1st attempt at independence from Spain.

Shopping

Riobamba

Camping gear
Some of the tour operators listed below hire camping and climbing gear; also **Veloz Coronado** (Chile 33-21 y Francia, T03-296 0916, after 1900). **Marathon Explorer** (Multiplaza mall, Av Lizarzaburu near the airport). High-end outdoor equipment and clothing. **Protección Industrial** (Rocafuerte 24-51 y Orozco, T03-296 3017). Outdoor equipment, rope, fishing supplies, rain ponchos.

Handicrafts
Crafts sold at Plaza Roja on Wed and Sat. **Almacén Cacha** (Colón y Orozco, next to the Plaza Roja). A cooperative of indigenous people from the Cacha area, sells woven bags, wool sweaters, and other crafts, good value (closed Sun-Mon).

What to do

Riobamba

Mountain biking
Guided tours with support vehicle average US$50-60 pp per day.
Julio Verne, *see Tour operators*. Very good tours, equipment and routes.
Pro Bici, *Primera Constituyente 23-51 y Larrea*, T03-295 1759, www.probici.com. Tours and rentals.

Tour operators
Most companies offer climbing trips (US$240 pp for 2 days to Chimborazo or Carihuayrazo), trekking (US$100 pp per day) and day-hikes (US$50-60 pp).
Andes Trek, *Esmeraldas 21-45 y Espejo*, T03-2951275, www.goandestrek.com. Climbing and trekking, transport, equipment rental. Also runs an office and hostel in Quito.
Expediciones Andinas, *Vía a Guano, Km 3, across from Hotel Abraspungo*, T03-236 4278, www.expediciones-andinas.com. Climbing expeditions run by Marco Cruz, a guide certified by the **German Alpine Club**, operate **Chimborazo** Lodge (see Where to stay, above). Recommended.
Incañán, *Brasil 20-28 y Luis A Falconí*, T03-294 0508, http://incanian2011.blogspot.com. Trekking, cycling and cultural tours.
Julio Verne, *Brasil 22-40 between Daniel L Borja and Primera Constituyente*, T03-296 3436, www.julioverne-travel.com. Climbing, trekking, cycling,

jungle and Galápagos trips, transport, equipment rental, English spoken, Ecuadorean/Dutch-run, very conscientious and reliable. Uses official guides. Highly recommended.

The Devil's Nose Train

The Devil's Nose Train departs from Alausí, Tue-Sun at 0800 and 1100, 2½ hrs return, US$32, includes a snack and folklore dance. *Autoferro* from Riobamba to Urbina (Sat-Sun at 0800, US$27), dress warmly. Purchase tickets well in advance for weekends and holidays at any train station (Riobamba, T03-296 1038, Mon-Wed 0800-1630, Thu-Fri 0700-1630, Sat-Sun 0700-1300; Alausí, T03-293 0126, Tue-Sun 0700-1530), through the call centre (T1800-873637) or by email (info@trenecuador. com, then you have to make a bank deposit). Procedures change frequently, so enquire locally and check www.trenecuador.com.

Transport

Riobamba

Bus **Terminal Terrestre** on Epiclachima y Av Daniel L Borja for all long-distance buses including to Baños and destinations in Oriente. **Terminal Oriental**, Espejo y Cordovez, only for local services to Candelaria and Penipe. **Terminal Intercantonal**, Av Canónigo Ramos about 2.5 km northwest of the Terminal Terrestre, for Guamote, San Juan and Cajabamba (Colta). Taxi between terminals US$1.50-2. To **Quito**, US$4.75, 4 hrs, about every 30 mins; also shared taxis with: **Montecarlo Trans Vip**, T03-296 8758 or T09-8411 4114, 7 daily, US$18 (US$5 extra for large luggage) and **Delux**, T09-3920 9827 or T09-8343 0275, every 2 hrs, US$20. To **Guaranda**, US$2.50, 2 hrs (sit on the right). To **Ambato**, US$1.50, 1 hr. To **Alausí**, see below. To **Cuenca**, 8 a day via Alausí, 5½ hrs, US$8. To **Guayaquil** via Pallatanga, frequent service, US$7, 5 hrs, spectacular for the first 2 hrs. To **Baños**, 2 hrs, US$2. To **Puyo** US$4, 4 hrs. To **Macas** via Parque Nacional Sangay, 8 daily, 4 hrs, US$6.25 (sit on the left).

Guaranda

Bus Terminal at Eliza Mariño Carvajal, on road to Riobamba and Babahoyo; if you are staying in town get off closer to the centre. Many daily buses to: **Ambato**, US$2.50, 2 hrs. **Riobamba**, see above. **Babahoyo**, US$3.75, 3 hrs, beautiful ride. **Guayaquil**, US$5, 5 hrs. **Quito**, US$6.25, 5 hrs.

Reserva Faunística Chimborazo

There are no buses to the shelters. Take a tour or arrange transport with a Riobamba tour operator (US$35 one way, US$45 return with wait) or take a Riobamba–Guaranda bus, alight at the turn-off for the refuges and walk the remaining steep 8 km (5 km taking short cuts) to the 1st shelter. For the eastern slopes, take a trekking tour, arrange transport from an agency or take a bus between Riobamba and Ambato, get off at the turn-off for **Posada La Estación** and Urbina and walk from there.

Alausí

Bus To **Riobamba**, 1½ hrs, US$2.50, 84 km. To **Quito**, from 0600, 8 a day, 6 hrs, US$7.50, often have to change in Riobamba. To **Cuenca**, 4 hrs, US$6.25. To **Ambato** hourly, 3 hrs, US$3.75. To **Guayaquil**, 4 a day, 4 hrs, US$6.25. **Coop Patria**. Colombia y Orozco, 3 blocks up from the main street; **Trans Alausí**, 5 de Junio y Loza. Many through buses don't go into town, but have to be caught on the highway, taxi from town US$1.

Parque Nacional Sangay

To **Atillo** from Parque La Dolorosa, Puruhá y Primera Constituyente, 15 daily 0400-1845, US$2.50, 2 hrs. Also Riobamba–**Macas** service goes through Atillo, see above. To **Alao**, from Parque La Dolorosa, hourly 0700-2300, US$1.50, 1½ hrs. To **Guarguallá Grande** from Parque La Dolorosa daily at 1345 (return to Riobamba at 0545), US$2 (Grande), 2 hrs; also a milk truck from La Dolorosa to Guargualla at 0530, US$2. To **Candelaria**, from Terminal Oriental, daily 0600, 0800, 1100, 1500 and 1700, US$1.25, 1½ hrs. Alternatively, take a bus from the same terminal to Penipe, every 30 mins, US$0.40, 40 mins, and hire a pickup truck from there to Candelaria, US$15, 40 mins.

Cuenca
& around

★Founded in 1557 on the site of the Inca settlement of Tomebamba, much of Cuenca's colonial air has been preserved, with many of its old buildings renovated. Its cobblestone streets, flowering plazas and pastel-coloured buildings with old wooden doors and ironwork balconies make it a pleasure to explore. The climate is spring-like, but the nights are chilly. In 1999 Cuenca was designated a UNESCO World Heritage Site. It is home to the largest expat retiree community in Ecuador. The surrounding area is known for its crafts.

Cuenca *Colour map 1, C3.*

Inca remains, colonial buildings, museums

Sights

On the main plaza, **Parque Abdón Calderón**, are the Old Cathedral, **El Sagrario** ① *Mon-Fri 0900-1730, Sat-Sun 0900-1300, US$2*, begun in 1557, and the immense 'New' **Catedral de la Inmaculada**, started in 1885. The latter contains a famous crowned image of the Virgin, a beautiful altar and an exceptional play of light and shade through modern stained glass. Other churches which deserve a visit are **San Blas**, **San Francisco** and **Santo Domingo**. Many churches are open at irregular hours only and for services. The church of **El Carmen de la Asunción**, close to the southwest corner of La Inmaculada, has a flower market in the tiny **Plazoleta El Carmen** in front. There is a colourful daily market in **Plaza Rotary** where pottery, clothes, guinea pigs and local produce, especially baskets, are sold. Thursday is the busiest.

Museo del Monasterio de las Conceptas ① *Hermano Miguel 6-33 entre Pdte Córdova y Juan Jaramillo, T07-283 0625, Mon-Fri 0900-1830, Sat and holidays 1000-1300, US$3*, in a cloistered convent founded in 1599, houses a well displayed collection of religious and folk art, in addition to an extensive collection of lithographs by Guayasamín.

Pumapungo ① *C Larga y Huayna Capac, T07-283 1521, Mon-Fri 0830-1730, Sat 1000-1400*, is a museum complex on the edge of the colonial city, at the actual site of Tomebamba excavations. Part of the area explored is seen at **Parque Arqueológico Pumapungo**. The **Sala Arqueológica** section contains all the Cañari and Inca remains and artifacts found at this site. Other halls in the premises house the **Sala Etnográfica**, with information on different Ecuadorean cultures, including a special collection of *tsantsas* (shrunken heads from Oriente), the **Sala de Arte Religioso**, the **Sala Numismática** and temporary exhibits. There are also book and music libraries, free cultural videos and music events. Three blocks west of Pumapungo, **Museo Manuel Agustín Landívar** ① *C Larga 2-23 y Manuel Vega, T07-282 1177, Mon-Fri 0800-1300, 1500-1800, Sat 0900-1300, free*, is at the site of the small Todos los Santos ruins, with Cañari, Inca and colonial remains; ceramics and artifacts found at the site are also displayed.

Museo de las Culturas Aborígenes ① *C Larga 5-24 y Hermano Miguel, T07-283 9181, Mon-Fri 0900-1800, Sat 0900-1200, US$4, craft shop*, the private collection of Dr J Cordero Íñiguez, has an impressive selection of pre-Columbian archaeology. **Museo Remigio Crespo Toral** ① *C Larga 7-25 y Borrero, Mon-Fri 1000-1730, Sat 1000-1600, Sun 1000-1300, free*, in a beautifully refurbished colonial house, has important history, archaeology and art collections. **Museo del Sombrero** ① *C Larga 10-*

Best for
Arts & crafts ■ Colonial architecture ■ Lakes

Essential Cuenca

Finding your feet

The **Terminal Terrestre** is on Avenida España, 15 minutes' ride northeast of the centre, T07-284 2633. The **airport** is five minutes beyond the Terminal Terrestre, T07-286 7120, www.aeropuerto cuenca.ec. Both can be reached by city bus, but best take a taxi at all hours (US$1.50-2.50 to the centre). The **Terminal Sur** for regional buses within the province is by the Feria Libre El Arenal on Avenida Las Américas. Many city buses pass here.

The city is bounded by the Río Machángara to the north and the Ríos Yanuncay and Tarqui to the south. The Río Tomebamba separates the colonial heart from the newer districts to the south. Avenida Las Américas is a ring road around the north and west of the city and the *autopista*, a multi-lane highway bypasses the city to the south.

Getting around

The narrow streets of colonial Cuenca are clogged with cars on weekdays, detracting from the area's considerable charm. It is hoped that a new tram system projected for completion in 2017 (but delayed) will help alleviate the congestion. See Transport, page 1112, for further details.

Safety

Though safer than Quito or Guayaquil, routine precautions are advised. Outside the busy nightlife area around Calle Larga, the city centre is deserted and unsafe after 2300, taking a taxi is recommended. The river banks are OK while university students are around, until about 2200. The Cruz del Vado area (south end of Juan Montalvo), the Terminal Terrestre and all market areas are not safe after dark.

---

41 y Gral Torres, T07-283 1569, Mon-Fri 0900-1800, Sat 0900-1500, Sun 0930-1330, shop with all the old factory machines for hat finishing.

On Plaza San Sebastián is **Museo Municipal de Arte Moderno** ① *Sucre 1527 y Talbot, T07-283 1027, Mon-Fri 0830-1300, 1500-1830, Sat-Sun 0900-1300, free*, has a permanent contemporary art collection and art library. It holds a biennial international painting competition and other cultural activities. Across the river from the Museo Pumapungo, the **Museo de Artes de Fuego** ① *Las Herrerías y 10 de Agosto, T07-288 3061, Mon-Fri 0900-1300, 1500-1800, free except for special events*, has a display of wrought iron work and pottery. It is housed in the beautifully restored Casa de Chaguarchimbana. At the University of Cuenca is an **Orquideario** ① *Av Víctor Manuel Albornoz, Quinta de Balzay, Mon-Fri, 0800-1200, 1400-1800*. South of city, accessed via Avenida Fray Vicente Solano, beyond the football stadium, is **Turi church**, orphanage and mirador; a tiled panorama explains the magnificent views.

Listings Cuenca *map page 1106.*

Tourist information

To locate an establishment see www.ubicacuenca.com.

Cámara de Turismo
Terminal Terrestre, T07-284 5657.
Mon-Sat 0800-1300, 1500-1800.
Information about the city, including city and long-distance bus routes; also at the airport.

Fundación Municipal Turismo
Bolívar 8-44 y Benigno Malo, on Parque Calderón next to the Municipio, T07-284 0383, www.
cuencaecuador.com.ec. Mon-Fri, 0800-2000,
Sat 0830-1730, Sun 0900-1600.
Helpful. Free walking tours Tue-Sat 1000-1200, see Facebook: VisitCuencaEc to sign up.

Where to stay

$$$$ Carvallo
Gran Colombia 9-52, entre Padre Aguirre y Benigno Malo, T07-283 2063, www.hotel carvallo.com.ec.
Combination of an elegant colonial-style hotel and art/antique gallery. Very comfortable rooms all have bath tubs, buffet breakfast, cafeteria.

$$$$ Mansión Alcázar
Bolívar 12-55 y Tarqui, T07-282 3918,
www.mansionalcazar.com.
Beautifully restored house, a mansion indeed, central, very nice rooms, restaurant serves gourmet international food, lovely gardens, quiet relaxed atmosphere.

$$$$ Oro Verde

Av Ordóñez Lazo, northwest of the centre towards
Cajas, T07-409 0000, www.oroverdehotels.com.
Elegant hotel, buffet breakfast, excellent
international restaurant (buffet Sun lunch),
small pool, parking.

$$$$ Santa Lucía

Borrero 8-44 y Sucre, T07-282 8000,
www.santaluciahotel.com.
A stylish renovated colonial house, very nice
comfortable rooms, excellent Italian restaurant,
safe deposit box.

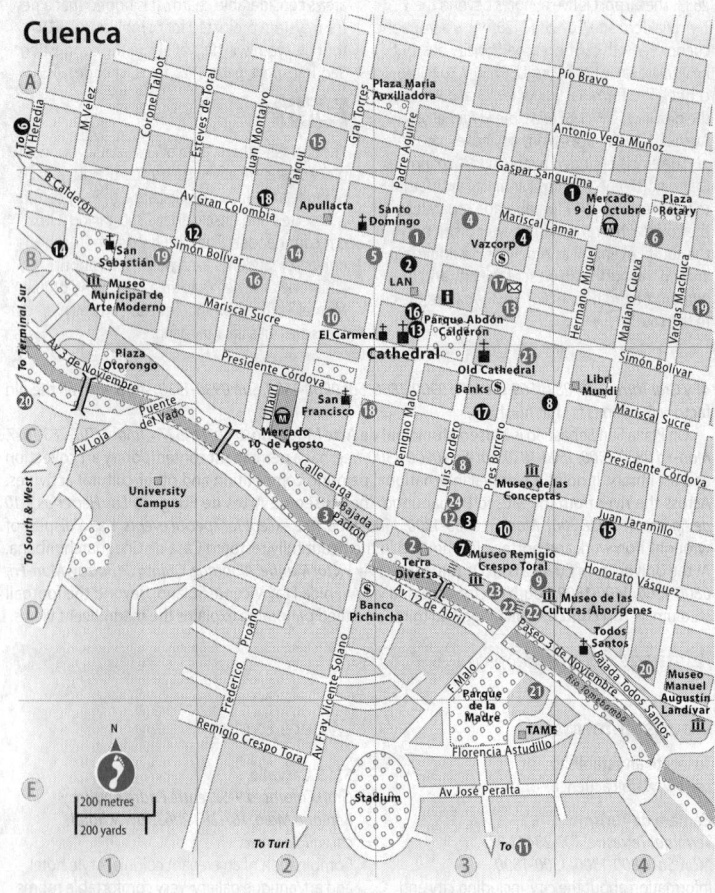

Cuenca

Where to stay

1 Carvallo *B3*
2 Casa del Barranco *D3*
3 Casa del Río *C2*
4 Casa Ordóñez *B3*
5 Colonial *B3*
6 El Cafecito *B4*
8 El Príncipe *C3*
9 Hogar Cuencano *D3*
10 Inca Real *B2*
11 La Casona *E3*
12 La Cigale *C3*
13 La Orquídea *B3*
14 La Posada Cuencana *B2*
15 Macondo *A2*
16 Mansión Alcázar *B2*
17 Mercure El Dorado *B3*
18 Milán *C2*
19 Posada del Angel &
    Mangiare Restaurant *B1*
20 Posada Todos Santos *D4*
21 Santa Lucía *C3*
22 Turista del Mundo *D3*
23 Victoria *D3*
24 Yakumama *C3*

Restaurants

1 Balcón Quiteño *B4*
2 Café Eucalyptus &
   Grecia *B3*
3 Cesare's *C3*
4 El Carbón *B3*
5 El Maíz *E5*
6 Good Affinity *A1*
7 Goza *D3*

\$\$\$ Inca Real
Gral Torres 8-40 entre Sucre y Bolívar,
T07-282 3636, www.hotelincareal.com.ec.
Refurbished colonial house with comfortable
rooms around patios, breakfast available, good
Spanish restaurant, parking.

\$\$\$ La Casona
Miguel Cordero 2-124 y Alfonso Cordero,
near the stadium, T07-410 3501, www.
lacasonahotel.com.ec.
Attractive refurbished family home in a
residential area, comfortable carpeted rooms,
buffet breakfast, restaurant, parking.

\$\$\$ Mercure El Dorado
Gran Colombia 787 y Luis Cordero, T07-283 1390,
www.eldoradohotel.com.ec.
Elegant modern hotel, rooms have safe and minibar, buffet breakfast, cafeteria, spa, gym, business
centre, parking.

\$\$\$ Posada del Angel
Bolívar 14-11 y Estévez de Toral, T07-284 0695,
www.hostalposadadelangel.com.
A nicely restored colonial house, comfortable
rooms, good Italian restaurant, parking, patio
with plants, some noise from restaurant, English
spoken, helpful staff. Recommended.

\$\$\$ Victoria
C Larga 6-93 y Borrero, T07-283 1120,
www.hotelvictoriaecuador.com.
Elegant refurbished hotel overlooking the river,
comfortable modern rooms, excellent expensive
restaurant, nice views.

\$\$\$-\$\$ Casa Ordóñez
Lamar 8-59 y Benigno Malo, T07-282 3297,
www.casa-ordonez.com.
Well-renovated colonial house with wood
floors and 3 inner patios, attractively decorated
rooms and common areas, down comforters,
no smoking.

\$\$ Casa del Barranco
Calle Larga 8-41 y Luis Cordero, T07-283 9763,
www.casadelbarranco.com.
Tastefully restored colonial house, some rooms
with lovely views over the river, cafeteria
overlooking the river.

\$\$ Casa del Río
Bajada del Padrón 4-07 y C Larga, T07-282 9659,
hostalcasadelrio@hotmail.com.
Pleasant quiet *hostal* on El Barranco overlooking
the river, private or shared bath, breakfast
available, nice views, attentive service.

\$\$ Colonial
Gran Colombia 10-13 y Padre Aguirre,
T07-284 1644.
Refurbished colonial house with beautiful patio,
carpeted rooms.

$$ El Príncipe
J Jaramillo 7-82 y Luis Cordero, T07-284 7287, www.hotelprincipe.com.ec.
A refurbished 3-storey colonial house, comfortable rooms around a nice patio with plants, restaurant, parking.

$$ La Orquídea
Borrero 9-31 y Bolívar, T07-282 4511, www.laorquidea.com.ec.
Refurbished colonial house, bright rooms, fridge, low season and long term discounts, good value.

$$ La Posada Cuencana
Tarqui 9-46 y Bolívar, T07-282 6831, www.laposadacuencana.com.ec.
Small family-run hotel with beautiful colonial-style rooms.

$$ Macondo
Tarqui 11-64 y Sangurima, T07-284 0697, www.hostalmacondo.com.
Nice restored colonial house, large rooms, buffet breakfast, cooking facilities, pleasant patio with plants, garden, very popular, US-run. Highly recommended.

$$ Milán
Pres Córdova 989 y Padre Aguirre, T07-283 1104, www.hotelmilan.com.ec.
Multi-storey hotel with views over market, restaurant, popular.

$$ Posada Todos Santos
C Larga 3-42 y Tomás Ordóñez, near the Todos Santos Church, T07-282 4247.
Tranquil hostel decorated with murals, good views of the river, very good, attentive service, English spoken, group discounts.

$$-$ El Cafecito
Mariano Cueva 11-28 y Lamar, T07-411 4765, http://elcafecitohostel.wixsite.com/elcafecito/cuenca.
Sister to hostel of same name in Quito, opposite Mercado 9 de Octubre, convenient, private rooms with bath and dorm with bath (US$10 pp), café with vegan options, teas, coffees, bar, tours booked.

$ Hogar Cuencano
Hermano Miguel 436 y C Larga, T07-283 4941, celso3515@yahoo.com.
Well-furnished family-run central *hostal*, private or shared bath, US$10 pp in dorm, cafeteria, breakfast available, cooking facilities.

$ La Cigale
Honorato Vasquez 7-80 y Cordero, T07-283 5308, www.hostallacigale.com.
Very popular hostel with private rooms and dorms (US$8 pp), breakfast available, very good restaurant ($$-$), hostel can be noisy until midnight.

$ Turista del Mundo
C Larga 5-79 y Hermano Miguel, T07-282 9125, esperanzab65@gmail.com.
Popular hostel with comfortable rooms, private or shared bath, no breakfast, cooking facilities, nice terrace, very helpful.

$ Yakumama
Cordero 5-66 y Honorato Vásquez, T07-283 4353, www.hostalyakumama.com.
Popular hostel, 2 private rooms and dorms with 2-6 beds US$7.50-10 pp, restaurant with Ecuadorean and Swiss dishes, bar, patio with plants and lounging area, terrace with skate ramp, can get noisy.

Restaurants

There is a wide selection and fast turnover of restaurants. Most places are closed on Sun evening. There are cheap *comedores* at the Mercados 9 de Octubre and 10 de Agosto.

$$$ Tiestos
J Jaramillo 4-89 y M Cueva, T07-283 5310. Tue-Sat 1230-1500, 1830-2200, Sun 1230-1500.
Superb international cuisine prepared on *tiestos*, shallow clay pans, comfortable feel-at-home atmosphere, very popular, reserve ahead.

$$$ Villa Rosa
Gran Colombia 12-22 y Tarqui, T07-283 7944, www.restaurantevillarosa.com. Mon-Fri 1230-1530, 1830-2200.
Very elegant restaurant in the centre of town, excellent international and Ecuadorean food and service. A meeting place for business people.

$$$-$$ Balcón Quiteño
Sangurima 6-49 y Hermano Miguel, and Av Ordóñez Lazo 311 y los Pinos, T07-283 1928. Daily 1000-0100.
Good Ecuadorean and international food and service, 1960s decor. Popular with locals after a night's partying.

$$$-$$ El Carbón
Borrero 10-69 y Lamar, in Hotel Cuenca, T07-283 3711, www.hotelcuenca.com.ec. Daily 0700-2300.

Excellent charcol-grilled meat served with a choice of fresh salads, seafood, wide choice of dishes and breakfasts, large portions enough for 2.

$$$-$$ El Maíz
C Larga 1-279 y C de los Molinos, T07-284 0224. Mon-Sat 1100-1600, 1830-2100.
Good traditional Ecuadorean dishes with some innovations, salads.

$$$-$$ Mangiare
Estévez de Toral 8-91 y Bolívar, at Posada del Angel, T07-282 1360. Mon-Sat 1200-1500, 1730-2230, Sun 1200-1500.
Excellent Italian food, home-made pasta, good value, very popular with locals.

$$$-$$ Pedregal Azteca
Esteves de Toral 8-60 y Bolívar, T07-282 3652. Tue-Sat 1200-1500, 1830-2300, Sun 1200-1500.
Nicely decorated restaurant with very good authentic Mexican food.

$$ Café Eucalyptus
Gran Colombia 9-41 y Benigno Malo. Mon-Fri 1700-2300 or later, Sat 1900-0200.
A pleasant restaurant, café and bar in an elegantly decorated house. Large menu with dishes from all over the world. British-owned, popular. Recommended.

$$ Cesare's
Honorato Vásquez 6-83 y Borrero, T09-9814 9651. Mon-Sat 1700-2200.
Mediterranean and international food, popular with expats.

$$ Raymipampa
Benigno Malo 8-59, at Parque Calderón. Mon-Fri 0830-2300, Sat-Sun 0930-2230.
Good typical and international food in a nice central location, inexpensive set lunch on weekdays, fast service, very popular, at times it is hard to get a table.

$$-$ Viejo Rincón
Pres Córdova 7-46 y Borrero. Mon-Fri 0900-2100, Sat 0900-1500.
Tasty Ecuadorean food, very good economical set lunch and à la carte, popular.

$ Good Affinity
Capulíes 1-89 y Gran Colombia. Mon-Sat 0930-1530.
Very good vegetarian food, vegan options, cheap set lunch, nice garden seating.

$ Grecia
Gran Colombia y Padre Aguirre. Mon-Sat 1200-1500.
Good quality and value set lunch and à la carte.

$ Moliendo Café
Honorato Vásquez y Hermano Miguel. Mon-Sat 0900-2100.
Tasty Colombian food including set lunch, friendly service.

Cafés

Goza
C Larga y Borrero, Plaza de la Merced. Mon-Thu 0800-2200, Fri-Sat 0800-2400, Sun 0800-2200.
Very popular café/restaurant with a varied menu; one of the few places in Cuenca with outdoor seating and open Sun evening.

Maria's Alemania
Hermano Miguel 8-09 y Sucre. Mon-Fri 0730-1800.
Excellent bakery and cafeteria, wide variety of whole-grain breads.

Mixx Gourmet
Parque San Blas 2-73 y Tomás Ordoñez.
A variety of fruit and liquor flavoured ice cream, popular. Several others nearby.

Monte Bianco
Bolívar 2-80 y Ordóñez and a couple of other locations.
Good ice cream and cream cakes, good value.

San Sebas
San Sebastián 1-94 y Sucre, Parque San Sebastián. Tue-Sun 0830-1500.
Outdoor café, popular for breakfast, good selection of giant sandwiches and salads.

Tutto Freddo
Bolívar 8-09 y Benigno Malo and several other locations. Daily 0900-2200.
Good ice cream, crêpes, pizza, sandwiches and sweets, reasonable prices, popular.

Bars and clubs

Calle Larga is a major destination for night life, with lots of bars with snacks and some restaurants. Av 12 de Abril, along the river near Parque de la Madre, and to the west of the centre, Plaza del Arte, Gaspar de Sangurima y Abraham Sarmiento, opposite Plazoleta El Otorongo, are also popular. Most bars open Wed-Thu until 2300, Fri-Sat until 0200.

La Mesa Salsoteca
Gran Colombia 3-36 entre Vargas Machuca y Tomás Ordóñez (no sign).
Latin music, salsa, popular among travellers and locals, young crowd.

MalAmado
C San Roque y Av 12 de Abril.
Pleasant atmosphere, good music, food, a good place for dancing, US$10-15.

Rue
At Parque de la Madre, Av 12 de Abril. Tue-Sat 2200-0200.
Nice bar/restaurant with outdoor seating, no cover charge.

Wunderbar
Entrance from stairs on Hermano Miguel y C Larga. Mon-Fri 1100-0200, Sat 1500-0200.
A café-bar-restaurant, drinks, good coffee and food including some vegetarian. Nice atmosphere, book exchange, German-run.

Entertainment

Cinemas
Multicines, *Av José Peralta.* Complex of 5 theatres and food court, also at Mall del Río.

Dance classes
Cachumbambe, *Remigio Crespo 7-79 y Guayas, p2, T07-288 2023.* Salsa, merengue and a variety of other rhythms, group and individual classes.

Festivals
Mar/Apr Good Friday. There is a fine procession through the town to the Mirador Turi.
12 Apr Foundation of Cuenca.
May-Jun Septenario, the religious festival of Corpus Christi, lasts a week.
Oct-Dec Bienal de Cuenca, an internationally famous art competition. The next one is due in late 2018. Information from Bolívar 13-89, T07-283 1778, www.bienaldecuenca.org.
3 Nov Independence of Cuenca, with street theatre, art exhibitions and night-time dances all over the city for 4 days.
24 Dec Pase del Niño Viajero, probably the largest and finest Christmas parade in all Ecuador. Children and adults from all the barrios and surrounding villages decorate donkeys, horses, cars and trucks with symbols of abundance. Little children in colourful indigenous costumes or dressed up as Biblical figures ride through the streets accompanied by musicians. The parade

starts at about 1000 at San Sebastián, proceeds along C Bolívar and ends at San Blas about 5 hrs later. In the days up to, and just after Christmas, there are many smaller parades.

Shopping

Books
BC Carolina, *Hermano Miguel 4-46 y C Larga.* Good selection of English books for sale and exchange. Friendly service.
Librimundi, *Hermano Miguel 8-14 y Sucre, www.librimundi.com.* Nice bookshop with good selection and a café/reading area.

Camping equipment
Bermeo Hnos, *Borrero 8-35 y Sucre, T07-283 1522.*
Explorer, *at Mall del Río.* Sporting goods, clothing.
Tatoo/Cikla, *Av Remigio Tamariz 2-52 y Federico Proaño, T07-288 4809, www.tatoo.ws.* Good camping, hiking, climbing and biking gear. Also rent bikes.
Several other shops near the university, on or near Av Remigio Crespo. Equipment rental from **Apullacta**, see Tour operators.

Handicrafts
There are many craftware shops along Gran Colombia, Benigno Malo and Juan Jaramillo alongside Las Conceptas. There are several good leather shops in the arcade off Bolívar between Benigno Malo and Luis Cordero. *Polleras*, traditional skirts worn by indigenous women are found along Gral Torres, between Sucre and Pres Córdova, and on Tarqui, between Pres Córdova and C Larga. For basketwork, take a 15-min bus ride from the Feria Libre (see Markets, below) to the village of **San Joaquín**.
Arte, Artesanías y Antigüedades, *Borrero y Córdova.* Textiles, jewellery and antiques.
Artesa, *L Cordero 10-31 y Gran Colombia, several branches.* Modern ceramic tableware, can visit Eduardo Vega's studio on the hill just below El Turi.
Centro Artesanal Municipal 'Casa de la Mujer', *Gral Torres 7-33.* Crafts market with a great variety of handicrafts.
Colecciones Jorge Moscoso, *J Jaramillo 6-80 y Borrero.* Weaving exhibitions, ethnographic museum, antiques and crafts.
El Barranco, *Hermano Miguel 3-23 y Av 3 de Noviembre.* Artisans' cooperative selling a wide variety of crafts.
El Otorongo, *3 de Noviembre by Plaza Otorongo.* Exclusive designs sold at this art gallery/café.
El Tucán, *Borrero 7-35.* Good selection. Recommended.

Galápagos, *Borrero 6-75*. Excellent selection.
La Esquina de las Artes, *12 de Abril y Agustín Cueva*. Shops with exclusive crafts including textiles; also cultural events.

Jewellery
Galería Claudio Maldonado, *Bolívar 7-75*. Has unique pre-Columbian designs in silver and precious stones.
Unicornio, *Gran Colombia y Luis Cordero*. Good jewellery, ceramics and candelabras.

Markets
Feria Libre, *Av Las Américas y Av Remigio Crespo, west of the centre*. The largest market, also has dry goods and clothing, busiest Wed and Sat.
Mercado 9 de Octubre, *Sangurima y Mariano Cueva*. Busiest on Thu. Nearby at **Plaza Rotary** (*Sangurima y Vargas Machuca*), crafts are sold, best selection on Thu. Note this area is not safe.
Mercado 10 de Agosto, *C Larga y Gral Torres*. Daily market with a prepared foods and drinks section on the 2nd floor.

Panama hats
Manufacturers have displays showing the complete hat making process, see also **Museo del Sombrero**, page 1104.

Homero Ortega P e Hijos, *Av Gil Ramírez Dávalos 3-86*, T07-280 1288, www.homero ortega.com. Good quality.
K Dorfzaun, *Gil Ramírez Dávalos 4-34, near bus station*, T07-286 1707, www.kdorfzaun.com. Mon-Fri 0800-1600. Good quality and selection of hats and straw crafts, nice styles, good prices. English-speaking guides.

What to do

Language courses
Rates US$6-7 per hr shared lessons, US$8-12 per hr private.
Centro de Estudios Interamericanos (CEDEI), *Gran Colombia 11-02 y General Torres*, T07-283 9003, www.cedei.org. Spanish and Quichua lessons, immersion/volunteering programmes, also run the attached **Hostal Macondo**. Recommended.
Estudio Internacional Sampere, *Hermano Miguel 3-43 y C Larga*, T07-284 2659, www. sampere.es. At the high end of the price range.
Sí Centro de Español e Inglés, *Bolívar 13-28 y Juan Montalvo*, T09-9918-8264, www. sicentrospanishschool.com. Good teachers, competitive prices, homestays, volunteer opportunities, helpful and enthusiastic, tourist information available. Recommended.

Tours

Day tours to Ingapirca or Cajas run about US$50 pp, to Gualaceo or Chordeleg US$55. Trekking in Cajas about US$60-100 pp per day, depending on group size.

Apullacta, *Gran Colombia 11-02 y Gral Torres, p 2, T07-283 7681, www.apullacta.com*. Run city and regional tours (Cajas, Ingapirca, Saraguro), also adventure tours (cycling, horse riding, canopy, canyoning), sell jungle, highland and Galápagos trips; also hire camping equipment.

Metropolitan Touring, *Sucre 6-62 y Borrero, T07-284 3223, www.metropolitan-touring.com*. A branch of the Quito operator, also sells airline tickets.

TerraDiversa, *C Larga 8-43 y Luis Cordero, T07-282 3782, www.terradiversa.com*. Lots of useful information, helpful staff. Ingapirca, Cajas, community tourism in Saraguro, jungle trips, horse riding, mountain biking and other options. The more common destinations have fixed departures. Also sell Galápagos tours and flights. Recommended.

Van Service, *T07-281 6409, www.vanservice.com.ec*. City tours on a double-decker bus. The 1¾-hr tour includes the main attractions in the colonial city and El Turi lookout. US$8, hourly departures 0900-1900 from the Old Cathedral. Also hire cars and vans with driver.

Transport

Air Airport is about a 20-min ride northeast of the centre. To **Quito** with **LATAM** (Bolívar 9-18, T07-283 8078) and **TAME** (Florencia Astudillo 2-22, T07-288 9581). Also to **Guayaquil** with TAME.

Bus City buses US$0.25. For the local **Baños**, city buses every 5-10 mins, 0600-2230, buses pass the front of the Terminal Terrestre, cross the city on Vega Muñoz and Cueva, then down Todos los Santos to the river, along 12 de Abril and onto Av Loja. A tram system is under construction and was expected to start operating in 2017 but was experiencing delays: many streets are closed due to the construction, taxis have to take detours, traffic is chaotic, allow extra time.

Regional Buses to nearby destinations leave from **Terminal Sur** at the Feria Libre on Av Las Américas. Many city buses pass here but it is not a safe area.

Long distance The **Terminal Terrestre** is on Av España, 15 mins by taxi northeast of centre. Take daytime buses to enjoy scenic routes. To **Riobamba**, 5½ hrs, US$8. To **Baños** (Tungurahua), transfer in Riobamba. To **Ambato**, 6½ hrs, US$10. To **Quito**, Terminal Quitumbe, US$12-15, 8-9 hrs. To **Alausí**, 4 hrs, US$6; all Riobamba-and Quito-bound buses pass by, but few enter town. To **Loja**, 4 hrs, US$7.50, see www.viajerosinternacional.com; transfer here for Vilcabamba. To **Saraguro**, US$5.40, 2½ hrs. To **Machala**, 3½ hrs, US$6, sit on the left, wonderful scenery. To **Huaquillas**, 5 hrs, US$8. To **Guayaquil**, via Cajas and Molleturo, 4 hrs, or via Zhud, 5 hrs, both US$8. To **Macas** via Paute and Guarumales or via Gualaceo and Plan de Milagro, 6-7 hrs, US$11; spectacular scenery but prone to landslides, check in advance if roads are open. To **Gualaquiza**, in the southern Oriente, via Gualaceo and Plan de Milagro or via Sígsig, 6 hrs, US$8.75.

International To **Chiclayo** (Peru) via Tumbes, **Máncora** and **Piura**, with **Super Semería**, at 2200, US$20, 11 hrs (US$17 as far as Piura or Máncora); also with **Azuay** at 2130; and **Pullman Sucre**, connecting with CIFA in Huaquillas; or go to Loja and catch a bus to Piura from there.

Long-distance taxis and vans Río **Arriba**, Del Batán 10-25 y Edwin Sacoto, near Feria Libre, T07-404 1790, to **Quito**, daily at 2300, US$25, 6½ hrs, from Quito, Páez N20-64 y Washington, T02-252 1336, at 1700; to **Guayaquil**, hourly 0400-2200, US$12, 3 hrs, several other companies nearby. To **Loja**, Elite Tours, Remigio Crespo 14-08 y Santa Cruz, T07-420 3088, also **Faisatur**, Remigio Crespo y Brazil, T07-404 4771, US$12, 3 hrs; taxi US$60. To **Vilcabamba**, van service daily at 1330 from **Hostal La Cigale**, Honorato Vásquez y Luis Cordero, US$15, 5 hrs, reserve ahead.

Car rental Bombuscaro, España 11-20 y Elia Liut, opposite the airport, T07-286 6541. Also international companies.

Taxi All taxis are required to use meters, US$1.50 is the minimum fare; approximately US$2 from the centre to the bus station; US$2.50 to airport; US$5 to Baños.

Baños

There are sulphur baths at Baños, with a domed, blue church in a delightful landscape, 5 km southwest of Cuenca. These are the hottest commercial baths in Ecuador, entry US$3-10. Above **Hostería Durán** (see Where to stay) are four separate complexes of warm baths with spa and lodging, **Agapantos** (www.agapantos.com, T07-289 2493), **Rodas** (www.hosteriarodas.com), **Durán** (www.hosteriaduran.com) and **Piedra de Agua** (www.piedradeagua.com.ec). The latter two are better maintained and more exclusive.

Ingapirca *Colour map 1, B3.*
Open 0800-1800, US$6, including museum and tour in Spanish; bags can be stored, small café.

Ecuador's most important Inca ruin, at 3160 m, lies 8.5 km east of the colonial town of **Cañar** (*hostales* in $ range). Access is from Cañar or **El Tambo**. The Inca Huayna Capac took over the site from the conquered Cañaris when his empire expanded north into Ecuador in the third quarter of the 15th century. Ingapirca was strategically placed on the Capac Ñan, the Great Inca Road that ran from Cuzco to Quito, see Inca Trail, below. The site shows typical imperial Cuzco-style architecture, such as tightly fitting stonework and trapezoidal doorways. The central structure may have been a solar observatory. Nearby is a throne cut into the rock, the **Sillón del Inca** (Inca's Chair) and the **Ingachugana**, a large rock with carved channels. A 10-minute walk away from the site is the **Cara del Inca**, or 'face of the Inca', an immense natural formation in the rock looking over the landscape. On Friday there is an interesting indigenous market at Ingapirca village.

A tourist *autoferro* (bus on rails) runs from El Tambo 7 km to the small Cañari-Inca archaeological site of **Baños del Inca** or **Coyoctor** ① *site open daily 0800-1700, US$1; 5 daily departures Wed-Sun, US$8, includes entry to El Tambo museum and Coyoctor site, excursion lasts 2 hrs*, a massive rock outcrop carved to form baths, showers, water channels and seats overlooking a small amphitheatre. There is an interpretation centre with information about the site, a hall with displays about regional fiestas and an audiovisual room with tourist information about all of Ecuador.

Inca Trail to Ingapirca

The three-day hike to Ingapirca starts at **Achupallas** (lively Saturday market, one hostel), 25 km from Alausí (see page 1098). The walk is covered by three 1:50,000 *IGM* sheets, Alausí, Juncal and Cañar. The Juncal sheet is most important, the name Ingapirca does not appear on the latter, you may have to ask directions near the end. Also take a compass and GPS. Good camping equipment is essential. Take all food and drink with you as there is nothing along the way. A shop in Achupallas sells basic foodstuffs. There are persistent beggars the length of the hike, especially children. Tour operators in Riobamba offer this trek for about US$360 per person (two passengers, less for a larger group), three days, with everything included; tours from Cuenca cost about US$520 per person (group of two).

East of Cuenca

Northeast of Cuenca, on the paved road to Méndez in the Oriente, is **Paute**, with a pleasant park and modern church. South of Paute, **Gualaceo** is a rapidly expanding modern town set in beautiful landscape, with a charming plaza and Sunday market. The **iTur** ① *at the Municipio, Gran Colombia y 3 de Noviembre, Parque Central, T07-225 5131, Mon-Fri 0800-1300, 1400-1700*, is very helpful, English spoken. A scenic road goes from Gualaceo to Limón in Oriente. Many of Ecuador's 4000 species of orchids can be seen at Ecuagénera① *Km 2 on the road to Cuenca, T07-225 5237, www.ecuagenera.com, Mon-Fri 0730-1600, Sat 0730-1700, Sun 0900-1700, US$5 (US$3 pp for groups of 3 or more)*.

South of Gualaceo is **Chordeleg**, a touristy village famous for its crafts in wood, silver and gold filigree, pottery and panama hats. At the **Museo Municipal** ① *C 23 de Enero, Mon-Fri 0800-1300, 1400-1700, Sat-Sun 1000-1600*, is an exhibition hall with fascinating local textiles, ceramics and straw work, some of which are on sale at reasonable prices. It's a good uphill walk from Gualaceo to Chordeleg, and a pleasant hour downhill in the other direction. South of Gualaceo, 83 km from Cuenca, **Sígsig**, an authentic highland town where women can be seen weaving hats 'on the move'. It has a Sunday market, two *residenciales* and an archaeology museum. A scenic road goes from Sígsig to Gualaquiza in Oriente, paved as far a Chigüinda, two-thirds of the way.

Parque Nacional Cajas
The park office is at Laguna Sorocucho, T07-237 0127, Mon-Fri 0800-1600. Entry free, overnight stay US$4 per night (see Where to stay, below).

Northwest of Cuenca, Cajas is a 29,000-ha national park with over 230 lakes. The park is being diligently conserved by municipal authorities both for its environmental importance and because it is the water supply for Cuenca. The *páramo* vegetation, such as chuquiragua and lupin, is beautiful and the wildlife interesting. Cajas is very rich in birdlife; 125 species have been identified, including the condor and many varieties of hummingbird (the violet-tailed metaltail is endemic to this area). On the lakes are Andean gulls, speckled teal and yellow-billed pintails. On a clear morning the views are superb, even to Chimborazo, some 300 km away.

There are two access roads. The paved road from Cuenca to Guayaquil via Molleturo goes through the northern section and is the main route for Laguna Toreadora, the visitors' centre and Laguna Llaviuco. Skirting the southern edge of the park is a gravel secondary road, which goes from Cuenca via San Joaquín to the Soldados entrance and the community of Angas beyond. (See Transport, below.) There is nowhere to stay after the *refugio* at Laguna Toreadora (see Where to stay, below) until you reach the lowlands between Naranjal and La Troncal.

The park offers ideal but strenuous walking, at 3150-4450 m altitude, and the climate is cold and wet. There have been deaths from exposure. The best time to visit is from August to January, when you may expect clear days, strong winds, night-time temperatures to -8°C and occasional mist. From February to July temperatures are higher but there is much more fog, rain and snow. Arrive in the early morning if possible since it can get very cloudy, wet and cool after about 1300. It is best to get the *IGM* maps in Quito (Chaucha, Cuenca, San Felipe de Molleturo, and Chiquintad 1:50,000) and take a compass and GPS. It is easy to get lost.

Listings Around Cuenca

Where to stay

Baños
There are also a couple of cheap *residenciales* in town.

$$$ Caballo Campana
Vía Misicata-Baños Km 4, on an alternative road from Cuenca to Baños (2 km from Baños, taxi US$5 from the centre of Cuenca), T07-412 8769, www.caballocampana.com.
Nicely rebuilt colonial hacienda house in 28 has with gardens and forest, heated rooms, suites and cabins, includes buffet breakfast, Ecuadorean and international cuisine, horse riding and lessons, sports fields, discounts for longer stays.

$$$ Hostería Durán
Km 8 Vía Baños, T07-289 2485, www.hosteriaduran.com.
Includes buffet breakfast, restaurant, parking, has well-maintained, very clean pools (US$3-7

for non-residents), gym, steam bath, transport from Cuenca, camping.

Ingapirca
There are a couple of simple places in the village. Also good economical meals at **Intimikuna**, at the entrance to the archaeological site.

$$$ Posada Ingapirca
500 m uphill from ruins, T07-221 7116, for reservations T07-283 0064 (Cuenca), www.grupo-santaana.net.
Converted hacienda, comfortable rooms, heating, includes typical breakfast, excellent but pricey restaurant and bar with fireplace, good service, great views.

$$-$ Cabañas del Castillo
Opposite the ruins, T09-9998 3650, cab.castillo@hotmail.com.
3 simple cabins, heating, restaurant with fireplace.

El Tambo

This is the nearest town to Ingapirca on the Panamerican Highway.

$ Chasky Wasy
Montenegro next to Banco del Austro,
1 block from the park, T09-9883 0013.
Nice hostel with ample rooms, no breakfast, parking nearby.

$ Sunshine
Panamericana y Ramón Borrero, at north end of town, T07-223 3394.
Simple, family-run, not always staffed, private or shared bath, restaurant nearby, traffic noise.

Inca Trail to Ingapirca

$ Ingañán
Achupallas, T03-293 0663.
Basic, with bath, hot water, meals on request, camping.

East of Cuenca

Paute

$$$$ Hostería Uzhupud
Km 32 Vía a Paute, T07-370 0860,
www.uzhupud.com.
Set in the beautiful Paute valley 10 km from town, deluxe, relaxing, rooms at the back have best views, swimming pools and sauna (US$15 for non-residents), sports fields, horse riding, gardens, lots of orchids. Recommended.

$ Cutilcay
Abdón Calderón, by the river, T07-225 0133.
Older basic hostel, private or shared bath, no breakfast.

Gualaceo

$$ Peñón de Cuzay
Sector Bullcay El Carmen on the main road to Cuenca, T07-217 1515.
In one of the weaving communities, spa and pool, no breakfast. Fills on weekends, book ahead.

$ Hostal El Jardín
On the corner next to bus terminal.
Very clean ample rooms with private or shared bath, no breakfast, a simple decent place.

Parque Nacional Cajas

There is a *refugio* at **Laguna Toreadora** (US$4 pp, reserve ahead at T07-283 1900), cold (take sleeping bag), cooking facilities, and camping at **Laguna Llaviuco**. Other shelters in the park are primitive.

$$$$-$$$ Hostería Dos Chorreras
Km 21 Vía al Cajas, sector Sayausí, T07-404 3108,
www.hosteriadoschorreras.com.
Hacienda-style inn outside the park. Heating, restaurant serves excellent fresh trout, buffet breakfast, reservations advised, horse rentals with advanced notice.

Transport

Ingapirca

Bus Direct buses **Cuenca** to Ingapirca with **Transportes Cañar** Mon-Fri at 0900 and 1220, Sat-Sun at 0900, returning 1300 and 1545, US$3.50, 2 hrs. Buses run from Cuenca to Cañar (US$2.15) and El Tambo (US$2.50) every 15 mins. From **Cañar**, corner of 24 de Mayo and Borrero, local buses leave every 15 mins for Ingapirca, 0600-1800, US$0.75, 30 mins; last bus returns at 1700. The same buses from Cañar go through **El Tambo**, US$0.75, 20 mins. If coming from the north, transfer in El Tambo. Pick-up taxi from Cañar US$10, from El Tambo US$6.25.

Inca Trail to Ingapirca

From **Alausí to Achupallas**, small buses and pickups leave as they fill between 1100 and 1600, US$1.50, 1 hr. Alternatively, take any bus along the Panamericana to **La Moya**, south of Alausí, at the turn-off for Achupallas, and a shared pick-up from there (best on Thu and Sun), US$0.50. To hire a pick-up from Alausí costs US$12-15, from La Moya US$10.

East of Cuenca

Bus From Terminal Terrestre in Cuenca: to **Paute**, every 15 mins, US$1.50, 1 hr; to **Gualaceo**, every 15 mins, US$1, 50 mins; to **Chordeleg**: every 15 mins from Gualaceo, US$0.35; 15 mins or direct bus from Cuenca, US$1.50, 1 hr; to **Sigsig**, every 30 mins via Gualaceo, US$2.15, 1½ hrs.

Parque Nacional Cajas

Bus From Cuenca's Terminal Terrestre take any **Guayaquil** bus that goes via Molleturo (not Zhud), US$2, 30 mins to turn-off for Llaviuco, 45 mins to Toreadora. **Coop Occidental** to Molleturo, 8 a day from the Terminal Sur/Feria Libre, this is a slower bus and may wait to fill up. For the Soldados entrance, catch a bus from Puente del Vado in Cuenca, daily at 0600, US$2.15, 1½ hrs; the return bus passes the Soldados gate at about 1600.

From Cuenca various routes go to the Peruvian border, fanning out from the pleasant city of Loja, due south of which is Vilcabamba, famous for its invigorating climate and lovely countryside.

South to Loja

The Pan-American Highway divides about 20 km south of Cuenca. One branch runs south to Loja, the other heads southwest through Girón, the Yunguilla valley (with a small bird reserve, see www. fjocotoco.org) and Santa Isabel (several hotels with pools and spas; cloudforest and waterfalls). The last stretch through sugar cane fields leads to Pasaje and Machala. The scenic road between Cuenca and Loja undulates between high, cold *páramo* passes and deep desert-like canyons.

Saraguro *Colour map 1, C3.*

On the road to Loja is this old town, where the local people, the most southerly indigenous Andean group in Ecuador, dress all in black. The men are notable for their black shorts and the women for their pleated black skirts, necklaces of coloured beads and silver *topos*, ornate pins fastening their shawls. The town has a picturesque Sunday market and interesting Mass, Easter and Christmas celebrations. Traditional festivities are held during solstices and equinoxes in surrounding communities, Inti Raymi (19-21 June) being the most important. Necklaces and other crafts are sold near the church. Saraguro has a community tourism programme with tours and homestay opportunities with indigenous families (US$33 pp full board). Contact **Fundación Kawsay** ① *18 de Noviembre y Av Loja, T07-220 0331, www.turismosaraguro.com*, or the **Oficina Municipal de Turismo** ① *C 10 de Marzo y Av Loja, T07-220 0100 ext 18, Mon-Fri 0800-1200, 1400-1800.* See also www.saraguro.org. **Bosque Washapampa** ① *entry US$3,* 6 km south has good birdwatching.

Loja *Colour map 1, C3.*

This friendly, pleasant highland city, encircled by hills, is an important transport hub, of particular interest to travellers on route to and from Peru. If spending any time in the area then the small town of Vilcabamba, 40 km to the south (see below), is a more interesting place to hang out but Loja makes a practical overnight stop with all facilities and services.

Housed in a beautifully restored house on the main park is the **Centro Cultural Loja** home of the **Museo de la Cultura Lojana** ① *10 de Agosto 13-30 y Bolívar, T07-257 0001, Mon-Fri 0830-1700, Sat-Sun 1000-1600, free*, with well-displayed archaeology, ethnography, art, and history halls and temporary exhibits. **Parque San Sebastián** at Bolívar y Mercadillo and the adjoining Calle Lourdes preserve the flavour of old Loja and are worth visiting. Loja is famed for its musicians and has a symphony orchestra. Cultural evenings with music and dance are held at Plaza San Sebastián, on Thursday 2000-2200. The **Museo de Música** ① *Valdivieso 09-42 y Rocafuerte, T07-256 1342. Mon-Fri 0830-1300, 1500-1800, free*, honours 10 Lojano composers.

Parque Universitario Francisco Vivar Castro (Parque La Argelia) ① *on the road south to Vilcabamba, Tue-Sun 0800-1700, US$1, city bus marked 'Capulí-Dos Puentes' to the park or 'Argelia' to the Universidad Nacional and walk from there*, has trails through the forest to the *páramo*. Across the road is the **Jardín Botánico Reynaldo Espinosa** ① *Mon-Fri 0730-1230, 1500-1800, Sat-Sun 1300-1800, US$1*, which is nicely laid out. On a ridge to the west of the city is the largest wind farm in Ecuador.

Parque Nacional Podocarpus

Headquarters at Cajanuma entrance, T07-302 4862. Limited information from Ministerio del Ambiente in Loja, Sucre 04-55 y Quito, T07-257 9595, parquepodocarpus@gmail.com, Mon-Fri 0800-1700. In Zamora at Sevilla de Oro y Orellana, T07-260 6606. Their general map of the park is not adequate for navigation, buy topographic maps in Quito.

Podocarpus (950 m to 3700 m) is one of the most diverse protected areas in the world. It is particularly rich in birdlife, including many rarities, and includes one of the last major habitats for the spectacled bear. The park protects stands of *romerillo* or podocarpus, a native, slow-growing conifer. Podocarpus is divided into two areas, an upper premontane section with many lakes, spectacular walking country, lush cloudforest and excellent birdwatching; and a lower subtropical section, with remote areas of virgin rainforest and unmatched quantities of flora and fauna. Both zones are wet (wellies are recommended) but there may be periods of dry weather October to January. The upper section is also cold, so warm clothing and waterproofs are indispensable year-round.

Entrances to the upper section: at Cajanuma, 8 km south of Loja on the Vilcabamba road, from the turn-off it is a further 8 km uphill to the guard station; and at San Francisco, 23 km from Loja along the road to Zamora. Entrances to the lower section: Bombuscaro is 6 km from Zamora, the visitor's centre is a 30-minute walk from the car park. Cajanuma is the trailhead for the demanding eight-hour hike to Lagunas del Compadre, a series of beautiful lakes set amid rock cliffs, camping is possible there (no services). Another trail from Cajanuma leads in one hour to a lookout with views over Loja. At San Francisco, the *guardianía* (ranger's station) operated by Fundación Arcoiris, offers nice accommodation (see below). This section of the park is a transition cloudforest at around 2200 m, very rich in birdlife. This is the best place to see podocarpus trees: a trail (four hours return) goes from the shelter to the trees. The Bombuscaro lowland section, also very rich in birdlife, has several trails leading to lovely swimming holes on the Bombuscaro River and waterfalls; Cascada La Poderosa is particularly nice.

Conservation groups working in and around the park include: Arcoiris ① *Macará 11-25 y Azuay, T07-2561830, www.arcoiris.org.ec*, and Naturaleza y Cultura Internacional ① *Av Pío Jaramillo y Venezuela, T07-257 3691, www.natureandculture.org*.

Routes to the Peruvian border

Of all the crossings from Ecuador to Peru, by far the most efficient and relaxed is the scenic route from Loja to Piura via Macará (see below). Other routes are from Vilcabamba to La Balsa (see page 1121), Huaquillas on the coast (page 1134) and along the Río Napo in the Oriente (see page 1158). There are smaller border crossings at Lalamor/Zapotillo, west of Macará, and Jimbura, southeast of Macará. The latter has immigration but no customs service. If arriving with a vehicle, cross at one of the other border posts.

Leaving Loja on the main highway going west, the airport at La Toma (1200 m) is reached after 35 km. La Toma is also called Catamayo, where there is lodging. At Catamayo, where you can catch the Loja-Macará-Piura bus, the Pan-American Highway divides: one branch runs west, the other south.

On the western road, at San Pedro de La Bendita, a road climbs to the much-venerated pilgrimage site of El Cisne, dominated by its large incongruous French-style Gothic church. Vendors and beggars fill the town and await visitors at festivals (see page 1119). Continuing on the western route, Catacocha is spectacularly placed on a hilltop. Visit the Shiriculapo rock for the views. There are pre-Inca ruins around the town; small archaeological Museo Hermano Joaquín Liebana ① *T07-268 3201, 0800-1200, 1400-1800*. From Catacocha, the road runs south to the border at Macará.

Another route south from Catamayo to Macará is via Gonzanamá, a small city (basic *hostales*), famed for the weaving of beautiful *alforjas* (multi-purpose saddlebags), and Cariamanga, a regional centre (various hotels and services). From here the road twists along a ridge westwards to Colaisaca, before descending steeply through forests to Utuana with a nature reserve (www.fjocotoco.org) and Sozoranga (one hotel), then down to the rice paddies of Macará, on the border. There is a choice of accommodation here and good road connections to Piura in Peru.

Macará–La Tina The border is at the international bridge over the Río Macará, 2.5 km from town, taxi US$1.50. An integrated border complex was being built on the Ecadorean side in 2017. Until its completion, immigration, customs and other services are housed in temporary quarters. The border is open 24 hours. Formalities are straightforward, it is a much easier crossing than at Huaquillas. In Macará, at the park where taxis leave for the border, there are money changers dealing in soles, but no changers at the bridge. On the Peruvian side, minivans and cars run to Sullana but it is safer to take a bus from Loja or Macará directly to Piura. Peruvian consulates in Loja ① *Zoilo Rodríguez 03-05, T07-258 7330, Mon-Fri 0900-1300, 1400-1800.*; in Macará ① *ZBolívar y 10 de Agosto, Barrio JM Cantón, T07-269 4030, consuladoperu-macara@rree.gob.pe; see www.consulado.pe*.

Tourist information

iTur
José Antonio Eguiguren y Bolívar, Parque Central, Loja, T07-257 0407 ext 202. Mon-Fri 0800-1300, 1500-1800, Sat 0800-1600.
Local information and map, monthly cultural agenda, English spoken, helpful.

Ministerio de Turismo
Bernardo Valdivieso y 10 de Agosto, Ed Colibrí, p2, Loja, T07-257 2964. Mon-Fri 0815-1700.
Regional information for Loja, Zamora and El Oro.

Where to stay

Saraguro

$$ Achik Huasi
On a hillside above town, T07-220 0058, or through Fundación Kawsay, T07-220 0331.
Community-run *hostería* in a nice setting, private bath, hot water, parking, views, tours, taxi to centre US$1.

$ Saraguro
Loja 03-2 y A Castro, T07-220 0286.
Private or shared bath, hot water, no breakfast, nice courtyard, family-run, basic, good value.

Loja
International chain hotels include **Howard Johnson** (www.hojo.com)

$$$$ Grand Victoria
B Valdivieso 06-50 y Eguiguren, ½ a block from the Parque Central, T07-258 3500, www.grandvictoriabh.com.
Rebuilt early 20th-century home with 2 patios, comfortable modern rooms and suites, restaurant, small pool, spa, gym, business centre, frigobar, safety box, parking, long-stay discounts.

$$ Bombuscaro
10 de Agosto y Av Universitaria, T07-257 7021, www.bombuscaro.com.ec.
Comfortable rooms and suites, includes buffet breakfast, cafeteria, parking, good service.

$$ Libertador
Colón 14-30 y Bolívar, T07-256 0779, www.hotellibertador.com.ec.
A very good hotel in the centre of town, comfortable rooms and suites, includes buffet breakfast, good restaurant, indoor pool (open to non-guests Sat-Sun 1000-1700, US$5), spa, parking.

$ Londres
Sucre 07-51 y 10 de Agosto, T07-256 1936.
Economical hostel in a well-maintained old house, shared bath, hot water, no breakfast, basic, clean.

$ Real Colón
Colón 15-54 entre 18 de Noviembre y Sucre, T07-257 7826.
Modern centrally located multi-storey hotel, parking, decent value for this price range.

$ Vinarós
Sucre 11-30 y Azuay, T07-258 4015, hostalvinaros@hotmail.com.
Pleasant hostel with simple rooms, private bath, electric shower, no breakfast, good value.

Parque Nacional Podocarpus
At **Cajanuma**, there are cabins with beds for US$4, bring warm sleeping bag, stove and food. At San Francisco, the *guardianía* (ranger's station), operated by **Fundación Arcoiris** offers rooms with shared bath, hot water and kitchen facilities, US$8 pp if you bring a sleeping bag, US$12 if they provide sheets. Ask to be let off at Arcoiris or you will be taken to Estación San Francisco, 10 km further east. At **Bombuscaro** there are cabins with beds US$4 and an area for camping (note that it rains frequently).

Routes to the Peruvian border

Catamayo

$$ MarcJohn's
Isidro Ayora y 24 de Mayo, at the main park, T07-267 7631, granhotelmarcjohns@hotmail.com.
Modern multi-storey hotel, rooms with fan or a/c, includes breakfast from 0700 or set dinner, restaurant, attentive service.

$$ Rosal del Sol
A short walk from the city on the main road west of town, T07-267 6517.
Ranch-style building, comfortable rooms with fan, restaurant not always open, small pool, parking, includes airport transfer, welcoming owner.

$ Reina del Cisne
Isidro Ayora at the park, T07-267 7414.

Simple adequate rooms, hot water, cheaper with cold water, fan, no breakfast, pool, gym, parking, good value.

Macará

$ Bekalus
Valdivieso y 10 de Agosto, T07-269 4043.
Simple hostel, a/c, cheaper with fan, cold water, no breakfast.

$ El Conquistador
Bolívar y Abdón Calderón, T07-269 4057.
Comfortable hotel, some rooms are dark, request one with balcony, includes simple breakfast Mon-Sat, electric shower, a/c or fan.

Restaurants

Saraguro
Several restaurants around the main plaza serve economical meals.

$$$ Shamuico
10 de Marzo, next to the tourist information office, at the main park, T07-220 0509. Wed-Sun 1230-2100.
Gourmet European-Ecuadorean fusion cuisine, run by a Saraguro-born chef who trained in Spain. Live music some Fri and Sat.

$ Tupay
10 de Marzo y Vivar, at the main park. Sun-Fri 0700-2200.
Very good set meals, also breakfast.

Loja

$$$ Riscomar
Rocafuerte 09-00 y 24 de Mayo, T07-257 4965, www.riscomarloja.com. Tue-Sat 1000-1600, 1900-2200, Sun 1000-1600.
Extensive choice of good seafood and meat dishes.

$$ Lecka
24 de Mayo 10-51 y Riofío, T07-256 3878. Mon-Fri 1700-2230.
Small quaint restaurant serving German specialities, very good food, friendly German/Ecuadorean owners. Recommended.

$$ Mama Lola
Av Salvador Bustamante Celi y Santa Rosa, T07-2614381. Mon-Sat 1200-2200, Sun 1200-1600.
Popular place for typical *lojano* specialities such as *cecina* and *cuy*.

$$-$ Casa Sol
24 de Mayo 07-04 y José Antonio Eguiguren. Daily 0830-2330.
Small place serving breakfast, economical set lunches and regional dishes in the evening. Pleasant seating on balcony.

$$-$ Pizzería Forno di Fango
24 de Mayo y Azuay, T07-258 2905. Tue-Sun 1200-2230.
Excellent wood-oven pizza, salads and lasagne. Large portions, home delivery, good service and value.

$ Angelo's
18 de Noviembre y José Félix de Valdivieso, at Hotel Floy's. Mon-Sat 0700-1500, 1800-2100.
A choice of good quality set meals, also breakfast, pleasant atmosphere, quiet (no TV), friendly service.

Cafés

Biscuit & Co.
24 de Mayo y Rocafuerte. Mon-Sat 1100-2100.
Nice café with good sandwiches, snacks, sweets and coffee. French-Ecuadorean run.

Jugo Natural
José A Eguiguren14-20 y Bolivar, near the main park. Mon-Fri 0700-1900, Sat 0800-1800, Sun 0800-1400.
Small popular café with a choice of fresh fruit juices, snacks (try their *empanadas*), coffee, salads, vegetarian soups and lunches, cake, ice-cream.

Festivals

Loja
Aug-Sep Fiesta de la Virgen del Cisne, thousands of faithful accompany the statue of the Virgin in a 3-day 74-km pilgrimage from El Cisne to Loja cathedral, beginning 16 Aug. The image remains in Loja until 1 Nov when the return pilgrimage starts. Town is crowded Aug-Sep.

What to do

Loja
Birdsexplore, *Lourdes 14-80 y Sucre, T07-258 2434, T09-8515 2239, www.exploraves.com.* Specializes in birdwatching tours throughout Ecuador, overnight trips to different types of forest, about US$150 pp per day. Pablo Andrade is a knowledgeable English-speaking guide.

Transport

Saraguro

Bus To **Cuenca** US$5.40, 2½ hrs. To **Loja**, US$2.10, 1½ hrs. Check if your bus leaves from the plaza or the Panamericana.

Loja

Air The airport is at La Toma (Catamayo), 35 km west (see Routes to the Peruvian border, page 1117): taxi from airport to Catamayo town US$2, to Loja shared taxi US$5 pp, to hire US$20 (cheaper from Loja) eg with Jaime González, T07-256 3714 or Paul Izquierdo, T07-256 3973; to Vilcabamba, US$40. There are 1-2 daily flights to **Quito** and **Guayaquil** with **TAME** (24 de Mayo y E Ortega, T07-257 0248).

Bus All buses leave from the Terminal Terrestre at Av Gran Colombia e Isidro Ayora, at the north of town, 10 mins by city bus from the centre; left luggage; US$0.10 terminal tax. Taxi from centre, US$1.50. To **Cuenca**, almost every hour (www.viajerosinternacional.com), 4 hrs, US$7.50. Van service with **Elite Tours**, 18 de Noviembre 01-13, near Puerta de la Ciudad, T07-256 0731 and **Faisatur**, 18 de Noviembre y Av Universitaria, T07-258 5299, US$12, 3 hrs; taxi US$60. **Machala**, 10 a day, 5-6 hrs, US$7 (3 routes, all scenic: via Piñas, for **Zaruma**, partly unpaved and rough; via Balsas, paved; and via Alamor, for **Puyango petrified forest**). **Quito**, Terminal Quitumbe, regular US$17; **Transportes Loja** *semi-cama* US$21, 12 hrs. **Guayaquil**, US$12 regular, US$15 *semi-cama*, 8 hrs. To **Huaquillas**, US$7.50, 6 hrs direct. To **Zumba** (for Peru, paved to Palanda),

10 daily including **Sur Oriente** at 0500 to make connections to Peru the same day and **Cariamanga** at 0900, US$10, 7 hrs; **Nambija** at 2400 direct to the border at La Balsa (only in the dry season), US$12.50, 8 hrs. To **Catamayo** (for airport) every 15 mins 0630-1900, US$1.30, 1 hr. To **Macará**, see below. To **Piura (Peru)**, Loja Internacional, via Macará, at 0700 and 2300 daily, US$14, 8-9 hrs including border formalities. Also **Unión Cariamanga** at 2400. To **Zamora**, frequent service, 1½-2 hrs, US$3.

Parque Nacional Podocarpus

For **Cajanuma**, take a Vilcabamba bound bus, get off at the turn-off, US$1, it is a pretty 8-km walk from there. Direct transport by taxi to Cajanuma, about US$10 (may not be feasible in the rainy season) or with a tour from Loja. You can arrange a pickup later from the guard station. Pickup from Vilcabamba, US$20. To the **San Francisco section**, take any bus between Loja and Zamora, make sure you alight by the Arcoiris *guardianía* and not at Estación Científica San Francisco which is 10 km east. To the **lower section**: Bombuscaro is 6 km from Zamora, take a taxi US$6 to the entrance, then walk 1 km to the visitor's centre.

Routes to the Peruvian border

Macará

Bus Transportes Loja and **Cariamanga** have frequent buses, daily from Macará to **Loja**; 5-6 hrs, US$7.50. Direct Loja-**Piura** buses can also be boarded in Macará, US$5 to Piura, 3 hrs. **Transportes Loja** also has service to **Quito**, US$19, 15 hrs, and **Guayaquil**, US$14, 8 hrs.

Vilcabamba to Peru

a beautiful, tranquil area popular with tourists and expats

★**Vilcabamba** *Colour map 1, C3.*
Once an isolated village, Vilcabamba (population around 5000) is today a colourful and eclectic cross between a resort town and a thriving expatriate community. It is popular with travellers and a good place to stop on route between Ecuador and Peru. The whole area is beautiful, with an agreeable climate. There are many nice places to stay and good restaurants. The area offers many great day-walks and longer treks, as well as ample opportunities for horse riding and cycling. A number of lovely private nature reserves are situated east of Vilcabamba, towards Parque Nacional Podocarpus. Trekkers can continue on foot through orchid-clad cloudforests to the high *páramos* of Podocarpus. Artisans from all over Latin America sell their crafts in front of the school on weekends and there is an organic produce market by the bus terminal on Saturday morning, in addition to the regular Sunday

Tip...
There are no banks, but there are ATMs by **iTur** and the church. Not all cards are accepted, however.

market. **Craig's Book Exchange** ① *in Yambuara, 1 km east of town, follow Diego Vaca de Vega*, has 2500 books in 12 languages and a small art gallery and pottery studio.

Rumi Wilco ① *10-min walk northeast of town, take C Agua de Hierro towards C La Paz and turn left, follow signs, US$2 valid for three visits*, is 40-ha private nature reserve with several signed trails. Many of the trees and shrubs are labelled with their scientific and common names. There are great views of town from the higher trails, and it is a very good place to go for a walk. Over 100 species of birds have been identified here. Volunteers are welcome. **Sacred Sueños** ① *1½-hr walk in the hills above town, T09-8931 3698, www.sacredsuenos.wordpress.com*, is a grassroots permaculture community which accepts volunteers, two weeks' minimum commitment.

Climbing **Mandango**, 'the sleeping woman' mountain is a scenic half-day walk. The signed access is along the highway, 250 m south of the bus terminal. Be careful on the higher sections when it is windy and enquire beforehand about public safety. South of Vilcabamba, 45 km on the road to Zumba is the 3500 ha bird and orchid rich **Reserva Tapichalaca** ① *T07-250 5212, www. fjocotoco.org, entry US$15*, with a lodge ($$$).

Border with Peru: La Balsa

Many daily buses run on the scenic road from Loja via Vilcabamba to **Zumba** (see Loja, Transport, page 1120), 112 km south of Vilcabamba. It is a 1½-hour rough ride by *ranchera* (open-sided bus)

Vilcabamba

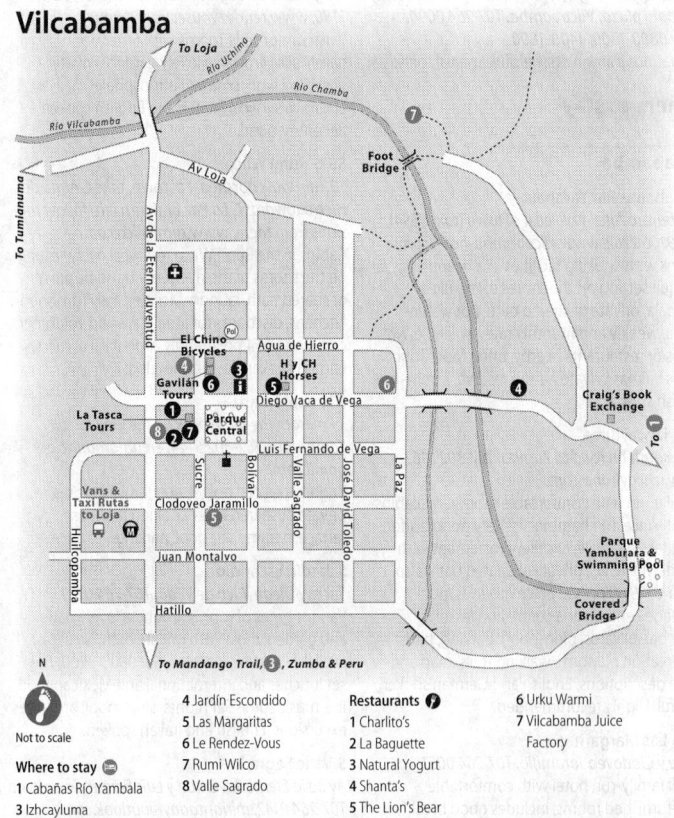

Not to scale

Where to stay 🛏
1 Cabañas Río Yambala
2 Izhcayluma

4 Jardín Escondido
5 Las Margaritas
6 Le Rendez-Vous
7 Rumi Wilco
8 Valle Sagrado

Restaurants 🍴
1 Charlito's
2 La Baguette
3 Natural Yogurt
4 Shanta's
5 The Lion's Bear

6 Urku Warmi
7 Vilcabamba Juice Factory

from Zumba to the border at La Balsa; there is a control on the way, keep your passport to hand. La Balsa is just a few houses on either side of the international bridge over the Río Canchis; there are simple eateries, shops, money changers (no banks here or in Zumba), and one very basic hotel on the Peruvian side. It is a relaxed border, Ecuadorean customs and immigration are officially open 24 hours. The Peruvian border post is open 0800-1300, 1500-2000; entering Peru, visit immigration and the PNP office (see page 1117 under Macará–La Tina for Peru's consulate in Loja). On the Peruvian side mototaxis run to **Namballe**, 15 minutes away, and cars run to Namballe and **San Ignacio** when full, two hours, from where there is transport to **Jaén**. This is a faster, more direct route between Vilcabamba and **Chachapoyas** (see the Chachapoyas to Ecuador section, in the Peru chapter) than going via the coast. Parts are rough but it can be done in two days; best take the bus passing Vilcabamba around 0600.

Listings Vilcabamba to Peru *map page 1121.*

Tourist information

iTur
Diego Vaca de Vega y Bolívar, on the corner of the main plaza, Vilcabamba, T07-264 0090. Daily 0800-1300, 1400-1800.
Has various pamphlets, helpful, Spanish only.

Where to stay

Vilcabamba

$$ Cabañas Río Yambala
Yamburara Alto, 4 km east of town (taxi US$4), T09-9106 2762, www.vilcabamba-hotel.com.
Cabins with cooking facilities in a beautiful tranquil setting on the shores of the Río Yambala, private or shared bath, hot water, sauna, weekly and monthly rates available. No shops or restaurants nearby, bring food. Tours to Las Palmas private nature reserve. Family-run, English spoken.

$$-$ Izhcayluma
2 km south on road to Zumba, T07-302 5162, www.izhcayluma.com.
Popular inn with comfortable rooms and cabins with terrace and hammocks. Very good buffet breakfast available, excellent restaurant with wonderful views, private or shared bath, also dorm US$9.50 pp, very nice grounds, pool, massage centre, yoga centre and lessons, lively bar, billiards, ping-pong, parking, bird observation platform, walking trails, map and route descriptions, English and German spoken, helpful. Highly recommended.

$$-$ Las Margaritas
Sucre y Clodoveo Jaramillo, T07-264 0051.
Small family-run hotel with comfortable well-furnished rooms, includes good breakfast,

intermittent solar-heated water, parking, pool, garden.

$$-$ Le Rendez-Vous
Diego Vaca de Vega 06-43 y La Paz, T09-9219 1180, www.rendezvousecuador.com.
Very comfortable rooms with terrace and hammocks around a lovely garden. Private or shared bath, pleasant atmosphere, attentive service, French and English spoken. Recommended.

$$-$ Rumi Wilco
10-min walk northeast of town, take C Agua de Hierro towards C La Paz and turn left, follow the signs from there, www.rumiwilco.com.
Cabins in the Rumi Wilco reserve. Lovely setting on the shores of the river, very tranquil, private or shared bath, laundry facilities, fully furnished kitchens, discounts for long stays and volunteers, camping US$4 pp, friendly Argentine owners, English spoken. Recommended.

$ Hostal Taranza
1 km from the main park on the way to Yamburara, T07-302 5144, erenatomauricio@ gmail.com.
Brightly painted hostel, economical rooms, private or shared bath, cooking facilities, terrace, hammocks, pool, parking.

$ Jardín Escondido
Sucre y Diego Vaca de Vega, T07-264 0281.
Various types of rooms around a lovely patio and garden, most with private bath, breakfast available, restaurant (Mon-Sat 0800-2200) has set lunches and international and Mexican food, live music some Sat nights, small pool, organizes excursions. English and Italian spoken.

$ Valle Sagrado
Av de la Eterna Juventud y Luis Fernando de Vega, T07-264 0142, miriantaday@outlook.com.

Simple economical rooms around a large garden, private or shared bath, electric shower, laundry and cooking facilities, breakfast extra, restaurant (open 0800-2200), parking, family-run.

Border with Peru

$$-$ Emperador
Colón y Orellana, Zumba, T07-230 8063.
Rooms with private bath, a/c, no breakfast.

$ San Luis
12 de Febrero y Brasil, Zumba, T07-230 8017.
Rooms on top floor are nicer, private or shared bath, no breakfast, attentive service.

Restaurants

Vilcabamba
Around the Parque Central are many café/bar/restaurants with pleasant sidewalk seating; too many to list, see map, page 1121.

$$$-$$ The Lion's Bear
Diego Vaca de Vega y Valle Sagrado, T09-5929 4323. Thu-Mon 1200-2100.
Fine European cuisine, especially French, weekly menu according to seasonal ingredients, live music Fri-Mon. British/French-run.

$$ Izhcayluma
At the hotel of the same name, see above. Daily 0800-2000.
Excellent international food, German specialities and several vegetarian options, served in a lovely open-air dining room with gorgeous views and attentive service. Highly recommended.

$$ Shanta's
Off Av Loja, 700 m north of the main park, T09-5949 1012. Wed-Sat 1300-2100, Sun 1300-2000.
Excellent pizza, trout, filet mignon and *cuy* (with advance notice). Also pasta and vegetarian options, good fruit juices and drinks. Nicely decorated rustic setting, pleasant atmosphere and attentive service. Recommended.

$ Charlito's
Diego Vaca de Vega y Sucre. Tue-Sun 1130-2100.
Salads, pasta, pizza, soup, sandwiches with tasty home-made wholemeal bread, microbrews and other drinks.

$ Natural Yogurt
Bolívar y Diego Vaca de Vega. Mon Sat 0800-2100.
Very popular economical restaurant, breakfast, home-made yoghurt, a variety of savoury and

Tip...
Try the local microbrew, **Sol del Venado** (www.soldelvenado.com/index.html), which is served by many establishments.

sweet crêpes, pasta, Mexican dishes, hamburgers, vegetarian options.

$ Vilcabamba Juice Factory
Sucre y Luis Fernando de Vega, Parque Central. Tue-Sat 0800-1600, Sun 0800-1400.
Healthy juices, soups and salads, vegan food available, waffles on weekends, run by a naturopath, sells natural food products, very popular with expats.

La Baguette
Diego Vaca de Vega y Av de la Eterna Juventud. Wed-Sat 0700-1700, Sun 0700-1400.
French bakery and café, great bread and pastries, crêpes, selection of breakfasts. Recommended.

What to do

Vilcabamba
See Where to stay, above, for more options.

Cycling
El Chino, *Sucre y Diego Vaca de Vega, T09-8187 6347, chinobike@gmail.com.* Mountain bike tours (US$25-35), rentals (US$2-3 per hr, US$10-15 per day) and repairs. Also see **La Tasca Tours**, below.

Horse riding
Prices pp for group of 2: 2 hrs US$20, half day US$30, full day with snack US$45, overnight trips US$70 per day all included.
Gavilán Tours, *Sucre y Diego Vaca de Vega, T07-264 0256 or 09-8133 2806 (Gavin Moore), gavilanhorse@yahoo.com.* Run by a group of experienced horsemen.
H y CH, *Diego Vaca de Vega y Valle Sagrado, T09-9152 3118.* Alvaro León, good horses and saddles.
La Tasca Tours, *Sucre at the plaza, T09-8556 1188, latascatours@yahoo.com.* Horse and bike tours with experienced guides, René and Jaime León.
Vilcabamba Exploring, *Diego Vaca de Vega y Bolívar, T09-9020 8824.* Julio Ocampo, horse riding tours, also guided hike to waterfall.

Language courses
Spanish classes with **Marta Villacrés** (T09-9751 3311).

Massage

Beauty Care, *Diego Vaca de Vega y Valle Sagrado, T09-8122 3456. Daily 0800-1200, 1400-1800.* Karina Zumba, facials, waxing, Reiki, massage 1 hr US$20.

Shanta's, *see Restaurants, above, T09-8538 5710, by appointment only.* Lola Encalada, very good 1½-hr therapeutic massage US$31, also does waxing. Recommended.

Transport

Vilcabamba

Loja to Vilcabamba, a nice 1-hr bus ride; from Loja's Terminal Terrestre, **Vilcabamaturis** minibuses, every 15-30 mins, 0545-2115, US$1.65, 1 hr; or *taxirutas* (shared taxis) from José María Peña y Venezuela, 0600-2000, US$2.25, 45 mins; taxi, US$20. To **Loja**, vans and shared taxis leave from the small terminal behind the market. For **Parque**

Nacional Podocarpus, taxis charge US$20 each way, taking you right to the trailhead at Cajanuma. To **Cuenca** vans at 0800 from **Hostería Izhcayluma**, US$15, 5 hrs, Cuenca stop at Hostal La Cigale. To **Zumba** buses originating in Loja pass Vilcabamba about 1 hr after departure and stop along the highway in front of the market (1st around 0600, next 1000), US$8.25, 5-6 hrs. To Catamayo airport, taxi US$40, 1½ hrs. To **Quito** (Quitumbe) **Transportes Loja** (tickets sold for this and other routes at Movistar office, Av de la Eterna Juventud y Clodoveo Jaramillo) at 1900, with a stop in Loja, US$22.50, 13-14 hrs.

Border with Peru

Terminal Terrestre in Zumba, 1 km south of the centre. From Zumba to **La Balsa**, *rancheras* at 0800, 1430 and 1730, US$2.25, 1-1½ hrs. From La Balsa to Zumba at 1200, 1730 and 1900. Taxi Zumba-La Balsa, US$30. To **Loja**, see above. In Zumba, petrol is sold 0700-1700.

Guayaquil
& south to Peru

Guayaquil is hotter, faster and louder than the capital. It is Ecuador's largest city, the country's chief seaport and main commercial centre, some 56 km from the Río Guayas' outflow into the Gulf of Guayaquil. Industrial expansion continually fuels the city's growth. Founded in 1535 by Sebastián de Benalcázar, then again in 1537 by Francisco de Orellana, the city has always been an intense political rival to Quito. Guayaquileños are certainly more lively, colourful and open than their Quito counterparts. Since 2000, Guayaquil has cleaned-up and 'renewed' some of its most frequented downtown areas, it boasts modern airport and bus terminals, and the Metrovía transit system.

Thriving banana plantations and other agro-industry are the economic mainstay of the coastal area bordering the east flank of the Gulf of Guayaquil. The Guayas lowlands are subject to flooding, humidity is high and biting insects are fierce. Mangroves characterize the coast leading south to Huaquillas, the main coastal border crossing to Peru.

Guayaquil *Colour map 1, B2.*

a lively city with fine hotels and restaurants

A wide, tree-lined waterfront avenue, the Malecón Simón Bolívar runs alongside the Río Guayas from the Palacio de Cristal, past Plaza Olmedo, the Moorish clock tower, by the imposing Palacio Municipal and Gobernación and the old Yacht Club to Las Peñas.

Sights

The riverfront along this avenue is an attractive promenade, known as **Malecón 2000** ① *daily 0700-2400*, where visitors and locals can enjoy the fresh river breeze and take in the views. There are gardens, fountains, childrens' playgrounds, monuments, walkways and an electric vehicle for the disabled (daily 1000-2000, US$2). You can dine at upmarket restaurants, cafés and food courts. Towards the south end are souvenir shops, a shopping mall and the **Palacio de Cristal** (prefabricated by Eiffel 1905-1907), originally a market and now a gallery housing temporary exhibits.

At the north end of the Malecón is an **IMAX** large-screen cinema, and downstairs the **Museo Miniatura** ① *Tue-Sun 0900-2000, US$1.50*, with miniature historical exhibits. Beyond is the **Centro Cultural Simón Bolívar**, better known as **MAAC, Museo Antropológico y de Arte Contemporaneo** ① *T04-230 9400, daily 0900-1630, free,* with excellent collections of ceramics and gold objects from coastal cultures and an extensive modern art collection.

North of the Malecón 2000 is the old district of **Las Peñas**, the last picturesque vestige of colonial Guayaquil with its brightly painted wooden houses and narrow, cobbled main street (Numa Pompilio Llona). It is an attractive place for a walk to **Cerro Santa Ana**, which offers great views of the city and the mighty Guayas. It has a bohemian feel, with bars and restaurants. A large open-air exhibition of paintings and sculpture is held here during the **Fiestas Julianas** (24-25 July). North of La Peñas is

Best for
Birdlife ▪ Hotels ▪ Museums ▪ Sightseeing

Essential Guayaquil

Finding your feet

José Joaquín de Olmedo international airport is 15 minutes north of the city centre by car. Not far from the airport is the **Terminal Terrestre** long distance bus station. Opposite this station is Terminal Río Daule, an important transfer station on the Metrovía rapid transit system.

A number of hotels are centrally located in the downtown core, along the west bank of the Río Guayas, where you can get around on foot. The city's suburbs sprawl to the north and south of the centre, with middle-class neighbourhoods and some very upscale areas in the north, where some elegant hotels and restaurants are located, and poorer working-class neighbourhoods and slums to the south. Road tunnels under Cerro Santa Ana link the northern suburbs to downtown.

Getting around

Metrovía is an integrated transport system of articulated buses running on exclusive lanes. The buses can be packed and so should be avoided if you are carrying a lot of belongings. The taxis are efficient, but although drivers should use the meter, they do not always do so. See also Transport, page 1132.

Safety

The Malecón 2000, parts of Avenida 9 de Octubre, Las Peñas and Malecón del Estero Salado are heavily patrolled and reported safe. The rest of the city requires precautions. Do not go anywhere with valuables, for details see page 1193. Parque Centenario is also patrolled, but the area around it requires caution. 'Express kidnappings' are of particular concern in Guayaquil; do not take a taxi outside the north end of the Malecón 2000 near the MAAC museum, walk south along the Malecón as far as the Hotel Ramada, where there is a taxi stand; whenever possible, call for a radio taxi.

When to go

From May to December the climate is dry with often overcast days and pleasantly cool nights, whereas the rainy season from January to April is oppressively hot and humid.

Puerto Santa Ana, with a luxury hotel, upmarket apartments, a promenade and three museums: to the romantic singer Julio Jaramillo, to beer in the old brewery, and to football.

By the pleasant, shady **Parque Bolívar** stands the **Cathedral** (Chimborazo y 10 de Agosto), in Gothic style, inaugurated in the 1950s. In the park are many iguanas and it is popularly referred to as Parque de las Iguanas. The nearby **Museo Municipal** ① *in the Biblioteca Municipal, Sucre y Chile, Tue-Sat 0900-1700, free, city tours on Sat, also free*, has paintings, gold and archaeological collections, shrunken heads, a section on the history of Guayaquil and a good newspaper library.

Between the Parque Bolívar and the Malecón is the **Museo Nahim Isaías** ① *Pichincha y Clemente Ballén, T04-232 4283, Tue-Fri 0830-1630, Sat-Sun 0900-1600, free*, a colonial art museum with a permanent religious art collection and temporary exhibits.

Avenida 9 de Octubre, the city's main artery, runs west from the Malecón. Halfway along it is **Parque Centenario** with a towering monument to the liberation of the city erected in 1920. Overlooking the park is the museum of the **Casa de la Cultura** ① *9 de Octubre 1200 y P Moncayo, T04-230 0500, Mon-Fri 0900-1800, Sat 0900-1500, free, English-speaking guides available*, which houses an impressive collection of prehispanic gold items in its archaeological museum; and a photo collection of old Guayaquil.

West of Parque Centenario, the **Museo Presley Norton** ① *Av 9 de Octubre y Carchi, T04-229 3423, Tue-Sat 0900-1700, free*, has a nice collection of coastal archeology in a beautifully restored house. At the west end of 9 de Octubre are **Plaza Baquerizo Moreno** and the **Malecón del Estero Salado**, another pleasant waterfront promenade along a brackish estuary. It has various monuments, eateries specializing in seafood, and rowing boats and pedal-boats for hire.

Around the city

Parque Histórico Guayaquil ① *Vía Samborondón, near Entrerríos, T04-283 2958, Wed-Sun 0900-1630, free; CISA buses to Samborondón leave from the Terminal Terrestre every 20 mins, US$0.25.* The park recreates Guayaquil and its rural surroundings at the end of the 19th century. There is a natural area with native flora and fauna, a traditions section where you can learn about rural life, an urban section with old wooden architecture, and eateries. A pleasant place for a family outing.

Botanical Gardens ① *Av Francisco de Orellana, in Ciudadela Las Orquídeas (bus line 63), T04-289 9689, daily 0800-1600, US$3, guiding service for up to 5 visitors US$10 (English available).* There are over 3000 plants, including 150 species of Ecuadorean and foreign orchids (most flower August to December). One area emulates the Amazon rainforest and has monkeys and other animals. It is northwest of the city.

Tip...
Outside downtown, addresses are hard to find; ask for a nearby landmark to help orient your driver.

Bosque Protector Cerro Blanco ① *Vía a la Costa, Km 16, T09-8622 5077 (Spanish), fundacionprobosque@ymail.com, http://bosquecerroblanco.org, US$4, additional guiding fee US$10-15 depending on trails visited, camping US$20 for group of 8, lodge available.* The reserve, run by **Fundación Pro-Bosque**, is set in tropical dry forest with an impressive variety of birds (over 200 species), many reptiles and with sightings of monkeys and other mammals. Unfortunately it is getting harder to see the animals due to human encroachment in the area. Reservations required during weekdays, for groups larger than eight at weekends, and for birders wishing to arrive before or stay after normal opening hours (0800-1600). Take a CLP bus from the **Terminal Terrestre**, a **Cooperativa Chongón** bus from Antepara y 10 de Agosto (hourly) or a taxi (US$8-10). On the other side of the road, at Km 18 is **Puerto Hondo**, where there are **rowboat trips** ① *through the mangroves are offered, T09-9140 0186, US$15 for a group of 7, 1 hr, reserve ahead.*

Guayaquil orientation

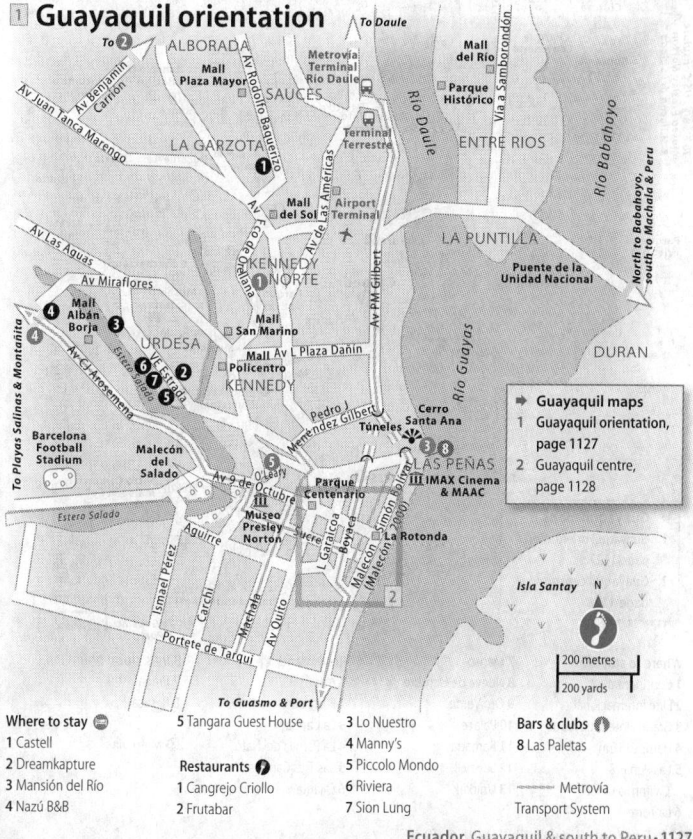

Where to stay 🛏
1 Castell
2 Dreamkapture
3 Mansión del Río
4 Nazú B&B
5 Tangara Guest House

Restaurants 🍴
1 Cangrejo Criollo
2 Frutabar
3 Lo Nuestro
4 Manny's
5 Piccolo Mondo
6 Riviera
7 Sion Lung

Bars & clubs 🍸
8 Las Paletas

━━━ Metrovía Transport System

➤ **Guayaquil maps**
1 Guayaquil orientation, page 1127
2 Guayaquil centre, page 1128

Area Nacional de Recreación Isla Santay ① www.islasantay.info, open 0600-1800, bicycle rental US$4. On the Río Guayas, opposite downtown Guayaquil is this Ramsar wetland rich in fauna and flora. Two pedestrian draw bridges (open 0600-2100) link the island with the mainland, one from Calle El Oro, south of Malecón 2000, the second from the city of Durán; a boardwalk/cycle path joins the two. By the local village, 2.8 km from the Guayaquil bridge and 5.3 km from the Durán bridge, is the Eco Aldea, with a crocodile breeding centre (open 0600-1700), a cabin and restaurant run by the local community. Boat service to the Eco Aldea from **Cooperativa las Palmeras** ① T09-8654 7034, US$4 pp return, minimum 10 passengers, depart from the Yacht Club.

② Guayaquil centre

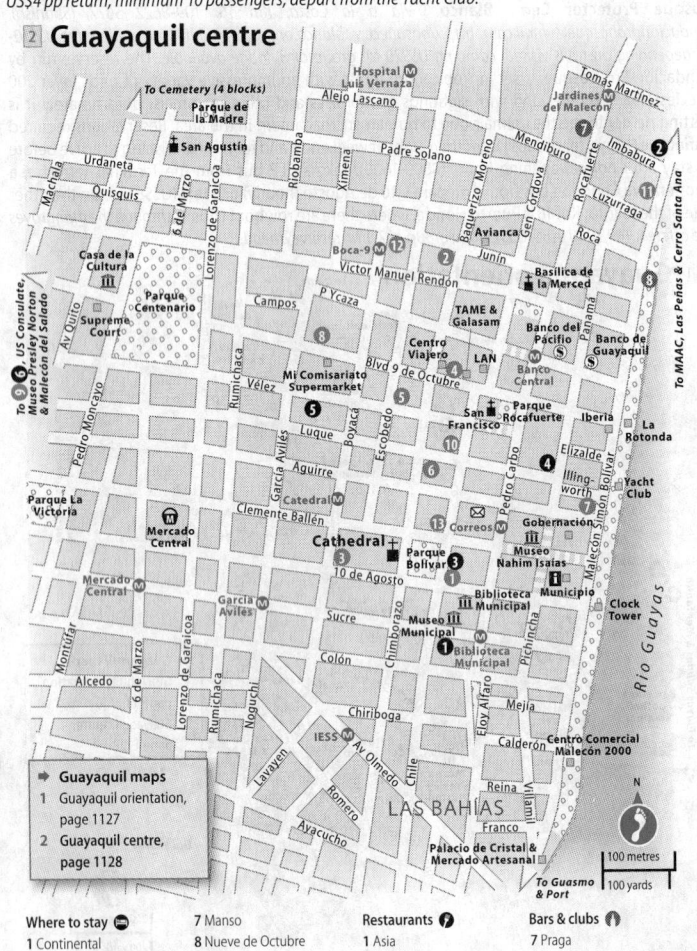

Where to stay 🛏
1 Continental
2 Elite Internacional
3 Grand Hotel Guayaquil
4 Hampton Inn
5 Las Peñas &
   California Café
6 La Torre
7 Manso
8 Nueve de Octubre
9 Oro Verde
10 Palace
11 Ramada
12 Savoy II
13 Unipark

Restaurants 🍴
1 Asia
2 Fruta Bar
3 La Canoa
4 La Parrilla del Ñato
5 Las Tres Canastas
6 Ollantay

Bars & clubs 🍸
7 Praga
8 Resaca

Ⓜ Metrovía

➡ **Guayaquil maps**
1 Guayaquil orientation, page 1127
2 Guayaquil centre, page 1128

Reserva Ecológica Manglares Churute ① *Free entry, camping and use of basic cabins; boat tour US$20-40, depending on group size (2-4 hrs recommended), arrange several days ahead through the Dirección Regional, Ministerio del Ambiente in Guayaquil, Parque de los Samanes, Bloque 7, north of the city, T04-372 9066. Buses (CIFA, Ecuatoriano Pullman, 16 de Junio) leave the Terminal Terrestre every 30 mins, going to Naranjal or Machala; ask to be let off at the Churute information centre. The reserve can also be reached by river.* Heading east then south from Guayaquil, 22 km beyond the main crossroads at Km 50 on the road to Machala, lies this rich natural area with five different ecosystems created to preserve mangroves in the Gulf of Guayaquil and forests of the Cordillera Churute. Many waterbirds, monkeys, dolphins and other wildlife can be seen. There is a trail through the tropical forest (1½ hours' walk) and you can also walk (one hour) to Laguna Canclón or Churute, a large lake where ducks nest. Near the park is **Monoloco Lodge ($)**, www.monoloco.ec, tours available.

Listings Guayaquil *maps pages 1127 and 1128.*

Tourist information

Empresa Pública Municipal de Turismo
C 10 de Agosto y Malecón, T04-259 4800, ext 3479. Mon-Fri 0930-1700, www.guayaquilesmidestino. com (in Spanish and English).
In the Municipio, 1st floor, has information about the city. There is also an information booth at the Terminal Terrestre.

Immigration
Av Río Daule, near the bus terminal, T04-214 0002.

Ministerio de Turismo
Subsecretaría del Litoral, Av Francisco de Orellana y Justino Cornejo, Edif Gobierno del Litoral, p 8 and counter on the ground floor, Ciudadela Kennedy, T04-268 4274, www.ecuador.travel. Mon-Fri 0900-1700.
Information about the coastal provinces of Ecuador and whale watching regulations.

Where to stay

Guayaquil has some of the best top-class accommodation in Ecuador.

For major chain hotels see: www.hilton.com (**Hilton Colón** and **Hampton Inn**, both excellent), www.ororverdehoteles.com (**Oro Verde** – see the brand new www.hoteldelparque.com.ec – and **Unipark**), www.hotelcontinental.com.ec, www. hojo.com (**Howard Johnson**), www.hdoral.com (**Best Western**), www.marriott.com, www. sheraton.com www.sonesta.com/guayaquil and www.wyndham.com (with excellent location and views of the river). There are several mid-range (**$$**) hotels on Junín between Gen Córdova and Escobedo but decent economy places are few and far between; the latter are concentrated around Parque Centenario, not a safe area.

$$$$ Mansión del Río
Numa Pompilio Llona 120, Las Peñas, T04-256 6044, www.mansiondelrio-ec.com.
Elegant boutique hotel in a 1926 mansion, period European style, river view, buffet breakfast, airport transfers, 10 mins from city centre.

$$$ Castell
Av Miguel H Alcívar y Ulloa, by Parque Japonés, Kennedy Norte, T04-268 0190, www.hotelcastell.com.
Modern comfortable hotel in a quiet location in the north of the city, includes buffet breakfast, restaurant, a/c, convenient for the airport (taxi US$2.50).

$$$ Grand Hotel Guayaquil
Boyacá 1600 y 10 de Agosto, T04-232 9690, www.grandhotelguayaquil.com.
A traditional Guayaquil hotel, central, includes buffet breakfast, good restaurants, pool, gym and sauna.

$$$ Nazú B&B
Ciudadela La Cogra, Manzana 1, Villa 2, off Av Carlos Julio Arosemena Km 3.5 (taxi from bus terminal or airport US$6-8, Metrovía '28 de Mayo' stop, best without luggage), T04-220 1143, www.nazuhouse.com.
Lovely suburban guesthouse with a variety of rooms and suites with a/c, includes dinner and breakfast, pool, parking, terrace with views of the city, English and German spoken.

$$$ Palace
Chile 214 y Luque, T04-232 1080, www.hotelpalaceguayaquil.com.ec.
Modern hotel, includes buffet breakfast, restaurant, 24-hr cafetería, traffic noise on Av Chile side, good value for business travellers.

$$$ Ramada
Malecón 606 e Imbabura, T04-256 5555,
www.hotelramada.com.
Excellent location right on the Malecón, rooms
facing the river are more expensive, includes
buffet breakfast, restaurant, a/c, pool, spa.

$$$-$$ Las Peñas
Escobedo 1215 y Vélez, T04-232 3355,
www.hlpgye.ec.
Nice hotel in a refurbished part of downtown,
ample modern rooms, cafeteria, a/c, quiet
despite being in the centre of town, good value.
Recommended.

$$ La Torre
Chile 303 y Luque, p 13-15, T04-232 1918,
http://hotellatorre.guayaquilgp.com.
Popular hotel in a downtown office tower,
long flight of stairs to get into the building,
comfortable rooms, cafeteria, a/c, nice views,
reasonably quiet for where it is, popular, advance
booking advised, good value.

$$ Manso
Malecón 1406 y Aguirre, upstairs, T04-252 6644,
www.manso.ec.
Nicely refurbished hostel in a great location
opposite the Malecón. Rooms vary from fancy
with a/c, private bath and river view, to simpler
with shared bath and fan, and 3- to 4-bed dorms
(US$17 pp), English spoken.

$$ Tangara Guest House
Manuela Sáenz y O'Leary, Manzana F,
Villa 1, Ciudadela Bolivariana, T04-228 4445,
www.tangara-ecuador.com.
Comfortable hotel in a nice area by the university
and near the Estero Salado, a/c, fridge, low season
discounts, convenient for airport and bus terminal
but also along the flight path, so it is noisy.

$$-$ Dreamkapture
Juan Sixto Bernal, Alborada Etapa 12, mz 2
villa 21, T04-227 1938, www.dreamkapture.com.
Hostel with private rooms and shared and single-
sex dorms (US$9.50-11 pp), some with bath and
a/c, fans, breakfast included, kitchen, garden and
plunge pool. Also has travel agency for mainland
and Galápagos tours, www.dreamkapturetravel.
com. US$5 taxi ride from bus and airport
terminals and centre.

$$-$ Elite Internacional
Baquerizo Moreno 902 y Junín, T04-256 5385/09-
9477 8901, Facebook: hoteleliteinternacional.
Completely refurbished old downtown hotel,
comfortable rooms with a/c and hot water, parking.

$$-$ Savoy II
Junín 627 y Boyacá, T04-231 0206,
http://hotelyhostalsavoy.amawebs.com.
Central location, simple rooms with a/c and
hot water.

$ Nueve de Octubre
9 de Octubre 736 y García Avilés, T04-256 4222.
Busy 8-storey hotel in a central location. Simple
functional rooms, those facing the street are larger
but noisy, restaurant, private bath, cold water, a/c,
cheaper with fan, parking extra. Fills early and
does not accept reservations. Good value.

Restaurants

Main areas for restaurants are the centre
with many in the larger hotels, around
Urdesa and the residential and commercial
neighbourhoods to the north.

$$$ Cangrejo Criollo
Av Rolando Pareja, Villa 9, La Garzota, T04-262
6708. Mon-Sat 0900-0100, Sun 0900-2300.
Excellent, varied seafood menu.

$$$ Lo Nuestro
VE Estrada 903 e Higueras, Urdesa, T04-238 6398.
Daily 1200-2300.
Luxury restaurant with typical coastal cooking,
good seafood platters and stuffed crabs,
colonial decor.

$$$ Manny's
Av Miraflores 112 y C Primera, Miraflores, T04-220
2754; also in Urdesa and Kennedy. Daily 1000-2400.
Well known crab house with specialities such
as *cangrejo al ajillo* (crab in garlic butter), good
quality and value.

$$$-$$ La Parrilla del Ñato
VE Estrada 1219 y Laureles in Urdesa; Av Francisco
de Orellana opposite the Hilton Colón; Luque y
Pichincha downtown; and several other locations,
T04-268 2338. Daily 1200-2300.
Large variety of dishes, salad bar, also pizza by
the metre, good quality, generous portions. Try
the *parrillada de mariscos*, available only at the
Urdesa and Kennedy locations. Recommended.

$$$-$$ Piccolo Mondo
Bálsamos 504 y las Monjas, Urdesa, T04-238 7079.
Mon-Sat 1230-2330, Sun 1230-2200.
Very exclusive Italian restaurant since 1980, the
best in food and surroundings, good antipasto.

$$$-$$ Riviera
VE Estrada 707y Ficus, Urdesa, and Mall del Sol,
T04-288 3790. Daily 1230-2330.

Extensive Italian menu, good pasta, antipasto, salads, bright surroundings, good service.

$$$-$$ Sion Lung
VE Estrada 621 y Ficus, Urdesa, also Av Principal, Entre Ríos, T04-288 8213. Daily 1200-2230.
Chinese food, a variety of rice (*chaulafán*) and noodle (*tallarín*) dishes.

$$ Asia
Sucre 321 y Chile, downtown, also VE Estrada 508 y Las Monjas, Urdesa and in shopping centres in the north. Daily 1100-2130.
Chinese food, large portions, popular.

$$ La Canoa
Hotel Continental, Chile y 10 de Agosto. Open 24 hrs.
Rare regional dishes, with different specials during the week, a Guayaquil tradition.

$$-$ Manso
Malecón 1406 y Aguirre, at the hotel. Mon-Fri 1230-2200, Sat 1830-2200.
Small dining area serving innovative set lunches, à la carte dishes and snacks. Tables overlooking the river are nice.

$ Ollantay
Tungurahua 508 y 9 de Octubre, west of downtown.
Good vegetarian food.

Cafés and snacks

California
Escobedo 1215 y Vélez, below Hotel Las Peñas. Mon-Sat 0700-2000, Sun 0800-1500.
Good and popular for breakfast, snacks, drinks, sweets and à la carte meals.

Fruta Bar
Malecón e Imbabura, VE Estrada 608 y Monjas, Urdesa.
Excellent fruit juices and snacks, unusual African decor, good music.

Las Tres Canastas
Vélez y García Avilés and several other locations.
Breakfast, snacks, safe fruit juices and smoothies.

Bars and clubs

Guayaquil nightlife is not cheap. There are clubs and bars in most of the major hotels, as well as in the northern suburbs, especially at the Kennedy Mall. Also in vogue are the Las Peñas area, and the Zona Rosa, bounded by the Malecón Simón Bolívar and Rocafuerte, C Loja and C Roca. Both these areas are considered reasonably safe but always take a radio taxi back to your hotel.

La Paleta
Escalón 176, Las Peñas. Tue-Sat from 2000.
Good music, great drinks and snacks. US$10-15 cover Fri and Sat, popular, reserve.

Praga
Rocafuerte 636 y Mendiburo. Tue-Sat from 1830.
US$10-16 cover, live music Fri-Sat. Pleasant atmosphere, several halls, varied music.

Resaca
Malecón 2000, at the level of Junín. Daily 1130-2400.
Lovely setting, live tropical music Fri-Sat night. Also serves set lunches on weekdays, regional dishes and pricey drinks.

Entertainment

Cinema
Cinemas are at the main shopping centres and cost US$4-8. The IMAX Cinema, Malecón 2000, projects impressive films on its oversize screen.

Theatre
Centro Cívico, *Quito y Venezuela.* Excellent theatre/concert facility, home to the Guayaquil Symphony which gives free concerts.

Festivals

24-25 Jul The foundation of Guayaquil.
9-12 Oct The city's independence.
Both holidays are lively and there are many public events; cultural happenings are prolonged throughout Oct.

Shopping

There are many shopping malls (eg **Malecón 2000**, south end of Malecón and the huge **San Marino**, Av Francisco de Orellana y L Plaza Dañín) which are noisy but have a/c for cooling off on hot days.

Handicrafts
In Albán Borja Mall are: **El Telar** with a good variety of *artesanías* and **Ramayana**, with nice ceramics. **Mall del Sol**, near the airport, also has craft shops.
Mercado Artesanal del Malecón 2000, *at the south end of the Malecón.* Has many kiosks selling varied crafts.
Mercado Artesanal, *Baquerizo Moreno between Loja and J Montalvo.* Greatest variety, almost a whole block of stalls with good prices.

What to do

Boat tours

The gulf islands and mangroves can be visited on tours from Guayaquil, Puerto Hondo or Puerto El Morro.

Isla Puná, the largest of the islands has a community tourism programme, contact the village of **Subida Alta**, T09-9156 4562.

Capitan Morgan, *Muelle Malecón y Sucre*. 1-hr tours on the river with nice city views, Tue-Fri at 1600, 1800 and 1930, Sat and Sun at 1230, 1400, 1600, 1800 and 1930, Fri and Sat also at 2130; US$7. Also 2-hr party cruises, Thu 2130-2330, Fri-Sat from 2330-0200, US$15, with live music, open bar and dancing.

Cruceros Discovery, *Muelle Malecón y Tomás Martínez*. 1-hr river cruises, US$7, Tue-Fri from 1600, Sat-Sun from 1300, and party trips.

Tour operators

A 3-hr city tour costs about US$14 pp in a group. Tours to coastal haciendas offer a glimpse of rural life.

Centro Viajero, *Baquerizo Moreno 1119 y 9 de Octubre, of 805, T04-230 1283, T09-9235 7745 24-hr service, www.centroviajero.com.* Custom-designed tours to all regions, travel information and bookings, flight tickets, car and driver service, well informed about options for Galápagos, helpful, English, French and Italian spoken. Recommended.

Galasam, *Edif Gran Pasaje, 9 Octubre 424, ground floor, T04-230 4488, www.galasam.com.ec.* Galápagos cruises, city tours, tours to reserves near Guayaquil, diving trips, also run highland and jungle tours and sell flight tickets.

Guayaquil Visión, *ticket booth at Olmedo y Malecón, T04-292 5332, Facebook: GuayaquilVision.* City tours on a double-decker bus, from US$7, departs from Plaza Olmedo and the Rotonda, Malecón at the bottom of 9 de Octubre. Also tours to attractions outside the city and night-time party tours.

La Moneda, *Av de las Américas 406, Centro de Convenciones Simón Bolívar, of 2, T04-292 5660, www.lamoneda.com.ec.* City and coastal tours, whale watching, also other regions.

Metropolitan Touring, *Francisco De Orellana, Edif. World Trade Center, CC Millenium Galery, PB, T04-263 0900, www.metropolitan-touring.com.* High-end land tours and Galápagos cruises.

Train rides

The train station is in Durán, across the river from Guayaquil, reservations T1800-873637, www.trenecuador.com, Mon-Fri 0800-1630, Sat-Sun 0700-0900. For information on the luxury *Tren Crucero* from Durán to Quito, see page 1046. Combined train/bus day trips to Bucay, 88 km away, Fri and every other Sat-Sun, cost US$30. Other fortnightly weekend itineraries go to Naranjito and San Antonio, US$53 and 112; snack included. Durán-Alausí on Sat, 0800, Alausí-Durán Sun at 0700, US$69, US$121 return. Tickets are also sold at the railcar in Malecón 2000, Malecón y P Icaza, Mon-Fri 0900-1230, 1330-1800, Sat-Sun 1000-1200, 1330-1600.

Transport

Air José Joaquín de Olmedo is a modern airport with all services (change only cash euros at poor rates) and luggage storage. The information booth outside international arrivals (T04-216 9000, open 24 hrs) has flight, hotel and transport information. It is 15 mins to the city centre by taxi, US$5, and 5-10 mins to the bus terminal, US$3. Fares from the airport to other areas are posted at exit doors and on www.taxiecuadorairport.com. Official airport taxis are more expensive but safer than those out on the street. It is along line 2 of the Metrovía, but neither the Metrovía nor buses to the centre (eg Línea 130 'Full 2') are safe or practical with luggage. For groups, there are van services such as **M&M**, T04-216 9294, US$15 to centre.

Many flights daily to **Quito** (sit on the right for the best views) and **Galápagos**, see page 1173, with **Avianca** (Junín 440 y Córdova, T04-231 1028, T1-800-003434), **LATAM** (Gen Córdova 1042 y 9 de Octubre, and in Mall del Sol, T1-800-101075) and **TAME** (9 de Octubre 424 y Chile, T04-268 9127 and Galerías Hilton Colón, T04-268 9135 or T1-700-500800). **TAME** also flies to **Esmeraldas** and **Loja**.

Bus Metrovía (T04-213 0402, www.metrovia-gye.com.ec, US$0.25) is an integrated system of articulated buses on exclusive lanes and *alimentadores* (feeder buses) serving suburbs from the terminuses. Line 1 runs from the Terminal Río Daule, opposite the Terminal Terrestre, in the north, to the Terminal El Guasmo in the south. In the city centre it runs along Boyacá southbound and Pedro Carbo northbound. Line 2 goes from the Terminal Río Daule along Av de las Américas past the airport, then through the centre and on to Integración Pradera in the southern suburbs. Line 3 goes from the centre (transfer points to line 1 at Biblioteca Municipal and IESS; to line 2 at Plaza La Victoria) along C Sucre to the northwest as far as Bastión. Provides access to neighbourhoods such as Urdesa, Miraflores, and Los Ceibos. The Metrovía is a good way of getting around without luggage or valuables. You need a prepaid card to board. **City buses** (US$0.25) are only permitted on a few streets in the centre; northbound buses go along Rumichaca or the Malecón, southbound along Lorenzo de Garaicoa or García Avilés. Buses and Metrovía get very crowded at rush hour.

Taxi Using a radio taxi, such as Samboroncar, T04-284 3883, or Vipcar, T04-239 3000, is recommended. Short trips costs US$2.50, fares from the centre to Urdesa, Policentro or Alborada are around US$4-5. Taxis are supposed to use a meter, but not all drivers comply.

Long distance The **Terminal Terrestre**, just north of the airport, is off the road to the Guayas bridge. The Metrovía, opposite the bus station, and many city buses (eg Línea 84 to Parque Centenario) go from to the city centre but these are not safe with luggage; take a taxi (US$3-4). The bus station doubles as a shopping centre with supermarket, shops, banks, post office, calling centres, internet, food courts, etc. Incoming buses arrive on the ground floor, where the ticket offices are also located. Regional buses depart from the 2nd level and long distance (interprovincial) buses depart from the 3rd level. The terminal is very large, so you need to allow extra time to get to your bus. Check the board at the entrance for the location of the ticket counters for your destination, they are colour-coded by region.

Several companies to **Quito**, 8 hrs, US$12.50, US$15for express buses which go at night; also non-stop, a/c services, eg **Transportes Ecuador**, Av de las Américas y Hermano Miguel, opposite the airport terminal, T04-292 5139. To **Cuenca**, 4 hrs via Molleturo/Cajas, 5 hrs via

Zhud, both US$8, both scenic; also hourly van service, 0500-2100, with **Río Arriba**, Centro de Negocios El Terminal, Bloque C, of 38, Av de las Américas y entrada a Bahía Norte, T09-8488 9269, US$12, 3 hrs, reserve ahead; several others at the same address, departures every 30-40 mins. **Riobamba**, 5 hrs, US$6.25. To **Santo Domingo de los Tsáchilas**, 5 hrs, US$6.25. **Manta**, 4 hrs, US$5. **Esmeraldas**, 8 hrs, US$10. To **Bahía de Caráquez**, 6 hrs, US$6.25. To **Ambato**, 6 hrs, US$7.50. Frequent buses to **Playas**, 2 hrs, US$3.25; and to **Salinas**, 2½ hrs, US$4.75. To **Santa Elena**, 2 hrs, US$3.25, change here for **Puerto López**. To **Montañita** and **Olón**, CLP, at 0520, 0620, 0900, 1300, 1500 and 1640, 3¼ hrs, US$7.25. For the Peruvian border, to **Huaquillas** direct, 4½-5 hrs, US$7.50; van service with **Transfrosur**, Chile 616 y Sucre, T04-232 6387, hourly 0500-2000, Sun 0900-2000, 4 hrs, US$13.50; to **Machala**, 3 hrs, US$5, also hourly vans with **Oro Guayas**, Luque y García Avilés, T04-252 3297, US$12, 3 hrs. To **Zaruma**, 8 buses daily, US$8.25, 6 hrs. To **Loja**, with **Trans Loja**, 8 daily, US$12, 9-10 hrs.

International (Peru) CIFA, T04-213 0379, www.cifainternacional.com, from Terminal Terrestre to **Tumbes** 8 daily, 6 hrs, US$10 *ejecutivo*, US$15 *bus-cama*; to **Piura** via **Máncora** (9 hrs, same price as Piura), *ejecutivo* service at 0720, and 2100, 10-11 hrs, US$15; and *bus-cama* at 1950 and 2330, US$20; also with **CIVA**, daily at 2130, *semi-cama* US$17, *cama* US$20. To **Chiclayo** with **Super Semería**, at 2200 daily, US$25, 12 hrs. To **Lima** with **Cruz del Sur**, of 88, T04-213 0179, www.cruzdelsur.com.pe, Tue, Wed, Fri, Sun at 1400, US$85 *semi-cama*, US$120 *cama* (including meals), 27 hrs (stops in Trujillo). With **Ormeño**, Centro de Negocios El Terminal (near Terminal Terrestre), Of C33-34, T04-213 0847, daily at 1130 to **Lima**, US$70.

South to Peru   Colour map 1, C2.

a few beaches, a lovely town and some archaeological sites

Machala
The capital of the province of El Oro (altitude 4 m) is a booming agricultural town in a major banana producing and exporting region. It is unsafe, somewhat dirty and oppressively hot. For the tourist, the only reasons for stopping here are to go to the beautiful tranquil uplands of El Oro, and to catch a through CIFA bus to Peru (also runs from Guayaquil) for the beaches around Máncora. **Tourist office** ① *25 de Junio y 9 de Mayo, Municipio, iturmachala@hotmail.com, Mon-Fri 0800-1300, 1430-1730, Spanish only.* Some 30 km south along the road to Peru is **Santa Rosa** with the regional airport.

Puerto Bolívar
Puerto Bolívar, on the Estero Jambelí among mangroves, is a major export outlet for over two million tonnes of bananas annually. From the old pier canoes cross to the beaches of **Jambelí** (every 30 minutes, 0730-1500, US$4 return) on the far side of the mangrove islands which shelter

Puerto Bolívar from the Pacific. The beaches are crowded at weekends, deserted during the week and not very clean. Boats can be rented for excursions to the **Archipiélago de Jambelí**, a maze of islands and channels just offshore, stretching south between Puerto Bolívar and the Peruvian border. These mangrove islands are rich in birdlife (and insects for them to feed on, take repellent), the water is very clear and you may also see fish and reefs.

☆Zaruma

Southeast from Machala is the delightful old gold-mining town of Zaruma (118 km). It is reached from Machala by paved road via Piñas, by a scenic dirt road off the main Loja–Machala road, or via Pasaje and Paccha on another scenic dirt road off the Machala–Cuenca road.

Founded in 1549, Zaruma is perched on a hilltop, with steep, twisting streets and painted wooden buildings. The **tourist office** ① *in the Municipio, at the plaza, T07-297 3533, Mon-Fri 0800-1200, 1400-1800, Sat 0900-1600*, is very friendly and helpful. They can arrange for guides and accommodation with local families. Next door is the small **Museo Municipal** ① *Wed-Fri 0800-1200, 1400-1800, Sat 0900-1600, Sun 0900-1300, free*, it has a collection of local historical artifacts.

The Zaruma area has a number of prehispanic archaeological sites and petroglyphs. Tours with **Oroadventure** ① *at the Parque Central, T07-297 2761*, or with English-speaking guide **Ramiro Rodríguez** ① *T07-297 2523, kazan_rodríguez@yahoo.com*. Zaruma is also known for its excellent Arabica coffee freshly roasted in the agricultural store basement, the proud owner will show you around if the store isn't busy. On top of the small hill beyond the market is a public swimming pool (US$1), from where there are amazing views over the hot, dry valleys. For even grander views, walk up **Cerro del Calvario** (follow Calle San Francisco); go early in the morning as it gets very hot. At **Portovelo**, south of Zaruma, is the largest mine in the area. Its history is told inside a mine shaft at the **Museo Magner Turner** ① *T07-294 9345, daily 0900-1730, US$2*. There are also archaeological pieces; the owner is knowledgeable about sites in this region.

Piñas and around

Piñas, 19 km west of Zaruma, along the road to Machala is a pleasant town which conserves just a few of its older wooden buildings. Northwest of Piñas, 20 minutes along the road to Saracay and Machala, is **Buenaventura**, to the north of which lies an important area for bird conservation, with over 310 bird species recorded, including many rare ones. The **Jocotoco Foundation** (www.fjocotoco.org) protects a 1500-ha forest in this region, with 13 km of trails, entry US$15, lodge $$$$, advance booking required.

Bosque Petrificado Puyango

110 km south of Machala, west of the Arenillas–Alamor road, T07-293 2106 (Machala), bosquepuyango@hotmail.com, 0900-1700, US$1.

At Puyango, a dry-forest reserve, a great number of petrified trees, ferns, fruits and molluscs, 65 to 120 million years old, have been found. Over 120 species of birds can be seen. There is a camping area, no accommodation in the village, but ask around for floor space or try at the on-site information centre. If not, basic accommodation is available in **Las Lajas**, 20 minutes north (one residencial) and **Alamor**, 20 km south (several hotels, eg $ Rey Plaza, T07-268 0256).

Huaquillas

The stiflingly hot Ecuadorean border town of Huaquillas is something of a shopping arcade for Peruvians. The border runs along the Canal de Zarumilla and is crossed by two international bridges, one at the western end of Avenida La República in Huaquillas and a second newer one further south.

Border with Peru: Huaquillas-Tumbes

The best way to cross this border is on one of the international buses that run between Ecuador and Peru. Border formalities are only carried out at the new bridge, far outside the towns of Huaquillas (Ecuador) and Aguas Verdes (Peru). There are two border complexes called CEBAF (Centro Binacional de Atención Fronteriza), open 24 hours, on either side of the bridge; they are about 4 km apart. Both complexes have Ecuadorean and Peruvian customs and immigration officers so you get your exit and entry stamps in the same place. There is a **Peruvian Consulate in Machala** ① *Urb Unioro, Mz 14, V 11, near Hotel Oro Verde, T07-298 1719, www.consulado.pe/es/Machala, Mon-Fri 0800-1300, 1500-1800, Sat 0800-1300*. If crossing with your own vehicle, you have to stop at both border complexes for customs and, on the Ecuadorean side, you also have to stop at the customs (*aduana*) post at Chacras, 7 km from the Ecuadorean CEBAF, on the road to Machala. If you do not take one of the international buses, the crossing is inconvenient. See details in the Peru chapter. A taxi from Huaquillas to the Ecuadorean CEBAF costs US$2.50, to the Peruvian CEBAF US$5. See Peru chapter for transport to Tumbes and beyond. Banks do not change money in Huaquillas. Many street changers deal in soles and US$ cash. Do not change more US$ than you need to get to Tumbes, where there are reliable *cambios*, but get rid of all your soles here as they are difficult to exchange further inside Ecuador. Only clean, crisp US$ bills are accepted in Peru. Those seeking a more relaxed crossing to or from Peru should consider Macará (see page 1117) or La Balsa (see page 1121).

Listings South to Peru

Where to stay

Machala

$$$$ Oro Verde
Circunvalación Norte in Urbanización Unioro, T07-298 5444, www.oroverdehotels.com.
Includes buffet breakfast, 2 restaurants, nice pool (US$13 for non-guests), beautiful gardens, tennis courts, full luxury. Best in town.

$$ Oro Hotel
Sucre y Juan Montalvo, T07-293 0032, www.orohotel.com.
Includes breakfast, pricey restaurant, a/c, fridge, parking, nice comfortable rooms but those to the street are noisy, helpful staff. Recommended.

$ San Miguel
9 de Mayo y Sucre, T07-292 0474.
Good quality and value, some rooms without windows, hot water (request), no meals, a/c, cheaper with fan, fridge, helpful staff.

Zaruma

$$ Hostería El Jardín
Av Ayora, Barrio Limoncito, 10-min walk from centre (taxi US$1.50), T07-297 2706, www.hosteriaeljardinzaruma.com.
Lovely palm garden and terrace with views, internet, parking, comfortable rooms, breakfast extra, family-run. Recommended.

$$-$ Roland
At entrance to town on road from Portovelo, T07-297 2800.
Comfortable rooms (some are dark) and nicer more expensive cabins around pool, no breakfast, parking.

$$-$ Zaruma Colonial
Sucre y Sesmo, T07-297 2742, on Facebook.
Colonial style hotel, ample rooms, those to the back have mountain views, no meals.

$ Blacio
C Sucre, T07-297 2045.
Modern, ask for rooms with balcony, no meals.

$ Romería
On the plaza facing the church, T07-297 3618.
Old wooden house with balcony, a treat, restaurant downstairs.

Huaquillas

$$$$ Hillary Nature Resort
Km 1 Vía Arenillas-Alamor, 25 km east of Huaquillas, T07-370 0260, www.hillaryresort.com.
Luxury resort and spa. Ample rooms with all amenities, pool, 2 restaurants, several meeting rooms and convention facilities for 600 people.

$$-$ Hernancor
1 de Mayo y 10 de Agostso, T07-299 5467, grandhotelhernancor@gmail.com.
Nice rooms with a/c, includes breakfast, parking.

$$-$ Sol del Sur
Av La República y Chiriboga, T07-251 0898, www.soldelsurhotel.com.
Attractive rooms, includes breakfast, a/c, small bathrooms, parking.

$ Vanessa
1 de Mayo y Hualtaco, T07-299 6263.
A/c, internet, fridge, parking, pleasant.

Restaurants

Machala
The best food is found in the better hotels.

$$ Mesón Hispano
Av Las Palmeras y Sucre.
Very good grill, attentive service, outstanding.

$ Chifa Gran Oriental
25 de Junio entre Guayas y Ayacucho.
Good food and service, clean. Recommended.

Zaruma

$$ Amalsi
C Pichincha s/n. Mon-Sat 1100-2100.
Good pizzas, hamburgers and meals.

$$-$ 200 Millas
Av Honorato Márquez, uphill from bus station.
Good seafood.

$ Cafetería Uno
C Sucre.
Good for breakfast and Zaruma specialities, best *tigrillo* in town.

Transport

Machala
Air The regional airport is at Santa Rosa, 32 km south of Machala. 1 or 2 flights a day to **Quito** with TAME (Montalvo entre Bolívar y Pichincha, T07-293 0139).

Bus There is no Terminal Terrestre. Do not take night buses into or out of Machala as they are prone to hold-ups. To **Quito**, with **Occidental** (Buenavista entre Sucre y Olmedo), 10 hrs, US$10, 8 daily, with **Panamericana** (Colón y Bolívar), 7 daily. To **Guayaquil**, 3 hrs, US$6, hourly with **Ecuatoriano Pullman** (Colón y Rocafuerte), **CIFA** (Bolívar y Guayas) and **Rutas Orenses** (Tarqui y Rocafuerte), half-hourly; also hourly vans with **Oro Guayas**, Guayas y Pichincha, T07-293 4382, US$15, 3 hrs. There are 3 different scenic routes to **Loja**, each with bus service. They are, from north to south: via **Piñas** and **Zaruma**, partly paved and rough, via **Balsas**, fully paved; and via **Arenillas** and **Alamor**, for **Puyango** petrified forest. Fare to **Loja**, US$7, 5-6 hrs daily with **Trans Loja** (Tarqui y Bolívar). To **Zaruma**, see below. To **Cuenca**, half-hourly with **Trans Azuay** (Sucre y Junín), 3½ hrs, US$6. To **Huaquillas**, with

CIFA, direct, 1½ hrs, US$2.50, every 20 mins. To **Piura**, in Peru, with **CIFA**, at 1100, 2300 and 2400, US$10-15, 6 hrs, via **Máncora**, US$9-1400, 5 hrs and **Tumbes**, 6 daily, US$5, 3 hrs.

Zaruma
Bus To/from **Machala** with **Trans Piñas** or **TAC**, half-hourly, US$4.50, 3 hrs. To **Piñas**, take a Machala bound bus, US$1.25, 1 hr. To **Guayaquil**, 8 buses daily US$8.25, 6 hrs. To **Quito**, 5 daily, US$13.75, 12 hrs; to **Cuenca**, 3 daily (**Trans Azuay** at 0730, US$8.75, 6 hrs and **Loja**, 4 daily, US$6.25, 5 hrs (may have to change at Portovelo).

Puyango
Puyango is west of the Arenillas-Alamor highway: alight from bus at turn-off at the bridge over the Río Puyango. Bus from **Machala**, **Trans Loja** at 0930 and 1300, **CIFA** at 0600, US$3.50, 2½ hrs. From **Loja**, **Trans Loja** 0900, 1400 and 1930, US$7, 5 hrs. From **Alamor**, **Trans Loja** at 0730, 1000 and 1300, US$1.50, 1 hr. From **Huaquillas**, CIFA at 0500, **Trans Loja** at 0740 and **Unión Cariamanga** at 1130, US$2.50, 1½ hrs. You might be able to hire a pick-up from the main road to the park, US$3. Pick-up from Alamor to Puyango US$25 return, including wait.

Huaquillas
Bus There is no Terminal Terrestre, each bus company has its own office, many on Teniente Cordovez. If you are in a hurry, it can be quicker to change buses in Machala or Guayaquil. To **Machala**, with **CIFA** (Santa Rosa y Machala), direct, 1½ hrs, US$2.50, every 20 min; via Arenillas and Santa Rosa, 2 hrs, every 10 mins. To **Quito**, with **Occidental**, every 2 hrs, 12 hrs, US$12.50; with **Panamericana**, 11½ hrs, 3 daily via Santo Domingo; 2 daily via **Riobamba** and **Ambato**, 12 hrs. To **Guayaquil**, frequent service with **CIFA** and **Ecuatoriano Pullman**, 4½-5 hrs, US$7.50, take a direct bus; van service to downtown Guayaquil with **Transfrosur**, C Santa Rosa y Machala, T07-299 5288, hourly 0500-2000, Sun 0700-2000, 4 hrs, US$13.50. To **Cuenca**, 8 daily, 5 hrs, US$7.50. To **Loja**, 6 daily, 6 hrs, US$7.50.

> **Tip...**
> There may be military checkpoints on the roads in this border area, so keep your passport to hand.

Pacific
lowlands

This vast tract of Ecuador covers everything west of the Andes and north of the Guayas delta. Though popular with Quiteños and Guayaquileños, who come here for weekends and holidays, the Pacific lowlands receive relatively few foreign visitors, which is surprising given the natural beauty, diversity and rich cultural heritage of the coast. Here you can surf, watch whales, visit archaeological sites, or just relax and enjoy some of the best food this country has to offer. Parque Nacional Machalilla protects an important area of primary tropical dry forest, pre-Columbian ruins, coral reef and a wide variety of wildlife. Further north, in the province of Esmeraldas, there are not only well-known party beaches, but also opportunities to visit the remaining mangroves and experience two unique lifestyles: Afro-Ecuadorean on the coast and indigenous Cayapa further inland. Coastal resorts are busy and more expensive from December to April, the *temporada de playa*.

Guayaquil to Puerto López
quiet beaches, popular resorts and small fishing villages

Southwest of Guayaquil is the beach resort of Playas and, west of it, the Santa Elena Peninsula, with Salinas at its tip. From the town of Santa Elena, capital of the province of the same name, the coastal road stretches north for 737 km to Mataje on the Colombian border; along the way are countless beaches and fishing villages, and a few cities. Puerto López is the perfect base for whale watching and from which to explore the beautiful Parque Nacional Machalilla.

Playas and Salinas *Colour map 1, B1/B2.*
The beach resorts of Playas and Salinas remain as popular as ever with vacationing Guayaquileños. The paved toll highway from Guayaquil divides after 63 km at El Progreso (Gómez Rendón). One branch leads to **Playas** (General Villamil), the nearest seaside resort to Guayaquil.

Playas Bottle-shaped ceibo (kapok) trees characterise the landscape as it turns into dry, tropical thorn scrub. In Playas a few single-sailed balsa rafts, very simple but highly ingenious, can still be seen among the motor launches returning laden with fish. In high season (*temporada* – December to April), and at weekends, Playas is prone to severe crowding, although the authorities are trying to keep the packed beaches clean and safe (thieving is rampant during busy times). Out of season or midweek, the beaches are almost empty especially north towards Punta Pelado (5 km). Playas has six good surf breaks. There are showers, toilets and changing rooms along the beach, with fresh water, for a fee. Many hotels in our \$\$-\$ ranges. Excellent seafood and typical dishes from over 50 beach cafés (all numbered and named). Many close out of season. **Tourist office** ① *on the Malecón, Tue-Fri 0800-1200, 1400-1800, Sat-Sun 0900-1600.*

Best for
Archaeology ■ Natural beauty ■ Relaxing ■ Wildlife

ON THE ROAD

2016 earthquake

On 16 April 2016, at the close of this edition, an earthquake measuring 7.8 on the Richter scale struck the coast of Manabí near Pedernales. Over 650 people were killed and nearly 5000 were injured, with heavy property damage from Manta north to Muisne. In the aftermath of the tragedy, Ecuadoreans throughout the country showed their solidarity with those in affected areas and considerable assistance was also provided by the international community. By the time you read this, reconstruction should be well underway. Many of the affected areas lived from tourism and tourists can play an important role in the economic recovery of the region. There may be specific opportunities for volunteers and anybody can help just by visiting.

The information in this section generally reflects the state of affairs prior to the earthquake. There will be many changes and advance enquiry is advised before travelling between Manta and Muisne. The Galápagos Islands were not affected by the earthquake.

Salinas and further south Salinas, surrounded by miles of salt flats, is Ecuador's answer to Miami Beach. **Turismo Municipal** ① *Eloy Alfaro y Mercedes de Jesús Molina, Chipipe, T04-293 0004, Tue-Fri 0800-1700, Sat 0800-1400*. There is safe swimming in the bay and high-rise blocks of holiday flats and hotels line the seafront. More appealing is the (still urban) beach of Chipipe, west of the exclusive Salinas Yacht Club. In December-April it is overcrowded, its services stretched to the limit. Even in the off season it is not that quiet. The ocean all along the south shore of the Santa Elena peninsula is a marine reserve. Built on high cliffs, 8 km south of La Libertad, is **Punta Carnero**, with hotels in the $$$-$$ range. To the south is a magnificent 15-km beach with wild surf and heavy undertow, there is whale watching in season.

North to Puerto López

The '**Ruta del Spondylus**' north to Puerto López in the province of Manabí parallels the coastline and crosses the Chongón-Colonche coastal range. Most of the numerous small fishing villages along the way have good beaches and are slowly being developed for tourism. Beware of rip currents and undertow.

Valdivia

San Pedro and Valdivia are two unattractive villages which merge together. There are many fish stalls. This is the site of the 5000-year-old Valdivia culture. Many houses offer 'genuine' artefacts (it is illegal to export pre-Columbian items from Ecuador). Juan Orrala, who makes excellent copies, lives up the hill from the **Ecomuseo Valdivia** ① *open daily, US$1.50*, which has displays of original artefacts from Valdivia and other coastal cultures. There is also a handicraft section, where artisans may be seen at work, and lots of local information. At the museum is a restaurant and five rooms with bath to let. Most of the genuine artefacts discovered at the site are in museums in Quito and Guayaquil.

Manglaralto *Colour map 1, B2.*

Located 180 km northwest of Guayaquil, this is the main centre of the region north of Santa Elena. There is a tagua nursery; ask to see examples of worked 'vegetable ivory' nuts. It is a nice place, with a quiet beach, good surf but little shade. **Pro-pueblo** is an organization working with local communities to foster family-run orchards and cottage craft industry, using tagua nuts, *paja toquilla* (the fibre Panama hats are made from), and other local products. They have a craft shop in town (opposite the park), an office in San Antonio south of Manglaralto, T04-278 0230, and headquarters in Guayaquil, T04-268 3569, www.propueblo.com. **Proyecto de Desarrollo Ecoturístico Comunitario** ① *contact Paquita Jara T09-9174 0143*, has a network of simple lodgings with local families (US$9 per person), many interesting routes into the Cordillera Chongón Colonche and whale-watching and island tours.

Montañita and Olón

About 3 km north of Manglaralto, **Montañita** has mushroomed into a major surf resort, packed with hotels, restaurants, surf-board rentals, tattoo parlours and craft/jewellery vendors. The murder of two tourists in Montañita in 2016 and the subsequent focus on public safety provoked the authorities to take measures to encourage visitors back to the town. At the north end of the bay, 1 km away, is another hotel area with more elbow-room, Baja Montañita (or Montañita Punta, Surf Point). Between the two is a lovely beach where you'll find some of the best surfing in Ecuador. Various competitions are held during the year. At weekends in season, the town is full of Guayaquileños. Beyond an impressive headland and a few minutes north of Montañita is **Olón**, with a spectacular long beach, still tranquil but starting to get some of the overflow from Montañita. Nearby is **El Cangrejal**, a 7-ha dry tropical forest with mangroves.

Tip...

There is an ATM at **Banco Bolivariano** in Montañita and one other but they do not always work, so take cash.

Ayampe to Salango

North of Montañita, by La Entrada, the road winds up and inland through lush forest before continuing to the tranquil village of **Ayampe**. Tourism is growing here, with many popular places to stay at the south end of the beach, but the village retains an especially peaceful atmosphere, carefully safeguarded by the local community. The surfing here is very good. North of Ayampe are the villages of **Las Tunas**, **Puerto Rico** and **Río Chico**. There are places to stay all along this stretch of coast. Just north of Río Chico is **Salango**, with an ill-smelling fish processing plant, but worth visiting for the excellent **Salango archaeological museum** ⓘ *at the north end of town, daily 0900-1200, 1300-1700, US$1*, housing artefacts from excavations right in town. It also has a craft shop and, at the back, nice rooms with bath in the $ range. There is a place for snorkelling offshore, by Isla Salango.

Puerto López *Colour map 1, B2.*

This pleasant fishing town is beautifully set in a horseshoe bay. The beach is best for swimming at the far north and south ends, away from the fleet of small fishing boats moored offshore. The town is popular with tourists for watching humpback whales from approximately mid-June to September, and for visiting Parque Nacional Machalilla and Isla de la Plata.

Tip...

Banco Pichincha is situated in a large building at south end of Malecón. It has the only ATM in town, so it is best to take some cash.

Puerto López

To Machalilla & Manta

To ❸❺❼ & Fish Market

Río Pital

Abdón Calderón

González Suárez

Lascano

Machalilla

Montalvo

Atahualpa ⓘ iTUR

Machalilla Nat Park Office

Eloy Alfaro

General Córdova

García Moreno

$ Banco Pichincha

Mariscal Sucre

To Pier

To Montañita & Guayaquil

N

Not to scale

Where to stay 🛏
1 Itapoa
2 La Terraza
3 Mandála
4 Máxima
5 Nantu
6 Sol Inn
7 Victor Hugo

Restaurants 🍴
1 Bellitalia
2 Carmita
3 Patacón Pisao

Parque Nacional Machalilla

Park office in Puerto Lópe, C Eloy Alfaro y García Moreno, daily 0800-1200, 1400-1600.

The park extends over 55,000 ha, including Isla de la Plata, Isla Salango, and the magnificent beach of **Los Frailes** and preserves marine ecosystems as well as the dry tropical forest and archaeological sites on shore. The beach is clean and well cared for, but gets busy on weekends and holidays. At the north end of Los Frailes beach is a trail through the forest leading to a lookout with great views and on to the town of Machalilla (don't take valuables). The land-based part of the park is divided into three sections which are separated by private land, including the town of Machalilla. The park is recommended for birdwatching, especially in the cloudforest of Cerro San Sebastián (see below); there are also howler monkeys, several other species of mammals and reptiles.

About 5 km north of Puerto López, at Buena Vista, a dirt road to the east leads to **Agua Blanca** (park kiosk at entry). Here, 5 km from the main road, in the national park, amid hot, arid scrub, is a small village and a fine, small **archaeological museum** ① *0800-1800, US$5 for a 2-hr guided tour of the museum, ruins (a 45-min walk), funerary urns and sulphurous lake, horses can be hired, camping is possible and there's a cabin and 1 very basic room for rent above the museum for US$5 pp; pick-up from Puerto López US$8,* containing some fascinating ceramics from the Manteño civilization. **San Sebastián,** 9 km from Agua Blanca, is in tropical moist forest at 800 m; orchids and birds can be seen and possibly howler monkeys. Although part of the national park, this area is administered by the Comuna of Agua Blanca, which charges an entry fee; you cannot go independently. It's five hours on foot or by horse. A tour to the forest costs US$40 per day including guide, horses and camping (minimum two people), otherwise lodging is with a family at extra cost.

About 24 km offshore is **Isla de la Plata.** Trips are popular because of the similarities with the Galápagos. Wildlife includes nesting colonies of Waved Albatross (April to November), frigates and three different booby species. Whales can be seen from June to September, as well as sea lions. It is also a pre-Columbian site with substantial pottery finds, and there is good diving and snorkelling, as well as walks. Take a change of clothes, water, precautions against sun and seasickness (most agencies provide snorkelling equipment). You can only visit with a tour and staying overnight is not permitted.

Puerto López to Manta

North of Machalilla, the road forks at **Puerto Cayo,** where whale-watching tours may be organized July-August. One road follows the coast, partly through forested hills, passing Cabo San Lorenzo with its lighthouse. The other route heads inland through the trading centre of **Jipijapa** to **Montecristi,** below an imposing hill, 16 km before Manta. Montecristi is renowned as the centre of the panama hat industry. Also produced are varied straw- and basketware, and wooden barrels which are strapped to donkeys for carrying water. Ask for José Chávez Franco, Rocafuerte 203, where you can see panama hats being made. Some 23 km east of Montecristi is **Portoviejo,** capital of Manabí province, a sweltering unsafe commercial city.

Listings Guayaquil to Puerto López *map page 1139.*

Where to stay

Salinas

$$ Francisco II and III
Malecón y Las Palmeras, T04-277 3751;
Malecó 231 y C 27, T09-9155 2127,
www.hotelfranciscoecuador.com.
Both are very nice, comfortable rooms,
restaurant, a/c, fridge pool.

$$ Travel Suites
Av 5 Y C 13, T04-277 2856, maguerra@
salinastravelsuites.com.
Modern, a/c, kitchenette with fridge,
very good value in low season.

Manglaralto
See also **Proyecto de Desarrollo Ecoturístico Comunitario,** page 1138.

$$-$ Manglaralto Sunset
El Oro y Constitución, 1 block from the Plaza, T04-290 1405, www.hotelmanglaraltosunset.com.

Nice modern place, comfortable rooms with a/c, hammocks, cafeteria bar, electric shower, parking.

Montañita

There are many places to stay in town; the quieter ones are at Montañita Punta. Prices are negotiable in low season.

$$$-$$ Balsa Surf Camp
50 m from the beach in Montañita Punta, T09-8971 4685, balsasurfcamp.com.
Very nice spacious cabins with terrace, hammocks in garden, fan, parking, surf classes and rentals, small well-designed spa, French/Ecuadorean-run. Recommended.

$$ La Casa del Sol
In Montañita Punta, T09-6863 4956, www.casadelsolmontanita.com.
A/c, some rooms are dark, fan, restaurant/bar, surf classes and rentals, yoga drop-in.

$$ Pakaloro
In town at the end of C Guido Chiriboga, T04-206 0092, www.pakaloro.com.
Modern 4-storey building with lots of wood, ample rooms with balcony and hammock ($ low season), dorm US$12-20 pp (US$9-12 low season), fan, shared kitchen, nice setting by the river, good value.

$$ Rosa Mística
Montañita Punta, T09-9798 8383, www.rosamisticahostal.com.
Tranquil place, small rooms, cheaper ones away from beach, a/c, garden.

$$-$ Las Palmeras
15 de Mayo y Ledesma, T06-696 2134, https://hostalpalmeras.jimdo.com.
Reasonably quiet, fan, laundry, family-run, English spoken.

$$-$ Sole Mare
On the beach at the north end of Montañita Punta, T04-206 0119, www.solem are-ecuador.com.
In a lovely setting on the beach, fan, garden, parking, run by an attentive father-and-son, both called Carlos, English spoken, good value.

Olón

$$$ Samai
10 mins from town by taxi (US$5), T09-9462 1316, www.samailodge.com.
Rustic cabins in a natural setting, great views, restaurant/bar, pool, jacuzzi, advance booking required.

$$ Isramar
Av Sta Lucia, ½ block from beach, T04-278 8096, http://hosteriaisramar.com.
Rooms with bath and fan, small garden, restaurant/bar, friendly owner Doris Cevallos.

$$-$ La Mariposa
13 de Diciembre y Rosa Mística, by church, T09-8017 8357, www.lamariposahostal.com.
3-storey building, nice ocean views from top floor, Italian-run, English and French also spoken, good value.

Ayampe to Salango

Ayampe

$$ Finca Punta Ayampe
South of other Ayampe hotels, Quito T09-9189 0982, www.fincapuntaayampe.com.
Bamboo structure high on a hill with great ocean views, restaurant, hot water, mosquito nets, helpful staff.

$$-$ Cabañas de la Iguana
Ayampe, T05-257 5165, www.hotelayampe.com.
Cabins for 4, mosquito nets, cooking facilities, quiet, relaxed family atmosphere, knowledgeable and helpful, organizes excursions, good choice.

Las Tunas–Puerto Rico

$$$-$$ La Barquita
By Las Tunas, 4 km north of Ayampe, T05-234 7051.
Restaurant and bar are in a boat on the beach with good ocean views, rooms with fan and mosquito nets, pool, nice garden, games, tours, Swiss-run.

Puerto López

$$$ La Terraza
On hill overlooking town, C San Francisoc s/n (moto-taxi US$0.50), T09-8855 4887, www.laterraza.de.
Spacious cabins, great views over the bay, gardens, restaurant (only for guests), crystal-clear pool and jacuzzi, parking, German-run.

$$$ Victor Hugo
North along the beach, T05-230 0054, www.victorhugohotel.com.ec.
Ample rooms with bamboo decor, balconies.

$$ Mandála
Malecón at north end of the beach, T05-230 0181, www.hosteriamandala.info.
Nice cabins decorated with art, fully wheelchair accessible, gorgeous tropical garden, good

restaurant only for guests, fan, mosquito nets, games, music room, Swiss/Italian-run, English spoken, knowledgeable owners. Highly recommended.

$$ Nantu
Malecón at north end of the beach, T05-230 0040, www.hosterianantu.com.
Ample modern well-maintained rooms, a/c, small pool and garden, restaurant and bar overlooking the beach.

$$-$ Itapoa
On a lane off Abdón Calderón, between the Malecón and Montalvo, T09-9314 5894, www.hosteriaitapoa.com.
Thatched cabins around large garden, hot water, cheaper in dorm, includes breakfast on a lovely terrace overlooking the sea, family-run, English spoken.

$ Máxima
González Suárez y Machallila, T05-230 0310, www.hotelmaxima.org.
Cheaper with shared bath, mosquito nets, laundry and cooking facilities, camping, parking, modern, English spoken, good value.

$ Sol Inn
Montalvo y Eloy Alfaro, T05-230 0234, http://hostalsolinn.machallilatours.com.
Bamboo and wood construction, private or shared bath, hot water, fan, laundry and cooking facilities, garden, pool table, popular, relaxed atmosphere, offers tours and Spanish classes.

Puerto López to Manta
There are other places to stay but many close out of season.

$$ Luz de Luna
5 km north of Puerto Cayo on the coastal road, T09-9708 8613 Quito T02-249 3825, www.hosterialuzdeluna.com.
On a clean beach, comfortable spacious rooms with balcony, a/c, cheaper with fan, cold water in cabins, shared hot showers available, mosquito nets, pool. Also in Salinas.

$$ Puerto Cayo
South end of beach, Puerto Cayo, T05-238 7119, T09-9752 1538.
Good restaurant, a/c or fan, comfortable rooms with hammocks and terrace overlooking the sea.

Restaurants

Salinas
A couple of blocks inland from the Malecón are food stalls serving good ceviches and freshly cooked seafood.

$$$ La Bella Italia
Malecón y C 17.
Good pizza and international food.

$$$-$$ Amazon
Malecón near Banco de Guayaquil, T04-277 3671.
Elegant upmarket eatery, grill and seafood specialities, good wine list.

$$ Oyster Catcher
Enríquez Gallo entre C 47 y C 50. Oct-May.
Restaurant and bar, friendly place, safe oysters, enquire here about birdwatching tours with local expert Ben Haase.

$ El Mayquito
Av 2 y C 12.
Simple, friendly place with good food.

Montañita

$$$-$$ Tikilimbo
C Guido Chiriboga 2, www.tikilimbo.com.
Good quality, vegetarian dishes available. Also has hotel, bar and surf shop.

$$ Hola Ola
In the center of town, by Rocío, Facebook: hola.ola.cafe.
Good international food and bar with some live music and disco, popular.

$$ Marea Pizzeria Bar
10 de Agosto y Av 2. Evenings only.
Real wood-oven pizza, very tasty. Recommended.

$$ Rocío
10 de Agosto y Av 2, inside eponymous hotel, www.rocioboutiquehotel.com.
Good Mediterranean food.

Salango

$$ El Delfín Mágico.
T09-9114 7555.
Excellent, order meal before visiting museum because all food is cooked from scratch, very fresh and safe.

Puerto López

$$$ Bellitalia
North toward the river, T09-9617 5183.
Mon-Sat 1800-2100.
Excellent authentic Italian food, home-made pasta, attentive owners Vittorio and Elena. Reservations required. Recommended.

$$ Carmita
Malecón y General Córdova.
Tasty fish and seafood, a Puerto López tradition.

$$ Patacón Pisao
Gen Córdova, half a block from the malecón.
Colombian food, giant *patacones* and *arepas*.

What to do

Salinas
Ben Haase, *at Museo de Ballenas, Av Enríquez Gallo 1109 entre C47 y C50, T04-277 7335, T09-8674 7607.* Expert English-speaking naturalist guide runs birdwatching tours to the Ecuasal salt ponds, US$50 for a small group. Also whale watching and trips to a sea lion colony.
Fernando Félix, *T04-238 4560, T09-7915 8079.* English-speaking marine biologist, can guide for whale watching and other nature trips, arrange in advance.

Montañita
Surfboard rentals all over town from US$4 per hr, US$15 per day.

Language courses
Montañita Spanish School, on the main road 50 m uphill outside the village, T04-206 0116, www.montanitaspanishschool.com.

Ayampe to Salango

Ayampe
Otra Ola, *beside Cabañas de la Iguana, www.otraola.com.* Surf lessons and board rental, yoga and Spanish classes. Enthusiastic Canadian owners.

Puerto López

Language courses
La Lengua, *Abdón Calderón y García Moreno, east of the highway, T09-233 9316 or Quito T02-250 1271, www.la-lengua.com.*

Whale watching
Puerto López is a major centre for trips from Jun to Sep, with many more agencies than we can list. Whales can also be seen elsewhere, but most reliably in Puerto López. There is a good fleet of small boats (16-20 passengers) running excursions, all have life jackets and a toilet, those with 2 engines are safer. All agencies offer the same tours for the same price. Beware touts offering cheap tours to "La Isla", they take you to Isla Salango not Isla de la Plata. In high season: US$45 pp for whale watching, Isla de la Plata and snorkelling, with a snack and drinks, US$25 for whale watching only (available Jun and Sep). Outside whale season, tours to Isla de la Plata and snorkelling cost US$40. Trips depart from the pier (US$1 entry fee) around 0800 and return around 1700. Agencies also offer tours to the mainland sites of the national park. A day tour combining Agua Blanca and Los Frailes costs US$25 pp plus US$5 entry fee. There are also hiking, birdwatching, kayaking, diving (be sure to use a reputable agency) and other trips.
Aventuras La Plata, *on Malecón, T05-230 0189, www.aventuraslaplata.com.* Whale-watching tours.
Cercapez, *at the Centro Comercial on the highway, T05-230 0173.* All-inclusive trips to San Sebastián, with camping, local guide and food at US$40 pp per day.
Exploramar Diving, *Malecón y Gral Córdova, T09-9724 0254, www.exploradiving.com.* Quito based, T02-256 3905. Have 2 boats for 8-16 people and their own compressor. PADI divemaster accompanies qualified divers to various sites, but advance notice is required, US$120 pp for all-inclusive diving day tour (2 tanks). Also diving lessons. Recommended.
Palo Santo, *Malecón y Abdón Calderón, T05-230 0312, palosanto22@gmail.com.* Whale-watching tours.

Transport

Playas
Bus Trans Posorja and Villamil to **Guayaquil**, frequent, 2 hrs, US$3.25; taxi US$25.

Salinas
Bus To **Guayaquil**, Coop Libertad Peninsular (**CLP**), María González y León Avilés, every 5 mins, US$4.75, 2½ hrs. For **Montañita**, **Puerto López** and points north, transfer at La Libertad (not safe, take a taxi between terminals) or Santa Elena. From La Libertad, every 30 mins to Puerto López, US$5, 2½ hrs; or catch a Guayaquil–Olón bus in Santa Elena.

Manglaralto

Bus To **Santa Elena** and **La Libertad**, US$1.50, 1 hr. Transfer in Santa Elena for Guayaquil. To **Guayaquil** direct, see Olón, below. To **Puerto López**, 1 hr, US$2.

Montañita and Olón

Bus Montañita is just a few mins south of Olón, from where **CLP** has direct buses to **Guayaquil** at 0445, 0545, 1000, 1300, 1500, 1700 (same schedule from Guayaquil), US$7.50, 3 hrs; taxi US$90; or transfer in Santa Elena, US$2, 1½ hrs. To **Puerto López**, Cooperativa Manglaralto every 30 mins, US$2.50, 45 mins.

Puerto López

Mototaxis all over town, US$0.50 pp.

Bus Bus terminal 2 km north of town. To **Santa Elena** or **La Libertad**, every 30 mins, US$5, 2½ hrs. To **Montañita** and **Manglaralto**, US$3.25, 1 hr. To **Guayaquil**, direct with **Cooperativa Jipijapa** via Jipijapa, 10 daily, US$5.75, 4 hrs; or transfer in Olón or Santa Elena. Pick-ups for hire to nearby sites are by the market, east of the highway. To/from **Manta**, direct, hourly, US$3.75,

2½ hrs; or transfer in Jipijapa. To **Quito** with **Reina del Camino**, office in front of market, daily 0800 and 2000; and **CA Aray** at 0500, 0900 and 1900, 9 hrs, US$16. To **Jipijapa**, Cooperativa Jipijapa, every 45 mins, US$2, 1 hr.

Parque Nacional Machalilla

Bus To **Los Frailes**: take a bus towards Jipijapa (US$0.75), mototaxi (US$5), or a pick-up (US$8), and alight at the turn-off just south of the town of Machalilla, then walk for 30 mins. No transport back to Puerto López after 2000 (but check in advance). **To Agua Blanca**: take tour, a pick-up (US$7), mototaxi (US$10 return with 2 hrs wait) or a bus bound for Jipijapa (US$0.75); it is a hot walk of more than 1 hr from the turning to the village. **To Isla de la Plata**: the island can only be visited on a day trip. Many agencies offer tours, see Puerto López, above.

Puerto López to Manta

Bus From Jipijapa (terminal on the outskirts) to **Manglaralto** (2 hrs, US$2.50), to **Puerto López** (1 hr, US$1.25, these go by Puerto Cayo), to **Manta** (1 hr, US$1.25), to **Quito** (10 hrs, US$9).

Manta and Bahía de Caráquez

busy centres separated by wildlife and sporting opportunities

These are two quite different seaside places: Manta a rapidly growing port city, prospering on fishing and trade; Bahía de Caráquez a relaxed resort town and a pleasant place to spend a few days. It is proud of its 'eco' credentials. Just beyond Bahía, on the other side of the Río Chone estuary, is the popular resort village of Canoa, boasting some of the finest beaches in Ecuador.

Manta and around *Colour map 1, B2.*

Ecuador's second port after Guayaquil is a busy town that sweeps round a bay filled with all sorts of boats. A constant sea breeze tempers the intense sun and makes the city's *malecones* pleasant places to stroll. At the gentrified west end of town is Playa Murciélago, a popular beach with wild surf (flags indicate whether it is safe to bathe), with good surfing from December to April. Here, the Malecón Escénico has a cluster of bars and seafood restaurants. It is a lively place especially at weekends, when there is good music, free beach aerobics and lots of action. Beyond El Murciélago, along the coastal road are San Mateo, Santa Marianita, San Lorenzo and Puerto Cayo, before reaching Machalilla and Puerto López. The **Museo Centro Cultural Manta** ① *Malecón y C 19, T05-262 6998, Mon-Fri 0900-1630, Sat-Sun 1000-1500, free*, has a small but excellent collection of archaeological pieces from seven different civilizations that flourished on the coast of Manabí between 3500 BC and AD 1530. Three bridges join the main town with **Tarqui**, which was flattened in the April 2016 earthquake. Manta has public safety problems, enquire locally about the current situation.

Crucita

A rapidly growing resort, 45 minutes by road from either Manta or Portoviejo, Crucita is busy at weekends and holidays when people flock here to enjoy ideal conditions for paragliding, hang-gliding and kite-surfing. The best season for flights is July to December. There is also an abundance of sea birds in the area. There are many restaurants serving fish and seafood along the seafront. A good one is Motumbo, try their *viche*, they also offer interesting tours and rent bikes.

North to Bahía

About 60 km northeast of Manta (30 km south of Bahía de Caráquez) are **San Clemente** and, 3 km south, **San Jacinto**. The ocean is magnificent but be wary of the strong undertow. Both get crowded during the holiday season and have a selection of *cabañas* and hotels. Some 3 km north of San Clemente is **Punta Charapotó**, a high promontory clad in dry tropical forest, above a lovely beach. Here are some nice out-of-the-way accommodations and an out-of-place upmarket property development.

☆Bahía de Caráquez and around *Colour map 1, B2.*

Set on the southern shore at the seaward end of the Chone estuary, Bahía has an attractive riverfront laid out with parks along the Malecón which goes right around the point to the ocean side. The beaches in town are nothing special, but there are excellent beaches nearby between San Vicente and Canoa and at Punta Bellaca (the town is busiest July-August). Bahía has declared itself an 'eco-city', with recycling projects, organic gardens and ecoclubs. Tricycle rickshaws called 'eco-taxis' are a popular form of local transport and keep the streets blissfully quiet. Information about the eco-city concept can be obtained from **Río Muchacho Organic Farm** in Canoa (see below) or the **Planet Drum Foundation** ① *www.planetdrum.org*. **Museo Bahía de Caráquez** ① *Malecón Alberto Santos y Aguilera, T05-269 2285, Tue-Sat 0830-1630, free,* has an interesting collection of archaeological artefacts from prehispanic coastal cultures, a life-size balsa raft and modern sculpture. Bahía is a port for international yachts, with good service at **Puerto Amistad** ① *T05-269 3112.* There was significant earthquake damage in April 2016.

The Río Chone estuary has several islands with mangrove forest. The area is rich in birdlife, and dolphins may also be seen. **Isla Corazón** has a boardwalk through an area of protected mangrove forest and there are bird colonies at the end of the island which can only be accessed by boat. The village of **Puerto Portovelo** is involved in mangrove reforestation and runs an ecotourism project (tour with *guía nativo* US$6 per person). You can visit independently, taking a Chone-bound bus from San Vicente or with an agency. Visits here are tide-sensitive, so even if you go independently, it is best to check with the agencies about the best time to visit. Inland near Chone is **La Segua** wetland, very rich in birds; Bahía agencies offer tours here. **Saiananda** ① *5 km from Bahía along the bay, T05-239 8331, owner Alfredo Harmsen, biologist, reached by taxi or any bus heading out of town, US$2,* is a private park with extensive areas of reforestation and a large collection of animals, a cactus garden and spiritual centre. Also offer first-class accommodation ($$ including breakfast) and vegetarian meals served in an exquisite dining area over the water.

San Vicente and Canoa *Colour map 1, B2.*

On the north side of the Río Chone, **San Vicente** is reached from Bahía de Caráquez by a long bridge. Some 17 km beyond, **Canoa**, once a quiet fishing village with a splendid 200-m-wide beach, has grown rapidly and is increasingly popular with Ecuadorean and foreign tourists. It was badly damaged in the April 2016 earthquake. There is no ATM in Canoa, but in San Vicente at Banco Pichincha. The beautiful beach between San Vicente and Canoa is a good walk, horse or bike ride. Horses and bicycles can be hired through several hotels. Surfing is good, particularly during the wet season, December to April. In the dry season there is good wind for windsurfing. Canoa is also a good place for hang-gliding and paragliding. Tents for shade and chairs are rented at the beach for US$3 a day. About 10 km north of Canoa, the **Río Muchacho Organic Farm** ① *www.riomuchacho. com, see What to do, page 1148,* accepts visitors and volunteers, it's an eye-opener to rural coastal (*montubio*) culture and to organic farming.

North to Pedernales *Colour map 1, A2.*

The coastal road cuts across Cabo Pasado to **Jama** (1½ hours; cabins and several *hostales*), then runs parallel to the beach past coconut groves and shrimp hatcheries, inland across some low hills and across the Equator to **Pedernales**, a market town and crossroads with nice undeveloped beaches to the north. It was heavily damaged in the 2016 earthquake. A poor unpaved road goes north along the shore to Cojimíes. The main coastal road, fully paved, goes north to Chamanga, El Salto and Esmeraldas. Another important road goes inland to El Carmen; it divides at Puerto Nuevo: one

Branch to Santo Domingo de los Tsáchilas, another to La Concordia. The latter is the most direct route to Quito.

Santo Domingo de los Tsáchilas

In the hills above the western lowlands, Santo Domingo, 129 km from Quito, is an important commercial centre and transport hub. It is capital of the eponymous province. The city is big, noisy and unsafe, caution is recommended at all times in the market areas, including the pedestrian walkway along 3 de Julio and in peripheral neighbourhoods. Sunday is market day, shops and banks close Monday instead. It was known as 'Santo Domingo de los Colorados', a reference to the traditional red hair dye, made with *achiote* (annatto), worn by the indigenous Tsáchila men. Today the Tsáchila only wear their indigenous dress on special occasions. There are less than 2000 Tsáchilas left, living in eight communities off the roads leading from Santo Domingo towards the coast. Their lands make up a reserve of some 8000 ha. Visitors interested in their culture are welcome at the **Complejo Turístico Huapilú**, in the Comunidad Chigüilpe, where there is a small but interesting museum (contributions expected). Access is via the turn-off east at Km 7 on the road to Quevedo, from where it is 4 km. Tours are run by travel agencies in town. The Santo Domingo area also offers opportunities for nature trips and sports activities, such as rafting.

Listings Manta and Bahía de Caráquez

Tourist information

Ministerio de Turismo (Paseo José María Egas 1034 (Av 3) y C 11, Manta, T05-262 2944, Mon-Fri 0900-1230, 1400-1700); **Dirección Municipal de Turismo** (C9 y Av 4, Manta, T05-261 0171, Mon-Fri 0800-1700); and **Oficina de Información ULEAM** (Malecón Escénico, Manta, T05-262 4099, daily 0900-1700); all helpful and speak some English.

Where to stay

Manta and around

All streets have numbers; those above 100 are in Tarqui (those above C110 are not safe).

$$$$ Oro Verde
Malecón y C 23, T05-262 9200,
www.oroverdehotels.com.
Includes buffet breakfast, restaurant, pool, all luxuries.

$$$ Vistalmar
C M1 y Av 24B, at Playa Murciélago, T05-262 1671,
www.hosteriavistaalmar.com.
Exclusive hotel overlooking the ocean. Ample cabins and suites tastefully decorated with art, a/c, pool, cabins have kitchenettes, gardens by the sea. A place for a honeymoon.

$$$-$$ Donkey Den
In Santa Marianita, 20 mins south of Manta, T09-9723 2026, www.donkeydenguesthouse.com.
Nice rooms right on the beach where kite-surfing is popular, private or shared bath, dorm for 5

US$15 pp, cooking facilities, breakfast available, popular with US expats, taxi from Manta US$10.

$$ Manakin
C 20 y Av 12, T05-262 0413.
A/c, comfortable rooms, small patio, nice common areas.

$$ YorMar
Av 14 entre C 19 y C 20, T05-262 4375,
www.hostalyormar.com.ec.
Attractive rooms with small kitchenette and patio, a/c, parking.

$ Centenario
C 11 No 602 y Av 5, enquire at nearby Lavamatic Laundry, T05-262 9245.
Pleasant hostel in a refurbished old home in the centre of town. Shared bath, hot water, fan, cooking facilities, nice views, quiet location, good value.

Crucita

$$-$ Cruzita
Towards the south end of beach, T05-234 0068.
Pleasant hostel right on the beach with great views, meals on request, cold water, fan, small pool, use of kitchen in the evening, parking, good value. Owner Raul Tobar offers paragliding flights and lessons. Recommended.

$$-$ Hostal Voladores
At south end of beach, T05-234 0200,
www.parapentecrucita.com.
Simple but nice, restaurant, private bath, cheaper with shared bath, hot water, small pool,

sea kayaks available. Owner Luis Tobar offers paragliding flights and lessons.

North to Bahía

San Jacinto and San Clemente

$$ Hotel San Jacinto
On the beach between San Jacinto and San Clemente, T05-267 2516, www. hotelsanjacinto.com.
Older refurbished place with a pleasant location right by the ocean, restaurant, hot water, fan.

Punta Charapotó

$$-$ Peñón del Sol
On the hillside near Punta Charapotó, T09-9941 4149, penondelsol@hotmail.com.
Located on a 250 ha dry tropical forest reserve, meals on request, shared bath, cold water, lovely atmosphere, great views, camping possible.

$ Sabor de Bamboo
On the ocean side of the road to Punta Charapotó, T09-8024 3562, see Facebook.
Nice simple wooden cabins with sea breeze, cold water, restaurant and bar, music on weekends, wonderfully relaxed place, friendly owner Meier, German and English spoken.

Bahía de Caráquez

$$$ La Piedra
Circunvalación near Bolívar, T05-269 0780, www.hotellapiedra.com.ec.
Modern hotel with access to the beach and lovely views, good expensive restaurant, a/c, pool, good service, bicycle rentals for guests.

$$$-$$ La Herradura
Bolívar e Hidalgo, T05-269 0446, www.laherradurahotelecuador.com.
Older well-maintained hotel, restaurant, a/c, nice common areas, cheaper rooms are good value.

$$ Bahía B&B
By Puente Las Caras and Paseo Shopping, 500m from Malecón, T05-269 1880, http:// ecuavacation.com.
A variety of different rooms in a modern building, a/c, parking, Canadian/Colombian owned.

Canoa

There are over 60 hotels in Canoa.

$$$ Hostería Canoa
1 km south of town, T09-9995 5401, www.hosteriacanoa.com.

Comfortable cabins and rooms, good restaurant and bar, a/c, pool, sauna, whirlpool.

$$-$ Amalur
C San Andrés, opposite football pitch, T09-8303 5039, www.amalurcanoa.com.
Rooms and apartments ($$), brightly furnished, all with bath, welcoming, restaurant (see below), garden.

$$-$ Baloo
On the beach at south end of the village, T09-8188 5048, www.baloo-canoa.com.
Wood and bamboo cabins, private or shared bath, British-run. Nice quiet location, being rebuilt after 2016 earthquake.

$ Casa Shangrila
On main road 200 m north of bridge, T09-9146 8470, http://casashangrila.com.
Inland, away from the buzz of the centre but only 5 min walk from a nice quiet stretch of beach. Rooms with fan and private bath, hot water, nice garden, small pool, attentive service, good value.

$ Coco Loco
On the beach toward the south end of town, T09-5910 4821, www.hostalcocoloco.weebly.com.
Pleasant breezy hotel with nice views, café serves breakfast and snacks, bar, private or shared bath, also dorm, hot showers, cooking facilities, surfboard rentals, party atmosphere, excellent horse riding, English spoken, popular. Under new ownership in 2017, being renovated.

North to Pedernales

Jama

$$$-$$ Punta Prieta Guest House
By Punta Prieta, T09-8039 5972, Quito T02-286 2986, www.puntaprieta.com.
Gorgeous setting on a headland high above the ocean with access to pristine beaches. Meals available, comfortable cabins and suites with fridge, balcony with hammocks, nice grounds.

Pedernales

$$ Cocosolo
On a secluded beach 20 km north of Pedernales (pickups from main park US$1, 30 mins), T09-9940 6048, http://cocosololodge.com.
A lovely hideaway set among palms. Cabins and rooms, camping possible, restaurant, horses for hire, French and English spoken.

Santo Domingo de los Tsáchilas

$$$$ Tinalandia
16 km from Santo Domingo, on the road to Quito, poorly signposted, look for a large rock painted white; T09-9946 7741, Quito T02-244 9028, www.tinalandia.com.
Includes full board, nice chalets in cloudforest reserve bordering on Bosque Protector Tanti, great food, spring-fed pool, good birdwatching, advance booking required.

$$$ Zaracay
Av Quito 1639, 1.5 km from the centre, T02-275 0316, www.hotelzaracay.com.
Restaurant, gardens and swimming pool (US$5 for non-guests), parking, good rooms and service. Advance booking advised, especially on weekends.

$ Safiro Internacional
29 de Mayo 800 y Loja, T02-276 0706.
Comfortable modern hotel, cafeteria, hot water, a/c, good value.

Restaurants

Manta and around
Restaurants on Malecón Escénico serve local seafood.

$$ El Marino
Malecón y C 110, Tarqui. Lunch only.
Classic fish and seafood restaurant, for ceviches, *sopa marinera* and other delicacies.

Bahía de Caráquez

$$ Puerto Amistad
On the pier at Malecón y Vinueza. Mon-Sat 1200-2400.
Nice setting over the water, international food and atmosphere, popular with yachties.

$$-$ Muelle Uno
By the pier where canoes leave for San Vicente. Daily 1000-2400.
Good grill and seafood, lovely setting over the water.

Canoa

$$ Amalur
See Where to stay, above. Daily 1200-2100.
Fresh seafood and authentic Spanish specialities, attentive service.

$$-$ Surf Shak
At the beach. Daily 0800-2400.
Good for pizza, burgers and breakfast, best coffee in town, Wi-Fi, popular hangout for surfers, English spoken.

What to do

Manta and around
Delgado Travel, *Av 6 y C 13, T05-262 2813, vtdelgad@hotmail.com.* City and regional tours, whale-watching trips, Parque Nacional Machalilla, run **Hostería San Antonio** at El Aromo, 15 km south of Manta.

Language courses
Academia Sur Pacífico, *Av 24 y C 15, Edif Barre, p3, T05-267 9206, www.surpacifico.k12.ec.* With a variety of programmes and activities.

Bahía de Caráquez

Language courses
Sundown, *at Sundown Inn, in Canoa, on the beach, 3 km toward San Vicente, contact Juan Carlos, T09-9364 5470, www.ecuadorbeach.com.* US$7.50-9 per hr.

Canoa
Surfboard rentals US$5 per hr.
Canoa Thrills, *at the beach next to Surf Shak, www.canoathrills.com.* Surfing tours and lessons, sea kayaking. Also rent boards and bikes. English spoken.
Río Muchacho Organic Farm, *J Santos y Av 3 de Noviembre, T05-302 0487, www.riomuchacho.com.* Bookings for the organic farm and ecocity tours. Also has an ecolodge ($ pp) with meals at US$5. Hikes from Canoa to Río Muchacho and around Río Muchacho. Knowledgeable and helpful with local information. Recommended.

Transport

Manta and around
Air Eloy Alfaro airport. **TAME** (T05-390 5052), **Avianca** (T05-262 8899) and **LATAM** to **Quito** several daily.

Bus Most buses leave from the terminal on C 7 y Av 8 in the centre. A couple of companies have their own private terminals nearby. To **Quito** Terminal Quitumbe, 9 hrs, US$10-12. **Guayaquil**, 4 hrs, US$5, hourly. **Esmeraldas**, 3 daily, 10 hrs, US$10. **Santo Domingo**, 7 hrs, US$7.50.

Portoviejo, 45 mins, US$1, every 10 mins.
Jipijapa, 1 hr, US$1.25, every 20 mins.
Bahía de Caráquez, 3 hrs, US$3.75, hourly.

Crucita

Bus Run along the Malecón. There is frequent service to **Portoviejo**, US$1.25, 1 hr and **Manta**, US$1.50, 1½ hrs.

North to Bahía

Bus From San Clemente to **Portoviejo**, every 15 mins, US$1.50, 1¼ hrs. To **Bahía de Caráquez**, US$0.75, 30 mins, a few start in San Clemente in the morning or wait for a through bus at the highway. Mototaxis from San Clemente to Punta Charapotó, US$0.75.

Bahía de Caráquez

Boat Motorized canoes (*lanchas* or *pangas*) cross the estuary to **San Vicente**, from the dock opposite C Ante, US$0.50.

Bus The Terminal Terrestre is at the entrance to town, 3 km from centre, taxi US$2. To **Quito** Terminal Quitumbe, **Reina del Camino** at 0620, 0800, 2145 and 2220, 8 hrs, US$12.50. To **Santo Domingo**, 5 hrs, US$7.50. To **Guayaquil**, hourly, 6 hrs, US$8.75. To **Portoviejo**, 2 hrs, US$2.50. To **Manta**, 3 hrs. US$3.75. To **Puerto López**, change in Manta, Portoviejo or Jipijapa.

Canoa

Bus To/from **San Vicente**, every 30 mins, 0600-1900, 30 mins, US$0.75; taxi US$5. Taxi to/from Bahía de Caráquez, US$7. To **Pedernales**, every 30 min 0600-1800, 2 hrs, US$3.25. To **Quevedo**, 4 daily, where you can get a bus to **Quilotoa** and **Latacunga**. To **Quito**, direct with **Reina del Camino** at 2145, US$12.50, 6 hrs; or transfer in Pedernales or Bahía.

Pedernales

Bus To **Santo Domingo**, every 15 mins, 3½ hrs, US$5, transfer to Quito. To **Quito** (Quitumbe) direct **Trans Vencedores**, 7 daily via Santo Domingo, US$7.75, 5 hrs; also starting in Jama at 0815 and 2300. To **Chamanga**, hourly 0600-1700, 1½ hrs, US$2.50, change there for **Esmeraldas**, 3½ hrs, US$4.50. To **Bahía de Caráquez**, shared vans from Plaza Acosta 121 y Robles, T05-268 1019, 7 daily, US$5.75.

Santo Domingo de los Tsáchilas

Bus The bus terminal is on Av Abraham Calazacón, at the north end of town, along the city's bypass. Long distance buses do not enter the city. Taxi downtown, US$1, bus US$0.25. A major hub with service throughout Ecuador.To **Quito** via Alóag US$3.75, 3 hrs; via San Miguel de los Bancos, 5 hrs; also **Sudamericana Taxis**, Cocaniguas y Río Toachi, p 2, T02-275 2567, door to door shared taxi service, frequent departures via Alóag or Los Bancos, 0400-1900, US$15-17, 3-4 hrs. To **Ambato** US$5, 4 hrs. To **Loja** US$16.25, 11 hrs. To **Guayaquil** US$6.25, 5 hrs. To **Esmeraldas** US$3.75, 3 hrs. To **Atacames**, US$5, 4 hrs. To **Manta** US$7.50, 7 hrs. To **Bahía de Caráquez** US$6.25, 6 hrs. To **Pedernales** US$5, 3½ hrs.

Northern lowlands

a lush area with an interesting cultural mix

A mixture of palm lined beaches, mangroves (where not destroyed for shrimp production), tropical rainforests, Afro-Ecuadorean and Cayapa indigenous communities characterize this part of Ecuador's Pacific lowlands as they stretch north to the Colombian border.

North to Atacames

North of Pedernales the coastal highway veers northeast, going slightly inland, then crosses into the province of Esmeraldas near **Chamanga** (San José de Chamanga, population 4400), a village with houses built on stilts on the freshwater estuary. It was devastated in the April 2016 earthquake. The town is 1 km from the highway. Inland and spanning the provincial border is the **Reserva Ecológica Mache-Chindul**, a dry forest reserve.

North of Chamanga by 31 km and 7 km from the main road along a paved side road (this intersection is not a safe place to wait) is **Mompiche** with a lovely beach and one of Ecuador's best surfing spots. There is an international resort complex and holiday real-estate development 2 km south at Punta Portete. The beach is being gradually eroded by the sea and a break-water has been built near the town. The nearest banks and ATMs are far away in Atacames and Pedernales. Take sufficient cash. The main road continues through El Salto, the crossroads for **Muisne**, a town on an island with a beach (strong undertow) and a few hostels.

The fishing village of **Tonchigüe** is 25 km north of El Salto. South of it, a paved road goes west and follows the shore to **Punta Galera**, along the way is the secluded beach of **Playa Escondida** (see Where to stay, below). Northeast of Tonchigüe by 3 km is Playa de **Same**, with a beautiful, long, clean, grey sandy beach, safe for swimming. The accommodation here is mostly upmarket, intended for wealthy Quiteños, but it is wonderfully quiet in the low season. There is good birdwatching in the area and some of the hotels offer whale watching tours in season. Ten kilometres east of Same and 4 km west of Atacames, is **Súa**, a friendly little beach resort, set in a beautiful bay (damaged in the April 2016 earthquake).

Atacames *Colour map 1, A2.*
One of the main resorts on the Ecuadorean coast, Atacames, 30 km southwest of Esmeraldas, is a real party town during the high season (July-September), at weekends and national holidays. Head instead for Súa or Playa Escondida (see above) if you want peace and quiet.

After the damage caused by the April 2016 earthquake, the area around Atacames and Esmeraldas was badly affected by a second major earthquake in December 2016.

Esmeraldas *Colour map 1, A2.*
Capital of the eponymous province, Esmeraldas is a place to learn about Afro-Ecuadorean culture and some visitors enjoy its very relaxed swinging atmosphere. Marimba groups can be seen practising in town, enquire about schedules at the tourist office. A bridge connects the city to Tachina, where the airport is located. Ceramics from La Tolita culture (see below) are found at the **Museo y Centro Cultural Esmeraldas** ① *Piedrahita 427 y Bolívar, T06-272 7076, Tue-Sun 0830-1630, US$1, English explanations.* Despite its wealth in natural resources, Esmeraldas is among the poorest provinces in the country. Shrimp farming has destroyed much mangrove, and timber exports are decimating Ecuador's last Pacific rainforest.

Insect-borne diseases including malaria are a serious problem in many parts of Esmeraldas province, especially in the rainy season (January to May). Most *residenciales* provide mosquito nets (*toldos* or *mosquiteros*), or buy one in the market near the bus station. Esmeraldas also suffered in the December 2016 earthquake.

North of Esmeraldas
From Esmeraldas, the coastal road goes northeast to Camarones and Río Verde, with a nice beach, from where it goes east to **Las Peñas**, once a sleepy seaside village with a nice wide beach, now a holiday resort. With a paved highway from Ibarra, Las Peñas is the closest beach to any highland capital, only four hours by bus. Ibarreños pack the place on weekends and holidays. From Las Peñas, a secondary road follows the shore north to **La Tola** (122 km from Esmeraldas) where you can catch a launch to Limones. Here the shoreline changes from sandy beaches to mangrove swamp; the wildlife is varied and spectacular, especially the birds. The tallest mangrove trees in the world (63.7 m) are found by **Majagual** to the south. To the northeast of La Tola and on an island on the northern shore of the Río Cayapas is **La Tolita**, a small, poor village, where the culture of the same name thrived between 300 BC and AD 700. Many remains have been found here, several burial mounds remain to be explored and looters continue to take out artefacts to sell.

Limones (also known as Valdez) is the focus of traffic downriver from much of northern Esmeraldas Province, where bananas from the Río Santiago are sent to Esmeraldas for export. The Cayapa people live up the Río Cayapas and can sometimes be seen in Limones, especially during the crowded weekend market, but they are more frequently seen at Borbón (see below).

Borbón and further north
Borbón, upriver from La Tola at the confluence of the Cayapas and Santiago rivers, is a lively, dirty, busy and somewhat dangerous place, with a high rate of malaria. The local fiestas with marimba music and other Afro-Ecuadorean traditions are held the first week of September.

From Borbón, the coastal road goes northeast towards **Calderón** where it meets the Ibarra-San Lorenzo road. Along the way, by the Río Santiago, are the nature reserves of **Humedales de Yalare**, accessed from **Maldonado**, and Playa de Oro (see below). From Calderón, the two roads run together for a few kilometres before the coastal road turns north and ends at **Mataje** on the border with Colombia. The road from Ibarra continues to San Lorenzo.

San Lorenzo *Colour map 1, A3.*

Hot and humid San Lorenzo stands on the Bahía del Pailón, which is characterized by a maze of canals. It is a good place to experience the Afro-Ecuadorean culture including marimba music and dances. There is a local festival 6-10 August and groups practice throughout the year; ask around. At the seaward end of the bay are several beaches without facilities, including San Pedro (one hour away) and Palma Real (1¾ hours). Note that this is a tense border area with many police and other patrols, but also armed civilians and much contraband activity. Enquire about current conditions with the police or Navy (Marina). From San Lorenzo you can visit several natural areas; launches can be hired for excursions, see Transport, page 1154. There are mangroves at **Reserva Ecológica Cayapas-Mataje**, which protects islands in the estuary northwest of town. **Reserva Playa de Oro** ① *www.touchthejungle.org, see Where to stay, page 1152*, has 10,406 ha of Chocó rainforest, rich in wildlife, along the Río Santiago. Access is from **Selva Alegre** (a couple of basic *residenciales*), off the road to Borbón.

Border with Colombia: San Lorenzo–Tumaco

The Río Mataje is the border with Colombia. From San Lorenzo, the port of Tumaco in Colombia can be reached by a combination of boat and land transport. Because this is a most unsafe region, travellers are advised not to enter Colombia at this border. Go to Tulcán and Ipiales instead.

Listings Northern lowlands

Tourist information

iTur
Bolívar y 9 de Octubre, Esmeraldas, T06-272 3150.

Ministerio de Turismo
Mejía y Sucre, p 4, Esmeraldas, T06-245 2242.
Mon-Fri 0900-1200, 1500-1700.

Oficina Municipal de Turismo
On the road into Atacames from Esmeraldas,
T06-273 1912. Mon-Fri 0800-1230, 1330-1600.

Where to stay

North to Atacames
Mompiche
There are several economical places in the town.
Camping on the beach is not safe.

$$ Gabeal
300 m east of town, T09-9969 6543, http://
hosteriagabeal.wixsite.com/turismoecuador.
Lovely quiet place with ample grounds and
beachfront. Bamboo construction with ocean
views, balconies, small rooms, cabins, camping
(US$3 pp), breakfast available, discounts in low
season, boat trips, surf lessons. Rooms 6 to 10 are
good choices.

Tonchigüe to Punta Galera

$$$-$$ El Acantilado
By the cliff, T06-302 7620, www.elacantilado.net.
Comfortable rooms and cabins, pool, nice views,
gardens, good restaurant, path to the beach. Also
operate a camping area at Tongorachí, US$30 pp
including 3 meals prepared in the community, a
private development project.

$$ Playa Escondida
10 km west of Tonchigüe and 6 km east of
Punta Galera, T06-302 7483, T09-9650 6812,
www.playaescondida.com.ec.
A charming beach hideaway set in 100 ha
with 500 m beachfront stretching back to dry
tropical forest. Run by Canadian Judith Barett
on an ecologically sound basis. Nice rustic
cabins overlooking a lovely little bay, excellent
restaurant, private showers, shared composting
toilets, camping US$10 pp, good birdwatching,
swimming and walking along the beach at low
tide. Also offers volunteer opportunities.

$$-$ La Terraza
On Same beach, T06-247 0320, pepo@hotmail.es.
Pleasant rooms and cabins for 3-4 with balconies,
hammocks and large terrace, spacious, hot water,
a/c, fan, mosquito net, some rooms have fridge,
good restaurant open in season, Spanish-run.

Súa

$$ Las Buganvillas
On the beach, T06-247 3008, see Facebook.
Nice, room 10 has the best views, pool,
helpful owners.

$ Chagra Ramos
On the beach, T06-247 3106, see Facebook.
Hotel with balconies overlooking the beach,
restaurant, cold water, fan, parking, good service.

Atacames

Prices rise on holiday weekends, discounts may
be available in low season. There are many more
hotels than we can list.

$$$ Juan Sebastián
*Towards the east end of the beach,
T06-273 1049, www.hoteles-embassy.com/
juansebastian/en/index.php.*
Large upmarket hotel with cabins and suites,
restaurant, a/c, 3 pools (US$5 for non-guests),
fridge, parking, popular with Quiteños.

$$ Carluz
*Behind the stadium, T06-273 1456,
www.hotelcarluz.com.*
Good hotel in a quiet location. Comfortable suites
for 4 and apartments for 6, good restaurant, a/c,
fan, pool, fridge, parking.

$$ Cielo Azul
*Towards the west end of the beach, near the
stadium, T06-273 1813, www.hotelcieloazul.com.*
Restaurant, fan, pool, fridge, rooms with
balconies and hammocks, comfortable
and very good.

Esmeraldas

Hotels in the centre are poor; better to stay in
the outskirts.

$$ Apart Hotel Esmeraldas
*Libertad 407 y Ramón Tello, T06-272 0622,
http://aparthotelesmeraldas.net.*
Good restaurant, a/c, fridge, parking,
excellent quality.

$$ Perla Verde
*Piedrahita 330 y Olmedo, T06-272 3820,
www.hotelperlaverde.ec.*
Good rooms with a/c and fridge, restaurant,
bar, ATM, parking, in the city centre.

North of Esmeraldas

Las Peñas

$$$-$$ Cabañas Mikey
*By the beach, north end, T06-279 3101, http://
laspeñasesmeraldas.com/cabanas_mikey.html.*
Cabins with kitchenettes, private bath,
hot water, pool.

San Lorenzo

$$$ Playa de Oro
*On the Río Santiago, upriver from Borbón,
contact Ramiro Buitrón at Hotel Valle del
Amanecer in Otavalo, T06-292 0990,
www.touchthejungle.org.*
Basic cabins with shared bath, includes
3 meals and guided excursion. Advance
booking required.

$$ Tunda Loma
*Km 17 on the road to Ibarra (taxi from
San Lorenzo US$5), T06-278 0367.*
Beautifully located on a hill overlooking the
Río Tululbí. Wood cabins, includes breakfast,
restaurant, warm water, fan, organizes tubing
trips on the river and hikes in the forest.

$$-$ Castillo Real
*Camilo Ponce y Esmeraldas, T06-278 0152,
see Facebook.*
Rooms with private bath and a/c, cheaper with
fan, good restaurant, parking.

Tip...
Arrive in San Lorenzo prepared! Expect to
be mobbed by children wanting a tip to
show you to a hotel or restaurant. Also take
insect repellent.

Restaurants

North to Atacames

Mompiche
Several other places serve cheap set meals.

$$ La Facha
*C La Fosforera, T06-244 8024,
www.lafachahostel.com.*
Great sea food and vegetarian (try their veggie
burgers), very creative and recommended.
Argentine chef. Also has a hostel with private
and shared rooms.

Same

$$$ Seaflower
By the beach at the entrance road.
Excellent international food.

$$-$ Azuca
By south entrance to village, T09-8882 9581,
Facebook: Same-Azuca-Restaurant.
Good creative food, also rents cheap rooms
with shared or private bath.

Súa

$ Kikes
On the Malecón, T09-9355 8406.
Good local food, generous portions, good value,
also rents rooms.

Atacames
The beach is packed with bars and restaurants
offering seafood, too many to list.

$$ Da Giulio
Malecón y Cedros. Weekdays 1700-2300,
weekends from 1100.
Spanish and Italian cuisine, good pasta.

$$-$ La Ramada
On the Malecón.
Specializes in ceviches and *encebollados*,
good value.

Esmeraldas
There are restaurants and bars on the Malecón at
Las Palmas beach offering regional specialities.

$$ Chifa Asiático
Cañizares y Bolívar, T06-272 6888.
Chinese and seafood, a/c, excellent.

$$ El Chacal
Manabí y Alfaro, T06-272 4436, Facebook:
La-Casa-Del-Chacal. Open 1700-2300.
Tasty à la carte meals, popular with locals.

$$-$ Ceviches Maranatha
Quito y Olmedo, T09-415 0681.
Good ceviche and other seafood.

$$-$ Parrilladas el Toro
Olmedo y 9 de Octubre, T06-272 3610,
Facebook: parrilladaeltoro. Open 1730-2300.
Popular meat and seafood grill.

North to Atacames
Bus Hourly from **Chamanga** to **Esmeraldas**,
US$4.50, 3½ hrs, and to **Pedernales**, US$2.50,
1½ hrs. **Mompiche** to/from **Esmeraldas**, 8 a
day, US$3.75, 3 hrs, the last one from Esmeraldas
about 1630. To **Playa Escondida**: take a *ranchera*
or bus from Esmeraldas or Atacames for Punta
Galera or Cabo San Francisco, 5 a day, US$2.50,
2 hrs. A taxi from Atacames costs US$15 and
a pick-up from Tonchigüe US$6.25. To **Súa**
and **Same**: Buses every 30 mins to and from
Atacames, 15 mins, US$0.50. Make sure it drops
you at Same and not at **Club Casablanca**.

Atacames
Bus To **Esmeraldas**, every 15 mins, US$1, 1 hr.
To **Guayaquil**, US$11.25, 8 hrs, **Trans Esmeraldas**
at 0830 and 2245. To **Quito**, various companies,
about 10 daily, US$10, 7 hrs. To **Pedernales**,
Coop G Zambrano, 4 daily, US$5, 4 hrs or change
in Chamanga.

Esmeraldas
Air The Airport is along the coastal road heading
north. A taxi to the city centre costs US$3, buses to
the Terminal Terrestre from the road outside the
airport pass about every 30 mins. If heading north
towards San Lorenzo, you can catch a bus outside
the airport. **TAME** (at Centro Comercial Multiplaza,
Maldonado entre Estupiñán y Manabí, T06-272
5203), 1-2 daily flights to **Quito**; to **Guayaquil**,
1 daily Mon, Wed, Fri.

Bus *Terminal terrestre* by Redondel CODESA,
taxi to town US$3, to airport US$6. **Trans-
Esmeraldas** (recommended) and **Panamericana**
have *servicio directo* or *ejecutivo* to Quito and
Guayaquil, a better choice as they are faster
buses and don't stop for passengers along
the way. Frequent service to **Quito** via Santo
Domingo or via Calacalí, US$8.75, 6 hrs; ask which
terminal they go to before purchasing ticket;
also shared vans via Los Bancos with **Esmetur
Express**, Espejo y Eloy Alfaro, T06-271 3488 or
T09-9226 0857, 4 vehicles daily, 5 hrs, US$30,
US$10-20 extra to/from the beaches. To **Ibarra**,
9 hrs, US$12.50, via Borbón. To **Santo Domingo**,
US$3.75, 3 hrs. To **Ambato**, 6 a day, US$10, 8 hrs.
To **Guayaquil**, hourly, US$10, *directo*, 8 hrs. To
Bahía de Caráquez, via Santo Domingo, US$10,
9 hrs. To **Manta**, US$10, 10 hrs. **La Costeñita** and
El Pacífico, both on Malecón, to/from **La Tola**,
8 daily, US$4.75, 3 hrs. To **Borbón**, frequent

service, US$4.50, 3 hrs. To **San Lorenzo**, 8 daily, US$5.75, 4 hrs. To **Súa**, **Same** and **Atacames**, every 15 mins from 0630-2030, to Atacames US$1, 1 hr. To **Chamanga**, hourly 0500-1900, US$4.50, 3½ hrs, change here for points south.

North of Esmeraldas
Ferry There are launches between **La Tola** and **Limones** which connect with the buses arriving from Esmeraldas, US$3.75, 1 hr, and 3 daily Limones-San Lorenzo, 2 hrs US$3. You can also hire a launch to **Borbón**, a fascinating trip through mangrove islands, passing hunting pelicans, approximately US$10 per hr.

Borbón
Bus To **Esmeraldas**, US$4.50, 3 hrs. To **San Lorenzo**, US$2, 1 hr.

San Lorenzo
Bus Buses leave from the train station or environs. To **Ibarra**, 10 daily, US$5, 4 hrs. To **Esmeraldas**, via Borbón, 8 daily, US$5.75, 4 hrs.

Ferry Launch service with **Coopseturi**, T06-278 0161; and **Costeñita**, both near the pier. All services are subject to change and cancellation. To **Limones**, 4 daily, US$3, 2 hrs. To **La Tola**, US$6, 4 hrs. To **Palma Real**, for beaches, 2 daily, US$3, 2 hrs. To hire a boat for 5 passengers costs US$20 per hr.

The
Oriente

East of the Andes the hills fall away to tropical lowlands. Some of this beautiful wilderness remains unspoiled and sparsely populated, with indigenous settlements along the tributaries of the Amazon. Large tracts of jungle are under threat, however: colonists are clearing many areas for agriculture, while others are laid waste by petroleum development. For the visitor, the Ecuadorean jungle, especially the Northern Oriente, has the advantage of being easily accessible and infrastructure here is well developed. The eastern foothills of the Andes, where the jungle begins, offer a good introduction to the rainforest for those with limited time or money. Further east lie the few remaining large tracts of primary rainforest, teeming with life, which can be visited from several excellent (and generally expensive) jungle lodges. Southern Oriente is as yet less developed for tourism, it offers good opportunities off the beaten path but is threatened by large mining projects.

Northern Oriente

waterfalls, cloudforests, lagoons and wildlife

★Much of the Northern Oriente is taken up by the Parque Nacional Yasuní, the Cuyabeno Wildlife Reserve and most of the Cayambe-Coca Ecological Reserve. The main towns for access are Baeza, Lago Agrio and Coca.

Quito to the Oriente

From Quito to Baeza, a paved road goes via the **Guamaní pass** (4064 m). It crosses the Eastern Cordillera just north of **Volcán Antisana** (5705 m), and then descends via the small village of **Papallacta** (hot springs, see page 1049) to the old mission settlement of Baeza. The trip between the pass and Baeza has beautiful views of the glaciers of Antisana (clouds permitting), high waterfalls, *páramo*, cloudforest and a lake contained by an old lava flow.

Baeza *Colour map 1, A4.*

The mountainous landscape and high rainfall have created spectacular waterfalls and dense vegetation. Orchids and bromeliads abound. Baeza, in the beautiful Quijos valley, is about 1 km from the main junction of roads from Lago Agrio and Tena. The town itself is divided in two parts: a faded but pleasant **Baeza Colonial** (Old Baeza) and **Baeza Nueva** (New Baeza), where most shops and services are located. The trail/road from Baeza Vieja to Las Antennas has nice views, two hours return. There are excellent kayaking and rafting opportunities in the area, tours offered by **Casa de Rodrigo** (see Where to stay, page 1159) and operators in Quito and Tena.

Best for
Adventure sports ▪ Jungle lodges ▪ Wildlife

Essential Oriente

Access

There are commercial flights from Quito to Lago Agrio, Coca and Macas; and from Guayaquil to Coca via Latacunga. From Quito, Macas and Shell, light aircraft can be chartered to any jungle village with a landing strip. Western Oriente is also accessible by scenic roads which wind their way down from the highlands. Quito, via Baeza, to Lago Agrio and Coca, Baños to Puyo, and Loja to Zamora are fully paved, as is the entire lowland road from Lago Agrio south to Zamora. Other access roads to Oriente include: Tulcán to Lago Agrio via Lumbaquí, Riobamba to Macas, and three different roads from Cuenca to Macas and Gualaquiza.

Getting around

Some roads are narrow and tortuous and subject to landslides in the rainy season, but all have regular bus service and all can be travelled in a 4WD or in an ordinary car with good ground clearance. Deeper into the rainforest, motorized canoes provide the only alternative to air travel.

Jungle travel without a guide is not recommended. Access to national parks and reserves is controlled, some indigenous groups prohibit the entry of outsiders to their territory, navigation in the jungle is difficult, and there is a variety of dangerous animals. For your own safety as well as to be a responsible tourist, the jungle is not a place to wander off on your own.

Jungle tours

These fall into four basic types: lodges, guided tours, indigenous ecotourism and river cruises. When staying at a jungle lodge, you will need to take a torch (flashlight), insect repellent, protection against the sun and a rain poncho that will keep you dry when walking and when sitting in a canoe. See also Lodges on the Lower Napo (page 1160) and the Upper Napo (page 1167). All jungle lodges must be booked in advance. **Guided tours** of varying length are offered by tour operators, who should be licensed by the Ecuadorean **Ministerio de Turismo**. Tour operators are mainly concentrated in Quito, Baños, Puyo, Tena, Misahuallí, Coca, and, to a lesser extent, Macas and Zamora.

A number of indigenous communities and families offer **ecotourism** programmes in their territories. These are either community-controlled and operated, or organized as joint ventures between the indigenous community or family and a non-indigenous partner. These programmes usually involve guides who are licensed as *guías nativos* with the right to guide within their communities. You should be prepared to be more self-sufficient on such a trip than on a visit to a jungle lodge or a tour with a high-end operator. Take a light sleeping bag, rain jacket, trousers (not only shorts), long-sleeve shirt for mosquitoes, binoculars, torch, insect repellent, sunscreen and hat, water-purifying tablets, and a first aid kit. Keep everything in waterproof stuff-sacks or several plastic bags to keep it dry. Ask if rubber books are provided.

River cruises offer an appreciation of the grandeur of Amazonia, but less intimate contact with life in the rainforest. Passengers sleep and take their meals on comfortable river boats, stopping on route to visit local communities and make excursions into the jungle.

Tip...
There may be police and military checkpoints in the Oriente, so always have your passport handy.

Safety

A yellow fever vaccination is required. Anti-malarial tablets are recommended, as is an effective insect repellent. In the province of Sucumbíos, enquire about public safety before visiting sites near the Colombian border.

When to go

Heavy rain can fall at any time, but it is usually wettest from March to September.

Beyond Baeza

From Baeza a road heads south to Tena, with a branch going east via Loreto to Coca, all paved. Another paved road goes northeast from Baeza to Lago Agrio, following the Río Quijos past the villages of **Borja** (8 km from Baeza, very good *comedor* **Doña Cleo** along the highway, closed Sunday) and **El Chaco** (12 km further, basic accommodation) to the slopes of the active volcano **Reventador**, 3560 m (erupting since 2002). Check www.igepn.edu.ec and enquire locally about volcanic activity before trekking here; simple $ **Hostería El Reventador** at the bridge over the Río Reventador; **Ecuador Journeys** offers tours, see page 1044. Half a kilometre south of the bridge is signed access to the impressive 145-m **San Rafael Falls** (part of **Reserva Ecológica Cayambe-Coca**), believed to be the highest in Ecuador. It is a pleasant 45-minute hike through cloudforest to a *mirador* with stunning views of the thundering cascade. Many birds can be spotted along the trail, including cock-of-the-rock, also monkeys and coatimundis. A large hydroelectric project has been built nearby. Although access to the falls is not restricted, the turbines use up to 70% of the water in the Río Quijos, leaving the remainder to go over the falls.

Lago Agrio *Colour map 1, A5.*

The capital of Sucumbíos province is an old oil town which now lives mainly from commerce with neighbouring Colombia. The name comes from Sour Lake, the US headquarters of Texaco, the first oil company to exploit the Ecuadorean Amazon in the 1970s. It is also called Nueva Loja or just 'Lago'. If taking a Cuyabeno tour from Lago Agrio, it is worth leaving Quito a couple of days early, stopping en route at Papallacta, Baeza and San Rafael falls (see above).

> **Tip...**
> Lago Agrio is 30 km from the Colombian border, the crossing here is not safe and routine precautions are advised in town as well; best return to your hotel by 2200.

Cuyabeno Wildlife Reserve

This large tract of rainforest, covering 603,000 ha, is located about 100 km east of Lago Agrio along the Río Cuyabeno, which eventually drains into the Aguarico. In the reserve are many lagoons and a great variety of wildlife, including river dolphins, tapirs, three species of caimans, ocelots, 11 species of monkeys and some 680 species of birds. This is among the best places in Ecuador to see jungle animals. The reserve is deservedly popular and offers a more economical jungle experience than many other areas in Oriente.

Access to most lodges is by paved road from Lago Agrio via Tarapoa as far as the bridge over the Río Cuyabeno, where there is a ranger station and visitors must register. Nobody is allowed to enter the reserve without a tour. From the bridge, transport is mainly by motorized canoe; **Magic River** also offers a worthwhile paddling alternative, see Cuyabeno jungle lodges, below. Most tours include a visit to a local Siona community.

The reserve can be visited year-round but the dry season (January-February) can bring low water levels and generally less wildlife, although certain species may be easier to see at this time. In order to see as many animals as possible and minimally impact their habitat, seek out a small tour group which scrupulously adheres to responsible tourism practices. Cuyabeno is close to the Colombian border and there have, in the past, been occasional armed robberies of tour groups. Do not take unnecessary valuables. Most Cuyabeno tours are booked through Quito agencies or online, see Cuyabeno jungle lodges, below.

Coca *Colour map 1, A5.*

Officially named **Puerto Francisco de Orellana**, Coca is a hot, noisy, bustling city at the junction of the Ríos Payamino and Napo, which has experienced exceptionally rapid growth from petroleum development. It is the capital of the province of Orellana and, for tourists, a launch pad to visit the lower Río Napo and jungle areas accessed from the Vía Auca, a road running south from the city. The view over the water is nice, and the riverfront **Malecón** can be a pleasant place to spend time around sunset; various indigenous groups have craft shops here. Hotel and restaurant provision is adequate but heavily booked and ironically for an oil-producing centre, petrol supplies are erratic.

Jungle tours from Coca The lower **Río Napo**, **Parque Nacional Yasuní** and **Huaorani Reserve**, all accessed from Coca, offer some of the finest jungle facilities and experiences in Ecuador. Wildlife in this area is nonetheless under threat, insist that guides and fellow tourists take all litter back and ban all hunting. Many tours out of Coca are booked through agencies in Quito but there are also a few local operators (see below).

The paved road to Coca via Loreto passes through **Wawa Sumaco**, where a rough road heads north to **Sumaco National Park**; 7 km along it is $$$$ Wildsumaco ① T06-301 8343, Quito office T02-333 1633, www.wildsumaco.com, reservations required, a comfortable birdwatching lodge with full board, excellent trails and over 500 birds including many rare species. Just beyond is the village of **Pacto Sumaco** from where a trail runs through the park to the *páramo*-clad summit of **Volcán Sumaco** (3732 m), six to seven days round-trip. Local guides must be hired, there are three nice shelters along the route and a community-run hostel in the village (T06-301 8324, www.sumacobirdwatching.com).

Coca to Nuevo Rocafuerte and Iquitos (Peru)

Pañacocha is halfway between Coca and Nuevo Rocafuerte, near a magnificent lagoon. Here are a couple of lodges (see Lodges on the Lower Napo, in Where to stay, below) and Coca agencies also run tours to the area (see Jungle tours, in What to do, below). Entry to Pañacocha reserve US$10. There are basic places to stay and eat in Pañacocha village.

Following the Río Napo to Peru is rough, adventurous and requires plenty of time and patience. There are two options: by far the more economical is to take a motorized canoe from Coca to **Nuevo Rocafuerte** on the border. This tranquil riverside town has simple hotels, eateries, a phone office and basic shops. It can be a base for exploring the endangered southeastern section of **Parque Nacional Yasuní**; local guides are available. Ecuadorean immigration is two blocks from the pier, next to the Municipio. Peruvian entry stamps are given in **Pantoja**, where there is a decent municipal *hospedaje*, $ Napuruna. Shopkeepers in Nuevo Rocafuerte and Pantoja change money at poor rates; soles cannot be changed in Coca. In addition to immigration, you may have to register with the navy on either side of the border so have your passport at hand. See Transport, page 1163, for Coca–Nuevo Rocafuerte boat services and onward to Pantoja and Iquitos.

The second option for river travel to Iquitos is to take a tour with a Coca agency, taking in various attractions on route, and continuing to Iquitos or closer Peruvian ports from which you can catch onward public river transport. These tours are expensive and may involve many hours sitting in small, cramped craft; confirm all details in advance.

Listings Northern Oriente

Tourist information

Lago Agrio

iTur
Av Quito y 20 de Junio, in the Parque Recreacional, T06-283 3951, iturlagoagrio@ hotmail.com. Mon-Fri 0800-1700.

Coca

iTur
Chimborazo y Amazonas, by the Malecón, T06-288 0532, www.orellanaturistica.gob.ec. Mon-Sat 0730-1630.

Ministerio de Turismo
Quito y Chimborazo, Ed Azriel Shopping, T06-288 1583.

The place to file any complaints regarding a jungle lodge or tour.

Where to stay

Baeza

$$-$ Gina
Jumandy y Batallón Chimborazo, just off the highway in the old town, T06-232 0471, restaurantgina@hotmail.com.
Hot water, parking, pleasant, popular restaurant.

$$-$ Quinde Huayco
By the park in the old town, T06-232 0649.
Nice ample rooms, garden, restaurant, quiet location away from the main road.

$ La Casa de Rodrigo
In the old town, T09-232 0467,
rodrigobaeza1@yahoo.com.
Modern and comfortable, hot water, cheaper
with shared bath, kitchen facilities, friendly
owner offers rafting trips, kayak rentals and
birdwatching. Good value and recommended.

$ Samay
Av de los Quijos, in the new town, T06-232 0170.
Very well-maintained older place with private
or shared bath, hot water, friendly, family-run,
good value.

Around Baeza

$$$$ Cabañas San Isidro
*Near Cosanga, 19 km south of Baeza, T02-289
1880 (Quito), www.cabanasanisidro.com.*
A 1200-ha private nature reserve with rich
birdlife, comfortable accommodation and
warm hospitality. Includes 3 excellent meals,
reservations required.

$$ Hostería El Reventador
*On main highway next to bridge over the
Río Reventador, turismovolcanreventador@
yahoo.com.*
Meals on request, hot water, pool, simple rooms,
busy at weekends, a bit run-down and mediocre
service but well located for San Rafael Falls and
Volcán Reventador.

Lago Agrio

$$$ Gran Hotel de Lago
*Km 1.5 Vía Quito, T06-283 2415,
granhoteldelago@grupodelago.com.*
Restaurant, a/c, pool, parking, cabins with nice
gardens, quiet. Recommended and often full.

$$ Arazá
*Quito 536 y Narváez, T06-283 1287,
www.hotel-araza.com.*
Nice comfortable rooms, restaurant, a/c,
pool, fridge, parking. Recommended.

$$ El Cofán
*12 de Febrero 3915 y Quito, T06-283 0526,
elcofanhotel@yahoo.es.*
Restaurant, a/c, fridge, parking,
older place but well maintained.

$$ Lago Imperial
*Colombia y Quito, T06-283 0453,
hotellagoimperial@hotmail.com.*
A/c, some rooms with hot water, ample common
areas, pool, patio, restaurant, central location,
good value.

$$-$ Gran Colombia
*Quito y Pasaje Gonzanamá, T06-283 1032,
hgrancolombia@yahoo.es.*
With a/c, cheaper with fan and cold water, more
expensive rooms in back are quieter and better,
indoor parking, central.

$$-$ Oasis
9 de Octubre y Orellana, T06-283 0879.
Modern hotel away from centre, a/c, cheaper
with fan, very clean, includes breakfast.

$ Casa Blanca
Quito 228 y Colombia, T06-283 0181.
Simple adequate rooms with electric shower
and fan.

Cuyabeno Wildlife Reserve

Lodges
There are over a dozen lodges operating in
Cuyabeno, more than we can list. The following
are all recommended. Prices range from
US$300-475 pp for 5 days/4 nights, including
transport from Lago Agrio, accommodation,
all meals and guiding. A small community fee
is charged separately.

Caiman Lodge
T09-9161 0922, www.caimanlodge.com.
On Quebrada La Hormiga near the lagoon. Well
maintained lodge with an observation tower.

Cuyabeno Lodge
*Operated by Neotropic Turis, Quito T02-292 6153,
www.neotropicturis.com.*
On the lagoon. This was the first lodge in the
reserve, operating since 1988. Very well organized
and professional. Ample grounds, comfortable
accommodation in several price categories,
observation tower, and paddle canoes for use
of guests.

Guacamayo Ecolodge
*Operated by Ara Expeditions, Quito, T02-290 4765,
www.guacamayoecolodge.com.*
On the Río Cuyabeno near the lagoon. Well
maintained lodge with an observation tower.

Magic River
Quito T02-262 9303, www.magicrivertours.com.
On the Río Cuyabeno downstream from the
lagoon. Specialize in paddling trips (great fun and
wildlife watching without engine noise) which
spend the first night in a tent camp in the jungle.
Friendly atmosphere at the lodge, good food
and service.

Nicky Lodge

Operated by Dracaena, Quito T02-290 6644, www.amazondracaena.com.
On the lower Río Cuyabeno near it's confluence with the Aguarico, far from all the other lodges. Good wildlife including some species not easily seen elsewhere.

Siona Lodge

Booked through Galasam, Quito T02-290 3909, www.galasam.net.
On the lagoon. Comfortable lodge with very good infrastructure.

Tapir Lodge

Quito T02-380 1567, www.tapirlodge.com.
On the Río Cuyabeno dowstream from the lagoon. Known for high-quality guiding.

Coca

Coca hotels are often full, best book in advance.

$$$ Heliconias

Cuenca y Amazonas, T06-288 2010, http://heliconiasgrandhotel.com.ec.
Spotless rooms, ample grounds, upmarket restaurant, includes buffet breakfast, pool and gym (US$5 for non-guests). Recommended.

$$$-$$ El Auca

Napo y García Moreno, T06-288 1554, www.hotelelauca.com.
Restaurant, a/c, parking, a variety of different rooms and mini-suites. Comfortable, nice garden with hammocks, English spoken. Popular, central, but can get noisy.

$$$-$$ Río Napo

Bolívar entre Napo y Quito, T06-288 0872, www.hotelrionapo.com.
Modern rooms with a/c, good but a bit overpriced.

$$ La Misión

By riverfront 100 m downriver from the bridge, T06-288 0260, hotelamision@hotmail.com.
A larger hotel, restaurant, disco on weekends, a/c and fridge, pool (US$3 for non-guests), parking, a bit faded but still adequate.

$$ Omaguas

Quito y Cuenca, T06-288 2436, h_omaguas@hotmail.com.
Very clean rooms with tile floors, a/c, restaurant, parking, attentive service.

$$-$ Amazonas

12 de Febrero y Espejo, T06-288 0444, hosteriacoca@hotmail.com.

Nice quiet setting by the river, away from centre, restaurant, electric shower, a/c, cheaper with fan, parking.

$$-$ San Fermín

Quito 75-04 y Bolívar, T06-288 0802, alexandragalarza@amazonwildlife.ec.
Variety of different rooms, some with a/c, cheaper with fan, ample parking, popular and busy, good value, owner organizes tours. Recommended.

$ Santa María

Rocafuerte entre Quito y Napo, T09-9761 7034.
Small adequate rooms with a/c or fan, private bath, cold water, good economy option.

Jungle tours from Coca

Lodges on the Lower Napo

All Napo lodges count travel days as part of their package, which means that a '3-day tour' spends only 1 day actually in the jungle. All prices given below are per person based on double occupancy, including transport from Coca. Most lodges have fixed departure days from Coca (eg Mon and Fri) and it is very expensive to get a special departure on another day. For lodges in Cuyabeno, see page 1159; for lodges on the Upper Napo, see page 1167, for southern Oriente lodges see page 1168.

Amazon Dolphin Lodge

Quito T02-250 3225, www.amazon dolphinlodge.com.
On Laguna de Pañacocha, 4½ hrs downriver from Coca. Special wildlife here includes Amazon river dolphins and giant river otters as well as over 500 species of birds. May be closed in dry season (Jan-Feb). Cabins with private bath, US$600-900 for 4 days.

La Selva

Quito T02-515 4000, www.laselva junglelodge.com.
An upmarket lodge and spa, 2½ hrs downstream from Coca on a picturesque lake. Surrounded by excellent forest, especially on the far side of Mandicocha. Bird and animal life is exceptionally diverse. Many species of monkey are seen regularly. A total of 580 bird species have been found, one of the highest totals in the world for a single elevation. Comfortable cabins, excellent meals, massage treatments available at extra cost. High standards, canopy tower, most guides are biologists. US$1215 for 4 days.

Napo Wildlife Center

Quito T02-600-5819, USA T1-800-250 1992, UK T0-800-032-5771, www.napowildlifecenter.com.
Operated by and for the local Añangu community, 2½ hrs downstream from Coca. This area of hilly forest is rather different from the low flat forest of some other lodges and the diversity is slightly higher. There are big caimans and good mammals, including giant otters, and the birdwatching is excellent with 2 parrot clay-licks and 2 canopy towers, 40 m high. From about US$1400 for 4 days. Recommended.

Sacha

Quito T02-256 6090, www.sachalodge.com.
An upmarket lodge 2½ hrs downstream from Coca. Very comfortable cabins, excellent meals. The bird list is outstanding; the local bird expert, Oscar Tapuy (Coca T06-2881486), can be requested in advance. Canopy tower and 275-m canopy walkway. Several species of monkey are commonly seen. Nearby river islands provide access to a distinct habitat. US$1050 for 4 days.

Sani

Quito T02-252 8226, www.sanilodge.com.
All proceeds go to the Sani Isla community, who run the lodge with the help of outside experts. It is located on a remote lagoon which has 4- to 5-m-long black caiman. This area is rich in wildlife and birds, including many species such as the scarlet macaw which have disappeared from most other Napo area lodges. There is accommodation and a 35-m canopy tower. An effort has been made to make the lodge accessible to people who have difficulty walking; the lodge can be reached by canoe (total 3½ hrs from Coca) without a walk. US$1058 for 4 days. Good value, recommended.

Lodges in the Reserva Huaorani

Otobo's Amazon Safari

www.rainforestcamping.com.
8-day/7-night camping expeditions in Huaorani territory, access by road from Coca then 2-day motorized canoe journey on the Ríos Shiripuno and Cononaco. All meals and guiding included. Excellent jungle with plenty of wildlife. US$200 pp per night.

Shiripuno

Quito T02-227 1094, www.shiripunolodge.com.
A lodge with capacity for 20 people, very good location on the Río Shiripuno, a 4-hr canoe ride downriver from the Vía Auca. Cabins have private bath. The surrounding area has seen relatively little human impact to date. From US$610 for 4 days, plus US$20 entry to Huaorani territory.

Coca to Nuevo Rocafuerte and Iquitos

$ Casa Blanca

Malecón y Nicolás Torres, T06-238 2184.
Rooms with a/c or fan, nice, simple, welcoming. There are a couple of other basic places to stay in town.

Restaurants

Baeza

$$-$ Kopal
50 m off the main road opposite the old town.
Good pizza, nice atmosphere, closes early.

$ El Viejo
East end of Av de los Quijos, the road to Tena in the new town. Daily 0700-2100.
Good set meals and à la carte.

Lago Agrio

There are good restaurants at the larger hotels (see above).

$$-$ D'Mario
Av Quito 2-63. Daily 0630-2200.
Set meals and à la carte, generous portions, popular, meeting place for Cuyabeno groups.

$$-$ La Casanostra
Guayaquil 500 y 9 de Octubre. Mon 1200-1500, Tue-Sat 1200-1500, 1830-2230.
Nice quiet place with open-air seating, good set lunch, à la carte at night.

$ El Buen Samaritano
12 de Febrero y Venezuela. Sun-Fri 0700-1930.
Cheap and simple vegetarian restaurant.

Coca

$$ Fuego y Carne
Fernando Roy y Amazonas.
Upmarket for Coca, good grill and Italian dishes.

$$-$ Pizza Choza
Rocafuerte entre Napo y Quito. Daily 1800-2200.
Good pizza, nice atmosphere.

$ La Casa del Maito
Espejo entre Quito y Napo. Daily 0700-2300.
Simple place serving *maitos* and other local specialities, good food, hopelessly chaotic service, go early before it gets crowded.

$ Media Noche
Napo y Rocafuerte (no sign). Daily 1700-2400.
Only chicken in various dishes, large portions,
quick service, very popular, a Coca institution.

$ Ocaso
Eloy Alfaro entre Napo y Amazonas.
Mon-Sat 0630-2030, Sun 0630-1400.
Simple set meals and à la carte.

Papa Dan's Bar
Napo y Chimborazo.
A landmark watering-hole by the Malecón.
Several other bars nearby.

What to do

Coca

Jungle tours
See also page 1158.

Amazon Travel, *Amazonas y Espejo, in Hotel
Safari*, T06-288 1805, www.ecuadortravelamazon.
com. Patricio Juanka runs jungle tours throughout
the region, very knowledgeable and helpful.
Luis Duarte, *at Casa del Maito (see Restaurants,
above)*, T06-288 2285, cocaselva@hotmail.com.
Regional tours and trips to Iquitos.
Sachayacu Explorer, *in Píllaro near Baños
(see page 1086)*, T03-287 5316. Although not based
in Coca, experienced jungle guide Juan Medina
offers recommended jungle tours and trips to
Iquitos. Advance arrangements required.
Wildlife Amazon, *Robert Vaca at Hotel San
Fermín (see Where to stay, above)*, T06-288 0802,
www.amazonwildlife.ec. Jungle tours and trips
to Iquitos.

River cruises on the lower Río Napo
Manatee, operated by Advantage Travel, Quito
T02-336 0887, www.manateeamazonexplorer.com.
This 30-passenger vessel sails between Pompeya
and Pañacocha, US$986 for 4 days. First-class
guides, excellent food, en suite cabins. They
also operate similar cruises onboard the
40-passenger luxury vessel **Anakonda** (www.
anakondaamazoncruises.com), US$1800 for 4 days.

Coca to Nuevo Rocafuerte and Iquitos
Juan Carlos Cuenca, *Nuevo Rocafuerte, T06-238
2257.* Is a *guía nativo* who offers tours to Parque
Nacional Yasuní, about US$60 per day.

Transport

Baeza
Bus Buses to and from **Tena** pass right through
town. If arriving on a **Lago Agrio** bus, get off at
the crossroads (La "Y") and walk or take a pick-up
for US$0.25. From **Quito**, Mon-Sat at 1130, 1245,
1520, 1645, with **Trans Quijos**, T02-295 0842,
from Chile E3-22 y Pedro Fermín Cevallos (near
La Marín, an unsafe area at night), US$4, 3 hrs.
These continue to **Borja** and **El Chaco**. To **Quito**
from El Chaco Mon-Sat at 0330, 0430, 0600, 0800,
pass Baeza about 20 mins later.

Lago Agrio
Air Airport is 3 km southeast of the centre,
taxi US$1.50. **TAME** (Orellana y 9 de Octubre,
T06-283 0113) flies once or twice a day to **Quito**.
Book several days in advance. If there is no space
available to Lago Agrio then you can fly to **Coca**
instead, from where it is only 2 hrs by bus on a
good road.

Bus Terminal terrestre, Manuela Sáenz y
Progreso, 8 blocks north of Av Quito, taxi US$1.25.
To **Quito** Terminal Quitumbe, frequent service
with several companies (**Trans Baños** is good),
US$10, 7-8 hrs; most buses go via Reventador
and El Chaco, but may take the slightly longer
route via Coca if there are disruptions. To **Baeza**
5 hrs, pay fare to Quito. To **Tena**, US$8.75, 6 hrs.
To **Tulcán** via La Bonita, US$8.75, 7 hrs. Several
companies offer service direct to **Guayaquil**,
without stopping in Quito, US$17.50, 14 hrs,
as well as other coastal cities. To **Coca**, every
15 mins 0800-1830, US$3.75, 2 hrs.

Coca
Air Flights to **Quito** with TAME (C Quito y
Enrique Castillo, T06-288 0768) and Avianca (at
the airport T06-288 1742), several daily, fewer on
weekends, reserve as far in advance as possible.

Bus Long distance buses, including those to
Lago Agrio, depart from the modern Terminal
Terrestre, 3 km north of centre, taxi US$1.50.
A small terminal on 9 de Octubre serves only
regional destinations. **Hotel San Fermin** (T06-288
0802, see above) will purchase bus tickets from
Coca for a small commission. To **Quito** Terminal
Quitumbe, US$12.50, 7 hrs via Loreto, 9 hrs via
Lago Agrio, several daily. To **Baeza**, pay fare to
Quito, 5 hrs. To **Tena**, US$8.75, 4 hrs. To **Baños**,
US$12.50, 7 hrs. To **Riobamba**, US$13.50, 9 hrs.
To **Guayaquil**, US$20, 15-16 hrs.

River Down the Río Napo to **Nuevo Rocafuerte** on the Peruvian border, 50-passenger motorized canoes leave Coca daily except Sat, 0700, 10-12 hrs; returning at 0500, 12-14 hrs; US$15. Details change, enquire locally, buy tickets at the dock a day in advance and arrive early for boarding. **Transportes Fluvial Orellana**, T06-288 2582, cfluvialorellana@yahoo.es, and 2 others.

From Nuevo Rocafuerte boats can be hired for the 30 km trip down river to the Peruvian border town of **Pantoja**, US$60 per boat, try to share the ride. Departure dates of riverboats from **Pantoja**

to **Iquitos** are irregular, about once a month, be prepared for a long wait. Try to call Iquitos or Pantoja from Coca, or check with Luis Duarte at **Casa del Maito** restaurant (see above), to enquire about the next sailing; full details are given under Iquitos, Transport, in the Peru chapter. For the journey, take a hammock, cup, bowl, cutlery, extra food and snacks, drinking water or purification, insect repellent, toilet paper, soap, towel, cash dollars and soles in small notes; soles cannot be purchased in Coca.

Central and southern Oriente
a whitewater rafting centre and off-the-beaten-track exploration

Quito, Baños, Puyo, Tena and Puerto Misahuallí are all starting points for central Oriente. Further south, Macas, Gualaquiza and Zamora are the main gateways. All have good road connections.

Archidona
Archidona, 65 km south of Baeza and 10 km north of Tena, has a striking, small painted church and not much else. Tours can be arranged to a private reserve on **Galeras Mountain** where there is easy walking as well as a tougher trek, the forest is wonderful; contact Elias Mamallacha, T09-8045 6942, mamallacha@yahoo.com.

Tena and around *Colour map 1, B4. See map, page 1164.*
Relaxed and friendly, Tena is the capital of Napo Province. It occupies a hill above the confluence of the Ríos Tena and Pano, there are nice views of the Andean foothills often shrouded in mist. Tena is Ecuador's most important centre for whitewater rafting and also offers ethno-tourism. It makes a good stop en route from Quito to points deeper in Oriente. The road from the north passes the old airstrip and market and heads through the town centre as Avenida 15 de Noviembre on its way to the bus station, nearly 1 km south of the river. Tena is quite spread out. A couple of pedestrian bridges and a vehicle bridge link the two halves of town.

Misahuallí *Colour map 1, B4.*
This small port, at the junction of the Napo and Misahuallí rivers, is perhaps the best place in Ecuador from which to visit the 'near Oriente', but your expectations should be realistic. The area has been colonized for many years and there is no extensive virgin forest nearby (except at Jatun Sacha and Liana Lodge, see Lodges

> **Tip...**
> Beware the troop of urban monkeys by the plaza, who snatch food, sunglasses, cameras, etc.

on the Upper Río Napo, page 1167). Access is very easy however, prices are reasonable, and while you will not encounter large animals in the wild, you can still see birds, butterflies and exuberant vegetation – enough to get a taste for the jungle.

There is a fine, sandy beach on the Río Misahuallí, but don't camp on it as the river can rise unexpectedly. A narrow suspension bridge crosses the Río Napo at Misahuallí and joins the road along the south shore. At Chichicorumi, outside Misahuallí, is **Kamak Maki** ⓘ US$3, T09-9982 7618, www.museokamakmaki.com, an ethno-cultural museum run by the local Kichwa community.

Puyo *Colour map 1, B4.*
The capital of the province of Pastaza feels more like a lowland city anywhere in Ecuador rather than a typical jungle town. Visits can nonetheless be made to nearby forest reserves and tours deeper into the jungle can also be arranged from Puyo. It is the junction for road travel into the northern and southern Oriente (80 km south of Tena, 130 km north of Macas), and for traffic heading to or

from Ambato and Riobamba via Baños; all on paved roads. The Sangay and Altar volcanoes can occasionally be seen from town.

Omaere ① *T06-288 3174, Tue-Sun 0900-1700, US$3, access by footbridge off the Paseo Turístico, Barrio Obrero,* is a 15.6-ha ethnobotanical reserve located in the north of Puyo. It has three trails with a variety of plants, an orchidarium and traditional indigenous homes. **Yana Cocha** ① *3 km from Puyo, 500 m off the road to Tena, T06-288 5641, daily 0800-1700, US$3,* is a rescue centre with good conditions for the animals, and you can see them close up. There are other private reserves of varying quality in the Puyo area and visits are arranged by local tour operators (see page 1170). You cannot however expect to see large tracts of undisturbed primary jungle here.

Macas *Colour map 1, B4.*

Capital of Morona-Santiago province, Macas is situated high above the broad Río Upano valley. It is a pleasant tranquil place, established by missionaries in 1563. **Sangay volcano** (5230 m) can be seen on clear mornings from the plaza, creating an amazing backdrop to the tropical jungle surrounding the town. The modern cathedral, with beautiful stained-glass windows, houses the much-venerated image of La Purísima de Macas. Five blocks north of the cathedral, at Don Bosco y Riobamba, the **Parque Recreacional**, which also affords great views of the Upano Valley, has a small orchid collection. The Sunday market on 27 de Febrero is worth a visit. **Fundación**

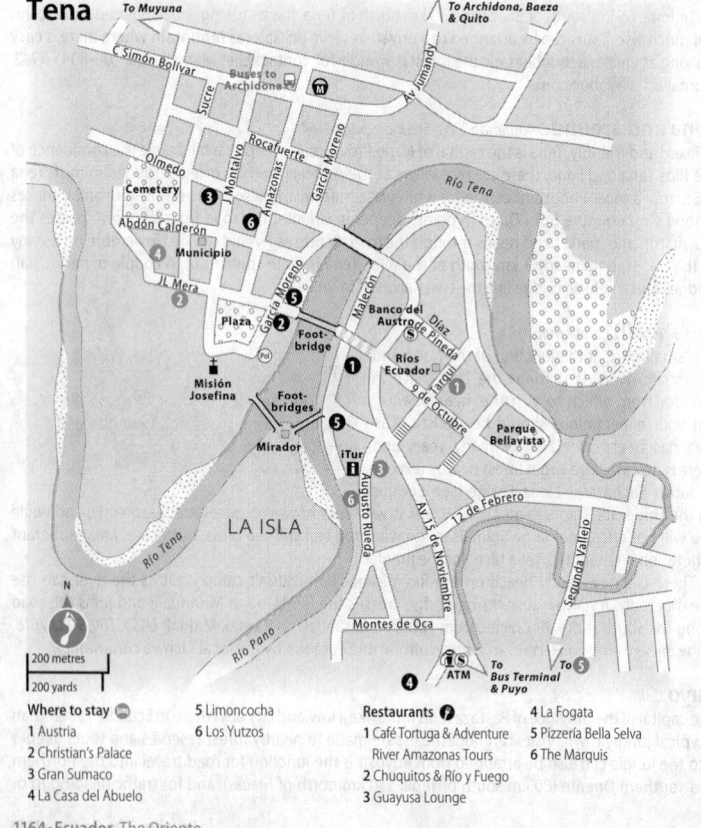

Tena

Where to stay 🛏
1 Austria
2 Christian's Palace
3 Gran Sumaco
4 La Casa del Abuelo
5 Limoncocha
6 Los Yutzos

Restaurants 🍴
1 Café Tortuga & Adventure River Amazonas Tours
2 Chuquitos & Río y Fuego
3 Guayusa Lounge
4 La Fogata
5 Pizzería Bella Selva
6 The Marquis

Chankuap ⓘ *Soasti y Bolívar, T07-270 1176, www.chankuap.org*, sells a nice variety of locally produced crafts and food products. **Ministerio de Turismo** ⓘ *Bolívar y 24 de Mayo, T07-270 1480, Mon-Fri 0800-1700*. Macas provides access to **Parque Nacional Sangay** ⓘ *Macas office, Juan de la Cruz y Guamote, T07-270 2368, Mon-Fri 0800-1300, 1400-1700*. The lowland area of the park has interesting walking with many rivers and waterfalls. See also Sangay Transport (page 1103) for notes on the road from Macas to Riobamba.

Macas to Gualaquiza

South of Macas lies one of Ecuador's least touristed areas, promising much to explore. **Sucúa**, 23 km from Macas, is the administrative centre of the Shuar indigenous people who inhabit much of southern Oriente. The town has most services and some attractions nearby; enquire at the **Tourist Office** in the Municipio. **Logroño**, 24 km further south, has a large limestone cave nearby; to visit contact Mario Crespo, T07-391 1013. It is another 31 km to (Santiago de) **Méndez**, a crossroads with a modern church. A paved road descends from Cuenca via Paute and Guarumales to Méndez, and another road heads east from Méndez via Patuca to Santiago and San José de Morona, near the Peruvian border. Some 26 km south of Méndez is **Limón** (official name General Leónidas Plaza Gutiérrez), a busy, friendly place, surrounded by impressive hills. From Limón the road climbs steeply 10 km to **Plan de Milagro**, another crossroads, where a great road for birdwatching (partly paved), descends from Cuenca via Gualaceo. Next are **Indanza**, 5 km south, then **San Juan Bosco**, 16 km further, with striking views of Cerro Pan de Azucar (2958 m) rising abruptly out of the jungle, before the road reaches Gualaquiza, 55 km ahead.

Gualaquiza *Colour map 1, C3.*

A pleasant town with an imposing church on a hilltop, Gualaquiza's pioneer-settlement charm is threatened by large mining projects in the area. Fortunately, tourism offers an alternative as there are also lovely waterfalls, good rivers for tubing, caves, and undeveloped archaeological sites nearby. Information and tours from the **Oficina Municipal de Turismo** ⓘ *García Moreno y Gonzalo Pesántez, Mon-Fri 0730-1230, 1330-1630*, and from Leonardo Matoche at Canela y Café.

At Gualaquiza a rough road forks northwest to climb steeply to Cuenca via **Sígsig**. The road south from Gualaquiza passes El Pangui and Yantzaza (55 km), 8 km south of which is **Zumbi**, with basic hotels on the plaza. At Zumbi, a bridge crosses the Río Zamora and a side road goes southeast to Guayzimi and the beautiful **Alto Nangaritza** region, with **Reserva El Zarza**. The upper Río Nangaritza flows through Shuar territory and a magnificent jungle-covered gorge with 200-m-high walls. There are also oilbird caves and other natural attractions. There is bus service to the area from Zamora, and tours are available form Cabañas Yankuam (see Where to stay, page 1169) and Zamora tour operators. South of Zumbi, the broad valley of the Río Zamora becomes progressively narrower, with forested mountains and lovely views. It is 35 km to Zamora.

Zamora *Colour map 1, C3.*

The colonial mission settlement of Zamora, at the confluence of the Ríos Zamora and Bombuscaro, today has a boom-town feeling due to large mining and hydroelectric projects in the area. It is reached by road from Gualaquiza (see above) or Loja, 64 km away. The road from Loja is beautiful as it wanders from *páramo* down to high jungle, crossing mountain ranges of cloudforest, weaving high above narrow gorges as it runs alongside the Río Zamora. The town itself is hilly, with a pleasant climate and a nice linear park along the river. It gives access to the **Alto Nangaritza** (see above) and is the gateway to the lowland portion of **Parque Nacional Podocarpus** (see page 1116). Between town and the park is **Copalinga**, a bird-rich private reserve (see Where to stay, page 1169). There are two private orchid collections that can be visited: **Pafinia** ⓘ *Av del Ejército Km 2*, run by Marco Jiménez, mmjimenez473@gmail.com; and another belonging to **Padre Stanislau** ⓘ *Av del Ejército, Cumbaratza, across from Hotel El Arenal.*

Tourist information

Tena

iTur and Ministerio de Turismo
Malecón, sector El Balnerio, T06-288 8046.
Mon-Fri 0730-1230, 1400-1700.

Puyo

iTur
Francisco de Orellana y 9 de Octubre, T06-288
5122. Daily 0800-1700. Also at Treminal Terrestre,
T06-288 5122, Wed-Sun 0900-1600.

Zamora

Ministerio de Turismo
José Luis Tamayo y Amazonas. Mon-Fri 0815-1700.
English spoken.

Unidad de Turismo
Municipio, Diego de Vaca y 24 de Mayo,
by the plaza, Zamora, T07-305 9386.
Mon-Fri 0800-1230, 1400-1730.

Where to stay

Archidona

$$$$-$$$ Hakuna Matata
Vía Shungu Km 3.9, off the road between
Tena and Archidona, T02-222 2119,
www.hakunamatata-acuador.com.
Comfortable cabins in a lovely setting by the Río
Inchillaqui. Includes 3 meals, walks, river bathing
and horse riding.

$$$ Huasquila
Vía Huasquila, Km 3.5, Cotundo, T02-237 6158,
T09-8764 6894, www.huasquila.com.
Wheel chair accessible bungalows and Kichwa-
style cabins, includes breakfast, various packages,
full board available, jungle walks, caving, rock art.

$$$ Orchid Paradise
2 km north of town, T06-288 9232.
Cabins in nice secondary forest with lots of birds.
Full board or cheaper with only breakfast, owner
organizes tours in the area.

$$-$ Hoteles Palmar del Rio
Circunvalacion E45 y Transversal 16, T06-287
7001; more economical branch on main street

4 blocks south of plaza, T06-287 7000;
www.hotelespalmardelrio.com.
Clean pleasant rooms with fan and parking.
Premium branch with pool, sauna, restaurant
and tour agency, includes breakfast.

Tena

$$$-$$ Los Yutzos
Augusto Rueda 190 y 15 de Noviembre,
T06-288 6717, Facebook: hostalosyutzos.
Comfortable rooms and beautiful grounds
overlooking the Río Pano, quiet and family-run.
A/c, cheaper with fan, parking.

$$$ Christian's Palace
JL Mera y Sucre, T09-9408 7020,
http://hotelchristianpalace.online.
Restaurant, a/c, pool, parking, modern and
comfortable. Also Christian Resort, Km 5 on road
to Puyo, http://hotelchristianresort.com, T02-515
4324 Quito for both.

$$ La Casa del Abuelo
JL Mera 628, T06-288 6318,
www.tomas-lodge.com.
Nice quiet place, comfortable rooms and suites,
small garden, hot water, ceiling fan, parking,
tours. Recommended.

$$-$ Austria
Tarqui y Díaz de Pineda, T06-288 7205.
Spacious rooms, with a/c, cheaper with fan,
ample parking, quiet, good value.

$$-$ Gran Sumaco
Augusto Rueda y 15 de Nov, T06-288 8434,
www.hostalgransumaco.net.
Nice hotel in a good location, quiet, clean, bright,
ample rooms, many with balcony and views. A/c,
cheaper with fan, very good value.

$ Limoncocha
Sangay 533, Sector Corazón de Jesús, on a hillside
4 blocks from the bus station, ask for directions,
T06-284 6303, www.hostallimoncocha.com.
Concrete house with terrace and hammocks,
some rooms with a/c, private or shared bath,
US$7 pp in dorm, hot water, fan, laundry
and cooking facilities, breakfast available,
parking, German/Ecuadorean-run, enthusiastic
owners organize tours. Out of the way in a
humble neighbourhood, nice views, pleasant
atmosphere, good value.

Misahuallí

\$\$\$\$ El Jardin Aleman
Jungle lodge on shores of Río Mishuallí,
3 km from town, T06-289 0122,
www.eljardinaleman.com.
Comfortable rooms with bath, hot water.
Price includes 3 meals and river tour, set in
protected rainforest.

\$\$\$\$ Hamadryade
Behind the Mariposario, 4 km from town, T09-
8590 9992, www.hamadryade-lodge.com.
Luxury lodge in a 64-ha forest reserve, 5 designer
wood cabins, packages include breakfast, dinner
and excursions, French chef, pool, lovely views
down to the river.

\$\$\$ Hostería Misahuallí
Across the river from town, T06-289 0063,
www.hosteriamisahualli.com.
Cabins for up to 6 in a nice setting, includes
breakfast, other meals on request, electric
shower, fan, pool and tennis court.

\$\$ Cabañas Río Napo
Cross the suspension bridge, then 100 m
on the left-hand side, T06-289 0071,
www.cabanasrionapo.blogspot.com.
Nice rustic cabins with thatch roof, private
bath, hot water, ample grounds along the
river, Swiss/Kichwa-run, enthusiastic.

\$\$ El Paisano
Rivadeneyra y Tandalia, T06-289 0027,
www.hostalelpaisano.com.
Restaurant, hot water, mosquito nets,
small pool, helpful.

\$\$-\$ Banana Lodge
500 m from town on road to Pununo,
T06-289 0190, www.bananalodge.com.
Nicely decorated hostel, ample rooms, huge
garden with hammocks, breakfast available,
cooking facilities, parking, US\$4 pp for
campervans, Russian/Ecuadorean-run.

\$ Shaw
Santander on the Plaza, T06-289 0163,
hostalshaw@hotmail.com.
Good restaurant, hot water, fan, simple rooms,
annexe with kitchen facilities and small pool,
operate their own tours, English spoken, very
knowledgeable. Good value. Recommended.

Lodges on the Upper Río Napo

Casa del Suizo
Quito T02-256 6090, www.casadelsuizo.com.
On north shore at Ahuano, resort with capacity
for 200, comfortable rooms, well-tended
grounds, pool, gift shop, great views. Swiss/
Ecuadorean-owned. US\$125 pp per night.

Cotococha Amazon Lodge
Km 10 on the road from Puerto Napo to
Ahuano, shore of Río Napo, T02-244 1721
(Quito office), www.cotococha.com.
Comfortable cabins. Packages with meals,
entrance fees and local guides, excursions by
dug-out canoe. US\$440 for 4 days.

Jatun Sacha Biological Station
East of Ahuano and easily accessible by bus,
Quito T02-243 2240, www.jatunsacha.org.
A 2500-ha reserve for education, research and
tourism. 507 birds, 2500 plants and 765 butterfly
species have been identified. Basic cabins with
shared bath, cold water, good self-guided trails,
canopy tower. US\$30 per night, day visit US\$6,
guiding US\$30 per group. Good value.

Liana Lodge
On Río Arajuno near confluence with the Napo,
Tena T06-301 7702, www.selvaviva.ec.
Comfortable cabins with terraces and river
views on a 1700-ha reserve. *Centro de rescate* has
animals on site. US\$387 for 4 days. Also arranges
stays at **Runa Wasi**, next door; basic cabins run by
the local Kichwa community, US\$32 pp per night
with 3 meals, guiding extra.

Yachana
Quito T02-252 3777, www.yachana.com.
Near the village of Mondaña, 2 hrs downstream
from Misahuallí or 2½ hrs upstream from Coca,
also accessible by road (about 6 hrs from Quito).
On a 2500 ha reserve, 14 cabins on a bluff
overlooking the Río Napo. Proceeds help support
community development projects. US\$366-456
for 4 days. Recommended.

Puyo

\$\$\$\$ Altos del Pastaza Lodge
access from Km 16 of Puyo-Macas road,
Quito T09-9767 4686.
Attractive lodge in 65-ha reserve overlooking the
Río Pastaza, pool. Don't expect much wildlife, but
a nice place to relax, 1- to 4-day packages include
meals and walking tours.

$$$$ Las Cascadas Lodge
Quito T02-250 0530, www.surtrek.com.
First-class lodge 40 km east of Puyo, 8 rooms
with terraces, includes full board, activities and
transport from/to Quito, waterfalls; 3- and 4-day
packages US$434-650.

$$$ El Jardín
Paseo Turístico, Barrio Obrero, T03-288 6101,
www.eljardinrelax.com.ec.
Nice rooms and garden, good upmarket restaurant.

$$ Delfín Rosado
Ceslao Marín y Atahualpa, T03-288 8757.
Pool, modern rooms with a/c, parking.

$$ Las Palmas
20 de Julio y 4 de Enero, 5 blocks from centre, T03-288 4832, hostal_laspalmas_puyo@yahoo.com.
Comfortable modern rooms with fridge, parking.

$ Colibrí
Av Manabí entre Bolívar y Galápagos,
T03-288 3054.
Hot water, private bath, parking, away from
centre, simple but nice, good value, offers tours.
Recommended.

$ San Rafael
Tte Hugo Ortiz y Juan de Velazco, 1½ blocks from
bus station, T03-288 7275.
Good choice for late arrivals or early departures.
Clean rooms with private bath, hot water,
good value.

Southern Oriente jungle lodges

Kapawi
Quito T02-316 1506, or 09-9140 5976,
http://achuarlodge.com.
A top-of-the-line lodge located on the Río
Capahuari near its confluence with the Pastaza,
not far from the Peruvian border. Run by the
local Achuar community and accessible only by
small aircraft and motor canoe. The biodiversity
is good, but more emphasis is placed on ethno-
tourism here than at other upmarket jungle
lodges. From US$1298 for 4 days includes land
transport from Quito to Shell, flight Shell-Kapawi
US$222 return.

Macas

$$$ Arrayán y Piedra
Km 7 Vía a Puno, T07-304 5949,
arrayanypiedra@hotmail.com.
Large resort-style lodging, nice rooms, pool and
spa, ample grounds, restaurant with very good
food, but variable service.

$$ Cabañas del Valle
Av 29 de Mayo, 1.5 km from town, T07-232 2393.
Comfortable rooms, pool, parking, sports areas.

$$ Casa Blanca
Soasti 14-29 y Sucre, T07-270 0195.
Hot water, small pool, modern and comfortable,
very helpful, good value, often full, book in
advance. Recommended.

$$ Nivel 5
Juan de la Cruz y Amazonas, T07-270 1240.
Nice modern multi-storey hotel, hot water, fan,
pool, parking, helpful staff.

Macas to Gualaquiza

Sucúa
There are several other hotels ($) in town.

$$ Arutam
Vía a Macas Km 1, north of town, T07-274 0851.
Restaurant, pool and sauna, parking, modern
comfortable rooms, nice grounds, sports fields,
well suited to families.

$$ Lucelinda
1 km vía a Cuenca, T07-274 2118.
Comfortable rooms with fans, pool, restaurant.

Méndez

$ Interoceánico
C Quito on the plaza, T07-276 0245.
Hot water, parking, smart, good value.

Limón

$ Dream House
Quito y Bolívar, T07-277 0166.
With restaurant, shared bath, hot water, adequate.

San Juan Bosco

$ Antares
On the plaza.
Restaurant, hot water, indoor pool, simple
functional rooms, helpful owner.

Gualaquiza

$ Gran Hotel
Orellana y Gran Pasaje, T07-278 0722.
Modern concrete building, hot water, fan,
parking, small rooms, some windowless.

$ Wakis
Orellana 08-52 y Domingo Comín, T07-278 0138.
Older simple place with small rooms, private
or shared bath, hot water, parking, enthusiastic
owner speaks English.

Alto Nangaritza

$$ Cabañas Yankuam
*3 km south of Las Orquideas, T07-260 5739
(Zamora), www.lindoecuadortours.com.*
Rustic cabins, includes breakfast, other tasty
meals on request, private or shared bath,
good walking in surrounding jungle-clad
hills, organizes trips up the Río Nangaritza.
Family-run. Reservations required.

Zamora

In addition to those listed below, there are several
other hotels in town.

$$$ Copalinga
*Km 3 on the road to the Bombuscaro entrance
of Parque Nacional Podocarpus, T09-9347 7013,
www.copalinga.com.*
Nice comfortable cabins with balcony in a
lovely setting, includes very good breakfast,
other delicious meals available if arranged in
advance, more rustic cabins with shared bath
are cheaper, excellent birdwatching, walking
trails. Belgian-run, English, French and Dutch
spoken, attentive service, reserve 3 days ahead.
Highly recommended.

$$ Samuria
*24 de Mayo y Diego de Vaca, T07-260 7801,
hotelsamuria@hotmail.com.*
Modern bright hotel, comfortable well furnished
rooms, a/c, cheaper with fan, restaurant, parking.

$$ Wampushkar
*Diego de Vaca y Pasaje Vicente Aldeán,
T07-260 7800, Facebook: wampushkarhotel.*
Nice modern hotel, ample rooms, a/c, cheaper
with fan, hot water, parking, good value.

$ Betania
*Francisco de Orellana entre Diego
de Vaca y Amazonas, T07-260 7030,
hotel-betania@hotmail.com.*
Modern, functional, breakfast available,
private bath, hot water.

Restaurants

Tena

$$$ The Marquis
*Amazonas entre Calderón y Olmedo.
Daily 1200-1600, 1800-2200.*
Upmarket restaurant serving good steaks.

$$ Chuquitos
*García Moreno by the plaza.
Mon-Sat 0700-2100, Sun 1100-2100.*
Good food, à la carte only, seating on a balcony
overlooking the river. Pleasant atmosphere,
attentive service, popular and recommended.
Araña Bar downstairs, Mon-Thu 1700-2400,
weekends to 0200.

$$ Pizzería Bella Selva
*Malecón south of the footbridge; 2nd location
on east side. Daily 1100-2300.*
Pizza and pasta.

$$ Río y Fuego
*JL Mera y García Moreno. Daily 0730-1100,
1700-2300.*
Good breakfast and dinner. Asian and
international dishes, Vietnamese/
Ecuadorean-run.

$$-$ Guayusa Lounge
Juan Montalvo y Olmedo. Tue-Sat 1500-2300.
Light meals, snacks and cocktails, good meeting
place, US-run.

$ La Fogata
*Serafín Guetiérrez entre Rafaela Segala and
Av Napo. Daily 1200-2200.*
Tasty set meals, large portions, good value.

Café Tortuga
*Malecón south of the footbridge.
Mon-Sat 0700-1930, Sun 0700-1330.*
Juices, snacks, book exchange, handy bus time-
table, Wi-Fi, nice location, friendly Swiss owner.

Misahuallí

$$$ El Jardín
*300 m past bridge to Ahuano.
Daily 1200-1600, 1800-2200.*
Variety of dishes, beautiful garden setting.

$$ Parrilería Fasage
*1 block from the plaza near Hotel El Paisano.
Daily 1200-2400.*
Good quality grill.

$$-$ Bijao
On the plaza. Wed-Sun 0900-2200.
Good set meals and *comida típica* à la carte.

Puyo

$$$-$$ Lagarto Juancho
Orellana y Sangay. Mon-Sat 1800-2400.
Ecuadorean *comida típica*, large portions,
very clean.

> **Tip...**
> In Puyo, there are several cheap *comedores* serving local dishes on Calle San Francisco near 10 de Agosto.

$$ Pizzería Buon Giorno
Orellana entre Villamil y 27 de Febrero. Mon-Sat 1200-2300, Sun 1400-2300.
Good pizza, lasagne and salads, pleasant atmosphere, very popular. Recommended.

El Fariseo Café
Atahualpa entre 27 de Febrero y General Villamil. Mon-Sat 0700-2200.
Good cakes and the best coffee in town.

Escobar Café
Atahualpa y Orellana. Mon-Sat 0630-2400.
Good for early breakfast, sandwiches, bar at night, attractive bamboo decor.

Macas

$$ Junglab
Bolívar entre Guamote y Amazonas, T07-270 2448. Tue-Sun 1200-2230.
Delicious creative meals using local produce.

$$-$ La Italiana
Soasti y Sucre. Mon-Sat 1200-2300.
Great pizzas, pasta and salads.

$ La Choza de Mama Sara
10 de Agosto y 9 de Octubre. Mon-Sat 0830-2100.
Traditional Macabeo cuisine such as *ayampacos* and *yuca* and palm tamales, served for breakfast. Also a choice of set lunches, good value.

$ Rincón Manabita
Amazonas y 29 de Mayo. Mon-Fri 0700-2200, Sat-Sun 1000-1600.
Good breakfasts and a choice of set meals which are delicious and filling. Also à la carte.

Zamora

$ Agape
Sevilla de Oro y Pje San Francisco. Mon-Fri for lunch only.
Good set lunch and à la carte.

$ Asadero Tío Bolo
Alonso de Mercadillo, across from the riverside park. Tue-Sat 1830-2130.
Small place with good grill, friendly service, very popular, go early.

Spiga Pan
Av del Maestro y Pío Jaramillo. Daily 0730-2230.
Great bakery with a variety of hot bread, cream cakes and fresh fruit yoghurt.

What to do

Tena
Rafting tours cost US$40-80 per day, safety standards vary between operators. Avoid touts selling tours on the street.
Adventure River Amazonas (ARA), *Francisco de Orellana 280 y 9 de Octubre, on the malecón,* T06-288 8648, www.riveramazonas.com. Rafting, adventure sports and community cultural tours. Ecuadorean/French run.
Caveman Tours, *no storefront,* T09-8420 0173, www.cavemanecuador.com. Water sports and tours.
Limoncocha, *at Hostal Limoncocha (see Where to stay, above).* Rafting, kayaking and jungle, English and German spoken.
Ríos Ecuador, *Tarqui 230 y Díaz de Pineda,* T06-288 6727; plans to move in 2016 to Hostal Tena Ñaui, *Vía a las Antenas, 10 mins from centre,* T06-288 7188, www.riosecuador.com. Rafting and kayaking.
River People, *no storefront,* T09-8356 7307, www. riverpeopleecuador.com. Rafting and kayaking.

Misahuallí
Jungle tours (US$45-80 pp per day) can be arranged by most hotels as well as:
Ecoselva, *Santander on the plaza,* T06-289 0019, www.ecoselvapepetapia.com. Recommended guide Pepe Tapia speaks English and has a biology background. Well organized and reliable. Bike rentals, US$10 per day.
Runawa Tours, *in La Posada hotel, on the plaza,* T06-289 0031. Owner Carlos Santander, tubing, kayak and jungle tours.
Teorumi, *between the plaza and malecón,* T06-289 0203, www.teorumimisahualli.com. Offers tours to the Shiripuno Kichwa community.

Puyo
Selvavida Travel, *Ceslao Marín y Atahualpa,* T03-288 9729, www.selvavidatravel.com. Specializes in rafting and Parque Nacional Yasuní.

Macas
Tours to indigenous communities and lowland portions of Parque Nacional Sangay, cost about US$50 per day.
Insondu, *Bolívar y Soasti,* T07-270 2533.

Real Nature Travel Company, *no storefront*, T07-270 2674, www.realnaturetravel.com. Run by RhoAnn Wallace and professional bird-watching guide Galo Real, English spoken.
Tsuirim Viajes, *Don Bosco y Sucre*, T09-9357 9003. Owner Leo Salgado.

Zamora
Cabañas Yankuam, *see page 1169*. Offer tours to the Alto Nangaritza.
Wellington Valdiviezo, T09-9380 2211, lindozamoraturistico@gmail.com. Tours to the Alto Nangaritza, Shuar communities, adventure sports, visits to shamans. Contact in advance.

Transport

Tena
Bus Run-down Terminal Terrestre on 15 de Noviembre, 1 km from the centre (taxi US$1). To **Quito**, US$7.50, 5 hrs. To **Ambato**, via Baños, US$6.25, 4½ hrs. To **Baños**, US$6, 3½ hrs. To **Riobamba**, US$7.50, 5½ hrs. To **Puyo**, US$3.75, 2 hrs. To **Coca and Lago Agrio**, fares given above. To **Misahuallí**, see below. To **Archidona**, from Amazonas y Bolívar by market, every 20 mins, US$0.35, 15 mins.

Misahuallí
Bus Buses run from the plaza. To **Tena**, hourly 0600-1900, US$1.25, 45 mins. Make long-distance connections in Tena. To **Quito**, 1 direct bus a day at 0830, US$8.75, 5 hrs.

River No scheduled passenger service, but motorized canoes for 8-10 passengers can be chartered for touring.

Puyo
Air The nearest airport to Puyo is at Shell, 13 km. Military flights to jungle villages are not open to foreigners, but light aircraft can be chartered starting around US$300 per hr.

Bus Terminal Terrestre on the outskirts of town, a 10- to 15-min walk from the centre; taxi US$1.

To **Baños**, US$2.50, 1½ hrs. To **Ambato**, US$3.75, 2½ hrs. To **Quito**, US$6.25, 5 hrs via Ambato; shared taxis with **Autovip**, T02-600 2582 or 09-9629 5406, US$40, 8 daily, fewer on weekends or **Delux**, T09-3920 9827or 09-8343 0275, every 2 hrs, US$25. To **Riobamba**, US$5, 3½ hrs. To **Tena**, see above. To **Macas**, US$6.25, 2½ hrs. To **Coca**, US$11.25, 8hrs. To **Lago Agrio**, US$15, 11 hrs.

Macas
Air Small modern airport within walking distance at Cuenca y Amazonas. To **Quito**, Mon, Wed and Fri with **TAME** (office at airport T07-270 4940). Sit on left for best views of Volcán Sangay. Air taxis to jungle villages, US$600 per hr for 9 passengers.

Bus Terminal Terrestre by the market. To **Puyo**, see above. To **Baños**, US$9, 4½ hrs. To **Quito**, via Puyo, Baños and Ambato, US$10, 8 hrs. To **Riobamba** through Parque Nacional Sangay, a beautiful ride, 6 daily, US$6.25, 4 hrs. To **Cuenca**, US$11, 6-7 hrs, via Guarumales and Paute or via Plan de Milagro and Gualaceo. To **Gualaquiza**, US$8, 8 hrs, where you can get a bus to Zamora and Loja (see below). To **Sucúa**, hourly, US$1.25, 30 min. To **9 de Octubre**, for PN Sangay, US$2, 45 mins.

Gualaquiza
Bus To **Macas**, see above. To **Cuenca**; via Sígsig, 4 daily, US$8.75, 6 hrs; or via Plan de Milagro and Gualaceo. To **Zamora**, US$4.50, 3½ hrs. To **Loja**, US$7.50, 5½ hrs.

Alto Nangaritza
To **Las Orquídeas**, with **Trans Zamora**, from Zamora at 0400, 0645, 1115 and 1230, US$4.75, 3½ hrs; from Yantzaza at 0440, 0740, 1150 and 1310, US$3.25, 3½ hrs; with **Unión Yantzaza**, from Yantzaza at 0430, 0930, 1130, 1430 and 1630; from Loja at 1415, 1510, US$7.75, 5½ hrs.

Zamora
Bus Leave from Terminal Terrestre. To **Loja**, frequent service, 1½-2 hrs, US$3; to **Gualaquiza**, US$4.50, 3½ hrs, where you can transfer for Macas.

Galápagos
Islands

★A trip to the Galápagos Islands is an unforgettable experience. The islands are world renowned for their fearless wildlife but no amount of hype can prepare the visitor for such a close encounter with nature. Here you can snorkel with penguins, sea lions and the odd hammerhead shark, watch giant 200-kg tortoises lumbering through cactus forest and enjoy the courtship display of the blue-footed booby and magnificent frigatebird, all in startling close-up.

Lying on the equator, 970 km west of the Ecuadorean coast, the Galápagos consist of six main islands, 12 smaller islands and over 40 islets. The islands have an estimated population of 27,000, but this does not include many temporary inhabitants. Santa Cruz has 16,600 inhabitants, with Puerto Ayora the main city and tourist centre. San Cristóbal has a population of 7900 with the capital of the archipelago, Puerto Baquerizo Moreno. The largest island, Isabela, is 120 km long and forms over half the total land area of the archipelago. Some 2500 people live there, mostly in and around Puerto Villamil on the south coast. Floreana, the first island to be settled, has about 160 residents.

Best for
Scenery ▪ Swimming ▪ Walking ▪ Wildlife

Essential Galápagos Islands

Finding your feet

Airports at **Baltra**, across a narrow strait from Santa Cruz, and **Puerto Baquerizo Moreno**, on San Cristóbal, receive flights from mainland Ecuador. The two islands are 96 km apart and on most days there are local flights in light aircraft between them, as well as to **Puerto Villamil** on Isabela. There is also speedboat service between Puerto Ayora (Santa Cruz) and the other populated islands. There are no international flights to Galápagos.

Avianca, **LAN** and **TAME** all fly from Quito and Guayaquil to Baltra or San Cristóbal. Baltra receives more flights but there is at least one daily to each destination. You can arrive at one and return from the other. You can also depart from Quito and return to Guayaquil or vice versa, but you may not buy a one-way ticket. The price of return fares varies considerably, depending on how far ahead and by what means you book. In 2017 regular low-season rates started at US$405 return from Guayaquil and US$445 from Quito (high-season fares are US$80-100 more). See also Fees and inspections, page 1176.

Buses meet flights from the mainland at Baltra: some run to the port or *muelle* (10 minutes, no charge) where the cruise boats wait; others go to Canal de Itabaca, the narrow channel which separates Baltra from Santa Cruz. It is 15 minutes to the Canal, free, then you cross on a small ferry, US$1. On the other side, buses (US$2, may involve a long wait while they fill) and pickup truck taxis (US$20 for up to four passengers) run to Puerto Ayora, 45 minutes. For the return trip to the airport, buses leave the Terminal Terrestre on Avenida Baltra in Puerto Ayora (2 km from the pier, taxi US$1) at 0700, 0730 and 0830 daily. See also Transport, page 1188.

Getting around

Emetebe Avionetas, Boyacá 916 y Victor Manuel Rendón, next to Hotel City Plaza, Guayaquil, T04-230 1277, www.emetebe.com.ec, see Transport for local offices, offers inter-island flights in light aircraft. Two daily flights except Sun between **Puerto Baquerizo Moreno** (San Cristóbal), **Baltra** and **Puerto Villamil** (Isabela). All fares US$165 one way; baggage allowance 25 lbs.

Lanchas (speedboats with three large engines for about 20 passengers) operate daily between Puerto Ayora and each of Puerto Baquerizo Moreno, Puerto Villamil, and Puerto Velasco Ibarra (Floreana); US$25-35 one way, two hours or more depending on the weather and sea. Tickets are sold by several agencies in Puerto Baquerizo Moreno, Puerto Ayora, and Puerto Villamil; purchase a day before travelling. This can be a wild ride in rough seas, life vests provided, take drinking water.

When to go

The Galápagos climate can be divided into a hot season (December-May), when there is a possibility of heavy showers, and the cool or *garúa* (mist) season (June to November), when the days generally are more cloudy and there is often rain or drizzle. July and August can be windy, force four or five. Daytime clothing should be lightweight. (Clothing generally, even on 'luxury cruises', should be casual and comfortable.) At night, however, particularly at sea and at higher altitudes, temperatures fall below 15°C and warm clothing is required. The sea is cold July to October; underwater visibility is best January to March. Ocean temperatures are usually higher to the east and lower at the western end of the archipelago. Despite all these climatic variations, conditions are generally favourable for visiting Galápagos throughout the year.

High season for tourism is June to August and December to January, when last-minute arrangements are generally not possible. Some boats may be heavily booked throughout the year and you should plan well in advance if you want to travel on a specific vessel at a specific time.

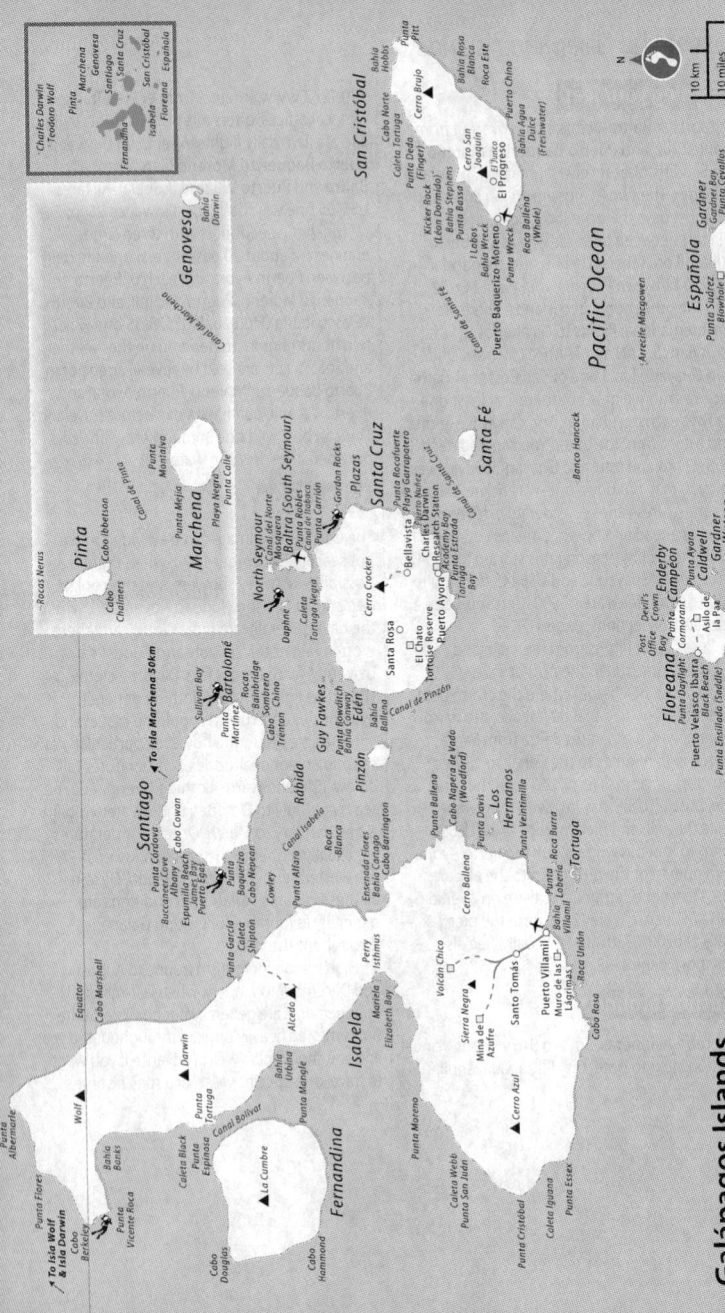

Galápagos Islands

Santa Cruz: Puerto Ayora *See map, page 1178.*

Santa Cruz is the most central of the Galápagos islands and the main town is Puerto Ayora. About 1.5 km from the pier is the **Charles Darwin Research Station** ① *at Academy Bay, www. darwinfoundation.org, office Mon-Fri 0700-1600, visitor areas 0600-1800 daily, free.* A visit to the station is a good introduction to the islands. Collections of several of the rare sub-species of giant tortoise are maintained on the station as breeding nuclei, together with tortoise-rearing pens for the young. The **Centro Comunitario de Educación Ambiental** ① *west end of Charles Binford, Mon-Fri 0730-1200, 1400-1700, Sat morning only, free,* has an aquarium and exhibits about the Galápagos Marine Reserve.

There is a beautiful beach at **Tortuga Bay**, 45 minutes' easy walk (2.5 km each way) west from Puerto Ayora on an excellent cobbled path through cactus forest. Start at the west end of Calle Charles Binford; further on there is a gate where you must register, open 0600-1800 daily, free. Make sure you take sun screen, drinking water, and beware of the very strong undertow. Do not walk on the dunes above the beach, which are a marine tortoise nesting area. At the west end of Tortuga Bay is a trail to a lovely mangrove-fringed lagoon, with calmer warmer water, shade, and sometimes a kayak for rent.

Las Grietas is a lovely gorge with a natural pool at the bottom which is splendid (crowded on weekends) for bathing. Take a water taxi from the port to the dock at Punta Estrada (five minutes, US$0.80). It is a 10-minute walk from here to the **Finch Bay hotel** and 20 minutes further over rough lava boulders to Las Grietas – well worth the trip.

The Puerto Ayora-Baltra road goes through the agricultural zone in the highlands. The community of **Bellavista** is 7 km from the port, and **Santa Rosa** is 15 km beyond. The area has National Park visitor sites, walking possibilities and upmarket lodgings. **Los Gemelos** are a pair of large sinkholes, formed by collapse of the ground above empty magma chambers. They straddle the road to Baltra, beyond Santa Rosa. You can take a taxi (US$15 return with wait) or airport bus all the way; otherwise take a bus to Santa Rosa, then walk one hour uphill. There are several **lava tubes** (natural tunnels) on the island. Some are at **El Mirador**, 3 km from Puerto Ayora on the road to Bellavista. Two more lava tubes are 1 km from Bellavista. They are on private land, it costs US$3-5 (US$10 with torch) to enter the tunnels (bring a torch) and it takes about 30 minutes to walk through them. Tours to the lava tubes can be arranged in Puerto Ayora.

The highest point on Santa Cruz Island is **Cerro Crocker** at 864 m. You can hike here and to two other nearby 'peaks' called **Media Luna** and **Puntudo**. The trail starts at Bellavista where a rough trail map is painted as a mural on the wall of the school. The round trip from Bellavista takes six to eight hours. A permit and guide are not required, but a guide may be helpful. Always take food, water and a compass or GPS.

Another worthwhile trip is to the **El Chato Tortoise Reserve**, where giant tortoises can be seen in the wild during the dry season (June to February). In the wet season the tortoises are breeding down in the arid zone. Follow the road that goes past the Santa Rosa school to 'La Reserva'. At the end of

Fees and inspections

A US$20 fee is collected at Quito or Guayaquil airport, where a registration form must be completed. It is best to pre-register on line at www.gobiernogalapagos.gob.ec, or ask your tour operator to do so for you. Bags are checked prior to flights to Galápagos, no live animals, meat, dairy products, fresh fruit or vegetables may be taken to the islands. On arrival, every foreign visitor must pay a US$100 National Park fee. All fees are cash only. Be sure to have your passport to hand at the airport and keep all fee receipts throughout your stay in the islands. Bags are checked again on departure, as nothing may be taken off the islands. Puerto Villamil charges a US$10 port fee on arrival in Isabela.

Basic rules

Do not touch any of the animals, birds or plants. Do not transfer sand, seeds or soil from one island to another. Do not leave litter anywhere; nor take food on to the uninhabited islands, which are also no-smoking zones. There is increasingly close contact between people and sea lions throughout Galápagos. Never touch them however, and keep your distance from the male 'beach-masters', they have been known to bite. Always take food, plenty of water and a compass or GPS if hiking on your own. There are many crisscrossing animal trails and it is easy to get lost. Also watch out for the large-spined opuntia cactus and the poisonwood tree (*manzanillo*) found near beaches, contact with its leaves or bark can cause severe skin reactions.

What to take

A remedy for seasickness is recommended. A good supply of sun block and skin cream to prevent windburn and chapped lips is essential, as are a hat and sunglasses. You should be prepared for dry and wet landings, the latter involving wading ashore; keep photo equipment and other delicate items in a waterproof stuff-sack or plastic bags. The animals are so tame that you will take far more photos than you expected; if you run out of memory cards they can be bought in Puerto Ayora, but best to take your own. Snorkelling equipment is particularly useful as much of the sea-life is only visible under water. The cheaper boats may not provide equipment or it may be of poor quality. If in doubt, bring your own. Good sturdy footwear is important, boots and shoes soon wear out on the abrasive lava terrain. Always take US$ cash to Galápagos as there are few ATMs and they may not always work. ATMs on Puerto Ayora, Puerto Baquerizo, no banks or ATMs in Puerto Villamil, but there is **MoneyGram**, in La Isla supermarket for international funds transfer. The ATM withdrawal limit is US$300-500 per day. Cash advances on credit cards cannot be obtained in Galápagos.

Tipping

A ship's crew and guides are usually tipped separately. Amounts are often suggested onboard or in agencies' brochures, but these should be considered in light of the quality of service received and your own resources.

Problems

Raise any issues first with your guide or ship's captain. Serious complaints are rare but may filed with iTur or **Ministerio de Turismo** offices in Puerto Ayora or Puerto Baquerizo Moreno, see Tourist information in Listings, below.

Choosing a tour

There are various options for visiting Galápagos but by far the best is the traditional **live-aboard cruise** (*tour navegable*), where you travel and sleep on a yacht, tour boat or cruise ship. These vessels travel at night, arriving at a new landing site each day. Cruises range from three to 14 nights, seven is recommended. Itineraries are controlled by the National Park to distribute cruise boats evenly throughout the islands. All cruises begin with a morning flight from the mainland on the first day and end on the last day with a midday flight back to the mainland. The less expensive boats are normally smaller and less powerful so you see less and spend more time travelling; also the guiding may be mostly in Spanish. The more expensive boats have air conditioning, hot water and private baths. All boats have to conform to certain minimum safety standards; more expensive boats are better equipped. Boats with over 20 passengers take quite a time to disembark and re-embark people, while the smaller boats have a more lively motion, which is important if you are prone to seasickness. Note also that there may be limitations for vegetarians on the cheaper boats. The least expensive boats (economy class) cost up to US$200 per person per day and a few of these vessels are dodgy. For around US$250-600 per day (tourist and tourist superior class) you will be on a better, faster boat which can travel more quickly between visitor sites, leaving more time to spend ashore. Over US$600 per day are the first-class and luxury brackets, with far more comfortable and spacious cabins, as well as a superior level of service and cuisine. No boat may sail without a park-trained guide.

The table on page 1180 lists tourist vessels; for dive boats see page 1187. The sailing vessels listed also have motors and many frequently operate under engine power. All details are subject to change. Captains, crews and guides regularly change on all boats. These factors, as well as the sea, weather and your fellow passengers will all influence the quality of your experience. Many overseas agencies sell cruises in the Galápagos Islands. Some are listed in Tour operators, in the Practicalities chapter, for instance Galápagos Classic Cruises, Galápagos Network, INCA, International Expeditions, Select Latin America and Wilderness Travel.

Island-hopping is another option for visiting Galápagos, whereby you spend a night or two at hotels on some of the four populated islands, travelling between them in speedboats. You cover less ground than on a cruise, see fewer wildlife sites, and cannot visit the more distant islands. Island-hopping is sold in organized packages but visitors in no rush can also travel between and explore the populated islands independently and at their leisure. **Day tours** (*tour diario*) are yet another alternative, based mostly out of Puerto Ayora. Some take you for day-visits to National Park landing sites on nearby unpopulated islands, such as Bartolomé, Seymour, Plazas and Santa Fe (US$100-220), and can be quite good. Others go for the day to the populated islands of Isabela or Floreana, with no stops permitted along the way. The latter require at least four hours of speedboat travel and generally leave insufficient time to enjoy visitor sites; they are not recommended. All forms of land-based tourism have grown rapidly, with a considerable impact on the Islands.

None of the above options is cheap. Galápagos is such a special destination for nature-lovers however, that most agree it is worth saving for and spending on a quality tour. If nature is not your great passion and you are looking mainly for an exotic cruise or beach holiday, then your money will go further and you will likely have a better experience elsewhere.

Booking a tour in advance

You can book a Galápagos cruise in several different ways: 1) over the internet; 2) from either a travel agency or directly though a Galápagos wholesaler in your home country; 3) from one of the many agencies found throughout Ecuador, especially in Quito (see page 1044) but also in other tourist centres and Guayaquil (page 1132); or 4) from local agencies, mostly in Puerto Ayora but also in Puerto Baquerizo Moreno. The trade-off is always between time and money: booking from home is most efficient and expensive, last-minute arrangements in Galápagos are cheapest but most time-consuming (and the cost of staying in Puerto Ayora is high), while Quito and Guayaquil are intermediate. It is not possible to obtain discounts or make last-minute arrangements in high season (see When to go, page 1173). Surcharges may apply when using a credit card to purchase tours on the islands, there are limits to ATM withdrawals and no cash advances in Galápagos, so take sufficient cash if looking for a last-minute cruise. Also, if looking for a last-minute sailing, it is best to pay your hotel one night at a time since hoteliers may not refund advance payments. Especially on cheaper boats, check carefully about what is and is not included (eg drinking water, snorkelling equipment, etc).

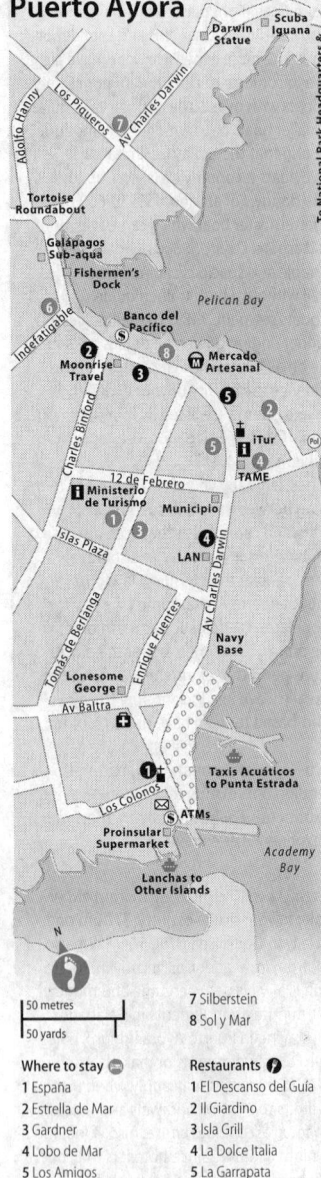

Puerto Ayora

Where to stay
1 España
2 Estrella de Mar
3 Gardner
4 Lobo de Mar
5 Los Amigos
6 Peregrina
7 Silberstein
8 Sol y Mar

Restaurants
1 El Descanso del Guía
2 Il Giardino
3 Isla Grill
4 La Dolce Italia
5 La Garrapata

the road (about 3 km) you reach a faded wooden memorial to an Israeli tourist who got lost here. Take the trail to the right (west) for about 45 minutes. There are many confusing trails in the reserve itself; take food, water and a compass or GPS. If you have no hiking experience, horses can sometimes be hired at Santa Rosa or arrange a tour from Puerto Ayora.

Tortoises can also be seen at **Cerro Mesa** and at several private ranches, some of which have camping facilities; eg **Butterfly Ranch** ① *Hacienda Mariposa, entry US$3, camping US$25 pp including breakfast, access at Km 16, just before Santa Rosa, walk 1 km from here, make previous arrangements at Moonrise Travel.*

San Cristóbal: Puerto Baquerizo Moreno

Puerto Baquerizo Moreno, on San Cristóbal island, is the capital of the archipelago. Electrical energy here is provided by wind generators in the highlands, see www.eolicsa.com.ec. The town's attractive *malecón* has many shaded seats shared by tourists, residents and sea lions. The **cathedral** ① *on Av Northía y Cobos, 0900-1200, 1600-1800,* has interesting artwork combining religious and Galápagos motifs.

To the north of town, opposite **Playa Mann** (suitable for swimming), is the Galápagos National Park highly informative visitor centre or **Centro de Interpretación** ① *T05-252 0138, ext 123, daily 0700-1700, free.* A good trail goes from the Centro de Interpretación to the northeast through scrub forest to **Cerro Tijeretas**, a hill overlooking town and the ocean, 30 minutes away. From here a rougher trail continues 45 minutes to **Playa Baquerizo**. Frigatebirds nest in this area; there are sea lions on the beaches below. To go back from Cerro Tijeretas, if you take the trail which follows the coast, you will end up at **Playa Punta Carola**, a popular surfing beach, too rough for swimming. To the south of Puerto Baquerizo Moreno, 30 minutes' walk past the stadium and high school (ask for directions), is **La Lobería**, a popular beach with sea lions, marine iguanas, many bathers at weekends, and a rough trail leading to beautiful cliffs with birds, overlooking the sea.

Four buses a day run the 6 km inland from Puerto Baquerizo Moreno to **El Progreso** US$0.50, 15 minutes, then it's a 2½-hour walk to **El Junco lake**, the largest body of fresh water in Galápagos. Pick-up trucks to El Progreso charge US$3, or you can hire them for touring: US$25 to

BACKGROUND

Unconnected islands

The Galápagos have never been connected with the continent. Gradually, over many hundreds of thousands of years, animals and plants from over the sea somehow migrated there and as time went by they adapted themselves to Galápagos conditions and came to differ more and more from their continental ancestors. Unique marine and terrestrial environments, due to the continuing volcanic formation of the islands in the west of the archipelago and its location at the nexus of several major marine currents, have created laboratory-type conditions where only certain species have been allowed access. The formidable barriers which prevent many species from travelling between the islands, has led to a very high level of endemism. A quarter of the species of shore fish, half of the plants and almost all the reptiles are found nowhere else. In many cases different forms have evolved on the different islands. Charles Darwin recognized this speciation within the archipelago when he visited the Galápagos on the *Beagle* in 1835 and his observations played a substantial part in his formulation of the theory of evolution.

This natural experiment has been under threat ever since the arrival of the first whaling ships and even more so since the first permanent human settlement. New species were introduced and spread very rapidly, placing the endemic species at risk. Quarantine programmes have since been implemented in an attempt to prevent the introduction and spread of even more species, but the rules are not easy to enforce. There have also been campaigns to eradicate some of the introduced species on some islands, but this is inevitably a very slow, expensive and difficult process.

One striking feature of the islands is the tameness of the animals. The islands were uninhabited when they were discovered in 1535 and the animals still have little instinctive fear of man.

Plant and animal species are grouped into three categories. **Endemic species** are those which occur only in the Galápagos and nowhere else on the planet. Examples of Galápagos endemics are the Galápagos marine and Galápagos land iguana, Galápagos fur sea lion, flightless cormorant and the 'daisy tree' (*Scalesia pedunculata*). **Native species** make their homes in the Galápagos as well as other parts of the world. Examples include all three species of boobies, frigate birds and the various types of mangroves. Although not unique to the islands, these native species have been an integral part of the Galápagos ecosystems for a very long time. **Introduced species** on the other hand are very recent arrivals, brought by man, and inevitably the cause of much damage. They include cattle, goats, donkeys, pigs, dogs, cats, rats and over 500 species of plants such as elephant grass (for grazing cattle), and fruit trees. The unchecked expansion of these introduced species has upset the natural balance of the archipelago. Any domestic animals must now be neutered before they can be brought to the islands. The number of tourists also has grown steadily: from 11,800 in 1979, to 68,900 in 2000, to over 224,755 in 2015. From 2007 to 2010, Galápagos was on the UNESCO list of endangered World Heritage Sites. Although it is now off the list, promoting environmental conservation and sustainable development in the face of growing tourism and population has proven to be an ever greater challenge.

El Junco (return with wait), US$50 continuing to the beaches at **Puerto Chino** on the other side of the island, past a man-made tortoise reserve. Camping is possible at Puerto Chino with a permit from the National Park, take all supplies. At El Junco there is a path to walk around the lake in 20 minutes. The views are lovely in clear weather but it is cool and wet in the *garúa* season. Various small roads fan out from El Progreso and make for pleasant walking. **Jatun Sacha** (www.jatunsacha. org) has a volunteer centre on an old hacienda in the highlands beyond El Progreso, working on eradication of invasive species and a native plant nursery; US$15 taxi ride from town, take repellent.

Boats go to **Punta Pitt** at the northeast end of San Cristóbal where you can see all three species of booby. Off the northwest coast is **Kicker Rock** (León Dormido), the basalt remains of a volcanic plug; many seabirds, including nazca and blue-footed boobies, can be seen around its cliffs (five-hour trip, including snorkelling, recommended).

ON THE ROAD

Galápagos tourist vessels

Name	Type	Capacity	Website	Class
Galapagos Legend	CS	100	gogalapagos.com	L
Silver Galapagos	CS	100	silversea.com	L
Xpedition	CS	100	galapagosxpedition.co.uk	L
Nat Geo Endeavour	CS	96	expeditions.com	L
Eclipse	CS	48	oagalapagos.com	L
Nat Geo Islander	CS	48	expeditions.com	L
Isabela II	CS	40	metropolitan-touring.com	F
Coral I	MY	36	gogalapagos.com	F
Evolution	MV	32	quasarex.com	L
La Pinta	CS	48	metropolitan-touring.com	L
Galaven	MY	22	various	TS
Coral II	MY	20	gogalapagos.com	F
Eric	MY	20	ecoventura.com	F
Letty	MY	20	ecoventura.com	F
Monserrat	MY	20	monserrat-cruise.info	TS
Grace	MY	18	quasarex.com	L
Aída María	MY	16	aidamariatravel.com	TS
Amigo I	MY	16	various	E
Anahi	MC	16	andandotours.com	F
Angelito	MY	16	cometatravel.com	TS
Archipel I	MY	16	galacruises.com	TS
Archipel II	MC	16	galacruises.com	F
Athala II	MC	16	various	L
Beluga	MY	16	enchantedexpeditions.com	F
Cachalote	2mSCH	16	enchantedexpeditions.com	F
Cormorant Evolution	MC	16	haugancruises.com	TS
Daphne	MY	16	various	TS
Darwin	MY	16	vigaltravel.com	TS
Eden	MY	16	aidamariatravel.com	TS
Estrella del Mar I	MY	16	gadventures.com	TS
Floreana	MY	16	yatefloreana.com	TS
Fragata	MY	16	yatefragata.com	TS
Galaxy I	MC	16	galagents.com	T
Galaxy II	MC	16	galagents.com	T
Golondrina	MY	16	golondrinaturismo.com	T
Grand Odyssey	MY	16	galapagosgrandodyssey.com	F
Integrity	MY	16	various	L
Majestic	MY	16	gadventures.com	F
Mary Anne	3mBarq	16	andandotours.com	F
Millennium	MC	16	galapagosexperience.net	F
Nemo III	MC	16	nemogalapagoscruises.com	T
Ocean Spray	MC	16	haugancruises.com	L
Odyssey	MC	16	yachtgalapagosodyssey.com	F
Origin	MY	20	origingalapagos.com	L
Petrel	MC	16	haugancruises.com	T
Queen Beatriz	MC	16	peakdmc.com	L
Queen of Galapagos	MC	16	gadventures.com	L

Name	Type	Capacity	Website	Class
Reina Silvia	MY	16	reinasilvia.com	F
San José	MY	16	various	F
Santa Cruz	CS	90	metropolitan-touring.com	F
Seaman Journey	MC	16	galapagosjourneycruises.com	F
Sea Star Journey	MY	16	latintrails.com	F
Stellamaris	MY	16	galasam.net	F
Tip Top III	MY	16	rwittmer.com	F
Tip Top IV	MY	16	rwittmer.com	F
Treasure of Galapagos	MC	16	treasureofgalapagos.com	F
Xavier	MY	16	various	TS
Yolita II	MY	16	yolitayacht.com	TS
King of the Seas	MY	14	various	E
Nemo I	MC	14	nemogalapagoscruises.com	T
Samba	SV	14	galapagosexperience.net	TS
Beagle	2mSch	13	galapagosexperience.net	F
Nemo II	MC	12	nemogalapagoscruises.com	F
Passion	MY	12	andandotours.com	TS
New Flamingo	MY	10	various	E

Type Key
CS = Cruise Ship
MY = Motor Yacht
MV = Motor Vessel
MC = Motor Catamaran
2mSch = 2-masted Schooner
3mSch = 3-masted Schooner
3mBarq = 3-masted Barquentine
SV = Sailing Vessel

Class Key
L = Luxury Class
F = First Class
TS = Tourist Superior Class
T = Tourist Class
E = Economy Class

Isabela: Puerto Villamil

This is the largest island in the archipelago, formed by the coalesced lava flows of six volcanoes. Five are active and each has (or had) its own separate sub-species of giant tortoise. Isabela is also the island which is changing most rapidly, driven by growing land-based tourism. It remains a charming place but is at risk from uncontrolled development. Most residents live in Puerto Villamil. In the highlands, there is a cluster of farms at Santo Tomás. There are several lovely beaches right by town, but mind the strong undertow and ask locally about the best spots for swimming and surfing.

It is 8 km west to **Muro de las Lágrimas**, built by convict labour under hideous conditions. It makes a great day-hike or hire a bicycle (always take water). Short side-trails branch off the road to various attractions along the way, and a trail continues from the Muro to nearby hills with lovely views. Inland from the same road, 30 minutes from town, is the **Centro de Crianza**, a breeding centre for giant tortoises surrounded by lagoons with flamingos and other birds. In the opposite direction, 30 minutes east toward the *embarcadero* (pier) is **Concha de Perla Lagoon**, with a nice access trail through mangroves and a small dock from which you can go swimming with sea lions and other creatures. Tours go to **Las Tintoreras**, a set of small islets in the harbour where white-tipped reef sharks and penguins may be seen in the still crystalline water (US$35 per person). There are also boat tours to **Los Túneles** at Cabo Rosa (US$80 per person, a tricky entrance from the open sea), where fish, rays and turtles can be seen in submerged lava tunnels.

Sierra Negra Volcano has the second-largest basaltic caldera in the world, 9 km by 10 km. Visits are only permitted with a guide. It is 19 km (US$20, 30 minutes) by pickup truck to the park entrance (take passport and National Park entry receipt), where you start the 1½-hour hike to the crater rim at 1000 m. It is a further 1½ hours' walk along bare brittle lava rock to **Volcán Chico**, with several fumaroles and more stunning views. You can camp on the crater rim but must take all supplies, including water, and obtain a permit the day before from the National Park office in Puerto Villamil. A tour including transport and lunch costs about US$50 per person. Highland tours are also available to **La Cueva de Sucre**, a large lava tube with many chambers; be sure to take a torch if visiting on your own. A bus to the highlands leaves the market in Puerto Villamil at 0700 daily, US$0.50, ask the driver for directions to the cave and return times.

Floreana: Puerto Velasco Ibarra

Floreana is the island with the richest human history and the fewest inhabitants, most living in Puerto Velasco Ibarra. You can reach the island with a day-tour boat from Puerto Ayora, but these do not leave enough time to enjoy the visit. A couple of days stay is recommended, but you must be flexible in case there isn't enough space in boats returning to Puerto Ayora. Services are limited, one shop has basic supplies and there are a handful of places to eat and sleep, none is cheap. Margaret Wittmer, one of the first settlers on Floreana, died in 2000, but you can meet her daughter and granddaughter.

La Lobería is a beautiful little peninsula (which becomes an island at high tide), 15 minutes' walk from town, where sea lions, sea turtles, marine iguanas and various birds can be seen. The climate in the highlands is fresh and comfortable, good for walking and birdwatching. A *ranchera* runs up to **Asilo de La Paz**, with a natural spring and tortoise area, Monday to Saturday 0600 and 1500, returning 0700 and 1600; Sun 0700 returning 1000. Or you can walk down in three to four hours, detouring to climb **Cerro Allieri**.

Post Office Bay, on the north side of Floreana, is visited by tour boats. There is a custom (since 1792) for visitors here to place unstamped letters and cards in a barrel, and deliver, free of charge, any addressed to their own destinations.

Tourist information

Santa Cruz

iTur
Av Charles Darwin y 12 de Febrero, Puerto Ayora,
T0-252 6153 ext 22. Mon-Fri 0730-1230, 1400-
1730, Sat-Sun 1600-1930. Also at Baltra airport.
Has information about Puerto Ayora and Santa
Cruz Island.

Ministerio de Turismo
Charles Binford y 12 de Febrero, Puerto Ayora,
T05-252 6174. Mon-Fri 0830-1300, 1430-1730.
An administrative office but receives complaints
about agencies and vessels.

San Cristóbal

Ministerio de Turismo
12 de Febrero e Ignacio Hernández,
Puerto Baquerizo Moreno, T05-252 0704.
Mon-Fri 0830-1230, 1400-1730.
Operates as in Santa Cruz, above.

Municipal tourist office
Malecón Charles Darwin y 12 de Febrero,
Puerto Baquerizo Moreno, T05-252 0119 ext 120.
Mon-Fri 0730-1230, 1400-1800.
Downstairs at the Municipio.

Isabela

Municipal tourist office
By the park, Puerto Villamil, T05-252 9002,
ext 113. Mon-Fri 0730-1230, 1400-1700.
Has local information.

Where to stay

Santa Cruz

Puerto Ayora

$$$$ Angemeyer Waterfront Inn
By the dock at Punta Estrada, T05-252 6561,
www.angermeyer-waterfront-inn.com.
Gorgeous location overlooking the bay south of
the centre. Includes buffet breakfast, restaurant,
comfortable modern rooms and apartments,
some with kitchenettes, a/c, attentive service.

$$$$ Silberstein
Darwin y Piqueros, T05-252 6277, Quito T02-292
1739, www.hotelsilberstein.com.

Modern and comfortable with lovely grounds,
pool in tropical garden, a/c, buffet breakfast,
restaurant (see page 1185), bar, spacious rooms
and common areas, very nice.

$$$$ Sol y Mar
Darwin y Binford, T05-252 6281,
www.hotelsolymar.com.ec.
Right in town but with a priviledged location
overlooking the bay. Includes buffet breakfast,
restaurant, bar, pool, jacuzzi and use of bicycles.

$$$ España
Berlanga y 12 de Febrero, T05-252 6108,
www.hotelespanagalapagos.com.
Pleasant and quiet, spacious rooms, a/c, small
courtyard with hammocks, good value.

$$$ Jean's Home
Punta Estrada, T05-252 6446, T09-9296 0347,
gundisg@hotmail.es.
Comfortably refurbished home in a lovely out-of-
the-way location (short water taxi ride south of
town), a/c, family-run, English and German spoken.

$$$ Lobo de Mar
12 de Febrero y Darwin, T05-252 6188, Quito
T02-250 2089, www.lobodemar.com.ec.
Modern building with balconies and rooftop
terrace, great views over the harbour. A/c,
small pool, fridge, modern and comfortable,
attentive service.

$$$ Peregrina
Darwin e Indefatigable, T05-252 6323,
peregrinagalapagos@yahoo.com.
Away from the centre of town, a/c, nice rooms
and common areas, small garden, family-run,
homey atmosphere.

$$ Estrella de Mar
By the water on a lane off 12 de Febrero,
T05-252 6427.
Nice quiet location with views over the bay.
A/c, fan, fridge, spacious rooms, sitting area.

$$-$ Gardner
Berlanga y 12 de Febrero, T05-252 6979,
hotelgardner@yahoo.com.
Comfortable rooms, cheaper with fan, kitchen
facilities, breakfast available, good value.

$$-$ Los Amigos
Darwin y 12 de Febrero, T05-252 6265.
Small place, basic rooms with shared bath,
cold water, fan, laundry facilities, good value.

Highlands of Santa Cruz

$$$$ Galápagos Safari Camp
T09-8296 8228, www.galapagossafaricamp.com.
Luxury resort with a central lodge and
comfortable, en suite tents. Includes breakfast
and dinner, swimming pool, organizes tours
and activities.

$$$$ Semilla Verde
T05-301-3079, www.gps.ec.
Located on a 5 ha property being reforested with
native plants, comfortable rooms and common
areas, includes breakfast, other meals available or
use of kitchen facilities, British/Ecuadorean-run,
family atmosphere.

San Cristóbal

Puerto Baquerizo Moreno

$$$$ Miconia
Darwin e Isabela, T05-252 0608,
www.hotelmiconia.com.
Restaurant, a/c, small pool, large well-equipped
gym, modern if somewhat small rooms, some
with fridge.

$$$ Blue Marlin
Española y Northia, T05-252 0253,
www.bluemarlingalapagos.ec.
Ample modern rooms are mostly wheelchair
accessible, bathtubs, a/c, pool, fridge.

$$$ Casablanca
Mellville y Darwin, T05-252 0392,
www.casablancagalapagos.com.
Large house with terrace and views of harbour.
Each room is individually decorated by the owner
who has an art gallery on the premises.

$$ Casa de Nelly
Tijeretas y Northia, T05-252 0112,
casadenellygalapagos.com.ec.
3-storey building, quiet, bright comfortable
rooms, a/c, kitchen facilities, family-run.

$$ Mar Azul
Northia y Esmeraldas, T05-252 0139.
Nice comfortable lodgings, electric shower, a/c
and fan, fridge, kitchen facilities, pleasant. Same
family runs 2 more expensive hotels.

$ San Francisco
Darwin y Villamil, T05-252 0304.
Simple rooms with private bath, cold water, fan,
kitchen facilities, good value.

El Progreso

$$ Casa del Ceibo
Pto Baquerizo Moreno T05-252 0248.
A single unique room in the branches of a huge
kapok tree. Private bath, hot water, US$1.50 to
visit, advance booking required.

Isabela

Puerto Villamil

Many hotels have opened in recent years.

$$$$ Albemarle
On the beachfront in town, T05-252 9489,
www.hotelalbemarle.com.
Attractive Mediterranean-style construction,
restaurant, bright comfortable rooms with
wonderful ocean views, a/c, small pool.

$$$$ La Casa de Marita
At east end of beach, T05-252 9238,
www.galapagosisabela.com.
Tastefully chic, includes breakfast, other meals on
request, a/c and fridge, very comfortable, each
room is slightly different, some have balconies.
A little gem and recommended.

$$$ Casa Isabela on the Beach
On the beachfront in town, T09-9856
3802, Quito T02-250 4002, http://
casaisabelaonthebeach.com.
Pleasant house on the beach, rooms with a/c,
nice ocean views.

$$$ IsaMar
On the beachfront in town, Book through Tropic
Ecuador, www.destinationecuador.com.
10 rooms with sea views, aq/c, Wi-Fi,
restaurant and bar, full range of activities
on land and on water.

$$$ La Laguna
Los Flamencos y Los Petreles, T05-349 7940,
www.gruposanvicentegalapagos.com.
Pleasant rooms with a/c, attractive balconies
and common areas, jacuzzi.

$$$ San Vicente
Cormoranes y Pinzón Artesano, T05-252 9140,
www.gruposanvicentegalapagos.com.
Very popular and well organized hotel which
also offers tours and kayak rentals, includes
breakfast, other meals on request or use of
cooking facilities, a/c, jacuzzi, rooms a bit
small but nice, family-run.

$ Hostal Villamil
10 de Marzo y Antonio Gil, T05-252 9180,
www.gruposanvicentegalapagos.com.
A/c, kitchen and laundry facilities, small patio
with hammocks, family-run and very friendly,
good value. Recommended.

$$ La Jungla
Off Antonio Gil at the west edge of town,
T05-301 6721, www.thejunglegalapagos.com.
Nice rooms with a/c, beach views, meals on
request, secluded non-central location.

Highlands of Isabela

$$ Campo Duro
T09-8545 3045, refugiodetortugasgigantes@
hotmail.com.
Camping (tents provided), includes breakfast and
dinner, nice ample grounds, giant tortoises may
be seen (US$2 to visit), friendly owner. Taxi from
Pto Villamil, US$7.

Floreana: Puerto Velasco Ibarra

$$$$ Lava Lodge
Book through Tropic Ecuador,
www.destinationecuador.com.
Wooden cabins on the beach a short distance
outside town, family-owned, full board, kayak,
snorkel and SUP equipment, guided tours to
wildlife and historic sites, popular with groups.

$$$ Hostal Santa María
Opposite the school, T05-253 5022.
Nice modern rooms with private bath, hot water,
fan, fridge, screened windows, friendly owner
Sr Claudio Cruz.

$$$ Hotel/Pensión Wittmer
Right on Black Beach, T05-253 5013.
Lovely location, simple comfortable rooms,
electric shower, fan, very good meals available,
family-run, German spoken, reservations required.

Restaurants

Santa Cruz: Puerto Ayora

$$$ Il Giardino
Charles Darwin y Charles Binford, T05-252 6627.
Open 0800-2230, closed Tue.
Very good international food, service and
atmosphere, excellent ice cream, very popular,
book in advance.

$$$ Isla Grill
Charles Darwin y Tomás de Berlanga,
T05-252 4461. Tue-Sun 1200-2200.
Upmarket grill, seafood and pizza.

$$$ La Dolce Italia
Charles Darwin y 12 de Febrero.
Daily 1100-1500, 1800-2200.
Italian and seafood, wine list, a/c,
pleasant atmosphere, attentive owner.

$$$-$$ La Garrapata
Charles Darwin between 12 de Febrero and
Tomás de Berlanga. Mon-Sat 0900-2200.
Good food, attractive setting and nice music.

$$$-$$ Silberstein
Darwin y Piqueros, T05-252 6277.
Serves a good range of both Ecuadorian and
international cuisine. Lovely setting with tables,
inside and outside, some overlooking the pool
area. In eponymous hotel; see page 1183.

$$ Kiosks
Along Charles Binford between Padre Herrera
and Rodríguez Lara.
Tasty local fare, including a variety of seafood,
outdoor seating, lively informal atmosphere,
busy at night. Also beside the fishermen's dock
at Pelican Bay, evenings only.

$ El Descanso del Guía
Charles Darwin y Los Colonos. Daily 0645-1945.
Good set meals, very popular with locals.

San Cristóbal: Puerto Baquerizo Moreno

$$$-$$ La Playa
Av de la Armada Nacional, by the navy base.
Daily 0930-2330.
Varied menu, fish and seafood.

$$$-$$ Olimpio
Northía y Isabela. Closed Sun.
Attractive restaurant, international food.

$$$-$$ Rosita
Ignacio de Hernández y General Villamil.
Daily 0930-1430, 1700-2230.
Old-time yachtie hangout, good food, large
portions, nice atmosphere, à la carte and
economical set meals. Recommended.

$$ Descanso del Marinero
Northía y Española. Wed-Mon 0800-2100.
Ceviches and seafood, outdoor seating.

$ Mi Grande
Villamil y Darwin, upstairs.
Popular for set meals and good breakfast.

$ Several simple places serving economical set meals on Northia between Española and 12 de Febrero. Also Sun lunch up at El Progreso, good *comida del campo*.

Mockingbird Café
Española y Hernández. Mon-Sat 0730-2330, Sun from 0930.
Fruit juices, brownies, snacks, internet.

Sabor Cuencano
Northía y Isabela. Closed Sun.
Good popular bakery.

Isabela: Puerto Villamil

$$$-$$ Various outdoor restaurants around the plaza feature seafood on the menu: **Cesar's**, **Los Delfines** and **Encanto de la Pepa**, which is very good.

$$-$ Isabela Grill
16 de Marzo y Flamencos.
Good choice for set lunch, dinner and à la carte.

$ El Faro
Las Fragatas ½ block from Plaza.
Daily 1200-1400, 1800-1930.
Simple set lunch, grill at night, popular.

Floreana: Puerto Velasco Ibarra

$$$-$$ Meals available at hotels or from a couple of restaurants catering to tour groups, all require advance notice.

$$ Lelia Restaurante
Opposite the school, T05-253 5041.
Good home cooking. Friendly owner also has 2 rooms for rent.

$ The Devil's Crown
100 m from the dock on road to the highlands.
Set lunch and dinner most days, ask in advance.

Shopping

Santa Cruz: Puerto Ayora
There is an attractive little **Mercado Artesanal** (craft market) at Charles Darwin y Tomás de Berlanga. **Proinsular**, opposite the pier, is the largest and best-stocked supermarket in Galápagos.

> **Tip...**
> Most items can be purchased on the islands but at a higher price than in mainland Ecuador. Do not buy anything made of black coral as it is an endangered species.

San Cristóbal: Puerto Baquerizo Moreno

Galamarket
Isabela y Juan José Flores.
A modern well-stocked supermarket.

What to do

Santa Cruz: Puerto Ayora

Cycling
Mountain bikes can be hired from travel agencies in town. Prices and quality vary, about US$15-20 for 3 hrs.

Diving
Only specialized diving boats are allowed to do diving tours. It is not possible to dive as part of a standard live-aboard cruise nor are dive boats allowed to call at the usual land visitor sites when they are diving. Some dive boats, however, might offer a week of diving followed by a week of cruising to land sites. For a list of dive boats, see table, opposite. National Park rules prohibit collecting samples or souvenirs, spear-fishing, touching animals, or other environmental disruptions. Experienced dive guides can help visitors have the most spectacular opportunities to enjoy the wildlife. There are several diving agencies in Puerto Ayora, Baquerizo Moreno and Villamil (see Tour operators, below) offering courses, equipment rental, and dives; prices and quality vary. On offer in Puerto Ayora are diving day trips (2 dives, US$175-250) and daily tours for up to 1 week in the central islands. There is a hyperbaric chamber in Puerto Ayora at **Centro Médico Integral** (Marchena y Hanny, T05-252 4576, www.sssnetwork.com). Check if your dive operator is affiliated with this facility or arrange your own insurance from home. To avoid the risk of decompression sickness, divers are advised to stay an extra day on the islands after their last dive before flying to the mainland, especially to Quito at 2840 m above sea level.

Dive Center Silberstein, *opposite Hotel Silberstein, T05-252 6028, www.divingalapagos. com.* Day tours in nice comfortable boat for up to 8 guests, English-speaking guides, good service, dive courses and trips for all levels of experience. Island-hopping dive tours and 8-day diving cruises are also organized.
Nautidiving, *Av Charles Darwin, T05-252 7004.* Offers day-trips to central islands as well as longer trips.

ON THE ROAD

Dive boats

Name	Type	Capacity	Website	Class
Aggressor III	MY	16	aggressor.com	L
Astrea	MY	16	various	TS
Deep Blue	MY	16	various	F
Galapagos Sky	MY	16	galapagossky.com	L
Humbolt Explorer	MY	16	galasam.net	F
Pingüino Explorer	MY	16	galacruises.com	TS
Encantada	2mSch	12	scubagalapagos.com	T
Nortada	MY	8	galapagosnortada.com	F

Type Key
MY = Motor Yacht
2mSch = 2-masted Schooner

Class Key
L = Luxury Class
F = First Class
TS = Tourist Superior Class
T = Tourist Class

Scuba Iguana, *Charles Darwin near the research station, T05-252 6497, www.scubaiguana.com*. Matías Espinoza runs this long-time reliable and recommended dive operator. Courses up to PADI divemaster.

Snorkelling
Masks, snorkels and fins can be rented from travel agencies and dive shops, US$5 a day, deposit required. Las Grietas is a popular place to snorkel near Puerto Ayora.

Surfing
There is surfing at Tortuga Bay and at other more distant beaches accessed by boat. Look for the surf club office at Pelican Bay. There is better surfing near Puerto Baquerizo Moreno on San Cristóbal. The **Lonesome George** agency rents surfboards, see below.

Tour operators
Lonesome George, *Av Baltra y Enrique Fuentes, T05-252 6245, lonesomegr@yahoo.com*. Run by Victor Vaca. Sells tours and rents: bicycles (US$3 per hr), surf-boards (US$30 per day) snorkelling equipment and motorcycles.
Moonrise Travel, *Av Charles Darwin y Charles Binford, T05-252 6348, www.galapagosmoonrise. com*. Last-minute cruise bookings, day-tours

Tip...
Avoid touts offering cheap tours at the airport or in the street. Also be wary of agencies who specialize in cut-rate cruises.

to different islands, bay tours, flights, enquire about horse riding at ranches, run guesthouse in Punta Estrada and rent chalets by Playa de los Alemanes. Owner Jenny Devine is knowledgeable and helpful.
Zenith Travel, *JL Mera N24-264 y Cordero, Quito, T02-252 9993, www.zenithecuador. com*. Good-value Galápagos cruises. All-gay Galápagos cruises available. Multilingual service, knowledgeable helpful staff, good value.

San Cristóbal: Puerto Baquerizo Moreno

Cycling
Bike rentals cost US$3 per hr, US$15 per day.

Diving
There are several dive sites around San Cristóbal, most popular being Kicker Rock, Roca Ballena and Punta Pitt, full day about US$200, see Tour operators, below.

Kayaking
Rentals US$10 per hr; from **Islander's Store** (Av J Roldós, above cargo pier, T05-252 0348); and **Galápagos Eco Expedition** (Av de la Armada, next to La Playa restaurant).

Surfing
There is good surfing in San Cristóbal, the best season is Dec-Mar. Punta Carola near town is the closest surfing beach; other spots are Canon and Tongo Reef, past the navy base. There is a championship during the local fiesta, the 2nd week of Feb.

Tour operators

Canon Point, *Armada Nacional y Darwin*. Rents bikes, skate boards and surfboards.

Chalo Tours, *Darwin y Villamil, T05-252 0953, chalotours@hotmail.com*. Specializes in diving and snorkelling.

Sharksky, *Darwin y Villamil, T05-252 1188, www.sharksky.com*. Highlands, diving, snorkelling, island-hopping, last-minute cruise bookings and gear rental. Also has an office on Isabela. Swiss/Ecuadorean-run, English, German and French spoken, helpful.

Wreck Bay Dive Center, *Darwin y Wolf, T05-252 1663, www.wreckbay.com*. Reported friendly and respectful of the environment.

Puerto Villamil

Hotels also arrange tours. Kayak rentals at **Hotel San Vicente**.

Galápagos Dive Center, *16 de Marzo y Cormoranes, T05-301 6570*. Dive trips, diving gear sale and rental.

Galapagos Native, *Cormoranes y 16 de Marzo, T05-252 9140, www.gruposanvicentegalapagos. com*. Mountain biking downhill from Sierra Negra, full day including lunch, US$42. Also rentals: good bikes US$3 per hr, US$20 per day; snorkelling gear US$5 per day; surf boards US$4 per hr.

Isabela Dive Center, *Escalecias y Alberto Gil, T05-252 9418, www.isabeladivecenter.com.ec*. Diving, land and boat tours.

Transport

Santa Cruz: Puerto Ayora
Airline offices Avianca, Rodríguez Lara y San Cristóbal, T05-252 6798. **Emetebe**, Darwin y Berlanga, T05-252 4978, Baltra airport T05-252 4755. **LATAM**, Av Charles Darwin e Islas Plaza, T1-800-101075. **TAME**, Av Charles Darwin y 12 de Febrero, T05-252 6527.

Sea *Lanchas* (speedboats) depart daily from the pier near the volleyball courts (see map) for the following islands: **San Cristóbal** at 0700 and 1400 (return 0700, 1500); **Isabela** at 0700 and 1400 (return 0600, 1500); **Floreana** at 0700; fares US$25-35.

Pick-up truck taxis These may be hired for transport throughout town, US$1. A *ranchera* runs up to the highlands from the **Tropidurus** store, Av Baltra y Jaime Roldós, 2 blocks past the market: to **Bellavista** US$0.50, 10 mins; **Santa Rosa** US$1, 20 mins. For airport transfers, see page 1173.

Water taxis (*taxis acuáticos*) From the pier to Punta Estrada or anchored boats, US$0.80-1 during the day, US$2 at night.

Yacht agents All yachts must use an agent by law. **Galápagos Ocean Services** (Peter Schiess), Charles Darwin next to Garrapata restaurant, T09-9477 0804, www.gos.ec. **Naugala Yacht Services** (Jhonny Romero), T05-252 7403, www.naugala.com.

Puerto Baquerizo Moreno
Airline offices Avianca, Northía y Av de la Armada, and at the airport, T05-252 1118. **Emetebe**, at the airport, T05-252 1183. **TAME**, Charles Darwin y Manuel J Cobos, T05-252 1351.

Puerto Villamil
Airline offices Emetebe, Antonio Gil y Las Fragatas, at the corner of the plaza, T05-252 9155.

Practicalities
Getting around

Air

Airlines operating within Ecuador include: **Avianca** ① *T1-800-003434, www.avianca.com*, serving Quito, Guayaquil, Coca, Manta and Galápagos and international routes to Bogotá and Lima; **LATAM** ① *T1-800-000527, www.latam.com*, for Quito, Guayaquil, Cuenca and Galápagos and international routes to the US, Madrid, Argentina, Chile, Colombia and Peru; and **TAME** ① *T1-700-500800 or Quito T02-397 7100, www.tame.com.ec*, serving Quito, Guayaquil, Cuenca, Latacunga, Loja, Coca, Lago Agrio, Esmeraldas, Manta, Santa Rosa (for Machala) and Galápagos and international flights to the US, Colombia and Peru.

TRAVEL TIP
Driving in Ecuador

Roads An excellent network of paved roads runs throughout most of the country. Maintenance of major highways is franchised to private firms, who charge tolls of US$1.15. Roads are subject to damage during heavy rainy seasons. Always check road conditions before setting out.

Safety Driving is safer during the daytime, especially on mountain roads, and it is best to stay off the road altogether at the beginning and end of busy national holidays. It's a sad fact that better roads have meant higher speeds and more serious accidents. Bus and truck drivers, in particular, are known for their speed and recklessness.

Documents To bring a foreign vehicle or motorcycle into the country, its original registration document (title) in the name of the driver is required. If the driver is not the owner, a notarized letter of authorization is required. All documents must be accompanied by a Spanish translation. A 90-day permit is granted on arrival, extensions are only granted if the vehicle is in the garage for repairs. No security deposit is required and you can enter and leave at different land borders. Procedures are generally straightforward but it can be a matter of luck. Shipping a vehicle requires more paperwork and hiring a customs broker. The port of Guayaquil is prone to theft and particularly officious. Manta and Esmeraldas are smaller and more relaxed, but receive fewer ships. A valid driver's licence from your home country is generally sufficient to drive in Ecuador and rent a car, but an international licence is helpful.

Car hire To rent a car you must be at least 21 (surcharges apply to drivers aged 21-25) and have an international credit card with embossed numbers. You will be asked to sign two blank credit card vouchers, one for the rental fee and the other as a security deposit for the vehicle, and authorization for a charge of as much as US$5000 may be requested against your credit card account if you do not purchase full insurance. We have received reports of newer credit cards without embossed number being accepted only for payments, but not deposits. The uncashed vouchers will be returned to you when you return the vehicle. Make sure the car is parked securely at night. A small car suitable for city driving costs around US$350 per week including unlimited mileage, tax and basic insurance. A 4WD or pickup truck (recommended for unpaved roads) costs about US$850 a week. Drop-off charges are about US$125.

Fuel There are two grades of petrol, 'Extra' (82 octane, US$1.48 per US gallon) and 'Super' (92 Octane, US$1.98-2.30). Both are unleaded. Extra is available everywhere, while Super may not be available in more remote areas. Diesel fuel (US$1.03) is notoriously dirty and available everywhere.

Rail

A series of mostly short tourist rides (some combining train and bus travel) have replaced regular passenger service along the spectacular Ecuadorean railway system, extensively restored in recent years. Some trains have two classes of service, standard and plus; carriages are fancier in the latter and a snack is included. On some routes, an *autoferro*, a motorized railcar runs instead of the train. The following routes are on offer: **Quito to El Boliche** (Cotopaxi and Machachi); **Riobamba to Alausí, Alausí to Sibambe** via the Devil's Nose; **Ambato to Urbina; Riobamba to Urbina; Otavalo and Ibarra to Salinas; El Tambo to Coyoctor** near Ingapirca; **Durán** (outside Guayaquil) **to Bucay**; and the **Tren Crucero**, an upmarket all-inclusive tour of up to four days along the entire line from Quito to Durán. Details are given under What to do, in the corresponding cities. For further information, see **Empresa de Ferrocarriles Ecuatorianos** ① *T1-800-873637, www.trenecuador.com.*

Road

Bus Most destinations in Ecuador have frequent bus service and bus travel is generally convenient except for the location of Quito's terminals very far from the city centre. Many itineraries are listed on http://andestransit.com and www.multipasajes.com, where tickets for some major routes can be purchased online (for a fee). In 2017 bus fares were approximately US$1.50 per hour of travel time. Throughout Ecuador, travel by bus is safest during the daytime.

Vans and shared taxis These operate between major cities and offer a faster, more comfortable and more expensive alternative to buses. Some provide pickup and drop-off at your hotel.

Hitchhiking Public transport in Ecuador is so abundant that there is seldom any need to hitchhike along the major highways. On small out-of-the-way country roads however, giving passers-by a ride is common practice and safe. A small fee is usually charged, check in advance.

Taxi In major cities, all taxis must in principle use meters. At especially busy times or at night drivers may nonetheless refuse to do so, in which case always agree on the fare before you get in.

Maps and guide books

Instituto Geográfico Militar (IGM) ① *Senierges y Telmo Paz y Miño, east of Parque El Ejido, Quito, T02-397 5100, ext 2502, www.geoportaligm.gob.ec, Mon-Thu 0730-1600, Fri 0700-1430, take ID.* They sell country and topographic maps in a variety of printed and digital formats. Prices range from US$3 to US$7. Maps of border and sensitive areas are 'reservado' (classified) and not available for sale without a permit. Buy your maps here, they are rarely available outside Quito.

Where to stay

Hotels

Higher-class hotels are found mainly in provincial capitals and resorts, where self-styled boutique hotels are common. The larger cities also have an array of international hotels. In the countryside, a number of *haciendas* have opened their doors to paying guests. A few are in the **Exclusive Hotels & Haciendas of Ecuador** group ① www.ehhec.com, and there are many other independent haciendas of good quality. Some are mentioned in the text. Larger towns and tourist centres have many more hotels than we can list. The hotels that are included are among the best in each category, selected to provide a variety of locations and styles. Additional hotels are found in www.hotelesecuador. com, www.ecuadorboutiquehotels.com and www.infohotel.ec. Many economical hotels do not include breakfast. Service of 10% and tax of 14% are added to better hotel bills. Some cheaper hotels apply only the 14% tax, but check if it is included. All but the most basic establishments have Wi-Fi in their rooms or common areas.

Camping

Camping in protected natural areas can be one of the most satisfying experiences during a visit to Ecuador. Organized campsites, car or trailer camping on the other hand are very uncommon. Because of the abundance of cheap hotels you should never have to camp in Ecuador, except for cyclists who may be stuck between towns. In this case the best strategy is to ask permission to camp on someone's private land, preferably within sight of their home for safety. It is not safe to pitch your tent at random near villages and even less so on beaches. Screw-on Camping Gas canisters are obtainable, but white gas, such as US Coleman fuel, is not. Unleaded petrol (gasoline) is available everywhere and may be an alternative for some stoves.

Food & drink

Restaurants

The large cities have a wide selection of restaurants with Ecuadorean, international and fashionable fusion cuisine. Upmarket restaurants add 24% to the bill, 14% tax plus 10% service. All other places add the 14% tax, which is also charged on non-essential items in food shops. The cuisine varies with region, the following are some typical dishes.

In the highlands *Locro de papas* (potato and cheese soup), *mote* (white hominy, a staple in the region around Cuenca, but used in a variety of dishes in the Sierra), *caldo de patas* (cowheel soup with *mote*), *llapingachos* (fried potato and cheese patties), *empanadas de morocho* (a fried ground corn shell filled with meat), *sancocho de yuca* (vegetable soup with manioc root), roast *cuy* (guinea pig), *fritada* (fried pork), *hornado* (roast pork), *humitas* (tender ground corn steamed in corn leaves), and *quimbolitos* (similar to *humitas* but prepared with wheat flour and steamed in *achira* lily leaves). *Humitas* and *quimbolitos* come in both sweet and savoury varieties.

On the coast *Empanadas de verde* (fried snacks: a ground plantain shell filled with cheese, meat or shrimp), *sopa de bola de verde* (plantain dumpling soup), ceviche (see below), *encocados* (dishes prepared with coconut milk, may be shrimp, fish, etc, very popular in the province of Esmeraldas), *cocadas* (sweets made with coconut), *viche* (fish or seafood soup made with ground peanuts), and *patacones* (thick fried plantain chips served as a side dish).

In Oriente Dishes prepared with yuca (manioc or cassava root) and river fish. *Maitos* (in northern Oriente) and *ayampacos* (in the south) are spiced meat, chicken or palm hearts wrapped in leaves and roasted over the coals.

Throughout the country If economizing ask for the set meal in restaurants: *almuerzo* at lunch time, *merienda* in the evening – cheap and wholesome; it costs US$2.50-5. *Fanesca*, a traditional Easter dish, is a filling fish soup with beans, many grains, ground peanuts and more; it is so popular that in Quito and main tourist spots it is sold throughout Lent, between Carnival and

Easter. Ceviche, marinated fish or seafood which is usually served with popcorn and roasted maize (*tostado*), is very popular throughout Ecuador. Only *ceviche de pescado* (fish) and *ceviche de concha* (clams) which are marinated raw, potentially pose a health hazard. The other varieties of ceviche such as *camarón* (shrimp/prawn) and *langostino* (jumbo shrimp/king prawn) all of which are cooked before being marinated, are generally safe. The vegetarian variety, *ceviche de chochos*, prepared with lupin beans, is excellent and cheap. *Langosta* (lobster) is an increasingly endangered species but continues to be illegally fished; please be conscientious. *Menestra* is a bean or lentil stew, served with rice and grilled meat, chicken or fish. Ecuadorean food is not particularly spicy. However, in most homes and restaurants, the meal is accompanied by a small bowl of *ají* (hot pepper sauce) which may vary in potency. In addition to the prepared foods mentioned above, Ecuador offers a large variety of delicious fruits, some of which are unique to South America.

Drink

The best fruit drinks are *naranjilla* (a tomato relative), *maracuyá* (passion fruit), *tomate de árbol* (tree tomato), *babaco* (highland papaya), *guanábana* (soursop), *piña* (pineapple), *taxo* (banana passion fruit) and *mora* (blackberry), but ask whether juices are prepared with purified water. The main beers are Pilsener and Club. Argentine and Chilean wines are available in cities and resorts areas, but are not cheap. *Aguardiente* (unmatured rum, many brands) is popular, also known as *puntas*, *trago de caña*, or just *trago*. The usual soft drinks, known as *colas*, are widely available. In tourist centres and many upscale hotels and restaurants, good cappuccino and espresso can be found. Try to purchase beer in reusable brown glass bottles, rather than green disposable ones. Bottled water is likewise best bought in large containers, as small plastic bottles create a great deal of rubbish.

Essentials A-Z

Accident and emergency

For all emergencies nationwide, T911.
Policía Nacional, T101.

Disabled travellers

Ecuador for All (www.ecuadorforall.com) is a tour operator catering to travellers with special needs.

Electricity

AC throughout, 110 volts, 60 cycles. Sockets are for twin flat blades, sometimes with a round earth pin.

Embassies and consulates

For all Ecuadorean embassies and consulates abroad and for all foreign embassies and consulates in Ecuador, see http://embassy.goabroad.com.

Health

Medical services

Cuenca Hospital Monte Sinaí, Miguel Cordero 6-111 y Av Solano, near the stadium, T07-288 5595, www.hospitalmontesinai.org, several English-speaking physicians. **Hospital Santa Inés**, Av Toral 2-113, T07-282 7888, Facebook: sisantaines. Dr Jaime Moreno Aguilar speaks English.
Galápagos Islands Puerto Ayora: Hospital, Av Baltra, Puerto Ayora. **Hospital**, Roldós y Flores, Puerto Baquerizo Moreno.
Guayaquil Kennedy hospital group has 3 facilities: Av del Periodista, Av 11 NO, Barrio Kennedy; C Crotos, off Av Rodolfo Baquerizo Nazur, Barrio Alborada; and in Samborondón, T1-800-536 6339, www.hospikennedy.med.ec. Reliable, with many specialists and a very competent emergency department. **Clínica Alcívar**, Coronel 2301 y Azuay, T04-372 0100, www.hospitalalcivar.com, and **Clínica Guayaquil**, Padre Aguirre 401 y General Córdova, T04-256 3555, www.clinicaguayaquil.com (Dr Roberto Gilbert speaks English and German) are also reliable.
Ibarra Instituto Médico de Especialidades, Egas 1-83 y Av Teodoro Gómez de La Torre, T06-295 5612, www.ime.amawebs.com.
Latacunga Clínica Latacunga, Sánchez de Orellana 11-79 y Marqués de Maenza, T03-281 0260, Facebook: Clin icaLatacunga. Open 24 hrs.
Quito For hospitals, doctors and dentists, contact your consulate or the tourist office for advice. **Clínica Pichincha**, Veintimilla E3-30 y Páez, T02-256 2296, emergencies 02-299

8777, http://hcp.com.ec/website/. Very good, but expensive. **Metropolitano**, Mariana de Jesús y N Arteta, T02-399 8000, http://hospitalmetropolitano.org. Very professional and recommended, but expensive. **Voz Andes**, Villalengua Oe 2-37 y Av 10 de Agosto, T02-397 1000 or 1-700-700700, www.hospitalvozandes.org. Quick and efficient, fee based on ability to pay, a good place to get vaccines.

Money

US$1 = €0.92 (Jun 2017).

The **US dollar** (US$) is the official currency of Ecuador. Only US$ bills circulate. US coins are used alongside the equivalent size and value Ecuadorean coins. Ecuadorean coins have no value outside the country. Many establishments are reluctant to accept bills larger than US$20 because of counterfeit notes or lack of change. There is no substitute for cash-in-hand when travelling in Ecuador; US$ cash in small denominations is by far the simplest and the only universally accepted option. Other currencies are difficult to exchange outside large cities and fetch a poor rate.

Credit cards, ATMs and banks

The most commonly accepted credit cards are Visa, MasterCard, Diners and, to a lesser extent, American Express. Paying by credit card may incur a surcharge. Cash advances on credit cards can be obtained through many ATMs (only **Banco de Guayaquil** for Amex), but daily limits apply. Larger advances on Visa, MasterCard and less frequently Amex are available from several banks. Their fees, procedures and the time required vary considerably and are subject to change, confirm all details locally. Among the more efficient banks for cash advances in Ecuador are: **Banco del Austro** (www.bancodelaustro.com), up to US$2000 a day on Visa or MC, 4% commission; **Banco Bolivariano** (www.bolivariano.com.ec), up to US$1000 a day on Visa or MC, no commission. Internationally linked ATMs are common, although not all machines work with all cards. Try to have cash with you at all times, but especially in the smaller towns and out of the way places. Credit cards are generally easier to use in ATMs than debit cards. ATMs are a focus for scams and robberies, use them judiciously. Funds may be rapidly wired to Ecuador by **Western Union** or **MoneyGram**, fees and taxes apply, enquire in advance.

Cost of living/travelling

The average budget is US$65-80 pp a day for travelling fairly comfortably, including transport. Your budget will be higher the longer you stay in big cities, Galápagos and resort areas (especially in high season) and depending on how many internal flights you take. A basic travel budget, using hotels with shared bath, simple meals, no flights and no tours would be US$25-30 a day. Rooms range from about US$10-15 pp for basic accommodation to about US$40-60 for mid-range places, to well over US$100 for upmarket hotels. The cost of using the internet is generally US$0.50-$1 per hr. An **International Student Identity Card (ISIC)** may help you obtain some discounts when travelling. ISIC cards are sold by **Grupo Idiomas**, Circunvalación Sur 501-c y Ebanos, Urdesa Central, Guayaquil, T04-238 0400, www.grupoidiomas.com. They need proof of full-time enrolment in Ecuador or abroad (minimum 20 hrs per week), 2 photos, passport, US$20 and the application form found in www.isic.com.ec.

Opening hours

Banks: Mon-Fri 0900-1700. **Government offices:** variable hours Mon-Fri, some close for lunch. **Other offices:** open 0900-1230, 1430-1800. **Shops:** open 0900-1900; close at midday in smaller towns, open till 2100 on the coast.

Public holidays and festivals

1 Jan: New Year's Day; **6 Jan**: Reyes Magos y Día de los Inocentes, a time for pranks, which closes the Christmas-New Year holiday season. **Carnival**: Mon and Tue before Lent, celebrated everywhere in the country (except Ambato) by throwing water at passers-by: be prepared to participate. **Easter**: Holy Thu, Good Fri, Holy Sat. **1 May**: Labour Day; **24 May**: Battle of Pichincha, Independence. **Early Jun**: Corpus Christi. **10 Aug**: first attempt to gain the Independence of Quito. **9 Oct**: Independence of Guayaquil. **2 Nov**: All Souls' Day. **3 Nov**: Independence of Cuenca. **6 Dec**: Foundation of Quito. **25 Dec**: Christmas Day.

Safety

Public safety is an important concern throughout mainland Ecuador; Galápagos is generally safe. Armed robbery and bag snatching and slashing are among the most significant hazards. 'Express kidnapping', whereby victims are taken from ATM to ATM and forced to withdraw money, is a threat in major cities, and fake taxis are often involved. Radio taxis are usually safer.

Secure your belongings at all times, be wary of con tricks, avoid crowds and congested urban transport, and travel during the daytime. It is the larger cities, especially Guayaquil, Quito, Cuenca, Manta, Machala, Esmeraldas and Santo Domingo which call for the greatest care. Small towns and the countryside in the highlands are generally safer than on the coast or in the jungle. The entire border with Colombia calls for precautions; enquire locally before travelling off the beaten path there. If robbed, a report can be filed online at www.gestiondefiscalias.gob. ec/rtourist/. For further information see Safety, in Essential Quito, page 1024, and other parts of the chapter.

Although currently uncommon, sporadic social unrest remains part of life in Ecuador and you should not overreact. Strikes and protests are usually announced days or weeks in advance, and their most significant impact on tourists is the restriction of overland travel. It is usually best to wait it out rather than insisting on keeping to your original itinerary.

In Ecuador, drug sale, purchase, use or growing is punishable by lengthy imprisonment.

Ecuador's active volcanoes are spectacular, but have occasionally threatened nearby communities. The **National Geophysics Institute** provides daily updates at www.igepn.edu.ec.

Tax

Airport tax
International and domestic departure tax is included in the ticket price.

VAT/IVA
12%. It may in principle be reclaimed on departure if you keep official invoices with your name and passport number; don't expect a speedy refund or bother with amounts under US$100. High surtaxes applied to various imported items make them expensive to purchase in Ecuador.

Telephone and Wi-Fi

International phone code: +593. There are independent phone offices, *cabinas*, in most cities and towns, but mobile (cellular) phones are by far the most common form of telecommunication. You can purchase a

SIM card (*un chip*) for US$5 for either of the 2 main mobile carriers: **Claro** and **Movistar**; in principle an Ecuadorean *cédula* (national ID card) is required but a passport is sometimes accepted or ask an Ecuadorean friend to buy a chip for you. The chips work with many foreign mobile phones, but enquire about your unit before purchasing. Mobile phone shops are everywhere, look for the carrier's logo. You get an Ecuadorean mobile phone number and can purchase credit (*recarga*) anywhere for as much or as little as you like. Calls cost about US$0.20 per min and only the caller pays. Mobile phone numbers have 10 digits starting with 09, landlines (*fijos*) have 7 digits plus an area code (eg 02 for Quito, 04 for Guayaquil). When calling a landline from a mobile, you must include the area code. Skype, WhatsApp and similar services on Wi-Fi-enabled devices are the most economical form of international communication from Ecuador. Cyber cafés are common in the cities and towns of Ecuador but are gradually being replaced by widespread Wi-Fi access. Wi-Fi is available in most hotels, at many cafés and in some public places.

Time

Official time is GMT -5 (Galápagos, -6).

Tipping

In upmarket restaurants 10% service may be included in the bill. In cheaper establishments, tipping is uncommon but welcome. It is not expected in taxis. Airport porters, about US$1 per bag.

Tourist information

Ministerio de Turismo, Av Gran Colombia y Briceño, Quito, T02-399 9333, www.turismo. gob.ec. Its web site www.ecuador.travel is a good general introduction. Their regional offices are given in the text. Most municipalities also have their own local tourist offices, quality of service varies. For information on parks and reserves, see national parks, page 1022.

Useful websites
www.ecuador.com; www.quitoadventure. com; and www.paisturistico.com General guides with information about services activities and national parks
www.ecuadorexplorer.com; www.ecuador travelsite.org; and www.ecuaworld.com

Are all travel guides; the latter includes volunteering options.
www.trekkinginecuador.com
For hiking information

Visas and immigration

All visitors to Ecuador must have a passport valid for at least 6 months and an onward or return ticket, but the latter is seldom asked for. Citizens of Afghanistan, Bangladesh, Cuba, Eritrea, Ethiopia, Kenya, Nepal, Nigeria, Pakistan, Senegal and Somalia require a visa to visit Ecuador, other tourists do not require a visa unless they wish to stay more than 90 days. Upon entry all visitors must complete an international embarkation/disembarkation card. Keep your copy, you will be asked for it when you leave.

Note You are required by Ecuadorean law to carry your passport at all times. Whether or not a photocopy is an acceptable substitute is at the discretion of the individual police officer, having it notarized can help. Tourists are not permitted to work under any circumstances.

Length of stay Tourists are granted 90 days upon arrival and there are no extensions except for citizens of the Andean Community of Nations. Visitors are not allowed back in the country if they have already stayed 90 days during the past 12 months. If you want to spend more time studying, volunteering etc, you can get a purpose-specific visa (category '12-IX', between US$100 and 400 and paperwork, allow extra time) at the end of your 90 days as a tourist. There is no fine at present (subject to change) for overstaying but you must request an exit permit 48 hrs before departure and may be barred from returning to Ecuador. There are immigration offices in all provincial capitals. If your passport is lost or stolen then, after it has been replaced by your embassy, you will have go to an immigration office to obtain a *movimiento migratorio* (a certificate indicating the date you entered Ecuador) in order to be able to leave the country. Visas for longer stays are issued by the Ministerio de Relaciones Exteriores (Foreign Office, http://cancilleria.gob.ec), through Ecuador's diplomatic representatives abroad.

Immigration Dirección Nacional de Migración, Amazonas N32-171 y República, Quito, T02-243 9408, www.ministeriointerior.gob.ec/migracion, Mon-Fri 0800-1200 and 1500-1800.

Weights and measures

Metric, US gallons for petrol, some English measures for hardware and weights and some Spanish measures for produce.

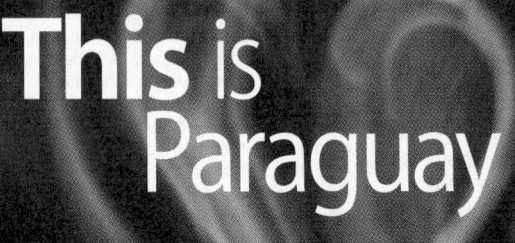

This is
Paraguay

Wedged between neighbours with higher-profile attractions and undervalued as a tourist destination this country of farmland, nature and folklore retains an air of mystery which is a significant part of its appeal. From the hot, wild and impenetrable Chaco in the northwest to the lush forests of the southeast, there is abundant birdlife, a number of rivers to navigate and fantastic opportunities to experience rural tourism. Although dwarfed by Brazil and Argentina, Paraguay covers some 407,000 sq km, roughly the same size as California.

Land-locked Paraguay has had a strange history of charismatic leaders, steadfastness and isolation. Paraguayans are proud of their Guaraní culture and heritage, evident in the widespread use of it as the officially recognized indigenous language, which is still taught in schools. Although difficult to pronounce for many outsiders, the Guaraní language cannot mask the warmth of Paraguayan hospitality. Music, too, marks Paraguay apart from its neighbours: emotive songs and European dances accompanied by virtuoso harp players and guitarists.

Yet in other ways, Paraguay is not so separate. It shares with Argentina and Brazil remains of the mission settlements (*reducciones*) built by Jesuits near the banks of the Río Paraná, testimony to one of the major social experiments on the continent. The contrast between the ever-expanding capital, Asunción, and little towns seemingly stuck in a different era is as marked as anywhere. And like many South Americans, Paraguayans are passionate about football and dedicated to the daily consumption of yerba mate (*Ilex paraguariensis*). Today the country is part of the Latin American and Caribbean Economic System, with trade routes to Argentina and Brazil well established and the road to Bolivia, the infamous Ruta 9, or Trans-Chaco Highway, fully open. The deeper it penetrates into the sparsely populated northwest, the bigger an adventure the Trans-Chaco becomes; it remains one of the great road trips in South America.

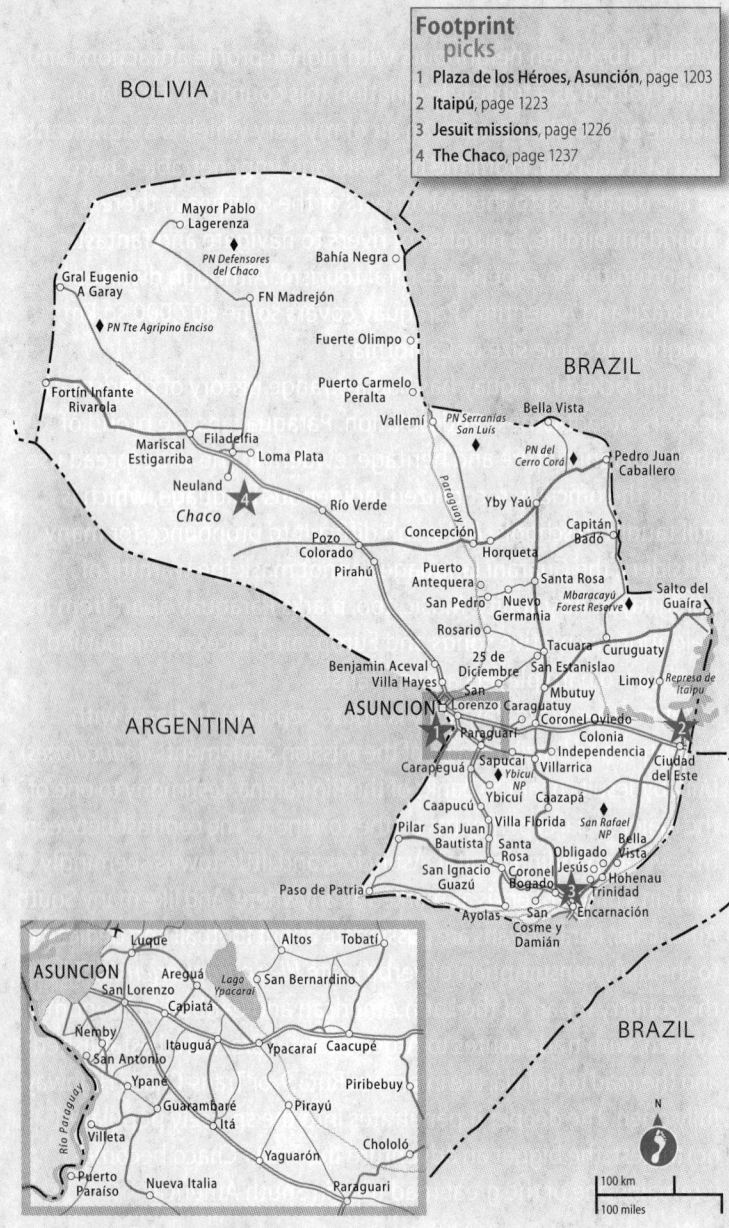

Footprint
picks

1 **Plaza de los Héroes, Asunción**, page 1203
2 **Itaipú**, page 1223
3 **Jesuit missions**, page 1226
4 **The Chaco**, page 1237

BOLIVIA

Mayor Pablo
Lagerenza

*PN Defensores
del Chaco*

Bahía Negra

Gral Eugenio
A Garay

FN Madrejón

PN Tte Agripino Enciso

Fuerte Olimpo

Fortín Infante
Rivarola

Puerto Carmelo
Peralta

Vallemí

Bella Vista

BRAZIL

Mariscal
Estigarriba

Filadelfia

Loma Plata

Neuland

*PN Serranías
San Luis*

*PN del
Cerro Cord*

Pedro Juan
Caballero

Chaco

Río Verde

Yby Yaú

Pozo
Colorado

Concepción

Capitán
Bado

Pirahú

Horqueta

Puerto
Antequera

Santa Rosa

*Mbaracayú
Forest Reserve*

Salto del
Guaíra

San Pedro

Nuevo
Germania

Rosario

Tacuara

Curuguaty

Benjamín Aceval
Villa Hayes

25 de
Diciembre

San Estanislao

Limoy

*Represa de
Itaipú*

ARGENTINA

San
Lorenzo

Mbutuy

Caraguatuy

ASUNCION

Paraguarí

Coronel Oviedo

Colonia
Independencia

Carapeguá

Sapucaí

*Ybicuí
NP*

Villarrica

Ciudad
del Este

Caapucú

Ybicuí

Caazapá

Pilar

San Juan
Bautista

Villa Florida

Santa
Rosa

*San Rafael
NP*

Bella
Vista

San Ignacio
Guazú

Obligado

Jesús

Hohenau

Paso de Patria

Coronel
Bogado

Trinidad

Ayolas

San
Cosme y
Damián

Encarnación

ASUNCION

Luque

Altos

Tobatí

Areguá

San Bernardino

San Lorenzo

*Lago
Ypacaraí*

Capiatá

Ñemby

Itauguá

Ypacaraí

Caacupé

San Antonio

Ypane

Piribebuy

BRAZIL

Guarambaré

Itá

Pirayú

Villeta

Yaguarón

Chololó

Nueva Italia

Paraguarí

100 km
100 miles

N

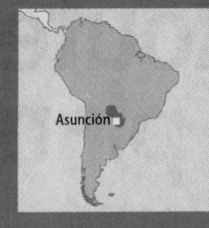

Asunción

Footprint
picks

★ Plaza de los Héroes,
Asunción, page 1203
This is the heart of the city and a great place to people-watch.

★ Itaipú, page 1223
The dam is gargantuan and the interesting tours on offer reveal panoramic views of the power plant.

★ Jesuit missions, page 1226
Built during the 17th and 18th centuries with a blend of indigenous styles and Christian attributes, some of the missions that remain are UNESCO World Heritage Sites.

★ The Chaco, page 1237
This wild area, dotted with estancias and filled with birdlife, is also the last homelands of Paraguay's indigenous peoples.

Route planner

The capital and eastern Paraguay
a city that means business in the fertile agricultural part of the country

Asunción, Paraguay's largest city, sits on a bay of the Río Paraguay. It is the political and commercial heart of the country and much of the architecture dates from the early 1800s. East of the capital, the towns and villages of the **Región Oriental** are quiet and traditional; many have unique crafts associated with them. Further to the south, there are many signs of Jesuit heritage close to the city of **Encarnación**. From here you can cross the Río Paraná to the Argentine city of **Posadas**. Paraguay's eastern border with Brazil has several frontier posts, but the main one is **Ciudad del Este**, where you can visit **Itaipú**, until recently the largest hydroelectric dam in the world. Across the Friendship Bridge from Ciudad del Este is Foz do Iguaçu in Brazil and the magnificent **Iguaçu Falls**.

North of the capital
river trips and routes to Brazil and Bolivia

North of Asunción there is one main town, **Concepción**, and the most interesting route there, if you have the time, is by river boat from the capital. The boat ride one way up the river takes at least a day, so quicker ways are via the Chaco, along part of the Trans-Chaco Highway or across the Cordillera and San Pedro Departments along Ruta 3. Beyond Concepción, the Río Paraguay leads to the Brazilian and Bolivian Pantanal; the former can also be reached by road.

Western Paraguay
the west, wild and under threat

Región Occidental, or Chaco, makes up the western half of the country. **The Chaco** begins as a marshy palm savannah, but becomes an increasingly impenetrable and dry scrub forest as it approaches the border with Bolivia. Large areas are being deforested. The Trans-Chaco Highway crosses the Chaco but apart from scattered military outposts, there are few urbanized areas for 400 km until you reach the Mennonite colonies of **Filadelfia**, **Loma Plata** and **Neuland** which make up the Chaco Central region. This is not a region in which to venture off the beaten track alone and unprepared.

Essential Paraguay

Finding your feet

Paraguay is divided into two main regions separated by the Río Paraguay. The capital, Asunción, sits between the two; to the east of the river lies the Región Oriental (approximately 40%) and to the west the Región Occidental (approximately 60%), better known simply as the Chaco. Unless coming from Buenos Aires or Santa Cruz, it is best to plan your travels to either of these regions from Asunción.

Getting around

Internal flights link up most main centres, and bus services run along main routes. The railways largely ceased operating in 2001 and the few remaining lines that were running have since stopped as well. In January 2017, Paraguay and Bolivia met to discuss establishing a railway line between Roboré, Bolivia and Puerto Carmelo

Fact file

Location 25.2667° S, 57.6667° W
Capital Asunción
Time zone GMT -4 hrs; October to March GMT -3 hrs
Telephone country code +5958
Currency Guaraní (PYG)

Peralta, where a new bridge is planned across the Río Paraguay to improve transport links with Brazil.

Safety

Paraguay is generally a safe place to visit.

When to go

The climate is sub-tropical, with a marked difference between summer and winter and often from one day to the next. December to February (summer) can be very hot and humid, with temperatures from 25°C to 40°C, and even higher in the Chaco. During winter (June-August) the temperature can range from 0°C at night to 28°C in the day. From March to May (autumn) and September to October/November (spring) the heat is less oppressive. Some rain falls each month, but the heaviest rains tend to occur from March to May. Temperatures below freezing are very rare; snow has been recorded only twice since metrological recordkeeping began. The best time to travel is August to October and the best time to see wildlife is June-July.

Time required

Anything between one to three weeks.

Weather Asunción

January	February	March	April	May	June
35°C	33°C	33°C	29°C	25°C	24°C
22°C	22°C	21°C	18°C	14°C	13°C
135mm	143mm	145mm	170mm	70mm	83mm

July	August	September	October	November	December
24°C	26°C	28°C	30°C	32°C	34°C
11°C	13°C	14°C	18°C	19°C	31°C
47mm	53mm	85mm	154mm	161mm	170mm

Asunción

Asunción was founded in 1537 on the eastern bank of a calm bay in the Río Paraguay. It is the longest continually inhabited area in the River Plate Basin and in colonial times was referred to as the 'Mother of Cities' because it was from here that missionaries and military expeditions alike set off to establish other cities. The historic centre is a testament to 19th-century ideals, with names reflecting its heroes and battles. Tree-lined avenues, parks and squares break up the rigid grid system. In July and August the city is drenched in colour with the prolific pink bloom of lapacho trees, which grow everywhere.

Sights *Colour map 6, C6.*

Paraguay's past radiates from the historic buildings of this city on a river bay

Historic centre

Asunción's historic centre (along with other sites throughout the city) has recently undergone a renaissance in terms of popularity and government support and there are now a number of tours that take in many of its best-known buildings and spaces. The restoration of several historically significant buildings in the centre (eg Palacio de Gobierno) and outside (eg Casa de las Artes Escénicas Edda de los Ríos) was supposed to coincide with Paraguay's independence bicentennial (2011), but work continues. As a result, opening hours may change without notice.

At the bottom of Avenida Colón, just before it joins El Paraguayo Independiente, are the colonial façades of **La Recova**, shops selling local arts and crafts (see Shopping, page 1211). The main river port and **Aduana** (Customs) are at this same junction. Every Saturday afternoon from 1500 there are cultural activities at the port (Puerto Abierto). Continue along El Paraguayo Independiente to a small plaza on your left with a statue of the former dictator, Alfredo Stroessner. After his deposition, the statue was crushed and placed inside a block of concrete, only his hands and face protruding. Next to this is the **Palacio de Gobierno** (1857), restoration completed in late 2016, built in the style of Versailles by Alan Taylor as a palace for Francisco Solano López (1860-1869). In later years Taylor was forced to use child labour as all adult men were enlisted to fight in the Triple Alliance War. It now houses government departments. At night it is beautifully illuminated and there may be guided tours on Fridays, 0800-1700, T021-414 0220 in advance to book. Down the side of the palace towards the river is a platform for viewing the back of the building. Directly opposite the Palace is the **Manzana de la Rivera** ① *Ayolas 129 y El Paraguayo Independiente, T021-442448, Mon-Sat 0700-2000, museum, cultural centre and library all Mon-Fri 0800-1900, Sat 0800-1800, Sun 0800-1200*, 10 buildings and a patio area, of which nine buildings are restored, dating from 1700s. They include **Casa Viola** with Museo Memoria de la Ciudad with historical photos and city information, **Casa Clari**, with exhibition halls and a bar, the Miguel Acevedo cultural centre, the Ruy Díaz de Guzmán auditorium, and **Casa Vertúa**, the municipal library. These collectively represent the most complete set of colonial era buildings in the city.

A block away from the Palace is the **Congreso Nacional**, built in steel and glass representing a huge ship moored on the river bank and incorporating part of the old congress building. On **Plaza de la Independencia** there is a small memorial to those who died in the struggle for democracy (also look out for statues of the frog and the dog). On the Plaza are the **Antiguo Colegio Militar** (1588) originally a Jesuit College, now home to government ministries, the **Cabildo** (1844-1854) ① *Mon-Fri 0900-1900, Sat 0800-1200, free*, since 2003 the **Centro Cultural de la República** ① *T021-443094, http://cabildoccr.gov.py*, with temporary exhibitions,

Tip...
Don't be confused! Plaza de la Independencia is often referred to as Plaza Constitución or Plaza Juan de Salazar.

indigenous and religious art, museum of music, film and video on the top floor, and the **Catedral Metropolitana** ① *T021-449512, Mon-Fri 0800-1100, 1400-1700, possible to view the interior before, after or during Sunday Masses (1100 and 1900)* (mid-17th century, rebuilt 1842-1849). The altar, decorated with Jesuit and Franciscan silver, is very beautiful. From the Plaza turn right onto Alberdi and to your right is the **Correos** (old post office), the Palacio Patri in colonial times, with a courtyard and a small museum (the building is reportedly being restored). At Alberdi and Presidente Franco is the **Teatro Municipal Ignacio Pane** ① *T021-445169, www.teatromunicipal.com.py, for information on events,* fully restored to its former belle époque glory. The **Estación Central del Ferrocarril Carlos Antonio López** ① *Eligio Ayala y México, just below Plaza Uruguaya, T021-446789,* was built 1861-1864 with British and European help. Paraguay had the first passenger carrying railway in South America. No trains now run from the station, which is now in a state of partial disrepair, but it has a small **museum** ① *Mon-Fri, 0800-1600, US$2,* featuring the old ticket office, machinery from Wolverhampton and Battersea and the first steam engine in Paraguay, the Sapucai (1861). **Plaza Uruguaya,** at the nexus of calles México, Eligio Ayala, 25 de Mayo and Antequera, with its shady trees and fountain is another spot to stop and rest in the daytime. From here take Mariscal Estigarribia towards Plaza de Los Héroes.

Mariscal Estigarribia becomes Palma at its intersection with Independencia Nacional (the names of all streets running east to west change at this point). On ★**Plaza de los Héroes** is the **Panteón Nacional de los Héroes** ① *Palma y Chile, open daily 0730-1830,* which is based on Les Invalides in Paris, begun during the Triple Alliance War and finished in 1937. It contains the tombs of Carlos Antonio López, Mariscal Francisco Solano López, Mariscal Estigarribia,

Essential Asunción

Finding your feet

Silvio Pettirossi International airport, T021-688 2000, www.dinac.gov.py, is in Luque, 16 km northeast of the city centre, from which taxis, buses and an airport-to-hotel minibus service run. It takes about one hour to go from the airport to the centre of the city. The bus terminal, **Terminal de Omnibus Asunción,** T021-551740, http://toa.asuncion.gov.py/, is south of the centre at the intersection of Avenidas Fernando de la Mora y República Argentina, 30-45 minutes away by taxi or bus. It is open 24 hours a day. See Transport, page 1212, for details.

Getting around

Most of the historical sights of interest are in a relatively small area by the river, so walking between them is not a problem. Likewise, many central hotels and restaurants are within walking distance of these sights. Places outside the city's centre, for example Villa Morra (see below), are easily reached by taxi or bus. The bus system is extensive and runs 0600-2200 (2400 on a few routes); buses stop at signs before every street corner. Asunción is very spread out and transport so slow that you need to allow 60-90 minutes to get beyond its limits.

Tip...

If going by taxi, give the driver the specific street address but also the name of the nearest intersection. The often-used 'casi' (near) and 'esquina' (corner) both mean 'at the corner of'. Almost all locations in Asunción are referred to in this manner (in this chapter 'y' is used).

the victor of the Chaco War, an unknown child-soldier, and other national heroes. The child-soldiers honoured in the Panteón were boys aged 12-16 who fought at the battle of **Acosta Ñu** in the War of the Triple Alliance, 15 August 1869. Most of the boys died and somewhere between 60%-70% of adult Paraguayan men were killed during the war. Plaza de los Héroes is made up of four separate squares with different names. These include Plaza Libertad and Plaza de la Democracia.

On weekdays in the Plaza at Chile y Oliva (Plaza Libertad) there are **covered market stalls** selling traditional Paraguayan arts and crafts in wood, cotton and leather. Along Palma indigenous women sell colourful woven bags, beads and baskets. You may be approached by indigenous men selling bags, whistles, bows and arrows or feather headdresses. A few blocks further along Palma near its intersection with Alberti is the tourist information office (address in the listings); it has craft stalls for those not wishing to buy on the street. On Saturday morning, till 1200, Palma becomes a pedestrian area, with stalls selling arts, crafts, clothes and during the summer there is entertainment outside the tourist office. On Sunday there are stalls selling second-hand or antique items around Plaza de los Héroes. (If looking for more handicraft and traditional items, visit also the nearby Plaza de la Democracia bordering Olivia and NS de la Asunción.) From Palma turn right at 14 de Mayo to the **Casa de la Independencia** (1772) ① *14 de Mayo y Pdte Franco, T021-493918, www. casadelaindependencia.org.py, Mon-Fri 0700-1730, Sat 0800-1300, free, has toilets,* with a historical collection; the 1811 anti-colonial revolution was plotted here. The **Iglesia de Encarnación** ① *14 de Mayo y Víctor Haedo, T021-490860, Mon-Fri 0830-1200 and 1530-1900; Sat 0830-1200; Sun 1000 (for Mass only),* partially restored after a fire in 1889 by an Italian immigrant who offered his services gratis on condition that he be free to select the best materials. Completely restored after a three-year effort, it is, when open, a tranquil place to end your tour.

Heading out of the centre along Avenida Mariscal López

Museo Nacional de Bellas Artes ① *E Ayala 1345 y Curupayty, T021-211578, www.cultura.gov.py, Mon-Fri 0700-1800, Sat 0800-1400, free, guided tour,* shows the development of Paraguayan art and its European precursors, largely the collection of Juan Silvano Godoy. The **Museo Histórico Militar** ① *in the Ministry of National Defence, Mcal López y 22 de Septiembre (surrender passport on entry), T021-223965, Mon-Fri 0700-1300, free,* has articles from both the Triple Alliance and the Chaco Wars. These include blood-stained flags from the Triple Alliance as well as clothes and personal

Asunción

Where to stay
1 Amalfi *C4*
3 Aspen Apart Hotel *C1*
4 Asunción Palace *B1*
5 Bavaria *A6*
6 Black Cat Hostel *A3*
8 Cecilia *B6*
9 Chaco *B4*
10 Crowne Plaza *B6*
11 El Nómada Hostel *C4*
13 El Viajero Asunción *C3*
14 Granados Park *B2*
15 La Casita de la Abuela
  Hostal Verde *C1*
16 La Española *C4*
17 Las Margaritas *B2*
18 Maison Suisse *A6*
19 Palmas del Sol *A6*
20 Paramanta *A6*
21 Portal del Sol *A6*
23 Sabe Center *B4*
24 Sheraton *A6*
25 Westfalenhaus *A6*
26 Zaphir *B1*

200 metres
200 yards

possessions of Franciso Solano López and his Irish mistress, Eliza Lynch. The national cemetery, **Cementerio Recoleta** ① *Av Mcal López y Chóferes del Chaco*, resembles a miniature city with tombs in various architectural styles. It contains the tomb of Madame Lynch (ask guide to show you the location), and, separately, the tomb of her baby daughter Corrine (Entrada 3 opposite Gran Unión supermarket). Beyond Chóferes del Chaco, between Avenida Mcal López and Avenida España, is **Villa Morra**, a smart residential and commercial zone with bars, restaurants and shopping centres. On the southeast outskirts of Asunción, at Km 12, is the fast-growing city of **San Lorenzo**. Reached via Ruta 2 (Mariscal Estigarribia Highway) or take buses 12, 18, 56, 26 and get off at central plaza with blue, 18th-century neo-Gothic cathedral. The **Museo Arqueológico y Etnográfico Guido Boggiani** ① *Bogado 888 y Saturio Ríos, 1½ blocks from plaza, T021-584717, see Facebook, Tue-Fri 1500-1800, Sat 0900-1200, 1500-1800, ring the bell if door is shut*, is staffed by a very helpful lady who explains the exhibits, which include rare Chamacoco feather art, and a well-displayed collection of tribal items from the northern Chaco from the turn of the 20th century. The shop across the road sells crafts at good prices. There's also a daily market.

Heading out of the centre along Avenida España

Museo Etnográfico Dr Andrés Barbero ① *España 217 y Mompox, T021-441696, www.museobarbero. org.py, Mon-Fri 0800-1700, free*, houses a good collection of tools and weapons of the various Guaraní cultures. The **Centro de Artes Visuales** ① *Grabadores del Cabichuí entre Cañada y Emeterio Miranda, T021-607996, Wed-Sat 0900-1200, 1530-2000, exhibitions open Thu-Sat 1530-2000, shop and café Wed-Sat 1530-2000, take bus 30 or 44A from the centre past Shopping del Sol, ask driver for Cañada*, also operates, under the umbrella of its Museo del Barro ① *www.museodelbarro.org*, two museums including contemporary art in its **Museo Paraguayo de Arte Contemporáneo** ① *T021-607996, www.museodelbarro.org/colecciones/ museo-de-arte-contemporaneo, Wed-Sat 0900-1200, 1530-2000, free, guided tours can be arranged 48 hrs in advance T0981-381735 or 021-607996 (US$25 for max 30 people)*, the most popular museum in the country by far, and the **Museo de Arte Indígena** ① *www.museodelbarro. org/exhibicion/museo-de-arte-indigena*, which contains indigenous art and outstanding displays of rarely seen colonial art. Highly recommended.

Luque, founded 1636, has an attractive central plaza with some well-preserved colonial buildings and a pedestrianized area with outdoor cafés. It is famous for the making of Paraguayan harps and guitars and for fine filigree jewellery in silver and gold at very good prices, many shops on the main street. Luque is aware of its colonial heritage: the partial demolition in 2012 of two colonial-era houses in its centre was halted by the government. There is tourist information at Plaza General Aquino, which also holds the mausoleum of José Elizardo Aquino, a hero of the disastrous War of the Triple Alliance. There are some fine musical instrument shops on the road to Luque along Avenida Aviadores del Chaco. **Guitarras Sanabria** ① *Av Aviadores del Chaco 2574 casi San Blas, T021-614974, www.arpasgsanabria.com.py, getting there: take bus 30*, is one of the best-known firms.

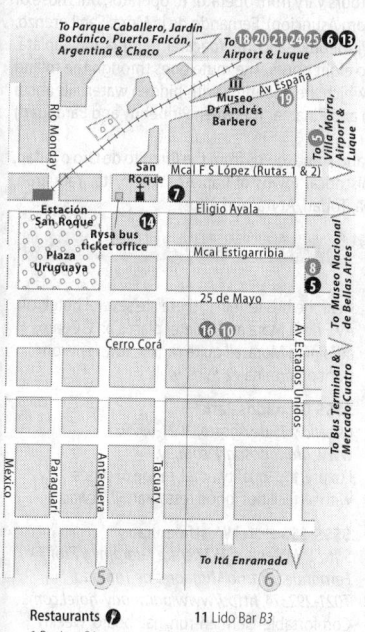

Restaurants
1 Bar Leo *B1*
2 Bellini *B2*
3 Bolsi *B3*
4 Café Literario *B4*
5 El Bar de la Preferida *B6*
6 El Molino *A6*
7 La Flor de la Canela *A5*
8 La Vienesa *B3*
11 Lido Bar *B3*
12 Munich *A4*
13 Paseo Carmelitas *A6*
14 San Roque *B5*
15 Taberna Española *C1*

Bars & clubs
16 Britannia Pub *B5*
17 Rivera *B2*

Other places in Asunción

Some 6 km east, the 245-ha **Jardín Botánico y Zoológico** ① *Av Artigas y Primer Presidente, T021-281389/281390, www.mca.gov.py/zoo.htm, daily 0700-1700, US$1*, lies along the Río Paraguay, on the former estate of the López family. The gardens are well-maintained, with signed walks, a rose garden and orchid nursery, and are bordered by the 18-hole Asunción Golf Club. In addition to claiming 490 species of flora and fauna, this is a good place to buy local crafts including jewellery and cloth bags, but you'll need insect repellent if taking any of the side trails. In the gardens are the former residences of Carlos Antonio López, a two-storey typical Paraguayan country house with verandas, now housing a **Museo de Historia Natural** and a library, and that of Solano López, a two-storey European-inspired mansion which is now the **Museo de Historia Natural e Indigenista y Herbario** ① *both museums and orchid nursery are free, Mon-Sat 0730-1130, 1300-1730, Sun 0900-1300. Getting there: by bus Nos 2, 6, 23, and 40, US$0.60, 35 mins from Luis A Herrera, or Nos 24, 35 or 44B from Oliva or Cerro Corá.* Neither museum is in good condition.

Around Asunción

Many villages close to Asunción can be visited on a day trip: eg Areguá and San Bernardino on Lago Ypacaraí (see pages 1216 and 1217), Altos, great views over the lake, Itauguá (traditional ñandutí 'spider web' lace and handicrafts centre).

Alternatively take a tour from any travel agent (see What to do, page 1212) of the **Circuito de Oro** or the Camino Franciscano. Destinations for both tours vary from operator to operator, but those of the Circuito de Oro tend to include (by distance from Asunción), Fernando de la Mora, San Lorenzo, Julián Augusto Saldivar, Itá, Yaguarón, Paraguarí, Piribebuy, Caacupé, Ypacaraí, Itauguá and Capiatá, 160 km on paved roads on Rutas 1 and 2, seven to eight hours. The route goes through the rolling hills of the Cordillera, no more than 650 m high, which are beautiful, with hidden waterfalls and a number of spas: Chololó, Piraretá (near Piribebuy) and Pinamar (between Piribebuy and Paraguarí) are the most developed.

The **Camino Franciscano** is similar, but longer and some towns from the Circuito de Oro overlap, but usually includes some combination of the historical towns of Capiatá, Ypané, Itá, Yaguarón, Villarrica, Valenzuela, Piribebuy, Caacupé, Caazapá, Tobatí, Atyrá, and Altos.

Listings Asunción *map page 1204.*

Tourist information

Secretaría Nacional de Turismo
Palma 468, T021-494110/441530, or 0800-11-3030, www.senatur.gov.py. Daily 0700-1900.
Staff have information on all parts of Paraguay, free map available; also has a bookstore. Both the airport and bus terminal have tourist information desks. Check for special tours being run from the tourist office, sometimes run by Senatur, sometimes in conjunction with agencies.
The city of Asunción's municipal website **www.asuncion.gov.py** also has up-to-date information in Spanish.

Where to stay

Hotel bills do not usually include service charge. Look out for special offers.

Asunción has a **Sheraton** ($$$$, see www.sheraton-asuncion.com.py) and a **Crowne Plaza** ($$$$, see www.ihg.com/crowneplaza/hotels/).

Near the bus terminal, there are several hotels on Av F de la Mora and quieter places on C Cedro, adjoining Mora, all quite similar; turn left from front of terminal, 2 mins' walk.

$$$$ Granados Park
Estrella y 15 de Agosto, T021-497921, www.granadospark.com.py.
Luxury, top-quality hotel, range of suites with all facilities, good restaurant *Il Mondo*.

$$$$-$$$ Hotel Westfalenhaus
Sgto 1° M Benítez 1577 entre Kuarajhy y Prof Fernández, Barrio Miraflores de Trinidad, T021-292374, http://www.paraguay-hotel.com.
Comfortable, German-run, half board, weekly rates and self-catering apartments, pool, safe deposit box, international restaurant, **Piroschka**, gym, massage and spa, English, German and Spanish spoken.

$$$ Aspen Apart Hotel
Ayolas 581 y Gral Díaz, T021-496066, www.aspen.com.py.

Modern, lots of marble, 50 suites and apartments, pool, sauna, gym, cheaper longer stays.

$$$ Cecilia
Estados Unidos 341 y Estigarribia, T021-210365, www.hotelcecilia.com.py.
Comfortable suites, weekend specials, pool with a view, sauna, gym, airport transfers, parking, medical service.

$$$ Chaco
Caballero 285 y Estigarribia, T021-492066, www.hotelchaco.com.py.
Central 1970s hotel, parking nearby, rooftop pool, bar, good restaurant (**$$$ Don Pedro**).

$$$ Las Margaritas
Estrella y 15 de Agosto, T021-448765, www.lasmargaritas.com.py.
Modern, central business hotel, safe in room, restaurant, terrace grill, gym, sauna, pool. English, German, Portuguese spoken. Recommended.

$$$ Sabe Center
25 de Mayo y México, T021-450093, www.sabecenterhotel.com.py.
Luxury hotel in modern tower, with all facilities, discounts available. English and Spanish spoken.

$$$-$$ Paramanta
Av Aviadores del Chaco 3198, T021-607053, www.paramantahotel.com.py.
Mid-way between airport and centre, buses stop outside, bar, restaurant, pool, gym, gardens, and many other services. English, German, Portuguese spoken.

$$ Amalfi
Caballero 877 y Manuel Domínguez, T021-441162, www.hotelamalfi.com.py.
Modern, comfortable, spacious rooms, frigobar, safe downstairs, small bar and comedor. Recommended.

$$ Asunción Palace
Colón 415 y Estrella, T021-492151, www.asuncionhotelpalace.com.
Historic building dating from 1858. 24 rooms, fridge, very helpful, elegant, laundry. English spoken.

$$ Bavaria
Chóferes del Chaco 1010, T021-600966, www.hotelbavariapy.com.
Comfortable, colonial style, beautiful garden, pool, good value rooms and suites with kitchens, fridge, English, German spoken, very helpful staff.

$$ La Española
Herrera 142 y F Yegros, T021-449280, www.hotellaespanola.com
Central, poor breakfast, credit cards accepted, airport pick-up, laundry, luggage storage, restaurant, parking.

$$ Maison Suisse
Malutín 482, Villa Morra, T021-600003, http://hotelcasasuiza.com.
Convenient for shops, restaurants and bars, rooms with disabled access, pool, garden, gym, buffet breakfast in 'Suizoguayo' style. Also has **Casa Suiza**, Sen Long 389, T021-603492, which is a little cheaper.

$$ Palmas del Sol
España 202, T021-449485, www.hotelportaldelsol.com.
Linked to Portal del Sol, very helpful, good buffet-style breakfast, a/c and fan, small pool, English, German spoken.

$$ Portal del Sol
Av Denis Roa 1455 y Santa Teresa, T021-609395, www.hotelportaldelsol.com.
Comfortable hotel, some rooms sleep 4, free airport pick-up, pool.

$$ Zaphir
Estrella 955 y Colón, T 021-490025, zaphir@pla.net.py.
Ideal location. Rather dingy looking but cosy, clean, and quiet, Wi-Fi accessible in rooms. Very friendly staff. Highly recommended.

$$-$ El Nómada
Iturbe 1156 y Rodríguez de Francia, T992-272946, www.hostel-asuncion-paraguay.com.
Popular hostel with private rooms and dorms (US$10-12 pp), some with bath, Wi-Fi, bar, restaurant, small pool, terrace and parking, airport pick-up can be arranged.

$ Black Cat Hostel
Eligio Ayala 129 casi Independencia Nacional, T021-449827, www.hostelblackcat.com.
Central backpacker hostel in a historic building, dorms for 8 and 16, private rooms for 1-2 (**$$**), shared bath, helpful with travel advice, breakfast included, English spoken. Recommended.

$ El Viajero Asunción
Alberdi 734, T021-444563, www.hostelasuncion.com.
Private and shared dorms all en suite with a/c. Breakfast included. Cable TV and DVDs. Wide common areas, swimming pool.

$ La Casita de la Abuela Hostal Verde
Hernandarias 1074 entre Jejui y Manduvira, T981-468090, Facebook: LaCasitaDeLaAbuelaHostalVerde.
New but already hugely popular with backpackers and NGO workers. Centrally located. Rooms for 4-8. Wi-fi, cable TV, a/c, kitchen, enclosed parking lot. Owner Javier speaks English and French and is very helpful.

Out of the city

$$$$ Resort Yacht y Golf Club Paraguayo
14 km from town, at Lambaré, on own beach on the Río Paraguay, T021-906121, www.resortyacht.com.py.
7 restaurants and cafés, super luxury, with pool, gym, spa, golf, tennis, airport transfers; many extras free, special deals.

$$$ Estancia Oñondivemi
Tourism farm, Km 27.5 on Ruta 1 just past the turn off to Ruta 2, Juan Augusto Saldivar, San Lorenzo 30 mins from Asunción, T029-5 20344 or T981-441460, www.onondivemi.com.py.
A pleasant escape from the city. Serves all meals, food organically grown on site. Horse riding, fishing, swimming, nature walks (they have a nearby property with a waterfall, lovely for swimming), attractive accommodation with a/c, cheaper with fan. Groups welcome.

Camping

If camping, take plenty of insect repellent. There is a pleasant site at the **Jardín Botánico**, tents and vehicles permitted, cold showers and 220v electricity, busy at weekends. Lock everything in vehicle.

Restaurants

Many restaurants are outside the scope of the map. A few restaurants close at weekends, but may open at night. A good meal in the food halls at the shopping malls, which you pay for by weight, as you do in some of the city centre restaurants, is about US$2.30-4. Average price of a good meal in quality restaurants: US$20-25. The following are open most days of the week, day and night. For Spanish-language reviews see asunciongourmet.blogspot.com.

$$$ Acuarela
Mcal López 4049 y San Martín, T021-601750, www.acuarela.com.py.
Very good *churrascaría* and other Brazilian dishes.

$$$ Bolsi
Estrella 399 y Alberdi, T021-491841, www.bolsi.com.py. Open 24/7.
One of Asunción's longest-operating eateries. Enormously popular. Wide choice of wines, good for breakfast, excellent food in large servings. Has great diner next door, lower prices, also popular.

$$$ Ciervo Blanco
José A Flores 3870 casi Radiooperadores del Chaco, T021-214504, Facebook: CiervoBlanco.
For meat dishes and *parrillada* and Paraguayan music shows.

$$$ La Pergola Jardín
Perú 240 y José Berges, T021-214014, www.lapergola.com.py.
Excellent restaurant for national and international food, lunchtime buffets including Sun. In same group as the Vitapan *confitería/panaderías*.

$$$ Mburicao
Antonio Riobó 737 y Chaco Boreal, T021-660048, www.mburicao.com. Daily 1200-1430 (except Sat), 2000-2400.
Mostly Mediterranean food, some with a local twist. Highly recommended.

$$$ Paulista Grill
San Martín casi Mcal López, T021-611501, www.paulistagrill.com.py.
A good *churrascaría*, good value, cheaper in the week, popular with groups.

$$$ Rolandi
Mcal López y Infante Rivarola, T021-610447, www.restauranterolandi.com.
Delicious pasta, steak and fish. Recommended.

$$$ Shangrila
Aviadores del Chaco y San Martín, T021-661618, www.shangri-la.com.py.
Very good food at upmarket Chinese.

$$$ Sukiyaki
Hotel Uchiyamada, Constitución 763 y Luis A de Herrera, T021-222038.
Good Japanese.

$$$ Taberna Española
Ayolas 631 y General Díaz, T021-443768.
Spanish food, very good.

$$$-$$ El Chef Peruano
General Garay 431 y Del Maestro, T021-605756.
Good-quality Peruvian food, popular with groups.

\$\$\$-\$\$ Tierra Colorada Gastro

Santísima Trinidad 784 y Tte Fernández, T021-663335, http://tierracoloradagastro.com.
Out of the centre in Barrio Mburucuya, toward Parque Ñu Guasu in Luque. Paraguayan-fusion dishes, deliberately healthy, many using indigenous recipes and produce from farms in the area; good reputation.

\$\$ Bellini

Palma 459 y 14 de Mayo, Facebook: belliniparaguay, has several branches including in shopping malls.
3-course pasta buffet or à la carte, good value and popular.

\$\$ Lido Bar

Plaza de los Héroes, Palma y Chile, T021-446171, http://lidobar.com.py. Daily 0700-2300.
An institution in Asunción, great location across from Panteón, loads of character. Good for breakfast, *empanadas* and watching the world go by. Good quality and variety, famous for fish soup, delicious, very popular. Recommended. Also has a branch in Villa Morra, Mcal López y Cruz del Chaco, open 0600-0100.

\$\$ Munich

Eligio Ayala 163, T021-447604.
Pleasant, old-fashioned, with a shady patio, popular with business people.

\$\$ San Roque

Eligio Ayala y Tacuary, T 021-446015, Facebook: barsanroquepy.
Traditional, 'an institution' and one of the oldest restaurants in town, relatively inexpensive. Recommended.

\$ La Vienesa

Alberdi y Oliva, T021-612793, www.lavienesa.com.py.
Wide menu, meat dishes, fish, pasta, pizza, Mexican, lots of breads and sweets, coffee. Also does by weight and take away. Popular at lunchtime. Also at Av España y Dominicana, Villa Morra, and 5 other branches.

\$ Tapei

Tte Fariña 1049 y Brasil y Estados Unidos, T021-201706.
Serves stylish Chinese and vegetarian by weight. Recommended.

Cafés and snacks

Most cheap lunch places close around 1600.

Bar Leo

Colón 462 y Olivia, T021-490333, www.barleo.com.py.
Small, clean place for lunch buffet, takeaway and *empanadas* and *tortas*.

Café Literario

Mcal Estigarribia 456, T021-491640. Mon-Fri 1600-2200.
Cosy café/bar, books and good atmosphere. Occasional cultural events with Alianza Francesa.

El Bar de la Preferida

Estados Unidos 341 y 25 de Mayo, T021-202222, www.hotelcecilia.com.py/restaurant-la-preferida.html.
Bar with meals served by kilo, Mon-Sat from 1200, different availability each day. Part of **Hotel Cecilia** and not to be confused with restaurant by the same name.

El Café de Acá

Tte Vera 390 casi Dr Mora, T021-623583, www.elcafedeaca.com. Open 0730-2400.
Serving coffee as in the old days.

El Molino

España 382 y Brasil, T021-225351.
Good value, downstairs for sandwiches and home-made pastries, upstairs for full meals in a nice setting, good service and food (particularly steaks) but pricey. Bakery as well. Recommended.

Heladería París

6 locations: Brasilia y Abelardo Brugada, Roca Argentina 982, Quesada y San Roque González, Felix Bogado y 18 Julio, Julio Correa y Molas López 143, and NS de Asunción y Quinta Avenida, www.hparis.com.py.
Café/bar/ice cream parlour. Popular.

La Flor de la Canela

Tacuary 167 y Eligio Ayala, T021-498928, https://es-la.facebook.com/laflordelacanelaPY/.
Cheap Peruvian lunches.

Michael Bock

Pres Franco 828, T021-495847.
Excellent bread and sweet shop, specializing in German pastries.

Quattro D (4D)

San Martín y Dr Andrade, 2nd location at Patio de Comidas del Shopping del Sol, T021-615168. www.quattrod.com.py.
Ice cream parlour offering great range of flavours, also weekday lunches from about US\$1 and up.

Bars and clubs

Bars

Online, the best sources are **Asunción Quick Guide** (www.quickguide.com.py) and **Turismo Internal Paraguay** (www.tip.com.py). *Asunción Viva* is a weekly listing of what's going on in the city; its monthly version costs US$1.65 (free at tourist office).

Paseo Carmelitas, Av España y Malutín, Villa Morra, http://paseocarmelitas.com.py, small but upscale mall has several popular bars, such as **El Bar, Kamastro, Kilkenney Irish Pub, Sheridan's** and others as well as restaurants and shops. To get there, take bus 30 from Oliva, which goes along Mcal López, but returns on España, or bus 31 to Mcal López.

Britannia Pub
Cerro Corá 851, T021-443990, www.britannia-pub.com. Evenings only, closed Mon.
Good variety of drinks, German spoken, popular expat hangout, book exchange.

Café Bohemia
Senador Long 848 casi España, T021-662191, see Facebook.
Original decor and atmosphere, Mon and Tue live blues/jazz, alternative at weekends.

Rivera
Estrella 442 y Alberdi.
Central bar on 2nd floor, balcony, good for drinks and music.

Clubs

Av Brasilia has a collection of clubs such as **Ristretto Café & Bar** (No 671 y Siria, T021-224614, http://ristrettocafebar.jimdo.com) and **Mouse Cantina** (No 803 y Patria, T021-228794).

Café Proa
Padre Juan Pucheú 549 casi España at same corner as French Embassy, T021-222456.
Tango classes every night, 1800-2130, light snacks and drinks, very pleasant.

Coyote
Sucre 1655 casi San Martín, T021-662114, www.facebook.com/CoyoteAsuncion/.
Several dance floors and bars, affluent crowd, see website for other events in different locations including Ciudad del Este and San Bernardino. Recommended.

Face's
Av Mcal López 2585 (technically in Fernando de la Mora), T021-671421/672768, https://faces.com.py. Also in Ciudad del Este.
Largest club in Paraguay, shows nightly.

Glam
Av San Martin 1155 y Agustín Barrios, T021-663121, www.glam.com.py (see Facebook while page is under construction –2017).
Along with Coyote and Face's (see above), one of Asunción's most popular clubs. Thu, Fri and Sat.

Entertainment

Cinema and theatre

See newspapers for films, performances of concerts, plays and ballets. For online listings, check **ABC Digital** (www.abc.com.py), **Última Hora** (www.ultimahora.com) and **La Nación** (www.lanacion.com.py). See also the monthly *Asunción Quick Guide* (www.quickguide.com.py) and the **Dirección General de Cultura y Turismo** (http://cultura.asuncion.gov.py). Cinema admission US$5 (Wed and matinées half price). Most shopping malls have modern cinemas; see Shopping centres, below. For the **Teatro Municipal**, see page 1203. Various cultural centres also put on films, theatrical productions and events:

Alianza Francesa, *Mcal Estigarribia 1039 y Estados Unidos, T021-210503, www.ambafrance-py.org/Alianza-Francesa-de-Asuncion.*
Centro Cultural Paraguayo Americano, *España 352 entre Brasil y Estados Unidos, T021-224831, www.ccpa.edu.py.*
Goethe-Zentrum Asunción, *Juan de Salazar 310 y Artigas, T021-209060, www.goethe.de/ins/pa/asu.*

Festivals

Jul Expo. An annual 2-week trade show at Mariano Roque Alonso, Km 14.5 on the Trans-Chaco Highway. The biggest fair in the country with local and international exhibitors. Packed at weekends. Bus from centre takes 30 mins.

Shopping

Bookshops

English-language books are expensive throughout Paraguay. Better prices and selections are had in Argentina and Brazil.
'Books', at Shopping del Sol, T021-611730, and Mcal López 3971, also opposite Villa Morra shopping centre, T021-603722, www.libreriabooks.com. Very good for English books, new titles and classics.
El Lector, *San Martín y Austria, T021-610639, Facebook: ElLectorPy.* Has a selection of foreign material and a range of its own titles on Paraguay. Also has café and internet connection.

Crafts

Check the quality of all handicrafts carefully; in the city, lower prices usually mean lower quality. Many leading tourist shops offer up to 15% discount for cash; many others will not accept credit cards, so ask even if there are signs in window saying they do. For leather goods there are several places on Colón and on Montevideo including: **Boutique Irene** (No 463); **Boutique del Cuero** (No 329); and **Galería Colón 185**, recommended. Also **La Casa del Portafolio** (Av Palma 302, T021-492431).

Artes de Madera, *Ayolas 222*. Wooden articles and carvings.

Casa Overall 1, *Mcal Estigarribia y Caballero, T021-448657*. Good selection. Also **No 2** at 25 de Mayo y Caballero, T021-447891.

Casa Vera, *Estigarribia 470, T021-445868, www.casavera.com.py*. For Paraguayan leatherwork, cheap and very good.

Doña Miky, *O'Leary 215 y Pres Franco*. Recommended.

Folklore, *Mcal Estigarribia e Iturbe, T021-494360*. Good for music, woodcarvings and other items.

La Recova, *near the waterfront*. Long Asunción's general-purpose market, has served as an open-air and covered emporium for all manner of handicrafts and traditional goods (including better-grade hammocks, leather and silver products) for more than 150 years. It takes some searching to find the best deals, but the markets here are endlessly colourful and vibrant, with wares usually cheaper than what are being sold in Plaza Libertad or along Av Palma.

Victoria, Arte Artesanía, *Iturbe y Ayala, T021-450148*. Interesting selection of wood carvings, ceramics etc. Recommended.

Markets

Mercado Cuatro, *in the blocks bounded by Pettirossi, Perú and Av Dr Francia*. A huge daily market selling food, clothing, electrical items, DVDs, CDs, jewellery, toys, is a great place to visit. Good, cheap Chinese restaurants nearby.

Shopping Mariscal López *(see below)*. Has a fruit and vegetable market, Tue, in the car park, and a small plant/flower market, including orchids, Wed, at the entrance.

Shopping centres

Asunción has a number of modern shopping malls with shops, ATMs, cafés, supermarkets, cinemas and food halls all under one a/c roof. Most also offer Wi-Fi coverage. In the centre is **Mall Excelsior** (Chile y Manduvirá, T021-443015, www.mallexcelsior.com). **Shopping Villa Morra** (Av Mcal López y San Gonzalo González, T021-603050, http://villamorrashopping.com.py). **Shopping Mariscal López** (Quesada 5050 y Charles de Gaulle, behind Shopping Villa Morra, T021-611272, www.shoppingmariscal.com.py). **Shopping del Sol** (Av Aviadores de Chaco y D F de González, T021-611780, www.delsol.com.py).

What to do

Football

Asunción (technically in Luque) is the permanent home of the **South American Football Confederation, CONMEBOL** (www.conmebol.com), on the *autopista* heading towards the airport, opposite Ñu Guazú Park. This imposing building with its striking 'football' fountain houses offices, a hall of fame, extensive football library and a new museum with interactive exhibits, T021-494628 in advance for visits. See also **Asociación Paraguaya de Futbol** (www.apf.org.py).

Estadio Defensores del Chaco, *Mayor Martínez 1393 y Alejo García, T021-480120*. Is the national stadium, hosting international, cup and major club matches.

Horse riding

Club Hípico Paraguayo, *Av Eusebio Ayala y Benjamín Aceval, Barrio San Jorge Mariano Roque Alonso, T021-756148, http://clubhipicoparaguayo.com*. Actually 9 different athletic clubs in one; scene of many Asunción society events. Members club open to the public (daily rates available). Friendly and helpful.

Language schools

Idipar (Idiomas en Paraguay), *Manduvirá 963, T021-447896, www.idipar.com.py*. Offers courses in Spanish or Guaraní. Private or group lessons available, also offers accommodation with local families and volunteer opportunities. Good standard.

IPEE, *Lugano 790 y Ayolas, T021-447482*. Spanish or Guaraní, in individual or group classes. Recommended.

Nature tourism

See box, page 1216.

River tours

Operators at the marina area of Náutica San Isidro run river tours: **Asociación de Lancheros Unidos de Chaco'I**, T0983-127965, ask for Tomás Benegas; **River Tours**, Dr Mazzel y Kannonikoff, T021-480313 or 0981-145542, rivertours@nsi.com.py.

Rural tourism

Turismo rural is an enjoyable way to visit the country and get a feel for a Paraguayan way of life that revolves around agriculture and ranching. It is not as advanced as rural tourism in Argentina, Chile or Uruguay, amenities are modest and there is little concerted promotion of estancias, but the sector is slowly growing in Paraguay, particularly in the southeast (in Paraguarí, Caaguazú, Guairá and Caazapá departments) and to the east and northeast of Asunción (in Cordillera and San Pedro departments). The **Touring y Automóvil Club Paraguayo (TACPy)** (25 de Mayo y Brasíl, p 2, T021-210550, www. tacpy.com.py), is a potential source of information on rural tourism, although it does not cover the whole country. Thanks to increased government support for its mission, however, the **Paraguayan Rural Tourism Association (APATUR)**, Don Bosco 881, T021-497028, http://turismorural. org.py, is taking over this role. With advance notice, it can help organize visits to ranches and farms throughout the country's more accessible regions (there is a list on the website). Visitors experience living on a ranch, can participate in a variety of activities, and enjoy typical food, horse riding, photo safaris and nature watching. 1-day tour prices are about US$60-95 pp including accommodation, food and drink (not alcohol). All the ranches promoted by APATUR supposedly have good facilities, although there is as yet no accepted standardization. Transport to and from these ranches from Asunción is sometimes included in the package. See also the **Ministry of Tourism (SENATUR)** rural tourism website, http:// visitparaguay.travel/v1/experiencia/8-rural, for a list of ranches that welcome tourists. All visits should be arranged at least 1 week in advance and confirmed prior to leaving Asunción.

Tours

Many agencies offer day tours of the **Circuito de Oro** or **Camino Franciscano** (from US$50), with the possibility of different stops for each agency, so ask in advance which locations are included on the itinerary. Trips to local estancias, Encarnación and the former Jesuit Missions, Itaipú and Iguazú or the Chaco region are all offered as 1-, 2- or 4-day tours. Most agencies will also provide personalized itineraries on request. Many more city tours, especially those focusing on architecture and culture, are also available. For more information contact **SENATUR** or the **Paraguayan Association of Travel Agencies and Tourism (ASATUR)** (Juan O'Leary 650, p 1, T021-494728, www.asatur.org.py). Also, Paraguay's official national cultural organ, the Cabildo (page 1202), offers several options for itineraries throughout the country and capital.

Canadá Viajes, *Rep de Colombia 1061, T021-211192, www.canadaviajes.com.py.* Good Asunción and Chaco tours.

Inter Tours, *Perú 436 y España, T021-211747, www. intertours.com.py.* One of Paraguay's biggest full-service tour agencies. Tours to Chaco, Iguazú and Jesuit missions. Highly recommended.

Klassen Tours, *Denis Roa 1455, T021-612035, www.klassentours.com.* Recommended for tours within Paraguay, including fixed departures, also transfers and car rental.

Menno Travel, *Rep de Colombia 1042 entre Brasil y EEUU, T021-441210/493504, www.mennotravelsrl. com.* German spoken.

Vips Tour, *México 782 entre Fulgencio R Moreno y Herrera, T021-441199, also at Senador Long 790 y Tte Vera, T021-615920, www.vipstour.com.* Asunción, estancia and Chaco tours.

Transport

Air

Silvio Pettirossi Airport, T021-688 2000, www. dinac.gov.py. Official taxis are white and charge US$22 to the centre or the bus terminal (pay in guaraníes or dollars); good service. Urban taxis are yellow and can be taken at a stand by the bus stop beyond the car park payment booth, about 200 m from the terminal doors. Bus 30A 'verde' or 'azul' goes every 15 mins from the same bus stop to Plaza de los Héroes, US$1, at least 1 hr, difficult with luggage; there are ordinary buses and a/c *diferenciales*. To the bus station take 30A 'verde' and change to No 31 or 18 at the junction of Mariscal López and San Martín/República Argentina; allow 1¼ hrs. Minibus service from your hotel to airport run by **Tropical**, T021-424486, book in advance, US$2.70 (minimum 2 passengers, or pay for 2). The terminal has a tourist office (helpful, information on Asunción and the rest of the country, free city map and hotel information), bank (turn right as you leave customs – better rates in town), *cambios* (ditto, but rates in baggage reclaim are much worse than in entrance hall, next to tourist office), post office (0800-1800), handicraft shop (good quality, expensive), restaurant and several travel agencies who arrange hotel bookings. Left luggage US$5 per day per item.

Bus

Local Journeys within greater Asunción US$0.75. Buses can be busy at rush hours. Turnstiles are awkward for large backpacks. Keep your ticket for inspection until you leave bus.

Long-distance The **Terminal de Omnibus, TOA**, is south of the centre at República Argentina y Fernando de la Mora, T021-551740, http://toa.asuncion.gov.py. Local bus No 8 is the only direct one from Oliva, which goes via Cerro Corá and Av Brasil from the centre, and stops on the opposite side of Av F de la Mora to the terminal, US$0.75. From the terminal to the centre it goes via Brasil, FR Moreno, Antequera, Plaza Uruguaya and E Ayala. Get out between Chile and Alberdi for Plaza de los Héroes. Other buses, eg No 31, follow more circuitous routes. Taxi to/from centre, recommended if you have luggage, US$8-10, journey time depends on the amount of traffic, about 45 mins. The terminal has a bus information desk, free city/country map, restaurant (quite good), café, many *casas de cambio*, ATM, post office, phone booths and shops. Better companies include **Nuestra Señora de la Asunción**, T021-289 1000, www.nsa.com.py, has booking office at main terminal and at Mcal Estigarribia y Antequera, off Plaza Uruguaya (mainly for its tours), and at Benjamin Constant 984, opposite Aduanas. Some of its buses are direct, ie they don't stop everywhere and anywhere. **RYSA**, T021-557201/557210, www.rysa.com.py, has a booking office at Ayala y Antequera y Plaza Uruguaya. Also recommended are **La Ovetense**, T021-551737, https://es-la.facebook.com/LaOvetense; **Nasa-Golondrina**, T021-551731, for domestic destinations. Bus company offices are on the top floor of the terminal; some are obvious which company they represent (eg the big companies), others less so. Allow yourself time to choose the company you want and don't be tricked into buying the wrong ticket. Bus fares within Paraguay are given under destinations, also available on TOA's website. Note that all journey times are approximate.

To Argentina There is a road north from Asunción (passing the Jardín Botánico on Primer Presidente) to a concrete arch span bridge (Puente Remanso – US$1.25 toll, pedestrian walkway on upstream side, 20 mins to cross) which leads to the border at Puerto Falcón (about 40 km) and then to **Clorinda** in Argentina. The border is open 24 hrs; local services are run by **Empresa Falcón** to **Puerto Falcón**: US$1.25, every hr, last bus from Falcón to the centre of Asunción 1830; from Falcón to **Clorinda** costs US$0.75, but direct from Asunción to Clorinda is US$1. **Note** Buses don't wait for you to go through formalities: if you cannot process in time, wait for the same company's next bus and present ticket, or buy a new ticket.

Buses to **Buenos Aires** (18 hrs) daily, many companies, via Rosario and Santa Fe (fares range from US$30-60). To **Resistencia** and **Corrientes**, many daily, US$9 to Resistencia, US$10.50 to Corrientes; many drug searches on this road. To **Salta**, take a bus to **Resistencia**, then change to **Flecha** or **La Veloz del Norte**, or take a bus on the route through the Chaco, as below.

To Brazil Many Paraguayan buses advertise that they go to destinations in Brazil, when, in fact you have to change buses and book again at the border. Services to **Campo Grande** and **Corumbá** via Pedro Juan Caballero and Ponta Porã do not stop for immigration formalities. Check all details carefully. **Nuestra Señora de la Asunción** and others, and the Brazilian company **Pluma** (T021-551196, www.pluma.com.br) have direct services via Ciudad del Este to **Foz do Iguaçu** (Brazil), US$25-30, 5-6 hrs. To **Curitiba**, with **Pluma** and others, daily, 15½ hrs, US$45. To **Florianópolis**, **Pluma** and **Catarinense**, US$60 (T021-551738, www.catarinense.net), you may have to change in Cascavel. To **Porto Alegre**, **Uneleste** (T021-442679), Tue, Thu, US$60. To **São Paulo**, **Pluma**, **Sol** and **Brújula**, 20 hrs, US$45-68. **Pluma** to **Rio de Janeiro**, US$76 (not Sat); **Transcontinental** (T021-557369) to **Brasília** 3 a week, US$100.

To Bolivia Via the Chaco, to **Santa Cruz**, **Yacyretá**, T021-551725, Mon, Wed, Fri, and Sat at 2030, **Pycazú**, T021-555235, Thu, Sat 2100, **Palma Loma**, T021-558196, and **Río Paraguay**, T021-555958. Fares from US$52-64. All buses normally travel via Mariscal Estigarribia, for Paraguayan immigration where foreigners must get an exit stamp; La Patria; Infante Rivarola at the border (no stamps are given here); Ibibobo, for Bolivian immigration; and Villamontes. From here buses go either to Yacuiba for Argentina (Pocitos and on to Salta on Ruta 54), or direct to Santa Cruz.

Advertised as 21 hrs, the trip can take 2 days to Santa Cruz if the bus breaks down. Some food provided on both Salta and Santa Cruz routes, but take your own, plus extra water just in case; also take toilet paper. The buses can be very crowded. In summer the route can be very hot and dusty, but in winter, it can be cold at night.

Unless specifically advertised, buses to Bolivia do not go through Filadelfia or the other Mennonite colonies, so take a local service from Asunción (see page 1213). After visiting the Chaco, you can usually get on a Bolivia-bound bus in Mariscal Estigarribia, where the bus companies have agents (see page 1243), but enquire in advance with their offices in Asunción.

Car hire

Fast Rent a Car, Prof Chávez 1276 y Santa Rosa, T021-605462, www.fastrentacar.com.py. Good, helpful. Many other companies at the airport. Note that all Paraguayan car hire agencies require payment in US dollars as well as a deposit secured by a credit card of between US$500-1000.

Taxi

Taxi meters start at US$1.15 and rise in US$0.10 increments. There is a late night surcharge after 2200 to 0500. There are many taxi ranks throughou the city. Taxis can either be hailed or call **Radiotaxi** (recommended), T021-550116/311080

River

A small launch leaves from the pier at the bottom of Montevideo to **Chaco-i**, a strip of land between the Ríos Paraguay and Pilcomayo (no facilities), US$0.75 each way. Also across the river is the **Mbiguá Club** (rather run down), Facebook: Club-Mbigua-Oficial, boat fare US$4.50. The Argentine town of Clorinda is just the other side of the Pilcomayo, but there are no ferries or immigration for crossing here.

For boat travel to **Concepción**, see under Concepción, Transport, page 1236.

Train

At the time of writing, no tourist steam trains were running from Asunción.

Región Oriental:
East of Asunción

To the east of the Río Paraguay lie the most fertile lands and the most populated region of the country. Of the vast rainforests that once covered it, only a few isolated patches have not been converted to farmland. Rutas 2, 3 and 7 (a continuation of 2) all head east towards the border with Brazil, taking the traveller near tranquil villages known for their arts and crafts, German colonies, the occasional Franciscan mission, and small towns associated with the country's bloody past. In contrast to the quiet of the countryside, Rutas 1 and 8 run south and east, and lead to the southern Paraneña (the country's breadbasket and home to its gauchos), the former Jesuit missions and then merge at Coronel Bogado before reaching the Río Paraguay in Encarnación. Ciudad del Este, a straight shot across Rutas 2 and 7, is a crossroads for all manner of merchandise, much of it illegal, and the world's largest stolen car market, while the giant Itaipú dam has irreversibly changed the landscape. Along the border (and shared with Brazil and Argentina) are the Iguazú Falls, still the top draw for most visitors to Paraguay.

Itauguá to San Bernardino

lace, ceramics, strawberries and a lakeside resort

Itauguá

At Km 30 on Ruta 2, founded in 1728, Itauguá, now Paraguay's fastest-growing city, is where the famous *ñandutí*, or spiderweb lace, is made. There are some 120 different designs. Prices are lower than in Asunción and the quality is better; there are many makers. Almost all of the best *talleres* are located directly off the highway and can be accessed by bus. To watch the lace being made, ask around. The old town lies two blocks from the main highway. Worth seeing are the **market** ① *0800-1130, 1500-1800, closed Sun*, the church of Virgen del Rosario and the **Museo de Historia Indígena** ① *Km 25, daily 0800-1130, 1500-1800, US$0.60*, a beautiful collection of carvings of Guaraní mythological creatures, and the **Museo Parroquial San Rafael** ① *daily 0800-1130, 1500-1800, free*, with a display of indigenous art and Franciscan artefacts. There is a four-day **Festival de Ñandutí** in early July, including processions and the crowning of Señorita Ñandutí. There are also musical evenings on **Viernes culturales** (Cultural Fridays) in January and February. Itauguá is also the birthplace of Juan Crisóstomo Centurión, the only Paraguayan military leader to win a battle in the War of the Triple Alliance and an architect of the country's rebirth.

> **Tip...**
> You can see many of Paraguay's best traditional musicians perform during the festival held in Itauguá in July.

Best for
Arts and crafts ▪ **History** ▪ **Waterfalls** ▪ **Wildlife**

National parks and nature tourism

The abundance of wildlife, particularly birds, is most visible in the Chaco, especially in its remote national parks, along the Río Pilcomayo, and the frontier with Bolivia. It has been estimated that the Pantanal has the highest concentration of fauna in the Americas. Current estimates include between 10,000-13,000 plant species, 100,000 invertebrates (including 765 of butterfly), 300 species of fish, 120 reptiles, 100 amphibians, 687 birds and 171 mammals. For more details, visit **Fauna Paraguay** (www.faunaparaguay.com). However, the most visited (and possibly most beautiful) of the 40 or so national parks is Ybycuí, famous for its waterfalls, and less than a day's drive from Asunción; see page 1226. Paraguay has an extensive network of state-protected areas, 94 in all, covering – on paper at least – almost 7% of the country's territory. Some fall within three biosphere reserves, Chaco Paraguayo, Bosque Mbaracayú and Río Apa. Exactly what constitutes a protected area is confusing at best and the criteria can change from year to year. To complicate matters further, of this number, 38 are private reserves which are maintained by outside entities (in some cases, the Itaipú and Yacyretá dam authorities) but which are supervised by Paraguay's **Secretaría Nacional de Turismo** (SENATUR, www.senatur.gov.py) or **Secretaría del Ambiente** (SEAM, www.seam.gov.py). Unfortunately many of these protected areas exist solely on paper, and the whole system is under-funded. As beautiful and unique as these areas are, infrastructure is in most cases rudimentary at best (if it exists at all), and visiting them is not always easy. Always contact the relevant institutions and authorities first, and never venture in without prior permission (and a good all-terrain vehicle). The most reliable online source is the National Parks of Paraguay blog (http://nationalparksofparaguay.blogspot.com). A 2014 map of SEAM's **Sistema Nacional de Areas Protegidas del Paraguay** (SINASIP) can be found on the home page of its website.

For the reserves managed by the Itaipú and Yacyretá authorities, contact the relevant environmental departments. For private reserves contact the following conservation NGOs: **Guyra Paraguay**, Gaetano Martino 215 y Tte Ross, Asunción, T021-223567, www.guyra.org.py, which has a wealth of information for birdwatchers, naturalists and biologists as well as the capacity, infrastructure and expertise to organize tailor-made ecotours to all parts of the country, including some of the more remote locations not provided by other tour operators (highly recommended); **Fundación Moisés Bertoni para la Conservación de la Naturaleza**, Prócer Carlos Argüello 208, Asunción, T021-608740, www.mbertoni.org.py, which manages the Mbaracayú Reserve, one of two remaining pristine Atlantic Forest reserves in the region, as well as the lesser-known Tapyta Reserve; **Pro Cosara**, Hohenau II, Itapúa, T0717-20300, http://procosara.org, which works for the protection of the San Rafael Nature Reserve in eastern Paraguay and which welcomes volunteers at the ecological station (www.faunaparaguay.com/ecosaravolunteers.html); **Para la Tierra**, San Pedro del Ycuamandiyú, T0985-260074, www.paralatierra.org, which works for the protection of the Laguna Blanca Reserve and also welcomes volunteers. **Desarrollo Turístico Paraguayo** (DTP, offices in Asunción, Encarnación and Ciudad del Este, www.dtp.com.py), the country's largest and best-known tourism agency, can organize adventure tours to different parts of the country.

Areguá

At **Capiatá** (Ruta 2, Km 20, fine colonial church), a left turn goes to Areguá, Paraguay's strawberry capital and a centre of better-grade crafts (lots of artesanías). Founded in 1541 this is a pretty colonial village, 30 km east of Asunción and also easily reached from Luque's main road. It sits on the slope above **Lago Ypacaraí**. Formerly the summer capital of the country's elite, from its attractive church at the highest point in town there is one of the best views of the lake, its two nearby *cerros* (Kõi and Ita'ï) and surroundings. It has an interesting ceramics cooperative, a museum, arts and crafts exhibition and on its outskirts a remarkable Dominican convent, originally a castle built for Francisco Solano López and his mistress Eliza Lynch and later purchased by one of Paraguay's grandes dames, **Carlota Palmerola** ① *open daily 0800-1700, US$2.15*. Guided tours of the convent and other sites in town leave

Sunday 0900, return 1500, from SENATUR's office in Asunción, T021-433500, US$6.50. There is also a memorial in the centre to its most famous son, Gabriel Casaccia Bibolini, who many consider the founder of modern Paraguayan literature. There is a good German-run restaurant in the centre of the village. From here boat trips run across the lake at weekends to San Bernadino.

San Bernardino and Lago Ypacaraí

At Km 48 on Ruta 2 a branch road, 8 km long, leads off to **San Bernardino**, originally a Swiss German colony settled by the eminent botanist Emilio Hassler and known locally as 'Samber', on the east bank of **Lago Ypacaraí**. In the past few decades it has replaced Areguá as the country's summer resort for the rich. The lake, 24 km by 5 km, has facilities for swimming and watersports and sandy beaches (ask locally about pollution levels in the water). There are frequent cruises from the pier during the tourist season. As well as for Paraguay's elite, it is now the main vacation spot for all of Asunción from December to February, which means that it is lively and crowded at weekends in the summer, with concerts, pubs and nightclubs, but as a result it is commercialized. During the week and off season it is a tranquil resort town, with lakeside tourism clearly the main draw.

In town itself, visit **Casa Büttner** ① Colonos Alemanes, T0984-933158, free, an estate built by the German immigrant Julio Büttner in 1882. It saw Paraguay's first automobile and bus and also was the site of the country's first formal carpentry and ice-making factories. The house is still owned by Büttner's descendants and part of it serves as the town's library, a tea house and a crafts centre. It also has a wealth of information for travellers. Boats can be hired on the lake and there is good walking in the neighbourhood, for example from San Bernardino to **Altos**, which has one of the most spectacular views of the lake, wooded hills and valleys (round trip three hours). Shortly after the turn off from the main road towards San Bernardino is a sign to **La Gruta**; turn right here to a secluded park (Ypacaraí). There are grottos with still water and overhanging cliffs. No buses run after 2000 and taxis are expensive. The town is one of the few in Paraguay to have an official tourist guide agency (**SanBer Tour** ① T0981-607829, sanber_tour_py@hotmail.com), which offers five different tours. Tourist information is in **Casa Hassler** ① between General Morinigo and Emilio Hassler, T0512-232974, http://sanbernardino.gov.py/casa-hassler, which is also the town's cultural centre.

Listings Itauguá to San Bernardino

Where to stay

San Bernardino

Other than those listed, there are plenty of hotels, many with good restaurants, from the super luxury Sol de San Ber down. Book hotels in advance during fiestas.

$$$ Del Lago
Tte Weiler 401 y Mcal López, near lake in town, T0512-232201, www.hoteldellago.org.
With breakfast, attractive 1888 building renovated as a museum, upgraded, safe, regional decor, restaurant, bar and grill, pool, lovely gardens.

$$$ Pueblo Hotel San Bernardino
C 8 entre C 5 y Mbocayá, T0512-232195, pueblohotel@gmail.com.
Swimming pool, a/c, by the lake.
Weekend packages also available.

$$ Los Alpes
Ruta General Morínigo Km 46.5, 3 km from town, T0512-232083/232399, losalpeshotel@gmail.com.

Lovely gardens, 2 swimming pools, excellent self-service restaurant, children's playground, beach 1 km away, frequent buses to centre.

Camping
Brisas del Mediterráneo, Ruta Kennedy a 2000 m from Copaco, T981-510555, www.paraguay-hostel.com. With campsite (US$10.25, Oct-Apr), rooms ($$-$), meals, beach and games.

What to do

San Bernardino
Aventura Xtrema, NS de la Asunción y Hassler, T981-682243, San Bernardino, www.aventura xtrema.com.py. Offers backpacker tours and a variety of adventure tours: horse riding, caving, canoes, hiking, cycling and more.

Transport

Itauguá
Bus Frequent from **Asunción**, 1 hr, US$0.75.

Areguá

Bus From **Asunción**, bus from Shopping del Sol, Nos 11 or 111, may take scenic route through villages, 45-60 mins (longer if traffic is heavy); alternatively take local bus to Capiatá and change.

San Bernardino

Bus From **Asunción**, 3 companies: **Altos**, **Loma Grande** and **Ciudad de San Bernadino**, every 10 mins, 45 km, 1-2 hrs, US$1.25.

Caacupé to Coronel Oviedo

shrines, springs, museums and nature reserves

Caacupé

At Km 54 on Ruta 2, this is a popular resort and religious centre on the Azcurra escarpment. The centre is dominated by the modern Basilica of Our Lady of the Miracles, with a copper roof, stained glass and polychrome stone esplanade, consecrated by Pope John Paul II in 1988 (small fee to climb the tower). There is an ATM on the plaza between the supermarket and **Hotel El Mirador**.

Thousands of people from Paraguay, Brazil and Argentina flock to the shrine, especially for the **Fiesta de la Inmaculada Concepción** on 8 December, known locally as the Fiesta de la Virgen de Caacupé, or 'the black virgin'. Besides fireworks and candlelit processions, pilgrims watch the agile gyrations of Paraguayan bottle-dancers; they weave in intricate measures whilst balancing bottles pyramided on their heads. The top bottle carries a spray of flowers and the more expert dancers never let drop a single petal. The bottles contained blessed water, which is believed to come from the nearby spring of Tupasy Ykuá, which the Virgin revealed to early settlers. Caacupé is also well known for its Carnaval celebrations.

Tobatí

Getting there: take a bus from the corner below the park on the main Asunción road in Caacupé.

Tobatí, a town 15 km north of Caacupé along a marked branch road, specializes in woodwork. The town's highly regarded **Villa Artesenal** is 1-km walk from the bus stop outside the house of the late Zenon Páez, a world famous sculptor. It produces wonderful masks (some reputedly of pre-Columbian ancestry), coca-fibre hammocks and furniture. The Villa also has a small permanent exhibition and annual traditional handicrafts fair. There are some amazing rock formations on the way to Tobatí.

Piribebuy and Pirareta

Beyond Caacupé, at Km 71 on Ruta 2, a paved road runs 13 km due south to the town of Piribebuy, founded in 1636 and noted for its strong local drink, *caña*. Fortín Ron runs a **Ruta de la Caña Paraguaya tour** ① *3 hrs, US$20 pp, T021-613471, www.fortin.com.py*, with tastings accompanied by traditional music and dances. In the central plaza is the church (1640), with fine sculptures, high altar and pulpit. The town is officially one of Paraguay's 'heroic cities' in recognition of its staunch defence during a major battle in the War of the Triple Alliance (1869), commemorated by the **Museo Histórico Pedro Pablo Caballero** ① *Mariscal Estigarribia y Yegros, free, getting there: buses from Asunción by Transportes Piribebuy*, which also contains pristine artefacts from the Chaco War.

Near the town are the attractive falls of Pirareta and more than 15 hot springs (popular on weekends). The branch road continues via Chololó, 13 km south, and reaches Ruta 1 at Paraguarí, 28 km from Piribebuy (see page 1225). Between Pirbebuy and Paraguarí is an outdoor and adventure centre, **Eco-reserva Mbatoví** ① *T021-444844, or T0971-659820, for reservations and information visit www.mbatovi.com.py, entry US$35 for foreigners*, with a visitor centre. It includes an outdoor pursuits course and a three-hour guided walk, taking in early settlements, local folklore and beautiful scenery.

Caraguatay

A turn-off from Eusebio Ayala (Km 73) on Ruta 2 goes 20 km northeast to Caraguatay, a singular town with a unique history. Founded by the Spanish in 1770, it later served as the summer residence of Francisco Solano López and his Irish mistress Eliza Lynch. The town's centre boasts several beautiful colonial-era buildings and on the 24 of September, it celebrates the feast day of its patron saint, the Virgen de las Mercedes, with traditional dances and music that are no longer seen elsewhere in the country. Remarkably for a town of less than 5000 inhabitants, it has given the country three residents. Caraguatay is also the centre of an interesting economic experiment: it sends more workers abroad than any other municipality in Paraguay and the remittances returned have gone into making it one of the country's more upscale communities, with amenities and public services not easily found elsewhere. For more historical information, see http://caraguatay-ciudad.blogspot.com.

Parque Nacional Vapor Cué

Some 5 km from Caraguatay is the Vapor Cué National Park, where boats from the War of the Triple Alliance are preserved. Although officially a national park, it is more of an open-air museum. Next to the (indoor) museum is a hotel with pool, **Hotel Nacional de Vapor Cué** ($$, T0517-222395, www. hotelenvaporcue.com). Frequent buses run from Asunción to Caraguatay.

Coronel Oviedo and around *Colour map 6, C6.*

Coronel Oviedo, at the junction of west-east highway Ruta 2 and the major north-south Ruta 8, is an important route centre, although hardly worth a stop. Buses drop passengers for connections at the junction (El Cruce). Ruta 8 runs north to Santa Rosa del **Mbutuy**, continuing as Ruta 3 to Yby Yaú, where it meets Ruta 5 (westward to Concepción and eastward to Pedro Juan Caballero). At Mbutuy (Km 56, parador, restaurant, petrol station) Ruta 10 branches off northeast to the Brazilian frontier on the Río Paraná at **Saltos de Guaíra**, named after the waterfalls now under the Itaipú lake. There is a 900-ha wildlife reserve, **Refugio Biológico Binacional Mbaracayú**, administered by the Itaipú dam company, www.itaipu.gov.py/es/sala-de-prensa/noticia/areas-silvestres-protegidas-de-itaipu. Saltos de Guaíra, a free port, can also be reached by a paved highway (the Supercarretera Itaipú) which runs north from Hernandarias, via Colonia Limoy to meet Ruta 10 at Cruce Carolina Andrea (Coronel Oviedo-Salto de Guaíra is about 415 km by this route).

Mbaracayú Forest Nature Reserve

To visit, first contact the Moisés Bertoni Foundation in Asunción for details (see National parks, page 1216 for address); entry US$7.50. 2 bus companies from Asunción to Villa Ygatimi, daily, 7-8½ hrs, US$10.25 (Canindeyú, T021-555991; Nasa-Golondrina, T021-558451) or Canindeyú to Curuguaty, US$8.50; from Curuguaty to Ygatimi local bus 2 hrs, not all paved, US$3.50. From Villa Ygatimi it is 25 km to the park on a dirt road, T0971-282850/0985-261080, reservasmbaracayu@gmail.com to arrange transport; US$42.

Not to be confused with the nearby Refugio Biológico Mbaracayú mentioned above, this federally protected reserve covers 64,406 ha of Paraguay's rapidly disappearing Interior Atlantic forest. It is the largest area representative of this ecosystem in good conservation status in Paraguay. It contains 53% of all mammal species (nearly 100) and 58% of all bird species (411) found in eastern Paraguay. Activities include trails for walking and cycling (guides available), canoes, birdwatching, waterfalls, spectacular view points and star-gazing. There are also two indigenous communities, the Aché and Guaraní. There is a visitor centre, 3-km walk from the entrance, and small museum at Villa Ygatimi, also lodging ($$$, 13 rooms, each with Wi-Fi and a/c, with bath, price is full-board with transport; camping available). Packages of seven, 15 and 30 days can be booked.

Listings Caacupé to Coronel Oviedo

Where to stay

Caacupé

Cheaper than Lago Ypacaraí. Prices increase during the Fiesta de la Inmaculada Concepción.

$$-$ Katy María
Eligio Ayala y Dr Pino, T0511-242860,
beside Basílica, www.katymaria.com.
Well kept, welcoming, a/c, Wi-Fi.

$ El Mirador
On plaza, T0511-242652.
With bath.

$ Virgen Serrana
Plaza, T0511-242366.
A/c, cheaper with fan.

Estancias

$$$$ Estancia Aventura
Km 61.5, Ruta 2, T981-441804,
www.estancia-aventura.com.

91 ha of countryside, 7-day packages. Owner speaks German, English, Spanish. Good, horse riding, tennis, swimming, tours, can arrange airport pick-up from Asunción. Expensive but worth it.

Piribebuy

$$$ La Quinta
10 km from Piribebuy, 19 km from Paraguarí, 82.5 km from Asunción along Ruta 1 and then branch road from Piribebuy (take bus to Piribebuy then bus to Chololó, bus passes in front of hotel), T971-11 7444, www.laquinta.com.py.
Price based on 4 sharing in cabins, also suites, also open for day visits, own stream and is close to falls at Pirareta and Chololó.

$ Viejo Rincón
Maestro Fermín López y Tte Horacio Gini, T0515-212251.
Reasonable.

Coronel Oviedo

$$-$ Quincho Porá
Aquidaban 235, Coronel Oviedo, T0521-202963/ 972-86 4236, www.2cv-tours.de/hostel.htm.

Owned by Walter Schäffer who runs Citröen 2CV and Land Rover tours in Paraguay and South America. Good hostel, German/Paraguayan, lots of information, hammock space, bar.

Transport

Caacupé
Bus From **Asunción**, US$1.25, get off at Basilica (closer to centre) rather than Caacupé station.

Coronel Oviedo
Bus **Asunción** to **Coronel Oviedo**, US$3.50. From Asunción to **Saltos del Guairá**, US$10.25-12, 4 companies, several daily; to **Ciudad del Este**, US$11.

To Brazil Regular launches cross the lake to **Guaíra**, 20 mins. Also hourly bus service, 30 mins, US$1.75. Buses run north of the lake to **Mondo Novo**, where they connect with Brazilian services. **Brazilian consulate** is at Canindeyú 980, casi Pasaje Morán, T046-242305.

Villarrica and around *Colour map 6, C6.*

the region's cultural hub

Villarrica
Villarrica, 42 km south of Coronel Oviedo on Ruta 8, is delightfully set on a hill rich with orange trees. Founded in 1570 and moved seven times before settling in its current location in 1682, it is a very pleasant, friendly place, with a fine cathedral, built in traditional style with veranda, and various pleasant parks. The **Museo Municipal Maestro Fermín López** ① *closed weekends*, behind the church in a wonderfully restored building dating from the War of the Triple Alliance has a foreign coin collection; please contribute. Products of the region are tobacco, cotton, sugar, yerba mate, hides, meat and wine produced by German settlers. There is a large student population and the town is the cultural hub of the region. Its Carnaval Guaireño is one of the most spectacular events in the nation and attracts large crowds every year. For more information, see www.villarrica.gov.py, o www.villarricache ciudad.com. There is an ATM at gas station at northern end of town.

German colonies
There are several German colonies near Villarrica. Some 7 km north is an unsigned turn off to the east, then 20 km to tiny **Colonia Independencia**, which has some beautiful beaches on the river (popular in summer). German-speaking travellers can also visit the German cooperative farms (these are not Mennonite communities, but rather German settlements established in the early 20th century). A great mate and wine producing area and, at harvest time, there is a wine festival. They also have a good beer festival in October.

East from Coronel Oviedo
The paved Ruta 7 runs 195 km through farmed areas and woods and across the Caaguazú hills. From here it continues to the spectacular 500-m singlespan 'Friendship Bridge' across the Paraná (to Brazil) at Ciudad del Este.

Where to stay

Villarrica

There are more hotels than can be listed here.
Book rooms in advance during fiestas.

$$$ Villarrica Palace Hotel
Ruta 8 Blas Garay, turn right on road entering
Villarrica, T0541-42832.
Large modern hotel, restaurant, parking,
pool, sauna.

$$ Musa
Gral Díaz y Curupayty, T0541-44007,
www.musa-hotel.com.
Modern hotel, rooms with bath, a/c and
Wi-Fi, restaurant.

$$ Ybytyruzú
C A López y Dr Bottrell, T0541-42390,
www.hotelybytyruzu.com.py.
Best in town, 3 types of room, breakfast, more
with a/c, restaurant.

Colonia Independencia

$$ Hotel Tilinski
Out of town, T0548-265240, www.hotel-tilinski.com.
Peaceful, German spoken, camping, swimming
pool (filled with river water), camping, meals
for residents.

Restaurants

Villarrica

Many eating places on CA López and
General Díaz. At night on the plaza with the
Municipalidad stands sell tasty, cheap steaks.

Transport

Villarrica

Bus To **Coronel Oviedo**, US$2.50. To **Asunción**,
frequent, US$3.75-5, 3½ hrs (La Guaireña). Also
direct service to **Ciudad del Este**, see below.

Colonia Independencia

Bus Direct to **Asunción**, 3 daily (US$5, 4 hrs),
as well as to **Villarrica**.

Ciudad del Este and around *Colour map 7, C1.*

duty-free shopping and an enormous dam

Ciudad del Este

Originally founded as Ciudad Presidente Stroessner in 1957 and 327 km from Asunción at the eastern terminus of Ruta 7, this was the fastest growing city in the country until the completion of the Itaipú hydroelectric project, for which it is the centre of operations. Ciudad del Este, the country's second-largest city, has been described as the biggest shopping centre in Latin America, attracting Brazilian and Argentine visitors who find bargain prices for electrical goods, watches and perfumes. However, it is a counterfeiter's paradise and can be quite dangerous; always take care when walking around, even in the centre, and take advice on which parts are to be avoided. Check everything properly before making a purchase and ensure that shops pack what you actually bought. The main shopping street is Avenida San Blas, lined with shopping malls and market stalls, selling a huge variety of goods. Almost any vehicle advertised for sale, should you be tempted, was stolen in Brazil or Bolivia. Many jewels and stones are also counterfeit; be especially careful with touts advertising amethysts or emeralds. Watch the exchange rates if you're a short-term visitor. Parts of the city are dirty and frantic during business hours, but away from the Avenidas San Blas and Adrián Jara the pace of life is more relaxed and the streets and parks are green and quiet. **Tourist office** ① *Adrián Jara y Mcal Estigarribia, by the urban bus terminal, T061-508810, open 0700-1900, helpful.*

Salto del Monday

The '**Monday Falls**' ① *0730-1800, US$1.20, taxi US$25 return*, where the Río Monday drops into the Paraná gorge near the town of Presidente Franco, are worth seeing. They were proclaimed a protected area by the government in 2012. Camping and meals available. North of the city is the popular beach resort and biological refuge called **Tatí Yupí** ① *open 0830-1630, www.itaipu.gov.py/ es/turismo/refugio-tati-yupi.*

Border with Brazil

The border crossing over the Friendship Bridge to Foz do Iguaçu is very informal, but is jammed with vehicles and pedestrians all day long. No passport stamps are required to visit Ciudad del Este for the day if coming from Brazil. Motorcycle taxis (with yellow helmets; helmet provided, hang on tight) are a good option if you have no luggage, US$4.75 from Paraguayan immigration to central Foz. There are lots of minibuses, too, and taxis (see Transport, below). On international buses, eg from Florianópolis to Ciudad del Este and Asunción, or from Foz to Asunción, the procedure is: non-Brazilians get out at immigration for an exit stamp, then take the bus across the bridge to Paraguayan immigration where everyone gets out for an entry stamp. On buses from Asunción to Foz and beyond, non-Paraguayans get out at Paraguayan immigration for an exit stamp, then the bus takes all passengers across the river to Brazilian immigration for the entry stamp. Make sure you get all entry and exit stamps.

If going to Foz for the day, note that buses marked 'Foz do Iguaçu' do not – in spite of both the law and what you may be told – always stop at Paraguayan immigration before crossing into Brazil. This is unlikely to cause problems with Brazilian authorities, but make absolutely certain to pick up a Paraguayan exit stamp and a Brazilian entry stamp to re-enter Paraguay later. On return to Paraguay you do not need a Brazilian exit stamp or Paraguayan entry stamp because your original entry stamp covers you till you finally leave the country. Without the stamps you may have some explaining to do upon returning to Ciudad del Este, but the problem is common. You shouldn't face difficulties as long as your paperwork is in order. For local bus services, see Transport, below.

Although Ciudad del Este is a tax-free shopping destination for Brazilians, the same is not true in reverse. Technically there is a Paraguayan import tax of up to 60% on anything purchased in Brazil costing more than US$300. This applies to Paraguayan citizens only (and even then is not usually enforced), but keep all receipts for any items purchased in Brazil and make sure the price is denominated in reais. There are local banks (open Monday-Friday 0730-1100) in town and many *casas de cambio* on Adrián Jara y Curupayty.

There are friendly tourist offices in the customs buildings on both sides of the road on the Paraguayan side, open 24 hours. You can get out of the bus here, rather than going to the bus terminal. Taxis wait just beyond immigration, US$4.50-5.50 to most places in Ciudad del Este, but settle price before getting in as there are reports of exorbitant fares. Remember to adjust your watch to local time (Brazil is one hour ahead, as is Argentina except during Paraguayan summer time – October-April). Although Paraguay observes daylight saving throughout the country, only some states in Brazil (including Paraná) do so (see Brazil chapter for details). **Brazilian consulate** ① *Ciudad del Este, Pampliega 205 y Pa'í Pérez, T061-500984, http:// deleste.itamaraty.gov.br, Mon-Fri 0800-1230 (and*

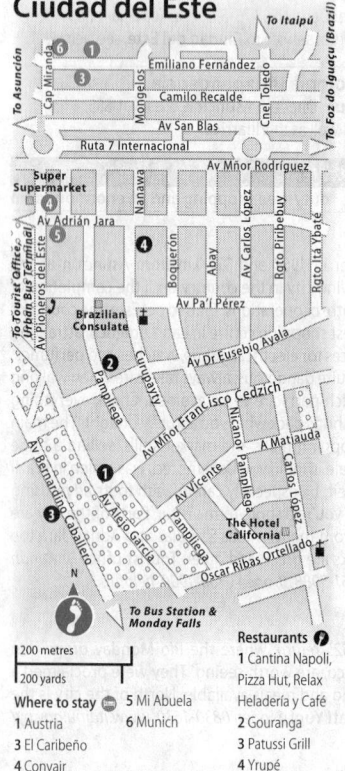

Ciudad del Este

To Itaipú
To Asunción
To Foz do Iguaçu (Brazil)

Cap Miranda
Emiliano Fernández
Mongelos
Camilo Recalde
Cnel Toledo
Av San Blas
Ruta 7 Internacional
Av Mñor Rodríguez

Super Supermaket
Nanawa
To Tourist Office/ Urban Bus Terminal/ Av Pioneros del Este
Av Adrián Jara
Boquerón
Abay
Av Carlos López
Av Carlos López
Rgto Piribebuy
Rgto Itá Ybaté

Brazilian Consulate
Av Pa'í Pérez

Curupayty
Pampliega
Av Dr Eusebio Ayala

Av Bernardino Caballero
Av Mñor Francisco Cedzich
Nicolás Fernández
Pampliega
A Matjauda
Carlos López

Av Julio García
Av Vicente
The Hotel California
Oscar Ribas Ortellado

To Bus Station & Monday Falls

N

200 metres
200 yards

Where to stay
1 Austria
3 El Caribeño
4 Convair
5 Mi Abuela
6 Munich

Restaurants
1 Cantina Napoli, Pizza Hut, Relax Heladería y Café
2 Gouranga
3 Patussi Grill
4 Yrupé

400-1600 to collect documents only), issues visas. **Argentine consulate** ① *Av Boquerón y Adrián Jara, dif China p 7, T061-500945, www.embajada-argentina.org.py/V2/consulados/consulado-gral-en-cde, Mon-Fri 0800-1300.*

★Itaipú and around

061-599 8040, www.itaipu.gov.py, daily 0800-1800. Take passport. Buses going to Hernandarias will drop you at the Centro de Recepción de Visitas.

The Itaipú project, a huge hydroelectric scheme covering an area of 1350 sq km and still subject to controversy among environmental groups, is close to Ciudad del Este (peaceful protests continue on an almost daily basis in Ciudad del Este as well as near the plant itself). It is currently the world's largest generator of renewable clean energy and well worth a visit. Tours of the plant offer panoramic views of the power plant featuring dam and spillway, run for 90 minutes and start hourly between 0800-1630, US$6.75. Tours of the exterior and internal workings of the plant run eight times a day and last 2½ hours, US$17. There is an interesting biological sanctuary, **Bella Vista**, that has successfully re-settled flora and fauna dislodged during the construction of the dam and offers 2½-hour guided tours Tuesday-Sunday 0830, 1000, 1430, 1530, US$5. There is a light show every Friday and Saturday, 2000 (2100 in summer), US$4, book in advance (phone as above, or call Brazilian side, +55-45-3529 2892, www.turismoitaipu.com.br).

On the way to Itaipú is **Zoológico Regional y Vivero Forestal** ① *on the Supercarretera Itaipú, 1.5 km from Ciudad del Este, T061-599 8632, www.itaipu.gov.py, guided visits on the hour Tue-Sat 0800-130, 1430-1700, free,* a zoo and nursery containing native animals and plants. The nursery has more than 500 species and annually plants some 200,000 ornamental, forest and fruit trees. Nearby is the **Museo de la Tierra Guaraní** ① *T061-599 8632, www.itaipu.gov.py/en/tourism/museum-guarani-and, Tue-Sun 0800-1700,* which offers a view of the science and culture of the Guaraníes via natural history displays and interactive screens.

Hernandarias, just north of Ciudad del Este, grew rapidly with the building of Itaipú. The supercarretera Itaipú runs north to Cruce Carolina Andrea, where it meets Ruta 10 for Saltos de Guaíra (see page 1219). This road gives access to two biological reserves on the Itaipú lake, **Itabó** (80 km) and, a further 80 km north, **Limoy**, www.itaipu.gov.py/es/medio-ambiente/reservas-y-refugios.

Listings Ciudad del Este and around *map page 1222.*

Where to stay

Ciudad del Este

$$$-$$ Convair
Adrián Jara y Pioneros del Este, T061-508555, www.hotelconvair.com.
In shopping district, comfortable, restaurant good, pasta festival on Thu, pool.

$$ Austria
R Fernández 165, T061-504213, www.hotelaustriarestaurante.com.
Above good restaurant, good breakfast, Austrian family, good views from upper floors, popular with shopping trips and groups. Warmly recommended.

$$ El Caribeño
Fernández 136, T061-512460, http://hotelcaribeno.com.py.
On 3 floors around central car parking area, plain rooms but spotless, helpful. Recommended.

$$ Mi Abuela
Adrián Jara y Pioneros del Este, T061-500333, http://miabuelahotel.com.
Small, off a central patio, restaurant, opposite **Convair**.

$$ Munich
Fernández 71 y Miranda, T061-500347, hotelmunich@hotmail.com.
A/c, frigobar, parking. Recommended.

Restaurants

Ciudad del Este

At the junction of Monseñor Francisco Cedzchiz y Av Alejo García, is **$$ Cantina Napoli**, pizzas and pastas. Also **Pizza Hut**, **Relax Heladería y Café**, T061-501671. Mon-Fri 1600-2400, Sat 1630-0100 (closed Sun) and **Librería El Foro**.

\$\$ Patussi Grill
*Av Bernardino Caballero y Yatayty Corá,
T061-502293, www.patussigrill.com.
Tue-Sun 1100-1500, Wed-Sat 1830-2330.*
Good churrasquería with a range of desserts, Wi-Fi.

\$ Gouranga
Pampliega y Eusebio Ayala, T061-510362.
Vegetarian restaurant with a menu that changes
daily, also juices, desserts, sandwiches, burgers, etc.

\$ Yrupé
*Curupayty y A Jara (part of Executive Hotel,
T061-512215, www.executivehotel.com.py/
restaurant.html), T061-509946.*
Good buffet lunch for US\$5.50 including
ice cream. Also desserts, coffee and Wi-Fi.

Supermarkets
Area Iris (A Jara y Av Pioneros del Este. Open
0700-1930, Sun 0800-1300). Serves good value
meals. **Shopping del Este** (by Puente de Amistad),
has several restaurants. Another good collection
of restaurants is at **Centro Gastronómico Epoca**
(on Rogelio Benítez), some distance southeast of
centre, near Lago de la República. Other shopping
centres, eg **Corazón**, have a Patio de Comidas.

What to do
Tour operators
Exchange Tour, *Edif Saba, Av Nanawa, pb Of 5,
T061-500766, http://exchangetour.webnode.es.*
Tours, transfers, car hire. Also at C Palma entre
14 de Mayo y 14 de Agosto, Galería Palma,
Loc 20, Asunción, T021-496469.

Transport
Ciudad del Este
Air International airport, Aeropuerto Guaraní,
T064-420844. To **Asunción**, **TAM** daily en route
from **São Paulo**. TAM, Av Nanawa 156, Ed SABA,
loc 10 pb, T061-506030-53.

Bus Terminal is south of the centre, T061-
510421 (No 4 bus from centre, US\$0.70, taxi
US\$5, recommended). Many buses to and from
Asunción, US\$13-16 rápido, 4½ hrs, at night
only; US\$6.75-8.50 común, 5 hrs minimum.
Nuestra Señora recommended (they also
have an office in Shopping Mirage, Pampliega
y Adrián Jara), **Rysa** (T061-510396) and others.
To **Villarrica**, many daily with **La Guaireña** and
La Carapagueña, US\$7, 4 hrs. To **Pedro Juan
Caballero**, 7 hrs, overnight US\$15, **García** and
others. To **Concepción**, **García**, 11 hrs, 2 per day.
To **Encarnación** (for Posadas and Argentina),

paved road, frequent, 4-5 hrs, US\$11 (this is
cheaper than via Foz do Iguaçu). There are
international services to **Argentina** and **Brazil**.

Border with Brazil and Argentina
To Brazil 4 bus companies cross the international
bridge between Ciudad del Este and Foz's bus
terminals, daily 0700-1830 each way every
10 mins, 30-40 mins, US\$2; speak to the driver
about waiting at the immigration posts at either
end of the bridge. Most buses will not wait at
immigration, so disembark to get your exit stamp,
walk across the bridge (15 mins) and obtain your
entry stamp; keep your ticket and continue to Foz
on the next bus free. Paraguayan taxis cross freely
to Brazil (US\$6.50-9.50 to central Foz depending
on destination, demand and time of day), or walk
across the bridge and then take a taxi. You can pay
in either currency (and often in Argentine pesos).
Obtain all necessary exit and entry stamps.

To Argentina Direct buses to **Puerto Iguazú**,
leave frequently from the end platform at the
terminal, US\$2.20 in guaraníes or pesos. The bus
leaves every 30-45 mins and crawls through
Ciudad del Este picking up passengers. It will let
you out at Paraguayan immigration if you need a
stamp, but will not wait. Catch the next bus outside
immigration – do NOT cross the bridge – and
use the same ticket. The bus then drives straight
through Brazil to Argentine immigration where
it waits for all passengers to get entry stamps.
2 companies, RISA and Río Uruguay, tickets not
interchangeable. The route ends at the bus terminal
in Puerto Iguazú. If overnighting in Puerto Iguazú
or continuing into Argentina, you need to get
Argentine and Paraguayan stamps (not Brazilian).
Also check what stamps you need, if any, if making
a day visit to Puerto Iguazú. It can take up to 2 hrs to
get from Ciudad del Este terminal to Puerto Iguazú
terminal; you cannot be in a hurry on this route.

Ferry to Argentina The Intercom/Balsa Iguazú
boat leaves from Presidente Franco, south of
Ciudad del Este, more or less hourly 0630-1700,
T061-554129. Take a Tres Fronteras bus from in front
of Arcoiris supermarket at the junction of Pioneros
del Este and Ruta Internacional. You can also catch
it at ER Fernández y Toledo, 2 blocks behind Casa
China, US\$0.50. Ask to be let out at the ferry. Fare
for a vehicle is US\$7.55, motorbike US\$3.75, foot
passengers US\$2.20. Immigration is open till 1700.

Itaipu
Bus Frequent services from **Ciudad del Este** to
Hernandarias, US\$1.

Región Oriental:
South of Asunción

Ruta 1 runs south from Asunción to Encarnación and the Argentine border. This is an attractive area of fertile landscapes, sleepy towns and the historically important Jesuits settlements, the ruins of some of which have been restored and now have interpretive and even multimedia exhibits.

Itá

Itá (Km 37 on Ruta 1), Paraguay's second-oldest town, settled as a Franciscan mission in 1539, is famous for rustic pottery, but also sells wood, leather and textile items including hammocks and exquisite cloth dolls. There is a **Centro de Artesanía** in the centre. At the town's entrance you can visit the workshop of **Rosa Brítez** (www.portalguarani.com/724_rosa_britez.html), a local ceramics artist and Paraguay's most famous artisan, recognized by UNESCO. Its Franciscan church, San Blas, also in the centre, was built in 1698 and has an interesting museum (free) featuring traditional crafts.

Yaguarón

Also founded in 1539, Yaguarón (Km 48) was a key centre of the Franciscan missions in colonial times. At the centre of the town, marooned on an island of green, mown grass, stands the church of **San Buenaventura** ① *daily 0700-1100, 1330-1630, on Sun morning only*, with its external bell-tower. The simplicity and symmetry of the exterior is matched by the ornate carvings and paintings of the interior. The tints, made by the *indígenas* from local plants, are still bright on the woodcarvings and the angels have Guaraní faces. Built in Hispano-Guaraní baroque style by the Franciscans between 1640 and 1775, it was reconstructed in 1885 and renovated in the late 20th century. Stations of the Cross behind the village lead to a good view of the surroundings.

Museo Dr José Gaspar Rodríguez de Francia ① *leaving the church, 500 m down the road to your left at Pirayú 325, T0533-177797, Tue-Sun 0930-1430, free guided tour in Spanish*, has artefacts from the life of Paraguay's first dictator, 'El Supremo', plus paintings and artefacts from the 18th century. The 18th-century single-storey adobe building with bamboo ceilings and tiled roof belonged to Francia's father. The fiesta patronal, San Buenaventura, is in mid-July. At the festivals for San Roque (16 August, first Sunday in September) music is provided by the Banda Peteke Peteke, a unique group that plays the mimby flute, the gualambáu (a musical bow) and two small drums.

Paraguarí and around   *Colour map 6, C6.*

the Jesuit missions are a highlight

Paraguarí

Founded 1775 and located at Km 63 along Ruta 1, this is the north entrance to the mission area, at the foot of a range of hills. Its restored church has two bell towers, separate from the main structure. Buses between Asunción and Encarnación stop here.

A kilometre from the centre is an interesting military museum, the **Museo Histórico de la Artillería** ① *www.portalguarani.com/detalles_museos_exposiciones.php?id=4&id_exposicion=59; free, but prior permission to visit is required*, inside the nearby military base with cannons and artefacts from the Chaco War. Its chapel holds a remarkable statue of Santa Bárbara, which is brought out on her feast day (4 December). You can stroll to the top of **Cerro Perõ** for views from the cross on top. More challenging is a one-hour climb through dense forest to the summit of

Best for
Arts and crafts ▪ Religious buildings ▪ Wildlife

Cerro Jhu, ask for directions in Barrio San Miguel behind the abandoned train station. Paraguarí is seen as Paraguay's capital of bullfighting.

Chololó and Sapucai

Northeast from Paraguarí 15 km is **Chololó** ① *bus US$1*, with a small but attractive series of waterfalls and rapids with bathing facilities and walkways, mainly visited in the summer.

    Sapucai, 25 km east of Paraguarí, is the location of the **workshops** ① *Mon-Fri, take a bus from Asunción at 0700, 1200, 88 km, 3 hrs, being restored*, where you can see – when the road is opened again after the floods of 2015 – old and abandoned wood-burning steam locomotives. There is also a small museum attached, T0539-263218 (currently closed – 2017). Close by is Paraguay's first viaduct, constructed by English engineers in 1897. The neighbourhood in which they lived is still known as Villa Inglesa and has several original houses constructed in late Victorian style. There are also some *hospedajes* ($).

Parque Nacional Ybycuí

Open 0800-1700, www.salvemoslos.com.py/pny.htm. For camping get a permit from the Secretaría del Ambiente (SEAM), Madame Lynch 3500, in Asunción, www.seam.gov.py (see also National parks, page 1216).

At **Carapeguá**, Km 84 on Ruta 1 (*hospedaje* on main street, basic, friendly; blankets and hammocks to rent along the main road, or buy your own, made locally and cheaper than elsewhere), a road turns off to Acahay, Ybycuí and the Parque Nacional Ybycuí, 67 km southeast. This is one of the most accessible national parks, if you have a car, and is one of the few remaining stands of Atlantic forest in eastern Paraguay. It contains 5000 ha of virgin forest and was founded in 1973. At the entrance is a museum, plus the reconstructed remains of the country's first iron foundry. Crowded on Sunday; guides available.

    Ruta 1 continues through **Villa Florida**, 162 km from Asunción, on the banks of the Río Tebicuary. It's a popular spot in January-February for its sandy beaches and the fishing is first-rate. The **Hotel Nacional de Villa Florida** ($$, T083-240207) and the **Touring y Automóvil Club's Hotel-Parador Villa Florida** (Km 156, T083-240205, www.tacpy.com.py) would make a convenient places to stop when travelling on this route.

★The Jesuit missions

In 1578 Jesuit missionaries came to what is now the border region of Brazil, Argentina and Paraguay to convert the Guaraníes to Christianity. The first mission in Paraguay was established in 1610 at San Ignacio Guazú. Together these two groups developed a pioneering economic and social system that emphasized collaboration and, to some extent, integration between the two societies. In 1767, by decree of Charles III of Spain, the Jesuits were expelled and local wealthy landowners took the Guaraníes as slave workers. More than thirty missions, or *reducciones*, were built. Eight of these remain in Paraguay and three have been inscribed as UNESCO World Heritage Sites. Numerous Asunción-based tour operators offer tours of these missions. For local tours, **Emitur** ① *T0782-20286, emitur.misiones@gmail.com*, offers area tours and visits to local ranches. Also see **Cámara Paraguaya de Turismo de las Misiones Jesuíticas** ① *Mcal Estigarribia 1031 y Curupayty, Encarnación T071-205021, rutajesuiticapy@hotmail.com*, for information.

Listings Paraguarí and around

Where to stay

Parque Nacional Ybycuí

$$$ Estancia Santa Clara
Km 141, Ruta 1, Caapucú, T021-605729, www.estanciasantaclara.com.py.
Tourism farm offering rural activites in a beautiful setting between Paraguarí and San Ignacio Guazú, full board or visit for the day (mini-zoo). Reserve in advance.

$$ Hotel Pytu'u Renda
Av General Caballero 509 y Quyquyho, Ybycuí, T0534-226364.
Good food, cooking facilities.

Restaurants

La Frutería
Ruta 1, Km 61, T0531-432406, about 2.5 km before Paraguarí.
Wide selection of fruit, outdoor seating and a restaurant serving *empanadas*, hamburgers, beer, fruit salad. Highly recommended.

Transport

Yaguarón
Bus Every 15 mins from **Asunción**, US$0.75.

Paraguarí and around
Bus City buses leave from Asunción terminal every 15 mins throughout the day, but much faster to take an Encarnación-bound bus, same fare US$1.

Parque Nacional Ybycuí
Bus There are 2 per day, 1000 and 1600 from **Ybycuí**, US$1.25, take bus going to the Mbocaya Pucú colony that stops in front of the park entrance. From Asunción take a bus to Acahay, **Transportes Emilio Cabrera**, 8 daily and change, or bus to Ybycuí, 0630, US$2.75.

San Ignacio Guazú and around

an area for fishing and mission art

San Ignacio Guazú

At Km 226 at the intersection of Rutas 1 and 4, this is a delightful town on the site of a former Jesuit *reducción* (*guazú* means big in Guaraní). Several typical Hispano-Guaraní buildings survive. Each Sunday night at 2000 a folklore festival is held in the central plaza, free, very local.

Museo de San Ignacio Guazú ① *T0782-232223, www.portalguarani.com, click on 'Museos y Centros Culturales' then 'Museos del Paraguay' and then scroll down, daily 0800-1130, 1400-1730, US$1,* housed in the former Jesuit art workshop, reputedly the oldest surviving civil building in Paraguay, contains a major collection of Guaraní art and sculpture from the missionary period. The attendant is very knowledgeable, but photos are not allowed.

Nearby is the **Museo Histórico Sembranza de Héroes** ① *T975-631352, Mon-Fri 0700-1200, 1300-1700, free,* with displays on the Chaco War.

Santa María de Fe

Santa María de Fe is 12 km northeast along a cobbled road. The **Museo Jesuítico** ① *T0781-283332, Tue-Sun 0830-1130, 1300-1700, US$1 (photos allowed),* in restored mission buildings contains 60 Guaraní sculptures among the exhibits. It is considered one of the country's finest museums for mission art. The modern church has a lovely altarpiece of the Virgin and Child (the key is kept at a house on the opposite side of the plaza). There is also the Santa María Cooperative and Educational Fund, begun by English journalist Margaret Hebblethwaite, which sponsors education and craftwork (notably appliqué) and organizes local activities for visitors. Santa María de Fe was between 1960-1976 the home of the radically utopian Ligas Agrarias Cristianas (Christian Agrarian League) until forcibly suppressed by Stroessner. There is a hotel on the plaza, see below.

Santa Rosa

At Santa Rosa (Km 248), founded 1698, only the Nuestra Señora de Loreto chapel of the original Jesuit church survived a fire. The current building dates from 1884. The chapel houses the **Museo Jesuítico de Santa Rosa** ① *T0858-285221, by appointment only, 0730-1130, 1430-1600 (ask at parroquia), free,* on the walls are frescoes in poor condition; exhibits include a sculpture of the Annunciation considered to be one of the great works of the Hispanic American Baroque. Daily buses from San Ignacio Guazú.

Southwest to Pilar

Ruta 4 (paved) from San Ignacio (see above) goes southwest to Pilar, on the banks of the Río Paraguay. Capital of Ñeembucú district, the town is known for its fishing (one of the largest fishing festivals in South America is held here during Holy Week), river beaches, manufacturing and historical Cabildo (now a museum). This area saw many bloody battles during the War of the Triple Alliance and you can visit **Humaitá**, with the Basílica de Nuestra Señora de Pilar, the old church of San Carlos, **Paso de Patria**, **Curupayty** and other historic battle sites. In early January the town's

Fiesta Hawaiana attracts tens of thousands of visitors. Pilar is unique in the country for having a successful youth tourism initiative. There are hotels in the $$-$ range and many restaurants serving fish (Las Cabañas has been recommended).

Ayolas, Santiago and San Cosme

At Km 262 on Ruta 1 a road leads to the former *reducción* at Santiago and the town of **Ayolas** founded 1840, although not by Jesuits, standing on the banks of the Aña Cuá river.

Santiago is an important former Jesuit centre (founded 1651) with a modern church containing a fine wooden carving of Santiago slaying the Saracens. More wooden statuary in the **Museo Tesoros Jesuíticos** ① T975-762008, Mon-Sat 0800-1100, 1400-1700, Sun 0900-1100, free (guided tour US$2.15), next door (ask around the village for the key-holder). There is an annual **Fiesta de la Tradición Misionera**, in January or February, with music, dance, horsemanship and other events.

Beyond is **Ayolas**, the area has been influenced by the construction of the Yacyreta dam and is good for fishing. There is the Museo Regional Yacyretá and, 12 km from Ayolas, the **Refugio Faunístico de Atinguy** ① free, Mon-Sat 0830-1130, 1330-1630, Sun and holidays 0830-1130, run as a research and educational facility by the **Entidad Binacional Yacyretá** (**EBY**) to study the fauna affected by the dam. EBY also has a reserve on the **island of Yacyretá** ① for visits to the project, T072-222141, or T021-445055, www.eby.gov.py.

Cross the river to Ituzaingó, Argentina (linked via road to Corrientes and Posadas). Follow the new paved road from Ayolas to the **San Cosme y Damián** former *reducción* or leave Ruta 1 at Km 333. This is the only ex-Jesuit mission in the country still used for religious services. When the Jesuits were expelled from Spanish colonies in 1767, the **church and ancillary buildings** ① 0700-1130, 1300-1700 US$5 (T0985-732956 for tickets), also valid for Trinidad and Jesús, see below, were unfinished. A huge project has followed the original plans. Some of the *casas de indios* are in private use for other purposes, such as the cultural centre and parts of the **Centro de Interpretación Astronómica Buenaventura Suárez** ① daily 0700-2000. For the tourist committee T0985-110047; guide Rolando Barboza T0985-732956.

Where to stay

$$ Hotel Rural San Ignacio Country Club
*Ruta 1, Km 230, T975-606631, gusjhave@
.com (Facebook: H.R.SIGNA).*
With full board and Wi-Fi in cabins. Also has shaded camping, US$6 pp, without tent or meals, but other services included, hot water, electricity, tennis, swimming pool, ping pong, pool, impressive place and very helpful owner.

$$ Parador Altamirano
Ruta 1, Km 224, T0782-232334.
Modern, on outskirts, with a/c ($ pp without), recommended, 24-hr restaurant.

$$ Santa María Hotel
Santa María de Fe, T0781-283311/981-861553, www.santamariahotel.org.
With breakfast, other meals extra, with a/c, internet, library. Activities offered include day tours of Santa María and 2-week tours to other Jesuit towns and the region.

$$-$ La Casa de Loly
Mcal López 1595, San Ignacio, T0782-232362, http://lacasadeloli.com.py, on outskirts.

Nice atmosphere, *cabañas* and rooms, pool, a/c, with breakfast, other meals on request.

Ayolas, Santiago and San Cosme

$$ Hotel Nacional de Turismo Ayolas
Av Costanera, Villa Permanente, T072-222273, www.hotelenayolas.com.
Overlooking the river, popular with fishing groups.

Transport

Bus Regular services to/from **Asunción**, US$4.50 *común*, up to 4½ hrs; to **Encarnación**, frequent, US$6 *común*.

Santa María

Bus From **San Ignacio** from the Esso station, 6 a day from 0500, 45 mins.

San Cosme y Damián

Bus From **Encarnación**, La Cosmeña and Perla del Sur, US$3.55, 2½ hrs, 0900 (Perla del Sur 0930 on Sun), return 1100, 1400 or 1600. Also **El Tigre** (T071-203973) at 1800. Bus goes via **Carmen del Paraná**.

Encarnación *Colour map 6, C6.*

A bridge connects this busy port (founded 1614, known as La Perla del Sur) with the Argentine town of Posadas across the Alto Paraná. The old town was flooded when the Yacyretá-Apipé dam was completed and what is not under water has been restored and a modern town has been built higher up with a pronounced emphasis on tourism and shopping. The town's pre-Lenten Carnival is the best known in the country. On the newly constructed Avenida Costanera is a **Sambódromo**, with a **Carnaval museum**. Of three popular man-made beaches, **San José** is in the town with a lovely view across the water at sunset and at night to the lights of Posadas (T985-842145, www.navegantes. com.py, for sailing, kayaks and boat trips, pedal kart hire US$5.30-19.50 per hour, beach seats US$0.35). The **Museo Casa de La Victoria** ① *Artigas esq Cerro Corá, Mon-Fri 0700-1120, 1400-1630, Sat 0700-1200, free,* is dedicated to the Guerra del Chaco with Bolivia. Encarnación is a good base for visiting nearby Jesuit missions. There are tourist offices on the **Costanera** ① *Av Costanera, Padre Bolik y RN1,*

Encarnación

Where to stay 🛏
1 Apart-Hotel Del Río
2 Casa de la Y
3 Cristal
4 De La Costa
5 De La Trinidad
6 Germano
7 Milord Boutique
8 Paraná
9 Viena

Restaurants 🍴
1 América Grill
2 Brasiliani Grill & Pasta
3 Heladería Mako
4 Hiroshima
5 Las Delicias
6 Paseo Gastronómico
7 Piccolo Italia
8 River Express 24 Horas

T071-202989, www.encarnacion.com.py, daily 0700-1900, in the building by Paraguayan immigration near the San Roque bridge① *same hours, but till 2200 Thu-Fri*, and at Trinidad, see below.

Border with Argentina

The San Roque road bridge connects Encarnación with **Posadas**. Formalities are conducted at respective ends of the bridge. Argentine side has different offices for locals and foreigners; Paraguay has one for both. The border is open 24 hours a day. **Argentine Vice Consulate** ① *is at Artigas 960, T071-201066, cenca@mrecic.gov.ar, Mon-Fri 0800-1300*. **Brazilian Vice Consulate** ① *Memmel 452, T071-206335 (see Facebook)*. There are moneychangers at the Paraguayan side of the bridge but it's best to change money in town: BBVA ① *25 de Mayo y Mcal Estigarribia*, **Banco Itapúa**① *14 de Mayo esq CA López*, **Banco Itaú**① *TR Pereira y CA López*. *Casas de cambio* for cash are on Mcal Estagarribia, eg **Cambios Chaco** (www.cambioschaco.com.py, Monday-Friday 0745-1715, Saturday 0800-1330) and **Cambios Visión** (Monday-Friday 0800-1645), just off the Plaza de Armas. **Note** Paraguay is one hour behind Argentina (except October-April).

☆Santísima Trinidad del Paraná

Northeast from Encarnación along Ruta 6 towards Ciudad del Este are the two best-preserved Jesuit former *reducciones*. These are both recognized as UNESCO World Cultural Heritage Sites. The hilltop site of **Trinidad** ① *US$4.50, joint ticket with Jesús and San Cosme y Damián, T0985-810053 (parroquia), Oct-May 0700-1900, Apr-Sep 0700-1730, light and sound show Thu-Sun 2000, summer, 1900, winter*, built 1706-1760, has undergone significant restoration. Note the partially restored church, the carved stone pulpit, the font and other masonry and relief sculpture. Also partially rebuilt is the bell-tower near the original church. You can also see another church, a college; workshops and indigenous living quarters. It was founded in 1706 by Padre Juan de Anaya; the architect was Juan Bautista Prímoli. For information or tours (in Spanish and German), ask at the visitor centre ① *T0985-753997, www.turismojesusytrinidad.com.py*, which is 500 m from the highway; a big sign to the ruins on the highway is 5 km beyond the Trinidad toll post. There are *artesanías* stalls nearby and craft demonstrations in the afternoon. One kilometre from Trinidad is **Parque Ecológico Ita Cajón** ① *T0985-726971, US$3.55*, an enormous clearing where the stone was quarried for the former *reducción*. Frequent folklore events are held here. The municipal office of Trinidad (T071-270165, Monday-Friday 0700-1300) in the centre of town also has information and a brochure. There is another tourist office on the highway, opposite the Hotel Parador Turístico Luján.

Northwest of Trinidad, 11.6 km along a paved road (which turns off 200 m north from Trinidad entrance) is **Jesús de Tavarangüé**, now a small town where another group of Jesuits settled in 1763. In the less than four years before they were expelled they embarked on a huge construction programme that included the church, sacristy, *residencia* and baptistry, on one side of which is a **square tower**① *phone and website as above, Oct-May 0700-1900, Apr-Sep 0700-1730*. There is a fine front façade with three great arched portals in a Moorish style. This leads into the huge church, with its 12-m-high walls intact and open to the sky. The church was unfinished at the time of the expulsion; the ruins have been restored. There are beautiful views from the main tower, which can only be climbed with a guide who has the key. At the entrance is a small museum. The municipal office of Jesús (T071-270150, Monday-Friday 0700-1300) in the centre of town also has information.

Colonies on the road to Ciudad del Este

From Trinidad the road goes through or near a number of German colonies, called the Colonias Unidas, including **Hohenau** (Km 36) and **Parque Manantial**① *Km 35, 500 m from main road, T0775-232250, Facebook: parque manantial, open 0900-2000*. The park is in a beautiful location and has three pools, a good restaurant, bar, lovely camping ground and complete facilities, horse riding, tour of the countryside by jeep and cross country tours to the nearby Jesuit ruins.

The next colony is **Obligado**, 35 km from Encarnación; (ATM in the centre of town). About 5 km further north is **Bella Vista** (Km 42, also has ATM), the yerba mate capital of Paraguay, with a giant replica of a mate *guampa* and *bombilla* at the main junction. The plantations, **Pajarito** ① *T0767-240240, www.pajarito.com.py*, and **Selecta** ① *T0767-240247, www.selecta.com.py*, accept visitors. From the roundabout at the main junction, Avenida Marcial Samaniengo goes 8.5 km unpaved to the port where you can cross the Río Paraná to Corpus in Argentina by ferry (five minutes, takes a few cars and foot passengers, US$2.50), making a good circuit between the Paraguayan and Argentine Jesuit missions. There are immigration and customs facilities on either side; hours change frequently (in late 2016, Monday-Friday 0700-1100, 1300-1600); no money changing facilities.

Listings Encarnación and around *map page 1229.*

Where to stay

Encarnación
There are several hotels on Av Gaspar Rodríguez de Francia, within easy reach of the Costanera, eg **Milord Boutique** (Av G R de Francia y 25 de Mayo, T071-206235, Facebook: milordrestaurant).

$$$-$$ De La Costa
Av Rodríguez de Francia 1240 con Cerro Corá, T071-205694, www.delacostahotel.com.py.
Smart hotel near the Costanera, with pool, garden, parking and restaurant.

$$$ De La Trinidad
Mcal Estigarribia y Memmel,T071-208099, www.hoteldelatrinidad.com.py.
Tower-block hotel of a good standard, close to bus station, 6 categories of room with all modern facilities, with spa, restaurant, pool, parking.

$$ Apart-Hotel Del Río
Wiessen y Artigas, T071-208288, delrioaparthotel@hotmail.com.
Spacious apartments with equipped kitchen and laundry area, comfortable beds, white tiled, cool, very helpful front desk, good value (out of season), convenient for centre and Costanera.

$$ Cristal
Mcal Estigarribia 1157 y Cerro Corá, T071-202371, www.hotelcristal.com.py.
City hotel with pool and restaurant, helpful staff.

$$ Paraná
Estigarribia 1414, T071-204440, hotelparanaenc@gmail.com, see Facebook.
Central, 2 standards of room, good breakfast, helpful reception. Recommended.

$$-$ Casa de la Y
Carmen de Lara Castro 422, entre Yegros y Molas, Barrio San Roque, T985-77 8198, http://casadelay.wix.com/casa-de-la-y.
Quiet location some way from most attractions (bus terminal transfer US$5), 1 double room (cheaper Sun-Thu), 1 dorm with bath (US$12 pp), garden, breakfast included, Wi-Fi, welcoming and attractive.

$$-$ Germano
General Cabañas y C A López, almost opposite bus terminal, T071-203346, www.hotelgermano.com.py.
Small, very accommodating, **$** without bath, TV or a/c, German and Japanese spoken, parking. Highly recommended.

$ Viena
PJ Caballero 568, T071-205981.
With breakfast, German-run, good food, garage, not always open.

Santísima Trinidad del Paraná and Jesús de Tavarangüé

$ Hotel Restaurant A Las Ruinas
At the ruins, T0985-828563.
Cheaper without breakfast, rooms have a/c, hot water, Wi-Fi; restaurant has daily menu for US$4.50.

$ Parador Turístico Dos Princesas
On a side street to left going towards ruins.
At a little shop, rooms cheaper without breakfast.

$ Posada María
150 m from ruins (turn right heading towards ruins), T0985-769812, posadamaria.trinidad@gmail.com.
Price per person, some rooms shared, with bath, breakfast, a/c, Wi-Fi, very friendly. Also have an *estancia* for guests, 5 km away, 2 well-equipped rooms, Wi-Fi, use of kitchen or full board, riding, trekking, vehicle trips in the region.

Colonies on the road to Ciudad del Este

$$$ Papillón
Ruta 6, Km 45, at south entrance to Bella Vista, T0767-240235, www.papillon.com.py.
A/c, pool, gardens, German, French, English, Flemish spoken, excellent restaurant, full and half-board available. Highly recommended. Organizes excursions in the area.

Restaurants

Encarnación
At the Wiessen end of Av Gaspar Rodríguez de Francia is the **Paseo Gastronómico**.

$$$-$$ Brasiliani Grill & Pasta
Ocampos y Ruta Internacional Roque González, by the road to Puente Internacional, T071-202181.
Brazilian buffet and pizzas in a popular restaurant.

$$ América Grill
Ruta Internacional y Av San Blas, T071-204829, www.americagrill.com.py. Closed Sun night.
Good *tenedor libre* with *parrilla*, fish, salad bar, cold meats, cheeses, desserts, all included for about US$10 pp. Drinks are not included. Live music Sat pm. Very good, very popular, especially on Sun (go early, like 1100). Recommended.

$$ Hiroshima
25 de Mayo y L Valentinas, T071-203505. Tue-Sun 1130-1400, 1900-2330.
Excellent Japanese, wide variety, fresh sushi.

$$-$ Piccolo Italia
Ruta 1 Av G de Francia near Av B Caballero, T071-202344. Opens lunchtime and from 1830.
Good food, home-made pastas, pizzas and other dishes, nice atmosphere, quite a walk along Av G de Francia, from beach end of Costanera.

$ Heladería Mako
Av Caballero 590 y Lomas Valentinas, T071-202116, www.makos.com.py. Open 0700-2400.
Clean and bright, *confitería*, ice creams, *empanadas*, sandwiches, burgers and more.

Las Delicias
Mallorquín 1028. Mon-Sat 0800-1200, 1500-1900.
Panadería and *confitería* for bread, cakes, cold drinks, lots of choice.

River Express 24 Horas
Mallorquín y Wiessen.
Self-service supermarket with tables on the street. Quite upmarket, but convenient.

Santísima Trinidad del Paraná and Jesús de Tavarangüé

$ La Misión Café
Next to the ticket office.
Smart, clean and new, meals, snacks, cakes, coffee, Wi-Fi, pricey, also sells souvenirs.

$ Parrilla Rincón Guaraní
At the car park outside the ruins.
Caters for groups, also has good-value lunch menu.

Transport

Bus City buses cost US$0.45, useful for getting to the commercial area, terminal and north of the centre. The bus terminal is at Mcal Estigarribia y Memmel (small, crowded and confusing), walking distance to centre, a bit further to the Costanera, but a long way from the new commercial area and international bridge. To/from **Asunción**, several companies including **La Encarnaceña** (recommended, T071-203448, www.laencarnacena.com.py), **Rysa** (T071-203311) at least 4 a day each, 6 hrs, US$15. Stopping (*común*) buses are much slower (6-7 hrs), US$10.50-11.50. To **Ciudad del Este**, US$11, several daily, 4 hrs. **La Encarnaceña** to Pilar at 1200, US$11. To Bella Vista, Itapúa Poty/Crucero del Sur, 8 a day, 1 hr, US$1.75, or take any stopping bus to Ciudad del Este. Many companies offer buses to Buenos Aires, US$45, and stops in between, and to Brazil.

Border with Argentina
Bus Take any 'Posadas/Argentina' bus over the bridge from opposite bus terminal, 0500-2200, to Posadas bus terminal, US$1.35 in guaraníes or pesos, 30 mins. Keep all luggage with you and retain bus ticket; buses do not wait. After formalities, use ticket on next bus.

Cycles are not allowed to use the bridge, but officials may give cyclists a lift. Pedestrians cannot walk across; take bus, taxi US$5.35-7, mototaxi US$3.50 (these 2 run 24 hrs), or train. This runs from 0600-1730, return from Posadas 0615-1715, 8 mins crossing, every 30 mins, US$1.25, must show passport. The entrance to station is through the market stalls on Juana de Lara at Padre Winkel in the new commercial zone. To get there take a **Circuito Comercial** bus on C A López at Plaza de Armas, or on Av B Caballero.

Santísima Trinidad del Paraná and Jesús de Tavarangüé
Bus Many go from **Encarnación** to Trinidad. They stop on the highway at the entrance to the town and to the ruins, which is a bit further along the road; take any bus from the terminal marked Hohenau or Ciudad del Este, US$1.50-1.75.

Bus direct **Encarnación–Jesús** 1800 with **Pastoreo** (this company goes every 30 mins to Trinidad, hourly on Sun, last back 1800) You can catch any Ciudad del Este to Encarnación bus from the highway back to Encarnación. Buses between the turn-off to Jesús and Jesús itself have an erratic schedule. From Trinidad ruins, walk to the highway and then 200 m to the service station at the Cruce. Ask here about the bus or taxi (US$11 return with wait at the site, can be shared). Staff at Jesús ruins will phone for a taxi for you, US$5.50 one way. There are no mototaxis, despite what they tell you in Encarnación bus terminal.

North of
Asunción

The winding Río Paraguay is 400 m wide and is still the main trade route for the products of northern Paraguay, in spite of a paved highway built to Concepción. With the start of the rainy season, most farms and rural communities lose their overland connection to the outside world. Boats carry cattle, hides, yerba mate, tobacco and timber.

Asunción to Concepción

Travelling north from Asunción by river (nowadays mostly done by *aquidaban*, a more upscale version of a cargo boat, usually with a few sleeping cabins), you first come across Puente Remanso in Mariano Roque Alonso, the bridge that marks the beginning of the Trans-Chaco Highway. Just further upstream is Villa Hayes, 31 km above Asunción, founded in 1786 but renamed in 1879 after the US president who arbitrated the territorial dispute with Argentina in Paraguay's favour. Further upstream at 198 km is Puerto Antequera and 100 km beyond that is Concepción. By road there are two routes: via the Trans-Chaco Highway (Ruta 9) and Pozo Colorado (146 km, five to seven hours) fully paved with spectacular views of birdlife. The other route, also paved, is Ruta 3 to Yby Yaú and then west along Ruta 5 (seven to nine hours).

At Santa Rosa del Aguaray, 108 km north of San Estanislao, there is petrol, *pensión* and restaurants. A paved road (Ruta 11) runs southwest for 27 km to **Nueva Germania** founded in 1866 by Bernhard Förster and Elisabeth Nietzsche (the philosopher's sister) to establish a pure Aryan colony (follow signs to **Hotel Germania**, $ with air-conditioning, very clean). From Nueva Alemania, this road goes on to San Pedro del Ycuamandiyú (48 km), and Puerto Antequera on the Río Paraguay (another 14 km). East of Santa Rosa, 23 km, is **$ Rancho Laguna Blanca** ① *T021-424760 or T0981-558671, www.lagunablanca.com.py, day visits US$3.50, camping US$5.25, dormitory US$17.50-13.75*, a nature reserve, family farm and rural tourism centre offering lots of activities including riding, trekking, kayaking and birdwatching (one of the few in this area open year-round). A further 23 km north of Santa Rosa, a dirt road runs northeast through jungle for 105 km to the interesting town of **Capitán Badó**, which forms the frontier with Brazil. About 50 km north of the turn off to Capitán Badó is Yby Yaú, see page 1234. From Capitán Badó a road follows the frontier north to Pedro Juan Caballero (another 119 km).

Concepción *Colour map 6, B6.*

Concepción, 422 km north of Asunción Via Ruta 9 and 5 (or 439 via Ruta 3), stands on the east bank of the Río Paraguay. It is known as La Perla del Norte for its climate and setting. Sunsets from the port are beautiful.

At Plaza La Libertad are the Catedral and Municipalidad. Main services are on Pdte Franco, such as post, telephone, internet, ATMs and exchange (eg **Norte Cambios** ① *Pdte Franco y 14 de Mayo, www. nortecambios.com.py, Mon-Fri 0830-1700, Sat 0830-1100, fair rates for US dollars and euros, cash only;* **Financiera Familiar** ① *Pdte Franco y General Garay, US$ cash only*). The town is the trade centre of the north, doing a considerable business with Brazil. The **Brazilian Vice Consulate** ① *Pdte Franco 972, T0331-242655, Mon-Fri 0800-1400, vc.concepcion@itamaraty.gov.br, issues visas, but go early to ensure same-day processing.* The market, a good place to try local food, is east of the main street, Agustín Pinedo (which is a kind of open-air museum). From here Avenida Presidente Franco runs west to the

Best for
River travel ▪ Scenery

port. Along Avenida Agustín Pineda is a large statue of María Auxiliadora with the Christ Child; it has viewing balconies. The **Museo Municipal Ex-Cuartal Militar** ① *Mcal López, in the Teatro Municipal building, diagonally opposite the Municipality, Mon-Sat 0700-1200, free*, contains a dusty collection of local items and faded photographs. You must ask for it to be opened and it's worth a look. The city historian, Sr Medina, offers good sightseeing tours; ask for him. Plaza Agustín Fernando de Pinedo has a permanent craft market. About 9 km south is a bridge across the Río Paraguay, which makes for an interesting walk across the shallows and islands to the west bank and the Chaco, about an hour return trip, taxi US$10. At weekends, the top of the bridge becomes a party venue for the city's youth. The island in the Río Paraguay facing Concepción is **Isla Chaco'i**, a planned free trade zone and tourism complex, but at present largely uninhabited, where you can stroll through the fields. Row boats take passengers to the island from the shore next to the port, US$0.50 per person. For more information visit the town's website, www.concepcion-py.com.

Tip...
To appreciate the colonial aspect of Concepción, walk away from the main commercial streets.

Heading north

Cargo boats go north of Concepción to Vallemí, Fuerte Olimpo, **Bahía Negra**, and intermediate points along the upper Río Paraguay, through the Pantanal de Nebileque (see Transport, below) Because of the time involved on this route from Paraguay to Bolivia, it is important to get a pre-dated exit stamp at **Immigration in Concepción** ① *Cnel Martínez y Cerro Corá, T0331-241937/982-964429, www.migraciones.gov.py/web/guest/oficinas-regionales*, if you wish to leave Paraguay this way. Near Bahía Negra on the banks of the Río Negro is **Los Tres Gigantes biological station** ① *contact Guyra Paraguay, T021-223567, www.guyra.org.py, in advance for details*. It can only be reached by boat (US$85 round trip, boat takes four people) and is a wonderful place to see Pantanal wildlife, including (with luck) jaguar and giant anteater. Accommodation with full board can be arranged for roughly US$35 per person per day.

East of Concepción

From Concepción Ruta 5 runs 215 km east to Brazil, fully paved and very scenic in parts.

Horqueta to Pedro Juan Caballero

This road goes through Horqueta, Km 50, a cattle and lumber town of 12,948 people. From **Yby Yaú** (junction with Ruta 8 south to Coronel Oviedo) the road continues to Pedro Juan Caballero.

Ten kilometres east of Yby Yaú Ruta 5 continues through the pleasant **Parque Nacional Cerro Corá** (12,038 ha, www.salvemoslos.com.py/pncc.htm), the site of Mariscal Francisco Solano López' death and the final defeat of Paraguay in the War of the Triple Alliance. To reach the park from the main entrance, however, take the left turn, a signed branch road, some 6 km out of Yby Yaú. Not far from the park's entrance is a monument to Solano López and other national heroes; the site is constantly guarded. It has hills and cliffs (some with pre-Columbian caves and petroglyphs), camping facilities, swimming and hiking trails. The rocky outcrops are spectacular and the warden is helpful and provides free guides. When you have walked up the road and seen the line of leaders' heads, turn right and go up the track passing a dirty-looking shack (straight on leads to a military base). The park's administration office (not a recommended entry point) is 5 km east of the main entrance at Km 180 back on Ruta 5.

Pedro Juan Caballero *Colour map 7, B1.*

This border town is separated from the Brazilian town of Ponta Porã by a road (Dr Francia on the Paraguayan side, on the Brazilian side either Rua Marechal Floreano or Avenida Internacional), which anyone can cross (see below for immigration formalities). Ponta Porã is the more modern and prosperous of the two towns; everything costs less on the Paraguayan side. Shopping China is a vast emporium on the eastern suburbs of town, reputed to have the best shopping in the Americas (has to be seen to be believed). Maxi is a large well-stocked supermarket with **Mr Grill** restaurant in the centre. You can pay in guaraníes, reais or US$, at good exchange rates. Arte Paraguaya, Mcal López y Alberdi, has a selection of crafts from all over the country. In recent years the town has attracted a prominent criminal element (based on drugs) so take care.

Border with Brazil

For day crossings you do not need a stamp, but passports must be stamped if travelling beyond the border towns (ask if unsure whether your destination is considered beyond). If you fail to get a stamp when entering Paraguay, you will be fined US$45 when you try to leave. **Paraguayan immigration** ① T0336-272195, Mon-Fri 0700-2200, Sat-Sun 0800-2200, take bus line 2 on the Paraguayan side, or any Brazilian city bus that goes to the Rodoviária, taxi US$7.50, is in the customs building on the eastern outskirts of town near *Shopping China*. Then cross bridge and report to Brazilian federal police in Ponta Porã (closed Saturday-Sunday). The **Brazilian vice consulate** ① Mcal Estigarribia 250, T0336-273562, Mon-Fri 0800-1300, issues visas, fees payable only in guaraníes, take passport and a photo, go early to get visa the same day. Many *cambios* on the Paraguayan side, especially on Curupayty between Dr Francia and Mcal López. Good rates for buying guaraníes or reais with US dollars or euros cash, better than inside Brazil; there is only one ATM. Banks on Brazilian side do not change cash but have a variety of ATMs. **BBVA** ① Dr Francia y Mcal Estigarribia, Mon-Fri 0845-1300, changes US dollars cash to guaraníes only, and has Cirrus ATM. **Norte Cambios** ① CA López entre Iturbe y C Domínguez (and other branches), Mon-Fri 0830-1630, Sat 0830-1100, fair rates for cash.

There is another crossing to Brazil at **Bella Vista** on the Río Apá, northwest of PJ Caballero; buses run from the Brazilian border town of Bela Vista to Jardim and on to Campo Grande. There is a Paraguayan immigration office at Bella Vista, but no Brazilian Policia Federal in Bela Vista. To cross here, get Paraguayan exit stamp then report to the local Brazilian police who may give a temporary stamp, but you must later go to the Policia Federal in either Ponta Porã or Corumbá. Do not fail to get the proper stamp later or you will be detained upon re-entering Paraguay.

Note If planning to go to Brazil or Bolivia by this route, you must enquire about exit and entry formalities before arriving at the border, preferably in Asunción, otherwise in Concepción or Pedro Juan Caballero – addresses above. Visas for those who need them for either country must be obtained in advance. They cannot be obtained at any of the smaller border crossings either in Paraguay or Brazil.

Listings North of Asunción

Where to stay

Asunción to Concepción

$$$ Estancia Jejui
Set on the Río Jejui, 65 km north of Tacuara on Ruta 3, address in Asunción, Telmo Aquino 4068, T021-600227, http://jejui.coinco.com.py.
Rooms have a/c, bath, hot water; full board, fishing, horse riding, tennis, boat rides extra.

Concepción

$$$ Concepción Palace
Mcal López 399 y E A Garay, T0331-241858, www.concepcionpalace.com.py.
By far the nicest hotel in town. With all mod cons, pool, restaurant, Wi-Fi throughout, large rooms.

$$-$ Francés
Franco y C A López, T0331-242383, info@hotelfrancesconcepcion.com.
With a/c, cheaper with fan, breakfast, nice grounds with pool (small charge for non-guests), restaurant, parking.

$$-$ pp Granja El Roble
In Dieciseis (16 km from Concepción on road to Belén), T985-898446, www.paraguay.ch.
Working farm and nature reserve with various sleeping options, full board with homegrown food, camping US$7, lots of activities including boat trips, tubing on Río Ypané, tours to the Chaco, aquarium, very good bird and wildlife-watching (special trips arranged, including for scientists), local information including on routes to Bolivia, internet, Wi-Fi. Excellent value, prices are not negotiable. Phone in advance to arrange transport if required.

$ Center
Presidente Franco e Yegros, T0331-242360.
More basic and cheaper than others, popular.

$ Concepción
Don Bosco y Cabral near market, T0331-242506.
With simple breakfast, a/c, cheaper with fan, family-run, good value.

$ Victoria
Franco y PJ Caballero 693, T0331-242256, hotelvictoria@hotmail.es.
Pleasant rooms, a/c, fridge, cheaper with fan, restaurant, parking.

Pedro Juan Caballero

$$$-$$ Eiruzú
Mcal López y Mcal Estigarribia, T0336-272435.
A/c, fridge and pool, starting to show its age but still good.

$$$-$$ Porã Palace
Alberdi 30 y Dr Francia, T0336-273021.
A/c, fridge, balcony, restaurant, pool, OK, rooms in upper floor are nicer.

$ Victoria
Teniente Herrero y Alberdi, near bus station, T0336-272733.
Cheapest decent lodgings, electric shower, a/c, cheaper with fan, family-run, simple, cash only.

Restaurants

Concepción

$ Hotel Francés
Good value buffet lunch, à la carte in the evening.

$ Hotel Victoria
Set lunches and à la carte, grill in *quincho* across the street.

$ Palo Santo
Franco y PJ Caballero, T0331-241454.
Good Brazilian food and value.

$ Ysapy
Yegros y Mcal Estigarribia at Plaza Pineda. Daily 1630-0200.
Pizza and ice cream, terrace or sidewalk seating, very popular.

Transport

Concepción
Bus The terminal is on the outskirts, 8 blocks north along General Garay, but buses also stop in the centre, Av Pinedo, look for signs Parada Omnibus. A shuttle bus (Línea 1) runs between the terminal and the port. Taxi from terminal or port to centre, US$4; terminal to port U$6. To **Asunción**, many daily with **Nasa-Golondrina** (T0331-242744), 3 with **La Santaniana**, plus other companies, US$10.50-12, 5½ hrs via Pozo Colorado, 9 hrs via Coronel Oviedo. To **Pedro Juan Caballero**, frequent service, several companies, US$10, 4-5 hrs. To **Horqueta**, 1 hr, US$2.50. To **Filadelfia**, Nasa-Golondrina direct

at 0730 Mon, Sat, US$12, 5 hrs, otherwise change at Pozo Colorado. To **Ciudad del Este**, **García** direct at 1230 daily, US$22, 9 hrs, or change at Coronel Oviedo.

Boat To/from **Asunción**, the only boat taking passengers is the *Guaraní*, which has a 2-week sailing cycle on the Asunción-Fuerte Olimpo route and is very slow, but nice and welcomes tourists. To make arrangements for the boat, speak to the owner and captain, Julio Desvares, T982-873436, or Don Coelo, T972-678695. To **Bahía Negra** and intermediate points along the upper Río Paraguay, the **Aquidabán** (T0331-242435) sails Tue 1000, arriving Bahía Negra on Fri morning and returns the same day to Concepción, arriving on Sun, US$17.50 to Bahía Negra, US$15 for a berth (book by the Fri of the week before, at least). If you don't want a berth, take a hammock. Meals are sold on board (US$2), but best to take food and water. Tickets sold in office just outside the port, T0331-242435, Mon-Sat 0700-1200. From Bahía Negra to **Puerto Suárez** (Bolivia) you must hire a boat to Puerto Busch, about US$60-70, then catch a bus.

There are sporadic ferries from Concepción to **Isla Margarita**, across from Porto Murtinho, Brazil. Standing room only. Ask for prices and times at dock. A regular ferry, for 1 vehicle and a few passengers, US$44 per vehicle, goes between Capitán Carmelo Peralta (customs and immigration service at west end of town, T984-331316, Mon-Fri 0700-1500) and Porto Murtinho (no immigration, head for Jardim, 3 hrs minimum by bus, then on to Ponta Porã, Campo Grande or Corumbá for entry stamp; obtain visa in advance, see note above).

Pedro Juan Caballero
Air From Asunción with **Sol del Paraguay**, T021-224555, daily except Wed and Sun, 1100, US$114 (US$112 from Pedro Juan Caballero), 12 passengers.

Bus To **Concepción**, as above. To **Asunción**, quickest route is via Yby Yaú, Santa Rosa and 25 de Diciembre, about 6 hrs. **La Santaniana** has nicest buses, *bus cama* US$17.50; *semicama* US$12; *común* US$10.50. Also **La Ovetense** and **Nasa-Golondrina** 2 a day on the quick route. To **Bella Vista**, **Perpetuo Socorro** 3 a day, US$8, 4 hrs. To **Campo Grande Amambay** 3 a day, US$21, 5 hrs, they stop at Policía Federal in Ponta Porã for entry stamp.

The Chaco

★West of the Río Paraguay is the Chaco, a wild expanse of palm savanna and marshes (known as Humid, or Bajo Chaco, closest to the Río Paraguay) and dry scrub forest and farmland (known as Dry, or Alto Chaco, further northwest from the river). The Chaco is one of the last homelands of Paraguay's indigenous peoples, who now number no more than 25,000 inhabitants. Birdlife is spectacular and abundant. Large cattle estancias dot the whole region and, until recently, agriculture was developed mainly by German-speaking Mennonites from Russia in the Chaco Central. Increasingly, though, large-scale deforestation to make way for cattle has been taking place. Through this vast area the Trans-Chaco Highway (Ruta 9) runs to Bolivia. Much of the region is perfect for those who want to escape into wilderness with minimal human contact and experience nature at its finest and who know the risks involved in traversing the terrain. Although the government has made much of its interest in promoting tourism in the Chaco, it is also considerably lacking in infrastructure, so travellers should prepare accordingly.

Reserva de la Biosfera del Chaco

This is the crown jewel of Paraguay's national park system, albeit one without infrastructure and nearly impossible to visit. **Guyra Paraguay**, which currently co-manages the national parks in this region, is possibly the best option for arranging a tour (see page 1243 and What to do, below). The 4.7-million-ha biosphere reserve in the Chaco and Pantanal ecosystems is a UNESCO Man and Biosphere Reserve and includes: **Parque Nacional Defensores del Chaco** (www.salvemoslos. com.py/pdchaco.htm), considered a pristine environment and the gateway to the seventh-largest ecosystem in Latin America. It is some 220 km from Filadelfia, has a biological station, but only one staffed ranger station at Madrejón in the southeastern corner with very limited facilities: some water, restricted electricity and a small shop for truckers. There were no other ranger stations in operation at the time of writing. **Parque Nacional Teniente Agripino Enciso** (www.salvemoslos. com.py/pntae.htm) is 20 km from La Patria. Nasa minibuses run from Filadelfia to Teniente Enciso via Mariscal Estigarribia and La Patria. The Reserve also contains Médanos del Chaco (www. salvemoslos.com.py/pnmc.htm) and Río Negro (www.salvemoslos.com.py/pnrn.htm) national parks; the Cerro Chovoreca monument; and the Cerro Cabrera-Timané reserve. All are north of the Trans-Chaco, mostly along the Bolivian border, and all face the threat of deforestation. Most of Paraguay's few remaining jaguars are found here. Puma, tapir and peccary also inhabit the area, as well as taguá (an endemic peccary) and a short-haired guanaco. **Cerro León** (highest peak 600 m) is one of the only hilly areas of the Chaco. It is located within PN Defensores del Chaco and in 2015 was the subject of intense lobbying to protect its wildlife, indigenous territory and historical importance from exploration and exploitation by extractive industries.

The Trans-Chaco Highway

To reach the Ruta Trans-Chaco, leave Asunción behind and cross the Río Paraguay to Villa Hayes. Birdlife is immediately more abundant and easily visible in the palm savanna, but other wildlife is usually only seen at night, and otherwise occurs mostly as road kills. The first service station

Best for
Birdlife ▪ Estancias ▪ Scenery

Essential The Chaco

Finding your feet

The Paraguayan Chaco covers more than 24 million ha, but once away from the vicinity of Asunción, the average density is far less than one person to the square kilometre. A single major highway, the Ruta Trans-Chaco (Ruta 9), runs in an almost straight line northwest towards the Bolivian border, ostensibly forming part of the *corredor bi-oceánico*, connecting ports on the Pacific and Atlantic oceans, although it has yet to live up to its expectations. The elevation rises very gradually from 50 m opposite Asunción to 450 m on the Bolivian border. Paving of the Trans-Chaco to the Bolivian border (the military outpost of Fortín Sargento Rodríguez) was completed in 2007, but in spite of being graded twice a year, several paved sections are showing signs of wear and tear, with repairs to potholes few and far between. Sand berms also form at will in some sections and must be avoided. Most travellers cross to Bolivia not through Sargento Rodríguez, but through another military base to the southwest, Mayor Infante Rivarola, which is gained by turning left from the Ruta Trans-Chaco in Estancia La Patria onto a hard-packed road. See also Transport, page 1243.

Tip...

Make sure you have enough fuel for your journey. Although there are service stations at regular intervals along the highway in the Bajo and Chaco Central, beyond Mariscal Estigarribia there is one stop for diesel only and no regular petrol at all until Villamontes in Bolivia, a long drive.

Getting around

Most bus companies have some a/c buses on their Chaco routes (a great asset December–March), enquire in advance. There is very little local public transport between the main Mennonite towns, you must use the buses heading to/from Asunción to travel between them as well as Mariscal Estigarribia.

Tip...

Be prepared. Any expedition to the reserve must be cleared with government authorities well ahead of time. Be aware it will also be a very costly undertaking.

Safety

Bus passengers and motorists should always carry extra food and especially water; climatic conditions are harsh and there is little traffic in case of a breakdown. No private expedition should leave the Trans-Chaco without plentiful supplies of water, food and fuel. No one should venture onto the dirt roads alone and since this is a major smuggling route from Bolivia, it is unwise to stop for anyone at night.

When to go

Winter temperatures are warm by day, cooler by night, but summer heat and mosquitoes can make it very unpleasant (pyrethrum coils, *espirales*, are sold everywhere). Any unusual insect bites should be examined immediately upon arrival, as Chagas disease is endemic in the Chaco.

after Asunción is at Km 130. **Pirahú**, Km 252, has a service station and is a good place to stop for a meal; it has a/c, delicious *empanadas* and fruit salad. The owner of the Ka-Í parador owns an old-fashioned carbon manufacturing site 2 km before Pirahú. Ask for him if you are interested in visiting the site. At Km 271 is **Pozo Colorado** and the turning for Concepción (see page 1233). There are two restaurants, a basic hotel ($ with fan, cheaper without), supermarket, hospital, a service station and a military post. The **Touring y Automóvil Club Paraguayo** provides a breakdown and recovery service from Pozo Colorado (T0981-939611, www.tacpy.com.py). At this point, the tidy Mennonite homesteads, with flower gardens and citrus orchards, begin to appear. At Km 282, 14 km northwest of Pozo Colorado, is **Rancho Buffalo Bill**, T021-298381, one of the most pleasant places to stop off or eat, beside a small lake. The estancia has limited but good accommodation (**$$-$**), ask at restaurant. Horse riding, nature walks and camping are good options here. At Km 320 is **Río Verde**, with fuel, police station and restaurant. The next good place to stay or eat along the Trans-Chaco is **Cruce de los Pioneros**, at Km 415, where accommodation (**$$-$** Los Pioneros, T0491-432170, hot shower, a/c), limited supermarket, vehicle repair shop, and fuel are available. A paved road runs from Cruce Boquerón, just northwest of Cruce de los Pioneros, to Loma Plata.

Mennonite communities

The Chaco Central has been settled by Mennonites, Anabaptists of German extraction who began arriving in the late 1920s. There are three administratively distinct but adjacent colonies: Menno (from Russia via Canada); Fernheim (directly from Russia) and Neuland (the last group to arrive, also from Russia, after

the Second World War). Among themselves, the Mennonites speak 'plattdeutsch' ('Low German'), but they readily speak and understand 'hochdeutsch' ('High German'), which is the language of instruction in their schools. Increasingly, younger Mennonites speak Spanish and some English. The people are friendly and willing to talk about their history and culture. Altogether there are about 80 villages with a population of about 18,000 Mennonites and 20,000 *indígenas* from eight distinct groups (they occupy the lowest rung on the socioeconomic ladder).

The Mennonites have created a remarkable oasis of regimented prosperity in this harsh hinterland. Their hotels and restaurants are impeccably clean, services are very efficient, large modern supermarkets are well stocked with excellent dairy products and all other goods, local and imported. Each colony has its own interesting museum.

The main towns are all very spread out and have no public transport except for a few expensive taxis in Filadelfia. Walking around in the dust and extreme heat can be tiring. Transport between the three main towns is also limited, see Transport, page 1243.

Filadelfia Also known as Fernheim Colony, Filadelfia, 466 km from Asunción, is the largest town of the region. The **Jacob Unger Museum** ① *C Hindenburg y Unruh, T0491-32151, US$1 including video*, provides a glimpse of pioneer life in the Chaco, as well as exhibiting artefacts of the indigenous peoples of the region. The manager of the Hotel Florida will open the museum upon request, mornings only. Next to the museum is **Plaza de los Recuerdos**, a good place to see the *samu'u* or *palo borracho* (bottle tree). A bookstore-cum-craft shop, **Librería El Mensajero**, next to Hotel Florida, is run by Sra Penner, very helpful and informative.

Apart from the website, www.filadelfiaparaguay.com, there is no tourist infrastructure in Filadelfia. General information may be obtained from the co-op office. Services in town include ATM at Banco Itaú ① *Av Hindenburg 775 y Caraya*; **Fernheim Cooperative Bank** ① *Hindenburg opposite the Cooperative building*, for US dollars and euro cash. **Internet** ① *Shopping Portal del Chaco and opposite Radio ZP30*. **Copaco phone office** ① *on Hindenburg, opposite supermarket, Mon-Sat 0700-2100, Sun 0700-1200, 1500-2000*.

Loma Plata The centre of Menno Colony, Loma Plata is 15 km east of Filadelfia. Although smaller than Filadelfia, it has more to offer the visitor, but few transport services. It has a good museum **Museo de la Colonia Menno** ① *Mon-Fri 0700-1130, 1400-1800, Sat 0700-1300, US$1.85*. **Balneario Oasis swimming complex** ① *Nord Grenze, 700 m past airport north of Loma Plata, T0492-52704,*

BACKGROUND

The three areas of the Chaco

The **Bajo Chaco** begins on the riverbank just west of Asunción across the Río Paraguay. It is a picturesque landscape of palm savanna, much of which is seasonally inundated because of the impenetrable clay beneath the surface, although there are 'islands' of higher ground with forest vegetation. Cattle ranching on huge, isolated estancias is the prevailing economic activity. Except in an emergency, it is not advisable to enter an estancia unless you have prior permission from the owner.

In the **Chaco Central**, the natural vegetation is dry scrub forest, with a mixture of hardwoods and cactus. The *palo borracho* (bottle tree) with its pear-shaped, water-conserving trunk, the *palo santo*, with its green wood and beautiful scent, and the tannin-rich *quebracho* (literally meaning axe-breaker) are the most noteworthy native species. This is the best area in Paraguay to see large mammals, especially once away from the central Chaco Mennonite colonies.

The **Alto Chaco** is characterized by low dense thorn and scrub forest which has created an impenetrable barricade of spikes and spiny branches resistant to heat and drought and very tough on tyres. Towards Bolivia cacti become more prevalent as rainfall decreases. There are a few estancias in the southern part, but beyond Mariscal Estigarribia there is little beyond the occasional military checkpoints. Summer temperatures often exceed 45°C.

US$2, Sep-Apr 1500-2100, except Sun and holidays, 1100-2100, has three pools with slides and snack bar, a welcome break from the summer heat. **Tourist office** (contact Walter Ratzlaff) ① *next to the Chortitzer Komitee Co-op, T0492-52301, turismo@chortitzer.com.py, Mon-Fri 0700-1130, 1400-1800, Sat 0700-1300,* very helpful. **Chortitzer Komitee Co-op** ① *Av Central, Mon-Fri 0700-1730, Sat 0700-1100,* changes US$ and euros at good rates. There is a Banco Itaú ATM outside. Other ATMs at bank at southern roundabout and by the Nasa bus office. **Internet** ① *at Microtec, Fred Engen 1207, Mon-Sat 0800-1130, 1400-2200, US$1 per hr.* **Telephone** ① *at Copaco, Av Central near supermarket, Mon-Sat 0700-2000, Sun 0700-1200, 1500-2000.*

☆Laguna Salada

To the southeast of Loma Plata is the Riacho Yacaré Sur watershed, with many salt water lagoons, generally referred to as Laguna Salada. This is a wonderful place to see waterbirds such as Chilean flamingos, swans, spoonbills and migratory shorebirds from the Arctic. There are extensive walks though the eerily beautiful landscape. **Laguna Capitán**, a 22-ha recreation reserve, 30 km from town, has several small lagoons, a swimming lake, basic bunk bed accommodation ($, shared bath), kitchen facilities, meals on request, camping. Reserve directly at T0983-344463, English and German spoken, also helpful for tour organizing, or through the Cooperative information office in Loma Plata. There is no public transport. Taxi US$30 one way; full-day tour combining Laguna Capitán with visit to the Cooperative's installations and museum, US$85 per group plus transport. Guides are required for visits. **Laguna Chaco Lodge** ① *70 km from town, T0492-252235,* a 2500-ha private reserve, is a Ramsar wetland site (no accommodation). The lovely Laguna Flamenco is the main body of water surrounded by dry forest. Large numbers of Chilean flamingos and other water birds may be seen here. **Campo María**, a 4500-ha reserve owned by the Chortitzer Komitee (www. chortitzer.com.py), some 90 km from town, also has a large lake and can be visited on a tour.

The **Indigenous Foundation for Agricultural and Livestock Development (FIDA)** ① *30 km from Neuland, Filadelfia and Loma Plata, T0491-432321, www.ascim.org,* located within Yalve Sanga, is a collective of 1762 indigenous inhabitants organized into 11 agricultural villages. The community has its own legal capacity and is the legal owner of 6000 ha of property. Yalve Sanga is the first indigenous version of the Mennonite cooperative colonies and provides an interesting insight into the lives of the communities. Limited handicrafts are sold in the Yalve Sanga supermarket (better selection in Neuland).

Neuland

Neuland, also known as Neu-Halbstadt, is 381 km northwest of Asunción. To the extent that the High Chaco has a tourism infrastructure at all, it is located squarely in Neuland, a well-organized town. There is a small **Museo Histórico** with objects brought by the first Mennonites from Russia, set in the building of the first primary school of the area. **Neuland Beach Park** ① *US$1.75*, has a pool, snack bar with air conditioning. **Parque la Amistad**, 500 m past pool, is 35 ha of natural vegetation where paths have been cleared for nature walks. Most spectacular are the wild orchids (September-October), cacti and birdlife. **Enrique (Heinz) Weibe** ① *T971-701634, hwiebe@neuland.com.py*, is the official guide of the Neuland colony; also ask for **Harry Epp** ① *contact through Neuland Co-op office, T0493-240201, www.neuland.com.py, Mon-Fri 0700-1130, 1400-1800, Sat 0700-1130*, who is very knowledgeable about the flora and fauna and is an informative and entertaining guide. He also gives tours of Neuland in a horse drawn carriage. Phone booths and post office are in centre of town next to the supermarket. **Neuland Cooperative** changes US dollars cash (Monday-Friday 0700-1130, 1400-1800, Saturday 0700-1130).

Around Neuland

Fortín Boquerón, 27 km from Neuland, was the site of the decisive battle of Chaco War (September 1932) and includes a memorial, a small, well-presented museum and walks around the remainder of the trenches. **Campamento Aurora Chaqueña** is a park 15 km from town on the way to Fortín Boquerón, there is simple accommodation with fan ($, take your own food and water). **Parque Valle Natural**, 10 km from Neuland on the way to Filadelfia, is an *espartillar*, a dry riverbed with natural brush around it and a few larger trees. Camping is possible although there is only a small covered area. All three sites are easily reached from Neuland as part of a package tour.

Mariscal Estigarribia and on to Bolivia *Colour map 6, B5.*

At 525 Km from Asunción, Mariscal Estigarribia's few services are spread out over 4 km along the highway: three gas stations, a couple of small supermarkets (La Llave del Chaco is recommended), two mediocre hotels, and one remarkably excellent restaurant. There are no banks, but the Shell station changes US$ cash. Copaco phone office is one street back from the highway. The immigration office (supposedly 24 hours, but often closed in the small hours) is at the southeast end of town near the Shell station. All buses stop at the terminal (**Parador Arami**), at the northwest end of town, where travellers entering from Bolivia are subject to thorough searches for drugs. The people are friendly and helpful.

There are no reliable services of any kind beyond Mariscal Estigarribia. At **La Patria**, 125 km northwest, the road divides: 128 km west to Infante Rivarola (no immigration post – use Mariscal Estigarribia) continuing to Villamontes, Bolivia, with Bolivian immigration at Ibibobo; 128 km northwest to Sargento Rodríguez continuing to Boyuibe, Bolivia (not used by public transport). There are customs posts at either side of the actual border in addition to the main customs offices in Mariscal Estigarribia and Villamontes.

On the Bolivian side, from the border to Villamontes (Ruta 11), the road is gravel and in good condition even after rain, and a 4WD is no longer indispensable. From Villamontes, a paved road runs north to Santa Cruz and south to Yacuiba on the Argentine border. Take small denomination US dollar notes as it is impossible to buy bolivianos before reaching Bolivia (if entering from Bolivia only *casas de cambio* in Santa Cruz or Puerto Suárez have guaraníes).

Tourist information

Consejo Regional de Turismo Chaco Central (CONRETUR)
Contact Hans Fast, T0492-52422, Loma Plata, fast@telesurf.com.py
Coordinates tourism development of the 3 cooperatives and the private sector.

The Fundación para el Desarrollo Sustentable del Chaco
Deportivo 935 y Algarrobo, Loma Plata, T0492-252235, fdschaco@telesurf.com.py.
Operates conservation projects in the area and has useful information but does not offer tours. Always examine in detail a tour operator's claims to expertise in the Chaco. For Tour operators, see page 1243. See also under individual towns for local tourist offices.

Where to stay

The Trans-Chaco Highway

$$$ pp Estancia Golondrina
José Domingo Ocampo, Km 235, San Luis, Asunción office, Pastor Ibáñez 2275 casi Av Artigas, T021-282704 (weekdays only), www.estanciagolondrina.com.
Take the unpaved road to the right, 15 km to the ranch. A good place for combining rural and ecotourism. The ranch has extensive agricultural land as well as 12,000 ha of protected virgin forest (Reserva Ypetí) and abundant wildlife. There are trails for walking or horse riding, boat trips on the river, picturesque accommodation (a/c, private bathroom, very comfortable) overlooking the river. Price includes all meals, activities and transportation from the main road.

Filadelfia

$$$-$$ Florida
Av Hindenburg 165-S opposite park, T0491-432151, http://hotelfloridachaco.com.
Fridge, a/c, breakfast, cheaper in basic annex with shared bath, fan and without breakfast. Pool (US$1.50 per hr for non-guests), restaurant ($) for buffet and à la carte.

$$-$ Golondrina-Avenida
Av Hindenburg 635-S at entrance to town, T0491-433111, www.hotelgolondrina.com.

Modern, 4 types of room with breakfast, a/c, fridge in the best (cheapest with fan, shared bath, no breakfast), restaurant.

$$-$ Golondrina-Centro
Industrial 194-E, T0491-432218, www.hotelgolondrina.com.
Modern, spacious common areas with game room. Spanish and German spoken.
   There is a **Touring y Automóvil Club Paraguayo** hotel at Transchaco Km 443, www.tacpy.com.py.

Loma Plata

$$-$ Loma Plata Inn
Eligio Ayala y Manuel Gondra, T0492-252166, www.lomaplata innhotel.com.
Near southern roundabout and Nasa bus office, with restaurant.

$$-$ Mora
Sandstrasse 803, T0492-252255.
With breakfast, a/c, Wi-Fi, new wing has spacious rooms with fridge, nice grounds, family-run, good value, good breakfast, basic meals on request. Recommended.

$$-$ Pensión Loma Plata
J B Reimer 1805, T0492-252829.
A/c, breakfast, comfortable rooms, homely atmosphere, very helpful, good value. Includes breakfast, other meals on request.

Neuland

$$-$ Hotel Boquerón
Av 1 de Febrero opposite the Cooperative, T0493-240306, www.neuland.com.py/en/services/hotel-restaurant-boqueron.
With breakfast, a/c, cheaper in older wing without TV, restaurant.

$ Parador
Av 1 de Febrero y C Talleres, T0493-240567.
With breakfast, a/c, cheaper with fan and shared bath, restaurant.

Mariscal Estigarribia

$ Parador Arami
Northwest end of town and far from everything, also known as la terminal, T0494-247277.
Functional rooms, a/c, meals on request, agents for Stel Turismo and Nasa buses.

Restaurants

Filadelfia

$$ El Girasol
Unruh 126-E y Hindenburg, T0491-320780.
Mon-Sat 1100-1400, 1800-2300, Sun 1100-1400.
Good buffet and *rodizio*, cheaper without
the meat.

Loma Plata

$$ Chaco's Grill
Av Dr Manuel Gondra, T0492-252166.
Buffet, *rodizio*, very good, patio, live music.

$ Norteño
3 Palmas 990, T0492-252447. Lunch till 1400 then
open for dinner.
Good, simple.

$ Pizzería San Marino
Av Central y Dr Gondra. Daily 1800-2300.
Pizza and German dishes.

$ Unión
Av Central, north of roundabout, halfway
to airport. Daily 0800-1300, 1700-2200.
Good standard food.

Mariscal Estigarribia

$$ Italiano
Southwest end of town behind Shell station,
T0494-247231.
Excellent, top quality meat, large portions,
an unexpected treat. Italian owner is friendly
and helpful, open for lunch and dinner.

What to do

Many agencies in Asunción offer Chaco tours.
Note that some are just a visit to Rancho Buffalo
Bill and do not provide a good overview of
attractions. Hans Fast and Harry Epp also run
tours to national parks. In Loma Plata ask around
for bicycle hire to explore nearby villages.

For more complete tailor-made tours, contact
Guyra Paraguay (www.guyra.org.py). This
birding organization does not offer tours of the
Chaco, but can make excellent referrals to those
operators that meet its high standards.

Transport

Filadelfia

Bus From **Asunción**, Nasa-Golondrina, 3 daily
except Sat, US$12; also **Stel Turismo**, 1 overnight;
6 hrs. To **Loma Plata**, Nasa-Golondrina 0800
going to Asunción, 0600 and 1900 coming
from Asunción, 1 hr, US$3.50. To **Neuland**, local
service Mon-Fri 1130 and 1800, 1 hr, US$3.50.
Also **Stel Turismo** at 1900 and **Nasa-Golondrina**
at 2130, both coming from Asunción. To
Mariscal Estigarribia, **Nasa** at 0500 Mon and
Fri, continuing to La Patria and Parque Nacional
Teniente Enciso (see page 1237), 5-6 hrs, US$12,
returns around 1300 same day (confirm all details
in advance).

Loma Plata

Bus **Asunción**, Nasa-Golondrina, daily 0600,
7-8 hrs, US$12. To **Filadelfia**, Mon-Fri 1300,
Sat 1100, Sun 1200, daily 2130, all continuing
to Asunción.

Neuland

Bus To **Asunción**, Stel Turismo at 1900 (1230
on Sat), via Filadelfia, 7-8 hrs, US$12. Local service
to **Filadelfia**, Mon-Fri 0500, 1230.

Mariscal Estigarribia

Bus From **Filadelfia**, Nasa-Golondrina 1100
daily; **Asunción**, Nasa-Golondrina, daily 1430,
and **Pycasu** 3 daily, US$12; **Stel**, 2 a day, US$13.75,
7-8 hrs. Buses from Asunción pass through town
around 0300-0400 en route to Bolivia: **Yaciretá**
on Tue, Thu, Sat, Sun (agent at Barcos y Rodados
petrol station, T0494-247320); **Stel Turismo** daily
(agent at Parador Arami, T0494-247230). You can
book and purchase seats in advance but beware
overcharging, the fare from Mariscal Estigarribia
should be about US$10 less than from Asunción.

Practicalities
Getting around

Air
There are scheduled services to most of the main parts of the country from Silvio Pettirossi airport. The local bus company, **Sol del Paraguay** (Eligio Ayala 988, Asunción T021-224555, www.viajaconsol.com), runs a domestic air service in 12-seater aircraft.

Rail
Most of the 441-km rail network closed in early 2001, with the last stretch sealed off in 2012. Neither freight trains to Encarnación, nor the tourist steam train service (*Tren del Lago*) from Asunción's Botánico station, to Sapucai via Areguá are now run. A large number of components of the historic railway system were dismantled and sold for scrap. Private-sector plans (which do not enjoy government funding) to recommence tourist trains have come and gone, but since 2015 Ferrocarriles del Paraguay (FEPASA) has been seeking investment for an electric light railway to run from Asunción to Ypacaraí via Luque, with a continuation eventually to the south of the country.

Road
Along all main roads, buses will stop at almost any junction to collect or drop off passengers, so all timetables are approximate.

Maps
A general map of the country can be purchased at most bookstores in Asunción and at bus terminals. The **Touring y Automóvil Club Paraguayo (TACPy)** ⓘ *www.tacpy.com.py*, publishes a guide in Spanish and English, with maps, US$15, but more detailed maps are available from **Servicio Geográfico Militar** ⓘ *Av Artigas 920, T021-204959*; take your passport.

TRAVEL TIP
Driving in Paraguay

Road Roughly 20% of roads are paved. Roads serving the main centres are in good condition and are continually being upgraded. A highway links Asunción with Iguazú Falls (six hours). Potholes are a hazard, especially in Asunción. Unsurfaced roads may not be passable in bad weather, especially November-April. There are regular police checks; it's advisable to lock doors.

Safety Beware of stray cattle on the road at night. Driving at night is not advisable.

Documents Neither a *carnet de passages* nor *libreta de pasos por aduana* is required for a car or motorcycle, but the carnet may make entry easier. Temporary admission for a private vehicle is usually 30 days.

Organizations Touring y Automóvil Club Paraguayo (TACP), 25 de Mayo 1086 y Brasil, piso 2, Asunción, T021-210550, www.tacpy.com.py, produces a road map and provides information about weather and roads. Information also from the office of the traffic police in Asunción, T021-493390/293387, Facebook: DIRECCIONPMT.

Car hire Weekly and free-km rates available. Rates from US$40 per day to US$130 for 4WD, which always should be used in lieu of a car.

Fuel Petrol/gasoline is called "nafta" and is unleaded. "Flex" is a mixture of petrol and alcohol. Petropar prices are Nafta econo (*regular*, 85 octane) US$0.70 per litre, eco especial (*supra*, 90 octane) US$0.85, and Nafta ecoplus (*suprema*, 95 octane) US$1; diesel US$0.75-0.90 per litre; *ecoflex* is US$0.70 per litre. There are few service stations in the Chaco.

Where to stay

Many hotels are in our $$-$ ranges, often good ones with private shower and toilet, but there are very few hostels with dormitory accommodation (US$10-15 per person). Most hotels have two rates – one for a room with a/c, the other without. Almost all include breakfast. See the Planning your trip chapter for our hotel price guide.

Food & drink

Restaurants

Lunch is usually served between 1130-1300 in most restaurants and bars. Evening meals are hard to find in small towns, but options exist in larger cities. See the Planning your trip chapter for our restaurant price guide.

Food

Typical local foods include *chipa*, a cheese bread that comes in a number of varieties: *almidón*, made with yuca flour; *barrero*, made with corn flour; *manduví*, made with peanuts (better warm than cold). *Chipa so'o* is maize bread with minced meat filling; *chipa guazú* is made with fresh corn; *sopa paraguaya* is a kind of sponge of ground maize and cheese. These make a great side dish, or can be enjoyed on their own. *Soyo* is a soup of different meats and vegetables; *albóndiga* a soup of meat balls; *bori bori* another type of soup with diced meat, vegetables, and small balls of maize mixed with cheese. The beef is excellent in the better restaurants (best cuts are *lomo* and *lomito*) and can be enjoyed with *chorizo* (sausage), *morcilla*, *chipa guazú*, *sopa paraguaya* and a variety of salads. *Parrillada completa* is recommended and there are many *churrascarías* (barbecues) serving huge quantities of meat, with salad, vegetables and pasta. River fish include *surubí* and *dorado*, which are prepared in many different ways. Although vegetarian restaurants are scarce, there are lots of fruits, salads and vegetables, as well as the non-meat varieties of *empanada*, such as *choclo*, *palmito* or *cuatro quesos*.

Drink

The most popular drink among Paraguayans is *tereré* (cold mate with digestive herbs) for warm days and hot mate for cold days. There is a **Festival de Tereré** in late February each year in Itakyry, Alto Paraná, during the **Feria Gastronómica y Artesanal**, Facebook: FestivalDelTerere. *Cocido* is a type of tea made by burning (traditionally with a red ember) the yerba with some sugar; this can be served with or without milk. Paraguayan beers are very good, the better brands being Baviera, Pilsen and Munich. These are lager-types, but you can sometimes find darker beers in the winter. The better brands of the national sugarcane-based spirit, *caña*, include Aristocrata (known as 'Ari'), Fortín and Tres Leones. You can find most global brand soft drinks, including Guaraná (originally from Brazil). *Mosto* is a very sweet but refreshing juice from sugarcane. And there is a wonderful variety of fresh fruit juices.

Essentials A-Z

Accident and emergency

Ambulance and police emergency T911. Medical emergency (SEME) T141. Fire services T131 (police); T132 (Cuerpo de Bomberos Voluntarios).

Electricity

220 volts AC, 50 cycles, but power surges and voltage drops are frequent. European 2 round pin plugs are used. Visitors from North America should bring an inexpensive adaptor, as few hotels outside Asunción offer 110-volt service.

Embassies and consulates

For Paraguayan embassies and consulates abroad and for all foreign embassies and consulates in Paraguay, see http://embassy.goabroad.com.

Health

Note: As of 17 October 2016, Paraguay's Ministry of Public Health and Social Welfare has confirmed the presence of zika-carrying mosquitoes in the country and has recommended that pregnant women do not travel to Paraguay. See www.mspbs.gov.py for all current health issues in Paraguay.

Medical services

Asunción Centro de Emergencias Médicas, Av Gral Santos y Teodoro S Mongelos, T021-204800, www.cem.gov.py. Public hospital. **Centro Médico Bautista**, Av Argentina y Cervera, T021-688 9000, www.cmb.org.py. **Sanatorio San Roque**, Eligio Ayala y Pa'í Pérez, T021-248 9000, www.sanroque.com.py, 24 hrs.

Money

US$1=₲5587; €1=₲6239 (Jun 2017).
The guaraní (plural guaraníes) is the unit of currency, symbolized by ₲ (the letter G crossed). There are bank notes for 2000, 5000, 10,000, 20,000, 50,000 and 100,000 guaraníes and coins for 50, 100, 500 and 1000 guaraníes. Get rid of all your guaraníes before leaving Paraguay; there is no market for them elsewhere.

Plastic/TCs/banks Asunción is a good place for obtaining US$ cash on MasterCard or Visa especially if heading for Brazil. ATMs for Visa and MasterCard are common in Asunción and offer good rates of exchange. They accept credit and debit cards and give dollars and guaraníes. Many banks in Asunción (eg **HSBC, Citibank, ABN AMRO, Interbanco**) give US$ cash, but charge up to 5.5% commission. Rates for most other foreign currencies are reasonable. Many *casas de cambio* on Palma, Estrella and nearby streets in the capital (Mon-Fri 0730-1200, 1500-1830, Sat 0730-1200). All rates are better than at frontiers. They change dollars, euros, Brazilian reais, Argentine pesos and a few will accept sterling notes or bolivianos. Visa and MasterCard cash advances are possible in Asunción, Ciudad del Este and Encarnación, but only for credit (not debit) cards. Note that account holders of international banks (eg **Citi, HSBC**) are not able to access their accounts in Paraguayan branches without incurring fees for withdrawals. Street dealers operate from early morning until late at night, even on public holidays, but double check their calculations and the cash they give you.

Cost of travelling Allow US$50-60 per person per day to cover main expenses, unless staying in the cheapest hotels and not moving around much. Average cost of internet in towns is US$0.75-1.25 per hr.

Opening hours

Banks: Mon-Fri 0845-1500. **Commercial office hours**: 0730-1100 or 1300, and 1430 or 1500-1800 or 1900. **Government offices**: 0700-1130 in summer, 0730-1200 in winter, open Sat. **Shops, offices and businesses:** open around 0700; some may close 1200-1500.

Post

The historic post office at Alberdi, between Benjamín Constant y El Paraguayo Independiente, in Ascunción does not have postal services. The main office is at 25 de Mayo 340 y Yegros, T021-498112, Mon-Fri 0700-2000, Sat 0700-1200. **Poste Restante** (ask at the Casillas section) charges about US$0.50 per item. Packages under 2 kg should be handed in at the small packages window, up to 20 kg at the 'Encomiendas' office. A faster and more reliable way to send parcels is by EMS, the post office courier service from the same office. Customs inspection of open parcel required. Register all important mail. There are sub-offices at **Shopping del Sol**, **Mall Excelsior** and in certain suburbs.

Public holidays and festivals

1 Jan; **1-3 Feb** (San Blas, patron of Paraguay and Day of Paraguayan Democracy); **1 Mar** (**National Heroes' Day**, on the anniversary of the death of former president Francisco Solano López); **Wed of Holy Week**; **Maundy Thu**; **Good Fri**; **1 May** (Labour Day); **14 May** (Independence); **12 Jun** (Paz del Chaco); **24 Jun** (San Juan); **15 Aug** (founding of Asunción); **16 Aug** (**Children's Day**, in honour of the boys who died at the Battle of Acosta Ñu, see page 1203); **29 Sep** (victory of Boquerón, decisive battle in the Chaco War); **8 Dec** (Virgen de Caacupé/ Inmaculada Concepción); **25 Dec**.

Safety

Paraguay is generally safe and visitors are treated courteously. At election times there may be demonstrations in the capital, but the country as a whole is very calm. Beware police seeking bribes, especially at Asunción bus station and at border crossings.

Tax

Airport tax US$40, payable on departure in US$ or guaraníes (cheaper) if not included in the ticket. US$4 on national flights.
VAT/IVA 10% (5% for some purchases).

Telephone and Wi-Fi

Country code +595.

Ringing: equal long tones with long pauses. Engaged: equal short tones with equal pauses. Directory enquiries and information: T112. To make calls between the provinces dial '0' followed by a 2- or 3- or, rarely 4-digit city code, then the 6-digit number (a few cities, eg Asunción, Ciudad del Este and Villarrica also have 7-digits). Mobile phone numbers have the 3-digit prefix of the carrier. These always start with 9. This is followed by 6 digits. You can use a prepaid SIM card, with prior registration at one of the official carrier's offices. The main providers are Tigo, Claro, Personal (Telecom) and Vox (state-run Copaco). Internet speed is relatively slow, but improving, and free Wi-Fi points were established in main cities in 2015 with more to follow.

Note The vast majority of websites offer information in Spanish only, with the secondary language more often being German or Portuguese than English.

Time

Standard time GMT -4 hrs begins early Apr. Summer time GMT -3 hrs begins early Oct.

Tipping

Restaurants, 10%. Taxis, 10%. In supermarkets, tip the check-out boys who pack bags; they are not paid.

Tourist information

Secretaría Nacional de Turismo Palma 468 y 14 de Mayo, Asunción, T021-494110/441530, www.senatur.gov.py. **SENATUR** makes available on its website for download a 32-page Spanish-only guide, *Jaha: Sitios imperdibles del Paraguay*, that provides a decent overview of tourism opportunities throughout the country, arranged by geography. (Although telephone numbers are given, website addresses are not.)

Useful websites

www.cabildoccr.gov.py Centro Cultural de la República El Cabildo, the government's official cultural website (in Spanish).
http://discoveringparaguay.com/home A blog about living and travelling in Paraguay (see also Facebook: discoveringparaguay).
www.portalguarani.com Portal to the arts and letters of Paraguay.
www.presidencia.gov.py The government's official website (in Spanish).

Visas and immigration

A passport valid for 6 months after the intended length of stay is required to enter Paraguay and tourist visas are issued at the point of entry for a stay of up to 90 days. Visas are extendable for an additional 3 months for US$52. Visitors are registered on arrival and proof of onward travel is required (although not always asked for). Citizens of the following countries do not require visas in advance: EU member states, Israel, Japan, Norway, Russia, South Africa, South Korea, Switzerland, countries of South and Central America.

Citizens of the following countries require visas either in advance or upon arrival (Visa en Arribo) only at Silvio Pettirossi International Airport: valid for 90 days only: Australia (US$135), Canada (US$150), New Zealand (US$140), Taiwan (US$100) and the United States (US$160). Fees are payable in these countries' respective national currencies or guaraníes; credit cards are not accepted. Citizens of all others countries other than the 2 groups above must apply previously at a Paraguayan embassy or consulate in person (not by mail) for a fee of US$21 for single entry, US$42 multiple entry. Present a valid passport, a passport photo, a covering letter and proof of onward travel and economic solvency. Always double-check at a consulate or www.mre.gov.py before arrival which nationalities need a visa, how much they cost and which Paraguayan consulates issue them. At the time of writing (Feb 2017) new legislation on visas was being prepared; T021-414 8771 for more information. Make sure you're stamped in and out of Paraguay to avoid future problems. If you do not get an entrance stamp in your passport you can be turned back at the border.

Weights and measures

Metric.

This is
Peru

Cuzco, capital of the Inca world, is now one of South America's premier tourist destinations, with its access to Machu Picchu and the Inca Trail, the Sacred Vilcanota Valley and a buzzing nightlife. On the border with Bolivia is Lake Titicaca, blessed with magical light and fascinating islands. But in Peru, the Egypt of the Americas, this is just the tip of the pyramid.

The coastal desert may seem uninhabitable, yet pre-Inca cultures thrived there. They left their monuments in sculptures etched into the surface of the desert, most famously at Nazca. Civilization builders welcomed gods from the sea and irrigated the soil to feed great cities of adobe bricks. After the Incas came the Spanish *conquistadores*, who left some of their own finest monuments. You can trek forever amid high peaks and blue lakes, cycle down remote mountainsides, look into bottomless canyons – deeper than any others on earth, or surf the Pacific rollers. There are enough festivals to brighten almost every day of the year, while the spiritual explorer can be led down mystical paths by a shaman.

East of the Andes the jungles stretch towards the heart of the continent with some of the richest biodiversity on earth. And, should you tire of nature, there is always Lima: loud, brash, covered in fog for half the year, but with some of the best museums, most innovative restaurants and liveliest nightlife in the country.

COLOMBIA

ECUADOR

Tumbes
Máncora
Talara
Piura
Bayovar
Mórrope
Chiclayo
Pacasmayo
Puerto Chicama
Huanchaco
Trujillo **3**
Chimbote
Casma
Huarmey
Patívilca
Barranca
Chancay
Ancón

La Tina
San Ignacio
Jaén
Sechura Desert

Saramériza

Nuevo Andoas
Andoas

Moyobamba
Chachapoyas **4**
Tingo
Leymebamba
Celendín
Cajamarca
Cajabamba
Huamachuco
Caraz
Yungay
Huaraz
Chavín de Huántar
Cerro de Pasco
La Oroya
Tarma
Junín

Pantoja

Puerto Arturo

Leoncia Prado

Iquitos
Amazonas
Nauta

Santa Rosa
Leticia
Tabatinga

Sta Cruz
Yurimaguas
Tarapoto
Juanjuí
Pampas del Sacramento

Uchiza
Tingo María
Huánuco
Puerto Bermúdez

Pucallpa
Ganzo Azúl
Abujao

BRAZIL

Esperanza

Iñapari
Iberia
Puerto Maldonado

Lagunas
Bretaña

Pacific Ocean

LIMA
Huancavelica
Cañete
Chincha Alta
Pisco
Paracas
Ica
Huacachina
Nazca
Nazca Lines

Huancayo
Ayacucho
Andahuaylas
Tambobamba
Challa
Cotahuasi

Atalaya
Pto Prado

Echarate
Machu Picchu
Ollantaytambo
Cuzco
Raqchi
Sta Rosa
Yauri
Ayaviri
Juliaca

Manu Biosphere Reserve
8
Boca Manu
Shintuya
Pilcopata
Mazuko
Ayapata

Chivay
Colca Canyon
Ocoña
Camaná
Mollendo
Ilo

Puno
Lake Titicaca
Arequipa
Desaguadero
Moquegua
Tacna

BOLIVIA

CHILE

Footprint picks

1 **Lima**, page 1256
2 **Cordillera Blanca**, page 1285
3 **Huaca de la Luna**, page 1309
4 **Chachapoyas**, page 1345
5 **Nazca Lines**, page 1368
6 **Colca and Cotahuasi canyons**, pages 1386 and 1391
7 **Cuzco and the Sacred Valley of the Incas**, pages 1415 and 1444
8 **Southern jungle**, page 1500

N

100 km
100 miles

Lima

Footprint picks

★ **Lima**, page 1256

Historic buildings and the best food and nightlife in the country.

★ **Cordillera Blanca**, page 1285

A region of jewelled lakes and dazzling mountain peaks.

★ **Huaca de la Luna**, page 1309

The remains of the once-mighty Moche Empire.

★ **Chachapoyas**, page 1345

Mysterious cities and cliff-side burial sites.

★ **Nazca Lines**, page 1368

Vast, enigmatic drawings etched into miles of barren southern desert.

★ **Colca and Cotahuasi canyons**, pages 1386 and 1391

See the majestic Andean condor, rising on the morning thermals.

★ **Cuzco and the Sacred Valley**, pages 1415 and 1444

Colonial churches, pre-Columbian ruins and unforgettable Machu Picchu.

★ **Southern jungle**, page 1500

Marvel at the diversity of habitats and wildlife.

Route planner

One to three weeks

a whistle-stop tour of the country's highlights

Southern highlights This circuit covers some of the most popular destinations in the country. Spend a couple of days in **Lima**, visiting the city's fascinating museums to gain an overview of the country's exceptionally rich history and culture. If your budget allows, you can also make the most of the capital's great gastronomy and vibrant nightlife. Then fly to **Cuzco** for a taste of its Inca and colonial heritage. On a short visit, you can catch the train from Cuzco directly to **Machu Picchu**, but if you prefer to hike the **Inca Trail** or any of the worthwhile alternatives, you need to consider additional time in the region. From Cuzco, travel to **Puno** to visit the shores and islands of beautiful **Titicaca**, the highest navigable lake in the world. Continue to the white city of **Arequipa** to take in its fine colonial architecture and more great dining opportunities. You can head out from the city to visit the awe-inspiring **Colca Canyon**, before flying back to Lima.

Northern highlights Alternatively, you might prefer to avoid the tourist honeypot of Cuzco and explore a different part of the country. Start, once again, in **Lima**, before travelling to **Huaraz** in the Cordillera Blanca. Only seven hours by road from the capital, it's one of the world's premier high-altitude recreation areas, with unparalleled ease of access. A few days hiking or climbing could easily be combined with the coastal archaeological sites and fine museums near the colonial city of **Trujillo** and further north around **Chiclayo** and **Lambayeque**. From here, continue to the **Chachapoyas** region, which also contains a bewildering number of prehispanic archaeological sites and the spectacular **Gocta waterfall**. For the final stage of your trip, either travel down the beautiful road that descends from the mountains to the subtropical city of **Tarapoto**, or take an even more spectacular ride to **Cajamarca**, surrounded by thermal baths, archaeological and historical sites and lovely countryside. From both Tarapoto and Cajamarca, you can catch a flight back to Lima.

Adding an extra two weeks to your trip would allow you to combine the two itineraries above into a more comprehensive tour of the country. Alternatively, try one of the following routes:

Extended southern route A trip to the **Central Andes** from **Lima** will take you off the beaten path, calling at **Huancayo**, **Huancavelica** and **Ayacucho** in a week to 10 days. Obviously the more time you allow, the more variety you'll see, especially in the **Mantaro Valley** near Huancayo and the places of historical interest around Ayacucho. These are also two of the best places to experience festivals and buy handicrafts. From Ayacucho, you can travel to Cuzco via **Andahuaylas** and **Abancay**. As an alternative to the highlands, head south from Lima on the Pan-American Highway for a week or so on the southern coast, taking in the **Paracas Peninsula**, with its marine birdlife, and the incredible **Nazca Lines**. A paved road runs from Nazca, via Abancay, to Cuzco. On this extended itinerary you should have time to see much more of **Cuzco** and its surroundings, especially the **Sacred Valley of the Incas**. Instead of the trek to Machu Picchu, you could try the more demanding and rewarding hike to the Inca city of **Choquequirao**. From Cuzco, make a trip to the southern jungle, either by flying or travelling overland to **Puerto Maldonado**. **Manu National Park** and the **Tambopata National Reserve** provide wonderful opportunities for nature enthusiasts to enjoy the highest levels of biodiversity in the world. Fly back to **Lima**, either from Puerto Maldonado or Cuzco.

Extended northern route Travel overland from **Lima** to **Huaraz** for trekking in the Cordilleras Blanca or Huayhuash. Both the **Huayhuash** and **Alpamayo circuits** are excellent long-distance high-altitude treks in this area. Head to **Trujillo** to visit the archaeological sites but break up a surfeit of sightseeing at the popular seaside resort of **Huanchaco**, before continuing to **Chiclayo** and **Chachapoyas** as above. Then descend from the mountains to **Tarapoto** and **Yurimaguas**, and travel by riverboat to **Iquitos**. The Amazonian city is the jumping-off point for the **northern jungle**, where there is a good network of jungle lodges. From Iquitos, catch a flight back to **Lima**.

Essential Peru

Finding your feet

Peru is the third largest South American country. Virtually its entire 2250-km Pacific coast is desert. From the narrow coastal shelf the Andes rise steeply to a high plateau dominated by massive ranges of snow-capped peaks, gouged with deep canyons. These heavily forested and deeply ravined mountains slope more gradually to the east, where the vast jungles of the Amazon Basin begin. Lima, the sprawling capital, is daunting at first sight, but worth investigating for its museums, colonial architecture and nightlife.

Fact file

Location 12.0433° S, 77.0283° W
Capital Lima
Time zone GMT -5 hrs
Telephone country code +51
Currency Nuevo sol (s/)

Getting around

With the exception of a very few regional connections, such as between Cuzco and La Paz (Bolivia), all international flights arrive at Jorge Chávez Airport near Lima. Major roads and good-quality bus services radiate out from Lima in every direction, including the Pan-American Highway which runs north–south along the coast. Travelling east, great steps have been taken to improve the road links between the Pacific and the highlands, including the completion of the fully paved Carretera Interoceánica, which runs from the

Pacific port of Ilo to Puerto Maldonado and on to the Brazilian border. However, more minor roads in the highlands and jungle regions can be poor and may be impassable during or after the rainy season. Travelling overland takes time, so if you're on a short visit, try to stick to one area or consider flying. Trips anywhere in the Amazon Basin will involve river transport. For further information, see Getting around, page 1514.

When to go

Each of Peru's geographical zones has its own climate. High season in the highlands is from May to September, when the weather is most stable for hiking and climbing. At this time the days are generally clear and sunny with temperatures around 20-25°C, though nights can be very cold at high altitude (often below freezing at night). During the wettest months in the highlands, November to April, average temperatures are 18°C, or 15°C at night. Some roads become impassable and hiking trails can be very muddy. April and May, at the end of the highland rainy season, is a beautiful time to see the Peruvian Andes, but the rain may linger, so be prepared.

On the coast, high season is September, and Christmas to February. The summer months from December to April are hot and dry, with temperatures of 25-35°C, but from approximately May to October much of this area (from the south to about 200 km north of Lima) is covered with *garúa*, a blanket of cloud and mist, caused by prevailing inshore winds picking up moisture over the cold Peruvian current. At this time only the northern

Weather Lima					
January	**February**	**March**	**April**	**May**	**June**
26°C 20°C 2mm	26°C 20°C 1mm	26°C 20°C 0.5mm	24°C 17°C 0mm	22°C 15°C 0mm	20°C 15°C 4mm
July	**August**	**September**	**October**	**November**	**December**
19°C 15°C 3mm	18°C 13°C 9mm	19°C 13°C 1mm	20°C 14°C 1mm	22°C 16°C 0.5mm	24°C 18°C 0mm

Tip...
Every bit as important as knowing where to go and what the weather will be like is Peru's festival calendar; check the website of **iPerú**, www.peru.travel. Local festivals are listed under each relevant town, and the major holidays are given in Essentials A-Z, page 1521.

beaches near Tumbes are warm and pleasant enough for swimming.

The best time to visit the jungle is during the dry season, from April to October, when temperatures reach 35°C (although a cold front can pass through at night in the south). During the wet season (November to April), it is oppressively hot (40°C and above) and while it only rains for a few hours at a time, which won't spoil your trip, it is enough to make some roads virtually impassable, making travel more difficult.

The high season for foreign tourism is from June to September (but year-round in Cuzco and Machu Picchu), while domestic tourism peaks on certain holidays, Christmas, Semana Santa and Fiestas Patrias. Prices rise and accommodation and bus tickets are harder to come by. If you know when you will be travelling, buy your tickets in advance.

Time required

A fortnight is enough time to focus on either the north or the south of the country for a tour of the major sites. Add another week or two to explore in more depth and to travel overland. You would need at least a month to cover the whole country; six weeks is preferable.

Best trekking destinations

Lima

★Lima's colonial centre and suburbs, shrouded in fog which lasts eight months of the year, are fringed by the *pueblos jóvenes* which sprawl over the dusty hills overlooking the city. It has a great many historic buildings and some of the finest museums in the country and its food, drink and nightlife are second to none. Although not the most relaxing of South America's capitals, it is a good place to start before exploring the rest of the country.

Central Lima   *Colour map 3, C2.*

the traditional heart of the city retains its colonial core

An increasing number of buildings in the centre are being restored and the whole area is being given a new lease of life as the architectural beauty and importance of the Cercado (as it is known) is recognized. Most of the tourist attractions are in this area. Some museums are only open 0900-1300 from January to March, and some are closed entirely in January.

☆Plaza de Armas (Plaza Mayor) and around

One block south of the Río Rímac lies the Plaza de Armas, or Plaza Mayor, which has been declared a World Heritage Site by UNESCO. Running along two sides are arcades with shops: Portal de Escribanos and Portal de Botoneros. In the centre of the plaza is a bronze fountain dating from 1650.

The **Palacio de Gobierno** ① *Mon-Fri 0830-1300, 1400-1730*, on the north side of the Plaza, stands on the site of the original palace built by Pizarro. The changing of the guard is at 1145-1200. The palace can be visited on a free 45-minute tour (Spanish and English); register two days in advance at the palace's tourist office (ask guard for directions).

The **Cathedral** ① *T01-427 9647, Mon-Fri 0900-1700, Sat 1000-1300; entry to cathedral US$3.65, ticket also including Museo Arzobispado US$11*, was reduced to rubble in the earthquake of 1746. The reconstruction, on the lines of the original, was completed 1755. Note the splendidly carved stalls (mid-17th century), the silver-covered altars surrounded by fine woodwork, mosaic-covered walls bearing the coats of arms of Lima and Pizarro and an allegory of Pizarro's commanders, the 'Thirteen Men of Isla del Gallo'. The remains of Francisco Pizarro, found in the crypt, lie in a small chapel, the first on the right of the entrance. The cathedral's **Museo de Arte Religioso** has sacred paintings, portraits, altar pieces and other items, as well as a café and toilets. Next to the cathedral is the **Archbishop's Palace and museum** ① *T01-427 5790, Mon-Sat 0900-1700*, rebuilt in 1924, with a superb wooden balcony. Permanent and temporary exhibitions are open to the public.

Just behind the Municipalidad de Lima is **Pasaje Ribera el Viejo**, which has been restored and is now a pleasant place, with several good cafés with outdoor seating. Nearby is the **Casa Solariega de Aliaga** ① *Unión 224, T01-427 7736, Mon-Fri 0930-1300, 1430-1745, US$11, knock on the door and wait to see if anyone will let you in, or contact in advance for tour operators who offer guided visits.* It is still occupied by the Aliaga family and is open to the public and for functions. The house contains what is said to be the oldest ceiling in Lima and is furnished entirely in the colonial style. The **Casa de la Gastronomía Nacional Peruana** ① *Conde de Superunda 170, T01-426 7264, www.limacultura.pe, US$1, behind the Correo Central*, has an extensive permanent collection of objects and displays on Peruvian food, historic and regional. It also has temporary exhibitions on the same theme. All signs are in Spanish.

Essential Lima

Finding your feet

All international flights land at Jorge Chávez airport in Callao, 16 km northwest of the centre; take a taxi into town. If arriving in the city by bus, most of the recommended companies have their terminals just south of the historic centre, many on Avenida Carlos Zavala. This is not a safe area so you should take a taxi to and from there. Downtown Lima is the historic centre of the city and retains many colonial buildings. Miraflores is 15 km south. It has a good mix of places to stay, parks, great ocean views, bookstores, restaurants and cinemas. From here you can commute to the centre by bus (45 minutes minimum) or taxi (30 minutes minimum). Neighbouring San Isidro is the poshest district, while Barranco, a little further out, is a centre for nightlife. Callao, Peru's major port, merges with Lima but is a city in its own right, with over one million inhabitants.

Getting around

Downtown Lima can be explored on foot by day; at night a radio taxi is safest. Buses, combis and colectivos provide an extensive public transport system but are not entirely safe. Termini are posted above the windscreens, with the route written on the side. There is also the Metropolitano rapid transit bus system and a limited metro service, neither of which is particularly useful for visitors. In most cases, taxis are the best way to travel between different districts. Bear in mind that Lima's roads are horribly congested at all times of day, so allow plenty of time to get from A to B and be patient. See also Transport, page 1282.

Tip...

Several blocks, with their own names, make up a long street, a jirón (often abbreviated to Jr). Street corner signs bear both names, of the jirón and of the block. In the historic centre blocks also have their colonial names.

When to go

Only 12° south of the equator, one would expect a tropical climate, but Lima has two distinct seasons. The winter is May-November, when a garúa (mist) hangs over the city, making everything look grey. It is damp and cold, 8-15°C. The sun breaks through around November and temperatures rise to 30°C or more. Note that the temperature in the coastal suburbs is lower than the centre because of the sea's influence. Protect against the sun's rays when visiting the beaches.

Time required

A few days are enough to see the highlights; a full week will allow more in-depth exploration.

East of Plaza de Armas

The first two blocks of Calle Ancash, from Calle Carabaya (on the east side of the Palacio de Gobierno) to San Francisco church, have been designated the 'tourist circuit of the Calles El Rastro y Pescadería'. (These are the colonial names of these two blocks.) The circuit starts from **Desamparados railway station** (which now houses fascinating exhibitions on Peruvian themes) and includes the open-air **Museo de Sitio Bodega y Quadra** ① *Ancash 213, Tue-Sun 0900-1700, free* (which displays the foundations of an old building), the **Casa de la Literatura** ① *Ancash 207, www. casadelaliteratura.gob.pe, Tue-Sun 1000-1900, free* (with an exhibit about Peruvian identity and holds cultural events) and several historic houses. The area is fully pedestrianized.

At the end of the circuit is the baroque church of ☆**San Francisco** ① *1st block of Jr Lampa, corner of Ancash, T01-426 7377 ext 111, www.museocatacumbas.com, daily 0930-1645, guided tours only, US$2.75, students half price, US$0.40 children,* which was finished in 1674 and withstood the 1746 earthquake. The nave and aisles are lavishly decorated in Mudéjar style. The monastery is famous for the Sevillian tilework and panelled ceiling in the cloisters (1620). The catacombs under the church and part of the monastery are well worth seeing. The late 16th-century **Casa de Jarava** or **Pilatos** ① *Jr Ancash 390,* is opposite. Close by, **Casa de las Trece Monedas** ① *Jr Ancash 536,* still has the original doors and window grills. **Parque de la Muralla** ① *daily 0900-2000,* on the south bank of the Rímac, incorporates a section of the old city wall, fountains, stalls and street performers. There is a cycle track, toilets and places to eat both inside and near the entrance on Calle de la Soledad.

The **Palacio Torre Tagle** (1735) ① *Jr Ucayali 363, Mon-Fri during working hours*, is the city's best surviving example of secular colonial architecture. Today, it is used by the Foreign Ministry, but visitors are allowed to enter courtyards to inspect the fine Moorish-influenced wood-carving in balconies and wrought ironwork. At Ucayali 391 and also part of the Foreign Ministry is the Centro Cultural Inca Garcilaso, which holds cultural events. **Casa de la Rada**, or **Goyeneche** ① *Jr Ucayali 358*, opposite, is a fine mid 18th-century French-style town house which now belongs to a bank. The patio and first reception room are open occasionally to the public. **Museo Banco Central de Reserva** ① *Jr Ucayali at Jr Lampa, T01-613 2000 ext 2655, Tue-Fri 1000-1630, Wed 1000-1900, Sat-Sun 1000-1300, free, photography prohibited*, houses a large collection of pottery from the Vicus or Piura culture (AD 500-600) and gold objects from Lambayeque, as well as 19th- and 20th-century paintings: both sections are highly recommended. **San Pedro** ① *3rd block of Jirón Ucayali, Mon-Sat 0930-1145, 1700-1800,* finished by Jesuits in 1638, has marvellous altars with Moorish-style balconies, rich gilded wood carvings in choir and vestry, and tiled throughout. Several Viceroys are buried here; the bell called La Abuelita, first rung in 1590, sounded the Declaration of Independence in 1821.

Between Avenida Abancay and Jr Ayacucho is **Plaza Bolívar**, where General José de San Martín proclaimed Peru's independence. The plaza is dominated by the equestrian statue of the Liberator. Behind lies the Congress building which occupies the former site of the Universidad de San Marcos and is now the **Museo del Congreso y de la Inquisición** ① *Plaza Bolívar, C Junín 548, near the corner of Av Abancay, T01-311 7777, ext 5160, www.congreso.gob.pe/museo.htm, daily 0900-1700, free.* The main hall, with a splendidly carved mahogany ceiling, remains untouched. The Court of Inquisition was held here from 1584; between 1829 and 1938 it was used by the Senate. In the basement there

① **Lima**

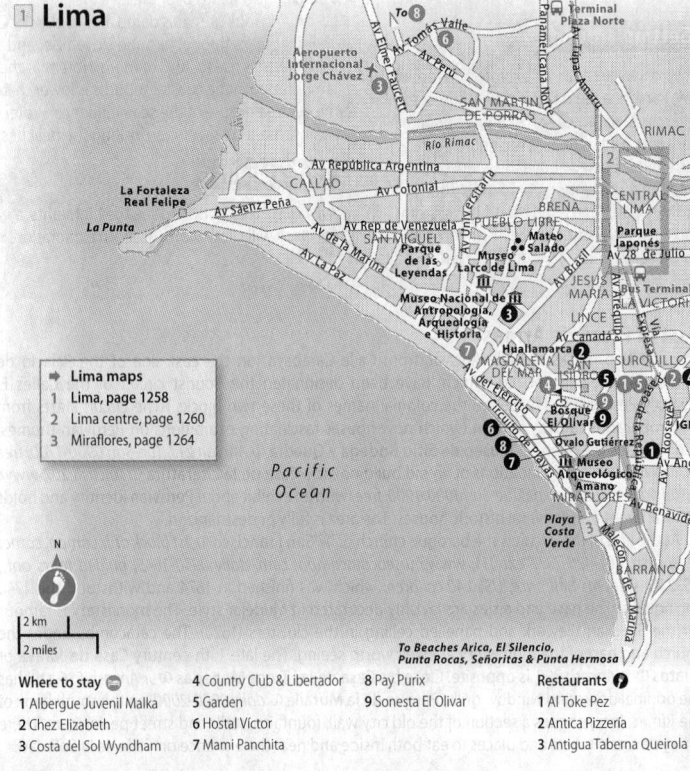

Where to stay 🛏
1 Albergue Juvenil Malka
2 Chez Elizabeth
3 Costa del Sol Wyndham
4 Country Club & Libertador
5 Garden
6 Hostal Víctor
7 Mami Panchita
8 Pay Purix
9 Sonesta El Olivar

Restaurants 🍴
1 Al Toke Pez
2 Antica Pizzería
3 Antigua Taberna Queirola

is a recreation *in situ* of the gruesome tortures. A description in English is available at the desk and students will offer to show round for a tip.

Behind the Congress is the Mercado Municipal (or Central) and the Barrio Chino, with many chifas and small shops selling oriental items. Block 700 of Ucayali is pedestrianized in `Chinese' style. The whole area is jam-packed with people.

West of Plaza de Armas

The 16th-century **Santo Domingo church and monastery** ① *T01-427 6793, monastery and tombs Mon-Sat 0900-1230, 1500-1800; Sun and holidays morning only, US$1.65*, is on the first block of Jr Camaná. The attractive first cloister dates from 1603. Beneath the sacristy are the tombs of San Martín de Porres, one of Peru's most revered saints, and Santa Rosa de Lima (see below). In 1669, Pope Clement presented the alabaster statue of Santa Rosa in front of the altar. Behind Santo Domingo is **Alameda Chabuca Granda**, named after one of Peru's greatest singers. In the evening there are free art and music shows and you can sample foods from all over Peru. A couple of blocks beyond Santo Domingo is **Casa de Osambela** or **Oquendo** ① *Conde de Superunda 298, T01-427 7987 (ask the caretaker if you can visit)*. It is said that José de San Martín stayed here after proclaiming independence from Spain. The house is typical of Lima secular architecture with two patios, a broad staircase leading from the lower to the upper floor, fine balconies and an observation tower. It is now the Centro Cultural Inca Garcilaso de la Vega and headquarters of various academies. A few blocks west is **Santuario de Santa Rosa** ① *Av Tacna, 1st block, T01-425 1279, daily 0930-1300, 1500-1800, free to the grounds*, a small but graceful church and a pilgrimage centre, consisting of the hermitage built by Santa Rosa herself, the house in which she was born, a section of the house in which she attended to the sick, her well and other relics.

Due west of the Plaza de Armas is **San Agustín** ① *Jr Ica 251, T01-427 7548, daily 0830-1130, 1630-1900, ring for entry*, whose façade (1720) is a splendid example of churrigueresque architecture. There are carved choir stalls and effigies, and a sculpture of Death, said to have frightened its maker into an early grave. The church has been restored since the last earthquake, but the sculpture of Death is in storage. Further west, **Las Nazarenas church** ① *Av Tacna, 4th block, T01-423 5718, daily 0700-1200, 1600-2000*, is built around an image of Christ Crucified painted by a liberated slave in 1655. This is the most venerated image in Lima and is carried through the streets on a silver litter, along with an oil copy of El Señor de los Milagros (Lord of Miracles) encased in a gold frame (the whole weighing nearly a ton), on 18, 19 and 28 October and again on 1 November (All Saints' Day). *El Comercio* newspaper and local pamphlets give details of times and routes.

South of Plaza de Armas

The Jr de La Unión, the main shopping street, runs southwest from the Plaza de Armas. It has been converted into a pedestrian precinct which teems with life in the evening. In the two blocks south of Jr Unión, known as Calle Belén, several shops sell souvenirs and curios. **La Merced** ① *Unión y Miró Quesada, T01-427 8199, Mon-Sat*

SAN JUAN DE LURIGANCHO

Cerro San ▲ *Cristóbal*

Av Independencia

SANTA ANITA

Cerro *El Agustino*

Av Aviación
Av Mexico
Av Nicolás Arriola

Av de Evitamiento

SAN BORJA

ATE

To Puruchuco

LA MOLINA

Museo de la Nación & Gran Teatro Nacional

Av Javier Prado Este

Hipódromo de Monterrico

MONTERRICO

Av Panamericana Sur

Av Aviación

Av Primavera

Av Alonso de Molina

Museo de Oro del Perú

Terminal Lima Sur Ñococongo

Av Los Héroes

To Chorrillos

El Tren Eléctrico ▬▬▬

Metropolitano bus line ▬▬▬

4 Chifa Titi
5 Como Agua Para Chocolate
6 Havanna
7 Pan de la Chola
8 San Antonio
9 Segundo Muelle

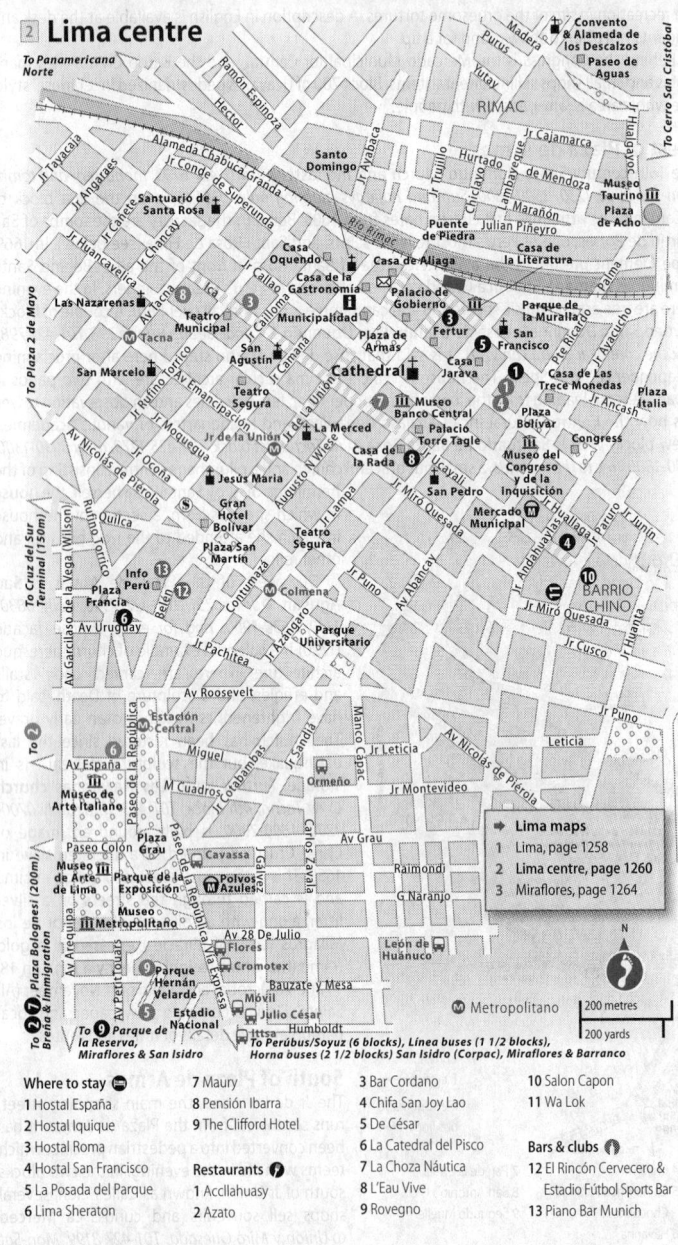

2 Lima centre

To Panamericana Norte

RIMAC

Convento & Alameda de los Descalzos
Paseo de Aguas

To Cerro San Cristóbal

Museo Taurino
Plaza de Acho

Santo Domingo

Santuario de Santa Rosa

Casa Oquendo
Casa de Aliaga
Puente de Piedra
Casa de la Literatura

Las Nazarenas
Teatro Municipal
Casa de la Gastronomía
Municipalidad
Palacio de Gobierno
Parque de la Muralla

To Plaza 2 de Mayo

San Marcelo
San Agustín
Plaza de Armas
Fertur
San Francisco

Cathedral
Casa Jarava
Casa de Las Trece Monedas
Plaza Italia

Teatro Segura
La Merced
Museo Banco Central
Plaza Bolívar
Congress

Jesús María
Palacio Torre Tagle
Museo del Congreso y de la Inquisición

Casa de la Rada
San Pedro
Mercado Municipal

To Cruz del Sur Terminal (150m)

Gran Hotel Bolívar
Plaza San Martín
Teatro Segura

BARRIO CHINO

Info Perú
Plaza Francia

Parque Universitario

To Plaza Francia

Estación Central

Museo de Arte Italiano

Av España

Plaza Grau

Paseo Colón
Museo de Arte de Lima
Museo Metropolitano

Parque de la Exposición

Polvos Azules
Cavassa

To Plaza Bolognesi (200m)

To Plaza Bolognesi
Breña & Immigration

Parque Hernán Velarde

Estadio Nacional

Flores
Cromotex
Móvil
Julio César

León de Huánuco

Metropolitano

To Parque de la Reserva, Miraflores & San Isidro

To Perúbus/Soyuz (6 blocks), Línea buses (1 1/2 blocks),
Horna buses (2 1/2 blocks) San Isidro (Corpac), Miraflores & Barranco

Ittsa

N

200 metres
200 yards

→ Lima maps
1 Lima, page 1258
2 Lima centre, page 1260
3 Miraflores, page 1264

Where to stay 🛏
1 Hostal España
2 Hostal Iquique
3 Hostal Roma
4 Hostal San Francisco
5 La Posada del Parque
6 Lima Sheraton
7 Maury
8 Pensión Ibarra
9 The Clifford Hotel

Restaurants 🍴
1 Accllahuasy
2 Azato
3 Bar Cordano
4 Chifa San Joy Lao
5 De César
6 La Catedral del Pisco
7 La Choza Náutica
8 L'Eau Vive
9 Rovegno
10 Salon Capon
11 Wa Lok

Bars & clubs 🍸
12 El Rincón Cervecero & Estadio Fútbol Sports Bar
13 Piano Bar Munich

0800-1245, 1600-2000, Sun 0700-1300, 1600-2000; monastery daily 0800-1200 and 1500-1730, is in Plazuela de la Merced. The first Mass in Lima was said here on the site of the first church to be built. The restored façade is a fine example of colonial Baroque. Inside are some magnificent altars and the tilework on some of the walls is noteworthy. A door from the right of the nave leads into the Monastery. The cloister dates from 1546.

Jr de la Unión leads to **Plaza San Martín**, which has a statue of San Martín in the centre. The plaza has been restored with colourful flower beds and is now a nice place to sit and relax. On its west side is the refurbished **Gran Hotel Bolívar** ① *Jr de la Unión 958, T01-619 7171, www.granhotelbolivar.com.pe*, which has a huge stained-glass dome over the entrance lobby. Its **El Bolivarcito** bar calls itself 'La Catedral del Pisco Sour'.

Further south, the **Museo de Arte Italiano** ① *Paseo de la República 250, T01-423 9932, Tue-Fri 0900-1900, Sat-Sun 1100-1700, US$1*, is in a wonderful neoclassical building, given to Peru on the centenary of its independence. Note the remarkable mosaic murals on the outside. It consists of a large collection of Italian and other European works of art and houses the **Instituto de Arte Contemporáneo**, which has many exhibitions.

Across Avenida 9 de Diciembre from here is the **Parque de la Exposición**, inaugurated for the Lima International Exhibition in 1872. **The Palacio de la Exposición**, built in 1868, now houses the **Museo de Arte de Lima** ① *Paseo Colón 125, T01-204 0000, www.mali.pe, Tue-Sun 1000-1900, Sat 1000-1700, US$9.35, students and over-65s half price, children under 8 free, reductions for Peruvians, free on Thu till 1500 and first Fri of month 1700-2200, bilingual guides available 1100-1600, signs in English*. There are more than 1200 exhibits from a collection of 17,000, giving a chronological history of Peruvian cultures and art from the Paracas civilization up to today. It includes excellent examples of 17th- and 18th-century Cuzco paintings, a beautiful display of carved furniture, heavy silver and jewelled stirrups and also pre-Columbian pottery. It also has theatre, film and concerts (see the website for details, or look in the museum itself), and a café.

The grounds now incorporate the **Gran Parque Cultural de Lima**. This large park has an amphitheatre, Japanese garden, food court and children's activities. Relaxing strolls through this green, peaceful and safe oasis in the centre of Lima are recommended. In the south of the park is the **Museo Metropolitano** ① *Av 28 de Julio, T01-433 7122, www.limacultura.pe, Tue-Sat 1000-2000, Sun from 1100, US$1.35*, which has audiovisual displays and temporary exhibitions about the history of Lima; it also hosts lectures and has a library.

In **Parque de la Reserva** ① *block 6 of Av Arequipa and Jr Madre de Dios opposite Estadio Nacional, Santa Beatriz, www.parquedelareserva.com.pe, Mon, Tue 0600-1300, Wed-Sun and holidays 0600-1300, 1500-2230*, is the **Circuito Mágico del Agua** ① *displays at 1915, 2015, 2130, US$1.50*, a display of 13 fountains, the highest reaching 80 m, enhanced by impressive light and music shows three times a night. It's great fun and very popular.

Inner suburbs

visit the major museums for an overview of Peru's history and culture

Rímac and Cerro San Cristóbal

The **Puente de Piedra**, behind the Palacio de Gobierno, is a Roman-style stone bridge built in 1610, crossing the Río Rímac to the district of the same name. Previously run-down and unsafe, Rímac is experiencing a revival. On Jr Hualgayoc is the bullring in the **Plaza de Acho**, inaugurated on 20 January 1766, with the **Museo Taurino** ① *Hualgayoc 332, T01-482 3360, Mon-Sat 0800-1600, US$1, students US$0.50, photography US$2*. Apart from matador's relics, the museum contains good collections of paintings and engravings, some of the latter by Goya. There are two bullfight seasons: October to first week in December and during July.

The **Convento de Los Descalzos** ① *Alameda de Los Descalzos, Rímac, T01-481 0441, Wed-Sun 1000-1300, 1500-1800, US$1, guided tour only, 45 mins in Spanish (worth it)*, was founded in 1592. It contains over 300 paintings of the Cuzco, Quito and Lima schools which line the four main cloisters and two ornate chapels. The chapel of El Carmen was constructed in 1730 and is notable for its baroque gold leaf altar. The museum shows the life of the Franciscan friars during colonial and early republican periods. The cellar, infirmary, pharmacy and a typical cell have been restored.

BACKGROUND

Lima

Lima, capital of Peru, is built on both sides of the Río Rímac, at the foot of Cerro San Cristóbal. It was originally named La Ciudad de Los Reyes, in honour of the Magi, at its founding by conquistador Francisco Pizarro in 1535. From then until the independence of the South American republics in the early 19th century, it was the chief city of Spanish South America. The name Lima, a corruption of the Quechua name Rimac (speaker), was not adopted until the end of the 16th century.

The Universidad de San Marcos was founded in 1551 and a printing press in 1595, both among the earliest of their kind in South America. Lima's first theatre opened in 1563, and the Inquisition was introduced in 1569 (it was not abolished until 1820). For some time the Viceroyalty of Peru embraced Colombia, Ecuador, Bolivia, Chile and Argentina. There were few cities in the Old World that could rival Lima's power, wealth and luxury, which was at its height during the 17th and early 18th centuries. The city's wealth attracted many freebooters and in 1670 a protecting wall 11 km long was built round it, then destroyed in 1869. The earthquake of 1746 destroyed all but 20 houses, killed 4000 inhabitants and ended the city's pre-eminence. It was only comparatively recently, with the coming of industry, that Lima began to change into what it is today.

Over the years the city has changed out of all recognition. The metropolitan area contains 8.6 million people, which equates to half the urban population of Peru and nearly one-third of the country's total population. Two-thirds of Peru's industries are located in the capital. Many of the hotels and larger businesses have relocated to the fashionable suburbs of Miraflores and San Isidro, thus moving the commercial heart of the city away from the Plaza de Armas. Modern Lima is seriously affected by haotic traffic and smog for much of the year and is surrounded by poor grimy neighbourhoods. Many of these former squatters' camps of shacks in the desert have evolved into bustling working-class districts, home to millions of inhabitants and much of the city's commercial activity. They are generally not safe to visit on your own, but going accompanied by a local friend or guide can provide an eye-opening insight into the reality of life in Lima.

Cerro San Cristóbal dominates downtown Lima. It can be visited on a one-hour **minibus tou** ① *Camaná y Conde Superunda, every 15 mins daily 1000-2100, US$3*, departing from in front of Santo Domingo. The tour includes a look at the run-down Rímac district, passes the Convento de lo Descalzos (see above), ascends the hill through one of the city's oldest shanties with its brightly painted houses and spends about 20 minutes at the summit, where there is a small museum and café. There are excellent views on a clear day. The second half of the trip is a historical tour. **Urbanito** buses ① *T01-424 3650, www.urbanito.com.pe,* also include Cerro San Cristóbal on their three-hou tour of central Lima, departing from the Plaza de Armas (weekends and holidays only).

San Borja

☆**Museo de la Nación** ① *Javier Prado Este 2465, T01-613 9393 ext 2484, www.cultura.gob.pe Tue-Sun 0900-1700, closed major public holidays. US$2.50, 50% discount with ISIC card.* Located in th huge **Banco de la Nación** building is the museum for the exhibition and study of the art and histor of the aboriginal races of Peru. There are good explanations in Spanish and English on Peruvia history, with ceramics, textiles and displays of many ruins in Peru. It is arranged so that you ca follow the development of Peruvian precolonial history through to the time of the Incas. A vis is recommended before you go to see the archaeological sites themselves. There are display of the tomb of the Señor de Sipán, artefacts from Batán Grande near Chiclayo (Sicán culture reconstructions of the friezes found at Huaca La Luna and Huaca El Brujo, near Trujillo, and of Sechí and other sites. 'Yuyanapaq' is a photographic record of the events of 1980-2000. Temporar exhibitions are held in the basement, where there is also a Ministerio de Cultura bookshop. Th museum has a cafetería.

To get there, take a taxi from downtown Lima or Miraflores US$3.20. From Avenida Garcilas de la Vega in downtown Lima take a combi with a 'Javier Prado/Aviación' window sticke Get off at the 21st block of Javier Prado at Avenida Aviación. From Miraflores take a bus dow

Avenida Arequipa to Avenida Javier Prado (27th block), then take a bus with a 'Todo Javier Prado' or 'Aviación' window sticker.

Surco

The neighbourhood has a pleasant, well tended, plaza with several restaurants and bars nearby.

Museo de Oro del Perú ① *Alonso de Molina 1100, Monterrico, Surco (between blocks 18 and 19 of Av Primavera), Lima 33, T01-345 1292, www.museoroperu.com.pe. Daily 1030-1800, closed 1 Jan, 1 May, 28 Jul, 25 Dec. US$11.55, children under 11 US$5.60; multilingual audioguides available.* This museum houses an enormous collection of Peruvian gold, silver and bronze objects, an impressive array of arms and military uniforms from Spanish colonial times to the present and textiles from Peru and elsewhere. Allow plenty of time to appreciate everything. More than one hundred of its pieces can be seen in the **Sala Museo Oro del Perú**, in Larcomar.

Breña and Pueblo Libre

Mateo Salado archaeological site ① *Corner of Avs Tingo María (Breña) and M H Cornejo (Pueblo Libre), T01-476 9887, tours Thu-Sun 0900-1600, US$3.35.* West of the centre, adjacent to Plaza de la Bandera, is this large administrative and ceremonial centre from the Ychma culture (AD 1100-1450) with five terraced pyramids made of rammed earth.

South of here, in the Pueblo Libre district is a trio of important museums.

Museo Nacional de Antropología, Arqueología e Historia ① *Plaza Bolívar, Pueblo Libre (not to be confused with Plaza Bolívar in the centre), T01-463 5070, Tue-Sat 0900-1700, Sun and holidays 0900-1600, US$4, students US$1.20, guides available for groups; taxi from downtown US$3; from Miraflores US$4.* The original museum of anthropology and archaeology has ceramics from the Chimú, Nazca, Mochica and Pachacámac cultures, a display on the Paracas culture, various Inca curiosities and works of art, and interesting textiles. **Museo Nacional de Historia** ① *T01-463 2009, Tue-Sat 0900-1700, Sun and holidays 0900-1600, US$3.65,* in a mansion occupied by San Martín (1821-1822) and Bolívar (1823-1826) is next door. It exhibits colonial and early republican paintings, manuscripts and uniforms.

To get there, take any public transport on Avenida Brasil with a window sticker saying 'Todo Brasil'. Get off at the 21st block called Avenida Vivanco. Walk about five blocks down Vivanco. The museum will be on your left. From Miraflores take bus SM 18 Carabayllo-Chorrillos, marked 'Bolívar, Arequipa, Larcomar', get out at block 8 of Bolívar by the Hospital Santa Rosa and walk down Avenida San Martín five blocks until you see a faded blue line marked on the pavement; turn left. The blue line is a pedestrian route (15 minutes) linking the Museo Nacional de Antropología, Arqueología e Historia to the Museo Larco de Lima.

☆**Museo Larco de Lima** ① *Av Bolívar 1515, T01-461 1312, www.museolarco.org, 0900-2200, 0900-1800 24 Dec-1 Jan, US$10.55 (half price for students, seniors US$8.75); texts in Spanish, English and French, disabled access, photography not permitted; taxi from downtown, Miraflores or San Isidro, 15 mins, US$4.* Located in an 18th-century mansion, itself built on a seventh-century pre-Columbian pyramid, this unmissable museum has a collection which gives an excellent overview on the development of Peruvian cultures through their pottery. It has the world's largest collection of Moche, Sicán and Chimú pieces. There is a Gold and Silver of Ancient Peru exhibition, a magnificent textile collection and a fascinating erotica section. Don't miss the storeroom with its vast array of pottery, unlike anything you'll see elsewhere. There is a library and computer room for your own research and has a good café open during museum hours, see below. It is surrounded by beautiful gardens, and has a park outside.

To get there, take any bus to the 15th block of Avenida Brasil. Then take a bus down Avenida Bolívar. From Miraflores, take the SM 18 Carabayllo-Chorrillos (see above), to block 15 of Bolívar.

San Isidro, Miraflores and Barranco are the hub of the capital's social life, with numerous hotels restaurants and night spots (see pages 1268-1277). There are also beaches further south and a number of sights worth seeing. Avenida Arequipa runs south for 52 blocks from downtown Lima to Parque Kennedy in Miraflores. Alternatively, the Vía Expresa, a six-lane urban freeway locall known as 'El Zanjón' (the Ditch) is the fastest route across the city.

San Isidro

To the east of Avenida La República, down Calle Pancho Fierro, is **El Olivar**, an olive grove planted b the first Spaniards which has been turned into a park. Some 32 species of birds have been recorde there. Between San Isidro and Miraflores is **Huallamarca** ① *C Nicolás de Rivera 201 and Av Rosario, T01-222 4124, Tue-Sun 0900-1700, US$1.75.* An adobe pyramid of the Maranga (Lima) culture, it date from about AD 100-500, but has later Wari and Inca remains. There is a small site museum. To ge there, take bus 1 from Avenida Tacna, or minibus 13 or 73 to Choquechaca, then walk.

Miraflores

Parque Kennedy and the adjoining Parque Central de Miraflores are located between Avenida Larco and Avenida Mcal Oscar Benavides (locally known as Avenida Diagonal). The extremely well-kept park area has a small open-air theatre with performances Thursday to Sunday and an arts and crafts market most evenings of the week. To the north is the former house and now museum of the author **Ricardo Palma** ① *Gral Suárez 189, T01-445 5836, http:// ricardopalma.miraflores.gob.pe, Mon-Fri 0915-1245, 1430-1700, US$2.20, includes video and guided tour.*

Tip...
To travel by public transport between Miraflores and central Lima, there is no shortage of Línea Azul buses along Avenida Arequipa. Buses to Barranco can be caught on Avenida Tacna, Avenida Wilson (also called Garcilaso de la Vega), Avenida Bolivia and Avenida Alfonso Ugarte.

At the southern end of Avenida Larco and running along the Malecón de la Reserva is the renovated **Parque Salazar** and the modern shopping centre called **Centro Comercial Larcomar**. Here you will find expensive shops, hip cafés and discos and a wide range of restaurants, all with

100 metres

100 yards

➡ **Lima maps**
1 Lima, page 1258
2 Lima centre, page 1260
3 **Miraflores, page 1264**

Ⓜ Metropolitano

a beautiful ocean view. The 12-screen cinema is one of the best in Lima and even has a 'cine-bar' in the 12th theatre. Don't forget to check out the Cosmic Bowling Alley with its black lights and fluorescent balls.

A few hundred metres to the north is the famous ☆**Parque del Amor**, a great place for a stroll where, on just about any night, you'll see at least one wedding party taking photos.

Museo Arqueológico Amano ① *Retiro 160, 11th block of Av Angamos Oeste, Miraflores, T01-441 2909, www.museoamano.org, by appointment only Mon-Fri 1500-1630, US$9 (photography prohibited)*, has artefacts from the Chancay, Chimú and Nazca periods, which were owned by the late Mr Yoshitaro Amano. It has one of the most complete exhibits of Chancay weaving and is particularly interesting for pottery and pre-Columbian textiles, all superbly displayed and lit. To get there, take a bus or *colectivo* to the corner of Avenida Arequipa y Avenida Angamos and another one to the 11th block of Avenida Angamos Oeste. Taxi from downtown costs US$3.20, from Parque Kennedy, US$2.25.

Turn off Avenida Arequipa at 45th block to reach **Huaca Pucllana** ① *General Borgoño, 8th block s/n, T01-445 8695, www.mirafloresperu.com/huacapucllana/, Wed-Mon 0900-1600, US$4.25, students US$2, includes small site museum and 45-min tour in Spanish or English*, a pre-Inca site which is under excavation. Originally a Lima culture temple to the goddesses of sea and moon (AD 200-700), it became a Wari burial site (AD 700-900) before being abandoned.

Lugar de la Memoria, la Tolerancia y la Inclusion Social (LUM) ① *Bajada San Martín 151, T01-719 2065, www.lum.cultura.pe*, is a museum and documentation centre devoted to the victims of political violence in Peru during 1980-2000, one of several memorial museums throughout the country (see Yalpana Wasi, Huancayo, page 1465, and Museo de la Memoria de ANFASEP, Ayacucho, page 1473).

☆Barranco

The 45-minute walk south from Miraflores to Barranco along the Malecón is recommended in summer. This suburb was already a seaside resort by the end of the 17th century. There are many old mansions in the district, in a variety of styles, several of which are now being renovated, particularly on Calle Cajamarca and around San Francisco church. Barranco is quiet by day but comes alive at night (see Restaurants and Bars pages 1276-1277).

> **Tip…**
> If you wish to walk down the paths or steps from Miraflores to the Costa Verde below, those below the Villena bridge and from Yitzah Rabin Park are said to be safest. Take care on any other descent.

The attractive public library, formerly the town hall, stands on the plaza. It contains the helpful **municipal tourist office** ① *T01-719 2046*. Nearby is the interesting *bajada*, a steep path leading down to the beach. The **Puente de los Suspiros** (Bridge of Sighs) crosses the *bajada* to the earthquake-damaged La Ermita church (only the façade has been restored) and leads towards the Malecón, with fine views of the bay. A number of artists have their workshops in Barranco and there are several chic galleries.

The **Museo de Arte Contemporáneo de Lima (MAC Lima)** ① *Av Miguel Grau 1511, beside the municipal stadium, near Miraflores, T01-514 6800, www.maclima.pe, Tue-Sun 1000-1800, US$2, Sun US$0.35, with guided tour*, has permanent Latin American and European collections and holds temporary exhibitions. **MATE (Asociación Mario Testino)** ① *Av Pedro de Osma 409, T01-251 7755, www.mate.pe, Tue-Sat 1100-2000, Sun 1100-1800, US$5.55, with audio tour (no other explanations)*, is the world-renowned fashion photographer's vision of modern art, with a shop and excellent café/restaurant. Next door, by contrast, and equally important is the **Museo de Arte Colonial Pedro de Osma** ① *Av Pedro de Osma 423, T01-467 0141, www.museopedrodeosma.org, Tue-Sun 1000-1800, US$6.75, students half price, guided tours in English or Spanish*, a private collection of colonial art of the Cuzco, Ayacucho and Arequipa schools.

☆Pachacámac

T01-430 0168, http://pachacamac.cultura.pe, Tue-Sat 0900-1700, Sun 0900-1600; closed public holidays except by appointment, US$3.50, students US$1.75, guide US$7.

When the Spaniards arrived, Pachacámac in the Lurín valley was the largest city and ceremonial centre on the coast. A wooden statue of the creator-god, after whom the site is named, is in the excellent site museum (opened 2016). Hernando Pizarro was sent here by his brother in 1533 in search of gold for Inca emperor Atahualpa's ransom. In their fruitless quest, the Spaniards destroyed images and killed the priests. The ruins encircle the top of a low hill, whose crest was crowned with a **Temple of the Sun**, now partially restored. Slightly apart is the reconstructed **House of the Mamaconas**, where the 'chosen women' spun fine cloth for the Inca and his court. An impression of the scale of the site can be gained from the top of the Temple of the Sun, or from walking or driving the 3-km circuit, which is covered by an unmade road for cars and tour buses.

The site is large and it is expected that tourists will be visiting by vehicle (there are six parking areas). However, there are also combis from the Pan-American Highway (southbound) to Pachacámac for US$0.85 (the window sticker reads 'Pachacámac/Lurín'; let the driver know you want to get off at the ruins. A taxi from downtown will cost approximately US$5.50; pay extra for the driver to wait as you'll struggle to find a taxi back into the city.

Lima's beaches

Even though the water of the whole bay has been declared unsuitable for swimming, Limeños see the beach more as part of their culture than as a health risk. On summer weekends (December-April) the city's beaches get very crowded and lots of activities are organized. The beaches of **Miraflores**, **Barranco** and **Chorrillos** are popular, but the sand and sea here are dirty. It's much better to take a safe taxi south along the Circuito de Playas to Playa Arica (30 km south of Lima). There are many great beaches for all tastes between here and San Bartolo (45 km south). If you really want the height of fashion head to **Asia**, Km 92-104, where there are some 20 beaches with boutiques, hotels, restaurants and condos.

> **Warning...**
> Robbery is a serious threat on the beaches.
> Don't take any belongings of value with you and don't leave bags unattended at any time.

Listings Lima maps p1258, p1260 and p1264

Tourist information

iPerú has offices at **Jorge Chávez international airport** (T01-574 8000, daily 24 hrs); **Casa Basadre** (Av Jorge Basadre 610, San Isidro, T01-421 1627/1227, Mon-Fri 0900-1800); and **Larcomar shopping centre** (La Rotonda nivel 2, stand 211-212, Miraflores, T01-445 9400, daily 1100-2100). The **Municipal tourist kiosk** is on Pasaje Escribanos, behind the Municipalidad, near the Plaza de Armas (T01-632 1542, www. visitalima.pe and www.munlima.gob.pe, daily 0900-1700); ask about guided walks in the city centre. There are 8 **kiosks** in Miraflores: Parque Central; Parque Salazar; Parque del Amor; González Prada y Av Petit Thouars; Av R Palma y Av Petit Thouars; Av Larco y Av Benavides; Huaca Pucllana (closed Sat pm); and Ovalo Gutiérrez. The **tourist police** (Jr Moore 268, Magdalena at the 38th block of Av Brasil, T01-460 1060/T0800-22221, daily 24 hrs) are friendly and very helpful if you have your property stolen, English spoken. Also at Av España y Av Alfonso Ugarte; Colón 246, Miraflores, T01-243 2190, and at the airport. For

English websites, see www.limaeasy.com and www.mirafloresperu.com and for an upmarket city guide see www.limainside.net.

Where to stay

If you are only staying a short time and want to see the main sites, Central Lima is the most convenient place to stay. However, it is not as safe at night as the more upmarket areas of Miraflores, San Isidro and Barranco. All hotels in the upper price brackets charge 18% state tax and service on top of prices. In hotels foreigners pay no tax and the amount of service charge is up to the hotel. Neither is included in the prices below, unless otherwise stated. All those listed below have received good recommendations.

Lima has several international chain hotels: **JW Marriott**, www.marriott.com; **Lima Sheraton**, www.sheraton.com; **Sofitel Royal Park**, www. sofitel.com; **Swissôtel Lima**, www.lima.swissotel. com; **Westin**, www.starwoodhotels.com.

There are dozens of hostels in Lima offering dormitory accommodation and charging

US$10-17 pp, usually including a simple breakfast, hot water in shared bathrooms, kitchen facilities, bar and living room. Double rooms with private bathrooms start at about US$30. Some hostels are linked to travel agents or adventure tour companies.

Central Lima

$$$ The Clifford Hotel
Parque Hernán Velarde 27, near 1st block of Av Petit Thouars, Sta Beatriz, T01-433 4249, www.thecliffordhotel.com.pe.
Nicely converted, republican town house in a quiet and leafy park. Rooms and suites, has a bar, café and conference room.

$$ La Posada del Parque
Parque Hernán Velarde 60, near 1st block of Av Petit Thouars, Sta Beatriz, T01-433 2412, www.incacountry.com.
A charmingly refurbished old house with a collection of fine handicrafts, in a safe area, comfortable rooms, breakfast 0830-0930, airport transfer 24 hrs for US$18 for 1-3 passengers (US$8 pp for larger groups), no credit cards, cash only. Always check the website for special offers and gifts. The owners speak good English. Excellent value. Gay friendly. Has an agreement with the nearby Lawn Tennis Club (Arenales 200 block) for guests to eat at the good-value **Set Point** restaurant and use the gym.

$$ Maury
Jr Ucayali 201, T01-428 8188.
Formerly an upmarket hotel in the historical centre, but past its heyday. Some non-smoking rooms, a/c, frigobar, restaurant, airport transfers, secure. The bar is reputed to be the home of the 1st-ever pisco sour (this is, of course, disputed!).

$$-$ Hostal Iquique
Jr Iquique 758, Breña, T01-433 4724.
Rooms on top floor at the back are best, from singles with shared bath to triples with private bath, well-kept if a bit noisy and draughty, use of kitchen, luggage storage, safe, airport pick up extra.

$ Hostal España
Jr Azángaro 105, T01-427 9196, www.hotelespanaperu.com.
A long-standing travellers' haunt, rooms or dormitories, fine old building, motorcycle parking, laundry service, roof garden, good café, can be very busy.

$ Hostal Roma
Jr Ica 326, T01-427 7576, Facebook: hostalromaperu.
Over 35 years in the business, rooms sleep 1-4, private or shared bath, hot water, often full, luggage deposit and safe box, motorcycle parking, airport transfers (**Roma Tours** arranges city tours, flight reservations). Next door is **Café Carrara**.

$ Hostal San Francisco
Jr Azángaro 127, T01-426 2735.
Dormitories with and without bathrooms, safe, Italian/Peruvian owners, good service, café.

$ Pensión Ibarra
Av Tacna 359, 1402 y 1502 (elevator to 14th/15th floors doesn't run all hours), no sign, T01-427 8603/1035, pensionibarra@gmail.com.
Basic, economical, breakfast US$4, discount for longer stay, noisy, use of kitchen, balcony with views of the city, helpful owners (2 sisters), hot water, full board available (good small café almost next door). Reserve in advance; taxis can't stop outside so book airport pick-up (US$18.50) for safe arrival.

Inner suburbs

San Miguel and Magdalena del Mar are on the seaward side of Pueblo Libre.

$$ Mami Panchita
Av Federico Gallessi 198 (ex-Av San Miguel), San Miguel, T01-263 7203, www.mamipanchita.com.
Dutch/Peruvian-owned, English, Dutch and Spanish spoken, includes breakfast and welcome drink, comfortable rooms with bath, hot water, living room and bar, patio, book exchange, airport transfers, 15 mins from airport, 15 mins from Miraflores, 20 mins from historical centre. Frequently recommended.

San Isidro

$$$$ Country Club
Los Eucaliptos 590, T01-611 9000, www.hotelcountry.com.
Excellent, fine service, luxurious rooms, good bar and restaurant, buisness centre, gym, spa, golf, classically stylish with a fine art collection.

$$$$ Libertador Hotels Peru
Los Eucaliptos 550, T01-518 6300, www.libertador.com.pe.
Overlooking the golf course, full facilities for the business traveller, large comfortable rooms in this relatively small hotel, jacuzzi, a/c,

heating, fine service, good restaurant, airport transfers extra.

$$$$ Sonesta El Olivar
Pancho Fierro 194, T01-712 6000,
www.sonesta.com/Lima.
Excellent, one of the top 5-star hotels in Lima overlooking El Olivar park, modern, good restaurant and bar, terrace, gym, swimming pool, quiet, very attentive, popular.

$$$ Garden
Rivera Navarrete 450, T01-200 9800.
Good beds, a/c, heating, small restaurant, ideal for business visitors, convenient, good value.

$$ Chez Elizabeth
Av del Parque Norte 265, San Isidro, T9980 07557,
http://chezelizabeth.typepad.fr.
Family house in residential area 7 mins' walk from Cruz del Sur bus station. Shared or private bathrooms, TV room, laundry, airport transfers.

$ Albergue Juvenil Malka
Los Lirios 165 (near 4th block of Av Javier Prado Este), San Isidro, T01-442 0162,
www.youthhostelperu.com.
Dormitory style, 4-8 beds per room, also private doubles ($$), English spoken, laundry, climbing wall, nice café, airport transfer.

Miraflores

$$$$ Belmond Miraflores Park
Av Malecón de la Reserva 1035, T01-610 4000,
www.mirafloorespark.com.
An **Orient Express** hotel, excellent service and facilities, beautiful views over the ocean, top class. Rooftop, open-air, heated pool and spa which looks out over the ocean, open to the public when you buy a spa treatment.

$$$$ Casa Andina Private Collection
Av La Paz 463, T01-213 4300,
www.casa-andina.com.
Top of the range hotel in this recommended Peruvian chain (see below), modern, wheelchair accessible, well-appointed large rooms with safe. Fine food in **Alma** restaurant and good value café, **Sama**, first class service, bar, pool and gym.

$$$$ Hotel de Autor
Av 28 de Julio 562B, T01-396 2740; 2nd location at Av de la Aviación 316, T01-383 4268,
www.hoteldeautor.com.
Artistically decorated small hotel in a refurbished town house, in a courtyard off the street (no sign),

4 well-appointed suites and pleasant common areas, personalized service, English spoken.

$$$$ Sonesta Posadas del Inca
Alcanfores 329, T01-241 7688,
www.sonesta.com/Miraflores/.
Part of renowned chain of hotels, convenient location, a/c, restaurant, airport transfer extra.

$$$ Alemán
Arequipa 4704, T01-445 6999,
www.hotelaleman.com.pe.
No sign, comfortable, quiet, garden, excellent breakfast, smiling staff.

$$$ Antigua Miraflores
Av Grau 350 at C Francia, T01-201 2060,
www.antiguamiraflores.com.
A small, elegant hotel in a quiet but central location, excellent service, tastefully furnished and decorated, gym, good restaurant. Recommended.

$$$ Casa Andina
Av 28 de Julio 1088, T01-241 4050,
www.casa-andina.com.
Also at Av Petit Thouars 5444, T01-447 0263, in Miraflores. The 'Classic' hotels in this chain have similar facilities and decor. Very neat, with many useful touches, comfortable beds, fridge, safe, laundry service, buffet breakfast, other meals available. Check website for discounts and for the more upmarket **Casa Andina Select** at Schell 452, T01-416 7500 ($$$$-$$$), with disabled facilities.

$$$ Casa de Baraybar
Toribio Pacheco 216, T01-652 2262,
www.casadebaraybar.com.
1 block from the ocean, extra long beds, a/c or fan, colourful decor, high ceilings, 24-hr room service, laundry, airport transfers free for stays of 3 nights. Bilingual staff. Recommended.

$$$ José Antonio
28 de Julio 398 y C Colón and C Colón 328,
T01-445 7743, www.hotelesjoseantonio.com.
Good in all respects, including the restaurant, large modern rooms, jacuzzis, swimming pool, business facilities, helpful staff speak some English.

$$$ La Castellana
Grimaldo del Solar 222, T01-444 4662,
www.castellanahotel.com.
Pleasant, good value, nice garden, safe, expensive restaurant, laundry, English spoken.

$$$ San Antonio Abad
Ramón Ribeyro 301, T01-447 6766,
www.hotelsanantonioabad.com.
Secure, quiet, helpful, tasty breakfasts, 1 free
airport transfer with reservation, justifiably
popular, good value.

$$$ Señorial
José González 567, T01-445 0139,
www.senorial.com.
90 rooms, with restaurant, room service,
comfortable, nice garden, parking, good services.

$$$-$$ Casa Rodas
Tarapacá 250, T01-242 4872,
www.casarodas.com.
Rooms for 2, 3 or 4, one with private bath, the rest
with shared bath, good beds, helpful staff.

$$$-$$ Hostal El Patio
Diez Canseco 341, T01-444 2107,
www.hostalelpatio.net.
Very nice suites and rooms, comfortable, English
spoken, convenient, *comedor*, gay friendly. Very
popular, reservations are essential.

$$$-$$ Inka Frog
Gral Iglesias 271, T01-445 8979,
www.inkafrog.com.
Self-styled "Exclusive B&B", comfortable, nice
decor, lounge with huge TV, rooftop terrace,
good value.

$$ El Carmelo
Bolognesi 749, T01-446 0575,
www.hotelelcarmelo.com.pe.
Great location a couple of blocks from the Parque
del Amor, small restaurant downstairs serving
criolla food and ceviche, good value, comfortable,
breakfast extra.

$$ Residencial Miraflores Bed and Breakfast
General Borgoño 280, T01-447 8004,
www.residencialmiraflores.com.
Refurbished old home in a good location, rooms
furnished with antiques, nice common areas,
quiet, family run, English spoken.

$$ Sipán
Paseo de la República 6171, T01-241 3758,
www.hotelsipan.com.
Very pleasant, on the edge of a residential area
next to the **Vía Expresa** (which can be heard
from front rooms). Economical meals available
in restaurant, 24-hr room service, security box,
secure parking. Airport transfers available.

$$-$ Albergue Turístico Juvenil Internacional
Av Casimiro Ulloa 328, San Antonio,
T01-446 5488, www.limahostell.com.pe.
Dormitory accommodation or a double private
room, basic cafeteria, travel information, laundry
facilities, swimming pool often empty, extra
charge for breakfast, safe, situated in a nice
villa; 20 mins' walk from the beach. Bus No 2
or *colectivos* pass Av Benavides to the centre.

$$-$ Condor's House
Martín Napanga 137, T01-446 7267,
www.condorshouse.com.
Award-winning, quiet hostel, 2 categories of
dorm rooms with lockers, good bathrooms, also
doubles, good meeting place, TV room with
films, book exchange, *parrillada* prepared once
a week, bar. Helpful staff.

$$-$ Explorer's House
Av Alfredo León 158, by 10th block of
Av José Pardo, T01-241 5002, http://
explorershouselima.com.
No sign, but plenty of indications of the house
number, dorm with shared bath, or double rooms
with bath, hot water, laundry service, Spanish
classes, English spoken, very welcoming.

$$-$ Flying Dog
Diez Canseco 117, T01-445 6745,
www.flyingdogperu.com.
Also at Lima 457 and Olaya 280, all with dorms,
doubles, triples, quads. All are on or near Parque
Kennedy, with kitchen, lockers, but all have
different features. There are others in Cuzco,
Iquitos and Arequipa.

$$-$ Hitchhikers B&B Backpackers
Bolognesi 400, T01-242 3008,
www.hhikersperu.com.
Located close to the ocean, mixture of dorms
and private rooms with shared or private bath,
nice patio, parking, bicycles to borrow, airport
transfers. Also has a hostel in Cuzco.

$$-$ HosteLima
Cnel Inclán 399, T01-242 7034,
www.hostelima.com.
Private double rooms and brightly painted
dorms, close to Parque Kennedy, helpful staff,
safe, bar/restaurant and snack shop, movie room,
travel information.

$$-$ The Lighthouse
Cesareo Chacaltana 162, T01-446 8397,
www.thelighthouseperu.com.

Near Plaza Morales Barros, British/Peruvian run, relaxed, small dorm or private rooms with private or shared bath. Good services, small indoor patio.

$$-$ Lion Backpackers
Grimaldo del Solar 139, T01-447 1827,
www.lionbackpackers.com.
Quiet hostel in a convenient location, private and shared rooms (with lockers), all en suite, those on upper floor are the nicest, clean kitchen facilities, book exchange, helpful owner and staff, bus terminal pick up.

$$-$ Loki Backpackers
José Galvez 576, T01-651 2966,
www.lokihostel.com.
In a quiet area, the capital's sister to the party hostel of the same name in Cuzco, doubles or dorms, good showers, cooked breakfast extra, Fri barbecues, lockers, airport transfers.

$$-$ Pariwana
Av Larco 189, T01-242 4350,
www.pariwana-hostel.com.
Party hostel with doubles and dorms in the heart of Miraflores, individual lockers with power outlets so you can leave your gadgets charging in a safe place. Always lots going on here.

$$-$ Pirwa
Coronel Inclán 494, T01-242 4059,
www.pirwahostels.com.
Members of a chain of hostels in Peru (Cuzco, Arequipa, Puno, Nazca), choice of dorms and double rooms, lockers, transfers arranged, bike rental.

$ Blue House
José González 475, T01-445 0476,
www.bluehouse.com.pe.
A true backpacker hostel, most rooms with bath including a double, basic but good value for the location, *terraza* with *parrilla*, films to watch.

$ Casa del Mochilero
Cesareo Chacaltana 130A, T01-444 9089,
pilaryv@hotmail.com (casa-del-mochilero
on Facebook).
Ask for Pilar or Juan, dorms or double room on terrace, all with shared bath, breakfast and internet extra, hot water, lots of information.

$ Friend's House
Jr Manco Cápac 368, T01-446 6248, Friends.
House.Miraflores.Lima.Peru on Facebook.
Very popular, reserve in advance. Near Larcomar shopping centre, dormitory accommodation

with shared bath and hot water, plenty of good information and help, family atmosphere. Highly recommended. They have another branch at José González 427, T01-446 3521. Neither branch is signed, except on the bell at No 427.

Barranco

$$$$ B
Sáenz Peña 204, T01-206 0800, www.hotelb.pe.
Boutique hotel in an early 20th-century mansion. Beautifully redesigned as a luxury hotel in the original building and a contemporary wing, eclectic design features and a large collection of mostly modern art, next to Lucía de la Puente gallery and convenient for others, blog and Facebook give cultural recommendations, highly regarded Mediterranean/Peruvian restaurant, cocktail bar, plunge pool, parking, excellent service. 1 room for disabled travellers. In **Relais y Châteaux** group.

$$$ Barranco 3B
Jr Centenario 130, T01-247 6915,
www.3bhostal.com.
Small, modern B&B, simple comfortable rooms with fan.

$$-$ Barranco's Backpackers Inn
Mcal Castilla 260, T01-247 1326.
Ocean view, colourful rooms, all en suite, shared and private rooms, tourist information.

$$-$ Domeyer
Jr Domeyer 296, T01-247 1413,
www.domeyerhostel.net.
Private or shared rooms sleeping 1-3 people in a historic house, secure, gay friendly.

$$-$ Safe in Lima
Alfredo Silva 150, T01-252 7330,
www.safeinperu.com.
Quiet, Belgian-run *hostal* with family atmosphere, single, double and triple rooms, very helpful, airport pick-up US$28, good value, reserve in advance, lots of information for travellers.

$ The Point
Malecón Junín 300, T01-247 7997,
www.thepointhostels.com.
Rooms range from doubles to large dormitories, all with shared bath, very popular with backpackers (book in advance at weekends), laundry, gay friendly, restaurant, bar, party atmosphere most of the time, but also space for relaxing, weekly barbecues, travel centre.

Callao (near the airport)

$$$$ Costa del Sol Wyndham
Av Elmer Faucett s/n, T01-711 2000,
www.costadelsolperu.com.
Within the airport perimeter. Offers day rates
as well as overnights if you can't get into the
city. Good service, buffet breakfast, pool, gym,
spa, jacuzzi, but high-priced because of lack of
competition and expensive extras.

$$ Hostal Víctor
Manuel Mattos 325, Urb San Amadeo de Garagay,
Lima 31, T569 4662, Facebook:hostelvictor.
5 mins from the airport by taxi, or phone or email
in advance for free pick-up, large comfortable
rooms, hot water, 10% discount for Footprint
book owners, American breakfast (or packed
breakfast for early departure), evening meals
can be ordered locally, 2 malls with restaurants,
shops, cinemas, etc nearby, very helpful.

$$-$ Pay Purix
Av Japón (formerly Bertello Bolatti), Mz F, Lote 5,
Urb Los Jazmines, 1a Etapa, Callao, T01-484 9118,
www.paypurix.com.
3 mins from airport, can arrange pick-up (taxi
US$6, US$2 from outside airport). Hostel with
doubles and dorms, convenient, English spoken,
CDs, DVDs, games and use of kitchen.

Restaurants

18% state tax and 10% service will be added to
your bill in middle- and upper-class restaurants.
Chinese is often the cheapest at around US$5
including a drink. For the rise of Peruvian
cuisine, see Gastronomic Lima, opposite.

Central Lima

$$$ Wa Lok
Jr Paruro 864 and 878, Barrio Chino, T01-427 2656.
Good dim sum, cakes and fortune cookies
(when you pay the bill). English spoken,
very friendly. Also at Av Angamos Oeste 700,
Miraflores, T01-447 1329.

$$$-$$ De César
Ancash 300, T01-428 8740. Open 0800-2300.
Old-fashioned atmosphere, apart from the 3 TVs,
breakfasts, snacks, seafood, meat dishes, pastas,
pizza, juices, coffees and teas. Good food.

$$ Chifa San Joy Lao
Ucayali 779.
A *chifa* with a good reputation, one of several
on the pedestrianized part of the Barrio Chino.

$$ L'Eau Vive
Ucayali 370, also opposite the Torre Tagle Palace,
T01-427 5612. Mon-Sat, 1230-1500 and 1930-2130.
Run by nuns, lunch *menú*, Peruvian-style in interior
dining room, or à la carte in either of dining
rooms that open on to patio, excellent, profits
go to the poor, Ave María is sung nightly at 2100.

$$ Salon Capon
Jr Paruro 819.
Good dim sum, at this recommended *chifa*.
Also has a branch at Larcomar shopping centre,
elegant and equally recommended.

$$-$ Bar Cordano
Ancash 202 y Carabaya (in Calles El Rastro y
Pescadería zone).
Historic tavern serving Peruvian food and drinks,
great atmosphere, favoured by politicians.

$$-$ Rovegno
Arenales 456 (near block 3 of Arequipa),
T01-424 8465.
Italian and Peruvian dishes, home-made pasta,
also serves snacks and sandwiches and has a
bakery. Good value.

$ Acllahuasy
Jr Ancash 400. Daily 0700-2300.
Around the corner from **Hostal España**.
Good Peruvian dishes.

$ La Catedral del Pisco
Jr de la Unión 1100 esq Av Uruguay 114,
T01-330 0079. Daily 0800-2200.
Comida criolla and drinks, including free Peruvian
coffee (excellent) or *pisco sour* for Footprint
Handbook owners! Live music at night, Wi-Fi.

Breña and Pueblo Libre

$$$ Café del Museo
At the Museo Larco, Av Bolívar 1515, T01-
462 4757. Daily 0900-2200, seating inside
and on the terrace.
Specially designed interior, selection of salads,
fine Peruvian dishes, pastas and seafood, a tapas
bar of traditional Peruvian foods, as well as
snacks, desserts and cocktails. Highly regarded.

$$ Antigua Taberna Queirolo
Av San Martín 1090, 1 block from Plaza Bolívar,
T01-460 0441, http://antiguatabernaqueirolo.
com. Mon-Sat 0930-2330, Sun 0930-1600.
Atmospheric old bar with glass-fronted shelves of
bottles, marble bar and old photos, owns bodega
next door. Serves lunches, sandwiches and
snacks, good for wine, does not serve dinner.

Gastronomic Lima   For locations, see map, page 1264.

Lima attracts terms such "gastronomic capital of South America", which is reflected in the fact that the **Mistura** festival (www.mistura.pe) each September attracts hundreds of thousands of visitors. There are several restaurants that are championed as the height of culinary excellence. They are often priced beyond the average traveller's budget, but a meal at one of these could be the ideal way to celebrate a special occasion. Most serve à la carte and a tasting menu. At the heart of much of today's Peruvian gastronomy are traditional ingredients, from the coast, the Andes and the jungle. The star chefs all recognize the debt they owe to the cooks of the different regions. Their skill is in combining the local heritage with the flavours and techniques that they have learnt elsewhere, without overwhelming what is truly Peruvian.

Gastón Acurio is usually credited with being the forerunner of the evolution of Peruvian cuisine. He is also recognized for his community work. With **Astrid y Gastón Casa Moreyra** (Avenida Paz Soldán 290, San Isidro, www.astridygaston.com), Acurio and his wife Astrid have moved their flagship restaurant from Miraflores to this historic house in San Isidro. It has been completely remodelled and opened in 2014. Other ventures include ceviche at **La Mar** (Avenida Lar 770, Miraflores, T01-421 3365), *anticuchos* at **Panchita** (Avenida 2 de Mayo 298, Miraflores, T01-242 5957, see Facebook page) and his chain of **T'anta** cafés, eg behind the Municipalidad in the city centre, at Pancho Fierro 115 in San Isidro and in Larcomar.

Central (Santa Isabel 376, Miraflores, T01-446 9301, www.centralrestaurante.com.pe) presents Virgilio Martínez award-winning, sophisticated recipes fusing Peruvian ingredients and molecular cuisine.

Manifiesto (Independencia 130, Miraflores, T01-249 5533, www.manifiesto.pe) is billed as "Tacna meets Italy", bringing together the birthplace and family roots of chef Giacomo Bocchio.

Rafael Osterling has two restaurants in the city: **Rafael** (San Martín 300, Miraflores, T01-242 4149, www.rafaelosterling.com), celebrated for its classic Peruvian dishes incorporating flavours from around the globe, especially the Mediterranean, and **El Mercado** (H Unanue 203, Miraflores, T01-221 1322), which concentrates on seafood, reflecting all the influences on Peruvian cooking.

At **IK** (Elias Aguirre 179, Miraflores, T01-652 1692, reservas@ivankisic.pe, see Facebook page), molecular gastronomy meets Peruvian ingredients at the late Ivan Kisic's restaurant.

Lima 27 (Santa Lucía 295 – no sign, T01-221 5822, www.lima27.com) is a modern restaurant behind whose black exterior you will find contemporary Peruvian cuisine. It's in the same group as **Alfresco** (Malecón Balta 790, T01-242 8960), **Cala on Costa Verde** (http://calarestaurante.com), and a new sandwich bar, **Manduca**, in Jockey Plaza.

Pedro Miguel Schiaffino's **Malabar** (Camino Real 101, San Isidro, T01-440 5200, http://malabar.com.pe) takes the Amazon and its produce as the starting point for its dishes, as does Schiaffino's **Amaz** (Av La Paz 1079, Miraflores, T01-221 9393). This eatery is in a group of four places under the Hilton Hotel. Also here is **Ache** (Avenida La Paz 1055, T01-221 9315, achecocinanikkei on Facebook) which specializes in Japanese fusion cuisine.

La Picantería (Moreno 388 y González Prada, Surquillo, T01-241 6676, www.picanteriasdelperu.com) serves excellent seafood, first-class *ceviche*, has a fish-of-the-day lunch menu and a good bar.

At **AlmaZen** (Federico Recavarrén 298 y Gálvez, T01-243 0474) you will find one of the best organic slow-food restaurants in Latin America.

Beyond Lima there are many excellent innovative restaurants in Arequipa (see www.festisabores.com), Cuzco, Ayacucho and elsewhere. Don't forget that the regional cooking that provided inspiration for Peru's growing international fame is still very much alive and well, often in much more modest surroundings than the fine dining settings of the capital. One such place that has moved to the capital is **Fiesta Gourmet** (Avenida Reducto 1278, T01-242 9009, www.restaurantfiestagourmet.com), which specializes in food from Chiclayo and the north coast: superb food in fancy surroundings.

$$ La Choza Náutica
Jr Breña 204 and 211 behind Plaza Bolognesi,
T01-423 8087, www.chozanautica.com.
Good *ceviche* and friendly service;
has 3 other branches.

$ Azato
Av Arica 298, 3 blocks from Plaza Bolognesi,
T01-423 0278. Open 1200-2300.
Excellent and cheap Peruvian dishes,
menú and à la carte.

San Isidro

$$$ Antica Pizzería
Av 2 de Mayo 732, T01-222 8437. 1200-2400.
Very popular, great ambience, excellent food,
Italian owner. Also in Barranco at Alfonso
Ugarte 242, www.anticapizzeria.com.pe.

$$$ Chifa Titi
Av Javier Prado Este 1212, Córpac, T01-224 8189,
www.chifatiti.com.
Regarded by many as the best Chinese restaurant
in Lima with over 60 years in operation.

$$$-$$ Como Agua para Chocolate
Pancho Fierro 108, T01-222 0297.
Mon-Sat 1200-1600, 1800-2200.
Dutch-Mexican owned restaurant, specializing
in Mexican food as the name suggests, also has
a very amusing Dutch night once a month, *menú*
and à la carte.

$$$-$$ Segundo Muelle
Av Conquistadores 490, T01-717 9998,
www.segundomuelle.com. Daily 1200-1700.
Ceviches and other very good seafood dishes,
including Japanese, *menú* and à la carte, popular.

Cafés

Havanna
Miguel Dasso 163, www.havanna.pe.
Mon-Sat 0700-2300, Sun 0900-2200.
Branch of the Argentine coffee and *alfajores*
chain, others in the city include **Larcomar**.

Miraflores

C San Ramón, known as **Pizza Street** (across from
Parque Kennedy), is a pedestrian walkway lined
with popular outdoor restaurants/bars/discos
that are open until the wee small hours. Good-
natured touts try to entice diners and drinkers
inside with free offers.

$$$ El Kapallaq
Av Reducto 1505. On Facebook.
Mon-Fri 1145-1630 only.

Prize-winning Peruvian restaurant specializing
in seafood and fish, excellent ceviches, also a
few treats for meat eaters.

$$$ El Rincón Gaucho
Av Armendáriz 580, T01-447 4778 and
Av Grau 540, Barranco.
Good grill, renowned for its steaks.

$$$ Huaca Pucllana
Gral Borgoño cuadra 8 s/n, alt cuadra 45
Av Arequipa, T01-445 4042, www.resthuaca
pucllana.com. Daily 1200-1600, 1900-2400.
Facing the archaeological site of the same name,
contemporary Peruvian fusion cooking, very good
food in an unusual setting, popular with groups.

$$$ La Gloria
Atahualpa 201, T01-445 5705, www.lagloria
restaurant.com. Mon-Sat 1300-1600, 2000-2400.
Popular upmarket restaurant serving Peruvian food,
classic and contemporary styles, good service.

$$$ La Preferida
Arias Araguez 698, T01-445 5180, http://
restaurantelapreferida.com. Daily 0800-1700.
Seafood restaurant and tapas bar, with delicious
ceviches, also has a branch in Monterrico.

$$$ La Trattoria
At Larcomar, T01-446 7002,
www.latrattoriadimambrino.com.
Italian cuisine, popular, good desserts.
Has another branch, **La Bodega**,
opposite entrance to Huaca Pucllana.

$$$ Las Brujas de Cachiche
Av Bolognesi 472, T01-447 1883,
www.brujasdecachiche.com.pe.
Mon-Sat 1200-2400, Sun 1230-1630.
An old mansion converted into bars and dining
rooms, fine traditional food (menu in Spanish
and English), live *criollo* music.

$$$ Rosa Náutica
T01-445 0149, www.larosanautica.com.
Daily 1200-2400.
Built on old British-style pier (Espigón No 4), in
Lima Bay. Delightful opulence, fine fish cuisine,
experience the atmosphere by buying a beer in
the bar at sunset.

$$$ Saqra
Av La Paz 646, T01-650 88 84, www.saqra.pe.
Mon-Sat 1200-2400.
Colourful and casual, indoor or outdoor seating,
interesting use of ingredients from all over Peru,
classic flavours with a fun, innovative twist,
inspired by street food and humble dishes,

vegetarian options, many organic products. Also good cocktail bar. Go with a group to sample as many dishes as possible.

$$$-$$ Chifa Internacional
Av Roosevelt (ex República de Panamá) 5915, T01-445 3997, www.chifainternacional.com. Mon-Fri 1230-1530, 1900-2330 (Fri until 0030), Sat 1230-1600, 1900-0030, Sun 1200-2315.
Great *chifa* in San Antonio district of Miraflores.

$$$-$$ Punto Azul
San Martín 595, 01-T445 8078, Benavides 2711, T01-260 8943, with other branches in San Isidro, Surco and San Borja, http://puntoazulrestaurante.com. Tue-Fri 1100-1600, Sat-Sun1100-1700 (San Martín 595 also open Mon-Sat 1200-2400).
Popular, well-regarded chain of seafood and ceviche restaurants.

$$ Café Tarata
Pasaje Tarata 260, T01-446 6330. Mon-Sat 0830-2200.
Good atmosphere, family-run, good varied menu.

$$ El Parquetito
Lima 373 y Diez Canseco, T01-444 0490. Daily 0900-0100.
Peruvian food from all regions, good *menú* and à la carte, serves breakfast, eat inside or out.

$$ La Estancia
Schell 385, 01-444 2558. Sun-Thu 0800-2200.
Café and restaurant, Peruvian dishes with a Mediterranean touch, salads, sandwiches, cocktails.

$$ Las Tejas
Diez Canseco 340, T01-444 4360. Daily 1200-2400.
Good, typical Peruvian food, especially ceviche, *menú* and à la carte.

$$ Lobo del Mar – Octavio Otani
Colón 587, T01-242 1871.
Basic exterior hides one of the oldest *cevicherías* in Miraflores, excellent, a good selection of other seafood dishes.

$$ Mama Olla
Pasaje Tarata 248. Daily 0700-2400.
Charming café on a pedestrian walkway, huge menu, also set meals, big portions.

$ Al Toke Pez
Av Angamos Este 886, Surquillo, across Paseo de la República from Miraflores. Tue-Sun 1130-1530.
Small popular economical ceviche bar, also serves other seafood dishes, tasty, a real find.

$ Govinda
Schell 630.
Vegetarian, from Hare Krishna foundation, lunch *menú* US$3.

$ Madre Natura
Chiclayo 815, T01-445 2522, www.madre naturaperu.com. Mon-Sat 0800-2100.
Natural foods shop and eating place, very good.

Cafés

Café Café
Martin Olaya 250, at the corner of Av Diagonal.
Very popular, good atmosphere, over 100 different blends of coffee, good salads and sandwiches, very popular with 'well-to-do' Limeños. Also in Larcomar.

Café de la Paz
Lima 351, middle of Parque Kennedy and Pasaje Tarata 227, www.cafedelapazperu.com. Daily 0800-2400.
Good outdoor café right on the park, expensive, great cocktails.

C'est si bon
Av Cdte Espinar 663. Daily 100-2100
Excellent cakes by the slice or whole, best in Lima.

Chef's Café
Av Larco 375 and 763. Daily 0700-2400.
Nice places for a sandwich or coffee.

Haiti
Av Diagonal 160, Parque Kennedy. Mon-Thu 0700-0200, Fri-Sat 0700-0300.
Great for people watching, good ice cream.

La Lucha
Av Benavides y Olaya (under Flying Dog), on Parque Kennedy, with small branches between Olaya and Benavides, on Ovalo Gutiérrez and at Larcomar.
Excellent hot sandwiches, limited range, choice of sauces, great juices, *chicha morada* and *café pasado*. Good for a wholesome snack.

La Tiendecita Blanca
Av Larco 111 on Parque Kennedy.
One of Miraflores' oldest, expensive, good people-watching, very good cakes, European-style food and delicatessen.

Pan de la Chola
Av La Mar 918, El-Pan-de-la-Chola on Facebook. Tue-Sat 0800-2200, Sun 0900-1800.
Café and bakery specializing in sourdough bread, Peruvian cheeses, teas, juices and sweets.

San Antonio
Av Angamos Oeste 1494.
Fashionable *pastelería* chain with hot and cold lunch dishes, good salads, inexpensive, busy. Other branches at Rocca de Vergallo 201, Magdalena del Mar, and Av Primavera 373, San Borja.

Barranco

$$$ Canta Rana
Génova 101, T01-247 7274. Sun-Mon 1200-1700, Tue-Sat 1200-2200.
Good ceviche, expensive, small portions, but the most popular local place on Sun.

$$$ La 73
Av Sol Oeste 176, casi San Martín, at the edge of Barranco, T01-2470780. Mon-Sat 1200-2400, Sun 1200-2200.
Mostly meat dishes, has a lunch menu, look for the Chinese lanterns outside, good reputation.

$$$ La Costa Verde
Bajada Armendáriz al lado del Salvataje on Barranquito beach, T01-247 1244, www.restaurantecostaverde.com. Mon-Sat 1300-2300, Sun buffet 1300-1600.
Excellent fish and wine, expensive but considered one of the best.

$$$ Sóngoro Cosongo
Ayacucho 281, T01-247 4730, at the top of the steps down to Puente de Suspiros, www.songorocosongo.com. Mon-Sat 1200-2300, Sun from 2200.
Varied *comida criolla*, "un poco de todo".

$$$-$$ Tío Mario
Jr Zepita 214, on the steps to the Puente de Suspiros.
Excellent *anticuchería*, serving delicious Peruvian kebabs, always busy, fantastic service, varied menu and good prices.

$$ Las Mesitas
Av Grau 341, T01-477 4199. Open 1200-0200.
Traditional tea rooms-cum-restaurant, serving *comida criolla* and traditional desserts which you won't find anywhere else, lunch *menú* served till 1400, US$3.

Cafés

Expreso Virgen de Guadalupe
San Martín y Ayacucho.
Café and vegetarian buffet in an old tram, also seating in the garden, more expensive at weekends.

La Boteca
Grau 310-312.
Smart-looking café-bar.

Tostería Bisetti
Pedro de Osma 116, www.cafebisetti.com.
Coffee, cakes and a small selection of lunchtime dishes, service a bit slow but a nice place.

Bars and clubs

See also Entertainment (below) for a list of *peñas* offering live music and dancing.

Central Lima

The centre of town, specifically Jr de la Unión, has numerous nightclubs, but it's best to avoid the nightspots around the intersection of Av Tacna, Av Piérola and Av de la Vega, as these places are rough and foreigners will receive much unwanted attention. For the latest gay and lesbian nightspots, check out www.gayperu.com.

El Rincón Cervecero
Jr de la Unión (Belén) 1045, T01-428 1422, www.rinconcervecero.com.pe. Mon-Fri 1230-2400, Fri-Sat 1230-0030.
German-style pub, fun.

Estadio Fútbol Sports Bar
Jr de la Unión (Belén) 1049, T01-427 9609. Mon-Wed 1215-2300, Thu 1215-2400, Fri-Sat 1215-0300, Sun 1215-1800.
Beautiful bar with a disco, international football theme, good international and creole food.

Piano Bar Munich
Jr de la Unión 1044 (basement), T01-5737390. Mon-Sat from 1700.
Small and fun.

Miraflores

La Tasca
Av Diez Canseco 117, very near Parque Kennedy, part of the Flying Dog group and under one of the hostels (see Where to stay, page 1270).
Spanish-style bar with cheap beer (for Miraflores). An eclectic crowd including ex-pats, travellers and locals. Gay-friendly. Small and crowded.

Media Naranja
Schell 130, at bottom of Parque Kennedy.
Brazilian bar with drinks and food.

Murphy's
Schell 619, T01-447 1082. Mon-Sat from 1600.
Happy hours every day with different offers, lots of entertainment, very popular.

The Old Pub
San Ramón 295 (Pizza St), www.oldpub.com.pe.
Cosy, with live music most days.

Treff Pub Alemán
Av Benavides 571-104, T01-444 0148 (hidden from the main road behind a cluster of tiny houses signed 'Los Duendes'). Mon-Thu 1200-0100, Fri-Sat 1800-0300, Sun 1900-0100.
A wide range of German beers, plus cocktails, good atmosphere, darts and other games.

Barranco

Barranco is the capital of Lima nightlife. The following is a short list of some of the better bars and clubs. The pedestrian walkway Pasaje Sánchez Carrión, right off the main plaza, has watering holes and discos on both sides. Av Grau, just across the street from the plaza, is also lined with bars, including **the Lion's Head Pub** (Av Grau 268, p 2) and **Déjà Vu** at No 294. Many of the bars in this area turn into discos later on.

Ayahuasca
San Martín 130. Mon-Sat 2000-0300 (opens 1800 Thu-Fri).
In the stunning Berninzon House, which dates from the Republican era, a chilled out lounge bar with several areas for eating, drinking and dancing. Food is expensive and portions are small, but go for the atmosphere.

Barranco Beer Company
Grau 308, T01-247 6211, www.barrancobeer.com. Sun-Wed 1100-2400, Thu 1100-0200, Fri-Sat 1100-0300.
Artisanal brewhouse.

El Dragón
N de Piérola 168, T01-221 4112.
Popular bar and venue for music, theatre and painting.

Juanitos
Av Grau, opposite the park. Daily 1600-0400.
Barranco's oldest bar, where writers and artists congregate, a perfect spot to start the evening.

La Noche
Bolognesi 307, at Pasaje Sánchez Carrión, T01-247 1012, www.lanoche.com.pe. Mon-Sat 2000-0200.
A Lima institution. High standard live music, Mon is jazz night, all kicks off at around 2200.

La Posada del Angel
3 branches, Pedro de Osma 164 and 214, T01-247 0341, see Facebook. Mon-Sat 1900-0300.
These are popular bars serving snacks and meals.

La Posada del Mirador
Ermita 104, near the Puente de los Suspiros (Bridge of Sighs), see Facebook.
Beautiful view of the ocean, but you pay for the privilege.

Santos Café & Espirituosos
Jr Zepita 203, Bajada de Baños, just above the Puente de Suspiros, T01-247 4609, also on Facebook. Mon-Thu 1700-0100, Fri-Sat 1700-0300.
Favourite spot for trendy young professionals who want to drop a few hundred soles, relaxed, informal but pricey.

Sargento Pimienta
Bolognesi 757, www.sargentopimienta.com.pe. Tue-Sat from 2200.
Live music, always a favourite with Limeños.

Victoria
Av Pedro de Osma 135.
Upmarket pub in the beautiful Casa Cillóniz, serving up a selection of beers, cocktails, snacks and live music.

Entertainment

Theatre and concert tickets can be booked through **Teleticket** (T01-613 8888, Mon-Fri 0900-1900, www.teleticket.com.pe). For cultural events, see **Lima Cultural** (www.limacultura.pe), the city's monthly arts programme.

Cinema
The newspaper *El Comercio* lists cinema information in the section called *Luces*. Mon-Wed reduced price at most cinemas. Most films are in English with subtitles and cost from US$7-8.75 in Miraflores and malls, US$3-4 in the centre. The best cinema chains in the city are **Cinemark**, **Cineplanet** and **UVK Multicines**. **Cinematógrafo de Barranco**, *Pérez Roca 196, Barranco, T01-264 4374.* Small independent cinema showing a good choice of classic and new international films.
Filmoteca de Lima, **Centro Cultural PUCP**, *Camino Real 1075, San Isidro, T01-616 1616, http://cultural.pucp.edu.pe.*

Peñas
Del Carajo, *Catalino Miranda 158, Barranco, T01-247 7977, www.delcarajo.com.pe.* All types of traditional music.
La Candelaria, *Av Bolognesi 292, Barranco, T01-247 1314, www.lacandelariaperu.com. Thu-Sat 2000 onwards.* A good Barranco *peña* with a regular dance presentation and other shows.

La Estación de Barranco, *Pedro de Osma 112, T01-247 0344, www.laestaciondebarranco.com, Mon-Sat 1900-0300.* Good, family atmosphere, varied shows.

Las Brisas de Titicaca, *Héroes de Tarapacá 168, at 1st block of Av Brasil near Plaza Bolognesi, T01-715 6960, www.brisasdeltiticaca.com.* A Lima institution with lunch shows Fri-Sat 1300-1730, evening shows Tue-Wed 2100-0015, Thu 2145-0135, Fri-Sat 2200-0200.

Sachún, *Av del Ejército 657, Miraflores, T01-441 0123, Facebook: SachunRestauranteTuristico. Thu-Sat 2100-0300.* Great shows.

Theatre

El Gran Teatro Nacional, *corner of Avs Javier Prado and Aviación, San Borja.* Capable of seating 1500 people, it hosts concerts, opera, ballet and other dance as well as other events.

Teatro Municipal, *Jr Ica 377, T01-315 1300 ext 1767, see Facebook.* Completely restored after a fire, with full programmes and a theatre museum on Huancavelica.

Teatro Segura, *Jr Huancavelica 265, T01-427 9491.* Stages professional performances.

There are many other theatres in the city, some of which are related to cultural centres. All have various cultural activities; the press gives details of performances: **CCPUCP** (see Cinemas, above); Instituto Cultural Peruano-Norteamericano (Jr Cusco 446, Lima Centre, T01-706 7000, central office at Av Angamos Oeste 160, Miraflores, www.icpna.edu.pe); **Centro Cultural Peruano Japonés** (Av Gregorio Escobedo 803, Jesús María, T01-518 7450, www.apj.org.pe).

Festivals

18 Jan Founding of Lima.
Mar/Apr Semana Santa, or Holy Week, is a colourful spectacle with processions.
28-29 Jul Independence, with music and fireworks in the Plaza de Armas on the evening before.
30 Aug Santa Rosa de Lima.
Mid-Sep Mistura, www.mistura.pe, a huge gastronomy fair in Parque Exposición, with Peruvian foods, celebrity chefs, workshops and more.
Oct The month of Our Lord of the Miracles; see Las Nazarenas church, page 1259.

Shopping

Bookshops

Crisol, *Ovalo Gutiérrez, Av Santa Cruz 816, San Isidro, T01-221 1010, below Cine Planet.* Large bookshop with café, titles in English, French and Spanish. Also in **Jockey Plaza Shopping Center** (*Av Javier Prado Este 4200, Surco, T01-436 0004, daily 1100-2300*, and other branches, www.crisol.com.pe).

Epoca, *Av Cdte Espinar 864, Miraflores, T01-241 2951.* Great selection of books, mostly in Spanish.

Ibero Librerías, *Av Diagonal 500, T01-242 2798, Larco 199, T01-445 5520, in Larcomar, Miraflores, and other branches.* Stocks Footprint Handbooks as well as a wide range of other titles.

Camping equipment

It's better to bring all camping and hiking gear from home. Camping gas (the most popular brand is **Doite**) is available from any large hardware store or bigger supermarket. White gas (*bencina*) is available from hardware stores.

Alpamayo, *Av Larco 345, Miraflores at Parque Kennedy, T01-445 1671. Mon-Fri 1000-1930, Sat 1000-1300.* Sleeping mats, boots, rock shoes, climbing gear, water filters, tents, backpacks etc, very expensive but top quality equipment. Owner speaks fluent English and offers good information.

Altamira, *Arica 880, Parque Damert, behind Wong on Ovalo Gutiérrez, Miraflores, T01-445 1286.* Sleeping bags, climbing gear, hiking gear and tents.

Camping Center, *Av Benavides 1620, Miraflores, T01-242 1779, www.campingperu.com. Mon-Fri 1000-1800.* Selection of tents, backpacks, stoves, camping and climbing gear.

El Mundo de las Maletas, *Preciados 308, Higuereta-Surco, T01-449 7850. Daily 0900-2200 and CC Shopping Cente, Av La Mar 2275, San Miguel.* For suitcase repairs.

Tatoo, *CC Larcomar, locs 123-125B, T01-242 1938, www.tatoo.ws. Daily 1100-2150.* For top-quality imported ranges and own brands of equipment.

Todo Camping, *Av Angamos Oeste 350, Miraflores, near Av Arequipa, T01-242 1318. Mon-Fri 1000-2000, Sat 1000-1700.* Sells 100% deet, blue gas canisters, lots of accessories, tents, crampons and backpacks.

Handicrafts

Miraflores is a good place for high quality, expensive handicrafts; there are many shops on and around the top end of Av La Paz (starting at Av Ricardo Palma).

Agua y Tierra, *Diez Canseco 298 y Alcanfores, Miraflores, T01-444 6980. Mon-Fri 1000-2000.* Fine crafts and indigenous art.

Alpaca 859, *Av Larco 859, Miraflores, T01-447 7163.* Good quality alpaca and baby alpaca products.

Arte XXI, *Av La Paz 678, Miraflores, T01-447 9777.* Gallery and store for contemporary and colonial Peruvian paintings.

Artesanía Santo Domingo, *Plazuela Santo Domingo, by the church of that name, in Lima centre, T01-428 9860.* Good Peruvian crafts.

Centro Comercial El Alamo, *corner of La Paz y Diez Canseco, Miraflores.* Artesanía shops with good choice.

Dédalo, *Paseo Sáenz Peña 295, Barranco, T01-652 5400, http://dedaloarte.blogspot.co.uk.* A labyrinthine shop selling furniture, jewellery and other items, as good as a gallery. It also has a nice coffee shop and has cinema shows. Other branches on Parque Kennedy and at Larcomar.

Kuna by Alpaca 111, *Av Larco 671, Miraflores, T01-447 1623, www.kuna.com.pe. Daily 1000-2000.* High-quality alpaca, baby alpaca and vicuña items. Also in Larcomar (loc 1-07), Museo Larco, the airport, Jockey Plaza, at hotels and in San Isidro.

Kuntur Wasi, *Ocharán 182, Miraflores, opposite Sol de Oro hotel, T01-447 7173. Mon-Sat 1000-1900.* English-speaking owners are very knowledgeable about Peruvian textiles; often have exhibitions of fine folk art and crafts.

La Casa de la Mujer Artesana, *Juan Pablo Ferandini 1550 (Av Brasil cuadra 15), Pueblo Libre, T01-423 8840, www.casadelamujerartesana.com. Mon-Fri 0900-1230, 1400-1630.* A cooperative run by the Movimiento Manuela Ramos, excellent quality work mostly from *pueblos jóvenes*.

Las Pallas, *Cajamarca 212, Barranco, T01-477 4629. Mon-Sat 0900-1900.* Very high quality handicrafts, English, French and German spoken.

Luz Hecho a Mano, *Berlín 399, Miraflores, T01-446 7098. Mon-Fri 1100-1330, 1400-1700, Sat 1030-1700.* Lovely handmade handbags, wallets and other leather goods including clothing which last for years and can be custom made.

Museo de la Nación (*see page 1262*). Often hosts specialist handicrafts markets presenting individual work from across Peru during national festivals. There are bargains in high-quality Pima cotton.

Jewellery

On Cs La Esperanza and La Paz, Miraflores, dozens of shops offer gold and silverware at reasonable prices.

Ilaria, *Av 2 de Mayo 308, San Isidro, T01-512 3530, www.ilariainternational.com, Mon-Fri 1000-1930.* Jewellery and silverware with interesting designs. There are other branches in Lima, Cuzco, Arequipa and Trujillo.

Maps

Instituto Geográfico Nacional, *Av Aramburú 1190, Surquillo, T01-475 9960, www.ign.gob.pe. Mon-Fri 0830-1645.* It has topographical maps of the whole country at 1:100,000, political and physical maps of all departments and satellite and aerial photographs. You may be asked to show your passport when buying these maps.

Lima 2000, *Av Arequipa 2625 (near the intersection with Av Javier Prado), T01-440 3486, www.lima2000.com.pe. Mon-Fri 0900-1800.* Has excellent street maps of Lima, from tourist maps, US$5.55, to comprehensive books US$18. Also has country maps (US$5.55-9.25), maps of Cuzco, Arequipa, Trujillo and Chiclayo and tourist maps of the Inca Trail, Colca area and Cordillera Blanca.

Limap, *T01-444 2685, www.limap.pe.* Publishes various thematic maps (dining, shopping, beaches, etc.) and has a useful website.

Markets

All are open 7 days a week until late(ish).

Feria Nacional de Artesanía de los Deseos y Misterios, *Av 28 de Julio 747, near junction with Av Arequipa and Museo Metropolitano.* Small market specializing in charms, remedies, fortune-telling and trinkets from Peru and Bolivia.

Mercado 1, *Surquillo, cross Paseo de le República from Ricardo Palma, Miraflores and go north 1 block.* Food market with a huge variety of local produce. C Narciso de la Colina outside has various places to eat, including **Heladería La Fiorentina** (No 580), for excellent ice creams.

Mercado Inca, *Av Petit Thouars, blocks 51-54 (near Parque Kennedy, parallel to Av Arequipa), Miraflores.* An unnamed crafts market area, with a large courtyard and lots of small flags. This is the largest crafts arcade in Miraflores. From here to C Ricardo Palma the street is lined with crafts markets.

Parque Kennedy, the main park of Miraflores, hosts a daily crafts market from 1700-2300.

Polvos Azules, *on García Naranjo, La Victoria, just off Av Grau in the centre of town.* The 'official' black market, sells just about anything; it is generally cheap and very interesting; beware pickpockets.

What to do

Cycling

BikeMavil, *Av Aviación 4023, Surco, T01-449 8435, see Facebook page. Mon-Sun 1000-2000.* Rental service, repairs, tours, selection of mountain and racing bikes.

Bike Tours of Lima, *Bolívar 150, Miraflores, T01-445 3172, www.biketoursoflima.com.*

Mon-Fri 0930-1800, Sat-Sun 0930-1400. Offer a variety of day tours through the city of Lima by bike, also bicycle rentals.

Buenas Biclas, *Domingo Elías 164, Miraflores, T01-241 9712, www.buenasbiclas.com. Mon-Fri 1000-2000, Sat 1000-1800.* Mountain bike specialists, knowledgeable staff, good selection of bikes, repairs and accessories.

Casa Okuyama, *Manco Cápac 590, La Victoria, T01-461 6435. Mon-Fri 0900-1300, 1415-1800, Sat 0900-1300.* Repairs, parts, try here for 28-in tyres, excellent service.

Cycloturismo Peru, *T99-9012 8105, www. cicloturismoperu.com.* Offers good-value cycling trips around Lima and beyond, as well as bike rental. The owner, Aníbal Paredes, speaks good English, is very knowledgeable and is the owner of **Mont Blanc Gran Hotel**.

Mirabici, *Parque Salazar, T01-673 3903. Daily 0800-1900.* Bicycle hire, US$7.50 per hr (tandems available); they also run bike tours 1000-1500, in English, Spanish and Portuguese. Bikes to ride up and down Av Arequipa can be rented on Sun 0800-1300, US$3 per hr, leave passport as deposit, www.jafibike.com.

Perú Bike, *Punta Sal 506, Surco, T01-260 8225, www. perubike.com. Mon-Fri 0930-1930, Sat 0930-1500.* Experienced agency leading tours, professional guiding, mountain bike school and workshop.

Diving
Peru Divers, *Av Defensores del Morro 175, Chorrillos, T01-251 6231, www.perudivers.com. Mon-Fri 0900-1700, call ahead.* Owner Lucho Rodríguez is a certified PADI instructor who offers certification courses, tours and a wealth of good information.

Hiking
Trekking and Backpacking Club, *Jr Huáscar 1152, Jesús María, Lima 11, T01-423 2515, T94-3866 794, www.angelfire.com/mi2/tebac.* Sr Miguel Chiri Valle, treks arranged, including in the Cordillera Blanca.

Paragliding
Aeroxtreme, *Trípoli 345, dpto 503, T01-242 5125, www.aeroxtreme.com, call ahead.* One of several outfits offering parapenting in Lima, US$70, 20 years' experience.

Andean Trail Perú, *T99-836 3436, www.andean trailperu.com.* For parapenting tandem flights, US$53, and courses, US$600 for 10 days. They also have a funday for US$120 to learn the basics. Trekking, kayaking and other adventure sports arranged.

Textiles/cultural tours
Puchka Perú, *www.puchkaperu.com.* Web-based operator specializing in textiles, folk art and markets. Fixed-date tours involve meeting artisans, workshops, visit to markets and more. In association with Maestro Máximo Laura, world-famous weaver, http://maximolauratapestries. com, whose studio in Urb Brisas de Santa Rosa III Etapa, Lima can be visited by appointment, T01-577 0952. See also Museo Máximo Laura in Cuzco.

Tour operators
Do not conduct business anywhere other than in the agency's office and insist on a written contract.

The Andean Experience Co, *Sáenz Peña 214, Barranco, T01-700 5100, www.andean-experience. com. Mon-Fri 0830-1815, Sat 0900-1200.* Offers tailor-made itineraries designed to match each traveller's personal interests, style and preferences to create ideal Peru trips.

Aracari Travel Consulting, *Schell 237, of 602, Miraflores, T01-651 2424, www.aracari.com. Mon-Sat 0800-1800.* Regional tours throughout Peru, also 'themed' and activity tours, has a very good reputation.

Coltur, *Av Reducto 1255, Miraflores, T01-615 5555, www.colturperu.com. Mon-Fri 0900-1800, Sat 0900-1200.* Very helpful, experienced and well-organized tours throughout Peru.

Condor Travel, *Armando Blondet 249, San Isidro, T01-615 3000, www.condortravel.com. Mon-Fri 0900-1800.* Highly regarded operator with tailor-made programmes, special interest tours, luxury journeys, adventure travel and conventional tourism. One-stop shopping with own regional network.

Dasatariq, *Av Reducto 1255, Miraflores, T01-447 2741, www.dasatariq.com.* Also in Cuzco. Well-organized, helpful, with a good reputation.

Domiruth Travel Service S.A.C, *Av Petit Thouars 4305, Miraflores, T01-610 6000, www.domiruth.com.* Tours throughout Peru, from the mystical to adventure travel. See also **Peru 4x4 Adventures**, part of Domiruth (Jr Rio de Janeiro 216-218, www.peru4x4adventures.com), for exclusive 4WD tours with German, English, Spanish, Italian and Portuguese-speaking drivers.

Ecocruceros, *Av Arequipa 4964, of 202, Miraflores, T01-226 8530, www.islaspalomino.com. Mon-Fri 0900-1900, Sat 0900-1300.* Daily departures from Plaza Grau in Callao (see page 1257) to see the sea lions at Islas Palomino, 4 hrs with 30-40 mins wetsuit swimming with guide, snack lunch, US$48 (take ID), reserve a day in advance.

Excursiones MYG, *T01-241 8091*. Offers a variety of tours in Lima and surroundings, including historic centre, nighttime, culinary tours, Caral, and further afield.

Explorandes, *C San Fernando 287, Miraflores, T01-200 6100, www.explorandes.com. Mon-Fri 0900-1750, Sat 0900-1200.* Award-winning company. Offers a wide range of adventure and cultural tours throughout the country. Also offices in Huaraz and Cuzco (see pages 1293 and 1435).

Fertur Peru Travel, *C Schell 485, Miraflores, T01-242 1900; and Jr Junín 211, Plaza de Armas, T01-427 2626; USA/Canada T1-877 247 0055 toll free, UK T020-3002 3811, www.fertur-travel.com. Mon-Fri 0900-1900, Sat 0900-1600.* Siduith Ferrer de Vecchio, CEO of this agency, is highly recommended for tour packages, up-to-date tourist information and also great prices on national and international flights, discounts for those with ISIC and youth cards. Other services include flight reconfirmations, hotel reservations and transfers to and from the airport or bus or train stations. Also in Cuzco at Av El Sol 803, Of 205, T084-221304.

Il Tucano Peru, *Elías Aguirre 633, Miraflores, T01-444 9361, 24-hr number T01-975 05375, www.iltucanoperu.com. Mon-Fri 0900-1800.* Personalized tours for groups or individuals throughout Peru, also 4WD overland trips, first-class drivers and guides, outstanding service and reliability.

Info Perú, *Jr de la Unión (Belén) 1066, of 102, T01-425 0414, www.infoperu.com.pe. Mon-Fri 0900-1800, Sat 0930-1400.* Run by a group of women, ask for Laura Gómez, offering personalized programmes, hotel bookings, transport, free tourist information, sale of maps, books and souvenirs, English and French spoken.

InkaNatura Travel, *Manuel Bañón 461, San Isidro, T01-203 5000, www.inkanatura.com. Mon-Fri 0900-1800, Sat 0900-1300.* Also in Cuzco and Chiclayo,

experienced company with special emphasis on both sustainable tourism and conservation, especially in Manu and Tambopata, also birdwatching, and on the archaeology of all of Peru.

Lima Mentor, *T01-243 2697, www.limamentor.com.* Contact through web, phone or through hotels. An agency offering cultural tours of Lima using freelance guides in specialist areas (eg gastronomy, art, archaeology, Lima at night), entertaining, finding different angles from regular tours. Half-day or full day tours.

Lima Tours, *N de Piérola 589 p 18, T01-619 6900, www.limatours.com.pe. Mon-Fri 0900-1745.* Very good for tours in the capital and around the country; programmes include health and wellness tours.

Peru For Less, *ASTA Travel Agent, Luis García Rojas 240, Urb Humboldt, T01-273 2486, US office: T1-877-269 0309, UK office: T+44-203-002 0571, Cuzco office: T084-254800, www.peruforless.com.* Will meet or beat any published rates on the internet from outside Peru. Good reports.

Peru Hop, *Av Larco 812, p 3, corner with San Martín, T01-242 2140, www.peruhop.com. Daily 0900-2100.* A hop-on, hop-off bus service from Lima to Cuzco via Paracas, Nazca, Arequipa, also to Puno and La Paz, daily departures, tours of places of interest, a variety of passes with different prices.

Peru Rooms, *Av Dos de Mayo 1545 of 205, San Isidro, T01-422 3434, www.perurooms.com.* Internet-based travel service offering 3- to 5-star packages throughout Peru, cultural, adventure and nature tourism.

Rutas del Peru SAC, *Av Enrique Palacios 1110, Miraflores, T01-445 7249, www.rutasdelperu.com.* Bespoke trips and overland expeditions in trucks.

Viajes Pacífico (Gray Line), *Av Paseo de la República 6010, p 7, T01-610 1911, www.graylineperu.com.* Tours throughout Peru and South America.

Viracocha, *Av Vasco Núñez de Balboa 191, Miraflores, T01-445 3986, peruviantours@viracocha. com.pe. Mon-Fri 0900-1800, Sat 0900-1300*. Very helpful, especially for flights, adventure, cultural, mystical and birdwatching tours.

Open-top bus tours Mirabús (*Diagonal Oscar Benavides, block 3, T01-242 6699, www.mirabus peru.com, daily 0900-1900*), runs many tours of the city and Callao (from US$3.50 to US$30) – eg Lima half day by day, Lima by night, Costa Verde, Callao, Gold Museum, Miraflores, Pachacámac with Paso horses display and dance show, Caral. Similar services concentrating on the city are offered by **Turibus**, from Larcomar, *T01-230 0909, www.turibusperu.com*.

Private guides The MITINCI (Ministry of Industry Tourism, Integration and International Business) certifies guides and can provide a list. Most are members of **AGOTUR** (Asociación de Guías Oficiales de Turismo) (*Av La Paz 678, Miraflores (for correspondence only), www. agotur.com*). Book in advance. Most guides speak a foreign language.

Transport

Air
For details of flights see under destinations. A list of airlines is found in Getting around, page 1514.

Jorge Chávez Airport (flight information T01-517 3500, www.lap.com.pe) is 16 km from the centre of Lima in Callao. It has all the facilities one would expect at an international airport. The **airport information desk** is by international Arrivals. **iPerú tourist information** desks at international arrivals, domestic departures and on the mezzanine (24 hrs, very helpful). The airport has car hire offices, public telephones, **Global Net** and other ATMs, *casas de cambio* and a bank (note that exchange rates are substantially poorer than outside, **Forex** exchange kiosk with fair rates in **Outlet Shopping Centre**, left of the airport as you step out, Mon-Sat 1100-1900, do not take any luggage with you). Internet facilities are more expensive than in the city, but there is Wi-Fi at departure areas and all gates (10 mins free). Smart shops, restaurants and cafés are plentiful.

Tip...
Do not go to the airport's car park exit to find a taxi without an airport permit outside the perimeter. Although these are cheaper, they are not safe even by day, far less so at night.

Purchase airline tickets at the airport, not across from it, were fake airline agents are located.

Transport from the airport Airport Express Lima, T01-446 5539, www.airportexpresslima. com, is a new (2017) bus service between the airport and **Miraflores** from 0700-2400, every 30 mins in the morning and evening, hourly 1200-1800, US$8 one way, US$15 return (discounts for children 4-15 and for Peruvians). There are 7 stops in Miraflores; website has map and "stop finder". Various taxi companies have desks at domestic and international arrivals, including **Taxi365** (T01 219 0271, taxi365@ cmv.pe), **Taxi Directo** (T01-711 1111, servicioenlinea@taxidirecto.com) and **Taxi Green** (T01-484 4001, www.taxigreen.com.pe). All charge the same fares: US$16.50 to the centre, US$18 to Miraflores, fares to other destinations are posted. **Mitsu** (T01-261 7788, www.mitsoo. net) is more expensive and only operates from international arrivals. Independent taxi drivers also tout for passengers in the airport terminal, they are at least as expensive as the above and generally less secure. The least safe options are taxis and buses that stop by pedestrian exits outside the airport perimeter and armed robbery is a serious hazard.

If you must travel by public transport, avoid rush hour and travelling at night and pay more for a non-stop bus service. Combis to the centre (Av Abancay), lines '9', C' or' Roma 1', charge US$0.60. Buses to Miraflores, line 'S' ('La S') or '18' and can be caught outside the airport on Av Faucett, US$0.85. Note that luggage is not allowed on public buses except very late at night or early in the morning.

Bus
Local Bus routes are shared by buses, combis (mid-size) and *colectivos* (mini-vans or cars). None is particularly safe; it is better to take a taxi (see below for recommendations). *Colectivos* run 24 hrs, although less frequently 0100-0600; they are quicker than buses and stop wherever requested. Buses and combis charge about US$0.40-0.45, *colectivos* a little more. On public holidays, Sun and from 2400 to 0500 every night, a small charge is added to the fare.

The **Metropolitano** (T01-203 9000, www. metropolitano.com.pe) is a system of articulated buses running on dedicated lanes south–south across the city from Naranjal in Comas to Estación Central (in front of the **Sheraton** hotel; estimated journey time 32 mins) and then south along the Vía Expresa/Paseo de la República to Matellini in Chorrillos (estimated journey time 32 mins); there are purpose-built stations along the route. The **Metropolitano** tends to be very crowded and is of limited use to visitors, but can be handy for reaching Miraflores (use stations between Angamos and 28 de Julio) and Barranco (Bulevar is 170 m from the Plaza). There are 2 branches through downtown Lima, either via Av Alfonso Ugarte and Plaza 2 de Mayo, or via Jr Lampa and Av Emancipación. Fares are paid using a prepaid and rechargeable card (minimum S/5, US$1.45), available from every station; each journey costs S/2.50 (US$0.70). Services run Mon-Sat 0500-2300 with shorter hours on Sun and on some sections. There are express services Mon-Fri 0600-0900 and 1635-2115 between certain stations.

Long distance There are many different bus companies, but the larger ones are better organized, leave on time and do not wait until the bus is full, many are open 0700-about 2200. Leaving or arriving in Lima by bus in the rush hour can add an extra hour or more to the journey. All bus companies have their own offices and terminals in the centre of the city, many around Carlos Zavala, but this is not a safe area. Many north-bound buses also have an office and stop at the Terminal Plaza Norte (http://granterminalterrestre.com, Metropolitano Tomás Valle), not far from the airport, which is handy for those who need to make a quick bus connection after landing in Lima. Many south-bound buses are at the Terminal Terrestre Lima Sur, at Km 11-12 on the Panamericana Sur by Puente Atocongo (Metro Atocongo).

Cruz del Sur (T01-311 5050, www.cruzdelsur.com.pe) has its main terminal at Av Javier Prado 1109, La Victoria, with *Cruzero* and *Cruzero Suite* services (luxury buses) and *Imperial* service (quite comfortable buses and periodic stops for food and bathroom breaks, a reasonable option with a quality company) to most parts of Peru. Another terminal is at Jr Quilca 531, Lima centre, for *Imperial* services to Arequipa, Ayacucho, Chiclayo, Cuzco, Huancayo, Huaraz, and Trujillo. There are sales offices throughout the city, including at Terminal Plaza Norte.

Ormeño (www.grupo-ormeno.com.pe) and its affiliated bus companies depart from and arrive at Av Javier Prado Este 1057, Santa Catalina, T01-472 1710, but the terminal at Av Carlos Zavala 177, Lima centre, T01-427 5679, is the best place to get information and buy any Ormeño ticket. **Ormeño** offers *Royal Class* and *Business Class* service to certain destinations. These buses are very comfortable with bathrooms and hostess, etc.

Cial, República de Panamá 2460, T01-207 6900 ext 119, and Paseo de la República 646, T01-207 6900 ext 170, has national coverage.

Flores (T01-332 1212, www.floreshnos.pe) has departures to many parts of the country, especially the south from terminals at Av Paseo de le República 683, Av Paseo de le República 627 and Jr Montevideo 523. Some of its services are good quality.

Other companies include:

Cavassa, Raimondi 129, Lima centre, T01-431 3200, www.turismocavassa.com.pe. Also at Terminal Plaza Norte. Services to **Huaraz**.

Cromotex, Av Nicolás Arriola 898, Santa Catalina; Av Paseo de La República 659, T01-424 7575, www.cromotex.com.pe. To **Cuzco** and **Arequipa**.

Ittsa, Paseo de la República 809, T01-423 5232, www.ittsabus.com. Also at Terminal Plaza Norte. Good service to the north, **Chiclayo**, **Piura**, **Tumbes**.

Julio César, José Gálvez 562, La Victoria, T01-424 8060, www.transportesjuliocesar.com.pe. Also at Terminal Plaza Norte. Good service to **Huaraz**; recommended to arrive in Huaraz and then use local transport to points beyond.

Línea, Paseo de la República 941-959, Lima centre, T01-424 0836, www.transporteslinea.com.pe. Also at Terminal Plaza Norte (T01-533 0739). Among the best services to destinations in the north.

Móvil, Av Paseo de La República 749, Lima centre (near the national stadium); Av Alfredo Mendiola 3883, Los Olivos, and Terminal Terrestre Lima Sur, T01-716 8000, www. moviltours.com.pe. To **Huaraz** and **Chiclayo** by *bus cama*, and **Chachapoyas**.

Oltursa, Aramburú 1160, San Isidro, T01-708 5000, www.oltursa.pe. A reputable company offering top-end services to **Nazca**, **Arequipa** and destinations in **northern Peru**, mainly at night.

Soyuz, Av México 333, T01-205 2370. To **Ica** every 7 mins, well organized. As **PerúBus**, www. perubus.com.pe, the same company runs north to **Huacho** and **Barranca**.

Tepsa, Javier Prado Este 1091, La Victoria; Av Gerardo Unger 6917, T01-617 9000, www. tepsa.com.pe. Also at Terminal Plaza Norte (T01-533 1524). Services to the north as far as **Tumbes** and the south to **Tacna**.

Transportes Chanchamayo, Av Nicolás Arriola 535, La Victoria, T01-265 6850, www. transporteschanchamayo.com. To **Tarma**, **San Ramón** and **La Merced**.

Transportes León de Huánuco, Av 28 de Julio 1520, La Victoria, T01-424 3893. Daily to **Huánuco**, **Tingo María**, **La Merced** and **Pucallpa**.

International Ormeño (see above) to **Guayaquil** (29 hrs with a change of bus at the border, US$56), **Quito** (38 hrs, US$75), **Cali** (56 hrs, US$131), **Bogotá** (70 hrs, US$141), **Caracas** (100 hrs, US$150), **Santiago** (54 hrs, US$102), **Mendoza** (78 hrs, US$159), **Buenos Aires** (90 hrs, US$148), **São Paulo** (90 hrs); a maximum of 20 kg is allowed pp. **Cruz del Sur** to **Guayaquil** (3 a week, US$85), **Buenos Aires** (US$201) and **Santiago** (US$130). **El Rápido** (Abtao 1279, La Victoria, T01-432 6380, www. elrapidoint.com.ar) to **Buenos Aires** Mon, Wed, Fri; connections in Mendoza to other cities in Argentina and Uruguay.

Car hire

Most companies have an office at the airport, where you can arrange everything and pick up and leave the car. It is recommended to test drive before signing the contract as quality varies. It can be much cheaper to rent a car in a town in the Sierra for a few days than to drive from Lima; also companies don't have a collection service. Cars can be hired from: **Paz Rent A Car**, Av Diez

Canseco 319, of, 15, Miraflores, T01-446 4395, T99-993 9853. **Budget**, T01-204 4400, www. budgetperu.com. Prices range from US$35 to US$85 depending on type of car. Make sure that your car is in a locked garage at night.

Metro

The 1st line of the **Tren Eléctrico** (www.linea uno.pe) runs from Villa El Salvador in the southeast of the city to Bayóvar in the northeast, daily 0600-2230. Each journey costs S/.1.50 (US$0.55); pay by swipe card S/.5 (US$1.75). Metro stations Miguel Grau, El Ángel and Presbítero Maestro lie on the eastern edge of the downtown area. Construction work has started on the next section.

Taxi

Taxis do not use meters although some have rate sheets (eg **Satelital**, T01-355 5555, http://3555555satelital.com). Agree the price of the journey beforehand and insist on being taken to the destination of your choice. At night, on Sun and holidays expect a surcharge of 35-50%. The following are taxi fares for some of the more common routes, give or take a sol. From downtown Lima to: Parque Kennedy (Miraflores), US$4; Museo de la Nación, US$3.75; San Isidro, US$3.75; Barranco, US$4.75. From Miraflores (Parque Kennedy) to: Museo de la Nación, US$2.75; Archaeology Museum, US$3.75; Barranco, US$4.80. By law, all taxis must have the vehicle's registration number painted on the side. They are often white or yellow, but can come in any colour, size or make. Licensed and phone taxis are safest, but if hailing a taxi on the street, local advice is to look for an older driver rather than a youngster.

There are several reliable phone taxi companies, which can be called for immediate service, or booked in advance; prices are 2-3 times more than ordinary taxis: to the airport, US$15; to suburbs, US$10. Try **Taxi Real**, T01-215 1414, www.taxireal.com; **Taxi Seguro**, T01-536 6956, www.taxisegurolima.com; **Taxi Tata**, T01-274 5151, www.tata-taxis.com. If hiring a taxi by the hour, agree on price beforehand, US$7-9. **Note** Drivers don't expect tips; give them small change from the fare.

Train

Details of the service on the Central Railway to Huancayo are given on page 1464.

Huaraz &
the cordilleras

★Apart from the range running along the Chile-Argentina border, the highest mountains in South America lie along the Cordillera Blanca. This is an area of jewelled lakes and snowy mountain peaks attracting mountaineers and hikers in their thousands. Huaraz is the natural place to head for: it has the best infrastructure and the mountains, lakes and trails are within easy reach. From town you can see more than 23 peaks over 5000 m, of which the most notable is Huascarán (6768 m), the highest mountain in Peru. Although the snowline is receding, the Cordillera Blanca still contains the largest concentration of glaciers found in the world's tropical zone and the turquoise-coloured lakes, which form in the terminal moraines, are the jewels of the Andes. Here also is one of Peru's most important pre-Inca sites, at Chavín de Huantar. Large multinational mining projects have brought some prosperity as well as social change and ecological damage to the area.

Towards Huaraz and the cordilleras

high-altitude pass and plateau

North from Lima the Pan-American Highway parallels the coast and a series of roads branch off east for the climb up to Huaraz in the Callejón de Huaylas, gateway to Parque Nacional Huascarán. Probably the easiest route to Huaraz is the paved road that branches off the highway north of Pativilca, 203 km from Lima. The road climbs increasingly steeply to the chilly pass at 4080 m (Km 120). Shortly after, Laguna Conococha comes into view, where the Río Santa rises. A road branches off from Conococha to Chiquián (see page 1303) and the Cordilleras Huayhuash and Raura to the southeast. After crossing a high plateau the main road descends gradually for 47 km until Catac, where another road branches east to Chavín and on to the Callejón de Conchucos on the eastern side of the Cordillera Blanca. Huaraz is 36 km further on. From Huaraz the road continues north between the towering Cordillera Negra, snowless but rising above 5000 m and the snow-covered Cordillera Blanca.

The alternative routes to the Callejón de Huaylas are via the Callán pass from Casma to Huaraz (fully paved, see page 1306), and from Chimbote to Caraz via the Cañón del Pato (partly paved, rough and spectacular; page 1306).

Huaraz Colour map 3, B2.

Peru's hiking and climbing centre

Located 420 km from Lima, Huaraz is the capital of Ancash department and the main town in the Cordillera Blanca, with a population of 115,000. It is expanding rapidly as a major tourist centre but is also a busy commercial hub, especially on market days. At 3091 m, it is a prime destination for hikers and a mecca for international climbers and trekkers.

Best for
Climbing ▪ Scenery ▪ Solitude ▪ Trekking

Essential Huaraz and the cordilleras

Finding your feet

Established in July 1975, Parque Nacional Huascarán includes the entire Cordillera Blanca above 4000 m, with an area of 3400 sq km. It is a UNESCO World Biosphere Reserve and part of the World Heritage Trust. Park fees are 10 soles (US$3) for 1 day, 20 soles (US$6) for three consecutive days (no overnight stays). Permits for 21 days (for trekking and climbing) cost 65 soles (US$20) and are valid for 21 days. All permits must be bought at the national park office in Huaraz (Jr Federico Sal y Rosas 555, by Plazuela Belén, T043-422086, pnhuascaran@sernanp.gob.pe, Monday-Friday 0830-1300, 1430-1700), or at rangers posts at Llanganuco and Huascarán (for the Llanganuco–Santa Cruz trek), or at Collón for Quebrada Ishinca.

Warning…

Huaraz has its share of crime, especially since the arrival of mining and during the high tourist season. Women should not go to surrounding districts and sites alone. Muggings have taken place on the way to Laguna Churup, on the way to the Mirador Rataquenua, and also between the Monterrey thermal baths and Wilcawain ruins; do not walk this way.

Current regulations state that local guides are mandatory everywhere in the park except designated 'Recreation Zones' accessible by car. Tourists must hire a licensed tour operator for all activities and those operators may only employ licensed guides, cooks, arrieros and porters. Fees, regulations and their implementation change frequently; always confirm details in Huaraz.

Getting around

The best way to explore the cordilleras is, of course, on foot (see Trekking and climbing in the cordilleras, page 1292). However, there are also numerous buses and minivans daily between Huaraz and Caraz, and more limited services to settlements on the eastern side of the Cordillera Blanca. The bus journeys through the Cahuish tunnel (4516 m), Punta Olímpica tunnel (4700 m), and over Portachuelo de Llanganuco Pass (4767 m), are all spectacular.

When to go

The months of May to September are the dry season and best for trekking, although conditions vary from year to year. From November to April the weather is usually wet, views may be restricted by cloud, and paths are likely to be muddy.

Sights

Huaraz's setting, at the foot of the Cordillera Blanca, is spectacular. The town was almost completely destroyed in the earthquake of May 1970. The Plaza de Armas has since been rebuilt, but the new **Cathedral** is still under construction. **Museo Arqueológico de Ancash** ① *Ministerio de Cultura, Plaza de Armas, Mon-Sat 0900-1700, Sun 0900-1400*, contains stone monoliths and huacos from the Recuay culture, well labelled. The main thoroughfare, Avenida Luzuriaga, is bursting at the seams with travel agencies, climbing equipment hire shops, restaurants, cafés and bars. A good district for those seeking peace and quiet is La Soledad, six blocks uphill from the Plaza de Armas on Avenida Sucre. Here, along Sucre and Jr Amadeo Figueroa, are many hotels and rooms for rent in private homes. The **Sala de Cultura SUNARP** ① *Av Centenario 530, Independencia, T043-421301, Mon-Fri 1700-2000, Sat 0900-1300, free*, often has interesting art and photography exhibitions by local artists.

Around Huaraz

About 8 km to the northeast is **Willkawain** ① *Tue-Fri 0830-1600, Sat-Sun 0900-1330, US$1.75, take a combi from 13 de Diciembre and Jr Cajamarca, US$0.75, 20 mins, direct to Willkawain*. The ruins (AD 700-1100, Huari Empire) consist of one large three-storey structure with intact stone roof slabs and several small structures. About 500 m past Willkawain is Ichicwillkawain with several similar but smaller structures. A well-signed trail climbs from Wilkawain to Laguna Ahuac (Aguak Cocha, 4580 m); it's a demanding acclimatization hike (12 km return), with no services along the way.

A popular excursion is to **Laguna Churup**, ① *inside PN Huascarán, see page 1286 for fees*, in a lovely setting beneath rocky peaks at 4500 m. This demanding 6-km full-day hike, climbs 600 m from the village of Pitec, 10 km east of Huaraz. There are no services in Pitec; take food, warm clothing, sun protection, etc. Most Huaraz operators offer this tour or take a taxi from to Pitec, US$15 one way (and hope for a ride back), US$35 with all-day wait.

There is extensive rock climbing at **Hatun Machay** ① *elevation 4300 m, 70 km south of Huaraz, off the road to Conococha, US$5 community fee*, with a comfortable shelter ($ in dorms, camping, meals available) and 400 climbing routes (see www.toposperu.com/2015/12/21/hatun-machay/). The area also offers great scenery, petroglyphs, and trekking to the village of Pampas Chico. Huaraz agencies sell tours, or take public transport to Catac and a taxi from there (US$15), or take a Lima- or Chiquián-bound bus to the turnoff at Km 131 (35 km south of Catac), and walk 4 km uphill.

Listings Huaraz *maps p1288 and p1290*

Tourist information

The national park office (see Essential box, opposite) is principally administrative, with no information for visitors.

Indecopi
Av Gamarra 671, T043-423899, www.indecopi.gob.pe.
Government consumer protection office. Very effective but not always quick. Spanish only.

iPerú
Pasaje Atusparia, of 1, Plaza de Armas, T043-428812, iperuhuaraz@promperu.gob.pe. Mon-Sat 0900-1800, Sun 0900-1300.
Also at Jr San Martín cuadra 6 s/n, daily 0800-1100, and at Anta airport when flights arrive.

Policía de Turismo
Av Luzuriaga on Plaza de Armas, around the corner from iPerú, T043-421351, divtueco_huaraz@yahoo.com. Mon-Sat 0730-2100.
The place to report crimes and resolve issues with tour operators, hotels, etc. All female officers, limited English spoken.

Where to stay

Hotels fill up rapidly in high season (May-Sep), especially during public holidays and special events when prices rise (beware overcharging). Touts meet buses and aggressively 'suggest' places to stay. Do not be put off your choice of lodging; phone ahead to confirm.

$$$$-$$$ Andino Club
Pedro Cochachín 357, some way southeast of the centre (take a taxi after dark), T043-421662, www.hotelandino.com.
Swiss-run hotel with very high standards, ample grounds, excellent restaurant, variety of rooms including panoramic views, balcony, fireplace, jacuzzi and sauna.

$$$ El Patio
Av Monterrey, 250 m downhill from the Monterrey baths, T043-424965, www.elpatio.com.pe.
Very colonial-style with lovely gardens, comfortable rooms, singles, doubles and triples, some with balconies, also 4 lodges with fireplaces. Meals on request, bar.

$$$ Hostal Colomba
Francisco de Zela 210, just off Centenario across the river, T043-421501, www.huarazhotel.com.
Lovely old hacienda, family-run, garden with playground and sports, safe parking, gym and well-equipped rooms sleeping 1-6, comfortable beds, restaurant.

$$$ The Lazy Dog Inn
30 mins' drive from Huaraz (US$10 by taxi), close to the boundary of Huascarán National Park, 3.1 km past the town of Marian, close to the Quebrada Cojup, T943-789330, www.thelazydoginn.com.
Eco-tourism lodge actively involved in community projects (see www.andeanalliance.org), water recycling systems and composting toilets. Beautifully designed in warm colours, great location gives access to several mountain valleys. Organizes horse riding and hiking trips. Excellent home-cooked breakfast and dinner included. Canadian owned, English spoken. Recommended.

$$$-$$ San Sebastián
Jr Italia 1124, T043-426960, www.sansebastianhuaraz.com.
Lovely out-of-the-way hotel, comfortable beds with duvets, bath tubs, restaurant, nice common areas, parking, helpful, good views. Recommended.

$$ Suiza Peruana
Jr Federico Sal y Rosas 843, T043-425263, www.suizaperuana.com.
Central location, comfortable rooms, nice design, great views, elevator, garage, 24-hr service.

$$-$ Albergue Churup
Jr Amadeo Figueroa 1257, T043-424200, www.churup.com.
13 rooms with private bath or 2 dorms with shared bath, hot water, fire in sitting room on 4th floor, cafeteria, use of kitchen 1800-2200, lots of information, laundry, book exchange, English spoken, Spanish classes, adventure travel tours, extremely helpful. Airport transfers and free pick-up from bus.

$$-$ Alojamiento Soledad
Jr Amadeo Figueroa 1267, T043-421196, info@quenualadventures.com.
Private and shared bath, US$12 pp in dorm, abundant hot water, good breakfast, use of kitchen, family home and atmosphere, trekking information and tours, bus station pick-up. Warmly recommended.

$$-$ Hatun Wasi
Jr Daniel Villayzán 268, T043-425055.

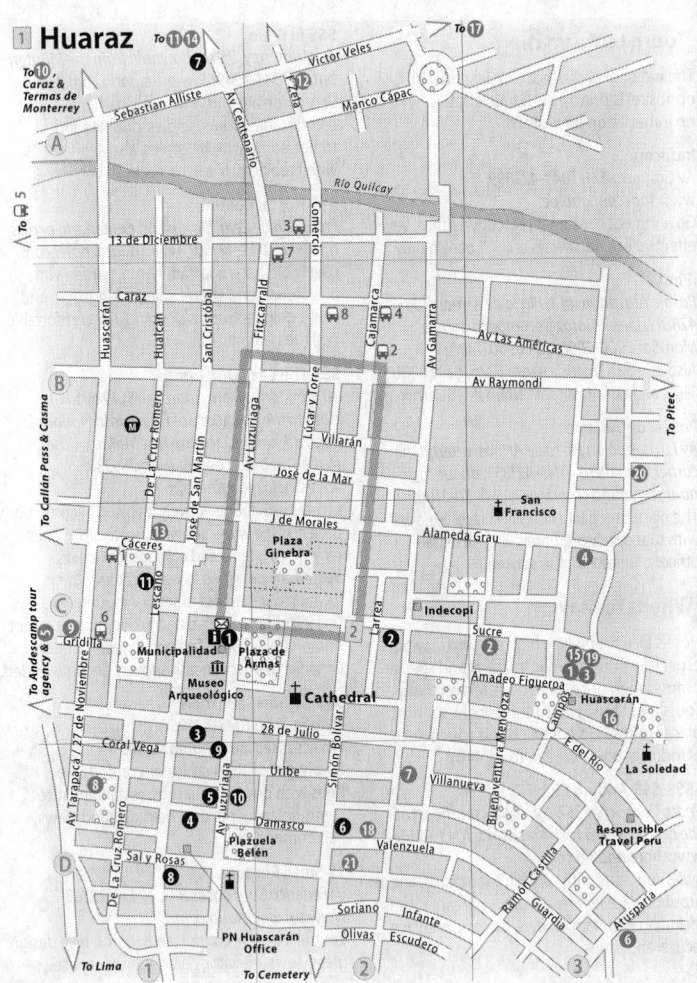

Family-run hotel next to **Jo's Place**. Spacious rooms, with hot water, pleasant roof terrace, ideal for breakfasts, with great views of the Cordillera.

$$-$ La Casa de Zarela
J Arguedas 1263, T043-421694,
www.lacasadezarela.hostel.com.
Hot water, use of kitchen, laundry facilities, popular with climbers and trekkers, owner Zarela who speaks English organizes groups and is very knowledgeable.

N

200 metres
200 yards

➡ **Huaraz maps**
1 Huaraz, page 1288
2 Huaraz centre, page 1290

$$-$ Residencial NG
Pasaje Valenzuela 837, T043-421831,
www.residencialng.com.
Breakfast, hot water, good value, helpful.

$ Alojamiento El Jacal
Jr Sucre 1044, T043-424612.
With or without shower, hot water, helpful family, garden, laundry facilities.

$ Alpes Huaraz
Jr Ladislao Meza 112, up a cobblestone street past the San Francisco church, T043-428896,
www.hostalalpeshuaraz.com.
Rooms with private bath, hot water, fireplace, kitchen, terrace with views, garden, arrange tours, friendly atmosphere, good value.

$ Andescamp Hostel
Jr Huáscar 615, T043-423842,
www.andescamphostel.com.
Hostel with dorms and private rooms, some with bath, and snack bar. Tour agency, see What to do, below.

$ Angeles Inn
Av Gamarra 815, T043-422205,
solandperu@yahoo.com.
No sign, look for **Sol Andino** travel agency in same building (www.solandino.com), laundry facilities, garden, hot water, owners Max and Saul Angeles are official guides, helpful with trekking and climbing, rent equipment.

$ Benkawasi
Parque Santa Rosa 928, 10 mins from centre, T043-423150, http://huarazbenkawasi.com.
Doubles, also rooms for 3, 4 and dorm, hot water, breakfast available, laundry, games room, pick-up from bus station.

$ Casa Jaimes
Alberto Gridilla 267, T043-422281, 2 blocks from the main plaza, www.casajaimes.com.
Dormitory with hot showers, laundry facilities, has maps and books of the region. Noisy but economical.

$ Familia Meza
Lúcar y Torre 538, behind Café Andino (enquire here, see Restaurants, below), T043-421203.
Shared bath, hot water, laundry facilities, popular with trekkers, mountaineers and bikers.

$ Hostal Quintana
Mcal Cáceres 411, T043-426060,
www.hostal-quintana.com.
English, French, Italian and Spanish spoken, mountain gear rental, 2 of the owner's sons are

certified guides and can arrange itineraries, laundry facilities, café popular with trekkers.

$ Jo's Place
Jr Daniel Villayzan 276, T043-425505.
Safe, hot water at night, nice mountain views, garden, terrace, English/Peruvian-run, warm atmosphere, popular.

$ La Cabaña
Jr Sucre 1224, T043-423428.
Shared and double rooms, hot showers, laundry, popular, safe for parking, bikes and luggage, English and French spoken, good value.

$ Lodging House Ezama
Mariano Melgar 623, Independencia, 15 mins' walk from Plaza de Armas (US$0.50 by taxi), T043-423490.
Light, spacious rooms, hot water, safe, helpful.

$ Residencial Sucre
Sucre 1240, T043-422264, filibertor@terra.com.pe.
Private house, kitchen, laundry facilities, hot water, English, German and French spoken, mountaineering guide, Filiberto Rurush, can be contacted here.

Restaurants

$$$ Créperie Patrick
Luzuriaga 422. Mon-Sat 1600-2230, Sun 1800-2230.
Excellent alpaca, *cuy*, crêpes, fish, quiche, spaghetti and good wine.

$$$ Pizza Bruno
Luzuriaga 834. Open from 1600-2300.
Best pizza, excellent crêpes and pastries, good service, French owner Bruno Reviron also has a 4WD with driver for hire.

$$$-$$ Mi Comedia
Av Centenario 351, T043-587954. Open 1700-2300.
Wood-oven pizzas, rustic European style, very good service.

$$$-$$ Trivio
Parque del Periodista, daily 0800-0030.
Creative international food, good coffee, nice view.

$$ Bistro de los Andes
Luzuriaga 702 y Sucre, Plaza de Armas, upstairs, T043-426249. Mon-Sat 1200-2200.
Great food, owner speaks English, French and German. Plaza branch has a nice view of the plaza. Wide range of international dishes.

$$ Chilli Heaven
Parque Ginebra, T043-396085. Mon-Sat 1200-2145, Sun 1700-2100.
Specializing in spicy food; Mexican, Indian and Thai.

$$ El Horno Pizzería Grill
Parque Ginebra, T043-424617. Daily 1200-2300.
Good atmosphere, fine grilled meats and pizza, very popular.

2 Huaraz centre

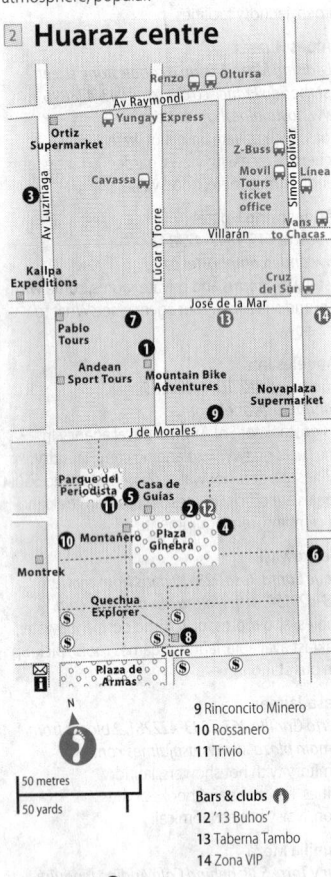

N

50 metres
50 yards

Restaurants
1 Café Andino & Familia Meza Lodging
2 Chilli Heaven
3 Créperie Patrick
4 El Horno Pizzería Grill
5 Encuentro
6 Frutelo
7 Pizza B&B
8 Pizzería Landauro
9 Rinconcito Minero
10 Rossanero
11 Trivio

Bars & clubs
12 '13 Buhos'
13 Taberna Tambo
14 Zona VIP

➡ Huaraz maps
1 Huaraz, page 1288
2 Huaraz centre, page 1290

$$ Encuentro
Parque del Periodista and Julian de Morales 650.
Daily 0800-2300.
Breakfast, lunch and dinners, very busy and
very good.

$$ Huaraz Querido
Bolívar 981. Lunch only.
Very popular place for great ceviche and other
fish dishes.

$$ Pizza B&B
La Mar 674, beside laundry of same name.
Excellent traditional sauces for pizza and pasta,
and desserts.

$$ Pizzería Landauro
Sucre, on corner of Plaza de Armas.
Closed 1200-1800 and Sun.
Very good for pizzas, Italian dishes, sandwiches,
breakfasts, nice atmosphere.

$$-$ Chifa Jim Hua
Teófilo de Castillo 556. Daily 1100-2330.
Large, tasty portions, economical lunch *menú*
Mon-Sat.

$$-$ El Fogón
Luzuriaga 928, upstairs, T043-421267. Mon-Sat
1200-1500, 1800-2400, Sun 1800-2400.
Good value *menú*, wide selection of tasty
Peruvian and international dishes, generous
portions, good service, very popular with
locals, go early.

$$-$ Rinconcito Minero
J de Morales 757. Open 0700-2300.
Breakfast, popular lunch *menú*, vegetarian
options, coffee and snacks.

$$-$ Sala de Estar
Luzuriaga 923, upstairs. Tue-Sun 1700-2300.
Pasta dishes, home-made desserts, fruit juices
and drinks. Good creative meals.

$$-$ Salud y Vida
Lescano 632. Mon-Sat 0800-2100, Sun 1230-1530.
Vegetarian *menú* and *à la carte*, sells
home-made yoghurt.

Cafés

Café Andino
Lúcar y Torre 538, 3rd floor, T043-421203,
www.cafeandino.com.
Peruvian/American-owned café-restaurant-bar
with book exchange and extensive lending
library in many languages. A great place to relax

and meet other travellers, warmly recommended.
Owner Chris Benway also runs **La Cima Logistics**,
see What to do, page 1294.

Cafetería y Juguería
Sucre 806.
Cheap café just above the Plaza. Serves excellent
yogurt and honey drinks, among other treats.

California Café
28 de Julio 562, T043-428354, http://huaylas.
com/californiacafe/california.htm. Mon-Sat
0700-1900, Sun 0700-1400.
Excellent breakfast, great sandwiches, falafel, coffee
and chocolate cake, book exchange. Californian
owner is a good source of information on trekking
in the Cordillera Huayhuash and security issues.

Frutelo
Bolívar y Sucre, upstairs.
Open 0800-1200, 1700-2200.
Fruit juices, coffee, creative sandwiches, burgers
and snacks.

Mi Comedia Gelatería
Jr San Martin 1213.
"The best home-made *gelato* this side of Milan."

Panadería Salazar
Av Luzuriaga 944, Gamarra 755 and other locations.
Good bakery and café, cheap, pleasant
atmosphere, good for a snack.

Rossanero
Luzuriaga 645 entre Sucre y J de Morales,
2nd floor, daily 0700-2300.
Café with extensive menu, coffee, sandwiches,
ice cream, reasonable prices.

Bars and clubs

13 Buhos Bar
Parque Ginebra.
Bar and restaurant. Afternoon, evening and
nightspot, very popular, owner makes his own
craft beer. Good music, games, nice ambience.

Taberna Tambo
José de la Mar 776. Open 1000-1600,
2000-early hours.
Folk music daily, disco, full on, non-stop dance
mecca. Very popular with both locals and gringos.

Zona VIP
José de la Mar y Bolívar.
Lively disco.

ON THE ROAD
Trekking and climbing in the cordilleras

The Cordillera Blanca offers popular backpacking and trekking, with a network of trails used by the local people and some less well-defined mountaineers' routes. Most circuits can be hiked in five days. Although the trails are easily followed, they are rugged with high passes, between 4000 m and 5000 m, so backpackers should be fit, acclimatized to the altitude and able to carry all equipment. Essential items are a tent, warm sleeping bag, stove, and protection against wind and rain. The weather is unreliable and you cannot rule out rain and hail storms even in the dry season. Less stamina is required if you hire mules to carry equipment.

Safety The height of the Cordillera Blanca and the Callejón de Huaylas ranges and their location in the tropics create conditions different from the Alps or even the Himalayas. Fierce sun makes the mountain snow porous and glaciers move more rapidly. Deglaciation is rapidly changing the face of the Cordillera. Older maps do not provide a reliable indication of the extent of glaciers and snow fields (according to some studies 15% of the range's glaciers have disappeared since the 1970s), so local experience is important. If the national park rules prohibiting independent treks or climbs have been lifted, move in groups of four or more, reporting to the Casa de Guías (see opposite) or the office of the guide before departing, giving the date at which a search should begin, and leaving your embassy's telephone number, with money for the call. International recommendations are for a 300 m per day maximum altitude gain. Be wary of agencies wanting to sell you trips with very fast ascents (but ask around if this is what you want).

It is imperative that all climbers carry adequate insurance (it cannot be purchased locally). Be well prepared before setting out on a climb. Wait or cancel your trip when the weather is bad. Every year climbers are killed through failing to take weather conditions seriously. Climb only when and where you have sufficient experience.

Rescue services, while better than in the past, may not be up to international standards. In the event of an emergency try calling the **Casa de Guías**, T043-421811 or 941-946818; **Edson Ramírez** at the national park office, T944-627946 or T943-626627; or the **Police**, T043-422487

Festivals

3 May Patron saints' day, **El Señor de la Soledad**, celebrations last a week.
Jun Festival del Andinismo, international climbing week.
Jun San Juan and **San Pedro** are celebrated throughout the region during the last week of Jun.
Aug Inkafest, mountain film festival, dates change each year.

Shopping

Clothing
For local sweaters, hats, gloves and wall hangings at good value, try Pasaje Mcal Cáceres, off Luzuriaga; the stalls off Luzuriaga between Morales and Sucre; Bolívar cuadra 6, and elsewhere. **Last Minute Gifts** (Lucar Y Torre 530, 2nd floor) sells hats, clothing, souvenirs and jewellery.

Markets
The central market offers various canned and dry goods, as well as fresh fruit and vegetables. Beware pickpockets in this area. There are also several supermarkets in town (see Huaraz centre map, page 1290), do not leave valuables in your bags while shopping.

What to do

Try to get a recommendation from someone who has recently returned from a tour, trek or climb. All agencies run conventional tours to Llanganuco (US$12 pp, very long day), Chavín (8-10 hrs, US$14 pp), Laguna Churup, Laguna 69, and Pastoruri. They all pool their clients and entry tickets are not included. Competition is fierce and the cheapest is not the best. Many agencies also hire equipment.

Horse riding
Posada de Yungar, *Yungar (about 20 km from Huaraz on the Carhuaz road)*, T043-421267/967-9836. Swiss-run. Ask for José Flores or Gustavo Soto. US$7.50 per hr on good horses; good 4-hr trip in the Cordillera Negra.

or 966-831514. Satellite phones can be rented through the Casa de Guías and some agencies, ask around. There is cell-phone coverage in some (but not all) parts of the Cordillera Blanca.

Personal security and responsibility Before heading out on any trekking route, always enquire locally about crime levels. The Cordillera Blanca is generally safe, but muggings are not unknown. On all treks in this area, respect the locals' property, leave no rubbish behind, do not give sweets or money to children who beg and remember that your cooking utensils and tent would be very expensive for a *campesino*, so be sensitive and responsible. Along the most popular routes, campers have complained that campsites are dirty, toilet pits foul and that rubbish is not taken away by groups. Do your share to make things better.

Information Casa de Guías, Plaza Ginebra 28-g in Huaraz, T043-421811. Monday-Saturday 0900-1300, 1600-1800. This is the climbers' and hikers' meeting place. It has a full list of all members of the Asociación de Guías de Montaña del Perú (AGMP) throughout the country and has useful information, books, maps, arrangements for guides, *arrieros*, mules, etc. It also operates as an agency and sells tours. Notice board, postcards and posters for sale. Also see www.trekkingperu.org.

Guides, arrieros and porters The Dirección de Turismo issues qualified guides and *arrieros* (muleteers) with a photo ID. Note down the name and card number in case you should have any complaints. Most guides are hired in Huaraz or, to a lesser extent, in Caraz. Prices apply across the region, with some minor variations in the smaller towns: *arriero*, US$18 per day; donkey or mule, US$8 per day; trekking guides US$40-70 per day (more for foreign guides); climbing guides US$90-200 per day (more for foreign guides), depending on the difficulty of the peak; cooks US$30-40 per day; all subject to change. You are required to provide or pay for food and shelter for all *arrieros*, porters, cooks and guides. Associations of *arrieros*: Humacchuco-Llanganuco (for porters and cooks), T943-786497, victorcautivo@hotmail.com. Pashpa Arrieros, T043-830540/83319. Musho Arrieros, T043-230003/814416. Collon Arrieros (for llama trekking), T043-833417/824146.

Sr Robinson Ayala Gride, *T043-423813*. Contact him well in advance for half-day trips, US$36; enquire at El Cortijo restaurant, on Huaraz-Caraz road, Km 6.5. He is a master *paso* rider.

Mountain biking
Mountain Bike Adventures, *Lúcar y Torre 530, T043-424259, www.chakinaniperu.com*. Contact Julio Olaza. US$60 pp for day trip, all inclusive, various routes, excellent standard of equipment. Julio speaks excellent English and also runs a book exchange, sells topo maps and climbing books.

Trekking and climbing
Trekking tours cost US$50-70 pp per day, climbing US$100-160 pp per day. Many companies close in low season.
Active Peru, *Gamarra 699 y Sucre, T043-423339, www.activeperu.com*. Offers classic treks, climbing, plus standard tours to Chavín and Llanganuco, among others, good in all respects, Belgian owner speaks Dutch, German and English.

Alpa-K, *Parque Ginebra 30-B, above Montañero, www.alpa-k.org*. Owner Bertrand offers tours throughout Peru and has a B&B ($) on the premises. French, Spanish and some English spoken.
Andean Footsteps, *Cra Huaraz-Caraz Km 14, Paltay, T943-121286*. David Maguiña specializes in treks, climbs and tours with a commitment to using local personnel and resources. Local projects are sponsored.
Andescamp, *Jr Huáscar 615, T043-423842, or T943-563424, www.andescamphostel.com*. Popular agency and hostel (see Where to stay, above), especially with budget travellers. Only qualified guides used for climbing trips. Variety of treks, mountaineering expeditions and courses, rafting, paragliding and other adventure sports.
Cordillera Blanca Adventures, *run by the Mejía Romero family, Los Nogales 108, T043-421934, www.cordillerablanca.org*. Experienced, quality climbing/trekking trips, good guides/equipment.
Explorandes, *Gamarra 835, T043-421960, www.explorandes.com*.

Galaxia Expeditions, *Parque del Periodista,
T043-425355, www.galaxia-expeditions.com.*
Usual range of tours, climbing, hiking, biking,
equipment hire, etc. Good budget option. Go to
the office to buy tours direct, do not buy from
unscrupulous sub-contractors.

Huascarán, *Jr Pedro Campos 711, Soledad, T043-
424504, www.huascaran-peru.com.* Contact Pablo
Tinoco Depaz, one of the brothers who run the
company. Good 4-day Santa Cruz trip. Good food
and equipment, professional service, free loan of
waterproofs and *pisco sour* on last evening.

Kallpa, *José de la Mar y Luzuriaga, p 2, T043-
427868.* Organizes treks, rents gear, arranges
arrieros (muleteers) and mules, very helpful.

La Cima Logistics, *at Café Andino (see
page 1291), www.cafeandino.com/lacima/.*
Christopher Benway makes custom
arrangements for climbing and trekking trips.

Montañero, *Parque Ginebra 30-B, T043-426386,
and at Hotel San Sebastián (see Where to stay,
page 1287), www.trekkingperu.com.* Run by
veteran mountain guide Selio Villón. German,
French and English spoken.

Monttrek, *Luzuriaga 646, upstairs, T043-421124,
monttrek@terra.com.pe.* Good trekking/climbing
information, advice and maps, ice and rock
climbing courses (at Monterrey), tours to Laguna
Churup and the 'spectacular' Luna Llena tour; also
hire mountain bikes, run ski instruction and trips,
and river rafting. Helpful, conscientious guides.
Next door in the Pizzería is a climbing wall, good
maps, videos and slide shows. For new routes/
maps contact Porfirio Cacha Macedo, 'Pocho',
at Monttrek or Jr Corongo 307, T043-423930.

Peruvian Andes Adventures, *José Olaya 532,
T043-421864, www.peruvianandes.com.* Run by
Hisao and Eli Morales, professional, registered
mountain and trekking guides. All equipment
and services for treks of 3-15 days, climbing
technical and non-technical peaks, or just day
walks. Vegetarians catered for.

Quechua Explorer, *Sucre 765 of 4, T043-
221445, www.quechuaexplorer.com.* Hiking,
mountaineering, rock and ice climbing,
rafting, biking, cultural and ecological
tourism, experienced and friendly guides.

Quechuandes, *Av Luzuriaga 522, T943-
562339, www.quechuandes.com.* Trekking,
mountaineering, rock climbing, ice climbing,
skiing, mountain biking and other adventure
sports, guides speak Spanish, Quechua, English
and/or French. Animal welfare taken seriously
with weight limits of 40 kg per donkey.

Responsible Travel Peru, *Jr Eulogio del Rio 1364,
Soledad, T956-125568, www.responsibletravelperu.
com.* Sustainable tourism initiatives, community
based, with trekking, homestays, tours,
volunteering and other responsible travel ideas.

Guides For details of the Casa de Guías,
see page 1293.

Aritza Monasterio, *through Casa de Guías.* Speaks
English, Spanish and Euskerra.

Augusto Ortega, *Jr San Martín 1004, T043-
424888.* Augusto has climbed Everest.

Filiberto Rurush Paucar, *Sucre 1240, T043-
422264 (Lodging Casa Sucre).* Speaks English,
Spanish and Quechua.

Genaro Yanac Olivera, *T043-422825.*
Speaks good English and some German,
also a climbing guide.

Hugo Sifuentes Maguiña, *Siex (Sifuentes
Expeditions), Jr Huaylas 139, T043-426529.* Trekking,
rock climbing and less adventurous tours.

Koky Castañeda, *T043-427213, or through Skyline
Adventures, or Café Andino.* Speaks English and
French, UIAGM Alpine certified.

Max, Misael and Saul Angeles, *T043-
456891/422205 (Sol Andino agency).*
Speak some English, know Huayhuash well.

Máximo Henostrosa, *T043-426040.* Trekking
guide with knowledge of the entire region.

Ted Alexander, *Skyline Adventures, Pasaje
Industrial 137, Cascapampa, Huaraz, T043-427097,
www.skyline-adventures.com.* US outward bound
instructor, very knowledgeable.

Tjen Verheye, *Jr Carlos Valenzuela 911, T043-
422569.* Belgian and speaks Dutch, French,
German and reasonable English, runs trekking
and conventional tours and is knowledgeable
about the Chavín culture.

Camping gear The following agencies
are recommended for hiring gear: **Galaxia
Expeditions**, **Monttrek**, **Kallpa** and **Montañero**.
Also **Skyline**, **Andean Sport Tours** *(Luzuriaga
571, T043-421612)*, and **MountClimb** *(Jr Mcal
Cáceres 421, T043-426060, mountclimb@
yahoo.com).* Casa de Guías rents equipment
and sells dried food. Check all camping and
climbing equipment very carefully before taking
it. Quality varies and some items may not be
available, so it's best to bring your own. All
prices are standard, but not cheap, throughout
town. All require payment in advance, passport
or air ticket as deposit and rarely give any
money back if you return gear early. Many
trekking agencies sell screw-on camping gas
cartridges. White gas (*bencina*) is available from

ferreterías on Raymondi below Luzuriaga and by Parque Ginebra.

Tour operators

Chavín Tours, *José de la Mar*, *T043-421578*, *www.chavintours.com.pe*. All local tours, long-standing agency with its head office in Lima.

Mony Tours, *San Martí n 643*, *T043-428949*, *www.monytoursperu.com*. Daily departures for local tours, uses its own vehicles, guiding in Spanish.

Pablo Tours, *Luzuriaga 501*, *T043-421145*, *www.pablotours.com*. For all local tours, also with many years of operation.

Quenual Adventures, *at Alojamiento Soledad (see Where to stay, page 1288), T943-603413, www.quenualadventures.com*. Custom tailored trekking and conventional tours with multilingual guides. Owner Francisco Romero is knowledgeable and helpful.

Transport

Air LC Peru (Luzuriaga 904, T043-222003) flies 3 times a week to/from **Lima**, US$120-155, 1 hr.

Bus Many of the companies have their offices along Av Raymondi, Jr Lúcar y Torre, and Bolívar (see map, page 1290). Some recommended companies are: **Cavassa**, Jr Lúcar y Torre 446, T043-425767; **Cruz del Sur**, Bolívar y La Mar, T043-728726; **Empresa 14**, Fitzcarrald 216, T043-421282, terminal at Bolívar 407; **Julio César**, Prol Cajamarca s/n, cuadra 1, T043-396443; **Línea**, Bolívar 450, T043-726666, **Móvil**, modern station at Av Confraternidad Internacional Oeste 451, T043-422555, ticket office on Bolívar 541, T043-429541; **Oltursa**, Av Raymondi 825, T043-423717; **Z-Buss**, Bolívar 410, T043-428327.

Long distance To **Lima**, 7-8 hrs, US$15-25 (**Móvil** prices), large selection of ordinary service and luxury coaches throughout the day. To

Trujillo via Callán pass (sit on left for great views), Pariacoto, Casma, and Chimbote, **Línea** at 0930, 2200 and 2300, US$9-15, 7 hrs. To **Chimbote** (US$6, 4½ hrs) via **Casma** (same fare, 3½ hrs), 8 daily buses with **Yungay Express**. You can make connections from Chimbote at the Terminal Terrestre outside town, no need to enter the city.

Within the Cordillera Blanca Frequent minivans run daily, 0500-2000, between Huaraz and **Caraz**, 1¼ hrs, US$2, from Jr Cajamarca y Av Raimondi; no luggage racks, you have to pay an extra seat for your bag. To **Chavín**, 110 km, 3 hrs (sit on left side for best views), US$6 with **Sandoval/Olguita Tours**, Mcal Cáceres 338, 3 a day. Also **Trans Río Mosna**, Mcal Cáceres 265, T043-426632, 3 a day; buses go on to **Huari**, 4 hrs, US$7.50.

Vans and shared taxis to **Chacas**, US$7.50, 2½ hrs; and **San Luis**, US$9, 3 hrs; an unforgettable ride via the 4700-m-high Punta Olímpica tunnel, throughout the day with **Turismo Lince**, Villarán y Bolívar. **Renzo**, Raymondi 821, T043-425371, daily buses to Chacas via Punta Olímpica at 0615 and 1400; some continue to **Piscobamba** and **Pomabamba**. To **Sihuas**, Sandoval/Olguita Tours, Tue/Fri 0800; **Perú Andino**, 1 a week, 8 hrs, US$11.

Colectivos to **Recuay**, US$0.75, and **Catac**, US$0.85, daily at 0500-2100, from Gridilla, just off Tarapacá (Terminal de Transportistas Zona Sur). To **Chiquián** for the Cordillera Huayhuash, US$9, 120 km, 3½ hrs, with **Nazario**, Bolognesi 216, T043-422887, at 1345. To **Huallanca** (Huánuco) on the paved road through Conococha, Chiquián, Aquia to Huansala, then by good dirt road to Laguna Pachacoto and Huallanca. Departs Huaraz twice a day, 1st at 1300, with **Nazario**, as before, US$8. Frequent daily service from Huallanca to **Huánuco**.

Taxi Standard fare in town is about US$1.20, more at night; radio taxis T043-421482 or 422512.

Chavín and the Callejón de Conchucos

don't miss this pre-Inca fortress temple

From Huaraz it is possible to make a circuit by road, visiting Chavín de Huantar, Huari, San Luis, Yanama and Yungay, but bear in mind that the road north of Chavín is gravel and rough in parts and the bus service is infrequent.

South of Huaraz

South of Huaraz is **Olleros**, from where the spectacular and relatively easy three- to four-day hike to Chavín, along a pre-Columbian trail, starts. Some basic meals and food supplies are available; for guides and prices, see Trekking and climbing in the cordilleras, above. Alternatively, if you're travelling by road to Chavín, head south from Huaraz on the main road for 38 km to **Catac** (two basic hotels and a restaurant), where a paved road branches east for Chavín.

Further south, the Pumapampa valley is a good place to see the impressive *Puya raimondii* plants. A 14-km gravel road leads from Pachacoto to a park office at 4200 m, where you can spend the night. Walking up the road from this point, you will see the gigantic plants, whose flower spike can reach 12 m in height and takes 100 years to develop. The final flowering (usually in May) is a spectacular sight. Another good spot, and less visited, is the **Queshque Gorge**, which is easy to find by following the Río Queshque from Catac.

From Catac to Chavín is a magnificent journey. The road passes Lago Querococha, and there are good views of the Yanamarey peaks. At the top of the route the road cuts through a huge rock face, entering the Cahuish tunnel at 4516 m. The tunnel has no light and is single lane with a small stream running through it. Cyclists must have powerful lights so that trucks and buses can see them. On the other side of the tunnel, the road descends into the Tambillo valley, then the Río Mosna gorge before Chavín.

☆Chavín de Huantar *Colour map 3, B2.*
Tue-Sun 0900-1600, US$3.50, students half price, guided tours in Spanish for groups available for an extra charge. You will receive an information leaflet in Spanish at the entrance.

Chavín de Huantar, a fortress temple, was built about 800 BC. It is the only large structure remaining of the Chavín culture, which, in its heyday, is thought to have held influence from Cajamarca and Chiclayo in the north to Ayacucho and Ica in the south. In 1985, UNESCO designated Chavín a World Heritage Trust Site. The site is in good condition despite the effects of time and nature but becomes very crowded in high season. In order to protect the site some areas are closed to visitors. All the galleries open to the public have electric lights. The guard is also a guide and gives excellent explanations of the ruins.

The main attractions are the marvellous carved stone heads (*cabezas clavas*), the designs in relief of symbolic figures and the many tunnels and culverts, which form an extensive labyrinth throughout the interior of the pyramidal structure. The carvings are in excellent condition, and the best are now in the Museo Nacional Chavín. The famous Lanzón dagger-shaped stone monolith of 800 BC is found inside one of the temple tunnels.

Just north of the ruins, the town of Chavín, painted colonial yellow and white, has a pleasant plaza with palm and pine trees. There are a couple of good, simple hotels and restaurants here and a local fiesta in mid July. The **Museo Nacional Chavín** ① *1 km north of town and 1.6 km from the site, Tue-Sun, 0900-1700, US$3.50*, has a comprehensive collection of items gathered from several deposits and museums, including the Tello obelisk dating from the earliest period of occupation of Chavín (c 100 BC), and many impressive *cabezas clavas*.

Chavín to Huari
The road north from Chavín descends into the Mosna river canyon. The scenery is quite different from the other side of the Cordillera Blanca, very dry and hot. After 8 km it reaches **San Marcos**, the town that has been most heavily impacted by the huge **Antamina** gold mine. Hotels may be full with mine workers and public safety is a concern, so press on for 32 km to Huari.

Huari is perched on a hillside at 3150 m and has various simple hotels ($ Huagancu 2, Jirón Sucre 335, T043-630434, clean and good value) and restaurants. The fiesta of Nuestra Señora del Rosario takes place on 7 October, with festivities during the first two weeks of the month. There is a spectacular two- to three-day walk from Huari to Chacas via Laguna Purhuay inside Parque Nacional Huascarán. Alberto Cafferata of Caraz writes: "The Purhuay area is beautiful. It has splendid campsites, trout, exotic birds and, at its north end, a 'quenual' forest with orchids. This is a microclimate at 3500 m, where the animals, insects and flowers are more like a tropical jungle, fantastic for ecologists and photographers." A pleasant alternative for those who don't want to do the longer walk to Chacas is a day walk to Laguna Purhuay, starting at the village of Acopalca; a taxi from Huari to Acopalca costs US$3.50, to Puruhuay, US$14. The lake has a visitor centre, food kiosk and boat rides.

San Luis to Huaraz
From Huari the road climbs to the Huachacocha pass at 4350 m and descends to **San Luis** at 3130 m, 60 km from Huari. Here you'll find the $ Hostal Puñuri (Ramón Castilla 151, T043-830408, with bath and hot water), a few basic restaurants, shops and a market.

Beyond San Luis there are a few options to take you back to Huaraz. The first is via **Chacas**, 10 km south of San Luis on a paved road. It has a fine church and celebrates the **Virgen de la Asunción** on 15 August, with bullfights, a famous carrera de cintas and fireworks. There are hostels ($), shops, restaurants and a small market. ☆A spectacular paved road and 4700-m-high tunnel through **Punta Olímpica** connect Chacas with Carhuaz in the Callejón de Huaylas north of Huaraz. Alternatively, it is a three-day hike west from Chacas to Marcará via the Quebradas Juytush and Honda (lots of condors to be seen). Quebrada Honda is known as the *Paraíso de las Cascadas* because it contains at least seven waterfalls.

The second road route heads some 20 km north of San Luis, to where a road branches left to **Yanama**, 45 km from San Luis, at 3400 m. It has a good comfortable hotel, **Andes Lodge Peru** ① *T043-943 847423, www.andeslodgeperu.com*, $$, full board available, excellent food and services, fabulous views. The village retains many traditional features and is beautifully surrounded by snow-capped peaks. There are superb views from the ruins above the town, reachable on a day hike. From Yanama the road continues west via the Portacheulo de Llanganuco pass to Yungay (see page 1298).

North of San Luis

A longer circuit to Huaraz can be made by continuing from San Luis for 62 km to **Piscobamba**, which has a couple of basic hotels, a few shops and small restaurants. Beyond Piscobamba by 22 km is **Pomabamba**, worth a visit for some very hot natural springs (the furthest are the hottest). There are various hotels ($) near the plaza and restaurants. Pomabamba is also the terminus of one the variations of the **Alpamayo Trek**, see page 1278.

From Pomabamba a dusty road runs up the wooded valley crossing the puna at Palo Seco, 23 km. The road then descends steeply into the desert-like Sihuas valley, passing through the village of Sicsibamba. The valley is crossed half an hour below the small town of **Sihuas**, a major connection point between the Callejón de Conchucos, Callejón de Huaylas, the upper Marañón and the coast. It has a few $ hotels and places to eat.

From Sihuas it is also possible to travel in the other direction, via Huancaspata, Tayabamba, Retamas and Chahual to Huamachuco along a road which is very poor in places and involves crossing the Río Marañón twice. Using this route, it is possible to travel from Cuzco to Quito through the Andes entirely by public transport. This journey is best undertaken in this direction, but it can take over two days (if it's not impassable) in the wet season.

Listings Chavín and the Callejón de Conchucos

Where to stay

Chavín

$$$ Tambo Konchukos
10 km north of Chavín, T043-709772.
A small ecolodge attached to a farm researching traditional Andean farming practices. Offers a variety of activities, rooms have wood burning stoves, restaurant serves Andean cuisine.

$$-$ La Casona
Wiracocha 130, Plaza de Armas, T043-454116.
In a renovated house with attractive courtyard, single, double and triple rooms, some with balcony overlooking Plaza or courtyard, nice breakfast, laundry, parking.

$$-$ R'ikay
On 17 de Enero 172N, T043-454068.

Set around 2 patios, modern, best in town, variety of room sizes, hot water, restaurant does Italian food in the evening. Recommended.

$ Inca
Wiracocha 170, T043-754021.
Rooms are cheaper without bath, good beds, hot water on request, nice garden.

Restaurants

Chavín

$$-$ Chavín Turístico
Middle of 17 de Enero.
The best in town, good *menú* and à la carte, delicious apple pie, nice courtyard, popular. Also run a *hostal* nearby.

$$-$ La Portada
Towards south end of 17 de Enero.

In an old house with tables set around a pleasant garden.

$ La Ramada
Towards north end of main street, 17 de Enero.
Regional dishes, also trout and set lunch.

Transport

Chavín
It is much easier to get to Chavín (even walking!) than to leave the place by bus. All buses to **Huaraz** (2 hrs from Chavín), originate in Huari or further afield. They pass through Chavín at irregular hours and may not have seats available. Buying a ticket at an agency in Chavín does not guarantee you will get a seat or even a bus. **Sandoval/Olguita Tours** goes through around 1200, 1600 and 1700 daily, **Río Mosna** at 0430 and then 4 between 1600-2200. There are also services to **Lima**, 438 km, 12 hrs, US$14, with **Trans El Solitario** and **Perú Andino** daily, but locals prefer to travel to Huaraz and then take one of the better companies from there.

In the other direction, buses from Huaraz or Lima (such as **El Solitario**, which passes through Chavín at 1800) go on to **Huari**, with some going on to **San Luis**, a further 61 km, 3 hrs; **Piscobamba**, a further 62 km, 3 hrs; and **Pomabamba**, a further 22 km, 1 hr. The other way to reach places in the Callejón de Conchucos is to hop on and off the cars and combis that leave regularly from Chavín's main plaza, every 20 mins and 30 mins respectively, to **San Marcos**, 8 km, and **Huari**, 38 km.

Huari
Terminal Terrestre at Av Circunvalación Baja. Bus to **Huaraz**, 4 hrs, US$5.50, **Sandoval/Olguita Tours** 3 a day. Also runs to **San Luis** and **Lima**.

San Luís to Huaraz
There are daily buses between Yanama and **Yungay** over the 4767-m Portachuelo de Llanganuco (3 hrs, US$7.50), stopping at Vaquería (at the end of the Santa Cruz valley trek) 0800-1400, US$4, 2 hrs.

North of San Luís

Pomabamba
To **Piscobamba**, combis depart hourly, 1 hr, US$1.50; also combis to Sihuas (see below). El Solitario has a service to **Lima** on Sun, Mon and Thu at 0800, 18 hrs, US$15, via **San Luis** (4 hrs, US$5), **Huari** (6 hrs, US$7.50) and **Chavín** (9 hrs, US$9); La Perla del Alto Mayo goes from Pomabamba to **Lima** via **Huaraz** on Wed, Thu, Sat, Sun, 16 hrs.

Sihuas
To **Pomabamba**, combi from Av 28 de Julio near the market at 1100, 4 hrs, US$7 (returns 0200). To **Huaraz**, via Huallanca, with **Cielo Azul**, daily at 0830, 10 hrs, US$11. To **Tayabamba**, for the Marañón route north to Huamachuco and Cajamarca: **Andía** passes through from Lima on Sat and Sun at 0100, **La Perla del Alta Mayo** passes through Tue, Thu 0000-0200; also **Garrincha** Wed, Sun around 0800; all 8 hrs, US$11, the beginning of a long wild ride. To **Huacrachuco**, **Andía** passes through Wed, Sat 0100. To **Chimbote**, **Corvival** on Wed, Thu and Sun morning, 9 hrs, US$9; **La Perla del Alta Mayo** Tue, Thu, Sun. To **Lima** (19 hrs, US$20) via Chimbote, **Andía** Tue, Sun 0200, Wed, Sat 1600; and 3 other companies once or twice a week each.

Callejón de Huaylas

hike to beautiful mountain lakes

Carhuaz and Mancos *Colour map 3, B2.*
Carhuaz is a friendly mountain town with a pleasant plaza. There is very good walking to thermal baths or up the Ulta valley. Market days are Wednesday and Sunday (the latter is much larger). The local fiesta of **Virgen de las Mercedes**, 14-24 September, is rated as among the best in the region. From Carhuaz it is 14 km to Mancos at the foot of Huascarán. The village has a dormitory at La Casita de mi Abuela, some basic shops and restaurants. After Mancos, the main road goes to **Yungay** (8 km north, 30 minutes).

☆Yungay *Colour map 3, B2.*
The town of Yungay was completely buried by a massive mudslide during the 1970 earthquake; a hideous tragedy in which 20,000 people lost their lives. The original site of Yungay, known as Yungay Viejo, is desolate and haunting; it has been consecrated as a *camposanto* (cemetery). The

new settlement is on a hillside just north of the old town. It has a pleasant plaza and a concrete market, good on Wednesday and Sunday. The **Virgen del Rosario** fiesta is celebrated on 17 October, and 28 October is the anniversary of the founding of the town. The tourist office is on the corner of the Plaza de Armas. The main road continues 12 km north of Yungay to Caraz.

Lagunas de Llanganuco

The Lagunas de Llanganuco are two beautiful lakes nestling beneath Huascarán and Huandoy. From Yungay, the first you come to is **Laguna Chinancocha** (3850 m), the second Laguna **Orconcocha** (3863 m). The park office is situated before the lakes at 3200 m, 19 km from Yungay. Accommodation is provided for trekkers who want to start the Santa Cruz Valley trek from here (see below). From the park office to the lakes takes about five hours (a steep climb). The last section is a nature trail, Sendero María Josefa (sign on the lake); it takes 1½ hours to walk to the western end of Chinancocha where there is a control post, descriptive trail and boat trips on the lake. Walk along the road beside the lake to its far end for peace and quiet among the quenual trees, which provide shelter for 75% of the birdlife found in the park. The trailhead for a popular hike to **Laguna 69** is at Cebollapampa, 4 km past Orconcocha. This pretty route to a lake at 4600 m gets crowded in high season with groups (US$18 per person, quality varies). There is also public transport from Yungay, see Transport, page 1302.

Caraz *Colour map 3, B2.*

This pleasant town at 2290 m is a good centre for walking and parasailing and is the access point for many excellent treks and climbs. Tourist facilities are expanding as a more tranquil alternative to Huaraz, and there are great views of Huandoy, Huascarán and surrounding summits in July and August. In other months, the mountains are often shrouded in cloud. In addition to its many natural attractions, Caraz is also developing a lively cultural scene. Events are organized by **Caraz Cultura** ① *contact Ricardo Espinosa, T991-996136, carazcultura@gmail.com.* On 20 January is the fiesta **Virgen de Chiquinquirá.** In the last week of July is **Semana Turística.**

The **Museo Arqueológico Municipal** is on San Martín, half a block up from the plaza. The ruins of **Tumshukaiko** are 1.5 km from the Plaza de Armas in the suburb of Cruz Viva, to the north before the turn-off for Parón. There are seven platforms from the Huaraz culture, dating from around 2000-1800 BC, but the site is in poor shape.

☆ Treks around Caraz

Caraz has a milder climate than Huaraz and is more suited to day trips. A good day walk goes from Caraz by the lakes of Miramar and Pampacocha to Huaripampa, where you can get a pickup back to Caraz. A longer full-day walk with excellent views of Huandoy and Huascarán follows the foothills of the Cordillera Blanca east along the main Río Santa valley, from Caraz south through the villages of Chosica and Ticrapa. It ends at Puente Ancash on the Caraz–Yungay road, from where frequent transport goes back to Caraz.

Laguna Parón ① *US$5.* From Caraz a narrow, rough road goes east 32 km to beautiful Laguna Parón in a cirque surrounded by several, massive snow-capped peaks, including Huandoy, Pirámide Garcilazo and Caraz. The gorge leading to it is spectacular. It is a long day's trek for acclimatized hikers (25 km) up to the lake at 4150 m, or a four- to five-hour walk from the village of Parón, which can be reached by combi (US$2). Camping is possible. There is no trail around the lake and you should not attempt it as it is slippery and dangerous, particularly on the southern shore; tourists have been killed here. Caraz agencies offer tours, US$15 per person.

Santa Cruz Valley One of the best known treks in the area is the beautiful three- to five-day route from Vaquería, over the 4750 m Punta Unión pass, to Quebrada Santa Cruz and the village of Cashapampa. It can be hiked in either direction. Starting in Cashapampa, you climb more gradually to the pass, then down to Vaquería or the Llanganuco lakes beyond. Along this 'clockwise' route the climb is gentler, giving more time to acclimatize, and the pass is easier to find, although, if you start in Vaquería and finish in Cashapampa you ascend for one day rather than three in the other direction. You can hire an *arriero* and mule in Cashapampa; see box, page 1293, for prices. Campsites are at Llamacorral and Taullipampa before Punta Unión, and Quenoapampa (or Huaripampa) after the pass. You can end the hike at Vaquería on the Yanama–Yungay road and take a minibus or, better, an open truck from there (a beautiful run). Or end the walk a day later with a night at the Yuraccorral campsite at the Llanganuco lakes, from where cars go back to Yungay. This trek is very popular and offered by all tour agencies in Huaraz and Caraz.

☆Puyas raymondii at Winchos

A large stand of *Puya raimondii* can be seen in the Cordillera Negra southwest of Caraz. Beyond Pueblo Libre is a paved road which heads west via Pamparomás and Moro to join the Panamerican highway south of Chimbote. The *Puya raymondii* plants are located at a place called **Winchos**, after 45 km (1½ hours). There are far-reaching views of the Cordillera Blanca and west to the Pacific. The plants are usually in flower May or October. Take warm clothing, food and water. You can also camp near the puyas and return the following day. The most popular way to visit is to rent a bike (US$18 per day), travel up by public transport (see below), and then ride back down in four or five hours. Or form a group (eg via the bulletin board at Pony's Expeditions, Caraz) and hire a car which will wait for you (US$60 for five). From Caraz, a minibus for Pamparomás leaves from Ramón Castilla y Jorge Chávez around 0830, two hours, US$3 (get there at about 0800 as they often leave early). From the pass (El Paso) or El Cruce it is a short walk to the plants. Return transport leaves between 1230 and 1300. If you miss the bus, you can walk back to Pueblo Libre in four hours, to Caraz in six to eight hours, but it is easy to get lost and there are not many people to ask directions along the way.

Listings Callejón de Huaylas

Tourist information

Caraz

The **tourist office** (Plaza de Armas, next to the municipality, T043-483860 ext 143), has limited information. There are 3 ATMs in the centre.

Where to stay

Carhuaz

$$ El Abuelo
Jr 9 de Diciembre 257, T043-394456,
www.elabuelohotel.com.
Modern, comfortable hotel, nicely decorated with local tapestries and ceramics. Restaurant, garden with organic fruit and veg, parking, credit cards accepted. Knowledgeable owner is map-maker, Felipe Díaz.

$ 4 family-run *hospedajes* operate as part of a community development project. All have private bath and hot water. The better 2 are: **Hospedaje Robri** (Jr Comercio 935, T043-224124), and **Alojamiento Las Torresitas** (Jr Amazonas 412, T043-394213).

Yungay

$ Rima Rima
Grau 275, T043-393257, www.hotelrimarima.com.
Ample rooms with private bath, hot water, nice views from terrace.

$ Sol de Oro
Santo Domingo 7, T043-393116.
Simple rooms with private bath, hot water, kitchen and laundry facilities, good value.

Lagunas de Llanganuco

$$$$-$$$ Llanganuco Mountain Lodge
Laguna Keushu, Llanganuco Valley, T976-592524,
www.llanganucomountainlodge.com.
Standard and luxury rooms in a beautiful location, includes full board, great trekking opportunities (local guides available), low season discounts. Enthusiastic British owner, Charlie Good. Contact well in advance.

Caraz

$$$-$$ Los Pinos Lodge
Parque San Martín 103 (also known as Plazuela de la Merced), T043-391130, www.lospinoslodge.pe.
Nice comfortable rooms, buffet breakfast, patio, gardens, parking, cosy bar, tourist information. Recommended. Also have a nearby annex nearby called **Caraz Backpacker** ($).

$$$-$$ O'Pal Inn
Km 265.5, 5 mins south of Caraz, T043-391015,
www.opalsierraresort.com.
Scenic, family bungalows, suites and rooms, swimming pool, includes breakfast, restaurant, games room.

$$-$ La Alameda
Av Noé Bazán Peralta 262, T043-391177,
www.hostallaalameda.com.
Comfortable rooms, hot water, ample parking,
pleasant gardens.

$ Chavín
San Martín 1135 just off the plaza, T043-391171.
Get a room overlooking the street, many others
have no window. Warm water, guiding service,
tourist info.

$ Edward's
San Martín 1245, T043-391631.
Good rooms with private bath, electric shower,
parking, good value.

$ Hostal La Casona
Raymondi 319, 1 block east from the plaza,
T043-391334.
With or without bath, hot water, lovely little
patio, noisy at night.

$ La Perla de los Andes
Daniel Villar 179, Plaza de Armas, next to the
cathedral, T043-391767.
Comfortable rooms, hot water, helpful.

$ San Marco
San Martín 1133, T043-391558.
Comfortable rooms with private or shared bath,
hot water, patio.

Restaurants

Carhuaz

$$$-$$ La Bicharra
Jr Comercio 1069, T943-780893.
Daily from 1900.
Innovative North African/Peruvian cooking.

$$ JR
Parque San Martín 165. Mon-Fri 1200-1500.
Good varied *menú*, terrace seating, clean
and popular.

Yungay

$$ Alpamayo
Av Arias Graziani s/n. Lunchtime only.
At north entrance to town, good for local dishes.

$ Café Pilar
On the main plaza. Open 1000-2100, closed Wed.
Good for juices, cakes and snacks, lunch *menú*.

Caraz

$$$-$$ Intirumi
Barrio Nueva Victoria, 15-min walk north of
centre, T964-964651, www.intirumi.com.
Tue-Sun 1200-2100.
Delicious creative cuisine, ingredients from their
own organic garden, lovely atmosphere for
relaxed dining, family run by Kelly and Mac from
the USA. Recommended.

$$-$ Entre Panes
Daniel Villar 211, half a block from the plaza.
Closed Tue.
Variety of excellent sandwiches, also meals.
Good food, service and atmosphere.

$$-$ La Pizza del Abuelo
Raimondi 425, T965-729489. Open 1800-2200.
Good pizzas, pastas, juices and desserts, warm
atmosphere, friendly owners. Recommended.

$$-$ La Punta Grande
D Villar 595, 10 mins' walk from centre. Closes 1700.
Good place for local dishes.

$$-$ La Terraza
Jr Sucre 1107, T043-301226. Sun-Fri 0800-2130.
Good *menú* as well as pizza, pasta, juices,
home-made ice cream, sandwiches, sweets,
coffee and drinks.

$ Jeny
Daniel Villar on the plaza next to the Cathedral.
Local fare at reasonable prices, ample variety.

Cafés

Café Cultura
Plazuela La Merced off D Villar, T980-990659.
Open after 1700.
Cultural events, coffee, sandwiches, juices and
desserts in a nicely refurbished old home.

Café de Rat
Sucre 1266, above Pony's Expeditions.
Breakfast, vegetarian dishes, good pizzas, drinks
and snacks, darts, travel books, nice atmosphere.

El Turista
San Martín 1117. Open 0700-2030.
Small, popular for breakfast, ham omelettes and
ham sandwiches are specialities.

Panificadora La Alameda
D Villar y San Martín.
Good bread and pastries, ice cream, popular with
locals. The excellent *manjar blanco* for which the
town earned its nickname 'Caraz dulzura' is sold
here and at several other shops on the same street.

Bars and clubs

Caraz

Airu Bar
At Los Pinos Lodge, Parque San Martín.
Open 1800-2200.
Café-bar serves wines and piscos.

Shopping

Caraz

Large market at Sucre y La Mar. Some dried camping food is available from **Pony's Expeditions**, who also sell Camping Gaz canisters.

What to do

Caraz

Agencies in Caraz arrange treks in the Cordilleras Blanca and Huayhuash, as well as more local destinations.
Apu-Aventura, *Parque San Martín 103, 5 blocks west of plaza, T043-391130, www.apuaventura.pe.* Range of adventure sports and equipment rental.
Pony's Expeditions, *Sucre 1266, near the Plaza de Armas, T043-391642, www.ponyexpeditions.com. Mon-Sat 0800-2200.* English, French, Italian and Quechua spoken. Owners Alberto and Aidé Cafferata are knowledgeable about treks and climbs. They arrange local tours, offer accommodation at **Pony's Lodge ($$)**, trekking, transport for day excursions, and rental of a 4WD vehicle with driver. Also maps and books for sale, equipment hire and mountain bike rental (US$15 for a full day). Well organized and reliable. Highly recommended.

Transport

Carhuaz

Transport leaves from Av La Merced between the plaza and the highway. To **Huaraz**, *colectivos* 0500-2000, US$0.90, 40 mins. To **Caraz**, 0500-2000, US$1, 1 hr. Buses from Huaraz to **Chacas**, 87 km, 3 hrs, US$5.75, pass through Carhuaz about 40 mins after leaving Huaraz. The road

works its way up the Ulta valley to the tunnel at Punta Olímpica from where there are excellent views. **Renzo** daily buses pass through en route to **San Luis** (see page 1296), 10 km past Chacas, 1½ hrs.

Yungay

From the small terminal vans run all day to **Caraz**, 12 km, 30 mins, US$0.50, and **Huaraz**, 54 km, 1 hr, US$1. To the **Llanganuco lakes**, cars leave when full, especially 0700-0900, from Av 28 de Julio 1 block from the plaza, 1 hr, US$2.50. Taxi to Llanganuco, US$50 with full-day wait. To **Yanama**, vans run via the Portachuelo de Llanganuco Pass, 4767 m, stopping at the trailhead for the Llanganuco–Santa Cruz trek, and Cebollapampa (for Laguna 69); leave 0700-0730, 58 km, 3½ hrs to Yanama, US$5.

Caraz

To **Lima**, 470 km, daily, US$11-30, 10-11 hrs via Huaraz and Pativilca, 9 companies: **El Huaralino** (T996-896607), **Huaraz Buss** (T943-469736), **Zbuss** (T043-391050), **Cooperativa Ancash** (T043-391126), all on Jr Cordova, also **Rochaz** (Pasaje Olaya, T043-794375), **Cavassa** (Ctra Central, T043-392042), **Yungay Express** (Av Luzuriaga, T043-391492), **Móviltours** (east end of town, www.moviltours.com.pe) and **Rodríguez** (Daniel Villar, T043-635631).

To **Chimbote**, Yungay Express, via Huallanca, Casma and Cañón del Pato, 3 daily, US$9, 7 hrs, sit on right for best views. To **Trujillo**, via Casma with Móviltours. To **Huaraz**, combis leave from a terminal on the way out of town, where the south end of C Sucre meets the highway, daily 0400-2000, 1¼ hrs, US$2, no luggage racks, you might have to pay an extra seat for your bag. To **Yungay**, 12 km, 15 mins, US$0.70. To **Huallanca** and **Yuramarca** (for the Cañón del Pato), combis and cars leave from Córdova y La Mar, 0700-1600, US$2.50. To **Cashapampa** (for the Santa Cruz valley) *colectivo*/minibus from Ramón Castilla y Jorge Chávez, Caraz, leave when full from 0600 to 1530, 1½ hrs, US$2. To **Parón** (for the walk to Laguna Parón), *colectivos* leave from Ramón Castilla y Jorge Chávez, close to the market, 1 hr, US$2.

Cordillera Huayhuash

remote mountains just waiting to be explored

The Cordillera Huayhuash, lying south of the Cordillera Blanca, has azure trout-filled lakes interwoven with deep quebradas and high pastures around the hem of the range. It is perhaps the most spectacular cordillera for its massive ice faces that seem to rise sheer out of the puna's contrasting green. You may see tropical parakeets in the bottom of the gorges and condors circling the peaks. The area offers fantastic scenery and insights into rural life.

The cordillera is approached from several points: **Chiquián** and **Llamac** in the north; **Oyón**, with links to Cerro de Pasco, lies to the southeast; **Churín** is to the south, and **Cajatambo**, a small market town with a beautiful 18th-century church and a lovely plaza, lies to the southwest. Note that the road out of Cajatambo is not for the faint-hearted. For the first three to four hours it is no more than a bus-width, clinging to the cliff edge.

☆Huayhuash trekking circuit

The complete circuit is very tough; allow 10 to 12 days. There are up to eight passes over 4600 m, depending on the route. Fees are charged by every community along the way, adding up to about US$80 for the entire circuit; take soles in small denominations and insist on getting a receipt every time. A half-circuit is also possible, and there are many other options. The trail head is at **Cuartel Huain**, between Matacancha and the **Punta Cacanan Pass** (which marks the continental divide at 4700 m).

Listings Cordillera Huayhuash

Where to stay

There are various hotels ($) and some good restaurants around the plaza in Cajatambo. The following are all in Chiquián:

$ Hostal San Miguel
Jr Comercio 233, T043-447001.
Nice courtyard and garden, clean, many rooms, popular.

$ Hotel Huayhuash
28 de Julio 400, T043-447049.
Private bathroom, hot water, restaurant, laundry, parking, modern, great views, information and tours.

$ Los Nogales de Chiquián
Jr Comercio 1301, T043-447121, http://hotelnogaleschiquian.blogspot.com.
Traditional design, with private or shared bath, hot water, cafeteria, parking. Recommended.

Restaurants

$ El Refugio de Bolognesi and Yerupajá
Tarapacá, Chiquián.
Both offer basic set meals.

$ Panificadora Santa Rosa
Comercio 900, on the plaza, Chiquián.
For good bread and sweets, has coin-operated phones and fax.

Transport

Coming from Huaraz, the road is now paved beyond Chiquián to Huansala, on the road to Huallanca (Húanuco). Private vehicles can sometimes be hired in Chiquián or Llamac (less likely) to take you to the trailhead at Cuartel Huain; otherwise you'll have to walk.

Chiquián

To **Huaraz**, buses leave the plaza at 0500 daily, US$1.75, except Trans **El Rápido**, Jr Figueredo 216, T043-447049, at 0500 and 1330, US$3.65. Also *colectivo* to Huaraz 1500, 3 hrs, US$2.45 pp. There is also a connection from **Chiquián to Huallanca** (Huánuco) with buses from Lima in the early morning and combis during the day, which leave when full, 3 hrs, US$2.50. From Huallanca there are regular combis on to **La Unión**, 1 hr, US$0.75, and from there transport to **Huánuco**.

Cajatambo

Buses to **Lima** daily at 0600, US$9, with **Empresa Andina** (office on plaza next to Hostal Cajatambo), **Tour Bello** (1 block off the Plaza) and Turismo Cajatambo (Jr Grau 120; or Av Carlos Zavala 124 corner of Miguel Aljovin 449, Lima, T01-426 7238).

North coast

The north of Peru has been described as the Egypt of South America, as it is home to many ruined pre-Inca treasures. Many tourists pass through without stopping on their way to or from Ecuador, missing out on one of the most fascinating parts of the country. Along a seemingly endless stretch of desert coast lie many of the country's most important pre-Inca sites: Chan-Chán, the Moche pyramids, Túcume, Sipán, Batán Grande and El Brujo. The main city is Trujillo, while Chiclayo is more down to earth, with one of the country's largest witchdoctors' markets. The coast is also famous for its deep-sea fishing, surfing and the unique reed fishing boats at Huanchaco and Pimentel. Inland lies colonial Cajamarca, scene of Atahualpa's last stand. Further east, where the Andes meet the jungle, countless unexplored ancient ruins await the more adventurous traveller.

North of Lima

awesome prehistoric ruins along the Panamericana

Huacho and around

The Pan-American Highway is four-lane (several tolls, about US$2.65) to Km 101. Here it by-passes both **Huacho** and **Puerto Huacho**, 19 km to the west. There are several hotels in Huacho. The beaches south of the town are clean and deserted.

☆Caral

25 km east of the Panamericana (Km 184); after 18.5 km, a track leads across the valley to the ruins (30 mins), though the river may be impassable Dec-Mar. Information: Proyecto Especial Caral, T01-205 2500 (Lima), www.caralperu.gob.pe. Daily 0900-1600. US$4, US$7 per group; all visitors must be accompanied by an official guide and not stray from the marked paths.

A few kilometres before Barranca, a signed turning to the east at Km 184 leads up the Supe valley to the UNESCO World Heritage Site of Caral. This ancient city, 26 km from the coast, dates from about 2600 BC. Many of the accepted theories of Peruvian archaeology have been overturned by Caral's age and monumental construction. It appears to be the oldest city in South America (a claim disputed by the Miravalles site, in the department of Cajamarca). The dry desert site lies on the southern fringes of the Supe valley, along whose flanks are 32 more ruins, 19 of which have been explored. Caral covers 66 ha and contains eight significant pyramidal structures. To date seven have been excavated by archaeologists from the University of San Marcos, Lima, who are undertaking careful restoration on the existing foundations to re-establish the pyramidal tiers.

It is possible to walk around the pyramids on marked paths. A viewpoint provides a panorama of the whole site. Allow at least two hours for your visit. Handicrafts are sold in the car park. You can stay or camp at the **Casa del Arqueólogo**, a community museum in Supe (at the turn-off to Caral), which provides information on the Caral culture and the progress of the excavations.

Best for
Archaeology ■ Seafood ■ Surfing

ON THE ROAD

2017 floods

Almost the entire Pacific coast was hit by flooding after torrential rains associated with El Niño in early 2017. As this chapter was being researched damage was reported from Tumbes in the north to Arequipa in the south, but most severely in Piura and Lambayeque. Travellers may still encounter disruption when the book is in use.

Barranca to Huarmey

Barranca is by-passed by the Highway but is an important transport hub for the region so you may find yourself there to change buses. Some 4 km beyond the turn-off to Huaraz at Pativilca, beside the Panamericana, are the well-preserved ruins of the Chimú temple of **Paramonga** ① *US$1.80; caretaker may act as guide.* Set on high ground with a view of the ocean, the fortress-like mound is thought to be of Huari origin and resembles a llama when seen from above.

Between Pativilca and Chimbote the mountains come down to the sea. The road passes by a few very small protected harbours in tiny rock-encircled bays, such as **Huarmey**, with a fine beach and active hostel.

☆Sechín

5 km north of Casma, off the road to Huaraz. Daily 0800-1700 (photography best around midday). US$1.80 (children US$0.35, students US$1.40); ticket also valid for the Max Uhle Museum by the ruins and other sites in the Casma Valley. Mototaxi from Casma, US$2.85 each way for 2 passengers, US$8.55 return including wait.

This archaeological site in the Nepeña Valley, north of Casma, is one of the most important ruins on the Peruvian coast. It consists of a large square temple completely faced with about 500 carved stone monoliths narrating, it is thought, a gruesome battle in graphic detail. The style is unique in Peru for its naturalistic vigour. The complex as a whole is associated with the pre-Chavín Sechín culture, dating from about 1600 BC. Three sides of the large stone temple have been excavated and restored, but you cannot see the earlier adobe buildings inside the stone walls because they were covered up and used as a base for a second storey, which has been completely destroyed.

Casma and around *Colour map 3, B2.*

Sechín is accessed from the city of Casma (population 22,600), which has a pleasant Plaza de Armas, several parks and two markets including a good food market. While safer than Chimbote, you should still take care if staying in Casma. Tortugas, 10 minutes away, is a better option and is a pleasant place to spend a day at the seaside and enjoy the seafood.

Chimbote to Callejón de Huaylas *Colour map 3, B2.*

The port of Chimbote (population 296,600) serves the national fishing industry; the smell of its fishmeal plants is overpowering. If that's not enough to put you off staying here, the city is also unsafe. Take extensive precautions; always use taxis from the bus station, and avoid staying overnight if possible.

Just north of Chimbote, a road branches northeast off the Pan-American Highway and goes up the Santa valley following the route of the old Santa Corporation Railway which used to run as far as **Huallanca** (not to be confused with the town southeast of Huaraz), 140 km up the valley. At Chuquicara, three hours from Chimbote

Tip...

If arriving in Chimbote from Caraz via the Cañón del Pato there is usually time to make a connection to Casma or Trujillo/Huanchaco and avoid overnighting in Chimbote. If travelling to Caraz from Chimbote, take the **Línea** 0600 service or earlier from Trujillo to make the 0830 bus up the Cañón del Pato. If overnighting is unavoidable, head south to Casma for the night, but buy your ticket to Caraz the day before.

(paved – very rough thereafter), is **Restaurante Rosales**, a good place to stop for a meal (you can sleep here, too, but it's very basic). There are also places to stay and eat at Huallanca, and fuel is available. At the top of the valley by the hydroelectric centre, the road goes through the very narrow and spectacular **Cañón del Pato**. You pass under tremendous walls of bare rock and through almost 40 tunnels, but the flow of the river has been greatly reduced by the hydroelectric scheme. After this point the road is paved to the Callejón de Huaylas and south to Caraz and Huaraz. For bus services along this route, see Transport, in Listings section, below.

A faster route to Huaraz, paved and also very scenic, branches off the Pan-American Highway at **Casma**. It climbs to **Pariacoto**, with basic lodging, and crosses the Cordillera Negra at the **Callán Pass** (4224 m). The descent to Huaraz offers great views of the Cordillera Blanca. This beautiful trip is worth taking in daylight; sit on the right for the best views. The road has many dangerous curves requiring caution. For bus services along this route, see Transport, opposite.

An alternative road for cyclists (and vehicles with a permit) is the 50-km private road known as the 'Brasileños', used by the Brazilian company Odebrecht which has built a water channel from the Río Santa to the coast. The turn-off at Km 482 on the Pan-American Highway is 35 km north of the Santa turning and 15 km south of the bridge in Chao. It is a good all-weather road via Tanguche. Permits are obtainable from the Chavimochic HQ at San José de Virú, US$7.50, or from the guard at the gate on Sunday.

Listings North of Lima

Where to stay

Barranca to Huarmey

$ Jaime Crazy
Manuel Scorza 371 y 373, Sector B-8, Huarmey, T043-400104, JaimeCrazyPeru on Facebook.
A hostel offering trips to beaches, archaeological sites, farming communities, volunteering and all sorts of activities.

Casma and around

Hotel prices are higher in Jan and Feb.

$$ Hostal El Farol
Túpac Amaru 450, Casma, T043-411064, www.elfarolinn.com.
Very nice, rooms and suites, swimming pool, pleasant garden, very good restaurant, parking, information.

$$ Hostal Gabriela
Malecón Grau Mz 6, Lt 18, Tortugas, T043-631302, misateinversiones@gmail.com.
Pleasant 10-room hotel, lounge with ocean views, good restaurant with extensive menu, seafood, local and international dishes.

$$ Tarawasi
1a Línea Sur, Centro, Tortugas, T043-782637, tarawasitortugas@hotmail.com.
Small family-run *hospedaje*, pleasant atmosphere, 2 terraces with ocean views, good restaurant serves Peruvian and Mediterranean food.

$ El Dorado
Av Garcilazo de la Vega Mz J, Lt 37, 1 block from the Panamericana, Casma, T043-411795, http://eldoradocasma.blogspot.com.
With fan, pool, restaurant and tourist information.

$ Las Dunas
Luis Ormeño 505, Casma, T043-711057.
An upgraded and enlarged family home, welcoming.

Chimbote to Callejón de Huaylas

There are plenty of hotels in Chimbote, so try to negotiate a lower rate.

$$ Cantón
Bolognesi 498, T043-344388.
Modern, higher quality than others, has a good but pricey *chifa* restaurant.

$$ Ivansino Inn
Av José Pardo 738, T043-321811.
Includes breakfast, comfortable, modern.

$ Hostal El Ensueño
Sáenz Peña 268, 2 blocks from Plaza Central, T043-328662.
Cheaper rooms without bath, very welcoming, safe.

$ Hostal Karol Inn
Manuel Ruiz 277, T043-321216.
Hot water, good, family-run, laundry, *cafetería*.

$ Residencial El Parque
E Palacios 309, on plaza, T043-345572.
Converted old home, hot water, nice, secure.

Restaurants

Huacho and around
Good restaurants in Huacho include **Cevichería El Clásico** (C Inca s/n, daily 1000-1800), and **La Estrella** (Av 28 de Julio 561).

Casma and around
The best restaurants are at **Hostal El Farol** and at the hotels in Tortugas. Cheap restaurants are on Huarmey. The local ice cream, *Caribe*, is available at Ormeño 545.

\$\$ Tío Sam
Huarmey 138.
Specializes in fresh fish, good ceviche.

What to do

Casma and around
Akela Tours, *Lima A3-3, T990-283145, Facebook: akelatours*. Good tours of Sechín, trips to the desert and beaches, sandboarding; run by Monika, an archaeologist.
Sechín Tours, *Hostal Monte Carlo, Casma, T043-411421, renatotours@yahoo.com*. Organizes tours in the local area. The guide, Renato, only speaks Spanish but has knowledge of local ruins.

Transport

Huacho and around
AméricaMóvil (Av Luna Pizarro 251, La Victoria, Lima, T01-423 6338; in Huacho T01-232 7631) and **Zeta** (Av Abancay 900, Lima, T01-426 8087; in Huacho T01-239 6176) run every 20-30 mins **Lima–Huacho**, daily 0600 to 2000, 2½ hrs, US\$6 (more expensive at weekends).

Caral
Empresa Valle Sagrado Caral buses to the site leave the terminal in Barranca (Berenice Dávila, cuadra 2), US\$2.75 shared, or US\$35 private service with 1½ hrs at the site. A taxi from Barranca to the ruins costs US\$10 one way. Tours from Lima usually allow 1½ hrs at Caral, with a 3-hr journey each way, stopping for morning coffee and for lunch in Huacho on the return. If you don't want to go back to Lima, you'll have to get to Barranca to continue your journey.

Barranca to Huarmey
Bus companies have their offices in Barranca, so buses tend to stop there (opposite El Grifo service station at the end of town) rather than at Pativilca or Paramonga. To **Lima**, 3½ hrs, US\$7.50. To **Casma**, 155 km, several daily, 2½ hrs, US\$6. To **Huaraz**, take a minibus from C Lima in Barranca to the gas station in Pativilca where you can catch a bus, *colectivo* or truck along the good paved road to Huaraz. From Barranca buses run only to Paramonga port (3 km off the Highway, about 15 mins from Barranca); from there you can get a taxi to the **Paramonga ruins**, US\$9 (including wait); otherwise it's a 3-km walk along the Panamericana.

Casma and around
América Express and **Tres Estrellas** run frequent services from **Lima** to **Chimbote** (see Chimbote below) stopping in Casma, 370 km, 6 hrs, US\$11-18; other companies going to Chimbote or Trujillo might drop you off by the highway. In the other direction, many of the buses to **Lima** stop briefly opposite the petrol station, block 1 of Ormeño or, if they have small offices, along blocks 1-5 of Av Ormeño.

To **Chimbote**, 55 km, it is easiest to take the **Los Casmeños** *colectivos*, which depart when full from between the Plaza de Armas and Banco de la Nación, 45 mins, US\$2.15. To **Trujillo** and Chiclayo, it is best to go first to Chimbote bus station and then take an **América Express** bus.

To **Huaraz,** 150 km via **Pariacoto**, 4 hrs, US\$9, with **Transportes Huandoy** (Ormeño 166, T043-712336) daily 0700, 1100 and 1400, or **Yungay Express** (by the Ovalo near the Repsol petrol station) daily 0600, 0800 and 1400; also *colectivos* from the same Ovalo, US\$11, 3 hrs.

Chimbote
The bus station is 4 km south of town on Av Meiggs. Under no circumstances should you walk to the centre: minibus, US\$0.50, taxi US\$1.50. There are no hotels near the terminal; some companies have ticket offices in the centre.

To/from **Lima**, 420 km, 5½ hrs, US\$15-20, frequent service with many companies, eg hourly with **América Express**, several daily with **Tres Estrellas**. To **Trujillo**, 130 km, 2 hrs, US\$6, **América Express** every 20 mins till 2100, these continue to **Chiclayo**.

To **Huaraz**, most companies, with the best buses, go the 'long way round': down the Panamericana to Pativilca, then up the main highway, 7 hrs, US\$14; the main companies start in Trujillo and continue to **Caraz**. The fastest route, however, is via Pariacoto, 5 hrs, US\$11, with **Trans Huandoy** (Etseturh, T043-354024) at 0600, 1000 and 1300, and **Yungay Express** at 0500, 0700 and 1300. Alternatively, you can travel to **Caraz** via the Cañón del Pato, 6 hrs,

US$12, with **Yungay Express** at 0830; sit on the left-hand-side for the best views.

Trujillo and around Colour map 3, B2.

a colonial city with ancient archaeology on its doorstep

☆ The capital of La Libertad Department, 548 km from Lima, Trujillo disputes the title of second city of Peru with Arequipa. It has an urban population of over 1.5 million, but the compact colonial centre has a small-town feel. The greenness surrounding the city is a delight against the backcloth of brown Andean foothills and peaks. Founded by Diego de Almagro in 1534 as an express assignment ordered by Francisco Pizarro, it was named after the latter's native town in Spain. Nearby are some of Peru's most important Moche and Chimú archaeological sites and a stretch of the country's best surfing beaches.

Sights

The focal point is the pleasant and spacious **Plaza de Armas**, whose buildings, and many others in the vicinity, are painted in bright pastel colours. The prominent sculpture represents agriculture, commerce, education, art, slavery, action and liberation, crowned by a young man holding a torch depicting liberty. Fronting it is the **Cathedral** ① daily 0700-1230, 1700-

> **Warning...**
> The city is generally safe, but take care beyond the inner ring road, Avenida España, as well as at bus stops, terminals, ATMs and internet cafés.

2000, dating from 1666, with religious paintings and sculptures displayed next door in the **museum** ① Mon-Fri 0900-1300, 1600-1900, Sat 0900-1300, US$1.45. Also on the Plaza are the Hotel Libertador, the colonial-style Sociedad de Beneficencia Pública de Trujillo and the Municipalidad (great views from Salón Dorado on second floor, ask at the gate, Mon-Fri 0800-1600). The **Universidad de Trujillo** ① Independencia y Almagro, second only to that of San Marcos at Lima, was founded in 1824. The colonial-style **Casa Urquiaga (or Calonge)** on the plaza now houses the **Banco Central de Reserva** ① Pizarro 446, Mon-Fri 0930-1500, Sat-Sun 1000-1330, free 30-min guided tour; take passport, which contains valuable pre-Columbian ceramics. Another beautiful colonial mansion is **Casa Bracamonte (or Lizarzaburu)** ① Independencia 441, which houses the Seguro Social de Salud del Perú and has occasional exhibitions. Opposite the Cathedral on Independencia, is the **Casa Garci Olguín** (Caja Nuestra Gente), recently restored but boasting the oldest façade in the city and Moorish-style murals. Two blocks from Plaza de Armas is the spacious 18th-century **Palacio Iturregui**, now occupied by the **Club Central** ① Jr Pizarro 688, restricted entry to patio, daily 0830-1000, US$1.85, an exclusive social club with a private collection of ceramics. **Casa Ganoza Chopitea** ① Independencia 630, which now houses a cafeteria, is considered architecturally the most representative of the viceroyalty in the city. It combines baroque and rococo styles and is also known for the pair of lions that adorn its portico.

Other mansions still in private hands include **Casa del Mayorazgo de Facalá** ① Pizarro 314 (Scotiabank), another entrance on Bolognesi, Mon-Fri 0915-1230. **Casa de la Emancipación** ① Jr Pizarro 610 (Banco Continental), Mon-Sat 0900-1300, 1600-2000, is the building where independence from Spain was planned and was the first seat of government and congress in Peru. The **Casa del Mariscal de Orbegoso** now houses the **Museo de la República** ① Orbegoso 553, daily 0930-2000. It is owned by the BCP bank and holds temporary exhibitions. **Museo Haya de la Torre (Casa del Pueblo)** ① Orbegoso 664, Mon-Sat 0900-1300, 1600-2000, is a small, well-presented museum about the life of the founder of the APRA party who was one of the leading 20th-century socialists in the Americas. He was born in the house, which now holds a cinema club once a week.

One of the best of the many churches is the 17th-century **La Merced** ① Pizarro 550, daily 0800-1200, 1600-2000, with picturesque moulded figures below the dome. The church and monastery of **El Carmen** ① Colón y Bolívar, Mass Sun 0700-0730, has been described as the 'most valuable jewel of colonial art in Trujillo', but is rarely open except for Mass. **La Compañía** ① near Plaza de Armas, is now an auditorium for cultural events.

Museo de Arqueología ① Junín 682 y Ayacucho, Casa Risco, T044-249322, Mon-Fri 0830-1430, US$1.85, houses a large and interesting collection of thematic exhibits of Moche and Chimú culture. The **Museo del Juguete** ① *Independencia 705 y Junín, Mon-Sat 1000-1800, Sun 1000-1300, US$1.85, children US$0.70*, is a toy museum containing examples from prehistoric times to 1950, collected by painter Gerardo Chávez. Downstairs is the **Espacio Cultural Angelmira** with a café bar ① *daily 0900-2300, jazz concerts Fri and Sat nights*; in a restored *casona*, worth a visit. **Museo de Zoología de Juan Ormea** ① *Jr San Martín 368, T044-205011, Mon-Fri 0900-1800, US$0.70*, has interesting displays of Peruvian animals.

Gerardo Chávez also opened the **Museo de Arte Moderno** ① *Av Industrial, 3.5 km from centre, T044-215668, Mon-Fri 0800-1300, 1345-1745, Sat-Sun 0800-1500, US$3, students half price*, which has some fine exhibits, a peaceful garden (Jardín de los Sentidos) and friendly staff. In the central square of the Moche district (6 km south of the centre) is the **Museo de Moche** ① *daily 0900-1600, US$1.65*, that houses the Cassinelli Collection of pre-Columbian art. There is also a **botanical garden** ① *Mon-Sat 0800-1700, free*, about half a block beyond the Ovalo Larco, southwest of the city centre.

★Huacas del Sol and de la Luna
Information: Proyecto Huaca de la Luna, Jr San Martín 380, Trujillo, T044-221269, www.huacas.com. Daily 0900-sunset (last entry 1600); access by 1-hr guided tour only (English, French or Spanish); groups can be up to 25 people and quite rushed. US$4 (students US$2, children US$0.40), booklet in English or Spanish US$2.85; all tickets are sold at the Museo Huacas de Moche – see below.

A few kilometres south of Trujillo are the huge and fascinating Moche pyramids, the Huaca del Sol and the Huaca de la Luna. Until the Spaniards destroyed a third of it in a vain search for treasure, Huaca del Sol was the largest man-made structure in the western hemisphere, at 45 m high. It consisted of seven levels, with 11 or 12 phases of construction over the first six centuries AD. Today, about two thirds of the pyramid have been lost and it is closed to the public.

Huaca de la Luna, 500 m away, received scant attention until extensive polychrome moulded decorations were uncovered in the 1990s. The colours on these remarkable geometric patterns and deities have faded little and it is now possible to view impressive friezes of the upper four levels on the northern exterior wall of the *huaca*. The highest mural is a 'serpent' which runs the length of the wall; beneath it are several levels of repeated motifs depicting victorious warriors, 'felines', 'fishermen' holding fish and huge 'spider/crab' images. Combined with intricate, brightly painted two-dimensional motifs in the sacrificial area atop the huaca, and with new discoveries in almost every excavation, Huaca de la Luna is now a truly significant site well worth visiting.

The **Templo Nuevo**, or Plataforma III, represents the period 600 to 900 AD and has friezes in the upper level showing the so-called Rebellion of the Artefacts, in which weapons take on human characteristics and attack their owners. Also visit the **Museo Huacas de Moche** ① *5 mins' walk from Huaca de la Luna, www.huacasdemoche.pe, daily 0900-1600, US$1, students US$0.75, children US$0.40*, the site museum. Three halls display objects found in the huacas, including beautiful ceramics, arranged thematically around the Moche culture, the cermonial complex, daily life, the deities of power and of the mountains and priests who worshipped them. In the nearby **Campiña de Moche** are craft workshops and an outdoor restaurant with swimming pools.

The **visitor centre** ① *T044-834901*, has a café showing videos and a souvenir shop and good toilets. In an outside patio, craftsmen reproduce ceramics in designs from northern Peru.

Chan Chán
5 km from Trujillo centre. Daily 0900-1600. Site may be covered up if rain is expected. Tickets cost US$3.80 (US$2 with ISIC card), children US$0.35, and are valid for Chan Chán (site and museum), Huaca El Dragón and Huaca La Esmeralda for 2 days. Official guides, US$10, wait by the souvenir shops; toilets here too.

The imperial city of the Chimú domains was once the largest adobe city in the world. The vast, crumbling ruins consist of 10 great

Warning...
There are police at the entrance to the site, but it is a 25-minute walk from there to the ticket office. If you're not on a tour, you are advised to take one of the vehicles that wait at the entrance as it is not safe to walk to the ticket office. On no account should you walk beyond Chan Chán to Buenos Aires beach, nor walk on the beach itself, as there is serious risk of robbery and of being attacked by dogs.

compounds built by Chimú kings, with perimeter walls up to 12 m high surrounding sacred enclosures with usually only one narrow entrance. Inside, rows of storerooms contained the agricultural wealth of the kingdom, which stretched 1000 km along the coast from near Guayaquil to the Carabayllo Valley, north of Lima. The Incas almost certainly copied this system and used it in Cuzco where the last Incas continued building huge enclosures. The Chimú surrendered to the Incas around 1471 after 11 years of siege.

Trujillo

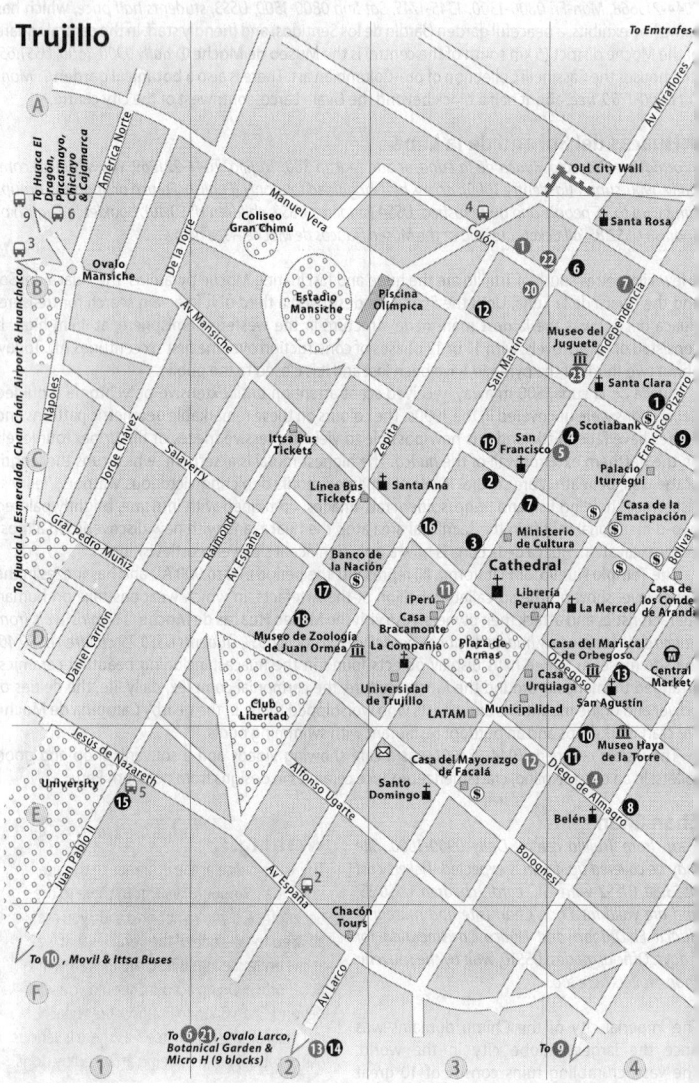

Most of the compounds contain a huge walk-in well which tapped the ground water, raised to a high level by irrigation further up the valley. Each compound also included a platform mound which was the burial place of the king, his women and his treasure, presumably maintained as a memorial.

The dilapidated city walls enclose an area of 28 sq km containing the remains of palaces, temples, workshops, streets, houses, gardens and a canal. What is left of the adobe walls bears either well restored or modern fibreglass fabrications of moulded decorations showing small figures of fish,

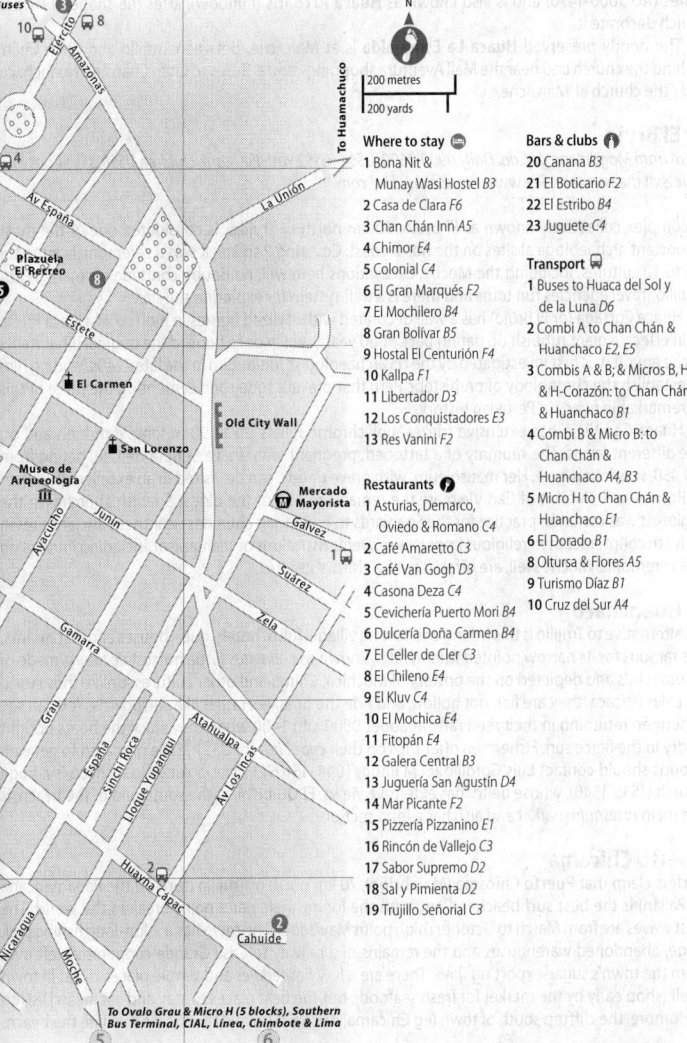

Where to stay 🛏
1 Bona Nit &
   Munay Wasi Hostel *B3*
2 Casa de Clara *F6*
3 Chan Chán Inn *A5*
4 Chimor *E4*
5 Colonial *C4*
6 El Gran Marqués *F2*
7 El Mochilero *B4*
8 Gran Bolívar *B5*
9 Hostal El Centurión *F4*
10 Kallpa *F1*
11 Libertador *D3*
12 Los Conquistadores *E3*
13 Res Vanini *F2*

Restaurants 🍴
1 Asturias, Demarco,
   Oviedo & Romano *C4*
2 Café Amaretto *C3*
3 Café Van Gogh *D3*
4 Casona Deza *C4*
5 Cevichería Puerto Mori *B4*
6 Dulcería Doña Carmen *B4*
7 El Celler de Cler *C3*
8 El Chileno *E4*
9 El Kluv *C4*
10 El Mochica *E4*
11 Fitopán *E4*
12 Galera Central *B3*
13 Juguería San Agustín *D4*
14 Mar Picante *F2*
15 Pizzería Pizzanino *E1*
16 Rincón de Vallejo *C3*
17 Sabor Supremo *D2*
18 Sal y Pimienta *D2*
19 Trujillo Señorial *C3*

Bars & clubs 🍸
20 Canana *B3*
21 El Boticario *F2*
22 El Estribo *B4*
23 Juguete *C4*

Transport 🚌
1 Buses to Huaca del Sol y
   de la Luna *D6*
2 Combi A to Chan Chán &
   Huanchaco *E2, E5*
3 Combis A & B; & Micros B, H
   & H-Corazón: to Chan Chán
   & Huanchaco *B1*
4 Combi B & Micro B: to
   Chan Chán &
   Huanchaco *A4, B3*
5 Micro H to Chan Chán &
   Huanchaco *E1*
6 El Dorado *B1*
7 Oltursa & Flores *A5*
8 Turismo Díaz *B1*
9 Cruz del Sur *A4*

birds, fishing nets and various geometric motifs. Painted designs have been found on pottery unearthed from the debris of a city ravaged by floods, earthquakes and *huaqueros* (grave looters). The **Ciudadela de Nik-An** (formerly called Tschudi) is the only palace open to visitors.

The **site museum** ① *on the main road, 100 m before the turn-off, daily 0830-1630, US$1*, has objects found in the area, with displays and signs in Spanish and English.

The partly restored temple, **Huaca El Dragón** ① *daily 0930-1630 (in theory); combis from Huayna Cápac y Los Incas, or Av España y Manuel Vera marked 'Arco Iris/La Esperanza', taxi US$2*, is on the west side of the Pan-American Highway in the district of La Esperanza. It dates from Huari to Chimú times (AD 1000-1470) and is also known as **Huaca Arco Iris** (rainbow), after the shape of friezes which decorate it.

The poorly preserved **Huaca La Esmeralda** is at Mansiche, between Trujillo and Chan Chán, behind the church and near the Mall Aventura shopping centre. Buses to Chan Chán and Huanchaco pass the church at Mansiche.

☆ El Brujo

3 km from Magdalena de Cao. Daily 0900-1600. US$4 (US$2 with ISIC card, children US$0.35). Shops and toilets at the entrance. See www.fundacionwiese.com.

A complex collectively known as El Brujo, 60 km north of Trujillo, is considered one of the most important archaeological sites on the north coast. Covering 2 sq km, it was a ceremonial centre for up to 10 cultures, including the Moche. Excavations here will, no doubt, continue for many years. Trujillo travel agencies run tours and there is a trail system for exploring the site.

Huaca Cortada (or El Brujo) has a wall decorated with stylized figures in high relief. Huaca Prieta is, in effect, a giant rubbish tip dating back 5000 years, which once housed the original inhabitants of the area. It was first investigated by the US archaeologist Junius Bird in the late 1940s, leading him to establish the chronology of prehistoric Peru that prevails today and cementing the place of this unremarkable *huaca* in Peruvian history.

Huaca Cao Viejo has extensive friezes, polychrome reliefs up to 90 m long, 4 m high and on five different levels. The mummy of a tattooed, pregnant woman, La Señora de Cao, dating from AD 450, was found here. Her mausoleum, with grave goods, can be visited in an excellent purpose-built museum. In front of Cao Viejo are the remains of one of the oldest Spanish churches in the region. It was common practice for the Spaniards to build their churches near these ancient sites in order to counteract their religious importance. Demonstrations of shamanism, including immersion in a ceremonial Moche well, are offered by the visitors' centre.

☆ Huanchaco

An alternative to Trujillo is this fishing and surfing village, full of hotels, guesthouses and restaurants. It is famous for its narrow pointed fishing rafts, known as *caballitos* (little horses) *de totora*, made of totora reeds and depicted on the pottery of Mochica, Chimú and other cultures. Unlike those used on Lake Titicaca, they are flat, not hollow, and ride the breakers rather like surfboards. You can see fishermen returning in their reed rafts at about 0800 and 1400 when they stack the boats upright to dry in the fierce sun. Fishermen offer trips on their *caballitos* for US$1.75; be prepared to get wet. Groups should contact Luis Gordillo (El Mambo, T044-461092). Overlooking Huanchaco is a huge church (1535-1540), whose belfry has extensive views. **El Quibishi**, at the south end of the beach, is the main *artesanía* market and also has a food section.

Puerto Chicama

Surfers claim that **Puerto Chicama** (Malabrigo), 70 km north of Trujillo (turn off the Panamericana at Paiján) is the best surf beach in Peru, with the longest left-hand point-break in the world. The best waves are from March to October (high point May/June). The town has a 1-km-long fishing pier, huge, abandoned warehouses and the remains of a railway to Casa Grande cooperative left over from the town's sugar-exporting days. There are a few *hospedajes* and simple places to eat in town itself (shop early by the market for fresh seafood), but the best places to stay and eat are in Distrito El Hombre, the clifftop south of town (eg **Chicama**, Arica 625); avoid the shacks that line the beach.

Pacasmayo and around *Colour map 3, B1.*

Pacasmayo, 102 km north of Trujillo, is the port for the next oasis north. It has a nice beachfront with an old Customs House and a very long pier. Away from the seafront Pacasmayo is a busy commercial centre. Resort El Faro is 1 km away, with surfing at the point and kite- and windsurfing closer to town. There are maritime festivals at New Year and Semana Santa. **Bosque de Cañoncillo**, 23 km northeast of Pacasmayo, (40 minutes by taxi, US$15 with one-hour wait, public transport also available) has trails through carob forests and lakes with endemic birds; two hours' walk from entrance to lakes, take water and sun protection. **Puemape** is a long beach with good waves and basic restaurants, 15 km south of Pacasmayo, 40 minutes by taxi, US$5.

Santuario y Reserva Nacional Calipuy

These two adjacent highland nature reserves are home to impressive stands of *Puya raimondii* and the largest herd of guanaco in Peru, respectively. Both reserves (sncalipuy@sernanp.gob.pe, rncalipuy@sernanp.gob.pe) reach elevations above 4000 m and are not easy to get to, but well worth the effort. Entry is free. Access is either through Chao (more direct), along the Panamericana south of Virú, or the regional centre of Santiago de Chuco, which has simple places to stay and eat, see Transport (page 1321).

Listings Trujillo *map p1310*

Tourist information

Useful websites include http://trujilloperu.
xanga.com and http://vivetrujillo.com.

Gobierno Regional de la Libertad
*Dirección de Turismo, Av España 1800,
T044-296221.*
Information on regional tourism.

Indecopi
*Santo Toribio de Mogrovejo 518, Urb San Andrés II
etapa, T044-295733, sobregon@indecopi.gob.pe.*
For tourist complaints.

Perú
*Jr Independencia 467, of 106, T044-294561,
iperutrujillo@promperu.gob.pe. Mon-Sat 0900-
1800, Sun 0900-1300. Also at Huaca de La Luna,
daily 0900-1300.*

Municipalidad de Trujillo
*Sub-Gerencia de Turismo, Av España 742,
T044-244212, anexo 119, sgturismo@
munitrujillo.gob.pe. Mon-Fri 0900-1600.*
Information about museums, official tour
agencies and cultural activities.

Tourist police
*Independencia 572, in the Ministerio de Cultura
building, policia_turismo_tru@hotmail.com.
Mon-Sat 0800-2000.*
Provide useful information and can help with
reports of theft, some staff speak English.

Where to stay

Trujillo

$$$$ Casa Andina Private Collection
*Av El Golf 591, Urb Las Flores del Golf III,
T01-213 9739, www.casa-andina.com.*
Large multi-storey luxury hotel, part of a nation-
wide chain, located outside the centre. All facilities.

$$$$ Libertador
*Independencia 485, Plaza de Armas, T044-232741,
www.libertador.com.pe.*
Modern hotel in historic building, lovely place
to stay. Comfortable rooms, excellent service,
swimming pool in a flower-filled patio, sauna,
cafetería and restaurant, breakfast extra,
excellent buffet lunch on Sun.

$$$ Chimor
Diego de Almagro 631, T044-202252.
A small modern hotel, comfortable and
welcoming, includes buffet breakfast.

$$$ El Gran Marqués
*Díaz de Cienfuegos 145-147, Urb La Merced,
T044-481710, www.elgranmarques.com.*
Price includes breakfast, modern, minibar,
pool, sauna, jacuzzi, restaurant.

$$$ Gran Bolívar
*Bolívar 957, T044-222090,
www.granbolivarhotel.net.*
In converted 18th-century house, restaurant and
room service, café, bar, laundry, gym, parking.

$$$ Kallpa
Díaz de las Heras s/n, Urb Vista Hermosa,
T044-281266, www.kallpahotel.pe.
A smart boutique hotel, welcoming, English
spoken, below usual boutique hotel prices.

$$$ Los Conquistadores
Diego de Almagro 586, T044-481650,
www.losconquistadoreshotel.com.
An elegant modern hotel with good
service, 1 block from Plaza de Armas.

$$ Colonial
Independencia 618, T044-258261,
www.hostalcolonial.com.pe.
Attractive but small rooms, hot showers, basic
breakfast, good restaurant, especially for set
lunch. Recommended.

$$ Hostal El Centurión
Paraguay 304, Urb El Recreo, T044-201526,
www.hostalelcenturion.com.
About 20 mins' walk from the Plaza, modern,
good rooms, well kept, safe but no a/c, simple
restaurant, good service.

$$-$ Residencia Vanini
Av Larco 237, outside Av España, T044-200878,
kikacarmelavanini@hotmail.com.
Youth hostel in a converted private house, nice
garden, basic rooms, some with bath.

$ Bona Nit
Colón 257, T044-298530, www.bonanithostal.com.
Well located economy hotel, rooms with fan and
frigobar, includes simple breakfast, good value.

$ Casa de Clara
Cahuide 495, T044-243347,
http://trujilloperu.xanga.com.
Friendly backpackers' *hostal*, hot water, good
food, helpful, information, lodging packages
with meals and tours, laundry service, use
of kitchen with permission and charge for
gas, meeting place and lots going on, many
languages spoken (see Clara Bravo and Michael
White, What to do, below). Restaurants nearby.
Good economy option.

$ Chan Chán Inn
Av Ejército 307, T044-791515,
chanchaninn@hotmail.com.
Close to several bus terminals so noisy, includes
breakfast, popular with backpackers, café,
laundry, money exchange, information.

$ El Mochilero
Independencia 887, T044-297842,
Elmochilerotrujilloperuoficial on Facebook.

A variety of basic dorms and rooms, only one with
bath, electric showers, breakfast available, fridge
for guests' use. Tours arranged, information.

$ Munay Wasi Hostel
Jr Colón 250, T044-231462,
www.munaywasihostel.com.
Family-run hostel within Av España, private and
shared rooms (US$10 pp with breakfast), shared
bath, book exchange, tourist information, fully
equipped kitchen.

El Brujo

$ Hospedaje Jubalu
Libertad 105, Magdalena de Cao, T995-670600.
With hot water. There's no internet in town and
limited shopping.

Huanchaco

$$$-$$ Bracamonte
Los Olivos 160, T044-461162,
www.hotelbracamonte.com.pe.
Comfortable, modern, contemporary decor,
pool and garden, secure, good restaurant offers
lunch *menú* and some vegetarian dishes, English
spoken, laundry service, games room, garage.
Highly recommended.

$$$-$$ Qhamar
Av Circunvalación 140, Urb. El Boquerón,
T044-462366, www.qhamarhotel.com.
Modern quiet hotel away from the centre.
All rooms with sea view, a bit small but
bright and comfortable. Small swimming
pool, pool table, table football, bar, garden,
airport pickup available.

$$ Hostal Huanchaco
Larco 185 on Plaza, T044-461272.
With hot water, pool, good but pricey cafeteria,
video, pool table.

$$ Hostal Huankarute
La Rivera 312, T044-461705,
www.hostalhuankarute.com.
On the seafront, with small pool, bar, sun terrace,
bicycle rental; some rooms larger, more luxurious
and more pricey, all with ocean view.

$$ Las Palmeras
Av Larco 1624, sector Los Tumbos, T044-461199,
Facebook: laspalmerasdehuanchaco.
Rooms with terrace, hot water, dining room, pool
and gardens. Rooms on top floor with sea view
cost more than ground floor rooms with pool
view. Basic breakfast.

$$ Residencial Sol y Mar
La Rivera 400, T044-461120.
Ample rooms, large pool, garden, terrace, event room, no breakfast but café next door.

$ Casa Amelia
Av Larco 1150, T044-46135, www.casaamelia.net.
Small quiet hostel with a big garden and homely atmosphere, kitchen facilities, 2 terraces, book exchange, good surfing information, parking, Dutch-run.

$ Casa Fresh
Av La Rivera 322, T945-917150, www.casafresh.pe.
Popular seafront hostel, basic rooms, roof bar/terrace with great views over the Huanchaco surf spot. Noisy weekend disco next door. Frequently organizes activities, has a collection of instruments to play and is connected to a surf school and tour agency.

$ Frogs
C El Pescador 308, Los Tumbos, www.frogsperu.com.
Located in a quiet area, big bright rooms, some with with sea view. Yoga area, terrace with hammocks and bean bags, sunset views, bar, pool table, ping pong, ample kitchen facilities and TV room. Popular meeting place, organize daily activities, Peruvian-German owned, opened in 2015.

$ Hospedaje My Friend
Los Pinos 533, T044-461080.
Dorm rooms with bath upstairs, hot water, TV room, information. Tours arranged but service is erratic. Popular with surfers, good meeting place, restaurant/bar open 0800-2230.

$ La Casa Suiza
Los Pinos 308, T044-639713,
www.lacasasuiza.com.
This Huanchaco institution has a variety of rooms with/without bath, breakfast US$3, BBQ on the roof, book exchange.

$ McCallum Lodging
Los Ficus 460, T044-626923, http://mccallumlodginghouse.wordpress.com.
Private rooms and dorms, hot water, hammocks, home-cooked meals available and recipes shared, laundry, baggage and surfboard storage, family atmosphere, highly considered by locals and tourists.

Ñaylamp
J Larco 1420, northern end of seafront El Boquerón, T044-461022,
www.hostalnaylamp.com.
Rooms set around a courtyard with garden, others have sea view, dorms, hammocks, good beds, hot water, kitchen facilities, camping, tents for hire, laundry, safe, Italian food, good breakfasts.

Puerto Chicama

The following are in Distrito El Hombre (several close out of season).

$$$ Chicama Surf Resort
T044-576206, www.chicamasurf.com. All year.
Exclusive, with surfing classes, boats to the waves, spa, restaurant, infinity pool.

$$ Hostal Los Delfines
T943-296662.
Owner is Tito Venegas. Guests can use well-equipped kitchen, rooms with balcony, hot water, spacious.

$$ Iguana Inn
C Progreso, Pto Malabrigo, T04-57622, www.hoteliguanainn.com.
Good mid-range option, well equipped rooms with fridge and coffee/tea maker.

$ Hostel El Hombre
C Arica 803, T044-576077.
Legendary surfers' hangout and meeting spot. Basic rooms. Owner Doris prepares food.
In town there are several cheaper places; **Hostal El Naipe**, Tacna 395, is arguably the best.

Pacasmayo

$$$ El Faro
Urb La Perla, T044-311802,
www.elfaropacasmayo.com.
Well known surf resort on the coast, simple rooms, large pool, good restaurant, bar, surfboard and other gear rentals, organizes tours.

$$ El Mirador
Aurelio Herrera 10, www.perupacasmayo.com.
Variety of rooms and prices, all with private bath, fan and safe box. Well located, popular and good value.

$$ Libertad
Leoncio Pardo 1-D, T044-521937,
http://hotellibertad.pe/pacasmayo/.
2 km from beach by petrol station, with breakfast, Wi-Fi and internet, safe, restaurant/bar, parking, efficient and nice.

$ Duke Kahanamoku
Ayacucho 44, T044-521889.
Backpackers' surfing place, with classes and board rental, breakfast extra, hot water, free internet.

Restaurants

A speciality is *shambar*, a thick minestrone made with pork. On sale everywhere is *turrón*, a nougat-type sweet. All along Pizarro are restaurants to suit all tastes and budgets. On the west side of the central market at Grau y Ayacucho are several small, cheap restaurants.

Trujillo

$$$ El Celler de Cler
Independencia 588, upstairs. Open 1830-0100.
One of the best restaurants of Trujillo, located in an old colonial house in the centre, some seating on a nice little balcony. Peruvian and international dishes, mostly meat, no fish.

$$$-$$ El Mochica
Bolívar 462.
Good typical food with live music on special occasions.

$$$-$$ Galera Central
Junín 235, T044-294142.
Good original *menú* as well as *à la carte* and upmarket *'cocina de autor'*.

$$ Café van Gogh
Independencia No 533. Open 0830-2130.
Small quiet restaurant half a block from Plaza de Armas. Very good coffee, vegetarian dishes and crêpes.

$$ Demarco
Pizarro 725.
Popular at midday for lunchtime *menús* and for its cakes and desserts, good service.

$$ Mar Picante
Húsares de Junín 412, T044-20846.
Very good local seafood in a family-run restaurant.

$$ Pizzería Pizzanino
Av Juan Pablo II 183, Urb San Andrés, opposite University. Evening only.
Good for pizzas, pastas, meats, desserts.

$$ Romano
Pizarro 747.
International food, good *menú*, breakfasts, coffee, excellent milkshakes, cakes.

$$-$ Cevichería Puerto Mori
Estete 482, T044-346752.
Very popular, they serve only good seafood. At the same location are 2 more fish restaurants, but not of the same quality.

$ Asturias
Pizarro 741.
Nice café with a reasonable *menú*, good pastas, cakes and sandwiches.

$ Juguería San Agustín
Bolívar 526.
Good juices, good *menú*, sandwiches, ice creams, popular, excellent value. Also at Av Larco Herrera y Husares de Junín.

$ Oviedo
Pizarro 737.
With soups, vegetarian options, good salads and cakes, helpful.

$ Rincón de Vallejo
Orbegoso 303.
Good *menú*, typical dishes, very crowded at peak times. 2nd branch at Av España 736.

$ Sabor Supremo
Diego de Almagro 210, T044-220437.
Menú and à la carte vegetarian food, vegan on special request.

$ Sal y Pimienta
Zepita 366.
Very popular for economical lunch, close to buses for Huanchaco and Chan Chán.

$ Trujillo Señorial
Gamarra 353, T044-204873. Mon-Sat 1300-1530.
Restaurant and hotel school, good *menú*, food nicely presented, good value.

Cafés

Café Amaretto
Gamarra 368.
Smart, good selection of real coffees, "brilliant" cakes, sweets, snacks and drinks.

Casona Deza
Independencia 630. Tue-Sun 1600-2300.
Comfortable café/bar selling home-made pasta and pizza and good coffee in an old mansion.

Dulcería Doña Carmen
San Martín 814.
Serves local specialities such as *alfajores*, *budín*, *king kong*, etc.

El Chileno
Ayacucho 408.
Café and ice cream parlour, popular.

El Kluv
Junín 527 (next to Metro Market).
Italian-owned, fresh, tasty pizzas at noon and in the late afternoon.

Fitopán
Bolívar 406, www.fitopan.com.
Good selection of breads, also serves lunches.
Has 3 other branches.

El Brujo

$ Café Antojitos
At entrance to Plaza de Armas, Magdalena de Cao.
Run by a women's cooperative, specializing in
sugar-based snacks.

$ El Brujo
Plaza de Armas, Magdalena de Cao.
Best place to eat in town and accustomed to
providing meals for tourists.

Huanchaco
There are about 30 restaurants on the beachfront.
Recommended on Av Larco are **Estrella Marina**
at No 740, **Los Herrajes** at No 1020, and **Lucho
del Mar** at No 750; all $$. Many close in the low
season and at night.

$$$ Big Ben
Av Larco 1884, El Boquerón, T044-461378,
www.bigbenhuanchaco.com. Daily 1200-1700.
Seafood and international cuisine, very good.

$$$ Club Colonial
La Rivera 514, on the beachfront, T044-461015.
Daily 1100-2300.
A smart restaurant and bar, French-speaking
Belgian owner.

$$$ El Mochica
Av Larco 700, T044-461963. Open 0900-2300.
Same owners and good quality as the restaurant
in Trujillo.

$$$ Huanchaco Beach
Av Larco 800, T044-461484. Open 1200-1700.
One of the best quality in town, popular with tours.

$$$-$$ El Sombrero
Av Larco 510, T044-462283, www.restaurant
elsombrero.com. Open 1100-2300.
Smart restaurant serving good ceviche and
seafood, most tables have great sea view. Has
another branch at Av Mansiche 267, Trujillo.

$$ Casa Tere
Plaza de Armas, T044-461197.
For best pizzas in town, also pastas, burgers
and breakfasts.

$$ La Barca
Raimondi 117, T044-461855.
Very good seafood, well-run, popular.

$ La Esquina
Jr Unión 120. Open 1200-2200.
Small place serving very good barbecued fish.

$ Otra Cosa
Av Victor Larco 1312. Open 0800-2200.
Dutch-Peruvian vegetarian restaurant serving a
variety of dishes including falafel, burritos and
menú. Good organic coffee, fruit salads, juices
and the best Dutch apple pie in Peru.

Cafés

Argolini
Av Rivera 400.
Convenient for people staying in the Los Pinos/
Los Ficus area for fresh bread, cakes, ice cream,
coffee and juices.

Chocolate
Av Rivera 752. Daily 0830-1800.
Swiss management, serves breakfast, also some
vegetarian food, coffee and cakes.

Bars and clubs

Trujillo

Bar/Café Juguete
Junín y Independencia. Until midnight.
An classic French-style café serving
good coffee as well as alcohol. Has a
pasta restaurant attached.

Canana
San Martín 788, T044-232503.
Bars and restaurant, disco, live music at
weekends (US$1.50-3), video screens
(also has travel agency). Recommended,
but take care on leaving.

El Boticario
Av Larco 962, T044-639346. Open from 2000.
A small but very elegant upmarket bar with great
service and original cocktails. You have to go well
dressed but it's worth it.

El Estribo
San Martín 809, T044-204053.
A club playing a wide variety of genres and
attracting a mixed crowd.

Huanchaco

Jungle Bar Bily
Av Larco 420. Open 1000-0200.
Well known popular cocktail bar, happy hour
1800-2200. Also a good restaurant.

Sabes?

*Av Larco 920, http://sabesbar.com.
Open 1900-0200.*
Well established British-owned pub, good pizzas and cocktails (happy hour 1900-2100), pool table and tranquil atmosphere. Popular with tourists and Trujillanos alike.

Festivals

End Jan National Marinera Festival.
Last week of Sep Festival Internacional de La Primavera.
Both festivals have cultural events, parades, beauty pageants and Trujillo's famous **Caballos de Paso.**

Huanchaco

1st week of May **Festival del Mar**, a celebration of the disembarkation of Taycanamo, the leader of the Chimú period. A procession is made in Totora boats.
29 Jun **San Pedro**, patron saint of fishermen. His statue is taken out to sea on a huge totora-reed boat. There are also surf competitions.
Carnival and **New Year** are also popular celebrations.

Shopping

Trujillo

Bookshops

Librería Peruana, *Pizarro 505, just off the Plaza.* Has the best selection in town, plus postcards; ask for Sra Inés Guerra de Guijón.

There are also 3 branches of **SBS**: on Jr Bolívar 714; in Mall Aventura, Av Mansiche block 20, and in Plaza Real Mall, Prol Av César Vallejo (behind UPAO University), California (take taxi or green California micro A).

Handicrafts

120 Artesanía por Descubrir, *Las Magnolias 403, California, www.tienda120.blogspot.com.* Art gallery designs and handmade crafts, near Real Plaza.
APIAT, *Av España y Zela*. The largest craft market in the city, good for ceramics, totora boats, woodwork and leather, competitive prices.
Artesanía del Norte, *at Dulcería La Libertad, Jr Pizarro 758, and at the Huacas del Sol y de la Luna*. Sells items mostly designed by the owner, Mary Cortijo, using traditional techniques.
Trama Perú, *Pizarro 754, T044-243948, www.tramaperu.com. Daily 1000-2200.*

High-quality, hand-made art objects, authorized Moche art replicas.

Markets

Mercado Central, *Gamarra, Ayacucho and Pasaje San Agustín.*
Mercado Unión, *between Av Santa and Av Perú.* A little safer than others; also repairs shoes, clothes and bags.

What to do

Trujillo

City tours

Mirabus, *tickets from Multidestinos, Orbegoso 311, of 36, T044-291861, US$4.50, departs from Plaza de Armas at 1000, 1200, 1700, 1800, 1900 in summer, 1200 and 1700 in winter.* 1-hr ride through the colonial centre in a double-decker bus with Spanish commentary.

Horse shows

Casa Campo Alcor, *Vía de Evitamiento Km 567, Víctor Larco, T948-315055. Open 1330-1430, US$9.* These horses, typical of northern Peru, have been bred for their special gait which makes them more comfortable to ride. In the show they dance to the sounds of *marinera*.

Tour operators

Prices vary and competition is fierce so shop around. During low season (Mar-Apr and Dec) some tours only run in the afternoon or with a minimum number of participants. During peak season (a week before and after Jul 28 and at Easter) English guides are scarce. At all times, groups are usually large and quality varies. To Chan Chán, El Dragón and Huanchaco, 4-4½ hrs for US$8-9 pp. To Huacas del Sol and de la Luna, 2½-3 hrs for US$8-9 pp. To El Brujo, 4-5 hrs for US$13-17 pp. Prices do not include entrance fees.
Chacón Tours, *Av España 106-112, T044-255212. Sat afternoon and Sun morning*. Recommended for flights etc, not local tours.
Colonia Tours, *Independencia 618 (Hotel Colonial), T044-25826*. Local tours including Chan Chán, Las Huacas and El Brujo.
Domiruth, *Diego de Almagro 539, T044-299 0952, www.domiruth.com.* For airline tickets.
North Perú Tours, *Gamarra 432, Of 301, T044-310423, www.north-peru.com.* Organizes tours around Trujillo and throughout northern Peru.
Trujillllo Tours, *Pizarro 478, Of 101, T044-200412*. Organizes good tours (more time, better guides) to Chan Chán and the Huacas for around US$25.

Tour guides

Many hotels work on a commission basis with taxi drivers and travel agencies. If you decide on a guide, make your own direct approach and always agree what is included in the price. The tourist police (see Tourist information) has a list of guides; average cost US$8 per hr. Beware of cowboy outfits herding up tourists around the plazas, especially Plaza de Armas, and bus terminals for rapid, poor quality tours. Also beware scammers offering surfing or salsa lessons and party invitations.

Alfredo Ríos Mercedes, *T949-657978, riosmercedes@hotmail.com*. Speaks English.
Clara Bravo and Michael White, *Cahuide 495, T044-243347, http://trujilloperu.xanga.com, microbewhite@yahoo.com*. Clara is an experienced tourist guide who speaks Spanish, English, German and understands Italian and runs small group tours daily: archaeological tour US$20 for 6 hrs, city tour US$7 pp, US$53 per car to El Brujo, with extension to Sipán, Brüning Museum and Túcume possible (tours in Lambayeque involve public transport, not included in cost). Clara works with **Michael White**, who provides transport and is very knowledgeable about tourist sites.
Henry Valiente, *T949-547132, ysaac_hnr9@hotmail.com*. An experienced English-speaking guide.
Jannet Rojas Sánchez, *Alto Mochica Mz Q 19, Trujillo, T949-344844*. Speaks English, enthusiastic. Also works for **Guía Tours** (*Av Nicolas De Pierola 1208, T998-460330*).
Luis Ocas Saldaña, *Jr José Martí 2019, T954-042086, guianorteperu@hotmail.com*. Very knowledgeable, helpful, covers all of northern Peru.
William Alvarado, *T947-006070, william_alvarado_gotur@hotmail.com*. An experienced English-speaking guide.

Volunteering

There are many social and volunteer projects in Trujillo, but not all are recommendable. Try to get a personal recommendation from other volunteers before signing up.
Supporting Kids in Peru, *www.skipperu.org*. Works with poor children and their families in Trujillo.

Huanchaco

Language classes

Sam Owen, *T967-992775, skypispanish@gmail.com*. Originally from Wales and married to a Peruvian, he offers unique and very practical Spanish lessons.

Surfing

There are plenty of surf schools. Equipment rental is US$8.75/day; single lesson, about US$15 for 2 hrs.
Indigan, *Deán Saavedra 582 (next to soccer field), T044-462591*. Jhon and Giancarlos Urcía for lessons, surf trips and rentals. Also offer lodging at their home.
Muchik, *Av Larco 650, T044-462535, www.escueladetablamuchik.com*. Instructors Chicho and Omar Huamanchumo are former surf champions. They arrange trips to other surf sites and also offer repairs. Recommended.

Volunteering

Fairmail, *www.fairmail.info*. An innovative social enterprise that teaches poor kids to use a camera, sells their photo-art and returns the profits to them.

Transport

Trujillo

Air The **airport** is west of the city; access to town is along Av Mansiche. Taxi to city hotels, US$7-9.

To **Lima**, 1 hr, several daily flights with **LATAM**, **LC Perú** and **Avianca/TACA**.

Bus Local Micros (small buses with 25 or more seats) and combis (up to 15 passengers) on all routes within the city cost US$0.50-0.60; *colectivos* (6 passengers) charge US$0.50 and tend to run on main avenues starting from Av España. In theory, they are not allowed in the city centre. For transport to the archaeological sites, see below.

To **Huanchaco**, there are 2 combi routes (A and B; both take 25 mins), run by the **Caballitos de Totora** company (white and black), and 4 micros (A, B, H and H-Corazón; 45-60 mins), run by **Transportes Huanchaco** (red, yellow and white). They run 0500-2030, every 5-10 mins, US$0.75. The easiest place to pick up any of these combis or micros is Ovalo Mansiche, 3 blocks northwest of Av España in front of the Cassinelli museum. Combi A takes the southerly route on Av España, before heading up Av Los Incas. Combi B takes the northerly route on Av España.

Long distance The **Terminal Terrestre de Trujillo** (TTT), or Terrapuerto, is to the southeast of the centre, on Km 558 on the Panamericana Norte, beyond Ovalo La Marina. It was completed in 2014 but bus companies continue to operate from their private terminals as well. Always ask where the bus leaves from when buying your ticket. On arrival, take a taxi from the terminal and insist on being taken to your hotel of choice.

To **Lima**, 561 km, 9-10 hrs in the better class buses, average fare US$22-32; 10 hrs or more in the cheaper buses, US$11-16. There are many bus companies doing this route, among those recommended are: **Cruz del Sur** (Amazonas 437, between Av Ejército and Miraflores, T044-720444; **Línea** (Av América Sur 2857, T044-297000), 3 levels of service; **Flores** (Av Ejército 346, T044-208250); **Ittsa** (TTT and Av Juan Pablo 1110, T044-284644), frequent service, good value; **Móvil** (TTT, T044-245523, and Av América Sur 3959, T044-286538); **Oltursa** (TTT, T044-263055), 3 *bus cama* services to Lima; **Ormeño** (Av El Ejército 233, T044-259782).

To **Puerto Chicama**, combis from Santa Cruz terminal (Av Santa Cruz, 1 block from Av America Sur), US$2, 1½ hrs; also **Dorado** buses (Av N de Piérola 1062, T044-291778), US$2, via Chocope

(US$0.75) and Paiján (US$0.60). Small **Pakatnamú** buses leave when full, 0400-2100 (from Av N de Piérola 1092, T044-206594), to **Pacasmayo**, 102 km, 1¼ hrs, US$5.50.

To **Chiclayo**, 4 hrs from Trujillo, from US$5.50, several companies, including **Emtrafesa** (Av Túpac Amaru 185, T044-471521) and **Ittsa** (see above), both hourly. To **Jaén**, 9 hrs. To **Piura**, 6 hrs, US$10-15 (**Ittsa**'s 0900, 1330, or **Línea**'s 1415 buses are good choices). **Ittsa** also goes to **Talara**, 2200, 9 hrs, US$16.

Direct buses to **Huaraz**, 319 km, via Chimbote and Casma (169 km), with **Línea**, 0900 and 2130, and **Móvil**, 2240 and 2300, 8 hrs, US$17-30. There are also several buses and *colectivos* to **Chimbote**, with **América Express** (from Av La Marina 315), 135 km, 2 hrs, US$6, departures every 30 mins from 0530 (ticket sales from 0500); leave Trujillo before 0600 to make a connection to Huaraz from 0800 in Chimbote (see page 1307). Ask Clara Bravo and Michael White (see Guides, above) about transport to Caraz avoiding Chimbote: a worthwhile trip via the Brasileños road and Cañon del Pato.

To **Cajamarca**, 300 km, 7-8 hrs, US$10-27, with **Línea** (1030, 2200, 2300), **Turismo Díaz** (1320, 2230) and **Emtrafesa** (2145). To **Huamachuco**, 170 km, 5-6 hrs, see page 1339.

Taxi Taxis in town charge US$1.30 within Av España and US$1.50 within Av América; always use official taxis, which are mainly black, or cooperative taxis, which have the company logo on the side (eg **Sonrisas**, T044-233000). Beware of overcharging; check fares with locals.

Huacas del Sol and de la Luna

There are combis every 15 mins from Ovalo Grau in Trujillo and, less safe, from Galvez y Los Incas, but they drop you a long walk from the site. Taxis charge about US$5; there are few at the site so ask your driver to wait.

Chan Chán

Take any transport between Trujillo and Huanchaco (see above) and ask to get out at the turn-off, US$0.50; then get onward transport from the entrance to the ticket office, US$1. Do not walk from the turn-off to the ticket office. A taxi from Trujillo to the site is US$5; from Huanchaco, US$3.

El Brujo

The complex can be reached by taking one of the regular buses from Trujillo to Chocope,

Tip...
On Friday to Sunday nights the better bus services must be pre-booked two to three days in advance.

US$1.25, every 10 mins, 1 hr, and then a *colectivo* to Magdalena de Cao, US$0.75 (leave when full), 15 mins, then a mototaxi taking up to 3 people to the site, US$7.50 including 1½-hr wait. Unless you particularly like Peruvian public transport, it is more convenient to go on a tour.

Huanchaco
From Huanchaco, micro A goes to the 28 de Julio/ Costa Rica junction in Trujillo where it turns west along Prolongación César Vallejo, passing the UPAO university and Plaza Real shopping centre, continuing to the Av El Golf (the terminus for the return to Huanchaco on almost the same route). On other routes from Huanchaco to Trujillo centre, ask the *cobrador* to let you off near C Pizarro on Av España. To reach the **Línea, Móvil Tours** and southern bus terminals in Trujillo, take

micro H from Huanchaco; it also goes to Ovalo Grau where you can catch buses to the Huacas del Sol and de la Luna. For **Cruz del Sur**, **Ormeño** and **Flores** bus services, take combi or micro B from Huanchaco.

Puerto Chicama
Buses stop just off Plaza Central, opposite the Comisaria.

Santuario y Reserva Nacional Calipuy
Buses from Terminal Santa Cruz in Trujillo to **Santiago de Chuco**, US$6, 4 hrs. Private 4WD from Santiago de Chuco to the reserves, about US$85 return. To hire a 4WD in Trujillo to the reserves via Chao, contact Manuel Rubio, T948-312400, about US$150 for 1 day, US$215 for 2.

Chiclayo and around   Colour map 3, B1.

witches' brews and Moche treasures

Lambayeque Department, sandwiched between the Pacific and the Andes, is a major agricultural zone, especially for rice and sugar cane. It boasts a distinctive cuisine and musical tradition, and an unparalleled ethnographic and archaeological heritage. Excavations at the region's adobe pyramid cities are uncovering fabulous treasures.

Chiclayo See map, page 1322.
Since its foundation in the 16th century, Chiclayo has grown to become a major commercial hub with a population of 800,000. Its witchcraft market is famous, but it is best known for the spectacular cache of prehispanic archaeological treasures found on its doorstep.

On the Plaza de Armas is the 19th-century neoclassical **Cathedral**, designed by the English architect Andrew Townsend. The private **Club de la Unión** is on the Plaza at the corner of Calle San José. Continue five blocks north on Balta, the busiest commercial street, to the **Mercado Modelo**, one of northern Peru's liveliest and largest daily markets. Don't miss the market stalls off Calle Arica on the south side, where ritual paraphernalia used by traditional curers and diviners (*curanderos*) are sold: herbal medicines, folk charms, curing potions and exotic objects, including dried llama fetuses, to cure all manner of real and imagined illnesses. At **Paseo Artesanal Colón**, south of the Plaza, shops sell handicrafts in a quiet, custom-built open-air arcade. Other relaxing spots are the **Paseo de las Musas**, with its gardens and imitation Greek statues, and **Paseo Yortuque**, with 80 fiberglass statues representing the history of the area.

Monsefú and the coast
The traditional town of **Monsefú**, southwest, is known for its music and handicrafts; there's a good market, four blocks from the plaza. The stalls open when potential customers arrive (see also Festivals, page 1328).

Beyond Monsefú are three ports serving the Chiclayo area. **Pimentel**, 8 km from Chiclayo, is a beach resort which gets very crowded on Sundays and during the summer (US$4 to rent a chair and sunshade). Most of the seafront has been bought up by developers, but the main plaza is an oasis of green. There are several seafood restaurants (El Muelle de Pimentel, Rivera del Mar cuadra 1, T074-453142, is recommended). You can walk along the restored pier for US$0.75. Sea-going reed boats (*caballitos de totora*) are used by fishermen and may be seen from the pier returning late morning or afternoon on the beach.

The surfing between Pimentel and the Bayovar Peninsula is excellent, reached from Chiclayo (14.5 km) by a road branching off from the Pan-American Highway. Nearby **Santa Rosa** has little to recommend it, other than to see the realities of fishing life, and it is not safe to walk there from Pimentel. The most southerly port, 24 km by road from Chiclayo, is **Puerto Eten**, a quaint place with some wooden buildings on the plaza. Its old railway station has been declared a national heritage monument. The adjacent roadstead, Villa de Eten, is a centre for panama hat-making, but is not as picturesque.

Chiclayo

100 metres
100 yards

Where to stay 🛏
1 Alfonso Ugarte B2
2 Costa del Sol Wyndham C3
3 Embajador A3
4 Gran Hotel Chiclayo B1
5 Hosp Concordia C3
6 Hosp San Eduardo C3
7 Inti B2
8 Paraíso A3

9 Pirámide Real C3
10 Santa Rosa B2
11 Sicán C2
12 Sol Radiante C2
13 Sunec C2

Restaurants 🍴
1 Balta 512 C3
2 Boulevar B2
3 Café 900 C3
4 Café Astoria C2
5 D'Onofrio C3
6 El Huaralino C1
7 Fiesta B1

8 Hebrón C3
9 Kaprichos A3
10 La Panadería B2
11 La Parra C3
12 La Plazuela B1
13 Las Américas B3
14 Roma C3
15 Sabores Peruanos C1
16 Tradiciones C3
17 Vichayo Restobar C1

Transport 🚌
1 Brüning Express to Lambayeque B1

2 Cial C1
3 Civa C3
4 Colectivos to Lambayeque A2
5 Colectivos to Puerto Etén A3
6 Cruz del Sur C3
7 Emtrafesa C3
8 Línea C2
9 Móvil C1
10 Oltursa B1
11 Tepsa C2
12 Transportes Chiclayo B1

☆Lambayeque

About 12 km northwest of Chiclayo is Lambayeque, a good base from which to explore the Chiclayo area. Its narrow streets are lined by colonial and Republican houses, many retaining their distinctive wooden balconies and wrought-iron grillwork over the windows, although many are in very bad shape. On Calle 2 de Mayo don't miss **Casa de la Logia o Montjoy**, whose 67-m-long balcony is said to be the

Warning…
Solo cyclists should not cross the desert as muggings have occurred. Take the safer, inland route to Piura via Olmos. In the desert, there is no water, fuel or accommodation. Do not attempt this alone.

longest in the colonial Americas. It has been restored and can be visited (free). At 8 de Octubre 345 is **Casona Descalzi** ① *T074-283433, daily 1100-1700*, which is well preserved as a good restaurant. It has 120 carved iguana heads on the ceiling. **Casona Iturregui Aguilarte**, at No 410, is, by contrast, seriously neglected. Also of interest are the 16th-century **Complejo Religioso Monumental de San Francisco de Asís** and the baroque **Iglesia de San Pedro**, which stands on Plaza de Armas 27 de Diciembre.

The reason most people visit is to see the town's two museums. The older of the two is the **Brüning Archaeological Museum** ① *daily 0900-1700, US$2.75, a guided tour costs an extra US$10*, in a modern building, which specializes in Mochica, Lambayeque/Sicán and Chimú cultures. Three blocks east is the more recent **Museo de las Tumbas Reales de Sipán** ① *Av Juan Pablo Vizcardo y Guzmán 895, T074-283977, www.museotumbasrealessipan.pe, Tue-Sun 0900-1700, US$3.55, guides US$13 (some speak English), mototaxi from plaza US$0.60*, shaped like a pyramid. The magnificent treasure from the tomb of the 'Old Lord of Sipán', and a replica of the Lord of Sipán's tomb are displayed here (see below). A ramp from the main entrance takes visitors to the third floor, from where you descend, mirroring the sequence of the archaeologists' discoveries. There are handicrafts outside and in the museum shop, also a branch of **Arte y Joyas Arqueológicas del Perú** ① *T9-8512 2539, ciecsipanarqueojoyas@gmail.com (also at Museo Amano in Lima and Museo Inkariy, Urubamba Km 53, Cuzco)*, selling jewellery inspired by pre-Inca and Inca art. There is also a **tourist office** ① *Tue-Sun 1000-1400*.

From Lambayeque the Pan-American Highway heads north for 190 km to cross the **Sechura Desert**, a large area of shifting sands separating the oases of Chiclayo and Piura. If you're travelling this route, stop off in **Mórrope**, 20 km north of Lambayeque, to see one of the earliest churches in northern Peru. **San Pedro de Mórrope** (1545), an adobe and *algarrobo* structure on the plaza, contains the tomb of the cacique Santiago Cazusol.

Sipán

Turn-off is well signposted in the centre of Pomalca. Daily 0900-1700. Tombs and museum, US$3.50; guide at site US$10 (may not speak English). To visit the site takes about 2-3 hrs. There are comedores outside the site.

At this imposing complex a short distance east of Chiclayo excavations since 1987 in one of three crumbling pyramids have brought to light a cache of funerary objects considered to rank among the finest examples of pre-Columbian art. Peruvian archaeologist Walter Alva, former leader of the dig, continues to probe the immense mound that has revealed no less than 16 elite tombs filled with 1800-year-old offerings worked in precious metals, stone, pottery and textiles of the Moche culture (circa AD 1-750). In the most extravagant Moche tomb El Señor de Sipán was discovered, a priest clad in gold (ear ornaments, breast plate, etc), with turquoise and other valuables.

In another tomb were found the remnants of what is thought to have been a priest, sacrificed llama and a dog, together with copper decorations. In 1989 another richly appointed, unlooted tomb contained even older metal and ceramic artefacts associated with what was probably a another warrior-priest, called 'The Old Lord of Sipán'. Three tombs are on display, with replicas of the original finds. **Museo de Sitio Huaca Rajada** ① *daily 0900-1700, US$2.85*, concentrates on the finds at the site, especially Tombs 14, 15 and 16 containing 'Priest-Warriors', the decorative techniques of the Moche and the roles that archaeologists and local communities play in protecting these precious discoveries. You can wander around the previously excavated areas of the Huaca Rajada to get an idea of the construction of the burial mound and adjacent pyramids. For a good view, climb the large pyramid across from the excavated Huaca Rajada.

Ventarrón

A 4000-year-old temple, Ventarrón, was uncovered about 20 km from Sipán in 2007 by Walter Alva; his son, Ignacio, is now in charge of the dig. It predates Sipán by some 2000 years and shows at least three phases of development. Its murals, which appear to depict a deer trapped in a net, are claimed to be the oldest in the Americas and there is evidence of cultural exchange with as far away as the Amazon. A project to build a site museum and improve access is underway; until then, entry with guide is US$4 (some speak English), open 0800-1700, allow one to two hours to visit the site.

Chaparrí Reserve

75 km from Chiclayo, for day visits T074-433194, www.chaparri.org. US$10.50 entry to the reserve; groups of 10 accompanied by a local guide. Mototaxi from Chongoyape to Chaparrí, US$15.

East from Pomalca, just before Chongoyape, is the turning to the Chaparrí private ecological reserve, 34,000 ha, set up and run by the Comunidad Muchik Santa Catalina de Chongoyape. Visitors can go for the day or stay at the **EcoLodge Chaparrí** (see Where to stay, page 1327). All staff and guides are locals, which provides work and helps to prevent littering. There are no dogs or goats in the area so the forest is recuperating; it contains many bird and mammal species of the dry forest, including white-winged guan and spectacled bear. There is a Spectacled Bear Rescue Centre where bears rescued from captivity live in semi-wild enclosures. The Tinajones reservoir is good for birdwatching.

Túcume

T978-977578. Daily 0830-1630. US$4.50, students US$1, children US$0.30, plus guide US$15. Mototaxi from highway/new town to ruins, US$0. 75. Allow at least 3 hrs to visit the whole site and museum.

About 35 km north of Chiclayo, not far from the old Panamericana and Túcume Nuevo, lie the ruins of this vast city built over 1000 years ago. A short climb to the two *miradores* on **Cerro La Raya** (or **El Purgatorio**) offers the visitor an unparalleled panoramic vista of 26 major pyramids, platform mounds, walled citadels and residential compounds flanking a ceremonial centre and ancient cemeteries. One of the pyramids, Huaca Larga, where excavations are still being undertaken, is the longest adobe structure in the world, measuring 700 m long, 280 m wide and over 30 m high. There is no evidence of occupation at Túcume before the Sicán or Lambayeque people who developed the site AD 1000-1375. Thereafter the Chimú conquered the region, establishing a short reign until the arrival of the Incas around 1470. The Incas built on top of the existing structure of **Huaca Larga** using stone from Cerro La Raya.

Among the other pyramids which make up this huge complex are: **Huaca El Mirador** (90 m by 65 m, 30 m high), **Huaca Las Estacas**, **Huaca Pintada** and **Huaca de las Balsas**, which is thought to have housed people of elevated status such as priests. A walkway leads around the covered pyramid and you can see many mud reliefs including fishermen on rafts.

Apart from the miradores and Huaca Las Balsas, not much of the site is open to view, as lots of archaeological study is still going on. However, a site museum displays many objects found here, including miniature offerings relating to the prehispanic gods and mythology of Lambayeque, items relating to the last Inca governor of Túcume and a room detailing the history of the region from pre-Columbian times to the present. There is also a shop.

The town of **Túcume Viejo** is a 20-minute walk beyond the site. Look for the side road heading towards a park, opposite which is the ruin of a huge colonial church made of adobe and some brick. The surrounding countryside is pleasant for walks through mango trees and fields of maize. Fiesta de la Purísima Concepción, the festival of the town's patron saint, takes place eight days prior to Carnival in February, and also in September.

> **Tip...**
> There is a pleasant dry forest walk to Huaca I, with shade and the chance to do some bird- and lizard-watching.

☆Ferreñafe

The colonial town of **Ferreñafe**, 20 km northeast of Chiclayo, is worth a visit, especially for the **Museo Nacional Sicán** ① *Av Batán Grande cuadra 9, T074-286469, Museo-Nacional-Sican-109965152373661 on Facebook, Tue-Sun 0900-1700, US$4, students half price, good explanations in Spanish, café and gift shop.* This excellent museum on the outskirts of town houses objects of the Sicán (Lambayeque) culture from near Batán Grande. To get there, take a mototaxi from the centre, five minutes, US$1.75, or, from Chiclayo, catch a combi from Avenida N de Piérola towards Batán Grande; these pass the museum every 15-20 minutes, taking 40 minutes, US$1.

Sicán (El Santuario Histórico Bosque de Pómac)

10 km beyond Ferreñafe along the road to Batán Grande (from the old Panamericana another entrance is near Túcume), dalemandelama@gmail.com. Daily 0900-1700. US$4; a guide (Spanish only) can be hired with transport, US$12, or horses for hire US$7. Food and drinks are available at the visitor centre, and camping is permitted.

El Santuario Histórico Bosque de Pómac includes the ruins of Sicán. Visiting is not easy because of the arid conditions and distances involved: it is 10 km from the visitor centre to the nearest *huaca* (pyramid). A two-hour guided tour of the area includes at least two *huacas*, some of the most ancient carob trees and a mirador that has a beautiful view across the emerald-green tops of the forest with the enormous pyramids dramatically breaking through.

Sicán has revealed several sumptuous tombs dating to AD 900-1100. The ruins comprise some 12 large adobe pyramids, arranged around a huge plaza, measuring 500 m by 250 m, with 20 archaeological sites in total. The city of the Sicán (or Lambayeque culture) was probably moved to Túcume (see above), 6 km west, following 30 years of severe drought and then a devastating El Niño-related flood in AD 1050-1100. These events appear to have provoked a rebellion in which many of the remaining temples on top of the pyramids were burnt and destroyed. The forest itself has good birdwatching possibilities.

Olmos and around

On the old Pan-American Highway 885 km from Lima, Olmos is a tranquil place surrounded by endless lemon orchards and vineyards; there are several hotels and a **Festival de Limón in the last week in June**. A paved road runs east from Olmos over the Porcuila Pass, branching north to Jaén and east to Bagua Grande (see page 1358). Olmos is the best base for observing the critically endangered white-winged guan, a bird thought extinct for 100 years until its rediscovery in 1977. The **Barbara d'Achille breeding centre** ① *0900-1700, US$1.75,* for the white-winged guan can be visited. The old Pan-American Highway continues from Olmos to Cruz de Caña and Piura.

Listings Chiclayo and around *map p1322*

Tourist information

Chiclayo

Indecopi
*Los Tumbos 245, Santa Victoria,
T074-206223, aleyva@indecopi.gob.pe.
Mon-Fri 0800-1300, 1630-1930.*
For complaints and tourist protection.

PerúU
*Palacio Municipal, C San José 823, T074-205703,
iperuchiclayo@promperu.gob.pe.
Mon-Sat 0900-1800, Sun 0900-1300.*

Also in Lambayeque at **Museo de las Tumbas Reales de Sipán**, Tue-Sun 1000-1400. There are tourist kiosks on the Plaza and on Balta.

Tourist police
Av Sáenz Peña 830. Daily 24 hrs.
Very helpful and may store luggage and take you to the sites themselves.

Ferreñafe

Mincetur
*On the Plaza de Armas, T074-282843,
citesipan@mincetur.gob.pe.*
Helpful.

Where to stay

Chiclayo

$$$ Costa del Sol Wyndham
Balta 399, T074-227272,
www.costadelsolperu.com.
Non-smoking rooms, smart, small pool, sauna,
jacuzzi, Wi-Fi, ATM. **Páprika** restaurant, good
value Sun buffets, vegetarian options.

$$$ Gran Hotel Chiclayo (Casa Andina Select)
Villareal 115, T511-2139739,
www.casa-andina.com.
Large, modern hotel for corporate and leisure
guests, pool, safe car park, changes dollars,
jacuzzi, entertainments, restaurant. Now
operated by **Casa Andina**.

$$$ Inti
Luis Gonzales 622, T074-235931,
www.intihotel.com.pe.
More expensive rooms with jacuzzi, family rooms
available, welcome cocktail, airport transfer
included, parking, safe and fridge in room,
restaurant, helpful staff.

$$$ Sunec
Izaga 472, T074-205110, www.sunechotel.com.pe.
Modern hotel in a central location, parking and
small pool.

$$ Embajador
*7 de Enero 1388, 1½ blocks from Mercado
Modelo, T074-204729, https://hotelchiclayo
embajador.com.*
Modern, bright, good facilities, 10 mins' walk
from centre, small comfortable rooms, small
restaurant, excellent service, free pick-up from
bus office, tours arranged.

$$ Paraíso
Pedro Ruiz 1064, T074-228161,
www.hotelesparaiso.com.pe.
Modern rooms with fan, restaurant, 24-hr
cafetería, meeting rooms, parking, very
good service.

$$ Santa Rosa
L González 927, T074-224411.
Rooms with windows are bright and spacious,
best at rear. Hot water, fan, laundry, good value.

$ Alfonso Ugarte
Alfonso Ugarte 1193, T074-222135.
No meals, small but comfortable double and
single rooms.

$ Hospedaje Concordia
7 de Enero Sur 235, Urb San Eduardo,
T074-209423.
Rooms on 2nd floor bigger than 3rd, modern,
pleasant, no meals, laundry service, view of
Parque San Eduardo.

$ Hospedaje San Eduardo
7 de Enero Sur 267, Urb San Eduardo,
T074-208668.
No meals, colourful decor, modern bathrooms,
fan, Wi-Fi, public phone, quiet, hot water.

$ Pirámide Real
MM Izaga 726, T074-224036.
Compact and spotless, good value, no meals,
safe in room, fan, very central.

$ Sicán
MM Izaga 356, T074-208741, hsican@hotmail.com.
With breakfast, hot water, fan, comfortable,
restaurant and bar, laundry, parking, welcoming
and trustworthy.

$ Sol Radiante
Izaga 392, T074-237858.
Hot water, comfortable, pleasant, family-run,
laundry, tourist information. Pay in advance.

Lambayeque

$$ Hostería San Roque
2 de Mayo 437, T074-282860,
www.hosteriasanroque.com.
In a fine, extensive colonial house, beautifully
refurbished, helpful staff, bar, swimming pool,
lunch on request. Single, double, triple, quad
rooms and dorm for groups of 6, **$**.

$ Hostal Libertad
Bolívar 570, T074-283561,
www.hostallibertad.com.
1½ blocks from plaza, big rooms, fridge, secure.

$ Hostal Real Sipán
Huamachuco 664, opposite Brüning Museum.
Modern, an option if arriving late at night.

Mórrope

$$-$ La Casa del Papelillo
*San Pedro 357, T955-624734, lacasadelpapelillo@
gmail.com, www.airbnb.es/rooms/89079.*
3 rooms in a remodelled 19th-century home,
1 with private bath, includes breakfast,
communal areas, cultural events, discounts
for community volunteer work. Owner Cecilia
is knowledgeable and helpful.

Chaparrí Reserve

$$$ EcoLodge Chaparrí
984-676249 or in Chiclayo T074-452299,
www.chaparrilodge.com.
A delightful oasis in the dry forest, 6 beautifully
decorated cabins (more being built) and 5 double
rooms with shared bath, built of stone and mud,
nice and cool, solar power. Price is for 3 meals and
a local guide for 1 day, first-class food. Sechuran
foxes in the gardens; hummingbirds bathe at the
pool about 0600 every day. Recommended.

Túcume

$ pp Los Horcones
951-831705, www.loshorconesdetucume.com.
Closed Feb-Mar.
Rustic luxury in the shadow of the pyramids,
adobe and *algarrobo* rooms set in lovely garden
with lots of birdlife, pool. Good food, pizza oven,
breakfast included. Note that if rice is being
grown nearby in Jan-May there can be a serious
mosquito problem.

Olmos

$$ Los Faiques
8 km from old Panamericana on road to Salas,
can arrange a taxi from Chiclayo or take Salas
combi from Chiclayo, T979-299932,
www.losfaiques-salas.com.
Very pretty place in a quiet forest setting,
buffet breakfast, dinner on request.

El Remanso
San Francisco 100, T074-427046,
Iremansolmos@yahoo.com.
Like a hacienda, with courtyards, small pool, white-
washed rooms, colourful bedding, flowers and
bottled water in room, hot water (supposedly). Price
is full board, good restaurant. Charming owner.
There are several other places to stay in town.

Restaurants

Chiclayo
For delicious, cheap ceviche, go to the **Nativo**
stall in the Mercado Central, a local favourite.
For ice cream, try **D'Onofrio**, Balta y Torres Paz.
La Panadería, Lapoint 847, has a good choice of
breads, including *integral*, snacks and soft drinks.

$$ El Huaralino
La Libertad 155, Santa Victoria.
Wide variety, international and creole,
but mixed reports of late.

$$$ Fiesta
Av Salaverry 1820 in 3 de Octubre suburb, T074-
201970, www.restaurantfiestagourmet.com.
Gourmet local dishes, excellent food and service,
beautifully presented, daily and seasonal specials,
fabulous juices, popular business lunch place.

$$$ Sabores Peruanos
Los Incas 136. Tue-Sun 1200-1700.
Great Peruvian seafood and meat dishes.

$$ Balta 512
Balta 512, T074-223598.
First-class local food, usually good breakfast,
popular with locals.

$$ Boulevar
Colón entre Izaga y Aguirre.
Good, friendly, *menú* and à la carte.

$$ Hebrón
Balta 605.
For more upmarket than average chicken, but
also local food and *parrilla*, good salads. Also
does an excellent breakfast and a good buffet
at weekends.

$$ Kaprichos
Pedro Ruíz 1059, T074-232721.
Chinese, delicious, huge portions.

$$ Las Américas
Aguirre 824. Daily 0700-0200.
Good service.

$$ Roma
Izaga 706. Open all day.
Wide choice, breakfasts, snacks and meals.

$$ Tradiciones
7 de Enero Sur 105, T074-221192. Daily 0900-1700.
Good variety of local dishes, including ceviche,
and drinks, pleasant atmosphere and garden,
good service.

$$ Vichayo Restobar
Los Alamos 230, Urb Santa Victoria, T074-227664.
Wed-Fri until 1630, longer hours Sat-Sun.
Excellent fish and seafood dishes.

$ Café 900
MM Izaga 900, www.cafe900.com.
Appealing atmosphere in a remodelled
old house, good food, popular with locals,
sometimes has live music.

$ Café Astoria
Bolognesi 627. Daily 0800-1200, 1530-2100.
Breakfast, good-value *menú*.

$ La Parra
Izaga 746.
Chinese and creole *parrillada*, very good, large portions, cheerful.

$ La Plazuela
San José 299, Plaza Elías Aguirre.
Good food, seats outside.

Lambayeque

A Lambayeque speciality is the 'King Kong', a giant *alfajor* biscuit filled with *manjar blanco* and other sweets. San Roque brand (www.sanroque.com.pe), sold throught Peru, is especially good.

$$ Casona Descalzi
Address above. Lunch only.
Good menu, including traditional northern dishes.

$$ El Cántaro
2 de Mayo 180. Lunch only.
For traditional local dishes, à la carte and a good *menú*.

$$ El Pacífico
Huamachuco 970, T074-283135. Lunch only.
Renowned for its enormous plates of *arroz con pato* and *causa norteña*.

$$ El Rincón del Pato
A Leguía 270. Lunch only.
Offers 40 different duck dishes and very good seafood.

$$-$ Sabor Norteño
Bolívar 440.
One of the few restaurants open in the early evening.

$ Café Cultural La Cucarda
2 de Mayo 263, T074-284155. Tue-Sun, evenings only.
Small alternative café, decorated with antiques, delicious pastries, pies and cakes. Recommended.

Festivals

6 Jan **Reyes Magos** in Mórrope, Illimo and other towns, a recreation of a medieval pageant in which pre-Columbian deities become the Wise Men.
4 Feb **Túcume** devil dances.
14 Mar and 14 Sep **El Señor Nazareno Cautivo**, in Lambayeque and Monsefú, whose main celebration of this festival is 14 Sep.
Mar/Apr **Holy Week**, traditional Easter celebrations and processions in many villages.
2-7 Jun **Divine Child of the Miracle**, Villa de Eten.
27-31 Jul **Fexticum** in **Monsefú**, traditional foods, drink, handicrafts, music and dance.

6 Aug Pilgrimage from the mountain shrine of **Chalpón** to **Motupe**, 90 km north of Chiclayo; the cross is brought down from a cave and carried in procession through the village.
24 Dec-1 Jan **Christmas** and **New Year** processions and children dancers (*pastorcitos* and *seranitas*) can be seen in many villages, including **Ferreñafe**, **Mochumi**, **Mórrope**.

What to do

Chiclayo

Tour operators
Lambayeque's museums, Sipán and Túcume can easily be visited by public transport (see below). Local operators run 3-hr tours to Sipán; Túcume and Lambayeque (5 hrs); Sicán is a full-day tour including Ferreñafe and Pómac. There are also tours to Zaña and coastal towns.
InkaNatura, *Manuel María Izaga 730, of 203, T979-995024, www.inkanatura.net. Mon-Fri 0915-1315, 1515-1915, Sat 0915-1315.* Historical and nature tours throughout northern Peru. Good service.
Julio Porras, *T979-710768, julio.porras.guide@gmail.com.* Julio organizes tours in an around Chiclayo. He knows the area well and speaks fluent English.

Sicán (El Santuario Histórico Bosque de Pómac)

Horse riding
Rancho Santana, *Pacora, T979-712145, www.cabalgatasperu.com. Mar-Dec.* Relaxing tours on horseback, half-day (US$15.50), 1-day (US$22.50) or 3-day tours to Santuario Bosque de Pómac, Sicán ruins and Túcume, Swiss-run (Andrea Martin), good horses. Also **$** a bungalow, a double room and camping (tents for hire) at the ranch with safe parking for campervans. Frequently recommended.

Transport

Chiclayo
Air José Abelardo Quiñones González airport 1 km from town, T074-233192; taxi from centre US$4. Arrive 2 hrs before flight; be prepared for manual search of hand luggage; no restaurant or bar in departure lounge.

Daily flights to/from **Lima** and **Piura** with **LATAM** (MM Izaga 770) and **StarPerú** (MM Izaga 459, T074-225204), direct or via **Trujillo**.

Bus Local Combis to **Monsefú** cost US$0.75 from Bolognesi y Sarmiento, or Terminal Epsel (Av Castañeda Iparraguirre s/n). Combis to **Pimentel** leave from Av L Ortiz and San José, US$1.10. *Colectivos* to **Lambayeque**, US$0.75, 25 mins, leave from Pedro Ruíz at the junction with Av Ugarte; also **Brüning Express** combis from Vicente de la Vega entre Angamos y Av L Ortiz, every 15 mins, US$0.50, or **Trans Lambayeque** *colectivo* from Plaza Elias Aguirre, US$0.90. Combis to Sipán leave from terminal Epsel, US$1, 1 hr. To **Chongoyape** for Chaparrí reserve, take a public bus from Leoncio Prado y Sáenz Peña (1¼ hrs, US$1.50), then a mototaxi to **Chaparrí**, US$10. Combis to Tucumé leave from Av Leguía, 15 m from Angamos, US$1, 45 mins. *Colectivos* to the centre of Ferreñafe leave from terminal Epsel every few mins, or from 8 de Octubre y Sáenz Peña, 40 mins, US$1. Combis to **Batán Grande** depart from Av N de Piérola, and pass the museum in Ferreñafe every 15-20 mins, 90 mins, US$1.

Long distance There is no central terminal; most buses stop outside their offices in Bolognesi. To **Lima**, 770 km, US$25-36, with **Civa** (Av Bolognesi 714, T074-223434); **Cruz del Sur** (Bolognesi 888, T074-225508); **Ormeño** (Haya de la Torre 242, 2 blocks south of Bolognesi, T074-234206); **Ittsa** (Av Bolognesi 155, T074-233612); **Línea** (Bolognesi 638, T074-22221), *especial* and *bus cama* service; **Móvil** (Av Bolognesi 195, T074-271940), goes as far as Tarapoto; **Oltursa** (ticket office at Balta e Izaga, T074-237789, terminal at Vicente de la Vega 101,

T074-225611); **Tepsa** (Bolognesi 504-36 y Colón, T074-236981) and **Transportes Chiclayo** (Av L Ortiz 010, T074-223632). Most companies leave from 1900 onwards.

To **Trujillo**, 209 km, with **Emtrafesa** (Av Balta 110, T074-600660), every 15 mins, 4 hrs, US$5.50, and **Línea**. To **Piura**, 4 hrs, US$5.50, **Transportes Chiclayo** leave 15 mins throughout the day; also **Línea** and **Emtrafesa** and buses from the **Cial/Flores** terminal (Bolognesi 751, T074-239579). To **Sullana**, US$8.50. To **Tumbes**, US$9, 9-10 hrs; with **Cial, Cruz del Sur** or **El Dorado**. To **Cajamarca**, 260 km, US$9-20, eg **Línea**, 4 a day; others from Tepsa terminal (Bolognesi y Colón, eg **Días**, T074-224448). To **Chachapoyas**, US$13.50-25, with **Civa**, 1730 daily, 10-11 hrs; **Transervis Kuelap** (Tepsa station), 1830 daily; **Móvil**, at 2000. To **Jaén**, US$7.75-9.60, many companies; **Móvil** charges US$11.55-15.50. To **Tarapoto**, 18 hrs, US$25-29, with **Móvil**, also **Tarapoto Tours** (Bolognesi 751, T074-636231). To **Guayaquil**, with **Civarun** at 1825, *semi-cama* US$34.75, *cama* US$42.50, also **Super Semería**, US$25, 12 hrs, via Piura, Máncora, Tumbes; they also go to Cuenca.

Taxi Mototaxis are a cheap way to get around: US$1 anywhere in city. Chiclayo to Pimentel, US$6, 20 mins. Taxi *colectivos* to Eten leave from Mariscal Nieto and José Quiñones.

Lambayeque
Some major bus lines have offices in Lambayeque and can drop you off there. There are numerous combis between Lambayeque and **Chiclayo** (see above). Combi to **Túcume**, US$1.25, 25 mins.

Piura and around *Colour map 3, A1.*

a proud and historic city

Piura was founded in 1532, three years before Lima, by the conquistadors left behind by Pizarro. The city has public gardens and two well-kept parks, Cortés and Pizarro (also called Plaza de las Tres Culturas); the latter has a statue of the man himself. Old buildings are kept in repair and new buildings blend with the Spanish style of the old city. Several bridges cross the Río Piura to Castilla, two are pedestrian.

Sights
In the Plaza de Armas is the **cathedral** ① *daily 0800-1200, 1700-2030*, with a gold-covered altar and paintings by Ignacio Merino. A few blocks away is **San Francisco** ① *Mon-Sat 0900-1200, 1600-1800*, where the city's independence from Spain was declared on 4 January 1821, nearly eight months before Lima. **Casa Museo Grau** ① *C Tacna 662, opposite the Centro Cívico, T073-326541, Mon-Fri 0800-1300, 1500-1800, Sat-Sun 0800-1200, US$0.70*, is the birthplace of Admiral Miguel Grau, hero of the War of the Pacific with Chile. The museum contains a model of the *Huáscar*, the largest Peruvian warship in the War of the

> **Tip...**
> The winter climate, May to September, is very pleasant although nights can be cold and the wind piercing; December to March is very hot.

Pacific, which was built in Britain. It also contains interesting old photographs. The small **Muse Municipal Vicús** ① *Sullana, near Huánuco, Tue-Sat 0900-1645, Sun 0900-1300*, includes a Sala de Ore (closed weekends, US\$1.45) with 60 gold artefacts from the local Vicús culture and an art section.

Catacaos

Twelve kilometres southwest of Piura, Catacaos is famous for its *chicha*, *picanterías* (local restaurants some with music) and for its crafts, including tooled leather, gold and silver filigree jewellery

Piura

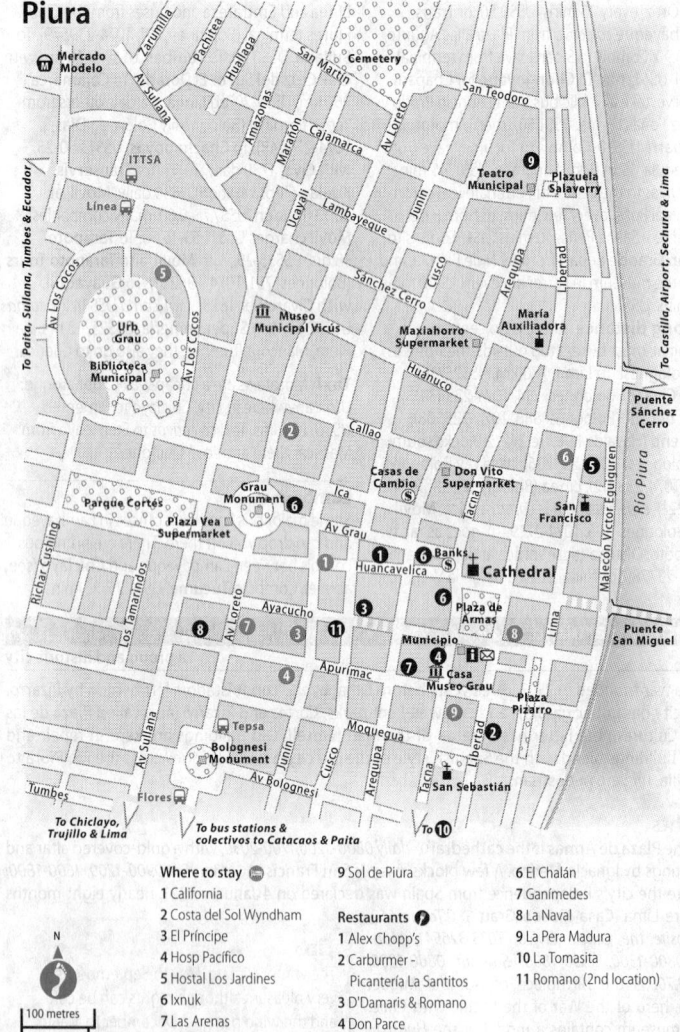

N

100 metres
100 yards

wooden articles and straw hats (expensive). The town has splendid celebrations during Holy Week. About 2 km south of Catacaos is the **Narihuala archaeological site** ① *Tue-Sun 0830-1630, US$0.70, children will guide you for a tip, mototaxi from Catacaos US$1.80*, which consists of deteriorated adobe pyramids of the Tallán culture (AD 900-1400) and a site museum.

Paita and around

Paita, 50 km from Piura, is the major fishing port for the area and is flanked on three sides by towering, sandy bluff. Looming over Paita is a small colonial fortress built to repel pirates, who attacked it frequently. Several colonial buildings survive. Bolívar's mistress, Manuela Sáenz, lived the last 24 years of her life in Paita, after being exiled from Quito. She supported herself until her death in 1856 by weaving, embroidering and making candy, after refusing the fortune left her by her husband. Nearby beaches include **Colán**, to the north, with various hotels, restaurants and a long sandy beach (beware the stingrays); and less developed **Yasila**, a fishing village to the south. **Isla Foca**, with a great diversity of sea birds and a pelican rookery (November-Dec ember), is reached from Paita. Fishermen offer boat tours around the island, 40 minutes, US$25 per boat, contact Asociación Cristo te Ama, T968-198924.

Tourist information

iPerú
Ayacucho s/n y C Libertad, edif Serpost, a lane off the Plaza de Armas, T073-320249, iperupiura@promperu.gob.pe. Mon-Sat 0900-1800, Sun 0900-1300; there's another office in arrivals at the airport.
Very helpful staff, English spoken.

Where to stay

$$$-$$$ Costa del Sol Wyndham
Av Loreto 649, T073-302864, www.costadelsolperu.com.
Centrally located, part of the Peruvian 1st class hotel chain, pool, restaurant.

$$$-$$$ Los Portales
Libertad 875, Plaza de Armas, T073-321161, www.losportaleshoteles.com.pe.
Elegantly refurbished *casona* in the heart of the city, luxurious suites and rooms, includes welcome cocktail, the city's social centre, pleasant terrace, nice pool.

$$ Ixnuk
Ica 553, T073-322205, www.ixnuk.com.
Modern hotel with bright ample rooms, a/c, fridge, airport transfers.

$$-$$ El Príncipe
Junín 930, T073-324868.
Comfortable suite and rooms with a/c, fridge, airport transfers.

$$ Las Arenas
Loreto 945, T073-305554.
Older well maintained hotel in a central location, variety of rooms, a/c, cheaper with fan, small pool, IYHF discounts.

$$ Sol de Piura
Tacna 761, T073-332395,www.soldepiura.com.
Centrally located modern hotel, comfortable rooms with a/c, fridge, airport transfers.

$$-$ Hostal Los Jardines
Av Los Cocos 436, Urb Club Grau, T073-326590, www.hotellosjardines.com.
Not far from the centre, rooms with ceiling fan, ageing but OK, parking, good value.

$ California
Jr Junín 835, upstairs, T073-328789.
Shared or private bath, own water-tank, mosquito netting on windows, roof terrace.

$ Hospedaje Pacífico
Apurimac 717, T073-303061.
Simple comfortable rooms with fan, the newer ones on the top floors are the nicest, no breakfast, good value.

Restaurants

$$$ Carbumer – Picantería La Santitos
Libertad 1001, T073-309475. Daily 1100-1900.
Very good fish, regional dishes and pizza in a renovated colonial house with a/c.

$$$ La Tomasita
Tacna 853, T073-321957. Daily 1100-1730.
Very good *picantería* serving regional dishes

including ceviche, *arroz con cabrito* (goat) and *seco de chavelo* (sun-dried meat). A/c.

$$$-$$ Don Parce
Tacna 642, T073-300842. Daily 0700-2400.
Upmarket restaurant serving varied international food. *Menú* Mon-Sat.

$$ Alex Chopp's
Huancavelica 538, T073-322568. Daily 1200-2400.
A la carte dishes, seafood, fish, and especially beer.

$$-$ Romano
Ayacucho 580, Mon-Sat 0730-2300, and Ayacucho 609. Tue-Sun 0900-1600.
Popular with locals, wide selection of *menú* options.

$ D'Damaris
Ayacucho 588. Daily 0720-2200.
Good value vegetarian *menú* and à la carte, pleasant atmosphere, no TV.

$ Ganímedes
Apurímac 468-B. Mon-Sat 0800-2230, Sun 0800-2100.
Vegetarian lunch *menú*, pizza and à la carte from 1800, very good bakery.

$ La Naval
Apurímac 836 (no sign). Mon-Sat 0700-1600.
Tasty economical *menú*, good selection, family run and friendly.

Cafés and snack bars

D'Pauli
Lima 541. Mon-Sat 0900-1400, 1600-2130.
Sweets, cakes and sandwiches.

El Chalán
Several branches including Tacna 520 on Plaza de Armas, Grau 173, Grau 452 and others.
Sandwiches, sweets, fruit salad, *cremoladas* and very good ice cream.

La Pera Madura
Arequipa 168, next to Teatro Municipal, no sign. Daily 1700-2300.
For turkey sandwiches, *tamales* and other local specialities.

Catacaos

Among the town's *picanterías*, **Chayo** (Jr San Francisco 497) and **El Ganso Azul** (Jr Josefina Ramos) are very good.

What to do

City tours, visits to craft towns, beaches, adventure sports (including surfing and sandboarding) and nature tours in the Piura highlands and desert are all available.

Canechi Tours, *C Tacna 349, p2, T073-311327, www.canechitours.com.*
Piura Tours, *C Arequipa 978, T073-326778, piuratours@speedy.com.pe.* For flight tickets, the manager Mario speaks good English.

Transport

Air Capitán Guillermo Concha airport is in Castilla, 10 mins from the centre by taxi (US$2-3, airport taxis charge more). It has gift shops and car rental agencies (see below). 10 daily flights to **Lima** with **Avianca/TACA** (Centro Comercial Rea Plaza), **LATAM** (Centro Comercial Open Plaza) or **Peruvian Airlines** (Libertad 777).

Bus Local *Colectivos* have their stops near the Piura stations; they leave as they fill up. To **Catacaos**, *colectivos* from Jr Loreto 1292, 1 block from Ovalo Bolognesi, US$0.90, 20 mins. To **Paita Trans Dora** (T968-158086) from Prolongación Sánchez Cerro, next to Club de Tiro, every 20 min 1 hr, US$1.50; also from **Terminal Gechisa** (Prolongación Sánchez Cerro, opposite Proyecto Chira, T073-399322) and *colectivos* from Av Loreto block 12, by Jr Tumbes. Transfer in Paita for **Colán** and **Yacila**. To **Chulucanas** from **Terminal Castilla**, every 30 mins (less often in wet season), US$1.20, 1 hr. To **Huancabamba**, with **San Pedro y San Pablo** (T073-349271), from **Terminal El Bosque**, Castilla, at 0730, 1330, 1830, 6 hrs; also **Civa** (T073-397991) from same terminal at 1030, 1800; and **Turismo Express Norte** (073-344330) from **Terminal Castilla**, at 0730, 1400, 1830.

Long distance Interprovincial bus companies are on Av Sánchez Cerro, blocks 11-13 and Av Loreto, blocks 11-14; the latter is in a more pleasant area and closer to the centre. Some regional services run from **Terminal Gechisa**, Prolongación Sánchez Cerro (the road to Sullana) west of the city.

To **Lima**, 973 km, 14-15½ hrs, US$30-48. Most buses stop at the major cities on route: **Cruz del Sur** (Av Circunvalación 160, T073-337094); Olturs (Bolognesi 801, T073-326666); **ITTSA** (Sánchez Cerro 1142, T073-333982); **Tepsa** (Loreto 1195, T073-306345); **Flores** (Av Loreto cuadra 12), 8 daily; several others.

To **Chiclayo** and **Lambayeque**, 209 km, 4 hrs, from US$5.50, with **Trans Chiclayo** (Sánchez

Cerro 1121, T073-308455), every 30 min; **Línea** (Sánchéz Cerro 1215, T073-303894, www.linea.pe), hourly; several others. To **Trujillo**, 7 hrs, 420 km, US$12.50-15, **Línea** at 1330 and 2300; to travel by day **ITTSA** at 0900 or change in Chiclayo; several others in the afternoon and around 2300.

To **Sullana**, 38 km, 30 mins, US$0.50, frequent service from **Terminal Gechisa** 0500-2200.
To **Ayabaca**, 6 hrs, with Transporte Vegas (Panamericana C1 Lt10, Urb San Ramón, T073-308729) at 0730, 0830 and 1400, or El Poderoso Cautivo (Sullana Norte 7, Urb San Ramón, T073-309888) at 0730, 0840 and 1500.

To **Tumbes**, 282 km, 4½ hrs, US$7-8.50, **El Dorado** (Sánchez Cerro 1119, T073-325875), every 1-2 hrs; several others originating in cities to the south eg **Cruz del Sur**, **Cial** (Bolognesi 817, T073-304250), **CIVA** (Av Loreto 1401, T073-345451) and **Emtrafesa** (Los Naranjos 255, T073-337093, also to Chiclayo and Trujillo); also *colectivos*, US$12. To **Máncora**, 187 km, US$5.50, 3 hrs, with **Eppo** (Av Panamericana 243, behind CC Real

Plaza, T073-304543, www.eppo.com.pe), every 30 mins; or buses to Tumbes or Ecuador; **SERTUR** *colectivos* from Sanchéz Cerro cuadra 11, US$11.
To **Cajamarca**, 467 km, US$18, 10 hrs, at 1845, 1930, 2130, 2230, with **Dias** (Av Loreto 1485, T073-302834), also to Lima at 1500; also to **Tarapoto**, 1230 daily, US$21, 16 hrs.

To Ecuador To Guayaquil via Tumbes, US$15-20, 10-11 hrs, with **CIFA**, from the same terminal as **Dias** (Av Loreto 1485, T972-894616), at 1030, 1800, 2030, 2200; also **Super Semeria** (from the same terminal), at 2200, and **CIVA**, from Av Loreto 140, at 1945. To **Loja** via Macará, with **Transportes Loja**, from the same terminal as Ronco (Av Loreto 1241, T073-333260), at 1300 and 2100, US$14, 8-9 hrs; or with **Unión Cariamanga**, from Dias terminal (T969-493907), at 2000.
To **Cuenca**, US$15, 10 hrs, with **Azuay**, from Ronco terminal (T976-900101), at 2030; or **Super Semeria**, from **Dias terminal**, at 2030.

Car hire Ramos, T073-348668; and Vicus, T073-342051, both outside the airport, several others.

North to Ecuador

beach resorts and nature reserves en route to the border

Sullana to La Tina

The Pan-American Highway forks at **Sullana**, 38 km north of Piura. Built on a bluff over the fertile Chira valley, the city is neither clean nor safe, so there is no reason to stop here. To the east the Panamericana crosses the Peru–Ecuador border at La Tina (see below) and continues via Macará to Loja and Cuenca. The excellent paved road is very scenic and is the best option if you want to visit the southern or central highlands of Ecuador.

Border at La Tina–Macará The border crossing is problem-free and both sides are open 24 hours. Immigration, customs and other services are currently on either side of the international bridge. An integrated border complex was under construction on the Ecuadorean side in 2017. On the Peruvian side, there is one *hospedaje* and several eating places on the road down to the bridge. On the Ecuadorean side, Macará is a small city with all services, 2.5 km past the bridge. There are no money changers or ATMs right at the bridge, only at the park in Macará where vehicles leave for the border.

Sullana to Máncora

The second branch of the Pan-American Highway is the coastal road which goes from Sullana northwest towards the Talara oilfields, and then follows the coastline to Máncora and Tumbes. From Talara, the Panamericana goes a few kilometres inland but the old Panamericana gives access to lovely beaches and fishing towns that are a peaceful alternative to Máncora.

Máncora

Máncora, a resort stretching along the Pan-American Highway, is popular with young Limeños, Chileans and Argentines and also as a stop-off for travellers, especially surfers, on the Peru-Ecuador route. Development here has been rapid and haphazard. The resort is crowded and noisy during the December-February high season; beaches can get dirty; drugs and scams (many involving mototaxis) abound. The centre is patrolled but outlying areas are not, enquire locally about safety. There is one bank and various ATMs in Máncora but take some cash, exchange rates are better in Piura. **Vichayito**, 7 km south of Máncora, is accessed from Km 1155 or from Las Pocitas and is a lovely beach well suited to swimming, kite-surfing (April to November) and diving. Separated by a headland from Vichayito is **Las Pocitas**, a stretch of beautiful beach with rocks, behind which little pools (or *pocitas*) form at low tide. It is another alternative to Máncora, just 4 km away, for those looking for tranquillity.

Punta Sal to Tumbes

At Km 1187, 22 km north of Máncora, is the turn-off for **Punta Sal**, marked by a large white arch (El Arco) over the road (2 km). Punta Sal boasts a 3-km-long white sandy beach and a more upmarket clientèle than Máncora, with accommodation (and prices) to match. There is no town centre and no banks, ATMs or restaurants independent of hotels, so it is very quiet in the low season.

Zorritos, 62 km north of Punta Sal and 27 km south of Tumbes, is an important fishing centre with a good beach. **Caleta La Cruz**, 16 km southwest of Tumbes, is the only part of the Peruvian coast where the sea is warm all year. It was here that Pizarro landed in 1532. There are regular *colectivos*, US$0.30 each way, from Tumbes.

Tumbes and around Colour map 3, A1.

The most northerly Peruvian city is Tumbes, 265 km north of Piura. Few tourists stop here since international buses take you directly north to Ecuador or south to the beaches or Piura.

The most striking aspect of the town itself is its bright and cheery modern public buildings: the **Malecón Benavides**, a long promenade beside the Tumbes river, has rainbow-coloured archways and a monstrous statue called El Beso (the Kiss); the Plaza de Armas sports a large structure of many colours, and even the **cathedral**, built in 1903 and restored in 1985, has green and pink stripes. Calles Bolívar and San Martín (Paseo de la Concordia) make for a pleasant wander, and there is a small artisans' market at the top end of San Martín (approaching Plaza Bolognesi). On Calle Grau, there are the tumble-down colonial houses, many of which are no longer in use.

☆ Tumbes provides access to important protected areas, administered by Sernanp ① *Panamericana Norte 1739, Tumbes, T072-526489; Los Cocos H-23, Urb Club Grau, Piura, T072-321668*, which, due to the latitude, are rich in fauna and flora found nowhere else in Peru. The best time to visit the parks is the dry season, April to December. On the coast, the **Santuario Nacional los Manglares de Tumbes** (permit required to visit) protects 3000 ha of Peru's remaining 4750 ha of mangrove forest. Inland, the **Parque Nacional Cerros de Amotape** protects 90,700 ha of varied habitat, but principally the best

> **Tip...**
>
> There is an Ecuadorean Consulate in Tumbes at Bolívar 129, piso 3, Plaza de Armas, T072-525949, cecutumbes@cancilleria.gob.ec, Monday-Friday 0800-1300.

preserved area of dry forest on the west coast of South America. Adjoining it is the **Zona Reservada de Tumbes** (75,000 ha), which protects dry equatorial forest and tropical rainforest. The Río Tumbes crocodile, which is a UN Red-data species, is found at the river's mouth, where there is a small breeding programme, and in its upper reaches.

Border with Ecuador The best way to cross this border is on one of the international buses that run between Peru (Piura, Máncora or Tumbes) and Ecuador (Huaquillas, Machala, Guayaquil or Cuenca). If travelling from further south in Peru, do not take a bus all the way to the border; change to an Ecuador-bound bus in Piura, Máncora or Tumbes. Formalities are only carried out at the new bridge, far outside the border towns of **Aguas Verdes** (Peru) and **Huaquillas** (Ecuador). There are two border complexes called CEBAF (Centro Binacional de Atención Fronteriza), open 24 hours on either side of the bridge. Both complexes have Peruvian and Ecuadorean immigration officers so you get your exit and entry stamps in the same place. If crossing with your own vehicle however, you may have to stop at both border complexes for customs.

If you do not take one of the international buses then the crossing is hot, harrowing and transport between the two sides via the new bridge and border complex is inconvenient and expensive (see Transport, page 1338). Travellers often fall victim to thefts, muggings, shakedowns by minor officials and countless scams on both sides. Never leave your baggage unattended and do your own arithmetic when changing money. Those seeking a more relaxed crossing to or from Ecuador should consider La Tina–Macará or Namballe–La Balsa.

Tourist information

Máncora

Municipio
Av Piura 532, T073-258061.
See also www.vivamancora.com.

Tumbes

iPerú
Malecón III Milenio, p3, T072-506721.
Mon-Sat 0900-1800, Sun 0900-1300,
iperutumbes@promperu.gob.pe.

Where to stay

Máncora

There are at least 50 hotels in and around Máncora, heavily booked in high season (Dec-Mar) when prices can increase by 100% or more and one-day bookings are not accepted. Many hotels have even higher rates for Christmas, New Year, Easter and Independence Day holidays when the resort is full to bursting. The main strip of the Panamericana is known as Av Piura from the bridge for the first couple of blocks, then Av Grau to the end of town. The better hotels are at the southern end of town, with a small concentration of mid-range hotels just over the bridge. Hotels to the left look onto the beach directly in front of the best surf and often have beach entrances as well as road entrances. They are the most popular with tourists and are all noisy at night from nearby discos, which last until around 0200 Mon-Thu and 0600 Fri-Sun. Cheaper hotels close to the village have no direct beach access. When checking into a cheaper hotel, expect to pay up front and make sure you get a receipt or you might be asked to pay again the next time the receptionist sees you. Take every precaution with your valuables, theft is common. Mosquitoes are bad Dec-Mar and dengue fever is a concern, so protect against bites day and night.

Máncora town

$$$ Don Giovanni
Pje 8 de Noviembre s/n, T073-258525,
www.dongiovannimancora.com.
3-storey Indonesian-style beachfront hotel, includes breakfast, restaurant and ice cream parlour, kitesurfing classes available.

$$ Del Wawa
Beachfront, T073-258427, www.delwawa.com.
This relaxed and spacious Spanish-owned hotel is popular with serious surfers and kitesurfers. Hotel service poor, rooms noisy, food average, but great location and nice restaurants round the corner.

$$ Kon Tiki
Los Incas 200, T073-258138,
www.kontikimancora.com.
On hill with lighhouse, great views, cabins with thatched roofs, hammocks, kitchen facilities, bar. Transport to/from bus station provided. Advance booking required.

$$ Las Olas
Beachfront, T073-258099,
www.lasolasmancora.com.
Smart, cabin-style rooms, top floor rooms have best view of ocean, hammocks and gardens, includes breakfast.

$$ Punta Ballenas Inn
Km 1164, south of Cabo Blanco bridge
at the south entrance to town, T072-
630844, www.puntaballenas.com.
Lovely setting on beach, garden with small pool, expensive restaurant.

$$-$ Kokopelli Beachpackers
Av Piura 209, T073-258091,
www.hostelkokopelli.com.
Popular hostel 3 mins' walk from beach, with pool, bar, good food, good meeting place, lots of facilities. Rooms for 2, 4 or 8, mixed or female only, all with bath, hot water.

$$-$ Laguna Surf Camp
T01-99 401 5628, www.vivamancora.com/
lagunacamp.
50 m from the sea, thatched roofs, cabins sleeping up to 6 people (US$11 pp), also cabins around small communal area with hammocks, pool and restaurant. Good surf lessons, helpful staff.

$$-$ Loki del Mar
Av Piura 262, T073-258484, www.lokihostel.com.
In the **Loki** group of hostels, seafront, bright white and modern muti-storey building, doubles with private bath or dorms with 4-6 beds and lockable closets, bar, restaurant, pool, lots of activities. Be ready for loud music and parties. Advance booking required.

$ Casa del Turista
Av Piura 224, T073-258126.
Family-run, TV, roof terraces giving sea views, good value and location. Recommended.

Quebrada Cabo Blanco

Crossing the bridge into Máncora, a dirt track leads downhill to the right, to the Quebrada Cabo Blanco, signed to **La Posada Youth Hostel**. The many hotels at the end of the track are badly lit for guests returning at night (robberies have occurred) but are relatively quiet and relaxing.

$$ Kimbas Bungalows
T073-258373, www.kimbasbungalows mancora.com.
Relaxed spot with charming thatched bungalows, Balinese influences, nice garden with hammocks, pool, some rooms have hot water, good value. Recommended.

$$ La Posada
T073-258328.
IYHF affiliated hostel, dorms (US$20 pp), camping (US$12 pp) and rooms with private bath, fan, garden with hammocks, pool, cooking facilities, parking,

Las Pocitas and Vichayito

There are over 40 hotels in this area, south of Máncora. Most are more upmarket than those in town.

$$$$ Las Arennas
Antigua Panamericana Norte, Km 1213, T073-258240, www.arennasmancora.com.
Smart, luxury pool or beachfront suites, all modern facilities, with central bar and restaurant serving imaginative dishes, beautiful pool, palm-lined beach frontage, very romantic.

$$$ Las Pocitas
Antigua Panamericana Norte, Km 1215, T998-139711, www.laspocitas.pe.
Great location, rooms with ocean views, lovely palm-lined beach, terrace, pool, restaurant and bar.

$$$ Máncora Beach Bungalows
Antigua Panamericana Norte, Km 1215, Lima T01-201 2060, www.mancora-beach.com.
Comfortable rooms with ceiling fan, terrace and hammocks, good restaurant, good value for this price range.

$$$ Puerto Palos
Antigua Panamericana Norte, 2 km south of Máncora (10 mins by mototaxi, US$2), T073-258199, www.puertopalos.com.

Variety of rooms, fan, suites have a/c. Excellent, nice pool overlooking ocean, hammocks, sunbeds, umbrellas, good restaurant. Friendly and hospitable.

$$ Marcilia Beach Bungalows
Antigua Panamericana Norte, Km 1212, T994-685209, www.marciliadevichayito.com.
Nice rustic bamboo cabins with ocean views, includes breakfast, family-run.

Punta Sal to Tumbes

There is a huge resort of the Colombian **Royal Decameron** group in Punta Sal, www.decameron.com.

$$$$ Punta Sal
Panamericana Norte, Km 1192, Punta Sal Chica, T072-596700/540088, www.puntasal.com.pe.
A beautiful complex of bungalows along a fine sandy beach, with pool, bar decorated with photos of big game fishing, fine restaurant. Most deals are all-inclusive, but massages and whale-watching trips are extra. Good food and service.

$$$-$ Waltako Beach Town
Panamericana 1199, Canoas de Punta Sal, T998-141976, www.waltakoperu.com.
Thatched cabins for 2, 4 or 6 people, with kitchenette, porch and hammock. Camping on the beach if you bring your own tent. Restaurant and bar, bicycles, quad bikes and horses for hire. Volunteers welcomed for conservation and reforestation work.

$$ Hospedaje El Bucanero
At the entrance to Playa Punta Sal, set back from the beach, T072-540118.
The most happening place in Punta Sal, popular with travellers, rates rise in high season, a variety of rooms, pool, restaurant, bar and gardens.

$$ Huá
On the beach at the entrance to Playa Punta Sal, T072-540023, www.hua-puntasal.com.
A rustic old wooden building, pleasant terrace overlooking ocean, hammocks, quiet, restful, good food, friendly service.

$$-$ Las Terrazas
Opposite Sunset Punta Sal, T072-507701.
One of the more basic and cheaper hotels in Punta Sal in operation since 1989, restaurant has sea view, some rooms better than others, those with own bath and sea view twice the price. Helpful owners.

$ Hospedaje Orillas del Mar
San Martín 496, Cancas.

A short walk from Punta Sal Chica beaches, this is the best of the basic *hostales* lining the beach and Panamericana.

$ Hostal Grillo Tres Puntas
Panamericana Norte, Km 1235, Zorritos, T072-794830, www.casagrillo.net.
On the beach, rustic bamboo cabins, quiet and peaceful. Great food prepared by Spanish chef-owner, León, who breeds Peruvian hairless dogs. Lukewarm showers, Wi-Fi in dining area, camping possible on the beach.

Tumbes

Note that Av Tumbes is still sometimes referred to by its old name of Teniente Vásquez. At holiday times it can be very difficult to find a room.

$$$ Wyndham Costa del Sol
San Martín 275, Plazuela Bolognesi, T072-523991, www.costadelsolperu.com.
The only high-class hotel in town, minibars, a/c, good restaurant, garden, pool, excellent service. Parking for an extra fee. Rooms which look onto the Plaza Bolognesi are noisy.

$$ Lourdes
Mayor Bodero 118, 3 blocks from main plaza, T072-522966.
Welcoming place. Narrow corridor leading to cell-like rooms which are plushly decorated with a mixture of antique and modern furniture. Good bathrooms, fans in each room.

$$-$ Asturias
Av Mcal Castilla 307, T072-522569.
Comfortable, hot water, a/c or fan, restaurant, bar and laundry. Accepts credit cards.

$ Hostal Tumbes
Filipinas s/n, off Grau, T072-522203, or T972-852954.
Small, dark, basic but cleanish rooms with fans and bath. Good cheap option.

Restaurants

Máncora

Máncora is packed with restaurants: plenty of sushi, pizza and grills. Most are pricey; the cheaper places are north along Av Piura.

$$$ Pizzería Mamíferos
Av Piura 346. Tue-Sun 1800-2300.
Wood-fired pizzas and lasagne.

$$$-$$ Josil
Av Piura, near The Birdhouse. Closed Sun.
Very good Sushi bar.

$$$-$$ Tao
Av Piura. Closed Wed.
Good Asian food and curries.

$$ Angela's Place/Cafetería de Angela
Av Piura 396, www.vivamancora.com/deangela. Daily 0800-2300.
A great option for a healthy breakfast or lunch and heaven for vegetarians and whole-food lovers: home-made bread, yoghurts, fresh fruit, etc.

$$ Don César
Hard to find, ask around or take a mototaxi. Closed Sun.
Good fresh seafood, very popular with locals.

$ The Birdhouse
Av Piura.
This small open-air commercial centre incorporates **Green Eggs and Ham**, daily 0730-1300 for great breakfasts (US$3.35), including waffles, pancakes or eggs and bacon, plus juice or coffee. Directly underneath is **Papa Mo's** milk bar, with comfy seats next to the sand and a selection of drinks.

$ Café La Bajadita
Av Piura.
Has an impressive selection of delicious home-made desserts and cakes.

Tumbes

There are cheap restaurants on the Plaza de Armas, Paseo de la Concordia and near the markets.

$$-$ Budabar
Grau 309, on Plaza de Armas, T072-525493.
One of a kind chill-out lounge offering traditional food and comfy seating with outdoor tables and cheap beer, popular in the evenings.

$$-$ Chifa Wakay
Huáscar 413. Evenings only.
A large, well-ventilated smart restaurant offering the usual Chifa favourites.

$$-$ Classic
Tumbes 185.
Look for it almost under the bridge over the river, heading south. Popular for local food.

$$-$ Los Gustitos
Bolívar 148.
Excellent *menús* and à la carte. Popular, good atmosphere at lunchtime.

$ Cherry
San Martín 116. Open 0800-1400, 1700-2300.
Tiny café offering an amazing selection of cakes and desserts, also fresh juices, shakes,

sandwiches, hot and cold drinks and traditional *cremoladas* (fruit juice with crushed ice).

$ Sí Señor
Bolívar 119 on the plaza.
Good for snacks, cheap lunch menus.

What to do

Máncora
Surfing on this coast is best Nov-March; boards and suits can be hired from several places on Av Piura, US$10 per day. Many agencies on Av Piura offer day trips to Manglares de Tumbes, as well as private transport in cars and vans.
Iguanas Trips, *Av Piura 306, T073-632762, www. iguanastrips.com*. Run by Ursula Behr, offers a variety of adventure tourism trips, horseriding and camping in the nearby national parks and reserve zones.
Samana Chakra, *in the eponymous hotel, T073-258604, www.samanachakra.com*. Yoga classes, US$5 per hr.
Surf Point Máncora, *on the beach next to Hostal del Wawa*. Surf lessons US$17.50 per hr, kitesurfing (season Mar-Sep) US$50 per hr. Surfboard, bodyboard and paddle-board rentals.

Transport

Sullana
Bus The long distance Terminal Terrestre is outside the centre; always take a taxi or mototaxi. To **Tumbes**, 244 km, 4-5 hrs, US$8, several buses daily. To **Chiclayo** and **Trujillo** (see under Piura). To **Lima**, 1076 km, 14-16 hrs, several buses daily, most coming from Tumbes, luxury overnight via Trujillo with **Ittsa** (T073-503705), also with **Ormeño** and **Tepsa** (José de Lama 236, T073-502120). To **Máncora**, **Eppo** (from its own terminal), frequent, 2½ hrs, US$4.50. To **Piura**, from **Terminal Gechisa**, José de La Mar, in the centre, US$0.50, 30 mins.

To the international bridge at **La Tina** (see page 1333), shared taxis leave when full from the Terminal Terrestre La Capullana, off Av Buenos Aires, several blocks beyond the canal, US$5.40 pp, 1¾ hrs. Once on the Ecuador side, buses leave frequently from Macará for Loja, so even if you are not taking the through bus (see Piura, page 1329), you can still go from Sullana to Loja in a day.

Máncora
Bus To **Sullana** with **Eppo**, every 30 mins, 0400-1830, US$3.50, 2½ hrs; continue to **Piura**, US$6, 3 hrs; also *colectivos* to Piura, 2 hrs, US$11. To **Tumbes** (and points in between), vans and *colectivos* leave when full, US$3.50, 1½ hrs. Several companies to **Lima**, US$28-70, 18 hrs. To **Chiclayo**, Tran Chiclayo, US$17.50, 6 hrs. To **Trujillo**, US$25, 9 hrs.

To **Ecuador** To **Machala** (US$14, 5 hrs) and **Guayaquil** (US$17.50, 8 hrs), with **CIFA** and **Supe Semería** at 0800, 1100 and 1300; Guayaquil direct at 2300 and 2330; several others, see Piura Transport. To **Cuenca**, **Super Semería** at 2300, US$20; or **Azuay** at 2330.

Punta Sal
Taking a taxi from Máncora to Punta Sal is the safest option, 20 mins, US$14; mototaxi 40 mins, US$10.

Tumbes
Air Daily flights to and from **Lima** with **LATAM** (Bolognesi 250).

Bus Daily to and from **Lima**, 1320 km, 18-20 hrs depending on stopovers, US$34-45 regular fare, or US$60 with **Cruz del Sur VIP** (Tumbes Norte 319, T072-896163). **Civa** (Av Tumbes 518, T072-525120) has several buses daily. Cheaper buses usually leave 1600-2100, more expensive ones 1200-1400. Except for the luxury service, most buses to Lima stop at major cities en route. Tickets to anywhere between Tumbes and Lima sell quickly, so if arriving from Ecuador you may have to stay overnight. Piura is a good place for connections in the daytime.

To **Sullana**, 244 km, 3-4 hrs, US$8, several buses daily. To **Piura**, 4-5 hrs, 282 km, US$7-8.50, with **El Dorado** (Piura 459, T072-523480) every 1-2 hrs; **Trans Chiclayo** (Tumbes 466, T072-525260) and **Cruz del Sur**. *Colectivos* **Tumbes/Piura** (Tumbes N 308, T072-525977) are a faster option, 3½ hrs, US$12 pp, leave when full. To **Chiclayo**, 552 km, 7-8 hrs, US$9, several each day with **Cruz del Sur**, **El Dorado** and others. To **Trujillo**, 769 km, 10-11 hrs, from US$15, with **Ormeño** (Av Tumbes s/n, T072-522228), **Cruz del Sur**, **El Dorado**, **Emtrafesa** (Tumbes Norte 596, T072-522894).

To **Ecuador** **CIFA** (Av Tumbes 958) runs to **Machala**, US$4, and **Guayaquil**, 5 hrs, 4 a day, luxury bus at 1000, US$8.50. For other options, see Piura Transport (page 1333). If you cannot cross on an international bus (the preferred option), then take a taxi from Tumbes to the new international bridge and border complex beyond Aguas Verdes, 17 km, US$12, and from there to **Huaquillas** across the border, US$2.50-5. See Border with Ecuador, page 1334.

Northern
highlands

Leaving the Pacific coast behind, you climb in a relatively short time up to the Sierra. It was here, at Cajamarca, that the defeat of the Incas by the Spaniards began, bringing about cataclysmic change to this part of the world. But, unlike this well-documented event, the history of the Incas' contemporaries and predecessors has to be teased out of the stones of their temples and fortresses, which are shrouded in cloud in the 'Eyebrow of the Jungle'.

Trujillo to Cajamarca

don't miss the extensive ruins at Marca Huamachuco

The main route from the coast to Cajamarca is via Ciudad de Dios, a junction some 20 km north of Pacasmayo (see page 1313) on the Panamericana. The 175-km paved road branches off the highway soon after it crosses the Río Jequetepeque. Terraced rice fields and mimosas may often be seen in bloom, brightening the otherwise dusty landscape. The old road (now paved) via Huamachuco and Cajabamba is longer and higher but more interesting, passing over the bare puna before dropping to the Huamachuco valley.

Huamachuco and around *Colour map 3, B2.*

This colonial town is located at 3180 m, 181 km from Trujillo. It was on the royal Inca Road and has the largest main plaza in Peru, with fine topiary and a controversial modern **cathedral**. On Sundays there is a colourful **market**, with dancing in the plaza. **Museo Municipal Wamachuko** ① *Sucre 195, Mon-Sat 0900-1300, 1500-1900, Sun 0900-1200, free*, displays artefacts found at nearby **Cerro Amaru** and **Marca Huamachuco** (see below). The extensive Huari ruins of **Wiracochapampa** are 3 km north of town (45 minutes' walk), but much of the site is overgrown. There are good thermal baths at **El Edén** with several open air pools, 45 minutes by combi via Sausacocha.

☆**Marca Huamachuco** ① *Access along a poor road, off the road to Sanagorán, 5 km from Huamachuco (there is an archway at the turn-off). Daily 0900-1700; a minimum of 2 hrs is needed, or 4 hrs to really explore. US$1. Carry all food and drink with you. Mototaxi from Huamachuco to the turn-off, US$2, or combi to Sanagorán.* These hilltop pre-Inca fortifications rank in the top 10 archaeological sites in Peru. They are 3 km long, dating back to at least 300 BC though many structures were added later. Its most impressive features are: El Castillo, a remarkable circular structure with walls up to 8 m high located at the highest point of the site, and El Convento complex, five circular structures of varying sizes towards the northern end of the hill. The largest one has been partially reconstructed.

Cajabamba

Cajabamba is a small market town and a useful stop-over point between Huamachuco and Cajamarca (places to eat include **Cafetería La Otuscana**, Grau 929, and **Don Lucho**, L Prado 227). A thermal bath complex, **La Grama**, is 30 minutes by combi (US$1) from Cajabamba, with a pool, very hot individual baths and an adjoining small *hostal*.

Best for
Archaeology ■ Birdlife ■ Trekking ■ Waterfalls

Where to stay

Huamachuco

$$ Real
Bolívar 250, T044-441402,
www.hotelrealhuamachuco.com.
Modern, sauna, majority of fittings are
wood, pleasant with good service.

$$ Santa María
Grau 224, T044-348334.
An enormous, sparsely furnished edifice offering
the best-quality rooms in town, with restaurant.

$$-$ Hostal Santa Fe
San Martín 297, T044-441019,
www.actiweb.es/luisnv83/.
Good value, hot water, parking, restaurant.

$ Hostal Huamachuco
Castilla 354, on the plaza, T044-440599.
With private or shared hot showers, small rooms
but large common areas, good value, has parking.

Cajabamba

$ Hostal Flores
Leoncio Prado 137, Plaza de Armas, T076-551086.
With electric shower, cheaper without bath, clean
but rooms are gloomy, nice patio; no breakfast.

Restaurants

Huamachuco

$$-$ Bull Grill
R Castilla 364.
Smart place specializing in meat dishes,
with a cool bar at the back.

$ Café Somos
Bolognesi 665.
Good coffee, large turkey/ham sandwiches and
excellent cakes.

$ Doña Emilia
Balta 384, on Plaza de Armas.
Good for breakfast and snacks.

$ El Viejo Molino
R Castilla 160.
Specializes in local cuisine, such as *cuy* (guinea pig).

Festivals

Huamachuco

1st weekend of Aug El Chaku, in which vicuñas
in the area are rounded up and shorn.
14 Aug Founding of Huamachuco, celebrated
for many days before and after the date.
Spectacular fireworks and amazing, aggressive
male dancers called *turcos*, bull-fighting in one
of the largest rings in Perú.

Transport

Huamachuco

Bus To/from **Trujillo**, 170 km, 5-6 hrs, US$9-15
(see page 1308): the best service is **Fuentes**
(best – J Balta 1090, Huamachuco, T044-441090
and Av R Palma 767, Trujillo, T044-204581); **Tunesa**
(Suárez 721, T044-441157). To **Cajabamba**, with
Trans Los Andes (Pje Hospital 109), 3 combis a
day, 2 hrs, US$7.50.

Cajabamba

Bus Several companies run buses and combis to
Cajamarca, 127 km, US$7.50-8, 3 hrs.

Cajamarca and around *Colour map 3, B2.*

follow in Atahualpa's fateful footsteps

Cajamarca is an attractive colonial town surrounded by lovely countryside. It was here in 1532
that Pizarro ambushed and captured Atahualpa, the Inca emperor. This was the first showdown
between the Spanish and the Incas and, despite being greatly outnumbered, the Spanish
emerged victorious. Change has come fast to Cajamarca: the nearby Yanacocha gold mine (www.
yanacocha.com.pe) has brought new wealth to the town but also major ecological disruption and
social problems. The city is also the hub of tourism development for the whole Circuito Turístico
Nororiental, which encompasses Chiclayo, Cajamarca and Chachapoyas.

City centre

The **Plaza de Armas**, where Atahualpa was executed, has a 350-year-old fountain, topiary and gardens. The **Cathedral** ① *daily 0800-1000, 1600-1800*, opened in 1776 and is still missing its belfry, but the façade has beautiful baroque carving in stone. On the opposite side of the plaza is the 17th-century church of **San Francisco** ① *Mon-Fri 0900-1200, 1600-1800*, older than the Cathedral and with more interior stone carving and elaborate altars. The attached **Museo de Arte Colonial** ① *entrance is behind the church on Amalia Puga y Belén, Mon-Sat 1430-1800, US$1*, is filled with colonial paintings and icons. The guided tour of the museum includes entry to the church's spooky catacombs.

The group of buildings known as **Complejo Belén** ① *Tue-Sat 0900-1300, 1500-1800, Sun 0900-1300. US$5 (valid for more than 1 day and for the Cuarto de Rescate; see below), guided tour for all the sites, US$2.85-8.50*, comprises the tourist office and Institute of Culture, two museums and the beautifully ornate church of Belén, considered the city's finest. The arches, pillars and walls of the nave are covered in lozenges (*rombos*), a design picked out in the gold tracery of the altar. Look up to see the inside of the dome, where eight giant cherubs support an intricate flowering centrepiece. The carved pulpit has a spiral staircase and the doors are intricately worked in wood. In the same courtyard is the **Museo Médico Belén**, which has a collection of medical instruments. Across the street on Junín and Belén is a maternity hospital from the colonial era, now the **Archaeological and Ethnological Museum**. It has a range of ceramics from all regions and civilizations of Peru.

To the east, the **Cuarto de Rescate (Ransom Chamber)** ① *entrance at Amalia Puga 750, Tue-Sat 0900-1800, Sun 0900-1300*, is the room where Atahualpa was held prisoner. A red line on the wall is

Cajamarca

Where to stay

1 Cajamarca
2 Costa del Sol Wyndham
3 El Cabildo
4 El Cumbe Inn
5 El Ingenio
6 El Portal del Marqués
7 Hosp Los Jazmines
8 Hostal Becerra
9 Hostal Perú
10 La Casona del Inca
11 Los Balcones de La Recoleta

Restaurants

1 Bella's Café Lounge
2 Casa Club
3 Cascanuez
4 De Buena Laya
5 Don Paco
6 El Pez Loco
7 El Zarco
8 Heladería Holanda
9 Om-Gri
10 Pascana
11 Pizzería El Marengo
12 Pizzería Vaca Loca
13 Querubino
14 Salas
15 Sanguchón.com

said to indicate where Atahualpa reached up and drew a mark, agreeing to have his subjects fill the room to that height, once with gold and twice with silver.

You can also visit the stone altar set high on **Santa Apolonia hill** ① *US$0.60, take bus marked Santa Apolonia/Fonavi, or micro A,* from where Atahualpa is said to have surveyed his subjects. There is a road to the top, or you can walk up from Calle 2 de Mayo, using the steep stairway. The view is worth the effort, especially at sunrise (but go in a group).

Around the city centre are many fine old houses, with garden patios and 104 elaborately carved doorways. Look out for the **Bishop's Palace**, across the street from the Cathedral; the **palace of the Condes de Uceda**, at Jr Apurímac 719 (now occupied by BCP bank, photography prohibited); and the **Casa Silva Santiesteban** (Junín y 2 de Mayo).

The Universidad Nacional de Cajamarca maintains an experimental arboretum and agricultural station, the **Museo Silvo-agropecuario** ① *Km 2.5 on the road to Baños del Inca,* with a lovely mural at the entrance.

Around Cajamarca

☆**Los Baños del Inca** ① *6 km from Cajamarca. Daily 0500-2000, T076-348385, www.ctbinca.com.pe, entry US$0.70, baths US$1.75-2.10, sauna US$3.50, massage US$7. Combis marked Baños del Inca cost US$0.20, 15 mins; taxis US$2.30.* These sulphurous thermal springs are where Atahualpa bathed to try to cure a festering war wound; his bath is still there. The water temperature is at least 72° C, and the main baths are divided into five categories, all with private tubs and no pool (take your own towel; soaps are sold outside); many of the facilities are open to men- or women-only at certain times. Obey the instructions and only spend 20 minutes maximum in the water. The complex is renewed regularly, with gardens and various levels of accommodation (see Where to stay, below). A nice 13-km walk downhill from the Baños del Inca will bring you **Llacanora** after two hours, a typical Andean village in beautiful scenery.

Ventanillas Head north from the baños to the **Ventanillas de Otusco** ① *8 km from Cajamarca, daily 0800-1800, US$1.10, combi US$0.20,* part of an old pre-Inca cemetery that has a deteriorating gallery of secondary burial niches. There are good day walks in this area and local sketch maps are available. From Otusco, a road leads 20 km to **Ventanillas de Combayo** ① *occasional combis on Mon-Sat; more transport on Sun when a market is held nearby, 1 hr.* These burial niches are more numerous and spectacular than those at Otusco, being located in an isolated, mountainous area and distributed over the face of a steep, 200-m-high hillside.

Cumbe Mayo This site, 20 km southwest of Cajamarca, is famous for its extraordinary, well-engineered pre-Inca channels, running for 9 km across the mountain tops at 3600 m. This hydraulic irrigation system is said to be the oldest man-made construction in South America. The sheer scale of the scene is impressive, backed by the huge rock formations known as Los Frailones ('big monks') and others. On the way to Cumbe Mayo is the Layzón ceremonial centre. It is possible to walk from Cajamarca to Cumbe Mayo in three to four hours, although you're advised to take a guide or join a tour group. The trail starts from the hill of Santa Apolonia (see above) and goes straight through the village and up the hill. At the top of the mountain, leave the trail and take the road to the right to reach the canal. The walk is not difficult and you do not need hiking boots, but it is cold (best weather May to September). Take warm clothing and a good torch. The locals use the trail to bring their goods to market. There is no bus service to Cumbe Mayo; taxi US$15. Guided tours run from 0830 to 1400 and are recommended in order to see all the pre-Inca sites.

Porcón The rural cooperative, with its evangelical faith expressed on billboards, is a popular excursion, 30 km northwest of Cajamarca. It is a tightly organized community, with carpentry, bakery, cheese and yoghurt-making, zoo and vicuñas. A good guide helps to explain everything. If you're not taking a tour, contact **Cooperativa Agraria Atahualpa Jerusalén** ① *Chanchamayo 1355, Fonavi 1, T076-825631.* At Km 8 along the road to Porcón is **Huambocancha**, a town specializing in stone sculptures. Combis run from Cajamarca market, US$0.75, 30 minutes.

Kuntur Wasi ① *21 km north of Chilete, site museum in San Pablo US$1.75, ruins US$2.50.* Some 93 km west of Cajamarca is the mining town of Chilete, near which is **Kuntur Wasi**, a site devoted to a feline cult. It consists of a pyramid and stone monoliths. There are two basic *hostales* in Chilete.

Tourist information

Information is available from: **iPerú** (Jr Cruz de Piedra 601, T076-365166, iperucajamarca@ promperu.gob.pe, Mon-Sat 0900-1800, Sun 0900-1300); **Dirección Regional de Turismo** and **Ministerio de Cultura**, in the Conjunto Monumental de Belén (Belén 631, T076-362601, Mon-Fri 0900-1300, 1500-1730), and the **Sub-Gerencia de Turismo** (Av Alameda de los Incas, Complejo Qhapac Ñan, opposite UNC university on the road to Baños del Inca, T076-363626, www.municaj.gob.pe). The **University tourist school** (Del Batán 289, T076-361546, Mon-Fri 0830-1300, 1500-2200) also offers free advice and leaflets.

Where to stay

$$$$ Costa del Sol Wyndham
Cruz de Piedra 707, T076-362472,
www.costadelsolperu.com.
On the Plaza de Armas, part of a Peruvian chain, with airport transfer, welcome drink; restaurant, café and bars, pool, spa, casino, business centre.

$$$ El Ingenio
Av Vía de Evitamiento 1611-1709,
T076-368733, www.elingenio.com.
Colonial style buildings 1½ blocks from El Quinde shopping mall. With restaurant, solar-powered hot water, spacious, quiet and relaxed, generous breakfast.

$$ Cajamarca
Dos de Mayo 311, T076-362532,
hotelcajamarca@gmail.com.
3-star in beautiful colonial mansion, sizeable rooms, hot water, food excellent in **Los Faroles** restaurant.

$$ El Cabildo
Junín 1062, T076-367025.
Includes breakfast, in historic monument with patio and modern fountain, full of character, elegant local decorations, comfortable, breakfast served.

$$ El Cumbe Inn
Pasaje Atahualpa 345, T076-366858,
www.elcumbeinn.com.
Includes breakfast and tax, comfortable, variety of rooms, hot water, evening meals on request, small gym, will arrange taxis, very helpful.

$$ El Portal del Marqués
Del Comercio 644, T076-368464,
www.portaldelmarques.com.
Attractive converted colonial house, laundry, safe, parking, leased restaurant **El Mesón del Marqués** has good lunch *menú*. Casino with slot machines.

$$ La Casona del Inca
2 de Mayo 458-460, Plaza de Armas, T076-367524,
www.casonadelinca.pe/turismo.html.
Upstairs, old building, traditional style, some rooms overlooking plaza, some with interior windows, good beds, breakfast in café on top floor, tours, laundry.

$$ Los Balcones de la Recoleta
Amalia Puga 1050, T076-363302,
http://hostalbalcones.jimdo.com.
Beautifully restored 19th-century house, central courtyard full of flowers, some rooms with period furniture, internet.

$ Hospedaje Los Jazmines
Amazonas 775, T076-361812, www.
hospedajelosjazmines.com.pe.
In a converted colonial house with courtyard and café, 14 rooms with hot water, all profits go to disabled children, guests can visit the project's school and help.

$ Hostal Becerra
Del Batán 195, T076-367867.
With hot water, modern, pleasant, will store luggage until late buses depart.

$ Hostal Perú
Amalia Puga 605, on Plaza, T076-365568.
With hot water, functional rooms in old building around central patio used by **El Zarco** restaurant, wooden floors, credit cards taken.

Los Baños del Inca

$$$$-$$$ Laguna Seca
Av Manco Cápac 1098, T076-584300,
www.lagunaseca.com.pe.
In pleasant surroundings with thermal streams, private hot thermal baths in rooms, swimming pool with thermal water, restaurant, bar, health spa with a variety of treatments, disco, horses for hire.

$$$ Hacienda Hotel San Antonio
2 km off the Baños road (turn off at Km 5),
T076-348237, Facebook: Hacienda-Hotel-
San-Antonio-258452027710.

An old *hacienda*, wonderfully restored, with open fireplaces and gardens, 15 mins walk along the river to Baños del Inca, riding on *caballos de paso*, own dairy produce, fruit and vegetables, catch your own trout for supper; try the *licor de sauco*.

\$\$-\$ Los Baños del Inca
See above, T076-348385.
Various accommodation: bungalows for 2 to 4 with thermal water, fridge; **Albergue Juvenil**, not IYFH, hostel rooms with bunk beds or double rooms, private bath, caters to groups, basic. Camping possible. Restaurant offers full board.

Restaurants

\$\$\$ Pascana
Av Atahualpa 947.
Well-known and recommended as the best in town, near the Qhapac Ñan Municipality. Their **Taberna del Diablo** is the top disco in town.

\$\$\$ Querubino
Amalia Puga 589, T076-340900.
Mediterranean-style decoration, a bit of everything on the menu, including pastas, daily specials, breakfasts, cocktails, coffees, expensive wines otherwise reasonable, popular.

\$\$ Casa Club
Amalia Puga 458-A, T076-340198.
Daily 0800-2300.
Menú, including vegetarian, and extensive selection à la carte, family atmosphere, slow but attentive service.

\$\$ Don Paco
Amalia Puga 390, T076-362655.
Opposite San Francisco. Typical, including *Novo Andino*, and international dishes, tasty food, desserts, drinks.

\$\$ El Pez Loco
San Martín 333.
Recommended for fish dishes.

\$\$ Om-Gri
San Martín 360, near the Plaza de Armas.
Opens 1300 (1830 Sun).
Good Italian dishes, small, informal, French spoken.

\$\$ Pizzería El Marengo
Junín 1201.
Good pizzas and warm atmosphere, T368045 for delivery.

\$\$ Salas
Amalia Puga 637, on the main plaza, T076-362867. Open 0800-2200.
A Cajamarca tradition: fast, attentive service, excellent local food (try their *cuy frito*), best *tamales* in town, very popular.

\$\$-\$ De Buena Laya
2 de Mayo 343.
With a rustic interior, popular with *hostales*, offers Novo Cajamarquino cuisine; lunchtime menú US\$3.50.

\$\$-\$ El Zarco
Jr Del Batán 170, T076-363421. Sun-Fri 0700-2300.
Breakfast, good vegetarian dishes, excellent fish, also has short *chifa* menu, very popular.

\$ Pizzería Vaca Loca
San Martín 330.
Popular, best pizzas in town.

Cafés

Bella's Café Lounge
Junín 1184, T076-345794.
For breakfasts, sandwiches, great desserts and coffee from Chanchamayo, Wi-Fi, a place to linger, check emails and relax, owner Raul speaks English. Popular with visitors to the city.

Cascanuez
Amalia Puga 554.
Great cakes, extensive menu including *humitas*, breakfasts, ice creams and coffees, highly regarded.

Heladería Holanda
Amalia Puga 657 on the Plaza de Armas, T076-340113.
Dutch-owned, easily the best ice creams in Cajamarca, 50 flavours (but not all on at the same time); try *poro poro*, *lúcuma* or *sauco*, also serves coffee. Four branches, including at Baños del Inca. Ask if it is possible to visit their factory.

Sanguchón.com
Junín 1137.
Best burgers in town, sandwiches, also popular bar.

Festivals

Feb Carnaval. Cajamarca's pre-Lent festivities are spectacular and regarded as among the best, if the most raucous, in the country.
Mar Palm Sun. The processions in Porcón, 16 km to the northwest, are worth seeing.
24 Jun San Juan in Cajamarca, Chota, Llacanora, San Juan and Cuturvo. Jul Agricultural fair is held at Baños del Inca

Oct Festival Folklórico in Cajamarca on the 1st Sun.

Shopping

Handicrafts
Specialities including gilded mirrors and cotton and wool saddlebags (*alforjas*). Items can be made to order. The **Mercado Central** at Amazonas y Apurímac is colourful and worth a visit for *artesanía*. There are also stalls at the Belén complex (Belén and/or 2 de Mayo) and along the steps up to Santa Apolonia hill. Other options for a good range of local crafts are the **Feria Artesenal** (Jr El Comercio 1045, next to the police office) and **El Molino** (2 de Mayo).

What to do

Agencies around the Plaza de Armas offer trips to local sites and further afield, trekking on Inca trails, riding *caballos de paso* and handicraft tours. Approximate prices: Cumbe Mayo, US$6.50-8.50, 4-5 hrs at 0930; Porcón, US$6.50-8.50, 4-5 hrs at 0930; Otusco, US$4.50-7, 3-3½ hrs at 1530; city tour, US$7, 3 hrs at 0930 or 1530. Kuntur Wasi is a full day trip. There are also 2 day/3 night tours to Kuélap and Cutervo National Park.

Cumbemayo Tours, *Amalia Puga 635 on the plaza, T076-362938*. Standards tours, guides speak English and French.
Mega Tours, *Amalia Puga 691 on the plaza, T076-341876, www.megatours.org*. Conventional tours, full day and further afield, ecotourism and adventures.

Air The airport is 5 km from town; taxi US$8. There are flights to/from **Lima**, with **LC Peru** (Comercio 1024, T076-361098), Sun-Fri, and **LATAM** (Cruz de Piedra 657).

Bus Buses in town charge US$0.35. Bus companies have their own ticket offices and terminals; many are on Av Atahualpa blocks 2-6, a 20-min walk from the Plaza de Armas.

To **Lima**, 870 km, 12-14 hrs, US$27-53, many daily with **Civa** (Ayacucho 753, T076-361460), **Cruz del Sur** (Atahualpa 606, T076-361737) and **Línea** (Atahualpa 318, T076-363956), **Móvil** (Atahualpa 405, T076-340873), **Tepsa** (Sucre y Reina Forje, T076-363306) and **Turismo Días** (Av Evitamiento s/n, T076-344322), including several luxury services.

To **Trujillo**, 295 km, 7 hrs, US$10-27, regular buses daily 0900-2230, with **Emtrafesa** (Atahualpa 315, T076-369663), **Línea** and **Turismo Días**; most continue to Lima via Chimbote. To **Chiclayo**, 265 km, 6 hrs, US$9-20, several buses daily with **Línea** and **Turismo Días**; change here for Piura and Tumbes. To **Celendín**, 107 km, 3½ hrs, US$6, usually 2 a day with **CABA** (Atahualpa 299, T076-366665), **Royal Palace's** (Reina Forje 130, T076-343063) and **Rojas** (Atahualpa 309, T076-340548). To **Chachapoyas**, 336 km, 11-12 hrs, US$18, with **Virgen del Carmen** (Atahualpa 333A, T983-915869), at 0500, via **Leymebamba**, US$11.55, 9-10 hrs; paved road through beautiful countryside.

Taxi US$2 within city limits. Mototaxis, US$0.75. Radio taxi: **El Sol**, T076-368897, 24 hrs; **Taxi Super Seguro**, T076-507090.

Chachapoyas region

uncover the mysteries of a once-mighty empire

★Cajamarca is a convenient starting point for the trip east to the department of Amazonas, which contains the archaeological riches of the Chachapoyans. Here lie the great pre-Inca cities of Vilaya (not yet developed for tourism) and the immense citadel of Kuélap, among many others. It is also an area of great natural beauty with waterfalls, notably Gocta, cliffs and caves. The road is paved but prone to landslides in the rainy season. It follows a winding course through the mountains, crossing the wide and deep canyon of the Río Marañón at Balsas. The road climbs steeply with superb views of the mountains and the valleys below. The fauna and flora are spectacular as the journey alternates between high mountains and low forest.

Celendín *Colour map 3, B2.*

East from Cajamarca, this is the first town of note, with a pleasant plaza and cathedral that is predominantly blue. The fascinating local market on Sunday is held in three distinct areas. From 0630 till 0730 there's a **hat market** by the

Tip...
The **Multired** ATM beside the **Banco de la Nación** on 2 de Mayo in Celendín may not accept all foreign cards; take cash.

Alameda, between Ayacucho and 2 de Mayo at Jorge Chávez, at which you can see hats at every stage of production. Then, at 0930 the **potato market** takes place at 2 de Mayo y Sucre, and, at the other end of town, there's a **livestock market** on Túpac Amaru. The Virgen del Carmen festival takes place from 16 July to 3 August. The most popular local excursion is to the hot springs and mud baths at **Llanguat**, 20 km away (US$2.75 by limited public transport).

Leymebamba and around *Colour map 3, B2.*

There are plenty of ruins – many of them covered in vegetation – and good walking possibilities around this pleasant town at the source of the Utcubamba River. **La Congona**, a Chachapoyan site, is well worth the effort, with stupendous views. It consists of three hills: on the vegetation-covered conical hill in the middle, the ruins are clustered in a small area, impossible to see until you are right there. The other hills have been levelled. La Congona is the best preserved of three sites in this area, with 30 round stone houses (some with evidence of three storeys) and a watch tower. The two other sites, **El Molinete** and **Cataneo**, are nearby. All three sites can be visited in a day but a guide is advisable. It is a brisk three hours' walk from Leymebamba, first along the rough road to Fila San Cristóbal, then a large trail. The road starts at the bottom of Jr 16 de Julio.

In 1996 six burial chullpas were discovered at **Laguna de los Cóndores**, a spectacular site in a lush cloudforest setting. The chullpas contained 219 mummies and vast quantities of ceramics, textiles, woodwork, quipus and everyday utensils from the late Inca period, now housed in the excellent ☆ **Museo Leymebamba** ① *outside San Miguel, on the road to Celendin, T041-816803, www.museoleymebamba.org, daily 0800-1700, entry US$5.75.* It is beautifully laid-out and very informative, and the collection of mummies and quipus is superb. To get there from Leymebamba, walk to the village of 2 de Mayo, ask for the trail to San Miguel, then take the footpath uphill; the road route is much longer (taxi from Leymebamba US$2.75, mototaxi US$2).

It is also possible to visit Laguna de los Cóndores itself; the trip takes 10 to 12 hours on foot and horseback from Leymebamba. An all-inclusive tour for the three-day muddy trek can be arranged at Leymebamba hotels (ask for Sinecio or Javier Farge) or with Chachapoyas operators, US$70 per person.

Around Yerbabuena

The road to Chachapoyas follows the Utcubamba River north. In the mountains rising from the river at **Yerbabuena** (important Sunday market, basic *hospedaje*) are a number of archaeological sites. Before Yerbabuena, a road heads east to **Montevideo** (basic hospedaje) and beyond to the small village of **San Pedro de Utac**, where you can hike up to the impressive but overgrown ruins of Cerro Olán.

On the other side of the river, west of Yerbabuena, are burial chullpas from the Revash culture (AD 1250), entry US$3. They are reached from either **San Bartolo** (30-45 minutes' walk, horses can be rented) or along a trail starting past **Puente Santo Tomás** (1½ to two hours' walk).

The town of **Jalca Grande** (or La Jalca), at 2800 m, is reached along a road going east at **Ubilón**, north of Yerbabuena. Jalca Grande has the remains of a Chachapoyan roundhouse, a stone church tower, a small **museum** with ceramics and textiles, and one very basic *hospedaje*.

Tingo to Kuélap *Colour map 3, B2.*

Situated at the junction of the Tingo and Utcubamba rivers, 40 km north of Leymebamba and 37 km south of Chachapoyas, Tingo (altitude 1800 m) is the access point for Kuélap. A road climbs steeply from Tingo to Nuevo Tingo and Choctámal, where it divides. The right branch provides access to the southern part of Gran Vilaya; the left branch climbs east to Lónguita, María, Quizango and Kuélap. It is also possible to walk to Kuélap from María (two to 2½ hours), Choctámal (four to five hours) and Tingo, although this last is a strenuous, five-hour uphill slog and only fit hikers should try to ascend and descend in one day on foot. Take waterproofs, food and drink, and start early as it gets very hot. In the rainy season it is advisable to wear boots; at other times it is hot and dry. Take all your water with you as there is nothing on the way up. See also Transport, page 1353. A **cable car** ① *US$5.75 pp including bus from car park at ticket office to cable car station every 10 mins 0900-1350, last bus down 1655, 10 mins. There may be queues for the first buses,* from Nuevo Tingo to Kuélap began operating in 2017, taking riders across the valley in 20 minutes.

☆Kuélap

Daily 0800-1700. US$6, guides available for US$9 per group (Rigoberto Vargas Silva has been recommended). The ticket office at the car park has a small but informative Sala de Interpretación.

Kuélap is a spectacular pre-Inca walled city at 3000 m which was re-discovered in 1843. It was built continuously from AD 500 up to Inca times and is said to contain three times more stone than the Great Pyramid at Giza in Egypt. The site lies along the summit of a mountain crest, more than 1 km in length. The massive stone walls, 585 m long by 110 m wide at their widest, are as formidable as those of any pre-Columbian city. Some reconstruction has taken place, mostly of small houses and walls, but the majority of the main walls on all levels are original, as is the inverted, cone-shaped main temple. The structures have been left in their cloudforest setting, the trees covered in bromeliads and moss, the flowers visited by hummingbirds.

Chachapoyas *Colour map 3, B2.*

The capital of the Amazonas Region was founded in 1538 and retains its colonial character. The city's importance as a crossroads between the coast and jungle began to decline in the late 1940s, but

Chachapoyas

Where to stay 🛏
1 Aventura Backpackers Lodge *A1*
2 Belén *A1*
3 Casona Monsante *B2*
4 Casona Revash *B2*
5 Chachapoyas Backpackers *B2*
6 El Dorado *A1*
7 La Casona de Chachapoyas *A1*
8 Las Orquídeas *A1*
9 Posada del Arriero *B1*
10 Puma Urco *B2*
11 Rumi Huasi *A2*
12 Vista Hermosa *A1*
13 Xalca *B1*

Restaurants 🍴
1 Amazonas 632 *B2*
2 Batán del Tayta *B2*
3 Chacha Restaurante *B2*
4 Dulcería Santa Elena *B2*
5 El Edén *A2*
6 El Tejado *A1*
7 Fusiones *A1*
8 Heladería San Antonio *B2*
9 La Candela *B2*
10 La Tushpa *B1*
11 Panadería Café San José *B2*
12 Paraíso de las Pizzas *A1*

Transport 🚌
1 Civa *A2*
2 GH Bus *A3*
3 Móvil Tours *B3*
4 Star Bus & Transervis Kuelap *B3*

archaeological and ecological tourism have grown gradually since the 1990s and have brought increasing economic benefits to the region.

The cathedral, with a lovely modern interior, stands on the spacious Plaza de Armas. **Ministerio de Cultura Museum** ① *Ayacucho 904, T041-477045, Mon-Fri 0800-1300, 1500-1700, free*, contains a small collection of artefacts and mummies, with explanations in Spanish. The **Museo Santa Ana** ① *Jr Santa Ana 1054, T041-790988, Mon-Fri 0900-1700, US$2*, has colonial religious art and prehispanic ceramics and textiles. Jr Amazonas, pedestrianized from the Plaza de Armas uphill to Plaza Burgos, makes a pleasant stroll.

Around Chachapoyas

Huancas ① *Autos leave from the terminal and from the corner of Av Aeropuerto and Evitamiento in Chachapoays, daily 0600-1800, 20 mins, US$1.15, or 2-hr walk*. Huancas is a small village to the north of Chacha where rustic pottery is produced. Walk uphill from the plaza to the **mirador** ① *1 km, US$0.70*, for magnificent views into the deep canyon of the Río Sonche, with tumbling waterfalls. There are crafts on sale here. At **Huanca Urco**, 5 km from Huancas, past the large prison complex, are ruins, remains of an Inca road and another mirador with fine views to Gocta waterfall in the distance.

Levanto Due south of Chachapoyas, Levanto was built by the Spaniards in 1538, directly on top of the previous Chachapoyan structures, as their first capital of the area. Nowadays Levanto is an unspoilt colonial village overlooking the massive canyon of the Utcubamba River. On a clear day, Kuélap can be seen on the other side of the rift. A 30-minute walk from Levanto towards Chachapoyas will bring you to the overgrown ruins of **Yalape**, which seems to have been a massive residential complex, extending over many hectares. Local people can guide you to the ruins.

Mendoza and around

A paved road heads east from Chachapoyas, reaching Mendoza after 2½ hours. The town is the centre of the coffee-producing region of Rodríguez de Mendoza. Close by are the caves at Omia, the Tocuya thermal baths, Mirador Wimba and the Santa Natalia waterfall. Also of interest is the Guayabamba Valley, where there is an unusually high incidence of fair-skinned people. It is a worthwhile four-hour hike from Mendoza to Huamanpata, a very pretty valley surrounded by forest; there's a lake here in the wet season, but this reduces down to a river in drier months. Robert Cabrerra (T949-305401) has cabins and camping, and he offers two-day tours from US$35 per person; contact him well in advance.

> **Tip...**
> South of the road from Chachapoyas to **Mendoza**, in the district of Soloco, is **Parjugsha**, Peru's largest cave complex, about 300 m deep and with some 20 km of galleries (10 km have been explored and connected). Spelunking experience is essential.

Lamud and around

At Km 37 on the Chachapoyas–Pedro Ruiz road an unpaved road leads to the village of **Luya** where it divides. One branch goes north to **Lamud**, a convenient base for several interesting sites, such as San Antonio and Pueblo de los Muertos. **EcoMuseo Molino de Piedra San Jose** ① *1 km north of Lamud, daily 0900-1600*, has a fascinating display of traditional rural life with demonstrations of milling, baking, weaving, etc. Also worth visiting is the **Quiocta cave** ① *30 mins by car from Lamud, then a 10-min walk, US$2, 0800-1600, closed Thu*. The cave is 560 m long, 23 m deep, and has four chambers with stalactites and stalagmites and a stream running through it. There are petroglyphs at the mouth, and partly buried human remains. Tours to the cave can be arranged in Chachapoyas or through the Lamud tourist office.

The second road from Luya goes south and west to Cruzpata for access to **Karajía** ① *2½ hrs' walk from Luya or 30 mins from Cruzpata, US$2, take binoculars*, where remarkable, 2.5-m-high sarcophagi are set into an impressive cliff-face overlooking the valley. Other sites nearby include **Chipuric**, 1½ hours' walk from Luya, and **Wanglic**, a funeral site with large circular structures built under a ledge in a lush canyon with a beautiful waterfall nearby: a worthwhile excursion (1½ hours). Ask for directions in Luya, or take a local guide (US$10 a day). The road to Luya and Lamud is unpaved; see Chachapoyas Transport for how to get there.

☆Gocta

…ccess from San Pablo de Valera or Cocachimba. Entry fee US$4, guides (compulsory), US$15 for up to 5 passengers.

…outh of Pedro Ruíz is the spectacular **Gocta waterfall**, …ne of the highest in the world at 771 m. (The upper …aterfall is 231 m; the lower waterfall is 540 m.) From …hachapoyas, take the Pedro Ruiz road for 35 km to …ocahuayco (about 18 km before Pedro Ruiz) where …here are two roads up to Gocta, along either bank …f the Cocahuayco River. The first turn-off leads to …he village of **San Pablo de Valera** at 1934 m (6 km …rom the main road, 20 minutes by car). From here, … is a one- to 1½-hour walk to a mirador, and then …0 to 60 minutes to the base of the upper falls, 6.3 km in total. The second turn-off, 100 m further …long the main road, leads to the village of **Cocachimba** at 1796 m (5.3 km from the main road, …0 minutes). From here, it is a 1½- to 2½-hour walk (5.5 km) to the base of the lower waterfall, of …hich there is an impressive view. Both routes go through about 2 km of lovely forest; the San Pablo …rail is somewhat flatter. A path connecting both banks starts on the San Pablo side at the mirador. …his is a much smaller trail, quite steep and not signposted past the mirador. There is a suspension …ootbridge over the main river before the trail joins the Cocachimba trail about three quarters of the …ay to the base of the lower falls. To see both sides in one day you need to start very early, but this … a great way to get the full experience. Each community offer similar services: horses can be hired …or US$12 (they can only go part of the way); rubber boots and rain ponchos are available for US$1.20 …t is always wet by the falls). The best time to visit is during the dry season from May to September; …n the wet season the falls are more spectacular, but it is cold, rainy and the trails may be slippery.

Several more waterfalls in this area are increasingly accessible, including **Yumbilla**, which … 895 m (124 m higher than Gocta) in eight tiers. For more information about expeditions … Yumbilla, other falls and related projects, see the Florida-based NGO, **Amazon Waterfalls …ssociation** ⓘ *www.amazonwaterfalls.org.*

> **Tip…**
> If you start the hike at San Pablo and finish at Cocachimba, arrange transport to return to San Pablo at the end of the day. Or, if you are staying in Cocachimba, arrange transport to San Pablo to begin the hike. The ride is about 30 minutes.

Listings Chachapoyas region *map p1347*

Tourist information

…hachapoyas

…Perú
…n the Plaza de Armas, T041-477292,
…peruchachapoyas@promperu.gob.pe.
…lon-Sat 0900-1800, Sun 0900-1300.

…lendoza

…or information on the area, ask for Michel
… cardo Feijoó Aguilor in the Mendoza municipal
…ffice, mifeijoo@gmail.com; he can help
…rrange guides and accommodation. A
…ecommended guide is Alfonso Saldana
…elaez, fotoguiaalsape@gmail.com.

…octa

…ommunity tourist information is available in
…oth San Pablo, T041-631163, daily 0800-1730,
…nd Cocachimba, T041-630569, daily 0800-1730.

Where to stay

Celendín

$$-$ Hostal Celendín
Unión 305, Plaza de Armas, T076-555041,
hcgustavosd1@hotmail.com.
Some rooms with plaza view, central patio
and wooden stairs, hot water, pleasant, has
2 restaurants: **Rinconcito Shilico** (2 de Mayo 816),
and **Pollos a la brasa Gusys**.

$ Hostal Imperial
Jr Dos de Mayo 568, 2 blocks from the plaza,
T076-555492.
Large rooms, good mattresses, hot water, Wi-Fi,
parking, decent choice.

$ Loyer's
José Gálvez 410, T076-555210.
Patio with wooden balcony all round, nice,
singles, doubles and family rooms.

$ Maxmar
Dos de Mayo 349, T076-555330.
Cheaper without bath, hot shower extra, basic, parking, good value, owners Francisco and Luis are very helpful.

$ Mi Posada
Pardo 388, next to Atahualpa bus, T074-979-758674.
Includes breakfast, small cheerful rooms, family atmosphere.

$ Raymi Wasi
Jr José Gálvez 420, T976-551133.
With electric shower, cheaper without, large rooms, has patio, quiet, parking, good value, restaurant and karaoke.

Leymebamba and around

$$$$-$$$ Kentitambo
Across the road from Museo Leymebamba, T971-118273, www.kentitambo.com.
Accommodation in 3 comfortable cabins, lovely grounds with hummingbirds, meals made from local produce. **Kentikafe** offers sandwiches, cake, tea and coffee.

$$ La Casona
Jr Amazonas 223, T041-630301, www.casonadeleymebamba.com.
Nicely refurbished old house with balcony, attractive common area, simple rooms with solar hot water, arrange tours and horses.

$$ La Joya Hostal Cafetín
Jr 16 de Julio, T990-168715.
Modern hotel, ample rooms, good café on 1st floor.

$ La Petaca
Jr Amazonas 426, on the plaza, T999-020599.
Good rooms with hot water, breakfast available, café, helpful.

Tingo to Kuelap

$$$ Estancia Chillo
5 km south of Tingo towards Leymebamba, T041-630510/979-340444.
On a 9-ha farm, dinner and breakfast included, with bath, hot water, transport, horse riding. Friendly family, a lovely country retreat.

$$ Choctámal Marvelous Spatuletail Lodge
3 km from Choctámal towards Kuélap at Km 20, T041-941-963327, www.marvelousspatuletail.com.
Book in advance. Heated rooms, hot showers, hot tub, telescope for star-gazing. Meals US$8-10. Offers horse riding and a chance to see the endangered marvellous spatuletail hummingbird

$ Albergue León
Along the south bank of the Río Tingo, just upriver from the highway, T941-715685, hildegardlen@yahoo.es.
Basic, private or shared bath, electric shower, guiding, arrange horses, run by Lucho León who is knowledgeable.

Chachapoyas

$$$ La Casona de Chachapoyas
Chincha Alta 569, T041-477353, www.casaviejaperu.com.
Converted old house with lovely courtyard, very nicely decorated, all rooms different, comfy beds, family atmosphere, good service, living room and *comedor* with open fire, includes breakfast, good café, Wi-Fi and library. Repeatedly recommended

$$$ Xalca
Jr Grau 940, T041-479106, www.laxalcahotel.com.
Built in colonial style with central patio, large comfortable rooms, parking, good service.

$$ Casona Monsante
Amazonas 746, T041-477702, www.casonamonsante.com.
Converted colonial house with patio, orchid garden, comfortable rooms decorated with antiques. Under new dynamic management in 2017.

$$ Las Orquídeas
Ayacucho 1231, T041-478271, www.hostallasorquideas.com.
Converted home, pleasantly decorated rooms, large garden.

$$ Posada del Arriero
Grau 636, T041-478945, www.posadadelarriero.net.
Old house with courtyard nicely refurbished in modern style, although rooms are a bit plain, helpful staff.

$$ Puma Urco
Amazonas 833, T041-477871, www.hotelpumaurco.com.
Comfortable rooms, includes breakfast, TV, frigobar, **Café Café** next door, hotel and café receive good reports, run tours with **Turismo Explorer**.

\$-\$ Casona Revash
Grau 517, Plaza de Armas, T041-477391,
revash9@hotmail.com.
Traditional house with patio, stylish decor,
steaming hot showers, breakfast available,
helpful owners, good local information,
popular. Operate tours and sell local crafts.

\$ Aventura Backpackers Lodge
r Amazonas 1416, T959-555939,
Facebook: AventuraBackpackersLodge.
Dorms with bunk beds, use of kitchen,
good value.

\$ Belén
r Ortiz Arrieta 540, Plaza de Armas, T041-477830,
www.hostalbelen.com.
With hot water, nicely furnished, pleasant sitting
room overlooking the Plaza, good value.

\$ Chachapoyas Backpackers
r Dos de Mayo 639, T041-478879,
www.chachapoyasbackpackers.com.
Simple 2- and 3-bed dorms with shared bath,
electric shower, a good budget option, same
owners as **Turismo Explorer** tour operator.
Lovely family-run place. Recommended.

\$ El Dorado
Ayacucho 1062, T041-477047,
vvanovt@hotmail.com.
With bathroom, electric shower, helpful staff,
a good economical option.

\$ Rumi Huasi
Ortiz Arrieta 365, T041-791100.
With and without bath, electric shower,
small rooms, simple and good.

\$ Vista Hermosa
Puno 285, T041-477526.
Pleasant ample rooms, some have balconies,
electric shower, good value.

Levanto

\$ Levanto Marvelous Spatuletail Lodge
Behind the church, T041-478838,
www.marvelousspatuletail.net.
2 circular buildings with tall thatched roofs,
4 bedrooms with 2 external bathrooms can
accommodate up to 12 people, hot shower,
lounge with fireplace and kitchen, meals
US\$8-10, must book ahead.

Lamud and around

\$\$\$ Tambo Sapalanchan
500 m north of Lamud, T987-936003,
tambosapalanchan@gmail.com.
Comfortable bungalows overlooking
attractive farmland, restaurant.

\$ Hostal Kuélap
Garcilaso de la Vega 452, on the plaza, Lamud.
With or without bath or hot water, basic.

Gocta

San Pablo

\$ Hospedaje Las Gardenias
T941-718660.
Basic rooms with shared bath, cold water,
economical meals available.

\$ Hotel Gocta Camping
T941-718660.
Camping with hot showers and lovely views at
the site of a hotel under construction.

Cocachimba

\$\$\$\$-\$\$\$ Gocta Natura Cabins
www.goctanatura.com.
Five spacious bungalows, each with private
terrace and fine views of Gocta waterfall.

\$\$\$ Gocta Andes Lodge
Cocachimba, T041-630552 (Tarapoto T042-
522225), www.goctalodge.com.
Beautifully located lodge overlooking the
waterfall, ample rooms with balconies,
lovely terrace with pool, restaurant. Packages
available with other hotels in the group.

\$ Hospedaje Gallito de la Roca
T041-630048.
Small simple rooms with or without bath,
hot water, economical meals available.

\$ Hospedaje Las Orquídeas
T041-631265.
Simple rooms in a family home, shared bath,
cold water, restaurant.

Restaurants

Celendín

\$\$-\$ La Reserve
José Gálvez 313.
Good quality and value, extensive menu,
from Italian to *chifa*.

$ Carbón y Leña
2 de Mayo 410.
For chicken, *parrillas* and pizzas.

$ Juguería Carolin
Bolognesi 384. Daily 0700-2200.
One of the few places open early,
for juices, breakfasts and *caldos*.

Chachapoyas

$$$ Batán del Tayta
La Merced 604. Closed Sun.
Excellent innovative local cuisine, generous
portions. Recommended.

$$ El Tejado
*Santo Domingo 424. Daily for lunch only,
but hours vary.*
Excellent upscale *comida criolla*. Large portions,
attentive service, nice atmosphere and setting.
Good-value *menú ejecutivo* on weekdays.

$$ La Candela
Dos de Mayo 728. Open till 2200.
Pizzas with local Chachapoyas ingredients, baked
in an adobe oven.

$$ La Tushpa
Ortiz Arrieta 753. Open 1800-2200, closed Sun.
A restaurant for carnivores. Great steaks and
chicken dishes.

$$ Paraíso de las Pizzas
Chincha Alta 355. Open till 2200.
Good pizzas and pastas, family-run.

$ Chacha Restaurante
Grau on Plaza de Armas. Daily.
Huge portions of typical Peruvian food.

$ El Edén
*Grau by the market. Sun-Thu 0700-2100,
Fri 0700-1800.*

Simple vegetarian, a variety of dishes à la carte
and economical set meals.

Cafés

Amazonas 632
Amazonas 632. Mon-Sat 1700-2300.
A nice hangout with good snacks, main courses
and desserts.

Dulcería Santa Elena
Amazonas 800. Daily 0900-2230.
Old-fashioned home-made desserts.

Fusiones
*Ayacucho 952, Plaza de Armas.
Mon-Sat 0700-2230.*
Breakfast, fair-trade coffee, juices, snacks,
Wi-Fi, book exchange, volunteer opportunities,
occasional live music.

Heladería San Antonio
2 de Mayo 521 and Amazonas 856.
Good home-made ice cream; try the *lúcuma* and
guanábana flavours.

Panadería Café San José
Ayacucho 816. Mon-Sat 0630-2200.
Bakery and café, good breakfasts, sweets
and snacks.

What to do

Chachapoyas
The cost of full-day trips depends on season
(higher Jul-Sep), distance, number of passengers
and whether meals are included. Several
operators have daily departures to Kuélap (US$15-
19, 3 hrs each way in vehicle, including lunch stop
on return, 3 hrs at the site; note that tour prices
and travel times will change once the cable car
is operational); Gocta, US$13.50-15; Quiocta and

Karajía, US$19-27, and Museo de Leymebamba and Revash, US$31-39. All-inclusive trekking tours to Gran Vilaya cost about US$46-50 pp per day. **Amazon Expedition**, *Jr Ortiz Arrieta 508, Plaza de Armas, T041-798718, http://amazonexpedition. com.pe*. Day tours and multi-day treks.
Andes Tours, *at Casona Revash*. Daily trips to Kuélap and Gocta, other tours to ruins, caves and trekking. Also less-visited destinations, combining travel by car, on horseback and walking.
Cloudforest Expeditions, *Jr Puno 368, T041-477610, www.kuelapnordperu.com*. Tours to ruins, trek to Yumbilla, English and German spoken.
Nuevos Caminos, *at Café Fusiones, T041-479170, www.nuevoscaminostravel.com*. Alternative community tourism, volunteer opportunities.
Turismo Explorer, *Jr Grau 509, T041-478162, www. turismoexplorerperu.com*. Daily tours to Kuélap, Gocta and other destinations, trekking tours including Laguna de los Cóndores and other archaeological sites, transport, good service.
Vilaya Tours, *Jr Amazonas 261, T941-708798, www.vilayatours.com*. All-inclusive treks to off-the-beaten-path destinations throughout northern Peru. Run by Robert Dover, a very experienced and knowledgeable British guide, book ahead.

Transport

Celendín

Bus To **Cajamarca**, 107 km, 3½ hrs, with **Royal Palace's** (Jr Unión y José Gálvez, by Plaza de Armas), 1400 daily; also **CABA**, 2 a day, and **Rojas**, 3 a day. Cars to Cajamarca leave when full from Ovalo Agusto Gil, Cáceres y Amazonas, 2½ hrs, US$9 pp. They also go from the same place to **Chachapoyas**, 6 hrs, US$18 pp. **Virgen del Carmen** (Cáceres 112 by Ovalo A Gil, T076-792918) to Chachapoyas, daily at 0900, US$11.55, via **Leymebamba**, 6 hrs, US$7.75.

Leymebamba and around

To **Chachapoyas** (fills quickly, book ahead), 2½-3 hrs, cars US$7.75, combis US$4, best with Raymi Express, at 0500, 0600, 0630, 1200, 1400; several other companies. To **Celendín**, US$7.75, and **Cajamarca**, US$11.55, 8 hrs, service originating in Chachapoyas.

Tingo to Kuélap

The easiest way to visit Kuélap is on a tour from Chachapoyas (see above) or by hiring a vehicle with driver (US$45 per vehicle, or US$54

with wait). Alternatively, **Trans Roller's** combis or cars depart from the Terminal Terrestre in Chachapoyas at 0400 to **Tingo** (US$3.10, 1 hr), **Choctámal** (US$4.50, 1½ hrs), **Lónguita** (US$5, 2 hrs), **María** (US$6, 2½ hrs) and **Kuélap**, US$8, 3 hrs (only if they have enough passengers). Note that the car returns from Kuélap straight away (around 0700), so you will have to spend the night in the area (see Where to stay, page 1350). There is also additional transport in combis or cars to María with **Sr José Cruz** at 0530 (returns from María at 0800) and to Lónguita with **Trans Shubet** around 1400-1500. Cars bound for Magdalena with **Brisas del Utcubamba** and transport going to/from Yerbabuena or Leymebamba also pass through **Tingo**. All of the above leave from the Terminal Terrestre in Chachapoyas.

Chachapoyas

Air To/from **Tarapoto**, 3 daily flights in a 9-seater aircraft with **SAETA** (Jr Chincha Alta 579, www.saetaperu.com), US$21, 10 kg luggage allowance. See also under Jaén, page 1359.

Bus Regional The **Terminal Terrestre**, a regional transport terminal, is 9 blocks from the Plaza de Armas, at Jr Triunfo, block 1. For services to **Tingo**, **Choctámal** and **Kuélap**, see above. To **Leymebamba**, 83 km, 3 hrs, US$4 (reserve ahead), the best service is with **Raymi Express**, at 0930, 1200, 1400, 1600, 1700; also **Mi Cautivo**, 4 a day. For **Revash**, to **Santo Tomás**, **Comité Santo Tomás** at 1000, 1300, 1500 (return at 0300, 0400, 0500), US$4.30, 3 hrs; get off at **Cruce de Revash** (near Puente Santo Tomás), US$4.30, 2½ hrs; or with the same company to **San Bartolo** at 1400 (return 0600), US$4.30, 3 hrs. To **Jalca Grande** with **Tours Tello**, 2 combis depart Mon-Fri from 1430 onwards, US$4.30, 3 hrs (return 0300-0400). To **Levanto**, **MW Megawil** at 0500 and 1100. To **Mendoza** (86 km), **Guayabamba** US$7.75, 2½ hrs, also combis US$6. To **Luya** and **Lamud**, cars 0400-1800, US$2.85; there are cars from Luya to Cruzpata, 0600-1700, US$3, 1 hr.

Also from the Terminal Terrestre, to **Pedro Ruiz** (for connections to Chiclayo, Jaén, or Tarapoto), cars depart as they fill 0600-2200, US$3.85, 1 hr; combis every 2 hrs 0600-1800, US$2; and **Diplomáticos** and **TED** vans, as they fill 0500-1900. To **Bagua Grande** (for connections to Jaén), cars US$8.50, 2 hrs; combis/vans with **Evangelio Poder de Dios**, US$6. This company also goes to **Moyobamba** (for connections to Tarapoto), at 0700, US$9.75, 5 hrs. To **Celendín** (8-9 hrs, US$11.55) and **Cajamarca** (11-12 hrs,

US$18) with **Amazonas Express**, at 0530 and 1930 daily; **Virgen del Carmen**, at 1930 to Cajamarca.

Long distance The recommended companies serving Chachapoyas are: **MóvilTours** (Libertad 464, T041-478545), **GH Bus** (tickets from Jr Grau entre Triunfo y Amazonas, T041-479200; station at C Evitamiento, take a taxi) and **Transervis Kuélap** (Jr Unión 330, T041-478128). To **Lima** (20-22 hrs, US$44-52) with **Móvil Tours** at 1300; with **GH Bus** at 1030. To **Chiclayo** (9 hrs, US$15-25) at 1930 with **Móvil Tours** or **GH Bus**; 2000 with **Transervis Kuélap**. Other options to Chiclayo are **Civa** (Salamanca y Ortiz Arrieta, T041-478048) at 1815 and **Star Bus** (Jr Unión 330) at 1930. To **Trujillo** (12 hrs, US$23-29), at 1930 with **Móvil Tours** or **GH Bus**.

Gocta

The easiest way to get to Gocta is with a tour from Chachapoyas; in high season there are also tours from Pedro Ruiz. A taxi from Chachapoyas costs US$30, or US$38 with 5-6 hrs' wait. A taxi from Pedro Ruiz costs US$2 pp (there are seldom other passengers to share) or US$10 for the vehicle. Sr Fabier, T962-922798, offers transport service to San Pablo; call ahead to find out when he will be in Pedro Ruiz. A mototaxi from Pedro Ruiz (5 Esquinas, along the road to Chachapoyas, 4 blocks from the highway) costs US$6, beware of overcharging and dress warmly; it is windy and cold. Arrange return transport ahead or at the tourist offices in San Pablo or Cocachimba, as it is difficult to get transport back from Cocahuayco to either Chachapoyas or Pedro Ruiz.

Chachapoyas to the Amazon

look out for birdlife on this dramatic journey to the jungle

From Chachapoyas the road heads north through the beautiful Utcubamba canyon for one hour to a crossroads at Pedro Ruíz, which has two hotels, other lodgings and some basic restaurants. From here, you can return to the coast, head to Jaén for Ecuador, or continue east to Tarapoto and Yurimaguas, making the spectacular descent on a paved road from high Andes to jungle.

☆Pedro Ruiz to Moyobamba

In the rainy season, the road east of Pedro Ruiz may be subject to landslides. This is a very beautiful journey, first passing Laguna Pomacochas, then leading to where the high Andes tumble into the Amazon Basin before your eyes. The descent from the heights of the Abra Patricia Pass to the Río Afluente at 1400 m is one of the best birdwatching areas in northern Peru. ECOAN ⓘ *T041-816814, www.ecoanperu.org*, has two private bird reserves: 20 minutes east of Pedro Ruiz before Pomacochas, protecting the marvelous spatuletail hummingbird (*Loddigesia mirabilis*), US$10, 0600-1800; and at Km 364.5 aimed at conserving the critically endangered long-whiskered owlet (*Xenoglaux loweryi*) and other rare species. Further along, Nueva Cajamarca (reported unsafe), Rioja (198 km, with several hotels) and Moyobamba are growing centres of population, with much forest clearance beside the road.

Moyobamba *Colour map 3, B2.*

Moyobamba, capital of the San Martín Region, is a pleasant town in the attractive Río Mayo valley. The area is renowned for its orchids: there is a **Festival de la Orquídea** over three days around 1 November. Among several places to see the plants is **Orquideario Waqanki** ⓘ *www.waqanki. com, daily 0700-1800, US$0.55*, where the orchids have been placed in trees. Just beyond are **Baños Termales San Mateo** ⓘ *5 km southeast, daily 0600-2200, US$0.55*, which are worth a visit. Boat trips can be taken **from Puerto Tahuishco**, the town's harbour, a pleasant walk north of the centre.

Morro de Calzada ⓘ *13.5 km west of Moyobamba via Calzada, combi to the Calzada turnoff, US$0.55, mototaxi to the start of the trail US$2.50*, is an isolated outcrop in white sand forest that is good for birdwatching. A path through forest leads to a lookout at the top (1½ hours), but enquire about safety beforehand.

Tarapoto and around *Colour map 3, B2.*

Tarapoto, the largest commercial centre in the region, with a population of 120,000, is a very friendly place. It stands at the foot of the forested hills of the **Area de Conservación Regional Cordillera Escalera** (149,870 ha), which is good for birdwatching and walking. Next to the conservation area and within easy reach of town is the 9-ha **El Amo del Bosque Sector** ⓘ *Urawasha, 5 km walk (9 km* *by car) from town, T042-524675 (after 1900),* where the knowledgeable owner, Sr José Macedo, offers guided tours, and 20-ha **Wayrasacha** ① *6-km walk (10 km by car) from the city, T042-522261,* run by Peruvian-Swiss couple César Ramírez and Stephanie Gallusser, who offer day trips, overnight stays in a basic shelter and volunteer opportunities (English and French spoken).

Lamas

Off the main road, 22 km northwest of Tarapoto, Lamas is a small hill town with a Quechua-speaking native community, descendants of the Chancas people from the distant central highlands. Lamas is known as 'la ciudad de los tres pisos' (the city of three storeys). On the top level is a lookout with good views, a hotel-restaurant and a *recreo turístico*. The main town occupies the middle level, where there is a small **Museo Los Chankas** ① *Jr San Martín 1157, daily 0830-1300, 1430-1800, US$1.15,* with ethnological and historical exhibits. Uphill from the museum is **El Castillo de Lamas** ① *Mon-Sat 0900-1230, 1400-1800, Sun 0930-1830, US$2,* an art gallery and café set in an incongruous medieval castle. On the lower level is the neighbourhood of **Wayku**, where the native Chancas live. Lamas' **Easter** celebrations draw many Peruvian visitors, as do the **Fiestas Patronales** in honour of Santa Rosa de Lima in the last week in August.

Tarapoto to Yurimaguas

From Tarapoto it is 129 km to Yurimaguas on the Río Huallaga (see page 1490), along a spectacular paved road. The road climbs through lush country reaching the 50-m **Ahuashiyacu Falls** ① *US$1.15,* within the **Cordillera Escalera** conservation area after 15 km. This is a popular place with locals. Tours are available or there's transport from La Banda de Shilcayo, a Tarapoto neighbourhood. Past Ahuashiyacu, the road climbs to a tunnel – stop at the police control for good birdwatching (mototaxi US$6) – after which you descend through beautiful forest perched on rocky cliffs to Pongo de Caynarachi (several basic comedores), where the flats start. From Yurimaguas launches go to Iquitos (see page 1492).

Listings Chachapoyas to the Amazon

Tourist information

Moyobamba
See www.moyobamba.net.

Dircetur
Jr San Martín 301, T042-562043.
Mon-Fri 0800-1300, 1430-1730.
Has leaflets and map, English spoken.

Oficina Municipal de Información
Jr Pedro Canga 262, at Plaza, T042-562191
ext 541. Mon-Fri 0800-1300, 1430-1715.
No English spoken.

Tarapoto

Dircetur
Jr Angel Delgado Morey, cuadra 1, T042-522567.

Oficina Municipal de Información
Jr Ramírez Hurtado, at plaza, T042-526188.
Mon-Sat 0800-1300, 1500-2000, Sun 0900-1300.

Where to stay

Moyobamba

$$$ Puerto Mirador
Jr Sucre, 1 km from centre, T042-562050,
www.hotelpuertomirador.com.
Buffet breakfast, lovely grounds, views
overlooking river valley, pool, good
restaurant, credit cards accepted.

$$ Orquídea del Mayo
Jr San Martín 432, T042-561049,
orquideadelmayohostal@hotmail.com.
Modern comfortable rooms with bath,
hot water.

$$ Río Mayo
Jr Pedro Canga 415, T042-564193.
Central, modern comfortable rooms, frigobar,
small indoor pool, parking.

$$-$ El Portón
Jr San Martín 449, T042-562900.
Pleasant modern rooms with fan, hot water,
nice grounds with hammocks, kitchen facilities.

$ Cobos
Jr Pedro Canga 404, T042-562153.
Private bath, cold water, simple but good.

$ La Cueva de Juan
Jr Alonso de Alvarado 870, T042-562488,
lacueva870@hotmail.com.
Small courtyard, private bath, hot water,
central but reasonably quiet, good value.

Lamas

$ Hosp Girasoles
Opposite the mirador in the upper part of town,
T042-543439, stegmaiert@yahoo.de.
Breakfast available, nice views, pizzeria and
friendly, knowledgeable owners.

Tarapoto and around

There are several **$** *alojamientos* on Alegría Arias
de Morey, cuadra 2, and cheap basic hotels by the
bus terminals.

$$$ Puerto Palmeras
Cra Belaúnde Terry, Km 614, T042-524100.
Private reserve outside town. Large, modern
complex, popular with families, lots of activities
and entertainment. Nice rooms, helpful staff,
good restaurant, pleasant grounds with
pool, mountain bikes, horses and small zoo,
airport transfers.

$$$ Puma Rinri Lodge
Cra Shapaja–Chasuta, Km 16, T042-526694,
www.pumarinri.com.
Lodge/resort hotel on the shores of the
Río Huallaga, 30 km east of Tarapoto.
Offers a variety of all-inclusive packages.

$$ Huingos Lodge
Prolongación Alerta cuadra 6, Sector Takiwasi,
T042-524171, www.huingoslodge.com.
Nice cabins in lovely grounds by the Río Shilcayo.
Fan, electric shower, frigobar, kitchen facilities,
hammocks, HI-affiliated, mototaxi from bus
stations US$1.55-2.

$$ La Patarashca
Jr San Pablo de la Cruz 362, T042-528810,
www.lapatarashca.com.
Very nice hotel with large rooms, cheaper
without a/c, rustic, restaurant, electric shower,
large garden with hammocks, tours arranged.

$$ Luna Azul
Jr Manco Capac 276, T042-525787,
www.lunaazulhotel.com.

Modern, central, includes breakfast and airport
transfers, with bath, hot water, a/c or fan, frigobar.

$$-$ El Mirador
Jr San Pablo de la Cruz 517, 5 blocks
uphill from the plaza T042-522177,
www.elmiradortarapoto.blogspot.com.
With bath, electric shower, fan, Wi-Fi, laundry
facilities, breakfast available, hammocks on
rooftop terrace with good views, tours arranged.
Family-run and very welcoming.

$ San Antonio
Jr Jiménez Pimentel 126, T042-525563.
Rooms with private bath, hot water and fan,
good value.

Moyobamba

$$-$ Kikeku
Jr Pedro Canga 450, next to casino. 24 hrs.
Good chifa, also comida criolla,
large portions, noisy.

$ El Avispa Juane
Jr Callao 583. Mon-Sat 0730-1600,
Sun 0800-1500.
Regional specialities, menu Mon-Sat and
snacks, popular.

$ La Buena Salud
25 de Mayo 227, by market. Sun-Fri 0800-1500.
Vegetarian set meals, breakfast and fruit juices.

Helados La Muyuna
Jr Pedro Canga 529.
Good natural jungle fruit ice cream.

Tarapoto

There are several restaurants and bars around
Jr San Pablo de la Cruz on the corner of Lamas –
a lively area at night.

$$$-$$ Chalet Venezia
Jr Alegría Arias de Morey 298. Tue-Sun 1200-2300.
Upmarket Italian-Amazonian fusion cuisine, wine
list, elegant decor, interior or terrace seating.

$$$-$$ Real Grill
Jr Moyobamba on the plaza. Daily 0830-2400.
Regional and international food. One of the best
in town.

$$-$ Chifa Cantón
Jr Ramón Castilla 140. Mon-Fri 1200-1600,
Sat-Sun 1200-2400.
Chinese, very popular and clean.

$ El Manguaré
Jr Moyobamba corner Manco Cápac.
Mon-Sat 1200-1530.
Good set meals or à la carte, good service.

Cafés

Café Plaza
Jr Maynas corner Martínez, at the plaza.
Daily 0730-2300.
Breakfast, coffee, snacks, juices, Wi-Fi, popular.

Helados La Muyuna
Jr Ramón Castilla 271. Sun-Thu 0800-2400,
Fri 0800-1700, Sat 1830-2400.
Good natural ice cream, fruit salads and drinks
made with jungle fruits.

Transport

Pedro Ruíz
Bus Many buses on the **Chiclayo–Tarapoto**
and Chiclayo–**Chachapoyas** routes pass
through town. Bus fare to Chiclayo, US$11.50-19;
to Tarapoto, US$11.50-15.50. Cars or combis are
more convenient for Chacha or Bagua. To **Jaén**,
Trans Fernández bus from Tarapoto passes Pedro
Ruiz about 1400-1500, or take a car to Bagua
Grande and transfer there.

Car, combi and van To **Chachapoyas**, cars
US$4, combis US$2, 1 hr. To **Bagua Grande**, cars
US$4.75, combis US$4, 1 hr. To **Moyobamba**,
cars US$10.70, 4 hrs. To **Nueva Cajamarca**,
cars US$9.75, combis US$7.75, 3-3½ hrs. From
Nueva Cajamarca it's a further 20 mins to **Rioja**
by car, US$1.15, or combi, US$0.75. From Rioja
to **Moyobamba**, 21 km, 20 mins, car US$1.15,
combi US$0.75.

Moyobamba
Bus The bus terminal is 12 blocks from the
centre on Av Grau (mototaxi US$0.55). No services
originate in Moyobamba; all buses are en route
to/from Tarapoto. Several companies head west
to **Pedro Ruiz** (US$9, 4 hrs), **Jaén** (US$9, 7 hrs),
Chiclayo (US$15-US$23, 12 hrs). To reserve a seat
on a long-haul bus, you may have to pay the fare
to the final destination even if you get off sooner.

Car, combi and van Empresa San Martín
(Benavides 276) and **ETRISA** (Benavides 244)
run cars (US$1.15) and vans (US$0.75) to **Rioja**,
20 mins; to **Nueva Cajamarca**, 40 mins (US$2,
US$1.55) and **Tarapoto**, 2 hrs (US$7.75, US$4);
combis cost about 50% less on all routes. To
Chachapoyas, **Evangelio Poder de Dios**
(Grau 640), at 1500, US$9.75, 5 hrs.

Tarapoto
Air Taxi to town, US$3; mototaxi US$1.15. To
Lima, daily with **LATAM** (Ramírez Hurtado 183,
on the plaza, T042-529318), **Avianca/TACA**,
Peruvian Airlines and **Star Perú** (San Pablo de
la Cruz 100, T042-528765). **Star Perú** to **Iquitos**
daily (Mon, Wed, Fri via Pucallpa), **LATAM** to
Iquitos Mon, Thu.

Bus Buses depart from Av Salaverry,
blocks 8-9, in Morales; mototaxi from centre,
US$1.15, 20 mins.

To **Moyobamba**, 116 km, US$3.85, 2 hrs; to
Pedro Ruiz, US$11.50-15.50 (companies going
to Jaén or Chiclayo), 6 hrs; to **Chiclayo**, 690 km,
15-16 hrs, US$25-29; and **Lima**, US$46-52,
cama US$64, 30 hrs. For **Chachapoyas**, go to
Moyobamba and take a van from there (see
above). To **Jaén**, US$13.50-15.50, 9-10 hrs, with
Fernández, 4 a day. To **Piura** US$23, 16 hrs, with
Sol Peruano, at 1200. To **Tingo María**, US$27,
and **Pucallpa**, US$35, Mon, Wed, Fri 0500, Tue,
Thu, Sat 0830, **Transamazónica** and **Transmar**
alternate days; there have been armed holdups
on this route.

Car, combi and van To Lamas, cars from
Av Alfonso Ugarte, cuadra 11, US$1.45, 30 mins.
To **Moyobamba**, cars with **Empresa San Martín**
(Av Alfonso Ugarte 1456, T042-526327) and
ETRISA (Av Alfonso Ugarte 1096, T042-521944);
both will pick you up from your hotel, US$7.70,
2 hrs; combis with **Turismo Selva** (Av Alfonso
Ugarte, cuadra 11), US$4, 2½ hrs. To **Yurimaguas**,
Gilmer Tours (Av Alfonso Ugarte 1480), frequent
minibuses, US$5.75, 2½ hrs; cars with **Empresa
San Martín**, US$7.75, 2 hrs; **Turismo Selva** vans,
US$4, 8 daily.

Bagua Grande and further west

This is the first town of note heading west from Pedro Ruiz. It has several hotels but is hot, dusty and unsafe; Pedro Ruiz or Jaén are more pleasant places to spend the night. From Bagua Grande the road follows the Río Chamaya, climbing to the Abra de Porculla (2150 m) before descending to join the old Pan-American Highway at Olmos (see page 1325). From Olmos you can go southwest to Chiclayo, or northwest to Piura.

Jaén *Colour map 3, B2.*

Some 50 km west of Bagua Grande, a road branches northwest at Chamaya to **Jaén**, a convenient stopover en route to the jungle or Ecuador. It is a modern city surrounded by rice fields, with a population of about 100,000. The **Museo Hermógenes Mejía Solf** ① *2 km south of centre, T976-719590, Mon-Fri 0800-1400, mototaxi US$0.60,* displays pre-Columbian artefacts from a variety of cultures. Newly discovered temples at Monte Grande and San Isidro, close to Jaén, are revealing more finds, dating back possibly to 3500 BC.

San Ignacio to the border

A road runs north for 109 km to **San Ignacio** (only the first 55 km are paved), a pleasant town with steep streets in the centre of a coffee-growing area. The nearby hills offer excursions to waterfalls, lakes, petroglyphs and ancient ruins. West of San Ignacio is the **Santuario Tabaconas-Namballe** ① *Sernanp, Huancabamba s/n, Sector Santiago, downhill from the centre in San Ignacio, T968-218439,* a 32,125-ha reserve at 1700-3800 m protecting the spectacled bear, mountain tapir and several ecosystems including the southernmost Andean *páramo*. From San Ignacio the unpaved road, being widened, runs 45 km through green hills to **Namballe**. The border is 15 minutes from Namballe at **La Balsa** (taxi or mototaxi, US$1.15), which has a simple lodging and comedor, a few small shops and money changers. To leave Perú, head directly to immigration (daily 0830-1300, 1500-2000; ask for the officer at his house if he is not at his desk). To enter Peru, visit immigration first, then get a stamp from the PNP (police), and return to immigration. *Rancheras* (open-sided buses) run from La Balsa to Zumba at 1200, 1700 and 1915 (US$1.75, 1¾ hours) and from Zumba to La Balsa at 0800, 1430 and 1700. From Zumba there is onward transport to Vilcabamba and Loja. There are Ecuadorean military controls before and after Zumba (keep your passport to hand), but in general this crossing is relaxed and straightforward.

Listings Chachapoyas to Ecuador

Where to stay

Bagua Grande

$$-$ Río Hotel
Jr Capac Malku 115, www.riohotelbaguagrande.blogspot.com.
A good choice if you can't avoid staying in Bagua Grande.

Jaén

$$ Casa del Sol
Mcal Castilla 140, near Plaza de Armas, T076-434478, hotelcasadelsol@hotmail.com.
Modern confortable rooms with frigobar, parking, suites with jacuzzi.

$$ El Bosque
Mesones Muro 632, T076-431184, hoteleraelbosque@speedy.com.pe.
On main road by bus terminals. Quiet rooms at back, gardens, frigobar, hot water, pool, restaurant.

$$ Prim's
Diego Palomino 1341, T076-431039, www.primshotel.com.
Includes breakfast, good service, comfortable, hot water, a/c or fan, frigobar, Wi-Fi, friendly, small pool.

$ Danubio
V Pinillos 429, T076-433110.
Older place, nicely refurbished, many different rooms and prices, some cheaper rooms have cold water only, fan, good.

San Ignacio to the border

$ Gran Hotel San Ignacio
Jr José Olaya 680 at the bottom of the hill, San Ignacio, T076-356544, granhotel-sanignacio@hotmail.com.
Restaurant for breakfast and good lunch *menú*, modern comfortable rooms, upmarket for here.

$ Hostal Maldonado
Near the plaza, Namballe, T076-830011 (community phone).
Private bath (cheaper without), cold water, basic.

$ La Posada
Jr Porvenir 218, San Ignacio, T076-356180.
Simple rooms which are cheaper without bath or hot water, restaurant.

$ Sol de la Frontera
1 km north of Namballe, 4 km from La Balsa, T997-827766, isabelayub@yahoo.es.
British-run by Isabel Wood. Comfortable rooms in bungalows, bathtubs, gas water heaters, continental breakfast, set in 2.5 ha of countryside. A good option if you have your own vehicle or bring some food. Meals only available for groups with advance booking. Camping and campervans.

Restaurants

Jaén

$$-$ La Cabaña
San Martín 1521. Daily 0700-0000.
Daily specials at noon, à la carte in the evening, popular.

$$-$ Lactobac
Bolívar 1378 at Plaza de Armas. Daily 0730-0000.
Variety of à la carte dishes, snacks, desserts, good *pollo a la brasa*. Very popular.

$ Ebenezer
Mcal Ureta 1360. Sun-Thu 0700-2130, Fri 0700-1600.
Simple vegetarian restaurant serves economical midday *menú* and à la carte.

$ Gatizza
Diego Palomino 1503. Mon-Sat 0830-1800.
Tasty and varied *menú*.

Transport

Bagua Grande

Many buses pass through **Bagua Grande** en route to/from Chiclayo, Tarapoto or Chachapoyas. Cars to **Jaén** from Mcal Castilla y Angamos at the west end of town, US$4, combis US$2.50, 1 hr. From R Palma 308 at the east end of town, cars leave to **Pedro Ruiz**, US$4.60, combis US$4, 1 hr; to **Chachapoyas**, US$9.75, combis US$5.75, 2½ hrs.

Jaén

Air To/from **Lima**, daily with **LATAM** (Mega Plaza Jaén, Av Mesones Muro 2003, T01-213 8200, Mon-Fri 0100-2200), US$99.

Bus, car and combi Terminals are strung along Mesones Muro, blocks 4-7, south of centre; there are many ticket offices, so always enquire where the bus actually leaves from. To **Chiclayo**: US$7.75-15.50, 6 hrs, many companies, **Móvil** more expensive than others. Cars to Chiclayo from Mesones Muro, cuadra 4, US$27, 5 hrs. To **Lima** (via **Trujillo**), with **Móvil** at 1500, 16 hrs, *bus cama* US$46, *semi-cama* US$38.50; with **Civa** (tickets from Mcal Ureta 1300 y V Pinillos; terminal at Bolívar 935), 1700, US$35-42. To **Piura** via Olmos, with **Sol Peruano**, at 2200, US$15.50, 8 hrs. To **Tarapoto**, 490 km, US$13.50-15.50, 9-10 hrs, with **Fernández**, 4 a day. To **Moyobamba**, US$11.50-13.50, 7 hrs, same service as Tarapoto, likewise to **Pedro Ruiz**, US$6-7.75, 3½ hrs. To **Bagua Grande**, cars from Mesones Muro cuadra 6, 0400-2000, US$4, 1 hr; combis from cuadra 9, US$2.50. To **Chamaya**, cars from Mesones Muro, cuadra 4, 0500-2000, US$1, 15 mins. To **San Ignacio** (for Ecuador), cars from Av Pacamuros, cuadra 19, 0400-1800, US$7.75, 2 hrs; combis from cuadra 17 and 20, US$4.60, 3 hrs.

San Ignacio to the border

Bus From San Ignacio to **Chiclayo**, with **Civa** (Av San Ignacio 386), daily at 1830, US$11.55, 10-11 hrs; with **Trans Chiclayo** (Av San Ignacio 406), 1945 daily. To **Jaén**, from *óvalo* at south end of Av Mariano Melgar. To **Namballe** and **La Balsa** (border with Ecuador), cars leave from Sector Alto Loyola at north end of town, way above the centre, US$6 to Namballe, US$6.55 to La Balsa, 1½ hrs.

South coast

The Pan-American Highway runs all the way south from Lima to the Chilean border. This part of Peru's desert coast has its own distinctive attractions. The most famous, and perhaps the strangest, are the mysterious Nazca Lines, whose origin and function continue to puzzle scientists the world over. But Nazca is not the sole archaeological resource here: remains of other pre-Columbian civilizations include outposts of the Inca empire itself. Pisco and Ica are the main centres before Nazca. The former, which is near the famous Paracas marine reserve, is named after the latter's main product, the pisco grape brandy, and a number of places are well known for their bodegas.

South from Lima

vineyards, seabirds and a forgotten valley

Beyond the beaches which are popular with Limeños the road passes near several towns, including Cañete and Chincha, with its Afro-Peruvian culture. The Paracas peninsula, near Pisco, is one of the world's great marine bird reserves and was home to one of Peru's most important ancient civilizations. Further south, the Ica valley, with its wonderful climate, is home to that equally wonderful grape brandy, pisco. Most beaches have very strong currents and can be dangerous for swimming; if unsure, ask locals.

Cañete and Quebrada de Lunahuana

About 150 km south of Lima, on the Río Cañete, is the prosperous market centre of **San Vicente de Cañete**. All the main services are within a few blocks of the plaza. A paved road runs inland, mostly beside the Río Cañete, through Imperial and Nuevo Imperial to **Lunahuaná** (40 km). This town is located 8 km beyond the Inca ruins of **Incawasi**, which used to dominate the valley. In the week **Lunahuaná** is very quiet, but on Sunday the town is full of life, with pisco tastings from the valley's bodegas, food and handicrafts for sale in the plaza and lots of outdoor activities. Throughout February and March you may still be able to see traditional methods of treading the grapes to the beat of a drum.

☆Upper Cañete Valley

Beyond Lunahuaná the road ascending the Cañete Valley leaves the narrow flood-plain and runs 41 km, paved, through a series of gorges to the San Jerónimo bridge. A side road heads to Huangáscar and the village of Viñac, where **Mountain Lodges of Peru** has its **Viñak-Reichraming Lodge** (see Where to stay, page 1363). The road beyond Huangáscar, from which you can see extensive areas of pre-Columbian agricultural terracing, is impassable from January to mid-March.

The main road carries on to the market towns of **Yauyos** (basic accommodation, 5 km off the road) and Llapay, a good base in the middle of the valley. Beyond Llapay, the Cañete valley narrows to an exceptionally tight canyon; the road squeezes between rock and rushing water. Near Alís, the road forks. The eastern branch climbs steeply to a 4600-m pass then drops down to Huancayo (see page 1465), while the northern branch follows the Río Cañete deeper into the **Reserva Paisajística Nor Yauyos-Cochas** ① contact Juan Carlos Pilco (pilco_traveler@hotmail.com) or the Sernanp regional office: RPNYC, Av Francisco Solano 107, San Carlos, Huancayo, T064-213064. After the attractive village of **Huancaya**, the valley is transformed into one of the most beautiful upper valleys in all Peru, on a par with Colca. The river passes through high Andean terrain and descends through a series of absolutely clear, turquoise pools and lakes, interrupted by cascades and white

Best for
Archaeological mysteries ▪ Birdwatching ▪ Pisco

water rapids. Culturally, the valley is fascinating for its dying indigenous languages and traditional ways of life, including perhaps the best pre-Columbian terracing anywhere in Peru.

Pisco and around *Colour map 3, C3.*

The largest port (population 82,250) between Callao and Matarani, Pisco is located a short distance west of the Pan-American Highway and 237 km south of Lima. In August 2007, an earthquake of 7.9 on the Richter scale struck the coast of Peru south of Lima, killing 519 people and injuring 1366; 58,500 homes were destroyed. In Pisco itself almost half of the buildings were destroyed. In October 2011, another earthquake, this time measuring 6.9 on the Richter scale, occurred just off the coast of Ica, leaving one dead, 1705 homeless and 515 damaged or destroyed houses.

Criollo culture is celebrated at local festivals (see page 1365) in **Chincha Alta**, 35 km north of Pisco, where African slave labour once allowed the great haciendas to thrive. Chincha is also a good place to sample locally produced wine and pisco.

From Pisco to the sierras

A 317-km paved road goes up the Pisco valley from the suburb of San Clemente to Ayacucho in the sierra, with a branch to Huancavelica. At Castrovirreyna it reaches 4600 m. The scenery on this journey is superb. The road passes one of the best-preserved Inca ruins in coastal Peru after 38 km: **Tambo Colorado** ① *see www.facebook.com/TamboColorado for details of a French research project here*, includes buildings where the Inca and his retinue would have stayed. Many of the walls retain their original colours. On the other side of the road are the public plaza, the garrison and the messengers' quarters. The caretaker will act as a guide and has a small collection of items found on the site. You can visit Tambo Colorado on a guided tour from Pisco (US$15, minimum two people) or travel independently by taxi, bus or *colectivo* (see Transport, page 1366).

Paracas National Reserve
Daily 1100-1500. US$1.75 pp. Tours (recommended) cost US$9 in a bus with 20 people.

Down the coast from Pisco is the bay of **Paracas**, sheltered by the Paracas peninsula to the south and west. The peninsula, a large area of coast to the south and the Ballestas Islands are protected as a national reserve, with the highest concentration of marine birds in the world.

Tip...

Paracas means 'sandstorm' in Quechua; these can last for up to three days, especially in August. The wind gets up every afternoon, peaking at around 1500.

Paracas can be reached by the coast road from San Andrés, passing the fishing port and a large proportion of Peru's fishmeal industry. Alternatively, go down the Pan-American Highway for 14.5 km past the Pisco turning and take the road to Paracas across the desert. In town is the **Museo Histórico de Paracas** ① *Av Los Libertadores Mz Jl Lote 10, T955-929514*, with exhibits from the pre-Columbian culture of the region.

The entrance to the reserve is at the south end of town on the main road. Just inside the reserve is the **Julio C Tello site museum** ① *museojuliotello@cultura.gob.pe, Tue-Sun 0900-1700, US$2.20* (named after the Peruvian archaeologist who first researched the Paracas culture), which reopened in 2016 after the 2007 earthquake. Tours follow a route through the reserve, including to a *mirador* overlooking **La Catedral** rock formation, which collapsed in 2007. Longer tours venture into the deserts to the south. The tiny fishing village of **Lagunilla** is 5 km from the museum across the neck of the peninsula. Eating places there are poor value (watch out for prices in dollars), but almost all tours stop for lunch here. About 14 km from the museum is the pre-Columbian image known as '**El Candelabro**' (the candelabra), which has been traced into the hillside. It's at least 50 m long and is best seen from the sea; sit on the left side of the boat.

Warning...

It's advisable to see the peninsula as part of a tour from either Pisco or Paracas: it is not safe to walk alone and it is easy to get lost.

☆Trips to the **Islas Ballestas** leave from the jetties in Paracas town. The islands are spectacular, eroded into numerous arches and caves which give the islands their name (*ballesta* means archer's bow) and provide shelter for thousands of seabirds. You will see, close up, guano birds, pelicans, penguins, hundreds of inquisitive sea lions and, if you're lucky, dolphins swimming in the bay. Birdlife here includes some very rare species. The book *Las Aves del Departamento de Lima* by Maria Koepcke is useful. Most boats are speedboats with life jackets, some are very crowded; wear warm clothing and protect against the sun. The boats pass Puerto San Martín and the Candelabra en route to the islands.

Ica *Colour map 3, C3.*

Ica, 70 km southeast of Pisco, is Peru's chief wine centre and is also famous for its *tejas*, a local sweet of *manjarblanco*. It suffered less damage than Pisco in the 2007 earthquake, but one side of the Plaza de Armas did collapse. The **Museo Regional** ① *Av Ayabaca, block 8 (take bus 17 from the Plaza de Armas, US$0.50), T056-234383 Mon-Wed 0800-1900, Thu-Sun 0900-1800, US$4, students US$2.15, tip guides US$4-5*, has mummies, ceramics, textiles and trepanned skulls from the Paracas, Nazca and Inca cultures. There's also a good, well-displayed collection of Inca quipus and clothes made of feathers. Behind the building is a scale model of the Nazca Lines with an observation tower, which is useful for orientation before visiting the lines themselves. The kiosk outside sells copies of motifs from ceramics and textiles.

Huacachina
From Ica, take a taxi for US$1.75 or colectivo from Bolívar block 2, return from behind Hotel Mossone, US$0.75.

About 5 km from Ica, round a palm-fringed lake amid amazing sand dunes, is the oasis and summer resort of Huacachina, a popular hang-out for people seeking a change from the archaeology and chill of the Andes. Plenty of cheap hostels and bars have opened, playing pop and grunge as opposed to pan-pipe music. Paddleboats can be rented, and sandboarding on the dunes has become a major pastime. For the inexperienced, note that sandboarding can be dangerous.

☆Bodegas around Ica

Local wine *bodegas* that you can visit include **La Caravedo** ① *Panamericana Sur 298, T01-9833 4729*, with organic production and sophisticated presentation, and **El Carmen**, on the right-hand side when arriving from Lima, which has an ancient grape press made from a huge tree trunk. **El Catador** ① *Fondo Tres Esquinas 102, Subtanjalla, 10 km outside Ica, T056-962629, elcatadorcristel@ yahoo.es, daily 1000-1800, US$1.50, combi from the 2nd block of Moquegua, every 20 mins, US$0.75, taxi takes 10 mins, good tours in Spanish*, has a shop selling wines, pisco and crafts associated with winemaking. In the evening there's a restaurant-bar with dancing and music. El Catador is best visited during harvest from late February to early April. Near El Catador is **Bodega Alvarez**, whose owner, Umberto Alvarez, is very hospitable. The town of Ocucaje is a popular excursion from Ica for tours of the **Ocucaje winery** ① *Ctra Panamericana Sur, Km 335.5, T01-251 4570, www.ocucaje.com*, which makes wines and pisco.

Listings South from Lima

Tourist information

Cañete and Quebrada de Lunahuana

For information on Cañete town, see www. municanete.gob.pe, or the Oficina de Turismo's Facebook page. There's a **tourist office** in Lunahuaná in the Municipalidad, opposite the church, T01-284 1006, daily.

Ica

Dircetur (Av Grau 148, T056-238710). Some tourist information is also available at travel agencies.

Where to stay

Cañete and Quebrada de Lunahuana

There are places to stay in San Vicente de Cañete, and a range of options in and around Lunahuaná, from large family resorts and *casas de campo* to campsites, plus many *restaurantes campestres*. Note that prices may rise at weekends and holidays.

Upper Cañete Valley

For details of accommodation in Huancaya, call T01-810 6086/7, or see www.huancaya.com.

$$$ Viñak-Reichraming Lodge
Mountain Lodges of Peru, T01-421 6952,
www.refugiosdelperu.com (see page 1435).
A wonderful place to relax or go horse riding or
walking, with superb views and excellent food.
Prices are pp for full board.

$ Hostal Llapay
Llapay. Will open at any hour.
Basic but very friendly, restaurant.

Pisco

$$ Posada Hispana Hostal
Bolognesi 222, T056-536363,
www.posadahispana.com.
Some rooms with loft and bath, also rooms
with shared bath, hot water, can accommodate
groups, comfortable, breakfast extra, **Café de
la Posada on site**, information service, English,
French, Italian and Catalan spoken.

$$-$ El Candelabro
Callao y Pedemonte, T056-532620,
www.hoteleselcandelabro.com.
Modern and pleasant, with restaurant.
All rooms have bath and fridge.

$$-$ Hostal San Isidro
San Clemente 103, T056-536471,
http://sanisidrohostal.com.
With or without bath, hot water, safe, welcoming,
nice pool and cafeteria, pizzeria, free laundry
facilities, games room, English spoken, parking.
Breakfast not included, free coffee in mornings,
use of kitchen. Arranges dune buggy tours and
other excursions.

$$-$ San Jorge Residencial
Jr Barrio Nuevo 133, T056-532885, Facebook:
Hotel-San-Jorge-Residencial-684121474997837.
Smart and modern. Hot water, secure parking,
breakfast is served in the restaurant, also
lunch and dinner, swanky and spacious,
café/bar in garden.

$ Hostal Los Inkas Inn
Prol Barrio Nuevo Mz M, Lte 14, Urb San Isidro,
T056-536634.
Affordable rooms and dorms with private bath,
fan, safes, rooftop games area, small pool.

$ Hostal Tambo Colorado
Av Bolognesi 159, T056-531379,
www.hostaltambocolorado.com.
Welcoming, helpful owners are knowledgeable
about the area, hot water, small café/bar, use
of kitchen.

Paracas

$$$$ Hotel Paracas Luxury Collection Resort
Av Paracas 173, T056-581333,
www.libertador.com.pe.
The famous Hotel Paracas has been reincarnated
as a resort, with spa, pools, excellent rooms in
cottages around the grounds, access to beach,
choice of restaurants, bar, kayaking.

$$$$ La Hacienda Bahía Paracas
Lote 25, Urb Santo Domingo, T01-213 1000,
www.hoteleslahacienda.com.
Next to **Doubletree** but not connected, rooms
and suites, some with access straight to pool,
spa, choice of restaurants, bar.

$$$$-$$$ Doubletree Guest Suites Paracas
Lote 30-34, Urb Santo Domingo on the outskirts,
T01-617 1000, www.doubletree.com.
Low rise, clean lines and a comfortable size, built
around a lovely pool, on beach, water sports, spa,
all mod cons and popular with families.

$$$ El Mirador
At the turn-off to El Chaco, T056-545086,
www.elmiradorhotel.com.
Hot water, good service, boat trips arranged, meals
available, large pool, tranquil gardens, relaxing.

$$$ Gran Palma
Av Principal Mz D lote 03, half block from plaza,
T01-665 5932, www.hotelgranpalma.com.
Central, convenient for boats, best rooms have
sea view, buffet breakfast on the terrace.

$$ Brisas de la Bahía
Av Principal, T056-531132,
www.brisasdelabahia.com.
Good, family-run *hostal*, convenient position for
waterfront and bus stops, ask for a back room,
good breakfast.

$$ Los Frayles
Av Paracas Mz D lote 5, T056-545141,
www.hostallosfrayles.com.
Variety of simple, well-kept rooms, ocean view,
breakfast extra, roof terrace, tourist information,
transfers to/from bus arranged.

$$ Mar Azul
Alan García Mz B lote 20, T056-534542,
www.hostalmarazul.com.
Family-run *hostal* overlooking the sea, although
most rooms face away from ocean, comfortable,
hot water, breezy roof terrace with sea view for
breakfast (included), helpful owner Yudy Patiño.
Also **Ballestas Expeditions** for local tours.

\$\$ Santa María
Av Paracas s/n, T056-545045,
www.hostalsantamariaparacas.com.
Smart rooms, hot water, no view. **El Chorito**
restaurant, mainly fish and seafood. Also has
Santa María 2, round the corner in lovely
converted house (same contact numbers), not all
rooms have view but has rooftop terrace. **Santa
María 3**, under construction on the approach
road, will have more facilities and pool.

\$ Backpackers House
Av Los Libertadores, beside museum, T056-
635623, www.paracasbackpackershouse.com.pe.
Rooms with and without bath, private and
dorms, at high season prices rise to **\$\$-\$**.
Good value, comfortable, tourist information.

\$ Hostal El Amigo
El Chaco, T056-545042,
hostalelamigo@hotmail.com.
Simple, hot water, no food, no internet but very
helpful staff.

Ica
Hotels are fully booked during the harvest festival
and prices rise. Many hotels are in residential
neighbourhoods; insist taxis go to the hotel
of your choice.

\$\$\$\$-\$\$\$ Las Dunas
Av La Angostura 400, T056-256224,
www.lasdunashotel.com.
Lima office: Av Vasco Núñez de Balboa 259,
Lima, T01-213 5000. Variety of rooms and suites.
Prices are reduced on weekdays. Packages
available. Complete resort with restaurant,
swimming pool, many sporting activities and
full-day programmes.

\$\$\$ Villa Jazmín
Los Girasoles Mz C-1, Lote 7, Res La Angostura,
T056-258179, www.villajazmin.net.
Modern hotel in a residential area near the sand
dunes, 8 mins from the city centre, solar heated
water, restaurant, buffet breakfast, pool, tours
arranged, airport and bus transfers, helpful staff,
tranquil and very good.

\$\$ Princess
Santa Magdalena D-103, Urb Santa María,
T056-215421, www.hotelprincess.com.pe.
Taxi ride from the main plaza, small rooms, hot
water, frigobar, pool, tourist information, helpful,
peaceful, very good.

\$ Arameli
Tacna 239, T056-239107.

1 block from the Plaza de Armas, is a nice place to
stay, good value, café on 3rd floor.

Huacachina

\$\$\$ Mossone
East end of the lake, T056-213630,
www.dmhoteles.pe.
Faded elegance, hacienda-style with a view of
the lagoon, full board available, good buffet
breakfast, large rooms, bilingual staff, lovely
courtyard, bicycles and sandboards, large, clean
swimming pool.

\$\$ Hostal Huacachinero
Av Perotti, opposite Hostal Salvatierra,
T056-217435, http://elhuacachinero.com.
Spacious rooms, sparsely furnished but
comfortable beds, nice atmosphere, pool,
outside bar and restaurant, parking, offers
tours and buggy rides.

\$\$ Hostería Suiza
Malecón 264, T056-238762,
hostesuiza@terra.com.pe.
Overlooking lake, lovely grounds, quiet,
safe parking.

\$ Carola del Sur (also known as
Casa de Arena II)
Av Perotti s/n, T056-237398.
Basic rooms, popular, small pool, restaurant/
bar, hammocks, access to Casa de Arena's bigger
pool, noisy at night, pressure to buy tours.

\$ Casa de Arena
Av Perotti s/n, T056-215274.
Basic rooms and dorms, thin walls, bar, small
pool, laundry facilities, board hire, popular
with backpackers but grubby, check your bill
and change carefully, don't leave valuables
unattended, disco next door.

\$ Desert Nights
Run by Desert Adventures (see What to do, below).
Good reputation, English spoken, food available.

\$ Hostal Rocha
T056-222256, kikerocha@hotmail.com.
Hot water, with or without bath, family-run,
kitchen and laundry facilities, board hire,
small pool, popular with backpackers, but
a bit run-down.

\$ Hostal Salvatierra
T056-232352, http://salvaturgroup.galeon.com.
An old building, with or without bath, not on
waterfront, charming, pool, relaxing courtyard,
rents sandboards, good value.

Restaurants

Pisco

$$-$ As de Oro
San Martín 472, T056-532010. Closed Mon.
Good food, not cheap but always full at
lunchtime, swimming pool.

$ Café Pirata
Callao 104, T056-534343.
Mon-Sat 0630-1500, 1800-2200.
Desserts, pizzas, coffee and lunch menu.

$ Chifa Lisen
Av San Martín 325, T056-535527.
Daily 1230-1530, 1800-2200.
Chinese food and delivery.

Paracas

There are several eating places on the Malecón
by Playa El Chaco, all with similar menus and
prices (in our **$$** range), vegetarian options and
open for breakfast, including **Bahía**; **Brisa Marina**
(varied menu, mainly seafood), and **Johnny y
Jennifer**. Better value *menús* are available at
lunchtime on the main road, eg at **Lobo Fino**.
Higher quality food within walking distance of
the centre can be found at the **Hotel Paracas'**
restaurant and trattoria, **$$$**, both of which are
open to the public.

Ica

$$-$ Anita
Libertad 133, Plaza de Armas.
Local dishes, breakfast, à la carte a bit expensive
for what's offered, but set menus at US$4.50 are
good value.

$ Carne y pescao
Av Juan José Elías 417, T056-228157.
Seafood and, at night, grilled chicken
and *parrilladas*.

$ D'lizia
Lima 155, Plaza de Armas, T056-237733,
www.delizia.com.pe.
Also in the Patio de comidas at Plaza Vea mall
and in Urb Moderna. Modern and bright, for
breakfasts, lunches, sandwiches, snacks, ice
cream, cakes and sweets, juices and drinks.

$ Plaza 125
C Lima 125, T056-211816.
On the plaza, regional and international food as
well as breakfast, good-value set lunches.

$ Tejas Helena
Cajamarca 137.
Sell the best *tejas* and locally made chocolates.

Huacachina

$ La Casa de Bamboo
Av Perotti s/n, next to Hostería Suiza,
T056-776649.
Café-bar, English breakfast, marmite, Thai curry,
falafel, vegetarian and vegan options, book
exchange, games.

$ Moroni
T056-238471. Open 0800 till late.
Only restaurant right on the lake shore, serving
a variety of Peruvian and international foods.

Festivals

Cañete and Quebrada de Lunahuana

Feb A festival of adventure sports is held
in Lunahuaná.
1st weekend of Mar Fiesta de la Vendimia
(grape harvest) in Lunahuaná.
Last week of Aug Cañete festival, with regional
music and dancing.

Pisco and around

End Feb Verano Negro. Famous festival in
Chincha Alta celebrating black and criollo culture.
Nov Festival de las Danzas Negras is held in
El Carmen, 10 km south of Chincha Alta.

Ica

**Early Mar Festival Internacional de la
Vendimia** (wine harvest).
Oct The image of **El Señor de Luren** draws
pilgrims from all Peru to a fine church in Parque
Luren on the 3rd Mon, when there are all-night
processions; celebrations start the week before.

What to do

Cañete and Quebrada de Lunahuana

Several agencies in Lunahuaná offer rafting and
kayaking on the Río Cañete, especially at the
anexo of San Jerónimo: Nov-Apr rafting is at
levels IV-V; May-Oct is low water, levels I-II only.

Paracas

There are agencies all over town offering trips
to the Islas Ballestas, the Paracas reserve, Ica,
Nazca and Tambo Colorado. A 2-hr boat tour
to the islands costs US$13-15 pp, including

park entrance fee and tax, departure 0800. Usually, agencies will pool 40 clients together in 1 boat. An agency that does not pool clients is **Huacachina**, based in Ica, with an office in Paracas, T056-215582, www.huacachinatours. com. Do not book tours on the street.

Zarcillo Connections, *Independencia A-20, Paracas, T056-536636, www.zarcilloconnections. com.* With long experience for trips to the Paracas National Reserve, Tambo Colorado, trekking and tours to Ica, Chincha and the Nazca Lines and surrounding sites. Agent for **Cruz del Sur** buses. Also has its own hotel, **Zarcillo Paradise**, in Paracas.

Ica

Agencies offer city tours, trips to the Nazca Lines, Paracas and Islas Ballestas, plus dune buggies and sandboarding.
AV Dolphin Travel, *C Municipalidad 132, of 4, T056-256234, www.av-dolphintravelperu.com.*
Desert Travel, *Lima 171, inside Tejas Don Juan on Plaza, T056-227215, desert_travel@hotmail.com.*
Ica Desert Trip, *Bolívar 178, T056-237373, www. icaeserttrip.com.* Roberto Penny Cabrera (speaks Spanish and English) offers 1-, 2- and 3-day trips off-road into the desert, archaeology, geology, etc. 4 people maximum, contact by email in advance. Take toilet paper, something warm for the evening, a long-sleeved loose cotton shirt for daytime and long trousers. Recommended, but "not for the faint-hearted".

Huacachina

Dune buggies do white-knuckle, rollercoaster tours for US$20 (plus a small municipal fee); some start at 1000 but most between 1600 and 1700 to catch the sunset, 2½ hrs.
Desert Adventures, *Huacachina, T056-228458, www.desertadventure.net.* Frequently recommended for sandboarding and camping trips into the desert by 4WD and buggies, French, English and Spanish spoken. Also to beaches, Islas Ballestas and Nazca Lines flights. Has **Desert Nights** hostel (see Where to stay, above).

Transport

Cañete and Quebrada de Lunahuana
Soyuz bus runs between Lima and **Cañete** every 7 mins, US$5. There are combis between Cañete and **Lunahuaná**, US$2.75.

Upper Cañete Valley
Cars run from the Yauyos area to **Huancayo**, US$7.50. Ask locally where and when they leave. Public transport between villages is scarce and usually goes in the morning. When you get to a village you may have to wait till the early evening for places to open up.

Pisco
Air Capitán RE Olivera airport, originally a military base, has a new passenger terminal and is expected to become an alternative airport to Callao (Lima), with connections also to southern Peru. **Aerodiana** (Av Casimiro Ulloa 227, San Antonio, Lima, T01-447 6824, www.aerodiana.com.pe) offers Nazca overflights from Pisco.

Bus Buses drop passengers at San Clemente on Panamericana Sur (**El Cruce**); many bus companies and tour agencies have their offices here. It's a 10-km taxi ride from the centre, US$8, or US$10 to Paracas. *Colectivos* leave from outside Banco Continental (plaza) for El Cruce when full, US$2.

To **Lima**, 242 km, 4 hrs, US$7.50. The best company is **Soyuz**, every 7 mins from El Cruce. **Ormeño** has an office in Pisco plaza and will take you to El Cruce to meet their 1600 bus. **Flores** is the only company that goes into Pisco town, from Lima and Ica, but buses are poor and services erratic. To **Ica**, US$1.25, 45 mins, 70 km, with **Ormeño**; also *colectivos*. To **Nazca**, 210 km, take a bus to Ica and then change to a *colectivo*. To **Ayacucho**, 317 km, 8-10 hrs, US$12-20, several buses daily leave from El Cruce; book in advance and take warm clothing as it gets cold at night. To **Huancavelica**, 269 km, 12-14 hrs, US$12, with **Oropesa**, coming from Ica. To **Arequipa**, US$17, 10-12 hrs, 2 daily.

To **Tambo Colorado**, buses depart from near the plaza in Pisco at 0800, US$2.50, 3 hrs; also *colectivos*, US$2 pp. Alight 20 mins after the stop at Humay; the road passes right through the site. For buses back to Pisco in the afternoon, wait at the caretaker's house.

Taxi To **Paracas** about US$3; combis when full, US$1.75, 25 mins. To **Tambo Colorado**, US$30 (return).

Paracas
Cruz del Sur has 2 direct buses a day to its Paracas terminal, regular bus from US$9, luxury services US$30-35 from **Lima**, US$15 to **Nazca**. Agencies in Paracas sell direct transfers between Paracas and Huacachina, with **Pelican Perú**, at 1100 daily, US$7, comfortable and secure.

Bus All bus offices are on Lambayeque blocks 1 and 2 and Salaverry block 3. To **Pisco**, US$1.25, 45 mins, 70 km, with **Ormeño**; also *colectivos*. To **Paracas junction**, US$1.15. To **Lima**, 302 km, 4 hrs, US$21-34, on upmarket buses, several daily including **Soyuz** (Av Manzanilla 130), every

7 mins, 0600-2200, and **Ormeño** (Lambayeque 180). To **Nazca**, 140 km, 2 hrs, several buses (US$3.50) and *colectivos* (US$5) daily, including **Ormeño**, **Flores**, 4 daily, and **Cueva** (José Elias y Huánuco), hourly 0600-2200; buses to **Arequipa** follow this route.

Nazca and around

mysterious and unmissable drawings in the desert

Set in a green valley amid a perimeter of mountains, Nazca's altitude puts it just above any fog which may drift in from the sea. Nearby are the mysterious, world-famous Nazca Lines and numerous other ancient sites.

Nazca town *Colour map 3, C3.*

Nazca town lies 140 km south of Ica via the Pan-American Highway (444 km from Lima) and is the tourist centre for visiting the Nazca Lines. **Museo Antonini** ① *Av de la Cultura 600, eastern end of Jr Lima (10-min walk from the plaza or short taxi ride), T056-523444, cahuachi@terra.com.pe or CISRAP@numerica.it, daily 0900-1900 (ring the bell), US$6 including guide,* houses the discoveries

> **Tip...**
> There is a small market at Lima y Grau, the Mercado Central at Arica y Tacna and a Raulito supermarket at Grau 245.

of Professor Orefici and his team from the huge pre-Inca city at Cahuachi (see page 1369), which, Orefici believes, holds the key to understanding the Nazca Lines. Many tombs survived the *huaqueros* (tomb robbers), and there are displays of mummies, ceramics, textiles, amazing *antaras* (pan pipes) and photos of the excavations. In the garden is a prehispanic aqueduct. Recommended.

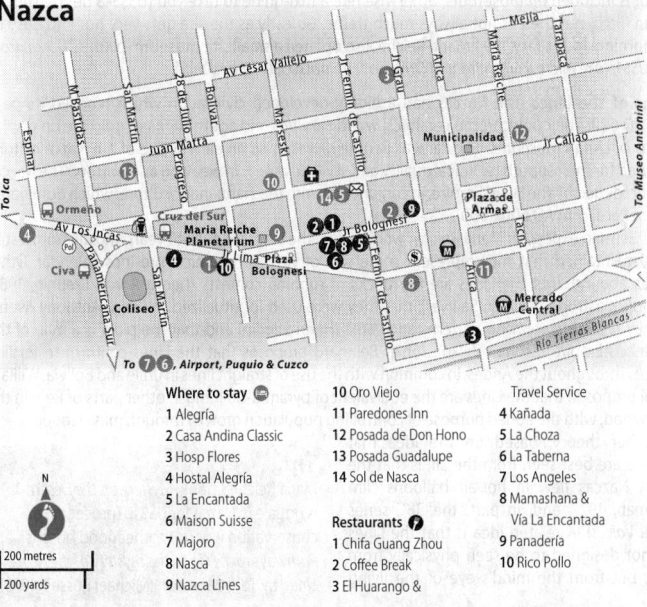

Nazca

Where to stay
1 Alegría
2 Casa Andina Classic
3 Hosp Flores
4 Hostal Alegría
5 La Encantada
6 Maison Suisse
7 Majoro
8 Nasca
9 Nazca Lines
10 Oro Viejo
11 Paredones Inn
12 Posada de Don Hono
13 Posada Guadalupe
14 Sol de Nasca

Restaurants
1 Chifa Guang Zhou
2 Coffee Break
3 El Huarango &

Travel Service
4 Kañada
5 La Choza
6 La Taberna
7 Los Angeles
8 Mamashana &
  Vía La Encantada
9 Panadería
10 Rico Pollo

N

200 metres
200 yards

The **Maria Reiche Planetarium** ① *Hotel Nazca Lines, T056-522293, show daily usually at 1915 in English, 2000 in Spanish, US$7 (students half price),* offers introductory lectures every night about the Nazca Lines, based on Reiche's theories, which cover archaeology and astronomy. The show lasts about 45 minutes, after which visitors are able to look at the moon, planets and stars through telescopes.

Viktoria Nikitzhi, a colleague of Maria Reiche, gives one-hour lectures about the Nazca Lines at **Dr Maria Reiche Center** ①*Av de los Espinales 300, 1 block from Ormeño bus stop, T965-888056, viktorianikitzki@hotmail.com, US$5.* She also organizes tours in June and December (phone in advance to confirm times or to ask about volunteer work).

Just south of town are the **Paredones ruins and aqueduct** ① *US$3.55 (including El Telar Geoglyphs, Acueductos de Cantayoc, Las Agujas Geoglyphs and Acueductos de Ocongalla).* The ruins, also called Cacsamarca, are Inca on a pre-Inca base but are not well preserved. However, the underground aqueducts, built 300 BC-AD 700, are still in working order and worth seeing. A 30-minute to one-hour walk through Buena Fe (or organize a taxi from your hotel) will bring you to the Cantayoc, Las Agujas and El Telar sites, which consist of markings in the valley floor and ancient aqueducts descending in spirals into the ground. The markings consist of a triangle pointing to a hill and a telar (cloth) with a spiral depicting the threads. Climb the mountain to see better examples.

★Nazca Lines

Cut into the stony desert above the Ingenio valley north of Nazca are the famous Nazca Lines, thought to have been etched onto the Pampa Colorada sands by three different groups: the Paracas people (900-200 BC), the Nazcas (200 BC-AD 600) and the Huari settlers from Ayacucho (about AD 630); see Origins of the Lines, below. There are large numbers of lines, not only parallels and geometrical figures, but also recognizable designs, including a dog, an enormous monkey, birds (one with a wing span of over 100 m), a spider and a tree. They are best seen from the air (see What to do, page 1372), but three of the huge designs – the Hands, the Lizard and the Tree – can also be viewed from the mirador, 17 km north of Nazca on the Pan-American Highway, paid for by Maria Reiche in 1976. (Travellers suggest the view from the hill 500 m back to Nazca is better.) The mirador is included on most tours; otherwise hire a taxi-guide to take you (US$5-8 per person), or you can hitch, but there is not always much traffic. Go early as the site gets very hot and busy by mid-morning. In January 1994 Maria Reiche also opened a small site **museum** ① *Km 421, 5 km from town, US$1; take micro from in front of Ormeño terminal (US$0.75, frequent).*

Origins of the Lines The Nazcas had a highly developed civilization which reached its peak about AD 600. Their polychrome ceramics, wood carvings and adornments of gold are on display in many of Lima's museums. The Paracas people represented an early phase of the Nazca culture, renowned for their superb technical quality and stylistic variety in weaving and pottery. The Nazcas were succeeded by the Huari Empire, in conjunction with the Tiahuanaco culture, which dominated much of Peru from AD 600-1000.

The German expert, Dr Maria Reiche, who studied the Lines for over 40 years, mostly from a step ladder, maintained that they represent some sort of vast astronomical pre-Inca calendar. Other theories abound: that the Lines are the tracks of running contests (Georg A von Breunig, 1980, and English astronomer Alan Sawyer); that they were used for ritualized walking (Anthony Aveni), that they represent weaving patterns and yarns (Henri Stierlin) and that the plain is a map of the Tiahuanaco Empire (Zsoltan Zelko). Johan Reinhard proposes that the Lines conform to fertility practices throughout the Andes, in common with the use of straight lines in Chile and Bolivia. William H Isbell proposed that the Lines are the equivalent of pyramid-building in other parts of Peru in the same period, with the added purpose of controlling population growth through mass labour.

Another theory, based on the idea that the Lines are best seen from the air, is that the ancient Nazcas flew in hot-air balloons (Jim Woodman, 1977, and, in part, the BBC series *Ancient Voices*). A related idea is that the Lines were not designed to be seen physically from above, but from the mind's eye of the flying

Tip...
Maria Reiche's book, *Mystery on the Desert*, is on sale in Nazca for US$10 (proceeds to conservation work). Another good book is *Pathways to the Gods: the mystery of the Nazca Lines*, by Tony Morrison (Michael Russell, 1978).

shaman. Both theories are supported by pottery and textile evidence which shows balloonists and a flying creature emitting discharge from its nose and mouth. There are also local legends of flying men. The depiction in the desert of creatures such as a monkey or killer whale suggests the qualities needed by the shaman in his spirit journeys.

Tip...
The best times to fly over the Nazca Lines are between 0800 and 1000 and again between 1500 and 1630, when there is less turbulence and better light (assuming there is no fog). Flights are bumpy with many tight turns; many people get airsick, so it's wise not to eat or drink just before a flight.

After six years' work at La Muña and Los Molinos near Palpa (43 km north of Nazca) using photogrammetry, Peruvian archaeologist Johny Isla and Markus Reindel of the Swiss-Liechtenstein Foundation deduced that the lines on both the Palpa and Nazca plains were offerings dedicated to the worship of water and fertility, two elements which also dominate on ceramics and on the engraved stones of the Paracas culture. Isla and Reindel believe that the Palpa lines predate those at Nazca and that these lines and drawings are themselves scaled-up versions of the Paracas drawings. This research proposes that the Nazca culture succumbed not to drought, but to heavy rainfall, probably during an El Niño event.

In all probability, there was no single, overriding significance to the Lines for the people who made them. Some of the theories attached to them may capture parts of their meaning, and, no doubt, more theories and new discoveries will be tested to cast fresh light on the puzzle.

Other excursions

Overlooking Nazca town to the east is **Cerro Blanco**, the highest sand dune in the world at 2078 m. Tours to the dune start very early in the morning and involve a three-hour hike to the summit. Descents can be made on dune buggies, or by sandboarding or parapenting.

The Nazca area is dotted with over 100 ancient cemeteries, where the dry, humidity-free climate has perfectly preserved invaluable tapestries, cloth and mummies. At **Chauchilla** ① *30 km south of Nazca, last 12 km a sandy track, US$3*, huaqueros ransacked the tombs and left bones, skulls, mummies and pottery shards littering the desert. A tour takes about two hours and usually includes a visit to a small family gold-processing shop where very old-fashioned techniques are still used.

One hour west of the Nazca Lines along a rough dirt track. **Cahuachi** ① *US$3.50 entry, US$17 pp on a tour, US$12-15 in private taxi*, is a Nazca ceremonial site comprising some 30 pyramids. Less than 5% of the site has been excavated so far, some of which has been reconstructed. Some believe it could be larger than Chan Chán, making it the largest adobe city in the world (see also Museo Antonini, above). Some 4 km beyond Cahuachi is a site called **El Estaquería**, thought to have been a series of astronomical sighting posts; more recent research suggests the wooden pillars were used to dry dead bodies and therefore it may have been a place of mummification.

On the coast west of Nazca, **Reserva Nacional de San Fernando** was established in 2011 to protect migratory and local land and oceanic wildlife, such as the Humboldt penguin, sea lions, the Andean fox, dolphins and whales. Condors and guanacos may also be seen, which is unusual for the coast. San Fernando is located in the highest part of the Peruvian coastal desert, where the Nazca Plate lifts the continental plate, generating moist accumulation in the ground with resulting seasonal winter flora and a continental wildlife corridor between the high coastal mountains and the sea. Full-day and two-day/one-night tours are offered by some agencies in town.

Towards Cuzco: Sondondo Valley

Two hours out of Nazca on the paved road to Abancay and Cuzco is the **Reserva Nacional Pampas Galeras** at 4100 m, which has a vicuña reserve and an interesting Museo del Sitio. There's also a military base and park guard here. Entry is free. At Km 155 is **Puquio**, an uninspiring commercial centre which provides access to **Andamarca** and the surrounding villages of the splendid **Sondondo Valley** in the south of the department of Ayacucho. Sondondo offers limitless ancient terraced slopes, a very good chance to see condors, *Puyas raimondii*, small friendly villages and great walking opportunities. This off-the-beaten-path area has modest infrastructure but is gradually opening up to tourism. Beyond Puquio, it's another 185 km to **Chalhuanca**. Fuel is available in both towns. There are wonderful views on this stretch, with lots of small villages, valleys and alpacas.

☆Puerto Inca
10 km north of Chala. Taxi, US$8, or colectivo towards Nazca as far as the turn-off at Km 610, about US$6.

On the coast southwest of Nazca, near the fishing village of **Chala**, are the large pre-Columbian ruins of **Puerto Inca**. This was the port for Cuzco. The site is in excellent condition: the drying and store houses can be seen as holes in the ground (be careful where you walk). On the right side of the bay is a cemetery; on the hill, a temple of reincarnation, and the Inca road from the coast to Cuzco is clearly visible. The road was 240 km long, with a staging post every 7 km so that, with a change of runner at every post, messages could be sent in 24 hours. The site is best appreciated when the sun is shining.

Listings Nazca and around *map p1367*

Tourist information

iPerú is located at the airport (iperunasca@
promperu.gob.pe, daily 0700-1300, 1400-1600).
The **tourist police** are at Av Los Incas cuadra 1,
T056-522105. The ordinary police are at Av Los
Incas, T056-522105 (T105 for emergencies).

Where to stay

If arriving by bus, beware of touts who tell you
that the hotel of your choice is closed, or full.
If you phone or email, the hotel should pick
you up at the bus station free of charge, day
or night.

$$$ Casa Andina Classic
*Jr Bolognesi 367, T01-213 9739,
www.casa-andina.com.*
This recommended chain of hotels' Nazca
property, offering standardized services in
distinctive style. Bright, modern decor, central
patio with palm trees, pool, restaurant.

$$$ Maison Suisse
*Opposite airport, T056-522434,
www.nazcagroup.com.*
Comfortable, safe car park, expensive restaurant,
pool, suites with jacuzzi, good giftshop, shows
video of Nazca Lines. Also has camping facilities.
Its packages include flights over Nazca Lines.

$$$ Majoro
*Panamericana Sur Km 452, T056-522490,
www.hotelmajoro.com.*
A charming old hacienda about 5 km from
town past the airstrip so quite remote, beautiful
gardens, pool, slow and expensive restaurant,
quiet and welcoming, good arrangements for
flights and tours.

$$$ Nazca Lines
Jr Bolognesi 147, T056-522293.
With a/c, rather dated rooms with private patio,
hot water, peaceful, restaurant, safe car park, pool

(US$9-10.50 pp includes sandwich and drink).
Can also arrange package tours which include
2-3 nights at the hotel plus a flight over the lines
and a desert trip.

$$$-$$ Oro Viejo
Callao 483, T056-521112, www.hoteloroviejo.net.
Has a suite with jacuzzi and comfortable standard
rooms, nice garden, swimming pool, restaurant
and bar. Recommended.

$$$-$$ Puerto Inka
*2 km along a side road from Km 610
Panamericana Sur south of Nazca (reservations
T054-778458), www.puertoinka.com.pe.*
Bungalows on the beautiful beach, hammocks
outside, indoor games room, disco, breakfast
extra, great place to relax, kayaks, boat hire,
diving equipment rental, pleasant camping US$5,
low season discounts, used by tour groups, busy
in summer.

$$ Alegría
Jr Lima 166, T056-522497, www.hotelalegria.net.
Rooms with hot water, cafeteria serving
breakfast, pool, garden, English, Hebrew, Italian
and German spoken, laundry facilities, book
exchange, restaurant, ATM, parking, bus terminal
transfers. OK but can be noisy from disco and
traffic. Also has a tour agency where guests are
encouraged to buy tours (see What to do), flights
and bus tickets.

$$ La Encantada
Callao 592, T056-522930.
Pleasant modern hotel with restaurant, laundry
and parking.

$$ Paredones Inn
Jr Lima 600, T056-522181.
1 block from the Plaza de Armas, modern,
colourful rooms, great views from roof terrace,
laundry service, bar, suites with minibar,
microwave, jacuzzi, helpful staff.

$$ Posada de Don Hono
Av María Reiche 112, T056-506822,
laposadadedonhono1@hotmail.com.
Small rooms and nice bungalows, good
café, parking.

$ Hospedaje Flores
Grau 550, T056-521040.
Pleasant, family-run place, hot water,
Wi-Fi, parking.

$ Hostal Alegría
Av Los Incas 117, opposite Ormeño bus terminal,
T056-522497.
Basic, hot water, hammocks, nice garden,
camping, restaurant.

$ Nasca
C Lima 438, T056-522085,
marionasca13@ hotmail.com.
Hot water, with or without bath, laundry facilities,
newer annexe at the back, nice garden, safe
motorcycle parking.

$ Posada Guadalupe
San Martín 225, T056-522249.
Family run, lovely courtyard and garden, hot
water, with or without bath, good breakfast,
relaxing. (Touts selling tours are nothing to do
with hotel.)

$ Sol de Nasca
Callao 586, T056-522730.
Rooms with and without hot showers,
restaurant, pleasant, but don't leave
valuables in luggage store.

Restaurants

There's a *panadería* at Bolognesi 387.

$$$-$$ Vía La Encantada
Bolognesi 282 (website as hotel above).
Modern, stylish with great food – fish,
meat or vegetarian, good-value lunches.

$$-$ La Choza
Bolognesi 290.
Nice decor with woven chairs and thatched
roof, all types of food, live music at night.
Single women may be put off by the crowds
of young men hanging around the doors
handing out flyers.

$$-$ La Taberna
Jr Lima 321, T056-521411.
Excellent food, live music, popular with gringos,
it's worth a look just for the graffiti on the walls.

$$-$ Mamashana
Bolognesi 270.
Rustic style with a lively atmosphere,
for breakfast, grills, pastas and pizzas.

$ Chifa Guang Zhou
Bolognesi 297, T056-522036.
Very good.

$ Coffee Break
Bolognesi 219. Sun-Fri 0700-2300.
For real coffee and good pizzas.

$ El Huarango
Arica 602.
National and international cuisine. Relaxed family
atmosphere and deliciously breezy terrace.

$ Kañada
Lima 160, nazcanada@yahoo.com.
Cheap, good *menú*, excellent *pisco sours*, nice
wines, popular, display of local artists' work,
email service, English spoken, helpful.

$ Los Angeles
Bolognesi 266.
Good, cheap, try the *sopa criolla*, and the
chocolate cake.

$ Rico Pollo
Lima 190.
Good local restaurant with great chicken dishes.

Festivals

29 Aug-10 Sep Virgen de la Guadalupe festival.

What to do

Land-based tours
All guides must be approved by the Ministry of
Tourism and should have an official identity card.
Touts (*jaladores*) operate at popular hotels and the
bus terminals using false ID cards and fake hotel
and tour brochures. They are rip-off merchants
who overcharge and mislead those who arrive
by bus. Only conduct business with agencies at
their office, or phone or email the company you
want to deal with in advance. Some hotels are not
above pressurising guests to purchase tours at
inflated prices. Taxi drivers usually act as guides,
but most speak only Spanish. Do not take just any
taxi on the plaza for a tour; always ask your hotel
for a reputable driver.
Air Nasca Travel, *Jr Lima 185, T056-521027.* Guide
Susi recommended. Very helpful and competitive
prices. Can do all types of tours around Nazca, Ica,
Paracas and Pisco.

Algería Tours, *Lima 186, T056-523431, http:// alegriatoursperu.com*. Offers inclusive tours. Guides with radio contact and maps can be provided for hikes to nearby sites. Guides speak English, German, French and Italian. They also offer adventure tours, such as mountain biking from 4000 m in the Andes down to the plain, sandboarding, and more.

Félix Quispe Sarmiento, 'El Nativo de Nazca'. He has his own museum, Hantun Nazca, at Panamericana Sur 447 and works with the Ministerio de Cultura to offer tours off the beaten track. Can also arrange flights. Knowledgeable. Ask for him at Kañada restaurant.

Fernández family, *Hotel Nasca (see above)*. Local tours; ask for the hotel owners and speak to them direct.

Huarango Travel Service, *Arica 602, T056-522141, huarangotravel@yahoo.es*. Tours around Ica, Paracas, Huacachina, Nazca and Palpa.

Mystery Peru, *Simón Bolívar 221, T01-435 0051, T956-691155, www.mysteryperu.com*. Owned by Enrique Levano Alarcón, based in Nazca with many local tours, also packages throughout Peru.

Nazca Perú 4x4, *Bolognesi 367 (in Casa Andina), T056-522928, or T975-017029*. Tubular 4WD tours to San Fernando National Reserve and other off-the-beaten-track locations.

Sightseeing flights

Small planes take 3-5 passengers to see the Nazca Lines. Flights last 30-35 mins and are controlled by air traffic personnel at the airport to avoid congestion. The price for a flight is around US$130 pp plus US$10 airport tax. Most tours include transport to the airport; otherwise it's US$5 by taxi or US$0.25 by bus. It is best to organize a flight with the airlines themselves at the airport. They will weigh you and select a group of passengers based on weight, so you

---

Warning...

Be aware that fatal crashes by planes flying over the Lines do occur. Some foreign governments advise tourists not to take these flights and some companies will not provide insurance for passengers until safety and maintenance standards are improved.

---

may have to wait a while for your turn. Make sure you clarify everything before getting on the plane and ask for a receipt. Also let them know in advance if you have any special requests.

Aero Diana, *Av Casimiro Ulloa 227, San Antonio, Lima, T01-447 6824, www.aerodiana.com.pe*. Daily flights over the Lines.

Aero Paracas, *T01-641 7000, www.aeroparacas. com*. Daily flights over the Lines.

Alas Peruanas, *T056-522444, http://alasperuanas. com, or through Hotel Alegría*. Experienced pilots offer flights over the Nazca Lines as well as 1-hr flights over the Palpa and Llipata areas, where you can see more designs and other rare patterns (US$130 pp, minimum 3); Nazca and Palpa combined, US$250. See the website for promotional offers. All **Alas Peruanas** flights include the BBC film of Nazca.

Transport

Air The airport caters only for sightseeing flights.

Bus It is worth paying extra for a good bus; there are reports of robbery on the cheaper services. Over-booking is common.

To **Lima**, 446 km, 7 hrs, several buses and *colectivos* daily, US$23-26. **Ormeño** (T056-522058) *Royal Class* at 0530 and 1330 from Hotel Nazca Lines, normal service from Av Los Incas, 6 a day; **Civa** (Av Guardia Civil, T056-523019), normal service at 2300; **Cruz del Sur** (Lima y San Martín, T056-720440), via Ica and Paracas, luxury service, US$39-55. To Ica, with **Ormeño**, 2 hrs, US$3.50, 4 a day. For **Pisco** (210 km), 3 hrs, buses stop 5 km outside town (see under Pisco, Transport), so change in Ica for direct transport into Pisco.

To **Arequipa**, 565 km, 9 hrs, US$19-22.50, or US$28-52 for *bus cama* services: **Ormeño**, from Av Los Incas, Royal Class at 2130, 8 hrs, also **Cruz del Sur** and **Oltursa** (Av los Incas 103, T056-522265), reliable, comfortable and secure on this route. Delays are possible out of Nazca because of drifting sand across the road or because of mudslides in the rainy season. Travel in daylight if possible. Book your ticket the previous day.

To **Cuzco**, 659 km, via **Chalhuanca** and **Abancay** (13 hrs), with **Ormeño**, US$50, and **Cruz del Sur**, 2015, 2100, US$50-70. The highway from Nazca to Cuzco is paved and is safe for bus travellers, drivers of private vehicles and motorcyclists.

Arequipa &
the far south

The colonial city of Arequipa, with its guardian volcano, El Misti, is the ideal place to start exploring southern Peru. It is the gateway to two of the world's deepest canyons, Colca and Cotahuasi, whose villages and terraces hold onto a traditional way of life and whose skies are home to the magnificent condor. From Arequipa there are routes to Lake Titicaca and to the border with Chile.

Arequipa *Colour map 6, A1.*
beautiful buildings and fascinating museums in the 'White City'

The city of Arequipa (population one million) stands in a beautiful valley 1011 km from Lima, at the foot of the perfect cone of El Misti volcano (5822 m), guarded on either side by the mountains Chachani (6057 m), and Pichu-Pichu (5669 m). The city has fine Spanish buildings and many old and interesting churches built of sillar, a pearly white volcanic stone almost exclusively used in the construction of Arequipa. The city was re-founded on 15 August 1540 by an emissary of Pizarro, but it had previously been occupied by Aymara peoples and the Incas. It is the main commercial centre for the south and is a busy place. Arequipeños resent the general tendency to believe that everything is run from Lima. It has been declared a World Cultural Heritage Site by UNESCO.

City centre
Plaza de Armas The elegant Plaza de Armas is faced on three sides by arcaded buildings with many restaurants, and on the fourth by the massive **Cathedral**, founded in 1612 and largely rebuilt in the 19th century. It is remarkable for having its façade along the whole length of the church (entrances on Santa Catalina and San Francisco 0700-0900, 1700-1900). Inside is the fine Belgian organ and elaborately carved wooden pulpit. The Cathedral has a **museum** ⓘ *www.museocatedralarequipa. org.pe, Mon-Sat 0900-1630, US$3*, which outlines the history of the building, its religious objects and art and the bell tower. Behind the Cathedral is an alley with handicraft shops and places to eat.

☆**Santa Catalina Convent** ⓘ *Santa Catalina 301, T054-2212132, www.santacatalina.org.pe. Mon, Wed, Fri-Sun 0800-1700 (last admission 1600), Tue and Thu 0800-2000, US$12, 1-hr tour US$6 for group up to 4, many guides speak English or German.* This is by far the most remarkable sight, opened in 1970 after four centuries of mystery. It is a complete miniature walled colonial town of over 2 ha in the middle of the city, where about 450 nuns lived in total seclusion, except for their women servants. The few remaining nuns have retreated to one section of the convent, allowing visitors to see a maze of cobbled streets and plazas bright with geraniums and other flowers, cloisters and buttressed houses. These have been painted in traditional white, orange, deep red and blue. The convent has been beautifully refurbished, with period furniture, paintings of the Cuzco school and fully equipped kitchens. On Tuesday and Thursday evenings the convent is lit with torches, candles and blazing fireplaces: very beautiful. There is a good café, which sells cakes, sandwiches, baked potatoes and a special blend of tea.

☆**Museo Santuarios Andinos** ⓘ *La Merced 110, T054-286614, ext 105. Mon-Sat 0900-1800, Sun 0900-1500, US$6 includes a 20-min video in English; 40-min guided tour US$3, discount with university student card (not ISIC).* This museum contains the frozen Inca mummies of child sacrifices found on Mount Ampato. To the Incas, Nevado Ampato was a sacred god, who claimed the highest tribute:

Best for
Architecture ▪ Food ▪ Scenery ▪ Trekking

Essential Arequipa

Getting around

Arequipa is the main commercial centre and transport hub for the south, with flights and long-distance buses to/from Lima and other major cities. In the city the main places of interest and the hotels are within walking distance of the Plaza de Armas. The centre is known as Cercado; the Río Chili, spanned by six bridges, separates it from the suburbs to the west, among them the colonial district of Yanahuara. If you are going to the suburbs, take a bus or taxi. Traffic can be chaotic, making the city noisy; perhaps a planned public transit system will help.

When to go

The climate in Arequipa is delightful, with a mean daytime temperature in the low 20s. The sun shines on 360 days of the year and average annual rainfall is just 100 mm.

Safety

There have been reports of taxi drivers colluding with criminals to rob both tourists and locals. Ask hotels, restaurants, etc, to book a safe taxi for you. Theft can be a problem in the market area and the park at Selva Alegre at quiet times. Be very cautious walking anywhere at night. The police are conspicuous, friendly, courteous and efficient, but their resources are limited.

human sacrifice. The mummy known as 'Juanita', found in 1995, is particularly fascinating as both the body and the Inca textiles it is wearing are so well preserved; it reveals a huge amount of information about Inca life and ritual practices. From January to April, Juanita is often jetting round the world and is replaced by other child sacrifices unearthed in the mountains.

Monasterio de Santa Teresa ① *Melgar 303, T054-281188, www.museocarmelitas.com, Tue-Sat 0900-1700, Sun 0900-1300, US$6, multilingual guides available (tip suggested).* Smaller, less known, but as impressive as Santa Catalina, is the Monastery of Santa Teresa, dating to 1710. This living monastery is the home of Carmelite nuns and one of Arequipa's hidden treasures. Housed in one cloister the **Museo de Arte Virreinal**, which also includes an exhibit about the techniques and materials used in colonial art. If you are there at noon, you can listen to the nuns singing Angelus and other prayers. Sweets, rose soap and other things made by the nuns are sold at the gift shop.

Colonial houses Arequipa is said to have the best preserved colonial architecture in Peru, apart from Cuzco. As well as the many fine churches, there are several seignorial houses with large carved tympanums over the entrances. Built as single-storey structures, they have mostly withstood earthquakes. They have small patios, no galleries, flat roofs and small windows, disguised by superimposed lintels or heavy grilles. Good examples are the 18th-century **Casa Tristán del Pozo**, or **Gibbs-Ricketts house** ① *San Francisco 108, Mon-Fri 0900-1800, Sat 0900-1200*, with its fine portal and puma-head waterspouts. It houses a bank and art gallery. **Casa de Moral** ① *Moral 318 y Bolívar, Mon-Sat 0900-1700, Sun 0900-1300, US$1.80, US$1 for students*, also known as Williams house is now a bank and has a museum. **Casa Goyeneche** ① *La Merced 201 y Palacio Viejo*, is also a bank office, but the guards will let you view the courtyard and fine period rooms.

The oldest district of Arequipa is **San Lázaro**, a collection of tiny climbing streets and houses quite close to the **Hotel Libertador**, where you can find the ancient **Capilla de San Lázaro** ① *daily 0900-1700, US$1.80*.

Arequipa's churches Among the many fine churches is **La Compañía** ① *General Morán y Alvarez Thomas*, whose main façade (1698) and side portal (1654) are striking examples of the florid Andean *mestizo* style. To the left of the sanctuary is the **Capilla San Ignacio de Loyola** or **Capilla Real** (Royal Chapel) ① *Mon-Sat 0900-1300, 1500-1800, Sun 0900-1300, Mass daily 1200, US$1.50*, with a beautiful polychrome cupola. Also well worth seeing is the church of **San Francisco** ① *Zela 103, Mon-Sat 0715-0900, 1500-2000, Sun 0715-1245, 1800-2000*. There are religious art **museums** ① *Mon-Sat 0900-1200, 1500-1800, US$1.80*, on either side of it, and also at the convent and at Templo de la Tercera Orden.

Opposite San Francisco is the interesting **Museo Histórico Municipal** ① *Plaza San Francisco 407, Mon-Sat 0800-1600, US$3*, with scale models of the façades of Arequipa's churches, much war memorabilia, some impressive photos of the city in the aftermath of several notable earthquakes,

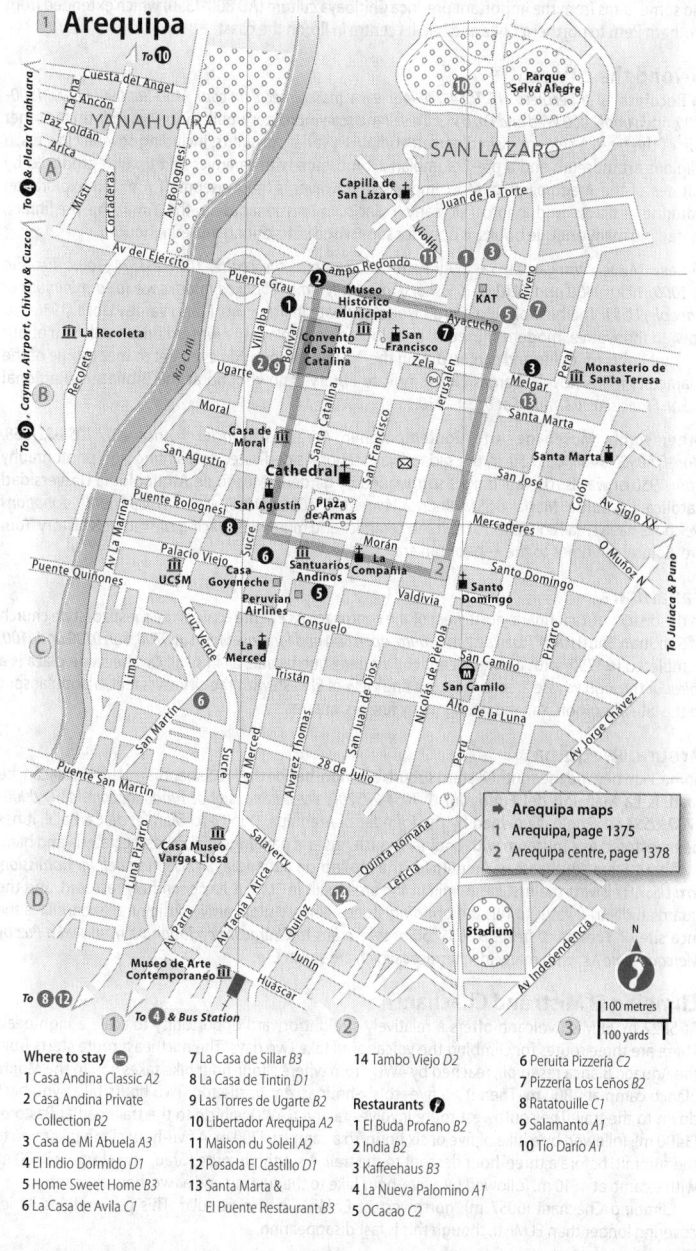

1 Arequipa

To ➓

Cuesta del Angel

YANAHUARA

Tacna
Ancón
Paz Soldán
Arica
Cortaderas
Mistí
Av Bolognesi

To ➒ & Plaza Yanahuara

Av del Ejército

Puente Grau

To ➒ • Cayma, Airport, Chivay & Cuzco

La Recoleta 🏛

Recoleta

Río Chili

Villalba
Bolívar

Ugarte

Moral

Casa de Moral 🏛

San Agustín

Puente Bolognesi

San Agustín

Palacio Viejo

UCSM 🏛

Puente Quiñones

Cruz Verde

La Merced 🏛

San Martín

Puente San Martín

Luna Pizarro

Av Parra

Casa Museo Vargas Llosa 🏛

Museo de Arte Contemporáneo 🏛

To ➑ ➓

To ➍ & Bus Station

Parque Selva Alegre

SAN LÁZARO

Capilla de San Lázaro ■

Juan de la Torre

Violín

Campo Redondo

Museo Histórico Municipal

Convento de Santa Catalina 🏛

San Francisco ✝

Zela

Ayacucho

KAT

Rivero

Peral

Melgar

Monasterio de Santa Teresa 🏛

Santa Marta

Santa Catalina

Santa Marta ✝

Jerusalén

Santa Marta

Cathedral 🏛

Plaza de Armas

Morán

San José

Mercaderes

Colón

Av Siglo XX

O Muñoz N

Casa Goyeneche 🏛

Santuarios Andinos 🏛

La Compañía ✝

Santo Domingo ✝

Valdivia

Consuelo

Peruvian Airlines

La Merced ✝

Tristán

28 de Julio

Álvarez Thomas

Nicolás de Piérola

San Camilo

San Camilo

Alto de la Luna

Perú

San Juan de Dios

To Juliaca & Puno

Santo Domingo

Pizarro

Av Jorge Chávez

Salaverry

Tacna y Arica

Quiroz

Junín

Huáscar

Quinta Romaña

Leticia

Stadium

Av Independencia

N

100 metres
100 yards

➡ **Arequipa maps**
1 Arequipa, page 1375
2 Arequipa centre, page 1378

Where to stay 🛏
1 Casa Andina Classic *A2*
2 Casa Andina Private Collection *B2*
3 Casa de Mi Abuela *A3*
4 El Indio Dormido *D1*
5 Home Sweet Home *B3*
6 La Casa de Avila *C1*
7 La Casa de Sillar *B3*
8 La Casa de Tintín *D1*
9 Las Torres de Ugarte *B2*
10 Libertador Arequipa *A2*
11 Maison du Soleil *A2*
12 Posada El Castillo *D1*
13 Santa Marta & El Puente Restaurant *B3*
14 Tambo Viejo *D2*

Restaurants 🍴
1 El Buda Profano *B2*
2 India *B2*
3 Kaffeehaus *B3*
4 La Nueva Palomino *A1*
5 OCacao *C2*
6 Peruita Pizzería *C2*
7 Pizzería Los Leños *B2*
8 Ratatouille *C1*
9 Salamanto *A1*
10 Tío Darío *A1*

and some items from the important pre-Inca Chiribaya culture (AD 800-1350) which extended from southern Peru to northern Chile and had its centre in Ilo, on the coast.

Beyond the city centre
La Recoleta ① *Jr Recoleta 117, T054-270966, www.museolarecoleta.com. Mon-Sat 0900-1200, 1500-1700, open until 2000 Wed and Fri. US$3.* This Franciscan monastery, built in 1647, stands on the other side of the river. A seldom-visited gem, it contains a variety of sights, including several cloisters, a religious art museum and a pre-Columbian art museum with ceramics and textiles produced by cultures of the Arequipa area. Most impressive however is the museum of Amazon exploration featuring artifacts and photos of early Franciscan missionaries in the Amazon. The library, containing many antique books, is open for supervised visits during museum hours.

☆**Casa Museo Vargas Llosa** ① *Av Parra 101, south of the centre, T054-283574. Tours Tue-Sun at 1000, 1030, 1400 and 1430 (3-10 visitors), or at any time if booked in advance for a minimum of 6 people, US$3.* The birthplace of Peru's Nobel laureate in literature, Mario Vargas Llosa (1936-) is now an innovative, modern museum. In holographic displays the writer himself tells you about the highlights of his life and career; during the 90-minute tour, you even get to meet some of the characters in his novels. Vargas Llosa's private library is now found at the **Biblioteca Regional** ① *San Francisco 308, Mon-Sat 0830-2030.*

Other sights Museo de Arte Contemporáneo Arequipa ① *Tacna y Arica 201, T054-221068, Mon-Fri 0900-1400, US$1.50,* in the old railway station, is dedicated to painting and photography from 1950 onwards. The building is surrounded by gardens. **Museo de Arqueología Universidad Católica de Santa María UCSM** ① *Cruz Verde 303, T054-221083, Mon-Fri 0830-1600, donations welcome,* has a small collection of textiles, ceramics and mummies, tracing the region's history from pre-Columbian times to the Republican era.

Yanahuara
In the district of Yanahuara, northwest of the centre across Puente Grau, is the mestizo-style church of **San Juan Bautista** ① *Plaza de Yanahuara, open Sun and for mass Mon-Sat 0700, Sun 0700 and 1100,* completed in 1750, with a magnificent churrigueresque façade, all in sillar. On the same plaza is a *mirador* through whose arches there is a fine view of El Misti with the city at its feet, a popular spot in the late afternoon. Yanahuara has many fine restaurants.

Around Arequipa
Some 3 km beyond the southwestern suburb of **Tingo**, beside the Río Sabandía on the Huasacanche road, is **La Mansión del Fundador** ① *T054-225200, www.lamansiondelfundador.com, daily 0900-1700, US$4.50.* Originally owned by the founder of Arequipa, Don Garcí Manuel de Carbajal, it has been restored as a museum with original furnishings and paintings; it also has a cafeteria and bar.

About 8 km southeast of Arequipa is the **Molino de Sabandía** ① *US$3, ring bell for admission; taxi US$7.* This was the first stone mill in the area, built in 1621. It has been fully restored, and the guardian diverts water to run the grinding stones when visitors arrive. Adjoining Sabandía is the Inca site of **Yumina** ① *free, taxi US$7.50 or take a bus to Characato or Sabandía from Av La Paz by Mercado Siglo XX,* with many Inca terraces which are still in use.

Climbing El Misti and Chachani
At 5822 m, El Misti volcano offers a relatively straightforward opportunity to scale a high peak. There are three routes for climbing the volcano; all take two days. The northeast route starts from the Aguada Blanca reservoir, reached by 4WD, from where a four-hour hike takes you to the Monte Blanco camp at 4800 m. Then it's a five- to six-hour ascent to the top. Two hours takes you back down to the trail. The southwest route involves taking a 4WD vehicle to the trailhead at Pastores (3400 m), followed by a hike of five or six hours to a camp at 4700 m. A five-hour climb takes you to the summit, before a three-hour descent to the trail. A southern route (Grau) also starts at 3400 m, with a camp at 4610 m, followed by a five-hour hike to the summit and a two-hour descent.

Climbing Chachani (6057 m), northwest of El Misti, is also popular. This peak retains its icy covering longer than El Misti, though this is fast disappearing.

Remember that both summits are at a very high altitude and that this, combined with climbing on scree, makes it hard going for the untrained. Great care must be taken on the unstable rock left by deglaciation; serious accidents have occurred. Be prepared for early starts, and take plenty of water, food and protection against the weather. Favoured months are May to September. Always contact an experienced guiding agency or professional guide in Arequipa as you should never climb alone. The price range is US$75-90 per person for a group of 3-5 people (see What to do, page 1383).

Tourist information

Indecopi
Hipólito Unanue 100-A, Urb Victoria, T054-212054, mlcornejo@indecopi.gob.pe.

iPerú
Portal de la Municipalidad 110, on the south side of Plaza de Armas, T054-223265, iperuarequipa@prompreu.gob.pe. Mon-Sat 0900-1800, Sun 0900-1300, also in the airport Arrivals hall, at flight times.

Municipal tourist office
Portal de la Municipalidad 112 next to iPerú. Mon-Fri 0830-1700.

Tourist police
Jerusalén 315, T054-201258. Daily 24 hrs.
Very helpful dealing with complaints or giving directions.

Where to stay

There are several economical *hostales* along Puente Grau and Ayacucho, near Jerusalén. Hostel chains include: **Flying Dog** (www.flying dogperu.com), **Pirwa** (www.pirwahostels.com) and **Wild Rover** (www.wildroverhostels.com).

$$$$ Casa Andina Private Collection
Ugarte 403, T054-226907, www.casa-andina.com.
Luxury hotel in a restored 18th-century mansion, former Casa de la Moneda. 5 large suites in colonial building, 36 rooms in modern extension off 2nd courtyard. Gourmet restaurant, room service, business centre, roof terrace with views.

Tip...
On arrival, do not believe taxi drivers who say the hotel of your choice is closed or full in order to take you to another hotel which pays them a high commission. Instead, phone your preferred hotel in advance, or ring the doorbell and check for yourself.

$$$$ Libertador Arequipa
Plaza Simón Bolívar, Selva Alegre, T054-215110, www.libertador.com.pe.
Large comfortable rooms, good service, swimming pool (cold), gardens, good meals, pub-style bar, cocktail lounge, squash court.

$$$ Casa Andina Classic
Jerusalén 603, T054-202070, www.casa-andina.com.
Part of the attractive **Casa Andina** chain, with breakfast, comfortable and colourful, central, modern, good restaurant, parking.

$$$ Casa Andina Select
Portal de Flores 116, T054-412930, www.casa-andina.com.
Remodelled 5-storey building on Plaza de Armas, modern rooms, buffet breakfast, restaurant, small pool, gym, caters to business travellers.

$$$ Santa Marta
Santa Marta 207, T054-243925, www.hostalsantamarta.com.
Pleasant, comfortable hotel with nice patio, modern rooms in back, arrange airport and bus terminal transfers. Renovated and under new management in 2017.

$$ Casablanca Hostal
Puente Bolognesi 104, a few metres from the Plaza de Armas, T054-221327, www.casablancahostal.com.
Super stylish *hostal*, lovely minimalist rooms in a colonial building. Ambient lighting, rooms with exposed stone walls, most with balcony.

$$ Casa de Melgar
Melgar 108, T054-222459, www.lacasademelgar.com.
18th-century building, excellent rooms, solar hot water, courtyard, good breakfast buffet, Italian restaurant next door.

$$ Casa de Mi Abuela
Jerusalén 606, T054-241206, www.lacasademiabuela.com.
An Arequipa tradition, in the same family for several generations, suites with bathtub and

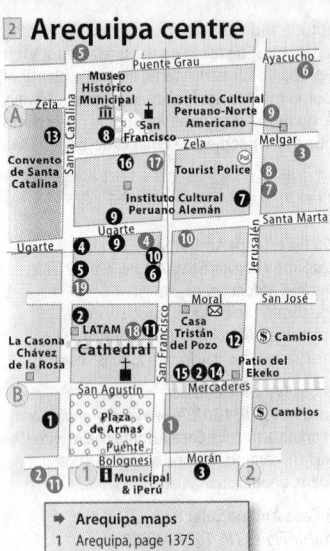

N

50 metres
50 yards

rooms, small swimming pool, therapeutic massage area, rooms at the back are quieter and overlook the garden, English spoken, parking, restaurant and piano bar, buffet breakfast or evening snacks on patio or in beautiful gardens, tour operator. Warmly recommended.

$$ Hostal Solar
Ayacucho 108, T054-241793,
www.hostalsolar.com.
Colonial building, newer rooms in back are bright, good breakfast served in nice patio, sun lounge on roof, very secure, multilingual staff.

$$ La Casa de Avila
San Martín 116, Vallecito, T054-213177,
www.casadeavila.com.
Rooms around spacious, sunny garden, computers for guests' use, can arrange airport/bus station pick-up, recommended Spanish courses held in the garden and other activities.

$$ La Casona de Jerusalén
Jerusalén 306-A, T054-205453,
lacasonadejerusalen@hotmail.com.
Centrally located colonial house with garden, ample bright rooms with or without bath, private bath rooms include breakfast, terrace, English, German and Italian spoken.

$$ La Casa de Margott
Jerusalén 304, T054-229517,
www.lacasademargott.com.
Family-run in a refurbished 19th-century house, bright with a massive palm tree in patio, spacious, convenient, small bar/café, sauna, security box, heaters in fancier rooms.

$$ La Casa de Tintin
Urbanización San Isidro F1, Vallecito,
T054-284700, www.hoteltintin.com.
20 mins' walk, 5 mins by taxi from the Plaza de Armas, Belgian/Peruvian-owned, garden, terrace, sauna, massage, laundry service, café and bar, very pleasant and comfortable.

$$ Las Torres de Ugarte
Ugarte 401A, T054-283532,
www.torresdeugarte.com.
Round the corner from Santa Catalina convent, some rooms are bungalow style in colonial part at the back, roof terrace, safe, luggage store, reflexology.

$$ Maison du Soleil
Pasaje Violín 102, Plazoleta Campo Redondo, San Lázaro, T054-212277, www.maisondusoleil.com.pe.

Nice hotel in a quiet, pleasant location, comfortable rooms, lovely common areas and terrace, includes buffet breakfast, attentive service, **Arthur** restaurant (closed Sun) features molecular cuisine and offers cooking lessons.

$$ Posada El Castillo
Pasaje Campos 105, Vallecito, T054-201828, www.posadaelcastillo.com.
Dutch/Peruvian-owned, in an old house decorated with utensils found in the renovation, 5 mins by taxi from city centre. Variety of rooms and suites, some with balcony and view of El Misti, wonderful breakfast in annexe, pool, lovely gardens, a good choice.

$ Cazorla Hostel
Ugarte 202, p2, T054-226111, see Facebook.
Nice hostel in a central location, private rooms with bath and 8-10-bed dorms, buffet breakfast included, kitchen facilities, terrace.

$ El Indio Dormido
Av Andrés Avelino Cáceres B-9, T054-427401, http://members.tripod.com/h_indio_dormido/.
Close to bus terminals, kitchen, cafeteria, parking, laundry, TV room, very helpful, family-run.

$ Home Sweet Home
Rivero 509A, T054-405982, www.homesweethome-peru.com.
Family-run, Cathy, who runs a travel agency speaks Spanish, English, French, very helpful, warm and inviting atmosphere, substantial fresh breakfast included. Private or shared bath, US$6 pp in dorm, hot water all day, simple rooms, kitchen and laundry facilities, parking.

$ Hostal Santa Catalina
Santa Catalina 500, T054-243705, www.hostalsantacatalinaperu.com.
On busy corner, simple rooms arranged around a courtyard, private or shared bath, kitchen facilities, security box, roof terrace with great views, helpful staff, organizes tours.

$ La Casa de Sillar
Rivero 504, T054-284249, www.lacasadesillar.com.
Nice refurbished 17th-century stone house, comfortable rooms, private or shared bath, nice patio with plants, ample kitchen facilities, terrace with views, tour operator.

$ La Posada del Cacique
Jerusalén 404, T054-202170, posadadelcacique@yahoo.es.
Well maintained, good value and helpful, with roof terrace.

$ Le Foyer
Ugarte 114, T054-286473, www.hlefoyer.com.
Nicely refurbished old house, pleasant common areas, terrace bar, colourfully decorated, private rooms and US$10 pp in dorm, book exchange, arrange tours, popular.

$ Los Andes Bed & Breakfast
La Merced 123, T054-330015, www.losandesarequipa.com.
Good value, kitchen use, hot water, large rooms with waxed wood floors and minimalist decor, TV rooms, pleasant roof terrace.

$ Lula's B&B
In Cayma, T054-272517, www.bbaqpe.com.
Same owners as **Ari Quipay** language school, Lula (Peruvian) and her husband (Swiss) speak Spanish, English, German and French, with airport/bus terminal pick-up, modern, charming, quiet, meals available.

$ Tambo Viejo
Av Mariscal Cáceres 107, IV Centenario, 5 blocks south of the plaza near the rail station, T054-288195, www.tamboviejo.com.
Noisy and less-than-safe area. 12-room guesthouse, quiet, English and Dutch spoken, walled garden, choice of 8 fresh breakfasts (extra), vegetarian restaurant, safe deposit, coffee shop, bar, book exchange (2 for 1), money changed, tourist information for guests, luggage store extra, tours and volcano climbs arranged, discounts for long stays. For a small fee, you can use the facilities if passing through. Free pick-up from bus terminal 0700-2300 (call when arriving).

Restaurants

Arequipa is proud of its gastronomy. Typical dishes, many of them spiced with the hot *rocoto* pepper, accompanied by a glass of local *chicha* or an Arequipeño wine, are available in *picanterías* and at San Camilo market. There are also regional sweets and excellent chocolate, see Shopping below. AGAR, the local gastronomy association, organizes a yearly event, see Festivals, page 1382.

$$$ Chicha
Santa Catalina 210,Casona Santa Catalina int 105, T054-287360. Mon-Sat 1200-2300, Sun 1200-1800.
The menu of mostly local and fusion dishes is created by Gastón Acurio, fine dining in a historic building opposite Santa Catalina. In the same patio and also with an Acurio menu is **Tanta**, serving breakfast and snacks.

$$$ La Trattoria del Monasterio
Santa Catalina 309, T054-204062, www.latrattoriadelmonasterio.com. Mon-Sat 1200-1600, 1900-2300, Sun 1200-1600.
A fusion of Italian and Arequipeño styles and ingredients, in a cloister in Convento de Santa Catalina.

$$$ Salamanto
Urbanización León XXIII, H-11, Cayma, T054-340607, www.salamanto.com. Mon-Sat 1900-2330.
Gourmet Peruvian cuisine, the menu changes every 3 months, bar, good service, popular among foreigners. Also **El Molle Café** next door (Tue-Sat 1200-2330, Sun 1230-1600, closed Jan-Feb).

$$$ Zig Zag
Zela 210, T054-206020, www.zigzagrestaurant.com. Daily 1200-2400.
Lovely atmosphere and decor in a colonial house with arched ceilings, gourmet European/Peruvian fusion cuisine, specializes in meat (alpaca is recommended) and fish cooked on volcanic rock. Also offer a choice of set meals at midday. Delicious, very popular, book in advance. Recommended.

$$$-$$ La Nueva Palomino
Pje Leoncio Prado 122, Yanahuara, T054-252393. Daily 1130-1730.
An Arequipa institution that has been in the same family for 3 generations, a very popular, large *picantería*, with a wide selection of local dishes, such as *rocoto relleno*, *cuy chactado* and *chupe de camarones*, accompanied by *chicha arequipeña*, made with purple corn, large portions. Expect queues at weekends. Recommended.

$$$-$$ Tío Darío
Pje del Cabildo 100, 2 blocks from the Yanahuara church, T054-270473. Daily 1100-1630.
Very good ceviche and other seafood specialities with an Arequipeño touch, also meat dishes, outdoor seating in pleasant gardens with views.

$$ Bóveda San Agustín
Portal San Agustín 127-129, T054-243596. Daily 0700-2300.
Attractive bar downstairs, with an upstairs balcony overlooking the Plaza de Armas. Good breakfasts, lunches and evening specials.

$$ Crepísimo
Santa Catalina 208, at Alianza Francesa, T054-206620, www.crepisimo.com. Daily 0800-2300.
Over 100 different sweet and savoury crepes with traditional and Peruvian flavours, plus salads, sandwiches, *menú* at lunch, great coffee and juices, drinks, magazines and board games, pleasant ambiance. Very tasty, recommended.

$$ Pizzería Los Leños
Jerusalén 407, T054-281818. Daily 1700-2300.
The first wood-fired pizza in the city, plus pasta, *empanadas* 0800-1300, original flavours with a touch of Peruvian home cooking, pleasant atmosphere and music.

$$-$ Gonzalette Asador
Zela 201-B. Mon-Sat 1730-2400, and Villa Hermosa 1009, Av Aviación. Sat-Sun and holidays 1100-1700.
Good value for alpaca steaks, *parrillada*, lamb, pleasant atmosphere, good music.

$$-$ Hatunpa
Ugarte 207 and 208 (across the street). Mon-Sat 1230-2130, Sun 1200-1600.
Small place serving tasty dishes prepared with Andean native potatoes with a choice of toppings, craft beer, warm personalized service, very popular.

$$-$ Peruita Pizzería
Palacio Viejo 321A, T054-212621. Mon-Fri 1230-1500, 1730-2230, Sat 1730-2230.
Set lunch at midday and à la carte in the evening, very good wood-fired pizza and Italian dishes, Italian run.

$ El Buda Profano
Bolívar 425, www.elbudaprofano.com. Daily 1200-2200.
Tasty vegan sushi bar, soups, drinks, desserts, English spoken.

$ El Puente
Santa Marta 207-A, Mon-Sat 0830-1700, and Bello Horizonte C-11B, across Puente Quiñones, behind Umacollo stadium. Daily 0830-1800.
A choice of tasty vegetarian dishes, good value.

$ El Turko
San Francisco 223-25. Sun-Thu 0800-2400, Fri and Sat 0800-0600.
Bright café/bar selling kebabs, coffee, recommended breakfasts and good sandwiches.

$ India
Bolívar 502. Mon-Sat 1200-2100.
Very small restaurant serving tasty Indian cuisine, prepared by an Indian cook, many vegetarian dishes.

$ Istanbul
San Francisco 231. Mon-Wed 0900-2400,
Thu-Sat 0900-0200, Sun 1100-2400.
Middle Eastern fast food, including a delicious
falafel and other vegetarian dishes Also good
coffee. In the same group as El Turko.

$ Ratatouille
Puente Bolognesi 214, T958-794192,
http://ratatouillearequipa.wix.com/home.
French/Peruvian-owned, colourful, serves typical
Mediterranean dishes, as the name implies, based
on fresh produce, good value, popular.

$ Sandwichería Mamut
Mercaderes 111 and Mamut Express at Morán
140, by Plaza de Armas. Daily 0900-2100.
Very tasty giant sandwiches with classic
and typical Peruvian flavours and many
different dressings.

Cafés

Café Capriccio
Mercaderes 121. Daily 0800-2200.
Not that cheap, but excellent coffee, cakes,
etc. Very popular with local business people.
Capriccio Gourmet, on Santa Catalina 120,
San Francisco 135 and at several shopping
centres, is also good.

Café Valenzuela
Morán 114 and other locations.
Mon-Sat 0800-2200, Sun 1630-2030.
Fantastic coffee (also sells beans and ground
coffee), locals' favourite.

Chaqchao
Santa Catalina 204, p2, T054-234572.
Daily 1100-2100.
Coffee, pizza, desserts, organic chocolate. At 1500
they offer fun chocolate-making classes (US$21),
reserve ahead.

Entre Libros y Café
Jerusalén 307. Mon-Sat 0930-2100.
Coffee from various regions of Peru, teas, juices,
fraps, sandwiches, library, books for sale, musical
and other cultural events.

Gud
Santa Catalina 206-A. Mon-Sat 0830-2130.
Paninis, salads, waffles, desserts, chocolates
and craft beer.

Kaffeehaus
Melgar 117, www.kaffeehaus.org. Mon-Fri 0730-
2000, Sat 0800-2000.

Variety of excellent coffees roasted on the
premises, waffles, sandwiches, German desserts.
German/Peruvian-run.

La Alemana
San Francisco 137 and at shopping centres.
Mon-Thu 0800-2400, Fri-Sat 0800-0300.
Wide choice of sausages, plus very good *empanadas*
and sandwiches. Good value and popular.

La Canasta
Jerusalén 115 in courtyard, no sign.
Mon-Sat 0830-2000.
Excellent bakery, great baguettes twice daily, also
serves breakfast and delicious apple and brazil
nut pastries, courtyard seating. Recommended.

OCacao
Palacio Viejo 205 A. Mon-Fri 0900-2130,
Sat 1000-2130.
Small café run by a Belgian *chocolatier*: coffee,
sweets, excellent truffles and bonbons.

Pura Fruta
Mercaderes 131 and Av Trinidad Morán 205,
Cayma. Mon-Sat 0800-2200, Sun 0900-1400.
A great variety of fruit juices and smoothies, coffee,
frappés, yoghurt, salads, sandwiches, desserts.

Bars and clubs

Casona Forum
San Francisco 317, www.casonaforum.com.
Entry US$7.50.
Huge complex incorporating the **Retro Bar**
(live music Tue-Sat from 1930), **Zero** pool bar for
rock music, **Club Latino** for salsa dancing, Club
de los 80 (Thu-Sat from 2200) for 1980s music
and lovely views, and **Forum**, an underground
club with imitation waterfall and plants (Thu-Sat
from 2200).

Déjà Vu
San Francisco 319-B. Daily 1900-0300.
Popular rooftop bar, hosts DJ electronic music
evenings and live music, weekend drinks
specials. During the day (1100-1800), **Deja Vu**
fish restaurant (**$$**) operates in the terrace, lovely
setting and food.

Farren's
Pasaje Catedral 107.
Good meeting place, great music.

Museo del Pisco
Moral 229A. Daily 1700-2400.
Bar where you can learn about the pisco culture
and history, also tastings and mixology classes.

Festivals

A full list of the region's many festivals is available locally from **iPerú**, see Tourist information, above.

10 Jan **Sor Ana de Los Angeles y Monteagudo**, festival for the patron saint of Santa Catalina monastery.

Mar-Apr **Semana Santa** celebrations involve huge processions every night, culminating in the burning of an effigy of Judas on Easter Sun in the main plazas of Cayma and Yanahuara, and the reading of his will, containing criticisms of the city authorities.

27 Apr The celebration of the apostle Santiago.

May Is known as the **Mes de Las Cruces**, with ceremonies on hilltops throughout the city.

3 Aug A procession through the city bearing the images of Santo Domingo and San Francisco.

6-31 Aug **Fiesta Artesanal del Fundo El Fierro** is a sale and exhibition of *artesanía* from all parts of Peru, taking place near Plaza San Francisco.

6-17 Aug Celebration of the city's anniversary on 15th, many events including a mass ascent of El Misti.

Oct-Nov FestiSabores, www.festisabores.com, gastronomical festival held at Plaza Yanahuara for 4 days around the last weekend in Oct. A good place to sample the local food, wine, pisco and music; check www.festisabores.com for exact dates.

2 Nov **Day of the Dead** celebrations in cemeteries.

Dec Hay Festival, www.hayfestival.org/arequipa, week-long cultural festival, offshoot of the UK literary festival.

Shopping

The central San Camilo market, between Perú, San Camilo, Piérola and Alto de la Luna, is worth visiting.

Alpaca goods, textiles and crafts

Claustros de La Compañía, *Morán 140*. Handicrafts shopping centre in a colonial setting, containing many alpaca knitwear outlets including a factory outlet in the 2nd patio.

El Ekeko, at *Patio del Ekeko, Mercaderes 141, www.elekeko.pe*. A variety of crafts, T-shirts, Panama hats, gourmet foodstuffs.

Fundo del Fierro, large handicraft market behind the old prison on Plaza San Francisco; it's worth a visit.

Ilaria, *at Patio del Ekeko.* Fine jewellery.

Kuna by Alpaca 111, *at Patio del Ekeko, www.kuna.com.pe or www.incalpaca.com*. High-quality alpaca and wool products. Also at Casona Santa

Catalina, Santa Catalina 210, Local 1-2; in **Hotel Libertador** and at the airport. Shops in Lima, Cuzco and Puno.

La Comercial, *Mercaderes 236 (no sign), opposite Teatro Municipal*. Recommended for knitted goods, bags, etc.

Michell y Cia, *Juan de la Torre 101, www.michell.com.pe*. Factory outlet, excellent place for alpaca and other wool yarn in huge variety of colours, also a clearance room for baby and adult alpaca yarn. Alpaca and pima cotton garments also for sale at **Sol Alpaca**, Casona Santa Catalina, Santa Catalina 210. 1920s machinery on display. Branches in Lima and Cuzco.

Millma's Baby Alpaca, *Pasaje Catedral 112 and 117, also at Santa Catalina 225, millmas@hotmail.com*. 100% baby alpaca goods, run by Peruvian family, high quality, beautiful designs, good prices.

Bookshops

Librería El Lector, *San Francisco 213*. Wide selection, including Peruvian authors, book exchange in various languages (2 for 1), stocks *Footprint*.

Librerías San Francisco *has branches at Portal de Flores 138 and San Francisco 102-106*. Books on Arequipa and Peru, some in English, also expensive regional topographical maps.

SBS Book Service, *San Francisco 125, T054-205317*. Has a good selection of travel books, etc.

Shopping centres

There are several international style malls in the suburbs of Cayma, Paucarpata, Cerro Colorado and others.

Patio del Ekeko, *Mercaderes 141*. A commercial centre with upmarket restaurants and shops.

Sweets

Antojitos de Arequipa, *Morán 129*. An Arequipa institution. Sells traditional sweets. Also at Jerusalén 120, Portal de Flores 144, the airport and all shopping centres.

La Ibérica, *Jerusalén 136, www.laiberica.com.pe*. Another Arequipa stalwart since 1909. Top-quality chocolate, but expensive. Outlets at Mercaderes 102, Morán 112, Portal de Flores 130, the airport and all shopping centres.

What to do

City tours

There are 4 guides' associations, one of which (**Adegopa**, Morán 118,Claustros de la Compañía, tienda 11http://adegopa.blogspot.com.) offers free promotional tours. **Panoramic bus tours** are offered by several companies (eg www.bustour. com.pe), US$10 for 2 hrs, US$13 for 4 hrs. Most depart from C Zela by Santa Catalina convent, several daily. **Free walking tours** are offered daily at 1000 and 1500 by tourism students from the Universidad Nacional San Agustín (UNSA), meet at Santa Catalina 204; information from Municipal Tourist office at Plaza de Armas; also with **Free Walking Tour Peru**, T998-959566, www.fwtperu. com, depart Plaza San Francisco at 1145; several others, tips expected.

Climbing, cycling, rafting and trekking

Be wary of agencies offering climbing trips with very fast ascents.

Beinhart Peru, T928 841740, www.beinhart-peru.page4.com (in German). Custom tailored multi-day or multi-week cycling and trekking expeditions for small groups. Run by Klaus Hartl, a very dynamic and knowledgeable guide based in Puerto Maldonado and Arequipa. German, English and Czech spoken, contact well in advance. Warmly recommended.

Carlos Zárate Aventuras, Jerusalén 505-A, T054-202461, www.zarateadventures.com/en. Run by Carlos Zárate of the Asociación de Guías de Montaña de Perú. Good family-run business that always works with qualified mountain guides. A specialist in mountaineering and exploring, with a great deal of information and advice and some equipment rental. Carlos also runs trips to one of the supposed sources of the Amazon, Nevado Mismi, as well as trekking in the Cotahuasi canyon, climbing tougher peaks such as Ampato and Coropuna, mountain biking, rock climbing and rafting.

Colca Trek, Jerusalén 401 B, T054-206217, www.colcatrek.com.pe. Knowledgeable and English-speaking Vlado Soto is one of the best guides for the Cotahuasi Canyon and is recommended for climbing, trekking and mountain biking in the Colca Canyon. He also rents equipment and has topographical maps.

Cusipata, Jerusalén 402-A, T054-203966, www. cusipata.com. Recommended as a very good local rafting operator, very popular half-day trips. Also 6-day trips on the Río Colca. Río Chili 1-day kayak courses, as well as mountain bike tours.

Expediciones y Aventuras, Rivero 504 at La Casa de Sillar, T958 326432, www.expedicionesy aventuras.com. Family-run adventure sports operator led by Gustavo Rondón. Experienced guides for rafting, kayaking, biking, climbing, trekking, sand-boarding, body-boarding and horse riding tours. Innovative 4WD routes and camping tours to Colca, Valle de los Volcanes, Cotahuasi, protected areas and the coast; very helpful.

Naturaleza Activa, Santa Catalina 211, T988 227723, naturactiva@yahoo.com. Experienced guides, knowledgeable, climbing, trekking and mountain biking.

Sacred Road Xtreme, Jerusalén 400 AB2, T054-212332, www.sacredroad.com. Arranges hiking, climbing, biking, and rock climbing in Colca Canyon and elsewhere, experienced guides led by Arcadio Mamani, equipment available.

Volcanyon Travel, Las Condes D2, Cayma, T958 021556,www.volcanyontravel.com; main office in Cuzco. Trekking and some mountain bike tours in the Colca Canyon, also volcano climbing.

Language classes

Centro de Intercambio Cultural Arequipa (**CEICA**), www.ceica-peru.com; **Escuela de Español Ari Quipay (EDEAQ)**, www.edeaq.com; **Instituto Cultural Peruano Alemán**, www.icpa. org.pe; **Llama Education**, www.arequipa spanish.com; **Spanish School Arequipa**, www.spanishschoolarequipa.com; **Carlos Rojas**, rojasnuezcarlosmiguel@yahoo.com.pe; **Silvana Cornejo**, silvanacor@yahoo.com.

Tour operators

Many agencies on Jerusalén, Santa Catalina and around Plaza de Armas sell air and bus tickets and offer tours of Colca, Cotahuasi, Toro Muerto and the city. Prices vary greatly so shop around; check carefully what is included in the cheapest of tours and that there are enough people for the tour to run. Travel agents frequently work together to fill buses. Many tourists prefer to contract tours through their hotel. If a travel agency puts you in touch with a guide, make sure he/she is official. The following have been recommended as helpful and reliable:

Andina Travel Service, Jerusalén 309-A, T054-285477. Good 1- to 4-day tours of Colca Canyon, climbing and other adventure sports, guide Gelmond Ynca Aparicio is very enthusiastic.

Colca Explorer, Mariscal Benavides 201, Selva Alegre (north of the centre), T054-282488, www. colca-explorer.com. Agency associated with

Amazonas Explorer in Cuzco, with many options in Colca and southern Peru: from classic local tours to horse riding, mountain biking, fishing in remote lakes, climbing, treks and visiting alpaca farms on the altiplano.

Colca Journeys, *C Rodríguez Ballón 533, Miraflores (northeast of the centre), T973-901010, www. colcajourneys.com*. Specializes in and operates tours to the Colca and Cotahuasi canyons as well as Valle de los Volcanes.

Giardino Tours, *at Casa de Mi Abuela (see above), T054-221345, www.giardinotours.com*. Professional company offering tours and transport, has own properties in Arequipa, Colca (eg delightful **La Casa de Mamayacchi** in Coporaque) and Valle de Los Volcanes, community tourism options, good information.

Kuntur Adventure and Tourism (KAT), *Jerusalén 524B, T054-281864, www.katperutours.com*. Offers a variety of standard and adventure tours (small groups, up to 7 persons) including Colca and half-day Ruta del Sillar. Run by Gerardo Pinto, very knowledgeable and helpful, English and German spoken.

Land Adventure, *Residencial La Peña A-20, Sachaca (southwest of the centre), 947 376345, www.landadventures.net*. 'Sustainable' tour operator with good guides for communities in Colca, trekking (including a 5-day Salkantay trek and Lares), climbing, downhill biking; private tours only.

Pablo Tour, *Jerusalén 400-AB-1, T054-203737, www.pablotour.com*. Family-run agency, has connections with several *hostales* in Cabanaconde and knows the area well, 3-day mixed tours in the Colca Canyon with mountain biking, trekking and rafting, also climbing and sandboarding, free tourist information, topographical maps for sale, bus and hotel reservation service. Son Edwin Junco Cabrera

can sometimes be found in the office; he speaks fluent French and English and is very helpful.

Tierra Ëtnica, *Jerusalén521B, T054-286927, www.tierraetnica.com*. Culinary tours, community tourism in Colca.

Vita Tours, *Jerusalén 302, T054-284211, www. vitatours.com.pe*. Good value tours in the Arequipa area, including to the coast, and in the Colca Canyon where they have a hotel, **La Casa de Lucila in Chivay**.

Volunteering

Paz Holandesa, *Villa Continental, Calle 4, No 101, Paucarpata, T054-432281, www.pazholandesa. com*. Dutch foundation dedicated to helping the impoverished (see their website if you are interested in volunteering). Also has a travel clinic for tourists, Dutch and English spoken, 24-hr service, highly recommended.

Volunteers Peru, *www.volunteersperu.org*. Runs social projects in a home for abandoned girls in the city and teaching English in Cotahuasi.

Transport

Taking a taxi from the airport or bus terminals to your hotel is recommended.

Air Rodríguez Ballón airport is 7 km from the centre, T054-434834. 2 desks offer hotel reservations; also car rentals. Take a taxi to/from your hotel, 30 mins. Airport taxis charge US$7-9 to the centre; other taxis charge US$4-6 to/from the centre; best to use a radio taxi company listed below. The stop for local buses and combis (eg 'Río Seco', 'Cono-Norte' or 'Zamacola') is about 500 m from the airport, but this is not recommended with luggage.

To **Lima**, 1½ hrs, several daily with **Avianca/ TACA** (Centro Comercial Real Plaza, Av del Ejército, Cayma), **LATAM** (Santa Catalina 118-C),

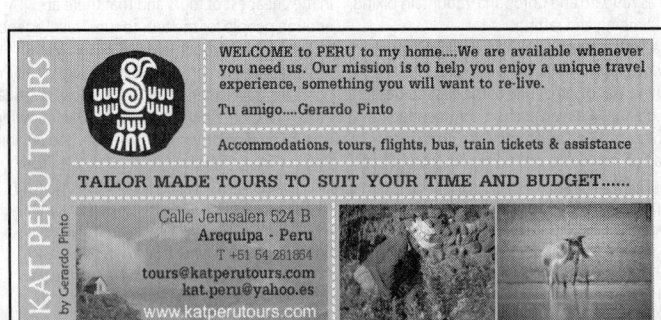

Peruvian Airlines (La Merced 202-B) and **LC Perú** (Moral 223-225, T054-214746). **LATAM** also serves **Juliaca**, 30 mins. **Avianca/TACA** and **LATAM** also serve **Cuzco**, 1 hr from Arequipa. **Peruvian Airlines** also serves **Tacna**. **Amazonas** (La Merced 121-B, www.amazonas.com) sells tickets between Cuzco and **La Paz**, Bolivia.

Bus There are 2 terminals at Av Arturo Ibáñez Hunter, south of the centre, 30 mins by city bus (not recommended with luggage, US$0.50), or 20 mins by taxi, US$2.50-3.60. The older **Terminal Terrestre**, T054-427792, has shops and places to eat. The newer **Terrapuerto**, across the car park, T054-348810, has a travel agency (T054-427852, daily 0600-1400, 2000-2300), which gives information and makes hotel reservations. Most luxury class services leave from the Terrapuerto. Terminal tax is US$0.55-0.90. Some companies have offices in both terminals. Flores, with frequent service to Lima and throughout southern Peru, is in both terminals and also has a private terminal nearby at Av Forga y Av Los Incas. Note that buses may not depart from the terminal where you bought your ticket.

To **Lima**, 1011 km, 15-18 hrs, standard services US$18-29, luxury US$36-56. Cruz del Sur (T054-427375), Enlaces (T054-430333), Tepsa (T054-608079), Oltursa (T01-708-5000) are recommended. The road is paved but drifting sand and breakdowns may prolong the trip.

To **Nazca**, 566 km, 9-11 hrs, US$19-22.50 (US$30-52 on luxury services), several buses daily, mostly at night; most buses continue to Ica (US$30-42) and Lima. Also US$12 to **Chala**, 400 km, 6 hrs. Note that some companies charge a full fare to Lima for intermediate destinations. To **Moquegua**, 213 km, 4 hrs, US$6.50-12, several buses (**Moquegua** is recommended) and colectivos daily. To **Tacna**, 320 km, 6-7 hrs, US$9-11, hourly with **Flores**, direct luxury service without stopping in Moquegua, US$16.

To **Cuzco**, all buses go via Juliaca, US$11-46, 10-11 hrs. Most companies go overnight (eg **Enlaces, Cial, Cruz del Sur, Oltursa**), but Flores and others travel in daytime, at 0715 and 1230.

To **Juliaca**, US$5.50 normal, US$7 *semi-cama*, US$9-27 *cama*, 5 hrs with **Julsa** (T054-430843), hourly 24 hrs a day, with **Flores**, 6-8 daily; some buses continue to Puno. To **Puno**, 297 km, 5-6 hrs, US$7-11, hourly with **Julsa** (poor safety record), 4 daily with **Flores**, at 0800 with **Cruz del Sur** (US$21-27), several others. **4M Express** (La Merced 125 Int 111, T054-452296, www.4m-express.com) offers a tourist service to Puno with stops at Pampa Cañahuas (vicuña observation), Vizcachani (rock formations) and Lagunillas (flamingo and other bird observation) daily at 1245, 6 hrs, US$30-35 (high season), includes bilingual guiding, snack and hotel pickup in Arequipa. They offer a similar service from Chivay to Puno and Cuzco (see Colca transport, page 1391), so you don't necessarily have to travel via Arequipa. To **Puerto Maldonado** via Juliaca, US$18-24, 16 hrs, at 1530 with **Julsa**, 1600 with **Power**, 1700 with **Wayra** (T959-390512) or 1630 with **Mendivil** (T974-210329); more frequent departures from Juliaca.

To **Chivay**, with **Andalucía** (Terrapuerto, T959 448412) at 0930*, 1500, 2400*, **Reyna** (Terminal Terrestre, T958 793712) at 0100*, 0830, 1100*,and **Trans Milagros** (T054-298090) at 0330*, 0530, 1400*, US$4, 3 hrs; those with an asterisk (*) continue to **Cabanaconde**, US$5.50, a further 56 km, 2 hrs. **4M Express** provide private transport between Arequipa and Chivay on request and tour vans will also take extra passengers, pickup starting 0300, arrange with a tour operator.

Taxi From US$1 for trips around town. Companies include: **Alo 45**, T054-454545; **Taxitel**, T054-266262; Real T054-426161; **Turismo Arequipa**, T054-458888.

Train The train station is 7 blocks south of the Plaza de Armas (Huáscar y Quiroz, www.perurail.com). The railway runs from Arequipa to Juliaca (279 km), where it divides, to Cuzco (381 km) and Puno (44 km). For **PeruRail**'s *Belmond Andean Explorer*, see page 1407. *Andean Plains and Islands of Discovery* service to **Cuzco** (2days/2 nights, US$1225-1755) departs Sat 2000, includes excursion on Lake Titicaca (Uros, Taquile and Playa Collata) and stops at Marangoni and Raqchi.

watch condors cruising above this spectacular canyon

★The Colca Canyon is deep: twice as deep as the Grand Canyon. The Río Colca descends from 3650 m above sea level at Chivay to 3287 m at Cabanaconde. In the background looms the grey, smoking mass of Sabancaya (5976 m), one of the most active volcanoes in the Americas, and its more docile neighbours, Ampato (6265 m) and Hualca Hualca (6025 m). Unspoiled Andean villages lie on both sides of the canyon, inhabited by the Cabana and Collagua peoples, and some of the extensive pre-Columbian terraced fields are still in use. High on anyone's list when visiting the canyon is an early-morning trip to the Cruz del Cóndor to see these majestic birds at close quarters.

Arequipa to Chivay

From Arequipa there are two routes to **Chivay**, the first village on the eastern edge of the canyon. The old dirt route goes through Cayma and then runs north between Misti and Chachani to the altiplano. The newer paved route is longer but quicker. It goes through Yura, following the railway. The two routes join at Cañahuas, one of the access points to Reserva Nacional Salinas y Aguada Blanca, where you will have to purchase or show your tourist ticket. Both routes afford fine views of the volcanoes Misti, Chachani, Ampato and Sabancaya; if you're lucky, you can see herds of vicuñas near the road. Cyclists should use the Yura road, as it's in better condition and has less of a climb at the start. At Cañahuas, you can change buses to/from Juliaca or Chivay if you want to bypass

Essential Colca Canyon

Finding your feet

To enter the canyon you must buy a tourist ticket for US$21 (S/70, valid for seven days) at a checkpoint on the road to Chivay; you may be required to show this ticket at Mirador Cruz del Cóndor. It is not always possible to join a tour in Chivay; it is best to organize it in Arequipa and travel with a group. Prices generally do not include the Colca entry ticket, meals other than breakfast nor entry to the baths. From Arequipa a one-day tour to the mirador costs US$20-25. It departs Arequipa at 0300-0330, arrives at the Cruz del Cóndor at 0730-0830, followed by an expensive lunch stop at Chivay and back to Arequipa by 1800-1900. For many, especially for those with altitude problems, this is too much to fit into one day (the only advantage is that you don't have to sleep at high altitude). Two-day tours are about US$25-35 per person with an overnight stop in Chivay or Yanque; more expensive tours range from US$45 to US$90. Most agencies will have a base price for the tour and then different prices depending on which hotel you pick.

Trekking around the canyon

There are many hiking possibilities in the area, with *hostales* or camping for longer treks. Make sure to take enough water, or purification tablets, as it gets very hot and there is not a lot of fresh water available. Sun protection is also a must. Ask locals for directions as there are hundreds of confusing paths going into the canyon. In Cabanaconde trekking and adventure sports can be organized quite easily at short notice. Buy food for longer hikes in Arequipa. Topographical maps are available at the **Instituto Geográfico Nacional** in Lima, and at **Colca Trek** or **Pablo Tour** in Arequipa. Economical trekking tours from Arequipa cost US$45-55 for two days, US$55-65 for three days; entry tickets and lunch on the last day are not included. Agencies pool their passengers and the tour quality is often poor. A private three-day trekking tour for two passengers costs about US$450 per person.

When to go

Conditions vary annually, but January to April is the rainy season, which makes the area green with lots of flowers. This is not the best time to see condors, however, or to go hiking as some treks are impossible if it rains heavily (this is very rare). May to December is the dry, cold season when there is more chance of seeing the birds.

Time required

Allow at least two to three days to appreciate the Colca Canyon fully, more if you plan on doing some trekking.

Arequipa; the road from Cañahuas to Puno via Patahuasi, Imata and Juliaca is paved and has a daily tourist transport service (see Transport, page 1391). It can be cold in the morning, reaching 4825 m in the Pata Pampa pass, but the views are worth it.

Chivay and around

Chivay (3650 m) is the gateway to the canyon, and its road bridge is the main link between the north and south sides (others are at Yanque and Lari). Crossing the river at Chivay going west to follow the canyon on the north side, you pass the villages of **Coporaque**, **Ichupampa** (a footbridge crosses the river between the two villages), **Lari**, **Madrigal** and **Tapay**.

In Chivay, the **Maria Reiche Planetarium and Observatory** ① *in the grounds of the Casa Andina hotel, 6 blocks west of the Plaza between Huayna Capac and Garcilazo, www.casa-andina.com, US$5.70, discounts for students,* makes the most of the Colca's clear Southern Hemisphere skies with a powerful telescope and two 55-minute presentations per day at 1830 (Spanish) and 2000 (English). There is a Globalnet ATM close to the plaza. Thse hot springs of **La Calera** ① *US$4.30 to bathe, half price to visit, regular colectivos (US$0.30), taxi (US$1.70) or a 1-hr walk from town,* are 4 km away and are highly recommended after a hard day's trekking.

Beyond the baths, the road continues northeast to **Tuti**, which has a small handicrafts shop and is the starting point for the trek to **Nevado Mismi** (5598 m). After Tuti is **Sibayo** (*pensión* and grocery store) from where a long circuit leads back to Arequipa, passing through **Puente Callalli**, **Chullo** and **Sumbay**. This is a little-travelled road, but the views, with vicuña, llamas, alpacas and Andean duck are superb.

Chivay to Cruz del Cóndor

From Chivay, the main road goes west along the south side of the Colca Canyon. The first village encountered is **Yanque** (8 km, excellent views), with an interesting church containing superbly renovated altar pieces and paintings; there's a museum on the opposite side of the plaza. A large thermal swimming pool is 20 minutes' walk from the plaza, beside the renovated colonial bridge that leads to the villages of Coporaque and Ichupampa on the other side of the canyon (US$0.75). The road west continues paved to **Achoma** and **Maca** (footbridge to Madrigal on the north side), which barely survived an earthquake in 1991. Then comes the tiny village of **Pinchollo**. From here it is a 30-minute walk on a dirt track to the **Hatun Infiernillo** geyser.

The Mirador at **Cruz del Cóndor**, where you may be asked to show your tourist ticket, overlooks the deepest point of the canyon. The view is wonderful and condors can be seen rising on the morning thermals (0900, arrive by 0800 to get a good spot) and sometimes in the late afternoon (1600-1800). Camping here is officially forbidden, but if you ask the tourist police in Chivay they may help. Reyna's 0430 bus from Chivay stops here very briefly (ask the driver), or try hitching with a tour bus at around 0600. Buses from Cabanaconde stop at about 0700 (**Andalucía**) or 0830 (**Reyna**); they leave Cabanaconde's plaza 30 minutes earlier.

Cabanaconde

From the Mirador it is a 20-minute ride in tourist transport or 40 minutes by local bus on a paved road to Cabanaconde at 3287 m. You can also walk: three hours by the road, or two hours via a short cut following the canyon. This is the last village in the Colca Canyon, friendly, smaller and less touristy than Chivay. The views are superb and condors can be seen from the hill just west of the village, a 15-minute walk from the plaza. You'll also see agricultural terraces, arguably the most attractive in the valley, to the south of the village. Cabanaconde is an excellent base for visiting the region, with interesting trekking, climbing, biking and horse riding.

Treks around Cabanaconde

Two hours below Cabanaconde is **Sangalle**, an 'oasis' of palm trees and swimming areas where there are three campsites with basic bungalows and toilets. It's a beautiful spot, recommended. (It's three to 4½ hours back up; ask for the best route in both directions. Horses can be hired to carry your bag, US$5.85.)

A popular hike involves walking east on the Chivay road to the Mirador de Tapay (before Cruz del Cóndor), then descending to the river on a steep track (four hours, take care). Cross the bridge to the village of San Juan de Chuccho on the north bank, where you can stay and eat at a basic family hostel, of which there are several. From here, pass **Tapay** (also possible to camp here, minivan to Cabanaconde at 0400 and 1100) and the small villages of Cosñirhua and Malata, all the time heading west along the north side of the Río Colca (take a guide or ask local directions). After about three hours' walking, cross another bridge to the south bank of the Río Colca, follow signs to Sangalle, spend the night and return to Cabanconde on the third day. This route is offered by many Arequipa and local agencies.

Another nice hike, which can be combined with the one above, goes west past the stadium to Mirador de Achachihua, then steeply downhill to a road and, along it to a pedestrian or a car bridge over the Río Colca (three to four hours). Before crossing, look for geysers upstream from the pedestrian bridge. On the north side, continue on the road for about 30 minutes. At a hairpin bend where the road turns northeast, go left and follow a large trail northwest, cross a pedestrian bridge over the Río Huaruro, just ahead is **Llahuar** (30 minutes from the road) with nice rustic thermal baths next to the Colca River and two places to stay. Minivans from Tapay to Cabanaconde pass the Llahuar turnoff around 0500 and 1200. From Llahuar, you can continue steeply uphill to the villages of Llatica and Fure and the Fure and Huaruro Falls (five to six hours). From Fure you can reach the Tapay–Cabanaconde road.

Tourist information

Tourist information and a map are available in Arequipa from the **Autoridad Autónoma del Colca** (Puente Grau 116, T054-203010, Mon-Fri 0900-1700, Sat 0900-1200). In Chivay, there is a very helpful **tourist office** in the Municipalidad on the west side of the plaza (closed at weekends). The tourist police, also on the plaza, can give advice about local guides. There's a traveller's **Medical Center (TMC)** (Ramón Castilla 232, T054-531037). There's also a friendly tourist information office in Cabanaconde (T054-280212) that is willing to give plenty of advice, if not maps. It's a good place to find trekking guides and muleteers (US$25 a day mule and guide).

Where to stay

Note that only the fancier hotels and *hostales* have Wi Fi and it is very slow.

Chivay and around

$$$ Casa Andina
Huayna Cápac s/n, Chivay, T054-531020,
www.casa-andina.com.
Attractive cabins with hot showers and a cosy bar/dining area, a member of the recommended hotel chain, heating, parking.

$$$ Pozo del Cielo
C Huáscar B-3, Sacsayhuaman–Chivay,
T054-531041 (Alvarez Thomas 309, Arequipa,
T054-346547), www.pozodelcielo.com.pe.

Very comfortable option, located over the Puente Inca from Chivay amid pre-Inca terraces. Warm rooms, good views, good service and restaurant.

$$ Casa de Lucila
M Grau 131, Chivay, T054-531109,
http://vitatours.com.pe.
Three-storey hotel, comfortable rooms, guides available, reserve ahead in high season.

$$ Colca Inn
Salaverry 307, Chivay, T054-531111,
www.hotelcolcainn.com.
Good mid-range option, modern, decent restaurant, basic breakfast included or US$2.50 for buffet breakfast, some rooms with heaters, nice views from upper rooms. Also run the more upmarket **Hotel Colcallacta**.

$$ La Casa de Mamayacchi
In Coporaque, 6 km from Chivay on the opposite side of the river, T054-531004,
www.lacasademamayacchi.com, reservations through Giardino Tours in Arequipa.
Part of the hotel is in an original Inca structure, nice rooms with heaters, lovely dining area, terraced garden, multi-day packages including transport.

$$ Posada del Colca
Salaverry 325, Chivay, T054-531040,
laposadadelcolca@hotmail.com,
also on Facebook.
Central, good rooms.

$ Hospedaje Restaurant Los Portales
Arequipa 603, Chivay, T054-531101,
losportalesdechivay@hotmail.com,
also on Facebook.
Good value, though beds have rather 'floppy'
mattresses. Restaurant downstairs.

$ La Pascana
Puente Inca y C Siglo XX 106, Chivay, T054-531001,
hrlapascana@hotmail.com.
Excellent value on the northwest corner of
the Plaza. Spacious en suite rooms overlook
a pleasant garden, hot water, parking and a
good restaurant.

$ Rumi Wasi
Sucre 714, 6 blocks from plaza
(3 mins' walk), Chivay.
Good rooms, hot water, helpful.

Chivay to Cruz del Cóndor

$$$$ Colca Lodge
Across the river from Yanque, T054-531191 (office:
Mariscal Benavides 201, Selva Alegre, Arequipa,
T054-202587), www.colca-lodge.com.
Very relaxing, with beautiful hot springs beside
the river, spend at least a day to make the most
of the activities on offer. Day passes available.
Rooms heated with geothermal energy, solar-
heated water.

$$$$ Las Casitas del Colca
Av Fundo La Curiña s/n, Yanque, T996 998355,
www.lascasitasdelcolca.com.
Luxury cottages made of local materials with
underfloor heating and plunge pools. Has a
gourmet restaurant, bar, vegetable garden and
farm, offers cookery and painting courses, the spa
offers a variety of treatments, swimming pool.

$$$ Collahua
Av Collahua cuadra 7, Yanque (office: Mercaderes
212, Galerías Gamesa, Arequipa, T054-226098),
www.hotelcollahua.com.
Modern bungalows just outside Yanque, with
heating, solar-powered 24-hr hot water and
plush rooms, restaurant.

$$$ Eco Inn
Lima 513, Yanque, T054-837112,
www.ecoinnhotels.com.pe.
Perched high on a bluff with incredible views
over the valley and restored Uyo Uyo ruins.
Large, comfortable rooms in cabins, restaurant
open from 0530 for buffet breakfast, Wi-Fi in
lobby and restaurant.

$$ Tradición Colca
Av Colca 119, Yanque, T054-781178 (office:
C Argentina 108, Urb Fecia JL Bustamante y
Rivero, T054-424926), www.tradicioncolca.com.
Adobe construction, gas stove, garden spa,
massages, sauna. Restaurant, bar, games room,
observatory and planetarium (free for guests),
horse riding from 2 hrs to 2 days, hiking tour to
Ullu Ullu, bike rentals, travel agency in Arequipa.

$ Casa Bella Flor Sumaq Wayta Wasi
Cuzco 303, Yanque, T054-774505,
www.casabellaflor.com.
Charming small lodge run by Sra Hilde Checca,
flower-filled garden, tasteful rooms, good meals
(also open to non-residents). Hilde's uncle,
Gregorio, guides visitors to pre-Columbian sites.

$ Hospedaje Refugio del Geyser
C Melgar s/n, behind municipality, Pinchollo,
T959-007441.
Basic with good local information.

$ Rijchariy Colca Lodge
On the track leading down to the footbridge
over the river, Yanque, T054-764610.
Great views, garden, comfortable
rooms, restaurant.

Cabanaconde

$$ Kuntur Wassi
C Cruz Blanca s/n, on the hill above the plaza,
T054-233120, www.arequipacolca.com.
Excellent 3-star, restaurant with fine traditional
meals. Creative design, with rooms with heaters
spaced between rock gardens and waterfalls.
Viewing 'tower' and conference centre above.
Owners Walter and María very welcoming and
knowledgeable about treks.

$$ La Casa de Santiago
Grau, 3 blocks from the plaza, T941 414048,
www.lacasadesantiago.com.
Upmarket small *hostal*, with views of the
mountains and a large garden.

$$ Posada del Conde
C San Pedro, T054-440197, pdelconde@yahoo.com.
Smart hotel and lodge. Cheaper in low season,
with hot shower, comfortable beds, good food.
Local guides and horses for hire.

$ Hostal Valle del Fuego
1 and 2 blocks from the plaza on C Grau y Bolívar,
T054-668910, www.valledelfuego.com.
Rooms with comfortable beds and dorms
(US$7 pp, breakfast extra), laundry facilities,

restaurant. Can arrange guides, pack animals, bike rentals. The Junco family have plenty of information and work with related establishments, including: **Pablo Tour** in Arequipa, where you can make reservations and get a Colca map; **Oasis Paraíso** in Sangalle (discounts for clients of Valle del Fuego and related hotels); **Casa de Pablo Club** at the end of the street, and **La Casa de Santiago** (see above). They usually meet the incoming buses. Popular.

$ La Posada de San Felipe
At Anglican Church, Camino al Mirador Achachihua, 4 blocks from the Plaza, T983 855648.
Nice ample rooms with bath and reliable hot water, quiet location.

$ Pachamama Home
San Pedro 209, T054-767277, www.pachamamahome.com.
Backpacker hostel, rooms with and without bath, family atmosphere, hot water, lots of information, good bar/pizzería **Pachamama** next door, try the Colca Sour, made from a local cactus. You can help with teaching and activities for village children.

$ Virgen del Carmen
Av Arequipa s/n, 5 blocks up from the plaza.
Hot showers, may even offer you a welcoming glass of *chicha*.

Trekking around Cabanaconde
Sangalle has 3 campsites with basic bungalows and toilets. In San Juan de Chuccho, **Hostal Roy** and **Casa de Rebelino** ($) are both good. US$2 will buy you a decent meal. Llahuar hostels ($) fill up, reserve ahead, **Llahuar Lodge**, T956 271333, llahuar.lodge@hotmail.com, rustic cabins with shared cold shower, nice camping area above hot pools (US$3 pp), good meals; next door and more economical is **Casa de Virginia**, T973 559851, rooms with shared bath with solar hot shower, camping (US$2.30 pp) meals on request, use of pools at Llahuar Lodge.

Restaurants

Chivay and around
Several restaurants serve buffet lunches for tour groups, US$5 pp, also open to the general public. Of the few that open in the evening, most have folklore shows and are packed with tour groups. When walking in the valley meals and drinks can be taken in any of the larger lodges. For local

cheeses and dairy products, visit **Productos del Colca** (Av 22 de Agosto), in the central market.

$$ El Balcón de Don Zacarías
Av 22 de Agosto 102 on plaza, T054-531108.
Breakfast, the best lunch buffet in town, à la carte menu, *Novo Andino* and international cuisine.

$$ Yaraví
Plaza de Armas 604.
Arequipeña food, vegetarian options and the most impressive coffee machine in town.

$$-$ McElroys's Irish Pub
On the plaza.
Warm bar, good selection of drinks (sometimes including expensive Guinness), sandwiches, pizza, pasta and music. Also buffet lunch and à la carte at night. Accepts Visa.

$ Innkas Café-Bar
Plaza de Armas 706.
Coffee, sandwiches, *menú*, pizzas, pool table, good atmosphere.

Cabanaconde

$$-$ Casa de Pablo Club
C Grau.
Excellent fresh juices and *pisco sour*, cable TV (football!), small book exchange and some equipment hire.

$ Café de Mirko
At Plaza de Armas. Opens early.
Small café serving coffee, herbal teas and snacks.

$ Rancho del Colca
On plaza.
Mainly vegetarian.

Festivals

There are numerous festivals in the Colca region, many of which last several days and involve traditional dances and customs.

2-3 Feb Virgen de la Candelaria, celebrated in Chivay, Cabanaconde, Maca and Tapay.
Feb Carnaval in Chivay.
3 May Cruz de la Piedra in Tuti.
13 Jun San Antonio in Yanque and Maca.
14 Jun San Juan in Sibayo and Ichupampa.
21 Jun Anniversary of Chivay.
29 Jun San Pedro y San Pablo in Sibayo.
14-17 Jul La Virgen del Carmen in Cabanaconde.
25 Jul Santiago Apóstol in Coporaque.
26 Jul-2 Aug Virgen Santa Ana in Maca.
15 Aug Virgen de la Asunta in Chivay.

8 Dec Immaculada Concepción in Yanque and Chivay.
25 Dec Sagrada Familia in Yanque.

What to do

It is not always possible to join a tour in Chivay; it is best to organize it in Arequipa and travel with a group. In Cabanaconde trekking and adventure sports can be organized quite easily at short notice. See also Essential Colca Canyon, page 1386.

Chivay

Ampato Adventure Sports, *Av Siglo 417, 2 blocks from the bus station, T054-489156, www.ampatocolca.com.* Offer information and rent good mountain bikes.
Pedro Samayani, *T958 034023, pedroscolca@ hotmail.com.* Local guide offers tours throughout the Colca area.
Zacarías Ocsa Osca, *T949 494866, zacariasocsa@ hotmail.com.* Local trekking guide offers Colca tours and more unusual routes such as Mismi, Inca road from Chivay to Apurímac, a 5-day tour to 3 canyons and llama trekking.

Cabanaconde

Local guides charge US$15 pp per day to Sangalle, US$20 pp per day to Llahuar, minimum 3 passengers. A muleteer with 1 mule charges US$25 per day.
Agotour Colca, *T951 526615 (Alejandro Maque).* An association of regional guides.
Chiqui Travel & Expeditions, *Plaza de Armas s/n, next to the Municipalidad, T958-063602.* Edizon Gomosio, private guide, professional and reliable, organizes trekking, biking and horse riding, can also arrange for pack animals and make reservations.

Transport

Bus The bus station in Chivay is 3 blocks from the main plaza, next to the stadium for service to Arequipa, Cabanaconde and Pinchollo. Vans and *colectivos* leave from the terminal behind the market to other villages in the area.

See Arequipa Transport, page 1385, for service originating there. To **Arequipa**, buses start at the Plaza de Armas in **Cabanaconde**, US$5.50, 5 hrs; **Reyna** at 0700 and 1400, **Andalucía** at 0815 and 0900 and **Trans Milagros** at 1130 and 2200; they pass **Cruz del Cóndor** (20 mins, US$2.20), then **Chivay** 2 hrs after departure; Chivay–Arequipa US$4, 3 hrs. Tour buses take extra passengers if they have room, enquire with tour operators. **4M Express** (see below) offers private transport to Arequipa on request. **Chivay** to/from **Cabanaconde**, 56 km, US$1.45, 2 hrs, through buses from/to Arequipa; also hourly minibuses depart half a block from the Chivay terminal. To **Cuzco**, take the **4M Express** tourist service (see below) or a regular bus to Cañahuas and change there for a bus to Juliaca, then carry on to Cuzco. Note, however, there are no bus stations in Cañahuas, it is cold and buses to Juliaca are often full.

Tourist service **4M Express**, www.4m-express.com, has several routes departing from Hotel La Pascana on Chivay's plaza, all stop at places of interest along the way and include a snack. To **Puno** Terminal Terrestre, daily 1315, US$50, 7 hrs, stopping at Patapampa lookout, Chucura Volcano and Lagunillas (birdwatching). To **Cuzco**, direct route along a paved road via Tuti, Sibayo and Sicuani, Mon, Wed and Fri at 0700, US$65 (lunch extra), 10½ hrs, stopping at Castillos de Callalli rock formations, Yauri rock forest, Laguna de Langui (25 km long), Sicuani (lunch break) and dropping off at **4M**'s private station.

Cotahuasi Canyon

how low can you go?

★At its deepest, at Ushua (just below the village of Quechualla), the Cotahuasi Canyon measures 3354 m from rim to river, making it 163 m deeper than the Colca Canyon and the deepest canyon in the world. From this point, the only way along the canyon is by kayak, and it is through kayakers' reports that the area has come to the notice of tourists. The Reserva Paisajística Cañón de Cotahuasi protects the extensive Cotahuasi drainage, from the icy summits of Solimana and Huanzo (5445 m) to where it joins the Río Ocoña at 950 m. The canyon is very dry, especially from April to October when the contrast between the desert slopes and the green irrigated oases along the wider sections of the river valley and on the hanging valleys of its tributaries is particularly striking. Grapes, organic kiwicha (amaranth) and quinoa for export, avocados, citrus and other fruits are grown here. The side canyons are very impressive in their own right. Despite the arid climate and rugged geography, the canyon has been populated for centuries. There are a number of pre-Inca and Inca remains perched on terraces cut into the vertical canyon walls and segments of Inca trade routes from the coast to the highlands can still be seen. The area has several thermal baths, waterfalls, impressive rock formations, cacti and *Puya raimondii* bromeliad forests, and amazing views. A good *turismo vivencial* programme with homestays in many villages allows you to access all the attractions.

Towards Cotahuasi: Río Majes Valley

Southwest of Arequipa, a paved road branches off the Pan-American to the impressive Siguas Canyon and on to the agricultural valley and canyon of the Río Majes, a rafting destination. At the linear roadside town of **Corire** are several hotels and restaurants serving excellent freshwater shrimp.

Nearby is the world's largest field of petroglyphs at **Toro Muerto** ① *6.5 km from Corire, US$1.45, van from the plaza in Corire to La Candelaria Mon-Fri 0700, returning 1400, US$0.60, or taxi, US$14 incl 2-hr wait, tours available from Arequipa.* Access to the UNESCO World Heritage Site is signposted off the main road 1.5 km south of Corire, where a road turns east to the village of La Candelaria, 2 km from the main road. One block above the plaza is the archaeological site's office where the entry fee is collected. From here it is 3 km on a dirt road to the site entrance which provides the only shade in the area; the immense field of 5000 sculpted rocks in the desert lies beyond. The sheer scale of the 5-sq-km site is awe-inspiring and the view is wonderful. The higher you go, the more interesting the petroglyphs, though some have been ruined by graffiti. Don't believe the guides who, after the first few rocks, say the others are all the same. The designs range from simple llamas to elaborate human figures and animals. There are several styles which are thought to be Wari (AD 700-1100), Chuquibamba (AD 1000-1475) and Inca in origin. An extensive review of the designs is found in *Memorias del Arqueólogo Eloy Linares Málaga* (Universidad Alas Peruanas, 2011). Take plenty of water, sunglasses and sun cream. At least an hour is needed to visit the site.

From Corire an unpaved road follows the Río Majes to Camaná on the coast. Upriver from Corire, the paved road goes past a park with dinosaur prints to the regional centre of **Aplao**, which has a small museum containing Wari cultural objects from the surrounding area. A side road to the north leads to **Andagua** (several places to stay) in the fascinating **Valle de los Volcanes**, while the main road continues northwest to **Chuquibamba** (several places to stay and eat) in a scenic terraced valley, where the paving ends. Beyond Chuquibamba, the road climbs steeply to traverse the *puna* between Nevado Coropuna (6425 m) and Nevado Solimana (6093 m). The views are awe-inspiring, so it is well worth the effort to travel this route by day.

Cotahuasi and the upper canyon

From Mirador Allhuay (3950 m) at the rim of the Cotahuasi Canyon, the road, now paved, winds down to the peaceful colonial town of **Cotahuasi**, nestled in a sheltered hanging valley at 2680 m, beneath Cerro Huinao. Its streets are narrow, with whitewashed houses. The Río Cotahuasi flows 1500 m below the town at the bottom of its great canyon.

Following the Río Cotahuasi to the northeast up the valley, you come to **Tomepampa** (10 km), a small town at 2700 m, with painted houses and a colonial church. The attractive hot springs of **Luicho** ① *16.5 km from Cotahuasi, daily 0330-2130, US$1.80, 1 simple room for rent,* are a short walk from the road, across a bridge. There are three pools (33° to 38°C). The paved road ends at **Alca**, 20 km from Cotahuasi, at 2750 m, with several simple places to stay and eat. Above it are the small ruins of Kallak, Tiknay and a 'stone library' of rock formations. All these places are connected by hourly mini-buses from Cotahuasi (see Transport). **Puyca** ① *23 km beyond Alca, bus from Alca at 0530, return at 1200, 1½ hrs, US$2.50, www.canyoncotahuasi.com,* is the last village of any significance in the valley, hanging on a hillside at 3560 m. Locals can guide you on treks in the area, and horses can be hired. Nearby, at 3700 m, are the extensive Wari ruins of Maucallacta (20-minute walk), the most important in the Cotahuasi area. Beyond is **Churca** ① *24 km from Puyca, van from Alca at 0530, return at 1200, 2-3 hrs, US$3.20,* from where you can walk to Lauripampa at about 4000 m in 20 minutes to see a vast prairie of *Puya raimondii* plants. On the opposite side of the river from Churca is Chincayllapa from where you can drive to the Occoruro geysers at 4466 m, also reached in a full-day walk from Puyca.

Along a tributary of the Cotahuasi, in a beautiful terraced side canyon north of Cotahuasi, is the village of **Pampamarca** ① *at 3397 m, 28 km from Cotahuasi, daily bus from Cotahuasi at 0500 and 1630, returning 0600 and 1330, US$2, 2 hrs, accommodation in homestays.* There are excellent walking possibilities here. Attractions include the Wito rock formations, 90 m high Uskune waterfall, Josla thermal baths and, a bit further afield, the Fuysiri waterfalls.

Downstream from Cotahuasi

A rough, narrow road follows the Río Cotahuasi downriver for 28 km to Mayo. At Km 13 is the access to the powerful, 150-m **Cataratas de Sipia** ① *2 km from the road, bus from Terminal Terrestre Tue-Thu and Sat 0630, Mon and Sun 0630 and 1330, Fri 0630 and 1400, US$1.45, 30 mins (return 2½-3 hrs later).* A good trail leads from the road to several lookouts over the three-tiered falls, which are the most visited attraction in the canyon; take care near the edge, especially if it is windy. The best light is at midday. You can also get an overview of the falls from the road, continuing past the turnoff to the top of the hill.

Beyond Sipia the road, carved into the canyon wall, leads to the hamlets of Chaupo and Rosariopampa and, at Km 23, the cactus forest of **Judiopampa**, with trails. The road ends at **Mayo** ① *return transport daily 0900, also 1600 Mon, Fri and Sun,* between two trails which climb to the village of **Velinga** (with homestays). A trail continues past the roadhead to the Niñochaca bridge over the Río Cotahuasi, beyond which is the dilapidated but extensive ruin of Huaña and, past another bridge, the charming village of **Quechualla** (9 km from Mayo, with homestays) at 1665 m. Ushua, the deepest part of the canyon, is below Quechualla, where you can also see two small waterfalls along a tributary stream.

Listings Cotahuasi Canyon

Tourist information

Tourist information is available from **CONSETUR**, represented in Cotahuasi by **Purek Tours** (C Arequipa 103, daily 0900-1300, 1400-2000). A map of Cotahuasi may be available at **iPerú** in Arequipa. See also www.municipiolaunion.com. There are no ATMs in Cotahuasi but **Banco de la Nación** (C Cabildo) changes US$ cash.

Where to stay

Río Majes Valley

$ Hostal Willy's
Av Progreso opposite the market, Corire, T054-472046 and Progreso y Morán, at the Plaza, Aplao, T959-476622.
Both modern buildings with comfortable rooms, no breakfast.

$ La Casa de Mauro
La Central, 12 km north of Aplao (combi service), T054-631076, www.star.com.pe/lacasademauro.
Simple cabins and camping (US$5.50 per tent) in a lovely rural setting, restaurant with 60 different shrimp dishes, run by the friendly Zúniga family, rafting, trekking and conventional tours.

$ Montano
Ramón Castilla s/n, Corire, T054-472122.
Best rooms are at the back away from the road, some rooms are small, no breakfast, good value.

Cotahuasi and the upper canyon
For information about homestays in the towns outside Cotahuasi, contact CONSETUR (see above).

$$ Valle Hermoso
Tacna 108-110, Cotahuasi, T054-581057, www.hotelvallehermoso.com.
Nice and cosy, includes breakfast, beautiful views of the canyon, comfortable rooms, large garden, meals with home-grown fruit and veg require advanced notice.

$ Casa Primavera
Main street, Tomepampa, T954-734056.
Family-run hostel with a flower-filled courtyard, some rooms with private bath, price includes breakfast, other meals on request, kitchen facilities, common areas, good value.

$ Don Justito
Arequipa110, ½ block below the plaza, Cotahuasi, T973-698053.
Ample functional rooms with and without bath, plenty of solar heated water, popular, good value economy option.

$ El Mirador
Centenario 100-A, Cotahuasi, T054-489417.
Pleasant rooms, great views, no breakfast.

$ Hatun Huasi
Centenario 309, Cotahuasi, T054-581054, www.hatunhuasi.com.
Popular *hostal* with a variety of rooms, nice small garden and common areas, parking, breakfast

extra, helpful owner Catalina Borda speaks some English. Recommended.

Restaurants

Cotahuasi and the upper canyon
There are many tiendas well-stocked with fruit, vegetables and local wine.

$$-$ Buen Sabor
C Arequipa, up from the plaza, Cotahuasi.
A la carte Peruvian dishes, caters to tourists.

$ La Chocita Cotahuasina
Av Independencia, ½ block from the church, Cotahuasi. Open 0700-2100, closed Wed.
Good set meals, pleasant patio seating.

What to do

Several tour operators in Arequipa (see page 1383), organize tours to Cotahuasi. Also see **Purek Tours** in Cotahuasi town, under Tourist information, above.
Amazonas Explorer, *in Cuzco, www.amazonas-explorer.com.* Can organize 5-day kayaking expeditions on the Cotahuasi for experienced kayakers only.

Río Majes Valley
La Casa de Mauro Tours, *see Where to stay, T959-362340, www.star.com.pe/lacasademauro.* Pancho Zúñiga offers rafting, trekking and 4WD tours in the Majes, Cotahuasi and Colca areas.

Cotahuasi and the upper canyon
Purek Tours, *C Arequipa 103, Cotahuasi, T054-698081, cotahuasitours@gmail.com.* Biking, horse riding and 2- to 3-day trekking tours.

Transport

Río Majes Valley
Empresa Del Carpio buses to **Corire** and **Aplao** leave from the Terrapuerto in **Arequipa** about every 1½ hrs 0430-1900, 3-4 hrs, US$4.30; to **Chuquibamba** at 0515 and 1615, return 0500 and 1200, US$7.50, 6-7 hrs. For **Toro Muerto**, ask to be let out at the turnoff to La Candelaria. Cotahuasi-bound buses from Arequipa stop at the plaza in Corire (near the Del Carpio station), at the highway in Aplao and at the terminal in Chuquibamba. To **Camaná** on the coast (transfer here for Nazca and Lima), van from Aplao at 0800, passes Corire 0830, US$5.40, 2 hrs; returns from Camaná at 0400-0500. To **Andagua**, Reyna from Arequipa at 1600, via Corire and Aplao, return about 1500. There is a daily minivan from Andagua to **Chacas**.

Cotahuasi and the upper canyon
Destinations along the canyon are connected Mon-Sat 0600-1800 by hourly combis from Cotahuasi, fewer on Sun. Cotahuasi has a modern bus station (terminal fee US$0.35) 10 mins' walk from the plaza. Buses daily from **Arequipa** Terminal Terrestre, 10-11 hrs, US$11: **Cromotex** at 1700 and 1800; **Reyna** at 1630; they stop for refreshments in Chuquibamba, about halfway. Both companies continue to **Tomepampa** and **Alca;** buses leave Alca for Arequipa around 1400 (you can get off at Cotahuasi). Return Cotahuasi to Arequipa, **Cromotex** at 1800 and 1900, **Reyna** at 1700. From **Lima**, Trans López (Sebatián Barranca 158, La Victoria, T01-332 1015), Sun at 0900, US$36, 20 hrs (passes Chuquibamba Mon 0500-0630); return Cotahuasi to Lima Tue 0700. This is the only public transport daytime option to/from Cotahuasi, offering magnificent views; you can board in Corire, Aplao or Chuquibamba.

South to Chile

Moquegua is a pleasant stopover on the route south or east

From Arequipa, the main road to the coast goes southwest for 37 km to Repartición where it divides. One branch goes west from here for 54 km through a striking arid landscape before dividing again: northwest to the Majes and Cotahuasi areas (see above) or southwest to Camaná (170 km from Arequipa) on the coast. The second branch from Repartición goes south and, in 15 km, divides south to Mollendo and southeast towards Moquegua.

Moquegua and around *Colour map 6, A1.*
This city lies 213 km from Arequipa in the narrow Moquegua river valley and enjoys a sub-tropical climate. The old centre, a few blocks above the Pan-American Highway, has winding, cobbled streets and 19th-century buildings. The Plaza de Armas, with its mix of ruined and well-maintained churches, colonial and republican façades and fine trees, is one of the most interesting small-city

plazas in the country. Within the ruins of Iglesia Matriz is the **Museo Contisuyo** ① *Jr Tacna 294, on the Plaza de Armas, T053-461844, www.museocontisuyo.com, Wed-Mon 0800-1300, 1430-1730, Tue 0800-1200, 1600-2000, US$0.50,* which focuses on the cultures that thrived in the Moquegua and Ilo valleys, including the Huari, Tiahuanaco, Chiribaya and Estuquiña, who were conquered by the Incas. Artefacts are well displayed and explained in Spanish and English.

A highly recommended excursion is to **Cerro Baúl** (2590 m) ① *30 mins by colectivo, US$2,* a tabletop mountain with marvellous views and many legends, which can be combined with the pleasant town of Torata, 24 km northeast.

One of the most breathtaking stretches of the **Carretera Binacional** from Ilo to La Paz runs from Moquegua to Desaguadero at the southeastern end of Lake Titicaca. The road is fully paved and should be travelled in daylight. It skirts Cerro Baúl and climbs through zones of ancient terraces to its highest point at 4755 m. On the altiplano there are herds of llamas and alpacas, lakes with waterfowl, strange mountain formations and snow-covered peaks. At Mazo Cruz there is a PNP checkpoint where all documents and bags are checked. Approaching Desaguadero the Cordillera Real of Bolivia comes into view.

Tacna *Colour map 6, A1.*

Thanks to its location, only 36 km from the Chilean border and 56 km from the international port of Arica, Tacna has free-trade status. It is an important commercial centre, and Chileans come here for cheap medical and dental treatment. Around the city the desert is gradually being irrigated to

Tacna

To Bus Station, Panamericana Norte & Alto de la Alianza
To Panamericana Norte & Stadium

□ Chilean Consulate

Cnl Albarracín
Presbítero Andía
Zarumilla
Julio Mac Lean

Museo Ferroviario ▥

2 de Mayo

Touring y Automóvil Club

Francisco Lazo
Cnl Inclán
Hipólito Unanue
28 de Julio
Gral Deustua
Arias Aragüez
P Méndez

Mercado 2 de Mayo

Teatro Municipal ▥

OGD Tur Tacna

Centro Cultural Miculla

de la Barca

Modesto Basadre

Gral Blondell

Francisco de Zela

Scotiabank Ⓢ

BCP Ⓢ

Vigil

San Martín

Cathedral ✝

Plaza de Armas

Casa de la Cultura

Arequipa
Mollendo
Ugarte
Apurímac
Ayacucho
Pasaje
Junín

Callao

Simón Bolívar

Av Bolognesi

Parque de la Locomotora

Av Grau

Mercado Central ▥

Pallardelli

Av Restauración

To Panamericana Sur, Airport & Arica

N

400 metres
400 yards

Where to stay 🛏
1 Copacabana
2 Dorado
3 El Mesón
4 Gran Hotel Tacna
5 Hostal Anturio
6 Hostal Bon Ami
7 La Posada del Cacique
8 Roble 18 Residencial

Restaurants 🍴
1 Café Zeit
2 Cusqueñita
3 Da Vinci
4 Fu-Lin
5 Il Pomodoro
6 Koyuki
7 Un Limón
8 Verdi

produce olives and vines; fishing is also important. Tacna was in Chilean hands from 1880 to 1929, when its people voted by plebiscite to return to Peru. Above the city (8 km away, just off the Panamericana Norte) is the **Campo de la Alianza**, scene of a battle between Peru and Chile in 1880. The cathedral, designed by Eiffel, faces the Plaza de Armas, which contains huge bronze statues of Admiral Grau and Colonel Bolognesi. They stand at either end of the Arca de los Héroes, the triumphal arch which is the symbol of the city. The bronze fountain in the Plaza is said to be a duplicate of the one in the Place de la Concorde (Paris) and was also designed by Eiffel. The **Parque de la Locomotora** ① *knock at the gate under the clocktower on Jr 2 de Mayo for entry, daily 0700-1700, US$0.30,* near the city centre, has a British-built locomotive, which was used in the War of the Pacific. There is a very good railway museum at the station.

Border with Chile

It is 56 km from Tacna to the Chilean city of Arica. The border post is 30 minutes from Tacna at Santa Rosa, open 0800-2300 Sunday to Thursday and 24 hours on Friday and Saturday. You need to obtain a Peruvian exit stamp at Santa Rosa before proceeding a short distance to the Chilean post at Chacalluta where you will get a Chilean entrance stamp. Formalities are straightforward and should take about 30 minutes in total. All luggage is X-rayed in both directions. No fruit or vegetables are allowed across the border. If you need a Chilean visa, get it from the Chilean consulate in Tacna (Presbítero Andía block 1, T052-423063, Monday-Friday 0800-1300). Money-changers can be found at counters in the international bus terminal; rates are much the same as in town. Remember that Peruvian time is one hour earlier than Chilean time from March to October; two hours earlier from September/October to February/March (varies annually).

Crossing by bus It takes one to two hours to travel from Tacna to Arica, depending on waiting time at the border. Buses charge US$2.50, and *colectivo* taxis, which carry five passengers, charge US$7.50 per person. All leave from the international terminal in Tacna throughout the day, although *colectivos* only leave when full. As you approach the terminal you will be grabbed by a driver or his agent and told that the car is "just about to leave". This is hard to verify as you may not see the *colectivo* until you have filled in the paperwork. Once you have chosen a driver/agent, you will be rushed to his company's office where your passport will be taken from you and the details filled out on a Chilean entry form. It is then 30 minutes to the Peruvian border post at Santa Rosa. The driver will hustle you through all the exit procedures. A short distance beyond is the Chilean post at Chacalluta, where again the driver will show you what to do. It's a further 15 minutes from Chacalluta to Arica's bus terminal. A Chilean driver is more likely to take you to any address in Arica.

Crossing by private vehicle Those leaving Peru by car must buy *relaciones de pasajeros* (official forms, US$0.45) from the kiosk at the border or from a bookshop; you will need four copies. At the border, return your tourist card to immigration (Migraciones), visit the PNP (police) office, return the vehicle permit to the SUNAT/Aduana office and finally depart through the checkpoints.

Listings South to Chile *map p1395*

Tourist information

Moquegua

Dircetur
Ayacucho 1060, T053-462236.
Mon-Fri 0800-1630.
The regional tourist office.

Tacna

Dircetur
Blondell 50, p 2, T052-246944, www.
turismotacna.com. Mon-Fri 0730-1530.
Provides a city map and regional information.

Immigration
Av Circunvalación s/n,
Urb El Triángulo, T052-243231.

iPerú
San Martín 491, Plaza de Armas, T052-
425514. Mon-Sat 0830-1800, Sun 0830-1300,
iperutacna@promperu.gob.pe.

Also in the Arrivals hall at the airport (usually open when flights are scheduled to arrive), at the Terminal Terrestre Internacional (Mon-Sat 0830-1500) and at the border (Fri-Sat 0830-1600).

OGD Tur Tacna
Deústua 364, of 107, T052-242777.

Tourist police
Pasaje Calderón de la Barca 353, inside the main police station, T052-414141 ext 245.

Where to stay

Moquegua
Most hotels do not serve breakfast.

$ Alameda
Junín 322, T053-463971.
Includes breakfast, large comfortable rooms, welcoming.

$ Hostal Adrianella
Miguel Grau 239, T053-463469.
Hot water, safe, helpful, tourist information, close to market and buses, bit faded.

$ Hostal Carrera
Jr Lima 320-A (no sign), T053-462113.
With or without bath, solar-powered hot water (best in afternoon), laundry facilities on roof, good value.

$ Hostal Plaza
Ayacucho 675, T053-461612.
Modern and comfortable, good value.

Tacna

$$$ Gran Hotel Tacna
Av Bolognesi 300, T052-424193, www.dmhoteles.pe.
Disco, gardens, safe car park. The pool is open to non-guests who make purchases at the restaurant or bar. English spoken.

$$ Copacabana
Arias Aragüez 370, T052-421721, www.copahotel.com.
Good rooms, also has a restaurant and pizzería.

$$ Dorado
Arias Aragüez 145, T052-415741, www.doradohoteltacna.com.
Modern and comfortable, good service, restaurant.

$$ El Mesón
H Unanue 175, T052-425841, www.mesonhotel.com.
Central, modern, comfortable, safe.

$ Hostal Anturio
28 de Julio 194 y Zela, T052-244258.
Cafetería downstairs, breakfast extra, good value.

$ Hostal Bon Ami
2 de Mayo 445, T052-244847.
With or without bath, hot water best in afternoon, simple, secure.

$ La Posada del Cacique
Arias Aragüez 300-4, T052-247424.
Antique style in an amazing building constructed around a huge spiral staircase.

$ Roble 18 Residencial
H Unanue 245, T052-241414, roble18@gmail.com.
1 block from Plaza de Armas. Hot water, English, Italian, German spoken.

Restaurants

Moquegua

$ Moraly
Lima y Libertad. Mon-Sat 1000-2200, Sun 1000-1600.
The best place for meals. Breakfast, lunches, *menú* US$1.75.

Tacna

$$ Da Vinci
San Martín 596 y Arias Araguez, T052-744648. Mon-Sat 1100-2300, bar Tue-Sat 2000-0200.
Pizza and other dishes, nice atmosphere.

$$ Il Pomodoro
Bolívar 524 y Apurimac. Closed Sun evening and Mon lunchtime.
Upscale Italian serving set lunch on weekdays, pricey à la carte in the evening, attentive service.

$ Cusqueñita
Zela 747. Daily 1100-1600.
Excellent 4-course lunch, large portions, good value, variety of choices. Recommended.

$ Fu-Lin
Arias Araguez 396 y 2 de Mayo. Mon-Sat 0930-1600.
Vegetarian Chinese.

$ Koyuki
Bolívar 718. Closed Sun evening.
Generous set lunch daily, seafood and à la carte in the evening. Several other popular lunch places on the same block.

$ Un Limón
Av San Martín 843, T052-425182.
Ceviches and variety of seafood dishes.

Cafés

Café Zeit
Deústua 150, CafeZeit on Facebook.
German-owned coffee shop, cultural events and live music as well as quality coffee and cakes.

Verdi
Pasaje Vigil 57.
Café serving excellent *empanadas* and sweets, also set lunch.

Moquegua
25 Nov **Día de Santa Catalina**. The anniversary of the founding of the colonial city.

Moquegua
Bus All bus companies are on Av Ejército, 2 blocks north of the market at Jr Grau, except **Ormeño** (Av La Paz casi Balta). To **Lima**, US$30-42, 15 hrs, many companies with executive and regular services. To **Tacna**, 159 km, 2 hrs, US$6, hourly buses with **Flores** (Av del Ejército y Andrés Aurelio Cáceres). To **Arequipa**, 3½ hrs, US$7.50-12, several buses daily. *Colectivos* for Tacna and Arequipa leave when full from Av del Ejercito y Andrés Aurelio Cáceres; they charge almost double the bus fare – negotiate. To **Desaguadero** and **Puno**, **San Martín-Nobleza**, 4 a day, 6 hrs, US$12; *colectivos* to Desaguadero, 4 hrs, US$20, with **Mily Tours** (Av del Ejército 32-B, T053-464000).

> **Tip...**
> If you're travelling to **La Paz**, Bolivia, the quickest and cheapest route is via Moquegua and Desaguadero; it involves one less border crossing than via Arica and Tambo Colorado. There is a **Bolivian Consulate** in Tacna (Avenida Bolognesi 175, Urb Pescaserolli, T052-245121, Monday-Friday 0830-1630).

> **Tip...**
> Bus passengers' luggage is checked at **Tomasiri**, 35 km north of Tacna. Do not carry anything on the bus for anyone else. Passports may be checked at Camiara, a police checkpoint some 60 km from Tacna. There is also a post where any fruit will be confiscated in an attempt to keep fruit fly out of Peru.

Tacna
Air The airport (T052-314503) is at Km 5 on the Panamericana Sur, on the way to the border. To go from the airport directly to Arica, call the bus terminal (T052-427007) and ask a *colectivo* to pick you up on its way to the border, US$7.50. Taxi from airport to Tacna centre US$5-6.
To **Lima**, 1½ hrs; daily flights with **LATAM** (Apurímac 101, esq Av Bolognesi, T01-213 8200) and **Peruvian Airlines** (Av Bolognesi 670, p2, T052-412699), also to **Arequipa**.

Bus There are 2 bus stations (T052-427007; local tax US$0.50) on Hipólito Unánue, 1 km from the plaza (*colectivo* US$0.35, taxi US$1 minimum). One terminal is for international services (ie Arica), the other for domestic; both are well organized, with baggage stores. It is easy to make connections to the border, Arequipa or Lima. To **Moquegua**, 2 hrs, US$6, and **Arequipa**, 6 hrs, frequent buses with **Flores** (Av Saucini behind the Terminal Nacional, T052-426691), **Trans Moquegua Turismo** and **Cruz del Sur**. Ask at the **Flores** office about buses along the Vía Costanera to Ilo. To **Nazca**, 793 km, 12 hrs, several buses daily, en route to Lima (fares US$3 less than to Lima). Several companies daily to **Lima**, 1239 km, 21-26 hrs, US$26-62 *bus-cama* with **Oltursa** or **Civa**; **Cruz del Sur** (T052-425729) charges US$43.
Buses to **Desaguadero**, **Puno** and **Cuzco** leave from Terminal Collasuyo (Av Internacional, Barrio Altos de la Alianz, T052-312538); taxi to centre US$1. **San Martín-Nobleza** in early morning and at night to **Desaguadero**, US$22, and **Puno**, US$18, 8-10 hrs.

Train The station is at Av Albaracín y 2 de Mayo. Following 5 years of interruption, service along the cross-border line to Arica was resumed in 2016, with 2 trains daily at 0600 and 1630, US$5.50, 1½ hrs.

Lake
Titicaca

★Straddling Peru's southern border with Bolivia are the sapphire-blue waters of mystical Lake Titicaca, a huge inland sea which is the highest navigable lake in the world. Its shores and islands are home to the Aymara and Quechua. Here you can wander through traditional villages where Spanish is a second language and where ancient myths and beliefs still hold true. Paved roads climb from the coastal deserts and oases to the high plateau in which sits Lake Titicaca (Arequipa-Yura-Santa Lucía-Juliaca-Puno; Moquegua-Desaguadero-Puno). The steep ascents lead to wide open views of pampas with agricultural communities, desolate mountains, small lakes and salt flats. It is a rapid change of altitude, so be prepared for some discomfort and breathlessness.

Puno and around   Colour map 6, A2. See map, page 1400.

Titicaca's tourist centre

Located on the northwest shore of Lake Titicaca at 3855 m, Puno is capital of its region and Peru's folklore centre, with a vast array of handicrafts, festivals and costumes and a rich tradition of music and dance. The city has a noticeable vitality, helped by the fact that students make up a large proportion of the 120,000-strong population.

Sights

The **Cathedral** ⓘ *Mon-Fri 0800-1200, 1500-1800, Sat-Sun 0800-1300, 1500-1900,* completed in 1657, has an impressive baroque exterior, but an austere interior. Across the street from the Cathedral is the **Balcony of the Conde de Lemos** ⓘ *Deústua y Conde de Lemos, art gallery open Mon-Fri 0830-1230, 1330-1730,* where

> **Tip...**
> Puno gets bitterly cold at night: from June to August the temperature at night can fall to -25°C, but is generally not below -5°C.

Peru's Viceroy stayed when he first arrived in the city. The **Museo Carlos Dreyer** ⓘ *Conde de Lemos 289, Mon-Fri 0900-1900, Sat 0900-1400, US$4.50 includes 45-min guided tour,* has eight halls with archaeological and historical artefacts from pre-Inca to republican times.

A short walk up Independencia leads to the **Arco Deústua**, a monument honouring those killed in the battles of Junín and Ayacucho. Nearby is a *mirador* giving fine views over the town, the port and the lake beyond. The walk from Jr Cornejo following the Stations of the Cross up Cerro Azoguini, with fine views of Lake Titicaca, has been recommended, but be careful and don't go alone or after dark; the same applies to any of the hills around Puno, including Huajsapata and Kuntur Wasi.

From the Plaza de Armas Avenida Titicaca leads 12 blocks east to the lakeshore and port. From its intersection with Avenida Costanera towards the pier, one side of the road is lined with the kiosks of the **Artesanos Unificados de Puno**, selling crafts. Closer to the port are food kiosks. On the opposite side of the road is a shallow lake where you can hire **pedal boats** ⓘ *US$0.60 pp for a short ride.* At the pier are the ticket counters for transport to the islands. The **Malecón Bahía de los Incas**, a lovely

Best for
Boat trips ■ Festivals ■ Handicrafts ■ Local customs ■ Scenery

promenade along the waterfront, extends to the north and south; it has a sundial and is a pleasant place for a stroll and for birdwatching.

The **Yavarí** ① *anchored off Isla Esteves (see Hotel Libertador, taxi from centre US$3.50), www.yavari.org, tours every 2 hrs, 0800-1600, US$12*, is the oldest ship on Lake Titicaca. It was built in England in 1862 and was shipped in kit form to Arica, then by rail to Tacna and by mule to Lake Titicaca, a journey that took six years. The *Yavarí* was finally launched on Christmas Day 1870. The ship offers Bed & Breakfast ($$$), see website or contact T051-367780. Berthed in Puno harbour, is the **MS Ollanta**, which was built in Hull (UK) and sailed the lake from 1926 to the 1970s. Another old ship is the **MN Coya**, built in Scotland and launched on the lake in 1892, it was being overhauled in 2016.

☆Sillustani

32 km from Puno off the road to Juliaca. Daily 0830-1730. US$3. Tours from Puno, US$10-15, last about 3-4 hrs, some stop at a Colla house on the way, to see local products. Or take a van towards Juliaca as far as the turnoff for Sillustani (US$0.75), where taxis wait (mostly in the morning), US$1 pp for the 14-km-ride to the site. It's cold and windy; make sure you have return transport.

Puno

To Juliaca, Cuzco & Arequipa
To ⑮⑲❶❶ & Yavari Ship/B&B

Where to stay
1 Casa Andina Private Collection Puno A4
2 Casa Andina Tikarani B2
3 Casona Colón Inn Puno centre
4 Conde de Lemos C2
5 El Buho Puno centre
6 Hacienda Plaza de Armas C2
7 Hacienda Puno Puno centre
8 Hostal Imperial & Los Uros B3
9 Hostal Los Pinos B2
10 Hostal Margarita B2
11 Hostal Pukara Puno centre
12 Inka's Rest B3
13 Intiqa B2
14 Italia B2
15 Libertador Lago Titicaca A4
16 Plaza Mayor Puno centre
17 Posada Don Giorgio B2
18 Posada Luna Azul C2
19 Sonesta Posadas del Inca A4
20 Tayka & Vylena Hostels C1
21 Tierra Viva Puno Plaza Puno centre

Restaurants
1 Cafetería Mercedes Puno centre
2 Casa del Corregidor C2
3 Chifa Nan Hua B2
4 Incabar Puno centre
5 La Casona Puno centre
6 La Cayma Puno centre
7 La Estancia Puno centre
8 La Hostería Puno Centre
9 Loving Hut C3
10 Machupizza Puno centre
11 Mojsa C2

Near Puno are the chullpas (pre-Columbian funeral towers) of Sillustani in a beautiful setting on a peninsula in Lake Umayo (3850 m). The scenery is barren, but impressive. John Hemming writes: "Most of the towers date from the period of Inca occupation in the 15th century, but they are burial towers of the Aymara-speaking Colla tribe. The engineering involved in their construction is more complex than anything the Incas built – it is defeating archaeologists' attempts to rebuild the tallest 'lizard' chullpa." Artefacts found in the tombs can be seen at the Museo Carlos Dreyer in Puno (see above). Handicraft sellers wait at the exit. There is community tourism at **Atuncolla**, near the lake, US$18 pp for homestays with full board, contact T951-905006.

There are more chullpas from the Lupaca and Colla kingdoms (AD 1100-1450) in **Cutimbo** ① *turn-off at Km 17 on the Puno–Moquegua road, daily 0830-1730, US$3*, where rock art and Inca ruins are also to be found.

Tip...
Photography at Sillustani is best in the afternoon light, though this is when the wind is strongest.

☆Península de Capachica

The Península de Capachica encloses the northern side of the Bahía de Puno and is a great introduction to Lake Titicaca. The scenery is very pretty, with sandy beaches, pre-Inca terracing, trees and flowers. It is also good for hiking and mountain biking, and sailing boats can be hired. The view of the sunset from Auki Carus hill rivals that from Taquile (see page 1408). At the eastern end of the peninsula, the pretty farming villages of **Llachón**, **Santa María** and **Ccotos** have become a focus of community-based tourism. There are currently six organizations, each with a dozen or more families and links to different tour operators in Puno, Cuzco or abroad. Visitors share in local activities and 70% of all produce served is from the residents' farms. Throughout the peninsula the dress of the local women is very colourful, with four-cornered hats called *monteras*, matching vests and colourful *polleras*. Off the east coast of the peninsula is the island of **Ticonata**, whose community tourism association offers accommodation in round houses and various activities. It's a short boat ride from Ccotos, or from Amantaní (see page 1409); motorboats from Puno take 3½ hours.

☆Western shore: Chucuito to the border

An Inca sundial can be seen near the village of **Chucuito** ① *19 km from Puno, vans from 1 de Mayo y Banchero Rossi, US$0.50, 25 mins*, which has houses with carved stone doorways and two interesting colonial churches: 16th-century Santo Domingo, the first in the region, and 17th-century La Asunción. Also here is the Inca Uyo, a fertility plaza filled with stone phalli. Further south is the larger town of **Acora** (34 km), which provides access to a lovely

Puno centre

12 Pizzería/Trattoria El Buho *Puno centre*
13 Ricos Pan *C2, centre*
14 Tradiciones del Lago *Puno centre*
15 Tulipan's *Puno centre*
16 Ukukus *Puno centre*

Bars & clubs 🍸
17 Positive *Puno centre*

peninsula with luxury hotels and the Charcas beaches. The important commercial centre of **Ilave** is 55 km from Puno.

Juli ① *www.munijuli.gob.pe, 80 km, colectivo from Terminal Zonal Sur in Puno, US$1.50, 1½ hrs; returns from outside Juli market at Ilave 349*, has some fine examples of religious architecture. **San Pedro church** ① *on the plaza, daily 0800-1700, free, donations appreciated*, contains a series of paintings of the saints, with the Via Crucis scenes in the same frame, and gilt side altars above which some of the arches have baroque designs. **San Juan Letrán** and **La Asunción** ① *both daily 0800-1700, US$2.50 each*, are now museums containing paintings by artists from the Cuzco School of Art and from Italy. San Juan has two sets of 17th-century paintings of the lives of St John the Baptist and St Teresa, contained in sumptuous gilded frames, as well as intricate *mestizo* carving in pink stone. The nave at La Asunción is empty, but its walls are lined with unlabelled paintings. The original murals on the walls of the transept can be seen. Its fine bell tower was damaged by earthquake or lightning. Outside is an archway and atrium which date from the early 17th century. Needlework, other weavings, handicrafts and antiques are offered for sale in town.

A further 20 km along the lake, atop a hill, is **Pomata** ① *bus from Juli US$0.90, US$2.50 from Puno*, whose red sandstone church of **Santiago Apóstol** ① *daily 0800-1200, 1300-1600, US$1 (if guardian is not there, leave money on table)*, has a striking exterior and beautiful interior, with superb carving and paintings from the Escuela Cusqueña.

Past Pomata, the road south along the lake divides; one branch continues straight towards the Bolivian border at Desaguadero, via **Zepita**, where the 18th-century Dominican church is worth a visit. **Desaguadero** is a bleak place with simple restaurants and accommodation. Friday is the main market day, when the town is packed. There is a smaller market on Tuesday but at other times it is deserted.

The other branch of the road from Pomata follows the lakeshore to the border crossing at Kasani near **Yunguyo** (see page 1414 for border crossings). Vans depart from Yunguyo to Punta Hermosa, where you can catch a boat to Anapia in Lago Menor (see page 1409).

Listings Puno and around *map p1400*

Tourist information

Useful websites include www.munipuno.gob.pe (the municipal site) and www.titicaca-peru.com (in Spanish and French).

Indecopi
Jr Ancash 146, T051-363667.
Consumer protection bureau.

iPerú
Jr Lima y Deústua, near Plaza de Armas, T051-365088, iperupuno@promperu.gob.pe. Mon-Sat 0900-1800, Sun 0900-1300. Also at Juliaca airport.
Helpful English- and French-speaking staff, good information and maps.

Tourist police
Jr Deústua 588, T051-352303. 24 hrs.
Report robberies here, and scams (such as unscrupulous price changes) to Indecopi and iPerú.

Where to stay

There are over 80 places to stay in Puno, including a number of luxury hotels in and around the city. Prices vary according to season. Many touts try to persuade tourists to go to a hotel not of their own choosing. Be firm.

$$$$ Casa Andina Private Collection Puno
Av Sesquicentenario 1970, T051-363992, www.casa-andina.com.
This recommended chain's luxury lakeshore property.

$$$$ Libertador Lago Titicaca
On Isla Esteves linked by a causeway 5 km northeast of Puno (taxi US$3), T051-367780, www.libertador.com.pe.
Modern hotel with every facility, built on a Tiahuanaco-period site, spacious, good views, bar, restaurant, disco, good service, parking.

$$$$ Sonesta Posadas del Inca
Av Sesquicentenario 610, Huaje, 5 km from Puno on the lakeshore, T051-364111, www.sonesta. com/laketiticaca/.

62 rooms with heating, facilities for the disabled, local textile decorations, good views, **Inkafé** restaurant has an Andean menu, folklore shows.

$$$ Hacienda Plaza de Armas
Jr Puno 419, T051-367340, www.hhp.com.pe.
Tastefully decorated modern hotel overlooking the Plaza de Armas, small comfortable rooms, all with bathtub or jacuzzi, heater, safety box, restaurant.

$$$ Hacienda Puno
Jr Deústua 297, T051-356109, www.hhp.com.pe.
Refurbished colonial house, with buffet breakfast, rooms and suites with good bathrooms, restaurant with local specialities, comfortable.

$$$ Intiqa
Jr Tarapacá 272, T051-366900, www.intiqahotel.com.
Built around a sunny courtyard. Stylish, rooms have heaters, dinner available, professional staff.

$$$ Plaza Mayor
Deústua 342, T051-368728, www.plazamayorhotel.com.
Comfortable, well-appointed, good big beds, buffet breakfast, heating, restaurant.

$$$ Tierra Viva Puno Plaza
Jr Grau 270, 1 block from plaza, T051-368005, www.tierravivahoteles.com.
Regional decor, heating, all rooms non-smoking, central, business centre.

$$$-$$ Casona Colón Inn
Tacna 290, T051-351432, www.coloninn.com.
Colonial style, good rooms, some with bathtub, heating, good service. **Le Bistrot** serves international and Peruvian cuisine.

$$ Casa Andina Tikarani
Independencia 185, T051-367803, www.casa-andina.com.
A central option. Heating, non-smoking rooms, business centre.

$$ Conde de Lemos
Jr Puno 681, T051-369898, www.condelemosinn.com.
Convenient, comfy suites and rooms with bathtubs, heating, elevator, buffet breakfast, restaurant.

$$ El Buho
Lambayeque 142, T051-366122, www.hotelbuho.com.
Nice carpeted rooms, most with bathtubs, heating, discount for *Footprint* book owners, buffet breakfast, tour agency, parking extra.

$$ Hostal Imperial
Teodoro Valcarcel 145, T051-352386, www.hostalimperial.com.
Basic but big rooms, good hot showers, safety box, helpful, stores luggage, comfortable.

$$ Hostal Pukara
Jr Libertad 328, T051-368448, www.pukaradeltitikaka.com.
Excellent, English spoken, helpful service, heating, central, quiet, free coca to drink in evening, American breakfast included, dining room on top floor, lots of stairs.

$$ Italia
Teodoro Valcarcel 122, T051-367706, www.hotelitaliaperu.com.
Cheaper in low season, good restaurant, buffet breakfast, small rooms, helpful staff.

$$ Posada Don Giorgio
Tarapacá 238, T051-363648, Facebook: Posada-Don-Giorgio-Puno-199808310121923.
Comfortable large rooms, nicely decorated, traditional architecture, heater extra.

$$ Posada Luna Azul
Cajamarca 242, T051-364851, www.posadalunaazul.com.
Comfortable carpeted rooms, heating, parking, luggage storage.

$ Hostal Los Pinos
Tarapacá 182, T051-367398, hostalpinos@hotmail.com.
Family-run, helpful, breakfast available, cold rooms, heater on request, reliable hot water, laundry facilities, small book exchange, tours organized, good value. Recommended.

$ Hostal Margarita
Jr Tarapacá 130, T051-352820.
Large building, family atmosphere, cold rooms, private or shared bath, heaters on request, helpful owner, tours can be arranged.

$ Hostal Vylena
Jr Ayacucho 503, T051-351292, hostalvylena20@hotmail.com.
Functional rooms, hot water during limited hours, breakfast available, luggage storage, economical.

$ Inka's Rest
Pasaje San Carlos 158, T051-368720.
Several sitting areas, heating, double or twin rooms with private or shared bath and US$9 pp in dorm, cooking and laundry facilities, a place to meet other travellers, reserve ahead.

$ Los Uros
Teodoro Valcarcel 135, T051-352141.
Private or shared bath, breakfast available, quiet at back, small charge to leave luggage, laundry, heating costs extra.

$ Tayka Hostel
Jr Ayacucho 515, T051-351427, www.taykahostel.com.
Simple lodging, private rooms include breakfast, shared rooms (US$9 pp) do not, electric showers, luggage storage.

Península Capachica

Local families offer accommodation in their homes, lists available from iPerú in Puno and the Municipalidad in Capachica town. All hosts can arrange private boat transport (US$25 per boat) to Amantaní and Uros Titino, a less visited, more authentic, part of the Uros Islands; public boat service from Llachón to Amantaní, US$2.50 pp. Among those who offer lodging in Llachón ($ per bed, meals extra) are: **Tomás Cahui Coila** (T951-691501); **Felix Turpo Coila** (T951-664828); **Valentín Quispe** (T951-821392, llachon@yahoo.com); other families also accept guests.

Western shore: Chucuito to the border

$$$$ Castillo del Titicaca
Playa de Charcas, 45 mins from Puno, T950-308000, www.castillo.titicaca-peru.com.
Exclusive 5-room hotel on a rocky promontory overlooking the lake and surrounded by extensive terraced gardens. Luxurious apartments and rooms, 1 inside a castle, restaurant with lake views, full board. Belgian manager Christian Nonis is known for his work on behalf of the people of Taquile.

$$$$ Titilaka Lodge
Comunidad de Huencalla s/n, on a private peninsula near Chucuito, T01-700 5111 (Lima), www.titilaka.com.
Luxury boutique hotel in Relais et Châteaux group offering all-inclusive packages in an exclusive environment on the edge of the lake. Plenty of activities available on land and on the water; works with local Uros communities.

$$$ Taypikala Lago
Sandia s/n, Chucuito, T051-792266, www.taypikala.com.
Upmarket hotel near the lakeshore, suites with jacuzzi, fridge and fireplace, and heated rooms with bathtub and safety box; restaurant, pool, spa, water sports, gym, meditation and yoga areas.

$$ Las Cabañas
Jr Tarapacá 538, Chucuito, T951-751196, www.chucuito.com.
Rooms and ample cottages in nice grounds, breakfast included, other meals available. Owned by Sr Juan Palao, a knowledgeable local historian, busy at weekends, events held here; will collect you from Puno if you phone in advance.

$ Hostal Isabel
San Francisco 110, near Plaza de Armas, Yunguyo, T951-794228.
With or without bath, nice rooms and courtyard, electric shower, parking, friendly. A few other cheap places to stay.

$ Sra Nely Durán Saraza
Chucuito Occopampa.
2 nice rooms, 1 with lake view, shared bath, breakfast and dinner available, very welcoming and interesting.

Restaurants

Tourist restaurants and their touts, all offering alpaca, trout, *cuy* and international dishes, are clustered along Jr Lima.

$$$-$$ La Casona
Lima 423, p2, T051-351108, www.lacasona-restaurant.com. Daily 1200-2130.
Upmarket tourist restaurant serving a wide choice of international dishes.

$$$-$$ Mojsa
Lima 635 p 2, Plaza de Armas, www.mojsarestaurant.com. Daily 1200-2130.
Good international and *Novo Andino* dishes, also has an arts and crafts shop.

$$$-$$ Tradiciones del Lago
Lima 418, T051-368140, www.tradiciones delago.com. Daily 1200-2200.
Popular tourist restaurant serving a great variety of à la carte dishes.

$$ Incabar
Lima 348, T051-368031. Daily 0800-2200.
Open for breakfast, lunch and dinner, interesting dishes in creative sauces, fish, pastas, curries, café and couch bar, nice decor.

$$ La Estancia
Libertad 137. Daily 1100-2200.
Grilled meat and à la carte Peruvian dishes, large portions, very popular.

$$ La Hostería
Lima 501, T051-365406. Mon-Sat 1100-2200, Sun 1700-2200.

Good set meal and à la carte dishes including local fare like alpaca and *cuy*, pizza, also breakfast.

$$ Tulipan's
Lima 394. Daily 1000-2200.
Sandwiches, juices and a lunchtime menu are its staples. One of the few places in Puno with outdoor seating in a pleasant colonial courtyard, a good option for lunch.

$$-$ Chifa Nan Hua
Arequipa 378. Daily 1200-2200.
Tasty Chinese, big portions.

$$-$ La Cayma
Libertad 216, T051-634226. Open 0900-2200, closed Sat.
Good pizza, Peruvian and international dishes, tasty set lunch, pleasant atmosphere, good service.

$$-$ Loving Hut
Pje Choquehuanca 188. Mon-Sat 0900-1800.
Daily choice of very tasty, creative vegan dishes and salad bar, good value *menú* 1200-1500. Popular and recommended.

$$-$ Machupizza
Arequipa 409, T951-246001. Mon-Sat 1800-2200.
Tasty pizza and other Italian dishes, good value, popular with locals.

$$-$ Pizzería/Trattoria El Buho
Jr Libertad 240, T051-356223. Daily 1700-2230.
Excellent pizza, lively atmosphere.

$$-$ Ukukus
Pje Grau 146, T051-369504, Sun-Fri 1000-2200.
Good combination of Andean and *Novo Andino* cuisine as well as pizzas and some Chinese *chifa* style.

Cafés

Cafetería Mercedes
Jr Arequipa 144.
Good *menú*, bread, cakes, snacks, juices.

Casa del Corregidor
Deústua 576, aptdo 2, T051-365603.
In restored 17th-century building, sandwiches, good snacks, coffee, good music, great atmosphere, nice surroundings with patio. Also has a Fairtrade store offering products directly from the producers.

Ricos Pan
Jr Arequipa 332 and Jr Moquegua 334. Mon-Sat 0600-2130, Sun 1500-2130.

Café and bakery, great cakes, excellent coffees, juices and pastries, breakfasts and other dishes.

Bars and clubs

Dómino
Libertad 443.
Happy hour Mon-Thu 2000-2130.
"Megadisco", good.

Pachas
Lima 370.
Innovative bar.

Platinum
Libertad 521.
Club, popular with local youth.

Positive
Lima 382. Daily 0600-0100.
Drinks, snacks, large-screen TV, reggae and rock. Also serves breakfast all day.

Festivals

1st 2 weeks in Feb Virgen de la Candelaria. On the 1st Sun, some 100 communities compete in an indigenous dance contest. The dances include *llameritos*, *wifala* and *ayarachis*. The following Sun and Mon colourfully attired dancers participate in a contest of *mestizo* folk dances such as *diablada*, *morenada*, *llamerada*, *caporales* and *saya*. A large procession takes place on 2 Feb, the main day. The nighttime festivities on the streets are better than the official functions in the stadium. The dates of the festival until 2020 are posted on www.titicaca-peru.com.
Mar/Apr Good Fri. A candlelit procession through darkened streets.
3 May Festividad de las Cruces. Celebrated with masses, a procession and the Alasitas festival of miniatures.
29 Jun Colourful festival of **San Pedro**, several venues, including Ichu (between Puno and Chucuito) and Zepita (see page 1402).
4-5 Nov Pageant dedicated to the founding of Puno and the emergence of Manco Cápac and Mama Ocllo from the waters of Lake Titicaca.

Shopping

Puno is the best place in Peru to buy alpaca wool articles; bargaining is appropriate. There are numerous outlets selling alpaca garments, paintings and other handicrafts in the centre. You will be hassled to buy along Jr Lima, so keep your wits about you.

Markets

Mercado Artesanal Asociación de Artesanos Unificados, see above (daily 0700-1800). Closer to the centre is **Central Integral de Artesanos del Perú** (CIAP; Jr Deústua 792, Mon-Sat 0900-2100). The **Mercado Central**, in the blocks bound by Arbulú, Arequipa, Oquendo and Tacna, has all kinds of food, including good cheeses as well as a few crafts. Beware pickpockets.

What to do

To avoid paying above the odds for a tour by a *jalagringo*, ask to see their ID card. Only use agencies with named premises, compare prices and never hand over money on the street.

Agencies organize trips to the Uros floating islands (½ day from US$7.50), the islands of Taquile (full day including Uros from US$18, US$36 on a fast boat) and Amantaní (2 days), as well as to Sillustani (½ day from US$9) and other places. The standard tour is 2 days, 1 night, visiting the Uros, staying in either Taquile or Amantaní and then visiting the other island the next day (US$27-36 pp). Choose an agency that allows you to pay direct for your lodging so you know that the family is benefiting. Some agencies pool tourists, especially in low season. We have received good reports on the following:

All Ways Travel, Casa del Corregidor, Deústua 576, p 2, T051-353979, T051-355552, www.titicacaperu. com. Good quality tours, very helpful, kind and reliable, speak German, French, English and Italian, towards the upper end of the price range. Among their tours is a unique cultural tour to the islands of Anapia and Yuspique in Lake Wiñaymarka, beyond the straits of Tiquina.
CEDESOS, Centro para el Desarrollo Sostenible, Jr Moquegua 348 Int p 3, T051-367915, www. cedesos.org. A non-profit NGO which offers interesting tours of Capachica peninsula with overnight stops in family homes, going to the less visited islands where there are few tourists.
Cusi Expeditions, Jr T Varcarcel 155, T051-369072, cusitravel@hotmail.com. Experienced operator that runs most of the standard tour boats to the islands. Good prices, accurate information.
Edgar Adventures, Lima 328, T051-353444, www.edgaradventures.com. English, German and French spoken, very helpful and knowledgeable, work with organized groups. Constantly exploring new areas, lots of off-the-beaten-track tours. Community-minded, promote responsible tourism. Consistently recommended.

Inca Lake Travel, Jr Cajamarca 619, Of 4, T956-060988, www.incalake.com. Standard tours as well as bike tours and rentals.
Kontiki Tours, Jr Melgar 188, T051-353473, www. kontikiperu.com. Large tour agency specializing in spiritual tourism and special interest excursions.
Nayra Travel, Lima 419, of 105, T051-337934, www.nayratravel.com. Small agency run by Lilian Cotrado and her helpful staff, traditional local tours and a variety of options in Llachón. Can organize off-the-beaten track excursions for a minimum of 2 people. Recommended.
Pirámide Tours, no storefront, www.titikakalake. com. Sells out of the ordinary and classic tours, flexible, personalized service, modern fast launches, very helpful, works only via internet.
Titikaka Explorers, Jr Puno 633 of 207, T951-522633, www.titikaka-explorer.com. Good service, helpful, works with organized groups.

Transport

Air The regional airport is in Juliaca (see Transport page 1413). Airport transfers from/to **Puno** US$4.50 pp with hotel pickup: **América Tours** (Jr Tacna 313, T951-568624) and **Rossy Tours** (Jr Tacna 308, T051-366709); many hotels also offer airport transfers. Taxi from Puno to the airport, about US$20-25. Alternatively, take regular public transport to Juliaca (see below) and then a taxi to the airport from there, but allow extra time. **LATAM** office in Puno at Jr Tacna 299, T051-367227.

Boat Boats to the islands (see page 1410) leave from the terminal at the harbour; *trici-taxi* from centre, US$1.

To Bolivia Crillon Tours, Camacho 1223, La Paz, T+591 2-233 7533, www.titicaca.com, run luxury services by bus and hydrofoil between La Paz and Puno, with onward tours to Cuzco and Machu Picchu. Similar services, by catamaran, are run by **Transturin** (Ayacucho 157, p2, T051-353319, Puno, www.transturin.com).

Bus Local Small buses and vans for Juliaca, Ilave and towns on the lakeshore as far as Desaguadero and Yunguyo, leave from the **Terminal Zonal Sur** (Av Costanera Sur; taxi to the centre, US$1.50). To **Juliaca**, 44 km, 1 hr, vans US$1.25, also from **Terminal Fátima** (Jr Ricardo Palma 225) and **Dorado** (Jr Lampa y Pje Ilo); they all go to the *Salida a Cuzco*, outside the centre of Juliaca; for long-distance bus services to Juliaca, see below. To **Yunguyo**, 0600-1900, 2½ hrs, US$3; if there are enough passengers, they may continue to the border at **Kasani**, US$3.60 (taxi from Puyo to Kasani US$55). To **Desaguadero**, vans 0300-1900, 2½ hrs, US$3.60 (taxi US$50).

Long distance All long-distance buses leave from the **Terminal Terrestre** (1 de Mayo 703 y Victoria, by the lake). It has a tourist office. Platform tax, US$0.50. Taxi to the centre, US$1.50.

To **Puerto Maldonado**, direct with Santa Cruz at 1930, US$12-15, 13 hrs, or change in Juliaca (see below). To **Arequipa**, 5-6 hrs via Juliaca, 297 km, US$6-11, hourly with **Julsa** (poor safety record); 4 daily with **Flores**; at 1500 and 2230, with **Cruz del Sur** (city office at Jr Lima 394, T051-368524, *busca cama* US$22); several others. **Tourist service** with 3 stops (see Arequipa transport, page 1385), with **4M Express**, www.4m-express.com, from the Terminal Terrestre at 0600, 6 hrs, US$27-35 includes bilingual guiding, snack and hotel drop-off in Arequipa. The same company offers service with 3 stops direct to **Chivay** on the **Colca Canyon** (see Transport, page 1391), without going to Arequipa, from the Terminal Terrestre at 0600, US$50, 7 hrs. To **Moquegua**, 5 hrs, US$9-18, and **Tacna**, 7 hrs, US$11-18. To **Lima**, 1011 km, 21-24 hrs, US$36-57, all buses go through Arequipa, sometimes with a change of bus.

To **Cuzco**, 388 km, 6-7 hrs, there are 3 levels of service, all via Juliaca: Regular, stopping in Juliaca, US$7-12; Direct, US$15-27, from Terminal Terrestre with **Tour Perú** (city office at Jr Tacna 285, www.tourperu.com.pe) at 0800 and 2200, with **Cruz del Sur** at 2200 and with **Transzela** (www.transzela.com.pe) at 0815 and 2200; Tourist service with 5 stops (Pucará, La Raya, Sicuani for lunch, Raqchi and Andahuaylillas), US$65 (includes lunch, may or may not include entry tickets), 10 hrs. Several companies offer the tourist service; all depart from the Terminal Terrestre (except Turismo Mer): **Inka Express** (Terminal Terrestre and Jr Tacna 346, T051-365654), leaves 0700; **Turismo Mer** (Jr Tacna 336, T051-367223, www.turismomer.com) leaves from private terminal at Av Costanera 430, past the Terminal Zonal Sur, at 0730; **Wonder Perú** (Terminal Terrestre and Jr Tacna 344, T051-353388) leaves 0715. In high season, reserve 2 days ahead.

To Bolivia To **Copacabana** (via **Kasani border**), US$5.40-7, 3½ hrs, departures at 0700 or 0730 and 1430; continuing to **La Paz**, US$10-12.50 (from Puno), 10 hrs (including border and lunch stops); most services involve transferring to a Bolivian company in Copacabana. All companies have offices at the Terminal Terrestre from where they leave; some also have offices in the centre; some provide hotel pick-up. The better companies include: **Tour Perú** (Jr Tacna 285, of 103, T951-604189, www.tourperu.com.pe);

Panamericano (Jr Tacna 245, T051-354001); **Huayruro Express** (Jr Arequipa 624, T051-366009), and **Titicaca** (Jr Tacna 285, of 104, T051-363830, www.titicacabolivia.com), which also has a 0600 departure. **Litoral**, at the Terminal Terrestre, is cheaper, but thefts have been reported on its night buses. To **La Paz**, direct via Desaguadero with **Tour Peru** at 0700, US$16, 5 hrs.

Taxi In addition to regular cabs, and *moto-taxis*, Puno also has 3-wheel rickshaw *trici-taxis*.

Train The train station is 3 blocks from Plaza Pino (La Torre 224, T051-369179, www.perurail.com, Mon-Fri 0700-1200, 1500-1800, Sat 0700-1500). The railway runs from Puno to Juliaca (44 km), where it divides, to Cuzco (381 km) and Arequipa (279 km). **PeruRail's** *Belmond Andean Explorer* luxury sleeper trains with private bath and shower operate on this route (no service in Feb). Includes stops at points of interest, optional excursions at extra cost. Buy tickets well in advance; passport required. To **Cuzco** (1 day/1 night, US$480-695 double occupancy) departs Wed 1200, stopping at La Raya and Cusipata.

Península Capachica

Boat Boats from Amantaní to Puno stop in Chifrón (near Capachica village) 0800-1200, US$2.50 one way. The daily 0800 boat from Puno to Amantaní may drop you off at Colata (at the tip of the peninsula), a 1-hr walk from Llachón. Confirm all details locally. Returning to Puno, you can try to flag down the boat from Amantaní which passes Colata between 0830 and 0930. In Santa María (Llachón), boats can be hired for trips to **Amantaní** (US$29 return, 40 mins) and **Taquile** (US$32 return, 50 mins), minimum 10 passengers.

Road Vans run daily 0700-1600 from Av Costanera y Jr Lampa in Puno to **Capachica**, 1½ hrs, US$1.45, where you get another van to **Llachón**; these leave when full, 30 mins, US$1; by mototaxi costs US$5, by taxi US$7.

Western shore

Minibuses to **Puno** depart from Jr Cusco esq Arica, 1 block from Plaza 2 de Mayo, in Yunguyo, hourly 0600-1900, 2½ hrs, US$2.90. Don't take a taxi from Yunguyo to Puno without checking its reliability first; the driver may pick up an accomplice to rob passengers.

> **Tip…**
> It is advisable to travel between Puno and Cuzco by day, for safety as well as for the views.

The Uros
US$2.50 to land, 5 km northeast of Puno.

Of the estimated 80 Uros or 'floating islands' in Puno Bay, only about 15 are regularly visited by tourists. Today we can talk about two kinds of Uros people; those close to the city of Puno and easily accessible to tourism, and those on islands that remain relatively isolated. On the more far-flung islands, reached via narrow channels

Tip...
The Uros people cannot live from tourism alone, so it is better to buy their handicrafts or pay for services rather than just to tip them.

through the reed beds, the Uros do not like to be photographed and continue to lead relatively traditional lives outside the monetary economy. They hunt and fish and depend on trade with the mainland for other essentials. They also live off the lake's plants, the most important of which are the reeds they use for their boats, houses and the very foundations of their islands.

Visitors to the floating islands will encounter more Uros women than men. These women wait every day for the tour boats to sell their handicrafts, while most of the men are out on the lake, hunting and fishing, although you may see some men building or repairing boats or nets. They glean extra income from tourists offering overnight accommodation in reed houses, selling meals and providing Uro guides for two-hour tours. Organized tour parties are usually given a boat-building demonstration and the chance to take a short trip in a reed boat. Some islanders will also greet boatloads of tourists with a song and will pose for photos. The islanders, who are very friendly, appreciate gifts of pens, paper, and other items for their two schools. This form of tourism on the Uros Islands is now well-established and, whether it has done irreparable harm or will ultimately prove beneficial, it takes place in superb surroundings. Take drinking water as there is none on the islands.

Taquile
US$2.50 to land, 37 km east of Puno. Contact Munay Taquile, the island's community-based travel agency, Titicaca 508, Puno, T051-351448, www.taquile.net.

Isla Taquile is just 1 km wide but 6-7 km long. It has numerous pre-Inca and Inca ruins, and Inca terracing. The sunset from the highest point of the island (3950 m) is beautiful. Full-day tours usually include a stop in Taquile along with Uros, and two-day tours to Amantaní also stop here either on the way there or back. This means there are lots people on the island around midday. For a more authentic experience, get a tour that stays overnight in Taquile, or go independently to have time to explore the island's six districts or *suyos* and to observe the daily flurry of activity around the boatloads of tourists: demonstrations of traditional dress and weaving techniques, the preparation of trout to feed the hordes. When the boats leave, the island breathes a gentle sigh and people slowly return to their more traditional activities.

On Sunday, people from all the districts gather for a meeting in the main plaza after Quechua mass. There is an (unmarked) **museum of traditional costumes** on the plaza and a co-operative shop that sells exceptional woollen goods; they are not cheap, but of very fine quality. Each week different families sell their products. Other shops on the plaza sell postcards, water and dry goods. If you are staying over, you are advised to bring some food with you, particularly fruit, bread and vegetables, as well as water, plenty of small-value notes, candles, a torch, toilet paper and a sleeping bag. Take precautions against sunburn and take warm clothes for the cold nights.

Tip...
There are four docks at the island, so if you have trouble walking up many steps at high altitude, ask to be taken to a landing stage which requires less climbing.

☆Amantaní

US$2.50 to land, 44 km northeast of Puno.

Another island worth visiting is Amantaní. It is very beautiful, peaceful and arguably less spoiled and friendlier than Taquile. There are three docks; the one on the northwest shore is closest to Pueblo de Amantaní, the main village. There are seven other villages on the island and ruins on both of its peaks, **Pacha Tata** (4115 m) and **Pacha Mama** (4130 m), from which there are excellent views. There are also temples. On the northwest shore, 30 minutes from the Pueblo, is the **Inkatiana**, a throne carved out of stone, eroded from flooding. The residents make beautiful textiles and sell them quite cheaply at the Cooperativa de Artesanos. They also make basketwork and stoneware. The people are Quechua speakers, but understand Spanish. Islanders arrange dances for tour groups for which visitors are invited to dress up in local clothes and join in. Small shops sell water and snacks.

Anapia and Yuspique

18 km from Punta Hermosa, contact Asociación de Turismo Anapia, Sra María Chávez Segales, T951-991164.

In the Peruvian part of the Lago Menor or Huiñamarca (see Lake Titicaca, Bolivia), are the islands of **Anapia**, inhabited by a friendly, Aymara-speaking community which maintains its traditions, and **Yuspique**, on which are ruins and vicuñas. The community has organized committees for tourism, motorboats, sailing boats and accommodation with families (from US$9 per person). You can visit Anapia independently (see Transport, below) or take a tour with All Ways Travel, see page 1406. On the island ask for José Flores, who is very knowledgeable about Anapia's history, flora and fauna. He sometimes acts as a guide.

Listings The islands

Where to stay

The iPerú office in Puno has a list of families offering accommodation in their homes.

The Uros

Accommodation costs from US$14 pp with simple meals extra or US$60 pp full board including tour. **René Coyla Coila** (T951-743533), is an official tour guide who can advise on lodgings. Some families you can contact are: **Elsa Coila Coila** (Isla Aruma Uros, T951-607147); **Cristina Suaña** (Kantati Uros, T951-695121); **Luis Carvajal** (Qhanan Pacha, T951-835264); and **Silverio Lujano** (**Kamisaraki Inn Lodge**, Kamisaraki, T951-049493).

Taquile

The Community Tourism Agency **Munay Taquile** (T051-351448, www.taquile.net) can arrange accommodation on the island. Someone will approach you when you get off the boat if you don't have anything booked in advance. Rates are from US$9 pp for bed only, from US$21 pp full board, or US$43 pp including transport and guiding. Some families have become popular with tour groups and so have been able to

build bigger and better facilities (with showers and loos), classified as Albergue Rural or Hotel Rural. As a result, families with more basic accommodation (Casa Rural) are often losing out on valuable tourist income. Instead of staying in the busy part of the island around the main square, consider staying with the Huayllano community on the south side of the island; contact **Alipio Huatta Cruz** (T951-668551 or T951-615239) or arrange a visit with **All Ways Travel**, see page 1406.

Amantaní

The **Presidente del Comité Turístico de Amantaní** is Gerardo Yanarico (T951-848548). Rates are US$11-30 pp full board, or from US$29 pp including a tour. If you are willing to walk to more distant communities, you might get a better price and you are helping to share the income. Options include: **$$ Kantuta Lodge** (T051-630238, 951-636172, www.kantutalodge. com), run by Richard Cari and family, full board; **Hospedaje Ccolono** (Occosuyo, T951-675918); **Eduardo Yucra Mamani** (**Jatari**, Comunidad Pueblo, T951-664577); or **Victoriano Calsin Quispe** (T051-360220/363320).

Restaurants

Taquile
There are many small restaurants around the plaza and on the track to the Puerto Principal, including Gerardo Huatta's **La Flor de Cantuta**, on the steps, and **El Inca** in the main plaza. Meals are generally fish, rice and chips, omelette and *fiambre*, a local stew. Meat is rarely available and drinks often run out. Breakfast consists of pancakes and bread.

Amantaní
The artificially low price of tours allows families little scope for providing anything other than basic meals, so take your own supplies.

Festivals

Taquile
Jun-Aug The principal festivals are **2-7 Jun** and the **Fiesta de Santiago 25 Jul-2 Aug**, with many dances in between.

Amantaní
15-20 Jan Pago a la Tierra or **San Sebastián** is celebrated on the hills of the island. The festivities are very colourful, musical and hard-drinking. **9 Apr Aniversario del Consejo** (the local council). **8-16 Aug Feria de Artesanías**.

Transport

Purchasing one-way tickets gives you more flexibility if you wish to stay longer on the islands, but joining a tour is the most convenient way to visit, especially as it will include transport between your hotel and the port. 2-day tours to Uros, Amantaní and Taquile, including simple lodging and meals, start at US$27.

The Uros
Asociación de Transporte los Uros (T051-368024, aeuttal@hotmail.com, daily 0800-1600) runs motorboats from Puno to the islands, daily 0630-1630 or whenever there are 10 people, US$3.60. Agencies charge US$5.50-7 for a ½-day tour.

Taquile
Operaciones Comunales Taquile (T051-205477, daily 0600-1800) has boats at 0730 and 0800 in high season, stopping at the **Uros** on the way, returning at 1400 and 1430; in low season only 1 boat travels, US$7 return. Organized tours cost US$21-25.

Amantaní
Transportes Unificados Amantaní (T051-369714, daily 0500-1800) has 2 boats daily at 0815, 1 direct at Uros; they return at 0800 the next day, 1 direct to **Puno**, the 2nd stopping at **Taquile** and continuing to Puno at 1200. Rates are US$7.50 Puno to Amantaní direct one way; US$11 return including stops at **Uros** and Taquile; US$3 Amantaní to Taquile one way. If you stop in Taquile on the way back, you can choose to continue to Puno at 1200 with the Amantaní boat or take a Taquile boat at 1400 (also 1430 in high season).

Anapia
Take a van from Parque Primero de Mayo in **Yunguyo** towards Tinicachi and alight at **Punta Hermosa**, just after Unacachi, US$0.55, 35 mins. Boats leave **Anapia** for Punta Hermosa on Sun and Thu at 0600, returning from Punta Hermosa to Anapia on the same days between 1200 and 1300, US$1.25, 1½ hrs each way. To hire a boat from Punta Hermosa to Anapia costs US$29.

North of Puno

routes to Cuzco, the jungle and Bolivia

Heading north from Puno, the road crosses a range of hills to another coastal plain, which leads to Juliaca. This town is the main transport hub for journeys north to Cuzco or the jungle, west to Arequipa or east along the unspoiled northern shores of the lake.

Juliaca *Colour map 6, A2.*
Freezing cold at night, hygienically challenged and less than safe, Juliaca, 289 km northeast of Arequipa, is not particularly attractive. As the commercial focus of an area bounded by Puno, Arequipa and the jungle, it has grown very fast into a noisy chaotic place with a large, impermanent population of over 100,000, lots of contraband and more *trici-taxis* than cars. Monday, market day, is the most disorganized of all.

Lampa

The unspoiled friendly little colonial town of **Lampa**, 31 km northwest of Juliaca along an old road to Pucará, is known as the 'Pink City'. Being so close to Juliaca, it is a fine alternative place to stay for those seeking tranquility. It has a splendid church, **La Inmaculada** ① *daily 0900-1200, 1400-1600, US$3.60*, containing a copy of Michelangelo's 'Pietà' cast in aluminium, many Cuzqueña school paintings and a carved wooden pulpit. A plaster copy of the 'Pietà' and a mural depicting local history can be seen in the Municipalidad. **Kampac Museo** ① *Jr Alfonso Ugarte 462 y Ayacucho, T951-820085, daily 0700-1800, US$1.80*, a small private museum featuring an eclectic collection of sculptures and ceramics from a number of Peruvian cultures; the owner, Profesor Jesús Vargas, can be found at the shop opposite. Lampa has a small Sunday market and celebrates a fiesta of **Santiago Apóstol** on 6-15 December. There is a fine colonial bridge just south of the town and La Cueva del Toro cave with petroglyphs at Lensora, 4 km past the bridge. The Tinajani rock formations and stands of *Puya raimondii* plants south of Ayaviri (see below) can also be accessed from Lampa.

Juliaca to Cuzco

The road Puno–Juliaca–Cuzco is fully paved. There is much to see on the way, but neither the regular daytime buses nor the trains make frequent stops. Tourist buses stop at the most important attractions, but to see these and other sights at a more relaxed pace, you will need to take local transport from town to town, or use your own car. There are plenty of places to stay and eat en route.

The road and railway cross the altiplano, gradually climbing. Along the way is **Pucará**, 65 km northwest of Juliaca, which has pre-Inca ruins, a museum and produces ceramic bulls which are placed on roofs throughout the region. Accessed from **Ayaviri** (33 km from Pucará), whose speciality is a mild, creamy cheese, are the Tinajani rock formations, stands of *Puya raimondii* plants and Laguna Orurillo. Knitted alpaca ponchos and pullovers and miniature llamas are made in **Santa Rosa** (42 km from Ayaviri), which has access to Nuñoa where more *Puyas raimondii* can be seen.

At **La Raya** (4350 m), the highest pass between Juliaca and Cuzco, there is a crafts market by the railway. Trains stop here so passengers can admire the scenery. Up on the heights breathing may be a little difficult, but the descent along the Río Vilcanota is rapid. At **Aguas Calientes**, 10 km from La Raya along the railway, are steaming springs reaching 40°C, with thermal pools for bathing; the beautiful deposits of red ferro-oxide in the middle of the green grass is a startling sight. At **Maranganí**, the river is wider and the fields greener, with groves of eucalyptus trees.

Located 38 km beyond La Raya pass at 3690 m is **Sicuani**, the main city in eastern Cuzco and good base from which to visit the easternmost attractions of the region. It is an important commercial and agricultural centre and a transport hub. Excellent llama and alpaca wool products and skins are sold next to the pedestrian walkway and at the Saturday market. Around Plaza Libertad there are several hat shops. The tourist office (see Tourist information, below) has an excellent display of traditional outfits from all the districts of Canchis, which are among the most colourful in Cuzco. For information about places between Sicuani and Cuzco, see Raqchi and around, page 1440.

Puno to the jungle

A branch of the Interoceanic Highway, fully paved, runs together with the Juliaca–Cuzco road, before branching north across the vast alpaca-grazed altiplano. **Azángaro** (73 km from Juliaca) has the Templo de Tintiri, an adobe colonial church rich in art. Beyond is the cold regional centre of **Macusani**, 192 km from Juliaca, at 4400 m. The dramatic road then descends past the mining supply towns of **Ollachea** (with simple accommodation and eateries, a waterfall, thermal baths and pre-Inca ruins) and **San Gabán** (with petroglyphs and waterfalls) to **Puente Iñambari** (or Loromayo), where it converges with the other branches of the Interoceánica from Cuzco and Puerto Maldonado (see page 1502). **Mazuko** (360 km from Juliaca), another mining town, is 5 km north of the junction. This off-the-beaten-path route through the **Cordillera Carabaya** connects Lake Titicaca and the southern jungle (see Transport, below).

This is an excellent area for those who want to explore. Along the way are rock formations, petroglyphs and the glaciated summits of Allin Cápac surrounded by lakes and valleys ideal for trekking. Richar Cáceres (T942-989821) in Macusani, is a recommended English-speaking mountaineer and guide, who is knowledgeable about the area.

Further east, leading north from the northeastern shore of Titicaca near Huancané, another road goes towards the jungle. At **Putina**, 92 km from Juliaca, are **thermal baths** ① *Tue-Sun 0400-2100, US$0.70*. Vicuñas can be seen at Picotani nearby, and *Puya raimondii* plants at Bellavista, 5 km from town. The road then crosses the beautiful Cordillera Apolobamba to **Sandia** (125 km from Putina), **San Juan del Oro** (80 km from Sandia) and **Putina Punco** (40 km ahead. Beyond lies the remote **Parque Nacional Bahuaja-Sonene** ① *Sernanp, Libertad 1189, Puno, T051-363960*, with restricted access requiring a Sernamp permit (US$54). It is difficult to reach the park from this side and involves paddling a canoe through serious rapids; access is easier from the Río Tambopata side, see page 1503.

Huancané to Bolivia

A paved road goes northeast from Juliaca across the *puna* for 56 km to **Huancané** (altitude 3825 m), which has a massive adobe church by its attractive plaza and good birdwatching possibilities nearby in the **Reserva Nacional del Titicaca**, where the road crosses the Río Ramis. Nearby, a road goes north to Putina and the jungle, see above. East of Huancané, the shore of Titicaca is beautiful, with terraced hills rising above coves on the lake. There are many Inca and pre-Inca ruins as well as pre-Inca roads to follow. In the warmer coves, where the climate is tempered by the lake, people lead traditional lives based on fishing and subsistence farming. There is access from the shore to idyllic **Isla Suasi** (www.islasuasi.pe) and to the Bolivian border. Lodging and eateries in the towns along this route are generally basic; there are also water shortages.

Puno–La Paz via Tilali and Puerto Acosta See page 1414.

Listings North of Puno

Tourist information

Juliaca

Information is available from **Dircetur** (Jr Noriega 191, p 3, T051-321839, Mon-Fri 0730-1530) and **iPerú** (at the airport, iperupunoapto@promperu. gob.pe, open when flights arrive).

Juliaca to Cuzco

The **Sicuani tourist information office** (at the Municipio, Plaza de Armas, T084-509257, Mon-Fri 0800-1300, 1430-1800) has pamphlets and very helpful staff.

Where to stay

Juliaca

The town has water problems in dry season.

$$$-$$ Hotel Don Carlos
Jr 9 de Diciembre 114, Plaza Bolognesi,
T051-323600, www.hotelesdoncarlos.com.
Comfortable, modern facilities, heater, good service, breakfast, restaurant and room service. Also has **Suites Don Carlos** (Jr M Prado 335, T051-321571).

$$ Royal Inn
San Román 158, T051-321561,
www.royalinnhoteles.com.
Rooms and suites with heater and bathtub, good restaurant ($$-$).

$$ Sakura
San Román 133, T322072,
hotelsakura@hotmail.com.
Quiet, basic rooms in older section with shared bath.

$$-$ Hostal Luquini
Jr Brasesco 409, Plaza Bolognesi, T051-321510.
Comfortable, patio, helpful staff, reliable hot water in morning only, motorcycle parking.

$ Yurac Wasi
Jr San Martín 1214.
Near Terminal Terrestre, good simple economical rooms, private or shared bath.

Lampa

$$ La Casona
Jr Tarapacá 271, Plaza de Armas, T999-607682,
patronatolampa@yahoo.com.
Lovely refurbished 17th-century house, nice ample rooms with heaters and duvets, advanced booking required, tours arranged.

$ Hospedaje Estrella
Jr Municipalidad 540, T980-368700,
juanfrien@hotmail.com.
Appealing rooms, with or without private
bath, solar hot water, very friendly, breakfast
available, parking.

Huancané to Bolivia

$$$$ Hotel Isla Suasi
T051-351102 (office), T941-741347,
www.islasuasi.pe.
The hotel is the only house on this tiny, tranquil,
private island. There are beautiful terraced
gardens, best Jan-Mar. The non-native eucalyptus
trees are being replaced by native varieties.
You can take a canoe around the island to see
birds and the island has vicuñas, a small herd
of alpacas and vizcachas. The sunsets from the
highest point are beautiful. Facilities are spacious,
comfortable and solar-powered, price includes
buffet breakfast, guided walk, birdwatching,
canoe tour and sauna. Transport costs US$100
op return, either by land from the airport or by
private boat from Puno, including stops in Uros
and Taquile, or a combination of the two.

Restaurants

Juliaca

$$ El Asador
Unión 113. Daily 1200-0100.
Regional dishes, chicken, grill and pizza, good
food and service, pleasant atmosphere.

$ Delycia's
M Núñez 168. Closed Fri evening and Sat.
Good vegetarian set lunch with small salad bar.

$ Nuevo Star
Bolívar 121. Daily 0600-2000.
Decent set meals.

$ Ricos Pan
Jr San Román y Jorge Chávez.
Good bakery with café, popular.

Shopping

Juliaca
La Dominical, *near the exit to Cuzco. Held on Sun.*
A woollens market.
Las Calceteras, *Pl Bolognesi.* Handicrafts gallery.
Túpac Amaru market, *on Moquegua 7 blocks
east of railway line.* Cheap.

Transport

Juliaca
Air Manco Cápac airport, is small but well
organized. To/from **Lima**, 1¾ hrs, 5 a day with
LATAM (Jr San Román 125, T051-322228, airport
T051-328485) via **Arequipa** (30 mins), **Cuzco** and
direct; and 2 a day direct with **Avianca/TACA**
(Real Plaza mall, Jr Tumbes 391, T051-326415,
airport T051-327966). Beware over-charging for
ground transportation. If you have little luggage,
regular taxis and vans stop just outside the
airport parking area. Taxi from Plaza Bolognesi,
US$2.75; taxi from airport to centre US$3.60, or
less from outside airport gates. For transfers to/
from **Puno**, see page 1406.

Bus Local To **Puno**, minibuses leave when
full from Jr Brasesco near Plaza Bolognesi
throughout the day, US$1.25, 1 hr. To **Capachica**,
they leave when full from Cerro Colorado
market, 0500-1700, US$2, 1½ hrs. To **Lampa**,
cars (US$1.25) and vans (US$0.90) leave when
full from the Mercado Santa Bárbara area,
eg **El Veloz** (Jr Huáscar 672 y Colón) or **Ramos**
(2 de Mayo y Colón), others nearby, 30 mins. Vans
to **Pucará** (US$1.25, 45 min), **Ayaviri** (US$1.80,
1½ hrs) and **Azángaro** depart from Terminal
Virgen de Las Mercedes (Jr Texas, corner San
Juan de Dios); they also stop at Paseo Los Kollas
by the exit to Cuzco to pick up passengers. To
Sicuani, take a bus bound for Cuzco (see below)
or **Chasquis** vans leave when full from 8 de
Noviembre 1368, by Paseo de Los Kollas, US$5.40,
2½-3 hrs. Minibuses for **Moho** via **Huancané**
depart when full 0500-1800 from Jr Moquegua y
Circunvalación, north of Mercado Tupac Amaru,
US$2.15, 1½ hrs. Minibuses for **Conima** and
Tilali depart when full from Jr Lambayeque y
Av Circunvalación Este, also near the market,
US$3.60, 3 hrs; these continue to the Bolivian
border on market days.

Long distance The Terminal Terrestre is at
the east end of San Martín (cuadra 9, past the
Circunvalación). To **Lima**, US$38 normal, US$43-
70 cama, 20-22 hrs; with **Ormeño** 1630, 2000,
Flores or **Civa** at 1500, several others. To **Cuzco**,
US$5.40 normal, US$9 semi-cama, US$12.50-17
cama, 5-6 hrs, with **Power** (T051-322531) every
2 hrs, 0530-2330, **Flores** at 1200 and 1700, several
others. To **Arequipa**, US$5.50 normal, US$7 semi-
cama, US$9-27 cama, 4-5 hrs, with **Julsa** (T051-
331952) hourly 0300-2400, with **Flores** 6-8 daily,
several others. To **Moquegua** (7 hrs) and **Tacna**
(8-9 hrs), US$9-11 semi-cama, US$12.50-15

cama, most depart 1930-2030, with **San Martín** also at 0745. To **Puerto Maldonado** along the Interoceanic Highway, US$10.60-15, 12 hrs; several companies leave from the Terminal Terrestre and then pick up passengers at private terminals around M Nuñez cuadra 11, 'El Triángulo', by the exit to Cuzco: **Santa Cruz** (M Núñez y Cahuide, T051-332185) at 1500 and 1800; **Julsa** (Ferrocarril y Cahuide, T051-326602) at 1600; **Wayra** at 1730; **Realeza** at 1930. Buses originating in Arequipa only stop at their own stations. To **Macusani**, **Alianza** (Av Ferrocarril y Cahuide) 1300, 1700, 1815, US$3.50, 3 hrs; **Jean** (M Núñez y Pje San José), 0845, 1330, 1800; also minibuses from Pje San José, leave when full, US$4.25.

Borders with Bolivia

Puno–La Paz via Yunguyo and Copacabana The most frequently travelled route is along the southwest coast of Titicaca, from Puno to La Paz via **Yunguyo** (Peru) and **Copacabana** (Bolivia). The border villages on either side are called Kasani. This route is very scenic and involves crossing the Straits of Tiquina on a launch (there are barges for the vehicles) between Copacabana and La Paz. Almost all the tourist class bus services use this route.

Peruvian immigration (daily 0700-1930, Peruvian time) is five minutes' drive from **Yunguyo** and 500 m from the Bolivian immigration post (daily 0830-2000, Bolivian time). Minibuses go from the Terminal Zonal Sur in Puno to Yunguyo may continue to the border at Kasani if there are enough passengers; there are also shared taxis (US$0.40 per person) and private taxis (US$2.50) from Yunguyo (Jr Titicaca y San Francisco, one block from Plaza de Armas) to Kasani. Minibuses (US$0.50) and taxis (US$3 or US$0.60 per person) run from Kasani to Copacabana (8 km, 15 minutes). Peruvian time is one hour behind Bolivian time. If you need a visa for Bolivia (eg US citizens) go to the **Bolivian consulate** in Puno (Jr Aymaraes G-5, Urb APROVI, Barrio Llaviri, T051-205400, Monday-Friday 0800-1600; allow about 48 hours), or ask at the Yunguyo border crossing.

There is one ATM at Plaza 2 de Mayo in Yunguyo and a couple in Copacabana, as well as *cambios* at the Plaza de Armas in Yunguyo and on the Peruvian side of the border.

Puno–La Paz via Desaguadero A more direct route between Puno and La Paz is via the bleak town of **Desaguadero** (same name on both sides of the border), on the southwest coast of the lake. The Carretera Binacional, which joins La Paz with Moquegua and the Pacific port of Ilo, goes through Desaguadero, see page 1402, but there is no need to stop here, as all roads to Desaguadero are paved and, if you leave La Paz, Moquegua or Puno early enough, you should be at your destination before nightfall. This particular border crossing allows you to stop at the ruins of Tiahuanaco in Bolivia along the way. The **Peruvian border office** is open daily 0700-1930; the Bolivian office, daily 0800-2030 (both local time). It is easy to change money on the Peruvian side where there are many changers by the bridge.

Puno–La Paz via Tilali and Puerto Acosta
The most remote route to Bolivia is along the northeast shore of the lake, via Huancané, Moho, **Tilali** (Peru) and **Puerto Acosta** (Bolivia). The Peruvian immigration office for entry and exit formalities is in Tilali, on the plaza. Customs control is 2 km further on and Bolivian immigration is across the border. From Juliaca there are minibuses to Tilali, the last village in Peru; these may continue to the border on market days (Wed and Sat). At other times you may have to hitch or walk 4 km from Tilali to the frontier and then a further 10 km to Puerto Acosta in Bolivia. From Puerto Acosta buses run to **La Paz**, with more frequent services from Escoma, 25 km further into Bolivia. Confirm all details locally.

Juliaca to Cuzco

Sicuani

The bus terminal is in the newer part of town, which is separated from the older part and the Plaza by 3 bridges, the middle one has a pedestrian walkway. To **Juliaca**, Chasquis vans leave when full, US$5.40, 2½-3 hrs. To **Cuzco**, 137 km, US$3.60, 3 hrs. (The Sicuani terminals in Cuzco are at Av Huayruropata, Wanchaq, near Mercado Tupac Amaru.)

Puno to the jungle

From Macusani to **Juliaca**, US$3.50, 3 hrs; also minibuses US$4.25. Vans go as they fill from Macusani to San Gabán; some continue to Puente Iñambari.

Cuzco

★Cuzco stands at the head of the Sacred Valley of the Incas and is the jumping-off point for the Inca Trail and famous Inca city of Machu Picchu. It's not surprising, therefore, that this is the prime destination for the vast majority of first-time visitors to Peru. The ancient Inca capital is said to have been founded around AD 1100, when the Sun sent his son, Manco Cápac, and the Moon sent her daughter, Mama Ocllo, to find a suitably fertile place to found their kingdom. The Spanish transformed the navel of the Inca civilization into a jewel of colonial achievement. In more recent times Cuzco has developed into a major commercial and tourism centre of 450,000 inhabitants, most of whom are Quechua. Colonial churches, monasteries and convents and extensive pre-Columbian ruins are interspersed with countless hotels, bars and restaurants that cater to the over one million tourists who visit every year. Almost every central street has remains of Inca walls and doorways; the perfect Inca stonework now serves as the foundations for more modern dwellings. This stonework is tapered upwards and every wall has a perfect line of inclination towards the centre, from bottom to top (battered). The curved stonework of the Temple of the Sun, for example, is probably unequalled in the world.

Sights *Colour map 6, C4.*

Inca stones, colonial churches and 21st-century crowds

Since there are so many sights to see in Cuzco city, not even the most ardent tourist would be able to visit them all. Those with limited time, or who want a whistle-stop tour, should visit the cathedral, Qoricancha, La Compañía de Jesús, San Blas, La Merced, San Cristóbal (for the view) and Sacsayhuaman. If you visit one museum make it the Museo Inka, which has the most comprehensive collection.

City centre

Plaza de Armas The heart of the city in Inca days was Huacaypata (the Place of Tears) and Cusipata (the Place of Happiness), divided by a channel of the Saphi River (no longer visible). Today, Cusipata is Plaza Regocijo and Huacaypata is the Plaza de Armas. This was the great civic square of the Incas, flanked by their palaces, and was a place of solemn parades and great assemblies. Around Plaza de Armas are colonial arcades and four great churches. To the northeast is the early 17th-century baroque **Cathedral** ① *US$9 or CRA ticket, daily 1000-1800.* It was built on the site of the Palace of Inca Wiracocha (Kiswarcancha). The high altar is solid silver and the original altar *retablo* behind it is a masterpiece of Andean woodcarving. The Cathedral contains two interesting paintings: the first is the earliest surviving painting of the city, depicting Cuzco during the 1650 earthquake; the second, at the far right-hand end of the church, is a local painting of the Last Supper replete with Peruvian details, including *cuy* and *chicha*. In the sacristy are paintings of all the bishops of Cuzco. The choir stalls, by a 17th-century Spanish priest, are a magnificent example of colonial baroque art.

Best for

Colonial architecture ▪ Festivals ▪ Inca archaeology ▪ Museums

Essential Cuzco

Finding your feet

Respect the altitude: rest for several hours after arrival; eat lightly; don't smoke; avoid alcohol; drink plenty of water, and remember to walk slowly. There are too many sights in the city to see on a single visit; limit yourself to the highlights or to areas of particular interest. Note that many churches close to visitors on Sunday, and photography inside churches is generally not allowed.

> **Tip...**
> The best place for an overall view of the Cuzco Valley is from the top of the hill of Sacsayhuaman.

Getting around

The **airport** is to the southeast of the city; the road into the centre passes close to Wanchaq station, at which **trains** from Arequipa and Puno arrive. The **bus terminal** is near the Pachacútec statue in Ttio district. If transport has not been arranged by your hotel on arrival, you are advised to travel by taxi from the airport, train or bus stations. You are also strongly advised to take a taxi when returning to your hotel at night. During the day, the centre of Cuzco is quite small and easy to explore on foot. Agencies offer guided tours of the city and surrounding archaeological sites, but visiting independently is not difficult. There are regular buses from Cuzco to villages and towns throughout the region.

Visitors' tickets

A combined entry ticket, called *Boleto Turístico de Cusco (BTC)*, is available to most of the main sites of historical and cultural interest in and around the city, and costs as follows: 130 soles (US$39.40) for 16 sites for 10 days; or 70 soles (US$21.20) for either the included city sites (three museums, two archaeological sites and one monument) (valid for two days); or Sacsayhuaman, Qenqo, Puka Pukara and Tambo Machay (one day); or Pisac, Ollantaytambo,

Chinchero and Moray (two days). The BTC can be bought at **iCusco** (Portal Mantas 117-A, Monday-Saturday 0800-2000, Sun 0800-1300) and **Cosituc** (Avenida El Sol 103, of 102, Galerías Turísticas, T084-261465, daily 0800-1800, www.cosituc.gob.pe), or at any of the sites included in the ticket. For students with an ISIC card the 10-day BTC costs 70 soles (US$25), only available at the Cosituc office upon presentation of the ISIC card. Take your ISIC card when visiting the sites, as some officials may ask to see it.

Two other combined entry tickets apply to churches and religious museums, and can be purchased at any of the included sites. The *Circuito Religioso Arzobispal (CRA, http://cra.org.pe)* costs 30 soles (US$12 for 30 days) and includes the Cathedral, Museo Arzobispal, San Blas and San Cristóbal. The *Ruta del Barroco Andino (RBA, http://rutadelbarrocoandino.com)* costs 25 soles (US$7.60 for seven days) and includes La Compañía in Cuzco and churches in Adahuaylillas, Huaro and Canincunca, all southeast of Cuzco. To visit only La Compañía the cost is 10 soles (US$3); to visit the three out-of-town churches or any one of them, you need the RBA Valle Sur Este ticket for 15 soles (US$4.55). Other churches and museums have individual entry fees.

Machu Picchu entrance tickets are sold electronically at www.machupicchu.gob.pe, and at the Cuzco ticket office (C Garcilaso, s/n, next to Museo de Historia Regional, T084-582030, Monday-Saturday 0700-1930).

Security

Police patrol the streets and stations, but still be vigilant. On no account walk back to your hotel late at night from a bar or club: strangle muggings and rapes do occur. Pay for the club's doorman to call you a taxi, and make sure that it is licensed. You should also take care at San Pedro market (otherwise recommended), in the San Cristóbal area and at out-of-the-way ruins. Also take precautions during Inti Raymi. Always go to the police when robbed, even though it will take you some time to go through the necessary procedures.

The elaborate pulpit is also notable. Much venerated is the crucifix of El Señor de los Temblores, the object of many pilgrimages and viewed all over Peru as a guardian against earthquakes.

The tourist entrance to the Cathedral is through the church of **La Sagrada Familia** (also known as Jesús, María y José; 1733), which stands to the left of the Cathedral as you face it. Its gilt main altar has been renovated. The far simpler **El Triunfo**, on the right of the Cathedral, was the first Christian church in Cuzco, built on the site of the Inca Roundhouse (the Suntur Huasi) in 1536. It has a statue of the Virgin of the Descent that is reputed to have helped the Spaniards repel Manco Inca when he besieged the city in 1536.

On the southeast side of the plaza is the beautiful **La Compañía de Jesús** ① *US$3, students US$1.50, or RBA ticket, Mon-Fri 0900-1700, Sat 0900-1115, 1300-1700, Sun 0900-1030, 1245-1700*, built in the 17th century on the site of the Palace of the Serpents (Amarucancha), residence of Inca Huayna Capac. Its twin-towered exterior is extremely graceful, and the baroque interior is rich in fine murals and paintings, with a resplendent altar decorated in gold leaf. Outside the church, look for the **Inca stonework** in the Callejón Loreto, running southeast past La Compañía de Jesús from the main plaza, with the walls of the Acllahuasi (see below) on one side, and the **Amarucancha** on the other.

Santa Catalina and around The church, convent and museum of **Santa Catalina** ① *Arequipa at Santa Catalina Angosta, Mon-Sat 0830-1730, Sun 1400-1700*, were built upon the foundations of the *Acllahuasi*, where Inca women chosen for their nobility, virtue and beauty were housed in preparation for ceremonial and domestic duties. The convent is a closed order, but the church and museum are worth visiting. Guided tours by English-speaking students (tip expected) will point out the church's ornate gilded altarpiece and beautifully carved pulpit and the museum's collection of Cuzqueño art.

Around the corner, **Museo Machupicchu** (Casa Concha) ① *Santa Catalina Ancha 320, T084-255535, Mon-Sat 0900-1700, US$7*, features objects found by Hiram Bingham during his initial excavations of Machu Picchu in 1912, which were returned by Yale University to the Peruvian government in 2011-2012.

If you continue down Arequipa from Santa Catalina you come to Calle Maruri. Between this street and Santo Domingo is **Cusicancha** ① *free, Mon-Fri 0715-1300, 1400-1600, sometimes open at weekends*, an open space showing the layout of the buildings as they would have been in Inca times.

Santo Domingo and Qoricancha ① *Mon-Sat 0800-1730, Sun 1400-1700 (closed holidays), Museo Qoricancha US$3.60; church free, multi-lingual guides charge US$11 for a 40-min tour*. This is one of the most fascinating sights in Cuzco. Behind the walls of a 17th-century Catholic church are the remains of Qoricancha, a complex that formed the centre of the vast Inca society. Its Golden Palace and Temple of the Sun were filled with such fabulous treasures of gold and silver that it took the Spanish three months to melt it all down.

The first Inca, Manco Cápac, is said to have built the temple when he left Lake Titicaca and founded Cuzco with Mama Ocllo. However, it was the ninth Inca, Pachacútec, who transformed it. When the Spaniards arrived, the complex was awarded to Juan Pizarro, the younger brother of Francisco, who willed it to the Dominicans when he was fatally wounded in the Sacsayhuaman siege. The Dominicans ripped much of the complex down to build their church. The baroque

cloister has since been excavated to reveal four of the original chambers of the great Inca Temple of the Sun – two on the west have been partly reconstructed in a good imitation of Inca masonry. The finest stonework is in the celebrated curved wall beneath the west end of Santo Domingo. This can be seen (complete with a large crack from the 1950 earthquake) when you look out over the Solar Garden. Excavations have revealed Inca baths below here and more Inca retaining walls. Another superb stretch of late Inca stonework is in Calle Ahuacpinta outside the temple, to the east, or left as you enter.

Around the corner from the site (but not part of it), **Museo de Sitio Qorikancha** (formerly Museo Arqueológico)① *Av El Sol, Mon-Sun 0900-1800, entrance by BTC*, contains a limited collection of pre-Columbian items, Spanish paintings of imitation Inca royalty dating from the 18th century, and photos of the excavation of Qoricancha.

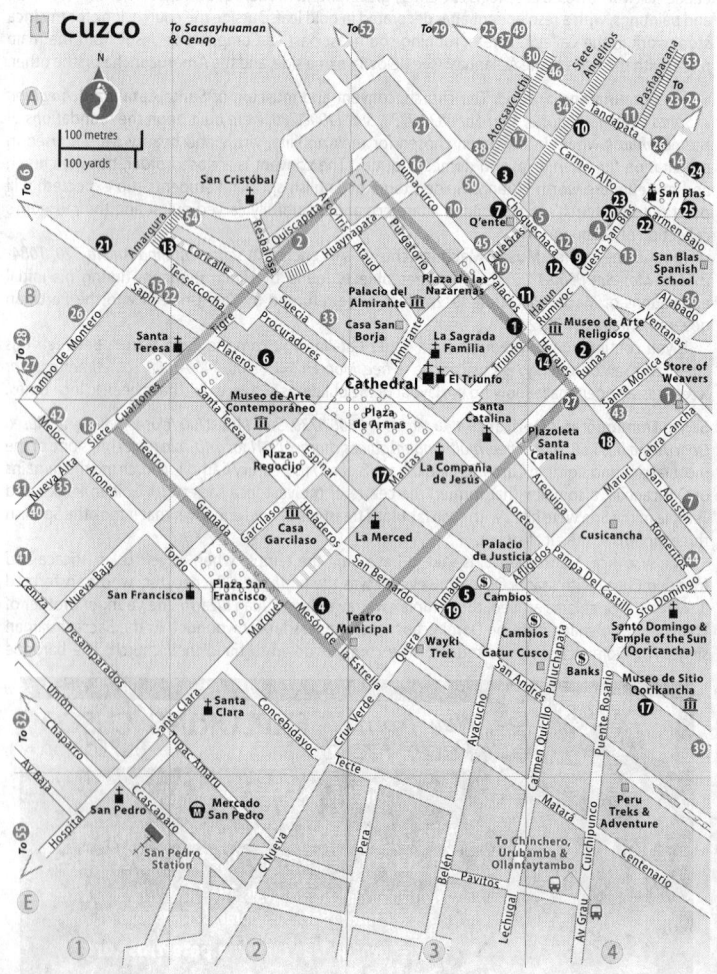

Cuzco

Southwest of the Plaza de Armas **The church of La Merced** ① *Plazoleta Espinar, C Mantas, church Mon-Sat 0700-0800, 1700-2000, Sun 0700-1200, 1800-2000; monastery and museum Mon-Sat 0800-1230, 1400-1730, US$3.50,* was first built in 1534 and rebuilt in the late 17th century. Attached is a very fine monastery with an exquisite cloister. Inside the church are buried Gonzalo Pizarro, half-brother of Francisco, and the two Almagros, father and son. The church is most famous for its jewelled monstrance, which is on view in the monastery's museum during visiting hours.

Museo de Historia Regional ① *in the Casa Garcilaso, C Garcilaso y Heladeros, daily 0800-1700, entrance by BTC,* tries to show the evolution of the Cuzqueño school of painting. It also contains Inca agricultural implements, colonial furniture and paintings.

San Francisco ① *on Plaza San Francisco, 3 blocks southwest of the Plaza de Armas, museum open daily 0900-1700, US$3,* is an austere church reflecting many indigenous influences.

➡ **Cuzco maps**

Where to stay 🛏
1 Albergue Casa Campesina *B4*
2 Albergue Municipal *B2*
3 Amaru Colonial *B5*
4 Amaru Hostal *B4*
5 Andenes al Cielo *B4*
6 Andenes de Saphi *A1*
7 Casa Andina Koricancha *C4*
8 Casa Andina Private Collection Cusco *C5*
9 Casa Andina San Blas *B5*
10 Casa Cartagena *A3*
11 Casa de la Gringa *A4*
12 Casa Elena *B4*
13 Casa San Blas & Tika Bistro *B4*
14 Casona Les Pleiades *A4*
15 Cusco Plaza - Saphi *B1*
16 El Arqueólogo & Divina Comedia Restaurant *A3*
17 El Grial *A3*
18 El Mercado *C1*
19 El Monasterio *B3*
20 Estrellita *C5*
21 Flying Dog Hostel *A3*
22 Hitchhikers B&B Backpackers Hostel *B2*
23 Hosp El Artesano de San Blas *A4*
24 Hosp Inka *A4*
25 Hostal Casa de Campo *A3*
26 Hostal El Balcón *B1*
27 Hostal Killipata *B1*
28 Hostal Loki *B1*
29 Hostal Kuntur Wasi *A3*
30 Hostal Pakcha Real *A4*
31 Hostal Qorichaska *C1*
32 Hostal Quipu *D1*
33 Hostal Suecia *B2*
34 Hostal Tikawasi *A4*
35 Hostal Wayras *C1*
36 Hostería de Anita *B4*
37 La Encantada *A3*
38 Los Apus Hotel & Mirador *A3*
39 Maison de la Jeunesse *D4*
40 Mallqui Hostal *C1*
41 Mamá Simona Hostel *C1*
42 Niños/Hotel Meloc *C1*
43 Novotel *C4*
44 Palacio del Inka Luxury Collection *C4*
45 Palacio Nazarenas *B3*
46 Pensión Alemana *A4*
47 Pirwa Backpackers San Blas *A5*
48 Pirwa Garcilaso *D6*
49 Quinua Villa Boutique *A3*
50 Rumi Punku *A3*
51 Sonesta Posadas del Inca *E6*
52 Supertramp *A3*
53 The Blue House *A4*
54 The WalkOn Inn *B2*
55 Tu Casita *E1*

Restaurants 🍴
1 A Mi Manera *B3*
2 Baco *B4*
3 Blue Alpaca *A3*
4 Café Cocla *D2*
5 Café El Ayllu *D3*
6 Café Morena *B2*
7 Café Punchay *A3*
8 El Paisa *E5*
9 Jack's Café *B4*
10 Juanito's Sandwich Café *A4*
11 Justina *B3*
12 Kushka...fé *B4*
13 Kusikuy *B1*
14 La Bodega 138 *B4*
15 La Chomba *C5*
16 La Cusqueñita *E6*
17 La Valeriana *D4, C3*
18 Le Soleil *C4*
19 Los Toldos *D3*
20 Macondo *A4*
21 Mr Soup *B1*
22 Pachapapa *B4*
23 Panadería El Buen Pastor *A4*
24 Tacomanía *A4*
25 The Meeting Place *A4*

Bars & clubs 🍸
26 Km 0 (Arte y Tapas) *A4*
27 Museo del Pisco *B4*

ON THE ROAD

Inca society

Cuzco was the capital of the Inca empire – one of the greatest planned societies the world has known – from its rise during the 11th century to its death in the early 16th century. (See John Hemming's *Conquest of the Incas* and B C Brundage's *Lords of Cuzco* and *Empire of the Inca*.) It was solidly based on other Andean civilizations which had attained great skill in textiles, building, ceramics and working in metal. Immemorially, the political structure of the Andean *indígena* had been the *ayllu*, the village community; it had its divine ancestor, worshipped household gods, was closely knit by ties of blood to the family and by economic necessity to the land, which was held in common. Submission to the *ayllu* was absolute, because it was only by such discipline that food could be obtained in an unsympathetic environment.

All the domestic animals, the llama and alpaca and the dog, had long been tamed, and the great staple crops, maize and potatoes, established. What the Incas did – and it was a magnificent feat – was to conquer enormous territories and impose upon the variety of *ayllus*, through an unchallengeable central government, a willing spiritual and economic submission to the State. The common religion, already developed by the classical Tiwanaku culture, was worship of the Sun, whose vice-regent on earth was the absolute Sapa Inca. Around him, in the capital, was a religious and secular elite which never froze into a caste because it was open to talent. The elite was often recruited from chieftains defeated by the Incas; an effective way of reconciling local opposition. Even the idol-gods of conquered peoples were brought to Cuzco, at once a form of homage and captivity.

The mass of the people were subjected to rigorous planning. They were allotted land to work, for their group and for the State; set various tasks (the making of textiles, pottery, weapons, ropes, etc) from primary materials supplied by the functionaries, or used in enlarging the area of cultivation by building terraces on the hill-sides. Their political organization was simple but effective. The family, and not the individual, was the unit. Families were grouped in units of 10, 100, 500, 1000, 10,000 and 40,000, each group with a leader responsible to the next largest group. The Sapa Inca crowned the political edifice; his four immediate counsellors were those to whom he allotted responsibility for the northern, southern, eastern and western regions (*suyos*) of the empire.

Equilibrium between production and consumption, in the absence of a free price mechanism and good transport facilities, must depend heavily upon statistical information. This the Incas raised to a high degree of efficiency by means of their quipus: a decimal system of recording numbers by knots in cords. Seasonal variations were guarded against by creating a system of state barns in which provender could be stored during years of plenty, to be used in years of scarcity. Statistical efficiency alone required that no one should be permitted to leave his home or his work. The loss of personal liberty was the price paid by the masses for economic security. In order to obtain information and to transmit orders quickly, the Incas built fine paved pathways along which couriers sped on foot. The whole system of rigorous control was completed by the greatest of all their monarchs, Pachacútec, who also imposed a common language, Quechua, as a further cementing force.

☆ Two blocks south of here, **San Pedro market** is popular with tourists but has only been slightly sanitized for their benefit. It remains a working market and is a pleasant and reasonably safe place to purchase local produce and crafts. In front of the market, the church of **San Pedro** was built in 1688. Its two towers were made from stones brought from an Inca ruin.

☆**Calle Hatun Rumiyoc** This street, running northeast from the Plaza de Armas, contains some of the most imposing Inca masonry in Cuzco, including the famous 'Stone of 12 angles' (halfway along its second block, on the right-hand side going away from the Plaza). The huge stone has been precisely cut into a 12-sided polygon in order for it to fit perfectly with the surrounding stones.

The **Museo de Arte Religioso** ① *Hatun Rumiyoc y Herrajes, daily 0800-1800, US$3.60 or CRA ticket*, is housed in the **Palacio Arzobispal**, which was built on the site of the palace occupied in 1400 by the Inca Roca. The museum contains a collection of colonial paintings and furniture, including the paintings by the indigenous master, Diego Quispe Tito, of a 17th-century Corpus Christi procession that used to hang in the church of Santa Ana.

☆**San Blas** The San Blas district, uphill from the centre to the northeast, is now firmly on the tourist map, thanks to its shops, galleries and good-value hotels and restaurants. Its main sight is the small, simple church of **San Blas** ① *Plazoleta San Blas, Carmen Bajo, daily 0800-1800, US$3.60 or CRA ticket*, which has a beautiful *mestizo* pulpit, carved from a single cedar trunk; well worth seeing. **Museo Máximo Laura** ① *Carmen Alto 133, T084-227383, http://museomaximolaura.com, Mon-Sat 0930-2000, Sun 1330-2000*, displays 24 prize-winning exhibits by this celebrated textile artist, with workshop, gallery and shop.

☆**Museo Inka** ① *Cuesta del Almirante 103, T084-237380, Mon-Sat 0800-1830. US$4*. The impressive **Palacio del Almirante**, just north of the Plaza de Armas, houses the Museo Inka, run by the Universidad San Antonio de Abad. The museum exhibits the development of culture in the region from pre-Inca, through Inca times to the present day, with displays of textiles, ceramics, metalwork, jewellery, architecture and technology. Don't miss the collection of miniature turquoise figures and other offerings to the gods. Weaving demonstrations are given in the courtyard.

☆**Museo de Arte Precolombino** ① *Pl de las Nazarenas 231, daily 0900-2200, US$7, US$3.50 with student card; under same auspices as the Larco Museum in Lima, MAP Café (see Restaurants, below)*. Housed in the **Casa Cabrera** on the northwest side of the Plaza de las Nazarenas, this beautiful museum is set around a spacious courtyard and contains many superb examples of pottery, metalwork (largely in gold and silver), woodcarvings and shells from the Moche, Chimú, Paracas, Nazca and Inca cultures. There are some vividly rendered animistic designs, giving an insight into the way Peru's ancient people's viewed their world and the creatures that inhabited it. Every exhibit carries explanations in English and Spanish. Highly recommended.

Elsewhere on the plaza, the **Convento de las Nazarenas** is now a hotel. You can see the Inca-colonial doorway with a mermaid motif, but ask permission to view the lovely 18th-century frescos inside.

☆Sacsayhuaman
30-min walk from Plaza de las Nazarenas. Daily 0700-1730. Entry with BTC ticket. Students offer free guided tours; give them a tip.

There are some magnificent Inca walls in this ruined ceremonial centre, on a hill in the northern outskirts. The massive rocks weighing up to 360 metric tons are fitted together with absolute perfection. Three walls run parallel for over 360 m and there are 21 bastions. Sacsayhuaman was thought for centuries to be a fortress, but the layout and architecture suggest a great sanctuary and temple to the Sun, which rises exactly opposite the place previously believed to be the Inca's throne; this was probably an altar, carved out of the solid rock, with broad steps leading to it from either side. The hieratic, rather than the military, hypothesis was supported by the discovery in 1982 of the graves of priests, who would have been unlikely to be buried in a fortress. The precise functions of the site, however, will probably continue to be a matter of dispute as very few clues remain, owing to its steady destruction.

The site survived the first years of the conquest. Pizarro's troops had entered Cuzco unopposed in 1533 and lived safely at Sacsayhuaman, until the rebellion of Manco Inca in 1536 caught them off guard. The bitter struggle that ensued became the decisive military action of the conquest: Manco's failure to hold Sacsayhuaman cost him the war and the empire. The destruction of the hilltop site began after the defeat of Manco's rebellion. The outer walls still stand, but the complex of towers and buildings was razed to the ground. From then until the 1930s, Sacsayhuaman served as a kind of unofficial quarry of pre-cut stone for the inhabitants of Cuzco.

The site can be reached in 30 minutes by walking up Pumacurco from Plaza de la Nazarenas, or from the church of **San Cristóbal**, just north of the centre. The church was built by Cristóbal Paullu Inca to honour his patron saint. North of San Cristóbal, you can see the 11 doorway-sized niches of the great Inca wall of the **Palacio de Colcampata**. This was Paullu's residence and where, legend has it, the founding Inca Manco Cápac had lived centuries before.

Beyond Sacsayhuaman

Take a guide to the sites and visit in the morning for the best photographs. Entry by BTC ticket; carry it with you as there are roving ticket inspectors. To get there take the Pisac bus or the Señor del Huerto city bus from Mercado Rosaspata up to Tambo Machay (US$0.70).

Along the road from Sacsayhuaman to Pisac, past a radio station, is the temple and amphitheatre of **Qenqo**, which has some of the finest examples of Inca stone carving *in situ*, especially inside the large hollowed-out stone that houses an altar. Four kilometres furthter on the same road is **Puka Pukara**, known as the Red Fort, but more likely to have been a *tambo*, or post-house; it's worth coming here for the wonderful views alone. Nearby is the spring shrine of **Tambo Machay**, which is in excellent condition. Water still flows by a hidden channel out of the masonry wall, straight into a little rock pool traditionally known as the Inca's bath. You can visit the sites on foot, a pleasant walk of at least half a day through the countryside; enquire about safety beforehand, take water and sun protection, and watch out for dogs. Alternatively, catch a bus up, and walk back.

Rainbow Mountain

This tour is offered by all low-end agencies in Cuzco, departing 0300 daily, returning 1900, US$25 plus US$3 community entrance fee, typical group size 20-25.

Since 2016 this previously seldom-visited area has become a must for budget travellers seeking surreal selfies. It features a trek along a high ridgeline (up to 5000 m), accessed from the community

② **Around Plaza de Armas**

of Chilca in the Cordillera Vilcanota. The ridge is traversed by colourful mineral bands and there are fine views of Ausangate in good weather. The area is beautiful but has already been impacted by mass tourism. The trek is demanding; you should be acclimatised to altitude before undertaking it. To visit this area safely and responsibly, look for an agency which runs smaller groups and takes more time, such as **Apus Perú** (page 1436) and others.

Listings Cuzco maps p1418 and below

Tourist information

iPerú is the most reliable source of information. Their main office and information desk is at the airport (T084-237364, daily 0600-1700). There is also an iPerú desk on Plaza de Armas (Portal de Harinas 177 at BCP Traveller Point, T084-596159, Mon-Fri 0900-1900, Sat-Sun 0900-1300) and a kiosk next to La Compañía church (T084-216680, Mon-Sat 0900-1300, 1400-1800). Information also available from **iCusco/Dircetur** (Portal Mantas 117-A, next to La Merced church, T084-222032, Mon-Sat

0800-2000, Sun 0800-1300). See also www.aboutcusco.com and www.cuscoonline.com.

The **tourist police** (Plaza Túpac Amaru, Wanchaq, T084-512351/235123) will prepare a *denuncia* (report for insurance purposes) for you. **Indecopi** (Urbanización Constancia Mz A-11-2, Wanchaq, T084-252987, toll-free 24-hr T0800-44040, paragon@indecopi.gob.pe) is the consumer protection bureau.

Where to stay

Cuzco has hundreds of hotels in all categories but the more expensive ones should nonetheless be booked several months in advance, particularly for the week around Inti Raymi, when prices are greatly increased. Prices given are for the high season in Jun-Aug. When there are fewer tourists, hotels may drop their prices by as much as half. Always check for discounts. Be wary of unlicensed hotel agents for medium-priced hotels who are often misleading about details; their local nickname is *jalagringos* (gringo pullers), or *piratas*. Many places will store your luggage when you go trekking, but always check valuables and possessions before and after depositing them with hotel/hostel staff.

International chain hotels in Cuzco include **Best Western** (www.bestwestern.com), **JW Marriott** (www.marriott.com), **Novotel** (www.novotel.com) and **Sonesta** (www.sonesta.com). There are also several hostel chains: **Flying Dog** (www.flyingdogperu.com), **Pirwa** (T084-244315, www.pirwahostelscusco.com) with 4 properties, and **The Point** (www.thepointhostels.com).

Where to stay 🛏
1 Andean Wings *A1*
2 Casa Andina Catedral *C3*
3 Casa Andina Classic - Cusco Plaza *C2*
4 Cusco Plaza - Nazarenas *B3*
5 EcoPackers *A1*
6 El Procurador del Cusco *A2*
7 Hostal Resbalosa *A3*
8 Hostal Royal Frankenstein *B1*
9 Inkaterra La Casona *B3*
10 Loreto Boutique Hotel *C2*
11 Marqueses *B1*
12 Pariwana *C1*
13 Pirwa Hostels *B1, B2*
14 Sonesta Posadas del Inca *B2*
15 The Point *C1*
16 Tierra Viva Cusco Plaza *A3*

& Guesthouse *B3*
12 Fusi Chicken and Grill *C2*
13 Greens Organic *C3*
14 Incanto *C3*
15 Kión *C3*
16 Kushka...fé *B1*
17 La Bondiet *C1*
18 Limo *B3*
19 MAP Café *B3*
20 Morena Peruvian Kitchen *A2*
21 Museo del Café *B2*
22 Papacho's *C3*
23 Pucará *B2*
24 Sara *C3*
25 Tunupa *B2*
26 Tupananchis *C1*
27 Víctor Victoria *A2*
28 Yajúú! Juice Bar *B2*

Restaurants 🍴
1 Barrio Ceviche *B2*
2 Café El Ayllu *C1*
3 Café Halliy *A2*
5 Café Perla *C3*
6 Chicha *B1*
7 Cicciolina *C3*
8 Dolce Vita *C3*
9 Dos por Tres *C1*
10 El Encuentro *A2, C3*
11 Fallen Angel restaurant

Bars & clubs 🎵
29 El Garabato & Ukuku's *B2*
30 Indigo *A2*
31 Los Perros Bar *A2*
32 Mama Africa & Inca Rail Ticket Office *B2*
33 Mythology *B3*
34 Norton's Pub *C3*
35 Paddy's Pub *C3*
36 Temple *A2*

> **Tip...**
> Since it is cold in Cuzco and many hotels have no heating, ask for an *estufa*, a heater which some places will provide for an extra charge.

Around the Plaza de Armas

$$$$ Inkaterra La Casona
Pl Las Nazarenas 211, T084-234010,
www.inkaterra.com.
A private, colonial-style boutique hotel in
a converted 16th-century mansion. 11 exclusive
suites, all facilities, concierge service with
activities and excursions, highly regarded
and the height of luxury.

$$$$ The Fallen Angel Guest House
Pl Las Nazarenas 221, T084-258184,
www.fallenangelincusco.com.
A 4-room luxury hotel above the restaurant
of the same name. Each suite is decorated in
its own lavish style (with living room, dining
room, bathroom, feather duvets, heating),
very comfortable and a far cry from the usual
adaptation of colonial buildings elsewhere in
the city. With all amenities, excellent service,
LGBT friendly.

$$$ Andean Wings
Siete Cuartones 225, T084-243166,
www.andeanwingshotel.com.
In a restored 17th-century house, intimate
suites, some with jacuzzi, are individually
designed (one is accessible for the disabled),
spa, restaurant and bar.

$$$ Casa Andina Classic – Cusco Plaza
Portal Espinar 142, T084-231733,
www.casa-andina.com.
40-room hotel near plaza, ATM and safe
deposit box. Equally recommendable are **Casa
Andina Koricancha** (San Agustín 371, T084-
252633), **Casa Andina Catedral** (Santa Catalina
Angosta 149, T084-233661), and the **Casa Andina
San Blas** (Chihuampata 278, San Blas, T084-
263694), all of which are in the same vein.

$$$ Loreto Boutique Hotel
Pasaje Loreto 115, T084-226352,
www.loretoboutiquehotel.com.
Great location; 12 spacious rooms with original
Inca walls, upgraded to boutique status. Laundry
service, will help organize travel services
including guides and taxis, free airport pick-up.

$$$ Marqueses
Garcilaso 256, T084-264249,
www.hotelmarqueses.com.
Spanish colonial style, with 16/17th-century
style religious paintings and 2 lovely courtyards.
Rooms have heavy curtains and some are a
little dark; luxury rooms have bath and shower.
Buffet breakfast.

$$$ Sonesta Posadas del Inca
Portal Espinar 108, T084-227061; and Av el Sol
954, T084-581200; www.sonesta.com.
Includes buffet breakfast, warmly decorated
rooms with heating, safe, some rooms on 3rd floor
have view of Plaza, very helpful, English spoken,
restaurant with Andean food, excellent service.

$$$ Tierra Viva Cusco Plaza
Suecia 345, T084-245858,
www.tierravivahoteles.com.
Boutique hotel in the former residence of
Gonzalo Pizarro. Rooms and suites have
comfortable beds, heating, minibar, safe,
with excellent breakfast. Exemplary service,
airport transfers.

$$ EcoPackers Hostel
Santa Teresa 375, T084-235460,
www.ecopackersperu.com.
Ecologically friendly, well-regarded *hostal* in a
colonial *casona*, double rooms with en suite
or dorms for 4-18 people, communal kitchen,
games room, bar, large-screen TV room, garage
for bicycles or motorcycles.

$$ Pariwana
Mesón de la Estrella 136, T084-233751,
www.pariwana-hostel.com.
Variety of rooms in a converted colonial mansion
with courtyard, from doubles with bath to dorms
sleeping 14, also girls only dorm, restaurant,
bar/lounge, English spoken, lots of activities.

$$-$ Hostal Resbalosa
Resbalosa 494, T084-224839,
www.hostalresbalosa.com.
Private or shared bath, hot water all day, ask for a
room with a view, dorm beds, laundry facilities,
full breakfast extra.

$ El Procurador del Cusco
Coricalle 425, Prolongación Procuradores,
T084-243559, http://hostelprocuradordelcusco.
blogspot.com.
Youth hostel. Basic rooms with or without
bath, upstairs is better, use of the basic kitchen
and laundry area, helpful, good value.

$ Hostal Royal Frankenstein
San Juan de Dios 260, 2 blocks from
the Plaza de Armas, T084-236999,
www.hostal-frankenstein.net.
Eccentric place but a frequent favourite, with
private or shared bath, hot water, safe, kitchen,
includes breakfast, small charge for computer,
heater and laundry, medical services, German-
owned, German and English spoken.

Beyond the Plaza, including San Blas

$$$$ Casa Andina Private Collection Cusco
Plazoleta de Limacpampa Chico 473,
T084-232610, www.casa-andina.com.
The most upmarket and comfortable in
this group, in a 16th-century mansion with
4 courtyards, enriched oxygen available
in the rooms, plus a gourmet restaurant
serving local cuisine and a bar with an
extensive pisco collection.

$$$$ Casa Cartagena
Pumacurco 336, T084-224356,
www.casacartagena.com.
In a converted monastery and national heritage
building, super-deluxe facilities with Italian
design and colonial features, 4 levels of suite,
La Chola restaurant, extensive complimentary
Qoya spa, enriched oxygen system, and all
services to be expected in a Luxury Properties
group hotel.

$$$$ El Mercado
C Siete Cuartones 306, T084-582640,
www.elmercadotunqui.com.
On the site of a former market close to the
Plaza de Armas, owned by **Mountain Lodges
of Peru**, superior rooms and suites, restaurant,
bar, helpful staff.

$$$$ El Monasterio (Belmond)
C Palacios 140, Plazoleta Nazarenas, T084-
604000, www.monasteriohotel.com.
5-star, beautifully restored Seminary of San
Antonio Abad (a Peruvian National Historical
Landmark), including the baroque chapel,
spacious comfortable rooms with all facilities
(some rooms offer an oxygen-enriched
atmosphere), very helpful staff (buffet breakfast
open to non-residents, will fill you up for the rest
of the day), good restaurants, lunch and dinner
à la carte, business centre.

$$$$ Palacio del Inka Luxury Collection
Plazoleta Santo Domingo 259, T084-231961,
www.libertador.com.pe.
5-star, good, especially the service, warm and
bright, **Inti Raymi** restaurant, excellent, live music
in the evening.

$$$$ Palacio Nazarenas (Belmond)
Plazoleta Nazarenas 276, T084-582222,
www.palacionazarenas.com.
Boutique hotel in a beautifully restored former
convent. Outdoor swimming pool, spa, history
booklet and cooking classes.

$$$$-$$$ Casa San Blas
Tocuyeros 566, just off Cuesta San Blas,
T084-237900, www.casasanblas.com.
An international-standard boutique hotel with
bright, airy rooms decorated with traditional
textiles. Breakfast, served in the **Tika Bistro**
downstairs. Pleasant balcony with good views,
attentive service.

$$$$-$$$ Quinua Villa Boutique
Pasaje Santa Rosa A-8, parallel to Tandapata,
T084-242646, www.quinua.com.pe.
A beautiful living museum, 5 different
apartments, each with a different theme and
kitchen, low season discounts.

$$$ El Arqueólogo
Pumacurco 408, T084-232522,
www.hotelarqueologo.com.
Helpful, French and English spoken, heating
extra, will store luggage, garden, cafetería and
kitchen. Same group as **Vida Tours** (Ladrillo 425,
T084-227750, www.vidatours.com). Traditional
and adventure tourism.

$$$ La Encantada
Tandapata 354, T084-242206,
www.encantadaperu.com.
Good beds, rooftop spa, fabulous views of the
city. Swiss-Peruvian owned.

$$$ Los Apus Hotel & Mirador
Atocsaycuchi 515 y Choquechaca, San Blas,
T084-264243, www.losapushotel.com.
Includes airport transfer, full of character, very
clean and smart, central heating, disabled
facilities, two restaurants, fourth floor terrace.

$$$ Pensión Alemana
Tandapata 260, San Blas, T084-226861,
www.hotel-cuzco.com.
Colonial-style modern building. Swiss-owned,
welcoming, comfortable, discount in low season.

$$$ Rumi Punku
Choquechaca 339, T084-221102,
www.rumipunku.com.
An Inca doorway leading to a sunny courtyard,
comfortable rooms, helpful staff, safe, spa
(US$15 per day).

$$$-$$ Amaru Hostal Group
Cuesta San Blas 541, T084-225933,
www.amaruhostal.com.
Private or shared bath. Price includes airport/
train/bus pick-up. Oxygen, kitchen for use in
the evenings, book exchange. Rooms around a
pretty courtyard, good beds, pleasant, relaxing.

Same price category and services at: **Amaru Colonial** (Chihuampata 642, San Blas, T084-223521, www.amaruhostal2.com), and **Hostería de Anita** (Alabado 525-5, T084-225499, www.hosteriadeanita.com), safe, quiet, good breakfast. Also has the more economical **Mallqui Hostal** (Nueva Alta 444, T084-231294), with private rooms and gendered dorms.

$$$-$$ Andenes al Cielo
Choquechaca 176, T084-222237, www.andenesalcielo.com.
At the foot of the San Blas district, 15 rooms and a penthouse in renovated historic home, most expensive rooms have fireplaces, all with either balconies or patios, heating. Buffet breakfast, rooftop patio, safe deposit box, free airport pick up.

$$$-$$ Casona Les Pleiades
Tandapata 116-829, T084-506430, www.casona-pleiades.com.
Small guesthouse in renovated colonial house, cosy and warm, generous hosts, video lounge and book exchange, café, free airport pickup with reservation, lots of info, low season discounts.

$$$-$$ Cusco Plaza – Nazarenas
Plaza Nazarenas 181, T084-246161, www.cuscoplazahotels.com.
Friendly service and good location. Buffet breakfast and café with coffee and snacks. Also runs **Cusco Plaza – Saphi**, Saphi 486, T084-263000.

$$$-$$ Hostal Casa de Campo
Tandapata 298 (at the end of the street), T084-244404, www.hotelcasadecampo.com.
Some of the top rooms have many steps up to them, includes bus/airport/rail transfer with reservations, 10% discount for *Footprint* book owners, safe deposit box, sun terrace, quiet, relaxing, all rooms have great views, Dutch and English spoken, take a taxi after dark.

$$$-$$ Hostal El Balcón
Tambo de Montero 222, T084-236738, www.balconcusco.com.
Warm atmosphere, very welcoming, quiet, laundry, meals on request, English spoken, wonderful views, beautiful garden.

$$$-$$ Hostal Tikawasi
Tandapata 491, T084-231609, www.tikawasi.com.
Includes heating, family-run, lovely garden overlooking the city. Stylish, modern rooms with good views, comfortable beds.

$$ Albergue Casa Campesina
Av Tullumayo 274, T084-233466, www.hotelescbc-cusco.com/casacam/.
Private or shared bath, lovely place, funds support the **Casa Campesina** organization (www.cbc.org.pe), which is linked to local *campesino* communities (see also **Store of Weavers** under Shopping, below).

$$ Andenes de Saphi
Saphi 848, T084-227561, www.andenesdesaphi.com.
Set around 3 Inca terraces. Rooms nicely decorated with animal themes. Common room, bright reception area.

$$ Casa Elena
Choquechaca 162, T084-241202, www.casaelenacusco.com.
French/Peruvian hostel, very comfortable, helpful staff, good choice.

$$ El Grial
Carmen Alto 112, T084-223012, www.hostalelgrial.com.
Family-run, 2 star hostel, in a 17th-century building, coffee shop, laundry service.

$$ Hostal Kuntur Wasi
Tandapata 352-A, San Blas, T084-227570, www.hospedajekunturwasi.com.
Great views, cheaper without bath, use of basic kitchen and laundry (both extra), owner speaks a bit of English and is very helpful and welcoming, a pleasant place to stay.

$$ Hostal Qorichaska
Nueva Alta 458, T084-228974, www.qorichaskaperu.com.
Rooms are clean and sunny, the older ones have traditional balconies. Also has dorms, mixed and gendered. A good choice.

$$ Hostal Quipu
Fierro 495, T084-236179, www.hostalquipu.com.
Small pleasant rooms with private bath and reliable hot water, sunny patio, modern kitchen facilities, helpful staff, good value.

$$ Hostal Suecia
Suecia 332, T084-233282, www.hostalsuecia1.com.
Central location in a beautiful colonial building, private bath, hot showers, laundry.

$$ Niños/Hotel Meloc
Meloc 442, T084-231424, www.ninoshotel.com.
Modern decor in colonial building. Excellent breakfast extra, restaurant, laundry service, luggage store, English spoken, run as part of the

Dutch foundation **Niños Unidos Peruanos** and all profits are invested in projects to help street children. Also has **Niños 2/Hotel Fierro** (C Fierro 476, T084-254611), with all the same features.

$$-$ Casa de La Gringa
Tandapata y Pasñapacana 148, T084-241168, www.casadelagringa.com.
Uniquely decorated rooms, lots of art and colour, 24-hr hot water, kitchen, common areas, heaters, safe homely feeling. See also **Another Planet** (Tour operators), below.

$$-$ Hostal Loki
Cuesta Santa Ana 601, T084-243705, www.lokihostel.com/en/cusco.
Huge bustling hostel in a restored viceroy's residence on the steep Cuesta Santa Ana, dorms and rooms set around a beautiful courtyard, comfortable beds. A great meeting place.

$$-$ Mamá Simona Hostel
Ceniza 364, near San Pedro market, T084-260408, www.mamasimona.com.
Traditional old house with rooms around a courtyard, doubles (heating extra) and dorms, duvets, shared bathrooms, towel rental, includes breakfast, laundry service, helpful.

$$-$ Supertramp
Sapantiana 424B, T084-225783, www.supertramphostel.com.
In a quiet area, built using recycled materials. 2 rooms with bath (1 has jacuzzi) and several dorms, bunk beds with privacy curtains and lockers with electric outlets. Outdoor common area for breakfast (included) and parties.

$$-$ The WalkOn Inn
Suecia 504, T084-235065, www.walkoninn.com.pe.
2 blocks from the Plaza, dorms and rooms with private or shared bathrooms, breakfast extra, laundry service, airport/bus station pick-up extra.

$ Albergue Municipal
Quiscapata 240 (between Resbalosa and Arcoiris), T984-252506.
Youth hostel. Dormitories and double rooms with shared bath, great views, small cooking facilities, laundry, luggage store, very clean, pleasant and good value.

$ Estrellita
Av Tullumayo 445, parte Alta, T084-234134.
Most rooms with shared bath, 2 with private bath, basic but excellent value, safe parking available for bikes.

$ Hitchhikers B&B Backpackers Hostel
Saphi 440, T084-260079, www.hhikersperu.com.
Located close to the plaza, mixture of dorms and 1- to 3-bed private rooms with private or shared bath, includes breakfast, hot water, kitchen, lockers.

$ Hospedaje El Artesano de San Blas
Suytuccato 790, San Blas, T084-263968, http://hospedaje-el-artesano-de-san-blas-guest-house-cusco.bedspro.com.
Many bright and airy rooms overlooking courtyard, quiet, taxis leave you at Plaza San Blas, then it's a steep walk uphill for 5-10 mins.

$ Hospedaje Inka
Suytuccato 848, San Blas, T084-231995, http://hospedajeinka.weebly.com.
Spacious rooms with private or shared bath, wonderful views, very helpful owner, Américo. Taxis leave you at Plaza San Blas, walk steeply uphill for 5-10 mins, or phone the *hostal*.

$ Hostal Killipata
Killichapata 238, just off Tambo de Montero, T084-236668, hostalkillipata@hotmail.com.
Family-run lodging with variety of room sizes, private or shared bath, good showers, hot water and fully equipped kitchen. Breakfast is extra.

$ Hostal Pakcha Real
Tandapata 300, San Blas, T084-237484, www.hostalpakchareal.com.
Family-run, hot water, relaxed, with or without bath. Breakfast included, laundry facilities extra. Airport/train/bus pick-up, but call ahead if arriving late.

$ Hostal Wayras
Nueva Alta 451, T084-237930, wayrashouse@hotmail.com.
Small quiet place, best rooms on top floor, cheaper with shared bath, solar hot water, small kitchen, attentive owner.

$ Maison de la Jeunesse
Av El Sol, Cuadra 5, Pasaje Grace, Edif San Jorge (down a small side street opposite Museo de Sitio de Qoricancha), T084-235617, hostellingcusco@hotmail.com.
Double rooms with bath or a bed in a dorm with shared bath; TV and video room, lockers, cooking facilities and hot water. Affiliated to HI (www.hihostels.com).

$ The Blue House
Kiskapata 291 (parallel and above Tandapata), T084-242407, see Facebook.

Cosy family *hostal*, good value. Reductions for longer stays, includes breakfast, hot shower, views.

$ Tu Casita
C Hospital 787, interior 5 (entrance down an alley near San Pedro market), T984-754519, tucasitacusco@gmail.com.
Dorms, shared bath, 2 kitchens, balcony. Friendly owner Delcy.

Restaurants

Around the Plaza de Armas
There are many good cheap restaurants on Procuradores, Plateros and Tecseccocha.

$$$ A Mi Manera
Triunfo 393, T084-222219.
Imaginative *Novo Andino* cuisine with open kitchen. Great hospitality and atmosphere.

$$$ Barrio Ceviche
Portal de Harinas 181, Plaza de Armas, T084-226334.
Coastal Peruvian cuisine, with fresh fish flown in daily from Lima. Fitting marine decor and great service.

$$$ Chicha
Plaza Regocijo 261, p 2 (upstairs), T084-240520. Daily 1200-2400.
Specializes in regional dishes created by restaurateur Gastón Acurio (see under Lima, Restaurants), Peruvian cuisine of the highest standards in a renovated colonial house, at one time the royal mint, tastefully decorated, open-to-view kitchen, bar with a variety of *pisco sours*, good service.

$$$ Cicciolina
Triunfo 393, 2nd floor, T084-239510.
Reservations required for dinner.
Sophisticated cooking focusing largely on Italian/Mediterranean cuisine, impressive wine list. Good atmosphere, great for a special occasion.

$$$ Fallen Angel
Plazoleta Nazarenas 221, T084-258184.
Sun from 1500.
International and *Novo Andino* gourmet cuisine, great steaks, genuinely innovative interior design, worth checking out their events.

$$$ Fusi Chicken and Grill
Av El Sol 106, T084-233341. Open 1100-2300.
In the La Merced commercial centre, 2nd floor. *Novo Andino* and international cuisine in a chic contemporary setting, fine wines.

$$$ Greens Organic
Santa Catalina Angosta 135, upstairs, T084-254753.
Largely organic, but not wholly vegetarian, ingredients in fusion cuisine, very good.

$$$ Incanto
Santa Catalina Angosta 135, T084-254753. Daily 1100-2400.
Restaurant has Inca stonework and serves Italian dishes (pastas, grilled meats, pizzas), and desserts, accompanied by an extensive wine list. Also Peruvian delicatessen.

$$$ Kión
Triunfo 370, T084-431862. Open 1100-2300.
Traditional *chifa* and regional flavours using Chinese techniques.

$$$ Limo
Portal de Carnes 236, p2, T084-240668.
On 2nd floor of a colonial mansion overlooking the Plaza de Armas, Peruvian cuisine of the highest standard, with strong emphasis on fish and seafood, fine pisco bar, good service and atmosphere.

$$$ MAP Café
In Museo de Arte Precolombino, Plaza de las Nazarenas 231, T084-242476. Open for lunch and dinner.
Haute cuisine approach to traditional dishes using Andean crops, innovative children's menu, minimalist design and top-class service.

$$$ Papacho's
Portal de Belén 115, upstairs, off Plaza de Armas, T084-245359. Daily 1200-2400.
Gastón Acurio's upmarket US-style diner with a Peruvian twist. Emphasis on burgers.

$$$ Tunupa
Portal de Confitería 233, p 2, Plaza de Armas.
Large restaurant, small balcony overlooking Plaza, international, Peruvian and *Novo Andino* cuisine, good buffet US$15, nicely decorated, cocktail lounge, live music and dance at 1930 and 2130.

$$$ Tupananchis
Portal Espinar 180-184, T084-231198.
Tasty *Novo Andino* and fusion cuisine in a sophisticated atmosphere.

$$$-$$ Morena Peruvian Kitchen
Plateros 348B, T084-437832. Mon-Sun 1200-2200.
Modern takes on Peruvian food in a nicely decorated setting, generous portions, good service. Recommended.

\$\$ Pucará
Plateros 309, T084-222027. Mon-Sat 1230-2200.
Peruvian and international food (no language skills required as a sample plate of their daily menu is placed in the window at lunchtime), nice atmosphere.

\$\$ Sara
Santa Catalina Ancha 370, T084-261691.
Vegetarian-friendly organic café bistro, stylish and modern setting, menu includes both traditional Peruvian dishes as well as pasta and other international dishes.

\$\$ Víctor Victoria
Tecseccocha 466, T084-252854. Daily 0700-2200.
Set lunch with salad bar, Peruvian dishes and a few vegetarian options.

\$ El Encuentro
Tigre 130and Santa Catalina Ancha 384. Daily 0800-2200.
Breakfast, economical *menú* and à la carte. Good vegetarian food, very busy at lunchtime.

Cafés

Café Cocla
Mesón De La Estrella 137.
Excellent coffee, also sells organic coffee beans, works with several cooperatives in the Cuzco region.

Café El Ayllu
Almagro 133, and Marqués 263.
Classical/folk music, good atmosphere, superb range of milk products, wonderful apple pastries, good selection for breakfast, great juices, quick service. A Cuzco institution.

Café Halliy
Plateros 357.
Popular meeting place, especially for breakfast, good for comments on guides, has good snacks and 'copa Halliy' (fruit, muesli, yoghurt, honey and chocolate cake), also good *menú* including vegetarian.

Café Perla
Santa Catalina Ancha 304, on the plazoleta.
Extensive menu of light meals, sandwiches, desserts and coffee, including beans for sale roasted on the premises. Popular.

Dolce Vita
Santa Catalina Ancha 366. Open 1000-2100.
Delicious Italian ice cream.

Dos por Tres
Marquez 271.
Popular for over 20 years, great coffee and cakes.

La Bondiet
Heladeros 118. Open 0730-2300.
Upmarket French café with a good selection of sweet and savoury pastries, *empanadas*, good sandwiches, juices and coffee. A local favourite.

Museo del Café
Espaderos 136, around a beautifully restored colonial courtyard.
Coffee, snacks, sweets and a chance get to know the coffee making process. Coffee accessories for sale.

Yajúú! Juice Bar
Portal Confituría 249 and Ayacucho 178-2. Daily 0700-2300.
Fresh inexpensive juices and smoothies as well as sandwiches.

Beyond the Plaza, including San Blas

\$\$\$ Baco
Ruinas 465, T084-242808.
Wine bar and bistro-style restaurant, same owner as Cicciolina. Specializes in BBQ and grilled meats, also veggie dishes, pizzas and good wines. Unpretentious and comfy, groups welcome.

\$\$\$ Kusikuy
Amargura 140, T084-262870.
High quality Peruvian food with good ambience. Good for *cuy* (guinea pig); reserve an hour in advance for this.

\$\$\$ Le Soleil
C San Agustin 275, in La Lune hotel, T084-240543, www.restaurantelesoleilcusco.com. Closed Wed.
Excellent restaurant using local products to make classic French cuisine.

\$\$\$ Pachapapa
Plazoleta San Blas 120, opposite church of San Blas, T084-241318.
A beautiful patio restaurant in a colonial house, good Cusqueño and other dishes, at night diners can sit in their own, private colonial dining room, attentive staff.

\$\$\$-\$\$ Divina Comedia
Pumacurco 406, T084-437640. Daily 1200-1500, 1800-2200.
An elegant restaurant just 1 block from El Monasterio hotel, diners are entertained by classical piano and singing. Friendly atmosphere with comfortable seating, perfect for a special night out, reasonable prices.

$$ Blue Alpaca
Choquechaca 278, T084-233565. Daily 1100-2200.
Variety of national and international dishes, many vegetarian options, hearty alpaca burgers, lunch and dinner *menú*.

$$ El Paisa
Av El Sol 819, T084-501717. Open 0900-1700.
Typical northern Peruvian dishes including ceviche and goat.

$$ Jack's Café
Choquechaca y Cuesta San Blas, T084-254606.
Excellent varied menu, generous portions, relaxed atmosphere, can get very busy at lunchtime, expect a queue in high season.

$$ Justina
Palacios 110. Mon-Sat from 1800.
Good value, good quality pizzería, with wine bar. It's at the back of a patio.

$$ Kushka...fé
Choquechaca 131-A and Portal Espinar 159. Daily 0700-2300.
Great food in a nice setting, English spoken.

$$ La Bodega 138
Herrajes 138, T084-260272.
Excellent pizza, good salads and pasta. Warm and welcoming. Craft beer.

$$ La Cusqueñita
Tullumayo 227 y Av Garcilaso, T084-227314.
A traditional *picantería* serving Cuzco specialities, live music and dance show daily.

$$ Los Toldos
Almagro 171, T084-229829 (deliveries).
Grilled chicken, fries and salad bar, also *trattoria* with home-made pasta and pizza, delivery.

$$ Macondo
Cuesta San Blas 571, T084-227887.
Interesting restaurant with an imaginative menu, good food, well-furnished, gay friendly.

$$ Tacomanía
Tandapata 917, T984-132032. Dinner only.
Serving tacos cooked to order with freshly made Mexican fillings. Owned by Englishman Nick Garret.

$$-$ Mr Soup
Saphi 448, T084-253806. Open lunch and dinner, closed Mon.
Huge bowls of soup from all over the world: udon, goulash, tom ka gai, various Peruvian classics.

$ Café Punchay
Choquechaca 229, T084-261504.
German-owned vegetarian restaurant, with a variety of pasta and potato dishes, good range of wines and spirits, projector for international sports and you can bring a DVD for your own private movie showing.

$ La Chomba
Tullumayo 339. Open lunch and dinner.
Large portions of traditional Peruvian food. Popular with locals, good for tourists seeking a genuine experience.

Cafés

Juanito's Sandwich Café
7 Angelitos 638, San Blas.
Great grilled veggie and meaty burgers and sandwiches, coffee, tea and hot chocolate. Juanito himself is a great character and the café stays open late.

La Valeriana
Av El Sol 576, and Mantas near Plaza de Armas. Mon-Sat 0700-2200, Sun 0730-2100.
Good coffee and pastries.
Try the *lúcuma* cupcakes.

Panadería El Buen Pastor
Cuesta San Blas 579.
Very good bread, *empanadas* and pastries, proceeds go to a charity for orphans and street children.

Qucharitas
Procuradores 385 and Plaza San Francisco 148.
Ice cream made right in front of you, with a wide variety of flavours and toppings.

The Meeting Place
Plazoleta San Blas 630.
Good coffee, waffles and pastries. Supports various social projects. Popular.

Bars and clubs

Bars

Indigo
Tecseccocha 415, T084-260271.
Lounge, cocktail bar and serves Asian and local food. A log fire keeps out the night-time cold.

Km 0 (Arte y Tapas)
Tandapata 100, San Blas.
Mediterranean themed bar tucked in behind San Blas, good snacks and tapas, with live music every night (around 2200).

Los Perros Bar
Tecseccocha 436. Open 1100-0100.
Great place to chill out on comfy couches, excellent music, welcoming, good coffee, tasty meals available (including vegetarian), book exchange, English and other magazines, board games.

Museo del Pisco
Santa Catalina Ancha 398, T084-262709, www.museodelpisco.org. Daily 1100-0100.
A bar where you can sample many kinds of pisco; tapas-style food served.

Norton's Pub
Santa Catalina Angosta 116. Daily 0700-0300.
On the corner of the Plaza de Armas, fine balcony, microbrews, sandwiches and light meals, cable TV, English spoken, pool, darts, motorcycle theme. Very popular.

Paddy's Pub
Triunfo 124 on the corner of the plaza. Open 1000-0100.
Irish theme pub, deservedly popular, good grub.

Clubs

El Garabato Video Music Club
Plateros 316. Daily 1600-0300.
Dance area, lounge for chilling, bar, live shows 2300-0030 (all sorts of styles) and large screen showing music videos.

Mama Africa
Portal de Panes 109.
Cool music and clubber's spot, good food with varied menu, happy hour till 2300, good value.

Mythology
Portal de Carnes 298, p 2.
Mostly an early '80s and '90s combination of cheese, punk and classic, popular.

Temple
Tecseccocha y Tigre. Open 2100-0600.
A big nightclub set in a covered courtyard with large bar and pool table. Live bands some nights.

Ukuku's
Plateros 316. Entry US$1.35.
Very popular, good atmosphere, good mix of music including live shows nightly.

Entertainment

Centro Qosqo de Arte Nativo, *Av El Sol 604, T084-227901.* Regular nightly folklore show from 1900 to 2030, entrance on BTC ticket.

La Esencia, *Limacpampa Chico 400, upstairs, T984-169134, www.facebook.com/laesenciacusco.* Nightly music, storytelling, theatre or movies. Serves tea and light snacks.

Teatro Municipal, *C Mesón de la Estrella 149 (T084-226203 for information 0900-1300 and 1500-1900).* Plays, dancing and shows, mostly Thu-Sun. They also run classes in music and dancing Jan-Mar which are great value.

Festivals

Feb or Mar Carnival in Cuzco is a messy affair with flour, water, cacti, bad fruit and animal manure being thrown about in the streets.
Mon before Easter El Señor de los Temblores (Lord of the Earthquakes). Procession starting at 1600 outside the Cathedral. A large crucifix is paraded through the streets, returning to the Plaza de Armas around 2000 to bless the tens of thousands of people who have assembled there.
2-3 May Vigil of the Cross takes place at all mountaintops with crosses on them, a boisterous affair.
Jun Corpus Christi (Thu after Trinity Sun). All the statues of the Virgin and the saints from Cuzco's churches are paraded through the streets to the Cathedral. The Plaza de Armas is surrounded by tables with women selling *cuy* (guinea pig) and a mixed grill called *chiriuchu* (*cuy*, chicken, tortillas, fish eggs, water-weeds, maize, cheese and sausage) and lots of Cusqueña beer.
24 Jun The pageant of **Inti Raymi**. The Inca festival of the winter solstice, is enacted in Quechua at 1000 at the Qoricancha, moving on to Sacsayhuaman at 1300. Tickets for the stands can be bought a week in advance from the Emufec office (Santa Teresa 142), US$100-140, less if bought Mar-May. Travel agents can arrange the whole day for you, with meeting points, transport, reserved seats and packed lunch. Those who try to persuade you to buy a ticket for the right to film or take photos are being dishonest. On the night before Inti Raymi, the Plaza de Armas is crowded with processions and food stalls. Try to arrive in Cuzco 15 days before Inti Raymi.
28 Jul Peruvian Independence Day. Prices shoot up during these celebrations.
Aug On the last Sun is the **Huarachicoy** festival at Sacsayhuaman, a spectacular re-enactment of the Inca manhood rite, performed in dazzling costumes by boys from a local school.
8 Sep Day of the Virgin is a colourful procession of masked dancers from the church of Almudena,

at the southwest edge of Cuzco, near Belén, to the Plaza de San Francisco. There is also a splendid fair at Almudena, and a free bull fight on the following day.

1 Nov All Saints' Day, celebrated everywhere with bread dolls and traditional cooking.

8 Dec Day of the Immaculate Conception. Churches and museums close at 1200.

24 Dec Santuranticuy, 'the buying of saints', with a big crafts market in the plaza, very noisy until early hours of the 25th. This is one of the best festivals with people from the mountains coming to celebrate Christmas in Cuzco.

Shopping

Arts and crafts
In the Plaza San Blas and the surrounding area, authentic Cuzco crafts still survive. A market is held on Sat. Many leading artisans welcome visitors. Among fine objects made are Biblical figures from plaster, wheatflour and potatoes, reproductions of pre-Columbian ceramics and colonial sculptures, pious paintings, earthenware figurines, festive dolls and wood carvings.

Cuzco is one of the great weaving centres of Peru and excellent textiles can be found at good value. Be very careful of buying gold and silver objects and jewellery in and around Cuzco. Do not buy condor feathers, painted or unpainted, as it is illegal to sell or purchase them. Condors are being killed for this trade. The prison sentence is 4 years.

Agua y Tierra, *Cuesta San Blas 595, T084-236466.* Excellent quality crafts from rainforest communities and Ayacucho.

Factoria La Vicuñita, *Saphi 818, T084-233890.* Huge selection of alpaca clothing, textiles, ceramics, rugs and jewellery. They can show you how to distinguish between fake and real alpaca items.

Feria Artesanal Qoricancha, *Av El Sol, block 4.* Good for cheap crafts.

Mendívil, *Plaza San Blas 619 and Hatunrumiyoc 486.* Known for its long-necked statues of saints. Also sells a wide assortment of other crafts.

Pedazo de Arte, *Plateros 334B.* A tasteful collection of Andean handicrafts, many designed by Japanese owner Miki Suzuki.

Seminario, *inside Museo de Arte Precolombino, Plaza Nazarenas.* Sells the ceramics of Seminario-Behar (see under Urubamba, page 1445), plus cotton, basketry, jewellery, etc.

Books and maps
Centro de Estudios Regionales Andinos Bartolomé de las Casas, *Limacpampa Grande 571, T084-234073, www.cbc.org.pe. Mon-Sat 1100-1400, 1600-1900.* Good books on Peruvian history, archaeology, etc.

Librería Jerusalén, *Heladeros 143, T084-235428. 1030-1400, 1630-1830.* English and Spanish books, maps, guidebooks, postcards, book exchange (2 for 1). Helpful owner.

Maratón, *Av de la Cultura 1020, across the street from San Antonio Abad university, T084-225387.* Wide selection of IGN topographical maps, of interest to trekkers and cyclists.

SBS Librería Internacional, *Av El Sol 864, T084-248106, www.sbs.com.pe. Mon-Fri 0900-2030, Sat 0930-1330, 1600-2000.* Good selection of books and maps.

Camping equipment
For renting equipment, check with tour agencies. Check the equipment carefully as it is common for parts to be missing or damaged. A deposit is asked, plus credit card, passport or plane ticket. White gas (*bencina*), US$3 per litre, can be bought at hardware stores and **Camping Rosly** below. Stove spirit (*alcohol para quemar*) is available at some pharmacies; cooking gas canisters can be found at camping shops.

Camping Rosly, *Procuradores 394, T084-248042.* New and second-hand gear sales and rentals; repairs. Owner speaks English.

Tatoo, *Espinar 144, T084-236703, www.tatoo.ws.* High-quality hiking, climbing and camping gear, not cheap, but international brand names and their own lines.

Fabrics and alpaca clothing
Alpaca Golden, *Portal de Panes 151, T084-262914, alpaca.golden@terra.com.pe.* Also at Plazoleta Nazarenas 175. Designer, producer and retailer of fine alpaca clothing.

The Center for Traditional Textiles of Cuzco, *Av El Sol 603, T084-228117, www.textilescusco.org.* A non-profit organization that seeks to promote, refine and rediscover the weaving traditions of the Cuzco area. Tours of workshops, weaving classes, you can watch weavers at work. Also run 3-day weaving courses. Over 50% of the price goes direct to the weaver. Recommended.

Hilo, *Carmen Alto 260, T974-222294.* Fashionable items designed individually and handmade on-site. Run by Eibhlin Cassidy, she can adjust and tailor designs.

Josefina Olivera, *Portal Comercio 173, Plaza de Armas. Daily 1100-2100.* Sells old textiles and weavings, expensive but worth it to save pieces being cut up to make other item.

Kuna by Alpaca 111, *Plaza Regocijo 202, T084-243233, www.kuna.com.pe*. High-quality alpaca clothing with outlets also in hotels **Mariott** and **Palacio del Inka**.

Store of Weavers (Asociación Central de Artesanos y Artesanas del Sur Andino Inkakunaq Ruwaynin), *Av Tullumayo 274, T084-233466*. Store run by 6 local weaving communities, some of whose residents you can see working on site. All profits go to the weavers themselves.

Food and natural products

Choco Museo, *Garcilaso 210, 2nd floor, also in Ollantaytambo, T084-244765, www.chocomuseo. com*. Offers chocolate-making classes and runs trips to their cocoa plantation.

Coca Museum, *Plaza San Blas 618, T084-501020. Daily 0800-2000*. Shop/museum offers a free tour and sells coca-based products. Information about the history and nutritional value of coca; also about cocaine production.

Frutas Secas Emilia, *San Pedro Market, Kiosk 1077, southwest side of the market next to one of the entrances. Daily 0900-1800*. Large selection of dried fruit and nuts with good prices; also found at stands in **Wanchaq Market**.

La Cholita, *Los Portales Espinar 142B*. Special chocolates made with local ingredients.

San Isidro, *San Bernardo 134. Mon-Sat 0900-1300, 1600-2000*. Excellent local dairy products (great natural yoghurt and a variety of cheeses), honey and jams.

Jewellery

Cusco Ink, *Choquechaca 131*. Tattoo and piercing studio. Also sells Peruvian clothing and jewellery including a wide variety of gauges.

Esma Joyas, *in the courtyard at Triunfo 393*. Handmade jewellery with interesting designs distinct from other local options.

Ilaria, *Portal Carrizos 258, T084-246253*. Branches in hotels **Monasterio**, **Marriott** and at the airport. Recommended for jewellery and silver.

Inka Treasure, *Plazoleta Nazarenas 159, T084-262914*. With branches at Portal de Panes 139 and 163. Also at the airport and the airport in Juliaca. Fine jewellery including goldwork, mostly with pre-Columbian designs, and silver with the owner's designs. Tours of workshops at Av Circunvalación, near Cristo Blanco.

Spondylus, *Plazoleta San Blas 617 and Cuesta San Blas 505, T084-235227*. A good selection of interesting gold and silver jewellery and fashion tops with Inca and pre-Inca designs.

Markets

Wanchaq (Av Garcilaso, southeast of centre) and **San Pedro Market** (see page 1420) sell a variety of goods. **El Molino**, beyond the Terminal Terrestre, sells everything under the sun at knock-down prices, but quality is not guaranteed and there are no tourist items; it's fascinating but crowded, so go there by *colectivo* or taxi and don't take valuables.

Music

Sabino Huamán, *Tandapata 370, T984-296440*. Shop and workshop featuring traditional Andean instruments. With advance notice, he can help you create your own custom pan pipe. Recommended for anyone interested in Andean music.

What to do

There are many travel agencies in Cuzco. The sheer number and variety of tours on offer is bewildering and prices for the same tour can vary dramatically. In general you should only deal directly with the agencies themselves. Do not deal with guides who claim to be employed by agencies listed below without verifying their credentials. Be sure to ask whatever questions you may have in advance. Doing so by email offers the advantage of getting answers in writing but it may also be worth visiting a prospective operator in person to get a feeling for their organization. Competition among agencies can be fierce, but remember that the cheapest option is often not the best. For the latest information, consult other travellers returning from trips. Student discounts are only obtainable with an ISIC card.

City tours cost about US$10-15 for 4 hrs; check what sites are included and that the guide is experienced. Open sightseeing bus tour, about 1 hr, US$7; tickets sold by walking vendors at the Plaza de Armas and the intersection of Heladeros and Mantas. Various 'free' walking tours of Cuzco meet at the Plaza de Armas around midday, the guides expect a minimum tip, ask how much in advance.

In general visitors to Cuzco are satisfied with their tours. Independent travellers should keep in mind, however, that you can do any trek and visit any archaeological site on your own, except for the Inca Trail to Machu Picchu. Visiting independently requires more time, effort and greater language skills than taking a package tour, but it opens the door to a wealth of authentic experiences beyond the grasp of mass tourism.

For a list of recommended Tour operators for Manu, see page 1510.

Cultural tours

Faces of Cusco, *Portal de Carnes 216, Plaza de Armas, T084-225745, www.facesofcusco.com*. Cultural tours including the San Pedro Market, chocolate making, cocktail classes, pisco and craft beer tasting. A good place to hang out and meet people. Friendly owner Vinay is a good source of information.

Milla Tourism, *Urb Lucrepata E16, T084-231710, www.millaturismo.com. Mon-Fri 0800-1300, 1500-1900, Sat 0800-1300*. Mystical tours to Cuzco's Inca ceremonial sites such as Pumamarca and the Temple of the Moon. Guide speaks only basic English. They also arrange cultural and environmental lectures and courses.

Rooftop Kitchen, *T960-17 835, www.rooftop kitchenperu.com*. Gastronomic tours, include a visit to San Pedro Market and cooking lessons where you prepare your own lunch or dinner using regional ingredients. Cost includes transfers.

See also **Choco Museo**, page 1433.

Inca Trail and general tours

Only a restricted number of agencies are licensed to operate **Inca Trail** trips. **Sernanp** (Oswaldo Baca 402, Urb Magisterial, 1 etapa, T084-229297, www.sernanp.gob.pe) verifies operating permits (see Visitors' tickets, above, for Dirección de Cultura office). Unlicensed agencies will sell Inca Trail trips, but pass clients on to the operating agency. This can cause confusion and booking problems at busy times, so book your preferred dates as early as possible in advance. Note also that many companies offer treks as alternatives to the trails to Machu Picchu. These treks are unregulated, so it is up to clients to ensure that the trekking company does not employ the sort of practices (such as mistreating porters, not clearing up rubbish) which are now prohibited on the trails to Machu Picchu. See Essential Inca Trail, page 1459.

Action Valley Adventure Park, *C Santa Teresa 325, Plaza Regocijo, T954-777400, www.action valley.com*. Paragliding, rafting, bungee jumping and other tours and adventure activities.

Amazon Trails Peru, *Tandapata 660, T084-437374, or T984-714148, www.amazontrailsperu.com*. Trekking tours around the area, including the Inca Trail, Salkantay and Choquequirao. Also well-equipped and well-guided trips to Manu.

Amazonas Explorer, *see under Rafting, mountain biking and trekking, below*. Run a high-quality 5-day/4-night Inca Trail trek, every Tue, Mar-Nov.

Andean Treks, *US company, no Cuzco storefront, www.andeantreks.com*. Manager Peter Robertson uses high-quality equipment and satellite phones. Organizes itineraries, from 2 to 15 days with a wide variety of activities in this area and further afield.

Andina Travel, Treks & Eco-Adventure, *Plazoleta Santa Catalina 219, T084-251892, www.andinatravel.com*. Eco-agency with more than 10 years' experience operating all local treks. Has a reputation in Cuzco for local expertise and community projects.

Big Foot, *Triunfo 392 (oficina 213), T084-233836, www.bigfootcusco.com*. Tailor-made hiking trips, especially in the remote corners of the Vilcabamba and Vilcanota mountains; also the Inca Trail.

Chaska, *Garcilaso 265 p 2, of 6, T084-240424, www.chaskatours.com*. Dutch-Peruvian company offering cultural, adventure, nature and esoteric tours. They specialize in the **Inca Trail**, but also llama treks to Lares and treks to Choquequirao.

Culturas Peru, *Tandapata 354A, T084-243629, www.culturasperu.com*. Swiss/Peruvian company offering adventure, cultural, ecological and spiritual tours. Also specialize in alternative Inca trails.

Destinos Turísticos, *Portal de Panes 123, oficina 101-102, Plaza de Armas, T084-228168, www. destinosturisticosperu.com*. The owner speaks Spanish, English, Dutch and Portuguese and specializes in package tours from economic to 5-star budgets. Advice on booking jungle trips and renting mountain bikes. Very helpful.

EcoAmerica Peru, *C Marquez 259, of 8, 2nd floor, T999-705538, www.ecoamericaperu.com*. Associated with **America Tours** (La Paz, Bolivia). Owned by 3 experienced consultants in responsible travel, conservation and cultural heritage. Specializes in culture, history, nature, trekking, biking and birding tours. Knowledgeable guides, excellent customer service for independent travellers, groups or families. Also sell tours and flights to Bolivia.

Enigma Adventure, *C Fortunato L Herrera 214, Urb Magisterial 1a Etapa, T084-222155, www. enigmaperu.com*. Run by Spaniard Silvia Rico Coll. Well-organized, innovative trekking expeditions including a luxury service, Inca Trail and a variety of challenging alternatives. Also cultural tours to weaving communities, Ayahuasca therapy, climbing and biking.

Explorandes, *Paseo Zarzuela Q-2, Huancaro, T084-238380 ext 116, www.explorandes.com.* Experienced high-end adventure company. Arrange a wide variety of mountain treks; trips available in Peru and Ecuador, book through website. Also arranges tours across Peru for lovers of orchids, ceramics or textiles. Award-winning environmental practices.

Fertur Peru Travel, *El Sol 803, Of 205, T084-221304, www.fertur-travel.com.* Cuzco branch of the Lima tour operator, see page 1281.

Gatur Cusco, *Puluchapata 140 (a small street off Av El Sol 3rd block), T084-245121, www. gaturcusco.com.* Esoteric, ecotourism, and general tours. Owner Dr José (Pepe) Altamirano is knowledgeable in Andean folk traditions. Excellent conventional tours, bilingual guides and transportation. Guides speak English, French, Spanish and German. They can also book internal flights.

Habitats Peru, *Condominio La Alborada B-507, Wanchaq, T084-246271, www.habitatsperu.com.* Birdwatching and mountain biking trips offered by Doris and Carlos. They also run a volunteer project near Quillabamba.

Hiking Peru, *Mantas 113, T984-651414, www. hikingperu.com.* 8-day treks to Espíritu Pampa; 7 days/6 nights around Ausangate; 4-day/3-night Lares Valley Trek.

Inca Explorers, *C Peru W-18, Ttio, T084-241070, www.incaexplorers.com.* Specialist trekking agency for small group expeditions in socially and environmentally responsible manner. Also 2-week hike in the Cordillera Vilcanota (passing Nevado Ausangate), and Choquequirao to Espíritu Pampa.

InkaNatura Travel, *Ricardo Palma J1, T084-243408, www.inkanatura.com.* Offers tours with special emphasis on sustainable tourism and conservation. Knowledgeable guides.

Inkayni Tours, *Triunfo 392, of 214, T084-232817, www.inkayniperutours.com.* Offers trips and treks to Machu Picchu, city tours in Cuzco and alternative treks, such as Salkantay, Lares, Huchuy Qosqo.

Llama Path, *Cuichipunco 257, T084-265134, www.llamapath.com.* A wide variety of local tours, specializing in Inca Trail and alternative treks, involved in environmental campaigns and porter welfare. Many good reports.

Mountain Lodges of Peru, *T084-243636 (North America T1-877-491-5261, Europe T+44-0-800-014-8886), www.mountainlodgesofperu.com.* Offer lodge-to-lodge treks from one purpose-built lodge to another, including a 7-day Salkantay to Machu Picchu trek and a 5- or 7-day route from Lamay to Ollantaytambo via the Lares valley (http://laresadventure.com), with flexible options for activities.

Peru Treks & Adventure, *Av Pardo 540, T084-222722, www.perutreks.com.* Professional, high-quality tour operators specializing in trekking and cultural tours in the Cuzco region. They pride themselves on good treatment of porters and support staff and have been consistently recommended for professionalism and customer care; a portion of profits go to community projects.

Q'ente, *Choquechaca 229, p 2, T084-222535, www.qente.com.* Their Inca Trail service is recommended. Also private treks to Salkantay, Ausangate, Choquequirao and Vilcabamba. Horse riding to local ruins costs US$35 for 4-5 hrs. Very good, especially with children.

Sky Travel, *Santa Catalina Ancha 366, interior 3-C, T084-240141, www.skyperu.com.* English spoken. General tours around city and Sacred Valley. Inca Trail with good-sized double tents and a dinner tent (the group is asked what it would like on

the menu 2 days before departure). Other trips include Vilcabamba and Ausangate (trekking).

Southamerica Planet, *Garcilaso 210, of 201, T084-241424, www.southamericaplanet.com.* Peruvian/Belgian-owned agency offering the Inca Trail, other treks around Cuzco and packages within Peru, as well as Bolivia and Patagonia.

Tanager Tours, *no storefront, T084-387254, Lima T01-669 0825, www.tanagertours.com.* Specializes in birdwatching tours throughout Peru but will also arrange other tours. Book via internet.

T'ika Trek, *no storefront, UK T07824-377292, www.tikatrek.com.* UK contact Fiona Cameron lived for many years in Peru and is a keen hiker and biker. With over 10 years in the Cuzco tourism business, Fiona provides high-quality personalized tours all over Peru as well as to the Galápagos Islands (Ecuador). Focus is on small groups and families.

Trekperu, *Av República de Chile B-15, Parque Industrial, Wanchaq, T084-261501, www.trekperu. com.* Experienced trek operator as well as other adventure sports. Offers 'culturally sensitive' tours. Cusco Biking Adventure includes support vehicle and good camping gear (but providing your own sleeping bag).

United Mice, *Av Pachacútec 424 A-5, T084-221139, www.unitedmice.com.* Inca Trail and alternative trail via Salkantay and Santa Teresa, well-established and reputable. Good guides who speak languages other than Spanish. Discount with student card, good food and equipment. City and Sacred Valley tours and treks to Choquequirao.

Valencia Travel Cusco, *Portal de Panes 123, Centro Comercial Ruiseñores, of 306-307, T084-255907, www.valenciatravelcusco.com.* Specialize in adventure trails, both the classics and the roads less travelled, and immersion homestays.

Wayki Trek, *Quera 239, T084-224092, www.waykitrek.net.* Budget travel agency recommended for their Inca Trail service. Owner Americo Aguilar knows the area very well. Treks to several almost unknown Inca sites and interesting variations on the 'classic' Inca Trail with visits to porters' communities. Also treks to Ausangate, Salkantay and Choquequirao.

Language courses

Academia Latinoamericana de Español, www.latinoschools.com; **Acupari**, www.acupari.com; **Amauta Spanish School**, www.amautaspanish.com; **Amigos Spanish School**, www.spanishcusco.com; **Centro Tinku**, www.centrotinku.com (Spanish and Quechua); **Fair Services Spanish School**, www.fairservices-peru.org; **San Blas Spanish School**, www.spanishschoolperu.com.

Rafting, mountain biking, paragliding and trekking

When looking for an adventure operator please consider more than just the price of your tour. Competition between companies in Cuzco is intense and price wars can lead to compromises in safety. Check the quality of safety equipment (lifejackets, etc) and ask about the number and experience of rescue kayakers and support staff. On large and potentially dangerous rivers like the Apurímac and Urubamba (where fatalities have occurred), this can make all the difference. Always use a licensed operator.

Amazonas Explorer, *Av Collasuyo 910, T084-252846, www.amazonas-explorer.com.* Experts in rafting, standup paddleboarding, catamaran sailing, mountain biking, horse riding and hiking. Rafting routes include expeditions to the Apurimac, Cotahuasi and Tambopata rivers. Owner Paul Cripps has great experience. Also offer the classic Inca Trail and alternatives. Group and tailor-made trips. All options are at the higher end of the market. Highly recommended.

Apumayo, *Jr Ricardo Palma Ñ-II, Santa Mónica, Wanchaq, T084-246018, www.apumayo.com. Mon-Sat 0900-1300, 1600-2000.* Urubamba rafting (from 0800-1530 every day); 3- to 4-day Apurímac trips. Also mountain biking to Maras and Moray in Sacred Valley, or from Cuzco to the jungle town of Quillabamba. This company also offers tours for disabled people, including rafting.

Apus Perú, *Cuichipunco 366, T084-232691, www.apus-peru.com.* Conducts most business by internet, specializes in alternatives to the Inca Trail, strong commitment to sustainability, well organized. Associated with **Threads of Peru** NGO which helps weavers.

Pachatusan Trek, *Villa Union Huancaro G-4, B 502, T084-231817, www.pachatusantrek.com.* Offers a wide variety to treks, as alternatives to the Inca Trail, professional and caring staff, "simply fantastic".

River Explorers, *Urb Kennedy, Av Los Brillantes B36, T084-431116, www.riverexplorers.com.* An adventure company offering mountain biking, trekking and rafting trips (on the Apurímac, Urubamba and Tambopata). Experienced and qualified guides with environmental awareness.

Terra Explorer Peru, *T084-237352, Urb Santa Ursula D4, Wanchaq, www.terraexplorerperu.com.* Offers a wide range of trips from high-end raftingand expeditions to the Apurímac,

Colca and Cotahuasi canyons, to trekking the Inca Trail and others, mountain biking, kayaking (including on Lake Titicaca) and jungle trips. All guides are bilingual.

Shamans and mystical plant experiences

San Pedro and Ayahuasca have been used since before Inca times, mostly as a sacred healing experience. If you choose to experience these plants, only do so under the guidance of a reputable agency or shaman and always have a friend with you who is not partaking. If the medicine is not prepared correctly, it can be highly toxic and dangerous. Never buy from someone who is not recommended; never buy off the streets, and never try to prepare the plants yourself.
Another Planet, *Tandapata y Pasñapakana 148, San Blas, T084-241168, www.anotherplanet peru.org*. Run by Lesley Myburgh, who operates mystical and adventure tours in and around Cuzco, and is an expert in San Pedro cactus preparation. She arranges San Pedro sessions for healing in the garden of her house outside Cuzco. Tours meet at **La Casa de la Gringa**, see Where to stay, above.
Etnikas Travel & Shamanic Healing, *Av la Cultura 2122 and Recoleta 674, T084-244516, www.etnikas.com*. A shamanic centre offering travel for mind, body and spirit. Offers ayahuasca sessions in their proper ceremonial context. Expensive but serious in their work.
Sumac Coca Travel, *San Agustín 245, T084-260311, www.sumaccoca.com*. Mystical tourism, offering Ayahuasca and San Pedro ceremonies, and also more conventional cultural tourism. Professional and caring.

Private guides

As most of the sights do not have any information or signs in English, a good guide can really improve your visit. Either arrange this before you set out or contract one at the sight you are visiting. A tip is expected at the end of the tour. Tours of the city or Sacred Valley cost US$50 for half-day, US$65 full day plus transport and entrance fees; a guide to Machu Picchu charges US$80 per day. A list of official guides is held by **Agotur Cusco** (C Heladeros 157, Of 34-F, p 3, T084-233457). See also www.leaplocal.org.

Transport

Air The airport (open 0500-2030) is at Quispiquilla, near the bus terminal, 1.6 km from centre, airport information T084-222611/601. There are plans to build a new airport at Chinchero, 23 km northwest of the city (see page 1446). The airport can get very busy; check in at least 2 hrs before your flight. Flights may be delayed or cancelled during the wet season. The Arrivals area has ATMs, money exchange booth (poor rates), a medical post, an **iPerú** desk (open 0700-1300, 1400-1600), **Peru Rail** booth, a **Dircetur** desk, restaurant, cafeteria (Oxishot oxygen canisters available here) and a **Tourist Police** booth (open 0500-2000). In the main lobby is the **iPerú** office (open 0600-1700). Hotel representatives and travel agents operate at the airport offering transport to particular hotels for arriving visitors without prior bookings; take your time to choose a hotel at a price you can afford. If you already have a booking, taxis and tourist minibuses meet new arrivals and (should) take you to the hotel of your choice: be insistent. A taxi to and from the airport costs US$5-7 (US$9-12 from the official taxi desk). *Colectivos* (not safe with luggage, white and yellow *Liebre* or blue *Correcaminos*) cost US$0.20 between Plaza Regocijo and the airport; to go to the airport, get on at block 2 of C Ayacucho, by Av El Sol.

To **Lima**, 55 mins, over 40 daily flights with **Avianca/TACA**, **Star Perú**, **LATAM**, **Peruvian Airlines** and **LC Perú**. To **Arequipa**, 30 mins daily with **LATAM**. To **Juliaca** (for Puno), 1 hr daily with **LATAM**. To **Puerto Maldonado**, 30 mins, with **Avianca/TACA**, **LATAM** and **Star Perú**. To **La Paz**, **Peruvian Airlines** and **Amaszonas** (www.amaszonas.com), 1 hr, daily.

Bus Long distance The busy, often crowded Terminal Terrestre is on Av Vallejo Santoni, block 2 (Prolongación Pachacútec). *Colectivo* from centre US$0.20 (not safe with luggage), taxi US$2-3. Platform tax US$0.50.

To **Lima,** US$35-65, a long ride (20-24 hrs) and worth paying for a comfortable bus. The route is via **Abancay** (US$7, 5 hrs) and **Nazca** (US$30, 13 hrs) on the Panamerican Highway. It is paved, but floods in the wet season often damage large sections. At night, take a blanket or sleeping bag to ward off the cold. Better companies to Lima include: **Molina**, daily at 2000; **Cruz del Sur** at 1400, 1600 and 1800; **Móvil Tours** at 1700 and **Oltursa** at 1600. **Bredde** has most frequent service (5 daily) to Abancay; others include

> **Tip...**
> If you're prone to travel sickness, take precautions on the way from Cuzco to Abancay; there are many curves but the scenery is magnificent.

Expreso Sánchez and Celajes. Los Chankas to Abancay at 0730, 1930 and 2000 continues to **Andahuaylas** (US$13.50, 9 hrs) and **Ayacucho** (US$25, 16 hrs).

To **Juliaca**, 344 km, US$5 normal, US$9 semi-cama, US$12.50-17 cama, 5-6 hrs, with **Power** every 2 hrs, 0400-2300; several others. The road is fully paved, but after heavy rain buses may not run. To **Puno**, 388 km, 6-7 hrs; there are 3 levels of service, all via Juliaca: regular, stopping in Juliaca, US$7-12; direct, US$15-27, with **Tour Perú** (www.tourperu.com.pe); **Cruz del Sur** or **Transzela** (www.transzela.com.pe); and tourist service with 5 stops (Andahuaylillas church, Raqchi, Sicuani for lunch, La Raya and Pucará), US$45-50 (includes lunch, may or may not include entry tickets; ask), 10 hrs. Several companies offer the tourist service; all leave from private terminals: **Inka Express** at 0700 from Av 28 de Julio 211, 5th stop Urb Ttio, T084-247887, www.inkaexpress.com; **Turismo Mer** at 0700 from Av La Paz A-3, Urb El Ovalo, Wanchaq, T084-245171, www.turismomer.com; and **Wonder Perú** at 0700 from Av 28 de Julio R2-1, Urb Ttio, Wanchaq, www.wonderperuexpedition.com. In high season, reserve 2 days ahead. **Note** It is advisable to travel by day on the Cuzco-Juliaca-Puno route, the views are great.

To **Arequipa (via Juliaca)**, 521 km, 10-11 hrs, with **Cruz del Sur** at 2000 and 2030, US$37-47; **Cromotex** at 1900 and 2000, US$11-36; **Flores** at 0645 and 2030, US$11; **Power** at 0500 and 1700, US$11; many others, mostly at night. A tourist service direct to **Chivay** on the **Colca Canyon** is offered by **4M Express** (Av 28 de Julio, Urbanización Ttio, Wanchaq, T054-452296, www.4m-express.com), Tue, Thu and Sat at 0700, US$65 (lunch extra); see Colca Canyon Transport, page 1391, for details.

Several daily buses between Cuzco and **Puerto Maldonado** bus terminals; **Cruz del Sur** departs from its private terminal at Av Industrial 2126, Santiago; there is also van service, see page 1513.

To the **Sacred Valley** There are 2 routes to Urubamba and Ollantaytambo: 1 via Pisac and Calca, the other via Chinchero. It is worth going on one and returning on the other. To **Pisac** (32 km, 1 hr, US$1.50-3), **Calca** (50 km, 1½ hrs, US$1.50) and **Urubamba** (72 km via Pisac and Calca, 2 hrs, US$3), *colectivos* (transfer in Pisac) and minibuses from C Puputi near Av la Cultura (see map, page 1418, C6), leave when full 0600-1800. Buses returning from Pisac are often full; last one back leaves around 2000. Taxis charge about US$20 one way to Pisac.

To **Chinchero** (23 km, 45 mins US$2), **Urubamba** (50 km via Chinchero, 1½ hrs, US$2.50), **Ollantaytambo** (70 km via Chinchero and Urubamba, 2 hrs, US$3.50-5), *colectivos* and minibuses from C Pavitos near Av Grau (see map, page 1418, E4). Taxi to Ollantaytambo US$22 one way.

Taxi In Cuzco taxis are recommended when arriving by air, train or bus. They have fixed prices but you have to stay alert to overpricing (always agree on the price in advance): in the centre US$1.50 (50% more after 2100 or 2200). Safer and more expensive are radio-dispatched taxis with a sign on the roof, including **Aló Cusco** T084-222222, **Ocarina** T084-255000, and many others. With wait time, trips to **Sacsayhuaman**, US$10; to ruins of **Tambo Machay** US$15-20 (3-4 people); day trip US$50-85.

Train PeruRail uses Estación Wanchaq (Av Pachacúteq, T084-238722, www.perurail.com, ticket sales for all PeruRail services Mon-Fri 0700-1700, Sat, Sun and holidays 0700-1200). There are also **PeruRail** offices at Portal de Carnes 214 and Plaza Regocijo 202, both open daily 0700-2200, and sales points at the Lima and Cuzco airports (in domestic departures and arrivals, respectively). Purchase tickets well in advance, take your passport or a copy when buying tickets. **Inca Rail** uses Estación San Pedro (Ccascaparo opposite San Pedro Market) for a bus-rail combined service to Machu Picchu, when Poroy station is closed; ticket sales at Portal de Panes 105, Plaza de Armas, T084-581860, www.incarail.com, Mon-Fri 0700-2200, Sat, Sun and holidays 0700-2000.

The *Belmond Andean Explorer*, PeruRail's luxury sleeper trains with cabins with private bath and shower, leave from Wanchaq station. The service includes stops at points of interest; there are also optional excursions at extra cost. These trains do not operate in Feb. The following prices are based on double occupancy. *Spirit of the Water* service to **Puno** (1 day/1 night, US$565-815 pp) departs Tue 1100, stops at Raqchi and La Raya, optional boat tour on Lake Titicaca; *Peruvian Highlands* to **Arequipa** via Titicaca (3 days/2 nights, US$1440-2065 pp), departs Thu 1100, stops at Raqchi, La Raya, excursion on Lake Titicaca (Uros, Taquile and Playa Collata), Saracocha, Sumbay Caves, optional trip to Colca, and Arequipa city tour. Trains to **Machu Picchu** and the **Sacred Valley** leave from Poroy (7.5 km east of the centre) or Ollantaytambo, depending on the season and service, see page 1457.

The main road from Cuzco to Lake Titicaca and Arequipa follows the Río Vilcanota upstream to La Raya, the border with the neighbouring department of Puno. Along the route are archaeological sites, fascinating colonial churches, beautiful lakes and the majestic Ausangate massif, where you can do some serious high-altitude trekking.

Southeast of Cuzco

Between the villages of Saylla and Oropesa are the extensive **Tipón ruins** ① *5-km climb from village, daily 0800-1630, entry only with BTC; take a combi to Oropesa, then a taxi*, which include baths, terraces, irrigation systems, possibly an agricultural laboratory and a temple complex, accessible from a path leading from just above the last terrace. **Oropesa**, whose church contains a fine ornately carved pulpit, is the national 'Capital of Bread'; try the delicious sweet circular loaves known as *chutas*.

Paucartambo and around

At **Huambutío**, north of the village of Huacarpay, the road divides, with one branch leading northwest to Pisac and the other (being paved in 2017) heading north to **Paucartambo**, in the deep valley of the Río Mapacho, on the eastern slope of Andes. At 2850 m, this pleasant colonial town, 80 km east of Cuzco, has an excellent museum and interesting surroundings (helpful tourist office in the Terminal Terrestre). In the Centro Cultural is the **Museo de los Pueblos** ① *daily 0800-1300, 1500-1800, US$3*, with exhibits on the history, culture and textiles of the region, including the famous **Fiesta de la Virgen del Carmen** (Mamacha Carmen; 15-19 July and smaller one 2-4 Feb), at which masked dancers enact rituals and folk tales. **Watoqto**, a Killke archaeological site (AD 1200), later occupied by the Incas, is 15 km upriver (taxi US$15 return) and 11 km downstream are the **Chimur** thermal baths (public transport Sat-Sun at 0400, US$5 return) and Inca road remnants. You can travel 44 km from Paucartambo, to **Tres Cruces**, at the southern edge of **Parque Nacional Manu** ① *entry US$3*, along the Pilcopata road, turning left after 25 km at the Ajcanaco park control point. Come here for the sunrise in May to mid-August, when peculiar atmospheric conditions make it appear that two suns are rising. Tour agencies in Cuzco can arrange transport and lodging or ask at Acjanaco rangers' station (past the control point) to use the Tres Cruces shelter, take warm clothing and sleeping bag. **Trocha Ericson** is a 4-km trail from the Acjanaco control point to Pillahuato, downhill on the road to Pilcopata. **Trocha Unión**, a pre-Hispanic trail, runs 12 km from Tres Cruces to Mirador San Pedro, further along the road to Pilcopata; camping is possible about half way down.

Piquillacta

Daily 0800-1630, entry only with BTC. Buses to Urcos will drop you near the entrance.

Further on from Huacarpay are the extensive pre-Inca ruins of Piquillacta (which translates as the City of Fleas). This was an administrative centre at the southern end of the Huari Empire. The whole site is surrounded by a wall encompassing many enclosed compounds with buildings of over one storey; it appears that the walls were plastered and finished with a layer of lime. On the opposite side of the highway from Piquillacta is Laguna de Huacarpay (also known as Moina) and the ruins that surround it: Kañarakay, Urpicancha and the impressive Huari aqueduct and Inca gateway of Rumicolca, at the pass just beyond Piquillacta. A guide will help to find the more interesting structures. It's good to hike or cycle and birdwatch around the lake.

Andahuaylillas to Urcos

Buses from Cuzco to Urcos leave when full from Av de la Cultura y Pje Carrasco, opposite the Hospital Regional, US$1, 1½ hrs, passing Andahuaylillas en route.

Andahuaylillas, 32 km southeast of Cuzco, has a lovely shady plaza and beautifully restored early 17th-century **church** ① *daily 0730-1730, on RBA ticket*. It's known as the 'Andean Sistine Chapel', due to its fabulous frescoes. There's also a splendid doorway and a gilded main altar. The next village,

Huaro, also has a **church** ① *daily 0800-1700, on RBA ticket*, whose interior is entirely covered with colourful frescoes. Urcos, meanwhile, is a chaotic commercial centre and transport hub; beware overcharging for everything here. South of Urcos, stop off at the villages of **Cusipata**, which has an Inca gate and wall, and **Checacupe**, which has a lovely church.

Cordillera Vilcanota

A spectacular road from Urcos crosses the Eastern Cordillera to Puerto Maldonado in the jungle (428 km, see page 1502). Some 82 km from Urcos, near the base of Nevado Ausangate, is the town of **Ocongate**, a friendly regional centre with most services and a good place to prepare for trekking. Beyond Ocongate, **Tinqui** is a smaller, colder town with basic places to stay and eat; it's the starting point for hikes around Ausangate, which, at 6384 m, is the loftiest peak in the Vilcanota range. From Mahauyani, 12 km beyond Tinqui, a wide trail runs 8.5 km up to the sanctuary of Señor de Q'Olloriti at 4700 m, where a massive pilgrimage is held during the two weeks leading up to Trinity Sunday (8 weeks after Easter Sunday) and culminating on the following Tuesday. Above the Christian sanctuary are the glaciers of Nevado Cinajara, the original object of devotion and still considered a sacred site. There is good trekking in the area and few visitors outside the festival.

Continuing east, some 47 km after passing the snow line on the Hualla-Hualla pass, at 4820 m, the super-hot thermal baths of **Marcapata** ① *173 km from Urcos, US$0.20*, provide a relaxing break. Beyond this point, what is arguably the most spectacular road in Peru descends the eastern flank of the Andes towards Puerto Maldonado (see page 1502).

☆**Ausangate Trek** ① *entry US$3.50 at Tinqui plus US$3.50 at each of 3 communities along the route.* The hike around the mountain of Ausangate (6348 m) is spectacular. There are two popular routes requiring three to six days. It is hard going, with two passes over 5000 m and camping above 4000 m, so you need to be fit and acclimatized. Temperatures in high season (April-October) can drop well below zero at night. It is recommended to take a guide and/or *arriero*. Arrieros and mules can be hired in Tinqui: US$12 per day for a guide, US$10 per mule, more for a saddle horse. *Arrieros* also expect food. Make sure you sign a contract with full details. Buy supplies in Cuzco or Ocongate. Maps are available at the IGN in Lima and Maratón in Cuzco (see Shopping, above). Cuzco agencies and **Hostal Ausangate** (see Where to Stay, below) run tours from about US$120. Bring your own warm sleeping bag. **Miguel Pacsi** (T984-668360, mpacsi1@hotmail.com) has been recommended as a private guide and can help with logistics.

Q'eswachaka

At Combapata (about 50 km from Urcos on the road to Sicuani) a paved road climbs west for 16 km, through a region of large highland lakes, to the cold regional centre of **Yanaoca** at 3950 m. Yanaoca has simple places to stay and eat, and provides access to the village of Quehue, 20 km further south. Near the village an Inca bridge spans the upper Río Apurímac at Q'eswachaka. The bridge, a UNESCO World Heritage Site, is 28 m long and is made entirely of q'oya (a flexible straw), woven and spliced to form cables which are strung across the chasm. The bridge is rebuilt each year in June, during a unique and spectacular four-day event. Cuzco operators offer tours during the festival or you can go on your own at any time of the year, although it's not safe to cross the bridge between December and June.

Raqchi and around

Continuing on the main road to Sicuani, **Tinta**'s church has a brilliant gilded interior and an interesting choir vault. **Raqchi** is the scene of the region's great folklore festival and also the site of the **Viracocha Temple** ① *daily 0800-1600, US$6, take a bus from Cuzco towards Sicuani, US$3.50.* John Hemming wrote: "What remains is the central wall, which is adobe above and Inca masonry below. This was probably the largest roofed building ever built by the Incas. On either side of the high wall, great sloping roofs were supported by rows of unusual round pillars, also of masonry topped by adobe. Nearby is a complex of barracks-like buildings and round storehouses. This was the most holy shrine to the creator god Viracocha, being the site of a miracle in which he set fire to the land – hence the lava flow nearby. The landscape is extraordinary, blighted by huge piles of black volcanic rocks."

You can do a homestay here with pottery classes and a walk to the extinct Quimsachata volcano. There is also simple accommodation in the nearby town of **San Pedro**, along the main road to Sicuani. Beyond San Pedro, the road continues southeast to Sicuani, La Raya and the department of Puno.

Listings Upper Vilcanota Valley

Where to stay

Paucartambo
There are several simple accommodations in town, all are booked a year ahead for the Jul fiesta.

$ Anka Hostal
Prolongación Ericson, opposite the terminal, T952-412461.
Simple rooms with private bath and hot water, no breakfast.

$ Hospedaje Tres Cruces
Plazoleta Cuculi, opposite the church, T084-612655.
Simple rooms with bath, cheaper with shared bath, hot water, covered patio, no breakfast.

Andahuaylillas to Urcos
These are all in Andahuaylillas; the 1 decent hostal in Urcos ($ **El Amigo**, C Carpintero y Jr César Vallejo, T084-307064) is often full.

$ Hostal Chiss
C Quispicanchis 216, T984-857294.
Economical accommodation in a family home with kitchen and washing facilities, private or shared bath, electric shower, some mattresses are poor. Effusively friendly owner, Sr Ladislao Belota.

$ Hostal El Nogal
Plaza de Armas, T084-771164.
Small place with 3 warm bright rooms, shared bath, electric shower, restaurant.

Cordillera Vilcanota

$ Hospedaje Janmarco
On the left-hand side as you enter Tinqui from Ocongate.
Simple clean rooms, shared bath with electric shower. Owner Ernesto Jancco is knowledgeable and can arrange guides and pack animals for excursions. **La Casa de Xiomana** next door has good set meals.

$ Hostal Ausangate
On the right-hand side as you enter Tinqui from Ocongate, T974-327538, Cuzco T084-227768, ausangate_tour@outlook.com.
Basic rooms with shared bath, cold water, meals available. Sr Cayetano Crispín, the owner, is knowledgeable and can arrange guides, mules, etc. A reliable source of trekking and climbing information.

$ Hostal Siesta
C Libertad 320, Ocongate, T996-030606.
Pleasant rooms with shared bath, patio, very clean and good value. Helpful owner Sr Raúl Rosas changes US$ at fair rates.

Festivals

Jun Confirm all dates locally. **Q'eswachaka**, during the 1st or 2nd weekend of the month, is a 4-day festival centred on the reconstruction of the Inca rope bridge; **Q'Olloriti**, the multitudinous Snow Star Festival, is held at a sanctuary at 4700 m near Ocongate and Tinqui. It lasts 2 weeks and culminates on the Tue after Trinity Sun; several Cuzco agencies offer tours; on the 2nd or 3rd weekend the **folklore dance festival** in Raqchi draws participants from all over Peru.

Transport

Paucartambo
Vehicles to Paucartambo leave as they fill (0300-2000) from the *Paradero Control* in the San Jerónimo neighbourhood of Cuzco: vans, US$3, 2½ hrs; and cars, US$3.60, 2 hrs. **Gallito de las Rocas**, also from San Jerónimo, several daily buses, US$2.45, 3 hrs. From Paucartambo terminal to **Pilcopata**, buses pass 0700-0900, US$3, 5 hrs; also trucks originating in Cuzco. There is more transport to the lowlands on Mon, Wed and Fri, returning Tue, Thu, Sat. To **Tres Cruces**, a taxi from Paucartambo costs about US$40, alternatively take a bus from Cuzco or Paucartambo bound for Pilcopata to Acjanaco

and walk from there. Acjanaco can also be reached taking a combi from Paucartambo to Challabamba (leave when full, US$1, 30 mins) and a pickup taxi from there, (US$12, 45 mins).

Cordillera Vilcanota
Buses to **Oconate** (some continue to **Tinqui**) leave from a small terminal on Av Tomasatito Condemayta, corner of the Coliseo Cerrado in Cuzco, every 30 mins, 0430-1800, 3 companies, US$3.25, 3 hrs. Cars are also available from Urcos.

Cuzco to Choquequirao

stunning views from a 'lost city'

Abancay road

West of Cuzco a road heads towards Abancay (see page 1479) for access to Ayacucho and the central highlands, or Nazca and the coast. There are enough Inca sites on or near this road to remind us that the empire's influence spread to all four cardinal points. Two kilometres before Limatambo a few hundred metres from the road, are the ruins of Tarahuasi (76 km from Cuzco, US$6), comprising a very well-preserved Inca temple platform, with 28 tall niches, and a long stretch of fine polygonal masonry. The ruins are impressive, enhanced by the orange lichen which gives the walls a honey colour.

Further along the Abancay road, 100 km from Cuzco, is the exciting descent into the **Apurímac canyon**, near the former Inca suspension bridge that inspired Thornton Wilder's *The Bridge of San Luis Rey*.

☆Choquequirao

Entry US$18, students US$9.

Choquequirao is another 'lost city of the Incas', built on a ridge spur almost 1600 m above the Apurímac at 3100 m. It is reckoned to be a larger site than Machu Picchu, but the constructions are more spread out. The main features of Choquequirao are the **Lower Plaza**, considered by most experts to be the focal point of the city. The **Upper Plaza**, reached by a huge set of steps or terraces, has what are possibly ritual baths. A beautiful set of slightly curved agricultural terraces run for over 300 m east-northeast of the Lower Plaza.

The **usnu** is on a levelled hilltop, ringed with stones and giving awesome 360° views. The **Ridge Group**, mostly cleared, is a large collection of unrestored buildings some 50-100 m below the usnu. The **Outlier Building**, thought to be the priests' residence, is isolated and surrounded on three sides by steep drops of over 1.5 km into the Apurímac Canyon. It has some of the finest stonework in Choquequirao. The **Llama Terraces** are 200 m below and west of the Lower Plaza, a great set of agricultural platforms beautifully decorated with llamas in white stone. East of the Lower Plaza are two other very large and impressive groups of terraces built on nearly vertical slopes; there is a **Waterfall Temple** located along the southeastern edge of these terraces.

Part of what makes Choquequirao so special is its isolation. At present, the site can only be reached on foot, a tough and exceptionally rewarding trek which attracts fewer than 50 hikers a day in high season and far fewer at other times. Sadly, there are plans to build a cable car to Choquequirao which would convert it into a mass tourism alternative to Machu Picchu, although construction had not yet begun in early 2017.

The route to Choquequirao begins in (San Pedro de) **Cachora**, a village on the south side of the Apurímac, reached by a side road from the Cuzco–Abancay highway, shortly after Saywite. Take an Abancay-bound bus from Cuzco, four hours to the turn-off called Ramal de Cachora, where cars wait for passengers, then it's a 30-minute descent from the road to Cachora village. From the village you need at least a day to descend to the Río Apurímac then another day or two to climb up to Choquequirao, depending on your condition and how much weight you are carrying. Horses can be hired to carry your bags. Allow one or two days at

Tip...
Some tours allow insufficient time at Choquequirao (at least one full day is highly recommended), so enquire before you sign up.

the site. The route is well signed and in good condition, with several nice campsites (some with showers) en route.

You can either return to Cachora the way you came or continue two to four days from Choquequirao to Yanama, and then on to either Huancacalle (see page 1461) or to Totora, Santa Teresa and Machu Picchu (see page 1453). These treks are all long and demanding. Cuzco agencies offer all-inclusive trekking tours to Choquequirao; some continue to Yanama and Santa Teresa, fewer to Huancacalle.

Listings Cuzco to Choquequirao

Where to stay

$$ Casa de Salcantay
200 m below the Plaza, Cachora, T984-281171, www.salcantay.com.
Price includes breakfast, dinner available if booked in advance, very nice comfortable rooms, fantastic views. Dutch/Peruvian-run, Dutch, English, German spoken. Very helpful owners Jan and Giovana can organize treks.

$$ Casa Nostra
500 m below Cachora off the road to Capuliyoc, T958-349949, www.choquequiraotrekk.com.
Rooms with private bath and dorms, includes breakfast, other meals available, superb views, Italian/Peruvian-run by Matteo and Judith.

$$ Los Tres Balcones
Jr Abancay, Cachora, www.choquequirau.com.
Hostel designed as start and end-point for the trek to Choquequirao. Breakfast included,

comfortable, hot showers, restaurant and pizza oven, camping. They run an all-inclusive 5-day trek to Choquequirao. May be closed when there is no group, book in advance.

$ Hospedaje Salcantay
1 block above the Plaza, Cachora, T958-303055.
Simple rooms with clean shared bathrooms, warm water, large yard, good value.

Transport

From the Terminal Terrestre in Cuzco take any bus towards Abancay; **Bredde** has 5 daily, 0600-2030, US$7, 4 hrs, to **Ramal de Cachora**. *Colectivos* from Ramal de Cachora to **Cachora** village, US$1.80, 30 mins, beware overcharging. *Colectivos* also run all day from Prolongación Núñez in Abancay to Cachora, US$3.50, 1½ hrs. **Note** when travelling to Cachora, avoid changing vehicles in Curahuasi, where drivers have attempted to hold up tourists.

Sacred Valley
of the Incas

★As the Río Vilcanota (in places called the Río Urubamba) flows north and west, it waters the agricultural heartland that provided the context for the great city of Cuzco. Here the Incas built country estates, temples, fortresses and other monumental works and, in the process, it became their 'Sacred Valley'. The name conjures up images of ancient, god-like rulers who saw the landscape itself as a temple; their tributes to this dramatic land survive in places such as Machu Picchu, Ollantaytambo, Pisac and countless others. For the tourist, the most famous sights are now within easy reach of Cuzco and draw massive crowds, but there remains ample scope for genuine exploring, to see lost cities in a less 21st-century setting. If archaeology is not your thing, there are markets to enjoy, birds to watch, trails for mountain-biking and a whole range of hotels to relax in.

Pisac, Urubamba and Ollantaytambo

markets and monuments

The road from Cuzco that runs past Sacsayhuaman and on to Tambo Machay (see page 1422) climbs up to a pass, then continues over the pampa before descending into the densely populated Vilcanota valley. This road then crosses the river by a bridge at Pisac and follows the north bank to the end of the paved road at Ollantaytambo. It passes through Calca, Yucay and Urubamba, which can also be reached from Cuzco by the beautiful, direct road through Chinchero, see page 1446.

☆Pisac *Colour map 3, C4.*

Pisac, 30 km north of Cuzco, has a traditional Sunday morning **market**, at which local people sell their produce in exchange for essential goods. It is a major draw for tourists who arrive in their droves throughout the day. Pisac has other, somewhat less crowded but more commercial markets every second day. Each Sunday at 1100 there is a Quechua Mass in the church on the plaza, where there is also a small, interesting **Museo Folklórico**. Elsewhere, the **Museo Comunitario Pisac** ① *Av Amazonas y Retamayoc K'asa, museopisac@gmail.com, 0800-1300, 1400-1700, closed Sat, free but donations welcome,* has a display of village life, created by the people of Pisac. At dusk you will hear, if not see, the *pisaca* (partridges), after which the place is named. There are many souvenir shops on Bolognesi. Local fiesta: 15 July.

High above the town on the mountainside is Pisac's superb **Inca fortress** ① *1½- to 2-hr walk from the plaza (1 hr descent), daily 0800-1630, you must show your BTC multi-site ticket to enter; combi US$0.75, taxi US$8 each way from near the bridge.* Walking up, although tiring, is recommended for the views and location. It's at least one hour uphill all the way, starting from the plaza and continuing past the Centro de Salud and a control post. The path goes through working terraces, giving the ruins a context. On the eastern side of the ridge, the first group of buildings is Pisaqa, with a fine curving wall. Climb then to the central part of the ruins, the Intihuatana group of temples and rock outcrops in the most magnificent Inca masonry. Here are the Reloj Solar ('Hitching Post of the Sun') – now closed because thieves stole a piece from it, palaces of the moon and stars, solstice markers, baths and water channels. From Intihuatana, a path leads around the hillside through a tunnel to Q'Allaqasa, the military area. At this point, a large area of Inca tombs in holes in the hillside can be seen across the valley. The end of the site is Kanchisracay, where the agricultural workers were housed. Road transport approaches from the Kanchisracay end; the drive up from town takes about 20 minutes. Even if you're going by car, do not rush as there is a lot to see and a lot of walking to do.

☆Calca and Huchuy Cuzco

The second village on the road from Pisac towards Urubamba is **Lamay**, 7 km away, which has simple places to stay and warm springs nearby that are highly regarded for their medicinal properties. Next is **Calca**, 11 km beyond Lamay at 3000 m, which has a fancier hotel and several simpler ones and eating places around its large plaza and a bus terminal along the highway. The **Fiesta de la Vírgen Asunta** is held here on 15-16 August.

Dramatically located at 3700 m on a flat esplanade on the opposite side of the river (not visible from the valley) are the impressive ruins of a small Inca town, **Huchuy Cuzco** (Little Cuzco) ① *access by car from Calca or along walking trails from Lamay (good steep 4-km trail), Calca (difficult 10.5 km), Tambo Machay (about 20 km, 1-2 days) and Chinchero (18 km, 1-2 days), entry US$7, accommodation with families near the ruins and at Pucamarka, towards Tambo Machay.* The views are magnificent. The ruins themselves consist of extensive agricultural terraces with high retaining walls and several buildings made from finely wrought stonework and adobe mud bricks.

Valle de Lares

The Valle de Lares is renowned for its magnificent mountains, lakes and small villages, which make it perfect for trekking and mountain biking, although parts are undergoing rapid development. One route starts near an old hacienda in Huarán (6 km west of Calca at 2830 m), crosses two passes over 4000 m and ends at the hot springs near Lares. From this village, transport runs back to Calca. Alternatively, you can add an extra day and continue to Ollantaytambo, or start in Lares and finish in Yanhuara (between Urubamba and Ollantaytambo). Several agencies in Cuzco offer trekking and biking tours to the region (see page 1436).

Yucay

About 3 km east of Urubamba, Yucay has two grassy plazas divided by the restored colonial church of Santiago Apóstol, with its oil paintings and fine altars. On the opposite side from Plaza Manco II is the adobe palace built for Sayri Túpac (Manco's son) when he emerged from Vilcabamba in 1558.

Urubamba *Colour map 3, C4.*

Like many places along the valley, Urubamba is in a fine setting at 2863 m with snow-capped peaks in view. The main road along the valley skirts the town, and the bridge for the road to Cuzco via Chinchero is just to the east. The large market square is one block west of the main plaza. Calle Berriózabal, on the west edge of town, is lined with pisonay trees and cafés. There

are many pottery studios in town, including **Seminario-Bejar Ceramic Studio** ① *Berriózabal 405, T084-201002, www.ceramicaseminario.com.* Pablo Seminario and his workshop have researched pre-Columbian techniques and designs and now use them in their distinctive pottery. The tour of the workshops is highly recommended.

Chinchero
Church and archaeological site daily 0800-1600, BTC ticket (see page 1416).

Chinchero (3762 m) is southeast of Urubamba along the more direct (western) road to Cuzco. It is a friendly town with an attractive church built on an Inca temple. The church has been restored to reveal the full glory of its interior paintings: ceiling, beams and walls are covered in beautiful floral and religious designs. Excavations have revealed many Inca walls and terraces around the town's plaza. Groups from Cuzco come to visit the church, ruins and several touristy textile centres in the town. Much of the area's character will change when the new airport for Cuzco is built nearby.

☆Moray and around
9 km by road west of Maras, BTC ticket (see page 1416).

The remote but beautiful site of Moray comprises three 'colosseums', used by the Incas, according to some theories, as a sort of open-air crop nursery; it is known locally as the 'laboratory of the Incas'. The great depressions contain no ruined buildings, but are lined with fine terracing. Each level is

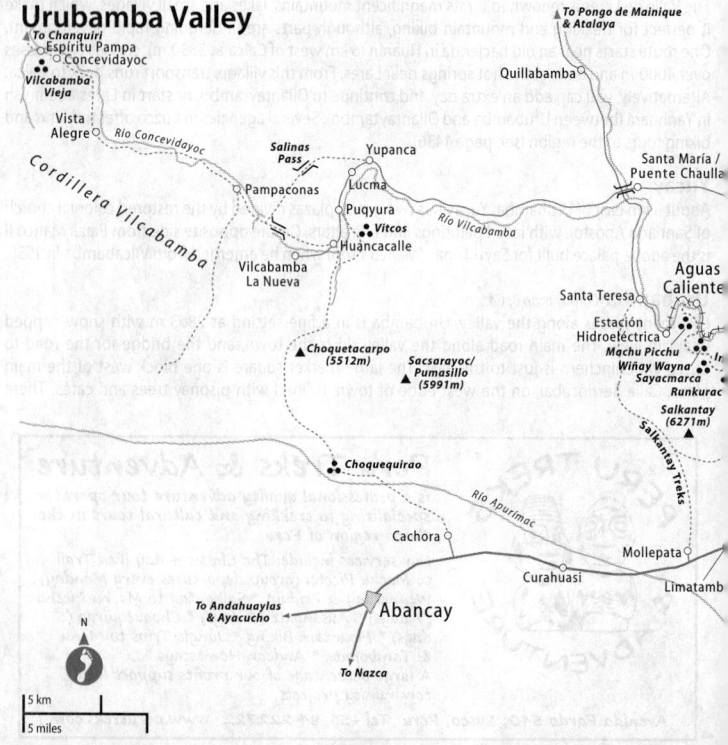

Urubamba Valley

said to have its own microclimate. It is a very atmospheric place which, many claim, has mystical power, and the scenery is absolutely stunning.

The most interesting way to get to Moray from Urubamba is to walk from **Tarabamba**, 6 km west, where a bridge crosses the Río Urubamba. Turn right after the bridge to reach **Pichingoto**, a tumbled-down village built under an overhanging cliff. Just over the bridge and before the town to the left of a small, walled cemetery is a salt stream. Follow the footpath beside the stream to Salineras, a small village below which are a mass of terraced **Inca salt pans** ① *entry US$3, taxi from Urubamba, US$11*. There are over 5000 *salineras* and they are still in operation. The village of **Maras**, with basic hostels and eateries, is 7 km beyond the salt pans (two-hour walk or 15-minute taxi ride), from where it's 9 km by unmade road or 5 km through the fields to Moray; ask in Maras for the best walking route. Tour companies in Cuzco offer cycle trips to Moray; see Transport, for further details on how to get there. If you're walking to the salt pans and Moray, take water as this side of the valley can be very hot and dry.

Ollantaytambo *Colour map 3, C4.*

The attractive but touristy town of Ollantaytambo is located at 2800 m at the foot of some spectacular Inca ruins and terraces and is built directly on top of an original Inca town. A great many visitors arrive by road from Cuzco to see the ruins and take the train from here to Machu Picchu.

> ### Tip...
> Traffic around Ollantaytambo train station is chaotic every evening; take care not to be run over on Avenida Ferrocarril.

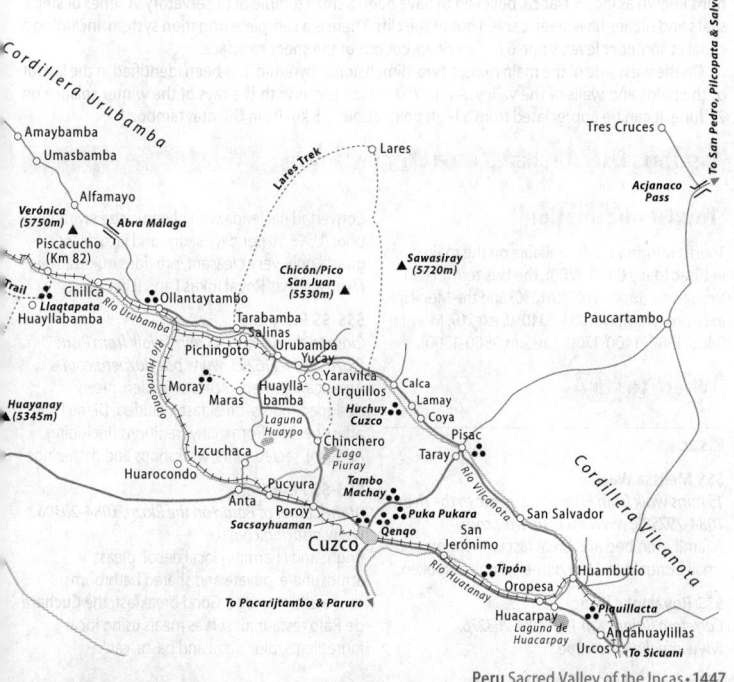

Entering Ollantaytambo from the east, the road is built along the long Wall of 100 Niches. Note the inclination of the wall, which leans towards the road. Since it was the Incas' usual practice to build their walls leaning towards the interior of the building, it has been deduced that the road, much narrower then, was built inside a succession of buildings. The road leads into the Plaza de Armas. The Inca town, or *Llacta*, on which the present-day town is based, can clearly be seen behind the north side of the plaza, where the original Inca *canchas* (blocks of houses) are almost entirely intact and still occupied. The road out of the plaza leads across a bridge to the colonial church with its enclosed *recinto*. Beyond are Plaza Araccama and the entrance to the archaeological site

☆**Ollantaytambo temple fortress** ① *Daily 0800-1600; if possible arrive at 0800, before the other tourists. Admission by BTC visitor's ticket, which can be bought at the site. Guides are available at the entrance.* After crossing the great high-walled trapezoidal esplanade known as 'Mañariki', visitors to Ollantaytambo are confronted by a series of 16 massive, stepped terraces of the very finest stonework. These flights of terraces leading up above the town are superb, and so are the curving terraces following the contours of the rocks overlooking the river. Ollantaytambo was successfully defended by Manco Inca's warriors against Hernando Pizarro in 1536. Manco Inca built the wall above the site and another wall closing the Yucay valley against attack from Cuzco. Beyond these imposing terraces lies the so-called Temple of Ten Niches. Immediately above this are six monolithic upright blocks of rose-coloured rhyolite, the remains of what is popularly called the Temple of the Sun. The temple was started by Pachacútec, using Colla *indígenas* from Lake Titicaca – hence the similarities of the monoliths facing the central platform with the Tiahuanaco remains. The massive, highly finished granite blocks at the top are worth the climb to see. The Colla are said to have deserted halfway through the work, which explains the many unfinished blocks lying about the site.

There are more Inca ruins in the small area behind the church, between the town and the temple fortress. Most impressive of these is the so-called Baño de la Ñusta (bath of the princess) carved from the bedrock. Some 200 m behind the bath, along the face of the mountain, are some small ruins known as Inca Misanca, believed to have been a small temple or observatory. A series of steps, seats and niches have been carved out of the cliff. There is a complete irrigation system, including a canal at shoulder level, some 6 inches deep, cut out of the sheer rock face.

On the west side of the main ruins, a two-dimensional 'pyramid' has been identified in the layout of the fields and walls of the valley. A fine 750 m wall aligns with the rays of the winter solstice on 21 June. It can be appreciated from a high point about 3.5 km from Ollantaytambo.

Listings Pisac, Urubamba and Ollantaytambo

Tourist information

Tourist information is available on the main plaza in Pisac (daily 0800-1700), the bus terminal in Urubamba (Mon-Fri 0745-1630) and the Municipio in Ollantaytambo (T084-204030, ext 207, Mon-Fri 0800-1300, 1400-1700, Sat-Sun 0800-1300).

Where to stay

Pisac

$$$ Melissa Wasi
15 mins walk from Pisac Plaza, close to the river, T084-797589, www.melissa-wasi.com.
A family-run bed and breakfast with rooms and small bungalows. Very homely, English spoken.

$$$ Royal Inka Pisac
Carretera Ruinas Km 1.5, T084-263276, www.royalinkahotel.pe.

Converted hacienda with olympic-size swimming pool (US$3.50 per day), sauna and jacuzzi for guests only, very pleasant, provides guides. This chain also has **Royal Inkas I** and II in Cuzco.

$$$-$$ Paz y Luz
Close to the river, 10-15 mins' walk from Pisac Plaza, T984-216293, www.pazyluzperu.com.
American-owned, pleasant garden, nicely designed rooms, breakfast included. Diane Dunn offers healing from many traditions (including Andean), sacred tours, workshops and gatherings.

$$$-$$ Pisac Inn
At the corner of Pardo on the Plaza, T084-203062, www.pisacinn.com.
Bright and charming local decor, pleasant atmosphere, private and shared bathrooms, sauna and massage. Good breakfast, the **Cuchara de Palo** restaurant serves meals using local ingredients, plus pizza and pasta, café.

\$\$ Hostal Varayoc
Mcal Castilla 380, T942-338130,
luzpaz3@hotmail.com.
Renovated hotel around a colonial courtyard.
Decor is smart, modern private bathrooms.
Ask to see the guinea pig house.

\$ Res Beho
Intihuatana 114, T084-203001.
Ask for room in main building, good
breakfast available.

Valle de Lares

\$\$\$ The Green House
Km 56.8 Huarán, T941-299944,
www.thegreenhouseperu.com.
A charming retreat, only 4 rooms, breakfast
included, comfortable lounge, restaurant, small
kitchen for guests, beautiful garden, restricted
internet. No children under 12. Information on
walks and day trips in the area. Activities include
hiking, biking, horse riding and rafting. Intimate,
beautiful and relaxing.

Yucay

\$\$\$\$-\$\$\$ Sonesta Posadas del Inca
Sacred Valley
Plaza Manco II de Yucay 123, T084-201107,
www.sonesta.com.
Converted 300-year-old monastery is like a
little village with plazas, chapel, 88 comfortable,
heated rooms, price includes buffet breakfast.
Many activities, canoeing, horse riding,
mountain biking, etc. **Inkafe** restaurant
is open to all, serving Peruvian, fusion and
traditional cuisine with a US\$15 buffet.

\$\$\$ La Casona de Yucay
Plaza Manco II 104, T084-201116,
www.hotelcasonayucay.com.
This colonial house was where Simón Bolívar
stayed during his liberation campaign in 1824.
With heating, 2 patios and gardens, **Tika**
restaurant and **Apus** bar.

Urubamba

\$\$\$\$ Casa Andina Private Collection
Sacred Valley
Paradero 5, Yanahuara, between Urubamba
and Ollantaytambo, T984-765501, www.casa-
andina.com.
In its own 3-ha estate, with all the facilities
associated with this chain, plus **Valle Sagrado
Andean Cottage** for family and long-stay

accommodation, 'Sacred Spa', gym, planetarium,
good restaurant, adventure options.

\$\$\$\$ Río Sagrado (Belmond)
Km 76 Cuzco–Ollantaytambo Road, 4 km from
Urubamba, T084-201631, www.belmond.com.
Rooms and villas set in beautiful gardens
overlooking the river with fine views.
Mayu Wilka spa, restaurant and bar,
offers various packages.

\$\$\$\$ Sol y Luna
Fundo Huincho, west of town, T084-608930,
www.hotelsolyluna.com.
Award-winning bungalows and suites set off
the main road in lovely gardens, pool, excellent
gourmet restaurant, wine tastings, spa,
handicrafts shop. Also has **Wayra** lounge bar
and dining room, open to non-guests, for freshly
cooked, informal lunches. Entertainment includes
paso fino horse shows, contemporary arts and
circus shows (open to all). Arranges adventure
and cultural activities and traditional tours.
Profits go to **Sol y Luna** educational association,
www.colegiosolyluna.com.

\$\$\$\$ Tambo del Inka
Av Ferrocarril s/n, T084-581777, www.
luxurycollection.com/vallesagrado.
A resort and spa on the edge of town, in gardens
by the river. Completely remodelled with a
variety of rooms and suites, fitness centre,
swimming pools, **Hawa** restaurant, bar, business
facilities and lots of activities arranged.

\$\$\$ Casa Colibrí
2.5 km from town on road to Ollantaytambo,
T084-205003, www.casacolibriecolodge.com.
Delightful, spacious rooms and *casitas*
made of local stone, wood and adobe, set in
beautiful gardens to attract bees, butterflies
and hummingbirds. Very restful, hammocks,
meditation room, excellent homegrown food,
swings and table tennis, popular with couples,
families and yoga groups.

\$\$ Las Chullpas
Querocancha s/n, 3 km from town, T084-201568,
www.chullpas.pe.
Very peaceful, excellent breakfast, vegetarian
meals, English spoken, natural medicine, treks,
riding, mountain biking, camping US\$3 with hot
shower. Mototaxi from town US\$2.50, taxi (ask for
Querocancha) US\$4.

\$\$ Urubamba Homestay
C Pisagua s/n, T084-201562,
www.urubambahomestay.com.

3 rooms with bath in a private home, includes breakfast, roof terrace, gardens, support community projects. British-run by Keith and Joan Parkin.

$$-$ Mauru'sTambo del Sol
Av La Convención 113-B, T084-201352, www.hostaltambodelsol.com
Ample modern rooms with bathtubs and suite with cooking facilities, beautiful garden, parking, good value.

$ Hospedaje Buganvilla
Jr Convención 280, T084-205102, bukanvilla@hotmail.com.
Sizable rooms with hot water, breakfast on request, quiet, bright, lovely gardens, lively owners Raul and Mónica, good value, very pleasant.

$ Hospedaje Los Jardines
Jr Convención 459, T084-201331, www. hospedajelosjardines.blogspot.co.uk.
Attractive guesthouse with comfortable rooms, hot water, delicious breakfast US$3.25 extra (vegans catered for), safe, lovely garden, laundry. **Sacred Valley Mountain Bike Tours** also based here.

Chinchero

$$$ La Casa de Barro
Miraflores 147, T084-306031, www.lacasadebarro.com.
Modern hotel, with heating, bar, restaurant serving 'fusion' food using organic local produce, tours arranged.

$$ Mi Piuray
C Garcilaso 187, T084-306029, www.hospedajemipiuraycusco.com.
Simple rooms around a patio with flowers, private or shared bath, electric showers, kitchen facilities, meals on request, knowledgeable owner.

Ollantaytambo

There are many hotels but they are often full, so it's best to book ahead in high season.

$$$$ Pakaritampu
C Ferrocarril 852, T084-204020, www.pakaritampu.com.
Modern, well-appointed rooms, buffet breakfast, restaurant and bar, laundry, safe and room service. Adventure sports can be arranged. Lunch and dinner are extra. Excellent quality and service, but room 8 is next to the railway station car park.

$$$$-$$$ El Albergue Ollantaytambo
Within the railway station gates, T084-204014, www.elalbergue.com.
Owned by North American artist Wendy Weeks. Also has **Café Mayu** in the station and a very good restaurant using ingredients from their own organic farm. Characterful rooms, rustic elegance, some larger than others, safety boxes, lovely gardens and a eucalyptus steam sauna. Books and crafts for sale. Private transport arranged to nearby attractions and Cuzco airport.

$$$ Apu Lodge
Calle Lari, T084-797162, www.apulodge.com.
On the edge of town, great views of the ruins and surrounding mountains. Run by Scot Louise Norton, good service, quiet, nice garden, good buffet breakfast, can help organize tours and treks.

$$$ Hostal Sauce
C Ventiderio 248, T084-204044, www.hostalsauce.com.pe.
Smart, simple decor and views of the ruins from 3 of the 6 rooms as well as from the dining room, food from own farm.

$$$ Sol Ollantay
C Ventiderio 226 by the bridge between the 2 plazas, T084-204130, www.hotelsolollantaytambo.com.
Tastefully renovated with good views from most rooms, ample rooms with heaters, some with balcony or terrace, buffet breakfast.

$$$-$$ Picaflor Tambo
Larricalle s/n, T084-436758, www.picaflortambo.com.
6 comfortable rooms set around a courtyard, charming, a good choice.

$$$-$$ Tika Wasi Valley
C Convencion s/n, T084-204166, www.tikawasivalley.com.
Great location close to the archaeological site, garden, good service and comfortable rooms decorated in 'Inca style'.

$$ Casa de Wow
C Patacalle 840, T084-204010, www.casadewow.com.
Dorms, kitchen facilities, balcony with great view of ruins, English spoken. Organizes tours.

$$ Full Moon Lodge
Cruz Esquina s/n, T989-362031, http://fullmoonlodgeperu.com.
Quiet place away from the centre, rooms with private bath set around a large garden with

hammocks and fire pit, also has camp site on Av Estudiantil (US$5 pp). Offers San Pedro experiences.

$$ Hostal Andean Moon
Calle del Medio s/n, 3 blocks from Plaza de Armas, T084-204080, www.andeanmoonhostal.com.
Rooms with wood floors, some with bathtub, heaters, beautiful garden and rooftop views, jacuzzi, bar, luggage storage.

$$ Hostal Iskay II
Patacalle 722, T084-434109, www.hostaliskay.com.
In the Inca town. Great location but car access is difficult. Only 7 rooms, free tea and coffee, use of kitchen. Good reports.

$$ Las Orquídeas
Av Ferrocarril 406, T084-204032, www. lasorquideasollantaytambo.com.
Fairly small but nice rooms, flower-filled patio, discounts for 2 or more nights, luggage storage.

$ Hostal El Tambo
C Horno, north of the plaza, T984-489094, hostaleltambo.com.
Once past the door you emerge into a lovely garden full of fruit trees and flowers. Small basic rooms for up to 4 people, shared bath downstairs in the courtyard, hot water, breakfast available, good value. Friendly owner.

$ Hostal Chaska Wasi
C Principal s/n, Plaza de Armas, T084-204045.
Private rooms and dorms, hammocks, hot showers, free hot drinks, laundry, popular. Owner Katy is very friendly.

$ Hostal Plaza Ollantaytambo
C Principal s/n, beside the police station on Plaza de Armas, T084-436741, hostalplazaollantaytambo@gmail.com.
Small modern rooms with private bath and reliable hot water. Variable service, all a bit improvised but great location and value.

Restaurants

Pisac

$$$ Mullu
Plaza de Armas 352, T084-203073, and Mcal Castilla 375, T084-203182. Tue-Sun 0900-1900.
Café/restaurant with Peruvian and Asian fusion menu. Has a gallery promoting local artists.

$$$-$$ Cuchara de Palo
In Pisac Inn on Plaza de Armas, T084-203062.

Gourmet restaurant using local ingredients to make traditional Peruvian food. Cosy atmosphere.

$$ Sapos Lounge
Espinar y Arequipa, T994-647979. Tue-Sun 1500-2300.
Good pizza and drinks, produce from a local organic farm. Good nightlife spot.

$ Apus Organic
Grau 584, T988-338141.
Small restaurant serving good organic, vegetarian and vegan food.

Cafés

Blue Llama Café
Corner of the plaza opposite Pisac Inn, T084-203135.
Cute, colourful café with a huge range of teas, good coffee, breakfasts, daily *menús*, and board games.

Horno Colonial San Francisco
Mcal Castilla 572.
Good wholemeal bread and cheese *empanadas*.

Ulrike's Café
C Pardo 613, T084-203195. Daily 0800-2100.
The best apple crumble with ice cream, excellent coffee, smoothies and many international dishes. Good value 3-course daily *menú*. Book exchange.

Urubamba

$$$ El Huacatay
Arica 620, T084-201790, www.elhuacatay.com. Mon-Sat 1230-2130.
A small restaurant with a reputation for fine, creative fusion cuisine (local, Mediterranean, Asian). Lovely garden setting.

$$$ El Maizal
Av Conchatupa, the main road before the bridge, T984-705211. Daily 1200-1600.
Country-style restaurant, buffet service with a variety of *Novo Andino* and international choices, beautiful gardens, caters to tour groups.

$$$ Tres Keros
Av Señor de Torrechayoc, T084-201701.
Novo Andino cuisine, try the lamb chops.

$$$ Tunupa
On road from Urubamba to Ollantaytambo, on riverbank, T974-782163. Open 1200-1500.
Buffet lunch US$15. Same owners as Tunupa in Cuzco, colonial-style hacienda, excellent food and surroundings, pre-Columbian and colonial art exhibitions.

$$$-$$ Paca Paca
Av Mcal Castilla 640, T084-201181.
Tue-Sun 1300-2100.
Varied selection of dishes including Peruvian
fusion, also pizza, pleasant inviting atmosphere.

$$-$ Guyin
Comercio 453, T084-608838 for delivery.
Daily 1600-2300.
Pizza, pastas and grill. Popular with local expats.

$$-$ Pizza Wasi
Av Mcal Castilla 857, Plaza de Armas,
T084-434751 for delivery. Daily 1200-2300.
Good pizzas and pastas. Mulled wine served in
a small restaurant with nice decor, good value.

$ El Edén
Av Mcal Castilla 960, T984-850095.
Mon-Sat 0900-2100.
Pastries, sandwiches, coffee and juices. Jams and
bread to go. Some gluten-free products.

Ollantaytambo
There are restaurants all over town offering *menú
turístico*, pizzas, pastas, juices and hot drinks.

$$$ Papa's
C Horno at the plaza, T974-787191. Daily 1100-2100.
Restaurant and lounge serving Tex-Mex, local
dishes, pizzas, soups, salads, and desserts.

$$$-$$ Puka Rumi
Av Ventiderio s/n, next to Heart's Café,
T084-204151. Daily 0700-2100.
Serves a variety of international dishes, pizza,
salads, upmarket *menú*.

$$ Coffee Tree
Plaza de Armas, T084-436734.
Good coffee and a variety of Peruvian and
international dishes. Popular.

$$ Heart's Café
Av Ventiderio s/n, T084-436726, www.
livingheartperu.org. Open 0700-2100.
International and Peruvian dishes including
vegetarian, box lunch and takeaway available,
good coffee. All profits to education and self-help
projects in the Sacred Valley. Popular, tasty food
but disappointing service.

$$ Huatakay
Av Occobamba s/n, 2nd block, T984-397305.
Daily 0600-2100.
Large restaurant serving *menú* and regional
specialities à la carte. Pleasant setting. Owns
Quechuas Lodge on the same street, guests
get a discount at the restaurant.

$$ Il Piccolo Forno
C del Medio 120, T084-625492.
Tue-Sun 1200-2100.
Very good Italian food and take-away pizza, as
well as home baked bread, pies and cookies.
Gluten free options.

$$ La Esquina
C Principal at the corner of Plaza de Armas,
T084-204078. Mon-Sat 0700-2100.
Variety of international dishes, wide selection
of pastries and sweets, popular.

$ Doña Eva
C Ollantay facing the market. Sun-Fri 0700-2100,
Sat 0700-1900.
Economical *menú* and à la carte, one of the few
unpretentious places in town, popular with locals
and travellers alike.

Festivals

Urubamba
May-Jun Harvest months, with many
processions following ancient schedules.
Urubamba's main festival, **El Señor de
Torrechayoc**, takes place around 20 May.
8 Sep Chinchero celebrates the **Day of
the Virgin**.

Ollantaytambo
6 Jan **Bajada de Reyes Magos** (Epiphany) is
celebrated with dancing, a bull fight, local food
and a fair.
End-May/early-Jun **Fiesta del Señor de
Choquekillca**, patron saint of Ollantaytambo,
has his festival 50 days after Easter, with several
days of dancing, weddings, processions, masses,
feasting and drinking.
Jun **Ollanta-Raymi**. A colourful festival on the
Sun following Inti Raymi.
29 Oct The town's anniversary, with lots of
dancing in traditional costume and many local
delicacies for sale.

What to do

Urubamba
Perol Chico, *5 km from Urubamba at Km 77, T950-
314065/950-314066, www.perolchico.com.* Dutch/
Peruvian-owned and operated stables offering
1- to 11-day horse riding trips. Good horses,
riding is Peruvian paso style.

Ollantaytambo

Awamaki, *C La Convención across from the church, T084-436744, www.awamaki.org*. Cultural tours and artisan workshops (dying, weaving, woodcarving) which can be integrated with homestays in local communities. Also adventure tours, volunteering, Spanish and Quechua classes.

Transport

Pisac

To **Urubamba**, US$1, 1 hr. To **Cuzco**, 32 km, 1 hr, US$1.50, last one back leaves around 2000; these buses are often full. There are also *colectivos* and minibuses; all leave from C Amazonas near the main bridge.

Urubamba

The Terminal is on the main road, 3 blocks west of the centre. To **Calca**, US$0.50, 30 min; and **Pisac**, US$1, 1 hr. To **Cuzco**, by bus, US$1.50, 1½ hrs via Chinchero or 2 hrs via Pisac; by van US$2; by car US$2.50. Frequent vans to **Ollantaytambo**, US$0.50, 30 mins, all leave when full throughout the day.

Moray and around

Any bus between Urubamba and Cuzco via Chinchero passes the clearly marked turning to Maras; from the junction taxi *colectivos* charge US$2.50 pp to Maras, or you can walk all the way from here to Moray (see above). There is also public transport from Chinchero to Maras until 1700. A taxi to Moray and the salt pans (from where you can walk back to the Urubamba–Ollantaytambo road) costs US$25, including 1-hr wait.

Ollantaytambo

Bus Vans leave all day for Urubamba from the produce market, 1 block east of the main plaza, US$0.50, 30 mins. Vans to Cuzco leave frequently from Av Ferrocarril above the railway station and from the main Plaza near the information centre, US$3.50, 1½ hrs. Taxi to Cuzco, US$22.

Train Ollantaytambo is the point of departure for most trains to Machu Picchu (see Transport, page 1457). The station is a 10- to 15-min walk from the Plaza, longer in the early evening when Av Ferrocarril is clogged with vehicles. There are **Perú Rail** and **Inca Rail** ticket offices outside the station and you must have a ticket to be allowed onto the platform unless you are staying at El Albergue Hotel.

Machu Picchu *Colour map 3, C4.*

iconic and unmissable

★There is a tremendous feeling of awe on first witnessing Machu Picchu. The ancient citadel (42 km from Ollantaytambo by rail) straddles the saddle of a high mountain (2380 m) with steep terraced slopes falling away to the fast-flowing Vilcanota river snaking its hairpin course far below in the valley floor. Towering overhead is Huayna Picchu, and green jungle peaks provide the backdrop for the whole majestic scene. Machu Picchu is a complete Inca city. For centuries it was buried in jungle, until Hiram Bingham stumbled upon it in 1911. It was then explored by an archaeological expedition sent by Yale University. The ruins require at least a day to explore. Take time to appreciate not only the masonry, but also the selection of large rocks used for foundations, the use of water in the channels below the Temple of the Sun and the beauty of the surrounding mountains.

Main site

The **main entrance** to the ruins is set at the eastern end of the extensive **terracing** that must have supplied the crops for the city. Above this point to the south is the final stretch of the Inca Trail leading down from **Intipunku** (Sun Gate). From the **Watchman's Hut** you get the perfect view of the city (the one you've seen on all the postcards), laid out before you with Huayna Picchu rising above the furthest extremity. The main path into the ruins comes to a **dry moat**; from here a long staircase goes to the upper reaches of the city, past quarries on the left and roofless buildings on the right which show the construction methods used. Above the main plazas are the **Temple of the Three Windows**, the **Principal Temple** and the **Sacristy**. These buildings were clearly of great importance, given the fine stonework involved. Beyond the Sacristy is the **Intihuatana** or 'hitching-post of the sun', one of the highlights of Machu Picchu. Carved rocks (*gnomons*) such as this are found at all major Inca sites and were the point to which the sun was symbolically 'tied' at the winter solstice, before being freed to rise again on its annual ascent towards the summer solstice. Below the Intihuatana is the **Main Plaza** and, at its northern end a small plaza fronted by the **Sacred Rock**.

Essential Machu Picchu

Getting there

The easiest way to get to Machu Picchu is by train from Poroy (near Cuzco) or Ollantaytambo to Aguas Calientes, from where you can walk or catch a bus to the ruins. Santa Teresa provides alternative access for those who have travelled by road from Ollantaytambo, either by train or walking from Estación Hidroeléctrica. The most strenuous but rewarding way to Machu Picchu is to hike one of the Inca trails (see page 1458).

Tickets

The entrance fee for Machu Picchu only is 152 soles (US$46), 77 soles (US$23) for university students with some ISIC cards (see www.machupicchu.gob.pe/items/estudiantes.html for regulations), or 70 soles (US$21) for students 8-18 years, younger children free. Afternoon tickets starting 1300 cost 100 soles (US$30.30), 50 soles (US$15.15) for university students, or 40 soles (US$12.12) for younger students. To climb Huayna Picchu or Machu Picchu Mountain, visitors of all ages pay an additional 48 soles (US$14.60). When you purchase your ticket for one of the climbs, you must also specify the time you will start. Only 200 people during a time slot are allowed up at Huayna Picchu (access 0700-0800 or 1000-1100) and 400 people during slot at Machu Picchu Mountain (0700-0800 or 0900-1000). It is wise to reserve your ticket online in advance at www.machupicchu.gob.pe. You can also pay online (unless you need to show an ISIC card) with Visa or at branches of **Banco de la Nación**; **Centro Cultural de Machu Picchu** (Avenida Pachacútec cuadra 1) in Aguas Calientes; Dirección Regional de Cultura in Cuzco (C Garcilaso s/n, Mon-Sat, 0700-1930); AATC (C Nueva Baja 424) in Cuzco; offices of **PeruRail** and **Inca Rail** in Cuzco, and **Hotel Monasterio**

in Cuzco. Other websites offer tickets for sale at an inflated price. The only place to buy tickets without a previous on-line reservation is at Dirección Regional de Cultura (see above). Do not buy (fake) tickets on the street in Cuzco.

On arrival

The site is open from 0600 to 1600. Officially, only 2500 visitors are allowed entry each day, but there may be more in high season, April through August. It is best to arrive early, although it is not possible to walk up to the ruins before the first buses arrive. You can deposit your luggage at the entrance for a small fee. Guides are available at the site, US$80 for one to 10 people. Site wardens are also informative.

Regulations

In an attempt to mitigate crowding, the authorities announced new regulations in 2014, but these were only beginning to be implemented in mid-2017. They will require that all visitors be accompanied by a guide, that they follow one of three established routes without turning back and that they limit stops at certain places to three to five minutes. The first new measure, from 1 July 2017, is that entry will be limited to morning (0600-1200) or afternoon (1200-1730) tickets.

Advice and precautions

Take your own food, if you don't want to eat at the Sanctuary Lodge self-service restaurant, and take plenty of drinking water. Note that food is not officially allowed into the site and drink can only be carried in canteens/water bottles, not disposable containers. Toilets are only at the entrance. Take insect repellent and wear long clothes. Also take protection against the sun and rain.

The outline of this gigantic, flat stone echoes that of the mountains behind it. Southeast of the Main Plaza to the left are several groups of closely packed buildings that were probably **living quarters** and workshops; also in this area are the **Condor Temple** and a cave called **Intimachay**. A short distance to the south is a series of **ceremonial baths**, probably used for ritual bathing. The uppermost, **Principal Bath**, is the most elaborate. Next to it is the **Temple of the Sun**, or Torreón, which was almost certainly used for astronomical purposes. Underneath the Torreón is the **Royal Mausoleum**, which combines a natural cave-like opening with fine masonry. Ascend the stairs south of the Mausoleum to come across a finely constructed two-storey building known as the **Palace of the Princess**; this is likely where priests prepared for ceremonies in the Torreón. North across the stairway from the Torreón is the group of buildings known as the **Royal Sector**.

Around Machu Picchu

Huayna Picchu ① *Access to the main path daily 0700-0800 and 1000-1100; latest return time 1500; max 200 people per departure. Tickets US$60 (includes entry to Machu Picchu). Check on www. machupicchu.gob.pe or with the Ministerio de Cultura in Aguas Calientes or Cuzco for current departure times and to sign up for a place.* The mountain overlooking the site (on which there are also ruins) has steps to the top for a superlative view of the whole site, but it is not for those who are afraid of heights, and you shouldn't leave the path. The climb takes up to 90 minutes but the steps are dangerous after bad weather. Another trail to Huayna Picchu is via the **Temple of the Moon**, which consists of two caves, one above the other, with superb Inca niches inside. To reach the Temple of the Moon, take the marked trail to the left of the path to Huayna Picchu. It is in good shape, although it descends further than you think it should and there are very steep steps on the way. After the Temple it is safest to return to the main trail to Huayna Picchu, instead of taking a difficult shortcut. The round trip takes about four hours. Before doing any trekking around Machu Picchu, check with an official which paths may be used, or which are one-way.

Machu Picchu Mountain ① *Two daily departures, 0700-0800 and 0900-1000, maximum 400 people per departure but they are seldom fully booked. Tickets US$60 (includes entry to Machu Picchu). Check on www.machupicchu.gob.pe or with the Ministerio de Cultura in Aguas Calientes or Cuzco for current departure times and to sign up for a place.* Climbing this mountain is another excellent option and is generally less crowded than Huayna Picchu. It gives a completely different view of the site and surrounding valleys. The route is steep and takes up to three hours.

Other sights and trails The famous **Inca bridge** is about 45 minutes along a well-marked trail south of the Royal Sector. The bridge (on which you cannot walk) is spectacularly sited, carved into a vertiginous cliff-face. East of the Royal Sector is the path leading up to **Intipunku** on the Inca Trail (60 minutes, fine views; see page 1458).

Aguas Calientes

The terminus of the tourist rail service to Machu Picchu, Aguas Calientes (official name Machu Picchu Pueblo) has grown from a handful of tin shacks along the railway in the 1980s, into an international resort village with countless multi-storey luxury hotels, restaurants advertising four-for-one happy hours, persistent massage touts and numerous services for the over one million tourists who visit every year. Although it is not to every traveller's taste, it may be worth spending the night here in order to visit the ruins early in the morning. Avenida Pachacútec leads from the plaza to the **thermal baths** ① *at the upper end of town, daily 0500-2000, US$3.50*, which have a communal pool smelling of sulphur that's best early in the morning. There are showers for washing *before* entering the baths; take soap and shampoo, and keep an eye on valuables. The **Museo Manuel Chávez Ballón y Jardín Botánico** ① *near the bridge to Machu Picchu, 25-min walk from town, daily 0900-1600, US$6*, displays objects found at Machu Picchu and local plants. There is also a **Butterfly House** ① *access from Camping Municipal, see below, US$3.50*.

Listings Machu Picchu

Tourist information

iPerú
Av Pachacútec, by the plaza, Aguas Calientes, T084-211104.
Provides tourist information Mon-Sat 0900-1300, 1400-1800, Sun 0900-1300.

Where to stay

Machu Picchu

$$$$ Machu Picchu Sanctuary Lodge
Reservations as for the Hotel Monasterio in Cuzco, which is under the same management (Belmond), T084-211038, www.belmond.com.
Comfortable, good service, helpful staff, food well-cooked and presented. Electricity and water 24 hrs a day, prices are all-inclusive, restaurant for residents only in the evening, but the buffet

lunch is open to all. Usually fully booked well in advance, but try Sun night when other tourists find Pisac market a greater attraction.

Aguas Calientes

$$$$ Casa Andina Classic
Av Imperio de los Incas E-34, T084-582950, www.casa-andina.com.
Luxury chain hotel, rooms with heating and safety boxes, restaurant serving *Novo Andino* cuisine.

$$$$ Casa del Sol
Av Imperio de los Incas 608, on the railroad, T951-298695, www.casadelsolhotels.com.
5-storey hotel with lift/elevator, different room categories with river or mountain views, nice restaurant, beautiful spa. Shower service and changing room available after check out.

$$$$ Inkaterra Machu Picchu Pueblo
Km 104, 5 mins walk along the railway from town, T084-211122. Reservations T01-610 0400 in Lima, or Inkaterra La Casona in Cuzco, T084-234010, www.inkaterra.com.
Beautiful colonial-style bungalows in village compound surrounded by cloudforest, lovely gardens with a lot of steps between the public areas and rooms, spa, excellent restaurant, offer tours to Machu Picchu, several guided walks on and off the property. Good baggage service to coordinate with train arrivals and departures. Also has the Café Inkaterra by the railway line.

$$$$ Sumaq Machu Picchu
Av Hermanos Ayar Mz 1, Lote 3, T084-211059, www.sumaqhotelperu.com.
Award-winning 5-star hotel on the edge of town, between railway and road to Machu Picchu. Suites and luxury rooms with heating, restaurant, bar, spa.

$$$ Gringo Bill's
Colla Raymi 104, T084-211046, www.gringobills.com.
Pretty rooms, good beds, balconies, train-station pickup (on foot), lot of coming and going, good restaurant, breakfast from 0500, packed lunch available.

$$$ La Cabaña
Av Pachacútec 805, near thermal baths, T084-211048, www.lacabanamachupicchu.com.
Variety of rooms, café, laundry service, helpful, popular with groups.

$$$ Presidente
Av Imperio de los Incas, at the old station, T084-211034, www.hostalpresidente.com.

Adjoining **Hostal Machu Picchu**, see below, more upmarket but little difference.

$$$ Wiracocha Inn
C Wiracocha 206, T084-211088, www.wiracochainn.com.
Rooms and higher-priced suites, restaurant, helpful, popular with groups.

$$$-$$ Rupa Wasi
Huanacaure 105, T084-211101, www.rupawasi.net.
Charming 'eco-lodge' up a small alley off Collasuyo, laid back, comfortable, great views from the balconies, purified water available, organic garden, good breakfasts, half-board available, excellent restaurant, **The Tree House**, and cookery classes.

$$$-$$ Terrazas del Inca
Wiracocha M-18-4, T084-771529, www.terrazasdelinca.com.
Includes breakfast, safety deposit box, helpful staff.

$$ Hostal El Místico
Av Pachacútec 814, near thermal baths, T084-211051, www.elmisticomachupicchu.com.
Good breakfast, quiet, new-wave-ish, comfortable.

$$ Hostal Machu Picchu
Av Imperio de los Incas 135, T084-211095, hostalmachupicchu.com.
Functional, quiet, Wilber, the owner's son, has travel information, hot water, nice balcony over the Urubamba, grocery store.

$$ Hostal Pirwa
C Túpac Inka Yupanki 103, T084-244315, www.pirwahostelscusco.com.
In the same group as in Cuzco, Lima and elsewhere.

$$ Imperio de los Inkas
Av Pachacútec 602, T084-211105, www.hostalimperiodelosinkas.com.
Functional, quiet, family-owned *hostal*, group rates, good value.

$$ Jardines de Mandor
4 km from Aguas Calientes along the railway to Estación Hidroeléctrica, T940-188155, www.jardinesdemandor.com.
Relaxed rural lodging with simple rooms and a lovely garden. Camping possible, meals available, a delightful contrast to the buzz of Aguas Calientes.

$ Hostal Quilla
Av Pachacútec 705, T084-211009, namdo_28@hotmail.com.

Adequate functional rooms, small terrace, pizzeria downstairs.

$ Las Bromelias
Colla Raymi 102, just off the plaza, T084-211145, on Facebook.
Rooms with private bath and hot water, some are small, family-run, good value.

Camping
See **Jardines de Mandor**, above. There is also a campsite (US$6 per tent) in a field by the river, just below the former Puente Ruinas station. It has toilets and cold showers. There's an unpleasant smell from the nearby garbage-processing plant. Do not leave your tent and belongings unattended.

Aguas Calientes
The town is packed with eating places which double as bars, many of them are similar-looking *pizzerías*. Tax is often added as an extra to the bill. Simple economical set meals are served upstairs at the produce market, clean and adequate, daily 0600-1900. See also **The Tree House** restaurant at Rupa Wasi, above.

$$$ Café Inkaterra
On the railway, just below the Machu Picchu Pueblo Hotel.
US$15 for a great lunch buffet with scenic views of the river.

$$$ Chullpi
Av Imperio de los Incas 140, T084-211350
Traditional Peruvian food with good service.

$$ Indio Feliz
C Lloque Yupanqui 103, T084-211090.
Great French cuisine, excellent value and service, set 3-course meal for US$20, good *pisco sours*, great atmosphere.

$$ Inka Wasi
Av Pachacútec 112, T 984-110301.
Very good choice, has an open fire, full Peruvian and international menu available.

$$ Pueblo Viejo
Av Pachacútec 6th block (near plaza), T084-211072.
Good food in a spacious but warm environment. Price includes use of the salad bar.

$$ Toto's House
Av Imperio de los Incas 600, on the railway line across from the craft market, T084-211020.
Same owners as **Pueblo Viejo**. Good value and quality *menú*, buffet from 1130-1500.

Cafés

La Boulangerie de Paris
Jr Sinchi Roca by the footbridge. Open 0500-2100.
Coffee, sandwiches, quiche and great French pastries.

Bus Buses leave **Aguas Calientes** for Machu Picchu as they fill (long queues) daily 0530-1500, 25 mins, US$24 return, US$12 single, children US$12, valid 48 hrs. The bus stop and ticket office in Aguas Calientes is on Malecón Hermanos Ayar y Av Imperio de los Incas. Tickets can also be bought in advance at **Consettur** in Cuzco (Av Infancia 433, Wanchaq, T084-222125, www.consettur.com), which saves additional queuing when you arrive in Aguas Calientes. Buses return from the ruins to Aguas Calientes daily 0700-1730. The walk up from Aguas Calientes takes 1-2 hrs following a poor path and crossing the motor road (take care). The road is also in poor condition and landslides can cause disruptions.

Train 2 companies operate services to Machu Picchu, terminating at the station in Aguas Calientes (Av Imperio de los Incas): **PeruRail** (Wanchaq Station, Av Pachacúteg, T084-581414, www.perurail.com) runs trains from Poroy (near Cuzco), from Urubamba (available only to clients of **Hotel Río Sagrado**) and from Ollantaytambo. **Inca Rail** (Portal de Panes 105, Plaza de Armas, Cuzco, T084-581860, www.incarail.com) runs mostly from Ollantaytambo and one daily train from Poroy. Prices vary, depending on the time of year and convenience of the time of departure. Return tickets are generally more economical than two one-way tickets; you can combine service classes and you can return to a different station from the one where you originated your trip. You require a passport (or copy) to purchase tickets and your original passport to travel to Machu Picchu. High season fares are listed below, they are slightly cheaper in low season, and all are subject to change; see company websites. All carriages have a/c and heating, those in more expensive services have larger panoramic windows. Hot and cold drinks are served in all services, meals only in the more expensive ones.
Note Services may be disrupted in the rainy

season, especially Jan-Feb, when trains to some stations may not operate (see below). Tourists may not travel on the local trains to Machu Picchu, except from Santa Teresa, see page 1461.

There are 3 classes of **PeruRail** tourist train: **Vistadome** (recommended, US$102-105 one-way from Poroy, US$98 from Urubamba, US$72-94 from Ollantaytambo); **Expedition**, similar to above but with less visibility and does not include meals (US$93 one-way from Poroy, US$70-80 from Ollantaytambo); and the luxurious **Belmond Hiram Bingham** service with meals, drinks and entertainment (US$505 one way from Poroy, US$884 round trip). Vistadome and Expedition services are more frequent from Ollantaytambo than from Poroy or Urubamba. For additional **PeruRail** ticket offices, see page 1438.

Inca Rail has 8 trains a day from Ollantaytambo and one from Poroy (at 0555, return at 1612) to Machu Picchu. If Poroy is closed, a combined bus-rail service departs San Pedro station in Cuzco at 0450 and continues on the 0720 train from Ollantaytambo; the combined return service starts with the 1612 train from Machu Picchu (US$155 return). Inca Rail offers 2 classes of service: **First Class**, which includes a cocktail and meals (from Ollantaytambo at 1115, from Machu Picchu at 1900, US$121 one-way); and **Executive Class**, simpler, more frequent service (US$79 one-way from Poroy, US$61-79 from Ollantaytambo). In high season (1 Apr-31 Oct, Christmas and New Year), 1st class carriages may be added to some Executive trains and an exclusive **Presidential Class** carriage can also be chartered at any time of the year.

Inca trails

follow in the Incas' footsteps

☆ The most impressive way to reach Machu Picchu is via the centuries-old Inca Trail that winds its way from the Sacred Valley near Ollantaytambo, taking three to five days. What makes this hike so special is the stunning combination of Inca ruins, unforgettable views, magnificent mountains, exotic vegetation and extraordinary ecological variety. This, the most famous trek in South America, is extremely popular and limited to 500 hikers a day (including guides and porters) and fully booked many months in advance. It can only be done with a licensed tour operator or licensed private guide (the majority of trekkers sign up with an operator); independent trekking is not permitted. The Inca Trail is rugged and steep and you should be in good physical shape. For most hikers, the magnificent views compensate for any weariness, but it is cold at night and weather conditions change rapidly.

The Classic Trail

The trek to Machu Picchu begins for most trekkers at Km 82 on the rail line, **Piscacucho**. In order to reach the trailhead, hikers are transported by their tour operator in a minibus on the road that goes from Ollantaytambo to Quillabamba. At Phiry the road divides; the left branch follows the north shore of the Río Vilcanota and

> **Tip...**
> Make sure your train ticket for the return to Cuzco has your name on it (spelt absolutely correctly), otherwise you will have to pay for any changes.

ends at Km 82, where there is a bridge. Equipment, food, fuel and field personnel reach Km 82 (depending on the tour operator's logistics) for the Sernanp staff to weigh each bundle before the group arrives. Since many groups leave every day, it is convenient to arrive early. An alternative starting point at Km 88, **Qorihuayrachina**, can only be reached by train; it is hardly used.

The walk to **Huayllabamba**, following the Río Cusichaca, needs about three hours and isn't too arduous. Huayllabamba is a popular camping spot for tour groups, but there is another camping place about an hour ahead at **Llulluchayoc** (3200 m). A punishing 1½-hour climb further is **Llulluchapampa**, an ideal meadow for camping. If you have the energy to reach this point, it will make the second day easier because the next stage, the ascent to the first pass, **Warmiwañuska** (Dead Woman's Pass) at 4200 m, is tough; 2½ hours.

Afterwards take the steep path downhill to the **Pacaymayo** ravine. Beware of slipping on the Inca steps after rain. Tour groups usually camp by a stream at the bottom (1½ hours from the first pass). Camping is no longer permitted at **Runkuracay**, on the way up to the second pass. This is a much easier climb to 3900 m, with magnificent views near the summit in clear weather. **Chaquicocha** camp (3600 m) is about 30 minutes past the ruins at **Sayacmarca** (3500 m), about an hour beyond the top of the second pass.

Essential Inca Trail

Equipment

Take strong footwear, rain gear and warm clothing, extra snacks, water and water-purification supplies, insect repellent, plastic bags, coverings, a good sleeping bag and a torch/flashlight. Equipment is provided by tour agencies, but always check what is included and what must be rented or brought from home. Maps of the Trail and area are available from Cuzco bookshops. On most tours, porters will take the heavy gear; you should carry a day-pack for your water, snacks, etc.

Tours

Tour operators taking clients on any of the Inca Trails leading to the Machu Picchu must be licensed and have to pass an annual test. **Sernanp** (Avenida José Gabriel Cosio 308, Urb Magisterial, 1 etapa, T084-229297, www.sernanp. gob.pe) verifies operating permits. Unlicensed agencies will sell Inca Trail trips, but pass clients on to the operating agency. This can cause confusion and booking problems at busy times. There have been many instances of disappointed trekkers whose bookings did not materialize. Don't wait to the last minute, and check your operator's cancellation fees. Tour operators in Cuzco include transport to the start, equipment and food, as part of the total price for all treks that lead to Machu Picchu. Prices start at about US$600 per person for a four-day/three-night trek on the Classic Inca Trail and rise according to the level of service given. If the price is significantly lower, you should be concerned, as the company may be cutting corners. Operators pay US$15 per day for each porter and other trail staff; porters are not permitted to carry more than 20 kg. In principle, groups of up to four independent travellers who do not wish to use a tour operator are allowed to hike the trails if they contract an independent, licensed guide to accompany them, as long as they do not contract any other persons such as porters or cooks. In practice it is hard to find a guide, becuase they are fully occupied working for agencies.

Tickets

Current advice is to book your preferred dates as early as possible, several months to a year in advance, depending on the season when you want to go, then confirm nearer the time. Don't wait to the last minute. Check your operator's cancellation fees before booking. Tickets cost US$88.50; university students US$44.60; younger students US$40.90. This is the price for all hiking trails (Km 82 or Km 88 to Machu Picchu, Salkantay to Machu Picchu, and Km 82 or Km 88 to Machu Picchu via Km 104) except for the Camino Real de los Inkas (from Km 104 to Wiñay-Wayna and Machu Picchu), for which the fee is US$67.30, university students US$34, younger students US$31.80. Tickets can only be purchased by tour operators or guides on behalf of their clients. They are non-refundable and cannot be changed, so make sure you provide accurate passport details to your operator. No tickets are sold at the entrance to any of the routes.

When to go

July and August is the height of the tourist season but the Trail is booked to capacity for most of the year. Check conditions in the rainy season from December to March (note that this can vary from year to year); the weather may be cloudy and the paths are very slippery and difficult in the wet. The Trail is closed each February for cleaning and repair.

Time required

Four days would make a comfortable trip (though much depends on the weather). Allow a further day to see Machu Picchu when you have recovered from the hike. Alternatively, you can take a five-day tour, which reaches Machu Picchu in the afternoon. The first two days of the Trail involve the stiffest climbing, so do not attempt it if you're feeling unwell.

Regulations and precautions

Littering is banned, as is carrying plastic water bottles (canteens only may be carried). Pets and pack animals are prohibited. Groups must use approved campsites only. You cannot take backpacks into Machu Picchu; leave them at the entrance. Leave all your valuables in Cuzco and keep everything inside your tent, even your shoes. Security has, however, improved in recent years. Always take sufficient cash to tip porters and guides at the end (S/.50-100 each, but at your discretion).

A gentle two-hour climb on a fine stone highway leads through an Inca tunnel to the third pass. Near the top there's a spectacular view of the entire Vilcabamba range, and another campsite. You descend to Inca ruins at **Phuyupatamarca** (3650 m), well worth a long visit.

From there steps go downhill to the magnificent ruins of **Wiñay-Wayna** (2700 m), with impressive views of the cleared terraces of Intipata. There is a campsite here that gets crowded and dirty. After Wiñay-Wayna there is no water and no camping till after Machu Picchu, near Aguas Calientes (see Where to stay, page 1456). The path from this point goes more or less level through jungle for two hours before it reaches the steep staircase up to the **Intipunku**, where there's a fine view of Machu Picchu, especially at dawn, with the sun alternately in and out, clouds sometimes obscuring the ruins, sometimes leaving them clear. Groups try to reach Machu Picchu as early as possible to avoid the crowds, but this is usually a futile endeavour and requires a pre-dawn start as well as walking along the edge of the precipice in the dark.

Camino Real de los Inkas and other options

The **Camino Real de los Inkas** or **Short Inca Trail** starts at Km 104, where a footbridge gives access to the ruins of Chachabamba and the trail, which ascends above the ruins of Choquesuysuy to connect with the main trail at Wiñay-Wayna. This first part is a steady, continuous ascent of three hours (take water). Many people recommend this short Inca Trail. It can be extended into a three-night trek by starting from Km 82, trekking to Km 88, then along the Río Urubamba to Pacaymayo Bajo and Km 104, from where you can join the Camino Real de los Inkas. Alternatively, good day hiking trails from Aguas Calientes run along the banks of the Urubamba.

Salkantay treks

Two treks involve routes from **Salkantay**: one, known as the **High Inca Trail** joins the classic trail at Huayllabamba, then proceeds as before on the main Trail through Wiñay Wayna to Machu Picchu. To get to Salkantay, you have to start the trek in Mollepata, three hours northwest of Cuzco in the Apurímac valley. Salkantay to Machu Picchu this way takes three nights and requires an Inca Trail permit and licensed operator.

The second Salkantay route, known as the **Santa Teresa Trek**, takes four days and crosses the 4600-m Salkanatay Pass to reach the Santa Teresa valley, which you follow to its confluence with the Vilcanota. The goal is the town of Santa Teresa (see page 1461). There was talk in 2017 that a trekking permit would also be introduced on this Santa Teresa trek, but no official announcement by the close of this edition.

Inca Jungle Trail

This route is offered by several tour operators in Cuzco and combines hiking with cycling and other activities. On the first day you cycle downhill from the Abra Málaga pass on the Ollantaytambo–Quillabamba highway to Alfamayo at 2300 m. This involves three to four hours of riding on the main road with speeding vehicles inattentive to cyclists; it's best to pay for good bikes and back-up on this section. Some agencies also offer white-water rafting in the afternoon or a van ride followed by a hike to Santa María. The second day is a hard 11-km trek from Santa María to Santa Teresa. It involves crossing three adventurous bridges and bathing in the Colcamayo hot springs near Santa Teresa. The third day is a six-hour trek from Santa Teresa to Aguas Calientes. Some agencies offer zip-lining near Santa Teresa as an alternative. The final day is a guided tour of Machu Picchu.

Vilcabamba and around

discover the last refuge of the Incas

Santa María

A paved road runs from Ollantaytambo to Santa María, sometimes called Puente Chaullay, an important crossroads with basic places to stay and eat. This is a very beautiful journey, with snowy peaks on either side of the valley. The climb to the **Abra Málaga pass** (4350 m), west of Ollantaytambo, is steep with many tight curves – on the right is a huge glacier. Soon on the left, Nevado Verónica begins to appear in all its huge and snowy majesty. After endless zig-zags and breathtaking views, you reach the pass. The descent to the Vilcanota valley around Santa María shows hillsides covered in lichen and Spanish moss. From Santa María, roads run to Quillabamba in the lowlands to the north; to Lucma, Pucyura, Huancacalle and Vilcabamba to the west, and to Santa Teresa to the south.

Huancacalle and around

West of Santa Maria, the tranquil little village of **Huancacalle** is the best base for exploring the last stronghold of the Incas, including the nearby ruins of **Vitcos**, which were the palace of the last four Inca rulers from 1536 to 1572. **Yurac Rumi**, the sacred white rock of the Incas is also here. It is 8 m high and 20 m wide and covered with intricate carvings. The 7-km loop from Huancacalle to Vitcos, the Inca terraces at **Rosaspata**, Yurac Rumi and back to Huancacalle makes a nice half-day hike. Several excellent longer treks begin or end in Huancacalle: from Choquequirao to Vilcabamba Vieja (Espíritu Pampa, see below), and to Machu Picchu via Santa Teresa.

Towards Vilcabamba Vieja

The road continues west from Huancacalle, 5 km up to the chilly little village of **Vilcabamba**; there's no regular transport but you can hike through the pleasant countryside. There is a mission here run by Italians, with electricity and running water, where you may be able to spend the night; ask for '*La Parroquia*'.

Beyond Vilcabamba the road runs a further 12 km to **Pampaconas**, start of the trail to the **Vilcabamba Vieja** ruins at **Espíritu Pampa**, a vast pre-Inca site with a neo-Inca overlay set in deep jungle at 1000 m. This is where the last Incas held out against the Spanish for nearly 40 years. From Huancacalle a trip to Espíritu Pampa will take three or four days on foot. Give yourself at least a day at the site to soak up the atmosphere before continuing to **Chuhuanquiri** (San Miguel) for transport back to Quillabamba and Cuzco. It is advisable to take local guides and mules, and to enquire in Cuzco and Huancacalle about public safety along the route. Distances are considerable and the going is difficult. The best time of year is May to November. Outside this period it is dangerous as the trails are very narrow and can be thick with mud and very slippery. There are no services along the route; bring all food and supplies including plenty of insect repellent, and take all rubbish with you back to Cuzco for disposal.

Santa Teresa

South of Santa María, this relaxed little town provides alternative access to Machu Picchu (via Estación Hidroeléctrica; see Transport, below) for those who do not wish to ride the train from Cuzco or Ollantaytambo, and makes a good base for activities in the area. Santa Teresa is located at the confluence

> **Tip...**
> Many Cuzco agencies sell '**Machu Picchu By Car**' tours that go through Santa Teresa. You can also reach it by road on your own.

of the Ríos Sacsara, Salkantay and Vilcanota, and its lower elevation at 1600 m creates a warm climate that is a pleasant change from the chill of Cuzco and trekking at high altitude. Many tour groups and independent travellers pass through or spend the night en route to or from Machu Picchu, and several popular treks go through here (see page 1458). There are plenty of hotels, restaurants and most services. The **Colcamayo Thermal Baths** ⓘ *2 km from town along the Río Vilcanota, Wed, Thu, Sat-Mon 0500-2300, Tue and Fri 1600-2300, US$1.75*, have crystal-clear warm pools in a pretty setting and an ice-cold waterfall; free camping nearby (the bugs can be fierce here). There are several zip-lines around town, including **Cola de Mono** (www.canopyperu.com), which is part of various tour itineraries.

Listings Vilcabamba

Where to stay and eat

Huancacalle

Huancacalle has a few basic shops and eateries, although these are not always open; there's a better selection in Pucyura, 2 km north.

$ Sixpac Manco
Huancacalle, T971-823855.
A good simple *hostal*, with shared bath, electric shower, large garden, meals on request. It is managed by the Cobos family, who are very knowledgeable about the area and can arrange for guides and pack animals for trekking.

Santa Teresa

There is a **tourist information office** in the Municipio, Mon-Sat 0800-1700.

$ Casa de Judas
Av Calixto Sánchez by the Plaza, T974-709058.
Rooms with private bath and dorm, solar hot water, good value economy option.

$ Hospedaje El Sol
Av Av Calixto Sánchez, T989-606591,
https://hospedajesol.com.
Rooms of various sizes, all with private bath and hot water.

$ Hostal Yacumama
C Julio Tomás Rivas, T974-290605.
Rooms with private bath, hot water, breakfast available, restaurant next door.

Transport

Santa María

To reach Santa María from Cuzco, take a Quillabamba-bound van from Av Antonio Lorena by an unnamed street 3 blocks uphill (west) of C Almudena, in the Santiago district, US$9, 4 hrs to Santa María. Cars leave Santa María as they fill throughout the day for **Santa Teresa**, US$3.50, 45 mins. There are also vans from Santa María to **Cuzco** and **Quillabamba** (US$1.75, 1 hr).

Huancacalle

Take a van to Santa María (see above) and a *colectivo* from there to Huancacalle, US$5.50, 2 hrs; *colectivos* start in Quillabamba, so if they are full, you might have to go to Quillabamba to catch one there. When travelling from Huancacalle to Cuzco you can get off the *colectivo* at Santa María and catch Cuzco-bound transport from there.

Santa Teresa

From Santa Teresa market, vans leave for the **Estación Hidroeléctrica** at 0530-0700 and 1200-1430, US$1.75, 30 mins, to meet the local train which runs to Aguas Calientes, at 0754, 1500 and 1635; from Aguas Calientes to Hidroeléctrica at 0644, 1235 1330; US$31, 40 mins. There is a **PeruRail** office at Santa Teresa market (daily 0500-0720, 1200-1600), but tickets are only sold at the Estación Hidroeléctrica (daily 0500-0720, 1200-1600), which is not much more than a railway siding; tickets are also sold at the Ollantaytambo and Aguas Calientes train stations. You can also walk 11 km along the tracks from Estación Hidroeléctrica to Aguas Calientes, a pleasant 3- to 4-hr hike with great views and many birds, but mind the passing trains.

Central highlands

The Central Andes have many remote mountain areas with small typical villages, while larger cities of the region include Ayacucho and Huancayo. The vegetation is low, but most valleys are cultivated. Secondary roads are often in poor condition, sometimes impassable in the rainy season; the countryside is beautiful with spectacular views and the people are friendly. Huancayo lies in a valley which produces many crafts; the festivals are very popular and not to be missed.

Lima to Huancayo

ride the rails into the hills

The Central Highway more or less parallels the course of the Central Railway between Lima and Huancayo (335 km). With the paving of roads from Pisco to Ayacucho and Nazca to Abancay, there are now more options for getting to the Sierra and the views on whichever ascent you choose are beyond compare. You can also reach the central highlands from Cuzco and Huaraz so Lima is not the sole point of access overland.

Marcahuasi

3 hrs' walk from San Pedro de Casta. Entry US$4, pack donkey US$8, horse US$10.

Up the Santa Eulalia valley, 40 km beyond **Chosica** (a chaotic town, 45 km east of Lima), is Marcahuasi, a table mountain about 3 km by 1 km at 4000 m, near the village of **San Pedro de Casta**. There are three lakes, a 40-m-high Monumento a la Humanidad and other mysterious lines, gigantic figures, sculptures, astrological signs and megaliths. Their origin is a mystery, although a widely accepted theory is that the formations are the result of wind erosion. The trail to Marcahuasi starts south of the village of San Pedro and climbs southeast. It's three hours' walk to the *meseta*; guides are advisable in misty weather. At shops in San Pedro you can buy everything for the trip, including bottled water. Take all necessary camping equipment for the trek. Tourist information is available at the municipality on the plaza and tours can be arranged with travel agencies in Lima.

Towards La Oroya

For a while, beyond Chosica, each successive valley looks greener and lusher, with a greater variety of trees and flowers. Between Río Blanco and **Chicla** (Km 127, 3733 m), Inca contour-terraces can be seen quite clearly. After climbing up from **Casapalca** (Km 139, 4154 m), there are glorious views of the highest peaks and of mines at the foot of a deep gorge. The road ascends to the Ticlio Pass, before the descent to **Morococha** and **La Oroya**. A large metal flag of Peru can be seen at the top of Mount Meiggs; this is not by any means the highest peak in the area, but through it runs the Galera Tunnel, 1175 m long, in which the Central Railway reaches its greatest altitude, 4782 m.

   La Oroya (3755 m) is the main smelting centre for the region's mining industry. It stands at the fork of the Yauli and Mantaro rivers. Any traveller, but asthmatics in particular, should beware the pollution from the heavy industry, which can cause breathing difficulties. For destinations to the east and north of La Oroya, see page 1481.

Jauja and around

The town of Jauja, founded 1535, 80 km southeast of La Oroya at 3400 m, was Pizarro's provisional capital until the founding of Lima. It has a colourful Wednesday and Sunday market. The **Museo Arqueológico Julio Espejo Núñez** ① *Jr Cusco 537, T064-361370, Mon and Wed 1500-1900, Sun 0900-*

Best for
Crafts ▪ Festivals ▪ Hair-raising journeys ▪ Scenery

ON THE ROAD

☆Central Railway

Constructed in the late 19th and early 20th centuries, this is the second-highest railway in the world and is a magnificent feat of engineering, with 58 bridges, 69 tunnels and six zigzags, passing beautiful landscapes. It's a great way to travel to the central highlands. The main line runs from **Lima**, via La Oroya, to Huancayo, and is run as an irregular tourist service, operated mostly on national holidays by **Ferrocarril Centro Andino** (Avenida José Gálvez Barrenechea 566, piso 5, San Isidro, Lima, T01-226 6363, www.ferrocarrilcentral.com.pe). The train leaves Lima at 0700, reaching Huancayo 11 hours later; the return journey begins at 0700 or 1800, three or four days later; see the website for the next departure date. There are *turístico* (US$224 single, US$299 return) and *clásico* fares (US$149 single Lima–Huancayo, US$209 return), sold online and by Lima and Huancayo agencies. Price is for foreigners; Peruvians pay less. Coaches have reclining seats and heating; there's also a restaurant, tourist information, toilets and a nurse with first aid and oxygen.

Beyond Huancayo trains run on a narrow gauge (3 ft) line 128 km to **Huancavelica**. They depart from a small station in the Huancayo suburb of Chilca (15 minutes by taxi from the centre, US$2). The train runs daily and has two classes of service, Primera Clase (US$3) and Bufet (US$4). This authentic Andean train journey on the *Tren Macho* takes six long, uncomfortable hours and navigates 38 tunnels and 15 bridges. There are fine views as it passes through typical mountain villages where vendors sell food and crafts. In some places, the train has to reverse and change tracks.

1200, 1400-1700, donations welcome, knock on door of La Casa del Caminante opposite where the creator and curator lives, is a quaint but endearing mix of relics from various Peruvian cultures, including two mummies, one still wrapped in the original shroud. The **Cristo Pobre** church is supposedly modelled on Notre Dame and is something of a curiosity. On a hill above Jauja there is a fine line of Inca storehouses, and, on hills nearby, the ruins of Huajlaasmarca, with hundreds of circular stone buildings from the Huanca culture. There are also ruins near the **Laguna de Paca** ① *3.5 km from Jauja; colectivos from the Terminal, US$0.50*. The western shore is lined with restaurants, many of which offer weekend boat trips, US$1.

On the road south to Huancayo is **Concepción** at 3251 m, with a market on Sunday. From Concepción a branch road (6 km) leads to the **Convent of Santa Rosa de Ocopa** ① *Wed-Mon 0900-1200 and 1500-1800, 45-min tours start on the hour, US$1.25; colectivos from the market in Concepción, 15 mins, US$0.50*, a Franciscan monastery set in beautiful surroundings. It was established in 1725 in order to train missionaries for the jungle. It contains a fine library with over 25,000 volumes, a biological museum and a large collection of paintings.

Listings Lima to Huancayo

Tourist information

Jauja
Subgerencia de Turismo (at the Municipalidad on the Plaza, T064-362075, Mon-Fri 0800-1300, 1400-1700), has pamphlets and general information.

Where to stay

Marcahuasi
Locals in San Pedro de Casta will put you up ($); ask at tourist information at the municipality.

The best hotel in town is the **$ Marcahuasi**, just off the plaza. Rooms with private or shared bath; it also has a restaurant. There are 2 other restaurants in town.

Jauja

$ Hatun Wasi
Jr Junín 1072, T064-362416.
Modern multi-storey hotel, good simple rooms, solar hot water after 1100, no breakfast, good value.

$ Hostal María Nieves
Jr Gálvez 491, behind school, 1 block from Plaza de Armas, T064-362543.

Safe, helpful, large breakfast available, hot water on request, small patio, parking. Family run, older place but well cared for.

Restaurants

Towards La Oroya

$$ El Tambo
2 km before town on the road from Lima.
Good trout and frogs legs, local cheese and *manjar*; recommended as the best in and around town; buses on the Lima route stop here.

Jauja

$ Quickly's
Jr Junín 1100. Sun-Fri 0900-2300, Sat 1700-2300.
Menú for lunch, à la carte and sandwiches at night. Clean and friendly.

$ Yuraq Wasi
Jr Bolognesi 535. Sun-Fri lunch only.
Selection of tasty *menús*, pleasant garden seating, good service, a 'find' for Jauja.

Transport

Most buses on the Lima–La Oroya route are full when they pass through Chosica.

Marcahuasi

Bus *Colectivos* for Chosica leave from Av Grau, **Lima**, when full, between 0600 and 2100, US$1. Minibuses to San Pedro de Casta leave **Chosica** from Parque Echenique, opposite market, 0900 and 1500, 4 hrs, US$3.50; return 0700 and 1400.

Towards La Oroya

Bus To Lima, 4½ hrs, US$8. To **Jauja**, 80 km, 1½ hrs, US$2. To **Tarma**, 1½ hrs, US$2.50. To **Cerro de Pasco**, 131 km, 3 hrs, US$3. To **Huánuco**, 236 km, 6 hrs, US$7.50. Buses leave from Zeballos, adjacent to the train station. *Colectivos* also run on all routes.

Jauja

Air Francisco Carle airport is located just outside Jauja. **LC Peru** has 2 daily flights from **Lima**, 45 mins; price includes transfer to Huancayo.

Bus The old train station serves as the bus station. To **Lima,** US$15, or with **Cruz del Sur** (Pizarro 220), direct, 6 hrs, US$22-29 *bus cama*. To **Huancayo**, 44 km, 1 hr, US$2.25; combis to Huancayo from 25 de Abril y Ricardo Palma, 1¼ hrs, US$2.50. To **Cerro de Pasco**, with **Turismo Central**, 5 hrs, US$6. **Turismo Central** also goes to **Huánuco**, 8 hrs, US$15. To **Tarma**, US$3, hourly buses from Junín y Tarma, about 10 blocks north of the centre. Also *colectivos* to Tarma from the same corner.

Huancayo and the Mantaro Valley *Colour map 3, C3.*

a nexus of traditional crafts and culture

Huancayo is the capital of the Junín Region and the main commercial centre for central inland Peru, with a population of over half a million. This busy, over-extended city lies in the Mantaro Valley at 3271 m, surrounded by villages that produce their own original crafts and celebrate festivals all year round. People flock in from far and wide to the important festivals in Huancayo, with an incredible range of food, crafts, dancing and music.

Sights

There is a large neo-classical **Cathedral** on the always-busy Plaza de Armas/de la Constitución. The weekly Sunday market gives a taste of Huancayo at festival time; it gets going after 0900. Jiron Huancavelica, 3 km long and four stalls wide, sells clothes, fruit, vegetables, hardware, handicrafts and traditional medicines and goods for witchcraft. There is also an impressive daily market behind the railway station and a large handicrafts market on Plaza Huanamarca, between Ancash and Real. For an even wider selection, go to the villages themselves for local handicrafts.

Yalpana Wasi ① *Mariscal Castilla 851, Chilca district, T064-365318, Mon-Sat 0900-1300, 1500-1800, free admission,* the 'Place of Memory', is a moving modern museum honouring victims of political violence during the Sendero Luminoso campaign (1980-2000). The exhibits and prologue, written by Mario Vargas Llosa, are a "compelling wake-up call to Peruvian society" (Jaime García Heras). The **museum** ① *at the Salesian school, Pje Santa Rosa 229, north of the river in El Tambo, Mon-Fri 0900-1300, 1500-1800, Sat 0900-1200, US$1.75,* has a good collection of ceramics from various cultures, as well as stuffed animals and miscellaneous curiosities. The **Parque de Identidad Wanka** ① *on Jr San Jorge in the Barrio San Carlos northeast of the city, daily 0800-2000, entry free,* is a mixture of surrealistic construction interwoven with native plants and trees and the cultural history of the Mantaro Valley.

It also has restaurants and craft stalls. On a hillside on the outskirts of town are the impressive, eroded sandstone towers of **Torre-Torre**; take a bus to Cerrito de la Libertad and walk up.

☆Mantaro Valley

The whole Mantaro Valley is rich in culture. Near the small town of Huari are the ruins of **Warivilca** ① *5 km from Huancayo, daily 1000-1200, 1500-1700 (museum mornings only), US$1.75, take a micro for Chilca from Av Ferrocaril*, with the remains of a pre-Inca temple of the Huanca tribe. The Museo de Sitio on the plaza houses deformed skulls and the modelled, painted pottery of successive Huanca and Inca occupations of the shrine.

East of the Río Mantaro, the villages of **Cochas Chico** and **Cochas Grande** ① *11 km north of Huancayo, micros from the corner of Huancas and Giráldez, US$0.50*, are famous for *mate burilado*, or gourd carving. You can buy samples cheaply direct from manufacturers such as Pedro Veli or Eulogio Medina; ask around. There are beautiful views of the Valle de Mantaro and Huancayo from here.

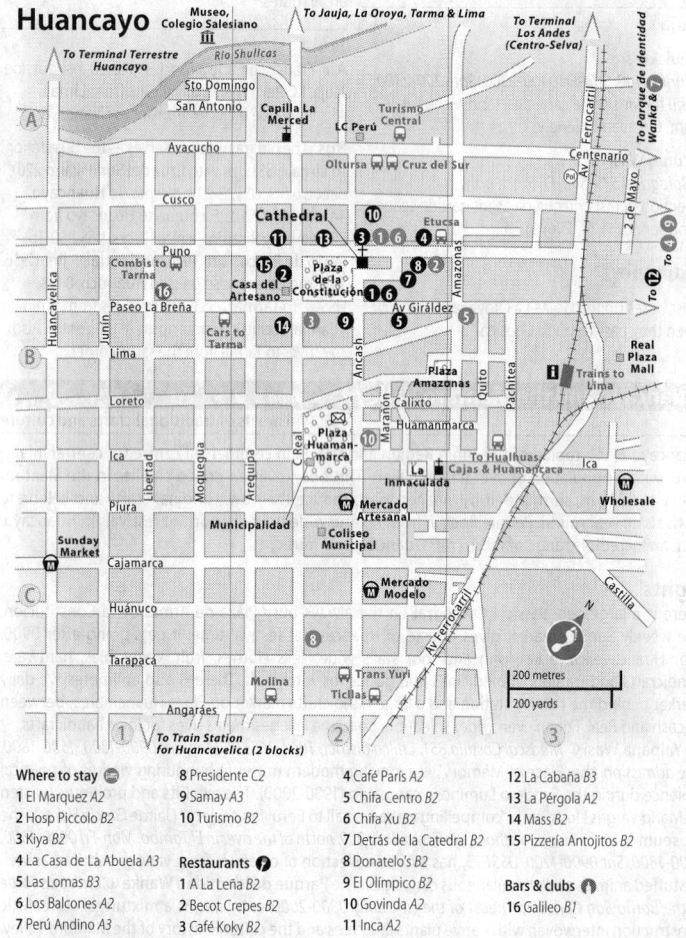

Huancayo

Where to stay
1 El Marquez *A2*
2 Hosp Piccolo *B2*
3 Kiya *B2*
4 La Casa de La Abuela *A3*
5 Las Lomas *B3*
6 Los Balcones *A2*
7 Perú Andino *A3*
8 Presidente *C2*
9 Samay *A3*
10 Turismo *B2*

Restaurants
1 A La Leña *B2*
2 Becot Crepes *B2*
3 Café Koky *B2*
4 Café París *A2*
5 Chifa Centro *B2*
6 Chifa Xu *B2*
7 Detrás de la Catedral *B2*
8 Donatelo's *B2*
9 El Olímpico *B2*
10 Govinda *A2*
11 Inca *A2*
12 La Cabaña *B3*
13 La Pérgola *A2*
14 Mass *B2*
15 Pizzería Antojitos *B2*

Bars & clubs
16 Galileo *B1*

Hualahoyo, near Cochas, has a little chapel with 21 colonial canvases. **San Agustín de Cajas** (8 km north of Huancayo) makes fine hats, and **San Pedro** (10 km) makes wooden chairs. **Hualhuas** (12 km) is known for its fine alpaca weavings which you can watch being made. The weavers take special orders, and small items can be finished in a day; negotiate a price.

The town of **San Jerónimo de Tunan** is renowned for the making of silver filigree jewellery. It has a Wednesday market and a fiesta on the third Saturday in August. There are ruins two to three hours' walk above San Jerónimo, but seek advice before hiking to them.

Between Huancayo and Huancavelica, **Izcuchaca** is the site of a bridge over the Río Mantaro. On the edge of town is a fascinating pottery workshop whose machinery is driven by a water turbine. There is also a small shop. It's a nice hike to the chapel on a hill overlooking the valley (one to 1½ hours each way).

Huancayo to Ayacucho via Huanta

There is a fully paved route to Ayacucho from Huancayo which involves not so much climbing for cyclists. Cross the pass into the Mantaro valley on the road to **Quichuas**. Then to **Anco** and **Mayocc** (lodging). From here the road crosses a bridge after 10 km and in another 20 km reaches **Huanta** in the picturesque valley of the same name. Huanta celebrates the **Fiesta de las Cruces** during the first week of May. Its Sunday market is large and interesting. The area is notable as the site of perhaps the oldest known culture in South America, dating from 20,000 years ago. Evidence was found in the cave of **Pikimachay**, 24 km from Ayacucho, off the road from Huanta. The remains are now in Lima's museums.

Listings Huancayo and Mantaro Valley *map p1466*

Tourist information

The regional office is in Jauja (see page 1463). For city info contact **DIRCETUR** at the train station (T064-222575). **Indecopi** (Pje Comercial 474, El Tambo, T064-245180, abarrientos@indecopi. gob.pe) is the consumer protection office.

Where to stay

Huancayo

$$$ Presidente
C Real 1138, T064-231275, http://huancayo. hotelpresidente.com.pe.
Helpful, classy, safe, serves breakfast, restaurant, convention centre.

$$$ Turismo
Ancash 729, T064-231072, http://turistases. hotelpresidente.com.pe/.
Restored colonial building, same owner as Presidente, with more atmosphere, elegant, rooms quite small, Wi-Fi extra, quiet. Restaurant ($$-$) serves good meals, fine service.

$$$-$$ El Marquez
Puno 294, T064-219202, www.elmarquezhuancayo.com.
Good value, efficient, popular with local business travellers, safe parking.

$$ Kiya
Giráldez 107, T064-214955, www.hotelkiya.com.pe.
Comfortable although ageing, hot water, helpful staff. Spectacular view of Plaza.

$$-$ Posada Junco y Capulí
Julio Tello 414, El Tambo neighbourhood, T064-244368, www.posadajuncoycapuliperu.com.
Small charming place located about 2 km from Plaza de la Constitución, convenient to shops and services. Simple, comfortable, quiet rooms, includes very good breakfast.

$ Hospedaje Piccolo
Puno 239.
With hot water, good beds, well-kept.

$ La Casa de la Abuela
Prolongación Cusco 794 y Gálvez, T064-234383, www.incasdelperu.org/casa-de-la-abuela.
Doubles with or without private bath and dorms, 10-min walk from town. Hot shower, breakfast, laundry facilities, meals available, sociable staff, owner speaks English, good meeting place, games room, free pickup from bus station if requested in advance. Discount for Footprint readers.

$ Las Lomas
Giráldez 327, T064-237587.
Central location, basic rooms, hot water, good value, can arrange tours.

$ Los Balcones
Jr Puno 282, T064-214881.
Comfortable rooms, restaurant, hot water, helpful staff, elevator (practically disabled-accessible). View of the back of the Cathedral.

$ Peru Andino
Pasaje San Antonio 113-115, near Parque Túpac Amaru, in 1st block of Francisco Solano (left side of Defensoría del Pueblo), 10-15 mins' walk from the centre (if taking a taxi, stress that it's Pasaje San Antonio), T064-223956.
Hot showers, several rooms with bath, laundry and kitchen facilities, breakfast and other meals on request, safe area, cosy atmosphere, run by Sra Juana and Luis, who speak some English, organize trekking and mountain bike tours, bike hire, Spanish classes. Can pick up guests at Lima airport with transfer to bus station.

$ Samay
Jr Florida 285 (cdra 9 de Giráldez), T064-365259.
Hostel with shared bath, quiet (unless the little football field next door is being used), breakfast, laundry and kitchen facilities, garden, nice terraces on 3rd floor, helpful staff.

Huancayo to Ayacucho

$ Hostal Recreo Sol y Sombra
Quichuas.
Charming, small courtyard, helpful, basic.

Restaurants

Huancayo

Breakfast is served in Mercado Modelo from 0700. Better, more expensive restaurants serve typical dishes for about US$6, drinks can be expensive. Lots of cheap restaurants along Av Giráldez, and a large food court in Real Plaza mall.

$$ Detrás de la Catedral
Jr Ancash 335 (behind Cathedral as name suggests), T064-212969.
Pleasant atmosphere, excellent dishes. Charcoal grill in the corner keeps the place warm on cold nights. Considered by many to be the best in town.

$$ El Olímpico
Giráldez 199.
Long-established, one of the more upscale establishments offering Andean and *comida criolla*; the real reason to go is the owner's model car collection displayed in glass cabinets.

$$ La Cabaña
Av Giráldez 675, T064-223303. Daily 0900-2400.
Pizzeria, restaurant and bar, pastas, grill, juices and ice cream, wide variety of dishes, excellent atmosphere, Wi-Fi, home delivery US$2.

$$ Pizzería Antojitos
Puno 599.
Attractive, atmospheric pizzería with live music some nights.

$$-$ Chifa Xu
Giráldez 208.
Good food at reasonable prices, always a bustling atmosphere.

$ A La Leña
Ancash on Plaza Constitución.
Good rotisserie chicken and salads, popular.

$ Chifa Centro
Giráldez 238, T064-217575. Another branch at Av Leandra Torres 240.
Chinese food, good service and atmosphere.

$ Donatelo's
Puno 287.
Excellent pizza and chicken place, with good atmosphere, popular.

$ Govinda
Jr Cusco 289.
Vegetarian restaurant and café, good service, sells natural products. Nice tranquil atmosphere with no blaring TV, good concert videos instead.

$ La Pérgola
Puno 444, overlooking the plaza.
An oldie with a pleasant atmosphere, 4-course *menú*.

$ Mass
Real 549 and on block 10 of Real.
A clean place for *pollo a la brasa* with fast service.

Cafés

Becot Crepes
Av Real 471.
Savoury and sweet crêpes to go, tasty and cheap.

Café Koky
Ancash y Puno, Ancash 235, and Real Plaza Mall. Daily 0700-2300, lunch 1230-1530.
Good breakfasts, lunches, sandwiches, capuccino and pastries, fancy free Wi-Fi.

Café París
Puno 254 and Arequipa 265.
Sofá-café and restaurant, good food and atmosphere, many sweets, *menú* at midday.

Inca

Puno 530.
Popular *fuente de soda*, with coffee, Peruvian food, desserts, milkshakes.

Bars and clubs

Huancayo

Galileo Disco-Pub
Paseo La Breña 376.
Live music Wed through Sat, good atmosphere.

Festivals

There are so many festivals in the Mantaro Valley that it is impossible to list them all. Nearly every day of the year there is some sort of celebration in one of the villages. See also Public holidays and festivals in Essentials A-Z.

1-6 Jan New Year has many celebrations, including **La Huaconada** dance festival in Mito.
20 Jan San Sebastián y San Fabián, recommended in Jauja.
Feb There are carnival celebrations for the whole month, with highlights including **Virgen de la Candelaria** and **Concurso Nacional de Huaylash**.
Mar-Apr Semana Santa, with impressive Good Fri processions.
3-8 May Fiesta de los Shapis in Chupaca.
May Fiesta de las Cruces throughout the whole month.
13 Jun Virgen de las Mercedes.
22-30 Jun San Juan Bautista.
24-25 Jul Santiago.
4-15 Aug San Juan de Dios.
16 Aug San Roque.
30 Aug Santa Rosa de Lima.
8 Sep Virgen de Cocharcas.
15-18 Sep Virgen de la Natividad.
23-24 Sep Virgen de las Mercedes.
4th week of Sep Tourism week.
18-30 Oct Celebrations for **El Señor de los Milagros**.

Shopping

All crafts are made outside Huancayo in the many villages of the Mantaro Valley, or in Huancavelica. The villages are worth a visit to learn how the items are made.

What to do

Huancayo

Tour operators
American Travel & Service, *Plaza Constitución 122, of 2 (next to the Cathedral)*, T064-211181, T964-830220. Wide range of classical and more adventurous tours in the Mantaro Valley and the central jungle. Transport and equipment rental possible. Most group-based day tours start at US$8-10 pp.
Hidden Perú, *no storefront*, T964-164979, andinismo_peru@yahoo.es, *Facebook: Eco Mountain trek – Peru*. Marco Jurado Ames is a mountain guide who organizes adventure and cultural trips in the Andes and Amazon Basin, for 1-12 days with trekking in the Mantaro valley, Huaytapallana and Pariacaca ranges; mountain biking, walking and mountaineering in Cuzco and Huaraz.
Incas del Perú, *Av Giráldez 675*, T064-223303, www.incasdelperu.org. Jungle, biking and hiking trips throughout the region as well as day trips to the Mantaro Valley. Also arranges flight/train tickets and language and volunteer programmes (Spanish for beginners, US$50 for 5 days or US$185 per week, including accommodation at Hostal La Casa de La Abuela and all meals at La Cabaña); also home-stays and weaving, traditional music, Peruvian cooking and lots of other things. Very popular and recommended.
Peruvian Tours, *Plaza Constitución 122, p 2, of 1*, T064-213069. Next to the Cathedral and American Travel & Service. Classic tours of the Mantaro valley, plus day trips up to the Huaytapallana Nevados above Huancayo, plus long, 16-hr excursions to Cerro de Pasco and Tarma.

Transport

Huancayo

For train services, see Central Railway, page 1464.

Bus Terminal Terrestre Huancayo for buses to most destinations is 3 km north of the centre in the Parque Industrial. **Terminal Los Andes** (also known as **Terminal Centro-Selva**; Av Ferrocarril 151, T064-223367) serves mainly the central highlands and the jungle. Some companies have their own terminal in the centre, including **Turismo Central** (Jr Ayacucho 274, T064-223528). Most buses to the Mantaro Valley leave from several places around the market area, and from Av Ferrocarril. Buses to **Hualhuas** and **Cajas** leave from block 3 of Pachitea. Buses to **Cochas** leave from Amazonas y Giráldez.

There are regular buses to **Lima**, 6-7 hrs on a good paved road, US$13-25 with **Oltursa**. Other recommended companies with frequent service include **Etucsa, Turismo Central, Mega Bus** (Ancash 385, T064-225432) and **Cruz del Sur** (Terminal Los Andes). Travelling by day is recommended for the fantastic views and for safety, although most major companies go by night (take warm clothing).

To **Ayacucho**, 319 km, 9-10 hrs, US$13 with **Molina** (C Angaráes 334, T064-224501), 3 a day, recommended; 1 a day with **Turismo Central** (via Huanta) US$10-22; also **Ticllas** and **Etucsa** from Terminal Terrestre, US$5-10. There are 2 routes: one via Huanta, mostly paved; and the other via Huancavelica, partly paved with the remainder in poor condition, very difficult in the wet. Take warm clothing.

To **Huancavelica**, 147 km, 3 hrs, US$5. Many buses daily, including **Transportes Yuri** (Ancash 1220), 3 a day. The road is paved and offers a delightful ride, much more comfortable than the train (if you can find a driver who will not scare you to death). Shared taxis from Av Real cuadra 12, US$8 (US$10 on weekends), negotiable.

To **Cerro de Pasco**, 255 km, 5 hrs, US$7.50. Several departures. Alternatively, take a bus to La Oroya, about every 20 mins from Terminal Los Andes, or a shared taxi, US$5, 2 hrs. From La Oroya there are regular buses and *colectivos* to Cerro, US$8. The road to La Oroya and on to Cerro is paved and in good condition. To **Huánuco**, 7 hrs, **Turismo Central**, twice daily, US$20, good service.

To **Tarma**, **Lobato** and **America** from Terminal Los Andes, 5 hrs, US$10; some continue to **La Merced**. Also **Turismo Central** to La Merced, US$19. Minibuses and cars from outside the terminal, to Tarma US$6, to La Merced US$12, 3 hrs.

To **Yauyos**, cars at 0500 from Plaza de los Sombreros, El Tambo, US$7.50. It is a poor road with beautiful mountain landscapes before dropping to the valley of Cañete; cars go very fast.

To **Jauja**, 44 km, 1 hr. *Colectivos* and combis leave every few mins from Terminal Los Andes, US$2.50. Taxi to Jauja US$15, 45 mins.

To **Tingo María** and **Pucallpa**, daily with **Turismo Central**, US$27.

Huancavelica   *Colour map 3, C3.*

a colonial mountain town

Huancavelica is a tranquil, friendly and attractive town at 3676 m, surrounded by huge, rocky mountains. It was founded in the 16th century by the Spanish to exploit rich deposits of mercury and silver, but it remains predominantly an indigenous town. There are beautiful mountain walks in the surrounding area.

Sights

On the Plaza de Armas, the **Catedral de San Antonio**, built in 1673, has an altar considered to be one of the finest examples of colonial art in Peru. Also very impressive are the five other churches in town, including **Santo Domingo** built in 1601 (Toledo y Carabaya), **San Francisco** (Plaza Bolognesi) built in 1774, with no less than 11 altars, and **San Sebastián** (Plaza Bolognesi). Unfortunately, most are closed to visitors outside early-morning mass. The **Ministerio de Cultura** ① *Plazoleta San Juan de Dios, Arica y Raimondi, T064-453420,* is a good source of information on festivals, archaeological sites, history, etc. It also runs courses and lectures on music and dancing, and has a small but interesting **Museo Regional** ① *T064-753420, Mon-Sat 0830-1300, 1430-1800,* with exhibits of archaeology, anthropology and popular art.

Bisecting the town is the Río Ichu. South of the river is the main commercial centre. On the hillside north of the river are the **San Cristóbal thermal baths** ① *Av Escalinata y 28 de Abril, daily 0600-1700, US$0.50 for private rooms, water not very hot (26° C), US$0.30 for the hot public pool, also hot showers, take a lock for the doors.* The pedestrian walkway up to the baths on Av Escalinata is full of figures illustrating the village festivals of the region and their typical characters. There are also thermal baths in Secsachaca, 1 km from town. The Potaqchiz hill, just outside the town, gives a fine view; it's about one hour walk up from San Cristóbal.

Excursions from Huancavelica include the abandoned **Santa Bárbara mine** and nearby village of **Sacsamarca**, 4 km southwest the city and accessible by vehicle or on foot, a demanding day-hike. The small town of **Yauli**, 14 km east of Huancavelica, has an interesting Saturday market (*colectivo* from Terminal Pampa Amarilla, Av Huancavelica y Sebastián Barranca, leave as they fill, US$1.50).

Huancavelica to Ayacucho

The fully paved route from Huancavelica to Ayacucho (247 km) is one of the highest continuous roads in the world. The journey is a cold one but spectacular, as the road rarely drops below 4000 m for 150 km, with great views and many lakes en route. It goes via Santa Inés (4650 m), which is located 78 km south of Huancavelica on the main Pisco–Ayacucho road.

Out of Huancavelica the road climbs steeply with switchbacks between herds of llamas and alpacas grazing on rocky perches. Around Pucapampa (Km 43) is one of the highest habitable altiplanos (4500 m), where the rare and highly prized ash-grey alpaca can be seen. Snow-covered mountains are passed as the road climbs to 4853 m at the Abra Chonta pass, 23 km before Santa Inés. By taking the turn-off to Huachocolpa at Abra Chonta and continuing for 3 km you'll reach one of the highest drivable passes in the world, at 5059 m. Nearby are two lakes (Laguna Choclacocha) which can be visited in 2½ hours. The Abra de Apacheta at 4750 m is 52 km beyond Santa Inés, on the main road 98 km from Ayacucho. The rocks here are all the colours of the rainbow, and running through this fabulous scenery is a violet river. You can combine a tour to Santa Inés with the trip to Ayacucho (eg with Paccari Tours, see below).

A more adventurous route to Ayacucho is via Lircay and Julcamarca, along dirt roads with beautiful scenery all the way; see Transport, below, for bus services and accommodation options.

Listings Huancavelica

Tourist information

Dircetur
Pje Miraflores 280, p4, T064-452938, www. dirceturhuancavelica.gob.pe. Mon-Sat.
Good maps and leaflets, very helpful.

Where to stay

$$$ Presidente
Plaza de Armas, T064-452760, http:// huancavelica.hotelpresidente.com.pe.
Lovely colonial building, higher-priced suites available, heating, parking, safe, laundry, buffet breakfast, very good restaurant (small and old-fashioned) and café.

$$ Illariy
Jr Carabaya 344, T064-369028, Illariyhotel@hotmail.com.
Convenient near Plaza de Armas, clean and quiet, good rooms, excellent buffet breakfast, helpful.

$ Ascensión
Jr Manco Capac 481 (Plaza de Armas), T064-453103.
Very comfortable, wooden floors, with or without bath, hot water, good value.

$ La Portada
Virrey Toledo 252, T064-453603.
Large rooms with private bath or small, basic rooms with shared bath with extra charge for TV. Lots of blankets, unlimited coca tea, helpful staff, good value, secure metal doors.

$ Montevideo
Av Malecón Santa Rosa 168, T967-980638.
Clean basic rooms. 4th floor terrace has great views of the river and *malecón*.

$ Victoria
Virrey Toledo 133, next to the plaza.
Basic, functional, modern and clean.

Restaurants

$$ Los Farolitos
Jr Arica 202, Plazoleta San Juan de Dios, Mon-Sat 0800-2200.
Restaurant, café and bar serving good food, juices and drinks. Small place with tables on the pedestrian street, nice atmosphere. Recommended.

$$-$ Roma II
Manco Capac 580, T064-452608. Open 1800-2300.
Pizzas, smells delicious, friendly staff, delivery available.

$ Chifa El Mesón
Manchego Muñoz 153, T064-453570.
Very popular, standard *chifa* fare. Delivery available.

$ Frutas
Manchego 279.
Clean modern place serving fruit salads, juices and sandwiches.

$ Joy Campestre
Av de los Incas 870.

Comida criolla and regional dishes served in a leisurely country environment.

$ Killa Café
Virrey Toledo, on Plaza de Armas opposite the Cathedral, evenings only.
Good coffee, sandwiches and wine, no noisy TV, free Wi-Fi, paintings for sale, nice and cosy.

$ Los Portales
Virrey Toledo 158, on Plaza de Armas.
Good breakfast, sandwiches and coffee, giant fruit extracts (try the apple extract).

Festivals

4-8 Jan Fiesta de los Reyes Magos y los Pastores.
2nd Sun in Jan Fiesta del Niño Perdido.
20 Jan-mid Mar Pukllaylay Carnavales, celebration of the 1st fruits from the ground (harvest).
Mar/Apr Semana Santa (Holy Week).
End May-Jun Toro Pukllay festival.
May and Aug Fiesta de Santiago in all communities.
22-28 Dec Los Laijas or **Galas** (scissors dance). This event is on UNESCO's World Heritage list.

Shopping

Huancavelica is a major craft centre, with a wide variety of goods produced in surrounding villages. Handicraft sellers congregate on the 4th block of Victoria Garma and under Plaza Santa Ana (*sótano*). Most handicrafts are transported directly to Lima, but you can still visit craftsmen in neighbouring villages.

What to do

Cielo Azul, *Jr Manuel Ascencio Segura 140, on the plaza (former municipal tourism office), T967-718802.* City tours and many others, US$10-30 pp for a group of 6.
Paccari Tours, *Av Ernesto Morales 637, T978-978828, www.paccaritours.com.* Offers city tours (also by bike), visits to Uchkus Inkañan archaeological site, boating on one of the lakes, alpaca herding on the Puna, and historic mine tours. Owner Daniel Páucar is very helpful.
Willka Tours, *Jr Carabaya 199, T967-758007, www.willkatours.com.* Variety of local tours.

Transport

Bus There is a Terrapuerto bus terminal in Ascensión, next to the Esalud Hospital II in the west end of town. Many bus companies also have offices on, and leave from the east end of town, around Parque M Castilla (Santa Ana), between Manchego and O'Donovan.

To **Huancayo**, 147 km, 5 hrs, US$4, paved road, **Transportes Ticllas** (Manchego 686, T064-452787). Also shared taxis all day from Av Machego y González Prada and from the Terrapuerto, US$8 Mon-Thu, US$10 Fri-Sun, 3½ hrs. Most buses to Huancayo go on to **Lima**, 445 km, 13 hrs, minimum, US$14; there are several a day including **Molina** (Manchego 608, T064-454244). The other route is via **Pisco**, 269 km, 12 hrs, US$12, and **Ica**, US$13, 1730 daily, with **Oropesa** (Manchego 612, T064-369082), continuing to Lima. Buy your ticket 1 day in advance. The road is poor until it joins the Ayacucho–Pisco road, beyond which it is paved. Most of the journey is done at night; be prepared for sub-zero temperatures in the early morning as the bus passes snowfields, then for temperatures of 25-30°C as the bus descends to the coast.

Train Station at Av Ferrocarril s/n, T064-452898. *Tren Macho* to **Huancayo**, 3-4 times a week (see Central Railway, page 1464).

Huancavelica to Ayacucho

There is no direct transport from Huancavelica to Ayacucho, other than with **Molina** which passes through from Huancayo daily between 2230 and 2400, US$13. Otherwise you have to go to **Rumichaca** just beyond Santa Inés on the Pisco–Ayacucho road, with **San Juan Bautista**, 0430, 4 hrs, then take a minibus to Ayacucho, 3 hrs. Rumichaca has only a couple of foodstalls and some filthy toilets.

The alternative route to Ayacucho is to take a taxi or *colectivo* from Huancavelica with **Transportes 5 de Mayo** (Av Sebastián Barranca y Cercado) to the small village of **Lircay**, US$7.55, 2½ hrs. The village has an unnamed *hostal* ($) at Sucre y La Unión, with bath and hot water (much better than **Hostal El Paraíso**, opposite). **Transportes 5 de Mayo** continues from Lircay Terminal Terrestre hourly from 0430 to Julcamarca, 2½ hrs, US$6, where there is a colonial church and the very basic **Hostal Villa Julcamarca**, near the plaza (no tap water). From Julcamarca plaza, take a minibus to Ayacucho, US$4, 2 hrs.

The final, slow option to Ayacucho is to take the train to Izcuchaca, stay the night and continue by *colectivo* from there (see page 1467).

☆ The city of Ayacucho, the capital of its department, is famous for its hugely impressive Semana Santa celebrations, its splendid market and, not least, its plethora of churches – 33 of them no less – giving the city its alternative name La Ciudad de las Iglesias. A week can easily be spent enjoying Ayacucho and its hinterland. The climate is lovely, with warm, sunny days and pleasant balmy evenings. It is a hospitable, tranquil place, where the inhabitants are eager to promote tourism. It also boasts a large, active student population. Ayacucho is a large city but the interesting churches and colonial houses are all fairly close to the Plaza Mayor. Barrio Santa Ana is further away to the south; you can take a taxi or walk.

The decisive Battle of Ayacucho was fought on the Pampa de Quinua (see page 1475), on 9 December 1824, bringing Spanish rule in Peru to an end. In the middle of the festivities, the Liberator Simón Bolívar decreed that the city be named Ayacucho, 'Place of the Souls', instead of its original name, Huamanga.

Sights

Plaza Mayor The city is built round the Plaza Mayor, with the Cathedral, Municipalidad, Universidad Nacional de San Cristóbal de Huamanga (UNSCH) and various colonial mansions facing on to it. The **Cathedral** ① *open for Mass Mon-Sat 1730, Sun 1000 and 1730,* built in 1612, has superb gold-leaf altars. It is beautifully lit at night. On the north side of the Plaza Mayor, at Portal de la Unión 37, is the **Casona de los Marqueses de Mozobamba del Pozo**, also called Velarde-Alvarez. Recently restored as the **Centro Cultural de la UNSCH**, it hosts frequent artistic and cultural exhibitions; see the monthly Agenda Cultural. Jr Asamblea is pedestrianized for its first two blocks north of the plaza; on a parallel street is **Santo Domingo** (1548) ① *9 de Diciembre, block 2, Mass daily 0630-0730.* Its fine façade has triple Roman arches and Byzantine towers.

Beyond the plaza Jr 28 de Julio is pedestrianized for two blocks south of the plaza. A stroll down 28 de Julio leads to the prominent **Arco del Triunfo** (1910), which commemorates victory over the Spaniards. Through the arch is the church of **San Francisco de Asís** (1552) ① *28 de Julio, block 3, daily for morning Mass.* It has an elaborate gilt main altar and several others. Across 28 de Julio from San Francisco is the **Mercado de Abastos Carlos F Vivanco**, the packed central market. As well as household items and local produce, look out in particular for the stalls dedicated to cheese, breads and fruit juices. West of the market, **Santa Clara de Asís** ① *Jr Grau, block 3, open for Mass 0600-0800,* is renowned for its beautifully delicate coffered ceiling and for housing an image of Jesús Nazareno, patron of Huamanga. It is open for the sale of sweets and cakes made by the nuns; go to the door at Nazareno 184, which is usually open.

One block east of Jr 28 de Julio, the 16th-century church of **La Merced** ① *2 de Mayo, open for Mass 0600-0800 and 1700-1900,* is the second oldest in the city. The high choir is a good example of the simplicity of churches in the early period of the Viceroyalty. **Casona Jáuregui**, opposite, is also called **Ruiz de Ochoa** after its original owner. Its outstanding feature is its doorway, which has a blue balcony supported by two fierce beasts with erect penises.

On the fifth block of 28 de Julio is the late 16th-century **Casona Vivanco**, which houses the **Museo Andrés A Cáceres** ① *Jr 28 de Julio 508, Mon-Fri 0900-1300, 1500-1700, US$0.70.* The museum has baroque painting, colonial furniture, republican and contemporary art, and exhibits on Mariscal Cáceres' battles in the War of the Pacific. Further south still, on a pretty plazuela, is **Santa Teresa** (1683) ① *28 de Julio, block 6, daily Mass 0600-0800, usually 1600,* with its monastery. The nuns here sell sweets and crystallized fruits and a *mermelada de ají*, made to a recipe given to them by God; apparently it is not *picante* (spicy). **San Cristóbal** ① *Jr 28 de Julio, block 6, rarely open,* was the first church to be founded in the city (1540), and is one of the oldest in South America. With its single tower, it is tiny compared with Santa Teresa, see above.

> **Tip...**
>
> For a moving insight into the recent history of this region and the violence surrounding the Sendero Luminoso campaign, visit **Museo de la Memoria de ANFASEP**, Prolongación Libertad 1229 (cuadra 14), in the north of the city, T066-317170, www.anfasep.org.pe, Mon-Fri 0900-1300, 1500-1800, Sat 0900-1300, US$0.70.

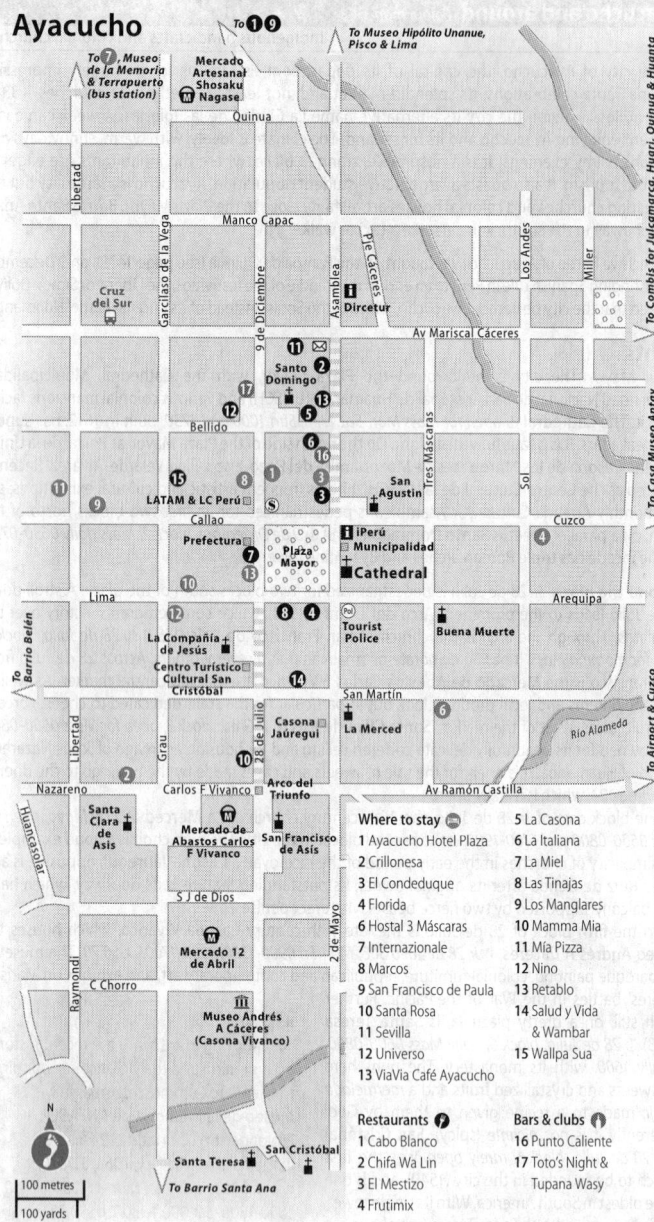

Ayacucho

To ① ⑨

To *Museo Hipólito Unanue,*
Pisco & Lima

To ⑦, Museo
de la Memoria
& Terrapuerto
(bus station)

Mercado
Artesanal
Shosaku
Nagase

Quinua

Manco Capac

Libertad

Garcilaso de la Vega

9 de Diciembre

Asamblea

Pie Cáceres

Los Andes

Miller

To Combis for Julcamarca, Huari, Quinua & Huanta

Cruz
del Sur

🅸 Dircetur

Av Mariscal Cáceres

⑪ ✉
Santo Domingo ②
⑰ ⑬
⑫ ⑤

Bellido

⑥
⑯

⑮ ⑧ ① San Agustín
③ ③
⑨ Ⓢ
LATAM & LC Perú

Callao

Tres Máscaras

Sol

Cuzco

To Casa Museo Antay

Prefectura ⑦
⑬

Lima

① ③
⑧ ④

🅸 iPerú
Municipalidad
✝ Cathedral

Plaza
Mayor

Arequipa

④

To Barrio Belén

La Compañía
de Jesús
Centro Turístico
Cultural San
Cristóbal

⑫

⑧ ④
🅿 Tourist
Police

Buena Muerte

⑭

San Martín

Casona
Jáuregui

⑩ ✝ La Merced ⑥

Río Alameda

To Airport & Cuzco

Libertad

Grau

28 de Julio

Arco del
Triunfo

Av Ramón Castilla

Nazareno
Carlos F Vivanco

Huamanga

Santa
Clara
de Asís

Mercado de
Abastos Carlos
F Vivanco

San Francisco
de Asís

S J de Dios

Raymondi

C Chorro

Mercado 12
de Abril

Museo Andrés
A Cáceres
(Casona Vivanco)

2 de Mayo

N

100 metres
100 yards

Santa Teresa ✝ San Cristóbal

To Barrio Santa Ana

Where to stay 🛏

1 Ayacucho Hotel Plaza
2 Crillonesa
3 El Condeduque
4 Florida
6 Hostal 3 Máscaras
7 Internazionale
8 Marcos
9 San Francisco de Paula
10 Santa Rosa
11 Sevilla
12 Universo
13 ViaVia Café Ayacucho

5 La Casona
6 La Italiana
7 La Miel
8 Las Tinajas
9 Los Manglares
10 Mamma Mia
11 Mía Pizza
12 Nino
13 Retablo
14 Salud y Vida
 & Wambar
15 Wallpa Sua

Restaurants 🍴

1 Cabo Blanco
2 Chifa Wa Lin
3 El Mestizo
4 Frutimix

Bars & clubs 🍸

16 Punto Caliente
17 Toto's Night &
 Tupana Wasy

Inaugurated in 2016, the **Casa Museo Joaquín López Antay** ① *Jr Cuzco 424, T956-695466, open 0600-2000,* is located in the home of a well-known local artist who excelled in the creation of *retablos*. **Museo de Antropología y Arqueología Hipólito Unanue** ① *Av Independencia 508, T66-318305,* is a small, very well organized private museum with Wari ceramics and other artefacts.

Barrio Santa Ana For a fascinating insight into Inca and pre-Inca art and culture, a visit to Barrio Santa Ana is a must. Here, about 200 families have workshops making *artesanías*: textiles, *retablos*, ceramics and work in stone. Their work is distributed through the galleries in the barrio. A good grasp of Spanish is essential to appreciate the galleries fully. Note that the galleries in the barrio are closed on Sunday. Visit **Julio Gálvez** ① *Plazoleta Santa Ana 120, T066-314278,* for remarkable jewellery and sculptures in alabaster (*piedra de huamanga*). Also see Handicrafts, page 1478.

North of Ayacucho

A good road north from Ayacucho leads to **Huari** ① *22 km from Ayacucho, daily 0800-1700, US$1;* vans leave from Paradero a Huari Quinua (Jr Ciro Alegría, 3ra cuadra), when full from 0700, 40 mins, US$1.50; or take a tour. This site dates from the 'Middle Horizon' (AD 600-1000), when the Huari culture spread across most of Peru. This was the first urban walled centre in the Andes. The huge irregular stone walls are up to 3-4 m high, and rectangular houses and streets can be made out. The most important activity here was artistic: ceramics, gold, silver, metal and alloys such as bronze, which was used for weapons and for decorative objects. The ruins now lie in an extensive *tuna* cactus forest (don't pick the fruit). There is a museum at the site.

Vans to Huari continue to **Quinua** ① *37 km northeast of Ayacucho, a further 25 mins, US$0.75, or US$1.50; ask the driver to go all the way to the 'Obelisco' for an extra US$0.75.* This village has a charming cobbled main plaza and many of the buildings have been restored. There is a small market on Sunday. The village's handicrafts are recommended, especially its ceramics; San Pedro Ceramics, at the foot of the hill, and Mamerto Sánchez (Jr Sucre) should be visited, but there are many others. Most of the houses have miniature ceramic churches on the roof. The **Fiesta de la Virgen de Cocharcas** is celebrated around 8th September. Nearby, on the **Pampa de Quinua** (part of a 300-ha Santuario Histórico), a 44-m-high obelisk commemorates the Battle of Ayacucho in 1824. A reenactment of the battle is held on 9 December, with college students playing the roles of Royalist and South American soldiers.

Trips of about six hours can be arranged to Huari, La Quinua village and the Santuario Histórico for US$18 per person (minimum three people).

Vilcashuamán and around

Full-day tours to these sites cost US$23 pp for 8 passengers, departing 0500. Alternatively, travel by van from Terminal Zona Sur, Av Cuzco 350 (daily 0200-1600, return 0700-1700, 4 hrs, US$4.50) and stay overnight in one of the 3 basic but clean hotels ($).

The Inca ruins of **Vilcashuamán** are 120 km to the south of Ayacucho. Vilcashuamán was an important Inca provincial capital at the crossroads where the main road from Cuzco to the central coast met the empire's north–south highway. There are several monumental Inca buildings, including an intact *usnu*, a flat-topped pyramid which was used for religious ceremonies. The village of Vischongo is one hour from Vilcashuamán; it has a market on Wednesday. Other attractions in the area include **Intihuatana**, Inca baths of fine masonry, near a lake about one hour uphill from the village, and Puya Raimondi plants at Titankayuq, one hour's walk from Vischongo.

Listings Ayacucho and around

Tourist information

Dirección Regional de Industria y Turismo (Dircetur)
Asamblea 481, T066-312548. Mon-Fri 0730-1430.
Friendly and helpful.

iPerú
Jr Cusco 108, T066-318305, iperuayacucho@ promperu.gob.pe. Mon-Sat 0900-1800, Sun 0900-1300.
Very helpful. Also has an office at the airport, open mornings only.

Tourist police
Arequipa cuadra 1, T066-312055.

Where to stay

$$$ Ayacucho Hotel Plaza
Jr 9 de Diciembre 184, T066-312202,
www.dmhoteles.pe.
Spacious and elegant in a colonial *casona*,
comfortable rooms, some suites have balconies
overlooking the plaza. With restaurant, bar,
cafetería, games room, conference rooms,
parking. Helpful staff, organizes tours.

$$$-$$ Internazionale
Urb María Parado de Bellido Mz O, Lt 1, Emadi,
T066-314701, www.internazionalehotel.pe.
Business-orientated, 5 mins drive from the centre,
modern, junior suites with jacuzzi and roof
terrace with great view of the city. Restaurant,
helpful staff.

$$$-$$ ViaVia Café Ayacucho
Portal Constitución 4, Plaza de Armas, T066-
312834, www.viaviacafe.com/en/ayacucho.
Single, double and triple rooms with private
bath, solar hot water 24 hrs, TV room, Spanish,
Dutch and English spoken. The attached **ViaVia**
restaurant and travellers' café overlooks the
Plaza, offering international and Peruvian food,
a lunch *menú*, lounge and live music Fri-Sat.
Has a 2nd property, **Via Via Alameda** (Alameda
Valdelirios 720), slightly cheaper, with bar-
restaurant, ice cream parlour.

$$ San Francisco de Paula
Jr Callao 270, T066-312353, www.
hotelsanfranciscodepaula.com.
A bit like a museum with hallways filled with
handicrafts and a nice patio, mirador (terrace
with views), restaurant, parking, popular choice.
Comfortable rooms and some suites with jacuzzi.

$$ Santa Rosa
Jr Lima 166, T066-314614,
www.hotelsantarosa.com.pe.
Lovely colonial courtyard in building with
historical associations, roof terrace, warm
rooms, attentive staff, car park, computers
for guests, cash only, good restaurant with
good value *menú*.

$$ Sevilla
Jr Libertad 631, T066-314388,
www.hotelsevillaperu.com.
Convenient location, comfortable rooms with
fridge, microwave and abundant hot water, nice

courtyard and common areas, includes buffet
breakfast, friendly helpful staff.

$$ Universo
Jr Grau 101, 1 block from the plaza, T066-313888.
Modern rooms, parking, laundry, meeting room,
tour desk, helpful.

$ Crillonesa
C Nazareno 165, T066-312350,
hotelcrillonesa@outlook.com.
Good rooms, hot water, laundry facilities, great
views from roof terrace, near produce market but
reasonably quiet, volunteer opportunities. Good
value, warmly recommended. Owner Carlos
Manco is very friendly, helpful and has loads of
information. He will act as a local tour guide and
knows everyone.

$ El Condeduque
Jr Asamblea 159, T066-316231,
elcondeduquehotel@hotmail.com.
Ample rooms with private bath, hot water, nice
common areas, good central location, includes
breakfast, good value.

$ Florida
Jr Cuzco 310, T066-312565.
Small, central location, pleasant, quiet, patio with
flowers, electric showers, no breakfast.

$ Hostal 3 Máscaras
Jr 3 Máscaras 194, T066-312921,
www.hoteltresmascaras.galeon.com.
Newer rooms with bath better, but with
less character, than the old ones without,
nice colonial building with patio, hot water,
breakfast extra, car park.

$ Marcos
9 de Diciembre 143, T066-316867.
Comfortable, modern, in a cul-de-sac half a block
from the Plaza, quiet, hot water, laundry, includes
breakfast in the cafetería.

Restaurants

Ayacucho has its own regional gastronomy, a
speciality is *cuy chactado* (fried guinea pig). For
a cheap, healthy breakfast, try *maca*, a drink of
maca tuber, apple and quinoa, sold outside the
market opposite Santa Clara, 0600-0800.

$$ Las Flores
Jr José Olaya 106, Plaza Conchopata, east of city
in the 'gourmet neighbourhood', T066-316349.
Daily 1100-1900.
Specializes in *cuy chactado*. Taxi US$1.50
from centre.

$$ Las Tinajas
Portal Independencia 65, T066-310128.
Open 1200-2400.
Chicken grill and bar, large balcony overlooking the main square, very popular, good service.

$$ Mamma Mia
Jr 28 de Julio 262.
Excellent pizza, elegant and cosy, located on Plaza More, a nice spot where there are other restaurants and cafés, boutiques, jewellers and 4 karaoke pubs.

$$-$ La Casona
Jr Bellido 463. Open 0800-2230.
Dining under the arches and in dining room, regional specialities, try their *puca picante*, *mondongo* and *cuy*, and a wide menu.

$$-$ Los Manglares
Av 26 de Enero 415, T066-315900. Open 1030-1600.
The best-established *cevichería* of several on this avenue, also does home delivery.

$$-$ Nino
Jr 9 de Diciembre 205, on small plaza opposite Santo Domingo church, T066-814537.
Daily 1700-2300.
Quaint decor, terrace and garden; serves chicken and *parrillas*, including take-away.

$ Cabo Blanco
Av Maravillas 198, close to Shosaku Nagase market (see Shopping). Open 0800-1800.
Ceviches, seafood and fish dishes, small place with personal service. Also serves beers, wines and cocktails.

$ Chifa Wa Lin
Asamblea 257.
Very popular Chinese, variety of *menús* said to be the best in town.

$ La Italiana
Jr Bellido 486, T066-317574. Daily 1700-2300.
Pizzeria with a huge wood-burning oven.

$ Mía Pizza
Av Mcal Cáceres 1045, T066-313273.
Open 1800-0200.
Pizzas *a la leña*, pastas and karaoke (also has a bar to get you in the mood for singing). Good atmosphere, like an old tavern.

$ Retablo
Jr Asamblea 219, T066-528453.
Chicken, meat, burgers and more in a large modern locale. Always full with locals, good value.

$ Salud y Vida
San Martín 439, Mon-Sun 0700-1600.
Vegetarian *menú*, generous portions, good service. Lunches are better than breakfasts.

$ Wallpa Sua
Jr Garcilazo de la Vega 240.
A good chicken place, also with *parrillas*.

$ Wambar
San Martín 403, upstairs. Daily.
Generous portions of grilled chicken with native Andean potatoes and *quapchi*. Live music Sat-Sun.

Cafés

Centro Turístico Cultural San Cristóbal
28 de Julio 178.
Has some expensive cafés including **Lalo's** (café, pizza delivery service and bar) and **Café Express** (coffee specialists) other restaurants and craft shops. There are tables in the pleasant courtyard.

El Mestizo
Upstairs at Portal Unión 37, Plaza Mayor.
Mon-Sat 0800-2300.
Restaurant, café and art gallery serving regional specialities, vegetarian and international dishes. Tranquil atmosphere in a colonial *casona*.

Frutimix
Portal Independencia 56, and Jr 9 de Diciembre 427.
Shakes, frapps (Baileys, chocolate or frapuccino), modern and tasty.

La Miel
Portal Constitución 11-12, on the Plaza.
Daily 1000-2300.
Good coffee, hot drinks, juices, shakes, cakes and snacks, also ice creams.

Bars and clubs

Punto Caliente
Jr Asamblea 187. Daily from 1830 until the night is over.
Music, drinks, pizzas and karaoke, upscale.

Tupana Wasy
Jr 9 de Diciembre 213, 3rd floor.
Live contemporary and traditional Andean music. On the 2nd floor is **Toto's Night**, another pub.

Festivals

The area is well known for its festivals throughout the year. Almost every day there is a celebration in one of the surrounding villages; check with the tourist office.

Feb Carnaval. Reported to be a wild affair.
Mar/Apr Semana Santa begins on the Fri before Holy Week. There follows one of the world's finest Holy Week celebrations, with candle-lit nightly processions, floral 'paintings' on the streets, daily fairs (the biggest on Easter Sat), horse races and contests among peoples from all over central Peru. Prices double and all accommodation is fully booked for months in advance. Many people offer beds in their homes during the week. Look out for notices on the doors and in windows of transport companies.
25 Apr Anniversary of the founding of Huamanga province.
1-2 Nov Todos Los Santos and **Día de los Muertos**.
9 Dec Reenactment of the Battle of Ayacucho on the Pampa de Quinua.

Shopping

Handicrafts
Ayacucho is a good place to buy local crafts including filigree silver, which often uses *mudéjar* patterns. Also look out for little painted nativity scenes, carvings in local alabaster, harps, or the pre-Inca tradition of carving dried gourds. The most famous goods are carpets and retablos. In both weaving and retablos, scenes of recent political strife have been added to more traditional motifs. For carpets, go to Barrio Santa Ana (see page 1475). Also recommended is **Familia Pizarro** (Jr Perú 102, Barrio Belén), who produce textiles, *piedra huamanga* (sculptures in local alabaster) and carnival masks of good quality; all pieces are individually made. They also have rooms for visitors to stay and take classes. Edwin Pizarro (T966-180666) creates amazing altar-pieces.

Markets
Mercado 12 de Abril, *Chorro y San Juan de Dios*. For fruit and vegetables.
Shosaku Nagase, *Jr Quinua y Av Maravillas, opposite Plazoleta de María Parado de Bellido.* A large handicraft market.

What to do

A&R Tours, *Jr 9 de Diciembre 130, T066-311300, www.viajesartours.com. Daily 0800-2000.* Offers tours in and around the city.

Fly Travel, *Jr 9 de Diciembre 118, T066-313282, flytravel_ayp@hotmail.com.* Offers tours along 2 main circuits. To the north: Wari-Quinua-Huanta; south: Vilcashuamán-Cangallo.
Morochucos Rep's, *Jr 9 de Diciembre 136, T066-317844.* Dynamic company in business for over 30 years, with tours locally and to other parts of Peru, flight, train and bus tickets.
Urpillay Tours, *28 de Julio 262 (Plaza More), of 8, T066-315074, urpillaytours@ terra.com.* All local tours and flight tickets.
Wari Tours, *Lima 138, T066-311415.* Local tours.
Willy Tours, *Jr 9 de Diciembre 209, T066-314075.* Personal guides, also handles flight and bus tickets.

Transport

Air The airport is to the east of the city along Av Castilla. Taxi from airport to city centre, US$3. To/from **Lima**, 55 mins, with **LATAM** (Jr 9 de Diciembre 107), daily; **LC Peru** (Jr 9 de Diciembre 119, T066-312151), 2 daily; **StarPerú** (Portal Constitución 17, T066-316676).

Bus Long distance Bus terminal **Terrapuerto "Libertadores de América"** (Av Javier Pérez de Cuéllar s/n, T066-312666) is 10 mins northwest of centre. All bus companies are here, and **Cruz del Sur** also has its own terminal in the centre (Av Mcal Cáceres 1264, T066-312813).

To **Lima**, 8 hrs on a good paved road, via Ica, several companies US$14-22, including Expreso **Molina** (Jr 9 de Diciembre 459, T066-312984), 7 daily, 5 in the evening; **Cruz del Sur**, US$26 *regular*, US$37 *suite* and *VIP* services; **Tepsa**, US$37, presidencial; **Internacional Palomino** (Jr Manco Cápac 216, T066-313899), morning service, US$13-26; **Los Chankas** (Jr Manco Cápac 450, T066-401943), at 2000 hrs, US$10-16. For **Pisco**, 332 km, take an Ica/Lima bus and get out at San Clemente (10 mins from Pisco), 5 hrs, same fare as Ica; then take a bus or van.

To **Cuzco**, with **Los Chankas**, vans at 0720 to Andahuaylas, US$9, transfer there; buses at 2000 direct to Cuzco, US$18, some continue to Puerto Maldonado. Also **Señor De Huanca** (Pasaje Cáceres 166).

To **Huancayo**, 319 km, 9-10 hrs, US$10-13, 3 daily with **Molina**, also **Turismo Central** (Jr Manco Cápac 513, T066-317873), US$13 at 2030. The views are stunning.

For **Huancavelica**, **Expreso Molina** at 2100, US$13, 3 hrs, continuing to Huancayo, you must pay the full fare to there; also **Turismo Central** at 2030.

stop to stretch your legs on the journey to Cuzco

Beyond Ayacucho are two highland towns, Andahuaylas and Abancay, which are possible stopping or bus-changing places on the road to Cuzco. The road towards Cuzco climbs out of Ayacucho and crosses a wide stretch of high, treeless *páramo* before descending through Ocros to the Río Pampas. It then climbs up to Chincheros, 158 km from Ayacucho, and Uripa, which has a good Sunday market. Ayacucho to Andahuaylas is 261 km on a paved road. It's in good condition when dry, but landslides may occur in the wet. The scenery is stunning. Daytime buses stop for lunch at Chumbes, which has a few restaurants, a shop selling fruit, bread and *refrescos*, and some grim toilets.

Andahuaylas

Andahuaylas is about 80 km further on, at 3000 m in a fertile valley. It offers few exotic crafts, but beautiful scenery, great hospitality and a good market on Sunday. On the north side is the Municipalidad, with a small **Museo Arqueológico**, which has a collection of pre-Columbian objects, including mummies. A worthwhile excursion is to the **Laguna de Pacucha** ① *colectivo from Av Los Chankas y Av Andahuaylas, at the back of the market, US$1, 40 mins*. On the shore is the town of Pacucha, which has a family-run *hostal* ($) on the road from the plaza to the lake and various places to eat. A road follows the north shore of the lake and climbs to **Sóndor** ① *8-10 km from Pacucha, US$0.65; taxi from Andahuaylas, US$10, or colectivo towards Argama*. This Inca archaeological site at 3300 m has various buildings and small plazas leading up to a conical hill with concentric stone terracing and, at the summit, a large rock or *intihuatana*. **Sóndor Raymi** is celebrated here each year on 18-19 June. With any form of public transport, you will have to walk back to Pacucha, unless you are very lucky.

Abancay

Nestled between mountains in the upper reaches of a glacial valley, the town of Abancay is first glimpsed when you are many kilometres away. It is capital of the department of Apurimac, an important mining area. **Santuario Nacional de Ampay** ① *5 km north of town on a paved road (take a colectivo to Tamburco and ask the driver where to get off), US$1.50*, has two lakes called Ankasccocha (3200 m) and Uspaccocha (3820 m), a glacier (receding rapidly) on Ampay mountain at 5235 m and a forest of endemic *Intimpa* trees (*Podocarpus glomeratus*). It's a two-day trek to the glacier, with overnight camping.

Saywite

3 km from the main road, Km 49 from Abancay. US$4, students US$2.

Beyond the town of Curahuasi, 126 km before Cuzco, is the large carved rock of Saywite. It is a UNESCO World Heritage Site. The principal monolith is said to represent the three regions of jungle, sierra and coast, with the associated animals and Inca sites of each. It is fenced in, but ask the guardian for a closer look. It was defaced, allegedly, when a cast was taken, breaking off many of the animals' heads. Six further archaeological areas stretch away from the stone and its neighbouring group of buildings.

Listings Ayacucho to Cuzco

Tourist information

Abancay
Information is available from the **tourist office** (Lima 206, daily 0800-1430) or Dircetur (Av Arenas 121, p1, T083-321664 in Abancay).

Where to stay

Andahuaylas

$ El Encanto de Apurímac
Jr Ramos 401 (near Los Chankas and other buses), T083-723527.
With hot water, very helpful.

$ El Encanto de Oro
Av Pedro Casafranca 424, T083-423066, www.encantodeoro.4t.com.

Modern, comfy, hot water, laundry service, restaurant, organizes trips on request. Reserve in advance.

$ Las Américas
Jr Ramos 410, T083-721646.
Near buses, bit gloomy in public areas, rooms are fine if basic, cheaper without bath, hot water, helpful.

$ Sol de Oro
Jr Juan A Trelles 164, T083-721152.
Good value, good

Abancay

$$-$ Turistas
Av Díaz Barcenas 500, T083-321017,
www.turismoapurimac.com.
The original building is in colonial style, rooms a bit gloomy, breakfast not included. Newer rooms on top floor (best) and in new block are more expensive, including breakfast. Good restaurant ($$), wood panelled bar, parking.

$ Hostal Arenas
Av Arenas 192, T083-322107.
Well-appointed rooms, good beds, hot showers, helpful service, restaurant.

$ Imperial
Díaz Barcenas 517, T083-321538.
Great beds, hot water, spotless, very helpful, parking, good value, cheaper without bath or breakfast.

Restaurants

Andahuaylas

$ El Dragón
Jr Juan A Trellas 279.
A recommended chifa serving huge portions, excellent value (same owner as Hotel El Encanto de Apurímac).

$ Il Gatto
Jr G Cáceres 334.
A warm pizzeria, with wooden furniture, pizzas cooked in a wood-burning oven.

$ Nuevo Horizonte
Jr Constitución 426.
Vegetarian and health food restaurant, breakfast.

Abancay

$ Focarela Pizzería
Díaz Bárcenas 521, T083-322036.

Simple but pleasant decor, pizza from a wood-burning oven, fresh, generous toppings, popular.

$ Pizzería Napolitana
Díaz Barcenas 208.
Wood-fired clay oven, wide choice of toppings.

What to do

Abancay

Apurimak Tours, *at Hotel Turistas, see Where to stay.* Run local tours and 1- and 2-day trips to Santuario Nacional de Ampay: 1-day, 7 hrs, US$40 pp for 1-2 people (cheaper for more people). Also a 3-day trip to Choquequirao including transport, guide, horses, tents and food, just bring your sleeping-bag, US$60 pp. The hotel can also put you in touch with Carlos Valer, a very knowledgeable and kind guide.

Transport

Andahuaylas

To **Ayacucho**, with **Los Chankas** (Av José María Arguedas y Jr Trelles, T083-722441) 6 hrs, at 0600 and 1800 or 1840 (bus from Cuzco). To **Abancay**, 138 km, paved, 3-4 hrs, with **Señor de Huanca** (Av Martinelli 170, T083-721218), 3 a day, US$6, or **Los Chankas** at 0630, US$7.50. To **Cuzco**, with **San Jerónimo** (Av José María Arguedas 425, T083-801767), via Abancay, 1800 or 1830, also 1900 Sun, US$22, or **Los Chankas**. To **Lima**, buses go via Ayacucho or Pampachiri and Puquio, US$20. On all night buses, take a blanket.

Abancay

The Terminal Terrestre is on Av Pachacútec, on the west side of town. Taxi to centre, US$1, or it's a steep walk. All buses leave from Terminal Terrestre but several companies have offices on or near the El Olivo roundabout at Av Díaz Bárcenas y Gamarra; others are on Av Arenas.

To **Cuzco**, 195 km, 4½ hrs, US$14-18, with **Bredde** (Gamarra 423, T083-321643), 5 a day; **Molina** (Gamarra 422, T083-322646), 3 a day; **San Jerónimo**, at 2130; **Los Chankas** (Díaz Bárcenas 1011, El Olivo, T083-321485) and several others. To **Lima**, **Oltursa**, US$66, or **Tepsa** US$71; several others. The scenery en route is dramatic, especially as it descends into the Apurímac valley and climbs out again. To Andahuaylas, **Molina** at 2330; **San Jerónimo** at 2130; **Señor de Huanca** (Av Arenas 198, T083-322377), 3 a day; also Los Chankas.

A paved road heads north from La Oroya towards Cerro de Pasco and Huánuco. Just 25 km north of La Oroya a branch turns east towards Tarma, then descends to the little-visited jungles of the Selva Central. This is a really beautiful run. North of La Oroya the road crosses the great heights of the Junín pampa and the mining zone of Cerro de Pasco, before losing altitude on its way to the Huallaga Valley. On this route you can connect by road to the Cordillera Blanca via La Unión.

☆Selva Central

Founded in 1534, **Tarma** (60 km from La Oroya) has a charming Plaza de Armas and is notable for its Semana Santa celebrations (see Festivals, below) and its locally made fine flower-carpets. The town is noisy and dirty, mainly of interest as a transport hub, but the surrounding countryside offers some worthwhile excursions. **Acobamba**, a small town 9 km along the road to San Ramón (see below), provides access to the **Santuario de Muruhuay**, 2 km away, which has a venerated image of Christ painted on the rock behind the altar. High quality weavings are produced in **San Pedro de Cajas**, about 27 km northwest of Tarma, where you can visit the workshop of the Ulloa Bailón family (C San Pedro 1007, T964-243816), among others. There are petroglyphs at **Pintish Machay**, a good day-hike from the village of **Huaricolca**, 15 km south of Tarma along the road to Jauja.

Beyond Tarma the road is steep and crooked but there are few places where cars cannot pass one another. In the 80 km from Tarma to La Merced the road runs between great overhanging cliffs as it drops 2450 m and the vegetation changes dramatically from temperate to tropical. The first town in Chanchamayo Province is **San Ramón**, 11 km before La Merced. It has several hotels ($$$-$) and restaurants, and there are regular combis and *colectivos* between the two towns. **La Merced** lies in the fertile Chanchamayo valley. Asháninka *indígenas* can usually be found around the central plaza selling bows, arrows, necklaces and trinkets. There is a festival in the last week of September. There are several hotels ($$-$) and restaurants.

About 25 km from La Merced along the road to **Oxapampa**, a road turns northeast to Villa Rica, centre of an important coffee-growing area. From here, a poor dirt road continues northeast to **Puerto Bermúdez**. This authentic jungle town, at the geographic centre of Peru, has grown up along the now seldom-used airstrip. It lies on the Río Pichis, an affluent of the Pachitea, and is a great base for exploring further into the Selva Central, with trips upriver to the Asháninka community. Tours are arranged by **Albergue Cultural Humboldt** (see Where to stay, below). To go further downriver to Pucallpa, there is road transport via Ciudad Constitución, about US$20 over two stages.

Pampas de Junín

The road north from La Oroya runs up the Mantaro Valley through canyons to the wet and mournful Junín pampa at over 4250 m, one of the world's largest high-altitude plains. An obelisk marks the battlefield where the Peruvians under Bolívar defeated the Spaniards in 1824 (celebrated on 6 August annually). Blue peaks line the pampa in a distant wall. This windswept sheet of yellow grass is bitterly cold and the only signs of life are the youthful herders with their sheep and llamas. The road follows the east shores of Lago Junín. The town of **Junín** lies some distance south of the lake and has the desolate feel of a high *puna* town, bisected by the railway; it has several basic hotels. The **Junín National Reserve** ① US$5, ticket from Sernanp in Junín, Jr San Martín 138, T064-344146, protects one of the best birdwatching sites in the central Andes where the giant coot and even flamingos may be spotted. It is easiest to visit from the village of Huayre, 5 km south of Carhuamayo, from where it is a 20-minute walk down to the lake. Fishermen are usually around to take visitors out on the lake.

Cerro de Pasco and around *Colour map 3, B3.*

This long-established mining centre, 130 km from La Oroya, is not attractive, but is nevertheless very friendly. Copper, zinc, lead, gold and silver are mined here, and coal comes from the deep canyon of Goyllarisquisga, 42 km north of Cerro de Pasco. It is the highest coal mine in the world and its name translates as the 'place where a star fell'. The town is sited between Lago Patarcocha and the huge abyss of the mine above which its buildings and streets cling precariously. Nights are bitterly cold here at 4330 m. Southwest of Cerro de Pasco by 40 km is **Santuario Huayllay (Bosque de Piedras)**

① *information from Sernanp in Junín, US$1; camping permitted; minibuses to Huallay depart from Cerro de Pasco's terminal throughout the day, about 1 hr, US$1; last return 1800.* These unique weathered limestone formations at 4100-4600 m are in the shape of a tortoise, elephant, alpaca, and more. They can be explored on 11 tourist circuits through the rock formations. The village of **Huallay** is 6 km southwest of the sanctuary; it has a municipal hostel and other hotels. A festival of sports and music is held here on 6-8 September.

Huánuco and around

The Central Highway from Cerro de Pasco continues northeast another 528 km to Pucallpa, the limit of navigation for large Amazon river boats. The first part of this road has been rebuilt into an all-weather highway, and the sharp descent along the nascent **Río Huallaga** is a tonic to travellers suffering from *soroche*. The road drops 2436 m in the 100 km from Cerro de Pasco to Huánuco, most of it in the first 32 km. From the bleak high ranges the road plunges below the tree line offering great views. The only town of any size before Huánuco is **Ambo**. Huánuco itself is an attractive Andean town on the Upper Huallaga with an interesting market. Situated between the highlands and jungle at 1894 m, it has a particularly pleasant climate.

Located 5 km west of Huánuco on the road to La Unión is **Kótosh** ① *US$0.75, including a guide (in Spanish); taxi from Huánuco, US$5 including a 30-min wait.* Investigations suggest that this archaeological site, at an altitude of 1912 m, was occupied for over 2000 years. Six distinct phases of occupation have been identified, the oldest of which dates back some 4000 years. The Temple of Crossed Hands dates from 2000 BC and was once regarded as the 'oldest temple in the Americas'. Further afield in the **Alto Marañón** region of the departments of Huánuco and Ancash are the widely dispersed sites of the little-known **Yarowilca** culture, with many impressive multi-storey stone structures. For more information contact **High Tours** in Huánuco (page 1484).

La Unión and around

From Huánuco, a spectacular but poor dirt road leads to **La Unión**, capital of Dos de Mayo district. It's a fast-developing town with a couple of simple hotels ($) and restaurants, but electricity can be a problem and it gets very cold at night. On the pampa above La Unión are the Inca ruins of ☆**Huánuco Viejo** (or **Huánuco Pampa**) ① *2½ hrs' walk from La Unión, entry US$1.50; taxi from La Unión, US$6.50-9.50 with wait*, a temple-fortress with residential quarters. The site has examples of very fine Inca stonework comparable with anything to be seen in Cuzco. It is the only major Inca settlement on the royal highway not to have been built over by a colonial or modern town.

> **Tip...**
> One of the finest stretches of the Royal Inca Road, or Capaq Ñan, runs from Huánuco Viejo to the **Callejón de Conchucos**. Some tour operators in Huaraz (page 1292) offer this trek.

Listings East and north of La Oroya

Tourist information

Selva Central
There is a **tourist office** on the plaza in Tarma (Arequipa 259, T064-638750, Mon-Fri 0800-1300, 1500-1800) is very helpful, mostly Spanish spoken; see also www.tarma.info. In La Merced, visit **Dircetur** (Pardo 110, San Ramón, T064-331265).

Huánuco and around
The **tourist office** is on the plaza (Gen Prado 716, T062-512980). A website giving local information is www.webhuanuco.com.

Where to stay

Selva Central

Tarma

$$$ Hacienda Santa María
2 km out of town at Vista Alegre 1249, Sacsamarca, T064-321232.
A beautiful (non-working) 17th-century hacienda, beautiful gardens and antique furniture. Includes breakfast. Excellent guides for local day trips.

$$$ Los Portales
Av Castilla 512, T064-321411,
www.losportaleshoteles.com.pe.
On the edge of town, hot water, heating, 1950s
building with old furnishings, includes breakfast,
good restaurant.

$$$-$$ Hacienda La Florida
6 km from Tarma, T064-341041,
www.haciendalaflorida.com.
18th-century working hacienda owned by
German-Peruvian couple Inge and Pepe, who
also arrange excursions. Variety of rooms
sleeping 1-4, adjoining family rooms, dorm for
groups and an independent house; all with
hot water, meals available, lots of home-grown
organic produce. Also camping for US$5.

$$ Los Balcones
Jr Lima 370, 064-323600.
Good location near the plaza, all rooms are
non-smoking, some with balcony and frigobar,
indoor parking.

$$ Normandie
Beside the Santuario de Muruhuay,
Acobamba, T064-341028, Lima T01-365 9795,
www.hotelnormandie.com.pe.
Rooms with hot water, bar, restaurant,
tours offered.

$ Hospedaje Residencial El Dorado
Huánuco 488, T064-321914, www.
hospedajeeldoradotarma.com.
Hot water, ample rooms set round a patio, 1st floor
better, includes simple breakfast, safe, welcoming,
secure parking. Older place but well cared for.

$ Tampu Wasi
*Jr Amazonas 798, T064-321744, and Jr Huánuco
235, T064-323128.*
Rooms with private bath, electric shower,
parking. Nice place, good value.

Puerto Bermúdez

$ Albergue Cultural Humboldt
By the river port (La Rampa), T063-963-722363,
http://alberguehumboldt.free.fr.
The owner, Basque writer Jesús, has created a
real haven for backpackers, with maps, library
and book exchange. Rooms sleep 1-3, or there
are hammocks and tents. Meals available,
Spanish and Peruvian food. Jesús arranges
tours, from day trips to camping and trekking
in primary forest.

Pampas de Junín

Carhuamayo is the best place to stay when
visiting the reserve. **Gianmarco** (Maravillas 454)
and **Patricia** (Tarapacá 862) are the best of several
basic *hostales*. There are numerous restaurants
along the main road.

Cerro de Pasco and around

$ Hostal Arenales
Jr Arenales 162, near the bus station,
T063-723088.
Modern, TV, hot water in the morning.

$ Señorial
Jr San Martín 1, in the district of San Juan,
5 mins north of Cerro by taxi, T063-422802,
hotelsenorial@hotmail.com.
The most comfortable in town, hot water,
fine view across the mine pit.

$ Welcome
*Av La Plata 125, opposite the entrance to the bus
station, T063-721883.*
Some rooms without window, hot water 24 hrs.

Huánuco and around

$$$ Grand Hotel Huánuco (Inka Comfort)
Jr D Beraún 775, T062-514222,
www.grandhotelhuanuco.com.
With restaurant, pool, sauna, gym and parking.

$ El Roble
Constitución 629, T062-512515.
Without bath, cheap and good value.

$ Hostal Miraflores
Valdizán 560, T062-512848,
www.granhostalmiraflores.com.
Hot water, private bathroom, quiet, safe,
laundry service.

$ Imperial
Huánuco 581, T062-518737.
With hot showers, quiet and helpful.

$ Las Vegas
28 de Julio 940, on Plaza de Armas, T062-512315.
Small rooms, hot water, restaurant next door. Good.

Restaurants

Selva Central

Tarma

$ Chavín
Jr Lima 270 at Plaza de Armas. Daily 0730-2230.

Very good quality and variety in set meals (weekdays only), also à la carte.

$ Chifa Roberto Siu
Jr Lima 569 upstairs.
A good option for Chinese food, popular with locals.

$ Comedor Vegetariano
Arequipa 695. Open 0700-2100, but closed Fri after lunch and Sat.
Vegetarian, small and cheap, sells great bread.

Cerro de Pasco and around

$ Los Angeles
Jr Libertad, near the market.
Excellent *menú* for US$1.50. Recommended.

$ San Fernando
Bakery in the plaza. Opens at 0700.
Great hot chocolate, bread and pastries.

Huánuco and around

$ Chifa Men Ji
28 de Julio, block 8.
Good prices, nice Chinese food.

$ Govinda
Prado 608.
Reckoned to be the best vegetarian restaurant.

$ La Olla de Barro
Gral Prado 852, close to main plaza.
Serves typical food, good value.

$ Pizzería Don Sancho
Prado 645.
Best pizzas in town.

Festivals

Selva Central
Mar/Apr The **Semana Santa** celebrations at Tarma are spectacular, with a very colourful Easter Sun morning procession in the main plaza. Accommodation is hard to find at this time, but you can apply to the Municipalidad for rooms with local families.

Pampas de Junín
6 Aug Colourful ceremony to commemorate the **Batalla de Junín** (1824), which was fought on the nearby Pampas de Junín, marking a decisive victory in favour of the independence of Peru and South America. The town fills with visitors, prices rise and hotel rooms are scarce.

Huánuco and around
20-25 Feb Carnaval Huanuqueño.
3 May La Cruz de Mayo.
16 Jul Fiesta de la Virgen del Carmen.
12-18 Aug Tourist week.
28-29 Oct Fiesta del Señor de Burgos, the patron of Huánuco.
25 Dec Fiesta de los Negritos.

La Unión and around
27 Jul Fiesta del Sol. Major annual festival at Huánuco Viejo. Lodgings in La Unión are almost impossible to find at this time.

What to do

Selva Central

Tarma
Max Aventura, *Jr 2 de Mayo 682, T064-323908, www.maxaventuraperu.com.* Reliable operator offering tours around Tarma, Lago Junín, and into the Chanchamayo region. Uses good vehicles.

Huánuco and around
High Tours, *Jr Dámaso Beraún 849, T062-517203, www.hightoursperu.com.* Local, regional and Peru-wide tours including trekking, rafting and Yarowilca archaeological sites.

Transport

Selva Central

Tarma
Bus Most buses and vans leave from the Terminal Terrestre at the west end of Jr Lima. Some companies also have private terminals. Beware overcharging by *colectivo* drivers. To **Lima**, 231 km (paved and congested with heavy traffic), 6-9 hrs, US$10-15, with the following companies: **Transportes Junín** (Amazonas 669; in Lima at Av Nicolás Arriola 198, T01-224 9220), 6 a day, with *bus cama* at night; **Trans La Merced** (in Lima at Av 28 de Julio 1581, La Victoria), 3 a day; **Trans Los Canarios** (Jr Amazonas 694), 2 daily starting in Tarma; **Transportes Chanchamayo** (Callao 1002, T064-321882), 2 a day, en route from Chanchamayo. To **Jauja**, US$2, and **Huancayo**, US$3, from the stadium, 0800-1800, every 1½ hrs; also **Trans Los Canarios** about 1 per hr, 0500-1800, and **Trans Junín** at 1200 and 2400; *colectivos* depart when full from Callao y Jauja, 2 hrs, US$4, and 3 hrs, US$6, respectively. To **Cerro de Pasco**, **Empresa Junín**

(Amazonas 450), 4 a day, 3 hrs, US$2.50; also *colectivos* when full, 2 hrs, US$4. To **La Oroya**, **buses** leave from opposite the Terminal, 1 hr, US$1.50, while *colectivos* leave from petrol station on Av Castilla block 5, 45 mins, US$2. To **San Ramón**, US$1.75, 1½ hrs, with **Trans Junín**, 4 a day, continuing to La Merced, US$2.75, 2 hrs; vans US$1.75, and *colectivos*, US$4, depart from the stadium to La Merced. Combis and *colectivos* run along Jr Huánuco by the Mercado Modelo to **Acobamba** and up to **Muruhuay**, 15 mins, US$0.30 and US$0.45 respectively.

Chanchamayo

Air Flights leave from San Ramón. There is a small airstrip where **Aero Montaña**, T064-331074 has air taxis that can be chartered (*viaje especial*) to the jungle towns, with a maximum of 3 people, but you have to pay for the pilot's return to base. Flights cost US$250 per hr. **Puerto Bermúdez** takes 33 mins. You can also just go to the air base, across the river, on the east side of town.

Bus Many buses go to La Merced from **Lima**: **Expreso Satipo**, **Junín**, **La Merced** and **Chanchamayo** each have several buses during the day, US$8 *regular*, US$11 *cama* upper level, US$12.50 *cama* lower level, 7-8 hrs. To **Tarma**, with **Transportes Angelitos/San Juan**, hourly, 2½ hrs, US$1.75, or *colectivos*, just over 1 hr, US$4. To **Puerto Bermúdez**, **Empresa Transdife** and **Villa Rica** have 4WD pick-ups between 0400 and 0600 and may pick up passengers at their hotels. You must purchase tickets in advance, the vehicles get very full, US$14 in front, US$8 in the back (worth spending the extra money), 8-10 hrs or more.

Cerro de Pasco and around

Bus There is a large bus station. To **Lima** several companies including **Carhuamayo** and **Transportes Apóstol San Pedro**, hourly 0800-1200, plus 4 departures 2030-2130, 8 hrs, US$8. If there are no convenient daytime buses, you could change buses in La Oroya. Buses leave when full, about every 20-30 mins, to **Carhuamayo** (1 hr, US$1), **Junín** (1½ hrs, US$1) and **La Oroya** (2½ hrs, US$2); *colectivos* also depart with a similar frequency, 1½ hrs, US$2.50, to La Oroya. To **Tarma**, **Empresa Junín**, at 0600, 1500, 3 hrs, $2.50; *colectivos* also depart hourly, 1½ hrs, US$4. To **Huancayo**, various companies leave throughout the day, 5 hrs, US$4. To

Huánuco, buses and cars leave when full, about half hourly, 2½ hrs and 1½ hrs, US$2 and US$4 respectively.

Huánuco and around

Air The airport (T062-513066) is served by flights from **Lima**, with **StarPerú** and **LCPeru** (2 de Mayo 1355, T062-518113), daily, 55 mins.

Bus To **Lima**, US$18-25, 8 hrs, with **León de Huánuco** (Malecón Alomía Robles 821), 3 a day; also **Bahía Continental** (Valdizán 718), recommended, and **Transportes El Rey**. The majority of buses of all companies leave 2030-2200, most also offer a bus at 0900-1000. A *colectivo* to Lima, costing US$23, leaves at 0400, arriving at 1400; book the night before at Gen Prado 607, 1 block from the plaza; recommended. To **Cerro de Pasco**, 3 hrs, US$2, *colectivos* under 2 hrs, US$4; all leave when full from the Ovalo Carhuayna on the north side of the city, 3 km from the centre. To **Huancayo**, 7 hrs, US$6, with **Turismo Central** (Tarapacá 530), at 2100. *Colectivos* run to **Tingo María**, from block 1 of Prado close to Puente Calicanto, 2½ hrs, US$5; also **Etnasa**, 3-4 hrs, US2. For **Pucallpa**, take a *colectivo* to Tingo María, then a bus from there.

To **La Unión**, **Turismo Unión**, daily 0730, 7 hrs, US$5; also **Turismo Marañón**, daily 0700; this is a rough road operated also by El Niño *colectivos* (Aguilar 530), which leave when full, US$7.15.

La Unión and around

Bus To **Huánuco** with **Turismo Unión** (Jr Comercio 1224), daily at 0600, US$8, 7 hrs; also **Turismo Marañón** (Jr Comercio 1309), daily at 0700 (no afternoon/evening departures), and El Niño *colectivos* (Jr Comercio 12, T062-515952), 5 hrs. To **Huallanca** (for access to Huaraz and the Cordillera Blanca), combis leave from the market, about hourly, when full and follow the attractive Vizcarra valley, 1 hr, US$2. **El Rápido** runs to **Huaraz** 0400, 4½ hrs, US$8, or change in Huallanca.

Amazon Basin

The Amazon Basin covers a staggering 4,000,000 sq km, but despite the fact that 60% of Peru is covered by this green carpet of jungle, less than 14% of its population lives here, meaning that much of Peru's rainforest is still intact. It is home to 2000 species of fish, 300 mammal species, over 10% of the world's 8600 bird species and, together with the adjacent Andean foothills, 4000 butterfly species. This incredible biological diversity is coupled with acute ecological fragility: petroleum exploitation, gold mining and colonization from the highlands are perennial threats.

The principal means of communication in the jungle is by its many rivers, the most important being the Amazon, which rises high up in the Andes as the Marañón, then joins the Ucayali to become the longest river in the world. The two major tourist areas in the Peruvian Amazon are the northern and southern jungles. Wildlife-viewing in these two areas is quite different. Northeastern Peru is dominated by flood plains and vast rivers, with much of the land regularly submerged. There are chances of seeing manatees, giant otters and pink and grey Amazonian dolphins. The Southern Amazon has faster-running rivers and rapids unsuited to dolphins and manatees, but a huge variety of habitats mean there are more bird species here. Moreover, in protected areas such as Manu and Tambopata, tapir, giant anteaters, otters and primates are fairly easy to spot due to the lack of hunting pressure.

From Huánuco to Pucallpa

experience the transition from Andes to Amazon

Huánuco to Tingo María
The journey to Tingo María from Huánuco, 135 km, is very dusty but gives a good view of the jungle. Some 25 km beyond Huánuco the paved road begins a sharp climb to the heights of Carpish (3023 m). A descent of 58 km brings it to the Río Huallaga again; it then continues along the river to Tingo María. Landslides along this section are frequent and construction work causes delays. On this route it is advisable to travel only by day.

Tingo María
Tingo María is situated on the Río Huallaga, in the Ceja de Montaña (literally 'eyebrow of the mountain'). The Cordillera Azul, the front range of the Andes, covered with jungle-like vegetation to its top, separates this transition zone from the jungle lowlands to the east. The meeting here of highlands and jungle makes

Tip...
If you're venturing into the Peruvian Amazon, make sure you are properly equipped. Take a long-sleeved shirt, waterproof coat and shoes or light boots on jungle trips, plus binoculars and a good torch, as well as espirales to ward off the mosquitoes at night. 'Premier' is the most effective local insect repellent.

Best for
Ecotourism ▪ River trips ▪ Wildlife watching

the landscape extremely striking. Tingo María is isolated for days in the rainy season. Annual rainfall here is 2642 mm, but the altitude prevents the climate from being oppressive. Bananas, sugar cane, cocoa, rubber, tea and coffee are grown, but the main crop of the area is coca, grown on the *chacras* (smallholdings) in the countryside, and sold legitimately and otherwise in Tingo María.

The mountain that can be seen from all over the town is called La Bella Durmiente (the Sleeping Beauty). A small university outside the town, beyond the **Hotel Madera Verde**, has a little **museum-cum-zoo** ① *free but a small tip is appreciated*; it also maintains botanical gardens in the town. About 6.5 km from Tingo, on a rough road, is a fascinating cave, the **Cueva de las Lechuzas** ① *US$1 for the cave, take a torch, and do not wear open shoes; to get there, take a motorcycle-taxi from town, US$1.75,* crossing the Río Monzón by new bridge. There are many oilbirds in the cave and many small parakeets near the entrance.

Tingo María to Pucallpa

From Tingo María to the end of the road at Pucallpa is 255 km, with a climb over the watershed – the Cordillera Azul – between the Huallaga and Ucayali rivers. The road is in poor shape for most of the journey, but some paving has been completed and the entire route is scheduled to be improved. Travel by day: it is safer and the views are tremendous as you go from the high jungle to the Amazon Basin; sit on the right-hand side of the bus. When the road was being surveyed it was thought that the lowest pass over the Cordillera Azul was over 3650 m high, but then an old document was discovered, stating that a Father Abad had found a pass through these mountains in 1757. As a consequence, the road goes through the **Boquerón del Padre Abad**, a gigantic gap 4 km long and 2000 m deep. At the top of the pass is a Peruvian customs house – the jungle land to the east is a free zone – beyond which the road bed is along the floor of a magnificent canyon. It is a beautiful trip through luxuriant jungle, ferns and sheer walls of bare rock, punctuated by occasional waterfalls plunging into the roaring torrent below. East of the foot of the pass the paved road goes over the flat pampa, with few bends, to the village of **Aguaytía**, where there is a narcotics police outpost, fuel station, accommodation and restaurants. From Aguaytía the road, paved in parts, continues for 160 km to Pucallpa – five hours by bus. There is a service station three hours before Pucallpa.

Pucallpa *Colour map 3, B3.*

Pucallpa is a rapidly expanding jungle town on the Río Ucayali, navigable by vessels of 3000 tons from Iquitos, 533 nautical miles away. Different 'ports' are used depending on the level of the river; they are all just mud banks without any facilities (see Transport, below). The economy of the area includes sawmills, plywood factories, oil refinery, fishing and boat building. Large discoveries of oil and gas are being explored. The town is hot and dusty between June and November and muddy from December to May. **Museo Regional in the Parque Natural de Pucallpa** ① *Cra Federico Basadre Km 4.2, Mon-Fri 0800-1630, Sat and Sun 0900-1730, park entry US$1.10,* has examples of Shipibo ceramics, as well as some delightful pickled snakes and other reptiles.

Lago Yarinacocha

Northeast of Pucallpa, 20 mins by colectivo or bus along Jr Ucayali, US$0.50, or 15 mins by taxi.

The main attraction in this area is **Lago Yarinacocha**, an oxbow lake linked to the Río Ucayali by a canal at the northern tip of its west arm. River dolphins can be seen here. **Puerto Callao**, also known as **Yarinacocha** or Yarina, is the main town at the southern tip, reached by road from Pucallpa. There are a number of restaurants and bars here and it is popular at weekends. From the town, a road continues along the western arm to **San José**, **San Francisco** and **Santa Clara** (bus US$0.75). The area is populated by the Shipibo people, who make ceramic and textile crafts. The area between the eastern arm of the lake and the Río Ucayali has been designated a reserve and incorporates the beautifully located **Jardín Botánico Chullachaqui** ① *free, reached by boat from Puerto Callao to Pueblo Nueva Luz de Fátima, 45 mins, then a 1-hr walk.* For more information ask at Moroti-Shobo on the Plaza de Armas in Puerto Callao.

Tourist information

Tingo María

The **tourist office** is at Av Ericson 158, T062-562310, perucatapress@gmail.com. The **municipality** (Alameda Perú 525, T062-562058) also provides information, and the tourist police has an office in the municipal offices.

Pucallpa

Tourist information is available from **Dircetur** (Jr 2 de Mayo 111, T061-575110, Mon-Fri 0730-1300, 1330-1515) and from **Gobierno Regional de Ucayali** (GOREU; Raimondi block 220, T061-575018).

Where to stay

Tingo María

$$ Albergue Ecológico Villa Jennifer
Km 3.4 Carretera a Castillo Grande, 10 mins from Tingo María, T962-603509, www.villajennifer.com.
Danish-Peruvian owned, includes breakfast, 2- to 4-night packages, US$50-90, and tours to local sites, pool, mini-zoo, birdwatching, restaurant, laundry service, phone ahead to arrange bus station pick-up. Rooms are surrounded by local flora, with lots of birdlife.

$$ Madera Verde
Av Universitaria s/n, out of town on the road to Huánuco, near the University, T062-561800, www.maderaverdehotel.com.pe.
Wooden chalets, cabins and rooms in beautiful surroundings, breakfast included, restaurant, 2 swimming pools, butterfly farm, free entry to wildlife rescue centre.

$$ Nueva York
Av Alameda Perú 553, T062-562406, joferjus@hotmail.com.
Central and noisy, cheaper without bath and TV, laundry, good value, restaurant.

Pucallpa

$$$ Casa Andina Select
Jr Sucre 198, T06-586600, www.casa-andina.com.
Centrally located luxury hotel, rooms and suites with a/c, frigobar, safety box, restaurant, pool. Part of the Casa Andina hotel chain.

$$$-$$ Grand Hotel Mercedes
Raimondi 610, T061-575120, www.granhotelmercedes.com.
Pucallpa's 1st hotel, still family-run, with some refurbished rooms, modern facilities with old-fashioned ambiance, includes breakfast, hot water, a/c, fridge, pool, restaurant.

$$ Antonio's
Jr Progreso 545, T061-573721, www.antonioshotel.com.pe.
A variety of rooms and prices, garden, pool, jacuzzi, parking, airport pick-up.

$$ Komby
Ucayali 360, T061-571562, http://kombypucallpa.com.
Cold water, fan or a/c, ample rooms, pool, very noisy street but back rooms are quiet, good value, free airport pick-up.

$$-$ Arequipa
Jr Progreso 573, T061-571348, www.hostal-arequipa.com.
Good, a/c or fan, breakfast, comfortable, safe, restaurant, pool.

$ Barbtur
Raimondi 670, T061-572532.
Cheaper without bath, central, good beds, cold water, friendly but noisy.

Lago Yarinacocha

$$$ pp Yarina Ecolodge (Pandisho Amazon Ecolodge)
North of the village of 11 de Agosto, towards the northern tip of the eastern shore of the west arm, T061-799214 (in Pucallpa, Pasaje Bolívar 261, T961-994227).
Full board, good resort with cabins by the lakeshore, includes packages of varying length and rainforest expeditions. Also has a lodge in Pacaya-Samiria, Amazon Green.

Restaurants

Pucallpa

$$-$ C'est si bon
Jr Independencia 560 y Pasaje Zegarra, Plaza de Armas. Daily 0800-2400.
Chicken, snacks, drinks, sweets, ice cream.

Shopping

Pucallpa

Many Shibipo women carry and sell their products around Pucallpa and Yarinacocha. For local wood carvings visit the workshop of **Agustín Rivas** (Jr Tarapacá 861/863, above a small restaurant; ask for it), whose work is made from huge tree roots. **Artesanías La Anaconda** (Pasaje Cohen by Plaza de Armas) has a good selection of indigenous crafts.

Festivals

Pucallpa

Local festivals are **Carnival** in **Feb**, **San Juan** on **24 Jun**, and the Ucayali regional fair in **Oct**.

What to do

Pucallpa

Usko Ayar Amazonian School of Painting, *Jr LM Sánchez Cerro 465-467, T958-623871, see Facebook page*. Located in the house of artist and healer Pablo Amaringo, who died in 2009, the renowned school provides art classes for local people and is dependent upon selling their art. It welcomes overseas visitors for short or long stays to study painting and learn Spanish and/or to teach English to Peruvian students.

Transport

Tingo María

Air To/from **Lima** Mon-Fri, 1 hr 10 mins, with **LCPerú** (Av Raymiondi 571, Rupa Rupa, T062-561672).

Bus To **Huánuco**, 119 km, 3-4 hrs, US$2 with **Etnasa** (not recommended due to theft and drug-trafficking); instead take a micro, US$2, or *colectivo*, US$5, 2 hrs, several daily. Direct buses continue to Lima, 10 hrs, with **Turismo Central** (Raimondi cuadra 9, T062-562668; in Lima at Av N Arriola 515, La Victoria, T01-472 7565, www.turismocentral.com.pe); **Transmar** (Av E Pimentel 147, T062-564733; in Lima at Av 28 de Julio 1511 and Av N Arriola 197, T01-265 0190, www.transmar.com.pe); **GM Internacional** (Av Raimondi 740, T062-561895; in Lima at Av 28 de Julio 1275, T01-715 3122, www.gm

internacional.com.pe), and **Bahía Continental** (recommended, T01-424 1539), US$18-30.

To **Pucallpa**, 5 hrs, US$15 with **Ucayali Express** *colectivos* (Raimondi y Callao) and **Selva Express** (Av Tito Jaime 218, T062-562380). Buses take 7-8 hrs, US$9.

Pucallpa

Air To **Lima** and **Iquitos**, daily 1 hr, with **LATAM** (Jr Tarapacá 805, T061-579840), **Peruvian** (Independencia 324, T061-505655) and **Star Perú** (7 de Junio 865, T061-590585). To **Tarapoto**, 3 weekly with **North American** (Av Aeropuerto, T961-717276, www.northamerican.pe), they also fly to regional destinations. Airport taxis charge US$6 to town; other taxis charge US$3.

Bus There are regular bus services to **Lima**, several companies, 18-20 hrs (longer in the rainy season, Nov-Mar), including **Transmar** (Av Raimondi 793, T061-579778); fares range from US$17.50 *regular* to US$43 for top level *bus cama*. To **Tingo María**, bus US$9, 7-8 hrs, bound for Lima, also **Etposa** (7 de Junio 843) at 1700; or by combi, 5 hrs, US$15, with **Turismo Ucayali** (7 de Junio 799, T061-593002) and **Selva Express** (Jr 7 de Junio 841, T061-579098). Take blankets as the crossing of the Cordillera at night is bitterly cold.

Ferry Boats to all destinations dock around Puerto Inmaculada, 2 blocks downriver from the Malecón Grau, at the bottom of Jr Inmaculada, unless the water level is very high, in which case they dock at Puerto Manantay, 4 km south of town. A mototaxi to any of the ports costs US$0.75 from the Plaza de Armas; taxis charge US$3.

To **Iquitos** down the Ucayali and Amazon rivers, 3-4 days, longer if the water level is low when larger boats must travel only by day, hammock US$40, berth US$140 double. **Henry** is a large company with departures Mon, Wed, Fri and Sat from Puerto Henry at the bottom of Jr Manco Capac, by Jr Arica; their newer boats, *Henry 6* and *7*, have some cabins with private bath. Another good boat is *Pedro Martín 2* sailing from Puerto Inmaculada. You must ask around for the large boats to Iquitos. Departure times are marked on chalk boards on the deck. Schedules seem to change almost hourly. Do not pay for your trip before you board the vessel, and only pay the captain. Some boat captains may allow you to live on board for a couple of days before sailing. Bottled drinking water can be bought in Pucallpa, but not cheaply. See also Getting around, page 1514.

The Río Huallaga winds northwards for 930 km from its source to the confluence with the Marañón. The Upper Huallaga is a torrent, dropping 15.8 m per km between its source and Tingo María. In contrast, the Lower Huallaga moves through an enervation of flatness. Its main port, Yurimaguas, lies below the last rapids and only 150 m above the Atlantic Ocean yet is distant from that ocean by over a month's voyage. Between the Upper and Lower rivers lies the Middle Huallaga, the third of the river that is downstream from Tingo María and upstream from Yurimaguas.

Yurimaguas *Colour map 3, A2.*

Yurimaguas is connected by road with the Pacific coast, via Tarapoto (120 km) and Moyobamba (see page 1354). It's a very relaxed jungle town and, as the roadhead on the lower Río Huallaga, is an ideal starting point for river travel in the Peruvian Amazon. A colourful Mercado Central is open every morning, full of fruit and jungle

> **Tip...**
> There are several banks with ATMs in town and **Casa de Cambio Progreso** (Progreso 117) changes US$ cash.

animals, many, sadly, for the pot. The town's patron saint, La Santísima Virgen de las Nieves, is celebrated from 5 to 15 August each year, which coincides with tourism week. Excursions in the area include the gorge of Shanusi and the lakes of Mushuyacu and Sanango.

☆ Reserva Nacional Pacaya-Samiria

SERNANP, Jorge Chávez 930/942, Iquitos, T065-223555, Mon-Fri 0700-1300, 1500-1700. Entry US$2 for 1 day, US$23 for 3 days, US$46 for 7 days, payable at the ranger stations.

Northeast of Yurimaguas, this vast reserve is bounded by the rivers Marañón and Ucuyali, narrowing to their confluence near the town of Nauta. At 2,080,000 ha, it is the country's second-largest protected area. The reserve's waterways and wetlands provide habitat for several cats (including puma and jaguar), manatee, tapir, river dolphins, giant otters, black cayman, boas, 269 species of fish and 449 bird species. Many of the animals found here are in danger of extinction. There are 208 population centres in the area of the reserve, 92 within the park, the others in the buffer zone. Five native groups plus colonos live in the region.

The reserve can only be visited with an authorized guide arranged through a tour operator or a local community tourism association. Native guides generally speak only Spanish and native tongues. Most of the reserve is off-limits to tourists, but eight areas have been set up for visitors. These have shelters or camping areas; conditions are generally simple and may require sleeping in hammocks. Trips are mostly on the river and often include fishing. Four circuits are most commonly offered. All are rich in wildlife.

The basin of the Yanayacu and Pucate rivers is the most frequently visited area and includes Laguna El Dorado, an important attraction. This area is accessed from **Nauta** on the Marañón, 1½-2 hours by paved road from Iquitos. It's three hours by *peque peque* or 1½ hours by *deslizador* from Nauta to the reserve. Note that Nauta has pirate guides, so it's best to arrange a tour with an operator.

The middle and lower Samiria is accessed from **Leoncio Prado** (which has a couple of *hospedajes*), 24 hours by *lancha* from Iquitos along the Marañón. Several lakes are found in this area.

The lower Pacaya, mostly flooded forest, is accessed from **Bretaña** on the Canal de Puinahua, a shortcut on the Ucuyali, 24 hours by lancha from Iquitos. This area is less frequently visited than others.

The Tibilo-Pastococha area in the western side of the park, also in the Samiria basin, is accessed from **Lagunas**, on the Río Huallaga. It's 10-12 hours by lancha or three hours by *deslizador* from Yurimaguas, 17 hours by *deslizador* from Nauta and 48 hours by *lancha* from Iquitos. All river traffic from Yurimaguas to Iquitos stops here.

Another way of visiting the reserve is on a cruise, sailing along the main rivers on the periphery of the park. These tours are offered by some Iquitos operators.

Tourist information

Yurimaguas

Ask for information at the **Municipalidad Provincial de Alto Amazonas** (Plaza de Armas 112-114, T065-351213), or see www.yurimaguas.net.

Pacaya-Samiria Reserve

General information and a list of authorized community associations and operators is found on the reserve's web page, at the reserve office in Iquitos and at iPerú in Iquitos.

Where to stay

Yurimaguas

$$$-$$ Río Huallaga
Arica 111, T065-353951,
Facebook: RioHuallagaHotel.
Pleasant modern hotel overlooking the river, safety box, pool, bar, cinema, rooftop restaurant with lovely views.

$$-$ Hostal Luis Antonio
Av Jaúregui 407, T352062, hostal_luis_antonio@ hotmail.com (also on Facebook).
Cold water, small pool, a/c at extra cost, breakfast, very helpful.

$$-$ Posada Cumpanama
Progreso 403, T065-352905, http:// posadacumpanama.blogspot.com.
Rooms cheaper with shared bath, breakfast extra, tastefully decorated, pool, very pleasant.

$ Hostal Akemi
Jr Angamos 414, T065-352237,
www.hostalakemi.com.
Decent rooms with hot water, cheaper without a/c, some with frigobar, restaurant, pool, helpful owner, good value.

$ Hostal El Caballito
Av Jaúregui 403, T065-352427.
Cold water, small bathroom, fan, pleasant, good value.

$ Hostal El Naranjo
Arica 318, T065-352650.
A/c or fan, hot water, frigobar, small pool, with restaurant.

Pacaya-Samiria Reserve

$$$$ Pacaya Samiria Amazon Lodge
www.pacayasamiria.com.pe; office at Urb Las Palmeras 09, Iquitos, T065-225769.
Hatuchay hotel group. Beautifully designed lodge on a hill overlooking the Marañón, just inside the reserve but close to road and town. All buildings in indigenous style, with balconies and en suite bathrooms, restaurant, bar. Community visits and specialist birdwatching trips included in the price, but boat trips (also included) can be long. Camping trips can be arranged deeper inside the reserve. Packages start at US$520 pp for 3-day/ 2-night programme.

$$$ Ecological Jungle Trips & Expeditions Tours
www.ecologicaljungletrips.com;
office at Putumayo 163 p 2, Iquitos,
T965-783409/942-643020.
Delfín Lodge, 2½ hrs from Nauta on the Río Yarapa, is the base for tours to Pacaya-Samiria, 10 rooms. Programmes from 3 days to 7 days, tailored according to the interests of the guests.

$ Basic places in Nauta include **Nauta Inn** (Manuel Pacaya by Laguna Sapi Sapi, T065-411025) and **Plaza Inn** (Marañón 365, T65-411735, with bath, some rooms with a/c).

$ Basic places in Lagunas include **Eco** (Jr Padre Lucero, near cemetery, T065-503703); **Hostal Paraíso Verde** (Carrión 320, ½ block from the plaza, T941 809988, www.hostalparaisoverde. com, with fan and electric shower); **Samiria** (Jr José Cárdenas, near the market).

What to do

Yurimaguas

Huayruro Tours, *Río Huallaga Hotel, Yurimaguas; also at Alfonso Aiscorbe 2 in Lagunas, T065-401186, www.peruselva.com.* Tours to lakes, day and multi-day trips to Pacaya-Samiria.

Pacaya-Samiria

Community associations in many of the villages around the reserve run tours. Community tours cost about US$70 pp per day, compared to US$80 minumum for agency tours arranged in Iquitos. Make sure you know exactly what is included (park fees, lodging, food, transport, guide), what the trip involves (canoeing, walking, hunting, fishing) and the type of accommodation. In the community of San Martín de Tipishca in the Samiria Basin are **Asiendes** (Asociación Indígena en Defensa de la Ecología Samiria), T965-861748, asiendesperu@hotmail.com (asiendes.peru on Facebook) and **Casa Lupuna**. 5 associations operate in Lagunas; a tour operator is **Huayruro Tours** (see above). In Bretaña, the **Gallán family** offer tours.

Yurimaguas

Bus The road to Tarapoto is paved. To Lima, with **Paredes Estrella** (Mariscal Cáceres 220), 0830 daily, 32-34 hrs, US$38.50, via **Tarapoto** (US$4), **Moyobamba** (US$7.75, 5-6 hrs), **Pedro Ruiz** (US$17.50), **Chiclayo** (US$27) and **Trujillo** (US$33). Also **Ejetur**, 0500 to Lima. Faster than the bus to Tarapoto are: **Gilmer Tours** (C Victor Sifuentes 580), frequent mini-buses, US$5.75, 2½ hrs; cars (eg **San Martín**) US$7.75; and combis (**Turismo Selva**, Mcal Cáceres 3rd block) US$4.

Ferry There are 6 docks in all. To **Iquitos**, *lanchas* from Embarcadero La Boca, 3 days/2 nights, best is **Eduardo/Gilmer** (Elena Pardo 114, T065-352552; see under Iquitos, Transport). To **Lagunas** for Pacaya Samiria Reserve, from Embarcadero Abel Guerra at 0900, US$11.55, 10 hrs. Also *rápidos* to Lagunas and Nauta (1½ hrs by *colectivo* from Iquitos, US$4), see Iquitos Transport, page 1499.

Iquitos and around *Colour map 3, A4.*

unique jungle city and gateway to the Amazon

☆Iquitos stands on the west bank of the Amazon and is the chief town of Peru's jungle region. Some 800 km downstream from Pucallpa and 3646 km from the mouth of the Amazon, the city is completely isolated except by air and river. Its first wealth came from the rubber boom in the late 19th century and early 20th century, but now the main economic activities are logging, commerce, petroleum and tourism. The atmosphere of the city is completely different from the rest of Peru: hot, dirty, colourful, noisy and congested with the tens of thousands of mototaxis and motorcycles that fill the streets. Iquitos is the main starting point for tourists wishing to explore Peru's northern jungle. Here you can experience the authentic Amazon, from the lively streets of the city to the pink dolphins and Victoria regia water lilies of the river and its waterways. The city has many good restaurants.

Sights

The incongruous **Iron House/Casa de Fierro** stands on the Plaza de Armas, designed by Eiffel for the Paris exhibition of 1889. It is constructed entirely of iron trusses and sheets, bolted together and painted silver and was is supposedly transported from Paris by a local rubber baron. It now houses a pharmacy. Of special interest in the city are the older buildings, faced with azulejos (glazed tiles). They date from the rubber boom of 1890 to 1912, when the rich merchants imported tiles from Portugal and Italy and ironwork from England to embellish their homes. **Museo Amazónico** ⓘ *Malecón Tarapacá 386, T065-234221, Mon-Sat 0800-1300, 1430-1730, Sun 0800-1230, free, some guides speak English, tip expected*, in the Prefectura, has displays of native art and sculptures by Lima artist Letterstein. Also worth visiting is the **Museo de Culturas Indígenas Amazónicas** ⓘ *Malecón Tarapacá 332, T065-235809, daily 0800-1930, US$5.25*, the private museum of Dr Richard Bodmer, who owns the **Casa Morey** hotel (see below). It celebrates cultures from the entire Amazon region; ask here about historic Amazonian boats, such as **Barco Ayapua** ⓘ *Plaza Ramón Castilla, T065-236072, US$5*, an early 20th-century vessel from the rubber boom era, fully restored for visits, expeditions and short trips. The waterfront by Malecón Maldonado, known as 'Boulevard', is a pleasant place for a stroll and gets busy on Friday and Saturday evenings.

Belén, the picturesque, lively waterfront district, is an authentic part of Amazon river life, but is not safe at night. Most of its huts were originally built on rafts to cope with the river's 10 m change of level during floods from January to July; now they're more commonly built on stilts. Arrive by 0700 to see people arriving with their forest fruits and fish to sell in the **Belén** market. On Pasaje Paquito are bars serving local sugar cane rum and places where shamans buy medicinal plants and other items for their ceremonies. The main plaza has a bandstand made by Eiffel. In the high season canoes can be hired on the waterfront for a tour of Belén, US$3 per hour. To get there take a mototaxi to Los Chinos and walk down to the port.

Iquitos

Where to stay 🛏
1 Best Western Plus Samiria
2 Casa Andina Classic
3 Casa Linda
4 Casa Morey
5 Double Tree by Hilton
6 El Sitio
7 Green Track Hostel
8 Hostal El Colibrí
9 La Casa Fitzcarraldo
10 La Casona
11 Las Amazonas Inn
12 Marañón
13 Nativa Apartments
14 Victoria Regia

Restaurants 🍴
1 Amazon Bistro
2 Antica Pizzería
3 Chef Paz
4 Chez Maggy Pizzería
5 El Carbón
6 El Sitio
7 Espresso Café
8 Festejo
9 Fitzcarraldo
10 Helados La Muyuna
11 Huasaí
12 La Gran Maloca
13 La Mona
14 María's Café
15 Mitos y Cubiertos
16 Norma Mía
17 Panadería Tívoli
18 Yellow Rose of Texas

Bars & clubs 🍸
19 Arandú
20 Ikaro
21 Karma
22 Noa Noa

Around Iquitos

When the river is low (June-September), there is a pleasant beach, with white sand and palms, at **Tipishca** on the Río Nanay, reached in 20 minutes by boat from Puerto de Santa Clara near the airport; it gets quite busy at weekends. **Santa Rita**, reached from Puerto de Pampa Chica, on a turnoff from the airport road, is quieter. Also near the airport is the village of **Santo Tomás** ① *turn left just before the airport, then take another left 300 m further on, then it's about 4 km to the village; mototaxi from Iquitos US$5*. It has a nice lake for swimming and renting canoes; beaches appear when the river is low, from July to September. The restaurants at the lake are very basic, so it's best to take your own food.

Pilpintuhuasi Butterfly Farm ① *near the village of Padre Cocha, T065-232665, www.amazonanimalorphanage.org, Tue-Sun 0900-1600, guided tours at 0930, 1100, 1330 and 1500, US$5, students US$3, includes guided tour*, has butterflies, a small, well-kept zoo and a rescue centre, run by Austrian biologist Goody Sperrer. (Next door is another butterfly farm run by Goody's ex-husband.) To get there catch a *colectivo* from Bellavista to Padre Cocha (20 minutes), then walk 15 minutes from there. If the river is high, speedboats can reach Pilpintuhuasi directly from Iquitos, US$25 return including waiting time; pay at the end.

The **Centro de Rescate Amazónico** ① *Km 4.5 on the road to Nauta, www.centroderescate amazonico.com, Mon 1200-1500, Tue-Sun 0900-1500, 1-hr guided tour US$6, students US$3, must show ID*, is where orphaned and injured manatees and other aquatic mammals and wildlife are nursed until they can be released. It's a good place to see these endangered species. Further along the road to Nauta are several balnearios.

Allpahuayo-Mishana Reserve

SERNANP, Jorge Chávez 930/942, Iquitos, T065-223555, Mon-Fri 0700-1300, 1500-1700, reserve fees US$8.50, students US$6.25.

On the Río Nanay, some 25 km south of Iquitos by the Nauta road or two hours by boat from Bellavista, this reserve protects the largest concentration of white sand jungle (varillales) in Peru. Part of the Napo ecoregion, it has one of the highest levels of biodiversity in the Amazon basin. Among several endangered species are two primates and several endemic species. The area is rich in birds: 475 species have been recorded. Within the reserve at Km 25 is Zoocriadero BIOAM, a good birdwatching circuit in land belonging to the Instituto Nacional de Innovación Agraria (INIA). Just beyond is the **Jardín de Plantas Medicinales y Frutales** ① *Km 26.8, daily 0800-1600, guiding 0800-1000*; with over 2400 species of medicinal plants. At Km 28, El Irapay interpretation centre ① *Mon-Sat 0830-1430*, has a trail to Mishana village by the river.

Border with Brazil and Colombia

Lanchas and rápidos make the journey downriver to the tri-border. Details on exit and entry formalities seem to change frequently, so when leaving Peru, check in Iquitos first at **Immigration** ① *Mcal Cáceres 18th block, T065-235371, Mon-Fri 0800-1615*, or with the Capitanía at the port. Boats stop in Santa Rosa for Peruvian exit formalities. Santa Rosa has six simple hotels (**Bellavista**, ½ block past immigration, with private bath, **Diana** and **Las Hamacas** are reported better than the others, price around US$15 for a double). All other details are given in the Brazil chapter. **Consulates in Iquitos**: Brazil ① *Sargento Lores 363, T065-235151, cg.iquitos@itamaraty.gov.br. Mon-Fri 0800-1400*, visas issued in two days; **Colombia** ① *Calvo de Araújo 431, T065-231461, http://iquitos.consulado.gov.co, Mon-Fri 0800-1400*.

Listings Iquitos and around *map p1493*

Tourist information

iPerú (Jr Napo 161, of 4, T065-236144, iperuiquitos@promperu.gob.pe, Mon-Sat 0900-1800, Sun 0900-1300) also has a desk at the airport, open at flight times. If arriving by air, go to this desk first to get a list of hotels, a map and advice about the touts outside the airport. Both www.iquitosnews.com and www.iquitostimes. com have articles, maps and information. If you have a complaint about service, contact **Indecopi** (Putumayo 464, T065-243490, Mon-Fri 0830-1630); to report a crime, contact the **tourist police** (Sargento Lores 834, T065-242081).

Where to stay

Information on jungle lodges is given under What to do, below, as many work closely or exclusively with particular tour operators. Around Peruvian Independence Day (27 and 28 Jul) and Easter, Iquitos can get crowded and flight prices rise at this time.

International luxury chain hotels include: **Best Western Plus Samiria** (www.bestwestern.com), **Double Tree by Hilton** (www.hilton.com).

$$$ Casa Morey
Raymondi y Loreto, Plaza Ramón Castilla,
T065-231913, www.casamorey.com.
Boutique hotel in a beautifully restored historic rubber-boom period mansion. Great attention to detail, includes airport transfers, ample comfortable rooms, pool, good library, good service, an excellent choice.

$$$ Victoria Regia
Ricardo Palma 252, T065-231983,
www.victoriaregiahotel.com.
Free map of city, safe deposit boxes in rooms, good restaurant, indoor pool.

$$$-$$ Casa Andina Classic
Aguirre 793 at Plaza 28 de Julio,
www.casa-andina.com.
The ex-Royal Inn Hotel is being refurbished in 2017, a new addition to the prestigious Peruvian hotel chain.

$$$-$$ La Casa Fitzcarraldo
Av La Marina 2153, T065-601138,
http://casafitzcarraldo.com.
Prices vary according to room. Includes breakfast and airport transfer, with Wi-Fi, satellite TV, minibar, 1st-class restaurant, treehouse, pool in lovely gardens, captive animals. The house is the home of Walter Saxer, the executive-producer of Werner Herzog's famous film, lots of movie and celebrity memorabilia.

$$$-$$ Marañón
Fitzcarrald y Nauta 289, T065-242673,
http://hotelmaranon.com.
Multi-storey hotel, spotless comfortable rooms, a/c, convenient location, small pool.

$$$-$$ Nativa Apartments
Nanay 144, T065-600270, https://
nativaapartments.com.
Bright suites with kichenette and apartments, a/c, no breakfast, complementary tea and coffee. Very attentive owner and staff.

$$ La Casona
Fitzcarald 147, T065-234 394,
www.hotellacasonaiquitos.com.pe.
In building dating from 1901, now modernized, hot water, fan or a/c, breakfast extra, kitchen facilities, small patio, pool, popular with travellers. Opposite, at Fitzcarald 152, is **Hostal La Casona Río Grande**, with smaller rooms, fan. Transport to either from the airport with advance reservation.

$$ Las Amazonas Inn
Ricardo Palma 460, T065-225367,
www.lasamazonasinn2.com.
Simple rooms with electric shower, a/c, kitchen facilities, breakfast available, airport transfers included, friendly owner.

$$-$ Casa Linda
Napo 818, T065-231533, http://
residenciacasalinda.com.
Good hotel in a quiet area, rooms with a/c, private bath, hot water, frigobar.

$$-$ Hostal El Colibrí
Raymondi 200, T065-241737,
hostalelcolibri@hotmail.com.
1 block from Plaza and 50 m from the river so can be noisy, nicely refurbished house, a/c or fan, hot water, gym, secure, good value, breakfast extra, helpful staff.

$ El Sitio
Ricardo Palma 541, T065-234932.
Fan, private bath, cold water, good value.

$ Green Track Hostel
Ricardo Palma 516, T950-664049,
www.greentrack-hostel.com.
Pleasant hostel, 4-6-bed dorms with a/c or fan, private rooms with and without bath, free pick up with advanced booking, terrace, Brazilian breakfast, English spoken, helpful owners, tours arranged to Tapiche Reserve (see below).

Restaurants

Local specialities include *a la Loretana* dishes (prepared with local spices), *inchicapi* (chicken, corn and peanut soup), *cecina* (fried dried pork), *tacacho* (fried green banana served with meat or chicken, mashed into balls and eaten for breakfast or tea), *juane* (chicken, rice, olive and egg, seasoned and wrapped in bijao leaves and sold in restaurants) and the *camu-camu*, an acquired taste fruit, said to have one of the highest vitamin C concentrations in the world. Avoid eating endangered species, such as paiche, caiman, turtle or chonta (wild palm heart) which are sometimes on menus.

For a good local breakfast, go to the Mercado Central, C Sargento Lores, where there are several kiosks outside, popular and cheap. Try the local *jugo de cocona*, a tart fruit juice.

$$$ Al Frío y al Fuego
On the water, go to Embarcadero Turístico (El Huequito) and a boat will pick you up, T065-224862. Mon 1830-2300, Tue-Sat 1130-1600 and 1830-2300, Sun 1130-1600.
Good upscale floating restaurant with regional specialities and a pool.

$$$ Fitzcarraldo
Malecón Maldonado 103 y Napo.
Smart, typical food, also pizza, good pastas and salads.

$$$ La Gran Maloca
Sargento Lores 170, opposite Banco Continental. Closes 2000 on Sun, other days 2300.
A/c, high class regional food.

$$$-$$ Amazon Bistro
Malecón Tarapacá 268, T065-242918. Mon-Sat 0600-0100, Sun 0700-1400.
Upscale French bistro/bar on the waterfront, drinks, snacks, breakfasts and meal of the day. Goof food, trendy and popular. Belgian/Peruvian-run. Live music at weekends.

$$$-$$ Chef Paz
Putumayo 468, T065-241277. Mon-Sat 0800-midnight.
Excellent food including fish, shellfish, meat dishes, local specialities and their own jungle sushi.

$$$-$$ Festejo
Morona 287, T065-242660. Tue-Sat 1200-2200, Sun1200-1700.
Very good Peruvian cooking, modern decor, a/c.

$$ Yellow Rose of Texas
Putumayo 180. Open 24 hrs so you can wait here if arriving late at night.
Varied food including local dishes, Texan atmosphere, good breakfasts, lots of information, also has a bar, Sky TV and Texan saddle seats.

$$-$ Antica Pizzería
Napo 159. Sun-Thu 0700-2400, Fri-Sat 0700-0100.
"The best pizza in town" and Italian dishes, pleasant ambiance especially on the upper level.

$$-$ Chez Maggy Pizzería
Raymondi 177. Daily 1800-0100.
Wood-fired pizza and home-made pasta.

$ El Carbón
La Condamine 115. Open 1900-2300 only.
Grilled meats, salads, regional side dishes such as *tacacho* and *patacones*.

$ El Sitio
Sargento Lores 404. Mon-Sat 1930-2230.
A simple place for *anticuchos* for all tastes including vegetarian, popular.

$ Huasaí
Fitzcarrald 131. Open 0715-1615, closed Mon.
Varied and innovative menu, popular, good food and value, go early.

$ Mitos y Cubiertos
Napo 337, by the Plaza. Mon-Sat midday only.
Generous lunches, good value.

Cafés

Espresso Café
Jr Próspero 418, p2, http://espressocafe.com.pe. Daily 1700-2400.
Upscale café-bar in a nicely decorated rubber-boom-era house. A variety of coffees and teas, gourmet sandwiches and snacks, desserts, art exhibits.

Helados La Muyuna
Jr Próspero 621 and on Napo near Malecón.
Good natural jungle fruit ice cream.

La Mona
Jr Nauta 656. Mon 1630-2300, Tue-Sat 0730-1200, 1630-2300, Sun 0800-1200, 1700-2300.
Café with a peaceful terrace with plants. Serves coffee, juices, sandwiches. Nice atmosphere and decor.

María's Café
Nauta 292. Tue-Sun 0800-1230.
Breakfasts, sandwiches, burgers, coffee and cakes, with desserts of the day.

Norma Mía
La Condamine 153.
Doña Norma has been making delicious cakes for over 30 years, also sells ice cream.

Panadería Tívoli
Ricardo Palma, block 3.
A variety of good bread and sweets.

Bars and clubs

Local drinks include: *chuchuhuasi*, made from the bark of a tree, which is supposed to have aphrodisiac properties (for sale at Arica 1046), *cola de mono* (a cocktail with milk and coffee) and *siete raíces* (aguardiente mixed with the bark of 7 trees and wild honey), sold at **Musmuqui** (Raymondi 382), Mon-Sat from 1900.

Arandú
Malecón Maldonado.
Good bar with nice views of the river.

Ikaro
Putumayo 341.
Good bar, Spanish rock music. Also has internet.

Karma
Napo 138.
Cocktails and rock music, has a happy hour.

Noa Noa
Pevas y Fitzcarrald.
Popular disco with cumbia and Latin music.

Festivals

5 Jan Founding of Iquitos.
Feb-Mar Carnival.
Jun Tourist week is the 3rd week.
24 Jun San Juan, the most important festival.
28-30 Aug Santa Rosa de Lima.
8 Dec Immaculate Conception (La Purísima), celebrated in Punchana, near the docks, Bellavista and Nanay.

Shopping
Handicrafts

Hammocks in Iquitos cost about US$20. **Mercado Artesanal Anaconda**, by the waterfront at Napo is good for Amazon handicrafts, but be sure not to buy items that contain animal products. Also try the **Asociación de Artesanos El Manguaré**, which has kiosks on Jr Pevas, block 1. **Mercado Artesanal de Productores** (4 km from the centre in the San Juan district, on the road to the airport; take a *colectivo*) is the cheapest in town with more choice than elsewhere.

For jungle clothing and equipment, visit **Comisesa** (Arica 348), and **Mad Mick's Trading Post** (Putumayo 163, top floor, next to the Iron House).
La Restinga, *Raymondi 254, T065-221371, larestinga@gmail.com*. This association sells t-shirts, books and soaps made by children. It also runs literacy workshops in Belén on Tue and Thu from 1430-1800, at which you can volunteer.

Jungle tours

Agencies arrange 1-day or longer trips to places of interest with guides speaking some English. Take your time before making a decision, research what is on offer and don't be bullied by the hustlers at the airport or on the street. Buy your tour at the operator's office. Find out all the details of the trip and food arrangements before paying (a minimum of US$50 per day). Several companies have their own lodges, providing various levels of accommodation in the heart of the jungle (see below). Downriver from Iquitos you find more comfort (electricity, air conditioning, swimming pool, internet, cell phone coverage) and tours often include visits to native communities and to Isla de los Monos, where monkeys and other animals can be seen. Upriver along the Amazon and its tributaries conditions are more primitive (solar powered or no electricity, no internet or phone). In this more scarcely populated area, there are better chances of seeing animals in the wild.

River cruises

There are several agencies that arrange river cruises in well-appointed boats with large picture windows. Most go to the Pacaya-Samiria region and depart from Nauta, very few go towards Brazil. There are 3-to 7-night cruises. Day tours and charters are also available. Luxury cruises cost about US$2400-4000 for 3 nights/4 days, more economical vessels about US$1400-1900 for the same period. Among the luxury boats are the *Aria* (www.aquaexpeditions.com), *Delfín I, II and III* (www.delfinamazoncruises.com), *Cattleya* and *Zafiro* (www.junglexperiences.com). More economical boats include *Amatista* and *La Perla* (same group as *Zafiro*), *Arapaima* (www. amazonexpeditioncruises.com), *Dawn on the Amazon I* (see Tour operators below, cruises to Allpahuayo Mishana Natural Reserve, US$225 pp per day), *La Estrella Amazónica* and *Queen Violeta*. Contact companies like **Amazon River Expeditions** (www.amazonriverexpeditions.com) **Amazon Voyagers** (www.amazoncruise.net) or **Rainforest Cruises** (www.rainforestcruises. com), for options. Alternatively, speed boats for river trips can be hired by the hour or day at the **Embarcadero Turístico**, at the intersection of Av de la Marina and Samánez Ocampo in Punchana (closed for renovations in 2017). Prices vary greatly, usually US$15-20 per hr, US$80 for speedboat, and are negotiable.

Shaman experiences

Iquitos is an important place for ayahuasca tourism. There are legitimate shamans as well as charlatans. **Karma Café** (Napo 138; see above) is the centre of the scene in town. See also the work of Alan Shoemaker (**Soga del Alma**, Rómulo Espinar 170, Iquitos 65, alanshoemaker@hotmail.com), who holds an International Amazonian Shamanism Conference every year (www.vineofthesoul.com).

Tour operators and jungle lodges

Cumaceba Amazonia Tours, *Putumayo 184 in the Iron House, T065-232229, www.cumaceba.com*. Overnight visits to Cumaceba Lodge, 35 km from Iquitos, and tours of 1-4 nights to the Botanical Lodge on the Amazon, 80 km from Iquitos, birdwatching tours, ayahuasca ceremonies.
Curuhuinsi Eco Adventure Tours & Expeditions, *T965-013225, www.facebook.com/ CuruhuinsiEcoAdventureToursExpeditions*. **Gerson Pizango** is a local, English-speaking and award-winning guide who will take you to his village 2½ hrs by boat, from where you can trek and camp or stay and experience village life. Expert at spotting wildlife and knowledgeable about medicinal plants, he offers interesting and varied expeditions benefitting the community. In the village, accommodation is in a hut by the riverside where there are pink and grey dolphins. A private room with mosquito net costs US$50-70 pp per day depending on length of trip and size of party, includes food, water, camping gear, boots, raincoats, torches, binoculars, fishing rods, machetes.
Dawn on the Amazon, *Malecón Maldonado 185 y Nauta, T065-223730, www.dawnontheamazon. com*. Offers a variety of day tours around Iquitos by land or r iver (US$85 pp per day) and custom-made cruises. Also has a good café/restaurant in town (http://dawnontheamazoncafe.com).
Explorama Tours, *by the riverside docks on Av La Marina 340, T065-252530, www.explorama.com*.

The biggest and most established operator, with over 40 years' experience. Frequently recommended. Their lodges are:
Ceiba Tops, 40 km (1½ hrs) from Iquitos, a comfortable resort with 75 a/c rooms with electricity, hot showers, good food, pool with hydromassage and beautiful gardens. Walks and excursions, a recommended jungle experience for those who want their creature comforts, US$340 pp for 1 night/2 days.
Explorama Lodge at Yanamono, 80 km from Iquitos, 2½ hrs from Iquitos, has palm-thatched accommodation with separate bathroom and shower facilities connected by covered walkways, cold water, no electricity, good food and service. US$455 for 3 days/2 nights.
Explornapo Lodge at Llachapa on the Sucusai creek (a tributary of the Napo), is in the same style as Explorama Lodge, but is further away from Iquitos, 160 km (4 hrs by river or a 15-min ride from Mazán), and is set in 105,000 ha of rainforest, so is better for seeing wildlife, US$1,120 for 5 days/4 nights. Nearby is the impressive canopy walkway 35 m above the forest floor and 500 m long. It is associated with the Amazon Center for Tropical Studies (ACTS), a scientific station, only 10 mins from the canopy walkway.
Explor Tambos, 2 hrs from Explornapo, offer more primitive accommodation, 8 shelters for 16 campers, bathing in the river.
Heliconia Lodge, Ricardo Palma 242; contact T01-421 9195, www.heliconialodge.com.pe. On the Río Amazonas, 80 km downriver from Iquitos, surrounded by rainforest, islands and lagoons, this is a beautiful place for resting, birdwatching, looking for pink dolphins, jungle hikes. Organized packages 3 days/2 nights, US$282. Good guides, food and flexible excursions according to guest's requirements. The lodge has hot water, electricity for 5 hrs each day, pool and a traditionally rustic yet comfortable design.

Muyuna Amazon Lodge, Putumayo 163, ground floor, T065-242858, T995-918964, www.muyuna.com. 140 km upstream from Iquitos on the Río Yanayacu, before San Juan village. 1- to 5-night packages available. 2 nights/3 days is US$400 pp all-inclusive for 2-10 people. Trusted guides, high-quality accommodation, solar electricity, hot water, good food and service, kayak and paddle-boards; very well organized, flexible and professional. Amenities are constantly updated with new ecological considerations. Birdwatching (400 species might be seen in a 4 day tour) and camping trips into the forest. This area is less spoilt than some other parts of the forest downstream. **Centro de Rescate Amazónico** (see page 1494) has released manatees here. Highly recommended. **Tapiche Reserve**, *Ricardo Palma 516, T065-600805/950-664049, office at Green Track Hostel (see above), www.tapichejungle.com*. On the Río Tapiche, a tributary of the Ucayali, 11 hrs up river from Iquitos. Fully screened wood cabins with thatched roofs, custom designed trips according to the visitor's interests, 4-day/3-night and 5-day/4-night tours offered.

Transport

Air Francisco Secada Vigneta airport, T065-260147 is southwest of the city; a taxi to the airport costs US$10; *mototaxi* (motorcycle with 2 seats), US$3.25. Most buses from the main road outside the airport go through the centre of town, US$0.75. To **Lima**, daily, with **LATAM** (direct or via Tarapoto), **Peruvian Airlines** and **Star Perú** (direct or via Tarapoto, also daily to Pucallpa) and Avianca/TACA. The military **Grupo Aéreo 42** fly occasionally to Santa Rosa.

Bus To **Nauta**, **Trans del Sur** from Libertad y Próspero, daily 0530-1900, US$3.10, 2 hrs; also vans from Av Aguirre cuadra 14 by Centro Comercial Sachachorro, which leave when full, US$4, 1½ hrs.

Ferry For general hints on river travel, see page 1514. For information about boats, go to the corresponding ports of departure for each destination, except for speed boats to the Brazil/Colombian border which have their offices clustered on Raymondi block 3. When river levels are very high departures may be from alternative places.

Lanchas leave from Puerto Henry and Masusa, 2 km north of the centre, a dangerous area at night. The 1st night's meal is not included. Always deal directly with boat owners or managers, avoid touts and middle-men. All fares are negotiable.

If arriving in Iquitos on a regular, slow boat, take extreme care when disembarking. Things get very chaotic at this time and theft and pickpocketing is rife. Some of the newer boats have CCTV to deter theft. *Deslizadores* or *rápidos* leave from Embarcadero Turístico or Nauta (see below).

To **Pucallpa**, 4-5 days upriver along the Amazon and Ucayali (can be longer if the water level is low), larger boats must travel only by day, hammock US$40, berth US$140 double. **Henry** (T065-263948) is a large company with 4 departures per week from Puerto Henry; *Henry 5, 6* and *7* have some cabins with bath. Another good boat is *Pedro Martín 2* from Puerto Masusa.

To **Yurimaguas** by *lancha*, 3-4 days upriver along the Amazon, Marañón and Huallaga, hammock space US$40, berth US$119-134 double. The **Eduardo/Gilmer** company, T065-960404, with 8 boats is recommended, sailing from Puerto Masusa several times a week, except Sun; *Eduardo I* and *Gilmer IV* have berths with bath for US$192. By *rápido* from Nauta, with **Rápido NR** (C Puerto Principal, Nauta, T953-998980), 20 hrs navigation upstream, US$40 includes a meal, snack and overnight lodging in Lagunas; all basic. The reverse, downstream, journey is 12 hrs, US$38, no overnight in Lagunas.

To **Santa Rosa** (on the border with Brazil and Colombia), the most convenient way to travel is by *rápido*, 8-10 hrs downriver, US$60, from the Embarcadero Turístico (always confirm departure point in advance) at 0530 Tue-Sun; be at the port 0445 for customs check, board 0500-0530. (In the opposite direction, boats leave Santa Rosa Tue-Sun at 0400 and take 10-12 hrs upstream; if you're coming from Brazil or Colombia get your immigration entry stamp the day before.) *Rápidos* carry life jackets and have bathrooms; a simple breakfast and lunch are included in the price. Luggage limit is 15 kg. Purchase tickets in advance from company offices in Iquitos: **Golfinho** (Raymondi 378, T065-225118, www.transportegolfinho.com) and **Transtur** (Raymondi 384, T065-221356). *Lanchas* to Santa Rosa, which may continue to Islandia, leave from the Puerto Pesquero or Puerto Masusa (enquire at T065-250440), Mon-Sat at 1800, 2-3 days downriver, US$31 in hammock, US$50 in cabin; in the other direction they depart Santa Rosa Mon-Sat at 1200.

To reach the border with Ecuador you go to **Pantoja**, 5-7 days upriver on the Napo, a route requiring plenty of time, stamina and patience. There are irregular departures once or twice a month, US$38, plus US$3 per day for a berth if you can get one; for details call **Radio Moderna** in Iquitos (T065-250440), or T065-830055 (a private phone in Pantoja village). The vessels are usually cargo boats that carry live animals, some of which are slaughtered en route. Crowding and poor sanitation are common. Once in Pantoja, there is no public transport to **Nuevo Rocafuerte** (Ecuador), so you must hire a private boat, US$60. To shorten the voyage, or to visit the jungle towns along the way, go to **Indiana**, daily departures from **Muelle de Productores** in Iquitos, US$5, 45 mins, then take a mototaxi

Tip...
There is no Ecuadorean consulate in Iquitos; if you need a visa, get it in Lima or in advance in your home country.

to **Mazán** on the Río Napo. From Mazán, there are *rápidos* to **Santa Clotilde**, US$31 includes a snack, 4-5 hrs, information from **Familia Ruiz** in Iquitos (T065-251410).

Southern jungle

Peru's premier wildlife-watching destination

★The southern selva is mostly in Madre de Dios department, which contains the Manu National Park (2.04 million ha), the Tambopata National Reserve (274,690 ha) and the Bahauja-Sonene National Park (1.1 million ha). The forest of this lowland region (altitude 260 m) is technically called Sub-tropical Moist Forest, which means that it receives less rainfall than tropical forest and is dominated by the floodplains of its meandering rivers. The most striking features are the former river channels that have become isolated as oxbow lakes. These are home to black caiman and giant otter and a host of other species. Other rare species living in the forest are jaguar, puma, ocelot and tapir. There are also howler monkeys, capybara, macaws, guans, currasows and the giant harpy eagle.

As well as containing some of the most important flora and fauna on Earth, the region also harbours gold-diggers, loggers, hunters, drug smugglers and oil-men, whose activities endanger the unique rainforest. Moreover, the construction of the Interoceánica, a road linking the Atlantic and Pacific oceans via Puerto Maldonado and Brazil, has brought more uncontrolled colonization in the area, as seen so many times before throughout the Amazon.

☆Manu Biosphere Reserve

Few other reserves on the planet can compare with Manu for the diversity of life forms; it holds over 1000 species of birds and covers an altitudinal range from 200 m to 4100 m above sea-level. Giant otters, jaguars, ocelots and 13 species of primates abound in this pristine tropical wilderness; uncontacted indigenous tribes are present in the more remote areas, as are indigenous groups with limited access.

The reserve is one of the largest conservation units on Earth, encompassing the complete drainage of the Manu River. It is divided into the **Manu National Park** (1,716,295 ha), which only government-sponsored biologists and anthropologists may visit with permits from the Ministry of Agriculture in Lima; the **Reserved Zone** (257,000 ha) within the national park, which is set aside for applied scientific research and ecotourism; and the **Cultural** or **Multiple Use Zone** (92,000 ha), a buffer area which contains acculturated native groups and colonists along the Alto Madre de Dios and its tributaries, where the locals still employ their traditional way of life. Among the ethnic groups in the Cultural Zone are the Mashco-Piro and the Yine, while the Harakmbut and Matsiguenka are mostly in the Reserved Zone. Also within the biosphere reserve are the **Nahua-Kugapakori Reserved Zone**, set aside for these two nomadic native groups, which is the area between the headwaters of the Río Manu and headwaters of the Río Urubamba, to the north of the Alto Madre de Dios; the **Megantoni Sanctuary**, in the foothills of the Ausangate range, north of Quillabamba and to the west of the national park; and, to the east of the national park, the **Amarakaeri Community Reserve**, see below. Associated with Manu are other areas protected by conservation groups, or local people (for example the Blanquillo and Manu Wildlife Center reserves) and some cloudforest parcels along the road.

Cuzco to Boca Manu and Puerto Maldonado

Cuzco to Boca Manu The trip over the Andes from Cuzco to the lowlands is long, the road is in places hair-raising and breathtaking, and the scenery is magnificent. Check about road conditions in the rainy season. From Cuzco you climb up to the Huancarani pass (very cold at night) then drop to Paucartambo (see page 1439) in the valley of the Río Mapacho. The road then ascends to the Acjanaco pass (also cold at night), one access to the highland section of Manu (see Tres Cruces, page 1439), after which it follows the Río Cosñipata down to the cloudforest around **San Pedro** (part of Manu's Cultural Zone, includes a 5060 ha **Perú Verde Reserve**, excellent birding including a cock-of-the-rock lek, several lodges), before reaching the lowlands at **Patria**, an area of coca production, followed by **Pilcopata**, at 650 m, a supply town on the border between the departments of Cuzco and Madre de Dios. Beyond Pilcopata is the turnoff for **Atalaya**, the first village on the Alto Madre de Dios River and tourist port from where tours depart for Boca Manu and the park; there are basic lodgings and restaurants here.

The route continues to **Salvación** (575 m), with some simple *hostales* and restaurants, the most pleasant town along this road. Just north of town is a national park office. **Cocha Machuhuasi** ① *1.5 km from town, entry US$1.50,* a municipal nature reserve with many birds, caymans and some mammals, has a small lake with punts and walking trails around it. From Salvación the road continues north, always along the east bank of the Alto Madre de Dios to Santa Cruz, with a park ranger station; nearby is the access for the Río Palotoa and the **Pusharo Petroglyphs** ① *entry US$15,* within the national park. Next is the turnoff for **Shintuya**, with thermal baths and community tourism and volunteering opportunities run by Proyecto Oteri (T082-812966 ask for Wili Corisepa, oteriproyect@gmail.com). Continuing on the road is **Itahuanía**, centre of an agricultural area with basic services and *hostales*. Next is **Shipitiari** (a couple of restaurants and a very basic lodging on the southeast shore of the river). In 2017, a poor road reached **Nuevo Edén** and the road cut, not yet transitable, reached **Diamante**. Where river transport starts depends on the road condition at

Essential Manu

Access to Manu

The Multi-Use Zone of Manu Biosphere Reserve is accessible to anyone and several lodges exist in the area. The Reserved Zone is accessible by permit only, available from the Manu National Park office in Cuzco; entry is strictly controlled and visitors must visit the area under the auspices of an authorized operator with an authorized guide. Permits are limited and reservations should be made well in advance. There is very little permanent accommodation in the Reserved Zone but several companies have tented safari camp infrastructures, some with shower and dining facilities, but all visitors sleep in tents. The entrance fee to the Reserved Zone is 150 soles pp (about US$45) and is included in package tour prices.

Tours to Manu usually enter by road, overnighting in a lodge in the cloudforest,

Tip...

It is not possible to arrange trips to the Reserved Zone of the national park from Itahuanía or Boca Manu, owing to park regulations. All arrangements, including permits, must be made in Cuzco.

and continue by boat (the route is described below). It is this journey from the highlands down through the various strata of habitat that sets it apart from many other visits to the jungle. At the end of the tour, passengers either return overland or fly back to Cuzco from Puerto Maldonado. There is an airstrip at Diamante, near Boca Manu, but there are no regular flights from Cuzco. Ask the tour operators in Cuzco if your tour will go overland or by air.

When to go

The climate is warm and humid, with a rainy season from Novemer to March and a dry season from April to October. Cold fronts from the South Atlantic, called friajes, are characteristic of the dry season, causing temperatures to drop to 15-16°C during the day and to 13°C at night. Always bring a sweater at this time. The best time to visit is during the dry season when there are fewer mosquitoes and the rivers are low, exposing the beaches. This is also a good time to see birds nesting and to view animals at close range, as they stay close to the rivers and are easily seen. A pair of binoculars is essential and insect repellent is a must.

the time, as rain often disrupts wheeled transport. There is no scheduled boat service to continue downriver. There may be cargo boats leaving for either Boca Manu or Boca Colorado on the Río Madre de Dios, but only when the boat is fully laden.

Boca Manu and the Reserved Zone
Boca Manu (365 m) is the connecting point between the rivers Alto Madre de Dios, Manu and Madre de Dios. It is a friendly village with basic places to stay and eat and reasonably supplied shops. On the south bank across the river, by an indigenous community, is an airstrip. La Isla del Valle is a Matsiguenka community (1 km from town) and La Cocha (2 km away) is an oxbow lake with giant otters, birds and other fauna.

Boca Manu is the entrance to the **Manu Reserved Zone** and to go further you must be part of an organized group. The park ranger station and an interpretation centre are located in Limonal, upstream along the Río Manu. You need to show your permit here. Upstream on the Río Manu you pass Cocha Juárez after three or four hours. You can continue to Cocha Otorongo in 2½ hours and Cocha Salvador, a further 30 minutes. The latter is the biggest lake with plenty of wildlife. From here it is two to three hours to Pakitza, the entrance to the National Park Zone, only accessible to biologists with a special permit. Beyond is Cocha Casu with a biological station.

Boca Manu to Puerto Maldonado via Boca Colorado   There is no regular passenger service between Boca Manu and Boca Colorado from where there is transport to Puerto Maldonado; see Transport page 1512.

The Madre de Dios River flows southeast from Boca Manu. South of the river is the 402,335 ha **Amarakaeri Communal Reserve** ① *headquarters at Jr Cajamarca 946, Puerto Maldonado, T082-571505, rcamarakaeri@sernanp.gob.pe*, protecting a variety of ecosystems in the watersheds of the Madre de Dios and Colorado rivers. Adjacent to Amarakaeri, in an area very rich in wildlife, with important macaw and mammal clay licks and several oxbow lakes, are a couple private reserves: **Manu Wildlife Center** ① *www.inkanatura.com/manu-tours-and-lodges*, with 16,190 ha, and **Tambo Blanquillo** ① *http://tamboblanquillo.com*, with 10,000 ha; both have lodges (see Where to stay) and canopy observation towers. Visitors get here on packaged tours. Downstream from the reserves the devastation from informal gold mining becomes evident until you reach **Boca Colorado**, a mining supply centre with accommodation, restaurants (**Milenium** is good), shops, internet and boats for hire; lone women travellers should be careful here. From Colorado you can take a van to Puerto Carlos (one hour, basic accommodation), cross the Inambari river (10 minutes), then take another van to Puerto Maldonado (two hours, see Transport) or Mazuko (1½ hours).

Cuzco to Puerto Maldonado via Mazuko
One branch of the Interoceánica highway runs Cuzco–Urcos–Quincemil–Mazuko–Puerto Maldonado. The changing scenery en route is magnificent.

Quincemil, 240 km from Urcos, is a centre for alluvial gold-mining with many banks. Hunt Oil is building a huge oil and gas facility here; its exploration controversially overlaps the Amarakaeri Communal Reserve.

Puente Inambari is the junction of three sections of the Interoceanic Highway, from Cuzco, Puerto Maldonado and Juliaca (see Puno to the jungle, page 1411). However, this is only a small settlement and transport stops 16 km further north at **Mazuko**. In the evenings, Mazuko is a hive of activity as temperatures drop and the buses arrive.

The Highway beyond Mazuko cuts across lowland rainforest, large areas of which have been cleared by migrants engaged in small-scale gold mining. Their encampments of plastic shelters, shops and prostibars now line the Highway for several kilometres around La Pampa (known as Km 108). A worthwhile stop on the route is the **Parador Turístico Familia Méndez** ① *Km 410, 85 km (1 hr) from Puerto Maldonado, T962-352668*, which prepares local dishes from home-grown ingredients and has wood cabins ($), camping and a trail network in the surrounding forest (walking tour available).

Puerto Maldonado *Colour map 3, C5.*
Puerto Maldonado (approximate population 200,000), overlooking the confluence of the Tambopata and Madre de Dios rivers, is an important base for visiting the southeastern jungles of

the Tambopata Reserve or departing for Bolivia or Brazil. Because of the gold mining and timber industries, it is a busy town and the immediate surrounding jungle is now cultivated. A bridge, part of the Interoceánica highway which continues north to the borders with Brazil and Bolivia, spans the Río Madre de Dios. Lovely sunsets are seen from the bridge and especially from the 47 m-high **Mirador** ① *Av Madre de Dios y Av Fitzcarald, 15 blocks west of the plaza, 0700-2030, closed Wed, US$1.* In town are a butterfly farm (www.perubutterfly.com) and a serpentarium (Serpentario Tropifauna on Facebook).

> **Tip...**
> Try the locally grown Brazil nuts (*castañas*) sold in the markets and shops of Puerto Maldonado. Many inhabitants of the Madre de Dios region are involved in their production. The harvest is from March to June, and the crop tends to be good on alternate years.

Jungle tours from Puerto Maldonado

A multi-day trip to a jungle lodge is the best way to experience the forest and see fauna. There are also many community tourism projects around Puerto Maldonado accessed by road and/or river. Attractions in the buffer zone of the Tambopata Reserve, include **Lago Tres Chimbadas** ① *entry US$4.50, 0600-1700, access from Puerto Vicente in the village of Infierno, then a 45-min boat ride and a 30-min walk,* a small oxbow lake (2 km long) rich in wildlife including giant river otters (best chance to see them in early morning), caymans and many birds.

Along the **lower Madre de Dios**, also in the national reserve's buffer zone, are small private reserves with lodges in all price categories. In this area is **Lago Valencia**, 60 km from Puerto Maldonado near the Bolivian border (four hours there, eight hours back, or by road). It is a large oxbow lake, 15 km long, with lots of wildlife and many excellent beaches and islands within an hour's boat ride. Mosquitoes are voracious, though. If you're camping, take food and water. For a cycling tour to Lago Valencia, see Lupuna Lodge, page 1508.

To the north of Puerto Maldonado, the **Río Las Piedras** drainage also offers opportunities to visit rich forest. The area is reached by a five-hour drive followed by boat travel. Several NGOs work in the region; see www.arbioperu.org, http://conservetheamazon.org and www.tamanduajungle.com.

☆ Tambopata National Reserve

Sernanp, Jr Cajamarca 946, Puerto Maldonado, T082-571247, rntambopata@sernanp. gob.pe.

The 274,690 ha Tambopata National Reserve (TNR) lies between the rivers Madre de Dios, Tambopata and Heath. The area was first declared a reserve in 1990 and is a very reasonable alternative for those who do not have the time or money to visit Manu. It is a close rival in terms of seeing wildlife and boasts some superb oxbow lakes. Other highlights are the famous clay licks or *collpas*, where macaws and parrots gather to eat minerals which allow them to digest otherwise toxic seeds and fruits; most renowned are **Collpa Chuncho** ① *entry US$20* and **Collpa Colorado** ① *entry US$30,* visited in five-day tours. There are a number of lodges here which are excellent for lowland rainforest birding and fauna observation. The reserve must be visited with an authorized tour operator (see What to do, page 1512).

Within the park and relatively close to Puerto Maldonado is the beautiful and tranquil **Lago Sandoval** ① *entry US$9,* a 30-minute boat ride along the Río Madre de Dios, and then a 3-km walk into the jungle; the first kilometre on a raised wooden walkway, but boots are advisable. You must go with a tour operator and start very early in order to have a chance to see giant river otters. The 3-km-long lake is very rich in fauna and it is surrounded by beautiful forest including *aguaje* palms and very tall kapoks. Around the lake are a few lodges.

Bahuaja Sonene National Park

Sernanp, Libertad 1189, Puno, T051-363960, daranibar@sernanp.gob.pe, fee US$54 for 7-day visit.

The Bahuaja-Sonene National Park, declared in 1996, stretches from the Heath River on the border with Bolivia across the Tambopata and includes the Pampas del Heath tropical grasslands. There are no facilities in the park. Visits only with tour operators who offer seven-day rafting trips along the Río Alto Tambopata, down river from Putina Punco, in the department of Puno (see page 1412), camping on the shore of the river and finishing at the Tambopata Research Centre (TRC). It is an adventurous trip involving paddling through grade III and IV rapids. Sernanp has a list of authorized operators, it includes **Amazonas Explorer** and **River Explorers**, see Cuzco operators, page 1436. **Collpa Heath** ① *entry US$6*, salt lick can be accessed by boat from Puerto Maldonado, along the lower Madre de Dios then up-river on the Heath; InkaNatura and Manu Tambopata Travel arrange tours. There are lodges in the park's buffer zone, InkaNatura has a lodge on the Río Heath, the **Heath River Wildlife Center** ① *www.inkanatura.com*.

To Iberia and Iñapari

Frequent public transport runs to **Iberia** and **Iñapari** on the border with Brazil. No primary forest remains along this section of the Interoceánica, only secondary growth and small chacras (farms). There are lumber towns and a few picturesque caseríos (settlements) that serve as processing centres for the brazil nut.

Iberia, Km 168, a small, quiet town, has a few simple hotels, including $ Casa Blanca (José Aldamis 848, T972-702204, with private bath, cold water, fan and a small garden); Las Castañuelas serves good breakfasts and lunches. Many birds and, at times, monkeys can be seen along the road across the Río Tahuamanu at dawn.

Iñapari, at the end of the road, Km 235, is a tranquil spread out border town with all services, connected by a suspension bridge to Brazil.

Crossing to Brazil Public transport stops near immigration (open 0700-1900 daily), 1 km before the centre of Iñapari and the international bridge (mototaxi US$0.30). Brazilian entry/exit stamps are given by Polícia Federal (open 0700-1900), just outside **Assis Brasil** (mototaxi from Iñapari US$1.20). The only exchange facilities at the border are in Iñapari: opposite immigration and around the plaza, and at Banco de la Nación, at the plaza, which also has an ATM, but rates are better in Cobija (Bolivia) and Puerto Maldonado. There is a paved road from Assis Brasil to Brasiléia, where you can cross to Cobija (Bolivia), or carry on to Rio Branco. There is no official crossing from Peru to Bolivia here, you must continue to Brasiléia.

> **Tip...**
> You can get your exit stamp in advance from Peruvian immigration in Puerto Maldonado (28 de Julio 465).

Listings Southern jungle

Tourist information

Manu Biosphere Reserve

Manu National Park Office
Av Cinco los Chachacomos F2-4, Larapa Grande, San Jerónimo, Cuzco, T084-274509, www.visitmanu.com. Mon-Fri.
Issues permits for the Reserved Zone.

NGOs working in the area which provide information include: **Amazon Conservation Association** (ACCA, Cuzco, T084-222329, Puerto Maldonado, T082-573543, www.amazon conservation.org); **Perú Verde** (Cuzco, T084-226392, www.peruverde.org); **Pronaturaleza** (Lima T01-271 2662, Puerto Maldonado T082-571585, www.pronaturaleza.org).

Puerto Maldonado

Immigration
Av 15 de Agosto 658, T082-571069.
Mon-Fri 0800-1600, Sat 0800-1200.

iPerú
Jr Loreto 390, at the plaza, T082-571830, iperuptomaldonado@promperu.gob.pe.
Mon-Sat 0900-1800, Sun 0900-1300. Also has a desk at the airport, Mon-Fri at flight times.
Very helpful. See also www.gotambopata.com.

Where to stay

Manu Biosphere Reserve

Most jungle lodges are booked as package deals for 3 days, 2 nights, or longer, with meals, transport and guides; see websites for offers. Some lodges in the Cultural Zone, including those in the cloud forest area accept independent travellers. Many lodges in the Cultural Zone use generators to provide a few hours of electricity for light and charging batteries, a few use solar power. In the Reserved Zone, solar power is used, tent camps may not have electricity.

Cuzco to Boca Manu and Puerto Maldonado

Cloud forest lodges

Cock of the Rock Lodge
South of Puente San Pedro, www.inkanatura.com.
Very nice cabins with private or shared bath, hot water, lovely grounds and common areas, camping platform with shower. The fanciest lodge in the area.

Manu Paradise Lodge
Km181.6, just north of Puente San Pedro, T084-224156, www.manuparadiselodge.com.
Nice setting by the river, well-kept grounds and rooms with bath and hot water, includes dinner and breakfast.

Orquídeas de San Pedro Lodge
On a trail 10 mins upriver from the bridge along the Río San Pedro, www.manuadventures.com.
Rustic basic cabins with mosquito nets, shared bath.

Posada San Pedro Lodge
1.5 km north of Puente San Pedro, http://pantiacolla.com
Rustic but very clean wood cabins with mosquito nets, shared bath with hot showers, pleasant common areas and grounds.

Tambo Paititi
On a trail 20 mins upriver from the bridge along the Río San Pedro, www.perudiscovery.com/en/.
Rustic basic cabins with mosquito nets, shared bath.

Alto Madre de Dios lodges

Amazonia Lodge
Just across the river from Atalaya, T084-816131, www.amazonialodgeperu.com; in Cuzco at Calle Tandapata 660, San Blas T084-437374. Tours through Amazon Trails Peru.
An old tea hacienda established by the Yabar Calderón family, famous for its bird diversity and fine hospitality, a great place to relax, meals included (price range **$$$** pp), birding or natural history tours available, contact in advance to arrange a pick-up.

Erika Lodge
25 mins from Atalaya, www.manuadventures.com.
Set in a 900 ha reserve with a range of altitudes. Offers basic accommodation and is cheaper than the other, more luxurious lodges. Also has a canopy zipline. Contact **Manu Adventures** (see page 1511).

Manu Learning Centre
Fundo Mascoitania, 45 mins by boat from Atalaya, www.crees-manu.org.
A 600-ha reserve within the Cultural Zone, see **Crees Tours**, under What to do, below.

Pantiacolla Lodge
30 mins downriver from Shintuya, http://pantiacolla.com.
Set in 900 ha of forest with great altitude range in a transition zone between cloud forest and rainforest. Owned by the Moscoso family. Book through **Pantiacolla Tours** (see page 1511).

Yanayacu Lodge
On the southeast bank of the river, about 1 hr by boat upstream from Diamante village.
Using local river transport to arrive at the lodge rates are very reasonable, prices depend on length of stay. Nearby is a small parrot *collpa*. The lodge also offers several different itineraries in Manu.

Cuzco to Boca Manu

$ Don Pocho
At the north end of town, Itahuanía, T996-547050.
Simple with shared bath and cold water. Owner offers transport.

$ Gallito de las Rocas
Av Cusco s/n, Pilcopata, T952-490712, gallitorocas@hotmail.com.
Bright rooms in clean wooden house, private or shared bath, cold water, a good option.

$ Hospedaje Sulema
In the centre, Itahuanía, T082-830674.
Simple place, friendly owner Sra Eulogia.

$ Los Amigos
Los Amigos s/n, behind the hospital, Salvación, T974-907909.
Simple but clean rooms, private or shared bath, cold water, quiet location.

$ Oteri
Shintuya, T082-812966, Oteriote on Facebook.
Homestay with Wili Corisepa and Isabel Poo, part of community project.

Boca Manu

Community phones: T082-834099, 082-830600. Several basic family-run *hospedajes*, ask at the shops by the plaza.

$ El Albergue
2 blocks from the river.
Simple rooms with shared bath, cold water, courtyard, caters to groups.

$ Yine Lodge
Next to Boca Manu airport.
A cooperative project run between **Pantiacolla Tours** and the Yine community of Diamante, who operate their own tours into their community and surroundings.

Manu National Park Reserved Zone

Several tour operators have camp tents around Cocha Salvador or Cocha Otorongo.

Casa Matsiguenka (Machiguenga)
Near Cocha Salvador, http://matsiguenka. weebly.com. In Cuzco, Av El Sol 627B, of 305, T084-225595.
Traditional Matsiguenka-style cabins each with 3 rooms with private bath, shared showers, solar lighting. Run by two local communities which also offer 4- to 7-day tours.

$ Romero Lodge
Near Limonal, www.crees-manu.org
Traditional wooden lodge with thatched roof, rooms with bath and hot shower.
See **Crees Tours**, page 1511.

Boca Manu to Boca Colorado

Madre de Dios Lodges

Manu Wildlife Center
On the left (northeast) bank, 2 hrs down the Río Madre de Dios from Boca Manu, 3 hrs up from Boca Colorado.
Book through **Manu Expeditions** (www.manu expeditions.com), which runs it in conjunction with the conservation group **Perú Verde**. 22 double cabins, with private bathroom and hot water. Also canopy towers for birdwatching and a tapir lick.

Tambo Blanquillo Lodge
On the right bank of the Madre de Dios, 30 mins downstream from Manu Wildlife Center (see above). In Lima: Av Nicolás de Piérola 265, Barranco, T01-249 9342, http://tamboblanquillo.com.
Comfortable wooden cabins with bath, hot shower and fan and a traditional style *maloca* with 20 rooms with shared bath, solar electricity.

A 10-min boat ride to the access trail to the famous Blanquillo macaw lick, 4- to 6-day tours.

Boca Colorado

$ Hospedaje Colorado
Across from the high school, past the bus station.
A new hotel built in 2016.

$ Hospedaje Fiori
Av Madre de Dios s/n, 1 block from the plaza, T997-277668.
Simple rooms with mosquito nets, private or shared bath, cold water.

Cuzco to Puerto Maldonado via Mazuko

Accommodation is available in Quincemil at **$ Hotel Toni**, friendly, clean, cold shower, good meals. There are more options in Mazuko; **$ Hostal Valle Sagrado** is the best.

Puerto Maldonado

Several new hotels cater to business travellers.

$$$-$$ Centenario
Av Dos de Mayo 744, T082-574731, www.hotelcentenario.com.pe.
Modern hotel 7 blocks from the plaza, bright ample rooms with a/c or fan and frigobar, good views from upper floors, restaurant, terrace with pool, parking, English spoken.

$$$-$$ Wasaí Puerto Maldonado Ecolodge
Jr Guillermo Billinghurst s/n, T082-572290, www.wasai.com.
In a beautiful location overlooking the Madre de Dios, with forest surrounding bungalows and suites, with a/c, also simpler double rooms with bath and dorms (US$12 pp), small pool with waterfall, good restaurant (local fish a speciality), bar. Includes buffet breakfast and transfers, bicycles. Helpful, family run, they can organize local tours and also have a lodge on the Río Tambopata (see page 1509).

$$ Cabañaquinta
Jr Moquegua 422, T082-571045, www.cabanaquinta.com.
A/c or fan, frigobar, laundry, free drinking water, good restaurant, garden with pool, very comfortable, airport transfers. Request a room away from the Interoceanic Highway.

$$ Paititi Hostal
Jr González Prada 290 y Av León Velarde, T082-574667, www.paititihostal.com.

Ample rooms with a/c or fan, those in front are bright but get street noise, good breakfast, gym, attentive staff.

$$ Perú Amazónico
Jr Ica 269, T082-571799,
www.peruamazonico.com.
Very nice modern hotel, comfortable rooms with a/c, fan and frigobar, parking, bicycle rentals. A good choice.

$$-$ Amarumayo
Av Ernesto Rivero 1550, 10 mins from the centre, T982-327375.
Comfortable rooms with a/c, pool and garden, good restaurant.

$$-$ Anaconda Lodge
600 m from airport, T982-728518,
www.anacondajunglelodge.com.
With private or shared bath, Swiss/Thai-owned bungalows, hot showers, swimming pool, Thai restaurant, pizza workshop (arrange a day ahead), tours arranged, camping (US$6 pp, no breakfast), very pleasant, family atmosphere.

$ Hospedaje El Bambú
Jr Puno 837, T082-639399.
Basic and small but well-kept rooms with bath and fan, family atmosphere, breakfast and juices not included in price but served in dining room. A good budget option.

$ Hospedaje Español
González Prada 670, T082-572381.
Simple economical rooms with or without fan, set back from the road, in a quiet part of town.

$ Tambopata Hostel
Jr González Prada 161, T082-574201.
www.tambopatahostel.com.
The only real backpacker hostel in town, private rooms with or without bath and unisex or mixed dorms, terrace with hammocks, kitchen facilities. Nice atmosphere, they also organize 1- to 5-day tours to Tambopata.

Around Tambopata National Reserve
Most jungle lodges are booked as package deals for 3 days, 2 nights, or longer, with meals, transport and guides; see websites below for offers.

Lodges on the lower Río Madre de Dios

Casa de Hospedaje Mejía
Close to Lago Sandoval, T082-573372; contact Sandoval en Tambopata Travel, see Local tour operators, page 1512.

Attractive but basic rustic lodge, full board can be arranged, canoes are available. In the same family and also by the lake is **Maloka Sandoval Lodge**, www.malokasandovallodge.com.

Eco Amazonia Lodge
1 hr down-river from Puerto Maldonado. Office at Av 26 de Diciembre 435, T082-573491; also have offices in Lima and Cuzco, www.ecoamazonia.com.pe.
Basic bungalows and dormitories set in a 4450-ha private reserve with trails, good for birdwatching, has its own Monkey Island with animals taken from the forest.

El Corto Maltés Amazonia
On south shore of the river, Billinghurst 229, Puerto Maldonado, T082-573831, www.cortomaltes-amazonia.com.
On the Madre de Dios, halfway to Sandoval which is the focus of most visits, private reserve with trails and clay lick. Thatched cabins with water, huge dining room, pool, ayahuasca ceremonies, well run.

Estancia Bello Horizonte
18 km northeast of Puerto Maldonado towards the border, Loreto 252, T082-572748, www.estanciabellohorizonte.com.
In a nice stretch of forest overlooking the old course of the Madre de Dios, now a huge *aguajal* (swamp) populated with macaws. A small lodge with bungalows for 30 people, with private bath, hot water, pool. Transport, all meals and guide (several languages offered) included, US$250-280 for 3 days/2 nights. The lodge belongs to **APRONIA**, an organization that trains and provides employment for orphaned children. Suitable for those wanting to avoid a river trip.

Inkaterra Reserva Amazónica Lodge
45 mins by boat down the Madre de Dios, Calle Asunción Nicole s/n – ex ENAPU, T082-573534, Puerto Maldonado, in Lima T01-610 0400, in Cuzco, T084-234010, www.inkaterra.com.
Tastefully redecorated hotel in the jungle with suites and bungalows, solar power, good food in huge dining room supported by a big tree. Jungle tours in its own 10,000 ha reserve, 30-40 m-high canopy walk; also tours to Lago Sandoval. In the same group and with the same high standards and style is **Inkaterra Hacienda Concepción**, 30 mins by boat from Puerto Maldonado (before Isla de los Monos), with cabins and a 6 room lodge. They also run **Inkaterra Guides Field Station**, 1 hr from Puerto Maldonado, a guides training centre and more rustic lodge for visitors and researchers.

Lupuna Lodge

On the south shore of the river, 13 km (40 mins by boat) from Puerto Maldonado, can also be reached by road and a short walk, T943-524714 (Spanish), 928-841740 (English, German), www. lupunavacations.com.

Small private reserve (90 ha) and family farm, 3 rustic screened cabins with bath and cold water, mosquito nets, tasty food with home grown produce. Spanish, English or German guiding in forest trails and nearby attractions including a clay lick, a good economy option with personalized service. Also offer half- to 3-day cycling tours, including a trip to Lago Valencia.

Monte Amazónico Lodge Lago Sandoval

On the south shore of the river, near Lago Sandoval, 60 min by boat from Puerto Maldonado, reserve through Carlos Expeditions, see Local tour operators below, http://carlosexpeditions.com.

Screened rooms and cabins with mosquito nets and bath, ample common areas include a pool.

Sandoval Lake Lodge

1 km beyond Mejía on Lago Sandoval. Book through InkaNatura, www.inkanatura.com.

Usual access is by canoe after a 3-km walk or rickshaw ride. Lodge overlooking the lake, huge bar and dining area, electricity, hot water. InkaNatura also has a lodge on the Río Heath, the **Heath River Wildlife Center**, about 4½ hrs from Puerto Maldonado by boat, but journey times depend on river levels. Just 10 mins from the lodge is a large macaw and parrot clay lick. In the vicinity you can visit both jungle and savannah and in the latter are many endemic bird species. **InkaNatura** runs tours which combine both lodges.

Lodges on the Río Tambopata

Lodges on the Tambopata are reached by vehicle to Puerto Nuevo port, 20 km upriver from Puerto Maldonado by the community of Infierno, then by boat. Over 20 small lodges and *casas de hospedaje* along the Tambopata river are grouped together under the names: **Tambopata Ecotourism Corridor** and **Tambopata Homestays, iPerú** has a current listing for these. See lodge websites for prices of packages offered, check whether entry fees to the reserve are included.

Explorers Inn

58 km from Puerto Maldonado (2½ hrs up the Río Tambopata; 1½ hrs return); Av Circunvalación, Terminal Terrestre, p2, of 111, Puerto Maldonado, T082-573029, www.explorersinn.com.

Just before the La Torre control post, adjoining the TNR, in the part where most research work has been done, this is one of the best places in Peru for seeing jungle birds (580 plus species have been recorded, they have their own clay lick and a 42-m viewing tower) and butterflies (1230 plus species). There are also giant river otters, but you probably need more than a 2-day tour to benefit fully from the location. Tours through the adjoining community of La Torre. The guides are biologists and naturalists undertaking research in the reserve. They provide interesting wildlife-treks.

Monte Amazónico Lodge Tambopata

On the north shore of the river, near Collpa Chuncho, 60 min by boat from Puerto Maldonado, reserve through Carlos Expeditions, see Local tour operators below, http://carlosexpeditions.com.

Screened rooms and cabins with mosquito nets and bath.

Rainforest Expeditions Lodges
3 lodges on the Tambopata River, Av Aeropuerto Km 6, La Joya, Puerto Maldonado, T082-572575, in Lima T01-7196422, in Cuzco T984-705266, USA and Canada T1-877-231 9251, www.perunature.com:

Posada Amazonas Lodge
2 hrs from Puerto Maldonado, 45 mins from Puerto Nuevo.
A collaboration between the tour operator and the local native community of Infierno. Attractive rooms with hot showers, visits to Lake Tres Chimbadas, with good birdwatching including the Tambopata *collpa*. Offers trips to a nearby indigenous primary healthcare project where a native healer gives guided tours of the medicinal plant garden. Service and guiding is very good.

Refugio Amazonas Lodge
3½ hrs from Puerto Maldonado, 2 hrs from Puerto Nuevo, close to Lago Condenados.
Bungalows within a private reserve, large en suite rooms with mosquito nets, hot water, well-designed and run, large open dining area, atmospheric with a resort feel. Visits to El Chuncho clay lick, 30-m observation tower. There are many packages and lots of add-ons at the larger lodges.

Tambopata Research Centre
7 hrs from Puerto Maldonado, 4 hrs from Refugio Amazonas.
The company's more intimate, but comfortable lodge, inside the Tambopata Reserve. Rooms are smaller than at the other lodges, with shared showers, hot water (a few more luxurious rooms under construction in 2017). The lodge is next to the famous Colorado macaw clay lick and a visit to El Chuncho lick is also included. Surrounded by outstanding jungle (includes 5 habitats).

Tambopata Eco Lodge
On the Río Tambopata; reservations office at Nueva Baja 432, Cuzco, T084-245695; operations office Jr Javier Heraud, Urb Los Lirios, Puerto Maldonado, T082-571392, www.tambopatalodge.com.
Rooms with solar-heated water, good guides, excellent food. Trips go to Lake Condenado, some to Lake Sachavacayoc, and to the Collpa de Chuncho, guiding mainly in English and Spanish, naturalists programme provided.

Wasaí Tambopata Lodge
Río Tambopata, 120 km (4½ hrs by boat) upriver from Puerto Maldonado or 1½ hrs by van and 1 hr walking; In Lima T01-436 8792, or Jr Guillermo Billinghurst, Puerto Maldonado, T997-516352, www.wasai.com.
Rustic cabins with bath, cold water, kayaking, zip-line, fishing, photography tours, mystic tours, wildlife observation, volunteering, tours to the Colllpa de Chuncho and Lago Sandoval, guiding in English and Spanish. Also run a tent camp further upstream and a hotel in Puerto Maldonado (see above).

To Iberia and Iñapari

$ Hospedaje Casa Blanca
Av José Aldamiz 848, Iberia, T972-702204.
Simple rooms with or without bath, electric shower, fan, small garden, breakfast available, helpful owners, a good choice.

$ Hospedaje Delta
Jr Jaime Troncoso 439, Iberia, T987-332968.
Multi-storey building, small rooms with bath, cold water, no breakfast.

$ Hospedaje Milagritos
Av León Velarde, near the international bridge, Iñapari, T965-041533.
Very clean functional rooms with bath, cold water, a/c, cheaper with fan.

$ Iñapari
Av Acre s/n, Iñapari, T948-573604.

A variety of rooms and prices, with or without bath, a/c or fan, Wi-Fi in common area.

Restaurants

Puerto Maldonado

\$\$ Burgos's
26 de Diciembre 195, 1 block from the plaza, T082-573653, www.burgosrestaurant.com. Daily 1100-2300.
Serves a choice of regional and international dishes, wine list. Groups should reserve ahead.

\$\$-\$ El Asadazo
Arequipa 209, east side of Plaza.
Popular *menú* at lunchtime, great sandwiches later in the day, cool bar in the evening.

\$\$-\$ El Horcón
Av León Velarde 361, T082-574029. Daily 1800-0100.
Good pizza, also Italian and Mexican dishes and grill, delivery.

\$\$-\$ El Hornito
Jr Carrión on the plaza and 2 other locations. Open from 1800.
Cosy, good pizzas, busy at weekends.

\$ La Estrella
Av León Velarde 480 and 3 other locations. Open 1700-2300.
Popular chicken place.

\$ Vegetariano
Jr Piura 426. Sun-Thu 0800-2100, Fri 0800-1600.
Good vegetarian set meals. Also wholemeal bread and biscuits.

Gustitos del Cura
Loreto 258, Plaza de Armas. Thu-Tue 0800-2300.
Ice cream and juice parlour offering unusual flavours, snacks, sweets, vegetarian dishes. Run by the NGOAPRONIA working with homeless teenagers. Also at Ucayali y 28 de Julio (closed Mon) and at C José María Grain 105, with river views.

Magdalena's
Loreto 300, Plaza de Armas. Daily 0600-2300.
Café, choice of bread, *empanadas*, sweet and savoury pastries, sandwiches, coffee, juices. A popular breakfast spot among tourists.

Bars and clubs

Puerto Maldonado

Casa de la Cerveza
On the plaza adjoining El Hornito. Daily 1000-0100.
Nearest thing to a pub in Puerto Maldonado, rock music, sports on large screen TV.

T-Saica
Loreto 335. Daily from 1800.
An atmospheric bar with live music some weekends.

Witite
Av León Velarde 151. Daily from 2200.
A popular disco playing varied music.

What to do

Manu Biosphere Reserve

Beware of pirate operators on the streets of Cuzco who offer trips to the Reserved Zone of Manu and end up halfway through the trip changing the route "due to emergencies", which, in reality means they have no permits to operate in the area. Some unscrupulous tour guides will offer trips to see the uncontacted tribes of Manu; on no account make any attempt to view these very vulnerable people.

The following companies in Cuzco organize trips into the Multiple Use and Reserved Zones;

contact them for more details. See also **Manu Tambopata Travel**, listed with Local (Puerto Maldonado) tour operators, below.

Amazon Trails Peru, *Tandapata 660, San Blas, Cuzco, T084-437374, or T984-714148, www.amazon trailsperu.com.* Operated by ornithologist Abraham Huamán, who has many years' experience guiding in Manu, and his German wife, Ulla Maennig. Well-organized tours to the National Park and Blanquillo clay lick, with knowledgeable guides, good boatmen and cooks, small groups, guaranteed departure dates. Runs 2 lodges in Manu. Also offers trekking in the Cuzco area.

Bonanza Tours, *Suecia 343, Cuzco, T084-507871, www.bonanzatoursperu.com.* 4- to 8-day tours to Manu with local guides, plenty of jungle walks and camp-based excursions with good food. Tours are high quality and good value.

Crees Tours, *Urb Mcal Gamarra B-5, Zona 1, Cuzco, T084-262433, and 7/8 Kendrick Mews, London SW7 3HG, T+44 (0)20-7581 2932, www. crees-manu.org.* Tours from 4 days/3 nights to 9 days/8 nights to the Manu Learning Centre, a lodge accommodating 24 guests, 45 mins from Atalaya by boat. The lodge has all en suite rooms with hot showers; food is produced locally in a bio-garden. All tours spend the 1st night at the **Cock of the Rock Lodge**, on the road from Paucartambo to Atalaya. Tours are associated with the **Crees Foundation** (www.crees-foundation.org), a fully sustainable organization which works with immigrant and indigenous communities to reduce poverty and protect biodiversity in the rainforest.

Expediciones Vilca, *Plateros 359, Cuzco, T084-244751.* Offers tours at economical prices.

Greenland Peru, *Celasco Astete C-12, Cuzco, T084-246572, www.greenlandperu.com.* Fredy Domínguez is an Amazonian and offers good-value trips to Manu with comfortable accommodation and transport and excellent food cooked by his mother.

Experienced, knowledgeable and enthusiastic, and he speaks English.

InkaNatura, *Ricardo Palma J1, Cuzco, T084-243408; in Lima T01-203 5000, UK T0800-234 8659, USA/ Canada T1-888-870 7378, www.inkanatura.com.* Tours to **Manu Wildlife Centre** (see Madre de Dios Lodges, above) and to **Sandoval Lake Lodge** and **Heath River Wildlife Center** in the Tambopata Reserve (see Lodges on the lower Río Madre de Dios, above) with emphasis on sustainable tourism and conservation. Knowledgeable guides. They also run treks in Cuzco area and tours in the Titicaca area and northern Peru.

Manu Adventures, *Plateros 356, Cuzco, T084-261640, www.manuadventures.com.* This company operates one of the most physically active Manu programmes, with options for 1 hr of whitewater rafting on the way to **Erika Lodge** on the Río Alto Madre de Dios, where they operate a canopy walkway and zipline.

Manu Expeditions and Birding Tours, *Jr Los Geranios 2-G, Urb Mariscal Gamarra, 1a Etapa, Cuzco, T084-225990, www.manuexpeditions.com.* Owned by ornithologist Barry Walker, 3 trips available to Manu National Park and **Manu Wildlife Center**, plus specialized birding tours in several South American countries and trekking and horse riding tours in the Cuzco area.

Oropéndola, *Av Circunvalación s/n, Urb Guadalupe Mz A Lte 3, Cuzco, T084-241428, www.oropendolaperu.org.* Guide Walter Mancilla Huamán is an expert on flora and fauna. 5-, 7- and 9-day tours. Good reports of attention to detail and to the needs of clients.

Pantiacolla Tours, *Garcilaso 265, interior, p 2, of 12, Cuzco, T084-238323, www.pantiacolla.com.* Run by Marianne van Vlaardingen and Gustavo Moscoso. They have tours to the cloud forest, the **Pantiacolla Lodge** (see Where to stay, page 1505) and also 7- and 9-day tours to the Reserved Zone.

Pantiacollaworks with indigenous communities and supports the Federación de Nativos de Madre de Dios.

Puerto Maldonado

Boat hire
Boat hire may be arranged at Puerto Capitanía.

Local tour operators
Many operators are located on the pedestrian section of Av León Velarde between the plaza and the bridge.

Carlos Expeditions, *Av León Velarde 141,T082-571320, www.carlosexpeditions.com*. Run by Carlos Borja Gama who speaks several languages, offers traditional tours and specialist birdwatching and photography tours. Also runs the Monte Amazónico lodges near Laguna Sandoval and along the Río Tambopata. Popular with backpackers.

Manu Tambopata Travel, *Jr San Martín 775, T082-573755, http://manutambopatatravel.com*. 3- to 8-day tours in Manu and Tambopata reserves. Include a trip to the Río Heath area.

Paquetes Turísticos Municipales, *a t the Municipalidad, Av LeónVelarde 230, Plaza de Armas,T983-336618*. Medioambiente y Turismo at the Municipalidad organizes group day tours to nearby attractions (including Lago Sandoval) on weekends and holidays. A good choice for those who have little time.

Sandoval en Tambopata Travel, *Av León Velarde 230, Plaza de Armas, T082-573372, www.malokasandoval.com*. Run by the Mejía brothers who speak English and French and offer tours to Sandoval Lake and their lodges: **Casa de Hospedaje Mejía** and **Maloka Lodge**.

Tambopata Expeditions, *Av León Velarde 160, T987-590164*. Tours to attractions in the Tambopata Reserve and surroundings including Salvador, Valencia and Tres Chimbadas lakes, also adventure tours like kayaking, canopy and ziplines. Operate **Tambopata Hostel** in town and **Collpas Tambopata Inn**, http://tambopatajungle.com, abutting the Tambopata Reserve. Popular with backpackers.

Tambopata National Reserve
For tours to the Tambopata Reserve, see Lodges on the lower Río Madre de Dios, Lodges on the Río Tambopata and Local tour operators, all above.

Cuzco to Boca Manu and Puerto Maldonado
Tour companies usually use their own vehicles for the overland trip from Cuzco to Manu, but it is possible to do it independently. Some companies offer the option to fly from Cuzco to Boca Manu in a charter flight, at an additional cost.

Air There is an airfield at the indigenous community across the river from Boca Manu. There are no commercial flights from Cuzco, only those chartered by tour operators. Irregular light-aircraft flights from Boca Manu to **Puerto Maldonado**, operated by the Pucallpa based company **North American** (T995-734281, www.northamerican.pe) are intended for the local population and subsidized by the government; they may take tourists if they have space. Ask at the Municipalidad in Boca Manu, the flights are scheduled one month at a time, according to demand (about 2 flights per week).

Road and river In 2017, the road from Cuzco was paved almost to Paucartambo, beyond is a good dirt road. It is passable in the rainy season, but there are usually some landslides that close the road for a few hours, a day, occasionally longer. Take repellent and some food and water. Most transport to this area leaves from Control de San Jerónimo, across from the police station, south of Cuzco (reached by Satélite city bus from San Francisco or by taxi, about US$6, 1 hr). Transport that starts elsewhere also passes the San Jerónimo stop. The following leave from San Jerónimo unless otherwise noted. To **Pilcopata** Gallito de las Rocasbus at 0500, **Apu Coñahuay** at 1700, US$7.50, 8 hrs; vans bound for Salvación (see below) take passengers to Pilcopata, US$9, 6 hrs. Trucks to Pilcopata run Mon, Wed, Fri, returning Tue, Thu, Sat, 9 hrs in wet season, less in the dry. To **Salvación**, vans leave from PRONAA, Av República del Perú, Primer Paradero, San Sebastián, south of Cuzco, most at 1100 and a few at 1600, US$12, 7-8 hrs; **Villa Salvación** (T990-420222), **Amazon Tours** (T984-802628, also has a kiosk at Control San Jerónimo), **Corazón Serrano** (T957-698111) and **Manu Express** (T932-756510). Book ahead; return to Cuzco at the same times. Salvación to **Shintuya**, Sr Cotayo, bus at 0600, US$2.45, 1½ hrs, return around 0730. Between Pilcopata and Salvación, Sr Yuyo, van, US$6 pp, 1½ hrs; also on Mon, Wed, Fri, Sr Cotayo's bus from Salvación at 1100, return from Pilcopata at

1600, US$2.45. Other than the bus to Shintuya, there is no scheduled service to continue north from Salvación. Depending on demand, Don Pocho (T996-547050, Itahuanía), offers transport north, most reliably in the evening Mon, Wed, Fri, enquire with Silvia at Transportes Villa Salvación (T942-144622); to **Itahuanía**, US$7.60, 2½ hrs; to **Shipitiare**, US$10.60, 3 hrs; to **Nuevo Edén** about US$12.60, 3½ hrs; beware of overcharging. Pickups can also be hired, enquire at **Transportes Corazón Serrano**.

To reach **Boca Manu**, enquire in Salvación which port is being used at the time (it depends on the state of the road). Time and patience are required at the port to get a boat, ask around and be attentive, sometimes they stop briefly. If they are taking cargo, you will have to wait for the boat to be fully laden. Itahuanía–Boca Manu in a shared boat is US$7.50; a private, chartered boat would be over US$100; Shipitiare-Boca Manu, US$6, 3 hrs; Diamante-Boca Manu, about US$4, 45 mins-1 hr. Boats may also leave from the port at the roadhead directly for Boca Colorado on the Río Madre de Dios (from Itahuanía, about 9 hrs, US$20).

There is no scheduled boat service from Boca Manu to **Boca Colorado**. Shared service costs US$9-12 and to charter a boat about US$300. Boats can be hired to go upriver from Boca Colorado with **Express Wari** (Av El Puerto, T958-966014) and others.

To reach **Puerto Maldonado** from Boca Colorado, vans leave the bus terminal for Puerto Carlos, US$6, 1 hr, for the ferry across the Inambari River, US$1.50, 10 mins; vans then run on an unpaved road to Santa Rosa (basic accommodation), the junction with the Carretera Interoceánica, to go either northeast to Puerto Maldonado, US$7.60, 2 hrs, or south to Mazuko, US$4.55, 1½ hrs. In Puerto Maldonado, contact **Turismo Boca Colorado** (Tacna 342, T082-573435) or **Expediciones Colorado Manu** (Av Ernesto Rivero 952, T946-693201). From Mazuko there is transport to Cuzco and Juliaca-Puno.

Cuzco to Puerto Maldonado: via Urcos and Mazuko

Bus The Interoceánica is paved all the way. There are many daily buses between the Cuzco and Puerto Maldonado bus terminals, US$9-12 económico, US$12-21 semi-cama, US$21-24 cama, 10-11 hrs. The more reliable companies include **Cruz del Sur** (from its private terminal in Cuzco at 2100), **Móvil** (0900, 1800, 2030), and

Transzela (2100); there are many others (2000-2100). Van companies that run to Mazuko, also offer service to Cuzco (US$18). Vans run between **Mazuko** and Puerto Maldonado 0300-2200, with **Express Turismo** (Av Tacna con Piura, Puerto Maldonado, T973-581284; Av Inambari in Mazuko) and **Expediciones Colorado Manu** (see above; in Cuzco, Av Alameda Pachacútec 427, T946-693203), US$7.60, 3 hrs. Several buses also run daily along the Interoceanic Highway from Arequipa and Juliaca, crossing the altiplano and joining the Cuzco–Puerto Maldonado section at Puente Inambari, south of Mazuko.

Puerto Maldonado

Air To **Lima**, daily with LATAM (León Velarde 503, T082-573677), direct and via Cuzco, Avianca/TACA (2 de Mayo 313), via Cuzco and Star Perú (León Velarde 505) direct and via Cuzco. Mototaxi from town to airport, US$3, taxi US$4.55, 8 km.

Bus and van The Terminal Terrestre is at Jr Atahualpa and Circunvalación Norte, 4 km northwest of the plaza; taxi to the centre US$2.75, mototaxi US$1.80. The better companies are listed, there are others. To **Cuzco**, see Cuzco to Puerto Maldonado via Mazuko, above; buses leave Puerto Maldonado at same time as departures from Cuzco. To **Juliaca**, via Mazuko, San Gabán and Macusani, US$10.60-15, 12 hrs, with **Santa Cruz** (T951-289800) at 1430, 1730; **Realeza** (T984 901945) at 1900; **Julsa** at 1530; **Mendivil** at 1630; **Wayra** (T940-213859) at 1700; **Power** (T977-648208) at 1600; the last 4 continue to **Arequipa**, US$18-24, 16 hrs. To **Puno**, with **Santa Cruz** at 1900, US$12-15, the only direct bus, otherwise change in Juliaca.

For **Boca Manu** and **Salvación** take a colectivo to **Boca Colorado** and then hire a boat or take a cargo boat to Boca Manu and further to Nuevo Edén or beyond (no fixed schedule). From Salvación there is transport to Cuzco.

To **Brazil**: to **Iberia**, 2½ hrs, US$4.55, and **Iñapari**, 3½ hrs, US$7.60, vans 0330-1900 daily, from Jr Ica block 5 y Jr Piura, by Mercado Modelo; recommended companies are **Turismo Imperial** and **Turismo Real Dorado**.

Car and motorcycle hire Las Anclas, Gonzales Prada 380, T983-766618, motorcycles cost US$1.50-3 per hr plus US$15 security deposit, pickup including 300 km costs US$280 per day, plus US$300 security deposit. Passport and driver's licence plus copies must be shown. English and German spoken.

Practicalities
Getting around

Air

Carriers serving the major cities are **Star Perú** ① T01-705 9000, www.starperu.com, **LATAM** ① T01-213 8200, www.latam.com, **Avianca/TACA** ① T01-511 8222, www.avianca.com, and **Peruvian Airlines** ① T01-716 6000, www.peruvianairlines.pe. For destinations such as Andahuaylas, Ayacucho, Cajamarca, Jauja, Huánuco, Huaraz and Pisco flights are offered by LC Peru ① T01-204 1313, www.lcperu.pe. Flights start at about US$100 one-way anywhere in the country from Lima, but prices vary greatly between airlines, with LATAM being the most expensive for non-Peruvians. Prices often increase at holiday times (Semana Santa, May Day, Inti Raymi, 28-29 July, Christmas and New Year), and for elections. During these times and the northern hemisphere summer, seats can be hard to come by, so book early. Flight schedules and departure times may change. In the rainy season delays and cancellations are more common. Flights to jungle regions may also be less reliable. It is best to allow an extra day between national and international flights, especially in the rainy season. Be at the airport well ahead of your flight.

Rail

There are four lines of interest to most travellers. The first is Cuzco–Machu Picchu, on which two companies operate services: **PeruRail** ① www.perurail.com, and **Inca Rail** ① www.incarail.com; the second and third are Puno–Cuzco and Cuzco–Arequipa, run by **PeruRail**. The other railway that carries passengers is the line from Lima to Huancayo, with a continuation to Huancavelica in the central highlands. The service runs on an irregular basis, so check www.fcca.com.pe for the latest schedule. Train services may be cut in the rainy season.

River

On almost any trip to the Amazon Basin, a boat journey will be required at some point, either to get you to a jungle lodge, or to go between river ports. Large passenger and cargo vessels are called *lanchas*; smaller faster craft are called *rápidos* or *deslizadores* (speedboats). *Yates* are small to medium wooden *colectivos*, usually slow, and *chalupas* are small motor launches used to ferry passengers from the lanchas to shore. Jungle lodges invariably have their own motorized canoes with a canopy for transporting guests.

On *lanchas* you can pay either to sling your hammock on deck, or for a berth in a cabin sleeping two to four people. Bear in mind that it's safer to club together and pay for a cabin in which to lock your belongings, even if you sleep outside in a hammock. A hammock is essential. A double hammock, of material (not string), provides one person with a blanket. Board the boat many hours in advance to guarantee hammock space. If going on the top deck, try to be first down the front; take rope for hanging your hammock, plus string and sarongs for privacy. On all boats, hang your hammock away from lightbulbs (they aren't switched off at night and attract all sorts of strange insects) and away from the engines, which usually emit noxious fumes. Guard your belongings from the moment you board. There is very little privacy; women travellers can expect a lot of attention. There are basic washing and toilet facilities, but the food is rice, chicken and beans (and whatever can be picked up en route) cooked in river water. Stock up on drinking water, fruit, tinned food and snacks before boarding. Vegetarians must take their own supplies. There is usually a bar on board. Take plenty of prophylactic enteritis tablets; many contract dysentery on the trip. Also take insect repellent and a good book or two.

Rápidos carry life jackets and have bathrooms; a simple breakfast and lunch are included in the price.

Driving in Peru

Documents You must have an international driving licence and be over 21 to drive in Peru. If bringing in your own vehicle you must provide proof of ownership; a *libreta de pasos por aduana* or *carnet de passages* is accepted, although not officially required. You cannot officially enter Peru with a vehicle registered in someone else s name. On leaving Peru there is no check on the import of a vehicle. All vehicles are required to carry Peruvian insurance (SOAT, Seguro Obligatorio para Accidentes de Tránsito) and spot checks are frequent, especially in border areas. SOAT can be purchased for as little as one month (US$10) at larger border crossings, but only during office hours (Monday-Friday 0800-1800).

Organizations The Touring y Automóvil Club del Perú, Avenida Trinidad Morán 698, Lince, Lima, T01-611 9999, www.touringperu.com.pe, with offices in several provincial cities, offers help to tourists and particularly to members of the leading motoring associations.

Car hire The minimum age for renting a car is 25. If renting a car, your home driving licence will be accepted for up to six months. Car hire companies are given in the text. Always check that the vehicle you rent has a spare wheel, toolkit and functioning lights etc.

Fuel and tolls From 84 octane to 97 octane petrol/gasoline is sold, as well as diesel. Unleaded fuel (90, 95 and 97 octane) is available in large cities and along the Panamericana, but rarely in the highlands or jungle. Current prices and availability throughout the country are posted on www.facilito.gob.pe. Tolls, US$1.50-3.70, are charged on most major paved roads.

Road

Most of Peru's main roads are paved, including the Pan-American Highway which runs north–south through the coastal desert. Mountain roads that are unpaved can be good, but some are very bad. Each year they are affected by heavy rain and mud slides, especially on the east slopes of the mountains. Some of these roads can be dangerous or impassable in the rainy season. Check with locals (not with bus companies, who only want to sell tickets), as accidents are more common at these times.

Bus Services along the coast to the north and south as well as inland to Huancayo, Ayacucho and Huaraz are generally good, but on long-distance journeys it is advisable to pay a bit extra and travel with a reliable company. Whatever the standard of service, accidents and hold-ups on buses do occur, especially at night; it is best to travel by day whenever possible, both for safety and to enjoy the outstanding views. All major bus companies operate modern buses with two decks on interdepartmental routes. The first deck is called *bus cama*, the second *semi-cama*. Both have seats that recline, *bus cama* further than *semi-cama*. These buses usually run overnight and are more expensive than ordinary buses which tend to run earlier in the day. Many buses have toilets and show endless movies. Each company has a different name for its regular and *cama* or *ejecutivo* services. **Cruz del Sur**, **Móviltours**, **Oltursa**, **Flores** and **Ormeño** are among the better bus lines covering large parts of the country. **Cruz del Sur**, generally regarded as a class above the others, accepts Visa cards and gives 10% discount to ISIC and Under 26 cardholders (you may have to insist). There are many smaller but still excellent bus lines that run only to specific areas. An increasing number accept internet bookings and you may find good deals on their websites. For bus lines, see page 1282. For a centralized information and booking site, visit www.busportal.pe. Most bus terminals charge a usage fee of about US$0.50 which you pay at a kiosk before boarding. Many also charge a small fee for use of the toilet. Take a blanket or warm jacket when travelling in the mountains.

> **Tip...**
> Prices of bus tickets are raised by 60-100% two or three days before Semana Santa, on 28 July (Independence Day – Fiestas Patrias), at Christmas and for special local events. Tickets are sold out two or three days in advance at this time and transport is hard to come by.

Where buses stop it is possible to buy food on the roadside. With the better companies you will get a receipt for your luggage, which will be locked under the bus. On local buses watch your luggage and never leave valuables on the luggage rack or floor, even when on the move. If your bus breaks down and you are transferred to another line and have to pay extra, keep your original ticket for refund from the first company.

Light vehicles operate on many shorter routes, up to about four hours; these may be minibuses, modern vans, older combis, or cars. The latter are called *colectivos* or *autos* and are usually faster (sometimes too fast) and more expensive than the others. Luggage space is more limited than on buses, but these light vehicles make it possible, in many cases, just to turn up and travel within an hour or two. They leave only when full. They go almost anywhere in Peru; most firms have offices. Book a day in advance and they may pick you up at your hotel or in the main plaza.

Hitchhiking Hitchhiking is difficult. Try toll points, but these are often far from towns. You are usually expected to pay for a ride, always ask in advance.

Taxi Taxi prices are fixed in most towns, about US$1-1.50 in the urban area. Fares are not fixed in Lima although some drivers work for companies that do have standard fares. Ask locals what the price should be and always set the price beforehand; expect to pay US$3-5 in the capital. The main cities have taxis that can be hired by phone; these charge a little more, but are usually reliable and safe. Many taxi drivers work for commission from hotels. Choose your own hotel and get a driver who is willing to take you there. Taxis at airports are much more expensive; seek advice about the price in advance. In most places it is cheaper to walk out of the airport to the main road and flag down a cab; but this may not be safe, especially at night (never do so in Lima). Another common form of public transport is the mototaxi, a three-wheel motorcycle with an awning covering the double-seat behind the driver. Fares are about US$1.

Maps

The **Instituto Geográfico Nacional** in Lima sells a wide selection of maps, see page 1279. Another official map source is the **Ministerio de Transporte** ① *Jr Zorritos 1203, Lima centre, T01-615 7800, www. mtc.gob.pe*. Mapa Vial del Perú by **Lima 2000** (www.lima2000.com.pe) is a very useful road map. A good travel map of the Callejón de Huaylas and Cordillera Huayhuash, by Felipe Díaz, is available in many shops in Huaraz. Trekking maps from the **Österreichischer Alpenverein** (www.alpenverein.at, in German) include: *Cordillera Blanca Nord 0/3a, Cordillera Blanca Süd 0/3b*, and *Cordillera Huayhuash 0/3c*; also available at **Café Andino** in Huaraz, and **Pony's Expeditions** in Caraz. Trekking maps for several regions of Peru can be downloaded from www.trekkingperu.org.

Where to stay

Hotels

All deluxe and first-class hotels charge 18% in state sales tax (IGV) and 10% service charges. Foreigners should not have to pay the sales tax on hotel rooms. Neither is given in the accommodation listings, unless specified. Places that offer accommodation should (but may not) have a plaque outside bearing the letters H (Hotel), Hs (Hostal), HR (Hotel Residencial) or P (Pensión) according to type.

A hotel has 51 rooms or more, a *hostal* 50 or fewer; the categories do not describe quality or facilities. Many hotels have safe parking for motorcycles. iPerú ① *www.peru.travel*, advises that all accommodation registered with them is listed on their website. See the Planning your trip chapter for our hotel price guide.

> **Tip...**
> All hotels seem to be crowded during Christmas and Easter holidays, Carnival and at the end of July; Cuzco in June is also very busy.

Camping

Camping in Peru is delightful and best suited to trekking routes and wilderness areas. There can be problems with robbery when camping near towns or villages. Avoid such a location, or ask

Camping gas in screw-top containers is available in the main cities. Those with stoves designed for white-gas should use *bencina*, available from hardware stores (*ferreterías*) in larger towns.

Youth hostels

Contact **Asociación Peruana de Albergues Turísticos Juveniles** ① *Av Casimiro Ulloa 328, Miraflores, Lima, T01-446 5488, www.limahostell.com.pe or www.hostellingperu.com.pe.*

Food & drink

Restaurants

A normal lunch or dinner costs US$5-8, but can go up to about US$80 in a first-class restaurant, with drinks and wine. (See box, page 1273, for information on high-end dining.) Middle- and high-class restaurants may add 10% service, but not include the 18% sales tax in the bill (which foreigners do have to pay); this is not shown on the price list or menu, check in advance. Lower-class restaurants charge only tax, while cheap, local restaurants charge no taxes. Lunch (*almuerzo*) is the main meal and most restaurants serve one or two set lunch menus, called *menú ejecutivo* or *menú económico* (US$2-3). The *menú* has the advantage of being served almost immediately and it is usually cheap. The *menú ejecutivo* costs US$2.50-4 or more for a three-course meal with a drink and it offers greater choice and more interesting dishes. *Menú* may also be available for the evening meal (*cena*) but is usually less inspired. Some Chinese restaurants (*chifas*) serve good food at reasonable prices. Many cheaper restaurants have blaring TVs, a must for local patrons but not conducive to relaxed dining. See the Planning your trip chapter for our restaurant price guide.

Peruvian cuisine

Coast The best coastal dishes are seafood-based, the most popular being ceviche. This is a dish of raw white fish marinated in lemon juice, onion and hot peppers. Traditionally, ceviche is served with corn-on-the-cob, *cancha* (toasted corn), yucca and sweet potatoes. *Tiradito* is ceviche without onions made with plaice. Another mouth-watering fish dish is *escabeche* – fish with onions, hot green pepper, red peppers, prawns (*langostinos*), cumin, hard-boiled eggs, olives, and sprinkled with cheese (it can also be made with chicken). For fish on its own, don't miss the excellent *corvina*, or white sea bass. You should also try *chupe de camarones*, which is a shrimp stew made with varying ingredients. Other fish dishes include *parihuela*, a popular bouillabaisse which includes *yuyo de mar*, a tangy seaweed, and *aguadito*, a thick rice and fish soup said to have rejuvenating powers. A favourite northern coastal dish is *seco de cabrito*, roasted kid (baby goat) served with the ubiquitous beans and rice, or *seco de cordero* which uses lamb instead. Also good is *ají de gallina*, a rich and spicy creamed chicken, and duck is excellent. *Humitas* are small, stuffed dumplings made with maize. The *criollo* cooking of the coast has a strong tradition and can be found throughout the country. A dish almost guaranteed to appear on every restaurant menu is *lomo saltado*, a kind of stir-fried beef with onions, vinegar, ginger, chilli, tomatoes and fried potatoes, served with rice. Other popular examples are *cau cau*, made with tripe, potatoes, peppers, and parsley and served with rice, and *anticuchos*, which are shish kebabs of beef heart with garlic, peppers, cumin seeds and vinegar. *Rocoto relleno* is a very spicy hot pepper stuffed with beef and vegetables, often served with *pastel de papas*, potato slices baked with eggs and cheese, to cool the fire. *Palta rellena* is avocado filled with chicken or Russian salad. *Estofado de carne* is a stew that often contains wine, and *carne en adobo* is a cut and seasoned steak. Two good dishes that use potatoes are *causa* and *carapulca*. On coastal menus *causa* is made with mashed potato wrapped around a filling, which often contains crabmeat. On other occasions, *causa* has yellow potatoes, lemons, pepper, hard-boiled eggs, olives, lettuce, sweet cooked corn, sweet cooked potato, fresh cheese, and is served with onion sauce.

Highlands The staples of highland cooking, corn and potatoes, come in a variety of shapes, sizes and colours. A popular potato dish is *papa a la huancaína*, which is topped with a spicy sauce made with *Leche Glória* (the ubiquitous tinned evaporated milk) and cheese. The most commonly eaten corn dishes are *choclo con queso*, corn on the cob with cheese, and *tamales*, boiled corn dumplings filled with meat and wrapped in a banana leaf. Most typical of highland food is *pachamanca*, a combination of meats (beef, lamb, pork, chicken), potatoes, sweet potatoes, corn, beans, cheese and corn humitas, all slow-cooked in the ground, dating back to Inca times. A delicacy in the highlands is *cuy*, guinea pig.

Jungle The main ingredient in jungle cuisine is fish, especially the succulent, dolphin-sized *paiche*, which comes with the delicious *palmito*, or palm-hearts, and yucca and fried bananas. *Tocacho* is green banana, cooked and ground to a chunky paste, usually served with pork (*cecina*) and sausage (*chorizo*). *Juanes* are a jungle version of tamales, stuffed with chicken and rice.

Other dishes Meat dishes are many and varied. *Ollucos con charqui* is a kind of potato with dried meat, *sancochado* is meat and all kinds of vegetables stewed together and seasoned with ground garlic and *lomo a la huancaína* is beef with egg and cheese sauce. Others include *fritos*, fried pork, usually eaten in the morning, *chicharrones*, deep fried chunks of pork ribs and chicken or fish, and *lechón*, baked pork. Very filling and good value are the many soups on offer, such as *caldos* (broths): eg *de carnero, verde*, or *de cabeza*, which includes a sheep's head cooked with corn and tripe. Also *yacu-chupe*, a green soup made from potato, with cheese, garlic, coriander, parsley, peppers, eggs, onions and mint, and *sopa a la criolla,* containing thin noodles, beef heart, egg, vegetables and pleasantly spiced.

Fruits Peruvian fruits are of good quality: they include bananas, the citrus fruits, pineapples, dates, avocados (*paltas*), eggfruit (*lúcuma*), custard apple (*chirimoya*) which can be as big as your head, quince, papaya, mango, guava, the passion-fruit (*maracuyá*) and the soursop (*guanábana*).

Drink

The most famous local drink is pisco, a clear brandy which, with egg whites and lime juice, makes the famous *pisco sour*. The most renowned brands come from the Ica valley. The best wines are also from Ica, Tabernero, Tacama (especially its Selección Especial and Terroix labels), Ocucaje and Santiago Queirolo (in particular its Intipalka label). Beer is of the lager type, the best known brands being Cusqueña and Arequipeña brands (lager) and Trujillo Malta (porter). In Lima only Cristal and Pilsen are readily available. Other brands, including some Brazilian beers, are coming onto the market, but there is little difference between any of them, Seek out the microbreweries which are springing up, eg in Huaraz. *Chicha de jora* is a maize beer, usually home-made and not easy to come by, refreshing but strong, and *chicha morada* is a soft drink made with purple maize. The local rival to Coca Cola (but now owned by that US multinational) is the fluorescent yellow Inca Cola; some say it tastes like boiled lollipops. Peruvian coffee is good, but the best is exported and many cafés only serve coffee in liquid form or Nescafé. There are many different kinds of herbal tea (*mates*): the commonest are *manzanilla* (camomile), *menta* (mint) and *anís*. *Mate de coca* is frequently served in the highlands to stave off the discomforts of altitude sickness.

Essentials A-Z

Accident and emergency

Police T105, www.pnp.gob.pe (Policía Nacional del Perú); **Emergency medical attention (Cruz Roja)** T115; **Fire** T116; these are meant to be nationwide but do not work in all locations.
Tourist police, Jr Moore 268, Magdalena, 38th block of Av Brasil, Lima, T0800-22221 nationwide toll-free; Lima T01-460 1060/0844, daily 24 hrs. They are friendly, helpful and speak English and some German.

Electricity

220 volts AC, 60 cycles throughout the country, except Arequipa (50 cycles). Most 4- and 5-star hotels have 110 volts AC. Plugs are American flat-pin or twin flat and round pin combined.

Embassies and consulates

For all Peru embassies and consulates abroad and for all foreign embassies and consulates in Peru, see http://embassy.goabroad.com.

Health

Medical services
Arequipa Clinic Arequipa SA, Puente Grau y Av Bolognesi, T054-599000, www. clinicarequipa.com.pe, fast and efficient with English-speaking doctors and all hospital facilities; **Paz Holandesa**, Villa Continental, C 4, No 101, Paucarpata, T054-432281, www. pazholandesa.com, Dutch and English spoken, 24-hr service. Highly recommended.
Cuzco Hospital Regional, Av de la Cultura, T084-227661, emergencies T084-223691; **Clínica Pardo**, Av de la Cultura 710, T084-240387, www. clinicapardo-cusco.com, 24 hrs daily, highly regarded and expensive, works with international insurance companies, some English-speaking staff; **Clínica Paredes**, Calle Lechugal 405, T084-225265, www.sos-mg.com. 24 hrs daily, excellent service, emergency doctors speak good English.
Iquitos Clínica Ana Stahl, Av la Marina 285, T065-252535.
Lima Clínica Anglo Americano, Alfredo Salazar 350, San Isidro, T01-616 8900, www. angloamericana.com.pe, stocks Yellow Fever and Tetanus; **Clínica Internacional**, Jr Washington 1471 y Paseo Colón (9 de Diciembre), T01-619 6161, www.clinicainternacional.com.pe, good,

clean and professional, consultations up to US$35, no inoculations; **Instituto de Medicina Tropical**, Av Honorio Delgado 430 near the Pan American Highway in the Cayetano Heredia Hospital, San Martín de Porres, T01-482 3903, www.upch.edu. pe/tropicales/, good for check-ups after jungle travel. **Clínica Good Hope**, Malecón Balta 956, Miraflores, T01-610 7300, www.goodhope.org. pe, has been recommended, will make visits to hotels; prices similar to US; **International Health Department**, at Jorge Chávez airport, T01-517 1845, daily 24 hrs for vaccinations.
Trujillo Clínica Peruano Americana, Av Mansiche 810, T044-231261, English spoken, good.

Money

US$1 = S/3.28; €1 = S/3.67 (Jun 2017).

Currency
The sol (s/) is divided into 100 céntimos. Notes in circulation are: S/200, S/100, S/50, S/20 and S/10. Coins: S/5, S/2, S/1, S/0.50, S/0.20, S/0.10 and S/0.05 (being phased out). Some prices are quoted in dollars (US$) in more expensive establishments, to avoid changes in the value of the sol. You can pay in soles, however. Try to break down large notes whenever you can as there is a shortage of change in museums, post offices, even shops. Taxi drivers are notorious in this regard – one is simply told 'no change'. Do not accept this excuse.

Checking for forgeries
Forged US$ notes and forged soles notes and coins are in circulation. Always check your money when you change it, even in a bank (including ATMs). Hold sol notes up to the light to inspect the watermark and that the colours change according to the light. The line down the side of the bill spelling out the bill's amount should appear green, blue and pink. Fake bills are only pink and have no hologram properties. There should also be tiny pieces of thread in the paper (not glued on). In parts of the country, forged 1-, 2- and 5-sol coins are in circulation. The fakes are slightly off-colour, the surface copper can be scratched off and they tend to bear a recent date. Posters in public places explain what to look for in forged soles. See also www.bcrp.gob.pe, under **Billetes y Monedas**.

Credit cards, ATMs and banks

Visa (by far the most widely accepted card in Peru), MasterCard, American Express and Diners Club are all valid. There is often an 8-12% commission for all credit card charges. Bank exchange policies vary from town to town, but as a general rule the following applies (but don't be surprised if a branch has different rules): **BCP** (Mon-Fri 0900-1800, Sat 0900-1300) changes US$ cash to soles; cash advances on Visa in soles only; VíaBCP ATM with US$2 surcharge for Visa/Plus, MasterCard/Cirrus, Amex. **BBVA Continental** changes US$ cash to soles; B24 ATM for Visa/Plus has US$5 charge. **Interbank** (Mon-Fri 0900-1815, Sat 0900-1230) changes US$ cash to soles for US$5 per transaction up to US$500; branches have **Global Net** ATMs (see below). **Scotiabank** (Mon-Fri 0915-1800, Sat 0915-1230) changes US$ cash to soles, cash advances on MasterCard; ATM for Visa, MasterCard, Maestro and Cirrus. There are also **Global Net** and **Red Unicard** ATMs that accept Visa, Plus and MasterCard, Maestro and Cirrus (the former makes a charge per transaction). ATMs usually have a maximum withdrawal limit of between US$140 and US$200. It is safest to use ATMs at bank branches during banking hours. At public places like shopping malls, at night and on Sun there is more chance of the transaction going wrong, or false money being in the machine. Most ATMs allow you to request either soles or US$ and their use is widespread. Availability decreases outside large towns. In smaller towns, always take some cash. Businesses displaying credit card symbols may not necessarily accept the cards.

Currency exchange

All banks' exchange rates are considerably less favourable than *casas de cambio* (exchange houses). Long queues and paperwork may be involved. US$ and euros are the only currencies which should be brought into Peru from abroad (take some small bills). There are no restrictions on foreign exchange. Few banks change euros. Some banks ask to see 2 documents with your signature for changing cash. Always count your money in the presence of the cashier. A repeatedly recommended *casa de cambio* is **LAC Dolar**, Jr Camaná 779, 1 block from Plaza San Martín, p 2, T01-428 8127, also at Av La Paz 211, Miraflores, T01-242 4069. Open Mon-Sat 1000-1800, good rates, very helpful, safe, fast, reliable, 2% commission on cash, will come to your hotel if you're in a group. Another recommended *casa de cambio* is **Virgen**

No one, not even banks, will accept US$ bills that look 'old', damaged or torn.

P Socorro, Jr Ocoña 184, T01-428 7748. Open daily 0830-2000, safe, reliable and friendly. In Lima, there are many *casas de cambio* on and around Jr Ocoña off the Plaza San Martín. You can check the current exchange rate at www.bcrp.gob.pe, but remember that it will be a little lower outside Lima. **Moneygram**, Ocharan 260, Miraflores, T01-447 4044, is a safe and reliable agency for sending and receiving money. Locations throughout Lima and the provinces. Exchanges most world currencies, but check their rates and commissions. Soles can be exchanged into US$ at the exchange desks at Lima airport (poor rates), and you can change soles for US$ at any border.

There is no real advantage in changing money on the street, but should you choose to do so, it does avoid paperwork and queuing. Use only official street changers, such as those around Parque Kennedy and down Av Larco in Miraflores (Lima). They carry ID cards and wear a green vest. Check your soles before handing over your US$ or euros, check their calculators, etc, and don't change money in crowded areas. If using their services, think about taking a taxi after changing to avoid being followed.

Cost of travelling

The average budget is US$45-60 pp a day for living fairly comfortably, including transport. Your budget will be higher the longer you stay in Lima and Cuzco and depending on how many internal flights you take. Rooms range from US$7-11 pp for the most basic *alojamiento* to US$20-40 for mid-range places, to over US$90 for more upmarket hotels (more in Lima or Cuzco). Living costs in the provinces are 20-50% below those in Lima and Cuzco. The cost of using the internet is generally US$0.35-0.70 per hr, but where there is little competition, rates are higher.

Students can obtain very few reductions in Peru with an international students' card, except in and around Cuzco. To be any use in Peru, it must bear the owner's photograph. An ISIC card can be obtained in Lima from **Intej**, Av San Martín 240, Barranco, T01-247 3230; also Portal de Panes 123, of 303, Cuzco, T084-256367; Mercaderes 329, p 2, of 34, Arequipa, T054-284756; Av Mariscal Castilla 3909-4089, El Tambo, 7o piso del Edif de

Administración y Gobierno de la UNCP, anexo 6056, Huancayo, T064-481081; www.intej.org.

National parks

Peru has 190 protected natural areas, including national parks and private reserves, covering 17% of the country's surface area. For information about national parks see **El Servicio Nacional de Areas Naturales Protegidas por el Estado** (Sernanp), C Diecisiete 355, Urb El Palomar, San Isidro, Lima, T01-717 7500, www.sernanp.gob.pe. See also Sernamp's app.

Opening hours

Banks: see under Money, above. Outside Lima and Cuzco banks may close 1200-1500 for lunch. **Government offices**: Jan-Mar Mon-Fri 0830-1130; Apr-Dec Mon-Fri 0900-1230, 1500-1700, but these hours change frequently. **Offices**: 0900-1700; most close on Sat. **Shops**: 0900 or 1000-1230 and 1500 or 1600-2000. In the main cities, supermarkets do not close for lunch and Lima has several that are open 24 hrs. Some are closed on Sat and most are closed on Sun.

Post

The central Lima post office is on Jr Camaná 195 near the Plaza de Armas. Mon-Fri 0730-1900, Sat 0730-1600. In Miraflores the main post office is on Av Petit Thouars 5201 (same hours). There are many small branches around Lima and in the rest of the country, but they are less reliable. For express service: **EMS**, next to central post office in downtown Lima, T01-533 2020.

Public holidays and festivals

A full list of local festivals is listed under each town; these are some of the most important: 1 Jan **New Year**, public holiday; 6 Jan **Bajada de Reyes**, public holiday; Feb **Carnaval**, major festival celebrated in most of the Andes over the weekend before Ash Wed; Mar/Apr **Semana Santa** (Holy Week), celebrated throughout Peru; 1 May Labour Day, public holiday, **Fiesta de la Cruz** is celebrated on this day in much of the central and southern highlands and on the coast; Jun Around Cuzco, the entire month is one huge fiesta, culminating in **Inti Raymi** on 24 Jun, one of Peru's prime tourist attractions; 28-29 Jul **Independence** (Fiestas Patrias), public holiday; 1 Aug **National Day of the Alpaca**, with events in major alpaca-rearing centres across the country;

7 Oct **Battle of Angamos**, public holiday; 1 Nov **Todos los Santos** (All Saints); 8 Dec **Festividad de la Inmaculada Concepción**. 24-25 Dec **Christmas**, public holiday.

Most businesses close for the official holidays but supermarkets and street markets may be open. Sometimes holidays that fall mid-week will be moved to the following Mon (enquire locally).

Safety

For general hints on avoiding crime, see the main Practicalities chapter at the end of the book; all the suggestions given there are valid for Peru.

The following notes on personal safety should not hide the fact that most Peruvians are hospitable and helpful. There is adequate police presence in Lima, Cuzco and most tourist areas. Nevertheless, be aware that assaults may occur in Lima and centres along the Gringo Trail. Also watch for scammers who ask you, "as a favour", to change dollars into (fake) soles and for strangers who shake your hand, leaving a chemical which will knock you out when you next put your hand to your nose. Outside Lima, the main tourist centres and the Jul-Aug peak holiday period, there is less tension, less risk of crime, and more genuine friendliness.

Although certain illegal drugs are readily available, anyone carrying any is almost automatically assumed to be a drug trafficker. If arrested on any charge the wait for trial in prison can take a year and is particularly unpleasant. If you are asked by the narcotics police to go to the toilets to have your bags searched, insist on taking a witness.

Tricks employed to get foreigners into trouble over drugs include slipping a packet of cocaine into the money you are exchanging, being invited to a party or somewhere involving a taxi ride, or simply being asked on the street if you want to buy cocaine. In all cases, a plain clothes 'policeman' will discover the planted cocaine and will ask to see your passport and money. He will then return them, minus a large part of your cash. Do not get into a taxi, do not show your money, and try not to be intimidated. Being in pairs is no guarantee of security, and single women may

Warning...

Drug use or purchase is punishable by up to 15 years' imprisonment. There are a number of foreigners in Peruvian prisons on drug charges.

be particularly vulnerable. Beware also thieves dressed as policemen asking for your passport and wanting to search for drugs; searching is only permitted if prior paperwork is done.

Many places in the Amazon and in Cuzco offer experiences with Ayahuasca or San Pedro, often in ceremonies with a shaman. These are legal, but always choose a reputable tour operator or shaman. Do not go with the first person who offers you a trip. Single women should not take part. There are plenty of websites for starting your research. See also under Iquitos, page 1498.

In Cuzco many clubs and bars offer coupons for free entry and a free drink. The drinks are made with the cheapest, least healthy alcohol; always watch your drink being made and never leave it unattended. Sadly, the free entry-and-drink system doesn't appear to apply to Peruvians who are invariably asked to pay for entry to a disco, even if their tourist companions get in for nothing. We have also received reports of nightclubs and bars in Lima and Cuzco denying entrance to people solely on the basis of skin colour, assumed economic status or sexual orientation. This discrimination should be discouraged.

For up-to-date public safety information contact the **tourist police** (see Accident and emergency, above), your embassy or consulate, and fellow travellers.

Tax

Airport tax Both international and domestic airport taxes should be included in the price of flight tickets, not paid at the airport. 18% state tax is charged on air tickets; also included in the price of the ticket. When making a domestic connection in Lima, you don't have to pay airport tax; contact airport personnel to be escorted to your departure gate.

VAT/IGV/IVA 18%.

Telephone and Wi-Fi

Country code+51.
There are independent phone offices, *locutorios*, in Lima and other cities as well as coin-operated payphones, but mobile (cellular) phones are by far the most common form of telecommunication. You can easily purchase a SIM card (*un chip*) for US$5.50 (much more at Lima airport) for either of the two main mobile carriers: **Claro** and **Movistar**. You must show your passport. The SIM cards work with many foreign mobile phones, but enquire about your unit before purchasing. Mobile phone shops are everywhere; look for *chip* signs with the carrier's logo. You get a Peruvian mobile phone number and can purchase credit (*recarga*) anywhere for as much or as little as you like. Calls cost about US$0.20/min and only the caller pays. Mobile phone numbers (*celulares*) have 9 digits, landlines (*fijos*) have 7 digits in Lima, 6 elsewhere, plus an area code (e.g. 01 for Lima, 084 for Cuzco). When calling a landline from a mobile phone, you must include the area code.

Free Wi-Fi is standard at even the most basic hotels in tourist areas and at better hotels everywhere. Some cafés and public areas also have connectivity. Skype, WhatsApp, and similar services on Wi-Fi-enabled devices are the most economical form of international communication from Peru.

Time

GMT -5.

Tipping

Restaurants: service is included in the bill, but tips can be given directly to the waiter for exceptional service. **Taxi drivers**: none (bargain the price down, then pay extra for good service). If going on a trek or tour, it is customary to tip the guide as well as the cook and porters.

Tourist information

Tourism promotion and information is handled by **PromPerú**, Edif Mincetur, C Uno Oeste 50, p 13 y 14, urb Córpac, San Isidro, T01-616 7300, or Av República de Panamá 3647, San Isidro, T01-616 7400, www.promperu.gob.pe. See also www. peru.travel. **PromPerú** runs an information and assistance service, **iPerú**, T01-574 8000 (24 hrs). Main office: Jorge Basadre 610, San Isidro, Lima, T01-616 7300 or 7400, iperulima@promperu. gob.pe, Mon-Fri 0830-1830. Also a 24-hr office at Jorge Chávez airport, and throughout the country. Service is generally excellent. For PromPerú apps, see www.peru.travel.

There are tourist offices of varying quality in most towns, either run by the municipality, or independently. Outside Peru, information can be obtained from Peruvian embassies/consulates. **Indecopi** T01-224 7777 (in Lima), T0800-44040 (in the Provinces), www.indecopi.gob.pe, is the government consumer protection and tourist complaint bureau. They are friendly, professional and helpful.

Useful websites

www.caretas.com.pe The most widely read weekly magazine, *Caretas*.

www.leaplocal.org Recommends good quality guides, helping communities benefit from socially responsible tourism.

www.minam.gob.pe Ministerio del Ambiente (Spanish).

www.peruthisweek.com Informative guide and news service in English for people living in Peru.

www.peruviantimes.com The *Andean Air Mail & Peruvian Times* internet news magazine.

www.terra.com.pe TV, entertainment and news (in Spanish).

Visas and immigration

Tourist cards

No visa is necessary for citizens of EU countries, most Asian countries, North and South America, and the Caribbean, or for citizens of Andorra, Belarus, Finland, Iceland, Israel, Liechtenstein, Macedonia, Moldova, Norway, Russian Federation, Serbia and Montenegro, Switzerland, Ukraine, Australia, New Zealand and South Africa. A Tourist Card (TAM – Tarjeta Andina de Migración) is free on flights arriving in Peru, and at border crossings for visits up to 183 days. The form is in duplicate, the original given up on arrival and the copy on departure. A new tourist card must be obtained for each re-entry. If your tourist card is stolen or lost, get a new one from **Migraciones** (Digemin, Av España 730, Breña, Lima, T01-200 1081, www.migraciones.gob.pe, Mon-Fri 0830-1300). There are also Migraciones offices in Cuzco (Av El Sol 612, T084-222741, Mon-Fri 0800-1600) and all departmental capitals but they offer few services of interest to tourists.

Tourist visas

For citizens of countries not listed above (including Turkey), visas cost US$37.75 or equivalent, for which you require a valid passport, a departure ticket from Peru (or a letter of guarantee from a travel agency), 2 colour passport photos, 1 application form and proof of economic solvency. Tourist visas are valid for 183 days. In the first instance, visit the Migraciones website (as above) for visa forms.

Keep ID, preferably a passport, on you at all times. You must present your passport when reserving travel tickets. To avoid having to show your passport, you can photocopy the important pages of your passport – including the immigration stamp, and have it legalized by a 'Notario público'.

Business visas

If receiving money from Peruvian sources, visitors must have a business visa: requirements are a valid passport, 2 colour passport photos, return ticket and a letter from an employer or Chamber of Commerce stating the nature of business, length of stay and guarantee that any Peruvian taxes will be paid. The visa allows the holder to stay 183 days in the country. On arrival business visitors must register with the Dirección General de Contribuciones for tax purposes.

Student visas

These must be requested from Migraciones (address above) once you are in Peru. In addition to completing the general visa form you must have proof of adequate funds, affiliation to a Peruvian educational institution, a letter of consent from parents or tutors if you are a minor. Full details are on the Migraciones website (in Spanish).

Extensions and changes of visas

Once in Peru tourists may not extend their tourist card or visa under any circumstances. It's therefore important to insist on getting the full number of days to cover your visit on arrival (it's at the discretion of the border official). If you plan to return to Peru later in your trip don't ask for much more than you will need, as the full number of days you are granted (not the days you actually stay) is deducted from your 183-day limit. If you exceed your limit, you'll pay a US$1-per-day fine.

If you wish to change a tourist visa into another type of visa (business, student, resident, etc), you may do so without leaving Peru. Visit Migraciones or their website to obtain the relevant forms.

Weights and measures

Metric.

This is
Uruguay

Uruguay is a land of rolling hills, best explored on horseback, or by staying at the many estancias that have opened their doors to visitors. It also has its feet in the Atlantic Ocean, and one of the best ways to arrive is by ferry across the shipping lanes of the Río de la Plata. Montevideo, the capital and main port, is refurbishing its historical centre to match the smart seaside neighbourhoods, but its atmosphere is far removed from the cattle ranches of the interior.

West of Montevideo is Colonia del Sacramento, a former smuggling town turned gambling centre, and a little colonial treasure, where race horses take their exercise in the waters of the Río de La Plata. Up the Río Uruguay there are pleasant towns, some with bridges to Argentina, some with hot springs. Also by the river is Fray Bentos, the town that lent its name to corned beef for generations, now home to an industrial museum.

Each summer, millions of holidaymakers flock to Punta del Este, one of the most famous resorts on the continent, but if crowds are not your cup of *mate* (the universal beverage), go out of season. Alternatively, venture up the Atlantic coast towards Brazil for emptier beaches and fishing villages, sea lions, penguins and the occasional old fortress. And anywhere you go, take your binoculars because the birdwatching is excellent.

Footprint
picks

1 Mercado del Puerto, page 1531
2 Estancia tourism, page 1541
3 Colonia del Sacramento, page 1544
4 Punta del Este, page 1560
5 Punta del Diablo, page 1566

Bella Unión   Río Quaraí   Artigas

Termas del
Arapey   Rivera

Salto   Minas de
Termas   Corrales
de Daymán   Tacuarembó   Aceguá
Termas de   Tambores   Ansina
Guaviyú   Melo
Paysandú   Guichón   Curtina   Las Toscas
Paso de   Río Branco
los Toros   Rincón del
Bonete   Quebrada de
Tres Bocas   (Lago Artificial)   los Cuervos
Río Negro
Fray
Bentos   Mercedes   Carlos Reyes   Cerro Chato   Treinta y Tres
Soriano   José R Varela
Palmitas   Durazno   Sarandí
Dolores   del Yi   Pirajá   Chuy
Trinidad   Lascano
Nueva   Sarandí   Velásquez
Palmira   Calera de las   Grande   Punta del
Carmelo   Huérfanas   Nueva   Florida   Cerro   Castillo   Diablo
Conchillas   Helvecia   San José   Colorado
Rosario   de Mayo   Aiguá
Colonia del   Colonia   Minas
Sacramento   Valdense   Canelones   Sta Rosa   Solís
Libertad   San   La Paloma
Río de la Plata   Atlántida   Carlos
MONTEVIDEO   Piriápolis   Maldonado
Punta del Este

Atlantic Ocean

N

20 km
20 miles

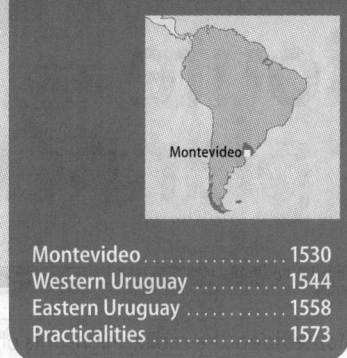

Montevideo

Footprint
picks

★ Mercado del Puerto, page 1531

At the heart of the port district, an old market building filled
with restaurants serving grills, tapas and *medio medio* (half still,
half sparkling white wine).

★ Estancia tourism, page 1541

Throughout the country, farms welcome visitors just for a day or
for longer to enjoy the produce and hospitality of rural Uruguay.

★ Colonia del Sacramento, page 1544

Uruguay's tiny colonial gem on the shore of the Río de la Plata,
with picturesque corners and museums; a great place to arrive
by boat from Argentina.

★ Punta del Este, page 1560

One of the premier tourist destinations in South America,
packed out in mid-summer, quiet the rest of the year.

★ Punta del Diablo, page 1566

The other side of Atlantic beach tourism, with wild beaches and
low-key lodgings. It's busy in high summer, but out of season is
a delightful retreat.

Route planner

The capital

modern malls and historic houses

In **Montevideo**, the capital, highlights of the Ciudad Vieja (old city) are Mercado del Puerto, the former dockside market, which has become an emporium for traditional food and drink, the magnificent Teatro Solís and the pedestrianized Calle Sarandí. Within the city limits are a number of beaches, which extend along the north shore of the Río de la Plata.

Western Uruguay

hot springs and springboards

West of the capital is **Colonia del Sacramento**, a well-preserved remnant of colonial architecture. It has one of the principal ports for ferries from Buenos Aires. West is the confluence of the Río Uruguay and the Plata estuary. Upstream are the UNESCO-recognized industrial complex at Fray Bentos and towns such as **Paysandú** and the historic **Salto**, from where you can cross to Argentina, and hot spring resorts.

Many estancias in western and central Uruguay accept visitors. Day trips usually involve a meal, handicraft shopping and an educational element. Many offer lodging and participation in the daily tasks, as these are working farms. Horse riding is the main activity but also fishing, hunting and wine-tasting are offered.

Eastern Uruguay

beaches, dunes and more beaches

The most famous Atlantic resort is **Punta del Este** which, in season (December to February), is packed with Argentines, Brazilians and locals. Beyond Punta del Este, there are quieter beaches with less infrastructure, but with sand dunes and other natural features.

Central Uruguay

an area of livestock and crops

Two main roads cross rolling hills on the way to Brazil. There are provincial towns with historic associations, cultural events and opportunities for walking, cycling and riding, especially around the artificial lakes formed by dams on the Río Negro, which divides Uruguay north from south.

Essential Uruguay

Finding your feet

Carrasco International airport is east of Montevideo, with easy connections by bus or taxi (20-30 minutes to downtown). Many visitors arrive at the port by boat from Buenos Aires, or by boat to Colonia and then bus to the Tres Cruces bus terminal just north of downtown. Both port and terminal have good facilities and tourist information.

Tip...

Don't trust the few black market money changers in Montevideo offering temptingly good rates. Many are experienced confidence tricksters. See Money, page 1575, for exchange information.

Getting around

There is a good bus network. All the main cities and towns are served by bus companies originating from the Tres Cruces Terminal in Montevideo. The few trains tend to be slow.

When to go

The climate is temperate, often windy, with summer heat tempered by Atlantic breezes. Winter (June to September) is damp; temperatures average 10-16°C but can sometimes fall to freezing. Summer (December to March) temperatures average 21-28°C. There is always some wind and the nights are relatively cool. The rainfall, with prolonged wet periods in July/August, averages about 1200 mm at Montevideo and some 250 more in the north, but the amount varies yearly.

Most tourists visit during the summer, which is also high season, when prices rise and hotels and transport need advance bookings. In the low season on the coast many places close, although increasingly they're staying open longer to encourage international and local visitors.

Carnival and Holy Week are the biggest festivals, particularly in Montevideo.

Time required

One to two weeks is recommended.

Safety

Personal security offers few problems in most of Uruguay. Petty theft does occur in Montevideo, most likely in tourist areas or markets.

Fact file
Location 34.8833° S, 56.1667° W
Capital Montevideo
Time zone GMT -3 hrs
Telephone country code +598
Currency Uruguayan peso (UYU)

Weather	Montevideo				
January	**February**	**March**	**April**	**May**	**June**
28°C 18°C 68mm	27°C 18°C 92mm	24°C 17°C 116mm	22°C 13°C 79mm	18°C 10°C 74mm	15°C 8°C 81mm
July	**August**	**September**	**October**	**November**	**December**
15°C 7°C 71mm	17°C 8°C 61mm	18°C 9°C 61mm	21°C 12°C 91mm	24°C 14°C 106mm	26°C 16°C 80mm

Montevideo

Montevideo, the capital, is a modern city that feels very much like a town. Barrios retain their personality but gel to form an appealing whole. The main areas, from west to east are: the shipping port, downtown, several riverside and central neighbourhoods (Palermo, Punta Carretas, Pocitos), the suburbs and Carrasco International airport, all connected by the Rambla. Everything blends together – architecture, markets, restaurants, stores, malls, stadiums, parks and beaches – and you can find what you need in a short walk.

Montevideo, officially declared a city in 1726, sits on a promontory between the Río de la Plata and an inner bay, though the early fortifications have been destroyed. Spanish and Italian architecture, French and art deco styles can be seen, especially in Ciudad Vieja. The city not only dominates the country's commerce and culture, it accounts for 70% of industrial production and handles almost 90% of imports and exports. In January and February many locals leave for the string of seaside resorts to the east. The first football World Cup was held in Centenario Stadium and was won by Uruguay in 1930.

Sights Colour map 8, B6.

a neighbourly, creative city best explored on foot

City centre

In the **Ciudad Vieja** is the oldest square in Montevideo: the **Plaza de la Constitución** or **Matriz**. On one side is the **Catedral** (1790-1804), with the historic **Cabildo** (1804) ① *JC Gómez 1362, T2915 9685, Mon-Fri 1200-1745, Sat 1100-1700, free,* opposite. It contains the **Museo y Archivo Histórico Municipal.** The Cabildo has several exhibition halls. On the south side is the **Club Uruguay** (built in 1888), which is worth a look inside. See also the unusual fountain (1881), surrounded by art and antiques vendors under the sycamore trees.

West along Calle Rincón is the small **Plaza Zabala**, with a monument to Bruno Mauricio de Zabala, founder of the city. North of this Plaza are: the **Banco de la República** ① *Cerrito y Zabala* and the **Aduana** ① *Rambla 25 de Agosto.* Eight historic houses belong to the Museo Histórico Nacional (see www.mec.gub.uy, or www.museohistorico.gub.uy for a full list): **Museo Histórico Nacional (Casa de Rivera)** ① *Rincón 437, T2915 1051, Wed-Sun 1100-1645, free,* is an early 19th-century mansion of the first president of the republic. Its rooms are dedicated to various stages of Uruguayan history. **Palacio Taranco, Museo de Artes Decorativas** ① *25 de Mayo 376, T2915 1101, Mon-Fri 1230-1740, free,* whose garden overlooks Plaza Zabala, a palatial mansion in turn-of-the-20th-century French style, with sumptuously decorated rooms, and a museum of Islamic and Classical pottery and glass. It was first built as a theatre in 1793 and rebuilt in 1908 after it was bought by the Ortiz de Taranco family. Also in the Ciudad Vieja is the **MAPI, Museo de Arte Precolombino e Indígena** ① *25 de Mayo 279, T2916 9360, www.mapi.uy, Mon-Sat 1030-1800, US$3, or US$7 including Museo Torres García, Museo Gurvich and Museo del Carnaval,* in a 19th-century mansion, bringing together public and private collections of local and non-Uruguayan artefacts.

The main port is near the Ciudad Vieja, with the docks three blocks north of Plaza Zabala. Three blocks south of the Plaza is the Río de la Plata. Cross the Rambla from the docks to visit the ★Mercado del Puerto (see Restaurants, page 1537) and the adjacent **Museo del Carnaval** ① *Rambla 25 de Agosto 1825, T2915 0807, www.museodelcarnaval.org, daily 1100-1700 (closed Mon-Wed, Apr-Nov), US$3.50*, a small exhibition with colourful pictures and costumes from the February celebrations. Proceed south one block to Cerrito, east two blocks to the **Banco de la República** and church of **San Francisco** (1864) ① *Solís 1469*, south across Plaza Zabala to Peatonal Sarandí (pedestrianized street) and east to Plaza de la Independencia (see below), stopping at the aforementioned historical sites as desired. On the Peatonal is the **Museo Gurvich** ① *Pasaje Sarandí 522-524, T2915 7826, www.museogurvich.org, Mon-Fri 1000-1800, Sat 1100-1500, US$5.25, Tue free*, dedicated to the life and work of painter José Gurvich (1927-74). Restoration of the Ciudad Vieja is slow but steady. Although safe by day, with many tourist police, common sense, even avoidance, is recommended at night.

Housed in a 19th-century building in the centre is **Museo Andes 1972** ① *Rincón 619, T2916 9461, www.mandes.uy, Mon-Fri 1000-1700, Sat 1000-1500*, a small museum commemorating the 1972 plane crash in which a Uruguayan rugby team survived 72 days in the Andean mountains. Not recommended for children under 12.

Between the Ciudad Vieja and the new city is the largest of Montevideo's squares, **Plaza de la Independencia**, a short distance east of Plaza de la Constitución. Numerous cafés, shops and boutiques line Peatonal Sarandí. Two small pedestrian zones full of cafés, live music (mostly after 2300) and restaurants, Peatonal Bacacay and Policía Vieja, lead off Sarandí. Below his statue (1923) in the middle of Plaza de la Independencia is the subterranean marble mausoleum of Artigas. Just west of the plaza is **Museo Torres García** ① *Sarandí 683, T2916 2663, www.torresgarcia.org.uy, Mon-Sat 1000-1800,*

Finding your feet

Street names are located on buildings, not street signs. Some plazas and streets are known by two names: for instance, Plaza de la Constitución is also called Plaza Matriz. It's a good idea to point out to a driver the location you want on a map and follow your route as you go. Also, seemingly direct routes rarely exist owing to the many one-way streets and, outside the centre, non-grid layout.

Getting around

The Ciudad Vieja can be explored on foot. From Plaza de la Independencia buses are plentiful along Avenida 18 de Julio, connecting all parts of the city. Taxis are also plentiful, affordable and generally trustworthy, although compact. *Remises* (private driver and car) can be rented by the hour. See Transport, page 1541.

Best street maps of Montevideo are at the beginning of the *Guía Telefónica* (both white and yellow page volumes). Free maps in all tourist offices and some museums. *Guía Eureka de Montevideo* is recommended for streets, with index and bus routes (US$8-9.50 from bookshops and newspaper kiosks). Pick up a copy of *Descubrí Montevideo*, useful city guide with an English version, downloadable from the municipal website, www.montevideo.gub.uy, or www. descubrimontevideo.uy, which also has a map and details of tourist buses and guided walks.

Tip...

Tango dancing by Joventango, a not-for-profit cultural institution, occurs three evenings a week in Mercado de la Abundancia.

US$4.20, bookshop. It has an exhibition of the paintings of Joaquín Torres García (1874-1949), one of Uruguay's foremost contributors to the modern art movements of the 20th century, and five floors dedicated to temporary exhibitions of contemporary Uruguayan and international artists. At the eastern end is the **Palacio Salvo** ① *Plaza Independencia 846-848, T2900 1264; open daily 1030-1330 for guided tours, Spanish and English, US$7*. Built 1923-1928, this was the first skyscraper in Uruguay and the tallest South American structure of its time; currently it houses a mixture of businesses and residences. The famous tango, *La Cumparsita*, was written in 1915, in a former café at its base. On the southern side is the **Museo de la Casa de Gobierno** ① *Palacio Estévez, Plaza Independencia 776, Mon-Fri 1000-1700*, with an exhibition of Uruguay's presidential history. Just off the plaza to the west is the splendid **Teatro Solís** (1842-1869) ① *Reconquista y Bartolomé Mitre, T2-1950 3323, www.teatrosolis.org.uy, guided visits vary according to theatre schedules, US$1.30 in Spanish (US$1.75 for tours in other languages); all tours free on Wed.* It has been entirely restored to perfection, with added elevators, access for disabled people, marble flooring and impressive attention to detail. Built as an opera house, Teatro Solís is now used for many cultural events, including ballet, classical music, even tango performances. Check press for listings. Tickets sold Tuesday-Saturday 1300-2000, Sunday-Monday and holidays, 1500-2000, closed January.

Avenida 18 de Julio runs east from Plaza de la Independencia. The **Museo de Arte Contemporaneo** ① *18 de Julio 965, 2nd floor, T2900 6662, Tue-Sat 1400-2000, free,* holds temporary exhibitions. In the **Museo del Gaucho y de la Moneda** ① *Av 18 de Julio 998, Palacio Heber Jackson, T2900 8764, Mon-Fri 1000-1600, free,* the Museo de la Moneda has a survey of Uruguayan currency and a collection of Roman coins. Museo del Gaucho is a fascinating history of the Uruguayan gaucho and is highly recommended. Between Julio Herrera and Río Negro is the **Plaza Fabini**, or **del Entrevero**, with a statue of gauchos engaged in battle, the last big piece of work by sculptor José Belloni. Beneath the plaza is the **Centro Municipal de Exposiciones – Subte** ① *T2908 7643, www.subte.montevideo.gub.uy, Tue-Sun 1400-2100, free,* temporary exhibitions of contemporary art, photography, etc. In the **Plaza Cagancha** (or Plaza Libertad) is a statue of Peace. The restored **Mercado de la Abundancia** ① *San José 1312,* is an attractive old market with handicrafts and good local restaurants plus the tango dancing by Joventango. The **Palacio Municipal** (La Intendencia) is on the south side of Avenida 18 de Julio, just before it bends north, at the statue of **El Gaucho**.

Montevideo Ciudad Vieja & Centre

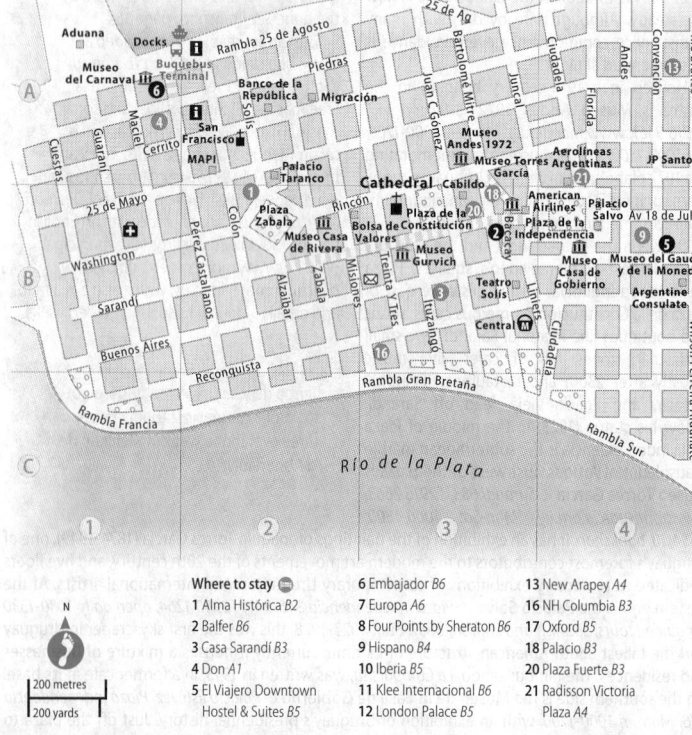

Where to stay		
1 Alma Histórica *B2*	6 Embajador *B6*	13 New Arapey *A4*
2 Balfer *B6*	7 Europa *A6*	16 NH Columbia *B3*
3 Casa Sarandí *B3*	8 Four Points by Sheraton *B6*	17 Oxford *B5*
4 Don *A1*	9 Hispano *B4*	18 Palacio *B3*
5 El Viajero Downtown Hostel & Suites *B5*	10 Iberia *B5*	20 Plaza Fuerte *B3*
	11 Klee Internacional *B6*	21 Radisson Victoria Plaza *A4*
	12 London Palace *B5*	

It often has interesting art and photo exhibitions and there is a huge satellite image of the city displayed on the main hall's floor. The road which forks south from the Gaucho is Constituyente, and leads to the beach at Pocitos. **Museo de Historia del Arte** ① *Ejido 1326, T1950 2191, Tue-Sun 1330-1900 (mid-Mar to mid-Dec 1200-1730), free*, is also in the Palacio Municipal. **Centro de Fotografía** ① *18 de Julio 885, T1950 7960, http://cdf.montevideo.gub.uy), Mon-Fri 1000-1930, Sat 0930-1430, free*, has photography exhibitions.

The immense **Palacio Legislativo** ① *from Plaza Fabini head along Av del Libertador Brig Gen Juan Lavalleja (known as Av Libertador), 5 blocks east of Plaza de la Independencia (buses 173, 175 from C Mercedes), guided visits Mon-Fri 1500 in English, 1030 and 1430 in Spanish, 1030 Portuguese, US$3*, was built 1908-1925 from local marble: there are 52 colours of Uruguayan marble in the Salón de los Pasos Perdidos, 12 types of wood in the library. Other rooms are also beautiful. Not far, and dramatically changing the city skyline, is the 160-m-high Torre **Antel telecoms building** ① *Paraguay y Guatemala, Aguada, T2928 8517, free guided visits Mon, Wed, Fri 1530-1700; Tue, Thu 1030-1200*, with a public terrace on the 26th floor for panoramic bay views.

Outside the centre

Centro Cultural y Museo de la Memoria ① *Av de las Instrucciones 1057, Prado, T2355 5891, http://mume.montevideo.gub.uy, Mon-Sat 1300-1900 (1200-1800 low season), free*, is a fascinating space commemorating the horrors of Uruguay's 1970s-80s dictatorship. **Museo Municipal de Bellas Artes Juan Manuel Blanes** ① *Millán 4015, Prado, T2336 2248, http://blanes.montevideo.gub.uy/, Tue-Sun, 1200-1800, free, take buses 148 or 149 from Mercedes*, in the ex-Quinta Raffo (a late 19th-century mansion) is dedicated to the work of the artist Blanes (1830-1901). It also has a room of the works of Pedro Figari (1861-1938), a lawyer who painted strange, naive pictures of peasant life and ceremonies of the Afro-Uruguayans, also other Uruguayan artists' work. **Museo Zoológico** ① *Rambla República de Chile 4215, Buceo, T2622 0258, daily 1000-1545, free, take bus 104 from 18 de Julio*, is well displayed and arranged, recommended, great for children.

In the **Puerto del Buceo**, following the coast eastwards away from the centre, the ship's bell of *HMS Ajax* and rangefinder of the German pocket-battleship, *Graf Spee*, can be seen at the **Naval Museum** ① *Rambla Charles de Gaulle y Luis A de Herrera, Buceo, T2622 1084, 0900-1200, 1400-1800, closed Thu, free*. Both ships were involved in the Battle of the River Plate (13 December 1939) after which *Graf Spee* was scuttled off Montevideo. The museum also has displays of documentation from this battle, naval history from the War of Independence onwards and on the sailing ship *Capitán Miranda*, www.capitanmiranda.org.uy, which circumnavigated the globe in 1937-1938.

Parque Battle y Ordóñez (reached eastwards of Avenida 18 de Julio), has numerous statues: the most interesting group is the well-known **La Carreta** monument, by José Belloni, showing three yoke of oxen drawing a wagon. In the grounds is the **Estadio Centenario**, the national 65,000-seater football stadium and a football museum, an athletics field and a

To Train Station
To Palacio Legislativo
Julio Herrera y Obes
Río Negro
Libertador
Lavalleja
G Rondeau
Yaguarón
Yaguarón
Paysandú
Uruguay
Yí
To Feria Dominical Tristán Narvaja
Iberia
Centro de Exposiciones
Automóvil Club del Uruguay
Mercedes
Colonia
Plaza Fabini
de los Artesanos
Museo de Arte Contemporáneo
Plaza Cagancha
Palacio Municipal/Intendencia
San José
❶❾❹❺
❷
❸
❿
❽
❻
Río Branco
Soriano
Mercado de la Abundancia
❼
Zelmar Michelini
Carlos Quijano
Canelones
Aquiles Lanza
To El Gaucho (200m) & Tres Cruces Bus Terminal
❿
Maldonado
❷❷
Paraguay
Durazno
Carlos Gardel
Isla de Flores
Río
To Rambla República Argentina
Panteón Nacional
❻
Cementerio Central

22 Sur Hotel C5

Restaurants ❼
1 Bosque Bambú B5
2 Café Bacacay B3
4 El Fogón B5
5 Los Leños Uruguayos B5

6 Mercado del Puerto A1
8 Subte Pizzería B6
9 Tartar B5
10 Viejo Sancho B6

bicycle race-track (bus 107). The **Planetarium** ① *next to the Jardín Zoológico, at Av Rivera 3275, T2622 9109, Mon-Fri 1000-1800, Sat-Sun 1430-1830, free, take bus 60 from Av 18 de Julio, or buses 141, 142 or 144 from San José,* gives good, 40-minute shows on Saturday and Sunday afternoons, free (also extra events on holidays, US$7).

From the Palacio Legislativo, Avenida Agraciada runs northwest to **Parque Prado** ① *Mon-Fri 1000-1600,* the oldest of the city's many parks, about 5 km from Avenida 18 de Julio (bus 125 and others). Among fine lawns, trees and lakes is a rose garden planted with 850 varieties and the monument of **La Diligencia** (the stage coach). Part of the park is the adjacent **Jardín Botánico** ① *daily summer 0700-1800, winter 0700-1700, museum Mon-Fri 1000-1600, guided tours, T2336 4005. It is reached via Av 19 de Abril (bus 522 from Ejido next to Palacio Municipal), or via Av Dr LA de Herrera (bus 147 from Paysandú).* The most popular park is **Parque Rodó**, on Rambla Presidente Wilson, with an open-air theatre, an amusement park, and a boating lake. At the eastern end is the **Museo Nacional de Artes Visuales** ① *Tomás Giribaldi 2283 esq Herrera y Reissig, T2711 6054, http://mnav.gub.uy, Tue-Sun 1400-1700, free,* one of the country's most important contemporary art collections, with some 6,000 works, plus a room devoted to Blanes. Recommended.

Within the city limits, the **Punta Carretas**, **Pocitos** and **Buceo** neighbourhoods are the nicest, with a mix of classical homes, tall condos, wonderful stores, services, restaurants, active beaches, parks, and two major malls: the **Montevideo Shopping Center** ① *on the east edge of Pocitos (Herrera 1290 y Laguna, 1 block south of Rivera), www.montevideoshopping.com.uy, daily 1000-2200,* and **Punta Carretas Shopping** ① *Ellauri 350, close to Playa Pocitos in the former prison, www.puntacarretas. com.uy.* Outside the city along Rambla Sur, the affluent **Carrasco** suburb has large homes, quieter beaches, parks and services. **Parque Roosevelt**, a green belt stretching north, and the international airport are nearby. The express bus D1 (US$0.80) runs every 20 minutes Monday to Saturday (about every hour Sunday and holidays) along Avenida 18 de Julio and the Rambla and is about 30 minutes quicker, and more comfortable, to Carrasco.

At the western end of the bay is the hill from which Montevideo gets its name, **El Cerro** ① *getting there: bus from centre to Cerro: 125 'Cerro' from Mercedes,* 139 m high, with the Fortaleza General Artigas, an old fort, at the top. It is now the **Museo Militar** ① *T2313 6716, Wed-Sun 1000-1800, free (fort visit US$0.90).* It houses historical mementos, documentation of the War of Independence and has one of the only panoramic views of Montevideo. The Cerro is surmounted by the oldest lighthouse in the country (1804).

Bathing **beaches** stretch along Montevideo's waterfront, from Playa Ramírez in the west to Playa Carrasco in the east. The waterfront boulevard, **Rambla Naciones Unidas**, is named along its several stretches in honour of various nations. Bus 104 from Aduana, which goes along Avenida 18 de Julio, gives a pleasant ride (further inland in winter) past Pocitos, Punta Gorda and all the beaches to Playa Miramar, beyond Carrasco, total journey time from Pocitos to Carrasco, 35 minutes. The seawater, despite its muddy colour (sediment stirred up by the Río de la Plata), is safe to bathe in and the beaches are clean. Lifeguards are on duty during the summer months.

Listings Montevideo *map page 1532.*

Tourist information

Tourist information for the whole country is at the **Tres Cruces bus terminal** (T2401 8998, trescruces@mintur.gub.uy, daily 0700-2300); at the **Ministry of Tourism** (Rambla 25 de Agosto de 1825 y Yacaré (next to the port), T21885, ext111); and at **Carrasco international airport** (T2604 0386, carrasco@mintur.gub.uy, 0800-2000); which has good maps. For information on Montevideo, at **Mercado del Puerto** (Piedras 252 y Pérez Castellano, T2916 8434, 1000-1600); **Intendencia de Montevideo** (Av 18 de Julio esq Ejido, 0900-1700); at airport and Tres Cruces, all helpful.

Where to stay

High season is 15 Dec-15 Mar, book ahead; many beach hotels only offer full board during this time. After 1 Apr prices are reduced and some hotel dining rooms shut down. During Carnival, prices go up by 20%. The city is visited by Argentines at weekends: many hotels increase prices. Midweek prices may be lower than those posted.

The tourist office has information on the more expensive hotels. **Holiday Inn** (www.holidayinn. com.uy), **Hyatt** (https://montevideo.centric. hyatt.com), **Ibis** (www.ibis.com), and others, are represented. For more information and reservations contact **Asociación de Hoteles y Restaurantes del Uruguay** (Gutiérrez Ruiz 1215, T2908 0141, www.ahru.com.uy). All those listed below have been recommended.

City centre

$$$$ Alma Histórica
Solís 1433, T2914 7450,
www.almahistoricahotel.com.
In an elegant, converted building on Plaza Zabala, this "boutique" hotel has 15 rooms designed in three themes, named after prominent Uruguayan cultural figures, with all modern services, terrace, *salón de té* and lounge bar.

$$$$ Four Points by Sheraton
Ejido 1275, T2901 7000,
www.fourpointsmontevideo.com.
Stylish hotel in the heart of Montevideo with all the mod cons. Indoor pool on the 10th floor, overlooking the city, spa treatments, cosy bar and fine dining.

$$$$ Radisson Victoria Plaza
Plaza Independencia 759, T2902 0111,
www.radisson.com/montevideouy.
Excellent restaurant (rooftop, fine views, Mon-Fri, lunchtime only), less formal restaurant in lobby, luxurious casino in basement, with new 5-star wing, art and antiques gallery, business centre (for guests only), pool, spa.

$$$$-$$$ Don
Piedras 234, T2915 9999, www.
donhotelmontevideo.com.uy.
Boutique hotel in 1930s building opposite Mercado del Puerto. With breakfast, 3 standards of room, all modern services including safe in room, restaurant.

$$$ Balfer
Z Michelini 1328, T2902 0073,
www.hotelbalfer.com.
Good, safe deposit, modern, business-style, excellent breakfast.

$$$ Casa Sarandí
Buenos Aires 558, T2400 6450,
www.casasarandi.com.
This gem of a guesthouse is in the heart of the historic quarter, run by Welsh expat Karen Higgs, author of the Guru'guay travel blog and guides (see page 1577, an excellent source of information. Comfortable rooms with antique furniture, reading room, use of kitchen. Highly recommen ded.

see page 1577

$$$ Embajador
San José 1212/14, T2902 0012,
www.hotelembajador.com.
Sauna, swimming pool in the summer, parking, medical services, free computer use, excellent all round.

$$$ London Palace
Río Negro 1278, T2902 0024, www.lphotel.com.
Well-established, convenient, excellent breakfast, parking. Associated with restaurant **El Fogón** (see below).

$$$ NH Columbia
Rambla Gran Bretaña 473, T2916 0001,
www.nh-hotels.com.
First class, overlooking the river in Ciudad Vieja. Well-appointed rooms, restaurant, sauna, fitness room.

$$$ Plaza Fuerte
Bartolomé Mitre 1361, T2915 6651,
www.capitalhoteles.com.
Restored 1913 building, historical monument, safe, business centre, car and bike rental.

$$$-$$ Europa
Colonia 1341, T2902 0045,
www.hoteleuropa.com.uy.
Comfortable, spacious rooms, good choice in this price range, buffet breakfast, restaurant, parking.

$$$-$$ Hispano
Convención 1317, T2900 3816,
www.hispanohotel.com.
Comfortable with good services, continental breakfast, parking.

$$$-$$ Klee Internacional
San José 1303, T2902 0606, www.klee.com.uy.
Very comfortable, good value in standard rooms, spacious, buffet breakfast, laundry service, parking, good view.

$$$-$$ Oxford
Paraguay 1286, T2902 0046,
www.hoteloxford.com.uy.
Good buffet breakfast, safes, multilingual staff, parking.

$$ Iberia
Maldonado 1097, T2901 3633,
www.hoteliberia.com.uy.
Modern, very helpful staff, bike rental, 1 room
with jacuzzi, minibar. US$5 for breakfast.

$$ New Arapey
Av Uruguay 925, near Convención, T2900 7032,
www.arapey.com.uy.
In a 1920s building, in central location.
Fully remodelled rooms with a/c, heating,
no breakfast, safe in reception, 10% discount
for long stay.

$$ Palacio
Bartolomé Mitre 1364, T2900 7032,
www.hotelpalacio.com.uy.
Classic old hotel, recently renovated, superior
rooms with balconies, TV and a/c, laundry service,
stores luggage, no breakfast, frequently booked,
good value.

$$ Sur Hotel
Maldonado 1098, T2908 2025, www.surhotel.com.
Colourful, welcoming, some rooms with
balconies. Good continental breakfast for US$5,
24-hr room service, jacuzzi in 2 rooms.

$$-$ El Viajero Downtown Hostel and Suites
Soriano 1073, T2908 2913,
www.elviajerohostels.com.
Private en suite with a/c and TV, dorms en suite
($), breakfast included, BBQ area, bar, outdoor
terrace, free Wi-Fi, bike rental.

Outside the centre
Tres Cruces, Palermo

$$$ Tres Cruces
Miguelete 2356 esq Acevedo Díaz, T2402 3474,
www.hoteltrescruces.com.uy.
Safe, café, decent buffet breakfast, medical
service. Disabled access.

$$$-$$ Days Inn
Acevedo Díaz 1821, T2400 4840,
www.daysinn.com.uy.
Buffet breakfast, safe, coffee shop and
health club, look for promotional offers.

Pocitos

$$$$-$$$ Ermitage
Juan Benito Blanco 783, T2710 4021,
www.ermitagemontevideo.com.
Near Pocitos beach, remodelled 1945 building,
rooms, apartments and suites, some with great
views, buffet breakfast.

$$$$-$$$ Pocitos Plaza
Juan Benito Blanco 640, Pocitos, T2712 3939,
www.pocitosplazahotel.com.uy.
Modern building in pleasant residential district,
next to the river, with large functional rooms,
buffet breakfast, gym with views. Wheelchair/
disabled access.

$$-$ pp Pocitos Hostel
Av Sarmiento 2641 y Aguilar, T2711 8780,
www.pocitos-hostel.com.
Rooms for 2 to 6 (mixed), use of kitchen, *parrilla*,
organic produce, towels extra (US$2).

$$-$ Unplugged Hostel
Luis de la Torre 930, near Pocitos Beach,
T2712 1381, www.unpluggedhostel.com.
HI-affiliated, beach towel and bike rental,
BBQ terrace, breakfast included.

Carrasco

$$$$ Belmont House
Av Rivera 6512, T2600 0430,
www.belmonthouse.com.uy.
Elegant 5-star mansion-style hotel, 28 beautifully
furnished rooms and suites, top quality, excellent
restaurant, bar, tea room Sat-Sun 1700-2000,
sauna, gym, 3 blocks from beach.

$$$$ Cottage
Miraflores 1360, T2600 1111,
www.hotelcottage.com.uy.
In a prime location next to wide beaches
and in quiet residential surroundings, very
comfortable, simply furnished rooms with
minibar, restaurant **Rambla**, bar **1940**, pool
in a lovely garden, excellent.

$$$$ Regency Suites Boutique Hotel
Gabriel Otero 6428, T2600 1383,
www.regency.com.uy.
Good boutique-style hotel with all services,
fitness centre, pool, restaurant **Cava** and
pub/wine bar, a couple of blocks from the
beach. In same group and price range is
the contemporary **Regency Rambla Design
Apart Hotel** (Rep de México 6079, T2601 5555,
www.regencyrambla.com.uy).

$$$$ Sofitel Montevideo Casino Carrasco & Spa
Rambla México 6451, T2604 6060,
www.sofitel.com.
This 100-year-old hotel and casino has been
beautifully restored and offers 93 rooms and
23 suites on the Carrasco waterfront. State-
of-the-art relaxing **So Spa**, fantastic bar and
excellent restaurant. Recommended.

Restaurants

There is a 22% tax on restaurant bills that may be included, plus a charge for bread and service (*cubierto*) that varies from US$1-3 pp.

City centre

$$$ Café Bacacay
Bacacay 1306 y Buenos Aires, T2916 6074, www.bacacay.com.uy. Closed Sun.
Good music and atmosphere, food served, try the specials.

$$$ El Fogón
San José 1080 (also at Punta Carretas), T2900 0900, www.elfogon.com.uy. Open 1200-1500 and 2000-2200.
Good value typical food, always full, arrive by 2000.

$$$ El Mercado del Puerto
Opposite the Aduana, C Piedras, between Maciel and Pérez Castellanos (take 'Aduana' bus), www.mercadodelpuerto.com.uy.
Don't miss eating at this 19th-century market building. Choose from delicious grills cooked on huge charcoal grates or more international fare like Spanish tapas and pasta. Best to go at lunchtime, especially Sat; the atmosphere's great, open until 1800 (last orders 1700). Inside the Mercado del Puerto, those recommended are: **Roldós** (T2915 1520), sandwiches, most people start with a *medio medio* (half still, half sparkling white wine). **El Palenque** (T2917 0190, www.elpalenque.com.uy), famed as the finest restaurant, try their excellent *cleric* , white wine cocktail. **La Estancia del Puerto**, **Cabaña Verónica**, **La Chacra del Puerto**. By far the busiest at lunchtime any day of the week is **Empanadas Carolina** (T2915 9917, www.empanadascarolina.com) with over 40 varieties to choose from.

$$$ Los Leños Uruguayos
San José 909, T2900 2285, www.parrilla.com.uy.
Good and smart *parrilla*, with an extensive and varied menu, including rice and pasta dishes, fish and seafood.

$$$ Viejo Sancho
San José 1229. Closed Sun, T2900 4063.
Excellent, popular, set menus for US$12.50 pp.

$$ Bosque Bambú
San José 1060, T2902 7720.
Asian, vegan and vegetarian buffet, eat-in or take-away. Also food shop.

$$ Subte Pizzería
Ejido 1327, T2902 3050.
An institution for *chivitos* and other fast-food on the go, cheap and good.

$ Tartar
San José 1096, T2902 3154.
Tiny café selling fresh fruit juices, *empanadas*, savoury pies and *chivitos*. Cheap and good-value set lunches.

Outside the centre

Pocitos

$$$ Bar Tabaré
Zorrilla de San Martín 154, T2712 3242, www.bartabare.com.
Wonderful restaurant in a converted old *almacén* (grocery shop). Great wines and entrées.

$$$ Da Pentella
Luis de la Torre 598, esq Francisco Ros, T2712 0981.
Amazing Italian and seafood, artistic ambience, great wines.

$$$ El Viejo y el Mar
Rambla Gandhi 400 y Solano García, Punta Carretas, T2710 5704.
Fish and seafood specialists, with a great location by the river.

$$$ Fellini Pocitos
José Marti 3408, T2706 9252.
Delicious Italian and Mediterranean cuisine, lively with bright and colourful décor, live music on Sun lunchtime.

$$$ Francis
Luis de la Torre 502 esq JM Montero, Punta Carretas, T2711 8603, http://francis.com.uy.
Wide-ranging menu, including *parrilla*, sushi, pastas and seafood, fashionable with prices to match, LGBT-friendly. Has another branch at Av Arocena 1692, in Carrasco, T2601 6626.

$$$ La Otra
Tomás Diago 758 y Juan Pérez, Pocitos, T2711 3006, www.laotraparrilla.com.
Specializes in meat *a la parrilla*, lively, very popular with neighbourhood locals.

$$$ Panini's Boutique
26 de Marzo 3586, T2622 1232, www.paninis.com.uy. Thu-Sun evenings till midnight.
Refined Italian cuisine and traditional Uruguayan steaks.

$$$ Pantagruel
Obligado 1199 esq Maldonado, T2709 1436.
Closed Sun evening and Mon.
Varied menu including *parrilla* and
Mediterranean, good quality and value.

$$ Club Natural y Popular
Blvr España 2643, Facebook: naturalypopular.
Vegan/vegetarian café with tasty, healthy daily
menu with a token system for dishes and drinks,
café open from 0930, lunch Mon-Fri 1200-1500,
English spoken, free Wi-Fi, shop has organic
products and treatments, yoga, pilates, etc.

$$ Pizzería Trouville
Gabriel Pereira 3151 y 26 de Marzo, T2709 3619,
www.pizzeriatrouville.com.uy.
A traditional pizza place with an extensive and
varied menu.

$$ Tranquilo Bar
21 de Septiembre 3000, esq Roque Graseras,
T2711 2127.
Very popular restaurant/bar, great lunch menu,
some outdoor tables.

Carrasco/Punta Gorda
Several restaurants on Av Arocena close to the
beach, packed Sun midday.

$$$ Café Misterio
Costa Rica 1700, esq Av Rivera, T2601 8765,
www.cafemisterio.com.uy. Closed Sun.
Lots of choice on international menu, including
vegetarian options and sushi, cocktails.
Completely new menu every 6 months.

$$$ García
Arocena 1587, T2600 2703, www.garcia.com.uy.
Spacious, indoor and outdoor seating, large
wine selection, baby beef and rack of lamb
are specialities.

$$$ Hemingway
Rambla México 5535, on west side of Punta
Gorda, T2600 0121, www.hemingway.com.uy.
Tue-Sun 0900 'til late, closed Mon.
Decent food, worth going for amazing sunset
views of river and city, great outdoor seating.

Confiterías

Café Brasilero
Ituzaingó 1447, half a block from
Plaza Matriz towards the port,
T2917 2035, www.cafebrasilero.com.uy.
Small entrance; easy to miss. A must, one of the
oldest cafés in Montevideo and a former hangout

of one of the greatest Latin American writers,
Eduardo Galeano (1940-2015).

Others include:

Amaretto
21 de Septiembre y Roque Graseras, Punta
Carretas, T2711 9934, www.amaretto.com.uy.
Excellent Italian coffee and pastries.

Bar Iberia
Uruguay esq Florida.
Locals' bar, no frills but friendly and lively.

Manchester Bar
18 de Julio 899.
Good for breakfasts and snack lunches,
retro décor.

Oro del Rhin
Convención 1403 (also at Pocitos riverfront,
on Plaza Cagancha and at shopping malls),
T2902 2833, www.orodelrhin.com.uy. Mon-Sat
0830-2000 (closed Sun).
Open since 1927 it retains the feel of an elegant
confitería serving good cakes and sandwiches or
vegetable pies for lunch, also a bookshop.

Options with multiple locations
Several good restaurants and establishments
have locations in many neighbourhoods and
serve typical Uruguayan fare. Among these are
family restaurants: **La Pasiva**, **Don Peperone**
and **Il Mondo della Pizza**. A popular bakery
chain is **Medialunas Calentitas**, great for coffee
and 2 popular *heladerías* are **La Cigale** and
Las Delicias.

Bars and clubs

Boliches
Head to Sarandí, Bacacay or Bartolomé Mitre in
Ciudad Vieja, or to Pocitos and Punta Carretas.
Discos charge US$5-10. Bars/discos/pubs offering
typical local nightlife:

503 Bar
Aguilar 832, just north of Ellauri.
Pool tables, only steel tip dart bar in town,
small wood frame entrance, no sign.

Baar Fun-Fun
Soriano 922 esq Convención, T2904 4859,
www.barfunfun.com.
Hangout of local artists, founded in 1895, used to
be frequented by Carlos Gardel, where *uvita*, the
drink, was born. Great live tango and local music
Tue-Sat. Recommended.

El Lobizón
Zelmar Michelini 1264, T2901 1334,
www.ellobizon.com.uy. Closed Sun.
Popular restaurant open till very late with rock
and fusion live performances.

El Pony Pisador
Bartolomé Mitre 1326, Ciudad Vieja, T2915 7470.
Popular with the young crowd. Live music. Also at
Av Dr Luis Alberto de Herrera e Iturriaga, Pocitos.

La Ronda
Ciudadela 1182 y Canelones, T2901 5659.
Open from 1800 till late all week.
Drinks, snacks, loud music and arty crowd, with
Cheesecake Records next door (see Facebook).

The Shannon Irish pub
Bartolomé Mitre 1318, T2916 9585,
www.theshannon.com.uy.
Pub with almost daily live shows, from '80s rock to
modern jazz, with DJs on Thu, US$3-4 cover charge.

Viejo Mitre
Bartolomé Mitre 1321, Ciudad Vieja, T2916 8259.
Open till late all week.
Irish-themed pub, with mixed live music, pizzas
and snacks, outside tables.

Outside the centre

At or near Parque Rodó

El Mingus
San Salvador 1952 esq Jackson, T2410 9342, www.
elmingus.com. Mon-Sat 2000 till late, closed Sun.
Jazz and blues, home-made food, drinks,
great atmosphere.

Living
Paullier y Hugo Prato, T2402 3795 (Elliving on
Facebook). Wed-Sun 2100-0500.
Popular corner bar, with electronica and
beatbox music.

Entertainment

Cinema
See www.cartelera.com.uy for listings.
Blockbusters often appear soon after release in
US, most others arrive weeks or months later.
Most films are in English (except non-English and
animated features). Modern malls (Montevideo
Shopping, Nuevocentro, Punta Carretas, Portones)
house several cine-theatre companies each,
including 3D halls. Independent art theatres:
Cine Universitario, *Canelones 1280, http://cine*
universitariodeluruguay.org.uy. 2 halls: Lumière
and Chaplin, also for classic and serious films.

Cinemateca film club, *www.cinemateca.org.uy.*
Has 4 cinemas: **Cinemateca 18** (18 de Julio
1280, T2900 9056); **Sala Cinemateca y Sala Dos**
(Dr L Carnelli 1311, T2419 5795/2412 8516); and
Sala Pocitos (A Chucarro 1036, T2707 4718).
The Cinemateca shows great films from all
over the world and has an extended archive.
It organizes film festivals. Tickets US$7; members
free or US$1.20.

Tanguerías
El Milongón, *Gaboto 1810, T2929 0594, www.*
elmilongon.com.uy. Mon-Sat 2100. A show that
may include dinner beforehand. For tango,
milonga, candombe and local folk music.
Recommended.
Joventango, *at Mercado de la Abundancia,*
Aquiles Lanza y San José 1312, T2901 5561, www.
joventango.com. Daily except Thu and Sat, 2130.
Cheap and atmospheric venue, also offers a
range of dance classes.
Museo del Vino, *Maldonado 1150, T2908 3430,*
www.museodelvino.com.uy. Wine bar with
various shows and live music, plus wine-tasting
and wine courses.
Sala Zitarrosa, *18 de Julio 1012, T2901 7303, www.*
salazitarrosa.com.uy. Very popular music venue.
Tango a Cielo Abierto, *Tango Under the Open Sky,*
in front of Bar Facal, Paseo Yi and 18 de Julio,
T2908 7741, www.facal.com.uy, for information.
Free and very good Uruguayan tango shows
Mon-Sat at 1330, next to a statue of Carlos Gardel.
Highly recommended.

Theatres
Montevideo has a vibrant theatre scene. Most
performances are only on Fri, Sat and Sun,
others also on Thu. Apart from **Teatro Solís**
(see page 1532), recommended are **Teatro del
Centro Carlos E Sheck** (Plaza Cagancha 1164,
T2902 8915), and **Teatro Victoria** (Río Negro
1479 y Uruguay, T2901 9971). See listings in the
daily press and *La Brecha* (www.brecha.com.uy).
Prices range from around US$5-75; performances
are almost exclusively in Spanish starting around
2100 or earlier on Sun. **Teatro del Anglo** (at the
Instituto Cultural Anglo-Uruguayo (known as
the 'Anglo'), San José 1426, T2902 3773, www.
anglo.edu.uy), puts on occasional productions,
as do the **Alianza Cultural
Uruguay-Estados Unidos** (Paraguay 1217,
T2902 5160, www.alianza.edu.uy), good library,
and the **Alliance Française** (Blvr Artigas 1271,
T2400 0505, www.alianzafrancesa.edu.uy),
concerts, library, excellent bookshop. Many
theatres close Jan-Feb.

Shopping

The main commercial street is Av 18 de Julio, although malls elsewhere have captivated most local shoppers.

Bookshops

The Sun market on Tristán Narvaja and nearby streets is good for secondhand books. Every December daily in the evening is **Feria IDEAS +**, a book, photography and crafts fair, at Plaza Florencio Sánchez (Parque Rodó), with readings and concerts (www.ideasmas.com). The selection of English and American books in Montevideo is poor. The following specialize in foreign publications:
Al Libro Inglés, *Cerrito 481, Ciudad Vieja, T2915 6818*.
Bookshop SRL, *JE Rodó 1671 (at Minas y Constituyente), T2401 1010, www.bookshop.com.uy*. Also has 11 other branches across Montevideo and in other parts of the country.
Librería Ibana, *International Book and News Agency* bookshop, *Convención 1485 (also Benito Blanco 845)*. Some foreign magazines and newspapers.
Librería Papacito, *18 de Julio 1409 and 888, T2908 7250/2900 2872, www.libreriapapacito.com*. Good selection of magazines and books, wide range of subjects from celebrity autobiographies to art.
Puro Verso, *Yi 1385, T2901 6429, www.libreria puroverso.com*. Very good selection in Spanish, small second-hand section in English, excellent café, chess tables. It has another branch on Sarandí 675, **Más Puro Verso** and **PV Lounge**, with good restaurant on 2nd floor.

Tip...

Many international newspapers can be bought on the east side of Plaza Independencia.

Galleries

There are many good art galleries.
Galería Latina, *Juan C Gómez 1420, Paseo de la Matriz, T2916 3737*. One of the best, with its own art publishing house. Several art galleries and shops lie along C Pérez Castellanos, near Mercado del Puerto.

Handicrafts

Suede and leather are good buys. There are several shops and workshops around Plaza Independencia. Amethysts, topazes, agate and quartz are mined and polished in Uruguay and are also good buys. For authentic, fairly priced crafts there is **Mercado de los Artesanos**

(www.mercadodelosartesanos.com.uy, on Plaza Cagancha, No 1365 (Mon-Sat 1000-2000, closed Sun), at Piedras y Pérez Castellano (daily) and at Mercado de la Abundancia, San José 1312 (closed Sun), T2901 8355). For leather goods, walk around C San José y W Ferreira Aldunate. **Montevideo Leather Factory** (Plaza Independencia 832). Recommended. **Manos del Uruguay** (San José 1111, and at Shopping Centres, www.manos. com.uy). A non-profit organization that sells very good quality, handwoven woollen clothing and a great range of crafts, made by independent craftsmen and women from all over Uruguay.

Markets

Calle Tristán Narvaja (and nearby streets, opposite Facultad de Derecho on 18 de Julio). On Sun, 0900-1600, there is a large, crowded street market here, good for silver and copper, and all sorts of collectibles. **Plaza de la Constitución**, a small Sat morning market and antique fair are held here. **Villa Biarritz** (on Vásquez Ledesma near Parque Rodó, Punta Carretas). A big market selling fruit, vegetables, clothes and shoes (Tue and Sat early – 1600, and Sun in Parque Rodó, 0800-1400).

What to do

Language schools

Academia Uruguay, *Juan Carlos Gómez 1408, T2915 2496, www.academiauruguay.com*.
International House, *Av Brasil 2831, T2709 6774, www.studyabroadcourses.com*.

Sports

Rugby (www.rugbynews.com.uy), volleyball, tennis, cycling, surfing, windsurfing and kitesurfing, lawn bowling, running, and walking are popular.

Basketball is increasingly popular; games can be seen at any sports club (**Biguá** or **Trouville**, both in Punta Carretas/Pocitos neighbourhoods). See www.fubb.org.uy for schedules.

Football (soccer) is the most popular sport. Seeing a game in **Centenario Stadium** is a must, located in Parque Batlle. If possible, attend a game with Uruguay's most popular teams, **Nacional** or **Peñarol**, or an international match. General admission tickets (US$5-20) can be bought outside before kickoff for sections Amsterdam, América, Colombes, Tribuna Olímpica. Crowds in Uruguay are much safer than other countries, but it's best to avoid the *plateas*, the end zones where the rowdiest fans chant and

★Estancias

Some of these grand estates have opened their doors to tourists, and a stay on an estancia can be a highlight of any trip to Uruguay. Information on estancias can be found at **Lares** (see Tours), which represents many estancias and *posadas*; at the tourist offices in Montevideo; or general travel agencies and those that specialize in this field (see below). More information on estancias is available at www.estancias-uruguay.com and some information is also given on http://turismo.gub.uy. Where to stay listing sections throughout the chapter also give details of recommended estancias.

cheer. Sit in Tribuna Olímpica under or opposite the tower, at midfield. **Parque Central** (just north of Tres Cruces), **Nacional**'s home field, is the next best venue. Other stadiums are quieter, safer and also fun. For information try www.tenfieldigital. com.uy, but asking a local is also advisable.

Golf Uruguay has 12 golf courses in total, between Fray Bentos and Punta del Este. Apart from Jan-Feb, Jul-Aug, you should have no problem getting onto the course, T2711 5285, www.asociacionuruguayadegolf.net.

Tours

The **Asociación de Guías de Turismo de Montevideo** (T099-629325, http://uruguias.com. uy), runs historical and architecture tours. Check times and availability in English. Tours of the city are organized by the **Municipalidad** (see www. montevideo.gub.uy), go to Ciudad y cultura, calendario de paseos, for details.

For visiting the several wineries around Montevideo, see www.loscaminosdelvino. com.uy. Also **The Wine Experience** (T097-348445, http://thewine-experience.com), offering a variety of tours in Montevideo, Colonia and Punta del Este.

Day tours of Punta del Este are run by many travel agents and hotels, US$50-100 with meals.

Cecilia Regules Viajes, *Bacacay 1334, Plaza Independencia, T2916 3011/12, www.ceciliaregules viajes.com*. Very good, knowledgeable, specialist in estancias, variety of tours in Uruguay, and skiing in Argentina.
Estancias Gauchas, *Cecilia Regules Viajes*. Agent for an organization of 280 estancias offering lunch and/or lodging, English, French and Portuguese spoken.
Fanáticos Fútbol Tours, *Pablo de María 1592 bis, T099-862325, www.futboltours.com.uy*. Tour operator dedicated to Uruguay's national sport. Bilingual tours of several football stadiums, organizes tickets to matches. Free walking tours.

Jetmar, *Plaza de la Independencia 725, T2902 0793, www.jetmar.com.uy*. A helpful tour operator. Many branches.
JP Santos, *Colonia 951, T2902 0300, www.jpsantos. com.uy*. Helpful agency, also has branch in Pocitos.
Lares, *Wilson Ferreira Aldunate 1322 L14, T2901 9120, www.larestours.com*. Specializes in nature and upscale cultural tours, including birdwatching, wine and gastronomy, art, trekking, horse riding and estancia tourism. Very experienced. Recommended.
Odile Travel, *Plaza Independencia 723 of 102, T2902 3736, www.odiletravel.com*. ISO-certified agency offering personalized service in a variety of fields, including sports (marathons, too), city cycling tours, gourmet and wine, bird and whale watching.
Rumbos, *WTC, L A de Herrera 1248 of 330, T2628 5555, www.rumbosturismo.com*. Caters specifically for independent travellers, very helpful.
TransHotel, *Acevedo Díaz 1671, T2402 9935, www.transhotel.com.uy*. Accommodation, eco-tourism, sightseeing and tailor-made itineraries.
Turisport Ltda, *San José 930, T2902 0829, www.turisport.com.uy (also in Pocitos)*. American Express for travel and mail services, good.

Transport

Air

The main airport is at Carrasco, 21 km outside the city, T2604 0329, www.aeropuertodecarrasco. com.uy; 24-hr exchange facilities. If making a hotel reservation, ask them to send a taxi to meet you; it's cheaper than taking an airport taxi. To Montevideo 30 mins by taxi or *remise* (official fares US$22-52, depending on destination in the city, US$140-200 to Punta del Este), by van US$15 (payable in Uruguayan or Argentine pesos, Brazilian reais, US$ or euros, credit cards also accepted), T2604 0323, www.taxisaeropuerto.com; about 50 mins by bus. Buses, Nos C1 and C3 from Terminal Baltasar Brum, Río Branco y Galicia, go to the airport US$1.50 (crowded before and after school hours); dark brown **Copsa** bus, www. copsa.com.uy, terminates at the airport. **COT** buses, www.cot.com.uy, connect city and airport, US$6, and Punta del Este, US$9.50.

Air services to Argentina: for the Puente Aéreo to Buenos Aires airport, check in at Montevideo airport, pay departure tax and go to immigration to fill in an Argentine entry form before going through Uruguayan immigration. Get your stamp out of Uruguay, surrender the tourist card you received on entry and get your stamp into Argentina. There are no immigration checks on arrival at Aeroparque, Buenos Aires.

Bus

Local City buses are comfortable and convenient, see **Sistema de Transporte Metropolitano (STM)** pages on www. montevideo.gub.uy and www.cutcsa.com.uy. A single fare, US$0.95, may be paid on the bus, otherwise you can buy a rechargeable smart card for multiple journeys at designated places throughout the city. Buses D1 (see Carrasco, page 1534), D2, D3, 5, 8, 9, 10 and 11 charge US$1.60. There are many buses to all parts from 18 de Julio; from other parts to the centre or old city, look for those marked 'Aduana'. For Punta Carretas from city centre take bus No 121 from C San José.

Remises Fares from US$35 from airport to city; **Remises Carrasco**, T2606 1412, www.remises carrasco.com.uy; **Urbana Remises**, T2400 8665, www.urbanaremises.com.uy.

Long distance (within Uruguay) During summer holidays buses are often full; it is advisable to book in advance (also for Fri and weekend travel all year round). Excellent terminal, **Tres Cruces**, Bulevar Artigas 1825 y Av Italia, T2401 8998 (10-15 mins by bus from the centre, Nos CA1, 64, 180, 187, 188 – in Ciudad Vieja from in front of Teatro Solís); it has a shopping mall, tourist office, internet café, restaurants, left luggage US$2 for up to 4 hrs, US$3 up to 8 hrs, US$4 up to 12 hrs and US$5 up to 24 hrs (extra fee if heavier than 20 kg), post and phone offices, toilets, good medical centre, **Banco de Montevideo** and **Indumex** *cambio* (accepts MasterCard). Visit www.trescruces.com.uy for bus schedules. Fares and journey times from the capital are given under destinations.

Summerbus T4277 5781, www.summer bus.com is a hop-on hop-off, door-to-door backpackers' service, taking travellers from hostel to hostel, with stops in Montevideo and all along the coast up to **Punta del Diablo**. Single tickets from US$12-45, or the full ticket of up to 12 stops for US$95 can be bought online or at hostels.

To Argentina (ferries and buses) You need a passport when buying international tickets. Direct to **Buenos Aires**: Buquebus, at the docks, in old customs hall, Terminal Fluvio-Marítima; Terminal Tres Cruces, Local 28/29, and Punta Carretas Shopping, Local Miranda; in all cases T130, www.buquebus.com. 1-3 daily, 3 hrs, from US$100 tourist class, one way (much cheaper if booked online; 3 classes of seat); departure tax included in the price of tickets. At Montevideo dock, go to Preembarque 30 mins before departure, present ticket, then go to Migración for Uruguayan exit and Argentine entry formalities. The terminal is like an airport and the seats on the ferries are airplane seats. On board there is duty-free shopping, video and poor value food and drinks. **Services via Colonia**: bus/ferry and catamaran services by **Buquebus**, from 5 crossings daily from about 1 to 4 hrs from Colonia, depending on vessel, fares: US$34 tourist class one way on slower vessel, US$50 tourist class on faster vessel (very good last minute deals available online in low season). All have 2½-hr bus connection Montevideo-Colonia from Tres Cruces. There are also bus connections to **Punta del Este**, 2 hrs, and **La Paloma**, 5 hrs, to/from Montevideo. Cars and motorcycles are carried on either route. Schedules and fares can be checked on www.buquebus.com, who also have flights between Uruguay and Argentina. Fares increase in high season, Dec-Jan, when there are more sailings. If you want to break your journey in Colonia, you will have to buy your own bus ticket on another company to complete the trip to/from Montevideo. **Colonia Express**, at Tres Cruces bus terminal local 31A, T2401 6666, and at the dock in Colonia, www.coloniaexpress.com, makes 4-5 crossings a day between Colonia and Buenos Aires in fast boats (no vehicles) with bus connections to/from Montevideo, Punta del Este and other Uruguayan towns. Fares range from US$22 to US$45 one way, depending on type of service and where bought, or US$22-52 with bus connections to/from Montevideo. **Seacat**, www. seacatcolonia.com, 3 fast ferries to **Colonia**, 1 hr, US$34-67 one way, with bus to **Montevideo** US$36-74. Offices: Río Negro 1400, at Tres Cruces locales 28/29, T2915 0202, and in Colonia, Punta del Este and Piriápolis. **Bus de la Carrera/Cita** (T2402 1313, www.busdelacarrera.com.uy, or www.cita.com.uy), **Belgrano** (T2402 5129, www.gralbelgrano.com.ar), **El Cóndor** (T2401 4764) and **Cauvi** (T2401 9196) run road services to **Buenos Aires** for US$48-53, 7½-8½ hrs.

Services to **Carmelo** and **Tigre** (interesting trip): bus/motor launch service by **Cacciola**, 1 a day, www.cacciolaviajes.com, US$32. Advanced booking is advisable on all services at busy periods. On through buses to Brazil and Argentina, you can expect full luggage checks both by day and night.

To Paraguay, Brazil, Chile If intending to travel through Uruguay to Brazil, do not forget to have Uruguayan entry stamped into your passport when crossing from Argentina. Without it you will not be able to cross the Brazilian border. To **Asunción**, Paraguay, US$150-183, 20-22 hrs, Wed, Sat (also Mon in high season) at 1300 with **EGA**, T2402 5165, www.ega.com.uy (and Río Branco 1417, T2902 5335), recommended, meals served. The through bus route is via Paysandú, Salto, Posadas, Encarnación, to Asunción (there are passport checks at Salto, Posadas and Encarnación). There are comfortable daily buses to **Porto Alegre** with EGA and TTL (Tres Cruces local B 27, T2401 1410, www.ttl.com.br), US$55-62, 12 hrs, and **São Paulo** (US$197-248, 30 hrs, 1 a week each via Florianópolis, US$140-164, and Curitiba, US$170-198, 23 hrs). Some private tour companies in Montevideo offer excellent deals on overland bus tours to places like Iguazú, Rio de Janeiro, Salvador, Bariloche and Santiago (eg **MTUR Viajes**, T2408 1516, www.mturviajes.com.uy, recommended).

Car hire

It is wise to hire a small car (1.3 litre engine) as Uruguay is relatively flat and gas prices are high. A small car can be negotiated for between US$40-80 per day depending upon season, free mileage, including insurance and collision damage waiver, if you are hiring a car for at least 3 days. Cheaper weekly rates available. Best to make reservations before arrival. **Autocar**, Mercedes 863, T2908 5153, www.autocar.com.uy. Economical, helpful. **Punta Car**, Cerro Largo 1383, T2900 2772, www.puntacar.com.uy, also at Aeropuerto Carrasco and other locations nationwide. **Snappy**, Andes 1363, T2900 7728, www.snappy.com.uy. **Sudancar**, Paysandú 1401, T2901 3780, www.sudancar.com.uy. Most car companies don't allow their cars to be taken abroad.

Taxi

The meter starts at about US$1.25 in *fichas*, which determine fares as shown on a table in taxi. Tipping is not expected but welcomed, usually by rounding up the fare. Do not expect change for large peso notes. Prices go up on Sat, Sun, holidays and late at night.

Train

Uruguayan railways, **AFE**, use outdated trains, but interesting rides for enthusiasts. The old train station has been abandoned, replaced by a nice terminus next to the Antel skyscraper, known as **Nueva Estación Central** at Paraguay y Nicaragua (Aguada), T2924 8080, www.afe.com.uy. Passenger trains currently only run Mon-Sat along the 25 de Agosto line. Most commuter trains run north between Montevideo and Progreso (about 5-10 a day), passing some of the country's poorest areas. Fewer services go beyond Progreso. To **Progreso** (55 mins, US$1.30), to **Canelones** (1 hr 20 mins, US$1.75), to **Santa Lucía** (1 hr 40 mins, US$2.10), to **25 de Agosto** (1 hr 45 mins, US$2.75). Occasionally, long distance services and a steam-engine run for special events, such as the 48-hr celebration of the **Día del Patrimonio (Heritage Day)** on 1 Oct, US$2.40 return ticket. More information T2924 3924.

Western
Uruguay

West of Montevideo, Route 1, part of the Pan-American Highway, heads to the UNESCO World Heritage Site of Colonia del Sacramento and the tranquil town of Carmelo. Off the road are the old British mining town of Conchillas and the Jesuit mission at Calera de las Huérfanas. Other roads lead to the Río Uruguay: Route 2 from Rosario to Fray Bentos, and Route 3 via San José de Mayo and Trinidad to the historic towns of Paysandú and Salto. The latter passes farms, man-made lakes and the river itself. There are also many hot-spring resorts.

To Colonia del Sacramento

parks, river ports and Uruguay's colonial treasure

Colonias Valdense and Suiza

Route 1 to Colonia de Sacramento is a four-lane highway. At Km 121 from Montevideo the road passes Colonia Valdense, a colony of Waldensians who still cling to some of the old customs of the Piedmontese Alps. For tourist information, T4558 8412. A road branches off north here to Colonia Suiza, a Swiss settlement also known as **Nueva Helvecia**, with lovely parks, gardens and countryside. In the town is the Santuario de Nuestra Señora De Schönstatt, all walls are covered by plants, and the first steam mill in Uruguay (1875). The Swiss national day is celebrated with great enthusiasm. There is a Centro Artesanal on Plaza Los Fundadores, with tourist information.

The highway skirts Rosario (130 km from Montevideo, 50 km before Colonia del Sacramento), called 'the first Uruguayan Museum of Mural Art'. Dozens of impressive murals are dotted around the city, some with bullfights, some abstract designs.

★Colonia del Sacramento *Colour map 8, B5.*
All museums Sat-Sun 1115-1645, closed either Tue, Wed, Thu or Fri, except Museo Archivo Regional (shut Sat-Sun) and Museo Naval (shut Mon-Wed), combined tickets US$1.60. See www.museos.gub.uy.

Founded by Portuguese settlers from Brazil in 1680, Colonia del Sacramento was a centre for smuggling British goods across the Río de la Plata into the Spanish colonies during the 18th century. The small historic section juts into the Río de la Plata, while the modern town extends around a bay. It is a lively place with

Tip...
The old town is best explored on foot but wear comfortable shoes for ease on the uneven cobbles.

streets lined with plane trees, a pleasant Plaza 25 de Agosto and a grand Intendencia Municipal (Méndez y Avenida General Flores, the main street). The town is kept very trim. The best beach is Playa Ferrando, 1.5 km to the east, easily accessible by foot or hired vehicle. There are regular connections by boat with Buenos Aires and a free port.

The **Barrio Histórico**, with its narrow streets (see Calle de los Suspiros), colonial buildings and reconstructed city walls, is charming because there are few such examples in this part of the continent. It has been declared Patrimonio Cultural de la Humanidad by UNESCO. The old town

Best for
Hot springs ▪ Ranches ▪ Sightseeing

ON THE ROAD

Gaucho life

Uruguay's passion for rural life began in 1603 with Hernando Arias and the first shipment of cattle and horses to the Banda Oriental.

Today, a typical day on an estancia begins at the hearth, perhaps with a warming *mate*, before a horseride. The fireplace may be decorated with signs of present and past ownership, each brand burnt into the fireplace representing a personal history, but one element unites them all: the myth of the gaucho.

You might be forgiven for imagining yourself a latter-day gaucho as you put your foot in the *copa* (a cupped stirrup) and mount a sturdy Uruguayan horse, perhaps of the same breed as the one that Napoleon had shipped back to carry him around a wintry Europe. However, your thick poncho might well be the only piece of gaucho gear that you are wearing. Gauchos sometimes used ponchos as shields in knife fights, but on the ride you probably won't be needing a *facón* (a large dagger), nor a pair of *bombachas* (baggy trousers gathered at the ankle) or *culero* (an apron of soft leather tied around the waist, open on the left side) to avoid lacerations from a lasso during branding and gelding. Horses on tourism estancias are used to novice riders, and *rebenques* (short whips) are best kept unused by your side. You'll find the Uruguayan horse a compliant platform for launching your *boleadoras* (three stones, covered with hide, on ropes tied at the middle, are used for entangling the legs of cattle). At this point you may learn whether your horse is a *pingo*, a gaucho's favourite horse, or *flete*, an ordinary cargo beast.

Riding along extensive *cuchillas* (ridges) and crossing rivers will bring to mind the nomadic gaucho lifestyle, and the revolutionary (largely gaucho) guerrilla bands. A *montonera* was a band of gauchos organized to drive the Brazilians and Argentinians out of Uruguay. Patriot leader Artigas was a *gaucho-caudillo* (boss).

Uruguayan life is built from livestock, sometimes quite literally. Houses were occasionally made from cattle hide. And cattle were put to other uses: coastal ranchers in Maldonado Department in the 19th century placed lights on the horns of their cows to lure ships onto the rocks for plunder.

can be easily seen on foot in a day, but spend one night there to experience the illuminations by nostalgic replica street lamps. The **Plaza Mayor** is especially picturesque and has parakeets in the palm trees. Grouped around it are the **Museo Municipal**, in a late-18th-century residence, rebuilt in 1835 (with indigenous archaeology, historical items, natural history, palaeontology), the **Casa Nacarello** next door (18th century; depicting colonial life), the **Casa del Virrey** (in ruins), the **Museo Portugués** (1717) with, downstairs, an exhibition of beautiful old maps, the ruins of the Convento de San Francisco, to which is attached the **Faro** ⓘ *lighthouse, entry US$0.90, daily 1300-sunset, from 1100 at weekends, on a clear day you can see Buenos Aires*, and the **Museo Naval** ⓘ *C Enríquez de la Peña y San Francisco, T2622 1084*, opened in the historic Casa de Lavalleja in 2009. At the Plaza's eastern end is the **Portón del Campo**, the restored city gate and drawbridge. Just north of the Plaza Mayor is the **Museo Archivo Regional** (1750), collection of maps, police records 1876-1898 and 19th-century watercolours. The **Iglesia Matriz**, on Calle Vasconcellos (beside the Plaza de Armas/Manuel Lobo), is the oldest church in Uruguay (late 17th century). Free concerts are held occasionally. At the end of Calle Misiones de los Tapes, the tiny **Museo del Azulejo** (1740-1760, rebuilt 1986), houses a collection of Portuguese, French and Catalan tiles, plus the first Uruguayan tile from 1840. At Calles de San José y España, the **Museo Español** (1720, rebuilt 1840), displays Spanish colonial items plus modern paintings by Uruguayan Jorge Páez Vilaró (temporarily closed until 2018). At the north edge, the fortifications of the **Bastión del Carmen** can be seen; nearby is the **Centro Cultural Bastión del Carmen** ⓘ *Rivadavia 223, T4522 7201*, in a 19th-century glue and soap factory, with frequent theatre productions. In the third week of January, festivities mark the founding of Colonia. The **Feria de la Ciudad** ⓘ *Campus Municipal, Fosalba y Suárez*, is a crafts fair worth a visit. Kids will love the **Acuario** ⓘ *C Virrey Cevallos 236, esq Rivadavia, www.acuario.com.uy, Wed-Mon 1600-2000, US$1.75*, in the Barrio Histórico.

Around the bay is **Real de San Carlos** ① *5 km, take 'Cotuc' or 'ABC' buses from Av Gral Flores, leaving Barrio Histórico, US$0.80,* an unusual, once grand but now sad tourist complex, built by Nicolás Mihanovich 1903-1912. The elegant bullring, in use for just two years, is falling apart (closed to visitors, bullfighting is banned in Uruguay). The casino, the nearest to Buenos Aires then (where gambling was prohibited), failed when a tax was imposed on Mihanovich's excursions; also disused is the huge Frontón court. Only the racecourse (Hipódromo) is still operational (free, except three annual races) and you can see the horses exercising on the beach and in the water.

Colonia del Sacramento

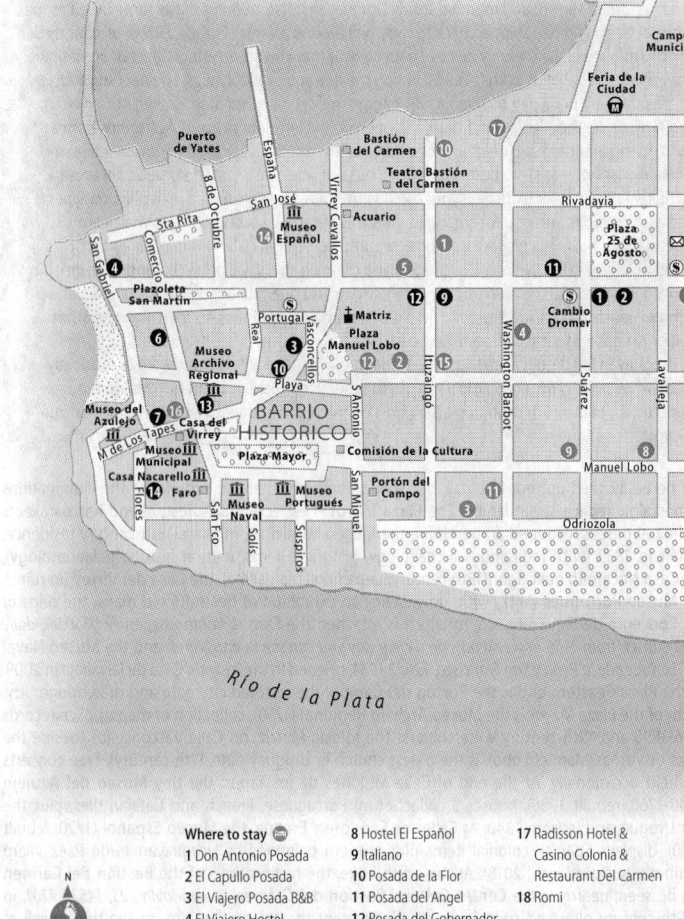

Where to stay
1 Don Antonio Posada
2 El Capullo Posada
3 El Viajero Posada B&B
4 El Viajero Hostel
5 Esperanza & Artemisa Spa
6 Hostal de los Poetas
7 Hostel Colonial

8 Hostel El Español
9 Italiano
10 Posada de la Flor
11 Posada del Angel
12 Posada del Gobernador
14 Posada del Virrey
15 Posada Manuel de Lobo
16 Posada Plaza Mayor

17 Radisson Hotel &
   Casino Colonia &
   Restaurant Del Carmen
18 Romi

Restaurants
1 Arcoiris
2 Club Colonia

Conchillas

Conchillas, 50 km from Colonia and 40 km from Carmelo, is a former British mining town from the late 19th century. It preserves dozens of buildings constructed by C H Walker and Co Ltd. Tourist information is available at the **Casa de la Cultura** ① *at C David Evans casi Dr Kyle, T4577 2809, Mon-Fri 0800-1400, with library*. The police station is also a good source of information. Direct buses from Colonia; road well marked on Route 21.

Carmelo

From Colonia, Route 21 heads northwest to Carmelo (77 km) on the banks of Arroyo Las Vacas. A fine avenue of trees leads to the river, crossed by the first swing bridge built 1912. Across the bridge is the Rambla de los Constituyentes and the Fuente de las Tentaciones. The church, museum and archive of El Carmen is on Plaza Artigas (named after the city's founder). In the **Casa de la Cultura Ignacio Barrios (IMC)** ① *19 de Abril 246, T4542 3840*, is a museum. Historically a mining centre, it is said that many luxurious buildings in Buenos Aires were made from the grey granite of Cerro Carmelo (mines flooded and used for watersports). It is one of the most important yachting centres on Río de la Plata and its microclimate produces much wine. There is a **tourist information kiosk** on Plaza Independencia, Uruguay y Roosevelt and another in the port building.

Calera de Las Huérfanas (Estancia Belén or de las Vacas) is the remains of one of the area's main Jesuit missions. Vines were introduced and lime was exported for the construction of Buenos Aires. After the expulsion of the Jesuits, its production sustained an orphanage in Buenos Aires. It's in relatively good state and is best reached by car (exit from Route 21 clearly marked, some 10 km before Carmelo, on to Camino de San Juan Martín, see www.caleradelashuerfanas.org).

Between Carmelo and Nueva Palmira, another river port, is the colonial monument, **Capilla de Narbona** (Route 21, Km 263), built in the early 18th century. At **Bodega y Granja Narbona** ① *Ruta 21, Km 268, T4540 4160, www.narbona.com.uy*, wine, cheese and other produce are available, as well as a fine restaurant and exclusive boutique hotel rooms.

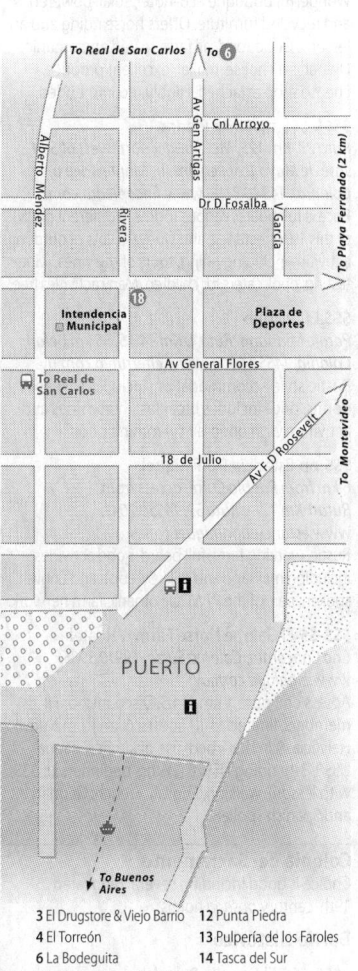

3 El Drugstore & Viejo Barrio
4 El Torreón
6 La Bodeguita
7 La Casa de Jorge Páez Vilaró
9 Mercosur
11 Mesón de la Plaza
12 Punta Piedra
13 Pulpería de los Faroles
14 Tasca del Sur

Tourist information

Visit www.guiacolonia.com.uy. If leaving Uruguay for Argentina here, the Argentine consulate is at the Argentine Cultural Centre (Flores 209, T4522 2093, http://ccolo.cancilleria. gov.ar, open weekdays 1300-1800).

Centro BIT
C Odriozola 434 (next to the port), T4522 1072, www.bitcolonia.com.
A large building complex with an official **tourist information centre** (T4522 4897, colonia@mintur. gub.uy, daily 1000-1800), restaurant, terrace, gift shop and a permanent exhibition on the country and region (show entry US$1.75).

Terminal Colonia
Av Buenos Aires, esq Manuel de Lobo, T4523 0288, www.coloniaturismoterminalcolonia.com.uy. Daily 0800-2000 (0900-1900 in winter).
Tourist information desk at bus terminal (daily 0900-2000, year-round).

> **Tip…**
> Banks open in the afternoon only. *Casas de cambio* can be found on Avenida Flores (eg Dromer, No 350, Colonia, Avenida Flores y Lavalleja). Most museums and restaurants accept Argentine pesos or US$, but rarely euros.

Where to stay

Colonia Suiza (Nueva Helvecia)

$$$$ Nirvana
Av Batlle y Ordóñez, T4554 4081, www.hotelnirvana.com.
Restaurant (Swiss and traditional cuisine), half- and full-board available, see website for promotions, sports facilities, 25 ha of park and gardens, poolside bar. Recommended.

Camping
Several campsites south of Route 1 on Río de la Plata. A good one at Blancarena is **Camping Enrique Davyt** (access from La Paz village east of Colonia Valdense), T4587 2110, campinged@adinet.com.uy, US$2.25 pp (discount for longer stays).

Tourism farms

$$$$ La Vigna
T4558 9234, Km 120 Ruta 51 to Playa Fomento, www.lavigna.com.uy.
Wonderful boutique eco-hotel, solar-powered and recycled furniture. Offers horse riding and art lessons. Good food, all farm reared and organic. Owner is a cheese-maker, excellent produce, cheese shop attached. Highly recommended.

$$$$-$$$ pp Finca Piedra
Ruta 23, Km 125, Mal Abrigo, northwest of San José de Mayo (convenient for Montevideo or Colonia), T4340 3118, www.fincapiedra.com.
Price is full board, various rooms in different parts of this 1930s estancia and vineyard, lots of outdoor activities including riding, tours of the vines, wine-tasting, pool, caters for children. Many activities free.

$$$ El Terruño
Paraje Minuano, Ruta 1, Km 140.5, 35 km before Colonia, T4550 6004, www.elterrunio.com.uy.
Rustic-style accommodation, including cheaper dorms, price includes breakfast, horse rides and activities, with open-air swimming pool.

$$$ pp Estancia Don Miguel
6 km from Pueblo Cufré, access from Ruta 1 Km 121 y Ruta 52, T4550 2041, www.estanciadonmiguel.com.
Rustic, working farm, full board, good activities including massage and reiki, Swedish and English spoken, part of the WWOOF organic farm network.

$$$-$$ El Galope Horse Farm & Hostel
Cno Concordia, Colonia Suiza, T9910 5985, www.elgalope.com.uy.
Access on Route 1 Km 114.5. Discounts for HI members, limited to 10 guests, 6 km from Nueva Helvecia, $ in bunk bed, use of kitchen, sauna US$8, 3-hr riding US$70 (1½ hrs beginners US$35 with lesson), walking, English, French, German and Spanish spoken.

Colonia del Sacramento
Choice is good including several renovated 19th-century *posada* hotels.

Barrio Histórico

$$$$-$$$ El Capullo Posada
18 de Julio 219, T4523 0135, www.elcapullo.com.
Spacious living area, English and American owners, stylish boutique-style rooms, outdoor pool and *parrilla*.

$$$ Posada Plaza Mayor
C del Comercio 111, T4522 3193,
www.posadaplazamayor.com.
In a 19th-century house, beautiful internal patio
with lemon trees and Spanish fountain, lovely
rooms with a/c or heating, English spoken.

Centre

$$$$-$$$ Don Antonio Posada
Ituzaingó 232, T4522 5344,
www.posadadonantonio.com.
1850 building, buffet breakfast, garden, pool,
excellent. Free guided walks organized Sat.

$$$$-$$$ Hotel Esperanza & Artemisa Spa
Gral Flores 237, T4522 2922,
www.hotelesperanzaspa.com.
Charming, with buffet breakfast, sauna,
heated pool, gym and treatments.

$$$$-$$ Radisson Hotel and Casino Colonia
Washington Barbot 283, T4523 0460,
www.radissoncolonia.com.
Great location overlooking the jetty,
contemporary architecture, casino attached,
price depends on room and season. 2 pools,
sauna, highly regarded restaurant **Del Carmen**,
very good.

$$$ El Viajero Posada B&B
Odriozola 269, T4522 8645,
www.elviajerohostels.com.
Very well located modern building with river
views, bike rental, 13 private rooms with a/c and
TV. Part of the Latin American El Viajero hostel
chain, with sister hostel, below.

$$$ Italiano
Intendente Suárez 103-105, T4522 7878,
www.hotelitaliano.com.uy.
Open since 1928, it has been renovated with
comfortable rooms, cheaper rates Mon-Thu
(low season). Large outdoor and indoor pools,
gym, jacuzzi, good restaurant. Recommended.

$$$ Posada del Angel
Washington Barbot 59, T4522 4602,
www.posadadelangel.net.
Early 20th-century house, pleasant,
warm welcome, gym, sauna, pool,
occasional entertainment.

$$$ Posada de la Flor
Ituzaingó 268, T4523 0794,
www.posada-delaflor.com.
At the quiet end of C Ituzaingó, next to the river
and to the Barrio Histórico, simply decorated

rooms on a charming patio and roof terrace
with river views, bike hire.

$$$ Posada del Gobernador
18 de Julio 205, T4522 2918, www.del
gobernador.com. Cheaper for longer stays.
Charming, with open-air pool, garden.

$$$ Posada del Virrey
España 217, T4522 2223,
www.posadadelvirrey.com.
Large rooms, some with view over bay (cheaper
with small bathroom and no balcony), with buffet
breakfast, guided walks on Sat. Recommended.

$$$ Posada Manuel de Lobo
Ituzaingó 160, T4522 2463,
www.posadamanueldelobo.com.
Built in 1850. Boutique hotel with 8 large rooms,
huge baths, limited parking, some smaller rooms,
nice breakfast area inside and out.

$$$-$$ Romi
Rivera 236, T4523 0456, www.hotelromi.com.
19th-century *posada*-style downstairs, with
lovely tiles at entrance. Airy modernist upstairs
and simple rooms. Recommended.

$$ El Viajero Hostel Suites Colonia (HI affiliate)
Washington Barbot 164, T4522 2683,
www.elviajerohostels.com.
Private en suite with a/c and TV, dorms en suite
with a/c, fireplace for winter, terrace and BBQ area
for the summer, breakfast included, free Wi-Fi.
Quirky art on walls.

$$ Hostal de los Poetas
Mangarelli 677, T4523 1643.
Some distance from the Barrio Histórico but one
of the cheapest, a few simple bedrooms with
a/c and TV and a lovely breakfast room, tiny
exuberant garden.

$$ Hostel Colonial
Gral Flores 440, T4523 0347,
www.hostelcolonial.com.uy.
HI affiliated. Pretty patio and quirky touches,
such as barber's chair in reception. $ in dorm.
Kitchen, bbq, common room, free use of bikes
(all ancient), run down and noisy, but popular.

$$ Hostel El Español
Manuel Lobo 377, T4523 0759,
www.hostelelespaniol.com.
Good value, $ pp with shared bath in dorms,
breakfast included, TV room. Part of the **HoLa**
network of hostels (www.holahostels.com).
Recommended.

Carmelo

$$ Timabe
19 de Abril y Solís, T5401 4725,
www.ciudadcarmelo.com/timabe.
Near the swing bridge, with a/c or fan,
dining room, parking, good.

Camping
At Playa Seré, hot showers.

Restaurants

Colonia Suiza (Nueva Helvecia)

$-$$ Piccolino
19 de abril, corner of main plaza.
Pizzas, snacks and ice-cream, open-air tables
on square, good value.

Colonia del Sacramento

$$$ El Drugstore
Vasconcellos 179, T4522 5241.
Hip, fusion food: Latin American, European,
Japanese, good, creative varied menu, good
salads and fresh vegetables. Music and show.

$$$ La Bodeguita
Del Comercio 167, T4522 5329. Tue-Sun 1930,
Sat-Sun from lunchtime.
Its terrace on the river is the main attraction
of this lively pizza place that also serves
good *chivitos* and pasta. Celebrated its
20th anniversary in 2014.

$$$ La Casa de Jorge Páez Vilaró
Misiones de los Tapes 65, T4522 9211,
www.arteamericano.com. Closed Tue-Wed.
Attractively set at an artist's former residence,
it offers a varied and fine menu, only 8 tables.

$$$ Mesón de la Plaza
Vasconcellos 153, T4522 4807.
140-year-old house with a leafy courtyard,
elegant dining, good traditional food.

$$$ Parrillada El Portón
Gral Flores 333, T4522 5318.
Excellent *parrillada*. Small, relatively smart,
good atmosphere. House speciality is offal
and great sausages.

$$$ Pulpería de los Faroles
Misiones de los Tapes 101, T4523 0271.
Inviting tables (candlelit at night) on the cobbled
plaza, for a varied *menú* that includes tasty
salads, seafood and local wines.

$$$ Punta Piedra
Ituzaingó y Gen Flores 248, T4522 2236.
Daily 0900-0000.
Set in a stone building, smart, great range of
meat dishes, local wines, *parrilla*, *chivitos*, pastas.

$$$ Viejo Barrio (VB)
Vasconcellos 169, T4522 5399.
Open from 2000, closed Wed.
Very good for home-made pastas and fish,
renowned live shows.

$$$-$$ El Torreón
End of Av Gen Flores, T4523 1524.
One of the best places to enjoy a sunset meal
with views of the river. Set in a historic tower
with indoor and outdoor seating. Also serves
toasties and cakes.

$$$-$$ Mercosur
Flores y Ituzaingó, T4522 4200,
www.restaurantemercosur.com.
Popular, varied dishes. Also café serving home-
made cakes. All you can eat buffet US$18. Cash
only, but accepts 5 currencies including euros.
Live shows.

$$ Club Colonia
Gen Flores 382, T4522 2189.
Good value, frequented by locals, good sturdy grub,
traditional Uruguayan fare and some Italian dishes.

$$ Tasca del Sur
Las Flores s/n. Daily from 1200 until late in
high season.
For a change from *parrilla* and pasta, this tiny
place does excellent tacos, quesadillas and fajitas.
The chef takes his time about things, but it's
worth the wait. Recommended.

Arcoiris
Av Gral Flores at Plaza 25 de Agosto. Open till 0130.
Very good ice cream.

Shopping

Colonia del Sacramento
This place is good for shopping with a large artist
community displaying wares, Uruguayan and
international, in galleries and shops.

El Almacén (Real 150), creative gifts. **Paseo
del Sol** (Del Comercio 158, www.paseodelsol.
com.uy), is a small commercial centre selling
local gifts, snack bar with occasional live music.
Oveja Negra (De la Playa 114), recommended
for woollen clothes. Leather shops on C Santa
Rita, next to Yacht Club. At **Arteco** (Rambla de las

Américas y Av Mihanovich, Real de San Carlos) and **Gadec** (C San Miguel, opposite Puerta de la Ciudadela) local artisans sell their produce.

What to do

Colonia Suiza (Nueva Helvecia)
Finca La Rosada, *Federico Fisher s/n, Nueva Helvecia, T4554 7036, www.larosada.com.uy.*
A soft-fruit and pecan nut farm, famous for its blueberries, pick-your-own in season, offers tours with lunch or tea, plus local sites, cooking classes, produce shop.

Colonia del Sacramento
City tours available with **Destino Viajes** (General Flores 341, T4522 5343, destinoviajes@adinet.com.uy).

A hop-on, hop-off city tour bus, run by **Buquebus**, stops at 10 different stops in and around Colonia, with a walking tour, US$25 valid all day, 1st bus 1100, last 1900. It can be included in some ferry packages from Buenos Aires.

Transport

There are plenty of filling stations between Colonia and the capital.

Colonia Suiza (Nueva Helvecia)
Bus Montevideo–Colonia Suiza, frequent, with **COT**, 2-2½ hrs, US$7.30; **Turil**, goes to Colonia Suiza and Valdense; to **Colonia del Sacramento**, frequent, 1 hr, US$3.35. Local services between Colonia Valdense and Nueva Helvecia connect with Montevideo/Colonia del Sacramento buses.

Colonia del Sacramento
Bus All leave from bus terminal on Av Buenos Aires y Manuel de Lobo, 7 blocks east of the Barrio Histórico, between the ferry port and the petrol station (www.terminalcolonia.com.uy, free luggage lockers, tourist info desk, ATM, exchange, café and internet). To **Montevideo**, several services daily, 2¼-2¾ hrs, **COT**, T4522

3121, **Chadre**, T4522 4734, and **Turil**, T4522 5246, from US$15-19. **Turil** to **Col Valdense**, 1 hr, US$4. **Berrutti** to **Conchillas**, 50 mins-1 hr, US$3.50. To **Carmelo**, 1½ hrs, **Chadre** and **Berrutti**, T4522 5301, www.berruttiturismo.com, US$5.50. **Chadre** to **Mercedes**, 3½ hrs, US$15, **Fray Bentos**, 4 hrs, US$17.50, **Paysandú**, 6 hrs, US$23.50 and **Salto**, 8 hrs, US$30.50. **Nossar**, T4522 2934, to **Durazno**, 2 ½-3 hrs, US$16.50.

Car hire In bus terminal: **Avis** (main hall), T4522 9842, from US$120 per day, **Hertz** (50 m from entrance), T4522 9851, from US$65 per day. **Thrifty** by port, www.thrifty.com.uy, T218488, also at Flores 172, T4522 2939, where there are bicycles too (US$6 per hr), scooters (US$12 per hr) and electric golf buggies (US$17 per hr) for hire, recommended as traffic is slow and easy to navigate.

Ferry Book in advance for all sailings in summer. Fares and schedules given under Montevideo, Transport. To **Buenos Aires**: from 5 crossings daily, with **Buquebus** (T130), cars carried. **Colonia Express**, office at the port, T2401 6666, www.coloniaexpress.com, makes 2-3 crossings a day between Colonia and **Buenos Aires** (50 mins) in fast boats (no vehicles carried) with bus connections to/from **Montevideo**, **Punta del Este** and Uruguayan towns. **Seacat**, www.seacatcolonia.com, T4314 5100, 3 fast ferries to **Buenos Aires**, 1 hr, office in Colonia, T4522 2919. **Note** Passports must be stamped and Argentine departure tax paid even if only visiting Colonia for 1 day.

Taxi A Méndez y Gral Flores, T4522 2920. Taxi in the centre US$1.50 flat fee.

Carmelo
Bus To **Montevideo**, US$16-19, Intertur, Chadre and **Sabelín**. To **Fray Bentos** (US$10), **Salto** (US$22.50), with **Chadre** from main plaza 0655, 1540. To **Colonia**, see above. To **Buenos Aires**: via Tigre, across the Paraná delta, an interesting bus/boat ride past innumerable islands: **Cacciola** 2 a day, approx US$56 return; T4542 4282, www.cacciolaviajes.com, see Montevideo page 1543.

Mercedes to Paysandú
bully beef, relaxing thermal springs and the River Uruguay

Mercedes *Colour map 8, B5.*
This livestock centre, known as 'the city of flowers', is best reached by Route 2 from the main Colonia-Montevideo highway. Founded in 1788, it is a pleasant town on the Río Negro, which during the season becomes a yachting and fishing centre. Its charm derives from its Spanish-colonial appearance, although it is not as old as the older parts of Colonia. There is an attractive

costanera (riverside drive) and a jazz festival in January and other events during the year (tickets from Soriano Turismo: www.sorianoturismo.com, check www.jazzalacalle.com.uy or Jazz a la Calle's Facebook page for future dates).

West of town 5 km is the **Parque y Castillo Barón de Mauá** ① *T4532 2201*, dating from 1857. It has a mansion which contains the **Museum of Palaeontology** ① *T4532 2201, museoberro@gmail.com, daily 1100-1700, free, on the ground floor*. The building is worth wandering around to see the exterior, upper apartments and stable block. Cheese, wine and olive oil are produced. It takes 45 minutes to walk to the park, a pleasant route passing Calera Real on the riverbank, dating back to 1722, the oldest industrial ruins in the country (lime kilns hewn out of the sandstone). At the **tourist office** ① *EE Giménez 643, T4532 2201, http://soriano.gub.uy*, maps and hotel lists are available.

Fray Bentos *Colour map 8, B5.*

Route 2 continues westwards (34 km) to Fray Bentos, the main port on the east bank of Río Uruguay. Here in 1865 the Liebig company built its first factory producing meat extract. The original plant, much extended and known as **El Anglo**, has been restored as the **Museo de la Revolución Industrial** ① *T4562 2918/3690, Tue-Sun 0930-1700, US$1.40, 1½-hr guided tour 1000 and 1500 in Spanish US$3.15, leaflet in English*, and the whole industrial landscape was added to the UNESCO World Heritage list in 2015. The office block in the factory has been preserved complete with its original fittings. Many machines can be seen. Within the complex is the Barrio Inglés, where workers were housed, and La Casa Grande, where the director lived (guided tours of Casa Grande Tuesday, Thursday, Sunday 1200). Bicycles are available for touring the site. There are **beaches** to the northeast and southwest. **Tourist office** ① *25 de Mayo 3400, T4562 2233, turismo@rionegro.gub.uy, Mon-Fri 0900-1800, Sat 0900-1500*.

Crossing to Argentina About 9 km upriver from Fray Bentos is the San Martín International Bridge (cars US$8, motorbikes US$1.70; pedestrians and cyclists may cross only on vehicles, officials may arrange lifts).

☆Paysandú *Colour map 8, A5.*

This undulating, historic city, 110 km north of Fray Bentos, is on the east bank of the Río Uruguay. Along Route 3, it is 380 km from Montevideo. There is a 19th-century **basilica** ① *daily 0700-1145, 1600-2100*. The **Museo Histórico Municipal** ① *Zorrilla de San Martín y Leandro Gómez, open*

> **Tip...**
> Bring a hat! Summer temperatures can get to 42°C.

afternoons only, has good collection of guns and furniture from the time of the Brazilian siege of 1864-1865. **Museo de la Tradición** ① *Av de los Iracundos, north of town at the Balneario Municipal, 0900-1400 daily, Sun also 1500-2000, reached by bus to Zona Industrial*, gaucho articles, is also worth a visit.

Crossing to Argentina The José Artigas international bridge connects with Colón, Argentina (US$6 per car, return), 8 km away. Immigration for both countries is on the Uruguayan side in the same office. If travelling by bus, the driver gets off the bus with everyone's documents and a list of passengers to be checked by immigration officials. There is a **tourist office** ① *T4722 7574, paysandu@mintur.gub.uy*, at the bridge. For money exchange, casas de cambio on 18 de Julio in town. **Argentine consulate** ① *L Gómez 1034, T4722 2253, http://cpays.cancilleria.gov.ar, Mon-Fri 1300-1800*.

Around Paysandú

The **Central Termal Guaviyú** ① *Ruta 3 Km 431.5, T4755 2023, www.termasguaviyu.com, US$3.20-3.75, getting there: 50 mins by bus, US$3, 6 a day*, thermal springs 60 km north, with four pools, restaurant, three motels (\$\$\$-\$\$ for four to six people) and private hotel with own thermal pools (\$\$\$, **Villagio**) and excellent cheap camping facilities. Along Route 90, 83 km east, is the **Centro Termal Almirón** ① *Ruta 90 Km 83, T4740 2891, termas.almiron@paysandu.gub.uy, US$2*, with camping, apartments and motels. The **Meseta de Artigas** ① *110 km north of Paysandú, 15 km off the highway to Salto, no public transport, free*, is 45 m above the Río Uruguay, which here narrows and at low water forms whirlpools at the rapids of El Hervidero. It was used as a base by General Artigas during the struggle for independence. The terrace has a fine view, but the rapids are not visible from the Meseta. The statue topped by Artigas' head is very original.

Tourist information

Paysandú

Tourist office
Plaza Constitución, 18 de Julio 1226, T4722 6220, www.paysandu.gub.uy. Mon-Fri 0900-1900, Sat-Sun 0800-1800 (2000 in summer). And at Plan de la Costa, Balneario Municipal.

Where to stay

Mercedes

$$$ Rambla Hotel
Av Asencio 728, T4532 4671, www.mercedesramblahotel.com.
Riverside 3-star hotel with crisp, businesslike rooms and buffet breakfast.

$$ Ito
Eduardo V Haedo 184, T4532 4919.
Basic though decent rooms in an old house with cosy inner patio.

Tourism farm

$$$ pp La Sirena Marinas del Río Negro
Ruta 14, Km 4, T9953 2698, www.lasirena.com.uy.
Estancia dating from 1830, picturesque, on the river, birdwatching, fishing, waterskiing, accommodation, meals, full board (**$$$-$$** double room with breakfast) friendly owners Rodney, Lucia and Patricia Bruce. Warmly recommended.

Fray Bentos

$$-$ Colonial
25 de Mayo 3293, T4562 2260, www.hotelcolonial.com.uy.
Attractive old building with patio. A/c and breakfast extra, **$** without bath.

$$ Plaza
18 de Julio y 25 de Mayo, T4562 2363, www.plazahotelfraybentos.com.uy.
Comfortable, a/c, internet, with breakfast, on the Plaza Constitución.

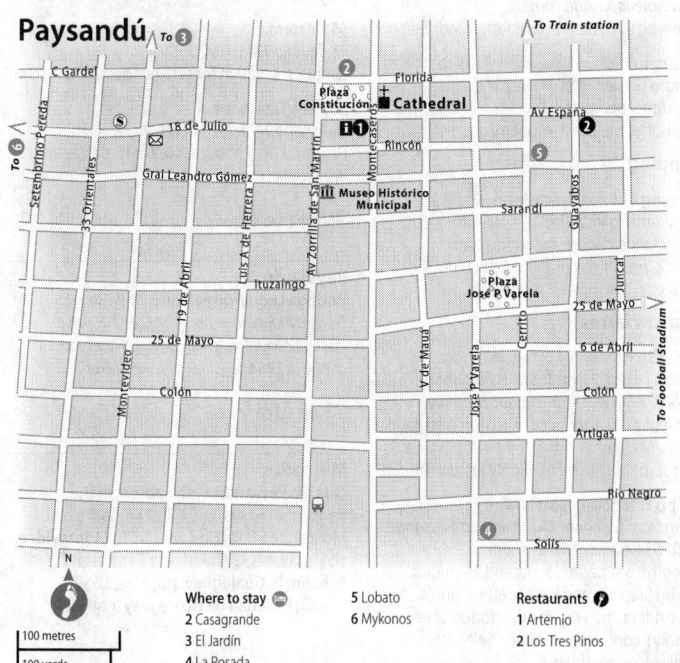

Paysandú — To 3, To Train station

C Gardel, Florida, Plaza Constitución, Cathedral, Av España, 18 de Julio, Rincón, Graf Leandro Gómez, Museo Histórico Municipal, Sarandí, Guayabos, Setembrino Pereda, 33 Orientales, Luis A de Herrera, Av Zorrilla de San Martín, Montecaseros, Ituzaingó, Plaza José P Varela, 25 de Mayo, 19 de Abril, Montevideo, 25 de Mayo, V de Maua, José P Varela, Cerro, 6 de Abril, Colón, Colón, Artigas, To Football Stadium, Río Negro, Solís

To 6

N, 100 metres, 100 yards

Where to stay
2 Casagrande
3 El Jardín
4 La Posada
5 Lobato
6 Mykonos

Restaurants
1 Artemio
2 Los Tres Pinos

Camping

At the **Club Remeros** on Rambla Costanera, opposite Parque Roosevelt, www.clubremerosmercedes.com.uy, T4532 2534.

Paysandú

Book hotels in advance during Holy Week.

$$$ Casagrande
Florida 1221, Plaza Constitución, T4722 4994, www.hotelcasagrande.com.uy.
Welcoming, buffet breakfast, parking, garden, very good.

$$$ El Jardín
Montevideo 1085, T4722 3745, www.hoteljardin.com.
Comfortable family-run residence with private parking, and a neat garden.

$$$ Mykonos
18 de Julio 768, T4722 0255.
Buffet breakfast, mostly a business hotel with good services.

$$ La Posada
José Pedro Varela 566, T4722 7879, www.hotellaposada.com.uy.
Patio with BBQ, buffet breakfast, laundry service.

$$ Lobato
Leandro Gómez 1415, T4722 2241, www.hotellobato.com.uy.
With buffet breakfast, modern, good.

Camping

Camping Club de Pescadores
Av Baldomero Vidal 1581, T4722 2885, www.clubpescadorespaysandu.com.
US$3.50 pp per day plus US$6 per tent, electricity, hot showers after 1800.

Tourism farms

$$$$-$$$ Hostería y Estancia La Paz
Colonia La Paz, 15 km south of Paysandú, T4720 2272, www.estancialapaz.com.uy.
Excellent rustic rooms, pool, customized gaucho experiences, horse riding, birdwatching. Half- and full-board available. Highly recommended.

$$$ pp Estancia Resort La Calera
60 km from Guichón, 150 km east of Paysandú, T2601 0340, www.lacalera.com.
44 rooms, 6 superior rooms and 24 studios, all with fireplace and kitchenette, 2 pools, horse riding and wagon rides, rodeo, sheep shearing, conference facilities. Self-catering. Highly recommended.

Restaurants

Mercedes

$$$-$$ Parador La Rambla
Rambla Costanera y 18 de Julio, T4532 7337.
For good Spanish-influenced meals on the riverside.

$ Príncipes del Sur
Giménez 747, T4532 8836.
Central, good cafe for snacks and icecreams.

Fray Bentos

Several other cafés and pizzerias on 18 de Julio near Plaza Constitución.

$$$ Wolves
At Barrio Anglo, T4562 3604.
Good home-made pastas next to the museum.

$$$-$$ Juventud Unida
18 de Julio 1130, T4562 3365.
The restaurant of a local football club is a popular place for varied meals.

Paysandú

$$$ Artemio
18 de Julio 1248, T072 36092.
Simple, reputation for serving "best food in town"

$$$ Los Tres Pinos
Av España 1474, T4724 1211.
Parrillada, very good, as well as its pastas and fish. Wine cellar, events.

What to do

Paysandú

Bodega Leonardo Falcone, *Av Wilson Ferreira Aldunate y Young, T4722 7718, www. bodegaleonardofalcone.com.uy.* Winery tours at one of Uruguay's finest wine makers.

Transport

Mercedes

Bus To **Paysandú**, with **Sabelín**, in bus terminal, 1½-2 hrs, US$7-8; also **Chadre** on the Montevideo-Bella Unión route. To **Montevideo**, US$16, 3½ hrs, **CUT**, **Agencia Central** and **Sabelín**. To **Gualeguaychú**, 2 hrs, US$9, **ETA CUT**, **Ciudad de Gualeguay** (not Sun).

Fray Bentos

Bus Terminal at 18 de Julio y Blanes. To/from **Montevideo**, **CUT**, 4-5 hrs, US$17.50, also **Chadre** and **Agencia Central**. To **Mercedes**, **ETA**, US$1.75, 5 daily (fewer Sun).

To Argentina To **Buenos Aires**, 4 hrs, US$34.50, **CITA**. To **Gualeguaychú**, 1½ hrs, US$5.75, **ETA CUT** (not Sun).

Paysandú

Bus It can be hard to get a seat on buses going north. Terminal at Zorrilla y Artigas, T4722 3225.

To/from **Montevideo**, US$22.50 (Núñez, Copay, T4722 2094, 6 a day), 5-6 hrs, also **Chadre**, US$21, and **Agencia Central**. To **Salto**, **Agencia Central**, **Alonso**, T4733 3969, 1½-2 hrs, 8 a day (Mon-Fri), US$8. To **Rivera**, US$18-21, **Copay**, 0400 Mon-Sat and 1200 daily, via Tacuarembó. To **Fray Bentos**, 2 a day with **Chadre**, 2 hrs direct, US$7.50. To **Colonia** by **Chadre**, 0750, 1750, 6 hrs, US$18.50.

To Argentina To **Colón**, Copay, Río Uruguay, 45 mins-1 hr, US$5.

Salto and the north

citrus fruits, thermal springs and metre-long lizards

☆**Salto** *Colour map 8, A5.*
A centre for cultivating and processing oranges and other citrus fruit, Salto is a beautifully kept town, 120 km by paved road north of Paysandú with a population of more than 100,000. The town's commercial area is on Calle Uruguay, between Plazas Artigas and Treinta y Tres. There are lovely historic streets and walks along the river, but the riverside location suffered some damage from flooding late 2015/early 2016. See the beautiful **Parque Solari** (northeast of the centre) and the **Parque Harriague** (south of the centre) with an open-air theatre.

The **Museo María Irene Olarreaga Gallino de Bellas Artes y Artes Decorativas** ① *Uruguay 1067, T4732 9898 ext 148, Tue-Sat 1400-2000, Sun 1700-2000, free*, in the French-style mansion of a rich *estanciero* (Palacio Gallino), is well worth a visit. **Museo del Hombre y La Tecnología** ① *Brasil 511, T4732 9898, ext 151, daily 1400-1900, free entry and free guided tours in Spanish*, is very interesting, with a small archaeological museum. There is a Shrove Tuesday carnival.

The most popular tourist site in the area is the large dam and hydroelectric plant **Represa de Salto Grande** ① *taxi to dam US$20.50; guided tours 0700-1600 (museum 0700-1500) arranged by Relaciones Públicas office, T4732 7777, www.saltogrande.org; visitors centre at the plant*, 13 km from Salto, built jointly by Argentina and Uruguay. A road runs along the top of the dam to Argentina. By launch to the **Salto Chico** beach, fishing, camping.

Near the dam (2 km north on ex-Route 3) is **Parque Acuático Termas de Salto Grande** ① *open all year 1000-1800 (longer Jan and Feb), US$11.50, T4734 0870, www.hotelhoraciooquiroga.com*, 4 ha, in a natural setting. There are several pools, slides, hydro massages, water jets and a man-made waterfall.

Crossing to Argentina North of the town, at the Salto Grande dam, there is an international bridge to Concordia, Argentina, which is open 24 hours a day, all year. Passengers have to get off the bus to go through immigration procedures. Buses don't go on Sundays. Both Argentine and Uruguayan immigration offices are on the Argentine side. **Argentine consulate** ① *Artigas 1162, T4733 2931, http://cslto.cancilleria.gov.ar, Mon-Fri 0900-1400.*

Termas del Daymán and other springs
About 10 km south of Salto on Route 3, served by bus marked 'Termas' which leave from Calle Brasil every hour, are Termas del Daymán, a small town built around curative hot springs. It is a nice place to spend a night, though it is crowded in the daytime; few restaurants around the beautifully laid out pools. **Complejo Médico Hidrotermal Daymán** ① *T4736 9090, www.viatermal. com/spatermaldayman, use of facilities US$3.75, multiple different treatments at additional cost*, has a spa and separate pools (external and internal), showers and jacuzzis. There is also Acuamania, a theme park, nearby.

The road to **Termas del Arapey** (T4768 2019, www.termasarapey.com and destinotermas.gub.uy) branches off Route 3 to Bella Unión, at Km 548, 80 km north of Salto, and then runs 19 km east and then south. Pampa birds, rheas and metre-long lizards in evidence. Termas del Arapey is on

ON THE ROAD

National pride

The indigenous Charrúas were remarkably brave, but they were also inhospitable and rallied against European explorers. They killed Spaniard Juan Díaz de Solís, the navigator who first charted Montevideo in 1515. Between early explorer visits, they learned to ride captured horses, still slinging stones on suede straps in defiance of and indifference to the superior Spanish swords. Their aggression, despite the impossible odds, led to their eradication when the last remaining natives were massacred in 1831. Nevertheless, their legacy lives on. *Mate*, the native tea, is now the national beverage, proudly sipped and shared throughout Uruguay. And the national soccer team is nicknamed *Los Charrúas* because, after winning the first and fourth FIFA World Cups in 1930 and 1950, against powerhouses Argentina and Brazil, people recognized that 'fight to the finish' attitude in the players. In fact, in Uruguay, it is a great compliment to be described as having *garra Charrúa*, meaning strength, resourcefulness, bravery and determination.

the Arapey river south of Isla Cabellos (Baltasar Brum). The waters at these famous thermal baths contain bicarbonated salts, calcium and magnesium.

To the Brazilian border *Colour map 8, A5/A6.*

Route 3 goes north to the small town of **Bella Unión**, from where an international bridge 5 km away crosses to the Brazilian town of **Barra de Quaraí**. This village lies next to a unspoilt area of densely wooded islands and beautiful sandbanks on the Río Uruguay, at the triple frontier point. About 80 km northwest is **Uruguaiana** which takes the main international bus traffic between Brazil and Argentina.

From near Bella Unión Route 30 runs east to **Artigas**, a frontier town in a cattle raising and agricultural area. The town is known for its good quality amethysts, and if you fancy a dip there is excellent swimming upstream from the bridge. The bridge across the Río Cuareim leads to the Brazilian town of **Quaraí**. The Brazilian consul is at Lecueder 432, T4772 5414, http://artigas.itamaraty.gov.br.

Listings Salto and the north

Tourist information

Salto

Tourist office
Uruguay 1052, T4733 4096, http://turismo. salto.gub.uy. Mon-Sat 0800-1900. And at the international bridge, T4732 8933, salto@mintur.gub.uy.
Provides a free map.

Where to stay

Salto

$$$$ Hotel Horacio Quiroga
At Parque del Lago, T4733 4411, www.hotelhoracioquiroga.com.

Best in town although some distance from centre, at the Termas complex, sports facilities, spa treatments, staffed by nearby catering school, special packages in season.

$$$-$$ Los Cedros
Uruguay 656, T4733 3984, www.loscedros.com.uy.
In centre, comfortable 3-star hotel, buffet breakfast, conference room.

$$ pp Concordia
Uruguay 749, T4733 2735.
Oldest hotel in Uruguay, founded 1860, Carlos Gardel stayed here, fine courtyard, pleasant breakfast room.

$$ Español
Brasil 826, T4733 4048, www.hotelespanolsalto.com.
Central, functional, with regular services, café and parking.

Termas del Daymán

$$$ Del Pasaje
Near Ruta 3, T4736 9661,
www.hoteldelpasaje.com.uy.
Hotel rooms, apartments for 2, 4, 6 or 7 people
and *cabañas*. Situated in front of the Parque
Acuático Acuamania.

$$$ La Posta del Daymán
Ruta 3, Km 487, T4736 9801,
www.lapostadeldayman.com.
A/c, half- and full-board or breakfast only,
thermal water in more expensive rooms,
thermal pool, good restaurant, gym, library,
long-stay discounts, camping. Recommended.
Also hydrothermal complex.

$$ Bungalows El Puente
C 6 y Circunvalación, near the bridge
over Río Dayman, T4736 9876, includes
discount to thermal baths.
13 bungalows for 2 to 7 people, cheaper without
a/c, kitchen.

$$ Estancia La Casona del Daymán
Ruta 3 Km 473, 3 km east of the bridge at
Daymán, T4733 2735.
Well-preserved colonial-era farm, horse riding
and many other rural pursuits.

$$ Hostal Canela
Los Sauces entre Los Molles y C 1, T4736 9121,
www.hostalcanela.com.uy.
HI affiliated. Good value, with kitchenette,
pool, gardens.

Termas del Arapey

$$$-$$ Hotel Termas del Arapey
T4768 2441, www.hoteltermasdelarapey.com.
Safe, indoor/outdoor pool, restaurant.

Camping
US$5-7 pp (low/high season), good facilities.

Artigas

There are a few hotels in town and the **Club
Deportivo Artigas** (Pte Berreta 451 and LA de
Herrera, 4 km from city, T4772 2532), open all year,
rooms ($) and camping (US$2.50 pp plus US$1.50
per tent), restaurant, no cooking facilities.

Camping
At **Club Zorrilla, Route 30, 5 km from Artigas**
(T4772 4341), with swimming pools, café, and
good facilities.

Restaurants

Salto

$$$ La Caldera
Uruguay 221, T4732 4648. Closed Mon lunchtime.
Good *parrillada* and local wines, also seafood.

$$$ La Casa de Lamas
Chiazzaro 20, T4732 9376.
Fish and home-made pasta.

$$$ La Trattoria (at Club de Uruguay)
Uruguay 754, T4733 6660.
Breakfast and good-value meals, excellent pasta.

Transport

If driving north to Paysandú and Salto, especially
on Route 3, fill up with fuel and drinking
water at every opportunity, stations are few
and far between. From Colonia to Punta del
Este by-passing Montevideo: take Ruta 11 at
Ecilda Paullier, passing through San José de
Mayo, Santa Lucía and Canelones, joining the
Interbalnearia at Km 46.

Salto
Bus Terminal 15 blocks east of centre at Batlle
y Blandengues, café, shopping centre, *casa de
cambio*. Take taxi to centre. To/from **Montevideo**,
5½-7½ hrs, US$28-35 (**Norteño, Núñez, Agencia
Central** and **Chadre**). **Argentur, Cotabu** and
Hernández to **Termas del Arapey**, 1¼ hrs, daily,
US$5. To **Bella Unión**, 2 hrs, US$8, 2 a day, Chadre.
To **Colonia**, 0555, 1555, 8 hrs, US$25; to **Fray
Bentos**, same times, US$13.

To Argentina To **Concordia**, **Chadre** and
Flecha Bus, 2 a day each Mon-Fri, 2 on Sat, no
buses Sun, US$5.50, 1¼-1½ hrs. To **Buenos Aires**,
US$38, **Flecha Bus**.
  To **Concordia**, US$5, 15 mins, 4 launches a day
(not Sun), depart port on C Brasil; immigration
either side of river, quick and easy.

Artigas
Bus To **Salto**, COA, T4772 2268, US$12. **Turil**
and **COT** from **Montevideo** 7-8 hrs, US$35 via
Durazno, Paso de los Toros and Tacuarembó.

Eastern
Uruguay

Resorts line the coast from Montevideo to Punta del Este, the ultimate magnet for summer holidaymakers, especially from Argentina. Out of season, it is quieter and you can have the beaches to yourself, which is pretty much the case year round, the closer you get to Brazil. Inland are cattle ranches, some of which welcome visitors, quiet lagoons and hills with expansive views.

East from Montevideo

natural attractions, resorts and public art

This beautiful coast consists of an endless succession of small bays, beaches and promontories, set among hills and woodlands. The beach season runs from December to the end of February. An excellent four-lane highway leads to Punta del Este and Rocha, and a good two-lane highway to Chuy, near the Brazilian border. This route takes in the most important Uruguayan beach resorts, as well as Parque Nacional Santa Teresa and other natural attractions.

Piriápolis *Colour map 8, B6.*

This resort set among hills, 101 km from Montevideo, is laid out with an abundance of shady trees, and the district is rich in pine, eucalyptus and acacia woods. It has a good beach, a yacht harbour, a country club, a motor-racing track (street circuit) and is particularly popular with Argentines. It was, in fact, founded in the 1890s as a bathing resort for residents of Buenos Aires. Next to the marina is a small cable car (with seats for two) to the top of **Cerro San**

> **Tip...**
>
> If driving, it's worth taking the coastal route. Although there are three tolls each way on the Interbalnearia (US$3 each – see Driving in Uruguay, page 1573), it is the easiest and most comfortable road in Uruguay with sufficient service stations along the way.

Antonio ① *US$4.75 return or US$3 one way, 10 mins ride, free car park and toilets at lower station (also reached by car, bus or on foot).* Magnificent views of Piriápolis and beaches, several restaurants. Recommended, but be careful when disembarking. North of the centre, at **Punta de Playa Colorada**, is a marine rescue centre, that looks after injured sea creatures before releasing them into the wild. **Tourist office**, Asociación de Turismo ① *Rambla de los Argentinos y Freire, T4432 5055, www.destinopiriapolis.com, summer 0900-2400, winter 1000-1800.*

About 6 km north on the R37 is **Cerro Pan de Azúcar** (Sugar Loaf Hill) ① *getting there: take bus 'Cerro Pan de Azúcar' and get off after 6 km,* crowned by a tall cross with a circular stairway inside, fine coastal views. There is only a steep path, marked by red arrows, up to the cross, about 1½ hour's walk. Just north of Piriápolis R 37 passes the **La Cascada** municipal park (open all year, small waterfall, old woodlands, picnic area, toilets) which contains the house of Francisco Piria, the founder of the resort, **Museo Castillo de Piria** ① *Mon-Fri in summer, 1000-1800, Sat-Sun 1000-1500 (winter Tue-Sun 1000-1530).* About 4 km beyond Cerro Pan de Azúcar is the village of Pan de Azúcar, which has a **Museo al Aire Libre de Pintura** where the walls of the buildings have been decorated by Uruguayan and Argentine graffiti artists, designers and writers with humorous and tango themes, known as the Mural Circuit (direct bus every hour from Piriápolis).

Best for
Beaches ■ Relaxing ■ Views

Portezuelo and Punta Ballena

R93 runs between the coast and the Laguna del Sauce to Portezuelo, which has good beaches. The **Arboreto Lussich** ① *T4257 8077, 0800-2000 (in winter Sat-Sun 1000-1800), free,* on the west slope of the Sierra de la Ballena (north of R93) contains a unique set of native and exotic trees. There are footpaths, or you can drive through; two *miradores*; worth a visit. From Portezuelo drive north towards the R9 by way of the R12 which then continues, unpaved, to Minas. Just off R12 is **El Tambo Lapataia** ① *1 km east from Solanas, then 4 km north, T2200 4976, http://lapataiapuntadeleste.com,* a dairy farm open to the public, daily 1200-2130 (shorter hours in winter), selling cheese, ice cream, *dulce de leche,* home-made pizzas and pastas. Also farming activities and organic garden.

At Punta Ballena there is a wide crescent beach, calm water and very clean sand. The place is a residential resort but is still quiet. At the top of Punta Ballena there is a panoramic road 2.5 km long with remarkable views of the coast. **Casa Pueblo**, the house and gallery of Uruguayan artist Carlos Páez Vilaró who died in 2014, is built in a Spanish-Moroccan style on a cliff over the sea. Now also a hotel with multiple facilities (see Listings, below) the gallery and museum can be visited (daily, 1000-1800, US$8.50), there are paintings, collages and ceramics on display, and for sale; open all year. Walk downhill towards the sea for a good view of the house.

Listings East from Montevideo

Where to stay

Piriápolis

Many hotels along the seafront, most close end-Feb to mid-Dec. Book in advance in high season. Many others than those listed here.

$$$ pp Argentino Hotel, Casino and Resort
Rambla de los Argentinos y Armenia, T4432 2791, www.argentinohotel.com.uy.
A fine hotel and landmark designed by Piria with casino, 2 restaurants, medicinal springs, sauna and good facilities for children and teenagers.

$$$ Escorial
Rambla de los Argentinos 1290, T4432 2537, www.hotelescorial.com.uy.
With mini-bar, sea or hill views, pool, parking, medical service.

$$$-$$ Rivadavia
Rambla de los Argentinos y Trápani, T4432 2532, www.hotelrivadavia.com.
Seafront hotel, rooms with and without sea view, restaurant, parking. Open all year (much cheaper in winter).

$ pp Hostel Piriápolis
Simón del Pino 1136 y Tucumán, T4432 0394.
Rooms for 2-4 (open all year), private rooms **$$**, 240 beds, non-HI members pay more, hot showers, cooking facilities, student cards accepted.

Camping

El Toro
Av de Mayo y Fuente de Venus, T4432 2332/0957 35114
Doubles in bungalows, and tents, 900 m from the beach.

Also **Piriápolis Fútbol Club** (at Misiones y Niza, just behind bus station, T4432 3275, piriapolisfc@adinet.com.uy, US$6.50).

Portezuelo and Punta Ballena

$$$$ Casa Pueblo
T4257 8611, www.clubhotelcasapueblo.com.
Highly recommended hotel and apartments, fantastical design, with spa and, lower down the hill, **Restaurant Las Terrazas**. Famous gallery and artist's studio adjacent.

$$$$ Hotel-Art & Spa Cumbres
Ruta 12 Km 3.5, 4 km inland, T4257 8689, www.cumbres.com.uy.
Themed as an artist's house-studio, on a wooded hill with great views over Laguna del Sauce and the coast, highly regarded, pool, restaurant and fully equipped spa and gym.

Camping

Punta Ballena
Km 120, Parada 45, T4257 8902, www.campingpuntaballena.com.
US$12.50 pp per night (US$10 in low season), many facilities, very clean. Also has tents for hire, US$12.50, and cabins for 4-8 people (**$$$-$$**).

Restaurants

Portezuelo and Punta Ballena

$$$ Medio y Medio
Cont Camino Lussich s/n, Punta Ballena,
T4257 8791, www.medioymedio.com.
Jazz club and restaurant, music nightly
and good food.

$$$-$$ Las Vertientes
Camino de Los Ceibos, 2 km on the Route 9,
T4266 4444, www.lasvertientes.com.uy.
Country gourmet restaurant, fresh food which all
comes from own farm, good salads and sweets.

Transport

Piriápolis may be reached either by following
the very beautiful R10 from the end of the
Interbalnearia, or by taking the original access
road (R37) from Pan de Azúcar, which crosses
the R93.

Piriápolis

Bus Terminal on Misiones, 2 blocks from
Hotel Argentino, T4432 4141 (**COT**). To/from
Montevideo, US$7, 1½ hrs. To **Punta del Este**,
US$6, 50 mins. To **Maldonado**, US$5, 40 mins. For
Rocha, **La Paloma** and **Chuy**, take bus to Pan de
Azúcar and change.

Punta del Este and around

the quintessential South American holiday destination

Maldonado *Colour map 8, B6.*
The capital of Maldonado Department, 140 km east of Montevideo, is a peaceful town, sacked by
the British in 1806. It has many colonial remains and the historic centre has been restored. It is also
a dormitory suburb of Punta del Este. Worth seeing is the **El Vigia watch tower** ① *Michelini y Pérez
del Puerto*; the Cathedral (started 1801, completed 1895), on Plaza San Fernando; the windmill; the
Cuartel de Dragones exhibition centre ① *Pérez del Puerto y 18 de Julio, by Plaza San Fernando*, and
the **Cachimba del Rey** ① *on Av Cachimba del Rey (the continuation of 3 de Febrero, almost Artigas,
an old well – legend claims that those who drink from it will never leave Maldonado.* **Museo
Mazzoni** ① *Ituzaingó 789, T4222 1107, summer 0800-2200, winter 1300-1800, free,* has regional items,
indigenous, Spanish, Portuguese and English. **Museo de Arte Americano** ① *Treinta y Tres 823 y
Dodera, T4222 2276, http://maam-uruguay.blogspot.com, open Dec-Feb only, phone in advance to see
if it's open,* a private museum of national and international art, interesting. **Tourist office** ① *Dirección
General de Turismo, Edif Municipal, Acuña de Figueroa y Burnett, T4222 3333, www.maldonado.gub.uy.*

★Punta del Este *Colour map 8, B6.*
About 7 km from Maldonado and 139 km from Montevideo (a little less by dual carriageway), facing
the bay on one side and the open waters of the Atlantic on the other, lies the largest and best
known of the resorts, Punta del Este (population 9200), part of the municipality of Maldonado,
particularly popular among Argentines and Brazilians. The narrow peninsula of Punta del Este has
been entirely built over. On the land side, the city is flanked by large planted forests of eucalyptus,
pine and mimosa. Two blocks from the sea, at the tip of the peninsula, is the historic monument
of El Faro (lighthouse); in this part of the city no building may exceed its height. (45 m) On the
ocean side of the peninsula, at the end of Calle 25 (Arrecifes), is a shrine to the first mass said by
the Conquistadores on this coast, 2 February 1515. Three blocks from the shrine is Plaza General
Artigas, which has a *feria artesanal* (handicraft market with 200 stalls)); along its side runs Avenida
Gorleno, the main street. There are two casinos, a golf course, and many beautiful holiday houses.
Museo Ralli of Contemporary Latin American Art ① *Curupay y Los Arrayanes s/n, Barrio Beverly
Hills, T4248 3476, www.museoralli.com.uy, Jan-Feb Tue-Sun 1700-2100, Mar, Dec, and Holy Week Tue-
Sun 1400-1800, Apr-May and Oct-Nov Sat-Sun 1400-1800, closed Jun-Sep, free.* Worth a visit but a car
(or bike – cycle path all the way from Punta del Este) is needed.

Punta del Este has excellent bathing **beaches**, the calm Playa Mansa on the bay side, the rough
Playa Brava on the ocean side. There are some small beaches hemmed in by rocks on this side of
the peninsula, but most people go to where the extensive Playa Brava starts. Papa Charlie beach on
the Atlantic (Parada 13) is preferred by families with small children as it is safe. Quieter beaches are
at La Barra and beyond.

There is an excellent yacht marina, yacht and fishing clubs. There is good fishing both at sea and in three nearby lakes and the Río Maldonado.

Isla de Gorriti, visited by explorers including Solís, Magellan and Drake, was heavily fortified by the Spanish in the 1760s to keep the Portuguese out. The island, densely wooded and with superb beaches, is an ideal spot for campers (0800-1830, 0900-1700 in winter, entry US$13.50; boats every 30 minutes from 0900-1700, return 1015-1800 (last boat), US$14, eg **Nautical Events**, T9862 9166, www.nauticalevents.com.uy). On **Isla de Lobos**, which is a government reserve within sight of the town, there is a huge colony of an estimated 300,000 sea-lions; public boat US$20 per person (leaves 1200), tour US$30-50, daily, also at 1200. Tickets should be booked in advance (T4244 1716, or Nautical Events, as above, or **Dimartours**, T4244 4750, www.dimartours.com.uy).

Punta del Este

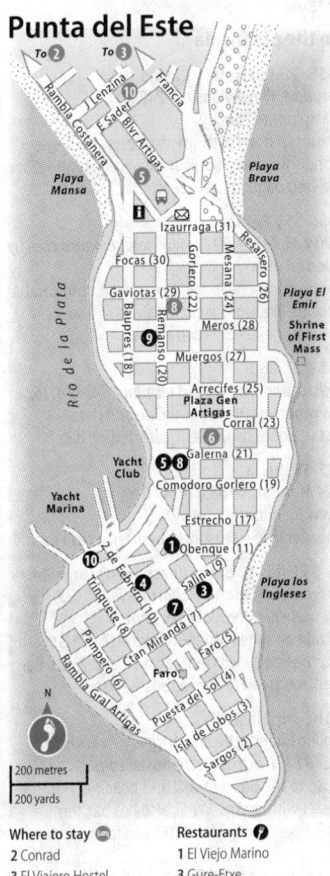

Where to stay 🛏
2 Conrad
3 El Viajero Hostel
5 Gaudi
6 Iberia
8 Remanso
10 The Trip Hostel

Restaurants 🍴
1 El Viejo Marino
3 Gure-Etxe
4 Il Baretto
5 Isidora
7 Lo de Charlie
8 Lo de Tere
9 Los Caracoles
10 Yatch Club Uruguayo

☆Beaches east of Punta del Este

Between the Peninsula and the mouth of the Río Maldonado, a road runs along the coast, passing luxurious houses, dunes and pines. Some of the most renowned architects of Uruguay and Argentina design houses here. Several of the beaches east of Punta del Este are excellent for surfing, more so the further east towards Brazil you travel. First in line after the main resort is **La Barra**, a fashionable, very hip and happening place, especially for summer nightlife. Punta del Este 'downtown', on the peninsula, is increasingly turning into a service centre and many visitors are choosing to base their stay in other, less built-up beach resorts. La Barra has a good collection of beaches, art galleries, bars and restaurants (take a bus from Punta del Este terminal or taxi US$20). **Museo del Mar Sirenamis** ① *1 km off the coast road, watch for signs, T4277 1817, www.museodelmar.com.uy, daily 1030-1830 year-round, US$7,* has an extensive collection on the subject of the sea, its life and history and on the first beach resorts. The coast road climbs a headland here before descending to the beaches further north, Montoya and **Manantiales** (reached by Condesa bus; taxi US$35-45). Some 30 km from Punta del Este is the former fishing village of **José Ignacio**, now increasingly luxurious, alternative and arty. It has an old lighthouse ① *summer daily 1100-2030, winter 1700-2000, US$1,* excursions with Novoturismo from Punta del Este, US$30, T4249 6554, http://novoturismo.com.uy, a beach club and other new developments, now the road is paved. Coastal R10 continues east of José Ignacio to the new circular bridge spanning Laguna Garzón, opened at the end of 2015. This unusual architectural feature was created by Uruguayan Rafael Viñoly and took just over a year to complete. R10 carries on to Laguna de Rocha, across which is La Paloma.

Tourist information

Punta del Este
See the websites www.puntaweb.com, www.puntadeleste.com and www.vivapunta.com.

Liga de Fomento
Parada 1, T4244 0514. Summer 0800-2000, winter 1100-1700.
Tourist information also in bus station (T4249 4042); at Rambla Claudio Williman (Mansa side, T4244 0514); at Av Gorlero 942 (T4244 6510, puntadeleste@mintur.gub.uy); and at airports.

> **Tip...**
> For exchange, there are many ATMs at banks on the peninsula and at Punta Shopping (Roosevelt). Best rates of exchange from BROU, which opens earlier and closes later than the other banks and accepts MasterCard.

Where to stay

Maldonado
Hotel accommodation is scarce in summer; cheaper than Punta del Este, but you will have to commute to the beach.

Mid-range places (**$$$-$$**), open all year, include: **Catedral** (Florida 830 casi 18 de Julio, T4224 2513, www.hotelcatedral.com.uy), central, and **Colonial** (18 de Julio 841 y Florida, T4222 3346, www.colonialhotel.com.uy). There are also more basic places.

$$ Isla de Gorriti
Michelini 884, T4224 5218.
Nice courtyard. Recommended.

Camping

El Edén
Balneario Las Flores, T4438 0565, www.eledencamping.com, US$8.50, also has cabañas for 2-6 people (US$11.50-15 pp).
Not open all year.

Punta del Este
Hotels are plentiful but expensive: we list recommended ones only. Rates in the few hotels still open after the end of Mar are often halved. Visitors without a car have to take a hotel on the

> **Fact...**
> Streets on the peninsula have names and numbers; the lowest numbers at the tip.

peninsula, unless they want to spend a fortune on taxis.

On the peninsula

$$$$ Conrad Hotel y Casino
Parada 4, Playa Mansa, T4249 1111, www.conrad.com.uy.
Luxurious hotel with spa, concerts and events, wonderful views. Book in advance in high season; see web page for special offers.

$$$$-$$$ Remanso
C 20 y 28, T4244 7412, www.hotelremanso.com.uy. Open all year.
Some rooms cheaper in low season, comfortable, businesslike, pool, jacuzzi, safe (also 2 suites in **$$$$** range). 2- to 4-bed rooms.

$$$-$$ Gaudi
C Risso, parada 1, by bus terminal, T4249 4116, www.hotelgaudi.com.uy. Open all year.
2-star. Good, convenient, safe, fridge, bar.

$$$-$$ Iberia
C 24 Mesana, No 685, T4244 0405, www.iberiahotel.com.uy.
Cheaper in low season, babysitter, safe in rooms.

$$-$ El Viajero Brava Beach Hostel and Suites
Av Francisco Salazar y Charrúa, T4248 0331, www.elviajerobravabeach.com.
Private en suite with TV, dorms en suite (**$**) with a/c, breakfast included, cable TV and DVDs, bar, fireplace, free Wi-Fi, near bus station.

$ The Trip Hostel
Emiliio Sader entre Blvr Artigas y Av Francia, T4248 8181, http://thetriphostel.com.
Close to the bus terminal and beaches. Popular hostel with dorms, Wi-Fi, also has bar, terrace, BBQ, bike rental, information on tours.

Beaches east of Punta del Este

San Rafael (Parada 12)

$$$$ La Capilla
Viña del Mar y Valparaíso, behind San Marcos, T4248 4059, www.lacapilla.com.uy. Open all year.

$$$ in low season, gardens, pool, popular restaurant, good. LGBT-friendly.

$$$$-$$$ San Rafael
Lorenzo Batlle y Pacheco, Parada 11 Playa Brava, T4248 2161, www.hotelsanrafael.com.uy. Open all year.
Large hotel, heating, safe, spa. Business and events facilities.

La Barra

$$$$ Hostal de la Barra
Ruta 10, Km 161.300, Playa Montoya, T4277 1521, www.hostaldelabarra.net. Open all year.
In low season prices $$$. A small hotel, not a hostel, with sea view, forest view and loft rooms, neat, Christmas, Carnival and Semana Santa require 7 or 4-night minimum stays.

$$$$ Kalá
Pedregal s/n, Altos de Montoya, T4277 3500, www.kalahotel.com.
A boutique hotel with 12 rooms, including 2 suites, with breakfast, bars, pools and jacuzzi, bicycles.

$$$$ La Posta del Cangrejo
hotel/restaurant, Ruta 10 Km 160, T4277 0021, www.lapostadelcangrejo.com.
Nice location, smart, prices reduced in low season ($$$). Recommended.

$$$$ Punta del Este Resort
Ruta 10, Parada 48, T4277 1000, www.puntadelesteresort.com. Open all year.
Very good and award-winning, but you will need a car to move around, great pool, spa, casino, restaurants, concerts, own cinema and wine bar.

$$-$ pp Backpacker de La Barra
C 9, No 2306, 0.5 km off main road, T4277 2272, www.backpackerdelabarra.com.
Youth hostel style, price depends on dates and class of room ($$$ in luxury double, high season), café, pool, gardens, parking, breakfast on terrace included.

Camping San Rafael
Camino Aparicio Saravia, 1 km from Barra bridge,T4248 6715, www.campingsanrafael.com.uy. Dec-Apr.
Good facilities, US$11 pp, also has 4-bed *cabañas* (US$120), Wi-Fi, bus 5 from Maldonado.

José Ignacio

$$$$ Estancia Vik
Camino Eugenio Saiz Martínez, Km 8, José Ignacio, T9460 5212, http://estanciavikjoseignacio.com.
Owned by the Vik family, this impeccable haven of laidback luxury offers one of the finest estancia stays in Uruguay. Excellent green credentials, extensive views across the José Ignacio Lagoon, exquisite *asados*, modern and traditional art in the rooms and suites. Horse riding and other activities offered. Highly recommended.

$$$$ Playa Vik
C Los Cisnes, T9370 4866, http:/playavik.com.
6 luxurious beach Casas, as well as accommodation in the main building, the Sculpture, all overlooking the sea and gardens. Fabulous modern art throughout the property, infinity pool, gym, spa and dining room. Also has the separate property **Bahía Vik** ($$$$) at José Ignacio further down the beach, www.bahiavik.com.

$$$$ Posada del Faro
C de la Bahía y Timonel, T4486 2110, www.posadadelfaro.com.
Exclusive hotel overlooking the sea, 12 rooms in 3 standards, pool, bar, restaurant.

Restaurants

Maldonado

$$$-$$ Lo de Rubén
Santa Teresa 846 y Florida, T4222 3059, www.loderuben.com.uy. Open every day.
Parrillada, best restaurant in town.

$$$-$$ Taberna Patxi
Dodera 944, T4223 8393, www.tabernapatxi.com.
Very good Basque food with authentic recipes, fish and seafood.

Punta del Este
Many enticing ice cream parlours on Gorlero. There are many more excellent restaurants beyond the peninsula.

$$$ El Viejo Marino
C 11 entre 14 y 12, Las Palmeras, T4244 3565.
Fish restaurant, busy, go early.

$$$ Gure-Etxe (also in La Coronilla)
C 9 y 12, T4244 6858.
Seafood and Basque cuisine.

$$$ Isidora
Rambla del Puerto, esq 21, T4244 9646, www.isidora.com.uy. Open year-round from 1100.
Smart, by the port, international cuisine beautifully presented.

$$$ Lo de Charlie
C 12 y 9, T4244 4183.
Mediterranean dishes, pasta and *parrilla* standards.

$$$ Lo de Tere
Rambla del Puerto y 21, T4244 0492,
www.lode tere.com. Open all year.
Good local food, various discounts, check
website for updates. Highly recommended.

$$$ Los Caracoles
C 20 y 28, T4244 0912.
Excellent food (international, *parrilla*, seafood)
at good prices.

$$$ Yatch Club Uruguayo
Rambla Artigas y 8, T4244 1056, www.ycu.org.uy.
Very good, fish, seafood, views over the port,
Mon-Fri lunch specials (not to be confused
with the Yacht Club Punta del Este, C 10 y 13,
with expensive restaurant).

$$ Il Baretto
C 9 y 10, T4244 5565, www.ilbarettopunta.com.
Daily year-round.
Traditional Italian gourmet, fish and seafood
specialities, good value.

Beaches east of Punta del Este
La Barra

$$$ Baby Gouda Deli Café
Ruta 10, Km 161, T4277 1874.
Alternative food, with some veggie options,
and cocktails.

José Ignacio

$$$ La Huella
Los Cisnes on Playa Brava, T4867 5432,
www.paradorlahuella.com. Daily till 1700.
Excellent, award-winning seafood, on the beach,
also has a bar.

$$$ La Susana
Ruta 10 Km 182.5, T9519 2555,
www.lasusana.com.
A beach club, bar and eatery during the day and
gourmet restaurant at night. Fabulous location
right on the beach for sunset cocktails (excellent
range). Delicious, easy-going international
cuisine. Recommended.

$$$ Marismo
Ruta 10 Km 185, T4486 2273,
http://restaurantmarismo.com.
Romantic, outdoor tables around a fire,
highly regarded.

$$$ Mostrador Santa Teresita
C Las Garzas y Los Tordos, T4486 2861.
A long table with main courses on one side,
desserts on the other, you can choose what
size of plate you want, good food.

Manantiales

$$$ Cactus y Pescados
Primera Bajada a Playa Bikini y Ruta 10,
T4277 4782.
Very good seafood, international menu.

Bars and clubs

Punta del Este

Capi
C 27 No 580, T4243 8103.
Small bar and restaurant, good local craft beers
and live music.

Moby Dick
Rambla Artigas 650, T4244 1240, www.mobydick.
com.uy. Open until the early hours.
Mock English-style pub by the port, very popular.

Ocean Club
Parada 12 de la Playa Brava, T4248 4869.
Very fashionable and smart club playing mostly
pop and house. Dress up.

Transport

The shortest route from Piriápolis to Punta del
Este is by the Camino de las Bases which runs
parallel to the R37 and joins the R93 some 4 km
east of the R37 junction.

Maldonado
Bus Av Roosevelt y Sarandí, T4222 0289. To/
from **Montevideo**, 2 hrs, US$8; to **Minas**, 2 hrs,
10 a day, US$6.50. To **San Carlos** take a local bus
3 blocks from the main bus station, US$3.

Punta del Este
Air Direct daily flights from Buenos Aires to
the new Punta del Este airport during the high
season. **Capitán Curbelo** (formerly Laguna del
Sauce, T4255 9777), handles flights to Buenos
Aires, 40 mins. Airport tax US$31. Exchange
facilities, tax-free shopping. Regular bus service
to airport from Punta del Este (will deliver to and
collect from private addresses and hotels), US$5,
90 mins before departure, also connects with
arriving flights. Taxi US$35-50; *remise* around

US$40 depending on destination (T4255 9100). El Jagüel airport is used by private planes.

Bus Local Traffic is directed by a one-way system; town bus services start from C 5 (El Faro), near the lighthouse.

Long distance Terminal at Av Gorlero, Blv Artigas and C 32, T4249 4042 (served by local bus No 7); has toilets, newsagent, café, free luggage storage and Casa de Cambio. To/ from **Montevideo** via Carrasco airport, COT (T4248 3558), US$8.10, just over 2 hrs, many in the summer; at least hourly in winter. To **Piriápolis**, US$6. To **San Carlos** (US$3.50) for connections to Porto Alegre, Rocha, La Paloma, Chuy. Direct to **Chuy**, 4 hrs, US$15-18. Local bus fare about US$1. For transport Montevideo-

Buenos Aires, **Buquebus** T130, at bus terminal, loc 09, buses connect with ferries. Also **Colonia Express** and **Seacat**.

The hop-on, hop-off **Summerbus** (www. summerbus.com, see Montevideo transport page 1542) also stops in Punta del Este and many other parts of the coast.

Car hire Punta Car, Artigas 101 y Risso, T2900 2772, www.puntacar.com.uy. And others.

Scooter hire US$51 per day, with drivers licence (US$50 fine if caught without it) and ID documents. Bicycle rental US$3.50 per hr, US$7.50 per half day, US$10 per day, includes padlocks. Several companies, including **Filibusteros**, Av Artigas y Parada 5, T4248 4125.

La Paloma to Brazil

beaches and birdwatching en route to Brazil

☆La Paloma and around Colour map 8, B6.

Protected by an island and a sandspit, this is a good port for yachts. The surrounding scenery is attractive, with extensive wetlands nearby. You can walk for miles along the beach. The pace is more relaxed than Punta del Este. **Tourist office** ① *in La Paloma bus station, T4479 6088*, very helpful. **Department of Rocha office** ① *Rutas 9 y 15, T4472 3100, www.turismorocha.gub.uy, daily 0800-2000*. There is one bank; also internet, a supermarket and post office. Bike rental from El Tobo (T4479 7881, US$3.50 a day).

Coastal R10 runs to Aguas Dulces (regular bus services, **Rutas del Sol**, cover the whole coast). About 10 km from La Paloma is **La Pedrera**, a beautiful village with stunning views and sandy beaches (tourist office on Calle Principal, T9927 9362). Beyond La Pedrera the road runs near pleasant fishing villages which are rapidly being developed with holiday homes, for example **Barra de Valizas**, a small, very laid-back hide-away, 50 minutes north. At **Cabo Polonio** (permanent population 80), visits to the islands of Castillos and Wolf can be arranged to see sea lions and penguins. It has two great beaches: the north beach is more rugged, while the south is tamer by comparison. Both have lifeguards on duty (though their zone of protection only covers a tiny portion of the endless stretches of beach). The village is within the Parque Nacional Cabo Polonio (www.mvotma.gub.uy). This limits the number of people who are allowed to stay there since the number of lodgings is limited and camping is strictly forbidden (if you arrive with a tent, it may be confiscated). During January or February (and especially during Carnival), you have to reserve a room in one of the few *posadas* or hotels, or better yet, rent a house (see Where to stay, below). From Km 264 on the main road all-terrain vehicles run 8 km across the dunes to the village (several companies, around US$5; tourist office by the terminal, open 0930-2000, T4472 3100). Day visitors must leave just after sundown (see Transport, below). Ask locally in Valizas about walking there, three to four hours via the north beach (very interesting, but hot, unless you go early). There are also pine woods with paths leading to the beach or village.

The **Monte de Ombúes** ① *open in summer months, from Jan, free, basic restaurant with honest prices*, is a wood containing a few *ombú* trees (Phytolacca dioica – the national tree), coronilla (Scutia buxifolia) and canelón (Rapanea laetevirens). It has a small circuit to follow and a good hide for birdwatching. To reach the woods from Km 264, go 2 km north along R10 to the bridge. Here take a boat with guide, 30 minutes along the river (**Monte Grande** recommended as they visit both sides of the river, T9929 5177). You can also walk from Km 264 across the fields, but it's a long way and the last 150 m are through thick brush. The bridge is 16 km from Castillos on R9 (see next paragraph): turn onto R16 towards Aguas Dulces, just before which you turn southwest onto R10.

From **Aguas Dulces** the road runs inland to the town of **Castillos** (ATM, shops, taxi rank and bus terminal on the main plaza, easy bus connections to Chuy), where it rejoins R9. A **tourist office** ① *C de Acceso y Gorlerito, T9959 1662, open 0900-1300, 1700-2200*, has details on hotels.

★Punta del Diablo

At Km 298 there is a turn to a fishing village in dramatic surroundings, with three fine beaches, Playa de la Viuda to the south, Playa del Pescador in the centre and Playa del Rivero to the north. Punta del Diablo is very rustic, good for surfing and popular with young people in high season, but from April to November the solitude and the dramatically lower prices make it a wonderful getaway for couples or families. Increased popularity has brought more lodging and services year round, although off-season activity is still extremely low compared to summer. **Municipal tourist office** ① *on access road, T4477 2412, daily 0800-2200*. See www.portaldeldiablo.com. For bicycle hire in this area, contact BiciUruguay ① *http://biciuruguay.com.uy, US$12 per day*.

Parque Nacional Santa Teresa

100 km from Rocha, 308 km from Montevideo, T4477 2103, open 0900-1900 to day visitors (open 24 hrs for campers), interpretation centre open daily 1300-1900.

This park has curving, palm-lined avenues and plantations of many exotic trees. It also contains botanical gardens, freshwater pools for bathing and beaches which stretch for many kilometres (the surf is too rough for swimming). It is the site of the impressive colonial fortress of Santa Teresa, begun by the Portuguese in 1762 and seized

> **Tip...**
> Practically every amenity is closed off-season.

by the Spanish in 1793. The fortress houses a **museum** ① *Wed-Sun 1300-1900 (winter Fri-Sun 1000-1700), US$1.50*, of artefacts from the wars of independence. Old cemetery nearby, several cafés and snack bars open high season. On the inland side of Route 9, the strange and gloomy Laguna Negra and the marshes of the Bañado de Santa Teresa support large numbers of wild birds. A road encircles the fortress; it's possible to drive or walk around even after closing. From there is a good view of Laguna Negra.

There are countless campsites (open all year), and a few cottages to let in the summer (usually snapped up quickly). At the *capatacia*, or administrative headquarters, campers pay US$4 pp per night. The park (entrance free) is well-kept and has numerous facilities attached to the different campsites, including cafés, supermarkets, telephones, post office, laundry services and several small restaurants. Beautiful isolated beaches also abound (six main beaches, several smaller ones). The bathing resort of **La Coronilla** is 10 km north of Santa Teresa, 20 south of Chuy; it has the **Karumbé marine-turtle center** ① *Ruta 9, Km 314, T09-991 7811, www.karumbe.org, Jan-Apr 1000-1900*. There are several hotels and restaurants, most closed in winter (tourist information T4472 3100). Montevideo–Chuy buses stop at La Coronilla.

Chuy *Colour map 8, B6.*

At Chuy, 340 km from Montevideo, the Brazilian frontier runs along the main street, Avenida Internacional, which is called Avenida Brasil in Uruguay and Avenida Uruguaí in Brasil. The Uruguayan side has more services, including supermarkets, duty-free shops and a casino. **Tourist office** ① *on the plaza, T4474 3627, infochuy@turismorocha.gub.uy, 0900-2100*. See www.chuynet.com. For details of Chuí in Brazil see the Brazil chapter.

On the Uruguayan side, on a promontory overlooking Laguna Merín and the gaúcho landscape of southern Brazil, stands the restored fortress of **San Miguel** ① *daily 1000-1900 (high season), Wed-Sun 1000-1700 (low season), US$1.50, bus from Chuy US$1.50, Rutas del Sol buses from Montevideo go here after passing through Chuy*, dating from 1734 and surrounded by a moat. It is set above a 1500-ha wetland park, which is good for birdwatching and is 10 km north of Chuy along Route 19 which is the border. There is a small museum of *criollo* and *indígena* culture (entrance included in the fortress ticket), displaying, among other artefacts, old carriages and presses. Not always open in low season. A fine walk from here is 2 km to the Cerro Picudo. The path starts behind the museum, very apparent. Tours (US$10 from Chuy) end for the season after 31 March.

Border with Brazil

Uruguayan passport control is 2.5 km before the border on Ruta 9 into Chuy, US$2 by taxi, 20 minutes walk, or take a town bus; officials friendly and cooperative. **Ministry of Tourism** kiosk here is helpful, especially for motorists (T4474 4599, chuy@mintur.gub.uy). Tourists may freely cross the border in either direction as long as they do not go beyond either country's border post. Taking a car into Brazil is no problem if the car is not registered in Brazil or Uruguay. (Uruguayan rental cars are not allowed out of the country. Although you can freely drive between Chuy and Chuí, if you break down/have an accident on the Brazilian side, car rental insurance will not cover it: park in Chuy, even if only one metre from Brazil, and walk.) From the border post, Ruta 9 bypasses the town, becoming BR-471 on the Brazilian side, leading to Brazilian immigration, also outside town. **Brazilian consulate** ① *Tito Fernández 147, T4474 2049, Chuy, open 0900-1300.* For buses to Brazilian destinations, go to the rodoviária in Chuí (details in the Brazil chapter). The bus companies that run from Chuy into Brazil ask for passports – make sure you get yours back before boarding the bus.

Entering Uruguay You need a Brazilian exit stamp and a Uruguayan entry stamp (unless visiting only Chuí), otherwise you'll be turned back at customs or other official posts. Those requiring a visa will be charged around US$80 depending on the country.

There is no problem spending reais in Chuy or pesos in Chuí. If not to change money there are several *cambios* on Avenida Brasil. All give similar rates, charging US$1 plus 1% commission on US dollars, pesos and reais. On Sunday, try the casino, or look for someone on the street outside the *cambios*.

Listings La Paloma to Brazil

Where to stay

La Paloma

$$$$-$$$ Palma de Mallorca
On Playa La Aguada, in nearby La Aguada, T4479 6739, www.hotelpalmademallorca.com.
Right on the ocean. Discounts for longer stays, heated pool, parking.

$$$ Bahía
Av del Navío s/n, entre Solari y Del Sol, T4479 6029, www.elbahia.com.uy.
Breakfast, double or triple rooms, clean and simple, quite old-fashioned, laundry, half-board available. Also has **Bahía Restó** restaurant.

Camping Parque Andresito
Ruta 15, Km 1500, T4479 6081, complejoandresito@adinet.com.uy.
Overpriced, thatched *cabañas* for rent, from US$52-110 per day with maid and kitchen facilities, sleep 2-5. **Grill del Camping** for *parrillas*.

Youth hostels

$ pp Altena 5000
At Parque Andresito, T4479 6396. Open all year.
50 beds in 4 rooms, HI discounts, good meals, kitchen.

$ pp Ibirapitá
Av Paloma s/n, near bus station and beach, T4479 9303, www.hostelibirapita.com.
Cheaper in mixed dorm and for HI members, doubles $$. Buffet breakfast, surf boards, bicycles.

Northeast of La Paloma

At Cabo Polonio you cannot camp. There are *posadas*, some listed below, or you can rent a house; see www.cabopolonio.com or www. portaldelcabo.com.uy for all options. Water is drawn from wells (*cachimbas*) and there is no electricity (some houses have generators, some gas lamps, otherwise buy candles). There are 4 shops for supplies, largest is **El Templao**. At **La Pedrera**, **Aguas Dulces** and **Barra de Valizas** there are various places to stay and lots of cheap cabins for rent.

$$$ La Perla
Cabo Polonio, T4470 5125, http://laperla delcabo.net. Open all year.
Restaurant and snack bar, spa, visits to lighthouse.

$$$ Posada Mariemar
Cabo Polonio, T4470 5164, mariemar@cabopolonio.com.
Nice 2nd-generation owners, own electricity generator, hot water, with breakfast, restaurant, open all year.

$$$ Posada Valizas
C Tomás Cambre, 1 block from Plaza de los Barcos, Barra de Valizas, T4475 4067, www.posadavalizas.com.
Tranquil and lovely, small-scale *posada*, 6 homely rooms. Peaceful garden setting, attentive service. Highly recommended.

$$$-$$ La Pedrasanta
C Cabo Polonio (Cedron), La Pedrera, T4479 2179, www.posadalapedrasanta.com.
Lovely, arty Italian/Argentine-run *posada* and restaurant. Pleasant garden, Tuscan cuisine, friendly owners, yoga classes. Recommended.

$$-$ pp Cabo Polonio Hostel
T9944 5943, www.cabopoloniohostel.com.
Small wooden hostel, hot showers, shared rooms, doubles available outside high season, kitchenettes, solar power, bar, good fresh food, can arrange whale-watching tours and riding.

$$-$ pp Reserva Ecológica La Laguna
2 km north of Aguas Dulces, T4475 2118/9960 2410, http://lalagunauruguay.blogspot.co.uk.
Rustic cabins on the shore a lake (on recently paved road), also hostel lodging, day rates for adults and children, full and half-board available, close to beach, horse riding, trekking, sailing, hydrobikes, meditation. Always phone in advance for directions and reservation.

Youth hostels

$ pp El Viajero La Pedrera Hostel
C 11 y C13 esquina, La Pedrera, T4479 2252, www.elviajerohostels.com.
Private en suite, dorms en suite, breakfast included, bar, wide common areas, gorgeous garden, free Wi-Fi.

Punta del Diablo
In high season you should book in advance; www.portaldeldiablo.com gives a full list of choices.

$$$$ Aquarella
Av No 5, ½ block from beach, T4477 2400, www.hotelaquarella.com.
Pool, jacuzzi, great views, gourmet restaurant.

$$$$-$$$ Terrazas de la Viuda
C del Indio, T9968 1138, www.terrazasdelaviuda.com.
Pleasant hotel with spacious rooms and pool, overlooking the beach. Also nearby sister hotel **La Viuda del Diablo**, on the beach itself, with restaurant and beach bar open to the public, Good, fresh seafood. Another sister hotel, Viuda

de José Ignacio, in José Ignacio (all 3 with same phone number).

$$$ Hostería del Pescador
On road into village, Blv Santa Teresa, T4477 2017, www.portaldeldiablo.com.
Rooms for 2-6, prices vary for season and day of week, restaurant, pool.

$$$-$ El Diablo Tranquilo Hostel and Bar
Av Central, T4477 2647, www.eldiablo tranquilo.com. Open year-round.
Shared and private rooms, breakfast and cooking facilities. Separate bar that is one of the nightlife hotspots. Highly recommended. Also **El Diablo Tranquilo Playa Suites** on the beach, run by the same team, double suites with fireplaces (**$$$-$$**).

$$$-$ Unplugged Hostel
C 9 esq 10, www.unpluggedhostel.com.
Dorm-only hostel not far from the beach. sociable place, outdoor communal area for *asados* and pizzas, free computer, good place to meet other travellers. Has another branch in Pocitos, Montevideo.

Parque Nacional Santa Teresa: La Coronilla

$$$$-$$$ Hotel Parque Oceánico
Ruta 9 km 312.5, T4476 2883, www.hotelparque oceanico.com.uy. Open year-round.
4-star hotel in stunning beachside location. 3 pools, 1 indoor, 2 outdoor, games room, full- and half-board options. Good restaurant also open to the public. Extensive grounds, short walk to endless beaches. Hiking, birdwatching, horse riding on the beach, forest walks. Highly recommended.

Chuy
All hotels are open the year round.

$$$ Parador El Fortín de San Miguel
Paraje 18 de Julio, near San Miguel fortress, T4474 6607, www.elfortin.com.
Excellent, full and half-board available, colonial-style hotel. Beautiful rooms, gym, 2 pools, restaurant. Recommended. You don't have to go through Uruguayan formalities to get there from Brazil.

$$$-$$ Nuevo Hotel Plaza
C Arachanes 565, T4474 2309, www.hotelplaza.chuynet.com.
On plaza, bath, good buffet breakfast, very helpful, good, restaurant El Mesón del Plaza.

$$ Alerces
Laguna de Castillos 578, T4474 2260,
hotelalerceschuy@adinet.com.uy.
4 blocks from border. Bath, breakfast, heater, pool.

$$ Victoria
Zenona Lima 143, T4474 3547,
www.hotelvictoriachuy.com.
Price includes breakfast, simple and clean, a/c.

Camping
From Chuy buses run every 2 hrs to the
Complejo Turístico Chuy campsite, Ruta 9
Km 331, turn right 13 km, T4474 9425, www.
complejoturisticochuy.com. Good bathing,
many birds. *Cabañas* and hostal accommodation
for 2-6 people start at **$$$-$$**, depending on
amenities, camping from US$14 pp.

Restaurants

La Paloma

$$$ La Marea
Av Solari y Av Paloma, near tourist office,
T4479 7456.
Very popular, has outstanding seafood.

$$ Arrecife
Av Solari y C de la Virgen, T4479 6837.
First class, serving pizzas, *parrilla* and a good
range of salads.

$ Somo's
Av Sagitario y Antares, T4479 8287.
Good and inexpensive pizzas, snacks and
chilled beer.

Northeast of La Paloma
In **Cabo Polonio**, there are a few restaurants,
some with vegetarian options, so you don't have
to bring any food with you. Fish is on the menu
when the sea is calm enough for the fishermen
to go out. The most expensive and fashionable
is **La Perla**, on the south beach. At weekends
during the summer there are DJs, dancing
and live music. For self-catering, the stores sell
fruit, vegetables, meat, etc. There are several
restaurants in **Castillos** including **$$$ La Strada**,
19 de Abril, and several restaurants in **Punta del
Diablo**, mostly colourful huts grouped around
the sea front serving excellent fish. A couple of
pizza places too.

$$ Chivito Veloz
Av Cachimbas y Av Faroles, Aguas Dulces.
Good, large portions for US$4-6.

Parque Nacional Santa Teresa

$$ La Ruta
L Fernández Tunón, La Coronilla, T4476 2788.
This small round restaurant at the entrance to
town may be your only option if you are driving
in the evening and off season from Chuy to
Punta or Montevideo. Good meat dishes. Off
season, most restaurants in La Coronilla and
around are closed.

Chuy

$$-$ Fusion
Av Brasil 387 y Numancia, T9904 7775.
Good food, local beer, traditional Uruguayan fare
and pizzas. Recommended

$$ Tango
Av Brasil 321, T4474 2751
Traditional local fare, and recommended for
good paella.

Transport

La Paloma
Bus Frequent to and from **Rocha**, US$3.75,
30 mins, and to and from **Montevideo** (4 hrs,
US$13.50). 4 buses daily to **Chuy**, US$10, 3½ hrs,
2 a day to **San Carlos**, **Pan de Azúcar** and **Aguas
Dulces**, all with Rutas del Sol, www.rutasdel
sol.com.uy. Northeast of La Paloma, some
Montevideo–Chuy buses go into **Punta del
Diablo**, 4 km from the main road (taxi to the centre
US$5.50, 'golf cart taxi' much cheaper at US$1.10).

To **Cabo Polonio**, Rutas del Sol from
Montevideo, US$17, 4-5 hrs, and any of the
coastal towns to Km 264, where you catch
the truck to the village (see above).

Chuy
Bus To **Montevideo** (COT, Cynsa, Rutas del
Sol) US$20-24, 4¾-6 hrs, may have to change
buses in San Carlos; to **Maldonado** US$12; to
Rocha, US$8-10. International buses passing
through en route from Montevideo to Brazil
either stop in Chuy or at the border. Make sure
the driver knows you need to stop at Uruguayan
immigration. Sometimes everybody must get
off for customs check. If looking for onward
transport, if there is a free seat, most companies
will let you pay on board.

Two roads run towards Melo, heart of cattle-ranching country: Route 8 and Route 7, the latter running for most of its length through the Cuchilla Grande, a range of hills with fine views. Route 8 via Minas and Treinta y Tres is the more important of these two roads to the border and it is completely paved.

Minas and around *Colour map 8, B6.*

This picturesque small town, 120 km north of Montevideo, is set in wooded hills. Juan Lavalleja, the leader of the Thirty-Three who brought independence to the country, was born here, and there is an equestrian statue to Artigas, said to be the largest such in the world, on the Cerro Artigas just out of town. The church's portico and towers, some caves in the neighbourhood and the countryside are worth seeing. Good confectionery is made in Minas; you can visit the largest firm, opposite **Hotel Verdun**. Banks are open 1300-1700 Monday to Friday. There is a tourist office at the bus station, Calle Treinta y Tres y Claudio Williman, T4442 9796. See www.lavalleja.gub.uy.

The **Reserva Natural Parque Salus** ① *daily 0900-1700, T9191 5617, www.salus.com.uy, free*, on the slopes of Sierras de las Animas, is 8 km to the south and very attractive; take the town bus marked 'Cervecería Salus' from plaza to the Salus brewery, then walk 2 km to the mineral spring and bottling plant (**$$$ Parador Salus**, T4443 1652, www.paradorsalus.com.uy, check website to see if open). It is a lovely three-hour walk back to Minas from the springs. The Cascada de Agua del Penitente waterfall, 11 km east off Route 8, is interesting and you may see wild rheas nearby. It's hard to get to off season. The Minas area is popular for mountain biking.

To the Brazilian border

Route 8 continues north via **Treinta y Tres** to Melo (also reached by Route 7), some 60 km south of Aceguá, which is on the border. In **Melo**, there are places to stay and exchange rates are usually better than at the frontier. If crossing to Brazil at Aceguá, Brazilian immigration is at Bagé, 63 km north of the border. At 12 km southeast of Melo is the Posta del Chuy (2 km off Route 26). This house, bridge and toll gate (built 1851) was once the only safe crossing place on the main road between Uruguay and Brazil. It displays gaucho paintings and historical artefacts.

Río Branco was founded in 1914, on the Río Yaguarón. The 1-km-long Mauá bridge across the river leads to Jaguarão in Brazil. The Brazilian vice-consulate in Río Branco is at Ismael Velázquez 1239, T4675 2003, vc.riobranco@itamaraty.gov.br, Monday-Friday 0800-1200 and 1400-1800. For road traffic, the frontier at Chuy is better than Río Branco or Aceguá.

An alternative route to Brazil is via Route 5, the 509-km road from Montevideo to the border town of Rivera, which runs almost due north, bypassing Canelones and Florida before passing through Durazno. The road is dual carriageway as far as Canelones. Running east from Florida, Route 56 traverses the countryside to Cerro Colorado on Route 7, also known as Alejandro Gallinal, which has an unusual clock tower. From Durazno, Route 5 crosses the Río Negro and goes to Tacuarembó.

Durazno *Colour map 8, B6.*

On the Río Yí 182 km from Montevideo, Durazno is a friendly provincial town with tree-lined avenues and an airport. There is a good view of the river from the western bridge. In February the town holds the annual Festival Nacional de Folclore, a major three-day event, featuring musicians from Uruguay and the rest of Latin America. See http://durazno.gub.uy.

South of the Río Negro is gently rolling cattle country, vineyards, orchards, orange, lemon and olive groves. North is hilly countryside with steep river valleys and cattle ranching. Dams on the Río Negro have created an extensive network of lakes near **Paso de los Toros**, 66 km north of Durazno ① *getting there: bus from Montevideo, 3½ hrs, US$14*. There are camping and sports facilities, and walking opportunities. Some 43 km north of Paso de los Toros a 55-km road turns east to **San Gregorio de Polanco**, at the eastern end of Lago Rincón del Bonete. The beach by the lake is excellent, with opportunities for boat trips, horse riding and other sports.

Tacuarembó *Colour map 8, B6.*

This is an agro-industrial town and major route centre, 390 km north of Montevideo (www.
tacuarembo.gub.uy). The nearby Valle Edén has good walking possibilities. Some 23 km west of
Tacuarembó, along Route 26, is the **Carlos Gardel Museum** ① *T4632 4898, daily 1000-1700, US$1*,
a shrine to the great tango singer who was killed in an air crash in Medellín (Colombia). Uruguay,
Argentina and France all claim him as a national son. The argument for his birth near here is
convincing. Large-scale gaucho festival in March/April, www.patriagaucha.com.uy.

Brazilian border

Rivera is divided by a street from the Brazilian town of Santana do Livramento. Points of interest are
the park, the Plaza Internacional, and the dam of Cañapirú. Uruguayan immigration is at the end of
Calle Sarandí y Presidente Viera, 14 blocks, 2 km, from the border (take bus along Agraciada or taxi
from bus terminal for around US$2). There is also a tourist office here, T4623 1900, rivera@mintur.
gub.uy. Luggage is inspected when boarding buses out of Rivera; there are also three checkpoints
on the road out of town. The Brazilian consulate is at Ceballos 1159, T4622 4470, consbrasrivera@
itamaraty.gov.br. Remember that you must have a Uruguayan exit stamp to enter Brazil and a
Brazilian exit stamp to enter Uruguay.

Listings *Montevideo north to Brazil*

Where to stay

Minas

$$ Posada Verdún
W Beltrán 715, T4442 4563,
www.hotelposadaverdun.com.
Good, simple rooms, with tiny internal courtyard,
à la carte restaurant with wood-fired oven on
the premises.

Camping

Arequita
Camino Valeriano Magri, T4440 2503,
www.lavalleja.gub.uy.
Beautiful surroundings, *cabañas* (for 2 people with
shared bathroom from US$14), camping US$5
each. Well-equipped. Pool use US$2.50 per day.

To the Brazilian border

Treinta y Tres

$$-$ La Posada
Manuel Freire 1564, T4452 1107,
www.hotellaposada33.com/indexb.html.
With breakfast, Wi-Fi, good overnight stop, basic
but clean, central location.

$ pp Cañada del Brujo
Km 307.5, Ruta 8, Sierra del Yerbal, 34 km
north of Treinta y Tres, T9929 7448, www.
pleka.com/delbrujo.
Isolated hostel, no electricity, basic but "fantastic",
dorm, local food, meals extra, owner Pablo Rado

drives you there (US$10.50), cycling, trekking
on foot or horseback, trips to Quebrada de los
Cuervos. Recommended.

Melo

$$ Virrey Pedro de Melo
J Muñiz 727/31, T4642 2673, www.
hotelvirreypedrodemelo.com.
Better rooms in new part, 3-star, minibar,
Wi-Fi, parking, laundry service.

Cerro Colorado

$$$$-$$$ San Pedro de Timote
Km 142, R7, 14 km west of Cerro Colorado, T4310
8086/2902 5869, www.sanpedrodetimote.uy.
A famous colonial-style estancia, working
ranch, landscaped park, 3 pools, cinema,
gym, horse riding, family-friendly 'petting
enclosure', good restaurant.

Durazno

There are a few hotels (**$$-$**).

Camping

At 33 Orientales, in park of same name by river,
T4362 2806, info.camping@durazno.gub.uy. Nice
beach, hot showers, toilets, laundry sinks, bike,
horse and canoe hire, bus shuttle to town.

Tourism farm

Estancia Albergue El Silencio
Ruta 14 Km 166, 10 km west of Durazno,
T4362 2014 (or T4360 2270, HI member),
silencio@adinet.coom.uy.

About 15 mins' walk east of bridge over Río Yí where bus stops, clean rooms, riding, swimming, birdwatching. Recommended.

Paso de los Toros

$$-$ Sayonara
Sarandí 302 y Barreto, T4664 2535.
2 blocks from centre, renovated old residence, rooms with bath, a/c and cable TV. With restaurant, breakfast extra.

San Gregorio de Polanco

$$ Posada Buena Vista
De Las Pitangueras 12, T4369 4841.
Overlooking lake, breakfast extra, snack bar, good, prices rise Dec-Easter.

Tacuarembó

$$$ Carlos Gardel
*Ruta 5 Km 387,500, T4633 0306,
www.hotelcarlosgardel.com.uy.*
Internet, pool, spa, restaurant, meeting room.

$$$ Tacuarembó
*18 de Julio 133, T4632 2105,
www.tacuarembohotel.com.uy.*
Breakfast, central, Wi-Fi, safe, restaurant, large pool, conference facilities.

$$ Central
Gral Flores 300, T4632 2341.
Ensuite bathrooms, rooms with or without a/c, parking, basic but clean and reasonable value.

Camping

Campsites 1 km out of town in the Parque Laguna de las Lavanderas, T4632 4761, and 7 km north on R26 at Balneario Iporá, T4632 9144, with cabins nearby at Complejo Sepe (**$$**) T4642 9244.

Brazilian border: Rivera

$$$-$$ Casablanca
*Agraciada 479, T4622 3221,
www.casablanca.com.uy.*
Comfortable and pleasant, stylish rooms contrast with the rough exterior, with Wi-Fi, room service and laundry.

$$$-$$ Uruguay Brasil
*Sarandí 440, T9107 3050,
www.hoteluruguaybrasil.com.uy.*
Buffet breakfast, minibar, Wi-Fi area, laundry service, restaurant, duty-free shop and secure car park.

Camping

Municipal site near AFE station, C Agraciada and Presidente Viera, and in the Parque Gran Bretaña 7 km south along R27, T4625 23083.

Restaurants

Minas

Restaurants include **Complejo San Francisco de las Sierras** (Ruta 12 Km 347.500, 3 km from Minas, T9802 5122); **Ki-Joia** (D Pérez in front of Plaza Libertad, T4442 1105).

Irisarri
C Treinta y Tres 618.
Best pastry shop, with high local reputation in lovely old Art Deco building, specialities include *yemas* (egg candy), *alfajores* (dulce de leche sandwich biscuits) and *damasquitos* (apricot sweets).

Transport

Minas

Bus To **Montevideo**, US$8, several companies, 2 hrs. To **Maldonado**, US$6.50, 7 a day, 1½-2 hrs (**COOM**).

Melo

Bus To **Montevideo** US$21-25, 5-7 hrs (**Núñez, EGA**); to **Treinta y Tres** from Montevideo, US$15-18. 3-5 buses daily to **Río Branco**, via **Lago Merín** US$8 (**La Flotta**, T4642 7668).

Durazno

Bus To **Montevideo** US$11, 2½-3½ hrs.

Tacuarembó

Bus From **Montevideo**, US$20-23, 4-5 hrs.

Brazilian border: Rivera

Bus Terminal at Uruguay y Viera (1.5 km from the terminal in Santa Ana). To/from **Montevideo**, US$28, 5½-7 hrs (**Agencia Central, Turil, Núñez**). To **Paysandú, Copay**, T4622 3733, at 0400 (Mon-Sat), 1600 (daily), US$21 To **Tacuarembó**, US$8 (**Núñez, Turil**), no connections for Paysandú. To **Salto**, Mon and Fri 1630, 6 hrs, US$27. For **Artigas**, take Brazilian bus from Santana do Livramento to Quaraí, then cross border bridge.

Practicalities
Getting around

Air

If flying from Uruguay to make an international connection in Buenos Aires, make sure your flight goes to Ezeiza International Airport (eg **American Airlines** or **Air Europa**), not Aeroparque (almost all **Aerolíneas Argentinas** and **Alas Uruguay** flights). Luggage is not transferred automatically to Ezeiza and you will have to travel one hour between the airports by taxi or bus. If you need a visa to enter Argentina, you must get a transit visa (takes up to four weeks to process in Montevideo), just to transfer between airports. See also Tax, page 1576, for airport taxes.

Rail

The passenger services are slow commuter services from Montevideo.

Road

Bus All main cities and towns are served by good companies originating from the Tres Cruces Terminal in Montevideo (www.trescruces.com.uy, for schedules and fares, but purchase must be made in person and early if travelling to popular destinations at peak holiday time). There are good services to neighbouring countries. Details are given in the text.

Car Driving your own or a rented vehicle (see page 1543) is a viable way to explore Uruguay, as it allows flexibility and access to further destinations. **Hitching** is not easy.

Maps

Automóvil Club del Uruguay ① *http://acu.com.uy, see box, below*, publishes road maps of the city and country, as do Esso and Ancap. **ITMB** of Vancouver also publishes a country map (1:800,000). Official maps are issued by **Servicio Geográfico Militar** ① *Av 8 de Octubre 3255, T2487 1810, www. ejercito.mil.uy/cal/sgm*.

TRAVEL TIP
Driving in Uruguay

Road Driving is expensive by South American standards: fuel costs are high and many roads have tolls (passenger vehicles US$3, payable by smart card or by credit or debit card in advance or afterwards: see https://telepeaje.com.uy). Roads are generally in good condition, with a significant proportion paved or all-weather. In rural areas, motorists should drive with their headlights on even in daylight, especially on major roads. Uruguayans are polite drivers: outside Montevideo, trucks will move to let you pass and motorists will alert you of speed traps.

Documents 90-day admission is usually given without any problems. Entry is easier and faster with a *carnet de passages*, but it is not essential. Without it you will be given a temporary import paper which must be surrendered on leaving the country. Insurance is required by law. For more information, see www.aduanas.gub.uy.

Organizations Automóvil Club del Uruguay, Av del Libertador 1532 (Estación Central, Colonia esq Yi), T1707, www.acu.com.uy. Reciprocity with foreign automobile clubs is available; members do not have to pay for affiliation.

Fuel All gasoline is unleaded: 97 octane, US$1.71 per litre; 95 octane, US$1.65 per litre; diesel, US$1.50-1.90 per litre depending on grade. Filling stations may close weekends.

Where to stay

There is an increasingly wide range of accommodation in all categories (slightly fewer mid-range hotels). Luxury accommodation and estancias are particularly good. See www.ahru.com.uy for hotels, www.estancias-uruguay.com (a useful listings of some 40 estancias) and text for further information.

There are lots of **camping** sites. Most towns have municipal sites (quality varies). Many sites along the Ruta Interbalnearia, but most of these close off season. The Tourist Office in Montevideo issues a good guide to campsites and youth hostels; see references in main text. See also www.solocampings.com/uruguay.Many good quality **hostels** can be found in Montevideo and other cities and towns (see recommendations in Where to stay sections). **Hostelling International** ① *Colonia 1086 p9 Of 903, Montevideo, www.hosteluruguay.org*, has 12 member hostels. See the Planning your trip chapter for our hotel price guide.

Food & drink

Restaurants

Dinner hours are generally 2000-0100. Restaurants usually charge *cubierto* (bread and place setting), costing US$1-3, and more in Punta del Este. Lunch is generally served from 1230-1500, when service often stops until dinner. A *confitería* is an informal place which serves meals at any time, as opposed to a *restaurante*, which serves meals at set times. Uruguay does not as yet have a great selection of international restaurants, although this is slowly changing. Vegetarians may have to stick to salads or pasta, as even the 'meatless dishes' may contain some meat. There are a few more vegetarian restaurants in Montevideo and, surprisingly, in some of the smaller beach resorts, attracting a more 'alternative' crowd. See the Planning your trip chapter for our restaurant price guide.

Food

In most places, you have two choices: meat or Italian food. Beef is eaten at almost all meals. Most restaurants are *parrilladas* (grills) where the main cuts are *asado* (ribs); *pulpa* (no bones), *lomo* (fillet steak) and entrecote. Steak prices normally indicate the quality of the cut. Also very popular are *chorizos* and *salchichas*, both types of sausage. More exotic Uruguayan favourites include *morcilla* (blood sausage, salty or sweet), *chinchulines* or *chotos* (small or large intestines), *riñones* (kidneys) and *molleja* (sweetbreads). *Cordero* (lamb) and *brochettes* (skewers/kebabs) are also common. Grilled *provolone*, *morrones* (red peppers), *boniatos* (sweet potatoes), and *chimichurri* sauce are also omnipresent. *Chivitos* (large, fully loaded steak sandwiches) and *milanesa* (fried breaded chicken or beef) are also popular; usually eaten with mixed salad (lettuce, tomato, onion), or chips. All Italian dishes are delicious, from bread to pastas to raviolis to desserts. Pizza is very common and good. Seafood includes squid, mussels, shrimp, salmon, and *lenguado* (sole). For snacks, *medialunas* (croissants) are often filled with ham and/or cheese, either hot or cold; toasted sandwiches and quiches/pies are readily available; *frankfurters*, known as *panchos* are hot dogs; *picada* (crackers or breads, cheese, olives, coldcuts) is a common afternoon favourite. Desserts, mostly of Italian origin, are excellent. *Dulce de leche* (similar to caramel) and *dulce de membrillo* (quince paste) are ubiquitous ingredients. As in Argentina, *alfajores* are a favourite sweet snack. Ice cream is excellent everywhere. High quality olive oil is produced near Punta del Este, see www.colinasdegarzon.com for tours and tastings. Punta del Este and surroundings also host an annual food and wine festival (http://puntafoodandwine.com).

Drink

The beers are good (**Patricia** has been recommended), and some new craft breweries are popping up, such the Montevideo Brewhouse (MBH: www.mbh.com.uy), producing some excellent 'artisan ales'. Local wines vary, but tannat is the regional speciality (eg **Don Pascual, Pisano**) and several bodegas offer tours. See www.bodegasdeluruguay.com.uy and www.uruguaywinetours.com. Whisky is the favourite spirit in Uruguay, normally Johnny Walker. There is also a national brand,

Dunbar whisky Uruguayo, a blended whisky that still has a little way to go before reaching international standards, but worth a sample. The local spirits include *uvita*, *caña* and *grappamiel* (honey liquor). In the Mercado del Puerto, Montevideo, a *medio medio* is half still white wine, half sparkling white (elsewhere a *medio medio* is half *caña* and half whisky). *Espillinar* is a type of Uruguayan rum. Try the *clericó*, a mixture of white wine and fruit juices. Very good fresh fruit juices and mineral water are common. *Mate* is the drink of choice between meal hours. Coffee is good, normally served espresso-style after a meal. Milk, sold in plastic containers, is excellent, skimmed to whole (*descremada* to *entera*).

Essentials A-Z

Accident and emergency

Emergency T911. **Ambulance** T105 or 911.
Medical emergencies T1727. **Fire service** T104.
Road police T108/109. Road information: T1954.
Tourist Police in Montevideo, at Colonia 1021, T0800-8226(information) or T1909 ext 2446.

Electricity

220 volts 50 cycles AC. Various plugs used: round 2-pin or flat 2-pin (most common), oblique 2-pin with earth, 3 round pins in a line.

Embassies and consulates

For all Uruguayan embassies and consulates abroad and for all foreign embassies and consulates in Uruguay, see http://embassy.goabroad.com.

Health

Medical services
Montevideo Hospital Británico, Av Italia 2420, T2487 1020, www.hospitalbritanico.com.uy. Recommended. Also Médica Uruguaya, Av 8 de octubre 2492, T2487 0525, www. medicauruguaya.com.uy.

Money

US$1=28.3; €1=31.5 (Jun 2017).
The currency is the *peso uruguayo*. Bank notes: 20, 50, 100, 200, 500, 1000 and 2000 pesos uruguayos. Coins: 1, 2, 5 and 10 pesos. Any amount of currency can be taken in or out.

There's no restriction on foreign exchange transactions (so it is a good place to stock up with US$ bills, though AmEx and some banks refuse to do this for credit cards; most places charge 3% commission for such transactions).

Dollars cash can be purchased when leaving the country. Changing Argentine pesos into Uruguayan pesos is usually a marginally worse rate than for dollars. Brazilian *reais* get a much worse rate. US$, Argentina pesos or Brazilian reais notes are accepted for some services, including hotels and restaurants in the main tourist centres.

Cost of travelling Prices vary considerably between summer and winter in tourist destinations, Punta del Este being one of the most expensive summer resorts in Latin America. In Montevideo, allow US$70-80 daily for a cheap hotel, eating the *menú del día* and travelling by bus. Internet price varies, around US$1 per hr at Antel *telecentros*.

Credit cards In some places there is a 10% charge to use Visa and MasterCard. **Banred**, www.banred.com.uy, is the largest ATM network from where you can withdraw US$ or pesos with a Visa or MasterCard. **HSBC**, **Lloyds TSB**, **BBVA**, **Citibank** all have Banred ATMs. **Banco de la República** (BROU) branches have Banred, Link and Cirrus ATMs. ATMs can also be found in supermarkets. Most cheaper hotels outside major cities do not accept credit cards.

Opening hours

Banks: Mon-Fri 1300-1800 (some till 1700).
Businesses: 0830-1200, 1430-1830 or 1900.
Government offices: Mon-Fri 0900-1800 in summer; Mon-Fri 1000-1700 (rest of the year).
Shops: Mon-Fri 1000-1900; Sat 1000-1300; **shopping malls**: daily 1000-2200. In small towns or non-tourist areas, there is a break for lunch and siesta, between 1300 and 1600.

Post

The main post office in Montevideo is at Misiones 1328 y Buenos Aires; 0900-1800 Mon-Fri, 0900-1300 Sat and holidays. **Poste restante** at main post office will keep mail for 1 month. Other branches in the capital: on Av Libertador 1440, next to Montevideo Shopping Center, 0900-1800, and under the Intendencia at corner of Av 18 de Julio and Ejido, Mon-Fri 1000-2000, Sat 1700-2200.

Public holidays and festivals

1 Jan, 6 Jan; Carnival; Easter week (Tourism Week); 19 Apr; 1 and 18 May, 19 Jun; 18 Jul; 25 Aug (the night before is **Noche de la Nostalgia**, when people gather in *boliches* to dance to old songs); 12 Oct; 2 Nov; 25 Dec.

Carnival begins in late Jan/early Feb and lasts for some 40 days until Carnival week, officially Mon and Tue before Ash Wed (many firms close for the whole week). The most prominent elements in Carnival are Candombe, representing the rituals of the African slaves brought to Río de la Plata in colonial times, through drumming and dance. The complex polyrhythms produced by the mass of drummers advancing down the street in the 'Llamadas' parades are very impressive. The other main element is Murga, a form of street theatre with parody, satire, singing and dancing by elaborately made-up and costumed performers.

Business also comes to a standstill during **Holy Week** (or Tourism Week), which coincides with La Semana Criolla del Prado (horse-breaking, stunt riding by gauchos, dances and song) Department stores close only from Good Fri. Banks and offices close Thu-Sun. Easter Mon is not a holiday. Also in Mar/Apr Tacuarembó, in the north, hosts gaucho festival **Patria Gaucha**. A weekend of Oct is chosen annually for celebrating the **Día del Patrimonio** (Heritage Day) throughout the country: hundreds of buildings, both public or private, including embassies, are open to the public for that day only. Also special train services run.

Safety

Personal security presents few problems in most of Uruguay. Petty theft does occur in Montevideo, most likely in tourist areas or markets. Beggars are often seen trying to sell small items or simply asking for money. They are not dangerous. The Policía Turística patrols the streets of the capital. In Dec 2013, Uruguay became the first country in the world to legalize cannabis/marijuana, as a drug-fighting measure. By 2017, the measure did not appear to have had any significant impact on visitors. Foreign tourists can visit Cannabis Social Clubs and participate in tours related to the production of cannabis, but they are not officially allowed to buy cannabis. Bear in mind also that crossing borders while in possession of drugs is still a serious offence.

Tax

Airport tax US$20 on all air travellers leaving Uruguay for Buenos Aires, Aeroparque, but US$44 to Ezeiza and all other countries; boarding fees are included in the cost of flight tickets. There is a tax of 3% on all tickets issued and paid for in Uruguay. Domestic airport tax is US$2.
VAT/IVA 22%, 10% on certain basic items.

Telephone and Wi-Fi

Country code +598.
Ringing: long equal tones, long pauses.
Engaged: short tones, short pauses.

In Uruguay, fixed line numbers are 8 digits long. There are no area codes. Mobile phone numbers are prefixed by 9 if calling from outside Uruguay and 09 if calling within the country. **Antel** *telecentros* in cities are good places to find phone, internet and other means of communication. If you wish to use your own phone with a Uruguayan SIM card, you should register your phone with customs on arrival. Antel, Movistar and Claro provide prepaid SIM card packages. Roaming with your own SIM should present no problems and does not require registration. Uruguay is at the top of the league in South America for internet speed and access, especially in urban areas.

Time

GMT -3 hrs all year (as of 2017 Uruguay is not observing DST).

Tipping

Restaurant and cafés usually include service, but an additional 10% is expected. Porters at the airport: US$1 per piece of luggage. Taxis: 5-10% of fare.

Tourist information

Ministry of Tourism, Rambla 25 de Agosto de 1825 y Yacaré, 1885, www.turismo.gub.uy. For birdwatching, contact: **Avesuruguay/ Gupeca**, Canelones 1198, Montevideo, T2902 8642, www.avesuruguay.org.uy, Mon-Tue, Thu-Fri 1300-1700, Wed 1600-2000. Uruguay is creating a system of national parks under the heading **Sistema Nacional de Areas Protegidas (SNA)**,

www.mvotma.gub.uy/snap (Spanish only).
By 2017, 14 parks had been created.

Useful websites

www.welcomeuruguay.com Excellent bilingual regional guide to all tourist related businesses and events.

www.brecha.com.uy *Brecha*, a progressive weekly listing films, theatres and concerts in Montevideo and provinces, US$2 (special editions sometimes free). Recommended.

http://guruguay.com Useful personal guide (in English) by Welsh expat Karen Higgs, who also publishes her own 'Guru' guidebooks, with handy tips for specialist tours and events.

Visas and immigration

A passport is necessary for entry except for nationals of most Latin American countries, who can get in with national identity documents for stays of up to 90 days. Nationals of the following countries need a visa for a tourist visit of less than 3 months: China, Egypt, Guyana, Morrocco and the majority of Caribbean, African, Middle Eastern, Central Asian and Asian states. Visas cost US$42, and you need a passport photo, hotel reservations or letter of invitation and a ticket out of Uruguay. Visa processing may take 2-4 weeks. Visas are valid for 90 days and usually multiple entry. Tourist cards (obligatory for all tourists, obtainable on entry) are valid for 3 months, extendable for a similar period at the **Migraciones office**, C Misiones 1513, T2916 0471. If entering and leaving Uruguay overland (bus or ferry), you may on departure be asked to show the ticket with which you arrived in the country.

Weights and measures

Metric.

This is
Venezuela

Venezuela is where the Andes meet the Caribbean. The Orinoco river separates the great plains from the table-top mountains of the Gran Sabana, where waterfalls tumble into the forest and lost worlds are easy to imagine. More recent innovations – cable cars up to the high peaks, hang gliders for jumping off them – are now part of the scene at Mérida, capital of Venezuela's Andes.

Lying at the heart of the country – geographically and spiritually – are the *llanos* (plains), a vast area of flat savannah the size of Italy that is home to an immense variety of exotic birds, mammals and reptiles, including caiman, anacondas, anteaters, pumas, jaguars and giant otters, to name but a few. These plains flood seasonally, but when the waters retreat, the birds and animals share their territory with cattle and the *llanero* cowboys, renowned for their hospitality towards visitors. A few *hatos* (cattle ranches) welcome tourists or there are budget tours from Mérida.

If the sea is more to your taste, head for the country's seductive coastline – the longest in the Caribbean at over 2500 km. Venezuela's waters have some of the best (and least known) dive sites in the region, with three marine national parks. Pick of the bunch are Islas Los Roques, an archipelago of emerald and turquoise lagoons and dazzling white beaches.

At the other end of the country, the Amazon is home to humid rainforests and rare plants and animals, as well as over 20 different ethnic groups. This part of Venezuela is very much frontier territory and remains as wild and untamed as it was when the country received its first foreign visitor back in 1498. So overwhelmed was Columbus by what he saw that he described it as "Paradise on Earth".

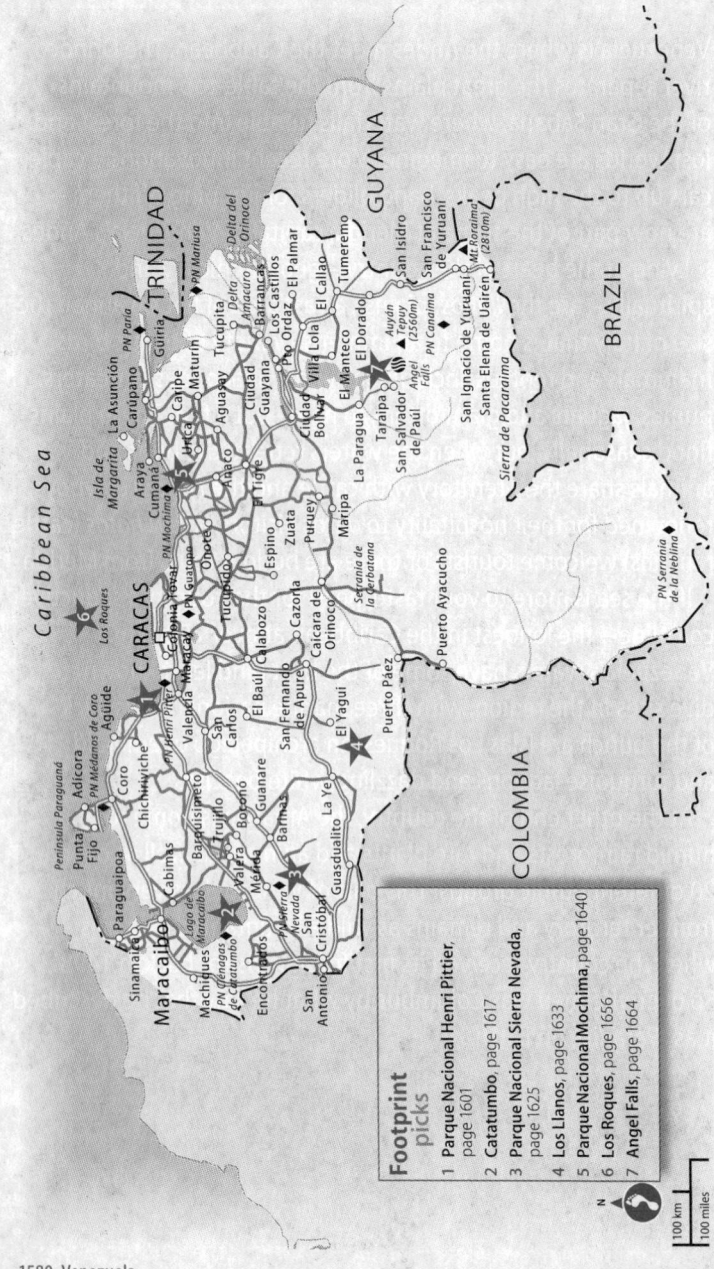

Caribbean Sea

TRINIDAD

GUYANA

BRAZIL

COLOMBIA

CARACAS

Maracaibo

Footprint picks

1 **Parque Nacional Henri Pittier**, page 1601
2 **Catatumbo**, page 1617
3 **Parque Nacional Sierra Nevada**, page 1625
4 **Los Llanos**, page 1633
5 **Parque Nacional Mochima**, page 1640
6 **Los Roques**, page 1656
7 **Angel Falls**, page 1664

100 km
100 miles

N

Footprint
picks

⭐ **Parque Nacional Henri Pittier**, page 1601

A birdwatcher's paradise of tumbling streams and steep hillsides that stretch down to the Caribbean.

⭐ **Catatumbo**, page 1617

The fabulous lightning displays over this swampy delta have earned it the name, the 'Lighthouse of Maracaibo'.

⭐ **Parque Nacional Sierra Nevada**, page 1625

Mérida has popular tourist sites and rugged adventures on its doorstep.

⭐ **Los Llanos**, page 1633

The Orinoco plains are one of the best places to see wildlife.

⭐ **Parque Nacional Mochima**, page 1640

The most accessible of Venezuela's Caribbean beaches are in this park.

⭐ **Los Roques**, page 1656

Coral reefs surround turquoise lagoons and dazzling white-sand islands.

⭐ **Angel Falls**, page 1664

The world's highest waterfall has a drop of almost 1 km.

Route
planner

One to two weeks

beaches, waterfalls, mountains and plains

A two-week visit would allow time on the beaches of either the eastern or western coasts, and a visit to the interior. If time is short there are flights between most cities and Caracas for the first or last leg of your trip.

East of Caracas is **Parque Nacional Mochima**, with some excellent beaches and a multitude of islets. Further east are unrivalled beaches on the **Paria Peninsula**, as well as **Isla de Margarita**, one of the country's principal tourist destinations. From the coast, take a bus to historic **Ciudad Bolívar** and then fly to the **Gran Sabana**, among whose wonders are the **Angel Falls**. There are many other falls in this region and a few places to stay, the most popular being **Canaima Camp** on a lagoon on the Río Carrao.

West of Caracas, some 320 km west of the capital, is the **Parque Nacional Morrocoy**, with many islands close to the shore. Northwest of Morrocoy is the historic town of **Coro**, surrounded by sand dunes, and the **Paranaguá Peninsula**. From here, head south by road to the **Andean Sierra Nevada** where the main centre for adventure is **Mérida**. It has plentiful accommodation and tour companies, who can arrange treks, climbing and excursions to **Catatumbo** on Lake Maracaibo and to ecotourism ranches on the plains to the east.

Three to four weeks

diving, exploring and trekking

With an extra week or two, you could spend some time diving and relaxing on the beautiful archipelago of **Islas Los Roques**, reached by plane from Caracas. Then explore the west coast and sierras. Travel west to east from the Andes across the **Llanos** to **Ciudad Bolívar**, from where you can explore the **Gran Sabana**, not just at **Canaima**, but also from the road south to **Santa Elena de Uairén**. Where Venezuela meets Brazil and Guyana is **Mount Roraima**; to reach its summit is one of the country's most adventurous excursions.

Essential Venezuela

Getting around

The country's main airport for international and domestic flights is Maiquetía, www.aeropuerto-maiquetia.com.ve, 28 km from Caracas near the port of La Guaira; it has two terminals: Maiquetía (national) and Simón Bolívar (international). There are flights from Maiquetía to major cities throughout the country. These are useful for covering large distances, but be prepared for unexplained cancellations, lost luggage and delays. Alternatively, long-distance buses run to all major towns and cities; many routes bypass Caracas. On shorter journeys, minibuses and shared taxis are fast and convenient but road safety is not a priority. For further details, see Transport, page 1597.

When to go

The climate is tropical, with changes between the seasons being a matter of wet and dry, rather than hot and cold. Temperature is determined by altitude. The dry season in Caracas is December to April, with January and February the coolest months (there is a great difference between day and night temperatures at this time). The hottest months are July and August. The Caribbean coast is generally dry, and rain is particularly infrequent in the states of Sucre, in the east, and Falcón, in the northwest. The lowlands of Maracaibo are very hot all year round, but especially so from July to September. South of the Orinoco, in the Gran Sabana and Parque Nacional Canaima, the dry season is November to May. The best time to visit Los Llanos is just after the rains, when the rivers and channels are still full of water and the humidity is not too high. In the Andes, the dry season is October to May; this is the best time for climbing or hiking. The days are clear, but the nights are freezing cold. The rains usually begin in June, but in the mountains the weather can change daily. High season, when it is advisable to book in advance includes: Carnival, Easter, 15 July to 15 September and Christmas to New Year.

Fact file
Location 105000° N, 669667° W
Capital Caracas
Time zone GMT -4½ hrs
Telephone country code +58
Currency Bolívar fuerte (BsF)

Time required

Two to three weeks will allow you to get a feel for the country and see the main sights. Allow more time if you want to flop on a beach for a few days or go diving.

Money

Venezuela officially has a two-tier exchange rate (see Money, page 1680) and foreigners are entitled to use the floating Dicom rate of about BsF 701 = US$1 (at the time of research). There is, however, a black market which is many times more favourable than the official rate. You may be able to use this if you know someone trustworthy to exchange money for you. The black market is illegal and in practice you may not find safe access to it. The prices quoted in this chapter are converted at the official Dicom rate, but visitors may find that establishments have a different pricing policy for foreigners, so it is best to phone in advance to check. Inflation, shortages and government regulations have all caused instability in the costs of goods and services in recent years.

Weather Caracas

January	February	March	April	May	June
25°C 17°C 16mm	26°C 18°C 18mm	27°C 18°C 12mm	27°C 20°C 59mm	27°C 21°C 80mm	26°C 20°C 139mm

July	August	September	October	November	December
26°C 20°C 121mm	26°C 20°C 124mm	27°C 20°C 114mm	26°C 20°C 123mm	26°C 19°C 73mm	25°C 18°C 42mm

Caracas
& around

Founded in 1567, Caracas is situated in a rift in thickly forested mountains which rise abruptly from a lush green coast to heights of 2000 m to 3000 m. The capital lies in a small basin at 960 m, which runs some 24 km east and west. For all its Caribbean appeal, it is not the gentlest of introductions to South America. Some enjoy its pleasant, year-round climate, its parks and cosmopolitan nightlife. Others have been drawn to experience the Bolivarian revolution. But others find this city of three million people, loud, congested and unsettling. By way of escape, there are several nearby excursions to mountain towns, the colonial district of El Hatillo, the Parque Nacional El Avila/Waraira Repano, beaches and Los Roques, a beautiful Caribbean atoll reached by a short flight.

Caracas *Colour map 1, A6.*

learn about Bolívar, then escape to the mountains or the sea

Plaza Bolívar and around

The shady **Plaza Bolívar**, with its fine equestrian statue of the Liberator and pleasant colonial cathedral, is still the official centre of the city, though no longer geographically so. The **Capitolio Nacional**, the National Assembly, consists of two neoclassical-style buildings, the **Legislative Palace** and the **Federal Palace** ① *Tue-Sun, 0900-1100, 1400-1600*. The Elliptical Salon has some impressive paintings and murals by the Venezuelan artist Martín Tovar y Tovar. The present **Cathedral** dating from 1674 has a beautiful façade, the Bolívar family chapel and paintings by Michelena, Murillo and an alleged Rubens 'Resurrection'. Bolívar was baptized in this Cathedral, and the remains of his parents and wife are here. The **Museo Sacro** ① *Plaza Bolívar, de la Torre a Gradillas, T0212-861 6562, Mon-Sat 0900-1600, US$0.05*, has colonial religious paintings and images, plus an art gallery, handicrafts, café and bookshop. Concerts and other cultural events are held at weekends.

The **Consejo Municipal** (City Hall) on Plaza Bolívar contains the **Museo Caracas** with three sections ① *open Tue-Fri 0930-1200, 1500-1800; Sat and Sun 0930-1800*. The first features a collection of paintings by Venezuelan artists, including Emilio Boggio; the Raúl Santana Museum of the Creole Way of Life has a collection of miniature figures in costumes, all handmade by Raúl Santana; and a collection of historical, pre-independence objects.

Casa Natal del Libertador ① *Sur 1 y Este 2, Jacinto a Traposos, opposite Plaza El Venezolano, T0212-541 2563, Tue-Fri 0900-1600, Sat, Sun and holidays 1000-1600, free*, is a fascinating reconstruction of the house where Bolívar was born on 24 July 1783. Interesting pictures, furniture and murals tell Bolívar's life story. The first house, of adobe, was destroyed by an earthquake. The second was later pulled down. The **Museo Bolivariano** is next door and contains the Liberator's war relics.

San Francisco ① *Av Universidad y San Francisco (1 block southwest of Plaza Bolívar)*, the oldest church in Caracas, rebuilt 1641, should be seen for its colonial altars. **Santa Teresa** ① *between La Palma and Santa Teresa, just southeast of the Centro Simón Bolívar*, has good interior chapels and a supposedly miraculous portrait of Nazareno de San Pablo; there are popular devotions here on Good Friday.

Best for
Excursions ■ Museums ■ Nightlife ■ Parks

Essential Caracas

Finding your feet

Maiquetía airport is 28 km from Caracas; if you're arriving or leaving at night, you are advised to stay in one of the nearby hotels on the coast rather than travelling to/from the city. For those travelling by bus, there are three main terminals in different parts of the city, each serving different regions of the country.

In the centre, each street corner has a name: addresses are generally given as 'Santa Capilla and Mijares' (*Santa Capilla y – sometimes a – Mijares*), rather than the official 'Calle Norte 2, No 26'. In the east, 'y' or 'con' are used for street intersections. Modern multi-storeyed edifices dominate and few colonial buildings remain intact. A 10-km strip from west to east, fragmented by traffic-laden arteries, contains several centres: Plaza Bolívar, Plaza Venezuela, Sabana Grande, Chacaíto, Altamira, La California and Petare. The Avila mountain is always north.

Tip...
Many museums are closed on Monday and at lunchtimes.

Getting around

The metro is air-conditioned, clean, safe, comfortable and quick, although poorly signed and often packed, especially at rush hours. It is supplemented by numerous bus services (again, crowded at rush hour), cable cars and taxis. Only ever use official taxi cabs or private taxis owned by your hotel.

When to go

Caracas has a pleasant Caribbean climate, although it can be hot and humid from June to September. If you're in the city on 3 May, look out for festivities associated with the **Velorio de la Cruz de Mayo**, which is still celebrated with dances and parties in some areas.

Security

Safety in Caracas has deteriorated in recent years and crime rates and kidnappings have risen significantly. You should be on your guard as soon as you arrive: there are many pirate taxis and rip-off merchants at the international airport. It is best not to arrive in Caracas at night. Avoid certain areas, such as all western suburbs from the El Silencio monument to Propatria; the areas around the Nuevo Circo and La Bandera bus stations; the area around the *teleférico*; Chapellín near the Country Club, and Petare. It is not advisable to walk at night in the city, except in the municipality of Chacao (Altamira, Chacao and Los Palos Grandes) and in Las Mercedes. Street crime is common, even armed robbery in daylight. Carry handbags, cameras and other valuables on the side away from the road, as motorcycle bag-snatchers are notorious. Police checks are frequent, thorough and can include on-the-spot searches of valuables; bribes are sometimes asked for. See also Safety, page 1682.

Tip...
Saturday and Sunday mornings and public holidays are bad for travel into/out of Caracas because traffic is so heavy.

Panteón Nacional and around
Av Norte y Av Panteón, T0212-862 1518, Tue-Sun 0900-1200, 1330-1600.

The remains of Simón Bolívar, the Liberator, lie in isolation in the new Mausoleo del Libertador, a 54-m high, white sweeping edifice which dwarfs the original Panteón Nacional (inaugurated 1875) in front of it. Bolívar's casket is made of caoba wood, decorated with gold and pearls. Tombs of other national heroes and heroines remain in the Panteón. That of Francisco Miranda (the Precursor of Independence), who died in a Spanish prison, has been left open to await the return of his body; likewise the tomb of Antonio José de Sucre, who was assassinated in Colombia.

Museo Histórico Fundación John Boulton ⓘ *Final Av Panteón, Foro Libertador, Casa N 3, next to the Panteón Nacional, T0212-861 4685, www.fundacionboulton.com, Tue-Sat 1000-1600*, contains good collections of 19th-century art and objects, furniture, maps, metals and coins and objects and documents relating to the life of Simón Bolívar.

San Bernardino

A delightful house in the beautiful suburb of San Bernardino houses the **Museo de Arte Colonial** ① *Quinta Anauco, Av Panteón, San Bernardino, T0212-551 8190, www.quintadeanauco.org.ve, Tue-Fri 0900-1200 and 1400-1600, Sat-Sun and holidays 1000-1600, closed 11 Dec to 11 Jan, US$1.25.* It was built in 1720 and was formerly the residence of the Marqués del Toro. Everything from the roof to the carpet has been preserved and the house contains a wealth of period furniture and sculpture and almost 100 paintings from the colonial era.

Parque Central

There are two good museums located at the Parque Central, a jungle of concrete edifices between Avenida Bolívar and Avenida Lecuna. The **Museo de Arte Contemporáneo** ① *Parque Central, Cuadra Bolívar, T0212-573 8289, www.fmn.gob.ve, Tue-Fri 0900-1700, Sat-Sun 1000-1700, free,* has some 3000 works on display, including modern sculptures and works by, among others, Miró, Chagall, Matisse and Picasso; it's one of the finest collections of modern art in South America. The **Museo de los Niños** ① *Parque Central, next to east Tower, Nivel Bolívar, T0212-575 0695, www. maravillosarealidad.com, Mon-Fri 0900-1700, Sat-Sun and holidays 1000-1700, US$0.08, children US$0.07,* is an extremely popular and highly sophisticated interactive science museum. It also has exhibits on the dangers of drugs, on colours and a planetarium (US$1.35; tickets for all four exhibits US$5.50, children US$5).

Plaza de los Museos

Parque Los Caobos is a peaceful place to wander if you are visiting the **Plaza de los Museos**, which is located at the western end of the park. Nearby is the **Bosque de las Esculturas**, an open-air sculpture exhibition. **Museo de Bellas Artes** ① *Plaza de los Museos, T0212-578 0275, www.fmn.gob.ve, free, Tue-Fri 0900-1700, Sat-Sun and holidays 1000-1700,* is the oldest museum in Caracas, designed by Carlos Raúl

1 Caracas

To Hotel Humboldt

To Simón Bolívar International Airport

PUERTA DE CARACAS

Gato Negro

COTIZA

Plaza Sucre Ⓜ

Av Sucre

Agua Salud

Panteón Nacional & Museo Histórico John Boulton

Quinta Anauco & Museo de Arte Colonial

Mariperez Cable Railway Station

Propatria

CATIA

Caño Amarillo

Ⓜ

SAN BERNARDINO

MARIPEREZ

Pérez Bonalde

23 DE ENERO

Capitolio

Av Urdaneta

Museo de la Revolución Bolivariana

Parque Ezequiel Zamora

El Silencio

La Hoyada

Parque Carabobo

Colegio de Ingenieros

3

Ⓜ Capuchinos

Av San Martín

Ⓜ

Av Bolívar

Bellas Artes

2

Plaza Venezuela

Artigas Ⓜ

Ⓜ Maternidad

SAN AGUSTÍN

QTA CRESPO

Autopista Fco Fajardo

CIUDAD UNIVERSITARIA

Sabana Grande

La Paz Ⓜ

EL PARAISO

Ciudad Universitaria Ⓜ

To La Yaguara & Las Adjuntas

N

EL CEMENTERIO

Los Símbolos

SANTA MONICA

Av Guzmán Blanco

Autopista Norte-Sur

Autopista El Valle

1 km

1 mile

To Caricuao

La Bandera Ⓜ

Paseo los Próceres

To Valles del Tuy, Maracay & Valencia

El Valle

To Valles del Tuy, Maracay & Valencia

Where to stay 🛏

1 Avila
2 Eurobuilding
3 Paseo Las Mercedes

Restaurants 🍴

1 Coco Thai & Lounge
2 Franca
3 La Castañuela
4 La Montanara
5 Mokambo

Villanueva. It contains a permanent collection of contemporary and 19th-century works by mainly Venezuelan and South American artists and also has a good café surrounded by outdoor sculptures. Adjacent is the **Galería de Arte Nacional** ① *T0212-576 8707, www.fmn.gob.ve, Tue-Fri 0900-1700, Sat-Sun and holidays 1000-1700*, which displays the history of Venezuelan art, with nearly 7000 artworks, and also houses the **Cinemateca Nacional** ① *T0212-482 2371, www.cinemateca.gob.ve*, an arts and experimental cinema complex. **Museo de Ciencias** ① *Plaza de los Museos, Los Caobos, T0212-573 4398, www.fmn.gob.ve, Tue-Fri 0900-1700, Sat-Sun and holidays 1000-1700*, has archaeological (particularly pre-Columbian), zoological and botanical exhibits, plus interesting temporary shows.

University and botanic gardens
Universidad Central de Venezuela ① *Ciudad Universitaria, near Plaza Venezuela, www.ucv.ve*, is one of the most successful expressions of modern architecture in Latin America. Designed by Carlos Raúl Villanueva, it was declared a World Heritage Site by UNESCO in 2000. Among its important works of art are Floating Clouds by Alexander Calder in the auditorium, murals by Victor Vasarely, Wilfredo Lam and Fernand Léger, and sculptures by Jean Arp, Baltasar Lobo and Henri Laurens.

Jardín Botánico ① *near Plaza Venezuela, entrance by Ciudad Universitaria, T0212-662 9254, Tue-Sun 0800-1700*, has collections of over 2000 species; 10,000 trees from 80 species grow in the arboretum alone. Here is the world's largest palm tree (*Corypha Sp*) and the elephant apple tree with its huge edible fruit.

Sabana Grande *See map page 1591.*
East of Plaza Venezuela, the mid-town neighbourhood of Sabana Grande is bisected by the pedestrianized Boulevard Sabana Grande (actual name Avenida Abraham Lincoln), which connects with eastern Caracas. It has been cleaned up in recent years and is now a popular commercial district filled with shops, eateries and a book market – a great place to observe everyday Caraqueño life.

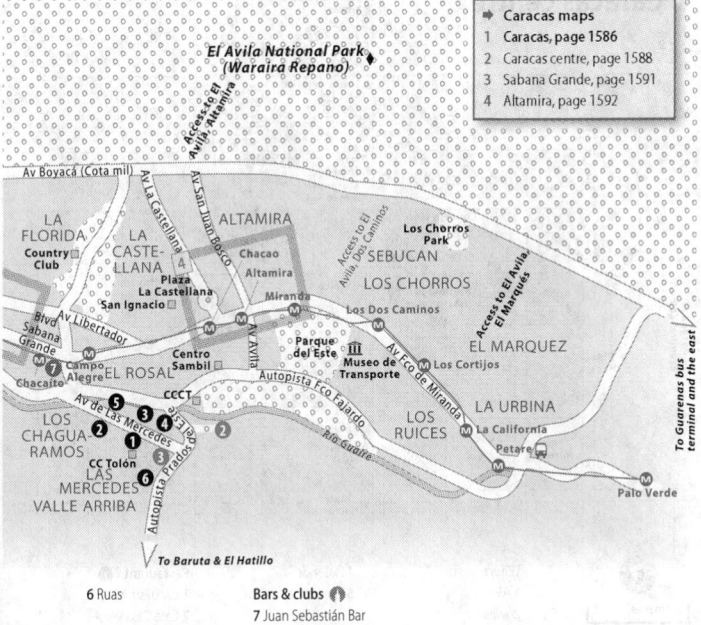

➡ Caracas maps
1 Caracas, page 1586
2 Caracas centre, page 1588
3 Sabana Grande, page 1591
4 Altamira, page 1592

6 Ruas

Bars & clubs 🍸
7 Juan Sebastián Bar

Eastern Caracas

The safest and most fashionable area of the city lies to the east of Sabana Grande in an area known as the 'golden belt of Caracas'. It includes Country Club, Las Mercedes, Valle Arriba, Chacao, La Castellana, Altamira, Los Palos Grandes and Sebucán, and it has the best hotels and residential districts. **Plaza Alfredo Sadel** is an open space where public events take place all year round. It's on Avenida Principal of Las Mercedes, an old residential neighbourhood that has been transformed into an exclusive commercial zone.

Plaza Bolívar de Chacao ① *Av Mohedano, entre Ribas y Páez*, marks the spot where the town of Chacao was born, in the grounds of the Hacienda San Diego. Opposite is Iglesia San José, its patron saint. It's a popular meeting place and a stage for art exhibitions and folklore shows. **Plaza Francia** ① *Av Francisco de Miranda, entre Av Luis Roche y Av San Juan Bosco, Altamira*, commonly called Plaza Altamira, is a well-known landmark with an obelisk, a fountain and a Metro station. **La Estancia** ① *Av Santa Ana, just along from the Altamira metro exit, www.pdvsalaestancia.com, Mon-Sat 0900-1630*, is a cultural centre with good exhibitions, regular activities and events including free yoga and music. It is set in a lovely park with beautiful trees and manicured lawns, the perfect place to escape from the hectic city. **Plaza Los Palos Grandes** ① *3a Av entre 2a y 3a Transversal, Los Palos Grandes*, at the heart of the fashionable neighbourhood of the same name, has a library, a coffee shop and mural. It is a good place to start a tour of the area and has an open market on Saturdays.

Parque Nacional del Este (officially Parque Francisco de Miranda) ① *Mon 0500-0900, Tue-Sun, 0500-1700, Miranda metro station*, is the largest park in Caracas and a popular place to relax, especially at weekends. It has a boating lake, cactus garden, tropical birds, some caged animals and reptiles as well as the **Humboldt Planetarium** ① *T0212-234 9188*. **Museo de Transporte** ① *Parque Nacional del Este (to which it is connected by a pedestrian overpass), T0212-234 2234, www.automotriz. net/museo-del-transporte, Sun 0900-1700*, has a large collection of vintage locomotives, aeroplanes, cars and carriages.

2 Caracas centre

Where to stay 🛏
1 Alex
2 Avila
3 Dal Bo Hostel
4 El Conde
5 Limón

Restaurants 🍴
1 Bar Basque
2 Café Casa Veroes
4 La Cita

West of the centre

The refurbished **Parque Ezequiel Zamora/El Calvario**, west of El Silencio, with the Arch of Confederation at the entrance, has a good view of Centro Simón Bolívar. It has a small Museo Ornitológico, botanical gardens and a picturesque chapel. Near here is the Cuartel 4 de Febrero (4-F), the barracks in 23 de Enero district, also known as the Cuartel de la Montaña. It is now home to the **Museo de la Revolución Bolivariana** ① *T0212-672 1719, Tue-Sun 0900-1600 (there is a special Metro Bus route from Metro El Silencio, or take a taxi, sketchy neighbourhood)*, the final resting place of the body of President Hugo Chávez, who died in March 2013. His body is entombed within a sombre, temperature-controlled marble sarcophagus. The Bulevar de la Dignidad connects the site of the museum with the Plaza 4 de Febrero.

Other parks and urban excursions

At the foot of the Avila mountain, the **Parque Los Chorros** ① *Tue-Sun 0830-1730, take bus from Los Dos Caminos station to Lomas de Los Chorros*, has impressive waterfalls and forest walks.

Paseo Los Próceres ① *Metro Los Símbolos*, not far from the Escuela Militar, is a monument to the Venezuelan Independence heroes and is popular with walkers, runners and cyclists. The densely wooded **Parque Caricuao** ① *Tue-Sun 0900-1630; take metro to Caricuao Zoológico, then 5-min walk up Av Principal La Hacienda*, is at the southwest end of the Metro line, and part of Parque Nacional Macuro. It makes a pleasant day out.

El Hatillo ① *take a bus or taxi from central Caracas, about 20-30 mins' drive, depending on traffic*, once a separate village now subsumed by the city sprawl, is one of the few places in Caracas that has retained its colonial architecture. Built around a central plaza, its peaceful streets of multi-coloured houses offer a fine selection of cafés, restaurants, shops and small galleries. It is a wonderful spot to escape from the city and to shop for handicrafts, but it's busy at weekends. It holds an annual international music festival, usually in October-November, but dates vary.

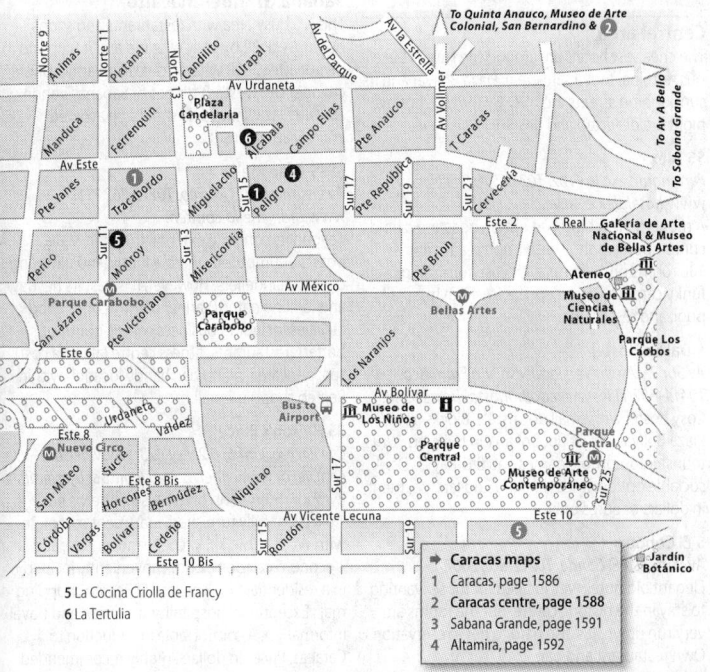

5 La Cocina Criolla de Francy
6 La Tertulia

Tourist information

The main tourist office is **Corpoturismo** (Parque Central, Torre Oeste, p 35, 36 y 37, T0212-576 5696). Online local guides in Spanish include http://laguiadecaracas.net and www. ciudadccs.info. Information can also be found on the Alcaldía's website, www.caracas.gob.ve.

Where to stay

The cheapest hotels are in the downtown area, but this is not a safe part of town at night, or even in the day with a backpack. Sabana Grande, which has a wide range of hotels, is not safe after 2000. If you don't want to stay in the suburbs or centre, spend a little more and go to the upmarket Chacao, Altamira, La Castellana districts (all easily reached by metro), where it is relatively safe to stroll around during the day. There are hotels on the coast, close to the airport, if you do not want to go into the city. If you book from abroad, make sure you receive written confirmation before beginning your journey.

Central area

The cheapest hotels are around the Nuevo Circo bus terminal (not a safe area). Plaza Bolívar and its surrounding streets are busy by the day, but by night are deserted and unsafe.

$$ Alex
Ferrenquín esq la Cruz, T0212-578 0437, www.hotelalex.com.ve.
A modern, new high-rise option boasting a bold contemporary lobby with tropical aquariums, 100 rooms on 14 floors with crisp furnishings and funky carpets, flatscreen TVs, Wi-Fi, gym, small pool, and restaurant.

$ Dal Bo Hostel
Av Sur 2 y Av Universidad, esq San Francisco, T0414-652 1136, www.dalbohostal.hostel.com.
Cosy hostel with small dorms, 1½ blocks from Plaza Bolívar, on 1st floor of an old building. Wi-Fi, tourist info, console games and Blu-Ray DVDs. A sociable option. Prices are in US dollars, payment in dollars or euros only.

$ El Conde
Av Sur 4 esq El Conde, T0212-862 2007.
Elegant old hotel, well located for those wanting to stay in the historic centre, but the rooms are very run down. It's also hard to get a reservation. Own restaurant and bar.

$ Limón
Av Lecuna, Frente Parque Central, T0212-571 6457/576 7822, Bellas Artes metro.
Red-brick building with a restaurant attached. Safe, parking, well located for museums and galleries.

San Bernardino

This residential area is 2 km north of Bellas Artes metro.

$$$ Avila
Av Jorge Washington, T0212-555 3000, www.hotelavila.com.ve.
Founded by Nelson Rockerfeller in 1942, now a bit past its heyday but a pleasant and tranquil retreat set in lush tropical gardens. Most staff speak English and German, there are fans, mosquito screens, pool, Metrobus nearby, a good restaurant and poolside bar, and travel agency. A 20-min drive from the centre, handy for close access to Avila National Park.

Sabana Grande/Chacaíto

This is a busy area with restaurants and shops, but most close by early evening and it is unsafe to be out after 2000 when crowds and atmosphere change. The western fringes of Sabana Grande around Plaza Venezuela should be avoided entirely after sunset.

$$$$ Gran Meliá
Av Casanova y El Recreo, T0212-762 8111, www.gran-melia.com/en.
Beyond its concrete exterior, the Gran Meliá boasts a sumptuous marble lobby, and glittering crystal chandeliers. However, it is past its heyday, and looking dated. Variety of rooms and good facilities including business centre, gourmet buffets, restaurants, fitness centre (at extra cost), spa, pool area, piano bar; handy location within Recreo shopping mall.

$$ Nelson's Place
C El Recreo, Edif 6, p 2, Apt 623, www.nelson. com.ve, or www.agelvis.com (contact by email).
By prior reservation only, Nelson Agelvis has 1 excellent fully furnished apartment complete with Wi-Fi, cable TV, kitchen, and lounge, and 1 economical room, both conveniently located in a residential block next to El Recreo shopping mall. Exceptional hospitality, attention and travel information. A comfortable introduction to Caracas. Prices in dollars. Highly recommended.

$$ Plaza Palace

Av Los Mangos, Las Delicias, T0212-762 4821,
plaza_palace_hotel@hotmail.com.
A secure building located on a quiet residential
street. Amenities include parking and business
facilities. Helpful, English spoken.

Chuao/Las Mercedes

An upmarket commercial district southeast
of the centre and Sabana Grande, no
metro station.

$$$$ Eurobuilding Hotel & Suites

C La Guarita, Chuao, T0212-902 1111,
www.hoteleuro.com.
A modern 5-star hotel that's part of an
international chain. It has a well-furnished
all-suite wing, large pool, gym, spa, barber,
restaurants, weekend rates.

$$$$-$$$ Hotel Paseo Las Mercedes

CC Paseo Las Mercedes, Las Mercedes,
T0212-993 1244, www.hotelpaseolas
mercedes.com.ve.
Located in the shopping mall with fine
restaurants and bars on the doorstep.
Comfortable, spacious rooms with good service.

Chacao, Altamira, La Castellana

These 3 districts, east of Gran Sabana and the
centre, are adjacent to each other, and are a
respectable commercial and residential zone.

$$$$ Renaissance

Av Eugenio Mendoza con C Urdaneta,
La Castellana, T0212-578 3922,
www.marriott.com/ccsbr.
A well-located hotel with bright contemporary
decor, tasteful and well-equipped rooms, Asian
restaurant, lounge bar, pool and gym. Good reports.

$$$$-$$$ Caracas Palace

Av Luis Roche con Av Francisco Miranda, Altamira,
T0212-771 1000, www.caracaspalace.com.
A popular luxury hotel well-located at the heart
of Chacao on the Plaza Francia. It boasts a crisp
white marble lobby and sweeping staircase,
2 restaurants, pool, spa, gym and business centre.

$$$$-$$$ Hotel Chacao and Suites

Av Francisco de Miranda y Av José Félix Sosa,
T0212-956 6900, www.hotelchacaosuites.com.
A smart luxury option with modern, stylish,
minimalist decor, spacious carpeted rooms and
well-equipped suites to suit executive travellers.
Amenities include Wi-Fi and restaurant.

3 Sabana Grande

➡ **Caracas maps**
1 Caracas, page 1586
2 Caracas centre, page 1588
3 Sabana Grande, page 1591
4 Altamira, page 1592

Where to stay
1 Gran Meliá
2 Nelson's Place
3 Plaza Palace

Restaurants
1 Da Guido
2 Jaime Vivas
3 La Huerta

$$$$-$$$ Pestana Caracas
1 Av Urb Santa Eduvigis, T0212-208 1900,
www.pestana.com.
Luxury hotel near Miranda metro station and
Parque del Este, business-oriented with all facilities,
fitness centre, pool, restaurant and penthouse bar.

$$$$-$$$ The VIP
3 Transversal con Av San Juan Bosco, Altamira,
T0212-319 4300, www.thevipcaracas.com.
Young, stylish boutique hotel with good sized,
crisply attired rooms, some with balconies,
as well as a fine gourmet restaurant and slick
lounge bar.

$ La Floresta
Av Avila Sur, T0212-263 1955/2253.
Simple, reasonable, generic rooms with cable
TV, hot water and Wi-Fi. A bit dated and the
remodeled rooms are better; some have a nice
view over the park. Good location near Altamira
metro and Plaza Francia. Parking.

$ Residencia Montserrat
Av Avila Sur, T0212-263 3533.
A good 3-star option with a range of reasonable
rooms and apartments, but a little run down.
Near Plaza Francia and Altamira metro. Pleasant,
clean, helpful, parking. Wi-Fi in lobby.

4 Altamira

➡ **Caracas maps**

N
100 metres
100 yards

Where to stay 🛏	Restaurants 🍴	9 El Alazán
3 Caracas Palace	1 Aprile	10 El Presidente
4 Chacao & Suites	2 Arepa Factory	11 Lee Hamilton
5 La Floresta	3 Avila Burger	12 Miga's
6 Pestana Caracas	4 Café Arabica	
7 Renaissance &	5 Catar	**Bars & clubs** 🍸
Restaurant La Estancia	6 Chez Wong	13 360º
8 Residencia Montserrat	7 Chirú	
9 The VIP	8 Come a Casa	

Near airport

See Litoral Central, page 1600.

Restaurants

Thanks to the creative input of generations of immigrants, Caracas' restaurant scene is extensive and diverse. There are more decent establishments than can be listed here, but an excellent online guide in Spanish is www.miropopic.com.

Central area

There are lots of classic Spanish haunts in the downtown area, full of atmosphere and history. You should use taxis at night as it is unsafe. Call ahead for reservations.

$$ Bar Basque
Alcabala a Peligro, La Candelaria, T0212-572 4857.
Intimate and well-established, this is a renowned family-run Caracas favourite that has been serving fine home-cooked Basque cuisine for 3 generations. Just a handful of tables and an excellent menu of fresh seafood, poultry and meat dishes. One of the best.

$$ Café Casa Veroes
Veroes a Jesuítas, T0212-564 7457.
Mon-Fri 0900-1600.
Sophisticated traditional Venezuelan food in a colonial house built in 1759 (www.casadela historiadevenezuela.com). A bastion of elegance in an otherwise shabby neighbourhood. Great ambiance and a changing menu.

$$ La Cita
Esq de Alcabala, La Candelaria, T0212-573 8819.
Serving traditional Spanish food for nearly 60 years, including seafood, fish stews and paella. Bustling, festive and packed at lunchtime. Book ahead.

$$ La Cocina Criolla de Francy
Av Este 2 y Sur 11, La Candelaria, T0212-576 9849.
Open 0900-1800, closed Sun.
Founded by Francy Moncada, his kitchen serves wholesome Venezuelan *criolla* cuisine, including rabbit, lamb, and *arepitas*. A good place to sample local flavours.

$$ La Tertulia
Alcabala a Urapal, La Candelaria, T0212-574 1476.
Family-run tapas restaurant with an extensive menu and daily specials. Famous for its lamb chops, octopus, tapas and Spanish-style fresh fish. Busy at noon.

Sabana Grande

This area has some cafés, bars (*tascas*) and restaurants. Places on the Sabana Grande Boulevard are good for people watching. There is also an array of fast-food joints in CC El Recreo (Av Casanova con Calle El Recreo, Sabana Grande, http://elrecreocc.com), most of them on the 6th floor.

$$ Da Guido
Av Fco Solano, T0212-763 0937.
A long-running Italian restaurant and Sabana Grande institution, as reliable as it was 50 years ago. It has a small menu of hearty home-cooked fare, simple, fresh, and authentic, the way good Italian food should be. Has a 2nd branch at 6 Av con 5 Transversal, Altamira, T0212-266 9927, equally popular.

$$ La Huerta
Av Fco Solano con 1ra Av de Las Delicias, T0212-762 5228.
Spanish *tasca* with a dash of Venezuelan, including tapas, seafood paella, rabbit, goat, and lamb. Popular with locals watching Spanish football. A good stock of wine.

$ Jaime Vivas
C San Antonio, T0212-763 4761.
The place for hearty local Caracas food, especially *pabellón*. Simple, no frills, and a bit dated, but maintains loyal clientele.

Chuao/Las Mercedes

The area has a good selection of upmarket restaurants and US-style steakhouses and chains.

$$$ Ruas
C Orinoco, Quinta Cujisal, Las Mercedes, T0212-992 1104/6904.
Busy Spanish restaurant specializing in fish and seafood, with paellas and other risottos, live music upstairs Thu and Sat, pricey but well-rated.

$$ Coco Thai and Lounge
CC Tolón, piso 3, Las Mercedes, T0212-300 8573, www.cocothai.com.ve.
Excellent Thai, Vietnamese, and Japanese cuisine, including tasty chicken in coconut curry, duck spring rolls and sashimi. Excellent presentation and flavours, great ambience, open-air terrace and striking eastern decor.

$$ La Castañuela
C Trinidad con C París, T0212-993 2205.
Good paella and seafood in generous portions. Popular and festive at weekends with live music and dancing. Attentive service.

$$ La Montanara
C Caroní con Madrid, Las Mercedes,
T0212-991 2812.
An authentic Italian trattoria (some say the best in
the city) and one of the most popular restaurants
in the district. Great atmosphere, often buzzing
and full with diners, so be prepared to wait.

$$ Mokambo
C Madrid con Monterrey, Las Mercedes,
T0212-991 2577.
A pleasant brunch, lunch and dinner spot
frequented by well-to-do crowds. They serve
creative Mediterranean cuisine, small menu
but with high-quality ingredients.

Cafés and bakeries

Café Olé
C California con C Jalisco, Las Mercedes,
T0212-993 9059
Tasty pastries and creative snacks at the best
branch of this local café chain, particularly
recommended for breakfast.

Franca
Av Principal de Las Mercedes, Qta Franca, T0212-
991 8376, https://franca.com.ve. Mon-Fri 0700-
2000, Sat 0800-2000, Sun 0800-1900).
Popular upscale café famous for its brownies
made with locally-sourced chocolate, also
delicious pastries, burgers and snacks. Other
branches in Los Naranjos and Palos Grandes.

St Honoré
Prol Av José M aría Vargas, Valle Arriba
(south of Las Mercedes), T0212-976 4550,
www.sthonore.com.ve.
Popular café and French-style patisserie, good
for lunch. Some of the best bread in town, often
recommended. Also runs coffee barista courses.

Altamira, La Castellana

$$$ Aprile
4 Av con 5 Transversal, Altamira, T0212-264 5775.
Upscale and fashionable Italian restaurant serving
ceviche, pastas, steak and fries. Smart interior,
cosmopolitan vibe. Reservations a must.

$$$ La Estancia
Av Principal, La Castellana, T0212-261 1874,
Facebook: restLaEstancia.
This Argentine ranch-style, long-standing
Caraqueño establishment has been serving
up great slabs of succulent steak for over
50 years, popular with business folk from
nearby **Renaissance Hotel**.

$$$ Lee Hamilton
Av San Felipe, La Castellana, T0212-261 0511.
Superb meat, served with old-fashioned charm
and elegance, often rated as the best steakhouse
in the city. Live music several times a week and a
buzzing bar.

$$ Chez Wong
Edif IASA, Plaza La Castellana, T0212-266 5015,
www.chezwong.com.ve.
Family run for two generations, Chez Wong
serves creative but simple and tasty Chinese
food, including good dimsum and Peking duck.
Minimalist decor.

$$ El Alazán
Av Luis Roche, entre 5 y 6 Transversal, Altamira,
T0212-285 0275.
Carnivores should not miss this place, one of the
best places in Caracas to enjoy a slab of prime
beef. Big, noisy, popular and an institution for
3 decades. Good wines.

Los Palos Grandes

$$ Avila Burger
6 Transversal entre 3 y 4, Cuadra Gastronómica,
T0212-285 6640.
Buzzing gourmet burger joint with an enticing
array of hearty options. Fun and casual. Also has
a branch in the Centro Comercial El Hatillo, p 5,
T0212-211 5498.

$$ Catar
Cuadra Gastronómica, 6 Transversal,
T0212-285 0649.
Relaxed, stylish café/restaurant with an eclectic
menu. Try the delicious thin crust pizzas and a
melt-in-the-mouth chocolate pudding. Good
selection for vegetarians. Several other good
restaurants in this gastronomic block.

$$ Chirú
2 Av entre 4 y 5 Transversal, CC Las Cúpulas,
T0212-285 1960.
Modern fusion of Peruvian-Asian gourmet cuisine,
signature dishes include squid risotto, ceviche
and tacutacu, Peruvian-style beans and rice.

$$ Come a Casa
1 Av con 1 Transversal, T0212-283 1707.
Low-key Sicilian-style trattoria serving
wholesome home-cooked pasta. Cosy
atmosphere and outdoor terrace.

$ Arepa Factory
2 Transversal entre Av Andrés Bello y 2 Av,
T0212-285 1125.

Don't be put off by the name, this fast-food joint serves Venezuelan gourmet *arepas* with sophisticated fillings; can get packed so don't expect snappy service.

$ El Presidente
3 Av entre 1 y 2 Transversal, T0212-286 3932. Closed Sun.
An unpretentious local institution serving wholesome home-cooked fare. Ideal for a quick lunch.

Cafés and bakeries

Café Arabica
Av Andrés Bello con 1 Transversal, T0212-286 3636
Good Venezuelan coffee, sourced from organic coffee cooperatives around the country, with great pastries, the best *empanadas* in the city. Small and cosy.

Miga's
Av Luis Roche con 1 Transversal, opposite Altamira Suites Hotel, www.migascafe.com.
Busy café/bakery/deli chain with a dozen or so outlets selling fresh breads, cakes, salads, sandwiches and meat dishes, some vegetarian options, open late. Good reliable quality, with extensive menu.

Caracas has a vibrant nightlife, though things are quieter now because of the recent economic problems and power cuts. Clubs don't usually come to life until after 2300, and then go on to the early hours. Las Mercedes district is full of busy, trendy bars. Always take care when leaving in the small hours.

Bars

360°
19th floor of Altamira Suites Hotel, 1 Av con 1 Transversal, Los Palos Grandes, T0212-284 1874.
Hip, sophisticated rooftop wine bar with panoramic views of the city, snack on pizza or sushi and sip delicious cocktails. A must just for the views.

Centro Comercial San Ignacio
See Shopping.
Has many fashionable, though pricey bars and the occasional nightclub, popular with wealthy young Venezuelans. Nivel Blandín has several, including **Samoa**, **Montaitos**, **Pisko Bar** and **Suka**, with giant hammock and good cocktails.

Clubs

Juan Sebastián Bar
Av Venezuela entre C Sorocaima y C Mohedano, El Rosal, T0212-951 0595. Facebook: JSebastianBar. Closed Sun and Mon.
Caracas' temple of jazz and salsa, live music.

Moulin Rouge
Av Fco Solano, Sabana Grande, T0212-761 1990.
Club famous for its live rock music and 2 dancefloors, one with DJs playing electronica.

For details of cinemas and other events, see the newspapers, *El Universal* (www.eluniversal.com) and *El Nacional* (www.el-nacional.com).

Ateneo de Caracas, *Av La Salle, Quinta La Colina, Colinas de Los Caobos, T0212-793 7015, https://ateneodecaracas.wordpress.com.* Concerts, ballet, theatre and film festivals.
Centro de Acción Social para la Música, *Blvd Amador Bendayán de Quebrada Honda, Los Caobos (metro Colegio de Ingenieros), T0212-508 0211.* Concert hall built for the Youth and Children's Orchestras of Venezuela. See the web page of *El Sistema* (FundaMusical Bolívar) for forthcoming concerts and events: http://fundamusical.org.ve.
Centro de Estudios Latinoamericanos Rómulo Gallegos (CELARG), *Av Luis Roche con 3ra Transversal, Altamira, T0212-285 2721, www.celarg.org.ve.* Cultural centre with cinema showing alternative and classic films, theatre, exhibitions, talks.
Trasnocho Cultural, *Urb Las Mercedes, Centro Comercial Paseo Las Mercedes, Nivel Trasnocho, T0212-993 1910, www.trasnochocultural.com.* Theatre, cinemas, exhibitions, lounge bar, bookshop, café and yoga centre.

Chocolate
Blue Moon, *Local 20 Calle Bolívar, El Hatillo, T0212-963 3023, www.bluemoonchocolates.com.* Divine chocolatier with small café selling hot chocolate mixes.
Kakao, *Centro Comercial Paseo Las Mercedes, T0212-993 5583, kakaovenezuela.com.* Currently the most popular chocolate maker in the city. Has various branches but this is probably the best, hand-crafted chocolates, teas, cakes and hot chocolate. Supporter of the **Bean-to-Bar** cacao origin movement.
La Praline Chocolatier, *Av Andrés Bello con 3ra Transversal, Los Palos Grandes, T0212-284 7986, www.lapraline.com.ve.* Ultimate heaven for

chocaholics, delicious chocolates crafted from Venezuelan cacao. The packets of hot chocolate make great gifts. Another branch at CC Galerías Los Naranjos in El Hatillo and in Caracas airport.

Handicrafts

Hannsi, *C Bolívar, El Hatillo, T0212-963 5577, http://hannsi.com.ve/web/*. A superstore of Venezuelan crafts and products made up of numerous small rooms.

Malls

For many Caraqueños, malls are not just popular for the shops, but have replaced plazas as more pleasant places to socialize in comfort and safety. There are plenty all over the city, such as **Centro Sambil** (Av Libertador, 1 block south of Chacao Metro), one of the largest in South America; **CC Galerías Sebucan** (Av Los Chorros, Los Dos Caminos, Los Anaucos), small but in a quiet and good neighbourhood; **CC Tolon** and **Paseo Las Mercedes** (both on Av Principal de Las Mercedes), and the exclusive **San Ignacio** (several blocks north of Chacao Metro).

Markets

Mercado de Chacao, *Av Avila, 3 blocks north of Chacao metro. Wed-Fri and Sun 0530-1430, Sat 0530-1600*. Good food, fruit and veg market.
Mercado Peruano, *Colegio de Ingenieros metro, Blvd Amador Bendayán. Daily 1000-1500*. Popular small Peruvian food market with ceviche stalls (go early to be sure of its freshness).
Mercado Quinta Crespo, *off Av Baralt, El Silencio metro. Daily, except Mon, 0600-1300*. One of the largest central food markets, shabby but vibrant.

What to do

Baseball

The popular baseball season is from late Sep to Jan. The capital's local team, Los Leones del Caracas, plays at the Estadio Universitario, Los Chaguaramos. Tickets can be bought at the stadium's box office, T0500-226 7366, www.leones.com.

Tour operators

Akanan, *C Bolívar, Edf Grano de Oro, pb loc C, Chacao, T0212-264 2769, www.akanan.com*. Excellent and professionally managed eco-tour operator with an emphasis on nature and adventure with riding, cycling, climbing, rafting, hiking and other outdoor activities outside Caracas. Small groups, personalized service and years of experience working with documentary film crews. Recommended.

Alborada Venezuela, *Plaza La Castellana, Torre IASA, oficina 101, T0212-263 1820, www.alboradavenezuela.com*. Tours focusing on nature conservation, also specialist interest, adventure trips and tours beyond Venezuela.
Alpiviajes, *Av Sucre, Centro Parque Boyacá, Torre Centro, of 11, Los Dos Caminos, T0212-285 0410, www.alpiviajes.com*. Tours throughout Venezuela, including fishing trips and adventure sports, English spoken, good for flights and advice. Flying safari tours in private plane. Recommended.
Ascanio Birding Tours, *Apartado Postal 78006, La Urbina 1074 Caracas, T0212-242 4949, www.abtbirds.com*. Specialists in birdwatching tours in Venezuela and neighbouring countries and the Caribbean.
Candes Turismo, *Av Francisco de Miranda, Edif Roraima, p 3, of 3C, T0212-953 1632, www.candesturismo.com*. Well-established tour operator, range of destinations, helpful, efficient, English, Italian, German spoken.
Cóndor Verde, *Av Caura, Torre Humboldt, M 3, Prados del Este, T0212-655 0101, www.condorverdetravel.com*. Operate throughout the country, well-established, German run.
Kayaman, *T0414-124 2725, www.kayaman.com*. Dedicated to kayaking, courses and construction. See related company, **Rafting Barinas**, page 1635.
Natoura Travel & Adventure Tours, *T0274-252 4216 (in US T303-800 4639; in Germany T05906-303364), www.natoura.com*. Tailor-made tours throughout Venezuela. Specialists in adventure tours and ecotourism. See also page 1625.
Osprey Travel, *Av Casanova, Sabana Grande, 2 Av de Bello Monte, Edif La Paz, p 5, of 51, T0414-310 4491, www.ospreyexpeditions.com*. Tours in Venezuela (also Colombia and Panama), diving, language courses, advice from English speaking staff. Office opens by appointment. Recommended.
Tucaya, *Quinta Santa Marta, 1 Av Urbanización Campo Claro, Los Dos Caminos, T0212-234 9401, www.tucaya.com*. Small company with good reputation, popular with French speakers, wide range of tours, from ecotourism to diving, also cover Colombia, Costa Rica and Panama.
Venezuela X, *T0212-234 4106, www.venezuelax.com*. Adventure tours of all types, on land, water and in the air, for all levels. Have a base camp south of Barinas for rafting, trekking and mountain biking trips, T0273-400 3625.

Transport

Air

The **airport** for international and domestic flights, Maiquetía, www.aeropuerto-maiquetia.com.ve, is 28 km from Caracas near the port of La Guaira, and has 2 terminals: Maiquetía (national) and Simón Bolívar (international), 5 mins apart via an a/c walkway from international to national, but an open-air sidewalk from national to international (less secure after dark). International passengers must check in at least 3 hrs before departure or they may lose their seat. National flights need 2 hrs check in. Always allow plenty of time to get to the airport as the route can be very congested (minimum 30 mins, up to 2-3 hrs in heavy traffic). It is unsafe to travel between Maiquetía and the city in the hours of darkness, so for evening or pre-dawn flights, it is recommended you stay in one of the hotels near the airport (see Litoral Central listings, below).

Taxis are the safest form of transport to and from the airport. It is best not to arrive at the airport without having pre-arranged a pick up. There have been incidents of foreigners getting taken in what seem to be marked taxis, only to be driven off, robbed and left in the middle of nowhere. If the hotel does not have its own taxis, ask them to contact a driver. On no account go with one of the freelance or unlicensed drivers who crowd the terminal. Official taxis are all black with a yellow logo and from 4 companies: **Astrala**, **Taxi Tours**, **Taxib** and **Utac**. You buy tickets from official counters and will be accompanied to the taxi by a member of staff. Double check the driver's ID. The fare varies depending on time of day and district (see www.aeropuerto-maiquetia.com.ve). There is also the private firm, **Taxi to Caracas**, www.taxitocaracas.com, US$40 one way for 1-3 people, book in advance, also books accommodation, bus tickets and flights.

Airport **shuttle buses** are run by Sitssa, T0212-242 0110/0800-7487720, www.sitssa.gob.ve, from national terminal, level 2, to the Alba Caracas Hotel, 0600-1900, BsF 200 (US$0.30), 2 blocks from Bellas Artes metro. Also **UCAMC**, from the national terminal exit. If heading for a hotel in Chacao or Altamira on arrival, get off at Gato Negro metro station (same fare) and take metro from there (with luggage only at off-peak times). To get to the airport, catch the shuttle buses under the flyover at Bolívar and Av Sur 17, Parque Central, 250 m from Bellas Artes metro (poorly lit at night, not safe to wait here in the dark), or at metro stations such as Parque Central and Gato Negro. (Watch your

Tip...
In both terminals, many people offer to change money on the black market. There is no way of knowing if they are trustworthy.

belongings around Gato Negro.) The service runs 0500-2200, every 30 mins, 1-2 hrs, depending on traffic. An alternative is to take a Sitssa bus from El Silencio to Catia La Mar (BsF 65) and get out at the airport. Taxis are the safest option.

Bus

Local TransMetrópoli buses (www.transmetropoli.com.ve) run on 24 routes mostly from El Silencio or Chacaíto to the suburbs, 0500-2100; they have wheelchair access. Also being introduced is a mass transport system, **BusCaracas**, using magnetic cards, single journey BsF4, 0600-2000. Regular buses are overcrowded in rush hour and charge extra after 2100. *Por puesto* minibuses, known as *busetas, carmelitas* or *carritos* run on regular routes; fares are about BsF 20-50, but depend on the distance travelled within the city.

Long distance Always take identification when booking a long-distance journey. Times and fares of buses are given under destinations.

The Terminal Oriente at Guarenas for eastern destinations is clean, modern and relatively safe. It can be reached by numerous buses from the city centre and Petare. Take a taxi at night.

The La Bandera terminal for all western destinations is a 500 m, unsafe walk from La Bandera metro station on Line 3. City buses that pass are prominently marked 'La Bandera'. Give yourself plenty of time to find the bus you need although there are bus agents who will assist in finding a ticket for your destination. Tickets are sold in advance except for nearby destinations such as **Maracay** and **Valencia**. Those first on get the best seats so it is advisable to arrive an hour before departure. There is a left luggage office, cash machines, restaurant and many food and drink kiosks.

The more upscale **Aeroexpresos Ejecutivos**, Av Principal De Bello Campo, Quinta Marluz, Bello Campo, Chacao, T0212-266 2321, www.aeroexpresos.com.ve (timetables and prices available online), a private bus company, runs regular services to **Barquisimeto**, **Maracaibo**, **Maracay**, **Maturín** and **Valencia**. Prices are more expensive than others, but worth it for the more comfortable and modern buses and for the extra security. **Sitssa**, see above, also runs nationwide bus services – see website for prices. Buses to places near Caracas leave from the old Nuevo Circo bus station (eg **Los Teques** – US$0.15, **Higuerote** – US$0.25, **Catia La Mar**, **La Guaira**).

Car
Car hire Self-drive cars are available at both airport terminals (offices daily 0600-2100) and in town. Some major hotels also have counters.

Metro
The metro (www.metrodecaracas.com.ve) operates 0530-2300. No smoking, no heavy luggage. There's a good selection of transport maps at shops in Altamira and La California stations. The lines are: **Line 1** (west–east) from Propatria to Palo Verde; **Line 2** (north–south), from El Silencio to Las Adjuntas, with connection to Caricuaoand Zoológico and a continuation from Las Adjuntas to Los Teques (Alí Primera); **Line 3**, south from Plaza Venezuela via El Valle to La Rinconada; **Line 4**, extending Line 2 west–east from Capuchinos to Plaza Venezuela/Zona Rental. **Line 5**, running east through Las Mercedes to Warairarepano, is being built (the first stage, to Bello Monte, opened in Nov 2015, with more stations to follow). A railway will continue east from Warairarepano to Guarenas and Guatire. **Line 6**, from Zoológico to La Rinconada is planned. **Line 7** is a bus route from Las Flores via La Hoyada and La Bandera to Los Ilustres.

A single ticket costs BsF4, BsF8 return, whereas a 10-journey (*multi abono*) ticket is BsF36.

Student discounts are available with ISIC card; apply at Parque del Este station. There are also *Metrotarjetas* (pre-paid cards) for 20, 30 and 40 trips. Metrobuses connect with the Metro system: get transfer tickets (*boleto integrado*, BsF6) for services to southern districts, route maps displayed at stations; retain ticket after exit turnstile. Metrobuses are modern, comfortable, recommended but infrequent. Metrocable systems run from Parque Central (Line 4) to San Agustín barrio, from Petare to La Cruz del Morro and from Palo Verde to Mariche and to La Dolorita.

> **Tip...**
> Never tell a driver it's your first visit to Caracas.

Taxi
Even though they are a legal requirement, meters are never used. Negotiate fares in advance; always offer 10% less than the driver's 1st quote and bargain hard. Taxi drivers are authorized to charge an extra 20% on night trips after 1800, on Sun and all holidays, and extra for answering telephone calls. After 1800 drivers are selective about destinations. Beware of taxi drivers trying to renegotiate fixed rates because your destination is in 'a difficult area'. See warning about pirate taxis under Air, above. See also under Air (or in Yellow Pages) for radio taxis.

Around Caracas
over Caracas' great national park to the sea

Between the capital and the Caribbean coast is the national park of Waraira Repano, not only a popular recreational area for Caraqueños, but also a refuge for wildlife within earshot of the city and a good place for birdwatching and hiking. The coast itself is also a favourite weekend escape, although it can get busy. Nor, at weekends, can you expect to have Colonia Tovar to yourself, a German immigrant town to which city folk flock for the local produce and mild climate.

Parque Nacional Waraira Repano and Monte Avila *Colour map 1, A6.*
Inparques, Av F de Miranda, Parque Generalísimo Francisco de Miranda (opposite Parking 2), Caracas, T0212-273 2807, https://twitter.com/inparquesgob. Closed Mon and Tue morning.

The 85,192-ha **Parque Nacional Waraira Repano** (formerly **El Avila**) forms the northern boundary of Caracas. The green slopes rise steeply from both the city and from the central Caribbean coast. Despite being so close to the capital, fauna includes red howler monkeys, jaguar and puma. There are also several species of poisonous snake. Access is from Caracas, with several marked entrances along the Cota Mil (Avenida Boyacá), designed for hikers.

A **cable railway**, the **Teleférico Warairarepano**① *Final Av Principal de Maripérez (Simón Rodríguez), T0212-339 4192, eventoswaraira@gmail.com, www.ventel.gob.ve, Tue-Thu 1000-1700, Fri-Sat 0830-2100, Sun 0830-2000, return ticket for foreigners US$14 (price may vary), reductions for Venezuelans, students with card, children 4-12, over 60s and disabled; take a taxi from Colegio de Ingenieros metro station,* runs up to Monte El Avila (2175 m). The 20-minute ride offers fantastic views of Caracas on clear days and is highly recommended. It's a popular spot, with a restaurant, food stalls and skating rink at El Avila station on the summit. From here you can look down the other side of Monte Avila over the village of Galipán all the way to the Caribbean Sea. The **Humboldt Hotel** on the summit is being refurbished.

If you're not taking the cable car, El Avila station can also be reached in 45 minutes by shared 4WD *carritos* that leave regularly from the entrance to the park at San Bernardino (on the edge of sketchy barrios, take care). Alternatively, trucks leave from the Avila hotel, about US$1 per person. A recommended trip is to ride up in a vehicle and hike back down (note that it is cold at the summit, around 13°C, take a sweater).

From El Avila station you can take a 4WD *carrito* to the village of Galipán, www.galipan.net, founded by Spanish immigrants from the Canary Islands and today a popular weekend excursion for *caraqueños*. The village has plenty of good restaurants serving excellent pork sandwiches and rich hot chocolate, as well as stone-built cabins and stalls selling strawberries and cream, jams and flowers. There are *posadas* for overnight stays. Also worth visiting is the old coffee hacienda Los Venados ① *Senderos Aéreos, T0424-200 6169, www.senderosaereos.com, Thu-Sun 1000-1530 (Sat-Sun only in low season)*, where there are picnic areas and a **zip-wire** (known as 'canopy').

Hiking in the national park
Hikers should go in groups of at least three, for mountain and personal safety. If you want to camp, inform any Puesto de Guardaparques of your route, where you intend to stay and get their permission; also leave a mobile phone number with them. Always take water and something for the cold at altitude. The unfit should not attempt any of the hikes.

Pico Naiguatá (2765 m) This is a very strenuous hike. Take the metro to La California, then a bus going up Avenida Sanz, ask for the Centro Comercial El Marqués. From there walk up Avenida Sanz towards Cota Mil (Avenida Boyacá), about four blocks. At the end of Avenida Sanz, underneath the bridge, is the entrance to the Naiguatá trail. In about 40 minutes you reach La Julia *guardaparques* station.

Pico Oriental (2600 m) From the Altamira metro station take a bus to 'La entrada de Sabas Nieves', where the **Tarzilandia** restaurant is. From here a dirt road leads up to the **Sabas Nieves** *guardaparques* station, a steep 20- to 40-minute hike with good views of the city, popular with keep-fit *caraqueños*. The path to Pico Oriental starts at the back of Sabas Nieves and is extremely easy to follow. **Note** Paths beyond Sabas Nieves are shut in dry season (roughly February-June depending on the year) to prevent forest fires.

Hotel Humboldt (2150 m) This is a relatively easy route of three hours. Take the Metro bus from Bellas Artes station to El Avila stop; opposite is a grocery. Turn the corner and walk two blocks up towards the mountain. At the top of the street turn left; almost immediately on your right is the park entrance. **Note** This area is not safe before 0800 or after dark. Plenty of people take this route, starting 0830-0900, giving enough time to get up and down safely and in comfort.

Litoral Central
The Litoral Central is the name given to the stretch of Caribbean Coast directly north of Caracas. A paved road runs east from Catia La Mar, past the airport and then through the towns of Maiquetía, **La Guaira**, Venezuela's main port, dating back to 1567, and Macuto. This became the state of Vargas in January 1999 and in December that year was the focus of Venezuela's worst natural disaster of the 20th century. Prolonged heavy rains on deforested hillsides caused flash floods and landslides, killing an estimated 30,000 people, many of whose bodies were never recovered, and leaving 400,000 homeless. From La Guaira a panoramic road runs to the beaches at Chichiriviche de la Costa, Puerto Cruz (nice beach, no shade, bars) and Puerto Maya (very nice beach with shade and services).

Colonia Tovar
1½ hrs from Caracas on Ruta 4, www.colonia-tovar.com.

This picturesque mountain town was founded in 1843 by German immigrants from Kaiserstuhl in the Black Forest; a small **museum** ① *Sat, Sun and hols 0800-1800*, tells the history of the founding pioneers. They retained their customs and isolation until a paved road reached the settlement in 1963. It is now very touristy, attracting hordes of weekend visitors, but the blond hair, blue eyes and Schwartzwald-accented German of the inhabitants remain, as do many traditions and dances. Local produce includes breads, blackberry jam, bratwurst and beer. Colonia Tovar offers delightful landscapes, a mild climate, old architecture and dignified hospitality in its many restaurants, cafés and hotels. However, the winding drive up from Caracas on Ruta 4, through La Yaguara, El Junquito and the Parque Nacional Macarao, is murder (up to four hours) at weekends, with long traffic jams, few picnic spots and little accommodation.

Listings Around Caracas

Where to stay

Litoral Central

If you're arriving or leaving the airport at odd times, there are some good choices in Catia La Mar and Macuto as an alternative to Caracas. These places often provide free transfers, or a taxi costs about US$5, 5-20 mins depending on traffic.

$$$$ Olé Caribe
Final Av Intercomunal, El Playón, 1160, Macuto, T0212-620 2000, www.hotelolecaribe.com.
A good, if expensive bet near the airport, safe in room, breakfast, pool, several restaurants and sports facilities.

$$$$-$$$ Express Maiquetía
Av La Armada, T0212-902 2222, www.hoteleuro.com.
Useful business hotel with 224 rooms and suites, with two restaurants, pool, gym, tennis, airport transfer.

$$ Buena Vista Inn
Av el Hotel y C 4, Qta Buenavista Inn, Urb Playa Grande, Catia la Mar, T0212-352 9163, http://buenavistainn.com.ve.
Convenient for airport, pick-up extra, small and homely, with a/c, cable TV and Wi-Fi.

$$ Catimar
Urb Puerto Viejo Av Principal, Catia La Mar, T0212-351 7906, www.hotelcatimar.com.
Price includes transfers to and from airport (you may have to phone them from Asistencia al usuario desk), nice bar, restaurant, basic rooms, reasonable value. Near small Puerto Viejo beach, said to be safe, with a few restaurants, snack bar.

$$ Posada Doña Alcinda
Av Principal La Atlántida C 7, T0212-619 1605, www.posadaalcinda.com.
Small hotel with suites and standard rooms, bar, airport transfer, diving courses and other activities can be arranged.

$$ Posada Il Prezzano
Av Principal de Playa Grande c/c 5, Catia La Mar, T0212-351 2626, www.ilprezzano.com.
Italian-run, spotless, pleasant, good value, restaurant.

$$ Santiago
Av La Playa, Urb Alamo, Macuto, T0212-213 3500, www.hotelsantiagodemacuto.com.
Comfortable, restaurant with live music, pool, secure parking, 15 mins' drive to airport.

Restaurants

Parque Nacional Waraira Repano

$$$ Casa Pakea
Ctra San Antonio de Galipán, Sector Manzanares (a la derecha de la Rosa Mística), T0416-714 4854.
Special transport from **Hotel Avila**, San Bernardino, or from the cable car station in Galipán. Fabulous restaurant in a wonderful location at the top of Monte Avila, small menu, traditional Basque food. Highly recommended.

$$$ Le Galipanier
Galipán, T0414-249 1978.
French onion soups, seafood and Swiss-style fondues. A classy and very romantic setting overlooking the valley.

Transport

Colonia Tovar

Travelling to Colonia Tovar is definitely not recommended at weekends, with huge traffic jams from Caracas, although it is generally easy to get a lift if there are no buses.

Bus Take the metro to **La Yaguara** and from there take a *por puesto* to **El Junquito** (1 hr if no traffic, US$0.50), then change for **Colonia Tovar** (1 hr, US$0.50). Last public transport back to Caracas 1800, later at weekends.

West from
Caracas

The Central Highlands run through this varied region. North of the highlands is the Caribbean, with secluded coves and popular resorts, such as Puerto Colombia. Straddling the mountains is the birders' paradise of Parque Nacional Henri Pittier. Two coastal national parks, Morrocoy, which lies offshore, and Los Médanos, around the old city of Coro, are further highlights of this area. West of Coro is the city and lake of Maracaibo; for most Venezuelans this region is summed up in three letters – oil. For others, it can be summed up in four letters – heat. Both are certainly true. To the south, though, are the eastern extremities of the Andean mountain chain, with quaint villages, lakes and high passes on the way to the Sierra Nevada de Mérida.

Maracay and around

busy city with a national park on its doorstep

Maracay is a hot, thriving industrial city and is the gateway to Henri Pittier National Park. The city has some pleasant leafy residential neighbourhoods and is the centre of an important agricultural area.

Maracay Colour map 1, A6.

In its heyday Maracay was the favourite city of Gen Juan Vicente Gómez (dictator, 1909-1935) and some of his most fantastic whims are still there. **Jardín Las Delicias** ① Av Las Delicias, en route to Choroní; take an Ocumare bus from terminal, with a zoo (closed for renovation at the end of 2016), park and fountain, was built for his revels. The heart of the city is **Plaza Girardot**, on which stands the attractive, white **Cathedral**, dating back almost to the city's foundation in 1701. There is an interesting collection of prehispanic artefacts in the **Museo de Antropología e Historia** ① South side of the plaza, T0243-711 5157, Mon-Sat 0800-1200, 1300-1530, free. The opposite end of the same building has rooms dedicated to Gómez and Bolívar. **Plaza Bolívar**, said to be the largest such-named plaza in Latin America, is 500 m east. The **Museo Aeronáutico de las Fuerzas Aéreas Venezolanas** ① C Junín con Av 19 de Abril, 1 block from Plaza Bolívar, T0243-233 3812, Mon-Thu 0930-1130, 1330-1530, Fri 0830-1100, has an interesting collection of aircraft and memorabilia. The **San José** festival is on 16-25 March.

★Parque Nacional Henri Pittier See map, page 1602.

A land of steep, lush, rugged hills and tumbling mountain streams, the 107,800-ha park rises from sea-level in the north to 2430 m at Pico Cenizo, descending to 450 m towards the Lago de Valencia. Named after Swiss conservationist and engineer Henri Pittier, the park was established in 1937 and is the oldest in the country. Estimates of bird species range from 20 to 50 (about 42% of all species in Venezuela), including seven different eagles and eight kites. The park extends from the north of Maracay to the Caribbean and south to the valleys of Aragua. The dry season is December to March and the rainy season (although still agreeable) is April to November. The variation in altitude produces a great range of vegetation, including impressive lower and upper cloudforests and bamboo.

Best for
Beaches ▪ Birdwatching ▪ Colonial towns

Two paved roads cut through the Park. The Ocumare (western) road climbs to the 1128-m-high Portachuelo pass, guarded by twin peaks (38 km from Maracay). At the pass is Rancho Grande, the uncompleted palace/hotel Gómez was building when he died (in a state of disrepair) and the **Estación Biológica Alberto F Yépez** ① bioestacion@gmail.com. It is close to the bird migratory routes; September and October are the best months. There are many trails in the vicinity. Permits to visit the park, walk the trails or stay at the station are available from the offices at the Facultad de Agronomía, Universidad Central de Venezuela, Maracay campus.

Aragua Coast

To Cata and Cuyagua The road to the coast from Rancho Grande goes through **Ocumare de la Costa** (48 km from Maracay), to **La Boca de Ocumare** and **El Playón** (hotels and restaurants at both places). The road is very busy at weekends. Some 20 minutes west by boat is **La Ciénaga**, a pretty place that has little shade. A few kilometres east is **Bahía de Cata**, now overdeveloped, particularly at the west end. The smaller beach at **Catita** is reached by fishing boat ferries (10 minutes, US$1.50), or a 20-minute walk, tricky over rocks at the start. In Cata town (5 km inland) is the small colonial church of San Francisco; devil dancers here fulfil an ancient vow by dancing non-stop through the morning of 27 July each year. **Cuyagua** beach, unspoilt, is 23 km further on at the end of the road. It has good surfing but dangerous rips for swimmers. There are devil dancers here too, on movable date in July/August.

To Choroní

The second twisty and narrow (eastern) road through the Parque Nacional Henri Pittier is spectacular and goes over a more easterly pass (1830 m), to **Santa Clara de Choroní**, a small colonial town with attractive, pastel single-storey houses. The **Fiesta de San Juan** on 31 May is worth seeing. Choroní is a good base for walking, with many opportunities for exploring the unmarked trails, some originating in picturesque spots such as the river pools (*pozos*) of El Lajao (beware of the dangerous whirlpool) and Los Colores, 6 km above Choroní. Other recommended *pozos* are La Virgen, 10 km from Choroní, and La Nevera, 11 km away.

☆Puerto Colombia and around *Colour map 1, A6.*

Just beyond Choroní is the popular fishing village of **Puerto Colombia**, a laid-back place with several narrow streets lined with colonial buildings. During high season, its small main bay attracts arts and crafts sellers. It is a good place to stay and spend a couple of days beach-hopping with boat rides to different bays. Five minutes' walk across the river lies Puerto Colombia's main attraction, the dazzling long stretch of white beach known as **Playa Grande**, lined with

> **Tip...**
> Take enough cash because there are no ATMs in Choroní or Puerto Colombia and credit cards are accepted in few places. The nearest banks and Italcambio (www.italcambio.com) are in Maracay.

Parque Nacional Henri Pittier

palm trees beneath mountains. There is a row of good fish restaurants at the beach entrance. At weekends drummers drum and dancers gyrate and the beach gets crowded with campers and families. At other times it's more peaceful, with brightly painted fishing boats (available for hire) and frigate birds wheeling overhead. If swimming, beware the strong undertow. There are public showers at the entrance.

A very bumpy, 30-minute boat ride east goes to **Cepe**, another beautiful long beach with good swimming, popular with campers. Boats usually take six to 10 people. From the beach, there is a delightful 25-minute walk to **Pueblo de Cepe** through the Henri Pittier park. Several places on the beach serve fish, salad and *tostones*. Most locals bring their own supplies in the obligatory beer cooler. From the beautiful unspoiled beach there are fishing and scuba diving trips. The latter, with guide and equipment, explore the only bit of coral on this stretch of the coast. At Cepe's west end, you can climb the hill and descend to **Playa Escondida**, a deserted but more rocky beach.

Other beaches include: to the east, before Cepe, **Valle Seco** (some shade, natural pool protected by reef) and **Chuao**. To the west are: **Diario** (small, no shade), **Aroa** (lovely, with river and palms, rough sea but one safe bathing area, no services, take everything with you, three hours' hike from Choroní, go early) and **Uricao** (also isolated).

Listings Maracay and around *map page 1602.*

Tourist information

Tourist information for the state is provided by **Inatur** (Hotel Golf Maracay, Urb Las Delicias, Final Urb Cantarrana, T0243-242 2420 – due to reopen as a Marriott hotel in 2017).

Where to stay

Maracay
Budget hotels are in streets around Plaza Girardot.

$$ Princesa Plaza
Av Miranda Este entre Fuerzas Aéreas y Av Bermúdez, T0243-232 0177, www.hotelprincesaplaza.com.ve.
Large hotel, 1 block east of Plaza Bolívar, convenient, inexpensive restaurant, **Ibiza**, for hotel guests only.

$ Caroní
Ayacucho Norte 197, Bolívar, T0243-554 4465, hotelcaroni@cantv.net.
Hot showers, comfortable, cheap. Recommended.

$ Mar del Plata
Av Santos Michelena 23, T0243-246 4313, mardelplatahotel@gmail.com.
Central, with hot water, excellent.

$ Posada El Limón
C El Piñal 64, El Limón suburb, near Parque Nacional Henri Pittier, T0243-283 4925, www.posadaellimon.com.
Dutch owned, in the grounds of a former mango plantation, some way from centre, relaxed and pleasant, family atmosphere, spacious rooms

(up to 4-5 beds), laundry, pool, good restaurant, parking, trips to Parque with guide.

Aragua Coast
Ocumare de la Costa

$$ De La Costa Eco-Lodge
California 23, T0243-217 7966, www.ecovenezuela.com.
Comfortable, upmarket lodge near beach, with outdoor bar serving food, restaurant, roof terraces with good sea views, pool, landscaped gardens, excursions, equipment hire, specialist bilingual guides.

Most *posadas* are in El Playón; websites like www.turismodeplaya.com give a selection. Expect to pay $$-$. Recommendations change annually.

La Ciénaga

$$$ pp all-inclusive Coral Lagoon Lodge
La Ciénaga, T0243-217 7966, www.ecovenezuela.com.
A dive resort accessible only by boat. Beautiful location on waterfront with view of mountains. 6 rooms in 2 cabins sleeping 2-4 people, fans, solar power with back-up generator, rainwater and seawater used. Hammocks, deckchairs, kayaks and snorkelling. Diving with PADI and SSI instructors to underwater grottos, canyons, reefs and wrecks.

Choroní
See www.choroni.info for listings and locations of many hotels and *posadas*.

$$ Hacienda El Portete
C El Cementerio, T0243-991 1255,
www.elportetechoroni.com.
Restored cocoa plantation, colonial-style large
grounds, pool, restaurant, many children's
facilities, excursions.

$$ Hacienda La Aljorra
1 km south in La Loma, T0243-218 8841,
laaljorra.hacienda@gmail.com,
Facebook:hacienda.choroni
On roadside, out of town, breakfast included,
hot water, 300-year old cacao hacienda in
62 ha of wooded hillside. Large rooms, relaxing
and peaceful. Also offer beach excursions and
mountain hikes

$ Posada Colonial El Picure
C Miranda No 34-A, T0243-991 1296,
www.hosteltrail.com/posadaelpicure.
Colonial house in village centre, backs onto river.
Popular with travellers, welcoming, 5 rooms,
4-6 beds, restaurant with vegetarian options.

Puerto Colombia and around
There are dozens of *posadas* for all budgets
in town, but most are fully booked during
high season when prices rise by around 40%.

Camping is possible on Playa Grande,
no permission needed and there are
showers on the beach; beware of theft.
Crowded during high season.

$$ Hostal Casa Grande 1
Morillo 33, T0243-991 1251,
www.hostalcasagrande.com.ve.
One of the best in town, attractive colonial
decor, pool, gardens, parking, spa at weekends,
games room, private generator. Excellent. Also
has **Casa Grande 2**, same street, equally stylish,
with restaurant.

$$ Posada Pittier
*On road to Choroní, 10-min walk from
Puerto Colombia, T0243-991 1028,*
www.posadapittier.com.
Small, immaculate rooms around central
garden with small pool, $$$ at weekends,
cheaper without breakfast, good meals, helpful,
Recommended.

$$-$ Posada Doña Enriqueta
Color 3, T0243-991 1158, just off the seafront,
www.hosteltrail.com/posadadonaenriqueta.
Basic rooms, but great location very close to
seafront, prices double on Fri and Sat, books
tours, helpful.

$ Costa Brava
C Morillo 9, near Malecón, T0243-991 1057,
suarezjf@cantv.net.
Basic, only 8 rooms, cheaper without bath, fans,
laundry, good food, parking, English spoken,
family-run. Recommended.

$ Hostal Nova Colonial
C Morillo 37, opposite bus stop,T0243-951 5321,
www.jungletrip.de.
Recently renovated merger of former hostals
Colonial and Casa Luna, some rooms with a/c,
lovely pool and mini waterfall, German and
English spoken, tourist information. Ask here
for **Casa Nova** and **Posada Alfonso**, both $$-$,
most rooms with bath, and for Jungle Lodge,
in the rainforest, where you can stay in
hammocks. Tours to Pittier park, diving
trips and airport transfers.

$ Hostal Vista Mar
C Colón at western end, T0243-991 1250,
http://hostalvistamar.net.
On seafront, pleasant, terraces with hammocks,
some rooms with sea view, a/c, helpful,
secure parking.

$ La Posada de Choroní
*C Principal, 2 blocks from Malecón, T0243-
991 1191, http://laposadadechoroni.com.*
Colonial building with rooms off central garden,
a/c, cable TV, hot water and outside showers for
washing off from beach, helpful, safe parking
space for 1 vehicle.

$ Posada Alonso
Near checkpoint, T0416-546 1412,
alons0243@hotmail.com.
Quiet, small hotel, a/c, hammocks, laundry, pool,
trips to nearby beaches. Recommended.

$ Posada Turpial
José Maitin 3, T0243-991 1123,
www.posadaturpial.com.
Colonial house, well-organized, cosy, attractive,
nice atmosphere, good restaurant, rooms around
patio, safety deposit box, German and English
spoken. Book in advance. Owners run travel
agency www.turpialtravel.com and organize local
tours, dive trips, airport transfers. Recommended.

Cepe and Chuao
Several *posadas* in Chuao, but they are some
distance from the beach (those listed are closer).
Camping is permitted on Chuao and Cepe
beaches, though no facilities or security.

$ El Gran Cacao
200 m up the hill from the port at Chuao,
T0243-872 4680.
Comfortable, with a/c or fan, family atmosphere.
Recommended.

$ La Luzonera
On the plaza, T0416-040 5499.
The best of the cheaper options, with a/c,
restaurant (**$$** half board), also has 2 houses
for rent, and camping area.

$ La Terraza del Morocho
Av Principal Las Tejerías 44, Chuao, T0414-450 3341.
Tiny, only 4 rooms, run by helpful couple, Osvaldo
and Yeldy, ask about guides for excursions.

Restaurants

Maracay
Many excellent restaurants in the Av Las Delicias
area and a variety of cheap restaurants in streets
around Plazas Girardot and Bolívar.

Puerto Colombia
Several places in town serve fish and seafood.

$$$-$$ Paco's Fish
C Los Cocos.
Gourmet fish restaurant in arty setting, with a/c.

$$ Madera Fina
Bahía Tipire, opposite Posada La Bokaina, between
Puerto Colombia and Choroni, T0412-039 2265.
Good food and cocktails, with great sea views from
terrace bar, not cheap but highly recommended.

What to do

Puerto Colombia
Jungle Trip Choroni, *see Hostal N ova Colonial,*
Where to stay, above. Good trips in the national park.

Posada Puerto Escondido, *Cepe, T0243-241 2114,*
www.puertoescondido.com.ve. Offers courses and
trips to a variety of dive sites.

Transport

Maracay
Bus The bus station is 2 km southeast of the
centre, taxi US$2.50. It has 2 sections: Terminal
Oriente for long distance and Terminal Nacional
for regional buses. *Por puestos* are marked
'Terminal' for the bus station and 'Centro' for
the centre (Plaza Girardot). To **Maracaibo**,
AeroExpresos, US$5.50 (US$2.50 regular). To
Valencia, US$1.50, 1 hr, and **Caracas**, US$1 by
autobus, US$1.25 by *microbus*, 1½-2 hrs. **Ciudad
Bolívar**, US$4, 10 hrs. To **Coro**, US$2.50, 5½ hrs.

Parque Nacional Henri Pittier
Bus Depart from Maracay Terminal; pay full fare
to **Ocumare** or hitch from the *alcabala* at El Limón.

Aragua Coast
Bus From **Maracay** to El Playón, 2-2½ hrs,
US$1.50. To **Cata** from El Playón US$1 from plaza,
from **Ocumare de la Costa** to El Playón, US$1.

Choroní
Bus The bus station between Choroní and Puerto
Colombia, next to the PDV filling station, serves
both towns. **Maracay-Choroní**, beautiful journey
through Henri Pittier park, every 2 hrs from 0630-
1700, more at the weekend, US$1.50, 2½-3 hrs.
Road congested at holidays and weekends.

Puerto Colombia
Bus From **Maracay** terminal buses leave from
platform 5. Buses to Maracay depart every hour
0500-1700, US$1.50, 2-3 hrs.

Taxi From **Maracay** US$5 pp, 1-1½ hrs.

Valencia and around

oranges, petroglyphs and beautiful beaches

The great basin in which lie the Lago de Valencia and the industrial town of Valencia is 100 km
west of Caracas. The basin, which is only 450 m above sea-level, receives plenty of rain and is
one of the most important agricultural areas in the country. Near the city are several groups
of petroglyphs while the coast has some very popular beach areas. Best known of these is the
Morrocoy national park, but you have to seek out the quiet spots.

Valencia *Colour map 1, A5.*
A road through low hills thickly planted with citrus, coffee and sugar runs 50 km west from Maracay
to the valley in which Valencia lies. It is hot and humid with annual rainfall of 914 mm. Like its
Spanish namesake, Valencia is famous for its oranges.

Founded in 1555, Valencia is the capital of Carabobo State and Venezuela's third largest city. It's the centre of its most developed agricultural region and the most industrialized. The **Cathedral**, first built in 1580, is on the east side of **Plaza Bolívar**. The statue of the Virgen del Socorro (1550) in the left transept is the most valued treasure; on the second Sunday in November (during the Valencia Fair) it is paraded with a richly jewelled crown. The city's handsome **Plaza de Toros** ① *South end of Av Constitución beyond the ring road*, is the second largest in Latin America after Mexico City (it is also used for shows). The magnificent former **residence of General Páez** ① *Páez y Boyacá, open Tue-Sun at 0900, closed for lunch Tue-Fri and at 1400 Sat-Sun, free*, is now a museum. Páez was the hero of the **Carabobo** battle, the site of which is 30 km southwest of Valencia on the highway to San Carlos (bus from Avenida Bolívar Sur y Calle 75 or Avenida 5 de Julio). The monument surrounded by splendid gardens and the view over the field from the *mirador* where the Liberator directed the battle in 1814 is impressive. Other attractive buildings are the **Casa de los Celis** (1766) ① *Av Soublette y C Comercio, T0241-617 6867, Tue-Sun 0900-1600*, a well-restored colonial house and National Monument which also houses the **Museo de Arte e Historia**, and the **Casa Estrella** (1766) ① *Av Soublette y C Colombia, Tue-Fri 0900-1700, Sat-Sun from 1000*, now a historical museum and cultural centre. There is also **MUVA** ① *Av Bolívar Norte y C Salom, T0241-858 0046, muva.fmn.gob.ve/el-museo, Mon-Fri 0900-1700, Sat 1000-1600, free*, a modern art museum with an impressive collection of 20th-century Venezuelan paintings and sculptures. **Tourist office** ① *Sector San José, Centro Comercial y Profesional, Av Bolívar Norte, p 4, of 30 y 32.*

Around Valencia
Most important of the region's petroglyphs can be found at the **Parque Arqueológico Piedra Pintada** (part of Parque Nacional San Esteban), where lines of prehispanic stone slabs, many bearing swirling glyphs, march up the ridges of Cerro Pintado. At the foot of Cerro Las Rosas is the **Museo Parque Arqueológico Piedra Pintada** ① *Sector Tronconero, vía Vigirmia, Guacara, T0416-446 5059, http://vildalys.wix.com/petroglifos-vigirima, Tue-Fri 0900-1600, Sat-Sun by appointment, free*, has 165 examples of rock art and menhirs (tours, parking, café).

Other extensive ancient petroglyphs have been discovered at **La Taimata** near Güigüe, 34 km east of Valencia on the lake's southern shore. There are more sites on rocks by the Río Chirgua, reached by a 10 km paved road from Highway 11, 50 km west of Valencia. About 5 km past Chirgua, at the **Hacienda Cariaprima**, is a remarkable 35-m-tall geoglyph, a humanoid figure carved into a steep mountain slope at the head of the valley.

Coast north of Valencia
Puerto Cabello, 55 km from Valencia, was one of the most important ports in the colonial Americas, from which produce was transported to the Dutch possessions. Puerto Cabello has retained its maritime importance and is Venezuela's key port. Plaza Bolívar and the colonial part of town are by the waterfront promenade at Calle 24 de Julio.

To the east is **Bahía de Patanemo**, a beautiful, tranquil horseshoe-shaped beach shaded by palms. It has three main sectors, Santa Rita, Los Caneyes and Patanemo itself, with the village proper, further from the beach than the other two. All three have lodging, but it may be difficult to find meals midweek (try at *posadas*). Offshore is the lovely **Isla Larga** (no shade or facilities), best reached by boat from Quizandal, 15 minutes. There are several cafés along the beachfront. Nearby are two sunken wrecks that attract divers. From Puerto Cabello, take a *por puesto* from the terminal, 20 minutes, US$1, a taxi US$4.

Parque Nacional Morrocoy *Colour map 1, A5.*
Palm-studded islets and larger islands (*cayos*) with secluded beaches make up Parque Nacional Morrocoy. The largest and most popular of the islands within the park is **Cayo Sombrero**, with two over-priced fish restaurants. No alcohol is sold on this or other islands; be aware of hidden extra costs and take your own supplies. It is very busy at weekends and during holidays and is generally dirty and noisy. But there are some deserted beaches, with trees on which to sling a hammock. For peace and quiet, take boats to the farthest cayos. **Playuela** is beautiful and is considered to have one of the nicest beaches of all. It has a small restaurant at weekends and there's a nice walk to Playuelita. **Boca Seca** is also pleasant, with shade and calm water suitable for children, but it can be windy. **Cayo Borracho**, one of the nicest islands, has become a turtle-nesting reserve, closed to

visitors. **Playa Azul**, a nice small cayo, has shallow water. The water at **Pescadores** is very shallow. **Los Muertos** has two beaches with shade, mangroves and palms. **Mero**'s beach is beautiful, with palms, but is windy. With appropriate footwear it is possible to walk between some of the islands. Calm waters here are ideal for waterskiing while scuba diving is best suited to beginners. Only by diving to deeper waters will you see coral, although in all locations there are still fish to watch. Take insect repellent against *puri puri* (tiny, vicious mosquitoes) and flies.

Adjoining the park to the north is a vast nesting area for scarlet ibis, flamingos and herons, the **Cuare Wildlife Sanctuary**, a Ramsar site. Most of the flamingos are in and around the estuary next to Chichiriviche, which is too shallow for boats but you can walk there or take a taxi. Birds are best watched early morning or late afternoon.

Tucacas and Chichiriviche *Colour map 1, A5.*
Tucacas is a hot, busy, dirty town, where bananas and other fruit are loaded for Curaçao and Aruba. Popular and expensive as a beach resort, it has garish high-rise blocks and casinos. A few kilometres beyond Tucacas, towards Coro, is **Chichiriviche**, smaller, more relaxed, but lined with tacky shops, also dirty and not that attractive. Both provide access to Parque Nacional Morrocoy, each town serving separate *cayos*, but only as far as Cayo Sombrero. Apart from this and the diving options, few have a good word to say about Tucacas or Chichiriviche.

Listings Valencia and around

Where to stay

Valencia
There are several business hotels, also ones for all budgets along the very long Av Bolívar.

$$ Dinastía
Av Urdaneteo y Av Cedeño, T0241-858 8139, www.dinastiahotel.com.ve
Central, just off Av Bolívar, all services, including jacuzzi and safe parking, restaurant.

$ Marconi
Av Bolívar 141-65, T0241-823 4843.
Small, modern hotel, simple rooms, helpful, safe, laundry, recommended, take bus or *colectivo* from bus station to stop after 'El Elevado' bridge, parking available in nearby shopping mall.

Coast north of Valencia
At **Patanemo** there are hotels and *posadas* in the village (eg María Lucía and **La Fortaleza**, both on Av Los Caneyes).

$$ Posada Santa Margarita
Bolívar 4-36, Puerto Cabello, T0242-361 4112, www.posadasantamargarita.com.ve.
Converted colonial house in historic district, 2 blocks from waterfront promenade, day trips, attractive rooms, cheaper with fan, roof terrace, restaurant, small pool. Book in advance.

$$ Villa Jarana
At entrance to Caneyes sector, 400 m from turn-off to Bahía de Patanemo, T0242-205 1712, villajarana.com.ve
Pleasant rooms and chalets, with pool, gardens and playground, restaurant (advance bookings for groups only).

$$-$ Posada Edén
Final Av Principal Los Caneyes, T0416-442 4955.
The best *posada* in the region, small, comfortable, hot water, restaurant and pool.

Parque Nacional Morrocoy
Camping is allowed at **Cayo Paiclá** and **Cayo Sol** but not year round and you must first make a reservation with **Inparques** (National Parks), Av Libertador, Tucacas, T0259-812 0053 (Falcón office: Intercomunal Coro-La Vela, sector Sabana Larga, Jardín Botánico Dr León Croizat, Coro, Estado Falcón, T0268-277 8451); reserve at least 8 working days in advance; 7 nights max, pay in full in advance (very complicated procedure). Very few facilities and no fresh water at **Paiclá**. **Playa Azul** and **Paiclá** have ecological toilets. At weekends and holidays it is very crowded and litter-strewn (beware rats).

$$$-$$ Villa Mangrovia
On Lizardo Spit between Tucacas and Chichiriviche, T0414-581 7207.
One of few places in the park itself. 6 rooms, superb food and service (all-inclusive, including boat trips), charming owner, Irina Jackson, good birdwatching.

Book via http://morrocoy.travel, or **Last Frontiers**, in UK, T01296-653000, www.lastfrontiers.com.

Tucacas

Chichiriviche has a wider choice of budget places. Most hotels and restaurants in Tucacas are on the long Av Libertador, the main street.

$$ Aparto Posada del Mar
Av Silva, T0259-812 0524,
www.apartoposadadelmar.com.
Variety of rooms with a/c, pool, restaurant, Wi-Fi, private jetty and windsurfing centre.

$ Manaure
Av Silva (opposite Posada del Mar), T0259-818 6121, parador_manaure@hotmail.com.
Modern, low-rise hotel, a/c, hot water, pool, good.

Chichiriviche

There are plenty of reasonably priced *posadas*, eg **Casa Manantial**, Playa Sur, 50 m from beach, T0259-818 6248, www.posadacasamanantial. com.ve ($) and **Morokkue**, Playa Norte, T0414-343 2764, www.morokkue.com.ve ($).

$$ Posada Alemania
Av Cuare, T0259-881 1283,
www.karibik-pur-venezuela.de.
German-run, also has rooms in a small house and an apartment, runs tours, rents snorkel gear, 200 m from Playa Sur, nice garden.

$$ Posada Kanosta
Av Principal de Playa Norte, T0259-818 6246, www.kanosta.com/en
Comfortable *posada*, spacious rooms, with garden and sofas on the porch, excellent restaurant, English and Italian spoken, boat trips.

$ Morena's Place
Sector Playa Norte, 10 mins walk from bus stop, T0259-815 0936, posadamorenas@hotmail.com.
Beautifully decorated house, fan, hammocks, very helpful hosts with travel advice and transfers, English spoken, laundry, breakfast and dinner on request; also has adjoining apartment for 4-6, US$3 per person, recommended.

$ Posada El Profe
2 C Playa Norte, T0259-416 1166,
www.posadaelprofe.com.
Welcoming B&B, several languages spoken, tours and information, contact Aminta in advance for best deals.

$ Posada Sol
Mar y Arena, Mariño y Partida, T0259-815 0306.

Small rooms, welcoming, upstairs terrace with a grill, 1 block from sea, tours and all-inclusive packages offered.

What to do

Tucacas
Diving
Frogman Dive Center, *CC Bolívar, Plaza Bolívar, T0414-340 1824, www.frogmandive.com.*
Introductory, Open Water and Advanced courses, dive trips to Morrocoy, shop.
Submatur, *C Ayacucho 6, near Plaza Bolívar, T0259-812 0082, morrocoysubmatur1@cantv.net.*
Experienced owner, runs 4-day PADI courses and day trips with 2 dives; also rents rooms, $, fan and kitchen, and trimaran trips to Bonaire and other offshore islands.

Transport

Valencia
Air The airport is 6 km southeast of centre. Taxi airport-bus terminal US$3.50. Daily flights to **Maracaibo**, **Porlamar**, **Caracas**, **Puerto Ordaz** and other cities (often via Caracas). Direct flights to **Curaçao** with Insel Air, T0241-824 3342, www. fly-inselair.com.

Bus Terminal is 4 km east of centre, part of shopping mall **Big-Low** (24-hr restaurants). Entry to platforms by *ficha* (token), US$1. Left luggage. Minibus to centre, frequent and cheap, but slow and confusing route at peak times; taxi from bus station to centre, US$5 (official drivers wear ID badges). To **Caracas**, frequent buses with **Aeroexpresos Ejecutivos** and others, 2½ hrs, US$3-5. Likewise to **Maracaibo**, US$3-4, 8 hrs. **Mérida**, 10-12 hrs, US$3-4 (regular bus US$2.50). **Puerto Cabello**, US$0.40, 1 hr. To **Coro**, US$1.50-3, 4½ hrs. To **Ciudad Bolívar**, US$4-6, 10 hrs.

Around Valencia
Bus To **Vigírima** 20 km northeast of Valencia at regular intervals (US$1.25), ask to get off at the 'Cerro Pintado' turn-off.

Parque Nacional Morrocoy
Ferry From **Tucacas**: prices per boat from US$10 return to **Paiclá** to US$25 return to **Cayo Sombrero** (max 7 per boat). The ticket office is on the left of the car entrance to the Park. Boats to Boca Seca and Playuelita only leave from Tucacas, day excursions also available, US$44 pp,

including food, with www.turismodeplaya.com.
From **Chichiriviche**: tickets are per boat and vary according to distance, around US$15-30. Prices are set for each *cayo* and there are long and short trips. There are 2 ports: one in the centre, one at Playa Sur. Ask for the ticket system to fix the price and to ensure you're picked up on time for return trip.

Tucacas
Bus Frequent *por puesto* from **Valencia**, US$4, bus US$2.50. To **Coro**, US$2, 3 hrs.

Chichiriviche
Bus To **Coro**, take a bus from the station on Av Zamora to **Sanare**, US$0.50, every 20 mins, then another to Coro, US$2.75, 3 hrs.

Coro and around

a colonial town with dunes, flamingos and a picturesque sierra nearby

The relaxed colonial city of Coro, with its sand-dune surroundings, sits at the foot of the arid, windswept Paranaguá Peninsula. Inland from Coro, the Sierra de San Luis is good walking country in fresher surroundings.

Coro *Colour map 1, A5. See map, page 1610.*
Coro, the capital of the Falcón state and former capital of the country, is a UNESCO World Heritage Site. Founded in 1527, it became an important religious centre for Christians and Jews alike. The city, 177 km from Tucacas, is relatively clean and well-kept and its small colonial part has several shaded plazas and beautiful buildings, many of which date from the 18th century. Recently, efforts have been made to preserve and restore its colonial heritage. In the rainy season the centre may flood. **Corfaltur tourist office** ① *Paseo Alameda entre Falcón y Palmasola, T0268-253 0260, http://corfaltur. blogspot.co.uk,* English spoken, helpful. **State tourist office** Fondo Mixto de Turismo ① *C Bolívar, CC Don Salim, of 3 y 4, T0268-251 3698.*

The **Cathedral**, a National Monument, was begun in 1583. **San Clemente church** ① *Mass Mon-Sat 1930,* has a wooden cross in the plaza in front, which is said to mark the site of the first Mass said in Venezuela; it is believed to be the country's oldest such monument. There are several interesting colonial houses, such as **Los Arcaya** ① *Zamora y Federación,* one of the best examples of 18th-century architecture, with the **Museo de Cerámica**, small but interesting, with a beautiful garden. **Los Senior** ① *Talavera y Hernández,* where Bolívar stayed in 1827, houses the **Museo de Arte de Coro** ① *T0268-251 5265, www.fmn.gob.ve/museos/museo-arte-coro, Tue-Fri 0900-1700, Sat-Sun 1000-1700, free,* exhibiting some interesting modern artwork. Opposite is the **Museo Alberto Henríquez** ① *T0268-252 5299,* which has the oldest synagogue in Venezuela (1853), if not South America. Built 1764-1765, **Las Ventanas de Hierro** ① *Zamora y Colón, Tue-Sat 0900-1200, 1500-1800, Sun 0900-1300, US$0.20,* is now the **Museo de Tradición Familiar**. Just beyond is the **Casa del Tesoro** (or del Obispo) ① *C Zamora, T0268-252 8701, free,* an art gallery showing local artists' work. There are other handicraft galleries in the centre, such as **Centro Artesanal Generalísimo Francisco de Miranda** ① *C Zamora, near Plaza San Clemente.* The **Jewish cemetery** ① *C 23 de Enero esq C Zamora, visit by prior arrangement only, enquire at the Museo Alberto Henríquez or your hotel,* is the oldest on the continent, founded by Jews who arrived from Curaçao in the early 19th century.

The **Museo de Coro 'Lucas Guillermo Castillo'** ① *C Zamora by San Francisco, T0268-251 5645, Tue-Sat 0900-1230, 1500-1830, Sun 0900-1400,* is in an old monastery, and has a good collection of church relics.

Coro is surrounded by sand dunes, **Los Médanos de Coro**, which form an impressive **national park** ① *0800-1700; outside town on the main road to Punto Fijo: take bus marked 'Carabobo' from C35 Falcón y Av Miranda, or up Av Los Médanos and get off at the end, just after Plaza Concordia, from there walk 500 m to entrance, or take a taxi.* The place is guarded by police and is generally safe, but stay close to the entrance and on no account wander off across the dunes. Kiosk at entrance sells drinks and snacks.

The historic part of the town's port, **La Vela de Coro**, is included in the UNESCO World Heritage Site, with some impressive colonial buildings, lovely sea front, wooden traditional fishing boats and historic church. It has an unmistakable Caribbean feel, but it is in urgent need of facelift (taxi from Coro US$4). On the road to La Vela, near the turning, is the interesting **Jardín Botánico Xerofito Dr León Croizat** ① *Sector Sabana Larga, T0268-277 8451, drfalcon@inparques.gov.ve, Tue-Fri 0800-1200,*

1300-1600, Sat and Sun 0900-1700, free, getting there: take Vela bus from corner of C Falcón, opposite Banco Coro, and ask to be let off at Pasarela del Jardín Botánico – the bridge over the road. It is backed by UNESCO and has plants from Africa, Australia, etc. Tours in Spanish.

Paraguaná Peninsula *Colour map 1, A5.*

Punto Fijo and around This area is a must for windsurfers and is a great place for walking and flamingo spotting. The western side of the peninsula is industrialized, with oil refineries at Cardón and Amuay connected by pipeline to the Lago de Maracaibo oilfields. The main town is **Punto Fijo**, a busy, unappealing place, whose duty-free zone attracts shoppers with cheap electrical goods and alcohol. It has a range of hotels and *posadas*, but the residential area of **Judibana**, about 5 km away, is better, with shopping centre, cinema and restaurants.

Adícora A quiet if run-down little resort on the east side of the peninsula. The beaches are very windswept and not great but they are popular with wind- and kite-surfers. There are three windsurfing schools in town. Adícora is also a good base for exploring the beautiful, barren and wild peninsula where goats and wild donkeys roam.

Coro

Callejón Aeropuerto
Av Josefa Camejo
C 23 Vuelvan Caras
C 25 Norte
C 25 Norte
C 27 Miranda
C 11 Miranda
C 8A Hernández
C 5A Toledo
C 31 Urdaneta
Casa del Tesoro
Museo de Cerámica
San Clemente
San Francisco
Museo de Coro
Las Ventanas de Hierro
C 33 Zamora
Alameda
Buses to Los Médanos
Plaza Falcón
Casa de Los Senior
C 35 Falcón
C 39 Palmasola
Cathedral
Plaza Bolívar
Paseo Talavera
Museo Alberto Henríquez
To Kuriana Travel
C 6 Federación
C 5 Comercio
C 41 Garcés
To Bus Terminal (9 blocks)
C 7 Andes
C 45 Buchivacoa
To Jewish Cemetery
To Bus Terminal (9 blocks)
To Los Médanos
To Colón

N
200 metres
200 yards

Where to stay
1 Casa Tun Tun
2 El Gallo
3 Intercaribe
4 Miranda Cumberland
5 Posada Don Antonio
6 Posada La Casa de los Pájaros
7 Villa Antigua

Restaurants
1 Barra del Jacal
2 Beirut Café y Grill
3 Panadería La Costa Nova

Cerro Santa Ana (830 m) is the only hill on the peninsula and commands spectacular views. The entrance is at El Moruy; take bus to Pueblo Nuevo (0730-0800), then take one to Punto Fijo and ask to be dropped off at the entrance to Santa Ana. From the plaza walk back to the signpost for Pueblo Nuevo and take the dirt road going past a white building; 20 m to the left is **Restaurant La Hija**. Walk 1 km through scrubby vegetation (watch out for dogs) to the **Inparques** office (closed Monday to Friday but busy at weekends). Register here before attempting the steep three-hour climb. It's safer to go on Saturday or Sunday. Some *posadas* in Coro arrange trips to the peninsula.

Laguna Boca de Caño (also called Laguna Tiraya) is a nature reserve north of Adícora, inland from Supi, along a dirt track that is usually fit for all vehicles. There is abundant birdlife, particularly flamingos. It is the only mangrove zone on the east of the peninsula.

Sierra de San Luis

South of Coro, on the road to Barquisimeto, the Sierra includes the **Parque Nacional Juan C Falcón**, with tropical forest, caves and waterfalls. Visit it from the picturesque village of **Curimagua**; jeeps leave from Coro terminal, US$3.50, one hour. The lovely colonial town of **Cabure** is the capital of the Sierra. Jeeps leave from Coro terminal, 58 km, 1¼ hours, US$3-4. As well as hotels, Cabure has restaurants, bars, a bakery, supermarket and pharmacy. A few kilometres up the road is a series of beautiful waterfalls, called the Cataratas de Hueque. **The Camino de los Españoles** is a fantastic three-hour walk through orange groves and tropical forest from Curimagua to Cabure. You will see many butterflies along the way. The path, approximately 20 km, is not well marked, so it is best to hire a guide. Take water. It's very muddy in rains; take insect repellent and good shoes and be prepared to get wet. Ask at any of the hotels listed below. To walk the **Camino de los Españoles** from Coro in one day, take transport to Cabure, ask to be dropped at the turn-off for the Hotel El Duende (see below) and walk uphill 1 km to the Posada, where you begin the trek. The path eventually comes out to the Curimagua-Coro paved road, where you can take transport back to Coro.

Listings Coro and around *map page 1610.*

Where to stay

Coro

Coro has several excellent *posadas* catering for travellers; book well in advance, especially in Dec.

$$ Intercaribe
Av Manaure entre Zamora y Urdaneta, T0268-251 1955, http://hotelintercaribe.jimdo.com.
Bland, modern, pool, a/c, small rooms.

$$-$ Miranda Cumberland
Av Josefa Camejo, opposite old airport, T0268-252 2111, www.hotelescumberland.com.
Large modern hotel, good value, restaurant, good pool area, travel agency.

$ El Gallo
Federación 26, T0268-252 9481, www.hosteltrail.com/posadaelgallo.
In colonial part, French/Venezuelan-owned, relaxed, spacious, shared baths, courtyard with hammocks, dorms and private rooms, some English spoken, sandboarding, manager Eric offers sandboarding tours in the Médanos, renting surfboards or sleds on the dunes.

$ Casa Tun Tun
Zamora 92, entre Toledo y Hernández, T0268-404 4260, www.hosteltrail.com/hostels/casatuntun.
Run by knowledgeable and welcoming Belgian couple. Restored colonial house with 3 attractive patios, free Wi-fi, kitchen facilities, laundry, relaxing hammock and sofa lounge areas, dorms and rooms with and without bath and lovely decor. Good value, nice atmosphere, free morning coffee, changes US$. Highly recommended.

$ Posada Don Antonio
Paseo Talavera 11, T0268-253 9578, Facebook: posadaturisticadonantoniocoro.
Central, small rooms, colonial-style patio, cable tv, a/c, parking.

$ Posada La Casa de los Pájaros
Monzón 74 entre Ampies y Comercio, T0268-252 8215.

Colonial house 6 blocks from centre, restored by the owners with local art and antiques, rooms with and without bath, hammock space, meals available, use of kitchen for small fee, laundry service, trips to local sights. Recommended.

$ Villa Antigua
C 58 Comercio 46, T0268-252 7499/0414-682 2924.
Colonial style, fountain in courtyard, restaurant.

Camping

About 30 km east of Coro at **La Cumara**, nice, good beach and dunes.

Adícora

$$$-$$ Archie's Surf Posada
Playa Sur, T0269-988 8285, www.kitesurfing-venezuela.com.
At entrance to Adícora, 5 mins' walk to centre. German-run, well established, organizes wind and kite surfing lessons. Also trips, horse riding and airport pick-ups. Furnished bungalows for 4-12, apartments for 2-4, hammocks. Prices in euros/dollars. Good reports.

$ Hacienda La Pancha
Vía Pueblo Nuevo, 5 km from Adícora in the hills, T0414-969 2649.
Beautiful, old, colonial-style house set in countryside, nice owners, restaurant, pool, no children.

$ Posada La Casa Rosada
C Comercio de Adícora, on Malecón, T0269-988 8004, www.posadala casarosada.com.
Pleasant, cosy, rooms for 2-8 people, garden and hammocks, breakfast extra, good restaurant. Recommended.

Sierra de San Luis

Curimagua

$ Finca El Monte
Vía La Soledad, 5 km from the village, T0268-404 0564, www.hosteltrail.com/fincaelmonte/.
Run by a Swiss couple on an eco-friendly basis. Peaceful, beautiful views, colonial style, hot water,

meals, hammocks. Tours round the park include birdwatching and cave tours. English, German and French spoken. Highly recommended.

Cabure

In town are several budget options, including **Posada Los Bucares** (T0416-653 9172), and **Posada Amaneceres** (T0416-806 0949).

$ Hotel El Duende
20 mins uphill from village, T0268-661 1079.
A beautiful 19th-century *posada* and garden, price depends on size of room, fan, cold water, good restaurant, horse riding, walking, peaceful.

Restaurants

Coro

$ Barra del Jacal
Av Manaure y C 29 Unión.
Outdoors, pizza and pasta.

$ Beirut Café y Grill
Av Independencia, near the tennis courts.
Nice bar with tasty Arabic snacks and drinks on the terrace.

Cafés

Panadería La Costa Nova
Av Manaure, opposite Hotel Intercaribe.
Good bread, empanadas and pastries, coffee and freshly-squeezed juices, open late.

Festivals

Coro

26 Jul Coro Week.
Oct Cine en la Calle, programme of open-air films on Paseo Talavera.
Nov-Dec Tambor Coriano in many places.
28 Dec Los Locos de La Vela (La Vela).

What to do

Coro

Contact *posadas* in town for tours, eg **La Casa de los Párajos**.

Transport

Coro

Air Airport open for domestic flights; see also Las Piedras, below, for flights.

Bus Terminal is on Av Los Médanos, entre Maparari y Libertad, buses go up C 35 Falcón, US$0.25, taxi US$2. To/from **Caracas** US$2-4, 6-8 hrs; **Mérida**, US$3-4 (regular bus), 9-10 hrs; **Maracaibo**, US$2-3, 4 hrs, *por puesto* US$4; **Tucacas**, every 20 mins, US$1.50-3, 3-4 hrs; **Punto Fijo**, *por puesto* US$1.50.

Punto Fijo

Air Airport at **Las Piedras**: *por puestos* from C Garcés y Av Bolívar (don't believe taxis who say there are no *por puestos* from airport to town); taxi from Punto Fijo US$3, from bus terminal US$2. Daily flights to **Curaçao** with **Insel Air**, www.fly-inselair.com.

Bus Terminal is in Carirubana district; *por puestos* to **Pueblo Nuevo**, **Adícora**, **Coro**, **Valencia** and **Maracaibo**. To **Maracay**, **Barquisimeto**, **Maracaibo** (US$2.50-4) and **Caracas** (US$8), 6-7 hrs. **Expresos Occidente** has a terminal on C Comercio entre Ecuador y Bolivia.

Adícora

Bus Several daily to and from **Coro**, 0630-1700, US$1.25-2, 1 hr; to and from **Pueblo Nuevo** and **Punto Fijo**, several daily from 0600-1730, US$0.50-1.25.

From Maracaibo to Colombia

sweltering oil capital of Venezuela on the route to the border

Not many tourists find their way to the heart of Venezuela's oil business on the shores of Lake Maracaibo. Those that do are usually on their way to Colombia via the border crossing on the Guajira Peninsula to the north. If you've got the time to stop and can handle the heat, Maracaibo is the only town in Venezuela where occasionally you'll see indigenous people in traditional dress going about their business and nearby are reminders of prehispanic and oil-free customs.

Maracaibo *Colour map 1, A4.*

Maracaibo, capital of the State of Zulia, is Venezuela's second largest city and oil capital, with a population of over two million. The region is the economic powerhouse of the country with over 50% of the nation's oil production coming from the Lago de Maracaibo area and Zulia state. The lake is reputedly the largest fresh water reserve in South America. A long cement and steel bridge,

Puente General Rafael Urdaneta, crosses Lago de Maracaibo, connecting the city with the rest of the country. Maracaibo is a sprawling modern city with wide streets. Some parts are pleasant to walk around, apart from the intense heat (or when it is flooded in the rainy season), but as in the rest of the country, security is becoming an issue. The hottest months are July to September, but there is usually a sea breeze from 1500 until morning.

Sights The traditional city centre is **Plaza Bolívar**, on which stand the **Cathedral** (at east end), the **Casa de Gobierno**, the **Asamblea Legislativa** and the **Casa de la Capitulación** (or Casa Morales) ① *Mon-Fri 0800-1600, free,* a colonial building and national monument. The Casa houses libraries, a gallery of work by the Venezuelan painter, Carmelo Fernández (1809-1887), several exhibition halls and a stunning interior patio dedicated to modern art. Next door is the 19th-century **Teatro Baralt**, hosting frequent subsidized concerts and performances.

Running west of Plaza Bolívar is the **Paseo de las Ciencias**, a 1970s development which levelled all the old buildings in the area. Only the **Iglesia de Santa Bárbara** stands in the Paseo. The Paseo de La Chinita continues west from Santa Bárbara to the Basílica de Nuestra Señora de Chiquinquirá. **Calle Carabobo** (one block north of the Paseo de las Ciencias) is a very good example of a colourful, colonial Maracaibo street. One block south of the Paseo is **Plaza Baralt** ① *Av 6,* stretching to Calle 100 and the old waterfront market (**Mercado de Pulgas**). The impressive **Centro de Arte de Maracaibo Lía Bermúdez** ① *T0261-723 3881, Mon-Sat 0930-1300, 1400-1600, Sun 1000-1400,* in the 19th-century Mercado de Pulgas building, displays the work of national and international artists. It is a/c, a good place to escape the midday heat and for starting a walking tour of the city centre. Its walls are decorated with beautiful photographs of Maracaibo. The Centro holds frequent cultural events, including the **Feria Internacional de Arte y Antigüedades de Maracaibo (FIAAM)**. The new part of the city round **Bella Vista** and towards the university is in vivid contrast with the small **old town** near the docks. The latter, with narrow streets and brightly painted, colonial style adobe houses, has hardly changed from the 19th century, although many buildings are in an advanced state of decay. The buildings facing **Parque Urdaneta** (three blocks north of Paseo de las Ciencias) have been well-restored and are home to several artists. Also well preserved are the church of **Santa Lucía** and the streets around. This old residential area is a short ride (or long walk) north from the old centre. **Parque La Marina**, on the shores of the lake, contains sculptures by the Venezuelan artist, Jesús Soto (1923-2005).

Paseo de Maracaibo, or Vereda del Lago, 25 minutes' walk from Plaza Bolívar, is a lakeside park near the **Hotel del Lago**. It offers walks along the shores of the lake, stunning views of the Rafael Urdaneta bridge and of oil tankers sailing to the Caribbean. The park attracts a wide variety of birds. To get there take a 'Milagro' *por puesto* or a 'Norte' bus northbound and ask the driver to let you off at the entrance. Opposite is the **Mercado de los Indios Guajiros** (see Shopping, below).

Maracaibo to Colombia

About one hour north is the **Río Limón**. Take a bus (US$1, from terminal or Avenida 15 entre Calle 76 y 77) to **El Moján**, riding with the Guajira people as they return to their homes on the peninsula. From El Moján, *por puestos* go to **Sinamaica** (US$2; taxi US$4.50).

Sinamaica is the entry point to the territory of Añu people (also known as Paraujanos) who live in stilt houses on Sinamaica lagoon (these houses inspired the invading Spaniards to christen the place 'Little Venice'). Some 15,000 Añu live in the area, although official numbers say there are only 4000. Their language is practically extinct (UNICEF has supported a project to revive it). The Añu use fibres to make handicrafts. To get to the lagoon, take a truck (US$0.50) from Sinamaica's main plaza on the paved road to Puerto Cuervito (five minutes), where the road ends at the lagoon. You can hitch a ride on a shared boat to one of the settlements for a few bolívares, or you can hire a boat by the hour (ask for Víctor Márquez, recommended). Main settlements on the lagoon are El Barro, La Bocita and Nuevo Mundo. **Parador Turístico de la Laguna de Sinamaica** has decent food, clean bathrooms and an excellent handicraft shop with local produce.

Beyond Sinamaica, the paved road past the Lagoon leads to the border with Colombia. Along the way you see Guajira people, the men with bare legs, on horseback; the women with long, black, tent-shaped dresses and painted faces, wearing the sandals with big wool pom-poms which they make and sell, more cheaply than in tourist shops. The men do nothing: women do all the work, tending animals, selling slippers and raising very little on the dry, hot, scrubby Guajira Peninsula.

Border with Colombia *Colombia is 1 hr behind Venezuela.*

If you travel on the road between Maracaibo and the border, even if you are planning to visit just Sinamaica and its lagoon, carry your passport with you. Police and army checkpoints are numerous. They are friendly but can get tough if you don't have your documents, or don't cooperate. The border is closed to traffic between 1800 and 0500 and from 2200 for pedestrians. You need an exit card and stamp to leave Venezuela, payable in bolívares only. For verification of procedures, there is a SAIME office (immigration) in Maracaibo at Destacamento 35, Avenida 2 El Milagro (diagonal al antiguo Banco Mara). Ask for 90 days on entering Colombia and make sure you get an entry stamp from the Colombian authorities. The Colombian consulate in Maracaibo is at Avenida 17 Baralt, Calle 69A No 17-64, Sector Paraíso, T0261-751 1750, http://maracaibo.consulado.gov.co, Monday-Friday 0730-1330. From the frontier to Maicao, it's a 15-minute drive. Also see Colombia chapter.

Listings From Maracaibo to Colombia

Tourist information

Maracaibo
The **tourist office** is **Corzutur** (Av 18, Edif Lieja, p 4, Urb Dr Portillo, T0261-783 5108). For what's going on in the city, see www.quehaymaracaibo. com and for some information http:// pamaracaibo.com.ve.

All banks shut at 1530 and exchange money in the morning only. Best for dollars is **Casa de Cambio de Maracaibo** (C 78 con Av 9B). **Italcambio** has branches at the Lago Mall (by Hotel Venetur Maracaibo), Centro Sambil (Av Guajira, Zl Norte), CC Aventura (Av 12 y 13 con C 74 y 75) and the airport.

Where to stay

Maracaibo
It is best to reserve well in advance.

$$$ Kristoff
Av 8 Santa Rita con C 68 No 68-48, T0261-796 1000, www.hotelkristoff.com.
In the north of the city some distance from centre. Large hotel, with all services, fully refurbished, nice pool open to non-residents, disco, laundry service, restaurant.

$$ Hotel El Paseo
Av 1B y C 74, Sector Cotorrera El Milagro, T0261-400 0000, www.hotelelpaseo.com.ve.
All rooms with breathtaking view of the lake, good, top of the range. **Girasol**, a revolving restaurant on the top floor with great view, serves international dishes.

$$ Venetur Maracaibo
Av 2 (El Milagro), near Club Náutico, T0261-794 4222, www.venetur.gob.ve.
With 360 rooms, some overlooking the lake.

$ Acuario
C 78 (Dr Portillo) entre Av 9 y 9-B, Bella Vista, T0261-797 1123, https://twitter.com/HotelAcuario.
Safe, small rooms, safe parking.

$ Doral
C 75 y Av 14A, T0261-797 8385, www.hoteldoral.com.
North of the city. Safe, decent rooms, helpful. Recommended.

$ Posada Oleary
Av Padilla, C 93 No 2A-12, Santa Lucía, T0261-723 2390, http://posadaoleary.com.ve
Small *posada* across from Hospital Central, rundown location, basic but adequate for the price, safe parking.

$ Trece 27
C 79 (Dr Quintero) entre Av 13 y Av 13A, T0261-935 5544, www.hotelmaracaibotrece27.com.
Hotel north of the centre with modern facilities, parking, near services on Av Delicias and 5 de Julio.

Restaurants

Maracaibo
A range of US chains and Chinese restaurants (mostly on Av 8 Santa Rita) and pizzerias in the north of town. There are many good restaurants around the Plaza de la República, C77/5 de Julio and Av 31, in Bella Vista. Many places to eat and bars on C 72 and 5 de Julio. Most restaurants are closed on Sun. Many restaurants on *palafitos* (stilts) in Santa Rosa de Agua district, good for fish (*por puesto* US$0.50 to get there); best to go at lunchtime.

$$-$ Koto Sushi
Av 11 entre C 75 y 76, Tierra Negra, T0261-798 8954.
Japanese food, very good and authentic-tasting dishes (ie lightly fried).

$$-$ Mi Vaquita
Av 3H con C 76-22, T0261-791 1990,
www.mivaquita.com.
Texan steak house, popular with wealthy
locals, bar area for dancing to DJs and live music,
pricey drinks, sports games on giant screens.
No sandals allowed.

$$-$ Peruano Marisquería
Av 15 (Delicias) y C 69, T0261-798 1513.
Authentic Peruvian seafood dishes and
international cuisine, highly rated.

$ Bambi
Av 4, 78-70, https://twitter.com/bambicafemcbo.
Italian run with good cappuccino, pastries,
recommended. Has other branches.

$ Pizzería Napolitana
*C 77 near Av 4, CC América, T0261-792 2736, and
Av 5 de Julio, diagonal a Plaza de la República,
https://twitter.com/pnapolitana. Closed Tue.*
Excellent food, pizzas and pastas.

$ Yal-la
*Av 8 C 68, Santa Rita, opposite Hotel Kristoff,
T0261-797 8863.*
Excellent, authentic Lebanese/Middle Eastern
restaurant at very reasonable prices. Great
vegetarian food.

Festivals

Maracaibo
5 Oct Virgen del Rosario.
18 Nov NS de Chiquimquira (La Chinita),
processions, bullfights – the main regional
religious festival.

Shopping

Maracaibo
There are several modern malls with all services
and amenities, including multiplex cinemas.
The most luxurious is **Centro Lago Mall** (Av El
Milagro, Mon-Sat 0900-2200, Sun 1200-2000).

Handicrafts and markets
El Mercado de los Indios Guajiros, *C 96 y Av 2,
El Milagro.* Open market, a few crafts, some
pottery, hammocks, etc.
Las Pulgas, *South side of C 100 entre Av 10 y 14.*
The outdoor market, enormous, mostly clothes,
shoes, and household goods.
   Most of the shops on **C Carabobo** sell
regional crafts, eg **La Salita** (C Carabobo, T0261-

723 1270). **El Turista** (C 72 y Av 3H, in front of
Centro Comercial Las Tinajitas, T0261-792 3495).

Transport

Maracaibo
Air La Chinita airport is 25 km southwest of
city centre (taxis US$10, no *por puestos*). Good
bookshop in arrivals sells city map; several good
but overpriced eateries; **Italcambio** for exchange,
daily 0600-1800, no commission; car hire
outside. Frequent flights to **Caracas**, **Valencia**,
Barquisimeto, **San Antonio**, and **Porlamar**.
International flights to **Miami**.

Bus The bus station is at Av 15 Las Delicias/
Av 17 Los Haticos, 1 km south of the old town.
It is old and chaotic, unsafe at night. *Cambio* at
bus terminal will change Colombian pesos into
bolívares at a poor rate. Taxi to the city US$3.
Ask for buses into town, local services are
confusing. Several fast and comfortable buses
daily to **Valencia**, US$3-4, 8 hrs. **San Cristóbal**,
US$5-8, 6-8 hrs. **Barquisimeto**, 4 hrs, US$3-5.
Coro, US$2-3, 4 hrs. **Caracas**, US$10-12, 10-13 hrs
(**Aeroexpresos Ejecutivos** from Av 15 con C 90 –
Distribuidor Las Delicias, T0261-783 0620); regular
bus US$5.50. **Mérida**, from US$4, 5-7 hrs.

   Local *Por puestos* go up and down Av 4 from
the old centre to Bella Vista. Ruta 6 goes up and
down C 67 (Cecilia Acosta). The San Jacinto bus
goes along Av 15 (Las Delicias). Buses from Las
Delicias also go to the centre and terminal. From
C 76 to the centre *por puestos* marked 'Las Veritas'
and buses marked 'Ziruma'. Look for the name of the
route on the roof, or the windscreen, passenger's
side. Downtown to Av 5 de Julio in a 'Bella Vista' *por
puesto* costs US$1-1.50, depending on distance. Taxis
minimum US$1.50; from north to centre US$2
(beware overcharging, meters are not used).
Public transport is being completely overhauled,
with a series of rapid transit (BTR) TransMaracaibo
integrated bus routes, some connecting with
the Metro. New large and small red public buses
(government-owned) connect the north, centre
and other parts of the city at US$0.10-0.25.

Metro An elegant light-rail system is being
developed, www.metrodemaracaibo.gob.ve.
6 stations of the 1st line are in operation, from
Altos de la Vanega, southwest of the centre,
to **Libertador**, via **Sabaneta** and **Urdaneta**:
Mon-Fri 0600-2000, Sat-Sun 0800-1800. Basic fare
US$0.10. An extension to Línea 1 and Línea 2 are
planned (no further progress at time of research).

Border with Colombia
Maracaibo-Maicao

Bus Services to Maicao are currently unreliable, hampered by the illegal trafficking of contraband gasoline into Colombia. There may be *colectivos* from Maracaibo bus terminal (5 passengers), US$7 pp; shop around, plus US$1 road toll, 2-3 hrs.

Some drivers are unwilling to stop for formalities; make sure the driver takes you all the way to Maicao and arrive before the last bus to Santa Marta or Cartagena (1630). To **Cartagena** with **Expresos Amerlujo**, T0261-787 7872, at 0630, Tue and Fri, 12-14 hrs, US$10-12, would appear to be the safest bet if you have to use this route.

From the lowlands to Mérida

take the high road to the Andes

The arid, fruit-growing area around the city of Barquisimeto leads to the lush Andean foothills of Trujillo state.

Barquisimeto *Colour map 1, A5.*
There are good air and road connections: buses from Caracas take 5½ hrs, from Coro 7 hrs and from Barinas in the Llanos, 5 hrs.

The heart of old Barquisimeto is **Plaza Bolívar**, with a statue of the Liberator, the white-painted **Iglesia Concepción** and the **Palacio Municipal** ① *Cra 17 y C 25*, an attractive modern building. It is now Venezuela's fourth largest city and capital of Lara state. For information contact: **Corporación de Turismo de Lara** ① *Cra 19 esq C 25, Palacio de Gobierno, T0251-231 4089, www.cortulara. com.ve*. On 28 December (morning) is the fiesta of **La Zaragoza**, when colourfully clad people are accompanied by music and dancing in the street. Huge crowds watch **La Divina Pastora** procession in early January, when an image of the Virgin Mary is carried from the shrine at Santa Rosa village into the city.

Barquisimeto to Mérida
Buses to Mérida (eight hours) take the Panamericana, which runs at the foot of the Andes near the border with Zulia state, via Agua Viva and El Vigía. More scenic routes take roads which climb towards the mountains, passing colonial towns and entering an increasingly rugged landscape. One such passes is the busy agricultural centre of **Quíbor**, 24 km southwest of Barquisimeto. Festivals on 18 January (NS de Altagracia) and 12 June (San Antonio de Padua).

Some 165 km southwest of Quíbor is **Boconó**, built on steep mountain sides and famed for its crafts. The **Centro de Acopio Artesanal Tiscachic** is highly recommended for *artesanía* (turn left just before bridge at entrance to town and walk 350 m). From Boconó there is a high, winding, spectacular paved road to Trujillo (see below).

Niquitao, a small town one hour southwest of Boconó, is still relatively unspoilt. Excursions can be made to the Teta de Niquitao (4007 m), two hours by jeep, the waterfalls and pools known as Las Pailas, and a nearby lake. Southwest of Niquitao, by partly paved road is **Las Mesitas**; continue up towards **Tuñame**, turn left on a good gravel road (no signs), cross pass and descend to **Pueblo Llano** (one basic hotel and restaurant), from where you can climb to the Parque Nacional Sierra Nevada at 3600 m, passing Santo Domingo (see also below). Good hiking in the area.

Valera *Colour map 1, A5.*
From the Panamericana in the lowlands, a road goes to the most important town in Trujillo state, Valera. Here, you can choose between two roads over the Sierra, either via Boconó and down to the Llanos at Guanare and Barinas, or via Timotes and Mucuchíes to Mérida. There are several upmarket business hotels, few decent budget ones, and lots of good Italian restaurants on the main street.

Trujillo *Colour map 1, A5.*
From Valera a road runs via the restored colonial village of **La Plazuela** to the state capital, Trujillo. This beautiful historic town consists of two streets running uphill from the Plaza Bolívar. It's a friendly place with a warm, subtropical climate. The **Centro de Historia de Trujillo**, on Avenida Independencia, is a restored colonial house, now a museum. Bolívar lived there and signed the

ON THE ROAD

☆The Lighthouse of Maracaibo

In the south and southwest of the Lago de Maracaibo is the Catatumbo delta, a huge swamp with fast-flowing, navigable rivers, luxurious vegetation and plentiful wildlife, making it one of the most fascinating destinations in the whole country. It is most famous, however, for the nightly displays of lightning over the lake, which are best seen from April or May to November or December. The phenomenon is yet to be explained. Indigenous people thought that it was produced by millions of fireflies meeting to pay the homage to the creator gods. Early scientific thought was that the constant silent flashing at three- to 10-second intervals was caused by friction between hot air moving south from Zulia and Falcón and cold currents from the Andes. Latest theories suggest it is the result of clashes between the methane particles from the marsh and the lake system between the Catatumbo and Bravo rivers. It has been proved that this phenomenon is a regenerator of the planet's ozone layer.

Whatever its origin, the spectacle is truly unique. Several operators run tours from Mérida (see page 1624) with transfers to Puerto Concha from where boats cross the lake to Ologa for overnight stays to see the lightning. They provide bilingual nature guides, who have information about birds, butterflies and flora. Several operators run tours from Mérida with boat transport (see page 1624) and bilingual nature guides, who have information about birds, butterflies and flora.

Another observation place is Congo Mirador on the edge of the Parque Nacional Ciénagas del Catatumbo, at the southwestern end of the lake. To get to the Mirador independently is a real tropical adventure involving three to four hours on a motorboat from the port of **Encontrados**, a small town with basic services. It is not fully safe because of illegal immigration and contraband coming from Colombia. Travel should be arranged in a group, and security can be hired in town. If staying overnight on the boat, take plenty of water and food, mosquito repellent and antiseptics.

Encontrados lies at the entrance to the **Parque Nacional Ciénagas de Juan Manuel de Aguas Blancas y Aguas Negras** (daily 0700-1600), known for its impressive vegetation and migrating birds. If you're not going on a tour, you must get a permit from Inparques to enter the park. The Catatumbo lightning can be seen from some parts of the park and even from Encontrados itself. In town basic accommodation ($) is available at Hostería Juancho (Calle Piar 74, T0275-615 0448) and at the central Hotel La Nona Magdalena (Avenida Principal, near Plaza Bolívar, T0275-414 2951). Restaurants close around 1600.

To get to Encontrados takes about four hours by car from Maracaibo, or three to four hours from San Cristóbal. Drive south from Maracaibo on the Machiques–Colón road then, at El Manguito, take a road to Encontrados, over 70 km from the intersection.

'proclamation of war to the death' in the house. A 47-m-high monument to the **Virgen de la Paz** ① daily *0830-1630, US$0.10*, with lift, was built in 1983; it stands at 1608 m, 2½ hours with town and gives good views to Lake Maracaibo but go early. Jeeps leave when full from opposite Hotel Trujillo (20 minutes, US$0.75 per person). For tourist information, visit the **Corporación Trujillana de Turismo** ① *Av Principal La Plazuela, Trujillo, T0272-236 1455, www.trujillotierramagica.gob.ve.*

Road to the high Andes

After **Timotes** the road climbs through increasingly wild, barren and rugged country and through the windy pass of **Pico El Aguila** (4118 m) in the Sierra de la Culata, best seen early morning, otherwise frequently in the clouds. This is the way Bolívar went when crossing the Andes to liberate Colombia, and on the peak is the statue of a condor. At the pass is the tourist restaurant **Páramo Aguila**, reasonably priced with open fire. People stop for a hot chocolate or a *calentado*, a herb liquor drunk hot. There are also food and souvenir stalls, and horses for hire (high season and weekends). Across from the monument is a small chapel with fine views. A paved road leads from here 2 km to a CANTV microwave tower (4318 m). Here are tall *frailejones* plants. Continuing north as a lonely track the road goes to the **Piñango lakes** (45 km) and the traditional village of **Piñango** (2480 m), 1½ hours. Great views for miles before the road reaches the Panamericana and Lago de Maracaibo.

Santo Domingo (altitude 2178 m), with good handicraft shops and fishing, is on the spectacular road up from Barinas to Mérida, before the Parque Nacional Sierra Nevada. Festival: 30 September, San Gerónimo. The tourist office is on the right leaving town, 10 minutes from the centre.

Listings From the lowlands to Mérida

Where to stay

Barquisimeto to Merida

Boconó

$ Estancia de Mosquey
Mosquey, 10 km from Boconó towards Biscucuy, T0272-414 8322, T0414-723 4246, estanciamosquey@hotmail.com.
Family-run, great views, rooms and *cabañas*, good beds, good restaurant, recommended. There are other hotels and *posadas* in town, some on or near Plaza Bolívar, 1 opposite the bus station.

Niquitao

$ Posada Turística de Niquitao
T0271-885 2042, or0416-771 7860, www.ciberexpo.com/posadaniquitao/.
Rooms around a patio in a restored old house, some with bunks, price is for room only, restaurant, tours arranged with guide, also has small museum.

Trujillo

$ Los Gallegos
Av Independencia 5-65, T0272-236 3193.
With hot water, a/c or fan, with or without TV. As well as several other places.

Road to the high Andes

Timotes

$ Caribay
Av Bolívar 41, T0271-828 9126.
Basic, with bar and restaurant.

$ Las Truchas
North entrance to town, T0271-808 0500, www.andes.net/lastruchas.
Hotel with 8 rooms and 44 cabins, with fireplace, with and without kitchen. Also has a restaurant, trout (*trucha*) its speciality.

Santo Domingo

$$$ La Trucha Azul
East end of town, C Nacional Barinas-Mérida, T0274-898 8111, www.latruchaazul.com.
Rooms with open fireplace, also suites, cabins and villas for up to 8 (US$330 per night).

$$-$ Los Frailes
Between Santo Domingo and Laguna Mucubají at 3700 m. T0274-417 3440, or T0212-976 0530, reservacioneshlf@gmail.com, Facebook: hotellosfrailesmerida'.
Cheaper in low season, includes breakfast. Beautiful former monastery, specializes in honeymoon packages, rooms are simple, international menu and wines.

$$-$ Moruco
T0274-898 8155/8070, out of town.
Good value, beautiful, also cabins, good food, bar.

$ Paso Real
On the other side of the river from Los Frailes, T0212-287 0517, 0414-974 7486.
A good place to stay, heating, restaurant.

Transport

Valera

Bus The terminal is on the edge of town. To **Boconó**, US$1-1.50, 3 hrs; to **Trujillo**, *por puestos*, 30 mins, US$0.50; to **Caracas**, 9 hrs, US$3.50-5 (direct at 2230 with **Expresos Mérida**); to **Mérida**, 4 daily with **Trans Barinas**, US$1.50-2.50, 4½ hrs; *por puestos* to **Mérida**, 3 hrs, US$4.50, leave when full (travel by day for views and, especially in the rainy season, safety); to **Maracaibo**, *micros* every 30 mins till 1730, 4 hrs, US$3 (bus US$2).

Road to the high Andes

Santo Domingo

Bus Buses or *busetas* pass in both directions every 2 hrs all day. **Mérida** 2 hrs, US$1.50 *por puesto*; **Barinas** 1½ hrs, US$1.75.

Mérida
& around

Venezuela's high Andes offer hiking and mountaineering, and fishing in lakes and rivers. The main tourist centre is Mérida (674 km from Caracas), but there are many interesting rural villages. The Transandean Highway runs through the Sierra to the border with Colombia, while the Pan-American Highway runs along the foot of the Andes through El Vigía and La Fría to join the Transandean at San Cristóbal.

The Sierra Nevada de Mérida, running from south of Maracaibo to the Colombian frontier, is the only range in Venezuela where snow lies permanently on the higher peaks. Several basins lying between the mountains are actively cultivated; the inhabitants are concentrated mainly in valleys and basins at between 800 m and 1300 m above sea level. The towns of Mérida and San Cristóbal are in this zone.

Mérida   *Colour map 1, A4.*

the base for exploring the Venezuelan Andes

Mérida stands on an alluvial terrace – a kind of giant shelf – 15 km long, 2.5 km wide, within sight of Pico Bolívar, the highest mountain in Venezuela. The mountain is part of the Five White Eagles group. The summits are at times covered in snow, but the glaciers and snow are retreating. Founded in 1558, the capital of Mérida State retains some colonial buildings but is mainly known for its 33 parks and many statues. For tourists, its claims to fame are the great opportunities for adventure sports and the buzz from a massive student population.

Sights

In the city centre is the attractive **Plaza Bolívar**, on which stands the **cathedral**, dark and heavy inside, with **Museo Arquidiocesano** beside it, and **Plaza de Milla**, or Sucre ① *C 14 entre Avs 2 y 3*, always a hive of activity. The **Parque de las Cinco Repúblicas** ① *C 13, entre Avs 4 y 5, beside the barracks*, is renowned for having the first monument in the world to Bolívar (1842, replaced in 1988) and contains soil from each of the five countries he liberated (photography strictly prohibited). Three of the peaks known as the Five White Eagles (Bolívar, 5007 m, La Silla del Toro, 4755 m, and León 4740 m) can be clearly seen from here.

Plaza Las Heroínas, by the lowest station of the *teleférico* (see below) is busy till 2300, an outdoor party zone, with artists exhibiting their work. Many cheap hotels, restaurants and tour operators are also located here.

Less central parks include **Plaza Beethoven** ① *Santa María Norte*, a different melody from Beethoven's works chimes every hour, but the site is now very neglected and run-down; *por puestos/busetas*, run along Avenida 5, marked 'Santa María' or 'Chorro de Milla', US$0.45. The **Jardín Botánico** ① *located on the way to La Hechicera, T0274-417 3290, Facebook: Fundación-Jardín-Botánico-de-Mérida, daily 0800-1700, 360 days a year, free Mon, US$0.75 Tue-Fri, US$1 Sat-Sun*, has been remodeled and contains the largest collection of bromeliads in South America, sculptures,

Essential Mérida

Getting around

Mérida's **airport** is on the main highway, 5 km southwest of the centre. The **bus terminal** is 3 km from the centre of town on the west side of the valley, linked by a frequent minibus service to Calle 25 entre Avenidas 2 y 3, US$0.50. City bus fares rise at weekends. A trolley bus system, www.tromerca.gob.ve, from the southern suburb of Ejido to La Hechicera in the north has been opened as far as Estación Mercado Periférico at Calle 38, but as yet does not connect the downtown area. The second line north of the centre to La Hechicera is still projected, but a cable car, Trolcable, from Los Conquistadores, Avenida Domingo Peña, to San Jacinto is in operation; both services run Monday-Saturday 0600-2000 (from 0700 on Saturday). Mérida may seem safe, but theft does occur. Avoid the Pueblo Nuevo area by the river at the stairs leading down from Avenida 2, as well as Avenida 2 itself.

a canopy walkway, and botanical specimens from a range of eco-systems. The **Jardín Acuario** ① *beside the aquarium, high season daily 0800-1800, low season closed Mon, US$0.25; (busetas leave from Av 4 y C 25, US$0.25, passing airport)*, is an exhibition centre, mainly devoted to the way of life and the crafts of the Andean *campesinos*.

Mérida has several museums: the small **Museo Arqueológico** ① *Av 3, Edif del Rectorado de la Universidad de los Andes, just off Plaza Bolívar, T0274-240 2344, http://vereda.ula.ve/museo_arqueologico, Mon-Fri 0830-1130, 1400-1730, US$0.50*, with ethnographic and pre-Columbian exhibits from the Andes. **Museo de Arte Moderno** ① *Av 2 y C 21, T0274-252 4380, Tue-Sat 0900-1200, 1300-1700, free*, is in the Centro Cultural Don Tulio Febres Cordero, which is a run-down but still impressive concrete building with political murals in front of its main entrance, and has several galleries and theatres.

Listings Mérida *map page 1622.*

Tourist information

Corporación Merideña de Turismo
Av Urdaneta beside the airport, T0800-637 4300, www.meridatudestino.com (with an associated app). Mon-Sat low season 0800-1200 and 1400-1800, high season 0800-1800.
They supply a useful map of the state and town. Also in the bus terminal, same hours, have a map of the city (free), at Parque Las Heroínas and at the Mercado Principal, low season 0800-1200, 1400-1800, high season 0830-1830.

Inparques
National Parks, Sector Fondur, Parcelamiento Albarrega, C 02, paralela a Av Las Américas, T0274-262 1529.
Map of Parque Nacional Sierra Nevada (mediocre) US$1; also, and easier, at Teleférico for permits.

Useful addresses

If you need to register a theft for insurance purposes, ask at the tourist office first. The **CICPC** will provide a *constancia* reporting the crime and listing the losses. Their office is on Av Las Américas, at Viaducto Miranda, T0274-262 2855. Open daily but they won't issue a *constancia* on Sun. To get there, take any bus marked 'Terminal Sur' or 'Mercado' leaving from C 25.
Immigration office: SAIME (Av 4 y C 16, quinta San Isidro N0 4-11, Parroquia Sagrario, T0274-251 8588, Mon-Fri 0800-1700). For those heading to Colombia, the Colombian consulate is at Final Av Universidad Quinta Noevia, Casa No 80, Sector Vuelta de Lola, T0274-245 9724, http://merida.consulado.gov.co, open 0730-1330.

Where to stay

Book ahead in school holidays and Feria del Sol. High season is mid-Jul to mid-Jan.

$$-$ Posada Casa Sol
Av 4 entre C15 y C16, T0274-252 4164, www.posadacasasol.com.
Renovated colonial-era house with lovely rooms in distinctive, tasteful style, modern art on walls, hot water, Wi-Fi, beautiful garden, large breakfast included. Very helpful, English, German and Italian spoken. Limited parking. The best in town, highly recommended.

$$-$ Posada Suiza
Av 3 entre C 17 y 18, No 17-59, T0274-252 4961, http://posada-suiza.net.
A 19th century colonial home converted to a guesthouse. Private rooms for 2 to 6 people, Wi-Fi in communal areas, internal patios. Adventure tours (trekking, rafting, riding, expeditions) with **Colibrí Tours**, same phone, www.colibri-tours.com.

$ El Escalador Andino
C 23 entre Avs 7 y 8, T0274-252 2563, el_escalador_ andino@hotmail.com, Facebook: Elescaladorandino.
A very simple little guesthouse run by a kindly old lady. Doubles or rooms with bed and bunks, hot water, Wi-Fi, free coffee, tourist information.

$ El Tisure
Av 4 entre C 17 y 18, T0274-252 6061, www.venaventours.com/hoteltisure.
A well-maintained colonial-style option, centrally located with 28 simple, calm, attractive rooms, including one enormous Presidential suite with a jacuzzi. Helpful and hospitable.

$ La Montaña
C 24 No 6-47 entre Av 6 y 7, T0274-252 5977, www.posadalamontana.com.
A friendly little *posada* with 19 rooms set around a courtyard, all with hot water, safe, fan, fridge, and Wi-Fi. Very helpful, English spoken, excellent restaurant. Mountain views from the sun terrace/ reading lounge. Recommended.

$ Los Bucares de Mérida
Av 4 No 15-5, T0274-252 2841, info@losbucares.com.
Colonial-style with tranquil inner courtyards, attractive wood beams and red tile roofs. Simple white-washed rooms with hot water, cheaper (and noisier) at the front. Amenities include parking and *cafetín*.

$ Montecarlo
Av 7 entre C 24 y C 25, T0274-252 5981, www.andes.net/hotelmontecarlo.
Simple rooms painted a calming sky blue. Ask for back one with view of mountain, safe, parking, hot water, restaurant.

$ Posada Alemania
Av 2 entre C 17 y 18, No 17-76, T0274-252 4067, www.posadaalemania.com.
Relaxed family atmosphere, cosy rooms with and without bath, leafy patio, laundry service, kitchen, communal areas, book exchange, and a good tourist information and eco-tourism office. Popular with backpackers, discounts for long stays, breakfast included. English and German spoken, German owner. Recommended.

$ Posada Casa Alemana-Suiza
El Encanto, Av 2 No 38-130, T0274-263 6503, www.casa-alemana.com.
Stylish guesthouse with a nice family atmosphere. Rooms are spacious, including a suite overlooking Pico Bolívar. Amenities include breakfast salon, kitchen, living room and bar, billiard room, chimney room, and roof top-terrace overlooking the Andes. Bus station pick-up available, parking, discount in low season and for long stays, laundry service, English and German spoken. Also runs good tours and activities.

$ Posada Doña Pumpa
Av 5 y C 14, T0274-252 7286, info@donapumpa.com.
6 simple, spacious, well-maintained rooms with good showers at this quiet guesthouse. English-speaking owner, parking.

$ Posada Guamanchi
C 24, No 8-86, T0274-252 2080, www.guamanchi.com.
Owned by tour operator of same name, if on a tour you are will receive a discount. Rooms and dorms of varying size, including 7 double rooms with private terrace and hammock and Wi-Fi. Good communal areas, including terraces overlooking the plaza, shared fridges, kitchens, TV room. Recommended.

$ Posada Luz Caraballo
Av 2 No 13-80, on Plaza de Milla, T0274-252 5441.
Colonial-style building with antique typewriters in the lobby, hot water, restaurant, good bar, parking, secure.

Restaurants

Good restaurants in Centro Comercial La Hechicera, Av Alberto Carnevalli, northeast of the centre.

$$ El Chipen
Av 5, No 23-67, T0274-252 5015.
Established 50 years ago, El Chipen is the oldest restaurant in Mérida and often recommended by locals. They serve Spanish and Venezuelan food, excellent trout and cordon bleu. Lots of character and old world style.

$$ El Encuentro
Av 4 y C 29, at Hotel Chama, T0274-252 4851, www.hotelchama.com.ve. Open 1200-2200 (till 2300 Fri-Sat, Sun till 1800).
Smart joint, moderately classy, serving gourmet international and Venezuelan cuisine, including seafood starters, fish, meat, chicken, pasta and risotto, wines and cocktails. Good presentation, the place for an intimate evening meal.

$$ La Abadía

*Av 3 entre C 17 y 18, T0274-251 0933,
www.abadiarestaurante.com. Closed Mon, Tue*
Kitsch and atmospheric old restaurant set in
an early 20th-century abbey and attended by
waiters wearing monks' habits. Good varied
menu of salads, soups, meat, pasta, and chicken.
Romantic and recommended. Also here is
Abadía Tours travel agency and boutique
Hotel La Abadía ($$$), same address.

$$ Orígenes Bistro y Bar

*Pasaje Ayacucho, Zona Las Heroínas, T0274-
252 9555, Face book: origenesbistroybar.
Closed Mon and Tue.*
Good and un-fussy Italian food, with friendly family
welcome, bar shows major live sports events.

$$-$ La Astilla

C 14, No 2-20, Plaza de Milla, T0274-251 0832.
Colourful pizzería filled with hanging plants and
nostalgic music, varied menu, frequented by

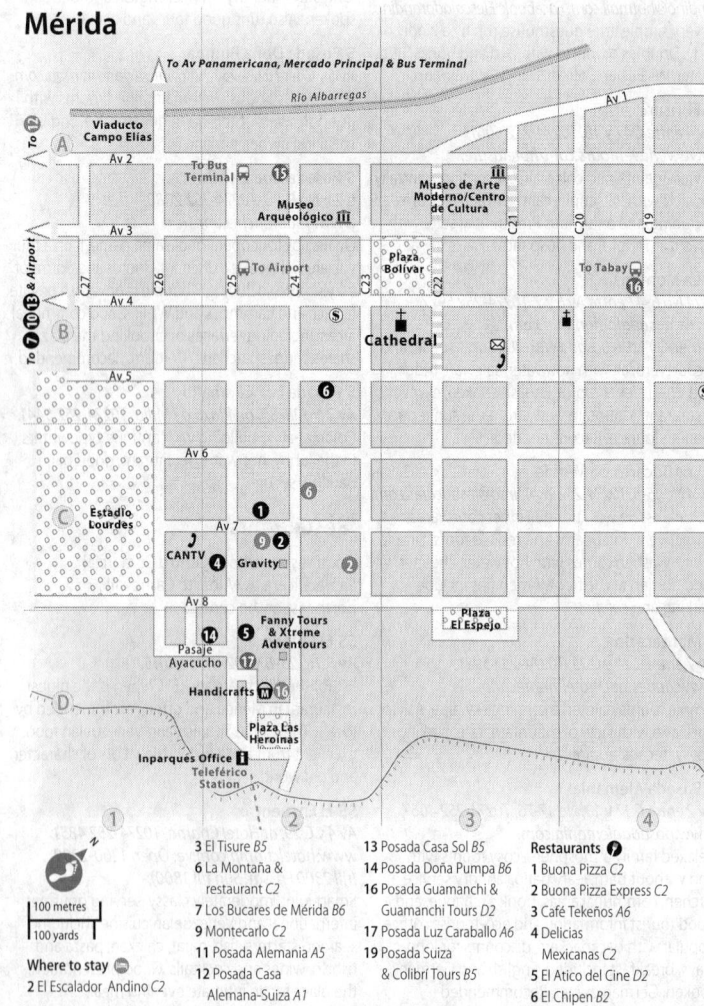

Mérida

Where to stay
2 El Escalador Andino *C2*

3 El Tisure *B5*
6 La Montaña & restaurant *C2*
7 Los Bucares de Mérida *B6*
9 Montecarlo *C2*
11 Posada Alemania *A5*
12 Posada Casa Alemana-Suiza *A1*

13 Posada Casa Sol *B5*
14 Posada Doña Pumpa *B6*
16 Posada Guamanchi & Guamanchi Tours *D2*
17 Posada Luz Caraballo *A6*
19 Posada Suiza & Colibrí Tours *B5*

Restaurants
1 Buona Pizza *C2*
2 Buona Pizza Express *C2*
3 Café Tekeños *A6*
4 Delicias Mexicanas *C2*
5 El Atico del Cine *D2*
6 El Chipen *B2*

locals and groups. Good vibe, reasonable food, average service.

$$-$ La Ciboulette
Av 4 y C 29, T0274-252 4851, next to Hotel Chama. Mon-Sat 1800-2300.

A sophisticated European-style bistro with eclectic gastronomic offerings, including tapas and fine wine. Occasional live music.

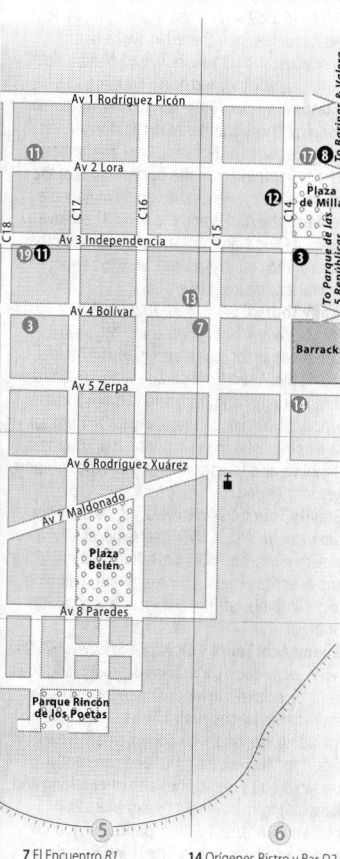

$ Buona Pizza
Av 7 Maldonado entre C 24 y 25, T0274-251 1274. Daily 1200-2300.

Thick-crust pizzas, popular with the locals and often buzzing in the evening. Express branch opposite and 2 other branches.

$ Café Tekeños
C 14 y Av 3, just of Plaza Milla, T0274-251 0241.

A casual, bohemian eatery in a lovely rustic colonial building, liberally adorned with interesting art and antiques. They serve hot chocolate, juices and snacks, particularly *tequeños* – tasty fried dough sticks with a variety of sweet and savoury fillings. Recommended.

$ Delicias Mexicanas
C 25, entre Av 7 y 8, next to Hotel Altamira.

Authentic Mexican joint with colourful furniture and art work by Diego Rivera. They serve old favourites from the homeland including *burritos*, fajitas, tacos, and *chilaquiles*. Not really gourmet, but servings are massive.

$ El Atico del Cine
C 25 entre Av 8 y Plaza Las Heroínas, T0274-252 9426/0414-747 5522.

Movie-themed restaurant, bar, and café set in a cosy upstairs attic. They serve pizza and other international fare. Casual place, sociable vibe.

$ El Sabor de los 4 Quesos
C 13 entre Av 1 y 2, by Plaza de Milla, T0274-1094, www.pizzeria4quesos.com.ve. Mon,Thu 1600-2200,Fri-Sun 1130-2200, closed Tue-Wed.

Cheap and popular locals' pizzeria, very busy, painted green and white with an inner patio.

Ice cream parlours

Heladería La Coromoto
Av 3 y C 29, T0274-252 3525. Tue-Sun 1415-2100.

Proud Guinness record holder serving the most ice cream flavours in the world, over 860 at the time of research, at least 60 choices daily, eg trout, avocado.

Bars and clubs

There is no cover charge for nightclubs but always take your passport or a copy. Use taxis to get back as the streets are deserted.

Birosca Carioca
Av 2 y C 24, T0424-7823161, Facebook: Birosca-Carioca.

Popular alternative hang-out, with live music, grunge, rock, metal, Indie music. Take care outside.

7 El Encuentro *B1*
8 El Sabor de los 4 Quesos *A6*
10 Heladería La Coromoto *B1*
11 La Abadía *B5*
12 La Astilla *A6*
13 La Ciboulette *B1*
14 Orígenes Bistro y Bar *D2*

Bars & clubs
15 Birosca Carioca *A2*
16 El Hoyo del Queque *B4*
17 La Botana *D2*

El Hoyo del Queque
C 19 y Av 4, T0274-252 4306, Facebook: El-Hoyo-del-Queque. Open 1200-2400.
Usually packed, good meeting place, youthful student crowd, also serves snacks and burgers. The best local bands play here, some nights free. Recommended.

La Botana
Plaza las Heroínas, C 24 y 25.
Raucous reggae bar that's packed with drinkers on a Fri and Sat night. Live music and DJs. They also serve pizza.

Festivals

1-2 Jan Paradura del Niño.
Feb/Mar Feria del Sol, held on the week preceding Ash Wed. This is also the peak bullfighting season.
15 May San Isidro Labrador, a popular festival nationwide, but especially in Mérida.
Dec For 2 weeks leading up to Christmas there are daily song contests between local students on Plaza Bolívar, 1700-2200.

Shopping

Camping shops
5007, *Av 5 entre C 19 y 20, CC Mediterráneo, T0274-252 6806, http://5007.freeservers.com.* Recommended.
Eco Bike, *Av 7 No 16-34, T0274-252 8650.* For mountain bikes and equipment. Many tour operators rent equipment.

Handicrafts
Handicraft market on La Plaza de Las Heroínas, opposite *teleférico.*
Mercado Principal, *Av las Américas (buses for bus station pass by).* Has many small shops, top floor restaurant has regional *comida típica,* bargaining possible.

What to do

Language schools
Iowa Institute, *Av 3 y C 18, Edif 17-71, T0274-935-9775, Ilinguainstitute@gmail.com, Facebook: Iowa LanguageInstitute. Open 0800-1200, 1430-1800.* Competitive prices, fully qualified teachers, homestays arranged. Recommended.

Parapenting
All agencies offer jumps. Conditions in Mérida are suitable for flying almost all year round. It takes on average 50 mins to get to a launch site and tandem jumps last 25-40 mins. There are 7 main sites. Can take own equipment and hire a guide.
Xtreme Adventours, *Av 8, C24, Plaza Las Heroínas, T0274-252 7241, xatours@hotmail.com.* Specializes in parapenting (latest equipment, safety) and many other adventure options, plus tours in the region. Also offers tours from Mérida to Canaima, Margarita and Los Roques.

Tour operators
Arassari Trek, *C 24 No 8-301 (beside the teleférico), T0414-746 3569, www.arassari.com.* Run by Tom and Raquel Evenou (based in Switzerland), mostly for rafting tours, but also Roraima, Los Llanos, canyoning, and horse-trekking.
Catatumbo Tour, *T0414-725 0315, www.catatumbo tour.com.* Photographer Alan Highton and his team specialize in 2-day trips to Catatumbo to see the lightning, visit the communities of the region and experience the variety of habitats between the Andes and the delta. They have a camp at Ologa lagoon. Naturalist tours to other parts of the country offered. Very experienced, several languages spoken.
Fanny Tours, *C 24, No 8-31, T0274-252 2952, T0414-747 1349, www.fanny-tours.com.* Patrizia Rossi, José Albarrán for parapenting (the first to do it), reliable. Apart from parapenting, specializes in mountain biking, with and without jeep support, bike hire, rafting; Llanos, Catatumbo, canyoning, trekking to mountains and some climbing; also tours combining all types of sport. Recommended.
Gravity Tours, *C 24 entre Av 7 y 8, 1 block from cable car, T0274-251 1279, T0424-760 8327, www. gravity-tours.com.* Bilingual guides, natural history and adventure tours, some extreme, including rock climbing, rafting, biking, Llanos trips and Gran Sabana.
Guamanchi Tours, *C 24, No 8-86, T0274-252 2080, www.guamanchi.com.* Owned by John and Joëlle Peña. Specializes in mountaineering and safari tours to Los Llanos, with 22 years' experience, including working with documentary crews. Good service, ethical ethos and constantly updated equipment. They also offer rafting and kayaking from beginner to extreme, biking, birdwatching, paragliding, pendulum jumping and tours of Amazonas. They have **Posada Guamanchi** in town (see page 1621) and at Los Nevados (see below) and an adventure camp with rooms with bath by the Río Siniguis in Barinas. German, French, Italian and English spoken. Recommended.

Natoura Travel & Adventure Tours, *C 31 entre Av Don Tulio y prol Av 6 No 5-27 (Diagonal Bomberos ULA), Mérida 5101, T0274-252 4216, in US T303-800 4639, www.natoura.com. Daily 0830-1800.* Friendly, award-winning company organizing tours throughout Venezuela, run by José Luis Troconis and Renate Reiners, English, French, German and Italian spoken, climbing, trekking, rafting, horse riding, mountain biking, birdwatching and equipment hire. Their self-drive option allows you to rent a car and they will reserve accommodation for your route. Repeatedly recommended.

Transport

Air Scheduled flights have been suspended since 2008 and remain so at time of research. Alternatively, there are frequent flights between Caracas and airports at **San Antonio** (3-5 hrs by road), or **El Vigía** (1½-2½ hrs away, shared taxi US$5.50 per car, an official will direct you to a taxi and set the price); both are served by several airlines.

Bus The terminal has 2 levels, the upper one for small buses, minivans and cars to nearby places, the lower for interstate buses, www.terminalde merida.com.ve. Taxis line up outside the main entrance; you will be shown to a taxi. A small exit tax is charged for journeys in the state and for long distance, payable at one of 2 kiosks leading to buses. Make sure you pay, officials check buses before departure. On interstate buses, it is essential to book in advance; for buses within the state you pay on board. The terminal has a tourist office, phones, toilets, luggage store and places to eat. Fares: **Caracas**, US$4.25, 10 hrs (regular buses, several companies); **Maracay**, US$3-4; **Valencia**, US$3-4 **Maracaibo**, US$4; **Coro**, US$3-4.

Transportes Barinas (T0274-263 4651), to **Barinas** (US$2) via **Apartaderos** (US$0.35), to **Guanare** (US$1) and **Valera** (US$1.50-2.50). From upper level of terminal: **Táchira Mérida**, T0414-712 5913, to **San Cristóbal** (US$2.50, 6 hrs) and **San Antonio**. Also to Jají, Chiguará, Apartaderos, Barinas, El Vigía. **Líneas Unidas**, T0274-263 8472, *por puesto* microbus with TV, and car, to **Maracaibo**, every 2 hrs, US$2.60-4. If heading for **Ciudad Bolívar**, change buses in Valencia or Maracay.

Taxi In town US$1.50.

Sierra Nevada de Mérida
climb the peaks or take the cable car, plus the Andean route to Colombia

The Sierra is a mixture of the wild and isolated and the very touristy. In the latter group fall the cable car up Pico Espejo and villages designed to lure the shopper, but it is not difficult to escape the tour groups. There are routes from the mountains to the Llanos and to Colombia. This area is the heart of Venezuelan mountaineering and trekking. There are several important peaks and some superb hikes. Bear in mind that high altitudes will be reached and acclimatization is essential. Suitable equipment is necessary; you may consider bringing your own. Other activities in the Sierra Nevada include mountain biking, whitewater rafting, parapenting and horse riding. See What to do, opposite.

★Parque Nacional Sierra Nevada (South)
Close to Mérida is the popular hiking area around Los Nevados, with the added attraction of the highest cable car in the world. The further you go from Mérida, the greater the off-the-beaten-track possibilities for hiking and exploration that arise.

Since this is a national park, you need a permit from the **Inparques** (National Parks) offices in Mérida (see page 1620) to hike and camp overnight. Permits are not given to single hikers (except to Los Nevados), a minimum of two people is needed. Have your passport ready. Return permit after your hike; park guards will radio the start of the trek to say you've reached the end. If camping, remember that the area is 3500-4200 m so acclimatization is necessary. The night temperatures can fall below freezing an a -12°C sleeping bag is necessary, plus good waterproofs. Conditions are much more severe than you'd think at balmy Mérida.
Don't leave litter. Some treks are very difficult so check with the tourist office before leaving. Water purification is also recommended. See Mérida Tour operators in What to do, opposite.

Warning...
Do not attempt Pico Espejo alone; go with a guide, it is easy to get lost.

Pico Espejo The world's highest and longest aerial cableway (built by the French in 1957-1960) runs to **Pico Espejo** (4765 m) in four stages. It is called **Teleférico de Mérida Mukumbarí**. The **Teleférico** ① *T274-252 7560, www.telefericodemerida.travel, Wed-Sun 0700-1300, US$50, payment in US$ only or with credit/debit card, passport/ID also required, only sold on day of travel from 0700-1100*, was reopened in 2016, following modernisation work, along with improved hiking trails. The final station is at Pico Espejo, with a change of car at every station, all of which have cafés, toilets and advice. Beware altitude sickness: there is oxygen and a nursing station at higher points. **Barinitas** is the ground level station, Plaza de las Heroínas; you can hire, or buy, hats, gloves and scarves here, the Venezuelans all do. **La Montaña** (2442 m) is the second station with a small Museo del Montañismo. You pass over various levels of forest. Next is **La Aguada** (3452 m), then **Loma Redonda** (4045 m). From here you can start the trek to Los Nevados (see below); you must inform Inparques if trekking to Los Nevados. Pause for 10 minutes at Loma Redonda before the last stage to Pico Espejo, where there is a statue of Nuestra Señora de las Nieves. Next door to Pico Espejo is **Pico Bolívar** (Mukumbarí, where the sun sleeps) with Humboldt behind. It has remnants of a glacier. In the other direction, closest is **La Silla del Toro** and you can see a statue of Francisco Miranda with the Venezuelan flag on an outcrop. On a clear day you can see the blue haze of the Llanos to the east and, west, as far as Sierra de Cocuy and Guicán in Colombia. Across Río Chama you can see Sierra de la Culata. It is advisable to spend only 30 minutes at Pico Espejo. Apart from Los Nevados trek, the only safe part to walk down is Loma Redonda to La Aguada; a rough but clear trail, two hours; wear boots, not for children or the elderly, take water.

It is possible to hike from Pico Espejo to the cloudforest at **La Mucuy** (see below), two to three days walking at over 4000 m altitude, passing spectacular snow peaks and Lagos Verde and Coromoto. A tent and a warm sleeping bag are essential, as is a good map. If you start at Pico Espejo you will be at the highest point first, so although you will be descending, you may have altitude sickness from the word go.

Los Nevados Los Nevados (altitude 2711 m) is a colonial town with cobbled streets, an ancient chapel and a famous fiesta on 2 May. From here, it is a very testing two-day trek to **Pico Espejo**, with a strong chance of altitude sickness as the ascent is more than 1600 m. It is best done November-June early in the morning (before 0830 ideally), before the clouds spoil the view. In summer the summit is clouded and covered with snow and there is no view. Reputable trekking companies provide suitable clothing; temperatures can be 0° C. August is the coldest month.

From Los Nevados to **Loma Redonda** takes five to seven hours, four hours with mules (14 km). The hike is not too difficult; breathtaking views; be prepared for cold rain in the afternoon, start very early. The walk from Los Nevados to the village of **El Morro** (24 km) takes seven to nine hours (very steep in parts). (It's 47 km to Mérida; jeeps do the trip daily.) Sr Oviller Ruiz provides information on the history of the church of San Jacinto (the patron saint, whose fiesta is on 16 August) and the indigenous cemetery. The town, with its red tiled roofs, is an interesting blend of the colonial and the indigenous.

★Parque Nacional Sierra Nevada (North) and Sierra de La Culata

The Transandean highway snakes its way through the rugged mountain landscape, past neat, little towns of red-tiled roofs, steep fields and terraces of maize and potatoes. Just outside Mérida a side road goes to **El Valle**, known for *pasteles de trucha, vino de mora* and handicraft shops. The snow-tipped peaks of the high sierras watch over this bucolic scene, with Pico Bolívar lording it over them all. Throughout the park you will see a plant with felt-like leaves of pale grey-green, the *frailejón* (or great friar, *espeletia*), which blooms with yellow flowers from September to December. There are more than 130 species; tall ones grow at less than 1 cm a year.

Tabay and around At 12 km from Mérida, Tabay (30 minutes, altitude 1708 m) is named after an indigenous tribe. Its Plaza Bolívar has an attractive church, trees and plants. Around it are mini mercados, Pizzería Valentina (best in town), Pastelitos (at bus stop from Mérida, for *empanadas* in the morning), and other transport stops. Jeeps run a regular service to **La Mucuy** cloudforest, 0600-2200, they are labelled (US$1 one way if five passengers). They drop you at the Guardaparques. There is nothing to pay for a day visit, but you pay per night if making the Travesía to Pico Espejo and the Teleférico (or alternative route) down to Mérida. When going back to Tabay, you may have to wait for a jeep; the driver will charge extra for backpacks. Jeeps also go to the **Aguas Termales**

(from a different stop, just off Plaza Bolívar, US$0.50). It is possible to walk and there are signs. The man-made pool has 38°C water. The area is also good for walking and horse riding; all Mérida agencies go here.

Beyond Tabay the road goes through **Mucurubá** (2400 m) with a pleasant Plaza Bolívar and blue and white church, colonial buildings and handicrafts, and passes the **Monumento al Perro Nevado**. It depicts Simón Bolívar; the young *indígena* boy, Tinjacá; the Mucuchíes dog, Snowy, and the father and son who gave Bolívar the dog in 1813. According to legend, both Tinjaca and Nevado were devoted to Bolívar until their death on the same day at the Battle of Carabobo, 1821. At **Mucuchíes** (altitude 2983 m) the statue of the Liberator on Plaza Bolívar also features Tinjaca and Snowy. Also on the Plaza is a wooden statue of San Isidro, patron saint of farmers; all rural communities honour him on 15 May. The patron saint of Mucuchíes is San Benito; this festival (and several others) on 27-30 December is celebrated by participants wearing flower-decorated hats and firing blunderbusses. **Tourist office** on Calle 9 as you enter from Mérida; internet at Calle 9 Independencia.

The road leads up from Mucuchíes to **San Rafael de Mucuchíes** (altitude 3140 m, fiesta 24 October). You should visit the remarkable church, pieced together from thousands of stones, by the late Juan Félix Sánchez (born 1900), nationally renowned as a sculptor, philosopher and clown. The chapel is dedicated to the Virgen de Coromoto; it was blessed by Pope John Paul II. The tombs of Sánchez and his companion of 50 years, Epifania Gil, are inside. Next door is his house, now a museum with photos, weavings and sculptures. Opposite is the library given by him to the community. He built a similar chapel at El Tisure. The picturesque road continues to **Apartaderos** (two hours from Mérida). It follows the Río Chama valley in the heart of the cultivated highlands and the fields extend up to the edge of the *páramo*, clinging to the steep slopes. Main crops are potatoes (four harvests a year) onions, garlic and carrots. East of the Río Chama is the Sierra Nevada; to the west is the Sierra de La Culata. There are handicrafts, *posadas* and eateries.

Apartaderos (altitude 3342 m) is at the junction of Route 7 and the road over the Sierra Nevada to Barinas. About 3 km above Apartaderos, a narrow paved road (signposted) turns west off the highway at Escuela Estatal 121 and winds its way to **Llano del Hato** (3510 m) and on to the **Centro de Investigaciones de Astronomía** (3600 m) ① *T0274-245 0106/888 0154, www. cida.gob.ve, Wed-Sat 1500-1900, Wed-Sun 1300-1900 in high season (Carnaval, Holy Week, Jul-Sep and Christmas); check website for details, US$1.40 for adults, seniors and under-6s free.* Guided tours cover the museum, two videos, two of the observatories and, if the weather permits, use of a telescope at nightfall. At least two view-points on the way in give great views of the Lake Mucubají plateau. A good paved road descends 7 km from Llano del Hato to the Mérida highway at La Toma, just above Mucuchíes. Many prehispanic terraces and irrigation systems, adobe houses and ox-ploughed fields (*poyos*) are visible from the road.

Three kilometres beyond the junction of the roads from Barinas and Valera is the entrance to the **Parque Nacional Sierra Nevada** (Línea Cultura bus from Mérida ends at the junction, two hours; taxis run from bus stop to park, US$2). At the turn-off to the park is a motel and restaurant. Near the entrance is **Laguna Mucubají**, at 3600 m, with free campsite; visitors' centre, bookshop, good maps, interesting museum. A two- to 2½-hour walk takes you to **Laguna Negra** and back (1½ hours on horseback, US$6 to hire a horse, guide US$3). A further 1½-hour walk from Laguna Negra is the beautiful **Laguna Los Patos**. There are many *frailejón* plants here. Guides (not always necessary) are at Laguna Mucubají or the hotels in Santo Domingo. *Páramo* tours to this area usually include Pico El Aguila (see Road to the high Andes, page 1617).

From Mérida to the Panamericana

There are three routes from Mérida to the Panamericana which runs at the foot of the Andes near the border with Zulia state. The most northerly of them is the most interesting.

Via La Azulita This beautiful journey, starting in the highlands from Mérida, heads west. It passes La Chorrera waterfall on the way to **La Encrucijada** (restaurant and service station), where a side road leads to **Jají**, a pretty, restored colonial village with white-washed houses, cobbled streets, arches on the exits to the plaza and a white and blue church. Most houses are given over to handicrafts shops. There are a few hotels and others in the hills, where there is good walking. *Buseta* from Mérida bus terminal, hourly, 50 minutes, US$0.50.

From La Encrujidada the road passes dairy farms before its descent through cloudforest. Towns passed on the way are San Eusebio and Mirabel. This is prime birdwatching territory as the road, paved but rough in parts, twists down through several habitats. **La Azulita**, 73 km, four hours from Mérida, is the base for birdwatching tours, with several lodges nearby. A modern cathedral stands on the Plaza. From La Azulita, the road meets the Panamericana at **Caño Zancudo**, passing en route the Cascada Palmita. Turn south for El Vigía, one of the hottest zones in South America, and routes to Lago de Maracaibo and Catatumbo.

Via El Ejido **El Vigía** is where the second route from Mérida meets the Panamericana. Transandean Route 7 leaves Mérida and passes through **El Ejido**, originally known as Las Guayabas, or 'the city of honey and flowers'. El Ejido and surrounding villages in the sugar cane zone are known for handicrafts and ceramics. One such historic town is **Mesa de los Indios** (www.andes.net/mesadelosindios), where sugarcane is produced, 5 km from El Ejido towards Jaji, 1¼ hours from Mérida. It is famous for its musical traditions and for its artists. Every Saturday La Retreta de Antonio Valero, a youth group band, plays wind and percussion instruments in the plaza at 2000. Travellers may donate a wind instrument to the youngsters. Buses to La Mesa leave the plaza in El Ejido.

The main road follows the Chama valley, to Lagunillas and Tovar. **Lagunillas** was founded in the 16th century by Spaniard Juan Rodríguez Suárez on the site of a prehispanic ceremonial centre. Its elaborately choreographed dances honouring a beautiful indigenous princess can be seen at festivities taking place on 15 May. More can be learned at **Museo Arqueológico Julio César Salas** ⓘ *on Parque Sucre*. **San Juan de Lagunillas**, 2 km away, is where Mérida was originally supposed to be built. Locals (and allegedly doctors) say that the climate is one of the healthiest in the world. There are botanical gardens and a colourful fiesta on 24 June.

Near **Estanques**, a winding road leads towards **Chiguará**, one of the best-preserved coffee towns in Venezuela. Bizarrely, it contains a theme park: La Montaña de los Sueños ⓘ *www.montanadelossuenos.com, 1400-2100, daily (Wed-Sun only in low season), ticket office open 1400-1700, US$14, children US$13 and senior citizens US$12, food available*, devoted to the history of the Venezuelan film industry (1950s to 1970s), complete with sets, old aeroplanes, limousines, cameras and posters. There are also displays of local television, commercial music and theatre. Chiguará is 45 km from Mérida: take bus or *por puesto* towards El Vigía and ask to be dropped at junction for Chiguará, from where you have to hitch or wait for infrequent bus or *por puesto*.

Beyond Estanques the main highway for bus and heavy traffic turns off Route 7. Near the intersection on the right is 19th-century **Hacienda La Victoria** with an interesting coffee museum. The highway descends from the grey, scarred mountains before the thickly wooded tropical hillsides above the plains. Buses between Mérida and San Cristóbal then belt along the Panamericana to **La Fría** from where a four-lane motorway goes to San Cristóbal.

Via Tovar and La Grita The third route leaves the Transandean road at **Tovar** (96 km from Mérida), passing through Zea, a pleasant town in the foothills. From Tovar the road continues to **Bailadores** (fiesta from Christmas to Candlemas, 2 February), and **La Grita**, a pleasant town in Táchira state (Sunday market, fiesta 6 August). Near Bailadores is the pleasant **Parque La Cascada India Carú**, named after a legendary princess whose tears at the death of her warrior lover created the waterfall. This route takes the wild and beautiful old mountain road over Páramo de La Negra to San Cristóbal. Mérida–San Cristóbal buses go via La Fría, not this road; by public transport change in Tovar and La Grita.

San Cristóbal *Colour map 1, B4.*

The capital of Táchira State was founded in 1561. Today it's a large, busy, but friendly place built over hills and ravines, although a few blocks in historic centre, around the cathedral, retain a colonial air. You need to know which district you are in for orientation, eg La Concordia for the bus station. The **Fiesta de San Sebastián** in second half of January is a major international event, with parades, trade shows, and much more; book ahead, prices rise.

On Sunday, take a taxi to **Peribeca** (US$11 one way), a tiny colonial village with handicraft shops, restaurants and sellers of dairy products, fruit desserts and bewildering variety of liqueurs and infusions. The pretty handicraft alley is next to the modern church. There are four *posadas* and many restaurants open for Sunday lunch (the best is **El Solar de Juancho**). Alternatively, on Monday, go to the wholesale vegetable market of **Táriba**, just off highway going north. The town's huge white Basílica de la Virgen de la Consolación (1959) can be seen from the highway.

San Cristóbal to San Antonio *Colour map 1, B4.*

The border town of San Antonio is 55 km from San Cristóbal by a paved, congested road. At **Capacho** (25 km from San Antonio) is an interesting old Municipal Market building, with lions at the four corners.

San Antonio is connected by international bridge with Cúcuta on the Colombian side (16 km); continue by road or air to Bogotá. San Antonio has a colonial cathedral and some parks, but is not tourist-oriented. Avenida Venezuela leads to Venezuelan customs. You can catch most transport here, to Cúcuta, San Cristóbal, even to Caracas, but the bus terminal is off the road to the airport: at the roundabout at end of Avenida Venezuela, turn left (Calle 11), take a Circunvalación combi marked Terminal (US$0.50). Also buses to airport. There is a festival on 13-20 May.

Border with Colombia This is the main crossing point between the two countries and the border formalities are geared towards locals. Few foreigners travel overland here. Make sure you get a Venezuelan exit stamp at SAIME ① *Urb Las Castras, Calle Principal Concordia, Antiguo FONCAFE, San Cristóbal, T0276-347 3434, Mon-Fri 0800-1600 (till 1700 on Tue).* You will have to fill out a departure

> **Fact…**
> Venezuelan time is 30 minutes ahead of Colombian.

card and pay departure tax across the street. **Colombian consulate** ① *Cra 2 No 7-61, entre C 5 y 6, T0276-347 1960, open Mon-Fri 0700-1300.* The border is open 0500-1800 for vehicles, till 2200 for pedestrians. Colombian formalities are taken care of right after the bridge: immigration procedures are straightforward with only a passport check and stamp. Foreigners can arrange exit and entry stamps 0800-1800, often much later. If you only travel to Cúcuta (even to spend the night), no immigration formalities are needed. Just cross the bridge by bus, taxi or *por puesto* and return the same way. If you plan to travel further to Colombia, however, you will need both Venezuelan exit stamp and Colombian entry stamp. Many *casas de cambio* on Avenida Venezuela near the international bridge will change Colombian pesos, but not all change cheques or even US$ cash. The exchange rate for bolívares to pesos is the same in San Antonio as in Cúcuta.

Entering Venezuela, get your passport stamp at immigration and take bus, *por puesto* or taxi across the bridge. Ask the driver to take you to Venezuelan immigration, otherwise you will be taken to the centre of San Antonio and will have to backtrack. You can also cross the bridge on foot. Information centre is at the end of the bridge on Venezuelan side. Go to **SAIME** for entry formalities then look for a bus or *por puesto* to San Cristóbal on Av Venezuela, or go to the bus station (taxi from SAIME US$1.50). If Venezuelan customs is closed at weekends, it is not possible to cross from Cúcuta. There is a customs and Guardia Nacional post at Peracal outside San Antonio; be prepared for luggage and strip searches. There may be more searches en route.

If crossing by private vehicle, car documents must be stamped at the SENIAT office at the Puente Internacional, just before San Antonio. Two different stamps are needed at separate **SENIAT buildings** ① *Mon-Fri 0800-1200, 1300-1630, final Av Venezuela, Edif Nacional San Antonio de Táchira, T0276-771 1145/1620, http://declaraciones.seniat.gob.ve.* It's essential to have proof of car/motorbike ownership. You must check in advance if you need a visa and a *carnet de passages* (see box, page 1677). See Cúcuta, Colombia chapter, for details on exit formalities. Once in Venezuela, you may find police are ignorant of requirements for foreign cars.

Note The border was reopened in December 2016, having been closed by the Venezuelan authorities in an effort to stop contraband and other illegal activities. At the time of research, it remains open to pedestrians, although money-changing facilities may be restricted. Seek advice locally before crossing this border.

Tourist information

Cormetur
C 45 con Av Urdaneta, next to airport, T800-637 4300.

Inparques
*Parque Metropolitano, Av 19 de Abril,
T0276-346 6544.*

Where to stay

Los Nevados

$$-$ pp Posada Florencia
Calle Principal, top end of town, T0416-078 6192.
Big dorms with 7-11 beds, good food, run by very
friendly and knowledgeable local family.

$ pp Posada Bella Vista
Behind church.
Hot water, hammocks, great views, restaurant.

$ pp Posada Guamanchi
T0274-252 2080, www.guamanchi.com.
Solar power, great views, with and without
bath, 2 meals included. Recommended.

El Morro

$ Posada run by Doña Chepa
As you enter from Los Nevados. T0274-271 4241.
Warm. Recommended.

$ pp Posada El Orégano
Including meals, basic, good food.
Recommended.

Tabay

$$ Posada Casa Vieja I
*Transandina via Páramo, San Rafael de Tabay,
inside the Parador Turístico El Paramito, T0273-
611 6634, www.casa-vieja-merida.com.*
Plant-filled colonial house, German and Peruvian
run, good doubles, hot water, breakfast and
dinner available, good food, relaxing, very
helpful, information on independent trips from
Tabay and transport, English, French and German
spoken. Travel agency, **Caiman Tours**, for Llanos,
wildlife and adventure tours, see also www.
birds-venezuela.de. From the bus terminal in
Mérida take a bus via Mucuchíes or Apartaderos,
30 mins to Tabay, get off exactly 1.5 km after the
gas station in Tabay village (just after you pass
Plaza Bolívar); the bus stop is called Cauchera/
El Paramito. There is a sign on the road pointing

left. Free pick-up from the airport or terminal
with reservation. They also have a 2nd *posada* in
the village of Altamira de Cáceres, Posada Casa
Vieja 2 (**$$**). Warmly recommended.

$ La Casona de Tabay
*On the Mérida road 1.5 km from the plaza,
T0274-283 0089, posadalacasona@cantv.net.*
A beautiful colonial-style hotel, surrounded by
mountains, comfortable, home cooking, family-
run. Take *por puesto*, 2 signposts.

Mucuchíes

$$-$ Los Conquistadores
*Av Carabobo 14, T0274-872 0350,
www.losconquistadoreshotelresort.com.*
Nice decor, modern, heating, lots of facilities like
pool tables and other games, garden, parking,
restaurant 0800-2200, *tasca* bar, and bike hire.
Arranges transport for tours, ATM.

$ Posada Los Andes
*Independencia 25, T0274-872 0151,
T0414-717 2313.*
Old house on street above plaza, run by Las
Hermanas Pironi Belli, 5 cosy rooms, hot water,
shared bathrooms, TV in living room, excellent
restaurant (breakfast extra, *criollo* and Italian
food, 0800-2030). Highly recommended.

San Rafael de Mucuchíes

$ El Rosal
Bolívar 37, T0274-872 0331, T0426-574 1130.
Hot water, good, also cabins with kitchenette,
no breakfast, café nearby, restaurant for groups,
tasca at weekends.

$ Posada San Rafael del Páramo
*Just outside San Rafael, 500 m from the
Capilla de Piedra, on road to Apartaderos,
T0274-872 0938/1161.*
Charming converted house with lots of
interesting sculpture and paintings, hot water,
heating, also cabin with kitchenette, walking
and riding tours (guide extra). Recommended.

Apartaderos

$ Hotel y Restaurante Mifafí
*On main road, T0274-888 0131,
www.refugiomifafi.com.*
Cheaper without heating, pleasant rooms and
cabins, hot water, good food served all day.
A welcoming, reliable choice.

From Mérida to the Panamericana

Jají

$$$ Estancia La Bravera
18 km from Jají towards La Azulita, T0212-978 2627, 0414-293 3306, www.estancialabravera.com.
Cabins in relaxing gardens in the cloudforest, great for birdwatching (self-guided tours offered) hot water, includes breakfast and dinner, lunch extra, uses home produce, non-Venezuelans should consult in advance for prices. Recommended.

$$$ Hacienda El Carmen
Aldea La Playa, 2 km from Jají (there is public transport), T0414-639 2701, T0414-630 9562, www.haciendaelcarmen.com.ve.
On a working dairy and coffee plantation, built 1863, fascinating buildings, lovely rooms, 1 with jacuzzi, some simpler rooms, breakfast included, coffee tours and nature trails, owner Andrés Monzón. Must reserve in advance.

$$-$ Posada Restaurant Aldea Vieja
C Principal, just off Plaza, T0274-266 0072/ 0426-926 0367.
Colonial-style main building, also cabins for 4-8, lovely views, simple rooms, hot water, meals extra, playground.

La Azulita

$ El Tao
On a side road beyond Remanso, 4-5 km, 6 mins in car from La Azulita, T0274-511 3088, T0416-175 0011, www.eltaomerida.com.
Taoist owners and oriental-style spa with saunas, and natural therapies, many birds, favoured by birders, lovely gardens, very safe and peaceful, nice public areas. Cabins for 2-7, also dorms, packages for 3-10 days available, restaurant, boxed lunches and early breakfast for birding groups, with guided walks, horse rides and excursions.

$ Remanso del Quebradón
Close to junction, T0416-289 1081, www.remanso.com.ve.
4 rooms, on a small coffee farm with fruit trees in the gardens, restaurant, games room, badminton, popular with birdwatchers.

San Cristóbal
Cheapest hotels around the bus station (eg **Río de Janeiro**, C 1, No 7-27, Urb Juan Maldonado, La Concordia, by bus station, and **Tropical**, Prol 5ta Av No 7472, opposite bus station, T0276-347 2932), **$$** business hotels in the centre and more upmarket places in the northwestern suburbs.

$$$ Lidotel
Sambil San Cristóbal Mall, Autopista Antonio José de Sucre, Las Lomas, T0276-510 3333, www.lidotelhotelboutique.com.
Attached to an enormous, posh shopping mall, with all the luxuries of 4-star hotel, pool, very well run. Recommended.

$$ Del Rey
Av Ferrero Tamayo, Edif El Rey, T0276-343 0561.
Good showers, fridge, kitchenette, laundry, no breakfast but *panadería* in building, pizzas.

$ Posada Rincón Tachirense
Av Ferrero Tamayo con C 3, N Ft-19, La Popita, T0276-341 8753, www.posadarincontachirense.com.
Not central, down hill from **Del Rey**, cheaper with shared bath, comfortable, has **Restaurant Clementina**, serving typical dishes. Recommended.

$ Posada Turística Don Manuel
Cra 10 No 1-104, just off Av 19 de Abril, Urb La Concordia, T0276-347 8082.
Rooms are across street; Sra Carmen will direct you. Hot water, family-run, fridge, fan, limited kitchen facilities, no breakfast, parking. Sleeps 8, always book in advance, convenient.

San Cristóbal to San Antonio

Capacho

$ La Molinera
20 mins from San Cristóbal at Capacho, municipalidad de Independencia, T0276-788 3117.
Rooms and suites in a beautiful, traditional *posada* with swimming pool and handmade furniture. Good Tachirense food in its restaurant.

San Antonio
Many hotels near town centre.

$ Adriático
C6 y Cra 6, T0276-771 5757.
Not far from Av Venezuela, 3-star, functional, a little rundown but handy for border.

$ El Gran Neveri
C 3, No 3-13, esq Carrera 3, T0276-771 5702.
Safe, parking nearby, 1 block from Customs, opposite Guardia Nacional barracks. No food, dated.

Restaurants

San Cristóbal
El Barrio Obrero has the main concentration of eateries, bars and discos. Try **Rocamar**, Cra 20 y C 14, for seafood. Also pizza places and *pastelerías*.

$$-$ La Olleta
Cra 21, no 10-171, just off plaza, Barrio Obrero,
T0276-356 6944.
Smart, simple decor, Venezuelan and international
with creative touches, well presented.

Around town there are many *panaderías* and
pastelerías for snacks as well as bread and cakes,
coffee and other drinks, eg **América**, Cra 8, Edif
La Concordia, no 4-113, La Concordia (several on
Cra 8 y C 4, La Concordia); also **Táchira** branches.

San Antonio

$ Da Cecilio
Cra 20, edge of town, beyond Mercado municipal,
T0276-771 0826.
Canteen-like décor but good pizzas.

Transport

Los Nevados
Jeep Los Nevados-**Mérida**, late afternoon
(depart 0700 from Plaza Las Heroínas in Mérida),
5-6 hrs, US$5 pp, US$20 per jeep, very rough and
narrow but spectacular.

Tabay
Regular bus service from **Mérida**, C 19 entre
Avs 3 y 4, every 10 mins, US$1.35; taxi US$4
(more at night).

Apartaderos
Bus To **Mérida** from turn-off to Barinas; bus to
Barinas on the road over the Sierra Nevada is
unreliable, best to catch it in Mérida.

San Cristóbal
Air Airport at Santo Domingo, 40 km away.
Helpful tourist kiosk with leaflets, map of San
Cristóbal US$0.50. Taxi to San Cristóbal US$6, can
take as little as 35 mins, but normally much more,
lots of traffic, nice scenery (tourist office says
no other option). Daily flights to/from **Caracas**.
Alternatively, fly to **San Antonio** (see below) for
better public transport links.

Bus Local buses cost US$0.25. **intercomunal**
goes from Av Ferrero Tamayo (northwest) to
Bus Terminal. **Tusca** from Av Ferrero Tamayo
to centre. Taxis US$2 for a short run.

The bus station is in La Concordia, in the
southeast. It is a bus terminal, shopping mall,
market, phone exchange and food court all
lumped together. Terminal tax US$0.10, paid
on bus before departure. Company offices are

grouped together, but **Expresos Occidente** have
their own terminal nearby. To **Mérida**, US$2.50,
5 hrs, with **Táchira-Mérida** (buy ticket on bus);
also **Expreso Unido**. Buses to Mérida go via the
Panamericana, not over the Páramo. National
Guard Control at La Jabonesa, just before San
Juan de Colón, be prepared for luggage search.
To **Maracaibo**, 6-8 hrs, US$3-4. To **Caracas**, US$4,
7½ hrs; **Valencia**, US$3.50, 6 hrs. To **Barinas**,
US$2, 4 hrs. To **San Fernando de Apure** via
Guasdualito, US$2, 4 hrs. To **San Antonio**,
1¼ hrs (but San Cristóbal rush hour can add lots
of time), US$1.50, **Línea San Antonio**, T0276-347
0976 (San Antonio 0276-771 2966) and **Unión de
Conductores**, T346 0691 (San Antonio 771 1364).
To **Cúcuta**, **Línea Venezuela**, T0276-347 3086
(Cúcuta T0270-583 6413) and **Fronteras Unidas**,
T0276-347 7446 (Cúcuta T0270 583 5445), US$2,
Mon-Fri 0800-1200, 1400-1800. Opposite terminal
on Rugeles, **Coop de Conductores Fronterizos**
cars, T0276-611 2256, to **San Antonio**.

San Antonio
Air The airport has exchange facilities (mainly
for Colombian pesos). Taxis run to SAIME
(immigration) in town, and on to Cúcuta airport.
Flights to **Caracas**.

Bus From terminal several companies to
Caracas, via the Llanos, Valencia and Maracay.
Caracas US$7 (*bus-cama*). **Expresos San
Cristóbal** have office on Av Venezuela, close to
Customs, 1800 to Caracas, 13-14 hrs; **Expresos
Mérida**, Av Venezuela, No 6-17, at 1900. **Táchira-
Mérida** to **Mérida** and **Barquisimeto**; **Expresos
Unidos** to Mérida. To **San Cristóbal**, catch a bus
on Av Venezuela.

Border with Colombia
Air It is cheaper, but slower, to fly **Caracas–
San Antonio**, take a taxi to Cúcuta, then take
an internal Colombian flight, than to fly direct
Caracas–Colombia. The airport transfer at San
Antonio is well organized and taxi drivers make
the 25-min trip with all stops.

Bus On Av Venezuela *por puestos/colectivos*
to **Cúcuta** charge US$0.50, and buses US$0.25
payable in bolívares or pesos, 30 mins. Some say
to terminal, others to centre. Taxi to Cúcuta, US$4.
On any transport that crosses the border, make
sure the driver knows you need to stop to obtain
stamps. *Por puesto* drivers may refuse to wait. Taxi
drivers will stop at all the offices.

Los Llanos
& Amazonas

A spectacular route descends from the Sierra Nevada to the flat Llanos, one of the best places in the world to see birds and animals. This vast, sparsely populated wilderness of 300,000 sq km – one third of the country's area – lies between the Andes to the west and the Orinoco to the south and east.

Southwest of the Guayana region, on the banks of the Orinoco, Puerto Ayacucho is the gateway to the jungles of Venezuela. Although it takes up about a fifth of the country, Amazonas and its tropical forests are for the most part unexplored and unspoilt.

Los Llanos
wildlife abounds on these extensive flood plains

★The Llanos are veined by numerous slow-running rivers, forested along their banks. The flat plain is only varied here and there by *mesas*, or slight upthrusts of the land. About five million of the country's 6.4 million cattle are in the Llanos, but only around 10% of the human population. When the whole plain is periodically under water, the *llaneros* drive their cattle into the hills or through the flood from one *mesa* to another. When the plain is parched by the sun and the savanna grasses become inedible they herd the cattle down to the damper region of the Apure and Orinoco. Finally they drive them into the valley of Valencia to be fattened.

In October and November, when the vast plains are still partially flooded, wildlife abounds. Animals include capybara, caiman, monkeys, anacondas, river dolphins, pumas and many bird species. Though you can explore independently, towns are few and distances are great. It's better to visit on a tour from Mérida (page 1624), or stay at one of the ecotourism *hatos* (see below).

> **Tip...**
> Motorists travelling east to Ciudad Bolívar can go either across the Llanos or via San Carlos, Tinaco, El Sombrero, Chaguaramas, Valle de la Pascua (see below) and El Tigre. The latter route requires no ferry crossings and has more places with accommodation.

Valencia to Barinas

A good road goes to the western *llanos* of Barinas from Valencia. It goes through **San Carlos**, **Acarigua** (an agricultural centre and the largest city in Portuguesa state) and **Guanare**, a national place of pilgrimage with a cathedral containing the much venerated relic of the Virgin of Coromoto. The **Santuario Nacional Nuestra Señora de Coromoto** ① *25 km form Guanare on road to Barinas, www.santuariobasilicacoromoto.com, open 0800-1700*, is on the spot where the Virgin appeared to Cacique Coromoto in 1652. An imposing modern basilica dedicated to the Virgin, it was inaugurated by Pope John Paul II in 1996. Buses run from Calle 20 y Carrera 9, Guanare, every 15 minutes (US$0.40). Pilgrimages to Coromoto are 2 January and 11 September and Candlemas is 2 February.

The road continues to **Barinas**, the capital of the cattle-raising and oil-rich state of Barinas. A few colonial buildings remain on the plaza: the **Palacio del Marqués** and the **Casa de la Cultura**. Also here is the beautifully restored, 19th-century **Escuela de Música**; the cathedral is to the east. The

Best for
Birdwatching ▪ Ranches ▪ Wilderness ▪ Wildlife

shady Parque Universitario, just outside the city on Avenida 23 de Enero, has a botanical garden. **Tourist office (Corbatur)** ① *C Arzobispo Méndez, edif Vifran, p 1, diagonal al Banco Exterior, T0273-552 7091, https://twitter.com/corbatur.* Helpful, maps, no English spoken; kiosks at airport and bus station. From Barinas there is a beautifully scenic road to Apartaderos, in the Sierra Nevada de Mérida (see page 1627).

Towards San Fernando de Apure *Colour map 1, A6.*
At Lagua, 16 km east of Maracay, a good road leads south to San Fernando de Apure. It passes through **San Juan de los Morros**, with natural hot springs; **Ortiz**, near the crossroads with the San Carlos-El Tigre road; the Guárico lake and **Calabozo**. Some 132 km south of Calabozo, San Fernando is the hot and sticky capital of Apure state and a fast-growing trade and transport hub. From San Fernando travel east to Ciudad Bolívar (page 1659) or south to Puerto Ayacucho (see below).

San Fernando to Barinas
From San Fernando a road heads west to Barinas (468 km). It's a beautiful journey, but the road can be in terrible condition, eg between Mantecal, La Ye junction and Bruzual, a town just south of the Puente Nutrias on the Río Apure. In the early morning, many animals and birds can be seen, and in the wet season caiman (alligators) cross the road. **Mantecal** is a friendly cattle-ranching town with hotels and restaurants. **Fiesta**, 23-26 February.

Listings Los Llanos

Where to stay

Barinas
Business hotels include Eurobuilding Express, T0273-500 3120, www.hoteleuro.com/home/8-barinas, and Living hotel, T0273-517 6000, www.livinghotel.com.

$ Posada El Toreño
Av vieja San Silvestre, T0273-541 3367.
Cabins in spacious grounds on outskirts, with small pool and play area, restaurant, parking, good for families and groups.

$ Varyná
Av 23 de Enero, near the airport, T0273-533 3984.
Hot water, restaurant, parking. Recommended.

Staying at a tourist ranch
An alternative to travelling independently or arranging a tour from Mérida is to stay at a tourist ranch. Most *hatos* are in Apure state and can be reached from Barinas or San Fernando de Apure.

$$ Ecoposada La Fe
Km 51 between Calabozo and San Fernando de Apure at Corozopando in Guárico state, T0414-272 4205, www.ecoposadalafe.com.
All-inclusive tours include animal-watching trips and horse riding. 8 bedrooms in a colonial-style house, swimming pools, restaurant.

$$ Hato El Cedral
About 30 mins by bus from Mantecal (see above, T0416-502 4064). Address: Av México con Sur 25, El Conde, Edif Hotel El Alba, Caracas, T0240-808 3108, http://hatoelcedral.com.ve.
A 53,000-ha ranch, where hunting is banned. Fully inclusive price, tax extra (high season Nov-Apr), a/c, hot water, land and river safaris, guides, pool. The government has nationalized the ranch, see www.venetur.gob.ve for nationalized ranches.

$$ pp Hato Piñero
A safari-type lodge at a working ranch near El Baúl (turn off Tinaco-El Sombrero road at El Cantón), T0273-541 8900 or 0426-746 0343, www.venetur.gob.ve.
2-night, 3-day packages, including food, lodging, tours with local guides, but not return transport from Caracas. Bird- and animal-watching trips. The ranch has been bought by the government, but still accepts visitors and tour groups. From Caracas, 6 hrs; from Ciudad Bolívar, 9 hrs.

$ pp Rancho Grande
Close to Mantecal, T0416-873 1192.
Run by very friendly and knowledgeable Ramón Guillermo González. All inclusive, good wildlife spotting and horse riding trips, 4-day packages.

San Fernando de Apure
Several hotels are within 1 block of the intersection of Paseo Libertador and Av Miranda.

$$ Soleos
Av Intercomunal Los Centauros, T0247-341 0034,
http://hotelsoleos.com.
Modern Best Western hotel with various types
of room, restaurant, bar, pool, parking, Wi-Fi,
southwest of centre.

$ Gran Hotel Plaza
C Bolívar, T0247-342 1746.
Safe hotel with parking.

$ La Torraca
Paseo Libertador near C Bolívar, T0247-342 2777.
Rooms have balcony overlooking centre of town.
Recommended.

$ Nuevo Boulevard
Paseo Libertador, Monumento A Páez,
T0247-342 2280.
A/c rooms with bath in modern block,
fairly central.

What to do

Barinas
Campamento Colibrí, *Sector Caño Grance,
La Acequia, T0274-252 4961, T0414-748 0064, www.
colibri-tours.com.* Rafting trips in association with
Colibrí Tours in Mérida (www.colibri-tours.com).
Grados Alta Aventura, *Altamira de Cáceres,
T0416-877 4540, www.grados.com.ve/2011.*
Rafting, kayaking, birdwatching and other
adventure pursuits.

Rafting Barinas, *T0273-311 0388, www.
raftingbarinas.com.* With Campamento Aguas
Bravas, Carretera Nacional vía San Cristóbal,
Km 416, La Acequia, for rafting excursions.

Transport

Barinas
Air Aeropuerto Nacional, Av 23 de Enero. Flights
to **Caracas**.

Bus To **Mérida**, 6 a day with **Transportes
Barinas**, US$2, spectacular ride through the
mountains, 5-7 hrs (sit on right for best views);
also to **Valera** at 0730, 1130, US$2, 7 hrs. To
Caracas, US$3.50-5, 8 hrs, a few companies
go direct or via **Maracay** and **Valencia**. To
San Cristóbal, several daily, US$2, 5 hrs; to
San Fernando de Apure, US$8.50, 9 hrs with
Expresos Los Llanos at 0900, 2300; the same
company also goes to **Maracaibo** at 2000 and
2200, US$7.50, 8 hrs.

San Fernando de Apure
Air Aeropuerto Las Flecheras, Av 1 de Mayo,
T0247-341 0139. Flights to **Caracas**.

Bus Terminal is modern and clean, not far from
centre; US$1.50 taxi. To **Caracas**, US$9-12, 7 hrs;
to **Maracay**, US$9; to **Puerto Ayacucho**, US$4-6,
8 hrs; to **Calabozo**, 1½ hrs, US$3.50.

San Fernando to Barinas
Bus San Fernando de Apure–Mantecal 3½ hrs,
US$3; Mantecal–Barinas, 4 hrs, US$4.50.

Amazonas

a remote, riverine region for determined travellers

Much of Amazonas is stunningly beautiful and untouched, but access is only by river. The more
easily accessible places lie on the course of the Orinoco and its tributaries. The best time to visit
is October to December after the rains, but at any season, this is a remote part of the country.

San Fernando to Puerto Ayacucho
Route 2 runs south from San Fernando to Puerto Páez, crossing several major rivers. Between
the Capanaparo and Cinaruco rivers is the **Parque Nacional Cinaruco-Capanaparo** (also called
Santos Luzardo), reached only from this road. Puerto Páez lies at the confluence of the Meta and
Orinoco rivers. On the opposite bank of the Meta is **Puerto Carreño** in Colombia. A ferry (US$1.50)
crosses the Orinoco from Puerto Páez to **El Burro**, which lies just west of the paved Caicara-Puerto
Ayacucho road. From the El Burro turn-off it is 88 km to Puerto Ayacucho; taxi two hours, US$6. If
Route 2 is closed, the journey to Puerto Ayacucho from San Fernando involves a minimum 15-hour
detour via the Caicara ferry.

Puerto Ayacucho *Colour map 1, B6.*
The capital of the State of Amazonas is 800 km via the Orinoco from Ciudad Bolívar, but no direct
boats journey up river. At the end of the dry season (April), it is very hot and humid. It is deep in the

wild, across the Orinoco from Casuarito in Colombia. **Museo Etnológico Monseñor Enzo Ceccarelli** ① *Av Río Negro 30, Tue-Sat 0830-1200, 1430-1830, Sun 0900-1300, US$0.50,* has a library and collection of regional exhibits, recommended. In front of the museum is a market, Plaza de los Indios, open every day, where *indígenas* sell handicrafts. One block away is the cathedral. Prices in Puerto Ayacucho are generally higher than north of the Orinoco.

> **Warning...**
> Malaria is prevalent in this area; so make sure you take precautions.

Excursions November to December is the best time, when rivers are high but the worst of the rains has passed. In the wettest season, May-June, it may be difficult to organize tours for only a few days. At any time of year, permission from the military may be required to travel independently on the rivers.

You can walk up **Cerro Perico** for good views of the town, or go to the Mirador, 1 km from centre, for good views of the Ature rapids. A recommended trip is to the village of Pintado (12 km south), where petroglyphs described by Humboldt can be seen on the huge rock **Cerro Pintado**. This is the most accessible petroglyph site of the many hundreds which are scattered throughout Amazonas.

Some 35 km south on the road to Samariapo is the **Parque Tobogán de la Selva**, a pleasant picnic area based around a steeply inclined, smooth rock over which the Río Maripures cascades. This waterslide is great fun in the wet season; crowded on Sunday, take swimsuit and food and drink. A small trail leads up from the slide to a natural jacuzzi after about 20 minutes. Enquire at agencies in town about tours.

The well-paved road from Puerto Ayacucho to **Samariapo** (63 km) was built to bypass the rapids which here interrupt the Orinoco, dividing it into 'Upper' and 'Lower'; the powerful Maripures Rapids are very impressive.

Listings Amazonas

Tourist information

Puerto Ayacucho
Ask in the Gobernación building, Av Orinoco, T0248-521 0578/0340, https://twitter.com/gobamazonas.

Where to stay

Puerto Ayacucho

$$ Gran Hotel Amazonas
Av Evelio Roa y Amazonas, T0414-260 4411, www.amazonas.travel.
Recently refurbished, with tasteful ethnic-style décor, a/c, fridge, pool, restaurant and bar.

$$-$ Orinoquia Lodge
On the Río Orinoco, 20 mins from airport, book through Wao Turismo, T0212-214 1027, www.waoturismo.com, Cacao Travel, www. cacaotravel-venezuela.com, or through, T0212-977 1234, www.casatropical.com.ve.
Nice setting, comfortable lodgings in thatched huts, full board.

$ Posada Manapiare
Urb Alto Parima, 2da entrada, casa 1, T0248-521 3954, Facebook: PosadaTuristicaManapiare.
Pleasant, well-run, with rustic thatch-roofed cabins, lots of information, excellent choice, with restaurant, small pool, safe parking.

$ Res Internacional
Av Aguerrevere 18, T0248-521 0242.
A/c (cheaper without), comfortable, shower, locked parking, safe but basic, good place to find tour information and meet other travellers, if no room available you can sling up your hammock, bus drivers stay here and will drive you to the terminal for early starts.

Río Manapiare area

$$$ Campamento Camani
In a forest clearing on the banks of the Río Alto Ventuari, 2 hrs by launch from San Juan de Manapiare, T0416-338 9448.
From Puerto Ayacucho daily aerotaxi takes 50 mins. Maximum 26 at any one time, mosquito nets, all amenities, excursions available. Has 2-, 3- and 4-night packages including transport, full board and jungle excursions.

What to do

It is strongly recommended to go on tours organized by tour agents or guides registered in the **Asocación de Guías**, in the Cámara de Turismo de Puerto Ayacucho, Casa de la Piedra, on the Arteria Vial de la Av Orinoco with Av Principal (the house on top of the large rock). Some independent guides may not have permission to visit Amazonas.

Transport

Puerto Ayacucho
Air Airport 7 km southeast along Av Orinoco.

Bus Expresos del Valle to **Ciudad Bolívar** (US$4-6, 10 hrs; take something to eat, bus stops once for early lunch), **Caicara**, **Puerto Ordaz** and **San Félix**; Cooperativa Cacique to **San Fernando de Apure**, US$4-6, 8 hrs; both companies in bus terminal. **Expresos La Prosperidad** to **Caracas** and **Maracay** from Urb Alto Parima. Bus from **Caracas**, daily, US$4.50, 12 hrs (but much longer in wet season).

Ferry Ferry service across the Orinoco to Casuarito, US$1.50.

East
coast

Beautiful sandy bays, islands, forested slopes and a strong colonial influence all contribute to make this one of the most visited parts of the country. The western part, which is relatively dry, has the two main cities, Puerto La Cruz and Cumaná, which is possibly the oldest Hispanic city on the South American mainland. As you go east, you find some splendid beaches.

Off shore are two of Venezuela's prime holiday attractions, Isla de Margarita, a mix of the overdeveloped and the quiet, and the island paradise of the Los Roques archipelago.

Caracas to Puerto La Cruz

beach life east of Caracas

Very much a holiday coastline, the first part takes its name from the sweeping Barlovento bay in Miranda state. Onshore trade winds give the seaboard a lusher aspect than the more arid landscape elsewhere.

Caracas to Higuerote

It is some five hours from Caracas to Puerto La Cruz through Caucagua, from which there is a 58 km road northeast to **Higuerote**; the best beaches are out of town. A coastal road from Los Caracas to Higuerote has many beaches and beautiful views.

Parque Nacional Laguna de Tacarigua

At 14 km before Higuerote on the road from Caucagua is Tacarigua de Mamporal, where you can turn off to the **Parque Nacional Laguna de Tacarigua**. The 39,100-ha national park is an important ecological reserve, with a lagoon separated from the sea by a landspit, mangroves, good fishing and many water birds, including flamingos (usually involving a day-long boat trip to see them, the best time to see them is 1700-1930; permit required from Inparques at the *muelle*, US$4.50, open 0500-1830). Around 20,700 ha of the park are offshore. Boat trips leave from the Inparques *muelle* and cost about US$18 per person in a group of four. For kayaking see http://kayakvenezuela.com, one-day tours. The beaches beyond here are unspoilt and relaxing, but mosquitoes are a problem after sunset.

Puerto La Cruz and around *Colour map 2, A1.*

Originally a fishing village, Puerto La Cruz is now a major oil refining town and busy, modern holiday resort. Tourist facilities are above average, if expensive, and the sea is polluted.

The seafront avenue, Paseo de La Cruz y El Mar (formerly Paseo Colón), extends to the eastern extremity of a broad bay. To the west the bay ends at the prominent El Morro headland. Most hotels, restaurants, bars and clubs are along Paseo de La Cruz y El Mar, with excellent views of Bahía de Pozuelas and the islands of the Parque Nacional Mochima (see below). Vendors of paintings, jewellery, leather and hammocks are on Paseo de La Cruz y El Mar in the evening.

Best for
Beaches ▪ Diving ▪ Idyllic islands ▪ Marine life

The **Santa Cruz** festival is on 3 May, while 8 September is the **Virgen del Valle**, when boats cruise the harbour clad in palms and balloons; afternoon party at El Faro, Chimana, lots of salsa and beer.

The main attractions of Puerto La Cruz lie offshore on the many islands of the beautiful Parque Nacional Mochima and in the surrounding waters. For details of how to get there, see below. The tourist office for the state is **Coranztur** ① *Av 5 de Julio, Ed Gral José Antonio Anzoátegui, pb, Barcelona, T0281-275 0474, www.coranztur.gob.ve.*

Listings Caracas to Puerto La Cruz *map below.*

Where to stay

Puerto La Cruz
Newer, upmarket hotels are at Lechería and El Morro; cheaper hotels are concentrated in the centre, though it's not easy to find a cheap hotel.

$$$ Venetur Puerto La Cruz
Paseo de La Cruz y El Mar, east edge of the centre, T0281-500 3611, www.venetur.gob.ve.

5-star hotel with all facilities, including gym, spa, marina and beach access.

$$-$ Rasil Cumberland
Paseo de La Cruz y El Mar y Monagas 6, T0281-262 3000, www.hotelrasil.com.ve.
Rooms, suites and bungalows, 3 restaurants, bar, pool, tour office, gym, money exchange, car rental, convenient for ferries and buses.

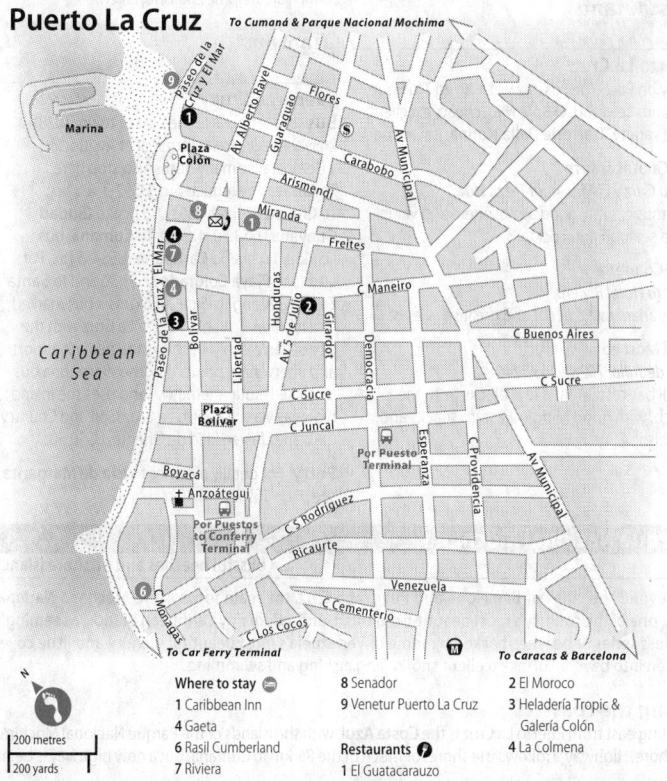

Puerto La Cruz

Where to stay 🛏
1 Caribbean Inn
4 Gaeta
6 Rasil Cumberland
7 Riviera
8 Senador
9 Venetur Puerto La Cruz

Restaurants 🍴
1 El Guatacarauzo
2 El Moroco
3 Heladería Tropic & Galería Colón
4 La Colmena

$$-$ Riviera
Paseo de La Cruz y El Mar 33, T0281-267 2111/2562, www.hotelriviera.com.ve.
Seafront hotel, some rooms have balcony, bar, watersports, very good location, restaurant.

$ Caribbean Inn
Freites entre Libertad y Honduras, T0281-267 4292, hotelcaribbean@cantv.net.
Big rooms, small pool, very good service.

$ Gaeta
Paseo de La Cruz y El Mar y Maneiro, T0281-265 0411.
Modern, good location but small, basic rooms, restaurant.

$ Senador
Miranda y Bolívar, T0281-267 3522.
Decent, if basic rooms, restaurant with view, parking, handy for nearby ferry terminal.

Restaurants

Puerto La Cruz
Many on Paseo de La Cruz y El Mar, eg **Tío Pepe**, delicious sea food. **O Sole Mio**, cheap, excellent, wide variety. **Trattoria Dalla Nonna**, Italian food.

$ El Guatacarauzo
De La Cruz y El Mar, near Pizza Hut.
Live music, salsa, good atmosphere and value, good seafood and cocktails.

$ La Colmena
Next to Hotel Riviera.
Vegetarian, rustic décor and great sea views.

$$ El Moroco
Av 5 de Julio, T0281-365 3240
Small bar-restaurant a few blocks from the beach, with good Middle-Eastern snacks and rice dishes.

Cafés

Heladería Tropic
Galería Colón on Paseo de La Cruz y El Mar.
Good ice cream.

What to do

Puerto La Cruz
Several companies, mostly on Paseo de La Cruz y El Mar, run **diving courses**. They're a bit pricier than Santa Fe and Mochima. Hotels and travel agents also organize trips. The nearest recompression chamber is on Isla Margarita. **Jakera**, www.jakera.com. Sea kayaks for rent from their lodge at Playa Colorada (T0293-808 7057), trips to whole country arranged (lodge in Mérida too, office C 24, No 8-205, Plaza Las Heroínas, Mérida, T0274-252 9577, 0416-887 2239), also Spanish lessons and volunteering. Chris and Joanna are helpful, English spoken.

Transport

Puerto La Cruz
Bus Bus terminal to the east of town, T0281-265 4949; *por puesto* terminal at Av Juncal y Democracia, many buses also stop here. To **Caracas** by regular bus, US$2-3, 4½ hrs; To **Ciudad Bolívar** US$3, 7½ hrs; to **Ciudad Guayana** US$3.50, 4½ hrs. To **Cumaná**, bus US$150, 1½ hrs. To **Carúpano**, bus US$4, 5 hrs. *Por puesto* to **Playa Colorado** US$1.50 and to **Santa Fe** US$2. Along Av 5 de Julio runs a bus marked 'Intercomunal'. It links Puerto La Cruz with the city of Barcelona (which has the nearest airport) and intervening points. Another Barcelona bus is marked 'Ruta Alternativa' and uses the inland highway via the Puerto La Cruz Golf and Country Club and Universidad de Oriente, US$0.50.

Ferry For details of ferries to **Isla de Margarita**, see page 1655.

Parque Nacional Mochima

blissful beaches and offshore islands

★Beyond the cities of Barcelona and Puerto La Cruz, the main focus is the Mochima National Park, one of the country's most beautiful regions. Hundreds of tiny Caribbean islands, a seemingly endless series of beaches backed by some of Venezuela's most beautiful scenery and little coves tucked into bays, all offer excellent snorkelling, fishing and swimming.

Along the coast
Starting east from Puerto La Cruz is the **Costa Azul**, with the islands of the Parque Nacional Mochima offshore. Highway 9 follows the shore for much of the 85 km to Cumaná, but a new highway is being

Essential Parque Nacional Mochima

Getting there

The highway between Puerto La Cruz and Cumaná runs through the park with access to many beautiful beaches. Tour companies offer trips to the islands from Puerto La Cruz, but you can also go independently with the cooperative boatmen, *peñeros*. One dock, **Transtupaco**, is next to **Venetur Puerto La Cruz**. The other **Embarcadero de Peñeros**, is on the point at the southwest end of Paseo de La Cruz y El Mar, by Calle Anzoátegui. Departures from 0900-1000, return at 1600-1630; US$10 per person. If beaches are full, the authorities will stop boats leaving. Tourist office in Puerto La Cruz provides tour operators for day trips to various islands for swimming or snorkelling; six-hour trip to four islands costs US$40 per person, including drinks. The islands to the east (Isla de Plata, Monos, Picuda Grande and Chica and the beaches of Ña Cleta, Conoma and Conomita) are best reached from the ports at **Guanta**, called Barinita and Valle Seco, US$6.50 (taxi from town, or *por puesto* from C Freites between Avenida 5 de Julio and C Democracia, and ask to be dropped off at the Urb Pamatacualito). Boat trips to the islands can also be taken from **Santa Fe** or **Mochima** (see below).

When to go

At Christmas, Carnival and Easter this part of the coast becomes extremely congested so patience is needed as long queues of traffic can develop. Accommodation is very hard to find and prices increase by 20-30%. Try to visit at quieter times of year.

Advice and regulations

To prevent littering and pollution, especially on the islands, carry out all your rubbish (no alcohol in glass bottles may be taken). Camping on the islands in Parque Nacional Mochima is possible, but not advisable. To stay overnight you need a permit from Inparques, Parque Andrés Eloy Blanco, US$2.50. Only camping gas cookers allowed. On day trips, take your own food as the island restaurants are expensive. When hiring a parasol for the day, make sure exactly what is included in the price and beware 'extra services'.

built. The road is spectacular but if driving take great care between Playa Colorada and Cumaná. It passes the 'paradise-like' beaches of **Conoma** and **Conomita**. Further along is **Playa Arapito**, where boats can be hired to **La Piscina**, a beautiful coral reef near some small islands, for good snorkelling (with lots of dolphins); boat ticket US$4.

Playa Colorada is a popular beach (Km 32) with beautiful red sands and palm trees (take a *por puesto* from corner of terminal in Puerto La Cruz, US$1.50). Nearby are **Playa Vallecito** (camping free, security guard, bar with good food and bottled water on sale, plenty of palm trees for slinging a hammock) and **Playa Santa Cruz**. At **Playa Los Hicacos** is a lovely coral reef.

In Sucre State 40 km from Puerto La Cruz is **Santa Fe**, larger and noisier than Mochima, but a good place to relax. The attractive beach is cleaned daily. It has a market on Saturday. Jeep, boat or diving tours available. Fishermen offer boat trips to Playas Colorada or Blanca; there are also boats for hire.

The little village of **Mochima** beyond Santa Fe, is 4 km off the main road. It's busy at weekends but almost deserted through the week. Boats take tourists to nearby beaches, such as **Playa Marita** and **Playa Blanca** (excellent snorkelling, take own equipment). Both have restaurants, but take food and water to be safe. Boats go to the nearby beaches, but arrange with the boatman what time he will collect you. There are also five- to six-island trips. Kayaking trips are available and walks on local trails and to caves (ask for information, eg from Carlos Hernández, or Rodolfo Plaza, see Diving, below).

Where to stay

Along the coast

Playa Colorada

$$ Sunset Inn
Av Principal, T0416-887 8156.
Clean, comfortable, pool, hot water, bar and restaurant, but all food extra. Reserve in advance.

$ Quinta Jaly
C Marchán, T0293-808 3246/0416-681 8113.
Hot water, very quiet, also 1 bungalow sleeps 6, family atmosphere, English and French spoken, use of kitchen, laundry facilities, good breakfast extra, multilingual library. Recommended.

Santa Fe

$$$-$$ Playa Santa Fe Resort and Dive Center
T0293-231 0051, www.santaferesort.com.
Renovated *posada* with rooms and suites, laundry service, owner Howard Rankell speaks English, can arrange transport to beaches, kitchen.

$ Bahía del Mar
T0293-231 0073, www.capvenezuela.fr.
Pleasant rooms with a/c or fan, upstairs rooms have a cool breeze, owners María and Juan speak French and some English, can arrange diving.

$ Café del Mar
1st hotel on beach, T0293-231 0009, T0414-779 3082.
A/c or cheaper with fan, good restaurant. Rogelio Alcaraz speaks English and Italian, arranges tours to islands.

$ La Sierra Inn
Near Café del Mar, T0293-383 5148.
Self-contained garden suite with fridge and cooker, run by Sr José Vivas, English spoken, helpful, tours to islands. Recommended.

$ Las Palmeras
T0293-231 0008, palmeras@mochima.org, www.laspalmerassantafe.blogspot.com.
Behind Cochaima, fan, room for 5 with fridge and cooker. Price negotiable, ask about light work in exchange for longer stays. English, German, Italian and Portuguese spoken.

$ Petit Jardin
Behind Cochaima, T0293-231 0036/T0416-387 5093, www.lepetitjardin-mochima.com.

A/c or fan, hot water, kitchen, pool, helpful.

Mochima

Various apartments are available for larger groups, look for signs.

$ Posada Doña Cruz
Calle Principal, T0293-416 6114, Facebook: posadacasacruzmochima.
A/c, cable TV. There is also **Posada Casa Cruz** on C Wolfgang Larrazábal, T0426-215 6809, with a/c and living room, bright and cheerful with arts café.

$ Posada El Embajador
Av W Larrazábal, by the jetty, T0293-416 3437, or 0426-184 4509.
Good value, comfortable, breakfast, restaurant, boat trips arranged.

$ Posada Gaby
At end of road with its own pier next to sea, T0293-431 0842/0414-773 1104, gaby@mochima.org.
A/c or fan, breakfast available, lovely place.

$ Posada Mochimero
On main street in front of Restaurant Mochimero, T0414-773 8782, mochimero@mochima.org.
A/c or fan, rooms with bath.

$ Villa Vicenta
C Principal, T0293-416 0916, or 0416 501 4382, villavicenta@mochima.org or posadavillavicenta@gmail.com.
Basic rooms with cold water and larger rooms with balcony, also cold water, dining room, owner Otilio is helpful.

Restaurants

Along the coast

Santa Fe

$ Club Naútico
Open for lunch and dinner.
Fish and Venezuelan dishes.

$ Los Molinos (Julios)
Open from 0800.
Beach bar serves sandwiches, hamburgers and cocktails.

Mochima

$ El Mochimero
On waterfront 5 mins from jetty.
Highly recommended for lunch and dinner.

$ Puerto Viejo
Calle La Marina.
Good food, if a bit pricey, good views.

What to do

Mochima

Diving **Rodolfo Plaza**, www.extreme-sports.com.ve, runs a diving lodge and school (**La Posada de los Buzos**, T0414-311 3968) and hires equipment, also walking, rafting, kayaking, canoeing trips and adventure sports around the country.

Transport

Santa Fe

Getting there from **Cumaná**, take *por puesto* 1 block down from the Redonda del Indio, along Av Perimetral, US$1.50. It may be difficult to get a bus from **Puerto La Cruz** to stop at Santa Fe, take a *por puesto* (depart from terminal, US$2, 1 hr), or taxi, US$3.50 including wait.

Mochima

Bus From **Cumaná** to Mochima take a bus from outside the terminal and ask to be let off at the street where the transport goes to Mochima, US$1.50; change here to crowded bus or jeep (US$0.50). No buses between Santa Fe and Mochima, take a *por puesto*, bargain hard on the price, US$10-15 is reasonable. Bus to Cumaná, 1400, US$1.50.

Cumaná   *Colour map 2, A1.*

a charming riverside town

Cumaná was founded in 1521 to exploit the nearby pearl fisheries. It straddles both banks of the Río Manzanares. Because of a succession of devastating earthquakes (the last in 1997), only a few historic sites remain. Like any other city it is not safe at night, the port area (1.5 km from the centre) especially so. Main festivals are 22 January, Santa Inés, a pre-Lenten carnival throughout the state of Sucre and 2 November, the Santos y Fideles Difuntos festival at El Tacal.

Sights

A long public beach, **San Luis**, is a short bus ride from the centre of town; take the 'San Luis/Los Chaimas' bus. The least spoilt part is the end by the old **Hotel Los Bordones**.

The **Castillo de San Antonio de la Eminencia** (1686) has 16 mounted cannons, a draw-bridge and dungeons from which there are said to be underground tunnels leading to the Santa Inés church. Restored in 1975, it is flood-lit at night (but don't go there after dark, it's not safe). The **Castillo de Santa María de la Cabeza** (1669) is a rectangular fortress with a panoramic view of San Antonio and the elegant homes below. **Convento de San Francisco**, the original Capuchin mission of 1514, was the first school on the continent; its remains are on the Plaza Badaracco Bermúdez facing the beach. The **Church of Santa Inés** (1637) ① *C Sucre, T0293-431 0722*, was the base of the Franciscan missionaries; earthquakes have caused it to be rebuilt five times. A tiny 400-year-old statue of the Virgen de Candelaria is in the garden. The **home of Andrés Eloy Blanco** (1896-1955) ① *Sucre 79, T0293-431 2895, Mon-Fri 0800-1200, 1430-1730, free*, one of Venezuela's greatest poets and politicians, on Plaza Bolívar, has been nicely restored to its turn-of-the-century elegance. On the opposite side of the plaza is **La Gobernación** around a courtyard lined by cannon from Santa María de la Cabeza; note the gargoyles and other colonial features. There are markets selling handicrafts and food on both sides of the river.

The **Museo Gran Mariscal de Ayacucho** ① *Consejo Municipal, Av Humboldt, in Parque Ayacucho, T0293-432 1896, Mon-Fri 0800-1700, Sat-Sun 0900-1700; free tours*, commemorates the battle of Ayacucho: with portraits, relics and letters of Bolívar and José Antonio Sucre (Bolívar's first lieutenant). **Museo del Mar** ① *C Vela de Coro, Complejo Cultural Luis Manuel Peñalver, T0293-400 8420, www.udo.edu.ve, Mon-Sat 0900-1600, US$2, getting there: take San Luis minibus from the cathedral*, has exhibits of tropical marine life.

Tourist information

Corsotur
*C Sucre 49, T0293-441 0136, http://sucrecorsotur.
blogspot.co.uk. Mornings only.*
This office is very helpful, English spoken.
See also http://turismosucre.com.ve.

Where to stay

$$$-$$ Nueva Toledo Suites
*End of Av Universidad, close to San Luis beach,
T0293-451 8118 ext 425, www.nuevatoledo.com.*
Pool, beach bar, good value all-inclusive deals.

$ Posada San Francisco
*C Sucre 16, near Santa Inés, T0293-431 3926,
laposada.sanfrancisco@gmail.com.*
Renovated colonial house, courtyard, spacious
rooms, hot water, cheaper rooms with fan, very
helpful, bar, restaurant. Recommended.

$ Posada Tempera
*C Páez 7, behind the Cathedral, T0293-431 2178,
or 0414-189 1874, www.tempera-posada.com.*
Charming, comfortable small *posada* in historic
centre, hot water, a/c, Wi-Fi, good breakfast
extra, laundry service, parking outside or in
nearby guarded parking lot, full-board packages
available, incl excursions. Also here is **Topaz** tour
operator, www.topaz.com.fr.

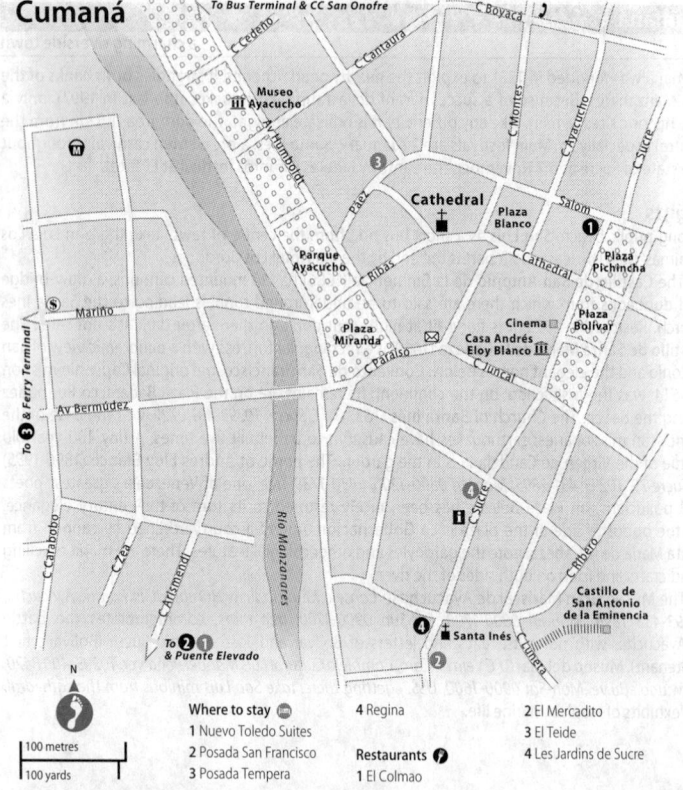

Cumaná

To Bus Terminal & CC San Onofre

C Boyaca
C Cedeño
C Cantaura
C Montes
C Ayacucho
C Sucre

Museo Ayacucho

Humboldt

Parque Ayacucho

Páez

Cathedral

Plaza Blanco

Salom

Plaza Pichincha

Ribas

C Cathedral

Mariño

Plaza Miranda

C Paraíso

Cinema

Casa Andrés Eloy Blanco

Plaza Bolívar

Av Bermúdez

C Juncal

C Sucre

C Ribero

To 3 & Ferry Terminal

Rio Manzanares

C Carabobo
C Zea
C Armendi

Castillo de San Antonio de la Eminencia

To 2 1
& Puente Elevado

Santa Inés

C Cumana

N

100 metres
100 yards

Where to stay
1 Nuevo Toledo Suites
2 Posada San Francisco
3 Posada Tempera

4 Regina

Restaurants
1 El Colmao

2 El Mercadito
3 El Teide
4 Les Jardins de Sucre

$ Regina
Arismendi y Av Bermúdez, T0293-431 1073.
Hot water, restaurant, helpful.

Restaurants

All central restaurants close Sun lunchtime.
After dark take a taxi.

$$ Les Jardins de Sucre
Sucre 27, in front of the Santa Inés church.
Delicious French cuisine, good service, outdoor
seating. Recommended.

$ El Colmao
C Sucre on Plaza Pichincha.
Serves very good fish, with charming
service, live music and dancing.

$ El Mercadito
Av Aristides Rojas (Perimetral) con Vargas y
Méjico, by the Puente Elevado
Lots of market food stalls for excellent cheap
lunches, fish and seafood.

$ El Teide
Av Aristides Rojas, opp C Buenos Aires

Spanish food, live music, long-standing
establishment with good local reputation.

What to do

Posadas San Francisco and **Tempera** can
help arrange local tours, as well as sailing and
diving trips.

Transport

Bus Terminal 3 km northwest of the centre on
Av Las Palomas, just before the junction with
Av Perimetral. Local bus into centre US$0.50,
taxi US$2-3. To **Puerto La Cruz**, US$1.50, 1½ hrs.
To **Güiria**, US$2, 4 hrs, **Expresos Los Llanos**
once a day, *por puesto* US$6-8 (6-7 hrs),
beware of overcharging, often stop in Irapa.
To **Carúpano**, US$1.50, 2-3 hrs. To **Caripe**, you
have to go to **Santa María**, south of Cariaco,
and change to *por puesto* there. To **Caracas**,
US$4-6 (6-7 hrs), frequent service; many daily
to **Ciudad Guayana** and **Ciudad Bolívar**, US$3
and US$2.50 respectively.

Ferry For ferries to **Isla de Margarita**, see
page 1655.

Araya to Paria

don't miss the detour from the coast to the Cueva del Guácharo

This section is bounded by two peninsulas, Araya, which is an area of desert landscapes
and pink salt lakes, and Paria, a finger of land stretching out to the most easterly point on
Venezuela's Caribbean coast and a place of peaceful, coastal towns, beaches and forest. The
eastern mountains, rising to 2000 m at their highest point, receive abundant rainfall in their
tropical forest.

Araya Peninsula

The main settlement is Araya which has an airport and a ferry dock. The major sight is the **Fortaleza
de Santiago de León**, built by Spain to protect the salt mines, but of which very little now remains.
Construction began in 1622 and it took 47 years to complete. Entry is free, but the only facilities are
a refreshment stand and a picnic area. Today the mines are exploited by a state-owned corporation,
ENSAL. Windsurfing is excellent, but only for the experienced.

Carúpano *Colour map 2, A1.*

This is a colonial town dating back to 1647, from which 70% of Venezuela's cocoa is shipped. The
area around Plaza Santa Rosa has been declared a national heritage site. Buildings include the
Museo Histórico, containing a comprehensive database on the city, and the **Iglesia Santa Rosa**.
The **Casa del Cable** ① *T0294-331 3847, www.fundacionthomasmerle.org.ve*, location of the first
telecommunications link with Europe, is the headquarters of the Fundación Thomas Merle, run
by his father, Wilfried Merle, who has been instrumental in setting up ecotourism and economic
development projects, with volunteering opportunities, in the Paria Peninsula. Carúpano is famous
throughout Venezuela as the last place still celebrating a traditional pre-Lenten Carnival: days of
dancing, rum drinking, with masked women in black (*negritas*). Book well ahead for places to stay
at this time (February). Other local festivals are 3 May, Velorios de la Cruz (street dances); 15 August,
Asunción de la Virgen. On the outskirts of Carúpano is **Playa Copey** (ask the *por puesto*/bus to

drop you at Playa Copey if arriving from Cumaná or other westerly points, or take a taxi from town, US$10. It is not easy to change foreign currency in Carúpano.

Caripe and around

A paved road runs inland from Carúpano to Caripe via Cariaco and Santa María. Between Cariaco and Casanay, **Las Aguas de Moisés** ① *T0294-416 8184, www.lasaguasdemoises.com, open 0800-1600, US$6.50, US$5 for seniors and children, ask to be let off from bus or por puesto on Cariaco-Carúpano route,* is a tourist park containing 11 large thermal pools. The waters are said to be curative and there are lots of sporting and other activities. Camping ($) is available, or **Hotel La Fuente** (T0294-414 6810).

Caripe is an attractive town set in gorgeous mountain scenery. There is a lively daily market. It is 12 km from the famous Cueva del Guácharo and a good place to escape from the beaches. It's especially good for walking and biking. At San Francisco, on the Maturín-Cumaná road (212 km, all paved but twisty; beautiful tropical mountain scenery), is a branch road running 22.5 km northeast to Caripe. **Feria de las Flores** is on 2-12 August and NS del Pilar is 10-12 October. See http://caripe.net. To get to Caripe from Caracas you must go to **Maturín** (the capital of Monagas state, offering relatively expensive accommodation), then take a *por puesto*. Alternatively go to Cumaná and then to Santa María for *por puesto* services.

Cueva del Guácharo

Open 0800-1630, US$12 with compulsory guide in Spanish, speak some English and German (give a tip). Leave backpacks at the ticket office, photography is not allowed. To go further into the caves permits from Inparques in Caracas are needed.

This remarkable cave was discovered by Humboldt and has since been penetrated 10.5 km along a small, crystal-clear stream. In the first caves live around 18,000 *guácharos* (oil birds) with an in-built radar system for sightless flight. Their presence supports a variety of wildlife in the cave: blind mice, fish and crabs in the stream, yellow-green plants, crickets and ants. For two hours at dusk (about 1900) the birds pour out of the cave's mouth. Through a very narrow entrance is the **Cueva del Silencio** (Cave of Silence). About 2 km in is the **Pozo del Viento** (Well of the Wind).

Wear old clothes, stout shoes and be prepared to get wet (rubber boots can be hired). In the wet season it can be a bit slippery; tours in the cave may be closed in August-September because of rising water level. There is a caving museum with good cafeteria. Opposite the road is a paved path to **Salto Paila**, a 25-m waterfall, about 30 minutes' walk, guide compulsory, pay by giving a tip. A beautiful path, built by Inparqes, starts at the caving museum, with some nice shelters for picnics. Camping may be allowed by the cave, but fires may not be lit.

Paria Peninsula

Río Caribe This lovely fishing village (20 km east of Carúpano) used to be a major cacao-exporting port. It is a good jumping-off point for the beautiful beaches of **Playa Medina** (in an old coconut plantation, 25 km east) and **Pui Puy**, both famous for their crystal-clear water and golden sands. Playa Medina is safe, has shade for rent and stalls selling food and drink; it is crowded at weekends and holidays. Cabins at the beach are expensive ($$ per person). To get to Playa Medina, take a taxi, US$10 return trip per car, US$11 to Pui Puy, as *camionetas* do not go to the beaches, only to the entrance, from where it's two hours' walk or more (not safe). Surfing at Playas Pui Puy and Querepare; visit **Querepare** between May and August to watch sea turtles laying their eggs.

Further east is the delightful village of **San Juan de las Galdonas** and some great beaches. Near Chacaracual, 15 minutes' drive from Río Caribe is **Paria Shakti** ① *T0294-611 8767/T0416-517 9676, pariashakti@gmail.com, see Facebook: HaciendaPariaShakti,* a 1.6-ha cacao plantation and holistic health centre that offers factory tours and massages. Next door, visit **Aguasana**, a hacienda with mineral-rich hot springs and mud pools (see Where to stay, below). Near Bohordal is **Campamento Hato Rio de Agua**, a buffalo ranch available for day visits and milk factory tours; many species of birds can be seen (also see Where to stay). Day trips are also available to **Caño de Ajíes** with a visit to a waterfall and the estuary which flows into the Golfo de Paria; you can see crocodiles, birds and snakes. It is part of the Parque Nacional Turuépano.

Güiria At Bohordal, the paved road from Río Caribe across the mountains meets Route 9, which continues to the pleasant town of **Irapa** (hotels, bus connections). The paved highway continues 42 km to **Güiria** (colour map 2, A2, www.guiria.com.ve), a friendly, peaceful town and a badly littered beach. **Feria de la Pesca**, 14 July.

Macuro A quiet town on the tip of the Peninsula, Macuro is accessible by boat (two hours from Güiria) and by a new road from Güiria (20 km paved, the remainder passable by 4WD). It was around here that Columbus made the first recorded European landing on the continent on 5 August 1498. Locals like to believe the landing took place at Macuro, and the town's official new name is Puerto Colón. There is a small **Museo de Macuro** on Calle Bolívar, 1 block from **Posada Beatriz**; ask here about walking tours and boat trips. A big party is held here every year on 12 October to mark the official 'discovery' of America. Restaurants only open at weekends. There are also a few basic shops and a pharmacy. The boat to Güiria leaves at 0500, arrive early, US$2.50 per person.

The beach is unattractive but the coast on the north side of the peninsula is truly wonderful; crystal-clear water and dazzling sands backed by dense jungle. A highly recommended trip for the adventurous is the hike to **Uquire** and **Don Pedro** on the north coast; four to six hours' walk, places to hang a hammock or pitch a tent. **Note** This part of the peninsula is a national park; you need a permit from Inparques in Caracas, page 1681.

Listings Araya to Paria

Where to stay

Araya

$ Araya Mar
El Castillo, T0293-437 1382/T0414-777 3682.
Hot water, good restaurant, arranges car and boat tours to the Salinas and around Araya, parking. Good restaurant serves Venezuelan food. Recommended.

$ Lagunasal
C El Progreso, T0293-437 1290/T0414-389 1549.
Modern *posada*, 100 m from the dock, with good services.

$ Posada Araya Wind
Beside the Fortaleza in front of beach, T0293-437 1132.
Some rooms with bath, cold water.

Carúpano

$$-$ Hotel Euro Caribe Internacional
Av Perimetral Rómulo Gallegos, T0294-331 3911, hoteleurocaribe@cantv.net.
Well located, some rooms with sea view, attentive staff, parking, good Italian restaurant.

$$-$ La Colina
Av Rómulo Gallegos 31, behind Hotel Victoria, T0294-332 0527, colinahotel@gmail.com.
Restaurant on terrace, beautiful view, comfortable rooms. Recommended.

$ Lilma
Av Independencia, 3 blocks from Plaza Colón, T0294-331 1361, hotellilma161@hotmail.com.
Hot water, restaurant, *tasca*, cinema.

$ Victoria
Av Perimetral Rómulo Gallegos, T0294-331 1554, hotelvictoriacarupano@hotmail.com.
Safe but basic and getting run down, hot water, pool.

Playa Copey

$ Posada Casa Blanca
Av Principal, 5 mins from Posada Nena, T0294-331 6896, josemcarrion@cantv.net.
Hot water, safe, good family atmosphere, private stretch of beach illuminated at night, Spanish restaurant, German spoken, discounts for long stays.

$ Posada Nena
1 block from the beach, T0294-331 7297, www.venezuela-vacaciones.com.
Hot water, games room, good restaurant, public phone, good service, German spoken, owner Volker Alsen offers day trips to Cueva del Guácharo, Mochima, Medina and other Venezuelan destinations. Recommended.

Caripe

$$-$ Finca Agroturística Campo Claro
At Teresén, T0292-555 1013, or 0414-7708043, see Facebook: Cabañas-Hacienda-Campo-Claro-235626746495606.

Cabins for 4-15 people with cooking facilities and hot water, also rooms ($), restaurant for residents, horse riding, coffee plantation and fruit orchard.

$$-$ Samán
Enrique Chaumer 29, T0292-545 1183.
Also has more expensive suites, comfortable, pool, parking, not so welcoming to backpackers.

Río Caribe

As well as those listed, there are other *posadas* and private, unmarked pensions; ask around.

$$ Posada Caribana
Av Bermúdez 25, T0212-263 3649/265 9150, www.parquenivaldito.com.
Beautifully restored colonial house, tastefully decorated, a/c or fan, restaurant, bar, excursions. Also owns Villas Playa Uva.

$ La Posada de Arlet
24 de Julio 22, T0294-646 1290.
English and German spoken, bar, arranges day trips to local beaches. Recommended.

$ Pensión Papagayos
14 de Febrero, 1 block from police station, opposite liceo, T0294-646 1868.
Charming house and garden, shared bath with hot water (single sex), use of kitchen, nice atmosphere, owner Cristina Castillo.

$ Posada Shalimar
Av Bermúdez 54, T0294-646 1135, www.posada-shalimar.com.
Francisco González speaks English, very helpful, can arrange tours to and provide information about local beaches and other areas. Beautiful rooms situated around pool have a/c. Recommended.

San Juan de las Galdonas

$ pp Habitat Paria
T0294-511 9571, www.soaf.info/hp/.
With breakfast and supper, rooms decorated with zodiac theme, fan, bar/restaurant, terraces, garden. The *posada* is right behind Barlovento beach on the right-hand side of San Juan. Can arrange boat tours. Recommended.

$ Posada Las Tres Carabelas
T0294-511 2729/0416-894 0914, lastrescarabelas3@gmail.com.
Fans and mosquito nets, restaurant, wonderful view, owner is knowledgeable about local area.

Outside Río Caribe

$$ Hacienda Posada Aguasana
Carretera El Pilar-Güiria, 5 km from Tunapuy, T0416-607 1913, www.posadaaguasana.com.
Attractive rooms with fans near hot springs, price does not include meals or use of hot springs (US$1.50 adults, US$1 under-12s and seniors). 2-6 night packages available, with and without transfers.

$$ Hato Río de Agua
T0294-332 0527.
Rustic cabins with fans, private bathrooms, restaurant on a buffalo ranch (see above), price includes breakfast and tours of dairy factory.

Güiria

$ Rincón Güireño
C Juncal y C Valdez, corner of Plaza Sucre.
Rooms with a/c, cable TV, parking. Good for breakfast.

Restaurants

Araya

Eat early as most places close before 2000. Hamburger stalls around the dock and 2 *panaderías*.

$ Eugenía
Calle Castillo, opposite Playa El Castillo.
For good value meals.

$ Las Churuatas de Miguel
On the beach near dock.
Fish and typical food.

Carúpano

$$-$ El Fogón de La Petaca
Av Rómulo Gallegos, on Boulevar Bermúdez, T0294-331 2555.
Traditional Venezuelan dishes, fish.

$$-$ La Madriguera
Av Perimetral Rómulo Gallegos, in Hotel Eurocaribe.
Good Italian food, some vegetarian dishes, Italian and English spoken.

$ Victor's Pub
C Acosta 33, esq C 2. Open till late, closed Sun.
Lively music bar with good food, pizzas, steaks and seafood, and live bands.
  Other options include the **food stalls** in the market, especially the one next to the car park, and the *empanadas* in the Plaza Santa Rosa.

Caripe

$$ Tasca Mogambo
Next to Hotel Saman.
Good, local food.

$ Alfredo Pizzería
C Rivera, 1 block south of main street
Good pizzas and other Italian dishes.

Río Caribe

$$ Mi Cocina
C Juncal, by Av Bermúdez, 3 mins' walk from Plaza Bolívar.
Very good food, large portions.

Transport

Carúpano

Air The airport is 15 mins' walk from the centre, US$1 by taxi. Check with **Rutaca** (T0501-788 2221), which occasionally offers flights to Caracas through Porlamar.

Bus To **Caracas**, US$3.50, 8-9 hrs, to Terminal de Oriente. For other destinations *por puestos* are a better option, eg **Cumaná**, US$2.50, 2 hrs, **Puerto La Cruz**, US$4, 4 hrs (Mochima/Santa Fé), **Güiria**, US$2.50, 3 hrs. They run more frequently and make fewer stops. Buses do not go from Carúpano to Caripe, you have to take a *por puesto* to **Cariaco**, US$1, then another to **Santa María**, US$1.50, then another to Caripe, US$1.

Caripe

Bus Terminal 1 block south of main plaza. For **Carúpano**, take *por puestos* to Santa María and Cariaco (see above), similarly for **Río Caribe** and **Las Aguas de Moisés**. To get to **Cumaná**, go to Santa María and catch transport from there. Bus to **Maturín** several daily, 2½ hrs, US$2; Maturín-

Caracas costs US$3.50, 7½ hrs. *Por puestos* run from Maturín to Ciudad Bolívar.

Cueva del Guácharo

Bus Frequent from **Caripe** to the caves. If staying in Caripe, take a *por puesto* (a jeep marked Santa María-Muelle), at 0800, see the caves and waterfall and catch the Cumaná bus which goes past the caves between 1200 and 1230 (but you will leave before the birds leave the cave). Taxis from Caripe US$1. *Por puesto* from Cumaná US$2.50, 2 hrs. Private tours can be organized from Cumaná for about US$10 pp, with guide.

Río Caribe and San Juan de las Galdonas

Bus Direct from **Caracas** (Terminal del Oriente) to Río Caribe, US$3.50, 8½ hrs, and from **Maturín**, US$2. *Por puesto* **Carúpano**-Río Caribe, US$1.50, or taxi US$4. Buses depart Río Caribe from the other Plaza Bolívar, 7 blocks up from pier. Jeep Carúpano-San Juan de las Galdonas 1100, 1½ hrs; *camioneta* from Río Caribe from stop near petrol station, 0600 till 1300, US$2.50.

Güiria

Bus Depart Plaza Sucre, at top end of C Bolívar: to **Maturín** (0400, US$2, 5½ hrs), **Caripito**, **San Félix**, **Cumaná**, US$2, Puerto La Cruz, US$2.50, and **Caracas**, US$4.50.

Ferry To **Macuro**: daily 1100-1200 from the Playita, US$1-2, return 0500, 2 hrs. To **Trinidad** The ferry between Chaguaramas, Trinidad, and **Güiria**, operated by **Pier 1 Cruises**, www.pier1tt.com, has been suspended indefinitely. Check with Pier 1 Cruises for resumption of service. Should the ferry run again, note that visas can't be arranged in Güiria, should you need one. Check all formalities in advance in Caracas or at another Trinidad and Tobago consulate.

Isla de Margarita *Colour map 2, A1.*

Venezuela's premier holiday island

Margarita is the country's main Caribbean holiday destination and is popular with both Venezuelans and foreign tourists. The island's reputation for picture-postcard, white-sand beaches is well-deserved. Some parts are crowded but there are undeveloped beaches and colonial villages. Porlamar is the most built up and commercial part of the island while Juan Griego and La Restinga are much quieter.

Despite the extensive building on much of the coast and in Porlamar, much of the island has been given over to natural parks. Of these the most striking is the **Laguna La Restinga**.

Tip...
It is advisable to reserve ahead, especially in high season, to get the best value for accommodation.

Finding your feet

The capital of the island is La Asunción on the eastern side. Porlamar, to the south, is the most developed area. If you're seeking sun and sand, then head for the north coast towns where the beaches tend to be lined with low-rise hotels and thatched restaurants. A 22-km sandbar known as La Restinga joins the eastern part of Margarita to the barren Peninsula de Macanao via a road bridge.

Getting there and around

There are many national, international and charter flights to Isla de Margarita. There also frequent ferries from Puerto La Cruz and Cumaná. Car hire is a good way of getting around (see Transport, page 1655). Women should avoid walking alone at night on the island and no one should go to the beaches after dark, except El Yaque (see below).

The western part, the **Peninsula de Macanao**, is hotter and more barren, with scrub, sand dunes and marshes. Wild deer, goats and hares roam the interior, but 4WDs are needed to penetrate it. The entrance to the Peninsula de Macanao is a pair of hills known as **Las Tetas de María Guevara**, a national monument covering 1670 ha. There are mangroves in the **Laguna de las Marites** natural monument, west of Porlamar.

Other parks are **Cerro El Copey**, 7130 ha, and **Cerro Matasiete y Guayamurí**, 1672 ha (both reached from La Asunción). The climate is exceptionally good and dry. Roads are good and a bridge links the two parts. Nueva Esparta's population is over 491,610 (2011 census), of whom 195,000 live in the Porlamar and Pampatar urban complex. The capital is La Asunción.

Porlamar

Most of the island's high-rise hotels are at Porlamar which is 20 km from airport and 28 km from Punta de Piedra, where ferries dock. Porlamar's beaches are nothing special, but it makes up for what it lacks in this department

Isla de Margarita

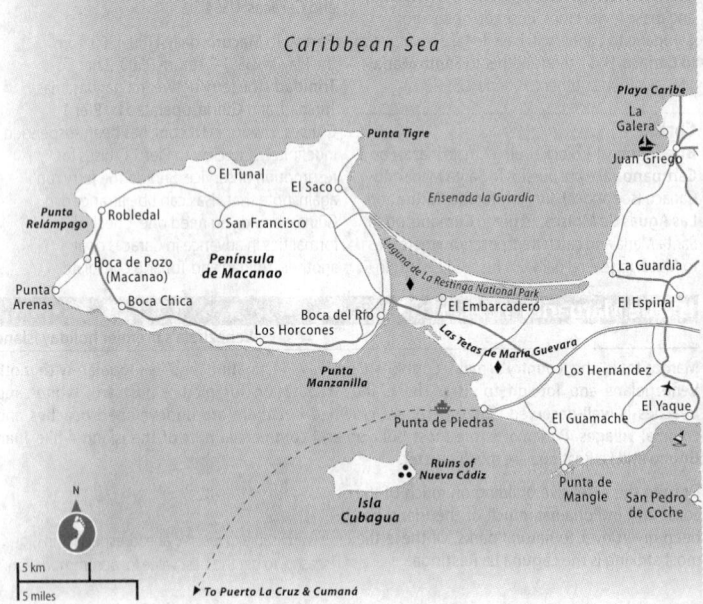

with its shops (see Shopping, page 1654). At Igualdad y Díaz is the **Museo de Arte Francisco Narváez**, which has some good displays of the work of this local sculptor and other Venezuelan artists. At night everything closes by 2300.

The **Bella Vista** beach is busy but clean and has lots of restaurants lining the seafront. **Playa Concorde** is small, sheltered and tucked by the marina. **Playa Morena** is a long, barren strip of sand for the Costa Azul hotel zone east of the city. **La Caracola** is a popular beach for a young crowd.

Pampatar

For a more Venezuelan atmosphere go northeast to Pampatar, which is set around a bay favoured by yachtsmen as a summer anchorage. Pampatar has the island's largest fort, **San Carlos de Borromeo**, which was built in 1662 after the Dutch destroyed the original. Jet skis can be hired on the clean and pretty beach. A fishing boat can be hired for 2½ hours, four to six passengers; shop around for best price; it's good fun and makes for a worthwhile fishing trip.

South coast

Playa El Yaque on the south coast, near the airport, is a mecca for wind- and kitesurfers. The winds are perfect from mid-June to mid-October and the water is shallow enough to stand when you fall off (see What to do, page 1655). After dark it becomes an open-air disco, the safest beach on the island at night. Most visitors come on package deals and therefore accommodation is expensive, but cheaper places to stay can be found. There is no public transport; a taxi from Porlamar costs US$8-10. Cholymar travel agency will change money and there is a *casa de cambio* in the Hotel California.

Boats go from Punta de Piedra, El Yaque and La Isleta to the **Isla de Coche** (11 by 6 km), which has 4500 inhabitants and one of the richest salt mines in the country (see Transport, page 1655). They also go, on hire only, to **Isla de Cubagua**, which is totally deserted, but you can visit the **ruins of Nueva Cádiz** (which have been excavated). Large private yachts and catamarans take tourists on day trips to Coche.

La Asunción

The capital of La Asunción located a few kilometres inland from Porlamar. It has several **colonial buildings**, a **cathedral**, and the **fort of Santa Rosa** ① *daily 0800-1800*, which features a famous bottle dungeon. There is a **museum** in the Casa Capitular, and a good local **market**, worth browsing for handicrafts. Nearby is the **Cerro Matasiete** historical site, where the defeat of the Spanish on 31 July 1817 led to their evacuation of the island.

Eastern and northern beaches

Playa Guacuco, reached from La Asunción by a road through the Guayamurí reserve, is a local beach with a lot of surf, fairly shallow, palm trees, restaurants and car park. Playa Parguito further up the east coast is best for surfing (strong waves; full public services).

Playa El Agua has 4 km of white sand with many kiosks and shady restaurants on the beach and on Calle Miragua. The sea is very rough in winter (dangerous for children), but fairly shallow; beware the strong cross current when you are about waist deep. This beach gets overcrowded at Venezuelan holiday times. The fashionable part is at the south end. The beach is 45 minutes by bus from Porlamar. See also www.playaelagua.info.

Manzanillo is a picturesque bay between the mountains on the northeast point of the island with apartments, beach houses and good places to eat (cheaper than Playa El Agua). Playa Escondida is at the far end. Puerto Fermín/El Tirano is where Lope de Aguirre, the infamous conquistador, landed in 1561 on his flight from Peru.

The coast road is interesting, with glimpses of the sea and beaches to one side. There are a number of clifftop look-out points. The road improves radically beyond Manzanillo, winding from one beach to the next. **Playa Puerto la Cruz** (wide and windy) adjoins **Pedro González**, with a broad sweeping beach, running from a promontory (easy to climb) to scrub and brush that reach down almost to the water's edge. **Playa Caribe** is a fantastic curve of white sand with moderate surf. Chairs and umbrellas can be hired from the many beach bars.

Juan Griego is further west, a fast-expanding town whose pretty bay is full of fishing boats. The little fort of La Galera is on a promontory at the northern side, beyond which is a bay of the same name with a narrow strip of beach lined with many seafront restaurants.

La Restinga

This is the 22-km sandbar of broken seashells that joins the eastern and western parts of Margarita. Behind the *restinga* is the eponymous **national park**, designated a wetland of international importance. More than 100 species of birds live here, including the blue-crowned parakeet, which is endemic to Margarita. There are also marine turtles and other reptiles, dolphins, deer, ocelots, seahorses and oysters. *Lanchas* can be taken into the fascinating lagoon and mangrove swamps to the beach from landing stages at the eastern end (US$3 for 30 minutes, US$14 for an hour trip in a boat taking five, plus US$3.50 entrance fee to park). Bus from Porlamar US$1.50. On La Restinga beach you can look for shellfish in the shallows (sun protection is essential) and delicious oysters can be bought here.

Península de Macanao

The Península de Macanao, over the road bridge from La Restinga, is mountainous, arid, barely populated and a peaceful place to get away from the holidaymakers on the main part of Isla Margarita. It also has some good beaches that are often deserted and is a good place for horse riding. **Punta Arenas** is a very pleasant beach with calm water and is the most popular. It has some restaurants, chairs and sunshades. Further on is the wilder **Playa Manzanillo**. It's best visited in a hire car as public transport is scarce. **Boca del Río**, near the road bridge, has a **Museo Marino** ① *T0295-291 3231, www.museomarino.com, daily 0900-1630, US$1.50, US$1 children and seniors*, which has interesting collections of marine life, organized by ecosystem, and also features a small aquarium.

Listings Isla de Margarita *map page 1650.*

Tourist information

Travel agencies can also provide a tourist guide to Margarita. The best map is available from **Corpoven**. See also www.islamargarita.com and http://margaritaislandnews.blogspot.co.uk.

Many offices close for lunch.

Cámara de Turismo
2da Entrada Urb Jorge Coll, Av Virgen del Valle, Qta 6, Pampatar, T0295-262 0683, www.ctene.org. Private company, have free maps and are very helpful.

Corpotur
Av Jóvito Villalba, Centro Artesanal Gilberto Menchini, Los Robles, T0295-262 2322, https://twitter.com/corpotur
The state tourism department.

Where to stay

Porlamar
Many luxury hotels are grouped in the Costa Azul suburb east of Porlamar, but they now pepper most of the northeast coast of the island. Most hotels and tour operators work on a high season/low season price system. High season prices (Christmas, Easter and Jun-Aug) can be up to 35%

higher. Flights and hotels are usually fully booked at this time. In low season, bargaining is possible.

$$$ Bella Vista
Av Santiago Mariño, T0295-261 7222, www.hbellavista.com.
Large hotel with all services, pool with sea views, beach, car hire, travel agency, 3 restaurants and bar.

$$ Imperial
Av Raul Leoni, via El Morro, T0295-261 6420, www.hotelimperial.com.ve.
Modern, best rooms have sea view, parking, balcony, safe, restaurant, small pool, parking.

$$ Margarita Princess
Av 4 de Mayo, T0295-263 6777, www.hotelmargaritaprincess.com.ve.
Large, comfortable rooms, balcony, restaurant, small pool.

$$-$ María Luisa
Av Raúl Leoni entre Campos y Fermín, T0295-261 0564, www.hotelmarialuisa.com.ve.
Good location between seafront and shopping district, with a pool and some beach views.

$ For You
Av Santiago Mariño, T0295-263 8635, foryouhotel@hotmail.com.
Modern, rooms a bit threadbare but adequate, with good service, roof restaurant, bar.

$ Posada Casa Lutecia
Final C Campos Cedeño y Marcano, T0295-263 8526, posadacasalutecia@cantv.net.
Lovely bright rooms with personal touch, French-owned, café with outdoor seating near beach.

South coast

$$ El Yaque Motion
Playa El Yaque, T0295-263 9742, T0416-596 5139, www.elyaquemotion.com.
400 m from beach. German run, popular with wind- and kitesurfers (lessons and equipment hire available), well-established, kitchen, laundry, roof terrace, cheaper with shared bath, rents 3 apartments for 4-8 people, English spoken, good.

$ Sail Fast Shop
Playa El Yaque, T0295-263 3449, www.sailfastshop.de.
Basic rooms 300 m from the beach, ask for Herbert Novak at the Sail Fast Shop opposite Hotel Yaque Paradise. Rooms with private bath, some with a/c, kitchen facilities.

La Asunción

$$ Ciudad Colonial
C La Margarita, T0295-416 7647, isbeeliasur@hotmail.com.
Upmarket appartments minimum 4 people, swimming pool, accepts credit cards, restaurant.

$ Posada Restaurant Ticino Da´Rocco
Crucero de Guacuco, vía Playa El Agua, C San Onofre, sector Camoruco, T0295-242 2727, posadaticino@gmail.com.
Pool, restaurant, accepts credit cards.

Eastern and northern beaches

Playa Guacuco

$$ Guacuco Resort
Vía Playa Guacuco, T0295-242 5546, www.guacucoresort.com.
Stylish, comfortable apartments for up to 4 people with balcony or terrace, 1 km from the beach and 300 m off the road, self-catering, tranquil, beautiful tropical gardens with birds, spa, pool and bar.

Playa El Agua
Most *posadas* are on C Miragua, which is near the beach.

$$$-$$ Coco Paraíso
Av Principal, T0295-249 0117/415 8452.
Pleasant, large rooms, pool, 3 mins from beach, English and German spoken.

$$ Costa Linda
C Miragua, T0295-249 1303/415 9961, www.hotelcostalinda.com.
Lovely rooms in colonial-style house, relaxing, safe, pool, restaurant and bar, accepts credit cards, English and German spoken.

$$ Margarita Tropical Villa
C Díaz Ordaz, T0295-249 0558, or 0416-695 3704, www.casatrudel.com.
Canadian/Venezuelan run, small place, patio with hammocks, 5 mins from beach, Wi-Fi, king-size beds, use of kitchen, hot water shower, minimum booking 4 nights.

$$-$ Doña Romelia
Av 31 de Julio (1 km before Playa Manzanillo), 10-min walk to Playa El Agua, T0295-249 0238.
Very attractive rustic-style hotel, bright rooms with balconies and hammocks, nice pool area and garden. Well-run, helpful staff. Recommended.

$ Chalets de Belén
Miragua 3, T0295-249 1707, jesush30@yahoo.com.
2 chalets for 4 and 6, kitchen, good value,
parking, no hot water, also 2 double rooms
(with discounts in the low season).

$ Hostería El Agua
Av 31 de Julio vía Manzanillo, T0295-249 1297.
Simple, hot water, safe, restaurant/bar, kitchen,
on road-side 4 mins' walk from beach, off-road
parking, English spoken.

Juan Griego

$$ The Sunset Posada Turística
*T0295-253 2168, losavila@verizon.net,
on Facebook.*
Apartments sleep 4-8, good value,
some with beachfront balconies.

$ Hostel El Caney
*Giulliana Torrico 17, Rue Guevara,
T0295-253 5059, http://elcaney.free.fr.*
Shared kitchen, larger rooms up to 5 people, no
breakfast, small pool, English and French spoken,
weekly and monthly rentals.

$ Patrick
El Fuerte, T0295-253 6218.
Good travellers hostel, rooms with fine sunset
views, excellent restaurant and bar, near beach.
English spoken, will arrange salsa and Spanish
lessons. Recommended.

Peninsula de Macanao

$$ Makatao
T0412-092 7187.
Run by Dr Alexis Vásquez, price includes transfer,
food, some therapies, natural drinks and lodging
in the singular rooms. The doctor runs health,
'eco-relax' and therapy programs, and there
are mud baths at the *campamento*.

Restaurants

Porlamar
The upmarket dining is in Urb Costa Azul on
Av Bolívar. There are plenty of eating places
on Campos and 4 de Mayo.

$$ La Casa del Mero
Av Raúl Leoni, opposite Hotel María Luisa.
Good place for a cocktail on the water,
serves seafood, steaks and chicken.

$$ La Pimienta
C A Manrique, T0295-264 1805. Closed Sun.

Good seafood and local dishes, new location.

$ Dragón Chino
Av Principal, 4 de Mayo, T0295-261 8253.
Great Chinese, good value, clean and quick service.

$ El Pollo de Carlitos
Marcano y Martínez.
Pleasant location, good food.

$ El Punto Criollo
Igualdad near Hotel Porlamar.
Excellent value *comida margariteña*, gets packed
at lunchtimes. Highly recommended.

Bars and clubs

Porlamar
Several bars, and live music in the Centro
Comercial Parque Costazul.

Pampatar
The seafront La Caranta area of Pampatar is lively
with bars and music clubs, including Beach Bar
and Guayoyo. Others include **Samoa cocktail bar**
(Av Jóvita Villalba, Pampatar, T0295-500 2673).

South coast
Several beach bars in Playa El Yaque; best bar is
Los Surf Piratas, drinks and dancing from 2130.

Festivals

Many religious festivals, including:
19 Mar Paraguachí (Feria de San José, 10 days).
26 Jul Punta de Piedras.
31 Jul Batalla de Matasiete.
15 Aug Asunción de la Virgen at La Asunción.
1-8 Sep El Valle.
4-11 Nov Boca del Río.
4-30 Nov Boca del Pozo.
5-6 Dec Porlamar.
27 Dec-3 Jan Juan Griego.

Shopping

Porlamar
Margarita's status as a duty-free zone attracts
Venezuelan shoppers, who go in droves for
clothing, electronic goods and other items. Street
sellers lay out their handicrafts on Av Santiago
Mariño in the afternoon. When buying jewellery,
bargain, don't pay by credit card (surcharges are
imposed) and get a detailed guarantee of the
item. Av Santiago Mariño and surroundings are
the place for designer labels, but decent copies

can be found on Blv Guevara and Blv Gómez and around Plaza Bolívar in the centre. For bargains on denims, T-shirts, shorts, swimming gear and bikinis, take a bus to Conejeros market (from Fraternidad, Igualada a Velásquez). Av J A Rodríguez, open Mon-Fri 0800-1700, Sat-Sun 0900-1400, also good restaurants for breakfast.

Pampatar
Centro Comercial La Redoma, *Av Jóvito Villalba*. A good small mall for food, clothing, medicines, and more.

What to do

Porlamar
Sailing
The motor yacht **Viola Festival** can be hired for mini cruises to the island of Coche. There are other yachts offering island cruises, fishing trips, etc. Contact local tour operators eg **Feliz Viaje** (*C Marcano, Porlamar, T0414-793 5605, www.felizviaje.com*).

La Asunción
Language schools
CELA Spanish School, *C Guayacanes con El Colegio, Quinta Los Cone, Urb Palo Santo, T0295-242 1920, http://cela-ve.com*. The website has information about tours in Margarita and other parts of the country.

Eastern and northern beaches
Tour shops in **Playa El Agua** are the best places to book scuba diving and snorkelling trips: most go to Los Frailes, a small group of islands to the north of Playa Agua, and reputedly the best diving and snorkelling in Margarita, but it's also possible to dive at Parque Nacional La Restinga and Isla Cubagua. Prices from US$75 pp for an all-inclusive full day (2 dives). Snorkelling is about two-thirds the price of scuba diving.
Enomis Divers, *Av 31 de Julio, CC Turístico, Playa El Agua, loc 2, sector La Mira, T0295-249 0366, www. divemargarita.com*. PADI school, diving trips, many programmes and certifications offered.

South coast
Sailboards, **kite surf** and **kayaks** can be hired on Playa El Yaque from at least 5 well-equipped companies, who also offer lessons. An hour's lesson costs US$55. English, German, French and Portuguese spoken. Enquire at

El Yaque Motion (see Where to stay, above) for more information about wind and kite surfing. A 20-min boat ride to Isla Coche leaves from next door to **El Yaque Motion**, a recommended spot for advanced kiters. Rescue service available at Playa El Yaque.

Peninsula de Macanao
Horse riding
You can ride on the peninsula at **Ranch Cabatucan**, including full-moon night rides, and children's workshops (2 km from Guayacancito on the road to Punta Arenas, T0295-808 5147, www.cabatucan.com).

Transport

Porlamar
Air There are too many flight options to list here: check with local offices for details. **Gen Santiago Mariño Airport**, between Porlamar and Punta de Piedras, has the international and national terminals at either end. Taxi from Porlamar US$3.50, 20-30 mins. All national airlines have routes to **Margarita**. Many daily flights to/from **Caracas**, 45-min flight; tickets are much cheaper if purchased in Venezuela. To **Canaima** and to **Los Roques** with **LTA**.

Bus Local Buses and *por puestos* serve most of the island, buses US$0.50-1, *por puestos* minimum fare US$1.50, few services at night when you should take a taxi anyway.
Long distance Several bus companies in Caracas sell through tickets from **Caracas** to Porlamar, arriving about midday, US$3. Buses return to Caracas from La Paralela bus station in Porlamar.

Car hire Several offices at the airport and at the entrance to **Hotel Bella Vista**, others on Av Santiago Mariño. Check the brakes, bodywork and terms and conditions of hire thoroughly. Scooters can also be hired. Motor bikes may not be ridden 2000-0500. **Note** Fill up before leaving Porlamar as service stations are scarce. Roads are generally good and most are paved. Signposts are often nonexistent. Free maps are confusing, but it's worth having one with you. Avoid driving outside Porlamar after dark. Beware of robbery; park in private car parks.

Ferry From **Puerto La Cruz** to Margarita (**Punta de Piedras**): **Conferry**, Terminal de Ferrys Eulalia Buroz, Puerto La Cruz, T0281-267 7221, and Terminal de Ferrys at Guanta, from where most ferries depart, www.conferry.com, open 0600-2030. Price varies according to class of seat, website gives departure times (extra ferries during high season), T0501-2663 3779 freephone for availability of tickets. Photocopy of passport required to purchase tickets. Fast ferry from Guanta, 3 hrs, slow ferry, 5 hrs, to Punta de Piedras also takes vehicles. Conferry from Punta de Piedras to Isla Coche. **Conferry** office in **Punta de Piedras**, Av J B Arismendi, Terminal de Ferrys, T0295-297 6473, daily 0600-1930.

Gran Cacique, 2-3 fast ferries a day **Puerto la Cruz**–Punta de Piedras, US$8-15 one way, also takes cars, US$27, and motorbikes, US$12-14, T0281-263 0935 (Puerto La Cruz ferry terminal), T0295-239 8339 (Punta de Piedras, T0295-239 8339, or Av Santiago Mariño, Edif Blue Sky, loc 3, Porlamar, T0295-264 2945). It is most advisable to book in advance, especially if travelling with a car or motorbike during high season. To get to terminal in Puerto La Cruz, take 'Bello Monte' *por puesto* from Libertad y Anzoátegui, 2 blocks from Plaza Bolívar. From **Cumaná** ferry terminal, El Salado, **Gran Cacique**, T0293-433 0909, 2-3 a

day, US$7.50-10 one way (children 3-7 and over-60s half price), and **Naviarca**, T0293-432 0011, continuous service, US$5 one way for passengers (children 3-7 and over-60s half price), motorcycles US$6, cars US$17.50. **Navibus**, T0295-500 6284, www.navibus.com.ve, has 2 sailings a day from Puerto la Cruz and Cumaná: US$9.50 and 7.50 respectively (children 2-7, over-60s and disabled half price), motorcycles US$16 and 13, cars US$21-25 and US$17.50.

Taxi Taxi for a day is US$3.50 per hr, minimum 3 hrs. Always fix fare in advance; 20% extra after 2000 and on Sun. Taxi from Porlamar to Playa El Agua, US$3.

Los Roques *Colour map 1, A6.*

the Caribbean of your imagination

★The turquoise and emerald lagoons and dazzling white sands of the Archipiélago de Los Roques make up one of Venezuela's loveliest national parks. For lazing on an untouched beach, or for snorkelling and diving amid schools of fish and coral reefs, these islands cannot be beaten. Diving and snorkelling are best to the south of the archipelago.

The islands of Los Roques, with long stretches of white beaches and over 20 km of coral reef in crystal-clear water, lie 166 km due north of La Guaira; the atoll, of about 340 islets and reefs, constitutes a national park of 225,153 ha. There are many bird nesting sites (eg the huge gull colonies on Francisqui and the pelicans, boobies and frigates on Selenqui); May is nesting time at the gull colonies. For information about the conservation of the marine environment, visit https://fundacionlosroques.wordpress.com.

This is one of the least visited diving spots in the Caribbean. There are at least seven main dive sites offering caves, cliffs, coral and, at Nordesqui, shipwrecks. There are many fish to be seen, including sharks at the caves of Olapa de Bavusqui. Prices are higher than the mainland and infrastructure is limited but the islands are beautiful and unspoiled.

Gran Roque

Gran Roque (population 3100) is the only permanently inhabited island. The airport is here, as is the national guard, a few grocery stores, public phones (offering expensive internet), a bank with an ATM (but take cash from the mainland), medical facilities, dive shops, a few restaurants and accommodation. Park Headquarters are in the scattered fishing village. Tourist information is available from the very helpful Oscar Shop (T0237-221 1043), directly in front as you leave the airstrip. Try also Veni a Los Roques (T0424-295 8043, http://venialosroques.com), who also arrange packages to other islands, including day (US$25) and overnight trips (US$70 for two, including meals). Boat trips to other islands can be arranged here or at *posadas* (round trip US$3-17, depending on distance), which are worthwhile as you cannot swim off Gran Roque. Prices are fixed by the boat

Essential Los Roques

Access and information

National park entry for foreigners US$1.25 (BsF900, at the DICOM rate at time of research), Venezuelans half price, children under four and seniors over 65 free. Prices are subject to change. You can pay in dollars, but it is not known at what exchange rate. Camping is free, but not allowed on Gran Roque; campers need a permit from Inparques (T0212-273 2811 in Caracas, or the office on Plaza Bolívar, Gran Roque, Monday-Friday 0830-1200 and 1400-1800, weekends and holidays 0830-1200 and 1430-1730); also the small office by the runway where you pay the entry fee. See www.los-roques.com and www.los-roques.com. Also look out for the excellent *Guía del Parque Nacional Archipiélago Los Roques* (Ecograph, 2004).

When to go

The average daytime temperature is 29°C with coolish nights. The islands tend to be very busy in July-August and at Christmas. At other times the islands are best visited midweek, as Venezuelans swarm here on long weekends and at school holidays, after which there is litter on every island. Low season is Easter to July.

Tip...

You will need strong sunblock as there is no shade and an umbrella is recommended.

owners' cooperative and are set in dollars for foreigners (if foreigners wish to pay in bolívares the exchange rate is most unfavourable).

Other islands

You can negotiate with local fishermen for transport to other islands: you will need to take your own tent, food and (especially) water. You may also have to take your own snorkeling equipment, unless it is provided by your package tour operator. **Madrisqui** has a good shallow beach and joins Pirata Cay by a sandspit. **Francisqui** is three islands joined by sandspits, with calm lagoon waters to the south and rolling surf to the north. You can walk with care from one cay to the other, maybe swimming at times. There's some shade in the mangrove near the bar at La Cueva. **Crasqui** has a 3-km beach with beautiful water and white sand. **Cayo de Agua** (one hour by fast boat from Gran Roque) has an amazing sandspit joining its two parts and a nice walk to the lighthouse where you'll find two natural pools.

Listings Los Roques

Where to stay

In most places on Islas Los Roques, breakfast and dinner are included in the price.

There are over 60 *posadas* on Gran Roque. Those listed below are all here.

$$$ pp El Botuto
On seafront near Supermercado W Salazar, T0416-622 0061, www.posadaelbotuto.com.
Nice airy rooms with fan, some with a/c, good simple food, locally owned. Trips to other islands and watersports arranged.

$$$ pp Piano y Papaya
Near Plaza Bolívar towards seafront, T0414-281 0104, www.losroques.com.

Very tasteful, run by Italian artist, with fan, $$ pp for bed and breakfast, credit cards accepted, Italian and English spoken, laundry service.

$$$ pp Posada Acquamarina
C 2 No 149, T0412-310 1962, www.posada-acquamarina.com.
All-inclusive, rooms have a/c, private bathrooms with hot water, terrace. Owner Giorgio very helpful, speaks Italian and some French, can arrange flights from Caracas. Excursions to other islands.

$$$ pp Posada Caracol
On seafront near airstrip, T0414-373 0101, or 0237-414 5566, www.caracolgroup.com.
Delightful, small *posada* with 4 double rooms, full-board with excursions, credit cards accepted,

Italian and English spoken, good boats. Also owns Villa Caracol.

$$$ pp Roquelusa
C 3 No 214, behind supermarket, T0212-287 0517, roquelusa@los-roques.org.
A cheaper option, basic but clean rooms, with cold water, a/c, good food, well run and friendly.

$$$-$$ pp Posada Doña Magalis
Plaza Bolívar 46, T0414-299 8550, www.magalis.com.
Simple place, locally owned, with a/c, cheaper with shared bath, includes trips to other islands, soft drinks, breakfast and dinner, delicious food, mostly fish and rice.

What to do

Many *posadas* arrange water sports such as windsurfing and kitesurfing (especially good at Francisqui), diving, sailing and fishing.

Diving
For health reasons you must allow 12 hrs to elapse between diving and flying back to the mainland. Lots of courses and packages available. **Cayo de Agua** and **Francisqui** recommended for snorkelling. Boats and equipment rentals can be arranged.
Ecobuzos, *3 blocks from the airstrip, T0295-262 9811/0416-595 0464/0414-395 4208 (English), www.ecobuzos.com.* Very good, new equipment, modern boats, experienced dive masters.

PADI courses, US$250 for standard scuba PADI certificate, other add-ons and beginner dives also available.

Sailing
Fully equipped yachts can be chartered from about US$140 per person per night for 2 people, all inclusive, highly recommended as a worthwhile way of getting some shade on the treeless beaches. Ask at **Angel & Oscar Shop**, or see websites such as www.los-roques.com and http://venialosroques.com.

Transport

Air Flights from **Maiquetía**, **Higuerote** or **Porlamar**. LTA (T0212-212 3110, www.tuy.com), **Chapi Air** (T0414-311 1117, www.chapiair.com), **Blue Star** (T0412-310 1962, www.bluestar.us) and **Los Roques Airlines** (T0212-833 8654/0414-332 0055, www.losroques-airlines.com) all fly from Maiquetía (Aeropuerto Auxiliar) once a day, 40 mins, from about US$250 round trip, more expensive if booked outside of Venezuela, but foreigners may not be able to book online. Tax of about US$10 is payable. Some carriers charge more at weekends. Remember that small planes usually restrict luggage to 10 kg. They offer full-day (return flight, meals and activities) and overnight packages. It's best to buy a return to the mainland as buying and confirming tickets and finding offices open on the islands is difficult.

Canaima &
the Orinoco Delta

In Parque Nacional Canaima, one of the largest national parks in the world, you'll find the spectacular Angel Falls, the highest in the world, and the mysterious 'Lost World' of Roraima (described under South to Brazil). Canaima is the tourist centre for the park, but indigenous communities are now accepting tourists. The historic Ciudad Bolívar on the Río Orinoco is a good starting place for the superb landscapes further south. Further east, beyond the industrial city of Ciudad Guayana, the Orinoco Delta is developing as a tourist destination.

Guayana, south of the Orinoco River, constitutes half of Venezuela, comprising rounded forested hills and narrow valleys, rising to ancient flat-topped tablelands on the borders of Brazil. These savannahs interspersed with semi-deciduous forest are sparsely populated. So far, communications have been the main difficulty, but a road that leads to Manaus passes through Santa Elena de Uairén on the Brazilian frontier (see page 1670). The area is Venezuela's largest gold and diamond source, but its immense reserves of iron ore, manganese and bauxite are of far greater economic importance.

Ciudad Bolívar Colour map 2, A1.
beautiful and historical colonial town

Ciudad Bolívar is on the narrows of the Orinoco, some 300 m wide, which gave the town its old name of Angostura, 'The Narrows'. It is 400 km from the Orinoco delta. It was here that Bolívar came after defeat to reorganize his forces, and the British Legionnaires joined him. At Angostura he was declared President of the Gran Colombia he had yet to build and which was to fragment before his death. With its cobbled streets, pastel buildings and setting on the Orinoco, it is one of Venezuela's most beautiful colonial towns.

Towards Ciudad Bolívar
Ciudad Bolívar can be reached easily by roads south from Caracas and Puerto La Cruz. The Caracas route, via Valle de la Pascua, and the Puerto La Cruz route, via Anaco, meet at **El Tigre**, which has good hotels and services. From the Llanos, from **Chaguaramas** turn south through Las Mercedes (hotel $) to **Cabruta**, 179 km, road in very bad shape, daily bus to Caracas, US$3.75, basic hotel. Then take a ferry from opposite the airport to **Caicara** (car ferry 1½ hours, *lanchas* for pedestrians 25 minutes). An 11.2-km bridge across the Orinoco is being built between Cabruta and Caicara (still incomplete at the start of 2017). Alternatively, from San Fernando de Apure take a bus to **Calabozo** and *por puesto* to **El Sombrero**, where you can catch the Ciudad Bolívar bus.

Sights
At the Congress of Angostura, 15 February 1819, the representatives of the present day Venezuela, Colombia, Panama and Ecuador met to proclaim Gran Colombia. The building, on **Plaza Bolívar**, built

Best for
Adventures ▪ Isolation ▪ Scenery

1766-1776 by Manuel Centurión, the provincial governor, houses a museum, the **Casa del Congreso de Angostura**, with an ethnographic museum in the basement. Guides give tours in Spanish only. Also on this plaza is the **Cathedral** (which was completed in 1840), the **Casa de Los Gobernadores de la Colonia** (also built by Centurión in 1766), the **Real Intendencia**, and the **Casa de la Cultura**. Also here, at Bolívar 33, is the house where Gen Manuel Piar, the Liberator of Guayana from the Spanish, was held prisoner before being executed by Bolívar on 16 October 1817, for refusing to put himself under Bolívar's command. The restored **Plaza Miranda**, up Calle Carabobo, has an art centre. The present legislative assembly and **Consejo Municipal** are between Plaza Bolívar and Plaza Miranda. In 1824, when the town was still known as Angostura a Prussian physician to Bolívar's troops invented the bitters; the factory moved to Port of Spain in 1875.

Museum at **Casa del Correo del Orinoco** ① *Paseo Orinoco y Carabobo, Mon-Fri 0930-1200, 1430-1700*, houses modern art and history exhibits of the city. **Museo Casa San Isidro** ① *Av Táchira, Tue-Sun 0900-1700, free, knowledgeable guides*, is a colonial mansion where Simón Bolívar stayed for two weeks. It has antique furniture and an old garden. **Museo de Arte Moderno Jesús Soto** ① *Av Germania, 0930-1730, weekends and holidays 1000-1700, free, guide in Spanish only*, is located some distance from the centre in pleasant gardens. It has works by Venezuela's celebrated Jesús Rafael Soto and other modern artists from around the world. Recommended. The best views of the city are from **Fortín El Zamuro** ① *C 28 de Octubre y Av 5 de Julio, daily except Mon, free, guides available*, dating from 1902, strategically located at one of the tallest points of the city, near to the **Botanical Gardens** ① *Av 5 de Julio, Mon-Fri 0830-1600, free*.

The **Paseo Orinoco** skirts the riverbank and heads west out of town; it is a relaxing place to stroll but unsafe after dark. Speedboats go across the river to the small, picturesque town of **Soledad**

Ciudad Bolívar

| 100 metres | |
| 100 yards | |

Where to stay 🛌
1 Amor Patrio
3 La Cumbre
4 Laja Real
5 Posada Angostura
6 Posada Casa Grande
7 Posada Doña Carol
8 Posada Don Carlos

Restaurants 🍴
1 Bambú Sushi Bar
2 La Ballena
3 Mercado La Carioca
4 Mirador Angostura
5 Tepuy

(US$0.50, one way, five minutes) on a journey that offers great views of colonial centre, the bridge and the river itself. Security can be an issue at either end; don't cross at night. There are no other passenger boat services. The **Angostura Bridge** can be seen from the waterfront *paseo*. This is the first bridge across the Orinoco, 1668 m long, opened in 1967, again with great views (cyclists and walkers are not allowed to cross, you must flag down a car or truck).

West of the centre is **El Zanjón**, an area of vegetation typical of the region. East is **Parque El Porvenir**, with botanical gardens (entrance on Calle Bolívar), but it is unsafe to wander unless accompanied by staff. Outside the airport is the *Río Caroní* aeroplane, which Jimmy Angel landed on top of Auyán Tepuy (see page 1664).

Going further…

Tours, usually starting from Ciudad Bolívar (see What to do, below), can be made into the area south of the Río Orinoco from **Maripa** (colour map 2, A1), travelling on the Río Caura. These include visits to indigenous villages, river bathing, jungle treks to waterfalls with explanations of wildlife and vegetation.

Listings Ciudad Bolívar *map page 1660*

Tourist information

Dirección de Turismo
*Av Bolívar, Quinta Yeita 59, T0285-632 6493, www.ciudadbolivar.gov.co.
Mon-Fri 0800-1200, 1400-1730.*
Helpful, English spoken.

Where to stay

\$\$ Laja Real
Av Andrés Bello y Jesús Soto, opposite airport, T0285-632 7911, www.hotellajareal.com.
A reasonable 1980s hotel, good for early morning flights, excellent pool (small charge for non-residents), sauna, gym, parking, restaurant.

\$\$ Posada Casa Grande
C Boyacá 8, T0285-632 4639, www.cacaotravel-venezuela.com (the HQ of Cacao Travel is here, with a chain of \$\$\$-\$\$ hotels, posadas and lodges around the country, including Posada Angostura, below).
A handsome colonial building converted to a tasteful 4-star hotel. Well-attired rooms overlook a central patio; upstairs there's a rooftop terrace with a bar and small pool. Professional service, good meals by prior arrangement, breakfast included. Recommended.

\$\$-\$ Posada Doña Carol
Libertad 28, T0285-634 0989, jmaury2008@hotmail.com, www.hosteltrail.com/hostels/posadadonacarol.
Basic and hospitable guesthouse with a mixture of rooms, including 1 large quadruple with an outdoor patio-balcony. Very helpful, breakfast extra, can prepare meals, organizes bus tickets and tours. Communal fridges and kitchen, refreshments, and laundry.

\$ Amor Patrio
Amor Patrio 30, T0414-854 4925.
A simple, friendly guesthouse with a tranquil little patio. 5 rooms have fan and shared bathroom, a/c is extra. No Wi-Fi but an internet terminal is available. Also laundry service and runs tours. Run by Gerd Altmann, highly respected for his travel expertise, German and English spoken. Recommended.

\$ La Cumbre
Av 5 de Julio, T0285-632 7709, lacumbre@cantv.net.
Secluded hill-top retreat with commanding views. Rooms are large and simple, some overlook the town and Orinoco river below. Resort-style facilities include a great pool, restaurant, bar, and terraces, maybe noisy at weekends. Take a taxi – not on bus route – or a steep uphill walk.

\$ Posada Angostura
Same contact details as Posada Casa Grande above, also on C Boyacá.
Handsome rooms in old colonial house, some rooms have river view, hot water, travel agency. Excellent food.

\$ Posada Don Carlos
C Boyacá 26 y Amor Patrio, just 30 m from Plaza Bolívar, T0285-632 6017, www.posada-doncarlos.com.
Stunning colonial house. 4 double rooms with a/c, or 6 cheaper rooms with fan, all with private bath. Breakfast and dinner available, lovely patio, bar, tours. Good vibe, helpful, popular. Recommended.

Outside town

$ Posada La Casita
Av Ligia Pulido, Urb 24 de Julio, T0285-617 0832,
www.posada-la-casita.com.
Beautiful leafy grounds at this secluded hotel, also
home to a small private zoo. Lodging is in spacious
and immaculately clean apartments or in tasteful
garden *casitas*, campsite for tents and caravans.
Amenities include pool, laundry service, hammocks,
food and drink at extra cost. Free pick up from
airport or bus terminal (ring in advance), free shuttle
service into town. The owner runs **Gekko Tours**.
German and English spoken, helpful. Prices in Euros.

Restaurants

Many restaurants close at 1700.

$$ Bambú Sushi Bar
Av 5 de Julio, inside Hotel La Cumbre, take a taxi.
Authentic sushi rolls served up at this breezy
hilltop restaurant overlooking the city. In the
same hotel, **Restaurante El Mirador**, serving
grilled fish and meat, isn't bad either.

$$ Tepuy
Av Andrés Bello y Jesús Soto, opposite airport and
inside Hotel Laja Real.
Slightly formal place with very attentive service.
Good pasta with prawns, as well as meat, chicken
and fish, wines and cocktails, live jazz some nights.

$$-$ Mercado La Carioca
Octava Estrella y Paseo Orinoco, on the banks of
the river. Daily from 0600-1500.
The best place for eating tasty local food. Great
view. Various stalls and excellent local food with
a range of prices.

$ La Ballena
C Urica y Zea T0285-632 0231.
Small *tasca* bar-restaurant, serving good paellas,
grilled fish and steaks, central, good value.

$ Mirador Angostura
Paseo Orinoco.
Un-pretentious *comida criolla* with views over
the river.

Cafés and fast food

Several fast food restaurants around **Museo de
Arte Moderno Jesús Soto**.

What to do

Competition is stiff in Ciudad Bolívar. Do not agree
to, or pay for a tour in the bus station or on the
street. Always ask to be taken to the office. Always

ask for a receipt (and make sure that it comes on
paper bearing the company logo) and only take a
tour that starts in Ciudad Bolívar. If you fall prey to
a con artist, make a *denuncio* at the police station
and inform genuine travel agents.

Ciudad Bolívar is the best place to book a tour
to Canaima, but you will pick up cheaper deals for
trips to Roraima and the Gran Sabana from Santa
Elena. Most agents in Ciudad Bolívar sell tours run
by just a handful of operators, but sometimes add
commission. Always ask who will be running the
actual tour; it may be cheaper to book from them
directly. Get independent recommendations
on standards of guiding, food, time-keeping,
etc. For 3 days/2 nights tours to Canaima
including flights, you pay around US$300-400 pp
depending on accommodation, or US$150-300
for 1-day tour that includes flights to Canaima,
flight near the Angel Falls, and activities around
Canaima lagoon (price depends on the activities)
and food (see below for flights to Canaima).

Bernal Tours, *T0285-632 5254, T0414-854 8234
(mob in Spanish), T0414-899 7162 (in English),
www.bernaltours.com.* Run by descendents of
Peruvian adventurer Tomás Bernal from Arequipa
(see Warning, opposite). They use *indígena*
guides and their own eco lodge at Canaima
lagoon overlooking the falls.
Gekko Tours, *run by Peter Rothfuss and María
Teresa de Rothfuss at airport (also Posada La Casita),
T0285-632 3223, T0414-854 5146/856 2925, www.
gekkotours-venezuela.de.* Established family
business with 18 years of experience.
Soana Travel, *run by Martin Haars at Posada Don
Carlos, Boyacá 26, T0285-632 6017, T0414-864 6616,
www.posada-doncarlos.com.* English and German
spoken. Professional and reliable.
Tiuna Tours, *at airport, T0285-632 8697/0416-686
1192, tiunatoursca@gmail.com.* Cheapest option
for Canaima, have a camp that takes 180 people.

Transport

Ciudad Bolívar
Air It's possible to fly to **Canaima**
independently, but an organized tour is highly
recommended. Several flights leave daily
with **Transmandú** (T0285-632 1462, www.
transmandu.com), **Sundance Air** (Gekko Tours,
T0285-632 3223) and, less frequently, with other
charter airlines. One-way tickets cost around
US$100; try to book at least 24-48 hrs in advance.
Arrange a 20-person charter to **Santa Elena**
with **Transmandú**, subject to weather. Puerto

Ordaz/Ciudad Guayana is a busier flight hub than Ciudad Bolívar and some tours start from there. Taxi from airport to Ciudad Guayana US$5, to historic centre US$1.20.

Bus Terminal at junction of Av República and Av Sucre. Left luggage. To get there take bus marked Terminal going west along Paseo Orinoco (US$0.15). Buy bus tickets in advance. Hourly to **Caracas** US$3.50-5, 7-8 hrs. 10 daily to **Puerto La Cruz**, US$3, 5 hrs. 1 daily to **Cumaná**, US$2.50, 5-6 hrs. Daily to **Valencia**, via Maracay, US$4-6,

8-9 hrs. **El Dorado** US$2.50, 5 hrs. To **Santa Elena de Uairén** with several companies, **Occidente** and **Línea Los Llanos** recommended for comfort, US$4.50, 9-10 hrs. To **Ciudad Guayana** hourly from 0700, US$1, 1½ hrs. 2 daily to **Caicara**, US$3 (including 2 ferry crossings), 6-7 hrs, with **Coop Gran Mcal Sucre**. 2 daily to **Puerto Ayacucho**, US$4-6, 10-12 hrs with **Línea Amazonas** or **Coop Gran Mcal Sucre**, take food.

Taxi US$2 to virtually anywhere in town. US$1.50 from bus station to town centre.

Parque Nacional Canaima and Angel Falls *Colour map 2, B1.*
jaw-dropping waterfalls and dramatic landscapes

★Canaima National Park, a UNESCO World Heritage Site since 1994, is one of the most unspoilt places on earth. At over 3 million ha, it is the second largest national park in Venezuela, the sixth largest on the planet. It is a world apart, with its fantastic table mountains, waterfalls which include the world's highest (Angel Falls), caves, deep forests and indigenous cultures.

Canaima Camp

At Canaima Camp, the Río Carrao tumbles spectacularly over Ucaima, Golondrina and Hacha Falls into the lagoon, which has beautiful tannin-stained water with soft beige beaches. It's a lovely spot, but it also has the air strip and is the centre of operations for river trips to indigenous areas and to Angel Falls. The falls are named after Jimmie Angel, the US airman who first reported their existence in 1935. Two years later he returned and crash landed his plane, the *Río Caroní*, on top of Auyán Tepuy. The site is marked with a plaque. Ruth Robertson, an American photojournalist, led the first overland expedition to establish the Falls' height in 1949. The sheer rock face was climbed in 1971 by three Americans and an Englishman, David Nott, who recounted the 10-day adventure in his book *Angels Four* (Prentice-Hall). Hugo Chávez said that the falls should be called by an indigenous name: Kerepakupai Merú. A second indigenous name is Parekupa Vena.

Excursions There is a famous 'tunnel' between Sapo and Sapito Falls (where Río Carrao passes behind Isla Anatoliy), where one can walk behind the huge waterfall – a must for any visitor. It is essential to be accompanied by a guide. The easiest way to get there is from Tomás Bernal Camp on Isla Anatoliy (five minutes boat ride from Canaima Camp). It's a 25-minute walk from there. Plastic raincoats are usually provided by the guide, or wear a swim suit. Wrap your camera and other belongings in a plastic bag. No matter what, you will get completely soaked in the middle of the tunnel. The path behind the waterfall is extremely slippery and should be taken only by the reasonably fit. Wrap your hand in an extra plastic bag, so it's not cut by the rough rope. When taking photos from behind the wall of water, experiment with camera speeds for the best effects.

There is one more, invisible, waterfall on Canaima Lagoon, at the opposite end from Canaima Camp. It is called Salto Ara. The lagoon is a terrace and at Salto Ara all the water goes

Essential Parque Nacional Canaima

Park entry is US$2.85 per person (BsF2000; Venezuelans pay BsF450, reductions for children) and is paid to Inparques on arrival in Canaima. There are several tourist lodges at Canaima and many package tours visit on two-day/one-night and three-day/two-night trips from Ciudad Bolívar or Ciudad Guayana. These offer a variety of activities and longer ones usually include a day-trip to the Angel Falls (a long, bottom-numbing day). There is also a great variety of prices, depending on the class of lodging chosen (US$300-400; also available from Ciudad Guayana and Caracas). Do not forget swimwear, insect repellent and sun cream; waterproof clothing may be advisable. Do not walk barefoot because there are chiggers, or niguas, in the lagoon's sand beaches. See also Trips to the Angel Falls.

down one step. It is invisible from the surface, the only indicator is foam rising as if from nowhere. This fall is extremely dangerous: do not swim or take a boat near it. This is where Tomás Bernal, the Peruvian discoverer of the above tunnel, lost his life in 1998 after the engine of his boat broke down. He is buried on Isla Anatoliy.

★Trips to the Angel Falls

The Angel Falls, the highest in the world (979 m – its longest single drop is 807 m), 70 km downriver from Canaima, are best reached by plane to Canaima from Ciudad Bolívar or Ciudad Guayana. Trips by boat upriver to the Angel Falls operate May-January, depending on the level of the water in the rivers, and cost about US$140-170. Boats literally fly up and down river over the boulders (not for faint-hearted), but even during the rainy season you may have to get out and push in places. Most trips starting from Canaima make an overnight stop on one of the islands, continuing to the Falls the next day. More relaxing, with more stops at beauty spots, are 44-hour, 'three-day' trips. Inparques ① *Av Guayana, Edif Centro Empresarial Alta Vista, p 8, Puerto Ordaz, Ciudad Guayana, T0286-966 2033*. Ask here if you need a *permiso de excursionistas* to go on one tour and come back with another, giving yourself more time at the Falls. You may have to pay extra to do this, up to US$10 (take all food and gear). Trips can be arranged with agencies in Ciudad Bolívar (see What to do, above) or at Canaima airport. All *curiaras* (dugouts) must carry first aid, life jackets, etc. Take wet weather gear, swimwear, mosquito net for hammock and insect repellent and a plastic bag to protect your camera/day bag. The light is best in the morning.

The cheapest way to fly over the falls is on scheduled flights from Ciudad Bolívar. From Canaima a 45-minute flight costs around US$75-85 per person and does some circuits over and alongside the falls; departures only if enough passengers.

Kamarata

The largest of the *tepuis*, **Auyán Tepuy** (700 sq km) is also one of the more accessible. Kamarata is a friendly indigenous settlement with a Capuchin mission on the plain at the east foot of the tepuy. It has a well-stocked shop but no real hotels; basic rooms can be found for under US$10 per person, camping also possible at the mission (mosquito nets necessary and anti-malarial pills advised). Take food, although there is one place to eat, and locals may sell you dinner. The whole area is within the Parque Nacional Canaima.

Pemón families in Kamarata have formed co-operatives and can arrange *curiaras*, tents and porters for various excursions: see What to do, below.

Kavác

About a two-hour walk northwest of Kamarata, this is an indigenous-run resort consisting of a dozen thatched huts (*churuatas*) for guests, a small shop, and an excitingly short airstrip serviced by Cessnas from Ciudad Bolívar, Santa Elena, and Isla Margarita; flights from the north provide excellent views of Angel Falls and Auyán Tepuy. There is a vehicle connection with Kamarata but it is expensive because all fuel has to be flown in.

The prime local excursion is to **Kavác Canyon** and its waterfall known as La Cueva, which can be reached by joining a group or by setting out early west up the Río Kavác. A natural jacuzzi is encountered after a 30-minute wade along the sparkling stream, after which the gorge narrows dramatically until the falls are reached. Go in the morning to avoid groups of day-trippers from Porlamar. The sun's rays illuminate the vertical walls of the canyon only for a short time around 1100. Be prepared to get wet; swimwear and shoes with good grip, plus a dry change of clothing are recommended; also insect repellent, as there is a mosquito and midge invasion around dusk. Late afternoon winds off the savannah can make conditions chilly. Most visitors to Kavác are on tours from Canaima, or elsewhere, so it may be difficult to book lodging at the camp (basic rooms or hammocks). If you go independently, take food with you. There is an entry charge for visitors.

Uruyén

South of Auyán Tepuy and west of Kamarata, Uruyén is similar to Kavác, only smaller and more intimate. It also has a beautiful canyon and is the starting point for treks up Auyán Tepuy. The camp is run by the Ceballo family, supported by **Eposak**, tourism NGO foundation: http://eposak.org/site/. Contact: reservaciones_uruyen@hotmail.com, for details.

Where to stay

Canaima

Most lodges and camps are booked up by package tour companies.

$$$$ Wakü Lodge (Canaima Tours)
T0286-962 0559, www.wakulodge.com.
The best option in Canaima, 4-star luxury, romantic, comfortable, a/c, good food, right on lagoon, free satellite/Wi-Fi for guests. Specializes mainly in all-inclusive packages. Recommended.

$$$ pp Campamiento Canaima
T0289-540-2747, www.venetur.gob.ve.
Run by **Venetur** as a luxury resort with 105 rooms, restaurant, meeting room. Superb views of the lagoon.

$$$ pp Campamiento Ucaima Jungle Rudy
T0414-861 5263/0289-808 9241, T0286-952 1529 in Puerto Ordaz, www.junglerudy.com.
Run by daughters of the late 'Jungle' Rudy Truffino, full board with a variety of tour packages, with its own cabins at Angel Falls, 1-hr walk from Canaima above Hacha Falls, bilingual guides.

$$$ pp Kusari
Close to Parakaupa Lodge, near airport, T0286-962 0443.
Basic but clean, with bath, fan, hammock on front porch, food available, ask for Claudio at **Tienda Canaima**.

$$$ pp Parakaupa Lodge
5 mins from airport, on southwestern side of lagoon, T0289-808 9080, Puerto Ordaz T0286-741 1497, parakaupa@angelfalls.travel.
Attractive rooms with bath, hammocks views over the lagoon and falls, restaurant, full board, full range of tours.

$$ Campamento Morichal
On lagoon shore, T0416-985 4630.
Small, rustic-style lodge with thatched roof, 12 rooms, hot water, fan, restaurant serving local dishes, excellent service.

$$ pp Tapuy Lodge
50 m from Canaima beach, T0212-977 1234 (reservations), www.casatropical.com.ve.
Next to the beach with expansive views of the mountains. Rooms are pleasant and include bath and a/c. Facilities include restaurant and bar. Attentive service and good reputation. One of the best. Recommended.

Camping and hammocks

Camp for free in Canaima, but only around the *fuente de soda*; fires are not permitted. No tents available for hire. Otherwise, best place to rent a hammock or camp is at **Campamento Tomás Bernal (Bernal Tours)** on Isla Anatoliy, T0414-854 8562 Spanish, T0414-899 7162 English, www.bernaltours.com. Camp has capacity for 60 hammocks. Also 4 beds in open for elderly travellers, 4 rooms with private bath. Clean bathrooms. Package ($$$ pp) includes flight, bilingual guide, hammock, mosquito repellent, all meals, boat trip across lagoon, raincoat. Bernal Tours also has a camp on Ratoncito Island by Angel Falls.

Campamento Tiuna (Tiuna Tours) has camping space and lodging ($ pp). Some families in the village rent hammocks ($ pp).

Restaurants

Canaima

Food is expensive at the lodges. A cheaper option is **Simon's** restaurant in the village which is used by many agencies. It is advisable to take food, though there are various stores, both on the west side, **Tienda Canaima**, or in the *pueblo indigena*, selling mainly canned foods. A *fuente de soda* overlooks the lagoon. There is an expensive snack bar at the airport selling basic food, soft drinks and coffee; also souvenir shop.

What to do

Canaima

You can do walking expeditions into the jungle to indigenous villages with a guide, but negotiate the price. Other excursions are to the Mayupa Falls, including a canoe ride on the Río Carrao (US$15, half day), to Yuri Falls by jeep and boat (US$40-45 full day); to Isla Orquídea (US$25, full day, good boat ride, beach barbecue); to Saltos de Sapo and Sapito (3 hrs, US$10, US$35 full day).

Guides in Canaima

Fierce competition at the airport but agencies offer the same things at the same prices. Some package tours to Canaima are listed on pages 1596 and 1662. Agents may tell you that guides speak English: some do, but many don't. **Bernal Tours** *(see page 1662).*
Excursiones Kavác, *T0414-857 8560, 0416-285 9919, excursioneskavac@gmail.com, https://twitter.com/kavacexcursione.* Several local companies use or

otherwise recommend Excursiones Kavác as a well-structured and economical option. In Canaima, they operate a basic lodge, **Campamento Churúm**, along with a rustic camp near the falls.

Kamaracoto Tours and **Tiuna Tours** for trips to Salto Sapo, Kavác, Salto Angel; they will also help with finding accommodation.

Kamarata

Macunaima Tours (Tito Abati), **Excursiones Pemón** (Marino Sandoval), and **Jorge and Antonio Calcaño II** run local tours.

For details on climbing Auyán Tepuy and many other tours in the region, contact **Kamadac** in Santa Elena, run by Andreas Hauer (T0289-995 1408, T0414-094 4341, www.abenteuer-venezuela.de).

Transport

Canaima

Air There are flights from **Caracas** to Canaima with **Conviasa**, but these require a change in Puerto Ordaz. Many travelers prefer to go independently to **Puerto Ordaz** or **Ciudad Bolívar** and have their chosen tour operator or lodging organize onward flights to Canaima.

The flight to Canaima from **Ciudad Bolívar** is spectacular and takes 1 hr each way, overflying mining towns of San Isidro and Los Barrancos, as well as the vast artificial lake at Guri and the Yuri Falls. For more information see page 1662.

Kamarata

Air Transmandú from Ciudad Bolívar (2 hrs).

Kavác

Air A day excursion by light plane to Kavác from **Canaima** (45 mins' flight) can be made with any of the tour operators at the airport, US$180. There are also flights from **Ciudad Bolívar** with **Transmandú**. Trips from Ciudad Bolívar can be arranged for 5 days/4 nights including Kavác and Angel Falls for US$625 (4 passengers).

Ciudad Guayana and the Orinoco Delta

take a boat trip into a watery world

Ciudad Guayana *Colour map 2, A2.*

In an area rich in natural resources 105 km downriver from Ciudad Bolívar, Ciudad Guayana was founded in 1961 with the merger of two towns, San Félix and Puerto Ordaz, on either bank of the Río Caroní where it spills into the Orinoco. Today, they are technically a single city, but most locals to refer to them as if they were separate settlements. Ciudad Guayana is hot, humid, sprawling and futuristic. Its wide avenues, lack of sidewalks and public transport reflect the functional vision of the US-owned Orinoco Mining Company, which had its headquarters here and was nationalized in 1976. The city lacks any aesthetic charm and is unsuitable for casual strolling.

East of the Caroní is the commercial port of **San Félix** and the Palúa iron-ore terminal. It is a very dangerous part of the city and there is no reason for you to visit it. Across the Caroní by the 470 m concrete bridge is the wealthier settlement of **Puerto Ordaz** (airport), the iron-ore port connected by rail with the Cerro Bolívar open-cast iron mine. The second bridge across the Río Orinoco, Puente Orinoquia, 3156 m long, was opened in Ciudad Guayana in 2006.

Excursions Unlike elsewhere in Venezuela, there is little emphasis on arts and culture. However, beyond the urban functionality are some pleasant parks, all well kept and free to enter. Just up the Caroní at Macagua, some truly beautiful cataracts called Salto Llovizna are in the **Parque Nacional La Llovizna** ① *open from early morning till 1630, taxi, US$3*, which covers 26 islands separated by narrow waterways and connected by 36 footbridges. Also in the park are hydroelectric plants, but these do not spoil the views of the larger and smaller falls, diverse fauna, including monkeys, and magnificent plants growing from the falling water. There are several trails. A facility on the **hydroelectric dam** ① *Tue-Sun 0900-2100*, houses an ecological museum, the Ecomuseo del Caroní, with art exhibitions and displays on the dam's construction, now sadly neglected and run down. Near La Llovizna, the iron-tinted waterfall in the pretty **Parque Cachamay** (about 8 km from centre, near the Guayana Hotel; open

Warning...

Visitors should be particularly careful while exploring Ciudad Guyana: it is surrounded by some desperately poor neighbourhoods. Violent crime, including rape, is unfortunately very common. And so is police unwillingness to answer 171 calls, let alone to investigate.

Tuesday-Sunday, from early morning till 1700) is worth a visit. A third park, adjoining Cachamay, is **Loefling Wildlife Park**, with tapirs, capybaras and capuchin monkeys.

Los Castillos, supposedly where Sir Walter Raleigh's son was killed in the search for El Dorado, are two old forts down the Orinoco from San Félix (one hour by *por puesto*, US$1.50, or take a tour).

Tucupita *Colour map 2, A2.*

A worthwhile side trip along asphalted roads can be made to Tucupita, on the Orinoco delta. Though capital of Delta Amacuro state and the main commercial centre of the delta, there's a one-horse feel about it. **Tourist office, Cortudelta** ① *Av Arismendi diagonal al INCES, T0287-721 3211/0414-879 0212, https://cortudelta.wordpress.com, Mon-Fri 0800-1700.* Tourists should go there first for tour information. There is some information on www.deltamacuro.gob.ve.

For a three- to four-day trip to see the delta, its fauna and the indigenous Warao, either arrange boats through the tourist office (see above). Boats are not easy to come by and are expensive except for large groups. Bargain hard and never pay up front.

Excursions often only travel on the main river, not in the *caños* where wildlife is most often seen. To avoid disappointment, be sure to determine where your guide intends to take you before you leave. If the river level rises after a downpour, arrangements may be cancelled. On all trips agree in advance exactly what is included, especially that there is enough food and water for you and your guide. Hammocks and mosquito repellents are essential.

Barrancas *Colour map 2, A2.*

An interesting and friendly village, founded in 1530, Barrancas is one of the oldest villages in the Americas, but its precolonial past dates back to 1000 BC. Situated on the Orinoco, it can be reached by road from Tucupita (63 km), or from Maturín. It has two basic hotels ($). The village has a large community of Guyanese people who speak English. It is possible to take a boat to the Warao villages of **Curiapo** and **Amacuro** (near Guyana border), check at harbour.

Listings Ciudad Guayana and the Orinoco Delta

Where to stay

Ciudad Guayana
The following options are in Puerto Ordaz.

$$$ Doral Inn Hotel
C Neverí, opposite the airport, T0286-952 6803, doralinn@bolivar.travel.
A good option for early morning flights. Generic rooms are massive and spotless with white marble floors, a/c, cable TV, and Wi-Fi. Next door, **Hotel Mara** is good too, but more expensive.

$$$ Venetur Orinoco
Av Guayana, Parque Punta Visat, T0286-713 1000, www.venetur.gob.ve.
It overlooks La Llovizna and Parque Cachamay, far from centre, great location but poor value. Get one of the newer rooms with a good view.

$$ Residencias Tore
C San Cristóbal y Cra Los Andes, T0286-923 1389, residenciastore@hotmail.com.
Ecologically aware hotel with solar heated water, restaurant, laundry and Wi-Fi. Simple, pleasant, quiet rooms have flat screen TVs and sparkling bathrooms.

$ Casa del Lobo
Of Wolfgang Löffler of Lobo Tours, C Zambia 2, Africana Manzana 39, T0286-961 6286/0414-871 9339, www.lobo-tours.de.
Homely *posada* with room for 8 people, free transfer from airport. 'El Lobo' speaks English and German. See also What to do, below.

$ Posada Turística Alonga
Urb La Corniza, Av Canadá, manz 10, casa 14, T0286-923 3154, Facebook: posadaturisticaalonga.
Family-run *posada* in a quiet residential area, Wi-Fi, with communal kitchen, breakfast and laundry service extra.

Tucupita

$$ Salma Suites
Urb Delfín Mendoza Petión diagonal a la UE María Auxiliadora, T0287-721 0659, www.hotelsalmasuitesvip.com.
Comfortable, modern business hotel with café, laundry service, Wi-Fi, taxi service and parking.

$$ Tucupita Suite
C Petión entre La Paz y Arismendi, T0287-621 2017, http://tucupitasuitehotel.com.

Modern hotel with clean rooms, a/c, Wi-Fi, restaurant and parking.

$ Saxxi
On main road into Tucupita, 10 mins from centre, T0287-721 2112.
Comfortable, hot water, a/c, bar/restaurant, disco Fri-Sat, pool. Also has camps **Mis Palafitos Lodge, $$**, T0287-721 1733. All inclusive.

Restaurants

Ciudad Guayana
There are plenty of restaurants and cafés on Cras Tumeremo and Upata, off Av Las Américas. Fast food and upmarket eateries in Ciudad Comercial Altavista.

El Arepazo Guayanés
C La Urbana, Puerto Ordaz, T0286-922 4757. 24 hrs.
The oldest and best *arepería* in Ciudad Guyana.

Mall Orinokia
On Av Guayana, Altavista, close to the bus terminal.
Huge, super-modern shopping mall with restaurants, food court, cafés, supermarket and travel agencies. Multi-screen cinema.

Mi Rinconcito
Across the street from Mall Orinokia (Altavista), T0286-962 1554.
Famous for its *cachapas* and live music at the end of the week.

What to do

Ciudad Guayana
Lobo Tours, *see Casa del Lobo, Where to stay.*
Wolfgang Löffler will tailor his tours to fit your demands. Trips organized to the Gran Sabana and Orinoco Delta, but will put together other excursions. Very helpful, all-inclusive, excellent cooking. English and German spoken.

Tucupita
Some boat owners visit hotels in the evenings looking for clients and may negotiate a price. Ask Pieter Rothfuss at **Gekko Tours/Posada La Casita** in Ciudad Bolívar about a trip through the southern part of the delta and into the Sierra Imataca highlands. The following (and **Mis Palafitos** – see Hotel **Saxxi**) are registered with the tourist board and have insurance (this does not necessarily guarantee a good tour).

Aventura Turística Delta, *C Centurión 62, T0414-879 5821, and at bus station, a_t_d_1973@ hotmail.com, www.hosteltrail.com/atd.* 2 camps in the northern part of the delta, all-inclusive tours, English and French spoken.
Orinoco Delta Lodge/Tucupita Expeditions, *El Guamal, T0287-808 4735, T0414-879 0044/794 0172, http://orinocodelta.net.* 2- to 5-night tours to its lodge and camps in the delta, also runs a school for Warao children.

Transport

Ciudad Guayana
Air Daily flights from Puerto Ordaz to **Caracas**, **Maracaibo**, **Porlamar** and short-haul destinations. Walk 600 m to gas station on main road for buses to San Félix or Puerto Ordaz.

Bus Terminals at San Félix and close to Puerto Ordaz airport; long-distance buses at both. Public transport in Ciudad Guayana is very limited. Free local buses are infrequent. Minibuses are fast and cheap; San Félix–Puerto Ordaz, US$0.75; buses run until 2100. Several buses daily to **Santa Elena de Uairén** (via El Callao), US$3.50, 8-9 hrs, night buses with **Los Llanos** (T0286-974 0767/951 8755) and **Occidente** recommended for comfort, but you'll miss the scenery. **El Callao** (US$2, **Tumeremo** (US$2), **El Dorado** (US$2.50) and Km 88 with **Turgar**. **Ciudad Bolívar** US$1, 1 hr. 8 daily to **Caracas**, US$4.50, 8½ hrs. 8 daily to **Puerto La Cruz**, US$3.50, 6 hrs. 2 daily to **Cumaná**, US$3, 5 ½-7 hrs. To **Tucupita**, US$2, 3 hrs, leaving from San Félix bus terminal with **Expresos Guayanesa**, booking office opens 1 hr before departure, be there early, passport check just before Tucupita. San Felix bus terminal is not a safe place, especially at night.

Car hire Many agencies at airport. A car is very useful here, eg for local excursions, or taking a road trip through the Gran Sabana to Brazil.

Taxi San Félix–Puerto Ordaz US$1.50 minimum, Puerto Ordaz–airport US$2.50, San Félix bus terminal-Puerto Ordaz bus terminal US$2.50, bus terminal–centre US$2, centre-San Félix bus terminal US$2.

Tucupita
Bus *Por puesto* from **Maturín** US$3.50, 2-3 hrs; bus to Maturín, US$2.50, 3-4 hrs. 2 daily to **San Félix**, US$2, see above. 3 daily to **Caracas**, US$4.50, 9-10 hrs.

Barrancas
Bus **Tucupita**–Barrancas, US$0.50, return at 0945 and 1700.

Travelling south from Ciudad Guayana to the Brazilian border is popular with Venezuelans, as well as for overland travellers heading in or out of Brazil via Boa Vista. The road to the border at Santa Elena de Uairén passes across the beautiful Gran Sabana and is paved, with all bridges in place.

To Tumeremo

South from Ciudad Guayana Highway (Troncal) 10 is a four-lane *autopista* as far as **Upata**. Fill up with fuel here and buy provisions opposite the petrol station. At 18 km beyond **Guasipati** is **El Callao** on the south bank of the Río Yuruari, off the highway, a small, clean, bright town whose renowned pre-Lenten carnival has a touch of calypso from British Caribbean immigrants who came to mine gold in the late 19th century (all prices rise for carnival). The town has many jewellery shops and restaurants. On another 41 km is **Tumeremo** (colour map 2, A2), which is recommended as the best place to buy provisions and gasoline.

El Dorado *Colour map 2, B2.*

This hot, dirty and noisy town is 76 km from Tumeremo, 278 km from Ciudad Guayana, and 7 km off the road on the Río Cuyuní. On a river island is the prison made famous by Henri Charrière/Papillon's stay there in 1945.

El Dorado to Santa Elena de Uairén

The turn-off to El Dorado is marked Km 0; distances are measured from here by green signs 2 km apart. The wall of the **Gran Sabana** looms above Km 88 (also called Las Claritas, or **San Isidro**), where expensive supplies and gasoline can be bought – expect queues for fuel. The highway climbs steeply in sharp curves for 40 km before reaching the top. The road is in very good condition and presents no problem for conventional cars. 4WDs may be better in the wet season (May-October). At Km 98 the huge **Piedra de la Virgen** is passed before the steepest climb (La Escalera) enters the beautiful **Parque Nacional Canaima** (see page 1663).

The landscape is essentially savannah, with clusters of trees, moriche palms and bromeliads. Typical of this area are the large abrupt *tepuis* (flat-topped mountains or mesas), hundreds of waterfalls, and the silence of one of the oldest plateaus on earth. At Km 119 (sign can only be seen going north) a short trail leads to the 40 m **Danto ('Tapir') Falls**, a powerful fall wreathed in mosses and mist. The falls are close to the road (about five minutes slippery walk down on the left-hand side), but not visible from it. The **Monumento al Soldado Pionero** (Km 137) commemorates the army engineers who built the road from the lowlands, finally opened in 1973; barbecues, toilets, shelters are now almost all in ruins. Some 4 km beyond is **Luepa**; everyone must stop at the military checkpoint

Essential Gran Sabana

Getting around

A 4WD is only necessary off the main road, especially in the rainy season. You may need spare tanks of fuel if spending a lot of time away from the main road (eg in Kavanayen and El Paují) and have a fuel-guzzling vehicle. Carry extra water and plenty of food. Small eating places may close out of season. There are Guardia Nacional checks at the Río Cuyuní (Km 8), at Km 126, and at San Ignacio de Yuruaní (Km 259); and a military checkpoint at Luepa (Km 143); all driving permits, car registration papers, and ID must be shown. See also Transport, page 1673.

Advice

In the towns as far as El Dorado, there are hotels, but many cater for locals, legitimate or otherwise, and for short-stay clients. Water is rationed in many places and hot water in hotels is rare south of Ciudad Guayana, except in better hotels in Santa Elena. Towns usually have a bank, but don't rely on them. Camping is possible but a good waterproof tent is essential. A small fee is payable to the *indígenas* living around Kaui, Kama and similar villages (see also under Essential Parque Nacional Canaima, page 1663, and Kamarata, page 1664). Insect repellent and long-sleeved/trousered clothes are needed against *puri-puri* (small, black, vicious biting insects) and mosquitoes (especially in El Dorado, at Km 88 and at Icabarú). See www.lagransabana.com.

a little way south. There is a popular camping place at Luepa, on the right going south. You may be able to rent a tent or you can hang a hammock in an open-sided shelter (very cold at night, no water or facilities, buy meals from a tour group, but pricey). There is a petrol station in Luepa. The Inparques station at Luepa has guestrooms for visitors of Inparques, but they may let you stay for a small fee. You can camp at a site on Río Aponwao on the left hand side of the road going south.

Some 8 km beyond Luepa, a poor, graded gravel road leads 70 km west to **Kavanayén** (little traffic, best to have your own vehicle with high clearance, especially during the wet season, take snacks; the road can be cycled but is slow, lots of soft, sandy places). Accommodation is at the Capuchin mission, $, also in private homes. One of the two grocery stores will prepare food, or the restaurant opposite serves cheap breakfasts and dinners, order in advance.

The settlement is surrounded by *tepuis*. Off the road to Kavanayén are the falls of **Torón Merú** and **Chinak-Merú** (also called Aponwao), 105 m high and very impressive. Neither is a straightforward detour, so get full instructions before setting out. Chinak-Merú is reached via the Pemón village of **Iboribó**. A day's walk west of Kavanayén are the lovely falls on the **Río Karuay**.

For the remaining 180 km to Santa Elena de Uairén few people and only a few indigenous Pemón villages are to be seen. San Juan and San Rafael de Kamoiran and **Rápidos de Kamoiran** are passed (fuel available at the falls, expect queues here too). The 5-m Kawí falls on the **Kaüi** River are at Km 195, while at Km 201.5 are the impressive 55 m high **Kama Merú** falls (US$1.50 to walk to bottom of falls). Also a small lake, handicrafts, a small shop, canoe trips. Cabins and *churuatas* can be rented, also camping. Buses can be flagged down going south or north three times a day; check times in advance.

At Km 237 the Río Arapán cascades over the charming **Quebrada Pacheco** (Arapán Merú); pools nearby where you can swim. Tour groups often stop here. A path up the opposite side of the main falls leads to an isolated natural pool 20 minutes' walk away, in the middle of the savannah. **Warning** Do not go beyond the red line at Pacheco: there is a hidden fall which has claimed lives. There is a Campamento at Arapán. Next is **Balneario Saro Wapo** on the Río Soruapé (Km 244), a good place for swimming and picnics, natural whirlpool, restaurant, 10 minutes downriver is a natural waterslide. At Km 250 is the Pemón village of Kumarakapai, San Francisco de Yuruaní (see page 1674), whose falls (Arapena-merú) can be seen from the bridge, followed, 9 km of bends later, by the smaller **San Ignacio de Yuruaní** (strict military checkpoint; excellent regional food).

A trail at Km 275 leads to the **Quebrada de Jaspe** where a river cuts through striated cliffs and pieces of jasper glitter on the banks. Visit at midday when the sun shines best on the jasper, or at 1500 when the colour changes from red to orange, dazzlingly beautiful.

Santa Elena de Uairén *Colour map 2, B2.*
This booming, pleasant frontier town was established by Capuchin monks in 1931. The mid-20th-century **cathedral** ① *daily 0530-1900, Mass Mon-Sat 0630 and 1830, Sun 0630 and 2030*, built from local stone, is a famous landmark. Thanks to its relaxed atmosphere and many hotels, Santa Elena is an agreeable place in which to spend time. It has Arab and Chinese communities and you are as likely to hear Portugese spoken as you are Spanish.

Border with Brazil
The 16 km road to the border is paved. The entire road links Caracas with Manaus in four days with hard driving; see Northern Brazil, in Brazil chapter, for a description of the road from the border and Brazilian immigration formalities. Modern customs and immigration facilities are at the border

Tip...
Note that banks in Ciudad Guyana will not exchange Brazilian reais.

and the crossing is straightforward on both sides (for more information, see Transport, page 1674). The SAIME office (immigration) is in the Municipio in Santa Elena, open Monday-Saturday 0900-1530. Staff at the Ministry of Justice and the Guardia Nacional headquarters ① *T0289-960 3765/995 1189/995 1958*, have been recommended as helpful with entry and exit problems. You can get a visa at the **Brazilian consulate** ① *Edif Galeno, C Los Castaños, Urbanización Roraima del Casco Central, T0289-995 1256/0426-392 1461; open 0800-1400*. The **Brazilian consulate in Ciudad Guyana** ① *Cra Tocoma, Edif Eli-Alti, of 4, Alta Vista, Ciudad Guyana, T0286-961 2995/0416-183 6135, 0800-1400*, is helpful, visa issued promptly.

For entry to Venezuela, some nationalities who cross the border from Boa Vista, Brazil, need a visa. It is not required by western Europeans, whose passport must be valid for a year, but check with a consulate before leaving home. A yellow fever vaccination certificate is required. Ask well in advance for other health requirements (eg malaria test certificate). Entering by car, keep photocopies of your licence, the Brazilian permission to leave and Venezuelan entry stamp. Allow two hours for formalities when crossing by private vehicle and don't cross during the lunch hour. Fresh fruit and vegetables may not be brought into Venezuela. There are frequent road checks when heading north from Santa Elena. SENIAT (the customs authority; T0800-736428) has its Aduana Principal Ecológica outside the town and there may be up to eight more thorough searches, mainly for drugs. Luggage will be sealed before loading into the bus hold in Santa Elena. These checks may mean you arrive in Ciudad Bolívar after dark. There is no public transport on the Venezuelan side, hitch or take a taxi from Brazil.

ATMs are unlikely to accept non-Venezuelan credit cards. Try shops in the centre on Calle Urdaneta, for dollars cash, or Brazilian reais. Try at the border with Brazilians entering Venezuela. Ask the bus driver on the Santa Elena–Boa Vista bus the best place for favourable bolívares/reais rates: in Santa Elena at Sucre y Perimetral; in Brazil at the first stop after the border. Check with travellers going in the opposite direction what rates should be.

El Paují

A road leaves the highway 8 km south of Santa Elena and after passing through a tunnel of jungle vegetation emerges onto rolling savannah dotted with *tepuis*. The road has been considerably improved and has been paved for 20 km. The rest is graded, but deteriorating. It can take between two to four hours to reach El Paují. Take advice before setting out, as rain can rapidly degrade the road. At Km 58 is a Guardia Nacional checkpoint at Paraitepuí, waterfall nearby.

El Paují, 17 km further on, is an agricultural settlement with a growing foreign population. It is a lovely area, with good walking. Excellent sights: **Chirica Tepuy**, huge, beautiful, jet black, set in rolling savannah; **Río Surucún**, where Venezuela's largest diamond was found; **Salto Catedral** (61 km off the road), beautiful small hollow, lovely falls, excellent swimming (camping, shop); **Salto La Gruta**, impressive falls; and **Pozo Esmeralda**, 1.5 km outside El Paují towards Icabarú (400 m south of road), fine rapids, waterfall you can stand under and pools. At Los Saltos de Paují are many powerful falls; going from El Paují towards Santa Elena, before crossing the first bridge, take track on left for about 500 m. A good walk is to the small hill, 2 km from El Paují beyond the airfield; views from the crest over **El Abismo**, the plunging escarpment marking the end of Gran Sabana highlands and the start of the Amazon rainforest. It takes an hour to reach the top, and the walk is highly recommended. Guides, though not necessary, are in the village. A recommended guide is German-speaking Marco. Small campsite (lovely early morning or sunset).

Apiculture is the main activity of El Paují and there's an **International Honey Festival** every summer. The honey made in this area is delicious; buy it at the shop in El Paují or Salto Catedral.

Listings Ciudad Guayana to Santa Elena de Uairén

Where to stay

To Tumeremo

$ Andrea
Plaza Miranda, Upata, T0288-221 3656.
Decent rooms, a/c, hot water, fridge in some rooms. Credit cards accepted, Chinese restaurant, safe parking.

El Dorado to Santa Elena de Uairén

$$ pp La Barquilla de Fresa
At Km 84.5. Book via Alba Betancourt in Caracas T0288-808 8710, T0426-991 9919.

English and German spoken at this small but immaculate and tranquil posada. Birdwatching tours; inventory of bird species here has reached more than 300 species, owner Henry Cleve is a renowned expert. Full board lodging, reservations and deposit required.

Rápidos de Kamoiran

$ Campamento Rápidos de Kamoiran
Km 172, T0289-540 0009, www.rapidosdekamoiran.blogspot.com.
Clean, with fan, cold water, also has camping, service station, Wi-Fi, also restaurant and picnic spot by rapids.

Santa Elena de Uairén

$$-$ Cabañas Friedenau
Av Ppal de Cielo Azul, off Av Perimetral, T0289-995 1353, Facebook: friedenau.cabanas.
Self-contained chalets, nice grounds, vegetarian food, parking, transfer to Puerto Ordaz, bikes, horseriding, trips to Roraima (see below), English spoken. Recommended.

$$-$ Gran Sabana
Carretera Nacional Via Brasil, 10 km from border, T0289-995 1810, www.hotelgransabana.com.
Large resort-style hotel with 58 rooms, one of the most upscale in town but past its heyday. Pool, parking, café, tours.

$$-$ Posada L'Auberge
C Urdaneta, T0289-995 1567, www.l-auberge.net.
Brick-built guesthouse with good rooms and shared balcony, a/c, Wi-Fi, cable TV, hot water, parking, tourist information. Family-run. Recommended.

$$-$ Villa Fairmont
Urb Akurimá, T0289-995 1022, at north edge of town, www.lagransabana.com/villafairmont.
Large place up on a hill with pool, jacuzzi, restaurant, parking, bar. Reasonable rooms but check before accepting.

$$-$ Ya-Koo Ecological Camp
2 km on unpaved road to Sampai indigenous community, up mountain behind Santa Elena, T0289-995 1742, www.ya-koo.com.
Cabañas in beautiful 10-ha site, full and half-board available, spacious rooms, hot water, natural pool. Cheaper in low season. Recommended if you have a car.

$ Kiamantí
Outside town 1 km from bus terminal, T0289-995 1952, http://kiamanti.blogspot.com/.
Very simple little cabins, full board, fan, hot water, parking, pool, games and play area.

$ Lucrecia
Av Perimetral, T0289-995 1385, near old terminal.
Motel-style lodgings with a small pool, parking and restaurant. Rooms have a/c or fan, hot water, cable TV, Wi-Fi. Helpful.

$ Michelle
C Urdaneta, T0289-416 1257, www.hosteltrail.com/posadamichelle.
Popular backpacker place, helpful. Basic rooms have fan, hot water, Wi-Fi. Shower and changing room available if you're waiting for a night bus.

$ Villa Apoipó
On the road to the airport, turn left at the Hotel Gran Sabana, T0289-995 2018, www.lagransabana.com/villaapoipo.
Very nice rooms, hot water, fan. For groups but will take independent travellers if you ring ahead. Use of kitchen or full board. Bunk beds or hammocks available in large *churuata*.

El Paují

$$-$ pp Campamento Amaribá
3.5 km outside El Paují on road from Santa Elena, transport available from airstrip, T0416-533 4270/0212-753 9314, amaribapauji@yahoo.com.
Comfortable cabins with mosquito nets, good facilities, full board, kitchen, tours arranged, very hospitable. Also dance, healing and therapy centre.

$ Campamento El Paují
3.5 km outside El Paují on road from Santa Elena, transport available from airstrip, T0289-995 1431, T0426-691 8966, dianalez@gmail.com, or contact through Maripak.
Beautiful cabins with spectacular views over the Gran Sabana, food available, camping US$6 per tent. Recommended.

$ Cantarana tourist camp
25 km from town, T0415-212 0662 (or try T0298-808 1026 and ask to leave a message; in Caracas T0212-234 0255), www.gran-sabana.info.
Basic accommodation, breakfast and dinner included, owners, Alfonso and Barbara Borrero, speak German, English and Spanish, waterfall and lovely surroundings.

$ Maripak
near the airstrip and small store, T0298-808 1033/0414-772 3070, or reserve in Caracas T0212-234 3661.
Cabins for 2/3 with bath, meals extra, good food, tours, camping.

$ Weimure
2 km outside El Paují on road from Santa Elena, pauji0@yahoo.com.
Beautiful cabin close to river, dynamic architect owner, meals available or use of kitchen.

Restaurants

Santa Elena de Uairén
Several restaurants on Mcal Sucre. The local river fish, Lau Lau, is good. Avoid seafood.

$ Alfredo's
Av Perimetral, at the end of C Urdaneta.
Tasty pizzas, pasta and soup at reasonable prices.

$ Tumá Serô
A cheap and bustling gastronomic market where you can pick up wholesome arepas, soup, pizzas, burgers.

$ Venezuela Primero
Av Perimetral, T0289-995 1149.
Dated interior but often recommended for its chicken, meat and fish.

Gran Sabana Deli
C Bolívar, T0289-995 1158.
A large café with pavement seating selling good hot coffee, imported ham, cheese, salami, fresh bread, olives, cakes, and pastries.

What to do

Santa Elena de Uairén
Santa Elena is the most economical place to book tours of the Gran Sabana, Roraima, and other *tepuis*. Many interesting attractions lie along the highway and can be covered in an undemanding day-trip. Trips to Roraima typically last 5-6 days, but it can be done in 4. An all-inclusive package (transport, guide, sleeping bag, mattress, map, food, tent, and porter) costs from about US$350 for two people (less if the tour is priced in BsF). There are cheaper options depending on how much equipment of your own you carry.
Alvarez Treks, *office in the bus station, T0414-385 2846, www.saltoangelrsta.com.* An excellent range of Gran Sabana tours by Francisco Alvarez. The 'traditional' tour is physically undemanding, follows the highway, a good trip for families and seniors. The moderately demanding 'non-traditional' tour offers a more intimate experience of the landscape with hikes through rivers and rainforests. The combination tour offers a bit of both, while the Extreme Tour is a 6-hr day with stops at waterfalls and swimming holes; 4-people minimum. Also tours of Roraima, Canaima and the Río Caura. Knowledgeable, helpful, recommended.
Backpacker Tours, *C Urdaneta, T0289-995 1430, T0414-886 7227, www.backpacker-tours.com.* 1- to 5-day, all-inclusive jeep tours through the Gran Sabana, visiting little-known falls in the Kavanayen area. Trekking to nearby Chirikayen Tepuy, 3-4 days and to Roraima (minimum 4 persons), plus more. German and

English spoken. Recommended. Also have own **$$ Posada Los Pinos**, *just outside Santa Elena, Kamadac, C Urdaneta, T0289-995 1408, T0414-094 4341, www.abenteuer-venezuela.de.* Run by Andreas Hauer, with German and Pemón staff, tours of Gran Sabana, all-inclusive tour to Roraima, and also more adventurous tours to Auyán Tepuy from which Angel Falls cascades and other mountains, difficult. Recommended.
Roberto's Mystic Tours, *Urdaneta, casa 6, T0289-416 1081, www.mystictours.com.ve.* As the author of several books about Roraima and the Gran Sabana, Roberto is very knowledgeable about the local environment and culture. His tours include a complete briefing of the region's ecological, botanical and energetic properties. Excellent tours, very helpful, highly recommended.
Ruta Salvaje, *C Mcal Sucre, at the junction opposite the petrol station, T0289-995 1134, www.rutasalvaje. com.* Well-established adventure tour specialists offering white-water rafting, parapenting and paramotoring, traditional and non-traditional day tours of the Gran Sabana, treks to Roraima, and tours of Angel Falls.

Transport

To Tumeremo
Bus From Upata to **Ciudad Bolívar**, US$1.50; to **San Félix** (Ciudad Guayana), US$0.75; to **Santa Elena**, US$4.

Tumeremo
Bus To **Caracas**, US$5, 10½-11 hrs. To **Ciudad Bolívar**, US$4, 6 a day, 5½ hrs. To **Santa Elena**, US$2.50, 6-8 hrs, with **Líneas Orinoco**, 2 blocks from plaza. **El Dorado**, US$0.75, 1 hr.

El Dorado
Bus All buses stop on main plaza. From **Caracas**, **Expresos del Oriente**, at 1830 daily, US$6, 12-14 hrs (950 km). The **Orinoco** bus links with **Ciudad Bolívar** (5 hrs, US$2.50) and **Santa Elena**, as does **Transmundial** (better, leaving 1100, US$2.50 to **Santa Elena**, US$2.50 to **San Félix**, 4 hrs).

El Dorado to Santa Elena de Uairén

Km 88 (San Isidro)
Bus Frequent *por puestos* from **El Dorado** to Km 88, 1 hr, US$2. Most non-luxury buses stop at the petrol station to refuel. Or get a ride with jeeps and trucks (little passes after 1030).

Santa Elena de Uairén

Air Airport, 8 km from the centre. Scheduled flights from Puerto Ordaz with **Conviasa** only, 2 a week (unreliable); infrequent charters from **Ciudad Bolívar** subject to weather conditions.

Bus The bus terminal on road to Ciudad Bolívar is 2-km/30 mins' walk from town, taxi US$2. Get to terminal 30 mins in advance for SENIAT baggage check for contraband. From **Caracas** there are direct buses (eg Expresos Los Llanos), US$8, 16 hrs, or you can go to Ciudad Bolívar or to Ciudad Guyana and then take a bus direct to Santa Elena. 10 buses daily from Santa Elena to **Ciudad Bolívar**, US$4.50, Expresos Los Llanos (T0289-995 1339) and **Expresos Occidente** recommended for comfort, 9-10 hrs. 10 daily to **Ciudad Guayana** and **San Félix**, US$3.50, 8-9 hrs.

To the border The best way to reach the border is with a *por puesto* taxi, US$1.50. They depart from the intersection of C Roscio and C Icabarú. Check that they drop you at the 2 immigration offices, 750 m apart, before going onward to the town of Pacaraima, where you can pick up connections to Boa Vista (eg **Rival Tur**, twice a day, US$8 in reais). Alternatively, from the bus station, there are daily buses to **Boa Vista**, about US$10 equivalent in reais (maybe less in BsF), 3½ hrs, **Amatur**. Also shared taxis to Boa Vista for US$14.50.

El Pauji

Road From **Santa Elena** by jeep, US$4 if full, more if not, daily at around 0600-0700 and 1500-1600 from Plaza Bolívar. Also at **Panadería Gran Café**, C Icabarú. To get further than El Paují, 4WD vehicle is necessary: **Cantarana**, US$6, and **Icabarú**, US$7.50.

Mount Roraima

An exciting trek is to the summit of Mount Roraima (altitude 2810 m), at one time believed to be the 'Lost World' made famous by Arthur Conan Doyle's novel. 'Roroima' is a word in the Pemón language meaning 'The great blue-green'. Due to the tough terrain and extreme weather conditions, this hike is only suitable for the fit. Supplies for a week or more should be bought in Santa Elena. If a tour company is supplying the food, check what it is first; vegetarians may go hungry.

San Francisco de Yuruaní

The starting point is this Pemón village, 9 km north of the San Ignacio military checkpoint (where you must register). There are three small shops selling basic goods but not enough for Roraima hike. Meals are available and tents can be hired, about US$10 each per day, quality of tents and stoves is poor; better equipment is available in Santa Elena.

Paraitepui

The road to Paraitepui (which is signposted), the nearest village to the mountain, leaves the highway 1 km south of San Francisco. It is in good condition, with three bridges; the full 25 km can be walked in seven hours. You can sleep for free in the village if hiring a guide; camping is permitted. Few supplies are available; a small shop sells basics. The villagers speak Tauripán, the local dialect of the Pemón linguistic group, but now most of them also speak Spanish.

Climbing Roraima

The foot trail winds back and forth on a more direct line than the little-used jeep track; it is comparatively straightforward and adequately marked descending from the heights just past Paraitepui across rolling hills and numerous clear streams. The goal, Roraima, is the mountain on the right, the other massive outcrop on the left is Mata Hui (known as Kukenán after the river which rises within it). If leaving the village early in the day, you may reach the Río Cuquenán crossing by early afternoon (good camping here). Three hours' walk brings you to a lovely bird-filled meadow below the foothills of the massif, another perfect camping spot known as *campamento base* (10 hours to base camp from Paraitepui). The footpath now climbs steadily upwards through the cloudforest at the mountain's base and becomes an arduous scramble over tree trunks and damp rocks until the cliff is reached. From here it is possible to ascend to the plateau along the 'easy' boulder-strewn slope which is the only route to the top. Walkers in good health should take about four hours from the meadow to the top. The summit is an eerie world of stone and water, difficult to move around easily. There are not many good spots to camp; but there are various overhanging ledges which are colourfully known as 'hoteles' by the guides, with just enough subsoil to take tent pegs. Red painted arrows lead the way to the right after reaching the summit for the main group of these. A marked track leads to the survey pillar near the east cliff where Guyana, Brazil and Venezuela meet; allow a day as the track is very rough. Other sights include the Valley of the Crystals, La Laguna de Gladys and various sinkholes, encrusted with carnivorous plants.

The whole trip can take anywhere between five days and two weeks. The dry season for trekking is November-May (with annual variations); June-August Roraima is usually enveloped in cloud. Do not remove crystals from the mountain; on-the-spot fines up to US$100 may be charged. Thorough searches are made on your return. Take your rubbish back down with you.

Listings Mount Roraima

Where to stay

San Francisco de Yuruaní

$ Arapena Posada
T0241-866 4339 or 0416-095 7613.
Small and basic, information on treks and adventure tourism, half-board available.

$ El Caney de Yuruaní
T0416-289 2413.
Clean, basic rooms, fan, restaurant.

Camping

Permitted just about anywhere, free. Plenty of mosquitos at night (and other creepy-crawlies at all times).

Climbing Roraima

Camping

Full equipment including stove is essential (an igloo-type tent with a plastic sheet for the floor is best for the summit, where it can be wet), wear thick socks and boots to protect legs from snakes, warm clothes for the summit (much mist, rain squalls and lightning at night) and effective insect repellent – biting *plaga* (blackflies) infest the grasslands. The water on the summit and around the foot of Roraima is very pure, but as more do the trek, the waters are becoming dirtied. Bring bottled water or a purifier for the savannah. Fires must not be lit on top of Roraima, only gas or liquid fuel stoves. Litter is appearing along the trail; please take care of the environment.

What to do

Climbing Roraima

Guides and tours

The National Guard requires all visitors to have a guide beyond Paraitepui; you will be fined. Go with a guide or tour operator from Santa Elena or from San Francisco; ask at **Arapena**, or **El Caney de Yuruaní**. Those hired on the street or in Paraitepui have no accident insurance cover. Guides can help for the hike's final stages (easy to get lost) and for finding best camping spots. Guides in San Francisco de Yuruaní cost US$18 a day, more if they carry your supplies. Check the camping gear for leaks, etc, and be clear about who is providing the guide's food.

Guides in Paraitepui cost US$15 a day, Spanish-speaking guides. The **Ayuso** brothers are the best-known guides. Ask for El Capitán, he is in charge of guides. Parking at Inparques US$1. There is no admission charge to enter the park, but a donation to the village is appreciated.

Transport

San Francisco de Yuruaní

Bus From **Santa Elena** bus will let you off here and pick up passengers en route northwards (no buses 1200-1900). Jeep to **Paraitepui** US$35. Cheapest is Oscar Mejías Hernández, ask in village.

Practicalities
Getting around

Venezuela's most important cities are served by domestic flights from Caracas. The most extensive coverage is offered by state-owned carrier **Conviasa** ① *http://portal.conviasa.aero*. Other lines include **Aeropostal** ① *www.aeropostal.com*, **Aserca** ① *www.asercaairlines.com*, **Avior** ① *aviorair.com*, **Rutaca** ① *www.rutaca.com.ve*, **Laser** ① *www.laser.com.ve*, and **Venezolana** ① *www.ravsa.com.ve*. **LTA (Aereotuy)** ① *www.tuy.com*, connects Caracas with Porlamar, Los Roques and camps at Boral (Maturín) and Arekuna (Canaima). None of Venezuela's airlines is great. Lost luggage, delays and cancellations without compensation are common. Beware of overbooking during holidays, especially at Caracas airport; check in at least two hours before departure. If you book a ticket online with a credit card, you may be told at check-in that your tickets is 'reserved but not purchased'. Check with your card company that you have not been charged twice. It is essential to reconfirm all flights, international and domestic, 72 hours in advance.

Road

Bus and taxi

Buses on most long-distance routes come in three standards, *tradicional*, *ejecutivo* and *bus-cama*. Fares are set by the authorities and you should see them posted on bus office windows, or in the **Gaceta Oficial**. There are numerous services between the major cities and many services bypass Caracas. Bus timetables may be found on http://busvenezuela.com. Buses stop frequently, but there may not always be a toilet at the stop. For journeys in a/c buses take a sleeping bag or similar because the temperature is set to freezing. This is most important on night journeys, which otherwise are fine. Also take earplugs and eyemask to protect against the loud stereo and violent Hollywood screenings. For journeys longer than six hours, it is essential to buy your ticket in advance, although they may not always be available until the day of departure. Sometimes hoteliers and tour operators have inside connections which can save a lot of hassle. The *colectivo* taxis and minibuses (jitneys), known as *por puesto*, seem to monopolize transport to and from smaller towns and villages. For longer journeys they are normally twice as expensive as buses, but faster, often breaking local speed limits. They are sometimes an unreliable and risky mode of transport, but great places to meet the locals and learn about the area. If first to board, wait for other passengers to arrive. Do not take a *por puesto* on your own unless you want to pay for the whole vehicle. Outside Caracas, town taxis are relatively cheap, and they are becoming popular for tourists and locals, for security reasons. Phone *Líneas de Taxi* and ask for interstate trip fares.

Hitchhiking

Hitchhiking (*cola*) is not recommended as it is unsafe. It is illegal on toll roads and, theoretically, for non-family members in the back of pick-up trucks. Avoid hitchhiking around Guardia Nacional posts (see also Safety, page 1682).

Maps

The best country map is **International Travel Maps'** *Venezuela Travel Reference Map* (Vancouver, Canada, www.itmb.ca); buy directly or at a good travel agency. They also print on demand a *Caracas (Venezuela) ITM City Map*. Also see **Google Maps** and the Caracas Street Map by http://mobile-streetmaps.com, pre-loaded on your iPhone before you leave home (download can take time).

Where to stay

Hotels and posadas

Using the Dicom/Simadi exchange rate (or the parallel market – see Money, below), value for money is quite high. For the thrifty, there are foreign-run, no-frills places catering for backpackers. The major cities, Isla Margarita, Los Roques, Guayana and Amazonas have higher room rates (eg US$20-60). Rooms are cheaper without a/c. In the Andean region prices are lower, starting at around US$5-10 per person. If comfort and cleanliness is what you are after, the price of a basic three-star (Venezuelan 'four star') hotel room with a/c, private bath and breakfast will be in our $$-$ range, depending on location and whether it's a hotel or *posada*. A prior reservation will not guarantee you a room. If you can, insist on seeing the room before paying; if you don't, you will probably be given the worst possible room.

A group of 22 *posadas*, mostly in the west of the country, have joined together under the banner **El Circuito de la Excelencia**, www.circuitodelaexcelencia.com, to offer high quality, distinctive lodging, food and service. **Casa Tropical** (main office) ① *CC Paseo Las Mercedes, Sector La Cuadra, Local 26, Caracas, T212-993 2939, http://casatropical.com.ve/*, offers interesting accommodation in seven properties on the central coast, in Ciudad Bolívar, Canaima and Amazonas. See the Planning your trip chapter for our hotel price guide.

Hostal Trail ① *www.hosteltrail.com*, is a Latin America-wide network of backpackers' hostels, with a dozen or so good-value budget places to stay throughout Venezuela.

Camping

Camping in Venezuela is risky because of crime. Camping, with or without a vehicle, is not possible at the roadside. If camping on the beach, for the sake of security, pitch your tent close to others, even though they play their radios loud.

Guidebooks

Elizabeth Kline's Guide to Camps, Posadas and Cabins in Venezuela 2015-16 (BsF 1500, in Spanish and English, available from principal bookshops in Venezuela, or purchasing information from klineposada1944@gmail.com) is incredibly detailed, covering some 1030 places in over 800 pages, and doesn't pull its punches. *La Guía Valentina Quintero* also covers the whole country, suggesting routes, where to stay and eat, published biannually, www.valentinaquintero.com.ve.

Food & drink

Restaurants

As with lodging, eating out is cheap if you change dollars using Dicom/Simadi; see Money, below. Midday used to be the best time to find a three-course *menú ejecutivo* or *cubierto*, but increasingly many places offer only à la carte, quoting scarcity of supplies. Minimum price for a basic meal is US$2, not including drinks. Hotel breakfasts are likely to be poor. It is better and cheaper in a *fuente de soda* and cheaper still in a *pastelería* or *arepería*. See the Planning your trip chapter for our restaurant price guide.

Food

There is excellent local fish (such as *pargo* or red snapper, *carite* or king fish), crayfish, small oysters and prawns. Although it is a protected species, turtle may appear on menus in the Península de Paraguaná as *ropa especial*. Of true Venezuelan food there is *sancocho* (vegetable stew with meat, chicken or fish); *arepas*, bland white maize bread; toasted *arepas* served with various fillings or the local salty white cheese, are cheap, filling and nutritious; *cachapas*, a maize pancake wrapped around white cheese; *pabellón*, of shredded meat, beans, rice and fried plantains; and *empanadas*, maize-flour pies of cheese, meat or fish. At Christmas there are *hallacas*, maize pancakes stuffed with chicken, pork, olives, boiled in a plantain leaf. A *muchacho* (boy) on the menu is a cut of beef. *Ganso* is not goose but beef. *Solomo* and *lomito* are other cuts of beef. *Hervido* is chicken or beef with vegetables. On the Península de Paraguaná roast kid (*asado de chivo*) and kid cooked in coconut are served. *Contorno* with a meat or fish dish is a choice of fried chips, boiled potatoes, rice or yuca. *Caraotas* are beans; *cachitos* are filled *croissants*. *Pasticho* is what Venezuelans call Italian lasagne. The main fruits are bananas, oranges, grapefruit, mangoes and pineapple. *Lechoza* is papaya, *patilla* water melon, *parchita* passion fruit, and *cambur* a small banana. Excellent strawberries are grown at Colonia Tovar, 90 minutes from Caracas, and in the Andes. Delicious sweets are *huevos chimbos*, egg yolk boiled and bottled in sugar syrup, and *quesillo*, made with milk, egg and caramel.

Drink

Venezuelan rum is very good; recommended brands are **Cacique**, **Pampero** and **Santa Teresa**. There are four good beers: **Polar** (the most popular, sold as Polar, Ice, Solera and Solera Light), **Regional**, **Cardenal** and **Zulia** (a *lisa* is a glass of keg beer; for a bottle of beer ask for a *tercio*). Brazilian **Brahma** beer is brewed in Venezuela. There is a good local wine in Venezuela. The *Polar* brewery joined with Martell (France) to build a winery in Carora. Bodegas Pomar also sells a champagne-style sparkling wine. Look out for Pomar wine festivals in March and September. Liqueurs are cheap, try the local *ponche crema*. Coffee is very cheap (*café con leche* is milky, *café marrón* much less so, *café negro* is black); it often has sugar already added, ask for "sin azúcar". Try a *merengada*, a delicious drink made from fruit pulp, ice, milk and sugar; a *batido* is the same but with water and a little milk; *jugo* is the same but with water. A *plus-café* is an after-dinner liqueur. *Chicha de arroz* is a sweet drink made of milk, sugar and vanilla. Fruit juices are very good, ask for "jugo natural, preparado en el momento" for the freshest juice.

Essentials A-Z

Accident and emergency

Dial T171 for the integrated emergency system. **CICPC (Cuerpo de Investigaciones Científicas, Penales y Criminalísticas)**, Av Leonardo Ruíz Pineda, San Agustín del Sur; Edif CICPC San Agustín, Caracas, T0800-272 4224 (0800-cicpc-24), www.cicpc.gob.ve. For registering crimes throughout the country.

Electricity

120 volts, 60 cycles. Plugs are US-style 'A' and 'B' types, 2-pin flat and 2-pin flat with optional D-shaped earth. Unpredictable power cuts are common.

Embassies and consulates

The Ministry of Foreign Affairs website is www.mppre.gob.ve. For Venezuelan embassies and consulates abroad and for all foreign embassies and consulates in Venezuela, see http://embassy.goabroad.com.

Health

Medical services

Caracas Clínica Avila, Av San Juan Bosco con 6ta Transversal, Altamira, T0212-276 1111, www.clinicaelavila.com. **Mérida Dr Aldo Olivieri**, Av Principal La Llanita, La Otra Banda, Centro Profesional El Buho, 09, T0274-244 3834, T0414-374 0356, aldrolia250@cantv.net, very good, gastroenterologist, speaks English and Italian.

Money

US$1= BsF 10 (Dipro); US$1= BsF 720 (Dicom) (Jun 2017).

The unit of currency is the bolívar fuerte (BsF), introduced in 2008. There are coins for 1, 10, 50 and 100 bolívares fuertes, 50, 25, 12.5, 10, 5 and 1 céntimos, and notes for 2, 5, 10, 20, 50, 100, 500, 1,000, 2,000 5,000, 10,000 and 20,000 bolívares fuertes. Have small coins and notes to hand, since in many shops and bars and on public transport large notes may be hard to change. Further new notes and coins may be introduced, and smaller denominations withdrawn, in an attempt to keep up with the rampant inflation; check locally on arrival.

Official and unofficial currency exchange
Venezuela has had an exchange control regime since 2003 to prevent capital flight. In Jun 2017, 2 official rates were in operation. Applicable to 'priority sectors' of food, medicine and staples, the official rate set by the **Centro de Comercio Exterior (Cencoex)** was US$1 = BsF 10 (in force in Jun 2017 and called **Dipro** – Tipo de Cambio Protegido). The second official exchange rate, **Dicom**, Tipo de Cambio Complementario, was a version of the floating forex system introduced in Feb 2015 (Simadi) which allows US dollars to be bought and sold according to supply and demand. In Jun 2017 it was US$1 = BsF 720, but continually rising. This rate is available to tourists and is used for international credit card transactions, including at ATMs, and in approved *cambios*, such as **Italcambio** (see below). You must present your passport and a photocopy; daily limit US$300. Prices in this book have been calculated where possible on its basis. Note that on Isla Margarita and Los Roques payment is required in dollars. In 2017 the government introduced new rules requiring hotels and tourist businesses in Caracas and other large cities to receive only dollars from foreigners, but at the time of research this was not being fully implemented. Check on arrival which currency you have to use.

Prices at anything other than the Dicom rate are extremely high, but since foreign visitors can use this rate they should not find the country expensive. At the time of writing, Dicom had not eliminated the 'parallel' (ie black) market in foreign currencies. According to unofficial reports this was around US$1 = BsF 5114 in Jun 2017, but since the unofficial exchange of dollars is illegal in Venezuela and since it is difficult for a visitor to find such a rate, the safest option is to use the Dicom rate. Whatever you decide to do, always consult a trusted and senior member of staff at a hotel or tour operator, never ask a stranger on the street. The unofficial rate can be checked on the internet before you enter Venezuela, but once inside the country you will find those websites blocked (search Twitter instead). Remember, the parallel exchange is illegal and involves risk to the changer. You will also be fined if caught in the act.

You can investigate wiring money to a foreign-based account which will release cash in Venezuela, or, if you have friends living in

Venezuela with an overseas bank account, sending money there.

Plastic and cash *Casas de cambio* and most ATMs and credit card transactions use Dicom, although commission charges might apply. ATMs are widespread but highly unreliable and not recommended. Some require a Venezuelan ID number and you should speak to your card issuer about this before leaving home. Despite the security risks, it is best to bring all the cash you need for your trip in US dollars, or as much as your insurance policy covers, and change small amounts at a time. Only bolívares purchased officially can be converted back, up to 25% of the amount originally changed, and you will need the original exchange receipt. For money exchange and other services including travel, go to **Italcambio**, www.italcambio.com, the official government exchange office and take ID. Offices at Av Urdaneta, esq Animas a Platanal, Edif Camoruco, Nivel Pb, El Centro, T0212-565 0219 and others in the capital and around the country. Italcambio also at national and international terminals at airport (open public holidays).

Cost of travelling If using the Dicom rate, you will need a daily budget of around US$20-40 for 'mid-range' lodging and dining, depending on the region. On a basic budget, you can get by on less than US$15 per day. First class travel can be had for US$50-70 daily, often for much less, and multi-day treks and all-inclusive packages to Angel Falls and Roraima are quite reasonable. Please bear in mind that Venezuela's economic situation is extremely unpredictable. In consequence, prices quoted in this book may be unreliable. Visitors should also note that some establishments have different prices, or methods of payment for Venezuelans and foreigners. It is advisable to phone in advance if unsure what you will be charged. Exchange regulations are subject to change at any moment and you can check the official rates at www.bcv.org. ve, the Banco Central's website (click on Tipo de Cambio). All rates, official and unofficial, can be found on www.venezuelaecon.com. At the time of writing it appeared that stability had not been brought to consumer markets so you may find shortages of basic shopping items. Before you travel, find out what the current situation is, by contacting your travel agent/tour operator, or visit the Britishgovernment's travel advice website: www.gov.uk/foreign-travel-advice (or similar for other countries).

National parks

Encompassing 16% of the national territory, Venezuela has 43 national parks, 30 national monuments and various other refuges and reserves, some of which are mentioned in the text. A full list is published by the **Instituto Nacional de Parques (Inparques)**, Salida del Distribuidor Santa Cecilia, Edif Sur del Museo de Transporte, Caracas, T0212-273 2811 (Caracas), www.inparques.gob.ve (site not active in Jun 2017). Each park has a regional director and its own guards (*guardaparques*). Permits are required to stay in the parks (up to 5), although this is not usually necessary for those parks visited frequently. A few parks charge a fee on arrival, such as Los Roques and Canaima. For more details, visit the **Ministerio del Poder Popular para Ecosicialismo y Aguas**, Centro Simón Bolívar, Torres del Silencio, Plaza Caracas, Distrito Capital, T0212-408 1111/273 2811, http://www.minea.gob.ve/ministerio/entes-adscritos/inparques/. See also https://twitter.com/inparquesgob?lang=en and www.facebook.com/instituto.nacionaldeparques/timeline.

Opening hours

Banks: Mon-Fri 0830-1530 only. **Businesses**: 0800-1800 with a midday break. **Government offices**: 0800-1200 are usual hours, although they vary. Officials have fixed hours, usually 0900-1000 or 1500-1600, for receiving visitors. **Shops**: Mon-Sat 0900-1300, 1500-1900.

Generally speaking, Venezuelans start work early, and by 0700 everything is in full swing. Most firms and offices close on Sat.

Post

Post offices are run by **Ipostel**, whose main branch is at Urdaneta y Norte 4, near Plaza Bolívar, Caracas, see www.ipostel.gob.ve, for branches, Mon-Fri 0800-1630. (The Galerías Avila office is open Mon-Sun 1000-2100.) It has an overseas package service; packages should be ready to send, also at airport. **MRW**, throughout the country, T0800-304 0000, see www.mrw.com.ve, for branches. 24-hr service, more reliable than Ipostel.

Public holidays and festivals

1 Jan; Carnival on the Mon-Tue before Ash Wed (everything shuts down Sat-Tue; book a place to stay in advance). Thu-Sat of Holy Week. 19 Apr (Declaration of Independence). 1 May.

Early Jun at **Corpus Christi** (the 8th Thu after Thu of Semana Santa) in San Francisco de Yare, 90 km from Caracas, some 80 male 'Diablos' of all ages, dressed all in red and wearing horned masks, dance to the sound of their drums and rattles. **24 Jun, Battle of Carabobo** and the feast day of **San Juan Bautista**, celebrated on the central coast where there were once large concentrations of plantation slaves who considered San Juan their special saint; the best-known events are in villages such as Chuao, Cata and Ocumare de la Costa. **5 Jul (Independence). 24 Jul (Bolívar's birthday). 12 Oct, Día de la Resistencia Indígena. 25 Dec.** From 24 Dec-1 Jan, museums are closed, most restaurants close 24-25 Dec (except for fast-food outlets) and there is no long-distance public transport on 25 Dec, while other days are often booked solid. On New Year's Eve, everything closes and does not open for at least a day.

Business travellers should not visit during Holy Week or Carnival. There are extra holidays only for banks which are set every year according to religious festivals, dates vary.

Safety

Venezuelans are generally honest, helpful, and hospitable people. The vast majority of visitors to the country do not encounter any problems, but you should be aware that street crime in big cities has soared in recent years. Most of the trouble occurs at night in poor barrios, but nonetheless caution is strongly advised when navigating the downtown and bus station districts of Caracas, Maracaibo and Valencia. Carry only as much money as you need, kept safely out of sight in a money belt whenever travelling. Dress like the locals, don't wear jewellery or expensive sunglasses, don't take out smartphones in the street, or expensive cameras in crowded places, such as markets. During the day is mostly trouble-free, as long as you are aware of where you are going. Ask your hotel about any unsafe areas. It is not advisable to walk after dark: always take a taxi from a well-marked, recognizable

Warning…

The British Foreign and Commonwealth Office currently advises against all travel to within 80 km of the Colombian border due to the risk of kidnapping by drug traffickers and paramilitaries.

company with a number, or get someone to recommend a driver. This applies even to tourist centres like Mérida and Ciudad Bolívar. You **must** speak at least basic Spanish to be able to get yourself around. Few people in the street will speak English, and even fewer in rural areas. Outside the big cities you will feel less unsafe, but still need to be careful in quieter rural areas. The more popular destinations (such as beaches and national parks) are used to having travellers. You still need to watch out for scams, cons and petty thieving. If you are seeking an isolated beach, make enquiries about which are safe beforehand. Stay away from political rallies and protest marches, as they can turn violent. Foreigners may find themselves subject to harassment or abuse, or to thorough police identity and body searches. Carry a copy of your passport and, if searched, watch the police like a hawk, in case they try to plant drugs to your bags. Do not photograph people without permission. Carry a mobile (but don't display it), keep the number of a trusted Venezuelan contact handy, and be prepared to call him or her, or your embassy if a police search becomes threatening.

Tax

Airport tax International passengers do not pay airport tax at Maiquetía International Airport as it is included in the price of tickets. At all other airports, a tax of BsF 708 (US\$1.10) is levied on domestic flights, BsF 1770 (US\$2.53 at Dicom rate) on international flights, which must be paid after check-in and before proceeding to security. The rate changes annually, for the latest check www. aeropuerto-maiquetia.com.ve. Exit stamps are payable by overland travellers at some borders. Correct taxes are not advertised and you may be overcharged. Under 2s do not pay tax.
VAT/IVA 12%.

Telephone and Wi-Fi

Country code +58.
Ringing: long equal tones with equal long pauses. Engaged: short equal tones, with equal pauses. The national phone carrier is **CANTV**, which has offices country-wide, many of which also have internet. Everywhere there are independent phone offices, sometimes just tables, offering landline and mobile calls. Phone cards for local calls are sold in multiples of BsF 5. Mobile phone codes are generally 0412, 0414, 0416, 0424 or 0426. Digitel, Movilnet and Movistar are the main

mobile providers. Visitors can use foreign phones with roaming, or purchase a local SIM card (phone must be unlocked).

The government has introduced a Wi-Fi for All programme, which is to include connectivity in public areas. Nevertheless, internet connection, while common, is among the slowest in Latin America.

Time

4 hrs behind GMT.

Tipping

Taxi drivers do not expect to be tipped. Hotel porters, US$1-2; airport porters US$4 per piece of baggage. Restaurants add 10% of bill for staff wages; tip a further 5-10%.

Tourist information

In charge of tourism is the **Ministerio del Poder Popular para el Turismo**, Av Francisco de Miranda con Av Principal de La Floresta, Edif Mintur (Frente al Colegio Universitario de Caracas), Chacao, Caracas, T0212-208 4651, www.mintur.gob.ve. Its promotional arm is Inatur, same address and website, T0212-208 7918. **Venetur** is the state-owned and operated travel agency, aimed at facilitating travel for nationals and foreigners, making reservations and arranging tours. It has offices at Maiquetía and Porlamar airports and in its hotels, eg lobby of Hotel Alba Caracas, Av México y Sur 25, El Conde, T0212-503 4359, www.venetur.gob.ve.

Outside Venezuela, contact Venezuelan embassies and consulates. Read and heed the travel advice at websites below.

Useful websites

www.venezuelatuya.com region-by-region travel guide, online hotel booking, with some history, geography, cuisine and traditions, in Spanish.

www.audubonvenezuela.org Site of the not-for-profit conservation organization, background details about national parks, but no practical information (Spanish only)

www.think-venezuela.net Information-packed tourism directory, with useful travel tips, hotels, restaurants, travel features and news stories (in English).

http://eposak.org/site/ Eposak is a tourism NGO foundation, supporting various lodges around the country (see Uruyén, page 1664).

Visas and immigration

Entry is by passport, or by passport and visa. Immigration forms are issued by airlines to visitors from all EU and other Western European countries, Australia, Canada, New Zealand, South Africa, USA and some South and Central American and most Caribbean countries. Forms are processed for an entrance stamp upon arrival. Valid for 90 days, entrance stamps cannot be extended. At some overland border crossings (including San Antonio) visitors are given only 30 days. Overstaying will lead to arrest and a fine when you try to depart. For citizens of some countries, tourist, transit, student, and business visas must be sought in advance. To check if you need a visa, see www.mppre.gob.ve. Requirements vary and include 2 passport photos, passport valid for 6 months, references from bank and employer, proof of foreign residence, demonstration of non-emigration to a consular official, proof of economic conditions, documentation of assets, and an onward or return ticket. The fee is US$30-60, depending on the type of visa. For a 90-day extension go to the Servicio Administrativo de Identificación, Migración y Extranjería, **SAIME**, Av Baralt, Edif Mil, p 3, on Plaza Miranda in Caracas, T0800-SAIME00 or T0800-724 6300 (Mon-Fri 07800-1900), www.saime.gob.ve (go to Extranjería, Prórroga de Visa); take passport, tourist visa, photographs and return ticket; passport with extension returned at end of day. SAIME offices in many cities do not offer extensions. If coming from Manaus or travelling onward to other countries in Latin America, you will need a yellow fever inoculation certificate. Carry your passport with you at all times as police do spot checks and anyone found without ID is immediately detained. You may also be asked to provide passport number in some restaurants and shops. Military checkpoints are common, especially in border zones, where all transport is stopped and you may be searched very thoroughly. Have documents ready and make sure you know what entry permits you need; soldiers may not know rules for foreigners. Business visitors on short visits are advised to enter as tourists, otherwise they'll have to obtain a tax clearance certificate (*solvencia*) before they can leave. Do not lose the carbon copy of your visa as this has to be surrendered when leaving.

Weights and measures

Metric.

This is
the Guianas

The geography of Guyana's coastal region was transformed during the struggles of European colonial powers to dominate this once inhospitable part of South America: old forts, Dutch drainage systems, sugar plantations, rice paddies , and the places of worship of those who were brought in to work the land. Leaving the sea behind, travelling by boat or by plane, it is a land of rivers, waterfalls and rainforests which give way to wildlife-rich savannahs, isolated ranches and indigenous communities. Suriname, too, has an equally intriguing combination of Dutch, Asian and African, which influences the culture, food and street life. And, like its neighbour, when you head inland, you enter a different world of bronze-tinted rivers, jungles and Maroon and Amerindian villages.

Despite having geographical features shared by other South American countries, Suriname and Guyana are classed as Caribbean states. Guyane, on the other hand, is an overseas department of France. It has a famous penal colony – now closed – circled by sharks, a European space programme whose launches can be witnessed and nature tourism in the undeveloped interior. All this within the context of a corner of South America where coffee and croissants are served and the prices match those of Paris.

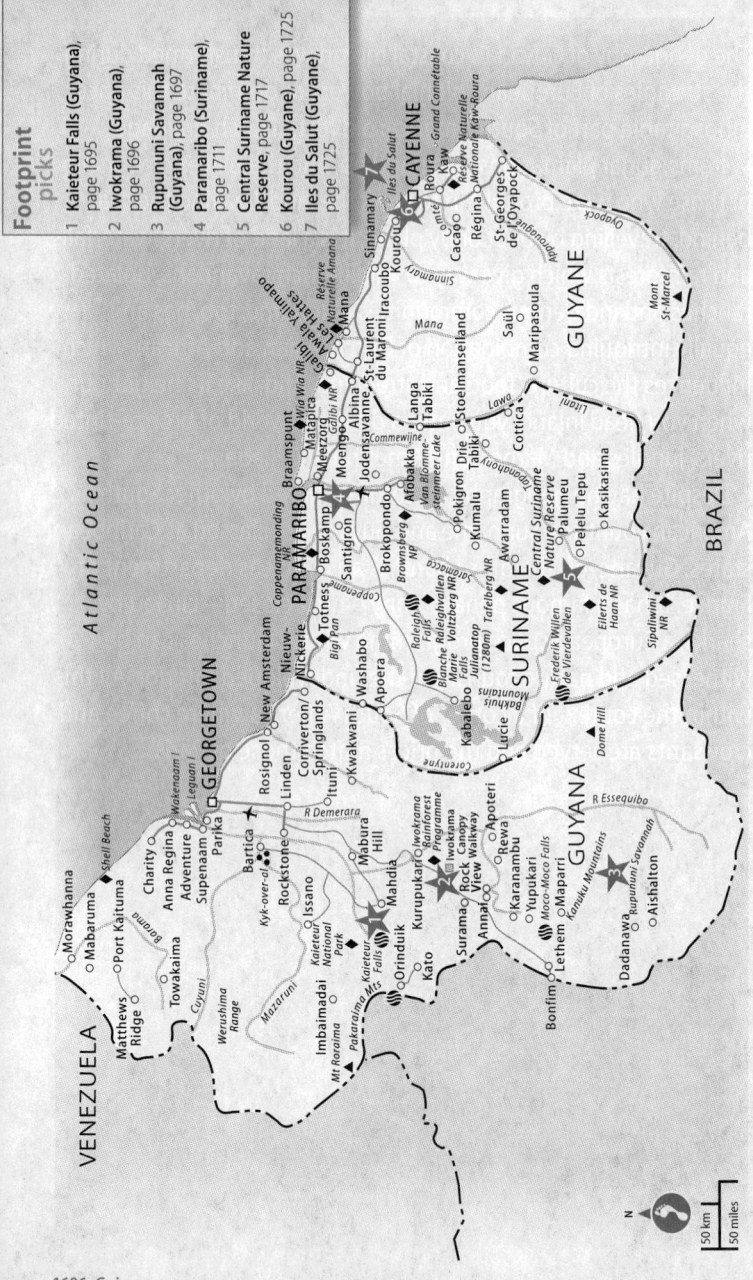

Footprint picks

1 Kaieteur Falls (Guyana),
   page 1695
2 Iwokrama (Guyana),
   page 1696
3 Rupununi Savannah
   (Guyana), page 1697
4 Paramaribo (Suriname),
   page 1711
5 Central Suriname Nature
   Reserve, page 1717
6 Kourou (Guyane), page 1725
7 Iles du Salut (Guyane),
   page 1725

Atlantic Ocean

VENEZUELA

GUYANA

SURINAME

GUYANE

BRAZIL

CAYENNE

GEORGETOWN

PARAMARIBO

Morawhanna
Shell Beach
Mabaruma
Port Kaituma
Matthews Ridge
Towakaima
Charity
Anna Regina
Adventure
Wakenaam I
Leguan I
Supenaam
Parika
New Amsterdam
Rosignol
Linden
Corriverton
Springlands
Nieuw Nickerie
Totness
Coronie
Washabo
Apoera

Bartica
Kyk-over-al
Issano
Rockstone
Itun
Kwakwani

Orinduik
Kato
Kaieteur Falls
Kaieteur National Park
Imbaimadai
Mt Roraima
Pakaraima Mts
Kurupukari
Iwokrama Rainforest Programme
Iwokrama Rock Canopy View Walkway
Surama
Annai
Rewa
Karanambu
Yupukari
Apoteri
Mapari
Moco-Moco Falls
Kanuku Mountains
Lethem
Bonfim
Dadanawa
Rupununi Savannah
Aishalton

Mahdia
Mabura Hill

Kabalebo
Lucie
Bakhuis Mountains
Dome Hill
Raleigh Falls
Blanche Marie Falls
Juliantop
Tafelberg NR
Eilerts de Haan NR
Sipaliwini NR

Santigron
Brownsberg NP
Brokopondo
Afobakka
Pokigron Dre
Van Blommesteinmeer
Tabiki
Kumalu
Awarradam
Palumeu
Central Suriname Nature Reserve
Pelelu Tepu
Kasikasima

Frederik Willem de Vierdeviken

Coppename

Boskamp
Baambspunt
Meerzorg
Moengo
Albina
Matapica
Jodensavanne
Commewijne

Galibi NR
Wia Wia NR
St-Laurent du Maroni
Iracoubo
Mana
Sinnamary
Kourou
Iles du Salut
Sinnamary
Réserve Naturelle Amana
Awala Yalimapo
Les Hattes

Cacao
Régina
Roura
Kaw
Grand Connétable
Réserve Naturelle Kaw-Roura
Montsinéry
St-Georges de l'Oyapock
Oyapock

Saül
Maripasoula
Stoelmansiland
Langa Tabiki
Cottica
Litani

Mont St-Marcel

R Demerara
Essequibo
Mazaruni
Cuyuni
Berbice
Corentyne
Coppename
Suriname
Maroni
Mana
Approuague

Werushima Range

50 km
50 miles
N

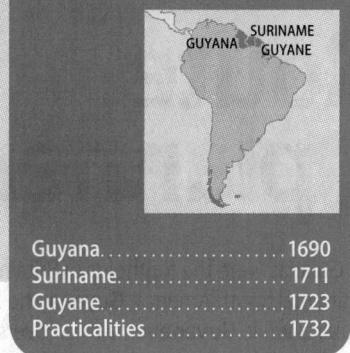

Footprint
picks

★ **Kaieteur Falls (Guyana)**, page 1695

Five times the height of Niagara and surrounded by unspoilt forest.

★ **Iwokrama (Guyana)**, page 1696

A conservation project where you can trek, take boat trips and stay
in camps deep in the jungle.

★ **Rupununi Savannah (Guyana)**, page 1697

Dry grassland scattered with Amerindian villages and brimming
with birdlife.

★ **Paramaribo (Suriname)**, page 1711

A wonderful blend of European architecture and South American
craft has led to the historic centre gaining UNESCO status.

★ **Central Suriname Nature Reserve**, page 1717

This immense protected area of pristine primary tropical forest teems
with life.

★ **Kourou (Guyane)**, page 1725

The space centre is the big draw, but fishing, bathing and other
excursions are on offer when in the area.

★ **Iles du Salut (Guyane)**, page 1725

A former prison island brought to the attention of the world by its
famous escapee, Henri Charrière, author of *Papillon*.

Route planner

The Guianas were the footholds of Britain, the Netherlands and France on continental South America. **Guyana** and **Suriname** are now independent republics while **Guyane** remains an overseas department of France. Even though language and colonial legacies separate them, they share a landscape dominated by bronze-tinted rivers which flow from wildlife-rich mountains and forests to a populated coastal strip on the Atlantic Ocean. Also, for such small countries their cultural mix is markedly varied.

Guyana

waterfalls, river routes, rain forest and savannah

Guyana's coast is a blend of coconut palms and Caribbean music, Dutch place names and drainage systems, Hindu Temples, Islamic mosques and Demerara sugar, all of which reflect the chequered history of the country. Despite being on the Atlantic, **Georgetown**, the capital, is known as the 'Garden City of the Caribbean'. This gives some idea of the country's orientation in trade and cultural terms. In the thinly populated interior waterfalls tumble over jasper rocks, or, at **Kaieteur**, into a chasm almost five times the height of Niagara. Life revolves around Amerindian communities beside the rivers in the tropical forest, or, further south, the scattered ranches of the **Rupununi Savannah**.

Suriname

a multi-cultural capital and a largely uninhabited hinterland

Like its neighbours, Suriname has been influenced by a variety of cultures, Amerindian, African, European and Asian. Markets, customs, festivals and food all reflect this. In Paramaribo, the capital, there is some fine wooden architecture, dating from the Dutch colonial period, and there are important Jewish monuments. The Maroons, descendants of escaped slaves, have maintained traditional African culture for centuries and, together with the Amerindians, have a special bond with the tropical rainforest and its biodiversity. Nature reserves include the combined parks of the **Central Suriname Nature Reserve**, **Brownsberg**, **Wia-Wia** and **Galibi**. The last two protect nesting ground for marine turtles. There are no beaches to speak of, but some recreational facilities and resorts have improvised beaches on the riverbanks.

Guyane

a space centre, a former prison and a forested interior

Guyane is heavily dependent on France. **Cayenne**, the capital, is on a peninsula at the mouth of the river of the same name. The department is known internationally for its space station at **Kourou**, home to the European Ariane space programme. The site has been used to launch over half the world's commercial satellites. An unusual attraction is the remains of the former penal colony, notably the **Iles du Salut**, made famous by Henri Charrière's book *Papillon*. Much of the country remains sparsely populated and underdeveloped despite French aid. Two million hectares of the interior, however, comprise the **Parc Amazonien de Guyane** which, with neighbouring reserves in Brazil, forms the world's largest protected tropical forest.

Guyana

Highlights of Guyana include the Kaieteur Falls, among the highest in the world, the Orinduik Falls on the border with Brazil and the Iwokrama Rainforest Reserve, with the Iwokrama Canopy Walkway. Travelling on any of the rivers, many with excellent beaches, is the most interesting way to get around. On the coast there are few beaches for bathing, but in the far northwest is Shell Beach, a protected area for marine turtles and birdlife.

Georgetown Colour map 2, B3.

tree-lined streets and traditional wooden great houses

Guyana's capital (population 200,000) and chief town and port is on the east bank of the mouth of the Demerara river. The climate is tropical, with a mean temperature of 27°C, but the trade winds provide welcome relief. The city is built on a grid plan, with wide tree-lined streets and drainage canals following the layout of the old sugar estates. Parts of the city are very attractive, with a profusion of flowering trees and white-painted wooden 19th-century houses raised on stilts. In the evening the sea wall is crowded with strollers, and at Easter it is a mass of colourful kites.

Sights

Although part of the old centre was destroyed by fire in 1945, there are some fine 19th-century buildings, particularly on or near High Street and the Avenue of the Republic. **St George's Anglican Cathedral**, which dates from 1889, is 44 m high and is said to be the world's tallest free-standing wooden building. It was designed by Sir Arthur Blomfield, who placed the supporting columns either side of the altar, leaving nothing but open space between ceiling and floor. Above the altar is a chandelier given by Queen Victoria. Other fine buildings on High Street are the Gothic-style **City Hall** (1888), the **City Engineer's Office**, the **Victoria Law Courts** (1887) and the **Magistrates' Court**. The **Public Buildings**, on Brickdam, which house Parliament, are an impressive neoclassical structure built in 1839. Opposite is **St Andrew's Presbytery** (18th century). **State House** on Main Street is the residence of the president. Much of the city centre is dominated by the imposing tower above **Stabroek market** (1881). At the head of Brickdam is an aluminium arch commemorating independence. Nearby is a monument to the 1763 slave rebellion, surmounted by an impressive statue of Cuffy, its best-known leader. Near the Pegasus hotel on Seawall Road is the **Umana Yana**, a conical thatched structure built by a group of Wai Wai Amerindians using traditional techniques for the 1972 conference of the Non-Aligned Movement (it burnt down in 2014 and was rebuilt in 2016). The **National Museum** ① North Rd, opposite the post office, T225 7191, Mon-Fri 0900-1600, Sat 0900-1400, free, has exhibits from Guyana and elsewhere, including a model of Georgetown before the fire and a good natural history section. The **Walter Roth Museum of Anthropology** ① 61 Main St, T225 8486, Mon-Thu 0800-1630, Fri 0800-1530, has artefacts from Guyana's nine Amerindian tribes and serves as a research centre for indigenous people.

The **Botanical Gardens** ① 20 mins' walk east from the Anglican Cathedral, free, covering 50 ha, have Victorian bridges and pavilions, palms and lily ponds (undergoing continual improvements). The gardens are safe in daylight hours, but keep to the marked paths. Do not go there after dark. Near the southwest corner is the former residence of the president, **Castellani House** ① Vlissengen Rd and Homestretch Av, T225 0579, Mon-Fri 1000-1700, Sat 1400-1800, which now houses the renovated **National Art Collection**, and there is also a large **mausoleum** containing the remains of the former president, Forbes Burnham, which is decorated with reliefs depicting scenes from his political career. Look out for the rare cannonball tree (*Couroupita guianensis*), named

Essential Guyana

Finding your feet

Cheddi Jagan International Airport is at Timehri, 40 km south of Georgetown, while **Ogle International Airport** is 8 km from the city. Taxis and minibuses run to Georgetown from both.

Getting around

There are domestic flights, some scheduled, some charters, to several parts of the country. The main roads from Georgetown to Linden and to Springlands for the ferry to Suriname are paved. The unpaved road that continues from Linden to Lethem gives access to places along the way to Brazil, but many other places are only reachable by boat.

Safety

Georgetown is a beautiful city, but check with your hotel, tour operator, the police or government authorities about unsafe areas. Don't walk the streets at night: always take a taxi, especially if going to Sheriff Street for the nightlife. At all times, avoid Albouystown (south of the centre) and the Tiger Bay area, just one block west of Main Street. Leave your valuables in your hotel. These problems are restricted to

Fact file

Location 5.0000° N, 58.7500° W
Capital Georgetown
Time zone GMT -4 hrs
Telephone country code +592
Currency Guyanese dollars (GYD)

Tip...

There are ATMs in Georgetown, but as a back up you are advised to take cash dollars or euros.

Georgetown and nearby villages; the interior remains as safe as ever.

When to go

Although hot, the climate is not unhealthy. Mean shade temperature throughout the year is 27°C; the mean maximum is about 31°C and the mean minimum 23°C. The heat is tempered by cooling breezes from the sea and is most appreciated in the warmest months, August to October. There are two wet seasons, from May to June, and from December to the end of January, although they may extend into the months either side. In the south and the Rupununi the wet season is May to July or August. Rainfall averages 2300 mm a year in Georgetown. Note that the Republic Day celebrations (23 February, float parade) last for one day, but there are other activities (Children's Costume Competition, etc) which take place during the preceding days. Also, in the two weeks prior to 23 February, many large companies hold Mashramani Camps at which public participation is encouraged. Hotels in Georgetown are very full, as they are also during international cricket. See also Public holidays and festivals in the A-Z, below.

Time required

One to two weeks to explore.

Weather Guyana

January	February	March	April	May	June
30°C 22°C 263mm	30°C 22°C 96mm	31°C 22°C 86mm	31°C 23°C 178mm	31°C 23°C 310mm	31°C 23°C 305mm

July	August	September	October	November	December
31°C 23°C 262mm	32°C 23°C 139mm	33°C 23°C 96mm	33°C 23°C 114mm	32°C 23°C 151mm	30°C 23°C 238mm

Georgetown

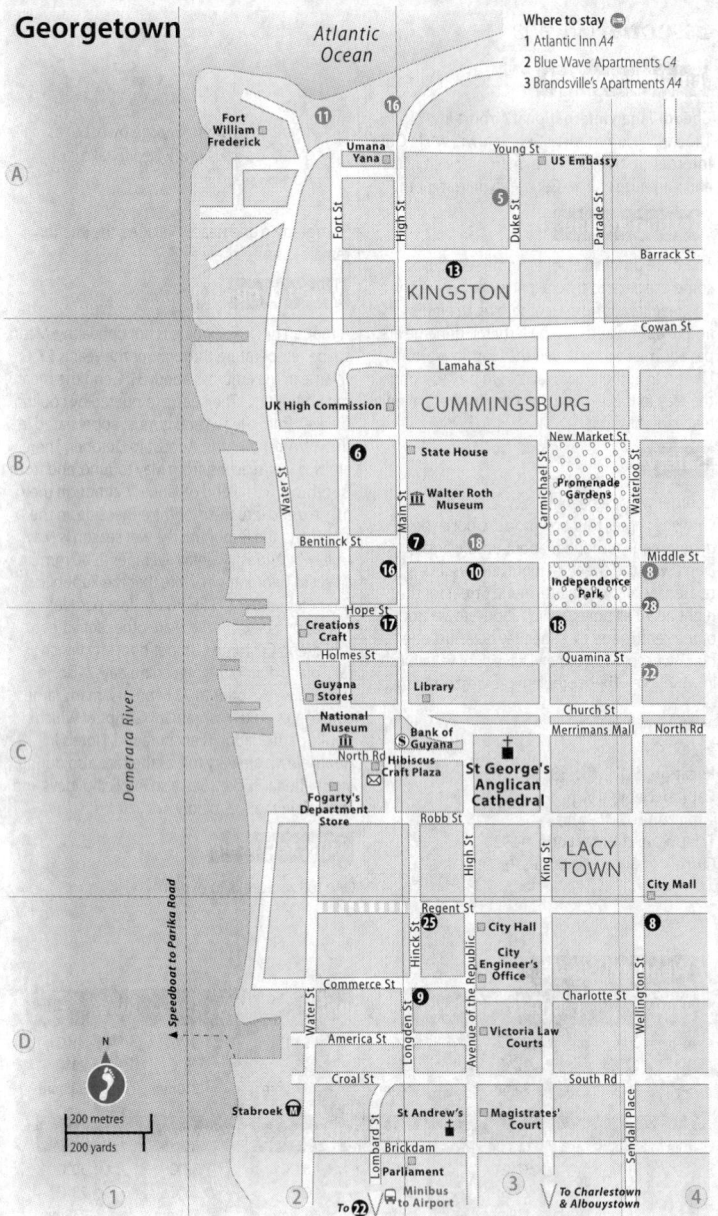

Atlantic Ocean

Fort William Frederick

Umana Yana

Young St

US Embassy

Fort St

High St

Duke St

Parade St

⑤

Barrack St

⑬

KINGSTON

Cowan St

Lamaha St

CUMMINGSBURG

UK High Commission

New Market St

Water St

⑥

State House

Carmichael St

Promenade Gardens

Waterloo St

Main St

Walter Roth Museum

Bentinck St

⑦

⑱

Middle St

⑯

⑩

Independence Park

⑧

⑱

㉘

Hope St

⑰

Creations Craft

Holmes St

Quamina St

㉒

Guyana Stores

Library

Church St

National Museum

Bank of Guyana

Merrimans Mall

North Rd

Demerara River

Hibiscus Craft Plaza

St George's Anglican Cathedral

North Rd

Fogarty's Department Store

Robb St

High St

King St

LACY TOWN

City Mall

Regent St

⑳

City Hall

⑧

Hinck St

City Engineer's Office

Wellington St

Commerce St

⑨

Avenue of the Republic

Charlotte St

Water St

Longden St

Victoria Law Courts

America St

Sendall Place

Croal St

South Rd

N

Speedboat to Parika Road

Stabroek

Lombard St

St Andrew's

Magistrates' Court

200 metres
200 yards

Brickdam

Parliament

Minibus to Airport

To Charlestown & Albouystown

To ㉒

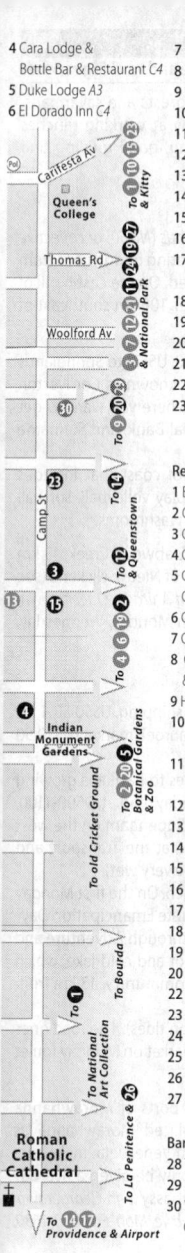

4 Cara Lodge &
  Bottle Bar & Restaurant *C4*
5 Duke Lodge *A3*
6 El Dorado Inn *C4*

7 Grand Coastal Inn *B4*
8 Halito Hotel, Bistro 176 *B4*
9 Herdmanston Lodge *B4*
10 Hotel Glow *A4*
11 Guyana Marriott *A2*
12 Melbourne Inn *A4*
13 Midtown *B4*
14 Millenium Manor *D4*
15 Ocean Spray International *A4*
16 Pegasus Guyana *A2*
17 Ramada Georgetown
  Princess *D4*
18 Rima Guest House *B3*
19 Roraima Residence Inn *B4*
20 Sleepin Guesthouse *C4*
21 Tropical View International *A4*
22 Waterchris *C4*
23 Windjammer International
  Cuisine & Comfort Inn *A4*

Restaurants 🍴
1 Brazil Churrascaria *D4*
2 Café Tepuy *C4*
3 Church's Chicken *B4*
4 Coalpot *C3*
5 Coffee Bean
  Café and Eatery *C4*
6 German's *B2*
7 Golden Coast *B3*
8 Gravity Lounge
  & United Cinema Mall *D4*
9 Hacks Halaal *D3*
10 Hibiscus Restaurant
  and Lounge *B3*
11 JR Burgers &
  Altitude Lounge *A4*
12 Juice Power *B4*
13 Lily's *A3*
14 Maggie's Snackette *B4*
15 Mario's Pizza & Quizno's *B4*
16 New Palm Court *B2*
17 New Thriving *C2*
18 Oasis Café *C3*
19 Play Land *A4*
20 Popeye's *B4*
21 Rayman's Halaal *D2*
22 Shanta's *B4*
23 Upscale *D3*
24 Tuma Sàlà *A4*
25 Upscale *D3*
26 White Castle Fish Shop *D4*
27 Xie Xie *A4*

Bars & clubs 🍸
28 The 592 Hub *B4*
29 704 Sports Bar *B4*
30 The Vintage Wine and
  Cheese Lounge *B4*

after the appearance of its poisonous fruit. The Botanical Gardens offer great birdwatching. The city has 200 bird species from 39 families, many of which can be seen in the gardens. Flycatchers, tanagers, hummingbirds and many migrating species such as peregrine falcons and warblers can be found around the capital, but the true stars are the blood-coloured woodpecker, which is endemic to the Guiana Shield, and the festive parrot. Both are regularly spotted in the gardens. Tour operators offer birdwatching tours.

The **zoo** ① *Vlissengen Rd and Regent Rd, T225 9142, 0930-1730, US$1.50 for adults, half price for children; US$11 to use personal video*, is being upgraded, together with the Botanical Gardens and National Park. It carries the WWF logo and has educational programmes. It has a collection of local animals including manatees, which can be seen throughout the day. The zoo also boasts a breeding centre for endangered birds which are released into the wild. Nearby is the **National Cultural Centre**, an impressive air-conditioned theatre with a large stage. Performances are also given at the **Theatre Guild Playhouse** in Parade Street. There are also beautiful tropical plants in the **Promenade Gardens** ① *Middle St, open 0830-1630*. Also in the centre are the **Indian Monument Gardens** ① *Camp and Church St*, with the **Indian Heritage Monument** representing the *Whitby*, one of the ships that transported indentured labourers from India to Guyana in 1838. **Indian Arrival Day** is celebrated here on 5 May and it is the site for other Hindu festivals such as **Phagwah** and **Divali**. More tropical gardens are in the **National Park** on Carifesta Avenue, which has a good public running track. At the Kitty Seawall, Carifesta Avenue, is the **1823 Slave Rebellion Monument** commemorating the 1823 Demerara slave uprising, with a sculpture by Ivor Thom of an African slave holding a cutlass, chain and cross to represent rebellion, revolution and religion.

The **Georgetown Cricket Club** at Bourda is one of the finest cricket grounds in the tropics. For the ICC World Cup in 2007, a new stadium was built at Providence on the east bank of Demerara right next to **Ramada Georgetown Princess Hotel** (8 km from the city on the airport road; take bus 42 or a taxi). It has fine modern stands but not enough protection from sun and rain.

The interior of Guyana is a land of great rivers, dramatic waterfalls, rainforests and savannahs. On the coast are turtle-nesting grounds and sea defences. You can stay at working ranches and community-run lodges. At all times, expect superb nature watching, good guiding and welcoming service.

Southeast to Suriname

New Amsterdam and the Berbice river ① *From Georgetown, take a minibus (No 50) or collective taxi to Rosignol on the west bank of the Berbice, US$6, then cross the river.* A floating bridge goes from Cotton Tree to Palmyra Village (5 km from New Amsterdam); a toll is charged. On the east bank of the Berbice river, near its mouth, is picturesque New Amsterdam, just over 100 km southeast of the capital.

Corriverton The road continues east from New Amsterdam (minibus No 50, US$3) to Springlands and Skeldon at the mouth of the Corentyne river. The towns are officially known as Corriverton (Corentyne River Town). Springlands is 2 km long, so you need to know where you want to get off the bus. You'll find the **Republic Bank** and **Guyana National Commercial Bank**, and Suriname dollars can officially be changed into Guyanese dollars here.

Near Corriverton is **No 63 Beach** (**Berbice**), part of a 16-km stretch of coast that includes 12 villages. Thousands of visitors come here each weekend to swim and play volleyball, softball cricket and other sports. There are changing facilities, *benabs* (shelters) and washrooms.

Border with Suriname A ferry sails once or twice daily from Moleson, or Crabwood Creek, 13 km south of Springlands, to South Drain/Canawaima in Suriname, 40 km south of Nieuw-Nickerie (see Transport, below). **Suriname Embassy** ① *in Georgetown: 54 New Garden and Anira St, Queenstown, T226 7844, or 225 2631, surnmemb@gol.net.gy.* The consular section is open Monday, Wednesday, Friday morning only, but visa applications can be handed in at any time.

West from Georgetown

The road crosses the 2-km-long floating **Demerara bridge** (opens often for shipping, US$0.50-1 for private vehicles, pedestrians free). Speedboats cross the Demerara from Stabroek market (US$0.50 every 30 minutes).

The road continues 42 km, past rice paddies, kokers and through villages to **Parika**, a growing town on the east bank of the Essequibo river (minibus US$2.50). It has a Sunday market, 0600-1100, and three banks. Two ferries, the *Kanawan* and *Sabanto*, cross the river to **Supenaam** on the west bank at high tide, mostly twice a day, US$1.50 (schedules can be checked at the **Transport and Harbours Department**, T225 9355, or T225 9350); or speedboat US$5 (can be very wet).

On **Tiger Island** at the mouth of the Essequibo is popular **Hamburg Beach**. On the first Monday in August some 15,000 people arrive for the **Hamburg Beach Fête**, to celebrate **Emancipation Day**.

From Supenaam, minibuses or taxis (US$7.50 per person) go to **Charity** through **Adventure** and **Anna Regina**. Nearby there is a resort at **Lake Mainstay**. You can visit a hot and cold lake, which varies in temperature according to depth, and the **Whyaka Amerindian Community**, 13 km from Anna Regina.

Mainstay is 2¾ hours by road and ferry from Georgetown (depending on tides). The road goes on to **Charity**, a pleasant town with loud bars, various hotels and a lively market on Monday (quiet at other times).

Border with Venezuela Near the border with Venezuela are the small ports of **Morawhanna** (Morajuana to the Venezuelans) and **Mabaruma**. Mabaruma has replaced Morawhanna as capital of the region since it is at less at risk from flooding. If arriving from Venezuela, make sure that the official who stamps your passport is not an imposter. You may only be given a five-day temporary visa, to be renewed on arrival in Georgetown. **Venezuelan Embassy** ① *in Georgetown: 296 Thomas St, South Cummingsburg, T226 6749, http://guyana.embajada.gob.ve, Mon-Fri 0830-1630.* It is not normally possible to cross from Guyana to Venezuela.

Shell Beach Part of a protected area of Atlantic coastline, Shell Beach is some 145 km long, from the Pomeroon river to the Venezuelan border. It safeguards the nesting grounds of leatherback, green, hawksbill and olive ridley turtles. Nesting activity begins in late March and continues, with hatching, until mid-August. Former turtle

Tip...
At the time of writing there were no tours to Shell Beach as the area was experiencing problems with flooding and erosion.

hunters have been retrained to patrol and identify nest sites, which are logged using global positioning satellite equipment. The project receives support from the WWF. The coast consists of areas of mangrove swamps with beaches formed entirely of eroded shell particles. There are large flocks of scarlet ibis. Other birds include Amazon parrots, macaws, toucans, woodpeckers and crab hawks. Iguanas are usually seen in the mangroves, with sightings of rare river dolphin on the narrower stretches of river.

The camp consists of a thatched dining area and huts for the staff and igloo-type tents for guests, with fly-sheets and mosquito netting (vital in the rainy season, when there are 'blizzards' of mosquitos). Showers and toilets are basic. Food is very good. An Arawak family runs the camp and offers daily activities of fishing and birdwatching. They are excellent English-speaking guides. Turtle watching is available in season.

Fort Island and Bartica From Parika (see page 1694) a vehicle ferry runs up the Essequibo river to Bartica daily at 0400 (returns 1200), US$2.50 one way. The 58-km journey takes six hours, stopping at **Fort Island**; boats come out from riverside settlements to load up with fruit. River taxis run from Parika to Bartica all day, US$12.50 per person. There are also flights from Ogle five days a week (see Transport, page 1709). On Fort Island is a **Dutch fort** (built 1743, restored by Raleigh International in 1991) and the **Dutch Court of Policy**, built at the same time. There is also a small village; the rest of the island is dairy farms.

Bartica, at the junction of the Essequibo and Mazaruni rivers, is the 'take-off' town for the gold and diamond fields and the interior generally. Opposite Bartica, at the mouth of the Mazaruni, is **Kaow Island**, with a lumber mill. The *stelling* (wharf) and **market** in Bartica are very colourful. Bars flank the main street. The annual Easter **regatta** is a boisterous affair featuring watersports, mostly power-boat racing, other sports, a parade and a beauty pageant. There are several resorts nearby; see Where to stay, page 1700.

Southwest of Bartica The Essequibo is navigable to large boats for some miles upstream of Bartica. The Cuyuni flows into the Mazaruni three miles above Bartica, and above this confluence the Mazaruni is impeded for 190 km by thousands of islands, rapids and waterfalls. To avoid this stretch of treacherous river a poor road runs from Bartica to Issano, where boats can be taken up the more tranquil upper Mazaruni. At the confluence of the Mazaruni and Cuyuni rivers are the remains of the early 17th-century Dutch stronghold **Kyk-over-al**, once the seat of government for the Dutch county of Essequibo. Nearby are the **Marshall Falls** (30-60 minutes by boat from Bartica, included in Essequibo river day trips, otherwise you have to hire a boat, US$250 per boat for a group of six to eight, return), which are beautiful, but too dangerous for swimming. You can swim in the nearby bay, part of the **Rainbow River Marshall Falls** property (day trippers may have to pay an entrance fee).

★**Kaieteur National Park** ① *Permission to enter the park must be obtained from the National Parks Commission, Georgetown, T225 9142, entry costs US$15 (both arranged by tour operators); a guide costs US$22.50.* The **Kaieteur Falls**, on the Potaro river, nearly five times the height of Niagara, with a drop of 228 m, are almost 100 m wide. Ranking with the Victoria and Iguazú Falls in majesty and beauty, they have the added attraction of being surrounded by unspoilt forest. Lying within a national park, there is also plenty of wildlife: tapirs, ocelots, monkeys, armadillos, anteaters and birds. At the falls themselves, one can see the magnificent silver fox, the Guianan cock-of-the-rock and the white-collared swift, also known as Makonaima bird, which lives behind the falls. At dusk the swifts swoop in and out of the gorge before passing through the deluge to roost behind the water. The golden rocket frog lives in the giant tank bromeliad and is endemic to this area. In the dry months, April and October, the flow of the falls is reduced; in January and June/July the flow is fullest. In the height of the wet season (June), the overland route is difficult and not recommended.

The **Pakaraima Mountains** stretch from Kaieteur westwards to include the highest peak in Guyana, **Mount Roraima**, once believed to be the inspiration for Conan Doyle's *Lost World*. Roraima is very difficult to climb from the Guyanese side, but **Wilderness Explorers** offer trips via Brazil and Venezuela.

Orinduik Falls Orinduik Falls are on the Ireng river, which forms the border with Brazil; the river pours over steps and terraces of jasper, with a backdrop of the Pakaraima Mountains. There is good swimming at the falls which are a 25-minute flight from Kaieteur.

South from Georgetown: to Brazil

Linden The second-largest town in Guyana is a bauxite mining town on the banks of the Demerara river. The road from the capital is good (slow for the first part to Timehri); police checks are to stop drug and gun running. Linden's opencast mine is 60-90 m deep and is said to have the world's longest boom walking dragline. The town is dominated by a disused alumina plant and scarred by old bauxite pits. In town is the lovely colonial guesthouse on the Demerara river, run by the mining company.

From Linden, rough roads suitable for 4WD vehicles run south to the bauxite mining towns of Ituni and Kwakwani. A good road goes west from Linden to Rockstone ferry on Essequibo river. From Rockstone roads run north to Bartica and southwest to Issano. The main road south to the logging centre at Mabura Hill is in excellent condition; from here a good road runs west to Mahdia, with a pontoon crossing of the Essequibo, and another road continues south from Mabura Hill to Kurupukari, the Essequibo river crossing on the route to Lethem.

⭐**Iwokrama** ① *For information and prices, which change frequently, contact the administrator, Iwokrama International Centre for Rainforest Conservation and Development, 77 High St, Kingston, Georgetown, T225 1504, http://iwokrama.org. Rates for lodging and tour packages are given on http:// iwokramariverlodge.com. The northern entrance is open 0600-1800; the southern entrance 0430-1630, see Transport, page 1710.* This is a 371,345-ha project set up by Guyana and the Commonwealth to conserve tropical forest primarily, but other habitats as well. As well as conservation, the programme involves studies on the sustainable use of the rainforest and ecotourism. It is hoped that the results will provide a database for application worldwide. The **Field Station** is at **Kurukupari**, near the Arawak village of **Fairview**, on the northeastern boundary of the reserve. You can meet research teams, take boat trips and stay at satellite camps deep in the forest (**Clearwater** on the Burro-burro, **Kabocalli** and **Turtle Mountain** on the Essequibo). Well-trained rangers, who speak their native language and English, escort visitors through the forest on many trails. One goes to **Turtle Mountain** (45 minutes by boat, then 1½ hours' walk), go early for great views of the forest canopy. Another trek is to the top of **Mount Iwokrama**, a difficult 20-km round trip; for the less fit there is a 10-km trail to the foot of the mountain to a pleasant stream and Amerindian petroglyphs. There are set rates for boat and Land Rover use and for field assistants to accompany you.

There is a 33-m-high **Iwokrama Canopy Walkway** ① *US$25 pp (children under 13, US$18) for a day visit including entry to the walkway and qualified guide with good birding knowledge, www. iwokramacanopywalkway.com*, managed by **Wilderness Explorers, Surama, Rock View Lodge** and **Iwokrama International Centre**, under the name of **Community And Tourism Services** (**CATS**); but any tour operator can make bookings. The walkway allows visitors to walk among the treetops and see the birds and monkeys of the upper canopy. Night excursions are available on the walkway. There is a library with birding books and a small arts and crafts shop. See **Atta Rainforest Lodge**, page 1701, which gives good access to wildlife in addition to the canopy walkway, with lots of guides.

Just beyond the southern entrance to Iwokrama a road turns west to the Makushi Amerindian village of **Surama** which organizes its own ecotourism activities through the village council and can accommodate guests in the Eco-Lodge ① *http://suramaecolodge.com, bookings through the website or through the CATS partnership (see above).* It is in a lovely location some distance from the village, overlooking both savannah and forest. The lodge has en suite benabs and, in the main building, good food in the restaurant and a handicrafts and hammock area upstairs. The office, 150 m away, has Wi-Fi. Overnight accommodation is $ per person and there are tours ranging from two days/ one night to six days/five nights (US$209-660, all options listed on website). Birdwatching, night trekking and boating are arranged and guides are included in the price. The staff are very helpful and knowledgeable. A harpy eagle nest nearby has proven very reliable over the last five years, with good sightings. The forest is beautiful, with many animals especially at dawn on the dirt road between Surama and the Lethem–Georgetown road.

★**Rupununi Savannah** This is an extensive area of dry grassland in the far southwest of Guyana, with scattered trees, termite mounds and wooded hills. The rivers, creeks and ponds, lined with Ite palms and other trees, are good for seeing wildlife. Among a wide variety of birds, look out for macaws, toucan, parrots, parakeets, osprey, hawks and jabiru storks (take binoculars). Many of the animals are nocturnal and seldom seen. The region is scattered with Amerindian villages and a few large cattle ranches which date from the late 19th century: the descendants of some of the Scottish settlers still live here. Links with Brazil are much closer than they are with the Guyanese coast; many people speak Portuguese and most trade is with Brazil. See http://rupununi.org.

In the wet season (May to July/August), much of the savannah may flood and malaria mosquitoes and kabura/sandflies are widespread. The best time to visit is October to April. River bathing is good, but beware of dangerous stingrays and black caiman. For visiting many parts of the interior, particularly Amerindian districts, permits are required in advance from the village council. If on a tour, the operator will take care of this. If travelling independently you can book with one of the many lodges as most work directly with the village councils. To conduct scientific, anthropological or archaeological research, permission is needed from the village council and the **Ministry of Indigenous People's Affairs** ① *251-252 Quamina St, South Cummingsburg, Georgetown, T227 5067, http://indigenouspeoples.gov.gy*. If in doubt, check beforehand with the ministry.

Annai Some 25 km south of Surama, this Amerindian village is located in the northern savannahs, south of the Iwokrama Rainforest Programme. Annai's airstrip is close to **Rock View Lodge**, which is most convenient for visiting the North Rupununi owing to its proximity to the Georgetown–Lethem road and the Rupununi river (see Where to stay and Transport, pages 1701 and 1710). It is possible to trek from Annai over the plains to the Rupununi river, or through dense jungle to the mountains. **Kwatamang Landing**, east of Annai, is a suitable access point to the Rupununi river for all the lodges from Iwokrama to Rewa, Karanambu and Caiman House at Yupukari.

Lethem A small but scattered town on the Brazilian border (see below), this is the service centre for the Rupununi and a shopping centre with supermarkets, shoe and clothing stores for the people of the savannah and for Brazilians. There are ATMs, a small **hospital** ① *T772 2006*, a **police station** ① *T772 2011*, and government offices. Prices are about twice as high as in Georgetown.

> **Fact...**
> In Lethem, a big event at Easter is the rodeo, from the Tuesday of Holy Week until the Wednesday after, visited by cowboys from all over the Rupununi.

From Lethem, transport can be hired for day-trips to the **Moco-Moco Falls** and the **Kumu Falls** (4WD and driver to Moco-Moco US$60-70, long, rough ride and walk, but worth it). The nearby **Kanuku mountains**, about two hours away, are recognized by **Conservation International** as one of the few remaining pristine Amazonian areas. There is good bird and mammal watching and there are waterfalls to visit.

Border with Brazil The **Takutu river** separates Lethem from Bonfim in Brazil. The crossing is about 1.6 km north of Lethem and 2.5 km from Bonfim. The river is crossed by a bridge, before which one lane of the road crosses over the other so that traffic is on the correct side of the road for the neighbouring country. It is important to observe formalities on both sides as people not having the correct papers and stamps will have problems further into either country. At Guyanese immigration (usually closes 1800), have your passport stamped and then go to the police desk in the same building to be signed in or out. In Brazil, go to Polícia Federal on the Brazilian side of the bridge, open 0800-1200, 1400-1800, to get your entry stamp. If you need a visa for Brazil you can apply in Georgetown at the **Brazilian Embassy** ① *308 Church St, Queenstown, T225 7970, http://georgetown.itamaraty.gov.br/en-us/, Mon-Fri 0900-1400*. You must have a yellow fever certificate. When entering both Guyana and Brazil, make sure you get a stamp for the number of days you need for your visit. See also Transport, page 1710.

Tourist information

For details of the **Guyana Tourism Authority** (National Exhibition Center, Sophia, Georgetown), **Ministry of Business** and the **Tourism and Hospitality Association of Guyana (THAG)**, see page 1739.

Where to stay

If you plan to stay in Georgetown, it's best to book your lodgings in advance. There isn't much choice in the lower price categories and many small hotels and guesthouses are full of long-stay residents, while some are rented by the hour. If in doubt, go to a larger hotel for the 1st night and look around next day in daylight.

There are several business hotels, near the north shore, eg **$$$-$$ Ocean Spray International** (46 Stanley Pl, Kitty, T227 3763/5, www. oceanspray.co.gy); and **$$$ Atlantic Inn** (56 Church Rd and First Av, Soubryanville, T225 5826, www.atlanticinngy.com), and apartments, eg **$$$$ Blue Wave Apartments** (8 North Rd, Bourda, T226 1418); and **$$$-$$ Brandsville's Apartments** (88-90 Pike St, Campbellville, T227 0989, www.brandsvillegy.com).

Georgetown

$$$$ Cara Lodge
294 Quamina St, T225 5301, http://caralodge.com.
A **Heritage House** hotel, converted 1840s mansion, with 36 superb rooms, good service, restaurant (see page 1703), bar, broadband (DSL) internet in rooms, taxi service, laundry, business centre with internet and conference room.

$$$$ Guyana Marriott
Block Alpha, Battery Rd, Kingston, T231 2480, www.marriott.com.
Impressive member of the international chain opened in 2015 with 9 floors and 192 rooms. Excellent amenities.

$$$$ Pegasus Guyana
Seawall Rd, T225 2856, www. pegasushotelguyana.com.
Very safe, a/c, comfortable, fridge, lovely pool, gym, tennis, business centre, massage and yoga, restaurants (**Aromas, El Dorado** serving Italian cuisine and **The Oasis** tea room) and bars (**Ignite, Latino** and **Aura Sky Lounge**). Check internet for special offers. 24-hr back-up electricity.

$$$$ Ramada Georgetown Princess
Providence, East Bank Demerara, next to Cricket World Cup Stadium, 15-20 mins' drive out of the city, T265 7009, www.ramada.com.
250 rooms all with a/c, huge pool with 2 poolside bars, restaurants, including **Providence** for international and local food, **Club Next** and casino.

$$$$-$$$ Duke Lodge
Duke St, Kingston, opposite US Embassy, T227 3807, http://roraimaairways.com.
Beautiful antique-style guesthouse 5 mins from central Georgetown, with breakfast, Wi-Fi, swimming pool and fine restaurant.

$$$$-$$$ Halito Hotel
176 Middle St, T226 1612/5, Facebook: Halito Hotel & Residence.
Luxurious, secure, self-contained rooms with kitchen, grocery, laundry, internet access, airport pick-up, restaurant (see page 1703).

$$$$-$$$ Roraima Residence Inn
R8 Eping Av, Bel Air Park, T225 9648, http://roraimaairways.com.
A small hotel with good standards, a/c and pool.

$$$ El Dorado Inn
295 Thomas and Quamina Streets, T225 3966, www.eldorado-inn.com.
Good hotel with nicely appointed rooms in central location. Also has **$$$$** suites.

$$$ Herdmanston Lodge
65 Peter Rose and Anira Streets, Queenstown, T225 0808, www.herdmanstonlodge.com.
In a lovely old house, pleasant district, breakfast, restaurant with daily buffet, Wi-Fi throughout, very comfortable.

$$$-$$ Grand Coastal Inn
Lot 1 & 2 Area M Plantation, Le Ressouvenir, 5 km out of city, T220 1091, www.grandcoastal.com.
3 standards of room, with breakfast and drinking water, dining room, bar, laundry, business centre with internet, car rental, tours, good.

$$$-$$ Midtown Hotel
176 Middle St, T623 5011, www.midtownhotelgy.com/.
Fans and a/c. Includes small breakfast, also has a **Hibachi** restaurant and bar. Good, but can be noisy from music and nightclub next door.

$$$-$$ Millenium Manor
43 Hadfield St, T223 0541,
http://milleniummanor.com.
3 standards of room with all facilities including
$$$$ suites, modern, comfortable, helpful staff.

$$$-$$ Tropical View International
33 Delph St, Campbellville, T227 2216/7, https://
tropicalviewinternationalhotel.shutterfly.com.
Smart, modern hotel in a residential
area, rooms with windows, all mod
cons, Wi-Fi, breakfast included.

**$$$-$$ Windjammer International Cuisine
and Comfort Inn**
27 Queen St, Kitty, T227 7478,
www.windjammer-gy.com.
30 very comfy rooms in 2 standards, plus bridal
and apartment suites, breakfast included, a/c,
hot water, Créole and West Indian restaurant,
swimming pool.

$$ Sleepin Guesthouse
151 Church St, Albertown, T223 0991,
www.sleepinguesthouse.com.
A/c, cheaper with fan, some rooms with
kitchenette, Wi-Fi, meals served, also has
car hire. Also $$$ **Sleepin International**,
24 Brickdam, Stabroek, T227 3446, www.
sleepininternationalhotel.com. Slightly better.

$$ Waterchris
184 Waterloo St, T227 1980, waterchris@mail.com.
A/c (supposedly), TV, hot water, phone ($ with
fan), simple and run-down wooden rooms,
some with shared bath next to a noisy TV
lounge, poor plumbing.

$$-$ Hotel Glow
23 Queen St, Kitty, T227 0863.
Clean, a/c or fan, some with TV, 24-hr **Amigo**
restaurant, breakfast extra, taxi or minibus
to centre.

$$-$ Melbourne Inn
29B Sheriff St, Campbellville, T226 7050,
sattie_naraine@yahoo.com.
On this famous street, rooms with and without
a/c, some with kitchen, all with bath, car hire.

$ Rima Guest House
92 Middle St, T225 7401, rima@networksgy.com.
Good central area, well run, modern, popular
with backpackers, no a/c, hot, communal bath
and toilets, good value, internet, safe, mosquito
nets, restaurant (breakfast US$6, lunch/
dinner US$8). Mrs Nellie Singh is very helpful.
Highly recommended, book ahead.

Resorts near Georgetown

$$$$ Arrowpoint Nature Resort
*Contact at R8 Eping Av, Bel Air Park, Georgetown,
T225 9648, or 94-95 Duke St, Kingston,
Georgetown, T231 7220, www.roraimaairways.
com, Facebook: ArrowPointResort.*
In the heart of the Santa Mission Amerindian
reservation, offers a "back to nature experience",
excellent birdwatching, with numerous other
activities such as mountain biking and canoeing.
Transport, meals and activities are all included in
the price. Reserve through **Roraima Airways** or
tour operators (see page 1705).

$$ Pandama Retreat and Winery
*Plot 9 Madewini, Soesdyke/Linden Highway
(just before Splashmin's Fun Park), T654 1865/
627 7063, www.pandamaretreat.com.*
Tucked away in sand forest along the Madewini
Creek, good for relaxation, offers a wide range
of programmes with a spiritual, educational and
artistic focus, aimed at small groups. Breakfast
included. Produces quality wines from local fruit.
Day visit US$5, camping US$15, cabins US$50,
meals US$7.50-10.

New Amsterdam and the Berbice river

$$$-$$ Little Rock Suites
*10 Main St and Church St, T333 2727,
littlerocksuitesgy@yahoo.com.*
Central, rooms of various sizes, a/c, fridge, with
restaurant and **Wine Tavern** and **Eclipse Bar**.

$$ Church View Guest House
*3 Main St and King St, T333 2880,
churchviewhotel@networksgy.com.*
Breakfast extra, room rate includes 1 hr in gym,
a/c, cheaper without, phone, TV, Wi-Fi.

$$ Parkway
4 Main St, T333 6438.
Clean, a/c, safe, with bath, breakfast, lunch and
dinner extra. Recommended.

Berbice resorts

$$ pp Dubulay Ranch
A working ranch on the Berbice river, 147 km
from the river mouth, has forest, savannah and
swamp habitats, with some 300 bird species,
deer, large cats, water buffalo and Dutch colonial
remains. Activities include boat trips, riding,
birdwatching, jeep tours, night-time wildlife
trips. Cheaper rates for scientists or students,
includes 3 meals and soft drinks/juices, but not
transport to the ranch (US$230 return from/to

Georgetown) or activities. Small parties preferred; advance booking essential. Can be booked through any tour operator.

Corriverton

$$ Mahogany
50 Public Rd, Springlands, T335 3525, vicgreene72@yahoo.com.
With bath, TV, fridge, hot water, clean, lunch/dinner available. Recommended.

Others include **$$ Malinmar** (13 Public Rd, Springlands, T333 3328, sandramuniram@yahoo. com), **$$ Riverton Suites** (Lot 78 Springlands, T335 3039, hotelriverton@hotmail.com), and **$ Paraton Inn** (K & L 78, Corriverton, T339 2413).

West from Georgetown: Lake Mainstay

In Charity are **Hotel Purple Heart, Restaurant and Bar** (103-104 Charity, *T771 5209, hotelpurpleheart@yahoo.com)*, and **Xenon** (*190 Charity, T771 4989/629 6231*).

$$$-$$ Lake Mainstay Resort
T226 2975, http://lakemainstayonline.com.
40 cabins with a/c, cheaper without lake view, also single rooms, beachfront on the lake, **Horoshi Restaurant**, bars, swimming, boating, other sports, birdwatching and nature trails, entertainment. All meals available and various all-inclusive packages for 2 to 3 days. The resort can arrange road and boat transport, otherwise go with own transport.

Adel's Rainforest Resort
Akawinni Creek, Pomeroon river, T771 5391/ 696 0574, www.adelresort.com.
In a pristine location 3 hrs from Georgetown, ideal for relaxation and tours of the Pomeroon river and Akawinni Creek, fishing, etc. All-inclusive accommodation with fruit and veg from organic garden.

Border with Venezuela: Mabaruma

$ Kumaka Tourist Resort
Maburama, contact Somwaru Travel Agency, 35 North Rd, Lacytown, Georgetown, T225 9276, or 777 5140, somwarutravelgy@ymail.com.
Meals, bath; offers trips to Hosororo Falls, Babarima Amerindian settlement, rainforest, early examples of Amerindian art.

$ Regional Guest House
T777 5091.
2 rooms with bath or shared bath, clean, book in advance.

Bartica

$$$-$ Platinum Inn International
Lot 7, First Av, T455 3041.
Range of rooms from suite with a/c, cable TV and fridge, to fan and TV, weekend packages available, internet, tours arranged, restaurant and bar.

$$-$ The New Modern Hotel & Nightclub
9 First Av, T455 2301, near ferry.
2 standards of room, with bath and fan. Recommended. Good food, best to book ahead.

Resorts near Bartica

$$$$-$$$ Baganara Island Resort
Beautiful house on Baganara Island in Essequibo river a few miles south of Bartica, T222 8053, http://baganara.net.
Price depends on season and standard of room, full board, private beach, watersports, airstrip; day trips US$85 pp (minimum 12), includes road and boat transport, snacks, lunch, local soft drinks, VAT, activities and guide. Transport to resort from Bartica US$30 pp return.

$$$$-$$$ Hurakabra River Resort
On the west bank of the Essequibo, 5 km from Bartica, about 2 hrs from Georgetown, booking office 1687 Century Palm Gardens, Durban Backlands, Lodge, T226 0240, www. hurakabra.com.
This nature resort has a choice of 2 lodgings, the grand **Mango Tree Villa**, which can sleep 8-10, and **Bamboo Cottage**, for 2 people, both on the waterfront with tropical forest behind, bamboo groves, mango trees and abundant birdlife, many activities included in price, arranges local tours.

Sloth Island Nature Reserve
5 mins by boat from Bartica, T227 5575, www.slothisland.com.
On a forested island with good birdwatching and other wildlife, large, fan-cooled rooms, also hammocks, restaurant, bar, excursions.

Kaieteur National Park

The (**$**) basic guesthouse near the top of the falls, 15 mins' walk from the airstrip, has beds with mosquito nets, hammocks, a kitchen, toilet and cold shower. Enquire and pay first at the **National Parks Commission** (Georgetown, T225 9142). If planning to stay overnight, you must be self-sufficient, whether the guesthouse is open or not; take your own food (and a hammock if the guesthouse is closed), it can be cold and damp at night; the warden is not allowed to collect money.

Linden

$$ Barrow's
82 Dageraad and Manni St, Mackenzie,
T444 6799, dunbarr@networksgy.com.
All double/twin, hot water, a/c, TV, fridge,
popular restaurant and bar below.

$$ Watooka Guesthouse
130 Riverside Drive, Watooka, T444 2162,
watookacomplex@yahoo.com.
In a historic building, old British charm with
a tropical flavour, comfortable a/c rooms
on ground and 1st floors, swimming pool,
restaurant and bar.

$$-$ Morning Star: Star Bonnett Restaurant & Hotel
*671 Industrial Area, 1.5 km out of
town on Georgetown Rd, T444 6505,
morningstar671industrialarea@gmail.com,
see Facebook.*
Various standards of room, all with a/c and TV,
clean, breakfast US$4, good lunches (US$6-12.50).

Iwokrama
There are places to stay at each end of the
Iwokrama reserve, used mainly by bus passengers
on the Georgetown-Lethem route. At the
northern entrance is **Charlie's Rainforest Lodge**
and at the southern end, at the Surama road
junction, is **Madonna's**. At each you can hire a
hammock in a benab for US$2.55, or a simple
room with fan for US$25 (Charlie's) or US$21
(Madonna's, which also serves meals, including
vegetarian, has a shop and electricity). Guests stay
for a few hours' rest on the journey and leave in
time to catch the 1st ferry across the Essequibo.

Note Wi-Fi is available in most of the lodges
in Iwokrama and the Rupununi, but it is supplied
on a monthly basis by satellite and solar power
and use for guests is strictly limited. Follow
instructions given to you by the staff.

$$$$ pp Atta Rainforest Lodge
*http://iwokramacanopywalkway.com
(booking office 141 4th St, Georgetown,
T227 7698, Wilderness Explorers.*
For visits to the Iwokrama Canopy Walkway,
8 rooms with bath, with a bar, dining area and
Wi-Fi, US$5 per hr. Mosquito nets provided,
comfortable beds, good bathrooms. Restaurant
serves breakfast, lunch and dinner, excellent food
(US$15, 20 and 25 respectively if not staying at
the lodge). The overnight trip rate includes entry
to the **Iwokrama Canopy Walkway**, trained
guide, 3 meals.

$$$$ Iwokrama River Lodge
*77 High St, Kingston, Georgetown, PO Box 10630,
T225 1504, http://iwokrama.org and http://
iwokramariverlodge.com.*
The River Lodge is one of the most comfortable
in South America in a beautiful setting on the
banks of the Essequibo, next to pristine forest.
It has 2 types of accommodation, in 8 free-
standing cabins or in rooms in the research
building ($$ or $ pp). The cabins are comfortable,
with bath and veranda. Meals are served in huge
dining research area with a library and bar which
offers alcoholic beverages at extra cost; breakfast
US$8, lunch US$12, dinner US$15. 2-day/1-night
packages are available from US$379-608 pp; price
depends on the number of activities included.

$ Michelle's Island
*On the Georgetown side of the Essequibo ferry
crossing, T639 5716.*
Michelle has a bar serving food and drinks and
she also owns an island bearing her name in the
river where you can stay in cabins if you want to
break the journey, arranges boat trips.

Surama
See page 1696, above.

Rupununi Savannah
The following can be booked independently
online or by phone. Because of limited
communication and the shortage of scheduled
flights, it may be helpful to engage a tour
operator to arrange all transport.

Annai

$$$$ The Rock View Lodge
*Between Annai and Rupertee,
http://rockviewlodge.com.*
Relaxing, comfortable lodge with 8 self-contained
rooms, price includes all meals, all drinks, hot
water, fans, Wi-Fi, laundry and guided tours (horse
riding is extra). Room only is $$$ but Wi-Fi and
meals can be paid for separately (breakfast US$10,
lunch US$15, dinner US$25 without drinks). There
is a natural rock swimming pool and a lookout
point on a rock in attractive gardens. The lodge
is owned and operated by the Edwards family
(Amerindian, Brazilian, British and Basque) who
are proud to represent Guyana's heritage, skills,
local knowledge and personalities. Activities
include nature tours for painting, photography
and birding, regional Amerindian and other local
cooking, culture and agrotourism. Recommended.
Transport can be arranged to/from the
Georgetown–Lethem road and Surama.

Lodges in the Rupunini

$$$$ pp Dadanawa Ranch
Duane and Sandy de Freitas, 96 km south of Lethem, one of the world's largest ranches, each bedroom has a verandah (being upgraded).
Their tour operator, **Rupununi Trails** (T+44-796-152 1951, www.rupununitrails.com), can organize trekking, birding, horse riding and fishing trips, rainforest adventures and camping with *vaqueros*. One of the most spectacular wildlife destinations in South America. Very remote and expensive but a high chance of seeing big cats, other large mammals and the harpy eagle.

$$$$ pp Karanambu Lodge
On the Rupununi river, www.karanambutrustandlodge.org/.
96 km northeast of Lethem, unique old home, 5 cottages with bath (1 suitable for a family), mosquito net, toiletries, good meals, solar energy, small shop selling local handicrafts, fishing, excellent birdwatching and boat rides with guides, including to see Victoria Amazonica flowers which open at dusk, daily giant-anteater spotting trip. 24 km from Yupukari Amerindian village, trips possible. For many years the late Dianne McTurk reared and rehabilitated orphaned giant river otters, and, thanks to her, the population on the river is now healthy. The lodge is now run by Jerry and Melanie McTurk, but there are no otters in residence at Karanambu (2017).

$$$$ Rewa Eco-Lodge
Rewa Village, on the Rupununi river at its junction with the Rewa river, contact through the website, http://rewaecolodge.com.
This lodge is 2-3 hrs by boat from Kwatamang Landing. It is run by the Rewa community and visitors are encouraged to visit the nearby village. 4 bedrooms in 2 *benabs* (shelters) with shared bath and toilets; 4 cabins with en suite facilities (3 more under construction); 1 *benab* with dining room; hammocks, solar lighting. Quietly efficient, immaculately kept, good food. Packages include sport fishing, harpy eagle or wild cats viewing (best Nov-Apr), arapaima spotting, excellent birdwatching, trek up Awarmie Mountain (900 m). 2- and 3-night packages available.

$$$ pp Caiman House Field Station
At Yupukari village on the Rupununi river, www.rupununilearners.org.
A centre principally for black caiman, but also giant river turtle research, plus projects with the community, such as public library and furniture

making. The field station has a guesthouse with simple rooms, the majority en suite. It also has hammock space for US$60 per day. All prices include 3 meals a day, good local food. Guests can go on and participate (in a minor way) in night research trips, walk local trails, go birdwatching and on boat trips and get to know the Yupukari community. All transport and activities cost extra.

Lethem

$$$ Maipaima Eco-Lodge
56 km from Lethem in Nappi village, Kanuku Mountains, T772 2085, http://maipaimaecolodge.com.
Community-run lodge with plenty of wildlife-viewing opportunities, hikes in rainforest and to waterfalls. One of the best activities is the hike to Jordon Falls where you can camp, 4-6 hrs through pristine forest to a waterfall. 2 cabins (with more being built) and a large dining hall, each cabin sleeps up to 8, buildings are elevated and connected by walkways. Hammock accommodation **$**.

$$$ Manari Ranch
20 mins' drive north of Lethem on Manari Creek, T668 2006, Facebook: manariranch, or contact through Wilderness Explorers (page 1706).
Great atmosphere, comfortable rooms and good food, savannah treks, drifts down river and out into the Ireng river, bird- and wildlife watching provided.

$$$ Ori Hotel and Restaurant
118 Lethem, T772 2124, http://origuyana.com.
Self-contained cabins and rooms with Wi-Fi, also has a guesthouse, fridge, restaurant and bar, excellent view of mountains from upper balcony, changes reais to Guyana dollars.

$$$-$$ Rupununi Eco Hotel
51-53 Commercial Area, T623 3060 (Daniel), 644 3201 (Michelle), http://www.rupununiecohotel.com.
Economy, standard and luxury rooms, with breakfast and Wi-Fi, all with a/c, microwave, fridge, luxury rooms have better bathrooms and carpet.

$ pp Savannah Inn
T772 2035 (Georgetown T227 4938), www.savannahguyana.com.
Including breakfast, a/c cabins and rooms with bath, fridge, benab with hammocks, garden, dining room with free fruit, juice and hot drinks,

changes reais into Guyanese dollars, tours arranged, will pick you up from airport or border with prior notice. Advance bookings only.

$ Takutu
430 Lethem, T772 2034.
Simple a/c and fan-cooled rooms, also hammock space, US$5, good value, fridge, clean, all meals extra.

Camps

$$$ Maparri Wilderness Camp
Contact Wilderness Explorers (page 1706) for rates and bookings. It can only be reached by air and river. See also www.rupununitrails.com.
On the Maparri river, in the Kanuku mountains (see page 1697), it is easy to watch macaws, herons, toucans, kingfishers, maybe harpy eagles from this camp. With luck, you can see tayra, labba, ocelot, agouti, monkeys, tapir and even jaguar. Various treks are arranged. Built of wood, with open sides, it has hammocks with mosquito nets. The site overlooks a waterfall; the river water is crystal clear (unlike most rivers in Guyana) and the fall and surrounding pools are safe for swimming. Simple, nutritional meals, and fish from the river, are prepared over an open fire.

Restaurants

Georgetown
A 10% service may be added to the bill. Many restaurants are closed on public holidays. Restaurants are categorized according to their most expensive dishes. All have much cheaper options on the menus.

Sheriff St is some way east of the centre but is 'the street that never sleeps' full of late-night Chinese restaurants, eg **Buddy's Mei Tung Restaurant** (No 137, T231 4100), very good, with nightclub and pool hall, and has some good bars including **Club Monaco** (No 63A, T223 3915) and **Royal Castle** (No 52 at Garnett St), for chicken burgers. Also **Aagman's** (No 28-A, T219 0161) and **Maharaja Palace** (No 207, T219 4346), serve Indian food; while **Antonio's Grille** (No 172 and 5th St, T225 7933) serves both international and local cuisine and **Kamboat** (No 51, T225 8323, delivery T225 8090) is recommended for Chinese.

$$$ Bistro 176
At Halito Hotel, see page 1698.
Restaurant and bar offering local and international cuisine.

$$$ Bottle Bar and Restaurant at Cara Lodge
Very good, pleasant surroundings, must book, also open for breakfast.

$$$ Café Tepuy
R 8 Eping Av, Bel Air Park, T225 9648.
Serves both international and local cuisine.

$$$ Golden Coast
62 Main St and Middle St, T231 7360.
Chinese, good food, huge portions, classy.

$$$ Gravity Lounge
United Center Mall, Camp St and Regent St, T226 8858.
Top-end restaurant and VIP lounge on the 6th floor, panoramic views, popular at weekends, often has Caribbean artistes.

$$$ New Palm Court
35 Main St, T231 8144, Facebook: palmcourtgy. Open 1100-0200.
Bar and restaurant with international and vegetarian food as well as drinks.

$$$ Play Land
American Italiano Family Restaurant, Lot 70, Park St, Enterprise, East Coast Demerara, T229 7100, http://playlanditaliano.net.
Out of town, but a good place to enjoy Italian food in a Guyanese setting.

$$$-$$ Lily's
87C Barrack St, T231 9804, lilysfastfoodcafe@gmail.com.
A whole range of different dishes, from breakfast to traditional, Cajun/Creole, Caribbean, Asian, burgers and sandwiches.

$$$-$$ Tuma Sàlà
249 BB Eccles EBD, T663 2818, Facebook: Tuma Sàlà. Open 0800-2000.
Specializing in Amerindian dishes, including fish, wild meat, cassava bread, vegetables, fruit, juices and indigenous wines and teas. Also has a craft shop.

$$$-$$ Xie Xie
159A West Barr St and Alexander St, T225 7769, Facebook: xiexiecafe.
High-quality food with a great atmosphere, daily lunch specials Mon-Sat from 1130.

$$$-$ Coalpot
Camp St, between Quamina St and Church St.
Good lunches starting at US$1.80, up to US$13.15 (no shorts allowed, cheaper *cafetería*).

$$$-$ New Thriving
Main St, the building before Customs House, T225 0038.
A/c, buffet restaurant with large, oily portions.

$$ Brazil Churrascaria
208 Alexander St, Lacytown, T225 6037.
All you can eat for US$15. Great food.

$$ Church's Chicken
Camp St and Middle St, T225 7546.
For chicken and fries.

$$ Coffee Bean Café and Eatery
133 Church St, South Cummingsburg, T223 2222, Facebook:coffeebean.gy.
For coffees, teas, juices, pastries, breakfasts and lunches of wraps, sandwiches and pastas.

$$ Hibiscus Restaurant and Lounge
91 Middle St, T231 5866, Facebook: HibiscusRestaurantLounge.
Typical sports bar, varied Western menu, outdoor area, popular hang-out bar.

$$ JR Burgers
3 Sandy Babb St, Kitty, T226 6614.
Popular. Also in the City Mall. In the same building is **Silhouette** restaurant and **Altitude Lounge and Bar**, on 3rd floor, same phone, a cocktail bar serving local food. Also a drive-through section next door.

$$ Mario's Pizza
Camp St and Middle St, T231 2639.
Opposite **Church's Chicken**. Variety of pizza.

$$ Popeye's
1e Vissengen Rd and Duncan St, T223 6226.
Serves chicken.

$$ White Castle Fish Shop
21 Hadfield and John St, Werk-en-rust, T223 0921.
Casual open-air bar, for great fried fish and chips. Delivery available.

$$-$ German's
8 New Market St, North Cummingsburg, T227 0079.
Creole food with an emphasis on its traditional soups.

$$-$ Hacks Halaal
5 Commerce St, T226 1844.
Specializes in Creole foods and snacks, local juices.

$$-$ Rayman's Halaal
11-14 Lombard and Princess St, T225 0399.
Halaal restaurant and sweetmeat shop.

$$-$ Shanta's
The Puri Shop, 225 Camp and New Market St, Cummingsburg, T226 4365.
Local cuisine, a wide variety of Indian and African dishes, casual in-house dining or take-away.

$ Oasis Café
125 Carmichael St, South Cummingsburg, T226 9916, www.oasiscafegy.com.
Fashionable and safe, has Wi-Fi access. Serves Creole food, mainly lunch, and has a Fri evening restaurant, **Oasis Paradiso**, T681 1648 for reservations, open 1930-2300 Probably the best coffee in Georgetown. Recommended. Also **Oasis Express** at the Cheddi Jagan International Airport, T261 3016. Sandwiches, snacks, drinks, etc.

$ Upscale
Regent St and Hinck St, T225 4721.
Popular, poetry night Tue, comedy night Fri.

Cafés

Juice Power
Middle St, past the hospital.
Excellent fruit juices, also sells drinking water.

Maggie's Snackette
224 New Market St, Cummingsburg, T226 2226.
Authentic Guyanese food, cakes, pastries and fruit drinks, very popular.

Quizno's
Camp St and Middle St, T225 1527.
Lunches, sandwiches, salads and soups.

Rupununi Savannah

Annai

The Oasis
On the Lethem–Georgetown road, T644 8101, ask for William.
Bar and *churrascaria* restaurant serving Brazilian and Guyanese food, shop. Interesting nature trail in front of the Oasis up a forest-covered hill – sweeping views of the savannah – channel-billed toucans very common.

Lethem
There are a number of eating places, including at hotels and guesthouses. Several sell Brazilian-influenced dishes.

By the airport are **Shirley & Sons**, which is a gift shop and bar, and **Touch Down Bar & Lounge**.

Bars and clubs

Georgetown

There are a number of modern bars, clubs and lounges hosting a variety of parties most nights, popular with Georgetown residents and Guyanese from outside the city. Most nightclubs sell imported, as well as local Banks beer. Don't walk home at night; take a taxi. See under Restaurants, above, for Sheriff St.

704 Sports Bar
Lamaha St and Albert St, Queenstown, T225 0252.
Sports, entertainment and food, also has a night club and **Sky Lounge** on different floors of the building.

The 592 Hub
177 Waterloo St, T227 5701.
With performing arts.

The Vintage Wine and Cheese Lounge
218 Lamaha and Camp St, T231 9631.
Wine and cheese bar with other meals and drinks.

Entertainment

Cinema

2 cinemas also at the **Fun City Arcade** at the **Princess Hotel** (see Ramada Georgetown Princess, page 1698, T265 7212, princessfuncity@ yahoo.com). The Arcade has more than 80 games.

Theatre

There are 2 theatres.

Shopping

Georgetown

The main shopping area is Regent St.

Crafts

Items that are a good buy: Amerindian basketwork, hammocks, wood carvings, pottery, and small figures made out of *balata*, a rubbery substance tapped from trees in the interior. Look for such items in the markets (also T-shirts), or craft shops. **Creations Craft** (Water St); **Amerindian Hostel** (Princess St), **Hibiscus Craft Plaza** (outside General Post Office). Others are advertised in the papers.

Department stores and other shops

Fogarty's and **Guyana Stores** (Church St), both stock a wide range of goods (good T-shirts at the latter).

City Mall, *Regent St and Camp St, T225 6644.* Is a small mall with everything from food to jewellers.

Footsteps Mega Store, *141 Camp St and Regent St, in the United Center Mall.* For a wide range of goods, from clothing to furniture and household items (also at Camp St and Charlotte St and America St and Longden St).

Georgetown Reading and Research Centre, *Woolford Av, in the Critchlow Labour College.* A wide range of books, used and new, at really great prices.

Giftland Mall, *in Turkeyen.* The largest mall in Guyana with 120 concessions, 8 cinemas, restaurants and the largest department store in the Caribbean.

Gold

Gold is sold widely, often at good prices but make sure you know what you are buying. Do not buy it on the street.

Markets

Most Guyanese do their regular shopping at the 4 big markets: **Stabroek** (don't take valuables), **Bourda**, **La Penitence** and **Kitty**.

What to do

Georgetown

The tourism sector is promoting ecotourism in the form of environmentally friendly resorts and camps on Guyana's rivers and in the rainforest. There is much tropical wildlife to be seen. Tours to Amerindian villages close to Georgetown cost US$95-160.

Tour operators

Dagron Tours, *91 Middle St, T223 7921, www. dagron-tours.com.* Well-established company offering adventure and eco-tours within Guyana, including to the Rupununi, to resorts near Bartica, Kaieteur and Orinduik; programmes to the 3 Guianas; tours to Brazil, Venezuela and the Caribbean. Also offer day tours, birdwatching and student field trips.

Evergreen Adventures, *Ogle Aerodrome, Ogle, East Coast Demerara, T222 8053, www.evergreen adventuresgy.com.* Tours on the Essequibo river to Baganara Island, plus bookings for other lodges and tours. Sister company to **Trans Guyana Airways**.

Old Fort Tours, *91 Middle St, T260 4536, www.angcamgy.com/old-fort-fours [sic]*. Tours of Georgetown, Kaieteur, Shell Beach, road and river trips throughout the country.

Rainforest Tours, *5 Av of the Republic and Robb St, T231 5661, www.rftours.com*. Frank Singh, day and overland trips to Kaieteur, Santa Mission, Essequibo/Mazaruni; also Pakaraima Mountain trip, Kukubara to Orinduik, 5 days from one Amerindian village to another.

Roraima Airways, *R8 Eping Av, Bel Air Park, T225 9647, www.roraimaairways.com*. Day trips to Kaieteur and Arrowpoint.

Splashmin's, *48 High St, Werk-en-rust, Georgetown, T223 7301, www.splashmins.com*. A water fun park on the Linden highway, 1 hr from the city, entrance and transportation from Georgetown: adult US$5.10, child US$2.55, children 4 and under free. Also has a resort (**$$$**) and camping grounds.

Torong Guyana, *56 Coralita Av, Bel Air Park, T225 0876/226 5298, toronggy@networksgy.com*. Air, land and river advice and logistical support to all destinations in Guyana, bespoke tours country-wide and excellent trips to Kaieteur.

Wilderness Explorers, *141 Fourth St, Campbellville, T227 7698, www.wilderness-explorers.com. (In London: c/o Claire Antell, 46 Melbourne Rd, London SW19 3BA, T020-8417 1585.)* Offer ready-made or custom-designed itineraries. Tours to all of Guyana's interior resorts, day and overland tours to Kaieteur Falls, horse trekking, hiking and general tours in the Rupununi (agents for **Ranches of the Rupununi**)

and rainforest (trips to **Iwokrama Rainforest Programme** and joint managers of **Iwokrama Canopy Walkway**, see page 1696). Tours also in Suriname, Guyane, Brazil, Venezuela, Barbados, Dominica, St Lucia and Trinidad and Tobago. Specialists in nature, adventure and birdwatching tours. Self-drive 4WD adventures in combination with **Europcar** (see below and page 1722 under Paramaribo), 14 days from US$5565 including all lodges, meals, drinks, excursions and activities as well as the vehicle (can drop vehicle in Lethem and fly back to Georgetown); driver/guide can also be provided. Free tourism information, booklet and advice available. General sales agents for **Air Services Ltd** and **Trans Guyana Airways**. Representatives: North America: T202-630 7689. Europe: Claudia Langer, claudia@wilderness-explorers.com.

Wonderland Tours, *85 Quamina St and Carmichael St, T225 3122, www.wonderland toursgy.com*. Day trips to Kaieteur and Orinduik Falls, Santa Mission, Essequibo and Mazaruni rivers, city tours; special arrangements for overnight stays available, recommended.

Travel agents

Connections Travel, *6 Av of the Republic*.
Frandec, *126 Quamaina St and Carmichael St, opposite Beacon Snackette, T226 3076, www.frandec.com*. Mr Mendoza. Repeatedly recommended (no tours to the interior).
Muneshwers Ltd, *45-47 Water St*.
Survival, *173 Sheriff St, Campbellville, T227 8506, survivaltravelagency@networksgy.com*.

New Amsterdam and the Berbice river

Cortours, *33 Grant, 1651 Crabwood Creek, Berbice, T335 0853/339 2430, cortoursinc@yahoo.com.* Offers package tours to Orealla village, Cow Falls and Wanatoba Falls for overnight visits and peacock bass fishing.

Bartica

B Balkarran, *2 Triangle St, T455 2544.* A good boatman and guide.

Essequibo Adventure Tours, *52 First Av, T455 2441, sbell@guyananet.gy.* Jet boat and tours on the Essequibo/Mazaruni and Cuyuni rivers.

Lethem

Bushmasters Ltd, *Rupununi Whistler, T682 4175, www.bushmasters.co.uk.* Adventure tours, safaris and survival courses, Guyanese guides and British staff.

Georgetown

Minibuses run regularly to most parts of the city, mostly from Stabroek market or Av of the Republic. Collective taxis ply set routes at a fixed fare; they stop at any point on request. Taxis can be taken within and outside the city limits.

Air

Cheddi Jagan International Airport, www. cjairport-gy.com, is at Timehri, 40 km south of Georgetown (a new Arrivals terminal is being built and there are plans to expand the runway). From the airport, take minibus No 42 to Georgetown US$2, 1-1½ hrs (from Georgetown it leaves from next to the Parliament building); for a small charge they will take you to your hotel (similarly for groups going to the airport). A taxi costs from US$25 (use approved airport taxis, T261 2281). Check in 3 hrs before most flights and contact the airline the day before your flight to hear if it has been delayed, or brought forward. Check-in queues can be long and the terminal overcrowded if several flights are scheduled for the same time. There is 1 small canteen and 3 duty-free shops. There is also an exchange house, open usual banking hrs; if closed, there are plenty of parallel traders outside (signboard in the exchange house says what the rate is).

Ogle International Airport, www. ogleairportguyana.com, for internal flights, **LIAT** international flights and most flights to **Suriname**, has immigration and customs facilities. It is 15 mins from Georgetown; taxi US$7.50-10, minibus from Market to Ogle US$0.50. (**Suriname Airways** also have flights to Suriname on Tue and Sat from Cheddi Jagan.)

Flights are often booked up weeks in advance (especially at Christmas and in Aug) and are frequently overbooked, so it is essential to reconfirm an outward flight within 72 hrs of arrival; it is difficult to change your travel plans at the last minute. Foreigners must pay for airline tickets in US$ (most airlines do not accept US$100 bills), or other specified currencies. Luggage should be securely locked as theft from checked-in baggage is common.

Airline offices Caribbean Airlines, 91-92 Av of the Republic and Regent St, T1-800-744 2225, or 261 2202, www.caribbean-airlines.com (to **Port of Spain**, Trinidad, with connections to the **Caribbean** and to **Miami**, direct to **New York** and **Toronto**, plus to **London** in a codeshare with **BA**). **Surinam Airways**, 110 Duke and Barrack St, Kingston, T225 4249, www.flyslm.com (**Suriname–Guyana–Miami** 3 times a week). **TGA**, Ogle, T222 2525, http://transguyana.net, with **GUM Air** (**Georgetown–Paramaribo** daily).

Bus

Within the city, minibuses run regularly to most parts, mostly from Stabroek market or Av of the Republic, fare G$80-140 (US$0.40-0.70, depending on destination) very crowded. It is difficult to get a seat during rush hours. There are regular services by minibuses and collective taxis to most coastal towns from the Stabroek market. Minibuses leave early; arrive before 0700. To **Rosignol**, No 50, US$2; to **Parika**, No 32, US$2.50; to **Linden**, No 43, US$5. Ask other passengers what the fare is.

Car hire

Car hire is available through numerous companies (the Guyana telephone book lists some of them and the rest can be found in the Yellow Pages). **Europcar**, 141 Fourth St, Campbellville, T225 1019/623 0495, www. europcar.com. Rent 4WD and SUVs (see above under **Wilderness Explorers**, page 1706, for fly/ drive packages). **Shivraj**, 98 Hadfield St, Werken-Rust, T226 0550/225 4785, carl@solution.com. US$54.65 plus US$220 deposit.

Taxi

Taxis charge US$2 for short journeys, US$5 for longer runs, with higher rates at night (a safe option) and outside the city limits. Collective taxis ply set routes at a fixed fare; they stop at any point on request. Certain hand signals are used on some routes to indicate the final destination (ask). Special taxis at hotels and airports, marked 'special' on the windscreen, charge about a 3rd more than regular taxis, or you can negotiate a 'by the hour' deal.

Southeast to Suriname

Boat

To **Suriname** A ferry from Moleson, or Crabwood Creek, 13 km south of Springlands, to **South Drain** (40 km south of Nieuw-Nickerie, paved road) the **Canawaima**, T339 2744, runs once or twice daily depending on demand, at 0900 and 1300 (1100 if once a day), check-in 0630-0800 and 1030-1200, US$10 single (US$15 return for 21 days), bicycles free, motorbikes US$5, cars US$30, pick-ups US$40, 30-min crossing. Immigration forms are handed out on board. At the ferry point is a hut/bar where you can buy Suriname dollars.

Bus

To Moleson Creek from the capital for the crossing to **Suriname**, No 63 from opposite Georgetown City Hall, Av of the Republic between Regent St and Charlotte St, leaves when full, US$12.75. This is not a safe area early in the morning, if there are no other passengers waiting take a taxi to Moleson Creek from Georgetown, US$125. **Champ Bus & Taxi Service**, T629 6735, runs taxi service to **Moleson Creek** and a bus to **Paramaribo**. If, by mistake, you get on a bus going only as far as **Springlands**, US$10.25, 15 mins before Moleson Creek, 3-4 hrs, the driver will probably take you for a little extra money (check with the driver in Georgetown where his bus is going); you can also break the journey at New Amsterdam. Entering Guyana, you may be able to join a Paramaribo–Georgetown minibus at Immigration. You have to change buses once across the border; you are given a card to hand to the bus driver in the next country. Direct buses Georgetown–Paramaribo are operated by **Dougla**, T226 2843; they pick up and drop off at hotels. Minibuses to Paramaribo by **Bobby's**, T226 8668, **Lambada**, **Bin Laden**, T264 2993/624 2411, and **Champ** (see above). Fares are US$50-60, not including the ferry crossing; they pick up and drop off at hotels. Check visa requirements for Suriname before travelling.

Border with Venezuela: Mabaruma

Air

ASL flies from Georgetown daily at 0700, return 0800 (in Mabaruma T664 2940/777 5003).

Boat

A ferry runs every other Tue from Georgetown at 1500 (US$8.35) to **Mabaruma**. The journey is surprisingly rough and "you will have to fight for hammock space and watch your possessions like a hawk". For assistance with transport contact Mr Prince through the **Government Guest House**. Boats also go from **Charity** (see page 1694) when there is demand. Ask for Peanut or Gavin. Boats go out to sea so you will get very wet and it can be rough, 6 hrs, costs up to US$100 per boat.

Shell Beach

Air/boat

Fly Georgetown–**Mabaruma**, then take a motorized canoe to **Shell Beach**, 1 hr (good trip in the early morning for birdwatching); lasting 20 mins, it goes from the mouth of the Waini river along coast to Shell Beach camp, which

can be a jolting ride. An alternative route crosses the Demerara and Essequibo rivers, continuing to Charity then taking various boat rides on the Pomeroon and Waina rivers to the Atlantic. Allow 3-4 days. Contact **Wilderness Explorers** and other Georgetown operators, see page 1706. Note that tours to Shell Beach were not running in 2017 owing to flooding.

Bartica

Air

Flight from Ogle to **Bartica** with **TGA** Wed, Fri 0700, 1600, Sun 1600, return 30 mins later (in Bartica T600 9100). The morning flight lands at Baganara only, with a boat connection to Bartica; the afternoon flight lands at Bartica only, with a boat to Baganara if there are passengers to or from Baganara.

Kaieteur and Orinduik Falls

Organized tours

A trip to the **Kaieteur Falls** alone costs US$220-260 with most operators, minimum 5, 8 or 12 people, depending on the aircraft. The other most popular day trip includes 2 hrs at Kaieteur Falls, lunch, drinks, park entrance fee and guide, plus 2 hrs at Orinduik Falls for US$260-290; take swimming gear. Trips depend on the charter plane being filled; there is normally at least 1 flight per week. Cancellations only occur in bad weather or if there are insufficient passengers. Operators offering this service are **Wilderness Explorers** (guarantees flight to Kaieteur Falls for flights booked as part of a package), **Rainforest Tours**, **Air Guyana Tours** and **Wonderland Tours**. Other options are Kaieteur Falls with **Baganara Island Resort** for US$245 pp or with **Arrowpoint** for US$275 pp. To charter a plane privately costs US$1200 to Kaieteur and Orinduik. Scheduled flights are the cheapest but are difficult to organize because you have to ask the airlines in person and the itinerary outward and return depends on what other stops are being made en route. **Air Services Ltd** is most frequent with a shuttle to **Mahdia**, from where flights go to other outlying destinations, eg Kaieteur every 3-4 days; you may have to wait a couple of hours in Mahdia while other destinations are served. A tour without transfers or food, but a local guide, costs US$130-145 pp; flight must be full, last-minute cancellations are not uncommon. Tour operators such as **Dagron Tours** (page 1705), **Rainforest Tours** (page 1706) and **Wilderness Explorers** (page 1706) in Georgetown offer overland trips to Kaieteur. Contact them for details of the route and what is included. Minibuses run daily from Georgetown as far as Mahdia, via Mabura Hill.

Iwokrama

Road

1¼ hrs by road from **Annai** or **Surama**. Coming from **Georgetown**, you have to cross the Essequibo at Kurupukari; ferry runs 0600-1700, hoot for service, US$35 for a car, pick-up or small minibus, US$55 for 15-seat minibus, US$125 truck. The entrances open to coincide with the Georgetown–Lethem buses. At each a passenger manifest is checked to ensure that no one has left the bus in the reserve to hunt. The northern entrance also has a customs point.

On the Rupununi

In 2016 local airlines only provided flights between Georgetown and Lethem, with no intermediate stops. In 2017 **Air Services Ltd** reintroduced a twice-weekly flight to Annai, but on a trial basis only. Transport around the Rupununi is difficult; there are a few 4WD vehicles and some lodges have their own converted Bedford trucks, but moped, bicycle and horse are more common on the rough roads. You can take the Lethem–Georgetown minibuses and get off at Annai, about US$20, 3 hrs from Lethem, or the **Surama** junction (see above).

Annai

Road

The **Rock View Lodge** is an ideal hub for the North Rupununi as it is beside the Annai airstrip, 2 km off the Georgetown–Lethem road, and close to the Rupununi river, offering air, road and river transportation. Rock View–Georgetown by minibus (see under Lethem), or Land Rover US$50-60 return. From Karanambu to Rock View by boat and jeep costs US$380 for up to 4 people, fascinating trip.

Lethem

At the **Rupununi Eco Hotel** (see page 1702), ask for Daniel, the owner, who rents 4WDs and minibuses for charters in the area; phone numbers and email as above.

Air

TGA flies **Georgetown**–Lethem–Georgetown daily at 0800, return 1000, plus Mon, Fri, Sat 1300, return 1500, 1 hr, US$142 one way, US$268 return. It does not make stops on the way. **ASL** have a scheduled service to Lethem daily at 0930, 1½ hrs. **Air Guyana/Wings** flies Georgetown–Lethem–Georgetown Tue, Thu and Sat. Taxis await flight arrivals at Lethem airport.

Road

The road from **Georgetown** to Lethem, 585 km, via Mabura Hill and Kurupukari is now all-weather, but only the 1st 105 km out of Georgetown are paved. It provides a through route from Georgetown to **Boa Vista** (Brazil). After Linden, it runs 100 km to **Mabura Hill**, then 50 km to **Frenchman's Creek** and on to the Essequibo. After the river and Iwokrama the road goes through jungle to the **Surama** road junction, then on to **Wowetta**, the 1st village in the Savannah. Then the road crosses the **Rupununi**. Minibuses leave when full for Lethem at 1800 (check in at 1700), US$50-60 one way; most can be found on Church St between Cummings St and Light St. Reliable service is provided by **P and A**, and by **Carlie's** (Robb St and Oronoque St, T699 1339, or 616 5984 (Carly), 617 1339 (Cindy). Most are Mon-Sat, but **Guy Braz**, 28 Sheriff St, Campbellville, T231 9752/3, guybraz_cindy@yahoo.com, operate every day. They take the 0600 ferry over the Essequibo and reach Lethem in the early afternoon. They leave Lethem from their own depots at 1800, stop at **Madonna's** (see page 1701) at 2100, then depart at 0330 to catch the first ferry at **Kurupakari**.

Border with Brazil

The simplest way to cross the border from Lethem is to take a taxi from the town or airport to Guyanese immigration. The vehicle waits while you get your stamp and then takes you across the bridge to Polícia Federal, US$10 for the journey. Guyanese cars are not allowed to go further into Brazil. Taxi drivers may help with changing money from Guyanese dollars to reais (rates for US dollars are poor). If there is no bus waiting at Polícia Federal going to **Boa Vista**, there are cars going to **Bonfim Rodoviária**, or to the **CoopBom** shared taxi company.

Suriname

The main attractions of Suriname are the tropical Amazonian flora and fauna, historic Paramaribo and the ethnic diversity in this sparsely populated country. Much of the interior is untouched and largely uninhabited. Infrastructure is limited, so most tourist lodges, Amerindian and Maroon villages can only be reached by small boat or plane.

Paramaribo *Colour map 2, B5. See map, page 1714.*

historic buildings and a colourful market

★The capital and main port lies on the Suriname river, 12 km from the sea. There are many beautiful colonial buildings in Dutch (neo-Normanic) style on the waterfront and central streets whose fusion of European architecture and South American craft led to the historic centre's UNESCO listing. Much of the historic centre, dating from the 19th century, and the religious buildings have been restored. The city has an intriguing mixture of cultures and an energetic nightlife.

Sights

Fort Zeelandia houses the **Suriname Museum** ① *T425871, www.surinaamsmuseum.net, Tue-Fri 0900-1400, Sun 1000-1400, US$2.75, free guided tours Sun 1030, 1200, has a café and shop.* All the historic buildings in the complex are open to the public. The fort itself now belongs to the **Stichting (foundation) Surinaams Museum** and is part of the Guiana Shield exchange programme ① *http://amazonian-museum-network.org.* It is full of interesting items, archaeological and cultural, up to the present day. The wooden officers' houses in the same complex have been restored as well. The 19th-century Roman Catholic **St Peter and Paul Basilica** (1885), built entirely of wood, is one of the largest wooden buildings in the Americas. This twin towered neo-Gothic building with rose windows is both impressive and beautiful. The interior is a delightful play of light on different tones of bare timber. One of the Caribbean's largest **mosques** is on Keizerstraat (make an appointment to visit). Next to it is one of the city's two synagogues: **Neve Shalom** (1835-1837), at Keizerstraat 88 (appointment needed to visit), and **Zedek v' Shalom** (1735) on the corner of Klipstenstraat and Heerenstraat. The latter is no longer used as a synagogue, but houses businesses; see www.surinamejewishcommunity.com/synagogues. Also worth seeing are the **Hindu temples** of **Arya Dewakar** on Wanicastraat and **Shri Vishnu Mandir** on Koningstraat. The **Numismatisch Museum** ① *Mr FHR Lim A Postraat 7, T520016, www.cbvs.sr/museum/numis-intro.htm, Mon-Fri 0800-1400,* displaying the history of Suriname's money, is operated by the Central Bank.

On Onafhankelijkheidsplein (Independence Square, originally called Oranjeplein), near Fort Zeelandia, stand the **Presidential Palace** (formerly the Governor's Mansion) and the **Ministry of Finance**, with an octagonal tower. On Sunday mornings you can see birdsong competitions here, a popular custom throughout Suriname. Men carrying their songbird (usually a small black *twa-twa*) in a cage are frequently seen; they may be on their way to and from work or just taking their pet for a stroll. Behind the Presidential Palace is the palm-tree-filled **Palmentuin** ① *0700-2200,* with a bandstand.

From Fort Zeelandia you can walk past the fine buildings on Water Kant to an area by the waterfront with handicraft stalls and the food stands known as *warungs* (see page 1719). Beyond is De Waag restaurant at the foot of Keizerstraat and the area where buses congregate and pirogues wait to ferry people over the river to Meerzorg. Further still is the **Central Market** ① *Mon-Fri 0700-1700, Sat*

> **Tip...**
> Head for Mr F H R Lim A Postraat if you wish to see what Paramaribo looked like only a comparatively short time ago.

Best for

Multiculturalism ▪ Tropical scenery ▪ Turtles

Essential Suriname

Finding your feet

The airport is 47 km south of Paramaribo. Most buses congregate in a chaotic area near the Central Market.

Getting around

There are a few regular bus services from Paramaribo. Private taxis can be expensive; shared taxis are a common way to get around. Car hire is available. Beyond the road network, river boats are the only means of transport, except where charter flights serve communities.

Tip...

In Paramaribo there are many ATMs and cambios for changing euros and dollars into Suriname dollars.

Safety

In Paramaribo, although it is reasonably safe, it's still wise to be cautious after dark and take care around the markets and docks.

Fact...

National dress is normally only worn by the Asians on national holidays and at wedding parties, but some Javanese women still go about in sarong and klambi.

Fact file
Location 5.8333° N, 55.1667° W
Capital Paramaribo
Time zone GMT -4 hrs
Telephone country code +597
Currency Suriname dollar (SRD)

When to go

The climate is tropical and moist, but not very hot, since the northeast trade wind makes itself felt throughout the year. In the coastal area the temperature varies on an average from 23° to 31°C, during the day; the annual average is 27°C and on a monthly basis it ranges from 26° to 28°C. The average annual rainfall is about 2340 mm for Paramaribo and 1930 mm for the western division. The seasons are: small rainy season from November to February; small dry season from February to April; large rainy season from 3pril to August; large dry season from August to November. Neither one of these seasons is, however, either very dry or very wet. The degree of cloudiness is fairly high and the average humidity is 82. The climate of the interior is similar but with higher rainfall. The high seasons, when everything is more expensive, are 15 March to 15 May, July to September and 15 December to 15 January.

Time required

Allow one to two weeks to explore.

Weather Paramaribo					
January 30°C 23°C 198mm	**February** 30°C 22°C 126mm	**March** 31°C 22°C 111mm	**April** 31°C 23°C 186mm	**May** 31°C 24°C 286mm	**June** 31°C 23°C 316mm
July 31°C 23°C 226mm	**August** 32°C 23°C 186mm	**September** 32°C 23°C 100mm	**October** 33°C 23°C 106mm	**November** 32°C 23°C 112mm	**December** 31°C 23°C 192mm

till 1400, with fruit, vegetables, fish, etc, downstairs, clothes and hardware upstairs. Almost next to it is the **Vreedzaam Market** (witches' or Maroon market) for medicinal herbs, remedies and potions. It's best to go with a local to explain things. There is a **Javanese market** area on Jozef Israelstraat in northern Paramaribo and a **Chinese market** on Tourtonnelaan, both on Sunday morning.

An interesting excursion for a half or full day is to take a city bus, or taxi, past Stinasu and the Courtyard Marriott to **Leonsberg**, a northeastern suburb of Paramaribo on the Suriname river (restaurants overlook the water). Here you can take a dolphin tour (see What to do, page 1721) or other river tours.

Alternatively, a ferry crosses the river to Nieuw-Amsterdam, the capital of the predominantly Javanese district of **Commewijne** at the confluence of Suriname and Commewijne rivers. There's an open-air **museum** ① *open Mon-Fri 0900-1700, weekends 1000-1800, US$0.85, over 60s and under 9s half price*, inside the old fortress that guarded the rivers' confluence. The Leonsberg ferry goes to within walking distance of the fort. From Nieuw-Amsterdam you can return to Paramaribo over the spectacular, steeply raked **Jules Wijdenbosch bridge** at **Meerzorg**, which has wonderful views eastwards by day and over the city lights at night. Below is the city's main port for commercial shipping. To get to Nieuw-Amsterdam by bus, take any bus from Paramaribo over the Meerzorg bridge, US$0.15, ask to be let out at the junction of Commissaris Thurkowweg and then catch a bus towards Mariënburg, US$0.20. Again, ask where to get off and walk 1 km to the fort. There are also ferries from Paramaribo, near the bus station, to Meerzorg. A taxi between Paramaribo and Nieuw-Amsterdam costs US$10.

Outside Paramaribo

old plantations and wildlife encounters aplenty

West of Paramaribo

A narrow but paved road leads through the citrus- and vegetable-growing areas of **Wanica** and **Saramacca**, linked by a bridge over the Saramacca river. At Boskamp (90 km from Paramaribo) is the **Coppename river**. The Coppename bridge crosses to **Jenny** on the west bank. The Coppename Estuary is the 12,000-ha Coppenamemonding Nature Reserve, a RAMSAR site protecting many shorebird colonies, mangrove and other (see www.ramsar.org and www.whsrn.org).

A further 50 km is **Totness**, where there was an early 19th-century Scottish settlement. It is the largest village in the Coronie district, along the coast between Paramaribo and Nieuw-Nickerie on the Guyanese border. There is a good government guesthouse. The road (liable to flooding) leads through an extensive forest of coconut palms. The **Bigi-Pan** area (68,320 ha, see www.whsrn. org) comprises lagoons, mangroves and mudflats and is a birdwatchers' paradise. Boats may be hired from local fishermen. METS includes Bigi Pan in its two-day tours to **Nickerie**, US$252, other agencies US$105-160 for two days, US$165-190 for three days.

Nieuw-Nickerie on the south bank of the Nickerie river 5 km from its mouth, opposite Guyana, is the main town and port of the Nickerie district, distinguished for its rice fields. It's a clean, ordered town with a sizeable East Indian population and a lot of mosquitoes.

Border with Guyana

Ferry to Moleson Creek (for Springlands) From South Drain/Canawaima (Suriname, 40 km from Nieuw-Nickerie, excellent road) to Moleson/Crabwood Creek (Guyana), it's a 30-minute trip on the ferry. Immigration forms are handed out on the boat. Queues can be long and slow to enter Suriname. Suriname is one hour ahead of Guyana. If entering Suriname from Guyana, you can change money at a hut at the ferry point or, failing that, at one of several banks in Nieuw-Nickerie. On departure, you can change Suriname dollars into Guyanese or US dollars at Corriverton or in Georgetown. The Guyanese embassy in Paramaribo is at Henck Arronstraat 82, T477895, guyembassy@sr.net, and the consulate in Nieuw-Nickerie is at Gouveneur Straat and West Kanaal Straat 10, T211019, guyconsulnick@sr.net.

Blanche Marie Falls, 320 km from Paramaribo on the road to Apoera on the Corantijn river, is a popular destination. **Washabo** near Apoera, which has an airstrip, is an Amerindian village. No public transport runs from Paramaribo to the Apoera-Bakhuis area, but operators run tours to Blanche Marie and Apoera, from US$345-370 per person for four days, US$475 for five days, minimum five people (www.blanche-marie.com) and there are charter flights to the Washabo airstrip. Irregular small boats sail from Apoera to Nieuw-Nickerie and to Springlands (Guyana).

East of Paramaribo to Guyane

Leaving the traffic jams of Paramaribo behind, the main highway crosses the Meerzorg bridge (see page 1713) and runs through eastern Suriname to Albina on the border with Guyane, passing through the districts of Commewijne and Marowijne. There are some interesting plantation estates left in the Commewijne district. A popular site near the junction of main road to Albina and the road to Nieuw-Amsterdam is the **Peperpot Nature Park** ① *T354547, Facebook: peperpotnaturepark, open daily 0800-1700, US$3.20*, a former cacao and coffee estate with nature trails and a historic plantation village. Tours from Paramaribo cost US$41-77, by bus or bicycle; buses from Meerzorg daily 0600-0900 and 1300-1800, none on Sunday, US$0.15, 10 minutes.

Frederiksdorp ① *www.frederiksdorp.com*. Dating from around 1760, Frederiksdorp is a beautiful plantation close to the Commewijne river. It can be reached by ferry from Mariënburg (US$4 for the boat); journey time from Paramaribo one hour. The old buildings are a World Heritage Site and have been converted into hotel accommodation. New bungalows have also been built. The restaurant serves local food with a European touch. There is a swimming pool with a wooden deck. About 10 minutes' walk away is the Hindustani and Moslem village of **Johanna en Margaretha**, with bars and eating places. From here boat trips go into the 'swamps', or former paddy fields, which is a great area for birdwatching. Beyond the swamps boats can go all the way to the beach at Matapica (see below), where turtles can be seen nesting (mosquitoes can be a problem at dusk). A three-day/two-

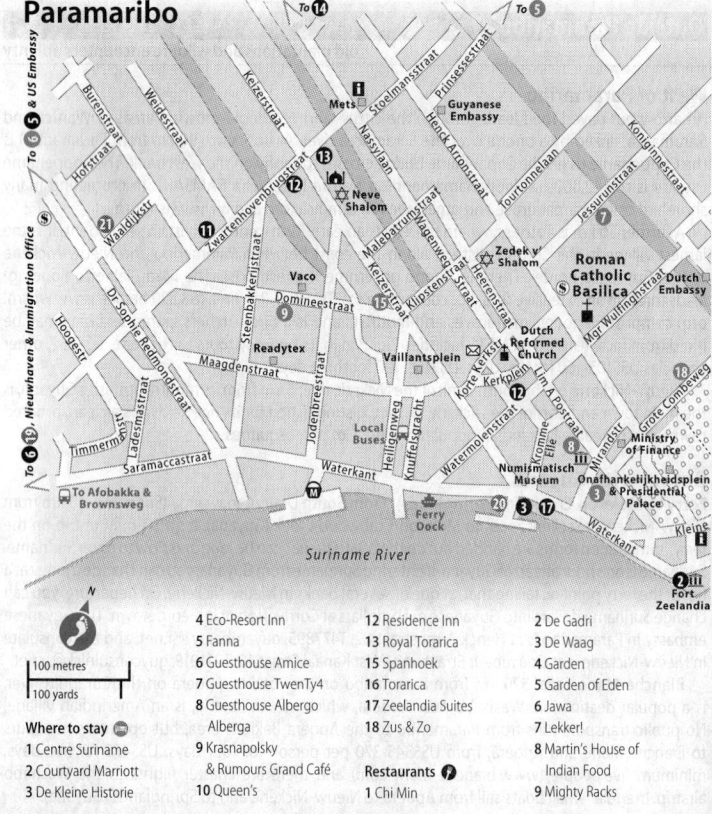

Paramaribo

To ⑭   To ⑤

To ⑥ ⑤ & US Embassy

To ⑥ ⑤ & Nieuwhaven & Immigration Office

Mets

Guyanese Embassy

Neve Shalom

Zedek y' Shalom

Roman Catholic Basilica

Dutch Embassy

Vaco

Domineestraat

Readytex

Maagdenstraat

Vaillantsplein

Dutch Reformed Church

Kerkplein

Local Buses

Ministry of Finance

To Afobakka & Brownsweg

Saramaccastraat

Waterkant

Numismatisch Museum

Onafhankelijkheidsplein & Presidential Palace

Ferry Dock

Suriname River

Kleine

Fort Zeelandia

N

100 metres
100 yards

Where to stay 🛏
1 Centre Suriname
2 Courtyard Marriott
3 De Kleine Historie
4 Eco-Resort Inn
5 Fanna
6 Guesthouse Amice
7 Guesthouse TwenTy4
8 Guesthouse Albergo Alberga
9 Krasnapolsky & Rumours Grand Café
10 Queen's
12 Residence Inn
13 Royal Torarica
15 Spanhoek
16 Torarica
17 Zeelandia Suites
18 Zus & Zo

Restaurants 🍴
1 Chi Min
2 De Gadri
3 De Waag
4 Garden
5 Garden of Eden
6 Jawa
7 Lekker!
8 Martin's House of Indian Food
9 Mighty Racks

night package costs US$370, including all transfers, meals, excursions and activities (except turtle watching). If you don't want to stay at Frederiksdorp, there are day cycle tours costing about US$60.

Wia-Wia Nature Reserve The northeast coast of Suriname is known as a major nesting site for sea turtles (five species including the huge leatherback turtle come ashore to lay their eggs). Wia-Wia Nature Reserve protects 36,000 ha and is especially rich in nesting grounds for local and migratory birds (see www.whsrn.org). Sea turtles used to nest here, but the beaches and turtles have shifted westwards out of the reserve to the Matapica area. Turtles can be observed from February to mid-August, but different species arrive at different times (April to June are the best months to visit as you can see adults coming ashore to lay eggs and hatchlings rushing to the sea at high tide). **Jenny Tours** ① *Waterkant 5c (in Broki), Paramaribo, T885 8495, http://suriname-tour.com,* offers two-day tours which cost US$100 per person, minimum two people. Suitable waterproof clothing should be worn.

The main road goes through **Tamanredjo** to the bridge over the Commewijne near Sigaripabo. Just beyond is a police checkpoint at **Stolkertsijver**. The road is in good condition, continuing through forest to **Albina** on the Marowijne river, a small town with shops, a market and restaurants.

Galibi Nature Reserve ① *US$2.75 entrance fee, local guide US$10/day.* From Albina it is a two-hour boat trip (including 30 minutes on the open sea) to **Galibi**. Here you can stay at **Stinasu's Warana Lodge**, which has cooking facilities, a refrigerator, rooms with shower and toilet, powered mostly by solar energy. Make arrangements through Stinasu or operators who run all-inclusive, two- and three-day tours from February to September, US$160-200 per person, minimum three (see Stinasu, page 1721, www.galibi-suriname.com or tour operators' websites); METS charges US$245 for two days, US$294 for three days; **Myrysji Tours** ① *Crommelinstraat 31, Paramaribo, T422550, www.galibi-tours.com,* have tours staying at their own lodge at **Christiaankondre** at the mouth of the Marowijne river.

Border with Guyana Customs and immigration on both sides close at 1900, but in Albina staff may leave by 1700. Boats across the river to St-Laurent du Maroni, Guyane, leave from two places: the Bac car ferry is the official crossing; unofficial pirogues leave from another dock close by (see Transport, page 1722). Whatever craft you take to enter Suriname, you must get your passport stamped at immigration at the Bac terminal. **Note** You must obtain a tourist card in advance from the consulate in Cayenne or St-Laurent; if you need a visa, check regulations before arrival. Likewise in St-Laurent, where there are two different docks, immigration is at the Bac terminal. There is an official *cambio* in Albina, Imex, outside the Bac/immigration terminal, which changes dollars, euros and Suriname dollars (opens at 0800). Since there is no legal money exchange in St-Laurent, if you have no euros get them here when crossing to Guyane. Suriname dollars are not recognized in Guyane.

South of Paramaribo

About 5 km from the **International Airport** there is a resort called **Colakreek** ① *Facebook: colakreek,*

10 Pannekoek en Poffertjes Café	**18** Zanzibar
11 Power Smoothie	
12 Roopram Rotishop	**Bars & clubs** 🎵
13 Roti Joosje	**19** Ballroom Energy
14 Spice Quest	**20** Broki
15 't Vat	**21** Touché
16 Tangelo	**22** Zuid
17 Warungs	

US$2.75 day visit for adults, reductions for children, pay extra for picnic sites, cabins, etc, so named for the colour of the water, but good for swimming (busy at weekends), lifeguards, water bicycles, children's village, restaurant, bar, tents or huts for overnight stay. It is managed by METS and there are plenty of package tours and combinations available; www.mets.sr. The village of **Bersaba**, 40 km from Paramaribo close to the road to the airport, is a popular area for kayaking trips at Coropina.

Santigron About 30 km southwest of Paramaribo, via **Lelydor**, is the Maroon village of **Santigron**, on the east bank of the Saramacca river. A community tourism project, **Santigron Experience** ⊕ *T874 6610, www.santigron.com*, organizes one-day tours, with a boat trip on the Saramacca river, or a cultural dance performance, US$60-85. They also offer two-day tours for US$170. You can also stay in B&B accommodation with dinner for US$48 per person. Minibuses leave Paramaribo for Santigron at 0530 and 1500, two hours, US$0.40. They return as soon as they have dropped off passengers in the village, so make sure you will have a bus to return on. Nearby is the Amerindian village of **Pikin Poika**. These two villages make a good independent day trip.

Jodensavanne and around Jodensavanne (Jews' Savannah, established 1639), south of Paramaribo on the opposite bank of the Suriname river, is where three cemeteries and the foundations of one of the oldest synagogues in the Western Hemisphere, have been restored (www.jodensavanne.sr.org). You can also visit the healing well. It is one to 1½ hours with a suitable vehicle; the road can be bad in the rainy season. The route is via the Martin Luther Kingweg to **Powakka**, about 90 minutes south of the capital, an Amerindian village of thatched huts and a small church. The road goes east to the ferry across the Suriname river at **Carolina**, then to **Redi Doti** near Jodensavanne. Tours to Jodensavanne cost from US$87 by boat, or US$75-115 by bus or car. **Blakawatra** is a beautiful creek with recreational facilities, not far from Jodensavanne, included in some tours (full day about US$100). Cassipora bus from Saramaccastraat in Paramaribo goes by Blakawatra and near the Carolina ferry at 0830 daily except Saturday, two hours one way, return also at 0830.

Brokopondo Reservoir You can continue by bus or car to **Afobakka**, south of Powakka, where there is a large dam on the Suriname river. Behind it is the Brokopondo reservoir, or W J van Blommestein Meer, built in the 1960s to provide electricity for the bauxite industry. Bus Paramaribo (Saramaccastraat, near Tropicana Casino) to Afobakka, three hours, US$1.05, at 0600 and 1300, 0830 on Sunday, and to Brokopondo at 0700 and 1330, none on Sunday, US$1.20, three hours. Near Brokopondo is the **Bergendal Eco & Cultural River Resort** ⊕ *Domineestraat 39, Paramaribo, T475050, www.bergendalresort.com;* book online, or via the Hotel Krasnopolsky, 85 km/1½ hours by road and river from the capital. Day visits and overnight stays in three types of comfortable cabins are offered. Activities include canopy zip-line, hiking, mountain bikes, kayaking and nature tours.

Brownsberg National Park ⊕ *US$2.75, guide US$9.75.* An hour by car from Brokopondo, are the hills of Brownsberg National Park which overlook the **Brokopondo lake**. It features good walking to four waterfalls. There are ample chances to see wildlife (it includes 400 species of bird). Stinasu manages the facilities and it, and other tour operators, run all-inclusive tours from Paramaribo (two-day tours from US$150, price includes transport, accommodation, food and guide; one-day tour with an agency costs from US$65-94). Independent visits are possible, but you must pay the entrance fee, and arrange accommodation in advance at Stinasu's guesthouses, campsite or hammock place (from US$5.50 camping to US$8.50 for a bed). Take your own food. If not in your own car, take the Afobakka bus, as above, to the village of **Brownsweg** (US$1.05, three hours) and ask for a car to take you to Brownsberg, or walk 7 km. **Tukunari Island** is a two-hour canoe ride from the Afobakka dam. The island is near the village of **Lebi Doti**, where Aucaner Maroons relocated when the reservoir waters rose.

The road south of Brownsberg ends at **Pokigron** (also called Atjoni). Beyond here progress up the Suriname river is by boat. Several tour operators organize stays in lodges (see page 1721).

Saramacca villages and Awarradam There are many **Saramacca villages** along the Gran Rio and Pikin Rio, both Suriname river tributaries. These are fascinating places, set up in the 17th and 18th centuries by escaped slaves, originally from Ghana, who preserve a ceremonial language, spirituality and traditions. METS has a comfortable lodge on the Gran Rio at **Awarradam**, in front of a beautiful set of rapids in thick forest, and many other agencies organize culturally sensitive tours to the villages. Independent visitors are also welcome.

In the far south of Suriname are a series of dramatic granite mountains rising out of pristine forest. The highest is **Mount Kasikasima** (718 m), near the Trio and Wajana Amerindian village of **Palumeu** on the Upper Tapanahony river. METS has a comfortable river lodge here and visitors learn about the lifestyle of the villagers. They and other operators also organize expeditions to the mountain, which involve a two-day boat trip and a strenuous six- to seven-hour climb, rewarded by incredible views over the rainforest. METS tours to Awarradam are four to five days, US$645 per person (from US$570 with other agencies); Awarradam and the Gran Rio river jungle camp, five days US$675; Palumeu, four to five days, US$645 with METS, from US$570 with other agecies; Kasikasima, five days, US$845; Kasikasima, eight days, US$895. Combinations of Awarradam and Palumeu and Awarradam and Kasikasima are available.

★**Central Suriname Nature Reserve** This reserve (1.592 million ha – 9.7% of Suriname's total land area) is now part of the UNESCO's World Heritage list. Raleigh/Voltzberg Reserve has been joined with Tafelberg and Eilerts de Haan reserves to create this enormous area, some of which is yet to be explored. **Raleighvallen/Voltzberg Nature Reserve** ① *US$2.75 for the 1st night, US$1.35 for each following night*, covering 78,170 ha, is a rainforest park, southwest of Paramaribo, on the Coppename river. It includes **Foengoe (Fungu) Island** in the river and **Voltzberg** peak. Climbing the mountain (240 m) at sunrise is an unforgettable experience. The reserve can be reached by air or by road (180 km, four hours) followed by a three- to four-hour boat ride. Tourist facilities are on Foengoe Island, to which **Stinasu** do four-day tours, all-inclusive with transport, food and guides from US$320 (www.raleighvallen.com). Other operators go through Stinasu.

Listings Suriname *map p1714*

Tourist information

Suriname Tourist Foundation
Main office JF Nassylaan 2, T424878, www. surinametourism.sr. Mon-Fri 0730-1500. Branch offices at the Zeelandia Complex, T479200. Mon-Fri 0800-1330, and Johan Adolf Pengel airport.

Where to stay

Service charge at hotels is 5-10%.

Paramaribo

$$$$-$$$ Courtyard Marriott
Anton Dragtenweg 52-54, T456000, www.marriott.com/pbmcy.
About 1 km from Torarica on the road towards Leonsberg, not possible to walk beside the river, so take a taxi or the hotel's shuttle bus to Krasnapolsky. 5 types of room, all spacious and comfortable, with pool, gym, live music, both restaurants have a dedicated kitchen, **Martini'Bar** cocktail lounge, popular.

$$$$-$$$ Krasnapolsky
Domineestraat 39, T475050, www.krasnapolsky.sr.
A/c, in business district, 4 standards of room, travel agency, shopping centre, good breakfast and buffet, 5 eating options, swimming pool with bar with view over city, business centre and conference facilities, airport shuttle.

$$$$-$$$ Torarica
Mr Rietbergplein 1, T471500, www.torarica.com.
One of the best in town, pleasant, family-oriented resort, book ahead, swimming pool and other sports facilities, sauna, casino, tropical gardens, pier over the river, a/c, 2 restaurants (**Plantation Room** for lunch and dinner, local and international food; **The Edge**, for drinks and snacks, open 0900-0100), also has **The Lounge** for drinks and snacks, Sun-Thu 1000-2400, Fri-Sat 1000-0130; good poolside buffet on Fri evening, superb breakfast.

$$$ Eco-Resort Inn
Cornelis Jongbawstraat 16, T425522, www.ecoresortinn.com.
Part of **Torarica** group with use of the resort facilities, good atmosphere and value, breakfast included, restaurant (**$$**), bar, helpful staff, business centre.

$$$ Queen's
Kleine Waterstraat 15, T474969, www.queenshotelsuriname.com.
Including breakfast, service charge and tax. A/c, 3 types of room, fitness centre, minibar, Garden restaurant and bar below (10% discount for guests) and **Euphoria** nightclub.

$$$ Residence Inn
Anton Dragtenweg 7, T521414, www.residenceinn.sr.

Minibar, laundry, including breakfast, in a residential area, pool, tennis court, a/c bar and **Matutu** restaurant, European and Surinamese food (**$$**), airport transfer.

$$$ Royal Torarica
Kleine Waterstraat 10, T473500,
www.royaltorarica.com.
Sister hotel of **Torarica**. More for business than leisure, but comfortable rooms, river view, pool and other sports facilities, lobby restaurant.

$$$ Spanhoek
Domineestraat 2-4 (entrance on Keiserstraat),
T477888, www.spanhoekhotel.com.
Boutique hotel in business district, funky, trendy decor, lovely bathrooms, continental breakfast with Surinamese delicacies, restaurant on 1st floor. Always ask about discounts if visiting in person, also long-term rentals. Has sidewalk café, **Terras**, for drinks and snacks. There is a cambio in the same building.

$$$-$$ Zeelandia Suites
Kleine Waterstraat 1a, T424631,
www.zeelandiasuites.com.
Smart, business-style suites with comfy rooms and all mod cons in same precinct as **'t Vat**.

$$ Guesthouse Albergo Alberga
Lim A PoStraat 13, T520050, www.
guesthousealbergoalberga.com.
Central, in a 19th-century house, pleasant, terrace and TV area, simple, spotless rooms, a/c or fan (cheaper), breakfast extra, pool, good value, book in advance. Steep spiral staircase to 1st floor.

$$ Guesthouse Amice
Gravenberchstraat 5 (10 mins from centre),
T434289, www.guesthouse-amice.sr.
Quiet area, room with balcony more expensive, a/c, comfortable, breakfast, airport transfer and tours available.

$$ Hotel Centre Suriname
Van Sommelsdijck-straat 4, T426310,
www.hotelcentresuriname.com.
A/c, good value, convenient, several places to eat nearby, parking.

$$ Zus & Zo
Grote Combeweg 13a, T520905, www.
twenty4suriname.com/zusenzo.html.
In a large green colonial building opposite Palmentuin, small but functional rooms, shared bath, cheaper with fan, use of washing machine, no kitchen but has a popular café open daily 0800-2300, arts and crafts centre, special events

most nights. In same group as **Guesthouse TwenTy4** and **Fiets** cycle agency.

$$-$ De Kleine Historie
Dr JC De Mirandastraat 8, T521007,
www.dekleinehistorieguesthouse.com.
Guesthouse with rooms for up to 6 with a/c and one dorm for 6 in bunks with fan (US$12 per bed), shared bath, breakfast included. Balconies, sitting room, cooking lessons (but no kitchen), very convenient for historic centre, clean, simple, very welcoming and helpful.

$$-$ Guesthouse TwenTy4
Jessurunstraat 24, T420751,
http://twenty4suriname.com.
Big pale blue-and-white house, simple but well-maintained rooms, cheaper with shared bath and fan, bar, buffet breakfast extra, Wi-Fi, pleasant, "backpackers' paradise".

$ Fanna
Prinsessestraat 31, T476789,
www.appartementsuriname.com.
From a/c with bath to basic, breakfast extra, safe, family-run, pool, kitchen, washing machine, English spoken.

West of Paramaribo

$$$ Residence Inn
R P Bharosstraat 84, Nieuw Nickerie, T210950,
www.residenceinn.sr.
Best in town, prices higher at weekend, central, a/c, bath, hot water, laundry, good restaurant (**Matutu, $$**), bar.

$ Ameerali
Maynardstraat 32-36, Nieuw Nickerie, T231212.
A/c, good, restaurant (**$$**) and bar.

South of Paramaribo

$$$$ De Plantage
Km 23.5 on the east–west road at Tamanredjo,
Commewijne, 40 mins from Paramaribo, T356567,
www.deplantagecomme wijne.com.
Price is for 2-night stay. Lovely chalets for 2-4 on an old cocoa plantation, restaurant, pool, jungle walks and observation tower, bicycles for rent. Transfer from Paramaribo US$21.50.

$$$ Overbridge River Resort
1 hr south of the capital, via Paranam (30 km),
then 9.5 km to Powerline mast 20-21, then 7.5 km
to resort, or 60 km by boat down Suriname
river. Reservations, Oude Charlesburgweg 47,
Paramaribo, T422565, www.overbridge.net.

Cabins by the river and a white-sand beach, price includes breakfast, weekend and other packages available and tours to nearby sights such as Jodensavanne and Brownsberg.

Lodges on the Upper Suriname river

$$$ Anaula Nature Resort
Wagenwegstraat 55, Paramaribo, T410700, www.anaulanatureresort.com.
A comfortable resort near the Ferulassi Falls about 1 hr's boat trip from Pokigron village, 4 hrs' drive from Paramaribo (or reached by air). It has lodges for 2-5 people, cold water, restaurant and bar, swimming pool; activities include forest and Maroon village excursions; 3- and 4-day packages from US$255-300 pp, all inclusive.

$$$ Danpaati River Lodge
Prinsessestraat 37, T471113, www.danpaati.net (in the same group as Access Suriname Travel and Frederiksdorp – see page 1721).
On an island, 345 km south of Paramaribo, Danpaati offers 3- and 4-day packages, from US$356-420 in bungalows ranging from luxury to family and double cabins. Closely associated with the village of Dan, where visitors can get involved in workshops, etc, genuine community experience, very friendly, excursions to the forest and on the river, yoga classes, swimming pool.

Restaurants

Paramaribo
There are some good restaurants, mainly Indonesian and Chinese. Most international-style places and several bars are in the Kleine Waterstraat/Van Sommelsdijkstraat area, opposite the Torarica.
Blauwgrond, north of the city, near Leonsberg, is the area for typical, cheap, largely Indonesian food, served in *warungs* (Indonesian for restaurants). Try a *rijsttafel* in a restaurant such as **Sarinah** (open-air dining), Verlengde Gemenelandsweg 187, T430661, see Facebook. Foodstalls on Waterkant serve mostly Javanese food on polystyrene plates with plastic cutlery; cheap and cheerful. Try *bami* (spicy noodles) and *petjil* (vegetables), recommended on Sun when the area is busiest. In restaurants, a dish to try is *gadogado*, an Indonesian vegetable and peanut concoction.

$$$ Spice Quest
Dr Nassylaan 107, T520747, SpiceQuest on Facebook. Open 1100-1500, 1800-2300, closed Mon.
Creative menu, open-air and indoor seating, Japanese-style setting. Recommended.

Tip...
Meat and noodles from stalls in the market are very cheap.

$$$-$$ De Waag
Waterkant 5, T474514, www.dewaag.sr. Breakfast, lunch and dinner.
Upmarket bodega and grill in a historic building where slaves were weighed and sold, indoor and outdoor eating, daily and weekly specials, tapas and wines.

$$ Chi Min
Cornelis Jongbawstraat 83, T412324, http://chimin-restaurant.com.
For well-prepared Chinese food, best to book ahead. Recommended.

$$ Garden
Opposite Torarica, next to 't Vat, T474979, Facebook: TheGardensu. Open 1700-0100.
Local and international cuisine, part of **Queen's Hotel**, shows in **Euphoria** nightclub (euphoriaparamaribo on Facebook).

$$ Garden of Eden
Virolastraat via Johannes Mungrastraat, T499448.
Attractive garden area and lounge bar/restaurant serving Thai food.

$$ Jawa
Kasabaholoweg 7, T492691.
Famous Indonesian restaurant.

$$ Martin's House of Indian Food
Hajarystraat 19, T473413, www.appartement enbina.com/restaurant/. Open 1100-2300.
Good value and tasty Indian food with friendly service and covered outside dining, plenty of vegetarian options.

$$ 't Vat
Kleine Waterstraat 1, Facebook: 't Vat Sidewalk Café. Daily early till late.
Sidewalk café and sports bar with light meals, snacks and drinks, very popular after work for early evening meeting and drinking. The place to be for the New Year street parties.

$$ Zanzibar
Van Sommelsdijkstraat 1, next to Multi Track Cambio, T471848. Tue-Sun 2000 till late.
Surinamese and international cuisine, entertainment.

$$-$ Lekker!
Van Sommelsdijkstraat22, T472722, www. lekkerparamaribo.com. Open 0800-1600.

For upmarket sandwiches, salads, soup, pasta, desserts and drinks, popular for business lunch, good service.

$$-$ Rooprram Rotishop
Zwartenhovenbrugstraat 23, T478816, and Watermolenstraat 37. Mon-Sat 0800-1500.
Rotis and accompanied fillings in fast-food style dining rooms, generous portions. Has several other outlets in the city.

$$-$ Tangelo
Kleine Waterstraat, between Torarica and Royal Torarica, part of same group. Open 0800-0100.
Coffee shop with snacks, cakes and desserts, has outside terrace, good.

$ De Gadri
Zeelandiaweg 1, T420688. Open 0800-2200.
Good location, view of river and close to Fort Zeelandia. Surinamese main dishes and snacks and sandwiches.

$ Pannekoek en Poffertjes Café
Van Sommelsdijckstraat 11, T422914. Thu, Sun 1000-2300, Fri-Sat 1000-0100.
Specializes in 200 different sorts of pancakes; other dishes too. Under same ownership is **Mighty Racks**, Sommelsdijckstraat 16, T520458, with a dinosaur at the front, specializing in beef ribs.

$ Power Smoothie
Zwartenhovenbrugstraat 62 (Mon-Fri 0800-2100, Sat 0800-1500) and in Hermitage Mall, Lalla Rookhweg (Mon-Sat 0900-2100, Sun 1600-2100), www.powersmoothiesuriname.com.
Healthy fast food and juice bars in centre and Hermitage Mall, east of centre.

$ Roti Joosje
Zwartenhovenbrugstraat 9, T472606, Facebook: rotishopjoosje. Open 0800-2200.
Well-known, well-liked roti shop in centre of town, a/c, long-established. Has other branches.

Bars and clubs

Paramaribo
For nightly activity, go to the Kleine Waterstraat/ Van Sommelsdijckstraat area.

Ballroom Energy
L'Hermitageweg 25, T497534.
Younger crowd.

Broki
Waterkant 5C, next to the Ferry Docks, T880 5472, Facebook: BrokiCafe.

Hammock bar, terrace overlooking river, good food and atmosphere.

Rumors Grand Café
In the lobby of Hotel Krasnapolsky, T475050. Open 0900-2200 (from 1400 on Sun).
Every Fri live entertainment (jamming) with Time Out.

Touché
Waaldijk/Dr Sophie Redmondstraat 60, T401181, Facebook: clubtouche. Fri-Sat only 2300.
Small restaurant, the best disco.

Zuid
Van Sommelsdijckstraat 17, T422928, see Facebook.
Bar with a good reputation, also has a grill serving burgers, pizzas.

Shopping

Paramaribo

Arts and crafts
Readytex, *Maagdenstraat 44-48, behind Hotel Krasnapolsky, www.readytexartgallery.com, Mon-Fri 0800-1630, Sat 0830-1330.* An arts, craft and souvenir shop on several floors, with its own art gallery, huge selection of items, including maps.

Bookshops
Vaco, *Domineestraat 26, T472545, Facebook: BoekhandelVACO, opposite Krasnapolsky.* A large, well-stocked bookshop, also sells English books; try here for maps.

Shopping centres
Hermitage Shopping Mall (Vieruurbloemstraat and Lalla Rookhweg), 5 mins in taxi south of centre. The only place open until 2100, with chemists, money exchange, top-quality boutiques, coffee shops and music stores.
Maretraite Mall (Jan Steenstraat, Blauwgrond, north of the city. There are several others.

What to do

Paramaribo

Cycling
Cardy Adventures and Bike Rental, *see Tour operators, below.*
Fietsen, *Grote Combeweg 13a, behind Zus & Zo and in same group, T520781, www.fietsein suriname.com.* Good-quality bikes for rent from US$3.75 for a city bike to US$26.50 per day for top-of-the-range racer; US$53-106 deposit

depending on bike. Tours with knowledgeable guides, good value, bike repair. Recommended.

Tour operators

Look for boards all over the centre advertising tours and special offers. Tours often require a minimum of 2 or 3 people, sometimes more. Prices of some tours are given in the text above. Others include: city tour by bus from US$30, by bike US$25; Commewijne boat tour; cookery workshops from US$32.

Access Suriname Travel, *Prinsessestraat 37, T424522, www.surinametravel.com*. Sells all major tours in Suriname, partner in Frederiksdorp and Danpaati (see Where to stay, above) and can supply general travel information on the country, good guides, manager Sirano Zalman is most helpful. Recommended.

Cardy Adventures and Bike Rental, *Cornelis Jongbawstraat 31 (near Eco-Resort Inn), T422518, www.cardyadventures.com)*. Bike rental (bike rental@cardyadventures.com) and standard and adventure tours throughout the country, English spoken, very helpful, efficient, excellent food.

Discover Suriname Tours, *Kleine Waterstraat 1a, T421818, www.discoversurinametours.com*. At same address as **Zeelandia Suites**, regular tours, adventure and nature tours, jeep safaris and trips to Guyana and Guyane.

METS Travel and Tours (Movement for Eco-Tourism in Suriname), *Dr JF Nassylaan 2, T477088, www.surinamevacations.com. Mon-Fri 0800-1600*. Runs a variety of tours and is involved with various community projects. Several of their trips to the interior are detailed above. They also offer city and gastronomy tours.

Moen's Dolphin Tours, *at Leonsberg dock, T08893063, or through tour operators*. Small boat tours to see brackish water or Guiana dolphin, the profosu (*Sotalia Guianensis*), at the confluence of the Suriname and Commewijne rivers, US$42 per boat; daytime and sunset tours. Boats are operated by Moen (pronounced 'Moon') and his sons. Moen is a recognized expert on the dolphins. Other boats offer the tour, but they all follow Moen if he is on the water as his success rate is second-to-none. Recommended.

Stinasu (Foundation for Nature Conservation), *Cornelis Jongbaw-straat 14, T476597, www.stinasu.sr. Mon-Thu 0700-1500, Fri 0700-1430*. Offers reasonably priced accommodation and provides tour guides in the Brownsberg, Raleigh Falls and Galibi nature reserves. Prices on page 1716.

Suriname Experience, *Chopinstraat 27, Ma Retraite 3, Paramaribo North, T453083, www.surinameexperience.com*. Very knowledgeable agency about Suriname.

Waldo's Travel Service, *Kerkplein 10, T422540, www.waldostravel.sr*. Mostly tours in the Caribbean and worldwide, some local, plus airport transfer service.

Waterproof Tours, *Venusstraat 26 (by appointment), T454434, www.waterproofsuriname.com*. Tours of the waters in and around Suriname, dolphin and caiman watching, birdwatching, river trips, also land-based tours in the country.

Wilderness Explorers, *see page 1706, www.wilderness-explorers.com*. Offer a wide range of tours to Suriname, Guyana and French Guyane. They have a UK office (T020-8417 1585) for advice and a list of UK operators who sell trips to the 3 Guianas.

Transport

Paramaribo

Air

Johan Pengel International Airport, www. japi-airport.com, is 47 km south of Paramaribo. Arrivals and Departures are in separate buildings. Be prepared for long queues at immigration and when getting your tourist card. There are food shops outside Departures. Minibus to town costs US$15-20 pp, eg **De Paarl**, Kankantriestraat 42, T403610, Facebook: garagedepaarl; **Buscovery/ Le Grand Baldew**, who have a booth in the Arrival hall, Tourtonnelaan 59, T474713, www. buscoverytours.com/www.legrandbaldew.com, **Waldo's**, see above, US$7 pp; bus costs US$10.50 with **Ashruf** taxi company, T454451 (it makes many stops), taxi proper costs US$25-28, but negotiate. Many hotels offer transfers to and from the international airport for guests with room reservation. There is a guesthouse near the airport (**$$ Sonja Guesthouse**, T680 6105, Facebook: zanderij.guesthouse, some 5 mins away by car). Internal flights and some flights to **Georgetown** leave from **Zorg en Hoop** airfield in a suburb of Paramaribo (on Doekhieweg Oost).

Airline offices Surinam Airways, Dr Sophie Redmondstraat 219, T432700, www.flyslm.com (to/from **Amsterdam**, with **KLM**, Burenstraat 33, T411811 ext 3; **Miami** via **Aruba** and via **Georgetown** twice a week; **Belém** via **Cayenne**; **Port of Spain** and **Curaçao**. Caribbean Airlines, Wagenwegstraat 36, T520034, www.caribbean-airlines.com (to/from **Port of Spain**). Gum Air, Doekhieweg 03, Zorg en Hoop Airport, T498760, info@gumair.com, with **Trans Guyana**, T433830

(Paramaribo–**Georgetown** daily). For **Air France** (flights between **Cayenne** and **Europe**), as for **KLM**, above.

Bus and taxi

There are few regular buses. The majority of services, short- and long-distance, leave from the **bus station** between Heiligenweg and Knuffelsgracht in the centre of Paramaribo, near the market. There is a sales office/waiting room, T472450, www.nvbnvsuriname.com; both office and website have timetables. The buses themselves are poorly marked and the whole place is chaotic. More buses wait on Waterkant, near Broki nightclub. Also near here is the dock for **pirogues** across the river to Meerzorg. There are privately run 'wild buses', also known as 'numbered buses' which run on fixed routes around the city; they are minivans and are severely overcrowded. Buses have no luggage space.

To Nickerie Mon-Sat 0600, 1300 each way, US$1.75. Shared taxis leave from the Central Market, about US$30-35.

Small bus to **Albina** from the bus station daily at 0700, 0830, 1230, except Sun 0830 only, US$1.20, 4 hrs; return from Albina at same times. A shared taxi costs US$22 per person, while a private taxi will charge US$128, about 2 hrs.

Direct minibuses to **Georgetown** via South Drain (fare does not include ferry crossing), are run by many small companies, US$50-60, pick up and drop off at hotels: **Bobby's**, T498583; **Lambada Bus Service**, Keizerstraat 162, T411 073, and **Bin Laden**, T0-210944/0-8809271. You have to change buses once across the border; you are given a card to hand to the bus driver in the next country. **Buscovery/Le Grand Baldew** (address above), organizes 3- and 4-day trips to **Georgetown** and **Cayenne** respectively, US$635 (they also do tours around Suriname).

Car hire

Avis, Kristalstraat 1, T551158, www.avis.com (also at hotels Torarica and Marriott); **De Paarl** (see above under Air); **Europcar**, Kleine Waterstraat 1 (behind 't Vat), T424631, www.europcar.sr, has a fly-drive programme including Guyana – in combination with Wilderness Explorers, see page 1706. **Hertz at Real Car**, Van 't Hogerhuysstraat 23, T400409, www.hertz.com; **SPAC**, Verl Gemenelandsweg 139A, T490882. **Wheelz**, HD Benjaminstraat 20, T442929, 08802361 after 1600 and at weekends, www.wheelzcarrental.com.

Taxi

Taxis generally have no meters, average price US$2.50 (agree it beforehand). If you're a hotel guest, let the hotel make arrangements.

Tourtonne's Taxi, Tourtonnelaan 142, T475734/425380, www.tourtonnestaxi.com, is recommended. Reliable and good value, also taxi tours, will collect from airport with advance notice.

West of Paramaribo

Bus

See under Paramaribo, above. The Nieuw Nickerie bus station is next to the market on G G Maynardstraat. **Paramaribo–South Drain** costs US$7.

Border with Guyana

Boat

From Nieuw Nickerie to Moleson Creek: the Canawaima ferry sails once or twice a day from South Drain, near Nieuw Nickerie, to **Moleson/Crabwood Creek** depending on demand, US$10 (US$15 with return within 21 days), cars US$30, pick-ups US$40. T212331, or T085 4008 to check when the ferry is running. Taxi bus from Nickerie market to South Drain at 0730, but can pick you up from your hotel.

Border with Guyane

Boat

The vehicle and passenger ferry to **St-Laurent du Maroni**, **Bac International** *La Gabrielle* (bac.gabrielle@orange.fr) has 3-4 crossings a day, 6 on Sat, 30 mins. Passengers US$5/€4.50 one way, car US$36.75/€34.20, payable only in euros. Service can change at any time. This is the official crossing. Unofficial pirogues cross from another dock nearby, US$5/€4.50 (or US$10.75/€10 for 1 person). See page 1740 for immigration details.

Minibuses and taxis

Transport to **Paramaribo** waits at the Bac and pirogue docks in Albina (see Transport, Paramaribo, for fares). There is a police check at Stolkertsijver (see page 1715). Some taxi drivers will check that you have a stamp in your passport; without it, you'll be in trouble.

Guyane

Tourism is slowly being developed in Guyane, as in all the Guianas, with the main draws being 'space tourism' at Kourou, birdwatching and adventure trips into the forests.

Cayenne *Colour map 2, B6.*

parks, mansions and museums

The capital and the chief port of Guyane is on the island of Cayenne at the mouth of the Cayenne river. Founded by French traders in the 16th century, but taking its name from an Amerindian prince, Cayenne remained relatively isolated until after the Second World War when Guyane became part of metropolitan France and Rochambeau airport (now called Félix Éboué) was constructed. It retains some of its 18th-century layout.

Sights

There are three main parks: the **Place des Palmistes** is a large open space with a variety of palms. Adjoining it is the open **Place de Grenoble** and **Place L Héder**, on which stands the Jesuit-built residence (circa 1890) of the Prefect (La Préfecture), as well as other official buildings. The **Place des Amandiers**

Cayenne

Where to stay
1 Best Western Amazonia
2 Central
3 Des Amandiers
4 Des Palmistes
5 Éclipse
6 Ker Alberte
7 Ket Taï
8 La Belle Étoile & Villa Soleil
9 Le Dronmi & Le Bistro

Restaurants
1 Café de la Gare
2 La Marina
3 La Petite Maison
4 Le Café Crème
5 Le Patriarche
6 Milles Pâtes
7 Nath, Café, Thé & Go
8 Paris-Cayenne

Best for
French culture ■ Rocket launches ■ Tropical forest ■ Wildlife

(also known as the Place Auguste-Horth) is by the sea; it is a nice place to go at dusk when birds are roosting in the trees and feeding at the water's edge, men play boules and dominoes and people fish and stroll in the fading light. An interesting museum, the **Musée Départemental Alexandre-Franconie** ① *1 ave Général de Gaulle, near the Place de Palmistes, T295913, http://musee.cg973.fr/ws/collections/app/report/index.html, different hours every day, closed Tue, Sun, Thu afternoon and Sat afternoon, US$3.35,* exhibits among other things pickled snakes and the trunk of the 'late beloved twin-trunked palm' of the Place de Palmistes. There is a good entomological collection and excellent paintings of convict life. The **Musée des Cultures Guyanaises** ① *54 rue Mme Payé, T314172, mcg87@wanadoo.fr, Mon, Tue, Thu 0800-1300, 1500-1745, Wed, Fri 0800-1300, US$2.50, 18-25 year-olds US$1, children free,* has a small collection of crafts from tribal communities. The **market** on Wednesday, Friday and Saturday mornings has a great Caribbean flavour, but is expensive. More appealing f the bathing beaches around the island, the best is **Montjoly**. Bus B from the gare routière goes to Montjoly and Rémire, US$2.20, Monday-Saturday (last return from Montjoly 1840); Line 6 buses run from Cité Mirza, Cayenne (near Hotel Ket Taï) to Montjoly for beaches, US$2.20, Monday to Saturday. The last one returns about 1925, earlier at weekends (times vary). There is a walking trail called **Rorota** which follows the coastline and can be reached from Montjoly or the **Gosselin beaches**. Another trail, **Habitation Vidal** in Rémire, passes through former sugar cane plantations and ends at the remains of 19th-century sugar mills.

Some 43 km southwest of Cayenne is **Montsinéry**, with a nearby **zoo** ① *Macouria, T317306, www.zoodeguyane.com, daily 0930-1730, US$18, children US$11,* featuring Amazonian flora and fauna, a walking trail, canopy walkway, zip-line and other activities. To get there, take bus E from Place du Marché, US$5.50.

Essential Guyane

Getting around

Domestic flights are heavily booked up, so make your reservations early. The roads are much improved, and *combos* (minivans) ply the coastal roads. See also the box, Driving in the Guianas, in Getting around, page 1733.

Tip...

Most banks have ATMs for cash withdrawals on Visa, sometimes MasterCard. It is almost impossible to change dollars outside Cayenne or Kourou.

When to go

The best months to visit are between August and November. The climate is tropical with heavy rainfall. Average temperature at sea level is fairly constant at 27ºC. There is often a cool ocean breeze. Night and day temperatures vary more in the highlands. The rainy season is November to July, sometimes with a dry period in February and March. The great rains begin in May.

Time required

One week, or two weeks if exploring beyond the coast.

Fact file
Location 4.0000° N, 53.0000° W
Capital Cayenne
Time zone GMT -3 hrs
Telephone country code +594
Currency Euro (EUR)

Weather Cayenne

January	February	March	April	May	June
28°C	28°C	29°C	29°C	29°C	29°C
22°C	22°C	23°C	23°C	23°C	22°C
456mm	305mm	402mm	405mm	592mm	462mm

July	August	September	October	November	December
31°C	31°C	31°C	31°C	30°C	29°C
22°C	20°C	20°C	20°C	22°C	22°C
238mm	172mm	98mm	103mm	163mm	360mm

The European space centre at Kourou is one of the main attractions, especially when a rocket is being launched. In stark contrast are the abandoned penal settlements. Beyond is largely unexplored jungle. Also in this section are the routes to Suriname and Brazil.

West to Suriname

★**Kourou** This is where the main French space centre (**Centre Spatial Guyanais**), used for the European Space Agency's Ariane programme, is located, 56 km southwest from Cayenne. It is also used by the Russians to launch Soyuz and Vega (a joint mission with other European countries). The site employs about 1500 personnel, with 7000 related jobs. Tourist attractions include bathing, fishing, sporting and a variety of organized excursions.

The space centre occupies an area of about 750 sq km along 50 km of coast, bisected by the Kourou river.

The **Musée de l'Espace** ① *T326123, Mon-Fri 0800-1800, Sat 1400-1800, US$7.60 (US$4.35 on Sat and for those visiting the space centre the same day, and groups of 20 or more), can be visited without reservation.* It has a small planetarium. To watch a launch you must apply on line at www.cnes-csg.fr; CNES at the **Centre Spatial Guyanais** will then send you an invitation if successful. You must present your invitation and ID to attend. Full details on the website. Alternatively, you can watch the launch for free, from 10 km, at **Montagne Carapa** at Pariacabo. Some launches are shown on a big screen in Cayenne and Sinnamary. Also see www.esa.int/Education and www.arianespace.com.

★**Iles du Salut** The Iles du Salut (many visitors at weekends), opposite Kourou, include the **Ile Royale**, **Ile Saint-Joseph**, and **Ile du Diable**. They were the scene of the notorious convict settlement built in 1852; the last prisoners left in 1953. One of their most famous residents was Henri Charrière, who made a miraculous escape to Venezuela. He later recounted the horrors of the penal colony and his hair-raising escape attempts in his book *Papillon* (some say Charrière's book is a compilation of prisoners' stories). There is a museum in the **Commander's House** on Ile Royale; brochures for sale. The **Ile du Diable** (**Devil's Island**), a rocky islet almost inaccessible from the sea, was where political prisoners, including Alfred Dreyfus, were held (access to this island is strictly forbidden). You can see monkeys, agoutis, turtles, hummingbirds and macaws, and there are many coconut palms on Ile Royale. Paintings of prison life by François Lagrange (the inspiration for Dustin Hoffman's character in the film *Papillon*) are on show in the tiny church. Visit the children's graveyard, mental asylum and death cells. These are not always open, but the church is open daily. Conservation work is underway. Three guided tours in French are given weekly.

Sinnamary and St-Laurent du Maroni Between Kourou and Iracoubo, on the road west, to St-Laurent (N1), is **Sinnamary** (116 km from Cayenne, bus US$22.50, 1 hour 20 minutes, no bus Sunday, US$11.25 from Kourou), a pleasant town where Kali'na (Galibi) Amerindians at a mission make artificial flowers, for sale to tourists. Carvings and jewellery are on sale here. **Tourist information** ① *28 rue Constantin Verderosa, T346883, 0730-1230 (1500-1800 Mon, Wed).* There are three- to five-day excursions up the Sinnamary river. Scarlet ibis can be seen in numbers on the Sinnamary estuary at **Iracoubo**.

St-Laurent du Maroni, formerly a penal transportation camp, is now a quiet, spread-

Essential Kourou

Finding your feet

There is no public transport to the space station so you'll need to take a taxi or hitch.

Tourist information

1 avenue de l'Anse, front de mer, T329833, ot-kourou@orange.fr, Mon, Tue, Thu 0900-1400, 1500-1630, Wed, Fri 0900-1400.

Tours

Public guided tours of the space station are given Monday to Friday 0800 and 1300, arrive 30 minutes early. Tours last three hours, but are only in French; under eights are not admitted. Reservations should be made 48 hours in advance, T326123, visites.csg@cnes.fr, Monday to Thursday 0800-1200, 1300-1700, Friday 0800-1200. No tours during a launch or on the days before or after.

out town with a few colonial buildings, 250 km from Cayenne on the river Maroni, which borders Suriname. Market days are Wednesday and Saturday, 0700-1400. The old **Camp de Transportation** (the original penal centre) can be visited on a 1¼-hour **guided tour** ① *T278596, Jul-Aug daily 0930, 1100, 1500, 1630, rest of year Mon 1500, 1630, Tue-Sat as Jul-Aug, Sun 0930, 1100, buy tickets from tourist office US$6.65.* There are also chilling guided tours of **Les Bagnes** (prison camps) ① *same times as above, US$13.35, which includes and exhibition (open Tue-Sat 0900-1200, 1430-1730, Sun 0900-1230, closed Mon and holidays); see also www.bagne-st-jean.com,* on the **Camp de la Relégation** at St-Jean du Maroni. On the riverfront by the Camp de Transportation, the **Office du Tourisme** ① *1 esplanade Laurent Baudin, 97320 St-Laurent du Maroni, T342398, www.ot-saintlaurentdumaroni.fr, Tue-Sat 0800-1200, 1430-1800, Mon 1430-1800, Sun and holidays 0830-1230, but Jul-Aug Mon-Fri 0800-1800, Sat 0800-1230, 1430-1800 (Sun opens 0830),* has lots of helpful information, list of local events, bicycles for hire, free Wi-Fi for one hour, and information on Ariane rocket launches (and bus to view it).

Border with Suriname The port, with customs and immigration, is 2 km south of the centre of St-Laurent du Maroni. The offices close at 1900. The Bac car ferry across the river to Albina, Suriname, is the official crossing; countless unofficial pirogues leave from a different dock nearby (see Transport, below, for details). Whatever craft you take, you must get your exit stamp from immigration at the Bac terminal. Likewise in Albina, immigration is at the Bac terminal. There is no legal money exchange in St-Laurent, but there is an official cambio in Albina (see page 1715). Otherwise, there is a **Banque BRED** ATM beside Hotel Star (nine blocks from the dock) for withdrawing euros, and other ATMs in the centre. You will need euros for the buses and taxis. **Surinamese consul** ① *6 rue Victor Schoelcher, T344968, Mon-Fri 0900-1200, 1400-1600. In Cayenne: 3 avenue L Héder (see Cayenne map, page 1723), T282160, cg.sme.cay@foreignaffairs.gov.sr, Mon-Fri 0900-1200.* At the Cayenne consulate, hand in your passport with €30 in cash, wait 25 minutes then pick up your tourist card (no onward flights or other documents asked for); English spoken. See Visas and immigration, page 1740.

Around St-Laurent About 3 km from St-Laurent, along the Paul Isnard road, is **Saint-Maurice**, where you can visit the **rum distillery** ① *T340909, www.rhumssaintmaurice.com, Mon-Fri 0730-1130.* At Km 73 on the same dirt road is access to **Voltaire Falls**, 1½ hours' walk from the road. Some 7 km south of St-Laurent on the road to St-Jean du Maroni is the Amerindian village of **Terre Rouge**. Several companies in St-Laurent offer half-day, full-day and longer trips by boat up the Maroni river.

Some 40 km north of St-Laurent du Maroni is **Mana**, a delightful town with rustic architecture near the coast (tourist office ① *rues M Bastie and Javouhey, T278409, Mon-Sat 0800-1300, 1500-1800*).

Some 20 km west of Mana following the river along a single-track access road is **Les Hattes**, or **Yalimapo**, an Amerindian village. About 4 km further on is **Les Hattes beach** where leatherback and other turtles lay their eggs at night. The season runs from April to August with May/June peak. There is no public transport to Les Hattes and its beach, but hitching is possible at weekends; take food and water and mosquito repellent. The freshwater of the Maroni and Mana rivers makes sea bathing pleasant. It is very quiet during the week.

Awala Yalimapo (or **Aouara**), a Kali'na Amerindian village with hammock places, is 16 km west of Les Hattes. It also has a beach where marine turtles lay their eggs. Take mosquito nets, hammock and insect repellent. Both turtle-nesting beaches are within the **Réserve Naturelle Amana** ① *270 avenue de 31 décembre 1988, 97319 Awala Yalimapo, T348404, amana2@wanadoo.fr, also on Facebook,* 14,800 ha of coastal and estuarine habitat protecting birds, mammals and reptiles. For more details see www.reserves-naturelles.org/amana and www.guyane-parcregional.fr/les-reserves-naturelles/reserve-naturelle-nationale-amana/.

There are daily flights from Cayenne to **Maripasoula**; details in Air transport, page 1731, local office T372141. It is up the Maroni from St-Laurent (about four days' journey up river in a *pirogue*). There may be freight canoes that take passengers or private boats from St-Laurent (ask at the St-Laurent tourist office, or see its website for names of operators); also four-day tours with Guyane-Évasion or other Cayenne operators. **Tourist office** ① *Passage Vignon, T371509, www.maripasoula.fr, Mon 0900-1300, Tue-Sat 0900-1300, 1500-1700.*

South to Brazil

Some 6 km past the airport, route D6 turns off the main road to the east, N2, to the small town of **Roura**, about 28 km southeast of Cayenne (bus D, US$5.50 from gare routière in Cayenne). It has an interesting church. Just outside Roura is the Laotian village of **Dacca**, by the Crique Gabriel. This is one of the main starting points for boat trips to the coast and island nature reserves of **Grand Connétable** (www.reserve-connetable.com) and **Ilet la Mère** and trips by pirogue inland to the **Fourgassier Falls** (12 km away by road in the dry season), and further still along the Comté river to **Cacao**. For information about the area contact the **Roura tourist office** ① *rue Georges Edmée Labrador, T270827, communication@roura.gf and visit the www.guyane-amazonie.fr pages*.

From Roura, the paved D6 runs southeast towards the village of **Kaw** (bus D, US$7.15 from Roura), on an island amid swamps which are home to much rare wildlife including black caimans and birds such as hoatzin and, in the Kaw estuary, scarlet ibis. There are basic rooms available, but most visits are on tours locally or from Cayenne, staying on houseboats. Take insect repellent. The **Réserve Naturelle Nationale Kaw-Roura**, 94,700 ha, is administered by the **Parc Naturel Régional de la Guyane** ① *www.guyane-parcregional.fr*.

At Km 53 on the main road southeast (N2) to Régina is the turn-off to Cacao (a further 13 km), a small, quiet village, where Hmong refugees from Laos are settled; they are farmers and produce fine traditional handicrafts. The Sunday morning market has local produce, Laotian food and embroidery. Ask the **Comité du Tourisme de la Guyane** for gîtes and river trips in the area.

Régina, on the Approuague river southwest of Kaw, is reached by the paved N2 road from Cayenne. The Service Tourisme de Régina-Kaw is on rue Gaston Monnerville in Régina, T280589, or you can ask for information at the Mairie in Régina. A good two- to three-day trip is on the river to the Athanase falls (US$260-300 with Jal-Voyages); see also www.escapade-carbet.com/carbet/village-de-saut-athanase/. The road continues paved from Régina to **St-Georges de l'Oyapock** (difficult in the rainy season).

Saül This remote gold-mining settlement in the 'massif central' is the geographical centre of Guyane. The main attractions are for the nature-loving tourist. Beautiful undisturbed tropical forests are accessible by a very well-maintained system of some 75 km of marked trails, including several circular routes. There is running water and electricity; the tourist office is in the town hall. There are a couple of places to stay and eat in town (see A Ke Nou, http://gite-restaurantakenou-saul.com, and **Chez Lulu**, www.chezlulu-saul.com, for example). Two markets sell food.

Saül and Maripasoula (see above) are within the contact zone (*zone d'adhésion*) of the **Parc Amazonien de Guyane** which covers two million hectares of the interior. Together with neighbouring reserves in Brazil such as Tumucumaque, Maricuru and Grão-Pará, this forms the world's largest protected tropical forest.

St-Georges de l'Oyapock This small town, with its small detachment of the French Foreign Legion who parade on **Bastille Day**, is 15 minutes downriver from Oiapoque in Brazil, €5/US$5.50 per person by motorized canoe, bargain for a return fare. A bridge between the two countries was completed in 2011, but remains closed until various infrastructure projects on the Brazilian side are finished. Ask in the Mairie, rue Jean Cedia, T370997, for tourist information. There are bars, restaurants, supermarkets with French specialities, a post office and public telephones which take phonecards. Oyapock Évasion ① *T272683 or mobiles T694-961961 or T694-946962, www.oyapock-evasion.com*, offers guided river and forest tours, trips to Brazil and transport. A day trip can be made to the **Saut Maripa rapids** (not very impressive with high water, but strewn with treacherous rocks), located about 30 minutes upstream along the Oyapock river, past the Brazilian towns of Oiapoque and Clevelândia do Norte. Hire a motorized *pirogue* (canoe) to take you to a landing downstream from the rapids. Then walk along the trolley track (used to move heavy goods around the rapids) for 20 minutes. In dry season 4WDs can get there. There are more rapids further upstream on the way to and beyond Camopi.

Border with Brazil For entry/exit stamps, look for PAF (Police Federal), set away from the river about 10 minutes' walk behind the Mairie; fork left at 'Farewell Greeting' sign from town (this may change when the border bridge is in service). Open daily 0700-1200, 1500-1800 (often not open after early morning on Sunday, so try police at the airport); French, Portuguese and English spoken. The Brazilian consulate in Cayenne is at 444 chemin St Antoine, T296010, cg.caiena@itamaraty.gov.br, Monday-Friday 0730-1300, 1330-1500. One of the **Livre Service** supermarkets and **Hotel Chez Modestine** will sometimes change dollars cash into euros at poor rates; if entering the country here, change money before arriving in St-Georges. Brazilian reais are accepted in shops at poor rates.

Tourist information

Cayenne

Comité du Tourisme de la Guyane
12 rue Lallouette, BP 801, 97300 Cayenne,
T296500, www.guyane-amazonie.fr. Mon, Wed,
Fri 0730-1330, Tue, Thu 0730-1300, 1400-1700.
Helpful, lots of brochures, but little in English.

Municipal tourist office
12 rue Louis Blanc, T396883, www.ville-cayenne.
fr/a-la-decouverte-de-cayenne/. Mon-Fri 0830-
1200, 1400-1700, Sat 0830-1300.

Where to stay

Cayenne

Most hotels have to add a small municipal tax to
the bill: it is charged daily, per person and varies
from hotel to hotel. Service is rarely added to the
bill. Hotels rarely include breakfast in the price
either, but B&B accommodation with breakfast
(gîte) is available from €45/US$50 a night.

$$$$ Ker Alberte
4 rue de Docteur Sainte-Rose, T257570,
www.hotelkeralberte.com.
Lovely hotel in a converted old house in the heart
of the city, the courtyard pool area has rooms
behind and above it, also 3 rooms in the older
villa, some with kitchen, good service, decorated
with modern art, restaurant with daily lunch
menu ($$$), café and tapas bar.

$$$$-$$$ Best Western Amazonia
28 Av Général de Gaulle, T288300,
www.hotel-amazonia.com.
A/c rooms in 4 categories, pool, central location,
good buffet breakfast extra, also buffet lunch,
dinner à la carte in **L'Outre-mer** restaurant.

$$$$-$$$ Hotel des Palmistes
12 Av Général de Gaulle, T300050, www.palmistes.co.
Fine 19th-century building with comfortable rooms
and suites overlooking the Place des Palmistes.
Restaurant ($$$) is open 7 days a week for all meals,
good food, music at weekends, popular bar.

$$$$-$$$ Le Dronmi
42 Av Général de Gaulle, T317770, www.ledronmi.com.
Spacious suites on 2 floors with kitchen, also smaller
rooms with microwave, helpful, secure entrance,
keys held behind the bar at **Le Bistro**, downstairs,
where breakfast (included in price) is served.

$$$ Central Hotel
Corner rue Molé and rue Becker, T256565,
www.centralhotel-cayenne.fr.
Good location, 2½ blocks from the Place de
Palmistes, a/c rooms. Special prices at weekends.
Bar François on 1st floor. Book in advance online.

$$$ Hotel des Amandiers
Place Auguste-Horth, T289728,
www.hoteldesamandiers.com.
Pleasant, across from the Place des Amandiers,
a/c, cheapest on ground floor, most expensive
with sea view, café serves breakfast and is open
all day for drinks, good service.

$$$ La Belle Étoile and Villa Soleil
74 rue Lt Goinet, T257085, www.prestigelocations.fr.
The first is a brand new building with 6 deluxe
suites on 3 floors, while the latter is the ground
floor of a Creole villa, quaint, old style. All suites
with kitchen, safe, a/c, washing machine. Very
good. In the same group is **Éclipse**, 47 rue
Lt Goinet, same phone, website and price.

$$$-$$ Ket Taï
72 Av Nelson Mandela, T289777,
g.chang@wanadoo.fr.
The best cheap hotel in town, by the canal
at the corner of the central area, simple a/c
rooms, en suites. If you can, look at a few rooms
before deciding.

Around Rémire-Montjoly

$$$ Motel du Lac
22 rue Poupon, Route de Montjoly, T380800,
moteldulac@orange.fr.
In a protected area, very peaceful, garden,
pool, bar, restaurant.

Near Matoury and the airport

$$$ La Chaumière
Chemin de la Chaumière (off the road
to Kourou), 97351 Matoury, T255701,
www.lachaumierecayenne.com.
Set in gardens, rooms, bungalows, a studio and a
villa, restaurant, pool, at bottom end of this price
band, good value, but cabs to town push up cost.

Kourou

Hotel rooms and rates are at a premium when
there's an Ariane rocket launch (once a month).

$$$$ Hôtel des Roches
Av des Roches, T320066, www.hoteldesroches.com.

Fair, a/c, includes breakfast, pool with bar, **Le Paradisier** and **Le Créolia** restaurants, buffet breakfast included, Wi-Fi.

$$$$ Mercure Ariatel
Av de St-Exupéry, Lac Bois Diable, T328900, www.accorhotels.com.
Overlooking a lake, 9-hole golf course nearby and pool. Has **Snack Ti Gourmet** for grills and salads and **Mahogany Bar**.

$$$$-$$$ Atlantis
Lieu dit Bois Diable, T321300, www.atlantiskourou.com.
A/c, modern, pool, best value for business visitors.

$$$-$$ Le Ballahou
1 et 3 rue Amet Martial, T220022, www.hotel-ballahou.com.
Small apart-hotel, some rooms with cooking facilities, also studios, a/c, TV, modern, massage and other therapies. Book ahead.

Iles du Salut

$$$$-$$$ Auberge Iles du Salut
Ile Royale (BP 324, 97310 Kourou, T321100, sothis2@wanadoo.fr).
Full board. 60-bed hotel, hammock space (US$11); former guard's bungalow (**$$$**), main meals are excellent; pricey gift shop (especially when cruise ship is in).

Sinnamary

$$$ Hôtel du Fleuve
11 rue Léon Mine, T345400, infohoteldufleuve@orange.fr.
On the main highway, by the roundabout into Sinnamary, with gardens, restaurant, internet access, pool, breakfast extra.

St-Laurent du Maroni

$$$$-$$$ Le Relais des 3 Lacs
19-21 allée des Toucans, T340505, reservationr3l@yahoo.fr.
Bungalows with kitchen, studios and rooms, a/c, shuttle to town centre, restaurant, gardens, pool.

$$$ Amazonia du Fleuve
20 rue Thiers, T341010, hotelamazonia@orange.fr.
Quite smart, Wi-Fi, safe in rooms, buffet breakfast.

$$$ La Tentiaire
12 av Franklin Roosevelt, T342600, tentiaire@wanadoo.fr.
A/c, the best, breakfast extra, phone, pool, secure parking. Must reserve in advance. If full, they will ring round other hotels.

$$$ Star
2 bis rue Thiers, T341084, hotelstar973@yahoo.fr.
Functional, tiled rooms, a/c, pool Wi-Fi not always available in rooms, safe in more expensive rooms.

$$ Chez Julienne
Rue Gaston Monnerville, 200 m past Texaco station, some way out of town on main road, T341153.
A/c, TV, a/c, shower, good value.

Around St-Laurent
The following gîtes are all at **Commune Awala-Yalimapo** (http://awala-yalimapo.mairies-guyane.org): **Ailumi Weyulu** (T347245, www.giteailumiweyulu.com); **Chez Rita** (Awala, T344914, gitechezrita@gmail.com); **Kudawyada** (260 av du 31 décembre 1988, T342060). Shared accommodation: **Auberge de Jeunesse Simili** (T341625, ajs.simili@wanadoo.fr).

$$$$-$$$ Auberge des Chutes Voltaires
Voltaire Falls, www.aubergechutesvoltaire.com.
Price is for half-board. Double rooms with bath or shared bath, hammock space US$66 half-board, US$11 to hire hammock (more with mosquito net), other meals available.

South to Brazil

$$ Auberge des Orpailleurs
8 km after the Cacao turn-off on the road from Cayenne to Régina, by the Orapu river, T0970-447855 (net phone), www.aubergedesorpailleurs.com.
6 rooms and also hammock spaces, breakfast extra. Canoes, trails and butterfly and moth collecting. Restaurant.

$$ Auberge de l'Approuague
Lieu-dit Corossony, 97390 Régina, T0694-446979, www.approuague.com.
Price is for double room, hammock space costs US$17.25, cheaper with own hammock, a 3-course meals costs US$27, great views of the forest.

Border with Brazil: St-Georges de l'Oyapock
Accommodation is cheaper on the Brazilian side.

$$$ Chez Modestine
Rue E Elfort, on the main square, T370013, modestine@wanadoo.fr.
A/c or fan, rooms in a traditional house, Wi-Fi, restaurant.

$$ Caz Cale
Rue E Elfort, 1st back from riverfront, just east of the main square, T370054.
A/c rooms with TV, cheaper with fan.

Restaurants

Cayenne

Many restaurants close on Sun. There are several small Chinese restaurants serving the same fare: noodles, rice, soups, etc.

$$$ La Marina
24 bis rue Molé, T301930. Open 1145-1430, 1900-2230, closed Sun.
Mainly for seafood, but also beef and chicken dishes.

$$$ La Petite Maison
23 rue Féliz Eboué, T385839, www.restaurantla petitemaison.com. Mon-Sat 1200-1400, 2000-2200.
Old building, on 2 floors, with a good varied menu.

$$$ Le Patriarche
12 rue Samuel Lubin, T317644.
Excellent classical French and Creole cooking, one of the best in Guyane and very good value for this country. Reserve in advance.

$$$ Paris-Cayenne
59 rue de Lallouette, T317617, www.pariscayenne.fr.
French cooking with tropical twist, also with bar, nice decor.

$$$-$$ Café de la Gare
42 rue Léopold Héder, T285320.
Great little restaurant with classy live music every Thu and weekend. Good atmosphere.

$$$-$$ Le Café Crème
42 rue Justin Catayée, T281256.
Pastries, sandwiches, juices and coffee; open for breakfast and lunch only, friendly.

$$$-$$ Mille Pâtes
52 rue J Catayée, T289180, www.millepates-guyane.com. Daily 1130-2230 (2300 Fri, Sat and night before a holiday).
Meat and fish dishes, mixed menu of pizza, pasta, burgers and daily specials, also take-away and delivery, a little English spoken.

$$ Nath, Café, Thé & Go
33 rue J Catayée.
Coffees, teas, smoothies and cakes. Pleasant.

Kourou

$$$-$$ Le P'tit Café
11 Place Monnerville, T326856.
A good value set lunch and a respectable à la carte menu.

$ Chinatown
66 rue Duchesne.
Cheap Chinese (also takeaway). Recommended.

$ Le Glacier des 2 Lacs
68 Av des 2 Lacs, T321210.
Ice cream, cakes, teas, very good.

St-Laurent du Maroni

$$$ Ti Pic Kréol's
24 rue Thiers (next to Star Hotel), T340983, www.tipickreols.com. Restaurant 1200-1430, 1900-2200, bar open all the time, closed Sun evening.
Excellent restaurant/bar, Créole menu including local game, popular for lunch, good service, pool table. Recommended.

$$ Le Mambari
7 rue Rousseau, T343590. Open till late.
French cuisine using local ingredients served in a traditional building.

What to do

Cayenne

Look under **Espace Pro** on www.guyane-amazonie.fr for listings of local tour operators. Full details on the company websites, some in English.
Guyane-Évasion, *ZI Degrad des Cannes, Montjoly, T294164, info@guyane-evasion.com, or see Facebook.* New company in 2016 offering day trips (2 to 5 days), river trips, visits to tourist camps and longer excursions to the interior.
JAL-Voyages, *26 Av Général de Gaulle, T316820, www.jal-voyages.com.* Range of river tours, eg on the Approuague (US$220), on a houseboat on the Kaw marshes (from US$90 for day visit to US$175 for day and night, full board, very good, Amerindian villages, little English spoken. Recommended.

Transport

Cayenne

Air

Cayenne Airport – Félix Éboué (T353882/89) 17 km south of Cayenne. There is a virtual tourist office with direct phone and an information office with little information. Bars, cafés, car hire and an ATM for Visa and Mastercard. Taxis wait outside and use meters (a card shows the rates per metre): US$35 to town by day, US$50 at night and on Sun, 20 mins. Cheapest route to town is taxi to Concorde, then bus F to gare routière in the centre US$3.65 (every 1 hr 15 mins, 0655-1855, far fewer on Sat, none on Sun), or taxi to **Matoury** US$10, then bus C, US$2 (more frequent service, none on Sun). Cheapest return to airport is by bus C to Matoury, or F to Concorde, then hitch or walk.

Airline offices Air Caraïbes, Félix Éboué airport, T308450, www.aircaraibes.com (to **France** and the **French Caribbean islands**); also **Air France**, T298785, www.airfrance.com. **Surinam Airways**, 15 rue Louis Blanc, T293000, www.flyslm.com (to **Paramaribo** and to **Belém**). **Azul**, www.voeazul.com.br (also to **Belém**).

Bus

Regular local services run by **SMTC**, most from the Place du Marché, US$1.20 (ticket office 2682 route de la Madeleine, T254929, Mon-Fri 0800-1200, 1500-1700; see www.ville-cayenne.fr/transports-lignes-horaires-tarifs/ – has maps). Interurban terminal, Gare routière is at corner of rue Molé and Av de la Liberté. To **St-Laurent du Maroni**, direct minibuses, 3¼ hrs, US$38, leaves when full from the opposite side of the canal from gare routière, or a bigger bus at 0800, 1100, 1300, 1500 via Kourou and Iracoubo US$27.50. To **St-Georges del' Oyapock**, US$44 (with Didier, T0694-437851, Dudu, T916998, Marcio, T130040), or US$33.50 via **Régina** (US$22.50, 1½ hrs, Cayenne-Régina, US$11 Régina-St-Georges).

Shared taxi (*collectifs*) From the gare routière, corner of Av de la Liberté and rue Malouet by the Canal Laussat, early morning, ask around as they are not signed. They leave when full. Other taxis at the stand on Place des Palmistes, corner of Av Gen de Gaulle and Molé.

Car hire

There are 11 agencies in Cayenne; those at the airport open only for flight arrivals. **Avis** (www.avis.fr), **Hertz** (www.hertzantilles.com) and **Ucar** (www.ucar-guyane.com). **Budget** (www.budget-guyane.com), **Europcar** (http://en.europcar-guyane.com) and **Sixt** (www.sixt.com) have offices. All types of car available. Cheapest rates are about €40/US$45 a day, km and insurance extra. The excess is very high.

Kourou

Bus

To/from **Cayenne**, US$11. To **St-Laurent du Maroni**, US$27.

Taxi

Shared taxi to **Cayenne**, US$16. Taxi to Cayenne or airport, US$90, more at night. To **St-Laurent du Maroni** US$30 by *taxi collectif* (irregular).

Iles du Salut

Boat

Sailing boats and motorboats go from Kourou to the islands: *Iles du Salut* catamaran, 100 passengers, from Ponton des Boulourous in Kourou, T284236, www.promaritimeguyane.fr, at 0830 daily, return at 1630 (embark 45 mins before departure), US$46.25 return, children under 12 US$24, 1 hr each way (book in advance online). The 12-seater *St Joseph* sails between Ile Royale and Ile Saint-Joseph, weather permitting, for US$6. Tickets may be obtained direct or from agencies in Cayenne or Kourou. Catamarans such as *Tropic-Alizés* (T0694-402020, www. ilesdusalut-guyane. com) and *La Hulotte* (T323381, www.lahulotte-guyane.fr) run sailing excursions to the islands, US$55 for a full day; 2-day trips also offered. No sailings between Ile Royale and Ile du Diable.

St-Laurent du Maroni and around

Air

Service with **Air Guyane** from **Cayenne**, daily, US$95. **Air Guyane** flies from Cayenne to **Maripasoula**, daily, 1 hr, US$99; minibus airport to town US$5.50, awaits flight arrival.

Bus

To **Cayenne**, Transports Best, T341400, 0600, from St-Laurent gare routière, US$27.50. Minibuses meet the ferry from Suriname, leaving when full from rue du Port, 3 hrs, US$38. If none direct, change in **Iracoubo**. To **Mana** and Awala with **Van Els**, T0694-236602, 4 daily, 2 on Sun, US$10. To **Kourou**, Antoinette et Frères from La Glacière, T0694-167322, US$27.50. There are several *taxis collectifs* (US$38 to Cayenne from gare routière, plus US$6 for hotel pick-up) and regular taxis; tourist office has phone numbers.

Border with Suriname

Boat

The vehicle and passenger ferry to **Albina**, Bac International *La Gabrielle* (T279129, bac.gabrielle@orange.fr), has 3-4 crossings a day, 6 on Sat, 30 mins. Passengers US$5 one way, car US$36.75, payable only in euros. Service can change at any time. Unofficial pirogues cross from a different port nearby, US$5 (or US$10.75 for 1 person). See page 1741 for immigration details.

South to Brazil

Air

Service with **Air Guyane** from Cayenne to Saül, daily except Sat, US$82. Try airport even if flight full.

Minibus

From Cayenne to **Cacao**, Mon-Fri 0725, 1600, return Mon-Fri 0600, 1725, US$18.

Practicalities
Getting around

Guyana

Most flights to the interior leave from Ogle, some 15 minutes from Georgetown. For scheduled flights between Georgetown and Lethem see page 1710, and services to Kaieteur, see page 1709. For Rupununi, see page 1710. Scheduled services to many parts of Guyana and charters are offered by **Trans Guyana Airways (TGA)** ⓘ *Ogle, T222 2525, http://transguyana.net;* **Air Services Limited (ASL)** ⓘ *Ogle, T222 1234, www.aslgy.com;* **Sky West Travel** ⓘ *Ogle, T225 4206, Facebook:skywestcharter (to northwestern Guyana),* and **Air Guyana–Wings** ⓘ *Ogle, T222 6513, www.airguyana.biz.* **Roraima Airways** ⓘ *RAL, Lot 8 Eping Av, Bel Air Park, Georgetown, T225 9647, www.roraimaairways.com,* and **Golden Arrow Airways** ⓘ *64 C Middle St, Georgetown, T226 0378, reservations@goldenarrowairways. com,* operate only charter flights out of **Ogle.** Domestic airlines are very strict on baggage allowance on internal flights: 20 lb per person.

Suriname

Internal services are run by **Gum Air** (page 1721), a small air charter firm. There are no scheduled flights, only charters. Most Amerindian and Maroon villages have an airstrip, but flights are on demand only.

Guyane

Air Guyane ⓘ *Félix Éboué airport, T293630, www.airguyane.com,* handles all domestic flights.

Guyana

There are over 960 km of navigable river. In addition to the ferries and river boats also contact the Transport and Harbours Department, Water St, Georgetown. Six-seater river boats are called *ballahoos,* three- to four-seaters are *corials;* they provide the transport in the forest.

Suriname

Cruises can be taken on the Suriname and Commewijne rivers near Paramaribo and some agencies make long-distance expeditions by boat. Where the road network ends, south of the Brokopondo reservoir, river boat is the only mode of transport, other than to the few places with an airstrip.

Guyane

The Maroni river (border with Suriname) has frequent boat services upriver from St-Laurent. There is a more limited river service on the Oyapock (border with Brazil). The other places where boat trips can be taken are Roura and Kaw.

Guyana

Minibuses and collective taxis

run between Georgetown and the entire coast from Charity to Corriverton; also to Linden. Minibuses run daily from Georgetown to Lethem. All taxis have an H on the number plate and it is recommended that you only use those painted yellow.

TRAVEL TIP

Driving in the Guianas

Guyana

Roads Most coastal towns are linked by a good 296-km road from Springlands in the east to Charity in the west; the Essequibo river is crossed by ferry, the Berbice by a toll bridge and the Demerara by a toll bridge, which, besides closing at high tide for ships to pass through (2-3 hours) is subject to frequent closures. Apart from a good road connecting Timehri and Linden, continuing as dirt to Mabura Hill and then on to Lethem on the border with Brazil, most other roads in the interior are very poor.

Safety Traffic drives on the left.

Documents No *carnet de passages* is required for driving a private vehicle. If you are bringing a private car into Guyana, policy differs over how many days you are given. You may be given 30 days at Springlands, but only three at Lethem.

Car hire Several companies in Georgetown (most are listed in the Yellow Pages of the phone directory). A permit is needed from local police; it can be applied for at Cheddi Jagan International Airport or at the Guyana Revenue Authority office, 200-201 Camp St, Georgetown. Rental agencies can advise.

Fuel Gasoline (Mogas) costs US$0.91 a litre; diesel US$0.79.

Suriname

Roads 26% of roads are paved. East–west roads: From Albina to Paramaribo to Nieuw–Nickerie is paved. North-south roads: the road Paramaribo–Paranam–Afobakka–Pokigron is open. The road to the western interior, Zanderij–Apura, crosses the Coppename River; thereafter small bridges are in poor shape (take planks to bridge gaps). On the unpaved Moengo–Blakawatra road (eastern Suriname), the bridge across the Commewijne River is closed to traffic. **Note** The Surinaamse Auto Rally Klub, www.sarkonline.com, has information on rallying and other motoring events.

Road safety Driving is on the left, but some vehicles have left-hand drive. There is a 24-hour emergency service for motorists: Wegenwacht, Sr Winston Churchillweg 123, T484691/487540.

Documents All driving licences accepted; you need a stamp from the local police and a deposit. To drive a foreign-registered vehicle requires no carnet or other papers. You must have two years on your driving licence. A surcharge is made on drivers under 21. People wishing to travel from Suriname to either Guyana or Guiane by car need special vehicle insurance, available from Assuria Insurance Company, Grote Combeweg 37, Paramaribo, T473400, www.assuria.sr. Although an international driver's licence is accepted in Suriname and Guyana, a special permit is required to drive for longer than one month.

Car hire There are several car rental companies in Paramaribo (see page 1722). Rates start at about US$40 for 1-2 days for the smallest car (US$210 for a week), rising to US$92 (US$500 per week) for a pick-up.

Fuel Gasoline is sold as diesel, 'regular', unleaded, or super unleaded (more expensive): US$0.65-0.70 per litre.

Guyane

Roads The main road, narrow, but paved, runs for 270 km from Pointe Macouris, on the roadstead of Cayenne, to Mana and St-Laurent. It also runs to Régina and St-Georges de l'Oyapock on the Brazilian border.

Safety Traffic drives on the right.

Documents There are no formalities for bringing a private car across the Guyane–Suriname border, but you must ensure that your insurance is valid.

Car hire The most popular way to get around.

Fuel Gasoline/petrol costs about €1.50/US$1.65 per litre. Diesel/gazole €1.27/US$1.40 per litre.

Suriname
Details of buses and taxis are given in the text in Transport sections. Hitchhiking is possible but neither common nor advisable.

Guyane
The bus and shared taxi terminal in the capital is the Gare routière at corner of rue Molé and Avenue de la Liberté beside the Canal Laussat. Transport is expensive. Hitchhiking is reported to be easy and widespread.

Maps

There is a recommended *ITMB* (International Travel Maps and Books) map that includes Guyana, Suriname and Guyane; they also publish a separate map on "Surinam and French Guiana".

Guyana
Maps of country and Georgetown (US$20) from **Department of Lands and Surveys** ① *Homestreet Av, Durban Backland (take a taxi), T226 0524 in advance*, poor stock. Rivers and islands change frequently, so maps only give a general direction. A local guide can be more reliable. Free country and city maps are available from most tour operators and hotels. Georgetown and Guyana maps can be found in *Explore Guyana magazine*.

Suriname
Some maps can be found in **Readytex** and at **Vaco bookshop** (see Paramaribo Shopping, page 1720).

Guyane
The **IGN** publishes a 1:400,000 country map with details of towns and a series of maps covering the coast at 1:25,000. Another map is available at www.map-france.com or www.cartesfrance.fr. The **Comité du Tourisme de la Guyane** also has a tourist map.

Where to stay

Guyana
Georgetown has the widest range of accommodation in the country. There are many mid-price hotels (our $$$-$$ range), but fewer at the cheaper end. It is advisable to make a reservation in advance. When booking an air-conditioned room, ensure it also has natural ventilation. Towns outside the capital have reasonable places to stay, but less choice.

In the interior, accommodation is in lodges. These mostly cater for small groups. Rooms are generally comfortable, with a shower attached. They may be quite rustic, with thatched roofs, and it is likely that you will share with some forms of wildlife (insects and bats, mostly). Beds have mosquito nets and many places provide insect repellent (although you should still bring your own), drinking water and emergency whistles. Meals are served communally. Lodges are invariably owned and operated by, or are closely associated with a community (Amerindian in Guyana, Maroon or Amerindian in Suriname). Many of the activities are tied to the community, guides are local and that the village's culture is shared and preserved.

Suriname
Paramaribo has the greatest choice, from a couple of backpacker-style hostels to top-of-the-range hotels and resorts. Most, even the hostels, are in our $$$-$$ range. Hotels (and restaurants) are rare outside Paramaribo, but accommodation in the interior is excellent if organized through a tour operator. In some cases, you can choose to go independently rather than all-inclusive. You still have to reserve accommodation, maybe supply your own hammock and mosquito net, but you must take all your food and drink and arrange transport. A tent is less useful in this climate.

Guyane

There are few hotels under our \$\$\$ bracket and almost no restaurants below the \$\$\$ bracket. Accommodation in Guyane is more expensive than Paris, but food is better value. The **Comité du Tourisme de la Guyane**, see page 1740, has addresses of furnished apartments for rent (*locations clévacances*) and gîtes, with accommodation in hammocks or *carbets* (imitation Amerindian huts), *carbets d'hôtes*, which include breakfast, and *camps touristiques*.

Food & drink

Guyana

The blend of different influences – Indian, African, Chinese, Creole, English, Portuguese, Amerindian, North American – gives distinctive flavour to Guyanese cuisine. One well-known dish is pepper-pot: meat cooked in bitter cassava juice (*casareep*) with peppers and herbs.

Some popular local dishes are cook-up-rice, curry (chicken, beef, mutton) with rice, dhal pouri or roti and metagee. Seafood is plentiful and varied, as are tropical fruits and vegetables. The staple food is rice. In the interior wild meat is often available, eg wild cow, or *labba* (a small rodent).

Rum is the most popular drink. There is a wide variety of brands, all cheap, including the best which cost US\$3.50 a bottle. **Demerara Distillers Ltd** produces several prizewinning brands, from 3- to 21-year-old rums. The 15-year-old El Dorado has frequently been voted the best rum in the world. Demerara Distillers have a distillery tour and visit to their rum heritage, US\$15. High wine is a strong local rum. There is also local brandy and whisky (*Diamond Club*), which are worth trying. *D'Aguiar's Cream Liqueur*, produced and bottled by **Banks DIH Ltd**, is excellent (and strong). The local beer, *Banks*, made partly from rice is good and cheap. There is a wide variety of fruit juices produced by **Topco**. *Mauby*, a local drink brewed from the bark of a tree, and natural cane juice are delightful thirst quenchers available from Créole restaurants and local vendors.

Suriname

Surinamese cuisine is as rich and varied as the country's ethnic makeup. High-quality rice is the main staple. Cassava, sweet potatoes, plantain and hot red peppers are widely used. *Pom* is a puree of the tayer root (a relative of cassava) tastily spiced and served with chicken. *Moksie Alesie* is rice mixed with meat, smoked chicken and fish, white beans, tomatoes, peppers and spices. *Pindasoep* (peanut soup with plantain dumplings or noodles) and *okersoep met tayerblad* (gumbo and cassava soup) are both worth a try. *Petjil* are cooked vegetables served with peanut sauce. Well-known Indonesian dishes include *bami* (fried noodles) and *nasi goreng* (fried rice), both spicy and slightly sweet. Among the Hindustani dishes are *roti*, *somosa* and *phulawri* (fried chickpea balls). Among Suriname's many tropical fruits, palm nuts such as the orange-coloured awarra and the cone-shaped brown maripa are most popular.

The local beer is called Parbo and the best-selling rums are Borgoe, Mariënburg and Black Cat, all distilled by **Suriname Alcoholic Beverages** (SAB, www.sabrum.com). There are many fruit juices to sample, as well as the various non-alcoholic drinks of the different ethnic communities.

Guyane

Different cultures have given an individual character to the cuisine, although the French influence is ever-present. The main ingredients are seafood, shrimp, rice, vegetables and spices. Many restaurants in Cayenne serve a varied menu of seafood, meat and chicken dishes, but also pizza, pasta, burgers, etc. Other influences are Chinese (often the cheapest), Vietnamese, Indonesian, Indian, Créole and Spanish. Some dishes to look out for are *bouillon d'aoura*, a slow-cooked stew containing crab meat and other seafood, chicken, vegetables and palm fruit; *blaff*, a spicy fish soup, usually served at the start of the day; *fricassée*, rice, beans and meat (often wild game); *couac*, grated, dried yucca served as an accompaniment. *Boucanage* is meat or fish steamed in banana leaves.

The most popular drink is Ti' Punch, a cocktail of rum, lime and sugar syrup. Cayenne has several French-style patisseries and cafés. Rhum Saint-Maurice, from near Saint-Laurent-du-Maroni, is the local rum distillery. The local artisanal beer is brewed by Jeune Gueule, www.jeunegueule.com.

Essentials A-Z

Accident and emergency

Guyana
Police: T911 (24-hr emergency response T225 6411); **Fire**: T912; **Ambulance**: T913.

Suriname
Police: Emergency T115; other police numbers in Paramaribo T471111/7777, www.politie.sr. **Medical emergency**: T113. **Fire Brigade**: T110.

Guyane
General emergency number: T112; also **police**: T17, **medical emergency**: T15, **fire**: T18.

Electricity

Guyana
220-240 volts, but 110 volts in Georgetown; 60 cycles. In lodges with their own generators, ask if unsure of the voltage. Plugs as in US: 2 flat pin, or 2 flat pin and a half-round earth pin. You may also find 3 round pin and 3 flat pin, UK-style plugs.

Suriname
110/127 volts AC, 60 cycles. Plug fittings: usually 2-pin round (European continental type).

Guyane
220 volts, 50 cycles. Plugs are the same as mainland Europe.

Embassies and consulates

For a full list of these countries' overseas representatives and of foreign embassies and consulates in each, visit http://embassy.go abroad.com. For France, see al so www.mfe.org.

Health

Medical services
For hospitals, doctors and dentists, ask at your hotel or else contact your consulate or the tourist office for advice.

Guyana
Well-equipped private hospitals in Georgetown include: **Balwant Singh**, 314 East St, South Cummingsburg, T225 4279/227 1087, http://drbalwantsinghshospital.com; **Prashad's**, Middle St and Thomas St, doctor on call at weekends, 24-hr malaria clinic, T226 7214/9 (US$2 to US$8 per day; medical consultations US$8 to US$15);

St Joseph Mercy, 130-132 Parade St, Kingston, T227 2073/5. If admitted to hospital you must bring sheets and food (St Joseph's provides these). **Georgetown Hospital** is understaffed even though facilities have improved.

Suriname
Academic Hospital (Academisch Ziekenhuis), Flustraat, Paramaribo, T442222, www.azp.sr. **Sint Vincentius Ziekenhuis**, Koninginnestraat 4, Paramaribo, T471212, www.svzsuriname.org.

Guyane
Centre Hospitalier Andrée Rosemond, Av des Flamboyants, 97300 Cayenne, T395050, www.ch-cayenne.net. Health information and list of other clinics can be found on www.guyane-amazonie.fr/infos-pratiques.

Money

Guyana
US$1 = G$198; €1 = G$221 (Jun 2017).
Exchange The unit is the Guyanese dollar. There are notes for 20, 50, 100, 500, 1000 and 5000 dollars. Coins are for 1, 5 and 10 dollars. Official exchange rate is adjusted weekly in line with the rate offered by licensed exchange houses (*cambios*). Rates vary slightly between *cambios* and from day to day and some *cambios* offer better rates for changing over US$100. There are ATMs in Georgetown. Also take cash dollars or euros. **Republic Bank** and *cambios* accept euros at best rates. A reputable, safe *cambio* in Georgetown is **Hand in Hand Trust Corporation**, Middle St, T226 9781, next to **Rima Guest House**. Take care with the roving *cambios* at the entrance to Stabroek market. To buy Suriname dollars, go to **Swiss House**, 25a Water St, a *cambio* in the unsafe market area around Water St and America St, known locally as 'Wall St'. There are others that will change Suriname dollars. Note that to sell Guyanese dollars on leaving, you will need to produce your *cambio* receipt. The black market on America St in Georgetown still operates, but rates offered are no better than the *cambio* rate. To avoid being robbed on the black market, or if you need to change money when *cambios* are closed, go by taxi and ask someone (preferably a friend) to negotiate for you. The black market also operates in Molson Creek/Springlands, the entry point from Suriname, and in Lethem at the Brazilian border (ask taxi drivers).

Cost of travelling Devaluation means that, for foreigners, prices for food and drink are low at present. Even imported goods may be cheaper than elsewhere and locally produced goods such as fruit are very cheap. Hotels, tours and services in the interior are subject to energy and fuel surcharges, making them less cheap.

Suriname

US$1 = SRD7.47; €1 = SRD8.36 (Jun 2017).

Exchange The unit of currency is the Suriname dollar (SRD), divided into 100 cents. There are notes for 1, 2.50, 5, 10, 20, 50 and 100 dollars. Coins are for 1 and 2.50 dollars and 1, 5, 10 and 25 cents (the 25-cent coin is usually known as a *kwartje*, 10-cent *dubbeltje* and 5-cent *stuiver*). Euros are readily exchanged in banks and with licensed money changers (*cambios*). The main banks that offer exchange are: **de Surinaamsche Bank; Finabank** (www.finabanknv.com, open on Sat 0900-1200); **Hakrinbank** (www.hakrinbank. com); **Republic Bank** (www.republicbanksr. com). There are ATMs throughout the city. On arrival at the Johan Adolf Pengel airport, you can exchange a wide variety of currencies into Surinamese dollars, including reais, Trinidad and Tobago dollars and Barbados dollars. In Paramaribo *cambios* at various locations are open till late and on Sat, but only accept US dollars and euros. A good, helpful one is **Multi Track Exchange**, van Sommelsdijkstraat at corner of Kleine Waterstraat, near the Torarica. Officially visitors must declare foreign currency on arrival. When arriving by land, visitors' funds are rarely checked, but you should be prepared for it. To check daily exchange rates for US dollars, euros, pounds sterling and other currencies, visit the **Central Bank** site, www.cbvs.sr. Prices can be quoted in SRD, US dollars or euros; check carefully as there seems to be no logic to it.

Guyane

US$1 = €0.89 (Jun 2017).

Exchange The currency is the euro. Take euros with you; many banks do not offer exchange facilities, but ATMs are common. Good rates can be obtained by using Visa or MasterCard (less common) to withdraw cash from any bank in Cayenne, Kourou and St-Laurent du Maroni. It is possible to pay for most hotels and restaurants with a Visa or MasterCard. American Express, Eurocard and Carte Bleue cards are also accepted. There's an exchange facility at the airport. A convenient cambio is **Global – Changes Caraïbes**, 68 av Général de Gaulle, Cayenne, open Mon-Fri 0730-1200, 1500-1730, changes US$ and reais into euros. It's almost impossible to change dollars outside Cayenne or Kourou.

Opening hours

Guyana

Banks: Mon-Thu 0800-1400, Fri 0800-1430. **Markets**: Mon-Sat 0800-1600, except Wed 0900-1200, Sun 0800-1000. **Shops**: Mon-Fri 0830-1600 or 1700, Sat 0830-1200.

Suriname

Banks: Mon-Fri 0900-1400 (airport bank is open when flights operate). **Government offices**: Mon-Thu 0700-1500, Fri 0700-1430. **Shops and businesses**: Mon-Fri 0800-1630 (some shops till 1900 on Fri), Sat 0800-1300. Asian supermarkets tend to keep longer hours.

Guyane

Hours vary widely between different offices, shops and even between different branches of the same bank. There seem to be different business hours for every day, but they are usually posted. Most shops and offices close for a few hours around midday.

Post

Guyana

The main post office is on Robb St, Georgetown, http://guypost.gy. There is another on Regent St, opposite Bourda market. There are postal centres in Lethem and at Rock View, Annai. Post offices are open Mon-Fri 0700-1500, some close 1130-1230; some open Sat 0700-1100.

Suriname

Surpost, Kerkplein 1, Paramaribo, T477 524, www.surpost.com.

Guyane

The main post office is on Route de Baduel, 2 km from the centre of Cayenne (take a taxi or 20 mins on foot).

Public holidays and festivals

Hindu and Muslim festivals

Hindu and Muslim festivals follow a lunar calendar, and dates should be checked as required: **Phagwah**, or **Holi**, usually in Mar, date varies each year, is the Hindu spring festival, when everyone is a target for coloured powder and coloured water; **Diwali**, or **Deepavali**, celebrated in the northern hemisphere autumn, is the **Hindu Festival of Light**, representing the triumph of knowledge, light and goodness over the darkness of ignorance and evil.

Significant dates in the Muslim calendar that are public holidays are **Eid al-Fitr**, end of Ramadan, the 1st day of the month of Shawwal (10th month of the lunar calendar); **Eid al-Adha** is the **Feast of Sacrifice** on the 10th day of the month of Dhu al-Hijjah, celebrating Ibrahim's (Abraham's) willingness to sacrifice his son; **Youman Nabi**, or **Mawlid al-Nabi**, commemorates the birthday of the Prophet Muhammad on the 12th day of the month of Rabi al-Awwal.

Guyana

The **Republic Day** celebrations (23 Feb) last for 1 day, but there are other activities (children's costume competition, etc) which take place during the preceding days. **Mashramani** (Mash) is the Guyanese equivalent of carnival and coincides with Republic Day. There are float parades, calypso and soca music, dancing and other events. Also, in the 2 weeks prior to 23 Feb, many large companies hold Mashramani Camps at which public participation is encouraged. Hotels in Georgetown are very full, as they are also during international cricket matches. At Eastertime the main event in the **Rupununi**, the Rodeo at Lethem, is held. Around 21-28 Aug, **Jam Zone Summer Break** is held at the Guyana National Stadium and HJ Water World in Providence, East Bank Demerara (Facebook: JamzoneSummerBreak) with concerts, pageants, fashion shows and sporting events. Also in Aug is the **Bartica Regatta**. Sep is **Heritage month** for indigenous communities, with games, food and drink in each village. 1 community is selected each year as the central point for a joint festival.

1 Jan New Year's Day.
23 Feb **Republic Day** and **Mashramani** festival.
Mar (usually) Phagwah.
Mar/Apr Good Fri, Easter Sun and Mon.
1 May Labour Day.
5 May Indian Arrival Day.
26 May Independence Day.
1st Mon Jul Caricom Day.
1st Mon Aug Emancipation Day.
Late Oct-early Nov Diwali (Deepavali). See above.
25-26 Dec Christmas Day and Boxing Day.

Suriname

The main tourist seasons are 19 Dec to Mar and Jul and Aug. Mid-Oct to end-Nov is also popular.

Surifesta (http://surifesta.com) is a year-end festival, from mid-Dec to the 2nd week of Jan, with shows, street parties and flower markets, culminating in a massive parade outside 't Vat and the igniting of giant strings of red *pagara* firecrackers in the centre of Paramaribo on 31 Dec. **Avondvierdaagse** (Four-Day Walk), starting on the 1st Wed after Easter, is a carnival parade of the young and old dressed in traditional costumes or just simple outfits; it is organized by **BVVS-Fernandes** (Johannes Mungrastraat 5, Paramaribo, T475623, www. bvss.sr or see Facebook). At the **Suriname Jazz Festival** (www.jazzfestivalsuriname. com) local and international jazz musicians perform in Paramaribo; it is held annually in October. **Nationale Kunstbeurs/National Art Fair/National Art Exhibition**, is held at various locations in Paramaribo in Oct/Nov (see Facebook: nationalekunstbeurssuriname).

1 Jan New Year's Day.
25 Feb Day of Liberation and Innovation.
Mar (usually) Phagwah (see above).
Mar/Apr Good Fri, Easter Sun and Mon.
1 May Labour Day.
1 Jul Emancipation Day.
9 Aug Indigenous People's Day, Javanese Immigration Day.
10 Oct Day of the Maroons.
Late Oct-early Nov Diwali (Deepavali).
25 Nov Independence Day.
25-26 Dec Christmas Day and Boxing Day.

Guyane

Guyane's Carnaval is joyous and interesting. It is principally a Créole event, but with some participation by all the different cultural groups (best known are the contributions of the Brazilian and Haitian communities). Celebrations begin in Jan, with festivities every weekend, and culminate in colourful parades, music and dance during the 4 days preceding Ash Wed. Each day has its own motif and the costumes are very elaborate. On Sat night, a dance called *Chez Nana – Au Soleil Levant* is held, for which the women disguise themselves beyond recognition as *Touloulous*, and ask the men to dance. They are not allowed to refuse. Since 1988 an additional dance has been added to Carnaval, *Le Bal Tololo*, on Fri night, the day before *Chez Nana*, in which the men disguise themselves with masks and fancy costumes and invite the women to dance. On Sun there are parades in downtown Cayenne. There are also street parades in other places, like Kourou and St-Laurent du

Maroni, usually earlier in the year than in Cayenne. **Lundi Gras** is the day to ridicule marriage, with mock wedding parties featuring men as brides and women as grooms. *Vaval*, the devil and soul of Carnaval, appears on **Mardi Gras** with dancers sporting red costumes, horns, tails, pitch-forks, etc. He is burnt that night (in the form of a straw doll) on a bonfire in the Place des Palmistes. **Ash Wednesday** is a time of sorrow, with participants dressed in black and white.

A full list of events can be found on **www.guyane-amazonie.fr**, but look out for the **Kali'na Amerindian Games** in early December, held in Awala Yalimapo. International teams take part in traditional sports. Public holidays are mostly the same as in Metropolitan France:

1 Jan   New Year's Day.
Feb/Mar   Carnival.
Mar/Apr   Good Fri, Easter Sun and Mon.
1 May   Labour Day.
8 May   Victory in Europe Day.
25 May   Ascension Day.
4-5 Jun   Whitsun.
10 Jun   Abolition of Slavery Day.
14 Jul   Bastille Day.
15 Aug   Assumption of Mary.
1 Nov   All Saints' Day.
11 Nov   Armistice Day.
25-26 Dec   Christmas Day and Boxing Day.

Tax

Guyana
Airport tax The G$6000 (US$30, €28.60) tax, made up of a security fee and a departure tax, is included in flight tickets. For international departures from Ogle airport, tax is G$3500 (US$17.70, €16.75). **VAT** 16%.

Suriname
Airport tax Departure tax is included in the air fare.

Guyane
Airport tax None.

Telephone and internet

In all 3 countries internet outside the cities, if available at all, is usually provided by satellite and use is restricted. Mobile reception is similarly unreliable. In the capital cities Wi-Fi can be found in many places and mobile reception is widespread.

Guyana *Country code +592.*
Ringing: a double ring, repeated regularly.

Engaged: equal tones, separated by equal pauses. Mobile phone reception outside Georgetown is patchy. In the Rupununi, for instance, few lodges have reception although at Annai there is GT&T reception and at Lethem GT&T and Digicel.

Suriname *Country code +597.*
Ringing: equal tones and long pauses.
Engaged: equal tones with equal pauses. **Telesur**, Heiligenweg 14, Paramaribo, T474242, www.sr.net, with branches nationwide. All **Telesur Dienstencentrum** offices offer email, fax, local and international phone and computer services. Phone cards for cheap international calls are available in newsagents, shops and hotels in Paramaribo, a better deal than Telesur card. In Nieuw Nickerie the telephone office is with the post office on Oost-Kanaalstraat, between Gouverneurstraat and R P Bharosstraat. If phoning within the city, omit 0 from the prefix. Mobile services are provided by **Telesur** and **Digicel**.

Guyane *Country code +594.*
Ringing: equal tones with long pauses.
Engaged: equal tones with equal pauses. Mobile services are operated by **Digicel** and **Orange**.

Time

Guyana
GMT -4 hrs; 1 hr ahead of EST (but the same as EST during US daylight saving).

Suriname
GMT -3 hrs.

Guyane
GMT -3 hrs.

Tourist information

Guyana
Guyana Tourism Authority, National Exhibition Center, Sophia, Georgetown, T219 0094, www.guyana-tourism.com, promotes the development of the tourism industry.
Ministry of Business, 229 South Rd, Lacytown, Georgetown, T226 2505, http://minbusiness.gov.gy/tourism/ creates tourism policy.
Tourism and Hospitality Association of Guyana (THAG), 157 Waterloo St, T225 0807, www.exploreguyana.org, is a private organization covering all areas of tourism, with an 80-page, full-colour magazine called *Explore Guyana*, available from the Association office.

Useful websites:

www.guyana.org For information and lots of useful links.

www.guyanabirding.com For birdwatching; see its associated newsletter, *Guyana Birding News*.

www.wwfguianas.org WWF Guianas Programme, the conservation initiative covering the 3 Guianas; offices in Georgetown, Paramaribo and Cayenne, Lotissement Katoury No 5, Route Montabo 97300, T313828.

Suriname

Suriname Hospitality and Tourism Association SHATA, Kristalstraat 1, Paramaribo, T710 0823, www.shata.sr, is a private organization including hotels and **Surinam Airways**, combining all the private organizations that used to exist independently.

Suriname Tourism Foundation, Dr J F Nassylaan 2, T424878, www.surinametourism.sr (in English). It publishes *The Official Tourist Destination Guide*.

Useful websites:

http://suriname.conservation.org Conservation International site with information on Suriname including the **Central Suriname Nature Reserve**. **www.whsrn.org** Western Hemisphere Shorebird Reserve Network, in which are the Bigi Pan, Wia Wia and Coppenamemonding reserves.

Guyane

The French Government tourist offices can usually provide leaflets on Guyane; also **Comité du Tourisme de la Guyane**, 1 rue Clapeyron, 75008 Paris, T33-1-4294 1516, bureauparisien@guyane-amazonie.fr, Mon-Fri 0900-1600. **Comité du Tourisme de la Guyane**, 12 rue Lallouette, BP 801, 97300 Cayenne, T05-94-296500, www.tourisme-guyane.com. See also www.ctguyane.fr. **Note** The Amerindian villages in the Haut-Maroni and Haut-Oyapock areas may only be visited with permission from the Préfecture in Cayenne *before* arrival in Guyane.

Protected areas:

The French government site **www.reserves-naturelles.org** has information on all Guyane's national parks. **www.guyane.developpement-durable.gouv.fr** has an *Atlas des Sites et Espaces protégés de Guyane* to download. Contact also **PNR de Guyane**, 31 rue François Arago, Cayenne, T289270, www.guyane-parcregional.fr, for Kaw-Roura and Amana, and **www.parc-amazonien-guyane.fr**, for the Parc Amazonien de Guyane.

Visas and immigration

Guyana

The following countries do not need a visa to visit Guyana: Australia, Argentina, Brazil, Canada, Colombia, Ecuador, Japan, New Zealand, Norway, Peru, Switzerland, Uruguay, USA, EU countries (except Cyprus, Czech Republic, Estonia, Hungary, Latvia, Lithuania, Malta, Poland, Slovak Republic and Slovenia) and the Commonwealth countries. Visitors are advised to check with the nearest embassy, consulate or travel agent for changes to this list. All visitors require a passport with 6 months' validity and all nationalities, apart from those above, require visas.

To obtain a visa you will need 2 photos, a letter of sponsorship and sponsor's contact number or email address, evidence of sufficient funds and, if coming from a country with yellow fever, a yellow fever certificate. Visa application forms can be found at **www.minfor.gov.gy** on the consular services pages. If Guyana has no representation in your country, apply to the Guyana Embassy in Washington DC, or the Guyana Consulate General in New York. Tourist visas cost US$25 for a period of 1 month initially, then US$25 for each additional month. Employment and student visas cost US$140 for 3 years in the first instance and an additional US$140 for each 3-year renewal. Business visas cost US$140 for 5 years in the first instance and US$140 for each 5-year renewal. Visitors from those countries where they are required arriving without visas are refused entry, unless a tour operator has obtained permission for the visitor to get a visa on arrival. To fly into Guyana, an exit ticket is required; at land borders an onward ticket is not usually asked for.

Suriname

Visitors must have a valid passport. Nationalities that do not need a visa or tourist card include: Israel, Japan, Malaysia, Philippines, South Korea, Gambia, Argentina, Brazil, Chile, Belize, Guyana and other Caricom member states. Nationals of the following countries may apply for a tourist card: the majority of EU countries (not Bulgaria, Cyprus, Ireland, Poland, Romania), Canada, Cuba, Indonesia, Mexico, Norway, Singapore, Switzerland, Turkey, USA, South American countries (except Argentina and Brazil – see above), Central American countries and foreigners of Surinamese origin. The card is valid for one entry by air of 90 days (but after 30 days you must apply to the Immigration Department, address below, for an extension); it costs €30/

US$35 (exact cash only) and can be obtained at a Surinamese embassy or consulate, the tourist card counter at **Schiphol Airport**, Amsterdam, T020-622 6717 (closed Sunday), or on arrival at Johan Adolf Pengel Airport (there may be long queues here). You need a passport valid for 6 months and a return flight ticket. See under St-Laurent du Maroni, Border with Suriname, page 1726, for details of the consulate in Cayenne. If your flights into and out of South America land at and depart from Johan Adolf Pengel Airport and you intend to visit countries in addition to Suriname, you must check whether you need to get a new tourist card to re-enter Suriname for your flight home.

For all other nationals, to obtain a visa in advance, you must apply to a Surinamese embassy or consulate up to 6 weeks before your scheduled departure to Suriname. You need to fill in an application form (which can be obtained online on consular websites) and submit it with a copy of your passport photo page, valid for 6 months, and a computer-generated itinerary or round-trip ticket. You will then be issued with a letter and another form to be completed with a passport photo and presented on arrival at Johan Pengel Airport where the visa fee must be paid. A 3-month tourist visa, single entry: €40; multiple entry: €40/US$42 for 3 months, €150 (US$158) for 12 months. A visa for US passport holders is US$100 for 5 years, multiple entry. A transit visa costs €10 (US$10.55). A business visa costs from €50 (US$53) (2 months) to €300 (US$316 – 2 years). See the websites of the Suriname consulate in The Netherlands, www.consulaatsuriname.nl, the embassy in the US, www.surinameembassy.org, or consulate in Miami, surcgmia@bellsouth.net, for latest details (prices vary in some cases). If arriving by land or sea, you cannot use a Visa on Arrival document; you must obtain a visa sticker from a consulate. Procedures at consulates vary: in Cayenne visa applications normally take 1 day, 2 passport photos are required. In Georgetown visa applications can be submitted at any time, but only collected when the consular section is open on Mon, Wed and Fri morning. If applying when the consulate is open, visas are usually processed on the same day. On entry into Suriname (by land or air) your passport will be stamped by immigration for 30 days. If you wish to stay in Suriname longer than 3 months, you must apply within 2 weeks of arrival in Suriname (at least 3 months if you are visa holder) for **Authorization of Temporary**

Stay (Machtiging Kort Verblijf, MVK) which is subject to a €10 administration fee, a €40 or US$42 fee and a US$150 finalization charge. MVK applications must be sent to a Suriname consulate or embassy. An exit stamp is given by the Immigration office at the airport or land border. If you want a multiple-entry visa or have any other enquiries, go to the **Immigration Department/Registration of Foreigners**, Mr J Lachmonstraat 166-8, Paramaribo, T597-490666, Mon-Fri 0700-1430, or **the Ministry of Foreign Affairs**, consular section, Lim A Po Straat and Watermolen straat, Paramaribo, T473575, sec. conza@foreignaffairs.gov.sr.

Note If you are arriving from Guyana, Guyane or Brazil in theory you need a certificate of vaccination against yellow fever to be allowed entry. It is not always asked for.

Guyane

Passports are not required by nationals of France and most French-speaking African countries carrying identity cards. For EU visitors, documents are the same as for Metropolitan France (that is no visa, no exit ticket required – check with a consulate in advance). EU passports must be stamped if arriving overland from Suriname or Brazil; be sure to visit Immigration, it is easy to miss. If arriving by air, EU citizens are not required to get an entry stamp, although you can join the queue for non-EU citizens to get one, or at least ask if you should have one. There is nowhere in Cayenne to get an entry stamp, only at the airport.
Note Whether or not you have an entry stamp, you must get an exit stamp. No visa required for most nationalities (except for those of Guyana, Suriname, some Eastern European countries – not Croatia – and Asian – not Japan – and other African countries) for a stay of up to 3 months. A flight ticket out of the country is required in theory (a ticket out of one of the other Guianas is also in theory not sufficient); a deposit is required otherwise. It is not always asked for, especially for EU citizens. Likewise, a yellow fever vaccination certificate is also required if arriving from Brazil, Suriname or Guyana, but it is not always asked for. If you stay more than 3 months, income tax clearance is required before leaving the country. A visa costs €60, or equivalent (US$63).

Weights and measures

All 3 countries are officially metric, although imperial is still widely used in Guyana.

This is
Falkland Islands/
Islas Malvinas

These remote South Atlantic outposts where there are more penguins than people may be windswept, but the islands are a haven for wildlife and a paradise for those who wish to see it: albatrosses nest in the tussac grass, sea lions breed on the beaches and dolphins cruise off the coast. About 640 km (400 miles) east of the South American mainland, the Falklands Islands/Islas Malvinas are made up of two large islands and over 748 smaller ones. Together with distant neighbours South Georgia and the South Sandwich Islands, they are the only part of South America where the British monarch's head appears on the stamps. The islands' remoteness adds to the charm of being able to see marine wildlife and, above all, penguins at close range. Based on 2010 census figures from Falklands Conservation, there are about 400,000 breeding pairs of five species of penguin (king, magellanic, gentoo, rockhopper, macaroni) in the islands. This compares with a human population of just 2844 (according to preliminary results from the 2016 census). The capital, Stanley, is a small, modern town, with reminders of its seafaring past in the hulks of sailing ships in the harbour. To visit the camp, as the land outside Stanley is known, 4WD vehicles make tours and you can fly to farming and island outposts for warm hospitality, huge skies and unparalleled nature watching.

In accordance with the practice suggested by the UN, we are calling the islands by both their English and Spanish names.

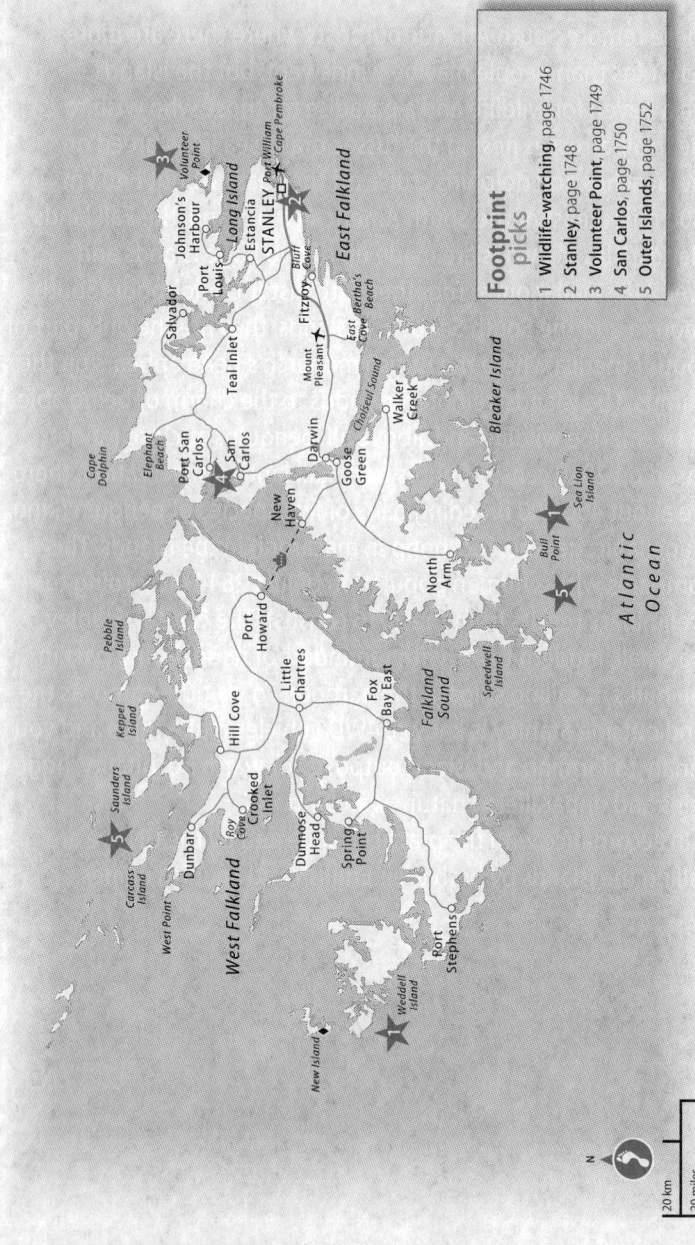

Footprint picks

1 **Wildlife-watching**, page 1746
2 **Stanley**, page 1748
3 **Volunteer Point**, page 1749
4 **San Carlos**, page 1750
5 **Outer Islands**, page 1752

Volunteer Point

Port William
Cape Pembroke

Johnson's Harbour
Long Island
STANLEY
Estancia
Port Louis
Bluff Cove
Salvador

East Falkland

Teal Inlet
Fitzroy
East Bertha's Cove Beach
Mount Pleasant
Choiseul Sound
Cape Dolphin
Walker Creek
Elephant Beach
Bleaker Island
Port San Carlos
San Carlos
Darwin
Goose Green
Pebble Island
New Haven
North Arm
Sea Lion Island
Keppel Island
Port Howard
Bull Point
Saunders Island
Hill Cove
Little Chartres
Fox Bay East
Falkland Sound
Speedwell Island
Carcass Island
Dunbar
Roy Cove
Crooked Inlet
Dunnose Head
Spring Point

West Falkland

West Point
Port Stephens
Weddell Island
New Island

Atlantic Ocean

N

20 km
20 miles

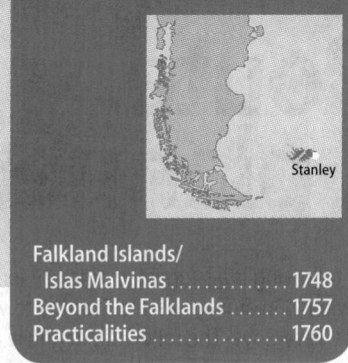

Footprint
picks

★ Wildlife-watching, page 1746

There are countless opportunities to see seabirds, penguins and marine
mammals at close range. This will be the main purpose of your visit.

★ Stanley, page 1748

The capital and main port has interesting public buildings,
a fascinating walk through maritime history and a variety
of places to stay, eat and drink.

★ Volunteer Point, page 1749

An exciting off-road journey will take you to the most accessible
nesting colony of king penguins in the world, plus plenty of other birds.

★ San Carlos, page 1750

One of several sites with strong associations with 1982, but also an
easily accessible view of Falklands' community life and a good base
for exploring East Falkland.

★ Outer Islands, page 1752

Not only do the smaller islands offer great wildlife spotting, they also
provide warm hospitality and, what's more, the flight getting there is
an essential part of the experience.

Route planner

The following is a suggested itinerary for a one-week stay in the Falklands/Malvinas. On arrival, head to **Stanley** to visit the Falkland Islands Museum and Gypsy Cove. The following day, take a 4WD tour to **Volunteer Point**, the world's most accessible King Penguin colony. Then head west to **San Carlos**, where Kingsford Valley Farm is a great base for exploring upper East Falkland. If flight itineraries allow, spend a couple of days at **Pebble Island Lodge** to admire the island's semi-precious pebbles and diverse marine and wetland birdlife. **Saunders Island** is another good option for more wildlife-spotting, either on foot or by 4WD, including four species of penguin and black-browed albatross at the Neck. After returning to Stanley visit the **1982 battlefield sites** on your way to Mount Pleasant Airport. An additional week would allow you to visit **West Falkland** and some more of the Outer Islands, such as **Carcass** or **Wedell**.

★Wildlife calendar

For wildlife enthusiasts, especially ornithologists, the islands are an exceptional destination. King and gentoo penguins are present the year round. Rockhoppers are on land October to May, magellanic penguins September to April. The black-browed albatross breeding season is September to May. Elephant seals are ashore September-December; adults haul out late January/early February to moult for 25 days. Sea lions can be seen December-March. Sei whales usually arrive in Falkland waters in January/February and remain till May/June. Other whale species may be seen in the same period, but not usually close to shore. Orcas are best seen on Sea Lion Island when sea lion pups are going to sea. Commerson's and Peale's dolphins are present the year round, but the former are less evident in winter. The most common birds are upland geese; other frequently seen geese are kelp and ruddy-headed. The flightless steamer duck (logger duck) can be seen in many places, as can Falkland skuas, southern giant petrels, Patagonian crested duck, speckled teal, grebes, shags, gulls and shorebirds such as magellanic and blackish oystercatchers. The rarest bird of prey in the world, the striated caracara (Johnny Rook) can easily be seen in several places (Sea Lion, Carcass, Weddell). Smaller birds that are easy to see include the striking long-tailed meadowlark, dark-faced ground tyrant, Falkland thrush and pipit. In islands unaffected by introduced predators you'll see the friendly tussacbird and the rarer Cobb's wren. There are many other common bird species (227 recorded in total) and, for botanists, plants of interest. For wildlife calendar, booklists, checklists and reports: **Falklands Conservation**, Jubilee Villas, corner of Philomel Street and Ross Road (access from Philomel Street), Stanley, T22247, FIQQ 1ZZ (David Spivack, The Gatehouse, The Lodge, Sandy, Bedfordshire, SG19 2DL, UK, T01767-693710), www.falklandsconservation.com, Monday-Friday 0800-1200, 1300-1630, also sells clothing, badges and books.

Getting around

To explore East Falkland requires a 4WD; many places are best visited as part of a tour. The outer islands are reached by short flights from Stanley Airport. There is a car ferry linking East and West Falkland. See Getting around, page 1760.

When to go

Best months to visit are October to April; some places to stay are only open in these months. This is the best time for most wildlife watching, too; see Wildlife calendar, opposite. The islands are in the same latitude south as London is north. The climate is cool and oceanic, dominated by persistent westerly winds which average 16 knots. Long periods of calm are rare except in winter. Though not always inclement, weather is very changeable but temperatures vary relatively little. At Stanley, the capital, the mean temperature in summer (January/February) is 15.4°C, but temperatures frequently exceed this on the islands. Stanley's annual rainfall is slightly higher than London's. In the drier camp, outside Stanley, summer drought sometimes threatens local water supplies. A dusting of snow may occur at any time of the year. Always wear water and windproof clothing; wear good boots and a peaked hat to protect the eyes from rain or hail. Sunblock is essential.

Time required

As flights from Chile only go once a week, stays in multiples of seven days are the only option. In one week you can see Stanley and a couple of nearby attractions, plus a bit of West Falkland or one or two islands, but the inter-island flight schedules will determine how much time you can stay on the outer islands. In two weeks you can see much more of East and West Falkland and several outer islands. The airbridge from the UK offers more flexibility. Cruise ship passengers do not disembark for more than a few hours.

Fact file
Location 51.2888° N, 2.3772° W
Capital Stanley
Time zone GMT -3 hrs (September-April) or -4 hrs (May-August)
Telephone country code +500
Currency Falklands pound (£)

Weather Falklands/Malvinas

January	February	March	April	May	June
14°C 7°C 57mm	14°C 7°C 53mm	12°C 6°C 53mm	8°C 3°C 51mm	6°C 2°C 43mm	3°C 1°C 42mm

July	August	September	October	November	December
4°C 1°C 42mm	5°C 1°C 29mm	6°C 1°C 32mm	9°C 2°C 31mm	11°C 4°C 39mm	13°C 6°C 57mm

Falkland Islands/
Islas Malvinas

★Stanley

The capital, Stanley, on East Falkland, is the major population centre. Its residents live mostly in houses painted white, many of which have brightly coloured corrugated iron roofs. Surrounded by rolling moorland, Stanley fronts the enclosed **Harbour**. The outer harbour of Port William is larger but less protected.

Relocated in 2014, the new **Historic Dockyard Museum** ① *The Dockyard, Stanley, T27428, www.falklands-museum.com, Tue-Fri 1000-1600, Sat 0900-1100, 1400-1700, Sun 1400-1700 (closed Sat morning in winter, from late Apr), extended hours on cruise ship days, admission £5 (concessions for children and seniors)*, covers all aspects of Falklands life, with galleries dedicated to social and maritime history, the war in 1982 and Antarctic heritage (featuring an authentic Antarctic refuge). A blacksmith's shop, a printing office and the R/T & Telephone Exchange are also part of the site, which itself dates from the founding of Stanley. It also has a gift shop and the Teaberry Café. The ticket includes a visit to **Cartmell Cottage** ① *by prior appointment only*, one of the original pioneer houses, whose interior reflects life in the late 19th century and the 1940s.

You can walk the length of the harbour front, from the wreck of the *Jhelum* (built in 1839 for the East India Company, now beginning to collapse) in the west, to the iron-built *Lady Elizabeth* at the far eastern end of the harbour (228 ft, with three masts still standing). A **Maritime History Trail** along the front has interpretive panels; a book describing the Stanley wrecks is sold at the museum. On the way you will pass **Government House**, the **Anglican Cathedral** (most southerly in the world, built in 1892) with a whalebone arch outside, several monuments commemorating the naval battle of 1914, the Royal Marines and the 1982 liberation. Among the latter is the **Memorial Wood**, off Ross Road East, where every tree is named for a British and Falkland casualty. Where Ross Road East turns inland, you can carry on east along the coastal path, past the FIPASS floating harbour and around the head of the bay to *Lady Elizabeth*. At low tide you can walk out to her.

> **Tip...**
> Visit the **public library**, T27147, in the Community School, for a good selection of books on travel and flora/fauna.

Around Stanley

Follow the bay round from the wreck and eventually you will come to **Gypsy Cove**, four miles, two hours' walk each way from centre (10 minutes by car). It features a colony of magellanic penguins, black-crowned night herons and other shorebirds. Occasionally, visitors can also spot orca, elephant seals, sea lions and variable hawks. There are minefield fences which prevent close inspection of the penguins; Yorke Bay, where the Argentine forces landed in 1982, is off limits.

Cape Pembroke lighthouse sits on the end of Cape Pembroke Peninsula and is open to the general public (an access key is available from the Museum for a £5 charge). The Cape itself offers great day walking, with plenty of wildlife watching: dolphins, whales and numerous bird species. There is also an impressive memorial to the crew of the *Atlantic Conveyor*, a supply ship sunk by Argentine forces during the 1982 Conflict.

Sparrow Cove, **Kidney Cove** and adjacent areas, only a short distance from Stanley by boat, are good areas to see four species of penguin and other wildlife. Tours are the only way to get there.

Long Island Farm, 20 miles from Stanley, is a 22,000-acre sheep farm belonging to a sixth generation Falkland Island family, whose traditional way of life, with a dairy and using sheep dogs and island-bred horses to gather sheep, is popular with cruise passengers and day trippers. There are excellent hikes along the beach and shore of Berkeley Sound, with rockhopper, gentoo and magellanic penguins.

★Volunteer Point

Track open 1 Nov-30 Apr. Admission £15; children £7.50; under-6s free (admission may be included in tour price). All visitors must obtain permission to visit the area from the wardens, Derek and Trudi Pettersson, T32000, drp@horizon.co.fk. Camping is possible by prior arrangement. Chemical toilets and a shelter near the penguins.

Volunteer Point, on the peninsula north of Berkeley Sound, is a **wildlife sanctuary** and the most accessible king penguin colony in the world with an estimated 2000 penguins (January 2017). There are also over 5000 gentoo penguins, about 2000 magellanic penguins, upland geese, ruddy-headed geese and many small birds. Sealions and dolphins are sometimes seen from the beautiful white-sand beach. The area can get quite busy on cruise-ship days. Visitors must remain outside the no-entry areas, marked with white stones, to avoid disturbing the breeding penguins. Visitors are advised to use local guides as the journey is about 2½ to three hours from Stanley. The first 35 miles are on all-weather road and the remaining 14 miles on off-road tracks where 4WD vehicles must be used.

Volunteer Point is part of a private farm (Johnson's Harbour) and is owned by Mrs Jan Cheek, jancheek@horizon.co.fk. The farm is approximately 36,000 acres and runs around 10,000 sheep. Photos of the area may be seen on **Facebook** (www.facebook.com/volunteershouse) and at www.volunteerpoint.co.fk.

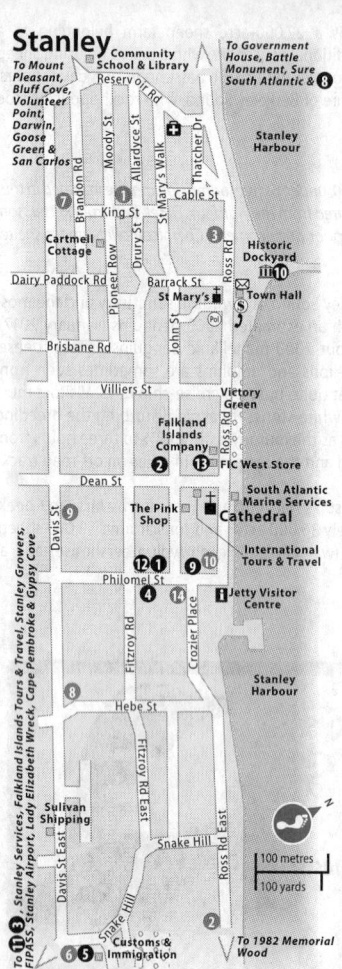

Stanley

To Mount Pleasant, Bluff Cove, Volunteer Point, Darwin, Goose Green & San Carlos

To Mount Pleasant School & Library

To Government House, Battle Monument, Sure South Atlantic & 🚤

Community

Stanley Harbour

Historic Dockyard

Town Hall

Victory Green

Falkland Islands Company

FIC West Store

South Atlantic Marine Services

The Pink Shop

Cathedral

International Tours & Travel

Jetty Visitor Centre

Stanley Harbour

Sulivan Shipping

To 1982 Memorial Wood

Customs & Immigration

To Stanley Services, Falkland Islands Tours & Travel, Stanley Growers, FIPASS, Stanley Airport, Lady Elizabeth Wreck, Cape Pembroke & Gypsy Cove

100 metres
100 yards

Where to stay
1 Bennett House B&B
2 Lafone Guest
3 Malvina House
6 Shorty's Motel
7 Susana Binnie's
8 The Paddock B&B
9 The Pale Maiden
10 Waterfront Hotel & Kitchen Café

3 Lighthouse Seaman's Centre
4 Michele's Café
5 Shorty's Diner
8 Stanley Arms Bar
9 Tasty Treat
10 Teaberry Café
11 The Narrows Bar
12 Victory Bar
13 West Store Café

Restaurants 🍴
1 BitterSweet
2 Deano's Bar

Bars & clubs 🍸
14 Globe

West of Stanley
Bertha's Beach, a 10-minute drive from Mount Pleasant Military Complex, is popular for its beautiful white sand beach with abundant bird life. Dolphins often come close to shore as they hunt in the shallows. To get through the locked gate to the beach, ask for the key from the farm manager at Fitzroy (T32384).

Beyond Mount Pleasant, the road divides, one branch turning north to San Carlos (see below), the other going to **Darwin** (1½ hours from Stanley), where an original iron barque ship, the *Garland*, can be seen across the bay. Within the settlement a section of mast from the *SS Gt Britain* stands on a hill alongside a gaucho corral built in 1874. Just before Darwin is the Argentine cemetery for those killed in the 1982 conflict, and just beyond, the larger settlement of **Goose Green**. Here the skeletal remains of the *Vicar of Bray*, last survivor of the California Gold Rush fleet, can be seen attached to the end of the jetty.

Lafonia
Lafonia forms the southern half of East Falkland. From Goose Green a road runs to the ferry dock for West Falkland at New Haven (35 minutes). Apart from a gentoo colony, there is nothing at the ramp. **North Arm** is one of four settlements in the flat expanses of Lafonia, a three-hour drive from Stanley. It has a small museum (T32080). **Bull Point** is the most southerly point of East Falkland; its wildlife includes 32 species of birds. Also near North Arm are **Tweeds Valley**, with 53 species of flora and fauna, and **Fanny Cove**, with some great rock formations. These locations can only be reached off-road so a tour guide is necessary.

★San Carlos and upper East Falkland
The road to **San Carlos** is hilly, with lovely views of higher mountains inland and the bays and inlets of Falkland Sound to the west. San Carlos (two hours from Stanley) is a picturesque waterside settlement and an excellent base for exploring upper East Falkland. Here is the English cemetery from the 1982 conflict and a museum covering the conflict and the local way of life. At **Kingsford Valley Farm** there is accommodation at the **White Grass Cottage** (see Where to stay), an attractive place by the water. You can also enjoy 'smoko' – tea and cake – at the White Grass Café.

The new road network makes it possible to head north to **Port San Carlos**, **Elephant Beach Farm** (see Where to stay for both) and Cape Dolphin. At **Elephant Beach Farm**, a 1½-hour drive from Stanley, gentoo penguins and many other bird species, sea lions, Commerson's and Peale's dolphins can be seen. The private property offers fishing for Falkland mullet in the tidal lagoon, and fossicking among the whale skeletons on the coast. **Cape Dolphin**, at the northernmost tip of East Falkland, supports three species of penguin, storm petrels, sea lions, the occasional whale and large numbers of ducks and birds on Swan Pond. Allow a full day to make the most of the cape; camping is also possible by prior arrangement. You can return to Stanley on the North Camp road via Teal Inlet and Estancia.

★East Falkland: outer islands

Bleaker Island Owned by Phyl and Mike Rendell, T32491, mrendell@horizon.co.fk, www. bleakerisland.com; see Cobb's Cottage and Cassard House, below. Hardly bleak, this island has a wonderful coastline with white sandy beaches and sheltered coves. Bird species include rockhoppers, magellanic and gentoo penguins, waterfowl, ruddy-headed geese, Falkland skuas and an impressive imperial shag colony of some 8000 pairs. The island's annual survey recorded 3,300 gentoo and 700 rockhopper breeding pairs in 2016. The area north of the settlement was declared a National Nature Reserve in 1972. One of the key features of the island is Big Pond, where you can spot black-necked swan, Chiloe wigeon, silvery and white-tufted grebes, speckled and silver teal and occasionally the rare flying steamer duck.

Sea Lion Island In the southeast, 35 minutes' flight from Stanley, Sea Lion Island is a wildlife sanctuary, a delightful place to explore and relax. The lodge (see Where to stay), open in the austral summer, is within easy reach of the wildlife. Many southern sea lions breed on the beaches; it is also the largest breeding ground for southern elephant seals in the islands. Up to three pods of orca whales are resident around the island and can be seen cruising the shore in search of elephant seal and sea lion pups risking their first swim (summer months). The island also has magnificent bird life: gentoo, magellanic and rockhopper penguins, giant petrels (known locally as stinkers; these can be seen but no longer breed here), imperial shag, flightless steamer and other ducks, black-crowned night herons, tussacbird, Cobb's wren, oystercatcher (magellanic and blackish) and striated caracara. Also on the island is the *HMS Sheffield* memorial.

West Falkland

Fewer than 50 people live on West Falkland. **Port Howard** is one of the principal settlements, a neat, picturesque place, and the largest privately owned farm in the Islands with approximately 42,000 sheep and 1000 cattle running across 200,000 acres. The original settlement is 3.5 km south and Bold Cove is the site of the first British landing by Captain John Strong in 1690. It's an excellent base to explore West Falkland (see **Port Howard Lodge**, page 1754). Activities include trout fishing; 4WD tours to wildlife and flora, 1982 war relics, fossil beds; hiking to Mount Maria.

About an hour west of Port Howard a road branches northwest to **Hill Cove** settlement, another 30 minutes' drive. You can visit the largest forest in the Falklands (an experiment in shelter planting). Further west is **Crooked Inlet Farm** at Roy Cove. Joy and Danny Donnelly run the sheep farm and still use horses for sheep work (see Where to stay, page 1754). The settlement is very photogenic, particularly in late spring when the yellow gorse blooms; commanding views over King George Bay to Hammock and Middle Islands.

In the centre of West Falkland is **Little Chartres**. West is a beautiful road to **Dunnose Head**, a centre for Falklands wool craft (ask if staying locally) and **Shallow Harbour**, passing the Narrows and Town Point nature reserves. To the south is **Fox Bay**, the largest settlement; half is government-owned, half, Fox Bay West, is private. The road passes Hawksnest Ponds, where swans may be seen, in a region of 2000 lakes and ponds. **Port Stephens** is a spectacular piece of country at the southwestern tip of West Falkland. Accessible by road and air, the area has rugged headlands, home to rockhopper and gentoo penguins, as well as many unusual geological formations at Indian Village and breathtaking coastal scenery; see also Where to stay, page 1754.

★West Falkland: outer islands

Pebble Island This is the third largest offshore island and is named after the semi-precious agates found on its beaches. Pebble is home to more than 40 species, including rockhopper, macaroni, gentoo and magellanic penguins, imperial shags, caracara and hawks. Sea lions can also be found on the coast. The eastern half of Pebble Island contains the Falklands' longest sand beach as well as extensive wetlands full of waterfowl and wading birds including black-necked swans.

Saunders Island Besides a representative sample of wildlife, Saunders contains the ruins of the 18th-century British outpost at **Port Egmont**. There is a small group of king penguins at the **Neck**, a three-hour walk or 45 minutes by Land Rover from the settlement. Gentoo, magellanic, rockhoppers, imperial shag and black-browed albatross can also be seen here, as well as dolphins wave surfing and whales spouting. A further 1½ to two hours' walk goes to the point where elephant seals can be seen. At the **Rookery**, on the north coast, you can see rockhoppers, imperial shag and black-browed albatross. Another good place is the bay just north of the Settlement with many gentoo and magellanic penguins. There are many other wildlife sites on this large island.

Carcass Island Taking its name from *HMS Carcass* which visited in the late 18th century, this island is west of Saunders. One of the most beautiful and attractive islands for wildlife and scenery, species include striated caracara, gentoo and magellanic penguins, gulls, geese and elephant seals. The island also has great examples of tussac grass. The island is cat, rat and mice free, allowing small bird species such as Cobb's wren to flourish. A recommended trip from Carcass is to **West Point Island**, to see a large colony of black-browed albatross and rockhoppers. Dolphins may be seen on the way. The crossing is about an hour each way; ask Rob McGill at Carcass Island farmhouse for details.

Weddell Island Named after explorer James Weddell, Weddell Island, in the southwest, is the third largest island of the archipelago, a little bigger than the island of Malta but with only two residents. It offers fully catered and self-catering accommodation, an interesting history, diverse flora and plenty of wildlife. This includes magellanic and gentoo rookeries, sea lions in the tussac grass, imperial shags, shore birds, geese and introduced species such as Patagonian grey fox and reindeer. In the surrounding waters are albatross, more sea lions, Peale's and Commerson's dolphins. There are good hikes straight out of the settlement.

New Island At the extreme western edge of the archipelago, New Island is a nature reserve owned by the **New Island Conservation Trust** ① *www.newislandtrust.co.uk*. The aim of the project, begun in 1973 by Ian Strange, is to ensure that the island operates as a reserve in perpetuity. There is a fully equipped field station in the settlement for scientific studies. The **Captain Charles Barnard Memorial Museum and Visitor Centre** is visited by passengers on cruise vessels. Contact can be made through the Trust's website.

Listings Falkland Islands/Islas Malvinas *map p1750*

Where to stay

Stanley

$$$$ Malvina House
3 Ross Rd, T21355, www.malvinahousehotel.com.
Very good, spacious executive and standard rooms, full board available, power showers, hot drinks, central heating, TV, nice restaurant, bar, sauna/jacuzzi, laundry, Wi-Fi for guests.

$$$$ Waterfront Hotel
36 Ross Rd, T21462, www.waterfronthotel.co.fk.

Comfortable en suite rooms, TV, modern facilities, welcoming, Wi-Fi. Waterfront kitchen café offers lunch and dinner, very helpful.

$$$$-$$$ The Pale Maiden
31 Davis St, T22660, www.thepalemaiden.com.
1 Oct-30 Apr.
Central, purpose-built, luxury B&B, with 4 individually decorated rooms, continental breakfast, lounge, good views. New in 2017.

$$$ pp Lafone House
Ross Road, T22891, arlette@horizon.co.fk,
Facebook: LafoneHouse.

Owned and run by Arlette Betts, luxury B&B, good harbour views, evening meals on request, very good food.

$$$-$$ The Paddock B&B
38 Davis St, T21466.
Central B&B with spacious rooms, welcoming, internet hotspot, parking, laundry, Spanish spoken. In same group as The Waterfront.

$$ pp Bennett House B&B
14 Allardyce St, T21191, celiastewart@horizon.co.fk.
Owned and run by Celia Stewart. Central, excellent home baking and breakfast, 3 rooms, 2 en suite, good views, welcoming. Camping £20 pp per night, including breakfast and use of house.

$$ pp Shorty's Motel
Snake Hill, T22861, marleneshort@horizon.co.fk.
All rooms en suite, laundry, internet, next to Shorty's Diner.

$$ pp Susana Binnie's
3 Brandon Rd, T21051.
Central B&B with 1 double room, shared bath, Spanish spoken.

Volunteer Point
The wardens, Derek and Trudi Pettersson (drp@ horizon.co.fk), offer full-board accommodation ($$$ pp) for up to 4 guests and transfers from Stanley or Mount Pleasant.

West of Stanley

$$$ Darwin House
Stanley Services Ltd, T31313, www.darwin-house.com. 1 Sep tp 31 May.
Comfortable accommodation in 6 en suite rooms, suitable for families, living room, conservatory, good walking in the area, tours can be arranged. Open daily for smoko (1100-1700) and lunch and dinner on request.

Lafonia
In North Arm 5 houses have self-catering, fully equipped, sleeping 5-10 people. The farm has a small shop for everyday items and frozen food, but take your own supplies. En route to Bull Point are 4 houses for rent, basic self-catering with peat stove and diesel generator (they are off-road, so a guide is needed). Take sleeping bags/ bedding, towels and food. A taste of old-style Falkland life. Contact Steven Dickson and Emma Reid (T32080).

San Carlos and upper East Falkland

$$$ pp Race Point Farm
Port San Carlos, John and Michelle Jones, T41012, jhjones@horizon.co.fk.
Full board and B&B available in a comfortable and modern 2-bedroom, self-catering cottage sleeping up to 8. TV, DVDs. Laundry, internet and phone on request. Gentoo, magellenic and rockhopper penguins are a short overland drive away at Fanning Head and Rookery Sands. 4WD guided tours are available. Good walks and excellent trout fishing on the San Carlos River. Horse riding available. Also have a flat for rent.

$$ pp Elephant Beach Farm (James Cabin)
T41020, benebf@horizon.co.fk.
Self-catering cottage sleeps up to 8. DVD, video, games etc, gas stove only for cooking. Tours of north coastline.

$$ pp White Grass Cottage at Kingsford Valley Farm
San Carlos settlement, East Falkland, T32044.
On a working farm, run by Andi Neate and Matthew McMullen. Close to trout fishing, San Carlos cemetery and museum.

East Falkland: outer islands

$$$$-$$$ pp Sea Lion Lodge
Sea Lion Island, T32004, sealion_lodge@horizon. co.fk or www.sealionisland.com. 1 Sep-31 Mar, high season prices Nov-end Feb.
Full board, some single rooms with shared bath, purpose-built, picture windows, comfortable, central heating, good bathrooms, good home cooking, packed lunches available for when you wish to go wildlife-watching, orientation tours, internet.

$$$ pp Cassard House
Bleaker Island, T21084 (Stanley), T32491 (Bleaker Island), mrendell@horizon.co.fk (Mike Rendell), www.bleakerisland.com. 30-min flight south from Stanley.
4 en suite bedrooms, well-equipped kitchen, local decorations, Wi-Fi, high standards.

$$$ pp Cobb's Cottage
Bleaker Island.
2 en suite bedrooms finished to a high standard throughout. Good wildlife. At both Bleaker Island properties full board is available 1 Oct to 30 Apr. Also wildlife tour £30.

West Falkland

$$$ pp Port Howard Lodge
Port Howard, West Falkland, T42187,
porthowardlodge@horizon.co.fk.
Sue Lowe and Wayne Brewer. Prices seasonal,
full board, all rooms en suite, central heating,
honesty bar, excellent food. Wayne takes Land
Rover tours (£30 for general interest) and will
drive to first class trout fishing spots, rod hire.
Has a small war museum, and the chance to see
the workings of a traditional large sheep station.

Crooked Inlet Farm
Roy Cove, Danny and Joy Donnelly, T41102,
j.d.donnelly@horizon.co.fk.
A comfortable self-catering property.
Also trout fishing, horse riding or
guided 4WD tours of the area.

Port Stephens
T42307, par@horizon.co.fk.
Self-catering accommodation in 2-bedroom
house, with kitchen/diner, central heating,
DVDs, in the settlement, a great base to explore
the region, very helpful hosts, Peter and Ann
Robertson, who run the farm here.

Shallow Bay Self Catering
25 mins from Hill Cove settlement,
contact Paul and Davina Peck, T41007,
psb@horizon.co.fk or daepeck@horizon.
Accommodation in the original stone home.
Meals available on request.

West Falkland: outer islands

$$$$-$$$ pp Pebble Island Lodge
Pebble Island, T41093, www.pebblelodge.com.
This cosy, well-appointed lodge is run by Riki
Evans ($$$ Oct and Mar). En suite rooms, central
heating, full board, lounge, TV and DVD, Wi-Fi
and island tours (£78 for a day).

$$$ pp Carcass Island
T41106, lorraine@horizon.co.fk.
Owned and run by Rob and Lorraine McGill.
Rooms are in the main farmhouse, full board,
excellent food, honesty bar, lounge with TV and
DVDs, gardens, open summer only. Tours to sites
on the island, perfect combination of hospitality
and wildlife.

$$$-$$ pp Saunders Island
Suzan and David Pole-Evans, T41298,
www.saundersfalklands.com.
At the settlement are 2 self-catering cottages, for
10 and 6, $$ pp per night. Self-catering **Portakabin**

sleeping 8 at the Neck, with 24-hr power, heating,
cooker ($$$ pp, camping £20 per night, transport
£70). Self-catering **Rookery Cabin**, within walking
distance of the Rookery, is modern, sleeps 4,
24-hr power, kitchen/diner, shower room, heating
($$$ pp, transport £30). Towels provided in all
lodgings. A shop at the settlement sells supplies.
Full board available on request.

Weddell Island
T42398, www.weddellisland.com. Oct-Mar.
Martin and Jane Beaton offer 2 charming
cottages sleeping 4 or 8 people, £170-
200 per night. Catering extra. All well-equipped
with central heating and modern appliances.
Free wildlife tour if you stay 3 nights or more.
Picturesque setting on an inlet.

Restaurants

Stanley
Most places are casual; for fine dining, try
Malvina House. At Sun lunchtime the pubs do
food, but in the evening **The Narrows**, **Shorty's
Diner** and **Stanley Arms** are open. Besides local
lamb, beef and fish (kingclip, toothfish, squid),
try diddle-dee berry jam and, in the autumn,
tea-berry buns.

BitterSweet
*3 Philomel St, T21888. Closed Mon (and
sometimes Tue in winter), open from 0900,
0800 on Fri, Sat 1000-1600, 1900-2330,
Sun 1100-1400 for brunch.*
Offers speciality coffees, handmade organic
chocolates, light refreshments and speciality
lunches or dinners. Café and wine bar, eat in
or take away.

Deano's Bar
40 John St, T22738.
Serving fresh local fish and chips and 100%
home-made local beef burgers as part of their
extensive menu; also popular are Saint Helenian
curries and fishcakes. Beers and spirits from
around the world, big screen satellite TV as
well as pool and darts.

Lighthouse Seaman's Centre
*Over the bridge next to FIPASS ('The Seaman's
Mission'). Open all day for seamen, 1000-1600
for general public, Sun 1200-1600.*
Tea/coffee, snacks. Internet and Wi-Fi hotspot.

Michele's Café
*Philomel St, T21123. Mon-Thu 0800-1600,
Fri 0800-0030, Sat 1030-0030.*

Home baking a speciality, all food cooked to order, eat in, take-away or delivery.

The Narrows Bar
39 Ross Rd East at Kelper Stores,
T22267, Facebook: TheNarrowsBar1.
Tue-Fri 1200-1400, 1700-closing, Sat-Sun
1200-closing, dinner served 1800-2100.
Daily specials, good pub food. Has Wi-Fi hotspot and internet centre, sells phone and Wi-Fi cards.

Shorty's
Snake Hill, T22855. See Facebook. Open 7 days
(seasonal), Mon-Fri 0900-2030, Sat-Sun till 2000.
Good fast food, lots of choice, eat in or take-away, good value.

Stanley Arms Bar
1 John Biscoe Rd, T21790, see Facebook.
Open 1130-1330, 1630-2300.
Good pub food, daily specials, eat in or take away.

Tasty Treat
Philomel St, T22500. Open 1100-1400, 1800-2030,
till 2100 Fri-Sat, closed Sun.
Hot and cold food, including fish and chips, Chilean and Saint Helenian dishes, breads, pastries, eat in or take-away.

Teaberry Café
Historic Dockyard. Mon-Fri 0730-1530, also on Sat
and extended hours on cruise ship days.
Offers speciality coffees, handmade organic chocolates and light refreshments.

Victory Bar
1A Philomel St, T21199. Daily for specials, lunch,
evening meals Mon, Tue and Thu 1600-2030.
Traditional English pub food, children welcome.

Waterfront Kitchen Café
36 Ross Rd at Waterfront B&B. All day Mon-Sat.
Coffee, tea, cakes, lunch with daily specials and dinner à la carte. Full bar and wine service.

West Store Café
FIC West Store, Ross Rd. Closed Sun.
Choice of coffees and other hot drinks, freshly made sandwiches, panini, pastries and cakes.

Bars and clubs

Stanley
The pubs include: **Beagle Bar** (at Malvina House Hotel); **Deano's Bar** (see above); **Narrows Bar** (see above); **Stanley Arms** (see above); **The Globe** (Philomel St, near the public jetty, Facebook: stanley.globetavern), open daily, bar menu, different entertainment every night; **The Trough** (Airport Rd), BYO, check Penguin News for opening dates (usually Sat night), live music and funky chill-out lounge, and **Victory Bar** (see above).

Shopping

Stanley

Gifts and souvenirs
The Boathouse, *Ross Rd.* Sells great underwater photography.
Capstan Gift Shop, *Ross Rd opposite West Store.* A wide selection of gifts, including books.
Cocoa Pod Organic, *next to the Jetty Visitor Centre.* Locally made organic chocolates and hand-crafted souvenirs.
Falklands Conservation Shop, *Jubilee Villas, Philomel St.* Good souvenirs.
Harbour View, *34 Ross Rd.* Souvenirs and local produce.
Jetty Visitor Centre, *Ross Rd (see Tourist information, page 1762).* Information, souvenirs and local handicrafts.
The Pink Shop, *John St.* Arts and crafts, books, pictures.
The Pod, *Philomel St, opposite The Globe.* Souvenirs and local produce.
Studio 52, *Ross Rd.* Local artwork and jewellery.

Groceries
FIC West Store (Ross Rd, Mon-Fri 0830-2000, Sat 0900-1800, Sun 0900-1700), also has an entertainment centre; **Kelper Family Stores** (39 Ross Rd East and 2 other locations, Mon-Fri 0730-2100, Sat-Sun 0900-2100); **Seafish Chandlery and Supermarket** (Stanley Airport Rd); **Stanley Growers Garden Centre** (Stanley Airport Rd); **Stanley Services** (Stanley Airport Rd).

Festivals

Feb/Mar The popular West and East Falkland Sports, at the end of the shearing season, rotate among the settlements.
Dec During the holidays in Dec, the sports meeting at the race course attracts visitors from all over the islands.

What to do

Fishing
Fishing for trout and mullet (South Atlantic cod) is superb. The main rivers are the Chartres and Warrah on West Falkland, and the San

Carlos on East Falkland. The season for trout is officially 1 Sep-30 Apr, but 2 distinct runs: Sep to mid-Nov and Mar/Apr. A licence is not required for rod and line fishing; catch and release is encouraged. Mullet may be caught at any time. Falkland Islands zebra trout are protected and must never be caught. Most land is privately owned, including rivers and streams; always get permission from the owner, some of whom charge a fee. Ask travel agents about regulations for specific areas and changes to daily bag limits.

Golf

Stanley's 18-hole course costs £5 a round; you can rent a set of clubs for £5.

Guided trips and tours

Comprehensive list at www.falklandislands.com. For more general travel services, see Tour operators, page 1763.

Adventure Falklands, *PO Box 223, T21383, pwatts@horizon.co.fk*. Patrick Watts offers tours of battlefield and other historical sights, ornithological trips and more. Recommended.

Beauchêne Fishing Company Ltd, *T22260, www.beauchenefishing.com*. Sightseeing tours, excursions, evening cruises and day charters out of Stanley on the *B-Mar* launch are all available.

Bluff Cove Lagoon Tours (Hattie and Kevin Kilmartin), *T21720, bluffcove@horizon.co.fk*. The Kilmartins offer wildlife excursions to Bluff Cove Lagoon and to the **Sea Cabbage Café** on their family farm, Bluff Cove, for cream tea and wonderful array of home-baking. Highly recommended.

Discovery Falklands, *33a Davis St, T21027, T51027 (mob), discovery@horizon.co.fk*. Tony Smith specializes in battlefield tours, wildlife, general interest, historical, also provides logistical support

and guidance for visiting TV crews and media personnel. Highly recommended.

Kidney Cove Safari Tours, *Murrell Farm, T54665, allowe@horizon.co.fk*. Adrian and Lisa Lowe, offer overland 4WD tours to see 4 species of penguins at Kidney Cove, close to Stanley, also fishing, battlefield and nature torus.

Penguin Travel, *Crozier Place, T27630, www.penguintravel-falklands.com*. Wildlife tours on foot, or by 4WD, Stanley tours, battlesite tours.

South Atlantic Marine Services, *Carol and Dave Eynon, Ross Rd, PO Box 140, T21145, dceynon@horizon.co.fk*. Overland tours, boat trips, safaris and have a dive centre with deck recompression chamber (PADI courses).

Transport

For air and ferry services, see page 1760.

Car hire

Rented vehicles may not be taken off road and may not travel on the ferry between East and West Falkland. On West Falkland Port Howard Farm may rent a vehicle if one is spare. **Falklands 4X4**, Crozier Place, Stanley, T27663, www.falklands4x4.com. Rents Land Rover Defender, Discovery and Freelander, and others. **Falklands Islands Tours and Travel**, Lookout Industrial Estate, Stanley, T21775, www.falklandtravel.com. For vans and minibuses, also vehicle hire with driver. **Moody Enterprises**, Moody Brook, Stanley, T22444, rkspink@hotmail.com. For 4WD and pick-ups. **Stanley Services Ltd**, Travel Division, Airport Rd, Stanley, T22622, info@falklandislandsholidays.com. Rents Mitsubishi Pajeros.

Taxis

Fares within Stanley, £3, to Stanley airport £6. **Town Taxis**, T52900.

Beyond the
Falklands

South Georgia

South Georgia, in the Southern Ocean in latitudes 54° to 55° south and longitude 36° to 38° west, has an area of 3755 sq km but no permanent residents.

South Georgia consists of a chain of high (almost 3000 m), snow-covered glaciated mountains. At King Edward Point, near sea level, snow falls on an average of nearly 200 days annually, but the coastal area is free from snow and partially covered by vegetation in summer. This is the port of entry and is 1 km from Grytviken. Wildlife consists of most of the same species found in the Falkland Islands/Islas Malvinas, but in much larger numbers, especially penguins, albatross, and seals. In 2011 a Habitat Restoration Programme (managed by the South Georgia Heritage Trust) to eliminate all non-native mammals began; it was primarily intended to eradicate rodents. The government's project to eradicate reindeer, which had been introduced in 1909, commenced in 2013 and was completed by 2015.

Sights

Points of interest are the abandoned whaling stations (although asbestos and other hazards restrict access to all except Grytviken), the little white whalers' church and several shipwrecks. The explorer, Sir Ernest Shackleton lies in the whalers' cemetery at Grytviken. A **South Georgia Museum** ① *http://sgmuseum.gs/index.php/South_Georgia_Museum*, managed by the Heritage Trust (www.sght.org) has been established where the whaling station has been cleaned and made safe to visit. Displays feature amazing steam industrial archaeology. Inside are artefacts, photographs and other items about the old Antarctic whaling and sealing industries with descriptions of the history of the island, including the Argentine invasion in 1982, and much about the wildlife. The museum has a shop which sells a good selection of books and many other items. The island issues distinctive stamps which are sold by the Post Office and museum. There is a South Georgia Association.

Essential South Georgia

There are two British Antarctic Survey stations, **King Edward Point** and **Bird Island**, and Government Officers at the former are the government's representatives who have responsibility for local administration (go@gov.gs). Their duties include those of Harbour Master, Customs and Immigration Officer, Fisheries Officer, Biosecurity Officer and Postmaster. Visitors normally arrive by cruise ship from Ushuaia, Punta Arenas or Stanley. Some also come by chartered yachts. Intending visitors, who are not part of tour groups, must submit a request through the **Government of South Georgia and the South Sandwich Islands**, Government House, Stanley, Falkland Islands, South Atlantic FIQQ 1ZZ, T+500-28200, email form on website (below). There is a landing fee of £125 for up to three days, plus £20 per day for visits over 72 hours, with a maximum of £205 for visits of up to a month. See also Information for Visitors on the **South Georgia website**: www.gov.gs. This contains important visitor briefing information including application forms and mandatory biosecurity protocols.

Best for
Adventure ■ Isolation ■ Wildlife

South Sandwich Islands

The South Sandwich Islands, some 500 km southeast of South Georgia, are uninhabited but administered by the same government as South Georgia. Although very rarely visited they are a spectacular chain of 11 volcanoes, several of which are active.

Antarctica

a unique land of ice and snow

Antarctica, the fifth largest continent, is 99.8% covered with perpetual ice. Although access is difficult, the annual number of tourists now exceeds the number of personnel on government research programmes. It is well known for its extraordinary scenery, wildlife, scientific stations, and historic sites. The weather may be spectacularly severe, thus visits are confined to the brief summer.

Presently some 30 countries operate over 60 scientific stations (45 remain open during winter). A wintering population of about 1200 lives in a continent larger than Europe. The **Antarctic Heritage Trust**, www.nzaht.org and www.ukaht.org, with headquarters in New Zealand and Britain, and some other organizations maintain several historic huts where organized groups are admitted. Many current research stations allow visitors for a couple of hours during a conducted tour. Of the historic huts, the one at **Port Lockroy**, established in 1944 and now a museum, has become the most-visited site. The historic huts used by Scott, Shackleton, Mawson, and Borchgrevink during the 'heroic age' of exploration are on the Australian and New Zealand side of Antarctica thus very distant from South America.

Antarctic Treaty Governance of Antarctica is principally through the Antarctic Treaty (1959) signed by all countries operating there; 53 countries were parties to the Treaty in 2017, representing over 80% of the Earth's population. Most visitors will be affected by several provisions of the Treaty, in particular those of the Environmental Protocol of 1991. These are principally for protection of wildlife (prohibiting harmful interference with animals or plants, especially when breeding), respecting protected areas and scientific research, alerting visitors to the need to be safe and prepared for rapid deterioration of weather, and keeping the environment pristine. Details will be found on www.iaato.org/visitor-guidelines. Seven countries have territorial claims over parts of Antarctica and three of these overlap (Antártida Argentina, British Antarctic Territory and Territorio Chileno Antártico); the Treaty has neutralized these with provision of free access to citizens of contracting states. Some display of sovereignty is legitimate and many stations operate a Post Office where philatelic items and various souvenirs are sold.

Further information There are many of specialist and general books about Antarctica, but the current best single source of information remains *Antarctica: Great Stories from the Frozen Continent* by Reader's Digest (first published Sydney 1985, with several later editions but out of print in 2017). General information may be found at the **Scott Polar Research Institute**, www.spri.cam.ac.uk, including links to other sites. Also useful is the website of **International Association of Antarctic Tour Operators, IAATO** (see below). Most national operators also have sites dedicated to their work but often with much more information. The **Council of Managers of National Antarctic Programmes**, in Christchurch, is the best source for these details: www.comnap.aq.

Visiting Antarctica

The region of the Antarctic south of South America is the most accessible, therefore over half the scientific stations are there or on adjacent islands. Coincidentally, it is also one of the most spectacular areas with many mountains, glaciers and fjords closely approachable by sea.

By sea Four ports are used: Stanley, Punta Arenas, Ushuaia and Puerto Williams; the last two are major bases for yachts. The **South Shetland Islands** and **Antarctic Peninsula** are most frequently visited, but ships also reach the **South Orkney Islands** and many call at South

Fact...
During the 2016-2017 austral summer an estimated 44,367 visitors reached Antarctica, of whom 33,237 landed on the continent from expedition ships and yachts.

Georgia at the beginning or end of a voyage. Most vessels are booked well in advance by luxury class passengers but sometimes late opportunistic vacancies may be secured by local agencies. Ships carrying 45-280 tourists land passengers at several sites during a couple of week's voyage. Some much larger vessels also visit; these generally do not land passengers but merely cruise around the coasts.

Voyages from South America and the Falkland Islands/Islas Malvinas involve at least two days each way crossing the Drake Passage where sea conditions may be very uncomfortable. No guarantee of landings, views or wildlife is possible and delays due to storms are not exceptional. Conversely, on a brilliant day, some of the most spectacular sights and wildlife anywhere may be seen. Visitors should be well prepared for adverse conditions with warm, windproof and waterproof clothing, and good boots for wet landings. The weather and the state of the sea can change quickly without warning.

In 1991 the **International Association of Antarctica Tour Operators** ① *320 Thames St, suite 264, Newport, Rhode Island, 02840, USA, T+1-401-841 9700, www.iaato.org*, was formed. It represents the majority of companies and can provide details of most offering Antarctic voyages. Many vessels have a principal contractor and a number of other companies bring smaller groups, thus it is advantageous to contact the principal.

Some private yachts carry passengers; enquire at Ushuaia or Puerto Williams, or the other ports listed. Travelling with the Argentine, Chilean, French or Russian supply ships may sometimes be arranged, but only at departure ports. These are much cheaper than cruise ships but have limited itineraries as their principal object is to supply stations and there is no guarantee of passage.

By air Antarctic Logistics and Expeditions (ALE)/Adventure Network International (ANI) ① *3478 South Main St, Salt Lake City, Utah 84115, USA, T+1-801-266 4876, https://antarctic-logistics.com*, provides flights to Antarctica from Punta Arenas where there is a **local office**. Wheeled aircraft fly as far as an inland summer camp at Union Glacier (79·46°S, 82·52°W), the only land-based tourist facility, whence ski-aircraft proceed to the South Pole, vicinity of Mount Vinson (4892 m, Antarctica's highest peak), and elsewhere. Other flights go from Punta Arenas and Cape Town. 'Flightseeing' is made by Qantas from Australia aboard aircraft which do not land but spend about four hours over the continent (and about the same getting there and back).

Practicalities

Getting there

Air

Flights from Santiago to Mount Pleasant, via Punta Arenas with **LATAM** ① www.latam.com, leave every Saturday and, once a month, stop at Río Gallegos in Argentina on both the outward and return flight. May 2017 fares: return from Santiago £950, Punta Arenas £632. Fares include Chilean airport taxes, but exclude Falklands embarkation tax: see Tax, page 1762. Passengers should confirm flights 24 hours before departure. For more information on LATAM flights, see the website (tickets may be bought online), or contact **International Tours and Travel Ltd** ① 1 Dean St, Stanley, FIQQ 1ZZ, T+500-22041, se.itt@horizon.co.fk or visit www.falklandislands.travel.

The UK Ministry of Defence operates an airbridge to the Falkland Islands twice a week (at the time of writing). They depart from RAF Brize Norton, Oxfordshire, and take about 20 hours including a refuelling stop in Ascension Island at the half way point (passengers can stop over if they wish). Fares: £2222 return. Falkland Islands residents and contract workers receive a discount. The £22 exit tax is not included in MoD flights. Luggage allowance for tourists is 27 kg, but this should be confirmed in advance. Confirm the flight itself 24 hours before departure. For the latest MoD schedules and prices, contact the **Falkland Islands Company Travel Department** ① T27633, info@fic.co.fk, or the **Falkland Islands Government Office** ① T020-7222 2542, travel@falklands.gov.fk, in London.

Airport information Mount Pleasant airport (code MPN) is 35 miles from Stanley. **Falkland Islands Tours and Travel** ① Lookout Industrial Estate, Stanley, T21775, admin@fitt.co.fk, book online at www.falklandtravel.com, and **Penguin Travel** (Falkland Islands Company) ① Crozier Place, Stanley, T27630, penguin.travel@fic.co.fk, www.penguintravel-falklands.com, transport passengers and luggage to and from the capital for £14/US$25 single. Arriving and departing passengers should make reservations. See also Taxis, page 1756.

Sea

Cruise ships en route to/from South America, South Georgia and the Antarctic are also a popular way to visit the Islands. Vessels typically visit between October and April each year. Passengers usually land for tours of Stanley and nearby sites, pub lunch, farmhouse tea, and call at outlying islands, such as Saunders, Carcass, West Point, New and Sea Lion Islands. Further details of companies that include the Falklands/Malvinas in their itineraries can be found on www.falklandislands.com and at www.iaato.org. Alternatively you can contact local port agents **Sulivan Shipping** ① T22626, www.sulivanshipping.com, and **Penguin Travel** (Falkland Islands Company) ① T27630, www.penguintravel-falklands.com.

Getting around

Air

The **Falkland Islands Government Air Service** ① FIGAS, T27219, www.fig.gov.uk/figas/, flies to farm settlements and settled outer islands on a shuttle service that varies daily according to demand. To book a seat, contact FIGAS with as much notice as possible; daily schedules are announced the previous afternoon on local radio and by fax and telephone. One-way airfares in 2017 cost up to £150 one way, but fares depend on distance (Visa and MasterCard accepted); luggage limit 20 kg. Services daily October-end March, six days a week otherwise; no flights on 1 January, Good Friday, 21 April, 14 June, 25 December. Services and fares are continually under review. FIGAS tickets are also available from **Falkland Islands Holidays** and **International Tours and Travel Ltd**, see Tour

ON THE ROAD

Landmines

During the 1982 conflict Argentine Forces declared that they had laid some 25,000 mines and numerous booby traps. 146 hazardous areas were identified, mapped and fenced with 29 areas being initially cleared. The UK government is committed to clearing all landmines from the islands. 30 minefields were made safe between 2009-2016. A further 46 will be cleared by 2018, with 27 more fields under survey for clearance. The fields are fenced, mapped and clearly marked and no civilian injuries or casualties have ever occurred. Should you spot anything unusual, make a note of its location and contact the Bomb Disposal Unit, T53939, or the police (see below). Please note, it is illegal to enter any area designated as minefield, or to remove minefield signage.

operators, below. Flights leave from Stanley Airport, 3 miles east of town on the Cape Pembroke peninsula, 10-15 minutes by car.

Road

The only paved roads are in Stanley. Outside Stanley, the major road to the airport at **Mount Pleasant** is part paved, but requires great care. Other roads are single track, of consolidated earth and stone. None should be driven at speed; look out for sheep or cattle, cattle grids and sudden hills, bends and junctions. On East and West Falkland, roads connect most of the settlements. Elsewhere, tracks require 4WD or quad bikes. Off-road driving in the boggy terrain is a skill not easily learned by short-term visitors and is not permitted by any car-hire company. Tour guides and drivers can be engaged to visit many places on the islands and taxis are readily available for journeys around Stanley. The **Jetty Visitor Centre** (see Tourist information, below) and the **Museum** (see page 1748) stock a range of maps, including the 1:50,000 map and A3 road maps.

Sea

A drive-on, drive-off ferry sails between New Haven (East) and Port Howard (West) on a variable schedule, usually twice a day. The same vessel, *MV Concordia Bay*, runs twice-monthly cargo services to the outer islands and when on this duty does not operate as a car ferry. For schedules T22300/55299, www.workboat.co.fk; office is on Philomel St, behind the Globe Tavern. If the wind is wrong it will not sail. Cars £50 (must be booked in advance), foot passengers £20, child under 16 £10, under 5 £5.

Where to stay & eat

Pre-booked accommodation is obligatory before being allowed entry. Advance reservation when travelling around is essential. The tourist board has introduced an accreditation scheme for places to stay, with star ratings 1-5 and gold and silver awards. Almost all places to stay in Stanley and on the islands have comfortable rooms, power showers, towels, heating, no smoking, honesty bars (where they have a bar) and, when not self-catering, good local food. For self-catering you can get supplies, including ready-prepared meals, in Stanley. Stores in Port Howard and Fox Bay on West Falkland open only at specified times, usually three days a week. See www.falklandislands.com.

On the outer islands bear in mind that the wildlife you will see is inextricably linked with where you stay because there is no choice of lodging. Fortunately this is not a hardship. See the Planning your trip chapter for our hotel and restaurant price guide.

Essentials A-Z

Accident and emergency

All emergencies T999. **Stanley Police Station** T28100.

Electricity

220/240 volts. Rectangular, 3-blade plug as in UK.

Health

Stanley has the excellent **King Edward Memorial Hospital (KEMH)**, dental service included. T28000.

Money

US$1 = £0.77; €1 = £0.87 (Jun 2017).
The Falklands pound (£) is at par with sterling. Local notes and coins are minted, but cannot be used outside of the islands. UK notes and coins are also legal tender. Currency from Ascension Island, where the airbridge flights stop, is not accepted. Foreign currency (including US$ and euros) can be changed at **Standard Chartered**, Ross Rd, Stanley, T22220, www.sc.com/fk/, which is the only bank on the islands. All establishments accept pounds sterling, some accept US$ and euros. Credit and/or debit cards are only accepted by a handful of establishments, including the bank. Otherwise use cash where possible. There are no ATMs on the islands.

Opening hours

Bank Standard Chartered Bank, Mon, Tue, Thu and Fri 0830-1500; Wed 0900-1500. **Offices** Mon-Fri 0800-1200, 1300-1630.

Post

From the UK there is direct air mail and heavy parcels come by sea every month. A weekly DHL service is operated via **Falkland Islands Chamber of Commerce**, West Hillside, Stanley, T22264, www.falklandislandschamberofcommerce.com. The **post office** is on Ross Rd in Stanley, T27159, www.falklandstam ps.com, Mon-Fri 0800-1630.

Public holidays and festivals

1 Jan, **Good Friday, 21 Apr** (Queen's birthday), **14 Jun** (Liberation Day), **1st Mon in Oct** (Peat Cutting Monday), **8 Dec** (Battle Day). The main social event is the Christmas period, **24 Dec, 25 Dec, 26 Dec.**

Tax

Airport tax Departing passengers by air on **LATAM** pay an embarkation tax of £22, payable in sterling, euros or dollars (there are no exchange facilities or ATM at Mt Pleasant).

Telephone and Wi-Fi

International dialling code +500.
Sure South Atlantic Ltd, Sure Shop, Ross Rd, Stanley, Mon-Fri 0800-1630, is the telecommunications provider.

You may be able to roam on the **Sure** network with your own SIM card. See the list of roaming partners at www.sure.co.fk. Local SIM cards, with £10 credit and 60 days validity, cost £30 from **Sure Shop** or at the **FIC**. Mobile phone coverage extends to most parts of East Falkland and some parts of West Falkland. Mobile help line locally is free phone 131.

Most hotels and guesthouses have Wi-Fi. Phone cards for international calls and Wi-Fi access cost £5 or £10. They can be purchased at **Sure, Kelper Stores, FIC** and a number of other local retailers. Calls to UK are 99p per min, to rest of world £1.10 (off peak £0.80 and £0.99 respectively). A £5 card will give you 50 mins of internet use. The **Jetty Visitor Centre** on Ross Rd also offers independent PC access.

For directory enquiries, dial T181. Operator services, T20800.

Time

GMT -4 in winter (May-Aug), -3 in summer. Some people use 'Camp time' (as opposed to 'Stanley time'), which does not use daylight saving.

Tourist information

Falkland Islands Tourist Board runs the **Jetty Visitor Centre,** at the head of the Public Jetty, Ross Rd, Stanley, open daily during summer 0930-1700, from 0900 Sat, 1000-1600 Sun, winter Mon-Sat 1000-1500, Sat-Sun 1100-1500, www.falklandislands.com. This has information on accommodation, tours, transport and activities, and offers internet, postal service and public telephones and access cards. It has a free visitor guide in English, Spanish and German. The **Falkland Islands Government London Office (FIGO)**, T020-7222 2542, www.falklands.gov.fk, will answer enquiries.

Useful websites

http://en.mercopress.com Merco Press, South Atlantic News Agency.
www.penguin-news.com *Penguin News* weekly newspaper.

Tour operators

See www.falklandislands.com for details of overseas operators.

Falkland Islands Company-Flights, T27633, info@fic.co.uk. Local booking agent for the MoD charter flight via Brize Norton, UK.

Falkland Islands Holidays (division of **Stanley Services**), Bypass Rd, Stanley, T22622, www.falkland islandsholidays.com. Offer inbound tourist services, FIGAS flights, overland 4WD excursions, bookings for lodgings and for fishing, riding and vehicle hire.

Golden Fleece Expedition Cruises, T42316, www.goldenfleecexp.co.fk. Specializes in film-work, scientific surveys or tourism around the Falklands, South Georgia or Antarctica.

International Tours and Travel Ltd, 1 Dean St, Stanley, T22041, www.falklandislands.travel. Handle inbound tourist bookings, book FIGAS flights, arrange tours, etc, and are the Falkland Islands' agents for **LATAM**. Recommended.

Visas and immigration

All visitors must have a full, current passport. Citizens of Britain, North America, Mercosur, Chile, Israel, Japan, South Korea, Switzerland, most Commonwealth countries and the EU may visit the islands without a visa, as may holders of UN and International Committee of the Red Cross passports. Other nationals should apply for a visa on line at www.visa4uk.fco.gov. uk and follow instructions. Travellers resident in the UK can apply direct to the **Customs and Immigration Department**, 3 H Jones Rd, Stanley, T27340, admin@customs.gov.fk. A visitor permit will be issued on arrival to those who have met the entry requirements. You must have a return ticket and confirm that you have accommodation, sufficient funds to cover the cost of your stay and evidence of medical insurance (including cover for aero-medical evacuation). Work permits are not available.

Weights and measures

Metric. On East Falkland miles are used; on West Falkland kilometres.

FALKLAND ISLANDS SOUTH AMERICA ANTARCTICA

www.falklandislands.travel

IATA
LAN

International Tours & Travel
Stanley, Falkland Islands   T +500 22041   se.itt@horizon.co.fk

Practicalities

Getting there

Air

Most South American countries have direct flights from **Europe**. In many cases, though, the choice of departure point is limited to Madrid and a few other cities (Amsterdam, London, or Paris, for instance). Argentina and Brazil have the most options: France, Germany, Italy, the Netherlands, Spain and the UK. Brazil also has flights from Lisbon to a number of cities. Since 2016 **British Airways** has introduced new direct services to Lima (Northern Hemisphere summer only) and Santiago. Latin American specialist **Air Europa** ℗ www.aireuropa.com, has an expanding network out of Madrid to all countries except Chile and the Guianas. Where there are no direct flights connections can be made in the USA (Miami, or other gateways), Buenos Aires, Rio de Janeiro or São Paulo. **Main US gateways** are Miami, Houston, Dallas, Atlanta and New York. On the west coast, Los Angeles has flights to several South American cities. If buying airline tickets routed through the USA, check that US taxes are included in the price. Flights from **Canada** are mostly via the USA, although there are direct flights from Toronto to Bogotá with **Air Canada** and **Avianca**. Likewise, flights from **Australia** and **New Zealand** are best through Los Angeles, except for the **LATAM** route from Sydney and Auckland to Santiago, and **Qantas'** non-stop route Sydney–Santiago, from where connections can be made. From **Japan** and from **South Africa** there are direct flights to Brazil.

Within **Latin America** there is plenty of choice on local carriers and some connections on US or European airlines. For airpasses, see below. To Guyana, the main routes are via the Caribbean (Port of Spain, Trinidad and Barbados) or New York, Miami and Toronto. Suriname is served by flights from Amsterdam and Port of Spain, while Guyane has flights from Paris and the French-speaking Caribbean. All three have air connections with northern Brazil.

Prices and discounts

Most airlines offer discounted fares on scheduled flights through agencies who specialize in this type of fare; some are listed in Tour operators, below. If you buy discounted air tickets always check the reservation with the airline concerned to make sure the flight still exists. Also remember the IATA airlines' schedules change in March and October each year, so if you're going to be away a long time it's best to leave return flights open. Peak times are 7 December-15 January and 10 July-10 September. If you intend travelling during those times, book as far ahead as possible. Between February and May and September and November special offers may be available. **Note** Using the internet for booking flights, hotels and other services directly can give you some good deals. But don't forget that a travel agent can find the best flights to suit your itinerary, as well as providing advice on documents, insurance, safety, routes, lodging and times of year to travel. A reputable agent will also be bonded to give you some protection if things go wrong.

TRAVEL TIP

Packing for South America

Everybody has their own preferences, but a good principle is to take half the clothes, and twice the money, that you think you will need. Listed here are those items most often mentioned. These include an inflatable travel pillow and strong shoes (footwear over 9½ English size, or 42 European size, is difficult to find in South America). Always take out a good travel insurance policy. You should also take waterproof clothing and waterproof treatment for leather footwear and wax earplugs, vital for long bus trips or in noisy hotels. Also important are flip flops, which can be worn in showers to avoid athlete's foot, and a sheet sleeping bag to avoid sleeping on dirty sheets in cheap hotels. Other useful things include: a clothes line, a nailbrush, a vacuum flask, a water bottle, a universal sink plug of the flanged type that will fit any waste-pipe, string, a Swiss Army knife, an alarm clock, candles (for power cuts), a torch/flashlight, pocket mirror, a padlock for the doors of the cheapest hotels (or for tent zip if camping), a small first-aid kit, sun hat, lip salve with sun protection, contraceptives, waterless soap, dental floss (which can also be used for repairs), wipes and a small sewing kit. Always carry toilet paper, especially on long bus trips. The most security conscious may also wish to include a length of chain and padlock for securing luggage to bed or bus/train seat, and a lockable canvas cover for your rucksack. Don't forget cables and adaptors for recharging phones, laptops and other electrical equipment. Contact lens wearers note that lens solution can be difficult to find in Bolivia and Peru. Ask for it in a pharmacy, rather than an opticians.

Sea

Travelling as a passenger on a cargo ship to South America is not a cheap way to go, but if you have the time and want a bit of luxury, it makes a great alternative to flying. There are sailings from Europe to the Caribbean, east and west coasts of South America. Likewise, you can sail from US ports to east and west coast South America. In the main, passage is round trip only. Agencies which specialize in this type of travel include: **Cargo Ship Voyages Ltd** ① *10 Westway, Cowes, Isle of Wight, PO31 8QP, T01983-303314, www.cargoshipvoyages.com.* **Globoship** ① *Neuengasse 30, CH-3001, Bern, Switzerland, T031-313 0004, www.globoship.ch.* **The Cruise People** ① *88 York St, London W1H 1QT, T020-7723 2450 or 0800 526 313, www.cruisepeople.co.uk,* also **Travltips Cruise and Freighter Travel Association** ① *25-37 Francis Lewis Blvd, Flushing, NY 11358, T800-872 8584, www.travltips.com.*

Getting around

Air

A few South American airlines offer flights between the countries of the region, for instance **LATAM**, **Avianca**, **Gol**, **Aerolíneas Argentinas** and some others who do not have as extensive networks. Using these airlines provides more scope than routes offered by non-South American carriers. Airlines within the same alliance as the carrier which took you to South America may not be the most cost-effective choice for flights within South America.

There is no hard-and-fast rule about flying between countries. In general, prices are determined by distance. Distances can be very great so flying a long way will be expensive, but you can find some good deals between neighbouring countries, for example Argentina and Chile. If you wish to cross a border and then fly long distance in the next country, it may be cheaper to cross the border overland and then fly within the next country, rather than fly all the way.

Note that some countries impose a high sales and other taxes on the purchase of flight tickets (eg Peru, Bolivia, Ecuador, Colombia), which will affect your travel budget. If considering using the internet to buy a ticket, bear in mind that some airlines require a locally issued credit card, or local ID to make a purchase. You will get the best advice from an authorized agent (such as **Journey Latin America** in the UK).

Air passes

Airpasses can offer savings on flying between different countries. These are normally bought in conjunction with an international flight to South America, but it is advisable to compare the cost of the individual legs within an airpass with the cost of a regular flight.

The **One World Visit South America** air pass links all South American countries except the Guianas for passengers arriving and leaving on airlines in the **One World Alliance** ① www. oneworld.com, and flights within South America must be with **American Airlines**, **British Airways**, **LATAM** or **Qatar Airways** or their affiliates. Prices are mileage-based; minimum three flights, maximum stay one year.

Gol's South America airpass covers flights in Argentina, Bolivia, Brazil, Chile, Dominican Republic, Paraguay, Uruguay and Venezuela. It is valid for five to 30 days, allows four to nine coupons and must include at least two countries in the area. Flights within Brazil are not allowed, but **Gol** has a Brazil Airpass for these (www.voegol.com.br). Fares range from US$629-1249, based on the number of destinations.

Rail

Where they still run, trains are slower than buses. They tend to provide finer scenery and you can normally see much more wildlife than from the road – it is less disturbed by one or two trains a day than by the more frequent road traffic.

Road

Bus

The continent has an extensive road system with frequent bus services. The buses are often comfortable; the difficulties of Andean terrain affect the quality of vehicles. In mountainous country do not expect buses to get to their destination after long journeys anywhere near on time. Do not turn up for a bus at the last minute; if it is full it may depart early. When the journey takes more than three or four hours, meal stops at roadside restaurants (usually with toilets), good and bad, are the rule. Usually, no announcement is made on the duration of a stop; ask the driver and

> **Tip...**
> Tall travellers are advised to take aisle rather than window seats on long journeys as this allows for more leg room.

Carnet de passages

There are two recognized documents for taking a vehicle through customs in South America: a *carnet de passages* issued jointly by the Fedération Internationale de l'Automobile (FIA – Geneva) and the Alliance Internationale de Tourisme (AIT – Geneva and Paris), and the *Libreta de Pasos por Aduana* issued by the Federación Interamericana de Touring y Automóvil Clubs (FITAC). The *carnet de passages* is recognized by all South American customs authorities (except Bolivia, Brazil and Guyana) but is not required by any. The *libreta* is a 10-page book of three-part passes for customs. Further information on the *carnet de passages* can be found here, www.fia.com/international-cpd-network. In the UK, the *carnet de passage* is available from CARS (Classic Automotive Relocation Services), www.carseurope.net; the document costs £210-250, depending on the number of pages. Information can be found here, http://www.fia.com/international-cpd-network. In the USA and Canada the *carnet* is issued by Boomerang Carnets, www.cpdcarnet.com, who can give full details; the fee is US$775. Also from the AAA of Australia, for a fee of AU$820, see www.aaa.asn.au. In all cases you have to add on administration fees, deposits and insurance premiums, which can take the cost into the thousands, depending on the value of the car.

---

follow him, if he eats, eat. See what the locals are eating and buy likewise, or make sure you're stocked up well on food and drink at the start. For drinks, stick to bottled water or soft drinks or coffee (black). The food sold by vendors at bus stops may be all right; watch if locals are buying, though unpeeled fruit is, of course, reliable.

Car

Type of car A normal car will reach most places, but high ground clearance is useful for badly surfaced or unsurfaced roads and for fording rivers. For greater flexibility in mountain and jungle territory 4WD vehicles are recommended. In Patagonia, main roads are gravel rather than paved: perfectly passable without 4WD. Consider fitting wire guards for headlamps, and for windscreens too. Diesel cars are cheaper to run than petrol ones and the fuel is easily available, although in Venezuela you may have to look hard for it outside Caracas. Standard European and Japanese cars run on fuel with a higher octane rating than is commonly available in North, South or Central America, and in Brazil petrol (*gasolina*) is in fact gasohol, with a 12% admixture of alcohol.

Security Spare no ingenuity in making your car secure, inside and out (even wing mirrors, spot lamps, wheels without locking nuts can be stolen). Try never to leave the car unattended except in a locked garage or guarded parking space. Lock the clutch or accelerator to the steering wheel with a heavy, obvious chain or lock. Street children will generally protect your car for a tip.

Documents To drive your own vehicle in South America, you must have an international driver's license. You must also have the vehicle's registration document in the name of the driver. In the case of a car registered in someone else's name, you should have a notarized letter of authorization. This may not be acceptable in all cases, for instance, according to legislation, in Peru, but practices may vary. Try to check before arriving at the border. Be very careful to keep **all** the papers you are given when you enter, to produce when you leave (see box, above).

Insurance Insurance for the vehicle against accident, damage or theft is best arranged in the country of origin. In Latin American countries it is very expensive to insure against accident and theft, especially as you should take into account the value of the car increased by duties calculated in real (ie non-devaluing) terms. If the car is stolen or written off you will be required to pay very high import duty on its value. Third-party insurance can be very difficult to find. Some countries may insist that it be bought at the border (Venezuela seems to be the only country where it is easy to obtain). If you can get the legally required minimum cover, so much the better. If not, drive with extreme caution and very defensively. If involved in an accident and you're uninsured, your car could be confiscated. If anyone is hurt, do not pick them up (you may become liable). Try to seek assistance from the nearest police station or hospital.

Car hire The main international car hire companies operate in all countries, but they tend to be very expensive, reflecting the high costs and accident rates. Hotels and tourist agencies will tell you where to find cheaper rates, but you will need to check that you have such basics as spare wheel, toolkit and functioning lights, etc. You'll probably have more fun if you drive yourself, although it's always possible to hire a car with driver. If you plan to do a lot of driving and will have time at the end to dispose of it, investigate the possibility of buying a second-hand car locally; since hiring is so expensive it may well work out cheaper and will probably do you just as well.

Car hire insurance Check exactly what the hirer's insurance policy covers. In many cases it only protects you against minor bumps and scrapes, not major accidents, nor 'natural' damage (eg flooding). Ask if extra cover is available. Also find out, if using a credit card, whether the card automatically includes insurance. Beware of being billed for scratches that were already on the vehicle. Also check the windscreen and ask what procedures are involved if a new one is needed.

Cycling

Unless you are planning a journey almost exclusively on paved roads – when a touring bike would suffice – a mountain bike is strongly recommended. The good quality ones (and the cast-iron rule is **never** to skimp on quality) are incredibly tough and rugged, with low gear ratios for difficult terrain, wide tyres with plenty of tread for good road-holding, V brakes, sealed hubs and bottom bracket and a low centre of gravity for improved stability. A chrome-alloy frame is better than aluminum as it can be welded. Although touring bikes, and to a lesser extent mountain bikes, and spares are available in the larger Latin American cities, remember that most locally manufactured goods are shoddy. Where imported components can be found, they are very expensive. (Shimano parts are the easiest to find.) Buy everything you can before leaving home.

> **Tip...**
> Get to know the bike before you go, ask the dealers in your country what goes wrong with it and arrange to get parts flown out to you.

Remember that you can always stick your bike on a bus, canoe or plane to get yourself nearer to where you want your wheels to take you. This is especially useful when there are long stretches of major road ahead. In almost any country it is possible to rent a bike for a few days, or join an organized tour for riding in the mountains. You should check, however, that the machine you are hiring is up to the conditions you will be encountering, or that the tour company is not a fly-by-night outfit without back-up, good bikes or maintenance. Visit www.warmshowers.org for a hospitality exchange for touring cyclists.

Motorcycling

Type of motorcycle The bike should be off-road capable. Buying a bike in the USA and driving down works out cheaper than buying one in the UK.

Security Try not to leave a fully laden bike on its own. An Abus D or chain will keep the bike secure. A cheap alarm gives you peace of mind if you leave the bike outside a hotel at night. Most hotels will allow you to bring the bike inside. Look for hotels that have a courtyard or more secure parking and never leave luggage on the bike overnight. Also take a cover for the bike.

Documents A passport, international driving licence and bike registration document are necessary. Riders fare much better with a *carnet de passages* (see box, opposite) than without.

Border crossings If you do not have a *carnet*, do not try to cross borders on a Sunday or a holiday as a charge is levied on the usually free borders. Customs and immigration inspectors are mostly friendly, polite and efficient. If in doubt ask to see the boss and/or the rule book.

Because air services have captured the lucrative end of the passenger market, passenger services on the rivers are in decline. Worst hit have been the upper reaches of rivers. The situation has been aggravated for the casual traveller by a new generation of purpose-built tugs (all engine-room and bridge), which can handle up to a dozen freight barges but have no passenger accommodation. In Peru passenger boats must now supplement incomes by carrying cargo, and this lengthens journeys. In the face of long delays, travellers might consider shorter 'legs' involving more frequent changes of boat; although the more local the service, the slower and more uncomfortable it will be. The introduction of fast boats on some major Amazon routes has speeded up journeys, but they cost a lot more than the regular passenger boats.

Hammocks, mosquito nets (not always good quality), plastic containers for water storage, kettles and cooking utensils can be purchased in any sizeable riverside town, as well as tinned food. Fresh bread, cake, eggs and fruit are available in most villages. Cabin bunks are provided with thin mattresses but these are often foul. Replacements can be bought locally but rolls of plastic foam that can be cut to size are also available and much cheaper. Eye-screws for securing washing lines and mosquito nets are useful, and tall passengers who are not taking a hammock and who may find insufficient headroom on some boats should consider a camp-chair. See also the special section on the Brazilian Amazon.

Maps and guidebooks

Those from the **Institutos Geográficos Militares** or **Nacionales** in the capitals are often the only good maps available in Latin America. It is therefore wise to get as many as possible in your home country before leaving, especially if travelling by land. A recommended series of general maps is that published by **International Travel Maps** (ITM) ① *12300 Bridgeport Rd, Richmond, Vancouver BC, V6V 1J5, Canada, T604-273 1400, www.itmb.ca*. As well as maps of South America Southern (1:2,600,000) and North (1:3,850,000), there are maps of most countries, the Amazon Basin, Easter Island, the Galápagos and several cities. **Stanford's** ① *12-14 Long Acre, Covent Garden, London WC2E 9LP, T020-7836 1321, www.stanfords.co.uk (another branch at 29 Corn St, Bristol, T0117-929 9966)*, also sells a wide variety of maps.

Essentials A-Z

Children

Travel with children can bring you into closer contact with South American families and, generally, presents no special problems. In fact the path is often smoother for family groups as officials tend to be more amenable where children are concerned. See Health below for specific information.

Food

Food can be a problem if the children are picky eaters. It is easier to take food such as biscuits, drinks and bread on longer trips than to rely on meal stops. Avocados are safe and nutritious for babies as young as 6 months and most older children like them too. A small immersion heater and jug for making hot drinks is invaluable, but remember that electric current varies. Try and get a dual-voltage one (110v and 220v).

Hotels

In all hotels, try to negotiate family rates. If charges are per person, always insist that 2 children will occupy 1 bed only, therefore counting as 1 tariff. If rates are per bed, the same applies. You can often get a reduced rate at cheaper hotels. Sometimes when travelling with a child you will be refused a room in a hotel that is 'unsuitable'. On river boat trips, unless you have large hammocks, it may be more comfortable and cost effective to hire a 2-berth cabin for 2 adults and a child.

Transport

People contemplating overland travel in South America with children should remember that a lot of time can be spent waiting for public transport. Even then, buses can be delayed on the journey. Travel on trains allows more scope for moving about, but trains are few and far between these days. In many cases trains are luxurious and much more expensive than buses. If hiring a car, check that it has rear seat belts.

On all long-distance buses you pay for each seat, and there are no half-fares if the children occupy a seat each. For shorter trips it is cheaper, if less comfortable, to seat small children on your knee. There may be spare seats which children can occupy after tickets have been collected. In city and local excursion buses, small children generally do not pay a fare, but are not entitled to a seat when paying customers are standing. On sightseeing tours you should always bargain for a family rate – often children can go free. All civil airlines charge half for children under 12, but some military services don't have half-fares, or have younger age limits. Note that a child travelling free on a long excursion is not always covered by the operator's travel insurance; it is advisable to pay a small premium to arrange cover.

Disabled travellers

In most of South America, facilities for the disabled are severely lacking. For those in wheelchairs, ramps and toilet access are limited to some of the more upmarket, or most recently built hotels. Pavements are often in a poor state of repair or crowded with street vendors. Most archaeological sites have little or no wheelchair access. Visually or hearing-impaired travellers are also poorly catered for, but there are experienced guides in some places who can provide individual attention. There are also travel companies outside South America who specialize in holidays which are tailor-made for the individual's level of disability. Some moves are being made to improve the situation and Ecuador's president (from 2017) Lenín Moreno, himself a paraplegic, has made huge strides in providing assistance at all levels to people with disabilities. At street level, Quito's trolley buses are supposed to have wheelchair access, but they are often too crowded to make this practical. In Chile all new public buildings are supposed to provide access for the disabled by law. PromPerú has initiated a programme to provide facilities at airports, tourist sites, etc. While disabled South Americans have to rely on others to get around, foreigners will find that people are generally very helpful.

Health

See your GP or travel clinic at least 6 weeks before departure for general advice on travel risks and vaccinations. Try phoning a specialist travel clinic if your own doctor is unfamiliar with health in the region. Make sure you have sufficient medical travel insurance, get a dental check, know your

How to avoid insect bites

Tropical insects are vectors for a number of diseases including zika, chikungunya, dengue and in some areas malaria and yellow fever. These are transmitted by mosquitoes (and some by sandflies) which bite both day and night. Here are a few tips to avoid getting bitten.

1. Be particularly vigilant around dawn and dusk when most diurnal and nocturnal mosquitoes bite. Cover ankles and feet and the backs of arms.

2. Check your room for insects and spray insecticide before you go out for the day to ensure an insect free night. Most hotels will have spray, otherwise it can be bought in pharmacies and supermarkets.

3. Use insect repellent – especially in beach and forested areas. No repellent works 100%, but most will limit bites. Repellent is available at most pharmacies and supermarkets. The Off! brand in Brazil is reliable. If you wish to make your own 'industrial-chemical-free' formula, one *Footprint* author finds the following recipe made with essential oils effective, including the Amazon: 70% jojoba oil, 30% citronella oil, 10-20 drops of Eucalyptus radiata, 10-15 drops of Wintergreen, 10-15 drops of Cajeput. Do not take this formula internally.

This insect repellent also works with sandflies who cannot land on the thick Jojoba oil.

4. Sandflies are not as widely present in South as in Central America but you will encounter them in some locations. Many DEET repellents and citronella-based repellents do not work on sandflies. The recipe above, Jojoba oil or 'Skin so Soft' baby oil does but you need to apply it thickly.

5. Bring a mosquito net. Bell nets are best. Lifesystems do treated models which repel and kill insects. Bring a small roll of duct tape, a few screw-in hooks and at least 5 m of string to ensure you can put the net up in almost all locations.

6. Sleep with the fan on. Fans are for stopping mosquitoes as much as they are for cooling.

7. Consider using insect-repellent treated shirts like those in the Craghoppers Nosilife range. Avoid black clothing. Mosquitoes find it attractive.

own blood group and, if you suffer a long-term condition such as diabetes or epilepsy, obtain a **Medic Alert** bracelet (www.medicalert.org.uk).

Vaccinations and anti-malarials

Confirm that your primary courses and boosters are up to date. It is advisable to vaccinate against polio, tetanus, typhoid, hepatitis A and, for more remote areas, rabies. Yellow fever vaccination is obligatory for most areas (once acquired the vaccine lasts for life). Cholera, diphtheria and hepatitis B vaccinations are sometimes advised. Specialist advice should be taken on the best antimalarials to take before you leave.

Health risks

The major risks posed in the region are those caused by insect disease carriers such as mosquitoes and sandflies. The key parasitic and viral diseases are malaria, South American trypanosomiasis (Chagas' disease) and dengue fever. Be aware that you are always at risk from these diseases. **Malaria** is a danger throughout the lowland tropics and coastal regions. **Dengue fever**, which is widespread, is particularly hard to protect against as the mosquitoes can bite throughout the day as well as night (unlike those that carry malaria). Since 2015 cases of the chikungunya virus, transmitted by the same mosquito that carries dengue, have been confirmed in all South American countries except Argentina, Chile and Uruguay. Cases of the **Zika virus**, similarly spread, have also been reported in many countries throughout the region. Try to wear clothes that cover arms and legs and also use effective mosquito repellent. Mosquito nets dipped in permethrin provide a good physical and chemical barrier at night. **Chagas' disease** is spread by faeces of the triatomine, or assassin bugs, whereas sandflies spread a disease of the skin called **leishmaniasis**.

Some form of **diarrhoea** or intestinal upset is almost inevitable. The standard advice is always to wash your hands before eating and to be careful with drinking water and ice; if you have any doubts about the water then boil it or filter and treat it. In a restaurant buy bottled water or ask where the water has come from. Food can also pose a problem, be wary of salads if you don't know whether they have been washed or not.

There is a constant threat of **tuberculosis** (TB) and although the BCG vaccine is available, it is still not guaranteed protection. It is best to avoid unpasteurized dairy products and try not to let people cough and splutter all over you.

One of the major problems for travellers in the region is **altitude sickness**. It is essential to get acclimatized to the thin air of the Andes before undertaking long treks or arduous activities. The altitude of the Andes means that strong protection from the sun is always needed, regardless of how cool it may feel.

Another risk, especially to campers and people with small children, is that of the **hanta virus**, which is carried by some forest and riverine rodents. Epidemics have occurred in Argentina and Chile, but do occur worldwide. Symptoms are a flu-like illness, which can lead to complications. Try as far as possible to avoid rodent-infested areas, especially close contact with rodent droppings.

If you get sick

Contact your embassy or consulate for a list of doctors and dentists who speak your language, or at least some English. Your hotel may also be able to recommend good local medical services.

Websites

www.cdc.gov Centres for Disease Control and Prevention (USA).

www.nhs.uk/nhsengland/Healthcareabroad/pages/Healthcareabroad.aspx Department of Health advice for travellers.

www.fitfortravel.scot.nhs.uk Fit for Travel (UK), a site from Scotland providing a quick A-Z of vaccine and travel health advice requirements for each country.

www.itg.be Institute for Tropical Medicine, Antwerp.

http://nathnac.net National Travel Health Network and Centre (NaTHNaC).

www.who.int World Health Organisation.

Books

Dawood, R, editor, *Travellers' health*, 5th ed, Oxford: Oxford University Press, 2012.

Johnson, Chris, Sarah Anderson and others, *Oxford Handbook of Expedition and Wilderness Medicine*, OUP 2008.

Wilson-Howarth, Jane. *The Essential Guide To Travel Health: don't let Bugs Bites and Bowels spoil your trip*, Cadogan 2009, and *How to Shit around the World: the art of staying clean and healthy while travelling*, Travelers' Tales, US, 2011.

Internet

Email is common and public access to the internet is widespread. In large cities an hour in a cyber café will cost between US$0.50 and US$2, with some variation between busy and quiet times. Speed varies enormously, from city to city, café to café. Away from population centres service is slower and more expensive. Remember that for many South Americans a cyber café provides their only access to a computer, so it can be a very busy place and providers can get overloaded.

Language

The official language of the majority of South American countries is Spanish. The exceptions are Brazil (Portuguese), Guyana and the Falklands/Malvinas (English), Suriname (Dutch) and Guyane (French). English is often spoken by wealthy and well-educated citizens, but otherwise the use of English is generally restricted to those working in the tourism industry. The basic Spanish of Hispanic America is that of southwestern Spain, with soft 'c's' and 'z's' pronounced as 's', and not as 'th' as in the other parts of Spain. There are several regional variations in pronunciation, particularly in the River Plate countries; see box, page 1774. Differences in vocabulary also exist, both between peninsular Spanish and Latin American Spanish, and between the usages of the different countries.

Without some knowledge of Spanish (or Portuguese) you will become very frustrated and feel helpless in many situations. English, or any other language, is absolutely useless off the beaten track. Some initial study, to get you up to a basic vocabulary of 500 words or so, and a pocket dictionary and phrase-book, are most strongly recommended: your pleasure will be doubled if you can talk to the locals. Not all the locals speak Spanish (or Portuguese); you will find that in the more remote highland parts of Bolivia and Peru, and lowland Amazonia, some people speak only their indigenous languages, though there will usually be at least one person in each village who can speak Spanish (or Portuguese).

Second languages and anomalies

Argentina English is the second most common language; French and Italian (especially in Patagonia) may be useful. In Spanish, the chief variant pronunciations are the replacement of the 'll' and 'y' sounds by a soft 'j' sound, as in 'azure' (though rarely in Mendoza or the northwest), the omission of the 'd' sound in words ending in '-ado', the omission of final 's' sounds, the pronunciation of 's' before a consonant as a Scottish or German 'ch', and the substitution in the north and west of the normal rolled 'r' sound by a hybrid 'rj'. In grammar the Spanish 'tú' is replaced by 'vos' and the second person singular conjugation of verbs has the accent on the last syllable eg *vos tenés, podés*, etc. In the north and northwest, the Spanish is closer to that spoken in the rest of Latin America.

Bolivia Outside the cities, especially in the highlands, Aymara and Quechua are spoken by much of the indigenous population. In the lowlands, some Tupi Guaraní is spoken.

Chile The local pronunciation of Spanish, very quick and lilting, with the 's' dropped and final syllables cut off, can present difficulties to the foreigner.

Colombia Colombia has arguably the best spoken Spanish in Latin America, clearly enunciated and not too fast. This is particularly true in the highlands. There are several indigenous languages in the more remote parts of the country.

Ecuador Quichua is the second official language, although it is little used outside indigenous communities in the highlands and parts of Oriente.

Paraguay Guaraní is the second official language. Most people are bilingual and, outside Asunción, speak Guaraní. Many people speak a mixture of the two languages known as *jopara*.

Peru Quechua, the Andean language that predates the Incas, has been given some official status and there is much pride in its use. It is spoken by millions of people in the Sierra who have little or no knowledge of Spanish. Aymara is used in the area around Lake Titicaca. The jungle is home to a plethora of languages but Spanish is spoken in all but the remotest areas.

Suriname The native language, called Sranan Tongo, originally the speech of the Creoles, is now a lingua franca understood by all groups, and English is widely used.

Guyane Officials do not usually (or deliberately not) speak anything other than French, but Créole is more commonly spoken.

In the Guianas, the Asians, Maroons and Amerindians still speak their own languages among themselves.

Language courses

If you are going to Brazil, you should learn some Portuguese. Spanish is not adequate: you may be understood but you will probably not understand the answers. Language classes are cheap in a number of centres in South America, for instance Quito. For details, see below and also in the main text in 'What to do'.

Academia Buenos Aires, C Hipólito Yrigoyen 571, p 4, CP 1086, Buenos Aires, Argentina, T+54 11-4345 5954, www.academiabuenosaires.com. A partner in the Tandem International group, www.tandem-schools.com. Also has schools in Bariloche and Montevideo.

AmeriSpan, T1-215-531 7917 (worldwide), T1-800-511 0179 (USA), www.amerispan.com, offers Spanish immersion programmes, educational tours, volunteer and internship positions throughout Latin America. Language programmes are offered in Argentina, Brazil, Chile, Colombia, Ecuador, Peru and Uruguay.

Cactus, UK T01273-830960, www.cactuslanguage.com.

Spanish Abroad, USA, T1-888-722 7623, or T602-778 6791, http://spanishabroad.com, run courses in Argentina, Bolivia, Chile, Colombia, Ecuador, Peru, Uruguay and Venezuela.

LGBT travellers

South America is hardly well known for its gay-friendliness, but recent years have seen a shift in public opinion and attitudes. There is still a definite divide between the countryside and the city, but at least in the latter there are now more gay bars, organizations and social networks springing up. The legal framework has also been changing and homosexuality is now legal across South America, with the exception of Guyana, where male homosexuality is still a crime. Many countries have anti-discrimination laws, civil partnerships are becoming more common and recognized, as are same-sex marriages in Argentina, Brazil, Colombia and Uruguay, and civil unions in Chile and Ecuador. There is also a slowly increasing acceptance and knowledge of transgender issues, particularly in Uruguay, Colombia and Brazil. That said, it is wise to use caution and avoid overt displays of affection in public, particularly in rural areas, where the population tends to be more conservative. In the often macho Latin culture, gay men are more likely to experience trouble or harassment than gay women, but men also have a much better developed support network of bars, clubs and organizations, while lesbian culture and communities remain more hidden.

Some of the best cities for gay life are Buenos Aires (Argentina), Santiago (Chile), Bogotá (Colombia), Quito (Ecuador) Rio de Janeiro and other cities in Brazil, Lima (Peru) and Quito (Ecuador). Useful websites include: **www.gaytravel.com**, **www.globalgayz.com**, **www.iglta.org** (International Gay an d Lesbian Travel Association), **www.lghei.org** (Lesbian and Gay Hospitality Exchange International) and **www.passportmagazine.com**. Argentina: **www.nexo.org** (in Spanish). Brazil: **www.riogayguide.com**. Chile: **http://santiago.gaycities.com** and the sites of movements such as **www.acciongay.cl**, **http://mums.cl** (Movimiento por la Diversidad Sexual) and **www.movilh.org** (Movimiento de Integración y Liberación Homosexual). Colombia: **www.guiagaycolombia.com**. Ecuador: **www.quitogay.net**; **www.hotelcasajoaquin.com/offers-tours/gaylife-in-quito.html**. Peru: **www.gayperu.com** (in Spanish). Uruguay: **www.gaysylesbianasdeuruguay.com**.

Local customs and laws

Appearance

There is a natural prejudice in all countries against travellers who ignore personal hygiene and have a generally dirty and unkempt appearance. Most Latin Americans, if they can afford it, devote great care to their clothes and appearance; it is appreciated if visitors do likewise. Buying clothing locally can help you to look less like a tourist. In general, clothing requirements in Brazil are less formal than in the Hispanic countries. As a general rule, it is better not to wear shorts in official buildings, upmarket restaurants or cinemas. Also, for Brazilians, it is normal to stare and comment on women's appearance, and if you happen to look different or to be travelling alone, you will attract attention. Single women are very unlikely to be groped or otherwise molested (except at Carnaval), but nonetheless Brazilian men can be very persistent, and very easily encouraged.

Courtesy

Remember that politeness – even a little ceremoniousness – is much appreciated. Men should always remove any headgear and say *"con permiso"* (*"com licença"* in Brazil) when entering offices, and be prepared to shake hands (this is much more common in Latin America than in Europe or North America); always say *"Buenos días"* (until midday) or *"Buenas tardes"* (*"Bom dia"* or *"Boa tarde"* in Brazil) and wait for a reply before proceeding further. Always remember that the traveller from abroad has enjoyed greater advantages in life than most Latin American minor officials and should be friendly and courteous in consequence. Never be impatient. Do not criticize situations in public; the officials may know more English than you think and they can certainly interpret gestures and facial expressions. Be judicious about talking politics with strangers. Politeness can be a liability, however, in some situations; most Latin Americans are disorderly queuers. In commercial transactions (eg buying goods in a shop), politeness should be accompanied by firmness, and always ask the price first (arguing about money in a foreign language can be difficult).

Politeness should also be extended to street traders. Saying *"No, gracias"* or *"Não, obrigado/a"* with a smile is better than an arrogant dismissal. Whether you give money to beggars is a personal matter, but your decision should be influenced by whether a person is begging out of need or trying to cash in on the tourist trail. In the former case, local people giving may provide an indication. On giving money to children, most agree don't do it. There are times when giving food in a restaurant may be appropriate, but find out about local practice.

Money

For more specific information, see the Essentials A-Z sections under Money in individual chapters.

Cash

The main ways of keeping in funds while travelling are with cash, either US$ or, in a growing number of places, euros; credit cards/debit cards; traveller's cheques are increasingly hard to exchange. Though the risk of loss is greater, the chief benefit of US$ notes is that better rates and lower commissions can usually be obtained for them. In many countries, US$ notes are only accepted if they are in excellent, if not perfect condition (likewise, do not accept local currency notes in poor condition). Low-value US$ bills should be carried for changing into local currency if arriving in a country when banks or *casas de cambio* (exchange shops) are closed (US$5 or US$10 bills). They are very useful for shopping: shopkeepers and *casas de cambio* tend to give better exchange rates than hotels or banks (but see below). If you are travelling on the cheap it is essential to keep in funds. At weekends, on public holidays and when travelling off the beaten track always have plenty of local currency, preferably in small denominations.

Approximate costs of travelling are given in the Practicalities section at the end of each chapter.

Plastic

It is straightforward to obtain a cash advance against a credit card. Many banks are also linked to one, if not both of the main international ATM acceptance systems, Plus and Cirrus. Coverage is not uniform throughout the continent, though, so it may be wise to take 2 types of cards. Moreover, do not rely on one card, in case of loss. Frequently, the rates of exchange on ATM withdrawals are the best available. Find out before you leave what ATM coverage there is in the countries you will visit and what international 'functionality' your card has. Check if your bank or credit card company imposes handling charges. With a credit card, obtain a credit limit sufficient for your needs, or pay money in to put the account in credit. If travelling for a long time, consider a direct debit to clear your account regularly. Transactions using credit cards are normally at an officially recognized rate of exchange. They are often subject to tax.

By using a debit card rather than a credit card you incur fewer bank charges, although a credit card is needed as well for some purchases and with a credit card you are better protected in cases of fraud, overcharging, etc. Obviously you must ensure that the account to which your debit card refers contains sufficient funds. Before travelling, it may be worth setting up 2 bank accounts: one with all your funds but no debit card, the other with no funds but which does have a debit card. As you travel, use the internet to transfer money from the full account to the empty account when you need it and withdraw cash from an ATM. That way, if your debit card is stolen, you won't be at risk of losing all your capital. If you do lose a card, immediately contact the 24-hr helpline of the issuer in your home country (keep this number in a safe place).

Another option is to take a prepaid currency card. There are many on offer, but it pays to check their fees and charges carefully.

Exchange

When changing money on the street if possible do not do so alone. If unsure of the currency of the country you are about to enter, check rates with more than one changer at the border, or ask locals or departing travellers. Whenever you leave a country, change any local currency before departing, because the further away you get, the less the value of a country's money.

Post

Postal services vary in efficiency and prices are quite high; pilfering is frequent. All mail, especially packages, should be registered. Some countries have local alternatives to the post office. Check before leaving home if your embassy will hold mail, and for how long, in preference to the **Poste Restante/General Delivery** (**Lista de Correos**) department of a country's **Post Office**. If there seems to be no mail at the Lista under the initial letter of your surname, ask them to look under the initial of your forename or your middle name. Remember that there is no W in Spanish; look under V, or ask. To reduce the risk of misunderstanding, use title, initial and surname only. If having items sent to you by courier (such as **DHL**), do not use poste restante, but an address such as a hotel: a signature is required on receipt.

Information on specific local problems is given in the Essentials A-Z sections under Safety in individual chapters.

Drugs

Users of drugs, even of soft ones, without medical prescription should be particularly careful, as some countries impose heavy penalties – up to 10 years' imprisonment – for even possession of such substances. The planting of drugs on travellers, by traffickers or police, is not unknown. If offered drugs on the street, make no response at all and keep walking. Note that people who roll their own cigarettes are often suspected of carrying drugs and subjected to intensive searches. Note that the sale of marijuana in Uruguay, which became legal in 2014, applies to Uruguayan citizens and permanent residents only.

Keeping safe

Generally speaking, most places in South America are no more dangerous than any major city in Europe or North America. In provincial towns, main places of interest, on daytime buses and in ordinary restaurants the visitor should be quite safe. Nevertheless, in large cities (particularly in crowded places, eg bus stations, markets), crime exists, most of which is opportunistic. If you are aware of the dangers, act confidently and use your common sense, you will lessen many of the risks. The following tips are all endorsed by travellers. Keep all documents secure; hide your main cash supply in different places or under your clothes: extra pockets sewn inside shirts and trousers, pockets closed with a zip or safety pin, moneybelts (best worn under rather than outside your clothes at the waist), neck or leg pouches, a thin chain for attaching a purse to your bag or under your clothes and elasticated support bandages for keeping money above the elbow or below the knee. Be extra vigilant when withdrawing cash from an ATM: ensure you are not being watched; never give your card to anyone, however smart he may look or plausible he may sound as a 'bank employee' wishing to swipe your card to check for problems. Keep cameras in bags; take spare spectacles (eyeglasses); don't wear expensive wristwatches or jewellery. If you wear a shoulder-bag in a market, carry it in front of you.

Ignore mustard smearers and paint or shampoo sprayers, and strangers' remarks

Tip...

Take local advice about being out at night and, if walking after dark, walk in the road, not on the pavement/sidewalk.

such as 'what's that on your shoulder?' Furthermore, don't bend over to pick up money or other items in the street. These are all ruses to distract your attention and make you easy prey for an accomplice.

It is worth knowing that genuine police officers only have the right to see your passport (not your money, tickets or hotel room). Before handing anything over, ask why they need to see it and make sure you understand the reason. Insist on seeing identification and on going to the police station by main roads. On no account take them directly back to your lodgings. Be even more suspicious if he seeks confirmation of his status from a passer-by. A related scam is for a 'tourist' to gain your confidence, then accomplices create a reason to check your documents. If someone tries to bribe you, insist on a receipt. If attacked, remember your assailants may be armed, and try not to resist.

Leave any valuables you don't need in safe-deposit in your hotel when sightseeing locally. Always keep an inventory of what you have deposited. If there is no safe, lock your bags and secure them in your room. Hostels with shared rooms should provide secure, clean lockers for guests. If you lose valuables, always report to the police and note details of the report – for insurance purposes.

When you have all your luggage with you, be careful. From airports take official taxis or special airport buses. Take a taxi between bus station/railway station and hotel. Keep your bags with you in the taxi and pay only when you and your luggage are safely out of the vehicle. Make sure the taxi has inner door handles and do not share the ride with a stranger. Avoid night buses; never arrive at night; and watch your belongings whether they are stowed inside or outside the cabin (roof top luggage racks create extra problems, which are sometimes unavoidable – make sure your bag is waterproof). Major bus lines often issue a luggage ticket when bags are stored in the hold of the bus. Finally, never accept food, drink, sweets or cigarettes from unknown fellow travellers on buses or trains. They may be drugged, and you would wake up hours later without your belongings.

Police

Law enforcement in Latin America is often achieved by periodic campaigns, for example a round-up of criminals in the cities just before Christmas. At such times, you may well be asked for identification and, if you cannot produce it, you will be jailed. If a visitor is jailed his or her friends should provide food every day. This is especially important for people on a diet, such as diabetics. In the event of a vehicle accident in which anyone is injured, all drivers involved are automatically detained until blame has been established, and this does not usually take less than 2 weeks. Never offer a bribe unless you are fully conversant with the customs of the country. (In Chile, for instance, it would land you in serious trouble if you tried to bribe a *carabinero*.) Wait until the official makes the suggestion, or offer money in some form which is apparently not bribery, for example "In our country we have a system of on-the-spot fines (*multas de inmediato*). Is there a similar system here?" Do not assume that an official who accepts a bribe is prepared to do anything else that is illegal. You bribe him to persuade him to do his job, or to persuade him not to do it, or to do it more quickly or slowly. You do not bribe him to do something which is illegal. The mere suggestion would make him very upset. If an official suggests that a bribe must be paid before you can proceed on your way, be patient (assuming you have the time) and he may relent.

Student travellers

Student cards must carry a photo if they are to be of any use in Latin America for discounts. If you are in full-time education you will be entitled to an International Student Identity Card, which is distributed by student travel offices and travel agencies in 133 countries. The ISIC gives you special prices on all forms of transport such as air, sea, rail, and access to a variety of other concessions and services. If you need to find the location of your nearest ISIC office contact the **ISIC Association**, www.isic. org, which has offices worldwide.

Telephone

The most common method of making phone calls is with a pre-paid card. These are sold in a variety of denominations, in or just outside, phone offices. Phone offices (*centros de llamadas*, *locutorios*) are usually private, sometimes with lots of cabins, internet and other services, at other times just a person at a table offering national and international calls, mobile phone calls through various providers and phone cards. Public call booths are also operated with phone cards, very rarely with coins or tokens. With privatization, more and more companies are competing on the market, so you can shop around. SKYPE can also be used. If you want to use a mobile phone, either take your own if your provider has an agreement with a local operator (these vary from country to country), or buy a local SIM card. Phones must be tri- or quad-band; again, this varies. Rental (not cheap) and buying a pay-as-you-go phone is possible, but you will have to check the range of the phone. The area covered is often small and rates rise dramatically once you leave it.

Tour operators

Amazing Peru and Beyond, Av Petit Thouars 5356, Lima, T1-800-704 2915, www.amazingperu.com. Wide selection of tours throughout Latin America.

Amazonia Expeditions, 10305 Riverburn Dr, Tampa, FL 33647, T1-800-262 9669 (in USA and Canada), 001-813-907 8475, http://perujungle. com. Specialist in ecotourism to the Peruvian Amazon, but also Andes, Galápagos and southern Argentina.

Andean Trails, 33 Sandport St, Leith, Edinburgh EH6 6EP, UK, T0131-467 7086, www.andeantrails. co.uk. Small group trekking, mountain biking and jungle tours in the Andes and Amazon.

Aston Garcia, Salters House, Salters Lane Industrial Estate, Sedgefield, Co Durham TS21 3EE, UK, T01740-582007, www.astongarcia tours.com. Escorted, private and tailor-made tours in Brazil, Chile, Ecuador and Peru.

Audley Travel, New Mill, New Mill Lane, Witney, Oxfordshire OX29 9SX, UK, T01993-838010, www.audleytravel.com. Tailor-made holidays to South America (and elsewhere).

Bespoke Brazil, The Union Building, 51-59 Rose Lane, Norwich NR1 1B Y, T01603-340680, www. bespokebrazil.com. Tailor-made holidays and private tours throughout Brazil.

Chile Tours, Suite 2, 56 Sloane Square, London SW1W 8AX, T020-7730 5959, www.chiletours.org.

Chimu Adventures, 1321 Blanshard St, Suite 301, Victoria BC, V8W 0B6, Canada, T(718) 473 0815, www.chimuadventures.com. Provide tours, treks, active adventures and accommodation throughout South America and the Antarctic.

Condor Travel, Armando Blondet 249, San Isidro, Lima 27, T01-615 3000, www.condortravel.com. In USA T1-855-926 2975. A full range of tours, including custom-made, and services in Argentina, Bolivia, Brazil, Chile, Colombia, Ecuador and Peru (offices in each country), with a strong commitment to social responsibility.

Discover South America, T01273-921655 (UK), www.discoversouthamerica.co.uk. British/Peruvian-owned operator offering tailor-made and classic holidays in South America. Specialist in off-the-beaten track destinations in Peru.

Discover the World, Artic House, 8 Bolters Lane, Banstead, Surrey SM7 2AR, T01737-214250, www.discover-the-world.co.uk. Includes Antarctica and the Falklands/Malvinas in its portfolio of destinations.

Dragoman, Camp Green, Debenham, Suffolk IP14 6LA, UK, T01728-861133, www.dragoman.com. Overland adventures.

Escaped to Latin America, T1-800-305 6543, http://escapedtoperu.com. Experienced team of local experts arranging custom-made tours throughout Latin America.

Exito Travel, 108 Rutgers Av, Fort Collins, CO80525, USA, T800-655 4053 (USA) T970-482 3019 (worldwide), www.exitotravel.com. International flight specialists, experts in multi-stop and airpass itineraries.

Exodus Travels, Grange Mills, Weir Rd, London SW12 0NE, T0203-131 2941, www.exodus.co.uk. Adventure travels worldwide.

Experience Chile, Clarendon House, 20-22 Aylesbury End, Beaconsfield, Bucks HP9 1LW, UK, T020-8133 6057, and Padre Mariano 236, of 102, Providencia, Santiago, T2-570 9436, www.experiencechile.org.

Explore, Nelson House, 55 Victoria Rd, Farnborough, Hampshire GU14 7PA, UK, T01252-883985, www.explore.co.uk.

Fairtravel4u, Jan van Gentstraat 35, 1755 PB Petten, The Netherlands, T+31-61-5292565; in Ecuador T593-09-9569 3342, www.fairtravel4u.org, www.amazon-rainforest-tours.org. Sells tours in Ecuador, Peru and Bolivia, specializing in economy trips.

Galápagos Classic Cruises with **Classic Cruises** and **World Adventures**, 6 Keyes Rd, London NW2 3XA, T020-8933 0613, www.galapagoscruises.co.uk. Specialists in tours to the Galápagos, Latin America and Antarctica for over 22 years. All trips are personalized to suit individual and group requirements. Special offers available.

Galápagos Network, 5805 Blue Lagoon Dr, Suite 160, Miami, FL 33126, T1-305-262 6264, www.ecoventura.com. Miami branch of Galágos specialists Ecoventura, with extensions to mainland Ecuador and Peru.

Geodyssey, 116 Tollington Park, London N4 3RB, UK, T020-7281 7788, www.geodyssey.co.uk. For tours to Latin America and the Caribbean.

HighLives Travel, 1 Empire Mews, Stanthorpe Rd, London SW16 2BF, T020-8144 2629, www.highlives.co.uk. Organized luxury, tailor-made tours in Latin America.

INCA, 1311 63rd St, Emeryville, CA 94608, T510-420 1550, www.inca1.com. Cruises and luxury tours to Galápagos, Antarctica, Patagonia and Peru.

International Expeditions, 1 Environs Park, Helena, Alabama, 35080, T1-855-231-3577, www.ietravel.com.

Journey Latin America, 401 King St, London W6 9NJ, UK, T020-3733 4413/8747 3108 (flights only), www.journeylatinamerica.co.uk. The specialists.

Last Frontiers, The Mill, Quainton Rd, Waddesdon, Bucks HP18 0LP, UK, T01296-653000, www.lastfrontiers.com. South American specialists offering tailor-made itineraries plus family holidays, honeymoons, Galápagos and Antarctic cruises.

Latin America for Less, 203 Valona Drive Round Rock, TX 78681, USA T1-817-230 4971 (USA toll free), www.latinamericaforless.com. Specialize in travel packages.

Latin American Travel Association, www.lata.travel. For useful country information and listings of all UK tour operators specializing in Latin America. Also has the **LATA Foundation**, www.latafoundation.org, supporting charitable work in Latin America.

Metropolitan Touring, Av de las Palmeras N45-74 y de las Orquídeas, Quito, T02-298 8312, with offices in Bogotá and Lima, www.metropolitan-touring.com. Long-established Ecuadorean company offering tours in Ecuador, Colombia and Peru.

Oasis Overland, The Marsh, Henstridge, Somerset BA8 0TF, UK, T01963-530113, www.oasisoverland.co.uk. Small group trips to Peru and Bolivia and overland tours throughout South America.

Rainbow Tours, 2 Waterhouse Square, 138-140 Holborn, London EC1N 2ST, UK, T020-7666 1250, www.rainbowtours.co.uk. Tailor-made travel throughout Latin America.

Reef and Rainforest Tours Ltd, Dart Marine Park, Steamer Quay, Totnes, Devon TQ9 5AL, UK, T01803-866965, http://reefandrainforest.co.uk. Tailor-made and group wildlife tours.

Revealed Travel, Terminal House, Station Approach, Shepperton TW17 8AS, T01932-424252, http://southamericarevealed.co.uk. Good-value, tailor-made holidays and honeymoons, plus small-group escorted tours.

Select Latin America, based in Central London, contact via website or phone, T020-7407 1478, www.selectlatinamerica.co.uk. Tailor-made holidays and small group tours, many years' experience.

South America Adventure Tours, 336 Kennington Lane, Suite 25, Vauxhall, London SE11 5HY, T0845-463 3389, http://southamericaadventuretours.com. Specialize in personalized adventure tours in Argentina, Brazil, Costa Rica, Ecuador and Peru.

The South America Specialists, 5 Saunders Piece, Ampthill, Bedfordshire, MK45 2QB, T01525-306555, www.thesouthamericaspecialists.com. Luxury travel itineraries throughout South America and Antarctica.

SouthAmerica.travel, www.SouthAmerica.travel, internet-based tour company with offices in Buenos Aires, Lima and Rio de Janeiro, UK T0800-011 9170 or T020-3026 9287, in Germany T0800-747 4540, US and Canada T1-800-747 4540, Australia T1-800-269979, worldwide phone T+1-206-203 8800. Experienced company offering 4- and 5-star luxury tours to South America (except the Guianas), with discount flights to South America from anywhere.

Steamond, 23 Eccleston St, London SW1W 9LX, T020-7730 8646, www.steamondtravel.com. Organizing all types of travel to Latin America since 1973, very knowledgeable and helpful.

Steppes Latin America, 51 Castle St, Cirencester, Glos GL7 1QD, T01285-601752, www.steppestravel.co.uk. Tailor-made itineraries for destinations throughout Latin America.

Swoop Patagonia, The Condor's Nest, Clifton Heights, Triangle West, Bristol BS8 1EJ, UK, T0117-369 0196, www.swoop-patagonia.co.uk. Specialists in adventure tours to Patagonia; also to Antarctica.

Tambo Tours, USA, T1-888-2-GO-PERU (246-7378), www.tambotours.com. Long-established adventure and tour specialist with offices in Peru and the US. Customized trips to the Amazon and archaeological sites of Peru, Bolivia and Ecuador.

Trailfinders, 194 Kensington High St, London W8 7RG, T020-7368 1200, www.trailfinders.com. 32 branches throughout the UK and in Ireland.

Tribes Travel, The Old Dairy, Wood Farm, Ipswich Rd, Otley, Suffolk IP6 9JW, UK, T01473-890499, www.tribes.co.uk. Tailor-made tours from ethical travel specialists.

Tropical Birding, 113 Wind Tree Valley Rd, Parkton, MD 21120, T1-409-515 9110, www.tropicalbirding.com. International tour operator specializing in birding, nature and nature photography tours.

Tucan, 316 Uxbridge Rd, Acton, London W3 9QP, T020-8896 1600, Av del Sol 616, of 202, AP 0637, Cuzco T51-84-241123, www.tucantravel.com.

Vaya Adventures, 2120 University Av, Berkeley, CA 94704, USA, T1-800-342 1796, www.vayaadventures.com. Customized, private itineraries throughout South America.

Wilderness Travel, 1102 Ninth St, Berkeley, CA 94710, T510-558 2488, T1-800-368 2794, www.wildernesstravel.com.

Yampu Tours, 6 Bruce Grove, London N17 6RA, T0800-011 2424, www.yampu.com. Personalized tours to suit any special interest from popular attractions to less-visited sights, from the historical to the culinary, spiritual and adventure. Named "South America's Leading Tour Operator" for 5 years running.

Tourist information

Local sources of information are given in the country chapters.

Finding out more
It is better to seek security advice before you leave from your own consulate than from travel agencies. You can contact:
Australian Department of Foreign Affairs, T+61-2-6261 3305, http://smartraveller.gov.au.
British Foreign and Commonwealth Office, Travel Advice Unit, www.gov.uk/browse/abroad. Footprint is a partner in the Foreign and

Commonwealth Office's **Know before you go** campaign, https://travelaware.campaign.gov.uk/.
US State Department's Bureau of Consular Affairs, Overseas Citizens Services, T1-888-407 4747 (from overseas: T202-501 4444), https://travel.state.gov.
Wanderlust, www.wanderlust.co.uk. The ultimate magazine for curious, independent-minded travellers.

Useful websites

Website addresses for individual countries are given in the relevant chapter's Practicalities section and throughout the text.
www.bootsnall.com/South-America
An online travel guide for South America, which is updated monthly.
www.lata.travel Lists tour operators, hotels, airlines, etc. Has a useful (free) guide which can also be ordered by phoning T020-3713 6688.
www.oas.org The Organization of American States site, with its magazine *Américas*.
www.rainforest-alliance.org Rainforest Alliance works for conservation and sustainability in South America and worldwide, including information on tour operators who promote sustainability.

Passports and other important documents

You should always carry your passport in a safe place about your person, or if not going far, leave it in the hotel safe. If staying in a country for several weeks, it is worthwhile registering at your embassy or consulate. Then, if your passport is stolen, the process of replacing it is simplified and speeded up. Keep photo- or digital copies of essential documents, including your flight ticket, and some additional passport-sized photographs, or send yourself before you leave home an email with all important details, addresses, etc, which you can access in an emergency. It is your responsibility to ensure that your passport is stamped in and out when you cross borders. The absence of entry and exit stamps can cause serious difficulties; seek out the proper immigration offices if the stamping process is not carried out as you cross. Also, do not lose your entry card; replacing one causes a lot of trouble and possibly expense. If planning to study in Latin America for a long period, get a student visa in advance. See the Practicalities section in each chapter for more specific information.

Footnotes

Index
Entries in bold refer to maps

FOOTPRINT
Features

About the author

Ben Box

One of the first assignments Ben Box took as a freelance writer in 1980 was subediting work on the *South American Handbook*. The plan then was to write about contemporary Iberian and Latin American affairs, but in no time at all the lands south of the Rio Grande took over, inspiring journeys to all corners of the subcontinent. Ben has contributed to newspapers, magazines and learned tomes, usually on the subject of travel, and became editor of the *South American Handbook* in 1989. He has also been involved in Footprint's Handbooks on *Central America & Mexico*; *Caribbean Islands*; *Brazil*; *Peru*; *Cuzco & the Inca Heartland*; *Bolivia*; *Peru, Bolivia and Ecuador*; and *Jamaica*. On many of these titles he has collaborated with his wife and Footprint Caribbean expert, Sarah Cameron.

Having a doctorate in Spanish and Portuguese studies from London University, Ben maintains a strong interest in Latin American literature. In the British summer he plays cricket for his local village side and year round he attempts to achieve some level of self-sufficiency in fruit and veg in a rather unruly country garden in Suffolk.

Acknowledgements

This new edition of the *South American Handbook* has, as ever, been written in collaboration with many people. Those who have helped with the individual chapters are acknowledged below, but Ben Box is also grateful to the following for their invaluable support during the preparation of this book: above all, the team at Footprint who put the book together: Felicity, Emma, Jo, Kevin, Debbie and Angus.

For specific chapter information, our warmest thanks go to the following contributors:

The Bolivia chapter was updated by Robert and Daisy Kunstaetter who would like to thank: Marcelo Apaza, Saúl Arias, Wolfgang Auer, Juan Carlos Gonzales, Fabiola Mitru, Carlos Morales, Derren Patterson, Mariana Sánchez, Soraya Sánchez, Martin Stratker, Viviana Ugarte, Remy van den Berg and Isabelle Verstraete.

For help with the Brazil chapter we are most grateful to Alex Robinson, author of Footprint's *Brazil Handbook*, and Robert and Daisy Kunstaetter.

The Chile chapter was updated by Lorraine Caputo.

The Colombia chapter was updated by Huw Hennessy, who wishes to thank Richard McColl.

For assistance with the Ecuador chapter we are grateful to Jean Brown, Robert and Daisy Kunstaetter, Patty Mothes and Popkje van de Ploeg.

The Paraguay chapter was updated by Geoffrey Groesbeck, author of Footprint's *Paraguay Handbook*.

Peru was updated by Robert and Daisy Kunstaetter, authors of Footprint's *Peru Handbook*. They wish to thank: Kristof De Rynck, Rob Dover, Leo Duncan, John and Julia Forrest, Jaime García, Klaus Hartl and Julio Porras.

The Uruguay and Venezuela chapters were updated by Huw Hennessy, who wishes to thank for help with Uruguay Anna Maria Espsäter and Paola Perelli; for help with Venezuela, José Luis Troconis, Juan Carlos Ramírez, Nelson Agelvis, Livio Leopardi of Delfino Tours, and Betsy Franco of Condor Verde Tour. And for assistance with both countries, Antonio Vaquero of Journey Latin America.

For the update of the Falkland Islas/Islas Malvinas chapter we wish to thank Kyle Biggs of the Falkland Islands Tourist Board in Stanley.

We are most grateful to the following travellers who have sent us their comments and suggestion over the past year: Dan Buck, US (Bol); Hugh Burton, UK (Bol); Alberto Cafferata, Peru (Per); Catalina (Chi); Clara Duffner (Bra); Cecilia Kamiche, Peru (Per); Mathilde Kettnaker (Col); Homero Kosiner (Arg, Chi, Col); Robert and Daisy Kunstaetter, Ecuador (in addition to their updating work in Peru and Bolivia), new information from Argentina, Brazil and Chile; Jaime García Heras, US (Arg, Per); Tim Lannan (Bol); Herbert Levi, Argentina (Arg, Uru); Steve Light, Peru (Per); Marilyn Longden (Bol, Uru); Robert Monks, Australia (Col); David Nichols, UK (Arg, Par); Sandra Rodríguez and family, Canada (Chi); Ekta Shah, Brazil (Bra); Emer Stevenson (Chi); Martijn Turksema, Colombia (Col); Rick Vecchio, Peru (Ecu, Per); Michael White, UK (Per); plus all the travellers who have written to Footprint with information for the individual country guidebooks.

In September/October 2016 the author travelled from Encarnación in Paraguay to Guyane, Suriname and Guyana via Brazil and, for their assistance, hospitality and generosity, he would like to thank most warmly the following people:

Sue Morkill and Edward Paine of Last Frontiers for arranging the complicated flight arrangements in Brazil, and Yuly Ospina of Air Europa. William H Coleman Inc and the staff at TMLA and Douglas Simões and the ATLAS team in Foz do Iguaçu.

In Guyane: Laurence Besançon, Chargée de l'Observation et de la gestion du Système d'Informations Touristiques, and Rolando at the Comité du Tourisme de la Guyane in Cayenne.

In Suriname: Jerry A-Kum, Director of the Suriname Tourism Foundation; Dave Boucke, General Manager, Torarica, and member of SHATA; Robbin Roemer of 't Vat and Country Manager for Europcar; Sirano Zalman of Access Suriname Travel and Frederiksdorp, Tessa Leuwsha, Henk Tjassing, Tony the guide and the staff at Frederiksdorp.

In Guyana: Tony Thorne and Claire Antell of Wilderness Explorers, plus the staff who helped organize and the trip to Suriname and Guyana: Teri O'Brien, Kenneth Shivdyal, Amarylis Lewis, Annie

Sonaram, and Ameer; and last but not least the tour guide Wally Prince. At Surama, Jackie Allicott and the staff and Kenneth Butler of Green Diamond Nature Tours. Rudy Edwards and the staff and community at Rewa. The staff at Atta, including Jonathan the guide. At Karanambu, Melanie and Jerry McTurk and staff. Colin Edwards and family at Rock View. At Caiman House, Peter Taylor, Fernando, Josie, Jenkins and the rest of the staff. Finally, thanks to the tour members Isak, Maddy, Naila, Diana, Federika and Paul, who were such great travelling companions.

Credits

Footprint credits

Editor: Jo Williams
Production and layout: Emma Bryers
Maps: Kevin Feeney, Robert Kunstaetter
Colour section: Angus Dawson

Publisher: John Sadler
Head of Publishing: Felicity Laughton
Marketing: Kirsty Holmes
Advertising and Partnerships: Debbie Wylde

Publishing information

Footprint South American Handbook
94th edition
© Compass Maps Ltd
October 2017

ISBN: 978 1 911082 23 1
CIP DATA: A catalogue record for this book is available from the British Library

® Footprint Handbooks and the Footprint mark are a registered trademark of Compass Maps Ltd

Published by Footprint
5 Riverside Court
Lower Bristol Road
Bath BA2 3DZ, UK
T +44 (0)1225 469141
footprinttravelguides.com

Printed in India by Thomson Press Ltd, Faridabad, Haryana

Every effort has been made to ensure that the facts in this guidebook are accurate. However, travellers should still obtain advice from consulates, airlines, etc about travel and visa requirements before travelling. The authors and publishers cannot accept responsibility for any loss, injury or inconvenience however caused.

Footprint Mini Atlas
South America

National highway
including Pan-American
Highway

Paved road

Unpaved all weather
including unpaved
Pan-American Highway

Seasonal unpaved road, track

Rail

Altitude in metres

4000
3000
2000
1000
500
200
0

Neighbouring
Country

9inset *Falkland Islands/
Islas Malvinas*

ECUADOR
*Galápagos
Islands*

500 km

500 miles

N

Map 1

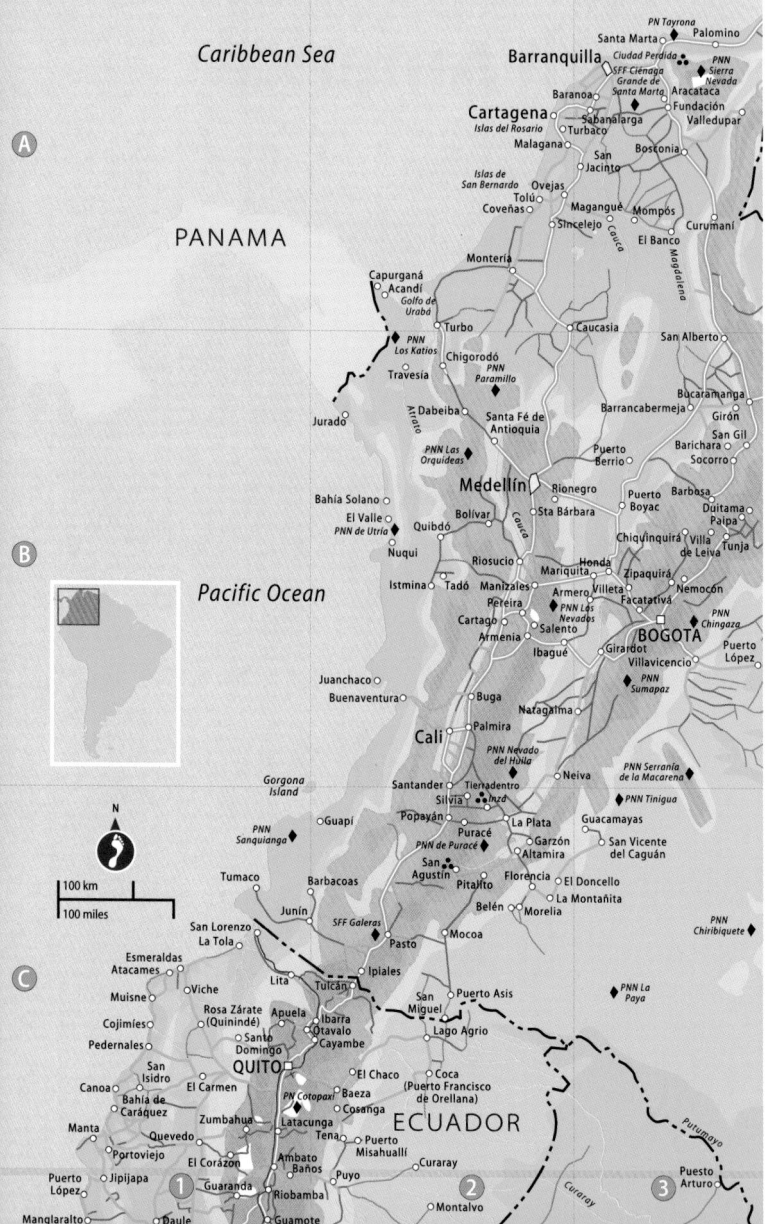

Caribbean Sea

PANAMA

Pacific Ocean

Gorgona Island

A

B

C

1　**2**　**3**

N

100 km
100 miles

PN Tayrona
Santa Marta　Palomino
Barranquilla
Ciudad Perdida　PNN
SFF Ciénaga　Sierra
Grande de　Nevada
Santa Marta　Aracataca
Baranoa
Cartagena　　　　Fundación
Islas del Rosario　Sabanalarga　Valledupar
Malagana　Turbaco
San
Jacinto　Bosconia
Islas de
San Bernardo　Ovejas
Tolú　Magangué　El Banco　Curumaní
Coveñas　Sincelejo　Mompós
Montería　　San Alberto
Capurganá
Acandí　Golfo de
Urabá
PNN　Turbo　Caucasia　Bucaramanga
Los Katios　Chigorodó　PNN
Travesía　　Paramillo　Barrancabermeja　Girón
Jurado　Dabeiba　Santa Fé de　San Gil
Atrato　Antioquia　Barichara
PNN Las　Puerto　Socorro
Orquídeas　Berrío　Barbosa
Bahía Solano　Medellín　Rionegro　Puerto　Duitama
El Valle　Quibdó　Bolívar　Sta Bárbara　Boyacá　Paipa
PNN de Utría　　　　　Chiquinquirá　Villa　Tunja
Nuquí　Riosucio　Cauca　Honda　de Leiva
Istmina　Tadó　Manizales　Mariquita　Zipaquirá
Pereira　Armero　Villeta　Facatativá　Nemocón
Cartago　PNN Las　Salento　PNN
Armenia　Nevados　BOGOTÁ　Chingaza
Juanchaco　Ibagué　Girardot　Puerto
Buga　Villavicencio　López
Buenaventura　Natagaima　PNN
Sumapaz
Cali　Palmira
PNN Nevado
del Huila
Santander　Tierradentro　Neiva　PNN Serranía
Silvia　Inzá　　de la Macarena
Guapi　Popayán　La Plata　Guacamayas　PNN Tinigua
PNN　Puracé　Garzón
Sanquianga　PNN de Puracé　Altamira　San Vicente
San　　del Caguán
Tumaco　Barbacoas　Agustín　Pitalito
Florencia　El Doncello
Junín　SFF Galeras　Pasto　Belén　La Montañita
San Lorenzo　　Morelia
La Tola　Ipiales　Mocoa　PNN
Esmeraldas　Lita　Tulcán　Chiribiquete
Atacames　Viche　San　Puerto Asis
Muisne　Rosa Zárate　Apuela　Miguel
Cojimíes　(Quinindé)　Ibarra　Lago Agrio　PNN La
Pedernales　Santo　Otavalo　Paya
San　Domingo　Cayambe
Isidro　El Carmen　QUITO　El Chaco　Coca
Canoa　Cosanga　(Puerto Francisco
Bahía de　PN Cotopaxi　de Orellana)
Caráquez　Zumbahua　Latacunga
Manta　Tena
Quevedo　Ambato　Puerto
Portoviejo　El Corazón　Baños　Misahuallí
Puerto　Jipijapa　ECUADOR
López　Guaranda　Riobamba　Puyo　Curaray
Daule　Guamote　Montalvo　Curaray　Puesto
Manglaralto　　Arturo
Putumayo

Map 2

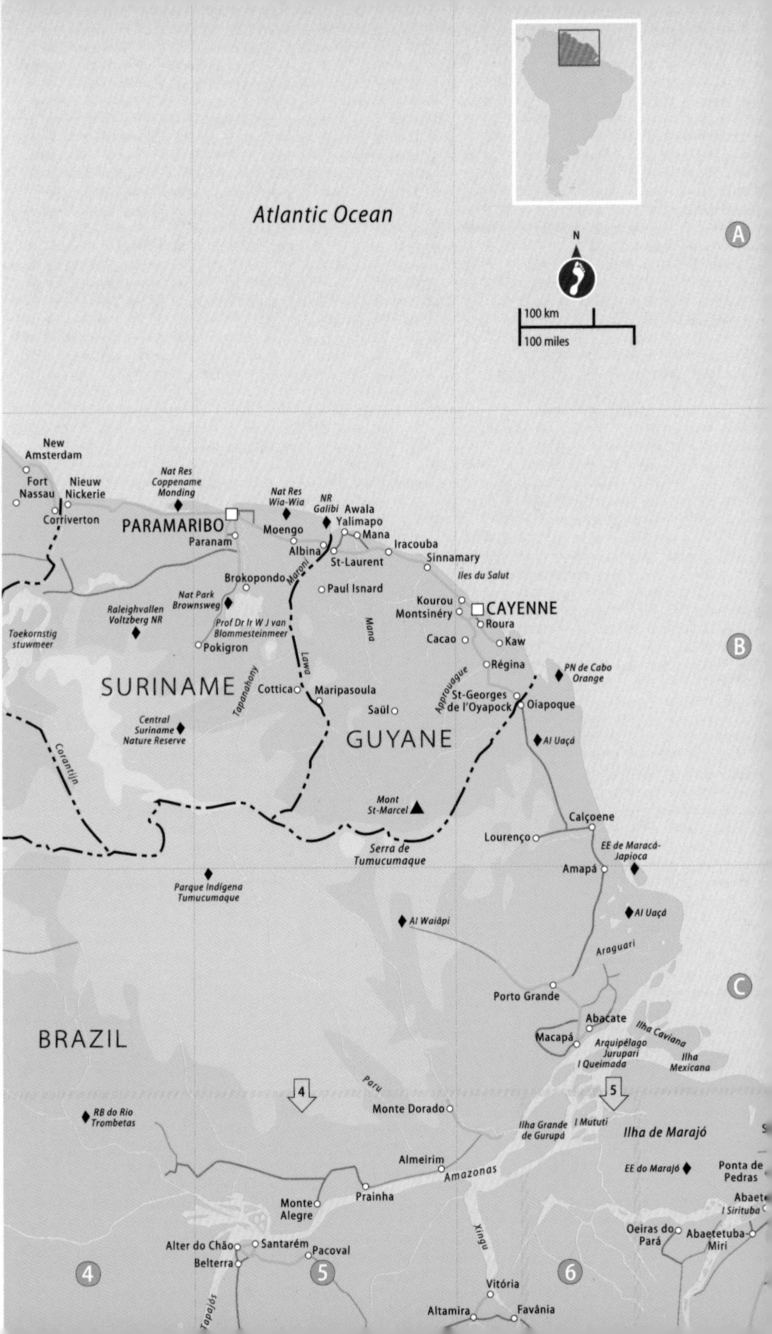

Atlantic Ocean

N

| 100 km |
| 100 miles |

New Amsterdam
Fort Nassau
Nieuw Nickerie
Corriverton

Nat Res Coppename Monding

PARAMARIBO
Paranam

Nat Res Wia-Wia
NR Galibi
Moengo
Awala
Yalimapo
Mana
Albina
St-Laurent
Iracouba
Sinnamary

Brokopondo
Paul Isnard
Iles du Salut
Kourou
Montsinéry
CAYENNE
Roura
Cacao
Kaw

Nat Park Brownsweg
Raleighvallen Voltzberg NR
Prof Dr Ir W J van Blommesteinmeer
Pokigron
Régina
PN de Cabo Orange

Toekornstig stuwmeer

SURINAME
Cottica
Maripasoula
Apatou
St-Georges de l'Oyapock
Oiapoque

Central Suriname Nature Reserve
Saül
GUYANE
AI Uaçá

Corantijn

Mont St-Marcel
Serra de Tumucumaque
Calçoene

Lourenço
EE de Maracá-Japioca
Amapá

Parque Indígena Tumucumaque
AI Waiãpi
AI Uaçá

Araguari

BRAZIL
Porto Grande
Abacate
Ilha Caviana
Macapá
Arquipélago Jurupari
I Queimada
Ilha Mexicana

Paru
④
Monte Dorado
Ilha Grande de Gurupá
I Mututi
⑤
Ilha de Marajó

RB do Rio Trombetas
Almeirim
Amazonas
EE do Marajó
Ponta de Pedras

Prainha
Xingu
Abaete
I Sirituba

Monte Alegre
Oeiras do Pará
Abaetetuba-Miri

Alter do Chão
Santarém
Pacoval
④
⑤
⑥
Belterra

Tapajós
Vitória
Altamira
Favânia

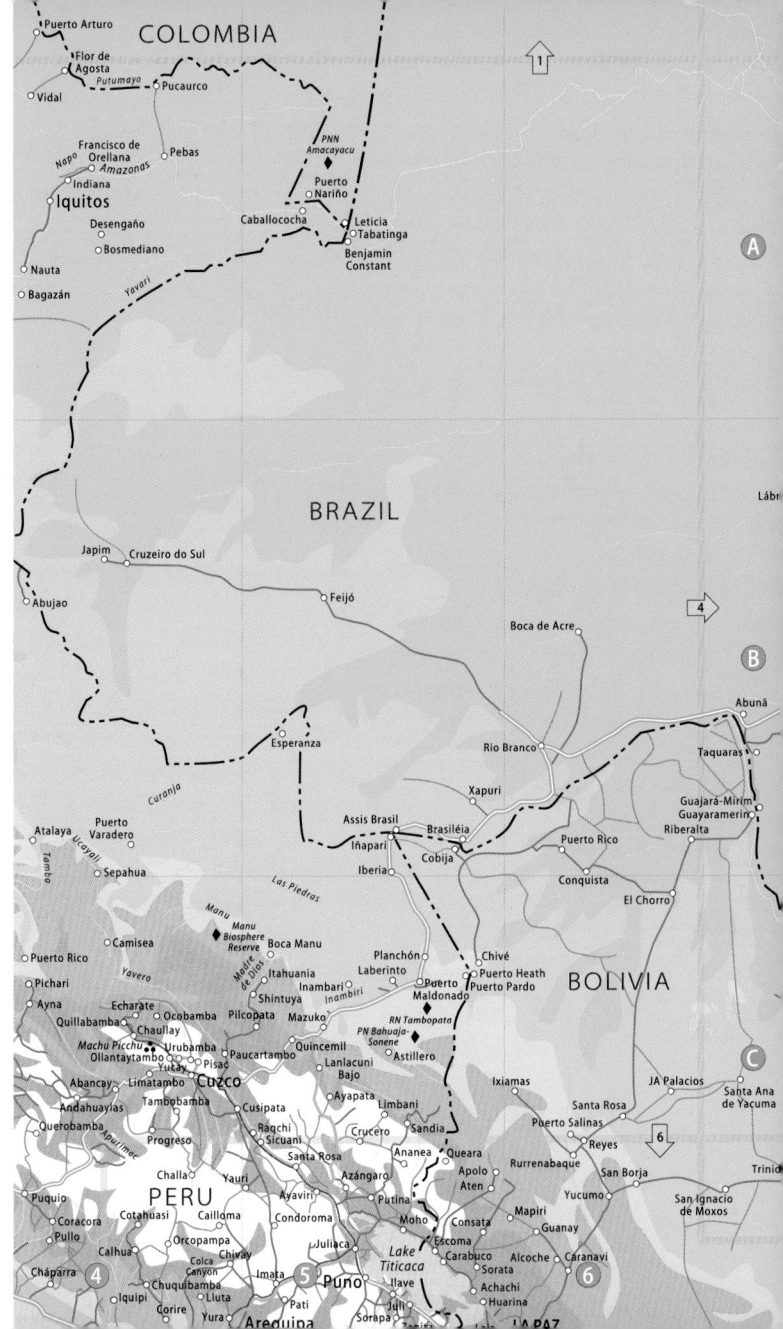

Map 4

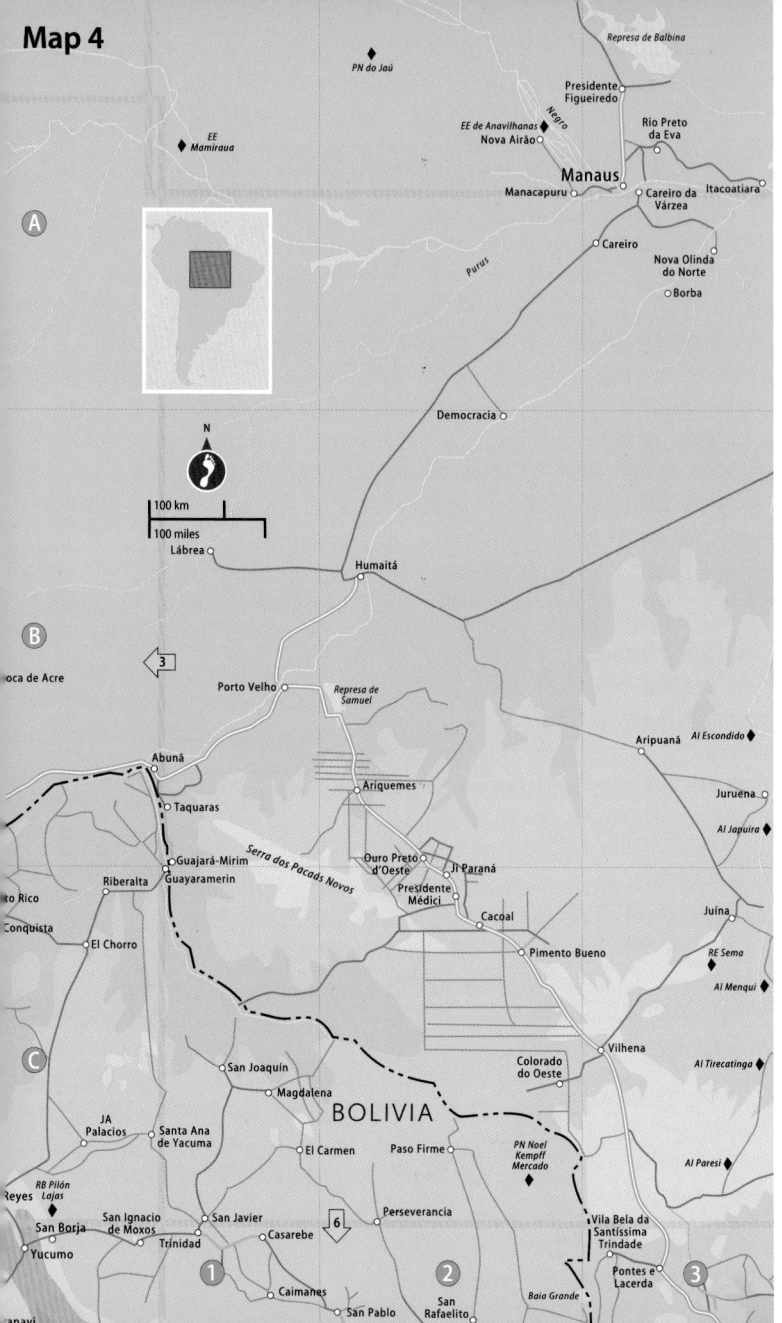

Map 5

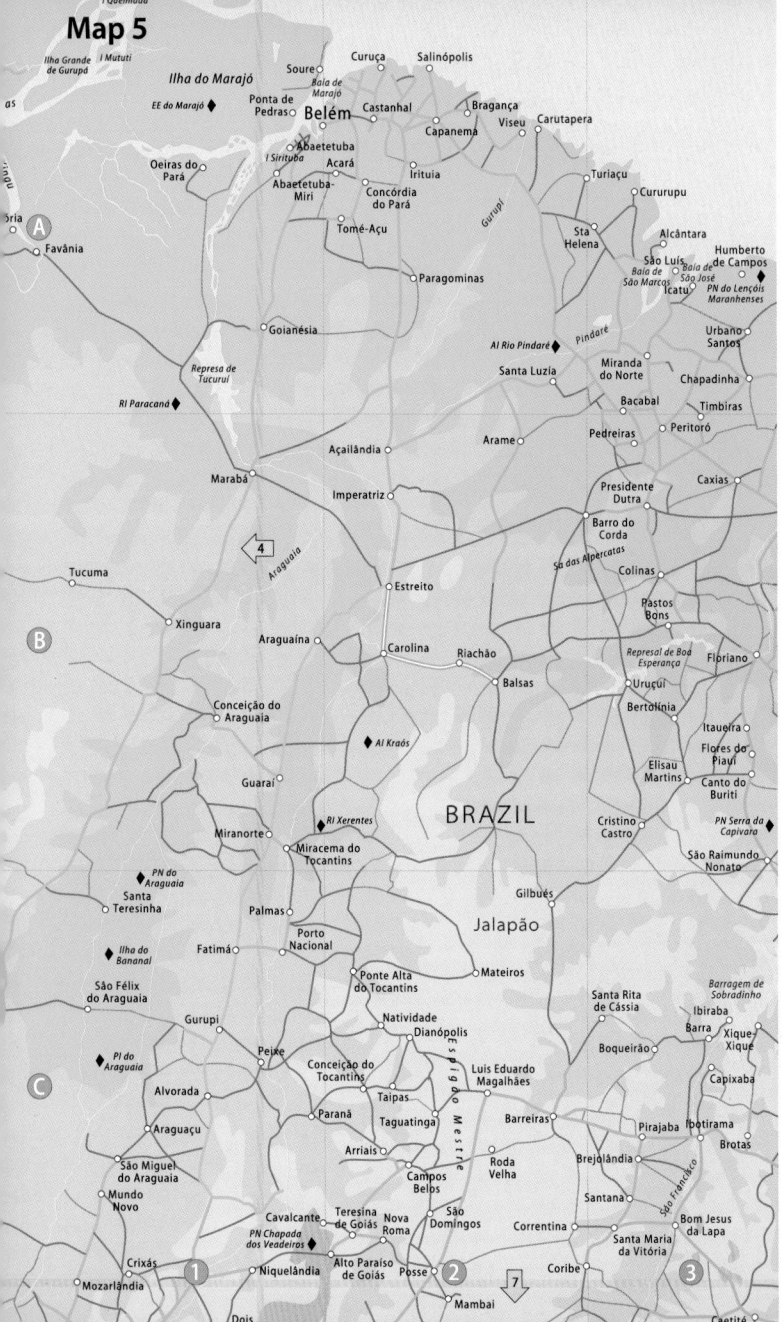

Ilha Grande de Gurupá
I Mútuti
I Queimada
Ilha do Marajó
EE do Marajó
Ponta de Pedras
Soure
Baía de Marajó
Curuçá
Salinópolis
Castanhal
Bragança
Viseu
Carutapera
Belém
Abaetetuba
I Sirituba
Acará
Abaetetuba-Miri
Oeiras do Pará
Favânia
Capanema
Irituia
Concórdia do Pará
Tomé-Açu
Paragominas
Goianésia
Turiaçu
Cururupu
Sta Helena
São Luís
Baía de São Marcos
Alcântara
Baía de São José
Humberto de Campos
PN do Lençóis Maranhenses
Icatu
Urbano Santos
AI Rio Pindaré
Santa Luzia
Miranda do Norte
Chapadinha
Bacabal
Timbiras
Peritoró
Caxias
Represa de Tucuruí
RI Paracaná
Açailândia
Arame
Pedreiras
Presidente Dutra
Barro do Corda
Sa das Alpercatas
Colinas
Pastos Bons
Floriano
Marabá
Imperatriz
Tucuma
Araguaia
4
Estreito
Riachão
Represa de Boa Esperança
Urucuí
Bertolínia
Itaueíra
Xinguara
Araguaína
Carolina
Balsas
Flores do Piauí
Conceição do Araguaia
AI Kraós
Elisau Martins
Canto do Buriti
PN Serra da Capivara
Guaraí
BRAZIL
Cristino Castro
São Raimundo Nonato
Miranorte
RI Xerentes
Miracema do Tocantins
Gilbués
PN do Araguaia
Santa Teresinha
Palmas
Jalapão
Ilha do Bananal
Fatimá
Porto Nacional
Santa Rita de Cássia
Barragem de Sobradinho
Ibiraba
São Félix do Araguaia
Ponte Alta do Tocantins
Natividade
Mateiros
Barra
Xique-Xique
PI do Araguaia
Gurupi
Dianópolis
Boqueirão
Capixaba
Alvorada
Peixe
Conceição do Tocantins
Luís Eduardo Magalhães
Pirajaba
Ibotirama
Brotas
Araguaçu
Paranã
Taipas
Taguatinga
Barreiras
Brejolândia
São Miguel do Araguaia
Arraias
Roda Velha
Santana
Mundo Novo
Cavalcante
Teresina de Goiás
Campos Belos
São Domingos
Correntina
Santa Maria da Vitória
Bom Jesus da Lapa
Crixás
PN Chapada dos Veadeiros
Nova Roma
1
Mozarlândia
Niquelândia
Alto Paraíso de Goiás
Posse
2
Mambaí
7
Coribe
3
Dois
Caetité

A B C
1 2 3

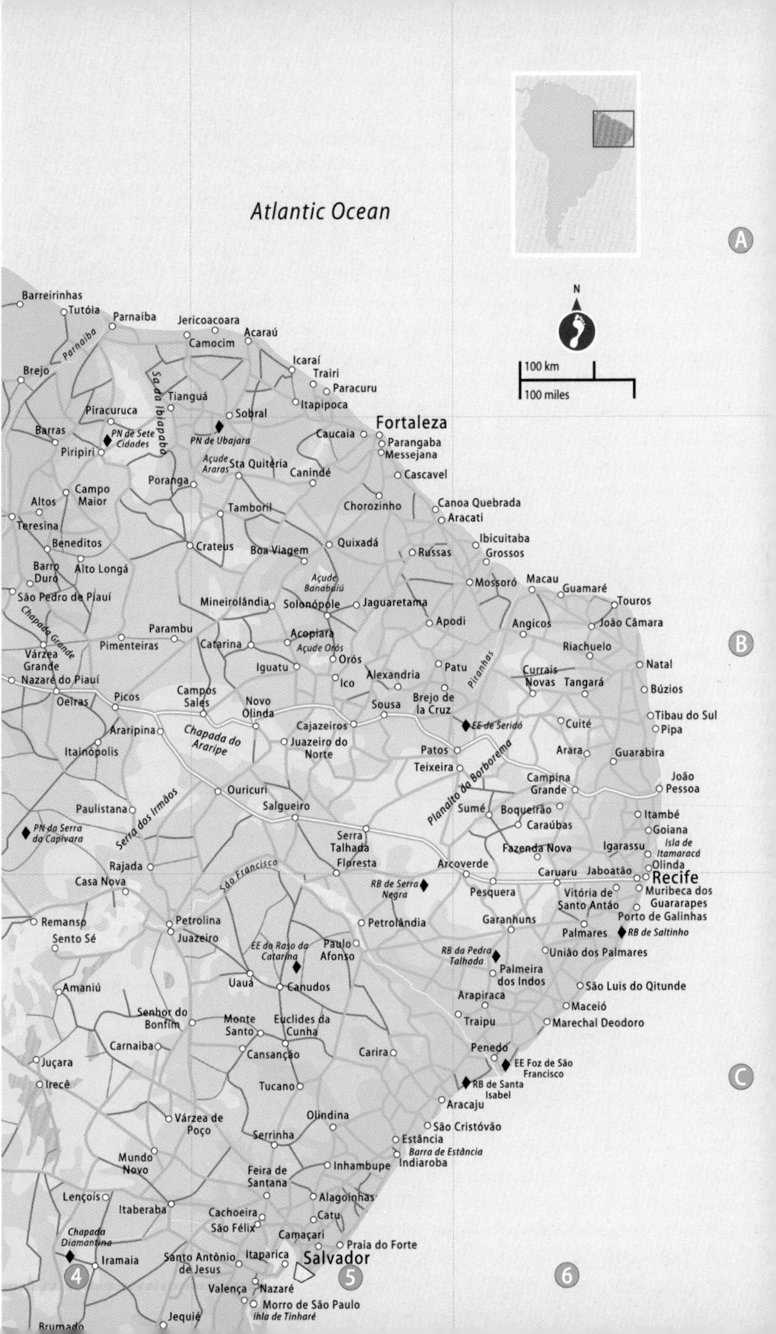

Atlantic Ocean
A
B
C
4
5
6
N
100 km
100 miles
Barreirinhas
Tutóia
Parnaiba
Jericoacoara
Acaraú
Camocim
Icaraí
Trairi
Paracuru
Itapipoca
Brejo
Sa da Ibiapaba
Tianguá
Piracuruca
Sobral
Barras
PN de Sete Cidades
PN de Ubajara
Piripiri
Fortaleza
Caucaia
Parangaba
Messejana
Açude Araras
Sta Quitéria
Canindé
Cascavel
Poranga
Altos
Campo Maior
Tamboril
Chorozinho
Canoa Quebrada
Aracati
Teresina
Benediti
Crateus
Boa Viagem
Quixadá
Russas
Ibicuitaba
Grossos
Barro Duro
Alto Longá
Açude Banabuiú
Mossoró
Macau
Guamaré
São Pedro de Piauí
Mineirolândia
Solonópole
Jaguaretama
Touros
Chapada Grande
Parambu
Apodi
Angicos
João Câmara
Pimenteiras
Catarina
Acopiara
Açude Orós
Riachuelo
Várzea Grande
Orós
Iguatu
Patu
Piranhas
Natal
Nazaré do Piauí
Ico
Alexandria
Currais Novas
Tangará
Búzios
Oeiras
Picos
Campos Sales
Novo Olinda
Sousa
Brejo de la Cruz
Tibau do Sul
Pipa
Araripina
Chapada do Araripe
Cajazeiros
EE de Seridó
Cuité
Itainópolis
Juazeiro do Norte
Patos
Arara
Guarabira
Teixeira
Planalto da Borborema
Campina Grande
João Pessoa
Ouricuri
Paulistana
Serra dos Irmãos
Salgueiro
Sumé
Boqueirão
Itambé
PN da Serra da Capivara
Serra Talhada
Caraúbas
Goiana
Fazenda Nova
Igarassu
Isla de Itamaracá
Rajada
Floresta
Arcoverde
Olinda
São Francisco
Caruaru
Jaboatão
Recife
Casa Nova
RB de Serra Negra
Pesquera
Vitória de Santo Antão
Muribeca dos Guararapes
Porto de Galinhas
Remanso
Petrolina
Petrolândia
Garanhuns
Palmares
RB de Saltinho
Sento Sé
Juazeiro
EE do Raso da Catarina
Paulo Afonso
RB da Pedra Talhada
União dos Palmares
Palmeira dos Indos
Uauá
Canudos
São Luis do Qitunde
Amaniú
Arapiraca
Maceió
Senhor do Bonfim
Monte Santo
Euclides da Cunha
Traipu
Marechal Deodoro
Carnaiba
Cansanção
Carira
Penedo
EE Foz de São Francisco
Juçara
Irecê
Tucano
RB de Santa Isabel
Aracaju
Várzea de Poço
Olindina
São Cristóvão
Serrinha
Estância
Barra de Estância
Mundo Novo
Inhambupe
Indiaroba
Feira de Santana
Lençóis
Itaberaba
Alagoinhas
Cachoeira
Catu
São Félix
Camaçari
Chapada Diamantina
Praia do Forte
Iramaia
Santo Antônio de Jesus
Itaparica
Salvador
Valença
Nazaré
Morro de São Paulo
Ihla de Tinharé
Jequié
Brumado

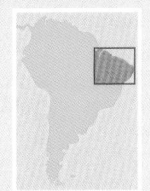

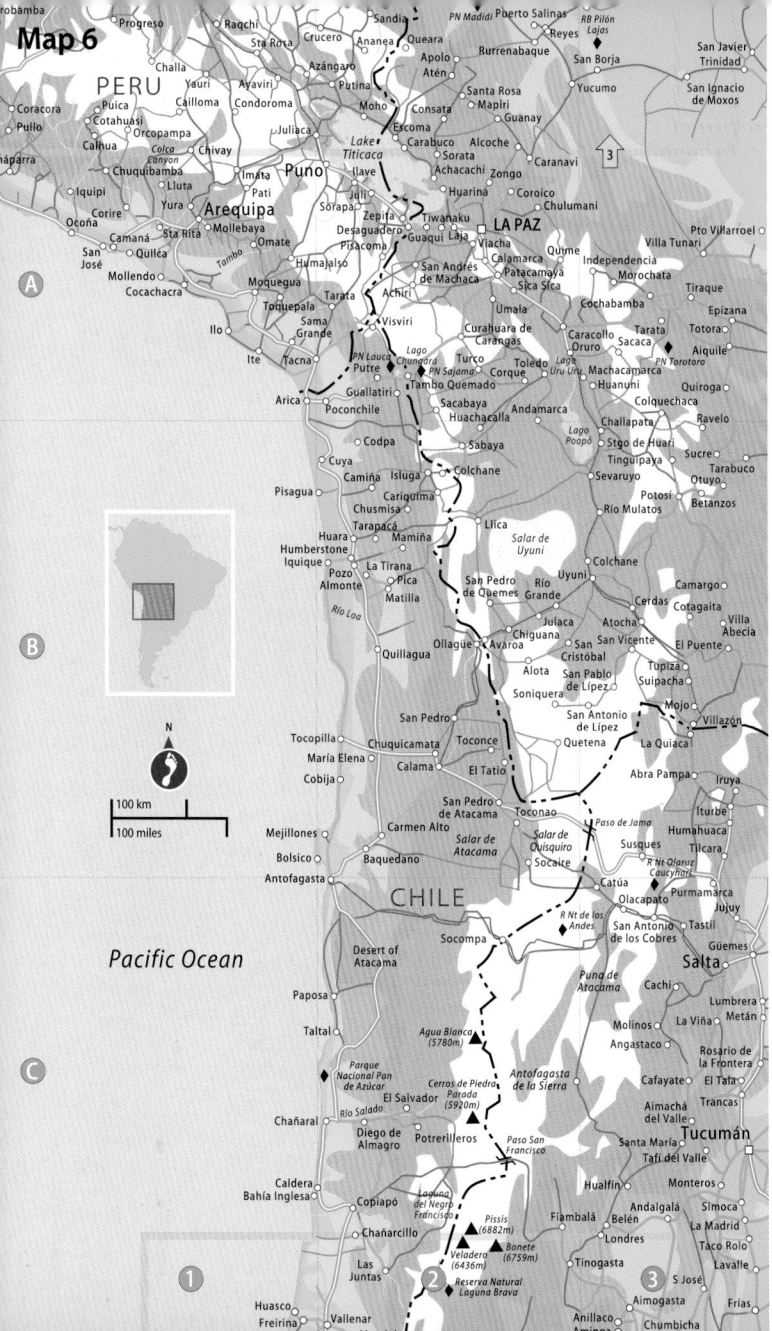

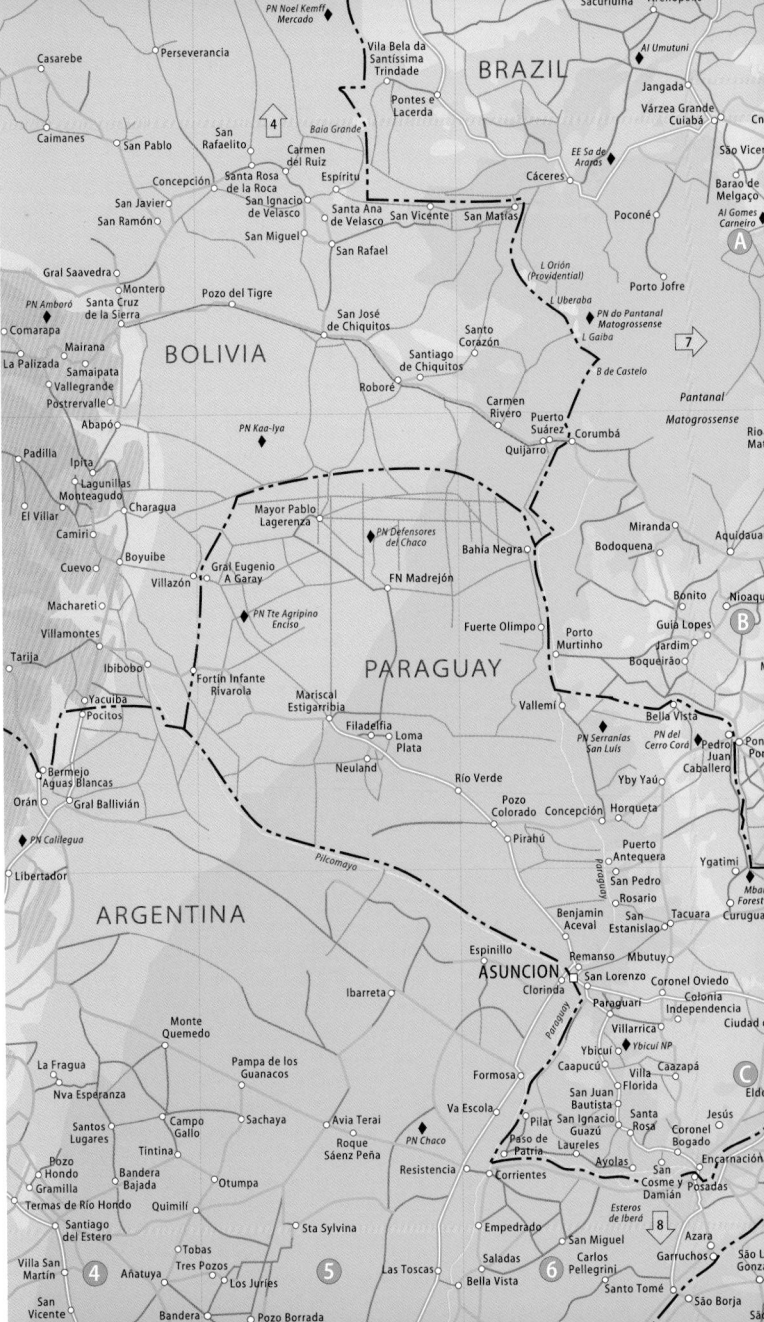

Map 7

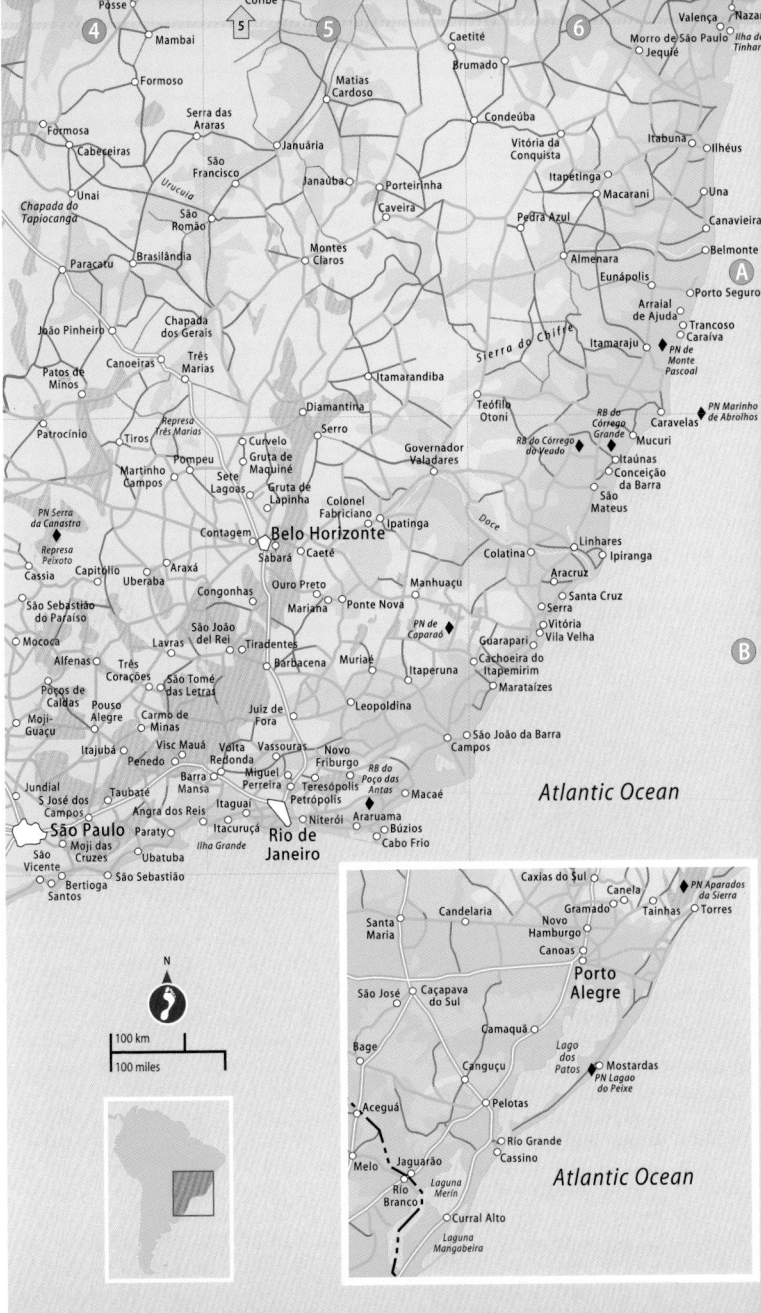

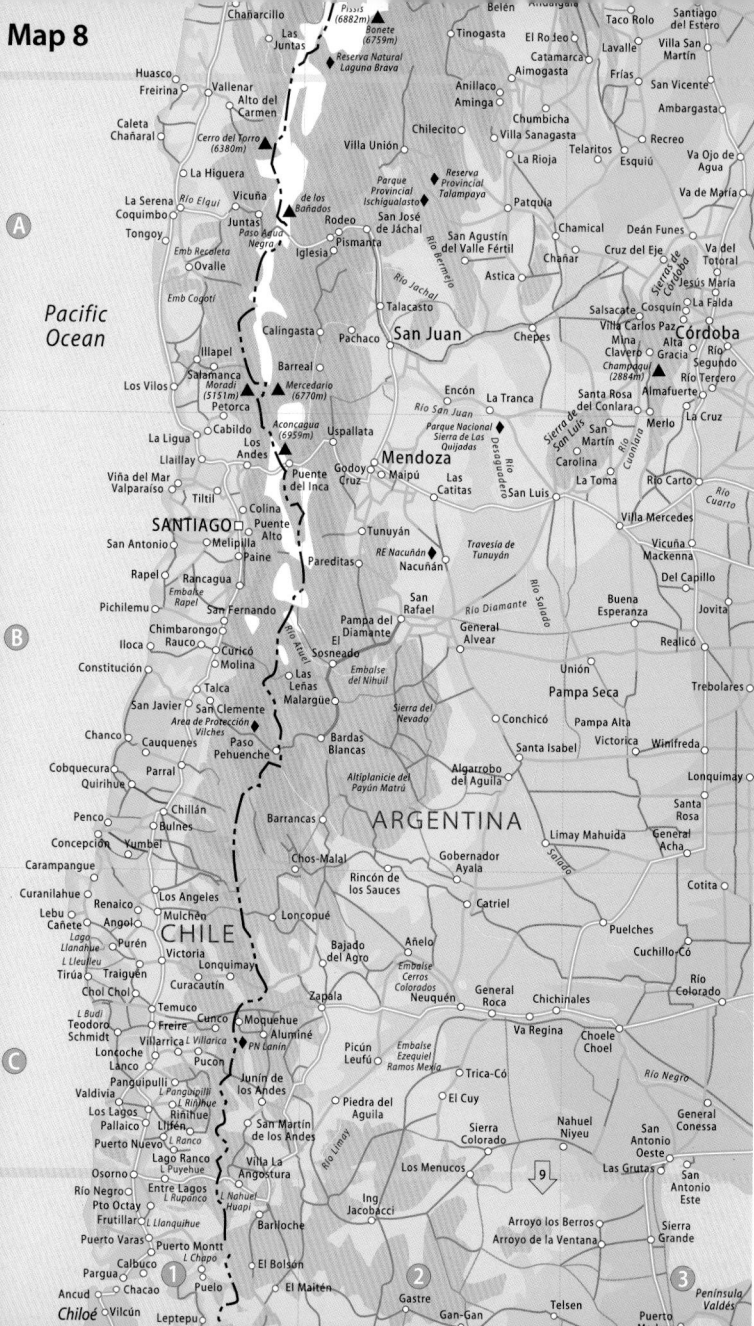

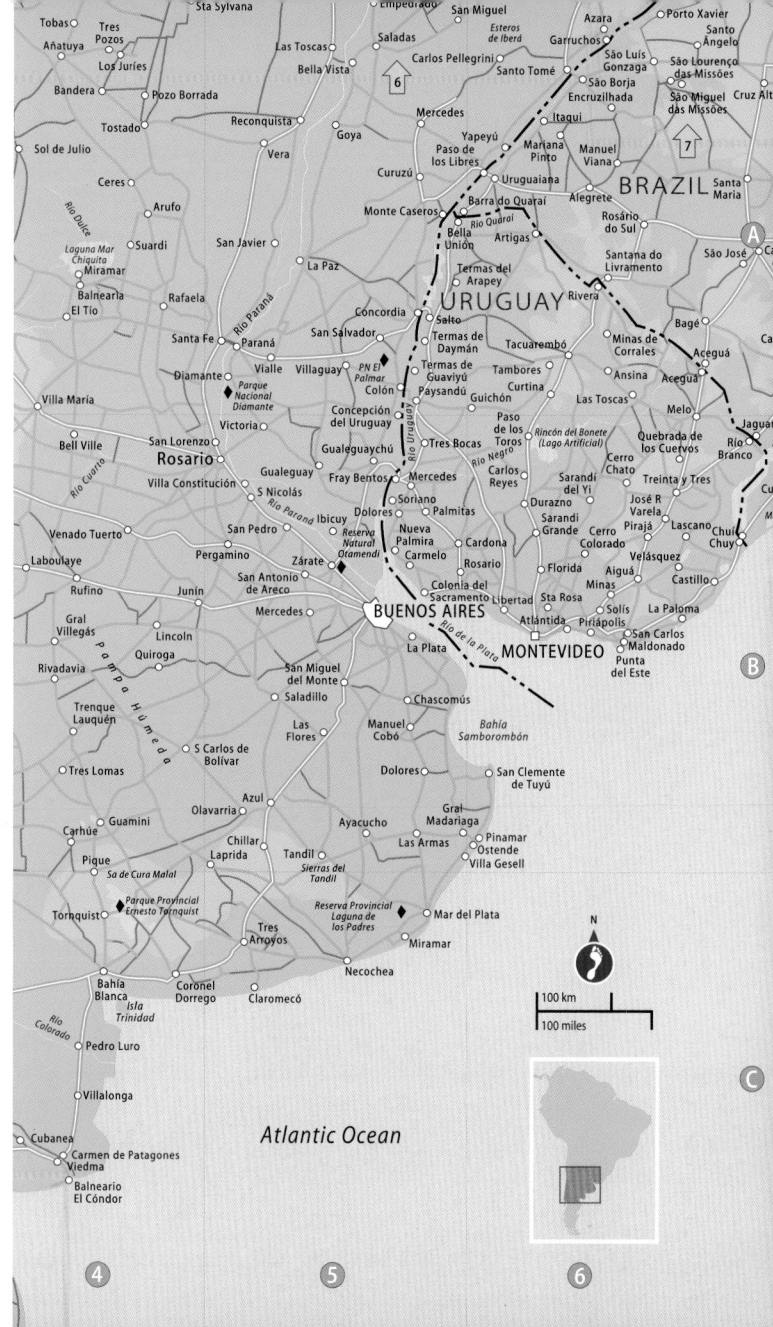

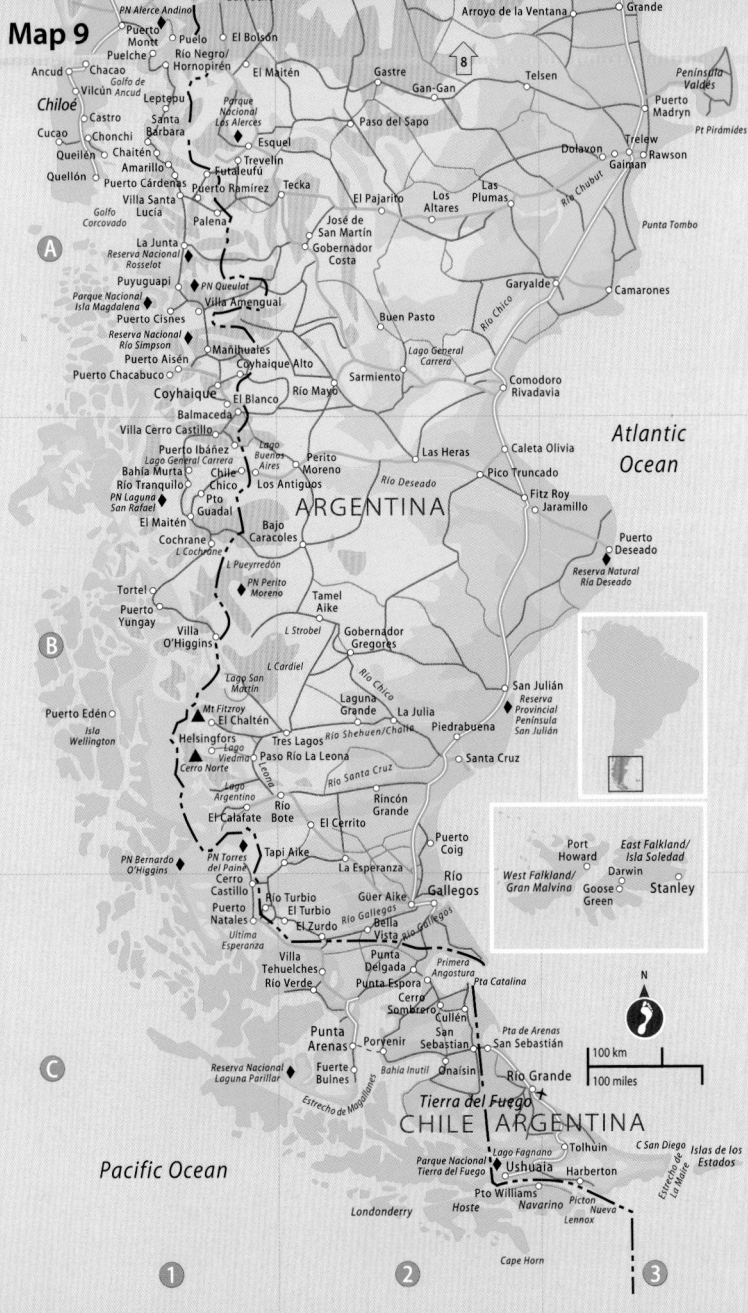

Map 9

Colour map index

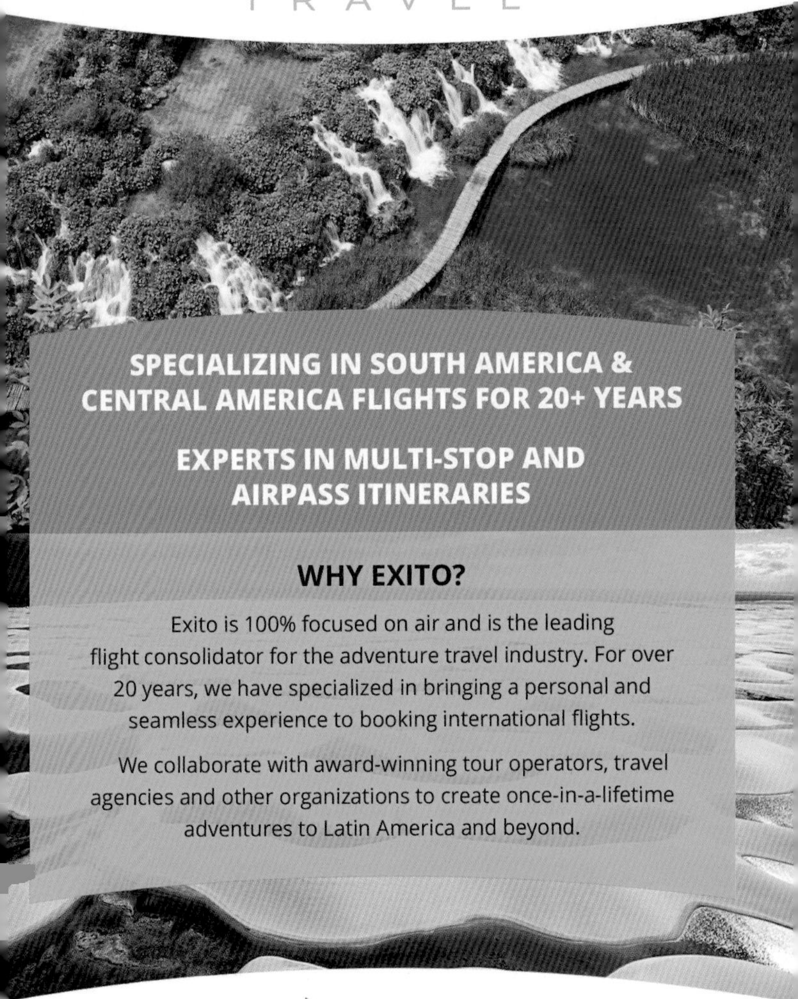

> Journey Latin America provided a couple of novice travellers in South America the security and comfort of having everything organised, with the adventure of discovering new and exciting locations and experiences.

TB, Grays, Essex

A pair of toco toucans, Brazil

As the UK's Nº1 specialist in travel to Latin America, we've been creating award-winning holidays to every corner of the region for over 36 years.

CALL **020 3733 4413**

JOURNEY
LATIN AMERICA

OR VISIT **JOURNEYLATINAMERICA.CO.UK**